CROSSWORD
PUZZLE
DICTIONARY

CROSSWORD PUZZLE DICTIONARY

ANDREW SWANFELDT

5th Edition

1817

HARPER & ROW, PUBLISHERS, New York
Cambridge, Philadelphia, San Francisco, London
Mexico City, São Paulo, Sydney

Designer: Sidney Feinberg

Library of Congress Cataloging in Publication Data
Swanfeldt, Andrew.
   Crossword puzzle dictionary.

   1. Crossword puzzles—Glossaries, vocabularies, etc.
   I. Title.
GV1507.C7S85   1984   793.73′2′03   83-48807
ISBN 0-06-181861-5
ISBN 0-06-181862-3 (thumb-indexed)

90 91 92 93 94 95 RRD/H 10 9 8 7 6 5
90 91 92 93 94 95 RRD/H 10 9 8   (IND)

Editor's Preface

Since its first appearance in 1940, the *Crossword Puzzle Dictionary*, compiled by the late Andrew Swanfeldt, has acquired a widespread and loyal following among crossword puzzle fans. Each successive edition improved and expanded the original. The third edition introduced the Instant Finder System, in which answer words are listed according to the number of letters. In this fifth edition, the editors have responded to many reader requests by providing separate lists for prefixes, suffixes, and combining forms, lists that can be found at the back of the book. To this fifth edition thousands of new words, both clue words and answer words, have been added and the book has been completely reset in larger type for easier reading. This fifth edition more than adequately reflects today's crossword puzzle clues and answers.

We are greatly indebted to Mr. John Willig, who began and completed a substantial amount of the revisions for this fifth edition. Mr. Willig died during his work on the book, and will be remembered with great fondness and deep gratitude. Ms. Ruth Adler took over the task of revising the book with admirable drive and attention to detail. She has our sincere thanks for a superb job.

Abbreviations Used in This Book

abbr.	abbreviation	It.	Italian
anc.	ancient	L.	Latin
Ar.	Arabic	mas.	masculine
c.	capital	O.T.	Old Testament
comb. form	combining form	pert. to	pertaining to
D.	Dutch	P.I.	Philippine Islands
F.	French	pl.	plural
fem.	feminine	Russ.	Russian
G.	German	Sc.	Scottish
Gr.	Greek	Sp.	Spanish
her.	heraldic	W.	Welsh
Ind.	Indian	Yid.	Yiddish
Ir.	Irish		

CROSSWORD
PUZZLE
DICTIONARY

A

aa: 4 lava 9 aphrolite

aal, al: 8 mulberry
   dye: 8 morindin

   aalii: 4 tree, wood

aardvark: 8 anteater, earth pig, edentate

Aaron: 10 high priest
   associate: Hur
   brother: 5 Moses
   builder of: 10 golden calf
   burial place: Hor
   father: 5 Amram
   sister: 6 Miriam
   son: 5 Abihu, Nadab 7 Eleazar, Ithamar

Aaron's rod: 7 mullein

aba: 4 robe 5 cloth 6 fabric 7 garment

abaca: 4 hemp 5 fiber, lupis

aback: 6 behind 8 unawares 10 by surprise

abaculus: 4 tile 7 tessera

abacus: 4 slab 10 calculator
   Chinese: 7 suan pan

abaddon: pit 4 hell 5 hades

Abadite, Ibidite: 6 Muslim

abaft: 4 back 5 arear 6 astern, behind 8 rearward

abalone: 5 awabi, ormer, shell 6 sea ear 7 mollusk

abandon: 4 drop, flee, junk, quit 5 ditch, leave, scrap, waive, yield 6 abjure, desert, disuse, give up, maroon, reject, resign, vacate 7 discard, forsake 8 abdicate, forswear, rashness, renounce 9 surrender 10 enthusiasm, exuberance, relinquish

abandoned: bad 4 left, lost 6 wanton 7 corrupt, forlorn 8 derelict, flagrant, forsaken, stranded 9 desolated, destitute, dissolute, shameless, unbridled 10 dissipated, profligate 12 unrestrained

abandonment instrument: 6 waiver

abase: 5 shame 6 defame, demean, demote, grovel, humble, lessen, reduce 7 degrade, put down 9 denigrate, humiliate 10 depreciate

abash: 5 shame, upset 6 dismay, put out 7 chagrin, mortify 8 bewilder, confound 9 discomfit, embarrass, humiliate 10 disconcert

abashed: 7 ashamed 8 sheepish, red-faced

abate: ebb, end 4 ease, fall, omit, slow, void, wane 5 allay, annul, let up, lower, quash, relax, remit, slake 6 deduct, lessen, reduce, recede 7 abolish, assuage, die down, nullify, slacken, subside 8 decrease, diminish, mitigate, moderate 9 alleviate

abatement: 6 rebate 8 decrease 9 allowance, deduction, reduction 10 diminution, relaxation, subsidence

abatis: 8 obstacle 9 barricade 13 fortification

abba: 6 father

abbey: 6 priory 7 convent, nunnery 8 cloister 9 monastery, sanctuary
   head: 5 abbot 6 abbess
   assistant: 5 prior 8 prioress
   pert. to: 8 abbatial

abbreviate: cut 4 clip, dock 5 prune 6 digest 7 abridge, curtail, cut back, shorten 8 contract, condense, truncate 9 make brief

ABC's: 6 basics 9 rudiments

abdicate: 4 cede, quit 5 demit, leave 6 disown, forego, resign, retire, vacate 7 abandon, lay down 8 disclaim, renounce 9 surrender 10 relinquish

abdomen: gut, pot 5 belly 6 paunch 7 midriff, stomach 9 bay window
   crustacean: 5 pleon
   pert. to: 6 pelvic 7 gastric, ventral 8 visceral

abduct: 5 seize 6 kidnap, snatch

abecedarian: 4 tyro 6 novice 7 learner 8 beginner, neophyte 9 fledgling 10 tenderfoot 12 alphabetical

abecedarium: 6 primer 12 alphabet book
   relative: 8 acrostic

abed: 4 sick 7 resting, retired 8 sleeping

Abel: *brother:* 4 Cain, Seth
   parent: Eve 4 Adam
   slayer: 4 Cain

Abelard's beloved: 7 Heloise

abele: 6 poplar

aberrant: odd 7 deviant, unusual 8 abnormal, atypical, peculiar, straying 9 unnatural, wandering

aberration: 4 slip 5 error, fault, lapse, mania, quirk 8 delusion, insanity 9 deviation 12 eccentricity 13 hallucination

abet: aid 4 back, goad, help 5 egg on 6 assist, foment, incite, second, uphold 7 espouse, further, support, sustain **8** befriend **9** encourage, instigate **11** countenance

abettor: 6 patron **8** advocate, promoter **9** accessory, auxiliary, supporter **10** accomplice **11** confederate, conspirator

abeyance: 4 stay **5** break, letup, pause **7** respite **10** on the shelf, suspension

abhor: 4 hate, shun **6** detest, loathe **7** despise, dislike **8** execrate **9** abominate

abhorrence: 5 odium **6** hatred **7** disgust **8** aversion **9** antipathy, revulsion **10** repugnance **11** detestation

Abi: *father:* **9** Zechariah
husband: **4** Ahaz
mother: **8** Hezekiah

abide: 4 bear, last, live, stay **5** await, brook, delay, dwell, exist, pause, stand, tarry **6** accept, endure, linger, remain, reside, submit, suffer **7** sojourn, sustain **8** continue, tolerate **9** acquiesce, withstand

Abiel's son: Ner

a bientot(F.): 6 so long

abies: 4 firs **5** trees **10** evergreens

Abigail: *husband:* **5** David, Nabal
son: **5** Amasa

ability: 5 force, knack, power, skill **6** energy, talent **7** caliber, faculty, knowhow, prowess **8** aptitude, capacity, facility, strength **9** dexterity, ingenuity **10** capability, competence, efficiency **11** proficiency

abject: low **4** base, mean, meek, poor **6** humble, paltry, sordid **7** hangdog, ignoble, servile, slavish **8** beggarly, contrite, cringing, degraded, wretched **9** miserable **10** submissive

abjure: 4 deny **5** avoid, spurn **6** eschew, give up, recall, recant, reject, resign, revoke **7** abandon, disavow, retract **8** abnegate, disclaim, forswear, renounce, take back, withdraw **9** repudiate

ablate: 8 melt away, vaporize **12** disintegrate

ablation: 7 erosion, removal **11** evaporation

ablaze: 5 afire, lit up **6** ardent, aflame **7** burning, glowing, ignited, radiant **8** inflamed

able: apt, fit **4** up to **5** adept, smart **6** au fait, clever, facile, strong, suited **7** capable **8** dextrous, skillful, suitable, talented, vigorous **9** competent, dexterous, effective, efficient, qualified, versatile **10** proficient

ablution: 4 bath **10** church rite

abnegate: 4 deny **5** forgo **6** abjure, forego, refuse, reject **7** disavow **8** disclaim, forswear, renounce **10** relinquish

Abner: *cousin:* **4** Saul
father: Ner

abnormal: 5 queer **7** deviant, erratic, offbeat, unusual **8** aberrant, uncommon **9** anomalous, eccentric, irregular, unnatural **9** out-of-line **10** exorbitant **11** exceptional **13** extraordinary

aboard: 4 onto **6** on deck **7** astride, present **9** alongside

abode: flat, home **5** house, manor **6** estate **7** cottage, mansion **8** domicile, dwelling, tenement **9** apartment, residence **10** habitation

animal: zoo **9** menagerie
of Dead: Dar **4** Aaru, Hell **5** Aralu, Hades, Orcus, Sheol **6** Heaven **9** Purgatory
of gods: **4** Meru **6** Asgard **7** Asgarth, Olympus **8** Asgardhr

abolish: end **4** kill **5** abate, annul, erase, quash **6** cancel, repeal, revoke, vacate **7** destroy, nullify, rescind, wipe out **8** abrogate **9** eradicate **10** annihilate, do away with, invalidate **11** discontinue, exterminate

aboma: boa **6** python **8** anaconda

abominable: 4 vile **6** horrid, odious **9** atrocious, execrable, loathsome, revolting **10** unpleasant **12** disagreeable

abominable snowman: 4 yeti **7** monster
habitat: **9** Himalayas

abominate: 4 hate **5** abhor **6** detest, loathe **8** execrate

abomination: 4 evil **5** crime, curse **6** infamy, horror, plague **7** outrage **8** anathema, atrocity, disgrace **9** antipathy **10** abhorrence, odiousness, repugnance **11** detestation

à bon marché(F.): 5 cheap

aboriginal: 5 first **7** endemic **8** primeval **9** primitive **10** indigenous

aborigine: 6 Indian, native, savage **10** autochthon

abortion: 7 failure **8** misbirth **11** miscarriage, monstrosity

abortive: 4 idle, vain **6** futile, no good **9** fruitless **12** unproductive, unsuccessful

abound: 4 teem **5** crawl, swarm **8** overflow

abounding: 4 rife **5** alive, flush **6** full of, jammed, packed **7** replete, teeming **8** abundant, thronged **9** plentiful

about: 4 as to, in re, near, some **5** anent, astir, circa **6** active, almost, around **7** apropos, close to **9** as regards **10** concerning, relative to, respecting, throughout **11** surrounding **13** approximately

about-face: 6 switch **8** flip-flop, reversal **9** turnabout **12** change of mind

above: oer **4** atop, over, past, upon **5** aloft **6** beyond, higher, on high **7** on top of **8** overhead, superior **9** exceeding **12** transcendent

above all: 6 indeed, mostly **7** chiefly **9** in the main, primarily

aboveboard: 4 open 5 frank, overt 6 honest, square 8 bona fide 9 in the open 10 on the level

above water: 4 safe 5 clear 7 solvent 9 out of debt

abracadabra: 5 charm, spell 6 jargon 10 hocus-pocus 11 incantation

abrade: rub 4 file, fret, gall, rasp, sand, wear 5 chafe, erode, grate, grind 6 scrape 7 corrode, eat away 8 irritate 9 excoriate

Abraham: 9 patriarch
bosom: 6 heaven 8 paradise
brother: 5 Nahor
concubine: 5 Hagar
father: 5 Terah
grandfather: 5 Nahor
grandson: 4 Esau
newphew: Lot
shrine: 5 Caaba, Kaaba
son: 5 Isaac, Medan, Shuah 6 Midian, Zimran 7 Ishmael
wife: 4 Sara 5 Hagar, Sarah 7 Keturah

abrasive: 4 sand 5 emery 6 pumice, quartz 8 annoying, corundum 9 sandpaper, provoking

abraxas: gem 5 charm

abreast: 4 even, up to 5 abeam 6 beside 8 parallel 9 alongside 10 side by side
of the times: 6 modern 7 popular 8 up to date 9 au courant(F.) 12 contemporary

abri: 6 dugout 7 shelter

abridge: cut 5 limit, 6 reduce, shrink 7 capsule, curtail, cut back, shorten 8 compress, condense, contract, diminish, retrench 10 abbreviate

abridgement: 4 brief 6 digest, precis, sketch 7 epitome, summary 8 abstract, synopsis 9 lessening 10 compendium, diminution

abroad: off 4 asea, away 5 astir 6 afield, astray 7 distant 8 overseas

abrogate: 4 undo, void 5 annul, quash, remit 6 cancel, repeal, revoke 7 abolish, nullify, rescind 8 overrule, set aside

abrupt: 4 curt, fast, rude 5 bluff, blunt, brief, brisk, gruff, hasty, jerky, quick, sharp, sheer, short, steep, terse 6 sudden 7 brusque, 8 headlong, vertical 9 impetuous 10 unexpected 11 precipitous 13 unceremonious

Absalom: *captain:* 5 Amasa
father: 5 David
sister: 5 Tamar
slayer: 4 Joab

abscess: 4 boil 5 ulcer 6 fester, lesion

abscond: fly, run 4 bolt, flee, quit, skip 5 scram 6 decamp, escape 7 make off 8 clear out 12 absquatulate

absence: 4 lack, void, want 5 leave 6 vacuum 7 truancy 8 furlough, omission 10 deficiency, withdrawal 13 nonappear-

ance, nonattendance

absent: off, out 4 away, gone 7 lacking, missing 10 not present

absent-minded: 7 bemused, far away 8 distrait, dreaming, unseeing 9 oblivious 10 abstracted 11 inattentive

absent without leave: 4 AWOL

absolute: 4 pure, rank, real, true 5 sheer, stark, total, utter, whole 6 actual, entire, simple 7 perfect, plenary 8 complete, despotic, explicit, implicit, outright, positive 9 arbitrary, downright, out and out, undoubted 10 autocratic, peremptory 11 categorical, unalienable 13 unconditional

absolutely: yea, yes 4 amen 5 quite, truly 6 wholly, for sure, utterly 8 of course 9 certainly, perfectly 10 positively, thoroughly 13 unequivocally

absolution: 6 pardon 7 amnesty 9 acquittal, cleansing, remission 11 exculpation, forgiveness

absolve: 4 free 5 clear, remit 6 acquit, excuse, exempt, let off, pardon, shrive 7 forgive, release 8 dispense, liberate, overlook 9 discharge, exculpate, exonerate, vindicate

absorb: 5 merge, unite 6 engage, imbibe, soak up, take in 7 combine, consume, drink in, engross, immerse, occlude 8 take over 10 assimilate 11 incorporate

absorbed: 4 rapt 6 intent, lost in 7 riveted 8 immersed, involved 9 engrossed, wrapped up 10 abstracted 11 preoccupied

absquatulate: 5 scram 6 decamp 7 abscond

abstain: 4 deny, fast 5 forgo, spurn, waive 6 desist, eschew, forego, pass up, refuse, reject 7 forbear, refrain 8 hold back, keep from, let alone, teetotal 9 do without

abstemious: 5 sober 7 ascetic, austere, sparing 8 moderate 9 abstinent, temperate

abstinence: 8 sobriety 10 self-denial 12 renunciation

abstract: 4 cull, deed, pure 5 brief, ideal, steal 6 deduct, divert, precis, remove 7 abridge, excerpt, purloin, summary 8 abstruse, detached, separate, synopsis, withdraw 9 difficult, epitomize, recondite, summarize 10 compendium 11 theoretical
art: 6 unreal 12 non-objective 13 expressionism
being: ens 4 esse 5 entia(pl.)

abstracted: 7 bemused, far away, pensive 8 absorbed 9 engrossed 11 preoccupied 12 absent-minded

abstruse: 4 deep 6 mystic, remote, subtle, 7 obscure 8 abstract, esoteric, profound

9 recondite 10 mysterious 11 hard to grasp

absurd: 4 wild 5 crazy, droll, inane, inept, silly, wacky 6 stupid 7 asinine, foolish 9 fantastic, ludicrous, senseless 10 irrational, ridiculous 11 meaningless, nonsensical 12 inconsistent, preposterous

abundance: 4 lots 5 store 6 oodles, plenty, riches, wealth 8 fullness, opulence, plethora 9 affluence, amplitude, plenitude, profusion 10 quantities

abundant: 4 lush, much, rich, rife 5 ample, thick 6 common, lavish 7 copious, fertile, profuse, replete, riotous, teeming 8 fruitful, generous, numerous, prolific 9 abounding, bountiful, luxuriant, plenteous, plentiful, prevalent 11 overflowing

abuse: mar, tax 4 flay, harm, hurt, maul, 5 curse, fault, scold, wrong 6 berate, defile, injure, insult, misuse, punish, revile 7 affront, bedevil, calumny, exploit, obloquy, outrage, pervert, slander, upbraid, violate 8 maltreat, misapply, mistreat, 9 blaspheme, contumely, desecrate, disparage, invective, objurgate 10 impose upon, manipulate, opprobrium, scurrility 12 vituperation

abusive: 4 foul 5 rough 6 savage 7 corrupt, profane 8 insolent, libelous 9 offensive, perverted 10 calumnious, scurrilous 11 blasphemous 12 vituperative

abut: 4 join 5 touch 6 adjoin, border, rest on 10 end against

abysmal: 4 deep 6 dreary 8 profound, unending, wretched 10 bottomless

abyss: pit 4 deep, gulf, hell, void 5 chasm, Hades 6 bottom, depths, vorago 7 gehenna, inferno 9 perdition

Abyssinia: See **Ethiopia**

acacia: 4 tree 5 babul, boree, cooba, myall 6 locust, wattle 7 catechu 9 boobyalla, gum arabic

academic: 5 rigid 6 formal, unreal 7 bookish, classic, erudite, learned 8 pedantic 9 scholarly, professor 11 quodlibetic, theoretical 12 conventional

division: 4 term 7 quarter 8 semester

academy: 6 lyceum, manege, school 7 college, society 8 seminary 9 institute 10 university

service: 4 Army (West Point), Navy (Annapolis) 8 Air Force (Colorado) 10 Coast Guard (New London) 14 Merchant Marine (Long Island)

Acadian: 5 Cajun

acajou: 6 cashew 8 mahogany 9 laurel oak

acaleph: 9 jellyfish

acarid: 4 mite, tick 6 insect

acaudal: 7 anurous 8 tailless

accede: let 5 agree, allow, grant, yield 6 assent, attain, comply, concur, give in 7

approve, consent 9 acquiesce 10 take office 11 acknowledge

accelerate: rev, gun 4 race, 5 hurry 6 hasten 7 advance, forward, further, quicken, speed up 8 dispatch, expedite, go faster, increase, step on it 9 move ahead, stimulate 11 precipitate

accelerator: 8 throttle 9 activator, cyclotron

accent: 4 beat, burr, mark, tone 5 ictus, drawl, pitch, pulse, sound, throb, twang 6 brogue, rhythm, stress 7 cadence 8 emphasis 9 underline 10 inflection, intonation

mark: 5 acute, grave 10 circumflex

accented: 7 marcato

syllable: 5 arsis

accentuate: 6 set off 7 sharpen 8 bring out 9 emphasize, intensify

accept: buy, see 4 take 5 admit, adopt, agree, allow, bow to, grant, honor 6 assent, endure, take in 7 approve, believe, embrace, espouse, receive 8 tolerate 9 acquiesce 10 understand 11 acknowledge

acceptable: 6 decent, not bad, viable 7 average, welcome 8 adequate, all right, pleasant, suitable 9 palatable 10 good enough 12 satisfactory

accepted: 5 valid 6 proper 7 correct, routine, popular 8 credited, orthodox, standard 9 canonical, customary, prevalent 10 sanctioned 12 conventional, countenanced

access: way 4 adit, door, gate, path, road 5 entry, onset, route, spell 6 attack, avenue, entree, portal, street 7 flare-up 8 approach, entrance, eruption, increase, outbrust, paroxysm 9 admission 10 admittance, passageway, right of way

accessible: 4 near, open 5 handy 6 at hand, patent, public 8 pervious 9 available, reachable 10 attainable, convenient, easy to meet, obtainable, procurable 12 approachable, unrestricted

accession: 5 enter 7 arrival 8 addition, approach, increase 9 adherence, agreement, inaugural, increment, induction 11 acquisition 12 installation

accessory: 4 aide, ally, tool 5 extra 6 helper 7 abettor, adjunct 8 additive, a party to, trapping 9 appendage, assistant, auxiliary, secondary 10 accomplice, attachment, incidental, subsidiary, supplement 11 additional, concomitant, confederate, contingency, subservient, subordinate, unessential 12 appurtenance, contributory 13 accompaniment

accident: hap 4 case, fate, luck 5 event, fluke, wreck 6 chance, hazard, mishap 7 fortune 8 calamity, disaster, incident

9 mischance 10 misfortune 11 catastrophe, contingency, contretemps 12 misadventure

accidental: 6 casual, chance, random 9 extrinsic, haphazard, secondary, unplanned, unwitting 10 extraneous, fortuitous, incidental, unexpected, unforeseen, unintended 11 conditional, inadvertent, subordinate 12 adventitious, nonessential 13 unintentional 14 unpremeditated

acclaim: 4 clap, fame, hail, laud 5 cheer, eclat, extol, honor, kudos 6 praise, repute, salute 7 applaud, approve, commend, glorify, root for, ovation 8 plaudits 9 pay homage 10 compliment 11 approbation

acclimate: 5 inure 6 harden, season 7 toughen 8 accustom 9 condition, habituate

acclivity: 4 hill, rise 7 incline 11 upward slope

accolade: 5 award, honor, medal 6 eulogy, salute 7 laurels, tribute 8 ceremony, citation, encomium 9 laudation, panegyric 10 decoration, salutation 11 distinction

accommodate: fit 4 give, hold, lend, suit 5 adapt, board, defer, favor, house, lodge, put up, serve, yield 6 adjust, attune, billet, change, comply, oblige, orient, settle 7 conform, contain, quarter 9 make agree, reconcile

accompany: 4 join, lead 5 add to, pilot 6 assist, attend, convey, convoy, escort, follow, go with, squire 7 coexist, conduct 8 chaperon 10 supplement

accomplice: 6 helper 7 abettor, cohort, partner 9 accessory, assistant, associate, colleague 11 confederate 12 participator 13 co-conspirator

accomplish: end, win 5 reach 6 attain, effect, finish, fulfil, manage, make it 7 achieve, execute, fulfill, furnish, perfect, perform, produce, realize, succeed 8 bring off, complete, dispatch, engineer 9 put across 10 consummate

accomplished: apt 4 able, done 5 adept, ended 6 expert 7 skilled 8 finished, talented 9 versatile 10 proficient

accomplishment: art 4 deed, feat 5 craft, skill 7 success 8 learning 10 attainment 11 achievement, performance

accord: 4 jibe 5 agree, allot, award, grant, tally, unity 6 accede, adjust, bestow, concur, treaty 7 concede, concert, consent, rapport 8 affinity, volition 9 give as due, harmonize, reconcile 10 compliance, conformity, correspond

accordant: 7 attuned 8 agreeing, coherent, suitable 9 congruous, consonant 10 compatible, consistent, harmonious

11 conformable 13 correspondent

accordingly: 4 ergo, then, thus 5 hence 9 therefore, thereupon, wherefore 12 consequently, in the same way

accost: 4 hail, meet 5 greet, speak 6 call to, halloo, salute, waylay 7 address, solicit, speak to 8 approach, bid hello, confront 9 encounter 10 button-hole

account: tab, use 4 bill, deem, item, rate, tale, view 5 basis, score, story, value, worth 6 client, detail, esteem, profit, reason, record, report, repute 7 history, invoice, recital 8 business, customer, estimate 9 advantage, chronicle, discourse, inventory, narrative, reckoning, statement 10 commentary, importance, recitation 11 description, explanation

book: 6 ledger

accountable: 6 liable 10 answerable, explicable 11 responsible 12 attributable

accountant: CPA 5 clerk 7 auditor 8 reckoner 10 bookkeeper, controller

accoutre, accouter: arm, rig 4 gird 5 array, dress, equip 6 attire, clothe, outfit 7 costume, furnish, turn out 8 decorate

accoutrements, accounterments: 4 gear 7 regalia 8 fittings, materiel 9 equipment, trappings

accredit: 4 okay 6 ratify 7 approve, ascribe, certify, confirm, empower, endorse, license 8 deputize, notarize, sanction, validate, vouch for 9 attribute, authorize 10 commission

accretion: 4 gain 6 growth 8 addition, increase 9 coherence, increment 11 enlargement 12 accumulation

accrue: add 4 earn, gain, grow 5 swell 7 collect, fall due, redound 8 cumulate, increase, multiply, snowball

accumulate: 4 grow, save 5 amass, hoard, lay in 6 accrue, garner, gather, muster, pile up 7 collect, compile, store up 8 assemble, increase 9 stockpile

accumulation: 4 bank, fund, heap, mass, pile 5 stack, store 7 backlog, cumulus, nest egg 8 dividend, interest, treasure 9 inventory 10 acervation 11 aggregation

accurate: 4 true 5 exact, right 7 certain, correct, precise 8 reliable 9 authentic, errorless, on the nose, veridical 10 dependable

accursed: fey(Sc.) 6 damned, doomed 7 hellish 9 abhorrent, execrable 10 abominable, detestable

accuse: tax 4 cite 5 blame 6 allege, attack, charge, defame, finger, indict 7 arraign, censure, impeach 8 denounce, reproach 9 inculpate 10 calumniate 11 bring to book, incriminate, recriminate

falsely: 5 libel

accuser: 7 charger, delator 8 libelant 9 plaintiff 10 prosecutor 11 complainant

accustom: use 5 adapt, enure, drill, inure, train 6 orient, season 7 toughen 9 acclimate, condition, get used to, habituate 11 familiarize

ace: jot, one, pip 4 a-one, atom, card, hero, mark, star, tops, unit 5 adept, basto, flyer, point 6 expert 7 aviator 8 particle, topnotch 9 first-rate, hole-in-one 11 crackerjack, hairbreadth, tennis score

acerbic: 4 acid, sour, tart 5 acrid, harsh, sharp, 6 bitter, severe 7 caustic 9 corrosive, sarcastic 10 astringent 11 acrimonious

acerbate: vex 7 envenom 8 embitter, irritate, infuriate 10 exasperate

acetaldehyde: 5 ethyl 7 ethanol

acetic acid: 7 vinegar
  salt: 7 acetate

acetylene: 5 tolan 6 alkyne, ethyne, tolane

ache: 4 hurt, long, pain, pang, pine 5 bleed, smart, throb, throe 6 desire, grieve, hunger, stitch, suffer, twinge 7 anguish 8 soreness, yearn for

achieve: get, win 4 earn, gain 5 reach 6 afford, attain, effect, finish, obtain 7 compass, execute, fulfill, produce, realize, succeed, triumph 8 complete, conclude, contrive 9 terminate 10 accomplish, consummate

achievement: act 4 coup, deed, feat 6 action 7 exploit 9 execution, 11 performance, tour de force 14 accomplishment

Achilles: *advisor:* 6 Nestor
  charioteer: 9 Automedon
  father: 6 Peleus
  fought in: 9 Trojan War
  friend: 9 Patroclus
  hero of: 5 Iliad
  horse: 7 Xanthus
  lover and captive: 7 Briseis
  mother: 6 Thetis
  slayer: 5 Paris
  soldier: 8 Myrmidon
  teacher: 6 Chiron 7 Centaur
  victim: 6 Hector
  vulnerable part: 4 heel

achromatic: 7 neutral 8 diatonic 9 colorless

acid: dry, LSD 4 keen, sour, tart 5 acerb, acrid, harsh, sharp 6 biting, bitter 7 acetose, acetous, pungent, vinegar 9 corrosive 11 acrimonious
  in fruit: 5 malic 6 citric 8 tartaric
  kind of: 5 amino, boric, iodic, oleic 6 acetic, cyanic, formic 7 stearic 8 carbolic
  neutralizer: 6 alkali
  nitric: 10 aquafortis
  radical: 4 acyl 6 acetyl 7 malonyl, benzoyl
  used in dyeing: 6 citric, oxalic 7 benzoic
  used in tanning: 6 lactic, tannic

acid rain: 7 fallout 12 air pollutant

Acis: *father:* 6 Faunus
  lover: 7 Galatea
  slayer: 10 Polyphemus

acknowledge: nod, own 4 aver, avow 5 admit, allow, grant, thank, yield 6 accept, affirm, answer, avouch, reveal 7 concede, confess, declare, divulge, own up to, profess 8 disclose 9 recognize

acme: cap, top 4 apex, peak 5 crest 6 apogee, climax, crisis, height, heyday, summit, vertex, zenith 8 pinnacle 11 culmination

acolyte: 6 helper, novice, server 8 altar boy, follower 9 attendant

aconite: 9 monkshood, wolfsbane
  poison from: 4 bikh

acorn: 4 mast 6 oak nut
  dried: 6 camata 8 camatina
  edible: 7 ballote, bellote

acouchi: 5 elemi, resin

acquaint: 4 tell 5 teach 6 advise, clue in, fill in, inform, notify 7 apprise, present 8 disclose 9 enlighten

acquaintance: 4 kith 6 friend 9 associate, companion, knowledge 11 familiarity

acquainted: 4 up on 6 au fait, versed 8 informed 9 in the know

acquiesce: bow 5 abide, agree, yield 6 accede, accept, assent, comply, concur, submit 7 concede, conform, consent

acquire: add, buy, get, win 4 earn, gain, grab, reap 5 amass, learn, reach 6 garner, gather, obtain, pick up, secure, take on 7 collect, develop, procure 8 contract 9 cultivate

acquisitive: 4 avid 6 greedy 8 covetous, grasping 10 avaricious

acquit: 4 free 5 clear 6 excuse, let off, pardon, parole 7 absolve, amnesty, comport, conduct, release 8 liberate 9 discharge, exculpate, exonerate, vindicate

acreage: 4 land 5 tract 6 realty 7 grounds 8 property 11 landholding

acrid: 4 sour 5 harsh, rough, sharp, 6 biting, bitter 7 caustic, pungent, reeking 8 unsavory, virulent 9 acidulous, corrosive 10 astringent, irritating

acrimonious: mad 5 angry, gruff, harsh, irate, sharp, surly, testy, wroth 6 biter, cranky 7 caustic 8 stinging 9 rancorous, resentful 11 contentious, quarrelsome

acroamatic: 4 oral 8 esoteric

acrobat: 7 gymnast, tumbler 8 balancer, stuntman 9 aerialist, trapezist 13 contortionist
  garment: 6 tights 7 leotard

acrogen: 4 fern, moss 9 liverwort

acropolis: 4 fort, hill 7 citadel

across: 4 over 6 beyond, facing 7 athwart

8 opposite 9 astraddle 10 transverse

the board: all 5 total 6 in toto, wholly 8 sweeping 10 altogether

acrostic: 4 game 6 phrase, puzzle 7 acronym 11 composition

act: law 4 bill, deed, fake, feat, move, skit, turn, work 5 doing, edict, emote, feign, put-on, serve, stunt 6 behave, bestir, decide, decree 7 comport, exploit, perform, portray, pretend, statute 8 function, play part, 9 dissemble, ordinance, represent 10 observance 11 impersonate, performance 12 have an effect

by turns: 9 alternate

act for: 5 front, spell 7 relieve 8 pinch-hit 9 represent

act like: ape 4 copy, echo 5 mimic 7 imitate 8 simulate

act on: 4 rule 6 affect 9 influence, take steps

act up: 7 carry on, show off 9 misbehave

action: fun 4 case, deed, fray, step, work 5 cause, fight, means 6 affair, battle 7 conduct, process 8 behavior, conflict, function, goings-on, maneuver, movement 9 animation, 10 deportment, enterprise, proceeding 11 transaction

field of: 4 bowl 5 arena, stage 7 stadium

legal: res 4 suit 6 trover 8 replevin 10 litigation

out of: 7 dormant 8 disabled, unused 9 sidelined 10 broken down, on the blink 11 inoperative

activate: 6 arouse, charge 7 start up 8 energize, mobilize, vitalize

active: 4 busy, spry 5 agile, alert, brisk, in use, quick, zippy 6 hearty, lively, moving, nimble 7 dynamic, kinetic, working 8 animated, athletic, spirited, vigorous 9 energetic, sprightly, 10 productive, up and about 11 functioning, industrious

activity: ado 4 life, stir, work 6 bustle, doings 8 business, exercise, function, movement 10 occupation

actor: 4 doer, mime 5 mimic 6 mummer, player, 7 artiste, histrio, trouper 8 comedian, stroller, thespian 9 performer, tragedian 11 barnstormer, entertainer

cue: 4 hint, word 6 prompt

group of: 4 cast 6 troupe 7 company

incompetent: ham 6 emoter

lines: 4 role, side

part: 4 hero, lead, role, star 5 heavy, 7 heroine, villain 8 juvenile

substitute: 7 stand-in 10 understudy

supporting: bit 5 extra, super 6 walk-on

actress: 4 diva 7 ingenue 9 soubrette 10 comedienne

actual: 4 real, true 6 extant 7 current, genuine 8 bona fide, concrete, existing, material, physical, positive, tangible 9 authentic, veritable 11 substantial

actuality: 4 fact 5 being 6 verity 7 reality 9 existence, substance

actuate: 4 move, stir 5 drive, enact, impel, spark, start 6 arouse, incite, set off 7 agitate, animate, enliven, inspire, provoke, trigger 8 motivate 9 instigate 11 put in motion

acumen: wit 7 insight 8 keenness, sagacity 9 acuteness, sharpness 10 astuteness, perception, shrewdness 11 discernment 12 perspicacity 14 discrimination

acupuncture: 7 therapy 11 anaesthesia, perforation

acute: 4 dire, keen 5 quick, sharp, smart 6 astute, severe, shrewd, shrill, subtle, urgent 7 crucial, extreme, intense, pointed 8 critical, incisive, piercing 9 ingenious, sensitive 10 discerning, perceptive 11 high-pitched, intelligent, penetrating, quick-witted 13 perspicacious

ad-lib: 9 improvise 11 extemporize

ad patres: 4 dead 8 deceased

adage: saw 5 axiom, maxim, motto 6 byword, dictum, homily, saying, truism 7 bromide, precept, proverb 8 aphorism, apothegm

Adah: *husband:* 4 Esau 6 Lamech

son: 5 Jabal, Jubal

Adam: *grandson:* 4 Enos 5 Enoch

rib: Eve

son: 4 Abel, Cain, Seth

teacher: 6 Raisel

wife, first: 6 Lilith

Adam-and-Eve: 9 puttyroot

Adam Bede author: 5 Eliot

adamant: 4 firm, hard 5 rigid, stony 8 obdurate 9 immovable, unbending 10 inflexible, relentless, unyielding

adapt: fit 4 suit 5 alter, inure, shape 6 adjust, change, comply, gear to, modify, tailor, temper 7 arrange, conform, convert, qualify 8 attemper, 9 acclimate, harmonize, reconcile 11 accommodate

adaptable: 6 pliant, supple 8 flexible 9 all-around, malleable, resilient, tractable, versatile 10 adjustable, changeable 11 conformable 12 reconcilable

add: sum, tot 4 fuse, join, tote 5 affix, annex, put in, tally, total, unite 6 append, attach, figure, reckon 7 augment, combine, compile, compute, connect, say more, subjoin 9 calculate

to: 5 mix in 6 blow up, expand, tack on 7 amplify 8 increase 9 strengthen 10 supplement

up: 5 recap 6 be okay, go over, 8 ring true 9 summarize

adda: 5 skink 6 lizard

adder: 5 krait, snake, viper 7 serpent

addict: fan 4 buff, user 5 hound, slave 6 votary 7 deliver, devotee, fanatic, habitue, hophead, pothead 8 acidhead 9 mainliner 10 aficionado, enthusiast

addiction: 5 habit 9 surrender 10 attachment 11 disposition, enslavement

addition: ell 4 plus, wing 5 annex, rider 6 prefix suburb, suffix 7 adjunct, codicil, joining 8 addendum, increase 9 accession, accretion, amendment, appendage, expansion, extension

in: 4 also, else 7 besides, further

additional: new 4 else, more 5 extra, fresh, other 9 auxiliary 12 supplemental

addled: 4 asea 5 dizzy, giddy, upset 7 mixed up 8 confused 9 befuddled, flustered 10 bewildered

address: aim, sue, woo 4 call, hail, home, tact, talk, 5 abode, court, greet, poise, skill 6 accost, adjust, aplomb, appeal, eulogy, manner, salute, speech 7 lecture, oration, speak to 8 approach, dispatch, harangue, mail drop, petition, presence 9 dexterity, discourse, residence, statement 10 allocution, peroration 11 take a stance

adduce: 4 cite, name 5 offer, quote 6 allege, submit, tender 7 advance, mention, present, suggest 11 give as proof

adeps: fat 4 lard

adept: ace, apt 4 A-one, able, deft, whiz, up on 5 handy, sharp 6 adroit, artist, expert, good at, master 7 capable, 8 skillful 9 dexterous, masterful, tolerable 10 acceptable, consummate, proficient

adequate: 4 fair, okay 5 ample, 6 decent, enough, not bad, plenty 8 all right, possible, suitable 9 competent, effective 10 answerable, sufficient 12 commensurate, satisfactory

a deux: 6 for two, 8 intimate

adhere: 5 cling, stick, 6 cleave, cohere 8 hold fast 12 stay together

adherence: 7 loyalty 8 devotion, fidelity 9 constancy 10 allegiance, attachment

adherent: 4 ally 6 votary 8 believer, disciple, follower, henchman, partisan, servitor, upholder 9 supporter

adhesive: gum, wax 4 bond, glue, tape 5 epoxy, paste 6 cement, gluten, mastic, sticky, viscum 7 stickum 8 birdlime, mucilage 9 tenacious

adhibit: 5 admit, affix, let in 6 attach

adieu: 5 adios, aloha 6 good-by, so long 7 good-bye 8 au revoir, farewell 11 leavetaking, valediction

adipose: fat 4 suet 5 fatty 6 tallow

adit: 5 stulm 6 access, tunnel 7 opening, passage 8 approach, entrance 9 admission, mine entry 10 passageway

adjacent: 4 near, next, nigh 5 close, handy 6 beside, hard by 7 against, meeting 8 abutting, touching 9 adjoining, bordering 10 contiguous, juxtaposed 11 neighboring 12 conterminous

adjective: 8 modifier 9 dependent, qualifier

demonstrative: 4 that, this 5 these, those

limiting: the

verbal: 9 gerundive

adjoin: add 4 abut, 5 touch, verge 6 append, attach, border, butt on 7 contact 8 be next to, neighbor 9 juxtapose

adjourn: end 4 stay 5 close, defer, delay 6 put off, recess 7 disband, suspend 8 dissolve, hold over, postpone, prorogue 9 terminate 11 discontinue

adjudge: 4 deem, find, rule 5 award, grant 6 decide, decree, settle 7 referee 9 arbitrate, determine

adjunct: 4 aide, part 5 annex 6 helper 7 quality 8 addition, appanage, appendix 9 accessory, appendage, associate, auxiliary, colleague 10 complement 11 subordinate 12 appurtenance

adjure: ask, beg, bid 5 plead, 6 appeal, charge 7 beseech, command, implore, entreat

adjust: fit, fix, set 4 bend, suit, trim, true, tune 5 adapt, align 6 attune, change, line up, settle, temper, 7 address, arrange, balance, conform, correct, justify, rectify, work out 8 modulate, regulate, set right 9 harmonize 10 concinnate, coordinate, straighten 11 accommodate, systematize

adjutage: 4 tube 5 spout 6 nozzle

adjutant: 4 aide, 5 stork 6 helper 7 officer 9 assistant, auxiliary

bird: 5 crane, stork 6 argala 7 marabou

admeasure: 5 allot 7 mete out, apportion

Admetus' wife: 8 Alcestis

administer: run 4 dose, rule 5 apply, issue, treat 6 direct, give to, govern, manage 7 conduct, control, deal out, execute, furnish, 8 carry out, dispense 9 look after, supervise 10 distribute 11 superintend

administrator: 7 manager, officer, trustee 8 director, executor 9 executrix

admirable: 5 brave, great 6 worthy 7 capital 8 laudable, splendid 9 deserving, estimable, excellent

name meaning: 7 Miranda

Admiralty Island: 5 Manus

capital: 8 Lorengau

admire: 4 like 5 adore, honor, prize, value 6 esteem, regard, revere, 7 approve, idolize, respect 8 venerate, look up to 11 think well of

admirer: fan 4 beau, buff 5 lover 6 backer, patron 7 booster, devotee, fancier

admission: fee 4 adit 6 access, charge, en-

tree, ticket **7** ingress **8** entrance **10** admittance, concession, confession, disclosure **15** acknowledgement
receipts: **4** gate, take **9** box-office
admit: own **4** avow **5** agree, allow, enter, grant, let in, own up **6** accept, avouch, enroll, induct, permit, take in **7** adhibit, concede, confess, include, profess, receive **8** initiate **9** come clean, recognize **11** acknowledge
admonish: **4** warn **5** alert, chide, scold **6** advise, enjoin, exhort, notify, rebuke, remind **7** caution, counsel, lecture, monitor, reprove **8** reproach **9** reprehend, reprimand, sermonize
ado: **4** fuss, stir, to-do **6** bother, bustle, flurry, hassle, hubbub, pother, ruckus **7** trouble, turmoil **9** commotion, confusion **10** excitement, hullabaloo
adobe: **4** clay **5** brick, house **6** mudcap
adolescence: **5** teens, youth **6** nonage **7** puberty **8** minority **9** salad days
adolescent: lad **4** girl, lass **5** green, minor, young, **6** subdeb **8** immature, juvenile, teenager, youthful **9** pubescent
Adonis: *beloved:* **9** Aphrodite
slayer of: **4** boar
adopt: **4** pass **5** enact **6** accept, assume, borrow, choose, employ, take up **7** approve, embrace, espouse, receive, support **8** advocate, maintain, practice **9** affiliate **10** naturalize **11** appropriate
adorable: **4** cute **5** sweet **6** lovely **7** angelic, lovable, winsome **8** charming, kissable **9** appealing **10** cuddlesome, delightful
adoration: **6** homage **8** devotion, idolatry
adore: **4** love **5** honor **6** admire, dote on, esteem, praise, revere **7** cherish, glorify, idolize, respect, worship **8** hold dear, venerate, **9** delight in
adorn: **4** deck, gild, trim **5** array, begem, grace, primp, prink **6** bedeck, doll up, emboss, enrich, set off **7** bedizen, dignify, dress up, enhance, furbish, garnish, **8** beautify, decorate, emblazon, ornament, trick out **9** bespangle, caparison, embellish, glamorize
ad rem: **8** relevant **9** pertinent **10** to the point
Adriana's servant: **4** Luce
Adriatic: *city:* **6** Venice
island: Bua, Eso **7** Lagosta, Lastovo
peninsula: **6** Istria
port: **4** Bari, Pola **5** Fiume **6** Ancona, Rimini **7** Trieste
resort: **4** Lido **5** Split
river into: **4** Reno **5** Adige, Bosna, Drini, Kerka, Piave
wind: **4** bora **10** tramontana, tramontane (pl.)
adrift: **4** asea, lost **5** loose **6** afloat, astray,

aweigh **8** derelict, homeless, unmoored **9** wandering **10** unanchored
adroit: apt **4** deft, **5** adept, handy, sharp, smart **6** artful, brainy, clever, expert, facile, habile **7** cunning **8** dextrous, skillful **9** dexterous, ingenious, masterful **10** proficient **11** quick-witted, resourceful
adulate: **7** idolize, lionize **8** enshrine, fawn upon, soft-soap **10** slaver over, overpraise
adulator: fan **5** toady **6** yes-man **9** flatterer, sycophant **10** bootlicker
adult: **4** aged, ripe **5** imago, **6** mature, nubile **7** grown-up, tempered **8** seasoned **9** developed, full-blown
adulterate: cut, mix **5** alloy, alter, spike **6** debase, dilute, doctor, weaken **7** falsify, thin out **8** denature **10** tamper with
adulterated: cut **6** impure **8** spurious **11** counterfeit, watered down
adumbrate: **4** bode **5** augur **6** darken, hint at, sketch **7** obscure, outline, portend, presage, suggest **8** indicate, intimate, rough out **10** foreshadow
adust: **6** burned, gloomy, sallow **7** parched **8** scorched **9** sunburned
advance: aid **4** cite, help, lend, loan, rise **5** boost, get on, raise, serve **6** adduce, allege, assign, better, foster, hasten, move up, prepay **7** bring up, elevate, forward, further, improve, proceed, promote, propose, upgrade **8** increase, overture, progress, put forth **9** encourage, get nearer, push ahead **10** accelerate, aggrandize, appreciate **11** improvement, make headway
guard: van **6** patrol **7** outpost
slowly: **4** inch, worm **5** crawl, creep
advanced: **5** ahead, early **7** liberal **8** tolerant **9** premature **10** avant-garde, precocious **11** enlightened, progressive
equally: **7** abreast
most: **8** farthest, foremost, headmost
advantage: use **4** boot, edge, gain, odds **5** asset, favor, start, stead **6** behalf, behoof, profit **7** account, benefit, **8** handicap, interest, leverage, overplus **9** upper hand **11** opportunity, superiority
advantageous: **6** useful **9** expedient, favorable, strategic **10** auspicious, beneficial, commodious, profitable, propitious **11** encouraging
advent: **6** coming **7** arrival **8** approach **11** incarnation
adventitious: **6** casual **7** foreign **8** acquired, episodic **9** extrinsic **10** accidental, fortuitous, incidental **12** nonessential
adventure: **4** feat, lark, risk **5** event, geste, quest **6** chance, danger, hazard **7** exploit **8** escapade **10** enterprise, expe-

rience 11 undertaking

adventurer: 7 gambler 9 daredevil, mercenary 13 fortune hunter

adventurous: 4 bold, rash 5 brash 6 daring, errant 8 intrepid, reckless 9 audacious, foolhardy, hazardous, imprudent

adversaria: ana 5 memos, notes 10 miscellany 12 commentaries

adversary: foe 5 enemy, rival 8 opponent 9 assailant 10 antagonist, competitor

adverse: con 4 anti 7 against, counter, harmful, hostile 8 contrary, critical, inimical, negative, opposing, opposite, untoward 9 diametric 11 conflicting, detrimental, disinclined, unfavorable 12 inauspicious, unpropitious

adversity: woe 5 trial 6 misery, sorrow 7 setback, tragedy, trouble 8 calamity, distress, hardship 9 suffering 10 affliction, ill-fortune, misfortune

advert: 4 note 5 refer 6 allude, attend 7 bring up, observe 8 consider, point out

advertise: 4 plug, puff, push 5 bruit 6 blazon, inform, notify, report 7 build up, declare, display, exploit, promote, publish 8 announce, ballyhoo, proclaim 9 broadcast, publicize 10 promulgate

advertisement: 4 bill, sign, spot 6 dodger, insert, notice, teaser 7 affiche, handout, leaflet, release, stuffer, placard 8 circular, handbill 9 broadside, throwaway 10 commercial

book jacket: 5 blurb 11 testimonial

outdoor: 5 flyer 6 banner, poster 9 billboard 10 skywriting 11 marquee sign

advice: tip 4 news, word 6 notice 7 caution, counsel, opinion, pointer, tidings 8 guidance 9 direction 10 admonition, suggestion 11 instruction 12 intelligence, word to the wise 14 recommendation

seek: 5 confer 6 huddle 7 consult

advisable: 4 wise 6 proper 7 politic, prudent 9 befitting, desirable, expedient

advise: 4 read, post, tell, warn 5 coach, guide 6 inform, notify 7 apprise, caution, counsel, suggest 8 acquaint, admonish, advocate, disclose 9 encourage, recommend

adviser, advisor: 4 tout 5 coach, guide 6 nestor 7 monitor, tipster 9 confidant, counselor 10 admonisher, consultant, Dutch uncle, instructor

advisory: 6 notice, report 7 warning 9 hortatory

body: 5 board, panel 7 cabinet, council 9 committee, think tank 10 brain trust

advocate: pro 4 abet, back, urge 5 favor, plead 6 advise, defend, friend, lawyer 7 endorse, espouse, promote, support 8 argue for, champion, hold with, partisan 9 counselor, paraclete, proponent,

recommend 11 intercessor

of new laws: 9 neonomian

adytum: 6 shrine 7 sanctum 9 sanctuary

adz, adze: axe 7 hatchet

relative: 6 pickax

Aeacus: *father:* 4 Zeus

son: 6 Peleus 7 Telamon

Aeetes: *kingdom:* 7 Colchis

daughter: 5 Medea

keeper of: 12 Golden Fleece

Aegean Sea: *ancient peoples:* 5 Psara, Psyra 6 Samian 7 Leleges, Samiote

gulf: 5 Saros 7 Argolis, Corinth, Saronic

island group: 8 Cyclades, Sporades 10 Dodecanese

river into: 6 Struma, Vardar 7 Marista

rock: Aex

Aegeon's wife: 7 Aemilia

Aegir's wife: Ran

aegis, egis: 6 shield 7 auspices, backing, control, defense 8 guidance 9 patronage 10 protection 11 sponsorship

Aegisthus: *father:* 8 Thyestes

mother: 7 Pelopia

slayer: 7 Orestes

victim: 6 Atreus 9 Agamemnon

Aegyptus: *brother:* 6 Danaus

father: 5 Belus

mother: 8 Anchinoe

Aello: 5 Harpy

Aeneas: *beloved:* 4 Dido

companion: 7 Achates

father: 8 Anchises

grandfather: 5 Capys

great-grandson: 4 Brut

mother: 9 Aphrodite

rival: 6 Turnus

son: Iulus 8 Ascanius

wife: 6 Creusa 7 Lavinia

Aeneid: *author:* 6 Vergil, Virgil

archer: 7 Acestes

first word: 4 arma

hero: 6 Aeneas

king slain by Aeneas: 6 Turnus

second word: 8 virumque

steersman: 9 Palinurus

third word: 4 cano

Aengus' mother: 5 Boann

Aeolian lyricist: 6 Sappho

Aeolus' daughter: 6 Canace 8 Halcyone

aeon, eon: age 5 kalpa(Ind.) 8 eternity 12 billion years 14 geologic period

aeonian, eonian: 7 eternal, forever 8 infinite 11 everlasting

aerate: 6 add air, aerify, charge 7 inflate 9 oxygenate, ventilate 11 expose to air

aerial: 4 aery, airy 5 lofty 6 high up, unreal 7 antenna 8 antennae(pl.), ethereal 9 imaginary 10 light as air 11 atmospheric 13 unsubstantial

aerie, eyrie: 4 nest 5 brood 9 penthouse 10 cliff house

aeriform: 6 unreal 7 gaseous 10 intangible

aerobatics: 4 loop, roll 5 stunt 11 flying feats

aerolite: 9 meterorite 10 brontolite

aeronaut: 5 pilot 7 aviator 10 balloonist

aerose: 6 brassy

aerostat: 7 airship, balloon 8 zeppelin 9 dirigible

aerugo: 4 rust 9 verdigris

aes: 4 coin 6 bronze

Aesculapius' teacher: 6 Chiron

Aeson: *brother:* 6 Pelias
son: 5 Jason

Aesop work: 6 Fables
character: ox; ant, ass, dog, fox 4 frog, hare, lion 5 eagle, mouse 8 tortoise 11 grasshopper

aesthete: 8 virtuoso 10 dilettante 11 cognoscente, connoisseur

aesthetic, esthetic: 8 artistic, pleasing, tasteful 9 beautiful 11 well-composed

aet, aetat(L.): 7 of an age

Aeta: Ita 8 Filipino 10 Philippino

Aether's father: 6 Erebus

Aetolian prince: 6 Tydeus

afar: off 4 away, 6 remote 7 distant

affable: 4 open 5 civil, 6 benign, genial, urbane 7 amiable, cordial, likable 8 charming, friendly, gracious, pleasant, sociable 9 agreeable, convivial, courteous 10 accessible 11 complaisant, good-natured 12 easy to talk to

affair: 5 event, issue, thing 6 action, matter 7 concern, lookout 8 business, endeavor, interest, intrigue, occasion 10 engagement, proceeding 11 transaction 12 circumstance
love: 5 amour, tryst 7 liaison, romance 8 intrigue 10 attachment
social: 4 ball, gala 5 party 6 at home, soiree 7 blowout, shindig 9 gathering 11 get together

affect: hit 4 move, stir, sway 5 act on, alter, fancy, feign, touch 6 assume, change, strike, 7 concern, impress, operate, pretend, profess 8 bear upon, frequent, interest, simulate, soften up 9 cultivate, influence 11 counterfeit, hypothecate
each other: 8 interact

affectation: 4 airs, pose, sham 5 put-on 6 facade, fakery 7 pietism 8 artifice, pretense 9 hypocrisy, mannerism 10 false front

affected: 5 moved, stagy 6 chi-chi, tootoo 7 mincing, stilted, studied, touched 8 disposed, involved, mannered, precious 9 unnatural 10 artificial, influenced 11 pretentious 13 grandiloquent

affection: 4 love 5 amour, fancy 6 liking, esteem, malady, regard 7 ailment, emotion, feeling 8 fondness, weakness 10 attachment, friendship, propensity, tenderness

affectionate: 4 fond, warm 6 ardent, doting, loving, soft on, tender 7 amorous, devoted 8 attached 11 sentimental

affianced: 7 engaged 8 intended, plighted, promised 9 betrothed, bride-to-be, groom-to-be 10 set to marry

affiant: 8 deponent

affidavit: 9 statement 10 deposition 11 attestation

affiliate: 4 ally, join, 5 merge, unite 6 attach, branch, relate 7 chapter, connect 9 associate, tie up with 10 subsidiary 11 combine with, group member

affinity: 4 bias 6 accord, liking 7 kinship, rapport 8 relation, sympathy 10 attraction, connection, fellowship, preference, similarity 11 propinquity, resemblance 12 predilection

affirm: 4 aver, avow 5 posit, swear 6 allege, assert, attest, avouch, depose, ratify, uphold, verify 7 declare, profess, testify 8 maintain, validate 9 predicate, pronounce 10 asseverate 11 state as true

affirmative: aye, nod, yea, yep, yes 4 amen, yeah 7 hopeful 8 dogmatic, thumbs up, positive 9 assertive 10 optimistic 11 declarative, predicative

affix: add 4 join, nail, seal 5 annex, pin on, stamp, unite 6 anchor, append, attach, clip to, fasten, staple 7 adhibit, connect, impress, subjoin

afflatus: 6 vision 10 creativity 11 inspiration

afflict: try, vex 4 hurt, pain, rack 5 beset, gripe, grill, harry, wound 6 burden, grieve, harass, pester, plague 7 oppress, torment, trouble 8 distress

afflicted: sad 6 ailing, woeful 7 grieved, doleful, put-upon 8 impaired, stricken, troubled 9 depressed, lacerated, suffering 10 in distress

affliction: rue, woe 4 care, evil, loss, pain 5 cross, grief, trial 6 duress, misery, ordeal, sorrow 7 anguish, disease, illness, scourge, trouble 8 calamity, distress, hardship, sickness 9 adversity, martyrdom 10 heartbreak, misfortune 11 tribulation 12 wretchedness

affluence: 4 flow 6 afflux, influx, riches, wealth 7 fortune 8 opulence 9 abundance, plenitude, profusion, substance 10 prosperity

affluent: fat 4 rich 5 flush, river 6 loaded, stream 7 copious, well off 8 in clover, well-to-do 9 flowing to, tributary 10 in the money, well-heeled 12 on easy street

afford: 4 bear, give, lend, risk 5 grant, in-

cur, spare, stand, yield **6** manage, supply **7** furnish, provide **10** pay the cost
affray: row **4** feud, riot **5** brawl, clash, fight, melee **6** attack, battle, fracas, ruckus, strife, tumult **7** assault, contest, quarrel, scuffle, **9** encounter **10** donnybrook, free-for-all **11** disturbance
affright: awe, cow **5** alarm, daunt, dread, scare, spook **7** startle, terrify **8** frighten **10** intimidate
affront: cut **4** defy, slap, snub **5** abuse, beard **6** insult, jeer at, nettle, offend, slight **7** outrage, provoke, put down **8** disgrace, illtreat, irritate **9** humiliate, indignity, stand up to **10** defamation
afghan: **5** shawl, throw **7** blanket **8** coverlet
Afghan fox: **6** corsac
Afghanistan: *capital:* **5** Kabul
city: **5** Herat, Qalat, Tagab, Tigri **6** Gardez, Ghazni, Kunduz, Maidan **7** Baghlan, Qala Nau **8** Charikar, Kandahar
language: **6** Pashto, Pashtu, Turkic **7** Persian
monetary unit: pul **7** afghani
mountain pass: **6** Khyber, Peiwar
mountain peak: **7** Sikaram **10** Shah Fuladi
mountain range: **8** Koh-i-Baba, Safed Koh **9** Hindu Kush
people: **5** Tajik, Uzbek **6** Hazara, Pathan **7** Pashtun, Sistani **8** Pashtoon
province: **4** Ghor **5** Balkh, Farah, Herat, Logar, Zabul **6** Bamian, Faryab, Ghazni, Kunduz, Paktia, Parwan, Takhar, Wardak
river: **5** Kabul, Kunar **7** Hari Rud, Helmand **8** Amu Darya
aficionado: fan **4** buff **5** freak **7** admirer, devotee **8** follower **10** enthusiast
afield: **4** away **6** abroad, astray, beyond **11** at a distance
afire: **5** aglow, eager **6** ablaze, alight, ardent **7** burning, flaming, ignited
afloat: **4** asea **5** awash **6** adrift, buoyed, natant **7** flooded, rumored **9** operating **10** above water, going about **11** circulating
afoot: **5** about, a pied, astir **6** abroad **7** brewing, walking **8** under way **9** happening **10** in the works, shanks mare
aforesaid: **5** ditto **10** prior named **13** last mentioned
aforethought: **7** planned **10** deliberate **12** premeditated
afraid: rad(Sc.) **4** wary **5** loath, timid **6** aghast, averse, craven, scared **7** alarmed, anxious, fearful **8** cowardly, hesitant, skittish **9** concerned, reluctant, terrified **10** frightened **12** apprehensive, fainthearted **13** pusillanimous
afreet, afrit, afrite: **4** ogre **5** demon, giant, jinni **7** monster
afresh: **4** anew, over **5** again, newly **6** de novo(L.), encore **8** once more **10** repeatedly **11** from scratch
Africa (see also specific countries):
city: **4** Oran **5** Accra, Cairo, Dakar, Lagos, Rabat, Tunis **6** Bangui, Durban, Harare, Ibadan **7** Algiers, Conakry, Mombasa, Nairobi, Tripoli, Yaounde **8** Cape Town, Freetown, Khartoum, Kinshasa, Monrovia, Pretoria **9** Salisbury, Timbuctoo **10** Addis Ababa, Alexandria, Casablanca **11** Brazzaville, Dar es Salaam **12** Johannesburg, Leopoldville **14** Elisabethville
country: **4** Chad, Mali, Togo **5** Benin, Congo, Egypt, Gabon, Ghana, Kenya, Libya, Niger, Sudan, Venda, Zaire **6** Angola, Gambia, Guinea, Malawi, Rwanda, Uganda, Zambia **7** Algeria, Burundi, Comoros, Lesotho, Liberia, Morocco, Nigeria, Senegal, Somalia, Tunisia **8** Botswana, Cameroon, Djibouti, Ethiopia, Tanzania, Transkei, Zimbabwe **9** Cape Verde, Mauritius, Swaziland **10** Ivory Coast, Madagascar, Mauritania, Mozambique, Seychelles, Upper Volta **11** Sierra Leone, South Africa **12** Guinea-Bissau
desert: **6** Libyan, Nubian, Sahara **8** Kalahari
gulf: **4** Aden **5** Gabes, Sidra **6** Guinea
island: **6** Azores, Djerba **7** Comoros, Madeira, Reunion **8** Canaries, St. Helena **9** Ascension, Cape Verde, Mauritius **10** Fernando Po, Madagascar, Seychelles
lake: **4** Chad, Tana **5** Abaya, Kyoga, Mweru, Ngami, Nyasa, Tumba **6** Albert, Chilwa, Dilolo, Kariba, Moeris, Rudolf, Shirwa **7** Leopold, Turkana **8** Victoria **9** Bangweulu **10** Tanganyika
language: Gur, Ibo, Kwa, Twi **4** Akan, Geez, Saho, Taal **5** Bantu, Fanti, Galla, Hausa, Tigre **6** Arabic, Berber, Gurage **7** Amharic, Argobba, Khoisan, Swahili **8** Cushitic, Kingwana, Tigrinya **9** Afrikaans
mountain: **4** Pare **5** Atlas, Elgon, Kenya **7** Cathkin **8** Cameroon **9** Champagne **11** Drakensberg, Kilimanjaro
people: Edo, Ewe, Fon, Ibo, Ijo, Kru, Vai, Vei, Yao **4** Agau, Agni, Akim, Akka, Akra, Alur, Arab, Asha, Bari, Beja, Boer, Boni, Copt, Efik, Egba, Ekoi, Fula, Hutu, Igbo, Kafa, Lozi, Luri, Madi, Moor, Nama, Nuba, Nupe, Qung, Riff, Saho, Sara, Yaka, Zulu **5** Bantu, Bassa, Batwa, Dinka, Fanti, Felup, Galla, Grebo, Gurma, Hausa, Inkra, Kafir, Masai, Mande, Mossi, Pygmy, Rundi, Shluh, Temne, Tutsi **6** Bariba, Basuto, Berber, Damara, Dorobo, Dyerma, Fu-

lani, Hamite, Harari, Herero, Kabyle, Kikuyu, Nilote, Senufo, Somali, Tuareg, Ubangi, Watusi, Yoruba, Zenaga **7** Akwapim, Ashango, Ashanti, Bedouin, Dahoman, Malinke, Sandawe, Songhai, Swahili **8** Hottentot, Mandingo

river: Nun, Omo **4** Athi, Geba, Nile, Ruvu, Tana **5** Benue, Binue, Chari, Chobe, Congo, Niger, Shari, Volta **6** Atbara, Bafing, Gambia, Joliba, Orange, Ruvuma, Sabaki, Ubangi, **7** Calabar, Limpopo, Lualaba, Luapula, Semliki, Senegal, Zambezi **9** Crocodile

Afrikaans: 4 Boer, Taal

Afro: 6 hair-do

aft: 4 back **6** astern, behind **9** posterior, to the rear

opposite of: **4** fore

after: for **4** next, past **5** since, apres(F.) **6** behind, beyond, hinder **8** in back of, rearward **9** following, in spite of **10** concerning, looking for, subsequent

a fashion: **6** in a way, partly **7** somehow **9** to a degree

all: but, yet **5** still **6** though **7** besides, however **9** in any case **10** just the same **11** nonetheless

awhile: **4** anon, soon **5** later

after-dinner: 12 postprandial

aftermath: 5 issue **6** effect, payoff, result, sequel, upshot **7** outcome **8** follow-up **11** consequence

afternoon nap: 6 siesta

afternoon performance: 7 matinee

afterthought: 9 added idea **10** double-take **15** late inspiration

in letter: **10** postscript

afterwards: 4 then **5** later **7** by and by **9** thereupon **11** in the future **12** subsequently

aga, agha: 4 lord **5** chief, title **6** leader **8** official **9** commander

wife: **5** begum

agacella: 8 antelope

Agag's slayer: 6 Samuel

again: bis(F.) **4** anew, more, over **6** afresh, de novo(L.), encore **7** besides, further **8** moreover, once more **12** additionally

against: con **4** anti, from, near, upon **6** beside, facing, next to, versus **7** opposed, vis-a-vis **9** counter to, in spite of **10** concerning, respecting

against the law: 7 illegal, illicit **12** unauthorized

agal: 4 cord, rope

agalloch: 5 garoo **8** calambac **9** aloeswood, calambour, eaglewood

Agamemnon: *avenger:* **7** Orestes

brother: **8** Menelaus

daughter: **7** Electra **9** Iphigenia

father: **6** Atreus

rival: **9** Aegisthus

son: **7** Orestes

wife: **12** Clytemnestra

agape: 4 agog, ajar, open **6** amazed **7** yawning **9** awestruck **10** bewildered, confounded, slack-jawed **11** dumb-founded, open-mouthed

agar, agar-agar: 6 gelose **12** algae extract **13** culture medium

agate: mib, taw **4** ruby **6** achate, marble, quartz **8** type size **10** chalcedony

agave: 4 aloe **5** amole, datil **6** maguey, mescal, pulque **9** amaryllis

fiber: **4** pita **5** istle, sisal

age: eld, eon, era **4** aeon, grow, time **5** cycle, epoch, ripen, years **6** mature, mellow, period, siecle(F.), wither **7** century, develop **8** blue moon, duration, eternity, lifetime, majority **10** generation

geological: See **geology:** *age*

modern: **5** space **6** atomic

of one's age: **5** aetat.(L.)

same: **6** coeval

aged: old **4** ripe **5** anile, dated, hoary, passe **6** feeble, infirm, mature, senile **7** ancient, elderly **8** seasoned, timeworn **9** senescent, up in years, venerable **10** antiquated

ageless: 7 eternal **8** enduring, timeless

agency: 4 firm, hand **5** cause, force, lever, means, proxy **6** bureau, medium, office **7** company, vehicle **9** influence, operation **10** instrument

agenda: 4 card, list **5** slate **6** record, docket **7** program **8** calendar, schedule **10** memorandum

Agenor: *daughter:* **6** Europa

father: **7** Antenor

son: **6** Cadmus

agent: fed, spy **4** doer, g-man, T-man **5** actor, buyer, cause, envoy, force, means, organ, proxy **6** broker, dealer, deputy, factor, medium, seller **7** bailiff, channel, facient, steward **8** assignee, emissary, executor, operator, promoter, salesman **9** go-between **10** commissary, instrument **11** facilitator **12** intermediary **14** representative

appoint: **6** depute **8** deputize

drug: **4** nark

insurance: **11** underwriter

agger: 4 road, tide **5** mound **7** rampart **9** earthwork **10** prominence

agglomerate: 4 heap, lump, mass, pile, **7** cluster **9** aggregate **10** collection **12** volcanic rock

agglutination: 5 union **8** adhesion

aggrandize: 4 lift **5** boost, exalt, raise **7** advance, augment, build up, dignify, elevate, enlarge, ennoble, glorify, magnify, promote **8** increase

aggravate: irk, nag, vex **4** gall, rile **5** anger, annoy, peeve **6** nettle, pester, worsen **7** enhance, enlarge, incense, magnify, provoke **8** aggrieve, heighten, increase, irritate **9** intensify, make acute **10** exacerbate, exasperate **11** fan the flame, get one's goat

aggregate: all, sum **4** bulk, mass **5** add up, bunch, gross, total, unite, whole **6** amount, volume **9** accretion, composite **10** accumulate **11** agglomerate

aggregation: 4 herd **5** flock, group, hoard **7** cluster, company **8** quantity **9** congeries, gathering **10** assemblage, collection, cumulation **11** association, combination

aggression: war **4** raid **6** attack, injury **7** assault, offense **8** invasion **9** intrusion **10** initiative **11** provocation **12** encroachment

aggressive: 4 bold **5** pushy **7** scrappy **8** militant, bellicose **10** pugnacious **11** hard-hitting **12** enterprising

aggressor: 7 invader **8** attacker **9** assailant

aggrieve: try **4** harm, hurt, pain **5** harry, wrong **6** injure, offend **7** afflict, oppress, trouble **8** distress **9** aggravate, persecute

aghast: 6 afraid **7** shocked, stunned **8** appalled **9** horrified, petrified, stupefied, terrified **11** scared stiff

agile: 4 deft, fast, spry, wiry **5** alert, brisk, light, lithe, quick **6** active, adroit, limber, lively, nimble, supple, valant **7** lissome, springy **8** dextrous

agio: 7 premium **10** banking fee

agitate: fan, irk, jar, vex **4** move, rile, rock, roil, seek **5** alarm, churn, drive, harry, rouse, shake, upset **6** debate, excite, foment, harass, incite, rattle, ruffle **7** discuss, disturb, fluster, inflame, perturb, provoke, push for, trouble **8** activate, convulse, disquiet, distress **9** make waves **10** discompose

agitation: 4 flap, stew **5** furor, storm **6** bustle, energy, flurry, tumult, unrest, uproar **7** ferment, flutter, rampage, tempest, turmoil **8** paroxysm, upheaval, violence **9** commotion, confusion **10** excitement, turbulence **11** trepidation
prone to: **9** emotional

Aglaia: 5 Grace

aglet, aiglet: pin, tag **8** metal tip **9** fancy stud **11** shoelace tip

agley: 4 awry **5** askew, wrong **6** aslant

agnate: 4 akin **6** allied **7** connate, kindred **8** paternal

agnomen: 5 alias **7** epithet **8** nickname

agnostic: 7 doubter, infidel, skeptic **8** nescient **10** unbeliever **11** freethinker

agnus dei: 4 hymn, lamb **6** prayer **8** mass part

ago: 4 back, erst, past, syne(Sc.), yore **5** since

agog: 4 avid, keen **5** eager **6** lively **7** all eyes, excited, popeyed **8** bursting, worked up **9** expectant, impatient **10** breathless

agon: 6 debate **7** contest **8** conflict, struggle **11** competition

agonize: 4 bear, rack **6** strain, writhe **10** excruciate

agony: 4 hell, pain **5** dolor, grief, throe, trial **6** misery **7** anguish, despair, torment, torture, travail **8** distress, **9** heartache, nightmare, suffering **11** tribulation

agora: 8 assembly **11** market place

agouti, agouty: 6 rodent
relative: **4** paca **9** guinea pig

Agra tomb: 8 Taj Mahal

agrafe, agraffe: 4 hook **5** clamp, clasp **6** eyelet **9** fastening, sculpture

agrarian: 5 rural **8** agrestic, pastoral **10** campestral **12** agricultural, land reformer

agree: fit **4** jibe, side, suit **5** admit, allow, grant, match, tally, yield, unite **6** accede, accord, assent, comply, concur, square, submit **7** arrange, comport, concede, conform, consent, promise **8** check out, coincide, get along, quadrate **9** acquiesce, be willing, congruous, cooperate, harmonize, reconcile **10** correspond, homologate

agreeable: 4 nice **5** ready, sweet **7** amiable, welcome, willing **8** amenable, charming, pleasant, pleasing, sociable, suitable **9** appealing, compliant, consonant **10** acceptable, compatible, convenient **11** consentient
render: **7** dulcify

agreement: nod **4** bond, deal, pact **5** lease **6** treaty, unison **7** bargain, compact, consent, entente, harmony, rapport **8** contract, covenant **9** concordat, indenture **10** accordance **11** arrangement, concordance, concurrence **13** understanding
in opinion: **9** consensus, unanimity
secret: **5** covin **9** collusion **10** conspiracy
written: **6** cartel **8** contract

agremens, agrements: 6 graces **8** niceties **9** amenities

agrestic: 5 rural **6** rustic **7** bucolic **10** unpolished

agriculture: 7 farming, tillage **8** agronomy **9** husbandry
area: **11** breadbasket
college student: **5** aggie
establishment: **4** farm **5** grove, ranch **7** orchard **8** vineyard
god: **4** Nabu, Nebo, Thor **6** Faunus,

Tammuz **8** Amaethon
goddess: Ops **5** Ceres **7** Demeter
machine: **4** disk, plow **5** baler, drill, mower **6** binder, harrow, header, reaper, seeder, tedder **7** combine, tractor **8** thrasher, thresher **9** separator **10** cultivator **11** caterpillar
pert to: **7** georgic **8** geoponic
science: **8** agrology **11** arviculture
agriculturist: 6 farmer, grower **7** planter, rancher **10** husbandman, orchardist
Agrippina: *brother:* **8** Caligula
husband: **8** Claudius
son: **4** Nero
aground: 6 ashore **7** beached **8** stranded
agrypnia: 8 insomnia **13** sleeplessness
agua: 4 toad
aguacate: 7 avocado
ague: 5 chill, fever **7** malaria
ague tree: 9 sassafras
agueweed: 7 boneset, comfrey, gentian **10** eupatorium
Ahab: *daughter* **7** Athalia **8** Athaliah
father: **4** Omri
wife: **7** Jezebel
Ahasuerus: *minister:* **5** Haman
wife: **6** Vashti
Ahaz: *son:* **8** Hezekiah
wife: Abi
Ahaziah's sister: 9 Jehosheba **11** Jehosobeath
ahead: 4 fore **5** early **6** before, onward **7** betimes, forward, in front, leading, one up on **8** advanced, anterior **9** in the lead, preceding **10** beforehand
Ahinoam: *husband:* **4** Saul **5** David
son: **5** Ammon
Aholibamah's husband: 4 Esau
Ahriman's angel: div **4** deev, deva
ahu: 5 mound **7** gazelle **8** boundary, memorial **9** stone heap
ahuehuete: 5 cedar **6** sabino **7** cypress
ai: 5 sloth **8** edentate
aid: 4 abet, back, help **5** allay, boost, coach, favor, grant, serve, treat **6** assist, relief, remedy, rescue, succor, uphold **7** advance, be of use, forward, further, subsidy, support **8** befriend **9** alleviate, auxiliary, give a hand **10** facilitate, go to bat for **11** collaborate
Aida: *composer:* **5** Verdi
father: **8** Amonasro
lover: **7** Radames
rival: **7** Amneris
aide: 6 deputy, second **7** officer, orderly **8** adjutant **9** assistant, attendant, man Friday **11** subordinate
aigrette: 5 egret, heron, plume, spray **8** feathers
ail: 4 ache, fail, pain **6** affect, bother, falter, suffer **7** decline, feel ill **8** take

sick **10** feel poorly
ailment (see also **disease**): **6** malady **7** disease, illness **8** disorder, sickness, weakness **9** affection, complaint, infirmity **10** affliction, disability **13** indisposition
aim: end, try **4** bent, goal, head, plan **5** essay, level, point, sight, train **6** aspire, design, direct, intend, intent, scheme, strive, target **7** address, attempt, go after, propose, purpose, resolve **8** ambition, consider, endeavor, estimate, shoot for, zero in on **9** calculate, intention, objective **11** destination
aimless: 4 idle **5** blind **6** chance, random **7** erratic **8** drifting **9** desultory, haphazard, hit-or-miss, senseless **10** undirected **11** to no purpose
aimlessness: 8 flanerie
aine: 5 elder **6** senior
air: sky **4** aria, aura, lilt, mien, pose, song, tell, tune, vent **5** ether, ozone, style, voice **6** aerate, aerify, allure, aspect, broach, cachet, expose, manner, melody, regard, vanity, welkin **7** bearing, display, exhibit, publish **8** attitude, behavior, carriage, demeanor, proclaim **9** broadcast, semblance **10** appearance, atmosphere, deportment **11** affectation, haughtiness
containing: **9** pneumatic
current: **4** wind **5** draft **6** breeze **7** draught
downward motion (pert. to): **9** katabatic
element: **4** neon **5** argon, xenon **6** helium, oxygen **7** krypton **8** nitrogen
up in the: **5** aloft, angry **8** agitated **9** unsettled **10** in suspense, not decided
overcast: **4** haze, smog **5** smaze **7** pea soup **10** cloudiness
air plant: 8 epiphyte
air pressure: 5 baric
air propeller: fan
air spirit: 5 Ariel, sylph
aircraft (see also **spacecraft**): **4** kite **5** blimp, plane **6** copter, glider **7** balloon, chopper **8** aerostat, airplane, autogyro, zeppelin **9** dirigible **10** helicopter
carrier: **7** flattop
group: **4** wing **5** fleet **6** flight **10** escadrille
fleet formation: **7** echelon
manufacturer: **4** Lear, Vega **5** Astra, Piper **6** Bendix, Boeing, Cessna, Hughes, United, Vultee, Wright **7** Convair, Curtiss, Douglas, Grumman, Tupolev **8** Ilyushin, Lockheed, Northrop, Republic **9** McDonnell **11** DeHavilland
motorless: **6** glider
part: fin **4** keel, tail, wing **5** cabin **6** cabane **7** aileron, cockpit, nacelle **8**

fusilage **9** empennage
pilotless: **5** drone
route: **6** skyway
route marker: **5** pylon
shelter: **6** hangar
vapor: **8** contrail
airing: 4 walk **6** pasear **8** exposure
airplane: jet, MIG, SST **4** gyro, zero **5**
avion(F., Sp.), liner **6** bomber, copter,
glider **7** clipper, fighter **9** transport
battle: **8** dogfight
dropper of A-bomb: **8** Enola Gay
inventor: **6** Wright
maneuver: dip **4** buzz, dive, loop, roll **8**
hedgehop, nosedive, sideslip, tailspin
10 barrel roll
operator: **5** flier, flyer, pilot **7** aviator **8**
aeronaut
Supersonic transport: **8** Concorde
airport: 5 drome **8** airdrome, airfield **9**
aerodrome
area: **5** apron, tower **6** runway **7** taxiway
Airport terminal:
Amsterdam: **8** Schiphol
Berlin: **5** Gatow, Tegel **9** Tempelhof
Boston: **5** Logan
Chicago: **5** O'Hare
Copenhagen: **7** Kastrup
Denver: **9** Stapleton
Dublin: **7** Shannon
London: **7** Croydon, Gatwick **8** Heathrow
Newfoundland: **6** Gander
New York: JFK **7** Kennedy **9** La Guardia
Paris: **4** Orly **8** De Gaulle **9** Le Bourget
Rome: **7** Da Vinci **8** Ciampino **9** Fiumicino
Tokyo: **6** Atsugi, Narita
Scotland: **9** Prestwick
Washington: **6** Dulles **8** National
airs: 4 show **7** hauteur **8** pretense **9** arrogance **10** uppishness, affectation
airtight: 6 sealed **8** hermetic **9** foolproof
12 impenetrable, invulnerable
airy: gay **4** cool, rare, thin **5** empty, light,
lofty, merry **6** aerial, breezy, jaunty, jocund, lively **7** haughty **8** affected, animated, debonair, delicate, ethereal, flippant, graceful, trifling, volatile **9**
sprightly, visionary, vivacious **11** atmospheric **13** insubstantial, unsubstantial
aisle: way **4** lane, path, walk **5** alley **7** passage **8** corridor **10** passageway
ait: oat(Sc.) **4** eyot, holm, isle **5** islet
ajar: 4 open **10** discordant
Ajax's father: 7 Telamon
ajonjoli: 6 sesame
akia: 5 shrub **6** poison
akimbo: 4 bent **6** angled **7** crooked
akin: sib **4** near **5** alike, close **6** agnate,
allied **7** cognate, connate, related, simi-

lar **9** analogous **10** comparable, correlated **11** consanguine
aku: 6 bonito **10** victorfish
akule: 4 fish, scad **7** goggler
ala: 4 axil, drum, wing **6** axilla, recess
Alabama: *capital:* **10** Montgomery
city: Opp **4** Elba, Troy **5** Ozark, Piper,
Selma **6** Dothan, Jasper, Mobile **7** Cullman, Gadsden, Opelika **8** Anniston **10**
Birmingham, Huntsville, Tuscaloosa
county: Lee **4** Bibb, Clay, Dale, Hale,
Pike **5** Coosa, Lamar **6** Blount, Elmore,
Etowah, Greene, Shelby, Sumter **7** Autauga, Chilton, Colbert, Marengo, Pickens, Winston **8** Escambia
explorer: **6** De Soto
Indian tribe: **5** Creek **6** Tohome **7** Choctaw, Koasati
motto: **21** We dare defend our rights
mountain: **6** Cheaha **7** Lookout, Raccoon
river: Pea **5** Coosa **6** Cahaba, Mobile,
Sipsey, Tensaw **7** Alabama, Conecuh,
Sepulga **9** Tennessee, Tombigbee
state bird: **12** yellowhammer
state fish: **6** tarpon
state flower: **8** camellia
state nickname: **12** Heart of Dixie
state tree: **4** pine
alabaster: 6 gypsum **7** calcite **9** aragonite
alacrity: 4 zest **5** haste, speed **8** celerity,
dispatch, rapidity **9** briskness, eagerness, readiness **10** enthusiasm, promptness **11** willingness
Aladdin's lamp spirits: 4 jinn **5** genni
a la diable: 7 deviled **8** seasoned
alameda: 4 mall, walk **9** promenade
Alamo: 4 fort **5** aspen **6** battle, poplar,
shrine **7** mission **10** cottonwood
hero: **5** Bowie **8** Crockett
a la mode: 4 chic **7** stylish **11** fashionable
alant: 10 sneezeweed
alar: 6 pteric, winged **8** axillary, winglike
10 wing-shaped
opposite of: **7** apteral
alarm: din, SOS **4** bell, fear **5** alert, clock,
noise, panic, scare, siren, upset **6** alarum, appall, buzzer, dismay, excite, outcry, signal, tocsin **7** disturb, startle,
warning **8** frighten, surprise **9** commotion **11** disturbance, trepidation **13**
consternation
alarmist: 9 Cassandra, pessimist, worrywart **11** scaremonger **13** prophet of
doom
alas: ach, woe **5** alack **6** ochone(Sc.) **8**
welladay, wellaway **9** alackaday **12** interjection
Alaska: *borough:* **5** Kenai, Sitka **6**
Haines, Juneau, Kodiak **10** Bristol
Bay, North Slope
capital: **6** Juneau
city: Eek **4** Nome **5** Sitka **6** Barrow,

Bethel, Chevak, Kodiak, Naknek **9** Anchorage, Fairbanks, Ketchikan
discovered by: **11** Vitus Bering
glacier: **4** Muir **8** Columbia
highway: **5** Alcan
island: **4** Adak, Atka, Attu **5** Kiska, Umnak **6** Agattu, Kodiak, Shuyak **7** Afognak, Baronof, Diomede, Nunivak
island group: Fox, Rat **4** Near **7** Fur Seal **8** Aleutian, Pribilof **9** Alexander, Andreanof
mountain peak: **4** Bona **5** Spurr **6** Katmai **7** Foraker, St. Elias **8** McKinley **9** Michelson
mountain range: **5** Baird **6** Brooks, De Long **7** Chugach **8** Wrangell
native: Auk **4** Dene, Tena **5** Aleut, Inuit **6** Ahtena, Eskimo, Innuit **7** Ingalik, Khotana, Koyukon, Tlingit
peninsula: **5** Kenai **6** Seward
purchase (1867): **12** "Seward's Folly"
river: **5** Chena, Kobuk, Yukon **6** Copper, Innoko, Noatak, Tanana **7** Koyukuk, Susitna **9** Kuskokwim, Matanuska, Porcupine
sea: **6** Bering **7** Chukchi
state bird: **9** ptarmigan
state fish: **6** salmon
state flower: **11** forget-me-not
state motto: **16** North to the future
state tree: **6** spruce
unofficial nickname: **12** Last Frontier
volcano: **5** Kukak **6** Griggs, Mageik, Seguam **7** Redoubt, Torbert
alate: ant **5** aphid **6** insect, winged
alb, albe: **7** camisia **8** vestment
albacore: **4** tuna **5** tunny **6** germon
Albania: *capital:* **6** Tirana
city: **5** Berat, Vlore **6** Avlona, Durres, Valona **7** Chimara, Coritza, Durazzo, Elbasan, Koritza, Prevesa, Scutari **8** Tepeleni
dialect: Geg **4** Cham, Gheg, Tosc, Tosk **7** Ghegish, Toskish
former king: Zog
lake: **5** Ohrid **6** Prespa **7** Scutari
monetary unit: lek **6** qintar
mountain: **4** Alps **6** Pindus
river: **4** Arta, Drin **5** Buene, Seman **6** Vijose
soldier: **7** palikar
albatross: **4** bird **5** nelly **6** fabric, gooney **9** hindrance, mallemuck **11** encumbrance
albeit: but, tho **5** altho, while **6** though **8** although **10** for all that **15** notwithstanding
Alberta: *capital:* **8** Edmonton
city: **4** Olds **5** Banff, Edson **7** Calgary **10** Lethbridge **11** Medicine Hat
lake: **4** Cold **5** Slave **6** Legend, Louise, Pigeon **8** Peerless

mountain peak: **5** Trout **6** Robson **7** Wallace **8** Columbia **10** Eisenhower
mountain range: **7** Rockies
province of: **6** Canada
provincial bird: **9** horned owl
provincial flower: **8** wild rose
resort: **5** Banff **6** Jasper **10** Lake Louise
river: Bow **4** Milk **5** Peace, Smoky **6** Battle, Oldman, Wapiti **7** Red Deer, Wabasca **9** Athabasca
Albion: **6** Anglia **7** England
albula: **5** chiro **8** bonefish
album: ana **4** book **6** record **8** register **9** anthology, scrapbook **10** collection
albumen 8 egg white
albuminoid: **7** elastin, keratin, protein **8** collagen
alburnum: **7** sapwood
alcazar: **6** castle, palace **8** fortress
Alcestis: *father:* **6** Pelias
husband: **7** Admetus
rescuer: **8** Heracles, Hercules
alchemy: art **5** magic **7** sorcery **11** thaumaturgy **13** transmutation
god: **6** Hermes
Alcidice: *husband:* **9** Salmoneus
daughter: **4** Tyro
Alcinous: *daughter:* **8** Nausicaa
wife: **5** Arete
Alcmaeon: *father:* **10** Amphiaraus
wife: **10** Callirrhoe
Alcmene's husband: **10** Amphitryon
alcohol: **5** booze, ethyl, vinyl **6** liquor, methyl **7** ethanol, spirits **8** methanol
aromatic: **8** farnesol, geraniol, linalool
crystalline: **6** guaiol, **7** menthol, talitol **8** mannitol
liquid: **5** allyl, butyl **6** pentyl **7** butanol **8** glycerol
radical: **4** amyl
solid: **5** cetyl **6** sterol **11** cholesterol
standard: **5** proof
alcoholic: **6** addict **9** spiritous **11** dipsomaniac **12** intoxicating
alcoholic drink: ale, gin, rum **4** beer, grog, wine **5** julep, lager, negus, toddy, vodka **6** brandy, liquor, whisky **7** liqueur, whiskey **8** cocktail, highball, vermouth
Alcott heroine: Amy, Meg **4** Beth
alcove: bay **4** nook **5** arbor, bower, niche, oriel **6** cranny, gazebo, recess **7** cubicle, dinette, pergola **8** alhacena(Sp.) **11** compartment
al dente: **13** firm to the bite, not over-cooked
alder: arn(Sc.) **4** tree **5** shrub
genus: **5** alnus
ale: mum **4** beer, bock, brew **5** lager, nappy(Sc.), stout **6** porter, stingo **8** beverage
mixed with sweetener: **4** flip **7** bragget

ale mug: 4 toby 5 stein
Alea: 6 Athena
alee: 5 ahead 7 leeward
opposite of: 5 stoss 8 windward
alehouse: bar, pub 4 cafe 6 bistro, saloon, tavern 7 taproom 8 grogshop 10 beer garden 11 rathskeller
alembic: 5 still 6 retort, vessel 7 refiner 9 distiller
Alençon product: 4 lace
alert: 4 gleg(Sc.), warn, wary 5 agile, alarm, alive, awake, brisk, eager, ready, sharp, siren 6 active, bright, lively, nimble, tocsin 7 wakeful 8 vigilant, watchful 9 observant, wide-awake 11 circumspect
alette: 4 wing 8 abutment
Aleutian Island: 4 Adak, Atka, Attu 5 Amlia, Kiska, Umnak 6 Akutan, Amukta, Kodiak, Seguam 7 Kagamil 8 Amchitka, Unalaska
group: Fox, Rat 4 Near 9 Andreanof
alewife: 4 fish 6 allice 7 herring, pompano, walleye
Alexander: *birthplace:* 5 Pella
father: 6 Philip
horse: 10 Bucephalus
kingdom: 9 Macedonia
mistress: 8 Campaspe
tutor: 9 Aristotle
victory: 4 Gaza, Tyre 5 Egypt, Issus 6 Arbela, Persia 7 Babylon
Alexandria: *bishop:* 10 Athanasius
magistrate: 8 alabarch
patriarch: 4 papa
theologian: 5 Arius
Alexandria Quartet: *author:* 7 Durrell
books: 4 Clea 7 Justine 9 Balthazar 10 Mountolive
narrator: 6 Darley
alfalfa: hay 6 fodder, lucern 7 lucerne
alforja: bag 5 pouch 6 wallet 9 saddlebag
alga: 4 kelp, nori 6 desmid, diatom, lichen 7 seaweed 8 plankton, rockweed 9 stonewort
genus: 5 dasya 6 alaria, nostoc, padina
study: 8 algology
algarroba: 5 carob 8 mesquite, raintree
Algeria: *capital:* 7 Algiers
city: 4 Oran 5 Blida, Medea, Setif 6 Biskra 7 Tlemcen 11 Constantine
department: 4 Oran 5 Alger, Batna, Oasis, Saida, Setif 6 Annaba, Saoura, Tiaret 7 Al Asnam 11 Constantine
desert: 6 Sahara
known to Romans as: 7 Numidia
measure: pik 5 rebis, tarri 6 termin
monetary unit: 5 dinar 7 centime
mountain: 5 Atlas
people: 5 Arabs 7 Berbers, Kabyles
river: 7 Cheliff, Sheliff

seaport: 4 Oran 6 Annaba 7 Algiers,
weight: 4 rotl
algid: 4 cold, cool 6 chilly, clammy
Alhambra: 6 palace 7 citadel
site: 7 Granada
Ali: *descendant:* 7 fatimid 8 fatimite
wife: 6 Fatima
Ali Baba: *brother:* 6 Cassim
password: 6 sesame
slave: 8 Morgiana 10 woodcutter
alias: AKA 7 epithet, pen name 9 pseudonym 10 nom de plume 11 assumed name
alibi: 4 plea 6 excuse 7 pretext 10 offer an out
Alice in Wonderland: *author:* 7 Carroll
cat of Alice: 5 Dinah
character: 5 Queen 6 Walrus 7 Duchess 8 Dormouse 9 Carpenter, Mad Hatter, March Hare 11 Cheshire cat, White Rabbit
alien: 5 fremd 6 exotic 7 foreign, hostile, invader, opposed, strange 8 outsider, stranger 9 different, extrinsic, foreigner, immigrant, outlander, unrelated
alienate: 4 part, wean 6 convey, devest 8 disunite, estrange, separate, transfer 9 disaffect 10 cause a rift
alienist: 6 shrink 12 psychiatrist
aliform: 8 winglike 10 wing-shaped
alight: sit 4 land, rest 5 aglow, lodge, perch, roost 6 arrive, bright, settle 7 deplane, descend, lighted, radiant 8 dismount 9 disembark, touch down
align, aline: 4 true 5 array, level 6 adjust, even up 7 marshal 8 regulate 10 straighten, join up with
alike: 4 akin, same 5 equal, twins 7 similar, uniform 8 of a piece 9 congruent, duplicate, identical 10 comparable
aliment: pap 4 food 6 viands 7 pabulum, rations 9 nutriment, substance 10 sustenance 11 nourishment
alimony: 4 keep 9 allowance 10 settlement 11 maintenance 12 support money
alive: 4 keen, spry, vive(F.) 5 alert, astir, aware, brisk, quick, vital, vivid 6 active, extant, living 7 dynamic, vibrant 8 animated, existent, swarming 9 breathing, sprightly, unexpired 10 not out of it, unforgotten
alkali: lye, reh 4 kali, salt, soda, usar
volatile: 7 ammonia
alkaline: *remedy:* 7 antacid
salt: 5 borax
alkaloid: 6 conine, heroin, eserin 7 caffein, cocaine, codeine 7 quinine 8 atropine, caffeine, morphine 10 strychnine
all: sum 5 gross, quite, total, whole 6 entire, in toto, solely, wholly 7 plenary 8

entirely, everyone, totality **9** aggregate, everybody **10** altogether, completely, everything, thoroughly **11** exclusively

all-fired: 7 extreme **9** excessive **10** inordinate

all in: 4 beat **5** tired, weary **6** bushed, pooped **7** worn out **9** exhausted

all-knowing: 10 omniscient

all out: 7 utterly **9** full scale **10** unreserved

all over: 4 done **5** ended **8** finished **9** universal **10** everywhere, throughout

all right: yes **4** okay **6** agreed **9** hunky-dory

all there: 4 sane

allay: 4 calm, cool, ease, lull **5** abate, quell, quiet, still **6** pacify, reduce, soften, soothe, temper **7** appease, assuage, comfort, compose, lighten, mollify, relieve **8** mitigate, palliate **9** alleviate

allege: 4 aver, avow, cite **5** claim, offer, plead, state **6** affirm, assert, charge **7** advance, ascribe, declare, present, profess **8** maintain **9** attribute **10** asseverate

allegiance: tie **4** duty **5** honor **6** fealty, homage **7** loyalty, tribute **8** devotion, fidelity **9** constancy, obedience **10** obligation

violation of: **7** treason **9** defection

allegory: 4 myth, tale **5** fable, story **7** parable **8** apologue

alleviate: aid **4** ease, help **5** abate, allay, salve, slake **6** lenify, lessen, soften **7** assuage, lighten, relieve **8** diminish, mitigate, moderate, palliate

alley: via, way **4** lane, mall, path, walk **5** byway **6** vennel(Sc.) **7** passage

back: **4** slum

blind: **7** dead end **8** cul-de-sac

alliance: 4 pact **5** union **6** accord, fusion, league, treaty **7** compact, entente, society **8** affinity, agnation, covenant **9** coalition **10** federation, fellowship **11** affiliation, association, confederacy, partnership

allice, allis: 4 shad

allied: 4 akin **6** agnate, in with, joined, linked, united **7** cognate, connate, germane, kindred, related, similar **9** analogous, connected

alligator: 6 caiman, cayman, jacare, yacare **9** crocodile

alligator pear: 7 avocado **8** aguacate

allium: 4 leek **5** onion **6** chives, garlic

allmouth: 6 angler

allocate: 5 allot, allow, award, share **6** assign **7** earmark, mete out **8** set aside **9** apportion **10** distribute

allonge: 5 rider **12** ballet stance

allot: tag **4** give **5** award, grant, share **6**

accord, assign, bestow, design, ordain, ration **7** deal out, dole out, let have, present, pro-rate, reserve, specify **8** allocate **9** apportion, parcel out, prescribe **10** distribute

allow let **4** bear, lend **5** admit, defer, grant, stand, yield **6** accept, assign, endure, permit, suffer **7** approve, concede, confess, own up to, suppose **8** consider, sanction, tolerate **9** authorize, give leave **11** acknowledge

allowance: fee **4** agio, edge, gift, odds, part **5** leave, quota, share **6** bounty, margin, salary **7** aliment, alimony, measure, pension, portion, stipend **8** discount, handicap, quantity, sanction **9** advantage, allotment, deduction, reduction, tolerance **10** concession, permission

short: **6** ration **9** scrimping

traveling: **7** mileage

weight: **4** tare, tret **7** scalage

alloy: mix **4** fuse **5** blend **7** mixture **8** compound **9** composite **10** adulterate, amalgamate

carbon and iron: **5** steel

Chinese: **7** paktong **8** packtong

copper and aluminum: **9** duralumin

copper, iron and zinc: **4** aich **7** rheotan

copper and tin: **6** bronze, oreide, ormolu, oroide, pewter

copper and zinc: **5** brass **6** tombac **8** arsedine

costume jewelry: **4** aich **6** oreide, ormolu, oroide, tombac **8** arsedine

fusible: **6** solder

gold and silver: **4** asem **8** electrum

gold-like: **4** aich **6** oreide, ormolu, oroide **8** arsedine

heat resistant: **6** cermet **7** ceramal

Japanese: **5** mokum

lead and tin: **5** calin, terne **6** pewter

mercurial: **7** amalgam

nickel and silver: **8** alfenide

nickel and iron: **7** elinvar

nonferrous: **4** tula

pewter-like: **5** bidri

silver with copper or tin: **6** billon

sulfuric: **6** niello

All's Well That Ends Well character: 5 Diana, Lafeu **7** Bertram

allspice tree: 7 pimento

allude to: 5 imply, infer **6** advert, hint at, relate **7** bring up, connote, mention, refer to, suggest, touch on **8** indicate, intimate, point out **9** insinuate

allure: air, woo **4** bait, draw, lead, lure, move, sway **5** angle, bribe, charm, court, decoy, snare, tempt **6** entice, entrap, glamor, induce, seduce **7** attract, beguile, ensnare **8** blandish, inveigle, persuade **9** captivate, fascinate, influence

allusion: 4 hint **7** mention **8** innuendo, instance **9** quotation, reference **10** intimation

alluvial: *clay:* **5** adobe

deposit: mud **4** sand, silt, wash **5** delta, drift, geest **6** gravel, placer

fan: **5** delta

alluvion: 4 flow, wash **5** flood **10** inundation

ally: pal **4** aide, join **5** unite **6** backer, friend, helper **7** connect, partner **8** adherent, relate to **9** affiliate, assistant, associate, auxiliary, colleague, supporter, take sides **10** accomplice **11** confederate

almanac: 4 ordo **8** calendar, yearbook **9** chronicle, ephemeris

almandine: 6 spinel, garnet

almighty: 5 great **7** extreme **8** powerful, puissant **10** omnipotent **12** irresistible

Almighty: God **7** Creator

almond: nut **5** badam **6** kanari

paste: **8** marzipan

pert. to: **10** amygdaline

served with: **8** amandine

syrup: **6** orgeat

almost: 4 nigh **5** about, close **6** all but, feckly(Sc.), nearly **8** as good as, not quite **9** virtually **13** approximately

alms: 4 dole, gift **6** aumous(Sc.) **7** charity, handout **8** donation, offering, pittance **11** benefaction **12** contribution

chest: **4** arca **7** poor box

dispenser: **7** almoner, almsman **11** eleemosynar

almsman: 6 beggar, pauper

almuce: 4 hood **6** tippet **9** headdress

aloe: 4 pita **5** agave **6** maguey

compound: **5** aloin

extract: **5** orcin **7** orcinol

powder: **5** picra

aloes: 5 tonic **8** agalloch **10** agallochum

aloft: 4 high **5** above **6** upward **7** skyward **8** airborne, in the air, overhead

aloha: 4 love **5** hello **7** goodbye **8** farewell, greeting, kindness **9** affection **10** salutation

alone: 4 bare, lorn, only, sole, solo **5** aloof, apart, solus **6** single, unique **8** desolate, detached, isolated, separate, solitary **9** matchless **11** exclusively **12** incomparable, unparalleled **13** unaccompanied

along: 4 near, with **5** ahead **6** as well, beside, onward **7** forward, in a line **8** advanced, on the way, together **10** lengthwise **11** approaching **12** in accord with

alongside: 6 beside, next to **7** abreast, against, close by **8** parallel

Alonso's son: 9 Ferdinand

aloof: shy **4** cold, cool **5** alone, apart,

proud **6** frosty, remote, silent **7** social, distant, removed **8** detached, reserved, reticent **10** withdrawn **11** at a distance, indifferent, standoffish

alopecia: 8 baldness **11** phalacrosis

alopecoid: 7 foxlike, vulpine

alouatte: 6 monkey

aloud: 4 oral **5** vocal **7** audible

alp: 4 peak **5** mount **8** mountain

alpaca: 4 paco, wool **5** cloth

habitat: **4** Peru **5** Andes **7** Bolivia

relative of: **5** llama **7** guanaco

alpha: 5 chief, first, start **11** Greek letter

and omega: all **5** whole **6** entire **15** beginning and end

alphabet (see also **Arabic, Greek, Hebrew**): **4** ABC's **5** order **6** basics, primer **7** letters **9** rudiments **10** abecedarium

character: **4** ogam, ogum, rune **5** ogham

pert. to: **11** abecedarian

Runic: **7** futharc, futhork

alpha rhythm: 9 brain wave

Alpine: *antelope:* **7** chamois

climber: **10** alpestrian

dance: **5** gavot

dress: **6** dirndl

dwelling: **6** chalet

goat: **4** ibex **8** steinbok

herdsman: **4** senn

pass: col **7** Brenner, Splugen **9** St. Bernard

plant: **9** edelweiss

primrose: **8** auricula

wind: **4** bise, bora **5** foehn

Alps: *Austrian:* **5** Tirol, Tyrol

division of: **5** Noric, Savoy **7** Bernese, Pennine **8** Maritime **9** Lepontine

Italian: **9** Dolomites

peak: **4** Rosa **5** Blanc, Eiger, Leone **7** Bernina **8** Jungfrau **10** Matterhorn

tunnel: **5** Blanc, Cenis **7** Arlberg, Simplon **10** St. Gotthard

Yugoslav: **6** Julian **7** Dinaric

already: now **6** before **7** earlier **8** even then, formerly **9** previously **10** beforehand, by this time

also: and, too, yet **4** erst, more, plus **5** again, ditto **6** as well **7** besides, further **8** likewise, moreover **9** similarly **10** in addition

also-ran: dud **5** loser **7** failure, washout

altar: 5 table **6** shrine **7** chantry **9** sanctuary

area: **4** apse **7** chancel

boy: **6** server **7** acolyte

cloth: **4** pall **7** frontal

curtain: **6** riddel, riddle

enclosure: **4** bema

hanging: **6** dorsal, dossal, dossel

ledge: **6** gradin **7** retable

platform: **8** predella

portable: **10** superaltar
screen: **7** reredos
top: **5** mensa
vessel: pyx **5** cruet, paten **7** chalice, pisci-na **8** ciborium **10** monstrance
alter: 4 geld, redo, spay, turn, vary, veer **5** adapt, amend, emend, reset, shift **6** adjust, change, modify, mutate, neuter, revamp, revise, temper **7** convert **9** transform
alter ego: 5 agent **6** friend **8** henchman **9** confidant, other self
altercation: row **4** spat, tiff **5** brawl, fight, scrap, set-to **6** strife, tussle **7** dispute, quarrel, wrangle **8** argument, squabble **10** contention, falling out **11** controversy
alternate: sub **4** else, sway, vary **5** other, proxy, recur, shift **6** change, deputy, rotate, seesaw **8** intermit **9** oscillate, take turns **11** interchange, reciprocate
alternative: 6 choice, either, option, way out **8** elective, loophole **10** preference
word introducing: **7** whether
Althaea's husband: 6 Oeneus
although: 5 while **6** albeit **7** despite, whereas **11** granted that **15** notwithstanding
altitude: 6 height **7** ceiling **9** elevation, loftiness
measuring device: **8** orometer **9** altimeter
altitude sickness: 7 soroche
alto: 4 part **6** singer **7** althorn, saxhorn **8** vocalist
altogether: 5 quite **6** in toto, wholly **7** en masse, totally, utterly **8** all in all, entirely **10** by and large, completely, thoroughly **12** collectively
in the: **4** bare, nude **5** naked **8** stripped **9** au naturel
altruism: 7 charity **10** generosity **11** benevolence **12** philanthropy **13** unselfishness
alum: 7 styptic **10** astringent
rock: **7** alunite
alumina: 4 clay **5** argil **8** corundum
aluminum: *calcium silicate:* **7** epidote
discoverers: **4** Davy **6** Wohler
hydrousphosphate: **9** wavellite
oxide: **7** alumina
sulfate: **4** alum
alumnus: 4 grad **5** pupil **8** graduate
alveolate: 6 pitted **11** honeycombed, having holes
always: e'er **4** ever **6** semper(L.) **7** forever, for good **8** evermore **9** eternally, uniformly **10** constantly, habitually, invariably **11** continually, perpetually, unceasingly **12** till doomsday **13** everlastingly
ama: 5 amula **9** candlenut
Amadis' beloved: 6 Oriana

amadou: 4 fuse, punk **6** tinder **9** touchwood
amah: 5 nurse **7** servant
amain: 7 greatly **8** forcibly, speedily **9** violently **10** vigorously **11** exceedingly
Amalekite king: 4 Agag
amalgamate: mix **4** fuse, join **5** alloy, blend, merge, unite **6** mingle **7** combine **8** coalesce, compound **11** consolidate
Amaltheia: 4 goat
horn: **10** cornucopia
nursling: **4** Zeus
amanita: 6 agaric, fungus
amanuensis: 6 penman, scribe, typist **8** recorder **9** scrivener, secretary **11** transcriber **12** stenographer
Amasa's father: 6 Jether
amass: 4 save **5** gross, hoard, stack, store **6** gather, heap up, pile up **7** collect, compile **8** assemble **9** stockpile **10** accumulate
amateur: ham **4** tiro, tyro **6** novice, votary **7** admirer, dabbler, devotee, fancier **8** beginner, neophyte **9** greenhorn **10** dilettante, aficionado **15** nonprofessional
Amati: 6 violin **11** violin maker
birthplace: **7** Cremona
amative: 6 ardent, erotic, loving **7** amorous **10** passionate
amaze: awe **4** stun **7** astound, stagger, stupefy **8** astonish, bowl over, confound, surprise **9** dumbfound, overwhelm **11** flabbergast
amazement: 6 wonder **8** unbelief **12** astonishment **13** consternation
Amazon: 5 river **12** woman warrior
discoverer: **6** Pinzon
early explorer: **8** Orellana, Teixeira
estuary: **4** Para
headstream: **7** Maranon
queen: **9** Hippolyta **12** Penthesileia
tributary: Ica **4** Napo, Paru **5** Jurua, Jutai, Negro, Xingu
amazon: ant **5** harpy, shrew, vixen, **6** parrot, virago **11** hummingbird
ambari: 4 hemp **5** fiber **7** cordage
ambassador: 5 agent, envoy **6** deputy, legate, nuncio **8** diplomat, emissary, minister **9** messenger **12** intermediary **14** representative **15** plenipotentiary
pert. to: **8** legatine
amber: 5 resin **6** yellow **8** amberoid
amberfish: 6 kahala **10** yellowtail
ambiance, ambience: 6 milieu **10** atmosphere **11** environment **12** surroundings
ambiguity: 7 duality, evasion, paradox **9** duplexity, duplicity, looseness, obscurity **10** hesitation **12** doubtfulness **13** inconsistency
ambiguous: 4 dark **5** vague **6** unsure **7**

cryptic, dubious, unclear **8** doubtful **9** equivocal, uncertain, unsettled **10** indefinite, indistinct **11** problematic **12** questionable **13** indeterminate

ambit: 5 limit, scope, space **6** bounds, extent, sphere **7** circuit, compass **8** boundary, precinct **13** circumference

ambition: aim **4** goal, hope, mark, wish **5** dream, drive **6** desire **7** purpose **9** intention, objective **10** aspiration

ambitious: 4 avid, bold, keen **5** eager, showy **7** emulous **8** aspiring **9** energetic, on the make **10** aggressive **11** power-hungry **12** enterprising

amble: 5 mosey **6** dawdle, stroll **7** meander, saunter **9** poke along

ambo: 4 desk **6** pulpit

Amboina button: 4 yaws

ambrosia: 5 honey **6** nectar **7** dessert **8** red-brown

ambrosial: 5 sweet, tasty **6** divine **8** fragrant, heavenly, luscious, perfumed **9** delicious **13** fit for the gods

ambry: 4 safe **5** chest, niche **6** closet, recess **10** repository

ambulatory: 7 movable, walking

ambush: mug **4** lurk, trap **5** await, blind, snare **6** lay for, waylay **7** assault **8** surprise **12** take unawares

ameliorate: 4 ease, help, mend **6** better, uplift **7** improve, promote **8** mitigate

amen: yea, yes **5** truly **6** assent, verily, so-be-it **7** exactly **8** approval, response, sanction **9** assuredly, certainly **10** that's right

Amen-Ra's wife: Mut

amenable: 4 open **6** docile, liable, pliant **7** willing **9** receptive, tractable **10** responsive **11** accountable **12** in the mood for

amend: 4 edit **5** alter **6** better, change, reform, remedy, repair, revise **7** correct, improve, rectify, redress **8** put right, work over

amends: 7 apology, redress **9** atonement, expiation **10** recompense, reparation **11** restitution **12** compensation **13** peace offering

amenities: 7 manners **8** agremens, comforts, niceties **9** agrements, etiquette **10** civilities, courtesies **11** formalities **12** conveniences, pleasantries

ament: 5 idiot, moron **6** catkin **7** cachrys, cattail, gosling **8** imbecile, nucament

amerce: 4 fine **6** punish **8** penalize

American: 4 Yank **6** Gringo, Yankee, Yanqui

colonists: **5** Dutch **8** pilgrims, puritans

American Indian: See **Indian (Americas)**

Amerind: 6 Eskimo, Indian

amethyst: gem **7** onegite

Amfortas' father: 7 Titurel

ami(F.): 5 lover **6** friend

amiable: 4 kind, warm **6** genial **7** affable, cordial, lovable, winsome **8** charming, engaging, friendly, gracious, sociable **9** agreeable, courteous **11** good-humored, good-natured, kind-hearted

amicable: 8 friendly **9** peaceable **10** harmonious, neighborly **12** well-disposed

amice: 4 cape, cowl, hood **5** ephod **6** almuce, tippet, vakass **8** vestment

amid: 5 among, midst **6** during **7** between **10** surrounded **11** encompassed

amino acid: 7 protein

amino compound: 7 diamide, diamine **8** triamine

amiss: ill **4** awry, bias **5** agley, askew, wrong **6** astray, faulty **7** haywire **8** improper **9** erroneous, incorrect **10** inaccurate

amity: 5 peace **6** accord **7** concord, harmony **8** goodwill **10** friendship **12** friendliness

ammonia: 9 hartshorn **11** refrigerant

derivative: **5** amide, amine **6** anilid **7** anilide, diamine

ammoniac: 8 gum resin

ammunition: 4 ammo, arms, shot **5** bombs **6** powder, shells **7** bullets rockets, weapons **8** grenades, materiel, missiles, ordnance, shrapnel **9** resources, artillery

case: **9** bandolier

depot: **4** dump **7** armory, arsenal **8** magazine

amnesia: 5 fugue **8** blackout **11** memory lapse **13** forgetfulness

amnesty: 6 pardon **10** absolution **11** forgiveness

amoeba, ameba: olm **7** proteus **8** organism **9** protozoon

amok, amuck: mad **5** crazy **6** crazed **7** violent **8** frenzied **12** uncontrolled

amole: 4 salt, soap **5** agave, plant

Amon's son: 6 Josiah

among: 4 amid, with **5** midst **7** between, betwixt **8** to each of **12** in the thick of

amor: 4 Eros, love **5** Cupid

amoral: 7 neutral **9** objective, shameless, unethical

amorous: 4 fond **6** ardent, erotic, loving, tender **7** amatory, fervent **10** passionate **12** affectionate

amorphous: 5 vague **8** formless, inchoate **9** irregular, shapeless, undefined **12** lacking unity **14** uncrystallized

amortize: 6 pay off **8** alienate, settle up, write off **9** liquidate **12** pay gradually

Amos: 6 O.T. book **7** prophet

amotion: 7 ousting, removal **11** deprivation

amount: gob, sum, tab **4** bulk, cost, dose,

part, unit **5** add up, chunk, equal, price, reach, stack, store, tally, total, whole **6** extent, number **7** measure, portion, signify **8** comprise, quantity **9** aggregate
fixed: **4** rate **8** set price **11** fixed charge
indefinite: any **4** some
made: lot **5** batch
relative: **5** ratio **6** degree
small: bit, jot, tot **4** dash, drop, iota, lick, mite, whit, wisp **5** grain, pinch, shred, speck, taste, trace **6** morsel, trifle **7** dribble, driblet, modicum, smidgen **8** fragment, molecule, particle
amour propre: **5** pride **6** egoism, vanity **7** conceit **8** self-love **10** narcissism
ampere unit: **4** volt, watt
ampersand: and **4** also, plus **9** character
amphetamine: **5** benny, upper **7** pep pill **8** inhalant **9** nose spray, stimulant
amphibian: eft, olm **4** frog, hyla, newt, rana, toad **7** caudate, proteus **8** tree toad **9** caecilian **10** salamander **14** land-water craft
family: **7** Hylidae, Pipidae, Ranidae **9** Bufonidae, Proteidae, Sirenidae
order of: **5** anura **6** eryops **7** aglossa, caudata **9** salientia
young: **7** tadpole **8** polliwog
amphibole: **7** edenite, oralite, uralite **9** tremolite **10** hornblende
Amphion: *father:* **4** Zeus **5** Iasus
mother: **7** Antiope
twin brother: **6** Zethus
wife: **5** Niobe
amphitheater: **4** bowl, oval **5** arena, cavea **6** circus **7** stadium **10** auditorium
Amphitrite: *father:* **6** Nereus
husband: **8** Poseidon
mother: **5** Doris
son: **6** Triton
Amphitryon's wife: **7** Alcmena, Alcmene
amphora: jar, urn **4** vase **6** pelike
ample: **4** full, good, much, rich, wide **5** broad, great, large, roomy **6** enough, plenty **7** copious, liberal, opulent **8** abundant, adequate, generous, handsome, spacious **9** bounteous, bountiful, capacious, extensive, plentiful, unstinted **10** munificent, sufficient
amplify: pad **5** swell, widen **6** dilate, expand, extend, stress **7** augment, enlarge **8** increase, lengthen, multiply **9** add detail **10** exaggerate
amputate: cut, lop **5** prune, sever **6** excise **7** chop off, curtail **9** eliminate
amula: ama **6** vessel **7** wine cup
amulet: gem **4** juju, mojo **5** charm, saffi, token **6** fetish, grigri, saphie **7** periapt **8** greegree, ornament, talisman **10** lucky piece, protection
Amulius' brother: **7** Numitor

amuse: wow **6** divert, engage, please, regale, tickle **7** beguile, delight, disport, enliven, gratify **8** distract **9** entertain, knock dead **10** exhilarate **11** play the fool
amusement: fun **4** game, jest, play **5** mirth, sport **7** pastime **8** pleasure **9** avocation, diversion, merriment **10** recreation, relaxation **13** divertisement, entertainment
place **4** fair, park **5** movie **6** casino, cinema, circus, midway **7** theater **8** carnival
amusing: **5** droll, funny **7** comical, risible **8** humorous, pleasant **9** laughable, ludicrous, priceless, quizzical **10** ridiculous **11** rib-tickling
Amy's sisters: Meg **4** Beth
Amycus: *enemy:* **5** Lycus **8** Dascylus
father: **8** Poseidon
friend: **8** Hercules
mother: **5** Melie
amyl: **6** pentyl, starch **7** alcohol
an: one **7** article
ana: **6** events **7** sayings **9** anecdotes, anthology **10** collection, miscellany **11** memorabilia
anabasis: **7** advance, headway, on-going **8** progress **10** expedition **11** forward march
anabatic: **9** ascending **12** upward moving
anaconda: boa **5** snake
Anacreon's birthplace: **4** Teos
anadem: **5** crown **6** diadem, fillet, wreath **7** chaplet, coronet, garland
anagogic: **6** occult **8** abstruse, mystical
anagram: **4** game **5** rebus **6** puzzle **9** logograph
analgesic: **5** opium **6** codein **7** anodyne, aspirin, codeine **8** sedative **10** anesthetic, pain-killer
analogous: **4** akin, like **5** alike **6** allied **7** cognate, related, similar **8** parallel **10** comparable, equivalent **11** correlative **13** correspondent
analogy: **8** metaphor **10** comparison, congruence, similarity, similitude **11** resemblance
analysis: **4** test **5** audit, study **8** exegesis **9** breakdown, criticism, reduction, titration **10** dissection **11** examination **14** interpretation
analyze: **4** sift **5** assay, parse, study, weigh **7** break up, dissect, examine **8** diagnose, separate **9** determine, reason out, take apart, subdivide
ananas: **7** pinguin **9** pineapple
Ananias: **4** liar **6** fibber **12** prevaricator
wife: **8** Sapphira
anarchist: **5** rebel **7** radical **8** mutineer, nihilist **9** insurgent **13** revolutionary
anarchy: **4** riot **5** chaos **6** revolt **7** license, misrule, mob rule **8** disorder, lynch law,

nihilism **9** confusion **11** lawlessness

anathema: ban **4** oath **5** curse **6** pariah, phobia **7** censure, outcast **9** bete noire **10** abhorrence, hated thing **11** imprecation, malediction **12** denunciation

anatomy: 4 body **8** analysis, skeleton **9** structure **10** dissection, morphology
animal: **7** zootomy
cell: **8** cytology
microscopic: **9** histology
plant: **9** phytotomy
research: **11** vivisection

Anaximander's principle: 7 apeiron

ancestor: 4 Adam, **8** forebear, **9** patriarch, precursor, prototype **10** forefather, forerunner, progenitor **11** predecessor
having common: **14** consanguineous
of a family branch: **6** stirps
worship: **6** manism

ancestry: 4 race **5** stock **6** family, origin **7** descent, lineage **8** breeding, heredity, pedigree **9** genealogy **10** bloodlines, extraction, family tree **11** antecedents
relating to: **6** atavic **9** atavistic

Anchises' son: 6 Aeneas

anchor: fix **4** bind, hook, moor **5** berth, bower, kedge, rivet **6** attach, drogue, secure **7** chaplet, connect, grapnel, killick, support **8** make fast **10** come to rest
bill: **4** peak
hoist: cat **7** capstan
part: arm **4** palm **5** fluke, shank, stock
position: **5** atrip
rest: **9** billboard
shaped: **8** ankyroid
timber: **7** grouser

anchorage: 4 dock, port, rade(Sc.) **5** haven **6** harbor, refuge **7** mooring **8** mainstay

anchorite: 4 monk **6** hermit **7** ascetic, eremite, recluse, stylite

anchorman: key **5** emcee **8** mainstay **11** commentator

anchovy: 6 sprat **7** herring

ancient: old **4** aged, auld(Sc.) **5** hoary **6** bygone, **7** antique, archaic, classic, elderly **8** historic, Noachian, obsolete, primeval **9** primitive **10** antiquated **11** patriarchal **12** along in years

ancilla: aid **6** helper **7** adjunct **8** handmaid **9** accessory

ancillary: 7 related **9** auxiliary **10** subsidiary **11** subordinate **13** supplementary

ancon: 5 elbow **6** corbel **7** console **9** olecranon

and: ant, too **4** also, plus **7** besides, further **8** moreover **10** connective **11** furthermore

and so forth: etc **4** more **6** others **8** etcetera

Andean: 5 grand, lofty **8** Peruvian

andiron: dog **7** firedog, hessian

Andorra: *capital:* **14** Andorra la Vella
language: **7** Catalan
monetary unit: **5** franc **6** peseta **7** centime, centimo
mountain: **8** Pyrenees
river: **6** Valira

andradite: 6 aplome, garnet

android: 5 robot **9** automaton

Andromache's husband: 6 Hector

Andromeda: 5 heath, plant **13** constellation
father: **7** Cepheus
husband: **7** Perseus
mother: **10** Cassiopeia

ane(Sc.): one **4** once

anecdote: 4 joke, tale, yarn **5** story **6** sketch **9** narrative
Collection: ana

anele: 5 bless **6** anoint, shrive

anemia: 4 fern **9** emptiness **11** lack of blood

anemic: wan **4** pale **6** watery **8** lifeless **10** exsanguine **12** without vigor

anemone: 9 buttercup **10** windflower

anent: 4 in re **5** about, as for **7** apropos **9** regarding **10** concerning **13** in reference to

aneroid: 9 barometer

anesthetic: gas **5** ether, **6** obtuse, opiate **7** anodyne, cocaine, dulling, menthol **8** morphine, sedative **9** analgesic, novocaine **10** chloroform, palliative **12** unperceptive

anew: 4 over **5** again **6** afresh **8** once more, recently

anfractuous: 6 spiral **7** turning, sinuous, winding **8** tortuous

angel: 4 dear, lamb **6** backer, cherub, patron, seraph, spirit, sponsor **8** guardian **9** harbinger, messenger **13** heavenly being
apostate prince: **5** Eblis **7** Lucifer
biblical: **5** Uriel **7** Chamuel, Gabriel, Jophiel, Michael, Raphael, Zadkiel
bottomless pit: **7** Abaddon **8** Apollyon
hierarchy: **6** Powers **7** Thrones, Virtues **8** Cherubim, Seraphim **9** Dominions
of death: **6** Azrael **7** Sammael
Paradise Lost: **5** Uriel **6** Belial **7** Ariocha
worship: **5** dulia

angelic: 4 pure **7** saintly **8** cherubic, heavenly, innocent **9** celestial, spiritual

angelus: 4 bell **6** prayer **8** devotion
painter: **6** Millet

anger: ire, irk, vex **4** bile, fury, gall, rile, roil **5** annoy, pique, wrath **6** choler, dander, enrage, nettle, offend, rancor, spleen, stir up, temper **7** burning, dudgeon, incense, inflame, passion, provoke **8** acrimony, irritate, vexation **9** aggravate, infuriate **10** antagonize, exasperate, resentment **11** displeasure, indignation

Angevin: 11 Plantagenet

angle: aim, ell, tee **4** bend, bias, fish, fork, hook **5** bevel, crook, facet, phase, point, quoin, slant, twist **6** aspect, jockey, scheme, zigzag **7** gimmick, perigon **8** fishhook, intrigue, position **10** standpoint

equal (pert. to): **8** isogonal, isogonic

external: **4** cant

having no: **6** agonic

mathematical: **5** acute, right **6** obtuse **7** oblique

measuring device: **6** octant **7** sextant **10** semicircle

of branch and leaf: **4** axil

of keel and bowsprit: **6** steeve

of ore vein: **4** hade

salient: **5** arris

angler: 7 lophiid, rodster, schemer, troller **8** allmouth, piscator **9** fisherman, goosefish, trickster

the compleat: **11** Izaak Walton

Anglo Saxon: *armor:* **7** hauberk **9** habergeon

army: **4** fyrd

assembly: **4** moot **5** gemot **6** gemote

coin: ora **5** sceat, styca **6** mancus

confederacy: **9** heptarchy

deity: Ing **4** Frey, Wyrd **5** Freyr

epic: **7** Beowulf

freeman: **5** thane, thegn

king: Ine **4** Edwy, Edred **6** Alfred, Egbert, Harold **8** Ethelred

king's council: **5** witan **11** witenagemot

letter: edh, eth, wyn **4** wynn **5** thorn

nobleman: **4** earl **8** atheling

poet: **4** scop

sheriff: **5** reeve **6** gerefa

slave: **4** esne

tax: **4** geld

village: ham

writer: **4** Bede

Angola: *capital:* **6** Luanda

city: **6** Lobito **7** Lubango, Malange **8** Benguela

monetary unit: **4** lwei **6** kwanza

mountain peak: **4** Moco

river: **5** Congo, Cuito, Kasai **6** Cuando, Cunene, Kwango

tribe: **5** Bantu, Kongo

angora: cat **4** goat, hair, wool, yarn **6** mohair, rabbit

angry: mad **4** grim, sore, **5** cross, huffy, irate, livid, vexed, wroth **6** fuming, ireful, put out **7** furious, painful, teed off, uptight **8** burned up, choleric, inflamed, **9** in a temper, indignant, irascible, resentful **11** exasperated, fit to be tied

anguilla: eel

anguish: rue, woe **4** ache, pain, pang **5** agony, dolor, grief, throe **6** misery, sorrow **7** torment, torture **8** distress **10** heartbreak

angular: 4 bony, lank, lean thin **5** gaunt, sharp **6** abrupt **7** jutting, pointed, scraggy, scrawny **8** rawboned **13** sharp-cornered

ani: 6 cuckoo **9** blackbird

anil: dye **6** indigo

anile: old **5** silly **6** doting, feeble, infirm, senile, simple **7** flighty, foolish **9** doddering **11** old-womanish

anima: 4 life, soul **6** psyche **9** inner self **10** vital force

animadversion: rap **4** slur **5** blame, knock **7** censure, obloquy, reproof **8** reproach **9** aspersion, criticism **10** perception, raking over **11** observation **12** faultfinding

animal (see also **amphibian, bird, carnivore, fish, insect, invertebrate, mammal, reptile, vertebrate**): **5** beast, biped, brute, gross, lusty **6** carnal, fleshy, mammal, rodent **7** sensual **8** creature, organism, physical **9** marsupial, quadruped

arboreal: **4** unau **5** chimp, koala, lemur, sloth **6** gibbon, marten, monkey **7** dasyure, opossum, raccoon, tarsier **8** kinkajou, marmoset, squirrel **10** orangutan

Biblical: **4** reem **8** behemoth

body: **4** soma

burrowing: **4** mole **6** badger, gopher, marmot, rabbit, wombat **7** echidna **9** armadillo, groundhog, woodchuck

class: **5** genus **6** genera(pl.)

coat: fur **4** fell, hair, hide, pelt, skin, wool **6** pelage

collection: zoo **9** menagerie

crawling: **4** worm **5** snake

cross-bred: **4** mule **5** hinny **6** hybrid

doctor: vet **12** veterinarian

draft: **4** mule, oxen(pl.) **5** horse **8** elephant

enclosure: pen, run, sty **4** barn, cage, coop, cote, fold, yard **5** hutch, kraal, stall **6** corral **7** pasture, paddock

equine: ass **5** horse, zebra

extinct: **4** dodo, urus **8** dinosaur, mastodon

fat: **4** lard, suet **5** cetin **6** tallow **7** lanolin

feline: cat **4** lion, lynx, puma **5** tiger **6** jaguar, ocelot **7** cheetah, leopard, panther

female: cow, dam, doe, ewe, gyp, hen, roe, sow **4** hind, mare, slut **5** bitch, filly, jenny, nanny, vixen **6** heifer **7** lioness, tigress

footless: **5** apoda

group: pod **4** herd, pack **5** drove, flock, pride, swarm **6** gaggle, school *hibernating:* 4 bear 9 groundhog, woodchuck

life: 4 bios 5 fauna

life (god of): 6 Faunus

lover: 8 zoophile 10 zoophilist

lupine: 4 wolf

male: cob, ram, tom 4 boar, buck, bull, cock, jack, stag, stud 5 billy, steer 6 gander 7 rooster 8 stallion

many-footed: 7 decapod, hexapod 8 multiped 9 centipede, millipede

marine: orc 4 brit, fish, inia, seal 5 coral, otter, polyp, salpa, whale 6 dugong, walrus 7 dolphin, manatee, rotifer 9 jellyfish 10 ctenophore, ctenophran

meat-eating: 9 carnivore

microscopic: 5 ameba, monad 6 acarid, amoeba 8 rhizopod 9 protozoan 10 animalcule

monkey-like: 5 lemur, loris

mythical: 4 faun, yeti 5 Hydra, snark 6 bagwyn, bunyip, dragon, garuda, Geryon, kraken, sphinx 7 centaur, griffin, mermaid, phoenix, unicorn 8 basilisk, Cerberus, Loch Ness, Minotaur 10 cockatrice

nocturnal: bat, owl 4 coon 5 lemur, ratel, tapir 6 possum 7 opossum 9 armadillo

one-celled: 5 ameba, monad 6 amoeba 9 protozoan

ovine: 5 sheep

pack: ass 4 mule 5 burro, camel, horse, llama 6 donkey

parasitic: 8 entozoon

plant-eating: 9 herbivore

porcine: hog, pig, sow 4 boar

pouched: 6 possum 7 opossum 8 kangaroo 9 marsupial

rabbit-like: 4 pika 6 marmot

ruminant: cow 4 deer, goat 5 camel, sheep 8 antelope

science: 7 zoology 8 ethology

symbol: 5 totem

track: pug 4 slot 5 spoor

undersized: 4 runt

ursine: 4 bear

vulpine: fox

young: cub, kid, pup 4 brit, calf, colt, fawn, foal, lamb, parr 5 bruin, chick, filly, puppy, shoat, whelp 6 cygnet, heifer, kitten 7 gosling 8 suckling, yearling 9 fledgling

animal and plant life: 5 biota

Animal Farm author: 6 Orwell

animalcule: 5 ameba, monad 6 amoeba 7 microbe, no-see-um, rotifer 9 protozoan

animate: 4 move, perk, stir 5 liven, rouse 6 ensoul, excite, fire up, living, vivify 7 actuate, enliven, inspire, quicken 8 activate, energize, vitalize 9 stimulate 10 exhilarate, invigorate 12 give motion to

animated: gay 5 brisk, peppy, vivid, vital

6 active, blithe, lively 7 buoyant, jocular 8 spirited, vigorous 9 sprightly, vivacious 10 full of zest 12 enthusiastic

animation: vim 4 dash, elan, life, zing 5 verve 6 esprit, spirit

anime: 5 copal, elemi, resin 9 oleoresin

animism: 8 naturism

animosity: 4 hate, 6 enmity, malice, rancor 7 dislike 9 antipathy, hostility 10 antagonism, resentment

animus: 4 mind, soul 6 effort, rancor, spirit, temper 7 ill will 8 attitude 9 intention, objective 10 antagonism 11 disposition, inclination

anion: ion 8 particle

opposed to: 6 cation

anisette: 7 cordial, liqueur

Anius' daughter: 5 Elais

ankle: 4 coot(Sc.) 5 talus 6 tarsus

pert. to: 6 tarsal

anlage: 4 base 6 embryo, source 8 blastema, rudiment 10 primordium

anna: 9 Hindu coin

annals: 6 record 7 history 8 archives 10 chronicles 11 publication 13 year by year log

annalist: 6 writer 7 diarist 8 recorder 9 historian 12 chronologist

Annapolis student: 4 pleb 5 plebe 10 midshipman

annatto, annotto, arnatto: dye 4 tree 5 urucu 6 salmon 7 achiote

derivative: 5 bixin 7 orellin

anneal: 4 bake, fuse, heat 5 smelt 6 temper 7 toughen 10 strengthen

annelid: 4 worm

fresh water: 4 naid

marine: 9 autolytus

annex: add, ell 4 wing 5 affix, seize, unite 6 append, attach, fasten, obtain, pick up, secure 7 acquire, preempt, procure 8 addition, arrogate, take over 9 extension 11 appropriate

Annie Oakley: 4 pass 6 ticket 7 freebie

annihilate: end 4 kill, raze, rout, slay 5 crush, erase, wreck 6 devour, murder, negate, squash 7 abolish, destroy, expunge, nullify, wipe out 8 decimate, demolish, massacre 9 eradicate, extirpate 10 extinguish, obliterate 11 exterminate 12 reduce to ruin

anniversary: 4 fete 7 jubilee 8 birthday, ceremony 11 celebration 13 commemoration

hundredth: 10 centennial

one hundred fiftieth: 16 sesquicentennial

tenth: 9 decennial

third: 9 triennial

thousandth: 10 millennial 11 millenniary

twentieth: 12 vigentennial

wedding: see **wedding:** *anniversary*

annotate: 4 edit, note 5 gloss 6 remark 7

comment, explain **9** elucidate **10** illustrate

announce: bid, cry **4** call, tell **5** bruit, state **6** assert, blazon, herald, inform, report, reveal **7** declare, divulge, publish, usher in **8** foretell, proclaim **9** advertise, broadcast, enunciate, introduce, make known **10** promulgate **11** give the word

announcement: **5** blurb, edict **6** decree, dictum, notice **7** message **8** bulletin **9** broadcast, manifesto, statement **11** declaration **12** notification, proclamation

of marriage: **5** banns

announcer: **4** page **5** crier, emcee

of coming events: **4** seer **6** herald **7** prophet **9** harbinger

annoy: bug, dun, ire, irk, nag, try, vex **4** bait, bore, fret, gall, nark, pain, rile **5** chafe, harry, peeve, pique, spite, tease, upset, worry **6** badger, harass, heckle, molest, needle, nettle, offend, pester, rattle **7** bedevil, disturb, provoke, trouble **8** distress, irritate **9** aggravate, displease, embarrass **10** exasperate **13** inconvenience

annoyance: **4** drag, pain, pest **5** thorn, trial, worry **8** headache, nuisance, vexation **11** disturbance **13** inconvenience

annual: **4** book **5** plant **6** flower, yearly **7** etesian **8** yearbook **11** publication

annul: **4** undo, void **5** blank, elide, erase, quash, remit **6** cancel, negate, recall, repeal, revoke **7** abolish, blot out, nullify, rescind **8** abrogate, derogate, dissolve, overrule **9** disaffirm **10** annihilate, extinguish, invalidate, neutralize, obliterate **11** countermand

annular: **6** banded, cyclic, ringed **8** cingular, circular

annulet: **4** ring **5** ridge **6** fillet **7** molding

anoa: **6** wild ox **8** sapiutan

relative: **7** buffalo

anode: **5** plate **8** terminal **9** electrode

deposit: **5** anion

anodic: **9** ascending

anodyne: **4** balm **6** opiate **7** soother **8** narcotic, sedative **9** analgesic **10** anesthetic, painkiller, palliative

anoesia, anoia: **6** idiocy

anoint: oil **5** anele **6** grease **9** apply balm **10** consecrate

anole: **6** lizard

anomalous: odd **6** off-key **7** deviant, foreign, strange, unusual **8** aberrant, abnormal, atypical, peculiar **9** eccentric, irregular **11** incongruous **12** out of keeping **13** contradictory

anomy: **7** miracle

anon: **4** soon, then **5** again, later **6** afresh **7** by and by, shortly **8** in a while **9** afterward, presently

anonym: **5** alias **10** nom-de-plume

anonymous: **7** unknown **8** nameless, unavowed, unsigned **9** incognito

anorexia: **7** fasting **14** self-starvation

another: new **4** more **5** fresh **6** second **7** further, one more **9** different **10** additional, not the same

anserine: **5** silly **6** stupid **7** foolish **9** gooselike

answer: **4** meet, plea, suit **5** avail, react, reply, serve **6** refute, result, retort, return **7** defense, fulfill, riposte, satisfy **8** rebuttal, repartee, response, solution **9** conform to, rejoinder **11** acknowledge

opposite of: ask **7** inquire **8** question

answerable: **6** liable **8** amenable **9** obligated **11** accountable, reponsible

ant: **5** emmet **7** pismire, termite

genus: **6** eciton **7** formica **8** myrmecia

kind: **4** army **6** amazon, driver **7** soldier **9** carpenter

leaf-cutting: **4** atta

male: **8** micraner **9** ergataner

nest: **4** hill **5** mound **6** colony **9** formicary

nonworker: **5** drone

queen: **4** gyne

stinging: **5** kelep **8** ponerine

worker: **6** ergate

ant bear: **8** aardvark, edentate, tamanoir

ant cow: **5** aphid

anta: **4** pier **5** tapir **8** pedestal, pilaster

Antaeus: *enemy:* **8** Hercules

father: **8** Poseidon

mother: **4** Gaea

antagonism: **6** animus, enmity, rancor **7** dislike **8** friction **9** animosity, antipathy, hostility **10** opposition

antagonist: foe **5** enemy, rival **7** battler, warrior **8** opponent **9** adversary **10** competitor

antagonistic: **4** anti **6** at odds **7** counter, hostile, opposed **8** contrary, inimical **9** dissonant **11** dead against

Antarctica: *bird:* **4** skua **7** penguin

explorer: **4** Byrd, Cook, Ross **5** Scott **6** Mawson **7** Wilkins **8** Amundsen

land areas: **5** Coats, Oates **6** Adelie, Graham, Wilkes **7** Enderby **8** Victoria **9** Queen Maud

mountain: **5** Siple **9** Admiralty

sea: **4** Ross **7** Weddell **8** Amundsen

seal: **4** Ross **9** sterrinck

ante: pay **5** price **9** poker term **10** come up with **11** initial cost

anteater: **5** tapir **6** animal **7** echidna **8** aardvark, aardwolf, edentate, tamandua, tamanoir

scaly: **5** manis **8** pangolin

antecedent: **4** fore **5** cause, prior **6** former, reason **7** premise **8** ancestor, anterior, previous **9** foregoing, precursor,

prototype **10** forerunner **11** predecessor
antedate: 7 precede **10** come before **11** make earlier
antediluvian: 10 antiquated
antelope: gnu 4 puku **5** eland, takin, yakin **6** dik-dik, impala **7** gazelle **8** steenbok **9** pronghorn **10** hartebeest
brown: **5** nagor
extinct: **7** blaubok
female: doe
forest: **5** bongo
four-horned: **6** chouka **7** chikara **10** chousingha
gazelle-like: **5** beira **7** gerenuk
genus: **4** oryx
goat-like: **5** goral, serow **7** chamois
golden: **6** impala
harnessed: **4** guib
large: gnu **4** aste, kudu, oryx **5** addax, beisa, bongo, eland **6** impala, koodoo, nilgai, nilgau **7** bubalis, defassa, gemsbok, sassaby **10** hartebeest
male: **4** buck
mountain: **7** chamois
mythical: **4** yale
pied: **8** bontebok
pronghorn: **6** cabrree, cabrie, cabret, cabrit
reddish: **7** grysbok
royal: **5** ipete **9** kleeneboc
sheep-like: **5** saiga
short-maned: gnu **6** nilgau
small: **6** duiker, grimme **7** grysbok **9** duikerbok
tawny: **5** oribi
tiger-like: **8** agacella
young: kid
antelope-like: 5 bovid **6** bovine
antenna: 4 palp **6** aerial, feeler, lead-in
insect: **5** clava
radar: **7** scanner
Antenor: *father:* **8** Aesyetes
son: **6** Agenor **11** Archelochus
wife: **6** Theano
anterior: 5 front, prior **6** atloid, former, before **7** earlier, ventral **8** atlantal, previous **9** foregoing, preceding **10** antecedent
anteroom: 4 hall **5** foyer, lobby **8** entrance **9** vestibule **11** antechamber
anthelion: 4 halo **6** nimbus **7** antisun, aureole **10** countersun
anthem: 4 hymn, song **5** motet, psalm **7** choral **9** antiphony, offertory **10** responsory
anther: 10 stamen part
anthesis: 9 full bloom **13** efflorescence
anthill: 4 bank **5** mound **9** formicary
anthology: ana **4** book **5** album **6** corpus **7** garland **8** excerpts **9** potpourri **10** collection, miscellany **11** compilation
Anthony Adverse author: 5 Allen

anthozoan: 5 coral, polyp **7** anemone
anthropoid: ape **5** orang **6** gibbon, monkey, simian **7** gorilla, primate, siamang **9** orangutan **10** chimpanzee, troglodyte
anthropophagite: 8 cannibal
anti: con, foe **6** contra **7** against, opposed
anti-aircraft: *fire:* **4** flack
gun: **5** archy **6** pom-pom
antic: 4 dido, lark **5** caper, comic, droll, prank, stunt **6** gambol **7** caprice, gambado **9** ludicrous **10** frolicsome, shenanigan, tomfoolery **11** monkeyshine
anticipate: 4 balk, hope **5** augur, await **6** divine, expect, prepay, thwart **7** counter, foresee, obviate, portend, prepare, presage, prevent **8** do before, forecast, outguess **9** apprehend, forestall, foretaste **10** enjoy ahead **11** precipitate **13** look forward to
anticipation: 6 augury **9** foresight, intuition **10** expectancy **12** presentiment
anticipating: 8 pregnant
antidote: 4 cure **6** remedy **10** corrective, preventive **11** neutralizer, restorative
Antigone: *father:* **7** Oedipus
mother: **7** Jocasta
sister: **6** Ismene
Antilles: *god:* **4** Zeme
native: **5** Ineri
pearl: **4** Cuba
antimacassar: 4 tidy **5** doily
antimony: 4 kohl **7** stibium
pert. to: **7** stibial
Antioch proselyte: 7 Nicolas
antipasto: 6 relish **9** appetizer **11** hors d'oeuvre
antipathy: 6 enmity, nausea, rancor **7** allergy, dislike **8** aversion, distaste, loathing **9** animosity, hostility **10** abhorrence, antagonism, repugnance
antipodal: 7 opposed **8** contrary, opposite **9** diametric **10** across from
antiquated: old **4** aged **5** fusty, hoary, passe **6** old hat **7** ancient, archaic **8** obsolete, outdated, outmoded **9** primitive **12** antediluvian **13** superannuated
antique: old **5** relic, virtu **7** classic, hasbeen **8** artifact, heirloom, type face **9** out of date, venerable **12** old-fashioned
antiseptic: 4 dull **5** vapid **6** iodine, phenol **7** alcohol, camphor, sterile **8** creosote, hygienic, peroxide, sanitary **9** boric acid, germicide, purifying **10** overly neat **12** disinfectant
powder: **6** formin
antisocial: 7 hostile **8** solitary **9** reclusive **11** anarchistic, stand-offish **12** misanthropic
antithesis: 7 reverse **8** antipode, contrast **10** opposition **13** exact opposite
antitoxin: 4 sera(pl.) **5** serum
antler: 4 horn

branch: bay **4** brow, snag, tine **5** crown, royal **7** speller **8** surroyal, trestine **9** bezantler
knob: **6** croche
main stem: **4** beam
skin surrounding: **6** velvet
unbranched: dag **5** spike **7** pricket **9** greenhorn
Antony and Cleopatra character: 4 Eros, Iras **5** Menas, Philo **6** Gallus, Taurus **7** Agrippa
anuran: 4 toad **10** salientian
anurous: 8 tailless
Anu's consort: 4 Anat
anvil: 5 forge **6** smithy, stithy **7** bickern **8** beakiron
bone: **4** amos **5** incus **7** incudes(pl.)
point: **4** horn, beak
tinsmith's: **5** teest
anxiety: 4 care, fear **5** alarm, anger, doubt, dread, panic, worry **7** caution, chagrin, concern, scruple, trouble **8** disquiet, suspense **9** misgiving **10** foreboding, perplexity, solicitude, uneasiness **12** apprehension
anxious: 4 agog **5** eager **6** uneasy **7** carking, unquiet **8** desirous, restless, watchful **9** disturbed, expectant, impatient
any: 4 much, part, some **8** quantity, whatever **9** one or more
anybody: one **7** someone
anyway: 11 at all events **12** nevertheless
Anzac: 10 Australian **12** New Zealander
A-OK: 4 fine **9** excellent **10** all in order
A-one: 4 tops **5** prime **8** superior **9** first rate, top-drawer
aorist: 9 verb tense
aoristic: 10 indefinite **12** undetermined **13** indeterminate
aorta: 6 artery
auodad: 4 arui **5** sheep
apa: 4 tree **7** wallaba
apace: 4 fast **7** quickly, rapidly, swiftly **8** speedily
Apache: 4 Yuma **6** Indian **10** Chiricahua
beverage: **6** tiswin
chief: **7** Cochise **8** Geronimo
jacket: **6** bietle
apar: 9 armadillo
apart: 4 away **5** alone, aloof, aside, riven, solus, split **7** asunder, enisled, removed **8** detached, divorced, in pieces, isolated, reserved, secluded, separate **9** divergent **10** abstracted **11** dissociated **12** individually
from: **6** but for **7** barring, save for **9** excepting, excluding, outside of
apartment: 4 digs, flat **5** abode, rooms, suite **6** rental, walk-up **7** chamber **8** building, dwelling, tenement
upper: **5** solar **6** sollar
apathetic: 4 dull, limp, logy **5** inert, stoic

6 torpid, supine **7** unmoved **8** listless, sluggish **9** impassive, incurious, unfeeling **10** insensible, phlegmatic **11** indifferent, unemotional **12** uninterested **13** dispassionate
apathy: 6 acedia, phlegm, torpor **7** languor **8** doldrums, lethargy **9** lassitude, unconcern **12** indifference
ape (see also **anthropoid**): **4** boor, copy, lout, mime **5** magot, mimic **6** baboon, gelada, gibbon, monkey, parrot, simian **7** emulate, imitate, portray, primate, take off **9** orangutan **10** chimpanzee **11** impersonate
family: **8** pongidae
largest: **7** gorilla
like animal: **5** lemur
apeak: 8 vertical
apeman: 6 Tarzan
aper: 4 boar, mime **5** mimic **7** buffoon, copycat
apercu: 6 digest, precis, sketch **7** insight, outline **10** conspectus **11** brief survey
aperitif: 4 whet **5** drink **8** cocktail **9** appetizer
aperture: gap **4** hole, leak, pore, rima, slit, slot, vent **5** chasm, cleft, crack, stoma **6** window **7** fissure, opening, orifice, ostiole **8** loophole, spiracle **11** perforation
apex: tip, top **4** acme, cusp, noon, peak **5** crest, crown, point, spire **6** apogee, climax, summit, vertex, zenith **8** meridian, pinnacle **9** fastigium **11** culmination, ne plus ultra **12** quintessence
covering: epi **6** finial
elbow: **5** ancon
pert. to: **6** apical
rounded: **6** retuse
Aphareus: *brother:* **7** Lynceus
son: **4** Idas
aphid: 5 louse **8** parasite
aphorism: saw **5** adage, axiom, gnome, maxim, motto **6** dictum, saying **7** epigram, precept, proverb **8** apothegm
Aphrodite: 5 Venus **8** Cytherea **9** butterfly
consort: **4** Ares
father: **4** Zeus
mother: **5** Dione
priestess: **4** Hero
son: **4** Eros **5** Eneas **6** Aeneas
temple site: **6** Paphos
apiary: 4 hive, skep **8** beehouse
apiece: per **4** each **6** singly **8** one by one **9** severally **11** for every one **12** individually, respectively
apish: 5 silly **7** foppish, slavish **8** affected
apishamore: 7 blanket
aplomb: 4 ease, elan, tact **5** nerve, poise **6** surety **8** coolness **9** assurance, composure, sangfroid **10** confidence, equanimity **11** nonchalance, savoir faire

apocalypse: 6 vision 8 prophecy 10 prediction, revelation
apocopate: 5 elide 7 shorten
apocryphal: 4 sham 5 false 6 unreal, untrue 7 dubious 8 doubtful, spurious 10 fictitious, not genuine 11 counterfeit, uncanonical, unauthentic
Apocryphal book: 5 Tobit 6 Baruch, Esdras, Judith 9 Maccabees
apodal: 8 footless
apogee: 4 acme, apex, peak 6 climax, summit, zenith 12 highest point
apograph: 4 copy 10 transcript
Apollo: 6 Delius 7 Phoebus
  abode of: 7 Helicon
  beloved of: 6 Cyrene, Daphne 8 Calliope
  birthplace: 5 Delos
  father: 4 Zeus 7 Jupiter
  festival: 5 Delia 6 Carnea
  instrument: 4 lute, lyre
  mother: 4 Leto 6 Latona
  oracle site: 6 Delphi
  priest: 7 Calchas
  sacred vale: 5 Tempe
  sister: 5 Diana 7 Artemis
  son: Ion 7 Orpheus
  traveler: 6 Abaris
  twin: 5 Diana
Apollyon: 5 Satan, devil 7 Abaddon, Lucifer 9 archfiend, Beelzebub
  evil spirit of: 16 Pilgrim's Progress
  vanquished by: 9 Christian
apologetic: 5 sorry 8 contrite, penitent 9 defensive, regretful 10 remorseful
apologue: 4 myth 5 fable, story 7 parable 8 allegory
apology: 4 plea 5 alibi 6 excuse, regret 7 defense 8 mea culpa 9 penitence 11 explanation, vindication 13 justification 14 acknowledgment
apostate: 7 traitor, seceder 8 deserter, disloyal, recreant, renegade, turncoat 9 faithless 10 recidivist
apostle: 4 John, Jude, Paul 5 James, Judas, Peter, Silas, Simon 6 Andrew, Philip, Thomas 7 Matthew, teacher 8 Barnabas, disciple, follower, Matthias, preacher 9 messenger 10 evangelist, missionary 11 Bartholomew
  of Indies: 6 Xavier
  pert. to: 7 petrine
  to Franks: 4 Remi
  to Gauls: 5 Denis
  to Goths: 7 Ulfilas
apothecary: 7 chemist 8 druggist, gallipot 10 pharmacist
  weight: 4 dram 5 grain, pound 7 scruple
apothegm: saw 5 adage, axiom, gnome, maxim 6 dictum, saying, truism 7 proverb 8 aphorism
apotheosize: 5 deify, exalt 7 ennoble, glorify, idolize 8 enshrine, idealize 10 consecrate
Appalachian range: 6 Ramapo
appall, appal: awe 4 stun 5 daunt, shock 6 dismay, 7 depress, horrify, terrify 8 frighten 10 scare stiff 11 make shudder 13 give the creeps
appalling: 5 awful 7 awesome, fearful 8 alarming, dreadful, terrible 9 frightful, unearthly 10 petrifying
appanage: 5 grant 7 adjunct 9 allowance, endowment, privilege 10 perquisite 11 prerogative
apparatus (see also **device, instrument**): rig 4 gear, tool 5 gizmo 6 dingus, gadget, outfit, system 7 utensil 8 material 9 appliance, equipment, machinery, mechanism, trappings 10 furnishing 11 contrivance 12 appurtenance
apparel (see also **dress, vestment**): 4 duds, garb, gear, robe, togs, wear 5 adorn, array, dress, equip 6 attire, clothe, outfit 7 costume, deck out, garment, raiment, vesture 8 clothing, wardrobe 9 embellish 11 furnishings, habiliments
apparent: 4 open 5 clear, overt, plain 6 patent 7 evident, glaring, obvious, seeming, visible 8 distinct, manifest, palpable, probable 9 easy to see, noticeable 10 ostensible, plain as day 11 discernible, perceptible, unconcealed 12 unmistakable
apparition: 5 ghost, haunt, shade, spook 6 shadow, spirit, sprite, wraith 7 eidolon, fantasy, phantom, specter, spectre 8 illusion phantasm, revenant 9 hobgoblin 10 appearance, phenomenon 13 hallucination
appeal: ask, beg 4 call, plea, seek, suit 5 charm, plead 6 adjure, allure, prayer, summon, turn to 7 address, beseech, entreat, glamour, implore, request, solicit 8 approach, petition 9 importune 10 attraction, supplicate
appealing: 4 cute 6 catchy 7 winsome 8 engaging, fetching, pleading, pleasant 9 agreeable, imploring 10 attractive, entrancing
appear: 4 come, look, loom, seem 5 arise, enter, issue, occur 6 arrive, emerge, show up 7 compear(Sc.), develop, emanate 11 materialize
appearance: air, hue 4 form, idea, look, mien, show, view 5 front, guise, sight 6 aspect, facade, manner, 7 arrival, bearing, display 8 demeanor, illusion, presence, pretense 9 semblance 10 disclosure, phenomenon 11 countenance 13 manifestation

first: **5** debut **8** premiere **9** unveiling

appease: 4 calm, ease, hush **5** allay, mease(Sc.), quiet, slake **6** buy off, pacify, please, soften, soothe **7** assuage, content, gratify, mollify, placate, satisfy **8** mitigate **9** sweet-talk **10** conciliate, propitiate **11** tranquilize

appellation: nom(F.), tag **4** name **5** label, title **7** epithet, moniker **8** cognomen, nickname **9** sobriquet **11** designation

appellee: 9 defendant **10** respondent

append: add **4** clip, hang **5** affix, annex, pin to, tag on **6** attach **7** subjoin **8** fasten to

appendage: arm, awn, ear, fin, leg, tab, tag **4** aril, barb, flap, limb, palp, tail, wing **5** canda, extra, rider **6** branch, suffix **7** adjunct, antenna, codicil **8** addition, hanger-on, offshoot, parasite, tentacle **9** accessory **10** dependency

appendix: 5 organ **7** addenda(pl.) **8** addendum, epilogue **10** supplement

appertain: 6 bear on, belong **7** apply to, concern, refer to **8** relate to **12** have to do with

appetite: yen **4** lust, urge, zest **5** gusto, taste **6** desire, hunger, liking, orexis, relish **7** craving, longing, passion, wanting **8** cupidity, penchant, tendency **10** preference, propensity

abnormal: **4** pica **7** bulimia

excessive: **5** greed **8** gluttony, gulosity **10** polyphagia

pert. to: **7** oretic

voracious: **7** edacity **8** rapacity

appetizer: 5 snack **6** canape, relish, savory, tidbit **8** aperitif, cocktail **9** antipasto **11** hors d'oeuvre

applaud: 4 clap, hail **5** cheer, extol **6** praise **7** acclaim, approve, commend, endorse, root for **10** compliment

applauders: 6 claque

applause: 4 hand **5** eclat, kudos **6** bravos, cheers, huzzas, salvos **7** hurrahs, ovation **8** clapping, plaudits **11** approbation

apple: 4 crab, pome **6** Esopus, pippin, russet **7** Baldwin, Fameuse, Winesap, Wealthy **8** Ben Davis, Cortland, Greening, Jonathan, McIntosh **9** Delicious, Oldenberg **10** Rome Beauty **11** Granny Smith, Gravenstein, Northern Spy, Spitzenburg **12** Yellow Newton, York Imperial **17** Yellow Transparent

acid: **5** malic

blight: **5** aphid **8** eriosoma

crushed pulp: **6** pomace

drink: **5** cider **8** Calvados

genus: **5** malus

immature: **6** codlin **7** codling

pastry: **7** strudel

ribbed: **7** costard

seed: pip

wild: **4** crab

apple knocker: 4 hick **5** yokel **6** rustic **7** bumpkin, hayseed **9** greenhorn

apple of one's eye: 7 darling **8** favorite

apple-polish: 4 fawn **5** toady **7** flatter **8** kowtow to **10** curry favor

applesauce: 4 bunk, pulp **5** hokum, hooey **6** relish **7** baloney, dessert, rubbish **8** nonsense **9** poppycock

appliance (see also **tool**)**: 4** gear **6** device, gadget **7** utensil **9** implement **10** instrument **11** contrivance

applicable: apt, fit **4** meet **5** ad rem(L.) **6** proper, useful **7** apropos, fitting, germane **8** apposite, relative, relevant, suitable **9** pertinent **10** to the point **11** appropriate

applicant: 8 prospect **9** candidate, solicitor

application: use **4** form **5** study **6** appeal, effort **7** request **8** dressing, industry, petition, sedulity **9** diligence, relevance **11** mental labor **12** perseverance

applique: 6 design **7** overlay **8** ornament, trimming **10** decoration

apply: ask, fit, use **5** put on, rub on **6** appeal, bear on, bestow, betake, devote, direct, employ, impose, relate **7** conform, overlay, pertain, request, solicit, utilize **8** carry out, petition, put in for, spread on **9** persevere **10** administer **11** superimpose **13** put into effect

appoggiatura: 9 grace note

appoint: fix, set **4** name **5** allot, elect, equip **6** assign, decree, detail, direct, outfit **7** confirm, furnish, mark out **8** delegate, nominate **9** authorize, designate, prescribe **10** commission

as agent: **6** depute **8** delegate, deputize

appointment: 4 date, post **5** berth, tryst **6** billet, office **7** meeting, station **8** position **9** selection **10** assignment, engagement, rendezvous **11** assignation

apportion: 5 allot, award, grant, share, split **6** assess, assign, divide, parcel, ration **7** divvy up, dole out, mete out, prorate **8** allocate **10** distribute

apportionment: 4 deal **8** dividend, division **9** allowance **12** distribution

appose: 9 place near **11** put opposite **13** put side by side

apposite: apt **6** timely **7** germane **8** relevant, suitable **9** pertinent **11** appropriate

appraise: 4 rate **5** assay, gauge, judge **6** assess, survey **7** analyze, examine **8** estimate, evaluate **10** adjudicate **11** put a price on

appreciable: 7 evident, obvious **8** apparent, palpable, tangible **10** noticeable **11** discernible, perceptible

appreciate: 4 feel, love **5** judge, prize, value **6** admire, esteem **7** advance, cherish, realize, respect **8** increase, treasure **9** be aware of **10** understand **11** go up in worth

appreciation: 5 gusto **6** thanks **7** tribute **8** judgment **9** enjoyment, gratitude **11** recognition, testimonial **12** gratefulness

apprehend: nab, see **4** know, view **5** catch, grasp, seize **6** arrest, detain, divine, fathom, wise up **7** capture, foresee, make out, realize **8** conceive, perceive **9** recognize **10** anticipate, comprehend

apprehensible: 5 lucid **6** noetic **7** sensate **8** knowable **12** intelligible

apprehension: 4 fear, idea **5** doubt, dread, worry **6** arrest, dismay, notion **7** anxiety, capture, concern **8** distrust, mistrust, suspense **9** misgiving, suspicion **10** conception, foreboding, perception, solicitude, uneasiness **11** premonition **12** anticipation, intellection, presentiment **13** understanding

apprehensive: apt **5** aware, jumpy **6** morbid **7** fearful, nervous **9** cognizant, conscious **10** discerning

apprentice: 4 tyro **6** novice, rookie **7** learner, trainee **8** beginner, neophyte **9** greenhorn, novitiate **10** tenderfoot

apprise, apprize: 4 tell, warn **5** value **6** advise, inform, notify, reveal **8** acquaint, disclose **10** appreciate

apprised: 5 aware **7** knowing

approach: try **4** loom, near **5** essay, verge **6** access, accost, advent, coming, impend **7** address, advance, close in, get warm, landing, solicit **8** overture **9** draw close, procedure **11** approximate, break the ice **12** narrow the gap

approbation: 4 okay **5** favor **6** assent, esteem, praise, regard, repute **7** plaudit, respect **8** applause, approval, blessing, sanction **10** admiration **12** commendation

appropriate: apt, due, use **4** grab, meet, take **5** annex, claim, right, steal, usurp **6** assign, assume, borrow, pilfer, pirate, proper, timely, worthy **7** apropos, condign, convert, fitting, germane, impound, preempt, purloin, related **8** accroach, arrogate, becoming, deserved, relevant, suitable **9** pertinent **10** applicable, confiscate, convenient, felicitous, plagiarize **11** set apart for

appropriation: 5 grant **7** stipend, subsidy **9** allotment, allowance **11** special fund

approval: 4 amen **5** eclat **6** assent **7** go

ahead, support **8** blessing, sanction **10** imprimatur **11** approbation, benediction

approve: 4 back, like, okay, pass **5** adopt, allow, clear, favor, value **6** accept, admire, concur, ratify **7** applaud, certify, commend, confirm, consent, endorse, initial, vote for **8** accredit, sanction **9** authorize **10** compliment **11** countenance, think well of

approximate: 4 near **5** about, circa, close **8** approach, resemble **9** come close

approximately: 4 nigh **5** about **6** almost, around, nearly **7** roughly **9** virtually **10** more or less **11** practically

appurtenance: 4 gear **5** annex **7** adjunct **8** appendix **9** accessory, apparatus, appendage, appliance, belonging

après: 5 after **10** afterwards

apricot: ume **4** ansu, tree **5** color, fruit **8** Blenheim

confection: **5** mebos **6** meebos

cordial: **7** perisco **8** periscot

vine: **6** maypop

a priori: 9 deductive **11** conditional, inferential, presumptive, reasoned out

apron: bib **4** tier **5** cover, smock **6** runway, shield, tarmac **8** pinafore **10** protection

leather: **4** dick **8** barmskin, lambskin **9** forestage

apropos: apt **4** as to, in re, meet **5** about, anent **6** timely **7** fitting, germane **8** by the way, relevant, suitable **9** opportune, pertinent **10** to the point **11** appropriate, in respect to

apse: 5 niche **6** recess **10** orbit point, projection

apt: fit, pat **4** able, deft, keen **5** adept, alert, prone, quick, ready **6** clever, liable, likely **7** apropos, capable, fitting **8** apposite, dextrous, disposed, inclined, skillful, suitable, tendency **9** competent, consonant, dexterous, pertinent **10** proficient **11** appropriate

apteral: 8 wingless

opposite of: **4** alar **5** alate

apteryx: 4 bird, kiwi

aptitude: art **4** bent, gift, turn **5** craft, flair, knack **6** genius, talent **7** ability, faculty, leaning **8** instinct **10** propensity **11** disposition

aquamarine: gem **4** blue **5** beryl, color

aquarium: 4 bowl, pool, pond, tank **5** globe

aquatic plant: 4 lily **5** coral, lotus **6** enalid, sugamo **7** elatine, seaweed **10** hydrophyte

aqueduct: 5 canal **7** channel, conduit, passage **9** conductor, water pipe

of Sylvius: **4** iter

aquila: 5 eagle
aquiline: 6 hooked 7 curving 9 eagle-like, prominent
Aquinas work: 5 Summa
aquosity: 7 wetness 8 moisture 10 wateriness
ara: 5 macaw
arab: 4 waif 5 gamin, nomad 6 urchin 8 wanderer
araba: cab 5 coach 6 monkey 8 carriage
Arabian: *abode:* dar 4 tent
   alphabet: See **Arabic:** *alphabet*
   antelope: 5 addax
   author: 6 lokman
   banquet: 5 diffa
   bazaar: suq
   bird: 7 phoenix
   caliph: Ali 6 sharif, sherif 7 shareef, shereef
   caravan: 6 cafila
   cloak: aba
   coffee: 5 mocha
   coin: 4 lari 5 carat, dinar, kabik, riyal
   cosmetic: 4 kohl
   demon: 4 jinn 5 afrit, genie, jinni 6 afreet, jinnee
   dish: 8 couscous
   drink: 4 bosa, boza 5 bozah 6 lebban
   drum: 9 tara-booka
   fabric: aba 4 haik
   father: abu 4 abba, abou
   flour source: 4 samh
   garment: aba 4 haik 6 cabaan 7 burnous 8 burnoose
   gazelle: 4 cora 5 ariel
   goddess: 5 Allat
   grammar: 7 ajrumya
   horse: 6 anezeh 8 kadischi, palomino
   infantryman: 5 askar
   jasmine: 4 bela 10 sampaquita
   judge: 4 cadi
   land: 6 feddan
   measure: den, saa 4 ferk, foot, kist 5 achir, barid, cadba, cafiz, covid, cuddy, makuk, mille, qasab, teman, woibe, zudda 6 artaba, assbaa, covido, feddan, gariba, ghalva 7 caphite, farsakh, farsang, kiladja, marhale, nusfiah
   palm: 4 doom, doum
   peasant: 6 fellah
   philosopher: 6 Farabi 8 Averroes
   plant: kat 5 retem
   prince (see also *ruler* below): 6 sherif 7 shereef
   raiders: 8 fedayeen
   river bed: 4 wadi, wady
   romance: 5 antar 6 antara
   ruler: 4 amir, emir 5 ameer, emeer, sheik 6 sultan
   shrub: kat 5 alhaj, retem
   tambourine: 4 taar 5 daira

   tea shrub: kat
   tent encampment: 5 douar
   vessel: 4 dhow 6 boutre, sambuk
   weight: 4 rotl 5 cheki, kella, nasch, nevat, ocque, oukia, ratel, toman, vakia 6 bokard, dirhem, miskal, tomand 8 farsalah
   wind: 6 simoom, simoon
Arabian Nights: *bird:* roc 4 aqib
   character: Ali 4 Sidi 5 Amina 7 Zobeide
   dervish: 4 Agib
   merchant: 7 Sindbad
   poet: Kab 5 Antar
   prince: 7 Alasnam
   sailor: 6 Sinbad 7 Sindbad
   sorceress: 5 Amine
   youth: 7 Aladdin
Arabic: *alphabet:* tha, jim, kha, dal, zay, sin, sad, dad, ayn, qaf, kaf, lam, mim, nun, waw 4 alif, dhal, shin 5 ghayn
   script: 5 cufic, kufic, neski 6 neshki
arable: 7 fertile 8 plowable, tillable
aracanga: 5 macaw
aracari: 6 toucan
arachnid: 4 crab, mite, tick 6 acarus, spider 8 scorpion 9 tarantula
Aram: 12 ancient Syria
Aramaic: 6 Syriac 9 Samaritan
araneous: 4 thin 8 delicate, gossamer 9 arachnoid 10 cobweblike
araphorostic: 7 unsewed 8 seamless
araponga: 8 bellbird
Arawakan: *Indian:* 4 Uran 5 Araua, Bares, Guana, Moxos, Piros 6 Campas 7 Atorais, Banivas, Jucunas, Lucayos, Tacanan, Ticunan 8 Lorenzan
   language: 5 Taino
arbiter: 5 judge 6 umpire 7 referee 8 dictator 9 moderator 11 adjudicator
arbitrary: 4 rash 6 random, thetic 7 willful 8 absolute, despotic 9 imperious 10 autocratic, capricious, highhanded, peremptory, tyrannical 11 dictatorial 12 unreasonable 13 irresponsible
arbitrate: 6 decide, settle 7 adjudge, mediate 9 determine, intercede
arbitrator: 8 mediator 9 ombudsman 11 conciliator
arbor: bar, rod 4 axle, beam 5 bower, shaft 6 gazebo 7 mandrel, pergola, retreat, spindle, trellis
arbustum: 5 copse 7 orchard 10 plantation
arc: bow 4 bend, halo 5 curve, orbit 7 rainbow 9 spotlight 10 circle part
   chord of: 4 sine
   horizon: 7 azimuth
arc lamp rod: 6 carbon
arca: box 5 chest, paten 9 reliquary
arcade: 6 loggia 7 gallery, portico 8 arcature 9 colonnade 10 passageway

Arcadia: 4 Eden 6 Arcady 8 paradise
  huntress: 8 Atalanta
  princess: 4 Auge
  town: 4 Alea
  woodland spirit: Pan
arcadian: 5 ideal, rural 6 rustic, simple 7 bucolic, idyllic 8 pastoral, shepherd
arcane: 6 hidden, occult 8 esoteric 10 cabalistic, mysterious
arcanum: 6 elixir, remedy, secret 7 mystery
Arcas: *father:* 4 Zeus
  mother: 8 Callisto
  son: 4 Azan 8 Apheidas
arch: bow, coy, sly 4 bend, hump, span 5 chief, curve, great, prime, saucy, vault 6 camber, clever, fornix, impish, instep 7 cunning, eminent, roguish, support, waggish 9 principal 11 mischievous
  inner curve of: 8 intrados
  kind of: 4 flat 5 round, Tudor 6 lancet 7 rampant, trefoil 9 horseshoe, primitive, segmental 10 shouldered 11 equilateral 12 basket-handle, four-centered 13 three-cornered
  memorial: 6 pailoo, pailou, pailow
  molding: 9 accoclade
  part: 8 keystone, springer, voussoir
  pointed: 4 ogee 5 ogive 6 Gothic
arch-enemy: 5 devil, Satan
archaic: old 7 ancient 8 historic, obsolete 9 venerable 10 antiquated 12 old-fashioned
archangel: 5 Satan, Uriel 7 Gabriel, Michael, Raphael
archer: 4 Clym, Egil, Tell 5 cupid 6 bowman 9 Robin Hood 11 Sagittarius
archery: *deity:* 6 Apollo 7 Artemis
  locker: 6 ascham
  lover: 11 toxophilite
  target: 4 wand 5 clout
archetype: 4 idea 5 ideal, model 7 example, paragon, pattern 8 exemplar, original, paradigm 9 prototype 10 pilot model
architect: 5 maker 6 artist, author 7 artisan, builder, creator, planner 8 designer 9 draftsman
architectural: 8 tectonic
architecture: *convexity:* 7 entasis
  order: 5 Doric, Ionic 10 Corinthian
  ornament: ove 5 gutta 6 dentil, rosace 7 rosette
  style: 5 Doric, Greek, Ionic, Tudor 6 French, Gothic, Lancet, Modern, Norman 7 Baroque, Cape Cod, English, Italian, Moorish, Spanish 8 Academic, Colonial, Egyptian, Etruscan, Georgian 9 Byzantine, Palladian 10 Corinthian, Romanesque 11 Renaissance
archive: 5 annal 6 museum, record 7 library 8 document, register 9 chronicle

archon: 5 ruler 8 dictator, official 10 magistrate
arctic: icy 4 cold, cool, shoe 5 gelid, polar 6 boreal, chilly, frigid, galosh 8 northern, overshoe
Arctic: *base:* 4 Etah
  bird: auk 9 ptarmigan
  canoe: 5 kayak, umiak 6 oomiak
  current: 8 Labrador
  dog: 5 husky 7 samoyed 8 malamute
  explorer: Nay, Rae 4 Byrd, Eric, Kane, Ross 5 Davis, Peary 6 Baffin, Bering, Button, Greely, Hudson, Nansen, Nobile 7 McClure, Wilkins, Wrangel 8 Amundsen 9 Frobisher, Rasmussen, Stefansson 10 Willoughby
  gull (genus): 4 xema
  headland: 5 Odden
  inhabitant: 4 Lapp 5 Aleut, Inuit 6 Eskimo, Indian 7 Alaskan 9 Laplander
  island: 5 Banks, Devon 6 Baffin 7 Wrangel 8 Bathurst
  jacket: 5 parka 6 anorak
  musk ox: 6 ovibos
  plain: 6 tundra
  plant: 5 ledum
  sea: 4 Kara 6 Laptev 7 Barents, Chukchi, Lincoln 8 Beaufort
  sea animal: 6 narwal, walrus 8 narwhale
  snowstorm: 5 purga
Arcturus: 4 star
arcuate: 4 bent 5 bowed 6 arched, curved, hooked
ardent: hot 4 avid, fond, keen, warm 5 eager, fiery, rethe(Sc.) 6 ablaze, fervid 7 amorous, earnest, feeling, fervent, flaming, intense, shining, zealous 8 desirous, vehement 9 impetuous, perfervid 11 inflammable 12 enthusiastic
ardor: 4 dash, elan, glow, heat, love, zest 5 gusto, verve 6 desire, fervor, mettle, spirit 7 passion 8 devotion, vivacity 9 animation, calenture 10 enthusiasm
arduous: 4 hard 5 lofty, steep 6 trying 7 onerous 8 exacting, tiresome, toilsome 9 difficult, laborious, strenuous 10 exhausting
area: 4 belt, size, zone 5 field, range, realm, scene, scope, space, tract 6 extent, locale, region, sector, sphere 7 expanse, purlieu 8 district, province 9 bailiwick, territory 12 neighborhood
  measure: are 4 acre, road 6 orpent 7 hectare
  pert. to: 7 spatial
areca: 4 palm 5 betel
arena: pit 4 bowl, oval, ring, rink 5 court, field, stage 6 sphere 7 stadium, theater 8 coliseum, province 10 hippodrome 12 amphitheater
  sports: See **field:** *athletic*
arenaceous: 5 sandy 6 gritty 8 sabulous

areola: pit **4** area, ring, spot **5** space **9** periphery **10** interstice
areometer: **10** hydrometer
Ares: **4** Mars
father: **4** Zeus
mother: **4** Enyo, Hera
sister: **4** Eris
son: **6** Cycnus
arete: **4** crag **5** crest, ridge, valor **6** virtue **9** manliness **10** excellence
argali: **5** sheep **6** aoudad
argent: **4** coin **5** money, white **6** silver **7** shining, silvery **9** whiteness
Argentina: *capital:* **11** Buenos Aires
capital suburb: **5** Lanus, Moron **7** Quilmes
city: **4** Azul, Goya **5** Jujuy, Salta **6** Parana **7** Cordoba, La Rioja, Mendoza, Posadas, San Juan, Santa Fe, Tucuman **8** Santiago
estuary: **7** La Plata
explored by: **5** Cabot **11** Juan de Solis
falls: **6** Iguacu, Iguazu **7** Iguassu
former dictator: **9** Juan Peron **11** Isabel Peron
Indian: **4** Lule **7** Guarani
measure: **4** sino, vara **5** legua **6** cuadra, fanega **7** manzana
monetary unit: **4** peso **7** centavo
mountain pass: **9** Uspallata
mountain peak: **4** Mayo **5** Cachi, Laudo **6** Bonete, Pissis, Rincon **9** Aconcagua, Incahuasi, Tupungato
mountain range: **5** Andes
port: **6** Rawson, Viedma **7** La Plata, Rosario **8** Gallegos **11** Bahia Blanca, Buenos Aires
province: **5** Chaco, Jujuy, Pampa, Rioja, Salta **6** Chubut **7** Cordoba, Formosa, Mendoza, Neuquen, Rio Negro, San Juan, San Luis, Santa Fe, Tucuman **8** Misiones, Santiago **9** Catamarca, Entre Rios
river: **4** Coig **5** Atuel, Chico, Dulce, Limay, Negro, Teuco **6** Chubut, Parana, Quinto, Salado **7** Bermejo **8** Colorado, Gallegos **9** Rio Grande
southern steppes: **9** Patagonia
volcano: **5** Lanin, Maipo **6** Domuyo **7** Peteroa
weight: **4** last **5** grano **7** quintal **8** tonelada
argil: **4** clay **7** alumina
argillaceous: **5** loamy **6** clayey, doughy, earthy, spongy
Argonaut: **5** Jason **8** wanderer **10** adventurer
Argos: *king:* **4** Abas **6** Danaus **7** Lynceus **8** Acrisius, Adrastus
princess: **5** Danae
argosy: **4** boat, ship **5** craft, fleet **6** supply, vessel **7** galleon **10** storehouse

argot: **4** cant **5** flash, lingo, slang **6** jargon, patois **7** dialect
argue: **4** moot, show, spar **5** cavil, claim, clash **6** bicker, debate, induce, reason **7** contend, contest, discuss, dispute, quarrel, wrangle **8** indicate, maintain, persuade **11** expostulate, remonstrate
argument: row **4** case, fuss, idea, plea, plot, text **5** set to, theme **6** combat, debate, hassle, reason **7** defense, polemic, rhubarb, summary **8** abstract **9** discourse, statement **10** difference **11** altercation, controversy
conclusive: **6** corker **7** crusher **8** clincher **9** knockdown **11** sockdolager, sockdologer
fallacious: **7** sophism
negative side: con
positive side: pro
specious: rot **8** claptrap, nonsense **9** sophistry **10** paralogism
starting point: **7** premise
argumentative: **7** eristic **8** forensic **10** rhetorical **11** indicative, contentious, presumptive **12** disputatious **13** controversial
Argus-eyed: **8** vigilant **10** on the alert
argute: **5** acute, sharp **6** shrewd, shrill **8** saw-edged **9** sagacious
arhat: **4** monk **5** lohan, saint
aria: air **4** solo, song, tune **6** melody **7** sortita
arid: dry **4** bald, bare, dull, lean **6** barren, jejune, meager **7** parched, sterile **8** withered **9** unfertile, waterless **10** desiccated, siccaneous **12** moistureless **13** uninteresting
ariel: **7** gazelle
Aries: ram
mother: **4** Enyo
aril: pod **7** coating **8** covering **9** appendage **10** integument
ariose: **7** melodic **8** songlike **9** melodious
arise: **4** flow, lift, rear, soar **5** begin, get up, issue, mount, raise, stand, surge, tower, waken **6** accrue, amount, appear, ascend, come up, derive, emerge, happen, spring **7** develop, emanate, proceed **8** stem from **9** come about, originate, take place
arista: awn **5** beard **9** appendage
aristocracy: **5** elite **8** nobility **9** oligarchy **10** ruling class, upper crust
aristocrat: **4** peer **7** Brahmin **8** nobleman **9** blue-blood, patrician **12** thoroughbred
Aristophanes work: **5** Birds, Frogs **6** Clouds, Plutus
Aristotle: **5** Greek **11** philosopher
birthplace: **6** Thrace **7** Stagira
category: **4** time **5** place **6** action **7** quality **8** position, quantity, relation **9** pas-

sivity, substance **10** possession
disciple: **11** Peripatetic
father: **10** Nicomachus
school: **6** Lyceum
teacher: **5** Plato
works: **7** De Anima, Organon, Poetico **8** Politics, Rhetoric
Arizona: *capital:* **7** Phoenix
city: Ajo **4** Mesa, Yuma **5** Tempe **6** Bisbee, Tucson **7** Nogales **8** Prescott **9** Flagstaff
county: **4** Gila, Pima **5** Pinal **6** Apache, Graham, Mohave, Navajo **7** Cochise, Yavapai **8** Coconino, Maricopa
dam: **6** Hoover **7** Boulder **8** Coolidge, Tailings **9** Roosevelt
desert: **7** Painted
early explorer: **6** De Niza **8** Coronado
forest: **6** Kaibab **9** Petrified
gorge: **11** Grand Canyon
Indian: **4** Hopi, Pima, Yuma **6** Apache, Navaho, Navajo, Papago
Indian war chiefs: **7** Cochise **8** Geronimo
lake: **4** Mead **6** Havasu **9** Roosevelt, San Carlos
mountain peak: **5** Lemon **6** Graham **7** Hualpai, Pastora **8** Mazatzal **9** Humphreys
mountain range: **5** Black **8** Gila Bend **13** Santa Catalina
river: **4** Gila, Salt **5** Verde **8** Colorado, San Pedro **9** San Carlos
site of noted battle: **8** O.K. Corral (Tombstone)
state bird: **10** cactus wren
state flower: **7** saguaro
state motto: **9** Ditat Deus (God enriches)
state nickname: **11** Grand Canyon
state tree: **9** paloverde
ark: bin, box **4** boat, ship **5** barge, chest, hutch **6** basket, coffer, refuge, wangan **7** retreat, shelter, wanigan **8** flatboat
builder: Noe **4** Noah
resting place: **6** Ararat
Arkansas: *capital:* **10** Little Rock
city: **4** Hope, Mena **5** Salem, Wynne **6** Des Arc, Lonoke, Searcy **7** De Queen **9** Fort Smith, Pine Bluff **10** Hot Springs
county: Lee **4** Clay, Drew, Pike, Poke, Pope, Yell **5** Izard, Sharp, Stone **6** Baxter, Chicot, Conway, Sevier **7** Pulaski **8** Poinsett
explored by: **6** de Soto, Joliet **7** La Salle **9** Marquette
Indian tribe: **5** Caddo **6** Quapaw
lake: **7** Greeson, Norfork
mountain: **4** Blue **6** Boston, Walker **8** Magazine
plateau: **5** Ozark
river: Red **5** Black, White **6** Saline **8** Arkansas, Cimarron, Ouachita **11** Mississippi

spa: **10** Hot Springs
state bird: **11** mockingbird
state flower: **12** apple blossom
state motto: **13** Regnat Populus (The people rule)
state nickname: **17** Land of Opportunity
state tree: **4** pine
unique mine product in U.S.: **8** diamonds
arkose: **9** sandstone
arm: bay, fin **4** limb, spur, wing **5** bough, equip, fiord, firth, fjord, force, inlet, might, power **6** branch, energy, member, outfit, sleeve, weapon **7** flipper, fortify, furnish, prepare, protect, provide, support **8** strength **9** appendage, extension **10** instrument, projection
bone: **4** ulna **6** radius **7** humerus
hollow at bend: **8** chelidon
joint: **4** ares **5** elbow, wrist
muscle: **6** biceps **7** triceps
part: **4** ares **5** elbow, wrist
pert. to: **8** brachial
armada: **4** navy **5** fleet **8** flotilla, squadron, warships **9** task force
armadillo: **5** poyou **6** mulita **7** tatouay **8** pangolin **10** pichiciago
giant: **4** tatu **5** tatou **6** peludo
small: **4** peba **11** quirquincho
three banded: **4** apar **5** apara **6** mataco
armament: **7** defense **8** ordnance, security, weaponry **9** munitions, safeguard **12** military gear
armamentarium: **4** data **5** store **6** armory **7** arsenal **9** apparatus, equipment **10** collection
armband: **7** maniple **8** brassard
Armenia: **14** Soviet Republic
ancient name: **5** Minni **8** Anatolia
capital: **7** Yerevan
lake: **5** Sevan
mountain: **7** Aragats
river: **5** Araks **6** Razdan (Zanga)
armet: **6** helmet
armistice: **4** lull **5** peace, truce **9** cessation **10** suspension
armoire: **8** cupboard, wardrobe **12** clothespress
armor: **4** egis, mail **5** guard, plate, byrnie, sheath, shield **7** cuirass, defense, hauberk **8** covering **10** protection
arm: **8** brassard, brassart **9** gardebras
armpit: **8** pallette
bearer: **6** squire **7** armiger, custrel
cap: **10** cerveliere
elbow guard: **9** cubitiere
face: **6** beaver **7** ventail **8** aventail
foot: **8** sabbaton, solleret
hand: **8** gauntlet
head: **4** coif **6** helmet **7** basinet
horse: **5** barde **6** crinet **7** peytrel, poitrel **8** chamfron
knee: **11** genouillere

leg: 4 boot, jamb 5 jambe 6 greave 7 chausse, jambeau

shoulder: 7 ailette 8 pauldron, pouldron 9 epauliere

skirt: 4 tace 5 tasse 6 taslet, tasset 11 braconniere

thigh: 5 cuish 6 cuisse, tuille 8 cuissard

throat: 6 camail, gorget

armored: 6 mailed, plated 8 ironclad, shielded 9 panoplied, protected 11 encuirassed

armpit: ala(L.) 5 oxter(Sc.) 6 axilla 7 axillae(pl.)

pert. to: 7 axillar

armory: 4 dump 5 depot 7 arsenal 8 magazine 9 warehouse

army: 4 here, host 5 array, crowd, force, horde 6 cohort, legion, number, throng, troops 7 militia 8 soldiers, warriors 9 multitude

chaplain: 5 padre

commission: 6 brevet

engineer: 6 sapper 7 pioneer

enlisted man: NCO 5 GI Joe 7 private 8 doughboy

mascot: 4 mule

meal: 4 chow, mess

NCO: PFC 8 corporal, sergeant

officer: 5 major 7 captain, colonel, general 8 sergeant 10 lieutenant

pert. to: 7 martial 8 military

post: 4 base, camp, fort

postal abbreviation: APO

school: OCS, OTS 7 academy 9 West Point

storehouse: 5 depot 6 armory 7 arsenal

unit: 5 corps, squad, troop 6 detail, outfit 7 brigade, company, platoon 8 division, regiment, battalion, task force 10 detachment

vehicle: 4 jeep, tank 9 half-track

army ant: 6 driver 9 legionary

aroid: 4 taro 5 apium, tania 6 tanier 8 araceous

aroma: 4 odor 5 nidor, savor, scent, smell 6 flavor 7 bouquet, perfume 9 fragrance, redolence

aromatic: 5 balmy, spicy, sweet 6 fruity, savory 7 odorous, piquant, pungent 9 ambrosial

gum: 5 myrrh

herb: 4 dill, mint, nard 5 anise, basil, clary, nondo, thyme 8 lavender, rosemary

seed: 5 anise, cumin 6 nutmeg

spice: 4 mace 5 clove 8 cinnamon

tree: 6 balsam, laurel 8 huisache 9 sassafras

weed: 5 tansy

around: 4 near 5 about, alive, circa 6 in turn 7 close by, through 10 encircling, enveloping, everywhere, on all sides

12 here and there

around-the-clock: 8 constant, unending 9 incessant, perpetual 10 continuous 11 day and night

arouse: 4 call, fire, move, spur, stir, whet 5 alarm, awake, evoke, pique, raise, rally, rouse 6 excite, foment, incite, kindle, revive, summon, thrill, work up 7 actuate, agitate, animate, enliven, incense, inflame 9 stimulate

arpeggio: 7 roulade, flourish 10 musical run

arraign: try 4 cite 6 accuse, charge, indict 7 impeach 8 denounce 9 challenge 11 incriminate 13 call to account

arrange: fix, set 4 edit, file, form, plan, sort 5 adapt, align, array, drape, frame grade, group, score, space 6 adjust, codify, design, devise, settle 7 catalog, compose, dispose, gradate, marshal, prepare, seriate, work out 8 classify, conclude, organize, regulate, tabulate 9 collocate 10 put in order 11 alphabetize, orchestrate

mutually: 5 agree 7 concert

arrangement: 4 deal 5 index, order, set-up 6 format, layout, scheme, system, treaty 7 pattern 8 contract, sequence 9 direction, structure 10 allocation 11 composition, disposition 12 dispensation

arrant: bad 5 utter 6 brazen 7 blatant, vagrant 8 rascally 9 confirmed, downright, itinerant, notorious, out and out, shameless 11 unmitigated 13 thoroughgoing

arras: 7 drapery, hanging 8 tapestry

array: 4 garb, host, robe, show 5 adorn, align, dress, habit, order 6 attire, bedeck, clothe, draw up, finery, series 7 apparel, arrange, company, deck out, display, furnish, marshal 8 accouter, grouping 10 assemblage

arrears: 4 IOU's 9 liability 11 unpaid bills 12 indebtedness

arrest: nab 4 curb, grab, halt, hold, jail, stay, stop 5 catch, check, delay, pinch, seize 6 collar, detain, hinder, lock up, retard, thwart 7 capture, custody, suspend 8 imprison, slow down, obstruct, restrain 9 apprehend, intercept, interrupt 11 incarcerate

arresting: 8 gripping, pleasing, striking 10 impressive, noticeable

arret: 5 edict 6 decree 8 decision, judgment

arrie: auk 5 murre 9 guillemot, razorbill

arris, aris: 4 pien 5 angle, piend

arrive: 4 come, land, show 5 reach 6 appear, attain, make it, turn up 7 prosper, succeed 8 get there

arrogance: 5 pride 6 hubris, hybris 7

conceit, disdain, egotism, hauteur **9** insolence **10** effrontery **11** affectation
arrogant: **5** lofty, proud **6** lordly, uppish **7** haughty **8** affected, assuming, cavalier, fastuous, insolent, superior **9** conceited, insulting, presuming **10** disdainful, hoity-toity **11** dictatorial, domineering, highfalutin, impertinent, overbearing, **12** contemptuous, contumelious, presumptuous, supercilious
arrogate: **4** grab, take **5** claim, seize, usurp **6** assume **7** preempt **8** take over **10** commandeer, confiscate
arrondissement: **4** ward **8** division
arrow: pin, rod **4** bolt, dart, reed **5** shaft **6** sprite, weapon **7** missile, pointer **9** indicator
case: **6** quiver
feathered: **4** vire
maker: **6** bowyer **8** fletcher
part: **4** barb, butt, head, nock **5** shaft, stele **7** feather
point: neb **4** barb
poison: **4** haya, inee, upas **5** urali **6** antiar, curare, sumpit, wagogo **7** woorali
rotating: **4** vire
arrow-shaped: **6** beloid **8** sagittal **9** sagittate
Arrowsmith author: **5** Lewis
arrowstone: **9** belemnite
arrowwood: **5** alder **9** buckthorn **10** burrobrush
arroyo: **5** brook, creek, gulch, gully, hondo, zanja **6** ravine, stream **7** channel **11** watercourse
ars artium: **5** logic
arsenal: **6** armory, supply **8** dockyard, magazine **10** storehouse **13** armamentarium
arsenate: *copper:* **7** erinite
hydrous zinc: **7** adamite
red manganese: **9** sarkinite
arsenic: **6** poison **8** chemical
antimony: **10** allemonite
sulfide: **7** realgar
trisulfide: **8** orpiment
arsenillo: **9** atacamite
arsenopyrite: **7** danaite
arsis: **4** beat **5** ictus **6** accent, rhythm
opposed to: **6** thesis
arson: **12** incendiarism
arsonist: **7** firebug **10** pyromaniac
art: ars(L.) **4** wile **5** craft, knack, magic, skill, trade **7** calling, cunning, faculty, finesse, science **8** business, learning **9** dexterity, duplicity, ingenuity **10** profession **11** contrivance, cultivation
black: **5** magic **7** alchemy **8** wizardry **9** diablerie **10** demonology, necromancy **11** conjuration
fancier of: **6** votary **7** esthete, devotee **10** dilettante **11** connoisseur
gallery: **5** salon **6** museum

manual: **5** craft, sloid, slojd, sloyd
school: **4** Dada **5** Dutch **6** ashcan, French, Paduan **7** Bauhaus, Flemish, Italian, Lombard, Umbrian **8** American, eclectic, Milanese, Scottish **9** Bolognese **10** Raphaelite
style: pop **4** Dada **5** genre **6** cubism **7** baroque, fauvism, realism **10** surrealism **11** objectivism, primitivism, romanticism **13** impressionism **14** abstractionism
Artemis: **5** Diana
birthplace: **5** Delos
brother: **6** Apollo
father: **4** Zeus
mother: **4** Leto
priestess: **9** Iphigenia
artel: **5** union **11** association, cooperative
artery: way **4** path, road **5** route **6** course, street, vessel **7** anonyma, conduit, highway **9** maxillary
trunk: **5** aorta **6** aortae(pl.)
head: **7** carotid
heart: **8** coronary
pulsation: **5** ictus
artful: apt, sly **4** foxy, wily **5** suave **6** adroit, clever, crafty, facile, shrewd, smooth, tricky **7** crooked, cunning, politic, vulpine **8** slippery, stealthy **9** deceitful, deceptive, designing, dexterous, practical
Artful Dodger: **7** Dawkins (Jack)
artfulness: **8** subtlety **9** diplomacy, duplicity, stratagem **10** refinement
arthritis: **4** gout
arthron: **5** joint **12** articulation
Arthur: See **King Arthur**
artichoke: **5** plant **6** Cynara **7** chorogi
leafstalk: **5** chard
relative: **7** cardoon
article: one, the **4** item, term **5** essay, paper, piece, plank, point, story, theme, thing **6** clause, detail, object, report **7** feature **8** causerie, doctrine **9** condition, statement **10** particular **11** composition, stipulation
French: les, une
German: das, der, die, ein
Spanish: las, los, una
articulate: say **5** speak, utter, vocal **6** fluent, verbal **7** express, jointed **8** distinct **9** enunciate, pronounce, talkative **10** formulated, meaningful, say clearly **12** intelligible
artificer: **4** hoax, plot, ploy, ruse, wile **5** blind, cheat, dodge, feint, fraud, guile, skill, trick **6** deceit, device, gambit **7** cunning, evasion, finesse **8** intrigue, maneuver, pretense **9** deception, expedient, ingenuity, invention, stratagem **10** subterfuge **11** machination
artificial: **4** mock, sham **5** bogus, faked, false **6** ersatz, forced, pseudo, unreal **7**

assumed, feigned **8** affected, falsetto, spurious **9** insincere, pretended, simulated, synthetic, unnatural **10** factitious, fictitious, theatrical **11** counterfeit

artillery: 4 arms, guns **6** cannon **7** rockets **8** missiles, ordnance
emplacement: **7** battery
fire: **5** salvo **6** rafale **7** barrage
wagon: **6** camion **7** caisson

artilleryman: 6 gunner, lascar **8** topechee **9** cannoneer **10** bombardier

artiodactyl: ox; pig **4** deer, goat **5** camel, sheep **6** artiad **7** giraffe **8** antelope **12** hippopotamus

artisan: 6 expert **9** craftsman **12** professional **13** skilled worker

artist: 4 star **5** actor **6** dancer, expert, master, singer, wizard **7** painter **8** designer, musician, sculptor, virtuoso **9** performer **12** professional

artless: 4 naif, open **5** frank, naive, plain **6** candid, rustic, simple **7** natural **8** innocent, trusting **9** childlike, guileless, ingenuous, untutored **10** unaffected **11** undesigning **15** unsophisticated

arty: 5 showy **9** imitative, overblown **11** pretentious, superficial

arui: 5 sheep **6** aoudad

arum: 4 taro **5** aroid, plant **10** cuckoopint
family: **7** araceae
water: **5** calla

arundinaceous: 5 reedy

Aryan: 11 Indo-Iranian **12** Indo-European
deity: **6** Ormazd, Ormuzd
god of fire: **4** Agni
language: **5** Latin **7** Persian **8** Sanskrit
of India: **5** Hindu

as: for, qua **4** like, that, thus, when **5** equal, since, while **7** because, equally, similar **9** therefore
a rule: **7** usually **8** commonly **9** generally **10** ordinarily
good as: **5** about **6** all but, almost, nearly
if: **5** quasi **9** seemingly
long as: **5** since **7** because **10** seeing that **11** considering

As You Like It character: 5 Celia, Phebe **6** Jaques, Oliver **7** Charles, Orlando **8** Rosalind
clown: **10** Touchstone
forest: **5** Arden
Rosalind's alias: **8** Ganymede

Asa: 6 healer **9** physician
father: **4** Abia
son: **11** Jehoshaphat

asafetida: 4 hing **6** ferula **8** gum resin

ascend: 4 rise, soar **5** climb, mount, scale, tower **7** clamber **8** escalate, progress **12** gain altitude

ascendancy: 4 sway **5** power **7** control, mastery, success **8** dominion, prestige,

whip hand **9** authority, dominance, influence, supremacy **11** sovereignty, superiority

ascent: 4 hill, ramp, rise **5** slope **6** stairs **7** incline, upgrade, upswing **8** eminence, gradient, progress **9** acclivity, elevation **11** advancement

ascertain: get **5** learn **6** dig out **7** find out, seek out, unearth **8** discover **9** determine

ascetic: nun **4** monk, yogi **5** fakir, stark, stoic, Yogin **6** Essene, severe, strict **7** austere, eremite, recluse, stylite **8** anchoret **9** abstinent, anchorite **10** abstemious **11** disciplined, self-denying
Buddhist: **7** bhikshu

ascot: tie **5** scarf **6** cravat **7** necktie **9** racetrack
relative: bib **6** choker **7** bolo tie

ascribe: lay **4** cite **5** blame, infer, refer **6** accuse, allege, assign, attach, charge, credit, impute **8** accredit **9** attribute

ascription: 6 prayer **11** declaration
of praise: **6** gloria
popular: **6** repute

ascus: bag, sac

asea: 4 lost **6** addled, adrift, in a fog **7** puzzled, sailing **8** confused **9** befuddled, uncertain **10** bewildered, ocean-going

aseptic: 4 cold **5** clean **6** barren **7** sterile **8** detached, lifeless **9** purifying

Asgard: *bridge to:* **7** Bifrost
watchman: **8** Heimdall

ash: ase(Sc.) **4** coke, tree **5** ember, rowan **6** cinder **7** clinker, residue
receptacle: bin, box, urn
reduce to: **7** cremate
tobacco: **6** dottel, dottle

ashamed: 7 abashed, hangdog **8** contrite, red-faced **9** mortified **10** humiliated, remorseful **11** embarrassed

Ashanti pepper: 5 cubeb

ashen: wan **4** gray, grey, pale **5** waxen **6** pallid **7** ghastly **8** blanched **9** cinereous

Asher: *daughter:* **5** Serah **6** Beriah
father: **5** Jacob
son: **4** Usui **6** Jimnah

ashkoko: 4 cony, hare **5** daman, hyrax

Asia: 6 Orient **9** continent
country: **4** Iran, Iraq, Laos, Oman **5** Burma, China, Egypt(part), India, Japan, Nepal, Qatar, Syria, Yemen **6** Bhutan, Brunei, Cyprus, Israel, Jordan, Kuwait, Russia(part), Taiwan, Turkey(part) **7** Bahrain, Lebanon **8** Cambodia, Malaysia, Maldives, Mongolia, Pakistan, Sri Lanka, Thailand **9** Indonesia, Singapore **10** Bangladesh, North Korea, South Korea **11** Afghanistan, Philippines, Saudi Arabia **12** Arab Emirates, North Vietnam, South Vietnam
desert **4** Gobi, Thar (India) **6** Syrian **7** Arabian **10** Takla Makan (China)

ethnic group: Han, Lao, Mon, Tai 4 Arab, Kurd, Shan, Thai, Turk 5 Karen, Khmer, Malay, Tajik, Tamil, Uzbek 6 Indian, Lepcha, Manchu, Mongol, Sindhi 7 Baluchi, Bengali, Persian, Punjabi, Tibetan 8 Armenian, Kanarese 9 Chungchia, Dravidian, Indo-Aryan, Sinhalese

lake: 6 Baikal 7 Aral Sea 8 Balkhash, Tungting 10 Caspian Sea

mountain pass: 6 Burzil 8 Baroghil

mountain peak: 4 Fang 5 Jannu, Kamet 6 Batura, Cho Oyu, Kailas, Kungpu, Nuptse, Pobeda, Trivor 7 Everest 9 Annapurna

mountain range: 5 Altai, Kumon, Sayan 6 Elburz, Kunlun, Pamirs, Zagros 7 Khingan, Kumgang 8 Tien Shan 9 Himalayas, Hindu Kush

river: Hsi, Ili 4 Amur, Lena, Onon, Ural, Yalu 5 Indus 6 Ganges, Irtysh, Mekong, Tigris, Yellow 7 Salween, Yangtze 8 Irrawaddy 9 Euphrates

Asia Minor (see also **Asia**): 8 Anatolia 9 peninsula

ancient city: 4 Myra, Myus, Teos, Troy 5 Issus, Perga 6 Mylasa, Patara, Priene, Sardis, Tarsus 7 Ephesus, Miletus 8 Colophon

ancient kingdom: 5 Caria, Ionia, Lydia, Mysia, Troad, Troas 6 Pontus 7 Cilicia, Phrygia, Pisidia 8 Bithynia, Pergamum

mountain: Ida

mountain range: 6 Sultan, Taurus

river: 5 Halys 8 Monderez

sea: 5 Black 6 Aegean 7 Marmara

aside: off 4 away, gone 5 aloof, apart 6 aslant 7 private, whisper 8 reserved, secretly, separate 9 obliquely, stage ploy 10 digression 11 parenthesis

aside from: 4 save 7 barring, besides 9 except for, excluding, outside of

asinine: 4 dull 5 crass, dense, inept, silly 6 absurd, obtuse, simple, stupid 7 doltish, fatuous, foolish, idiotic 9 gooselike, senseless

ask: beg, bid, sue 4 pray, quiz, seek 5 claim, crave, exact, plead, query, speer(Sc.), utter 6 adjure, demand, expect, invite 7 beseech, consult, entreat, implore, inquire, request, require, solicit 8 petition, question 11 interrogate

askance: 4 awry 5 askew 7 crooked 8 sideways 9 doubtfully, obliquely 11 skeptically 13 distrustfully, with suspicion

askew: 4 alop, awry 5 agley, amiss, atilt 6 aslant 7 asquint, cockeyed, crooked 9 distorted, out of line, to one side

asleep: out 4 dead, idle 6 dozing, latent, numbed 7 dormant, napping, unaware

8 off-guard 9 unfeeling 10 motionless, slumbering 11 not on the job, unconscious

asomatous: 10 immaterial 11 incorporeal

asp: 5 adder, aspen, snake, viper 7 serpent 8 ophidian

representative headdress: 6 uraeus

asparagus: 5 sprue

aspect: air 4 face, look, mien, side, view 5 angle, facet, guise, phase 6 manner, visage 7 bearing, feature, outlook 8 carriage, prospect 9 semblance 10 appearance 11 countenance

aspen: 4 tree 6 poplar 7 quaking 9 quivering, trembling, tremulous

asperity: ire 5 rigor 8 acerbity, acrimony, hardness, severity, sourness, tartness 9 briskness, harshness, roughness 10 bitterness, difficulty, unevenness 11 crabbedness 16 disagreeableness

asperse: 4 slur 5 abuse, decry, libel 6 defame, malign, revile 7 baptize, detract, slander, traduce 8 besmirch, christen, sprinkle 9 denigrate, discredit, disparage

aspersion: 7 baptism, calumny 8 innuendo 9 invective 12 vituperation

aspersorium: 4 font 5 basin, stoup

asphalt: 7 bitumen 8 blacktop, uintaite 10 wurtzilite

asphyxia: 5 apnea 6 apnoea 11 suffocation

aspic: gel 4 mold 5 jelly 7 gelatin 8 lavender

aspirant: 7 hopeful 9 applicant, candidate

aspiration: aim 4 goal, hope 5 ideal 8 ambition

aspire: try 4 hope, long, rise, seek, soar, wish 5 tower, yearn 6 ascend, desire 11 be ambitious

ass: 4 dolt, duff, fool 5 burro, chump, dunce, idiot, kiang, kulan 6 donkey, koulan, onager, quagga 8 imbecile 9 blockhead, simpleton 10 nincompoop

female: 5 jenny

male: 4 jack

assail: 4 beat, pelt 5 assay, beset, stone, storm, whack 6 accuse, attack, impugn, invade, malign, molest, scathe 7 assault, belabor, bombard 8 fall upon 9 encounter

assailant: 6 mugger 8 attacker 9 aggressor

Assam: 11 Indian state

capital: 8 Shillong

city: 4 Ledo 7 Gauhati, Nowgong

hills: 4 Abor, Garo, Miri, Naga 5 Khasi 6 Lushai

rubber: 7 rambong

silkworm: eri 4 eria

tribesman: Aka 4 Ahom, Garo, Naga 5 Lhota

assassin: gun **5** bravo **6** hit man, killer, slayer **8** murderer **9** cut-throat **10** hatchet man

Abel's: **4** Cain

Archduke Ferdinand's: **7** Princip

Gandhi's: **5** Godse

Garfield's: **7** Guiteau

J. F. Kennedy's: **6** Oswald

John Lennon's: **7** Chapman

Lincoln's: **5** Booth

Martin Luther King's: Ray

McKinley's: **8** Czolgosz

R. F. Kennedy's: **6** Sirhan

assault: mug **4** beat, raid, slug **5** beset, onset, pound, smite, storm **6** affray, assail, attack, buffet, breach, charge, fall on, invade **7** bombard, violate **8** outburst **9** incursion, onslaught **10** aggression **11** impinge upon

assay: try **4** test **5** prove **6** try out **7** analyze, examine **8** analysis, appraise, evaluate **9** determine **10** experiment

assemblage: **4** army, crew, herd, host, mass, pack **5** bunch, crowd, drove, flock, swarm **6** convoy, galaxy, hookup, throng **7** cluster, turnout **9** community **11** aggregation **12** congregation

art: **7** collage

assemble: fit **4** call, mass, meet **5** amass, piece, rally, unite **6** couple, gather, huddle, muster, summon **7** collect, convene, convoke, recruit **10** foregather **11** put together

assembly: hui **4** bevy, diet, feis, moot, raad **5** forum, group, junta, party, press, setup, troop **6** gemote, pow-wow, senate **7** comitia, company, council, husting, meeting, session, society **8** audience, conclave, congress, tribunal **10** convention, parliament **11** convocation, legislature

ecclesiastical: **5** synod **10** consistory

full: **5** plena

of witches: **5** coven

place: **5** agora

room: **4** hall **10** auditorium

assent: aye, bow, nod, yea, yes **4** amen **5** admit, agree, yield **6** accede, accept, accord, chorus, comply, concur, submit **7** approve, concede, conform, consent **8** adhesion, sanction **9** acquiesce, subscribe **10** compliance, condescend **11** acknowledge

assert: say **4** aver, avow, cite **5** claim, plead, posit, state, utter, vaunt, voice **6** affirm, allege, assure, avouch, defend, depone, depose, uphold **7** advance, betoken, contend, declare, protest, support **8** advocate, champion, maintain **9** predicate, vindicate

positively: **5** swear **10** asseverate

assertive: **8** dogmatic, positive **8** cocksure, forceful **9** defensive, pragmatic **10** aggressive **11** affirmatory

assess: tax **4** cess, levy, rate, scot, toll **5** price, value **6** charge, impose **7** measure **8** appraise, estimate **9** apportion

assessment: fee, tax **4** duty, levy **5** tithe **6** impost, surtax, tariff **7** scutage **9** valuation

assessor: **5** judge **11** adjudicator

asset: **9** advantage **11** distinction, strong point

assets: **5** goods, means, money, worth **6** credit, wealth **7** capital, effects **8** accounts, property **9** resources, valuables

assiduous: **4** busy **6** active **7** devoted **8** diligent, sedulous, studious **9** laborious, unwearied **10** persistent **11** hardworking, industrious, painstaking, persevering, unremitting **13** indefatigable

assign: fix, set **4** cede, give, rate, seal, sign **5** allot, allow, award, endow, order, refer **6** adduce, affect, allege, charge, convey, depute, detail, reckon, select, settle **7** adjudge, advance, appoint, ascribe, consign, dispose, mete out, specify, tribute **8** allocate, delegate, transfer **9** apportion, attribute, designate, determine **10** commission, distribute **11** appropriate

assignation: **4** date **5** tryst **7** meeting **10** rendezvous **11** appointment

assignment: job **4** duty, task **5** chore, stint **6** lesson **11** appointment

assimilate: **4** fuse **5** alter, blend, learn, liken, merge **6** absorb, digest, imbibe, take in **7** compare **8** resemble **9** transform **10** comprehend, metabolize, understand **11** appropriate, incorporate

assist: aid **4** abet, back, help **5** avail, boost, coach **6** back up, succor **7** benefit, be of use, relieve, support, sustain **8** befriend **9** give a hand **10** facilitate

assistant: **4** aide, ally, hand, zany **5** valet **6** deputy, lackey, minion, second **7** abettor, orderly, partner **8** adjutant, adjuvant, henchman, servitor **9** associate, auxiliary, secretary **10** accomplice **11** confederate, subordinate

to pastor: **6** curate

assistants: **4** crew **5** staff

assize: **4** rate, rule **5** court, edict, trial **6** decree **7** hearing, inquest, measure, precept, session, sitting, statute **8** assembly, standard, tribunal **9** enactment, ordinance **10** regulation

associate: mix, pal **4** aide, ally, chum, join, link, mate, peer, yoke **5** buddy, crony **6** cohort, fellow, friend, helper, hobnob, mingle, relate, spouse **7** adjunct, bracket, comrade, connect, consort, partner **8** copemate, federate, identify, intimate **9** affiliate, assistant, attendant, coadjutor, colleague, com-

panion, secondary, socialize **10** fraternize **11** concomitant
in crime: **10** accomplice
association: 4 body, bond, clan, club, coop **5** artel **6** cartel, league, pledge **7** company, consort, society **8** alliance, converse, intimacy, overtone, sodality **9** coalition, syndicate **10** assemblage, connection, fellowship, sisterhood **11** aggregation, brotherhood, combination, confederacy, conjunction, connotation, partnership
criminal: mob **4** gang, ring
literary: **6** lyceum **9** athenaeum
merchants': **5** hanse
political: **4** axis, bund **5** junta, party **7** machine
secret: **5** cabal, lodge
student: **7** council **8** sorority **10** fraternity
workers': **5** guild, union
assonance: pun **5** rhyme **8** paragram **11** resemblance
assort: 4 file, rank, type **5** group **8** classify **10** put in order
assortment: lot, set **4** olio **5** batch, group, suite **6** medley **7** melange, mixture, variety **8** pastiche **9** potpourri **10** collection, miscellany
assuage: 4 calm, ease **5** abate, allay, slake **6** lessen, modify, pacify, quench, reduce, soften, solace, soothe, temper **7** appease, comfort, mollify, relieve, satisfy **8** diminish, mitigate, moderate **9** alleviate **11** tranquilize
assuasive: 7 calming **8** soothing
as such: 5 per se **8** in itself **9** basically, in the main **11** in its own way
assume: don **4** dare, mask, sham **5** adopt, cloak, elect, feign, indue, infer, put on, raise, seize, usurp **6** accept, affect, clothe **7** believe, pretend, receive, suppose, surmise **8** accroach, arrogate, take over, simulate **9** undertake **11** appropriate, counterfeit
assumed: 5 alias, false **8** affected, supposed **9** fictional, uncertain **10** artificial, fictitious **12** hypothetical, supposititious
assumed name: 5 alias **9** pseudonym **11** nom de guerre
assuming: 5 lofty **8** arrogant, superior **11** pretentious **12** presumptuous
different form: **7** protean
assurance: 4 word **5** brass, faith, nerve **6** aplomb, belief, credit, pledge, safety, surety **7** courage, promise **8** audacity, boldness, coolness, security **9** certainty, certitude, cockiness, guarantee, impudence **10** confidence, effrontery **12** self-reliance
assure: 4 aver **6** assert, avouch, secure **7**

confirm, declare, hearten **8** convince, embolden **9** encourage, vouchsafe **10** asseverate, certiorate, strengthen, underwrite **13** say positively
assuredly: 4 amen **6** surely, verily **10** truthfully **11** indubitably, undoubtedly
Assyria: 5 Ashur, Assur **6** Asshur
capital: **5** Calah **7** Nineveh
city: **4** Hara, Opis **5** Al Sur **6** Arbela, Asshur, Kalakh **9** Dur Sargon
god: El, Zu; Ira, Sin **4** Adad, Anet, Nebo **5** Ashur, Hadad, Ninip **6** Asshur, Nergal, Shamas
goddess: **4** Nana, Nine **5** Istar **6** Allatu, Ishtar **9** Sarpanitu
king: Pul **5** Belus **6** Sargon **9** Sennacherib
measure: **4** cane, foot **5** makuk, gasab **6** artaba, gariba, ghalva **7** mansion
queen: **9** Semiramis
river: **6** Tigris
astart: 8 suddenly
asterisk: 4 star **13** reference mark
Asterius: 8 argonaut, minotaur
father: **10** Hyperasius
mother: **8** Pasiphae
wife: **6** Europa
astern: aft **4** back **6** behind **9** in the rear
asteroid: 4 Eros, Hebe, Iris, Juno **5** Ceres, Flora, Irene, Metis, Vesta **6** Astrea, Egeria, Europa, Hygeia, Pallas, planet, Psyche, Thetis **7** Eunomia, Fortuna, Lutetia **8** Massalia, starfish, starlike, Victoria **9** Melpomene, planetoid **10** Parthenope, star-shaped
first: **5** Ceres
nearest earth: **4** Eros
asthmatic: 5 pursy **6** wheezy **7** panting, puffing
astir: 5 about, afoot, alert **6** active, moving, roused **8** out of bed **10** up and doing
Astolat's Lily Maid: 6 Elaine
astonish: awe **4** daze **5** amaze **7** astound, impress, startle **8** bewilder, confound, surprise **11** flabbergast
astonished: 5 agape
astonishing: 8 fabulous **9** wonderful **10** incredible, stupendous **11** spectacular
astound: 5 amaze, appal, shock **6** appall **7** stagger, terrify **8** astonish, confound **9** overwhelm
astragalus: 5 talus **9** anklebone
astrakhan: 5 cloth **7** caracul, karakul
astral: 6 remote, starry **7** stellar **8** sidereal, starlike **9** visionary
astray: 4 awry, lost **5** agley, amiss, aside, wrong **6** abroad, afield, errant, erring, faulty **7** sinning **8** mistaken **9** wandering
astride: 4 atop **7** à cheval, mounted **8** bridging, spanning **9** astraddle **10** straddling

astringent: 4 acid, alum, sour, tart 5 acerb, harsh, stern 6 severe, tannin 7 austere, binding, styptic 11 acrimonious, compressive, contracting 12 constrictive
extract: 7 catechu
gum: 4 kino
astrologer: 4 Josh 6 Merlin 7 diviner 10 star reader 11 Nostradamus
astronaut: 9 cosmonaut
American: 4 Bean, Duke 5 Glenn, Irwin, Roosa, Scott, White, Young 6 Aldrin, Anders, Borman, Cernan, Conrad, Gordon, Kerwin, Lousma, Lovell, Worden 7 Collins, Grissom, Schirra, Shepard 8 McDivitt, Mitchell, Stafford 9 Armstrong, Mattingly 10 Cunningham
first in orbit: 5 Glenn
first on moon: 9 Armstrong
first space walker: 5 White
on longest mission: 4 Carr 5 Pogue 6 Gibson
on first space shuttle: 5 Young 7 Crippen
on rendezvous with Soviets: 5 Brand 7 Slayton 8 Stafford
Soviet: 7 Gagarin, Komarov
astromoner: 10 Hipparchus
astronomical: far 4 huge 5 great 6 uranic 7 distant, immense 8 colossal, infinite
instrument: aba 9 telescope 10 equatorial
measurement: 5 apsis 7 azimuth
Muse: 4 Clio 6 Urania
astute: sly 4 foxy, keen, wily 5 acute, canny, quick, sharp, smart 6 clever, crafty, shrewd 7 cunning, skilled 9 sagacious 10 discerning 14 discriminating
asunder: 5 apart, split 7 divided 8 divorced 9 separated
asylum: ark 4 home 5 altar, cover, haven 6 bedlam, harbor, refuge 7 alsatia, hospice, retreat, shelter 9 sanctuary 11 institution
asymmetric: 4 skew 9 distorted 10 unbalanced
asymmetry: 13 disproportion
at: 5 there 7 located
at all: 4 ever 5 aught, nohow 6 anyway
at hand: 4 near, nigh 7 close by, present
at last: 7 finally 10 ultimately
at once: now, PDQ 4 anon 5 amain 6 presto 9 forthwith, instantly, right away 11 immediately
Ata, Aeta: Ita 7 Negrito
Atahualpa: 4 Inca 6 Indian
ataman: 5 chief, judge 6 hetman 7 Cossack, headman
atap: 8 nipa palm
atavism: 9 reversion
atavus: 8 ancestor 11 grandfather
atelier: 6 studio 7 bottega 8 workshop
ates: 8 sweetsop
Athamas: *daughter:* 5 Helle

son: 7 Phrixos, Phrixus 8 Learchus
wife: Ino
athanor: 4 oven 7 furnace
Athapascan Indian: 4 Dene, Hupa, 5 Hoopa
atheist: 7 doubter 8 agnostic 11 nonbeliever
Athena, Athene: 4 Alea, Auge, Nike 5 Areia 6 Ergane, Hippia, Hygeia, Itonia, Pallas, Polias 7 Minerva 8 Apaturia, Athenaia 9 Parthenos, Poliuchos, Promachos 10 Chalinitis
pert. to: 9 Palladian
temple: 9 Parthenon
Athens (see also **Greece**): *alien resident:* 5 metic
ancient capital of: 6 Attica
assembly: 4 pnyx 5 boule
assembly platform: 4 bema
astronomer: 5 Meton
clan: obe
coin: 5 oboli 6 obolus 7 chalcus, chalkos
festival: 8 Apaturia, Athenaea 11 Scirophoria
founder: 7 Cecrops
general: 6 Nicias 7 Phocion 8 Zenophon
hill: 9 Acropolis 10 Lycabettus
hill where Paul preached: 9 Areopagus
historian: 8 Xenophon
king: 6 Codrus 7 Cecrops, Pandion
lawgiver: 5 Draco, Solon
magistrate: 5 draco 6 archon, dicast
marketplace: 5 agora
mountain: 6 Parnes
orator: 9 Isocrates
philosopher: 5 Plato 8 Socrates 9 Aristotle
platform: 4 bema 6 bemata(pl.)
rival: 6 Sparta
sculptor: 7 Phidias
seaport: 7 Piraeus
statesman: 8 Pericles 9 Aristides
temple: 4 Nike 9 Parthenon
theater: 5 Odeum
youth center: 6 Lyceum
athlete: pro 4 jock, star 5 boxer 7 amateur, acrobat, gymnast, tumbler 8 wrestler 9 aerialist
athlete's foot: 8 ringworm 10 skin fungus
athletic: 5 agile, burly, lusty, vital 6 brawny robust, sinewy, strong 8 muscular, powerful, vigorous 9 acrobatic, energetic, strapping
contest: 4 agon, game, meet, race 5 match 8 Olympics
field: 4 oval, ring, rink 5 arena, court, green 6 course 7 diamond, stadium 8 gridiron
prize: cup 5 medal, purse, 6 ribbon, trophy
athletics: 5 games, sport 8 exercise
athwart: 4 over 6 across, aslant 7

against, oblique **9** crosswise **10** perversely

atlantal: 6 atloid **8** anterior, cephalic

Atlantides: 8 Pleiades **10** Hesperides

atlas: 4 bone, book, list, maps, tome **5** titan **8** mainstay

Atlas: *daughter:* **4** Maia **6** Merope **7** Alcyone, Calypso, Electra, Kelaine, Taygete **8** Asterope, Pleiades

mother: **7** Clymeme

atmosphere: air **4** aura, mood, tone **5** ether **6** miasma, nimbus, welkin **7** climate, feeling **8** ambiance **10** background **11** environment

disturbance: **5** storm **6** static

gas: **5** argon **6** oxygen **8** nitrogen

phenomenon: **6** aurora, meteor

pressure: **10** barometric

atole: 4 mush **5** gruel **8** corn meal, porridge

atoll: 4 reef **6** island

Pacific: **4** Beru, Ebon, Mili **5** Makin, Wotho **6** Bikini, Canton, Jaluit, Likiep, Majuro, Tarawa **8** Eniwetok

atom: ace, bit, jot **4** iota, mite, mote, whit **5** monad, shade, speck, tinge **8** molecule, particle, quantity **9** corpuscle, scintilla

electrically charged: ion **5** anion **6** cation

nucleus: **6** proton **7** neutron

atomic: 4 tiny **6** minute **7** nuclear **9** molecular **13** infinitesimal

particle: **4** beta, pion **5** alpha, meson, quark **6** photon, proton **7** neutron **8** electron

physicist: **4** Bohr, Rabi **5** Fermi, Pauli **7** Compton, Meitner **8** Einstein

pile: **7** reactor

submarine: **5** Sargo, Skate **6** Triton **8** Nautilus

theory originator: **6** Dalton

atomize; 5 grate, spray **6** reduce **8** nebulize, vaporize **9** devastate, pulverize

atomy: 4 atom, mite, mote **5** pygmy **8** skeleton

atone: 6 repent **7** expiate **10** compensate, make amends

atonement: 7 penance **10** reparation **12** satisfaction

atonic: 7 unheard **9** voiceless **10** unaccented

atrabilious: 4 glum **6** gloomy, morose, sullen **10** melancholy

atramentous: 4 ebon, inky **5** black

Atreus: *brother:* **8** Thyestes

father: **6** Pelops

half brother: **10** Chrysippus

mother: **10** Hippodamia

slayer: **9** Aegisthus

son: **8** Menelaus **9** Agamemnon **11** Pleisthenes

wife: **6** Aerope

atrio: 6 valley **10** depression

atrip: 6 aweigh

atrium: 4 hall **5** court **6** cavity **7** auricle, chamber, passage **8** entrance

atrocha: 5 larva

atrocious: bad **4** dark, rank, vile **5** awful, black, cruel, gross **6** brutal, odious, savage, wicked **7** heinous, ungodly, violent **8** grievous, horrible, terrible **9** execrable, frightful, nefarious **10** abominable, villainous

atrophy: 6 shrink, starve, wither **9** waste away **10** emaciation **11** deteriorate

Atropos: 4 Fate

attach: add, fix, tag, tie **4** bind, glue, join, link, take, vest, weld **5** affix, annex, hitch, paste, seize, unite **6** accuse, addict, adhere, adjoin, append, arrest, cement, fasten, indict **7** adhibit, appoint, ascribe, connect, subjoin **9** affiliate, associate, garnishee

attached: 4 aide **8** diplomat

attached: 4 fond **6** doting

at base: **7** sessile

to the land: **8** praedial, agrarian

attachment: 4 love **8** devotion, fondness **9** accessory, addiction, adherence, affection **10** engagement, friendship **11** inclination

attack: fit **4** bout, fray, pang, raid, rush **5** assay, begin, beset, blitz, drive, fight, foray, ictus, onset, sally, spasm, storm **6** accuse, action, affray, assail, battle, charge, invade, onrush, pounce, sortie, strike, stroke, thrust **7** assault, censure, offense, potshot, seizure **8** paroxysm **9** incursion, onslaught **10** aggression

deceptive: **5** feint **9** diversion

suicidal: **8** kamikaze

attain: get, hit, win **4** earn, gain, rise **5** reach, touch **6** accede, amount, arrive, aspire, effect, secure, strike **7** achieve, acquire, compass, procure, succeed **8** overtake **10** accomplish, comprehend

attainment: 4 feat **5** skill **6** wisdom **14** accomplishment

attar: oil **7** essence, perfume

attempt: try **4** dare, seek, shot, stab, wage **5** assay, begin, essay, frame, start **6** effort **7** venture **8** endeavor, exertion **9** undertake **10** enterprise, experiment

attend: see **4** go to, hear, heed, mind, tend, wait **5** await, guard, nurse, serve, treat, visit, watch **6** assist, convoy, follow, harken, listen, shadow **7** care for, consort **8** champion, chaperon, minister **9** accompany

attendance: 4 gate **6** number, regard **8** presence **9** attention **11** application, expectation

attendant: aid **4** maid, page, zany **5** guide,

usher, valet **6** escort, helper, minion, porter, squire, waiter **7** courier, orderly, pageboy **8** chasseur, follower, henchman **9** assistant, associate, attentive, companion **10** consequent, subsequent **11** chamberlain, concomitant **12** accompanying

attendants: 5 suite, train **7** cortege, retinue **9** entourage

attention: ear **4** care, heed, hist, note **5** study **6** notice, regard **7** achtung(G.), respect **8** courtesy **9** diligence, obedience, vigilance **10** observance **11** observation **13** concentration, consideration

attentive: 4 wary **5** alert, awake, civil **6** intent, polite **7** careful, gallant, mindful **8** studious, watchful **9** advertent, assiduous, courteous, listening **10** interested **11** circumspect

attenuate: sap **4** thin **5** water **6** dilute, lessen, rarefy, reduce, weaken **7** slender **8** decrease, diminish, enfeeble, tapering **9** subtilize

attest: 5 prove, swear, vouch **6** adjure, affirm, invoke **7** certify, confirm, testify, witness **9** subscribe **12** authenticate

attic: 4 loft **6** garret **8** cockloft

Attic: 5 Greek **8** Athenian

Attic salt: wit

Attila: Hun **5** Etzel

attire: See **dress**

attitude: air, set **4** bias, mien, mood, pose **5** angle, phase, slant, stand **6** action, aspect, manner **7** bearing, feeling, posture **8** behavior, position **11** disposition

attorney: 5 agent, proxy **6** deputy, factor, lawyer **7** proctor **8** advocate **9** barrister, counselor, solicitor **10** counsellor

attract: 4 bait, draw, lure, pull **5** catch, charm, court, fetch, tempt **6** allure, engage, entice, invite, seduce **8** interest **9** captivate, fascinate, influence, magnetize

attraction: 4 card **6** magnet **7** gravity **8** affinity, penchant, witchery

attractive: 4 chic, cute, fair **5** bonny **6** lovely, pretty, taking **7** winning, winsome **8** alluring, charming, fetching, graceful **9** beautiful

attribute: fix, owe **4** mark, sign, type **5** asign, badge, blame, place, power, refer **6** allege, allude, assert, bestow, charge, impute, symbol **7** ascribe, pertain, quality **8** accredit, property **10** reputation **11** peculiarity **14** characteristic

attribution: 6 theory **8** etiology

attrition: 4 wear **5** grief **6** regret, sorrow **7** penance, remorse **8** abrasion, friction **9** weakening

attune: key **4** tune **5** adapt, agree **6** accord, adjust, temper **7** prepare **9** harmonize

atua: 5 being, demon **6** spirit

au fait(F.): 6 expert, versed **8** informed **9** competent, in the know **10** proficient

au fond(F.): 8 at bottom **9** basically

au naturel(F.): raw **4** nude **5** naked **6** unclad **8** stripped **9** in the buff

auberge: inn **7** albergo

auction: 4 cant, roup(Sc.), sale, sell, vend **5** trade **6** barter, bridge **8** disposal

hammer: **5** gavel

platform: **5** block

price: bid **5** upset

audacious: 4 bold **5** brash, hardy, saucy **6** brazen, cheeky, daring **7** forward **8** arrogant, fearless, impudent, insolent, intrepid, spirited **9** barefaced, imprudent, shameless **10** courageous **11** adventurous, impertinent, venturesome **12** presumptuous

audacity: 4 gall, grit, guts **5** brass, cheek, nerve, spunk, valor **7** courage **8** boldness, temerity **9** assurance, cockiness, derring-do, hardihood, impudence, insolence, sauciness **10** effrontery **12** impertinence

audible: 5 aloud, clear, heard **8** distinct

audience: 4 fans **5** house **6** public **7** gallery, hearing **8** assembly, audition, tribunal **9** following, interview, reception **10** spectators

audio-visual aid: 4 film, tape **5** slide **10** television

audit: 4 scan **5** check, probe **6** reckon, survey, verify **7** examine, inquire, inspect **8** analysis, estimate **10** accounting **11** investigate

audition: 4 test **5** trial **6** tryout **7** hearing

auditor: CPA **6** censor, hearer **8** listener **10** accountant, bookkeeper **11** comptroller

auditorium: 4 hall, room **5** cavea, odeum **7** theater

auditory: 4 otic **5** aural **8** acoustic

auger: bit **4** bore, tool **5** grill **6** gimlet, wimble

aught: 4 zero **5** zilch **6** cipher, **7** nothing **8** anything, goose egg

Augie March creator: 6 Bellow

augite: 8 pyroxene

augment: add, eke **4** grow **5** exalt, swell **6** append, dilate, expand, extend **7** amplify, enhance, enlarge, improve, magnify **8** heighten, increase, multiply **9** increment **10** aggrandize

augur: 4 bode, omen, seer **6** auspex, divine **7** betoken, foresee, portend, predict, presage, prophet, promise, signify **8** forebode, foreshow, foretell, forewarn, indicate, prophesy **9** auspicate **10** anticipate, conjecture, soothsayer **13** prognosticate

augury: 4 rite, sign **5** token **6** herald, ritual **7** warning **8** ceremony, forecast **9** harbinger, sortilege **10** divination, foreboding, forerunner

august: 5 awful, grand, noble **6** solemn **7** exalted, stately **8** imposing, majestic **9** dignified, venerable **11** magisterial

Augustus' death place: 4 Nola

auk: 4 loom **5** arrie, lemot, noddy **6** puffin, rotche **7** dovekey, dovekie **9** guillemot
family: **7** alcidae
genus: **4** alca, alle
razorbill: **4** falk **5** murre

aula: 4 hall, room **5** court **6** emblic

aumildar(Ind.): 5 agent **6** factor **7** manager **9** collector

aura: air **4** glow, halo, mood, odor **5** aroma **6** nimbus **7** essence, feeling, quality **8** mystique **9** emanation **10** atmosphere, exhalation

aural: 4 otic **7** audible **9** auricular
appendage: ear

aureate: 6 gilded, golden, ornate, rococo, yellow **8** splendid **9** brilliant

aureole: 4 halo **5** crown, glory, light **6** corona, nimbus **8** gloriole

auricle: ear **5** pinna **6** atrium, earlet **7** trumpet
part: **7** earlobe

auricular: 4 otic **7** hearsay **12** confidential

aurochs: 4 urus **5** bison **6** wisent

Aurora: Eos **4** dawn **7** morning, sunrise

auroral: 4 eoan, rosy **7** eastern, radiant

aurum: 4 gold

auscultate: 6 listen

auspex: 5 augur **7** diviner, prophet **10** forecaster, soothsayer

auspicate: 5 augur **7** portend, predict **8** initiate **10** inaugurate

auspices: 4 care, egis **5** aegis **7** backing, support **8** guidance **9** patronage **10** protection **11** sponsorship

auspicious: 4 fair, good **6** dexter **9** favorable, fortunate, opportune **10** propitious, prosperous **12** advantageous

Aussie: 10 Australian

austere: 4 cold, grim, hard **5** bleak, grave, gruff, harsh, rigid, rough, sharp, stern, stiff **6** bitter, formal, severe, simple, somber, strict **7** ascetic, earnest, spartan, serious **8** rigorous **9** unadorned, unsmiling **10** astringent, forbidding, relentless **13** unembellished

Australia: *capital:* **8** Canberra
city: Ayr **4** Yass **5** Dubbo, Perth, Weipa **6** Casino, Hobart, Mackay, Sydney **7** Kogarah, Mildura **8** Adelaide, Brisbane, Toowomba **9** Melbourne, Newcastle **10** Wagga Wagga
desert: **6** Gibson, Tanami **8** Victoria **10** Great Sandy

explored by: **13** Capt. James Cook
island: **5** Cocos, Heard **6** Fraser **7** Ashmore, Cartier **8** Kangaroo, Thursday **9** Christmas
lake: **4** Eyre **5** Carey, Cowan, Frome **6** Austin, Barlee, Mackay **7** Amadeus, Eyerard, Torrens **8** Carnegie
monetary unit: **4** cent **6** dollar
mountain peak: **4** Hale **5** Bruce **6** Cradle, Morgan **7** Bogong, Painter **9** Kosciusko
mountain range: **6** Stuart **7** Darling, Gregory **8** Flinders, Musgrave, St. George **9** Petermann
native: **6** Binghi **9** aborigine
peninsula: **4** Eyre **8** Cape York
port: **5** Pirie **6** Darwin, Kembia **7** Geelong, Jackson, Lincoln **8** Adelaide, Brisbane **9** Fremantle
river: Ord **4** Avon, Daly, Swan **5** Namoi, Paroo, Roper, Yarra **6** Barwon, Bulloo, Calgoa, Hunter, Isaacs, Murray **7** Darling, Fitzroy, Lachlan, Staaten **8** Burdekin, Flinders, Gascoyne, Georgina, Goulburn
sea: **5** Coral, Timor **6** Tasman **7** Arafura
state: **8** Tasmania, Victoria **10** Queensland **13** New South Wales
strait: **4** Bass **6** Torres

Australian: *animal:* **4** tait **5** koala, panda **6** bunyip, cuscus, wombat **7** dasqure, wallaby **8** duckbill, kangaroo, platypus **9** bandicoot, phalanger
apple: **6** colane
badger: **6** wombat
bag: **5** dilli
bear: **5** koala
beefwood: **5** belar
beverage: **4** kava
bird: emu **4** emeu, lory **5** arara, crake, grebe, stint **6** gannet, leipoa **7** bittern, boobook, bustard, figbird **8** berigora, dabchick, dotterel, lorikeet, lyrebird, morepork, whimbrel **9** bower-bird, cassowary, coachwhip, friarbird, stipiture **10** paradalote, partincole, sanderling
boomerang: **5** kiley, kilie
brushwood: **6** millee
bush: ake
bustard: **7** bebilya
cake: **6** damper **7** brownie
call: **5** cooee, cooey
cat: **7** dasyure
catfish: **6** tandan
cattle stealer: **6** duffer
cedar: **4** toon
clover fern: **6** nardoo
cockatoo: **5** galah
coin: **4** dump
colonist: **8** sterling
countryman: **8** Billijim
crayfish: **5** yabby **6** yabbie
cycad: **5** banga

dog: 5 dingo 6 Kelpie
duckbill: 8 platypus
eucalyptus: 6 bimbil, mallee 7 carbeen
fern: 5 nardu 6 nardoo
fish: 4 dart, mado, mako 5 yabby 6 tandan, yabbie
fruit: 5 nonda
gum tree: 4 kari 6 tewart, tooart, touart
herb: 8 piripiri
horse: 7 brumbee 8 yarraman
hut: 6 miamia
insect: 4 laap, lerp
kangaroo: 4 joey 5 tungo 7 bettong
kiwi: roa
lizard: 6 goanna
lorikeet: 6 parrot, warrin
mahogany: 6 jarrah 7 gunning
marsupial: 4 tait 5 koala 6 wombat 8
kangaroo
measure: 4 saum
mile: 4 naut
moth: 6 bogong
no: 4 baal, bail, bale
owl: 7 boobook 8 morepoke, morepork
palm: 8 bangalow
parakeet: 6 budgie 7 corella 10 budgeri-
gar
parrot: 4 lory 7 corella, lorilet 8 lorikeet 9
cockateel, cockatiel
pepper: 4 arva, kava, yava 6 ava-ava
petrel: 4 titi
phalanger: 5 ariel
plant: 5 lakea 6 correa 7 calomba, waratah 8 warratau
pine: 5 kauri, kaury
pond: 9 billabong
rat: 8 hapalote 9 hapalotis
ratite: 4 emeu
rifleman: 5 yager
rustler: 6 duffer
shark: 4 mako
shield: 8 heelaman, heilaman, hielaman,
yeelaman
snake: 6 elapid
soldier: 5 Anzac 6 digger, swaddy 8 Billijim
sorcerer: 5 boyla 6 boolya
spear: 7 wommera, woomera
talk: 6 yabber
thicket: 6 mallee
throwing stick: 5 kiley, kylie 7 wommera,
woomera 9 boomerang
toy: 8 weet-weet
tree: 4 toon 5 belah, belar, boree, gidya,
penda 6 gidgea, gidgee, gidyea, marara
7 alipata 8 beefwood, curajong, flindosa, flindosy, ironbark 9 koorajong 10
bunya-bunya
tulip: 7 waratah 8 warratau
war club: 5 waddy
weapon: 5 hulla, waddy 6 hullah 7 liangle
8 leeangle 10 hullanulla

wilderness: 7 outback
wombat: 5 koala
wood: emu
workman: 8 Billijim
Austria: *capital:* 6 Vienna
city: 4 Graz, Linz, Wels 5 Steyr 7 Bre-
genz 8 Salzburg 9 Innsbruck 10 Kla-
genfurt
ethnic group: 5 Croat 7 Slovene
lake: 5 Atter, Traun 9 Constance 10
Neusiedler
monetary unit: 8 groschen 9 schilling
mountain pass: 5 Loibl 7 Brenner,
Plocken 9 Semmering
mountain peak: 9 Hochstuhl, Hochvogel
10 Hochfeiler, Wildspitze 13 Gross-
glockner
mountain ranges of Alps: 6 Allgau, Carnic
8 Bavarian, Otztaler 10 Hohe Tauern
river: Inn, Mur 4 Enns, Lech, Murz, Raba
5 Drava, Steyr, Traun 6 Danube 7 Sal-
zach
state (lander): 5 Tirol 6 Styria, Vienna 8
Salzburg 9 Carinthia 10 Burgenland,
Vorarlberg 12 Lower Austria, Upper
Austria
Austrian: *coin:* 5 ducat, krone 6 florin,
heller, zehner
composer: 4 Berg 5 Haydn 6 Mahler,
Mozart, Webern 7 Strauss 8 Bruckner,
Schubert
conductor: 6 Mahler 7 Karajan
dance: 6 dreher
former ruling family: 8 Habsburg, Haps-
burg
measure: 4 fass, fuss, joch, mass, muth,
yoke 5 halbe, linie, meile, metze, pfiff,
punkt 6 achtel, becher, seidel 7 klafter,
viertel 8 dreiling 10 muthmassel 12
futtermassel
measure of weight: 4 marc, saum, unze 5
denat, karch, pfund, stein 7 centner,
pfennig 8 vierling 9 quentchen
nobility: 6 Ritter 9 Esterhazy
playwright: 7 Nestroy 10 Schnitzler 11
Grillparzer
psychiatrist: 5 Adler, Freud
violinist: 8 Kreisler
austringer: 8 falconer
Austronesian language: 4 Niue 7 Tagalog
autarch: 6 despot 8 autocrat
auteur: 8 director, virtuoso 9 film-maker
authentic: 4 pure, real, sure, true 5 exact,
right, valid 6 actual, proper 7 correct,
genuine 8 bonafide, credible, official,
original, reliable 9 veritable 10 authorized 11 trustworthy 13 authoritative
authenticate: 4 seal 5 prove 6 attest, verify 7 bear out, confirm, endorse 8 validate, vouch for
author: 4 doer 5 maker 6 father, framer,

parent, source, writer **7** creator, founder **8** ancestor, begetter, compiler, composer, inventor, novelist, producer **9** architect, initiator **10** playwright, instigator, originator

authoritative: 5 sound **7** factual, learned **8** dogmatic, official, oracular, positive **9** authentic, canonical, effectual, imperious, masterful, scholarly **10** conclusive, convincing, legitimate, peremptory **11** dictatorial, ex cathedra, magisterial

authority: 4 rule, sway **5** force, might, power, right **6** artist, expert, source, weight **7** command, control, warrant **8** dominion, prestige, sanction **9** influence **10** competence, importance, specialist **12** jurisdiction **13** justification

judicial: **4** banc

preponderant: **8** hegemony

symbol: **7** scepter

woman's: **7** distaff

authorize: let **4** vest **5** allow **6** clothe, permit, ratify **7** approve, empower, endorse, entitle, indorse, justify, license, warrant **8** accredit, delegate, legalize, sanction **10** commission, legitimize

authorless: 8 unsigned **9** anonymous

auto court: inn **5** motel

auto race: 4 drag **5** derby

driver: **4** Foyt **5** Petty, Sneva, Unser **8** Andretti **10** Rutherford, Yarborough

kind: **4** road **7** formula **8** stock car

notable: **7** Daytona **9** Grand Prix **12** Indianapolis

autobiography: 4 vita **5** diary **6** memoir

autochthonous: 6 native **7** edaphic, endemic **10** aboriginal, indigenous

autocrat: 4 czar, tsar, tzar **5** mogul **6** Caesar, despot **7** autarch, monarch **8** dictator **9** sovereign

autocratic: 8 absolute, arrogant, despotic **9** arbitrary **10** tyrannical

autograph: ink **4** name, sign **9** signature **11** John Hancock

automatic: 7 routine **8** habitual **10** mechanical, push-button, self-acting **11** instinctive, involuntary, spontaneous

automation: 5 golem, robot **7** android, machine

automobile: car **4** heap, jeep **5** coupe, crate, racer, sedan **6** jalopy **7** flivver, machine, phaeton **8** roadster **11** convertible

army: **4** jeep

British: AC, MG **5** Alvis, Riley, Rover **6** Allard, Anglia, Austin, Consul, Humber, Jaguar, Jowett, Morgan, Morris, Rapier, Singer, Zephyr **7** Bentley, Daimler, Hillman, Sunbeam, Triumph **8** Berkeley, Vauxhall **10** Rolls-Royce **11** Austin-Healy, Hillman-Minx, Morris-Minor **12** Metropolitan **13** Sunbeam-Talbot

Czech: **5** Skoda

early: EMF, Reo **4** Alco, Benz, Cord, Knox, Moon, Olds, Sear, Star **5** Brush, Regal, Stutz **6** Auburn, Dupont, Duryea, Graham, Haynes, Kissel, Lozier, Marmon, Mercer, Saxson, Thomas, Winton **7** Autocar, Bugatti, La Salle, Maxwell, Oakland, Premier, Rambler, Simplex, Stevens, Tourist **8** Apperson, Chalmers, Chandler, Franklin, Mercedes, National, Overland, Peerless **9** Hupmobile **10** Cunningham, Duesenberg, Jackrabbit, Locomobile **11** Graham-Paige, Pierce-Arrow **12** Crane-Simplex, Owen-Magnetic, Pope-Hartford, White-Streamer **13** Baker-Electric, Ofeldt-Steamer, Stevens-Duryea, Wills-St. Claire **14** Stanley-Steamer **16** Columbia-Electric **22** International Auto Buggy

Europe: BMW **4** Benz **5** Aston, Metro, Prinz, Skoda **6** Martin, Denzel, Isetta, Zodiac **7** Bugatti, Prefect **9** Facel-Vega

French: **5** Simca **7** Citroen, Panhard, Peugeot, Renault **8** Dauphine

German: DKW **4** Opel **6** Taunus **7** Goliath, Porsche, Weidner **8** Borgward, Rometsch, Wartburg **10** Golomobile, Lloyd-Wagon, Volkswagen **12** Mercedes-Benz

Italian: **4** Fiat **6** Lancia **7** Ferrari **8** Maserati **9** Alfa-Romeo

Japanese: **5** Honda, Mazda **6** Datsun, Subaru, Toyota **13** Pringe-Skylark

part: **4** hood **5** motor, trunk **6** engine **7** chassis, magneto, tonneau **8** ignition

Russian: Zim **6** Pobeda **9** Moskvitch

Swedish: **4** Saab **5** Volvo

supercharged: **6** hot rod

United States: **4** Ford, Jeep, Nash, Nova, Vega **5** Buick, Capri, Comet, Dodge, Pinto **6** Cougar, De Soto, Duster, Hudson, Impala, LeMans, Torino, Willys **7** Caprice, Lincoln, Mercury, Montego, Mustang, Packard, Pontiac, Rambler, Ventura **8** Cadillac, Chrysler, Corvette, Imperial, Maverick, Plymouth **9** Chevrolet **10** Oldsmobile, Studebaker **11** Continental, Thunderbird

autonomous: 4 free **8** separate **9** sovereign **11** independent **12** self-governed

autopsy: 8 necropsy **10** dissection **11** examination

autumn: 4 fall **6** season **8** maturity **11** harvest-time

auxiliary: aid, sub **4** aide, ally **6** backup, branch, helper **7** abetter, abettor, adjunct, partner, reserve **8** adjutant **9** accessory, adminicle, ancillary, assistant, coadjutor, secondary, tributary **10** additional, subsidiary, supporting **11** subordinate, subservient **13** supplementary

ava: 4 kava **5** shrub **6** pepper

avail: aid, use **4** help **5** serve, stead, value **6** profit **7** account, benefit, purpose, service, success, suffice, utilize **9** advantage **10** assistance

available: fit **4** free, open **5** handy, on tap, ready **6** usable **7** present **9** effectual, practical **10** accessible, attainable, convenient, obtainable, up for grabs **11** efficacious

avalanche: **4** heap, mass, pile **5** flood, slide **6** deluge **7** torrent **9** landslide, snowslide **10** inundation

Avalon, Avilion: **4** isle **6** island

tomb: **6** Arthur

avant-garde: new **7** leaders, offbeat **8** advanced, original, pioneers, vanguard **10** innovative **12** trendsetting, trailblazing

avarice: **7** avidity **8** cupidity, rapacity, venality **9** money-lust

spirit of: **6** Mammon

avaricious: **5** close **6** greedy, hungry, stingy **7** miserly **8** covetous, grasping **9** niggardly, penurious **12** parsimonious

avast: **4** halt, hold, stay, stop **5** cease

avatar: **8** epiphany **10** embodiment **11** incarnation

ave: **4** hail **8** farewell, greeting **10** salutation

Ave Maria: **6** prayer **8** Hail Mary **10** rosary bead

avenge: **5** repay **6** injure, punish **7** pay back, redress, requite, revenge **8** chastise **9** retaliate, vindicate **10** get even for

avenger: **7** nemesis **10** vindicator

avenue: rue(F.), way **4** gate, mall, pike, road **5** drive, entry **6** access, arcade, artery, course, outlet, street **7** opening **9** boulevard **10** passageway **12** thoroughfare

aver: say **5** claim, prove, state, swear **6** affirm, allege, assert, assure, avouch, depose, insist, verify **7** certify, contend, declare, justify, protest **8** maintain, proclaim **9** predicate **10** asseverate **11** acknowledge

average: par, sum **4** fair, mean, norm, so-so **5** ratio, usual **6** common, medial, median, medium, middle, normal, not bad **7** typical **8** mediocre, moderate, ordinary, standard **10** proportion **12** run-of-the-mill **13** approximation

averse: **5** balky, loath **7** against, opposed **8** hesitant, inimical **9** reluctant, unwilling **11** disinclined, ill-disposed, unfavorable **12** recalcitrant

aversion: **4** hate **5** odium **6** enmity, hatred, horror **7** disdain, disgust, dislike **8** distaste **9** antipathy **10** repugnance **11** abomination **12** estrangement **14** disinclination

avert: **4** bend, fend, foil **5** avoid, deter, dodge, evade, parry, twist **6** thwart **7** deflect, prevent, ward off **8** preclude, stave off **9** forestall, frustrate, keep at bay, turn aside

aviary: **4** cage **6** volary **8** dovecote, ornithon **9** birdhouse, columbary

keeper: **8** aviarist

aviation: **6** flying **10** airplaning **11** aeronautics

aviator: ace **5** flier, flyer, pilot **6** airman, fly-boy **7** birdman

notable: **7** Earhart **8** Corrigan **9** Chennault, Doolittle, Lindbergh **10** Richthofen (Red Baron), Rickenbacker

signal: out **4** over **5** roger

avid: **4** agog, keen, warm **5** eager, rabid **6** ardent, greedy, hungry **7** anxious, athirst, devoted **8** covetous, desirous, grasping **9** impatient, voracious

avidity: **7** avarice, craving, longing **8** cupidity **10** greediness

avifauna: **5** birds, ornis

avocado: **4** coyo, pear, tree **5** palta **6** chinin **13** alligator pear

avocation: **5** hobby **7** pastime **8** sideline **9** amusement, diversion **10** recreation

avocet: **4** bird **5** stilt **6** godwit

avoid: **4** duck, shun **5** annul, avert, dodge, elude, evade, hedge, parry, shirk, skirt, spair(Sc.) **6** bypass, escape, eschew **7** abstain, boycott, forbear, forsake, refrain **8** keep from, sidestep **10** steer clear **11** fight shy of

avoidance: **8** escapism **9** annulment **10** withdrawal

avoirdupois weight: ton **4** dram **5** ounce, pound **7** long ton

a votre sante(F.): **5** skoal, toast **6** prosit(G). **12** to your health

avow: own **5** admit, state, swear **6** affirm, assert, avouch, depose **7** confess, declare, justify, profess **8** maintain, proclaim **11** acknowledge

avowal: **4** word **8** averment **9** assurance **10** profession **14** representation

awa: **4** kava **8** milkfish

awabi: **8** abalone

await: **4** bide, pend, **5** abide, tarry **6** attend, expect, impend **8** mark time, watch for **10** anticipate, be ready for

awake: **5** alert, alive, astir, aware, rouse **6** active, arouse, excite, revive **7** careful, heedful **8** open-eyed, vigilant **9** attentive, conscious **10** up and about

awakening: **7** letdown **9** debunking, eye-opener **13** enlightenment

award: **4** give **5** allot, grant, honor, medal, prize **6** accord, assign, bestow, confer **7** adjudge, appoint, mete out, present, tribute **8** accolade, judgment, sentence **9** apportion, determine **10** decoration

academic: **6** degree **7** diploma **8** cum laude **9** sheepskin **12** Phi Beta Kappa **13** magna cum laude

broadcasting: **7** Peabody
cinema: **5** Oscar
detective story: **5** Edgar
Off-Broadway: **4** Obie
recording: **6** Grammy
science fiction: **4** Hugo
television: **4** Emmy
theatre: **4** Tony
aware: hep, hip **4** wary **5** alert, alive **7** knowing, mindful **8** apprised, apprized, informed, sensible, vigilant, watchful **9** au courant, cognizant, conscious **11** intelligent
away: awa(Sc.), fro, off, out, via **4** gone **5** along, apart, aside, forth, hence **6** abroad, absent, at once, begone, onward, thence **7** distant **8** directly, right off **9** elsewhere, forthwith
awe: cow **4** fear **5** alarm, amaze, daunt, scare **6** fright, regard, terror, wonder **7** buffalo, respect **8** astonish, bewilder, overcome **9** fascinate, overpower, reverence **10** intimidate, veneration
aweigh: **5** atrip
awesome: **4** eery **5** awful, eerie, weird **6** solemn **7** dreaded, ghostly, uncanny **8** imposing, terrible **9** appalling, unearthly **12** spell-binding
awful: bad **4** dire, ugly **6** august, horrid **7** awesome, fearful **8** dreadful, majestic, shocking, terrible **9** appalling, frightful **10** impressive, tremendous
awfully: **4** very **5** quite **7** greatly **9** extremely
awkward: **5** gawky, inapt, inept **6** clumsy, gauche, rustic, uneasy **7** boorish, loutish, stilted, uncouth, unhandy **8** bungling, lubberly, ungainly, untoward, unwieldy **9** difficult, graceless, ill at ease, inelegant, lumbering, maladroit, ponderous **10** backhanded, blundering, cumbersome, ungraceful, unskillful **11** heavyhanded **12** embarrassing, inconvenient
awl: **4** tool **5** punch **6** gimlet
awn: ear **4** barb **5** beard **6** arista **7** bristle **9** appendage

awning: **4** hood **6** canopy, screen, shield **7** shelter **8** velarium
fastening: **6** earing
relative: **7** marquee
awry: **5** agley(Sc.), amiss, askew, wrong **6** faulty, uneven **7** askance, asquint, crooked, haywire, oblique **8** cockeyed **9** distorted **11** out of kilter
ax: adz **4** adze, fire, sack **6** twibil **7** cleaver, dismiss, hatchet, kick out, twibill **8** tomahawk **9** discharge
blade: bit
butt: **4** poll
handle: **5** helve
axial: **7** central, midmost, pivotal
axilla: **6** armpit **8** shoulder
axiom: saw **5** adage, dicta(pl.), maxim, motto **6** byword, dictum, saying, truism **7** precept, proverb **8** aphorism, apothegm, sentence **9** principle **11** proposition
axis: **4** axle, deer, stem **5** pivot **6** chitra **7** fulcrum, spindle **8** alliance
axle: bar, cod, pin **4** axis **5** arbor, shaft **7** mandrel, spindel
axolotl: **4** newt **10** salamander
ayah: **4** maid **5** nurse **9** nursemaid
aye, ay: pro, yea, yes **4** ever, okay, vote **6** always, assent **7** forever **11** affirmative, continually
aye-aye: **5** lemur **6** will do **10** understood
Azerbaijan: *capital:* **4** Baku
Azores: *district:* **5** Horta **12** Ponta Delgada
island: **4** Pico **5** Corvo, Faial **6** Flores
port: **5** Horta
volcano: **4** Pico
Aztec: *ball game:* **8** tlachtli
emperor: **9** Moctezuma, Montezuma
god: **4** Xipe **9** Xipetotic **11** Xiuhtecutli
language: **7** Nahuatl
myth: **4** Nana, Nata
stone: **9** temelactl **12** chalchihuitl
temple: **6** teopan **8** teocalli
azure: **4** bice, blue **8** cerulean **9** cloudless, unclouded
azygous: odd **6** single

B

baa: 5 bleat
baahling: 4 lamb
Baal: 4 idol 5 deity 8 false god
  consort: 6 Baltis
baba: 5 child(Ind.) 7 rumcake
babacoote: 5 lemur
babassu: oil 4 palm, soap
Babbitt: 5 alloy, metal 9 bourgeois 10 philistine 11 materialist
  author: Lewis
babblative: 9 garrulous, talkative 10 loquacious
babble: yak 4 chat 5 prate, run on 6 cackle, drivel, gibber, gossip, murmur 7 blabber, blather, chatter, clatter, prattle, twaddle 8 nonsense 11 stultiloquy
babel: din 5 clang, tower 6 hubbub, jargon, medley, racket, tumult 7 discord 9 charivari, confusion 10 hullabaloo
babiche: 6 lacing, thongs
babillard: 4 bird 11 whitethroat
baboon: ape 4 papa 5 drill 6 chaema 7 babuina 8 mandrill
babul: gum, lac 4 tree, wood 6 acacia, mimosa
  pod: 5 garad
babushka: 5 scarf 8 kerchief 11 grandmother
  relative of: 8 bandanna
baby: tot 4 baba, babe, doll 5 bairn(Sc.), child, humor, spoil 6 coddle, fondle, infant, moppet, pamper, weanie(Sc.) 7 bambino(It.), papoose 9 youngster
  bed: 4 crib 6 cradle 8 bassinet
  carriage: 4 pram 5 buggy 6 gocart 8 stroller 12 perambulator
  christening robe: 7 chrisom, chrysom
  cry: mew 6 squall
  food: pap 4 milk 6 pablum
  outfit: 7 layette
  shoe: 6 bootee
babyish: 6 simple 7 puerile 8 childish
Babylonia: *abode of the dead:* 5 Aralu
  capital: 7 Babylon
  city: 5 Erech, Larsa 6 Calneh, Cunaxa, Cuthah, Lagash, Nippur, Sippar
  cycle of moon: sar 5 saros
  divison: 5 Akkad, Sumer
  god: Anu, Aya, Bel, Hea, Hes, Ira, Ler, Sin, Utu 4 Adad, Anat, Apsu, Baal, Gula, Irra, Nebo, Utug 5 Alala, Alalu, Dagan, Enlil, Etana, Ninib, Nusku, Siris, Urash 6 Ishtar, Nergal, Oannes, Tammuz 7 Ninurta, Shamash 8 Merodach 10 Adramelech 11 Adrammelech
  goddess: Aya 4 Erua, Nana, Nina 5 Belit, Istar 6 Belili, Beltis, Ishtar 7 Mylitta
  hero of myth: 5 Adapa, Etana 9 Gilgamesh
  king: 5 Gudea 6 Sargon 8 Naram-Sin 9 Hammurabi
  language: 8 Akkadian, Sumerian
  mountain: 6 Ararat
  New: 7 Chaldea
  priestess: 5 Entum
  river: 6 Tigris 9 Euphrates
  Jewish exile ruler: 8 Exilarch
  sun god's attendant: 6 Bunene
  tower: 5 Babel 7 zikurat 8 ziggurat
  waters: 4 Apsu
  weight: 4 mina 5 maneh
Babylonian: 6 lavish, wicked 7 opulent
bacalao: 5 murre 7 codfish, grouper 9 guillemot
bacca: 5 berry
baccalaureate: 6 degree, sermon 7 address, service 14 bachelor of arts
baccarat: 4 game
  player: 6 punter
  term: 5 banco
  variety of: 11 chemin-de-fer
baccate: 5 pulpy 7 berried
bacchanal: 4 orgy 7 debauch, reveler 8 carouser
Bacchanal's cry: 4 evoe 5 evohe
bacchante: 6 maenad 9 priestess
bachelor: 7 unmated 8 celibate
  recently married: 8 benedict
bachelor button: 8 milkwort 10 bluebottle
bacillus: 4 germ 5 virus 7 microbe
back: aid, tub, vat 4 abet, hind, nata, rear, tail 5 angel, bet on, dorsa(pl.), notum, spine, splat, stern 6 assist, dorsum, second, uphold, verify 7 endorse, finance, sponsor, support, sustain 8 bankroll, rearward 9 encourage, posterior, reinforce 10 strengthen
  at the: aft 5 abaft, arear 6 astern 7 postern
  lower part of: 4 loin
  of neck: 4 nape 6 scruff
  pain: 7 lumbago
  pert. to: 6 dorsal, lumbar, tergal

back off: ebb 6 recede, retire 7 retreat, reverse 10 give ground, retrograde

back out: 4 funk 5 welsh 6 renege 8 crawfish, withdraw

back scratcher: 7 strigil

back-street: 6 secret 8 on the sly 13 surreptitious

Back Street author: 5 Hurst

back talk: lip 4 guff, sass 9 insolence

backbite: 5 abuse 6 defame, vilify 7 asperse, slander

backbone: 4 grit, guts 5 nerve, pluck, spine, spunk 6 mettle, spirit 7 stamina, support 8 mainstay, vertebra

backer: 5 angel 6 patron 7 sponsor 8 promoter

backgammon: *old relative:* 7 pachisi
term: 4 blot 6 double
variation: 10 acey-deucey

background: 4 rear 6 offing 7 setting 8 distance, training 9 education

backing: aid 6 lining, refuse 7 support 9 financing 10 embankment 11 endorsement

backlash: 6 recoil 8 reaction

backlog: 7 reserve, surplus 12 accumulation

backslide: 4 fall 5 lapse 6 desert, revert 7 relapse 11 deteriorate

backup: 4 help 5 spare 9 alternate 10 substitute, supporting

backward: shy 4 dull, slow 5 arear, loath 6 astern, averse, behind, bygone, stupid 7 bashful, laggard, lagging, reverse 8 dilatory, hesitant 9 recessive, reluctant, to the rear, unwilling 10 behindhand, hesitating 11 into the past 13 retrogressive, retrospective

backwater: ebb 5 bayou 7 retract, retreat

backwoodsman: 4 hick 9 hillbilly

backwort: 7 comfrey

bacon: pig 4 pork 5 prize
Canadian: 4 loin
fat: 5 speck
side: 6 flitch, gammon
slice: 6 rasher, collop

Bacon work: 6 Essays, 11 New Atlantis 12 Novum Organum

bacteria, bacterium: 4 germ 6 aerobe 7 microbe 8 organism 10 aerobacter
chain: 6 torula 7 torulae(pl.)
culture: 4 agar 8 agar-agar
dissolver: 5 lysin
free from harmful: 7 asepsis, aseptic
rod-shaped: 7 bacilli(pl.) 8 bacillus
spherical: 5 cocci(pl.) 6 coccus
spiral: 8 spirilla(pl.) 9 spirillum
vaccine: 8 bacterin

bactrian: 5 camel

bad: big, ill, sad 4 evil, full, lewd, poor, sick, vile 5 nasty, sorry, wrong 6 arrant, faulty, rotten, severe, sinful, wicked 7

baleful, baneful, corrupt, harmful, hurtful, immoral, inutile, naughty, spoiled, tainted, unlucky, unsound, vicious 8 annoying, criminal, depraved, flagrant, inferior, unsuited 9 abandoned, atrocious, blemished, dangerous, defective, incorrect, injurious, offensive, perverted, worthless 10 aggravated, distressed, inadequate, iniquitous, pernicious 11 deleterious, displeasing, inopportune, unfavorable 12 disagreeable, inauspicious

bad blood: 4 hate 5 anger 6 enmity 10 bitterness, ill-feeling, resentment

bad debt: 7 default

bad habit: 4 vice 5 fault 7 frailty 8 weakness

bad luck: 7 ill wind 9 adversity 10 misfortune, tough break

badderlocks: 6 murlin 7 henware, seaweed

badge: pin 4 mark, sign 5 token 6 emblem, ensign, symbol 8 insignia 10 cognizance

badger: nag 4 bait, 5 annoy, brock, chivy, hound, tease, worry 6 bother, chivvy, harass, heckle, pester, teledu, wombat 7 torment 8 carcajou, huckster, irritate 9 bandicoot, mistonusk
group: 4 cete

Badger State: 9 Wisconsin

badigeon: 5 paste 6 cement 11 composition

badinage: 6 banter 7 joshing, kidding, teasing 8 raillery, repartee 11 give and take

badly: 4 illy 6 poorly, unwell 7 harshly 8 faultily, severely 9 seriously 10 shamefully 11 imperfectly 12 unskillfully 13 unfortunately

bad-mouth: 4 slur 7 run down 9 criticize, disparage

Baedeker: 9 guidebook 10 tourist aid

baffle: 4 balk, foil, pose 5 elude, evade, fling, stump 6 defeat, delude, outwit, puzzle, thwart 7 confuse, deceive, grating, mystify, nonplus 8 bewilder, confound 9 confusion, deflector, discomfit, frustrate 10 circumvent, disconcert

bag: cod, net, pod, pot 4 gain, poke, sack, trap 5 bulse, catch, forte, pouch, purse, seize, snare, steal 6 budget, cavity, entrap, hang-up, pocket, sachet, wallet 7 alforja, balloon, capture, reticle, satchel 8 reticule 9 cartridge, container, gladstone, haversack, specialty, way of life 10 collection, pocketbook 11 portmanteau
botanic: sac 4 asci 5 ascus, spore
canvas: 7 musette
fishing net: 4 bunt, fyke

hop: **7** sarpler
muslin: **6** tillot
traveling: **4** grip **6** valise **8** backpack, knapsack, suitcase
bagatelle: 4 game **5** verse **6** trifle
baggage: 4 arms, gear, minx **5** huzzy, nasty, tents, trash, wench **6** harlot, refuse, trashy, trunks **7** clothes, effects, rubbish, valises **8** carriage, rubbishy, utensils **9** munitions, viaticals, worthless **10** prostitute **11** impedimenta
baggy: 5 loose **6** flabby, puffed
Baghdad: *capital:* **4** Iraq
merchant; **6** Sinbad **7** Sindbad
river: **6** Tigris
bagnio: 4 bath **5** bagne **6** prison **7** brothel **8** hothouse
bagpipe: 5 drone **7** musette **8** zampogna **10** doodlesack, sordellina
mouthpiece: **4** muse
pipe: **6** drones **7** chanter
play: **5** skirl
player: **5** piper **7** doodler
sound: **5** skirl
tune: **4** port
bah: foh, pah, rot **5** faugh, pshaw **8** nonsense
Bahama Islands: Cat **4** Long **5** Abaco, Exuma, Grand, Turks **6** Andros, Bimini, Caicos, Inagua **7** Acklins, Crooked **9** Eleuthera
capital: **6** Nassau
native indian: **7** Lucayan
bahia: bay
Bahrain: 11 archipelago
capital: **6** Manama
gulf: **7** Persian
islands: **5** Sitra **7** Bahrain **8** Muharraq
monetary unit: **4** fils **5** dinar
bail: dip **4** bond, hoop, lade, lave, ring, rynd, yoke **5** ladle, scoop, throw, vouch **6** bucket, handle, secure, surety **7** custody, deliver, release **8** bailsman, bulwarks, security **9** guarantee
bailiff: 5 agent **6** deputy **7** steward **8** overseer **9** constable **10** magistrate **12** court officer
bailiwick: 4 area **6** domain, office **8** home base, province **9** territory **12** jurisdiction
bairn: 5 child
bait: bad **4** bite, chum, feed, halt, lure **5** decoy, tempt, worry **6** allure, attack, badger, entice, harass, repast **7** fulcrum, gudgeon, provoke, torment **9** persecute **10** allurement, enticement, exasperate, inducement, temptation **11** refreshment
artificial: **9** hackle fly
baize: 6 fabric **7** drapery
bake: dry **4** cook, fire **5** batch, broil, grill, parch, roast **6** anneal, harden **7** biscuit

baker: 4 oven **6** baxter **7** furnace, roaster, utensil
sheet: pan
shovel: **4** pale, peel
tool: **4** pale, peel
baker's dozen: 8 thirteen
baker's itch: 4 rash **9** psoriasis
baking chamber: 4 kiln, oast, oven
baking dish: 7 cocotte, ramekin
baking soda: 9 saleratus
Bakongo goddess: 6 Nyambe, Nzambi
Balaam's beast: ass **6** donkey
balance: 4 even, rest **5** poise, scale, weigh **6** adjust, equate, offset, sanity, stasis **7** residue **8** equality, equalize, serenity **9** composure, equipoise, remainder, stability **10** neutralize, steadiness **11** equilibrium **12** counterpoise
lose: **4** trip **7** stagger
weighing: **6** auncel
balancer: 7 acrobat, athlete, gymnast
balcony: 5 oriel, porch **6** piazza, sollar **7** balagan, gallery, mirador, pergola, terrace **8** brattice, verandah
church singer: **8** cantoria
projecting: **6** gazabo, gazebo
bald: 4 bare, base **5** crude, naked, plain, stark **6** callow, paltry, pilled, shaven, smooth **7** epilose, literal, sheared **8** glabrous, hairless **9** unadorned, uncovered **11** undisguised, unvarnished
Balder, Baldur: *father:* **4** Odin
mother: **5** Frigg
murder weapon: **9** mistletoe
slayer: **4** Hoth, Loke **5** Hothr
son: **7** Forsete, Forseti
wife: **5** Nanna
balderdash: rot **5** bilge, trash **6** drivel, jargon **8** claptrap, malarkey, nonsense **9** rigmarole **10** flumdiddle
baldicoot: 4 coot, monk
baldmoney: 7 gentian **8** spicknel
baldness: 8 alopecia **11** phalacrosis
baldric, baldrick: 4 belt **6** girdle, zodiac **7** balteus, support **8** baltheus, necklace
bale: woe **4** evil, harm **5** crate, death **6** bundle, sorrow **7** package **8** compress, disaster **9** influence, suffering
of wool: **7** sarpler
Balearic Island: 5 Ibiza **7** Cabrera, Majorca, Minorca **8** Mallorca **10** Formentera
language: **7** Catalan
measure: **5** palmo **6** misura, quarta, quarte **7** quartin **8** barcella, quartera
port: **5** Palma
weight: **5** artal, artel, cargo, corta, libra, mayor, ratel, rotel **8** quartano
baleen: 5 whale **9** whalebone
baleful: bad **4** evil **6** deadly, malign **7** noxious, ruinous **8** sinister, wretched **10** calamitous, pernicious **11** destructive

balk: jib, shy 4 beam, bilk, foil, loft 5 block, check, demur, hunch, rebel, reest(Sc.), ridge, waver 6 baffle, defeat, falter, hinder, impede, outwit, rafter, recoil, refuse, thwart 7 quibble 8 hang back 9 discomfit, frustrate, stop short 14 disappointment
Balkan: 9 Mountains, Peninsula
peak: 5 Botev
people: 4 Serb, Slav 5 Croat 8 Albanian, Romanian
states: 6 Greece, Turkey(part) 7 Albania, Romania 8 Bulgaria 10 Yugoslavia
balky: 6 mulish 8 stubborn 9 obstinate
ball: bal(F.), bob, orb, toy 4 bead, pill 5 dance, globe, glome 6 bullet, muddle, pellet, pompon, rundle, sphere 7 confuse, mandrel, ridotto 8 spheroid 11 glomeration
lofted: fly, lob
low: 5 liner
minced meat: 5 pinda 7 rissole
wooden: 4 knur
ball and chain: 4 wife 6 burden
ball club: 4 nine, team 6 eleven
ball game: cat 5 rugby 6 pelota, soccer, tennis 7 cricket
ball of fire: 4 whiz 6 genius, dynamo 7 hustler 8 go-getter, live wire 11 eager beaver
ball up: 5 snarl 7 confuse, perplex
ballad: lai(F.) 4 lied, lilt, poem, song 5 derry 6 sonnet 7 canzone
ballast: 4 load, trim 5 poise, stone 6 burden, gravel, weight 7 balance 9 saburrate
ballerina: 6 dancer 8 coryphee, danseuse
ballet: 5 dance, drama 9 pantomime 12 choreography
knee bend: 4 plie
leap 4 jete 9 entrechat, pas de chat
movement: pas 5 brise 8 glissade
posture: 6 pointe 9 arabesque
wear: 4 tutu 6 tights 7 leotard
whirl: 9 pirouette
ballistic missile: 4 ICBM, IRBM
balloon: bag 5 blimp 6 expand, gasbag 7 airship, distend, inflate 8 aerostat 9 dirigible
basket: car 7 gondola, nacelle
ballot: 4 poll, vote 5 elect, voice 6 billet, choice, ticket
ballyhoo: 4 plug, tout 6 hoopla, puff up 7 promote, trumpet 9 publicity
balm: oil 5 salve 6 lotion, relief, solace 7 anodyne, comfort, perfume, soother, unguent 8 ointment 9 fragrance
horse: 10 citronella
of Gilead: 6 balsam, poplar
balmy: 4 mild, soft 5 bland, daffy, moony, spicy, sunny, sweet 6 gentle, insane 7 healing, lenient 8 aromatic, fragrant,

soothing 9 assuaging 10 refreshing 11 odoriferous
baloney: 4 bunk 5 hooey 6 humbug 8 nonsense
balsa: 4 raft, tree, wood 5 float
balsam: 4 riga, tree, tolu 6 storay 7 copaiba 8 bdellium, ointment
apple: 4 vine 7 creeper 8 amargosa, amargoso, ampalaya
Baltic native: 4 Lett 7 Latvian 8 Estonian 10 Lithuanian
Baltic Sea: *canal:* 4 Kiel
gulf: 4 Riga 6 Danzig 7 Bothnia, Finland
island: 4 Dago 5 Faron, Oland, Visby 6 Karlso, Sarema 7 Gotland 8 Bornholm
port: Abo 4 Kiel, Riga 6 Gdansk, Gdynia 7 Tallinn 8 Klaipeda 9 Stockholm
river: 4 Oder, Odra 5 Dvina, Neman 7 Vistula
balustrade: 7 barrier, parapet, railing 8 banister
Balzac character: 4 Nana 6 Goriot
Bambi: 4 deer 7 animal
bambino: 4 baby 5 child 6 infant
bamboo: 4 cane, reed, tree
sacred: 6 nandin
sprouts: 5 achar
sugar: 9 tabasheer
woven: 6 sawali
bamboozle: 4 dupe 5 cheat, cozen, grill 6 cajole, humbug 7 buffalo, defraud, deceive, mystify, perplex 11 hornswoggle
ban: bar 4 tabu, veto 5 block, taboo 6 enjoin, forbid, hinder, invoke, outlaw 7 condemn, exclude 8 anathema, denounce, execrate, prohibit 9 proscribe 11 malediction 12 denunciation, interdiction 15 excommunication
Bana: *conqueror:* 7 Krishna
daughter: 4 Usha
banal: 4 flat 5 corny, inane, silly, stale, trite, vapid 6 jejune 7 insipid, trivial 9 hackneyed 10 pedestrian 11 commonplace 13 platitudinous
phrase: 6 cliche
banana: 4 musa 6 ensete 7 platano(Sp.) 8 plantain
bunch 4 hand, stem
family: 4 musa 6 pesang 8 musaceae
leaf: 5 frond
spider: 9 tarantula
wild: fei
banana fish: 6 albula 8 ladyfish
banana oil: 7 blarney 8 soft soap
bananas: mad 4 crazy 5 batty
band: tie 4 belt, cord, crew, fess, gang, girt, hoop, ring, zone 5 group, label, strap, strip, tribe, unite 6 armlet, bundle, collar, collet, fillet, girdle, streak, string, stripe, team up, troupe 7 binding, circlet, company, garland, orphrey 8 bracelet, cincture, ligament, sympho-

ny, tressure **9** aggregate, orchestra **10** collection

armed: **5** posse

armor: **6** tonlet

brain: **6** ligula **7** ligulae(pl.)

narrow: **4** tape **5** stria **6** striae(pl.)

small: **5** combo

bandage: 4 bind, tape **5** blind, clout, dress, sling, truss **6** fettle, fillet, ligate, swathe **8** cincture, ligature **9** blindfold

fastener: **7** ligator

nose: **9** accipiter

surgical: **5** spica **6** fascial, spicae(pl.) **7** fasciae(pl.)

bandeau: 5 strip **6** fillet **9** brassiere **10** hair ribbon

bandicoot: rat **6** badger

bandikai: 4 okra

bandit: 4 caco **5** bravo, thief **6** banish, outlaw, robber **7** bandido, brigand, ladrone **8** marauder, picaroon **10** highwayman

bandleader: 6 master **7** choragi, maestro **8** choragus **9** conductor

bandmaster: 5 Sousa

bandy: 4 cart, swap **5** trade **6** banter, bowed **7** chaffer, discuss **8** carriage, exchange **9** toss about, use glibly **11** give and take **12** treat lightly

bane: woe **4** evil, harm, kill, pest, ruin **5** curse, death, venom **6** injury, murder, poison, slayer **7** nemesis, scourge **8** mischief, murderer, nuisance

baneful: bad, ill **4** evil, vile **7** harmful, hurtful, noxious, ruinous **8** venomous **9** sinistral **10** pernicious

bang: rap **4** beat, blow, dash, dock, drub, slam **5** clash, drive, excel, force, impel, pound, sound, thump, whack, whang **6** bounce, cudgel, energy, strike, thrash, thwack **7** sardine, surpass **8** forelock **9** explosion

into: hit **5** crash **7** collide

bang-up: 5 crack **6** tiptop **9** first-rate

Bangladesh: *bay:* **6** Bengal

capital: **5** Dacca

city: **5** Bogra **6** Khulna, Mungla, Sylhet **7** Barisal **8** Chandput **10** Chittagong

language: **6** Bangla

monetary unit: **4** taka **5** paisa

river: **5** Padma **6** Ganges, Jamuna(Brahmaputra)

bangle: 4 flap, roam **5** droop, waste **7** circlet, fritter, trinket **8** bracelet, ornament

Bani's son: Uel **4** Amzi **5** Amram

banish: ban **5** eject, exile, expel, fleme **6** bandit, deport, dispel, forsay, outlaw **7** abandon, condemn, dismiss, exclude **8** displace, relegate **9** ostracize, proscribe, transport **10** expatriate, repatriate

banister: 7 railing **10** balustrade

bank: bar, bay, cop, rim, row **4** bink, brae, brew, caja, dike, dune, dyke, edge, hill, mass, pile, ramp, rive, sand, seat, tier, weir **5** banco, bench, bluff, brink, fence, levee, marge, mound, ridge, stack, share, shelf, shoal, shore, slope, stage, trust **6** causey, degree, depend, margin, reckon, rivage, strand **7** anthill, deposit, pottery, shallow **8** barranca, barranco, platform **9** acclivity, **10** depository, elevation, embankment

clerk: **6** teller

examiner: **10** accountant

requirement: **5** funds, money **6** assets **7** surplus **8** deposits

river: **4** ripa

bankroll: wad **4** back **5** funds **7** finance **8** currency **9** grubstake, subsidize

bankrupt: sap **4** bung **5** broke, drain, smash, strip **6** busted, devour, quisby, ruined **7** failure **8** beggarly, depleted **9** destitute, insolvent **12** impoverished

banner: 4 fane, flag, jack **5** color **6** ensign, fannon, pennon **7** leading, pennant, salient **8** banderol, foremost, gonfalon, standard, vexillum **9** banderole, exemplary, oriflamme **10** surpassing

banns: 6 notice **12** proclamation

banquet: 4 fete, meal **5** feast **6** dinner, junket, regale, repast **8** carousal, festival

room: **8** cenacula(pl.) **9** cenaculum

banquette: way **4** seat **5** shelf **7** footway **8** platform, sidewalk **10** embankment

banshee: fay **5** fairy, sidhe **6** goblin

bantam: 4 cock **5** saucy, small **6** little **7** chicken **9** combative **10** diminutive

breed: **8** Sebright

banter: kid, rag, rib **4** fool, jest, joke, josh, mock **5** chaff, jolly, tease **8** badinage, raillery **10** persiflage, pleasantry **11** give and take, playfulness

bantling: 5 child **6** infant

Bantu: *dialect:* **6** Chwana **8** Sechuana

language: Ila **4** Suto **5** Ronga **6** Thonga **7** Nyanaja **8** Nyamwezi **10** Wanymawezi

people: **4** Baya, Bihe, Bule, Fang, Gogo, Gola, Guha, Hehe, Jaga, Luba, Maka, Nama, Vira, Yaka, Zulu **5** Duala, Kafir **6** Banyai, Damara, Kaffir, Waguha, Yakala **7** Swahili, Wachaga **8** Bechuana

banxring: 6 mammal, tupaya **7** pentail **9** tree shrew

genus: **4** tana

look-alike: **8** squirrel

banzai: cry **6** attack

baobab: 4 tree **7** tebeldi

baptism: 9 aspersion, cleansing, immersion **11** christening

robe: **7** chrisom

vessel: **4** font **6** fontal, spring **7** piscina

water: **5** laver

baptize: dip **4** full, name **5** heave **6** purify

7 cleanse 8 christen, sprinkle

bar: ban, dam, fid, gad, law, rod 4 axle, band, bank, beam, bolt, cake, gate, hide, joke, lock, oust, pole, rail, reef, save, shut, stop 5 arbor, bench, bilco, block, close, court, deter, estop, fence, hedge, lever, perch, shade, shaft, strap, strip 6 billet, bistro, brooch, except, fasten, grille, hinder, meagre, saloon, stripe 7 barrage, barrier, confine, counter, leave out, exclude, pass over, prevent 8 conclude, handicap, obstacle, obstruct, preclude, prohibit, restrain, restrict, surround, tribunal 9 barricade, fastening, gatehouse, hindrance, interpose, ostracize 10 crosspiece, difficulty, impediment, inhibition, portcullis 11 obstruction

acrobat: 7 trapeze
bullion: 5 ingot
millstone: 4 rynd
resisting pressure: 5 strut
supporting: fid, rod 9 stanchion
tamping: 7 stemmer
window: 5 jemmy, jimmy 7 forcing

barb: awn, bur, jag, mow 4 burr, clip, file, flue, hair, herl, hook, jagg 5 beard, horse, point, ridge, shaft 6 pigeon 7 bristle 8 kingish 9 appendage 10 projection

anchor: 4 flue
feather: 4 harl, herl 5 ramus 7 pinnula, pinnule 8 pinnulae

Barbados: *capital:* 10 Bridgetown
bay: 4 Long 7 Oistins 8 Carlisle
liquor: rum
member: 12 Commonwealth
monetary unit: 4 cent 6 dollar
native: Bim
peak: 9 Mt. Hillaby
sovereign: 11 Elizabeth II
town: 5 Rouen 6 Kendal 7 Maxwell 8 Hastings

barbarian: Hun 4 boor, Goth, rude, wild 5 alien, brute 6 savage, vandal 7 ruffian 9 foreigner, untutored 10 Philistine, unlettered 11 uncivilized

barbarism: 4 cant 8 savagism, solecism 10 savageness

barbarity: 6 ferity 7 cruelty 8 ferocity, rudeness, savagery 9 brutality 10 inhumanity

barbarous: 4 fell, rude, wild 5 cruel 6 brutal 7 foreign, Hunnish, inhuman, slavish, uncivil 8 ignorant 9 ferocious, primitive 10 illiterate, outlandish, tramontane, unpolished 11 uncivilized 12 uncultivated

barbary ape: 5 magot 6 monkey
Barbary Coast States: 5 Tunis 7 Algiers, Morocco, Tripoli
barbecue: 4 bake 5 broil, grill

rod: 4 spit 6 skewer
barbed: 4 bent 6 hooked 8 uncinate
barber: 6 Figaro, poller, shaver, tonsor 7 scraper, tonsure 11 chirotonsor
barber's itch: 8 ringworm
bard: 4 poet, scop 5 druid, runer, scald 6 singer 8 minstrel, musician
India: 4 bhat
Bard of Avon: 11 Shakespeare
bare: 4 bald, mere, nude 5 alone, crude, empty, naked, plain, stark, strip 6 barren, callow, denude, divert, divest, expose, histie, meager, meagre, paltry, pilled, reveal, simple 7 divulge, exposed, unarmed, uncover 8 desolate, disclose, stripped 9 in the buff, unadorned, uncovered, worthless 10 threadbare 11 defenseless, unconcealed, unfurnished 13 unaccompanied
barefaced: 4 bold 6 brazen 7 blatant, glaring 8 impudent 9 audacious, out-and-out, shameless 11 undisguised
barefooted: 6 unshod 9 discalced
barely: 4 only 5 faint 6 hardly, merely, poorly 8 scantily, scarcely, slightly 13 unqualifiedly 14 insufficiently
barf: 5 vomit 7 upchuck
barfly: 5 drunk, stiff 8 carouser
bargain: 4 deal, huck, pact, sale 5 cheap, steal 6 barter, dicker, haggle, palter 7 chaffer, compact, contend, contest 8 contract, covenant, giveaway, struggle 9 agreement, negotiate, situation, stipulate 10 engagement 11 come to terms, transaction
bargain-basement: 5 cheap 6 tawdry
bargain for: 6 expect 7 count on
barge: ark, tow 4 bark, boat, raft, scow 5 lunge, lurch 6 barque, lumber, thrust, tender, vessel 7 lighter 8 flagship, flatboat 9 intrude on 12 move clumsily
charge: 10 lighterage
coal: 4 keel
bark: bag, bay, rub, wap, yap, yip 4 boat, coat, howl, husk, peel, pelt, pill, rind, ross, ship, skin, yawp 5 balat, barca, barge, cough, shell, shout, strip 6 abrade, cortex, girdle, vessel 7 solicit, tanbark 8 cortices, covering
aromatic: 6 sintoc 7 canella 9 sassafras
at: 5 scold 6 rebuke
cloth: 4 tapa 5 tappa 8 mulberry
covered with: 9 corticate 10 corticated
medicinal: 4 coto 5 casca, madar, nudar, niepa 7 quinine 8 cinchona 9 sassafras
outer: 8 periderm
pert. to: 8 cortical
remove: 4 ross 5 scale
resembling: 8 cortical
rough: 4 ross
tanning: 5 alder
up the wrong tree: err 5 stray

barker: dog 4 tout 7 spieler 8 pitchman 9 solicitor
barking deer: 7 muntjac, muntjak
barley: 5 grain
 ground: 6 tsamba
 pert. to: 11 hordeaceous
 steep: 4 malt
 variety: big 4 bere, bigg
barmy: 5 foamy, kooky, silly 6 frothy, screwy, yeasty 7 flighty, foolish, idiotic
barn: 4 byre 6 stable 10 storehouse
 part: bay, mow 4 loft 5 stall 7 hayloft
barn dance: 7 hoedown
 official: 6 caller
barnacle: 5 leech 8 hanger-on, parasite 9 appendage, shellfish 11 encumbrance
barnstorm: 4 tour 5 stump 6 troupe
barometric line: 6 isobar
baron: 4 peer 5 mogul 6 tycoon 7 magnate
baroque: 6 ornate, rococo 9 grotesque, irregular 11 extravagant 13 overdecorated
barrack: 4 camp 6 casern 7 cuartel(Sp.) 8 quarters
barracuda: 4 fish, kaku, spet 5 barry, pelon 6 becuna, picuda, sennet 10 guaguanche 12 guanchepelon
barrage: 4 hail 5 burst, salvo 6 attack, volley 7 barrier 9 broadside, cannonade, fusillade 10 obtruction, outpouring 11 bombardment
barranca, barranco: 4 bank 5 bluff 6 ravine
barrel: fat, keg, tun, vat 4 butt, cade, cask, drum, knag 6 runlet, tierce, vessel 7 cistern, rundlet 8 cylinder, hogshead 9 container, kilderkin
 herring: 4 cade
 maker: 6 cooper
 part: 4 side, hoop 5 stave
 raising device: 9 parbuckle
 stopper: 4 bung
 support: 4 hoop 6 gantry 7 gauntry
barren: dry 4 arid, bare, dull 5 empty, gaunt, stark, stern 6 desert, effete, fallow, jejune, meager 7 sterile 8 desolate, devoid of, impotent, treeless 9 childless, exhausted, fruitless, infertile 10 unfruitful 12 unproductive, unprofitable
barren oak: 9 blackjack
barren privet: 7 alatern 9 houseleek
barrette: bar 8 ornament
Barrie character: 5 Peter, Wendy
barrier: bar, dam 4 door, gate, line, wall, weir 5 bound, chain, fence, hedge, limit 6 abatis, hurdle, screen 7 barrage, defense, parapet, railing 8 boundary, fortress, frontier, stockade 9 barricade, palisades, restraint, roadblock 10 difficulty 11 obstruction
 movable: 4 bars, door 5 blind, shade 6

screen 7 curtain 8 shutters
barring: 6 save for 9 aside from, excepting, outside of
barrio: 4 slum 6 ghetto 7 village
barrister: 6 barman, lawyer 7 counsel 8 advocate, attorney 9 solicitor
barroom: pub 4 cafe 6 lounge, tavern, saloon 7 cantina(Sp.), doggery 8 dramshop
barrow: hod, hog 4 bank, dune, hill, mote 5 grave, gurry, mound 6 tumuli 7 hillock, trolley, tumulus 8 mountain
barter: 4 chap, chop, cope, coup, hawk, sell, swap, vend 5 corse, trade, troke, truck 6 dicker 7 bargain, cambium, permute, traffic 8 commerce, exchange 9 excambion 11 reciprocate
Bartered Bride composer: 7 Smetana
bas: low
bas-relief: 9 plaquette
basal: 5 basic 7 basilar 11 fundamental
basalt: 6 marble, navite 7 pottery
base: bed, low 4 clam, evil, foot, foul, lewd, mean, poor, root, stem, step, vile 5 basis, cheap, dirty, muddy, petty, snide 6 abject, bottom, common, ground, menial, paltry, podium, shabby, sordid, vulgar 7 bastard, bedrock, caitiff, comical, hangdog, housing, ignoble, lowdown, servile, slavish, support 8 degraded, infamous, inferior, pedestal, scullion, shameful, stepping, unworthy, wretched 9 absorbent, degrading, establish, predicate, worthless 10 despicable, foundation, villainous 11 ignominious 12 contemptible, dishonorable, disreputable 13 dishonourable
 architectural: 5 socle 6 plinth
 attached by: 7 sessile
 military: HDQ 4 camp 5 depot 12 headquarters
 structural: 6 plinth
base on balls: 4 pass, walk
baseball: *field:* 7 diamond
 founder: 9 Doubleday
 glove: 4 mitt
 hit: 4 bunt
 official: ump 5 coach 6 umpire 7 manager
 players: Ott (Mel) 4 Cobb (Ty), Dean (Dizzy), Ford (Whitey), Foxx (Jimmy), Mays (Willie), Rose (Pete), Ruth (Babe) 5 Aaron (Hank), Banks (Ernie), Bench (Johnny), Berra (Yogi), Brock (Lou), Grove (Lefty), Kiner (Ralph), Maris (Roger), Spahn (Warren), Young (Cy) 6 Feller (Bob), Gehrig (Lou), Gibson (Bob), Hunter (Catfish), Koufax (Sandy), Mantle (Mickey), Musial (Stan), Seaver (Tom), Wagner (Honus) 7 Hornsby (Rogers), Hubbell (Carl), Jackson (Reggie), Johnson (Walter), Speaker (Tris) 8 Clemente (Roberto),

DiMaggio (Joe), Robinson (Jackie), Williams (Ted) **9** Alexander (Grover), Killebrew (Harmon) **10** Campanella (Roy) **11** Yastrzemski (Carl)

team: **4** nine

teams (American League): **5** Twins (Minnesota) **6** Angels (Cal.), Red Sox (Boston), Royals (Kansas City), Tigers (Detroit) **7** Brewers (Milwaukee), Indians (Cleveland), Orioles (Baltimore), Rangers (Texas), Yankees (N.Y.) **8** Blue Jays (Toronto), Mariners (Seattle), White Sox (Chicago) **9** Athletics (Oakland)

teams (National League): **4** Cubs (Chicago), Mets (N.Y.), Reds (Cincinnati) **5** Expos (Montreal) **6** Astros (Houston), Braves (Atlanta), Giants (San Francisco), Padres (San Diego) **7** Dodgers (Los Angeles), Pirates (Pittsburgh) **8** Phillies (Philadelphia) **9** Cardinals (St. Louis)

term: bag, bat, box, fan, fly, hit, lob, low, out, peg, RBI, run, tap, top **4** ball, bean, beat, bunt, burn, deck, foul, high, hill, hole, home, hook, miss, pill, pole, sack, save, turn, walk, wild **5** alley, apple, bench, booth, clout, coach, count, curve, drive, error, field, first, force, frame, glove, homer, lined, mound, pitch, plate, popup, punch, score, slide, swing, third **6** assist, batter, bungle, bottom, charge, clutch, double, dugout, groove, hitter, inside, lifted, lumber, middle, popout, putout, rubber, runner, screen, second, series, single, sinker, stance, strike, string, target, triple, wind-up **7** arbited, arbiter, battery, blooper, bullpen, circuit, cleanup, diamond, fielder, floater, infield, manager, nothing, outside, pitcher, side-arm, squeeze, stretch, thumbed **8** delivery, grounded, grounder, knuckler, outfield, pinch-hit, powdered, soupbone, spitball **9** full-count, hot corner, sacrifice, smothered, strikeout, two-bagger **10** scratch-hit **11** three-bagger

baseless: 4 idle **9** unfounded, untenable **10** gratuitous, groundless **11** unsupported

bash: bat, lam **4** beat, blow, dent, mash, swat, wham, whop **5** party, smash **6** bruise, strike, wallop **7** blowout, hit hard **8** wingding

Bashemath's husband: 4 Esau

bashful: coy, shy **5** blate(Sc.), mousy, timid **6** demure, modest **7** daunted **8** backward, blushing, dismayed, retiring, sheepish **9** diffident, shrinking

Bashkir capital: Ufa

basic: 5 chief, vital **7** central **9** elemental, principal **10** underlying **11** fundamental, rudimentary **13** indispensable

basically: 8 at bottom **9** in essence, primarily **11** essentially

basil: 4 herb **5** plant, royal **6** fetter

basilica: 6 church, shrine, temple **7** Lateran

part of: **4** apse, nave

basin: cwm, pan **4** bowl, dish, dock, ewer, font, sink, tank **5** laver, stoup **6** cirque, crater, marina, valley, vessel **7** cuvette, piscina **8** lavatory, receptor, washbowl **9** reservoir **10** depression **11** aspersorium

geological: **4** tala

basis: 4 root **5** axiom **6** bottom, ground, reason **7** essence, footing, premise, support **10** foundation, groundwork

bask: sun **4** beek(Sc.), warm **5** acrid, bathe, enjoy, revel **6** bitter **7** rejoice **9** luxuriate

basket: ark, fan, ped **4** kipe, trug **5** cassy(Sc.), cesta, chest, crate, scull **6** cassie(Sc.), dosser, hamper, hoppet, panier **7** canasta, hanaper, pannier, scuttle **9** container **10** receptacle

coal mine: **4** corf

eel: **4** buck

fig: **4** caba **5** frail **6** tapnet

fire: **5** grate **7** cresset

fish: pot **4** caul, cawl, corf, hask, skip, weel **5** creel, crate, maund **6** courge

fruit: **6** pottle **7** prickle

material: **4** cane, rush **5** osier, otate **6** willow

twig: **6** wattle

water-tight: **7** wattape

wicker: cob **4** cobb, coop **5** willy **6** hamper **7** hanaper **8** bassinet

work: **4** caba **5** cabas, slath **6** slarth

basketball

inventor: **8** Naismith

official: ref **6** umpire **7** referee

players: **4** Reed (Willis), West (Jerry) **5** Cousy (Bob) **6** Baylor (Elgin), Pettit (Bob), Cowens (Dave) **7** Bellamy (Walt), Frazier (Walt) **8** Havlicek (John) **9** Robertson (Oscar) **11** Chamberlain (Wilt)

positions: **5** cager, guard **6** center **7** forward **8** hoopster

pro teams (NBA): **4** Jazz (Utah), Nets (New Jersey), Suns (Phoenix) **5** Bucks (Milwaukee), Bulls (Chicago), Hawks (Atlanta), Kings (Kansas City), 76ers (Philadelphia), Spurs (San Antonio) **6** Knicks (New York), Lakers (Los Angeles), Pacers (Indiana) **7** Bullets (Washington), Celtics (Boston), Nuggets (Denver), Pistons (Detroit), Rockets (Houston) **8** Clippers (San Diego), Warriors (Golden State) **9** Cavaliers (Cleveland), Mavericks (Dallas)

11 Supersonics (Seattle) **12** Trail Blazers (Portland)

team: **4** five **7** cagemen, quintet

term: gun, key **4** cage, dunk, pass **5** lay-up, stuff, tip-in **6** freeze, tap-off **7** dribble, rebound, time-out **8** jump ball **9** backboard, backcourt, field goal, free throw **11** ball control

Basque: *bay:* **6** Biscay

cap: **5** beret

city: **4** Irun **5** Eibar **6** Bermeo, Bilbao, Sestao, Tolosa **7** Vitoria

dance: **8** zortzico

game: **6** pelota **7** jai alai

language: **9** Euskarian

mountains: **8** Pyrenees **10** Cantabrian

petticoat: **8** basquine

province: **5** Alava **7** Vizcaya **9** Guipuzcoa

bass: low **4** deep, fish **5** voice **6** singer **7** achigan, jewfish

bassinet: **4** crib **6** cradle **7** baby bed

basswood: lin **4** bast **5** tilia **6** linden

bast: **4** bark, flax, hemp, jute **5** fiber, ramie **6** phloem **8** piassava

bastard: **4** base **5** false **6** cannon, galley, hybrid, impure **7** byspell, lowbred, mongrel **8** bantling, spurious **10** artificial **11** adulterated **12** illegitimate

baste: sew **4** beat, cane, cook, drub, lard, tack **6** cudgel, punish, stitch, thrash

bastion: *defensive:* **4** fort **13** fortification

shoulder: **6** epaule

bat: hit, wad **4** bate, beat, blow, club, gait, lump, mass, swat, wink **5** binge, brick, piece, speed, spree, stick **6** aliped, backie(Sc.), baston, beetle, cudgel, racket, strike, stroke, wander **7** flutter, noctule, vampire **8** bludgeon, serotine **9** reremouse **10** battledore, chiroptera, packsaddle **11** rattlemouse **12** chauvesouris, flittermouse

around: **4** roam **6** ponder **7** debate

European: **9** barbastel **11** barbastelle

species: **9** pipistrel **11** pipistrelle

Bataan: *bay:* **5** Subic

city: **7** Balanga

batch: lot **4** mass, mess, sort **5** group **6** bundle **7** mixture **8** quantity **10** collection

bate: **6** deduct, except **7** decrease, exclude

bateau: **4** boat

batfish: **6** diablo

bath: dip **4** bate, pert **5** therm **6** plunge, shower **7** balneum **8** ablution **10** natatorium

pert. to: **7** balneal

public: **7** piscine

sponge: **5** luffa **6** loofah

treatment by: **13** balneotherapy

Bath river: **4** Avon

bathe: bay, tub **4** bask, lave, stew, wash **5** embay **6** enwrap **7** immerse, pervade, suffuse **8** permeate

bathhouse: **6** cabana **8** balneary

bathing suit: **6** bikini, trunks **7** maillot

bathos: **8** comedown **10** anticlimax

bathroom: W.C.(abbr.) **6** hammam **8** sudatory **10** sudatorium **11** water closet

Bathsheba: *husband:* **5** Uriah

son: **7** Solomon

baton: rod **4** bend **5** staff, stick **6** baston, cudgel **7** bourdon, scepter, sceptre **9** truncheon

batrachian: **4** frog, toad

batten: **6** enrich, fatten, thrive **9** fertilize

batter: ram **4** beat, dent, maim **5** clour, dinge, frush, paste, pound **6** bruise, hammer, hitter, pummel **7** bombard, cripple, destroy, shatter, striker **8** demolish

battery: *floating:* **4** cell **5** praam **7** parapet **9** artillery **11** bombardment

plate: **4** grid

terminal: **5** anode **7** cathode

battle: war **4** duel, fray, meet, tilt **5** brush, fight, joust, onset **6** action, affray, combat **7** bombard, contend, contest, hosting, warfare **8** conflict, skirmish, struggle **9** encounter **10** engagement, tournament **11** competition, hostilities

area: **5** arena, front **6** sector **7** terrain

cry: **6** slogan **9** catchword

formation: **5** herse **6** deploy

line: **5** front

order: **7** regalia **8** battalia

royal: **5** melee **9** scrimmage

site: **6** Shiloh **7** Bull Run **8** Manassas **10** Armageddon, Gettysburg

trophy: **5** medal, scalp **6** ribbon

Battle Hymn of the Republic author: **4** Howe

battleship: **7** carrier **11** dreadnaught **16** superdreadnaught

batty: **5** crazy, silly **7** foolish

bauble: bow, toy **4** bead **6** button, gewgaw, trifle **7** trinket **8** gimcrack **9** plaything **10** knickknack

bauxite derivative: **8** aluminum

Bavaria: **6** Bayern(G.)

capital: **6** Munich

city: Hof **5** Furth **6** Passau **8** Augsburg, Bayreuth, Nurnberg, Wurzburg **9** Nuremberg **10** Regensburg

lake: **5** Ammer, Chiem **9** Starnberg

mountain: **10** Allgau Alps **11** Wetterstein **14** Bohemian Forest

peak: **5** Arber **9** Zugspitze

river: Alz, Ilz, Inn, Nab **4** Eger, Isar, Lech, Main **5** Amper, Iller, Regen, Saale **6** Danube **7** Altmuhl, Regnitz

Wagner festival site: **8** Bayreuth

bawd: **4** aunt, hare **5** dirty **6** defile **7** commode **8** procurer **9** procuress **10** fruitwoman

bawdy: 4 foul, lewd 5 dirty 7 obscene 8 unchaste

bawl: cry 4 howl 5 golly, shout 6 bellow, boohoo, outcry 8 glaister 10 vociferate
out: 5 scold 9 reprimand

bay: dam, ria, voe 4 bank, bark, cove, gulf, hole, hope, howl, loch(Sc.), roan, tree, yaup, yawp 5 bahia(Sp.), berry, bight, color, creek, fiord, fjord, fleet, haven, horse, oriel, sinus 6 laurel, recess, window 7 enclose, estuary, silanga, ululate 11 compartment, indentation
bird: 5 snipe 6 curlew, godwit, plover
camphor: 6 laurin

Bay of Biscay: *island:* Yeu 5 Belle, Groix 6 Oleron
resort: 7 Hendaye 8 Biarritz
river to: 5 Adour, Loire 7 Garonne

Bay State: 13 Massachusetts

bayard: 5 horse

Baylor University site: 4 Waco

bayonet: 4 stab 5 knife 6 pierce, weapon

bayou: 5 brook, creek, inlet, river 6 outlet, stream 7 rivulet 9 backwater

Bayou State: 11 Mississippi

bazaar, bazar: 4 fair, fete, sale 5 agora, burse 6 market 7 canteen 8 emporium 9 bezesteen 10 exposition

bazoo: 4 talk 5 kazoo, mouth

be: are 4 live 5 abide, exist, occur 6 remain 7 breathe, subsist 8 continue

beach: 4 bank, moor, ripa, sand 5 coast, plage(F.), playa(Sp.), shore 6 ground, shilla, strand 7 hardway, seaside, shingle

beachcomber: 7 vagrant 8 vagabond

beachhead: van 7 landing 8 foothold

beacon: 4 mark, sign 5 baken, fanal, guide, phare 6 ensign, pharos, signal 7 cresset, seamark, warning 8 signpost 10 lighthouse, watchtower
light: 7 cresset, lantern

Beaconsfield: 8 Disraeli

bead: 4 drop, foam 5 sewan, sight 6 bauble, bubble, prayer, wampum 7 globule, molding, sparkle, trinket
string: 6 rosary 7 chaplet 8 necklace

beady: 5 round, small 8 globular 10 glistening

beak: neb, nib 4 bill, nose, peak 5 snout, spout 7 rostrum 8 mandible 9 proboscis, schnozzle 10 promontory
ship's: bow, ram 4 prow
without: 9 erostrate

beaker: cup 4 tass 5 bocal, bouse, glass 6 bareca, bareka, vessel

be-all and end-all: 4 acme, A to Z 8 entirety, sum total, ultimate, whole bit 9 aggregate 10 everything 11 ne plus ultra 13 alpha and omega

beam: bar, ray 4 balk, emit, glow, I-bar, sile(Sc.), stud, T-bar 5 arbor, caber, flash, gleam, gleed, joist, light, shine, smile 6 binder, girder, rafter, timber, walker 7 bumpkin, chevron, radiate, support, trimmer 10 architrave

beaming: gay 4 rosy 6 bright, lucent, joyous 7 radiant, shining 8 all aglow, cheerful

beamy: 5 broad 7 massive 8 mirthful

bean: urd 4 chap, gram, head 5 brain, skull 6 caster, collar, fellow, kidney, lentil, nipple, noggin, strike, thrash, trifle 7 calabar, frijole(Sp.) 11 castigation
Asian: 4 gram, mung
climbing: 4 lima, pole
cluster: 4 guar
curd: 4 tofu
eye: 4 hila 5 hilum
kind: goa, soy, wax 4 lima, navy, snap 5 cacao, green, jelly, pinto 6 castor, coffee, kidney, string 7 calabar, jumping
lima: 4 haba 5 sieva
locust: 5 carob
lubricant: ben
Mexican: 6 frejol, frijol 7 frijole
poisonous 4 loco 7 calabar

bean shooter: 8 catapult 9 slingshot

Beantown: 6 Boston

bear: cub, lug 4 gest, tote 5 abide, allow, beget, breed, bring, brook, brown, bruin, carry, drive, geste, koala, Polar, press, stand, yield 6 afford, behave, endure, pierce, render, suffer, thrust, uphold 7 comport, conduct, forbear, grizzly, produce, support, sustain, undergo 8 forebear, tolerate 9 carnivore, transport 13 constellation
Alaskan: 6 kadiak, kodiak
genus: 5 ursus

bear bush: 8 inkberry

bear cat: 4 paud 9 binturong

bear down: 5 exert, press 6 stress 8 approach

bear-shaped: 8 ursiform

bear upon: 6 affect 7 concern

beard: 4 barb, defy 5 brave 6 arista, goatee 7 Vandyke 8 confront, face up to, hair tuft, whiskers 9 challenge 11 mutton chops
grain: awn

bearded: 5 hairy 6 barbed 7 barbate, hirsute 9 whiskered 11 barbigerous
grain: rye 5 awned, wheat 8 aristate

beardless: 5 young 6 callow

bearing: aim, air 4 gest, mien, port 5 birth, front, geste, habit, poise, trend 6 allure, apport, aspect, course, gerent, manner, orient, thrust 7 address, conduct, meaning, posture, purport, support 8 amenance, attitude, behavior, carriage, demeanor, pressure, relation, tendency, yielding 9 direction, gesta-

tion, influence, personage, producing **10** cognizance, deportment **11** comportment, countenance **12** significance
fine: **6** belair
heraldic: **4** ente, orle **5** pheon
plate: gib
beast: **4** bete(F.) **5** brute **6** animal, savage **7** monster **8** blighter **9** quadruped
mythical: roc **5** harpy, Hydra **6** dragon, Garuda, Geryon, gorgon, Kraken, Orthos, Scylla, Sphinx, Triton **7** centaur, chimera, Echidna, figfaun, griffin, griffon, Midgard, phoenix **8** Cerberus, chimaera, Minotaur **9** Charybdis, Sasquatch **10** Jabberwock
pertaining to: **7** leonine
royal: **4** lion
beast of burden: ass, yak **4** oxen(pl.) **5** burro, camel, horse, llama **6** donkey, onager
beastly: **5** feral, gross **6** animal, brutal **7** bestial, brutish, inhuman, swinish **9** offensive **10** abominable, disgusting
beat: bat, cob, dad(Sc.), fan, fib, tap, taw, tew **4** baff, bang, bash, bate, belt, best, blow, bolt, bray, cane, chap, club, daud, ding, dint, drub, dump, dunt, fell, flap, flax, flog, frat, haze, lash, lump, maul, mill, pant, pelt, prat, rout, scat, slam, tack, tick, whip, whop **5** baste, berry, churn, clink, douse, fight, filch, flail, knock, pound, pulse, round, scoop, strap, throb, thump, trump, whang, worst **6** accent, batter, beetle, buffet, cotton, cudgel, defeat, fettle, hammer, hamper, larrup, outrun, pummel, raddle, rhythm, squash, strike, stroke, swinge, switch, thrash, threap(Sc.), thresh **7** assault, battuta, belabor, blister, cadence, canvass, conquer, contuse, exhaust, fatigue, pulsate, shellac, surpass, trounce, vibrate **8** belabour, fatigued, lambaste, overcome, shellack, vanquish **9** exhausted, pulsation, throbbing **10** assignment
back: **5** repel **7** repulse **8** drive off
down: **5** crush **7** wear out **8** dispirit, suppress **10** make abject
into plate: **8** malleate
beat it: **4** scat **5** scram **7** vamoose
beater: rab **4** maul, seal **5** caner, lacer **6** dasher, mallet **8** thresher **9** scrutcher
beatify: **6** hallow **7** glorify **8** sanctify
beatitude: joy **5** bliss **7** benison **9** happiness **11** blessedness
beau: **5** beaux(pl.), blade, dandy, flame, lover, spark, swell **6** garcon, escort, fellow, steady, suitor **7** admirer, bravery, courter, coxcomb, cupidon, gallant **8** follower **9** boyfriend
Beau Brummell: fop **5** dandy **7** coxcomb
beau geste: **5** favor

beau ideal: **5** model **8** paradigm **14** shining example
beau monde: **7** fashion, society
beaut: **4** lulu
beautician: **10** beautifier, cosmetiste(F.) **11** cosmetician
beautifier: **8** cosmetic
beautiful: **4** fair, fine, glad, mear, meer, mere **5** belle, bonny **6** blithe, bonnie, choice, comely, decore, freely, lovely, poetic, pretty **7** elegant **8** charming, delicate, fairsome, gorgeous, graceful, handsome, stunning **9** exquisite **10** good-looking
people: **5** elite **6** jet set **9** haut monde **11** high society
beautify: **4** gild **5** adorn, grace, hight, preen, primp, prune **6** bedeck **7** adonize, garnish **8** decorate **9** embellish, glamorize
beauty: **5** belle, charm, grace **6** eyeful, looker, polish **8** knockout **10** comeliness, goodliness, loveliness **11** pulchritude
goddess: Sri **5** Freya, Venus **6** Freyja **7** Lakshmi **9** Aphrodite
lover: **7** esthete **8** aesthete
beaver: hat **4** coin **6** castor, rodent
cloth: **6** kersey
eater: **9** wolverine
skin: **4** plew
Beaver State: **6** Oregon
because: for **4** that **5** since **8** inasmuch, as long as
because of that: **7** thereby **9** therefore
becken: **7** cymbals
beckon: bow, nod **4** wave **6** curtsy, summon **7** bidding, command, curtsey, gesture **10** salutation
becloud: **4** hide **5** bedim **6** darken, perplex, puzzle **7** confuse, mystify, obscure **8** befuddle, overcast
become: get, wax **4** grow, pass, suit **5** adorn, befit, grace **6** accord, befall, beseem, betide, change **7** behoove, flatter
becoming: **4** good **5** right **6** comely, gainly **7** decorum, farrand, farrant **8** decorous, handsome, suitable, tasteful **10** attractive, convenient, flattering **11** appropriate
becscie: **9** merganser
becuna: **9** barracuda
bed: cot, pad **4** base, bunk, doss, lair, plot **5** basis, berth, couch, layer **6** bottom, couche(F.), cradle, litter, matrix, pallet, strata, tuck in **7** channel, lodging, stratum **8** matrices, plancher, rollaway **9** basegrave, stretcher **10** apishamore, foundation
feather: tye
small: cot **4** crib **6** cradle, pallet **7** hammock, truckle, trundle **8** bassinet

straw: **9** shakedown
bed stay: 4 slat
bedbug: 5 cimex **6** chinch **7** cimice(pl.) **8** conenose
bedding: 6 quilts, sheets **8** blankets **10** bedclothes
bedeck: gem **4** lard, trim **5** adorn, array, dight, grace **7** dress up **8** ornament **9** embellish
bedevil: 5 abuse, annoy, worry **6** muddle, pester **7** bewitch, confuse, torment
bedim: fog **4** mist **5** cloud **6** darken **7** becloud, obscure
bedizen: 4 daub **5** adorn, array, dizen **6** bedaub **9** overdress
bedlam: 4 riot **5** noise, rudas(Sc.) **6** asylum, madman, tumult, uproar **7** lunatic, madness **8** madhouse **9** confusion
Bedouin: 4 Arab, Moor **5** nomad
  head cord: **4** agal
  official: **4** cadi **5** sheik
  tribe: **4** Harb
bedridden: ill **6** ailing, laid up **8** confined **13** incapacitated
bedrock: 5 basis, nadir **6** bottom
bedroll: 6 bindle
bedroom: 4 flat **5** berth, cabin **7** boudoir **11** compartment
bee: dor, fly **4** apis, idea, ring **5** party **6** dingar, insect, notion, torque **7** caprice, stinger **9** gathering **11** hymenoptera **12** hymenopteron
  colony of: **5** swarm, yeast
  family: **5** apina **6** apidae
  female: **5** queen
  genus: **4** apis
  girl named for: **7** Melissa
  house: gum **4** butt, hive, scap, skep **6** apiary **7** alveary, bee-butt **9** alvearium
  house covering: **6** hackle
  male: **5** drone
  nose: **4** lora(pl.) **5** lorum
  pert. to: **8** apiarian
  pollen brush: **5** scopa **6** scopae(pl.) **9** sarothrum
beebread: 8 ambrosia
beech: 4 buck, tree **6** myrtle
  genus: **5** fagus
beechnut: 4 mast
beef: 4 meat **5** gripe **8** complain
  cut: **4** loin, rump, side **5** baron, chine, chuck, flank, roast, round, shank, steak **6** cutlet, muscle, saddle **7** brisket, knuckle, quarrel, quarter, sirloin **8** short-rib, shoulder **9** aitchbone, rattleran **11** porterhouse
  dried: **5** bucan, jerky, vifda, vivda **6** buccan **7** charqui
  pickled: **5** bully
  salted: **4** junk
  spiced: **8** pastrami, pastroma, pastromi
beefeater: 6 warden, yeoman

beefy: 5 hefty, heavy, husky **6** brawny, fleshy, stolid
Beehive State: 4 Utah
beekeeper: 8 apiarist, skeppist **12** apiculturist
beep: 4 tone, toot **6** signal
beer: ale, mum **4** bock, brew, grog, scud(Sc.) **5** kvass, lager, stout **6** liquor, porter, stingo, swanky **8** beverage
  barley: **5** chang
  cask: **4** butt
  ingredient: **4** hops, malt **5** yeast **6** barley
  king: **9** Gambrinus
  maize: **5** chica **6** chicha
  maker: **6** brewer
  mug: see *vessel,* below
  Russian: **5** kvass
  shop: pub **6** saloon, tavern
  unfermented: **4** wort
  vessel: mug **4** Toby **5** stein **6** flagon, seidel, tanker **8** schooner **9** blackjack
beer and skittles: fun **4** play
beery: 7 maudlin, muddled
beeswax substitute: 7 ceresin
beet: 5 chard, sugar **6** mangel **8** beetrave **9** vegetable
  genus: **4** beta
  soup: **7** borscht
Beethoven: *birthplace:* **4** Bonn
  opera: **7** Fidelio
  symphony: **5** fifth, first, ninth, sixth, third **6** Choral, eighth, Eroica, fourth, second **7** seventh **8** Pastoral
beetle: bat, bug, jut, ram **4** beat, goga, gogo, hang, maul, stag **5** amara, bulge, drive, gogga, hispa, meloe **6** chafer, golach, goloch, jutout, mallet, pestle, scarab, weevil **7** prinoid, project **8** lowering, overhang **9** prioninae(pl.) **10** battledore, projecting
  bark: **5** borer
  bright: **7** ladybug
  family: **10** elateridae **11** clavicornes, clavicornia
  fire: **6** cucuyo
  genus: **5** fidia
  grain: **7** cadelle
  grapevine: **6** thrips
  ground: **5** amara
  horny substance of: **6** chitin
  mustard: **9** blackjack
  rhinoceros: **4** uang
  sacred: **6** scarab
  wing cover: **5** shard
  wood: **6** sawyer
beetle-browed: 6 morose **8** scowling
beetle-head: 5 dunce **6** plover **9** blockhead
befall: hap **4** come **5** occur **6** astart, become, betide, happen **7** come off, pertain **8** bechance
befit: dow **4** suit **5** beset **6** become, be-

hove, beseem, betide **7** behoove **9** agree with **10** go together

befog: 5 cloud **6** obsane, puzzle **7** confuse, mystify

before: ere **4** said, up to **5** ahead, afore, avant, coram(L.), first, forby, front, prior **6** facing, forbye, former, rather, sooner **7** already, earlier, forward **8** anterior, hitherto, in advance **10** beforehand, heretofore, in time past, previously

before long: 4 anon, soon **9** presently

before now: ere **4** gone, over **6** erenow

befoul: 4 soil **5** dirty **6** bemire, defile, malign **7** pollute **8** entangle **11** contaminate

befriend: aid **4** abet, help **5** favor **6** assist, favour, foster, succor **7** benefit, support, sustain **11** countenance

befuddle: 4 daze **5** addle, besot **6** muddle **7** becloud, confuse, fluster, mystify, stupefy

beg: ask, bid, sue, woo **4** coax, pray, sorn(Sc.) **5** cadge, crave, mooch, plead **6** adjure, appeal **7** beseech, entreat, implore, request, solicit **8** petition **9** importune, panhandle **10** supplicate

beget: ean **4** bear, sire **5** breed, yield **6** author, create, father **7** acquire, engraff **8** engender, generate **9** germinate, procreate

begetter: 4 sire **6** author, father, mother, parent

beggar: 4 ruin **5** asker, randy, rogue **6** alsman, bacach, bidder, canter, devour, mumper, pariah, pauper, wretch **8** palliard, stroller **9** maunderer, mendicant, schnorrer, suppliant **10** impoverish, panhandler, petitioner, starveling, supplicant **12** hallan-shaker

saint: **5** Giles

speech: **4** cant

beggarly: 4 mean, poor **5** cheap, petty, sorry **6** abject, paltry **8** bankrupt, indigent, wretched **10** despicable **12** contemptible

Beggar's Opera author: Gay **6** Brecht

begin: 4 fang, lead, open, rise **5** arise, enter, start **6** attack, get off, spring **8** commence, embark on, inchoate, initiate **9** institute, introduce, originate **10** embark upon, inaugurate

begin again: 4 anew, over **5** renew **6** resume **7** restart

beginner: 4 boot, tiro, tyro **5** rooky **6** novice, rookie **7** amateur, entrant, noviate, recruit, trainee, student **8** freshman, neophyte **9** candidate, debutante, novitiate, postulate **10** apprentice

beginning: egg **4** dawn, edge, germ, rise, root, seed **5** alpha, birth, debut, start **6** outset, setout, source **7** genesis, gene-

ses(pl.), initial, nascent **8** entrance, exordium, inchoate, rudiment **9** day spring, embryonic, inception, incipient, the word go **10** conception, elementary, foundation, incunabula(pl.), initiation, opening gun **11** incunabulum **12** commencement

begone: off, out **4** away, scat, shoo **5** scoot, scram **6** aroint, avaunt, depart, get out **7** vamoose

begrudging: 6 loathe, grudge **7** envious, grumble **9** reluctant

beguile: fox **4** coax, foil, gull, lure **5** amuse, charm, cheat, cozen, elude, evade, trick **6** brique, delude, divert, entrap, seduce **7** deceive, ensnare, flatter, mislead **9** entertain **10** manipulate

behalf: 4 part, sake, side **5** stead **6** affair, matter, profit **7** benefit, defence, defense, support **8** interest **9** advantage

behave: act **4** bear, go on, quit, work **5** carry, react, treat **6** acquit, demean, deport, handle **7** comport, conduct, gesture, manager **8** function, regulate, restrain

behavior, behaviour: air **4** port, mien **5** guise, tenue **6** action, manner **7** bearing, comport, conduct, decorum **8** amenance, breeding, carriage **9** demeanour **10** deportment, governance

behead: 9 decollate **10** decapitate, guillotine

behemoth: 4 huge **5** beast, giant, hippo **7** monster

behest: bid, law **4** hest, rule **5** order **6** demand **7** command, mandate **9** prompting **10** injunction **12** solicitation

behind: aft **4** past, rear, ward, rump **5** abaff, abaft, after, ahind(Sc.), arear, later, passe, tardy **6** arrear, astern **8** backward, buttocks, dilatory **9** posterior **10** afterwards

behold: eye, see, spy **4** ecce, espy, gaze, hold, keep, look, scan, stop, view, wait **5** sight, voila, watch **6** descry, regard, retain **7** discern, observe, witness **8** consider, maintain, perceive

beholden: 7 obliged **8** indebted

behoof: use **6** profit **7** benefit **8** interest **9** advantage

behoove: dow, fit **4** need, suit **5** befit, ought **6** belong, proper **7** require **8** suitable **9** incumbent

beige: tan **4** ecru **5** color, grege(F.) **10** unbleached

being: ens **4** etre(F.), self **5** entia, gnome, human, thing, troll **6** animal, entity, extant, living, mortal, person **7** because, essence, present, reality **8** creature, ontology, standing **9** actuality, existence **11** subsistence **12** constitution

abstract: ens **5** entia

actual: **4** esse
celestial: **5** angel **6** cherub, seraph **8** divinity
in front: **6** anteal
physiological: **4** bion
science of: **8** ontology
Bela's son: Ard, Iri **4** Uzzi **5** Ezbon
Bel's wife: **5** Belit **6** Beltis
belabor, belabour: ply **4** beat, drub, lash, work **6** assail, batter, buffet, cudgel, hammer, hamper, thrash, thwack
belated: **5** tardy **7** delayed, overdue **12** old-fashioned
belay: **5** beset **6** invest, waylay **7** besiege **8** encircle
belaying pin: **5** kevel **7** bollard
belch: **4** boke, bolk, burp, galp, rasp **5** eruct **8** eructate **10** eructation
beldam, beldame: hag **4** fury **5** crone, jixen **6** alecto, erinys, virago **7** Jezebel **8** ancestor **9** Tisiphone **11** grandmother
beleaguer: **5** belay, beset **6** invest **7** assault, besiege **8** blockade, surround **9** encompass
belfry: **4** shed **5** tower **7** clocher **9** campanile
Belgian: **7** Fleming, Walloon
Belgium: *canal:* **5** Union **6** Albert **7** Campine
capital: **8** Brussels
city: Ans, Huy, Spa **4** Gand, Mons **5** Alost, Ciney, Eupen, Ghent, Ieper, Jumet, Liege, Namur, Ypres **6** Bruges, Brugge, Deurne, Lierre, Ostend, Turnai **7** Antwerp, Berchem, Herstal, Hoboken, Ixelles, Louvain, Malmedy, Mechlin, Roulers, Seraing **8** Bastogne, Courtrai, Muscron, Turnhout, Verviers, Waterloo
coin: **5** belga, franc **7** centime
commune: Ath, Ely, Hal, Mol, Spa **4** Aath, Boom, Geel, Genk, Lier, Niel, Roux, Zele **5** Aalst, Evere, Genck, Halle, Jette, Ronse, Uccle, Ukkel
endive: **7** witloof
Gaul tribe: **4** Remi **6** Belgae, Nervii
horse: **9** Brabancon
kings: **6** Albert **7** Leopold **8** Baudouin
language: **6** French **7** Flemish
marble: **5** rance
measure: vat **4** aune, last, pied **5** carat **6** perche **8** boisseau
province: **5** Liege, Namur **7** Antwerp, Brabant, Hainaut, Limburg **9** Luxemburg **12** East Flanders, West Flanders
river: Lys **4** Dyle, Leie, Maas, Yser **5** Demer, Dijle, Lesse, Meuse, Nethe, Rupel, Senne **6** Dender, Ourthe, Sambre **7** Ambieve, Schelde, Scheldt
seaport: **6** Ostend **7** Antwerp
tribe: **9** Bellovaci

violinist: **5** Ysaye
weight: **4** last **5** carat, livre, pound **6** charge **7** chariot **8** esterlin
Belial: **5** devil, Satan
belie: **4** hide **6** belong, defame **7** besiege, falsify, pertain, slander, traduce **8** disguise, negative, strumpet, surround **9** encompass **10** calumniate, contradict, contravene **11** counterfeit **12** misrepresent
belief: fay, ism **4** mind, sect, view **5** credo, creed, dogma, faith, tenet, troth, trust **6** credit **7** opinion **8** credence, doctrine, reliance **9** assurance, certainty **10** confidence, conviction, persuasion
liable to: **7** credent **9** credulous
believe: buy, wis **4** deem, trow, ween **5** judge, think, trust **6** accept, credit **7** suppose, swallow **8** accredit, consider, credence
believer: ist **8** adherent
in all religions: **7** omnist
in God: **5** deist **6** theist
in predestination: **13** particularist
Belili's brother: **6** Tammuz
belittle: **5** decry, dwarf, sneer **6** slight **7** detract **8** minimize **9** criticize, denigrate, discredit, disparage **10** depreciate, **13** underestimate
Belize: *capital:* **9** Belmopan
city: **10** Belize City
monetary unit: **6** dollar
peak: **8** Victoria
bell: **4** call, fair, gong, peal, ring, roar, toll **5** chime, cloak, codon, flare, knell, swell **6** bellow, bubble(Sc.), crotal, curfew, tocsin **7** blossom, campana, campane, corolla **9** beautiful **13** tintinnabulum
alarm: **6** tocsin
axle bearing: cod
clapper: **6** tongue
kind of: cow **4** door, gong, hand **5** ship's **6** church, jingle, school **8** electric
ringer: **6** sexton, toller **12** carillonneur
ringer of fiction: **9** Quasimodo
shaped: **10** campanular **11** campanulate
sound: **4** ding, dong, toll **5** knell **6** tinkle
tower: **7** belfry **9** campanile
bell, book, and candle: **15** excommunication
bell bottoms: **5** pants **8** trousers
bell ear: **6** cannon
Bell for Adano author: **6** Hersey
belladonna: **5** dwale, plant **6** remedy **7** manicon **8** narcotic **9** dwayberry **10** nightshade
extract: **7** atropin **8** atropine
bellbird: **6** shrike **8** arapunga
bellboy: **4** page **6** porter, redcap
Bellerophon: *father:* **7** Glaucus
spring: **7** Pelrene
belles-lettres: **10** literature

bellicose: mad 5 irate 7 hostile, warlike 8 militant 10 pugnacious 11 belligerent

belligerent: hot 7 hostile, warlike 8 choleric, fighting, jingoist 9 bellicose, combative, irascible, litigious, wrangling 10 pugnacious 11 contentious, hot-tempered, quarrelsome 12 disputatious, antagonistic

Bellini: *opera:* 5 Norma 9 I Puritani 12 La Sonnambula
sleepwalker: 5 Amina

bellow: cry, low, moo, yap 4 bawl, beal, bell, roar, rout, yaup, yawp 5 belve, blart, croon, roust(Sc.), shout 6 buller, clamor 7 bluster, ululate 10 vociferate

bellwether: 5 sheep 6 leader

belly: bag, cod, gie(Sc.), gut, pod 4 bouk, kyte(Sc.) 5 bingy, bulge, pleon 6 hunger, paunch 7 abdomen, stomach 8 appetite

belong: fit, set 4 bear, vest 5 apply, belie 6 inhere, relate 7 pertain 9 appertain

belongings: 4 gear 5 goods, traps 6 assets, estate 7 effects 8 chattels, property 9 household 10 appendages 11 possessions 13 appurtenances

beloved: 4 dear, idol 5 cheri(F.) 6 adored, cherie(F.) 7 darling 8 precious 9 boy friend, inamorata, valentine 10 girl friend, sweetheart

below: 4 down 5 infra, sotto(It.), under 7 beneath 8 downward, inferior 10 downstairs, underneath

belt: 4 area, band, beat, blow, cest, gird, mark, ring, sash, zone 5 girth, strap, strip, tract, whack, zonar 6 bodice, cestus, cingle, fettle, girdle, invest, region, strait, stripe, zonnar, zonule 7 baldric, circuit, passage 8 ceinture, cincture, encircle, surround 9 bandoleer, encompass 10 cummerbund
conveyor: 5 apron
ecclesiastical: 7 baldric, balteus 8 baltheus, baldrick
non-Mohammedan: 5 zonar

belted: 6 zonate 7 girdled 9 cinctured

bema: 4 pace, step 7 chancel

bemired: 5 dirty, muddy, stuck 10 bogged down

bemoan: 4 wail 6 grieve, lament, sorrow 7 deplore

bemuse: 5 addle 7 confuse 8 distract

bench: bar, pew 4 banc, seat 5 board, judge, ledge, stool 6 settee 7 discard
church: pew, pue 6 sedile(L.)

bench hook: 5 clamp

benchmark: 5 model 8 standard 13 comparison aid

bend: bow, nid, ply, sag 4 arch, flex, kink, turn 5 angle, baton, bulge, crimp, crook, curve, stoop, twist 6 buckle, cotice, cotise, crouch, direct, divert, fasten, inflex, submit 7 bendlet, incline, refract 9 genuflect
backward: 6 retort
in timber: sny

bender: leg 5 binge, drunk, spree 7 whopper 8 guzzling, sixpence

bending: 5 lithe 6 pliant, supple 7 anfract, crooked, flexion 8 flection

beneath: 5 below, lower, under 11 underground

Benedictine: 4 monk 7 Cluniac, liqueur
title: dom

benediction: 4 amen 5 grace 6 prayer 7 benison 8 approval, blessing 10 invocation

benefaction: 4 alms, boon, gift 5 grant 7 present 8 donation, gratuity 11 approbation

benefactor: 5 agent, angel, donor 6 friend, helper, patron, savior 8 promoter 14 philanthropist

beneficence: 6 bounty 7 charity 8 donation, goodness, kindness

beneficial: 4 good 6 useful 7 helpful 8 salutary 9 desirable, enjoyable, favorable, healthful, lucrative, wholesome 10 profitable, salubrious 11 serviceable 12 advantageous, remunerative

beneficiary: 4 heir, user 5 donee 6 vassal 7 legatee 9 feudatory

benefit: aid, use 4 boon, boot, gain, gift, help, prow, sake 5 avail, boost 6 assist, behalf, behoof, better, profit, usance 7 advance, bespeak, concert, deserve, improve, service, utility, welfare 8 befriend, interest 9 advantage, charity do, emolument 11 performance 12 contribute to

benevolent: 4 good, kind 6 benign, loving 7 amiable, liberal 8 generous 10 altruistic, charitable, munificent 13 philanthropic, tenderhearted

benign: 4 boon, good, kind, mild 5 bland 6 genial, gentle 7 affable 8 benedict, gracious, salutary 9 benignant, favorable, wholesome 10 benevolent, charitable, favourable, propitious, salubrious

Benin: *capital:* 9 Porto Novo
ethnic group: 4 Fons 5 Adjas, Mahis 7 Baribas, Yorubas
gulf: 6 Guinea
monetary unit: 5 franc 7 centime
mountain: 7 Atakora
port: 7 Cotonou
river: 4 Mono 5 Niger
town: 6 Abomey, Ouidah 7 Parakou

benison: 8 blessing, 9 beatitude 10 invocation 11 benediction

Benjamin: *descendant:* 4 Aher
grandson: Iri
son: Ehi 4 Gera, Rosh

benne: 6 sesame

bent: aim, bow, set **4** bias, gift, turn **5** bound, bowed, crank, crump, flair, knack, prone, taste, trend **6** akimbo, biased, braced, courbe, course, curved, energy, genius, hooked, swayed, talent **7** crooked, curvant, decided, flexion, flexure, impetus, leaning, leveled, pronate, purpose, stooped, tension **8** aptitude, declined, flection, penchant, tendency **9** curvature, direction, prejudice **10** determined, proclivity, propensity **11** disposition, inclination **13** prepossession **14** predisposition

benthonic plant: 6 enalid

benthos: 5 fauna, flora

benumb: nip **4** daze, dunt, numb, stun **5** daver **6** cumber, deaden **7** fretish, fretize, stupefy

benzine derivative: 6 phenol

Beowulf: 4 epic, poem

bequeath: 4 give, will **5** endow, leave, offer **6** bestow, commit, demise, devise, legate, quethe **7** bequest, commend **8** hand down, transmit **9** testament

bequest: 4 gift, will **6** legacy **8** bequeath, heritage, pittance **9** endowment

berate: jaw, nag **4** lash, rail **5** abuse, chide, scold, score **6** revile **7** censure, reprove, upbraid **8** chastise **10** vituperate

Berber: 4 Moor **6** Hamite, Kabyle **7** Haratin

chief: **4** caid, qaid

dialect: **6** Tuareg

tribe: **4** Daza, Riff, Tibu **6** Tuareg

bereave: rob **5** strip **6** divest, sadden **7** deprive, despoil **10** dispossess

bereft: orb **4** lorn, lost, poor **7** forlorn **8** bereaved **9** destitute **12** dispossessed

beret: cap, hat, tam **7** biretta, chapeau **8** berretta, chapeaux(pl.), headgear

berg: ice **4** floe **6** barrow **8** eminence, mountain

bergamot: 4 bose, mint, pear **5** snuff **6** orange **7** Bergama, essence, perfume

Berlin park: 10 Tiergarten

berm, berme: 4 bank, edge, path **5** ledge, shelf **7** terrace

Bermuda: 10 archipelago

capital: **8** Hamilton

monetary unit: **6** dollar

Bermuda cedar: 7 juniper

Bermuda grass: 4 doob

berry: bay, dew, haw **4** beat, cran, rasp **5** acini, bacca, black, fruit, mound, salal, savin **6** acinus, baccae, burrow, sabine, thresh **7** currant, hillock

disease: **8** bluestem

medicinal: **5** cubeb

oil: **5** olive

berry-like: 7 baccate

berserk: mad **5** bravo **6** pirate **7** enraged,

warrior **8** frenzied, maniacal

berth: bed, job **4** bunk, dock, slip **5** place, wharf **6** billet, office **7** lodging, mooring **8** position **9** anchorage, situation **11** appointment

bertha: 4 cape **6** cannon, collar

beryl: gem **5** jewel **7** emerald **10** aquamarine

green: **11** davidsonite

yellow: **8** heliodor

beseech: ask, beg, sue **4** pray **5** crave, plead **6** adjure, appeal, obtest **7** entreat, implore, solicit **9** impetrate, obsecrate **10** supplicate

beseeching: 9 precative

beset: ply **4** sail, stud **5** allot, belay, harry, siege, spend **6** assail, attack, harass, infest **7** arrange, bejewel, besiege, perplex **8** blockade, encumber, obstruct, surround **9** beleaguer

beside: by **4** hear **5** along, aside **6** next to **7** abreast **8** adjacent

comb. form: **4** para **5** juxta

besides: by; and, but, too, yet **4** also, else, over, then **6** beyond, except, withal **8** moreover **10** additional **11** furthermore

besiege: 4 gird, girt **5** belay, belie, beset, siege, storm **6** attack, invest, pester, plague **7** solicit **8** blockade, surround **9** beleaguer

besmirch: 4 soil **5** smear, sully, taint **7** asperse, blacken **8** discolor

besom: map **4** drab(Sc.) **5** broom, sweep **6** sloven(Sc.) **7** heather

besot: 4 dull **6** muddle, stupid **7** stupefy **8** befuddle **9** infatuate

bespangle: dot **4** star, stud **5** adorn **8** sprinkle

bespatter: 4 blot, dash, soil, spot **5** muddy, plash, stain, sully **6** malign, sparge **7** asperse, scatter **8** reproach, sprinkle

bespeak: ask **4** cite, hint, show **5** argue, imply, order, speak **6** accost, attest, engage, steven **7** address, arrange, benefit, betoken, discuss, exclaim, reserve **8** foretell, indicate, put in for **9** stipulate

best: ace **4** a-one, beat, most, pick, tops, wale **5** cream, elite, excel, worst **6** choice, defeat, finest, flower, outwit, utmost **7** conquer, largest, optimum, paragon, surpass **8** greatest, nonesuch, outmatch, outstrip, vanquish **9** excellent, overmatch **11** superlative

bestial: low **4** vile, wild **5** feral **6** brutal, filthy **7** brutish, inhuman **8** depraved

bestir: 5 rouse

bestow: add, put, use **4** deal, dote, give **5** allot, allow, apply, award, beset, grant, lodge, place **6** accord, beteem, confer, demise, devote, divide, donate, employ, entail, extend, harbor, impart, render **7** collate, dispose, instate, present, quarter, tribute **8** bequeath **11** communicate

bestride: 5 mount **6** stride **8** straddle

bet: lay, pot **4** ante, gage, play, plot, risk, wage **5** hedge, stake, wager **6** gamble, pledge
broker: **6** bookie **9** bookmaker
fail to pay: **5** welch, welsh
faro: **7** sleeper
roulette: bas **4** noir **5** carre **6** milieu **7** dernier, encarre, enplein

betake: hie **4** move **5** apply, catch, grant **6** assume, commit, repair, remove, resort **7** commend, journey

bete noire: 4 hate **5** dread **6** terror **7** bugaboo, bugbear **11** abomination

betel: 4 ikmo, itmo, siri **6** pupulo
leaf: pan **4** buyo

betel palm: 5 areca
extract: **7** catechu
masticatory: pan **4** buyo
seed: **8** betel nut

Betelgeuse: 4 star

bethel: 6 chapel

Bethesda: 4 pool **6** chapel

bethink: 5 think **6** devise, recall **7** reflect **8** consider, remember **9** recollect **10** deliberate

Bethlehemite: 4 Boaz

Beth's sister: Amy, Meg

Bethuel's son: 5 Laban

betide: hap **5** befit, occur, trite **6** become, befall, chance, happen **7** betoken, presage

betimes: 4 anon, rath, soon **5** early, rathe **8** speedily **9** forthwith, sometimes **10** seasonably **11** prematurely **12** occasionally

betise: 5 folly **9** silliness, stupidity

betoken: 4 mark, note, show **5** augur **6** assert, betide, denote, evince, import **7** bespeak, express, oblique, portend, presage, signify **8** forebode, foreshow, indicate **9** symbolize **10** foreshadow **13** prognosticate

betray: 4 blab, blow, boil, gull, sell, sile, sing, tell, undo, wray **5** peach, snare, spill **6** accuse, delude, descry, reveal, seduce, sell out, snitch, squeal, turn in **7** beguile, deceive, falsify, mislead **8** disclose, discover **11** double-cross

betrayer: rat **5** Judas, skunk **7** seducer, traitor **8** derelict, informer

betroth: 4 affy **6** assure, engage, ensure, pledge, plight **7** espouse, promise **8** affiance, contract, handfast

better: aid, top **4** good, mend, more **5** amend, emend, excel, safer, wiser **6** bigger, choice, exceed, reform **7** advance, choicer, correct, greater, improve, promote, rectify, relieve, support, surpass **8** increase, superior **9** desirable, melio-

rate, upper hand **10** ameliorate, preferable

better half: 4 wife

betting: *adviser:* **4** tout
figures: **4** odds
odds: **5** price

between: 4 amid **5** amell, among, entre(F.) **7** average, betwixt **12** intermediate
law: **5** mesne

between the lines: 6 latent, secret

bevel: 4 blow(Sc.), cant, edge, push(Sc.) **5** angle, bezel, miter, mitre, slant, slope **6** aslant **7** chamfer, incline, oblique **8** diagonal
corners: **5** splay
end of timber: **5** snape
out: **4** ream

beverage: ade, ale, nog, pop, tea **4** beer, grog, mead, milk, soda, wine **5** cider, cocoa, draft, drink, lager, leban, negus, morat, punch, treat, water **6** coffee, eggnog, liquid, liquor, nectar, posset **7** potable **8** cocktail, potation **9** metheglin **10** melicratum
alcoholic: See **alcoholic drink**
container: vat **6** kettle **7** charger **9** separator
extract: **4** kola
malted wheat: **6** zythem, zythum
mixed: **5** negus, punch, smash **6** bishop
mulberry and honey: **5** morat
Oriental: rak **4** sake **5** rakee **6** arrack
pepper: **4** kava
Polynesian: **4** kava
South American: **4** mate

bevy: 4 herd, pack **5** covey, drove, flock, group, swarm **6** flight, school **7** company **8** assembly **9** gathering, multitude **10** collection

bewail: cry, rue **4** keen, moan, sigh, wail, weep **5** mourn **6** bemoan, grieve, lament, plaint, sorrow **7** deplore **8** complain

beware: 4 cave, heed, shun **5** avoid, spend **6** eschew **7** look out, warning **8** take care, watch out

bewilder: fog **4** daze, foil, gaum **5** abash, addle, amaze, amuse, deave **6** baffle, bemist, bother, dazzle, muddle, puzzle **7** buffalo, confuse, fuddle, muddle, mystify, perplex, stagger, stupefy **8** astonish, confound, distract, entangle, surprise **9** embarrass, obfuscate **10** spiflicate **11** spifflicate

bewildered: 4 asea, lost, mang **5** agape, dazed **8** confused, helpless **9** perplexed

bewilderment: awe, fog **4** daze **9** amazement, confusion **10** perplexity **11** distraction **13** embarrassment

bewitch: hex **5** charm, fasci, spell, trick **6** enamor, entice, glamor, grigri, hoodoo,

thrill, voodoo **7** attract, bedevil, delight, enchant, glamour **8** ensorcel, forspeak, greegree **9** captivate, ensorcell, fascinate
Beyle's penname: 8 Stendhal
beyond: 4 free, over, past **5** above, after, aside, forby, ultra **6** forbye, yonder **7** besides, further, outside **8** superior **9** hereafter **10** too deep for
the sea: **11** ultramarine
the threshold: **12** ultraliminal
bezel, basil: rim **4** edge, ouch, seal **5** bevil, crown, facet **6** chaton, flange **8** template
bhagavat: 7 blessed
bhakta: 7 devotee **9** worshiper
bhalu: 4 bear
bhang, bang: 7 hashish **8** narcotic **10** intoxicant
product of: **6** majoon
bhangi: 6 mehtar **7** sweeper
bharal: tur **5** sheep **6** nahoor
bhat: 4 bard **8** minstrel
bhikku: 4 monk **5** friar **6** priest **9** mendicant
bhikshu: 5 friar **7** ascetic **9** mendicant
bhoosa: 5 chaff, husks, straw
b'hoy: 5 rowdy **8** gangster
bhut: 5 demon, ghost **6** goblin
Bhutan: *capital:* **6** Thimbu **7** Thimphu
ethnic group: **6** Bhotia, Lepcha
monetary unit: **8** chhetrum, ngultrum
mountain: **9** Himalayas
plain: **4** Duar
bias: 4 awry, bent, sway **5** amiss, color, slant, slope **7** bigotry, incline, leaning, oblique **8** clinamen, diagonal, tendency **9** clinamina(pl.), prejudice, procedure **10** favoritism, partiality, prepossess, propensity **11** declination, disposition, favouritism, inclination **12** predetermine, predilection **13** prepossession
biased 6 warped **7** partial **8** one-sided **9** jaundiced **11** tendentious
bib: sip **4** brat, fish **5** apron, drink **6** tipple, tucker **7** bavette(F.) **9** neckpiece **10** protection
bibelot: 5 curio **7** trinket **8** ornament **10** knickknack
Bible: *angel:* **5** Micah **7** Raphael
animal: **4** reem **5** daman **6** hydrax **8** behemoth
apocrypha: **5** Tobit **6** Baruch, Esdras, Jeremy, Judith, Syriac, Wisdom **7** Vulgate **8** Manasses **9** Maccabees **10** Septuagint **14** Ecclesiasticus
ascetic order: **6** Essene
battle scene: **10** Armageddon
book: Job **4** Acts, Amos, Ezra, Joel, John, Jude, Luke, Mark, Ruth **5** Hosea, James, Jonah, Kings, Micah, Peter, Titus **6** Daniel, Esther, Exodus, Haggai, Isaiah, Joshua, Psalms, Romans, Samu-

el **7** Ezekiel, Genesis, Hebrews, Matthew, Numbers, Obadiah, Timothy **8** Habakkuk, Jeremiah, Nehemiah, Philemon, Proverbs **9** Apocrypha, Ephesians, Galatians, Leviticus, Zechariah **10** Chronicles, Colossians, Revelation **11** Corinthians, Deuteronomy, Philippians **12** Ecclesiastes, Lamentations **13** Song of Solomon, Thessalonians
character: see *name* below
charioteer: **4** Jehu
city: Ain, Dan **4** Arad, Aven, Cana, Elim, Elon, Gath, Gaza, Geba, Maon, Rome, Tyre, Zoar **5** Akkad, Arvad, Ashur, Assur, Joppa, Sidon, Sodom **6** Bethel, Biblos, Gadara, Jerico, Tarsus **7** Babylon, Nineveh **8** Gomorrah, Nazareth **9** Jerusalem
clan: **6** Shelah
country: Nod, Pul **4** Aram, Bela, Edam, Elam, Gath, Hali, Moab, Seba, Seir **5** Ammon **6** Canaan **7** Galilee, Samaria
desert: **5** Sinai
garden: **4** Eden **8** Paradise
giant: **4** Anak, Emim **7** Goliath
giant killer: **5** David
hill: **4** Zion
hunter: **6** Nimrod
judge: **4** Agog, Elon **6** Gideon, Samson **8** Jephthah
king: Asa, Gog, Iva **4** Agag, Ahab, Ahaz, Amon, Bera, Jehu, Omri, Reba, Saul **5** David, Herod, Hiram, Joram, Nadab, Rezin, Tidal, Zimri **6** Birsha, Hezion, Japhia, Jotham, Uzziah **7** Jehoram, Solomon
kingdom: **4** Elam, Moab **5** Judea, Judah **6** Israel **8** Chaldeae
land of plenty: **6** Goshen
liar: **7** Ananias
money: **4** beka **5** bekah **6** shekel
mountain: Hor **4** Ebal, Nebo, Peor, Sina, Sion, Zion **5** Heres, Horeb, Sinai, Tabor **6** Ararat, Gilead, Moriah, Olivet, Pisgah
name: Ahi, Asa, Eri, Eve, Evi, Hor, Iri, Koa, Lot, Ner, Ono, Reu, Toi, Uel, Uri **4** Abel, Acan, Acub, Adam, Ader, Adna, Ador, Agee, Aher, Aman, Anak, Anam, Aner, Aram, Arem, Arie, Asan, Asom, Ater, Aven, Azal, Cain, Cana, Dura, Edar, Edec, Edes, Eker, Enan, Enos, Eran, Esau, Etam, Gera, Irad, Iram, Isac, Mary, Neri, Obal, Omar, Oreb, Oren, Paul, Reba, Sami, Sara, Seth, Suba, Ucal, Vale **5** Ahlab, Alian, Amasa, Aroer, Bedan, Besai, Caleb, Elias, Ephai, Esrom, Hadad, Hanes, Isaac, Mered, Nahum, Oseas, Peleg, Rahad, Tarah, Vania **6** Naaman, Pilate, Ramath **7** Abadias, Abigail, Antioch, Elmodam, Idithum, Sidrach, Tabitha

navigator: **4** Noah
ornament: **4** urim **7** thummin
patriarch: Reu **4** Seth, Shem **5** Jacob, Nahor, Peleg **6** Israel, Lamech
people: **4** Moab, Phut, Seba **5** Ammon **6** Hamite, Hivite, Kenite, Levite **7** Amorite, Dodanim, Moabite
plain: **4** Maab **5** Mamre **7** Jericho
plotter: **5** Haman
poem: **5** psalm
pool: **6** Siloam
priest: Eli **5** Aaron **6** Levite
pronoun: thy **4** thee, thou **5** thine
prophet: **4** Amos, Ezra **5** Elias, Hosea, Jonah, Micah, Nahum **6** Elijah, Isaiah **7** Ezekial **8** Jeremiah
psalmist: **5** David
queen: Abi **5** Sheba **6** Esther, Vashti **7** Jezebel
region: **4** Enon **5** Ophir, Perea **6** Bashan
reproach: **4** raca
river: Zab **4** Nile **5** Abana, Arnon **6** Kishon, Jordan
ruler: see *king* above
scholar: **7** Biblist **9** Biblicist
sea: Red **4** Dead **7** Galilee **8** Tiberias **10** Gennesaret
shepherd: **4** Abel **5** David
spice: **5** myrrh **6** cassia, stacte **12** frankincense
spy: **5** Caleb
stone: **4** ezel **6** ligure
tower: **4** Edar **5** Babel
town: see *city* above
tree: **5** cedar
tribe: see *people* above
valley: **4** Baca, Elah **6** Shaveh, Siddim
version: **4** Geez **5** Douay, Itala **6** Syriac **7** Vulgate **8** Bohairic **9** Apocrypha, King James **10** New English **15** Revised Standard
weed: **4** tare
witch's home: **5** Endor
Bible society: 7 Gideons
Biblical: 10 scriptural
bicker: war **4** bowl, spar, tiff **5** argue, brawl, cavil, fight **6** assail, attack, battle, rattle **7** contend, dispute, quarrel, wrangle **8** pettifog, skirmish, squabble **10** contention
bicycle: 4 bike **5** wheel **10** two-wheeler
for two: **6** tandem
rider: **7** cyclist
ten-speed: **10** derailleur
bid: beg **4** call, hist, pray **5** clepe, offer, order **6** adjure, charge, direct, enjoin, invite, reveal, summon, tender **7** command, declare, entreat, proffer, request **8** announce, proclaim, proposal
biddable: 6 docile **8** obedient
biddy: hen **7** chicken
bide: 4 face, stay, wait **5** abide, await,

dwell, tarry **6** endure, remain, reside, suffer **7** sojourn **8** continue, tolerate **9** encounter, withstand
bidonville: 10 shantytown
bier: 4 pyre **5** frame, grave **6** coffin, hearse, litter **7** support **10** catafalque, handbarrow
biff: 4 blow **6** strike
bifid: 6 forked
bifocal: 4 lens
bifold: 6 double **7** twofold
bifurcation: wye **4** fork **5** split **6** branch **8** division
big: 4 bold, huge, vast **5** bulky, chief, grand, great, gross, hefty, large **6** mighty **7** bumping, eminent, leading, massive, pompous, violent **8** boastful, bouncing, enormous, generous, gigantic, imposing, pregnant **9** notorious **10** tremendous **11** magnanimous, outstanding, pretentious, threatening
Big Dipper: *constellation:* **9** Ursa Major
star: **5** Alcor, Dubhe, Merak, Mizar **6** Alioth, Alkoid, Megrez, Phecda
big shot: VIP **5** mogul, wheel **6** tycoon **7** notable **8** brass hat **9** celebrity **11** heavyweight **13** high-muck-a-muck
big toe: 6 hallux
bigener: 4 mule **6** hybrid
bigfoot: 4 omah **9** sasquatch
bighorn: 5 sheep **6** argali, aoudad **8** cimarron
bight: bay **4** bend, coil, gulf, loop **5** angle, curve, inlet, noose **6** corner, hollow
bignou, biniou: bagpipe
bigot: 6 cafard, zealot **7** fanatic **9** hypocrite
bigoted: 6 biased, narrow **9** hidebound, illiberal, sectarian **10** intolerant, prejudiced **12** narrow-minded
bijou: 5 jewel **7** trinket
bile: 4 boil, gall, hump **5** venom **6** choler, growth
bilge: 4 scum **5** bouge, bulge **8** nonsense
bilingual: diglot
bilk: gyp **4** balk, hoax **5** cheat, cozen, dodge, shake, trick **6** delude, escape, fleece **7** deceive, defraud, swindle **9** frustrate **10** disappoint
bill: act, dun, law, neb, nib, tab **4** beak, note, peck, rise **5** libel, score, visor **6** caress, charge, indict, pecker, pickax, poster, strike **7** invoice, lampoon, mattock, placard, statute **8** billhook, document, headland, petition **9** memoranda(pl.), reckoning, statement **10** broadsword, memorandum, promontory **13** advertisement
anchor: pee
five dollar: fin, vee
one dollar: **4** buck **8** frogskin
ten dollar: **7** sawbuck

bill of fare: 4 card, menu 5 carte

billet: bar, gad, log 4 loop, note, pass, post 5 berth, enrol, house, lodge, order, put up, stick, strap 6 ballot, canton, enroll, harbor, letter, notice, ticket 7 bearing, epistle, harbour, missive, pollack, quarter 8 coalfish, document, firewood, ornament, position, quarters 11 appointment, requisition

billet-doux: 8 mash note 10 love letter
opposite: 12 Dear John note

billiards: 4 game, pool
player's turn: 6 inning
play to open: lag 6 string
shot: run 4 miss 5 break, carom, masse 6 cannon 7 bricole, cushion, scratch
stick: cue
term: 4 rack, spot 5 chalk 6 bridge, pocket 7 English 8 balkline, rotation 9 eight ball 10 object ball

billibi: 10 mussel soup
relative: 12 bouillabaise

billingsgate: 5 abuse 7 obloquy 8 ribaldry 12 vituperation

billow: sea 4 wave 5 bulge, float, surge, swell 6 ripple, roller 7 breaker 8 undulate

billowing: 5 tidal 7 surging

billy: caw 4 chap, club, goat, mate 6 cudgel, fellow 7 brother, comrade 8 billikin, bludgeon 9 blackjack

billycock: 5 derby 6 bowler

bin: ark, box, cub 4 bing, cart, crib, vina 5 frame, hutch, pungi, stall, store, wagon 6 basket, bunker, hamper, manger, trough, within 9 container 10 receptacle
coal: 6 bunker
fish: 5 canch, kench

binary: 6 hydrid 7 twofold

binate: 4 dual 6 double, paired 7 coupled, twofold

bind: jam, tie 4 gird, hold, tape 5 stick 6 cement, fetter, secure 7 confine 9 constrict, indenture, make stick 11 predicament
tightly: 4 frap
to secrecy: 4 tile, tyle
wings of a bird: 5 truss 6 pinion, skewer

binder: 4 band, beam, bond, cord, rope 5 baler, cover, frame, lever 6 fillet, folder, girder, header 9 bondstone

binding: 4 band, cord, rope, tape 5 valid 6 edging, ribbon 7 galloon, mousing, webbing 9 stringent 10 astringent, obligatory 11 restraining, restrictive
limp: 4 yapp

bindle stiff: 4 hobo 5 tramp 8 vagabond

binge: bat, bow, hit 4 blow, bust, soak, toot 5 beano, party, spree 6 bender, cringe 7 indulge 8 carousal 9 obeisance 10 indulgence

bingo: 4 game, keno 5 lotto 6 brandy

bioclean: 7 aseptic 8 germ-free

biography: 4 life, vita(It.) 6 memoir 7 account, history, memoire(F.), recount
saint's: 11 hagiography

biological class: 5 genus, order, phyla(pl.) 6 family, genera(pl.), phylum 7 species

bionomics: 7 ecology

biota: 13 flora and fauna

biotic community: 5 biome

biotite: 4 mica 7 anomite

birch: 4 cane, flog, tree, whip 5 canoe 6 betula 7 hickory

bird: ani, daw, nun, pie, tit 4 avis(L.), crow, kite, lark, ruff, tern, wren 5 egret, finch, hobby, pewee, pewit, raven, robin, snipe, terek, vireo 6 bulbul, dunlin, falcon, hoopoe, linnet, marten, mocker, oriole, phoebe, plover, shrike, thrush 7 bluejay, bustard, buzzard, catbird, flicker, halcyon, irrisor, jackdaw, kinglet, ortolan, peacock, redwing, skylark, sparrow, swallow, tanager, warbler, waxwing 8 airplane, bluebird, boatbill, bobolink, bobwhite, chicadee, grosbeak, kingbird, pheasant, redstart, starling, thrasher 9 blackbird, blackcock, brambling, bullfinch, goldfinch, partridge, phalarope, sandpiper 10 bufflehead, meadowlark, tropicbird, woodpecker 11 butcherbird, hummingbird 12 yellowhammer
adjutant: 5 stork 6 argala 7 hurgila, marabou
African: 4 taha 6 quelea 7 touraco 8 umbrette
American: 4 sora 5 robin, vireo 6 darter, fulmar, turkey 7 grackle, tanager 8 cardinal 10 bufflehead
Antarctic: 4 skua 7 penguin
aquatic: 4 duck, gull, loon, swan, tern 5 goose, grebe, small, terne 7 penguin 8 dabchick, flamingo
aquiline: 5 eagle
Arabian Nights: roc
Arctic: auk 6 fulmar
Asiatic: 4 mine, myna 5 pitta 7 hilltit 8 dotterel 9 brambling, feng-huang, fenghwang
Attic: 11 nightingale
Australian: emu, roa 4 emeu, lory 5 arara 6 leipoa 7 boobook, bustard, waybung 8 bellbird, lorikeet, lyrebird, manucode 9 cassowary, coachwhip, friarbird, pardalote
black: ani, ano, daw, pie 4 crow 5 merle, raven 6 oriole 7 jackdaw 8 starling
brilliant plumage: 4 tody 5 jalep 6 oriole, trogon 7 jacamar, tanager 8 pheasant
Central American: daw 4 crow, rave, rook 5 raven 6 magpie 7 corvine, jacamar 8 puffbird

crane-like: 5 wader 6 chunga
crocodile: 9 trochilus
crow-family: daw, jay, pie 4 craw 5 raven 6 magpie 7 jackdaw
crying: 6 ramage 7 limpkin
diving: auk 5 grebe
dressing of feathers: 5 preen
emu-like: 9 cassowary
European: ani, daw, emu, mew, qua 4 cirl, darr, emeu, gled, kite, mall, moro, osel, rook, stag, whim, yite 5 amsel, boonk, glede, mavis, merle, ousel, ouzel, sacer, saker, serin, tarin, terek, terin, whaup 6 avocet, avoset, cushat, gaylag, godwit, linnet, loriot, marten, merlin, missel, redcap, whewer, windle, winnel, wranny 7 bittern, bustard, haybird, kestrel, motacil, ortolan, sakeret, starnel, whiskey, winnard, witwall 8 bargoose, chepster, dotterel, garganey, redstart, wheybird, whimbrel, wrannock, yoldring 9 brambling, gallinule, goldfinch, goosander, peregrine, swinepipe, wheybeard 10 chiffchaff, lammegeyer, turtledove, whitterick 11 capercailie, lammergeier 12 capercailzie
extinct: moa 4 dodo, jibi, mamo 7 offbird
finch-like: 7 chewink, tanager
fish-catching: 6 osprey 9 cormorant
flightless: emu, moa 4 dodo, emeu, kiwi, rhea 7 apteryx, ostrich, penguin, ratitae 9 solitaire
fly-catching: 8 redstart 9 solitaire
flying backwards: 7 swallow, humming
food: hen 5 capon 6 pullet, turkey 7 chicken, rooster
frigate: ioa, iwa 6 tropic
gallinaceous: 6 peahen 7 peacock, peafowl
game: 5 quail, snipe 6 grouse, turkey 8 pheasant, woodcock 9 merganser
genus: 4 alca, crax, otis 7 certhia 9 apatornis
gull-like: 4 tern 6 jaeger
Hawaiian: ava, ioa, iwa 4 iiwi, koae, mamo, moho
heron family: 4 benu, ibis 7 bittern
honey eater: 4 moho
humming: ava 5 carib 7 colibri
insectivorous: owl 5 vireo
jay: gae 6 magpie
large: emu 4 emeu, guan, rhea 5 eagle 6 curlew, willet 7 bustard, megapod, ostrich, pelican, seriema 8 curassow, shoebill 11 lammergeier
largest: 7 ostrich
lark-like: 5 pipit
long-billed: 5 snipe 7 pelican
long-legged: io 4 sora 5 heron, snipe, stilt, wader 6 avocet, avoset, curlew 7 seriema
long-necked: 4 swan 5 agami, crane, goose, geese(pl.), stork 7 ostrich

male: cob, tom 4 cock 5 drake 6 gander 7 peacock, rooster 11 chanticleer
marsh: 4 sora 5 snipe, stilt
meadow: 8 bobolink
Mexican: 6 jacana, towhee 7 jacamar
mythological: roc 5 hansa 6 simurg 7 phoenix, simurgh
New Zealand: kea, moa 4 kaka, kiwi, kulu, ruru, titi, weka 6 kakapo 7 apterix, apteryx 8 morepork, notornis 10 blightbird
nonpasserine: 4 tody 6 hoopoe, motmot 8 hornbill 10 kingfisher
Northern: auk, 6 gannet, puffin
of Athena: owl
of Juno: 7 peacock
of paradise: 8 manucode
of peace: 4 dove
of prey: owl 4 hawk, kite 5 eagle, elant, owlet 6 eaglet, elanet 7 goshawk, vulture 9 accipeter
of Zeus: 5 eagle
oldest known: 13 archaeopteryx
oscine: 4 chat 6 dronge, oriole 7 tanager
ostrich-like: emu, moa 4 emeu, rhea 10 cassowarie
parrot-like: 11 budgereegah, budggerygah
parson: poe, tue, tui
parts of body: neb, nib 4 bill, cere, knee, lora, mala 5 lores 6 pecten, pileum, pinion, rostra, syrinx 7 ambiens 8 pectines(pl.)
passerine: 5 finch 7 sparrow, starnel 9 chatterer, coachwhip
pert. to: 5 avian, avine 8 ornithic 9 volucrine
pink: 8 flamingo
plover-like: 5 drome 7 lapwing
Poe's: 5 raven
predatory: owl 4 kite 5 yager 6 falcon, shrike 9 cormorant
protuberance at base of bill: 4 cere
rare: 8 rara avis
ratite: emu, moa 4 emeu 7 ostrich 9 cassowary
red-tailed: 4 koae
sacred: 4 ibis
sea: auk, ern 4 erne, gony, gull, smew, tern 5 eider, solan 6 gannet, petrel, puffin 7 pelican 9 albatross 10 shearwater
shore: ree 4 rail, sora 5 snipe, stilt, wader 6 avocet, avoset, curlew, plover, willet
Sindbad's: roc 4 rock, rukh
singing: 4 lark, wren 5 finch, mavis, robin, shama, veery, vireo 6 canary, linnet, mocker, oriole, oscine, thrush 7 mocking, robinet 8 bobolink, redstart 12 whippoorwill
small: tit 4 tody, wren 5 dicky, pipit, vireo 6 dickey, linnet, siskin, todies(pl.), tomtit 7 creeper, humming, sparrow, titlark, wheater 8 starling 9 didappers

South American: **4** guan, mina, myna **5** chaja, mynah **6** barbet, becard, toucan **7** cariama, oilbird **8** bellbird, boatbill, caracara, guacharo, hoactzin, puffbird
swallow-like: **4** cran **5** swift
swimming: **4** loon **5** grebe
talking: **4** crow, mina, mino, myna **5** mynah **6** parrot
tall: **6** avocet, avoset
tropical: ani **4** koae, tody **6** barbet, motmot, toucan, trogon
unfledged: gor **4** eyas **6** gorlin **8** bubbling, nestling
Vishnu's: **6** Garuda
wading: **4** hern, ibis, rail, sora **5** crane, heron, snipe, stilt, stork **6** avocet, jacana **8** flamingo, shoebill **9** sandpiper
web-footed: **4** duck, swan **5** drake, goose **6** avocet, avoset, gander
West Indies: ani **4** tody
white-tailed: ern **4** erne **5** egret
woodcock: **5** pewee
young: eya **4** gull **5** piper **7** flapper, nestler **8** birdikin, nestling **9** fledgling
bird cage: 6 aviary, pinjra, volary, volery **7** paddock
bird clapper: 9 scarecrow
bird crest: 4 tuft
bird eye: 12 cuckoo flower
bird nest: 4 aery, eyry **5** aerie, eyrie
bird of passage: 8 wanderer **9** transient
bird route: 6 flyway
birdman: 5 pilot **6** airman **7** aviator **13** ornithologist
birds: 4 aves
collective: **4** fowl
domesticated: **7** poultry
bird's-eye view: 6 apercu
bird-witted: 5 giddy
birdwoman: 8 aviatrix **9** aviatress, aviatrice
biretta, berretta: cap **5** beret **8** skullcap **13** clergyman's cap
biri: 9 cigarette
birl: 4 spin, toss, whir **5** whirr **6** rattle, rotate **7** revolve
birma: 6 calaba
birr: bur **4** blow, burr, push, rush, wind **5** force, storm, vigor **6** energy, thrust, onrush **7** impetus
birth: 4 bear **6** burden, origin, spring **7** descent, genesis, lineage **8** delivery, geniture, nascency, nativity **9** beginning, naissance, parentage **10** extraction
after: **9** postnatal
before: **8** prenatal
by: nee
goddess: **5** Parca
help with: **8** accouche
new: **10** renascence **11** Renaissance
nobleness: **6** eugeny
pert. to: **5** natal **13** primogenitive

birth control: 7 the pill **9** vasectomy **13** contraception
birth flower: *April:* **5** daisy
August: **9** gladiolus
December: **10** poinsettia
February: **8** primrose
January: **9** carnation
July: **8** sweet pea
June: **4** rose
March: **6** violet
May: **15** lily of the valley
November: **13** chrysanthemum
October: **6** dahlia
September: **5** aster
birth stone: *April:* **7** diamond **8** sapphire
August: **9** carnelian
December: **9** turquoise
February: **8** amethyst
January: **6** garnet
July: **4** ruby
June: **5** agate
March: **6** jasper **10** bloodstone
May: **7** emerald
November: **5** topaz
October: **5** beryl
September: **10** chrysolite
birthday: 11 anniversary, celebration
ode: **12** genethliacon
pert. to: **10** genethliac **12** genethliacal
birthmark: 4 mole **5** naeve, nevus **6** naveus **7** blemish, feature, spiloma **14** characteristic
pert. to: **7** naevoid
birthplace: 10 incunabula(pl.) **11** incunabulum
birthrate: 8 natality
birthright: 8 heritage
bis: 5 again, twice **6** encore, repeat **7** replica **9** duplicate
biscuit: bun **4** bake(Sc.), roll, rush, snap **5** scone, wafer **6** cookie **7** cracker, pentile, pretzel **8** hardtack **9** porcelain **11** earthenware
bisect: 4 fork **5** cross, halve, split **6** cleave, divide **8** separate
bisexual: 13 hermaphrodite
bishop: 4 pope **5** angel **6** archer, bustle, priest **7** pontiff, prelate, primate **8** director, overseer **9** clergyman, inspector **3** administrator **14** superintendent
apron: **7** gremial
assistant: **6** verger **9** coadjutor
buskin: **6** caliga **7** caligae(pl.)
cap: **4** hura **5** miter, mitre **7** biretta **8** berretta, mitrella
first year revenue: **5** annat **6** annate
jurisdiction: see **7** diocese
private room: **9** accubitus
robe: **6** chimar, chimer **7** chimere
staff: **7** crosier
stave: **6** baculi(pl.) **7** baculus
throne: **4** apse **8** cathedra

title: 4 abba, anba 7 prelate, primate

vestment: alb 4 cope 6 chimer, rochet 7 gremial, tunicle 8 dalmatic 10 omophorion

bishopric: see 7 diocese 10 episcopacy, episcopate

bishop's weed: 4 ammi 6 ammeos 8 bolewort, goutweed

bison: 6 bovine 7 aurochs, bonasus, buffalo

bisque: 4 soup 5 point 8 ceramics

bistro: bar 4 café 6 tavern 9 nightclub 10 restaurant

bisulcate: 6 cloven

bit: ace, end, jot, ort, wee 4 atom, bite, curb, doit, food, iota, item, mite, mote, part, snap, tool, whit 5 blade, check, crumb, drill, pezzo, piece, scrap, shred, speck, while 6 bridle, cannon, eating, morsel, smidge, splice, tittle, trifle 7 morceau(F.), portion, scatche, smidgen, smidgin, smigeon, snaffle 8 fraction, fragment, particle, quantity, restrain, smitchin, victuals 9 restraint

horse's curb: 6 pelham

Irish: 7 traneen

bit by bit: 9 gradually

bit part: 6 walk-on

bite: bit, cut, eat, nip 4 bait, cham, chew, food, gash, gnap, gnaw, hold, knap, meal, snap 5 chack, chamm, champ, cheat, chomp, pinch, seize, share, smart, snack, sting, trick 6 crunch, morsel, nibble, pierce 7 cheater, corrode, impress, partake, sharper, slander 8 lacerate, puncture, victuals 9 denticate, masticate

bite one's tongue: 6 regret

bite the bullet: 8 face up to 10 meet head-on 14 do it regardless

biting: 4 acid, hoar, keen 5 acrid, sharp, snell 6 bitter, rodent, severe 7 caustic, cutting, mordant, nipping, pungent 8 clear-cut, incisive, poignant, scathing, stinging 9 corrosive, sarcastic, trenchant, vitriolic

biting dragon: 8 tarragon

biting of nails: 12 phaneromania

bito: 4 balm, tree 7 hajilij

oil: 6 zachun

bitt: 4 post 5 block

bitter: bad 4 acid, bask, gall, keen, sore, sour, tart 5 acerb, acrid, amara, bleak, harsh, irate, sharp 6 biting, picric, severe 7 austere, caustic, crabbed, cutting, galling, hostile, painful, pungent, satiric 8 grievous, poignant, stinging, virulent 9 malicious, offensive 10 afflictive 11 acrimonious, distressful 12 antagonistic

bitter apple: 9 colocynth

bitter bush: 9 snakeroot

bitter-ender: 7 diehard

bitter gentian: 9 baldmoney

bitter grass: 9 colicroot

bitter oak: 6 cerris

bitter spar: 8 dolomite

bitter vetch: ers 5 vicia

bitter wintergreen: 10 pipsissewa

bitterly: 4 hard, sour 8 cursedly

bittern: 4 bump 5 boonk, heron 6 kakkak

bitterness: rue 4 acor, bile, fell, gall 5 atter 6 enmity, malice, rancor 7 amarity 8 acerbity, acrimony, severity 9 amaritude, hostility, poignancy, virulence 11 malevolence

bitters: 4 amer(F.) 5 tonic 6 liquor

pert. to: 9 amaroidal

bittersweet: 10 confection, nightshade

bitterweed: 7 ragweed 9 horseweed 10 sneezeweed

bitterwort: 7 felwort 9 dandelion

bitumen: tar 5 pitch 7 asphalt 8 alkitran 9 alchitran, elaterite

bivalve: 4 clam, spat 6 cockle, diatom, mussel, oyster 7 mollusk, Pandora, scallop 10 brachipod

genus: 5 pinna 6 anomia 7 toheroa 12 gastrochaena

bivocal: 9 diphthong

bivouac: 4 camp 5 etape, watch 6 encamp 7 shelter 10 encampment

biwa: 6 loquat

bizarre: odd 5 antic, dedal, outre, queer 6 quaint 7 curious, strange 8 fanciful 9 eccentric, fantastic, grotesque 10 ridiculous 11 extravagant

Bizet opera: 6 Carmen

blab: 4 chat 5 blart, blate, clack 6 babble, betray, gossip, reveal, tattle 7 blabber, chatter 8 telltale

black: jet 4 calo, dark, ebon, foul, inky, onyx 5 dirty, dusky, murky, Negro, noire(F.), raven, sable, slate, sooty 6 atrous, dismal, gloomy, pitchy, sullen 7 melanic, Negrito, piceous, swarthy, unclean 8 charcoal, mournful 9 atrocious 10 blackamoor, calamitous, forbidding

and white: 11 chiaroscuro

black and blue: 5 livid

spot: 6 bruise, shiner 10 ecchymosis

black art: 5 magic 7 alchemy 8 wizardry 10 necromancy 11 conjuration

black cod: 6 beshow

black death: 6 plague

black diamond: oil 4 coal 8 hematite

black earth: 4 mold 9 chernozem

black elder: 9 hackberry

black eye: 5 shame 6 bruise, shiner 7 scandal

black-eyed Susan: 6 ketmia 10 coneflower

black grunt: 10 tripletail

black hole: 4 cell 7 dungeon 8 solitary

13 collapsed star
black plague: 7 bubonic
Black Sea: *ancient name:* **6** Pontus
arms: **9** Sea of Azov **12** Sea of Marmara
connecting straits: **5** Kerch **8** Bosporus
11 Dardanelles
peninsula: **6** Crimea
ports: **5** Varna **6** Batumi, Burgas, Odessa
8 Istanbul **9** Constanta **10** Sevastopol
river to: Bug, Don **5** Kuban **6** Danube **7**
Dnieper, Sakarya **8** Dniester
black sheep: 7 deviate **9** reprobate
black widow: 6 spider **7** pokomoo
blackamoor: 5 bleck, Negro **7** negress
blackball: 4 pill, vets **6** ballot **7** boycott,
exclude, heeball **9** ostracize
blackberry: 6 agawam **8** dewberry
blackbird: ani, daw, pie **4** crow, merl **5**
amsel, colly, merle, ousel, ouzel, raven **6**
colley **7** jackdaw
blackboard: 5 slate
blackcap: 4 gull **7** warbler **8** chicadee, titmouse **9** raspberry
blackdamp: 9 chokedamp
blacken: ink, tar **4** char, soot **5** bleck,
cloud, japan, sully **6** darken, defame,
malign, vilify **7** asperse, slander, traduce **8** besmirch **10** calumniate
black eye: 5 mouse **6** shiner, stigma **9**
contusion
blackface: 5 actor, comic, sheep **8** boldface, minstrel
blackfin: 4 fish **5** cisco, sesis
blackfish: 5 whale **6** tautog **10** nigrescent
school: **5** grind
blackguard: 4 shag **5** gamin, guard, snuff
7 vagrant, villain **8** criminal, hanger-
on, vagabond **9** scoundrel
blackhead: 4 clam **6** comedo, mussel
blackjack: oak **4** club, duck, flag, game,
jack **5** billy **6** beetle, jerkin, vessel,
weapon **7** tankard
blackleg: 4 scab, snob **7** disease, gambler
8 apostate, swindler **13** strikebreaker
blacklist: ban **4** veto
blackmail: 5 bribe **6** coerce, extort **7** payment, tribute
blackmailer: 5 ghoul **7** leecher
blackmailing: 8 chantage **9** extortion
Blackmore heroine: 10 Lorna Doone
blackout: 5 faint **6** darken **8** darkness,
scrounge **11** suppression
blacksmith: gow **5** shoer, smith **6** plover,
smithy, stithy **7** farrier, striker **10**
horseshoer
shop: **5** anvil, stith **6** smithy, stithy **8**
smithery
blacksnake: 4 whip **5** racer, quirt
blackthorn: haw **4** sloe, tree
blackwort: 8 comfrey
bladder: sac **7** blister, inflate, vesicle

comb. form: **4** asco
blade: bit, fop, oar **4** blow, bone, edge, leaf,
shiv **5** blood, dandy, fluke, grain, knife,
spark, spear, spire, sword **6** cutter, lamina, scythe, sickle **7** gallant, lamin-
ae(pl.), scapula **9** propeller
blague: lie **4** hoax **6** humbug **8** claptrap,
nonsense, raillery
blah: 4 bunk, dull **8** nonsense
blahs: 5 dumps, ennui **7** boredom, malaise
8 doldrums
Blake's symbol: 4 Zoas
blamable: 6 faulty **8** culpable **11** blameworthy **13** reprehensible
blame: 4 call, hurt, onus, twit **5** chide,
fault, guilt, odium, shend **6** accuse,
charge, dirdum, impute, rebuke, revile,
scance **7** ascribe, censure, condemn, obloquy, reproof, reprove, upbraid **8** reproach **9** challenge, criticism, inculpate,
liability **10** accusation **11** culpability,
reprobation **12** reprehension **13** animadversion
deserving: **8** culpable
blameless: 4 good **7** perfect **8** innocent,
spotless **9** faultless, righteous **13** unimpeachable **14** irreproachable
blanch: 4 fade, pale **5** chalk, scald, white
6 argent, bleach, blench, whiten **8** etiolate **9** whitewash
bland: 4 kind, mild, oily, open, soft **5**
suave **6** benign, genial, gentle, smooth,
urbane **7** affable, amiable, insipid, lenient **8** gracious **9** benignant, courteous
10 wishy-washy **11** good-natured **12**
ingratiating
blandish: 4 coax **5** charm **6** allure,
blanch, cajole **7** beguile, flatter, wheedle
10 compliment
blank: 4 bare, flan, form, shot, void **5** annul, blind, break, clean, empty, range,
space **6** vacant **7** nonplus, unmixed,
vacuous **8** omission, unfilled **9** colorless, downright, fruitless, frustrate
blanket: 4 brot, wrap **5** cotta, cover, layer,
manta, quilt, sheet, throw **6** afghan,
poncho, serape **8** coverlet **10** barraclade
cowboy: **5** sugan **6** soogan, sougan, su-
gann
goat's hair: **6** cumbly
horse: **5** manta
Indian: **6** stroud
blare: 4 peal **5** blast, blaze, noise **6** blazon, scream **7** fanfare, tantara, trumpet
11 flamboyance
blarney: 4 coax **5** stone **6** butter **7** flatter,
wheedle **8** flattery
blasé: 5 bored, sated, weary **8** satiated **9**
surfeited **11** indifferent
blasphemy: 7 calumny, cursing, impiety
8 anathema, swearing **9** profanity, sac-

rilege **10** execration **11** imprecation, irreverence, malediction **12** vilification

blast: bub, nip, wap **4** bang, blow, gale, gust, ruin, wind **5** party, split, stunt **6** attack, blight, wither **7** blowout, bluster, explode, shatter, shindig, shrivel **8** dynamite, outburst, proclaim **9** criticize, discharge, explosion **10** detonation

blast furnace: *lower part:* **4** bosh
  nozzle: **6** tuyere

blat: **5** bleat, blurt **7** exclaim

blatant: **4** glib, loud **5** gaudy, gross, noisy, silly, vocal **6** coarse, vulgar **8** brawling **9** bellowing, clamorous, inelegant, obtrusive, shameless **10** vociferous

blather: **4** stir **5** bleat **6** babble **7** blither, prattle **8** nonsense **9** commotion

blaubok: **5** etaac **8** antelope

blaze: **4** burn, fire, glow, mark, shot **5** flame, flare, flash, glare, gleam, glory, shine, torch, **6** bleeze **7** bonfire, declare, pioneer, sparkle **8** splendor **9** firebrand **10** effulgence, illuminate **11** coruscation **13** conflagration

blazer: **6** jacket

blazon: **4** deck, show **5** adorn, blare, boast **6** depict, shield **7** declare, display, exhibit, publish **8** emblazon, inscribe **9** delineate, embellish **11** description, publication **14** representation

bleach: sun **5** chalk **6** blanch, blench, chlore, purify, whiten **7** decolor, lighten **8** etiolate

bleachers: **5** seats, stand **8** scaffold **10** grandstand

bleaching vat: **4** keir, kier

bleak: dim, raw **4** blae, blay, cold, gray grim, pale **5** sprat **6** bitter, bleach, dismal, dreary, frigid, gloomy, pallid **7** cutting **8** desolate **9** cheerless **10** depressing
  fish: **4** blay, bley **5** sprat

blear: dim **4** blur, dull **5** faint **6** darken **7** deceive, mislead **8** hoodwink, protrude

bleared: **4** inky **5** dusky **6** rheumy

bleat: baa **4** blat, blea **5** blart, gripe **7** blather, bluster, whicker

bleb: **4** blob **5** bulla **6** bubble **7** blister, pustule, vesicle **8** swelling

bleed: **4** flow, leak, shed **5** exude **6** escape, extort, fleece **7** agonize

bleeding heart: **8** dicentra

bleep, blip: **8** high note **10** TV deletion **11** shrill sound, video signal

blemish: mar **4** blot, blur, dent, flaw, gall, lack, mark, rift, scar, slur, spot, vice, want, wart **5** blame, breck, crack, fault, mulct, speck, sully, tache, taint **6** blotch, breach, defame, defect, impair, injure, macula, macule, smirch, stigma, blister **7** default, failing, fissure, macu-

lae(pl.) **8** pockmark **9** birthmark, deformity, discredit, disfigure **10** defacement, deficiency **12** imperfection **13** disfigurement
wood: **4** mote
wound: **4** scar **8** cicatrix **9** cicatrice

blend: mix **4** blot, fuse, join, meng **5** blind, cream, merge, shade, spoil, stain, tinge, unite **6** commix, dazzle, mingle **7** combine, confuse, corrupt, deceive, mixture, pollute **8** coalesce, tincture **9** admixture, associate, commingle, harmonize, integrate **10** amalgamate **11** incorporate

blended: **5** fondu, mixed **6** merged **7** mingled **9** confluent

blesbok: **5** nunni **8** antelope

bless: **4** keep, sain, wave **5** adore, anele, bensh(Yid.), extol, favor, guard, thank, wound **6** favour, hallow, praise, thrash **7** approve, beatify, glorify, protect **8** dedicate, macarize, preserve, sanctify **10** consecrate, felicitate

blessed: **4** holy **5** happy **6** divine, joyful, sacred **8** benedict, bhagavat, blissful, hallowed **9** beatified, benedight **11** consecrated

blessing: **4** boon, gift **5** bliss, grace **6** praise **7** benison, worship **8** felicity **9** beatitude **10** benedicite, beneficent **11** benediction

blight: nip **4** ruin, rust, smut **5** blast, frost **6** mildew, wither **7** destroy **9** frustrate

blimp: **7** airship, balloon, colonel

blind: bet, pot **4** ante, dark, daze, dull, hood **5** blank, blend, decoy, dunch, front, shade, stake, wager **6** ambush, bisson, dazzle, screen, secret **7** aimless, bandage, benight, eclipse, execate, eyeless, obscure, pretext, shutter **8** abortive, artifice, bayardly, blinding, hoodwink, ignorant, involved, jalousie, outshine, purblind, unseeing **9** benighted, concealed, deceitful, defective, insensate, intricate, senseless, sightless **10** incomplete, misleading, subterfuge **11** intoxicated **12** shortsighted
as a hawk: **4** seel
part of: **4** slat
printing for: **7** braille

blind alley: **7** dead end, impasse **8** cul-de-sac

blind god: **4** Hoth **5** Hoder, Hothr

blind spot: **6** hang-up **7** bigotry

blind staggers: gid **7** vertigo

blind worm: **5** orvet

blinder: **4** flap **5** bluff **7** blinker **8** hoodwink **9** blindfold **11** obstruction

blindfold: **4** dark **5** blink, bluff **7** bandage, blinder, obscure **8** heedless, hoodwink, reckless **9** concealed

blindness: 6 bisson, cecity 7 ablepsy, anopsia 8 oblepsia 9 ignorance
color: 13 achromatopsia 14 monochromatism
day: 11 hemeralopia
partial: 7 meropia 10 cecutiency
snow: 14 chiona-blepsia
blink: 4 shun, wink 5 blush, cheat, flash, gleam, shine, trick 6 glance, ignore, obtuse 7 blinter, condone, flicker, glimmer, glimpse, neglect, nictate, sparkle, twinkle 9 blindfold
at: 7 condone 8 overlook
on the: 7 haywire 10 out of order, out of whack 11 inoperative, in disrepair
blinker: eye 5 bluff, light 6 signal 7 blinder, goggles 8 coquette, hoodwink, mackerel
blinking: 5 utter 6 damned 8 blooming, complete
blintze: 7 pancake
blip: 4 echo
bliss: joy 4 Eden, kaif, seil(Sc.) 5 glory 6 heaven 7 delight, ecstasy, gladden, rapture 8 felicity, gladness, paradise, pleasure 9 happiness 11 contentment
place of: 4 Eden 6 Utopia 7 Elysium 8 Paradise
blissful: 4 holy 5 happy 6 blithe, elated 7 blessed, Elysian, Utopian 8 ecstatic, euphoric 9 beatified, glorified
blister: 4 beat, bleb, blob, lash 5 blain, bulge 6 bubble, scorch 7 vesicle 8 lambaste, vesicate 10 vesicatory
blithe: gay 4 glad 5 bonny, happy, jolly, merry 6 bonnie, jovial, joyous, lively 7 gaysome, jocular, winsome 8 cheerful, gladsome 9 sprightly
blitzkrieg: 4 raid 6 attack 11 bombardment
blizzard: 4 blow, gale, wind 5 purga 6 retort 9 snowstorm, squelcher
bloat: 5 puffy, swell 6 expand, tumefy 7 distend, ferment, inflate 8 drunkard
bloated: 5 bloat, cured 6 sodden, turgid 7 pompous
blob: lip, wen 4 bleb, blot, boil, daub, drop, lump, mark, mass 6 bubble, pimple, splash 7 blemish, blister, blossom, globule, pustule, splotch 8 globular
bloc: 4 ring 5 cabal, party, union 6 clique 7 faction 11 combination
block: ame, bar, cob, dam, hob, nog, row, vol 4 bloc, cake, clog, cube, fill, foil, head, mass, stop 5 annex, check, chump, deter, nudge, parry, shape, spike, stump 6 hamper, hinder, impede, oppose, outwit, square, street, stymie, taplet, thwart 7 buckler, inhibit, outline, prevent 8 blockade, obstacle, obstruct, stoppage 9 barricade, blockhead,

frustrate, hindrance, intercept 11 obstruction
architectural: 6 dentil, mutule
electrically insulated: 6 taplet
football: 4 clip
for shaping metal objects: ame
ice: 4 cube 5 serac
mechanical: 6 pulley
metal type: 4 quad, quod
nautical: 7 deadeye
perforated: nut
small: 7 tessera
blockade: bar, dam 5 beset, block, siege 6 whisky 7 embargo 8 obstruct 9 beleaguer, moonshine 11 obstruction, restriction
blockhead: ass, oaf 4 bust, coof, dolt, fool, mome 5 block, chump, cuddy, dunce, idiot, ninny 6 noodle 7 dizzard, halfwit, tomfool 8 beefhead, clodpate, gamphrel, hardhead 9 blockpate, grouthead, hoddy-peak, numbskull, screwball, simpleton 10 beetlehead, dunderhead, hoddy-doddy
blockhouse: 4 fort
bloke: guy, man 4 chap, toff 6 fellow 9 personage
blonde: 4 fair 5 light, straw 6 flaxen, golden, yellow 9 towheaded
blood: kin, sap 4 gore, life, mood, race 5 blade, fluid, serum, stock 6 claret, indred 7 gallant, kinship, kinsman, lineage, youstir(Sc.) 8 relation 9 lifeblood 14 consanguineous
cell: red 5 white 8 hemocyte 9 leukocyte 10 erythrocyte
clot: 8 thrombus
deficiency: 6 anemia 7 anaemia
disease: 8 leukemia
fluid part: 5 serum 6 plasma 7 opsonin
mixed: See **hybrid**
of the gods: 4 icor 5 ichor
particle in: 7 embolus
poisoning: 6 pyemia 7 pyaemia, toxemia 10 septicemia
pressure: 8 systolic 9 diastolic
serum: 6 plasma
stagnation: 4 clot 5 cruor, grume 6 stasis, stases
strain: 4 race 5 stock 6 family
testing instrument: 13 hemabarometer 14 haemabarometer
blood and thunder: 6 uproar 8 violence 9 melodrama
blood brother: 6 friend 8 intimate
blood feud: 8 vendetta
blood fine: cro(Sc.) 4 eric 7 galanas, wergild 9 bloodwite
blood horse: 12 thoroughbred
blood money: cro 7 breaghe
blood pudding: 7 sausage

blood relationship: 7 kinsman 8 relative 13 consanguinity

blood vessel: 4 vein 5 hemad 6 artery 9 capillary
comb. form: vas
rupture: 6 rhexis

bloodbath: 7 carnage 8 massacre 9 slaughter

bloodcurdling: 4 gory 8 horrible 10 terrifying

blooded: 9 pedigreed 12 thoroughbred

bloodhound: 4 lyam, lyme

bloodless: 4 dead, pale 6 anemic 7 anaemic, inhuman 8 lifeless 9 colorless, unfeeling 10 exsanguine

bloodroot: 7 puccoon 10 tetterwort

bloodshed: 5 death 7 carnage 8 violence 9 slaughter

bloodshot: red 8 inflamed

bloodstone: 10 chalcedony

bloodsucker: 5 leech 7 sponger, vampire 11 extortioner

bloodthirsty: 6 bloody, carnal 9 ferocious, murderous 10 sanguinary

bloody: 4 gory, grim 5 cruel 6 cruent 7 imbrued 8 bleeding, hematose, infamous 9 cruentous, ferocious, haematose, merciless, murderous, red-handed 10 sanguinary 11 ensanguined 12 bloodstained, bloodthirsty, contemptible

bloom (see also **flower**): dew 4 blow 5 flush 7 blossom, blowing 8 floreate, flourish 13 efflorescence

bloomer: 5 error 6 blower 7 blunder, failure

blooming: 4 rosy 5 flush, fresh, green 6 abloom, damned, florid

blooper: 5 error, radio 7 blunder, blowing, faux pas, roseate 8 blinking 10 prospering

blossom (see also **flower**): bud 4 blob, open 5 bloom 7 burgeon, prosper 8 flourish 9 efforesce 13 efflorescence
small: 8 floweret

blot: mar 4 blob, blue, daub, flaw, soil, spot 5 blend, erase, smear, speck, stain, sully 6 blotch, cancel, damage, defect, efface, impair, macula, shadow, smirch, smudge, smutch, stigma 7 blemish, eclipse, expunge, maculae(pl.), obscure, tarnish 8 disgrace, reproach 9 bespatter 10 obliterate, stigmatize 12 obliteration 13 disfigurement
out: 5 annul, erase 6 efface 7 abolish 10 annihilate

blotch: dab 4 blot, gout, spot 5 patch, smear, stain 6 macula, mottle, smirch, stigma 7 blemish, maculae(pl.), pustule, splotch 8 eruption, maculate

blotto: 11 intoxicated

blouse: 5 shirt, smock, tunic 7 casaque 10 shirtwaist
bushman's: 5 bluey

blow: bob, cob, cop, dub, fan, jab, pat, rap, tap, wap 4 ande, baff, bang, bash, beat, belt, biff, birr, blad, blaw, brag, buff, bump, chap, conk, crig, cuff, daud, dint, dird, drub, dunt, dush, fleg, gale, gowf, huff, jolt, knap, lash, mint, oner, pant, plug, puff, scud, slam, slap, slug, sock, wind 5 binge, blade, blast, blizz, bloom, boast, botch, break, brunt, burst, clink, clour, clout, clump, crump, curse, douse, dowse, filip, flack, flick, gowff, ictus, impel, knock, peise, shock, skite, slipe, sound, spend, storm, swipe, thump, treat, waste, whack, whang 6 bensel, bensil, betray, bounce, buffet, depart, dirdum, expand, fillip, flower, frolic, larrup, wallop 7 assault, attaint, bensail, bensall, bensell, blossom, blowout, bluster, boaster, destroy, inflate, publish, shatter, whample 8 boasting, calamity, confound, disaster, disclose 9 bastinado
in: 4 come 5 enter 6 arrive
mock: 5 feint
one's mind: 4 flip 5 go ape 6 turn on 8 freak out 10 overexcite 11 hallucinate
over: end 4 pass 7 subside
to: 5 treat
up: 4 bomb 5 scene 7 explode, inflate 8 dynamite, outburst

blow-by-blow: 8 detailed, itemized, thorough 10 particular

blower: fan 5 whale 6 puffer 7 bloomer 8 braggart 9 swellfish 11 sacheverell

blowfish: 6 puffer

blowfly: 10 bluebottle

blowgun: 10 peashooter

blowhard: 8 braggart

blowhole: 7 nostril 8 spiracle

blown: 5 stale, tired 6 opened 7 blossom, swollen, tainted 8 betrayed, flyblown, inflated 9 distended, exhausted, worthless

blowout: 4 blow, feed, meal 6 valley 7 shindig 10 depression

blowzy: 5 dowdy 6 frowzy 10 disheveled, slatternly

blub: 4 bulb 5 dwell 6 puffed 7 blubber, swollen

blubber: cry, fat 4 blub, foam, wail, weep 5 swell, thick, whine 6 bubble, flitch, medusa, nettle, seethe 7 blobber, bluster, swollen, whimper 9 disfigure
remove: 6 flense
whale: 5 fenks, speck 6 muktuk

blubbery: fat 5 obese 7 swollen 9 quivering 10 gelatinous 11 protuberant

bludgeon: bat, hit 4 club, mace 5 billy, stick 6 coerce, cudgel, weapon

blue: low, sad, sky **4** aqua, bice, glum **5** azure, livid, ocean, perse, risqué, small **6** cobalt, gloomy, indigo, severe **7** celeste, gentian, learned, lobelia **8** cerulean, cynanine, dejected, downcast, literary **9** turquoise **10** despondent, melancholy
asbestos: **11** crocidolite
gray: **5** merle, pearl, slate **7** cesious **8** caesious
green: **4** aqua, bice, teal **5** beryl **8** calamine **9** turquoise
red: **5** smalt **6** mallow **8** gridelin, mazarine **9** gris-de-lin
sheep: **6** bharal
sky: **5** azure **8** cerulean
blue blood: **5** noble **9** gentleman **10** aristocrat **12** bluestocking
blue boneset: **4** Scot **10** cornflower, mistflower
blue catalpa: **9** paulownia
blue-chip: **9** exemplary **11** prestigious
blue dandelion: **7** chicory
blue dye herb: **4** woad
Blue Eagle agency: NRA
blue earth: **10** kimberlite
Blue Grotto site: **5** Capri(Italy)
blue gum: **4** tree **10** eucalyptus
Blue Hen State: **8** Delaware
blue huckleberry: **11** tangleberry
blue jaundice: **8** cyanosis
blue jeans: **5** levis **6** denims
blue Joe: **8** bluegill
blue John: **4** milk
Blue Law State: **11** Connecticut
blue-pencil: **4** edit **6** delete, redact, revise
blue peter: **4** coot, flag **9** gallinule
blue-ribbon: top **4** best **6** Grade A **7** supreme **8** top-notch
Bluebeard's wife: **6** Fatima
bluebonnet: cap **4** Scot **7** bluecap **8** Scotsman **10** cornflower
bluebottle: **5** bluet **7** barbeau, blowfly **8** hyacinth
bluecap: **4** Scot **10** bluebonnet
bluefish: **4** bass, tuna **5** saury **8** weakfish
bluegill: **7** sunfish
bluegrass: **12** country music
Bluegrass State: **8** Kentucky
bluejacket: gob, tar **6** sailor
bluejoint: **6** redtop
bluenose: **4** snob **5** prude **8** moralist **11** Nova Scotian
bluepoint: **6** oyster
blueprint: map **4** plan, plot **5** chart, draft, trace **6** sketch **7** diagram, outline **8** game plan, strategy **9** cyanotype
bluer: **4** anil
bluerocket: **9** monkshood
blues: **4** song **5** dumps **6** cafard **7** megrims, sadness **10** melancholy, mulligrubs **11** despondency

bluestocking: **5** woman **12** intellectual
bluet: **5** plant **10** bluebottle **11** farkleberry
bluethroat: **7** warbler
bluff: **4** bank, brag, curt, fool, rude **5** blunt, burly, cliff, frank, gruff, short, surly, trick **6** abrupt, assume, crusty **7** blinder, blinker, brusque, deceive, uncivil **8** barranca, barranco, churlish, hoodwink, impolite **9** blindfold, outspoken, precipice **13** unceremonious
Bluff King Hal: **5** Henry
blunder: err, mix **4** balk, bull, flub, gaff, roil, slip, stir **5** boner, botch, break, error, fault, lapse, misdo **6** blotch, boggle, bumble, bungle, gazabo, gazebo, mingle, muddle, wallow **7** bloomer, confuse, derange, failure, faux pas, mistake, stumble **8** solecism **9** confusion, mismanage **11** disturbance
blunderbuss: gun **9** espingole **10** stumblebum
blunge: mix **5** blend **10** amalgamate
blunt: **4** bald, curt, damp, dull, flat **5** bluff, brusk, inert, plain, plump, stunt **6** clumsy, deaden, obtund, obtuse, stupid, weaken **7** brusque **8** hebetate **9** depressed, downright **10** point-blank **11** insensitive **13** unceremonious
mentally: **8** hebitate
blur: dim, hum **4** blob, blot, mist, soil, spot **5** blear, cloud, smear, stain, sully, taint **6** mackle, macule, smudge, stigma **7** blemish, confuse, obscure **9** disfigure
blurb: ad **4** puff, rove **5** brief **6** notice **7** write-up **12** announcement, commendation **13** advertisement
blush: **4** glow, look, rose **5** blink, color, flush, gleam, rouge, tinge **6** glance, mantle, redden **7** crimson **8** likeness **10** appearance, rubescence
blushing: red **4** rosy **5** ruddy **7** roseate **8** flushing **9** rosaceous **10** erubescent **11** embarrassed
bluster: **4** blow, huff, rage, roar, rant **5** blast, bleat, boast, bully, noise, storm, swank **6** babble, bellow, bounce, hector, huffle, tumult **7** blubber, bravado, gauster, roister, swagger **8** boasting, bullying, threaten **9** confusion, gasconade **10** intimidate, swaggering, turbulence **11** fanfaronade, rodomontade
boa: **5** aboma, scarf, snake **8** anaconda **9** neckpiece
boa contrictor: **5** snake **6** giboia, python
Boadicea's people: **5** Iceni
boar: hog, sus **4** aper **5** swine **6** barrow, hogget **8** sanglier **9** hoggaster
head: **4** hure
wound: **4** gore **5** ganch
board: **4** deal, diet, eats, fare, keep, lath, slat **5** enter, found, get on, house, lodge,

meals, panel, plank, stage, table **6** accost, embark, planch, shield **7** cabinet, council, duoviri, emplane, enplane, entrain, planche **8** approach, tribunal **9** authority, shipboard **10** commission, management, provisions **11** switchboard **13** entertainment

boast: gab **4** blaw, blow, brag, crow, pomp, rave **5** brave, extol, exult, glory, prate, roose, scold, skite, vapor, vaunt **6** bounce, clamor, extoll, flaunt, menace(Sc.), outcry, splore **7** bluster, clamour, display, glorify, show off, swagger **8** flourish, threaten **9** gasconade **11** rodomontade

boaster: skite **6** crower, gascon, pedant **7** bouncer, bravado, cracker, ruffler **8** blowhard, braggart, cacofogo, fanfaron, glorioso, jingoist, rodomont **9** cacafuego **11** braggadocio

boastful: big **6** parado **8** fanfaron **9** cock-a-hoop, gasconade, kompology **11** rodomontade, swellheaded, thrasonical

boat (see also **canoe, ship, vessel**): ark, cat, cot, gig, tub **4** bark, brig, carv, dory, junk, raft, scow, ship, skag, tack, trow, yawl **5** aviso, barca, barge, bully, canoe, coble, craft, dingy, ferry, ketch, liner, shell, skiff, skift, smack, xebec, zebec **6** baidak, bateau, carvel, chebec, cruise, cutter, dinghy, dugout, garvey, packet, vessel, zebeck **7** bateaus, chebeck, coracle, gondola, lighter, nacelle, pinnace, scooter, steamer **8** pessoner, schooner **9** submarine, transport **10** watercraft

Chinese: **4** junk **6** sampan
coal cargo: **7** collier
deck: **4** poop **5** orlop
fishing: **8** bracozzo
flat-bottomed: arc, bac **4** dory, keel, punt, scow **5** barge **6** bateau
freight: **7** lighter
front: bow **4** prow
garbage: **6** hopper
harbor: tug **5** barge **7** bumboat
Italian: **7** gondola
joint: **4** jerl
landing: LST
merchant: **6** argosy, holcad
ornamental: **9** navicella
part: bow **4** beam, deck, hold, keel, prow **5** bilge, cabin, stern **6** bridge, gunnel, kelson, saloon, thwart **7** capstan, gunwale, keelson, painter, scupper **12** companionway
pin: **5** thole
post: poy **4** biff **7** bollard, capstan **9** sternpost
power: tug
propellant: oar, row **4** pole **5** motor, scull
racing: gig **5** scull
ride: row **4** sail **6** cruise

round: **4** gufa **5** goofa **6** goofah
sailing: **4** pram, proa, yawl **5** praam, prahu, skiff, sloop, yacht
twin-hulled: **9** catamaran
undersea: sub **9** submarine **11** submersible

boatman: **5** poler **6** barger, Charon **7** hobbler, hoveler, huffler **8** hoveller **9** gondolier **10** barcajuolo

boatswain: **5** bosun **6** serang
whistle: **4** pipe

Boaz: *son:* **4** Obed
wife: **4** Ruth

bob: bow, cut, dab, job, rap, tap **4** ball, blow, buff, calf, clip, coin, cork, duck, grub, jeer, jerk, jest, knob, mock, worm **5** bunch, cheat, dance, filch, float, flout, shake, taunt, trick **6** bingle, buffet, curtsy, delude, pommel, strike, weight **7** bobsled, bobtail, cluster, curtesy, haircut, pendant, refrain **8** shilling **9** bobsleigh

bobac: **6** marmot

bobber: **4** cork, duck **5** float **6** bobfly **7** dropper **8** deadhead

bobbery: row **4** fray **5** brawl, fight, melee **6** hubbub, tumult **8** squabble **9** commotion **11** disturbance

bobbie, bobby: cop **4** bull **6** peeler **7** officer **9** policeman

bobbin: pin **4** cord, pirn, reel **5** braid, quill, spool **7** ratchet, spindle **8** cylinder **10** cuckoopint
frame: **5** creel
pin: **7** spindle

bobble: dib **4** mess **5** gum up **6** fumble

bobby: **7** officer **9** policeman

bobcat: **4** lynx

bobolink: **4** bird, reed **7** bunting, ortolan **10** butterbird

bobsled: bob **6** ripper

bobtail: bob, cur **4** dock **6** rabble, strunt(Sc.) **7** curtail **8** sheepdog **9** deficient **11** abbreviated

bobwhite: **4** bird **5** colin, quail **9** partridge

bocardo: **6** dokhma, **7** bokardo

Boccaccio work: **9** Decameron

bode: **4** omen, stop **5** augur, offer **6** herald **7** message, portend, presage **8** forebode, forecast, foreshow, foretell, indicate **9** messenger **10** inaugurate **13** foreshadowing, prognosticate

bodice: **4** jupe **5** choli, gilet, waist **6** basque, corset

bodiless: **9** trunkless **10** immaterial **11** incorporeal

bodily: **5** solid **6** actual, carnal **7** fleshly, sensual, somatic **8** corporal, entirely, material, physical **9** corporeal **10** completely **11** corporeally, substantial

bodily motion: **5** shrug **7** gesture

boding: 7 ominous 9 foretoken 10 foreboding, prediction, prognostic

bodkin: awl, pin 6 dagger, needle 7 hairpin, poniard 8 stiletto 9 eyeleteer

body: 4 bole, bouk, bulk, form, mass, nave, rupa, soma, stem 5 flesh, group, stiff, torso, trunk 6 corpse, corpus, extent, licham, object, person 7 cadaver, carcass, company 8 extensum, majority 9 aggregate, curcurbit, substance 10 assemblage, foundation 11 association, corporation

anterior part of: 7 prosoma

armor: 4 tace 6 corium

away from center: 6 distal

cavity: 5 sinus 6 coelom 7 coelome

fluid: 5 blood, lymph, serum 6 plasma, saliva

heavenly: sun 4 luna, moon, star 5 comet 6 meteor, planet 8 asteroid, luminary

joint: hip 4 knee 5 elbow, wrist 8 shoulder

motion: 7 gesture

of men: 5 posse 10 authorized

of persons: 5 corps, posse

of students: 5 class

of water: bay, sea 4 gulf, lake, pond, pool 5 ocean 6 lagoon, sealet 9 reservoir

path: 5 orbit

pert. to: 5 somal 8 physical, systemic

wagon: box

wall: 6 paries, septum

body politic: 4 weal 5 state 6 nation 9 community

bodyguard: 5 thane 6 escort 7 retinue, trabant 9 attendant, lifeguard, protector

Boeotia: *capital:* 6 Thebes

region: 5 Ionia

boeotian: 10 philistine

Boer: *dialect:* 4 Taal

general: 5 Botha

boffo: 10 successful 11 sensational 13 extraordinary 14 out of this world

bog: bug, car, fen, gog, hag 4 bold, carr, cess, mire, moor, moss, ooze, sink, slew, slue, syrt 5 marsh, saucy, swamp 6 morass, muskeg, slough 7 forward 8 quagmire 9 conceited

bog down: 4 mire 5 stall 6 bemire

bogey: bug, cow, hag 5 bogie, bogle, devil, gnome 6 boggle, booger, goblin 7 boggard, boggart, bugaboo, bugbear, gnomide, specter, spectre 9 hobgoblin, scarecrow 10 bullbeggar

in golf: 10 one over par

in the sky: UFO

boggle: jib, shy 4 balk, foil, stop 5 alarm, botch, demur, scare, start 6 baffle, bungle, goblin, shrink 7 bauchle, blunder, perplex, scruple, stagger 8 frighten, hesitate 9 dissemble, dumbfound, embarrass

boggy: wet 4 miry, soft 5 gouty, fenny, haggy, mossy 6 quaggy, swampy 7 boggish, queachy

bogus: 4 fake, sham 5 false, phony 6 forged 8 spurious 9 imitation 10 fictitious 11 counterfeit

bogy: See **bogey**

Bohemian: 4 arty 5 gipsy, gypsy 6 Picard 8 maverick 12 nonconformist

dance: 6 redowa

boil: sty 4 bile, blob, buck, coct, cook, rage, sore, stew, stye, teem 5 anger, botch, brede, poach, steam 6 betray, bubble, buller, burble, decoct, seethe, simmer 7 anthrax, estuate, inflame 8 aestuate, ebullate 10 ebbulliate, effervesce

almost: 5 scald

down: 6 decoct 8 simplify 10 streamline

boiler: 4 reef 6 copper, kettle, retort 7 alembic, caldron, furnace 8 cauldron

plate: 4 sput

tube scaler: 6 sooter

boisterous: 4 gurl, loud, rude 5 burly, gurly, noisy, rough, windy 6 coarse, stormy, strong, unruly 7 furious, massive, roaring, violent 8 cumbrous, strident, vehement 9 clamorous, excessive, excitable, turbulent 10 blustering, tumultuous, unyielding, vociferous

bold: big, bog, yep 4 derf, pert, rash, rude, wise, yepe 5 bardy, bield, brash, brave, brent, frack, freak, freck, gally, hardy, large, manly, nervy, peart, saucy, steep, stout 6 abrupt, audace, brassy, brazen, crouse, daring, fierce, heroic, strong 7 assured, dashing, defiant, forward, grivois, haughty, massive, valiant 8 arrogant, familiar, fearless, grivoise, immodest, impudent, insolent, intrepid, malapert, powerful, resolute 9 audacious, bodacious, confident, dauntless, imprudent, undaunted 10 courageous, forritsome 11 venturesome 12 enterprising, overassuming, presumptuous, stout-hearted 13 overconfident

boldness: 4 brow 5 bield, nerve, vigor 6 daring 7 bravery, chutzpa, courage 8 audacity, chutzpah, temerity 9 assurance, hardiesse, hardihood, hardiness 10 brazenness, confidence, effrontery 11 intrepidity, presumption 13 dauntlessness

bole: 4 clay, dose, stem 5 bolus, crypt, trunk 7 opening

bolero: 5 dance, waist 6 jacket

Bolero composer: 5 Ravel

bolide: 6 meteor 7 missile

Bolivia: *capitals:* 5 La Paz, Sucre

city: 5 Oruro, Uyuni 6 Camiri, Potosi, Robore, Viacha 8 Trinidad 9 Santa Cruz

district: 5 La Paz, Oruro, Pando 6 Elbeni,

Potosi, Tarija **9** Santa Cruz **10** Chu-
quisaca, Cochabamba
Indian: Uro, Uru **4** Iten, Moxo, Uran **6**
Arawak, Aymara, Charca, Chicha, Tacana **7** Aymaran, Puquina, Sirione **10**
Chiriguano
lake: **5** Poopo **8** Titicaca
liberator: **5** Sucre **7** Bolivar
measure: **6** league **7** celemin
monetary unit: **4** peso **7** centavo **9** bolivi-
ano
mountain: **5** Cuzco **6** Sajama, Sorata **7**
Illampu **8** Illimani
plateau: **9** Altiplano
river: **4** Beni **5** Abuna, Orton **6** Baures,
Mamore, Yacuma **7** Guapore, Madeira
9 Pilcomayo, San Miguel **11** Madre de
Dios
weight: **5** libra, macro
boll: pod **4** bulb, grow, knob **5** onion **6**
bubble **7** capsule, measure **8** pericarp
12 protuberance
boll weevil: 6 picudo
bollix: 4 flub, mess **5** botch, gum up **6**
bungle
bollard: 4 bitt, post
bolo: 5 knife **7** machete, sundang **8** pacifist **9** defeatist
Bolshevist: 7 Russian **9** socialist
leader: **5** Lenin
bolster: aid, pad **6** pillow **7** cushion, support **8** compress, maintain **9** reinforce
10 strengthen
bolt: bar, pen, pin, rod, run **4** beat, dart,
flee, gulp, lock, pawl, rush, sift **5** arrow,
bilbo, close, elope, flash, gorge, latch,
rivet, shaft **6** assort, decamp, desert,
fasten, flight, garble, pintle, purify, refine, secure, strong, toggle, winnow **7**
missile, shackle, thunder **8** fastener,
separate, stampede **9** lightning
bolus: cud **4** bole, clop, lump, mass, pill,
rock
bomb: dud, egg **4** flop **5** blare, shell **6** ashcan **7** bombard, failure, grenade, mar-
mite **8** fall flat **9** pineapple **10** projectile **11** blockbuster
guide: fin
hole: **6** crater
bombard: 4 bomb **5** blitz, crump, shell **6**
batter, bottle, strafe, vessel
bombardier: 6 gunner **12** artilleryman
bombardment: 5 blitz, siege **6** attack, rafale, strafe **7** barrage **9** cannonade
bombardon: 4 oboe, tuba **7** bassoon
bombast: gas, pad **4** rage, rant, rave **5**
stuff **6** padded **7** bluster, stuffed, tympany **8** boasting, rhetoric **9** turgidity
11 rodomontade **12** altiloquence **14**
grandiloquence
bombastic: 5 tumid, vocal **6** fluent, heroic, turgid **7** bombast, flowery, fustian,
orotund, pompous, ranting, stilted **8** in-

flated **9** expansive, flatulent, grandiose,
plethoric **10** lexiphanic, rhetorical **12**
magniloquent
bombinate: hum **4** boom
bombproof chamber: 8 casemate
bombyx: eri **4** eria, moth **8** silkworm
bon ami: 5 lover **6** friend **10** sweetheart
bon mot: 4 pun **4** jest, quip **9** witticism
bonafide: 7 genuine **9** authentic, veritable
bonanza: 4 mint **6** eureka **7** jackpot **8** eldorado, Golconda, gold mine
Bonanza State: 7 Montana
bonbon: 5 candy, cream **6** dainty **7** caramel **8** confetto, confetti **9** sugarplum
bond: tie, vow **4** bail, band, duty, glue,
knot, link, note, yoke **5** bound, chain,
nexus **6** binder, cement, connex, engage, escrow, fetter, league, pledge **7**
husband, manacle, shackle **8** adhesive,
contract, covenant, guaranty, ligament,
ligature, mortgage, security, vinculum **9**
agreement, composure, guarantee **10**
constraint, husbandman, obligation **11**
association, householder
chemical: **5** diene **7** valence
bondage: 4 yoke **7** helotry, peonage, serfdom, slavery **9** captivity, restraint, servitude, thralldom
bondsman: 4 carl, esne, peon, serf **5**
churl, Helot, slave **6** stooge, surety,
thrall, vassal **7** chattel, peasant, servant, villein
bone: rib **4** ossa(pl.), core, cram **5** blade **6**
fillet, radius **7** humerus, utterly
ankle: **5** talus **6** tarsus
anvil: **5** incus **7** incudes(pl.)
arm: **4** ulna **6** radius **7** humerus
back: **5** spine **8** vertebra
breast: **6** sterna(pl.) **7** sternum
cartilage: **6** ossein
cavity: **5** antra(pl.), sinus **6** antrum
cell: **10** osteoblast
change into: **6** ossify
collar: **8** clavicle
dorsal: **4** ilia(pl.) **5** ilium
elbow: **4** ulna
formation: **7** ostosis **10** parostosis
girdle: **12** sphenethmoid
manipulator: **9** osteopath
pert. to: **6** osteal **7** osseous
scraper: **6** xyster
thigh: **5** femur
bonefish: 8 ladyfish
bonelet: 7 ossicle
boner: 5 error **7** blooper, blunder, faux
pas, mistake
bones: 4 dice, ossa **8** skeletoa
boneset: 7 comfrey **8** hempweek **12** thoroughwort
boneyard: 5 stock, store **6** supply **9** scrap
heap
bonfire: 5 blaze
bongo: 4 drum **8** antelope

boniata: yam

boniface: 8 landlord **9** barkeeper, innkeeper **12** saloonkeeper

bonito: aku, atu **4** fish, nice **5** cobia **6** bonita, pretty, robalo **8** albacore, mackerel, skipjack

Bonjour Tristesse author: 5 Sagan

bonkers: mad **5** crazy **6** insane

bonne: 5 nurse **9** nursemaid **11** maidservant

bonnet: cap, hat **4** hood **5** cover, decoy, toque **6** capote, slouch **7** chapeau, coronet **8** headgear **9** headdress **10** accomplice, chinquapin
brim: **4** poke
string: **5** bride

bonnet monkey: 4 zati **5** munga

bonny, bonnie: gay **4** fine **5** merry, plump **6** blithe, pretty, strong **7** healthy **8** budgeree, handsome **9** beautiful **11** goodlooking

bonton: 5 elite

bonus: tip **4** gift, meed **5** award, bribe, bunce, pilon, prize, spiff **6** reward **7** cumshaw, premium, subsidy **8** dividend, lagnappe **9** allowance, lagniappe **12** compensation

bon vivant: 5 sport **7** epicure

bony: 4 hard, lank, lean, thin **5** stiff, tough **6** osteal, skinny **7** osseous **8** skeletal

boo: 4 hoot, jeer **5** decry, grass **9** marijuana

boob: ass **4** fool **5** dunce, goony, neddy **6** nitwit

boobook: owl **6** cuckoo

booby: 5 dunce, idiot, loser, prize **6** sleigh, stupid **8** goosecap **9** simpleton

booby hatch: 4 jail **6** asylum

boodle: 4 swag **5** cheat, crowd, graft **6** noodle **7** plunder **8** caboodle

boohoo: sob **4** hoot, weep **5** shout **8** sailfish

boojum: 5 snark

book: log, mss. **4** opus, text, tome **5** Bible, canto, diary, divan, enter, folio, liber, libri(pl.) **6** manual, record, volume **7** blotter, catalog, writing **8** brochure, document, libretto, register **9** catalogue, pot-boiler
accounts: day **5** bilan, liber **6** ledger **7** journal
alphabet: **9** abecedary
Apocrypha: **5** Tobit
back: **5** spine
best selling: **5** Bible
binding material: **5** cloth, paper **6** canvas **7** buckram, leather
blank: **5** album, diary **6** tablet
church music: **6** hymnal
collector: **12** bibliomaniac
cover ornamentation: **7** tooling
covering: **6** jacket **7** binding
design: **6** format, layout
destroyer: **11** biblioclast
devotional: **5** Bible **6** gospel, missal **7** diurnal, psalter
division: **7** chapter
elementary reading: **6** primer
fiction: **5** novel
group: **7** trilogy
Islam: **5** kitab, Koran
jacket notice: **5** blurb
kept in print: **8** backlist
large: **4** tome **5** folio
lover: **11** bibliophile
make-up: **6** format
manuscript: **5** codex, draft **7** codices(pl.)
map: **5** atlas
mass: **6** missal
navigator's: log **7** logbook **9** portolano
obscene: **11** pornography
of hours: **4** Hora **5** Horae(pl.)
of masses: **6** missal
of nobility: **7** peerage
of psalms: **7** psalter
of rules: **5** Hoyle
page: **5** folio
palm: **4** tara **7** taliera
part: **4** leaf, page **5** cover **7** binding, chapter, section **9** signature
pert. to: **13** bibliographic
school: **6** primer, reader **7** grammar, speller **9** geography **10** arithmetic
size: **6** octavo, quarto **8** twelvemo **9** duodecimo
title page: **6** rubric
translation: **4** pony
words of opera: **8** libretto
yearbook: **7** almanac
Zoroastrian: **6** Avesta

book dealer: 10 bibliopole **11** bouguiniste

bookbinder: 12 bibliopegist

bookcase: 5 forel **6** forrel

bookish: 8 highbrow, pedantic

bookkeeper: 7 auditor **10** accountant

bookkeeping term: 4 loss, post **5** audit, debit, entry **6** credit **9** statement

booklet: 8 brochure **10** literature

bookman: 6 bookie, dealer **7** scholar **9** publisher **11** litterateur

bookplate: 8 exlibris

bookworm: 6 reader **7** scholar **11** bibliophile

boom: jib **4** bang, bump, crib, pole, roar, spar **5** croon **7** bumpkin, resound, support **8** bowsprit, flourish **9** bombilate, bombinate **10** prosperity

boomerang: 5 kiley, kalie **6** recoil **7** rebound **8** backfire, ricochet

boon: gay **4** bene, gift, good, kind **5** favor, grant, merry, order **6** benign, bounty, favour, goodly, jovial, prayer **7** benefit, command, present **8** blessing, intimate, petition **9** congenial, convivial, favorable **10** concession, prosperous **11** benefaction

boon companion: pal **4** chum **5** buddy

boondocks: 6 sticks **9** backwoods **10** hinterland, wilderness

boondoggle: 6 trifle **7** goof off **9** goldbrick

boor: cad, oaf **4** Boer, carl, lout, pill **5** chuff, churl, clown, looby, slave, yokel **6** carlot, clunch, hoblob, lubber, lummox, rustic **7** cauboge, grobian, peasant, villein **8** bosthoon **9** barbarian, roughneck **10** clodhopper, countryman, husbandman, tramontane

boorish: 4 rude **5** gawky, rough, surly **6** clumsy, coarse, rustic, sullen, vulgar **7** awkward, crabbed, hoblike, ill-bred, loutish, roister, uncouth **8** churlish, cloddish, clownish, lubberly, ungainly **9** bourgeois **10** uncultured, unmannerly

boost: aid **4** abet, back, help, lift, plug, push, rise **5** coach, exalt, hoist, raise **6** assist, rear up **7** advance, commend, elevate, endorse, indorse, promote **8** increase **9** encourage **10** assistance **12** commendation

booster: 4 shot **9** injection **10** enthusiast

boot: pac, use **4** cure, gain, help, kick, shoe, sock **5** avail, booty, eject, jemmy, kamik, spoil **6** bootee, buskin, casing, crakow, enrich, fumble, galosh, novice, sheath, thrill **7** benefit, dismiss, galoshe **8** chassure(F.), covering **9** advantage, discharge, dismissal

half: pac **4** pack **6** buskin, cocker **7** blucher, bottine **8** cothurni(pl.) **9** cothurnus

heavy: pac **5** stogy **6** Brogan **8** Balmoral

high-water: **5** wader

loose-topped: **10** wellington

riding: **5** jemmy **7** gambado, jodhpur

small: **7** bottine **8** bottekin

Boot: 5 Italy

booted: 4 shod **7** ocreate

booth: 4 loge, shed, shop, sook, souk **5** bothy, cabin, crame, house, stall, stand **6** tienda **7** balagan

bootleg: 7 illegal, illicit, smuggle **11** clandestine **12** illegitimate **13** surreptitious

bootless: 6 futile **7** useless **9** incurable, worthless **10** remediless, unavailing **12** unprofitable

bootlick: 4 fawn **5** toady **7** flatter **9** brownnose **11** apple-polish

booty: 4 gain, loot, pelf, prey, swag **5** cheat, graft, prize **6** spoils **7** despoil, pillage, plunder **10** chevisance

booze: 4 bout **5** budge, drink, spree **6** fuddle, liquor

boozer: 4 pub **5** toper **6** bouser **8** drunkard

bora: 4 wind

borax: 6 tincal

Bordeaux wine (see also **wine**): **5** Bourg, cosne, medoc **6** claret **7** Margauz

border: hem, rim **4** abut, brim, dado, eave, edge, line, nark, orle, rand, roon, rund(Sc.), side, trim **5** bound, braid, brink, coast, costa, flank, forel, frame, limit, march, marge, plait, skirt, strip, touch, verge **6** adjoin, costae, edging, forrel, fringe, impale, margin, purfle, set off stripe **7** bordure, confine, outline, selvage **8** boundary, frontier, neighbor, surround, tressour, tressure **9** extremity, periphery **10** sidepieces **11** come close to

fluted: **5** frill

ornamental: **4** dado **5** frame **6** fringe

wall: **4** dado, ogee **7** cornice

bordering: 6 edging **8** abutting, adjacent

bore: bit, irk, tap **4** drag, gaze, hole, pall, poke, push, ream, size, tide, tire, tool **5** annoy, augur, chink, drill, eagre, ennui, gauge, prick, punch, tewel, trick, weary **6** befool, gimlet, pierce, thrust, tunnel **7** caliber, calibre, carried, crevice, opening **8** aiguille, diameter **9** annoyance, penetrate, perforate, terebrate **10** put to sleep **11** perforation **12** buttonholder

Boreas: 4 wind **7** norther

son: **5** Butes **6** Calais

borecole: 4 kail, kale

bored: 7 ennuyee(F.)

boredom: 5 ennui **6** tedium **7** fatigue **9** weariness

borer: 6 insect **7** hagfish, termite **8** shipworm

boric acid salt: 6 borate

boring: dry **4** flat **6** broach, tiring **7** tedious **8** irksome, piercing, tiresome **9** wearisome **11** displeasing, penetrating **13** uninteresting

boring tool: bit **5** auger, drill **6** gimlet, wimble

born: nee(F.) **6** innate **7** nascent, natural **8** inherent **9** delivered

dead: **9** stillborn

prematurely: **8** abortive

well: **4** free **5** noble **7** eugenic

borne (see also **bear**): **4** rode **6** narrow **7** carried, endured

by the wind: **6** eolian

boron 5 borax, boric **7** ulexite

borough: 4 burg, town **5** brush, burgh **6** burgus, castle **7** citadel, village **8** fortress, township

borrow: 4 copy, loan, take **5** adopt, steal **6** pledge, surety **7** chevise, hostage, tithing **11** frankpledge

bosc: 4 pear

boscage: 4 wood **5** grove **7** thicket

bosh: end, rot **4** joke, show, talk, tosh **5**

trash **6** bushwa, figure, flaunt, humbug, trivia **8** nonsense **9** poppycock

bosky: 5 bushy, tipsy, woody **7** fuddled **11** intoxicated

Bosnian native: 4 Slav **5** Croat

bosom: 4 barm(Sc.) **5** close, heart, sinus **6** breast, cavity, desire, recess **7** beloved, embrace, inclose **8** intimate **9** cherished **11** inclination, indentation **12** confidential

boss: bur, pad **4** baas, buhr, burr, knob, stud **5** bully, chief, empty, knosp, order, owner **6** brooch, button, direct, emboss, hollow, leader, manage, master, shield **7** capataz, cushion, foreman, hassock, headman, manager, phalera **8** director, domineer, overseer **9** supervise **10** politician, supervisor **12** protuberance **14** superintendent

African: **5** bwana

logging camp: **5** bully

political: **7** cacique

shield: **4** umbo

bossy: cow **4** calf **9** masterful **11** dictatorial, domineering

Boston: 4 game **5** waltz **8** Beantown

district: Hub **7** Back Bay

leader: **7** Brahmin

bot: 5 larva

botany: *angle:* **4** axil

cell: **5** spore

depression: **5** fovea **7** variole

botch: dub, mar, mux **4** boil, mend, mess, sore **5** bitch, bodge, spoil **6** boggle, bumble, bungle, cobble, jumble, repair **7** blunder, louse up **8** swelling **10** hodgepodge

botcher: 6 grilse, salmon **7** bungler, butcher, clouter, cobbler

both: two **7** equally

handed: **12** ambidextrous

bother: ado, ail, nag, vex **4** fuss **5** annoy, deave, tease, worry **6** badger, bustle, dither, flurry, gravel, harass, meddle, moider, molest, pester, pother, puzzle, tamper **7** confuse, disturb, perplex, trouble **8** bewilder, irritate, nuisance **10** discompose **13** inconvenience

Botswana: *capital:* **8** Gaborone

desert: **8** Kalahari

ethnic group: **5** Bantu **7** Bushmen

lake: **5** Ngami

monetary unit: **4** pula **5** thebe

river: **8** Okavango

town: Kanye **7** Mochudi

bottle: jug **4** vial **5** cruet, cruse, flask, glass, gourd, house, phial **6** bundle, carafe, carboy, corner, fiasco, flagon, magnum, vessel **7** canteen, costrel **8** building, decanter, demijohn, jeroboam, preserve, restrain **9** aryballos, aryballus, container

sealer: **6** capper

size: **4** pint, pipe **5** fifth, quart **6** magnum **8** jeroboam

small: **4** vial **5** ampul, cruet, phial **6** doruck, flacon **7** ampoule, costrel **8** decanter **11** vinaigrette

bottleneck: 7 barrier **8** blockade

bottom: bed **4** base, dale, foot, fund, holm, lees, root **5** abyss, basis, belly, dregs, floor, nadir **6** ground **7** bedrock, essence, grounds, lowland, support, surface **8** buttocks, sediment **10** foundation, groundwork **11** fundamental

bottom line: 12 crucial point, profit or loss **13** the whole story

boudoir: 4 room, cabin **7** bedroom, cabinet

bouffant, bouffante: 4 full **6** puffed **7** bulging

bough: arm, leg **4** limb, twig **5** shoot, spray, sprig **6** branch, ramage **7** gallows **8** offshoot, shoulder

bouillabaisse: 4 stew **7** chowder

bouillon: 4 soup **5** broth **8** consomme

boulder: 4 rock **5** stone

monument: **8** megalith

transported by ice: **7** erratic

boulevard: way **6** avenue, street **7** highway **12** thoroughfare

boulevardier: 4 roue **5** dandy, idler

bounce: 4 bang, blow, brag, bump, fire, jump, leap, sack **5** boast, bound, bully, carom, chuck, eject, knock, scold, thump, verve **6** spirit, spring, strike **7** address, bluster, dismiss, rebound, swagger **8** proclaim, ricochet **9** discharge, explosion, expulsion, terminate **10** resilience

bouncing: big **5** buxom, lusty, stout **7** healthy **9** excessive

bound: dap, end, hop **4** bent, bind, bond, brow, butt, dart, girt, jump, leap, mere, ramp, scud, skip, stem **5** ambit, bourn, going, limit, ready, stend, sting, tiled, vault, verge **6** border, bounce, bourne, curvet, define, domain, finish, finite, hurdle, oblige, prance, spring **7** barrier, certain, chained, closure, confine, costive, delimit, dressed, rebound, saltate, secured, trussed **8** boundary, confined, destined, enclosed, frontier, handfast, landmark, precinct, prepared, shackled **9** compelled, inhibited, obligated **10** borderland, indentured **11** apprenticed, constrained, termination **12** circumscribe **13** circumference

back: **5** carom **6** resile

by a vow: **6** votary

boundary: ahu, end, rim **4** dole, dool, edge, line, mear, meer, mere, meta, mete, term, wall **5** ambit, bourn, fence, hedge, limit, march, metae, mound, verge **6** border, bourne, define **7** barrier, bounder, termini(pl.), environs **8** frontier, precinct, terminus **9** demarcate, perimeter **11** termination **13** circumference

bounder: cad, cur **4** boor, rake, roue

boundless: 4 vast **6** untold **7** endless, eternal **8** infinite **9** limitless, unlimited **10** immoderate, unconfined, unmeasured **11** illimitable, measureless **12** immeasurable, interminable

bountiful: 4 good, lush, rich **5** ample **6** freely, lavish **7** liberal, profuse **8** abundant, generous **9** bounteous, plenteous, plentiful **10** munificent

bounty: 4 boon, gift, meed **5** award, bonus, grant, valor, worth **6** reward, virtue **7** largess, premium, present, prowess, subsidy **8** goodness, gratuity, kindness **9** allowance **10** generosity, liberality, recompense **11** beneficence, munificence

Bounty captain: 5 Bligh

bouquet, boquet: 4 aura, odor, posy **5** aroma, cigar, posey, spray **7** corsage, nosegay **9** fragrance **10** compliment **11** boutonniere

bourgeois: 6 common, stupid **7** boorish, burgher **8** mediocre **9** hidebound **12** capitalistic, conservative

bourn, bourne: 4 brook **6** stream **7** rivulet

bout: job **4** turn **5** booze, essay, fight, match, round, set-to, siege, spell, trial **6** attack, fracas **7** attempt, carouse, circuit, contest, debauch, outside, without **8** conflict **10** knobkerrie

drinking: bat **4** bust, toot **5** binge, spree **6** bender **7** carouse

boutique: 4 shop

boutonniere: 7 bouquet **10** buttonhole

bovine: bos, cow **4** bull, calf, dull, neat, slow, zebu **5** bison, steer **6** oxlike **7** patient, taurine **8** longhorn, sluggish

hybrid: **4** mule **6** catalo

genus: bos

bow: arc, nod, tie **4** arch, beck, bend, bent, duck, fold, knot, prow, stem, turn, wend **5** binge, conge, crush, curve, defer, kneel, noued, stoop, yield **6** archer, assent, bauble, buckle, curtsy, fiddle, ribbon, salaam, submit, swerve, weapon **7** depress, incline, inflict, rainbow **8** crescent, greeting **9** obeisance, prostrate **10** capitulate **11** buckle under

facing sea: **4** atry

of ship: **4** beak, prow, stem

oriental: **5** salam **6** salaam

toward: **5** afore

wood for: yew

bow-shaped: 6 arcate

bowdlerize: 6 censor, screen **9** expurgate

bowed: 4 bent **5** kneed **6** arcate, curved **7** bulging

bowels: gut **5** belly, colon **8** entrails **10** compassion **11** disembowels, eviscerates

bower: 4 jack, nook **5** abode, arbor, joker, knave **6** anchor **7** berceau, chamber, cottage, embower, enclose, pergola, retreat, shelter

bowfin: 4 amia **6** lawyer **7** grindle, mudfish

bowie: tub **4** bowl, cask, pail **5** knife

bowl: cap, cup, pan **4** coup **5** arena, basin, bowie, depas, phila, rogan **6** beaker, crater, syphus, tureen, vessel **7** stadium, whiskin

bowlegged: 5 bandy **6** curved **9** misshapen

bowler: hat **5** derby **6** kegler **8** trundler

bowling: 7 tenpins

division: **5** frame

pin: **7** ninepin, skittle

place: **5** alley

score: **5** spare **6** strike

bowman: 5 cupid **6** archer

box: bin, lug, pix, pyx **4** arca, cage, caja, case, cist, crib, cuff, cyst, loge, pack, scob, seat, slap, slug, spar, stow, till, tray **5** barge, boist, buist, buxus, caddy, chest, clout, crate, fight, hutch, punch, shrub, stall, trunk, TV set **6** arcana(pl.), buffet, bunker, carton, casket, coffin, hopper, shrine, strike **7** arcanum, cabinet, caisson, casquet, cassone, confine, enclose, fostell, hanaper, package, trummel **9** container, fisticuff **10** receptacle

alms: **4** arca

ammunition: **7** caisson **9** bandoleer, bandolier

document: **7** hanaper

tea: **8** canister

box office: 4 gate **6** income **8** receipts

boxcar: 7 carrier

boxer: dog, hat, pug **5** champ **6** bantam **7** bruiser, fighter, sparrer **8** pugilist **11** heavyweight

hand covering: **5** cesti, glove **6** cestus

boxing: 4 bout **5** match **8** pugilism **10** fisticuffs **13** prize-fighting

blow: jab **5** feint, punch

knockout: TKO

boxwood: 4 tree **5** seron

boy: bub, lad, son, tad **4** chap, nino(Sp.), page, puer(L.) **5** buddy, chabo, child, gamin, knave, rogue, valet, youth **6** garcon, nipper, rascal, shaver, urchin **7** gossoon, servant **8** henchboy **9** shaveling, stripling, youngster

boy friend: 4 beau **5** beaux(pl.), lover **6** steady **8** paramour **9** inamorato **10** sweetheart

boycott: 4 shun **5** avoid, debar **9** blackball **10** ostracized

brabble: 5 argue **7** chatter, quarrel

brace: leg, tie, two **4** bind, case, frap, gird, mark, pair, prop, stay **5** nerve, strut **6** clench, couple, crutch, fasten, fathom, splint **7** embrace, refresh, stiffen, support **8** buttress, encircle **9** reinforce, stimulate, suspender **10** strengthen **11** mantelpiece

bracelet: **4** band, ring **5** chain, charm, slave **6** armlet, bangle, grivna **7** armilla, circlet, manacle, poignet **8** handcuff **10** calombigas

bracer: **5** drink, tonic **6** breeze **9** stimulant

brachyuran: **4** crab **10** crustacean

bracing: **5** crisp, quick, tonic **10** salubrious **11** stimulating **12** invigorating **13** strengthening

bracken: **4** fern **5** plaid

bracket: **4** join **5** brace, class, level, shelf, strut **6** corbel, couple, sconce **7** console, fixture, spotted **8** category, speckled **9** merganser

brackish: **5** foist, salty **6** bracky, saline **7** saltish **8** nauseous **11** distasteful

bract: **5** glume, palea, palet **6** spadix, spathe

brad: pin **4** nail **5** rivet, sprig

brag: **4** blaw, blow, crow, defy, huff, yelp **5** bluff, boast, flird, preen, strut, vaunt **6** bounce, splore **7** display, gauster, roister, swagger **8** braggart, flourish, pretense, threaten **9** gasconade **11** rodomontade

braggadocio: **7** boaster **8** braggart, rodomont **9** swaggerer **10** cockalorum, pretension

braggart: **4** brag **5** boast **6** blower, crower, gasbag, gascon, potgun **7** boaster, cracker, ruffler, windbag **8** bangster, blowhard, fanfaron, rodomont **9** loudmouth, renommist **10** burgullian **11** braggadocio, rodomontade

Bragi's wife: **4** Idun **6** Ithunn

Brahma: **5** Hindu **7** creator

first woman created by: **6** Ahalya

Brahman: **4** zebu **5** Aryan, Hindu, **6** priest, pundit **9** Bostonian

land grant: **5** sasan

precept: **5** sutra, sutta

title: aya

Brahmin: **7** egghead **8** highbrow **12** intellectual

braid: cue **4** band, jerk, lace, plat, trim **5** brede, fancy, freak, jiffy, lacet, onset, plait, pleat, queue, start, tress, trick, twine, vomit, weave **6** bobbin, border, cordon, moment, plight, ribbon, sennet, snatch, string **7** caprice, entwine, upbraid **8** brandish, ornament, reproach, soutache, trimming **9** deceitful, interlace **10** interweave

gold and silver: **5** orris

hemp: **5** tagal

knotted: **5** lacet

brain: mad **4** bean, harn(Sc.), mind, utac, wits **5** skull **6** psyche **7** furious **8** cerebrum(L.), computer **9** intellect

box: pan **5** skull **7** cranium

layer: **4** obex **6** cortex

membrane: **4** tela **8** meninges

operate on: **6** trepan

orifice: **4** lura

part: **4** aula **8** cerebrum **10** encephalon **11** pericranium

passage: **4** iter

pert. to: **8** cerebral **10** cerebellar, encephalic

tumor: **6** glioma

white matter: pia **4** alba, dura

brain trust: **5** panel **7** council **8** advisers

brainchild: **4** opus, work **9** invention

brainless: **5** silly **6** stupid **7** foolish, witless **11** thoughtless

brainstorm: **4** idea **11** inspiration

brake: **4** cage, curb, drag, fern, rack, slow, trap **5** block, check, copse, delay, deter, stop, snare, vomit **6** bridle, harrow, hinder, retard **7** dilemma, thicket **9** brushwood

bramble: **5** brier, thorn **6** bumble **10** cloudberry

brambly: **5** spiny **6** thorny **7** prickly

bran: **5** treat **6** cereal, chisel

branch: arm, bow, **4** brog, bush, chat, fork, limb, part, rame, rami, snag, spur, stem, twig **5** bough, creek, ramus, shoot, spray, sprig, vimen, withe **6** divide, member, outlet, raddle, ramage, ramify, stolon, stream **7** diverge, tendril **8** district, offshoot **10** department **11** bifurcation **12** ramification

angle of: **4** axil

of nerves: **4** rami(pl.) **5** ramus

branched: **6** forked, ramate, ramose **7** cladose

branchia: **4** gill

brand: **4** birn, blot, burn, flaw, kind, mark, sear, smit, sort **5** buist, stain, stamp, sword, taint, torch **6** stigma **8** flambeau **9** cauterize, character, trademark **10** stigmatize

on stolen cattle: **4** duff

sheep: **4** smit

brandish: **4** dart, show, wave **5** bless, braid, shake, swing, wield **6** flaunt, hurtle **7** flutter, glitter, swagger, trot out, vibrate **8** flourish **9** coruscate, irradiate

brandling: **4** parr **9** earthworm

brandy: **4** marc **5** bingo **6** cognac **11** aguardiente(Sp.)

and soda: peg

cocktail: **7** sidecar, stinger **9** alexander

mastic: **4** raki **5** rakee

plum: **9** slivovitz

brannigan: 5 brawl, spree 6 bender, ruckus 10 falling out 11 altercation

brant: 4 rout 5 erect, goose, proud, quink, sheer, steep 7 steeply 8 straight

brash: 4 bold, rash 5 brazen, hasty, saucy, storm 6 attack 7 brittle, forward 8 cocksure, impudent, tactless 9 irascible 11 thoughtless 12 presumptuous

brass: 4 cash 5 alloy, money, nerve 6 brazen 7 officer 9 impudence, insolence 10 effrontery

brass hat (army slang): 7 general, officer 8 superior

brass tacks: 5 facts 10 essentials

brassard, brassart: 5 badge 6 bracer 7 armband

brassbound: set 5 rigid 10 inflexible

brassica: 4 cole, rape 6 turnip

brassy: 4 bold 6 aerose, brazen 8 impudent

brat: bib, imp 4 film, scum 5 apron, bairn, bilsh, child, cloak 6 infant, mantle, urchin 7 garment 8 clothing 9 offspring

bravado: 4 pomp 5 brave, pride, storm 6 bravor, hector 7 bluster, bombast, bravade, bravery, swagger 9 gasconade

brave: 4 bold, braw(Sc.), dare, defy, face, fine, game, good, prow 5 adorn, boast, bravo, bully, gutsy, hardy, manly, Roman, stout, vaunt 6 breast, chin-up, daring, heroic, manful, plucky 7 bravado, gallant, soldier, swagger, valiant, venture, warrior 8 cavalier, defiance, embolden, fearless, intrepid, stalwart, superior, valorous, virtuous 9 challenge, dauntless, excellent, undaunted 10 courageous 11 venturesome 12 stouthearted

Brave New World author: 6 Huxley

bravery: 4 grit 5 valor 6 spirit, valour 7 bravado, bravura, courage, heroism 8 boldness 9 fortitude, gallantry, gentleman, hardihood

bravo: ole(Sp.), rah 4 thug, viva 5 brave, bully 6 bandit, Indian 7 bravado, villain 8 applause, assassin 9 cutthroat, desperado

brawl: din, row 4 clem, fray, riot 5 broil, fight, melee, revel, scold 6 affray, bicker, fracas, habble, revile, rumpus, shindy, strife, tumult, uproar 7 brabble, discord, dispute, quarrel, scuffle, wrangle 8 complain, squabble 10 contention, donnybrook, free-for-all 11 altercation, disturbance

brawling: 5 noisy 7 blatant 9 clamorous 10 clamourous, vociferous 11 quarrelsome

brawn: 4 boar 5 flesh 6 fatten, muscle 8 strength 10 headcheese

brawny: 5 beefy 6 fleshy, robust, sinewy, strong, sturdy 7 callous 8 muscular, powerful, stalwart

bray: cry, mix, rub 4 beat, rout, tool 5 grind, noise, pound 6 bruise, heehaw, outcry, pestle, thrash, whinny

brazen: 4 bold, pert 5 brass, harsh, sassy 6 brassy 7 callous, forward 8 immodest, impudent, insolent, metallic 9 shameless

Brazil: *capital:* 8 Brasilia

city: 5 Belem, Natal 6 Cuiaba, Macapa, Maceio, Manaus, Santos 7 Aracaju, Goiania, Sao Luis 8 Boa Vista, Curitiba, Sao Paulo 10 Pernambuco 12 Rio de Janeiro

coffee plantation: 7 fazenda

dance: 5 samba 6 maxixe 9 bossa nova

discoverer: 6 Cabral

drink: 5 assai

emperor: 6 Pedro I 7 Pedro II

estuary: 4 Para

falls: 6 Iguacu 11 Paulo Afonso

fiber: 4 imbe

fish: 8 arapaima

forest: 5 matta, selva

grasslands: 6 campos

Indian: 4 Anta 5 Arara, Bravo, Carib, Guana 6 Arawak, Caraja, Tupian 7 Tariana 8 Araquaju, Botocudo

island: 6 Maraca, Marajo 7 Caviana, Mexiana

measure: pe 4 moio, pipa, sack, vara 5 braca, fanga, legoa, milha, palmo, passo, tonel 6 canada, covado, cuarta, league, quarto, tarefa 7 alquier, garrafa 8 alqueire 9 pollegada, quartilho

monkey: sai 6 miriki 9 belzebuth

monetary unit: 4 reis 5 conto, dolra 7 centavo, milreis 8 cruzeiro

mountain: Mar 5 Geral 6 Acarai, Orgaos, Parima 7 Paracis 8 Estrondo, Roncador, Tombador 10 Tumuc-Humac

palm: 4 jara 5 assai, inaja, tucum 6 babaca, jupati 7 babassu, cassava 9 barriguda

paste: 7 guarana

plant: 4 imbe, para, yage, yaje 5 caroa 7 ayapana, seringa 9 jaborandi

plateau: 8 planalto

promontory: 4 frio

river: 4 Para, Paru 5 Negro, Purus, Verde, Xingu 6 Amazon, Parana 7 Madeira, Tapajos, Uruguay 8 Paraguay, Parnaiba 9 Tocantins 12 Sao Francisco

rubber: ule 4 hule, Para 6 caucho

seaport: Rio 5 Belem, Natal 6 Recife, Santos 7 Pelotas, Vitoria 8 Salvador 9 Fortaleza, Rio Grande 11 Porto Alegre

state: 4 Acre, Para 5 Bahia, Ceara, Goias, Piaui 6 Parana 7 Alagoas, Sergipe, Paraiba 8 Amazonas, Maranhao, Sao Paulo 10 Mato Grosso, Pernambuco 11 Minas Gerais 13 Espirito Santo, Santa

Catarina **14** Rio Grande do Sul **16** Rio Grande do Norte

tree: apa, ule **4** anda, assu, uhle **5** araca, tingi **6** biriba, brauna, satine **7** araroba, becuiba, gomavel, paraiba, seringa, wallaba **8** bakupari **10** barbatimao, dal guarabu

weight: bag **4** onca **5** libra **6** arroba, oitava **7** arratel, quilate, quintal **8** tonelada

wood: **6** embuia **8** kingwood

breach: gap **4** chap, flaw, gool, rent, rift **5** brack, breck, chasm, cleft, crack, pause, split, wound **6** bruise, harbor, hernia, hiatus, inroad, schism **7** assault, blemish, dispute, fissure, opening, quarrel, rupture **8** breaking, fraction, fracture, interval, trespass **9** violation **10** disruption, infraction **12** infringement, interruption **14** nonfulfillment **16** misunderstanding

of etiquette: **5** gaffe **8** solecism

breach pin: **4** tige

bread: bun **4** diet, fare, food, loaf, pone, roll **5** dough, money **6** staple **7** aliment, bannock(Sc.) **10** livelihood, sustenance

boiled: **4** cush **6** panada

browned: **5** toast **6** sippet **7** crouton

communion: **4** azym, host **5** azyme, wafer

crust: **4** rind

dry and crisp: **4** rusk **8** zwieback **10** melba toast

leavened: **5** kisra **6** cocket

Passover: **5** matzo **6** matzoh, matzos(pl.), matzot(pl.) **7** matzoth(pl.)

pert. to: **6** panary

unleavened: **4** azym **5** azyme **6** matzos **7** bannock, matzoth **8** afikomen

bread-and-butter: **5** basic **8** everyday, ordinary

pert. to: **6** living **7** support **8** daily job **12** note of thanks

bread spread: jam **4** oleo **5** jelly **6** butter **9** margarine, marmalade **13** oleomargarine

breadth: **4** span **5** brede, scope, width **6** extent **8** diameter, distance, latitude **9** amplitude, dimension

breadwinner: **6** earner, worker

break: gap **4** boon, bust, dash, hint, knap, pick, plow, rend, rent, rift, rive, ruin, rush, slip, snap, stop, tear **5** alter, blank, burst, cleft, crack, craze, frush, lapse, pluck, sever, smash, wound **6** bruise, change, cleave, defeat, hiatus, impair, lacuna, pierce **7** blunder, caesura, crackle, crevice, crumble, destroy, disable, dispart, disrupt, exhaust, fissure, lacunae(pl.), opening, respite, rupture, shatter **8** caesurae, fraction, fracture, interval, separate **9** interrupt, penetrate **10** invalidate **12** interruption

14 discontinuance

down: **7** debacle, failure **8** collapse **9** cataclysm **10** catabolism

in: **5** stave, train **7** intrude **8** initiate **9** interrupt **13** enter forcibly

of day: **4** dawn, morn **5** sunup **7** morning

out: **5** erupt **6** escape **10** bring forth

up: **4** part **5** split **7** disband, disrupt **8** disperse, dissolve, separate **9** take apart **10** put a stop to

breakable: **7** brittle, bruckle, friable **8** delicate

breakbone fever: **6** dengue

breaker: **4** surf, wave **6** billow, comber, roller

breakwater: cob, dam **4** cobb, dike, mole, pier, pile, quay **5** jetty **6** refuge **11** obstruction

bream: tai **4** fish, scup **5** broom **7** sunfish

sea: **4** shad **6** sargus

breast: **4** crop **5** bosom, brave, chest **6** thorax **9** encounter

ornament: **8** pectoral

breastbone: **6** sterna(pl.) **7** sternum, xiphoid **9** gladiolus

pert to: **7** sternal

breastplate: *armor:* **4** urim **6** gorget, lorica, shield **7** poitrel, thummin **8** poitrail

ecclesiastical: **4** urim

breastwork: **4** fort **5** redan **7** brattle, bulwark, parapet, rampart **10** forecastle

breath: **4** ande, gasp, hint, huff, life, pant, pech, puff, sigh, wind **5** pause, scent, smell, vapor, whiff **6** breeze, pneuma **7** halitus, instant, respite **10** exhalation

breathe: **4** ande, live, pant, pech, puff, sigh **5** exist, speak, utter **6** aspire, exhale, inhale, wheeze **7** afflate, emanate, respire, suspire

hard: **4** gasp, pant

breather: **4** rest **5** break, pause, truce **6** recess **7** respite **9** armistice

breathing: **5** alive **7** gasping **9** spiration **11** respiration

difficult: **7** dyspnea **8** dyspnoea

harsh: **4** rale

impairment of: **9** emphysema

orifice: **4** nose, pore **5** mouth, nares **7** nostril **8** spiracle

smooth: **4** lene

sound: **4** rale **5** snore, snort **7** stridor

breathless: **4** dead **5** stale, tense **6** stuffy **10** motionless

Brecht (Bertolt): *play:* **7** Galileo **8** Man Is Man **9** Mahagonny **13** Mother Courage **15** Threepenny Opera

breech: **4** bore, butt, doup **5** block **7** droddum **8** buttocks, derriere **9** posterior

breeches: **5** chaps, jeans, levis **8** jodhpurs, knickers, trousers **10** pantaloons

breeching: **4** rope **7** harness

breed: ilk **4** bear, kind, race, rear, sort,

type **5** beget, brood, caste, cause, class, hatch, raise, stock, train **6** create, strain **7** educate, nourish, produce, progeny, species, variety **8** engender, instruct, multiply **9** offspring, originate, propagate **10** generation

breeding: 6 origin **7** culture, descent **8** behavior, civility, training **9** education, gestation **10** deportment, extraction **11** development, instruction

science: **8** eugenics

breeze: air, zip **4** aura, blow, flaw, gale, gust, pirr, stir, wind **5** blast, rumor, waltz **6** breath, report, zephyr **7** freshen, quarrel, whisper **11** disturbance

land: **6** terral

breezy: 4 airy **5** brisk, fresh, windy **6** airish **9** easygoing, vivacious

bressumer: 4 beam **6** girder, lintel **7** support

breve: 4 bird, mark, note, writ **5** brief, order **6** letter **7** compose, precept **8** syllable

brevet: 6 confer **9** promotion **10** commission

breviary: 4 ordo **6** digest, portas **7** coucher, epitome, summary **8** abstract **10** compendium **11** abridgement

brevity: 8 laconism **9** briefness, shortness, terseness **11** conciseness **12** succinctness

brew: ale, mix **4** beer, boil, loom, make, plot, pour **5** hatch **6** devise, dilute, foment, gather, liquor, seethe **7** concoct, incline, prepare **8** beverage, contrive **9** potpourri **10** miscellany

brewer: *grain:* rye **4** corn, malt **6** barley

vat: tun

yeast: **4** barm **6** leaven

briar: saw **4** pipe

bribe: fee, fix, oil, rob, sop, tip **4** bait, gift, hire, meed **5** bonus, cuddy, graft, offer, steal, sugar, tempt **6** buy off, extort, grease, payola, suborn **7** corrupt **8** gratuity **10** allurement

bric-a-brac: 5 curio, vertu, virtu **7** bibelot **11** knickknacks

brick: 4 pave, tile **5** block, quarl, stone **6** fellow, quarle

handler: **6** hacker

oven: **4** kiln

sun-baked: bat **5** adobe

tray: hod

vitrified: **7** clinker

wood: nog **4** dook **6** scutch

bridal: 7 nuptial, wedding **8** espousal, marriage

bride: bar, tie **4** loop, rein, rose **6** bridle, kallah

bridesmaid: 9 attendant

bridge: way **4** game, link, pons, pont, span **5** cross **6** ponton **7** auction, bascule,

connect, pontoon, trestle, viaduct **8** contract, traverse **9** alcantara, gangplank

combination: **6** tenace

forerunner: **5** whist

lever: **7** bascule

of musical instrument: **5** magas **10** ponticello

part: **4** arch, deck, pier **5** cable, pylon **7** caisson **8** spandrel

player: **4** east, west **5** north, south

pontoon plank: **5** chess

score: leg

support: **4** pier **5** truss

term: bid, bye, leg, set **4** book, game, pass, ruff, slam, suit, void **5** dummy, raise, trick, trump **6** double, renege, revoke, rubber **7** finesse, jump bid, no-trump, overbid **8** contract, redouble **9** grandslam, overtrick, part score, singleton **10** little slam, vulnerable

bridle: bit **4** curb, rein, rule **5** brake, brank, bride, check, guard, guide, strut **6** direct, govern, halter, master, simper, subdue **7** blinder, control, repress, snaffle, swagger **8** restrain, suppress **9** restraint

noseband: **6** musrol **8** cavesson

brief: few **4** curt, list, rife, writ **5** blurb, breve, charm, pithy, quick, short, terse **6** abrupt, common, letter **7** abridge, compact, compose, concise, invoice, laconic, mandate, outline, precept, summary **8** breviate, condense, fleeting, succinct, syllabus **9** catalogue, condensed, ephemeral, memoranda(pl.), prevalent **10** abridgment, compendium, memorandum, transitory **11** compendious **12** condensation

briefness: 7 brevity

brier, briar: 4 barb, pipe **5** erica, thorn **6** smilax

briery: 5 sharp, spiny

brig: 4 boat, jail **6** prison, vessel **8** stockade **10** guardhouse

brigand: 5 thief **6** bandit, pirate, robber **7** cateran, ladrone, soldier **8** marauder, picaroon **10** highwayman

bright: apt, gay **4** fine, glad, rosy **5** acute, aglow, alert, anime, beamy, clear, fresh, gemmy, light, lucid, nitid, quick, riant, sharp, smart, sunny, vivid, witty **6** cheery, clever, florid, garish, limpid, lively, lucent, orient **7** forward, fulgent, radiant, ringing, shining **8** animated, cheerful, colorful, flashing, gleaming, luminous, lustrous, splendid, splendor **9** brilliant, cloudless, effulgent, favorable, refulgent, sparkling **10** brightness, epiphanous, glistening, glittering, precocious **11** illustrious, intelligent, resplendent, transparent

brighten: 4 gild 5 cheer, clear, light, liven, shine 6 cantle, engild, polish 7 animate, burnish, enliven, furbish, lighten 8 illumine 9 irradiate

brightness: 5 eclat, flame, gleam, gloss, nitor, sheen 6 acumen, bright, fulgor, luster 7 clarity, fulgour, sparkle 8 splendor 9 clearness 10 brilliance, effulgence

brilliance: 4 fame 5 eclat, flame, glory 8 keenness, radiance, splendor 10 brightness, effulgence

brilliant: gay 4 good, keen, sage, wise 5 breme 6 bright, clever, signal 7 eminent, erudite, flaming, learned, radiant, shining 8 dazzling, glorious, luminous 9 effective, prismatic, refulgent, sparkling 10 glittering 11 prismatical, resplendent 13 distinguished

brim: lip, rim, rut, sea 4 edge 5 bluff, brink, marge, ocean, verge, water 6 border, margin 8 copulate, strumpet 9 periphery

brimming: big 4 full

brimstone: 6 sulfur, virago 7 sulphur 8 spitfire

brindled: 5 tawny 7 branded, flecked 8 streaked

brine: sea 4 main, salt 5 ocean, tears 6 pickle 8 marinade
preserve in: 4 corn, cure, salt

brine shrimp: 7 artemia

bring: 4 bear, sell, take 5 carry, fetch 6 convey, deduce 7 conduce, convert, procure, produce 9 accompany, transport
about: 5 cause 6 create, effect 7 achieve 10 accomplish
back: 6 effect, recall, return, revive 7 produce, restore 8 occasion, retrieve, transact 9 instigate 10 consummate
forth: ean(Sc.) 4 bear 5 educe, hatch, incur 6 adduce, beteem 7 produce
forward: 7 present 9 introduce
in: 4 earn 5 usher, yield 6 import, report, return 9 introduce
near to: 6 appose
off: 7 achieve, succeed 8 complete
on: 6 induce
out: 7 display, publish
to: 11 resuscitate
to earth: 4 land
to light: 6 elicit, reveal 7 unearth 8 disclose, discover
to naught: 4 dash 6 negate 7 confute 9 frustrate
together: 4 join 5 unite 7 compile 11 consolidate
up: 4 rear, stop 5 nurse, raise, refer, train, vomit 6 broach 7 educate 11 regurgitate
up to date: 4 post 5 brief 6 inform

brink: end, eve, lip, rim, sea 4 bank, brim, edge, foss 5 marge, shore, verge 6 border, margin

briny: 5 brack, ocean, salty 6 saline

brioche: 4 roll 6 stitch 7 cushion, pudding, savarin

Briseis' lover: 8 Achilles

brisk: gay 4 busy, fast, keen, pert, racy, spry, yern 5 agile, alert, alive, budge, crisp, fresh, frisk, peart, perky, quick, sharp, smart, yerne 6 active, adroit, breezy, cocket, crouse, lively, nimble, snappy 7 allegro 8 animated, friskful, spirited 9 energetic, sprightly, vivacious 11 stimulating 12 effervescing

bristle: awn 4 barb, hair, seta, tela 5 anger, birse, brush, parch, preen, setae, strut, toast 6 chaeta, palpus, ruffle, setula 7 chaetae, setulae, stubble
surgical: 4 seta 5 seton

bristled: 7 horrent 8 echinate

bristlelike: 5 setal 8 setiform

bristling: 5 rough 6 hispid, horrid, setose, thorny 7 horrent, scrubby

brit, britt: 5 sprat 7 herring 10 crustacean

Britain: See **England**

British Columbia: *capital:* 8 Victoria
city: 6 Duncan 7 Kitimat, Nanaimo, Quesnel 8 Kamloops, Smithers 9 Vancouver
explored by: 4 Cook 5 Drake 10 Juan de Fuca
Indian: 5 Haida 7 Shuswap
island: 9 Vancouver
lake: 6 Babine, Chilko, Fraser, Muncho, Stuart 7 Thutade
mountain: 5 Coast, Rocky 7 Cariboo, Purcell, Selkirk 8 Monashee
river: 4 Nass 5 Liard, Peace 6 Fraser, Skeena 7 Parsnip 8 Columbia
strait: 6 Hecate

Britomartis: 7 Artemis 8 Dictynna
mother: 5 Carme

brittle: 4 frow, weak 5 brash, candy, crisp, crump, eager, frail, frowy, frush, short 6 crispy, crumpy, feeble, fickle, frough, infirm, slight 7 brickle, bruckle, fragile, friable, froughy 8 delicate, snappish 9 breakable, crumbling, frangible, irritable 10 perishable

broach: air, awl, cut, pin, rod, tap 4 open, ouch, shed, spit, spur, stab, veer, vent 5 begin, dress, drift, prick, rimer, spool, voice 6 boring, brooch, launch, pierce, reamer 7 bring up, enlarge, publish, spindle, suggest, violate 8 approach, broacher, deflower, incision 9 introduce 11 perforation

broad: 4 deep, free, vast, wide 5 ample, beamy, large, plain, roomy, thick, woman 6 coarse, risqué 7 evident, general, grivois, liberal, obvious, platoid 8 grivoise, spacious, tolerant 9 capacious,

expansive, extensive, outspoken **12** unrestrained **3** comprehensive
broad-footed: 8 platypod
broad-minded: 7 lenient, liberal **8** catholic, tolerant
broadbill: 4 bird, gaya, raya **5** scaup **8** shoveler **9** swordfish
broadcast: sow **4** seed, send **5** radio, strew **6** spread **7** declare, publish, scatter **8** announce, televise, transmit **9** advertise
broadside: 4 bill **5** salvo **7** barrage **8** circular
broadsword: 4 bill, kris **6** glaive, spatha **7** cutlass, Ferrara **8** claymore, scimitar
brobdingnagian: big **4** huge **5** giant **8** colossal, gigantic
brocade: 5 cloth **6** broche, kincab **8** baudekin **9** baldachin
brocard: 4 gibe, rule **5** maxim, moral **6** speech **7** sarcasm **8** aphorism **9** principle
brochure: 4 book **5** tract **8** pamphlet, treatise
brocket: 4 deer, pita, stag **5** brock **7** spitter
brogue: 4 hose, shoe **5** fraud, trick **6** accent, brogan **7** dialect **8** trousers
broil: row **4** burn, char, feud, fray, heat **5** alarm, brawl, grill, melee, scrap **6** affray, birsle, braise, splore, tumult **7** brulyie(Sc.), contest, discord, dispute, embroil, garboil, quarrel **8** conflict, grillade **10** contention, dissension **11** altercation, disturbance
broiling: hot **6** torrid **8** sizzling, steaming **9** scorching **10** sweltering
broke: 4 poor **8** bankrupt **9** insolvent, penniless
broken: 4 rent, torn **5** burst, gappy, rompu(F.), rough, tamed **6** hackly, ruined, shaken **7** crushed, fracted, reduced, subdued **8** outlawed, ruptured, weakened **9** cashiered, dispersed, fractured, shattered **10** incoherent, incomplete **11** fragmentary **12** disconnected, intermittent
down: **6** shabby **7** haywire
broker: 5 agent **6** corser, dealer, factor, jobber **7** brogger, changer, courser, peddler, realtor, scalper **8** broacher, huckster, merchant **9** go-between **10** pawnbroker
brokerage: fee **4** agio **10** commission
brolly: 8 umbrella
bromide: 5 trite **8** compound, sedative **9** platitude **11** commonplace
bronco: 5 horse **6** cayuse **7** broncho, mustang **9** estrapade(Sp.)
bronco buster: 6 cowboy, ginete
Bronte: 4 Anne **5** Emily **9** Charlotte
hero: **9** Rochester **10** Heathcliff
novels: **8** Jane Eyre **16** Wuthering Heights
pen name: **9** Ellis Bell

Bronx cheer: boo **9** raspberry
bronze: aes(L.), tan **4** bust **5** alloy, brown **6** statue
film: **6** patina
gilded: **6** ormolu
nickel: **11** cupronickel
pert. to: **7** aeneous
brooch: bar, pin **4** boss, clip, ouch **5** cameo, clasp **6** fibula, plaque, shield **8** ornament **9** brochette
brood: fry, nye, set, sit **4** mope, nest, nide, race, weep **5** aerie, breed, covey, flock, group, hatch, issue, sedge, worry, young **6** cletch, clutch, family, litter, ponder **7** progeny, species **8** cogitate, incubate, meditate **9** multitude, offspring **11** contemplate
brook: run **4** bear, beck, burn, ghyl, gill, rill, rush, sike **5** abide, bayou, bourn, creek, stand **6** arroyo(Sp.), bourne, canada, endure, gutter, rindle, rivose, runlet, stream, suffer **7** comport **8** quebrada, tolerate **11** watercourse
brooklet: 4 beck, rill **6** rillet, runnel **7** rillock, rivulet **9** arroyuelo(Sp.)
broom: mop **4** fray, swab **5** besom, bream, brush, spart, sweep, whisk **8** splinter
broom plant: 5 hirse, spart **6** whisk **7** cyticus, genista, heather **8** deerweed
broomcorn millet: 5 hirse
broth: 4 bree, broo, soup **5** stock **6** brewis, jussal, jussel **7** pottage **8** bouillon, consomme, jusshell
brothel: 4 crib, stew **6** bagnio, bordel **8** bordello **10** bawdy house
brother: bub, fra, kin, pal, sib **4** mate, monk, peer **5** billy, buddy, cadet, frere(F.), friar **6** fellow, fraile, frater(L.) **7** comrade, sibling
pert. to: **9** fraternal
brotherhood: 4 gild **5** guild, lodge **6** friary **8** bratstro, sodality **10** fellowship, fraternity **11** association **13** brotherliness, companionship, confraternity
brotherly: 4 kind **6** tender **9** fraternal **12** affectionate
brougham: 8 carriage
brought up: 4 cade
brouhaha: din **5** babel, furor **6** furore, racket, rumpus, tumult **9** commotion **10** hullabaloo **11** pandemonium
brow: top **4** brae, bree, edge, mien, snab(Sc.) **5** bound, brink, crest, front, ridge, slope **8** boldness, forehead **9** acclivity, gangplank **10** effrontery **11** countenance
browbeat: 5 abash, bully **6** hector **7** depress **10** disconcert, intimidate
brown: dun, tan **4** coin, cook, dark, sear **5** dusky, penny, sedge, sepia, tawny, tenne, toast, umber **6** gloomy, russet, sennet, tanned **9** half-penny

cocoa: **6** sahara
dark: **5** sepia, umber **6** bister, bistre **9** chocolate
light: tan **4** ecru, fawn **5** beige, khaki, tenne
purple: **4** puce
red: bay **4** cuba, roan **5** henna, sepia **6** auburn, russet, sorrel **8** chestnut
yellow: **6** almond, bronze **12** butterscotch
brown Betty: 7 pudding **10** coneflower
brown study: 7 reverie **10** absorption **11** abstraction
brownie: elk, nis **4** cake **5** cooky, fairy, nisse, urisk **6** goblin, uruisg(Sc.) **9** sandpiper
brownnose: 9 sycophant
browse: 4 brut, crop, feed **5** graze **6** forage, nibble, peruse **7** dip into, pasture
bruin: 4 bear
bruise: 4 bash, bray, dent, dunt, hurt, maim, maul **5** black, break, crush, curry, delve, dinge, pound **6** batter, breach, hatter, injury, mangle, shiner **7** contuse, dammish, disable **9** pulverize, triturate
bruiser: 5 boxer **8** pugilist
bruit: din **4** fame, hint, rale, tell **5** noise, rumor, sound **6** blazon, clamor, report **7** declare, hearsay **8** intimate
brume: fog **4** haze, mist, smog **5** vapor
brumous: 5 foggy, misty **6** hiemal, sleety **7** wintery
brunette: 4 dark **5** brown, brune, gipsy, gypsy **7** swarthy
brunt: jar **4** blow, jolt **5** clash, force, onset, shock **6** attack, effort, impact **7** assault **8** outburst
brush: 4 comb, fray, skim **5** broom, clash, clean, copse, fight, graze, sweep, touch **6** badger, battle, brosse(F.), stroke **7** thicket **8** skirmish **9** brushwood, encounter, sideswipe **11** undergrowth
brushwood: 4 rone **5** brake, brush, copse, frith, scrog, scrub **6** rammel **7** coppice, thicket
brusque: 4 curt, rude **5** bluff, blunt, brusk, gruff, hasty, rough, short **6** abrupt **7** violent **8** cavalier, impolite **12** discourteous
brut: dry **6** browse
brutal: 5 cruel, feral, gross **6** carnal, coarse, savage, severe **7** bestial, beastly, brutish, caddish, inhuman **8** ruthless **9** atrocious, barbarous, ferocious, insensate
brute: 5 beast, yahoo **6** animal, savage **7** ruffian **9** scoundrel
bryophyte: 4 moss **5** plant **9** liverwort
Brython: 5 Welsh **6** Celtic **7** Cornish
god: Dea, Ler **4** Brian **5** Dylan, Lludd **8** Amaethon
goddess: Don **8** Rhiannon **9** Arianrhod
bubal: 4 topi **8** antelope

bubble: air, bub **4** bead, bell(Sc.), bleb, blob, boil, boll, dupe, foam, glob, seed, suds **5** caper, cheat, empty, slosh **6** burble, delude, seethe, trifle **7** blister, blubber, deceive, globule **8** delusive **9** pipe dream **10** effervesce **11** speculation
bubbling: gay **8** effusive **9** sparkling
buccal: 4 oral
buccaneer: 6 pirate, rifler, robber, viking **7** corsair, mariner, spoiler **8** Picaroon **10** freebooter
standard: **5** roger
Bucephalus: 5 steed **7** charger
buck: fob, ram **4** boil, butt, deer, dude, male, pass, prig, rear, soak, stag, toff, wash **5** carry, dandy, steep **6** basket, dollar, oppose, resist **7** sawbuck **8** antelope, prickett, sawhorse **9** buckwheat, pulverize
first year: **4** fawn
fourth year: **4** sore
buck up: 5 brace **7** comfort
buckaroo: 6 cowboy **8** horseman
buckboard: 8 carriage
bucket: tub **4** bail, bowk, cage, pail **5** cheat, hurry, scoop, skeel **6** bailer, barrel, drench, hoppet, situla(L.), vessel **7** swindle **8** cannikin
handle: **4** bail
molten glass: **7** cuvette
Buckeye State: 4 Ohio
buckle: bow **4** bend, curl, kink, tach, warp **5** clasp, marry, twist, yield **6** fibula(L.) **7** contend, fermail, fibulae(L.pl.), grapple **8** fastener, struggle **10** distortion
down: **5** set to **7** address, pitch in
part: **5** chape **6** tongue
under: bow **5** yield **6** cave in **10** capitulate
buckler: 4 crab **5** block **6** shield **7** rotella, roundel, shutter
buckram: 6 fabric **7** precise **10** cuckoopint, stiffening **11** muscle-bound
buckthorn: 5 rhamn **7** alatern, cascara **8** lotebush **9** alaternus, chaparral
buckwheat: 4 buck **8** sarrazin
buckwheat tree: 4 titi **6** teetee
bucolic: 4 idyl **5** local, naive, rural **6** farmer, rustic, simple **7** cowherd, ecologue **8** agrestic, herdsman, pastoral
bud: eye, gem, imp, pip **4** bulb, cion, germ, girl, grow, knop, seed **5** child, graft, scion, shoot, youth **6** button, flower, germin, sprout **7** blossom, brother, gemmule **8** bourgeon **9** germinate
arrangement: **11** aestivation
social: deb **8** debutant **9** debutante
Buddha: Foh **7** Gautama **10** Shakyamuni
cause of infinite existence: **6** nidana
center: **5** Lassa, Lhasa
chant: **6** mantra
church: **4** Tera

column: lat
disciple: **6** Ananda
doctrine: **7** trikaya
dryad: **6** Yaksha, Yakshi
enlightenment: **5** bodhi
evil spirit: **4** Mara
fate: **5** karma
fertility spirit: **6** Yaksha, Yakshi
festival: bon
final beatitude: **4** raga **7** nirvana
for justice: **6** dharna, dhurna
gateway: **5** toran, torii **6** torana
god: **4** deva
greater: **8** Mahayana
hatred: **4** dosa
hell: **6** Naraka
Japanese image: **8** Daibutsu
language: **4** Pali
lesser: **8** Hinayana
life cycle: **6** anicca
mendicant: **6** bhikku **7** bhikshu
monastery: **4** Tera **6** Vihara
monk: **4** lama **5** arhat, yahan, **7** poongee
  8 poonghee, poonghie, talapoin
monument: **5** stupa
mother: **4** Maya
novice: **5** goyim
paradise: **4** Jodo
passion: **4** raga
prayer: **4** mani
priest: **4** lama **7** mahatma
relic mound: **5** stupa
retribution: **5** karma
rock temple: **4** rath **5** ratha
sacred city: **5** Lassa, Lhasa
school: **5** ritsu
scripture: **5** sutra
sect: Zen **6** tendai **7** Jodo-shu
shrine: **4** tope **5** stupa **6** dagoba **7** chorten
son: **6** Rahula
spiritual leader: **4** guru **9** Dalai Lama
stupa site: **9** Amaravati
throne: **5** asana
title: **7** Mahatma
tree: **5** pipal **6** botree
will to live: **5** Tanha
buddy: boy, pal **4** chum, mate **5** crony **7**
  brother, comrade **9** companion
buddy-buddy: **4** cozy **5** close **8** intimate
budge: fur **4** move, stir **5** booze, brisk,
  stiff, thief **6** jocund, liquor **8** movement
  11 nervousness
budget: bag **4** body, boot, pack, plan, roll
  5 batch, bunch, stock, store **6** bottle,
  bundle, parcel, socket, wallet **7** program
  12 accumulation
buds: **8** burgeons, dehisces
pickled: **6** capers
buff: fan, rub **4** coat **5** shine **6** addict, polish **7** leather **8** nonsense **10** enthusiast
in the: **4** nude **5** naked
buffalo: ox **5** anoa, buff, stag **5** bison, bu-

gle **6** buffle, hamper **7** caribao, caribou,
  gazelle, nonplus, overawe, timarau, za-
  mouse **8** bewilder **9** bamboozle, frustrate
large: **4** arna, arni **5** arnee
meat: **7** biltong
wild: **4** arna, arni **5** arnee **8** seladang
buffalo gourd: **11** calabazilla
buffalo tree: **10** rabbitwood
buffer: dog, pad **6** bumper, fender, pistol
  7 cushion
buffet: bar, bob, box **4** beat, blow, buff,
  cuff, slap, toss **5** filip, smite, stool **6**
  abacus, batter, fillip, strike, strive,
  thrash **7** contend, counter, hassock **8**
  credence, credenza, cupboard, lambaste
  9 footstool, sideboard **10** affliction
bufflehead: **4** duck, fool **5** clown, dunce **6**
  buffle **9** merrywing
buffleheaded: **4** dull **6** simple, stupid
buffoon: dor, wag, wit **4** aper, fool, jape,
  mime, mome **5** actor, antic, buffo,
  clown, comic, drole, droll, mimer **6** harlot, jester, mummer, stooge **7** playboy **8**
  balatron, gracioso, humorist, merryman, ridicule **9** harlequin **10** harlequina, hobby-horse **11** merry-andrew,
  Punchinello
bug: bog, dor **4** flaw, germ, idea, mite, wire
  5 annoy, bogey, bulge, roach **6** beetle,
  chinch, elater, insect, scheme **7** bellied,
  bugbear, forward, pompous, wiretap **8**
  hemipter, hobbyist **9** conceited, hide a
  mike, hobgoblin, prominent **10** enthusiast, flashlight **11** hunchbacked
June: dor
lightning: **7** firefly
needle: **7** ranatra
bugaboo: **4** bogy, fear, goga, gogo, ogre **5**
  alarm, bogey, bogie, gogga **6** bodach,
  goblin **7** bugbear, specter, spectre **8**
  worricow(Sc.) **9** hobgoblin, scarecrow,
  worriecow(Sc.) **10** mumbo-jumbo
bugbane: **4** herb **9** hellebore **10** rattleroot
bugger: **4** chap **5** scamp **6** fellow, rascal
buggy (see also **carriage**): **4** cart, shay,
  trap **5** nutty **7** caboose, foolish, vehicle
  8 demented, infested, stanhope **9** gladstone
bughouse: **5** crazy, nutty **6** asylum, insane
bugle: **4** bead, horn **5** black **7** buffalo,
  bullock, clarion, trumpet
blare: **7** tanatara
call: **4** taps **6** alerte(F.), sennet, tattoo **7**
  retreat **8** reveille
note: mot
yellow: iva
bugleweed: **4** mint **6** indigo
bug off: **5** leave, scram **6** go away **7** buzz
  off, get lost
build: big **4** bigg, form, make, rear **5** edify,

erect, found, frame, raise, set up, shape
6 create, graith 7 fashion 8 assemble,
increase, physique 9 construct, establish, fabricate
nest: 6 nidify
up: 5 erect 7 enhance 8 increase 9 publicity 10 strengthen
builder: 5 maker 7 erector 8 tectonic 9
carpenter 11 constructor
labyrinth: 8 Daedalus
of wooden horse: 5 Epeus 6 Epeius
building: hut 4 casa(Sp.), pile 5 aedes,
hotel, house 6 biggin, bottle, fabric 7
edifice, factory 8 dwelling 9 apartment,
structure 10 storehouse 11 edification
addition to: ell 4 apse, wing 5 annex 6
lean-to
dilapidated: 7 rookery 8 firetrap, tenement
exhibition: 6 museum
farm: 4 barn, crib, shed, silo
gateway: 5 pylon
material: 4 iron, wood 5 brick, glass, steel
6 cement
medieval: 6 castle
part: ell 4 apse
projection: bay, ell 4 apse, wing 5 annex 6
dormer, lean-to 7 cornice
public: 5 edile 6 aedile, casino, church,
museum, temple 7 capitol, library, theater 10 auditorium
rib: 9 tierceron
round: 7 rotunda
sacred: 4 fane 6 church, mosque, temple 7
edicule 8 pantheon 9 cathedral
stately: 6 castle, palace 7 edifice, mansion
bulb: bud 4 blub, corm, knob, lamp, root,
seed 5 globe, onion, swell, tuber 6 bulbus, crocus 9 expansion 12 protuberance
edible: yam 4 sego 5 onion 6 garlic, potato
segment: 5 clove
bulbous: 5 round 7 swollen
bulbul: 4 bird, kala
Bulgaria: *capital:* 5 Sofia
city: 4 Ruse 5 Varna 6 Burgas, Pleven 7
Plovdiv
former kings: 5 Boris 6 Simeon 9 Ferdinand
monetary unit: lev 8 stotinka
mountain: 7 Balkans, Rhodope
peak: 6 Musala
province: 5 Vidin 6 Lovech, Pernik, Shumen, Sliven, Vratsa, Yambol 7 Gagrovo, Razgrad, Smolyan
river: 5 Mesta 6 Danube, Struma 7 Maritsa
weight: oka, oke 5 tovar
bulge: bag, bug, jut 4 bump, cask, hump,
knob, lump 5 belly, bilge, bloat, bouge,
flask, pouch, swell 6 billow, cockle, di-

late, extend, pucker, wallet 7 blister,
distend 8 protrude, swelling 9 convexity, gibbosity 10 projection 11 indentation 12 protuberance
bulging: 4 full 5 bombe, bowed, pudgy 6
convex 7 gibbous 8 bouffant
bulk: 4 body, heap, hold, hulk, hull, lump,
mass, pile, size 5 cargo, gross, might,
power, stall, swell 6 expand, extent, figure, volume 7 bigness 8 majority, quantity 9 aggregate, dimension, largeness,
magnitude 11 massiveness
bulkhead: 5 check 7 battery 9 partition,
structure
bulky: big 5 burly, gross, large, stout 6
clumsy, stody 7 hulking, massive,
weighty 8 unwieldy 9 corpulent, policeman, ponderous
bull: cop 4 apis, jest, male, seal, slip,
toro(Sp.), zebu 5 bobby, boner, drink,
edict, error 6 bovine, letter, peeler,
taurus(L.) 8 cajolery, document, flattery, nonsense 9 detective, policeman,
quadruped 10 zapaterito(Sp.)
angry: 5 gorer
castrated: 4 stot 5 steer 7 bullock
half man: 8 minotaur
hornless: 5 doddy 6 doddie
pert. to: 7 taurine
young: 4 stot(Sc.) 5 stirk 7 bullock
bull-like: taurine
Bull Run: *battle:* 8 Manassas
hero: Lee
bull session: 4 talk 7 rapping 10 discussion
bulla: 4 bleb, case, seal 5 blain 7 vesicle
bullate: 8 puckered
bulldoze: cow, dig, ram 5 bully, force,
push, scoop 6 coerce, menace, pistol 8
browbeat, restrain, threaten 10 intimidate
bulldozer: 5 bully 6 grader 7 machine
bullet: 4 ball, lead, shot, slug 5 hurry 6
pellet, sinker, tracer 7 missile
diameter: 7 caliber
fake: 6 pellet
bulletin: 4 memo 6 notice, poster, report
7 program 9 statement 11 publication
12 announcement
bullfight cheer: ole
bullfighter: 6 torero 7 matador, picador
8 capeador, matadore, toreador
foot: 6 torero
mounted: 8 toreador
bullfinch: alp, olp 4 monk, nope, olph,
pope 5 hedge
bullheaded: 6 stupid 8 stubborn 9 obstinate 10 headstrong
bullion: bar 5 ingot, metal 6 billot
bullock: 4 stot 5 bugle, steer, stirk 6 bovine 9 quadruped
bull's eye: 6 target

bully: 4 boat, boss, fine, good, huff, mate, punk 5 brave, bravo, great, tough 6 bounce, harass, hector, jovial, menace, tyrant 7 bluster, bouncer, bullock, darling, dashing, gallant, gauster, huffcap, roister, ruffian 8 bangster, barrater, barrator, browbeat, bulldoze, domineer, frampler, harasser 9 blusterer, bulldozer, companion, excellent, scrimmage 10 burgullian, intimidate, sweetheart

bulrush: 4 reed, rush, tule 5 sedge 6 bumble 7 cattail, papyrus, scirpus

bulwark: 4 bail, fort, wall 5 fence, mound 6 defend, shield 7 bastion, defence, defense, parapet, protect, rampart 10 breakwater, stronghold 12 propugnacula(L.pl.) 13 propugnaculum(L.)

bum: beg, din 4 hobo, idle 5 drink, drone, idler, mooch, tramp 6 frolic, guzzle, sponge 7 guzzler 8 vagaband

bumble: bee 4 veil 5 botch, drone, idler 6 beadle, bungle, jumble, muffle 7 bittern, blunder, bramble, bulrush, bungler

bummer: 4 flop 7 bad trip, washout 12 bad situation

bump: hit, jar 4 bang, blow, bust, jolt, lump, oust, thud, whop 5 bulge, clash, knock, thump 6 bounce, demote, nodule, strike 7 collide, pothole, replace 8 swelling 9 downgrade, hip thrust 12 protuberance

bump into: 4 meet 7 collide 8 come upon 9 encounter, run across, sideswipe

bump off: 4 do in, kill 6 murder, rub out 7 put away 9 liquidate

bumper: 4 fine 5 glass, large, guard 6 buffer, fender, goblet 8 carangid, doorstop 10 successful

bumpkin: oak, yap 4 clod, gawk, hick, lout, rube 5 churl, yahoo, yokel 6 lummox, rustic 7 hayseed 9 chawbacon

bumptious: 5 cocky 8 insolent 9 obtrusive

Bumppo, Natty: *alias:* 7 Hawkeye 10 Deerslayer, Pathfinder
companion: 12 Chingachgook
novels: 20 Leatherstocking Tales
writer: 6 Cooper

bumpy: 5 rough 6 uneven 7 jolting

bun: jag: 4 buzz, roll 7 biscuit, chignon 8 hair knot

bunch: lot, set 4 body, crew, herd, lump, pack, tuft 5 batch, clump, crowd, flock, group 6 bundle, circle 7 cluster 8 assemble, quantity, swelling 9 aggregate 10 collection

bunco: con, gyp 5 cheat, trick 7 defraud, swindle

bund: 4 band 6 league 7 society 10 embankment, federation 11 confederacy

bundle: lot, pot, wad 4 band, hank, pack, pile, roll 5 bunch, group 6 bindle, packet, parcel, wrap up 7 package 10 collection

bundle of: *arrows:* 5 sheaf 6 quiver
grain: 5 sheaf, shock
hay: 4 bale
sticks: 5 fagot 6 faggot 7 fascine
straw: 4 bolt

bung: 4 cork, plug 5 spile 7 stopper, stopple, tampion

bungle: err 4 flub, goof, muff 5 botch, fluff, gum up, spoil 6 boggle, bumble, foozle, fumble, mess up 7 blunder, louse up 9 mismanage 10 pull a boner

bungling: 6 clumsy 7 awkward 8 slipshod 9 maladroit, unskilled 10 blundering

bunk: bed, cot 5 berth, hokum, hooey, lodge, put up, sleep 6 billet, trough 7 baloney, twaddle 8 log truck, nonsense

bunker: bin 4 crib, hold 6 dugout, hazard 7 shelter 8 obstacle, sandtrap 10 difficulty 11 compartment

bunkum: rot 4 jazz 6 drivel, humbug 7 hogwash 8 buncombe 9 poppycock 10 balderdash, doubletalk

bunt: tap 4 butt, push 5 shove 6 strike 8 sail part 9 wheat smut, spearhead

bunting: 4 bird, flag, pape 5 finch 6 fabric, towhee 7 cowbird, garment, ortolan 8 bobolink

buoy: dan 5 elate, float, raise 6 hold up, marker, signal 7 support, sustain 8 deadhead
mooring: 7 dolphin

buoyant: gay 5 happy, light, on air 6 blithe, lively 7 elastic, hopeful, lilting, springy 8 animated, cheerful, floating, sanguine, spirited, volatile 9 resilient, vivacious 12 lighthearted

burble: yak 4 boil, gush 5 run on 6 bubble, gurgle, jabber 7 chatter, prattle

burbot: 4 fish, ling 6 lawyer 7 ellpout
genus: 4 lota
relative: cod

burden: tax, vex 4 birn(Sc.), care, cark, clog, duty, load, onus, 5 cargo, theme, worry 6 charge, hamper, impose, lading, saddle, weight 7 afflict, ballast, freight, oppress, refrain, trouble 8 capacity, encumber, handicap, overhead 9 aggravate, grievance 10 imposition 14 responsibility
of complaint: 8 gravamen

burden bearer: 5 Atlas 9 worry wart

burdensome: 5 heavy 7 arduous, irksome, onerous, weighty 8 cumbrous, grievous, grinding 9 demanding, difficult 10 oppressive 11 importunate, troublesome

bureau: 4 desk 5 chest 6 agency, office 7 dresser 10 chiffonier, department, escritoire

bureaucrat: 8 stickler 12 civil servant 13 petty official

bureaucratese: 4 cant 6 jargon 12 gobbledygook

burg: 4 city, town 6 hamlet 7 village 8
hick town 11 whistle-stop

burgeon: bud 4 grow 5 bloom 6 expand,
flower, sprout 7 shoot up 8 increase,
put forth

burglar: 4 yegg 5 crook, thief 6 cat man,
robber 8 peterman

burglary: 5 caper, heist, theft 7 break-in,
larceny, robbery 8 stealage

burgomaster: 4 gull 5 mayor 7 alcalde
10 magistrate

burgoo: 4 soup, stew 5 gruel 6 picnic 8
porridge

burial: 9 interment 10 deposition
case: box, urn 6 casket, coffin
ceremony: 7 funeral
litter: 4 bier
mound: low 6 barrow 7 tumulus
pile: 4 pyre
place: 4 tomb 5 grave 7 pyramid 8 catacomb, cemetery, golgotha 9 graveyard,
mausoleum, sepulcher 10 necropolis 12
potter's field

burin: 4 tool 6 graver

burl: 4 knot, lump 5 bulge 6 growth, veneer 11 excrescence
in mahogany: roe

burlap: 5 gunny 6 fabric 7 bagging, sacking 8 wrapping
fiber: 4 hemp, jute

burlesque: ape 4 mock, mime 5 farce,
mimic, revue 6 comedy, overdo, parody,
satire 7 ham it up, lampoon, overact,
takeoff 8 ridicule, travesty 9 slapstick
10 caricature, exaggerate comedian 9
top banana
serenade: 8 shivaree 9 charivari

burly: big 5 beefy, bulky, heavy, hefty,
husky 6 brawny, hearty, stocky, sturdy
8 muscular, thickset 9 strapping

Burma: *bay:* 6 Bengal 7 Hunter's 10
Combermere
canopy: 7 tauzaung
capital: 7 Rangoon
city: 4 Paan, Pegu 5 Falam, Manle,
Prome 6 Lashio, Loikaw, Sittwe 7 Bas-
sein, Henzada 8 Mandalay, Moulmein
coin: pya 4 kyat
dagger: dah, dao, dow 4 dout
deer: 6 thamin 7 thameng
demon: nat
district: 7 Toungoo
division: 4 Chin, Pegu 5 Magwe 6 Arakan 7 Rangoon, Sagaing 8 Mandalay 9
Irrawaddy 10 Tenasserim
garment: 6 tamein
gate: 5 toran
gibbon: lar
girl: 4 mima
gulf: 8 Martaban

hill dweller: Lai
language: Lai 4 Chin, Pegu 6 Kachin
measure: dha, lan, tha 4 byee, dain, seit,
taim, teng 6 palgat
musical instrument: 4 turr 5 tarau
official: wun 4 woon 6 sawbwa
peak: 4 Popa 8 Victoria
people: Lai, Mon, Tai 4 Chin, Kadu,
Naga, Shan 5 Karen, Lhota 6 Kachin,
Khamti, Peguan 7 Karenni 8 Ching-
paw
range: 4 Pegu 5 Dawna 6 Arakan
river: Uyu 4 Mali, Nmai, Pegu 6 Salwin,
Shweli 7 Kaladan, Myitnge, Salween,
Sittang 8 Chindwin 9 Irrawaddy
robber: 6 dacoit
ruined city: Ava
sash: 7 tubbeck
sea: 7 Andaman
states: 4 Shan 5 Kayah 6 Kachin 8
Kawthule
traveler's shed: 5 zayat
tree: 4 acle 7 yamanai
weight: mat, moo, vis 4 kait, ruay, viss 5
candy, tical, ticul

burn: 4 brew, char, fire, plot, raze, rill,
sear, sere 5 adust, anger, blaze, broil,
brook, cense, flame, parch, scald, singe,
waste, water 6 scorch, stream, tingle 7
combure, combust, consume, cremate,
flicker, oxidize, rivulet, smolder 8
squander 9 cauterize 10 incinerate
midnight oil: 6 stay up 9 lucubrate
surface: 5 singe 6 scorch 7 blister

burn up the road: 5 speed

burned: 5 baked 6 seared 7 charred 8 us-
tulate

burner: 6 Bunsen, censer 8 thurible

burning: hot 4 fire 5 afire, angry, blaze,
calid, eager, fiery, flame, gledy 6 ablaze,
ardent, fervid, torrid, urgent 7 caustic,
cautery, fervent, flaming, glaring, glowing, mordant, shining 8 ardurous, exciting, inustion 9 consuming, cremating,
inflaming 10 combustion, phlogistic 13
conflagration
bush: 5 wahoo
malicious: 5 arson
mountain: 7 volcano
taste: 5 acrid

burnish: rub 4 buff 5 glaze, gloss, shine 6
luster, patina, polish 7 furbish

burnisher: 4 tool 5 agate 6 buffer 7 frot-
tom 8 polisher

burnoose, burnous: 5 cloak 7 garment 8
albornoz

burnsides: 5 beard 8 whiskers

burnt work: 10 pyrography

burr: nut, pad, rib 4 barb, birr, boss,
buzz, halo, knob, ring, whir 5 briar,
whirr 6 banyan, circle, corona, tunnel,
washer 7 sticker 8 parasite 9 whet-

stone **10** sweetbread

burro: ass **6** donkey **9** quadruped **10** pack animal

burrow: den, dig **4** heap, hole, mine, mole, root, tube **5** berry, couch, mound **6** furrow, tunnel **7** passage, shelter **8** excavate

bursa: sac **4** hall, sack **5** pouch **6** cavity **9** residence

bursar: 6 purser, terrar **7** cashier **9** paymaster, treasurer **10** controller

burst: pop **4** blow, bust, loss, rend, scat **5** blast, break, erupt, flash, go off, salvo, split **6** broken, damage, injury, volley **7** explode, flare up, rupture, shatter **8** outbreak, sundered **9** interrupt

  forth: **5** erupt, sally **9** blasted
  inward: **7** implode
  out: **5** blurt **7** exclaim **9** ejaculate

bursting: 8 erupting **10** dehiscence

Burundi: *capital:* **9** Bujumbura
  ethnic group: Twa **4** Hutu **5** Tutsi
  lake: **10** Tanganyika
  monetary unit: **5** franc **7** centime
  town: **5** Ngozi **6** Gitega, Ruyigi

bury: 4 hide, sink **5** inter, inurn **6** cover, entomb, inhume, shroud **7** conceal, engross, immerse, repress, secrete **8** inundate, submerge **9** overwhelm, stash away

bus: 6 jitney **7** vehicle **9** charabanc

busby: cap, wig **6** fur hat **8** bearskin **9** headdress

bush: tod **4** buss, butt **5** bosch, clump, grove, shrub **6** branch, tavern **7** boscage, cluster, thicket **11** advertising

bushed: 4 worn **5** spent **8** dog-tired **9** exhausted

bushel: foo(Sc.), gob, lot **4** full
  quarter of: **4** peck
  forty: wey

bushing: 5 drill **6** collet, lining **7** padding
  machine: **6** sleeve

bush-league: 6 non-pro **7** amateur **8** inferior **10** second-rate

bushman: san(pl.) **4** gung, saan(pl.) **5** bushy **6** Abatoa, Abatua, Abatwa, rustic **8** woodsman
  blanket: **5** bluey

bushmaster: 5 snake, viper

bushwa: 4 bosh, bull, bunk **5** hooey, trash **7** baloney, hogwash, rubbish **8** nonsense

bushwacker: 5 papaw **6** pawpaw, scythe, sniper **8** guerilla

bushy: 5 bosky **6** dumose, dumous **7** bushman, queachy
  hair: **4** shag
  heap: tod

business: ado, art, job **4** care, firm, fuss, game, line, task, work **5** cause, trade **6** affair, custom, matter, metier, office **7** calling, concern, trading, traffic **8** activity, commerce, industry, vocation **9** diligence, following, patronage, rickmatic **10** employment, enterprise, occupation, solicitude **11** disturbance, importunity, intercourse, transaction **13** attentiveness, establishment
  custom: **9** patronage
  memorandum: **4** note **7** agendum
  place of: **4** mart, shop **5** store **6** market, office, shoppe **8** emporium

businessman: 9 executive
  powerful: **6** tycoon

buskin: 4 boot, shoe **7** bottine, tragedy **8** cothurni(L.pl.), half-boot, stocking **9** brodequin, cothurnus(L.)

buss: 4 boat, bush, calf, deck, kiss **5** dress, smack **6** vessel **9** transport

bussu: 4 palm **7** troolie

bust: 4 fail, raid, ruin, tame **5** bosom, break, burst, chest, flunk, lemon, loser, spree **6** arrest, bronze, demote, reduce, statue **7** degrade, dismiss, failure **8** bankrupt **9** blockhead, sculpture **10** depression

bust-up: 5 party, split **7** failure **8** collapse **11** dissolution

bustard: 4 bird, kori **5** crane, paauw **7** bebilya, houbara **8** gompaaum
  genus: **4** otis **6** otidae

buster: 4 crab, wind **5** blade, child **6** fellow

bustle: ado **4** fuss, stir, todo, whir **5** frisk, haste, whirr **6** clamor, fistle, flurry, hubbub, hustle, pother, racket, tumult, unrest, uproar **7** clatter, turmoil **8** activity, tournure **9** agitation, commotion, whirlwind **10** hurly-burly
  woman's: **6** bishop

busy: 4 nosy **5** brisk **6** active, at work, intent, lively, occupy **7** engaged, humming, on the go, operose **8** diligent, employed, occupied, sedulous, tireless, untiring **9** assiduous, attentive, detective, laborious, officious **11** distracting, industrious **13** indefatigable

busybody: 5 snoop, yenta(Yid.) **6** gossip **7** marplot, meddler, snooper **8** factotum, quidnunc **10** pragmatist, rubberneck

but: sed(L.), yet **4** mere, only, save **5** still **6** except, unless **7** besides, howbeit, however **11** nonetheless **12** nevertheless

butcher: 4 kill, slay **5** botch, spoil **6** bungle, murder **8** mutilate **9** slaughter **10** meat vendor **11** executioner
  hook: **7** gambrel
  rabbi: **8** shochtim
  tool: saw **5** knife, steel **7** cleaver

butcher-bird: 6 shrike

butchery: 6 murder **7** carnage **8** abattoir,

massacre, shambles **9** bloodbath, slaughter

butler: 7 servant, spencer, steward **8** factotum, retainer **9** major-domo **10** man-servant

butt: end, jut, pit, ram, tun **4** buck, bunt, cart, cask, fool, goad, goat, jolt, push, rump, stub **5** hinge, joint, mound, stump **6** adjoin, breech, target, thrust **7** fall guy, project **8** derriere, flatfish, flounder **13** laughing stock

cigar or cigarette: **5** snipe

in: **6** meddle **7** intrude **9** interfere, interrupt, intervene

butte: 4 hill **7** picacho **8** mountain

butter: fat, oil **4** food **6** beurre(F.), cajole, spread **7** blarney, flatter

artificial: **4** oleo **9** butterine, margarine **13** oleomargarine

serving of: pat

pert. to: **7** butyric

semifluid: ghi **4** ghee

shea: **5** galam **6** bambui, bambuk **7** bambara

tree: **4** shea **5** fulwa **8** phulwara

tub: **6** firkin

without solids: **5** drawn **9** clarified

butter-and-eggs: 6 clover **7** ransted **8** ramstead, ranstead, toadflax

butterball: 6 chubby **8** roly-poly

buttercup: 6 flower **7** anemone **8** crowfoot, reindeer **10** butter-rose

fruit: **6** achene

butterfingered: 6 clumsy **7** awkward **9** all-thumbs

butterfish: 5 coney **6** blenny, gunnel

butterfly: 4 kiho **5** satyr **6** idalia, morpho, ursula **7** admiral, buckeye, monarch, skipper, vanessa, viceroy **8** arthemis, cecropia, grayling **9** aphrodite, underwing **10** fritillary, lepidopter, swim stroke

expert: **13** lepidopterist

fish: **6** blenny, chiton **7** gurnard

genus: **8** melitaea **10** heliconius

larva: **11** caterpillar

lily: **4** sego **8** mariposa

butterwort: 9 steepweed

buttery: 6 larder, pantry, spence **9** storeroom, wheedling **10** flattering

button: bud: 4 boss, chin, hook, knob, knop **5** badge, catch, pearl **6** bauble, buckle **8** fastener, lapel pin

ornamental: **4** stud

part: **4** hole **5** shank

three jewel: **6** troche

button-down: 6 proper, square **8** orthodox, straight **10** unoriginal **12** conservative, conventional

buttonhole: 4 loop, slit **6** accost, detain, eyelet **11** boutonniere, get the ear of

buttress: 4 pier, pile, prop, stay **5** brace **7** support **8** abutment **11** counterfort

buxom: 5 busty, hefty, jolly, plump, prone, sonsy **6** bosomy, florid, sonsie **7** shapely **8** bouncing **10** curvaceous **11** full-figured

buy: 4 chap, coff(Sc.), coup, gain, shop **5** bribe, trade **6** market, ransom, redeem, secure **7** acquire **8** purchase

back: **6** redeem

cheaply: **5** steal **7** bargain

to sell at a profit: **7** regrate

buyer: 5 agent **6** client, patron **7** shopper **8** customer, prospect **9** purchaser

beware: **12** caveat emptor

stolen property: **5** fence

buzz: hum **4** burr, call, hiss, ring, whir **5** fancy, fling, phone, rumor **6** notion **7** whisper **9** bombinate, telephone

buzzard: 4 aura, hawk, **5** buteo, harpy **6** condor, curlew **7** vulture **9** senseless

bald: **6** osprey

honey: **4** pern

buzzer: bee **4** bell **5** alarm, badge **6** signal

buzz off: 5 leave **6** depart, pull out

by: ago, per, via **4** near, past **5** apart, aside, close **6** beside, nearby, next to, toward **7** besides, through **9** alongside **10** concerning **11** according to

and by: **4** anon, soon **5** later **7** shortly

means of: per **4** from, with **7** through

mouth: **4** oral

bypass: 4 miss, shun **5** evade, shunt, skirt **6** detour **7** circuit **8** sidestep

bygone: 4 past, yore **5** olden **6** former **7** ancient, elapsed **8** backward, departed

byname: 6 byword **7** surname **8** cognomen, nickname **9** sobriquet

bypath: 4 lane **5** byway

Byron character: 4 Inez, Lara **6** Haidee **7** Don Juan

bystander: 7 witness **9** spectator

byway: 4 lane, path **5** alley

byword: saw **5** axiom, motto **6** byname, phrase, saying **7** epithet, proverb **8** nickname **9** catchword

Byzantine: 6 tricky **7** devious **8** involved **9** intricate

C

C: **7** hundred
Caaba: **6** shrine
caama: fox **4** asse **10** hartebeest
cab: **4** hack, taxi **6** hansom
cab driver: **5** cabby **6** cabbie, cocher(F.) **7** cochero(Sp.)
cabal: **4** camp, plot, ring **5** junta, party **6** brigue, circle, clique, scheme **7** coterie, council, faction, in group **8** intrigue **10** conspiracy **11** machination
  pert. to: **9** factional
cabalistic: **6** mystic **10** mysterious
caballero: **6** escort, knight **8** cavalier, horseman **9** gentleman
cabana: **7** shelter **9** bathhouse
cabaret: **4** cafe **6** tavern **8** late spot **9** nightclub **10** restaurant, supper club
cabbage: **4** chou, crib, kale **5** filch, steal **6** pilfer, **7** bowkail(Sc.), purloin **8** borecole, colewort
  daisy: **11** globeflower
  salad: **4** slaw **8** coleslaw
  seed: **5** colza
  soup: **4** kale(Sc.) **7** borscht
  tree: **7** angelin **8** palmetto
  variety: **4** cale, kale **5** colza, savoy **8** colewort, kohlrabi
cabbagehead: **5** dunce **9** screwball
cabbageworm: **6** looper **7** cutworm
cabin: cot, den, hut **4** shed **5** booth, coach, hovel, lodge, shack **6** shanty **7** cottage **9** stateroom
cabin boy: **7** grummet
cabin car: **7** caboose
cabinet: box **4** case **5** habut, board, chest **6** bureau, closet, vanity **7** almirah (Ind.), armoire, commode, console, council, etagere, whatnot **8** cellaret, cupboard, ministry **10** chiffonier
cable: **4** boom, link, rope, wire **5** chain **6** stitch **8** telegram
  lifter: **7** wildcat
  post: **4** bitt
cable car: **4** tram **6** telfer **7** telpher
Cable TV: **13** shared antenna
cabochon: gem **5** stone **8** ornament **10** style of cut
caboodle: kit, lot **10** collection
caboose: cab, car **5** buggy **6** galley
cabotin: **5** actor **9** charlatan
cabotinage: **7** emoting **9** ham acting, theatrics

cabrilla: **4** bass **7** grouper
cacao: **4** bean, seed, tree **5** broma, cocoa **6** arriba **9** chocolate
cache: **4** bury, hide **5** store **7** conceal, secrete **8** treasure **10** storehouse, hiding place
cachepot: jar, urn **7** planter
cachet: **4** seal **5** stamp, wafer **6** status **8** prestige **11** distinction
cachexia: **7** illness, wasting **9** morbidity **2** malnutrition
cacholong: **4** opal
cackle: gab, jaw **4** blab, chat **5** clack, laugh **6** babble, gabble, giggle, gossip, titter **7** chackle, chatter, prattle, twaddle **8** laughter
cacoethes: **4** itch, mania **6** desire
cacography: **11** misspelling
  opposite: **11** orthography
cacophonous: **5** harsh **7** raucous **8** jangling, strident **9** dissonant **10** discordant **11** unmelodious
cactus: **4** bleo **5** dildo, nopal, plant **6** cereus, chaute, chende, cholla, mescal **7** airampo, opuntia, saguaro **8** chichipe **11** prickly pear
  drug: **6** peyote
  fruit: **6** cochal
  plantation: **7** nopalry
cad: cur **4** boor, heel **5** churl, creep **6** rascal, rotter **7** bounder, dastard **9** scoundrel
cadaver: **4** body **5** stiff **6** corpse **7** carcass **8** skeleton
cadaverous: **4** pale **5** gaunt **6** wasted **7** ghastly, haggard **9** emaciated
caddow: **5** quilt **7** jackdaw **8** coverlet
caddy: box, boy, can **4** case **5** chest **9** container
cade: keg, pet **4** cask, lamb **6** barrel, coddle **7** indulge, juniper
cadence: **4** beat, lilt, pace, tone **5** meter, metre, pulse, sound, swing, throb **6** rhythm **8** clausula **10** inflection, modulation
cadet: **5** plebe, youth **6** embryo, junior **7** student **10** midshipman **11** West Pointer
cadew: **4** worm
cadge: beg, bum **4** bind, hawk **5** carry, mooch **6** peddle, sponge **8** scrounge **9** panhandle

Cadmus: *daughter:* Ino **5** Agave **6** Semele **7** Autonoe
father: **6** Agenor
sister: **6** Europa
wife: **8** Harmonia
cadre: 4 cell, core, unit **5** frame, group **6** scheme, nucleus **9** framework
caduceus: 4 wand **5** staff **6** emblem, symbol **7** insigne, scepter, sceptre
caducity: 5 lapse **8** senility **10** feebleness **14** perishableness
Caesar: 6 tyrant **7** emperor
assassin: **6** Brutus **7** Cassius
capital: **4** Roma
colleague: **7** Bibulus
country conquered by: **4** Gaul
eulogist: **6** Antony
fatal day: **4** Ides
message: **12** veni, vidi, vici
place of victory: **6** Actium
river crossed by: **7** Rubicon
sister: **4** Atia
site of famous message: **4** Zela
wife: **7** Pompeia **8** Cornelia **9** Calpurnia
caesura: 4 rest, stop **5** pause **8** interval **10** verse break **12** interruption
cafard: 5 blues **6** apathy **7** boredom **10** depression **12** listlessness
cafe: 5 diner **6** saloon **7** barroom, cabaret **8** teahouse **9** nightclub **10** restaurant **11** coffeehouse
caffeine: 5 thein **6** theine **8** alkaloid **9** stimulant
cage: box, car, mew, pen **4** coop, jail **5** brake **6** aviary, basket, bucket, chapel, prison, shut in **7** chantry, confine **8** imprison, scaffold, strainer **9** enclosure, inclosure **11** incarcerate
cage hawk: mew **5** meute
cagey, cagy: sly **4** foxy, wily, wary **6** astute, shrewd **7** cunning
cahoots: 6 league **9** collusion **11** partnership
caiman: 6 jacare **9** crocodile
Cain: 8 murderer **10** fratricide
brother: Pur **4** Abel, Seth
descendant: **6** Lamech
father: **4** Adam
killer of: **4** Abel
land: Nod
mother: Eve
nephew: **4** Enos
son: **5** Enoch
Caine Mutiny: *author:* **4** Wouk (Herman)
character: **5** Queeg
ship: **11** mine sweeper
cairn: 8 landmark, monument **9** stone heap **11** trail marker
cairngorm: 6 quartz
caisson: box **5** chest, float, wagon **7** chamber, pontoon
disease: **5** bends

caitiff: 4 base, mean, vile **6** wicked **8** cowardly **10** despicable
cajole: con **4** coax **5** jolly, tease **6** entice, whilly(Sc.) **7** beguile, flatter, wheedle **8** blandish, butter up **9** sweet talk
cake: bar, bun set **4** lump, mass **5** block, crust, patty, wedge **6** harden, nacket(Sc.), pastry **7** bannock **8** solidify **9** coagulate
almond: **8** macaroon
boiled in honey: **8** teiglech
coffee: **6** kuchen
corn: **4** pone **7** fritter **8** tortilla
custard: **6** eclair **9** creampuff
dough: **6** batter
fat free: **9** angel food
filled: **4** flan **9** enchilada
fried: **7** cruller **8** doughnut
griddle: **7** bannock(Sc.), crumpet, hotcake, oatcake, pancake
plum: **4** baba
rich: **5** torte **7** stollen **8** madeline **9** madeleine
sacrificial: **6** hallah
seed: wig **4** wiff
small: bun **4** tart **6** cookie, muffin **7** cupcake
tea: **5** scone
thin: **5** scone, wafer
topping: **5** icing **8** frosting
unleavened: **5** matzo **6** damper **8** tortilla
cakewalk: 5 dance, march, strut **6** prance
calaba: 4 tree **5** birma
calabash: 5 gourd **6** curuba
calaboose: jug **4** brig, gaol, jail **5** clink **6** cooler, lockup, prison **8** hoosegow
caladium: 4 taro
calamanco: 6 fabric **7** garment
calamitous: sad **4** dire, evil **5** black, fatal **6** bitter, dismal, tragic, woeful **7** adverse, baleful, direful, hapless, ruinous, unhappy, unlucky **8** grievous, wretched **9** miserable **10** afflictive, deplorable, disastrous **11** distressful, unfortunate
calami: pen **5** quill **9** sweetflag
calamity: 4 blow, evil, ruin **5** storm **6** misery, sorrow **7** scourge, tragedy **8** accident, disaster, fatality **9** adversity, cataclysm **10** affliction, misfortune **11** catastrophe **12** misadventure, wretchedness
calangay: 8 cockatoo
calash: 6 calesa **8** carriage **10** woman's hood **11** Asian Seaman
calcar: 4 oven, spur **7** furnace
calced: 4 shod
calcite: *animal:* **8** skeleton
deposit: **4** spar, tufa **5** tatar **10** stalactite, stalagmite
soil with: **4** marl
calcium: *carbonate:* **4** tufa
oxide: **9** quicklime

sulfate: 6 gypsum 14 plaster of paris

calculate: aim 4 plan, rate, tell 5 count, think 6 assess, expect, figure, number, reckon 7 average, compute, prepare 8 consider, estimate, evaluate 9 determine, enumerate

calculation: 4 care 7 caution 8 forecast, prudence 9 deduction, logistics, reckoning 10 adjustment, estimation 11 computation

calculating: sly 4 wily 6 crafty, shrewd 7 cunning, guarded 8 cautious, scheming

calculator: 5 table 6 abacus 7 soroban 8 computer 10 accountant

Calder: 6 artist

work: 7 mobiles

caldron, cauldron: pot, vat 6 boiler, kettle, vessel 8 red color

Caleb's son: Hur, Iru

Caledonia: 8 Scotland

calefy: 4 heat, warm

calembour: pun

calendar: log 4 card 5 diary, slate 6 agenda, docket 7 almanac, journal, program 8 menology, register, schedule

church: 4 ordo

former: 6 Julian

French revolution: 6 Nivose 7 Floreal, Ventose 8 Brumaire, Fervidor, Gernubak, Messidor, Pluviose, Prairial 9 Fructidor, Thermidor 11 Vendemiaire

modern: 9 Gregorian,

calenture: 4 fire, glow, zeal 5 ardor, fever 7 passion 9 sunstroke

calf: boy, leg 4 dolt 5 bobby, bossy, youth 6 bovine, muscle 7 fatling

flesh: 4 veal, veau(F.)

hide: kip

motherless: 4 dogy 5 dogie

muscle: 9 plantaris

pert. to: 5 sural

unbranded: 8 maverick

Caliban: 5 beast, slave

adversary of: 8 Prospero

deity of: 7 Setebos

witch mother: 7 Sycorax

caliber: 4 bore, rank 5 class, worth, value 6 degree, talent 7 ability, breadth, compass, quality, stature 8 capacity, diameter

calibrate: 5 grade 7 measure 11 standardize

calico: 4 girl 5 cloth, woman 7 spotted 8 goldfish 9 womankind 12 multicolored

bass: 7 crappie

horse: 5 pinto 7 piebald

California: *capital:* 10 Sacramento

city: 7 Oakland, San Jose 8 San Diego 9 Long Beach 10 Los Angeles 12 San Francisco

county: 4 Napa 5 Butte, Glenn, Kings 6 Merced, Orange, Shasta, Sierra 7 Alameda 8 Del Norte, Monterey 9 Riverside, San Joaquin 10 Sacramento, Santa Clara 13 San Bernardino, San Luis Obispo

desert: 6 Mojave 8 Colorado

fault zone: 10 San Andreas

Indian tribe: 4 Hupa, Pomo, Seri, Juma 5 Hoopa, Yorok

lake: 5 Owens, Tahoe 6 Salton

motto: 6 Eureka

mountain peak: 6 Lassen, Shasta

national park: 8 Yosemite

nickname: 11 Golden State

observatory: 4 Lick 7 Palomar 8 Mt. Wilson

pass: 6 Donner, Sonora

peninsula: 8 Monterey

prison: 8 Alcatraz

state animal: 11 grizzly bear

state bird: 11 valley quail

state fish: 5 trout

state flower: 11 golden poppy

state tree: 9 butterfly

river: Eel, Mad, Pit 4 Kern 5 Kings, Smith 6 Merced, Salmon 7 Feather, Klamath, Russian, Salinas, Trinity 10 Sacramento, San Jacinto, Stanislaus

shrub: 5 salal 7 chamise, chamiso, tarbush 9 chaparral, manzanita

town: 4 Asti, Napa 5 Tracy 6 Arcata, Eureka, Fresno 7 Alameda, Arcadia, Salinas

tree: 6 torrey 7 redwood, sequoia 12 Wellingtonia

valley: 4 Napa

wine area: 4 Napa

caliginous: dim 4 dark 5 murky 7 obscure

Caligula's horse: 9 Incitatus

caliph, calif: Abu, Ali 4 Bekr, Imam, Omar 6 Othman 9 caliphate

descendant: 5 Alide 7 Fatamid 8 Fatamite

fourth: Ali

calix: cup 7 chalice

calk, caulk: nap 6 fill in 7 occlude 9 shoe plate, stop leaks 14 make water-tight

calking: 5 oakum

call: bid, cry, dub 4 cite, dial, hail, name, page, stop, term, yell 5 claim, clepe, clock, elect, phone, rouse, shout, style, utter, visit, waken, yodel, yodle 6 accuse, appeal, arouse, demand, invite, invoke, muster, quethe, summon 7 address, appoint, collect, command, convene, convoke, entitle, impeach 8 announce, assemble, nominate, proclaim, vocation 9 challenge, reprimand, telephone, terminate 10 denominate

back: 6 revoke 8 retrieve 10 phone again 11 ask to return

distress: S.O.S.

down: **5** scold **6** berate, invoke, rebuke **7** censure, reprove **8** denounce, execrate **9** reprimand

for: **4** page **5** exact **6** demand **7** predict, request, require

forth: **5** evoke **6** arouse, elicit, invoke, signal, summon **7** evocate

off: end **4** kill **5** count **6** cancel

on: ask, bid **4** urge **5** visit **6** drop in **8** appeal to

out: **5** ascry, shout **6** holler, muster **11** give voice to

to: **4** hail **5** ascry **6** accost, halloo **7** address

to attention: hop **6** remind

to mind: **4** cite **6** recall **8** remember

together: **6** muster **7** convene, convoke

call-in: **9** radio show **12** phone protest

Call of the Wild author: **6** London

calligrapher: **6** penman, writer **7** copyist **9** engrosser

calling: art, job **4** rank **5** trade **6** career, metier, naming, outcry **7** pursuit, station, summons **8** business, function, position, shouting, vocation **9** condition, summoning, utterance **10** employment, invitation, occupation, profession **11** appellation, convocation, undertaking **13** circumstances

Calliope's son: **7** Orpheus

Callisto's son: **5** Arcas

callous: **4** hard **5** horny, tough **6** brawny, obtuse, torpid **8** obdurate **9** indurated, unfeeling **11** hardhearted, indifferent **4** pachydermatous

callow: raw **4** bald, bare **5** crude, green **6** marshy **7** meadown **8** immature, juvenile, unformed, youthful **9** unfledged **13** inexperienced **15** unsophisticated

calm: lee **4** cool, dill, easy, fair, hush, lull, mees(Sc.), mild, rest **5** abate, allay, charm, mease, peace, quell, quiet, sober, still, stoic **6** defuse, docile, gentle, irenic, pacify, placid, sedate, serene, smooth, soothe, steady **7** appease, assuage, halcyon, mollify, pacific, patient, placate, restful, unmoved **8** composed, decorous, peaceful, restrain, tranquil **9** collected, impassive, temperate, unexcited, unruffled **10** halcyonian, phlegmatic, unconfused **11** complacence, tranquilize, undisturbed **13** dispassionate, imperturbable **15** undemonstrative

calmness: **5** poise **6** repose **8** ataraxia, serenity **9** composure, placidity, quietness, sang-froid, stillness **10** equanimity **11** self-control, tranquility **12** peacefulness **13** impassiveness

calorie, calory: **5** therm **10** energy unit

calotte: **6** ice cap **7** glacier **8** skull cap **11** snowy summit

calumet: **4** pipe

calumniate: **4** slur **5** belie, libel, smear **6** accuse, attack, defame, malign, revile, vilify **7** asperse, blacken, slander, traduce **9** blaspheme

calyx: **4** leaf **5** sepal

helmet-shaped: **5** galea

of flower: **8** perianth

cam: cog **4** awry, lobe **5** askew, catch, wiper **6** tappet **7** crooked, trippet **8** perverse

camalig (P.I.): hut **5** cabin **10** storehouse

camaraderie: **7** jollity **9** good cheer **10** fellowship **11** sociability **12** friendliness

camarilla: **4** cell, ring **5** cabal, junta **6** clique

Cambodia: *capital:* **9** Phnom Penh

city: **6** Angkor, Kratie **8** Siem Reap **10** Battambang

ethnic group: **5** Khmer

gulf: **4** Siam

lake: **8** Tonle Sap

monetary unit: sen **4** riel

one-time rulers: **6** Lon Nol, Pol Pot **8** Sihanouk

port: **6** Kampot

river: **6** Mekong

temple: **9** Angkor Wat

Cambria: See **Wales**

cambric: **5** linen **7** batiste

Cambridge: *boat races:* **4** Lent

college official: **6** bedell

council: **5** caput

honor examination: **6** tripos

student: **5** sizar, spoon **6** optime

camel: **6** mehari **8** ruminant **9** dromedary

driver: **6** sarwan **8** cameleer

two-humped: **8** Bactrian

camellia: **8** japonica

camelopard: **7** giraffe

Camelot: *lord:* **6** Arthur

magician: **6** Merlin

camel's hair: aba **5** cloth **6** camlet **8** cameline

garment: aba

cameo: gem **7** carving, relievo, rilievo, phalera **8** anaglyph **9** sculpture

cutting tool: **5** spade

stone: **4** onyx **8** sardonyx

camera: **7** chamber **10** department, instrument

part: **4** lens **6** finder **7** bellows, shutter

platform: **5** dolly

cameraman: **8** camerist, operator **12** photographer **13** projectionist

Cameroon: *Capital:* **7** Yaounde

city: **4** Buea, Edea **5** Kribi **6** Douala

ethnic group: **5** Bantu **7** Hamitic

gulf: **6** Guinea

monetary unit: **5** franc **7** centime

port: **6** Douala **8** Victoria

river: **5** Nyong **6** Sanaga

camion: bus **4** dray **5** truck, wagon **7** motorbus

camlet: **6** Angora, fabric, mohair **9** camelteen, camletine

Camorra: **5** Mafia

camouflage: **4** fake, hide **6** muffle, screen **7** conceal **8** disguise **9** deception

camp: **4** pest, tent **5** etape(F.), horde, siege, tabor **7** barrack, bivouac, shelter **8** quarters **10** settlement

follower: **5** bidar(Ind.) **6** gudget(Sc.)

pert. to: **7** castral

provision seller: **6** sutler

campaign: **5** drive, plain **7** canvass, crusade, solicit **9** champaign, operation

campanero: **8** arapunga, bellbird

campanile: **5** tower **6** belfry **7** clocher, steeple

camphol: **7** borneol

camphor: **7** menthol, asarone

campus: **4** quad **5** field **7** grounds

campy: **5** outre **7** extreme **8** affected **11** exaggerated

Camus work: **5** Rebel **6** Plague **8** Caligula, Stranger **12** State of Siege

can: cup, jug, may, tin **4** able, fire, jail **5** caddy, could eshin, skill **6** vessel **7** ability, capable, dismiss **8** conserve, preserve **9** competent, container, discharge, knowledge **10** cleverness, receptacle

Canada: *capital:* **6** Ottawa

bay: **5** Fundy, James **6** Baffin, Hudson, Ungava

city: **5** Banff **6** London, Oshawa, Regina **7** Calgary, Halifax, Toronto, Windsor **8** Edmonton, Montreal, Victoria, Winnipeg **9** Carstairs, Saskatoon, Vancouver

early explorer: **5** Cabot **7** Cartier, Erikson

emblem: **9** maple leaf

island: **5** Banks **6** Baffin **8** Victoria **9** Vancouver **11** Southampton

lake: **6** Louise **8** Winnipeg **9** Great Bear **10** Great Slave

measure: ton **5** minot, perch, point **6** arpent **7** chainon

monetary unit: **4** cent **6** dollar

mountain: **7** Cascade, Rockies **10** Laurentian

native group: **5** Inuit (Eskimo), Metis **6** Indian

peninsula: **5** Foxe, Gaspe **6** Ungava **7** Boothia **8** Melville

province: **6** Quebec **7** Alberta, Ontario **8** Manitoba **10** Nova Scotia **12** New Brunswick, Newfoundland, Saskatchewan **15** British Columbia **18** Prince Edward Island (see also entry for province)

river: Red **5** Yukon **6** Nelson, Ottawa **8** Columbia **9** Mackenzie **10** St. Lawrence

territory: **5** Yukon **9** Northwest (see also entry for province)

U.S. border lake: **4** Erie **5** Huron **7** Ontario **8** Superior

Canadian: **6** Canuck

canadine: **8** alkaloid

canaille: mob **5** flour **6** rabble **7** rifraff

canal: cut **4** cano, duct, tube **5** ditch, drain, fossa(L.), graff, zanje **6** fossae(L.pl.), groove, strait, trench **7** acequia(Sp.), channel, conduit, raceway, towpath **8** aqueduct **10** waterspout **11** watercourse

dredging machine: **7** couloir

famous: Soo **4** Erie, Kiel, Suez **6** Morris, Panama **7** Welland

footpath: **7** towpath

Canal Zone: *city:* **6** Balboa

lake: **5** Gatun

canape: **6** relish **9** appetizer **11** hors d'oeuvre

canard: **4** hoax **9** grapewine **11** fabrication

canary: **4** bird, fink **5** dance **6** singer, snitch, stoolie **8** informer, squealer

forerunner of: **5** serin

canary broom: **7** genista

Canary Islands: **4** Roca **5** Ferro, Lobos, Palma, Clara **6** Gomero **7** Inferno **8** Graciosa, Rocca Sta., Tenerife **9** Lanzarote, Teneriffe **10** Allegranza **11** Grand Hierro **13** Fuerteventura

city: **6** Laguna **9** Santa Cruz(c.)

commune: **4** Icod

measure: **8** fanegada

mountain: **6** La Cruz **8** El Cumbre, Tenerife **9** Teneriffe **11** Gran Canaria

canary yellow: **6** meline

canasta: **4** game **5** cards, crate **6** basket, hamper

play: **4** meld

cancel: **4** blot, dele, omit **5** annul, erase, quash, remit **6** delete, efface, recall, remove, revoke **7** abolish, call off, destroy, expunge, nullify, rescind, retract, scratch **8** abrogate **10** obliterate **11** countermand

cancer: **5** tumor **7** sarcoma **9** carcinoma

cancion: **4** song **5** lyric

candent: hot **7** fervent, glowing

candescent: **7** glowing **8** dazzling **11** luminescent

Candia: **5** Crete

candid: **4** fair, just, open, pure **5** blunt, clear, frank, naive **6** honest **7** artless, sincere **8** splendid **9** guileless, honorable, impartial, ingenuous, outspoken **10** aboveboard, immaculate **11** unconcealed **15** straightforward

candidate: **7** nonimee **8** aspirant, prospect **9** applicant

list: **4** leet **5** slate **6** roster

religious: **9** postulant
winning: **7** electee
Candiot, Candiote: 6 Cretan
candle: dip, wax **5** light, taper **6** cierge(F.)
9 chandelle
holder: **6** lampad, sconce, sconse, spider **7**
menorah **9** girandole **10** candelabra **11**
candlestick
kind of: **8** bayberry
place of keeping: **9** chandlery
wax: **5** taper **6** bougie
candlelight: 4 dusk **8** twilight **9** nightfall
candlelighter: 5 spill **7** acolyte
candlenut tree: ama **5** kukui **6** bankul
candlestick: 6 lampad, sconce **8** flambeau, standard **9** flambeaux(pl.)
bracket: **6** sconce, sconse
branched: **5** jesse **8** dicerion, dikerion **9**
girandole, tricerion, trikerion **10** chandelier **11** candelabrum
candlewood: 4 tree **5** shrub **9** coachwhip
candor, candour: 6 purity **8** fairness,
kindness **9** frankness, innocence, integrity, unreserve, whiteness **10** brightness, brilliance, kindliness **12** impartiality **13** outspokenness
candy: 5 fudge, gundy, lolly, sweet, taffy **6**
bonbon, comfit, nougate **7** brittle, caramel, congeal, fondate, flatter, sweeten **8**
lollipop, sourball **9** chocolate, granulate,
jelly bean, sweetmeat **10** confection **11**
crystallize
base: **7** fondant
medicated: **7** lozenge **9** cough drop
mixture: **6** fourre
nut: **7** praline
pulled sugar: **5** taffy **6** penide
sugar: **7** fondant **8** alphenic
candy striper: 10 nurse's aide
candytuft: 5 plant **6** flower, iberis
cane: rod **4** beat, dart, flog, pipe, reed,
stem, tube, whip **5** birch, lance, staff,
stick **6** bamboo, punish, rattan **7** calamus, hickory, malacca, scourge **9** crabstick
dense growth: **9** canebrake
knife: **7** machete
part: **7** ferrule
sugar: **7** sucrose
Canfield: 8 Klondike **9** solitaire
cangle: 7 dispute, quarrel, wrangle
canine (see also **dog**): cur, dog, fox, pup **4**
fisc, wolf **5** canis(L.), hound, pooch **7**
doglike
tooth: **7** laniary
caning: 6 rattan **8** birching
canister: box **9** container
canker: 4 rust **5** stain **6** infect **7** consume, corrode, corrupt, pervert, tarnish
9 verdigris
cannabis: 4 hemp
drug: **5** bhang **7** hashish **9** marijuana

Cannery Row author: 9 Steinbeck
cannibal: 6 savage **15** anthropophagite
cannikin: can, cup **4** pail **6** bucket
cannon: bit, gun **5** crack, thief **6** mortar,
pom-pom **7** bastard **8** howitzer, ordnance **9** artillery **10** pickpocket
breech-end knob: **8** cascabel
early: **5** aspic, saker **7** robinet
fire: **7** barrage
firing stick: **8** linstock
fodder: **8** infantry
handle: **4** anse
muzzle plug: **7** tampion
part: **4** bore **5** chase **6** breech, muzzle **7**
chamber, rimbase **8** cascabel, trunnion
shot: **5** grape
support: **8** trunnion
cannon fodder: 8 infantry, soldiers
cannonade: 5 blitz, burst, salvo **6** volley **7**
barrage
cannoneer: 12 artilleryman
cannot: 6 unable
cannular: 6 hollow **7** tubular
canny: sly **4** cozy, snug, wary, wily, wise **5**
lucky, pawky, quiet **6** clever, frugal,
gentle, shrewd **7** careful, cunning,
knowing, prudent, quietly, thrifty **8**
cautious, skillful, watchful **9** carefully,
dexterous, fortunate, sagacious **10** cautiously **11** comfortable, sharpwitted
canoe: 4 boat, kiak, pahi, proa, waka **5**
birch, kayak, prahu, skiff, umiak, waapa
6 ballam, dugout, oomiak, pitpan **7** al-
madia, bidarka, coracle, currane, pirogue
bark: **7** cascara
dugout: **5** banca **6** baroto, corial **7** pirogue, piroque **12** pambanmanche
large: pah **5** bungo
sailing: **4** proa **5** prahu
skin-covered: **4** kiak **5** bidar, kayak **7** bai-
dara
war: **4** proa
canon: law **4** code, hymn, laud, list, rule,
song **5** axiom, gorge, gulch, model, table, tenet **6** decree **7** precept, statute **8**
decision, standard **9** catalogue, clergyman, criterion **10** regulation **12** constitution
enigmatical: **4** nodi(pl.) **5** nodus
resident: **8** stagiary
canonical: 8 accepted, orthodox **10** sanctioned **13** authoritative
hour: **4** laud, none, sext **5** matin, prime **6**
tierce **7** vespers **8** compline
canonicals: alb **4** cope, cowl, robe **5** stole
9 vestments
canopy: sky **4** ceil, cope, dais, hood **5**
shade, vault **6** awning, celure, finial,
tester **7** marquee, shelter **8** covering **9**
baldachin, baldaquin, pavillion **11** baldacchino

altar: **7** ciboria(pl.) **8** baldakin, ciborium **9** baldachin, baldaquin **10** baldachino **11** baldacchino

bed: **6** tester **7** sparver

canorous: **5** clear **7** musical **8** sonorous **9** melodious **10** euphonious

cant: tip **4** coax, heel, lean, list, nook, sing, tilt, turn **5** argot, bevel, chant, hield, idiom, lingo, lusty, merry, niche, pitch, share, slang, slant, slope, whine **6** careen, corner, herald, intone, jargon, lively, patois, patter, snivel **7** auction, incline, portion, singing, wheedle **8** cheerful, pretense, vigorous **9** barbarism, hyprocrisy, vulgarism **10** intonation, vernacular **13** colloquialism **17** sanctimoniousness

cantabank: **6** singer **7** chanter

cantaloupe **9** muskmelon

cantankerous: **6** ornery **8** perverse **9** irritable, malicious **10** brabagious **11** contentious **12** crossgrained

cantata: **4** mote, poem **8** serenata **11** composition

cantatrice: **6** singer **9** chanteuse

canteen: K.T., P.X., bar **5** bazar, flask **6** bazaar **7** cantina

canter: jog, run **4** gait, lope, pace, rack **5** rogue **6** beggar, whiner **8** vagabond **10** street arab

Canterbury: *archbishop:* Odo **4** Lang **6** Anselm, Becket **7** Cranmer, Dunstan **9** Augustine

gallop: **5** aubin

canticle: ode **4** hymn, laud, song **5** canto **6** anthem, hirmos **7** bravura

church: **6** Te Deum, Venite **10** Magnificat

cantilena: **6** legato, melody **8** graceful

cantillate: hum **5** chant **6** intone, recite

cantina: bar, pub **5** pouch, store **6** pocket, pommel, saloon, tavern **7** canteen, gin mill **8** groggery

canting: **5** atrip, pious **12** hypocritical

cantle: **4** join, nook, part **5** cheer, piece, raise, slice **6** corner **7** portion, segment **8** brighten, fragment **11** cornerpiece

canto: air, fit **4** book, pace, song **5** verse **6** melody, passus

canton: **4** part **5** angle **6** billet, corner **7** portion, quarter, section **8** district, division

cantor: **5** hazan **6** leader, singer **7** chanter, chazzan, soloist **9** precentor

cantoria: **7** balcony, gallery

cantrip: **5** charm, spell, trick

cantus: **4** song **5** chant

canty: **6** lively **8** cheerful **9** sprightly

Canuck: **8** Canadian

canvas: **4** duck, sail, tarp, tent, tewk **5** scrim **6** burlap **7** picture, poldavy **8** painting

waterproof: **9** tarpaulin

canvasback: **4** duck **6** cheval

canvass: **4** beat, hawk, poll, sift **5** randy, study **6** debate, peddle, search **7** agitate, discuss, examine, solicit, trounce **8** campaign, consider **10** scrutinize **11** electioneer, investigate

canvasser: **5** agent **6** poller, rodman **7** counter **8** salesman

canyon: **5** cajon, chasm, gorge, gulch **6** arroyo, ravine

mouth: **4** abra

small: **6** canada

canzonet: air **4** song **5** canto **6** ballad **7** canzona, canzone **8** madrigal

caoba: **5** quira **8** mahogany, muskwood

caoutchouc: **6** rubber

source: ule **6** caucho

cap: fez, hat, lid, taj, tam, tip, top **4** acme, best, coif, cork, dome, eton, hood, hure, mate, pass, topi **5** beret, chief, cover, crown, excel, match, outdo, seize, topee, trump **6** arrest, beanie, bonnet, climax, cornet, helmet, puzzle, summit, top off, turban **7** commode, ferrule, overlie, overtop, perplex, surpass **8** headgear, surprise, tarboosh **9** detonator, headpiece **11** mortarboard

child's: **5** mutch, toque **6** biggin, bonnet

close-fitting: **4** coif **5** toque **6** cloche **7** calotte

covering: **8** havelock

ecclesiastical: **5** beret, miter **6** barret **7** biretta, galerum, galerus **8** barretta **9** zucchetto

hunter's: **7** montero

ignition: **4** fuse, fuze

knitted: **5** toque

military: **4** kepi **5** busby, shako

muslin: **5** mutch

part: **4** bill, peak **5** visor

Roman: **6** pileus

Scotch: tam **8** balmoral **9** glengarry **11** tamoshanter

sheepskin: **6** calpac **7** calpack

skull: **5** beame **6** callot, pileus **7** calotte, yamilke **8** yarmulka

steel: **10** cerveliere

cap-a-pie: **7** utterly **10** throughout

capa: **5** cloak **6** mantle

capability: art **5** craft, skill **6** stroil **7** ability **8** capacity **9** potential **10** competence, efficiency

capable: apt, can, fit **4** able **5** adept **6** expert **7** skilled **9** competent, effective, efficient, qualified **10** proficient **12** accomplished

of being cut: **7** sectile **8** scissile

of being defended: **7** tenable

of being heard: **7** audible

of being molded: **7** plastic

of being touched: **8** tangible

of endurance: **4** wiry **5** tough
of extension: **7** tensile
of flying: **6** volant
of suffering: **8** passible **9** sensitive
render: **6** enable
capacious: 4 full, wide **5** ample, broad, large, roomy **6** goodly **8** captious, spacious **9** extensive **10** commodious **12** considerable
capacitate: 7 qualify
capacity: 4 bent, gift, size, turn **5** knack, power, skill, space **6** burden, extent, spread, talent, volume **7** ability, caliber, calibre, content, faculty, fitness **8** aptitude, strength **9** continent, endowment, intellect **10** capability, competence
Capaneus: *father:* **9** Hipponous
  mother: **8** Astynome
  slayer: **4** Zeus
  son: **9** Sthenelus
  wife: **6** Evadne
caparison: 4 deck, trap **8** clothing, covering **9** adornment **10** decoation
cape: ras **4** cope, gape, head, look, neck, ness, writ **5** amice, cappa, cloak, fanon, fichu, orale, point, sagum, stare, stole, talma **6** bertha, chapel, mantle, sontag, tabard, tippet **7** leather, manteel **8** headland, lambskin, mantilla, pelerine **9** inverness, peninsula, sheepskin **10** projection, promontory
  crocheted: **6** sontag
  lace: **5** fichu **6** bertha **8** collaret
Cape anteater: 8 aardvark
Cape armadillo: 8 pangolin
Cape Colony plateau: 5 karoo **6** karroo
Cape Dutch: 9 Afrikaans
Cape elk: 5 eland
Cape gooseberry: 4 poha **12** ground cherry
Cape jasmine: 8 gardenia
Cape lancewood: 7 assagai
cape merchant: 10 supercargo
Cape polecat: 5 zoril **8** muishond
Cape Province: *people:* **4** Xosa **5** Pondo
Cape ruby: 6 garnet, pyrope
Cape Verde: *capital:* **5** Praia
  island: Sal **4** Fago
  native: **5** Brava, Serer
Capek: *play:* RUR
  creature: **5** robot
capel: 4 rock, wall **5** horse **6** quartz
capelin: 5 smelt **7** ice fish
caper: hop **4** dido, jump, lark, leap, romp, skip, skit **5** antic, brank, dance, flisk, frisk, prank, sauce, shrub **6** cavort, frisco, frolic, gambol, gamond, prance, spring, tittup, vagary **7** corsair, courant, friscal, gambado **8** capricci(pl.), capriole, devilment, marigold **9** capriccio, condiment, privateer **11** monkeyshine, waggishness

family: **13** capparidaceae
capercaillie: 4 cock **6** grouse
  courtship: lak
capernoited: 7 crabbed, peevish **9** irritable **11** intoxicated **12** muddleheaded
capernoitie: 4 head **6** noddle
capeskin: 7 leather **9** sheepskin
capful: 4 puff **8** quantity
capias: 4 writ **7** process
capillary: 6 minute **7** slender **8** filiform, hairlike **11** blood vessel
capillus: 4 hair
capilotade: 4 stew **5** sauce **6** ragout
capital: cap, top **4** cash, city, good, main, rare, seat **5** basic, chief, fatal, great, major, money, stock, vital **6** deadly, letter, mortal, primal, wealth **7** central, chattel, leading, radical, serious, weighty **9** copacetic, excellent, paramount, principal, prominent **10** first-class, pre-eminent **11** scrumptious
  ancient: **4** Roma
  gambler's: **5** stake
  impairment of: **7** deficit **9** depletion
  inadequate: **10** shoestring
  provide: **4** back **5** angel **7** finance
capital punishment: 7 hanging **8** shooting **12** death penalty **13** electrocution
capitalist: 8 investor **9** financier, plutocrat
capitalize: 4 back, fund, help **5** stake **7** finance, sponsor **8** bankroll **9** subsidize
capitano: 5 chief **7** captain, headman, soldier
capitate: 8 headlike, headshaped
Capitol Hill group: 5 House **6** Senate
capitulate: 4 fall **5** agree, title, yield **8** headline **9** enumerate, surrender **11** buckle under
caporal: 7 foreman, tobacco **8** overseer
capote: 4 hood **5** cloak **6** bonnet, mantle, topper **8** overcoat
cappuccino: 14 espresso coffee
capric acid salt: 6 rutate
caprice: fad **4** kink, mood, whim **5** antic, braid, fancy, freak, humor, quirk **6** maggot, notion, temper, vagary, whimsy **7** boutade, conceit, crochet, impulse, whimsey **9** capriccio **12** inconsistent
capricious: 5 dizzy, doddy, fluky, moody **6** fickle **7** comical, erratic, flighty, wayward **8** fanciful, freakish, humorous, unsteady, volatile **9** arbitrary, crotchety, fantastic, humorsome, whimsical **10** changeable, inconstant
Capricorn: 4 Goat **6** beetle **13** Constellation
  star within: **5** Deneb
capriole: 4 leap **5** caper **6** spring **9** headdress
capripede: 4 goat **5** satyr
caprylate: 4 acid, salt **5** ester **7** octoate

capsize: 4 coup, keel 5 upset 8 overturn
capstan: 4 drum 5 hoist, lever 8 cylinder, windlass
catch: 4 pawl
capstone: 4 acme, apex, peak 6 apogee, climax 8 pinnacle 11 culmination
capsule: pod 4 boll, case, pill 5 shell, theco, wafer 6 ampule, sheath 7 ampoule 8 pericarp 9 cartridge, detonator 10 repository
captain: boh 4 head 5 chief 6 leader, master 7 capitan, foreman, headman, manager, skipper 8 capitano, governor 9 centurion, commander, principal 14 superintendent
boat: gig
fictional: 4 Ahab, Nemo 5 Bligh, Queeg
pirate: 4 Kidd
caption: 5 title 6 leader, legend 7 cutline, heading 8 headline, overline, subtitle 9 underline
captious: 5 testy 6 crafty, severe 7 carping, cynical, fretful, peevish 8 alluring, caviling, contrary, critical, perverse, petulant 9 capacious, insidious, irascible 10 capricious, censorious 12 faultfinding 13 hypercritical
captivate: win 4 take 5 catch, charm 6 allure, enamor, please, ravish, subdue 7 attract, bewitch, capture, enamour, enchant 8 enthrall, overtake 9 enrapture, fascinate, infatuate
captive: 5 slave 6 enamor 7 caitiff, hostage 8 prisoner
captivity: 4 bond 6 duress 7 bondage, serfdom, slavery 9 servitude, thralldom 10 subjection 11 confinement 12 imprisonment
captor: 5 taker 6 victor 7 catcher
capture: bag, cop, get, nab, net, win 4 fang, grab, hook, land, prey, take, trap, tree 5 catch, prize, raven, seize 6 arrest, collar, obtain 9 apprehend, captivate 10 circumvent 12 apprehension
capuche: 4 cowl, hood
Capuchin: 5 friar 6 monkey, pigeon
caput: top 4 head 7 chapter, council, section 8 divison 9 paragraph
capybara: 6 rodent
car: (see also **automobile**): box, bus, van 4 auto, jeep, rath 5 buggy, coach, hutch, ratha, sedan, train, wrong 6 basket, hotrod 7 awkward, chariot, trailer, trolley, vehicle 8 roadster, sinister 10 automobile, left-handed 11 convertible 12 station wagon
aerial cable: 6 telfer 7 telpher
armored: 4 tank
railroad: box, oil 4 club, flat, mail, tank 5 chair, coach, diner 6 buffet, hopper, parlor 7 baggage, caboose, express, freight, gondola, pullman, sleeper, tourist 9 furniture, passenger 12 refrigerator
car barn: 5 depot
carabao: 5 mango 7 buffalo
caracara: 4 hawk
caract: See **character**
carafe: 6 bottle
caramel: 5 candy, sweet 6 bonbon 9 flavoring 10 confection
carapace: 5 crust, shell 6 lorica
carara: 9 coronopus
caravan: van 4 trek, trip 5 fleet 6 cafila, convoy, safari, travel 7 journey, vehicle
slave: 6 coffle
caravansary: inn 4 chan, khan 5 hotel, serai 6 hostel, imaret 8 choultry, hostelry 9 resthouse
carbine: gun 5 rifle 6 musket, weapon 7 escopet 9 escopette
carbohydrate: 5 sugar 6 starch 8 dextrose 9 cellulose
carbon: 4 coal, coke, copy, soot 6 crayon 7 replica 8 graphite
deposit: 4 soot
point: 6 crayon
carbonate: 4 burn, char, fizz 6 aerate, alkali 7 enliven 9 carbonize, energizer
carborundum: 5 emery 8 abrasive
carboy: jug 6 bottle
carbuncle: 4 boil 5 jewel 6 garnet 7 abscess, pustule
carcajou: 4 lynx 6 badger, cougar 9 wolverine
carcanet: 5 chain 6 collar 8 headband, necklace
carcass: 4 body 6 corpse 7 carrion
carcoon: 5 clerk 7 manager
card: map, pam, wag 4 comb, menu, plan 5 chart, fiche, joker, tease 6 cartel, ticket 7 program 8 schedule 9 character, eccentric 10 attraction, pasteboard
spot: pip
wool: tum 4 comb, rove, toom
card game: lu; gin, hoc, loo, pam 4 bank, faro, hock, keno, ruff, skat, slam, snap, solo, spin, vint 5 beast, chico, cinch, comet, crimp, decoy, gilet, gleek, monte, omber, ombre, pedro, pique, pitch, poker, rummy, stuss, trump, two-up, waist, whist 6 basset, boston, bridge, casino, commit, ecarte, euchre, fantan, flinch, hearts, masset, piquet, rounce, sledge, smudge 7 baccara, bezique, cayenne, Chicago, canasta, cooncan, old maid, sevenup 8 baccarat, commerce, conquian, contract, cribbage, handicap, Napoleon, patience, pinochle, tresillo, vederuff 9 Newmarket, panguinui, solitaire 10 blackstone 11 everlasting, speculation 14 spite and malice
bid: 4 slam 6 misere
fortune-telling: 5 tarot

holding: **6** tenace
old: hoc, loo, pam **4** brag, ruff **5** comet, gilet, omber, ombre, trump **7** primero, reversi **8** penneech, penneeck
player who cuts: **4** pone
playing card: ace, pam, ten **4** jack, king, trey **5** basto(Sp.), deuce, joker, knave, queen, taroc, tarot
term: bid, bue, cat, pic **4** book, card, deal, hand, meld, pair, pass, suit **5** flush, raise, trump **6** renege, tenace, tricon **8** sequence, straight **9** doubleton, singleton **10** Yarborough
widow: **4** skat
wild: **5** joker
cardigan: **6** fabric, jacket, wampus **7** sweater
cardinal: red **4** bird, main **5** basic, chief, cloak, color, vital **6** cleric **7** radical **9** principal **10** underlying
assembly at Rome: **7** college
hat: **8** gallerum
notification of elevation: **9** biglietto
office: hat **6** datary **7** dataria
title: **8** eminence
cards (see also **card game**): **4** deck, pack, suit
care: **4** cark, cure, duty, fret, heed, mind, reck, soin(F.), tend, wish, yeme **5** grief, guard, nurse, pains, worry **6** burden, desire, grieve, lament, regard, sorrow **7** anxiety, auspice, caution, cherish, concern, keeping, scruple, thought, tuition **8** business **9** attention, diligence, direction, oversight **10** management, solicitude **11** calculation, heedfulness **12** watchfulness **14** responsibility
for: **4** like, mind, tend **5** guard, nurse, treat **6** foster, relish
requiring: **7** fragile **8** ticklish
under another's: **4** ward **6** charge **7** protege **10** apprentice
careen: tip **4** cant, heel, keel, list, sway, tilt, veer **5** lurch, slope, swing, weave **7** incline
career: run, way **4** life, road **5** trade **6** charge, course, gallop **7** calling, pursuit, running **8** business, vocation **10** occupation, profession, racecourse **11** achievement
care for: **4** like, mind, tend **5** nurse **6** foster **7** nurture
carefree: **4** easy **5** frank, happy **6** breezy **8** reckless **10** insouciant **12** happy-go-lucky, lighthearted
careful: **4** wary **5** canny, chary, exact **6** frugal, intent **7** anxious, guarded, heedful, prudent, thrifty **8** accurate, cautious, diligent, discreet, dreadful, gingerly, mournful, troubled, vigilant, watchful **9** advertent, attentive, exquisite, observant, provident **10** economi-

cal, meticulous, respectful, respective, scrupulous, solicitous, thoughtful **11** circumspect, considerate, painstaking, punctilious
carefully: **7** charily **8** gingerly
careless: lax **4** cool, easy, lash, rash **5** slack **6** casual, overly, remiss, supine, untidy, unwary **7** languid **8** heedless, listless, reckless, slattern, slipshod, slovenly **9** forgetful, haphazard, negligent, unheeding, unmindful **10** delinquent, neglectful, nonchalant, regardless **11** inadvertent, inattentive, indifferent, perfunctory, spontaneous, thoughtless, unconcerned **13** irresponsible
caress: coy, hug, pat, pet **4** bill, dant(Sc.), kiss, neck **6** coddle, cosset, fondle, pamper, stroke **7** cherish, embrace **10** endearment
caretaker: **6** keeper **7** janitor **9** custodian **11** housekeeper
Carew's love: **5** Celia
careworn: **5** jaded, lined **7** haggard, pinched **8** troubled **10** distressed
carfuffle: **6** flurry, ruffle **8** disorder **9** agitation **10** disarrange
cargador: **6** porter **7** carrier **9** stevedore
cargo: **4** bulk, load **6** burden, lading **7** freight, payload **8** property, shipment **10** freightage
discarded: **6** jetsam
loader: **9** stevedore
space in ship: **4** hold
stabilizer: **7** ballast
take on: **4** lade, load
wrecked ship: **7** flotsam
Caribbean: *bird:* **4** tody
gulf: **6** Darien
island: **4** Cuba **5** Aruba, Haiti **6** Nassau, Tobago **7** Curacao, Grenada, Jamaica **8** Dominica, Trinidad **10** Hispaniola, Puerto Rico **12** Santo Domingo
island group: **7** Leeward **8** Antilles, Windward
caribe: **4** fish **6** pirana, piraya **7** piranha
caribou: **4** deer **8** reindeer
carica: **4** tree **6** papaya, pawpaw
caricature: ape **4** copy, mock, skit **5** farce, libel, mimic, squib **6** overdo, parody, satire **7** cartoon, lampoon **8** travesty **9** burlesque **12** exaggeration
caries: **5** decay **10** ulceration **11** saprodontia
carillon: **5** bells **6** chimes **9** bell tower **12** glockenspiel
cark: ail, vex **4** care, heed, load, stew **5** cavil, pains, worry **6** burden, charge, harass **7** anxiety, perplex, trouble **8** distress
carling: **6** rafter **7** support
Carmelite: **4** monk **5** friar
barefoot: **8** Teresian

carmen: 4 poem, song 11 incantation

Carmen composer: 5 Bizet

carmine: red 7 crimson, scarlet 8 coloring

carnage: 6 murder, pogrom 8 butchery, massacre 9 bloodshed, slaughter

carnal: 4 crow, lewd 6 animal, bodily, sexual, worldly 7 brutish, earthly, fleshly, secular, sensual 8 material, temporal 9 corporeal 11 unspiritual 12 bloodthirsty, unregenerate

carnation: 4 pink 5 flake 6 flower 7 picotee 9 grenadine(F.)

carnelian: 4 sard 10 chalcedony

carnival: 4 fete 7 revelry 8 festival 11 merrymaking

attraction: 4 ride 6 midway 8 sideshow 10 concession

performer: 4 geek

carnivore: cat, dog, fox 4 bear, coon, lion, lynx, mink, puma, seal, wolf 5 civet, coati, genet, hyena, otter, panda, pekah, ratel, sable, stoat, tiger 6 cougar, ermine, feline, ferret, jackal, jaguar, marten, ocelot, possum, serval, weasel 7 dasyure, genette, glutton, leopard, opossum, polecat, raccoon, tigress 8 mongoose 9 ichneumon

carnose: 6 fleshy

carob: 4 tree 6 locust 9 algarroba

carol: lay 4 noel, sing, song 5 ditty, yodel, yodle 6 alcove, ballad, warble 8 madrigal

Caroline island: Yap 4 Truk 5 Palau 6 Kusaie, Ponape

carom: 4 shot 6 bounce, glance, strike 7 rebound 8 ricochet

carousal: 4 lark, orgy, riot, romp, toot 5 binge, drunk, feast, randy, revel, spree 6 frolic, shindy, splore 7 banquet, carouse, wassail 8 festival, jamboree 9 bacchanal

carouse: 4 bout, hell, riot 5 birle(Sc.), bouse, drink, revel, quaff, spree, toast 7 wassail 8 carousal

carp: nag 4 fish, sing, snag, talk, yerk 5 cavil, prate, scold, speak 6 censor, nibble, peck at, recite 7 censure, chatter, henpeck, quibble 8 complain, goldfish 9 criticize, discourse

carpel: 9 carpophyl 10 carpophyll

carpenter: ant, bee 6 framer, joiner, wright 7 artisan, builder 8 tectonic 9 artificer 10 woodworker 12 cabinetmaker

machine: 5 lathe 6 planer, shaper

ship: 5 chips

tool: adz, awl, saw 4 adze 5 level, plane 6 gimlet, hammer, square 7 hatchet

carpet: mat, rug 4 kali 5 scold, tapet, tapis 6 fabric 8 covering

on the: 11 reprimanded

design: 9 medallion

variety: 4 Agra 6 velvet, Wilton 7 ingrain 8 Brussels, moquette, Venetian 9 Axminster, broadloom

carping: 6 jawing 7 blaming 8 captious, caviling, critical 10 censorious 12 faultfinding 13 hypercritical

carplike fish: 4 dace, rudd

carpus: 5 wrist

carr, car: bog, fen 4 pool 5 grove

carrack, carack: 4 boat 7 galleon

carrageen: 4 alga, moss 7 seaweed

carriage: air, gig 4 gait, garb, hack, load, mien, shay 5 bandy, brake, break, buggy, coach, front, midge, poise, wagon 6 burden, convoy, landau, manner, surrey 7 baggage, bearing, conduct, gesture, hackney, phaeton, vecture, vehicle 8 behavior, demeanor, dormeuse, equipage, portance 9 behaviour, execution 10 conveyance, deportment, management 14 administration

baby: 4 pram 5 buggy 6 gocart 8 stroller 12 perambulator

closed: cab 4 hack, taxi 6 calash 7 caleche 8 brougham, clarence

covered: 6 Berlin, landau 7 ricksha 8 carryall, dearborn, stanhope

driver: 4 hack 5 cabby 8 coachman

four-wheeled: 5 coupe 6 surrey, whisky 7 phaeton, whiskey 8 barouche, clarence, rockaway, victoria 9 chariotee, gladstone

French: 6 fiacre

one-horse: fly, gig 4 ekka(Ind.), shay, trap 5 sulky 6 dennet 7 cariole, dogcart 8 carriole

open: 7 dogcart, dos-a-dos 8 sociable

portable: 5 sedan

three-horse: 6 troika

two-seated: 6 tandem

two-wheeled: gig 4 shay, trap 5 essed, sulky, tonga 6 chaise, cisium, esseda, hansom 7 carreta, chariot, tilbury 8 carretta 9 caretella, carromata 11 jinrickshaw

carriage trade: 7 society

carried: 5 borne, giddy, toted 6 carted, lugged, wafted 8 drifting, ravished 10 abstracted 11 transported

carrier (see also **conveyance**): hod 4 ship 5 hamal, macer, plane 6 bearer, cadger, hamaul, hammal, khamal, porter 7 airline, courier, drayman, flattop, hammaul, postman, remover 8 cargador, portator, railroad, teamster 9 messenger

carrion: 4 vile 6 corpse, refuse, rotten 7 carcass, corrupt 9 loathsome

Carroll character: 5 Alice 6 hatter, rabbit 7 duchess 8 Dormouse 9 March Hare 10 Mock Turtle 11 White Rabbit 12 Humpty Dumpty

carrot: 4 root 5 plant 6 daucus 10 enticement
deadly: 5 drias
family: 8 ammaicea
genus: 5 carum
top: 7 red-head
wild: 8 hilltrot 10 laceflower
carrousel: 4 ride 12 merry-go-round
carry: hug, jag, lug 4 bear, cart, gest, hold, lead, take, tote, tump 5 bring, cadge, geste, guide, poise 6 behave, convey, convoy, delate, derive, extend 7 conduct, contain, produce, support, sustain, undergo 8 continue, transfer, transmit 9 prosecute, transport 11 comportment
away: 4 kill, take 5 eloin, reave, steal 6 eloign, remove 9 transport
off: win 4 kill 6 kidnap 7 succeed
on: 4 rant, rave, wage 6 manage 7 conduct, perform, proceed 8 continue, maintain, transact 9 misbehave, prosecute
out: 6 effect 7 execute, perform, sustain 8 complete
over: 4 tide 5 table 6 extend, shelve 8 contango, postpone, transfer
the day: win 7 prevail
carryall: bag, bus 4 case 8 carriage
carrying: 6 gerent 9 gestation
cart: 4 butt, char, dray, haul, tote, wain 5 araba, bandy, bogie, carry, sulky, tonga, wagon 6 charet, convey 7 chariot, hackery, trolley, trundle, tumbler, tumbrel, tumbril, vehicle 8 charette
farmer: 7 morfrey 8 morphrey
freight: 8 carreton
horse: 8 cartaver(Sc.)
license: 6 caroon 7 caroome, carroon
racing: 5 sulky
rope: 5 wanty(Sc.)
strong: 4 dray
two-wheeled: bin, gig 4 shay 5 dandy, sulky, tonga 6 reckla 7 tumbril 8 carretta(Sp.)
cartage: 7 drayage, haulage
carte: map 4 card, list, menu 5 chart 7 charter, diagram
carte du jour: 4 menu
cartel: 4 card, defy, pact, pool, ship 5 paper, trust 6 corner, letter, treaty 8 contract 9 agreement, challenge, syndicate 10 convention
carter: 7 drayman, trucker 8 horseman, teamster
Carthage: *citadel:* 5 Bursa, Byrsa
emblem: 4 palm
foe: 4 Cato
founder: 4 Dido
general: 5 Hanno 8 Hannibal
god: 6 Moloch
goddess: 5 Tanit 6 Tanith

language: 5 Punic
magistrate: 7 suffete
pert. to: 5 Punic
queen: 4 Dido
subject: 6 Libyan
victor at Zama: 6 Scipio
Carthusian: 4 monk 7 eremite
monastery: 5 Pavia 7 Certosa
noted: 4 Hugh
superior: 5 prior
cartilage: 6 tissue 7 gristle
ossified: 4 bone
cartload: 6 fother
cartograph: map 4 plat 5 chart
carton: box 4 case 9 container 10 receptacle
cartoon: 10 caricature
cartoonist: 4 Arno, Capp, Ding, Nast, Szep 5 Gould, Kelly, Young 6 Addams, Disney, Schultz 7 Mauldin, Trudeau 8 Goldberg
cartridge: bag 4 case 5 shell 7 capsule 8 cylinder
holder: 4 clip
cartwheel: 4 coin 6 tumble 10 handspring
carucate: 4 hide, land 5 carve, field
caruncle: 4 comb, gill 6 growth, wattle
carve: cut 5 sculp, sever, slice, split 6 chisel, sunder 7 dissect 9 sculpture
carving: *in stone:* 5 cameo 8 intaglio 10 engrailing
pert. to: 7 glyphic, glyptic
relief: 5 cameo
carya: 5 pecan 6 pignut 9 bitternut
caryatid: 6 figure 9 priestess
male: cap 7 telamon
casa: 5 house 8 building, dwelling
casaba: 5 melon 9 muskmelon
Casanova: 4 rake, roue, wolf 5 lover, Romeo 6 chaser 7 Don Juan 8 lothario, paramour 9 ladies' man
cascade: 5 falls, spout, force(Sc.) 8 cataract 9 waterfall
case: bag, box, hap, pod 4 bunk, burr, deed, file, pack, pair, suit 5 brace, bulla, burse, casus, cover, crate, event, folio, state, theca, trial 6 action, affair, binder, carton, chance, coffin, couple, matter, quiver, sheath, survey 7 cabinet, capcase, capsule, enclose, envelop, example, holster, inclose, lawsuit, oddball, satchel 8 accident, argument, cupboard, envelope, instance, pomander, situated 9 cartridge, condition, container, happening 10 occurrence, receptacle, sabretache 11 contingency
cigar: 7 humidor
cosmetic: 7 compact
document: 7 hanaper
explosive: 5 shell 6 petard 11 firecracker

grammatical: **6** dative **8** ablative, genitive, vocative **9** objective **10** accusative, nominative

small: tye **4** etui **5** bulla, etwee **6** trouse

toiletries: **4** etui **5** etwee

case history: 5 story **6** record **7** example **12** illustration

casement: 6 window **8** covering

cash: 4 coin, cush, dump, dust, jack, jake **5** blunt, brass, bread, clink, darby, dough, funds, money **6** specie **7** capital, hemlock **8** currency **10** ready money, spondulics

keeper: **6** bursar, teller **7** cashier **9** treasurer

cashbox: 4 till **6** coffer

cashew: nut **4** tree **7** maranon

cashier: 6 reject, purser **7** destroy, discard, dismiss, kick out **8** throw out **9** terminate

casing: 4 boot, shoe, tire **5** gaine **6** coffin, collet, lining, sheath **8** covering **9** framework

cask: keg, tub, tun, vat **4** butt, cade, cowl, knag, pipe **5** bowie, bulge, foist **6** bareca, bareka, barrel, cardel, casque, firkin, tierce **7** barrico, fostell **8** cassette, hogshead, puncheon **9** kilderkin

bulge: **5** bilge

oil: **4** rier

orifice: **8** bunghole

rim: **5** chimb, chime

stave: lag

wine: fat, tun **4** butt, fust, pipe **6** tierce

casket: 4 box, pix, tye **4** case, cask, cist, till, tomb **5** chest **6** Accera, chasse, coffer, coffin **7** casquet, fostell **8** cassette **9** reliquary

Caspian Sea: 5 Tates

ancient region: **7** Parthia

harbor: **4** Baku

river to: **4** Kura, Ural **5** Terek, Volga

casque: hat **4** cask **5** armor **6** helmet **9** headdress

Cassandra: 7 prophet, seeress

father: **4** Priam

husband: **9** Agamemnon

mother: **6** Hecuba

slayer: **12** Clytemnestra

cassation: 8 quashing **9** annulling, canceling **10** abrogation

cassava: 4 aipi, juca **5** aipim **6** casiri, manioc **7** tapioca

casserole: 4 dish **6** tureen

cassette: 6 casket, holder, sagger **9** cartridge **10** tape holder

cassia: 4 drug, herb, tree **5** senna, shrub

bark: **8** cinnamon

cassie: 6 basket **8** huisache

Cassiopeia: *daughter:* **9** Andromeda

husband: **7** Cepheus

kingdom: **8** Ethiopia

cassock: 4 gown **5** gippo **6** priest **7** pelisse, soutane **9** clergyman

cassone: box **5** chest

cassowary: emu **4** bird **5** murup **6** moorup

cast: 4 hurl, mold, molt, shed, spew, tint, toss **5** eject, fling, found, heave, mould, pitch, shade, sling, throw, tinge **7** cashier, deposit, discard

about: **4** hunt, seek **9** ferret out, search out

aside: see *away* below

away: **4** jilt, junk, shed **5** scrap, wreck **6** maroon, reject **7** abandon, discard, dismiss **8** squander **9** shipwreck

down: **5** abase **6** abattu, deject, sadden **7** abattue, depress, destroy **8** demolish, dispirit **9** woebegone **10** discourage, dispirited **11** crestfallen **12** disconsolate

lots: **5** cavel

off: **4** free **5** untie **6** disown, unmoor **7** discard **9** eliminate

out: **5** eject, expel **6** banish

up: add **5** total, vomit **6** reckon **7** compute, measure **8** reproach

castaway: 4 waif **5** tramp **6** pariah, reject **7** outcast **8** derelict, stranded **9** shipwreck

caste: 4 rank **5** breed, class, grade, order **6** degree, status

group: **5** varna

merchant: **6** banian, banyan

priestly: **4** magi(pl.) **5** magus

caster: 4 vial **5** cruse, cruet, phial, wheel **6** castor, hurler, roller **7** pitcher, trundle

castigate: 4 lash **5** emend, scare **6** berate, punish, revise, strafe, subdue **7** censure, chasten, correct, reprove **8** chastise, lambaste **9** criticize **10** tongue-lash

castigatory: 5 penal **8** punitive **10** corrective

Castile: *hero:* Cid

province: **5** Avila, Soria

river: **4** Ebro, Esla **5** Douro, Duero

Castilian: 7 Spanish

casting: *mold:* die **6** matrix **7** matrice

rough: pig

castle: 4 fort, rock, rook **5** abode, morro **7** bastile, chateau, citadel **8** bastille, castillo, fastness, fortress **10** stronghold **13** fortification

gate: **10** portcullis

in the air: **5** dream **6** vision **7** fantasy **8** daydream **9** imagining

ledge: **7** rampart

part: **4** bawn, moat **6** donjon **10** drawbridge

tower: **4** keep **6** turret

wall: **6** bailey **10** battlement

warden: **6** disdar, dizdar **9** castellan

castor: hat **4** bean, star **6** beaver **7** leather

Castor: *and Pollux:* **5** twins **6** Gemini **8** Dioscuri

brother: **6** Pollux **10** Polydeuces

father: **4** Zeus **9** Tyndareus

horse: **8** Cyllaros

mother: **4** Leda

sister: **5** Helen

slayer: **4** Idas

castor oil: 9 cathartic

castrate: gib **4** geld, spay, swig **5** alter, capon, prune **6** eunuch, neuter **7** evirate **8** caponize, mutilate **10** emasculate

casual: 5 stray **6** chance, random **7** cursory, natural, offhand **8** informal **9** easy-going, haphazard, uncertain **10** accidental, contingent, fortuitous, incidental, nonchalant, occasional **11** indifferent, low-pressure **14** unconventional, unpremeditated

casualty: 4 loss **5** death **6** chance, hazard, injury, mishap **8** accident, disaster **9** mischance **10** misfortune **11** contingency **12** misadventure

casus: 4 case **5** event **8** occasion

cat: 4 flog, lion, lynx, pard, puma, puss **5** civet, felid, gatol(Sp.), kitty, moggy, ounce, pussy, tiger **6** cougar, feline, jaguar, malkin, mawkin, ocelot, tibert **7** caracal, cheetah, leopard, panther, tigress, wildcat **8** baudrons(Sc.) **9** carnivore, grimalkin **11** caterpillar **12** catamountain, mountain lion

breed: **4** Manx **5** alley, tabby **6** Angora, Calico **7** Maltese, Persian, Siamese

civetlike: **5** genet

cry: mew **4** hiss, meow, miau, purr **5** miaou, miaow, miaul

disease: **9** distemper

Eugene Field's: **6** calico

female: **9** grimalkin

genus: **5** felis **7** felidae(pl.)

cat-o-nine-tails: 4 lash, whip **7** cattail

catachresis: 10 word misuse

cataclysm: 5 flood **6** deluge **7** debacle **8** disaster, overflow, upheaval **11** catastrophe

catacomb: 4 tomb **5** crypt, vault **8** cemetery

catafalque: 4 bier **6** coffin

cataian: 5 thief **7** sharper **9** scoundrel

catalepsy: 6 trance **7** seizure

catalog, catalogue: 4 book, list, roll, rota **5** brief, canon, flyer, index **6** record, roster **7** arrange, itemize **8** classify, register, schedule **9** enumerate, repertory **10** prospectus **11** systematize

of books: **11** bibliotheca

of goods: **9** inventory

of saints: **9** hagiology

Catalonia: *dance:* **7** sardana

marble: **8** brocatel **10** brocatelle

catalyst: 4 goad, spur **7** impetus **8** stimulus **9** incentive **10** motivation

catamaran: 4 raft, trow **6** balsa, float **6** vessel **8** auntsary

catamount: 4 lynx, puma **6** cougar

cataplasm: 8 poultice

catapult: 5 throw **6** launch, onager **7** bricole **8** ballista, crossbow **9** slingshot

cataract: lin **4** linn **5** falls, flood **6** deluge **7** cascade, Niagara **8** Victoria **9** waterfall **10** eye disease

cataria: 6 catnip

catarrh: 4 cold **5** rheum

catastrophe (see also **cataclysm**): **8** accident, calamity, disaster, fatality **10** denouement, misfortune

catbird: 7 mimidae

catcall: boo **4** hoot, razz **6** deride **8** pooh-pooh **10** Bronx cheer

catch: bag, cop, get, nab, net **4** draw, hasp, haul, hawk, hold, hook, land, nail, pawl, snap, stop, trap, tree **5** grasp, hitch, ketch, knack, seize, snare, trick **6** button, clutch, corner, detect, detent, engage, enmesh, entrap, snatch **7** attract, capture, ensnare, grapnel **8** entangle, overtake, surprise **9** intercept **12** come down with

fire: **6** ignite, kindle

one's breath: **4** gasp **5** chink

sight of: **4** espy, spot **6** descry

up with: **8** overtake

catchall: bag **6** basket **10** receptacle

catchfly: 5 plant **6** silence **7** campion

catching: 6 taking **8** alluring **10** contagious, entrapping, infectious **11** captivating

catchword: cue, tag **5** motto **6** byword, phrase, slogan

catchy: 6 fitful, tricky **9** appealing

cate: 4 food **6** viands **8** dainties **10** delicacies, provisions

catechism: 5 guide **6** manual **8** carritch **9** questions **10** carritches(Sc.)

catechumen: 5 pupil **7** audient, auditor, convert, student **8** beginner, neophyte

categorical: 8 absolute, explicit **11** dictatorial, unequivocal, unqualified

category: 4 rank **5** class, genus, genre(pl.), order **6** family **7** species **8** division **12** denomination **14** classification

catena: 4 link **5** chain **6** series **7** excerpt

cater: 4 feed **5** humor, serve, treat **6** pander, purvey, supply **7** provide

caterpillar: cat **4** muga **5** aweto, eruca, larva **6** canker, erucae(pl.), risper, woubit **7** tractor

caterwaul: cry **4** wail **5** miaul

catface: 4 scar

catfish: mud **4** cusk, elod, pout, raad, shal **5** bagre, raash **6** docmac, hassar,

raasch, tandau **7** candiru **8** bullhead **9** sheatfish
genus: **13** saccobranchus
catgut: 4 cord, ropp **5** tharm **6** string, violin
cathartic: 8 lapactic, laxative **9** cleansing, purgative
cathedral: dom **5** duomo **6** church
passage: **5** slype
cathode: 9 electrode
catholic: 5 broad, papal **6** cosmic, global **7** general, liberal **8** tolerant **9** universal **10** ecumenical
Catholic: See **Roman Catholic**
catkin: 5 ament, spike
catlike: 6 feline **8** stealthy **9** noiseless
catmint: nep, nip **4** herb
catnap: 4 doze **6** siesta, snooze
catnip: nep **6** catnep **7** cataria, catwort
Catoism: 9 austerity, harshness
Catreus: *daughter:* **6** Aerope **7** Clymene **9** Apemosyne
father: **5** Minos
mother: **8** Pasiphae
cat's-cradle: 7 ribwort
cat's-paw: 4 dupe, gull, pawn, tool **5** cully
cattail: 4 flag, musk, rush **5** ament, cloud, raupo, reree **6** catkin **7** bulrush, matreed
family: **9** typhaceae
cattle: 4 cows, dhan(Ind.), kine, neat, oxen **5** beefs, bulls, stock **6** beasts, beeves, steers **7** bovines
assemblage: **4** herd **5** drove
brand: **4** duff **5** buist
breed: **4** Nata, Zobo **5** Angus, Devon, Dutch, Niata(dwarf) **6** Durham, Belted, Jersey, Sussex **7** Brahman, Brangus, Kerries **8** Ayrshire, Bradford, Charbray, Guernsey, Hereford, Holstein, Longhorn **9** Red Polled, Shorthorn, Teeswater **10** Beefmaster, Brown Swiss **11** Charollaise, Dutch Belted **14** French Canadian, Santa Gertrudis
call: **4** sook
castrated: **5** steer
dealer: **6** drover, herder
dehorned: **5** muley **6** mulley
female: cow
genus: bos
goddess: **6** Bubona
group: **4** herd **5** drove **7** creaght(Ir.)
plague: **10** rinderpest
shelter: **4** byre **5** barth
tick: **8** carapato
yard: **6** cancha
cattleman: 6 cowboy **7** byreman **8** stockman
catty: 4 mean **8** spiteful **9** malicious
catwalk: 7 footway, walkway
catwort: 6 catnip
Caucasian: *goat:* tur

ibex: zac
language: Laz, Udi **4** Andi, Avar, Laze, Lazi, Udic **5** Udish **7** Semitic **9** Itranican
race: **5** Aryan, Osset **6** Ossete
rug: **4** baku, kuba **5** chila **7** derbend
tribe: **4** Imer, Kurd, Laze, Lazi, Svan **5** Pshav **7** Kubachi
caucho: ule **4** tree **6** rubber
caucus: 7 council, meeting, primary **8** election
caudal: 4 rear **9** posterior
appendage: **4** tail
caudata: 4 newt **5** snake **10** salamander
cauk: 5 chalk **9** limestone
caul: web **4** cawl, trug, veil **7** network, omentum **8** membrane, tressour, tressure
cauldron: See **caldron**
cauliflower: 7 cabbage **8** broccoli **9** disfigure
caulk, calk: 4 cork, fill, flag **6** chinse **7** chintze
cause: aim, gar(Sc.), key **4** case, chat, move, root, spur, suit **5** agent, basis, breed **6** create, effect, gossip, ground, induce, malady, motive, object, origin, reason, source, spring **7** concern, disease, lawsuit, produce, provoke **8** business, engender, movement, occasion **9** originate, wherefore **10** bring about, mainspring, prime mover
causerie: 4 chat, plea, talk **6** debate **10** discussion **12** conversation
causes, science of: 8 etiology
causeuse: 4 sofa **9** tete-a-tete
causeway: way **4** dike, road **7** chausse(F.), highway
causey: dam, way **4** bank, pave, road **5** mound **6** street **7** highway **8** sidewalk
caustic: lye **4** tart **5** acrid, sharp **6** biting, bitter, severe **7** burning, cutting, erodent, mordant, pungent, satiric **8** alkaline, scathing, snappish, stinging **9** corrosive, sarcastic, satirical, vitriolic **10** malevolent **11** acrimonious
agent: **7** cautery, erodent
cauterize: 4 burn, char, fire, sear **5** brand, inust, singe **9** sterilize
caution: 4 care, heed, warn **6** advice, cautel, caveat, exhort **7** anxiety, counsel, precept, proviso **8** admonish, forecast, monition, prudence, wariness **9** diligence, vigilance **10** admonition, precaution, providence **11** calculation, forethought, reservation **12** watchfulness
cautious: 4 wary **5** alert, canny, chary, siker **6** fabian, sicker **7** careful, guarded, prudent **8** discreet, vigilant **10** scrupulous **11** circumspect
cavalcade: 4 raid, ride **5** march **6** parade, safari **7** journey, pageant **10** procession

cavalier: gay 4 curt, easy, fine 5 brave, frank, lofty, proud, rider 6 escort, knight 7 brusque, gallant, haughty, offhand, soldier 8 Royalist 9 caballero, chevalier 10 disdainful 12 high-spirited, supercilious 13 high-and-mighty

Cavalleria Rusticana character: 4 Lola 5 Alfio 7 Turiddu

cavalry: 6 horses, troops 8 horsemen 10 knighthood

horse: 6 lancer

weapon: 5 lance, saber

cavalryman: 5 spahi 6 hussar, lancer, spahee 7 courier, dragoon, soldier, trooper 8 gendarme, horseman

cave: den, tip 4 café, cove, hole, lair, rear, sink, toss, weem 5 antre, cavea, crypt, speos, store, upset 6 beware, cavern, cavity, cellar, forgou, grotto, hollow, larder, luster, pantry, plunge 7 reserve, spelunk 8 collapse, overturn 9 storeroom 10 wine cellar

dweller: 10 troglodyte

researcher: 9 spelunker 12 speleologist

science of researching: 10 speleology

cave in: 5 stove, yield 6 submit 8 collapse

caveat: 6 beware, notice 7 caution, warning

cavern: den 4 cave, grot, hole, lair, weem 5 antra(pl.), croft 6 antrum, cavity, grotto, hollow 7 spelunk

cavernous: 4 vast 6 gaping, hollow 10 sepulchral 11 reverberant

cavetto: 5 gorge 7 molding

caviar: ova, roe 4 eggs, ikra 5 ikary 6 relish 8 delicacy

source: 6 beluga 7 sterlet 8 sturgeon

cavie: 4 cage, coop 7 hencoop

cavil: 4 cark, carp, haft 6 haggle 7 quibble 9 criticise, criticize, exception, objection

caviling: 4 mean 5 fussy, small 8 captious, picayune

cavity: bag, pit, sac 4 abri, cave, dalk, dent, hole, mine, vein, void 5 antra(pl.), atria(pl.), fossa, geode, lumen, mouth, sinus 6 antrum, atrium, camera, cavern, fossae(pl.), grotto, hollow, vacuum 7 cistern, vesicle 8 cul-de-sac 10 depression, excavation

anatomical: 5 antra(pl.), fossa 6 antrum, fossae(pl.)

brain: 6 coelia

gun: 4 bore

heart: 7 auricle 9 ventricle

lode: vug 4 voog, vugg, vugh

pert. to: 5 sinal 6 atrial, geodic

sac-like: 5 bursa 6 bursae(pl.)

skull: 4 aula 5 fossa, sinus

stone: 5 geode

cavort: 4 play, romp 5 bound, caper, cut up 6 curvet, gambol, prance 11 horse around

cavy: 4 paca, pony 6 agouti, aperea, cayuse, rodent 8 capybara 9 guinea pig

caw: cry 4 call, cawl 5 croak, quark, quawk 6 squall, squawk

cawl: 4 trug 6 basket

caxi: 4 fish 7 snapper

cay: See key

cayenne: 5 whist 6 canary, pepper 8 capsicum

cayuse: 4 cavy, pony 6 bronco 7 broncho

cease: end 4 halt, liss, quit, rest, stop 5 avast, douse, dowse, lisse, pause, peter 6 desist, devall, finish 7 abstain, refrain 8 intermit, knock off, leave off 9 terminate 11 discontinue

cease-fire: 5 truce 9 armistice

ceaseless: 4 ever 7 endless 8 unending 9 continual, incessant, unceasing 11 never-ending

ceasing: 9 cessation

Cecrops' daughter: 5 Herse 8 Aglauros

cecum: pit 4 pore 6 cavity

cedar: 4 toon, tree 5 savin 6 deodar, sabina, sabine, savine 7 waxwing

camphor: 6 cedrol

green: 5 cedre(F.), color

moss: 8 hornwort

cede: 4 cess, give 5 award, grant, leave, waive, yield 6 assign, resign, submit 8 hand over, renounce, sign over, transfer 9 surrender 10 relinquish

cedula: 8 document, schedule 11 certificate

ceil: 4 line 7 overlay 8 wainscot

ceiling: 6 lining, screen, soffit 7 curtain, testudo 8 covering, paneling 10 testudines(pl.) 11 wainscoting

covering: 9 calcimine, kalsomine

decorated: 7 plafond

division: 5 trave

mine: 5 astel

wooden: 8 plancher

Celebes: *bovine:* ox 4 anoa

island: 4 Muna

people: 6 toraja 7 toradja

celebrate: 4 keep, sing 5 extol, honor, revel 6 extoll, praise 7 glorify, observe 8 emblazon, eulogize, proclaim 9 solemnize 11 commemorate

celebrated: 4 kept 5 famed, noted 6 famous 7 eminent, feasted, renomme 8 glorious, observed, renowned 9 distingue, prominent 10 solemnized 11 conspicuous, illustrious 13 distinguished

celebration: 4 fete, rite 6 renown 7 jubilee 8 jamboree 9 celebrity, festivity

celebrity: VIP 4 fame, lion, name, star 5 eclat 6 renown, repute 9 superstar 11 celebration

celerity: 5 haste, hurry, speed 8 dispatch, rapidity, velocity 9 prestezza, quickness, swiftness

celery: *family:* **6** pascal
relative of: **6** carrot **7** parsnip
wild: **8** smallage
celestial: **4** holy **6** divine, uranic **7** angelic, Chinese, ethered **8** beatific, empyreal, ethereal, heavenly, Olympian
being: **5** angel **6** cherub, seraph **8** seraphim(pl.)
body: sun **4** moon, star **5** comet **6** meteor, nebula, planet **8** asteroid **9** satellite
elevation of mind: **7** anagoge
matter: **6** nebula
celibacy: **8** chastity
celibate: **6** chaste, single **8** bachelor, spinster **9** unmarried
cell: egg **4** cage, germ, jail **5** cabin, crypt, group, vault **6** cytode, prison **7** cellule, chamber, cubicle, dungeon **9** hermitage **10** ergastulum **11** compartment
blood: red **5** white **8** hemocyte **9** leukocyte **11** erythrocyte
bull: **5** toril **7** toriles(pl.)
coloring: **10** endochrome
colorless: **10** achroacyte, lymphocyte
connecting: **10** heterocyst
division: **7** spireme
generative: **6** gamete
group: **6** ceptor **7** cascade **8** blastema
layer: **8** blastula **10** blastoderm
lens-shaped: **8** lenticel
migratory: **9** leucocyte
pert. to: **6** cytoid
photoelectric: eye
star-shaped: **10** astroblast
structural unit: **7** energid, nucleus **10** protoplast
study of: **8** cytology
substance: **5** linin
cell-like: **6** cytoid
cella: **4** naos
cellar: **4** cave **5** vault **7** hypogee **8** basement **9** storeroom
cellaret: **4** case **7** cabinet **9** sideboard
cellophane: **7** wrapper **9** packaging
cellular: **6** porous **7** areolar **9** alveolate
celluloid: **4** film **6** plastic **8** xylonite
cellulose: *acetate:* **7** acetose
elastic: **5** rayon
Celsius: **10** centigrade **11** thermometer
Celt: **4** Gael, Gaul, Manx **5** Irish, Welsh **6** Breton, Briton, Eolith **7** Cornish
Celtic: **4** Erse, Gael **7** Scotch
abbot: **5** coarb
chariot: **5** essed
chieftain: **6** tanist
divinity: **7** Taranis
foot soldier: **4** kern
giant: **5** Fomor
god: Ler **4** Leir, Llyr
harp: **5** telyn **11** clairschach
hero: **5** Fionn
language: **4** Erse, Manx **5** Irish, Welsh **6**

Celtic, Cymric, Gaelic **9** Brythonic
peasant: **4** kern
priest: **5** Druid
sword: sax **4** seax
cembalo: **8** dulcimer **11** harpsichord
cement: fix **4** glue, join, knit, lime, lute **5** imbed, paste, putty, stick, unify, unite **6** cohere, fasten, gulgul(Ind.), mortar, solder **7** asphalt **8** adhesive, concrete, hadigeon(F.), solidify **11** agglutinate
hydraulic: **4** paar
infusible substance: **4** lute
mixer: **8** temperer
plastic: **8** albolite, albolith
quick-drying: **6** mastic
substance: **6** celite
window glass: **5** putty
cemetery: **6** litten **7** charnel **8** catacomb, Golgotha **9** graveyard **10** necropolis **11** polyandrium
underground: **8** catacomb
cenchrus: **5** grass **6** millet
cenobite: nun **4** monk **5** friar **6** essene **7** recluse **8** monastic **9** anchorite
cenoby: **5** abbey **6** priory **7** convent
cense: **4** rank **6** assess, rating **7** perfume, thurify **8** estimate, position
censer: **8** thurible
censor: **4** blip, edit **6** critic, cut out **7** clean up **8** restrict, suppress **9** detractor, blue-pencil
censorious: **6** severe **7** carping **8** blameful, captious, critical **9** satirical **10** denouncing **11** reproachful **12** fault finding
censurable: **5** amiss, wrong **8** blamable, culpable **13** reprehensible
censure: **4** carp, flay **5** blame, chide, decry, judge, slate **6** accuse, berate, charge, rebuff, rebuke, remord, targue(Scot.), tirade **7** chasten, condemn, impeach, inveigh, reprove **8** disallow, reproach **9** challenge, criticize, reprimand **10** animadvert, exprobrate, vituperate **11** disapproval **12** reprehension **13** animadversion **15** discommendation
census: **4** list, poll **5** count **11** enumeration
cent: **4** coin **5** penny **6** copper
centaur: **6** Chiron, Nessus **8** horseman
father: **5** Ixion
Centennial State: **8** Colorado
center, centre: cor, hub, mid **4** axis, core, foci(pl.), nave, seat **5** focus, heart, midst, pivot, spine **6** middle **7** lineman, nucleus **8** centrate **10** focal point **12** headquarters
away from: **6** distal
toward: **4** orad **5** entad **10** centerward
centerpiece: **7** epergne
centigrade: **5** scale **7** Celsius **11** thermometer
centipede: **4** veri **6** earwig, golach, goloch

8 chilopod, myriapod **9** arthropod, geophilus

central: key, mid **5** axial, basic, chief, focal, prime **6** median, middle **7** capital, centric, leading, pivotal, primary **8** dominant **11** equidistant **12** all-absorbing

Central Africa: See **Africa**

Central America: *agave:* **5** sisal
  ant: **5** kelep
  bird: **7** jacamar **8** puffbird
  canoe: **6** pitpan
  country: **6** Belize, Panama **8** Honduras, Salvador **9** Costa Rica, Guatemala, Nicaragua **10** El Salvador
  ethnic group: **6** Indian **7** Mestizo
  fishing boat: **6** cayuco
  gopher: **7** quachil
  Indian: **4** Maya **5** Carib
  language: **7** Nahuatl, Spanish
  measure: **7** cantaro, manzana
  monkey: **4** mono
  mullet: **4** bobo
  rodent: **4** paca
  snake: **10** bushmaster
  stockade: **4** boma
  tragon: **4** bird **6** quezal **7** quetzal
  tree: ebo, ule **4** eboe **5** amate **9** sapodilla
  village: **4** boma
  weight: **5** libra

Central Asia: See **Asia**

centric: **5** focal **6** middle, tarete **7** central **9** clustered **11** cylindrical **12** concentrated

centrifugal: **8** efferent **9** radiating

centripetal: **8** afferent, unifying **12** centralizing

century: age **6** siecle(F.)
  ten: **7** chiliad **10** millennium

century plant: **4** aloe **5** agave **6** maguey **7** tequila
  fiber: **4** pita, pito

ceorl: **5** churl, thane **7** freeman, villein

cepa: **5** onion

cephalagia: **8** headache

cephalic: **8** atlantal, cerebral

cephalopod: **5** squid **6** cuttle **7** inkfish, octopus
  secretion: ink

Cepheus: *daughter:* **9** Andromeda
  wife: **10** Cassiopeia

ceral: **4** waxy **7** waxlike

ceramics: **5** tiles **7** pottery **9** stoneware
  oven: **4** kiln
  sieve: **4** laun

cerate: wax **4** lard **5** salve **8** ointment

ceratoid: **5** horny

Cerberus: dog **7** monster **8** guardian **9** custodian

cere: wax **4** sere, wrap **6** anoint, embalm

cereal: rye **4** bean, bran, corn, mush, oats, rice **5** grain, maize, spelt, wheat **6** barley, farina, hominy **7** oatmeal, soybean **8** porridge **9** buckwheat
  coating: **4** bran
  grass: oat, rye **4** ragi, rice **5** grain, wheat **6** barley, raggee
  seed: **6** kernel
  spike: ear

cereal grass genus: **6** secale

cerebral: **6** mental **7** psychic **8** highbrow

cerebration: **7** thought **9** brainwork **10** reflection

cerement: **6** shroud **9** cerecloth

ceremonial fuss: **10** panjandrum

ceremonious: **5** grand, lofty, stiff **6** formal, proper, solemn **7** precise, stately, studied **10** respectful **11** punctilious **12** conventional

ceremony: **4** fete, form, pomp, rite, show, sign **5** state **6** augury, parade, powwow, review, ritual **7** display, pageant, portent, prodigy **8** accolade, function, marriage, occasion **9** formality, solemnity **10** observance **11** celebration

Ceres: **7** Demeter
  daughter: **10** Persephone, Proserpina
  father: **6** Cronus, Saturn
  mother: Ops **4** Rhea

cerise: red **6** cherry

cerite: **7** mineral **8** allanite

cernuous: **7** nodding **8** drooping **9** pendulous

cero: **4** fish **6** sierra **7** cavallo, pintado **8** mackerel

certain: **4** firm, real, sure, true **5** bound, clear, exact, fixed, plain, siker(Sc.) **6** actual, sicker, stated **7** assured, precise, settled **8** absolute, apparent, constant, official, positive, reliable, resolved, unerring **9** confident, steadfast, undoubted **10** dependable, inevitable, infallible,undeniable **11** determinate, indubitable, trustworthy **12** indisputable **13** incontestable **14** unquestionable **16** incontrovertible

certainly: **4** amen, ywis **5** iwiss, truly **6** certes, indeed, verily **7** hardily **8** forsooth

certainty: **8** firmness, sureness **9** assurance, dogmatism **10** confidence, conviction

certificate: **4** bond **5** check, libel, scrip **6** attest, ticket, verify **7** diploma, voucher **9** statement, testimony **10** credential **11** attestation, declaration, testimonial **13** certification
  cargo: **8** navicert
  debt: IOU **9** debenture
  land: **6** amparo(Sp.)
  medical, for ill student: **8** aegrotat
  money owed: **9** debenture

certify: **4** avow, vise **5** swear **6** affirm, assure, depose, evince, verify **7** endorse,

license, testify **9** determine, guarantee
under oath: **6** attest
certiorari: **4** writ **6** review
cerulean: **4** blue **5** azure **6** coelin **7** sky-
blue
cervine: elk **4** deer, stag **5** moose **6** cervid
8 cervidae(pl.), reindeer
cervix: **4** neck
cespitose: **6** matted, tufted **7** tangled
cess: bog, tax **4** cede, duty, levy, luck, rate,
tyrf **5** slope, yield **6** impost **7** measure
9 surrender **10** assessment, estimation
cessation: end **4** halt, liss, lull, rest, stay,
stop **5** letup, lisse, pause, truce **6** recess
7 ceasing, respite **8** interval, stoppage,
surcease **9** armistice, remission **10** conclusion **11** termination **12** intermission, interruption **14** discontinuance
of being: **8** desition
cession: **8** yielding **9** surrender **10** compliance, concession
cesspool: den, sty **4** sump **7** cistern
cetacean: orc **4** cete, orca **5** whale **6** beluga **7** dolphin, grampus **8** porpoise
blind: **4** susu
genus: **4** inia
cete: **5** whale **7** cetacea
Ceylon: *aborigine:* **4** Toda **5** Vedda **6**
Veddah
bay: **4** Palk
boat: **4** done, doni **5** balsa, dhoni, doney
11 warkamoowee
capital: **7** Colombo
coin: **4** cent
Dravidian: **5** Tamil
garment: **6** sarong
gooseberry: **10** ketembilla
governor: **6** disawa
hemp: **6** sina-wa
hill dweller: **4** Toda
language: **4** Pali **5** Tamil
measure: **4** para **5** parah **6** amunam, parrah
modern name: **8** Sri Lanka
monkey: **4** maha **5** toque **6** langur, rilawa,
rillow **10** wanderoock
moss: **4** agar, alga **5** jaffa **7** gulaman
native: **5** Vedda **6** Veddah
oak: **5** kusam
palm: **7** talipat, talipot
rat: **9** bandicoot
resthouse: **6** abalam
rice: **4** padi **5** paddy
rose: **8** cleander
seaport: **5** Galle
sedan: **6** tomjon, tonjon
skirt: **6** reddha
snake: **7** adjiger
soldier: **4** peon
tea: **5** pekoe
tree: **4** doon, hara, palu, tala **7** talipot
Chablis: **4** wine **8** Burgundy

chack: **4** bite, snap **5** clack, snack **8**
wheatear
chackle: **6** cackle, rattle **7** chatter
chacma: **6** baboon
chacra: **4** farm **5** milpa, ranch
Chad: *capital:* **8** N'Djamena
monetary unit: **5** franc
river: **5** Chari **6** Logone
chaeta: **4** seta **5** spine **7** bristle
chafe: irk, rub, vex **4** fret, frig, frot, fume,
gall, heat, josh, rage, warm, wear **5** anger, annoy, grind, scold **6** abrade, banter, excite, fridge, harass, injury, nettle
7 incense, inflame **8** friction, irritate,
raillery
chaff: guy, hay, kid, pug **4** bran, caff(Sc.),
guff, joke, josh, quiz, twit **5** borak,
chyak, dross, glume, hulls, husks, straw,
tease, trash **6** banter, bhoosa, chyack,
refuse **7** tailing **8** raillery, ridicule
chaffer: **5** bandy, sieve, wares **6** buying,
dicker, haggle, higgle, market **7** bargain,
chatter, selling, traffic **8** exchange **9** negotiate **11** merchandise
chaffinch: **7** robinet
chaffy: **5** scaly **7** acerose, acerous, paleate,
trivial **9** bantering, worthless **10** palea-
ceous
Chaillot resident: **8** madwoman
chain: guy, row, set, tew, tie, tye **4** bind,
bond, file, gyve, join, link **5** cable, leash,
suite, train **6** catena, chigon, collar, fasten, fetter, hobble, secure, series, string,
tether **7** bobstay, catenae(pl.), connect,
embrace, enslave, manacle, network,
shackle **8** bracelet, restrain **9** constrain
10 chatelaine **13** concatenation
collar: **4** tore **6** torque
key: **10** chatelaine
of quotations: **6** catena
of rocks: **4** reef
ornamental: **10** chatelaine
pert. to: **8** catenary
set with precious stones: **7** sautoir
chain-like: **8** catenate
chains: **7** bondage, serfdom
lady in: **9** Andromeda
chair: **4** seat **5** sedan, stool **6** office, pulpit, rocker **7** preside
back: **5** splat
bishop's official: **8** cathedra
cover: **4** tidy **12** antimacassar
decoration: **8** claw foot
easy: **6** morris, rocker
folding: **9** faldstool
litterlike: **4** kago
occupy: **7** preside
portable: **5** sedan
type: **4** club, easy **6** morris **7** rocking **8**
captain's **9** reclining
chairperson: **4** head **5** emcee **7** speaker **8**
director **9** moderator **10** supervisor

chaise: gig 4 shay 7 curicle 8 carriage
chaise longue: 6 daybed
chalcedony: 4 onyx, opal, sard 5 agate 6
jasper, quartz 7 opaline 9 carnelian 10
bloodstone 11 chrysoprase
orange: 4 sard
Chalcodon: *father:* 4 Abas
son: 9 Elephenor
Chaldea: 9 Babylonia
measure: 4 cane, foot 5 makuk, qasab 6
artaba, gariba, ghalva 7 mansion
river: 6 Tigris 9 Euphrates
chalet: hut 5 cabin, house 7 cottage 8 lavatory
chalice: ama, cup 4 bowl 5 calix, grail 6
goblet 7 calices(pl.)
cover: 4 pall 8 animetta
chalk: 4 cauk, pale, scar, talc, tick 5 creta,
score 6 blanch, bleach, crayon, credit,
rubble, whiten 7 account 9 limestone,
reckoning
out: 6 sketch 8 block out, rough out 11
skeletonize
up: get, win 6 pick up 7 acquire
challenge: 4 call, dare, defy, gage 5 blame,
brave, claim, query, stump 6 accuse, appeal, cartel, charge, dacker, daiker, demand, forbid, impugn, invite, take on 7
arraign, censure, impeach, provoke, reprove, summons 8 question, reproach 9
exception, objection 10 controvert 11
impeachment
judge: 6 recuse
to a duel: 6 cartel
challenger: 5 rival 7 duelist 8 pugilist 9
adversary, contender 10 competitor
chamber: oda 4 cell, flat, hall, kiva, room
5 atria(pl.), bower, solar, soler 6 atrium, camara, camera, hollow, sollar 7
bedroom, caisson, cubicle, lochlus 9
apartment, camarilla, vestibule 11
compartment
annealing: 4 leer
bombproof: 8 casemate
council: 10 consistory
drying: 4 kiln, oven
judge's: 6 camera
pert. to: 7 cameral
private: 5 adyta(pl.) 6 adytum 7 sanctum
8 conclave
underground: 4 cave 5 crypt 6 cavern 7
hypogee
chamberlain: 6 factor 7 officer, servant,
steward 9 attendant, chamberer, treasurer 10 camerlengo 14 superintendent
papal: 10 camerlengo, camerlingo
chambray: 5 cloth 6 fabric 7 gingham
chameleon: 5 anole, anoli 6 lizard
chameleonic: 6 fickle 10 changeable, inconstant
chamfer: 5 bevel, flute 6 furrow, groove 7
channel 11 countersink

chamois: 4 gems, skin 5 cloth, gemse 6
chammy, shammy, shamoy 7 leather 8
antelope, ruminant
male: 7 gemsbok
champ: 4 bite, chaw, firm, hard, mash 5
field, gnash 7 trample 8 ruminate 9
masticate 11 battlefield
champagne: 4 wine 5 color 6 bubbly
champignon: 6 fungus 8 mushroom
champion: ace, aid 4 abet, back, defy,
hero 6 assert, attend, defend, squire,
victor 7 espouse, fighter, protect 8 advocate, defender 9 challenge, combatant, firstrate 10 blue-ribbon, unexcelled
11 outstanding, titleholder
championship: 5 crown, title 7 defense,
pennant 8 advocacy 9 supremacy 10
leadership
champleve: 6 enamel, inlaid
chance: die, hap, lot 4 case, dint, fate,
luck, odds, risk, tide 5 ettle, stake 6 betide, casual, gamble, happen, hazard,
mishap, random 7 aimless, fortune,
stumble, venture 8 accident, casualty,
fortuity 9 adventure, haphazard, happening, mischance 10 contingent 11
contingency, opportunity, probability
by: 5 haply
even: 6 tossup
favorable: 4 odds
chancellor: 5 judge 7 adviser, officer 8
minister
chancery: 5 court 6 office 8 registry
chandelier: 6 pharos 7 fixture 11 candelabrum
chandler: 6 dealer 8 merchant, provider 9
tradesman
change: mew 4 move, swap, turn, vary,
veer 5 adapt, alter, amend, break, coins,
shift 6 modify, mutate, remove, revamp, revise, switch 7 commute, convert, deviate 8 castrate, revision, transfer 9 diversity, permutate, rearrange,
transform, transmute, transpose, variation 10 alteration, correction, difference, transition 11 desexualize, vicissitude 13 metamorphosis 15 diversi-
fication
appearance: 6 obvert
back: 6 return, revert
character of: 8 denature
color: dye 5 blush 6 redden
course: 4 tack, turn, veer 5 sheer
into: 6 become
music: 4 muta
subject to: 7 mutable 8 amenable, variable
sudden: 8 peripety
changeable: 5 eemis, giddy, immis 6 fickle, fitful, mobile 7 bruckle, erratic, mutable, protean, variant 8 amenable,
catching, unstable, volatile 9 alterable,

irregular, mercurial, uncertain, unsettled **10** capricious, inconstant, irresolute **11** chameleonic
in form: **9** metabolic
changeless: **5** fixed **6** steady **8** constant **9** steadfast **10** invariable
changeling: oaf **4** dolt, fool **5** child, dunce, idiot **7** waverer **8** imbecile, renegade, turncoat **9** simpleton **10** substitute
changeover: **5** shift **10** alteration, conversion
changing: *color:* **11** allochroous
pattern and color: **13** kaleidoscopic
channel: gat, ree, rut **4** cano, cava, dike, duct, dyke, gool, gote, gout, pipe, vein, wadi, wady **5** canal, chase, ditch, drain, drill, flume, flute, glyph, media(pl.), regal, rigol, river, sinus, stria **6** arroyo, artery, furrow, groove, gutter, medium, rabbet, rivose, sluice, strait, stream, striae(pl.), trough **7** conduct, conduit, passage, rivulet, silanga, tideway **8** aqueduct, guideway **10** instrument **11** watercourse
artificial: gat **4** leat **5** canal, drain, flume **6** sluice **7** drainer
brain: **4** iter
formed by cutting: **5** scarf
longitudinal: **6** rabbet
marker: **4** buoy
narrow: **6** furrow, strait
near port: **5** deeps
river: bed **6** alveni(pl.) **7** alvenus
ship: gat
vertical: **5** glyph
vital: **6** artery
water: gat **4** gote, gurt, leat, pipe, race **5** canal, drain, flume **6** sluice **7** conduit **8** aqueduct, millrace, tailrace
Channel Island: **4** Sark **8** Guernsey
measure: **4** cade **5** cabot
seaweed: **5** vraic
channelbill: **8** rainfowl
channeled: **6** fluted **7** voluted **8** furrowed **9** chamfered
channels: **5** media **6** striae
chanson: **4** song **5** lyric **6** ballad **7** refrain
chant: **4** cant, sing, song, tune **5** carol, psalm **6** anthem, cantus, intone, warble **7** introit, worship **8** vocalize **10** cantillate
Gregorian: **9** plainsong **12** cantus firmus
Jewish: **6** Hallel
chantage: **9** extortion **12** blackmailing
chanter: **6** cantor, singer **7** bagpipe **8** songster **9** chorister
chanteuse: **6** singer **10** cantatrice
chantey, chanty: **4** song
chanticleer: **4** cock **7** rooster
Chantilly: **4** lace
chantry: **4** cage **5** altar **6** chapel, shrine

chanty, chantey: **4** song
chaos: pie **4** gulf, mess, void **5** abyss, babel, chasm **6** jumble **7** anarchy, mixture **8** disorder, shambles **9** confusion **10** unruliness **11** lawlessness
primordial: **4** Apsu
utter: **6** tophet **7** topheth
Chaos: *Babylonian:* **4** Apsu
daughter: Nox, Nyx
Maori: **4** kore
son: **6** Erebus
chaotic: **5** snafu **7** muddled **8** confused, formless
chap: boy, buy, man, rap **4** bean, beat, blow, chip, chop, cove, duck, gent, kibe, mash **5** billy, bloke, bully, buyer, chink, cleft, crack, knock, lover, split, trade, youth **6** barter, breach, bugger, callan, choose, fellow, shaver, strike, stroke **7** callant, chapman, chappie, fissure, husband, roughen **8** blighter, customer, division
odd: **6** galoot
old: **6** geezer
young: **6** gaffer
chaparral: **7** thicket **9** buckthorn
chapel: **4** cage, cape, cope, cowl, hood **5** cloak **6** bethel, church, shrine **7** chantry, service **8** bethesda **9** reliquary, sanctuary
private: **7** oratory
sailor's: **6** bethel
chaperon: **4** hood **6** attend, duenna(Sp.), escort, matron **7** oversee, protect **8** guardian, trapping **10** escutcheon **11** gouvernante(F.)
chaplain: **5** padre **8** sky pilot **9** clergyman
chaplet: **4** bead, orle **5** crown **6** anadem, anchor, circle, fillet, rosary, trophy, wreath **7** coronal, coronet, garland **8** moulding, necklace, ornament
chapman: **5** buyer **6** dealer, hawker, trader **7** peddler **8** customer, merchant
chaps: **4** boys, jaws, lads **5** flews **8** breeches, leggings, overalls
chapter: **4** body, cell, post **5** caput, lodge **6** branch **7** correct, meeting, section **8** assembly **9** reprimand **10** contingent
char: **4** burn, cart, sear **5** broil, chark, chore, singe, trout **6** scorch **7** blacken, chariot **8** sandbank **9** carbonize
charabanc: bus **5** coach **7** vehicle
character: **4** bent, card, kind, mark, mold, note, part, rune, sign, sort, tone **5** brand, fiber, stamp, tenor, token, trait, write **6** caract, emblem, figure, letter, mettle, nature, repute, stripe, symbol **7** edition, essence, engrave, impress, quality **8** inscribe **9** agreement, ampersand **10** reputation **11** disposition
assumed: **4** role
bad: **5** drole(F.)

chief: 4 hero, lead, star 7 heroine 11 protagonist

group: 5 ethos

of a people: 5 ethos

vein: 6 streak

word-representing: 8 logogram 9 logograph

characteristic: 4 cast, mark, mien 5 trait 6 nature 7 feature, impress, quality, typical 8 property, symbolic 9 attribute, lineament 11 distinctive, pathognomic, peculiarity

individual: 9 idiopathy

characterize: 4 mark 6 define, depict 7 engrave, entitle, imprint, portray 8 describe, indicate, inscribe 9 delineate, designate, represent 11 distinguish

charade: 6 enigma, puzzle, riddle 7 pageant, picture, tableau 8 disguise, pretense 11 make-believe

charcoal: 5 carbo, chark 6 carbon, fusain, pencil 7 blacken, drawing

animal: 9 boneblack

reduce to: 4 char

chard: 4 beet 7 thistle 9 artichoke

chare, char: job 4 lane, task, turn 5 alley, chore 6 finish, street 7 perform

charge: fee 4 bill, cark, cost, duty, fill, lien, load, onus, rate, rush, toll, ward 5 debit, onset, order, price, refer 6 accuse, adjure, allege, assess, attack, burden, career, credit, defame, demand, enjoin, impute, indict, tariff, weight 7 arraign, ascribe, assault, average, censure, command, concern, custody, expense, impeach, keeping, mandate, mission 8 chastise, overload, price tag 9 challenge, oversight 10 commission, impetition, impregnate, injunction, management 11 arraignment, encumbrance, incriminate, instruction 14 responsibility

customary: 4 dues

grazing: 5 agist

with gas: 6 aerate

chargeable: 6 costly, liable 7 weighty 9 expensive, important, momentous 10 burdensome 11 responsible, troublesome

charged: 5 tense 9 emotional, on the cuff 10 purposeful

with electricity: 4 live

chargeman: 7 blaster, foreman 10 batteryman

charger: 4 dish 5 horse, mount, plate, steed 6 vessel 7 accuser, courser, platter 8 war-horse

charges: *boat carrying:* 7 boatage

legal: 4 dues, fees 5 costs 9 retainers

repairs to barrister's quarters: 9 detriment

charily: 8 frugally, gingerly 9 carefully 10 cautiously

chariness: 7 caution 8 prudence 9 frugal-

ity, integrity 11 heedfulness, sparingness

chariot: car 4 cart, char, wain 5 buggy, essed, wagon 6 charet, esseda, essede 7 vehicle 8 carriage, charette

for carrying image of god: 4 rath 5 ratha

Greek: 8 quadriga

Roman: 5 essed 6 esseda, essede

two-horse: 4 biga

charioteer: 5 pilot 6 auriga, driver 7 wagoner 9 charioter

charisma: 5 charm, power 6 allure, appeal, glamor, impact 8 urtchery 9 magnetism 11 fascination

charitable: 4 kind 6 benign, humane 7 lenient, liberal 8 generous 9 favorable, forgiving, indulgent 10 beneficent, benevolent 12 eleemosynary 13 compassionate, philanthropic

charity: 4 alms, dole, gift, love, pity, ruth 5 mercy 6 bounty 7 handout, largess 8 lenience 9 affection 10 almsgiving, generosity, liberality, tenderness 12 philanthropy

dispenser: 7 almoner

charivari: 5 babel 6 medley 8 serenade, shivaree 10 callithump 11 celebration

chark: cup 4 burn, char, coal, coke 5 glass 6 cinder, noggin 8 charcoal

charlatan: 4 sham 5 cheat, faker, fraud, quack 7 cabotin, empiric 8 imposter, magician 9 pretender 10 medicaster, mountebank

Charlemagne: *brother:* 8 Carloman

conquest: 5 Avars

court hero: 6 Roland

father: 5 Pepin

knight: 4 Gano 7 Ganelon, Paladin

nephew: 6 Roland 7 Orlando

peer: 6 Oliver 7 Paladin

pert. to: 8 Caroline

sword: 7 Joyeuse

Charles' Wain: 4 Bear, Ursa 9 Big Dipper

Charlie Chan creator: 7 Biggers

charlock: 4 weed 5 kraut 7 mustard, yellows

charlotte: 7 custard, dessert

Charlotte Corday's victim: 5 Marat

charm: obi 4 calm, juju, jynx, mojo, play, song 5 allay, freet, freit, grace, obeah, magic, saffi, safie, spell, weird 6 allure, amulet, beauty, caract, enamor, entice, fetich, fetish, glamor, grigri, melody, please, scarab, saphie, soothe, subdue, summon 7 assuage, attract, beguile, bewitch, cantrip, conjure, control, delight, enamour, enchant, enthral, flatter, glamour, periapt, singing, sorcery 8 breloque, enthrall, entrance, greegree, practice, talisman 9 agreeable, captivate, fascinate, seduction 10 attraction, demonifuge 11 incantation

protective: 6 amulet

charmer: 5 siren 8 exorcist, magician, sorcerer 9 sorceress 11 spellbinder

charming: 7 amiable, eyesome, winning, winsome 8 adorable, delicate 9 agreeable, beautiful, glamorous 10 attractive, glamourous

charnel: 7 ghastly 8 cemetery 10 sepulchral

house: 7 ossuary 8 mortuary

Charon: 7 boatman 8 ferryman

father: 6 Erebus

mother: Nox

payment to: 4 obol 6 obolus

river: 4 Styx

Charpentier opera: 6 Louise

charqui: 4 beef, meat 5 jerky 6 xarque

chart: map 4 card, plan, plat, plot 5 carte, graph 6 design, devise, record, scheme 7 diagram, dope out, explore, outline, project 8 document, platform 9 blueprint 10 cartograph

charter: let 4 deed, hire, rent 5 carte, chart, grant, lease 6 charta, permit 9 privilege 10 commission, conveyance

chary: shy 4 dear, safe, wary 5 chere, scant 6 frugal, prized, skimpy 7 careful, guarded, sparing 8 cautious, hesitant, precious, reserved, vigilant 9 diffident, reluctant, treasured 10 economical, fastidious, scrupulous 11 circumspect

Charybdis rock: 6 Scylla

chase: 4 hunt, shag, sick 5 annoy, catch, chevy, chivy, harry, score 6 chivvy, emboss, follow, frieze, furrow, gallop, groove, harass, hollow, indent, pursue, quarry, scorse, trench 7 channel, engrave, kick out, pursuit 8 ornament

away: 4 rout, shoo 5 drive

goddesss: 4 Dian 5 Diana

chaser: ram 4 wolf 5 drink 6 masher 7 Don Juan 8 airplane, engraver

chasm: gap, pit 4 gulf, rift 5 abyss, blank, canon, chaos, cleft, gorge 6 breach, canyon, hiatus 7 fissure 8 aperture, crevasse, interval

glacial: 7 crevass 8 crevasse

chasse: 4 slip, step 5 glide 6 liquor, sashay, shrine 7 dismiss 9 relinquary

chassepot: 5 rifle

chasseur: 6 hunter 7 footman 8 huntsman 9 attendant

chassis: 5 frame

chaste: 4 pure 5 clean, moral 6 decent, honest, modest, proper, severe, vestal 7 refined 8 celibate, innocent, virtuous 9 continent, undefiled 10 immaculate

chasten: 4 rate 5 abase, smite, smote, sober 6 humble, punish, refine, subdue, temper 7 afflict, censure, correct 8 chastise, moderate, restrain 9 castigate, humiliate, reprimand 10 discipline

chastise: 4 beat, flog, lash, slap, trim, whip 5 amend, blame, scold, spank, strap, taunt 6 accuse, anoint, berate, charge, punish, purify, rebuke, refine, swinge, temper, thrash 7 chasten, correct, reprove, scourge, suspect 9 castigate 10 discipline

chastity: 5 honor 6 purity, virtue 7 modesty 8 celibacy, goodness 9 innocence

chasuble: 6 deacon, planet 8 vestment

chat: mag 4 bird, chin, cone, coze, gist, talk, tove, twig 5 ament, cause, dally, point, prate, speak, spike 6 babble, branch, catkin, confab, gabble, gibber, gossip, jabber, potato, samara 7 chatter, prattle 8 causerie, converse, spikelet, strobile 9 dalliance 11 confabulate 12 conversation

chateau: 5 house, manor, villa 6 castle 7 mansion 8 fortress

Chateaubriand work: 4 René 5 Atala 10 Les Natchez

chatelaine: pin 4 etui, hook 5 chain, clasp, etwee, purse 6 brooch 8 mistress

chaton: 5 basil, bezel, bezil 7 setting

chattel: 4 gear 5 goods, money, slave, wares 7 capital 8 bondsman, property 9 livestock, principal

chatter: gab, jaw, mag, yap 4 blab, carp, chat, hack, rick, talk, tear, yirr 5 cabal, clack, garre, haver, prate, shake 6 babble, gabble, gibber, gossip, jabber, palter, rattle, shiver, tattle, yammer, yatter 7 blabber, brabble, chackle, chaffer, chipper, chitter, clitter, nashgob, prabble, prattle, shatter 8 schmoose, verbiage 9 small talk 11 goosecackle

conjurer's: 10 hanky-panky

chatterbox: jay, mag 4 piet 5 clack 6 gossip, magpie 8 quidnunc 10 chatterbag, chattermag 12 blabbermouth 13 chatterbasket

chattering: 8 babbling 9 prattling, talkative 10 loquacious

chauffeur: 5 drive 6 driver 8 operator 9 transport

chaussee: 4 road 6 street 7 highway 8 causeway

chaussure: 4 boot, shoe 7 slipper 8 footgear

chauvinism: 8 jingoism 10 patriotism 11 nationalism

chaw: jaw, vex 4 chew, envy, mull 5 champ, grind 6 ponder 7 portion 8 ruminate 9 chawbacon, masticate

chawbacon: 4 chaw, lout 5 yokel 6 rustic 7 bumpkin

cheap: low 4 base, poor, vile 5 close, gaudy, kitch, price, tacky, tight, tinny, value 6 abject, common, kitsch, plenty, shoddy, sordid, stingy, tawdry, trashy 7 bargain, dealing 8 inferior, purchase 9 innkeeper, low-priced 10 despicable 11 depreciated, inexpensive 12 contemptible cheap jack: 6 hawker, monger, pedlar, pedler, vendor 7 peddler 8 huckster 9 Cheap-John

cheat: do; bam, bob, cog, con, fob, gip, gum, gyp, nip 4 bilk, bite, clip, dupe, fake, flam, geck, gull, hoax, jilt, jouk, liar, mump, rook, sell, sham, skin 5 bunco, bunko, cozen, cully, dodge, faker, fling, foist, fraud, gouge, guile, knave, mulct, rogue, scamp, spoil, trick, welsh 6 baffle, chiaus, chisel, daddle, delude, deride, doodle, duffer, fiddle, fleece, grease, humbug, illude, jockey, outwit, raddle, renege, shaver 7 abusion, beguile, deceive, defraud, escheat, finesse, foister, gudgeon, juggler, mislead, plunder, quibble, sharper, swindle 8 artifice, delusion, dry-shave, hoodwink, imposter 9 bamboozle, hypocrite, imposture, scoundrel, strategem, victimize 10 mountebank 15 prestidigitator

cheater: 4 bite, gull 5 knave 6 bilker, topper 7 sharper 9 trickster

check: bit, dam, nab, nip, tab 4 balk, curb, damp, rein, snub, stay, stem, stop, stub, test, twit, were 5 abort, allay, block, brake, catch, chide, chink, choke, crack, daunt, delay, deter, draft, limit, quell, repel, stall, still, stunt, tally, taunt, token 6 arrest, attack, baffle, bridle, defeat, detain, detent, gravel, hinder, impede, oppose, outwit, quench, rabbet, rebate, rebuff, rebuke, scotch, stifle, ticket, verify 7 backset, command, control, inhibit, monitor, refrain, repress, reproof, reprove, repulse, setback 8 bulkhead, encumber, obstruct, restrain, withhold 9 constrain, frustrate, interrupt, overpower, reprimand, restraint, supervise 10 difficulty 11 certificate, counterfoil, examination

check growth of: 5 stunt 7 shorten

check in: 6 arrive 8 register

check out: die 5 leave 6 depart 7 confirm 11 investigate

check over: 5 study 7 examine, inspect 10 scrutinize

checkerboard: 7 dambrod 8 damboard
marked like: 10 tessellate

checkered: 4 pied, vair 5 diced, plaid 6 motley 10 changeable, variegated 11 diversified

checkers: 4 game 6 damrod, drafts 8 draughts
move: 4 dyke, fife, huff 5 cross 7 bristol
opening: 6 souter
term: 4 king 5 block, crown

checkerwork: 7 tessera 8 tesserae(pl.)
inlay: 6 mosaic

checklist: 7 catalog 9 catalogue, inventory

checkmate: 4 gain, lick, stop, undo 6 baf-

fle, corner, defeat, outwit, stymie, thwart 9 frustrate

checkrein: 4 curb 7 saccade

cheddar: 6 cheese

cheek: 4 chap, gall, gena, jole, jowl, leer, sass 5 bucca, chyak, crust, genae(pl.), nerve, sauce 6 chyack, haffet, haffit 8 audacity, temerity 9 brashness, impudence
bone: 5 malar 6 zygoma
distended: 7 buccate
muscle: 10 buccinator
pert. to: 5 genal, malar 6 buccal

cheep: pip, yap, yip 4 hint(Sc.), peep, pule 5 chirp, creak(Sc.), tweet 6 squeak, tattle 7 chirrup, twitter

cheer: ole(Sp.), rah 4 fare, food, root, viva, yell 5 bravo, elate, feast, heart, huzza, mirth, shout, whoop 6 cantle, gaiety, hurrah, huzzah, solace, viands 7 acclaim, animate, applaud, cherish, comfort, console, enliven, gladden, hearten, jollity, refresh, rejoice 8 applause, brighten, inspirit, pheasant, vivacity 9 animation, encourage, merriment 10 exhilarate, invigorate 11 acclamation, hospitality 13 entertainment, hospitability
burst: 5 salvo

cheerful: gay 4 cant, glad, gleg(Sc.), rosy 5 cadgy, canty, chirk, douce, happy, jolly, merry, peart, ready, sunny 6 blithe, bright, cheery, chirpy, crouse, genial, hearty, hilary, jocund, lively 7 buoyant, chipper 8 cheering, gladsome, homelike, sanguine 9 contented, lightsome, sprightly 10 enlivening 11 comfortable 12 lighthearted

cheerless: sad 4 cold, drab, glum, gray 5 bleak, drear 6 dismal, dreary, gloomy 7 forlorn, joyless 8 dejected 10 dispirited, melancholy 11 comfortless 12 disconsolate

cheerio: 5 adieu 6 bye-bye 7 good-bye

cheese: 4 Brie, Edam, Jack 5 cream, Gouda, Swiss, Ziega 6 Barrie, Dunlop, Glarus, mysost, Zieger 7 Cheddar, cottage, Gruyere, Stilton 8 American, Parmesan 9 Camembert, Gammelost, Limburger, Roquefort 10 Gorgonzola, Neufchatel 11 Liederkranz
brown: 6 mysost
curdy: 4 trip
dish: 4 cake 6 fondue, omelet 7 rarebit, souffle
green: 7 sapsago
large: 7 kebbock, kebbuck
milk whey: 5 ziega 6 zieger
Normandy: 7 angelot
pert. to: 6 caseic 7 caseous
poached: 10 gnocchetti
white: 11 Neufchatel

cheese maggot: 7 skipper
cheesecake: 7 dessert **10** photograph
cheeseparing: 6 penury **9** parsimony **10** stinginess
cheesy: 4 fine, poor **5** cheap, smart **6** shabby, sleazy **7** caseous **8** inferior **9** excellent, worthless
cheetah: cat **5** youse, youze **7** guepard **8** gueparde
chef: 4 cook **7** saucier **9** cuisinier **10** cuisiniere
chef d'oeuvre: 7 classic **9** showpiece, work of art **11** masterpiece, tour de force
chela: 4 claw **5** slave **6** pincer **7** servant **8** disciple
chelicera: 8 mandible **9** appendage
chelonian: 6 turtle **8** tortoise
chemical: 4 acid, salt **6** alkali **8** catalyst **10** alchemical **13** iatrochemical
agent: **8** catalyst
compound: **4** acid, base, diol, imin **5** amide, azine, ceria, ester, imine, purin **6** boride **7** inosite, leucine, metamer
element: See **element:** *chemical*
measure: **4** dram, gram **5** liter, titer
salt: sal
chemise: 5 shift, shirt, smock **6** camisa **8** lingerie
chemisette: 4 sham **6** guimpe
chemist: 7 analyst **8** druggist **9** alchemist **10** apothecary, pharmacist
vessel: **4** vial **5** ampul, cupel, flask, phial **6** aludel, ampule, beaker, retort **7** ampoule **8** bolt head, test tube
workroom: lab **10** laboratory
cheri, cherie: 4 dear **7** beloved, darling **9** cherished **10** sweetheart
cherish: aid, hug, pet **4** dote, hope, like, love, save **5** adore, cheer, cling, enjoy, nurse, prize, value **6** caress, esteem faddle, fondle, foster, harbor, nestle, pamper, pettle, revere **7** comfort, embosom, embrace, indulge, nourish, nurture, protect, support, sustain **8** enshrine, inspirit, preserve, treasure **9** cultivate, encourage, entertain
cheroot: 5 cigar
cherry: 4 bing, duke, gean **5** morel **7** capulin, chapman, lambert, morello, oxheart **8** amarelle, napoleon **9** bigarreau
acid: **7** cerasin
color: red **6** cerise
extract: **8** cerasein
sour: **8** amarelle
sweet: **4** bing **7** lambert, oxheart
wild: **4** gean **7** marasca, mazzard **10** maraschino
cherry finch: 8 hawfinch
cherry holly: 5 islay
cherry laurel: 7 cerasus
cherry orange: 7 kumquat

cherrystone: 4 clam **6** quahog
cherub: 5 angel **6** seraph, spirit **8** seraphim(pl.)
chervil: bun **4** herb
Cheshire district: 4 Hale **5** Hoole **6** Marple
chess: *draw game:* **9** stalemate
finish: **4** draw, mate **7** endgame **9** checkmate, stalemate
Japanese: **5** shogi
move: **5** debut **6** castle, fidate, gambit **10** fianchetto
opening: **5** debut **6** gambit **10** fianchetto
pert. to: **8** scacchic
piece: man **4** king, pawn, rook **5** horse, queen **6** bishop, castle, knight
chest: ark, box, kit **4** arca, bust, cist, cyst, fund, safe **5** ambry, bahut, front, hoard, hutch, trunk **6** basket, breast, bunker(Sc.), bureau, casket, coffer, coffin, hamper, locker, shrine, stripe, thorax **7** caisson, capcase, cassone(It.), commode, deposit, dresser, enclose, highboy **8** cupboard, treasury **9** container, strongbox **10** chiffonier, contention, receptacle, repository **11** controversy, gardeviance
alms: **6** almoin **7** almoign
animal: **7** brisket
bone: **5** costa
human: **6** breast, thorax
meal: **6** girnal, girnel
pert. to: **8** thoracic
sacred: ark **4** arca, cist
sound: **4** rale **7** rhonchi(pl.) **8** rhonchus
stone: **4** cist, kist
supply: **6** wangan, wangun **7** wanigan **8** wannigan
chesterfield: 4 coat, sofa **5** divan **8** overcoat **9** davenport
chestnut: 4 joke, ling, rata, tree **5** brown, horse **6** cliche, marron(F.), sativa **7** crenata, dentata
and gray: **4** roan
dwarf: **9** chincapin **10** chinquapin
genus of: **8** castanea
water: **4** ling **5** trapa
chevalier: 5 noble **6** knight **7** gallant **8** cavalier, horseman **9** gentleman **10** greenshank
cheverel, cheveril: 6 pliant **7** elastic, kidskin **8** flexible
chevet: 4 apse **11** termination
chevisance: 5 booty, issue, spoil **6** remedy, supply **8** chivalry, resource **9** expedient, substance **10** enterprise, provisions **11** achievement, transaction
chevron: 4 beam, mark **5** glove **6** rafter, stripe, zigzag **7** molding **10** gravystain
chevrotain: 4 napu **7** deerlet, kanchil, tragule
chew: cud **4** bite, cham, chaw, gnaw, quid

5 chamm, grind, munch, rumen 6 mumble 8 meditate, ruminate 9 denticate, manducate, masticate
inability to: 8 amasesis
on: 8 consider
out: jaw 5 scold 7 bawl out, tell off 10 tongue-lash
the rag: 6 gossip 7 chatter
chewing gum base: 6 chicle
chewink: 4 bird 5 finch, joree 6 towhee
chiastolite: 5 macle 10 andalusite
chiaus: 5 cheat 8 sergeant, swindler 9 messenger
Chibcha: 4 zipa 5 zaque 6 Indian, zacqua 7 muisca
chic: 4 pert, posh, trig, trim 5 natty, nifty, smart 6 dapper, modish 7 elegant, stylish
chicadee: 8 titmouse
Chicago district: 4 Loop
chicanery: 4 ruse, wile 5 feint, trick 8 artifice, intrigue, trickery 9 deception, duplicity, sophistry, stratagem
chichi: 5 showy, swank 7 splashy 8 affected 11 pretentious
chick: 4 girl, tick 5 child, natty 6 moppet, screen, sequin, sprout 7 chicken 8 young one
chick-pea: 4 gram, herb 5 chich, cicer 8 garbanzo, garvance, garvanzo 9 garavance
chickadee: 8 titmouse
chickaree: 8 squirrel
chicken: hen 4 cock, fowl 5 biddy, capon, chick, child, chuck, fryer, layer, manoc, poult 6 chicky, pullet 7 broiler, rooster 8 cockerel 11 chickabiddy
breed: 7 Leghorn 9 Wyandotte 11 Rhode Island
castrated: 5 capon
cooking: 5 fryer 7 broiler, roaster
pen: 4 coop
raising device: 7 brooder
young: 5 chick, fryer, poult 6 pullet 7 broiler
chicken out: 4 quit 6 renege
chicken snake: 4 boba
chickenhearted: 5 timid 8 cowardly
chickweed genus: 6 alsine
chicle: gum 5 latex
chicory: 4 bunk, root 5 plant 6 endive 7 succory, witloof
family: 12 cichoriaceae
chide: 4 rail, rate 5 blame, check, flite, flyte, scold 6 berate, rebuff, rebuke, threap, threep, threpe 7 censure, reprove, upbraid, wrangle 8 admonish, call down, reproach 9 objurgate, reprehend, reprimand
chief: aga, big, boh, cap, cob, dux, mir 4 agha, arch, boss, duce, duke, head, high, khan, main, rais, raja, reis, tyee 5 alder, elder, first, great, major, prime, rajah,

ruler, thane, titan, vital 6 adalid, cabeza, leader, master, rector, sachem, staple 7 capital, captain, central, eminent, foreman, overman, palmary, prelate, premier, supreme 8 big wheel, dominant, especial, foremost, intimate, sagamore 9 chieftain, commander, number one, paramount, principal, prominent 11 predominant
chiffonier: 5 chest 6 bureau 7 cabinet, commode, dresser
chigger: 4 mite 6 chigoe, insect, jigger, red-bug
chignon: bun 4 knot 5 chain, twist 6 collar
chigoe: 4 flea 7 chigger
chilblain: 4 kibe, mule(F.), sore 5 blain 6 pernio 8 swelling 12 inflammation
child (see also **children**): ben (Heb.), boy, bud, imp, kid, son, tad, tot 4 baba, babe, baby, bata, brat, chit, girl, page, tike, tyke 5 bairn(Sc.), chick, chiel(Sc.), gamin, issue, minor, youth 6 cherub, enfant, filius(L.), infant, moppet, urchin 7 bambino(It.), progeny 8 bantling, chiseler(Ir.), daughter 9 firstling, offspring, youngster 10 adolescent, descendant 11 chickabiddy
advancement: 9 precocity
chubby: 8 rolypoly 10 butterball
dainty: elf 5 fairy
gifted: 7 prodigy
homeless: 4 waif
illegitimate: 6 by-blow 7 bastard
killer: 11 infanticide
parentless: 6 orphan
patron saint: 8 Nicholas
pert. to: 6 filial
puckish: imp
roguish: 6 urchin
spoiled: 4 brat 5 mardy 7 cockney
street: 5 gamin
tiny: tot 4 babe, baby, tyke 6 infant, peewee
unmannerly: 7 smatche(Sc.)
childbirth: 5 labor 7 lying-in, travail 11 confinement, parturition
goddess: 4 Apet, Auge, Upis 5 Damia 6 Lucina 7 Auxesia
childish: 4 slow, weak 5 naive, petty, silly 6 puling, simple, weanly(Sc.), young 7 asinine, babyish, foolish, kiddish, puerile, unmanly 8 bairnish, brattish, immature, juvenile 9 credulous, childlike, infantile, kittenish
childish talk: 7 prattle
childish walk: 6 toddle
childless: 6 barren 7 sterile
childlike: 4 meek 6 docile, filial 7 babyish, dutiful 8 childish, innocent, trusting 9 confiding, frivolous 10 submissive
children: 7 progeny 9 offspring

dislike of: **9** misopedia **10** misopaedia
medical science: **10** pediatrics **11** paediatrics
room: **7** nursery
study: **8** pedology **9** paedology
tender of: **4** amah **6** sitter **9** nursemaid
Chile: *capital:* **8** Santiago
chief export: **6** copper
city: **6** Arauco, Cobija, Serena **7** Caldera, Copiapo **8** Coquimbo, Valdivia **10** Concepcion, Valparaiso
coastal wind: **5** sures
conqueror: **8** Valdivia
desert: **7** Atacama
Indian: Ona **4** Auca, Inca, Onan **6** Arauca, Chango
island: **5** Byron, Guafo, Hoste
measure: **4** vara **5** legua, linea **6** cuadra, fanega
monetary unit: **4** peso **5** libra **6** condor, escudo
mountain: **4** Maco, Toro **5** Maipu, Pular, Torre, Yogan
mountain range: **5** Andes
national police: **11** carabineros
province: **5** Arica, Aysen, Maule, Nuble, Talca **6** Bio-Bio, Cautin, Chiloe, Curico **7** Atacama
river: Loa **5** Itata, Maipu, Maule **6** Bio-Bio, Chuapa, Lontue **7** Illapel **8** Valdivia
rodent: **10** chinchilla
seaport: **4** Lota, Tome **5** Arica **8** Coquimba
shrub: **5** lithi **6** pepino
tree: **4** brea, pelu, ulmo **5** coleu, rauli, roble **6** alerce, alerse, coigue, muermo
volcano: **5** Lanin, Maipo **6** Antuco, Lascar, Llaima **7** Calbuco
weight: **5** grano, libra **7** quintal
workman: **4** roto
chill: ice, raw **4** ague, cold, cool, dazy(Sc.) **5** algor, gelid, rigor, shake **6** frappe, freeze, frigid, frosty, shiver **7** depress, frisson, glacial, malaria **8** coldness **11** refrigerate
chiller: **7** shocker **8** thriller
chilling: **4** eery **5** eerie **6** wintry **7** glacial
chills and fever: **4** ague **7** malaria
chilly: raw **4** cold, cool, lash **5** algid, bleak, hunch **6** arctic, frosty **9** cauldrife
chimaera: **7** ratfish
chime: din, rim **4** bell, edge, peal, ring, suit, ting **5** agree, prate **6** accord, cymbal, jingle, melody **7** concord, harmony **8** singsong
chime in: **4** tell **5** state, offer **6** chip in
chimera: **5** dream, fancy **6** mirage **8** illusion **9** pipe dream
chimerical: **4** vain, wild **6** absurd, unreal **7** utopian **8** delusive, fanciful, romantic **9** fantastic, imaginary, unfounded, visionary

chimes: **5** bells **8** carillon
chimney: lum **4** flue, pipe, tube, vent **5** gully, stack, tewel **6** funnel **7** fissure, opening, orifice **10** smokestack
cover: **4** cowl **7** turncap
deposit: **4** soot
piece: **5** parel **6** mantel
post: **5** speer
chimney corner: **8** fireside **9** inglenook
chimpanzee: ape **5** jacko, pigmy **10** anthropoid, troglodyte
chin: jaw, rap **4** chat **5** menta(pl.) **6** mentum
double: **4** fold **7** buccula
china: **4** ware **6** dishes **7** ceramic, pottery **8** Cinchona, crockery **9** porcelain **11** earthenware
fine: **5** Spode **6** Sevres **7** Dresden, Limoges, Meissen **8** Wedgwood
China: *aborigine:* Yao **4** Mans, Miao **6** Mantzu, Yaomin **7** Miaotse, Miaotze
alloy: **7** paktong **8** packtong
ancient name: **4** Tsao **5** Seres **6** Cathay
antelope: **6** dzeren
arch: **6** pailoo, pailou, pailow
artichoke: **7** chorogi
bamboo: **7** whangee
banker: **6** shroff
bean: soy **6** cowpea
black tea: **6** oolong
boat: **4** bark, junk **6** sampan
brigand: **9** hunghutze, hunghutzu
Buddha: Fo; Foh
Buddhist paradise: **7** Chingtu
cabbage: **7** pakchoi
calculator: **7** suan pan, swan pan
canton: Fu **5** Hsein
capital: **6** Peking **7** Beijing
city: Nom, Ude **4** Amoy, Luta, Tsin, Wuhu **5** Jehol, Macao, Macau, Pekin **6** Canton, Fachan, Fuchau, Hankau, Hankow, Huchau, Kalgan, Mukden, Nankin, Ningpo, Suchau, Swatow, Tsinan, Yunnan **7** Chengte, Chengtu, Chingtu, Fatshan, Foochow, Hanyang, Kaifeng, Lanchau, Nanking, Paoting, Taiyuen, Tunkuan, Wenchau, Wuchang, Yenping **8** Changsha, Chaochau, Fancheng, Hangchau, Hangchow, Kiaochau, Nanchang, Shanghai, Shenyang, Shaohing, Siangtan, Tengchau, Tientsin, Tungchau, Tunghwan, Yanphing **9** Changchau, Chinkiang, Chungking, Lienkiang **10** Chingkiang, Kingtechen
city (Pinyin spelling): **4** Luda (Luta) **7** Beijing (Peking), Chengdu (Chengtu), Nanjing (Nanking), Tianjin (Tientsin) **8** Quingdao (Tsingtao) **9** Chongqing (Chungking), Guangzhou (Canton)
civet: **5** rasse
clay: **6** kaolin
cloth: sha **4** moxa, pulo, silk **6** nankin **7** nankeen

cloth-stiffening gelatin: **7** haitsai

coin: le, pu; fan, neu, sen **4** cash, cent, mace, tael, tiao, yuan **5** liang, tsien **6** dollar, ticket **9** candareen **10** Kuping-tael **11** Haikwantael

cooking style: **5** Hunan **6** Fukien, Peking **8** Szechuan **9** Cantonese

cosmic order: tao

customs collector: **5** hoppo

deer: **8** elaphure

department: Fu **5** Hsien

desert: **4** Gobi

dialect: **4** Amoy **5** Hakka **6** Canton, Ningpo, Swatow **7** Foochow, Wenchow

dish: **4** rice **7** fooyung **8** fooyoung

divison: **4** chow, Miao **5** Hsien **6** canton **8** province

dog: **4** chow, peke

dragon: **6** chilin

drink: **6** samshu

duck eggs: **5** pidan

dulcimer: **7** yang-kin

dynasty: Han, Sui, Wei, Yin **4** Chin, Chou, Hsia, Ming, Sung, Tang, Tsin, Yuan **5** Shang **6** Manchu

exchange medium: **5** sycee

factory: **4** hong

festival: **9** Ching Ming

feudal state: Wei

figurine: **5** magot

fir: **5** nikko

fish: **7** trepang

flute: che **4** tche

fruit: **6** lichee, litchi

ginger: **9** galingale

god: **4** Ghos, Joss, Shen **5** Kuant

gong: **6** tamtam

gooseberry: **9** carambola

grass: bon **5** ramie

grass linen: **8** barandos

gruel: **6** congee, conjee

herb: tea **7** ginseng

herb genus: **7** nandina

houseboat: **5** tanka

idol: **4** joss **6** pagoda

indigo: **6** isatis

isinglass: **4** agar **8** agar-agar

island: **4** Amoy **5** Macao **6** Hainan, Taiwan **7** Formosa

jute: **7** chingma

laborer: **6** coolie

lake: **6** Po-yang **8** Tung-ting

language: **4** Shan **8** Mandarin **9** Cantonese

largest city: **8** Shanghai

leaders (Communist): Mao **9** Mao Zedong (Mao Tse-tung), Zhou Enlai (Chou Enlai) **10** Hua Guofeng (Hua Kuo-feng) **12** Deng Xiaoping (Teng Hsiao-ping)

leaders (Republic): **9** Sun Yat-sen **13** Chiang Kai-shek

lemon: **6** citron

magistrate: **8** mandarin

magnolia: **5** yulan

mandarin's residence: **6** oyamen

measure: cho, fen, tou, yan, yin **4** chih, fang, kish, quei, shih, teke, tsan, tsun **5** chang, ching, sheng, shing **6** kung ho, kung li, kung mu, tching, tchung **7** kung fen **8** kung chih, kung shih **9** kung ching, kung sheng

measure of distance: li

measure of weight: **4** chin **5** catty

money (see also *coin* above): fen **4** mace, tael, tiao, yuan **5** sycee, tsien

mountain: Omi **4** Omei, Sung **5** Tsins **6** Inshan, Kunlun, Pu-ling **7** Alashan, Kuliang **8** Tien Shan **9** Funiu-shan, Tsing-Ling

musical instrument: kin **5** cheng, sheng **7** samisen

Nationalist Party: **11** Kuomintang

noodles: **4** mein

nurse: ama **4** amah

official: **4** kuan, kwan **5** amban

oil: **4** tung

old name: **6** Cathay

orange: **7** kumquat **8** mandarin

ounce: **4** tael

ox: **4** zebu

pagoda: taa **4** taag

parasol tree: **6** aogiri

peony: **6** moutan

pert. to: **4** Sino

philosopher: **4** Moti **5** Motzu **6** Laotse, Laotzu **9** Confucius

plant: tea, udo **4** rice, tche **5** ramie **7** ginseng

poet: **4** Li Po **7** Li Tai-Po

pony: **7** griffin

porcelain: **7** Celadon, Nankeen

porcelain glaze: **7** eelskin

porgy: tai

port: **4** Amoy, Wuhu **5** Aigun, Shasi **6** Antung, Canton, Chefoo, Dairen, Harbin, Ichang, Ningpo, Pakhoi, Swatow, Szemao, Wuchow, Yochow **7** Foochow, Hangkow, Hunchun, Lungkow, Mengtsz, Nanking, Nanning, Samshui, Santuao, Soochow, Wenchow **8** Changsha, Hangchow, Kiukiang, Kongmoon, Lungchow, Shanghai, Tengyueh, Tientsin, Tsingtao, Wanhsien **9** Chinkiang, Chungking, Kiungchow, Newchwang **10** Chiankiang **12** Chingwangtao

port (Pinyin spelling): **6** Fuzhou (Foochow), Suzhou (Soochow), Xiamen (Amoy) **7** Qingdao (Tsingtao), Tianjin (Tientsin) **8** Hangzhou (Hangchow), Jiujiang (Kiukiang) **9** Chongqing (Chungking)

positive principle: **4** yang

pottery: **4** Kuan, Ming, Ting **5** Chien **7** boccaro, Tzuchou *pound:* 5 catty

prefecture: fu

province: 4 Amur 5 Chili, Honan, Hunan, Hupeh, Kansu 6 Fokien, Fukien, Shansi, Shensi, Yunnan 7 Kiangsi, Kiangsu, Kwangsi, Nganhui 8 Che-Kiang, Kweichau, Shantung, Szechuan 9 Kwangtung, Manchuria

province (Pinyin spelling): 5 Anhui (Anhwei), Gansu (Kansu), Hebei (Hopei), Henan (Honan), Hubei (Hupeh), Jilin (Kirin) 6 Fujian (Fukien), Shanxi (Shansi) 7 Guizhou (Kweichow), Jiangsu (Kiangsu), Jiangxi (Kiangsi), Ginghai (Chinghai), Shaanxi (Shensi), Sichuan (Szechwan) 8 Shandong (Shantung), Zhejiang (Chekiang) 9 Guangdong (Kwangtung) 12 Heilongjiang (Heilungkiang)

provincial chief: 6 taoyin

puzzle: 7 tangram

race: 4 Lolo 5 Sinic, Soyot 6 Mongol

region: 5 Tibet 7 Kwangsi, Ningsia 8 Mongolia, Sinkiang

religion: 6 Taoism 8 Buddhism 12 Confucianism

river: Han, Hsi, Ili, Kan, Min, Pei, Wei 4 Hwai, Tung, Yuan, Yuen 5 Hwang, Peiho, Pieho, Tarim 6 Yellow 7 Hoangho, Sikiang, Yangtze 12 Yangtsekiang

roller: 7 sirgang

salutation: bow 6 kowtow

sauce: soy

secret society: hui 4 tong

sedge: 4 mati

shrub: tea 5 ramie

silk: sha 5 pekin, tasar 6 pongee, tussah 7 taysaam, tsatlee 8 shantung

silkworm: 4 sina 6 tussah, tusser 10 ailanthus

silver: 5 sycee

skiff: 6 sampan

sky: 4 tien

sleeping platform: 4 kang

society: 4 Hoey, Huey, Hung, Tong 5 Triad

squash: 6 cushaw

state(anc.): 4 Tsao 6 Cathay

stocks: 6 cangue

strait: 6 Hainan, Taiwan 7 Formosa

street: 6 hutung

student: 9 sinologue

sugar cane: 5 sorgo

taa: 6 pagoda

Tartar tribe: 4 Toda

tax: 5 likin

tea: cha 4 Tsia 5 bohea, congo, congu, Emesa, hyson

temple: taa 6 pagoda

toy: 7 tangram

treaty port: 4 Amoy

tree: 5 nikko 6 kinkan, litchi 7 gingkgo, hagbush, kumquat 9 bandoline, soapberry

tribe: 4 Shan, Toba

vegetable: udo

vine: 5 kudzu 7 yangtao

walking stick: 7 whangee

warehouse: 4 hong

wax: 4 cere, pela

weight: fen, hao, kin, ssu, tan, yin 4 chee, chin, mace, shih, tael 5 catty, chien, liang, picul, tsien 6 kung li 7 haikwan, kung fen, kung ssu, kung tun 8 king chin 9 candareen 10 kuping tael 11 haikwan tael

wind instrument: 5 cheng, sheng

wormwood: 4 moxa

China Sea: *gulf:* 4 Siam

island: 6 Hainan 7 Formosa

Chinaberry: 5 lilac 9 soapberry

chinch: 6 bedbug

chine: 4 back, grow 5 chink, crack, crest, ridge, spine 6 cleave, ravine, sprout 7 crevice, fissure 8 backbone

Chinese (see also **China**): 5 Cerai, Seres, Seric, Sinic 6 Mongol, Sinico 7 Asiatic, Cataian, Sangley 9 Celestial

pert. to: 5 Seric 6 Serian 7 Sinitic 8 Senesian

chink: gap 4 bore, cash, coin, kink, rent, rift, rime 5 boore, check, chine, cleft, crack, grike, money 6 cranny, jingle, sprain 7 chinkle, crevice, fissure 8 aperture 9 chaffinch 10 interstice

chinky: 5 rifty 6 rimose

Chinook: 4 wind 6 indian 8 Flathead

chief: 4 Tyee

god: 8 tamanoas

people: 7 tilikum 8 tillicum

powwow: 4 wawa

salmon: 7 quinnat

woman: 10 klootchman

Chinook State: 10 Washington

chinquapin: oak 6 bonnet 8 chestnut, wankapin 9 rattlenut

chintzy: 4 mean 5 cheap, petty 6 stingy

chip: bit, cut, hew, nig 4 chap, clip, knap, nick, pare 5 crack, flake, piece, scrap, spale, spalt, waste 6 chisel 7 counter 8 fragment, splinter

in: 10 contribute 11 come through

of stone: 5 spall 6 gallet

chipmunk: 6 chippy, backee, rodent 8 squirrel

chipper: gay 4 spry 5 chirp, perky 6 babble, cockey, lively 7 chatter, chirrup, twitter 8 cheerful

chirk: gay 6 lively 7 chirrup 8 cheerful, embolden 9 encourage

chirm: din, hum 5 chirp, croon, noise 6 clamor

chirography: 6 script 7 writing 10 en-

grossing 11 handwriting
chiromancy: 9 palmistry 10 chirognomy
chirp: pip 4 peek, peep, pipe 5 cheep, chelp, chirk, chirl, chirm, chirt, tweet 7 chipper, chirrup, chitter, rejoice, twitter, wheetle
chirrup: 5 chirk, chirp, tweet 7 chitter, twitter
chisel: cut, gad, gyp 4 chip, form, pare, tool 5 burin, carve, cheat, gouge, hardy 6 gravel, haggle 7 bargain, defraud, engrave, quarrel, shingle 9 sculpture
ancient stone: 4 celt
engraving: 7 scooper, scorper
mine: gad 6 peeker
sculpture: 7 gradine 9 ebauchoir
stonemason's: 5 drove
toothed: 6 jagger
chiseler: 5 cheat, crook 6 gouger 9 bargainer
chiselled: 8 clearcut
chiselly: 6 gritty 8 gravelly 10 unpleasant 12 disagreeable
chit: dab, IOU, kid 4 bill, girl, mind, note, rice 5 child, draft, shoot 6 infant, letter, moppet, sprout 7 voucher 8 young one 9 offspring 10 memorandum
chitchat: 4 talk 6 banter, gossip 9 small talk 12 conversation
chiton: 4 gown, robe 5 tunic 7 mollusk
chitter: 4 peep 5 chirp 6 shiver 7 chatter, twitter
chivalrous: 5 brave, civil, noble 6 gentle, polite 7 gallant, genteel, valiant, warlike 8 knightly 9 courteous, honorable
chive: cut 4 stab 5 clout, clove, knive, onion 6 bulbet
chivy, chivvy: run, vex 4 hunt, race 5 chase, tease 6 badger, flight, harass, pursue 7 pursuit, scamper, torment 8 maneuver 9 confusion
chlamys: 5 cloak 6 mantle 7 garment
Chloe: 11 shepherdess
beloved: 7 Daphnis
chloride: 4 salt 5 ester 7 calomel, muriate 8 compound
chlorine: 6 bleach
chloroform: 4 kill 10 anesthetic
discoverer: 6 Liebig 7 Guthrie 9 Soubeiran
ingredient: 7 acetone
liquid used: 7 acetone
chobdar: 5 usher 9 attendant
chock: 5 block, chuck, cleat, wedge
chocolate: bar 5 candy, cocoa 8 beverage
family: 13 sterculiaceae
machine: 6 conche
powder: 5 cocoa 6 pinola
seed: 5 cacao
stick for mixing: 7 molinet
tree: 4 cola 5 cacao
choice: 4 a-one, best, fine, pick, rare, wale,

weal, will 5 cream, elite, prime, voice 6 chosen, dainty, flower, option, picked, select 8 delicate, druthers, election, eximious, uncommon, volition 9 excellent, exquisite, recherche 10 preferable, preference 11 alternative
choicy: 5 fussy, picky 6 choosy 7 finicky 10 fastidious 11 persnickety
choir: 5 quire 6 chorus
leader: 6 cantor 9 precentor
member: 4 alto, bass 5 basso 7 songman, soprano 9 chorister
vestment: 4 gown 5 cotta 8 surplice
choke: dam, gag 4 clog, fill, plug, quar 5 check, close, grane 6 hinder, impede, stifle 7 congest, querken, repress, silence, smother 8 obstruct, stoppage, strangle, suppress, throttle 9 constrict, neckcloth, suffocate 10 asphyxiate, extinguish
choler: ire 4 fury, rage 5 anger, wrath 6 spleen, temper 9 distemper, ill temper 10 resentment 11 biliousness 12 irascibility
choleric: mad 5 angry, cross, fiery, huffy, testy 6 fumish, touchy 7 bilious, enraged, iracund, peevish, peppery, waspish 8 wrathful 9 impatient, irascible 10 passionate 11 belligerent, hot-tempered, quarrelsome 13 quick-tempered
render: 6 enrage
chomp: 4 bite, chew 5 munch 6 crunch 8 ruminate 9 masticate
choose: opt 4 chap, cull, pick, vote, wale, weal 5 adopt, chuse, elect 6 prefer, select 7 embrace, espouse 9 single out
choosy, choosey: 7 finical, finicky 9 selective 10 fastidious
chop: cut, hew, jaw, lop 4 chap, dice, gash, hack, hash, jowl, rive, slit 5 carve, cleft, crack, knock, mince, slash, stamp, trade, truck, whang 6 barter, change, cleave, incise 8 exchange 9 cotolette
down: 4 fell, raze 5 level
off: lop 4 drib 5 prune 8 amputate
chop-chop: 7 quickly 8 promptly 9 posthaste 12 lickety-split
chophouse: 10 restaurant
Chopin: 7 pianist 8 composer
birthplace: 6 Poland
lover: 4 Sand (George)
chopping block: 7 hacklog
chopping tool: axe 7 cleaver, hatchet
choppy: 5 rough
choragus: 6 leader 10 bandleader
chord: 4 cord, tone 5 nerve, triad 6 string, tendon 7 harmony 8 filament 9 harmonize
arc: 4 sine
harplike: 8 arpeggio
musical: 5 major, minor
ninth: 4 none

seventh: **6** tetrad
succession: **7** cadence
chore: job **4** duty, task **5** stint **6** errand **9** housework **10** assignment
choreography: 7 dancing
chorister: 6 singer **7** chanter **8** choirboy
chorography: 9 map-making
chortle: 5 laugh, snort **7** chuckle
chorus: 4 song **5** choir **6** accord, assent, unison **7** concert, concord, harmony, refrain, singers **8** response
girl: **6** dancer, singer **7** chorine
leader: **7** choragi(pl.) **8** choragus **9** conductor
chosen: 5 elect, elite **7** elected **8** selected
Chosen: 5 Korea
chosen people: 10 Israelites
chough: 4 bird, crow
chouse: 4 dupe, gull, sham **5** chase, cheat, trick **6** harass **7** defraud, swindle **8** swindler **10** imposition
chow: dog **4** eats, food, grub, meal **6** fodder
chowchow: dog **4** bird, hash, olio **7** mixture **8** mishmash **10** hodgepodge, miscellany
chowderhead: 4 dope **5** dunce **6** noodle **7** schnook **9** lame-brain
Christ: 4 Lord **7** Messiah, Saviour
christen: 4 name **7** baptize **10** denominate
Christian: 7 Gentile **8** Nazarene
denomination: **6** Mormon, Quaker **7** Baptist **8** Anglican, Catholic, Lutheran **9** Calvinist, Methodist **12** Episcopalian
early **8** Galilean
Eastern: **6** Uniate
Egyptian: **4** Copt
persecuted: **6** martyr
unity: **7** irenics
Christian Science founder: 4 Eddy
Christiania: 4 Oslo
Christianity: *heretical sect:* **7** Docetae
love feast: **5** agape
martyr: **7** Stephen
symbol: **5** cross, orant **7** lehthus
theologian: **4** Kuhn **7** Aquinas, Niebuhr, Tillich **8** Bultmann **9** Augustine, deChardin **10** Bonhoeffer **11** Kierkegaard
writer: **6** Origen
Christmas: 4 noel, yule **7** holiday **8** festival, nativity, yuletide
carol: **4** noel **5** nowel
crib: **6** creche
decoration: **5** holly **6** tinsel **9** mistletoe
midnight mass supper: **9** reveillon
Christmas Carol: *author:* **7** Dickens
character: Tim **7** Scrooge
Christmas rose: 9 hellebore
Christ's thorn: 4 nabk, nubk **5** shrub **6** jujube

chromium: 7 element, mineral
group element: **7** uranium **8** tungsten **10** molybdenum
chromolithograph: 7 picture
chronic: 5 fixed, usual **6** severe **7** intense, routine **8** constant **9** confirmed, continual, customary, lingering, prolonged **10** continuous, inveterate **12** disagreeable
chronicle: 5 annal, diary, story **6** record **7** account, archive, history, recital **8** register **9** narrative
chronicler: 6 writer **8** compiler, recorder **9** historian **11** memorialist
chronology: 6 record **11** arrangement **14** classification
according to: **5** datal
error in: **9** prolepsis **11** anachronism
chronometer: 4 dial **5** clock, watch **9** metronome, timepiece **10** timekeeper
chrysalis: 4 kell, pupa **5** pupae(pl.)
chrysolite: 7 olivine, peridot
chrysoprase: 10 chalcedony
chthonian: 6 Hadean **8** infernal, plutonic **10** sulphurous
chub: 4 dace, dolt, fool, lout **5** chopa **6** chevin, shiner **8** fallfish, mackerel **9** hornyhead, squawfish
chubby: 5 chuff, fubsy, plump, pudgy, round, tubby **6** choaty, rotund **8** rolypoly
chuck: hen, log, pig **4** beef, cast, food, fowl, grub, hurl, jerk, lump, shed, toss **5** chock, cluck, ditch, pitch, throw **6** bounce **7** chicken, discard **9** dismissal
chuckle: 5 cluck, exult, laugh **6** giggle, titter **7** chortle
chuff: fat **4** boor, glum, ugly **5** brick, churl, cross, miser, proud, sound, sulky, surly **6** chubby, elated, rustic **7** swollen **9** conceited **11** ill-tempered
chug: 4 puff
chum: cad, pal **4** bait, mate, pard **5** buddy, butty, crony **6** cobber, copain, friend **8** roommate **9** associate, companion
around: **6** hobnob
chump: ass, oaf, sap **4** boob, dolt, head **5** block **7** fall guy **8** lunkhead **9** blockhead, schlemiel, schlemihl
chunk: dab, gob, pat, wad **4** junk, slug **5** claut, piece, throw, whang
chunky: 4 game **5** lumpy, plump, squat, stout, thick
church: 4 cult, sect, tera(Jap.) **5** creed, faith **6** temple **7** edifice **9** sanctuary, structure **10** house of God **13** house of prayer
adjunct: **6** belfry **7** steeple **9** bell tower
altar end: **4** apse
altar offering: **8** altarage
attendant: **8** altarboy, choirboy
balcony: **8** cantoria
bench: pew, pue **4** seat

bishopric: see **7** diocese **10** episcopacy, episcopate
body of: **4** nave
calendar: **4** ordo
caretaker: **6** sexton
chapel: **7** oratory
congregation: **7** synaxis
council: **5** synod **6** Nicene
court: **4** Rota
deputy: **5** vicar **6** curate
dignitary: **4** dean, pope **5** abbot, canon **6** bishop **7** prelate, primate
dissenter: **7** sectary
district: **6** parish **7** diocese
dominion of: **11** sacerdotium
doorkeeper: **7** ostiary
early Christian: **8** basilica
endowed: **8** benefice
entrance chapel: **7** galilee
episcopacy: **7** prelacy
field: **5** glebe
government: **9** hierarchy
home: **5** manse **7** deanery **8** convento **9** parsonage
law: **5** canon
member: **11** communicant
morning service: **5** matin
officer: **5** elder, vicar **6** beadle, deacon, lector, sexton, warden **7** prelate, sacrist **8** reverend **9** clergyman, moderator, presbyter, sacristan **11** headborough
part of: **4** apse, bema, nave **5** altar, solea **7** chancel, narthex **8** cantoria, transept **10** clearstory, clerestory
pertaining to: **9** ecclesial **14** ecclesiastical
prayer: **5** kyrie **12** kyrie eleison
property: **5** glebe
reader: **6** lector
recess: **4** apse
revenue: **5** tithe **8** benefice
Roman: **7** lateran **8** basilica
room: **6** vestry **7** galilee **8** sacristy
seat: pew, pue **5** bench **6** sedile **7** sedilia(pl.)
service: **4** mass, rite **5** matin **7** vespers, nocturn **8** evensong **9** communion
stand: **4** ambo
stipend: **7** prebend
vault: **5** crypt
vessel: ama, pyx **4** font **5** amula **7** columba, piscina **9** colymbion **10** monstrance
vestry room: **8** sacristy
wall: **6** cashel
warden's aide: **7** hoggler
wing: **5** aisle
churchgoer: 11 communicant
churchly: 9 religious, spiritual
churchyard: 6 litten **8** cemetery **9** graveyard
churl: cad, man **4** boor, carl, gnof, hind, lout, serf **5** carle, ceorl, chuff, gnoff, knave, miser **6** bodach, carlot, lubber,

rustic, vassal, yeoman **7** bondman, freeman, haskard, husband, niggard, peasant, villain, villein **10** countryman, curmudgeon
churlish: 4 mean **5** bluff, gruff, rough, surly **6** crabby, rustic, sordid, sulkly, sullen, vulgar **7** boorish, crabbed, uncivil, violent **9** illiberal **10** ungracious, unyielding **12** cross-grained
churn: 4 beat, kirn(Sc.), stir **5** drill, shake **7** agitate
part: **6** dasher
chute: 4 rush, tube **5** flume, hurry, rapid, shoot, slide **6** hopper, trough **7** cascade, decline, descent **8** downfall, stampede **9** waterfall
cibol: 5 onion **7** shallot
ciborium: pix, pyx **6** canopy, coffer, vessel
cicada: 6 cagale, cigala, locust **11** grasshopper
noise: **5** chirr
cicatrix: eye **4** mark, scab, scar, seam
cicatrization: 8 scarring
cicely: 5 myrrh
Cicero's target: 8 Catiline **10** Mark Antony
cicerone: 5 guide, pilot **6** mentor, orator **7** courier **9** conductor
cid: Ruy **4** epic, hero, poem **5** Bivar, chief, title **9** commander
sword of: **6** colada, tizona
cider: 5 perry **6** perkin, swanky **8** beverage
pulp: **6** pomace
cigar: 4 toby, weed **5** claro, smoke, stogy **6** boquet, Corona, maduro, stogie **7** bouquet, cheroot, culebra **8** perfecto **9** Belvedere
case: **7** humidor
crude: **7** cheroot, culebra
long thin: **8** panatela, panetela **9** panatella, panetella
cigarette: fag **4** biri, butt, pill **5** cubeb, smoke **6** gasper, reefer **9** cigarillo **10** coffin nail
cigarfish: 4 scad **8** quiaquia
cilium: 4 hair, lash **7** eyelash **8** barbicel
cima: See **cyma**
cimarron: 5 slave **6** maroon **7** bighorn
cimbia: 4 band **6** fillet
cimex: 6 bedbug, insect
cimmerian: 4 inky **5** black **6** gloomy **7** stygian **8** infernal **9** plutonian
cinch: 4 belt, gird, grip, pipe, snap **5** girth **6** fasten **8** sinecure **9** certainty
cinchona: 4 bark, tree
extract: **7** quinine
cinct: 4 girt **9** encircled
cincture: 4 band, belt, gird, halo, list, ring **5** girth **6** cestus, collar, fillet, girdle **7** baldric, compass **8** encircle **9** enclosure **11** environment, surrounding

cinder: ash **4** gray, slag **5** chark, dross, ember **6** scoria **7** clinker, lapilla, residue

cinders: 5 gleed, track

cinema (see also **motion picture**): **4** film, show **5** flick, movie **6** screen **7** picture **13** motion picture

cinerarium: urn **8** mortuary

cinerator: 6 ashery **9** crematory

cinerous: 4 gray **5** ashen

cingular: 7 annular **8** circular

cingulum: 4 band **5** ridge **6** girdle

cinnabar: ore **7** mineral **9** vermilion
  color: red
  derivative: **11** quicksilver

cinnamic acid derivative: 7 sinapic

cinnamon: 4 tree **5** canel, spice **6** canela, canell, canelo, cassia **7** canella, canelle **8** barbasco

cinnamon apple: 8 sweetsop

cinnamon oak: 8 bluejack

cinnamon stone: 6 garnet **8** essonite

cinquefoil: 6 clover **7** frasier **8** cowberry

cion: bud **5** graft, scion, shoot, uvula **10** descendant

Cipango: 5 Japan **6** Nippon

cipher: key, nil **4** code, null, zero **5** aught, ought **6** device, decode, figure, letter, naught, nought, number, symbol **8** goose egg **9** nonentity **10** cryptogram

cippus: 6 pillar **8** landmark **10** gravestone

circa: 5 about **6** around **13** approximation

Circassian: *dialect:* **6** Adighe **8** Cherkess **9** Abkhasian, Kabardian
  king: **9** Sacripant

Circe: 5 siren **7** tempter **9** sorceress **11** enchantress
  brother: **6** Aeetes
  father: Sol **6** Helios
  island: **5** Aeaea
  lover: **7** Ulysses **8** Odysseus
  niece: **6** Medea
  son: **5** Comus **9** Telegonus

circle: lap, set **4** disk, gyre, halo, hoop, loop, maru(Jap.), orbe, ring, rink, turn **5** class, crown, cycle, frame, group, monde, realm, rhomb, rigol, round, swirl, twirl **6** bezant, cirque, clique, collet, cordon, corona, diadem, girdle, rotate, rundle, spiral, system **7** chukkar, chukker, circlet, circuit, company, compass, coronet, coterie, enclose, revolve, ringlet **8** encircle, surround **9** circulate, encompass **10** associates, companions **13** circumference
  around sun or moon: **6** corona
  geographic: **6** tropic
  graph: **8** pie chart
  heraldry: **7** annulet
  inner: **5** bosom
  longest chord: **8** diameter
  luminous: **4** aura, halo **6** corona, nimbus

part of: arc **5** chord **6** degree, radius, secant, sector **7** segment

circlet: 4 band, hoop, ring **6** bangle, cirque **7** circuit **8** bracelet, headband
  of light: **7** aureola, aureole

circuit: lap **4** area, bout, iter, loop, tour, zone **5** ambit, cycle, orbit, round, route **6** ambage, circle, detour **7** compass, itinera(pl.) **8** district **10** revolution **13** circumference
  auxiliary: **5** relay
  court: **4** eyre

circuitous: 4 mazy **6** curved **7** crooked, devious, oblique, sinuous, twisted, vagrant, winding **8** circular, flexuous, indirect, rambling, tortuous **9** ambagious, ambiguous, deceitful, underhand, wandering **10** roundabout, serpentine **12** disingenuous, labyrinthine

circular: 4 bill **5** libel, orbed, round **6** ringed **7** annular, cycloid, discoid, perfect **8** cingular, complete, encyclic, globular, pamphlet **9** orbicular **10** circuitous, roundabout **11** publication
  indicator: **4** dial
  motion: **4** eddy, gyre **5** whirl **8** gyration
  plate: **4** disc, disk

circulate: air, mix **4** move, turn **6** rotate, spread **7** diffuse, publish **9** propagate **10** promulgate **11** disseminate
  publicly: **6** report **9** broadcast

circumference: arc, rim **4** ambi **5** girth **6** border, bounds, limits **7** circuit **8** boundary, surround **9** dimension, perimeter, periphery

circumlocution: 6 ambage **7** winding **8** verbiage **10** periphrase, redundancy, roundabout

circumscribe: 5 bound, fence, limit **6** define **7** confine, enclose, environ **8** encircle, restrain, restrict, surround **9** encompass

circumscribed: 6 narrow **7** insular, limited

circumspect: 4 wary, wise **5** alert, chary **7** careful, guarded, prudent **8** cautious, discreet, watchful **9** attentive **10** deliberate

circumstance: fix **4** fact, item **5** event, phase, state **6** affair, detail, factor, pickle **7** element, episode **8** incident, position **9** condition, situation **10** occurrence, particular **11** environment, opportunity **12** surroundings

circumstantial: 5 exact **6** minute **7** precise **8** detailed **9** pertinent **10** incidental, particular **11** inferential **12** nonessential

circumstantiate: 7 support **8** evidence

circumvent: 4 balk, dupe, foil **5** cheat, check, cozen, evade, trick **6** baffle, delude, entrap, outwit, thwart **7** capture,

deceive, defraud, ensnare, prevent **8**
surround **9** encompass, frustrate, overreach, underfong
circus: 4 ring **5** arena **6** circle, cirque **9**
spectacle **10** hippodrome **12** amphitheater **13** entertainment
arena wall: **5** spina
attraction: **5** freak **8** sideshow
column: **4** meta
employee: **5** clown, tamer
gear: **4** tent **5** rings **7** trapeze
rider: **8** desultor
cirque: 5 basin **6** circle, circus, corrie, recess **7** circlet, erosion
cirrus: 5 cloud **7** tendril **8** filament
cisco: 8 blackfin, whitefin
cist: box **4** tomb **5** chest **6** casket **7** chamber **9** cistavaen
cistern: sac, tub, vat **4** tank, well **6** cavity
7 cuvette **8** cisterna **9** reservoir, impluvium
cit: 8 townsman **9** tradesman **10** shopkeeper
citadel: arx **4** fort, hall **5** alamo, tower **6**
castle **7** borough **8** fastness, fortress **10**
stronghold **13** fortification
of Carthage: **5** Bursa, Byrsa
of Moscow: **7** Kremlin
citation: 6 notice **7** mention, summons **8**
encomium, monition **9** quotation, reference **10** allegation **11** enumeration
cite: 4 call, tell **5** allay, quote, refer **6** accite, accuse, adduce, allege, arouse,
avouch, excite, notify, repeat, summon
7 arraign, bespeak, excerpt, extract,
mention **8** indicate
citizen: cit **5** voter **6** native **7** burgess,
burgher, citoyen(F.), denizen, elector,
freeman, oppidan **8** civilian, commoner,
occupant, resident **9** citoyenne(F.) **10**
inhabitant
citizenship: *admission to:* **14** naturaliza-
tion **15** enfranchisement
pert. to: **5** civic
citrine: 5 color **7** rhubarb
citron: 4 lime **5** lemon **6** cedrat, yellow
citrullus: 7 pumpkin **10** watermelon
citrus: *belt:* **7** Florida **10** California
disease: **8** buckskin
drink: ade **5** juice
fruit: **4** lime, ugli **5** lemon **6** citron, orange **7** kumquat, tangelo **8** mandarin,
shaddock **9** tangerine **10** grapefruit
pest: **7** red mite
city: 4 burg, dorp, town, urbs(L.) **5** ville **6**
ciudad, staple **9** community **10** metropolis **12** municipality
celestial: **4** Zion
district: **4** slum **6** barrio, ghetto, uptown
8 business, downtown, red-light **11** residential **12** neighborhood
eternal: **4** Roma, Rome

hanging gardens: **7** Babylon
holy: **5** Mecca **6** Medina **9** Jerusalem
leaning tower: **4** Pisa
official: **5** mayor **7** manager, marshal **8**
alderman **10** councilman
oldest inhabited: **8** Damascus
pert. to: **5** civic, urban **7** oppidan **9** mu-
nicipal **12** metropolitan
planner: **8** urbanist
problem: **4** riot, slum, smog **5** crime **6**
ghetto **7** poverty, traffic
section: **4** slum, ward **5** block, plaza **6**
ghetto, square **8** downtown, red light
11 residential **12** neighborhood
slicker: **4** dude
wicked: **5** Sodom **8** Gomorrah
City: *of Bells:* **9** Strasburg **10** Strasbourg
of Bridges: **6** Bruges
of Brotherly Love: **12** Philadelphia
of Churches: **8** Brooklyn
of David: **9** Jerusalem
of God: **6** church, heaven **8** Paradise
of God author: **9** Augustine
of Hundred Towers: **5** Pavia
of Kings: **4** Lima
of Lilies: **8** Florence
of Masts: **6** London
of Rams: **6** Canton
of Refuge: **6** Medina
of Saints: **8** Montreal
of Seven Hills: **4** Rome
of Violet Crown: **6** Athens
of Victory: **5** Cairo
city-state: 5 polis **7** civitas
Cius: 6 Gemlik
civet: cat, cit **5** rasse, zibet **6** bondar, musang, zibeth **7** fossane, nandine
civet-like animal: 5 genet
civic: lay **5** civil, suave, urban **6** polite,
public, urbane **7** secular
civil: 4 hend **5** hende, suave **6** polite, urbane **7** affable, courtly, elegant, politic,
refined **8** discreet, gracious, obliging,
polished, wellbred **9** civilized, courteous
10 cultivated, respectful **11** complaisant **13** condescending
civil rights (extinction of): 9 attainder
Civil War: *admiral:* **8** Farragut
battle: **6** Shiloh **8** Antietam
commander: Lee **4** Pope **5** Ewell, Grant,
Meade, Sykes **7** Forrest, Jackson
civil wrong: 4 tort
civilian: cit **5** civvy **7** citizen, teacher **12**
noncombatant, practitioner
dress: **5** mufti
civility: 6 comity **7** amenity, decorum **8**
courtesy **9** propriety **10** affability, compliance, politeness **11** complacence **12**
complaisance
civilization: 6 kultur(G.) **7** culture **10** refinement **11** cultivation
civilize: 4 tame **5** teach, train **6** polish,

refine **7** educate **8** humanize, urbanize **9** cultivate **11** domesticate

clabber: mud **4** mire **6** curdle, lopper **12** bonnyclabber

clack: gab, jaw, yak **4** blab **5** chack, cluck, crack **6** cackle, gossip, rattle, tongue **7** chatter, clacket, clatter, prattle **10** chatterbox

clad: 5 drest, robed **6** beseen, decked **7** adorned, arrayed, attired, clothed, covered, dressed **8** sheathed

cladose: 6 ramose **8** branched

clag: mud **4** clog, clot, daub, mire **5** fault, stick **6** adhere, burden

claggum: 5 taffy **7** treacle **8** molasses **9** sweetmeat

claim: ask **4** aver, call, case, lien, mine, name **5** exact, right, shout, title **6** assert, demand, elicit **7** acclaim, derecho, pretend, profess, require **8** maintain, pretence, pretense, proclaim **9** challenge, homestead, postulate, vindicate **11** encumbrance

claimant: 7 usurper **9** pretender, arrogator

clairvoyance: ESP **7** insight **8** sagacity **10** divination **11** discernment, penetration

clairvoyant: 4 seer **6** omener **7** prophet, seeress

clam: 4 base, clog, daub, glam, hush, mean **5** clamp, crash, glaum, grasp, grope, smear, stick **6** adhere, clutch, sticky **7** bivalve, clangor, mollusk, steamer **8** adhesive

genus of: mya

kinds of: **4** mega **5** blunt, chama, razor, solen **6** gweduc, quahog **7** geoduck, quahaug **10** little neck

clamant: 4 dire, loud **6** crying, urgent **9** clamorous **10** imperative

clamber: 5 climb, scale **6** claver **7** rammack **8** scramble, struggle

clamjamfry: mob **5** crowd **6** rabble **7** rubbish

clammy: 4 damp, dank, soft, wack **5** moist, sammy **6** sticky, waughy

clamor: cry, din, hue **4** bere, bunk, roar, rout, to-do, wail **5** blare, boast, bruit, noise, shout **6** bellow, hubbub, outcry, racket, tumult, uproar **7** stashie **10** hullabaloo, hurly-burly, vociferate

clamorous: 4 loud **5** noisy **7** blatant, clamant, yelling **8** brawling, decrying **9** clamatory, turbulent **10** boisterous **11** openmouthed

clamp: lug, nip, pin **4** bolt, glam, grip, hold, nail, vise **5** block, clasp, glaum **6** fasten **7** grapple **8** fastener, holdfast **10** clothespin

clan: set, sib **4** cult, race, sect, sept, unit **5** class, group, horde, party, tribe **6** clique, family **7** coterie, society **8** division **10** collection, fraternity

emblem: xat **5** totem

head of: **5** chief, elder, thane

pert. to: **6** tribal

clancular: 6 secret **11** clandestine

clandestine: bye, sly **4** foxy **5** privy **6** artful, covert, hidden, secret **7** bootleg, furtive, illicit **8** phratria, stealthy **9** clancular, concealed **10** fraudulent **12** hugger-mugger **13** surreptitious, under-the-table

clang: din **4** ding, peal, ring **5** clank, clash, noise **6** jangle, timbre

clangor: din **4** clam, roar **5** clang **6** hubbub, uproar

clank: 4 ring **5** sound **6** rackle

clannish: 5 close **6** secret, tribal, united

clap: 4 bang, flap, peal, slap **5** cheer, clink, crack **6** poster, strike, stroke **7** applaud, chatter, plaudit **9** explosion **11** thunderpeal

clapper: 6 rattle, tongue **7** knacker, knocker

support: **7** baldric **8** baldrick

claptrap: 4 bull **5** hokum, trash **6** blague, device, drivel, humbug **7** fustian **8** malarkey, nonsense, trickery **10** pretension **11** insincerity

clarify: 5 clean, clear **6** purify, refine, render, settle **7** cleanse, explain, glorify **8** depurate, eliquate, simplify **10** illuminate **11** transfigure **13** straighten out

clarinet: 4 reed, wind **10** instrument

mouthpiece: **4** birn

snake charmer's: **4** been

clarion: 5 clear, sharp **7** ringing, trumpet

clarity: 5 glory **8** accuracy, literacy, splendor **9** clearness **10** brightness, brilliance **11** pellucidity

claro: 4 mild **5** cigar **12** light-colored

clash: jar **4** bang, bolt, dash, news, slam **5** brawl, brunt, crash, fight, occur, prate, shock **6** affray, differ, gossip, hurtle, impact, strife, strike, tattle **7** collide, discord, scandal **8** argument, conflict **9** collision, interfere

clasp: hug, pin **4** fold, grab, grip, hasp, hold, hook, hoop, ouch, tach **5** cling, grasp, morse, preen, seize, tache **6** agrafe, brooch, buckle, clench, clutch, enfold, enwrap, fasten, fibula, gimmer, gimmor, infold **7** agraffe, amplect, embrace, entwine, fermail, tendril **8** barette, fastener, surround **9** constrain, safety-pin **10** chatelaine

class: ilk **4** clan, kind, race, rank, sect, sort, type **5** breed, caste, genus, genre, grade, group, order, tribe **6** circle, family, gender, rating **7** seminar, species, variety **8** category, division **9** abteilung **11** description **12** denomination

animal: 5 genus 6 genera
biological: 5 genus 6 genera(pl.)
member: 4 coed 6 junior, senior 8 freshman 9 sophomore
middle: 11 bourgeoisie
pert. to: 7 generic
working: 11 proletariat
classic: top 4 book 5 model 7 ancient, vintage 8 standard, top-notch 9 venerable 11 composition, masterpiece, tour de force
classical: 4 pure 5 Attic, Greek, Latin, Roman 6 chaste 8 academic, masterly 9 firstrate
classification: 4 file, rank, rate, sort 5 genre, genra(pl.), genus, grade, order, taxis 6 genera(pl.), rating, system 8 analysis, category, division, taxonomy 12 confidential, distribution
classify: 4 list, rank, rate, size, sort, type 5 grade, group, label, range 6 assort, codify, divide, ticket 7 arrange, catalog, dispose, marshal 8 register 9 catalogue, segregate 10 categorize, distribute, pigeonhole
classy: 4 tony 5 nifty, slick, smart 7 stylish 11 fashionable
clatter: din, jar 5 clack, noise, rumor 6 babble, gabble, gossip, rackle, rattle, tattle, uproar 7 blatter, chatter, clutter, prattle, reeshie 9 commotion 10 hurlyburly 11 disturbance
Claudia's husband: 6 Pilate
claudicant: 4 lame 7 limping
Claudius: 7 emperor
 nephew: 6 Hamlet
 slayer: 6 Hamlet 9 Agrippina
 wife: 9 Messalina
 successor: 4 Nero
clause: 4 part 5 close, plank, rider 6 phrase 7 article, passage, proviso 8 sentence 9 condition, provision 10 conclusion 11 stipulation
 additional: 5 rider
claut: 4 hand, lump, rake, tear 5 chunk 6 clutch, scrape 7 handful, scratch
clavecin: 11 harpsichord
claver: 5 prate 6 clover, gossip 7 chatter, chamber
clavichord: 6 spinet
clavicle: 4 bone 10 collarbone
clavis: key 8 glossary
clavus: 4 band, corn 5 strip 6 bunion, callus
claw: dig 4 clee, fawn, hand, hook, nail, pull, sere, tear, unce 5 chela, cloof, clufe, court, grasp, griff, seize, talon, uncus 6 clutch, nipper, scrape, ungula 7 crubeen, flatter, scratch, wheedle 8 lacerate
clay: cob, pug 4 bole, galt, loam, lute, marl, mire 5 argil, brick, cloam, earth, gault,

loess, ochre, rabat, tasco 6 cledge, clunch, kaolin 8 lifeless 9 inanimate
bed: 5 gault
box: 6 saggar, sagger
building: 5 adobe, tapia
casting: 4 slip
constituent: 7 alumina
covered with: 6 lutose
deposit: 4 marl
fragment: bat
friable: 4 bole
layer: 4 lias 5 sloam
lump: 4 clag, clod
made of: 7 fictile
mineral: 7 nacrite
mold: dod
musical instrument: 7 ocarina
pert. to: 5 bolar
piece: 4 tile
pottery: 6 kaolin 7 kaoline
tropical: 8 laterite
claybrained: 4 dull 6 stupid
clayey: 5 bolar, heavy, malmy, marly 6 cledgy, lutose 9 argillous 12 argillaceous
clay pigeon: 6 target
clead: 6 attire, clothe
clean: fay, fey, hoe, mop 4 dust, fair, pure, smug, swab, trim, wash, wipe 5 bream, clear, curry, empty, feigh, grave, scour, scrub, smart 6 chaste, clever, kosher, purify 7 apinoid, cleanse, clearly, furbish, perfect 8 absterge, brightly, dextrous, entirely, renovate, spotless, unsoiled 9 destitute, dexterous, guiltless, speckless, undefiled 10 immaculate 11 butterworth, untarnished 12 spick-and-span, straighten up 13 unadulterated
 Hebrew: 6 kosher
cleaner: 4 soap 5 borax, purer 6 ramrod 8 cleanser 9 detergent 10 dentifrice
 fish: 6 scaler
cleaning implement: mop 4 swab 5 broom 6 ramrod, vacuum 7 sweeper
cleanly: 4 pure 6 adroit, artful, chaste 7 correct, elegant 8 innocent, skillful 9 dexterous
cleanse: 4 farm, heal, soap, wash 5 brush, clean, dight, purge, rinse, scour, scrub 6 purify, refine 7 baptize, clarify, deterge, sweeten 8 renovate 9 disinfect, expurgate, sterilize
cleanser: lye 9 detergent 10 clarifiant
cleansing: 4 bath 7 abluent, clysmic, washing 8 ablution, lavation 9 acquittal, cathartic, purgation 10 emundation 12 purification
cleansing process: 4 bath 7 washing
clear: net, rid 4 free, gain, open, over, pure, quit 5 atrip, breme, brent, clean, erase, lucid, plain, prune, sharp, vivid 6 acquit, assoil, bright, candid, clever, ex-

empt, fluted, limpid, lucent, patent, purify, settle, smooth 7 absolve, clarion, clarify, crystal, deliver, evident, glaring, graphic, lighten, obvious, release, rule out 8 apparent, brighten, definite, distinct, explicit, manifest, pellucid, relevant, scot-free, shake off 9 cloudless, discharge, disengage, elucidate, enigmatic, exculpate, exonerate, extricate, vindicate 10 see-through, unconfused 11 disentangle, open-and-shut, perspicuous, transparent 12 intelligible

as crystal: 7 evident, obvious

away: fay, fey 5 feigh 6 dispel 8 evacuate 9 eliminate, expurgate

out: 5 scram 6 decamp, desert 7 skidoo, take off

up: 5 solve 6 settle

clear-cut: 5 exact, lucid, sharp 7 concise 8 chiseled, definite, distinct, incisive 9 chiselled 10 unconfused 11 categorical 12 unquestioned

clear-eyed: 10 discerning

clear-headed: 10 perceptive

clear-sighted: 10 discerning 13 perspicacious

clearing: *in woods:* 5 glade, tract 8 slashing

of land: 4 sart 6 assart

cleat: 4 bitt 5 block, chock, kevel, wedge 6 batten 7 bollard, coxcomb, support 9 butterbur

cleavage: 5 chasm, cleft, split 6 schism 7 fission, fissure 8 division 9 partition 10 separation

cleave: cut, rip 4 chop, hold, join, link, part, rely, rend, rift, rive, slit, tear 5 break, carve, chawn, chine, clave, cleft, cling, clove, crack, sever, shear, split, stick 6 adhere, bisect, cohere, divide, pierce, sunder 7 dispart, fissure 8 separate

cleaver: axe 4 froe, frow

cleche: 4 urde 5 urdee 11 cross-shaped

cleek: 4 club, hook, link 5 crook, pluck, seize 6 clutch, snatch 8 fishhook, golf club

clef: key 9 character

bass: eff

treble: gee

cleft: gap 4 chap, chop, fent, flow, reft, rift, rima, rive 5 break, chasm, chawn, chink, clove, crack, crena, riven, split 6 breach, cleave, cloven, cranny, crotch, divide, recess 7 crevice, divided, fissure, opening 8 aperture, fracture

cleft-lip: 7 harelip

Cleite: *father:* 6 Merops

husband: 7 Cyzicus

clemency: 4 pity 5 mercy 6 lenity 7 quarter 8 kindness, leniency, mildness 10 compassion, indulgence

clement: 4 easy, kind, mild, soft, warm 6 gentle 7 lenient 8 merciful 9 forgiving, indulgent 10 benevolent 13 compassionate

clench: 4 fist, grip, grit, hold 5 brace, clasp, clint, close, grasp 6 clinch, clutch 9 interlock 10 strengthen

cleome: 5 caper

Cleopatra: *attendant:* 4 Iras 8 Charmian

killer: asp

lover: 6 Antony, Caesar 10 Mark Antony

river: 4 Nile

sister: 7 Arsinoe

Cleopatra's Needle: 7 obelisk

clepsydra: 9 timepiece 10 water clock

clergy: 4 cloth 8 ministry

body of: 6 pulpit 7 college

clergyman: 4 abba, abbe, dean, Papa 5 canon, clerk, padre, pilot, prior, rabbi, vicar 6 bishop, cleric, curate, deacon, divine, domine, parson, pastor, priest, rector 7 cassock, prelate 8 cardinal, chaplain, minister, preacher, reverend 9 blackcoat, dignitary, presbyter 12 ecclesiastic

office: 4 cure 6 curacy 8 ministry 9 pastorate, priorship, rectorate

residence: 5 manse 6 priory 7 rectory 8 vicarage 9 parsonage

traveling: 12 circuit rider

clergywoman: nun 8 rectress 9 priestess 10 religieuse

cleric: See **clergyman**

clerical: 10 of the cloth

clerical clothing: alb 5 rabat, stole, amice, cloth, fanon, orale 6 collar 7 biretta

clerk: nun 4 monk 5 agent, steno, write 6 cleric, commis, hermit, layman, priest, scribe, teller, yeoman 7 carcoon, compose, gomasta, scholar 8 employee, greffier(F.), recorder, salesman 9 assistant, clergyman, registrar, secretary 10 accountant 11 salesperson 12 ecclesiastic, stenographer

court: 11 protonotary 12 prothonotary

hotel: 7 deskman

passenger ship: 6 purser

clerkly: 7 learned, scribal 9 scholarly

clever: apt, sly 4 able, cute, deft, fine, gnib, hend, keen 5 agile, alert, clean, clear, handy, hende, lithe, quick, slick, smart, witty 6 active, adroit, artful, astute, bright, expert, habile, heppen, neatly, nimble, pretty, shrewd 7 amiable, cunning, parlous 8 dextrous, handsome, obliging, skillful, talented 9 dexterous, ingenious 10 well-shaped 11 clean-limbed, dexterously, intelligent, quick-witted 13 scintillating

cleverness: can 4 tact 5 skill 6 esprit 9 dexterity, ingenuity 10 adroitness, astuteness

clevis: 4 hake 5 copse 6 muzzle 7 fitting 10 connection

clew, clue: 4 ball, hint 5 globe, blome, skein 6 hurdle, thread

cliche: 6 truism 7 bromide 8 banality 9 hackneyed, platitude 11 stereotyped

click: 4 pawl, tick 5 agree, catch 6 detent 7 come off, ratchet

click beetle: 6 elater

client: 5 ceile 6 patron 7 patient 8 customer, henchman, retainer 9 dependent

clientele: 6 public 9 following

cliff: hoe 4 crag, hill, rock, scar 5 bluff, cleve, heuch, heugh, scarp, shore, slope 6 cleeve, height 7 clogwyn 8 hillside, palisade 9 precipice

cliff-hanger: 8 suspense 9 melodrama

climate: 4 mood 6 region, temper 8 attitude 9 condition

control chamber: 7 biotrin

climax: cap, top 4 acme, apex, near, peak, shut 5 mount, scale, tight 6 apogee, ascend, finish, opogee, summit, zenith 9 gradation 11 culmination

climb: gad 4 ramp, rise, shin 5 creep, grimp, mount, scale, speed(Sc.), twine 6 ascend, ascent, shinny 7 clamber

climb down: 7 descend 8 dismount

climb on: 5 mount, scale

climber: 6 rigger, scaler 11 mountaineer 12 alpenstocker

climbing device: 6 ladder

climbing plant: ivy 4 vine 5 liana, liane 7 creeper

clime: See **climate**

clinch: fix, get, hug 4 bind, grip, nail, seal 5 clamp, cling, clink, clint, grasp, rivet, seize 6 clench, clutch, fasten, secure, snatch 7 confirm, embrace, grapple, scuffle 8 complete, conclude, holdfast 9 establish

cling: hug 4 bank, hang, hold, rely 5 clasp, stick, trust 6 adhere, cleave, clinch, cohere, depend, fasten, shrink, wither 7 cherish, embrace, shrivel 8 contract 9 persevere

clingfish: 6 testar

clink: ale, jug, put, rap 4 beat, blow, brig, cash, clap, coin, jail, move, ring, slap 5 latch, money, rhyme, seize 6 clinch, jingle, lockup, moment, prison, strike, tinkle 7 instant 8 hoosegow 9 assonance, calaboose 10 guardhouse

clinker: 4 slag 5 waste

clinquant: 5 clink, showy 6 tinsel 8 tinseled 10 glittering

Clio: See **Muse**

clip: bob, cut, dod, hug, lip, lop, mow, nip 4 barb, chip, coll, crop, dock, dodd, hold, pace, pare, poll, snip, trim 5 clasp, force, prune, shear 6 clutch, fasten, hinder, holder 7 curtain, curtail, cut down,

embrace, scissor, shorten 8 diminish, encircle, mark down 9 encompass 10 abbreviate, overcharge

clipper: 4 boat, ship 6 vessel 7 shearer, workman

clique: cot, mob, set 4 bloc, clan, club, gang, ring 5 cabal, group, junto, write 6 circle, cletch 7 coterie, faction, in-group 8 conclave, sodality 9 camarilla 11 combination

clitter: 5 noise 6 rattle 7 chatter 10 stridulate

cloak: aba 4 brat, capa, cape, hide, mant, mask, pall, rail, robe, veil, wrap 5 capot, cover, guise, manta, manto, sagum 6 assume, bautta, capote, caster, chapel, dolman, mantle, mantua, pharos, screen, serape, shield, shroud, tabard, visite 7 bavaroy, chlamys, conceal, garment, manteau, manteel, pelisse, pretext, shelter, zimarra 8 albornoz, burnoose, disguise, intrigue, mantilla, palliate 9 dissemble 10 camouflage, roquelaure 11 portmanteau

African: 5 jelab 6 jellab

Arabian: 7 feridgi, ferigee, ferijee 8 feridjee

baptismal: 7 chrisom

bishop's: 10 mantelleta

ecclesiastical: 4 cope

Greek: 6 abolla 7 chlamys

hooded: 6 camail 8 burnoose

Indian: 5 choga

Jewish: 6 kittel 9 gaberdine

large-sleeved: 10 witzchoura

loose: 5 palla

monk's: 8 analabos

Punjabi: 5 choga

Roman: 5 sagum 7 alicula, paenula

Roman military: 10 paludamenta 11 paludamenta(pl.) 12 paludamentum

sleeveless: aba 6 dolman 7 paenula

Spanish: 4 capa 5 manta 6 mantle

Turkish: 6 dolman

waterproof: 6 poncho

worn over armor: 6 tabard

clobber: 4 beat, belt, slug 5 patch, pound, smear 6 cobble, defeat, strike, wallop

cloche: hat, jar 4 bell 5 cover

clocher: 6 belfry 9 bell tower, campanile

clock: nef 4 bell, call, dial, gong, time 5 cluck, hatch, hurry, meter, watch 6 beetle, Big Ben, crouch 8 horologe, incubate, ornament, recorder 9 clepsydra, hourglass, indicator, taximeter, timepiece 11 chronometer, speedometer

ancient water: 9 clepsydra

astronomical: 8 sidereal

maker: 9 horologer 10 horologist

part of: 4 dial 5 bundy 6 detent, foliot 8 pendulum, recorder

regulating body: 8 pendulum 10 escapement

ship-shaped: nef
water: **9** clepsydra
weight: **5** peise
clocker: 5 timer **8** railbird **11** embroiderer
clockmaker: 9 horologer
clockwise: 6 deasil, dessil **7** deiseal **8** positive
clod: sod **4** clat, clot, dolt, dull, lout, lump, turf **5** clout, clown, divot, earth, glebe, gross, knoll, yokel **6** dimwit, ground, stupid **7** bumpkin **9** blockhead, coagulate **10** clodhopper
cloddish: 5 gross **6** stupid **7** boorish, ill-bred
clodhopper: 4 boor, clod, shoe **6** rustic **7** bumpkin, plowman
clodpate: 4 clot, dolt, fool **7** ramhead **8** clodpole, clodpoll, imbecile **9** blockhead
clog: gum, jam, log **4** clag, clam, cloy, curb, load, lump, shoe, skid, stop **5** block, check, choke, dance, sabot **6** adhere, burden, chopin, fetter, galosh, hamper, hobble, hog-tie, impede, pattern, remora, sandal, secque, weight **7** galoshe, perplex, shackle, trammel **8** coalesce, encumber, obstruct, overshoe, restrain **9** embarrass, hindrance, restraint **10** difficulty **11** encumbrance
with mud: **4** daub **6** daggle
cloggy: 5 heavy, lumpy **6** sticky
clogwyn: 5 cliff **9** precipice
cloister: 4 hall, stoa **5** abbey, aisle, stoae(pl.) **6** arcade, friary, immure, piazza, priory **7** closter, convent, nunnery, seclude **9** cloistral, enclosure, hermitage, monastery, sanctuary, sequester **11** ambulatoria(pl.) **12** ambulatorium
pert. to: **9** claustral, cloistral
Cloister and the Hearth author: 5 Reade
cloistered: 7 recluse **11** sequestered
clone: 4 copy, dupe **6** double **7** replica **9** duplicate **13** identical twin
cloof, clufe: 4 claw, hoof **6** cleave
clop: 4 limp **5** sound **6** hobble
close: cap, end, hot **4** clit, firm, hard, hide, near, nigh, quit, seal, shut, slam, snug, stop **5** anear, block, cease, cheap, dense, finis, garth, gross, muggy, thick, tight **6** clause, clench, effect, expiry, finale, finish, narrow, nearby, period, stingy, strait **7** adjourn, compact, context, extreme, miserly, occlude, similar **8** accurate, adjacent, complete, conclude, familiar, imminent, intimate, taper off **9** barricade, extremity, niggardly, terminate **10** avaricious, conclusion, nip-and-tuck **11** termination **12** parsimonious
a hawk's eyes: **4** seel
firmly: bar **4** lock, seal **5** tight **6** batten, cement

closefisted: 4 near **6** stingy **7** miserly **8** handfast **9** niggardly
closely: 4 just **6** almost, barely, narrow, nearly **9** carefully, compactly
closemouthed: 6 secret, silent
closeness: 7 secrecy **8** fidelity, intimacy **9** parsimony, proximity **10** stinginess, strictness **11** conciseness, literalness **14** oppressiveness
closest: 4 next **7** nearest **9** proximate
closet: 4 ewry, room, safe **5** ambry, cuddy **6** armary, locker, pantry, secret **7** cabinet, conceal, private **8** conclave, cupboard, gardevin, wardrobe **9** gardevine **12** confidential
closing device: 4 lock **6** zipper
closure: end, gag **5** bound, limit **7** cloture **8** clausure **9** agreement, enclosure **10** conclusion **11** confinement, containment **12** entrenchment
clot: dot, gel **4** clag, clat, clod, gout, jell, lump, mass **5** clart, group, grume **6** balter, cotter **7** clodder, congeal, embolus, thicken **8** clodplate, coagulum, concrete, solidify **9** blockhead, coagulate **12** crassamentum
cloth (see also **fabric,** and name of individual fabrics: **cotton, linen, silk,** etc.): rag **5** bluet, toile(F.), tweed, twill **6** canvas, clergy, drapet, fabric, livery, napkin **7** acetate, drapery, garment, raiment, textile, worsted **8** dwelling, material, sheeting **10** cassinette
baptismal: **7** chrisom
bark: **4** tapa **9** tapa cloth
blemish: yaw **4** snag, tear **5** amper
camel's hair: aba **6** camlet
coarse: **4** duck **5** crash, gunny **6** burlap, linsey
crinkled: **5** crape, crepe **10** seersucker
dealer: **6** draper, mercer
decorative: see *ornamental* below
dryer: **6** tenter
dye method: tie **5** batik
fine-textured: **4** mull, pima, silk **7** percale
finisher: **7** beetler
flaw in: **4** rase
flaxen: **5** linen
glazed: **5** tammy
goat's hair: **5** tibet **6** camlet, mohair
heavy: **9** petersham
hemp: **4** jute **5** gunny **6** baline, burlap, canamo
homespun: **4** kelt
instrument: **8** ringhead
knitted: **6** jersey, tricot
light: **6** tissue **7** challis, etamine
lining: **5** serge **8** sarcenet, sarsenet
measure: ell **4** nail
mesh: net **5** super, tulle **11** cheesecloth
metallic: **4** acca, tash
mourning: **5** crape, crepe

muslin: **5** adati
narrow: **4** tape **5** braid **6** edging, ribbon
old kind: **4** acca, tuke **5** tewke **6** samite
ornamental: **4** gimp, lace **6** lampas, riband **8** tapestry
poplin: **7** tabinet **8** tabbinet
print: **6** calico **7** percale
printer: **7** candroy
raised design: **7** brocade
remnant: **4** fent
ridge in: **4** wale
roll: **4** bolt
rug: mat **7** matting
satin: See **fabric:** *satin*
shop: **7** mercery
silk: See **fabric:** *silk*
soft: **5** panne, plush, surah **6** fleece **9** montagnac
stiff: **7** taffeta **9** crinoline
stretcher: **6** tenter
synthetic: **5** nylon, rayon **6** dacron **7** acetate
toweling: **5** terry
twilled: rep **4** jean **5** denim, serge
used as a dressing: **5** stupe
velvet: **5** panne
weatherproof: **4** tarp **6** canvas
woolen: **6** kersey
clothe: don, dub, rig, tog **4** deck, dress, garb, gird, gown, robe, vest **5** adorn, array, clead, cleed, dress, endow, endue, frock, habit **6** attire, enrobe, invest, swathe **7** apparel, vesture **8** accouter, accoutre **9** authorize, represent
clothes (see also **dress**): **4** duds, garb, gear, suit, tack, wear **5** get-up, habit **6** attire **7** apparel, baggage, costume, raiment, regalia, toggery, vesture **8** clothing, frippery, garments **9** vestments **10** bedclothes **11** habiliments
basket: **6** hamper
civilian: **5** mufti
collection: **8** wardrobe
dealer: **6** ragman **7** fripper **9** fripperer
informal: **5** smock **6** halter, shorts, slacks, trunks
pert. to: **8** vestiary **10** habilatory
presser: **7** sadiron
clothesmoth: **5** tinea
clothespress: kas **5** chest **7** armoire **8** wardrobe
clothing: (see also **garment**): **4** wear **6** attire **7** apparel
coarse: **4** brat **5** burel
protective: **5** armor
woman's: **6** fardel
cloud: fog, nue(F.) **4** blur, dust, haze, hide, mist **5** bedim, befog, gloom, nubia, stain, sully, swarm, taint, vapor **6** cirrus, damage, darken, deepen, defame, nebula, nimbus, screen, shadow, stigma **7** blacken, confuse, cumulus, eclipse,

obscure, perplex, tarnish **8** befuddle, overcast **9** obfuscate **11** thunderhead
form: **6** nebule **7** stratus **9** mare's tail
morning: **4** velo
pert. to: **7** nebular **12** nephological
study of: **9** nephology
wind-driven: **4** rack, scud
cloudburst: **6** deluge **9** rainstorm
cloudless: **5** azure, clear **6** bright
cloudy: dim **4** dark, dull, hazy **5** filmy, murky, shady **6** gloomy, lowery, opaque **8** overcast **10** indistinct, lackluster
clough: **5** cleft **6** ravine, valley
clour: **4** blow, bump, dint **5** thump **6** batter
clout: bat, box, hit **4** beat, blow, bump, clod, club, cuff, join, mend, nail, pull, slap, slug, swat **5** patch, power, smite **6** strike, target, thrash, washer **7** bandage **8** bosthoon **9** influence **11** what it takes **12** handkerchief
clouter: **7** botcher, cobbler
clove: bud **4** bulb, tree **5** spice **6** ravine
cloven: **5** cleft, split **9** bisulcate
cloven-footed: **8** fissiped
clover: red **5** lotus, medic, nardu **6** alsike, luxury, nardoo **7** alfalfa, comfort, lucerne, melilot, trefoil **10** prosperity
cloverleaf: fan **7** freeway **8** crossway **11** interchange
clown: hob, oaf **4** aper, boor, fool, goff, joey, lout, mime, mome, zany **5** churl, comic, mimer, punch, zanni(It.) **6** august, bodach, hobbil, jester, lubber, rustic, stooge **7** buffoon, bumpkin, peasant, playboy **8** merryman **9** harlequin, joculator **10** bufflehead, countryman, harlequina **11** Emmet Kelly, merry-andrew, punchinello **13** pickle-herring
clownish: raw **4** rude, zany **5** gawky, rough **6** clumsy, coarse, rustic **7** awkward, boorish, hoblike, ill-bred, loutish, uncivil **8** ungainly **9** untutored
cloy: **4** clog, glut, nail, pall, sate **5** gorge, prick **6** pierce **7** satiate, satisfy, surfeit
club: bat, hit, set **4** beat, cane, join, mace, maul, polt, team **5** billy, bunch, clout, kebby, lodge, order, staff, stick, unite, yokel **6** clique, cudgel, kebbie, menage, weapon **8** bludgeon, sorority, spontoon **9** blackjack, truncheon **10** fraternity, knobkerrie, shillelagh **11** association
famous: **5** Lambs **6** Friars **7** Garrick
golf: **4** iron, wood **5** wedge **6** putter **7** sand wedge
club moss: **8** buckhorn
club-shaped: **7** clavate
clubfoot: **7** talipes **9** deformity
clubfooted: **7** taliped
clubs: **4** suit **5** cards, basto
clubstart: **5** stoat
cluck: hen **4** call, fuss **5** chuck, clack,

click, clock, sound **9** dumb bunny **13** featherweight

clue: key, tip **4** ball, clew, hint, idea **5** guide, twine **6** thread **7** inkling **8** innuendo **10** indication, intimation, suggestion **11** fingerprint

clump: tod **4** blow, bush, heap, lump, mass, mott, tope, tuft **5** bunch, group, grove, patch, tread **6** clunch, dollop **7** cluster, thicket **10** hodgepodge

clumsy: 4 rude **5** blunt, bulky, gawky, hulky, inapt, inept, stiff **6** gauche **7** awkward, boorish, ill-made, unhandy **8** bungling, tactless, ungainly, unwieldy **9** all thumbs, lumbering, maladroit **10** cumbersome **11** heavy-handed **13** inappropriate

Cluny product: 4 lace

cluster: bog **4** bush, cyme, knot, lump, tuft **5** bunch, clump, group **7** bourock, cluther, package **8** fascicle **9** glomerule **10** collection **11** agglomerate, aggregation

fern spore: **4** sori(pl.) **5** sorus

fiber: nep

flower: **4** cime, cyme **5** ament, umbel **6** raceme **7** panicle **8** anthemia

flower-like: **7** rosette

growing in: **8** acervate

of seven stars: **8** Pleiades

clustered: 6 tufted **8** racemose **9** aciniform, aggregate, glomerate **10** coacervate

clutch: nab **4** clam, claw, clem, clip, fist, glam, grab, grip, nest **5** brood, catch, clasp, claut, cleek, glaum, grasp, gripe, hatch, lever, power, seize, talon **6** cleach, clench, cletch, clinch, retain, snatch **7** control **8** coupling

clutter: 4 mess **6** bustle **7** clatter **8** disorder **9** confusion **10** disarrange, hodgepodge

Clymene: *father:* **7** Oceanus

husband: **7** Iapetus

mother: **6** Tethys

son: **5** Atlas **10** Prometheus

Clytemnestra: *daughter:* **7** Electra **9** Iphigenia

father: **9** Tyndareus

half-sister: **5** Helen

husband: **9** Agamemnon

mother: **4** Leda

paramour: **9** Aegisthus

son: **7** Orestes

victim: **9** Agamemnon, Cassandra

cnemis: 4 shin **5** tibia **7** legging

coach: bus, car **4** hack, help **5** araba, cabin, prime, teach, train, tutor **6** advise, direct, fiacre(F.), mentor, saloon **7** adviser, prepare, tallyho **8** carriage, dormeuse, instruct **10** instructor, stagecoach

railway: **7** Pullman, sleeper

coach dog: 9 Dalmatian

coachman: fly **4** fish, jehu, whip **5** pilot **6** driver **7** coachee, coacher **8** yemschik

assistant: **10** postillion

Russian: **7** yamshik **8** yemschik **9** yamstchik

coadjutor: 4 aide **6** bishop **7** partner **8** coworker **9** assistant, associate

coagulant: 4 curd **6** rennet **7** styptic **8** gelatine

coagulate: gel, set **4** cake, clod, clot, curd, jell **5** quail **6** cotter, curdle, posset **7** clabber, congeal, thicken **8** solidify

coagulation: 4 gout **7** clotter

coal: 4 bass, fuel **5** chark, ember, gleed, stoke **6** carbon, cinder

agent: **6** fitter

bed: **4** seam

block: jud

carrying box: hod **7** scuttle

constituent: **4** goaf **6** carbon, ethene, phenol, pyrene **7** benzene **8** creosote **11** naphthalene

distillate: tar

dust: **4** coom, culm, smut, soot, swad **5** coomb

immature form of: **7** lignite

kind of: jud **4** dant, hard, soft **6** cannel **7** lignite **9** tasmanite **10** anthracite, bituminous

lump: cob

mine explosive: **9** Bobbinite

miner: **7** collier

miner's disease: **11** anthrocosis

mining implement: **7** breaker

oil: **8** kerosene

refuse: **4** coke, dust, slag **6** cinder **7** backing, clinker

size: cob, egg, nut, pea **4** lump **5** slack, stove **6** broken **8** chestnut **9** buckwheat

wagon: **4** corb, carf, tram

worker: **7** collier, geordie **8** chaffman

coal car part: 6 hopper

coalbin: 6 bunker

coalesce: mix **4** fuse, join **5** blend, merge, unite **6** embody **7** combine **10** amalgamate

coalescence: 5 union **6** fusion, league **11** combination

coalfish: sey **4** parr **5** cuddy **6** beshow, billet, cudden, podler, sarthe **7** baddock, glashan, pollack

coalition: 4 bloc **5** trust, union **6** fusion, league, merger **8** alliance **11** combination, confederacy, conjunction **13** confederation

coarse: low, raw **4** dank, hard, hask, lewd, loud, rank, rude, vile **5** bawdy, broad, crass, crude, dirty, gross, harsh heavy, loose, randy, routh, thick **6** brutal, callow, common, earthy, impure, ribald, rustic, vulgar **7** blatant, fulsome, goatish, obscene, raucous, sensual **8** clownish, homespun, immodest, indecent, unchaste **9** inelegant, offensive, unrefined **10** boisterous, indelicate, unpolished **12** scatological

food: **6** fodder

coast: **4** bank, land, ripa **5** beach, blide, shore, slide **6** adjoin, border, rivage, strand **7** seaside **8** approach, littoral, seaboard, seashore

area: **7** seaside **8** seacoast **9** coastline, shoreline

dweller: **7** orarian

pert. to: **7** coastal, orarian **8** littoral, riparian

projection: **4** cape, ness **8** headland **9** peninsula

Coast Guard: *boat:* **6** cutter

service-woman: **4** Spar

coaster: mat **4** sled **5** trout **8** toboggan **9** container

coat (see also **cloak**): **4** bark, daub, husk, rind, zinc **5** cloth, cover, crust, glaze, habit, layer, paint, plate, shell, terve **6** enamel, jacket, mantle, parget, pelage, veneer **7** garment, incrust, overlay, plaster, vesture **8** membrane, tegument **9** petticoat **10** integument

animal: fur **4** hair, hide, pelt, wool **6** pelage

arctic: **5** parka

fastener: **4** frog **6** button

Irish: **9** coatamore

kind of: car, pea **4** cape, jupe, mail, robe, sack, toga **5** armor, simar, tails **6** coatie, duster, jerkin, kirtle, mantle, reefer, rocket, topper **7** cassock, cutaway, haubeck, paletot, pelisse, surcoat, surcote, surtout **8** benjamin, mackinaw, overcoat **9** gaberdine, newmarket, redingote **12** chesterfield

neck: **6** george

part: **4** cuff **5** lapel, skirt **6** collar, george, pocket, sleeve

seaman's: **5** grego

soldier's: **5** tunic

coat of arms: **5** crest

pert to: **8** heraldic

coati: **5** nasua **6** animal, narica

coating: **4** aril, film **6** patina, veneer **8** mucilage

coax: beg, coy, pet **4** cant, dupe, fawn, lure, urge **5** tease **6** cajole, cuitle, entice **7** beguile, cuittle, flatter, implore, wheedle **8** blandish, butter up, collogue, inveigle, persuade, soft soap **9** influence **10** manipulate

coaxial: **12** conterminous

cob: ear, mew **4** beat, blow, gull, loaf, lump, mole, mule, pier, pony, swan, toss **5** block, break, chief, excel, horse, outdo, piece, stump, throw, thump **6** basket, cobnut, leader, muffin, peapod, spider, strike **7** beating, seagull, surpass, threash **8** dumpling **10** breakwater

cobble: **4** darn, make, mend, pave **5** botch, patch, stone **6** bungle, repair **7** clobber, snarl up **11** cobblestone

cobbler: pie **4** snob **5** sheep, soler, sutor **6** souter **7** botcher, catfish, crispin, dessert, pompano, saddler **8** chuckler, scorpion **9** killifish, shoemaker

pitch: **4** code

cobia: **4** fish **6** bonito

cobra: asp, nag **4** naga, naja **5** snake, viper **6** uraeus

genus: **4** naja

tree: **5** mamba

cobweb: net **4** trap **5** snare, wevet **8** gossamer **9** intricacy

cocaine: **4** snow **8** alkaloid, narcotic **10** anesthetic

source: **4** coca

coccyx: **8** tailbone

cochleate: **6** spiral **11** shell-shaped

cock: tap **4** bank, fowl, heap, kora, pile, rick **5** fugie, fight, gallo, shock, stack, strut, valve, yowle **6** faucet, leader **7** chicken, contend, gorcock, rooster, swagger **8** gamecock, malemass **10** cockalorum **11** chanticleer

gun: nab

of the walk: **8** kingfish

weather: **4** vane

cock-a-hoop: **4** awry **5** askew **6** elated, lively **8** boastful, cockeyed

cock-and-bull story: lie **6** canard **7** untruth **9** falsehood

cockade: **4** knot **5** badge **7** rosette

Cockaigne: **6** utopia **8** paradise

cockatoo: ara **5** arara, cocky, galah, macaw **6** abacay, cockie, parrot **8** calangay, ganggang

genus: **7** cacatua, kakatoe

cockatrice: **7** serpent **8** basilisk

cockboat: cog **7** rowboat

cockchafer: **6** beetle

cocker: dog, pet **4** shoe **6** coddle, fondle, pamper, quiver, reaper **7** cater to, fighter, indulge, legging, nurture, spaniel

cockerel: **4** cock, slip **6** bantam

cockeyed: **4** alop, awry **5** askew **10** inebriated **11** intoxicated

cockfight: **4** game, spar **5** match **7** contest

cockfighting: **13** alectryomachy

cockhorse: **5** lofty, proud **7** astride, upstart **8** exultant

cockle: **4** boat, gall, gith, kiln, oast **5** bulge, shell, stove **6** darnel, pucker, ripple, wabble **7** mollusk, wrinkle **9** whimsical

cocklebur: **5** plant **7** burdock

cockpit: pit **4** ring, rink, well **5** arena, cabin, field **7** gallera

cocksure: 4 sure **5** cocky **7** certain **8** confident, positive

cocktail: 5 Bronx, drink **7** apertif, martini, sidecar **8** daiquiri **9** appetizer, Manhattan, Margarita **10** Bloody Mary

cocky: 4 pert **6** crouse, farmer, jaunty **8** arrogant, insolent **9** conceited **11** smart alecky

cocoa, coco: 4 head, palm, tary **5** broma **6** yuntia **9** chocolate

coconut: 7 coquito
dried meat: copra
fiber: **4** coir, kyar

cocoon: pod **4** clew, clue **5** shell **11** incunabulum

cod: bag, cor, pod **4** axle, bank, cusk, fish, fool, hoax, husk, rock **5** belly, pouch, scrod, torsk **6** burbot, codger, cultus, fellow, pillow **7** bacaloa, cushion
family: **7** gadidae
genus: **5** gadus
related fish: **7** rattail **9** grenadier
young: **5** scrod, sprag **7** codling

cod-like: bib **4** hake, ling **5** gadus

coda: 4 part **5** rondo **6** finale **10** conclusion

coddle: pet **4** baby, cade, cook **5** humor, nurse, spoil **6** caress, cocker, cosset, cotton, fondle, pamper, cater to **7** indulge, parboil

code: law **4** flag **5** canon, codex **6** cipher, digest, secret, signal **7** precept
inventor: **5** Morse
message: **6** cipher **10** cryptogram

coded message: 10 cryptogram

codex: 4 code **5** annal **9** formulary **10** manuscript

codger: cod **5** churl, crank, miser **6** fellow **7** niggard

codicil: 5 rider **6** sequel **8** appendix **10** supplement

codify: 5 index **6** digest **8** classify **11** systematize

coerce: cow **4** curb, make, urge **5** bully, check, drive, force **6** compel, menace **7** concuss, enforce, repress **8** bludgeon, bulldoze, restrain, restrict **9** blackmail, constrain, terrorize **10** intimidate

coercion: 5 force **6** duress

coeval: 12 contemporary

coffee: *after dinner:* **9** demitasse
alkaloid: **7** caffein
bean: nib
beverage: Rio **4** Java, Kona **5** Milds, Mocha **6** Bogota, Brazil, Santos **7** Sumatra **8** Medellin **9** Maracaibo
cake: **6** kuchen
French: **4** café
grinder: **4** mill
kind: **4** drip, java **5** mocha, Sanka **7** ara-

bica, instant **8** espresso
maker: urn **5** silex **10** percolator
refuse: **6** triage

coffee shop: 5 diner **8** snack bar **9** lunchroom **12** luncheonette

coffeeberry: 6 jojoba **7** cascara, soybean **8** peaberry **9** buckthorn, chaparral

coffeepot: 6 biggin **9** cafetiere

coffer: ark, box, dam **5** chest, hutch, trunk **6** casket, forcer, trench **7** caisson **8** ciborium, standard

coffin: 4 bier, case, cist, mold **6** basket, casing, casket **11** sarcophagus
cloth: **4** pall **5** cloak
support: **4** bier

cog: cam, lie **4** gear, jest **5** catch, cheat, cozen, tenon, tooth, trick, wedge, wheel **6** cajole **7** deceive, produce, quibble, wheedle **8** cockboat **9** fabricate, falsehood

cogent: 5 pithy, valid **6** potent, strong **7** telling **8** forcible, powerful **9** trenchant **10** conclusive, convincing, legitimate, persuasive

cogitate: 4 mull, muse, plan **5** think **6** ponder **7** connate, reflect **8** consider, meditate

cognate: kin **4** akin **5** alike **6** allied **7** kindred, related, similar **8** bandhava, relative

cognizance: ken **4** heed, mark **5** badge, crest **6** emblem, notice **7** bearing, cockade **9** knowledge **11** observation, recognition **12** apprehension

cognizant: 4 onto, ware **5** awake, aware **8** sensible **9** conscious **10** conversant **11** intelligent **12** apprehensive

cognize: 4 know **5** grasp **6** fathom **8** perceive **9** apprehend, recognize **10** appreciate, understand

cognomen (see also **name**): **4** name **5** style, title **6** byname **7** agnomen, moniker, surname **8** nickname, patronym **11** appellation

cognoscente: 5 judge **6** critic, expert **9** authority **10** specialist

cohabit: 4 live **5** dwell **6** occupy **8** accustom **9** accompany

cohere: fit **4** glue, suit **5** agree, cling, stick, unite **6** adhere, cement, cleave **7** connect **8** coincide **9** glutinate

coherence: 5 union **8** cohesion **9** congruity **10** accordance, connection, continuity **11** consistency

cohort: 4 band, mate **6** fellow **7** company **9** associate

coif, coiffe: cap **4** hood **6** beggin, burlet, hairdo **7** arrange **8** skullcap **9** headdress

coiffure: 6 hairdo **9** headdress

coign: 5 wedge **6** corner **8** position **10** projection

coil: ado, wip **4** ansa, clew, curl, fuss, hank, loop, roll, wind **5** helix, querl, tense, twine, twist **6** rundle, spiral, tumult, windup **7** haycock, ringlet, trouble **8** encircle **9** confusion, encounter **10** difficulty **11** convolution
electric: **6** teaser
coin: die, ori **4** cash, dime, make, mint **5** angle, brown, chink, clink, metal, money, quoin, shape, stamp, token, wedge **6** change, corner, create, invent, specie, strike **7** convert **8** currency **9** fabricate, neologize, originate **11** cornerstone
ancient: **4** obol **6** obolus
box: pyx **4** till **5** meter **8** register
collector: **11** numismatist
copper: **4** cent **5** penny, bodle, brown
counterfeit: **9** brummagem
difference: **5** value **11** seigniorage
edge corrugation: **7** reeding
front: **4** head **7** obverse
imperfectly minted: **8** brockage
kind of: lap, ora **4** dime, doit, mite, rial, rosa **5** cuyne, daric, disme, ducat, eagle, groat **6** bawbee, beaver, besant, bezant, cunzie **7** bezzant, carolus, crocard, louleau **8** bezantee, crockard **10** castellano
pert. to: **10** numismatic **12** numismatical
reverse side: **4** tail **5** verso
roll: **7** rouleau
science: **11** numismatics
silver: **4** batz, dime, dump, pina, tara **5** bezzo **6** tester, teston
stamper: **4** mill
weight: **6** shekel
coinage: **7** fiction, mintage **9** neologism
collector: **11** numismatist
coincide: gee **4** jibe **5** agree, tally **6** concur **9** harmonize **10** correspond
coincidence: **9** concourse **11** concurrence **12** concomitance, simultaneity
coincident: **4** even **8** together **9** consonant **10** concurrent **11** concomitant **12** contemporary **15** contemporaneous
coiner of new words: **9** neologian, neologist
coition: **7** meeting **10** attraction **11** conjunction
coke: aks **4** coal, core, dope **5** chark **7** cocaine
col: **4** pass **10** depression
colander: **5** sieve **7** utensil **8** strainer
Colchis: *king:* **6** Aeetes
princess: **5** Medea
cold: flu **4** dead, dull **5** algid, bleak, frore, gelid, rheum, virus **6** arctic, chilly, frigid, frosty, wintry **7** catarrh, chilled, distant, glacial **8** reserved, rhigosis, unheated **9** apathetic, cheerless **10** insensible, spiritless **11** hyperborean, indifferent, unemotional **12** unresponsive **13** dispassionate, marblehearted **15** undemonstrative

instrument to apply: **9** cryoprobe
pert. to: icy **5** gelid **6** frigid, frozen **10** frigorific
remedy: **13** antihistamine
cold and damp: raw **4** dank **5** bleak
cold-blooded: **7** callous **9** unfeeling
cold feet: **4** fear **5** alarm, doubt **9** cowardice **12** apprehension
cold mist: **4** drow
cold-shoulder: cut **4** snub **6** ignore, rebuff
cold steel: **5** sword **6** dagger **7** bayonet
cold sweat: **4** fear **5** shock **11** trepidation
colder: **4** husk **6** refuse **7** rubbish
coleoptera insect: **6** beetle, insect, weevil
Coleridge's sacred river: **4** Alph
Colette: **8** novelist
characters: **4** Gigi **5** Cheri **8** Claudine
colewort: **4** cole, kale **7** cabbage
colic: **5** gripe **9** bellyache **10** mulligrubs
coliseum: **4** bowl, hall **7** stadium, theater **8** building **12** amphitheater
collaborate: aid **9** cooperate
collagen: **7** protein **10** albuminoid
collapse: **4** cave, fall, fold **5** crash, slump, wreck **6** bust-up **7** crumple, debacle, deflate, failure, flummox, smashup **8** contract, downfall **9** breakdown, telescope **11** prostration
collar: nab **4** band, eton, gill, grab, ring, ruff **5** chain, fichu, ruche, seize **6** bertha, gorget, tackle, torque **7** capture, chignon, circlet, shackle **8** cincture, neckband, necklace **9** neckpiece
horse: **6** hounce
jeweled: **8** carcanet
kind of: **4** cowl, ruff **5** fanon, jabot, orale, phano, ruche, rabat, V-neck **6** cangue, carcan, rabato, rebato **7** bargham, panuelo **8** carcanet, Peter Pan **10** chevesaile, turtleneck
collarbone: **8** clavicle
collate: **6** bestow, confer, verify **7** arrange, bracket, compare, emamine **9** integrate
collateral: **4** side **8** indirect, parallel, security **9** ancillary **10** subsidiary **11** concomitant, subordinate
collation: tea **4** meal **5** lunch **6** repast, sermon **7** address, reading **8** dejeuner, parallel, treatise **10** collection, comparison, conference **12** consultation, contribution
colleague: **4** aide, ally **6** deputy **7** adjunct, consort, partner **8** confrere **9** assistant, associate
collect: tax **4** call, heap, levy, pile, pool, save **5** amass, glean, group, hoard, raise **6** accoil, accrue, confer, garner, gather, muster, prayer, sheave **7** compile, engross, impound, round up **8** assemble, contract **9** aggregate **10** accumulate, congregate, simmer down **11** agglomerate
collected: **4** calm, cool **5** sober **6** serene **8**

composed **9** aggregate, clustered **10** coacervate **11** agglomerate, unflappable
13 dispassionate

collection: ana **4** bevy, clan, olio **5** batch,
group, store, suite **6** bundle, conger, sorite **8** assembly, caboodle **9** aggregate,
anthology, collation, repertory **10** assemblage, assortment, cancionero

animals: zoo **9** menagerie

clothes: **8** wardrobe

facts: **4** data

literary: ana **7** library **8** analects

miscellaneous: **4** olio **6** fardel, jumble,
medley

poems: **5** divan, sylva **9** anthology **10**
cancionero

proper names: **11** onomasticon

collector: *bird egg:* **8** oologist

book: **11** bibliophile

coin: **11** numismatist

item: **5** curio **11** collectible

stamp: **11** philatelist

colleen: **4** girl, lass, miss **5** belle **6** damsel,
lassie, maiden

college (see also **university**): **5** lycee **6**
school **7** academy **8** seminary **10** assemblage, university **11** institution **12**
organization

accounts: **6** battel

building: gym, lab

campus: **4** quad **10** quadrangle

course: **5** major, minor **7** seminar

court: **4** quad

degree: B.L.S., B.Sc., LL.B., LL.D.,
M.Sc., S.C.B., Ph.D. **5** Litt.D.

girl: **4** coed

graduate: **6** alumna, doctor, master **7**
alumnus **8** bachelor

kind of: **9** electoral

living quarters: **4** dorm, hall **9** dormitory

official: **4** dean **5** prexy **6** beadle, bursar,
regent **7** proctor **9** president, registrar

pert. to: **8** academic **10** collegiate

professor: don **6** docent, doctor

session: lab **5** class **7** lecture, seminar **8**
tutorial

song: **9** alma mater

student group: **4** frat **8** sorority **10** fraternity

term: **8** semester

treasurer: **6** bursar

U.S. oldest: **7** Harvard

U.S. woman's oldest: **9** Mt. Holyoke

collet: **4** band, ring **5** chuck **6** casing, circle, collar, flange, socket **7** bushing, ferrule **8** neckband

collide: hit, ram **4** bump, dash, hurt **5** carom, clash, crash, wreck **6** hurtle, strike

collier: fly **4** boat **5** miner **6** plover, vessel
7 geordie

boy: **6** hodder

lung disease: **11** anthracosis

colliery: **4** mine

collision: **5** clash, crash, shock **7** crackup,
smashup **8** clashing **9** encounter **10** opposition, percussion **12** interference

collocate: set **5** place **7** arrange **8** position

colloquial: **6** patois **8** familiar, informal **9**
unstudied **10** vernacular **14** conversational

colloquy: **4** chat, talk **6** parley **8** dialogue
9 discourse **10** conference **12** conversation

colluctation: **8** struggle **10** contention

collude: **4** plot **6** scheme **7** connive **8** collogue, conspire

collusion: **6** deceit **7** cahoots, secrecy **9**
agreement, complicity **10** connivance

law: **5** covin

collusive: **8** convinous **10** fraudulent

Cologne: *German spelling:* **4** Koln

king: **6** Caspar, Jaspar

Colombia: *capital:* **6** Bogota

city: **4** Cali **5** Neiva, Pasto, Tunja **6** Cu-
cuta, Ibaque, Quibdo **7** Leticia, Po-
payan **8** Medellin **9** Cartagena, Mani-
zales, San Andres **10** Santa Maria **12**
Barranquilla

coin: **4** peso, real **6** condor, peseta **7** centavo

gulf: **6** Darien

Indian: **5** Boros **6** Betoya, Chitas, Ta-
hami, Yahuna **7** Tunebos

highest peak: **9** Cristobal

mahogany: **7** albarco

measure: **4** vara **7** celemin

monetary unit: **4** peso

mountains: **5** Andes

plant: **5** yocco

province: **5** Cauca, Choco, Huila, Valle **6**
Boyaca, Caldas, Narina, Tolima, Vau-
pes **7** Bolivar

river: **4** Sinu, Tomo **6** Atrato, Atroto,
Pattia, Yapura **7** Orinoco

seaport: **6** Lorica **9** Cartagena **10** Santa
Marta

volcano: **5** Huila, Pasto **6** Purace

weight: bag **4** saco **5** carga, libra **7** quilate,
quintal

colon: **4** coin **6** farmer **7** planter **8** colonist **10** husbandman

Colonel Blimp: **10** fuddy-duddy **12**
stuffed shirt

colonial teak: **8** flindosa

colonist: **7** pioneer, settler **8** emigrant

colonize: **5** found **6** gather, settle **7** migrate **9** establish

colonizer: ant **6** oecist **7** settler

colonnade: row **4** stoa **7** pergola, portico,
terrace **9** peristyle

colony: **5** swarm **9** community **10** dependency, settlement

colophon: **6** device, emblem

colophonite: **6** garnet **9** andradite

colophony: **5** resin, rosin

color: (see also next entry): dye, hue **4**

blee, cast, flag, tint, tone **5** badge, blush, paint, shade, stain, tenne, tinge **6** banner, ensign, redden **7** distort, pennant, pigment **8** standard, tincture **10** complexion

achromatic: **4** gray **5** black, white

change: **8** iridesce, opalesce

dull: dun **4** drab **5** terne

full of: **9** chromatic

graduation: **5** shade

healthy: tan

light: **4** tint

line of: **6** streak

malachite: **4** bice

mat white: **9** alabaster

mulberry: **7** morello

neutral: **4** ecru, gray **5** beige, black, white

painter: **6** Titian

pale: **6** pastel

primary: red **4** blue **5** black, white **6** yellow

quality: **4** tone

secondary: **5** green **6** orange, purple

shade of difference: **6** nuance

unhealthy **6** sallow

uniform in: **4** flot

value: see *quality* above

varying: **10** iridescent, opalescent

color: For colors see their names: **red, green, purple,** etc.; for shades see main color. EXAMPLES: "reddish brown": see **brown**; "grayish green": see **green.**

color bar: **11** segregation **14** discrimination

color blindness: **9** Daltonism **13** achromatopsia **14** monochromatism

color organ: **8** clavilux

color photography inventor: **4** Ives

Colorado: *capital:* **6** Denver

city: **5** Aspen, Delta, Lemar **6** Aurora, Pueblo **7** Boulder, Greeley, Manassa **8** Lakewood, Trinidad

county: Ada **4** Baca, Bent, Mesa, Yuma **5** Otero, Ouray, Routt **6** Custer, Gilpin, Moffat **7** Crowley, Chaffee

fort: **5** Logan

Indian: Ute **8** Arapahoe

motto: **13** Nil sine Numine

mountain peak: **5** Longs, Pikes **6** Elbert

mountain range: **5** Rocky

nickname: **10** Centennial

park: **5** Estes **9** Mesa Verde

resort: **4** Vail **5** Aspen **7** Manitou **15** Colorado Springs

river: **4** Bear **5** Green, White **7** Laramie **9** Rio Grande **11** South Platte

state bird: **11** lark bunting

state flower: **9** columbine

state tree: **10** blue spruce

colorant: dye **4** anil **7** pigment

coloratura: **6** singer **7** soprano **8** vocalist

colored: **6** biased **9** distorted, prismatic **14** misrepresented

partly: **4** pied **6** motley **7** piebald **10** variegated

colorful: gay **5** vivid **9** brilliant

colorimeter: **10** tintometer

coloring: *cell:* **10** endochrome

matter: dye **5** morin **7** pigment **8** clorofil **10** endochrome **11** chlorophyll

colorless: wan **4** drab, dull, pale **5** ashen, blake, blank, plain **6** pallid **7** hueless, neutral **8** blanched **9** impartial **10** achromatic **11** transparent **13** uninteresting

colors, set of: **7** palette

colossal (see also **huge**): big **4** huge, vast **5** great, large **7** immense, mammoth, titanic **8** enormous, gigantic **9** monstrous

colossus: **5** giant, titan **6** statue **7** monster, prodigy

colporteur: **6** hawker **7** apostle, peddler **10** evangelist, missionary **11** distributor

colt: gun **4** foal, tyro **5** filly **6** pistol **8** beginner, neophyte **9** quadruped, youngster

coluber: **5** snake **7** serpent

colubrine: **6** crafty **7** cunning **9** snakelike

Columbia River rapids: **6** Dalles

columbine: **4** bird, dodo **5** plant **6** flower **8** dovelike

Columbus: *birthplace:* **5** Genoa

burial place: **7** Seville

companion: **5** Ojeda

embarkation port: **5** Palos

patron: **8** Isabella **9** Ferdinand

ship: **4** Nina **5** Pinta **10** Santa Maria

son: **5** Diego

column: lat, row **4** file, line, post **5** shaft, stela, stele **6** pillar **7** support **8** cylinder, pilaster **9** formation

arrange in: **8** tabulate

base: **6** plinth **9** stylobate

female figure: **8** caryatid

male figure: **5** Atlas **7** telamon

part: **4** anta, fust **5** galbe, socle, scape, shank **6** plinth **7** entasis, capital **8** pilaster

pert to: **8** columnar

shaped like human figure: **7** telamon **8** atlantes, caryatid

small: **5** stele

support: **5** socle

type of: **5** Doric, Ionic **10** Corinthian

columnar: **6** terete **7** stelene **8** vertical

columnist: **6** writer **7** analyst

columns: *series of:* **9** colonnade

set in: **7** tabular

without: **7** astylar

coma: **4** tuft **5** bunch, carus, sleep **6** stupor, torpor, trance **7** cluster **8** lethargy **13** insensibility

comate: 5 hairy

comatose: out 6 drowsy 9 lethargic 10 insensible

comb: 4 card, lash, rake 5 brush, clean, crest, curry, tease 6 smooth 11 disentangle

flax: 6 hackle, heckle 7 hatchel

horse: 5 curry

comb-like: 8 pectinal 9 pectinate

combat: war 4 bout, cope, duel, fray, meet, rush, tilt 5 clash, fight, joust, repel, set-to 6 action, battle, oppose, resist, strife 7 contend, contest, counter, scuffle 8 argument, conflict, struggle 9 encounter, withstand 10 antagonize, contention

challenge to single: 6 cartel

code: 6 duello

place: 5 arena

combatant: 6 dueler 7 battler, fighter 8 champion 10 contestant

combative: 8 militant 9 agonistic 10 pugnacious 11 agonistical, belligerent

comber: 4 wave 7 breaker 11 beachcomber

combination: key 4 bloc, gang, pact, pool, ring 5 cabal, junto, party, trust, union 6 cartel, clique, corner, merger 7 combine, consort, coterie, faction 8 alliance, ensemble 9 aggregate, camarilla, coalition, composite, composure, synthesis 10 concoction, conspiracy 11 association, coalescence, composition, confederacy, conjunction, corporation, unification 12 undergarment 13 incorporation

combine: add, mix, wed 4 bloc, join, pool 5 blend, marry, merge, total, unite 6 absorb, concur, embody, merger, mingle, splice 7 conjoin, conjure, machine 8 coalesce, compound, concrete, condense, contract, federate 9 construct, cooperate 10 amalgamate 11 combination, consolidate 12 conglomerate

combining form: See list page 826

comboy: 6 sarong

combust: 4 burn 5 burnt 8 consumed 10 incinerate

combustible: 4 fuel, peat 5 fiery 9 irascible 10 accendible 11 inflammable

material: gas, oil 4 coal, coke, peat 6 tinder

combustion: 4 fire, heat 5 therm 6 tumult 7 burning 8 volatile 9 agitation, confusion, consuming, cremation, oxidation 12 inflammation

residue: ash, gas 7 clinker

come: 4 grow 5 arise, issue, occur, reach 6 accrue, appear, arrive, befall, emerge, happen, spring 7 advance, develop, emanate 8 approach, practice 9 eventuate

a cropper: 4 fail, fall

across: 4 find, meet 9 encounter 10 contribute

after: 5 ensue 6 follow 7 succeed

again: 6 return

along: 4 fare 7 improve 8 progress

apart: 5 break 12 disintegrate

at: 6 attack

before: 7 precede, prevene 8 antecede

between: 8 alienate 9 interpose

by: get 4 gain 6 obtain 7 acquire, inherit

clean: 7 confess

down with: 5 catch 8 contract

forth: 6 appear, emerge

from: 5 ensue 6 derive, result

in: 5 crash, enter 6 arrive 7 intrude

into view: 4 loom 6 appear, emerge

of age: 6 mature

off: 5 break, click, occur 6 go over, pan out 7 develop, succeed

on: 4 bait, lure 5 decoy, snare

out: 6 appear, emerge, emerse, extend 8 protrude

to: 5 total 6 arrive, awaken, revive 7 recover

to a head: 6 climax 9 suppurate

to nothing: end 4 stop 5 cease

to terms: 4 join 5 agree 6 assent, settle 7 approve, consent 8 coincide 9 acquiesce

together: 4 bump, join, meet 5 clash, merge 7 collide, convene 8 assemble, converge

under: 7 subvene

up: 5 arise, occur 6 appear

comeback: 5 rally 6 answer, retort, return 7 rebound 8 recovery, repartee

comedian: wag, wit 4 card 5 actor, antic, clown, comic 6 jester 7 buffoon

comedown: 4 fall, land 5 crash 6 alight, bathos 7 descend 8 collapse

comedy: 5 drama, farce, revue 8 comoedia(L.), travesty 9 burlesque, slapstick

muse: 6 Thalia

symbol: 4 sock

comely: 4 fair, hend, pert 5 bonny, hende 6 decent, goodly, liking, lovely, pretty, proper 7 farrant 8 becoming, decorous, graceful, handsome, pleasing, suitable 9 agreeable, beautiful 10 gratifying, personable 11 good-looking

comestible: 4 food 5 manna, viand 6 edible 7 eatable, victual 8 esculent

comet: 6 meteor

discoverer: 5 Biela, Encke, Swift 6 Donati, Halley, Olbers 8 Kohoutek

part: 4 coma

tail: 8 streamer

comeuppance: due 6 rebuke 7 deserts 12 chastisement

comfit: 5 candy 7 confect, praline 8 conserve, preserve 9 sweetmeat 10 confection

comfort: aid 4 ease, rest 5 bield(Sc.),

cheer **6** buck up, endure, relief, repose, solace, soothe, succor **7** animate, assuage, cherish, confirm, console, enliven, gladden, refresh, relieve, support, sustain **8** inspirit, nepenthe, pleasure, reassure **9** encourage, well-being **10** strengthen **11** consolation

comfortable: **4** bein, bien, cosh, cozy, easy, like, snug, trig **5** comfy **7** relaxed **8** cheerful, euphoric, well-to-do **9** contented **10** acceptable, commodious, complacent, gratifying **11** consolatory, encouraging

comforter: **4** puff **5** cover, quilt, scarf **6** tippet **7** cheerer **8** pacifier

comfortless: **7** forlorn **8** desolate **9** cheerless **12** inconsolable

comfrey: **5** daisy **9** blackwort

comic: wag, wit **5** droll, funny **8** comedian, farcical **9** burlesque, laughable, ludicrous

strip: **7** funnies

comical: low **4** base, zany **5** droll, funny, queer, witty **7** amusing, jocular, risible, strange, trivial **8** humorous, ticklish **9** diverting, laughable, ludicrous, quizzical, whimsical **10** capricious

coming: due **4** next **6** advent, future **7** arrival, forward **8** deserved **9** impending **11** approaching

coming out: **5** debut **8** issuance

comma: **4** lull **5** pause **8** interval

command: bid **4** beck, bode, boon, call, fiat, hest, rule, sway **5** beken, check, edict, exact, force, hight, order, power, ukase **6** adjure, behest, charge, compel, degree, demand, direct, enjoin, govern, impose, master, ordain **7** appoint, behight, bidding, control, dictate, mandate, officer, precept, require **8** domineer, restrain **9** authority, direction, influence, ordinance, prescribe **10** commission **11** appointment

supreme: **9** hegemony

to a horse: gee, haw, hup **4** whoa

to go: **4** mush **6** begone, giddap

to stop: **4** whoa **5** avast

commander: cid, cio **4** head **5** chief **6** leader, master, rammer **7** captain, drungar, emperor, general, officer **10** commandant **11** commendador(Sp.) **13** generalissimo

of a thousand men: **9** chiliarch

commanding: **8** dominant, imposing **9** imperious, masterful **10** imperative **13** authoritative

commandment: law **4** rule **5** edict, order **7** precept

commando: **6** raider, ranger

comme il faut: **6** proper **7** fitting

commemorate: **7** observe **9** celebrate, solemnize **11** memorialize

commemoration: **5** award, medal **6** plaque **7** service **8** memorial **11** celebration **13** solemnization

commence: **4** fall, open **5** arise, begin, found, start **6** incept, spring **7** take off kick off, lead off **8** initiate **9** institute, originate

commencement: **4** dawn **5** alpha, birth, onset, start **7** genesis, opening **9** beginning

commencer: **4** tyro **8** beginner

commencing: **7** initial, nascent **9** incipient

commend: pat **4** give, laud **5** adorn, boost, extol, grace, offer **6** bestow, betake, commit, praise, resign **7** applaud, approve, bespeak, deliver, entrust, intrust **8** bequeath **9** predicate, recommend **10** compliment, ingratiate

highly: **5** extol **8** eulogize **10** panegyrize

to favor: **10** ingratiate

commendable: **4** good **6** worthy **8** laudable **9** exemplary, honorable **12** praiseworthy

commensurate: **4** even **5** equal **6** enough **8** adequate **10** answerable, convenient **11** appropriate **12** proportional **13** corresponding, proportionate

comment: **4** note, talk, word **5** aside, gloss, gloze **6** notate, postil, remark **7** descant, discuss, explain, expound, observe **9** criticise, criticism, criticize, discourse **10** animadvert, annotation, commentary **12** obiter dictum **13** animadversion

commentary: **5** gloss **6** memoir **7** account **8** glossary, treatise

commentator: **6** critic, glozer **7** analyst **9** annotator, expositor, glossator, scholiast **10** glossarist **13** glossographer

commerce: **5** trade **6** barter **7** traffic **8** business, exchange **10** connection **11** interchange

vehicle: **5** truck

commercial: **9** mercature **10** mercantile **13** advertisement

commingle: mix **4** fuse, join **5** blend, merge, unite **7** combine, embroil **10** amalgamate

comminute: **4** mill **5** crush, grind **9** pulverize, triturate

commiseration: **4** pity **7** empathy **8** sympathy **10** compassion, condolence

commission: **4** send, task **5** board, trust **6** brevit, charge, demand, depute, errand, office, ordain, permit **7** command, consign, empower, mandate, mission, warrant **8** delegate, encharge **9** allowance, authority, authorize, brokerage, establish **10** constitute **11** instruction **12** compensation, dispensation, perpetration **13** authorization

commissioner: 5 envoy 7 officer 8 delegate

commissure: 4 seam 5 joint, miter, mitre 8 juncture 10 miter joint

commit: 4 give 5 allot, refer 6 assign, betake, remand 7 command, confide, consign, deposit, entrust, intrust 8 bequeath, delegate, imprison, relegate, turn over 9 recommend 10 perpetrate

committee: 4 body 5 board, group, junta 7 council 9 executors, guardians

commixture: 6 fusion 7 mixture 8 compound 9 composite

commode: cap 5 chest 8 cupboard 10 chiffonier

commodious: fit 5 ample, roomy 6 proper, useful 8 spacious, suitable 9 capacious 10 beneficial, convenient 11 comfortable, serviceable 12 advantageous

commodity: 4 item, ware 5 goods 6 staple 7 article

common: low 4 base 5 banal, brief, cheap, joint, stale, trite, usual 6 coarse, mutual, ornery, vulgar 7 average, current, general, generic, natural, popular, regular, trivial, unnoble 8 all right, familiar, frequent, habitual, mediocre, ordinary, pandemic, plebeian, trifling 9 bourgeois, customary, defective, hackneyed, prevalent, universal, unrefined 10 second-rate 11 commonplace 12 matter-of-fact

common effort: 8 teamwork

common fund: pot 4 pool 5 purse

common law: 6 custom 9 tradition

common man: 4 pleb 8 plebeian

common sense: 6 wisdom 8 gumption, judgment

common stock: 8 security

commoner: 5 ceorl, plebe 7 burgess, citizen, student 8 roturier 12 participator

commonly: *accepted:* 7 popular, vulgate
thought: 7 reputed 8 putative

commonplace: 4 dull, fade, worn 5 banal, daily, plain, prose, stale, trite, usual 6 common, garden, truism 7 humdrum, prosaic, tedious, trivial 8 ordinary 9 hackneyed 11 stereotyped, unimportant 13 unexceptional
remark: 6 cliche, truism 9 platitude

commonwealth: 5 state 6 public 9 community 10 federation, res publica

Commonwealth country: 6 Canada 8 Zimbabwe 9 Australia 10 New Zealand

commotion: ado, din 4 bree, fray, fuss, heat, riot, stir, to-do, whir 5 alarm, flare, hurry 6 bustle, cathro(Sc.), fracas, flurry, garray, mutiny, pother, tumult, unrest, welter 7 clatter, tempest, turmoil 8 brouhaha, disorder, upheaval, uprising 9 agitation, confusion 10 con-

cussion, convulsion, ebullition, excitement, turbulence 11 disturbance, pandemonium 12 perturbation

commune: 4 area, talk 5 argue, realm, share, treat 6 advise, confer, debate, import, parley, reveal 7 consult, discuss, divulge 8 converse, district, township 11 communicate, intercourse, participate 12 conversation
Israeli: 7 kibbutz
Russian: mir 7 kolkhoz

communicable: 4 open 5 frank 8 catching, sociable 9 expansive, garrulous, talkative 10 contagious, diffusible, infectious 13 communicative

communicant: 6 member 8 adherent 9 informant

communicate (see also **commune**): 4 tell 6 bestow, convey, impart, inform, reveal, signal 7 declare, dictate, divulge 8 converse

communication: 4 note 5 favor 6 favour, letter 7 message 8 telegram 9 directive 10 communique, connection 11 interchange 12 conversation
means: 4 drum, flag, note, post 5 phone, radio, smoke 6 letter, movies, speech, tomtom 9 telegraph, telephone 10 television

communion: 4 cult, host, mass, sect, talk 5 creed, faith, share, unity 6 church, homily 7 concord 8 antiphon, converse, viaticum 9 agreement, eucharist, sacrament 10 confession, fellowship 11 intercourse 12 conversation, denomination 13 communication, participation
case: 5 burse
cloth: 8 corporal 9 corporale
consecrated food: 5 hagia
cup: ama 7 chalice
plate: 5 paten
table: 5 altar
vessel: pyx

communique: 6 report 7 message 12 announcement 13 communication

communism: 8 Leninism 10 Bolshevism

communist: Red 5 pinko 6 Soviet 7 comrade, Marxist

community: mir 4 body, burg, city 5 firca, state, thorp 6 cenoby, colony, hamlet, nation, polity, public 7 enclave, society, village 8 district, likeness, province, township 9 frequency 10 commonness 12 commonwealth, neighborhood
pert. to: 8 societal

commute: 5 alter 6 change, travel 7 convert 8 exchange 10 substitute 11 interchange

Comoros: *capital:* 6 Moroni
island: 6 Moheli 7 Anjouan, Mayotte 12 Grande Comoro

monetary unit: franc

comose: 5 hairy **6** tufted

compact: 4 bond, case, firm, hard, knit, pact, plot, snug, trim **5** brief, close, dense, gross, pithy, solid, terse, thick **6** vanity **7** bargain, concise, concord, serried **8** alliance, condense, contract, covenant, solidify, succinct **9** agreement, concordat **10** compaction, compressed, conspiracy, federation **11** compendious, concentrate, confederacy, consolidate, sententious **13** understanding

compadre: pal 5 buddy **6** friend **9** companion

companion: pal **4** chum, fere, mate, peer, twin, wife **5** buddy, bully, butty, crony, cully, matey **6** comate, escort, fellow, friend, spouse **7** compeer, comrade, consort, husband, partner **8** compadre, helpmate **9** associate, attendant **11** concomitant **12** acquaintance

constant: **6** shadow

equal: **4** peer **7** compeer

faithful: dog **7** Achates

companionable: 6 social **7** amiable, cordial **8** gracious, sociable **9** agreeable

company: mob, set **4** band, bevy, body, core, crew, fare, fere, firm, gang, gest, ging, host, rout, team **5** coven, covey, crowd, flock, geste, group, guest, horde, party, squad, troop **6** actors, circle, clique, cohort, covine, curney(Sc.), throng, troupe **7** battery, college, consort, society, visitor **8** assembly **9** camarilla, cavalcade, concourse, gathering **10** fellowship **11** association, partnership **13** companionship

comparable: 4 like **7** similar **8** parallel **9** analogous

comparative: 4 than **5** equal, rival **7** compeer **8** relative **11** approximate

compare: vie **4** even **5** apply, liken, match, scale **6** confer, relate **7** collate, examine, senible **8** contrast, estimate **10** assimilate

comparison: 6 simile **7** analogy, parable **8** likeness, likening, metaphor **9** collation **10** conference, similitude **11** examination

compartment: bay, bin **4** cell, part **5** abode, stall, **6** alcove, bunker, region **7** cellule, chamber, section **8** division **9** apartment **10** pigeonhole

granary: **8** grintern

compass: 4 area, gain, room, size **5** admit, field, gamut, range, reach, scope **6** arrive, attain, bounds, circle, degree, device, effect, extent, sphere **7** achieve, caliber, circuit, confine, divider, enclose, environ, go round, horizon, pelorus **8** boundary, cincture, circuity, surround **10** accomplish, comprehend

beam: **7** trammel

card: **4** rose

housing: **8** binnacle

ink leg: pen

kind of: sun **4** gyro **5** solar

part: pen **4** airt, vane **5** rhumb **6** gimbal, needle **7** gimbals, trammel **8** trammels

pocket: **6** diacle

point: E.N.E., E.S.E., N.N.E., N.N.W., S.S.E., S.S.W., W.N.W., W.S.W. **4** airt **5** airth, rhumb **7** azimuth

sight: **4** vane

suspender: **6** gimbal

compassion: rue **4** pity, ruth **5** heart, grace, mercy, sorry **6** lenity **7** remorse **8** clemency, humanity, sympathy **10** condolence **12** misericordia **13** commiseration

compatible: 8 suitable **9** accordant, agreeable, congenial, congruous, consonant **10** consistent, harmonious **16** noncontradictory.

compatriot: 9 associate, colleague **10** countryman

compeer: 4 mate, peer, rank **5** equal, match **7** comrade **9** colleague, companion **11** comparative

compel: gar(Sc.) **4** make, move, urge **5** cause, drive, exact, force, impel, press **6** coerce, enjoin, extort, incite, oblige **7** actuate, command, dragoon, enforce, require **9** constrain, influence, instigate, overpower **11** necessitate, subjudicate

compelled: has **4** must **5** bound

compelling: 6 cogent **7** telling **8** forceful **9** demanding **10** conclusive, convincing, persuasive

compendious: 5 brief, short **6** direct **7** compact, concise **8** succinct **9** condensed **11** expeditious **13** comprehensive, short and sweet

compendium: 4 list **5** brief **6** apercu, digest, precis, sketch **7** catalog, compend, epitome, medulla, outline, summary **8** abstract, breviary, syllabus, synopsis **10** abridgment **11** compilation, composition, contraction **12** abbreviation

compensate: pay **4** jibe **5** agree, atone, repay, tally **6** recoup, reward, square **7** correct, redress, requite, restore, satisfy **9** idemnify **10** recompense, remunerate **11** contervail **12** counterpoise **14** counterbalance

compensation: fee, pay, utu **4** hire **5** bonus, wages **6** amends, angild, gersum, offset, reward, salary **7** damages, payment, redress, stipened **8** pittance, requital **9** emolument, indemnity **10** recompense **11** restitution **12** counterpoise, remuneration, satisfaction **15** indemnification

compete: pit, vie **4** cope, tend **5** match,

rival **6** strive **7** contend, contest, emulate

competent: apt, can, fit **4** able, good, meet, sane **5** adept, capax, smart **6** worthy **7** capable, endowed, skilled **8** adequate, suitable **9** effective, efficient, qualified **10** proficient, sufficient

competition: 4 game, heat **5** match, trial **7** contest, rivalry **8** conflict, tug-of-war **9** emulation **10** contention, free-for-all, opposition

competitor: foe **5** enemy, rival **6** player **7** entrant **8** opponent **9** adversary, candidate, combatant **10** antagonist, contestant

Compiegne's river: 4 Oise **5** Aisne

compilation: ana **4** book, code **5** cento **6** digest **9** accretion **10** collection, compendium, confection

compile: add **4** edit **5** amass **6** gather, select **7** arrange, collect, compose, prepare **8** assemble **11** anthologize

compiler: 6 author, editor

complacent: 4 calm, smug **7** fatuous **9** satisfied **11** comfortable **13** self-satisfied

complain: ail, yip **4** beef, carp, fret, fuss, kick, moan, rule, wail, yelp, yirn **5** brawl, croak, croon, gripe, whine **6** bewail, charge, cotter, grieve, grizze, grouse, murmur, repine, yammer **7** deplore, grumble, protest **9** bellyache **11** expostulate

complainant: 5 asker **7** accuser, querent, relator **9** plaintiff

complaining: 9 plaintive, querulous

complaint: ill **6** lament, malady, plaint **7** ailment, disease, illness, protest **8** disorder, gravamen, jeremiad **9** exception, grievance **10** accusation **11** lamentation

complaisant: 4 able, easy, kind **5** buxom, civil, suave **6** polite, smooth, urbane **7** affable, amiable, lenient **8** gracious, obliging, pleasing **9** compliant, courteous, favorable **10** favourable **12** ingratiating

complement: 4 crew, gang **5** force **6** amount **7** adjunct, obverse **10** completion, supplement **11** counterpart **13** accompaniment

complete: all, end **4** dead, deep, fill, full **5** close, every, plumb, quite, ripen, total, utter, whole **6** effect, entire, finish, intact, mature **7** achieve, execute, fullfill, germane, perfect, plenary, realize **8** absolute, blinking, circular, conclude, implicit, thorough **9** implement, surfeited, terminate **10** accomplish, consummate, effectuate **11** unqualified **12** wholehearted

completely: all **5** quite

completeness: 5 depth **9** entelechy

completion: end **6** finish **9** plenitude

complex: 4 hard, mazy **5** mixed **6** knotty **7** network, tangled, twisted **8** involved, manifold, syndrome **9** composite, difficult, entangled, intricate, perplexed **10** interlaced **11** complicated **12** labyrinthine **13** heterogeneous, sophisticated

complexion: hue **4** blee, look, rudd, tint **5** color, humor, state, tenor, tinge **6** aspect, temper **10** appearance

compliance: 7 harmony **8** civility **9** obedience **10** concession, submission **11** application **12** acquiescence, complaisance, tractability

compliant: 4 easy, oily **6** pliant, supple **7** ductile, dutiful, willing **9** indulgent **10** applicable, manageable, obsequious, sequacious **11** complaisant

complicate: 5 mix up **6** intort, puzzle, tangle **7** involve, perplex **8** bewilder

complicated: 4 hard **6** knotty, prolix **7** complex, gordian, snarled, tangled **8** involved **9** difficult, elaborate, embroiled, intricate, plexiform **10** disordered

complication: 4 node, plot **5** nodus, snarl **9** complexus, confusion, intricacy **10** difficulty, perplexity

compliment: 4 gift, laud **5** extol **6** boquet, eulogy, praise **7** adulate, applaud, bouquet, commend, flatter, tribute **8** encomium, flummery, gratuity **9** adulation, panegyric **12** blandishment, commendation, congratulate

comply: 4 cede, mind, obey **5** abide, adapt, agree, apply, yield **6** accede, accord, assent, enfold, submit **7** conform, embrace, observe **9** acquiesce **11** accommodate

component: 4 item, part, unit **6** factor, member **7** element **8** integral **10** compounder, ingredient **11** constituent

comport: act **4** bear, jibe, suit **5** agree, brook, carry, tally **6** accord, acquit, behave, demean, endure, square **7** conduct **9** behaviour, harmonize **10** correspond, deportment **11** comportance

comportable: 8 suitable **9** endurable, tolerable **10** consistent

comportment: 4 mien **7** conduct, dealing **8** behavior, demeanor **9** behaviour, demeanour **10** deportment

compose: pen, set **4** calm, dite, form, lull, make **5** allay, brief, clerk, dight, order, write **6** accord, adjust, create, design, indite, settle, soothe **7** arrange, compone, concoct, conform, dispose, fashion, produce **8** compound, comprise, comprize, regulate **9** alleviate, construct, formulate **10** constitute **11** tranquilize

compose type: set

composed: 4 calm, cool 5 quiet, sober, wrote 6 demure, placid, sedate, serene 7 written 8 compound, decorous, tranquil 9 collected, composite, unruffled 11 unflappable 13 dispassionate, self-possessed

composer: 4 bard, poet 5 odist 6 author, writer 7 elegist 8 monodist, musician 10 compositor, typesetter

composition (see also **musical composition**): ana 4 mass, opus, work 5 cento, ditty, drama, essay, paper, piece, poesy, theme 6 accord, lesson, make-up, thesis 7 article, compost, mixture, picture, writing 8 acrostic, compound, fantasia 9 admixture, aggregate, composure, congruity, formation, invention, structure, synthesis 10 adjustment, compendium, composture, confection, manuscript 11 arrangement, combination, compositure, conjunction 12 constitution, construction

art of: 8 rhetoric

for two: 4 duet 6 duetto

literary: 4 book 5 cento, drama, essay, novel, theme 6 satire, thesis 7 tragedy 8 treatise

metrical: 4 poem, rime 5 poesy, rhyme

mournful: 5 dirge

compositor: 7 caseman, printer 10 type setter

compos mentis: 4 sane 5 lucid 6 normal

compost: 4 soil 6 mingle 7 compote, mixture 8 compound 10 fertilizer 11 composition

composure: 4 bond, mien 5 quiet, union 6 repose 7 balance, posture 8 calmness, serenity 9 sangfroid 10 composture, equanimity, sedateness 11 combination, composition, tranquility

compote, compot: 4 bowl 5 fruit 7 dessert

compound: 4 fill, join 5 alloy, blend, ester, unite 6 adjust, jumble, medley, settle 7 amalgam, combine, complex, compone, compose, compost 8 ceromide 9 admixture, aggregate, composite, enclosure 10 amalgamate, commixture, compromise, concoction, confection, constitute, hodge-podge, settlement

alkaline: 4 soda

amorphous: 7 phenose

chemical: 4 amid, amin, azin, imid, imin 5 amide, amine, azine, azola, borid, ceria, ester, imide, imine, osone 6 borids 7 inosite, metamer, leucine 8 chloride

containing double bonds: 5 diene 6 triene

containing two hydroxyl groups: 4 diol

crystalline: 5 aloin, oscin 6 amarin, anisil, phenol 7 tropine

hypnotic: 7 trional

organic: 4 amin 5 amine, ester, ketol 6 ketole, ketone

compound interest: 9 anatocism

comprehend: get, see 4 know 5 grasp, imply, savvy, seize, sense 6 attain, digest, embody, fathom, follow, take in, uptake 7 contain, discern, embrace, enclose, imagine, include, involve, realize 8 comprise, comprize, conceive, conclude, perceive 9 apprehend 10 appreciate, understand

comprehensible: 8 exoteric, included 9 comprised, scrutable 11 conceivable 12 intelligible

comprehension: 4 hold 5 grasp 6 noesis 7 epitome, knowing, summary 9 inclusion, intension 10 conception 11 connotation

comprehensive: big 4 full, wide 5 broad, grand, large 7 concise, generic 8 encyclic, spacious 9 all-around, expansive, extensive, panoramic 11 compendious 12 encyclopedic

compress: nip, tie 4 bale, bind, firm, wrap 5 cling, cramp, crowd, crush, press 6 gather, shrink 7 abridge, bolster, compact, curtail, embrace, deflate, flatten, repress, squeeze 8 astringe, condense, contract, restrain 9 condense, constrain, epitomize 11 consolidate

medical: 5 stupe 7 bandage, pledget

compressor: 4 pump 6 device 7 machine 9 condenser

comprise, comprize: 4 hold 5 cover, imply, seize 6 attach, confer, embody 7 compose, contain, embrace, enclose, include, involve 8 conceive, perceive 10 comprehend, constitute

comprised: 4 rapt 8 included 9 engrossed 14 comprehensible

compromise: 8 compound, endanger 9 surrender 10 concession 12 middle ground

opposition to: 13 intransigence

comptroller: 7 auditor, officer 10 controller

compulsion: 4 need, urge 5 force 6 duress, stress 7 impulse 8 coaction, coercion 9 necessity 10 constraint

compulsory: 8 coercive, forcible 10 imperative, obligatory

compulsory service: 6 angary 7 angaria, slavery

compunction: 5 qualm 6 regret, sorrow 7 remorse, scruple 9 misgiving 10 conscience, contrition, repentance

compute: add, sum 4 cast, rate 5 count, tally 6 assess, figure, number, reckon 7 account 8 estimate 9 calculate, enumerate

computer: 5 brain 6 abacus, univac 7 machine 10 calculator 13 adding machine

algebraic language: **5** algol
bank: **6** memory
correct: **5** debug
data: **7** readout **8** software
information: **4** data **5** input **6** output
inventor: **7** Babbage
lag in getting information: **10** access time
plan for action: **7** program
program symbol: **5** block
symbol system: **4** code
type: **6** analog **7** digital
worker: **9** programer **10** programmer
comrade: pal **4** ally, chum, mate, peer **5** billy, buddy, crony **6** copain(F.), digger, fellow, frater, friend, hearty **7** brother **8** copemate **9** associate, companion
comte: 5 count
comtesse: 8 countess
con: rap **4** anti, know, lead, look, pore, read, scan **5** cheat, guide, knock, learn, steer, study **6** direct, peruse, regard, versus **7** against, deceive, examine, inspect, opposed, swindle **10** understand
conation: 4 will **8** tendency, volition **11** inclination
concatenate: 4 join, link **5** chain, unite **7** connect
concave: 4 void **6** arched, dished, hollow **7** bowlike, vaulted **8** incurved **9** depressed
concavity: dip, pit **4** bowl, dent, hole **6** crater, hollow **10** depression
conceal: 4 bury, hide, mask, sile, veil **5** cache, cloak, couch, cover, feign **6** closet, emboss, pocket, screen, shroud **7** secrete **8** bescreen, disguise, ensconce, withhold **9** dissemble **10** camouflage
goods: **5** cache, eloin **6** eloign
concealed: 4 dern(Sc.) **5** blind **6** buried, covert, hidden, latent, occult, perdue, secret, veiled **7** covered, larvate **8** abstruse **9** blindfold, disguised, insidious, recondite, withdrawn **11** clandestine
concealing: 9 designing **10** obvelation
concede: own **4** cede **5** admit, agree, allow, grant, own up, waive, yield **6** accord, assent **7** confess **9** surrender, vouchsafe **10** condescend **11** acknowledge
conceit: ego **4** idea **5** fancy, pride **6** notion, vagary, vanity **7** caprice, egotism, tympany **9** arrogance, conundrum **10** conception, self-esteem **11** swelled head
conceited: bug **4** fess, vain **5** chuff, cocky, flory, huggy, proud **6** clever **8** arrogant, dogmatic, priggish, snobbish **9** pragmatic, whimsical **11** coxcombical, egotistical, opinionated **12** narcissistic
conceive: 4 form, make, plan, ween **5** begin, brain, dream, fancy, frame, think **6** devise, ideate, ponder **7** imagine, realize, suppose, suspect **8** comprise, com-

prize, contrive **9** apprehend, formulate **10** comprehend, understand
concent: 9 agreement, harmonize **10** accordance **11** consistency
concentrate: aim, fix **4** mass, pile **5** coact, exalt, focus, unify **6** arrest, attend, center, gather **7** compact, essence, thicken **8** approach, assemble, condense, contract **9** intensify **10** centralize **11** consolidate **12** conglomerate
concentration: 7 extract **8** fixation **10** absorption **11** application
concentration camp: 6 prison, stalag
concept: 4 idea **5** fancy, image **7** opinion, thought **11** disposition
conception: ens **4** idea **5** fancy, fetus, image, start **6** belief, design, embryo **7** conceit, purpose **8** notation **9** beginning **10** cogitation, impression **12** apprehension **13** comprehension
conceptual: 5 ideal **8** abstract
concern: 4 bear, care, firm, reck, sake **5** apply, cause, event, grief, touch, worry **6** affair, affect, behold, charge, employ, matter, regard **7** anxiety, article, company, disturb, involve, pertain, respect, trouble **8** business, interest **9** implicate, rickmatic **10** solicitude **11** corporation, distinguish **12** apprehension **13** consideration, establishment
concerned: 6 intent **7** anxious, worried **8** affected, bothered, involved
concerning: for **4** in-re **5** about, anent, as for **9** regarding
concert: 4 plan, tune **5** unite **6** accord, chorus, concur, devise **7** arrange, benefit, concent, concord, consort, consult, harmony, recital **9** agreement **11** performance **13** entertainment
concert hall: 5 odeon, odeum **10** auditorium
concertina: 9 bandonion
concession: 4 boon **5** favor, grant, lease **6** assent, favour, gambit **7** cession **9** admission, allowance, privilege **10** compliance, compromise **12** acquiescence **13** condescension **15** acknowledgment
conch: 5 shell **6** cockle, mussel **7** mollusk
concierge: 6 porter, warden **7** doorman, janitor **9** attendant **10** doorkeeper
conciliate: get **4** calm, ease **5** atone **6** adjust, pacify, soothe **7** acquire, appease, concile, mollify, placate, satisfy **9** reconcile **10** propitiate **11** tranquilize
conciliatory: 4 mild, soft **6** gentle, giving, irenic **7** lenient, pacific, winning **8** irenical, lenitive **9** forgiving **10** mollifying **12** propitiating
concilium: 7 council
concise: 4 curt, neat **5** brief, crisp, pithy, short, terse **7** compact, laconic, pointed, precise, serried **8** mutilate, pregnant,

succinct **9** condensed **10** compedious, contracted **11** sententious **12** epigrammatic **13** comprehensive, short and sweet

concision: 6 schism **7** faction **8** division **10** cutting off, mutilation

conclave: 6 closet **7** chamber, meeting **8** assembly **13** secret meeting

conclude: bar, end **4** rest **5** close, estop, infer, judge, limit **6** clinch, deduce, figure, finish, gather, reason, settle, wrap up **7** achieve, arrange, confine, embrace, enclose, resolve, suppose **8** complete, dispatch, graduate, restrain **9** determine, speculate, terminate **10** comprehend

conclusion: end **4** amen, coda, last **5** finis **6** finale, finish, period, result, upshot **7** finding, outcome **8** epilogue, judgment **9** diagnosis, inference **10** conjecture, settlement **11** probability, termination

conclusive: 4 last **5** final, valid **6** cogent **7** certain, extreme, telling **8** decisive, definite, ultimate **10** convincing, peremptory **11** irrefutable **12** unanswerable **13** determinative

concoct: mix **4** brew, cook, plan, plot, vamp **5** fame, hatch **6** decoct, devise, digest, invent, refine, scheme **7** compose, dream up, perfect, prepare **8** compound, intrigue **9** fabricate, originate **10** assimilate

concomitant: 4 mate **6** fellow **7** consort **9** accessory, associate, attendant, attending, companion, conjoined, cooperant **10** coincident, concurrent **11** synchronous **12** accompanying **13** accompaniment, supplementary

concord: 4 pact **5** agree, amity, peace, union, unity **6** treaty, unison **7** compact, concert, consent, harmony, oneness **8** covenant **9** agreement, communion, congruity **10** accordance, consonance

concordant: 8 unisonal **9** agreeable, congruous, consonant **10** harmonious **13** correspondent

concourse: 5 crowd, place, point **6** throng **7** company **8** assembly **9** affluence, frequency, gathering **10** assemblage, confluence **11** coincidence, concurrence, conjunction, cooperation

concrete: 4 clot, firm, hard, knot, mess, real **5** beton, solid, unite **6** actual **7** combine, congeal, special **8** coalesce, compound, solidify, tangible **9** concresce **10** particular

component: **4** sand **5** water **6** gravel

construction: **6** tremie **7** caisson

concretion: 4 clot, mess **5** pearl **6** nodule **8** calculus

concubine: 5 woman **7** adalisk **8** mistress **9** odalisque

concur: 4 jibe, join **5** agree, chime, unite **6** accede, accord, assent **7** approve, combine, consent, go along **8** coincide, converge **9** acquiesce, cooperate **10** correspond

concurrence: 5 union **6** assent, bestow **7** consent, consort, meeting **8** adhesion **9** adherence, agreement, concourse **10** conspiracy **11** coincidence, conjunction

concurrent: 6 coeval, united **7** meeting **10** associated, coincident **11** concomitant, synchronous **12** accompanying, simultaneous

concuss: jar **4** jolt **5** clash, force, shake, shock **6** coerce **7** agitate

condalia: 9 chaparral

condemn: ban **4** damn, doom, file, fine **5** blame, decry, judge **6** amerce, attain, awreak, banish, detest **7** adjudge, censure, convict **8** denounce, reproach, sentence **10** confiscate, disapprove

condemnation: 4 doom **5** blame **7** censure, decrial **11** reprobation **13** animadversion **4** disapprobation

condense: cut **5** brief, unite **6** decoct, digest, harden, lessen, narrow, reduce, shrink **7** abridge, combine, compact, deflate, distill, shorten, thicken **8** compress, diminish, solidify **9** constrict, epitomize, evaporate, intensify **11** concentrate, consolidate

condensed: 4 curt **5** brief **7** compact, concise **8** absorbed **11** compendious

condenser: 4 cric **6** aludel

condescend: 5 deign, favor, grant, stoop **6** assent, oblige, submit, unbend **7** concede, descend **9** patronize, vouchsafe

condescension: 7 disdain **8** courtesy **10** affability, concession **12** complaisance

condiment: rea, soy **4** herb, kari, mace, sage, salt **5** caper, curry, sauce, spice, thyme **6** catsup, cloves, pepper, relish **7** chutney, cuminos, ketchup, mustard, paprika, vinegar **8** allspice, turmeric **9** appetizer, seasoning **10** mayonnaise

container: **5** cruet

stand: **6** caster

condisciple: 7 student **12** schoolfellow

condition: 4 case, mode, rank, rote, term **5** angle, birth, cause, class, estre, facet, place, stage, state **6** estate, fettle, gentry, morale, plight, status **7** article, calling, premise, proviso, station **8** covenant, occasion, position **9** agreement, exception, provision, requisite, situation **10** limitation, sine qua non **11** predicament, stipulation **13** circumstances

critical: **9** emergency

favorable: **4** odds

conditional: 4 iffy **9** qualified, tentative **10** accidental conditioned: 6 finite 7 limited

condolence: 4 pity, ruth 7 empathy 8 sympathy 10 compassion 13 commiseration

condone: 5 blink, remit 6 acquit, excuse, forget, ignore, pardon 7 absolve, forgive 8 overlook

condor: 4 coin 6 tiffin 7 vulture 8 gymnogyp

conduce: aid 4 help, hire, lead, tend 5 bring, guide 6 confer, effect, engage 7 advance, conduct, further, redound 10 contribute

conduct: act, run 4 bear, deed, gest, lead, mien, rule, wage 5 carry, geste, guard, guide, usher 6 action, attend, behave, convey, convoy, demean, deport, direct, escort, govern, manage, squire 7 bearing, channel, comport, conduce, conduit, control, execute, officer, operate 8 behavior, carriage, chaplain, demeanor, guidance, regulate, transact 9 accompany, behaviour, demeanour, supervise 10 administer, deportment, governance, government, proceeding 11 comportment, countenance, superintend

scandalous: 9 esclandre(F.)

conductor: cad 4 gude 5 guard 6 convoy, copper, escort, leader 7 cathode, maestro 8 aqueduct, cicerone, conveyor, director, employee 10 bandleader, impresario, propagator

stick: 5 baton

conduit: 4 duct, main, pipe, tube, wire 5 cable, canal, sewer 6 trough 7 channel, conduct, culvert, passage 8 aqueduct, pipeline

cone: 4 chat 5 crack, solid, spire 6 bobbin, object 7 cluster, fissure, strobil 8 strobile 9 container

section: 8 parabola

cone-shaped: 5 conic 6 pineal 7 conical

conenose: 6 bedbug

coney: See cony

confab: 4 chat, talk 6 powwow 7 prattle 10 conference 11 confabulate 12 conversation

confect: mix 4 form, make 6 pickle 7 prepare 8 preserve 9 construct

confection: 5 candy, dulce, sweet 6 bonbon, comfit, cimbal, dainty, nougat 7 caramel, confect, fondant, mixture, praline, sherbet, succade 8 compound, delicacy, marzipan, preserve, sherbert 9 confiture, marmalade, sweetmeat 10 concoction 11 bittersweet, compilation, composition, preparation

Confederacy: *banknote:* 8 blueback

capital: 8 Richmond

general: Lee 4 Hill, Hood 5 Bragg, Price 6 Morgan 7 Jackson, Pickett 10 Beauregard, Longstreet

guerrilla: 11 bushwhacker

president: 5 Davis

soldier: reb

vice-president: 8 Stephens

victory: 7 Bull Run 11 Chickamauga 16 Chancellorsville

confederate: aid, pal, reb 4 ally 5 rebel, stall, unite 6 league 7 abetter, abettor, conjure, fedarie, federal, partner 8 conspire, federate 9 accessory, assistant, associate, auxiliary 10 accomplice 12 collaborator

confederation: 4 band, body 5 union 6 league 7 compact, society 8 alliance, covenant 9 coalition 10 conspiracy, federation 11 association

confer: dub 4 give, meet, talk 5 award, endow, grant, treat 6 advise, bestow, donate, impart, invest, parley, powwow 7 commune, compare, conduce, consult, counsel, discuss, instate, present 8 comprise, converge 10 contribute, deliberate

conference: rap 4 talk 5 synod, trust 6 confab, huddle, parley, pow-wow 7 council, meeting, palaver 8 colloque, colloquy, congress 9 collation, comparing, discourse, interview 10 comparison, discussion 11 association 12 consultation, conversation

technique: 13 brainstorming

confess: own 4 avow, sing 5 admit, grant 6 attest, avouch, beknow, recant, reveal, shrive 7 concede, divulge 8 disclose, discover, manifest 11 acknowledge

confession: 5 credo, creed 6 avowal, shrift, shrive 9 admission, communion, statement 10 profession

confetti: 4 tape 5 candy 7 bonbons 9 sweetmeat 10 confection

container: 8 cascaron

confidant: 6 friend 8 intimate

confide: 4 rely, tell 5 trust 6 commit, depend 7 believe, consign, entrust, intrust 8 turn over

confidence: 4 hope 5 bield, faith, trust 6 aplomb, belief, credit, mettle, morale, secret, spirit 7 courage 8 affiance, boldness, credence, reliance, sureness 9 assurance, certitude, hardihood, hardiness 10 effrontery 11 presumption 12 impertinence

game: 4 scam 5 bunco, bunko 6 sting 7 swindle

lack: 10 diffidence

confident: 4 bold, smug, sure 5 hardy, siker 6 crouse, secure, sicker 7 assured, certain, hopeful, reliant 8 constant, fearless, impudent, sanguine, trustful 9 dependent, undaunted 10 dogmatical 11 trustworthy 12 presumptuous 13 self-possessed

confidential: 5 bosom, privy 6 covert, secret 7 private, subrosa 8 esoteric, intimate 9 auricular 11 trustworthy
law: 9 fiduciary
configuration: 4 cast, form 5 shape 6 figure 7 contour, outline 10 topography
confine: bar, box, dam, hem, new, pen, pin, sty, tie 4 bind, cage, coop, hasp, jail, keep, lock, seal 5 bound, cramp, delay, impen, limit, pinch, stint 6 border, compas, corral, fetter, forbar, hamper, hurdle, immure, impale, intern, pinion, pocket, tether 7 astrict, impound 8 boundary, conclude, imprison, restrain, straiten 9 carcerate, constrain, restraint 11 incarcerate 12 circumscribe
confined: ill 4 pent 5 bound, caged 6 sealed 7 cramped, cribbed, limited 8 impended, interned 9 impounded 10 cloistered 13 incommunicado
to select group: 8 estoeric
confinement: mew 7 lying-in 8 clausure, firmance 9 captivity, restraint 10 childbirth, constraint, internment 11 contraction 12 accouchement, imprisonment
place of: mew, pen 4 brig, cage, coop, goal, jail, stir 5 limbo 6 asylum, corral, prison 7 dungeon 9 calaboose 12 penitentiary
confirm: fix, set 4 firm, seal 5 prove 6 affirm, assent, assure, attest, avouch, clinch, ratify, settle, verify 7 approve, comfort, endorse, fortify, sustain 8 accredit, convince, sanction, validate 9 approbate, establish 10 comprobate, strengthen 11 corroborate, countersign 12 adminiculate, authenticate, substantiate
confirmed: set 5 fixed 6 arrant, stable 7 chronic 8 habitual, ratified 9 fortified, initiated 10 encouraged, inveterate 11 established
confiscate: 4 grab 5 seize, usurp 7 condemn, preempt 8 arrogate 9 sequester 11 appropriate
conflagration: 4 fire 5 blaze, fever 7 burning, inferno 9 holocaust 10 combustion 12 inflammation
conflict: war 4 bout, duel, fray, rift 5 broil, brush, clash, fight, grips, mix-up 6 action, battle, combat, mutiny, oppose, strife 7 contend, contest, discord, warfare 8 disagree, militate, struggle, tug-of-war 9 collision, encounter, rebellion 10 contentin 11 competition, controversy
final: 10 Armageddon
conflicting: 7 adverse, warring 8 clashing 10 contending 12 incompatible, inharmonious
confluence: 5 crowd 7 conflux, meeting 8

junction 9 concourse 12 assimilation
conform: fit 4 lean, obey, suit 5 adapt, agree, apply, yield 6 accede, adjust, assent, comply, settle, submit 7 compose 9 acquiesce, harmonize, reconcile 10 correspond 11 accommodate
conformist: 6 pedant 7 babbitt 9 precisian 10 philistine 11 reactionary
conformity: 7 decorum, harmony 8 affinity, likeness, symmetry 9 agreement, congruity, obedience 10 accordance, compliance, similarity, submission 11 affirmative 12 acquiescence, complaisance
to law: 6 dharma 8 legality
confound: mix 4 blow, dash, maze, rout, stam, stun 5 abash, addle, amaze, spend, spoil, waste 6 baffle, dismay, muddle, rattle 7 astound, confuse, confute, corrupt, destroy, flummox, perplex, stupefy 8 astonish, bewilder, distract, surprise 9 discomfit, dumbfound, embarrass, frustrate, overthrow 10 disconcert 11 intermingle
confraternity: 4 body 5 union 7 society 11 brotherhood
confrere: 6 fellow 7 comrade 9 colleague
confront: 4 defy, face, meet 5 beard, brave 6 oppose, resist 7 affront, compare 8 envisage, face up to, threaten 9 challenge, encounter
confuse: mix 4 dash, daze, maze, muss, rout 5 abash, addle, amaze, befog, blend, cloud, snarl 6 baffle, bemuse, bother, burble, caddle, flurry, fuddle, jumble, muddle, puzzle, rattle 7 bedevil, blunder, derange, fluster, mystify, nonplus, perplex, stupefy 8 befuddle, bewilder, confound, distract 9 barbulyie, discomfit, dumbfound, obfuscate 10 demoralize, disarrange, discompose, disconcert
confused: 4 asea, lost 5 foggy, muddy, vague 6 doiled, doited 7 chaotic, mixed up, obscure 8 deranged 9 chagrined 10 bewildered, hurly-burly, topsy-turvy, tumultuous 13 helter-skelter
confusion: din 4 coil, dust, fuss, harl, mess, moil, riot 5 babel, chaos, chevy, chivy, deray, mix-up, snafu, snarl, strow 6 babble, bedlam, caddle, chivvy, habble, hubbub, huddle, jabble, jumble, muddle, pother, rabble, rumpus, tophet, tumult, uproar, welter 7 blunder, bluster, clutter, farrage, flutter, garboil, topheth, turmoil, widdrim 8 disarray, disorder 9 agitation, commotion 10 hullabaloo, hurly-burly 11 disturbance, trepidation 12 hugger-mugger, perturbation, razzle-dazzle 13 embarrassment
confute: 4 deny 5 rebut 6 expose, refute 7 silence 8 confound, convince, disprove,

infringe, overcome **9** overwhelm

conge: bow **5** adieu **6** curtsy **7** license, molding **8** farewell, passport **9** clearance, dismissal **10** permission **11** leavetaking

congeal: gel, ice, set **4** jell **5** candy **6** cotter, curdle, freeze, harden **7** stiffen, thicken **8** concrete, solidify **9** coagulate **10** gelalinize **11** crystallize

congealing agent: **6** pectin **8** gelatine

congee: **9** departure **11** leave-taking

congener: **4** kind, race **5** class, genus

congenial: **4** boon **5** natal **6** native **7** connate, kindred **10** compatible **11** sympathetic

conger: eel **4** pike

congeries: **4** mass, ruck **5** group **6** muster **8** assembly **9** gathering **10** collection

congestion: jam **4** heap **8** crowding, stoppage **9** gathering **12** accumulation

conglobation: **4** ball

conglomerate: **4** heap, mass, pile, rock **5** stack **6** cartel **7** combine **9** clustered **10** assemblage **11** agglomerate **12** concentrated

Congo (see also **Zaire**): *capital:* **11** Brazzaville
  tribe: **4** Susa **6** Wabuma **7** Bangala
  monetary unit: franc
  tributary: **4** Uele **6** Ubangi **7** Aruwima

congou: tea

congratulate: **4** laud **5** greet **6** salute **8** macarize **10** compliment, felicitate

congregate: **4** herd, mass, meet, teem **5** group, swarm, troop **6** gather, muster **7** collect, convene **8** assemble

congregation: **4** body, fold, host, mass **5** flock, swarm **6** church, parish **7** meeting, synaxes **8** assembly, brethren **9** gathering **10** collection **11** convocation

congress: **4** dail, diet **5** synod **7** council, meeting **8** assembly, conclave **10** conference, convention, parliament **11** convocation, legislature

Congress: *building:* **7** Capitol
  member: **7** senator **14** representative
  upper house: **6** Senate

congressman: **7** senator **8** delegate **10** legislator **14** representative

congruity: **6** accord **7** concord, fitness, harmony **8** symmetry **9** agreement, coherence **10** conformity, consonance **11** composition, consistency, correctness, suitability **13** compatibility **14** correspondence

conical: **8** tapering

conifer: fir, yew **4** pine, tree **5** cedar, larch **6** spruce **7** pinacle, pinales

conium: **7** hemlock

conjecture: aim **4** plot, shot, view **5** augur, ettle, fancy, guess, opine **6** belief, divine, theory **7** imagine, opinion,

presume, suppose, surmise, suspect **9** inference, speculate, suspicion **10** conclusion, estimation **11** contrivance, speculation, supposition

conjoined: wed **6** joined, linked, united **7** related **8** conjunct, touching **11** concomitant

conjoint: **6** mutual, shared **8** combined **9** conjoined **10** associated **11** correlative **12** simultaneous

conjugal: **6** wedded **7** marital, nuptial **9** connubial **11** matrimonial

conjugate: **5** yoked **6** joined, united **7** coupled

conjunction: and, but, nor, tie **4** than **5** joint, since, union **6** either, hookup **7** coition, consort **9** coalition, concourse **10** connection **11** association, combination, composition, concurrence

conjuration: art **4** rune **5** charm, magic, spell, trick **6** voodoo **10** necromancy **11** incantation, legerdemain

conjure: beg **4** pray **5** charm, crave, halse **6** adjure, invent, invoke **7** beseech, combine, entreat, imagine **8** conspire, contrive, exorcise, exorcize **9** importune **10** supplicate **11** confederate

conjuror: **4** mage, sear **6** pellar, shaman, wizard **7** juggler, warlock **8** magician, sorcerer **9** coswearer, enchanter **15** prestidigatator

conk: die, hit **4** fail, head, nose, swat **5** faint, knock, stall **7** decease **8** pass away

Conlaech: *father:* **10** Cuchulainn
  mother: **5** Aoife

connate: **4** akin, born **5** fused **6** allied, inborn, innate **7** cognate, kindred, related **9** congenial **10** congenital, deep-seated

connect: tie, wed **4** ally, bind, glue, join, knit, link **5** affix, chain, marry, unite **6** attach, bridge, cement, cohere, connex, couple, fasten, relate **7** combine **8** continue **9** affiliate, associate, correlate, interlock **11** communicate

Connecticut: *capital:* **8** Hartford
  city: **4** Avon **6** Bethel, Darien **7** Meriden **8** New Haven, Stamford **9** Greenwich, Waterbury **10** Bridgeport
  county: **7** Tolland **8** Hartford **9** Fairfield, Middlesex
  Indian: **6** Pequot **7** Mohegan, Niantic
  nickname: **6** Nutmeg
  river: **10** Housatonic
  seaport: **6** Mystic
  state bird: **5** robin
  state flower: **6** laurel
  state song: **12** Yankee Doodle
  state tree: oak

connection: tie **4** bond, link **5** nexus, union **6** family **7** contact, kinship **8** affinity, alliance, commerce, intimacy, junction, relative, syndetic **9** coherence, reference, relevance **10** catenation, continuity **11** affiliation, association, conjunction, intercourse **12** articulation, relationship **13** communication

connective: and, nor **6** either **7** neither **8** syndetic **11** conjunction

connective tissue: 6 fascia

conniption fit: 7 tantrum

connive: 4 abet, plot, wink **5** blink, cabal **6** assent, foment, incite, scheme **7** collude **8** intrigue, overlook **9** machinate

connoisseur: 5 judge **6** critic, expert **7** epicure, gourmet **8** gourmand **9** collector **11** cognoscente

connotation: 4 hint **6** intent **7** meaning **10** denotation **13** comprehension, signification

connote: 5 imply **7** add up to **8** indicate

connubial: 6 wedded **7** marital **8** conjugal, domestic **11** matrimonial

conquer: get, win **4** beat, best, down, gain, lick, rout, tame **5** crush, daunt **6** defeat, evince, humble, master, reduce, subdue, victor **7** acquire, prevail, subject, triumph **8** overcome, surmount, vanquish **9** checkmate, discomfit, overpower, overthrow, overwhelm, subjugate

conqueror: 4 hero **6** victor, winner **12** conquistador

conquest: 7 mastery, triumph, victory

conquistador: 6 Cortez **9** conqueror

consanguineous: 4 akin **6** carnal **7** kindred, related

consanguinity: 5 blood, nasab **7** kinship **8** affinity **12** relationship

conscience: 5 grace, heart, inwit, qualm, sense **6** erinys, psyche, virtue **7** monitor, probity, scruple, thought **9** casuistry, punctilio **11** compunction

conscienceless: 6 amoral, shifty, tricky, unfair **7** devious **12** unprincipled

conscientious: 4 fair, just **5** exact, rigid **6** honest, strict **7** dutiful, upright **8** faithful **9** honorable **10** scrupulous **11** punctilious

conscious: 4 keen **5** alive, awake, aware **7** feeling, knowing **8** rational, sensible, sentient **9** attentive, cognizant, concerned **10** perceptive **12** apprehensive

consciousness: 9 awareness

loss of: **4** coma **5** faint **8** apoplexy

consciousness-altering: 11 psychedelic

conscript: 5 draft, enrol **6** enlist, muster **7** recruit

consecrate: vow **4** fain, seal **5** bless, deify, devot **6** anoint, hallow, ordain **8** sanctify, dedicate **10** inaugurate **11** apotheosize

consecrated: 4 holy **5** blest **6** oblate, sacred, votive **8** hallowed

cloth: **11** antimension

oil: **6** chrism

thing: **6** sacrum

consent: let **5** agree, allow, grant, yield **6** accede, accord, assent, beteem, comply, permit **7** approve **9** recognize **10** permission **11** concurrence **12** acquiescence **13** authorization

consequence: end **4** bore **5** event, fruit, issue, worth **6** effect, import, moment, repute, result, sequel, weight **7** concern, outcome **8** aftering, interest, occasion **9** aftermath, emanation, inference **10** importance **11** aftereffect, consecution **13** consideration

consequently: 4 ergo, then, thus **5** hence, later **8** pursuant **9** therefore **11** accordingly **12** subsequently **13** consecutively

conservative: 4 safe, Tory **5** staid **6** stable **7** diehard **8** moderate, old-liner **9** bourgeois **11** reactionary, right-winger **12** preservative

conservatory: 6 school **7** academy **10** glasshouse, greenhouse

conserve: can, jam **4** save **5** guard, jelly **6** defend, keep up, secure, shield, uphold **7** husband, protect, sustain **8** maintain, preserve **9** confiture, sweetmeat

consider: see **4** deem, heed, mull, muse, rate **5** ettle, judge, study, think, weigh **6** behold, debate, expend, impute, ponder, reason, reckon, regard **7** account, believe, canvass, examine, inspect, reflect, suppose **8** cogitate, estimate, look upon, meditate, ruminate **9** calculate, entertain, speculate **10** adjudicate, deliberate, think about **11** contemplate

considerable: 5 geyan(Sc.), large, smart, **7** notable, several **9** capacious, important **10** cognizable, noteworthy, remarkable **11** perceptible, significant

considerate: 4 kind, mild **6** gentle **7** careful, heedful, prudent, serious **8** delicate **9** attentive, observant, regardful **10** deliberate, reflective, respectful, thoughtful **11** sympathetic, warm-hearted

consideration: 4 sake **5** price, topic **6** aspect, esteem, motive, notice, reason, regard **7** respect, thought **9** attention, deference, incentive, influence **10** importance, inducement, recompense, reputation **11** consequence

considering: for **5** since **6** seeing

consign: 4 doom, give, mail, send, ship **5** allot, award, dight, remit, shift, yield **6** assign, commit, devote, remand, resign **7** address, confide, deliver, deposit, entrust, intrust **8** delegate, relegate, transfer, turn over **9** recommend **10** commission

consignee: 5 agent **8** receiver

consist: lie **4** hold **5** exist, stand **6** inhere, reside **7** contain, embrace **8** comprise, dovetail 9 harmonize

consistency: 4 body 5 union 6 degree 7 concord, harmony 8 firmness, solidity, symmetry 9 adherence, coherence, congruity 10 consonance, uniformity 11 composition, persistency 14 correspondence, substantiality

consistent: 4 firm 7 durable, logical, uniform 8 coherent, enduring, suitable 9 accordant, congruous, consonant, unfailing, unvarying 10 changeless, compatible, persisting

consociate: 9 associate 11 confederate

consolation: sop 4 fine 6 relief, solace 7 comfort 10 booby prize

console: 4 calm 5 allay, ancon, cheer, organ, table 6 buck up, solace, soothe 7 bracket, cabinet, comfort, relieve, support, sustain 9 alleviate, encourage

consolidate: mix 4 fuse, knit, mass, pool, weld 5 blend, merge, unify, unite 6 harden, mingle 7 combine, compact 8 coalesce, compress, condense, organize, solidify 10 amalgamate, strengthen 11 concentrate

consomme: 4 soup

consonance: 6 accord 7 harmony 9 resonance

consonant: 6 dental, fortis, letter, sonant 7 palatal, phoneme, spirant, unified 8 harmonic, in accord, suitable 9 accordant, agreeable, congruous 10 coincident, compatible, concordant, consistent, harmonious

hard: 6 fortis

hissing: 8 sibilant

pert. *to:* 7 palatal 9 fricative

smooth: 4 lene 5 lenis

voiceless: 4 lene, surd 6 atonic 7 spirate

consort: cot 4 aide, ally, join, mate, wife 5 agree, group, tally, unite 6 accord, attend, escort, mingle, spouse 7 company, concert, husband, partner 8 accustom, assembly 9 accompany, associate, colleague, companion, forgather 10 foregather 11 association, combination, concurrence, conjunction

consortium: 5 group, guild, order, union 8 alliance, congress

conspectus: 4 list 5 brief 6 survey 7 outline 8 synopsis 11 abridgement

conspicuous: 5 clear, famed, plain 6 extant, famous, marked, patent, signal 7 eminent, glaring, notable, obvious, pointed, salient, visible 8 apparent, manifest, striking 9 egregious, prominent 10 celebrated, noticeable 11 discernible, distinctive, illustrious, outstanding, perspicuous 13 distinguished

conspiracy: 4 coup, plan, plot, ring 5 cabal, covin, junto 6 scheme 7 compace 8 intrigue 9 agreement, champerty 11

combination, concurrence, confederacy, machination

conspire: 4 abet, plot 5 unite 6 league, scheme 7 collude, complot, conjure 8 contrive 9 cooperate 11 confederate

constable: cop 4 bull 6 beadle, harman, keeper, warden 7 bailiff, officer 8 tipstaff 9 policeman

constancy: 4 zeal 5 ardor 6 fealty 7 loyalty 8 devotion, fidelity 9 adherence, diligence, eagerness, integrity, stability 10 allegiance, attachment 11 earnestness 12 perseverance

symbol of: 6 garnet

constant: set 4 even, fast, firm, leal, true 5 fixed, loyal, solid, still, tried 6 stable, steady 7 certain, chronic, durable, forever, lasting, regular, staunch, uniform 8 enduring, faithful, positive, resolute 9 confident, continual, immovable, incessant, permanent, perpetual, steadfast, unvarying 10 consistent, continuous, invariable, persistent, unwavering

Constantine: *birthplace:* 4 Nish

mother: 6 Helena

son: 7 Crispus

victim: 6 Fausta 7 Crispus

wife: 6 Fausta

Constantinople: See **Istanbul**

constantly: 4 ever 6 always 10 invariably 11 perpetually 12 continuously

constate: 6 assert 9 establish

constellation (see also **star**): 5 group 6 dipper 7 cluster, pattern 10 assemblage 13 configuration

altar: Ara

archer: 11 Sagittarius

Argo division: 4 Vela

arrow: 7 Sagitta

balance: 5 Libra

Big Dipper: 9 Ursa Major

bird of paradise: 5 Apus

bull: 6 Taurus

Champion: 7 Perseus

charioteer: 6 Auriga

Charles' Wain: 6 Dipper

clock: 10 Horologium

compass: 5 Pyxis 8 Circinus

crab: 6 Cancer

crane: 4 Grus

cross: 4 Cruz

crow: 6 Corvus

crown: 6 Corona

dog: 5 Canis

dolphin: 9 Delphinus

dove: 7 Columba

dragon: 5 Draco

eagle: 6 Aquila

fish: 6 Pisces

goat: 9 Capricorn

herdsman: 6 Bootes

hunter: 5 Orion

lady, chained: 9 Andromeda
lady in the chair: 10 Cassiopeia
lion: Leo
Little Dipper: 9 Ursa Minor
lyre: 4 Lyra
maiden: 5 Virgo
northern: Leo 4 Coma, Lynx, Lyra, Ursa 5 Aries, Canes, Draco 6 Aquila, Auriga, Bootes, Cancer, Cygnus, Gemini, Taurus 7 Cepheus, Lacerta, Pegasus, Sagitta 8 Hercules 9 Andromeda, Delphinus, Vulpecula 10 Cassiopeia
peacock: 4 Pavo
rabbit: 5 Lepus
ram: 5 Aries
sails: 4 Vela
southern: Ara 4 Apus, Argo, Crux, Grus, Pavo, Vela 5 Canis, Cetus, Hydra, Indus, Lepus, Libra, Mensa, Musca, Norma, Virgo 6 Antlia, Carina, Corvus, Crater, Dorado, Fornax, Pictor, Pisces, Puppis, Tucana, Volans 7 Columba, Phoenix, Sextans 8 Aquarius, Circinus, Sculptor, Scorpius 9 Centaurus, Chameleon, Monoceros, Reticulum 10 Horologium 11 Capricornus, Sagittarius, 12 Microscopium
stern: 6 Puppis
swan: 6 Cygnus
twins: 6 Gemini
water bearer: 8 Aquarius
whale: 5 Cetus
winged horse: 7 Pegasus
wolf: 5 Lupus
consternation: 4 fear 5 alarm, dread, panic 7 dismay, fright, horror, terror 9 amazement, confusion, trepidity 11 distraction, trepidation 12 befuddlement
constituent: 4 item, part 5 piece, voter 6 detail, factor, matter, member 7 elector, element 9 component 10 ingredient
constitute: fix, set 4 form, make 5 enact, forge, found, set up, shape 6 depute, graith, ordain 7 appoint, compose, station 8 compound, comprise 9 determine, establish 10 commission
constitution: law 4 code 5 being, canon, humor, state 6 custom, health, nature, temper 7 charter 8 physique 9 enactment, ordinance, structure 11 composition, disposition 12 organization 13 establishment
Constitution: 9 Ironsides
Constitution State: 11 Connecticut
constitutional: 4 walk 6 inborn, innate 8 exercise 9 essential, organical 10 congenital, deep-seated
constrain: 4 bend, bind, curb, fain, urge 5 chain, check, clasp, cramp, deter, drive, force, impel, limit, press 6 coerce, compel, hold in, oblige, ravish, secure 7 as-

trict, confine, enforce, oppress, repress, violate 8 compress, distress, hold down, restrain 9 constrict 10 constringe 11 necessitate
constraint: 4 bond 5 force 6 duress, stress 7 reserve 8 coercion, distress, pressure 9 captivity, restraint, stiffness 10 compulsion, obligation 11 compression, confinement
constrict: tie 4 bind, curb, grip 5 choke, cramp, limit 6 hamper, shrink, strait 7 astrict, deflate, squeeze, tighten 8 astringe, compress, condense, contract, restrict 9 constrain 10 constipate, constringe
breath: 8 strangle
constrictor: boa 5 snake 6 muscle, python 8 anaconda 9 sphincter, strangler
construct: 4 form, make, rear 5 build, dight, erect, frame, model, set up 6 devise 7 arrange, combine, compose, confect, fashion 8 construe, engineer 9 fabricate, originate 11 put together
construction: 6 design, makeup 7 synesis 8 building, erection
constructive: 7 helpful 8 creative, implicit, inferred
construe: 5 infer, parse 6 render 7 analyze, dissect, explain, expound, resolve 8 spell out 9 construct, interpret, translate
consuetude: use 4 wont 5 habit, usage 6 custom 8 practice
consul's recognition: 9 exequatur
consult: ask 5 cabal, refer 6 advise, confer, decree, devise 7 concert, counsel, discuss, meeting 8 consider, contrive, decision 9 agreement, determine 10 deliberate
consultant: 6 expert 7 adviser, counsel
consultation: 6 advice 7 council, counsel 9 collation, interview 10 conference, discussion 12 deliberation
consume: eat, use 4 burn, fret, rust, wear 5 drink, raven, spend, use up, waste 6 absorb, absume, bezzle, canker, devour, engage, expend, feed on, perish 7 corrode, destroy, dwindle, engross, exhaust, swallow 8 gobble up, squander 9 dissipate 10 incinerate, monopolize
consumer: 4 usee, user
consummate: end 4 fine, full, ripe 5 ideal, sheer, utter 6 arrant, effect, finish, wind up, wrap up 7 achieve, consume, crowned, perfect, perform 8 absolute, complete 9 culminate, exquisite, out-and-out 10 accomplish
consumption: use 5 decay, waste 7 expense 8 phthisis 11 destruction, expenditure, white plague 12 tuberculosis
contact: 4 abut, join, meet 5 touch, union 6 arrive, impact, syzygy 7 meeting, rap-

port, taction **8** junction, tangency, touching **10** connection, contiguity **11** contingency **13** juxtaposition

contagion: pox **5** taint, virus **6** miasma, poison **7** disease **9** infection **13** contamination

preventative: **4** shot **8** antidote **10** alexiteric **11** prophylaxis

contagious: **7** noxious **8** catching **9** pestilent, spreading **10** infectious **12** communicable

contain: **4** have, hold, keep **5** carry, check, cover, house **6** embody, retain, take in **7** embrace, enclose, include, subsume, sustain **8** comprise, restrain **10** comprehend, simmer down

container: bag, bin, box, can, cup, jug, keg, pan, pod, pot, tin, tub, urn, vat **4** cage, case, cask, crib, ewer, sack, silo, tank, vase **5** crate, cruet, gourd, pouch **6** barrel, basket, bottle, carboy, carton, hamper, hatbox, holder, shaker **7** bandbox, capsule, hanaper, inkwell **8** canister, decanter, demijohn, hogshead, puncheon **10** receptacle

containing: For all phrases beginning with this word, see under the main word or phrase. EXAMPLE: "containing air": see **air** *containing.*

contaminate: **4** foul, harm, slur, soil **5** stain, sully, taint **6** befoul, debase, defile, infect, injure, poison **7** corrupt, debauch, pollute, tarnish, vitiate **8** dishonor **9** desecrate **10** adulterate

conte: **4** tale **5** story **9** narrative, novelette

contemn: **4** hate **5** flout, scorn, spurn **6** reject, slight **7** despise, disdain **8** contempt, look down

contemplate: **4** muse, plan, scan, view **5** deign, study, think, weigh **6** look at, ponder, regard, survey **7** propose, reflect **8** consider, meditate **9** speculate, think over

contemplation: **5** study **6** musing, prayer, regard, theory **7** request **8** petition **9** intention **10** meditation **11** speculation **12** deliberation **13** consideration

contemporaneous: **6** coeval, living, modern **7** current **8** existing, up-to-date **10** coincident **12** contemporary, simultaneous

contemporary: **6** coeval **7** current

contempt: **5** scorn, shame, sneer **6** slight **7** contemn, disdain, mockery **8** derision, disgrace **9** contumacy, contumely **10** disrespect **11** indignation

exclamation of: bah, foh **4** pooh

contemptible: low **4** base, mean, vile **5** cheap, petty, sorry **6** abject, paltry, scurvy, shabby, sordid, yellow **7** pitiful, scorned **8** beggarly, infamous, inferior, sneaking, unworthy, wretched **9** grovel-

ing, worthless **10** despicable **11** ignominious **12** dishonorable **13** insignificant

contemptuous: **7** haughty **8** arrogant, flouting, insolent, scornful **9** hubristic, insulting **10** despicable, disdainful **12** contemptible, supercilious

contend: say vie, war **4** cope, race, wage **5** argue, bandy, brawl, claim, fight **6** assert, battle, bicker, buffet, bustle, combat, debate, oppose, reason, strive **7** bargain, compete, contest, dispute, quarrel **8** conflict, contrive, cope with, maintain, militate, squabble, struggle

contender: **7** entrant **10** contestant **11** protagonist

content: **4** calm, ease, gist, paid **5** happy **6** amount, at ease, please **7** appease, gratify, replete, satiate, satisfy, suffice, willing **8** capacity **9** satisfied **12** satisfaction

contented: **4** cozy **5** sated **8** cheerful **9** satisfied

contention: war **4** bait, bate, feud, riot, tiff **5** broil **6** combat, debate, strife **7** contest, discord, dispute, opinion, quarrel, rivalry, wrangle **8** argument, conflict, squabble, struggle, variance **9** rebellion **10** dissension, litigation **11** altercation, competition, controversy **12** disagreement

contentious: **7** carping, peevish **8** perverse **9** bellicose, litigious, wrangling **10** pugnacious **11** belligerent, quarrelsome **12** cantankerous, disputatious

contentment: **4** ease **5** bliss **8** pleasure **9** happiness **11** complacence **12** satisfaction **13** gratification

conterminous: **4** next **8** adjacent, proximal, touching **9** adjoining, bordering

contest: bee, sue, try, vie **4** agon, bout, cope, duel, feud, fray, game, pitt, race, spar, tiff, tilt **5** broil, clash, fight, set-to, trial **6** action, adjure, affray, battle, combat, debate, defend, oppose, resist, strife, strive **7** bargain, brabble, compete, contend, dispute, protest, tourney, warfare **8** argument, conflict, skirmish, struggle, tug-of-war **9** champerty, encounter **10** controvert, tournament **11** altercation

kind of: **6** tryout **7** lawsuit **10** litigation

narrowly won: **8** squeaker

contestant: **4** vier **5** rival **6** player **7** agonist, entrant **8** finalist, prospect **9** combatant, candidate, contender, defendant, plaintiff **10** competitor **12** participator

contiguous: **4** next, nigh **6** nearby **7** close by **8** abutting, adjacent, touching **9** adjoining, immediate, proximate **10** contacting, near-at-hand **11** neighboring

continence: 6 virtue 8 chastity, sobriety 10 abstinence, moderation, temperance 13 self-restraint

continent: 4 Asia, land, mass 5 sober 6 Africa, chaste, Europe 7 content 8 capacity, mainland, moderate 9 Australia, Greenland, temperate 10 Antarctica, New Zealand receptacle, restrained 12 North America, South America

hypothetical: 8 Cascadia

lost: 8 Atlantis

contingency: 4 case 5 event 6 chance 7 adjunct, contact 8 fortuity, incident, prospect 9 accessory, emergency 10 crossroads 11 possibility, uncertainty

contingent: 6 casual, chance 8 doubtful, touching 9 dependent 10 accidental, fortuitous 11 provisional

on discretion: 9 arbitrary

continual: 7 endless, lasting, regular, undying, uniform 8 constant, enduring, unbroken 9 ceaseless, connected, incessant, perennial, permanent, unceasing 10 continuous, invariable 11 everlasting, unremitting 12 imperishable 13 unintermitted, uninterrupted

continually: aye 4 ever 6 always, hourly, steady 7 endless, eternal, forever 9 perpetual 10 constantly 11 incessantly, unceasingly

continuance: 4 stay 5 delay 6 sequel 8 duration 9 endurance, procedure 10 continuity 11 adjournment 12 postponement, perseverance

continue: be 4 bide, dure, go on, last, live, stay 5 abide, carry, exist, unite 6 beleve, endure, extend, remain, resume, take up 7 beleave, carry on, connect, persist, proceed, prolong, sustain 8 protract 9 persevere

continued: 5 still 6 serial 7 chronic 8 constant 9 extending 10 protracted

continuity: 6 script 8 cohesion, scenario 9 coherence 10 connection

contort: wry 4 bend, coil, turn, warp 5 gnarl, screw, twist, wrest 6 deform, writhe 7 distort, pervert 8 obvolute 9 convolute

contortionist: 7 acrobat

contour: 4 form, line 5 curve, graph, shape 6 figure 7 outline, profile 9 lineament 10 appearance, silhouette 13 configuration

contra: 6 offset 7 against, counter, opposed 8 opposite 9 opposed to, vice versa 11 contrasting 12 contrariwise

contraband: 6 banned 7 illegal, illicit 8 hot goods, smuggled, unlawful

contract: get 4 bond, knit, pact 5 catch, cramp, incur, lease, limit 6 cartel, engage, lessen, narrow, pledge, pucker, reduce, shrink, treaty 7 abridge, bargain, compact, crumple, curtail, promise, shorten, shrivel, wrinkle 8 condense, covenant, restrict 9 agreement, betrothal, constrict, indenture 10 abbreviate, constringe, convention, obligation, sicken with 11 arrangement, concentrate, stipulation 12 come down with

addition to: 5 rider 7 codicil

furnishing slaves: 8 assiento

maritime: 8 bottomry

part: 6 clause 7 article, proviso

unlawful: 10 chevisance

contraction: tic 5 cramp, spasm 6 intake, twitch 7 elision, epitome 9 gathering, reduction, shrinkage, stricture 10 abridgment, compendium, limitation 11 conciseness, confinement 12 abbreviation

common: een, eer, oer, oft, tis 5 arent, shant

heart: 8 systolic

contractor: 7 builder, remover 8 supplier

contradict: 4 deny 5 belie, rebut 6 forbid, impugn, negate, oppose, recant, refute 7 counter, dispute, gainsay 8 disprove 9 disaffirm 10 contravene, controvert

contradiction: 6 denial 7 paradox 8 antilogy, negation 10 gainsaying

contradictory: 6 oppose 8 antipode, contrary 9 dissonant 12 incompatible, inconsistent

contraption: rig 4 tool 6 device, gadget 7 machine 11 contrivance

contrary: 5 balky, polar, snivy 6 averse, contra, ornery, snivey 7 adverse, counter, hostile, opposed, reverse, wayward 8 captious, contrair, inimical, opposite, perverse, petulant 9 refactory, repugnant, unpopular, vexatious 10 discordant, discrepant 11 prejudicial, unfavorable 12 antagonistic, cantankerous, cross-grained 13 insubordinate

to fact: 5 false

to law: 7 illegal 16 unconstitutional

to reason: 6 absurd

contrast: 6 strife 7 compare, contend 8 opposite 9 diversity 10 difference, divergence

contravene: 4 defy, deny 6 hinder, oppose, thwart 7 dispute, violate 8 infringe, obstruct 9 disregard, repudiate 10 contradict, transgress

contravention: sin 4 vice 5 crime 6 breach 7 offense 9 violation 13 contradiction, transgression

contretemps: 4 slip 5 boner, hitch 6 mishap, scrape 8 accident 9 mischance 10 occurrence

music: 11 syncopation

contribute: aid 4 ante, give, help, tend 5

cause, grout **6** assist, bestow, chip in, concur, confer, donate, supply, tender **7** conduce, further, pitch in **9** cooperate, subscribe

contribution: sum, tax **4** alms, boon, gift **5** essay, share **6** impost **7** article, largess, payment, present, renewal, writing **8** donation, offering **9** collation **10** imposition

contrite: 4 worn **5** sorry **6** humble, rueful **8** penitent **9** repentant, sorrowful **10** apologetic, remorseful

contrition: 7 penance, remorse

contrivance: art, gin **4** gear, plan, tool **5** shift **6** deceit, design, device, gadget, scheme **7** fiction, machine, project **8** adaption, artifice, resource **9** apparatus, appliance, doohickey, invention **10** conjecture, instrument **11** contraption

contrive: 4 brew, make, plan, plot **5** frame, fudge, hatch, weave **6** afford, design, devise, divine, invent, make up, manage, scheme, wangle **7** achieve, agitate, concoct, consult, contend, dream up, fashion, procure, project, work out **8** conspire, engineer, intrigue **9** fabricate, machinate **10** accomplish

contrived: pat **5** hokey **10** artificial

contriver: 8 Daedalus **9** architect **10** originator

control: law, run **4** curb, hold, rein, rule, sway **5** charm, check, grasp, gripe, guide, power, skill, steer **6** bridle, direct, empire, govern, handle, manage, regime, subdue **7** command, conduct, mastery, preside **8** attemper, dominate, dominion, hegemony, regulate, restrain **9** influence, ordinance, prescribe **10** ascendancy, discipline, domination, manipulate, moderation, possession, regulation **11** predominate, superintend **12** jurisdiction

controversial: 7 eristic **9** debatable, polemical **12** disputatious **13** argumentative

controversy: row **4** spat, suit, tiff **5** chest **6** debate, strife **7** dispute, quarrel, wrangle **8** argument **10** contention, difference, difficulty, discussion, falling-out, litigation **11** altercation **12** disagreement

controvert: 4 deny, face, moot **5** argue **6** debate, oppose, oppugn, refute **7** contest, dispute, gainsay **9** challenge **10** contradict

contumacious: 6 unruly **7** riotous **8** insolent, mutinous, perverse, stubborn **9** obstinate, seditious **10** disdainful, headstrong, rebellious, refractory, unyielding **11** disobedient, intractable **13** insubordinate

contumely: 5 abuse, scorn **6** contek, insult **7** conteck, disdain **8** contempt, rudeness **9** arrogance **10** opprobrium **11** humiliation

contuse: 4 beat **5** pound **6** bruise, injure **7** squeeze

contusion: 4 blow, bump **6** bruise

conundrum: pun **4** whim **6** enigma, puzzle, riddle **7** conceit **8** crotchet

convalesce: 4 mend **7** improve, recover **10** recuperate

convene: sit **4** call, meet, open **5** unite **6** gather, muster, summon **7** convoke **8** assemble, converge **10** congregate, foregather

convenience: 4 ease **6** toilet **7** benefit, comfort **8** plumbing **9** appliance

convenient: fit **5** handy, ready **6** proper, useful **7** adapted, close-by, helpful **8** becoming, suitable **9** agreeable, available, congruous, favorable, opportune **10** accessible, commodious, near-at-hand **11** appropriate **12** commensurate

convent: 5 abbey **6** priory **7** meeting **8** cloister **9** community, monastery, sanctuary

head: **5** abbot **6** abbess **8** hegumene **10** hegumeness

member: nun **4** monk **8** cenobite

pert. to: **6** friary

reception room: **8** arlatory

room: **9** parlatory

superior: see *head* above

convention: 4 diet, feis, mise, rule **5** synod, usage **6** cartel, caucus, custom, treaty **7** decorum, meeting **8** assembly, congress, contract, covenant, practice **9** agreement, gathering, tradition **10** conference **11** convocation

conventional: 4 more **5** nomic, right, trite, usual **6** decent, formal, modish, proper **7** correct, regular **8** academic, accepted **9** customary, hidebound **10** ceremonial, stipulated **11** contractual

conventionalize: 5 adapt **7** conform, stylize

converge: 4 join, meet **5** focus **6** concur **8** approach, focalize

conversant: 5 adept, awake, aware **6** busied, expert, versed **7** skilled **8** familiar, occupied, up-to-date **9** concerned, practiced **10** acquainted, proficient

conversation: 4 chat, talk **6** confab, parley **7** conduct, palaver **8** behavior, chitchat, colloquy, dialogue, parlance **9** discourse, tete-a-tete **10** conference **11** association, interchange, intercourse **13** communication, interlocution

of three: **7** trialog **9** trialogue

private: **7** celidh(Sc.) **8** collogue **9** tete-a-tete

converse: 4 chat, chin, live, move, talk 5 dwell, speak 6 confer, homily, parley 7 commune, obverse, reverse 8 colloque, exchange, opposite 9 discourse 11 association, confabulate

convert: 4 turn 5 alter, amend, apply, renew 6 change, decode, direct, novice 7 restore, reverse 8 converse, neophyte, persuade 9 acetalize, proselyte, transform, translate, transmute, transpose 10 regenerate 11 proselytize 12 metamorphose, transmogrify

convertible: 4 auto 7 soft-top 10 automobile, changeable, equivalent, reciprocal, synonymous 15 interchangeable

convex: 5 bowed 6 arched, camber, curved 7 bulging, gibbous, rounded 9 cymbiform 11 protuberant

molding: 5 ovolo, torus

convey: 4 bear, cart, cede, deed, lead, mean, pass, send, take, tote, will 5 bring, carry, ferry, grant, guide, hurry, steal 6 assign, convoy, delate, demise, devise, eloign, impart, import, pass on, remove 7 auction, conduct, deliver, dispone, dispose 8 alienate, bequeath, transfer, transmit 9 accompany, transport 11 communicate

conveyance: bus, car, sak 4 auto, cart, deed, sled, taxi, tram 5 grant, stage, theft, train, wagon 6 demise 7 charter, conduct, rattler, trailer, trolley, vecture, vehicle, waftage 8 carriage, carrying, stealing, transfer 9 transport 10 automobile 11 transmittal

public: bus, cab, car 4 taxi, tram 5 train 6 subway 7 omnibus, ricksha, steamer 8 airplane, elevated, railroad, rickshaw 10 jinricksha, jinrikisha

convict: 4 find 5 argue, felon, lifer, prove 6 attain, termer, trusty 7 attaint, captive, condemn, culprit 8 criminal, jailbird, prisoner, sentence 10 malefactor

conviction: 4 mind, view 5 creed, dogma, faith, tenet 6 belief, credit 7 opinion 8 sentence 9 assurance 10 confidence

convince: get 4 draw 5 assure, prompt 7 win over 8 talk into 9 prevail on 11 bring around

convinced: 4 sold, sure 6 assure, subdue 7 certain 8 absolute, positive 9 persuaded

convincing: 5 sound, valid 6 cogent, potent 7 telling 8 forcible 10 conclusive, persuasive

convivial: gay 4 boon 6 festal, genial, jovial, lively, social 7 festive, jocular 8 reveling 9 vivacious

convocation: 4 diet 5 synod 7 calling, council, meeting 8 assembly, congress 9 gathering 10 convention 12 congregation

convoke: bid, sit 4 call, cite, meet 6 gather, muster, summon 7 convene 8 assemble 10 congregate

convolute: 4 coil, roll, wind 5 twist 6 tangle, writhe 7 contort 8 obvolute

convolution: 4 coil, curl, fold 5 gyrus, whorl 9 sinuosity

of brain: 5 gyrus

convolve: 5 twist 6 enwrap, enfold, infold, writhe

convolvulus: 4 vine 12 morning glory

convoy: 4 lead 5 carry, guard, guide, pilot, watch 6 attend, convey, escort, manage 7 conduct 9 accompany, conductor, safeguard

convulse: 4 rock, stir 5 shake 6 excite 7 agitate, disturb

convulsion: fit 5 shrug, spasm, throe 6 attack, tumult, uproar 8 laughter, paroxysm 9 agitation, commotion 11 disturbance

cony: das 4 hare, pika 5 daman, dassy, ganam, hutia, hyrax, lapen 6 burbot, dassie, gazabo, gazebo, rabbit 7 ashkoko

catcher: 5 cheat 7 sharper 8 swindler

coo: 4 curr(Sc.), woot 6 murmur

cook: fix, fry 4 bake, boil, chef, make, sear, stew 5 broil, grill, poach, roast, saute, shirr, steam 6 braise, decoct, seethe, simmer 7 dream up, prepare, process, servant 8 barbecue, contrive, cusinero, magirist 9 cuisinier

in simmering liquid: 4 poach

one's goose: 5 spoil 6 defeat

partially: 7 parboil

cooked: 4 done

cookery: 7 cuisine, science 8 magirics

cookie, cooky: 4 cake, snap 6 hermit 7 brownie, oatcake 8 seedcake 10 confection, gingersnap

cooking: *art:* 7 cuisine 8 magirics

device: 4 etna 5 range, stove 7 brazier, griddle 10 rotisserie

odor: 5 nidor

pert. to: 8 culinary

room: 5 cuddy 6 galley 7 kitchen

vessel: pan, pot 4 etna, olla 6 caster, chafer, spider, tureen 7 broiler, griddle, roaster, skillet, steamer 8 colander, fleshpot 9 autoclave

cool: air, fan, ice 4 calm, cold 5 algid, allay, chill, fresh, gelid, nervy, sober, staid, whole 6 chilly, go easy, placid, quench, sedate, serene 7 unmoved 8 careless, cautious, composed, mitigate, moderate, tranquil 9 apathetic, collected, officious, temperate, unruffled 10 deliberate, nonchalant, simmer down, unfriendly 11 indifferent, refrigerate, unconcerned 12 unresponsive 13 dispassionate, imperturbable, self-possessed 15 undemonstrative

one's heels: **4** wait
cooled: 6 frappe
cooler: fan **4** icer, jail, olla **5** drink **6** icebox, lockup, prison **11** refrigerant **12** refrigerator
coolie: 7 changar
cooling device: fan **7** freezer **12** refrigerator **14** air-conditioner
coolness: 5 nerve **6** aplomb **8** serenity **9** assurance **10** equanimity
coony: sly **4** cute, foxy **6** clever, crafty
coop: cot, cub, mew, pen, pot **4** cage, cote, jail **5** cramp, hutch **6** basket, corral **7** confine **9** enclosure **11** cooperative
cooperate: 4 tend **5** agree, coact, unite **6** concur **7** combine, conduce, connive **8** coadjute, conspire **10** contribute **11** collaborate
cooperation; 8 teamwork
cooperator: 9 auxiliary, colleague **10** accomplice
coordinate: 5 adapt, equal **6** adjust **7** arrange, syntony **8** classify **9** harmonize, integrate, reconcile **10** concurrent
coordination: 4 bond **5** skill **7** harmony, liaison **12** relationship
inability: **6** abasia
lack: **8** asynergy
coot: 4 duck, fowl, rail **5** smyth **6** beltie, person, scoter **7** henbil **13** phalacrocorax
cooter: 4 idle **6** loiter, turtle **8** tortoise
cootie: nit **4** bowl, game **5** louse **6** vessel **8** grayback
cop: bag, nab, rob **4** bank, blow, bull, head, heap, lift, pile, trap, tube **5** catch, crest, filch, mount, quill, shock, snare, steal, stock, swipe **6** peeler, spider, strike **7** capture **9** patrolman, policeman
cop-out: 6 excuse **7** retreat **9** defection
copacetic: 4 fine **5** dandy, prime **6** snappy **7** capital **12** satisfactory
copaiba: 4 tree **6** balsam **9** oleoresin
copal: 5 anime, resin
cope: vie, war **4** cape, duty, face **5** cappa, cloak, cover, dress, equal, flight, match, notch, rival, vault, wield **6** barter, canopy, chapel, combat, make do, mantel, muzzle, oppose, strike, strive **7** contend, contest **8** complete, deal with, exchange, struggle, vestment **9** encounter
Copenhagen: *park:* **6** Tivoli
shopping district: **7** Stroget
copestone: 5 crown, stone **6** coping **11** culmination
copier: 4 stat **5** Xerox **6** scribe
copious: 4 full, good, lush, rich **5** ample, large **6** fluent, lavish, plenty **7** diffuse, flowing, fulsome, profuse, replete, teeming, uberous **8** abundant, affluent, numerous **9** exuberant, plenteous, plentiful, redundant **11** overflowing

copper: cop **4** bull, cent **5** bobby, metal, penny **6** cuprum, peeler **9** butterfly, policeman
alloy: **5** brass **6** oroide **7** rheotan
arsenic sulfide: **8** enargite
coin: **4** cent **5** brown, penny
engraving: **9** mezzotint
sulfate: **7** vitriol
copperhead: 5 snake, viper
coppice: 4 bosk, wood **5** copse, firth, grove **6** forest, growth **7** thicket **9** brushwood, underwood
Corpreus: *father:* **6** Pelops
son: **10** Periphetes
victim: **7** Iphitus
copse: cut, hag **4** hasp, trim **6** clevis **7** coppice, shackle
Copt: 8 Egyptian **9** Christian **11** monophysite
dialect: **8** Bohairic
title: **4** anba
copula: 4 band, link **5** union **7** coupler
copy: ape **4** echo, edit, mime **5** dummy, image, mimic **6** ectype, effigy, follow, record **7** emulate, estreat, imitate, redraft, replica, reprint, tracing **8** apograph, likeness **9** abundance, antigraph, duplicate, imitation, reproduce **10** transcribe, transcript **11** counterpart **12** reproduction
exact: **5** tenor
kind of: **6** carbon, ectype **7** estreat, extract, pattern, replica **9** duplicate, facsimile
true: **7** estreat
copying: 7 mimicry **8** mimetism
copyist: 6 sribe **7** copycat **10** plagiarist **12** calligrapher
pert. to: **8** clerical
copyread: edit
copyright: 6 patent
infringe: **6** pirate **10** plagiarize
coque: bow **4** loop **8** trimming
coquet: toy **5** dally, flirt **6** lead on **11** string along
coquette: toy **4** vamp **5** dally, flirt **6** trifle **9** philander **11** hummingbird
coquetteish: coy **4** arch **7** roguish
cora: 7 gazelle
coral: red **4** pink **5** polyp **6** palule **8** skeleton, zoophyte **9** limestone, madrepore, millepore **10** stalactite
division: **7** aporosa
formation: **5** palus
island: key **4** reef **5** atoll
corbel: 4 knot **5** ancon **6** timber **10** projection
corbie: 4 crow **5** raven
cord: rib **4** band, bind, bond, welt **5** nerve, twine **6** bobbin, sennet, string, tendon, thread **7** amentum, measure **10** aiquilette, cordeliere

drapery: **7** torsade
goat's hair: **4** agal
parachute: **7** ripcord
twisted: **7** torsade
cordage: **4** rope, coir, eruc, feru, hemp, imbe, jute **5** fiber **6** sennit **7** rigging
Corday's victim: **5** Marat
corded: **4** tied **6** repped, ribbed, welted **7** stacked, twilled
Cordelia: *father:* **4** Lear
sister: **5** Regan **7** Goneril
cordelle: tow **4** cord, rope **7** towline, towrope
cordial (see also **liqueur**): **4** real, warm **5** shrub **6** ardent, elixir, genial, hearty **7** liqueur, sincere, zealous **8** anisette, friendly, gracious, vigorous **9** courteous, unfeigned **10** hospitable
apricot: **8** periscot
flavoring: **7** aniseed
cordiality: **5** ardor **6** regard, warmth **10** friendship, heartiness
cordon: **4** lace **5** braid, group, guard **6** ribbon
bleu: **4** chef, cook **6** ribbon **10** decoration
sanitary: **10** quarantine
core: cob, hub, nut **4** coke, gist, nave, pith **5** focus, heart, nowse, spool **6** cener, centre, kernel, matrix, middle, nodule **7** company, corncob, essence, nucleus **9** substance
corge: **5** score **6** twenty
coriander: **4** herb
corinne: **7** gazelle
corium: **5** layer **6** dermis
cork: oak **4** plug, seal, stop **5** float, shive **6** bobber **7** soberin, stopper, stopple
pert. to: **7** suberic
tissue: **5** suber
wax: **5** cerin
corker: **4** lulu **5** dandy **8** knockout **9** humdinger
corking: **4** fine **8** pleasing **9** excellent
corkscrew: **4** coil, wind **5** twist **6** spiral
corkwood: **5** balsa **6** blolly **8** harefoot
cormorant: **4** bird, shag **5** norie, scart **6** gormaw, scarth **7** glutton **8** ravenous **13** phalacrocorax
young: **7** shaglet
corn: zea **4** salt, samp **5** grain, maize, mealy **6** clavis, heloma, kernel **7** callous **8** preserve **9** granulate
bread: **4** pone
dealer: **10** cornmonger
ear: cob **5** mealy **6** mealie, nubbin
food: **6** hominy
ground: **4** meal **5** grist
hulled: **4** samp **6** hominy
Indian: zea
knife: **7** machete
spike: cob, ear
corn bread: **4** pone **8** tortilla
Corncracker State: **8** Kentucky

corndodger: **4** pone **5** bread **8** dumpling
corned: **6** salted
cornel: **4** tree **6** cherry **7** dogwood **8** redbrush
corner: box, get, wro **4** bend, cant, coin, nook, pool, trap, tree **5** angle, bight, catch, coign, elbow, herne, ingle, niche, quoin, trust **6** cantle, canton, coigne, cranny, recess **8** monopoly
cornerpiece: **6** bumper, cantle
cornerstone: **5** basis, coign **6** coigne **7** support **9** curbstone **10** foundation
cornet: **4** horn **8** woodwind **10** instrument
cornflower: **7** barbeau **10** bluebonnet, bluebottle
cornhouse: **7** granary **8** corncrib
Cornhusker State: **8** Nebraska
cornice: cap **4** band, drip, eave **5** crown **6** geison **7** molding **8** astragal
basket: **4** caul
diamond: **6** quartz
support: **5** ancon
underside: **6** soffit **8** plancier
wolframite: cal
cornmeal: **4** masa, samp **5** atole **7** hoecake **10** johnnycake
cornsilk: **5** floss
cornucopia: **4** horn **9** abundance **12** horn of plenty
Cornwall: *castle:* **8** Tintagel
mine: bal **5** wheal
ore: **5** whits
Cornwallis *adversary:* **6** Greene
surrender site: **8** Yorktown
corny: **5** banal, stale, trite **6** old hat **11** sentimental
corolla: **4** bell **8** perianth
part: **5** galea, petal
corollary: **5** dogma **6** result, truism **7** adjunct, theorem **9** deduction, inference, end product **11** consequence, proposition
geometric: **6** porism
corona: **4** halo **5** cigar, crown, glory **6** circle, fillet, rosary, wreath **7** aureole, circlet, garland, scyphus
coronation: **9** inaugural
stone: **5** Scone
coroner: **6** elisor **7** officer **8** examiner
coronet: **4** band, burr **5** crown, tiara **6** anadem, circle, diadem, timbre, wreath **7** chaplet
coronopus: **4** herb **6** carara
corporal: NCO **4** fano **5** fanon, fanum, phano **6** bodily
corporal punishment: **5** death **7** penalty **8** spanking, whipping
corporate: **6** united **8** combined **9** aggregate
corporation: **4** body, firm **5** trust **10** fellowship, foundation **11** association, combination

corporeal: 4 real **5** hylic, somal **6** actual, bodily, carnal **7** somatic **8** material, physical, tangible **11** substantial

corpse: DOA **4** body **5** mummy, relic, stiff **7** cadaver, carcass, carrion
fat of: **9** adipocere
pert. to: **7** deathly **10** cadaverous

corpulent: fat **5** bulky, burly, husky, obese, plump, stout **6** fleshy, portly, rotund **7** adipose, bellied, weighty **8** roly-poly **10** overweight

corpus: 4 body, bulk, mass **8** writings **10** literature

corpuscle: 4 cell **9** leucocyte
lack of red: **6** anemia
red blood: **7** hematid **8** haematid **11** polkilocyte, schistocyte

corral: pen, sty **4** coop **5** atajo, pound **7** confine, enclose **8** stockage, surround **9** enclosure, inclosure

correct: due, fit, fix **4** edit, lean, nice, okay, smug, true **5** amend, check, emend, exact, right **6** adjust, better, change, inform, proper, punish, rebuke, reform, remedy, repair, revamp, revise, strict **7** chasten, improve, perfect, precise, rectify, redress, reprove **8** accurate, chastise, definite, emendate, make over, regulate, rigorous, truthful **9** castigate, faultless **10** immaculate, particular, scrupulous **11** comme il faut, punctilious **12** conventional

correctable: 10 corrigible

correction: 10 discipline, punishment **11** castigation

correlated: 4 akin **7** matched, related

correlative: nor **4** then **5** equal, still **6** either, mutual **7** neither **8** analogue, conjoint **9** analogous **10** reciprocal **13** correspondent

correspond: fit, gee **4** jibe, suit **5** agree, match, tally, write **6** accord, concur, square **7** comport, respond **8** coincide, parallel, quadrate **9** analogous, harmonize **11** communicate

correspondence: 4 mail **7** analogy, letters, traffic **8** homology **9** assonance, congruity **10** similarity

correspondent: 5 match **6** pen pal, writer **8** quadrate, suitable **9** accordant, analogous, congruous **10** accomplice, concordant, equivalent **11** conformable, contributor, correlative

corresponding: 4 akin **5** alike **7** similar
in sound: **5** rimic **6** rhymic
part: **7** isomere

corrida: 9 bullfight
shout: olé

corridor: 4 hall **5** aisle, oriel **6** arcade **7** couloir, gallery **8** coulisse **10** passageway

corrie: 6 cirque, hollow

corrigible: 8 amenable **10** corrective,

punishable **11** correctable

corroborant: 5 tonic **10** supporting **12** invigorating **13** strengthening

corroborate: 5 prove **7** bear out, confirm, support, sustain **8** validate **9** establish **11** countersign **12** substantiate

corrode: eat **4** bite, burn, etch, gnaw, rust **5** decay, erode, waste **6** be-gnaw, canker, impair **7** consume, eat away **8** wear away

corrosive: 4 acid **6** ardent, biting **7** caustic, erosive, fretful, mordant **9** sarcastic **11** destructive **14** disintegrating

corrugate: 5 crimp **6** furrow, rumple **7** crinkle, crumple, wrinkle

corrugation: 4 fold **6** crease, pucker **7** wrinkle

corrupt: bad, low, rot **4** evil, vile **5** blend, bribe, spoil, stain, sully, taint, venal **6** augean, canker, debase, impure, poison, putrid, ravish, rotten **7** abusive, attaint, carrion, crooked, defiled, degrade, deprave, envenom, falsify, immoral, pervert, pollute, putrefy, violate, vitiate **8** confound, empoison, two-faced **9** abandoned, dishonest **10** adulterate, demoralize, flagitious, profligate **11** contaminate, purchasable **13** double-dealing

corsage: 5 waist **6** bodice **7** bouquet, flowers

corsair: bug **6** pirate, robber **8** picaroon, rockfish **9** buccaneer, sea robber **10** freebooter
body: **5** armor, cover

corset: 4 belt, busk **6** bodice, girdle **7** support
covering: **8** camisole
strip: **4** bone, busk

Corsica: *seaport:* **6** Bastia
town: **5** Calvi, Corte **7** Ajaccio(c.)

corslet: 6 bodice **8** corselet **11** breastplate

cortege: 4 pomp **5** suite, train **6** parade **7** retinue **10** procession

cortex: 4 bark, peel, rind **8** peridium

corundum: 4 ruby, sand **5** emeru, emery **7** alumina **8** abrasive, sapphire

coruscate: 5 blaze, flash, gleam, shine **7** glisten, glitter, radiate, sparkle **8** brandish **11** scintillate

corviform: 7 corvine **8** crowlike

corvine bird: daw **4** crow, rook **5** raven

coryza: 4 cold
symptom: **6** sneeze

cos: 7 lettuce, romaine

cosa nostra: 5 Mafia **9** syndicate

cosh: 4 neat, snug, tidy **5** happy, quiet, still **6** attack, lively, strike, weapon **7** assault **8** familiar, friendly **11** comfortable

cosher: pet **4** chat **5** feast, visit **6** pamper, sponge

cosmetic: 5 cream, henna, liner, paint, rouge **6** enamel, pomade, powder **7**

blusher, mascara **8** lipgloss, lipstick **9** eye shadow **10** nail polish
medicated: **6** lotion
paste: **4** pack
white lead: **6** ceruse
cosmic: 4 vast **6** global **7** orderly **8** catholic, infinite **9** universal **10** harmonious **12** cosmopolitan
opposed to: **7** chaotic
cosmonaut: See **astronaut**
cosmopolitan: 6 global, smooth, urbane **8** ecumenic **10** ecumenical **13** sophisticated
cosmos: 5 earth, globe, order, realm, world **6** flower, nature **7** harmony **8** creation, universe
opposed to: **5** Chaos
Cossack: 4 Turk **5** tatar **6** ataman, hetman, tartar **7** Russian **10** cavalryman
captain: **6** Sotnik
chief: **6** ataman, hetman
district: **6** voisko
mount: **5** steed **7** charger
regiment: **4** polk, pulk
squadron: **6** sotnia, sotnya
village: **8** stanitza
whip: **5** knout
cosset: pet 4 baby, love **6** caress, coddle, cuddle, fondle, pamper
cossette: 4 chip **5** slice, strip **9** schnitzel
cossid: 9 messenger
cost: 4 loss, pain **5** price, value **6** charge, outlay **7** expense **8** estimate **9** detriment, sacrifice, suffering **11** deprivation, expenditure **14** characteristic
business: **8** overhead
costa: rib **4** side, vein **5** ridge **6** border, mid-rib
Costa Rica: *capital:* San Jose
city: **7** Cartago, Heredia **8** Alajuela **9** Guadalupe
measure: **6** fanega, tercia **7** cajuela, manzana **10** caballeria
monetary unit: **5** colon **7** centimo
mountain: **6** Blanco **8** Chirripo
people: **6** Guaymi **7** Guaymie
port: **10** Puerto Limon **11** Punta Arenas
volcano: **5** Barba, Irazu
weight: bag **4** caja
costate: 6 ribbed
costly 4 dear, fine, high, rich **6** lavish **8** gorgeous, precious, prodigal, splendid **9** dearthful, expensive, priceless, sumptuous **10** exorbitant, invaluable **11** extravagant
costmary: 4 herb **5** plant, tansy **7** alecost
costume (see also **dress, vestment**): rig **4** garb, robe, sari, suit **5** dress, getup, habit **6** attire, outfit **7** apparel, clothes, raiment, uniform **8** clothing, ensemble **10** habiliment
costus root: 4 herb **6** pachak, pochok
cot: bed, hut, mat, pen **4** boat, coop, cote,

fold **5** abode, cabin, couch, cover, house, stall **6** pallet, sheath, tangle **7** charpai, charpoy, cottage, shelter **8** bedstead, dwelling **9** sheepfold, stretcher **11** fingerstall
cote: cot, hut **4** coop, fold, shed, wine **5** house, quote **7** cottage, shelter **8** hillside, outstrip, vineyard **9** inclosure, sheepfold
Cote d'Azur: 7 Riviera
coterie: set **4** ring **5** junto, monde **6** circle, clique, galaxy **7** platoon, society **9** camarilla
cothamore: 8 overcoat **9** greatcoat
cothurnus: 4 boot **6** buskin
cotillion: 5 dance **9** quadrille, solitaire
cotta: 5 stole **6** mantle **7** blanket **8** surplice, vestment
cottage: hut **4** bari, cosh **5** bower, cabin, house, lodge, shack **6** bohawn, cabana, chalet, shanty **7** shelter **8** bungalow **9** hosthouse **10** guesthouse
partition: **5** speer **6** hallan
Russian: **5** dacha
Swiss: **6** chalet
cottage cheese: 9 smearcase
cotter, cottar: mat, pin, vex **4** clot **6** fasten, potter, pucker, shrink, toggle, wither **7** congeal, cottier, peasant, shrivel, villein **8** cottager, cotterel, entangle **9** coagulate
cotton: 4 beat, flog **5** agree, fiber, toady **6** coddle, fabric **7** algodon, garment, succeed **8** perceive **9** harmonize **10** fraternize, understand
and linen: **7** fustian
cleaner: **5** willy **6** willow
cloth: **4** baft, jean, lawn, leno, susi **5** bafta, bluet, denim, doria, khaki, lisle, manta, surat, terry, vichy, wigan **6** baline, calico, cangan, hum-hum **7** camboye, cotonia, galatea, jaconet, nankeen, percale, silesia
cloth blemish: nit
Egyptian: sak **4** Pima **5** sakel
extraction: **5** bolly
fabric: **4** leno
fiber: **4** lint, noil **6** stapel
flowered: **6** chintz
fuzz remover: **6** linter
gauze: **4** leno
handkerchief: **7** malabar
knot in: nep **4** slub
lawn: **7** batiste
light: **7** etamine
long-staple: **4** maco
measure: lea **4** hank
printed: **6** calico
refuse: **8** grabbots
seed pod: **4** boll **5** bolly
seed remover: gin
sheeting: **5** manta **6** muslin **7** percale **8** drilling

striped: **5** bezan **7** express
strong: **4** duck **5** scrim **6** canvas
thread: **5** lisle
twilled: **4** jean **7** silesia
up to: **10** ingratiate
waste: **4** noil **6** linter
cotton gin inventor: 10 Eli Whitney
Cotton State: 7 Alabama
cottonseed kernel: 4 meat **7** oil cake
cottontail: 4 hare **7** leveret
cottonwood: 4 tree **5** alamo **6** poplar
couch: bed, cot, lie, put **4** hide, lair, lurk,
  sofa **5** divan, inlay, lodge, press, skulk,
  slink, sneak, squat, stoop, utter **6** burrow, litter, pallet, settee **7** conceal, express, overlay, recline **8** disguise **9** accu-
  bitus(L.), davenport, embroider
couch grass: 5 quack, quick **6** quitch,
  scutch
couchant: 4 abed **5** prone **6** supine **7**
  lurking **9** crouching, squatting
cougar: cat **4** puma **7** panther **9** catamount
cough: 4 bark, hack **5** hoast **6** tussis **9**
  pertussis
pert. to: **7** tussive
cough drop: 6 pastil, troche **7** lozenge **8**
  pastille
cough up: 4 ante **5** yield **10** contribute
coulee: 4 lava **5** gorge, gulch **6** cooley, ravine
couloir: 5 gorge, gully **7** hallway, passage
  8 corridor
council: 4 body, dael, diet, rede **5** board,
  boule, cabal, divan, junta, junto, synod
  6 senate **7** cabinet, consult, meeting **8**
  assembly, conclave, congress, hustling,
  ministry **10** conference, consistory, federation **11** convocation **12** consultation
church: **5** synod **10** consistory
pert. to: **7** cameral
political: **5** cabal, junta
table cover: **5** tapis
counsel: 4 lore, rede, rule, urge, warn **5**
  chide **6** advice, advise, confer **7** caution,
  suggest **8** admonish, advocate, attorney,
  prudence **9** barrister, counselor, recommend **10** counsellor **11** exhortation, instruction **12** consultation, deliberation
counselor, counsellor: 4 sage **6** lawyer,
  mentor, nestor **7** adviser, advisor, counsel, proctor **8** attorney **9** barrister
counselor-at-law: 9 barrister
count: add, sum, tot **4** bank, cast, earl,
  foot, graf, name, rely, tell, tote **5** com-
  te(F.), judge, score, tally **6** census, depend, esteem, figure, impute, number,
  reckon, rely on **7** account, ascribe, compute, trust in **8** numerate, sanction **9**
  ascertain, calculate, enumerate **10** depend upon
Count of Monte Cristo: 6 Dantes
count on: 4 lean, rely **6** depend, expect

count out: bar **6** except **7** rule out **9** eliminate
countenance: aid, mug **4** abet, brow, face,
  mien, puss, show, vult **5** favor, front **6**
  aspect, favour, visage **7** approve, bearing, conduct, endorse, feature, proffer,
  support **8** befriend, demeanor, hold
  with, sanction **9** demeanour, encourage,
  semblance **10** appearance **11** physiognomy
counter: bar, vie **4** chip, dump, eddy,
  pawn **5** shelf, stand, table **6** combat,
  marker, oppose **7** adverse, contend, current **8** contrary, opposite **10** contradict
  12 football play **13** contradictory
counter-irritant: 4 moxa **5** seton, stupe
  6 arnica, ginger, iodine, pepper **7** mustard **8** liniment
counteract: 5 annul, check **6** oppose, resist, thwart **7** balance, correct, destroy,
  nullify **8** antidote, negative **9** frustrate
  10 compensate, neutralize **11** countermand **12** counterpoise
counterattack: 6 answer, charge
countercurrent: 4 eddy **5** swirl **7** backset
  9 whirlpool
counterfeit: tin **4** base, copy, coin, duff,
  fake, mock, sham **5** belie, bogus, dummy, false, feign, forge, fudge, phony,
  queer **6** affect, assume, forged, pseudo,
  tinsel **7** falsify, feigned, imitate **8** deformed, simulate, spurious **9** brummagem, disguised, dissemble **10** adulterate, artificial, fictitious, fraudulent
counterfoil: 4 stub **5** check
countermand: 4 stop **5** annul **6** cancel,
  forbid, recall, revoke **7** abolish, rescind,
  reverse **8** abrogate, prohibit **9** frustrate
  10 counteract
counterpane: 6 spread **8** bedcover, coverlet **9** bedspread
counterpart: 4 copy, like, mate, twin **5**
  image, match **6** double **7** obverse, vis-á-
  vis **8** parallel **9** duplicate, facsimile **10**
  complement, equivalent, similitude
counterpoint: 4 foil **7** descant **8** contrast
  11 arrangement **13** juxtaposition
counterpoise: 6 make up, offset, set off **7**
  balance **8** equalize **10** compensate,
  counteract **13** counterweight **14** counterbalance
countersign: 4 mark, seal, sign **6** signal **7**
  confirm, endorse **8** consigne, password,
  sanction **9** signature, watchword **11**
  corroborate
countersink: 4 ream **5** bevel **7** chamfer
countertenor: 4 alto **8** falsetto
counting frame: 6 abacus
countless: 8 infinite **10** numberless **12**
  incalculable
country: 4 home, land, pais(Sp.) **5** realm,
  rural, state, tract, weald **6** ground, nation, people, region, sticks **7** bucolic,

outland **8** district, homeland **9** champaign, territory **10** fatherland **12** commonwealth

ancient: **4** Aram, Elam, Elis **5** Sheba

dance: **4** reel

home: **5** manor, ranch, villa **8** hacienda

man: **4** jake, rube **5** swain, yokel **6** farmer, rustic **7** bumpkin, hayseed, plowman **10** compatriot, inhabitant

mythical: **6** Utopia

open: **4** wold **5** heath, weald

pert. to: **5** rural **6** rustic **7** predial **8** agrestic, pastoral, praedial

place: **4** farm, peat **5** ranch, villa

reside in: **9** rusticate

road: **4** lane, path **5** byway

county: **4** seat **5** shire **6** domain, parish **7** borough **8** district

coup: buy **4** blow, plan, play **5** scoop, upset **6** attack, barter, putsch, strike, stroke **7** capsize, traffic **8** overturn, takeover **9** stratagem

coup de grace: end **7** quietus **9** deathblow

coup d'etat: **9** stratagem **10** revolution

couple: duo, tie, two **4** bond, case, dyad, join, link, mate, pair, span, team, twin, yoke **5** brace, leash, marry, twain, unite **7** bracket, connect **8** assemble

coupled: **5** yoked **6** joined, wedded **7** gemalad **8** geminate **9** conjugate

coupler: **4** link, ring **7** drawbar, shackle, tirasse

couplet: **4** pair, poem **5** brace **7** distich

coupon: **4** form, slip, stub **5** check, stamp **7** portion

courage: **4** grit, guts, prow, sand, soul **5** heart, nerve, pluck, spine, spunk, valor **6** daring, mettle, spirit **7** bravery, heroism, prowess **8** audacity, backbone, boldness, firmness, tenacity **9** assurance, fortitude, gallantry, hardihood **10** resolution

symbol of: **10** bloodstone

courageous: **4** bold, game **5** brave, hardy, manly, stout **6** daring, heroic, manful, plucky **7** gallant, spartan, staunch, valiant **8** fearless, intrepid, valorous **9** undaunted **11** adventurous **12** enterprising, high-spirited

courante: **4** romp **5** caper, dance, music **6** letter **7** current, gazette, running **9** messenger, newspaper

courier: **4** post **5** envoy, guide, scout **7** estafet, orderly, postboy, soilage **8** cicerone, dragoman, estafeet, horseman **9** attendant, go-between, messenger **10** cavalryman

courlan: **4** bird **7** limpkin

course: lap, run, way **4** bent, flow, game, heat, line, mode, path, race, rill, rink, road, rote, went **5** cycle, drift, orbit, route, tenor, track, trail, trend **6** artery,

career, cursus, gallop, manner, method, series, stream, street, system **7** beeline, conduct, highway, passage, pathway, process, routine, running, subject, traject **8** curricle, progress, sequence, tendency **9** direction **10** curriculum, proceeding, racecourse, succession **11** watercourse

alter: **4** veer **6** detour

dinner: **5** salad **6** entrée **7** dessert **9** blue plate

easy: **4** pipe, snap **5** cinch **8** sinecure

habitual: rut, way **4** rote **7** regimen, routine

of action: **6** career **8** demarche **9** procedure

of study: **7** seminar **8** syllabus **10** curriculum

roundabout: **6** detour **11** indirection

courser: **5** horse, racer, steed **7** charger **8** war-horse

court: bar, bid, see, sue, woo **4** area, body, quad, rota, seek, yard **5** arena, curea, curry, favor, forum, judge, patio, space, spark, tempt, train **6** allure, atrium, gemote, homage, invite, palace **7** address, attract, retinue, solicit **8** hustings, serenade, tribunal **9** attention, enclosure **10** quadrangle

action: **4** case, suit **5** trial

attendant: **5** staff **6** elisor, staves

bring into: sue **4** sist **6** arrest

calendar: **6** docket

call to: **4** oyes, oyez **7** summons **8** subpoena **11** arraignment

circuit: **4** eyre, iter

crier: **6** beadle

cry: **4** oyes, oyez

decision: **6** assize **7** finding, verdict **8** judgment

ecclesiastical: **5** Curia **10** consistory

exemption: **6** essoin

hearing: **4** oyer, suit **5** trial **6** action

inner: **5** patio

Mikado's: **5** dairi

minutes: **4** acta

of equity: **8** chancery

official: **5** clerk, crier, macer(Sc.) **7** bailiff

old: **4** leet **5** gemot **6** gemote **8** woodmote

order: **4** nisi, rule, writ **6** decree

panel: **4** jury

participant: **4** jury **5** crier, judge **6** elisor **7** pleader **8** advocate, talesman **9** defendant, plaintiff

pert. to: **5** aulic **10** fornaneous

session: set **4** oyer **6** assize **7** sitting **8** sederunt **11** downsitting

writ: **6** capias **7** summons **8** subpoena

court game: **6** tennis **9** badminton

court-martial: **8** drumhead

courteous: **4** fair **5** buxom, civil, suave **6** polite, urbane **7** affable, cordial, gallant, genteel, gentile, refined **8** debonair, gracious **9** attentive **10** complaisant, respectful **11** considerate, gentlemanly **12** well mannered

courtesan: 5 whore **6** geisha, madame **10** prostitute

courtier: 4 beau **5** beaux(pl.), wooer **7** courter **8** courtman **9** attendant, courtling, flatterer

courtly: 4 hend, prim **5** aulic, civil, hende, lofty **6** polite **7** elegant, refined, stately **8** gracious, polished **9** dignified

courtship: 4 suit **7** romance **8** sparking

courtyard: 4 area, quad **5** patio **7** cortile **9** curtilage **10** quadrangle

cousin: coz, kin **4** akin **6** allied **8** relative

couthie: 4 smug **6** kindly, smooth **8** friendly, pleasant **9** agreeable **11** comfortable

couturier, couturiere: 8 designer **10** dressmaker

cove: bay, den **4** cave, chap, gill, hole, nook, pass **5** basin, bight, creek, inlet **6** fellow, hollow, recess, valley **7** molding

covenant: 4 bind, bond, mise, pact **5** agree **6** accord, cartel, engage, pledge, treaty **7** bargain, compact, concord, promise **8** alliance, contract, document **9** agreement, concordat, condition, stipulate, testament, undertake **10** convention **11** confederacy, stipulation, transaction

cover: cap, lid **4** coat, hide, mask, pave, roof, span, veil **5** drape, hatch, put-on **6** mantle, screen, shield **7** obscure, overlay, shelter

a bet: **4** fade

a fire: **4** bank

a hatch: **6** batten

ground: **5** speed **7** advance

the eyes: **9** blindfold

up: **4** hide **7** conceal

up for: **6** shield **7** protect

with mud: **6** belute

with straw: **6** thatch

with strips of bacon: **4** lard

coverall: 4 gown **6** jumper **10** boiler suit

covered: 4 clad, shod **5** mossy **6** covert, hidden **7** encased **8** screened **9** cleithral, concealed, panoplied, sheltered

covering: fur, hap **4** aril, bark, boot, case, hood, hull, husk, mask, pall, roof, tarp, tile **5** apron, armor, crust, quilt, shell, testa **6** awning, canopy, drapet, facing, heling, helmet, jacket, pelage, screen, sheath, shroud **7** capsule, ceiling, healing, overlay, pericap, wrapper **8** casement, clothing, coverlet, umbrella **9** coverture, operculum **10** integument **11** smokescreen

defensive: **5** armor **6** helmut **10** camouflage **11** smokescreen

seed: **4** aril

thin: **4** film **6** veneer

coverlet: 5 quilt, rezai, throw **6** afghan, caddow, spread **7** blanket **8** coverlid **9** comforter **11** counterpane

covert: den, lie, sly **4** lair **5** niche, privy **6** asylum, harbor, hidden, latent, masked, refuge, secret **7** covered, defense, harbour, private, shelter, subrosa, thicket **8** hush-hush **9** concealed, disguised, insidious, shrubbery **10** underbrush **12** confidential **13** under-the-table

covet: 4 ache, envy, pant, want, wish **5** crave, yearn **6** desire, grudge, hanker

covetous: 4 avid, gair, gare, keen **5** eager, itchy **6** frugal, greedy, stingy **7** miserly **8** desirous, grasping **9** mercenary **10** avaricious **12** parsimonious

covey: 4 bevy **5** brood, bunch, flock, hatch **7** company **8** assembly

cow: awe **4** beef, bogy, cowl, cush, faze, kine, vaca **5** abash, alarm, bossy, brock, bully, daunt, dompt, moggy, scare **6** bovine, goblin, heifer, subdue **7** bluster, bugbear, depress, dragoon, overtop, squelch, terrify **8** browbeat, dispirit, frighten, threaten **9** quadruped, strongarm **10** intimidate

barn: **4** byre **7** vaccary

barren: **5** drape

cud: **5** rumen

dung: **4** upla

French: **5** vache

group: **4** herd, kine **6** cattle

hornless: not **4** moil **5** doddy, muley **6** doddie, mulley **7** pollard

hybrid: **7** cattabu, cattalo

pasture: **7** vaccary

pen: **6** corral

sound: low, moo

Spanish: **5** vaca

young: **4** calf **5** stirk **6** heifer

cow-headed deity: 4 Isis

cow pilot: 4 fish **9** chirivita **10** damselfish

coward: 6 pigeon **7** caitiff, chicken, quitter **9** jellyfish **10** scaredy-cat **11** lily-livered

cowardly: shy **4** argh **5** timid **6** afraid, cowish, craven, yellow **7** caitiff, chicken **11** lily-livered **12** fainthearted **13** pusillanimous

cowbird: 7 bunting **9** blackbird

cowboy: 5 rider, roper, waddi **6** drover, gaucho, herder **7** llanero, puncher, vaquero **8** buckaroo, buckayro, herdsman, wrangler **9** cattleman **10** cowpuncher **12** broncobuster

breeches: **5** chaps, levis **8** jodhpurs

contest: **5** rodeo

rope: **5** lasso, riata **6** lariat

cowcatcher: 5 guard, pilot

cowed: 8 downcast 11 crestfallen

cower: 4 fawn 5 quail, stoop, toady, wince 6 coorie, cringe, crouch, hurkle, shrink 11 apple-polish

cowfish: 4 toro 7 grampus, manatee, sirenia

cowherd: 8 herdsman, neatherd

cowl: cap, lid, tub 4 hood, monk 6 bonnet, vessel 7 capuche

cowled: 6 hooded 9 cucullate

cowpea: 5 sitao

cowpuncher: See **cowboy**

cowslip: 8 auricula, cyclamen, marigold, primrose

coxa: hip 6 haunch

coxcomb: fop, nob 4 buck, dude, fool, toff 5 cleat, dandy, hinge 7 princox 8 popinjay 12 lounge lizard

coy: pal, shy 4 arch, coax, nice 5 aloof, chary, decoy, quiet, still 6 allure, caress, demure, modest, proper 7 bashful, distant 8 reserved 9 diffident 10 coquettish, disdainful, hesitating 12 self-effacing

Coyote State: 11 South Dakota

coypu: 6 nutria, rodent

coze: 4 chat, talk 6 gossip 8 converse

cozen, cosen: cog, con, gyp 4 bilk, gull 5 cheat, trick 6 chisel 7 beguile, deceive, defraud, swindle 8 hoodwink 9 bamboozle 11 double-cross

cozy: 4 easy, safe, snug 5 bield 6 chatty, secure, toasty 8 covering, familiar, homelike, sociable 9 contented, gemutlich, talkative 10 buddy-buddy, palsywalsy 11 comfortable

cozy retreat: den 4 lair, nest, nook 5 ingle

crab: gin 4 beef, fuss, yawp 5 anger, gripe, maian, racer, winch 6 buster, cancer, grouse, hermit, peeler 7 buckler, fiddler, grumble 8 arachnid, irritate, windlass 9 horseshoe 10 crosspatch, crustacean, curmudgeon

abdomen: 5 apron

claw: 5 chela 6 nipper

constellation: 6 Cancer

fiddler: uca

genus: uca 6 birgus 7 limulus, squilla

resembling: 8 cancroid

suborder: 9 brachyura

crab apple: 5 malus, scrog

crabbed: 4 dour, glum, ugly 5 cabby, cross, testy 6 bitter, cranky, crusty, morose, rugged, sullen, trying 7 boorish, cramped, cornish, crooked, gnarled, knotted, obscure, peevish 8 churlish, contrary, petulant, vinegary 9 difficult, fractious, intricate, irregular 10 perplexing 11 intractable

crabgrass: 4 weed 9 digitaria

crabstick: 4 cane 5 crank, stick 6 cudgel

crabwood: 8 andiroba

crack: gag, pop 4 a-one, bang, blow, chap, chip, chop, clap, cone, flaw, jest, jibe, joke, kibe, leak, quip, rend, rift, rime, snap, yerk 5 brack, break, check, chine, chink, clack, cleft, craze, split 6 cleave, cranny 7 blemish, crackle, crevice, crevise, fissure 8 fracture 9 witticism 10 proficient

crack down on: 5 quash 6 attack 7 repress 10 discipline

crack up: 5 amuse, crash, extol, smash 8 collapse 9 break down

crackbrain: 8 crackpot 9 ding-a-ling, screwball

crackbrained: 5 crazy, kooky, nutty 7 erratic 12 unreasonable

cracker: 4 bake, liar 5 wafer 7 biscuit, boaster, breaker, burster, redneck, saltine, snapper 8 braggart, Georgian 11 firecracker

Cracker State: 7 Georgia

crackle: 4 snap 5 break, crack 7 brustle, crinkle, sparkle, sputter 9 crackling, crepitate

crackpot: nut 4 kook, loon 5 crank 7 erratic, lunatic 9 screwball

cracksman: 4 yegg 7 burglar, peteman

cradle: bed, cot 4 crib, rest, rock 5 cader, frame 6 creche 7 berceau, shelter 8 bassinet, cunabula 9 framework 11 incunabulum

song: 7 lullaby 8 berceuse

craft (see also **boat**): art, job 4 boat 5 fraud, guile, skill, trade 6 deceit, metier, talent, vessel 7 ability, know-how 8 aptitude, artifice, vocation 9 dexterity 10 employment, occupation 12 skillfulness

craftsman: 4 hand 5 navvy 6 artist, potter, weaver, writer 7 artisan, builder, workman 8 mechanic 9 artificer, carpenter

crafty: sly 4 arch, foxy, wily 5 adept 6 adroit, astute, callid, shrewd, subtle, tricky 7 cunning, vulpine 8 captious, fetching 9 cautelous, deceitful, ingenious 10 fallacious, fraudulent 13 Machiavellian 15 Mephistophelean

crag: tor 4 craw, neck, rock, scar, spur 5 arete, brack, cliff 6 throat 9 precipice

craggy: 5 harsh, rough 6 abrupt, knotty, rugged

crake: 4 bird, crow, rail, rook 5 raven 8 railbird

cram: wad 4 bone, fill, glut, pack, stow, urge 5 crowd, crush, drive, force, gorge, grind, learn, press, study, stuff, teach 6 bone up, review 7 jam-pack, squeeze

cramp: 4 coop, kink, pain 5 crick, crowd, pinch, stunt 6 hamper, hinder, knotty 7 confine 8 compress, contract, restrain, restrict 9 constrict, difficult 11 contraction

one's style: 5 queer 9 frustrate
cranberry: 7 pembina 8 bilberry, foxberry 9 mossberry, sourberry
habitat: bog
crane: job 4 bird, grus 5 davit, heron, jenny, raise, wader 6 sarsus 7 derrick, stretch 9 cormorant 10 wading bird
arm: gib, jib 6 gibbet 7 ramhead
charges: 7 cranage
genus: 4 grus
Malayan: 5 sarus
neck: 4 gaze 5 stare
pert. to: 6 gruine
ship: 5 davit
small: 10 demoiselle
traveling: 5 jenny, titan 7 goliath
crane fly: 6 tipula
cranial nerve: 4 vagi(pl.) 5 vagus
root: 5 radix 7 radices(pl.)
cranium: pan 4 head 5 skull 8 brainpan
nerve root: 5 radix
part: 7 calotte 8 calvaria
pert. to: 7 cranial
crank: wit 4 bent, crab, kook, sick, weak, whim, wind 5 brace, loose, rogue, shaky, winch 6 ailing, boldly, grouch, handle, infirm 7 awkward, bracket, fanatic, lustily 8 crackpot, grumbler, sourpuss 9 distorted, eccentric, sprightly 10 get started, monomaniac, vigorously
cranky: 4 ugly 5 crazy, cross, lusty, shaky, testy 6 ailing, infirm, sickly 7 crooked, grouchy 8 tortuous 9 crotchety, difficult, irritable 10 ill-humored 11 hot-tempered 12 disagreeable
cranny: 4 hole, nook 5 chink, cleft, crack, niche 6 corner 7 crevice, fissure
crap: 5 dregs, money 7 gallows, greaves, rubbish 8 nonsense, sediment
crape: 4 band, curl, friz 5 crepe, crimp, drape, gauze 6 shroud 8 mourning
crapehanger: 7 killjoy 10 spoilsport
crapulence: 7 surfeit 8 gluttony 11 overfeeding 12 intemperance, intoxication
crash: 4 fail, fall 5 blast, burst, cloth, crush, shock, smash, sound, wreck 6 fiasco 7 failure, shatter, smashup 8 collapse, splinter 9 collision
crass: raw 4 dull 5 crude, dense, gross, rough, thick 6 coarse, obtuse, stupid 9 unrefined
crate: box, car 4 case, crib 5 plane, seron 6 basket, cradle, encase, hamper, hurdle 7 canasta, vehicle 9 container 10 receptacle
bar: 4 slat
crater: cup, pit 4 cone, hole 5 fovea 6 cavity, hollow 7 caldera 10 depression
edge: lip
cravat: tie 4 neck 5 ascot, scarf, stock 7 bandage, necktie, overlay 8 crumpler 9

neckcloth 10 fourinhand 11 neckerchief
crave: ask, beg 4 long, need, pray, seek 5 covet, yearn 6 desire, hanker, hunger, thirst 7 beseech, entreat, implore, request, require, solicit 10 supplicate
craven: 6 afraid, coward, scared 7 dastard 8 cowardly, defeated, overcome, poltroon, recreant, sneaking 10 vanquished 11 lily-livered 12 fainthearted
craw: maw 4 crop 7 stomach 9 ingluvies
crawl: lag 4 drag, fawn, inch, ramp, swim 5 creep, kraal 6 cringe, grovel, scride 7 slither
crayfish: 4 crab 5 yabby 6 yabbie 7 crawdad, lobster 8 cambarus, crawfish 9 ecrevisse 10 crustacean
crayon: 4 plan 5 chalk 6 pastel, pencil, sketch 7 drawing
craze: fad 4 flaw, mode, rage 5 break, crack, crush, furor, mania, vogue 6 defect, impair, madden, weaken, whimsy 7 derange, destroy, fashion, shatter, whimsey 8 distract 9 bedlamize, infirmity 10 dernier cri 11 infatuation
crazed: mad, ree 4 amok, loco, wild, wood, zany 5 balmy, batty, daffy, dotty, manic, nutty, potty, wacky 6 coocoo, dottle, insane, looney 7 lunatic 8 deleerit, delieret, demented, deranged 10 crackbrain, distraught
crazy: mad 4 gaga, luny, nuts 5 batty, daffy, goofy, silly, wacky 6 absurd, cuckoo, insane, looney, maniac, teched 7 bananas, bonkers, cracked, lunatic 8 crackpot, demented 9 possessed 10 crackbrain, unbalanced 11 harebrained 12 preposterous
creak: gig 4 rasp, yirr 5 cheep(Sc.), croak, grind, groan 6 squeak 8 complain
cream: 4 beat, best, pick, whip 5 creme, elite, froth, sauce 6 bonbon 8 emulsion, ointment
cream of tartar: 5 argol
cream puff: 6 pastry 8 weakling
creamery: 5 dairy
creamy: 4 rich 5 reamy 6 smooth 8 luscious
crease: 4 fold, lirk, ruck, ruga, seam 5 crimp, pleat 6 furrow, rimple 7 crumple, wrinkle
create: 4 coin, form, make, plan 5 build, cause, forge, shape, write 6 design, invent 7 compose, fashion, imagine, produce 8 generate 9 establish, originate
creation: 5 world 6 cosmos, effect 7 fashion, product 8 creature, universe 9 macrocosm 10 production 11 masterpiece
creative: 9 demiurgic, inventive 10 innovative, productive 12 constructive
creativity: 6 genius

creator: 5 maker 6 author 7 founder 8 designer 9 architect 10 originator

creature (see also **animal**): man 4 tool 5 beast, being, slave, thing 6 animal, minion, person, wretch 8 hellicat(Sc.) 9 dependent 10 animalcule, individual

fabled: elf 4 puck 5 gnome 6 dragon, merman 7 centaur, mermaid

ogre: 5 pixie 6 wyvern

creche: 4 crib 6 manager 7 nursery

credence: 5 faith, trust 6 belief, buffet, credit 8 credenza 10 acceptance, confidence 11 reliability 15 trustworthiness

credential: 7 voucher 8 credence 11 certificate, testimonial

credenza: 5 niche, shelf, table 6 buffet 8 credence, cupboard 9 sideboard

credible: 6 likely 7 credent 8 probable 9 authentic, plausible, reputable 11 trustworthy 12 satisfactory

credit: 4 deem, feel, loan 5 asset, chalk, faith, honor, merit, tenet, trust 6 belief, charge, esteem, impute, renown, repute, weight 7 ascribe, believe 8 accredit, credence 10 estimation 11 recognition

credulous: 4 fond 5 naive 6 unwary 8 credible, gullible

creed: ism 4 cult, sect 5 credo, dogma, faith, tenet 6 belief 7 trowing 8 doctrine 10 confession

Christian: 6 Nicene 8 Apostle's

creek: bay, ria, rio 4 burn(Sc.), cove, kill, pill, rill, slue 5 bayou, bight, bogue, brook, crick, fleet, inlet, zanja 6 arroyo, estero, Indian, slough, stream 7 estuary, freshet, rivulet 11 watercourse

creel: 4 caul, cawl, rack, trap 6 basket, junket

creep: 4 fawn, inch, ramp 5 crawl, prowl, skulk, slink, steal 6 cringe, grovel, scride 7 cramble, gumshoe 9 pussyfoot

creeper: ivy 4 shoe, vine, worm 5 snake 6 ipecac, romper, tecoma

creeping: 4 slow 7 reptant, servile 9 reptilian 11 reptatorial

creese: 4 kris, stab 5 sword 6 dagger, weapon

cremate: 4 burn 9 incremate 10 incinerate

Cremona: 5 Amati 6 violin

crena: 5 cleft, notch 7 scallop 11 indentation

crenic acid salt: 7 crenate

creole: 6 patois 7 mestizo

Creole State: 9 Louisiana

crepe: 6 fabric 7 frizzed, pancake 8 crinkled, wrinkled

crepey cloth: 6 plissé

crepitate: 4 snap 6 rattle 7 crackle

crepuscule: 8 twilight

crescent: 4 horn, lune, moon, rool 5 curve, lunar 6 lunule 7 lunette, menis-

ci(pl.) 8 meniscus 10 semicircle

point: 4 cusp

crescent-shaped: 6 bicorn, lunate 7 lunated, lunular 9 semilunar

crescive: 7 growing 10 increasing

cresset: 5 torch 6 basket, beacon, signal 7 furnace 8 flambeau

crest: cop, tip, top 4 acme, apex, comb, edge, knap, peak, seal, tuft 5 chine, crown, plume, ridge 6 apogee, climax, copple, crista, finial, height, helmet, summit 7 bearing 8 pinnacle, whitecap 10 cognizance 11 culmination

rugged: 6 arete

crested: 6 muffed 7 crisate, crowned 8 pileated 9 coronated

crestfallen: low 4 blue, down 5 cowed 8 dejected 10 dispirited 11 downhearted 12 disconsolate

creta: 5 chalk

cretaceous: 6 chalky

Crete: 6 Candia

cape: 4 krio 5 krios

city: Hag 5 Canea(c.), Khora 6 Kisamo, Malemi, Mallia, Meleme, Retimo 7 Kasteli 8 Nikolacs, Sphakion 9 Heraclion, Tympakion 11 Palaiokhora

earth spirit: 6 Curete

flier: 6 Icarus

goddess: 8 Dictynna 11 Britomartis

king: 5 Minos 9 Idomeneus

language: 6 Minoan

man of brass: 5 Talos

maze: 9 labyrinth

monster: 8 minotaur

mountain: Ida 5 Dikte 9 Psiloriti

princess: 7 Ariadne

seaport: 5 Canea 6 Candia, Khania

Cretheus: *son:* 8 Amythaon

wife: 7 Biadice

cretin: 5 idiot

Creusa: *father:* 5 Priam

husband: 6 Aeneas

mother: 6 Hecuba

son: 8 Ascanius

crevasse: 5 chasm, split 8 cleavage

crevice: 4 bore, leak, nook, seam, vein 5 break, chine, chink, cleft, crack, grike 6 cranny 7 fissure, opening 8 cleavage, crevasse, peephole 10 interstice

crew: men, mob, set 4 band, gang, herd, oars, team 5 covey, group, hands, party, squad, staff 6 seamen, throng 7 company, faculty, members, retinue 8 equipage, mariners 10 assemblage, complement

crewel: 6 caddis 7 caddice 10 crewelwork, embroidery

crib: bed, bin, box, cab, cot, cub, hut, key 4 boom, dive, pony, rack, raft, trot 5 boose, boosy, cheat, crate, frame, hovel, stall, steal 6 bunker, cratch, creche,

manger, pilfer **7** purloin **8** cribbage **9**
enclosure **10** plagiarize, storehouse
cribbage score: nob, peg
crick: 4 kink **5** creek, hitch, spasm, twist
cricket: 4 game, grig **6** insect
  genus: **7** gryllus
  run: bye
  side: ons
  sound: **5** chirp **12** stridulation
  team: **6** eleven
  term: off, ons, rot **4** over **5** smick **6** yorker
crier: 4 huer **5** cryer **6** beadle, herald,
  wailer **7** muezzin
crime: act, sin **4** evil **5** abuse, arson,
  blame, wrong **6** felony, murder, piacle **7**
  misdeed, offense **8** iniquity **9** violation
  10 wickedness **11** abomination, malefaction, misdemeanor **13** transgression
  ecclesiastical: **6** simony
  goddess of: Ate
  organized: **10** underworld
  scene of: **5** venue
Crimea: 4 Krym
  capital: **10** Simferopol
  city: **5** Kerch, Yalta **10** Sevastopol
  people: **5** Tauri
  river: **4** Alma
  sea: **4** Azof, Azov
  seaport: **9** Balaklava
criminal: bad **4** yegg **5** crook, felon **6**
  guilty, inmate, nocent, slayer, wicked **7**
  convict, culprit, illegal **8** culpable, gangster **9** desperado, wrongdoer **10** blackguard, deplorable, flagitious, malefactor,
  malfeasant **11** blameworthy, disgraceful
  13 reprehensible
  habitual: **8** repeater **10** recidivist
  refuge: **7** Alsatia **11** Whitefriars
criminology branch: 8 penology
crimp: bit, rub **4** bend, curl, fold, friz,
  pote, wave, weak **5** cramp, flute, frizz,
  pinch, plait **6** goffer, hold in, ruffle **7**
  crinkle, friable, gauffer, wrinkle **8** hold
  back, obstacle **9** corrugate **12** inconsistent
crimson: dye, lac, red **4** pink, rose **5**
  blush, color, rouge **6** bloody, maroon,
  modena **7** carmine, scarlet
crine: 4 hair, mane **6** shrink **7** shrivel
cringe: bow **4** bend, fawn, jouk **5** binge,
  cower, crawl, quail, sneak, stoop, toady,
  wince, yield **6** crouch, grovel, shrink,
  submit **7** crinkle, distort, truckle **8**
  bootlick **11** apple-polish
cringing: 6 abject **7** hangdog
cringle: orb **4** disk **6** eyelet, terret **7**
  grommet
crinite: 5 hairy **6** fossil
crinitory: 5 hairy **7** crinose
crinkle: 4 bend, curl, kink, turn, wind **5**
  crimp, plica, ridge **6** pucker, ripple,
  ruck up, rumple, rustle **7** crackle, wrin-

kle **9** corrugate **11** convolution
cripple: mar **4** halt, harm, hurt, lame,
  main, wing **6** bacach, hobble, impair,
  injure, scotch, spavin, weaken **7** crap-
  ple, crumpet, disable, lamiter(Sc.) **8** enfeeble, handicap, mutilate, paralyze **9**
  hamstring **12** incapacitate
crisis: 4 acme, crux, pass, turn **5** panic,
  peril, pinch, trial **6** strait **8** decision,
  juncture **9** criterion, emergency, crossroads **11** conjunction **12** turning point
  having no: **9** acritical
crisp: new **4** cold **5** brisk, clear, curly,
  fresh, nippy, pithy, sharp, short, stiff,
  terse **6** biting, bright, lively **7** bracing,
  brittle, concise, cutting, friable **8** clear-
  cut **9** crackling, trenchant
crispin: 4 coat **9** shoemaker
crisscross: 4 awry **7** network **8** confused
  9 intersect
cristate: 6 ridged, tufted **7** crested
criterion: low **4** norm, rule, test, type **5**
  axiom, canon, gauge, nodel, proof **6**
  metric **7** measure **8** standard **9** yardstick **10** indication, touchstone
critic: 5 booer, judge, momus **6** carper,
  censor, expert, slater **8** collator, reviewer **9** detractor, literator, muckraker, nit-
  picker **11** connoisseur, criticaster,
  faultfinder
critical: 4 dire, edge **5** acute, exact **6** urgent **7** carping, exigent **8** captious, decisive, exacting **10** censorious, fastidious
  12 faultfinding **14** discriminating
  mark: **6** obelus **7** obelisk
  study: **6** examen **8** exegesis
criticism: 5 blame **6** review **7** comment **8**
  critique, diatribe, judgment **9** stricture
  10 assessment, commentary **13** animadversion
criticize: hit, pan, rap, rip **4** carp, flay,
  slam, slur, yelp **5** blame, blast, cavil,
  judge, knock, roast **6** jeer at, rebuke, review **7** censure, comment, examine **8**
  critique **9** castigate **10** animadvert
Crius: *father:* **6** Uranus
  mother: **4** Gaea, Gaia
  sister: **7** Eurybia
  son: **8** Astraeus
croak: caw, die **4** gasp, kill **5** creak, quark,
  speak, **6** grouch, grouse **7** forbode,
  grumble **8** complain
Croatia: *capital:* **5** Agram **6** Zagreb
  city: **5** Fiume, Rieka, Split **6** Osijek, Rijeka
  mountain: **6** Kapela
  people: **4** Serb, Slav, Sorb, Wend **5** Sclav **6**
  Hrvati **7** Hervati, Slovene **8** Croatian,
  European
crochet: 4 hoot, knit **5** braid, plait, weave
crock: jar, pig, pot **4** bull, smut, soil, soot
  5 stool **6** critch, smudge **8** potsherd **11**
  earthenware

crockery: 5 china, cloam 6 dishes, plates 11 earthenware

crocodile: goa 5 gator 6 cayman, gavial, jacare, mugger 7 reptile 9 alligator
genus: 11 goniopholis

crocus: 4 irid, lily 7 saffron

Croesus: 4 king 9 moneybags, plutocrat
country: 5 Lydia

croft: 4 farm 5 crypt, field, garth, vault 6 bleach, cavern

cromlech: 5 quoit 6 circle, dolmen 7 gorsedd 9 cyclolith

Cromwell: 4 Noll 6 Oliver
regiment: 9 Ironsides
son: 7 Richard
son-in-law: 6 Ireton
victory site: 6 Naseby

crone: hag 4 cive 5 biddy, witch 6 beldam 7 beldame 9 cailleach, cailliach

Cronus: 5 Titan
daughter: 4 Hera 6 Hestia 7 Demeter
father: 6 Uranus
mother: 4 Gaea
sister: 6 Cybele, Tethys
son: 4 Zeus 5 Hades 7 Jupiter, Neptune 8 Poseidon
wife: 4 Rhea 6 Cybele

crony: pal 4 chum 9 associate, companion

crook: 4 bend, turn, warp 5 cheat, cleek, crump, curve, pedum, staff, thief, trick 6 robber 7 crosier, crozier 8 artifice, swindler 10 camshachle(Sc.)

crooked: cam 4 agee, awry, bent 5 agley(Sc.), askew, false, gleed, lying, snaky, snide 6 akimbo, artful, aslant, crabby, crafty, curved, errant, shifty, tricky, zigzag 7 askance, asquint, corrupt, crabbed, oblique, turning, twisted, winding 8 tortuous 9 dishonest, distorted, irregular 10 circuitous, fraudulent, misleading 12 dishonorable, unscrupulous

croon: hum, low 4 boom, lull, sing, wail 5 chirm, whine 6 lament, murmur 8 complain

crop: cut, maw, top 4 clip, craw, knap, reap, trim, whip 5 fruit, quirt, shear 6 gather, gebbie, silage 7 curtail, harvest, tillage 8 gleaning, ingulies
goddess of: 6 Annona
second growth: 5 rowen
year's: 6 annona

cropper: 8 collapse, disaster

croquet: 5 roque

croquette: 5 cecil, 6 oyster

crosier, crozier: 5 crook, cross, staff

cross: go; mix 4 ford, rood, span 5 angry, testy, trial 6 bisect, crabby, cranky, crouch, emblem, gibbet, grumpy, outwit, signum, sullen, symbol, thwart, touchy 7 athwart, crabbed, fretful, froward, oblique, peevish, pettish, potence, sell out 8 crotched, crucifix, petulant, snappish, suastica, swastika, traverse, vexillum 9 frustrate, half-breed, intersect, irritable, plaintive 10 affliction, ill-humored, transverse 12 disagreeable 13 quick-tempered
barred: 11 trabeculate
fiery: 8 crantara 9 crostarie
Greek: 6 fylfot
stroke: 5 serif 6 ceriph
swords: 4 duel 5 fight 6 combat
tau: 4 crux 5 ankih
type: 5 Greek, Latin, Papal 6 Celtic, fleuré, formée, moline 7 Maltese 8 Egyptian
wires: 7 confuse

cross-examine: 5 grill 8 question 11 interrogate

cross-eye: 6 squint 9 esotropia 10 strabismus

cross-grained: 7 gnarled 8 churlish, perverse 9 irascible 12 cantankerous

cross out: 4 dele 5 blank, erase 6 cancel, delete 9 eliminate

cross-rib: 4 arch 6 lierne

cross section: 4 part 14 representation

crossbar: 4 axle, rung 5 round 10 horizontal

crossbeam: bar 5 trave 6 girder

crossbow: 6 weapon 8 arbalest

crossbreed: 5 husky 6 hybrid 9 hybridize

crosshatch: 7 engrave

crossing: 7 passage 8 opposing

crosspatch: 4 bear, crab 6 grouch

crosspiece: bar 4 spar, yoke 5 grill 8 crossarm 10 doubletree

crossroads: 4 pass 5 pinch 6 crisis 8 zero hour 9 carrefour 12 interaction, turning point
goddess: 6 Hecate, Hekate, Trivia

crossruff: 6 seesaw 9 alternate

crosswise: 6 across 7 athwart 8 acrostic, diagonal

crotch: 4 fork, pole, post 5 cleft, notch, stake 9 stanchion

crotchet: fad 4 hook, kink, whim 5 fancy 6 vagary 9 conundrum 11 peculiarity 12 eccentricity

crotchery: 6 cranky 10 capricious

crotch: 4 bend, fawn, ruck 5 cower, hunch, squat, stoop 6 cringe 7 scrooch

crouching: 8 couchant

crouton: bit 5 toast 7 garnish

crow: aga, caw, cry, daw, jay 4 bird, brag, rook 5 boast, exult, raven, vaunt 6 carnal, corvas, magpie 7 grapnel, jackdaw, swagger 9 blackbird
colony: 7 rookery
cry: caw
pert. to: 7 corvine

crow-like: 7 corvine

crowbar: pry 5 jemmy, jimmy, lever 7

gablock **8** gavelock

crowd: jam, mob, set **4** bike, cram, herd, host, pack, push, rock, rout, stow, swad **5** bunch, cramp, crush, drove, flock, group, horde, posse, press, serry, shoal, swarm, three, wedge **6** boodle, clique, hubble, huddle, jostle, rabble, throng **7** bourock(Sc.), company, squeeze **9** multitude **10** assemblage, clamjamfry(Sc.), confluence

penetrate: **5** elbow **6** needle

crowded: **4** full **5** close, dense, thick **6** filled, jammed, loaded, packed **7** bunched, compact, serried, stipate, stuffed, teeming **9** chock-full, congested

crowder: **6** loader **7** fiddler **8** thatcher

crown: cap, top **4** coin, pate, peak, poll **5** adorn, basil, bezel, bezil, crest, miter, mitre, tiara **6** anadem, circle, climax, corona(L.), diadem, fillet, invest, laurel, potong, reward, summit, trophy, wreath **7** aureole, chaplet, coronet, garland, install **8** coronate, enthrone, pinnacle, surmount **9** finish off, headdress, sovereign

pert. to: **8** coronal

crown prince: **4** heir **8** atheling

cru: **8** vineyard

crucial: **4** dire **5** acute, vital **6** severe, trying **7** pivotal, telling **8** critical, decisive **9** important, necessary

crucible: pot **4** dish, etna, test **6** cruset, ordeal, retort **7** furnace **10** affliction **11** climacteric

crucifix: pax **4** rood **5** cross

crucify: vex **4** hang, kill **5** harry **6** martyr **7** mortify, torment, torture **8** cruciate **9** persecute

crud: goo **4** curd, gook, gunk, junk **5** filth, slime, trash **6** refuse **7** thicken

crude: raw **4** bald, bare, rude **5** crass, green, harsh, rough **6** callow, coarse, savage, unripe, vulgar **7** uncouth **8** immature, impolite **9** primitive, unglossed, unrefined, untrained **10** incomplete, unpolished **11** undeveloped **13** inexperienced

cruel: **4** fell, hard **5** harsh **6** bloody, brutal, fierce, savage, severe, unjust, unkind **7** bestial, brutish, inhuman, neronic **8** barbaric, diabolic, fiendish, inhumane, pitiless, ruthless, sadistic, tyrannic **9** atrocious, draconian, ferocious, heartless, merciless, rapacious, unfeeling **10** diabolical, sanguinary, vindictive **11** hardhearted

cruet: ama, jar, jug **4** vial **5** cruse **6** bottle, caster, guttus, vessel **7** ampulla, burette **9** container

cruise: **4** boat, sail, trip **6** voyage **9** excursion

cruiser: **4** ship **6** vessel **7** warship **9** patrol car, powerboat

cruising: **4** asea

cruller: **7** olycook, olykoek **8** doughnut **9** friedcake

crumb: bit, ort **5** piece, scrap, shred **6** little, morsel **7** remnant, smidgen, smidgin **8** fragment, particle

crumb covered: **7** breaded

crumble: rot **5** break, crush, decay, slake, spoil **6** molder, perish **7** moulder **9** break down, decompose, pulverize **12** disintegrate

crumbly: **7** friable

crumpet: **4** cake **6** muffin **7** pikelet

crumple: **4** fold, muss **5** crush **6** crease, furrow, raffle, rumple **7** crunkle, wrinkle **8** collapse, contract **9** corrugate

crunch: **4** bite, chew **5** chomp, crump, crush, gnash, grind, munch, press **6** cranch **7** craunch, scrunch **8** ruminate **9** masticate

cruor: **4** gore **5** blood

crural joint: **4** knee

crus: **5** shank

crusade: war **5** jehad, jihad **8** campaign **10** expedition

crusader: **7** pilgrim, Templar **8** reformer

enemy: **7** Saladin, Saracen

port: **4** Acre

crush: bow, jam **4** cram, dash, mash, mill, mull **5** brake, break, crash, craze, crowd, force, grind, press, quash, quell, smash, tread, unman **6** bruise, burden, crunch, squash, subdue, thwack **7** conquer, crumple, depress, destroy, oppress, overrun, repress, scrunch, scrunge, shatter, squeeze, squelch **8** bear down, compress, demolish, overcome, suppress **9** overpower, overwhelm, pulverize **10** annihilate, obliterate

crust: **4** cake, hull, rind **5** shell **6** eschar, harden **7** coating **8** pellicle

crustacean: **4** crab, flea, scud **5** louse, prawn **6** endite, isopod, shrimp **7** lobster, squilla **8** barnacle **9** water flea **10** whale louse

appendage: **5** exite **6** endite **7** pleopod

claw: **5** chela **6** pincer

feeler: **7** antenna

genus: **5** eryon, hippa **6** tripos

group: **7** caridea

larva: **5** alima, **8** nauplius

limb: **6** podite **8** podomere

small: **6** isopod **7** copepod **8** barnacle

ten-footed: **4** crab

crusty: **4** curt **5** bluff, blunt, crisp, gruff, surly, testy **6** morose **7** crabbed, peevish, pettish **8** choleric, snappish **11** ill-tempered

crux: nub **4** ankh, core, gist, pith **5** cross, point **6** kernel, puzzle, riddle **7** problem **9** substance **10** difficulty

cry (see also **exclamation**): boo, caw, cri(F.), fad, hue, ole, sob, yip **4** bawl, bump, call, evoe, hawk, hoot, howl, keen, mewl, pule, rage, scry, wail, weep, yell, yelp **5** clepe, crede, greet, groan, rumor, shout, sound, utter, vogue, whewl, whine **6** bellow, boohoo, clamor, demand, lament, outcry, quethe, scream, shriek, slogan, snivel, squeal, squall, wimick, yammer **7** clamour, exclaim, fashion, screech **8** proclaim **11** acclamation, lamentation

court: **4** oyes, oyez

derisive: bah, boo **4** hiss, hoot **6** phooey **7** catcall

for: **4** need **6** demand, desire

gang's signal: **4** whyo

havoc: **8** mobilize

of approval: ole, rah **5** bravo

of pain: **4** ouch

of relief: **4** phew, whew

of sorrow: woe **4** alas **5** alack

of triumph: aha **6** hurrah

out: bay **4** bawl, hoot, howl **5** blame, crake, deery **7** censure, exclaim, protest **8** complain, denounce

political: **6** slogan **10** shibboleth

Cry the Beloved Country author: **5** Paton

crying: **4** dire **6** urgent **7** burning, clamant, heinous **8** pressing, recreant **9** notorious **11** exclamatory

crying bird: **7** limpkin

crying hare: **4** pika

crying out: **10** childbirth **11** confinement

crypt: pit **4** cave, cell **5** croft, vault **6** cavern, grotto, recess **7** chamber **8** follicle **10** depression

cryptic: **4** dark **5** murky, vague **6** hidden, occult, secret **7** obscure **9** enigmatic, recondite **10** mysterious **12** hieroglyphic

cryptogram: **4** code **6** cipher **11** cryptograph

crystal: ice **4** dial, hard **5** clear, glass, lucid **6** limpid, pebble **7** acicula, diamond **8** clear-cut, pellucid **11** crystalline, transparent

gazer: **4** seer **7** seeress

ice: **6** frazil

twin: **5** macle

crystalline: **4** pure **7** crystal **8** pellucid **11** transparent

acid: **7** alanine

compound: **5** alban **6** anisil, oscine **7** aconite, amarine **8** atropine

mineral: **4** mica, spar **6** quartz **7** apatite **8** boracite, elaterin

phenol: **5** orcin **6** orcine

pine tar: **6** retene

salt: **5** borax **8** analgene, racemate

structure: **6** sparry **8** siderite

substance: **4** urea **6** dulcin **9** scopoline

crystallize: **5** candy, sugar **7** congeal **8** solidify **9** granulate

cub: fry, pen **4** bear, coop, shed **5** stall, whelp **6** lionet, novice **7** codling **8** reporter **9** youngster

Cuba: *bay:* **4** Nipe, Pigs **10** Guantanamo

beverage: **4** pina

bird: **6** trogon **8** tocororo

capital: **6** Havana

carriage: **7** volante

castle: **5** Morro

chief export: **5** sugar

cigar: **6** Havana

city: **6** Guines **7** Palmira **8** Camaguey, Matanzas, Santiago **10** Cienfuegos, Santa Clara **14** Puerto Principe

dance: **5** conga, rumba **6** danzon, rhumba

dollar: **6** gourde

fish: **6** diablo **7** viajaca

hutia: **6** pilori

measure: **4** vara **5** bocoy, tarea **6** cordel, fanega **10** caballeria

monetary unit: **4** peso **7** centavo **8** cuarenta

mountain: **6** Copper **11** Pinar del Rio **12** Guaniguanico **13** Pico Turquinos

premier: **6** Castro

province: **6** Havana **7** Oriente **8** Camaguey, Matanzas **10** Santa Clara **11** Pinar del Rio

rodent: **5** hutia **6** pilori

root: **7** malanga

rum: **7** Bacardi

secret police: **5** porra

snake: **4** juba

storm: **6** bayamo

tobacco: **4** capa **6** vuelta

U.S. naval base: **10** Guantanamo

tree: **4** cuya **5** culla, jique

ward: **6** barrio

weapon: **7** machete

weight: **5** libra **6** tercio

cubbyhole: **4** nook

cube: cut, die **4** dice **5** block, solid **10** hexahedron

cube spar: **9** anhydrite

cubic: **5** solid **9** isometric

decimeter: **5** liter, litre

meter: **5** stere

shape: **6** cuboid

cubicle: bay **4** cell, room **5** booth, niche **6** alcove

cubitus: **4** ulna **7** forearm

Cuchulain, Cuchullin: **7** warrior

father: Lug

foe: **5** Maeve

kingdom: **6** Ulster

mother: **8** Dechtire

son: **8** Conlaoch

wife: **4** Emer **5** Eimer

cuckoo: ani 4 bird, fool, gowk, koel 5 clock, crazy, silly 7 boobook 8 rainfowl 10 road runner
  kind: 6 coucal, kobird 7 dowbird, wryneck 8 coccyzus

cuckoopint: 4 arum 5 aaron, plant 6 bobbin, dragon 7 buckram 8 mandrake 9 wake-robin

cucullate: 6 cowled, hooded 7 covered 10 hood-shaped

cucumber: 4 cuke, pepo, gourd 6 conger, pepino(Sp.), pickle 7 gherkin 9 elaterium

cud: chew, quid 5 bolus, rumen 6 cudgel

cuddle: hug, pet 6 caress, cosset, fondle, nestle 7 embrace, snuggle

cuddy: ass 4 lout 5 bribe, cabin 6 donkey, galley, pantry 9 blockhead

cudgel: bat 4 beat, cane, club, drub, rack 5 baste, drive, kebby, kevel, staff, stave, stick 6 alpeen, ballow, baston, kebbie, thrash, weapon 7 belabor, bourdon 8 bludgeon, shillala 9 bastinado, blackjack, crabstick, fustigate, truncheon 10 nightstick, shillelagh

cue: nod, tip 4 hint, mast, tail, wink 5 braid, cluff, plait, queue, twist 6 prompt, signal 7 pigtail 9 catchword 10 intimation

cuff: box 4 bank, blow, gowf, slam, slap, slug, swat 5 clout, fight, gowff, miser, smite, spank 6 buffet, codger, mitten, strike, wallop 7 scuffle 8 gauntlet, handcuff

cuirass: 4 mail 5 armor, loric, plate 6 lorica, thorax

cuisine: 4 food, menu 5 table 7 cookery

cul-de-sac: 6 pocket, strait 7 deadend, impasse 10 blind alley, difficulty

culicid: 8 mosquito

cull: opt 4 dupe, gull, pick, sift, sort 5 elect, glean, pluck 6 assort, choose, gather, remove, select 8 separate 9 single out

culm: 5 slack 6 refuse 7 deposit

culmen: top 4 acme 5 ridge

culmination: end 4 acme, apex, noon, peak 5 crown 6 apogee, climax, summit, vertex, zenith 10 completion 11 ne plus ultra 12 consummation

culpa: 5 fault, guilt 10 negligence 2 carelessness

culpable: 6 faulty, guilty, laches 7 immoral 8 criminal 10 censurable 11 blameworthy 3 reprehensible

culprit: 5 felon 7 convict 8 criminal, offender 10 malefactor

cult: 4 clan, sect 5 creed, faith 6 church, ritual, school 7 worship 8 religion 12 denomination

cultivate: ear, hoe 4 disk, farm, grow, plow, rear, tend, till, work 5 nurse, raise, study, train 6 affect, foster, harrow, plough 7 acquire, cherish, educate, husband, improve, nourish, prepare 8 civilize 9 encourage

cultivated: 5 civil 6 polite 7 genteel, refined 8 cultured, well-bred 12 domesticated
  land: 4 farm 5 arada, tilth

cultivation: 6 polish 7 culture, tillage 9 culturing, husbandry 10 refinement 12 civilization
  art: 9 geoponics

cultivator: 6 farmer, harrow, tiller 7 grubber, husband 10 husbandman

culture: art 4 agar 5 taste 6 polish 7 tillage 9 knowledge 10 discipline, refinement 11 savoir faire 12 civilization 13 enlightenment
  medium: 4 agar

culver: 4 dove 6 pigeon

culvert: 5 drain, sluit 6 bridge 7 conduit 8 overpass

cumbersome: 5 heavy 6 clumsy 7 awkward, onerous, weighty 8 cumbrous, unwieldy 10 burdensome

cumbrous: 8 clogging, unwieldy 9 difficult, vexatious 10 burdensome, cumbersome

cumin: 5 anise, cumic

cummerbund: 4 band, belt, sash

cumshaw: tip 5 bonus 6 thanks 7 present 8 gratuity

cumulate: 4 heap 5 amass, lay up 6 gather 7 combine 9 stockpile 10 accumulate

cunabula: 6 cradle

cuneal: 7 cuneate 11 wedge-shaped

cuneiform: 4 bone 6 wedged 7 writing 8 sphenoid

cunner: 5 canoe 6 nipper, wrasse

cunning: sly, wit 4 arch, cute, foxy, keen, wily 5 downy, guile, sharp, smart 6 adroit, artful, astute, callid, clever, crafty, deadal, deceit, shrewd, subtle, tricky, wisdom 7 curious, finesse, know-how, politic, vulpine 8 dextrous, skillful, stealthy 9 chicanery, colubrine, designing, dexterity, ingenious, knowledge, sagacious 10 fraudulent, witchcraft 3 Machiavellian

cup: ama, dop, mug, tyg 4 tass, toby 5 bouse, calix, cruse, glass, grail, phial, stein, tazza 6 beaker, crater, goblet, noggin, potion, vessel 7 chalice, stirrup, tankard
  assay: 4 test 5 cupel 6 beaker
  diamond cutting: dop
  eared: 6 quaich, quaigh
  earthenware: mug
  fungus: 6 aecium
  handle: ear, lug
  holder: 4 zarf

horn-shaped: 6 holmos
large: 5 grail, jorum
looped handles: 5 kylix 9 cantharus, kantharos
loving: tyg 5 award, prize
of tea: 5 forte, thing 6 metier
pastry: 7 dariole
resembling: 9 oalicular
small: 4 shot 5 chark, cruse 6 noggin 8 cannikin 9 demitasse
sports: 5 Davis, Ryder 6 Curtis 7 Stanley 8 America's, Wightman
two-handled: tig, tyg 5 depas
cup-shaped: 8 pezizoid, scypliate 10 cyathiform
cupbearer of the gods: 4 Hebe 8 Ganymede
cupboard: kas 4 case, safe 5 ambry, cuddy 6 buffet, closet, larder, pantry 7 armoire, cabinet, dresser 8 credenza 9 sideboard
cupel: 4 burn, test 6 refine
Cupid: Dan 4 Amor, Eros, love 7 Amorino
beloved of: 6 Psyche
mother: 5 Venus
cupidity: 4 lust 5 greed 6 desire 7 avarice, avidity, longing 8 appetite 12 covetousness
demon of: 6 Mammon
cupola: 4 dome, kiln 5 vault 6 turret 7 furnace, lantern, lookout
cur: cad, dog, yap 4 fice, mutt, tike, toad, tyke 5 feist 6 canine, messan, messin, rotter 7 bobtail, mongrel 9 goldeneye, yellow dog
curacao: 7 liqueur
Curacao island: 5 Aruba
curare: 5 urare, urari 6 oorali, poison
curassow: 4 crax, mitu 8 game bird
curate: cur 4 abbe 5 agent 7 dominie, vicaire 8 minister 9 assistant, clergyman
curative: 7 healing 8 remedial, salutary, sanative 9 medicinal 11 restorative, therapeutic 12 invigorating
curator: 6 keeper 7 manager, steward 8 guardian, overseer 9 custodian 14 superintendent
curb: bit 4 foil, rein 5 brake, check, curve, guard, limit 6 arrest, bridle, govern, hamper, thwart 7 control, inhibit, repress, shackle 8 hold back, hold down, moderate, restrain, restrict, withhold 9 constrain, hindrance 10 hamshackle
curculio: 4 turk 6 weevil
curd: See **curdle**
curdle: 4 clot, earn(Sc.), leep, quar, sour, yern 5 quail, quarl, spoil 6 posset, quarle 7 clabber, congeal, thicken 8 condense 9 coagulate
agent causing: 6 rennet
cure: age, 4 boot, care, heal, heed, help, jerk, salt, save 5 reest, smoke 6 charge,

curacy, physic, remedy, season 7 restore, therapy 8 antidote, preserve
by smoking: 6 gammon, smudge
in sun: 6 rizzar
skins: 5 dress
cure-all: 4 balm 5 avens 6 elixir, remedy 7 nostrum, panacea 10 catholicon
curfew: 4 bell 6 signal
curio: 5 relic, virtu 6 bauble, gewgaw 7 bibelot 8 keepsake, souvenir 9 bric-a-brac, curiosity, objet d'art 10 knickknack
curious: odd 4 nosy, rare 5 queer 6 prying, quaint 7 cunning, strange, unusual 8 freakish, meddling, peculiar, singular 9 intrusive, wondering 11 inquisitive
curl: 4 bend, coil, kink, lock, roll, wave, wind 5 acker, crisp, tress, twist 6 buckle, frowse, ripple, spiral, writhe 7 crimple, flexure, ringlet, tendril 11 convolution 12 heartbreaker
curled: 5 fuzzy, kinky 7 savoyed
curlew: 4 bird, fute 5 kioea, snipe, whaup 6 marlin, smoker 7 bustard
curlicue: ess 5 caper, curve 6 paraph, squirl 7 souggle 8 flourish, purlicue, squiggle
curling mark: tee
curly: 4 wavy 5 crisp 7 rippled 8 crinkled
curmudgeon: 4 crab 5 churl, miser 6 grouch 7 niggard
currant: 5 berry 6 raisin, rizzar
genus: 5 ribes
currency: 4 cash, coin 5 bills, lucre, money, scrip 6 specie 10 greenbacks 11 legal tender
current: now, way 4 eddy, flow, flux, ford, rife, tide 5 drift, going, rapid, tenor, trend, usual 6 coeval, common, course, living, motion, moving, recent, stream 7 counter, flowing, general, ongoing, present, running, thermal, torrent 8 frequent 9 prevalent 10 prevailing 11 electricity 15 contemporaneous
generator: electromotor
measuring device: 7 ammeter
ocean: 7 riptide 8 undertow 9 maelstrom, whirlpool
pert. to: 7 voltaic
currish: 4 base 7 cynical, ignoble 8 snarling 12 mean-spirited
curry: 4 comb, drub 5 clean, dress, groom 6 bruise, cajole, powder 7 prepare 9 condiment, seasoning
favor: 4 fawn 6 cajole, smooge
curse: ban 4 bane, blow, damn, oath 5 spell, swear 6 malign 7 beshrew, malison 8 anathema 9 blaspheme, imprecate, maranatha 10 execration, vituperate 11 deprecation, malediction 12 anathematize 13 excommunicate
cursed: bad 6 damned, odious 8 blighted,

virulent **9** execrable **13** blankety-blank

cursory: **4** fast **5** brief, hasty, quick, short **6** fitful, speedy **7** passing, shallow, sketchy **8** careless, rambling **9** desultory, irregular, transient **10** discursive, evanescent **11** superficial

curt: **4** rude, tart **5** bluff, blunt, brief, brusk, short, terse **6** abrupt **7** brusque, concise **8** cavalier, succinct **9** condensed

curtail: cut, lop **4** clip, crop, dock, pare, stop **5** abate, short, slash, stunt **6** lessen, reduce, teaser **7** abridge, bobtail, shorten **8** diminish, minorate, retrench **9** decurtate, epitomize **10** abbreviate

curtain: end **4** boom, drop, mask, veil, wall **5** blind, drape, shade **6** purdah, screen, shroud **7** ceiling, conceal, drapery **8** portiere

half: **4** bise, cafe **5** brise

holder: rod

raiser: **9** forepiece

curtains: end **5** death **6** demise **7** decease, drapery

curtilage: **4** quad, yard **5** court **9** enclosure **10** fenced area

curtsy, curtsey: bob, bow **4** beck **5** conge **9** obeisance

curvaceous: **7** endowed, rounded, shapely, stacked **9** well-built

curvature (see also **curve**): arc **4** bool, curl **8** kyphosis, lordosis **9** arcuation, scoliosis

center locus: **7** evolute

convex: **6** camber

surface: **5** plane

curve: arc, bow, ess **4** arch, bend, curb, ogee, turn, veer **5** ambit, bight, crook, crump, swirl, twist **6** bought, spiral **7** circuit, concave, contour, curvity, ellipse, flexure, inflect, sinuate **8** parabola, sinusaid, twisting **9** convexity, curvature

cusp: **7** spinode

double point of: **6** acnode

kind: **9** parabolic **10** memniscate

mathematical plane: **5** polar

parallel to an ellipse: **6** toroid

S-shaped: ess **4** agee **7** sigmoid

curved: **4** bent **5** round, wound **6** convex, hamate, turned **7** arcuate, arrondi, crooked, curvant **8** anchoral, aquiline, arciform

inward: **5** adunc **6** hooked **8** aduncous

curvet: hop **4** leap, turn **5** bound, caper, frisk, **6** cavort, frolic, gambol, gyrate, prance **8** corvetta(F.) **9** courbette, horse leap

Cush: *father:* Ham

son: **4** Seba **6** Nimrod

cushat: **4** bird, dove **6** pigeon

cushion: bag, cod, mat, pad **4** boss, seat **5**

gaddi, squab **6** buffer, insole, jockey, pillow, sachet **7** bolster, hassock **9** upholster

stuffing: **4** baru, down **5** kapok **8** feathers

cusk **4** fish, tusk **5** torsk **6** burbot

cusp: tip **4** apex, horn, peak **5** angle, point, tooth **6** corner **8** paracone **10** projection

cuspid: **11** canine tooth

custard: **4** flan **5** flawn **6** doucet, dowcet, dowset **8** flummery **9** charlotte

custard apple: **5** anona **6** annona, pawpaw **8** sweetsop

custodian: **5** guard **6** bailee, keeper, warden **7** curator, janitor **8** cerberus, guardian **9** caretaker, protector **10** supervisor

custody: **4** care, ward **5** trust **6** charge **7** control, durance, keeping, tuition **11** safekeeping **12** guardianship

custom: fad, law, mos(L.), tax, use **4** duty, form, garb, mode, more, rite, rote, rule, toll, wont **5** habit, haunt, usage, vogue **6** dastur, impost, ritual **7** costume, fashion, tribute **8** business, practice **9** costumbre, patronage **10** consuetude, convention, observance, tailor-made **12** constitution

of peoples: **5** mores

with force of law: mos

customary: **5** nomic, usual **6** common **7** general **8** familiar, habitual, orthodox **10** accustomed **11** traditional **12** conventional **14** consuetudinary

customer: **4** chap **5** buyer **6** client, patron **7** callant, patient, shopper **8** consumer, prospect **9** purchaser

group: **9** clientele

steady: **7** habitue, regular

customs: tax **4** cess, duty, levy, rate, toll **5** mores **6** impost, tariff **7** trewage

officer: **8** douanier

cut: bob, hew, lop, mow, nip, rit **4** bite, chip, chop, clip, crop, dock, fell, gash, hack, knap, mode, nick, pare, raze, slit, snee, snip, snub, trim **5** carve, flick, knife, lance, mince, notch, piece, prune, razee, scarp, sever, share, shear, shorn, slash, slice, snick, split **6** ablate, bisect, broach, chisel, cleave, dilute, divide, excise, haggle, ignore, incise, lessen, mangle, reduce, slight, swinge **7** affront, curtail, shorten, whittle **8** lacerate, mark down, retrench **9** engraving

a melon: **5** allot **8** dispense

a rug: **5** dance

across: **5** slice **8** transect **9** intersect, transcend

along: go **5** speed

back: **4** clip, pare, trim **5** lower, shave, slash **6** reduce **8** mark down

capable of being: **7** sectile

down: **4** pare **5** clear, slash **9** economize

in: mix **6** horn in **7** intrude **9** interpose, interrupt, introduce

in half: **5** halve **6** bisect, secant **8** dimidate

in small pieces: **4** dice, hash **5** mince **6** sliver

off: lop, nig **4** clip, crop, drib, poll **5** elide, roach, shave **7** deprive, divorce, exscind **8** amputate, truncate **9** apocopate, intercept **10** disinherit

out: **4** dele **5** elide **6** exsect, remove **7** exscind **9** eliminate

roughly: jag **4** hack, snag **7** butcher

short: bob **4** clip, crop, dock, poll **5** abort, check, clipt **6** arrest **7** curtail

slanting: **4** bias **5** bevel, miter, mitre

with die: **4** dink

with shears: **4** snip **5** shirl

wool: dod **4** dodd **5** shear

cut and dried: **5** trite **7** routine **8** foregone

cutaneous: **6** dermal

cutaway: **4** coat

cute: coy **4** keen **5** coony, dinky, sharp **6** clever, pretty, shrewd **7** cunning **8** affected **10** attractive

cuticle: **4** hide, skin **8** membrane, pellicle **9** epidermis **10** integument

blister: **4** bleb **5** bulla

ingredient: **5** cutin

cutis: **4** skin **6** corium, dermis

cutlass: **5** sword **6** dusack, tesack **7** machete

cutout: **9** decoupage

cutpurse: **5** thief **10** pickpocket

cutter: **4** beef, boat, sled **5** bravo, sloop, smack **6** cotter, editor, sleigh, slicer **7** clipper, incisor, ruffian **9** cutthroat, foretooth

cutthroat: **5** bravo, cruel **6** hit man **7** ruffian **8** ruthless

cutting: hag, raw **4** curt, keen, kerf, slip, tart, twig **5** acute, bleak, crisp, scion, scrap, scrow, sharp **6** biting, bitter, secant, severe **7** caustic, mordant, painful, satiric **8** chilling, incisive, piercing, poignant, wounding **9** sarcastic, trenchant **10** blustering **11** abridgement, curtailment **12** adulteration

edge: **5** blade

implement: ax, axe, bit, hob, saw **4** adze **5** knife, lathe, mower, plane, razor **6** chisel, reaper, scythe, shears **8** scissors

of last letter: **7** apocope

remark: dig **4** gibe **5** taunt **7** put-down

cuttlefish: **5** sepia, squid **7** octopus, scuttle

ink: **5** sepia

cutup: wag **5** devil, scamp **7** show off **9** prankster

cuvette: pot, tub **4** tank **5** basin **6** bucket, trench **7** cistern

Cybele: **4** Rhea

brother: **6** Cronus

father: **6** Uranus

mother: **4** Gaea

son: **4** Zeus **7** Jupiter, Neptune **8** Poseidon

sweetheart: **5** Attis

Cyclades Island: Ios, Zea **4** Keos, Milo, Nios, Sira, Syra **5** Delos, Melos, Naxia, Naxos, Paros, Syros, Tenos, Tinos **6** Andros **7** Amorgos

cycle: age, eon, era **4** aeon, bike **5** chain, epoch, pedal, round, saros, wheel **6** circle, course, period, series **7** bicycle, circuit, vehicle **8** tricycle **10** revolution, two-wheeler

cyclone: **4** gale, gust, wind **5** blast, storm **6** baguio **7** tornado, twister, typhoon **9** hurricane, whirlwind, windstorm

cyclopean: **4** huge, vast **6** strong **7** massive, titanic **8** colossal, gigantic **9** herculean

Cyclopes: **5** Arges **7** Brontes **8** Steropes **10** Polyphemus

Cyclops: **5** giant **7** monster

feature: **6** one eye

cyclostome: **7** hagfish, lamprey

cygnet: pen **4** fowl, swan

cylinder: **4** beam, drum, pipe, tube **6** barrel, bobbin, gabian, piston, platen, roller **8** lock part

cylindrical: **5** round **6** terete **7** centric, tubular

cyma: **4** gola, gula, ogee **7** molding

cymar, simar: **4** robe **5** shift

cymbal: tal, zel **8** doughnut **10** brass plate

cymbals: **6** becken, piatti

Cymbeline's daughter: **6** Imogen

Cymric: **5** Welsh

god of dead: **5** Pwyll

god of sky: **7** Gwydion

god of sun: **4** Lleu, Llew

god of underworld: **4** Gwyn

cynic: **5** Timon **7** doubter, knocker **9** pessimist **11** misanthrope

cynical: **6** ironic, sullen **7** currish, doglike **8** captious, downbeat, negative, sardonic, snarling

cynosure: **8** lodestar, polestar

cypress: **9** belvedere

Cyprus: *capital:* Nicosia

city: **6** Paphos **7** Limasol **9** Famagusta

measure: oka, oke, pik **4** cass **5** donum, kouza **6** gomari, kartos **7** medimno

monetary unit: **4** para **5** pound **7** piaster

mountain: **7** Troodos

weight: oka, oke **5** moosa **6** kantar

Cyrano: **4** poet **7** duelist

author: **7** Rostand

feature: **4** nose

cyrenaic: **7** hedonic **10** hedonistic

Cyrus: *daughter:* **6** Atossa

treasurer: **10** Mithredath

cyst: bag, sac, wen 5 pouch 6 ranula 7 vesicle

Cyzicus: *mother:* 6 Aenete
  slayer: 5 Jason
  wife: 6 Cleite

czar: 4 Ivan, king, Paul 5 baron, noble, Peter 6 prince, tycoon 7 emperor 8 Nicholas
  daughter: 8 czarevna, tsarevna
  son: 10 czarevitch, tsarevitch
  wife: 7 czarina, tsarina

Czechoslovakia: *capital:* 5 Praha 6 Prague
  city: 4 Asch, Brno, Eger, Hron 5 Opava, Plzen, Tuzla 6 Aussig, Kosice 7 Bud-weis, Ostrava, Teplitz 10 Bratislava
  coin: 5 ducat, haler 6 heller, koruna
  county: Ung
  dance: 5 polka 6 redowa 7 furiant
  leader: 5 Benes 7 Masaryk
  measure: lan, sah 4 mira 5 latro, liket, stopa 6 merice
  mountain: 5 Tatra
  munitions plant: 5 Skoda
  province: 7 Bohemia, Moravia
  reformer: 4 Huss
  river: Vag, Vah 4 Eger, Elbe, Gran, Hron, Isar, Iser, Labe, Oder, Ohre, Waag 5 Nitra 6 Moldau, Vltava

czigany: 5 gypsy

D

dab: hit, pat 4 blow, chit, lump, peck, spot 5 clout, smear 6 blotch, strike 7 portion, splotch 8 flatfish, flounder

dabble: dib 4 mess 5 dally 6 dibble, meddle, paddle, potter, splash, tamper, trifle 7 moisten, spatter 8 sprinkle

dabbler: 7 amateur 10 dilettante

dabchick: 5 grebe 9 helldiver

dace: 4 chub

dacoit: 6 robber 8 criminal 9 plunderer

dactyl: toe 6 finger 10 metric foot

dactylogram: 11 fingerprint

dactylopodite: 5 thumb 6 pollex

dactyloscopy: 14 classification, identification

Dadaism: 14 artistic revolt
  followers: Arp 4 Ball 5 Tzara 6 Aragon, Breton 7 Duchamp
  forerunner of: 10 surrealism

daddy longlegs: 5 stilt 7 spinner, tipulid 8 arachnid

dado: 6 groove 7 solidum 11 wall molding

daedal: 4 rich 6 varied 7 bizarre 8 artistic, skillful 9 ingenious, intricate 10 variegated

Daedalus: *son:* 6 Icarus
  constructor of: 9 labyrinth
  victim: 5 Talos

daemon (see also demon): 8 eudaemon

daffodil: 5 dilly

daft: mad 4 luny, wild 5 balmy, crazy, giddy, potty, silly 6 cuckoo, insane 7 cracked, foolish, idiotic 8 imbecile

Dag's horse: 8 Hrimfaxi 9 Skinfaksi

Dagda's kin: 5 Boann 6 Aengus, Brigit

dagger: 4 dirk, itac(P.I.), kris, snee 5 crise, katar(Ind.), skean(Ir.) 6 anlace, bodkin, coutel, creese, diesis, kreese, stylet, weapon 7 dudgeon, poniard 8 stiletto 10 misericord
  Burmese: dah, dow
  handle: 4 hilt
  Malay: 4 kris
  stroke: 4 stab 8 stoccado

daily: 4 a day 7 diurnal 9 hodiernal, newspaper, quotidian

daintily: 8 gingerly

dainty: 4 cate, nice, rare 5 acate, denty 6 bonbon, choice, costly, friand, mignon, minion, picked, scarce 7 elegant, finicky, minikin 8 delicacy, delicate, migniard 9 exquisite, squeamish 10 confection, fastidious

dairy: 7 vaccary 8 creamery
  food: 4 milk 5 cream 6 butter, cheese, yogurt
  tool: 9 separator

dais: 4 seat 5 bench, podia(pl.), stage, table 6 canopy, podium, settle 7 estrade, terrace 8 chabutra, platform

daisy: 5 gowan, oxeye 6 shasta 7 comfrey 10 moonflower

dak: 4 post
Dakota Indian: 4 Crow 5 Omaha, Osage, Sioux, Teton 6 Mandan 7 Arikara 8 Arikaree
Daksha's father: 6 Brahma
Dalai Lama: 5 ruler 13 reincarnation
dale: 4 dell, dene, glen, vale 5 spout 6 bottom, dingle, trough, valley
dalles: 6 rapids
dally: toy 4 chat, fool, idle, play, wait 5 delay, flirt, sport, tarry 6 dabble, dawdle, lead on, linger, loiter 10 trifle with 11 string along
dam: bar, bay 4 mare, stay, stem, stop, weir 5 block, check, choke, garth, mound 6 anicut, causey 7 annicut, barrier 8 blockade, obstacle, obstruct, restrain
dama: 5 addra 7 gazelle
damage: mar 4 blot, cost, harm, hurt, loss, ruin, teen 5 burst, cloud, spoil, wound 6 charge, deface, defect, impair, injure, scathe 7 expense, scratch 8 accident, disserve, mischief, sabotage 9 detriment, disprofit, vandalism 11 deleterious, impeachment 12 disadvantage
pert. to: 5 noxal
damages: 5 award 7 payment
daman: 5 hyrax
damask: 5 color 6 fabric 8 deep pink
dame: 4 lady 5 title, woman 6 matron
correlative: 4 sire
dammar: 5 resin, rosin
damn: 4 ruin 5 curse 7 condemn, swear at
damnable: 6 odious 8 infernal 9 execrable 10 detestable, outrageous
damnation: 9 perdition
damned: 4 lost 6 doomed 8 accursed
damnum: 4 harm, loss 9 detriment
damourite: 4 mica 9 muscovite
damp: deg, fog, wet 4 dank, dewy, dull, mist, roky 5 dabby, humid, moist, muggy, musty, rafty, rainy, soggy 6 clammy, deaden, muffle, quench, stupor 7 depress 8 dejected, dispirit 10 discourage
damper: 5 bread 7 checker 8 register
damsel: 4 girl, lass, miss 6 maiden 8 donzella, princess 10 demoiselle
Dan: *prince:* 7 Ahiezer
town: 4 Elon
Danae's kin: 4 Zeus 7 Perseus 8 Acrisius
dance: bal(F.), bob, hop, jig 4 ball, frug, haka, hoof, prom, shag 5 caper, frisk, rumba, tango, tread, stomp, twist, waltz 6 Boston, masque, minuet, monkey 7 foxtrot, saltate 8 fandango 9 cotillion, farandole, jitterbug 10 roundabout
ballroom: 5 polka, rumba, waltz 6 chacha 7 foxtrot, mazurka, twostep 10 Charleston, Turkey Trot
Brazilian: 5 samba 6 maxixe 9 bossa nova

ceremonial: 6 areito
chorus: 5 strut 6 cancan, kordax
college: hop 4 prom
country: hay 7 hoedown 8 haymaker 10 villanella
designer: 13 choreographer
drama: 6 ballet
English: 6 althea, morris
exhibition: tap 6 apache
fads: 4 frug, pony, shag 5 Lindy, twist 6 monkey 12 mashed potato
formal: 4 prom 5 pavan 7 mazurka 9 farandole
German: 9 allemande
gypsy: 7 farruca 8 flamenco 10 zingaresca
Hawaiian: 4 hula
Hebrew: 4 hora
India: 6 nautch
Italian: 8 courante 9 rigoletto 10 tarantella
Latin American: 5 conga, mambo, rumba, samba, tango 6 chacha, maxixe 7 carioca, criolla
lively: jig 4 juba, reel, trot 5 fling, galop, gavot, polka 6 bolero, branle, canary 8 galliard, rigadoon 9 cotillion, shakedown, tambourin 10 corybantic 11 schottische
masked: 7 ridotto
Muse: 11 Terpsichore
nineteenth-century: 7 tempete
old: 5 loure, rondo 6 bource, carole, cebell, corant, minuet 7 boutade, coranto, furlana, lavolta 8 chaconne 9 horedance, sarabande 10 tarantella
Peruvian: 5 cueca
shoes: 4 taps 5 pumps 8 slippers, toeshoes
slow: 6 adagio, minuet, valeta
Spanish: 8 fandango
square: 7 argeers, lancers 9 quadrille
strut: 8 cakewalk
sword: 8 matachin 11 Flamborough
voluptuous: 5 belly 8 habanera
dance of death: 7 macabre
dancer: 6 artist, hoofer 7 danseur 9 chorus boy 11 terpsichore
Biblical: 6 Salome
female: 4 pony 7 artiste, chorine 8 bayadere, coryphee, danseuse, devadasi 9 ballerina
dandelion: 7 chicory 10 bitterwort
stalk: 5 scape
dander: 5 anger, scurf 6 stroll, temper, wander 7 passion, saunter
dandle: pet 4 love 6 caress, fondle, pamper 9 knee-swing
dandruff: 5 scurf 6 furfur
dandy: fop 4 beau, buck, dude, fine, jake, prig, toff, yawl 5 nifty, swell 7 capstan, coxcomb, foppish, jessamy 8 popinjay,

sailboat **9** first-rate, exquisite **11** scrumptious **12** Beau Brummell, crackerjack

danger: **4** fear, risk **5** doubt, peril **6** hazard **7** pitfall, venture **8** distress, jeopardy **9** adventure
signal: **4** bell **5** alarm, siren **6** tocsin

dangerous: bad, rum **5** nasty, risky **6** unsafe **7** parlous **8** insecure **9** hazardous **10** precarious

dangle: lop **4** hang, loll **5** droop, swing **7** shoggle, suspend

Danish: **4** roll **6** pastry
anatomist: **5** Steno
astronomer: **5** Brahe
author: **8** Andersen
composer: **4** Gade
physicist: **4** Bohr
statesman: **5** Bajer, Brake

dank: wet **4** damp **5** humid, moist **6** clammy, coarse **7** drizzle

danta: **5** tapir

Dante: *beloved:* **8** Beatrice
birthplace: **8** Florence
circle of hell: **5** Caina
illustrator: **4** Dore
patron: **5** Scala
verse form: **7** sestina
work: **8** Commedia, Convivio, Eclogues, Epistles **9** Vita Nuova

Danube: *start:* **11** Black Forest
city on: Lom, Ulm **4** Baja, Linz, Ruse **6** Braila, Mohacs, Passau, Vienna **8** Belgrade, Budapest
delta: **8** Black Sea
tributary: Inn, Olt, Vah **4** Enns, Hrow, Isar, Lech, Naab, Prut, Raba, Sava **5** Arges, Drava, Iller, Iskur, Nitra, Tisza, Traun **6** Leitha, Morava **7** Altmuhl, Siretul

Danzig: *coin:* **6** gulden **7** pfennig
liqueur: **7** ratafia

dap: dab, dib, dip **4** skip **6** bounce, dibble **7** rebound

Daphne: **8** Mezereon
father: **5** Ladon
mother: **6** Creusa
pursued by: **6** Apollo
turned into: **10** laurel tree

Daphnis' lover: **5** Chloe

dapper: **4** neat, trim **5** natty **6** spruce **7** finical, foppish

dappled: **6** dotted **7** flecked, mottled, spotted **8** freckled **10** variegated

darbies: **8** manacles **9** handcuffs

Dardanelles: **10** Hellespont

dare: **4** dast, defy, face, osse, risk **5** brave **6** assume **7** attempt, venture **9** challenge, undertake

daredevil: **6** madcap **12** swashbuckler

daresay: **5** agree **7** believe, presume, suppose **13** think probable

dargah, durgah(Ind.): **4** tomb **5** court **6** mosque, shrine

daring: **4** bold, rash **5** brave, hardy, manly, nerve **6** heroic **7** courage **8** devilish, fearless **9** audacious **10** courageous **11** adventurous, venturesome

dariole: cup **5** shell

Darius: *father:* **9** Ahasuerus
prince: **6** Daniel

dark: dim, sad, wan **4** ebon **5** black, blind, brown, dingy, dusky, faint, murky, shady, sooty, unlit, vague **6** brunet, closed, cloudy, dismal, gloomy, opaque, wicked **7** melanic, obscure, rayless, stygian, swarthy **8** abstruse, ignorant, lowering, sinister **9** ambiguous, Cimmerian, infuscate, recondite, secretive, shuttered, tenebrous, uncertain **10** caliginous, indistinct, mysterious

dark-complexioned: **5** dusky **7** swarthy

dark horse: **7** unknown **9** candidate **10** contestant **14** unlikely winner

darken: dim **4** dull **5** bedim, shade, sully, umber **6** deepen, shadow **7** becloud, benight, blacken, eclipse, obscure, opacate, tarnish **8** overcast **9** obfuscate, overcloud **10** overshadow

darkness: **4** dusk, murk **5** gloom, night, shade **6** shadow **7** dimness, privacy, secrecy **8** gloaming, iniquity, twilight **9** blackness **10** wickedness
realm: Po **6** Erebus

darling: joe(Sc.), pet **4** cute, dear, duck **5** aroon(Ir.), deary, honey, sweet **6** cherie, cuddly, moppet **7** beloved **8** adorable, favorite **10** attractive, delightful, sweetheart

darn: **4** mend **5** patch **6** cussed, damned, repair **7** blasted, doggone

darnel: **4** tare, weed **5** grass **6** cockle

darner: **6** needle

dart: **4** bolt, flit, leap **5** bound, fling, scoot, shaft, speed, start **6** scurry, spring, sprint **7** missile **9** flechette **11** move quickly **12** stitched fold
barbed: **10** banderilla

dart-like: **8** spicular

D'Artagnan: *companion:* **5** Athos **6** Aramis **7** Porthos
creator: **5** Dumas

Dartmouth College location: **7** Hanover

Darwin: **10** naturalist
ship: **6** Beagle
theory: **9** evolution
teacher in evolution trial: **10** John Scopes
work: **12** Descent of Man **15** Origin of Species

das: **4** fish **6** dassie **9** blacktail **12** Hindu servant

Das Kapital author: **4** Marx

dash: pep **6** bang, ding, elan, gift, hurl, line, pelt, race, ruin, rush, show, slam **5**

abash, ardor, break, clash, crash, crush, fling, knock, smash, speed, spice, style, swash, throw **6** energy, hurtle, hyphen, shiver, spirit, splash, sprint, stroke, thrust **7** bravura, collide, depress, display, shatter, spatter, splotch **8** confound, gratuity, splinter **9** animation, bespatter, frustrate, overthrow

dasheen: 4 taro

dashiki: 7 garment **12** African shift
relative: **6** muu-muu

dashing: gay **4** bold, chic **5** bully, showy **6** jaunty, lively, swanky, veloce **7** stylish **8** spirited **11** fashionable

dastard: cad, sot **5** sneak **6** coward, craven **7** dullard **8** poltroon

dastardly: 4 base, mean, foul **5** nasty **6** rotten **10** despicable

data: 5 facts **8** material **11** information

date: age, day, era, woo **5** epoch, fruit **6** escort **7** take out **9** originate **10** engagement, extend from, rendezvous **11** anniversary, appointment
erroneous: **11** anachronism
on coin: **7** exergue

dated: 5 passe **6** demode, old hat **7** archaic **8** outmoded **12** old-fashioned **13** unfashionable

dateless: 8 timeless **10** immemorial

dating: 6 timing **8** courting

daub: 4 blob, blot, clag, clam, clat, coat, gaum, soil **5** clart, cleam, cover, paint, slake, smear **6** bedaub, grease **7** besmear, plaster, splotch **8** slaister

daughter: 4 bint **5** fille, filly **6** alumna **7** cadette
pert. to: **6** filial

Daughter of Moon: 7 Nokomis

daunt: awe, cow, daw **4** daze, faze, stun, tame **5** abash, break, check, deter **6** dismay, subdue **7** conquer, control, overawe, repress, stupefy, terrify **8** dispirit, overcome **10** disconcert, discourage, dishearten, intimidate

dauntless: 4 bold, good **5** brave, gutsy **7** aweless **8** fearless, intrepid, unafraid **10** courageous **11** indomitable, lionhearted

davenport: 4 desk, sofa **5** couch, divan **12** chesterfield
small: **8** love seat

David: *chief ruler:* Ira
companion: **6** Hushai
daughter: **5** Tamar
employer: **5** Nabal
favorite son: **7** Absalom
friend: **5** Ittai
kin: **5** Jesse, Tamar **6** Michal **7** Abigail, Absalom, Solomon
man of: Ira **4** Igal **7** Shammah
musician: **5** Asaph
prophet: **6** Nathan
scribe: **7** Shavsha

traitor to: **10** Ahithophel
valley of Goliath's death: **4** Elah

David Copperfield character: 4 Dora **5** Agnes, James **6** Barkis, Betsey, Dartle **8** Micawber, Peggotty, Traddles **9** Wickfield, Uriah Heep **10** Steerforth

Davy: 4 lamp

dawdle: lag **4** idle, loaf, poke **5** dally **6** diddle, linger, loiter, putter, trifle **8** lollygag **9** waste time **10** fool around

dawn: 4 morn **5** sunup **6** aurora **7** morning, sunrise **8** daybreak **9** beginning
goddess: Eos **5** Ushas **6** Aurora
pert. to: **4** eoan **7** auroral
symbol: dew
toward the: **8** eastward

day: yom(Heb.) **4** date, time **5** epoch **6** period **8** lifetime
before: eve **9** yesterday
father of: **6** Erebus
god of: **5** Horus
hot: **8** scorcher
joyful: **8** festival
judgment: **8** doomsday
of Atonement: **9** Yom Kippur
pert. to: **6** ferial

day blindness: hemeralopia

daydream: 4 muse **6** vision **7** reverie

days: *fateful:* **4** Ides
fifty: **13** quinquagesima
fourteen: **9** fortnight
gone by: **4** yore **7** long ago **8** old times **9** antiquity **10** yesteryear **11** past history

daze: fog **4** stun **5** daunt **6** bemuse, benumb, dazzle, muddle, trance **7** confuse, stupefy **8** befuddle, bewilder **9** dumbfound

dazed: 4 asea **5** dizzy, dopey, woozy **6** addled, groggy **7** stunned **9** in a stupor **10** punch-drunk

dazzle: 4 daze **5** blind, shine **7** eclipse **8** bewilder, outshine, surprise

dazzling: 5 vivid **6** bright, garish **7** fulgent, glaring, radiant **8** gorgeous **9** brilliant, sparkling **10** candescent, foudroyant **11** pyrotechnic

deaccession: 10 museum sale

deacon: 5 adept **6** cleric, doctor, layman, master **10** adulterate
prayers: **6** ectene
stole: **7** orarion

dead: 4 cold, dull, flat, gone, mort(F.), numb, tame **5** amort, inert, quiet, slain **6** asleep, lapsed **7** defunct, expired, extinct, sterile, tedious **8** absolute, complete, deceased, departed, inactive, lifeless, obsolete **9** apathetic, bloodless, inanimate, nerveless, unsalable **10** breathless, lusterless, monotonous, motionless, spiritless, unexciting **11** indifferent, ineffectual, inoperative **12** extinguished, unproductive, unprofitable

house of: 4 tomb 5 grave 6 morgue 7 ossuary 8 mortuary 9 crematory, ossuarium
mass for: 7 requiem
region of: Po 5 Hades 6 Erebus
dead duck: 5 goner 9 sure loser 13 hopeless cause
Dead Souls author: 5 Gogol
deadbeat: bum 7 sponger 8 parasite 10 free-loader
deaden: 4 dull, kill, mute, numb, stun 5 blunt 6 benumb, dampen, muffle, obtund, opiate, retard, weaken 7 petrify, repress, stupefy 8 paralyze 10 devitalize
dead end: 4 stop 7 impasse 8 cul-de-sac 9 blank wall 10 blind alley
deadfall: 4 trap 9 brush pile
deadhead: 6 bobber 8 non-payer 12 lacking cargo
deadline: 5 limit 8 boundary
deadlock: tie 4 draw 7 impasse 9 stalemate 10 standstill
deadly: 4 dire, fell 5 fatal 6 lethal, mortal 7 capital, fateful, ruinous 8 venomous, virulent 9 pestilent 10 implacable, pernicious 11 destructive, internecine
deadpan: 4 blank 6 vacant 9 impassive
deaf: 8 heedless 9 unmindful
deal: 4 dole, part, sale 5 allot, board, plank, sever, share, trade, wield 6 bestow, divide, handle, parcel 7 bargain, deliver, inflict, portion, scatter, wrestle 8 dispense, separate 9 apportion, negotiate 10 administer, distribute 11 transaction
great: 4 lots 5 loads 6 oodles 8 very much 9 big amount
with: 4 cope 6 handle 10 take care of
dealer: 5 agent 6 badger, broker, cadger, jobber, monger, seller, trader 8 merchant, operator 9 middleman, tradesman 10 negotiator, trafficker 11 distributor
secondhand goods: 10 pawnbroker
dealing: 7 trading, traffic 8 exchange 11 intercourse
shrewd: 6 deceit 9 chicanery
dean: 5 doyen 6 senior, verger 8 official
dear: pet 4 agra(Ir.), cara(It.), cher(F.), fond, high, lief, near 5 honey, loved 6 costly, scarce, worthy 7 beloved, darling, lovable 8 esteemed, glorious, precious, valuable 9 cherished, expensive, heartfelt, honorable, important 10 sweetheart 12 affectionate
dearly: 6 deeply, keenly, richly 8 heartily 9 earnestly
dearth: 4 lack, want 6 famine 7 paucity, poverty 8 scarcity 10 deficiency
death: end 4 bale, bane, doom, mort(F.) 5 decay 6 demise 7 decease, quietus 8

biolysis, curtains, rawbones 9 bloodshed, departure 10 expiration, extinction, grim reaper
after: 10 posthumous
angel of: 6 Azrael
aware of portending: fey
bringing: 6 funest
goddess: Hel 4 Dana, Danu
march: 7 cortege, funeral
meditation: 11 thanatopsis
mercy: 10 euthanasia
notice: 4 obit 8 obituary
personification: 4 Mors 5 Ankou 6 Charos, Charus
put to: gas 4 hang, kill, slay 5 choke, lynch 6 murder, starve, stifle 7 garrote 8 strangle 9 suffocate 11 assassinate, electrocute
rate: 9 mortality
rattle: 4 rale
register: 9 necrology
song: 5 dirge, elegy 8 threnody
symbol of: 5 orant
death-defying: 4 bold, rash 6 heroic 9 audacious, imprudent
deathless: 7 abiding, eternal, undying 8 immortal 12 imperishable
deathly: 5 fatal 6 deadly, grisly, lethal, mortal 7 ghastly, macabre 8 gruesome, moribund 10 cadaverous 11 destructive
debacle: 4 rout 5 wreck 6 defeat 7 beating, failure 8 collapse 9 breakdown, cataclysm
debar: 4 deny, tabu 5 estop, taboo 6 forbid, hinder, refuse 7 boycott, deprive, exclude, prevent, suspend 8 preclude, prohibit 9 foreclose, interdict 10 disqualify
debark: 4 land
debase: 5 alloy, lower, stoop 6 defile, demean, humble, impair, reduce, revile, vilify 7 cheapen, degrade, deprave, devalue, pervert, traduce, vitiate 8 dishonor 9 brutalize 10 adulterate, degenerate, depreciate 11 deteriorate
debased: low 4 vile 7 corrupt
debatable: 4 moot 8 arguable 9 uncertain 10 in question
debate: 4 agon, moot 5 argue, fight 6 reason, strife 7 agitate, canvass, contend, contest, discuss, dispute, examine, palaver, quarrel, wrangle 8 argument, consider, militate, question 9 dialectic, quodlibet 10 contention, deliberate 11 controversy 12 dissertation
pert. to: 8 forensic
place of: 5 forum 6 Lyceum
stoppage of: 7 cloture
debauch: 4 bout, orgy 5 spree, taint 6 defile, guzzle, seduce 7 corrupt, deprave, mislead, pollute, violate 9 bacchanal,

dissipate **10** hellbender, lead astray, saturnalia **11** contaminate

debauched: 4 lewd **6** wanton **9** dissolute

debauchee: rip **4** rake, roue **6** lecher **8** rake-hell **9** libertine

debilitated: 4 weak **5** seedy **6** feeble, infirm, sapped **9** burned out, enervated

debility: 5 atony **7** languor, malaise **8** weakness **9** infirmity, lassitude **10** feebleness

debit: 4 loss **6** charge

debonair: 4 airy **6** jaunty, polite, urbane **7** affable **8** graceful, gracious

Deborah's husband: 8 Lapidoth

debouche: 4 exit **6** outlet **7** opening, passage **9** emergence

debris: 5 scree, talus, trash, waste **6** refuse, rubble **7** rubbish **8** detritus

debt: sin **5** debit, fault **7** arrears **8** trespass **9** arrearage, liability **10** obligation

acknowledgment: IOU **4** bill, note

without: **7** solvent **11** unobligated

debunk: 6 expose, show up, unmask **8** disabuse **11** disillusion, set straight **12** tell the truth

debut: 7 opening **8** entrance, premiere **9** beginning, coming out **12** introduction

decad: ten

decade: 9 decennium

decadent: 6 effete, rotten, sinful, wicked **7** decayed **9** declining **10** degenerate, iniquitous, retrograde **12** deteriorated **13** retrogressive

decamp: 4 bolt **5** elope, scoot **6** depart, levant, mizzle **7** abscond, run away, take off, vamoose **8** clear out **9** skedaddle **10** hightail it

decant: 4 emit, pour **6** unload **8** transfer

decanter: 6 carafe

decapitate: 6 behead **10** guillotine

decapod: 4 crab **5** prawn, squid **7** lobster **10** crustacean

decay: ebb, rot **4** conk, dote, doze, fade, fail, ruin **5** death, spoil, waste **6** caries, mildew, wither **7** decline, failure **8** decrease **9** adversity, decadence, decompose **11** destruction, deteriorate, dissolution **12** dilapidation, disintegrate, putrefaction

dental: **6** caries

in fruit: **4** blet

deceased: 4 dead **7** defunct **8** departed

deceitful: shy **4** foxy **5** false, lying **6** fickle, hollow, shifty, sneaky **7** sirenic **8** tortuous **9** dishonest, faithless, insidious, insincere **10** circuitous, fallacious, mendacious **11** underhanded **13** machiavellian

deceivable: 8 gullible

deceive: con, lie **4** bilk, dupe, fool, gaff, gull, hoax, jilt **5** abuse, blind, bluff, catch, cheat, cozen, dodge, hocus, trick **6** baffle, betray, delude, humbug, illude **7** beguile, defraud, mislead **8** flimflam, hoodwink **9** bamboozle, frustrate **11** doublecross **12** misrepresent

deceiver: 6 trepan **7** juggler, sharper, warlock **8** magician

decelerate: 4 slow **5** brake **11** reduce speed

decency: 7 decorum **9** propriety

decennium: 6 decade

decent: 4 fair, good, pure **5** clean **6** chaste, comely, honest, modest, proper, seemly **7** correct, fitting, shapely **8** adequate, decorous **10** acceptable, conforming, sufficient **11** appropriate, respectable

deception: gyp **4** gaff, ruse, sham, scam, wile **5** cheat, covin, craft, fraud, guile, magic, trick **6** cautel, deceit, humbug **7** blaflum(Sc.), cunning, evasion, fallacy, fiction, knavery, pretext, sleight, slyness **8** artifice, falsedad(Sp.), intrigue, prestige, subtlety, trickery, trumpery **9** chicanery, collusion, duplicity, falsehood, hypocrisy, imposture, mendacity, sophistry, treachery **10** artfulness, camouflage, dishonesty, subterfuge **11** contrivance, counterfeit, dissembling **13** deceitfulness, dissimulation

deceptive: 5 false **8** delusive, illusory **10** fallacious, misleading

decided: 4 firm, flat, sure **5** fixed **6** all set, formed **7** certain, settled **8** clear-cut, decisive, definite, resolved **10** determined **11** established **14** unquestionable

decima: 5 tenth, tithe

decimal base: ten

decimate: 5 wreck **7** destroy, wipe out **8** demolish, massacre **9** slaughter **10** annihilate

decipher: 4 read **5** break, solve **6** decode, detect, reveal **7** analyze, unravel **8** discover, indicate **9** translate

decision: 4 fiat **5** arret, canon **6** crisis, decree, ruling **7** verdict **8** finality, judgment, sentence **9** precedent **10** conclusion, resolution **12** adjudication **13** determination

maker: **5** judge **6** umpire **7** referee **9** executive

sudden: **4** whim **7** impulse

decisive: 5 final **6** crisic **7** crucial **8** critical **10** conclusive, peremptory

deck: tog **4** buss, dink, heap, pink, trig **5** adorn, array, cover, dress, equip, floor, prink, store **6** blazon, clothe, fettle **7** apparel, bedight, bedizen, feather **8** beautify, decorate, platform **9** embellish **11** pack of cards

kind: gun **4** boat, main, spar **5** berth, upper **6** bridge **7** shelter **8** platform, splinter **9** hurricane, promenade **10** forecastle

high: **4** poop
lowest: **5** orlop
part: **7** scupper
deckle-edged: 5 erose
declaim: 4 rant, rave **5** orate, speak, spout **6** recite **7** elocute, inveigh **8** denounce, harangue, perorate **9** discourse
declaration: 4 word **6** oracle, placet **9** affidavit, assertion, statement **10** allegation, deposition, disclosure, exposition **11** affirmation **12** announcement, asseveration, proclamation **13** advertisement, pronouncement
declare: bid, say, vow **4** aver, avow, deny, tell **5** posit, state, voice **6** affirm, allege, assert, assure, avouch, blazon, depone, herald, indict, notify, relate **7** behight, express, profess, protest, signify, testify **8** announce, denounce, describe, indicate, maintain, manifest, proclaim **9** advertise, nuncupate, pronounce **10** annunciate, asseverate, promulgate **11** acknowledge, communicate
in cards: bid **4** meld
declination: 4 bias **5** slope **7** descent **8** swerving **9** deviation **10** declension **11** inclination **13** deterioration
decline: dip, ebb, set **4** bend, fade, fail, fall, flag, sink, turn, wane **5** chute, droop, lower, repel, slope, slump, stoop, stray **6** debase, refuse, reject, weaken **7** descend, descent, deviate, disavow, dwindle, failure, forbear **8** decrease, languish, withdraw **9** decadence, declivity, recadence, repudiate **10** retrograde **13** deterioration
declivity: dip **4** drop, fall **5** cliff, scarp, slope **6** calade **7** decline, descent **8** gradient **9** precipice
decoct: 5 smelt, steep **6** reduce, refine **7** extract **8** boil down, condense
decoction: 7 essence, extract
decode: 5 crack **8** decipher **9** figure out
decompose: rot **5** decay, spoil **7** putrefy
decor: 7 setting **10** background, design plan **11** furnishings, style scheme
decorate: 4 bind, cite, deck, pink, trim **5** adorn, dress, inlay, panel **6** emboss, parget **7** festoon, garnish, miniate **8** ornament, titivate **9** embellish
decorated: 6 ornate **7** damasse, honored, wrought **9** sigillate **10** beribboned
decoration: 4 bahl **5** medal **6** frieze, plaque, tinsel **7** epergne, garnish, regalis **8** applique, fretwork, ornament **9** furniture **10** chambranle, decorament
metalware: **4** tole
military: DSC, DSM, DSO **5** medal **6** ribbon
pert. to: **8** medallic
decorous: 4 calm, good, prim **5** grave, quiet, sober, staid **6** decent, demure, mod-

est, polite, proper, sedate, seemly, serene, steady **7** fitting, orderly, regular, settled **8** becoming, composed, mannerly **9** befitting, dignified, unruffled **11** appropriate
decorticate: 4 flay, hull, husk, pare, peel, pill, skin **5** strip **6** denude **9** excoriate
decorum: 7 decency **9** etiquette, propriety **10** convention
decoy: 4 bait, lure, tole **5** drill, plant, shill, tempt **6** allure, entice, entrap, pigeon **8** inveigle **9** shillaber
decrease: ebb **4** drop, fall, loss, sink, wane **5** abate, decay, taper, waste **6** impair, lessen, shrink **7** decline, dwindle, slacken, subside **8** diminish, moderate, retrench **9** decession, decrement **10** diminution
decree: act, law **4** rule, will **5** edict, enact, order, tenet, ukase **6** arrest, assize, decern(Sc.), dictum, indict, ordain **7** adjudge, appoint, command, mandate, statute **8** decision, rescript, sentence **9** determine, enactment, ordinance **10** adjudicate, plebiscite **12** adjudication, announcement
authoritative: **5** arret, canon
imperial: **4** fiat
Oriental: **5** irade **6** firman
papal: **4** bull
decrement: 4 loss **5** waste **8** decrease **10** diminution
decrepit: 4 lame, weak **6** feeble, infirm, senile, shabby **7** failing, invalid, rundown, unsound **9** bedridden **10** broken down **11** in disrepair
decretum: 4 rule **5** canon **7** precept **10** regulation
decry: boo **4** slur **5** lower **6** lessen **7** asperse, censure, condemn, degrade, detract **8** belittle, derogate **9** deprecate, discredit, disparage, down-grade, underrate **10** depreciate, undervalue
decuple: 7 tenfold
decussate: 5 cross **7** form an X **9** intersect
dedicate: vow **6** devote, direct, hallow, oblate **7** ascribe **8** inscribe **9** nuncupate **10** consecrate
deduce: 4 draw, lead **5** bring, drive, infer, trace **6** derive, elicit, evolve, gather **7** extract, make out **8** conclude
deduct: 4 bate, dock, take **5** abate, allow **6** defalk, remove **7** curtail **8** abstract, discount, separate, subtract, take away
deduction: 4 agio **6** rebate **7** reprise **8** illation, write-off **9** inference **10** conclusion
deed: act **4** case, fact, feat, fiat, gest **5** chart, doing, title **6** action, convey, escrow, pottah, remise **7** charter, exploit **8** document, contract, transfer **9** adven-

ture **10** instrument **11** achievement, performance, tour de force **14** accomplishment

benevolent: **4** boon **5** favor **8** benefice

evil: sin **11** malefaction

deeds: 4 acta **9** res gestae

deem: say **4** hope, reck, tell **5** judge, opine, think **6** esteem, expect, ordain, reckon, regard **7** account, adjudge, believe, surmise **8** announce, consider, judgment, proclaim **10** adjudicate

deep: low, sea **4** howe, rapt **5** abyss, grave, great, gruff, heavy, ocean **6** hollow, intent **7** abysmal, intense, serious, unmixed **8** absorbed, abstruse, complete, powerful, profound, thorough **9** entangled, insidious, recondite **11** far-reaching

deep-dyed: 6 rooted **7** long-set, old-line **9** colorfast, confirmed, hard-shell, indelible, ingrained **10** inveterate

deepen: 5 cloud **6** darken **7** enhance, thicken **9** intensify **10** strengthen

deep-seated: 6 inbred, innate, primal **8** inherent **9** intrinsic **10** congenital, entrenched, in the blood **11** instinctive

deer: 4 hind **6** animal, cervid, mammal **8** ruminant

Asian: **4** axis, maha, napu, shou, sika **5** maral **6** chitra, hangul, sambar **10** barasingha, chevrotain

barking: **7** muntjac, muntjak

cry: **4** bell

European: red **6** fallow **9** white-tail

fallow: **4** dama

family: **8** cervidae

female: doe **4** hind

genus of: **6** cervus

large: elk **5** moose **6** wapiti **7** caribou

male: **4** buck, hart, spay, stag **7** roebuck

meat: **5** jerky **7** charqui, venison

North American: elk **5** moose **6** wapiti

path: run **4** slot **5** trail

pert. to: **6** damine **7** cervine

small: roe **7** roebuck

South American: **4** pudu **6** guemal, vanada **7** brocket

young: kid **4** fawn, spay **7** spitter

de-escalate: 6 weaken **8** decrease, diminish, slow down

deface: mar **4** foul, ruin, scar **5** spoil **6** damage, defoil, deform, injure **7** blemish, detract, distort **8** mutilate **9** disfigure, vandalize

de facto: 7 in being **8** existing **10** unofficial

defalcation: 9 pilferage **10** peculation **12** embezzlement

defame: 4 foul **5** abase, cloud, libel, smear **6** injure, malign, vilify **7** asperse, blacken, blemish, detract, slander, traduce **8** dishonor **9** discredit, denigrate **10** calumniate

default: 4 fail, flaw, lack, omit, want **7** blemish, failure, forfeit, mistake, neglect **8** omission **10** negligence **11** delinquency, dereliction **12** imperfection **13** nonappearance

defeasance: 6 defeat **7** undoing **9** overthrow, annulment

defeat: win **4** balk, beat, best, drub, foil, loss, rout, ruin, undo **5** break, check, floor, skunk, worst **6** baffle, cumber, master, thwack **7** conquer, deprive, destroy, preempt, reverse, shellac **8** overcome, vanquish, Waterloo **9** discomfit, frustrate, overpower, overthrow, overwhelm **10** defeasance, disappoint **12** discomfiture

at chess: **4** mate **9** checkmate

narrowly: nip **4** edge **7** nose out

defeatist: 7 kill-joy **8** fatalist **9** Cassandra, pessimist

defect: 4 flaw, lack, vice, want **5** craze, fault, minus **6** damage, desert, injury **7** blemish, failing, forsake **8** drawback, renounce, weakness **10** deficiency **11** shortcoming **12** imperfection

in timber: **4** knot

without: **5** sound **7** perfect

defective: bad, ill **4** poor **6** faulty **7** halting, unsound **8** impaired, vitiated **9** deficient, imperfect **10** disordered, inaccurate, incomplete

defector: 6 bolter **8** apostate, deserter, renegade **9** turnabout **10** repudiator

defend: 4 back, hold, save, wear **5** guard, watch **6** assert, forbid, screen, secure, shield, uphold **7** contest, espouse, justify, prevent, protect, shelter **8** advocate, champion, conserve, maintain, preserve, prohibit **9** exculpate, vindicate

defendant: 7 accused **8** appellee

answer: **4** plea **14** nolo contendere

defender: 8 advocate, champion, guardian, upholder **9** proponent, protector

of the people: **7** tribune **9** ombudsman

defense: 4 egis, fort **5** aegis, alibi, fence, grith **6** answer, behalf, covert, excuse, sconce **7** bulwark, shelter **8** apologia, boundary, security **9** coverture, safeguard **10** protection **11** maintenance

position: **7** rampart **10** bridgehead

unit: AAF **4** army, NATO, navy **5** SEATO **7** marines

defenseless: 4 bare **5** naked **7** unarmed **8** helpless **9** unguarded

defensible: 7 tenable **9** excusable

defensive: 9 shielding **10** apologetic

defer: bow **4** wait **5** delay, yield **6** put off, shelve, submit **7** suspend **8** lay aside, postpone, prorogue, protract **9** hold off on **10** capitulate **12** knuckle under **13** procrastinate

deference: 6 homage, regard **7** respect **8**

courtesy **9** obeisance

defiant: 4 bold **5** brave **6** daring **8** insolent **11** challenging

deficiency: 4 lack, want **5** fault, minus **6** dearth, defect **7** absence **8** scarcity, shortage **10** inadequacy, scantiness **13** insufficiency

deficient: 5 short **6** meager **7** bobtail

deficit: 8 shortage **9** arrearage, income gap **11** debit excess **12** business loss

defile: 4 pass, soil **5** abuse, dirty, gorge, smear, sully, taint **6** debase, infect, ravish **7** corrupt, deprave, passage, pollute, tarnish, violate **8** dishonor, maculate **9** desecrate **11** contaminate

defiled: 6 impure **7** unclean **8** maculate

definable: 6 finite

define: end, fix, set **4** mere, term **5** bound, limit **6** decide **7** clarify, delimit, explain, expound **8** describe, discover **9** demarcate, determine, interpret, prescribe **11** distinguish **12** characterize, circumscribe

definite: 4 sure **5** clear, final, fixed, sharp **7** certain, limited, precise **8** distinct, explicit, limiting **10** conclusive **11** determinate, determining, unequivocal **12** determinable, unmistakable

definitive: 5 final **8** clear-cut, explicit, specific **10** conclusive

deflect: 4 bend, warp **5** parry **6** divert, swerve **7** deviate, refract **8** turn away

deflower: 6 ravage, ravish **7** despoil, violate

Defoe character: 4 Moll, Xury **6** Crusoe, Friday, Roxana **7** Mrs. Veal

deform: mar **4** maim, warp **6** deface **7** contort, cripple, distort **8** misshape **9** disfigure **10** disarrange

deformed: 7 crooked, hideous **8** formless **9** amorphous, loathsome, monstrous, shapeless, unshapely **11** counterfeit

deformity: 4 flaw **6** defect **7** blemish **13** disfigurement

of foot: **5** varus **7** talipes

defraud: rob **4** bilk, fake, gull, rook, trim **5** cheat, cozen, gouge, mulct, trick **6** chouse, fleece **7** swindle **9** bamboozle

defray: pay **6** expend, prepay **7** finance **10** stand treat **11** foot the bill, pay expenses **12** pick up the tab

deft: 4 neat, trim **5** agile, handy, quick **6** adroit, expert, nimble, spruce **8** dextrous, skillful **9** dexterous

defunct: 4 dead **7** extinct **8** deceased, departed, finished

defy: 4 dare, face **5** beard, brave, flout, scorn, stump **6** oppose, resist **7** affront, outface **8** champion **9** stand up to

dégagé: 6 casual **7** relaxed **8** detached, informal **10** uninvolved **11** free and easy **13** unconstrained

degenerate: rot **6** debase, effete, worsen **7** corrupt **8** decadent, depraved **10** go downhill **11** deteriorate

degradation: 7 descent **8** ignominy

degrade: 4 bust **5** abase, decry, lower, shame, strip **6** debase, demean, demote, depose, humble, reduce, vilify **7** corrupt, decline, depress **8** disgrace, dishonor **9** disparage, humiliate **10** degenerate, depreciate **11** deteriorate

degraded: 5 seamy **6** abject, fallen **7** debased **10** degenerate, diminished

degrading: 4 base **6** menial **8** shameful

degree: 4 bank, heat, rank, rate, rung, step, term, tier **5** class, grade, honor, order, pitch, point, stage, stair **6** extent, medium, soever **7** measure, station **8** quantity, standing **9** gradation **10** attainment

academic: B.L.S., B.Sc., L.L.B., L.L.D., M.Sc., Ph.D. **4** D.Lit. **5** Litt.D.

honorary: **8** laureate

kind of: nth **5** third

of academic excellence: **8** cum laude **13** magna cum laude, summa cum laude

seeker: **9** candidate

slight: ace, nth **4** hair, inch **5** shade **8** slightly **9** gradation

degust, degustate: 5 savor, taste **6** relish

dehydrate: dry **9** desiccate, evaporate

deific: 6 divine **7** godlike

deification: 10 apotheosis

deify: 5 exalt **7** glorify, idolize **10** consecrate **11** apotheosize

deign: 5 stoop **9** vouchsafe **10** condescend

deigning: 11 patronizing

deity (see also **god** and **goddess** under appropriate country or function): god **4** deva, idol, muse **6** genius **7** creator, demigod, godling, godhead **8** Almighty, divinity, **12** supreme being

half-fish: **6** Oannes

half-goat: **4** faun

hawk-eyed: **5** Horus **6** Sokari **7** Sokaris

jackal-headed: **6** Anubis

tutelary: **5** genie, lares, numen **7** Hershef, penates

deja vu: 8 illusion **10** paramnesia, seen before

de jure: 7 by right **8** lawfully

deject: 5 abase, lower **6** humble, lessen **7** flatten **8** dispirit **9** overthrow **10** demoralize, discourage, dishearten

dejected: low, sad **4** blue, down, glum, sunk **6** abased, gloomy, pining **7** humbled, unhappy **8** repining, wretched **9** cheerless, depressed, prostrate, woebegone **10** despondent, spiritless **11** crestfallen, downhearted **12** disconsolate, disheartened, fainthearted

dejection: 5 dumps **7** despair **10** melancholy

dejeuner: 5 lunch 9 breakfast, collation
Delaware: *capital:* 5 Dover
  bay: 8 Delaware, Rehoboth 11 Indian
  River
  city: 5 Lewes 6 Newark 7 Chester, Milford, Seaford, Smyrna 9 New Castle,
  10 Wilmington
  county: 4 Kent 6 Sussex 9 New Castle
  Indian: 6 Lenape
  river: 6 Indian 7 Leipsic 8 Delaware 9
  Broadkill, Christina, Nanticoke
  state bird: 7 blue hen
  state flower: 12 peach blossom
  state insect: 7 ladybug
  state nickname: 5 First 7 Diamond
  state tree: 5 holly
delay: lag 4 slow, stay, stop, wait 5 allay,
  check, dally, defer, demur, deter, dwell,
  stall, tarry 6 arrest, dawdle, detain, hinder, impede, linger, loiter, put off, retard, temper, weaken 7 assuage, prolong, respite 8 demurral, hesitate,
  macerate, mitigate, obstruct, postpone,
  reprieve, stoppage 9 detention, hindrance, lingering 10 cunctation, moratorium, suspension 13 procrastinate
delayed: 4 late 5 tardy 7 belated, overdue
delaying: 8 dilatory
dele: 4 omit 5 erase 6 cancel, delete, efface, remove 7 expunge 9 eradicate, extirpate 10 obliterate
delectable: 5 tasty 8 pleasing 9 delicious,
  desirable, diverting, enjoyable 10 delightful 11 pleasurable
delegate: 4 name, send 6 assign, commit,
  depute, deputy, legate, nuncio 7 appoint, consign, empower, entrust 8 emissary, transfer 9 authorize, surrogate
  10 commission 12 commissioner 14
  representative
delegation: 7 mission 9 committee 10
  deputation
delete: 4 dele, omit 5 erase, purge 6 cancel, remove 7 destroy, expunge 9 eliminate, eradicate 10 obliterate
  opposite of: 4 stet 7 put back, restore
deleterious: bad 7 harmful, hurtful, noxious 8 damaging 9 injurious, malignant
  10 pernicious 11 destructive, detrimental, prejudicial
Delian god: 6 Apollo
deliberate: 4 cool, pore 5 study, think,
  weigh 6 advise, confer, debate, ponder
  7 consult, planned, reflect, resolve 8
  consider, measured, meditate, mull over
  9 determine, leisurely, speculate, voluntary 10 purposeful, thought out 11 circumspect, intentional 12 premeditated
  13 dispassionate
deliberation: 7 counsel 10 reflection
  without: 4 rash 8 headlong 9 on impulse
Delibes ballet: 5 Naila 6 Kassya 8 Cop-
  pelia, La Source

  opera: 5 Lakme
delible: 10 eradicable
delicacy: roe 4 cate, ease, tact 5 taste 6
  caviar, dainty, luxury, nicety 7 finesse
  8 niceness, pleasure, subtlety 9 exactness, precision 10 daintiness, feminini-
  ty, refinement 11 savoir faire 13 gratification
  lacking: 5 gross 7 boorish 9 unrefined
delicate: 4 airy, fine, lacy, nice 5 frail,
  light, silky 6 dainty, minion, petite,
  puling, queasy, slight, tender 7 elegant,
  finical, fragile, minikin, refined, subtile
  tenuous 8 araneose, araneous, charming, ethereal, graceful, luscious, migniard, pleaseant 9 agreeable, beautiful,
  exquisite, sensitive 10 delightful, fastidious 11 comfortable, considerate
delicatessen: 11 charcuterie
delicious: 5 tasty, yummy 6 savory 8
  heavenly 9 ambrosial, exquisite, luxurious, nectarous, toothsome 10 delectable, delightful 11 scrumptious
delight: joy 4 glee, love 5 bliss, charm,
  feast, mirth, revel 6 admire, divert, liking, please, ravish, regale 7 ecstasy, enchant, gladden, gratify, rapture, rejoice
  8 entrance, gladness, pleasure, savoring
  9 delectate, enjoyment, enrapture, happiness 11 delectation
  in: 6 relish
delightful: 4 nice 6 dreamy 7 elysian 8
  adorable, delicate, glorious 9 delicious
  10 delectable, enchanting, entrancing
  11 pleasureful
Delilah's paramour: 6 Samson
delimit: See **define**
delineate: map 4 draw, limn, line 5 trace
  6 blazon, depict, design, sketch, survey
  7 outline, picture, portray 8 describe 9
  represent 12 characterize
delineation: 5 image 7 account 10 expression
delinquency: 7 default, failure, misdeed,
  offense 8 omission 9 violation 10 misconduct 11 dereliction, malfeasance,
  misdemeanor
delinquent: lax 6 remiss 7 overdue 8 behind in 9 negligent 12 teen offender
deliquesce: 4 thaw, melt 7 liquefy 8 dissolve
delirious: mad 4 wild 5 manic 6 insane,
  raving 7 frantic, lunatic 8 deranged, ecstatic frenetic, frenzied 9 rapturous 10
  irrational 11 lightheaded
delirium: 5 fever, mania 10 aberration
  13 hallucination
delirium tremens: 6 shakes 7 horrors
delitescent: 6 latent 10 obfuscated
deliver: rid 4 bail, deal, free, give, save,
  tell 5 bring, serve, speak, utter 6 commit, convey, redeem, render, rescue, resign, succor, unbind 7 consign, declaim,

dictate, present, release, relieve **8** dispatch, hand over, liberate **9** enunciate, pronounce, surrender **10** bring forth, emancipate **11** come through

delivery: 5 birth **6** rescue **7** address **8** shipment **9** rendition **11** deliverance, parturition **12** accouchement

dell: 4 dale, glen, vale **6** dingle, ravine, valley

Delphi: 6 oracle, shrine
god: **6** Apollo
priestess: **5** Pythia

Delphic: 5 vague **7** cryptic, obscure **9** ambiguous, enigmatic

delphinium: 8 larkspur

delta: 8 alluvium, triangle

delude: 4 bilk, dupe, fool **5** cheat, evade, trick **6** take in **7** beguile, deceive, mislead **8** hoodwink **10** circumvent, lead astray

deluge: sea **4** flow **5** flood, swamp **6** engulf **7** niagara, torrent **8** downpour, inundate, overflow, submerge **9** cataclysm, overpower, overwhelm **10** cloudburst

delusion: 5 dream, trick **6** mirage, vision **7** chimera, fallacy, fantasy **8** illusion, phantasm **9** deception **13** appersonation, hallucination
Buddhist: **4** moha
of grandeur: **11** megalomania
partner of: **5** snare

delusive: 5 false **6** unreal **7** seeming **8** fanciful, illusory **9** deceiving, imaginary

deluxe: 5 plush, super **6** choice **7** elegant, opulent **8** palatial **9** extra fine, luxurious, sumptuous

delve: dig, dip **4** mine, seek **5** plumb, probe **6** search **7** dig into, explore **11** investigate

demagogic: 8 factious

demagogue, demagog: 6 leader **8** agitator, fomenter **10** instigator **12** rabble rouser

demand: ask, cry **4** call, need **5** claim, exact, order, query **6** charge, elicit, expect, summon **7** command, inquire, mandate, request, require **8** question **9** challenge **10** commission **11** requisition

demandable: due

demarcate: 5 bound, limit **6** define **7** mark off **8** separate **12** circumscribe, discriminate

demean: 5 abase, lower **6** debase **7** degrade **8** belittle, maltreat **9** disparage, humiliate

demeanor: 4 mien, **5** habit **6** action **7** bearing, conduct **8** behavior, carriage, portance **9** treatment **10** deportment, management **11** comportment, countenance

demented: mad **4** luny **5** buggy, crazy, nutty **6** insane **7** fatuous **8** deranged

demerit: 5 fault **7** bad mark **11** short-

coming **12** imperfection

Demeter: 5 Ceres
daughter: **4** Kore **10** Persephone, Proserpina, Proserpine
headdress: **5** polos
mother: **4** Rhea
shrine: **9** anaktoron

demigod: 4 hero **7** godling
pert. to: **7** satyric
sylvan: **4** faun **5** satyr

demirep: 11 adventuress

demise: 5 death **7** decease **8** bequeath **13** pass by descent

demit: 5 lower **6** resign **8** abdicate, withdraw **10** relinquish **11** resignation

demiurgic: 8 creative **9** formative

demo: 5 model **7** display, protest **13** show of feeling, test recording

demobilize: 7 break up, disband **9** muster out **12** demilitarize

democratic: 7 popular **10** self-ruling **11** egalitarian, not snobbish

demode: 5 passe **8** outdated **12** old-fashioned

demoiselle: 5 crane **7** kaikara

demolish: 4 raze, ruin **5** level, waste, wreck **6** batter **7** destroy **9** devastate, overthrow

demon: hag, imp, nat **4** aitu, atua, ogre **5** devil, fiend, genie, lamia, Satan, witch **6** Abigor, afreet **7** villain, warlock **10** evil spirit
assembly of: **6** sabbat
drive out: **8** exorcize
female: **8** succubus
Hebrew: **8** Asmodeus
Iroquois: **5** otkon
person possessed by: **9** energumen
prince of: **9** Beelzebub
worship of: **9** diabolism
Zoroastrian: **5** daeva

demoniac: 7 satanic **8** devilish, diabolic, fiendish, infernal **10** diabolical

demonstrate: 4 show **5** prove **7** display, explain, portray **8** manifest

demonstration: 4 show, sign **5** proof **9** portrayal **10** apparition **11** mass protest **12** illustration **13** manifestation

demonstrative: 4 that, this **5** these, those **8** effusive, outgoing **9** emotional, expansive, ostensive **12** unrestrained

demoralize: 6 weaken **7** confuse, corrupt, deprave, pervert, unnerve **8** disspirit **9** undermine **10** discourage, dishearten **11** disorganize

Demosthenes: *follower:* **5** Bryan **6** orator
oration: **9** philippic

demote: 4 bust **6** reduce **9** downgrade

demotic: 6 common **7** popular

demulcent: 8 soothing **9** softening **10** mollifying

demur: 4 stay **5** delay, doubt, pause **6** boggle, linger, object **7** protest, scruple

8 hesitate, question 9 challenge 12 ir-resolution

demure: coy, shy 4 prim 5 grave, staid 6 modest, sedate 8 composed, decorous

den: mew 4 cave, cove, dell, dive, glen, hole, lair, nest, room 5 bield, cabin, couch, haunt, study 6 burrow, cavern, covert, grotto, hollow, ravine 7 retreat 8 hideaway, snuggery, workroom

denary: 7 tenfold

dendroid: 8 tree-like 11 arborescent

dendrophilous: 8 arboreal

denial: See **deny**

denigrate: 5 libel 6 defame, malign 7 disdain, put down, slander 8 ridicule 9 deprecate, disparage 10 speak ill of

denizen: 6 native 7 citizen, dweller, habitué 8 resident 10 inhabitant

Denmark: *capital:* 10 Copenhagen

city: 5 Arhus 6 Alborg, Odense 7 Esbjerg 8 Elsinore, Gentofte

county: Fyn 4 Ribe 5 Arhus, Vejle 6 Viborg 8 Bornholm

fjord: Ise, Lim 8 Mariager, Roskilde

flag: 9 Dannebrog

island: Als, Fyn 4 Aero 5 Samso 7 Falster, Lolland 8 Bornholm 9 Langeland

measure: ell, fod, mil, pot 4 alen, favn, rode 5 album, kande, linje, paegl, tomme 6 achtel, paegel, paegle, skeppe 7 landmil, oltonde, skieppe, viertel 8 fjerding 9 korntonde, ottingkar

monetary unit: ore 5 krone

parliament: 9 Folketing

peninsula: 7 Jutland

river: 4 Omme, Stor 5 Varde 6 Gudena

ruler: 4 Cnut, Eric, Knut 5 Sweyn 6 Canute 8 Waldemar 9 Christian, Margrethe

sea: 5 North 6 Baltic

sea inlet: 8 Kattegat 9 Skagerrak

territory: 9 Greenland 13 Faeroe Islands

weight: es; lod, ort, vog 4 eser(pl.), last, mark, pund, unze 5 carat, kvint, pound, quint, tonde 6 toende 7 centner, lispund, quintin 8 lispound, skippund 9 ship pound, skibslast 10 bismerpund

dennet: gig 8 carriage

denominate: 4 call, name 5 title 6 denote 8 christen, indicate, nominate 9 designate

denomination: 4 cult, sect 5 class, title, value 6 church 7 society 8 category 9 communion 10 persuasion 11 appellation

religious: 7 Baptist 8 Lutheran 9 Methodist, Unitarian 12 Episcopalian, Presbyterian 14 Congregational

denotation: 4 sign 5 token

denote: 4 give, mark, mean, name, show 6 import 7 betoken, express 8 indicate 9 designate, recommend, represent 10 denominate

denouement: end 6 answer, result 7 outcome 8 solution 11 explanation

denounce: 6 accuse, delate, descry, menace, scathe 7 arraign, condemn, upbraid 8 threaten 9 fulminate 10 stigmatize 13 inform against

de novo: 4 anew 5 again, newly 6 afresh 8 once more 12 from the start

dense: 4 firm 5 close, foggy, gross, heavy, murky, silly, solid, thick 6 obtuse, stupid 7 compact, crowded, serried 11 thickheaded 12 impenetrable

density: 4 mass 11 compactness

dent: 4 bash, dint, nick 5 dinge, notch, tooth 6 batter, hallow, indent 7 blemish, depress 10 depression, impression 11 indentation

dentate: 6 jagged 7 serrate, toothed

dentil: 5 block

dentin, dentine: 5 ivory 6 enamel

dentistry: *appliance:* dam 4 burr

branch: 9 exodontia 11 orthodontia 12 orthodontics

plastic: 6 cement

tool: 6 scaler 7 forceps

denture: 5 plate 10 set of teeth

denude: 4 bare 5 scalp, strip 6 divest 11 decorticate

denunciation (see also **denounce**): 7 censure 8 diatribe 9 philippic 10 accusation 11 malediction 12 condemnation

deny: nay 5 debar, repel 6 abjure, disown, forbid, impugn, negate, refuse, refute, reject, renege 7 confute, deprive, disavow, dispute, forsake, gainsay, protest 8 abnegate, disclaim, forswear, renounce, withhold 9 disaffirm 10 contradict, contravene, controvert

deodar: 5 cedar

depart: die 4 blow, exit, pass, quit, vary 5 found, leave, mosey, sever 6 begone, decamp, demise, desist, divide, perish, recede, retire, sunder 7 abscond, deviate, forsake, get away, pull out, retreat, take off, vamoose 8 farewell, separate, withdraw

department: 4 part 5 realm 6 branch, bureau, sphere 7 portion 8 division, province 11 subdivision

departure: 4 exit 5 death, going, twist 6 egress, exodus 7 decease 9 deviation 10 difference, divergence 11 abandonment, leavetaking

words of: 4 ta-ta 5 aloha 6 so long 7 goodbye 8 farewell

depend: 4 bank, hang, lean, rely, rest, turn 5 count, hinge, trust 7 confide

dependable: 4 sure 5 loyal, solid 6 secure, steady 7 certain 8 faithful, reliable 11 responsible, trustworthy

dependency: 6 colony 7 apanage, mandate 8 appanage

dependent: 4 ward 5 child 6 client, minion, vassal 7 subject 8 clinging, follower 9 reliant on 10 contingent, sequacious 11 conditional, provisional, subordinate

depict: 4 draw, limn 5 paint 6 blazon 7 picture, portray 8 describe 9 delineate, represent 12 characterize

depilate: 4 husk 5 shave

depilatory: 5 rusma

depilous: 8 hairless

deplete: 5 drain, empty, use up 6 reduce, unload 7 exhaust 8 diminish 10 impoverish

deplorable: sad 8 grievous, terrible, wretched 10 calamitous, lamentable 11 distressing, unfortunate

deplore: rue 4 moan, sigh, wail 5 mourn 6 bemoan, bewail, grieve, lament, regret 10 disapprove

deploy: 6 unfold 7 display 9 spread out

deplume: 5 pluck, strip

depone: 5 swear 7 testify 11 bear witness

deport: 5 evict, exile, expel 6 banish, behave, demean 7 bearing, conduct 8 send away 9 transport

deportment: air 4 gest, mien 5 geste, havit 6 action, manner 7 address, bearing, conduct 8 behavior, breeding, carriage, demeanor

depose: 4 aver, oust 5 abase 6 affirm, assert, divest, remove 7 degrade, dismiss, testify 8 dethrone, displace 10 dispossess

deposit: lay, set 4 bank, cast, dump, fund, hock, pawn 5 chest, lodge, place, store 6 entomb, pledge, repose, settle 7 consign, entrust, put down 8 security 11 part payment 12 accumulation
alluvial: 5 delta, geest
black: 4 soot
earthy: 4 gobi, marl, sand, silt 5 loess, trona 6 sludge 8 alluvium
geyser: 6 sinter 10 travertine
glacial: 4 kame 5 eskar, esker 7 moraine
gold-containing: 6 placer
gravel: 5 apron
marine: 5 coral
mineral: bed 4 lode, vein 5 manto
roric: dew
teeth: 6 tartar
wine cask: 6 tartar

deposition: 6 burial 7 deposit, opinion 8 sediment 9 affidavit, statement, testimony 10 allegation 11 declaration 12 displacement 13 precipitation

depository: 4 bank, safe 5 attic, chest, vault 6 locker 7 ossuary 9 strongbox

depot: 4 base, gare(F.) 6 aurang(Ind.), aurung 7 arsenal, station 8 magazine, terminal, terminus 9 warehouse 10 storehouse

deprave: 5 taint 6 debase, defile, malign, revile 7 corrupt, pervert, vitiate 10 degenerate, depreciate

depraved: bad 4 evil, ugly, vile 6 rotten, wicked 7 bestial, immoral, vicious 9 abandoned, graceless 10 profligate 11 demoralized 12 incorrigible

depravity: 4 vice 8 villainy

deprecate: 8 play down 9 denigrate, underrate 10 depreciate, disapprove

depreciate: 4 fall 5 abase, decry, slump 6 lessen, reduce, shrink 7 cheapen, degrade, depress, detract, devalue 8 belittle, derogate, diminish, minimize 9 disparage, dispraise, downgrade 10 undervalue

depredate: rob 4 prey, raze, sack 5 spoil 6 thieve, ravage 7 despoil, destroy, pillage, plunder 8 lay waste, prey upon

depress: bow, cow 4 dash, dent, fall, sink 5 abase, appal, chill, crush, lower, slump 6 appall, dampen, dismay, humble, indent, lessen, sadden, weaken 7 degrade, flatten 8 browbeat, diminish, dispirit, enfeeble 9 subjugate 10 depreciate, discourage, dishearten

depressed: low, sad 4 blue, down, glum 6 gloomy, hollow, lonely, oblate, somber, triste 8 dejected, downcast 9 afflicted, heartsore 10 in the dumps, spiritless 11 downhearted, melancholic

depressing: 5 bleak 6 dismal, dreary

depression: dip, pit 4 fall, foss, howe(Sc.) 5 atrio, basin, cowal, crypt, dinge, fossa, fosse, nadir 6 cafard, cavity, crater, dismay, gulley, ravine, valley 7 alveola, blowout 8 doldrums 9 dejection 11 despondency
between mountains: col
pert. to: 6 bathic

deprivation: 4 loss, want 6 penury 7 amotion, poverty 8 hardship 11 destitution

deprive: rob 4 deny 5 strip 6 depose, divest, hinder, remove 7 bereave, cashier, despoil 9 dismantle, relieve of 10 dispossess

deprived: 4 reft 5 needy 12 impoverished

depth: 5 abyss 8 deepness, strength 9 abundance, intensity 10 profundity 11 perspective 12 abstruseness, completeness, profoundness
in: 8 thorough 13 comprehensive
without: 4 thin 7 cursory, shallow, sketchy 11 superficial

depth charge: 4 bomb, mine 10 projectile

depths: 5 heart 7 lowness 10 inmost part

deputation: 7 mission 10 delegation

depute: 4 send 5 allot 6 asign, devote 7 appoint 8 delegate 10 commission, constitute

deputy: 4 aide 5 agent, envoy, proxy, vicar 6 commis, legate 7 bailiff 8 delegate

9 assistant, surrogate, vigilante 10 substitute

deracinate: 6 uproot 9 eradicate, extirpate

derange: 5 upset 7 confuse, disturb, perturb 8 disorder, displace, unsettle 9 interrupt 10 discompose 11 disorganize

deranged: mad 5 crazy 6 insane 8 demented, maniacal 10 distraught, unbalanced

derby: hat 4 race, town 5 shire 6 bowler

deregulate: 8 end curbs 9 decontrol 11 free of rules

derelict: bum, lax 4 hobo, wino 5 dingy, seedy, tramp 6 remiss, shabby 7 drifter, run down, vagrant 8 castaway, deserted, forsaken 9 abandoned 10 delinquent, neglectful

deride: 4 geck(Sc.), gibe, hoot, jape, jeer, mock, twit 5 fleer, rally, scoff, scorn, taunt 6 illude 8 ridicule 9 make fun of

de rigueur: 5 right 6 proper 7 correct 8 required 11 fashionable

derision: 8 contempt
sound of: boo 4 hiss 5 snort

derivation: 6 origin, source 9 etymology 10 wellspring

derivative: 7 spin-off 8 offshoot 9 outgrowth, traceable 10 unoriginal

derive: get 4 draw, stem 5 carry, infer, trace 6 deduce, evolve, gather, obtain 7 extract, proceed, receive 9 originate

derm: 4 skin 7 cuticle

dermal filament: 4 hair

dernier cri: 4 mode, rage 5 craze, style, vogue 7 fashion 8 last word

derogate: 5 annul, decry 6 lessen, repeal 7 detract, slander 8 restrict, withdraw 9 disparage 10 depreciate

derrick: rig 4 lift, spar 5 crane, davit, hoist 6 tackle
part: jib, leg 4 boom

derring-do: 7 bravado, courage 8 audacity

derringer: 6 pistol, weapon

dervish: 5 fakir 9 mendicant
cap: taj
of Arabian Nights: 4 Agib
practice: 7 dancing, howling 8 whirling

descant: 4 sing, song 6 melody, remark, warble 7 comment 9 discourse 11 observation 12 counterpoint, dissertation 13 accompaniment

descend: 4 fall, sink 5 avale, lower, stoop 6 alight, derive, go down 7 decline 9 originate 10 spring from
by rope: 6 rappel

descendant: son 4 cion, heir, seed 5 child, scion 7 spin-off 8 offshoot 9 offspring

descendants: 4 seed 5 issue 7 progeny 9 posterity 10 generation

descended from same mother: 5 enate 6 enatic

descent: 4 drop, fall 5 birth, chute, issue, scarp, slope, stock 6 escarp, strain 7 assault, decline, lineage 8 ancestry, breeding, downfall, pedigree 9 avalanche, declivity, onslaught 10 declension, derivation, extraction, generation 11 declination, degradation, inclination
airplane: 8 approach
skier's: 6 schuss

describe: 4 tell 6 define, depict, relate, report 7 declare, explain, express, narrate, outline, picture, portray, recount 9 delineate, designate, discourse, enumerate, represent 10 illustrate 12 characterize

description; ilk 4 kind, sort, type 7 account, recital, variety, version 9 chronicle 12 presentation

descry: see, spy 4 espy 5 sight 6 behold, detect, reveal, turn up 7 discern, display 8 disclose, discover, perceive 9 determine 11 distinguish

Desdemona: *husband:* 7 Othello
servant: 6 Emilia
slayer: 7 Othello
traducer: 4 Iago

desecrate: 5 abuse 6 defile 7 pollute, profane, violate 8 unhallow 11 contaminate

desecration: 9 blasphemy, sacrilege

desert: due, rat 4 bolt, fail, flee, sand 5 merit, waste 6 decamp, defect, go AWOL, renege, reward 7 abandon, abscond, badland, demerit, forsake, hornada 8 renounce 9 backslide, wasteland 10 punishment, relinquish, wilderness
area: 4 Gobi 6 Libyan, Mohave, Nubian, Sahara 7 Arabian, Painted
area of shifting sand: erg
beast: 5 camel 9 dromedary
dweller: 4 Arab 5 nomad 7 Bedouin
hallucination: 6 mirage
pert. to: 6 eremic
rat: 10 prospector
region: erg
science: 9 eremology
ship: 5 camel
shrub: 5 retem 6 alhagi, cactus, raetam 10 camel thorn
train: 7 caravan
valley: 6 bolson
vehicle: 9 dune buggy
watering spot: 5 oasis
wind: 6 samiel, simoom 7 sirocco

desert candle: 5 plant 8 ocotillo

desert-like: dry 4 arid, sere

deserted: 6 lonely 7 forlorn 8 desolate, forsaken 9 abandoned 11 uninhabited

deserter: rat 6 bolter 8 apostate, defector, fugitive, recreant, renegade

deserve: 4 earn, rate 5 merit 10 be worthy of

desiccate: dry 4 sear 5 drain, parch 6

wither **7** shrivel **9** dehydrate
desideratum: 4 need **6** desire
design: aim, end, map **4** draw, goal, idea, mean, plan, plot **5** allot, decor, drift, et- tle, model, motif, shape **6** device, in- tend, intent, invent, layout, object, sketch **7** destine, diagram, fashion, out- line, pattern, project, propose, purpose **8** contrive **9** calculate, delineate, inten- tion **10** conception **11** contemplate, contrivance
inlaid: **6** mosaic **8** intarsia
of scattered objects: **4** seme
open: **8** filigree, fretwork
perforated: **7** stencil
raised: **8** repousse **9** bas relief
skin: **6** tattoo
sunken: **8** intaglio
designate: set **4** mark, mean, name, show **5** label, style, title **6** assign, denote, in- tend, settle **7** appoint, entitle, specify **8** describe, identify, indicate **9** appellate, nuncupate **10** denominate **11** distin- guish **12** characterize
designed: 8 prepense **10** thought out **11** intentional **12** premeditated
designer: 7 planner, plotter, schemer **8** engineer **9** architect, couturier
designing: 6 artful, crafty **7** cunning **8** planning, plotting, scheming **10** fore- seeing, fraudulent
desinential: 8 terminal
desipient: 5 silly **7** foolish
desirable: 7 welcome **8** eligible, pleasing, salutary **9** agreeable, excellent **10** at- tractive, beneficial, worthwhile
desire: yen **4** care, hope, itch, lust, need, urge, want, will, wish **5** ardor, covet, crave, mania, yearn **6** affect, aspire, hanker, hunger, prefer, thirst, yammer **7** craving, fantasy, inkling, longing, passion **8** appetite, cupidity **9** appeten- cy, cacoethes **10** desiderium
want of: **11** inappetence
desirous: 4 fain, fond **5** eager **6** ardent, greedy **7** envious, wishful **8** covetous **10** solicitous **11** acquisitive
desist: 4 ease, halt, quit, stop **5** cease **7** abstain, forbear, hold off **11** discon- tinue, refrain from
desk: pew **4** ambo **5** board, table **6** pulpit **7** lectern **8** prie-dieu **9** davenport, monocleid, secretary **10** escritoire, monocleide
desman: 4 mole **7** muskrat
Desmanthus: 5 Acuan
desmid: 4 alga **5** algae(pl.)
desolate: sad **4** bare, lorn, ruin, sack, sole **5** alone, bleak, gaunt **6** dreary, gloomy, lonely, ravage **7** destroy, forlorn, lack- ing **8** deprived, deserted, forsaken, soli- tary **9** abandoned, destitute, dissolute,

woebegone **11** comfortless, uninhabited **12** disconsolate
desolation: woe **5** grief, havoc **6** sorrow **7** sadness **10** melancholy **11** destruction, devastation
area of: **5** waste **6** desert
Desmodium: 7 trefoil
despair: 5 gloom **6** give up **8** lose hope **10** melancholy **11** despondency **12** hope- lessness
desperado: 6 bandit, outlaw **7** ruffian **8** criminal **10** lawbreaker
desperate: mad **4** rash **7** extreme, frantic **8** headlong, hopeless, perilous, reckless **9** dangerous **10** despairing, despondent, infuriated, outrageous **11** precipitate **13** irretrievable
despicable: low **4** base, mean, vile **5** cheap, dirty **6** abject, paltry, scurvy, shabby, sordid **7** caitiff, ignoble **8** un- worthy, wretched **9** loathsome, miser- able **11** ignominious **12** contemptible, contemptuous
despise: 4 defy, hate **5** scorn, scout, spurn **6** detest, loathe, slight **7** contemn, dis- dain **8** misprize, vilipend **9** abominate, disregard **10** look down on
despite: 4 hate, snub **6** injury, insult, mal- ice **7** ill will **8** aversion, contempt **12** regardless of
despoil: rob **4** raid, ruin, sack **5** harry, reave, rifle, strip **6** divest, fleece, ravage, ravish, remove **7** bereave, deprive, dis- robe, pillage, plunder **8** deflower, disar- ray, unclothe **9** depredate
Despoina: 4 Kore **10** Persephone
despondency: 6 misery **7** despair **10** de- pression, melancholy **11** desperation
despondent: sad **4** blue **8** dejected, down- cast, hopeless **9** woebegone **10** dispirit- ed **11** discouraged **12** disconsolate, heavyhearted
despot: 4 czar, tsar, tzar **6** satrap, tyrant **7** autarch, monarch **8** autocrat, dictator **9** strong man
despotic: 6 lordly **8** absolute, dominant **9** arbitrary **10** tyrannical
dessert: ice, pie **4** cake **5** fruit, glace(Fr.) **6** eclair, mousse, pastry, sweets **7** ban- quet, pudding, sherbet, strudel **8** ice cream, Napoleon, sillabub **9** pound cake, sweetmeat **10** blanc-mange
destination: aim, end **4** fate, goal **7** ad- dress **8** terminus **9** objective **12** end of the line
destine: 6 decree, direct, doom to, intend **9** devise for, fix before, preordain **11** assign ahead, set aside for **12** predeter- mine
destiny: lot **4** doom, fate **5** karma **6** fu- ture, kismet **7** fortune **8** God's will **13** inevitability

destitute: 4 poor 5 clean, needy 6 bereft, devoid, wasted 7 forlorn, lacking, wanting 8 bankrupt, beggared, defeated, deprived, desolate, forsaken, helpless, indigent 9 abandoned, defaulted, driftless 10 devastated, frustrated 12 disappointed, impoverished

destroy: eat, end, gut 4 blow, full, raze, ruin, rush, slay, undo 5 break, craze, erase, erode, quell, smash, smite, spoil, wrack, wreck 6 blight, cumber, deface, defeat, efface, famish, ravage 7 abolish, consume, expunge, overrun 8 amortize, confound, decimate, demolish, desolate, dissolve, mutilate, overturn, sabotage 9 depredate, devastate, dismantle, eradicate, extirpate, liquidate, overthrow 10 annihilate, counteract, extinguish 11 assassinate, exterminate

destroyed: 5 kaput

destroyer: hun 6 vandal 7 warship 8 saboteur

Destroyer: 4 Siva

Destroying Angel: *fungus:* 7 amanita
Mormon: 6 Danite

destruction: end 4 bane, doom, loss, ruin 5 decay, havoc, waste 7 Abaddon(Heb.) 8 downfall, excision, shambles 9 holocaust, perdition 10 extinction, subversion
god: 4 Siva
goddess: Ara
of species: 8 genocide

destructive: 4 fell 5 fatal 6 deadly, mortal 7 baleful, deathly, fateful, harmful, hurtful, noisome, noxious, ruinous 8 wasteful 9 poisonous, truculent 10 catawampus, pernicious 11 deleterious, internecine

desuetude: 6 disuse 7 neglect 12 obsolescence 14 discontinuance

desultory: 4 idle 5 hasty, loose 6 casual, fitful, random, roving 7 aimless, cursory 8 rambling, unsteady, wavering 9 irregular, unsettled 10 discursive, incidental, inconstant 12 disconnected

detach: 5 sever 6 cut off 7 disjoin, divorce, isolate 8 disunite, separate, unfasten, withdraw 9 disengage 10 disconnect

detached: 4 free 5 alone, aloof, apart 7 neutral, removed 8 taken off, unbiased 10 impersonal 11 unconcerned, unconnected 13 disinterested, dispassionate

detail: 4 item 6 assign, nicety, relate 7 account, appoint, article, itemize, minutia, narrate, specify 8 rehearse, salience, spell out 9 enumerate, narrative 10 particular 11 stipulation 12 circumstance

detailed: 4 full 6 minute, prolix 8 itemized, thorough, tiresome 9 wearisome

10 meticulous, protracted

detain: 4 hold, keep, stay, stop 5 check, delay 6 arrest, hinder, retard 8 imprison, restrain, withhold
in time of war: 6 intern

detect: see, spy 4 espy, find, spot 5 catch 6 descry, divine, expose, reveal 7 develop, discern, nose out, uncover 8 decipher, discover

detection device: 5 radar, sonar 6 dowser 11 divining rod

detective: tec 4 bull, dick 6 sleuth, tracer 7 gumshoe, scenter, spotter 8 flatfoot, operator, Sam Spade, The Saint 9 James Bond, Nero Wolfe 10 Martin Kane, Miss Marple, Nick Carter, Perry Mason, Peter Salem, Philo Vance 11 Charlie Chan, Ellery Queen, Green Hornet, Nick Charles 12 investigator, Simon Templar 13 Hercule Poirot, Michael Shayne, Philip Marlowe 14 Sherlock Holmes
story writer: 8 Rex Stout 10 Ian Fleming 11 Ellery Queen 14 Agatha Christie 15 Dashiell Hammett, Raymond Chandler 16 Arthur Conan Doyle 18 Erle Stanley Gardner

detector: 7 reagent
storm: 7 sferics
weather change: 9 barometer

detent: dog 4 pawl 5 catch, click

detente: 8 easement 13 rapproachement

detention: 5 delay 7 capture 9 hindrance, restraint 10 arrestment

deter: bar 5 block, check, delay 6 hinder, retard 7 prevent 8 dissuade, keep from, restrain 9 constrain 10 discourage, dishearten, intimidate

detergent: 4 soap 7 purging, smectic, solvent 8 cleanser 9 cleansing

deteriorate: 4 fail 5 decay, spoil 6 debase, impair, weaken 7 decline, wear out 9 backslide 10 degenerate

determinable: 5 fixed 8 definite 9 judicable 10 mensurable

determinate: 7 certain 8 definite, resolute, resolved, specific 9 arbitrary 10 invariable 11 established

determinative: 5 final 7 shaping 8 limiting 9 directing 10 conclusive 13 authoritative

determine: end, fix, get 4 test 5 assay, award 6 assess, assign, decide, decree, define, descry, settle 7 adjudge, analyze, appoint, arrange, dispose, resolve 8 conclude 9 admeasure, arbitrate, ascertain, calculate 10 adjudicate, constitute, deliberate, predestine

determined: set 4 bent, firm 6 dogged, intent, mulish, sturdy 7 decided, settled 8 foregone, perverse, resolute, resolved, stubborn 9 obstinate, pigheaded 10 persistent, unyielding

deterrent: 5 block 6 hurdle 8 obstacle 9 hindrance 14 discouragement

detest: 4 damn, hate 5 abhor, curse 6 loathe 7 condemn, despise, dislike 8 denounce, execrate 9 abominate

detestable: 4 foul, vile 6 horrid, odious 7 heinous 8 infamous 9 nefarious 10 despicable 12 antipathetic

dethrone: 6 depose, divest

detonate: 4 fire 5 blast 6 blow up, set off 7 explode 9 fulminate

detonator: cap 7 torpedo 9 explosive

detour: 5 avoid, skirt 6 bypass 7 circuit 8 go around 9 deviation

detract: 5 decry 6 defame, divert, vilify 7 asperse, traduce 8 belittle, derogate, minimize 9 disparage 10 depreciate

detraction: 7 calumny, scandal, slander

detriment: 4 cost, hurt, loss 5 damna(pl.), wound 6 damage, injury 8 mischief 9 disprofit 10 impediment 12 disadvantage

detrimental: 7 adverse, harmful, hurtful 9 injurious 10 pernicious 11 deleterious

detritus: 4 tuff 5 chaff, scree, waste 6 debris 7 garbage, rubbish

de trop: 6 excess 7 too much, surplus 8 in the way, unwanted 11 superfluous

deva: 5 angel, deity

Devaki's son: 7 Krishna

devalue: See **depreciate**

devastate: 6 ravage 7 destroy, pillage, plunder, scourge 8 demolish, lay waste 10 depopulate

develop: 4 form, grow 5 arise, ripen 6 appear, detect, evolve, expand, flower, mature, reveal, unfold, unfurl 7 educate, enlarge, expound, uncover 8 disclose, discover, engender, generate, manifest 9 elaborate, germinate, transpire 11 come to light, materialize

development: 6 growth 7 stature 8 breeding, increase 9 evolution, expansion, formation, unfolding 11 elaboration

arrested: 7 aplasia

full: 8 maturity, ripeness

going back: 13 retrogression

Devi: *beneficent:* 5 Guari

consort: 4 Siva

fierce: 4 Kali

light: Uma

malignant: 5 Durga

riding a tiger: 6 Chandi

deviate: err, yaw 4 lean, miss, vary, veer 5 drift, lapse, sheer, stray 6 change, depart, detour, recede, squint, swerve, wander 7 decline, deflect, digress, diverge

from the norm: 6 mutate

from the vertical: 4 hade 5 angle, slant 10 out of plumb

deviation: 7 anomaly 11 declination

device: gin, mot 4 tool 5 drift, meter, motto, shift 6 design, emblem, gadget, scheme 7 compass, fiction, impresa, imprese, project, vehicle 8 artifice, fastener, gimcrack 9 apparatus, appliance, doohickey, expedient, invention, regulator, stratagem 10 concoction, instrument 11 contraption, contrivance

curve measuring: 9 rotameter

holding: 4 vise 5 clamp

devil: imp 4 Deil(Sc.), haze, mahu 5 annoy, bogey, demon, fiend, Satan, tease 6 dybbuk, pester 7 Amaimon, clootie, dickens, gremlin, Lucifer, Old Nick, torment, warlock 8 Apollyon, diabolus, Mephisto 9 archfiend, Beelzebub, cacodemon, scoundrel

Dante's: 8 Cagnazzo

pert. to: 7 satanic 10 diabolical

printer's: 10 apprentice

ruler: 10 diabolarch

tree: 4 dita

worship: 8 satanism

devil's bones: 4 dice

devil-may-care: gay 4 fast, rash 5 blasé 6 madcap 7 raffish 8 heedless, reckless 9 imprudent 10 nonchalant 11 harum-scarum

deviled: 9 a la diable

devilfish: ray 5 manta

devilish: 6 daring, rakish, wicked 7 demonic, extreme, hellish, inhuman, satanic 8 demoniac, diabolic, fiendish, infernal 9 excessive 10 diabolical 15 Mephistophelian

devilkin: imp

devious: sly 4 foxy 6 crafty, errant, roving, shifty, tricky 7 vagrant, winding 8 indirect, rambling, tortuous 9 eccentric, irregular 10 circuitous, farfetched, roundabout

devise: 4 plan, plot, will 5 array, frame, forge, weave 6 convey, cook up, design, invent, scheme 7 appoint, arrange, bethink, concoct, consult, dream up, prepare 8 bequeath, contrive 9 construct, fabricate, formulate 11 put together

devitalize: 6 deaden 10 eviscerate

devoid: 4 bare 5 empty 6 barren, free of, vacant 7 lacking, wanting 9 destitute

devoir: 4 duty, task 6 effort

devolve: 4 pass 8 overturn, transfer, transmit 11 change hands

devote: vow 4 ally, avow, doom, give 5 apply 6 addict, attach, bestow, depute, resign 7 address, consign, destine 8 dedicate, venerate 10 consecrate 11 appropriate

devoted: 4 true 5 liege, loyal, pious 6 devout, fervid **7** adoring, arduous, zealous **8** attached, constant, faithful **9** assiduous, religious **10** obsequious, venerating **11** whole-souled **12** affectionate, wholehearted

devotee: fan, nun **4** buff, monk **6** votary, zealot **7** admirer, amateur, fanatic **8** follower, partisan **9** supporter **10** aficionado, enthusiast

devotion: **4** aves(pl.) **6** fealty, prayer **7** loyalty, passion, worship **8** fidelity **9** adoration, reverence **10** allegiance
excessive: **13** ecclesiolatry
object of: **4** idol **5** totem **6** fetich, fetish
period of: **4** Lent **6** novena

devour: eat **4** fret **5** raven, waste **6** engulf **7** consume, engorge **10** annihilate

devout: **4** good, holy, warm **5** godly, pious **6** hearty, solemn **7** cordial, devoted, godlike, saintly, sincere **8** reverent **9** religious, righteous, spiritual **13** sanctimonious

dew: **4** rime **8** moisture **9** hoarfrost

dewlap: **4** jowl **7** wattles

dewy: **4** damp **5** moist, roric **6** gentle **9** sparkling **10** glistening, refreshing

dexter: **5** right **6** honest **9** fortunate **10** auspicious **15** straightforward

dexterity: art **5** craft, knack, skill **7** ability, address, agility, aptness, cunning, finesse, sleight **8** aptitude, deftness, facility **9** adeptness, diplomacy, quickness, readiness **10** adroitness, cleverness, expertness, nimbleness

dextral: **10** auspicious **11** right-handed

dey: **5** pasha, ruler

dhan: **6** cattle, wealth **8** property

diabetes remedy: **7** insulin

diablerie: **7** devilry, sorcery **8** mischief **10** black magic, demonology, witchcraft

diabolical, diabolic: **5** cruel **6** wicked **7** hellish, inhuman, satanic, violent **8** demoniac, devilish, fiendish, infernal

diacritic: **4** mark **5** tilde **6** umlaut **11** distinctive

diadem: **5** crown, tiara **6** anadem, circle, emblem, fillet **7** coronet **8** headband **11** sovereignty

diagnose: **7** analyze **8** identify, pinpoint

diagonal: **4** bias **7** slanted **13** catercornered

diagram: map **4** plan **5** chart, epure(F.), graph **6** design **7** outline, schema **9** blueprint

dial: **4** disk, face **6** tune in **7** control, crystal **8** horologe **9** indicator, telephone

dialect: **5** argot, idiom, lingo **6** brogue, debate, patois, patter, speech **8** language **10** vernacular **11** phraseology
Georgia: **6** Gullah
London: **7** cockney

Louisiana: **5** Cajun
most prestigious: **8** acrolect

dialogue: **4** chat, talk **6** parley **10** discussion **12** conversation
having nature of: **13** interlocutory

diameter: **4** bore **14** circle bisector
half: **5** radii(pl.) **6** radius

diametric: **7** counter **8** contrary, opposite

diamond: gem, ice **4** rock **5** field, jager, jewel **7** lozenge **8** corundum **9** brilliant, briolette, sparkling
crystal: **7** glassie
cutter: **12** brilliandeer
element: **6** carbon
famous: See **stone:** *famous*
fragments: **5** chips
glazier's: **6** emeril
holding device: dop **4** dopp
imitation: **5** paste **9** schlenter
industrial: **4** bort **5** bortz
necklace: **7** riviere(F.)
surface: **5** facet
unit of weight: **5** carat

diamond-hard: **7** adamant

Diamond State: **8** Delaware

Diana: **7** Artemis
father: **7** Jupiter
mother: **6** Latona
twin: **6** Apollo

diana monkey: **7** roloway

diaphanous **5** filmy, gauzy, sheer **8** gossamer **11** transparent

diaphragm: **7** midriff
pert. to: **7** phrenic

diary: log **6** record **7** journal **8** register **9** ephemeris

diaskeuast: **6** editor **7** reviser

diastase: **4** malt **6** enzyme

diatribe: **6** tirade **8** harangue **9** criticism, invective, philippic **12** denunciation

Diaz de Bivar's title: Cid

dibble: dib **7** dip bait **10** garden tool

dibs: **5** claim, share, syrup **6** rights

dice: **4** cube **5** bones **6** gamble **7** checker
game: **5** craps
losing throw: **5** three **7** boxcars **9** snake eyes
throw of six: **4** sice

dicey: **5** risky **6** chancy **9** uncertain

dichotomize: **4** part **5** sever **6** divide **7** break up **8** separate **10** split in two

dick: tec **6** copper **8** flatfoot **9** detective, policeman

Dickens: *character:* Pip, Tim **4** Dora, Nell **5** Fagin **6** Cuttle **7** Dorritt, Podsnap **9** Bill Sikes, Uriah Heep
pen name: Boz

dicker: **4** deal, swap **5** daker **6** barter, haggle **7** bargain, chaffer **8** exchange **9** agreement, negotiate

dickey: 4 weak 5 shaky 10 shirt front

dictate: say 4 tell 5 order, utter 6 decree, enjoin, impose, ordain 7 command, deliver, mandate, require 9 prescribe, principle 11 communicate

dictatorial: 6 lordly 7 pompous 8 arrogant, despotic, dogmatic, positive 9 imperious, masterful 10 autocratic, peremptory, tyrannical 11 doctrinaire, domineering, magisterial, opinionated, overbearing 13 authoritative

diction: 5 style 6 phrase 7 wording 8 language, parlance, verbiage 10 vocabulary 11 enunciation, phraseology

dictionary: 7 lexicon 8 wordbook 10 vocabulary 11 onomasticon

compiler: 13 lexicographer

geographical: gazetteer

poet's: 6 gradus

dictum: 5 adage, axiom, edict 6 decree, saying 7 opinion 8 apothegm 9 principle, statement 13 pronouncement

Dictynna: 11 Britomartis

didactic: dry 7 preachy 8 pedantic 10 moralistic 11 instructive

didacticism: 6 homily 8 pedantry

diddle: gyp 4 hoax 5 cheat 6 befool, dawdle, jiggle, loiter, trifle 7 swindle 9 waste time

dido: 5 antic, caper, frill, prank, trick 6 gewgaw 7 trinket 8 furbelow, gimcrack

Dido: *father:* 5 Belus

founder of: 8 Carthage

husband: 7 Acerbas

sister: 4 Anna

wooer: 6 Aeneas

die: ebb 4 cube, dado, fade, mold, seal, wane 5 abate, croak, stamp, yearn 6 chance, depart, expire, finish, perish, vanish, wither 7 decease, succumb 8 languish, puncheon 9 grow faint

loaded: 6 fulham, fullam

symbol: ace

die-hard: 4 Tory 7 old fogy 8 hardnose, mossback, rightist, stubborn 9 dogmatist, obstinate, pigheaded 11 reactionary 12 conservative

Dies Irae(L.): 4 hymn 8 mass part 10 day of wrath

diet: 4 fare, fast, food 5 board 6 reduce, viands 7 regimen 8 congress 10 convention 11 convocation, legislature

difference: 5 clash 6 change 7 discord, dispute 8 conflict, division, variance 10 alteration, dissension, unlikeness 11controversy, discrepancy, distinction 12 disagreement

different: 5 other 6 divers, sundry, unlike 7 diverse, several, unalike, unusual, variant, various 8 distinct, manifold, separate 9 disparate, divergent 10 dis-

similar, variegated 11 diversified

differentiate: 8 contrast 11 distinguish 12 discriminate

difficult: 4 hard 5 fussy, rough, tough 6 crabby, cranky, knotty, rugged, uphill 7 arduous, labored, not easy, obscure, painful, practic 8 abstract, puzzling, stubborn 9 intricate, laborious 11 complicated, troublesome

difficulty: ado, fix, jam, rub 4 snag 5 fight, nodus 6 hassle, pickle, plight, scrape, strait 7 barrier, dilemma, dispute, pitfall, problem, quarrel, trouble 8 asperity, obstacle, severity, struggle 9 hindrance, objection 10 impediment 11 controversy, obstruction, vicissitude 12 complication, disagreement

diffidence: 5 doubt 7 modesty, reserve, shyness 8 distrust, humility, timidity 9 suspicion 10 hesitation 11 bashfulness 12 apprehension

diffuse: 4 full, shed 5 strew, wordy 6 divide, expand, extend, prolix, spread 7 copious, pervade, pour out, publish, radiate, scatter, verbose 8 disperse 9 circulate, dissipate, expatiate, garrulous, irradiate, propagate 10 widespread 11 disseminate

diffusion: 7 osmosis 10 outpouring

dig: get, hoe 4 claw, gibe, grub, hole, like, mine, poke, root 5 delve, nudge, probe, spade, taunt 6 burrow, exhume, plunge, quarry, shovel, thrust 7 approve, unearth 8 excavate, scoop out 10 understand

dig out: 6 go into 7 uncover 10 do research 11 investigate

digest: 4 code 5 ripen 6 absorb, codify, mature, precis 7 concoct, epitome, pandect, summary 8 condense, synopsis 10 abridgment, assimilate, compendium, comprehend

digestion: 7 eupepsy 8 eupepsia

agent: 6 pepsin, rennin 7 maltase

ailment: 5 colic 6 gripes 7 pyrosis 9 dyspepsia 12 constipation

having good: 8 eupeptic

digging, fitted for: 7 fodient

digit: toe 4 unit 5 thumb 6 figure, finger, number 7 integer, numeral

podal: toe

shield for: cot 5 stall 7 thimble

vestigial: 7 dewclaw

diglot: 9 bilingual

dignified: 5 grand, lofty, noble, staid 6 august, sedate, solemn 7 courtly, stately 8 majestic 11 magisterial

dignify: 5 adorn, exalt, grace, honor 7 elevate, ennoble, promote

dignitary: VIP 5 nabob 6 big gun, leader 7 notable 8 brass hat, luminary, official

dignity: 4 rank 5 honor, pride, worth 6 repute 7 bearing, decorum, fitness, gravity, majesty, station 8 elegance, prestige, standing 9 nobleness 10 excellence

digress: 4 veer 5 drift, stray 6 swerve, wander 7 deviate, diverge 8 divagate 10 depart from

digression: 7 episode 8 excursus 9 excursion

dike, dyke: 4 bank, pond, pool 5 digue, ditch, levee 7 channel 8 causeway 10 embankment 11 watercourse

dilapidated: 5 dingy 6 beat-up, shabby 7 damaged, run-down 10 threadbare 12 falling apart

dilapidation: 4 ruin 5 decay 9 disrepair 10 raggedness 14 disintegration

dilate: 5 swell, widen 6 expand, extend 7 amplify, broaden, distend, enlarge, inflate, prolong, stretch 8 increase, lengthen, protract 9 discourse, expatiate

dilatory: 4 slow 5 slack, tardy 6 fabian, remiss 8 backward, delaying, inactive, sluggish 10 behindhand 15 procrastinating

dilemma: fix 4 node 5 poser 7 problem 8 quandary 10 perplexity 11 predicament 12 complication 13 Hobson's choice

dilettante: 5 lover 7 admirer, amateur, dabbler, dabster, esthete 8 aesthete

diligence: 4 heed 6 effort 7 caution 8 industry 9 constancy 11 application, earnestness, heedfulness

diligent: 4 busy 6 active, eident, steady 7 careful, earnest, heedful, operose 8 sedulous 9 assiduous 11 hardworking, industrious, painstaking, persevering

dill: 4 herb 6 pickle 9 flavoring, seasoning

dilly: pip 4 darb, lulu 5 beaut, dandy 9 humdinger

dillydally: lag, toy 4 loaf 5 stall 6 loiter, trifle 9 vacillate

dilute: cut 4 thin 5 alter 6 debase, modify, reduce, weaken 8 diminish 9 attenuate, water down

dim: wan 4 blur, dark, dull, fade, gray, hazy, mist, pale, veil 5 bleak, blear, dusky, faint, foggy, misty 6 cloudy, darken, gloomy, obtuse 7 eclipse, obscure, shadowy, tarnish 8 overcast 9 obfuscate 10 indistinct, mysterious 11 crepuscular

dime: 4 coin 5 disme

dimension: 4 bulk, size 5 scope 6 aspect, extent, height, length 7 breadth, quality 9 magnitude, thickness 10 importance, proportion
fourth: 4 time

diminish: ebb 4 ease, fade, melt, pare, sink, wane, wear 5 abate, lower 6 dilute, lessen, reduce, subdue, wither 7 abridge, assuage, curtail, deplete, dwindle, subside 8 condense, decrease, derogate, minimize, moderate, peter out, retrench, taper off 9 alleviate, epitomize, extenuate

diminution: 8 decrease 9 abatement, decrement, lessening 11 attenuation, curtailment

diminutive: wee 4 tiny 5 dwarf, petty, runty, small 6 bantam, little, petite 9 miniature, minuscule 11 lilliputian 12 teensy-weensy

dimness: 5 gloom 8 darkness 9 obscurity

dimple: 6 hollow, ripple 11 indentation

dim-witted: 4 dull, slow 5 dopey 6 obtuse 8 backward 11 thick-headed

din: bum 4 riot 5 alarm, bruit, clang, noise 6 clamor, hubbub, racket, rattle, steven, tumult, uproar 7 clangor, clatter, discord, turmoil 9 commotion, confusion 10 hullabaloo

dine: eat, sup 5 feast 6 regale

diner: 4 cafe 5 eatery 8 train car 10 coffee shop, restaurant 11 greasy spoon 12 luncheonette

dinette: 6 alcove 10 kitchen set

ding: 4 beat, dash, push, ring 5 clang, drive, excel, fling, knock, pound, thump 6 stroke, thrash, thrust

dingbat: 4 fool 5 dunce 6 dimwit 9 dumb cluck 12 featherbrain

dinge: 4 dent, dint 6 batter, bruise 10 depression

dinghy: 4 boat 5 skiff 7 rowboat, shallop

dingle: 4 dale, dell, glen, vale 6 valley

dingo: 7 wild dog

dingus: 5 gizmo 6 gadget 9 doohickey 11 thingamajig

dingy: dun 4 dark, drab, mean 5 dirty, dusky, grimy, seedy, smoky, tacky 6 gloomy, shabby 7 run-down, squalid 8 smirched 11 dilapidated

dinky: 4 cute, neat, poor, small 8 trifling 13 insignificant

dinner: 4 meal 5 feast 6 repast 7 banquet
after: 12 postprandial
course: 4 nuts, soup 5 fruit, salad 6 entree 7 dessert 9 appetizer
pert. to: 8 cenatory

dint: 4 beat, blow, dent, nick 5 clour, delve, dinge, force, notch, onset, power, press, shock 6 attack, chance, effort, strike, stroke 7 imprint 8 efficacy, striking 10 impression 11 indentation

diocese: see 8 district 9 bishopric
division: 6 parish

Dione: *consort:* 4 Zeus
daughter: 9 Aphrodite

Dionysus: *attendant:* 6 Maenad
festival: 7 Agrania 8 Agrionia

mother: **6** Semele
pert. to: **7** Bromian
diopside: 7 alalite **8** pyroxene
diorite: 7 diabase
Dioscuri: 5 twins **6** Anaces, Castor, Gemini, Pollux
father: **4** Zeus **9** Tyndareus
mother: **4** Leda
sister: **5** Helen **12** Clytemnestra
dip: sag, sop **4** bail, drop, dunk, lade, sink, soak **5** delve, ladle, lower, sauce, slope **6** candle, go down, hollow, plunge **7** decline, immerse, moisten **8** decrease, downturn, submerge **10** depression, pickpocket
in water: **5** douse, rinse, souse
diploma: 6 degree **7** charter **11** certificate
diplomacy: 4 tact **5** poise **7** finesse **8** delicacy **9** dexterity **10** artfulness
diplomat: 4 dean **6** consul **7** attache **8** minister **10** ambassador
office of: **7** embassy
dipody: 6 syzygy
dipper: 5 ladle, scoop **8** songbird
dippy: mad **5** silly, wacky **6** absurd **7** foolish **9** screwball
dipsomania: 9 potomania **10** alcoholism
dipteran: fly **4** gnat **8** mosquito
lobe of wing: **5** alula
dire: 4 dern, evil **5** awful, fatal **6** deadly, dismal, funest, tragic, woeful **7** doleful, drastic, fearful **8** dreadful, horrible, terrible, ultimate **10** calamitous, oppressive, portentous **12** overpowering
direct: aim, bid, con **4** airt, bain, bend, boss, edit, even, flat, head, helm, lead, open, rein, sway, turn **5** apply, blank, coach, frank, guide, order, point, refer, steer, teach, train, utter, write **6** ensign, govern, handle, honest, impart, lineal, manage **7** address, appoint, command, conduct, control, convert, execute, express, officer, preside **8** dedicate, instruct, marshall, regulate, straight **9** categoric, downright, immediate **10** administer, forthright, point-black **11** categorical, compendious, superintend, superscribe **15** straightforward
direction: way **4** bent, care, duct, east, road, rule, west **5** north, route, south, trend **6** course **7** address, bearing, command, control, mandate, precept **8** guidance, tendency **10** management, regulation **11** arrangement, inclination, information, instruction **13** determination
biblical: **5** selah
court: **5** order
line of: **5** range
musical: See **musical direction**
pole to pole: **5** axial
printer's: **4** stet

without: **7** astatic
direction finder: 7 compass
directive: 5 edict, order **6** decree, ruling **10** injunction, memorandum **13** pronouncement
directly: 4 now **6** at once **8** promptly **9** instantly, presently, right away **11** immediately, straightway
director: 4 boss, head **5** coach, guide, pilot **6** archon, bishop, leader, rector **7** manager, prefect, trainer **8** governor, producer **9** conductor **10** supervisor **13** administrator **14** superintendent
directory: 4 list, ordo **5** guide, index **9** phonebook
dirge: 4 keen, song **5** elegy **6** lament **7** requiem, epicede **8** epicedia(pl.), threnody **9** epicedium
dirigible: 5 blimp **7** airship **8** zeppelin
dirk: 4 snee, stab **5** skean, sword **6** dagger, weapon
dirndl: 5 dress, skirt
dirt: fen, mud **4** dust, gore, muck, nast, smut, soil **5** earth, filth, grime, trash **6** gossip, gravel, ground, refuse **7** lowdown, mullock, squalor **11** scuttlebutt
dirty: low **4** base, clat, foul **5** bawdy, cabby, dingy, foggy, grimy, gusty, horry, muddy, nasty, stain, sully **6** bemire, clarty, defile, filthy, greasy, grubby, impure, mussed, smutty, soiled, sordid, stormy **7** begrime, brookie, bruckle, clouded, muddied, obscene, squalid, sullied, tarnish, unclean **10** despicable
dirty dig: 4 gibe **5** taunt
dirty look: 5 frown, glare, scowl
dirty pool: 5 trick **8** foul play **9** chicanery, duplicity **10** unfairness **13** double-dealing
Dis: 5 Pluto
disability: 8 drawback, handicap **10** limitation **12** disadvantage
disable: 4 lame, maim **5** break, wreck **6** bruise, dismay, weaken **7** cripple **9** hamstring **10** disqualify **12** incapacitate
disabuse: 4 free **6** debunk, expose, show up **8** set right **9** enlighten **10** disenchant
disaccharide: 5 biose **7** lactose, maltose, sucrose **10** saccharose
disadvantage: 4 hurt, loss, risk **6** damage, injury **7** penalty **8** handicap **9** detriment
disadvantageous: 7 adverse, hurtful **11** detrimental, prejudicial, unfavorable
disaffected: 5 false **6** untrue **8** disloyal, forsworn, mutinous, perjured, recreant **9** estranged, faithless, insidious **10** perfidious, traitorous **11** treacherous
disaffection: 6 deceit **7** disease, disgust, dislike **8** disorder **9** distemper, hostility

10 disloyalty, alienation, discontent **13** indisposition **14** disinclination

disaffirm: 4 deny **5** annul **6** negate **7** reverse **9** repudiate **10** contradict

disagree: 4 vary **5** argue, clash **6** differ **7** dissent, quarrel **8** conflict

disagreeable: bad **4** sour, vile **5** cross, harsh, nasty **6** cranky **7** hateful, peevish **8** annoying, petulant **9** invidious, irritable, offensive, repugnant **10** forbidding, unpleasant **11** displeasing, distasteful

disagreement: 5 clash, fight **7** discord, dispute, dissent, wrangle **8** argument, variance **9** diversity **10** contention, difference, difficulty, dissension, divergence, unlikeness **11** contrariety, controversy, discrepancy, displeasure, incongruity **16** misunderstanding

disallow: 4 deny, veto **6** forbid, refuse, reject **7** censure **8** disclaim, prohibit **10** disapprove

disappear: fly **4** fade, flee **6** vanish **7** evanish **8** evanesce

disappoint: 4 balk, bilk, fail, fall, mock, undo **6** baffle, defeat, delude, outwit, thwart **7** deceive, destroy, nullify, let down **9** frustrate

disapproval: 7 censure, dislike, dissent **9** disliking **10** opposition **14** disapprobation

sound of: boo **4** hiss, hoot **7** catcall **9** raspberry **10** Bronx cheer

disapprove: 4 veto **6** reject, resent **7** condemn, protest **8** disallow, turn down **9** deprecate

disarm: 5 charm **6** defuse, subdue **7** win over **12** demilitarize, make harmless

disarming: 4 glib **5** suave **6** smooth **8** unctuous **10** soft-spoken **12** ingratiating

disarrange: 4 muss **5** upset **6** deform, ruffle **7** clutter, confuse, disturb **8** dishevel, unsettle **9** dislocate **10** discompose, disconcert **11** disorganize

disarray: 4 mess **5** strip **6** jumble, muddle **8** disorder **9** confusion **10** dishabille

disassociate: 4 part **7** break up, pull out **8** separate **11** cut ties with **12** withdraw from **14** sever relations

disaster: woe **4** bale, blow, evil, ruin **6** mishap **7** tragedy **8** accident, calamity, casualty, fatality **9** cataclysm, extremity, mischance **10** misfortune **11** catastrophe **12** misadventure

disavow: 4 deny **6** abjure, disown, recant, refuse, reject **7** decline, retract **8** abnegate, disclaim, renounce **9** repudiate

disband: part **7** break up, dismiss, release, scatter **8** disperse, dissolve, separate **9** discharge **12** disintegrate

disbelieve: 5 doubt **6** reject **7** suspect **8** question **9** discredit

disbeliever: 5 cynic **7** atheist, heretic, skeptic

disburden: rid **4** ease **7** relieve **8** get rid of, jettison **9** exonerate **11** disencumber

disburse: 5 spend **6** defray, expend, lay out, pay out **8** dispense **10** distribute

disc: See **disk**

discalced: 6 unshod **8** barefoot

discard: 4 dump, jilt, junk, omit, oust, shed **5** chuck, ditch, scrap, shuck, sluff **6** disuse, divest, reject **7** abandon, cashier, dismiss, forsake **9** cast aside, eliminate, repudiate, throw away

pile: **4** heap **5** trash **8** boneyard

discern: see **4** espy, read **6** behold, descry, detect, notice **7** observe **8** discover, perceive **10** understand **11** distinguish

discernible: 7 evident, visible **8** apparent, manifest **11** conspicuous, perceptible **15** distinguishable

discerning: 4 wise

discernment: 4 tact **5** flair, taste **6** acumen **7** insight **8** sagacity **9** sharpness **10** astuteness, divination, perception, shrewdness **11** penetration **12** clairvoyance, perspicacity **14** discrimination

discharge: can **4** boot, dump, emit, fire, free, pour, sack **5** eject, empty, expel, exude, shoot **6** acquit, bounce, defray, effect, exempt, let out, unlade, unload **7** absolve, cashier, disband, dismiss, execute, give off, release, relieve **8** disgorge, displace, evacuate **9** explosion, muster out, exculpate, exonerate, liquidate **10** liberation

disciple: ite **4** John, Jude, Mark **5** James, Judas, Peter, Simon **6** Andrew, Philip, Thomas **7** apostle, Matthew, scholar, student **8** adherent, believer, follower

disciplinarian: 4 czar, tsar **6** tyrant **7** trainer **8** martinet **10** taskmaster

discipline: 4 whip **5** drill, inure, teach, train **6** punish, school **7** chasten, control, scourge **8** chastise, instruct, regiment, regulate, restrain, training **9** obedience **10** keep in line, strictness **11** hold in check, self-control

disclaim: 4 deny **6** abjure, disown, refuse **7** disavow **8** abdicate, abnegate, disallow, renounce **9** repudiate

disclose: 4 bare, blow, open, tell **5** admit, utter **6** betray, descry, expose, impart, reveal, shrive, unseal, unveil **7** confess, develop, display, divulge, exhibit, uncover **8** discover, indicate **9** make known

disclosure: 6 expose **10** revelation

discolor: run **4** fade, spot **5** stain, smear, tinge **6** streak **7** tarnish **8** besmirch

discoloration: 4 mark, spot **5** stain

discomfit: irk, vex **4** rout **5** abash, annoy, upset **6** baffle, defeat, rattle **7** confuse, disturb, perturb **8** confound **9** embarrass, frustrate **10** disconcert

discomfort: **4** pain **6** dismay, grieve, sorrow, unease **7** disturb **8** distress **9** annoyance, embarrass **10** discourage, uneasiness **11** displeasure **13** inconvenience **14** discouragement

discommode: **5** upset **6** bother, put out **7** trouble **13** inconvenience

discompose: **4** fret **5** upset **6** flurry, ruffle **7** agitate, confuse, derange, disturb, fluster, perturb **8** disorder, displace, disquiet, unsettle **9** discharge **10** disarrange, disconcert

disconcert: **4** faze **5** abash, daunt, feeze, upset, worry **6** baffle, blench, rattle **7** confuse, disturb, nonplus, perplex, perturb **8** bewilder, confound **9** discomfit, embarrass **10** disarrange, discompose

disconnect: **4** undo **5** sever **6** unplug **7** disjoin **8** dissolve, disunite, separate, uncouple

disconnected: **6** abrupt, broken **7** cursory **8** rambling **9** desultory, scattered **10** abstracted, disjointed, incoherent

disconsolate: sad **6** gloomy, woeful **7** forlorn **8** dejected, desolate, hopeless **9** cheerless, miserable, sorrowful **10** dispirited, melancholy

discontent: **8** disquiet **9** dysphoria **10** uneasiness **11** displeasure, unhappiness **12** restlessness

discontinue: end **4** drop, quit, stop **5** break, cease, let up **6** desist, disuse, give up **9** terminate

discord: din, jar **5** clash **6** strife **7** faction **8** conflict, variance **9** cacophony, diversity **10** contention, difference, dissension, dissonance **12** disagreement
goddess of: Ate **4** Eris

discordant: **5** harsh **6** hoarse **7** jarring **8** contrary, jangling **10** discrepant, mismatched **11** incongruous, quarrelsome **12** antagonistic, incompatible, inconsistent, inharmonious
musically: **8** scordato
serenade: **9** charivari

Discordia: **4** Eris

discotheque: **7** cabaret **9** nightclub

discount: **4** agio **5** batta(Ind.) **6** ignore, rebate **7** dismiss **8** minimize **9** allowance, deduction, disregard, reduction **10** brush aside, disbelieve **11** sell for less **12** depreciation

discourage: **4** carp **5** daunt, deter **6** dampen, deject, hinder **7** depress, inhibit, prevent **8** dispirit, dissuade, restrain **10** discomfort, dishearten

discourse: **4** talk, tell **5** orate, paper, speak, tract **6** eulogy, homily, parley, preach, sermon **7** account, address, comment, declaim, discuss, dissert, lecture, oration, prelect **8** argument, colloquy, converse, parlance, treatise **9** expatiate, narration, panegyric, soliloquy **10** commentate **11** description **12** conversation, dissertation
art of: **8** rhetoric
long: **6** screed, tirade **7** descant **9** philippic

discourteous: **4** rude **6** scurvy **7** ill-bred, uncivil **8** impolite, ungentle **10** unmannerly **11** ill-mannered **13** disrespectful

discover: see, spy **4** espy, find **5** learn **6** define, descry, detect, expose, invent, locate, reveal **7** confess, discern, display, divulge, explore, find out, uncover, unearth **8** decipher, disclose, manifest, perceive **9** apprehend, ascertain

discoverer: spy **5** scout **8** explorer, inventor **10** originator

discovery: **4** find **5** trove **6** espial, strike **10** disclosure, revelation

discredit: **5** decry, doubt **6** damage, expose, show up **7** asperse, blemish, impeach, scandal, suspect **8** belittle, disgrace, dishonor, distrust, ignominy **9** disparage, disrepute **10** disbelieve

discreet: **4** wary **5** civil **6** polite, silent **7** careful, guarded, politic, prudent **8** cautious, reserved, reticent **11** circumspect

discrepant: **8** contrary **9** different, divergent **10** discordant **11** conflicting, disagreeing **12** inconsistent

discrete: **8** detached, distinct, separate **9** unrelated

discretion: **4** tact **6** wisdom **7** caution **8** judgment, prudence **9** restraint **13** secretiveness

discriminate: **5** favor **8** perceive, show bias **9** demarcate **10** place apart **11** distinguish **13** differentiate, play favorites

discriminating: **6** astute **7** careful, choosey **8** critical **9** selective **10** discerning, prejudiced

discrimination: **5** taste **6** acumen **8** inequity **10** partiality **11** discernment

discursive: **6** roving **7** cursory **8** rambling **9** desultory **10** digressive

discus: **4** disk **5** quoit
thrower: **10** discobolus

discuss: air **4** moot **5** argue, bandy **6** confer, debate, parley **7** agitate, bespeak, consult, dispute, examine **8** talk over **9** discourse **10** deliberate

discussion: rap **6** confab, huddle, parley, powwow **8** causerie **10** conference **11** bull session
group: **5** class, panel **7** seminar **10** round table
medium of: **5** forum

open to: **4** moot **9** debatable
disdain: **5** flout, scorn, spurn **7** contemn, despise, put down, ridicule, sneer at **8** contempt, derision **9** arrogance **11** haughtiness
disease: bug **4** harm **5** virus **6** malady **7** ailment, illness, trouble **8** debility, distress, sickness **9** complaint, infirmity **10** discomfort, pestilence, uneasiness **12** disaffection
animal: coe, pip **5** braxy, colic, farcy, hoose, hooze, mange **6** amoeba, garget **7** spavins **8** glanders, sacbrood **9** distemper, tularemia
local: **7** endemic
plant: fen **4** bunt, rust, scab, smut **5** ergot, speck **6** calico, coleur, mildew **7** erinose, viruela, walloon **8** brindled, melanose
prediction about: **9** prognosis
recognition of: **9** diagnosis
skin: **4** acne, rash **5** favus, hives, psora, tinea **6** dartre, eczema, herpes, lichen, tetter **7** scabies **8** impetigo, ringworm **9** psoriasis, xeroderma **11** scleroderma
wide-spreading: **8** epidemic
disembark: **4** land **6** alight **8** go ashore
disembodiment: **4** soul **6** spirit
disembowel: gut **4** hulk **6** paunch **8** gralloch **10** eviscerate
disembroil: **6** free of **8** untangle **9** extricate
disenchanted: **5** blase **7** knowing, let down, unhappy **9** turned off **11** enlightened, put straight, worldly-wise
disencumber: rid **4** ease **7** lighten, relieve **8** unburden **9** disengage
disengage: **4** free **5** clear, untie **6** detach, loosen **7** release, retreat, unravel **8** liberate, uncouple, unfasten **9** extricate
disentangle: **4** comb **5** clear, loose **6** evolve **7** unravel **8** separate **9** extricate **13** straighten out
disfavor: **5** odium **7** dislike, umbrage **9** bad repute, disesteem **11** displeasure
disfigure: mar **4** scar **5** spoil **6** deface, deform, injure, mangle **7** blemish **8** mutilate
disgorge: **4** spew, vent **5** eject, empty, expel, vomit **7** bring up **9** discharge **10** relinquish
disgrace: **4** blot, slur, soil, spot **5** abase, crime, odium, shame, stain **6** infamy, stigma **7** affront, attaint, degrade, scandal, slander **8** contempt, dishonor, ignominy, reproach **9** discredit, disesteem, humiliate **10** opprobrium **11** humiliation
disgruntled: **4** sore **5** upset **7** peevish
disguise: **4** hide, mask, veil **5** belie, cloak, feign **6** facade, masque **7** conceal, obscure, pretend **8** artifice, pretense **9** coverture, dissemble, incognito **10** cam-

ouflage, false front, masquerade **11** dissimulate
disgust: **5** repel, shock **6** degout(F.), horror, nausea, offend, revolt, sicken **8** aversion, distaste, loathing, nauseate **9** antipathy **10** abhorrence, repugnance **11** abomination **12** disaffection
disgusting: **4** foul, vile **5** nasty **6** filthy **7** beastly, fulsome, hateful, noisome, obscene **8** shocking
dish (see also **food**): cup **4** bowl, food **5** basin, nappy, paten, plate **6** critch, looker, patera, saucer, tureen **7** charger, plateau, platter, ramekin **8** favorite **9** casserole, container **10** preference
gravy: **4** boat
main: **6** entree
dishabille: **8** disarray, disorder **13** partly dressed
Dishan's son: **4** Aran
dishearten: **5** daunt **6** deject **7** depress, flatten, unnerve **8** dispirit **10** demoralize, discourage
disheartened: **6** gloomy **8** downcast **10** despondent **11** discouraged
disheveled: **5** messy **6** sloppy, untidy **7** ruffled, rumpled, tousled, unkempt **8** mussed up, slovenly, uncombed **10** disarranged, disorderly, in disarray
dishonest: **5** false, lying **7** corrupt, crooked, knavish **8** cheating, two-faced **9** deceitful **10** fraudulent, perfidious, untruthful **13** untrustworthy
dishonor: **5** shame, stain **6** defame, defile **7** degrade, obloquy, violate **8** disgrace, ignominy **9** discredit, disparage, disrepute **10** opprobrium
dishonorable: **4** base, foul **5** shady **7** corrupt, ignoble **8** infamous, shameful, unsavory **9** unethical **12** unscrupulous
disillusion: **10** disenchant
disinclination: **7** dislike **8** aversion, distaste **9** antipathy **10** reluctance, repugnance **12** disaffection
disinclined: **6** averse **9** reluctant, unwilling **10** indisposed
disinfect: **7** cleanse **9** sterilize
disinfectant: **5** iodin **6** iodine, phenol **9** germicide **10** antiseptic
disingenuous: **4** wily **5** false **6** artful, tricky **7** devious **8** indirect, specious **9** insincere **10** circuitous
disinherit: **6** cut off **7** deprive **10** exheredate
disintegrate: **4** melt **5** decay, erode **7** crumble, disband **8** dissolve, separate **9** decompose
disinter: **5** dig up **6** exhume **7** unearth
disinterested: **4** fair **8** unbiased, uncaring **9** apathetic, impartial **11** unconcerned
disjoin: **4** part, undo **5** sever **6** detach, sunder, break up **8** dissolve, disunite,

separate **10** disconnect, dissociate

disjointed: 7 muddled **8** inchoate, unhinged **10** disordered, incoherent **12** disconnected, lacking unity

disk: 4 chip, dial **5** cakra, medal, paten, plate, sabot, wheel **6** bezant, chakra, harrow, record, washer **7** medalet, phalera **9** cultivate, faceplate, medallion, millstone
hockey: **4** puck
metal: **4** flan, gong **6** ghurry, sequin **8** zecchino
pert. to: **6** discal **7** discoid
solar: **4** Aten

dislike: 4 loth, mind **6** detest, loathe **8** aversion, distaste **9** antipathy, disrelish, prejudice **10** repugnance **11** displeasure **12** disaffection
object of: **8** anathema
of children: **9** misopedia

dislocate: 5 splay **7** disrupt **8** disjoint, displace **10** disarrange

dislodge: 5 expel **6** remove **8** force out

disloyal: 5 false **6** untrue **9** faithless **10** inconstant, perfidious, traitorous, unfaithful **11** disaffected, treacherous

dismal: sad, wan **4** dark, dire, dull, glum, gray **5** black, bleak, drear, sorry **6** dreary, gloomy, triste **7** doleful, ghastly, joyless, ominous, unhappy **8** dolorous, funereal, lonesome **9** cheerless, sorrowful **10** acherontic, calamitous, lugubrious, melancholy **11** unfortunate

dismantle: 4 rase, raze **5** annul, strip **6** divest **7** deprive, destroy, rescind, uncloak **8** dismount, take down **10** do away with

dismay: 4 fear, ruin **5** alarm, appal, daunt, dread **6** appall, fright, subdue, terror **7** depress, deprive, horrify, terrify **8** affright, confound **9** dejection **10** depression, discomfort, discourage **11** trepidation **12** apprehension **13** consternation

dismember: 4 maim, part, rend **5** sever **6** mangle **7** dissect **8** disjoint, mutilate

dismiss: can **4** boot, bust, drop, oust **5** chuck, eject **6** banish, bounce, reject, remove **7** cashier, disband, discard **8** relegate **9** discharge, overthrow

dismissal: 5 conge **6** ouster **7** removal **9** discharge

dismount: 6 alight, get off **9** dismantle, take apart

Disney (Walt): 10 cartoonist
character: **4** Huey, Puff **5** Daisy, Dewey, Dumbo, Goofy, Louie, Pluto **6** Donald, Mickey, Minnie
film classic: **5** Bambi **8** Fantasia **9** Pinocchio, Snow White **15** Reluctant Dragon, Steamboat Willie

disobedient: 6 unruly **7** forward, naughty, wayward, willful **8** mutinous **10** rebellious, refractory **11** intractable **12** contumacious **13** insubordinate

disoblige: 6 offend **7** affront

disorder: 4 mess, muss, riot **5** chaos, snafu **6** burble, jumble, litter, malady, mucker, muddle, ruffle, tousle, tumult **7** ailment, clutter, confuse, derange, disturb, embroil, flutter, illness, misdeed, perturb, trouble **8** disarray, dishevel **9** commotion, complaint, confusion, distemper **10** disarrange, discompose, disconcert, misconduct **11** disorganize, misdemeanor **13** indisposition
visual: **10** strabismus

disorderly: 5 randy **6** unruly **8** slipshod, slovenly **10** topsy-turvy **12** huggermugger, ungovernable, unmanageable

disorganize: 5 upset **7** confuse, derange, disband, disrupt **8** disorder, dissolve **10** disarrange

disown: 4 deny **6** reject **7** disavow, retract **8** abdicate, disclaim, renounce **9** repudiate

disparage: 4 slur **5** abuse, decry, lower **6** slight **7** degrade, depress, detract, impeach **8** belittle, derogate, dishonor, disprize, minimize **9** discredit **10** depreciate

disparate: 7 unequal **8** separate **9** different **10** dissimilar **16** disproportionate

dispassionate: 4 calm, cool, fair **5** stoic **6** sedate, serene **8** composed, moderate **9** collected, impartial, temperate, unruffled **10** deliberate, unimpaired **12** unprejudiced

dispatch: rid **4** free, kill, mail, note, post, send **5** haste, hurry, speed **6** hasten **7** deliver, depeche(F.), dispose **8** celerity, conclude, expedite **9** quickness **10** accelerate, accomplish, promptness

dispatch boat: 5 aviso **6** packet

dispel: 7 scatter **8** disperse **9** dissipate, drive away **10** make vanish

dispendious: 6 costly **9** expensive **11** extravagant

dispensation: 4 plan **6** scheme **7** license, release **9** allotment, exemption **10** indulgence **12** distribution

dispense: 4 deal **5** forgo **6** effuse, excuse, exempt, forego, manage **7** absolve, arrange, dole out, hand out, provide **9** apportion **10** administer, distribute
with: **5** chuck, scrap **7** discard **8** get rid of **9** eliminate, toss aside

disperse: sow **4** rout **5** strew **6** dispel, spread, vanish **7** break up, diffuse, scatter **8** separate, squander **9** dissipate **10** distribute **11** disseminate

dispirit: cow **4** damp **5** daunt **6** deject **7** depress, flatten **10** discourage, dishearten, intimidate

dispirited: low, sad **4** blue **6** abattu(F.) **7**

abbattue(F.) **8** downcast **9** cheerless, woebegone **11** crestfallen **12** disconsolate

displace: 6 banish, depose, mislay, remove **7** push out **8** dislodge, take over, supplant **9** discharge, dislocate, supersede

display: air **4** pomp, show, wear **5** boast, scene, sight, sport **6** blazon, evince, expose, extend, flaunt, parade, reveal, unfold, unveil **7** etalage, exhibit, pageant, trot out, uncover **8** ceremony, disclose, discover, emblazon, exercise, flourish, indicate, manifest, splendor **9** spectacle, spread out **10** exhibition **11** affectation **13** demonstration

displease: vex **4** miff **5** anger, annoy, pique **6** offend **7** provoke **8** irritate **10** discontent, dissatisfy

displeasing: bad **7** irksome **9** offensive **10** unpleasant **11** distasteful **12** disagreeable

displeasure: ire **5** anger **6** injury **7** dislike, offense, umbrage **8** disfavor, distaste, vexation **10** discomfort, discontent, resentment, uneasiness **11** indignation

show: cry **4** pout **5** frown, scowl

disport: 4 play **5** amuse, frisk **6** divert, frolic, gambol

disposal: 4 sale **8** riddance **9** clearance **11** arrangement, transferral

dispose: set **4** bend, give, mind **5** array, order, place **6** adjust, attire, bestow, settle **7** appoint, arrange, prepare **8** dispatch, organize, regulate **9** determine **10** distribute

disposed: apt **5** fixed, prone, ready **7** tending **8** arranged, inclined

disposition: 4 bent, bias, mood, turn **5** humor **6** affect, animus, health, nature, temper **7** concept **8** aptitude, attitude, disposal **9** affection, character, diathesis **10** adjustment, management, proclivity, propensity **11** arrangement, inclination, temperament **12** constitution, distribution, organization **14** relinquishment

dispossess: 4 oust **5** eject, evict, expel, strip **6** depose, divest **7** bereave, deprive

dispraise: 5 blame **7** censure **9** disparage **10** depreciate **11** detract from

disproportion: 9 disparity **10** inequality

disproportionate: 6 uneven **7** unequal **8** lopsided **9** irregular, overblown **10** asymmetric, unbalanced

disprove: 5 rebut **6** negate, refute **7** confute, explode **8** overturn **9** discredit **10** controvert

disputable: 4 moot **5** vague **6** unsure **7** dubious, fallible **8** doubtful, insecure **9** uncertain **10** indefinite, precarious

disputant: 6 arguer **7** debater

disputation: 7 polemic **8** argument **9** dialectic **10** discussion **11** controversy

dispute: 4 deny, feud, fuss, moot, spat **5** argue, brawl, cabal **6** barney, bicker, debate, differ, haggle **7** brabble, contend, contest, faction, gainsay, quarrel, wrangle **8** argument, question, squabble **9** argy-bargy, encounter **10** contravene, controvert, litigation **11** altercation, controversy **12** disagreement

disqualify: 5 debar **6** outlaw **7** disable, rule out **8** prohibit **9** indispose **11** invalidate **12** incapacitate

disquiet: vex **4** fear, fret, pain **6** excite, stir up, unease, unrest **7** agitate, anxiety, disturb, fluster, trouble, turmoil **10** discompose, discontent **12** inconvenience, restlessness

disquisition: 5 essay **8** treatise **10** discussion

disregard: 4 omit **5** waive **6** forget, ignore, pass by, slight **7** neglect **8** discount, overlook **9** pretermit **10** contravene **11** inattention **12** indifference

disrelish: 7 dislike **8** distaste **9** antipathy

disreputable: low **4** base, hard **5** seamy, shady **7** raffish **8** shameful, unsavory **9** notorious **13** discreditable

disrepute: 5 odium **7** bad name **8** disgrace, dishonor, ignominy, reproach **9** disesteem

disrespect: 8 rudeness **9** insolence **10** incivility **11** discourtesy

disrespectful: 7 uncivil **8** impolite, impudent **10** irreverent **11** impertinent

disrobe: 5 strip **6** divest **7** take off, undress

disrupt: 4 rend, tear **5** break **7** disrump **11** discontinue, disorganize

dissatisfaction: 8 distaste **9** annoyance **10** discontent **11** displeasure

dissect: 5 carve, cut up **7** analyze **9** anatomize, dismember

dissemble: 4 hide, mask **5** cloak, feign **6** boggle **7** conceal **8** disguise, simulate **11** counterfeit, dissimulate

dissembler: 5 actor **9** hypocrite

disseminate: sow **5** stew **6** effuse, spread **7** diffuse, publish, scatter, send out **8** disperse **9** broadcast, circulate, propagate **10** distribute

dissent: 4 vary **6** differ **7** protest **8** disagree **9** exception, objection **10** dissidence **12** disagreement **13** nonconformity **14** nonconcurrence

signal of: nay

dissenter: 7 heretic, sectary **8** recusant **9** protestor **10** Protestant, schismatic, separatist, unbeliever **13** nonconformist

dissentious: 8 factious **11** contentious

dissert: 7 discuss 9 discourse

dissertation: 5 essay, theme, tract 6 debate, thesis, theses(pl.) 7 descant, lecture 8 treatise 9 discourse 10 discussion

Dissertation on a Roast Pig author: 11 Charles Lamb

disservice: 4 harm 6 damage, injury 8 mischief

dissever: 4 part 6 sunder 8 disunite

dissidence: 6 schism, strife 7 dissent 8 conflict 10 contention 12 disagreement 13 nonconformity

dissimilar: 6 unlike 7 difform, diverse 9 anomalous, different, disparate 13 heterogeneous

dissimulate: 5 feign 7 deceive, pretend 8 disguise 9 dissemble

dissipate: 5 spend, waste 6 dispel, expend 7 diffuse, scatter, shatter 8 disperse, dissolve, evanesce, squander 9 evaporate 11 fritter away, overindulge

dissocial: 10 unfriendly 11 standoffish

dissociate: 5 sever 7 disjoin 8 disunite, separate

dissolute: lax 4 wild 5 loose, slack 6 rakish, wanton 7 immoral, lawless 8 uncurbed 9 abandoned, debauched, unbridled 10 licentious, profligate 12 unrestrained

dissolution: end 4 ruin 5 decay 6 bust-up, demise 7 breakup, decease, divorce 10 abrogation 11 adjournment, termination 14 disintegration

comb. form: lys

dissolve: 4 fade, fuse, melt, thaw, void 5 annul 6 relent, unbind 7 adjourn, destroy, disband, disjoin, divorce, liquefy 8 discandy, disunite, separate 9 decompose, dissipate 10 deliquesce 12 disintegrate

dissolved: 6 solute

dissolving: 7 diluent

dissonant: 5 harsh 7 grating, jarring 8 jangling 10 discordant 11 cacophonous, incongruous, unmelodious 12 inconsistent, inharmonious 13 contradictory

dissuade: 5 deter 6 dehort, divert 10 discourage, disincline

distaff: 5 woman 6 female 12 maternal side

distal: 6 remote 7 distant 8 terminal
angle: 4 axil
opposite of: 8 proximal

distance: 4 step 5 depth, range, space 7 farness, mileage, reserve, yardage 8 interval, outstrip 10 background, remoteness
measuring device: 6 stadia 8 odograph, odometer, viameter 9 pedometer, telemeter

on earth's surface: 8 latitude 9 longitude

distant: far, off 4 afar, away, cold 5 aloof 6 remote, yonder 7 faraway, foreign, removed 8 reserved 9 separated 10 discrepant

distaste: 7 disgust, dislike 8 aversion 9 disrelish 11 displeasure 14 disinclination

distasteful: 7 hateful 8 brackish, nauseous, unsavory 9 loathsome, offensive, repugnant, repulsive 10 unpleasant 11 unpalatable 12 disagreeable

distemper: 4 soak 5 steep 6 choler, dilute, malady 7 ailment, disease, illness 8 disorder, sickness, unsettle 12 disaffection 13 indisposition

distend: 4 fill, grow 5 bloat, plump, swell, widen 6 dilate, expand, extend, spread 7 balloon, enlarge, inflate, stretch

distended: 4 wide 5 blown 8 patulous

distich: 7 couplet

distill, distil: 4 emit 6 infuse 7 trickle

distillation: 7 essence 10 refinement
device: 6 retort 7 alembic, matrass

distinct: 5 clear, plain, vivid 7 diverse, legible, obvious, special 8 apparent, separate 9 different 10 articulate, individual 11 well-defined 13 distinguished

distinction: 4 note, rank 5 glory, honor 6 laurel, luster, renown 9 variation 10 prominence, reputation, separation 14 discrimination 15 differentiation

distinctive: 8 peculiar, talented 9 prominent 11 conspicuous, outstanding 14 characteristic, discriminating
air: 6 cachet

distingué: 6 urbane 7 eminent 8 cultured, polished 10 cultivated

distinguish: 6 define, descry 7 discern 8 perceive, separate 9 designate, punctuate 10 discrepate 12 characterize, discriminate 13 differentiate

distinguished: 5 noted 6 famous, marked 7 eminent, notable, special 8 distinct, laureate, renowned 9 brilliant, prominent 10 celebrated 11 conspicuous, illustrious 13 extraordinary

distort: 4 warp 5 slant, twist 6 deform, garble 7 falsify, pervert 8 misstate 10 disfeature 12 misrepresent

distorted: 4 awry 5 askew 7 colored, crooked, deviant, gnarled 9 misshapen 10 anamorphic 11 anamorphous

distract: 5 addle, amuse, mix up 6 bemuse, divert, harass, puzzle 7 agitate, confuse, disturb, embroil, perplex 8 bewilder, confound

distraught: mad 6 crazed 7 frantic 8 deranged, harassed

distress: ail 4 hurt, need, pain 5 agony, anger, annoy, dolor, grief, gripe, worry, wound 6 danger, grieve, harass, harrow, misery, sorrow **7** afflict, anguish, anxiety, oppress, perplex, torture, trouble **8** aggrieve, calamity, straiten **9** adversity, constrain, martyrdom, necessity **10** affliction, constraint, discomfort **11** tribulation

call: SOS **6** mayday

signal: **5** alarm, flare, siren

distressing: sad **6** woeful **7** fearful, painful **9** sorrowful **10** deplorable, lamentable **11** troublesome

distribute: **4** deal, dole, mete, sort **5** allot, issue, share **6** assign, assort, divide, expend, impart, parcel **7** arrange, dispose, prorate **8** allocate, classify, dispense, disperse, separate **9** apportion, partition **10** administer **11** disseminate

distributively: **4** each **6** apiece **9** severally **10** separately **12** individually, respectively

distributor: **6** dealer, jobber **8** auto part **10** colporteur

district: **4** area, slum, ward **5** tract, vicus(L.) **6** canton, parish, region **7** circuit, country, demesne, diocese, quarter **8** locality, precinct, province **9** community, territory **12** neighborhood

theater: **6** rialto

District of Columbia: See **Washington, D.C.**

distrust: **4** fear **5** doubt **7** suspect **8** be wary of **9** suspicion **12** apprehension

distrustfully: **7** askance **11** skeptically

disturb: vex **4** rile, roil **5** alarm, annoy, freeze, rouse, upset **6** harass, molest, ruffle **7** agitate, derange, perturb, trouble **8** disquiet, distract, unsettle **9** discomfit, interfere, interrupt, make waves **10** disarrange, discompose, disconcert

disturbance: **4** riot, rout **5** alarm, brawl **6** affray, bother, fracas, hubbub, pother, rumpus, tumult, uproar **7** clatter, ferment, trouble, turmoil **8** disorder **9** agitation, annoyance, commotion, confusion **10** excitement **11** derangement, distraction, trepidation **12** discomposure, interruption, perturbation **13** collie-shangie(Sc.), inconvenience

atmospheric: **5** storm **7** cyclone, thunder, tornado **9** hurricane, lightning

emotional: **8** neurosis

ocean: **7** tsunami

disunite: **4** part **5** sever, untie **6** detach, divide, sunder **7** disband, disjoin, dissent, divorce, split up, unravel **8** alienate, dissever, dissolve, estrange, separate **10** disconnect, dissociate

disuse: **7** abandon, discard **9** desuetude **12** obsolescence

disyllabic foot: **7** trochee

ditch: rut, dike, junk, moat **5** canal, scrap **6** gutter, trench **7** abandon, channel **8** get rid of, jettison **9** throw away **10** excavation

side: **5** scarp

dither: **4** flap **5** panic, shake, waver **6** babble, shiver **7** tremble, twitter **9** vacillate **10** act nervous **12** shilly-shally

dithyrambic: **4** wild **10** boisterous

ditto: **4** same **6** repeat **8** likewise **9** duplicate

ditty: lay **4** poem, song **6** melody

diurnal: **5** daily **9** ephemeral

opposite: **9** nocturnal

divagate: **5** stray **6** wander **7** digress

divan: **4** sofa **5** couch **6** lounge, settee **9** davenport **11** smoking room **13** Muslim council

divaricate: **6** forked **7** diverge **11** spread apart

dive: den **4** dump, fall, jump, leap **5** joint, lunge, swoop **6** plunge **7** descend, hangout **8** submerge, tailspin

kind of: **4** swan **6** gainer **9** jackknife

dive into: try **5** begin, start

diver: **4** loon **7** pearler, plunger **9** submarine

disease: **5** bends **12** aeroembolism

gear: **4** mask, tank **5** scuba **7** flipper, snorkel, wet suit

diverge: **6** branch, differ, divide, ramify, spread **7** deviate, digress **8** disagree

divers: **4** many **6** sundry **7** several, various

diverse: **6** motley, sundry, unlike, varied **8** distinct, separate **9** different, multiform **10** dissimilar **13** heterogeneous

diversion: jeu **4** game, play **5** feint, hobby, sport **7** pastime **9** amusement, avocation, merriment **10** deflection, digression, recreation, relaxation **11** distraction **13** divertisement, entertainment

diversity: **6** change **7** variety **10** difference, unlikeness **11** variegation

divert: **5** amuse, relax **7** beguile, deflect, delight **8** dissuade, distract **9** entertain, turn aside

diverting: **5** droll **8** pleasant **9** laughable

divest: **4** bare, doff **5** spoil, strip **6** denude, depose **7** bereave, deprive, despoil, disrobe, uncover **8** denature, dethrone, take away, unclothe **9** dismantle **10** dispossess

of sham: **6** debunk

divide: cut, lot **4** deal, fork, part, rift, zone **5** cleft, divvy, ridge, sever, share, slice, space, split **6** branch, cleave, differ, parcel, ramify, sunder **7** aliquot, diverge, fissure, prorate **8** alienate, allocate, classify, disunite, graduate, separate **9** apportion, dismember, intersect, multisect, partition, watershed **10** distribute

into feet: **4** scan

into parts: **4** paly **6** bisect, gobbet **7** quarter, trisect **9** bifurcate, septinate

divided: 4 reft **7** fissate, partite **8** areolate, camerate **10** incomplete

dividend: 5 bonus **6** return, reward **12** extra portion

divider: 6 screen **7** compass **9** partition

divination: 4 omen **6** augury **8** prophecy **9** good guess **11** discernment **12** clairvoyance

ability: ESP

by dreams: **11** oneiromancy

by figures: **8** geomancy

by fire: **9** pyromancy

by the hands: **9** palmistry

by lots: **9** sortilege

by numbers: **10** numerology

by rods: **7** dowsing

by stars: **9** astrology

manual: **6** I Ching

divine: 4 holy **5** guess, pious **6** detect, devise, priest, sacred **7** blessed, foresee, godlike, portend, predict, presage **8** forebode, foreknow, foretell, heavenly, immortal, minister, perceive **9** ambrosial, celestial, clergyman, religious **10** anticipate, conjecture, superhuman, theologian **12** supernatural

artificer: **8** tvashtar, tvashtri

being: **4** deva

communication: **6** oracle

gift: **5** grace

messenger: **7** apostle

render: **5** deify

spirit: **5** numen

word: **5** logos

work: **7** theurgy

Divine Comedy author: 5 Dante

diviner: 4 seer **5** augur, sibyl **7** prophet **8** haruspex **10** soothsayer **11** clairvoyant **14** prognosticator

diving: 8 plunging **10** acrobatics, submerging

bird: auk **4** loon **5** grebe **6** osprey

divinity (see also **god, goddess**): **5** candy **8** theology

division: 4 chap, clan, dole, neat, part, rift **5** group, realm, share **6** canton, schism, sector **7** roulade, section **8** arpeggio, category, cleavage **9** Abteilung, allotment, concision, departure, partition **10** department **11** bifurcation, compartment, disjunction **13** apportionment, disconnection, dismemberment

athletic contest: lap, set **4** half, heat **5** round **6** inning, period **7** chukker, quarter

between torrid and temperate zones: **6** tropic

Bible: **4** book **5** verse

play: act **5** scene

poem: **5** canto **6** stanza

political: **4** city, ward **5** state **6** county, parish **7** borough **8** district, province

religious: **4** sect **6** schism

result: **8** fraction, quotient

social: **4** clan **5** caste, class, tribe

time: day, eon, era **4** aeon, hour, week, year **5** month, night **6** decade, minute, moment, second **7** weekend **9** fortnight

word: **8** syllable

divisional: 10 fractional, separative

divorce: 5 sever **6** sunder **7** break up **8** dissolve, disunion, disunite, separate **10** separation **11** dissolution

Jewish law: get **4** gett

mill: **4** Reno

divot: 10 lump of turf

divulge: 4 bare, show, tell **5** voice **6** impart, reveal, spread, unfold **7** publish, uncover **8** disclose, discover, give away, proclaim

divvy: 5 share **6** divide **7** portion

Dixie Land: 5 South

dizziness: 6 megrim **7** vertigo **9** giddiness

with headache: **10** scotodinia

dizzy: 4 daze **5** crazy, giddy **6** fickle, stupid **7** foolish **8** swimming, unsteady **10** capricious **11** lightheaded, vertiginous

Djibouti: *capital:* **8** Djibouti

city: **5** Obock **6** Dikhil

gulf: **4** Aden

monetary unit: **5** franc **7** centime

native: **5** Afars, Issas

DNA: 4 gene **11** nucleic acid **14** heredity factor

segment: **7** cistron

Dnieper: *tributary:* **4** Psel, Sozh, Sula **5** Desna, Psiol **7** Pripyat

cities on: **4** Kiev, **5** Orsha **7** Kherson, Mogilev, Nikopol **8** Smolensk

do: act **4** bilk, dost, make, suit **5** avail, cheat, guise, serve, trick **6** answer, finish, render, wind up, work at **7** achieve, arrange, clean up, execute, perform, produce, satisfy, suffice **8** carry out, transact **10** accomplish, administer

do away with: rid **4** drop **7** abolish **8** dissolve **9** liquidate **11** discontinue

do in: 4 kill **6** defeat **7** destroy, exhaust

do out of: 5 cheat, cozen **7** defraud

do-re-mi: 4 song **5** money

do up: tie **4** wrap **5** clean **7** arrange, prepare

do well: 7 prosper, succeed

do without: 5 forgo **6** forego, pass up, refuse

dobbin: 4 mare

docent: 5 guide **7** teacher **8** lecturer

docile: 4 calm, meek, tame **6** gentle **7** ductile, dutiful **8** biddable **9** tractable **10** manageable

dock: cut **4** bang, clip, moor, pier, quay **5** basin, wharf **6** marina **7** bobtail, cur-

tail, shorten **12** prisoner's box
post: **4** pile **7** bollard
ship's: **4** slip **5** basin, berth
worker: **9** stevedore
yard: **7** arsenal
docket: **4** card **6** agenda **7** program **8** calendar, schedule **13** police blotter
doctor: **4** dose **5** fix up, treat **6** healer, medico, repair **7** dentist, scholar **8** sawbones **9** internist, physician, adulterate **11** aesculapian
aide: **5** nurse
animal: vet **10** veterinary **12** veterinarian
oath of: **11** hippocratic
specialist: **7** oculist, surgeon **9** otologist **10** podiatrist **11** chiropodist, neurologist, optometrist, orthopedist **12** chiropractor, gynecologist, obstetrician, orthodontist, pediatrician, psychiatrist
doctrine: ism **4** doxy, lear, rule **5** credo, creed, dogma, maxim, tenet **6** belief, gospel, theory **7** article, opinion, precept **8** position **9** principle **10** discipline
pert. to: **10** dogmatical **12** teleological
secret: **7** esotery
single principle: **6** henism, monism
specific: **6** cabala, heresy, malism, Mishna **7** Mishnah **8** fatalism, hedonism **10** agathology, pragmatism **13** monarchianism
spreader: **12** propagandist
document: **4** bill, book, cite, deed, writ **5** lease, paper **6** record, verify **7** bear out, confirm, missive, precept, writing **8** contract, covenant, mortgage, validate **9** indenture **10** manuscript **11** corroborate
addition: **5** rider **7** codicil **9** amendment
file: **7** dossier
original record: **8** protocol
permissive: **7** license
provisional: **5** scrip
receptacle: **7** hanaper
signed by all parties: **8** syngraph
storehouse: **8** archives
travel: **8** passport
true copy: **7** estreat
Dodecanese Island: Kos **4** Syme **5** Kasos, Leros, Telos **6** Khalke, Lipsos, Patmos, Rhodes **7** Nisyros, Piscopi **8** Kalymnos **9** Karpathos
dodder: **5** shake **6** totter **7** tremble
doddering: old **5** inane **6** infirm, senile **7** foolish
dodge: **4** duck, jink, ruse **5** avoid, cheat, elude, parry, shift, shirk, trick **6** escape **7** deceive, evasion **8** artifice, sidestep **9** expedient **10** equivocate
dodger: **7** haggler **8** circular, handbill **13** advertisement
corn: **4** pone

dodo: **7** old fogy **8** mossback **10** back number, fuddy-duddy **11** extinct bird
doe: roe, teg **4** fawn, hind **6** female
doer: **6** dynamo, worker **7** hustler **8** activist, go-getter, live wire **9** performer **10** ball of fire
doff: **5** douse **6** remove **7** discard **8** put aside
dog: cur, mut, pug, pup **4** mutt, tyke **5** canis(L.), frank, lemon, pooch, puppy, trail, whelp **6** bowwow, canine, detent, rascal, shadow, wiener **7** mongrel **9** carnivore
African: **7** basenji
Australian: **5** dingo
breed: pug **4** Dane **5** boxer, hound, Husky, spitz **6** Afghan, basset, beagle, borzoi, Briard, collie, Eskimo, poodle, Saluki, setter **7** Basenji, bulldog, griffon, harrier, Maltese, mastiff, pointer, Scottie, Shih Tzu, spaniel, terrier, whippet **8** Airedale, Alsatian, chow chow, coach dog, Doberman, elkhound, foxhound, keeshond, Labrador, Malamute, Malemute, Malinois, papillon, Pekinese, Pyrenees, Samoyede, Sealyham, shepherd, springer **9** Chihuahua, dachshund, Dalmatian, deerhound, Great Dane, greyhound, kerry blue, Lhasa apso, St. Bernard, schnauzer, wolfhound, Yorkshire **10** Bedlington, bloodhound, Boston bull, Chesapeake, Manchester, otter hound, Pomeranian, Rottweiler, schipperke, weimaraner **11** bull terrier, Groenendael, ruby spaniel, Skye terrier **12** cairn terrier, Gordon setter, Newfoundland, water spaniel, Welsh terrier **13** Boston terrier, cocker spaniel, Great Pyrenees, Prince Charles **15** Brussels griffon, highland terrier, Riesenschnauzer **17** Bouvier de Flandres
close-haired: pug **5** boxer
Dorothy's: **4** Toto
Eskimo: **5** husky **7** Samoyed **8** Malamute, Malemute, Samoyede
famous: **4** Asta, Fala, King, Tige, Toby **5** Benji, Devil **6** Feller, Lassie **8** Checkers **9** Old Yeller, Rin-Tin-Tin **11** Strongheart
FDR's: **4** Fala
fox-like: **6** colpeo
genus: **5** canis
German origin: **5** boxer **8** Doberman **9** Drahthaar **10** Weimaraner
hauling: **5** husky **7** Samoyed **8** Malamute, Malemute, Samoyede **9** Dalmatian
house: **6** kennel
howling of: **9** ululation
hunting: **5** hound, toler **6** basset, beagle, borzoi, saluki, setter, talbot **7** courser, harrier, pointer **8** elkhound **9** retriever,

wolfhound **10** bloodhound
iron: **7** firedog
large: **4** Dane **5** boxer **6** briard, collie, police **7** mastiff **12** Newfoundland
long-haired: **4** alco, chow **7** spaniel
Orphan Annie's: **5** Sandy
small: Pom, pug, pup **4** alco, Peke **8** Pekinese **9** Chihuahua, Pekingese **10** Pomeranian
space traveler: **5** Leika
underworld: **8** Cerberus
upper lip: **5** flews
Welsh: **5** corgi **8** Sealyham
wild: **5** adjag, dhole, dingo **6** jackal **7** agouara **8** cimarron
dog days: 8 canicule
dog rose: 9 eglantine
fruit: hip
dog star: 6 Sirius
constellation: **10** Canis Major
dogfight: 5 brawl, melee, scrap **9** air battle **10** free-for-all
dogfish: 5 shark **6** bowfin
dogged: 8 stubborn **9** obstinate, tenacious **10** determined, persistent, purposeful **11** persevering
doggerel: 6 jingle **10** light verse
doggish: 5 showy, sulky **7** stylish **8** snappish, snarling
doggone: 4 damn, darn, drat **5** blast **6** shucks **9** son of a gun
dogie: 9 stray calf
dogma: 5 canon, credo, creed, tenet **6** belief, dictum **8** doctrine **10** conviction, philosophy
dogmatic: 6 biased **7** a priori **9** arbitrary, assertive, doctrinal **10** intolerant, peremptory, pontifical, prejudiced **11** dictatorial, opinionated
do-gooder: 8 altruist, idealist **9** soul saver **10** fixer-upper **13** bleeding heart
Dogpatch depicter: 4 Capp (Al)
dogs: 4 feet
dogwood: 5 osier, sumac **6** cornel
flowering: **7** boxwood
genus: **6** cornus
doily: mat **6** napkin
kin: **7** coaster
do in: 4 kill, ruin **6** finish, murder **7** exhaust, wear out **9** liquidate
doings: 5 deeds **6** events **7** actions **9** functions **10** activities
doldrums: 5 blues, dumps, ennui **6** apathy, tedium **7** boredom **10** depression, low spirits, ocean calms
dole: 4 alms **5** allot **6** relief **7** charity, deal out, handout, mete out **8** dispense **9** apportion **10** distribute
doleful: sad **5** drear, heavy **6** dismal, dreary, rueful **7** flebile **8** downcast, mournful **9** plaintive, sorrowful **10** lugubrious, melancholy **12** disconsolate

dolent: 9 sorrowful
doll: toy **4** babe, baby **5** array, puppe(G.) **6** maumet, moppet, muneca(Sp.), poupee(F.), puppet **8** mistress **9** golliwogg **10** sweetheart
doll up: 5 adorn, dress **11** put on the dog
dollar: one **4** buck **8** frogskin, simoleon
dollop: bit, tot **4** blob, dash, lump **5** snort **6** jigger, splash **10** tiny amount
Doll's House heroine: 4 Nora
dolly: car **4** cart **5** truck **7** carrier **12** wheeled frame **14** camera platform
dolor: 5 grief **6** sorrow **7** anguish, sadness **8** distress, mourning **11** lamentation
dolorous: sad **6** dismal **7** doleful **8** grievous **9** sorrowful
dolphin: 4 fish **6** dorado **7** bollard **8** moor spar, porpoise **10** bottlenose
movie: **7** Flipper
river: **5** bouto
dolt: ass, oaf **4** clod, fool **5** chump, dummy, dunce, idiot **7** bluntie(Sc.), dullard, half-wit **8** imbecile, numskull **9** blockhead, ignoramus, simpleton **10** dunderhead
doltish: 4 dull **5** dense, thick **6** stupid **7** foolish **8** blockish **11** thickheaded
domain: 4 area **5** realm, world **6** empire, estate, sphere **7** demesne **8** dominion, province **9** bailiwick, territory
Dombey and Son author: 7 Dickens
character: **4** Paul **5** Edith **6** Carker **9** Walter Gay
dome: cap **4** cima **6** cupola **7** calotte, edifice
domed: 7 vaulted
domestic: 4 cook, maid **6** native **7** servant **8** homebred, homemade **9** home-grown **11** housewifely
establishment: **6** menage
domesticate: 4 tame **5** train **6** master **7** reclaim **8** civilize **10** housebreak
domicile: 4 home **5** abode, house **6** menage **8** dwelling **9** residence **10** habitation
identification: **9** doorplate
dominant: 5 bossy, chief **6** ruling **7** central, regnant, supreme **8** superior **9** ascendant, imperious, paramount, prevalent, principal **10** commanding, preeminent, prevailing **11** outweighing **12** preponderant **13** overbalancing
dominate: 4 rule **5** reign **6** govern **7** control **8** stand out **9** tower over
domination: 4 sway **5** power **7** command, control, mastery **9** supremacy **11** sovereignty
domineer: cow **4** boss, rule **5** bully **7** command, oppress **8** bulldoze, ride over, walk over **12** crack the whip
domineering: 5 bossy **6** lordly **7** haughty **8** arrogant **9** imperious, masterful **10**

tyrannical **11** dictatorial, magisterial, overbearing

Dominica: *capital:* **6** Roseau
city: **6** Roseau **10** Portsmouth
island group: **8** Windward
member: **12** Commonwealth
monetary unit. **4** cent **6** dollar

Dominican: 9 Predicant

Dominican Republic: *bay:* **4** Ocoa, Yuma **5** Neiba **6** Rincon, Samana **7** Isabela **8** Escocesa
cape: **5** Beata, Falso, Viejo **6** Engano
capital: **12** Santo Domingo
city: **4** Bani, Moca **5** Neiba **8** Barahona, La Romana, Santiago
dictator: **8** Trujillo (Rafael)
ethnic group: **5** Negro **7** mulatto **9** Caucasian
Indian: **5** Carib **6** Arawak
island: **10** Hispaniola
island possession: **5** Beata, Saona **8** Catalina
lake: **10** Enriquillo
monetary unit: **4** peso **7** centavo
mountain peak: **4** Tina **5** Gallo **10** Pico Duarte
mountain range: **10** Cordillera
peninsula: **6** Samana
port: **11** Puerto Plata **12** Santo Domingo
province: **4** Azua **6** Duarte, La Vega, Samana **7** Dajabon, Peravia, Salcedo, San Juan **8** Bahoruco, Barahona, Santiago, Valverde
river: **4** Yuna **5** Yaque

dominie: 6 pastor **9** clergyman, pedagogue **12** schoolmaster

dominion: 4 rule, sway **5** realm, reign **6** domain, empire **7** control, dynasty, regency **9** authority, hierarchy, ownership, supremacy **10** ascendancy **11** sovereignty **12** jurisdiction
church: **11** sacerdotium
joint: **11** condominium

domino: die **4** mask

dominoes: 4 game **5** bones **7** ivories

domus: 4 home **5** house

don: 4 wear **5** array, dress, put on **6** assume, clothe, invest **7** get into **8** nobleman **9** gentleman, professor **10** instructor

Don Carlos: *author:* **8** Schiller
opera composer: **5** Verdi

Don Giovanni composer: 6 Mozart

Don Juan: 4 rake **6** masher **7** seducer **9** libertine **10** lady-killer, profligate

Don Quixote: *companion:* **11** Sancho Panza
steed: **9** Rosinante, Rozinante

Donar: 4 Thor

donate: gie(Sc.) **4** give **6** bestow **7** hand out, present, provide **10** contribute

donation: 4 gift **5** grant **7** bequest, present **8** offering **11** benefaction **12** contribution

done: 4 over **5** baked, ended **6** cooked **7** through **8** finished **9** completed, exhausted **12** accomplished

donee: 7 heritor **8** receiver **9** recipient **11** beneficiary

done for: 4 dead **5** goner, kaput **6** licked, ruined **7** wrecked **8** bankrupt **10** on the ropes

done in: 4 beat **5** spent **6** pooped, used up **7** worn out **8** frazzled **9** played out

donkey: ass **4** fool **5** burro, jenny, neddy **6** onager **8** imbecile, numskull
cry: **4** bray **6** heehaw

donkey engine: 6 yarder **10** locomotive **11** cargo lifter

donna: 4 lady, wife **5** madam, woman **8** mistress

donor: 5 giver **10** benefactor **11** contributor **14** philanthropist

doodle: 4 dolt, draw **5** cheat **6** putter **7** cartoon, trifler **8** scribble **10** nincompoop

doodlesack: 7 bagpipe

doohickey: 6 doodad, gadget **11** thingamabob

dooly, doolie: 6 litter **9** palanquin

doom: law, lot **4** damn, fate, ruin **5** death **6** decree, kismet **7** condemn, destine, destiny, fortune, statute **8** calamity, decision, judgment, sentence **9** ordinance, preordain **10** adjudicate, predestine **11** destruction **12** condemnation

doomed: fey **5** fatal **8** accursed **9** sentenced

door: 4 exit, gate **5** entry, hatch **6** portal **7** barrier, opening, passage **11** entranceway
back: **7** postern
crosspiece: **6** lintel
fastener: bar **4** bolt, hasp, lock **5** catch, latch
frame: **4** jamb
holder: **5** hinge
holy: **11** amphithyron
part: **4** jamb, knob, sill **5** panel **6** alette
storm: **6** dingle
trap: **4** drop

doorkeeper: 5 guard **6** porter, warden **7** ostiary **9** concierge(F.)

doormat: rug **8** weakling **10** pantywaist

dope: hop **4** drug **5** dunce, opium, paste **6** heroin, opiate **7** cocaine, predict, stupefy **8** narcotic **9** marijuana

doped: 4 high **6** stoned **7** drugged **8** hopped-up **9** spaced out

dope out: 5 crack, solve **6** decode, fathom **7** clear up **10** unscramble **12** get the answer

dopester: 4 tout **7** tipster **10** forecaster

dopey, dopy: 4 dull **5** dazed, woozy **6**

groggy, torpid **8** sluggish **9** lethargic **10** punch drunk
doppelganger: 6 double, spirit, wraith **10** apparition **11** counterpart
dor: bee **6** beetle **11** drumbledore
dorcas: 7 gazelle
dorian: 6 simple
Dorian festival: 6 Carnea **7** Carneia
doric: 6 rustic
Doric: *frieze bottom:* **6** taenia
frieze slab: **6** metope
Doris' king: 8 Aegimius
dormancy: 6 torpor **8** abeyance **10** quiescence
dormant: 5 fixed, quiet **6** asleep, latent, torpid **7** resting **8** inactive, sleeping **9** unaroused **10** stationary
dormer: 6 window **7** lucarne
dormitory: 12 sleeping room **13** residence hall
monastery: **6** dorter **7** dortour
dormouse: 4 loir **5** lerot
pert. to: **7** myoxine
dornick: 5 linen **6** damask
dorsal: 5 notal **6** aboral, tergal **7** abaxial **9** posterior
opposed to: **7** ventral
dorsum: 4 back
dose: 4 bole **5** draft, treat **6** doctor, drench, potion **7** draught **8** quantity
doss: 7 bed down **12** lodging house
dot: 4 clot, lump, mote, peck **5** dowry, point, speck **6** period **7** speckle, stipple **8** particle, sprinkle **9** bespangle **10** besprinkle, distribute
over the letter i: **6** tittle
dotage: 6 old age **7** anility **8** senility **10** feebleness **11** senectitude
dote on: 5 adore, fancy **6** pamper, revere **7** idolize, worship **10** love dearly **11** be partial to
doting: 4 fond **6** loving **7** devoted, doddery, fatuous **8** overfond **13** overindulgent
dotterel: 6 plover **7** lapwing **9** turnstone
dotty: 5 crazy, wacky, spotty **8** obsessed **9** eccentric **12** feebleminded
Douay Bible: 4 Aree
double: ply **4** dual, fold, twin **5** duple, fetch, twice **6** binary, binate, clench, duplex **7** twofold **8** geminate **9** ambiguous, duplicate, look-alike **11** counterpart
double-cross: 5 cheat **6** betray **7** deceive, sell out, swindle **9** treachery
double dagger: 6 diesis
double dealing: 6 deceit **8** trickery **9** duplicity
double-edged: 9 ancipital
doubled: 5 gemel **6** paired **7** twinned
doublespeak: 9 ambiguity, vague talk **12** equivocation **13** foggy language

double-talk: 5 hokum **7** twaddle **8** nonsense **9** gibberish **12** gobbledygook
doubt: 4 fear **5** demur, dread, qualm, query, waver **7** scruple, suspect **8** distrust, hesitate, mistrust, question **9** discredit, misgiving, suspicion **10** diffidence, disbelieve, indecision **11** uncertainty **12** apprehension
doubter: 5 cynic **7** skeptic **10** unbeliever
doubtful: 4 iffy **6** unsure **7** dubious, fearful **8** wavering **9** ambiguous, diffident, equivocal, uncertain, undecided **10** apocryphal, hesitating, irresolute, suspicious **11** distrustful, vacillating **12** apprehensive, questionable, undetermined **13** problematical
douceur: sop **4** gift **5** bonus **7** present **8** gratuity **9** pourboire
dough: 4 cash **5** money, paste **7** cabbage **10** green staff
doughnut: 6 sinker **7** cruller
relative: **7** fritter **9** friedcake
doughty: 4 fell **5** brave **7** valiant **8** intrepid
doughy: 4 ashy, soft **5** pasty **6** flabby, pallid **7** viscous
dour: 4 glum, grim, hard, sour **5** rough, stern **6** gloomy, morose, severe, strong, sullen **7** ominous **9** obstinate **10** inflexible
douse, dowse: 4 doff, duck, dunk, stow **5** rinse, slosh **6** drench, plunge, put out, strike **7** immerse **8** downpour **9** drenching **10** extinguish
douzepers: 4 Ivon, Otton **5** Ivory, Gerin, Ogier, peers **6** Anseis, Gerier, nobles, Oliver, Roland, Samson, Turpin **7** knights **8** Engelier, paladins **9** Berengier **17** Gerard de Rousillon
dove: 5 color **6** culver, pigeon **7** namaqua **8** pacifist **11** conciliator
home: **4** cote **9** columbary
pert. to: **9** columbine
political opposite: **4** hawk
sound: coo **4** curr
dovekey, dovekie: auk **9** guillemot
dovelike: 4 pure **6** gentle **7** lovable **9** columbine
dovetail: fit **4** jibe, mesh **5** agree, tally, tenon **6** go with **8** check out **10** correspond
dovish: 7 antiwar **9** peaceable **10** nonviolent
dowager: 6 matron **9** matriarch **10** grande dame
dowdy: 4 drab **5** seedy, tacky **6** blowzy, shabby, untidy **8** slovenly **9** unstylish **10** slatternly
woman: **5** frump
dowel: peg, pin **4** coak **6** pintle
dower: dot **5** endow **6** talent **9** endowment **13** bride's portion

dowitcher: 5 snipe
down: 4 dowl, fell, flix, flue, fuzz, hill, lint 5 below, dowle, floor, fluff 7 hillock, plumage 9 overthrow
down at the heel: 5 seamy, seedy
down in the mouth: 4 glum 7 unhappy 8 dejected 9 depressed 11 discouraged
down under: 8 Tasmania 9 antipodes, Australia 10 New Zealand
down with: 4 a bas
downbeat: 4 grim 5 bleak 6 dismal, gloomy 8 negative 11 pessimistic
downcast: sad 6 abject, gloomy, morose 7 forlorn 8 hopeless 10 despondent, dispirited, melancholy 11 discouraged 12 disheartened
downer: 6 bummer 7 bad trip 10 depressant 11 barbiturate
downfall: pit 4 fate, ruin, trap 5 abyss 7 descent, undoing 8 collapse 9 precipice, ruination 11 destruction, ecroulement 12 degringolade
downgrade: dip 4 bust, drop 5 lower 6 debase, demote, lessen, reduce 7 decline, descent, devalue 9 declivity
downpour: 4 rain 6 deluge 7 torrent 10 cloudburst
downright: 4 flat, pure, rank 5 blank, blunt, plain, plumb, sheer, stark 6 arrant, direct 8 absolute, complete, positive, thorough 9 out-and-out 10 forthright 11 unmitigated
downstairs: 5 below
downtrend: dip, sag 4 drop, fall, slip 5 slide, slump 7 decline
downwind: 7 leeward
downy: 4 soft 5 mossy, nappy, pilar, quiet 6 fluffy, placid 7 cunning, knowing 8 soothing
dowry: See **dower**
doxy: ism 5 wench 6 harlot 7 opinion 8 doctrine
doyen: 4 dean 6 expert 8 virtuoso 9 authority 10 past master 12 senior member
doze: nap, nod 5 decay, sleep 6 catnap, drowse, snooze 7 slumber, snoozle
drab: 4 bawd, dull 5 dingy, mousy, wench, whore 6 dreary 7 prosaic 8 lifeless 9 colorless 10 monotonous, prostitute 13 uninteresting
drachma: 4 coin, dram
one-sixth: 4 obol
draconian: 5 cruel 6 severe, strict
Dracula: 7 vampire
author: 10 Bram Stoker
draff: 4 lees 5 dregs, drink 6 refuse 7 hogwash
draft: nip, sip 4 dose, dram, gust, levy, plan, swig, toot 5 drink, epure, swipe 6 call up, devise, drench, potion, redact, scroll, sketch 7 draught, drawing, outline, pattern, project 8 beverage 9 conscript 10 air current

evader: 6 dodger
draftsman, draughtsman: 6 drawer 7 tippler 9 architect
drag: lug, tow, tug 4 bore, draw, haul, pull, swig, tear, tump 5 brake, delay, drawl, trail, trawl 6 anchor, burden, linger, taigle(Sc.) 7 grapnel 9 lag behind 10 wet blanket
out: 6 elicit, extend 7 prolong 8 protract
dragnet: 5 trawl 7 grapnel
dragoman: 5 agent, guide 11 interpreter
dragon: 7 monster 8 basilisk
biblical: 5 Rahab
biting: 8 tarragon
Chinese: 5 lung
French: 8 Tarasque
killer: 6 Cadmus, Sigurd 7 Beowulf, Perseus 8 St. George, St. Martha
Norse: 6 Fafner, Fafnir
Vedic: Ahi
dragonfly order: 8 odonata
dragoon: 6 coerce 9 force into 10 cavalryman
drain: dry, gaw, sap 4 fade, milk, pump, sink, tire, tube 5 canal, empty, gully, sewer, spout 6 burden, furrow, guzzle, outlet, siphon, trench 7 acequia, channel, deplete, draw off, exhaust 9 drink down, undermine 11 watercourse
arched: 7 culvert
drainage: 11 waste system
area: 5 basin
drained: 5 all in, spent 6 used up 7 worn out 8 depleted 10 cleaned out, gulped down
drainpipe: 6 leader
dram: nip 4 mite, slug 5 draft, drink 6 drachm 7 snifter 8 potation, quantity
drama: 4 play 5 opera 7 theater, tragedy 8 conflict, pastoral, the stage 11 composition
court: 5 trial
father of: 7 Thespis
Japanese: noh
main act: 8 epitasis
television: 9 soap opera
unspoken: 9 pantomime
dramatic: 4 wild 5 vivid 6 scenic 10 theatrical 12 melodramatic
expession system: 8 delsarte
dramatist: 5 actor 10 playwright
drape: 4 hang 5 adorn, cover 6 sprawl, swathe 7 curtain, hanging, valance 8 spraddle 10 fall in folds, wrap around
drapeau: 4 flag 8 standard
draper: 6 tailor
drastic: 4 dire 5 harsh 6 severe 7 extreme, radical 8 rigorous
draught: See **draft**
Dravidian (see also **India**): 4 Gond, Kota, Toda, Tulu 5 Arava, Gondi, Khond, Malto, Oraon, Tamil 6 Andhra,

Brahui, Kodagu, Kurukh, Telegu, Telegu **8** Kanarese **9** Malayalam
demon: **4** bhut
tribe: **6** Badaga **7** Collery
draw: lug, tie, tow, tug **4** drag, duct, hale, haul, lade, limn, lure, pull **5** catch, educe, train **6** allure, deduce, depict, derive, design, elicit, entice, induce, inhale, select, sketch **7** attract, detract, extract, inspire, portray **8** inveigle, standoff **9** allowance, delineate, reproduce, statement
again: **5** remap **6** replat
away from: **6** shrink
back: **5** wince **6** cringe, recede, recoil, resile, retire, shrink **7** retract, retreat
close: **4** near **8** approach, come nigh
finely: **4** etch
forth: **5** educe, evoke **6** elicit **7** pull out
off: sap **5** drain **6** siphon **7** extract **8** abstract
out: **4** pump **5** educe **6** elicit, extend **7** extract, prolong **8** lengthen, protract **11** interrogate **12** cross-examine
tight: **4** frap, furl, lace **5** brace, cinch
up: **4** halt, stop **5** frame **7** prepare **9** formulate
drawback: **6** defect **8** handicap **9** detriment, hindrance **12** disadvantage
draw game: **9** stalemate
drawer: **4** till
drawers: **5** pants **6** shorts **7** panties **9** long johns, underwear
chest of: **6** bureau **7** commode **10** chiffonier
drawing: **4** plan **5** draft, epure **7** hauling, picture, pulling **10** attracting, extracting **11** delineation, centripetal
absent-minded: **8** doodling
by number: **7** lottery
exaggerated: **7** cartoon **10** caricature
instrument: **9** eidograph **10** pantograph
watercolor: **4** wash
drawing room: **5** salon **6** parlor, saloon
drawl: **5** drant **6** loiter
drawn: wan **4** worn **6** peaked **7** haggard
drawstring: **5** latch
dray: **4** cart **5** wagon **6** camion
drayage: **7** cartage, haulage
drayman: **6** carter **7** carrier, wagoner
dread: awe **4** fear **5** alarm **6** dismay, horror, terror **7** anguish, anxiety **8** affright **12** apprehension
dreadful: **4** dire **5** awful **6** grisly, horrid **7** direful, fearful, ghastly, grimful, hideous **8** doubtful, horrible, shocking, terrible **9** frightful **10** formidable
dreadnaught, dreadnought: **4** tank **7** warship **8** fearless **10** battleship
dream: **4** hope, muse, reve(F.) **5** fancy **6** vision **7** chimera, fantasy, imagine, reverie, romance **8** illusion, phantasm **9** nightmare **10** apparition, aspiration

god of: **8** Morpheus
pert. to: **7** oneiric, somnial **9** oneirotic
dreamer: **4** poet **5** mystic **7** fantast **8** idealist **9** visionary **10** ideologist
dreaminess: **7** languor **8** euphoria
dreamy: kef **4** soft **5** great, super, vague **6** divine, groovy **7** faraway, pensive **8** fanciful, soothing **9** beautiful, marvelous **11** imaginative
dreary: sad **4** dire, dull, flat **5** bleak, cruel, ourie(Sc.) **6** boring, deadly, dismal, gloomy, somber, lonely **7** doleful **8** grievous **9** cheerless, sorrowful **10** depressing, monotonous, oppressive, pedestrian **11** distressful
dredge: dig, mop **4** coat, sift **5** scoop **6** deepen **8** excavate **9** search for
dredger: **6** duster **9** sprinkler
dregs: **4** lees, scum **5** draff, dross **6** bottom, dunder, rabble, refuse **7** deposit, grounds, residue **8** remnants, riffraff, sediment, settling **10** subsidence **12** crassamentum
drench: **4** dose, hose, sink, soak **5** douse, draft, drink, drown, souse, steep **6** imbrue **7** immerse **8** permeate, saturate, submerge
drenched: wet **4** asop **6** soaked **7** sopping
dress (see also **garment, gown, robe, vestment**): don, dub, fig, ray, rig, tog **4** garb, gear, gown, hone, knap, mill, rail, robe, suit, tire, trim, wear **5** adorn, array, curry, equip, fix up, frock, groom, guise, habit, prink, prune, treat **6** attire, clothe, enrobe, invest, outfit, revest, toilet **7** apparel, bandage, clothes, costume, deck out, garment, garnish, raiment, toggery, vesture **8** clothing, decorate, ornament, vestment **9** embellish, equipment, vestiture **10** habiliment **12** accouterment
clerical: **5** cloth
court: **4** robe
feathers: **5** preen
gaudily: **5** primp, prink **7** bedizen
in full armor: **7** panoply
informal: **6** shorts, slacks **8** negligee **9** blue-jeans
kind of: alb **4** huke **5** crape, crepe, ephod, mufti, tails, tenue, tunic, weeds **6** dirndl, finery, gaiter, kirtle, livery, tuxedo **7** regalia **8** lava-lava, peignoir **9** canonical, decollete, polonaise
leather: tan, taw, tew **5** curry
mean: **4** rags
odd: rig **5** getup
ornament: **4** frog, lace **5** jabot, ruche **6** sequin, zequin **7** ruching **8** chequeen, zecchino **10** embroidery
riding: **5** habit **8** breeches, jodhpurs
stone: nig **5** nidge, spall **7** scabble
trimming: **4** gimp, lace **5** braid
dress down: **5** scold **6** berate **7** bawl out,

tell off **9** castigate **10** tongue-lash
dressed: 4 clad **5** bound **7** habited
  well: **4** braw **5** smart **6** modish **7** soignee,
    stylish **9** spruced-up
dresser: 5 chest, rober **6** bureau **7** modiste **8** cupboard **10** chiffonier, escritoire
  leather: **7** currier **8** levanter
  scrupulous: fop **4** dude **5** dandy **8** macaroni **11** Beau Brummell
dressing: 5 sauce **7** bandage **8** stuffing
dressing stone: 9 scotching
dressmaker: 5 sewer **7** modiste **8** stitcher **9** couturier **10** couturiere, seamstress
  form: **7** manikin **8** mannikin **9** mannequin
dribble: 4 drip, drop **5** drool **6** bounce **7** slobber, trickle **11** fritter away
driblet: bit **6** trifle **8** pittance, small sum
drift: sag, **4** dene, dune, ford, herd, plot, tide, till **5** drove, fleet, float, flock, tenor, trend **6** broach, course, design, device, scheme, tunnel **7** impetus, impulse, pasture, purport **8** tendency **9** deviation **10** propulsion
  along: **4** tide **5** float **10** move slowly
  sidewise: **4** crab **8** crescent
driftage: 6 jetsam **7** flotsam **8** wreckage
drifter: bum **4** hobo **5** tramp **7** floater, vagrant **8** vagabond, wanderer **12** rolling stone
drill: gad, saw, tap **4** bore, spud **5** auger, borer, churn, decoy, train, tutor, twirl, whirl **6** allure, entice, furrow, pierce, school, seeder, stoper **7** channel **8** exercise, instruct, practice **9** perforate
drilling: 5 denim
drink (see also **beverage**): bib, lap, sip, tea **4** brew, grog, horn, swig, tiff, tope **5** booze, draft, punch, quaff, toast **6** absorb, bracer, chaser, coffee, drench, guzzle, hooker, imbibe, liquid, potion, tipple **7** draught, potable, swallow **8** beverage, cocktail, highball, libation, potation **10** intoxicant
  alcoholic: ale, gin, rum, rye **4** beer, beno, bosa, boza, chia, flip, mead, nipa, nogg, soma, swig **5** airah, bombo, bozah, bubud, bumbo, julep, lager, negus, posca, sling, vodka, zombi **6** brandy, casiri, caudle, fuddle, mescal, posset, rickey, zombie **7** cobbler, guarapo, martini, sidecar, tequila **8** aperitif, rumbarge, sangaree, tequilla **9** cointreau, margarita **11** screwdriver
  carbonated: pop **4** fizz, soda **9** ginger ale
  Christmas: nog **6** eggnog **7** wassail
  drugged: **6** mickey
  farinaceous: **6** ptisan
  frozen: **6** frappe
  fruit: ade **5** assai, bland, julep, morat **6** rickey **7** ratafia
  honey: **4** mead

  hot: **5** cocoa, negus, toddy **6** caudle
  magic: **8** nepenthe
  molasses and vinegar: **6** swanky
  of gods: **6** nectar
  Oriental: **4** sake
  portion: **4** shot **5** ounce **6** dollop, jigger
  Russian: **5** vodka
  sassafras: **6** saloop
  small: nip, peg, tot **4** dram, pony, shot, slug **5** snort **6** chaser, jigger **7** snifter
  Tatar: **6** kumiss
drinker: sot **4** lush **5** toper **7** imbiber, intaker, quaffer **8** drunkard **9** inebriate
drinking: 8 guzzling, tippling **9** carousing
  bout: bum **4** orgy, toot **5** binge, spree **6** bender
  horn: **6** rhyton
  salutation: **5** skoal **6** prosit **7** wassail **11** a votre sante
  vessel: cup, mug **4** bowl, tass(Sc.) **5** glass, gourd, hanap, jorum, stein **6** beaker, cappie(Sc.), dipper, goblet, noggin, patera **7** canikin, snifter, tankard **8** cannikin, schooner
drip: sie **4** bore, drop, leak, pill **5** eaves **7** dribble, trickle **10** wet blanket
  frozen: **6** icicle
drippy: 5 soupy **6** slushy **7** drizzly, insipid, maudlin **10** unpleasant **11** sentimental
drive: run **4** bang, bear, butt, goad, herd, push, ride, send, spur, urge **5** chase, crowd, force, hurry, impel, press, shove, sweep, vigor **6** attack, compel, cudgel, hasten, plunge, propel **7** impulse, operate, overtax **9** constrain **10** get-up-and-go
  away: **4** shoo **5** chase, repel **6** banish, dispel **7** repulse
  down: **4** tamp
  frantic: **7** bedevil
  out: **4** rout **5** exile, expel **8** exorcise **9** eradicate
  public: **9** esplanade
  too close: **8** tailgate
drive-in: 7 open-air **10** restaurant
drivel: 4 dote **5** drool **6** dotage, slaver **7** twaddle **8** claptrap, nonsense
driver: 4 jehu **5** drabi(Ind.) **6** cabbie, hackie, caller, jarvey, hammer, mallet **7** catcher, spanker **8** coachman, engineer, golf club, motorist, overseer, teamster **9** chauffeur, propeller **10** charioteer, taskmaster
  of golden chariot: **6** Helios
drizzle: 8 sprinkle **9** misty rain
droll: odd **5** comic, funny, merry, queer **6** jocose **7** amusing, comical, jocular, strange **8** farcical, humorous **9** diverting, laughable, ludicrous, whimsical **10** ridiculous
drollery: wit **4** jest **5** farce, humor **6** japery **10** buffoonery **11** waggishness

dromedary: 5 camel
dromond: 6 galley 7 warship
drone: bee, bum, hum 4 drum, slug 5 drant, idler, snail 6 bumble, draunt, lubber 7 bagpipe, humming, shirker, sleeper, speaker 8 loiterer, sluggard 9 bombilate
dronish: 4 slow 8 indolent, sluggish
drool: 6 drivel, slaver 7 slobber
droop: sag 4 bend, drop, flag, hang, loll, pine, sink, wilt 5 slump 6 slouch, wither 7 decline 8 languish
drooping: 4 limp 5 tired, weary 6 flaggy, 7 nodding 8 dejected, downcast 10 disspirited
of eyelid: 6 ptosis
on one side: 4 alop
drop: dap 4 bead, blob, drib, drip, fall, omit, shed, sink, stop 5 droop, lower, plump, plunk, slump 6 plunge 7 abandon, curtain, descent, dismiss, dribble, forsake, globule, plummet, release 8 decrease, quantity 10 relinquish 11 discontinue
lachrymal: 4 tear
syllable: 5 elide 7 elision
drop in: 5 enter, visit 6 arrive, call on, stop by 8 surprise
drop off: nap 4 doze 5 sleep 8 decrease
droplet: 7 globule
dropout: 6 misfit 8 maverick 11 social rebel 13 school quitter
dropped: 6 fallen 7 left off, lowered 8 released, went down 11 had done with
dropper: 7 pipette
dropsy: 5 edema
dross: 4 lees, scum, slag 5 chaff, dregs, sprue, waste 6 garble, refuse, scoria, sinter 7 cinders 8 leavings 9 recrement
iron: 6 sinter
drought, drouth: 6 thirst 7 aridity, dryness
drought plant: 9 xerophyte
drove (see also **drive**): mob 4 herd 5 atajo(Sp.), crowd, flock, horde 6 chisel, pushed, throng 7 steered 10 assemblage
drown: 5 flood 6 drench 8 get rid of, inundate 9 overwhelm
drowse: nod 4 doze 5 sleep 6 catnap, snooze 7 slumber
drowsiness: 8 dullness, lethargy 9 oscitancy 10 sleepiness 12 sluggishness
drowsy: 4 dull, logy 5 noddy 6 sleepy, stupid, supine 7 lulling 8 comatose, indolent, oscitant, sluggish 9 somnolent, soporific 11 heavy-headed
drub: tap 4 bang, beat, drum, lick, trim, whip 5 pound, stamp 6 berate, cudgel, pummel, thrash 7 belabor, shellac 8 lambaste
drubbing: 4 rout 7 debacle 9 thrashing, trouncing, walloping
drudge: 4 grub, moil, plod, toil 5 grind,

scrub, slave 6 digger, endure, slavey, suffer 7 plodder 9 workhorse
literary: 4 hack
drudgery: 4 moil, toil, work 5 labor 10 tedious job 11 irksome task
drug: 4 dope, dull, numb 5 hocus, opium 6 heroin, opiate 7 cocaine, stupefy 8 medicine, narcotic, sedative 9 analgesic, marijuana 10 pain killer, put to sleep 11 barbiturate
addict: 6 junkie 7 sniffer 8 snowbird 9 acid freak, mainliner
and ship: 8 shanghai
container: bag 4 deck 6 packet 7 capsule
depressant: 6 downer, heroin 7 cocaine, codeine 8 atropine
emetic: 5 senna 6 ipecac
hallucinogenic: LSD 4 hemp 6 mescal, peyote 7 cocaine 9 marijuana
of forgetfulness: 5 opium 7 hashish 8 nepenthe
stimulant: 7 pep pill, zedoary 9 digitalis 11 amphetamine
drugged: 4 high 5 hyped 6 zonked 7 freaked, on a trip 8 turned on 9 spaced out 10 insensible
drugget: mat, rug
druggist: 10 apothecary, pharmacist
bible: USP
drugstore: 8 pharmacy
druid: 6 priest
priestess of opera: 5 Norma
stone: 6 sarsen
symbol: 9 mistletoe
drum: 4 cask, drub 5 bongo, drone, gumbe, gumby, tabor 6 barrel, tambor, tom-tom, tympan 7 capstan, tambour, timbrel 8 bamboula, cylinder 9 reiterate, tambourin 10 tambourine
kettle: 5 naker 6 atabal, nagara, timbal 7 timpani(pl.), tympani(pl.) 9 darabukka, tambourone
string: 5 snare
tighten cords: 4 frap
drumbeat: 6 ruffle 8 berloque
at hour for sleep: 6 tattoo
drumbeater: 8 advocate, promoter 9 supporter 10 press agent, tub-thumper
drumfire: 5 salvo 6 volley 7 barrage 9 fusillade 11 bombardment
drummer: 8 salesman 13 percussionist
drumstick: 6 tampon
drunkard: sot 4 soak 5 dipso, rummy, souse, toper 6 boozer 7 fuddler, tippler, tosspot 8 borachio 9 alcoholic, inebriate 11 dipsomaniac
drunken: 4 gone 5 tight, tipsy 6 blotto, loaded 7 pickled, pie-eyed, sottish 8 squiffed 10 inebriated 11 intoxicated
drupelet: 5 acini(pl.) 6 acinus, kernel
dry: sec, ted 4 arid, brut, dull, sere, wipe 5 baked, drain, prosy, vapid, wizen 6 barren, boring, jejune 7 insipid, parched,

sapless, sub-arid, sterile, thirsty, xerotic **8** tiresome **9** dehydrate, drinkless, exsuccous, fruitless, pointless, sarcastic, waterless **10** evaporated, siccaneous, teetotaler **11** displeasing **12** moistureless, unprofitable **13** uninteresting

grass: hay

leather: sam

out: **5** steam, toast **6** rizzar(Sc.) **7** sober up **8** detoxify

up: **6** shrink, wither **7** shrivel **9** dehydrate, desiccate, evaporate, exsiccate, keep quiet **10** dehumidify

dry goods: 4 wear **6** linens, napery **7** fabrics **8** clothing, textiles

dry run: try **8** maneuver **9** rehearsal

dry shave: 5 cheat **7** defraud

dry spell: 7 drought

dryad: 5 nymph **6** yaksha, yakshi

dual: 4 twin **6** binary, double **7** twofold

dub: rub **4** call, flub, muff, name, poke **5** botch, fluff **6** duffer, goof up, thrust **7** entitle **8** add sound, beginner, nickname, rerecord **9** schlemiel **10** poor player

dubious: 8 doubtful **9** ambiguous, equivocal, uncertain, unsettled **10** disputable, precarious **12** questionable, undetermined

ducal: 5 noble

duck: bob, bow, pet **4** dive, dunk, fowl, jouk **5** avoid, dodge, douse, evade, shirk, souse **6** plunge **7** darling, odd chap **8** sidestep **11** shy away from

Asiatic: **8** mandarin

black: **9** blackjack

bluebill: **5** scaup

brood: **4** team

dead: **5** goner

diving: **4** smew **9** goldeneye **10** bufflehead, butterball

eating: **5** Pekin

eider: **4** colk, wamp

eggs in brine: **5** pidan

freshwater: **4** teal

freshwater genus: aix

genus: **4** anas **7** nettion

group: **4** sord, team **5** skein

heraldic: **6** cannet **8** cannette

hooked-bill: **9** merganser

hunter's screen: **5** blind

male: **5** drake

Muscovy: **4** pato

old squaw: **6** quandy

Old World: **7** pochard **9** sheldrake

pert. to: **7** anatine

pintail: **4** smee, smew **8** piketail **11** querquedule

rare: **5** merse

ring-necked: **5** bunty

river: **4** smee, teal **7** pintail, widgeon **8** piketail, shoveler **9** greenwing

ruddy: **6** bobber **9** blackjack

sea: **4** coot **5** eider, scaup **6** scoter **7** scooter **9** harlequin

tree: **7** yaguaza

wild: **4** teal **5** scaup **7** gadwall, mallard **10** canvasback

wooden: **5** decoy

yellow-billed: **7** geelbec **8** geelbeck

duck out: 4 flee **7** escape **9** disappear **10** go suddenly **11** take a powder

duckbill: 8 platypus **10** mallangong

duckweed: 5 lemna

duck soup: 4 snap **5** cinch **6** breeze **8** pushover **9** easy as pie **10** child's play

duct: vas **4** main, pipe, tube, vasa(pl.) **5** canal **7** channel, conduit, passage, trachea **8** aqueduct

ductile: 4 soft **6** docile, facile, pliant **7** plastic, pliable, tensile **8** flexible, tractile **9** compliant, malleable, tractable **10** manageable, sequacious

ductless gland: 6 pineal, thymus

dud: 4 bomb, bust, flop **5** lemon **6** fizzle, turkey **7** failure, washout

dude: fop **5** dandy, swell **7** coxcomb, peacock **8** macaroni **11** Beau Brummell **12** clotheshorse, fashion plate

rancher: **9** Easterner **10** tenderfoot

dudeen: 8 clay pipe

dudgeon: ire **4** fury, huff, rage **5** anger, pique, wrath **7** umbrage **8** ill humor **10** resentment

duds: 4 togs **6** attire **7** apparel, clothes **8** garments **10** belongings

due: 4 debt, just, meed, owed **5** merit, owing **6** extent, lawful, mature, proper, unpaid **7** deserts, exactly, fitting, payable **8** adequate, deserved, directly, rightful, suitable **9** scheduled **10** sufficient **11** appropriate **12** attributable

duel: 4 tilt **5** fence, fight **6** combat **7** contest, dispute **8** conflict **13** affair of honor

duelist: 9 combatant, principal

aide: **6** second

duende: 5 charm **6** allure **9** magnetism

duenna: 8 chaperon **9** governess

dues: 4 fees **5** taxes, tolls **7** charges **8** payments **11** assessments

duet: duo **4** pair **11** piece for two

ballet: **6** adagio

lower part: **7** secondo

upper part: **5** primo

duff: 5 humus, slack **7** pudding **8** coal dust

duffer: dub **4** dope **5** dunce **6** geezer **10** stumblebum **11** incompetent

dugong: 6 sea cow **7** manatee

dugout: 4 abri, boat, cave **5** banca, banka, canoe **6** cayuca, cayuco **7** foxhole, pirogue, shelter **10** excavation

dulcet: 5 sweet **8** pleasing, soothing **9** agreeable, melodious, organ stop **10** harmonious

dulcimer: 7 cembalo **9** pantaleon **10** instrument
Chinese: **7** yang-kin
gypsy: **8** cimbalom
Persian: **6** santir
dull: dim, dry, dun, sad **4** blah, dead, drab, dumb, flat, gray, logy, mopy, numb, poky, slow, tame **5** blear, blind, blunt, dingy, foggy, heavy, inert, mopey, murky, muted, prosy, stale, vapid **6** boring, cloudy, dampen, darken, deaden, dismal, dreary, drowsy, gloomy, leaden, lessen, muffle, obtund, obtuse, somber, stodgy, stolid, stuffy, stupid, torpid, weaken **7** doltish, humdrum, insipid, prosaic, tedious, vacuous **8** boeotian, lifeless, listless, overcast, sluggish, tiresome **9** apathetic, colorless, inanimate, lethargic, pointless **10** indistinct, insensible, lackluster, monotonous, pedestrian, slow-witted, uninspired **11** thickheaded **13** unimaginative
become: **4** fade, pall, rust **7** cloud up, tarnish **8** hebetate
finish: mat **5** matte
noise: **4** klop, thud
dullard: 4 clod, dolt, dope **5** dunce, idiot, moron **6** dimwit **8** dumbbell **9** lamebrain, simpleton
dullness: 6 apathy, torpor **7** languor **8** hebetude, lethargy, monotony **9** bluntness **10** mediocrity
dullsville: 4 drag **7** boredom, the pits **11** for the birds
dulse: 5 algae **7** seaweed
duly: 7 rightly **8** properly **9** fittingly, regularly **13** appropriately
Dumas fils: *character:* **7** Camille
Dumas père: *character:* **5** Athos **6** Aramis, Dantes **7** Porthos **9** D'Artagnan
dumb: mum **4** dull, mute **6** silent, stupid **7** asinine, idiotic **8** ignorant **9** senseless **10** speechless, tongue-tied **11** meaningless **12** inarticulate
dumbbell: 4 boob, dope, fool **6** nitwit **7** dullard, fathead **9** exerciser
dumbfound: 4 daze, stun **5** amaze **6** boggle **7** nonplus, stagger, surprise **8** astonish **11** flabbergast
dummy: 4 copy, dolt, fake, sham **5** dunce, front **6** effigy, layout **9** ignoramus, imitation, simpleton **10** fictitious, figurehead, substitute
in bridge: **11** exposed hand
magazine: **7** paste-up
window: **7** manikin **9** mannequin
dump: 4 beat, coin, drop, fire, junk **5** chuck, ditch, empty, hovel, let go, scrap **6** pigsty, unload **7** deposit **8** get rid of, jettison **11** storage area
dumpling: 5 blimp, knish **7** darling, gnoc-

chi(pl.) **8** doughboy, quenelle **10** butterball
dumps: 5 blues **8** doldrums, the blahs **9** dejection **10** depression, melancholy **11** despondency
dumpy: 5 pudgy, squat **6** stubby **8** thickset **9** shapeless
dun: tan **4** dark, drab, dull **5** annoy, brown, dingy, sepia **6** pester, plague **8** pressure **9** importune **13** demand payment
dunce: ass, oaf **4** boob, dodo, dope, fool **5** chump, idiot **6** dimwit **7** jackass **8** bonehead, dumbbell, imbecile, lunkhead, numskull **10** dunderhead, nincompoop
dune: 5 ridge **7** barchan, barkhan **8** sand hill
dungarees: 5 jeans, pants **6** slacks **8** overalls, trousers
fabric: denim
dungeon: 4 cell, jail **5** vault **6** donjon, prison **9** oubliette **10** ergastulum(L.)
of Calcutta: **9** Black Hole
dunk: dip, sop **4** soak **5** douse, steep **6** drench **7** immerse, moisten **8** saturate
dunlin: 4 stib **9** sandpiper
duo: 4 duet, dyad, pair **6** couple **7** twosome
dupe: con, fob, mug **4** bilk, fool, gull, hoax, tool **5** cheat, patsy, trick **6** delude, outwit, pigeon, sucker, victim **7** cat's-paw, deceive, defraud, mislead, swindle **8** flimflam, hoodwink **9** bamboozle
duple: 4 dual **6** binary, double **7** twofold
duplicate: 4 copy, mate, same **5** alike, ditto, spare **6** carbon, double, repeat **7** do again, estreat, replica **9** facsimile, identical, reproduce **10** transcript, bridge game **11** counterpart
genetic: **5** clone
duplicity: 5 fraud, guile **6** deceit **7** cunning, perfidy **8** trickery **9** deception, falsehood, treachery **13** dissimulation, double-dealing
durable: 4 firm **5** hardy, tough, stout **6** stable, staple, strong **7** lasting **8** constant, enduring **9** long-lived, permanent **10** consistent
duration: age, run **4** span, term, time **5** space **6** length, period **8** lifetime **9** longevity
denoting: **4** time **5** clock, timer **9** stopwatch
of ministerial charge: **9** pastorate
of position: **6** tenure
without beginning or end: **8** eternity
D'Urberville lass: 4 Tess
duress: 5 force **8** coercion, hardship, pressure **9** necessity **10** compulsion, constraint
durgah: See **dargah**

during: 4 amid 5 while 7 pending 10 throughout 11 at the time of

durra: 4 corn 6 millet 7 sorghum

durst: 8 ventured

dusk: eve 5 gloom 6 darken 7 dimness 8 darkness, gloaming, twilight

dusky: dim 4 dark 5 brown, murky, tawny 6 gloomy, somber 7 obscure, shadowy, swarthy, unclear 8 blackish, blue-gray 11 dark-skinned

dust: ash 4 coat, dirt, soot, smut 5 clean, earth, flour, pouce, stive(Sc.), strew 6 pollen, powder 7 eburine, fall-out, remains, turmoil, wipe off 8 levigate, sprinkle 9 commotion, confusion
measuring device: 9 koniscope
reduce to: 4 mull 9 pulverize
speck: 4 mote

dust off: 4 redo 8 renovate 9 bring back, refurbish

dusty: dim, dry 4 arid 7 clouded, powdery

dustup: row 4 tiff 7 quarrel 8 argument

Dutch: See **Netherlands**

Dutch ware: 5 delft

Dutch uncle: oom 6 mentor 7 adviser

dutiful: 5 loyal 6 docile 7 willing 8 faithful, obedient, reverent 9 compliant 10 respectful, submissive 11 reverential 13 conscientious

duty: job, lot, tax 4 care, onus, role, task, toll 5 chore, stint, trust 6 burden, charge, devoir, exitus(L.), impost, office, tariff 7 purpose, respect, service, station, tribute 8 function 10 allegiance, obligation
on commodities: 6 excise
shirk: 6 truant 7 goof off 8 goldbrick
tour of: 4 turn 5 hours, shift, trick, watch

dwarf: elf 4 grig, runt, tiny 5 crowl(Sc.), gnome, midge, pigmy, pygmy, scrub, stunt, troll 6 midget, peewee 7 manikin 8 belittle, decrease, diminish, minimize, Tom Thumb 9 make small, tower over 10 diminutive, homunculus, overshadow 11 lilliputian
in Snow White: Doc 5 Dopey, Happy 6 Grumpy, Sleepy, Sneezy 7 Bashful
king: 8 Alberich
male: 9 nannander
race: 8 Nibelung

dwarfish: 4 tiny 5 elfin, runty, small, squat 6 nanoid 7 stunted

dwarfishness: 6 nanism

dwell: lie 4 bide, live, stay 5 abide, delay, exist, lodge, pause, tarry 6 remain, reside 7 inhabit

dwell on: 5 brood, nurse 6 repeat 7 belabor, prolong 10 linger over

dweller: 5 liver 6 tenant 7 denizen 8 habitant, occupant, resident 9 addressee 10 inhabitant
around city: 11 suburbanite

cave: 10 troglodyte

city: 7 slicker 8 townsman, urbanite

desert: 4 Arab 5 nomad 7 Bedouin

earth: 9 tellurian

institutional: 6 inmate

lone: 6 hermit 7 eremite, recluse

monastic: nun 4 monk 5 abbot 6 abbess 8 cenobite

temporary: 6 lodger, roomer 7 boarder 9 transient

dwelling: hut 4 casa, digs, flat, home, slum, tent 5 abode, cabin, condo, hotel, house, hovel, motel, villa 6 castle, chalet, duplex, palace, shanty 7 chateau, cottage, lodging, mansion, trailer, triplex 8 building, bungalow, domicile, tenement 9 apartment, residence 10 habitation, pied-a-terre

dwindle: ebb 4 melt, pine, wane 5 abate, waste 6 lessen, shrink 7 decline 8 decrease, diminish, peter out, taper off

dye: aal 4 anil, tint 5 color, eosin, fucus, imbue, stain, tinge 6 litmus, madder 7 aniline, pigment, toluene 8 colorant
blue: 4 anil, woad 6 indigo
brown: 5 sumac 6 sumach
coal-tar: 7 magenta
hair: 5 henna 6 rastik
purple: 6 archil, orchil 8 murexide
quercitron bark: 6 flavin
red: 5 aurin, eosin 7 annatto, magenta 8 rhodamin 9 rhodamine 10 orseilline
red-brown: 5 henna
red-orange: 5 chica 7 fuchsin 8 morindin
source: 5 murex
violet: 7 gallein 8 thionine
yellow: 4 woad 5 arusa
yellow-red: 7 annatto

dyeing apparatus: vat 4 ager
scrape: 6 harass

dying 8 moribund

dynamic: 5 vital 6 active, potent 7 driving, intense 8 forceful, spirited, vigorous 9 energetic

dynamite: TNT 5 blast 6 blow up 9 explosive
kind of: 6 dualin 7 dualine 9 fulgurite 10 kieselguhr
inventor: 5 Nobel

dynamo: 7 hustler 8 go-getter, live wire 9 generator
in distributing system: 7 booster
inventor: 7 Faraday
part: 5 rotor 7 brushes 8 armature 10 commutator

dynast: 5 ruler 6 prince 8 governor

dynasty: 5 realm 8 dominion 10 line of rule

dyspeptic: 6 crabby 7 grouchy 10 ill-humored 11 bad-tempered

dysphoria: 7 anxiety 10 discomfort, discontent

dystopia: 10 living hell 13 dreadful place

E

Ea's daughter: 4 Nina
each: all, per 5 every 6 apiece 8 everyone
eager: hot 4 agog, avid, keen, sour, warm, wave 5 afire, agasp, itchy, ready, sharp 6 ardent, greedy, intent 7 anxious, athirst, brittle, burning, excited, fervent 8 desirous, spirited, vigorous, yearning 9 desireful, impatient, impetuous, strenuous 12 enthusiastic, forereaching
eagerness: 4 elan, zeal 5 ardor 6 fervor 7 ardency, avidity 8 alacrity, cupidity, fervency 9 alertness, constancy, readiness 10 enthusiasm, impatience 13 impetuousness
eagle: 6 aquila 8 allerion, bateleur, berghaan, insignia, U.S. emblem 9 golf score
biblical: 4 gier
constellation: 6 Aquila
genus of: 10 Haliaeetus
nest: 4 aery, eyry 5 aerie, eyrie
relative: 4 hawk 6 falcon
sea: ern 4 erne
eaglestone: 7 aetites
eagre: 4 bore, wave
ear: lug(Sc.) 4 hear, heed, obey, plow, till 5 auris(L.), spike 6 listen 7 auricle, hearing 8 audience 9 attention, cultivate
absence of: 6 anotia
bone: 5 ambos, incus 6 stapes 7 malleus, stirrup
canal: 5 scala
cavity: 6 meatus 7 cochlea
cleaning device: 8 aurilave
covering: lap 4 flap, muff
doctor: 9 otologist
inflammation of: 6 otitis
middle: 4 drum 8 tympanum
near: 7 parotic
part of: 4 burr, lobe 5 helix, pinna 6 tragus
pert. to: 4 otic 5 aural 7 entotic 9 auricular
plug: 7 stopple
science of: 7 otology
ear shell: 7 abalone
earache: 7 otalgia
eardrop: 7 earring, pendant
eared seal: 5 otary
earl: 4 peer 8 nobleman
wife of: 8 countess
earlier: ere 4 erst 5 elder 6 before, sooner

8 formerly, previous
early: old 5 prior 6 timely 7 ancient, betimes, too soon 9 in advance, matutinal, premature 10 beforehand
earmark: tag 5 allot, label, stamp, trait 7 feature 8 set aside 10 reserve for 14 identification
earn: get, win 4 gain, rate 5 gross, merit 6 obtain 7 achieve, acquire, deserve, realize 8 drag down
earner: 6 worker 11 breadwinner
earnest: 4 hard 5 grave, sober, staid 6 ardent, hearty, intent, sedate, solemn 7 engaged, forward, serious, sincere, zealous 8 diligent, emphatic 9 heartfelt 10 expressive, thoughtful 12 affectionate, wholehearted
earnest money: 5 token 6 pledge 7 deposit 8 security
earnings: pay 5 wages 6 income, salary 7 profits, returns 9 dividends
earring: 4 grip 8 ornament 9 girandole
earshot: 5 sound 7 hearing
earsplitting: 4 loud 5 shrill 8 piercing
earth: erd(Sc.), orb 4 bury, clay, dirt, fill, grit, land, loam, marl, muck, soil, turf 5 glebe, globe, loess, terra(L.), world 6 ground, planet 7 topsoil 10 terra firma
compound: 7 tierras
crust constituent: 6 silica
deposit: 4 marl, silt 5 loess 8 alluvium
dweller: 9 tellurian
god: Geg, Keb, Seb 5 Dagan
goddess: 4 Gaea 5 Ceres, Terra 6 Semele 7 Demeter
layer of: 5 sloam
lump of: 4 clod
metallic: ore
opposite side of: 9 Antipodes
pert. to: 4 geal 5 terra 8 telluric 9 planetary 11 terrestrial
pigment: 5 ochre, umber
prepare for seeding: 4 plow 5 spade 6 harrow 9 cultivate
ridge of: 4 kame 6 rideau
satellite of: 4 moon
science: 7 geodesy, geology 9 geography
earth bob: 4 grub 6 maggot
earth hog: 8 aardvark
earth lodge: 5 hogan
earthdrake: 6 dragon
earthenware: 4 delf 5 china, delft 7 bis-

cuit, faience, pottery **8** crockery **9** porcelain **10** terra-cotta
maker: **6** potter
piece of: **5** shard
earthfall: 9 landslide
earthling: 5 human **6** mortal
earthly: 6 carnal **7** mundane, secular, terrene, worldly **8** material, physical, possible, temporal **11** conceivable, terrestrial
earthnut: 5 arnot, chufa **6** peanut **7** truffle
earthquake: 5 seism, shock **6** tremor **7** temblor
intensity scale: **7** mercali, Richter
measuring device: **10** seisometer
pert. to: **7** seismic
point directly above: **9** epicenter
science: **10** seismology
earthstar: 6 fungus **7** geaster
earthwork: 5 agger **7** rampart **10** breastwork, embankment **13** fortification
earthworm: ess **7** annelid, ipomoea
earthy: low **5** gross **6** coarse, fleshy **7** sensual **9** practical, realistic, unrefined **11** terrestrial
earwax: 7 cerumen
earwig: 6 golach(Sc.) **9** centipede **12** eavesdropper
ease: 4 calm, rest **5** allay, knack, peace, quiet, relax **6** loosen, pacify, reduce, relief, repose, smooth, soften, soothe **7** appease, assuage, comfort, faculty, freedom, leisure, liberty, lighten, relieve, slacken **8** diminish, facility, mitigate, moderate, palliate, pleasure, security, unburden **9** alleviate, disburden, enjoyment **10** ameliorate, facilitate, relaxation, solicitude **11** contentment, naturalness, tranquility **12** satisfaction, tranquillity
at: **6** degage, otiose **7** relaxed, resting
ease off: 4 slow **5** slack
easel: 5 frame **7** support
easily: 6 gently, glibly **7** handily, readily **8** smoothly **13** without effort
east: 4 Asia **6** Levant, Orient
pert. to: **4** eoan **8** oriental
Easter: 5 Pasch **6** Eostre, Pascha
first Sunday after: **9** Quasimodo
pert. to: **7** paschal
Sunday before: **4** Palm
Eastern Church: *bishop:* **4** abba
choir platform: **5** solea
convent head: **8** hegumene
festival day: **8** apodosis
monk: **7** caloyer
prayer: **6** ectene, ektene
East Germany (see also **German, West Germany**): *capital:* **10** East Berlin
city: **5** Halle **6** Erfurt **7** Dresden, Leipzig, Rostock **9** Frankfurt

ethnic group: **5** Wends
island: **5** Rugen **6** Usedom
monetary unit: **4** mark **7** pfennig
mountain: **4** Harz **10** Erzgebirge **11** Fichtelberg
province: **4** Gera, Suhl **5** Halle **6** Erfurt **7** Cottbus, Dresden, Potsdam, Rostock **8** Schwerin **9** Frankfurt
river: **4** Elbe, Oder **5** Havel, Saale, Spree
easy: 4 calm, cozy, glib, mild **5** cushy, light, suave **6** facile, gentle, secure, simple **7** lenient, natural **8** carefree, careless, familiar, graceful, homelike, moderate, tranquil, unforced **9** compliant, indulgent, tractable, unhurried **10** manageable, unaffected **11** comfortable, complaisant, susceptible, unconcerned **13** unconstrained
easy job: 4 pipe, snap **5** cinch **8** sinecure
easy mark: 4 dupe **5** chump **6** pigeon, sucker **7** fall guy **9** soft touch
easygoing: 4 calm **5** homey **6** casual, placid **7** relaxed **8** carefree, informal **10** unaffected **11** low-pressure **12** happy-go-lucky
eat: sup **4** bite, dine, fare, feed, fret, gnaw, grub, rust **5** erode, feast, lunch, munch, taste **6** absorb, devour, ingest, ravage **7** consume, corrode, destroy, swallow **8** wear away **9** breakfast, partake of
between meals: **5** snack
by regimen: **4** diet
grass: **5** graze **6** forage **7** pasture
greedily: **4** cram, wolf **5** gorge, raven **6** gobble **10** gormandize
sumptuously: **5** feast **6** regale **7** banquet
eatable: 6 edible **8** esculent **10** comestible
eater: 8 consumer
big: **7** glutton **8** gourmand **11** trencherman
fastidious: **7** epicure, gourmet **8** Lucullus **10** gastronome
eating-place: inn **4** cafe **5** diner, grill, hotel **6** tavern **7** automat, beanery, tea-room **8** grubbery **9** cafeteria, chophouse, lunchroom **10** restaurant **11** greasy spoon **12** luncheonette
institutional: **9** refectory **10** dining hall
military: **8** mess hall
eave: 7 cornice
ebb: 4 fail, sink, wane **5** abate, decay **6** recede, reflux, retire **7** decline, subside **8** decrease, diminish **9** backwater
ebb and flow: 5 estus **6** aestus
Eber's son: 9 Joktan
Eblis: 5 Devil, Satan
before the fall: **6** Azazel
son: Sut, Tir **4** Awar **5** Dasim **8** Zalambur
ebon: 4 dark, inky **5** black, raven, sable
ebony: 5 black **8** hard wood
eboulement: 9 landslide
ebullience: 4 zest **6** gaiety **8** vitality **9**

animation **10** enthusiasm, exuberance **11** high spirits

ebullient: 5 brash **6** lively **7** boiling **8** agitated **12** effervescent

ebullition: 7 ferment **8** outburst **9** agitation, commotion **10** excitement **12** fermentation **13** effervescence

ecaudate: 8 tailless

ecce(L.): **6** behold

eccentric: odd **4** card, kook **5** crank, queer, weird **7** bizarre, devious, erratic, strange **8** abnormal, peculiar, singular **9** anomalous, character, irregular, quizzical, screwball

eccentricity: 5 quirk **6** oddity **8** crotchet **9** queerness **10** aberration **11** peculiarity, strangeness **12** idiosyncrasy

ecclesiastic: 4 abbe **5** abbot, clerk **6** divine, parson, pastor, priest **7** prelate **8** minister, reverend **9** clergyman
belt: **7** balteus **8** baltheus
council: **5** synod
court: **4** rota
garment: alb **4** cope **5** amice, fanon, orale, stole, cappa, rabat **6** callot **7** cassock, biretta, calotte **8** berretta
head: **6** rector
land: **5** glebe
living: **8** benefice
military: **5** padre **8** chaplain
ruler: **8** hierarch
service: **5** matin
unit: **6** parish

ecdysiast: 6 peeler **8** stripper **11** stripteaser

echelon: 4 rank **5** level **6** lineup **8** maneuver **9** formation

echidna: 8 anteater
three-toed: **6** nodiak

echinate: 5 spiny **7** bristly, prickly

echinoderm: 8 starfish **9** sea urchin

echo: 4 ring **6** repeat, second **7** imitate, iterate, resound, respond, revoice **8** response **9** imitation **10** repetition **11** reverberate **13** reverberation

eciton: ant

eclat: 4 fame, pomp **5** glory, kudos **6** praise, renown, repute **7** acclaim **8** applause, facility, splendor **9** notoriety **10** brilliancy **11** distinction, ostentation

eclectic: 5 broad, mixed **6** choosy, varied **7** blended, diverse, jumbled **8** catholic, combined **9** many-sided, selective

eclipse: dim **4** bind, blot, hide **5** blind, cloud, shade, sully **6** darken, dazzle, exceed **7** obscure, travail **8** outrival **10** extinguish, overshadow **11** obscuration, occultation
demon of: **4** Rahu
shadow: **8** penumbra **9** penumbrae(pl.)

eclogue: 4 idyl, poem **5** idyll **7** bucolic

ecology, oecology: 9 bionomics

economical: 5 chary **6** frugal, saving **7** careful, prudent, thrifty **9** provident

economics: *element:* **9** commodity
theoretical: **9** plutology

economize: 4 save **5** skimp, stint **6** scrimp **7** husband, utilize **8** retrench

ecostate: 7 ribless

ecru: 5 beige, linen **10** unbleached

ecstasy: joy **5** bliss **6** heaven, trance **7** delight, emotion, madness, rapture **8** euphoria, paradise **9** happiness **10** exaltation

ecstatic: 4 rapt **8** glorious **9** enchanted, entranced, rhapsodic **10** enraptured

ectad: 5 outer **7** outward **8** exterior
opposite of: **5** entad

ectype: 9 imitation

ecu: 4 coin **6** shield

Ecuador: *capital:* **5** Quito
city: **4** Loja, Nono, Puyo, Tena **5** Chone, Daule, Guano **6** Ambato, Cuenca, Ibarra, Pujili, Tulcan **7** Azogues, Cayambe, Machala, Pelileo, Pillaro **8** Babahoyo, Guaranda, Riobamba **9** Guayaquil
conquered by: **7** Pizarro
Indian: **4** Cara, Inca **5** Palta **6** Canelo, Jibaro
island: **4** Puna **9** Galapagos
measure: **5** libra **6** cuadra, fanega
monetary unit: **5** sucre **7** centavo
mountain peak: **5** Altar **6** Sangay **7** Cayambe **8** Cotopaxi, Illiniza
mountain range: **5** Andes
port: **5** Manta **7** Salinas **9** Guayaquil
province: **4** Loja, Napo **5** Azuay, Canar, El Oro **6** Carchi, Guayas, Manabi **7** Bolivar, Los Rios, Pastaza **8** Cotopaxi, Imbabura **9** Galapagos, Pichincha **10** Chimborazo, Esmeraldas, Tungurahua
river: **4** Coca, Napo **5** Daule, Paute, Tigre **6** Blanco, Guayas, Macuma, Zamora **7** Curaray, Pastaza **10** Esmeraldas
volcano: **8** Antisana

ecumenical: 6 global **7** liberal **8** catholic, tolerant, unifying **9** universal, worldwide **12** all-inclusive, cosmopolitan

ecumenical council: 4 Lyon **5** Lyons, Trent **6** Nicaea **7** Vatican **9** Chalcedon

eczema: 6 herpes, tetter **9** malanders **10** dermatitis

edacity: 8 appetite, gluttony, voracity **12** ravenousness

Edda: 4 saga

Eddaic god: 4 Odin

eddo: 4 taro

eddy: 4 purl, weel(Sc.) **5** gurge, shift, swirl, whirl **6** vortex **7** backset **9** maelstrom, whirlpool **12** contrary flow **14** countercurrent

edema: 5 tumor **6** dropsy **8** swelling **9** puffiness **12** intumescence

Eden: 6 heaven, utopia 7 arcadia, elysium
8 paradise

edentate: 5 sloth 7 ant bear 8 aardvark,
anteater, pangolin, tamandua 9 armadillo, toothless

Edessa's king: 5 Abgar

edge: hem, jag, lip, rim 4 bank, bite, brim,
brow, hone, rand, side, trim, whet 5 arris, bevel, blade, brink, crest, frill, ruler,
sidle, splay, sting, verge 6 adjoin, border, flange, fringe, impale, margin 7
nose out, sharpen, selvage 8 boundary,
keenness, selvedge 9 advantage, beginning, perimeter, periphery, sharpness
10 escarpment

run along: 5 skirt

sharp: 5 beard

uneven: 4 wany 5 waney

edged: 5 sharp, erose 7 crenate, cutting,
trimmed

edge in: 7 intrude, sneak by 9 gain entry
10 infiltrate 11 slip through

edging: hem 4 lace 5 frill, picot 6 border,
fringe 7 binding 8 rickrack 10 embroidery

loop: 5 picot

edgy: 5 sharp, tense 6 touchy 7 angular,
jittery, nervous, uptight 8 critical,
snappish 9 irritable

edible: 7 eatable 8 esculent 9 palatable
10 comestible

arum: 4 taro

fungus: 5 morel

gallingale: 5 chufa

mollusk: 4 clam 6 oyster 7 scallop

parts of fruit: 4 pulp

rush: 5 chufa

seaweed: 4 agar 5 dulse, laver 6 delisk 8
agaragar

seed: nut, pea 4 bean

tuber root: oca, uva, yam 4 beet, eddo,
taro 6 turnip 7 parsnip 8 rutabaga

edict: act, ban, law 4 bull, fiat 5 arret,
bando, bulla, irade, order, ukase 6 decree, dictum, notice 7 command, embargo, program, statute 9 ordinance,
programma 12 announcement, proclamation

papal: 4 bull

edifice: 4 dome 6 church 8 building 9
structure

kind: 6 castle, museum, palace, temple 7
capitol, mansion 8 monument 9 cathedral 10 tabernacle

edify: 5 teach 6 better, inform 7 educate,
improve 8 instruct 9 enlighten, make
clear 10 illuminate

edile: 10 magistrate

edit: 5 emend 6 direct, redact, review, revise 7 arrange, compile, correct, prepare, publish, rewrite 8 copyread 9 supervise

edition: 4 kind 5 issue, print, stamp 6
source 7 version 9 character 10 extraction

kind of: 5 extra 7 revisal, reprint

editor: 8 redactor 9 emendator, publisher,
redacteur 10 diaskeuast, journalist

room: 7 sanctum

Edom: 7 Idumaea

chieftain: 4 Iram

district: 5 Teman

king: 5 Hadad

mountain's Hor

Edomite's ancestor: 4 Esau

educate: 4 rear 5 teach, train 6 inform,
school 7 develop, nurture 8 instruct 9
cultivate, enlighten 10 discipline,
strengthen 12 indoctrinate

educated: 4 bred 6 taught 7 learned,
trained 8 lettered, literate, well-read 11
experienced 13 knowledgeable

education: 7 nurture 8 breeding, learning,
pedagogy, training 9 erudition 10 background, discipline 11 scholarship

institution: 6 school 7 college 8 seminary
10 university

organization: PTA 6 lyceum

educator: 5 tutor 7 teacher 9 pedagogue,
professor 10 instructor

educe: 5 evoke 6 elicit, evolve 7 extract 9
eliminate

eel: 4 grig 5 elver, moray, siren 6 conger 7
lamprey, muraena 8 anguilla, wriggler 9
snipefish

cut and cooked: 10 spitchcock

fish for: 7 sniggle

marine: 6 conger

migration: 7 eelfare

sand: 6 launce

young: 5 elver

eel-like: 10 anguilloid

eel-shaped: 12 anguilliform

eelboat: 6 schuit

eelpot: 4 trap

eelpout: 6 burbot, guffer, yowler 10 muttonfish

eelworm: 4 nema

eely: 7 elusive, evasive, wriggly 8 slippery,
slithery 9 wriggling

eerie, eery: 5 scary, timid, weird 6 dismal, gloomy, spooky 7 awesome, ghostly, macabre, strange, uncanny 8 eldritch, ghoulish 9 unearthly, unnatural,
unworldly 10 frightened 11 phantom-
like

efface: 4 dele, raze 5 erase 6 cancel, rub
out 7 blot out, destroy, expunge 9
eradicate, extirpate 10 obliterate

effacement: 7 erasure 10 withdrawal

effect: 4 make 5 cause, close, eclat, enact
6 intent, result, sequel 7 achieve, acquire, compass, conduce, emotion, execute, fulfill, operate, outcome, perform,

produce, purport, realize **8** complete **9** influence **10** accomplish, bring about, consummate, expression, impression **11** consequence **13** manifestation
of past experience: **5** mneme
effective: 4 able, real **5** sound **6** active, actual, causal, potent **7** capable, telling **8** adequate, forceful, powerful, striking, vigorous **9** brilliant, competent, effectual, efficient **10** perficient **11** efficacious, influential
effectiveness: 5 force, power, punch **8** strength, validity **10** efficiency
effects: 5 goods **7** baggage **8** chattels, movables property **10** belongings **11** possessions
effectual: 5 valid **6** useful **7** capable **8** adequate, workable **9** effective, efficient **10** does the job, functional, productive **13** authoritative
effeminate: 4 weak **5** timid **6** chichi, prissy **7** unmanly **8** oversoft, womanish **9** emolliate, not virile, sissified **12** nicenellyish, overdelicate **13** overemotional
effervesce: 4 fizz, foam, huff **6** bubble **7** enthuse, ferment, sparkle **8** rave over
effervescent: gay **4** airy **6** breezy, bubbly, frothy, lively, snappy, yeasty **7** buoyant **8** animated, bouncing, spirited, volatile **9** ebullient, exuberant, full of pep, vivacious
effete: 4 sere **5** spent **6** barren **8** decadent, moribund **9** exhausted
efficacious: 5 valid **6** mighty, potent **8** forcible, powerful, vigorous, virtuous **9** available, effective, officious, prevalent **10** legitimate **11** efficiently
efficient: 4 able **5** adept **6** expert **7** capable **8** powerful, skillful **9** competent, effective, effectual **11** efficacious
effigy: 5 dummy, image **8** likeness **9** jackstraw
efflorescence: 8 anthesis, blooming **9** flowering **10** burgeoning **11** fulfillment
effluvium: 4 aura, odor **5** vapor **9** emanation **10** exhalation
efflux: 7 outflow **8** effusion **9** effluence, emanation
effort: try **4** task, toil, work **5** chore, drive, essay, force, labor, nisus, pains, power, trial **6** energy, strain, stress **7** attempt, trouble **8** endeavor, exertion, struggle **9** diligence **11** application, undertaking
effortless: 4 easy **6** facile, simple, smooth **8** painless
effrontery: 4 gall **5** brass, cheek, nerve **8** audacity, boldness, temerity **9** hardihood, impudence, insolence, sauciness **10** confidence, incivility **11** presumption
effulgence: 5 blaze, glory **8** radiance,

splendor **10** brightness, brilliance
effulgent: 6 bright **7** radiant **8** luminous
effuse: 4 flow, gush, shed **7** emanate **9** pour forth, spread out **11** disseminate
effusive: 5 gushy **6** smarmy **7** cloying, profuse **8** bubbling **9** exuberant, rhapsodic **12** unrestrained **13** demonstrative
eft: 4 newt **6** lizard, triton **10** salamander
egad: 8 mild oath **9** expletive
egeran: 8 idocrase **11** vesuvianite
egeria: 12 woman adviser
egest: 4 void **7** excrete
egg: ova(pl.) **4** abet, goad, ovum, prod, seed, spur, urge **5** ovule, spore **6** incite **7** actuate, **9** instigate
before maturation: **6** oocyte
case: **5** shell **6** ovisac **7** ootheca
collector: **8** oologist
fertilized: **6** zygote **7** oosperm, oospore
fish: roe **5** berry **6** caviar
insect: nit
measuring device: **7** oometer
nest: **6** clutch
part of: **4** yolk **5** shell, white **7** albumen, latebra
Philippine duck: **5** balut
small: **5** ovule
tested: **7** candled
unfertilized: **8** oosphere
white of: **5** glair **7** albumen
yolk: **6** yellow **8** vitellus
egg-shaped: 4 ooid, oval **5** ovate, ovoid **6** ooidal **7** obovoid, ovaloid, oviform
egger: 4 moth
egghead: 7 Brahmin **8** highbrow **12** intellectual
eggnog: nog **8** beverage
eggplant: 7 brinjal **8** brinjaul **9** aubergine
eggshell: *confetti-filled:* **8** cascaron
Egil's brother: 6 Volund
egis: See **aegis**
Eglah: *husband:* **5** David
son: **7** Ithream
eglantine: 8 woodbine **10** sweetbrier **11** honeysuckle
Eglon's king: 5 Debir
ego: 4 self **6** psyche **7** conceit **9** number one **11** personality, selfishness
egotism: 5 pride **6** vanity **7** conceit **8** self-love **9** arrogance **10** self-esteem, narcissism
egotistic: 4 smug **5** cocky **7** selfish, stuck-up **8** boastful, superior **9** conceited **11** swell-headed **12** self-centered, vainglorious **13** self-important
egregious: 4 rank **5** gross **7** blatant, glaring, heinous **8** flagrant, shocking **10** deplorable, outrageous
egress: 4 exit **5** issue **6** outlet **7** outgate, passage **9** departure
egret: 5 heron, plume **6** gaulin **8** gaulding

Egypt: *capital:* 5 Cairo
  city: 4 Giza, Qena, Suez 5 Asyut, Benha,
    Luxor, Tanta 7 Al Arish 8 Port Said 9
    El Mansura 10 Alexandria
  dam: 5 Aswan
  desert: 6 Libyan 7 Arabian, Western
  ethnic group: 6 Nubian 7 Bedouin
  governorate: 4 Giza, Qena, Suez 5 Aswan,
    Asyut, Cairo, Minya, Sinai 6 Faiyum,
    Matruh, Red Sea, Sawhaj 7 Beheira 8
    Beni Suef, Damietta, Ismailia, Port
    Said
  lake: 6 Bitter, Nasser 7 Manzala 8 Burul-
    lus 11 Birket Qarun
  monetary unit: 5 pound 7 piaster
  mountain peak: 5 Sinai 6 Gharib, Nugrus
    9 Katherina
  mountain range: 9 Gebel Musa
  oasis: 4 Siwa 6 Dakhla, Dunqul, Kharga
    7 Farafra 8 Bahariya
  peninsula: 5 Sinai
  river: 4 Nile, Qena 7 Rosetta 8 Damietta
  waterway: 9 Suez Canal
Egyptian: 4 Arab, Copt 5 Nilot
  air god: Shu
  animal: fox 4 adda, lynx 5 genet, hyena 6
    jackal, jerboa 7 gazelle 9 ichneumon
  antelope: 5 bubal
  army chieftain: 6 sirdar
  beer: 6 zythum
  beetle: 6 scarab
  bird: 6 sicsac
  boat: 5 baris 8 dahabeah
  bottle: 6 doruck
  bull: 4 apis
  burial jar: 7 Canopus
  calendar: 4 Ahet, Apap, Tybi 5 Choik,
    Payni, Shemu, Thoth 6 Hathor, Me-
    chir, Mesore, Paophi 7 Pachons 9 Pha-
    menoth, Pharmuthi
  cap: fez
  cat-headed goddess: 4 Bast 5 Pakht
  Christian: 4 Copt
  civilization: 6 Tasian
  clover: 7 berseem
  cobra: 4 haje
  concubine: 5 Hagar
  cosmetic: 4 kohl
  cotton: Sak 4 pima
  crocodile-headed god: 4 Sobk 5 Sebek
  cross: 4 ankh
  crown: 4 atef
  dam: 4 sudd
  dancers: 7 ghawazi 8 ghawazee
  deity: Hor, Mut, Nut 4 Anta, Apet, Bast,
    Isis, Maat, Sati 5 Anaka 6 Hathor, Se-
    shat, Tefnut 7 Nepthys 8 Nechebit
  descendant: 4 copt 6 fellah
  dog: 6 saluki
  drink: 4 bosa, boza 5 bozah
  drug: 8 nepenthe
  elysium: 4 Aalu

  emblem: 4 aten 5 lotus
  gateway: 5 pylon
  god: Set 4 Ptah, Seth 5 Thoth 6 Anubis
    7 Serapis
  goddess: Mut, Nut 4 Bast, Isis 5 Pakht 6
    Sekhet 8 Nekhebet
  guard: 6 ghafir 7 ghaffir
  guide: 8 dragoman
  hawk-headed god: 5 Horus
  herb: 5 anise
  instrument: 7 arghool, arghoul, sistrum
  judge of the dead: 6 Osiris
  king: Tut 4 Fuad, Mena 5 Menes 6 Ram-
    ses 7 Ptolemy, Rameses 9 Amenhotep
    11 Tutankhamen
  laborer: 5 aperu
  lighthouse: 6 pharos
  lily: 6 calla, lotos, lotus
  lion-headed goddess: 4 Bast 5 Pakht 6
    Sekhet
  lizard: 4 adda 5 scink, skink
  love goddess: 6 Hathor
  lute: 5 nabla
  maternity goddess: 4 Apet
  measure: apt, dra, hen, rob 4 dira, draa,
    kada, khet, ocha, roub, theb 5 abdat,
    ardab, ardeb, cubit, farde, keleh, kilah,
    sahme 6 artaba, aurure, baladi, kantar,
    kedlah, robhah, schene 7 choryos, dari-
    bah, malouah, roubouh, toumnah 8 kas-
    sabah, kharouba 10 dira baladi, dira
    mimari, kerat kamel, nief keddah 11
    feddan nasri
  monarch: 7 Pharaoh
  monument: 7 obelisk
  official: 5 mudir
  paper: 6 papyri 7 papyrus
  peasant: 6 fellah
  Pharaoh's headdress: 7 pschent
  plant: 5 cumin 6 cummin, lentil
  pyramids at Giza: 6 Cheops (Khufu),
    Khafre 7 Menkure
  queen: 9 Cleopatra, Nefertiti, Nofretete
  relic: 5 mummy
  ruined cities: 5 Tanis 6 Abydos, Karnak,
    Thebes 7 Memphis
  sacred bird: 4 ibis
  sacred bull: 4 apis
  sacred flower: 5 lotos, lotus
  sanctuary: 5 secos, sekos
  seal: 6 scarab
  serpent: 5 apepi
  shrub: 5 kat
  solar disk: 4 Aten
  stone: 7 rosetta
  sun god: Tem, Tum 4 Atmu, Atum
  symbol: uta 4 ankh 6 scarab
  talisman: 5 angle
  temple: 4 Idfu 5 Luxor 6 Abydos, Kar-
    nak, Osiris 7 Dendera
  tomb: 7 mastaba, pyramid
  underworld: 4 Aaru, Duat 6 Amenti

vase: **7** canopic
viper: **8** cerastes
vulture-headed goddess: Mut **8** Nekhebet
weight: ket, oka, oke **4** dera, heml, khar, okia, rotl **5** artal, artel, deben, kerat, okieh, ratel, uckia **6** hamlah, kantar **7** drachma, quintal
wind: **6** kamsin **7** chamsin, kamseen, khamsin **8** khamseen
Ehud's son: 6 Naaman
eider duck: 4 colk
eidetic: 5 vivid
eidolon: 4 icon **5** ghost, image **7** phantom **10** apparition
eight: eta(G.) **6** ogdoad
group of: **5** octad, octet **6** octave **7** octette
eight-sided: 9 octagonal
eighth: *circle:* **6** octant
day after nones: **4** ides
note: **6** quaver
order: **5** octic
eighty: 9 fourscore
Eire: 4 Erin **5** Ierne **7** Ireland **8** Hibernia
Eireannach: 8 Irishman
ejaculate: 5 blurt, eject **7** exclaim
ejaculation: 7 begorra **8** uttering **11** exclamation
eject: 4 boot, cast, emit, oust, spat, spew, spit, void **5** erupt, evict, expel, spout, spurt, vomit **6** banish, bounce **7** dismiss, exclude, extrude, obtrude **8** disgorge **9** discharge, ejaculate **10** disembogue, dispossess
ejection: 6 ouster **8** eviction **9** expulsion
eke: 7 augment, enlarge, husband, stretch **8** increase, lengthen **10** supplement
el: 4 bend
El Salvador: *capital:* **11** San Salvador
city: **8** Santa Ana **9** San Miguel, Sonsonate **12** Villa Delgado
department: **5** La Paz **7** Cabanas, La Union, Morazan **8** Usulutan **9** Cuscatlan, Sonsonate **10** Ahuachapan, San Vicente
Indian: **5** Pipil
lake: **5** Guija **8** Ilopango
monetary unit: **5** colon **7** centavo
mountain peak: **8** Santa Ana **9** San Miguel **10** San Vicente **11** San Salvador
river: **5** Lempa
volcano: **6** Izalco
elaborate: 5 fancy **6** expand, ornate **7** amplify, develop, enlarge, explain **8** detailed **9** embellish, intricate **11** complicated, extravagant, painstaking
Elam: *capital:* **4** Susa
king: **12** Chedorlaomer
elan: 4 dash **5** ardor, gusto, verve **6** spirit, warmth **7** potency **9** eagerness **10** enthusiasm
elanet: 4 kite
elapse: 4 pass, slip **6** expire

elasmobranch fish: ray
elastic: 6 garter, spongy **7** buoyant, springy **8** cheverel, cheveril, flexible, stretchy **9** expansive, resilient **10** propulsive
fluid: gas
material from whales: **6** baleen
elastin: 10 albuminoid
elate: 4 buoy **5** cheer, exalt, exult, flush, lofty, raise **6** excite, please, thrill **7** elevate, gladden, inflate, success **8** elevated, heighten, inspirit **9** stimulate **10** exhilarate
elated: 5 happy, vogie(Sc.) **6** jovial **7** excited, jocular **8** exultant, jubilant **9** cock-a-hoop, overjoyed
elater: 6 beetle **8** skipjack
elaterite: 7 bitumen
Elatha's son: 4 Bres
Elatus' daughter: 6 Caenis **7** Caeneus
Elbe tributary: 4 Eger, Elde, Iser **5** Havel, Mulde, Saale **6** Elster
elbow: 4 bend **5** ancon, joint, nudge, shove **6** jostle
bend an: **5** drink **6** imbibe
bone: **4** ulna **5** ulnae(pl.)
pert. to: **5** ulnar **8** anconeal
elbowroom: 6 leeway **10** ample space
elcaja: 6 mafura
eld: 9 antiquity
elder: iva **4** aine(F.) **5** prior **6** senior **7** oldster **8** ancestor, danewort, superior, **9** presbyter **10** forefather
elderly: old **4** aged, gray **6** senile **7** ancient **9** up in years, venerable **11** over the hill
eldritch: 4 eery **5** eerie, weird **7** uncanny **9** frightful
Eleanor's husband: 7 Henry II
elect: 4 call, pick **6** assume, choose, chosen, decide, opt for, prefer, select, vote in **7** embrace, espouse, pick out **9** legislate
election: 6 choice **9** balloting **10** plebiscite **11** alternative
majority of votes: **9** plurality
nominating: **7** primary
to break the: **6** runoff
electioneer: 5 stump **8** campaign, politick **9** seek votes
elective: 8 optional **9** voluntary
elector: 5 voter **6** elisor **7** chooser **11** constituent
Electra: *brother:* **7** Orestes
father: **9** Agamemnon
husband: **7** Thaumas
mother: **1** Klytemnestra
son: **8** Dardanus
electric: 6 static **8** magnetic
appliance: **4** iron, oven **5** dryer, mixer, stove **6** heater, washer **7** blender, broiler, toaster

carrier: **9** conductor
circuit regulator: **7** booster
coil: **5** tesla
current: **6** direct **11** alternating
current meter: **7** ammeter **9** voltmeter
current moderator: **5** coder **9** rheometer
  10 attenuator
device: **4** plug **6** dynamo, switch **7** battery
  8 resistor, rheostat **9** amplifier, capacitor, condenser
generator: **6** dynamo
light: **4** neon **12** incandescent
measuring unit: amp, ohm, rel **4** volt, watt
  5 barad, farad, henry, joule **6** ampere,
  proton **7** coulomb **8** kilowatt
motor part: **10** commutator
particle: ion
pole: **5** anode **7** cathode
power: **7** wattage
resistance: **6** ohmage
safety device: **4** fuse
strength: **8** amperage
transmission: **5** radio
wave meter: **9** ondometer
electrify: jar **4** jolt **5** amaze **6** dazzle, fire
  up, thrill **7** astound, stagger, startle **8**
  astonish **9** galvanize
electronic tube: **6** triode **7** tetrode **8** kly-
  stron
electrum: **5** amber
Electryon: *brother:* **6** Mestor
daughter: **7** Alcmene
father: **7** Perseus
mother: **9** Andromeda
wife: **5** Anaxo
eleemosynary: **4** free **9** dependent **10**
  charitable, gratuitous
elegance: **4** chic **5** grace, style, taste **6**
  finery, luxury, polish **7** dignity **8** courtesy, grandeur, richness, splendor **9**
  propriety **10** concinnity, refinement **12**
  gracefulness
elegant: **4** chic, fine, posh **5** swank **6**
  dainty, dressy, superb, urbane **7** courtly, genteel, refined, stately **8** delicate,
  graceful, handsome, polished, tasteful **9**
  admirable, beautiful, excellent, exquisite, recherche, sumptuous **10** concinnous, fastidious
elegiac: sad **8** mournful **9** plaintive
elegist: **4** Gray, poet **6** Milton **10** Propertius
elegit: **4** writ
elegy: **4** poem, song **5** dirge **6** lament **7**
  epicede **9** epicedium **11** lamentation
element: air **4** fire **5** basic, earth, group,
  metal, water **6** matter **7** essence, quality
  8 rudiment **9** component **10** ingredient
  11 constituent, environment, fundamental
chemical: tin(Sn) **4** gold(Au), Iron(Fe),
  lead(Pb), neon(Ne), zinc(Zn) **5** argon(A),

boron(B), radon(Rn), xenon(Xe) **6** bar-
ium(Ba), carbon(C), cerium(Ce), ce-
sium(Cs), cobalt(Co), copper(Cu), er-
bium(Er), helium(He), indium(In), io-
dine(I), nickel(Ni), osmium(Os),
oxygen(O), radium(Ra), silver(Ag), so-
dium(Na), sulfur(S.) **7** arsenic(As), bis-
muth(Bi), bromine(Br), cadmium(Cd),
calcium(Ca), gallium(Ga), hafnium(Hf),
holmium(Ho), iridium(Ir), krypton(Kr),
lithium(Li), mercury(Hg), niobium(Cb),
rhenium(Re), rhodium(Rh), silicon(Si),
terbium(Tb), thorium(Th), thuli-
um(Tm), uranium(U), yttrium(Y) **8** ac-
tinium(Ac), aluminum(Al), antimo-
ny(Sb), astatine(At), chlorine(Cl),
chromium(Cr), Europium(Eu), fluo-
rine(F), hydrogen(H), illinium(Il), lute-
cium(Lu), masurium(Ma), nitrogen(N),
platinum(Pt), polonium(Po), rubi-
dium(Rb), samarium(Sm), scandi-
um(Sc), selenium(Se), tantalum(Ta),
thallium(Tl) titanium(Ti), tung-
sten(W), vanadium(V) **9** beryllium(Be),
columbium(Cb), germanium(Ge), lan-
thanum(La), magnesium(Mg), mangan-
ese(Mn), neodymium(Nd), palladi-
um(Pd), potassium(K), ruthenium(Ru),
strontium(Sr), tellurium(Te), virgin-
ium(Vi), ytterbium(Yb), zirconium(Zr)
10 dysprosium(Dy), gadolinium(Gd),
molybdenum(Mo), phosphorus(P) **12**
praseodymium(Pr) **13** protoactin-
ium(Pa)
combining power: **7** valence
decomposed: **5** anion
different weight: **7** isotope
even valence: **6** artiad
family: **7** halogen
minute: **5** monad
nonmetallic: **5** boron **6** bromin, iodine **7**
  bromine, silicon
nonvolatile: **6** barium
of air: **5** argon **6** oxygen **8** nitrogen
poisonous: **7** arsenic
rare earth: **6** erbium
elemental spirit: **5** genie
elementary: **5** basic, crude, plain **6** simple **7** initial, primary **8** inchoate, original **9** primitive **10** rudimental, uncombined **11** fundamental, rudimentary
organism: **5** monad
reader: **6** primer
elemi: **5** anime, resin **9** oleoresin
elephant: **5** hathi **6** tusker, muckna **7**
  mammoth **8** mastodon **9** pachyderm
call: **4** barr **7** trumpet
dentin: **5** ivory
driver: **6** mahout
ear: **4** taro
enclosure: **5** kraal
extinct: **8** mastodon

female: cow
goad: **5** ankus
group: **4** herd
male: **4** bull
maverick: **5** rogue
pert. to: **11** pachydermic
seat: **6** howdah
trap: **6** keddah
trappings for: **5** jhool
trunk: **9** proboscis
tusk: **5** ivory **9** scrivello
young: **4** calf
elephant boy: 4 Sabu
elephantine: 4 huge **6** clumsy **8** colossal, enormous, gigantic, ungainly **9** ponderous
goddess: **4** Sati
elevate: 4 lift, rear, rise **5** elate, erect, exalt, extol, heave, hoist, raise, setup, tower **6** uplift **7** advance, dignify, enhance, ennoble, glorify, promote **8** heighten, inspirit **10** exhilarate
elevated: 4 high **5** great, lofty, noble, risen, steep **6** elated, raised **7** boosted, exalted, moved up **8** majestic, towering, uplifted **9** dignified **10** high-minded
elevation: 4 bank, hill, rise **5** mound, ridge **6** ascent, height **8** altitude, eminence, highness, mountain **9** acclivity **10** exaltation, prominence **11** advancement
of mind: **7** anagoge
reference point: **9** benchmark
to sainthood: **12** canonization
elevator: bin **4** cage, lift, silo **5** hoist **9** ascenseur
elf: fay, hob, imp, pug **4** peri, pixy **5** dwarf, fairy, gnome, ouphe, pixie **6** goblin, sprite **7** brownie, incubus, succubi **8** succubus **10** changeling, leprechaun
elfin: 4 tiny **6** impish **7** puckish, tricksy **8** delicate, prankish **9** fairylike
elfwort: 10 elecampane
Elgin marbles: 10 sculptures
Eli: 4 Yale
son: **6** Hophni **8** Phinehas
Elia: 11 Charles Lamb
Eliam's daughter: 9 Bathsheba
Elian: 8 Eretrian
elicit: 4 draw, milk, pump **5** claim, educe, evoke, exact, wrest, wring **6** deduce, demand, entice, extort, induce **7** extract **8** bring out **9** call forth
elide: 4 omit, skip **5** annul **6** ignore **7** nullify **8** slur over, suppress **9** apocopate
eligible: fit **6** proper, worthy **8** suitable **9** desirable, qualified **10** acceptable
Elijah: 5 Elias **7** prophet **8** Tishbite
eliminate: 4 drop, oust **5** erase, expel, purge **6** cut out, delete, except, ignore, remove **7** abolish, exclude, silence, weed out **8** get rid of **9** eradicate

Eliot: *hero:* **6** Marner
heroine: **6** Romola
Elisha: *father:* **7** Shaphat
home: **11** Abelmeholah
servant: **6** Gehazi
elision mark: 10 apostrophe
Elissa: See **Dido**
elite: 4 best **6** choice, flower, gentry, select **7** quality, society **9** haut monde, top drawer **10** blue bloods, uppercrust **11** aristocracy **12** quintessence
gathering: **6** galaxy
elixir: 6 potion, spirit **7** arcanum, cordial, cure-all, nostrum, panacea
of life: **6** amrita **7** amreeta
Elizabeth I: 4 Bess **6** Oriana
mother: **6** Boleyn
elk: 4 deer **5** eland, moose **6** sambar, wapiti
genus of: **5** Alces
ell: 4 wing **5** annex **8** addition **9** extension
ellipse: 4 oval
elliptical: 4 oval **5** ovate **7** concise **8** abridged, cut short **10** contracted
elm: *family of:* **8** Ulmaceae
fruit of: **6** samara
rock: **5** wahoo
Elmo's fire: See **Saint Elmo's fire**
elocute: 7 declaim
elocution: 7 oratory **9** eloquence
elocutionist: 6 reader **7** reciter, speaker
eloge: 6 eulogy **7** oration **8** encomium **9** panegyric
elongate: 6 extend **7** draw out, stretch **8** lengthen, protract
elongated: 4 lank **6** linear **7** prolate, slender **9** stretched, strung out
elope: 4 flee **6** decamp **7** run away
eloquence: 7 fluency, oratory **8** rhetoric **9** elocution, facundity, loftiness
eloquent: 5 vivid **6** fervid, moving, poetic **8** stirring **10** expressive, meaningful, oratorical, persuasive **11** impassioned
else: 4 more **5** other **7** besides, further, instead **9** otherwise **10** additional
elsewhere: 4 away **7** not here **12** another place
elucidate: 5 clear **7** clarify, explain **8** simplify, spell out **9** interpret **10** illustrate
elude: 4 duck, flee, foil **5** avoid, dodge, evade **6** baffle, befool, delude, escape **7** beguile, deceive **9** frustrate
elusive: 4 eely **5** cagey **6** subtle, tricky **7** evasive **8** baffling **10** impalpable, lubricious **11** hard to grasp
elute: 5 rinse **7** cleanse, soak out **8** dissolve **10** use solvent
elver: eel
Elysian: 8 beatific, blissful **10** delightful
Elysium: 4 Eden **8** Paradise
elytrum of beetle: 4 wing **5** shard
emaciated: 4 lean **5** gaunt **6** peaked, skin-

ny, wasted **7** scrawny, wizened **8** starving, underfed **10** cadaverous

emanate: 4 flow **5** arise, issue **6** effuse **7** breathe, give off, proceed, radiate **8** stem from **9** come forth, originate

emanation: 4 aura **5** radon **6** efflux **7** outcome **8** emission **9** ectoplasm, effluence **10** exhalation **11** consequence

emancipate: 4 free **5** loose **6** unbind **7** manumit, release **8** liberate, unfetter **11** enfranchise

emancipator: 5 freer, Moses **7** Lincoln **9** deliverer

emasculate: 4 geld **6** soften, weaken **8** castrate, enervate **10** devitalize **12** make impotent

embalm: 7 mummify, perfume **8** preserve

embankment: 4 bund, dike, fill, quay **5** digue, levee, mound, revet **6** staith **7** backing **9** banquette

embargo: 5 edict, order **8** blockade, stoppage **9** restraint **10** impediment, inhibition **11** prohibition, restriction

embark: 5 begin, board, start **6** take up **7** enter on **8** commence, engage in **11** venture upon

embarrass: 4 faze **5** abash, annoy, shame, upset **6** hamper, hinder, impede **7** confuse, flummox, nonplus **8** bewilder, confound, dumfound, encumber, entangle, handicap, obstruct, straiten **9** discomfit, dumbfound **10** complicate, disconcert

embarrassment: fix 5 shame **6** unease **7** chagrin **8** distress **9** confusion **10** discomfort, perplexity **11** humiliation **12** bewilderment, discomposure, entanglement **13** inconvenience, mortification

embassy: 5 envoy **7** mission **8** legation **10** ambassador **13** foreign office

embattled: 8 fighting **9** embroiled, fortified **10** crenelated **11** hardpressed

embattlement: 7 parapet

embay: 7 shelter **8** encircle, surround

embed: 5 infix, inlay, set in **7** implant, ingrain **8** entrench

embellish: 4 deck, gild, trim **5** add to, adorn, dress, grace **6** bedeck, blazon, emboss, enrich, flower **7** apparel, bedrape, garnish, magnify **8** beautify, decorate, ornament **9** elaborate, embroider **10** exaggerate

embellished: 6 florid, gested, ornate

ember: ash 5 coal, slag **6** cinder **7** clinker

embezzle: 4 rook **5** steal **6** thieve **7** defraud, swindle **8** peculate

embitter: 4 sour **7** acidify, envenom **8** acerbate **9** acidulate **10** exacerbate, exasperate

emblaze: 5 adorn, honor **6** kindle **9** embellish

emblazon: 4 laud **5** adorn, extol **7** deck

out, display, exhibit, glorify **9** celebrate

emblem: bar 4 mace, orle, sign, star, type **5** badge, crest, image, token **6** device, figure, symbol **7** scepter **8** allegory, colophon, insignia **9** character, coat of arms

of authority: **4** mace

of Christianity: **5** cross

of clan: **5** totem

of U.S.: **5** eagle

emblematic: 7 typical **8** symbolic **10** figurative

emblic: 4 aula **5** aulae(pl.)

embodiment: map 6 avatar **7** epitome **11** incarnation **15** personification

of Ptah: **4** Apis

embody: 4 fuse **5** blend, merge, unite **6** mirror, take in, typify **7** contain, embrace, include **8** coalesce, organize **9** incarnate, personify, represent **10** comprehend **11** incorporate

embolden: 4 abet **5** brave, nerve **6** assure, buck up **7** bolster, hearten, inspire, support **9** encourage, enhearten

embolism: 8 stoppage **9** occlusion **11** obstruction **13** intercalation

embolus: 4 clot

embosom: 6 foster **7** cherish, embrace, enclose, shelter **8** surround

emboss: 5 adorn, chase **6** indent **8** ornament **9** embellish, embroider **10** do in relief

embossing: 8 celature

embouchure: 10 mouthpiece, river mouth

embowed: 6 arched **7** vaulted

embower: 6 enclose **9** shelter in

embrace: hug 4 clip, fold, love, neck, side **5** adopt, bosom, chain, clasp, cling, enarm, grasp **6** accept, caress, clinch, comply, cradle, cuddle, embody, enfold, huddle, inclip, infold, plight **7** cherish, contain, enclose, espouse, include, involve, welcome **8** comprise, encircle **9** encompass **10** comprehend **11** incorporate

embrangle: 7 confuse, perplex

embrocation: 6 arnica **8** liniment

embroider: tat 4 lace **5** couch, panel **6** emboss, frieze, pad out, stitch **7** build up **8** ornament **9** elaborate, embellish **10** exaggerate

embroidery: 4 lace **6** bonnaz, edging, hedebo **7** orphrey **8** arrasene **10** needlework

figure: **6** etoile

frame: **7** taboret

hole: **6** eyelet

machine-made: **6** bonnaz

thread: **5** floss

embroil: 5 mix up **6** muddle **7** confuse, involve **8** distract, entangle **9** commingle, implicate **12** get in trouble

embroilment: 4 spat, tiff **5** fight **6** fracas **7** dispute, quarrel **8** argument, squabble **11** altercation

embrown: tan **6** darken

embryo: 4 germ, seed **5** fetus, ovule **6** foetus **9** peritroch
young: **8** blastula

emcee: 4 host **8** director **9** moderator **10** run the show

eme(Sc.): 5 uncle **6** friend **8** relative

emend: 4 edit **5** alter **6** better, reform, repeal, revise **7** correct, improve, rectify, redress

emendator: 6 editor

emerald: gem **5** beryl, green **7** smaragd

Emerald Isle: 4 Eire, Erin **7** Ireland

emerge: 4 loom, rise **5** issue **6** appear, evolve **7** develop **9** come forth **10** come in view **11** materialize

emergence: 4 need **8** debouche, exigence **9** occurrence, outgrowth

emergency: fix **5** pinch **6** crisis, crises(pl.), crunch, strait **8** exigency, juncture **11** contingency
money: **5** scrip **8** reserves
signal: SOS **5** flare, siren

emergent: 6 rising

Emerson: *friend:* **7** Thoreau
philosophy: **17** transcendentalism
work: **6** Brahma, Merlin **8** Threnody

emery: 8 abrasive, corundum **11** carborundum

emetic holly: 6 yaupon

emeute: 4 riot **6** tumult **8** outbreak, uprising

emigrant: 7 exodist, settler **8** colonist, stranger

emigre: 5 alien, exile **7** evacuee, refugee **10** expatriate

eminence: 4 hill, note, rank, rise **5** knoll **6** ascent, esteem, height, renown, repute **8** standing **9** elevation, loftiness **10** projection, promontory **11** distinction

eminent: big **4** high **5** great, lofty, noble, noted **6** famous, marked, signal **8** glorious, renowned, singular, towering **9** egregious **10** celebrated, noteworthy **11** conspicuous, illustrious, outstanding **13** distinguished

emir, emeer: 5 noble, ruler, title **6** leader, prince **8** governor **9** chieftain, commander
province: **7** emirate

emissary: spy **5** agent, envoy, scout **6** deputy, legate **7** courier **8** delegate

emission: 4 flow **8** ejection, issuance **9** discharge, radiation

emissive: 8 exhalant

emit: 4 beam, cast, give, pour, send, shed, vent **5** eject, exude, fling, issue, utter **6** exhale, expire, let out **7** give off, radiate, release **8** throw off, transmit **9** discharge **10** disembogue
heat: **4** glow
light: **4** glow **9** luminesce
offensive odors: **4** reek

emmer: 5 spelt, wheat

emmet: ant **7** pismire **8** formicid

Emmy: 7 TV award **9** statuette

emolliate: 6 soften, weaken

emollient: 4 balm **5** salve **6** lotion **8** lenitive, soothing

emolument: 4 fees **5** wages **6** income, profit, salary **7** benefit, stipend **9** advantage **12** compensation

Emory University site: 7 Atlanta

emote: act, mug **4** gush, rant **7** ham it up, overact **12** be theatrical

emotion: ire, joy **4** fear, hate, love **5** agony, anger, grief, heart **6** relief, sorrow **7** ecstasy, feeling passion **8** jealousy, movement, surprise **9** affection, agitation, sensation, sentiment **11** disturbance, sensibility **14** susceptibility
without: **9** apathetic

emotional: 6 moving **8** stirring, touching **9** rhapsodic, sensitive **10** hysterical, passionate, responsive

emotionless: 4 cold **5** staid **6** frigid, torpid **7** deadpan, distant **8** reserved **9** apathetic, impassive, unfeeling **11** cold-blooded

empathy: 4 pity, ruth **6** accord **7** rapport **8** affinity, sympathy **13** understanding

emperor: 4 czar, king, tsar **5** ruler **6** caesar, sultan **7** monarch **9** imperator, sovereign
Holy Roman: **4** Otho, Otto

emphasis: 5 focus **6** accent, stress, weight **8** salience

emphasize: 6 play up **7** dwell on, feature **8** pinpoint, point out **9** highlight, punctuate **10** accentuate, underscore

emphatic: 7 certain, decided, earnest, marcato **8** absolute, decisive, definite, distinct, enfatico, forcible, positive **9** energetic

empire: 4 rule, sway **5** power, realm, reign, state **6** domain **7** control, kingdom **8** dominion **11** sovereignty

Empire State: 7 New York

empirical: 7 factual **12** experimental **13** observational, trial-and-error

emplacement: 7 battery **8** platform

employ: use **4** hire **5** apply **6** bestow, engage, occupy, retain, supply, take on **7** concern, enclose, involve, service, utilize **8** exercise

employed: 4 busy **6** unidle **7** engaged, working

employee: 4 hand, help **6** worker **8** hireling **9** jobholder **10** wage earner *bank:* **5** clerk, guard **6** teller **7** cashier **8** watchman **10** bookkeeper

minor: cog **6** helper, minion **7** servant **9** assistant, underling

slaughterhouse: **5** sider

employer: 4 boss, user **6** gaffer **7** manager **12** entrepreneur

employment: use **4** task, toil, work **5** craft, trade, usage **7** calling, purpose **8** business, vocation **10** engagement, occupation, profession

empoison: 7 envenom **10** make bitter

emporium: 4 mart, shop **5** bazar, store **6** bazaar, market

empower: 6 enable **7** entitle, license **8** accredit, delegate, deputize, sanction **9** authorize **10** commission

empress: 5 queen, ruler

Austrian: **12** Maria Theresa

Byzantine: **5** Irene **7** Endocia

French: **7** Eugenie **9** Josephine

of India: **8** Victoria

Russian: **4** Anna **7** czarina, tsarina **9** Catherine, Elizabeth

empress tree: 9 paulownia

emptiness: 4 void **6** hunger, vacuum **7** inanity, vacancy, vacuity

empty: rid **4** bare, dump, free, idle, pour, toom(Sc.), void **5** blank, drain, expel **6** barren, devoid, hollow, unload, vacant, vacate **7** deplete, exhaust, untaken **8** disgorge, evacuate, unfilled **9** discharge **10** unburdened, unoccupied

empty-headed: 5 silly, vapid **6** jejune, simple, stupid **7** fatuous, moronic, witless **8** ignorant **11** bird-brained

Empusa: 7 specter **9** hobgoblin

empyreal: 7 sublime **9** celestial

empyrean: 5 ether **7** heavens **9** firmament

emu: 4 rhea **6** ratite **9** cassowary

relative: **7** ostrich

emulate: ape, vie **4** copy **5** equal, excel, rival **7** compete, imitate

emulation: 6 strife **7** contest **10** contention **11** competition

emulsive: 9 softening

emyd: 6 turtle

enable: let **5** allow **6** permit **7** empower, entitle, qualify **9** authorize **12** make possible

enact: 4 pass **6** decree, effect, ordain **7** actuate, appoint, execute, perform, portray **9** legislate, personate, represent **10** bring about, constitute

enactment: law **6** assize, decree **7** passage, statute **9** ordinance **14** representation

enamel: 5 glaze, gloss, paint **6** aumail **7** dentine, schmelz **8** cosmetic, schmelze

enameled: 6 inlaid **10** variegated

enamored: 6 soft on **7** charmed, smitten **9** bewitched, entranced **10** captivated, crazy about, fascinated, infatuated, in love with

Enan's son: 5 Ahira

en bloc: 5 as one **8** as a whole **11** all together

en brochette: 8 skewered

encamp: 4 tent **5** lodge **7** bivouac

encase: box **5** cover **7** inclose

enceinte: 8 pregnant **9** expectant, with child

enchain: 4 bind **5** tie up **6** fetter

enchant: 5 charm **6** delude **7** bewitch, delight **8** ensorcel, enthrall **9** captivate, enrapture, fascinate, hypnotize, mesmerize, spellbind

enchantment: hex **5** charm, magic, spell **7** gramary, sorcery **8** gramarye, wizardry **10** necromancy, witchcraft **11** fascination, incantation

enchantress: 5 Circe, fairy, Medea, siren, witch **9** sorceress **11** Morgan le Fay

encharge: 7 entrust **10** commission

enchase: 5 inlay **7** engrave **8** decorate, ornament

enchiridion: 6 manual **8** handbook

enchorial: 6 native **7** demotic **8** domestic **11** of the people

encina: oak

encipher: 4 code

encircle: 4 band, belt, gird, girt, ring **5** embay, embow, hem in, inorb, orbit **6** emball, engirt, enlace, girdle **7** embrace, enclose, environ, wreathe **8** cincture, ensphere, surround **9** encompass, loop about **10** wrap around **12** circumscribe **13** circumference

encircling band: 4 halo, ring, zone **6** choker **8** bracelet, necklace

enclose: box, hem, mew, pen, rim **4** cage, gird, pale **5** bound, bower, fence, hedge, house **6** circle, corral, encase, encyst, enfold, enlock, enwrap, picket, pocket, shut in **7** contain, embosom, embrace, envelop, harness **8** comprise, conclude, encircle, imprison, palisade, surround **9** encompass, put inside **12** circumscribe

enclosure: haw, mew, pen, sty **4** bawn, cage, cell, coop, cote, fold, wall, weir, yair, yard **5** atajo, booly, court, crawl, fence, kraal, pound, stall **6** aviary, corral, cowpen, garden, hurdle, kennel, paling, prison, runway **7** paddock **8** cincture, cloister, sepiment, stockade **9** cofferdam **10** quadrangle

encomiast: 8 eulogist **10** panegyrist

encomium: 5 eloge **6** eulogy, praise **7** plaudit, tribute **8** accolade, citation **9** panegyric **10** compliment, salutation **12** commendation

encompass: 4 be-go, belt, clip, gird, ring, wall **5** belie, beset **6** begird, circle, embody, engird, take in **7** contain, embrace, enclose, environ, include **8** comprise, encircle, engirdle, surround **9** beleaguer, circulate **10** circumvent **12** circumscribe

encore: bis **5** again **6** recall, repeat **10** repetition
anti: boo **4** hiss **7** catcall

encounter: 4 bout, espy, face, meet **5** brush, fight, force, incur, onset **6** accost, affray, assail, attack, battle, breast, combat, oppose **7** address, affront, contest, dispute, hosting, run into **8** come upon, conflict, confront, skirmish **9** collision, forgather, interview **10** engagement, foregather, occurrence, tournament
courageously: **5** beard, brave **7** weather
group: **12** therapy sit-in **13** confrontation

encourage: 4 abet, back **5** boost, cheer, egg on, impel, nerve **6** advise, assure, buck up, exhort, foment, foster, incite, induce, second, uphold **7** advance, animate, cherish, comfort, confirm, console, enliven, forward, further, hearten, inspire, promote, support, sustain **8** embolden, inspirit, reassure **9** instigate, stimulate **10** give hope to, strengthen **11** countenance

encouragement: 4 lift, push **5** boost **6** praise **7** support **8** approval **9** incentive, patronage **12** pat on the back

encouraging: 4 good, rosy **6** likely **7** helping, hopeful **9** favorable, promising **11** comfortable, inspiriting **12** advantageous

encroach: 5 poach **6** invade **7** impinge, intrude **8** entrench, infringe, overstep, trespass

encroachment: 6 inroad **10** aggression, infraction

encuirassed: 7 armored **8** loricate

encumber: tax **4** clog, load **5** beset, check **6** burden, hamper, hinder, impede, retard, saddle **7** involve, oppress **8** entangle, handicap, obstruct, overcome, overload, slow down **9** embarrass, weigh down **10** overburden

encumbrance: 4 clog, lien, load **5** claim **6** burden, charge **7** trouble **8** handicap, hardship, mortgage **9** albatross **10** impediment **13** embarrassment, inconvenience

encyclic: 8 circular **13** comprehensive

encyclopedic: 7 erudite **8** complete **9** extensive, scholarly **10** exhaustive **11** wide-ranging **12** all-inclusive **13** comprehensive

end: aim, tip **4** fate, goal, heel, stop, tail **5** amend, cease, close, death, ensue, finis, issue, limit, napoo, omega, raise, scrap, stash **6** define, design, expire, finale, finish, napooh, object, period, upshot,

windup **7** abolish, achieve, closure, destroy, lineman, purpose, remnant **8** boundary, complete, conclude, dissolve, finality, surcease, terminal, terminus **9** cessation, determine, extremity, intention, objective, terminate **10** completion, conclusion, denouement, expiration **11** consequence, destruction, discontinue, termination **12** consummation **14** accomplishment
loose: tag **6** thread
musical: **4** coda, fine
on: **7** upright **8** vertical
remove: tip **4** clip
tending to: **5** telic
upper: tip **4** apex, head

End of World: 15 Gotterdammerung

end result: 7 outcome, product

end-all: 6 killer **7** quietus **8** clincher **9** last straw **11** coup de grace

endanger: 4 risk **6** hazard, menace **7** imperil **10** compromise, jeopardize

endearing: 5 sweet **7** lovable

endearment: 6 caress **9** sweet talk **10** loving word
term of: hon, pet **5** angel, lover, sugar **7** darling, sweetie **8** baby doll, precious

endeavor: aim, job, try **4** best, seek, work **5** assay, essay, exert, labor, study, trial **6** affair, effort, strife, strive **7** afforce, attempt **8** exertion, interest, struggle **9** undertake **10** enterprise

ended: 4 done, over, past **8** finished

endemic: 5 local

endive: 7 chicory **8** escarole

endless: 7 eternal, forever, undying **8** immortal, infinite **9** boundless, ceaseless, continual, incessant, perpetual, unceasing **10** continuous **11** everlasting, measureless **12** interminable **13** uninterrupted

endlong: 10 lengthwise **14** longitudinally

endmost: 4 last **8** farthest, remotest

endorse: 4 back, okay, sign **5** boost **6** second **7** approve, certify, stand by, support **8** advocate, sanction, vouch for **9** authorize, guarantee **11** countenance

endorsement: 4 fiat, visa **5** rider **7** backing **8** approval, sanction **9** signature

endow: 4 fund, will **5** award, bless, endue, equip, found, grace, grant, leave **6** clothe, enrich, invest, supply **7** furnish, provide **8** bequeath
with bodily form: **11** materialize
with power: **8** energize

endowment: 4 gift **5** dower, dowry **6** talent **7** ability, chantry **8** appanage, dotation **9** mentality **10** foundation

endue: 5 endow, teach **6** clothe, invest **8** instruct

endurable: 7 livable **8** bearable **9** tolerable **10** sufferable **11** supportable

endurance: 5 pluck 7 stamina 8 gameness, patience, strength, tenacity 9 fortitude, hardihood, suffering 10 resolution 11 continuance, persistence, resignation 12 perseverance

endure: 4 bear, bide, last, live, wear 5 abide, allow, brook, stand 6 drudge, harden, remain, suffer 7 comfort, forbear, persist, prevail, sustain, toughen, undergo, weather 8 continue, forebear, tolerate 9 withstand 10 strengthen 11 bear up under

endured: 5 borne

enduring: 4 fast 6 biding 7 durable, eternal, lasting, staunch 8 immortal 9 continual, perennial, permanent 11 everlasting 12 imperishable

Endymion: *mother:* 6 Calyce
son: 7 Aetolus
loved by: 6 Selene

enemy: fae, foe 4 Axis, feid 5 devil, fiend, Satan 6 foeman 7 hostile 8 opponent 9 adversary, ill-wisher 10 antagonist, backfriend

energetic: 4 fast, hard, spry 5 brisk, peppy 6 active, hearty, lively 7 arduous 8 emphatic, forceful, forcible, full of go, vigorous 9 dynamical, strenuous 10 expressive 11 hardworking 12 enterprising

energize: 7 animate 8 activate 10 invigorate

energumen: 7 fanatic 8 demoniac 10 enthusiast

energy: pep, vim, zip 4 bang, bent, birr, life 5 drive, force, might, nerve, power, steam, vigor 6 effort, intake, output, spirit 7 potency 8 activity, strength, vitality 9 animation
lack: 5 atony 7 inertia 9 lassitude
measuring device: 11 dynamometer
unit: erg 4 dyne 5 joule 7 quantum 8 watt hour 9 megajoule 10 horsepower

enervate: sap 6 weaken 7 exhaust, tire out, unnerve 8 enfeeble 10 debilitate, devitalize

enfant terrible: 4 brat 5 devil, scamp, whelp 6 terror 7 hellion 12 troublemaker

enfeeble: 4 numb 5 drain 6 deaden, deplete, impair, soften, weaken 8 enervate 9 attenuate, undermine 10 debilitate

enfilade: 4 rake

enfold: hug 4 wrap 5 clasp, cover 6 cuddle, enlace, enwrap, swathe 7 embrace, enclose, envelop, squeeze 8 encircle, surround

enforce: 5 exact 6 coerce, compel 7 execute, implant 8 carry out, insist on 9 constrain, prosecute 10 administer

enfranchise: 4 free 7 let vote, manumit, release 8 liberate 10 emancipate

engage: 4 book, hire, join, mesh, rent, sign 5 agree, catch, enter, lease, trade 6 absorb, arrest, embark, employ, enlist, induce, oblige, occupy, pledge, take on 7 bespeak, betroth, conduce, engross, involve, promise 8 contract, covenant, entangle, interest, persuade, set about 9 interlock, undertake

engaged: 4 busy 5 hired 6 bonded, meshed 7 assured, earnest, entered, pledged, versant 8 employed, involved, occupied, promised 9 affianced, betrothed

engagement: job 4 aval, date 5 fight 6 affair, battle, escrow 7 booking, contest, meeting 8 skirmish 9 betrothal, encounter 10 attachment, employment 11 appointment, involvement

engager: 6 surety

engaging: 5 sapid 6 taking 7 winning 10 attractive 11 interesting

engender: 5 beget, breed, cause 6 excite 7 develop, produce 8 generate, occasion 9 procreate, propagate

engine: gas 5 motor, steam 7 turbine 8 gasoline 10 locomotive
covering: 4 cowl
kind of: gin, ram 4 goat 5 dinky, mogul 6 diesel, helper, mallet, pusher 7 turbine 8 dollbeer 10 locomotive
military: ram 4 tank 6 onager 7 robinet 8 ballista, helepole 9 espringal 11 ribaudequin
part: cam 4 gear 6 boiler, piston, stator 8 cylinder 9 crankcase 10 carburetor 12 differential, transmission
speed up: rev

engineer: 4 plan 6 driver, manage 7 planner, plotter 8 contrive, designer, inventor, maneuver 9 construct 10 accomplish 11 constructor, superintend

engirdle: 8 surround 9 encompass

engirt: 7 envelop 8 encircle

England: 6 Albion 7 Britain 9 Britannia
capital: 6 London
city: 4 Bath, Hull, York 5 Derby, Leeds, Luton 6 Exeter, Oldham 7 Bristol, Croydon, Ipswich, Preston, Reading 8 Brighton, Coventry, Plymouth 9 Liverpool, Sheffield 10 Birmingham, Manchester
county: 4 Avon, Kent 5 Devon, Essex, Salop 6 Dorset, Durham, Surrey 7 Cumbria, Norfolk, Suffolk 8 Cheshire, Somerset 9 Cleveland, Hampshire, Wiltshire 10 Derbyshire, East Sussex, Humberside, Lancashire, West Sussex
invader of: 4 Dane 5 Norse, Roman, Saxon 6 Norman
island: Man 4 Holy 5 Farne, Lundy Wight 6 Scilly, Thanet, Walney 7 Sheppey

lake: **8** Coniston **9** Ullswater **10** Windermere

mountain peak: **7** Scafell, Snowdon **9** Cross Fell

mountain range: **7** Pennine **8** Cumbrian **9** Cotswolds **12** Cheviot Hills **13** Cotswold hills, Coniston Fells

port: **4** Hull **5** Dover **6** London **7** Preston **8** Plymouth **9** Liverpool **10** Portsmouth **11** Southampton

river: Exe, Lea **4** Aire, Avon, Foss, Hull, Nene, Ouse, Tyne **5** Stour, Trent **6** Humber, Kennet, Mersey, Severn, Thames **7** Derwent, Welland

English: 7 British

aborigine: **4** Pict

actor: **4** Tree **5** Donat, Evans **6** Arliss, Irving **7** Burbage, Gielgud, Olivier **8** Guinness

actress: **4** Gwyn **5** Leigh, Terry **6** Whitty **7** Langtry

admiral: **6** Nelson, Ramsey, Rodney, Vernon

admirer of: **10** anglophile

air force: RAF

Antarctic explorer: **5** Scott

apartment: **4** flat

apple: **6** beefin, biffin, coling, rennet **7** beaufin, costard **8** coccagee **9** guarenden, guarender

apron: **8** barmskin

archbishop: **4** Lang, Laud **6** Becket **7** Cranmer

architect: **4** Wren **10** Inigo Jones

bailiff: **5** reeve

bed: **4** doss

biologist: **6** Huxley

boat: **7** coracle

cattle tender: **7** byreman

charity school scholar: **8** blue coat

cheese: **7** stilton, truckle

chinaware: **5** Spode **8** Wedgwood

church caretaker: **6** verger

church officer: **6** beadle

circuit court: **4** eyre

class: **4** form

clergyman: **4** Inge **5** Donne, Oates **6** Becket, Newman **7** Latimer

coin: ora **4** rial, ryal **5** ackey, angel, crown, groat, pence, pound **6** bawbee, florin, guinea, seskin, teston **7** angelet, carolus **8** farthing, shilling, sixpence, twopence **9** dandiprat, fourpence, halfcrown, halfpenny, sovereign **10** threepence

composer: **4** Arne **5** Elgar, Neale **6** Delius, Handel **7** Britten, Stainer **8** Williams

conductor: **5** Boult **7** Beecham **10** Barbirolli

conservative: **4** Tory

conspirator: **6** Fawkes

court: **4** eyre, leet **5** gemot **6** gemote **8** hustling

crown tax: **4** geld

dance: **6** morris

dandy: **4** toff

diarist: **5** Pepys **6** Evelyn

dramatist: **4** Shaw **5** Peele, Reade, Wilde **6** Coward, Dryden, Pinero **7** Marlowe **8** Beaumont, Fletcher **11** Shakespeare

early conqueror: **5** Horsa **7** Hengist

economist: **4** Mill **6** Angell, Keynes **7** Gresham, Malthus, Ricardo

elevator: **4** lift

emblem: **4** lion

entertainment: **4** busk **7** ridotto

essayist: **4** Elia, Lamb, Lang **5** Bacon **6** Steele **7** Addison

estate: **4** este

explorer: **4** Cook, Ross **5** Cabot, Drake, Scott **6** Hudson

field: **5** croft

food dealer: **12** costermonger

forest: **5** Arden **8** Sherwood

freeman: **5** ceorl

game: **5** darts, rugby **6** soccer **7** cricket

gold: **4** rial, ryal

gun carrier: **4** bren

historian: **4** Bede **5** Acton, Grote **7** Toynbee **8** Macaulay

humorist: **4** Lear

jacket: **4** Eton

king: Hal, Lud **4** Bran, Brut, Cnut, Cole, Knut, Lear **5** Brunt, Henry, James, Sweyn **6** Alfred, Arthur, Bladud, Cnaute, Edward, Egbert, George **7** Artegal, Elidure, Richard, Stephen, William **8** Gorboduc

laborer: **5** navvy

land: **5** laine

law: **4** soke **6** esnecy **7** danelaw

lawyer: **7** bencher **9** barrister, solicitor

liberal: **4** Whig

lunch: **6** tiffin

machine gun: **4** Bren, Sten

magistrate: **4** beak

man: **6** Briton **8** John Bull **9** Britisher

measure: ell, pin, rod, ton, tun, vat **4** acre, bind, boll, comb, cran, foot, gill, goad, hand, hide, inch, last, line, mile, once, palm, peek, pint, pipe, pole, pool, rood, sack, span, trug, wist, yard, yoke **5** bodge, carat, chain, coomb, cubit, digit, float, floor, fluid, hutch, minim, perch, point, prime, quart, skein, stack, truss **6** barrel, bovate, bushel, cranne, fathom, firkin, gallon, hobbet, jugrum, league, manent, oxgang, pottle, runlet, strike, sulung, thread, tieree **7** furlong, hobbitt, quarter, quarten, rundlet, spindle, tertian, virgate **8** carucate, chaldron, hogshead, landyard, puncheon, quadrant, standard **9** kilderskin, shaftment, shaftmont **10** barleycorn, barn gallon, winchester **13** tablespoonful

minister: **4** Peel, Pitt **7** Walpole **8** Disraeli

molasses: **7** treacle

monk: **4** Beda, Bede **5** Baeda

news agency: **7** Reuters

novelist: **5** Arlen, Eliot, Hardy, Reade, Waugh, Wells **6** Austen, Bronte, Butler, Huxley, Sterne **7** Bennett, Dickens, Forster **8** Fielding, Forester, Trollope

officer's civilian dress: **5** mufti

old letter: wen **5** thorn

order: **6** Garter

painter: **4** Opie **6** Turner **7** Hogarth, Millais, Poynter **8** Reynolds **9** Constable **12** Gainsborough

pamphleteer: **5** Defoe, Swift

Parliament houses: **5** Lords **7** Commons

Parliament proceedings: **7** Hansard

party member: **4** Tory, Whig **7** Liberal **8** Laborite **9** Labourite **12** Conservative

patron saint: **6** George

peasant: **5** churl

pert. to: **8** Anglican **10** Anglo-Saxon

philosopher: **4** Hume **5** Bacon, Locke **6** Hobbes **7** Russell, Spencer **9** Whitehead

pirate: **4** Kidd **5** Drake **6** Morgan **7** Hawkins

poet: **4** Gray, Pope **5** Auden, Blake, Byron, Carew, Donne, Eliot, Keats **6** Brooke, Cowper, Dryden, Landor **7** Barrett, Caedmon, Chaucer, Shelley, Spenser **8** Browning **9** Coleridge, Masefield **11** Shakespeare

policeman: **5** bobby **6** copper, peeler

prairie: **4** moor **5** heath

printer: **6** Caxton

prison: **4** gaol

public school: **4** Eton **5** Rugby **6** Harrow **9** Sandhurst

queen: **4** Anne, Mary **8** Victoria **9** Elizabeth

racing town: **5** Ascot **10** Epsom Downs

rebel: **5** Essex, Tyler **8** Cromwell **10** Washington

resort: **4** Bath **8** Brighton

rifle: **7** Enfield

royal house: **4** York **5** Tudor **6** Stuart **7** Hanover, Windsor **9** Lancaster **11** Plantagenet

royal household officer: **7** equerry

royal residence: **7** Windsor

scientist: **6** Darwin, Huxley **7** Boyd-Orr

seaman: **5** limey **6** rating

serf: **6** thrall

settler: **4** Jute, Pict **5** Angle, Saxon **6** Norman

sheep: **8** cotswold

shoemaker: **4** snob

sixpence: **5** sprat

slave: **4** esne

socialist: **6** Fabian

soldier: **5** tommy **7** redcoat **8** fusileer, fusilier

spy: **5** Andre

stable: **4** mews

statesman: **4** Eden, Grey, Peel, Pitt **5** Bevin, Simon **6** Attlee **7** Asquith, Baldwin **8** Disraeli **9** Churchill, Gladstone, MacDonald, Macmillan **10** Walsingham **11** Chamberlain, Lloyd George

stone monument: **8** cromlech

streetcar: **4** tram

tavern: pub

tea muffin: **7** crumpet

thicket: **7** spinney

thrush: **5** mavis

title: **4** dame, duke, earl, king, lady, lord, peer **5** baron, noble, queen **6** knight, prince **7** baronet, duchess, marquis **8** baroness, countess, marquess, princess, viscount **11** marchioness, viscountess

tourist: **7** tripper

tribe: **5** Iceni

truck: **5** lorry

tutor: don

university: **5** Leeds **6** London, Oxford **9** Cambridge

uplands: **5** downs

weight: **5** stone

engorge: 4 glut **5** gorge **6** devour

engrave: cut **4** etch **5** carve, chase, print, sculp **6** chisel, incise **7** enchase, impress, imprint, stipple **8** inscribe, ornament **9** character, sculpture

by dots: **7** stipple

engraver: 6 chaser, etcher **7** artisan **13** siderographer

tool of: **5** burin

notable: **5** Durer **7** Hogarth

engraving: *wax:* **8** intaglio **9** cerograph, xylograph **11** glyptograph

instrument: **6** stylet

pert. to: **7** glyphic, glyptic

engross: 4 bury, grip, hold **6** absorb, engage, occupy **7** immerse **8** enthrall **9** fascinate, overwhelm, preoccupy

engrossed: 4 rapt **6** intent

engrosser: 7 copyist **12** calligrapher

engulf: 5 flood, swamp, whelm **6** deluge, devour **7** swallow **8** inundate, submerge **9** overwhelm

enhance: 4 lift **5** enarm, exalt, raise **6** deepen **7** augment, elevate, enlarge, greaten, improve, sharpen **8** heighten, increase **9** aggravate, intensify **10** exaggerate

enhearten: 8 embolden

enigma: 5 rebus **6** puzzle, riddle, sphinx **7** mystery, problem **9** conundrum

enigmatic: 6 mystic **7** cryptic, elusive,

obscure **8** baffling, mystical, puzzling **9** equivocal **12** inexplicable

enisle: 6 cut off **7** isolate **8** separate

enisled: 5 alone, apart **8** solitary

enjoin: bid **5** order **6** decree, forbid **7** command, dictate, require **8** admonish, prohibit

enjoy: own **4** have, like **5** eat up, fancy, savor **7** command, possess **11** think well of

enjoyment: fun, use **4** ease, zest **5** gusto **6** liking, relish **7** delight **8** felicity, pleasure **9** happiness **11** delectation **12** satisfaction **13** gratification

enkindle: 5 light **6** arouse, excite, ignite, stir up **7** incense, inflame **9** set on fire

enlace: tie **5** twine, twist, weave **6** enfold **7** entwine **8** encircle, entangle **10** interweave

enlarge: add, eke(Sc.) **4** grow, huff, ream **5** add to, swell, widen **6** broach, dilate, expand, extend, spread **7** amplify, augment, broaden, build up, develop, distend, enhance, greaten, magnify, stretch **8** increase, lengthen, **9** elaborate, expatiate, intumesce **10** aggrandize, exaggerate, make bigger

enlarged: 8 varicose

enlargement: 6 growth **8** addition, swelling **9** accretion, expansion, inflation **13** magnification

enlarging gradually: 5 evase

enlighten: 5 edify, teach **6** inform **7** apprise, educate **8** acquaint, instruct **9** irradiate **10** illuminate **11** disillusion

enlightened person: 10 illuminato

enlightenment: 5 bodhi **6** wisdom

enlist: 4 join **5** enter **6** embark, engage, enroll, induct, sign up **7** impress, recruit **8** register **9** volunteer

enlisted man: GI

enlistment: 5 hitch **11** service time

enliven: 4 warm **5** cheer, pep up, rouse **6** revive **7** animate, comfort, inspire, refresh **8** brighten, inspirit **9** encourage, stimulate **10** exhilarate, invigorate

enlivening: 5 vital **6** genial **9** sprightly

enlock: 7 enclose

en masse: 5 as one **8** as a whole, in a group **11** all together

enmesh: 4 trap **5** catch **7** ensnare **8** entangle

enmity: 5 spite **6** hatred, malice, rancor **7** dislike, ill will **8** aversion, bad blood **9** animosity, antipathy, hostility **10** antagonism, repugnance, resentment **11** malevolence

ennead: 4 nine **8** ninefold

ennoble: 5 exalt, honor, raise **6** uplift **7** dignify, elevate, glorify

ennui: 6 apathy, tedium **7** boredom, languor **8** doldrums **9** lassitude, weariness **12** indifference, listlessness

Enoch: *father:* **4** Cain **5** Jared
son: **4** Irad **10** Methuselah

enormous: big **4** huge, vast **5** great, large **6** heroic, mighty **7** immense, mammoth, massive **8** abnormal, colossal, gigantic **9** excessive, monstrous **10** gargantuan, prodigious, stupendous, tremendous **11** elephantine

Enos: *father:* **4** Seth
grandfather: **4** Adam
grandmother: Eve
uncle: **4** Abel, Cain

enough: 4 enow **5** ample, basta **6** fairly, plenty **8** adequate, passably **9** tolerably **10** sufficient **12** satisfactory

enounce: say **5** state, utter **8** proclaim **9** enunciate

enrage: 5 anger **6** grieve, madden **7** incense, inflame **9** infuriate **10** exasperate

enraged: 5 irate **7** berserk **8** choleric, maddened, wrathful

enrapture: 5 charm **6** ravish, thrill **7** beguile, bewitch, delight, enchant **8** enravish, enthrall, entrance **9** captivate, fascinate, transport

enrich: 5 adorn, endow **6** fatten **7** enhance, fortify, improve **8** decorate, ornament **9** embellish, fertilize **10** make better **11** add vitamins

enrobe: 6 attire, clothe

enroll, enrol: 4 join, list **5** enter, write **6** enfold, enlist, induct, record, sign up **7** impanel, recruit **8** inscribe, register **11** matriculate

enroot: 7 implant

en route: 8 on the way **9** in transit

ens: 5 being **6** entity **9** existence

ensconce: 4 hide **5** cover **6** settle **7** conceal, shelter **9** establish **11** place snugly

ensemble: 5 decor, getup, whole **6** outfit, troupe **7** company, costume **9** aggregate **11** combination

enshrine: 7 cherish **10** hold sacred

enshroud: 4 hide, veil, wrap **5** cloak **7** conceal, envelope, obscure

ensiform: 6 ensate **7** xiphoid

ensign: 4 flag, sign **5** badge **6** banner, signal, symbol **7** officer, pennant **8** gonfalon, standard **9** oriflamme
of Othello: **4** Iago
of sovereignty: **7** regalia
papal: **8** gonfalon

ensilage: 4 feed **6** fodder

enslave: 5 chain **7** shackle **8** enthrall **9** subjugate

enslavement: 7 bondage, serfdom **9** addiction, servitude, thralldom

ensnare: net, web **4** mesh, trap **5** benet, catch, noose, snarl **6** allure, enmesh, entoil, entrap **7** beguile, springe **8** entangle **10** intertwine

ensorcell, ensorcel: 5 charm **7** bewitch, enchant **9** fascinate

ensoul, insoul: 7 animate

ensuing: 4 next **9** following, resulting **10** subsequent, succeeding

ensure: 5 guard **6** clinch, secure **7** protect, warrant **8** make safe **9** guarantee

entad: 6 inward
opposite of: **5** ectad

entail: 6 demand, impose **7** call for, include, involve, require **11** necessitate

ental: 5 inner
opposite of: **5** ectal

entangle: knot, mesh, mire, trap **5** catch, ravel, snafu, snare **6** engage, enlace, enmesh, entrap, foul up, muddle, puzzle **7** confuse, embroil, ensnarl, involve, perplex **8** bewilder, encumber **9** embarrass, implicate **10** intertwine, interweave

entangled: 7 complex **9** intricate, twisted up **10** interwoven **11** complicated

entanglement: web **4** knot **6** affair **7** liaison **8** obstacle **13** embarrassment

entellus: 6 monkey **7** hanuman

entente: 6 treaty **8** alliance **9** agreement, coalition **13** understanding

enter: 4 join, post **5** admit, share **6** appear, arrive, engage, enlist, enroll, entrer(F.), pierce, record **7** get into, intrude **8** initiate, inscribe, register **9** introduce, penetrate, sign up for **11** matriculate
militarily: **6** invade

enter into: 8 take part **10** participate

enter upon: 5 begin **6** embark

enteric: 10 intestinal

enterprise: job **4** firm, push, task, zeal **5** drive, essay, vigor **6** action, effort, spirit **7** attempt, project, venture **8** business, endeavor, gumption **9** adventure, operation **10** initiative, management **11** undertaking

enterpriser: 12 entrepreneur

enterprising: 4 bold **5** alert **6** active, daring **7** driving **8** hustling **9** ambitious, energetic, wide-awake **10** aggressive, courageous **11** hardworking, industrious, progressive

entertain: 5 amuse, treat **6** divert, harbor, regale **7** beguile, cherish **8** consider, interest, play host **10** think about **11** contemplate

entertainer: 4 host, mime **5** actor **6** amuser, dancer, singer **7** actress, hostess, regaler, speaker, trouper **8** comedian, magician, minstrel **9** performer, soubrette(F.) **10** comedienne

entertainment: fun **4** fair, fete, gala, play **5** cheer, feast, opera, revue, sport, treat **6** kermis, shivvo **7** banquet, ceilidh(Ir.), concert, pastime, ridotto **8** function,

musicale **9** amusement, diversion, enjoyment, festivity, reception **10** recreation
place: **4** park **5** movie **6** casino, cinema, circus, midway, resort **7** cabaret, theater **10** playground

enthrall: 4 grip **5** charm **6** absorb **7** engross, enslave **8** intrigue **9** captivate, fascinate, spellbind

enthrone: 5 crown, exalt

enthusiasm: 4 elan, fire, zeal, zest **5** ardor, mania, verve **6** fervor, spirit **7** ardency, passion **9** animation, eagerness **10** ebullience, fanaticism

enthusiast: bug, fan, nut **4** buff **5** freak, lover **6** addict, maniac, rooter, zealot **7** devotee, fanatic **8** follower **9** supporter **10** aficionado

enthusiastic: 4 keen **5** rabid **6** ardent, gung ho **8** hipped on **10** forthgoing

enthymeme: 8 argument **9** syllogism

entice: 4 bait, coax, draw, lure, tole, wile **5** charm, decoy, tempt **6** allure, cajole, incite, induce, invite, seduce **7** attract, bewitch, wheedle **8** inveigle, persuade

entire: all **4** full **5** every, gross, sound, total, utter, whole **6** choate, intact **7** perfect, plenary **8** absolute, complete, integral, unbroken **9** undivided **10** unimpaired **11** unqualified **12** all-inclusive, undiminished

entirely: 4 only **5** alone, quite **6** solely, wholly **7** utterly **10** altogether, thoroughly **11** exclusively

entitle: dub **4** call, name, term **5** allow **6** enable, permit **7** empower, qualify **8** nominate **9** authorize, designate **10** denominate **12** characterize, make eligible

entity: ens **4** body, unit **5** being, thing **7** essence, integer **9** existence, structure **10** individual

entomb: 4 bury **5** inter, inurn **6** inhume

entourage: 5 court, staff, train **7** retinue **9** following, retainers **10** associates, attendants, sycophants

entracte: 8 interval **9** interlude **12** intermission

entrails: 6 vitals **7** giblets, innards, insides, viscera

entrain: 5 board

entrance: 4 adit, boca(Sp.), door, gate, hall **5** charm, debut, entry, foyer, mouth, stulm, toran, way in **6** access, atrium(L.), entree, portal, ravish, zaguan **7** delight, gateway, hallway, ingress, postern **9** admission, beginning, enrapture, fascinate, incursion, induction, overpower, threshold, vestibule **10** admittance, appearance **12** introduction

entranced: 4 rapt **8** ecstatic **10** mesmerized

entrant: **7** starter **8** beginner **10** competitor, contestant **11** participant

entrap: bag, net **5** catch, decoy, snare **6** allure, ambush, taigle(Sc.), trepan **7** beguile **8** entangle, inveigle

entre(F.): **7** between

entreat: ask, beg, bid, sue **4** pray, seek, urge **5** crave, plead **6** adjure, appeal, exhort, invoke **7** beseech, conjure, implore, prevail, request, solicit **8** persuade, petition **9** impetrate, importune **10** supplicate

entreaty: **4** plea, suit **8** petition **9** treatment **11** importunity, negotiation

entree: **5** entry **6** access **8** entrance **9** admission **10** acceptance, main course, permission

entrench, intrench: fix, set **5** dig in, embed **6** anchor, invade **7** implant **8** encroach, infringe, trespass **9** establish

entrenchment: **7** closure

entrepot: **5** depot **9** warehouse **10** storehouse

entrepreneur: **7** manager **8** employer, operator **10** impresario **11** enterpriser

entresol: **9** mezzanine

entrust: **4** give **6** assign, commit **7** address, commend, confide, consign, deposit **8** delegate, encharge, hand over **11** give custody

entry: **4** adit, hall, item, memo, note **5** debit **6** credit, entree, postea, record **7** ingress, passage **8** entrance, notandum, register **9** vestibule **10** adjustment, contestant, enlistment, enrollment

entwine: **4** coil, lace **5** braid, twist, weave **6** enlace **7** wreathe **9** interlace **10** interweave

enumerate: **4** tell **5** add up, count **6** detail, number, recite, reckon, relate **7** compute, itemize, recount, tick off **8** estimate **9** calculate **13** particularize

enumeration: **4** list **5** tally **6** census **7** account, catalog **9** catalogue

enunciate: say **5** state, utter, voice **7** declare, enounce **8** announce, proclaim **9** pronounce **10** articulate

enure: See **inure**

envelop: **4** hide, mask, veil **5** cloak, cover **6** bemist, encase, enfold, engirt, enwrap, invest, muffle, sheath, shroud, swathe **7** blanket, conceal, enclose, environ, obscure **8** surround **9** encompass

envelope: **4** coma, husk, rind **5** shell **6** jacket **7** wrapper **8** covering **10** integument

envenom: **6** poison **7** corrupt, vitiate **8** embitter **12** fill with hate

envious: **7** jealous **8** covetous **9** invidious, resentful **10** begrudging

environ: hem **4** gird **5** limit **6** girdle **7** envelop, inclose **8** encircle, surround **9** en-

compass **12** circumscribe

environment: **6** medium, milieu **7** climate, element, habitat, setting **8** ambiance, ambience **10** background **12** surroundings

science of: **7** ecology

environs: **7** suburbs **8** vicinity **9** outskirts **10** nearby area

envisage: **4** face **8** confront **9** visualize

envision: **5** dream **7** imagine, picture **8** conceive **9** conjure up **11** bring to mind

envoy: **5** agent, envoi(F.) **6** deputy, legate **7** courier **8** emissary **9** messenger **10** ambassador **12** commissioner **14** representative **15** plenipotentiary

envy: **5** covet **6** grudge **8** begrudge, jealousy

enwrap: **4** roll **5** clasp **6** enfold **7** enclose, envelop

enzyme: **6** cytase, lipase, olease, papain, pepsin, rennin, urease **7** adenase, amylase, casease, diatase, erepsin, guanase, inulase, maltase, pectase, pepsine, tannase **8** catalase, cytolist, eraptase, esterase, protease **9** biogenase, deamidase, deaminase, invertase, trehalase **10** amygdalase

leather-making: **7** tannase

opposite of: **5** azyme

eoan: **7** auroral

eolith: **4** celt **5** flint

eon: age **8** eternity

eonic: **4** eral

epee: **4** foil **5** blade, sword

epergne: **5** stand **11** centerpiece

ephah: **7** measure

one-tenth: **4** omer

ten: **5** homer

ephelis: **7** freckle

ephemeral: **5** brief, vague **7** passing **8** fleeting **9** temporary, transient **10** evanescent, short-lived, transitory **11** impermanent

Ephialtes' slayer: **6** Apollo **8** Hercules

Ephraim's descendant: **7** Resheph

epi: **6** final

epic: **4** Edda, epos, saga **5** grand, Iliad, noble **6** Aeneid, epopee, heroic **7** Beowulf, Odyssey **8** epyllion, imposing, majestic, Ramayana **9** narrative

epicarp: **4** husk, rind

epicedium: ode **4** song **5** dirge, elegy

epicene: **7** sexless, unmanly **10** effeminate

epichoric: **5** local

Epictetus: **4** Stoic **10** philosopher

birthplace: **10** Hierapolis

expelled from: **4** Rome

home: **6** Epirus

epicure: **7** glutton, gourmet **8** gourmand **9** bon vivant, high liver **10** gastronome **11** connoisseur

epicurean: 4 rich 6 lavish 7 Apician, sensual 8 hedonist, Lucullan 9 libertine, luxurious, sybaritic 10 voluptuous

epidemic: 4 rash 6 plague 8 outbreak 10 pestilence, widespread

epiderm appendage: 4 horn

epidermis: 4 skin 7 cuticle

epigram: 4 poem 6 bon mot, saying

epigramatic: 5 terse, witty 7 concise, piquant, pointed

epigraph: 5 motto 7 imprint 9 quotation 11 inscription

epilogue, epilog: 8 appendix, follow-up, postlude 10 conclusion

Epimetheus: *daughter:* 7 Pyrrha *wife:* 7 Pandora

epinard: 7 spinach

Epiphany: 10 Twelfth Day

episcopacy: 9 bishopric

Episcopal parish head: 6 rector

episode: 5 event, scene, story 8 incident 9 happening 10 occurrence

episperm: 5 testa

epistaxis: 9 nosebleed

epistle: 4 note 6 letter 7 message, missive

epitaph: 8 hicjacet 11 inscription

epithet: 4 name, term 5 title 6 insult, phrase 7 agnomen 9 expletive, sobriquet 11 abusive word, appellation

epitome: 5 brief 6 digest, precis, resume 7 summary 8 abstract, synopsis, ultimate 10 abridgment 12 condensation, quintessence

epitomize: 5 sum up 6 embody, typify 8 boil down, compress, condense 9 exemplify, summarize 10 abbreviate

epoch: age, era 4 date, time 5 event 6 period

epochal: 4 eral

epopee: 4 epic, epos

epoptic: 6 mystic, secret

epure: 5 draft 7 diagram, drawing, pattern

equable: 4 calm, even, just 6 placid, serene, smooth, stable, steady 7 regular, uniform 8 constant, tranquil, unvaried 9 easygoing, unruffled

equal: tie 4 cope, egal(F.), even, isos(Gr.), like, meet, peer, same 5 alike, match, rival 7 abreast, compeer, emulate, uniform 8 adequate, 9 identical 10 equivalent, tantamount 11 comparative, counterpart 12 commensurate, counterpoise

equal-angled figure: 6 isogon

equality: par 6 equity, parity 7 balance, egality 8 evenness, fairness 12 impartiality *legal:* 7 isonomy

Equality State: 7 Wyoming

equally: 5 alike 6 evenly, justly 8 likewise 9 similarly 10 fifty-fifty

equanimity: 4 cool 5 poise 6 aplomb 7 egality 8 calmness, evenness, serenity 9 composure 11 tranquility 12 tranquillity

equate: 5 match 7 balance, compare, even out 8 equalize

equatorial: 8 tropical

Equatorial Guinea: *capital:* 6 Malabo *city:* 4 Bata 11 Santa Isabel *ethnic group:* 4 Bubi, Fang 6 Pangwe *island:* 5 Bioko 6 Elobey, Pagalu 7 Corisco *mainland area:* 7 Rio Muni *monetary unit:* 6 ekuele 7 centimo *mountain peak:* 11 Santa Isabel *river:* 4 Ntem 6 Benito

equestrian: 5 rider 7 vaquero(Sp.) 8 horseman

equidistant: 7 central, halfway

equilibrium: 5 poise 7 balance 9 equipoise

equine: 4 colt, foal, mare 5 filly, horse, zebra

equine water sprite: 5 kelpy 6 kelpie

equip: arm, rig 4 deck, gear, gird, heel 5 array, dress, enarm, endow 6 attire, fit out, outfit 7 apparel, appoint, furnish, prepare, qualify, turn out 8 accouter, accoutre 10 habilitate

equipment: 4 gear 5 goods 6 attire, tackle 7 harness, panoply 8 armament, materiel 10 provisions 12 appointments 13 paraphernalia

equipoise: 7 balance 13 counterweight

equitable: 4 even, fair, just 5 equal, right 6 honest 7 upright 9 impartial, objective, righteous 10 reasonable

equitation: 12 horsemanship

equity: law 7 honesty, justice 8 equality, fairness 9 cash value, rectitude 10 investment 11 uprightness

equivalent: 4 akin, same 5 alike, match 8 of a piece, parallel 9 identical, the same as 10 comparable, synonymous, tantamount

equivocal: 4 hazy 5 vague 7 dubious, obscure 8 doubtful 9 ambiguous, enigmatic, uncertain 10 ambivalent, indecisive 11 problematic 12 questionable, undetermined 13 indeterminate, problematical

equivocate: fib, lie 5 dodge, evade, hedge, parry, shift, stall 6 escape, palter, weasel 7 quibble, shuffle 8 sidestep 9 pussyfoot 10 mince words 11 prevaricate

equivoque: mot, pun 4 quip 9 witticism 10 paronomasia

era: age 4 aeon, date, time 5 epoch, stage 6 period

eradicate: 4 dele, raze 5 erase 6 delete, remove, uproot 7 abolish, destroy, wipe out **8** demolish **9** extirpate **10** annihilate, deracinate **11** exterminate

eral: 7 epochal

erase: 4 blot, dele **5** annul **6** cancel, delete, efface, excise, remove, rub out **7** destroy, expunge, scratch **9** eliminate, eradicate **10** obliterate

ere: 6 before **10** sooner than, rather than

Erebus: *parent:* **5** Chaos
sister: Nox
son: **6** Charon

erect: 4 make, rear, step **5** build, exalt, raise, put up, set up **6** unbent **7** elevate, upended, upright **8** standing, straight, vertical **9** construct, establish, fabricate, institute **10** upstanding **13** perpendicular

erelong: 4 anon, soon

eremite: 6 hermit **7** ascetic, recluse **8** anchoret **9** anchorite
hut: **4** cell

Erewhon: 6 utopia
author: **6** Butler

ergo: 5 hence **9** as a result, therefore

ergot: 6 fungus **12** grain disease

Erin: 4 Eire **7** Ireland **8** Hibernia **9** Innisfail

Erinys: 4 Fury **6** Alecto **7** Megaera **9** Tisiphone

Eriphyle: *brother:* **8** Adrastus
daughter: **8** Eurydice
father: **6** Talaus
son: **7** Alcmeon

Eris: *brother:* **4** Ares
daughter: Ate
goddess of: **6** strife **7** discord
missile: **5** apple

eristic: 12 disputatious **13** controversial

ermine: fur **5** stoat **6** weasel **7** miniver
relative: **4** mink

erode: 4 rust **5** decay **6** abrade **7** corrode, destroy, eat into **8** wear away **9** undermine **11** deteriorate **12** disintegrate

Eros: 4 Amor **5** Cupid
beloved: **6** Psyche
brother: **7** Anteros
father: **6** Hermes **7** Mercury
mother: **5** Venus **9** Aphrodite

erose: 6 uneven **9** irregular

erotic: 4 lewd, sexy **5** bawdy **6** ardent, carnal, loving, ribald **7** amatory, amorous, sensual **8** immodest, indecent, prurient **9** salacious

err: sin **4** miss, slip **5** lapse, stray **6** bungle, wander **7** blunder, deviate, misplay, mistake **8** misjudge **10** transgress **12** miscalculate, misinterpret

errand: 5 chore **7** journey, mission

errand boy: 4 page **5** gofer **7** bellhop, courier **9** messenger

errant: 6 astray **8** shifting **9** deviating,

itinerant, wandering **10** journeying **11** adventurous

erratic: odd **4** wild **5** queer, wacky **6** fitful **7** strange, vagrant, wayward **8** aberrant, peculiar, unstable, variable **9** eccentric, irregular, wandering **10** capricious, changeable **12** inconsistent **13** unpredictable

erratum: 5 error **7** mistake

errhine: 6 sneeze

erroneous: 5 amiss, false, wrong **6** faulty, untrue **7** unsound **8** mistaken **9** incorrect, misguided **10** fallacious, inaccurate

error: sin **4** bull, flub, muff, slip **5** bevue, boner, fault, fluff, lapse **6** fumble, miscue **7** bloomer, blunder, default, erratum, fallacy, falsity, misplay, misstep, mistake, offense, rhubarb **8** solecism **9** violation **10** inaccuracy **12** irregularity, malformation
measuring device: **11** aberrometer

ers: 5 vetch **9** kersenneh

ersatz: 4 fake, sham **5** phony **9** imitation, synthetic **10** artificial, substitute **11** replacement

Erse: 5 Irish **6** Celtic, Gaelic **8** Scottish

erstwhile: 6 former, whilom **7** one-time **8** formerly **10** heretofore

eruca: 11 caterpillar

eruct: 4 burp, spew **5** belch **8** disgorge

erudition: 4 lore **6** wisdom **7** letters **8** learning, literacy **9** education, knowledge **11** instruction, scholarship

erupt: 4 emit, gush, spew **5** burst, eject, expel, spout **6** blow up **7** cast out, explode **8** throw off **9** discharge, pour forth

eruption: 4 rush **5** storm **7** flare-up **8** outbreak, outburst **9** commotion, explosion
skin: **4** acne, rash **5** rupia **6** blotch, pimple **9** festering

Eryx: *father:* **5** Butes
mother: **5** Venus **9** Aphrodite

Esau: 4 Edom
brother: **5** Jacob
country: **4** Edom
descendant: **7** Edomite
father: **5** Isaac
father-in-law: **4** Elon
grandson: **6** Amalek
mother: **7** Rebekah
son: **5** Korha, Reuel **7** Eliphaz
wife: **4** Adah **10** Aholibamah

escalate: 4 grow, go up, rise **5** climb, mount, swell **6** expand, extend, step up **7** advance, broaden **8** increase **9** intensify

escapade: 4 lark **5** antic, caper, fling, prank, sally **9** adventure, excursion

escape: lam **4** bolt, flee, jink(Sc.), miss,

skip, slip **5** avoid, dodge, elope, elude, evade, issue, spill **6** eschew, outlet **7** get away, leakage, outflow, take off **8** break out, get loose **9** disappear, diversion, evaporate **10** fly the coop **11** distraction
means: **8** loophole
escargot: 5 snail
escarole: 6 endive
escarp: 5 cliff, slope
eschalot: 5 onion
eschar: 4 scab **5** crust
eschew: 4 shun **5** avoid **6** escape **7** abstain
escolar: 8 mackerel
escort: see **4** beau, lead, show **5** guard, usher **6** attend, convoy, squire **7** conduct, consort, gallant **8** cavalier, chaperon **9** accompany, attendant, bodyguard, safeguard
escritoire: 4 desk **6** bureau **9** secretary
escrow: 4 bond, deed, fund **7** deposit
esculent: 6 edible **7** eatable **10** comestible
escutcheon: 6 shield
band: **4** fess **5** fesse
cord: **10** cordeliere
Esdras' angel: 5 Uriel
esker, eskar: 4 kame **5** mound, ridge
Eskimo: Ita **4** Yuit **6** Innuit
bird: **4** fute
boot: **5** kamik
canoe: **5** cayak, kayak, umiak **6** oomiac, oomiak **7** oomiack
coat: **5** parka **6** parkee, temiak
dog: **5** husky **8** malamute, malemute
dwelling: **4** iglu **5** igloo, topek, tupek, tupik **9** barrabora
goddess: **5** Sedna
knife: ulu
medicine man: **7** angakok, angakut, angekok, angekut **8** angekkok
mountain: **7** nunatak
settlement: **4** Etah
sledge: **7** komatik
esne: 4 serf **7** bondman **8** hireling
esodic: 8 afferent
esophagus: 6 gullet **7** pharynx
esoteric: 5 inner **6** mystic, secret **7** private **8** abstruse **9** recondite **10** acroamatic, mysterious **12** confidential
esoteric doctrine: 6 cabala
esoteric knowledge: 6 gnosis
ESP: 9 intuition **12** clairvoyance
espadon: 9 swordfish
espalier: 7 lattice, railing, trellis
Español: 7 Spanish
espantoon: 4 club **8** spontoon
esparto: 4 alfa **5** grass
especial: 4 dear **5** chief, close **8** intimate, peculiar, specific, uncommon **10** particular **11** exceptional, outstanding
especially: 6 mainly, really **7** notably **8** uniquely **9** expressly, primarily **10** sin-

gularly **11** exclusively
espial: 6 notice **9** discovery **11** observation
espionage: 6 spying **12** surveillance
agent: spy
esplanade: 4 walk **5** drive **6** maidan **7** roadway **9** promenade
espouse: wed **4** back, mate, tout **5** adopt, boost, marry **6** defend, take up **7** betroth, embrace, further, husband, promote, support **8** advocate, champion, maintain
esprit: wit **4** elan, zing **5** verve **6** spirit **10** cleverness **12** intelligence
esprit de corps: 9 team unity **10** group pride, solidarity
espy: see **4** spot **5** sight, watch **6** behold, descry, detect, locate, notice **7** discern, observe **8** discover
esquire: 7 armiger
ess: 4 worm **5** curve, sigma **7** sigmoid **8** curlicue, curlycue
essay: try **4** seek **5** chria(L.), paper, theme, tract, trail **6** effort, satire, take on, thesis **7** article, attempt, venture, writing **8** endeavor, exertion, treatise **9** undertake **10** enterprise, experiment **11** make a stab at **12** disquisition, dissertation
essayist: 4 Elia, Lamb **5** Paine **6** Holmes, Steele **7** Addison, Emerson
esse: 5 being **9** existence
essence: 4 ens **4** core, crux, gist, odor, pith, soul **5** attar, being, heart, ousia(G.) **6** entity, nature, spirit **7** element, extract, meaning, perfume **9** existence, principle, substance **10** extraction **11** concentrate
Essene: 6 mystic **7** ascetic
essential: key **4** main **5** basic, vital **7** crucial, leading, needful **8** cardinal, inherent **9** intrinsic, necessary, principal, requisite **10** sine qua non **11** fundamental **13** indispensable
essonite: 6 garnet
establish: fix, set **4** base, rear, rest, show **5** build, erect, found, plant, prove, setup, start **6** avouch, clinch, create, ground, locate, ordain, ratify, settle, verify **7** appoint, approve, confirm, install, instate, justify, provide, situate, sustain **8** colonize, constate, ensconce, identify, initiate, organize, radicate, regulate, validate **9** determine, institute, originate **10** accomplish, constitute **11** corroborate
established: 4 fast, firm, sure **7** certain
establishment: 4 mill **5** elite, house, plant **6** ecesis, menage **7** company, concern dounset(Sc.), factory **8** business, Old Guard **10** enterprise **11** institution, ruling class **12** control group
estancia(Sp.)**: 4** farm **5** ranch

estate: 4 fief, home, rank 5 acres, class, finca, manor, order, taluk 6 assets, domain, ground, legacy, status 7 demesne, dignity, fortune 8 allodium, freehold, hacienda, position, property, standing 9 condition, situation 10 belongings, plantation 11 latifundium
fourth: 5 press 9 newspaper
manager: 7 steward 8 executor, guardian
esteem: 4 deem 5 adore, count, favor, honor, pride, prize, value, worth 6 credit, regard, repute 7 account, cherish, opinion, respect 8 approval, venerate 9 deference, reckoning, reverence 10 admiration, appreciate, estimation 13 consideration
ester: 6 oleate 7 acetate, tropate 8 compound, stearate
estero: 5 inlet 7 channel, estuary
Esther: 8 Hadassah
festival: 5 Purim
foster father: 8 Mordecai
husband: 6 Xerxes 9 Ahasuerus
esthesiometer: 10 tactometer
esthetic: See **aesthetic**
estimable: 4 good 5 solid 6 worthy 8 laudable 9 admirable, honorable 10 worthwhile 11 meritorious, respectable
estimate: set 4 rank, rate 5 assay, gauge, guess, judge, prize, think, value 6 assess, figure, reckon 7 average, believe, surmise 8 appraise, consider, evaluate 9 calculate 11 computation
smallest: 7 minimum
too high: 8 overrate
too low: 10 undervalue
estimation: 4 fame, view 5 honor 6 belief, regard, repute 7 opinion 8 judgment
estivate: 6 summer
opposite of: 9 hibernate
estoc: 5 sword
estop: bar 5 debar 6 hinder, impede 7 prevent 8 preclude, prohibit
estrade: 4 dais 8 platform
estrange: part, wean 6 divert 7 break up 8 alienate, disunite 9 disaffect 10 antagonize, drive apart
estrangement: 6 schism 7 divorce 10 falling out, separation
estray: 4 waif 5 dogie
estreat: 4 copy, fine 5 exact 6 record 7 extract 9 duplicate
estuary: ria 5 firth, frith, inlet 6 estero 10 river mouth, tidal basin
esurient: 6 greedy, hungry 9 voracious
et al: 6 others 9 elsewhere
etaac: 7 blaubok 8 antelope
etagere: 7 whatnot 12 display stand
etat: 5 state ·
etch: 6 incise 7 engrave, impress 8 inscribe
Eteocles: *father:* 7 Oedipus
kingdom: 6 Thebes

mother: 7 Jocasta
son: 8 Laodamas
eternal: 6 eterne 7 ageless, endless, lasting, undying 8 constant, enduring, immortal, timeless 9 boundless, continual, deathless, immutable, perpetual, unceasing 10 perdurable 11 everlasting 12 imperishable, interminable, unchangeable 13 uninterrupted
Eternal City: 4 Rome
eternally: 6 always 7 forever 11 in perpetuum
eternity: age, eon 4 aeon 8 infinity 9 afterlife 12 the hereafter
etesian: 6 annual 8 periodic
pert. to: 4 wind
ethenol: 7 alcohol
etheostomoid: 4 fish 6 darter
ether: air, gas, sky 5 ozone 7 heavens, solvent 8 empyrean 10 anesthetic, atmosphere
ethereal: 4 aery, airy 5 filmy 6 aerial 7 fragile, slender 8 delicate, gossamer, heavenly 9 celestial, unearthly 10 spiritlike
ethical: 5 moral 7 upright 8 virtuous 9 righteous 10 aboveboard
ethics: 6 morals, values 9 moral code, standards 10 conscience, principles
Ethiopia: 9 Abyssinia
capital: 10 Addis Ababa
city: 4 Dese, Goba, Gore, Jima 5 Asela, Harer 6 Asmara, Gonder, Mekele 7 Nekemte 8 Dire Dawa
desert: 4 Haud 7 Danakil
emperor: 5 Negus 6 Memnon 7 Menelik 8 Selassie
ethnic group: 4 Afar, Arab 5 Galla, Tigre 6 Amhara, Harari, Sidama, Somali
lake: 4 Abbe, Tana, Zwai 5 Abaya, Chamo 6 Assale, Rudolf 8 Stefanie
measure: tat 4 cubi, kuba 5 derah, messe 6 cabaho, sinjer, sinzer, tanica 7 entelam, farsakh, farsang, ghebeta
monetary unit: 4 birr 6 santim
mountain peak: 9 Ras Dashan
mountain range: 5 Simen
old coin: 4 besa 6 talari
province: 4 Bale, Kefa, Welo 5 Arusi, Gojam, Harer, Shewa, Tigre 6 Sidamo, Welega 7 Eritrea 8 Gemu Gefa
river: Omo 4 Abay (Blue Nile) 5 Awash 6 Tekeze
weight: pek 4 kasm, natr, oket, rotl 5 alada, artal, mocha, neter, ratel, wakea 6 wogiet 8 farasula 9 mutagalla
etiolate: 4 pale 6 bleach, weaken
etiquette: 4 form, Post 5 usage 7 conduct, decorum, manners 8 courtesy, protocol 9 amenities, propriety 10 civilities 12 good behavior
breach of: 8 solecism
etna: 4 lamp 7 volcano

Etruria: *city:* 4 Veii
  god: 5 Tinia
  goddess: Uni 6 Menfra
  king: 4 Lars 7 Porsena
  pert. to: 8 Etruscan
  pottery: 8 bucchero
etui, etwee: 4 case 8 reticule 10 needle-case
etymology: 10 word change, word origin
etymon: 4 root 5 radix 7 radical
eucalyptus: 4 yate 6 jarrah 8 messmate, iron bark
  eater: 5 koala
  gum: 4 kino
  insect secretion: 4 laap, lerp
Eucharist: *box:* pix, pyx
  bread plate: 5 paten
  cloth: 4 fano 5 fanon
  cup: 5 calix 7 chalice
  wafer vessel: 8 ciborium
  wine vessel: ama 5 amula
eugenic: 8 wellborn
eulogistic: 9 laudatory 11 encomiastic, panegyrical 12 commendatory
eulogize: 4 laud 5 extol 7 glorify 9 celebrate
eulogy: 5 eloge, paean 6 hesped(Heb.), homage, praise 7 address, oration, tribute 8 encomium 9 panegyric 11 composition
eunuch: 5 spado 7 gelding 8 castrato
euphonium: 4 tuba
euphony: 5 meter 6 melody 7 harmony
euphorbia: 5 plant 6 spurge
euphoria: 4 ease 7 comfort, elation 9 well-being 12 exhilaration
Euphrates tributary: 6 Balikh, Khabur
euplexoptera: 6 earwig
Eurasia: *range:* 4 Ural 5 Urals
eureka red: 4 puce
Euripides: *play:* Ion 5 Helen, Medea 6 Hecuba 7 Electra, Orestes 8 Alcestis 10 Andromache, Hippolytus 11 Trojan Women
euripus: 6 strait 7 channel
Europa: *father:* 6 Agenor
  husband: 8 Asterius
Europe: See also **individual countries**
  countries: 5 Italy, Malta, Spain 6 Cyprus, France, Greece, Monaco, Norway, Poland, Russia (part), Sweden, Turkey (part) 7 Albania, Andorra, Austria, Belgium, Denmark, Finland, Hungary, Iceland, Ireland, Romania 8 Bulgaria, Portugal 9 San Marino 10 Luxembourg, Yugoslavia 11 East Germany, Netherlands, Switzerland, West Germany, Vatican City 12 Great Britain 13 Liechtenstein 14 Czechoslovakia
  islands: Fyn 5 Crete, Malta, Oland, Rugen 6 Aegean, Cyprus, Ionian, Orkney, Rhodes, Sicily 7 Britain, Corsica, Faer-oes, Falster, Gotland, Iceland, Ireland, Lofoten, Lolland, Vaigach 8 Balearic, Hebrides, Kolguyev, Sardinia, Shetland, Svalbard
  lake: 4 Como 5 Garda, Onega 6 Geneva, Ladoga, Peipus, Vanern, Zurich 7 Balaton, Malaren, Scutari, Vattern 8 Maggiore 9 Constance, Neuchatel
  mountain: 4 Alps, Ural 6 Balkan, Kjolen 7 Rhodope, Sudetic 8 Caucasus, Pyrenees 9 Apennines 10 Carpathian, Erzgebirge 14 Bohemian Forest
  peninsula: 6 Balkan 7 Crimean, Iberian, Italian, Jutland
  people: 4 Dane, Finn, Lapp, Lett, Pole, Serb, Slav, Turk, Wend 5 Croat, Czech, Dutch, Greek, Gypsy, Irish, Swede, Swiss, Welsh 6 Basque, French, German, Magyar, Scotch, Slovak 7 Catalan, Cypriot, English, Flemish, Italian, Russian, Slovene, Spanish, Walloon 8 Albanian, Andorran, Armenian, Romanian 9 Bulgarian, Hungarian, Icelander, Norwegian, Ukrainian 10 Monegasque 12 Byelorussian, Scandinavian
  river: Don 4 Ebro, Elbe, Oder 5 Dvina, Loire, Rhine, Rhone, Seine, Tagus, Tiber, Volga 6 Danube, Thames 7 Dnieper, Vistula 8 Dniester
  sea: 4 Azov 5 Black, North, White 6 Aegean, Baltic, Ionian 7 Barents, Caspian 8 Adriatic, Ligurian 9 Norwegian 10 Tyrrhenian 13 Mediterranean
Eurydice's husband: 7 Orpheus
Eurytus's daughter: 4 Iole
eutaxy: 4 form 8 dispatch, tidiness 9 good order 10 management
Euterpe: 4 Muse
  lover: 7 Strymon
  son: 6 Rhesus
evacuant: 6 emetic 8 diuretic, emptying 9 cathartic, purgative
evacuate: 4 void 5 empty, expel, leave 6 desert, remove, vacate 7 abandon, move out 12 withdraw from
evade: 4 bilk, duck, foil, shun 5 avert, avoid, dodge, elude, hedge, parry, shirk 6 baffle, escape, eschew 7 fend off 10 equivocate
evaluate: 4 rank, rate 5 class, grade 6 assess, ponder 8 appraise
evaluation: 5 assay, worth 8 critique, judgment 9 appraisal 10 estimation
evanesce: 4 fade 5 empty 6 vanish 9 disappear, dissipate, evaporate
evanescent: 7 cursory, evasive 8 fleeting, fugitive 9 ephemeral, fugacious, transient, vanishing 11 impermanent
evangel: 6 gospel
Evangeline's home: 6 Acadia
evangelist: 4 John, Luke, Mark 6 Graham, Sunday, writer 7 apostle, Ed-

wards, Matthew, Roberts **8** crusader, disciple **9** McPherson, patriarch **10** missionary, revivalist

evaporate: 5 dry up **8** condense, evanesce, fade away **9** dehydrate, disappear

evasion: 5 dodge, shift **6** escape **9** avoidance **10** subterfuge **12** equivocation

evasive: sly **4** eely **5** dodgy **6** shifty **7** devious, elusive, elusory, unclear **8** slippery **9** deceitful **12** tergiversate

eve: 4 dusk **6** sunset **7** sundown **9** threshold

Eve: rib **6** female

even: een, tie **4** fair, just **5** aline, equal, exact, flush, grade, level, match, plain, rival, suant **6** direct, placid, smooth, square, steady **7** abreast, balance, equable, flatten, regular, uniform **8** moderate, parallel **9** equitable, impartial **10** coincident **15** straightforward

even if: tho **8** although

even-tempered: 4 calm, mild **6** placid, serene **11** slow to anger, unflappable

evener: 7 leveler **9** equalizer **10** doubletree

evening: eve **4** ereb(Heb.), sera(It.), soir(F.) **5** abend(G.) **6** sunset **8** eventide, twilight

dress: tux **4** gown **5** tails **6** formal, tuxedo **8** black tie, white tie

party: **6** soiree

pert. to: **11** crepuscular

prayer: **7** vespers

primrose: **7** fuchsia

song: **8** serenade

star: **5** Venus **6** Hesper, Vesper **8** Hesperus

evenness: 7 balance **8** equality **10** equanimity, uniformity **11** consistency

event: hap **4** case, fact, fate, feat, tilt **5** casus(L.), doing, match **6** factum(L.), result **7** contest, episode **8** incident, landmark, occasion **9** adventure, happening, milestone **10** experience, occurrence, phenomenon **11** competition, consequence **12** circumstance

first: **5** debut **6** opener, prelim **8** premiere

eventful: 7 notable **8** historic **9** important, memorable, momentous **11** significant

eventide: 6 vesper **7** evening

eventual: 4 last **5** final, later **6** future **7** ensuing **8** ultimate

eventually: 6 one day **7** finally **8** in the end, sometime **10** ultimately **13** sooner or later

eventuate: 5 occur **6** happen, result

ever: aye, eer **6** always **7** forever **8** in any way **9** at any time **10** constantly **11** continually, perpetually

Everglades: 5 marsh, swamp

evergreen: fir, ivy **4** ilex **5** heath, holly,

savin **6** laurel, savine **7** jasmine **9** mistletoe **12** rhododendron

genus of: **4** Olax **9** Cupressus **11** Pittosporum

tree: fir, yew **4** pine **5** carob, cedar **6** balsam, calaba, larche

Evergreen State: 10 Washington

everlasting: 6 eterne **7** durable, endless, eternal, forever, lasting, tedious, undying **8** constant, enduring, immortal, infinite, timeless **9** continual, incessant, perpetual, unceasing, wearisome **10** perdurable **12** imperishable **13** uninterrupted

everlasting flower: 6 orpine

evermore: 6 always **9** eternally **10** constantly

every: all, ilk(Sc.) **4** each **6** entire **8** complete

everybody: all **8** everyone

everyday: 5 usual **6** common **7** mundane, prosaic, routine **8** ordinary

everything: all

evict: 4 oust **5** eject, expel **6** remove **7** kick out **10** dispossess

evidence: 4 show **5** proof, token, trace **6** attest, reveal **7** display, exhibit, support **8** argument, indicate, manifest, muniment **9** testimony **10** illustrate

evident: 5 broad, clear, plain **6** patent **7** glaring, obvious, visible **8** apparent, manifest, palpable **10** noticeable **11** discernible, indubitable, transparent **12** demonstrable

evil: bad, ill, sin **4** base, foul, harm, vice, vile **5** crime, malum(L.), wrong **6** menace, wicked **7** adverse, baleful, corrupt, heinous, hurtful, immoral, misdeed, noxious, satanic, vicious **8** calamity, depraved, devilish, disaster, iniquity, mischief, sinister **9** injurious, malicious, malignant, malignity, nefarious, offensive, worthless **10** malevolent, misfortune, pernicious **11** malefaction

incarnation of: **5** Satan

evil eye: hex **4** jinx **5** curse, Jonah **6** hoodoo, whammy **11** malediction

evil spirit: imp **5** demon, devil, fiend

Hebrew: **8** Asmodeus

Iroquois: **5** otkon

Zoroastrian: **5** daeva

evildoer: 5 cheat, crook, felon **6** sinner **7** culprit, villain **8** criminal **9** miscreant **10** malefactor

evince: 4 show **5** prove **6** subdue **7** conquer, display, exhibit **8** indicate, manifest

eviscerate: gut **10** devitalize, disembowel, exenterate

evocative: 6 moving **8** stirring **9** remindful **10** suggestive **11** reminiscent, stimulating

evoke: 5 educe, waken 6 arouse, elicit, excite, summon 9 stimulate 10 bring forth

evolution: 6 change, growth 7 biogeny 8 progress 11 development

evolve: 4 emit, grow 5 ripen 6 derive, expand, mature 7 develop, enlarge 8 increase 10 show change 11 disentangle

ewe: teg 5 sheep
old: 5 crone

ewer: jug 5 basin 7 pitcher 9 container

ewest: 4 next 7 nearest

ex: 6 former 9 strike out

ex cathedra: 8 official 13 authoritative

exacerbate: irk 5 tease 6 enrage, excite, worsen 7 provoke 8 embitter, increase, irritate 9 aggravate, infuriate 10 exasperate

exact: ask 4 even, fine, levy, true 5 wreak, wrest 6 compel, demand, elicit, extort, formal, minute, square, strict 7 careful, certain, command, correct, enforce, estreat, extract, literal, precise, regular, require 8 accurate, critical, explicit, rigorous, specific 9 identical 10 methodical, meticulous, scrupulous 11 painstaking, punctilious 13 hypercritical
satisfaction: 6 avenge 7 revenge

exacting: 5 fussy 6 severe, strict, trying 7 arduous, exigent, finicky, onerous 8 pressing, rigorous 9 demanding, stringent 10 burdensome

exactly: 4 just 5 fully, quite, spang, truly 6 evenly, just so, wholly 7 totally 8 entirely, of course 9 assuredly, certainly, on the nose 10 absolutely, altogether, positively

exactness: 8 accuracy 9 precision, rightness

exaggerate: 6 extend, overdo 7 amplify, enhance, enlarge, magnify, romance, stretch 8 increase 9 aggravate, embroider, overstate

exaggerated: 5 outre 6 padded 7 blown up, extreme 8 inflated, prodigal 11 extravagant

exaggeration: 9 hyperbole 10 caricature 13 embellishment, overstatement

exalt: 4 laud 5 extol, honor, raise 6 praise, uplift 7 acclaim, advance, dignify, elevate, enhance, ennoble, glorify, inspire, magnify, promote 8 enthrone, heighten 9 intensify 10 aggrandize

exaltation: 5 bliss 7 ecstasy, elation, rapture 9 elevation, transport 10 apotheosis 11 deification

exalted: 4 high 5 grand, noble 6 august, lordly 7 haughty, sublime 8 glorious 11 illustrious, high-ranking

examen: 7 inquiry 11 examination 13 investigation

examination: 4 exam, oral, quiz, test 5 assay, audit, check, trial 6 examen, review, survey 7 autopsy, inquest, inquiry 8 research, scrutiny 10 comparison, inspection 11 exploration, inquisition 13 consideration, investigation 14 reconnaissance
judicial: 13 interrogation
physical: 7 checkup
taker: 6 testee

examine: con, try 4 feel, scan, sift, view 5 assay, probe, quest 6 candle, ponder 7 analyze, canvass, explore, inspect, observe, palpate 8 look over, overhaul 10 scrutinize 11 inquire into, interrogate, reconnoiter

examiner 6 censor, conner 7 analyst, auditor, coroner 9 inspector 10 inquisitor

example: 4 case 5 ideal, model 6 sample 7 pattern 8 exemplar, foregoer, instance, paradigm, specimen 9 precedent 11 description, case history 12 illustration 15 exemplification

exanimate: 4 dead 8 lifeless 10 spiritless

exasperate: ire, irk 4 bait, gall, rile 5 annoy 6 enrage, excite, nettle, stir up 7 agitate, inflame, provoke, roughen 8 irritate 9 aggravate

exasperated: 5 wroth 9 indignant

excavate: dig 4 mine, mole 5 dig up, scoop 6 burrow, dredge, tunnel 9 hollow out

excavation: cut, pit 4 hole 5 grave 6 cavity, groove, trench
for ore: 4 mine 5 stope 6 quarry

exceed: top 4 best, pass 5 excel, outdo, outgo 6 better, outrun, outvie, overdo 7 eclipse, overtax, surpass 8 go beyond, outstrip, overstep, surmount 9 overshoot, transcend 11 predominate

exceedingly: 4 tres(F.), very 5 amain 7 parlous 9 extremely 10 remarkably, strikingly

excel: cap, top 4 best 5 outdo, shine 6 better, exceed 7 surpass 8 outclass, outrival 10 be expert at, tower above

excellence: 5 arete(Gr.), merit, worth 6 virtue 7 quality 8 goodness 10 perfection 11 distinction, superiority

excellent: 4 braw(Sc.), fine, good, tops 5 brave, bully, great, prime, super 6 choice, famous, grade A, select, spiffy, worthy 7 capital, corking, elegant 8 generous, peerless, sterling, superior, top-notch, valuable 9 admirable, first-rate 10 inimitable, preeminent, sans pareil 12 transcendent

except: bar, but 4 bate, omit, only, save 6 exempt, unless 7 besides, exclude, rule out 9 eliminate, other than

exception: 5 demur 7 dissent, offense 9 complaint, condition, objection

exceptional: 4 rare 7 notable, special, unusual **8** singular, superior, uncommon **9** wonderful **10** remarkable **11** outstanding **13** extraordinary

excerpt: 4 cite **5** quote, scrap **7** extract, pick out, portion, section **10** select from

excess: 4 glut, over, plus, riot **5** flood **7** nimiety, overage, surfeit, surplus **8** overmuch, plethora **9** profusion **10** exuberance, redundancy **11** prodigality, superfluity **12** intemperance **13** overabundance

of solar year: **5** epact

excessive: too **4** over **5** enorm(Sc.), undue **6** de trop(F.) **7** extreme, nimious **8** enormous, overmuch **9** exuberant **10** exorbitant, immoderate, inordinate **11** extravagant, intemperate **12** extortionate, unreasonable

exchange: set **4** mart, swap **5** bandy, store, trade, truck **6** barter, bourse, dicker, excamb(Sc.), market, rialto, switch **7** commute, traffic **9** tit for tat, transpose **10** quid pro quo, substitute **11** reciprocate **12** headquarters

exchequer: 5 funds, money **6** coffer **8** finances, treasury

excise: tax **4** duty, toll **6** cut out, impost, remove, resect **7** exscind, extract **8** alcabala(Sp.) **9** extirpate, surcharge

officer: **8** revenuer

excision: cut **7** erasure **9** exsection **10** amputation, rooting out **11** eradication, extirpation

excite: 4 fire, spur, stir, whet **5** elate, impel, pique, rouse **6** arouse, awaken, foment, incite, kindle, thrill, turn on **7** agitate, animate, inflame, provoke **8** disquiet **9** electrify, galvanize, stimulate, titillate

excited: hot **4** agog **5** eager, moved **6** heated **7** fevered, frantic **8** atwitter, worked up **9** steamed up **11** carried away

excitement: ado **4** stir, to-do **5** fever, furor **6** hubbub, warmth **7** turmoil **8** hysteria **9** commotion **10** hullabaloo **11** disturbance

exclaim: 6 cry out **8** burst out **9** ejaculate **10** vociferate **12** say violently

exclamation: aha, aie, bah, boo, fie, foh, hep, hey, hic, huh, och, oho, pah, poh, suz, tut, ugh, wow, yah **4** adad, ahem, alas, arra(Ir.), drat, egad, evoe, garn, hech, heck, hein(F.), hist, hoch(G.), hola, phew, pish, psha, pugh, rats, rivo, tush, wugg **5** alack, arrah(Ir.), bravo, faugh, feigh, heigh, holla, humph, ohone(Ir.), pshaw **6** clamor, hurrah, indeed, ochone(Ir.), outcry **7** hosanna **9** alackaday, expletive **12** interjection

of contempt: foh, pah

of disgust: ugh **4** rats
of exhilaration: **4** evoe
of pain: **4** ouch
of sorrow: **4** alas **9** alackaday
of surprise: aha, gee, oho, wow
of reproach: fie

exclude: ban, bar **5** debar, eject, expel **6** banish, except, exempt, reject **7** keep out **8** prohibit **9** blackball, eliminate, ostracize **13** excommunicate

exclusive: 4 only, rare, sole **5** alone, aloof, elite, scoop, whole **6** entire, select, single **7** private **8** cliquish, complete, snobbish **10** restricted

excommunicate: 8 unchurch

excoriate: 4 flay, gall **5** chafe, score, strip **6** abrade **8** denounce, lambaste **9** lash out at **11** decorticate

excrescence: 4 burl, lump, wart **6** pimple **8** tubercle **9** outgrowth

excruciating: 5 acute **6** fierce, severe **7** extreme, intense, painful, racking **9** agonizing, torturous **10** tormenting, unbearable **12** insufferable

exculpate: 4 free **5** clear, remit **6** acquit, excuse, pardon **7** absolve, forgive, justify, release **8** palliate **9** discharge, exonerate, vindicate

excursion: row **4** ride, sail, tour, trek, trip **5** jaunt, sally, tramp **6** cruise, junket, outing, ramble, safari, sortie, voyage **7** journey **8** campaign, escapade **10** digression, expedition

excusable: 6 venial **7** tenable **9** allowable **10** defensible, pardonable **11** justifiable

excuse: 4 plea **5** alibi, remit **6** acquit, copout, defend, let off, pardon **7** absolve, apology, condone, forgive, indulge, pretext **8** dispense, occasion, overlook, pass over **9** exculpate, exonerate, extenuate, vindicate, whitewash

execrable: bad **4** base, foul, vile **8** accursed, damnable, wretched **9** atrocious, monstrous, revolting **10** abominable, detestable, horrifying

execrate: 4 damn, hate **5** abhor, curse **6** detest, loathe, revile **8** denounce **9** imprecate, objurgate **12** anathematize

execute: act **4** hang, kill, obey, play, slay **5** lynch **6** direct, effect, finish, manage **7** conduct, enforce, perform **8** carry out, complete **9** discharge **10** accomplish, administer **11** electrocute

execution: 7 garrote, killing **8** garrotte **9** rendition, technique **10** completion **11** achievement, fulfillment, transaction

executive: 4 dean **5** mayor **7** manager, officer, premier **8** director, governor, official, overseer **9** president **10** supervisor **12** entrepreneur **13** administrator

executor: 4 doer **5** agent **8** enforcer **9** performer **13** administrator

exegesis: 10 exposition 11 explanation 14 interpretation

exegete: 6 critic 11 interpreter

exemplar: 5 model 7 example, pattern 9 archetype 12 illustration

exemplary: 5 ideal, model 6 worthy 7 typical 8 laudable, sterling 9 admirable, emulative 11 commendable 12 praiseworthy

exemplify: 6 embody, typify 9 epitomize, represent, symbolize 10 illustrate

exempt: 4 free 5 clear, spare 6 excuse, fidate 7 exclude, release, relieve 8 excepted 9 discharge 12 not subject to

exemption: 7 freedom 8 immunity 12 dispensation

exequy: 4 rite 7 obsequy 8 ceremony 10 procession

exercise: ply, use, vex 5 drill, etude, exert, train, wield 6 employ, harass, lession, parade, praxis, push-up, school 7 aufgabe, display, prepare, problem, provoke, utilize, work out 8 activity, maneuver, practice 9 athletics 10 exhibition, gymnastics, recitation 12 calisthenics 14 constitutional

system of: 8 aerobics

exerciser: 5 groom

exert: use 5 apply, wield 6 employ, strain 8 exercise, put forth

exertion: 4 toil, work 5 essay, labor, trial 6 action, effort, energy 7 trouble 8 endeavor, industry, strength, struggle 11 elbow grease

exfoliate: 5 scale 8 flake off 10 desquamate

exhalation: 5 steam 9 effluvium, emanation 10 expiration 11 evaporation

exhale: 4 emit 6 expire 7 blow out, respire 10 breathe out

exhaust: sap 5 drain, empty, use up 6 expend, overdo, weaken 7 deplete, fatigue, wear out 8 enervate 9 discharge 10 impoverish

exhausted: 4 beat, dead, done, worn 5 all in, spent, tired, weary 6 barren, beaten, bushed, effete, pooped 7 emptied 8 consumed, dog-tired 9 washed out

exhausting: 7 arduous

exhaustion: 7 fatigue 8 collapse 9 depletion, inanition, lassitude 11 prostration

exhaustive: 6 all-out 8 complete, sweeping, thorough 9 intensive 13 comprehensive

exheridate: 10 disinherit

exhibit: air 4 fair, show 5 stage 6 evince, expose, ostend, parade, reveal 7 display, perform, produce, trot out 8 disclose, evidence, manifest 9 represent 11 demonstrate

exhibition: 4 fair, show 5 sight 7 display, pageant 8 showcase 9 cosmorama,

spectacle 10 exposition 12 presentation 13 demonstration

exhilarate: 5 cheer, elate, pep up 6 excite, uplift 7 animate, enliven, gladden 10 invigorate

exhilaration: 6 gaiety 7 jollity 8 gladness, hilarity 9 merriment 10 joyousness

exhort: bid 4 goad, prod, spur, urge, warn 5 egg on, plead 6 advise, incite, preach 7 beseech, caution 8 admonish, appeal to 9 encourage

exhume: dig 5 delve 7 unearth 8 disinter

exigency: fix, jam 4 need, want 5 pinch 6 crisis, plight 7 urgency 8 juncture, pressure, quandary 10 difficulty 11 requirement

exigent: 5 vital 8 critical, exacting, pressing 9 demanding, necessary 10 imperative 13 indispensable

exiguity: 7 paucity

exiguous: 4 tiny 5 scant, small, spare 6 meager, sparse 7 slender 10 diminutive

exile: 4 oust 5 eject, expel 6 deport, outlaw, pariah 7 outcast, refugee 8 drive out, fugitive 9 nonperson, ostracize 10 banishment, expatriate 12 proscription

exist: am, are 4 live 6 endure, remain 7 breathe, survive

passively: 7 subsist 8 vegetate

existence: ens 4 esse, life 5 being 6 entity, inesse 7 essence, reality 9 actuality

beginning of: 5 birth, origin 9 nascency

having no: 4 dead, null, void 7 defunct

pert. to: 5 ontic

existent: 4 real 5 alive, being 6 extant 7 present 9 living now

at same time: 15 contemporaneous

in name only: 7 nominal, titular

Existentialist leader: 6 Sartre

exit: 4 door, gate 5 going, leave, split 6 egress, exodus, outlet, way out 7 buzz off, outgate, passage, pull out, retreat 8 debouche 9 departure 10 withdrawal

area without: 8 cul-de-sac 10 blind alley

exode: 5 farce 8 travesty 10 afterpiece

exodus: 9 migration 10 mass flight

Exodus author: 4 Uris (Leon)

exonerate: 4 free 5 clear 6 acquit, excuse, 7 absolve, relieve 9 disburden, discharge, exculpate, vindicate 12 find innocent

exorbitant: 5 undue 8 abnormal 9 excessive, out of line 10 immoderate, outrageous, overpriced 11 extravagant 12 extortionate, unreasonable

exorcism: 5 charm, spell 9 expulsion 11 incantation

exordium: 7 preface, prelude 8 foreword, preamble, prologue 9 beginning 12 introduction

exoteric: 6 layman 7 popular 8 external,

outsider **13** easily grasped

exotic: 5 alien **7** foreign, strange, unusual **8** enticing, striking **9** different, glamorous **10** extraneous, outlandish

expand: wax **4** grow, open **5** splay, swell, widen **6** dilate, extend, unfold, unfurl **7** amplify, augment, balloon, broaden, develop, distend, enlarge, inflate, magnify, stretch **8** increase, lengthen **9** expatiate, explicate, intumesce, spread out **10** make bigger

expanded: 8 patulous

expanse: 4 area, room **5** range, reach, space, sweep, tract **6** extent, spread **7** stretch **8** distance **9** magnitude

vast: **5** ocean **6** desert, empire

expansion: 6 growth **8** increase **9** extension **10** dilatation, distention **11** development, enlargement

expansive: 4 free, wide **5** ample, broad, large **6** genial **7** elastic, liberal **8** effusive, outgoing, spacious **9** bombastic, extensive, grandiose **11** extroverted **13** demonstrative

expatiate: 6 wander **7** descant, dwell on, enlarge **11** elaborate on **12** talk at length

expatriation: 5 exile **10** banishment

expect: 4 deem, hope **5** await, guess **6** assume, plan on, reckon **7** believe, foresee, look for, presume, suppose **8** envision **9** calculate **10** anticipate

expectant: 4 agog **5** alert, eager **7** hopeful, waiting **8** pregnant, sanguine **11** watching for

expectation: 4 hope **6** belief **7** surmise **8** prospect **10** confidence **12** anticipation

expectorate: 4 spit

expedient: 4 wise **5** dodge **6** proper **7** politic, stopgap **9** advisable, makeshift **10** profitable **12** advantageous

expedite: 4 hie **5** free **5** hurry, speed **6** hasten **7** quicken **8** dispatch **10** accelerate, facilitate **11** move quickly

expedition: 4 trek, trip **5** drave(Sc.), haste, hurry **6** safari, voyage **7** crusade, journey, mission **8** alacrity, progress **9** excursion

expeditious: 4 fast **5** hasty, quick, rapid, ready, swift **6** prompt, speedy **9** effective, immediate

expel: 4 oust **5** eject, evict, exile **6** banish, deport **7** cast out, exclude **8** dislodge, forjudge **9** discharge, eliminate, forejudge **10** dispossess, expatriate

expend: 5 spend, use up, waste **6** pay out **7** consume **8** disburse, dispense, shell out, squander **9** dissipate **10** distribute

expenditure: 4 cost **5** outgo **6** outlay **11** consumption **12** disbursement

expense: 4 cost, loss **5** batta(Ind.), price **6** charge, outlay **8** overhead **11** consump-

tion, expenditure **12** disbursement

expensive: 4 dear, high **6** costly, lavish **10** high-priced **11** dispendious, extravagant

experience: see **4** feel, have, know, live, meet, view **5** assay, event, skill, taste, trial **6** affair, endure, ordeal, suffer **7** calvary, feeling, know-how, undergo **8** training **9** adventure, encounter, go through, knowledge **10** background

experienced: met **4** able, wise **6** expert **7** veteran **9** practiced, qualified, underwent

experiment: try **4** test **5** assay, essay, trial **7** analyze **8** research

experimental: 9 empirical, tentative

expert: ace, pro **4** deft, good **5** adept **6** adroit, artist, au fait, clever, habile **7** artiste(F.), capable, skilled **9** authority **10** proficient **11** experienced **12** professional

expertness: 5 knack, savvy, skill **7** ability, mastery **8** facility **9** dexterity

expiate: 5 atone, avert **7** redress **10** make amends, propitiate

expiatory: 8 piacular **9** purgative

expiration: end **5** death **10** exhalation, extinction **11** termination

expire: die, end **5** cease, expel, lapse **6** run out, perish

expiry: 5 close, death **10** extinction **11** termination

explain: 5 solve **6** define, expand, unfold **7** clarify, expound, justify, unravel **8** describe, manifest, spell out **9** elucidate, explicate, interpret, make clear **10** account for, illuminate

explanation: key **5** cause **6** answer, motive, reason **7** account, apology, meaning **8** exegesis **9** rationale **10** exposition **11** description **13** clarification

expletive: 4 oath **5** curse **9** swear word **11** exclamation

explicate: 6 expand, unfold **7** amplify, explain, expound **9** interpret

explicit: 4 open **5** clear, exact, fixed, plain **7** express, obvious, precise **8** absolute, clear-cut, definite, positive, specific **9** categoric, outspoken **10** plain to see **11** categorical, unambiguous, unequivocal **13** unconditional

explode: 4 fire **5** blast, burst, erupt, go off **6** blow up, refute **7** deflate **8** detonate, disprove, dynamite **9** fulminate

exploding meteor: 6 bolide

exploding star: 4 nova

exploit: act **4** deed, feat, gest, milk **5** abuse, geste, stunt **6** misuse **7** utilize **8** impose on, profit by, put to use **9** adventure, heroic act **10** manipulate **11** achievement, tour de force

exploration: 5 probe **6** search **11** examination **13** investigation

explore: map, try **4** test **5** chart, probe, scout **6** search **7** examine, feel out **8** look into **9** range over **11** investigate

explorer: **4** Cook, Eric **5** Bruce, Cabot, Davis, diver, Drake **6** Baffin, Carter, Cortes, De Soto, Hearne, Hudson **7** pioneer, Pizarro, Raleigh **8** Amundsen, Columbus, Magellan, Vespucci **9** Frobisher **10** Chancellor, discoverer

explosion: pop **5** blast **6** blow-up, report **8** outburst **10** detonation

explosive: TNT **4** bomb, mine **5** tense **6** amatol, powder, tonite **7** ammonal, lyddite, melnite **8** cheddite, critical, dynamite, eruptive, unstable, volatile **9** fulminate, guncotton, plastique **10** ammunition, detonative **11** hot-tempered **13** nitroglycerin **15** trinitrotoluene

coal mine: **9** Bobbinite

device: cap **6** petard **9** initiator

high: TNT **7** cordite

igniter: **4** fuse

picric acid: **7** lyddite

projectile: **5** shell **6** rocket **7** grenade, missile **9** cartridge

sound: **4** bang, boom, chug **5** pluff, vroom

exponent: **6** backer **8** advocate, champion, promoter **9** expounder, supporter

expose: **4** bare, open, risk **5** strip **6** betray, detect, reveal, unmask **7** display, exhibit, pillory, publish, uncover, unearth **8** disclose, discover, muckrake, ridicule, satirize, unclothe **10** jeopardize

exposed: **6** unsafe **11** unprotected

exposition: **4** fair, mart, show **5** tract **6** bazaar **7** account **8** analysis, exegesis, treatise **10** exhibition **11** declaration, explanation **14** interpretation

ex post facto: **5** later **9** done after **10** subsequent **11** retroactive **12** after the fact

expostulate: **5** argue **6** object, oppose **7** discuss, dispute, examine, protest **8** complain **11** remonstrate

exposure: **5** vista **7** outlook **9** discovery, publicity, unmasking **10** divulgence, laying bare **11** orientation **12** helplessness

expound: **5** state, treat **6** define **7** develop, explain, exposit, express **8** construe **9** elucidate, explicate, hold forth, interpret

express: **4** vent **5** emote, opine, rapid, speak, state, utter, voice **6** convey, denote, direct, phrase, reveal **7** declare, dictate, expound, nonstop, testify **8** definite, describe, explicit, manifest **9** expatiate, high-speed **10** articulate, particular, peremptory

appreciation: **5** thank

approval: **6** praise **7** applaud

pity: **6** bemoan

regret: **9** apologize

expression: **4** form, pose, show, sign, term, word **5** idiom, token, voice **6** byword, oracle, phrase, symbol **8** laconism **9** euphemism, statement, utterance **10** holophrase **11** delineation, holophrasis **13** manifestation **14** representation

facial: **4** grin, leer **5** frown, scowl, smile, sneer, wince **7** grimace

hackneyed: **6** cliche **7** bromide **8** banality

mathematical: **8** equation

metaphorical: **6** figure

of approval: **4** clap **5** smile **7** ovation **8** applause

of assent: aye, nod, yea, yes **4** amen, okay **6** placet, righto, so be it **8** of course **9** sure thing

of contempt: bah, fie **4** geck, hiss **5** pshaw, sneer

of gratitude: **12** thanksgiving

of incredulity: **6** indeed

of opinion: **4** poll, vote

of sorrow: ay **4** alas **11** lamentation

of weariness: **4** sigh

expressionless: **5** stony **6** vacant **7** deadpan **9** impassive **11** inscrutable

expressive: **5** vivid **6** poetic **7** graphic **8** eloquent, emphatic **10** indicative **11** significant

expressly: **4** just **6** namely **7** clearly, plainly **9** specially

expressway: **4** road **7** freeway, highway **8** turnpike

expropriate: **4** take **5** seize **7** preempt **10** commandeer, confiscate

expulsion: **5** exile **7** ousting, removal **8** ejection, eviction **9** debarment, discharge **10** banishment

expunge: **4** dele **5** erase **6** cancel, delete, efface, excise **7** blot out, destroy, scratch **9** eradicate **10** annihilate, obliterate

expurgate: cut **4** blip **5** purge **6** censor, remove **10** blue-pencil

exquisite: fop **4** dude, nice **5** dandy, exact **6** choice, dainty **7** careful, elegant, refined **8** affected, delicate **9** beautiful, delicious, excellent, matchless, perfected, recherche **10** consummate, fastidious **12** accomplished **4** discriminating

exsanguine: **6** anemic **9** bloodless

exscind: **5** cut out **6** excise **9** extirpate

exsert: **8** protrude, stick out **11** thrust forth

exsiccate: dry **4** sear **5** parch **9** dehydrate

exsuccous: **7** dried up, sapless **8** withered **9** juiceless

extant: **5** alive, being **6** living **8** existing, manifest

extemporaneous: **6** ad-lib **7** offhand **9**

impromptu **10** improvised, off-the-cuff **11** unrehearsed **14** unpremeditated

extend: eke, lie, run **4** grow, rise, span **5** bulge, cover, offer, range, reach, renew, widen **6** accord, deepen, dilate, expand, spread, strain **7** amplify, broaden, display, distend, draw out, enlarge, overlap, overrun, proffer, prolong, radiate, stretch **8** continue, increase, lengthen, protract, protrude **10** exaggerate, generalize, outstretch

extension: 4 area **5** scope **8** addendum, addition, duration, increase **9** expansion **11** enlargement **12** augmentation **13** amplification

building: ell **4** wing, annex **6** lean-to

of time: **4**.stay **7** respite **8** reprieve

trench: sap

extensive: 4 vast, wide **5** ample, broad, large **7** immense **8** expanded **9** capacious **10** widespread **11** far-reaching, wide-ranging **13** comprehensive

extent: due, tax **4** area, body, bulk, levy, size, writ **5** ambit, limit, range, reach, scope, space, sweep **6** amount, degree, spread **7** acreage, breadth, compass, expanse **8** increase, latitude, duration **9** dimension, extension, magnitude, territory, valuation **10** assessment

extenuate: 4 thin **5** gloze **6** excuse, lessen, temper, weaken **7** justify **8** diminish, mitigate, palliate **9** alleviate, gloss over, whitewash **10** depreciate

exterior: 5 ectad, ectal, outer, shell **6** facade **7** outside, outward, surface **8** external

exterminate: 4 kill **6** uproot **7** abolish, destroy, wipe out **9** eradicate, extirpate **10** annihilate, extinguish

external: out **5** alien, outer **7** foreign, outside, outward **8** exterior **9** extrinsic **10** peripheral **11** superficial

extinct: 4 dead, gone, lost **7** defunct **8** quenched, vanished **11** disappeared, nonexistent **12** extinguished

extinction: 5 death **6** expiry **9** abolition **10** expiration **11** destruction **12** annihilation, obliteration

extinguish: end **5** choke, douse, quash, quell **6** cancel, put out, quench, stifle **7** destroy, expunge, smother **8** snuff out, suppress **9** suffocate **10** annihilate

extirpate: 4 dele **5** erase, expel **6** excise, uproot **7** destroy, exscind **8** demolish **9** eradicate **10** annihilate, deracinate **11** exterminate

extol: 4 laud **5** bless, exalt **6** praise **7** applaud, commend, elevate, enhance, glorify **8** emblazon, eulogize **9** celebrate

extort: 5 exact, force, wrest, wring **6** compel, elicit, wrench **7** extract **9** blackmail

extortion: 6 ransom **7** tribute **8** chantage,

coercion, exaction **9** shakedown **10** overcharge

extortionate: 9 excessive **10** exorbitant

extra: odd **4** more, orra(Sc.), over, plus **5** added, spare **7** adjunct, special, surplus **8** superior **9** accessory, lagniappe, unusually **10** additional, uncommonly **12** supplemental

extract: dig, pry **4** cite, draw **5** educe, exact, quote, steep, wring **6** decoct, deduce, derive, elicit, evulse, extort, obtain, pull out, remove, render **7** essence, estreat, excerpt, exhaust **8** separate, withdraw **9** decoction, quotation **11** concentrate

information: **4** pump, **5** grill **8** question

extraction: 5 birth, stock **6** origin **7** descent, essence **8** breeding, tincture **9** parentage

extraneous: 5 outer **6** exotic **7** foreign **9** extrinsic, unrelated **10** accidental, immaterial, irrelevant

extraordinary: odd **4** rare **6** signal **7** amazing, notable, special, strange, unusual **8** abnormal, singular, uncommon **9** irregular, monstrous, unheard of, wonderful **10** additional, incredible, phenomenal, remarkable, surprising, tremendous **11** exceptional **13** distinguished

extravagant: 4 wild **5** outre **6** costly, heroic, lavish **7** baroque, bizarre, fanatic, nimious, profuse, vagrant **8** prodigal, reckless, romantic, wanderer, wasteful **9** excessive, expensive, fantastic, luxurious **10** exorbitant, thriftless **11** dispendious **12** preposterous, unreasonable, unrestrained

extreme: end **4** last **5** final, great, limit, ultra, undue, utter **6** far out, heroic, severe, utmost **7** advanced, drastic, forward, howling, intense, outward, violent **8** devilish, farthest, greatest, terrible, terrific **9** desperate, excessive, nth degree, outermost, stringent, uttermost **10** avant-garde, conclusive, immoderate

extremely: 4 very **6** mighty **8** terribly **9** unusually **11** exceedingly

extremist: 5 basic **7** fanatic, radical **11** fundamental **13** revolutionary

extremity: arm, end, leg, tip, toe **4** foot, hand, limb, need, tail **5** limit, verge **6** border, finger, margin **8** boundary, disaster, terminus **9** bitter end

extricate: 4 free **5** clear, loose **6** rescue **8** liberate, untangle **9** disengage **10** disembroil **11** disentangle **12** wriggle out of

extrinsic: 5 alien **7** foreign, outward **8** external **10** accidental, extraneous, incidental **11** unessential **12** adventitious, nonessential

extroverted: 7 affable 8 friendly, outgoing, sociable 10 gregarious

extrude: 4 spew 5 eject, expel 7 project 8 force out

exuberance: 4 life, zest 5 vigor 6 energy, spirit 8 buoyancy, vivacity 9 animation 10 enthusiasm

exuberant: 6 lavish, lively 7 copious, fertile 8 effusive 9 abounding, excessive, luxuriant, plentiful, vivacious 10 flamboyant 11 uninhibited 12 unrestrained

exudation: gum, lac, sap, tar 5 pitch, resin, rosin 9 discharge, secretion

exude: 4 emit, ooze, seep, weep 5 sweat 7 secrete 8 perspire 9 discharge, percolate

exult: 4 brag, crow, leap 5 boast, gloat, glory 7 rejoice

exultant: 6 elated, joyous 8 jubilant 10 triumphant

exuviate: 4 molt, shed 5 moult 6 slough

eyas: 4 bird 8 nestling

eye: ee(Sc.); orb 4 disc, gaze, glim, lamp, loop, mien, ogle, scan, view 5 glare, watch 6 behold, goggle, oculus(L.), peeper, regard, vision 7 blinker, observe, witness 10 scrutinize 11 contemplate

black: 5 mouse 6 shiner

cavity: 5 oribt

colored portion: 4 iris

cosmetic: 4 kohl, kuhl 5 liner 6 shadow

covering: 6 eyelid 9 blindfold

defect: 4 cast 6 anopia, myopia 11 astigmatism

disease: 6 iritis 8 glaucoma, trachoma 14 conjunctivitis

doctor: 15 ophthalmologist

hollow: 5 orbit 6 socket

instrument for examining: 8 otoscope 14 ophthalmoscope

opening in: 5 pupil

part: 4 disc, iris, uvea 5 pupil 6 areola, cornea, retina

pert. to: 5 irian, optic 7 areolar, corneal, retinal 9 ocellated

protector: 5 patch, visor 7 blinker

pupil dilater: 8 atropine 10 belladonna

science: 13 ophthalmology

simple: 6 ocelli(pl.) 7 ocellus

eyebrow: 4 bree(Sc.) 11 supercilium

eye-catching: 6 marked 9 prominent 10 noticeable 11 conspicuous

eyedropper: 7 pipette

eyeglasses: 5 specs 6 lenses 7 lorgnon, nippers 8 monocles, pince-nez 9 lorgnette

eyelash: 5 cilia(pl.) 6 cilium

dye: 7 mascara

loss: 9 madarosis

eyeless: 5 blind 9 sightless

eyelet: 6 agrafe, gromet, oillet 7 agraffe 8 peephole 10 buttonhole 11 perforation

eyeleteer: 6 bodkin

eyelid: *drooping of:* 6 ptosis

pert. to: 9 blepharal

eye-popping: 7 amazing 8 exciting, stirring 9 thrilling 11 astonishing

eyer: 8 beholder 9 spectator

eyeshot: 5 range, reach

eyesight: 4 view 5 sight 11 observation

eyesore: 4 mess 6 defect 7 blemish

eyetooth: 6 cuspid

eyewash: rot 5 bilge 6 bunkum, drivel, excuse 8 claptrap, flattery

eyot: ait 5 islet

eyra: 7 wildcat

eyrie: See **aerie**

Ezekiel: *father:* 4 Buzi

four beasts: 5 Aniel 6 Azriel, Haniel 7 Kafziel

F

fabian: 8 cautious, dilatory
fabiform: 10 bean-shaped
fable: 4 myth, tale 5 story 6 legend 7 fiction, parable, untruth 8 allegory, apologue 9 falsehood, narrative
animal of: 6 dragon 7 centaur, unicorn
being of: 4 ogre 5 dwarf, giant, troll
bird of: roc 7 phoenix
collection: 8 bestiary
serpent of: 8 basilisk
fabric: rep, web 4 felt, repp 5 baize, beige, build, crepe, frame, lisle, rayon, serge, terry, tulle 6 creton, etoile 7 bunting, etamine, texture 8 cretonne, material 9 construct, cottonade, structure
calico: 5 sallo 6 sallco
coarse: mat 5 crash 6 burlap
corded: rep 4 repp 5 pique
cotton: 4 susi 5 pique, wigan 6 burrah 7 buckram, galatea, hickory 8 bourette
cotton knit: 10 balbriggan
cotton of light quality: 4 leno 7 jaconet, organza 9 silkaline
cotton mixture: 6 mashru 7 delaine, satinet, zanella 9 bombasine, bombazine, grusaille
cotton print: 6 calico 7 percale 8 cretonne
cotton twilled: 5 denim, sallo 6 salico 7 fustian, silesia
cotton with silk embroidery: 8 agabanee
curtain material: 4 leno 5 scrim 6 moreen, velvet 7 silesia
dealer: 6 draper, mercer
finisher: 6 beetle
flag material: 7 buntine, bunting
heavy: 5 denim 6 canvas
linen: 4 crea(Sp.), ecru 5 carde, crash 6 barras 7 buckram, drabbet, sinelon
linen and cotton: 9 huckaback
linen of light quality: 4 lawn 5 scrim
lustrous: 6 poplin, sateen
medieval: 4 acca 6 samite
metallic: 4 lamé
old: 9 ciclatoun
plaid: 6 tartan
printed: 5 batik 6 calico 7 challis
satin: 5 pekin 6 etoile
satin imitation: 6 sateen
sheer: 4 lawn 5 gauze, voile 6 dimity 7 batiste, chiffon, organdy
silk: 4 alma, gimp, gros, ikat 5 caffa, carde, crepe, ninon, rumal, satin, surah

6 blatta, camaka, patola, samite 7 alamode, chiffon, taffeta, Xmantua 8 barathea, bourette, sarcenet, sarsenet 9 charmeuse, levantine, matelasse 10 bombay-cine
silk (thin): 4 moff 5 tulle 6 pongee 7 hernani 8 eolienne
silk and cotton: 6 crepon, gloria 9 bombasine, bombazine
silk and linen: 8 brocatel 10 brocatelle
silk and wool: 6 crepon, gloria 7 challie, challis 8 eolienne
silk imitation: 5 rayon 7 satinet
silk mixture: kin 4 acca 5 balda 6 mashru 7 grogram 9 baldachin, baldaquin, farandine
silk-ribbed: rep 4 repp 6 faille 7 epingle 8 marocain
silk yarn: 7 schappe
straw: mat 7 matting
striped: aba 7 galatea, ticking
suiting: 6 dacron 7 acrilan, acrylic
surface: nap
synthetic: 5 nylon, orlon, rayon 6 dacron 7 acrilan, acrylic, plastic 9 polyester
textile: rep 5 moire 7 etamine
texture: 4 woof
thin: 5 gauze 8 gossamer, tarlatan 9 grenadine
towel: 4 huck 5 terry
Turkish: 6 agaric 7 chekmak 8 cottonee 10 terry cloth
twilled: 4 alma, jean 5 denim, sallo, serge, surah 6 coburg, sallco 8 corduroy, dungaree, shalloon, whipcord 9 bombasine, bombazine, gabardine, levantine, messaline, tricotine 10 broadcloth, kerseymere
unbleached: 5 beige
upholstery: rep 4 repp 6 frieze 7 tabaret
velvet-like: 5 panne 6 velure 8 duvetine 9 velveteen
waste material: 5 mungo
watered silk: 5 moire
waterproof: 8 burberry
white: 8 coteline
wide: 6 cotele
wool: 5 baize, beige, casha, serge, tweed 6 burnet, frisca, moreen 7 bolivia, debeige, delaine, droguet, frisado, frizado, hernani, worsted 8 cataloon, harateen, rattinet, zibeline 9 catalowne, gabar-

dine, grenadine, harrateen, montagnac, zibelline

wool (coarse): 6 djersa, duffel, kersey, witney 7 blocking

wool dress: 5 beige 7 delaine 8 wildbore 9 grenadine

wool mixture: 7 delaine, zanella 9 grisaille

wool-ribbed: rep 4 repp 8 marocain

worsted: 7 etamine

woven: 4 lamé 5 tweed, twill 6 tissue, tricot 7 blanket, damasse, textile

fabricate: 4 coin, form, make, mint 5 build, frame 6 devise, invent, make up 7 concoct, fashion, produce 8 contrive 9 construct 11 manufacture

fabrication: lie 7 fiction, forgery, untruth 8 pretense 9 falsehood

fabricator: 4 liar 6 forger 12 manufacturer

fabula: 5 story

fabulist: 4 liar 5 Aesop, Grimm 6 fabler 8 Andersen 10 parabolist

fabulous: 7 amazing, feigned 8 mythical, romantic 9 legendary 10 apocryphal, fictitious, incredible, phenomenal, remarkable 11 astonishing

facade: 4 face, mask 5 front, put-on 8 pretense

face: map, mug, pan 4 dare, defy, dial, leer, line, meet, moue 5 cover, front, stand 6 facade, oppose, veneer, visage 7 feature, grimace, surface 8 confront, envisage 9 encounter, semblance, stand up to 11 countenance, physiognomy

artery: 9 maxillary

bone: 5 malar 6 zygoma 7 maxilla 8 mandible

covering: 4 mask, veil

defect: 7 harelip

false: 4 mask

guard: 6 beaver

ornament: 4 veil 5 jewel, patch 9 cosmetics

paint: 4 fard 6 parget

part: eye, jaw, lid, lip 4 brow, chin, nose 5 cheek

with masonry: 5 revet

face eastward: 9 orientate

face-off: 8 showdown 13 confrontation

face-to-face: 7 affront, vis-a-vis

face value: par

facer: 6 bumper 7 tankard

facet: 4 side 5 angle, bezel, culet, phase 6 aspect

facetious: 5 comic, droll, funny, witty 6 jocose 7 amusing, jocular 8 humorous, polished 9 laughable 12 wisecracking

facia: 5 plate 6 tablet

facient: 4 doer 5 agent

facile: 4 able, easy, glib 5 adept, quick, ready, slick 6 expert, fluent 7 shallow

facilitate: aid 4 ease, help 5 speed 6 assist 8 expedite

facility: art 4 ease 5 eclat, knack, skill 7 address, freedom 9 dexterity, readiness 10 adroitness, expertness, pliability

facing: 5 front, panel 6 veneer 7 surface 8 covering, opposite

downward: 5 prone

inward: 8 introrse

outward: 8 extrorse

upward: 6 supine

facsimile: 4 copy 5 model 7 replica 9 duplicate, imitation 10 similitude 11 counterpart

fact: 4 data(pl.), deed, fait(F.) 5 datum, event, truth 7 keynote, lowdown, reality 9 actuality, thing done 12 circumstance

support: 15 circumstantiate

faction: 4 bloc, sect, side 5 cabal, junto, party 6 circle, clique, schism 7 coterie, dispute, quarrel 8 intrigue, offshoot 9 concision 11 combination

factious: 9 seditious 11 dissentious

factitious: 4 sham 9 unnatural 10 artificial

factor: gen 4 doer, gene 5 agent, cause, maker 6 author, detail 7 bailiff, steward 8 adherent, aumildar, gomashta, gomastah 11 chamberlain, constituent

factory: 4 mill, shop 5 plant 6 aurang, aurung 8 building, fabrique(F.), officina (Sp.), workshop 11 manufactory 13 establishment

book: 7 bindery

factotum: 5 agent 7 servant 8 handyman

factual: 4 real, true 7 genuine, literal

faculty: wit 4 ease, gift, flair, knack, power, skill, staff 6 talent 7 ability 8 aptitude, capacity

fad: 4 rage, whim 5 craze, fancy, hobby 7 crochet, fashion 9 amusement

faddle: 6 trifle 8 nonsense

fade: die, dim 4 dull, pale, wilt 5 decay 6 perish, vanish, wither 7 decline, lighten 8 diminish, discolor, dissolve, evanesce, languish 9 lose color 11 become faint

camera device: 4 iris 9 diaphragm

Faerie Queen: *author:* 7 Spenser

character: ate, Una 4 Alma 5 Guyon 6 Amoret 7 Artegal 8 Calidore, Florimel, Gloriana 11 Britomartis

Fafnir: *brother:* 5 Regin

slayer: 6 Sigurd 7 Sigurth 9 Siegfried

fag: 4 flag, tire, toil 5 droop, weary 6 drudge, menial 7 exhaust, fatigue, frazzle 9 cigarette

faik(Sc.): 6 lessen

fail: ebb 4 flag, fold, lose, sink, wane 5 flunk 6 desert, falter 7 exhaust, flicker, founder 8 languish, peter out

failing: 5 fault 6 foible 7 blemish, frailty, weakness 9 infirmity 10 deficiency 11 delinquency, diminishing 12 imperfection

fail-safe: 8 riskless 9 foolproof 10 error-proof

failure: dud 4 bust, flop, lack, loss, miss 5 bilge, decay, fault, lapse, lemon 6 fiasco, fizzle 7 bloomer, debacle, decline, default, neglect 8 abortion, collapse, omission 10 bankruptcy, deficiency 11 delinquency, miscarriage, shortcoming 13 deterioration 14 disappointment

fain: 4 fond, glad 5 eager 7 pleased, willing 8 desirous, inclined 11 constrained

faineant: 4 idle, lazy 5 idler 8 inactive, sluggard

faint: dim 4 dark, pale, pall, soft, weak 5 fuzzy, swoon, vague 6 evanid, feeble, hushed, sickly 7 blurred, languid, obscure, syncope 8 delicate, languish, listless, sluggish 9 simulated 10 indistinct

fainthearted: 5 timid 6 afraid, craven 8 cowardly, timorous

fair: 4 calm, even, just, mart 5 bazar, blond, clear, feria(L.), right 6 bazaar, blonde, decent, honest, kermis 7 exhibit, kermess 8 distinct, middling, unbiased 9 beautiful, equitable, impartial 10 auspicious, exhibition, reasonable 12 unprejudiced 13 disinterested, dispassionate

fair game: 4 butt, dupe 6 victim

fair-haired: 5 blond 6 blonde 8 favorite

fairest: 6 flower

fairly: 4 well 7 plainly 8 properly, suitably 9 favorably, tolerably 10 handsomely 12 legitimately

fairness: 6 equity 7 honesty, justice 8 equality 12 impartiality

fairy: elf, fay, hob, imp 4 peri, perl, pixy, puck 5 dwarf, gnome, pixie 6 goblin, spirit, sprite, yaksha, yakshi 7 banshee, gremlin, sylphid 10 leprechaun 11 enchantress

abode: 4 shee 5 sidhe

air: 5 sylph

chief: 4 Puck

king: 6 Oberon

of the Tempest: 5 Ariel

queen: Mab, Una 7 Titania

shoemaker: 10 leprechaun

spirit of death: 7 banshee

tricky: 4 Puck

fairy-like: 5 elfin

fait: 4 deed, fact

faith: 4 cult, sect 5 certy(Sc.), creed, troth, trust 6 belief, certie(Sc.), church, credit, pledge 7 promise 8 affiance, reliance, religion 9 bona fides 10 confidence, conviction

article: 5 tenet 9 credendum

faithful: 4 fast, feal, firm, leal, true 5 liege, loyal, pious, tried 6 honest, steady, trusty 7 devoted, sincere 8 accurate, constant 9 steadfast, veracious 13 conscientious

faithfulness: 8 fidelity

faithless: 5 false, punic 6 fickle, hollow, unjust, untrue 7 atheist 8 apostate, delusive, disloyal, shifting, unstable 9 deceptive, mercurial 10 inconstant, perfidious 11 disaffected, incredulous, treacherous 12 unsatisfying

faithlessness: 7 falsity, perfidy, untruth 8 betrayal 10 infidelity

fake: 4 hoax, sham 5 bogus, cheat, dummy, false, feign, fudge, phony 7 falsify, furbish, pretend, swindle, trump up 8 simulate, spurious 9 imitation 10 fictitious, fraudulent 11 counterfeit, manufacture

faker: 5 quack 6 humbug 7 peddler 9 charlatan, pretender

fakir: 4 monk, yogi 7 ascetic, dervish 9 mendicant

falbala: 7 flounce 8 furbelow, trimming

falcon: 4 hawk 6 hobby, saker 6 lanner, luggar, lugger, merlin, musket, tercel 7 kestrel 9 peregrine

bait: 4 lure

blind: 4 seel

genus: 5 Falco

male: 6 tercel 7 tiercel

nestling: 4 eyas

strap for: 4 jess

falconer: 6 hawker 8 ostreger 10 austringer

fall: sag 4 drip, drop, flop, plop, ruin, ruse, sile, sink, slip 5 abate, cloit(Sc.), crash, hance, lapse, plump, rapid, shoot, slump 6 autumn, happen, perish, recede, season, topple, tumble 7 cascade, decline, degrade, depress, descend, devolve, dribble, escheat, plummet, retreat, stumble, subside 8 cataract, collapse, commence, decrease 9 backslide, prostrate, surrender 10 capitulate, depreciate, disappoint 11 precipitate

back: 6 recede 7 relapse, retreat

behind: lag 5 lapse, trail 6 follow 8 straggle 10 lose ground

flat: die 4 fail, goof 6 bungle 7 misfire 9 fizzle out

in: 4 cave 5 agree 6 concur, line up 9 terminate

short: shy 4 fail, lack, miss

fall guy: 4 butt, dupe, gull 5 chump, patsy 6 pigeon, sucker 9 scapegoat

fallacious: sly 6 untrue 8 delusive, guileful, illusory 9 deceitful, deceptive, insidious 10 fraudulent, misleading 11 treacherous

fallacy: 4 flaw 5 error 6 idolum 7 mistake, pitfall 11 false notion

fallal: 4 ruff 6 finery, gewgaw

fallen: 5 loose, slain 6 ousted, sinful 7 debased, deposed, immoral

fallfish: 4 chub

fallible: 5 human 6 faulty, unsure 7 errable **9** imperfect **10** unreliable

falling: 6 cadent **8** prolapse, windfall **10** subsidence

fallout: 9 by-product, radiation **12** chance result

fall out: row **4** spat, tiff **5** scrap **6** bicker **7** wrangle **8** disagree

fallow: 4 pale **6** barren **9** yellow-red, yellowish **12** uncultivated

fallow deer: 6 damine

false: 4 fake, sham **5** bogus, fause(Sc.), paste, phony, wrong **6** fickle, hollow, pseudo, untrue **7** bastard, crooked, feigned **8** disloyal, illusive, recreant, spurious **9** deceitful, deceptive, dishonest, erroneous, faithless, incorrect, insincere, irregular, pretended **10** apocryphal, artificial, calumnious, fictitious, groundless, mendacious, misleading, perfidious, traitorous, untruthful **11** counterfeit, disaffected, treacherous, unveracious **12** hypocritical

falsehood: cog, fib, lie **4** flam, tale **5** fable, story **6** canard **7** fiction, perfidy, romance, untruth **8** roorback **9** deception, duplicity, imposture, mendacity, treachery **10** pseudology **11** fabrication

falsify: lie **4** fake **5** belie, feint, forge **6** betray, doctor **7** violate **9** dissemble **10** adulterate **11** counterfeit

Falstaff: *follower:* Nym
ancient: **6** Pistol
opera composer: **5** Verdi
play: **7** Henry IV
playwright: **11** Shakespeare
prince: Hal

falter: 4 fail **5** pause, waver **6** boggle, flinch, totter **7** fribble, stumble, tremble **8** hesitate

Fama: 5 rumor

fame: 5 bruit, glory, honor, kudos, rumor **6** renown, report, repute **7** hearsay **9** celebrity **10** reputation

familiar: 4 bold, cozy, easy, free, tosh **5** usual **6** common, homely, versed **7** affable **8** frequent, habitual, intimate, sociable **9** customary, household, presuming, well-known **10** accustomed, conversant **12** acquaintance **13** unconstrained

familiarize: 4 haft **8** accustom **9** habituate, make known **10** naturalize

family: kin **4** clan **5** class, flesh, group, house **6** cletch **7** kindred, lineage, progeny **8** category **9** household **10** generation
head: **7** goodman, husband **9** patriarch **11** householder **13** pater familias(L.)
pert. to: **7** nepotic **12** genealogical

famine: 6 dearth, hunger **8** scarcity **10** starvation **11** destitution

famished: 6 hungry **7** starved **8** ravenous

famous: 5 grand, known, noted **6** namely **7** eminent, namable, notable **8** renowned **9** excellent, notorious, prominent **10** celebrated **11** conspicuous, illustrious, outstanding **13** distinguished

famulus: 7 servant **9** attendant

fan: 4 beat, buff, cool **5** punka **6** basket, blower, colmar, punkah, rooter, shovel, spread, winnow **7** admirer, devotee **8** follower **9** flabellum, propeller **10** enthusiast
alluvial: **5** delta
form of: **7** plicate

fan-shaped: 10 flabellate

fanatic: mad **5** bigot, crazy, rabid, ultra **6** zealot **7** devotee **8** frenetic **9** energumen, extremist, phrenetic **10** enthusiast, monomaniac **11** extravagant

fancied: 6 unreal **7** dreamed **9** imaginary **10** fictitious

fanciful: odd **5** ideal, queer **6** dreamy, quaint, unreal **7** bizarre, strange **8** romantic **9** conceited, fantastic, grotesque, visionary, whimsical **10** capricious, chimerical, notionable **11** imaginative, unrealistic

fancy: fad **4** idea, love, maze, ween, whim **5** dream, freak, guess, humor **6** deluxe, ideate, liking, megrim, notion, ornate, vagary, vision, whimsy **7** caprice, chimera, conceit, elegant, fantasy, romance, suspect **8** conceive, illusion, phantasm, phantasy **9** capriccio **10** conception, conjecture, decorative, impression, ornamental **11** hanker after, imagination, inclination

fandango: 4 ball, tune **5** dance

fanfare: 4 pomp, show **5** salvo **7** display, panoply, tantara **8** flourish, ceremony

fanfaronade: 7 bluster **8** boasting, bragging **10** swaggering **11** ostentation

fanfoot: 5 gecko **6** lizard

fang: 4 earn, take, tusk, vang **5** begin, seize, snare, tooth **6** assume, obtain **7** capture, procure **9** undertake

fanion: 4 flag **6** guidon

fanlight: 7 transom

fanon: 4 cape **5** orale **7** maniple

fantast: 7 dreamer **9** visionary

fantastic: odd **5** queer, weird **6** absurd, quaint, unreal **7** bizarre **8** fanciful, freakish, romantic, singular **9** grotesque, whimsical **10** capricious, chimerical, ridiculous **11** extravagant, imaginative **12** unbelievable

fantasy: 4 idea, whim **5** dream, fancy **6** desire, vision **7** caprice, chimera, phantom, romance **8** illusion, phantasm **9** odd notion **10** apparition **11** imagination, inclination **13** hallucination

fantocinni: 5 shows **7** puppets

fantod: pet **4** fuss **7** anxiety

far: 4 long 6 remote 7 distant
across: 4 wide
down: 4 deep
far-out: 7 extreme, radical 8 advanced 10 avant-garde, unorthodox 11 in left field
far-reaching: 4 deep, vast 7 intense 8 profound
faraway: 6 dreamy, remote 7 distant, removed 9 oblivious 10 abstracted, stargazing
farce: 4 mime 5 stuff 6 comedy 7 mockery 8 drollery, pretense 9 forcemeat
farceur: wag 5 joker
farcical: 5 comic, droll 7 Atellan 9 ludicrous 10 ridiculous
fare: eat 4 diet, food, path, rate, wend 5 cheer, going, price, track, viand 6 happen, travel 7 journey, passage, proceed, prosper 8 progress 9 equipment, passenger, provision, sagaciate 10 expedition 11 nourishment 13 entertainment
farer: 8 traveler
farewell: ave(L.) 4 vale(L.) 5 adieu, adios, aloha, conge, final 7 goodbye, leaving, parting 9 bon voyage, departure 11 valedictory
farfetched: 6 forced 7 devious, dubious 8 doubtful, strained, unlikely 9 recherche 10 improbable, roundabout
farina: 4 meal 5 flour 6 starch
farinaceous food: oat, rye 4 meal 5 flour, grain, salep, spelt, wheat 6 barley, cereal 7 pudding 10 cornstarch
farm: 4 till 5 croft, ranch, range 6 grange, rancho, spread 7 hennery, potrero 8 estancia, hatchery, hacienda 9 cultivate, farmstead 10 plantation
building: 4 barn, crib, shed, silo
Israeli collective: 7 kibbutz
Russian collective: 7 kolkhoz
farm out: let 4 hire
farmer: 4 tate 6 grower, tiller, yeoman 7 granger, hayseed, planter, plowman, rancher 8 producer 9 hacendero(Sp.), ploughman 10 cultivator, husbandman 13 agriculturist
Egyptian: 6 fellah 8 fellahin(pl.)
migratory: 4 Okie
South African: 4 Boer
tenant: 6 cotter 7 cottier 12 sharecropper
farming: 9 husbandry
farnesol: 7 alcohol
faro: 5 monte
bet: 7 sleeper
card: 4 soda
card combination: 5 split 6 cathop
player: 6 punter
farouche: 4 wild 5 surly 6 fierce, savage 7 boorish 10 unsociable
farrago: 6 medley 7 mixture 10 hodgepodge
farrier: 5 shoer, smith 10 blacksmith,

horseshoer 12 veterinarian
farrow: 9 pig litter
farseeing: 10 telescopic
farsighted: 6 shrewd 9 hyperopia, provident, sagacious 13 hypermetropic
farther: 6 longer 7 remoter 10 in addition
farthest: 7 endmost, extreme, farmost, longest, outmost 8 remotest
farthing: 4 coin 8 quadrans
fascia: 4 band, sash 6 fillet 7 molding
fascicle: 6 bundle 7 cluster
fascinate: 5 charm 6 allure, enamor 7 attract, bewitch, enchant, engross 8 entrance, interest, intrigue 9 captivate, enrapture, spellbind
fascinating: 9 glamorous 10 attractive
fascination: 5 charm, spell 6 allure
Fascism: 6 Nazism 7 Falange 12 dictatorship
leaders of: 6 Franco, Hitler 9 Mussolini
fashion: fad, ton(F.) 4 form, make, mode, mold, rage 5 craze, forge, frame, guise, model, mould, shape, style, vogue 6 create, custom, design, fangle, invent, manner, method 7 compose, portray 8 contrive 9 construct, fabricate
fashionable: 4 chic 5 smart 6 modish, with it 7 a la mode, dashing, stylish 9 an courant
fashioned: 6 carved 7 wrought
fast: 4 diet, firm 5 agile, apace, bawdy, brisk, fixed, fleet, hasty, loose, quick, rapid, stuck, swift 6 lively, secure, speedy, stable, starve 7 abiding, settled 8 enduring, faithful, reckless 9 immovable, indelible, lecherous, steadfast, unfadable, velocious 10 abstinence, stationary, unyielding 11 expeditious
day of: 5 Ember
period of: 4 Lent
fasten: bar, fix, pen, pin, tag, tie 4 bend, bind, bolt, clip, gird, girt, glue, knit, lace, lash, link, lock, moor, nail, rope, seal, snib, soud, weld, wire 5 affix, annex, belay, brace, chain, clamp, clasp, cling, latch, paste, rivet, seize, strap, truss 6 anchor, attach, batten, cement, clinch, picket, secure, solder, staple, tether 7 connect, padlock 8 transfix
fastener: bar, big, nut, pin 4 agal, bolt, frog, hasp, lock, nail, snap 5 catch, clamp, clasp, latch, rivet, screw, strap, thong 6 buckle, button, hatpin, staple, zipper 7 latchet, padlock 8 staylace
fastidious: 4 fine, nice 5 chary, fussy, natty 6 choicy, choosy, dainty 7 choosey, elegant, finical, finicky, haughty, refined 8 critical, delicate, exacting, overnice, scornful 9 exquisite, squeamish 10 meticulous, particular
fastigate: 7 conical, pointed

fastness: 4 fort **6** castle **7** citadel, sanctum **8** fortress **10** stronghold

fastuous: 5 lofty **7** haughty **8** arrogant **11** pretentious **12** ostentatious

fat: oil, tub **4** lard, lipa, rich, suet **5** adeps, brosy, cetin, chuff, ester, fleck, gross, lipid, lipin, obese, plump, podgy, pudgy, pursy, squab, stout, thick **6** fleshy, grease, lipide, oleate, portly, pubble, stocky, tallow **7** adipose, blubber, fertile, fulsome, lanolin, opulent, pinguid, stearin **8** extended, fruitful, lanoline, stearate, stearine, unctuous **9** corpulent **10** profitable **11** flourishing
hard: **4** suet
liquid: **5** olein **6** oleine
wool: **7** lanolin **8** lanoline

fat farm: 9 health spa **10** diet resort

fat person: 4 lump **5** blimp, squab, tubby **8** roly-poly **12** humpty-dumpty

fata morgana: 6 mirage

fatal: fey **4** dire **6** deadly, doomed, lethal, mortal **7** ominous, ruinous **8** destined **9** condemned, prophetic **10** calamitous, disastrous, pernicious, portentous **11** destructive

fatality: 5 death **8** calamity, disaster

fatback: 8 menhaden, salt pork, sowbelly

fatbird: 8 guacharo

fate: end, lot **4** doom, ruin **5** event, karma **6** chance, kismet **7** destiny, fortune, outcome **8** downfall **14** predestination
goddess: Ker **4** Nona, Norn **5** Morta, Tyche **8** Adrastea **9** Adrasteia

fated: 6 doomed **7** decreed **8** destined **10** inevitable

fateful: 7 crucial **8** critical, decisive **9** momentous, prophetic **10** inevitable, portentous **11** destructive, predestined

Fates: *Greek:* **5** Moera, Moira **6** Clotho, Moerae **7** Atropos **8** Lachesis
Roman: **4** Nona **5** Decum, Morta, Parca **6** Parcae

fathead: oaf **4** boob, dolt **5** chump, dunce **6** dimwit **8** numskull

father: abu(Ar.), ama, dad, pop **4** abba, abou(Ar.), baba(Ar.), bapu, papa, pere(F.), sire **5** adopt, babbo, beget, daddy, friar, padre(Sp.), pater(L.), vader(Dan.) **6** author, create, old man, parent, priest **7** founder, tatinek (Czech.) **8** beaupere(F.), generate, inventor **9** confessor, originate, paternity, procreate **11** acknowledge
of English learning: **4** Bede
of geometry: **6** Euclid
of gods and men: **4** Zeus
of human race: **4** Adam
of plenty: **8** Abiathar
pert. to: **6** agnate **8** paternal
Father of Waters: 11 Mississippi

Father Time: *personified:* **6** old man
implements: **6** scythe **9** hourglass

fatherhood: 9 paternity

fatherly: 6 kindly **8** paternal **10** protective

fathom: 5 brace, delve, solve **7** measure **9** penetrate, ferret out **10** understand

fathomless: 7 abysmal **16** incomprehensible

fatidic: 9 prophetic

fatigue: fag **4** jade, tire **5** spend, weary **6** overdo, taigle(Sc.) **7** exhaust, wear out

fatigued: 4 beat **5** spent **7** drained **11** tuckered out

Fatima: *husband:* Ali **9** Bluebeard
descendant: **7** Fatimid **8** Fatimite
sister: **4** Anne
stepbrother: Ali

fatten: 4 lard **6** batten, enrich, thrive

fatty: 4 oily **5** suety **6** greasy **7** adipose **8** blubbery

fatuous: 5 inane, silly **6** stupid, unreal **7** foolish, idiotic, witless **8** demented, illusory, imbecile **9** frivolous, insensate

faucet: tap **4** cock **5** valve **6** spigot **7** hydrant

faugh: bah, fie, ugh

Faulkner: *character:* **4** Anse, Cash, Darl **5** Addie, Caddy, Jason, Jewel **6** Bayard, Dilsey, Popeye, Sutpen **7** Quentin **9** Dewey Dell
family: **7** Bundren, Compson **8** Sartoris
trilogy: **7** The Town **9** The Hamlet **10** The Mansion
work: **5** Pylon **6** A Fable **8** Sartoris **9** Sanctuary **11** As I Lay Dying **14** Absalom Absalom

fault: sin **4** debt, flaw, flub, lack, slip, vice **5** abuse, blame, culpa(L.), error, guilt, lapse, tache(Sc.) **6** defect, foible, vitium(L.) **7** blemish, blunder, default, demerit, failure, frailty, mistake, neglect, offense **10** peccadillo **11** culpability, delinquency, misdemeanor **12** imperfection **13** transgression
in mining: **4** hade

faultfinder: 5 momus **6** carper, critic **7** caption, knocker, nagster

faultless: 4 pure **5** right **7** correct, perfect, precise **8** flawless **9** blameless **10** impeccable **13** unimpeachable **14** irreproachable

faulty: bad, ill **5** amiss, unfit, wrong **9** incorrect **10** inaccurate

faun: 5 satyr
of Praxiteles: **6** marble

fauna and flora: 5 biota

Faunus: *grandfather:* **6** Saturn
son: **4** Acis

Faust: *author:* **6** Goethe
composer: **6** Gounod

faux pas: 4 bull, slip 5 boner, error, gaffe, lapse 6 boo-boo, bungle 7 blooper, misstep, mistake

faveolate: 9 alveolate 11 honeycombed

favonian: 4 mild 6 gentle

favor: aid, for, pro 4 boon, face, gree, help 5 bless, grace, leave, spare 6 esteem, letter, uphold 7 advance, feature, forward, support 8 advocacy, befriend, goodwill, kindness, resemble 9 party gift, patronage, privilege, subscribe 10 assistance, concession, indulgence, permission 11 accommodate, approbation, countenance 13 communication

pay: woo 5 court

favorable: 4 good, kind, rosy 5 clear 6 benign 7 benefic, optimal, popular 8 friendly, gracious, pleasing 9 approving, opportune 10 auspicious, charitable, convenient, propitious 12 advantageous

favored: 6 gifted 9 fortunate, preferred

favorite: pet 6 minion 7 darling, popular

favoritism: 4 bias 8 nepotism 9 prejudice

fawn: 4 buck, deer, jouk 5 color, cower, crawl, kotow, toady, whelp 6 cringe, grovel, kowtow, shrink 7 adulate, flatter, hangdog, servile, truckle 9 parasitic, sycophant 10 ingratiate

skin: 6 nebris

fay: elf 5 fairy, pixie 6 sprite

faze: 5 abash, daunt, worry 6 bother, rattle 7 confuse, nonplus, perplex 8 irritate 9 embarrass 10 disconcert

fealty: 6 homage 7 loyalty 8 fidelity 9 constancy, obeisance 10 allegiance

fear: awe 5 alarm, doubt, dread, panic 6 danger, dismay, fright, horror, phobia, terror 7 anxiety, suspect 8 affright, disquiet, distrust, venerate 9 agitation, reverence, revulsion 10 solicitude 12 apprehension 13 consternation

of animals: 9 zoophobia

of being alone: 10 monophobia

of burial alive: 11 taphephobia

of cats: 12 aelurophobia, ailurophobia

of crowds: 11 ochlophobia

of darkness: 11 nyctophobia

of dirt: 10 mysophobia

of drafts: 10 aerophobia

of enclosed places: 14 claustrophobia

of fire: 10 pyrophobia

of great heights: 10 acrophobia

of open spaces: 11 agoraphobia

of pain: 10 algophobia

of poisons: 10 toxiphobia

of strangers: 10 xenophobia

of thunder: 12 brontophobia 13 tonitrophobia

of water: 11 hydrophobia

fearful: 4 dire 5 awful, timid 6 afraid 7 ghastly, nervous, panicky, worried 8 cautious, doubtful, dreadful, grewsome, gruesome, horrible, horrific, shocking, terrible, timorous 9 appalling, frightful, trembling 10 formidable, horrendous, meticulous 11 distressing 12 apprehensive

fearless: 4 bold 5 brave 6 daring, heroic 8 intrepid 9 audacious, confident, dauntless, undaunted 10 courageous

feasible: 6 likely, viable 8 possible, probable, suitable 9 practical 10 reasonable

feast: eat, foy(Sc.), sup 4 dine, fete, luau, meal 5 festa, treat 6 regale, repast 7 banquet, delight, festino, gratify 8 festival, potlatch 10 burrakhana

January 6: 8 Epiphany

of lanterns: Bon

of lights: 7 Hanukka 8 Chanukah, Hanukkah

of lots: 5 Purim

of nativity: 9 Christmas

of tabernacles: 7 Succoth

of weeks: 8 Shabuoth

passover: 5 seder

feasting: 9 epulation

companion: 7 convive

feat: act 4 deed, gest 5 geste, stunt, trick 7 exploit miracle, venture 11 achievement, performance, tour de force 14 accomplishment

feather: 4 deck, down, vane 5 adorn, penna, pinna(L.), pluma(L.), plume, quill 6 clothe, fledge, fletch, hackle, pinion

barb: 4 harl, herl 7 pinnula

down: 4 dowl 5 dowle 7 plumule

mature: 10 teleoptile

quill: 5 remex 7 calamus

shaft: 5 scape

shank: 4 boot

shoulder: 4 cape

feather key: 6 spline

feather star: 8 comatula 9 comatulae(pl.), comatulid

featherbrained: 5 giddy, silly 7 flighty, foolish 9 frivolous 11 empty-headed

feathered: 7 pennate, pinnate

feathers: 5 dress 6 attire 7 plumage

shed: 4 molt 5 moult

featherweight: 5 dunce, light 7 trivial 10 of no matter

feathery: 4 soft 5 light 6 fluffy

featly: 6 neatly, nimbly 8 properly

feature: 4 face 5 favor, motif, token, trait 6 aspect, detail, play up, stress 7 amenity, element, outline 8 salience 9 attribute, character, emphasize, lineament 11 countenance 14 characteristic

natural: 9 geography

febris: 5 fever

feckless: 4 weak 8 careless 9 shiftless, worthless 10 unreliable 11 ineffective, thoughtless **13** irresponsible

fecund: 7 fertile **8** fruitful, prolific

fecundate: 9 fertilize, pollinate **10** impregnate

fed up: 5 bored **7** wearied **8** satiated **9** disgusted, surfeited

federation: 5 union **6** league **8** alliance **9** coalition **11** association, confederacy

fedora: hat

fee: 4 dues, cost, feal, feul(Sc.), fier, hire, rate, wage **5** price **6** charge, reward, salary **7** expense, payment, stipend, tribute, tuition **8** gratuity, malikana, retainer **9** allowance, bienvenne, emolument, pourboire **10** assessment, honorarium, perquisite, recompense **12** compensation

bridge: **4** toll

money-changing: **4** agio

trucking: **7** cartage

wharf: **7** quayage

feeble: 4 lame, mean, poor, puny, weak **5** faint **6** flabby, flimsy, infirm, scanty, sickly **7** fragile, invalid, languid **8** decrepit, impotent, inferior, thewless(Sc.), yielding **9** miserable **10** inadequate, indistinct **11** debilitated

feebleminded: 5 anile, dotty **7** moronic **10** irresolute **11** vacillating

feed: 4 eat, hay **4** bait, bran, fill, grub, meal, oats, sate **5** grass, graze, nurse **6** fodder, foster, repast, suckle, supply **7** blowout, furnish, gratify, herbage, indulge, nourish, nurture, satiate, satisfy, sustain **9** replenish

the kitty: **4** ante

to excess: **4** glut **5** gorge, stuff **7** surfeit **8** overfill **9** crapulate

feeder: 6 branch **9** tributary

fire: **6** stoker

feel: paw **4** deem **5** grope, probe, sense, touch **6** finger, fumble, handle **7** believe, examine, explore, texture **8** perceive **9** be moved by **10** appreciate, experience

feeler: 4 palp **6** palpus **7** antenna, smeller **8** proposal, tentacle **12** trial balloon

feeling: 4 pity, tact, view **5** humor, touch **6** morale **7** emotion, opinion, passion **8** attitude **9** affection, sensation, sentiment **10** atmosphere, experience, perception **11** sensibility **13** consciousness **14** susceptibility

capable of: **8** sentient

evocative of: **7** emotive

lack of: **6** apathy **8** numbness **9** unconcern **10** anesthesia **13** insensibility

feet (see also **foot**): **4** dogs

feign: act **4** fake, seem, sham **5** avoid, fable, shape, shirk **6** affect, assume, invent **7** conceal, fashion, imagine, pretend, romance **8** disguise, simulate **9** dissemble, personate **11** counterfeit, dissimulate, make-believe

ignorance: **7** connive

sickness: **8** malinger

feigned: 5 false, put on **6** pseudo **9** insincere **10** artificial, fictitious

feint: 4 hoax, ploy, ruse, wile **5** bluff, dodge, shift, trick **6** gambit **8** pretense **9** diversion

in fencing: **5** appel

feis: 8 assembly, festival **10** convention

feisty: 6 lively **8** snappish, spirited **9** energetic **10** aggressive **11** belligerent, quarrelsome

feldspar: 6 albite, gneiss **7** odinite, syenite **9** anorthite **11** labradorite

yield: **6** kaolin

felicitate: 6 salute **12** congratulate

felicitous: apt **5** happy **6** joyous **7** apropos, fitting **8** pleasing **11** appropriate

felicity: joy **9** happiness, well-being

felid: cat

feline: cat, sly, tom **4** lion, lynx, pard, puma **5** civet, tiger **6** jaguar **7** cheetah, leonine, leopard, sinuous, wildcat **8** stealthy **9** grimalkin **11** treacherous

breathing: **4** purr

fell: cut, fen, hew **4** down, hide, hill, moor, pelt, ruin, skin, very **5** cruel, eager, field, great, sharp **6** deadly, fierce, fleece, intent, mighty, savage, shrewd **7** brutish, crashed, doughty, hideous, inhuman, tumbled **8** mountain, spirited **9** barbarous, ferocious, marshland, momentous, prostrate **11** destructive

fellah: 7 peasant

fellow (see also **man, person**): guy, lad, man **4** bean, beau, bozo, chap, cove, dick, duck, hind, mate, peer **5** billy, bloke, match **6** bugger, codger, hombre(Sp.), person, sirrah **7** chappie, comrade, partner **8** neighbor **9** associate, companion **10** sweetheart **12** contemporary

awkward: oaf **4** lout **5** booby, clown **6** galoot **7** bumpkin **11** hobble-de-hoy

brutish: **5** yahoo

conceited: **7** egotist **8** braggart **9** know-it-all

craven: **6** coward

dissolute: **4** rake, roue **9** debaucher

dull: **4** drip, fogy **5** fogey

fat: **7** glutton

fine: **5** brick, bully **8** bonhomme(F.)

funny: wag, wit **4** card **5** clown

honest: **6** trusty

lazy: bum **6** loafer **9** drawlatch

little: bub **5** caddy **6** birkie, caddie, shaver **9** dandiprat

mean: cad **4** boor **5** bucko, churl **8** blighter

old: **6** geezer, gleyde

old-fashioned: **4** fogy
queer old: **6** geezer **10** curmudgeon
ragged: **10** ragamuffin **14** tatterdemalion
reckless: **4** buck **5** blade **9** daredevil, hell-raker
rowdy: **6** roarer **8** larrikin
shrewd: **6** gazabo, gazebo
silly: **8** dotterel
stupid: ass **4** clod, dolt, simp **5** dunce, moron **9** blockhead
tricky: **5** knave, scamp **6** rascal
vain: fop
worthless: bum, cur **5** rogue, scamp **7** brothel **9** schlemiel(Yid.), scoundrel
fellowship: **5** guild, union **7** company **8** alliance **9** communion **10** fraternity, membership **11** association, brotherhood, camaraderie, comradeship, corporation, familiarity, intercourse, partnership **12** friendliness **13** companionship
felly: **7** cruelly **8** savagely **11** barbarously **13** destructively
felo-de-se: **7** suicide
felon: **4** base **5** cruel **6** wicked **7** convict, culprit, whitlow **8** criminal, offender **10** lawbreaker, malefactor
felony: **5** crime **7** offense
felt: hat **6** fabric, sensed
felwort: **7** gentian
female: **4** girl **5** woman **7** womanly **8** feminine, ladylike, womanish **9** womanlike **10** effeminate
animal: cow, dam, doe, ewe, hen, sow **4** mare, slut **5** bitch, filly, jenny, tabby **6** heifer **7** lioness, tigress
assistant: **8** adjutrix **9** adjutrice
camel: **4** naga
figure: **5** orant **8** caryatid
fish: **4** raun
fox: **5** vixen
monster: **6** gorgon
principle: **5** Sakti
red deer: **4** hind
sandpiper: **5** reeve
sheep: ewe
slave: **7** odalisk **9** odalisque
spirit: **7** banshee
warrior: **6** Amazon
feminine: **4** soft, weak **6** female, tender **8** womanish **10** effeminate
femme fatale: **5** siren **7** Lorelei **9** temptress **10** seductress
femoral: **6** crural
femur: **9** thighbone
fen: bog **4** carr, fowl, moor **5** marsh, snipe, swamp **6** morass **8** quagmire
fence: bar **4** coop, duel, gird, rail, wall **5** dodge, guard, hedge, parry, pen in **6** paling, picket, rasper **7** barrier, bulwark, defense **8** encircle, palisade, surround **9** enclosure **12** circumscribe, dealer in loot **14** buy stolen goods

fish: net **4** weir
interwoven: **6** raddle
mending: **11** politicking
on the: **9** undecided **11** uncommitted
picket: **6** paling
sunken: **4** ha-ha
fencer: **7** duelist, parrier **9** gladiator, swordsman
cry of: **6** touche **7** en garde
fencing: **9** swordplay
attack: **7** reprise
breastplate: **8** plastron
cry: **4** sasa
hit: **5** punto
maneuver: **5** appel
movement: **4** volt
position: **5** carte, prime, sixte, terce **6** octave, quarte, quinte, tierce **7** seconde, septime
position of hands: **9** pronation **10** supination
redoubling of attack: **7** reprise
term: **4** bind **5** lunge **6** thrust, touche
thrust: **7** riposte
weapon: **4** epee, foil **5** saber, sabre, sword **6** rapier
fend: **4** ward **5** avert, avoid, parry **6** defend, manage, resist **7** keep off, provide, support **8** push away **10** take care of
fender: **5** guard **6** buffer, bumper, shield **8** mudguard **11** splashboard
fenestra: **6** window **7** foramen, opening **8** aperture, fontanel
fennel: **4** herb **9** seasoning
relative: **7** parsley
fer-de-lance: **5** snake
feracious: **8** fruitful
feral, ferine: **4** wild **6** deadly, savage **7** bestial, untamed **8** unbroken **11** uncivilized **14** undomesticated
Ferdinand's wife: **8** Isabella
feria: **4** fair **6** fiesta **7** holiday
fermail: **5** clasp **6** buckle
ferment: **4** barm, heat, turn, work, zyme **5** fever, yeast **6** enzyme, seethe, tumult, uproar **7** agitate **8** disorder **10** ebullition, exacerbate, excitement, turbulence
fermenting mixtue: bub
fern: **4** tara, weki **5** brake **7** bracken, woodsia **8** polypody **10** maidenhair
climbing: **4** nito
edible: roi **4** tara
genus: **7** Onoclea, Osmunda **8** Psilotum
leaf: **5** frond
royal: **6** osmund
scale: **7** ramenta(pl.) **8** ramentum
fern-like: **7** pteroid
ferocious: **4** fell, grim, wild **5** cruel, feral **6** bloody, brutal, fierce, raging, savage **7** inhuman, ominous, violent **8** pitiless, ravenous, ruthless **9** barbarous, malignant, merciless, murderous, rapacious,

truculent **10** implacable, malevolent, relentless, sanguinary **11** remorseless **12** bloodthirsty

ferret: 4 tape **6** weasel **7** polecat
male: hob

ferret out: 4 hunt, seek **5** probe **6** elicit **7** uncover **9** search for

ferric oxide: 5 rouge **6** powder

ferrotype: 7 tintype

ferrule: 4 cap **4** ring, virl(Sc.) **6** collet, pulley, verrel **7** bushing, verrell

ferry: 4 pont, scow **7** traject

ferryman: 6 Charon

fertile: fat **4** rank, rich **5** gleby **6** fecund, hearty **7** teeming **8** abundant, fruitful, generous, prolific **9** exuberant, feracious, inventive, luxuriant, plenteous, plentiful **10** productive, profitable
render: **6** enrich

fertility god: 4 Frey **5** Freyr

fertilize: 6 batten, enrich **8** fructify **9** fecundate **10** impregnate, inseminate

fertilizer: 4 marl **5** guano, humus **6** alinit, manure, pollen, potash **7** compost, nitrate **8** nitrogen **11** phosphorous **14** superphosphate

ferule: rod **5** ruler **6** fennel **10** discipline

fervent: hot **4** keen, warm **5** eager, fiery **6** ardent, bitter, fierce, raging, savage **7** boiling, burning, glowing, intense **8** vehement **9** impetuous, religious **10** passionate **11** impassioned

fervor: 4 fire, heat, love, rage, zeal **5** ardor **7** ecstasy, feeling, passion **8** candency **9** eagerness, vehemence **10** enthusiasm, excitement **11** earnestness

fess: bar **4** band

fester: rot **4** grow **6** rankle **7** blister, inflame, pustule, putrefy, smolder **8** embitter, ulcerate

festival: bee **4** fair, fete, gala **5** feast, feria, festa, revel **6** fiesta **7** banquet, holiday **8** carnival, carousal, jamboree **11** celebration
church: **4** Lent **6** Easter **9** Christmas
epiphany: **7** uphelya

festive: gay **4** gala **5** merry **6** festal, genial, joyous **7** jocular, playful **8** mirthful, sportive **9** convivial **10** frolicsome **11** celebratory

festivity: 4 gala **5** mirth, randy, revel **6** gaiety, splore **7** jollity, jubilee, whoopee **8** function **10** joyfulness **11** celebration, merrymaking **12** conviviality **13** entertainment, glorification
god: **5** Comus **7** Bacchus **8** Dionysus

festoon: 4 loop, swag **6** wreath **7** garland **8** decorate

fetch: get **4** gasp, tack, take **5** bring, sweep, trick **6** double, elicit, obtain, wraith **7** achieve, attract, go after, realize, sell for **8** artifice, interest, retrieve **9** stratagem

round: **6** revive **8** convince, persuade

fetching: 4 cute **8** alluring, charming, pleasing **10** attractive **11** fascinating

fete: 4 fair, gala **5** bazar, feast **6** bazaar, fiesta, regale **7** banquet, holiday **8** ceremony, festival **9** entertain **11** celebration

fetid: 4 foul, olid, rank **5** fusty, musty **6** putrid, rancid, rotten, virose **7** miasmic, noisome, noxious **8** mephitic, stinking **9** offensive **10** malodorous

fetish, fetich: obi **4** idol, joss, juju, obia **5** charm, huaca, image, obeah, obiah, totem **6** amulet, grigri, voodoo **7** sorcery **8** fixation, greegree, idee fixe, talisman **10** mumbo jumbo

fetter: 4 band, bind, bond, gyve, iron **5** basil, chain, tie up **6** anklet, garter, hamper, hobble, hog-tie, hopple, impede **7** confine, enchain, manacle, shackle, trammel **8** handcuff, restrain **9** restraint

fettle: 4 mend, trim **5** dress, groom, order, shape **6** repair, strike **7** fitness, harness, spirits **9** condition

feud: 4 fief, fray **5** broil **6** affray, enmity, strife **7** contest, dispute, quarrel **8** conflict **9** hostility **10** contention
blood: **8** vendetta

feudal: 6 lordly **8** manorial, medieval **9** imperious **10** oligarchic
estate: **4** fief **5** feoff
jurisdiction: soc **4** soke
lord: **7** vavasor **8** suzerain, vavasour
penalty: **7** sursise
pert. to: **5** banal
tenant: **6** vassal **7** homager
tenure: **6** socage

fever: 4 fire **6** febris(L.) **7** ferment **9** calenture **10** excitement **11** temperature **13** conflagration
kind of: **4** ague **5** octan, swamp **6** dengue, sextan, sodoku **7** malaria, quartan, scarlet, spotted **8** undulant
without: **8** apyretic

feverish: 5 fiery **6** hectic **7** excited, febrile, flushed, frantic, parched **8** inflamed, restless **9** overeager **11** impassioned

few: 4 less, some, thin **5** scant **6** scarce, skimpy **7** limited, not many, several **8** exiguous

fewness: 7 paucity

fey: odd **5** queer **7** puckish **9** eccentric, visionary, whimsical **12** otherworldly

fez: hat **8** tarboosh

fiacre: 4 hack **5** coach **8** carriage

fiance: 8 intended **9** betrothed

fiasco: 4 bomb, flop **6** fizzle **7** debacle, failure, washout **8** disaster

fiat: 5 edict, order **6** decree **7** comand **8** decision, sanction **9** ordinance **12** announcement, proclamation

fib: lie **5** hedge, story **7** untruth **9** falsehood **10** equivocate **11** prevaricate

fiber, fibre: 4 root **5** grain **6** nature, thread, tissue **7** quality **9** character

band: **6** fillet

bark: **5** olona, terap

hat: **5** datil

kind of: nap, nep, tal, tow **4** adad, aloe, bast, buri, coir, eruc, feru, flax, hemp, ixle, jute, kyar, lint, marl, noil, pita, silk, sola, wool **5** abaca, civil, erizo, floss, istle, istli, ixtle, kapok, linen, mudar, oakum, ramee, ramie, sisal **6** amiray, cotton, manila, raffia, staple **7** castuli, haurizo, sabutan **8** filament, fibrilla, keratose **9** gamelotte **10** anodendron, escobadura

knot: nep

palm: **4** eruc **6** raffia **7** coquita, coquito

synthetic: **5** nylon, orlon, rayon **6** dacron **7** acetate, acrilan

yarn: **6** strand

fibril: 4 hair **8** filament

fibrin: 6 gluten

fibrous: 4 ropy, wiry **6** sinewy **7** stringy

fibula: 5 clasp **6** brooch, buckle **7** leg bone

fickle: 5 dizzy, giddy **6** shifty **7** erratic, flighty **8** unstable, unsteady, variable, volatile, wavering **9** faithless, frivolous, mercurial, unsettled **10** capricious, changeable, inconstant, irresolute **11** vacillating **12** inconsistent

fictile: 6 molded **7** plastic

fiction: 4 tale, yarn **5** fable, novel **6** deceit, device, fabula, legend **7** coinage, fantasy, figment, forgery, romance **9** falsehood, invention **10** concoction, pretending **11** contrivance, dissembling, fabrication **14** counterfeiting

fictitious: 4 fake, sham **5** bogus, dummy, false, phony **6** untrue **7** assumed, feigned **8** fabulous, fanciful, mythical, spurious **9** imaginary, imitative, pretended, trumped up **10** apocryphal, artificial, not genuine **11** counterfeit

fid: 9 splice pin **10** topmast bar

fiddle: bow **4** viol **5** cheat **6** doodle, fidget, putter, tinker, trifle, violin **7** swindle **10** fool around

fiddler: 4 crab **7** scraper **8** sixpence **9** violinist

fiddler crab: uca

fiddlesticks: 4 bosh **5** pshaw **8** nonsense

Fidelio: *composer:* **9** Beethoven

hero: **9** Florestan

heroine: **7** Leonora

fidelity: 5 troth, truth **6** fealty **7** honesty **8** adhesion, devotion, veracity **9** adherence, closeness, constancy **10** allegiance **12** faithfulness

symbol of: **5** topaz **7** diamond

fidgety: 5 fussy, jumpy **6** uneasy **7** jittery, nervous, restive, twitchy, unquiet **8**

restless **9** impatient, irritable

fiducial: 4 firm **7** trusted **8** reliable **9** confident **11** trustworthy **12** solid as a rock

fiduciary: 7 trustee

field: lea, lot **4** acre, area, mead **5** campo, croft, paddy, plain, range, realm, rowen, sawah **6** campus, domain, ground, meadow, sphere **7** compass, entries, paddock, pasture, terrain **8** clearing **9** grassland **10** department

athletic: **4** oval, ring, rink **5** arena, court, green **6** course, stadia(pl.) **7** diamond, stadium **8** gridiron

common share: **4** dale

extensive: **7** savanna **8** savannah

god: **4** Faun

goddess: **5** Fauna

hand: **4** hoer **5** sower **6** picker, plower **7** laborer

pert. to: **8** agrarian, agrestic **10** campestral

questions: **11** reply glibly

Roman: **4** ager

stubble: **5** rowen

field mouse: 4 vole

field of blood: 8 Aceldama

fieldwork: 5 redan **7** lunette **13** fortification

fiend: 5 beast, brute, demon, devil, Satan **6** addict, expert, maniac, wizard **7** fanatic, monster **8** succubus **10** evil spirit

fiendish: 5 cruel **6** wicked **7** demonic, inhuman, vicious **8** demoniac, devilish, diabolic, infernal **9** barbarous **10** diabolical

fierce: 4 bold, fell, grim, wild **5** cruel **6** ardent, gothic, raging, savage **7** brutish, fervent, furious, intense, violent **9** ferocious, impetuous, truculent **10** catawampus, forbidding, passionate **12** disagreeable, uncontrolled

fiery: hot, red **5** adust **6** ablaze, ardent, fervid, torrid **7** burning, fervent, flaming, furious, glowing, igneous, parched, peppery, violent **8** choleric, feverish, inflamed, spirited, vehement **9** excitable, hotheaded, impetuous, irascible, irritable **10** mettlesome, passionate **11** combustible, inflammable

fiesta: 4 fete **5** feria, party **7** holiday **8** festival **9** festivity

fife: 4 pipe **5** flute

fifty-fifty: 4 even **7** equally **11** half and half

fig: rig **5** array, dress, fruit, shape **6** trifle **7** furbish **9** condition, little bit **10** tinker's dam

basket: **5** cabas

crate: **5** seron

family tree: **8** mulberry

genus: **5** ficus

sacred: **5** pipal

Smyrna: **5** eleme, elemi
fig-shaped: 8 ficiform
Figaro: 6 barber
author: **12** Beaumarchais
character: **6** Rosina **7** Susanna **8** Almaviva **9** Dr. Bartolo **10** Don Basilio
opera composers: **6** Mozart **7** Rossini
fight: box, war **4** bout, duel, fray, grit, spat, tiff, tilt **5** argue, brawl, clash, melee, pluck, scrap, set-to **6** affair, affray, battle, bicker, combat, debate, fracas, mettle, oppose, resist, spirit, strife, tussle **7** contend, contest, dispute, quarrel, ruction, scuffle, wrangle **8** conflict, militate, skirmish, squabble, struggle **9** encounter, pugnacity **11** altercation **12** disagreement
against the gods: **9** theomachy
fighter: pug **4** vamp **5** boxer **6** cocker **7** battler, duelist, soldier, warrior **8** andabata, barrater, barrator, champion, pugilist, guerilla, scrapper **9** combatant, guerrilla
fighting: 7 warlike **8** militant **10** pugnacious **11** belligerent
street: **4** riot **5** brawl **10** free-for-all
fighting fish: 5 betta
figment: 7 fiction **9** invention **11** fabrication
figuration: 4 form **5** shape **7** outline **9** symbolism **10** appearance
figurative: 6 florid **7** flowery **8** symbolic **9** allegoric **10** not literal, rhetorical **12** metaphorical
use of words: **5** trope
figure: sum **4** body, cost, form, rate **5** add up, build, digit, guess, image, judge, motif, price, shape, total, value **6** amount, design, emblem, number, reckon, symbol **7** chiffer, compute, contour, notable, numeral, outline **8** likeness **9** calculate, character, personage, play a part, quotation **13** configuration
geometrical: **4** cone, cube, lune **5** prism, rhomb, solid **6** circle, gnomon, oblong, sector, square **7** ellipse, lozenge, rhombus **8** crescent, pentacle, triangle **9** rectangle
human form: **4** nude **5** dummy **6** statue **7** manikin, telamon **8** atlantes, caryatid
many-sided: **4** cube **6** isogon **7** decagon, hexagon, nonagon, octagon, polygon **8** pentagon, tetragon **10** hexahedron, octahedron
of speech: **5** trope **6** aporia, simile **7** imagery **8** metaphor, metonymy
ornamental: **7** topiary **8** gargoyle
praying: **5** orant
symbolic: **6** emblem
figure out: 4 dope **5** crack, solve **6** decode **7** clear up, resolve, unravel **10** unscramble **12** get the answer

figured: 7 adorned, faconne(Fr.) **8** computed **9** patterned
figurehead: 4 tool **5** dummy, front **6** puppet, stooge **7** stand-in
figurine: 7 tanagra **9** statuette
motion picture: **5** Oscar
Fiji: *capital:* **4** Suva
cities: **5** Nandi **7** Lambasa, Lautoka
ethnic: **10** Polynesian
islands: **4** Koro, Ngau **8** Tavenuni, Viti-Levu **9** VanuaLevu
monetary unit: **6** dollar
mountains: **6** Nararu **8** Monavatu
filament: 4 hair, harl, wire **5** fiber, fibre **6** mantle, strand, thread
lamp: **8** tungsten
filbert: 8 hazelnut
filch: bob, nim, rob **4** lift **5** pinch, steal, swipe **6** pilfer **7** purloin
file: row **4** line, rank, rasp, tool **5** index, label **6** folder, record, smooth **7** arrange, cabinet **8** apply for, register **9** grind down **10** procession
combmaker's: **6** carlet
document: **7** dossier
nail: **10** emery board
filet: net **4** lace
filial: 9 childlike **10** respectful
filibeg: 4 kilt **5** skirt
filibuster: 9 talkathon **14** political stall **15** talk against time
filigree: 4 mesh **7** network, tracery **8** fretwork, lacelike
filing: 5 lemel **8** limation
Filipino: See **Philippines**
fill: pad **4** cram, feed, glut, heap, load, pack, sate **5** earth, gorge **6** blow up, charge, occupy, supply **7** distend, enlarge, execute, fraught, inflate, perfect, perform, pervade, satiate, satisfy, suffuse **8** complete, compound, permeate **9** replenish **10** accomplish, embankment, take care of **11** sufficiency
cracks: **4** calk, plug, shim **5** caulk, putty
in: **5** brief, spell **6** inform **7** put wise **8** acquaint **10** substitute **13** bring up to date
with zeal: **7** enthuse
fille: 4 girl **8** daughter
filled: SRO **4** full **5** sated, solid **6** loaded **7** replete **9** saturated **10** carried out
fillet: 4 band, bone, orle, orlo, tape **5** crown, miter, snood, stria, strip, tiara **6** anadem, binder, diadem, ribbon, striae(pl.), turban, wreath **7** bandeau, chaplet, garland, molding **8** headband, tressure **9** sphendone
architectural: **6** cimbia, fascia, listel, quadra, reglet, regula, taenia **8** bandelet, cincture
filling: *dental:* **5** inlay
fabric: **4** weft, woof

fillip: tap **4** blow, flip, snap **5** boost, twist **6** buffet, charge, jazz up **8** stimulus **9** extra dash, stimulate

filly: tap **4** colt, foal, girl, mare **9** youngster

film (see also **motion picture**): **4** blur, brat(Sc.), haze, mist, scum, skin, veil **5** flake, layer **6** lamina, patina **7** coating **8** beeswing, negative, pellicle **10** photograph

filmy: **4** hazy **5** gauzy, misty, wispy **6** cloudy **7** clouded **8** gossamer **13** unsubstantial

filter: **4** sift **5** drain, sieve **6** purify, refine, screen, strain **8** strainer **9** percolate
sugar: **4** clay

filth: **4** dirt, dung, muck, slop, smut **5** offal **6** ordure, refuse, vermin **7** garbage, squalor **9** obscenity

filthy: low **4** foul, miry, vile **5** dirty, gross, nasty **6** impure, rotten, sordid **7** bestial, immoral, obscene, raunchy, squalid, unclean **8** indecent, sluttish **9** polluting, repulsive, revolting **10** disgusting, licentious **11** disgraceful

fimbriate: **7** fringed

fin: arm **4** hand **5** fiver, pinna **7** acantha, airfoil, flipper **10** stabilizer

fin-footed: **8** pinniped

finagle: **5** cheat, trick **6** wangle **7** connive, deceive **9** machinate

final: **4** last **6** latter **7** dernier, extreme, outmost **8** decisive, definite, eventual, farewell, ultimate **9** uttermost **10** concluding, conclusive, definitive **11** terminating **13** determinating

final outcome: **5** issue **6** payoff, upshot

finale: end **4** coda **5** close, finis **6** ending, windup **7** closing **8** swan song **9** cessation **10** conclusion **11** termination

finally: **8** at length, in the end **10** ultimately **11** irrevocably **12** in conclusion **13** once and for all

finance: tax **4** back **5** endow, stake **6** pay for **7** banking **8** bankroll **9** subsidize **10** underwrite

finances: **5** funds, money **8** accounts, supports **9** economics, exchequer

financial: **6** fiscal **8** monetary **9** pecuniary

finch: **4** fink, moro, pape **5** serin, terin **6** burion, citril, linnet, siskin, towhee **7** chewink, redpoll, senegal, tanager **8** amadavat **9** snowflake

find: get **5** catch **6** locate **8** discover
by keen search: **5** probe **6** ferret

find fault: nag **4** carp, crab, fret **5** cavil, scold **8** complain **9** bellyache, criticize

find guilty: **7** convict

find out: **4** hear **5** learn **6** detect **7** unearth **8** discover **9** ascertain, determine

fine: rum, tax **4** good, jake, levy, nice, pure, thin **5** bonny, brave, bully, clear, dandy, frail, nifty, noble, sharp, sheer, silky, swell **6** amerce, bonnie, bright, choice, finish, ornate, proper, slight, spiffy, subtle, tender **7** elegant, forfeit, fragile, penalty, perfect, precise, tenuous **8** absolute, all right, delicate, handsome, penalize, pleasant, skillful, splendid, superior, top-grade, very well **9** beautiful, excellent, ingenious, sensitive **10** assessment, consummate, fastidious, pulverized, punishment, surpassing
for misdemeanor: **5** mulct
record of: **7** estreat

finery: **6** frills **7** clothes, gaudery, gewgaws, regalia **8** frippery, glad rags **9** showiness, trappings **10** fancy dress, Sunday best

finesse: art **4** tact **5** guile, skill, taste **7** cunning **8** artifice, delicacy, subtlety **9** dexterity, stratagem **10** artfulness, bridge play, manipulate, refinement, shrewdness **11** sensitivity **12** one-upmanship

Fingal's cave: *island:* **6** Staffa
kingdom: **6** Morven

fingent: **7** pliable **8** flexible, yielding

finger: paw, tap, toy **4** feel **5** digit, index, pinky, thumb, touch **6** handle, pilfer, pinkie **7** purloin **8** identify, indicate, inform on, point out
bone: **7** phalanx
guard for: cot **5** stall **7** thimble
little: **7** minimus
inflammation of: **5** felon **7** whitlow
pert. to: **7** digital **8** digitate
snap with: **6** fillip

finger board: **4** fret

fingerlike: **6** dactyl

fingerling: **4** parr **8** troutlet

fingernail moon: **6** lunule

fingerprint: **11** dactylogram
mark: **4** arch, loop **5** whorl **9** composite
science: **12** dactyloscopy

Finger Lakes: **5** Keuka **6** Cayuga, Owasco, Seneca **11** Skaneateles

finial: **4** epi **5** crest **8** ornament, pinnacle

finical: **4** nice **5** fussy **6** choosy, dainty, dapper, jaunty, prissy, spruce **7** choosey, finicky, foppish, mincing **8** delicate **9** squeamish **10** fastidious, meticulous **11** overprecise **14** overscrupulous

finis: end **4** goal **5** close **10** conclusion

finish: die, end **4** char, mill **5** bound, cease, chare, cheve, close, enden(G.), glaze, limit **6** fulfil, windup **7** achieve, execute, fulfill, perfect, surface **8** complete, conclude, terminal **9** erudition, terminate **10** accomplish, completion, conclusion, consummate, perfection
dull: mat **5** matte
glossy: **6** enamel

finished: did, oer, pau **4** done, fine, gone, over, ripe **5** ended, kaput **6** closed, ornate **7** refined, stopped **8** climaxed, lustered, polished **9** completed, concluded, perfected, performed **10** terminated **11** consummated **12** professional

finisher: **4** eyer **5** ender **7** beetler **8** enameler

finishing line: **4** tape

finite: **7** limited **9** definable **10** restricted, terminable **11** conditioned

fink: **8** informer, squealer **13** strikebreaker

Finland: **5** Suomi
  bathhouse: **5** sauna
  capital: **8** Helsinki
  city: **4** OuLu **5** Espoo, Lahti, Turku **7** Tampere
  composer: **8** Sibelius
  dialect: **5** Karel
  division: **5** Ijore **9** Villipuri
  forest god: **5** Tapio
  fortress: **11** Suomenlinna
  god: **6** Jumala
  harp: **7** kantele
  island: **5** Aland, Karlo **6** Kimito **9** Vallgrund
  isthmus: **7** Karelia
  lake: **5** Enare **6** Saimaa **7** Keitele **8** Piefinen **9** Oulujarvi
  language: **4** Avar, Lapp **5** Ugric **6** Magyar, Ostyak, Tarast **7** Samoyed **8** Estonian
  measure: **5** kannu, tunna, verst **6** fathom, sjomil **7** tunland **8** ottinger, skalpund, tunnland
  monetary unit: **5** peññi **6** markka
  mountain: **13** Haltiatunturi
  parliament: **9** Eduskunta
  pert. to: **6** Suomic **7** Suomish
  rivers: **4** Kemi, Oulu
  town: **5** Enare
  tribe: **4** Veps, Wote **5** Vepse **6** Ugrian

Finlandia composer: **8** Sibelius

Finnegan's Wake author: **5** Joyce

fiord, fjord: ise **5** inlet

fir: **9** evergreen
  genus: **5** abies

Firbolg queen: **6** Tailte **7** Talitiu

fire: can, feu(F.) **4** bale, burn, heat, zeal **5** ardor, arson, fever, gleed, light, shoot, stoke **6** arouse, excite, fervor, ignite, incite, kindle, spirit **7** animate, burning, dismiss, explode, fervour, glimmer, inflame, inspire **8** detonate, illumine, irritate, vivacity **9** calenture, cauterize, discharge, holocaust, terminate **10** combustion, enthusiasm, illuminate **12** inflammation **13** conflagration
  artillery: **7** barrage
  basket: **5** grate **7** cresset
  containing: **7** igneous

  fighter: **4** vamp
  god: **4** Agni, Loki **6** Vulcan **10** Hephaestus
  military: **4** flak **5** salvo **6** rafale **7** barrage
  particle: arc **5** spark
  pert. to: **7** igneous
  sacrificial: **4** agni
  set: **6** accend, ignite, kindle **7** inflame **8** enkindle, irritate
  worshiper: **5** Parsi **6** Parsee **9** pyrolater **10** ignicolist

firearm: gun **5** piece, rifle **6** musket, pistol **7** demihag **8** revolver

fireback: **7** reredos **8** pheasant

fireboat: **8** palander

firebrand: **5** blaze **6** bleery

firebug: **10** incendiary, pyromaniac

firecracker: **5** squib **6** petard **7** cracker, snapper **9** skyrocket

firedamp: gas **7** methane

firedog: **7** andiron

fireman: **4** vamp **6** stoker, tizeur **9** fireeater

fireplace: **5** focus, fogon, forge, foyer, ingle **6** heath **8** cheminee
  part: hob **6** mantel **9** ingleside **11** hearthstone

fireplug: **7** hydrant

firer: **6** stoker **10** incendiary

fireside: **9** ingleside **11** hearthstone

firestone: **5** flint

firewood: **4** lena **5** fagot **6** billet, billot

fireworks: **4** gerb **5** gerbe **7** fizgigs, rockets **9** sparklers **10** girandoles **11** tourbillion **12** pyrotechnics
  resembling: **11** pyrotechnic

firing: **4** fuel

firm: hui **4** buff, fast, hard, sure, trig **5** champ, dense, exact, firma, fixed, hardy, house, loyal, rigid, solid, sound, stith, stout, tight **6** hearty, secure, settle, sinewy, stable, stanch, steady, stolid, strong **7** adamant, certain, compact, company, confirm, context, decided, durable, staunch, unmoved **8** constant, faithful, fiducial, obdurate, resolute, unshaken **9** backboned, establish, immovable, immutable, standfast, steadfast **10** consistent, determined, unslipping, unwavering, unyielding **11** established, partnership, substantial, substantive, well-founded **13** establishment

firmament: sky **7** heavens **8** empyrean

firmly fixed: **6** rooted, stable

firmness: **4** iron **7** courage, resolve **8** solidity, strength, tenacity **9** constancy, stability **10** immobility, steadiness **11** consistency **13** determination **15** indissolubility

firn: ice **4** neve, snow

first: **4** erst, head, high, main **5** alpha, chief, forme, nieve, prime **6** primal, pri-

mus **7** highest, initial, leading, primary **8** earliest, foremost, original **9** primitive, principal **10** aboriginal, primordial
appearance: **5** debut **8** premiere
firstborn: 4 heir **5** eigne **6** eldest
first class: 5 prime **9** excellent, topdrawer **10** first-cabin
first-rate: 4 A-one, good, jake **5** prime **6** tiptop **7** skookum **8** clipping, top-notch **9** admirable, excellent
firth: 4 kyle **5** frith, inlet **7** coppice, estuary
Firth of Clyde island: 4 Bute
fiscal: 8 monetary **9** financial
fiscus: 8 treasury
fish: net **4** cast, quab **5** angle, drail, seine, troll **7** poisson(F.)
Alaska: **6** iconnu
ascending river from sea: **7** anadrom
Atlantic Coast: **4** opah, pogy **6** bunker, salema **7** alewife, bugfish, bughead, fatback, oldwife **8** bonyfish, menhaden **9** greentail **10** mossbunker
Australian: **4** mado **6** groper **7** grouper
bait: **5** killy **9** killifish
barbed tail: **8** stingray **9** stingaree
California: **4** rena **5** reina **6** rasher **8** bocaccio **9** garibaldi
carangold: **4** scad **5** jurel
carp: id; ide, orf
catfish: **6** hassar **9** sheatfish
caviar-yielding: **7** sterlet **8** sturgeon
cod: bib **4** cusk, hake, ling **5** torsk **6** gadoid **7** bacalao, beardie
colorful: **4** opah
cyprinoid: id; ide **4** dace
devil: ray **5** manta
eel-like: **4** link, opah **6** conger, cuchia **7** eelpout, lamprey
electric: **4** raad **7** torpedo
elongated: eel, gar **6** saurel
European: id; ide, rud **4** boce, dace, rudd, spet **5** alose, bleak, bream, sprat **6** angler, barbel, braice, meagre, plaice **7** gudgeon, lavaret, picarel
female: **4** raun **7** henfish
flat: dab, ray **4** butt, dace, sole **5** bream, fluke, skate **6** plaice, turbot **7** halibut, sanddab, sunfish, torpedo **8** flounder
Florida: **5** crunt **6** atinga, salema **7** burfish, tomtate **8** burrfish
food: cod, eel, gar, iki, sey **4** bass, boga, carp, haik, hake, scup, shad, sole, stew, tile, tuna **5** bolti, cisco, hilsa, jurel, siera, skate, smelt, trout **6** baleen, groupa, hilsah, mullet, pompon, salema, salmon, tautog, wahoon, weever, wrasse **7** alewife, escolar, garlopa, halibut, herring, pompano, pompoon, sardine, snapper **8** mackerel, sea trout **9** barracuda **10** barracouta
freshwater: id; gar, ide, orf **4** bass, carp,

chub, dace, orfe, pike, rudd **5** bream, loach, roach, tench **6** darter, redeye, sucker **7** crappie, mooneye
game: **4** bass, cero, pike, tuna **5** perch, trout **6** grilse, marlin, salmon, tarpon **8** grayling **9** swordfish
grunt: **5** ronco **10** bluestripe
Hawaiian: aku **4** ulua **5** akule, lania
herring: **4** shad, brit **5** sprat, sprot **7** alewife **8** pilchard
Japanese: tai, ayu
kind of: cat, cod, dab, eel, gar, ide, orf **4** bass, carp, chub, dace, dorn, hake, hiku, jocu, lant, lija, ling, mado, masu, meat, mero, mola, opah, orfe, pega, peto, pike, pogy, pout, rena, roud, rudd, ruff, scad, scup, shad, sier, skil, sole, spot, spet, tope, ulua **5** bream, lance, midge, otter, perch, pogie, porgy, prane, roach, ruffe, scrod, seine, skate, smelt, trout, umbra, wahoo **6** barbel, caribe, launce, mullet, porgie, sauger, saurel, shiner, timcod, turbot, wrasse **7** alewife, grunion, haddock, machete, pegador, pintado, piranha, poisson **8** gourhead, hardhead, pilchard, sturgeon **9** teleostei **10** candlefish
large: **4** cusk, opah **5** chiro, sargo, shark **6** bichir, tarpon **7** escolar, gourami, sennett **8** arapaima, sturgeon **10** blanquillo, maskalonge, maskinonge **11** muskellunge
little: see *small* below
long: eel, gar **7** lamprey
mackerel-like: **4** cero **5** tunny **6** coelho **7** escolar, pintado
Mediterranean: **5** porgy, sargo **6** chivey **9** menominee
nest-building: **5** acara **11** stickleback
New England: **4** hake
New Zealand: ihi **5** hikus
newly hatched: fry
Nile: **4** erse **5** saide
olive green: **7** lutfisk **8** ludefisk
one-horned: **9** monoceros
parasitic: **6** remora
pert. to: **7** piscine **8** ichthyic **9** piscatory
pike: gar **4** lude
pilot: **6** romero
raw: **7** sashimi
ray-like: **5** skate
river: **8** arapaima **10** barramunda
rock: **4** rena **5** reina **8** buccacio
scaleless: **9** alepidote
serpentine: eel
shark-eating: som **4** pega **7** catfish
shell: **7** abalone
small: fry, ide, ihi **4** brit, dace, goby, spet **5** saury, sprat **6** blenny, cunner, limpet, minnow, riggle, sennet, shiner **7** sardine **8** halfbeak, seahorse, spearing
small bait: **5** killy **9** killfish

South American: 4 gogy, mapo 5 acara 6 acoupa, aimara, almara, caribe
sparoid: tai 5 porgy, sargo
spear-snouted: gar
star: 7 asteria
sucking: 6 remora
teleost: eel 6 iniomi
toad: 4 sapo 6 slimer
toothed: 7 piranha
total haul: 4 mess 5 catch
tree-climbing: 6 anabas
tropical: 8 coachman
tunny: 4 tuna
voracious: 4 pike 5 shark 6 caribe 9 barracuda
West Indies: 4 Boga, cero, sier 5 chopa 6 Blanco 7 guapena 12 walleyed pike
young: fry 4 parr 6 alevin
fish basket: pot 4 caul 5 creel, slath
fish gig: 5 spear
fish handler: 4 icer
fish hawk: 6 osprey
fish hide: 7 eelskin
fish limb: fin
fish peddler: 6 ripier, ripper 7 rippier
fish pole: pew
fish preserve: 6 warren
fish relish: 7 botargo
fish roe: 6 caviar 7 caviare
fish sauce: 4 alec 5 garum
fish spear: gig 7 trident
fish trap: 4 coop, fyke, weel, weir 5 willy 6 eelpot
fisher: 5 eeler, pecan 6 seiner, wejack 7 trawler, troller
fisherman: 5 eeler 6 angler, seiner 7 prawner, trawler 8 peterman, piscator 9 harpooner 11 Izaak Walton
fishery: 7 piscary 9 piscation
fishhook: gig 5 angle, Kirby 6 Sproat 7 Kendall 8 Aberdeen, barbless, Carlisle, limerick
feathered: fly 5 sedge 6 hackle
fishing duck: 9 merganser
fishing gear: lam, rod, tew 4 cork, flew, flue, gaff, gimp, hook, line, reel, trot 5 cadar, cader, float, sedge, seine, snell, shood 8 trotline
fishing ground: 4 haaf
fishing vessel: 5 smack 6 seiner 7 trawler
fishlike: 8 ichthyic
fishline: 5 snell 7 boulter
fishmonger: 8 pessoner
fishnet: 4 bunt 5 seine, trawl 6 sagene
fishnet line: 5 meter
fishnet mender: 8 beatster
fishpond: 7 piscina
fishwife: 9 buttwoman
fishy: 4 dull 6 vacant 10 improbable, lusterless, suspicious, unreliable 11 extravagant

fissile rock: 5 shale
fission: 8 breaking, cleavage, cleaving 9 splitting 12 reproduction
fissure: gap 4 chap, cone, flaw, gool, leak, lode, rent, rift, rima, rime, seam, vein, vent 5 break, chasm, chine, chink, cleft, crack 6 cleave, cranny, divide, lesion 7 blemish, crevice, opening 8 aperture, cleavage, coloboma, crevasse, quebrada
fissured: 6 rimate 7 fissate, rimosed
fist: job 4 nave 5 grasp, nieve 6 clench, clutch, daddle, effort, strike 7 attempt 8 puffball, tightwad 11 handwriting
fistic: 10 pugilistic
fisticuffs: 4 ring 6 boxing 8 pugilism 13 prizefighting
fistula: 4 pipe, reed, tube 5 sinus 6 cavity
fit: apt, fay, gee, pan, rig 4 able, ague, good, hard, meet, ripe, suit, well, whim 5 adapt, adept, besit, chink, fancy, ictus, ready, right, spasm 6 adjust, attack, become, behove, besort, go with, habile, heppen, proper, seemly, stroke, strong, suited 7 adapted, behoove, capable, condign, conform, correct, healthy, prepare, qualify, tantrum 8 adequate, apoplexy, becoming, dovetail, eligible, glooming, idoneous(L.), outbreak, paroxysm, passable, suitable, syncopes 9 befitting, competent, congruous, convenable, opportune, pertinent, qualified 10 applicable, commodious, correspond, convenient, go together 11 accommodate, appropriate
out: 6 outfit 7 habille, prepare 9 equipment
together: fay 4 mesh, nest 5 panel 8 dovetail
fitful: 4 gery 7 cursory, flighty 8 restless, unstable, variable 9 impulsive, irregular, spasmodic, uncertain 10 capricious, convulsive 12 intermittent
fitly: pat 4 duly 6 gladly, meetly 7 happily 8 properly, suitably
fitness: 7 aptness, decency, decorum, dignity 8 aptitude, capacity, justness 9 rectitude 10 competence 11 suitability
fitout: 6 outfit 9 equipment
fitted: apt 4 able 6 suited 7 adapted 8 adjusted 9 qualified 10 convenient
for digging: 7 fodient, laniary
fitting: apt, due, pat 4 meet 5 happy 6 become, proper, seemly 8 decorous, graceful, suitable 9 befitting 10 adjustment, answerable, habiliment 11 appropriate
five: 4 cinq(F.), funf(G.) 6 cinque(It.) 7 epsilon(Gr.), quinque(L.)
group of: 6 pentad
five-dollar bill: "V"; fin, vee
five-finger: 4 fish 5 oxlip, plant 10 cinquefoil

Five Nations: 7 Cayugas, Mohawks, Oneidas, Senecas 9 Onondagas
founder: 8 Hiawatha
five-year period: 6 pentad 7 lustrum
fivefold: 9 quintuple
fix: peg, pin, set 4 glue, mend, moor, nail, seal 5 affix, allot, found, imbed, limit, tryst 6 adjust, anchor, arrest, assign, assize, attach, buy off, cement, clinch, define, fasten, ficche, freeze, make up, repair, revamp, settle, temper 7 appoint, arrange, confirm, delimit, dilemma, impress, imprint, prepare, station 8 renovate, transfix 9 determine, establish, stabilize 10 constitute 11 predicament, recondition, reconstruct 13 embarrassment
firmly: set 4 moor 5 brace, grave, imbed, stamp 6 anchor, cement, enroot 7 engraff
fixed: pat, set 4 fast, firm 5 siker, staid 6 frozen, intent, mended, sicker, stable 7 certain, dormant, settled, statary 8 arranged, attached, constant, definite, explicit, fastened, immobile, moveless, resolute, stubborn 9 immovable, indelible, inerratic, permanent 10 stationary 12 determinable, refrigerated
amount: 4 rate 6 ration 7 stipend 10 remittance
star: 4 Vega
fixer: 8 handyman
fixture: 5 annex 7 bracket, shelves 8 counters, shelving 10 furnishing
fizgig: 9 fireworks, whirligig
fizzle: 4 fuss 6 barney 7 failure, flivver, hissing 9 agitation
flabby: lax 4 fozy, lash, limp, weak 5 frush 6 feeble 7 flaccid
flabellate: 9 fan-shaped
flaccid: 4 limp 6 flabby, flaggy 8 yielding
flack: 4 blow, flap 5 throb 6 stroke 7 flutter
flag: fag, sag, sod 4 fail, fane, pine, tire, turf, waif, wilt 5 droop, woman 6 banner, colors, ensign, flower, pennon, signal 7 ancient, cattail, decline, drapeau, pennant 8 banderol, brattach, languish, standard, streamer, vexillum 9 banderole, flagstone, fourpence
kind of: 5 Roger 6 burgee, colors, danger, ensign, fanion, guidon, muleta 7 calamus, curtain, pennant 8 banderol, brattach, masthead, standard, streamer, vexillum 9 banderole, blackjack 10 Jolly Roger
flagellants: 4 albi
flagellate: 4 beat, flog, lash, whip 5 throw 6 thrash 7 flutter, scourge
flagellum: 4 whip 5 shoot 6 runner 7 scourge
flageolet: 4 pipe 6 zufolo 7 basaree, zuffolo

Hindu: 7 basaree
flagging: 4 weak 7 languid 10 spiritless
flagitious: 6 rotten, sinful, wicked 7 corrupt, heinous 8 criminal, flagrant, grievous 10 scandalous, villainous
flagon: cup, mug 5 stoup 6 bottle, vessel 7 flacket
flagrant: bad 4 rank 5 gross 6 odious, wanton, wicked 7 glaring, hateful, heinous, scarlet, violent 8 shameful 9 abandoned, atrocious, egregious, monstrous, nefarious, notorious 10 flagitious, outrageous, profligate, villainous
flagstone: 5 shale, slate
flagstone layer: 5 paver
flail: 4 beat, flog, whip 6 thrash, thresh
part: 7 swingle
flair: ray 4 bent, odor 5 skate, smell, taste 6 talent 7 leaning 8 aptitude 11 discernment
flak: 9 criticism 10 opposition
flake: nut 4 chip, film, flaw, rack, snow 5 fleck, flock, scale, strip 6 hurdle, lamina, paling 7 flaught 8 fragment 9 screwball
flaky: 5 scaly 7 laminar 8 laminose
flam: 4 whim 5 cheat, false, freak, trick 6 cajole, humbug, untrue 7 deceive, pretext, rubbish 8 drumbeat, illusory, nonsense, pretense 9 deception, deceptive, falsehood
flambeau: 5 torch 6 kettle 11 candlestick
flamboyant: 5 showy, swank 6 florid, ornate 7 flaming 9 flamelike 10 extravagant 11 resplendent
flame: 4 beau, fire, glow 5 ardor, blaze, flare, flash, glare, gleed, light 7 burning 9 affection 10 brightness, brilliance, sweetheart
fire without: 4 punk
movement: 4 dart, lick
flaming: 5 afire, fiery, vivid 6 ardent, flambe 7 blazing, burning, flaring 9 brilliant, consuming, flamelike 10 flamboyant, passionate 12 illuminating
Flanders capital: 5 Ghent
flanerie: 6 stroll 7 loafing 8 idleness 9 aimlessly, strolling 10 pillowcase
flaneur: 6 loafer 7 trifler
flank: 4 leer, side 5 thigh 6 border
flannel: 4 lana 6 stamin
flap: rob, tab, tag, wap 4 clap, flip, fuss, loma, slam, slap, waff 5 alarm, flack, flaff, flipe, lapel, skirt 6 bangle, faffle, lappet, strike, tongue 7 aileron, blinder, flounce, flutter, swindle 8 hang down 9 appendage, operculum 10 epiglottis
furnished with: 5 lobed
flapper: 7 snicket 9 backfisch 10 backfische
flare: 4 bell, flue 5 blaze, flame, flash, fleck, fusee, light, torch 6 signal, spread

7 flicker 8 outburst 10 illuminate 11 ostentation

flaring: 4 bell, flue 5 evase(F.), gaudy 7 flaming, glaring 8 dazzling

flash: 4 pool, rush 5 blash, blaze, burst, flare, flame, fluff, glaik, gleam, glent, glint, marsh, spark 6 bottle, fillip, glance 7 fouldre, glimmer, glimpse, glisten, glitter, instant, shimmer, sparkle 11 coruscation, fulguration, scintillate

flashing: 6 bright, flashy 7 forward 8 meteoric, snapping 9 fulgurant, fulgurous

flashy: gay 4 flat, gaud, loud 5 fiery, gaudy, showy 6 frothy, garish, ornate, slangy, sporty 7 insipid, tinhorn 8 dazzling, vehement 9 impetuous 10 spiritless

flask: 4 olpe 5 betty, bulge, girba 6 bottle, fiasco, flacon, guttus 7 ampulla, canteen, matrass 8 cucurbit 9 aryballos

flask-shaped: 10 lageniform

flat: 4 dead, dull, even, fade, plat, tame 5 abode, aflat, banal, bland, blunt, level, molle, plane, prone, vapid 6 boring, dreary, flashy 7 decided, insipid, platoid, prosaic, uniform 8 directly, dwelling, lifeless, unbroken 9 apartment, downright, prostrate, tasteless 10 homaloidal, horizontal, monotonous, unanimated 12 unmistakable 13 uninteresting

flat-nosed: 6 simous

flatboat: ark 4 scow 5 barge

flatfish: dab, ray 4 butt, dace, sole 5 bream, fluke 6 acedia, plaice, turbot 7 sanddab, sunfish, torpedo 8 flounder

flatiron: 7 sadiron

flatten: 4 even 5 level 6 deject, smooth 7 depress 8 compress, dispirit 9 prostrate 10 complanate, discourage, dishearten

flattened: 6 oblate 7 planate

flatter: 4 bull, claw, coax, fage, fume, palp 5 charm, float, gloze, honey, smalm 6 become, cajole, fickle, fleech, fraise, glaver, smooge, soothe 7 adulate, beguile, blarney, flether, flutter, wheedle 8 blandish, bootlick, butter up, collogue 10 compliment, ingratiate

flatterer: 6 cogger, glozer 7 soother 8 courtier 9 sycophant 10 assentator, greasehorn

flattering: 7 buttery, candied 11 assentatory

flattery: 4 bull, bunk 5 fraik, gloze, salve, taffy 6 butter, fleech 7 blarney, fawning, flether, palaver 8 cajolery 9 adulation 10 compliment 14 obsequiousness

flatulent: 5 gassy, windy 6 turgid 7 pompous, ventose 8 inflated 9 bombastic

flaunt: 4 bosh, wave 5 boast, vaunt 6 parade, trapes 7 display, flutter, traipse 8 brandish

flavor: 4 gamy, odor, rasa, salt, tang, zest 5 aroma, devil, sapid, sapor, sauce, savor, scent, taste, tinge 6 asarum, relish, season 7 perfume 8 hautgout, piquancy 9 fragrance

flavorable: 5 sapid, sipid 6 savory 9 palatable

flavoring material: 4 mint, sage 6 orgeat 7 cumarin 8 coumarin, cumarone 9 coumarone

flavorless: 5 stale, vapid 9 tasteless

flaw: fib, gap, lie, mar 4 gall, hole, rase, rift, spot, wind 5 brack, cleft, crack, craze, fault, flake 6 breach, defect 7 blemish, default, fissure, nullify, violate, whitlow 8 fracture, fragment, gendarme 10 intoxicate 12 imperfection

flawless: 5 sound 7 perfect 9 faultless

flax: pob, tow 4 card, harl, lint 5 hards, hurds, linen, linin, pouce 6 bobbin

filament: 4 harl

holder: 7 distaff

prepare: ret

refuse: pob

remove seed: 6 ribble

tool: 7 hatchel, swingle

flaxen: 5 blond, straw 6 golden

flaxen-haired: 4 bawn

flaxseed: 7 linseed

flay: 4 skin 5 slash, strip 6 assail, attack, fleece 7 censure, pillage, reprove 9 excoriate 11 decorticate

flea: 6 chigoe 10 sandhopper

genus: 5 pulex

fleck: fat 4 flea, flit, spot, tuft 5 flake, flare 6 dapple, streak, stripe 7 flutter, speckle 8 particle 9 variegate

fledgling, fledgeling: 5 squab

flee: fly, lam, run 4 bolt, fleg, loup, shun 5 elude, speed 6 escape, vanish 7 abandon, abscond, forsake 8 liberate 9 disappear, skedaddle

fleece: abb, jib, teg 4 bilk, fell, flay, gaff, wool 5 cheat, fleck, pluck, shear 6 toison 7 despoil

fleecy: 5 wooly 6 linten, woolly

fleeing: 7 fugient 8 fugitive

fleer: 4 gibe, grin, jeer, leer, mock 5 flout, laugh, scoff, sneer, taunt 7 grimace 8 derision

fleet: bay 4 fast, flit, navy, sail, skim, swim 5 creek, drain, drift, evand, float, flote, hasty, inlet, quick, rapid, swift 6 abound, argosy, armada, hasten, nimble, speedy 7 estuary 8 flotilla 10 evanescent, transitory

fleeting: 5 brief 6 caduke, volage 7 flighty, passing 8 caducous, fugitive, volatile 9 ephemeral, fugacious, tran-

sient **10** evanescent, short-lived, transitory **11** impermanent
Flemish: *geographer:* **8** Mercator
painter: **5** Bouts **6** Mabuse, Massys, Rubens **7** Gossart, Memling, Patinir, van Eyck **8** Breughel, Brueghel, Gossaert, van Cleve **12** van der Weyden
flesh: kin **4** body, meat, race **5** stock **6** family, muscle **7** kindred, mankind **8** humanity **9** mortality **10** sensuality
appendage: **5** palpi(pl.) **6** palpus
colored mineral: **9** sarcoline
formation: **8** sarcosis
kind of: **5** brawn **6** chevon, chiver **7** carrion
pert. to: **7** sarcoid
resembling: **7** sarcoid
fleshbrush: **7** strigil
flesh-eating: **11** carnivorous
fleshy: fat **5** beefy, gross, human, obese, plump, pulpy, stout **6** animal, bodily, brawny, carnal **9** corpulent
fruit: **4** pear, pome **5** berry, drupe, melon **6** tomato
fleur-de-lis: lis, lys **4** iris, liss, luce, lucy
fleuret: **4** epee **5** sword **6** flower
flex: **4** bend **5** tense
flexible: **4** limp, lush, soft **5** buxom, lithe, withy **6** limber, pliant, supple **7** ductile, elastic, flexile, lissome, plastic, pliable, springy, willowy **8** cheverel, cheveril, yielding **9** tractable, versatile **10** manageable
shoot: **4** bine
tube: **4** hose
flexuous: **5** snaky **6** zigzag **7** relaxed, sinuous, winding **8** softened, tortuous, wavering **9** adaptable **10** circuitous, flickering, serpentine, undulating
flexure: **4** bend, bent, curl, fold **5** curve
flick (see also **motion picture**): cut, hit **4** blow, flip, flit, snap, toss, whip **5** flisk, throw **6** flitch, propel **7** flutter
flicker: **4** fail, flit **5** flare, flunk, waver **6** fitter, shiver, yucker **7** blinter, flimmer, flitter, flutter, tremble, twinkle **8** flichter **9** flaughter, palpitate **10** woodpecker
flickering: **7** flabent, lambent **8** flexuous, unsteady
flier: ace **5** pilot **6** airman **7** aviator **8** operator
female: **8** aviatrix **9** aviatress, aviatrice
flight: hop, lam **4** bolt, rout **5** chevy, chivy, flock, floor, scrap, story, volee **6** chivvy, exodus, hegira, hejira **7** flaught, getaway, migrate, mission, scamper **8** stampede, swarming **9** agitation, migration **12** perturbation
in: **8** on the lam
of fancy: **5** sally

of steps: **4** rise **5** stoop **6** perron
of wild fowl: **5** skein
pert. to: **5** volar
put to: **4** rout
flightiness: **9** lightness
flightless bird: emu, moa **4** dodo, kiwi, weka **7** ostrich, penguin
flighty: **5** barmy, giddy, swift **6** fitful, nimshi, volage, whisky **7** foolish, giggish **8** fleeting, freakish **9** transient **10** capricious **11** harum-scarum **13** shuttlewitted
flim-flam: fob **5** freak, trick **6** humbug, tricky, trifle **7** swindle **8** nonsense, trifling **9** deception, deceptive **11** nonsensical
flimmer: **7** flicker, glimmer
flimsy: **4** limp, vain, weak **5** frail, gaudy **6** feeble, paltry, sleazy, slight **7** shallow, tenuous **10** gossamered **11** superficial **13** insubstantial, unsubstantial
flinch: **4** funk, game **5** feign, start, wince **6** blench, falter, flense, recoil, shrink
fling: **4** buzz, cast, dart, dash, ding, emit, fleg, gibe, hurl, kick, toss **5** cheat, dance, flirt, pitch, sling, sneer, throw, whang **6** baffle, effuse, hurtle, plunge, rebuff, spirit **7** flounce, repulse, sarcasm, scatter, swindle **9** overthrow
flint: **5** chert, miser, silex **6** quartz **9** firestone, skinflint
flintlock: **6** musket
flinty: **4** hard **5** cruel **8** obdurate
flip: tap **4** flap, glib, pert, snap, toss, trip **5** flick, flirt, slirt **6** fillip, limber, nimble, pliant, propel **7** journey **10** somersault
flippant: **4** airy, glib **6** fluent, limber, nimble **9** talkative
flipper: arm, fin, paw **4** hand
flip through: **4** scan **6** browse **7** dip into **8** glance at
flirt: tap, toy **4** dart, fike, flip, gibe, jeer, jest, joke, mash, mock, play, toss **5** dally, flick, fling, throw **6** coquet, fillip, lead on, masher, spring, trifle **7** trifler **9** philander
flirtatious: coy **4** arch **10** coquettish
flit: **4** dart, flow, scud **5** fleck, fleet, flick, float, flurr, hover, quick, scoot, swift **6** nimble **7** flicker, flutter, migrate
flitter: rag **5** droop, hover, piece, waver **6** tatter **7** flicker, flutter, shuffle **8** fragment
flittermouse: bat
float: bob, fly, sea **4** buoy, cork, flow, flux, hove, pont, raft, ride, sail, scow, soar, swim, waft, wave **5** balsa, drift, fleet, flood, hover, ladle **6** billow, bobber, bungey, ponton **7** flatter, flotter, pontoon **8** overflow **9** catamaran, negotiate, podoscaph

aloft: 4 soar

floating: 4 free 5 awash, loose 6 adrift, afloat, flying, natant 7 movable 8 drifting, fluitant, shifting, variable 9 wandering

flocculent: 6 woolly

flock: mob 4 bevy, fold, herd, pack 5 brood, bunch, charm, covey, crowd, drift, drove, flake, fleck, group, sedge, shoal, swarm 6 flight, hirsel 7 company 9 multitude 10 assemblage 11 aggregation

kind of: nid, nye, pod 4 nide, sord 5 covey, sedge, tribe

of geese: 6 gaggle

of lions: 5 pride

pert. to: 6 gregal

flocks (god of): Pan

floe: 4 raft

flog: cat, tan 4 beat, cane, hide, lash, toco, toko, wale, whip 5 birch, excel, fight, flail, linge, quilt, skeeg 6 cotton, larrup, strike, switch, thrash 7 baleise, belabor, scourge, sjambok, surpass, trounce 8 slaister 10 flagellate

flood: sea 4 bore, flow, flux 5 eagre, float, spate 6 deluge, excess 7 debacle, freshet, torrent 8 alluvion, inundate, overflow 9 cataclysm 10 inundation, outpouring 14 superabundance

flooded: 5 awash 6 afloat 10 surrounded

floodgate: 5 hatch 6 sluice

floodlight: 5 klieg

floor 4 drop, flat 5 level, story 6 defeat, ground, lay low 7 planche 8 bowl over 9 knock down

floor covering: mat, rug 4 tile 5 tapis(Fr.) 6 carpet, planks 8 linoleum, oilcloth

flop: dud 4 bomb, bust, fail, fall, whop 5 lemon, loser 6 fizzle 7 failure

flora: 6 plants 9 florilege 10 vegetation 11 florilegium

flora and fauna: 5 biota

floreate: 5 bloom

Florence: *bridge:* 12 Ponte Vecchio

cathedral: 5 Duomo

coin: 6 florin 7 ruspone

devotees: 4 neri

family: 6 Medici

gallery: 5 Pitti 6 Uffizi

iris: 5 ireos, orris

Florentine (see also **Florence**): 4 gold 6 finish

floret bract: 5 palea, palet

florid: 5 buxom, fresh, ruddy 6 ornate 7 flowery 8 blooming, rubicund, vigorous 10 figurative, flamboyant, rhetorical 11 embellished, full-blooded

Florida: *capital:* 11 Tallahassee

city: 5 Miami, Ocala, Tampa 7 Key West, Orlando, Palatka, Pompano 8 Sarasota

county: Bay, Lee 4 Dade, Gulf, Lake, Leon, Levy, Polk 5 Pasco

discoverer: 11 Ponce de Leon

key: 4 West 5 Largo 8 Biscayne

motto: 12 In God We Trust

nickname: 8 Sunshine

region: 10 Everglades

state bird: 11 mockingbird

state flower: 13 orange blossom

state tree: 8 palmetto

floss: 5 fluff, skein, waste 6 sleave, stream

flotage: 8 buoyancy

flotilla: 5 fleet

Flotow opera: 6 Martha

flotsam: 6 jetsam 8 driftage, wreckage 9 driftwood

flounce: 4 flap, slam 5 fling, frill 6 ruffle 7 falbala, falbelo 8 flounder, furbelow, struggle

flounder: dab 4 butt, keel, roll, toss 5 bream, fluke, megin 6 grovel, muddle, plaice, turbot, wallow 7 flounce, plounce, stumble, sunfish, topknot, vaagmar, vaagmer 8 flatfish, struggle, vaagmaer

flour: 4 atta, meal 5 clear 6 patent, powder, red dog

bleach: 5 agene

diabetic: 9 aleuronat

maker: 6 miller

sifter: 6 bolter

sprinkle with: 6 dredge

testing device: 11 farinometer

wheat: 4 atta

flourish: 4 boom, brag, grow, riot, rise, show, wave 5 adorn, bloom, boast, cheve, gloss, quirk, vaunt 6 parade, paraph, thrive 7 blossom, display, enlarge, fanfare, prosper, roulade 8 arpeggio, brandish, curlicue, curlycue, increase, ornament 9 embellish 10 decoration 11 ostentation

flourishing: fat 4 frim 5 green, palmy 7 florent 8 thriving 10 prosperous, successful

floury: 4 meal

flout: bob 4 gibe, jeer, mock 5 fleer, flite, flyte, frump, scoff, scorn, scount, sneer, taunt 6 deride, insult, quip at 7 jeering, mockery 8 betongue

flow: ebb, jet, run 4 bore, flit, flux, fuse, gush, hale, lava, lave, melt, pour, roll, shed, sile, teem, well 5 avale, drain, eagre, exude, fleam, float, flood, glide, issue, river, spill, spurt 6 abound, afflux, deluge, recede, stream 7 current, emanate, flutter, meander, spurtle 8 alluvion, inundate 9 streaming 10 menstruate, outpouring 12 menstruation

flower (see also **plant**): bud 4 best, blow, flag, iris, ixia, pink, posy, rose 5 aster, bloom, elite, lilac, pansy, tulip 6 azalia,

crocus, dahlia, orchid, posies(pl.), unfold **7** blethia, blossom, develop, fairest, gentian **8** camellia, choicest, daffodil, freshest, gardenia, geranium, hyacinth, ornament **9** carnation, embellish, gladiolus **10** upper class, upper crust **13** chrysanthemum
appendage: **5** bract
artificial: **7** rosette **8** gloxinia
band: **6** wreath
bell-shaped: **4** lily **5** tulip
blooming once a year: **6** annual
blue: **6** lupine **8** harebell
bud: **5** ament, caper **6** spadix
cluster: **4** cime, cyme **5** ament, bract, umbel **6** corymb, raceme **7** panicle **9** glomerule
of death: **8** asphodel
desert: **6** cactus
extract: **4** atar, otto **5** attar, ottar
fall: **5** aster **6** cosmos
of forgetfulness: **5** lotus
garden: **4** iris, ixia, lily, pink, rose **5** aster, canna, daisy, lilac, pansy, peony, phlox, tulip **6** asalia, olivia, orchid, violet **7** freesia, petunia, verbena **8** bletilla, camellia, daffodil, gloxinia, hyacinth, primrose **9** buttercup, carnation, gladiolus, narcissus **10** heliotrope, ranunculus **11** honeysuckle
goddess: **5** Flora
imaginary: **7** amarant **8** amaranth
large: **5** canna, peony
late-blooming: **5** aster
mass: **8** anthemia
meadow: **5** bluet
modest: **6** violet
obsolete: **5** pense
part: **5** calyx, sepal **6** anther, pistil, stamen **7** nectary, petiole **8** peduncle, perianth, pericarp
passion: **6** maypop
pink: **4** rose **7** rhodora
prickly: **4** burr
purple: **5** lilac, pense
receptacle: **4** vase **5** torus
spring: **4** iris **5** lilac, peony, tulip **7** arbutus **8** hepatica
stand: **7** epergne
stylized: lis
unfading: **7** amarant **8** amaranth
unknown kind: **8** belamour
white: **5** gowan
wild: **4** sage **5** bluet, daisy **6** lupine **7** anemone, arbutus **8** bluebell, hepatica **9** buttercup, innocence
wind: **7** anemone
yellow: **5** daisy, gowan, pense **7** jonquil **8** daffodil, marigold **9** buttercup
flower holder: pot **4** frog, vase **5** lapel
flowering: 7 flowery **8** anthesis, blooming **11** florescence

flowering plant: rue **4** arum **5** avens, calla, canna, orpin, phlox, yucca, zamia **6** azalea, bareta, cosmos, oxalis, spirea, teasel **7** barreta, gentian, lobelia, pavonia, petunia, rhodora, spiraea, tamarix, torenia, waratah **8** acanthus, ageratum, damewort, geranium, gerardia, valerian **9** candytuft, coreopsis, gloxinias, goldenrod, hollyhock, monkshood **10** pulsatilla, snapdragon
flowerless plant: 4 fern, moss **6** lichen **7** acrogen
flowerlike: 7 anthoid
flowerpot: 10 jardiniere
flowery: 6 florid **7** florent **9** flowering **10** figurative, flosculous
flowing: 4 flux **5** fluid, fluor, tidal **6** afflux, fluent **7** copious, current, cursive, emanent, fluxing **9** affluxion, emanation **10** transitive
together: **9** confluent
flu: 6 grippe
flub: 4 muff **5** boner, botch, error **6** bollix, bungle, goof up **7** blunder
fluctuate: 4 sway, vary, veer, wave **5** waver **7** vibrate **8** undulate, unsteady **9** oscillate, vacillate **10** irresolute **12** undetermined
fluctuating: 8 unstable, unsteady
flue: net **4** barb, down, open, pipe, thin **5** flare, fluff, fluke, stack **6** expand, feeble, funnel, sickly, tunnel **7** chimney, flaring, passage, shallow
fluency: 9 eloquence, profusion **10** smoothness
fluent: 4 glib **5** fluid, ready **6** facile, liquid, smooth, stream **7** copious, flowing, fluidic, renable, verbose, voluble **8** eloquent, flippant **9** talkative **12** smooth-spoken **13** talkativeness
fluff: nap **4** down, flue, lint, puff **5** flash, floss, whiff
fluffy: 4 soft **5** downy, drunk, fluey, fuzzy **6** linten **8** feathery, unsteady **12** undependable
fluid: ink **5** rasa **5** water **6** fluent, liquid, watery **7** flowing, fluible, fluxile, gaseous **8** floating, fluxible
kind of: gas, ink, oil, sap, tar **4** bile, icor, milk **5** blood, ether, grume, ichor, latex, nerol, plasm, serum **7** acetone, coal oil, naphtha, tearlet **8** gasoline, kerosene
measure: rhe
pert to: **7** humoral
without: **7** aneroid
fluidity unit: rhe
fluke: 4 fish, flue **5** blade **8** flounder
fluky: 8 unsteady **9** uncertain **10** capricious
flume: 4 leat **5** chute, gorge, water **6** ravine, sluice, stream **7** channel

flummox: 4 fail 7 confuse, perplex 8 confound 9 embarrass 10 disconcert

flunk: 4 bust, fail 7 flicker

flunky, flunkey: 4 snob 5 toady 6 cookee 7 footman, servant, steward

flurry: ado 4 gust, stir 5 haste, skirl 6 bother, bustle, scurry, squall 7 confuse, flusker, fluster, flutter, fooster 9 agitation, carfuffle 10 discompose

flush: 4 even, glow, pool, rose 5 blush, elate, rouge, vigor 6 aflush, excite, lavish, mantle, morass, redden, thrill 7 animate 8 abundant, affluent, prodigal, rosiness 9 abounding, encourage 10 prosperous

flushed: red 4 ruby 5 aglow 6 florid 7 scarlet 8 vigorous 10 prosperous

flushing: 8 blushing 9 rubescent

fluster: 5 shake 6 flurry, fuddle, muddle, pother, rattle 7 confuse, flusker, fooster 8 befuddle, flustrum 10 discompose

flute: nay 4 fife 5 crimp 6 flauto, goffer, zufolo 7 chamfer, channel, gauffer, magadis, piccolo, zuffolo 8 flautino

ancient: 5 tibia

Hindu: bin 5 pungi

player: 5 piper 6 aulete 7 flutist, tootler 8 auletris, flautist

stop: 7 ventage

wood for: 5 kokra

fluting: 5 strix 7 gadroon, godroon, strigil 10 gadroonage, godroonage

flux: 4 flow, fuse, melt 5 float, flood, resin, rosin, smear, smelt 6 fusion, stream 7 euripus, flowing, outflow

fly: bee, hop 4 flee, fleg, flit, leap, melt, scud, soar, solo, whir, whiz, wing 5 agile, alert, float, midge, pilot, quick, sharp, whirr 6 aviate, insect, nimble, spring, vanish 7 avigate, avolate, knowing 8 coachman 9 disappear

African: 4 zimb 5 zebub 6 tsetse

enemy: 6 spider

fishing: bee 4 lure 5 nymph, sedge 6 Cahill 7 Babcock, grannom, huzard 8 coachman, Ferguson, hare's ear 9 alexandra 10 Barrington

genus: 5 Dacus

kind of: bee, bot, fag, mau, plu 4 gnat, kivu, zimb 5 alder, cadew, horse, midge, whame 6 breeze, gadfly, seroot, tsetse 7 butcher, collier, tachina 8 housefly 9 shoemaker 10 bluebottle 11 caterpillar, trichoptera

small: 4 gnat 5 midge

two-winged: 8 dipteron

flyaway: 5 giddy 7 flighty 8 restless 12 unrestrained

flybane: 12 cinnamonroot

flyblow: 5 larva

fly-by-night: 6 unsure 7 dubious 10 unreliable 12 undependable 13 untrustworthy

flycatcher: 4 tody 5 pewee 6 phoebe, yetapa 7 fielder, grignet, grinder

flyer: ace 5 pilot 7 Pegasus 8 aeronaut, operator

flying: 5 awing 6 flight, volant, waving 8 aviation, floating 9 fugacious

pert to: 7 aviatic

flying adder: 9 dragonfly

flying boat: 8 seaplane 9 amphibian

flying body: 6 meteor

flying device: 4 kite 6 glider

Flying Dutchman heroine: 5 Senta

flying expert: ace

flying fish: 5 saury 7 gurnard

flying machine: 5 plane 8 aerostat 9 gyroplane 10 helicopter

flying mammal: bat

flying ship: 5 blimp 7 aeronat, biplane 8 airplane 9 amphibian, dirigible, monoplane 10 helicopter

Fo: 6 Buddha

foal: 4 colt 5 filly

foam: fob, sud 4 fume, head, scud, scum 5 frost, froth, spume, yeast 6 bubble, freath, lather 7 blubber

foaming: 5 nappy 6 yeasty 7 spumous

foamy: 5 barmy, spumy, sudsy 6 frothy

fob: 4 buck, foam 5 cheat, froth, trick 6 impose, pocket 8 flimflam, imposter, ornament, swindler

focal: 7 central, centric, nuclear, nucleus 13 concentrative

focus: 4 foci(pl.) 5 point, train 6 center, hearth 8 converge, polestar 9 fireplace 11 concentrate, nerve center

fodder: hay 4 feed, food, vert 5 mange 6 forage, silage 9 provender

kind of: ers, oat, rye 4 corn, rape 5 batad, maize, vetch, wheat 6 barley, clover, millet 7 alfalfa 8 deerweed 11 bitter vetch

storing place: 4 silo 5 bakie 6 haymow, silage 8 ensilage

trough for: 6 manger

foe: 5 enemy, fiend, rival 7 adverse, hostile, opposer, saracen 8 opponent 9 adversary, ill-wisher 10 antagonist

fog: dag, rag 4 damp, daze, haar, haze, mist, moke, moss, murk, prig, roke, smog 5 bedim, brume, cloud, grass, vapor 6 nebula, salmon, stupor 7 obscure, pogonip 8 bewilder, moisture 10 aftergrass 12 bewilderment

foggy: dim 4 dull, hazy, moky, roky 5 dense, dirty, misky, misty, murky, rooky 6 cloudy, marshy 7 brumous, muddled, obscure 8 confused, nubilous 9 beclouded

foghorn: 5 siren

fogy: 6 foozle

foible: fad 4 weak 5 fault, ferly 6 feeble 7 frailty 8 weakness 9 infirmity 11 shortcoming 12 imperfection

foil: 4 balk, soil, tain 5 blade, blunt, elude, evade, stain, stump, sword, track, trail 6 baffle, blench, boggle, defeat, defile, outwit, stigma, stooge, thwart 7 beguile, failure, pollute, repulse, trample 8 disgrace 9 frustrate, overthrow 11 frustration

foist: 4 cask, dupe, gull 5 barge, cheat, fudge, fusty 6 galley, suborn 7 palm off, swindle 8 brackish, hoodwink 9 rascality 11 interpolate

fold: bow, lap, pen, ply, wap 4 bend, cote, fail, flap, furl, loop, plie, ruga, tuck 5 clasp, crimp, drape, flipe, flock, layer, plait, pleat, plica, prank, sinus, yield 6 bought, crease, double, hurdle, infold, plight, pucker, rimple 7 crumple, embrace, flexure, placate, plicate 8 surround 9 enclosure, overthrow, plicature
kind of: 4 loop 5 bight, lapel, plica, quire 6 bought, dewlap, octavo 7 plicate 9 replicate
of skin: 4 ruga 5 plica

folded: 4 shut 6 closed 7 plicate

folder: 5 cover, folio 6 binder 7 leaflet 8 pamphlet

folderol, falderal: 8 nonsense

foliage: 6 leaves 7 leafage

foliated: 5 lobed 7 spathic

folio: fo 4 case, leaf, page

folk: 6 daoine, people 7 friends 9 intimates, relatives

folklore: 4 myth 6 custom, history, legend 9 tradition 12 superstition
genie of: 7 sandman

folks: 6 people

folkway: mos 5 mores(pl.) 6 custom 7 pattern

folletto: imp 5 fairy 6 goblin, spirit

follicle: sac, 5 crypt

follow: ape, dog, see, tag 4 copy, hunt, next, seek, shag, tail 5 adopt, after, chase, ensue, snake, spoor, trace, track, trail 6 attend, pursue, result, shadow 7 imitate, observe, replace, succeed 8 practice, supplant 9 accompany, alternate, supervene 10 comprehend, understand

follow behind: dog, lag, tag 4 heel, hunt, nose, tail 5 hound, trace 6 shadow, trail 7 draggle 9 supervene

follower: fan, ist, ite, son 4 aper, beau, zany 5 gilly 6 bildar, ensuer, gillie, gudget, sequel, sulter, votary 7 devotee, grifter, pursuer, retinue, spaniel 8 adherent, disciple, henchman, partisan, retainer, servitor 9 attendant, caudatory, cuadrilla, dependent, satellite, successor 10 aficionado, sweetheart 11 cuadrillero

following: 4 next, sect 5 after, below, suant, train 6 sequel 7 devotee, ensuing, sequent 8 business, trailing, vocation 9 clientele, supporter 10 posthumous, profession, sequential, subsequent, succeeding, successive 12 subsequent to
exact words: 7 literal
laws of arithmetical algebra: 6 scalor

follow-up: 6 sequel

folly: sin 4 whim 6 betise, dotage, lunacy 7 daffery, daffing, foolery, foppery, madness, mistake 8 fondness, idleness, lewdness, morology, nonsense, rashness 9 silliness 10 imprudence, wantonness 11 foolishness, witlessness 12 indiscretion

foment: 4 abet, brew, spur 5 rouse, stupe 6 arouse, excite, incite 7 agitate, ferment, provoke 9 encourage, instigate

fond: tid 4 dear, dote, fain, fool, fund, warm, weak 5 silly, stock, store 6 ardent, befool, caress, dearly, doting, loving, simple, tender 7 amatory, amorous, beguile, browden, devoted, foolish, insipid 8 desirous, enamored, sanguine, trifling, uxorious 9 credulous, enamoured, indulgent, savorless 10 curcuddoch, infatuated, passionate 12 affectionate
of dainties: 6 friand 9 friandise
of drink: 8 bibulous
of hunting: 7 venatic

fonda: inn 5 hotel

fondle: hug, pet 4 baby, coax, love, neck, waly 5 clasp, daunt, wally 6 caress, cocker, coddle, cosset, dandle, pamper, stroke 7 cherish, embrace 8 blandish, canoodle

fondly: 6 dearly 7 foolish 8 tenderly 9 foolishly 14 affectionately

fondness: gra 4 love 5 folly, taste 8 dearness, weakness 9 affection 10 attachment, tenderness 11 affectation, foolishness 12 predilection 15 Philotherianism

fondu: 6 cheese 7 souffle

fons: 6 origin, source 8 fountain

font: 4 pila 5 basin 6 source, spring 7 piscina 8 delubrum, fountain 10 aspersoria (pl.) 11 aspersorium

fontal: 6 source 8 original 9 baptismal

food: bit, pap 4 bite, cate, chow, diet, eats, fare, farm, gear, grub, meat, peck, prog 5 bread, broma, cheer, foray, scaff, tripe 6 fodder, foster, morsel, viands, wraith 7 aliment, edibles, handout, pabulum, vittles 8 flummery, grubbery, victuals 9 nutriment, provender 10 provisions, sustenance 11 comestibles, nourishment
animal: 4 feed 5 grain, grass 6 fodder, forage 9 provender
choice: 4 cake 6 pastry
container: jar 4 bowl, dish, olla 5 crock, plate 6 saucer

craving for: **4** pica **7** bulimia
devotee: **7** epicure, gourmet
dislike of: **6** asitia **9** sitomania **10** cibophobia
dressing: **5** sauce
element: **6** gluten **7** protein, vitamin
farinaceous: **4** sago
garnish: **5** sauce
heavenly: **5** manna
invalid: pap **5** broth
kind of: pap, poi, sop **4** ants, chum, crum, mess, mush, sago **5** acate, balut, bread, broma, cates, gruel, jelly, manna, puree, salep, scaff, souse, tripe **6** cagmag, cereal, farina, forage, hominy, vivres **7** abalone, boscage, pemican, tapioca **8** ambrosia, aperient, beebread,, pemmican **9** aperitive, rechauffe **10** rechauffee
list: **4** diet, menu **5** carte
of gods: **6** amrita **7** amreeta **8** ambrosia
pert. to: **8** cibarial **9** cibarious
protein: **4** fish, meat **6** cheese
provision of: **4** mess **6** ration **8** catering
scarcity: **6** famine
seller: **6** grocer **7** viander
semidigested: **5** chyme
soft: pap
storage pit: **4** cist
southern: **4** okra, pone **5** gumbo **6** hominy **7** hoecake **11** chitterling
special dish: **4** hogo, olla, stew **5** bredi, pilaf, pilau, pilaw, pizza **6** haslet, hominy, majoon, omelet, panada, pilaff, ragout, salmis, scouse, sundae, zimmis **7** chowder, custard, rarebit, ravioli, souffle **8** cabeliau, hautgout, omelette, sillabub, sukiyaki **9** cabilliau, colcannon, galantine, succotash **10** salmagundi, shishkebab
fool: ass, cod, cow, fop, fox, kid, mug, oaf, sap **4** boob, butt, dolt, dupe, gowk, gull, hoax, jape, jest, joke, simp, zany **5** bluff, clown, dunce, goose, idiot, moron, ninny, noddy, silly, spoof, trick **6** cuckoo, delude, dotard, gammon, jester, motley, nitwit, outwit, take in, tamper **7** buffoon, coxcomb, deceive, mislead, witling **8** hoodwink, imbecile, surprise **9** blockhead, simpleton **10** nincompoop
around: **4** play **5** cut up, dally **6** trifle **7** have fun, toy with, skylark **8** lallygag **9** philander, waste time
foolable: **5** naive **8** gullible
foolhardy: **4** rash **8** headlong, reckless **11** adventurous **12** presumptuous
foolish: mad **4** daft, rash, zany **5** anile, barmy, batty, buggy, crazy, dizzy, goofy, goosy, inane, inept, silly **6** absurd, harish, simple, stupid, unwise **7** asinine, fatuous, flighty, foppish, gullish, idiotic, puerile, witless **8** anserine, cockeyed, heedless **9** brainless, childlike, desi-

pient, doddering, imprudent, insensate, ludicrous, senseless **10** half-witted, indiscreet, irrational **11** nonsensical **12** preposterous
foolishness: **5** folly **6** levity **9** absurdity, horseplay, stupidity **10** insipience
foolproof: **4** sure **7** certain **8** risk free **10** infallible
fool's gold: **6** pyrite
fool's paradise: **7** chimera **8** illusion
fool's stitch: **6** tricot
foot: dog, pes **4** base **5** meter, speed **6** bottom, pay for, tootsy, trilby **7** measure **9** extremity
animal: pad, paw **4** hoof **7** fetlock, pastern
armor: **8** solleret
lever: **5** pedal **7** treadle
metric: **4** iamb **5** arsis, paeon **6** dactyl, iambus **7** anapest, pyrrhic, spondee, triseme, trochee **8** bacchius, epitrite, molossus, tribrach
pain **8** talalgia
part: toe **4** arch, heel, sole **6** instep, thenar
pert. to: **5** pedal, podal **6** pedate
foot bone: **6** cuboid, tarsus **7** phalanx **8** scaphoid **10** astragulus, metatarsus
foot doctor: **10** podiatrist **11** chiropodist
foot soldier: **4** kern(Sc.), peon **6** Zouave **7** dogface **8** doughboy **11** infantryman
football: **5** rugby **6** rugger, soccer **7** pigskin
famous coach: **4** Yost **5** Brown, Halas, Jones, Leahy, Hayes, Stagg **6** Bryant, Devine, Ewbank, Layden, Rockne **8** Lombardi **10** Parseghian
field: **8** gridiron
kick: **4** drop, place, punt **6** spiral
pass: **5** flare **6** shovel **7** forward, lateral **9** square out
position: end **5** guard **6** center, tackle **8** fullback, halfback, split end, tailback, tight end **10** cornerback, linebacker **11** quarterback, running back
pro teams (NFL): **4** Jets (New York), Rams (Los Angeles) **5** Bears (Chicago), Bills (Buffalo), Colts (Baltimore), Lions (Detroit) **6** Browns (Cleveland), Chiefs (Kansas City), Eagles (Philadelphia), Giants (New York), Saints (New Orleans) **7** Bengals (Cincinnati), Broncos (Denver), Cowboys (Dallas), Falcons (Atlanta), Oilers (Houston), Packers (Green Bay), Raiders (Oakland), Vikings (Minnesota) **8** Chargers (San Diego), Dolphins (Miami), Patriots (New England), Redskins (Washington, D.C.), Seahawks (Seattle), Steelers (Pittsburgh) **9** Cardinals (St. Louis) **10** Buccaneers (Tampa Bay) **11** Forty-Niners (San Francisco)
pro teams (USFL): **4** Gold (Denver) **5**

Blitz (Chicago), Stars (Philadelphia) **7** Bandits (Tampa Bay), Express (Los Angeles) **8** Breakers (Boston), Federals (Washington), Generals (New Jersey), Invaders (Oakland), Panthers (Michigan) **9** Stallions (Birmingham), Wranglers (Arizona)

score: **4** goal **6** safety **9** field goal, touchback, touchdown **10** conversion

team: **6** eleven (see *pro teams* above)

term: **4** down, sack, yard **5** block, flank, drive **6** fumble, huddle **7** defense, end zone, holding, kick-off, offense, offside, rushing **8** clipping, uprights **9** scrimmage, secondary **12** interception, interference

trophy: **7** Heisman (college)

footer: **6** walker **10** pedestrian

footfall: pad **4** step **5** tread **7** vestige

footing: **4** base, lace, rank **5** basis, track **6** status **7** balance, support, surface, toehold **8** standing **9** condition **12** relationship

footless: **5** inept **6** apodal, clumsy, futile, stupid **7** useless **13** unsubstantial

footloose: **4** free **7** nomadic **9** wandering **10** unattached

footman: **6** flunky, lackey, menial **7** servant **8** chasseur **9** attendant

footnote: **9** reference **11** explanation

footpad: **4** thug **5** thief **6** mugger, robber **9** holdup man **10** stickup man

footpath: **4** lane **5** trail **8** trottoir, sidewalk **9** banquette

footprint: **5** trace, track, tread

fossil: **9** ichnolite

rabbit: **5** prick

footrest: **4** pouf, rail **5** stool **7** cricket, hassock, ottoman

footstalk: **7** pedicel, petiole **8** peduncle

footwear (see also **shoe**): pac **4** boot, hose, pack, shoe, sock **5** kamik, sabot **6** arctic, galosh, kamika(pl.), patten, rubber **8** stocking

fop: **4** buck, dude, dupe, fool **5** dandy **7** coxcomb, jessamy **8** gimcrack, popinjay **9** exquisite **11** Beau Brummel **12** fashion plate, lounge lizard, man-about-town

foppery: **9** absurdity

foppish: **5** apish, dandy, silly **6** dapper, spruce, stupid **7** fangled, finical, foolish **8** dandyish

foppishness: **13** dandification

for: **7** because **8** favoring **9** favouring **10** concerning

for all voices: **5** tutti

for cash: **9** al contado(Sp.)

for each: per

for fear that: **4** lest

for nothing: **6** gratis, lanyap **8** gratuity **9** lagniappe

for shame: fie

for temporary use: **4** jury

for that reason: **4** ergo(L.) **9** therefore

for which reason: **6** whence

forage: ers, oat, rye **4** corn, mast, raid, rape **5** grass, maize, raven, spoil, wheat **6** barley, browse, clover, fodder, millet, ravage, russud **7** alfalfa **8** deerweed **9** pasturage **10** provisions **11** bitter vetch

foramen: **4** pore

foray: **4** rade, raid **5** melee **6** ravage, sortie **7** chappow, hership, pillage **9** incursion

forbear, forebear: **4** bear, help, shun, sire **5** avoid, forgo, spare **6** desist, endure, forego, parent **7** abstain, decline, refrain **8** ancestor **10** ancestress, forefather, foreparent

forbearance: **5** mercy **6** lenity **8** mildness, patience **9** tolerance **10** abstinence, self-denial **13** self-restraint

forbearing: **4** easy, mild **7** lenient, patient **8** tolerant **9** desisting, restraint

forbid: ban **4** defy, deny, fend, tabu, veto **5** debar, taboo **6** defend, enjoin, impede, refuse **7** forfend, forwarn, gainsay, inhibit **8** disallow, forefend, forspeak, preclude, prohibit **9** challenge, interdict, proscribe **10** contradict **11** countermand

forbiddance: ban **4** veto **12** interdiction, proscription

forbidden: **4** tabu **5** taboo **6** banned, denied **8** verboten **10** prohibited

Jewish law: **4** tref

Forbidden City: **5** Lhasa

forbidding: **4** grim **5** black, gaunt, stern **6** fierce, odious, strict **9** offensive, repellent **10** unpleasant **11** displeasing, prohibiting **2** disagreeable, interdicting

force: gar, gut, vim, vis **4** bang, birr, clip, cram, dint, feck, make **5** coact, drive, exert, farce, impel, might, peise, poach, power, press, repel, shear, stuff, wrest **6** coerce, compel, cudgel, energy, extort, oblige, ravish, stithy **7** ability, afforce, cascade, impetus, impulse, require, violate **8** coaction, coercion, efficacy, momentum, pressure, strength, validity, violence, virility **9** constrain, influence, puissance, restraint, waterfall **10** compulsion, constraint, constringe **11** necessitate

air upon: **4** blow

down: **4** tamp **5** stuff

into smaller space: **8** compress

kind of: **4** army, birr, dyne, elod, soul, task **5** agent, cadre, dynam, enemy, fohat, nerve, posse, steam, tonal **6** nature **7** voltage **8** battalia, sanction **9** bioenergy **13** reinforcement

onward: **4** urge **6** propel

out: **5** evict **6** banish, unseat
producing rotation: **6** torque
to do without: **7** deprive
with full: **5** amain
forced: 5 rigid, stiff **7** labored **8** spurious, strained **9** reluctant **10** artificial, compulsory, farfetched **11** constrained, involuntary, spontaneous **12** artificially
contribution: tax **4** duty, levy, toll **6** demand, excise, impost **7** tribute **8** exaction **10** assessment
feeding: **6** gavage
forceful: 6 mighty, strong, virile **7** dynamic, violent **8** eloquent, enfatico, forcible, vigorous **9** effective, energetic
forcemeat: 5 farce
forceps: 7 pincers **8** dentagra
forces: 4 army **6** troops
forcible: 5 stout, valid **6** cogent, mighty, potent **7** intense, violent, weighty **8** emphatic, forceful, powerful, puissant, vigorous **9** energetic, impetuous, necessary **10** compulsory, convincing, impressive, obligatory **11** efficacious, influential
forcibly: 5 amain **6** hardly **9** violently **10** vigorously
ford: 4 wade, wath **5** drift **6** stream **7** current **8** crossing **9** wathstead
Fordham's team: 4 Rams
fore: van, way **5** afore, ahead, front, prior, track **6** former **7** earlier, further, journey **8** advanced, formerly **10** antecedent, previously
forearm: arm
bone: **4** ulna
pert. to: **7** cubital
forebear: See **forbear**
forebode, forbode: 4 bode, omen **5** augur, croak **6** divine **7** betoken, portend, predict, presage **8** foretell **13** prognosticate **15** prognostication
foreboding, forboding: 4 omen **5** black **6** augury, boding, gloomy **7** anxiety **8** bodement, sinister **10** prediction **11** pessimistic, presagement **12** apprehension, presentiment
forecast: 4 bode **5** guess, infer **6** scheme **7** caution, foresee, fortune, predict, surmise **8** foredeem, foretell, prophesy **9** calculate, foregleam, forepoint, forescent, foretoken, prognosis **10** conjecture, foreordain, prediction, prognostic **11** calculation, foredestiny **12** predetermine **15** prognostication
forecaster: 4 seer **6** oracle **7** prophet **8** dopester **11** nostradamus **13** meteorologist
foreclose: 5 debar **6** hinder **7** prevent **8** preclude
foredoom: 7 destiny **10** predestine
forefather: 4 sire **5** elder **6** parent **7** for-

bear **8** ancestor **9** grandsire **10** forerunner, progenitor
forefinger: 5 index
forefoot: paw, pud
forefront: van **5** front
foregather: 4 meet **7** consort, convene **8** assemble **9** encounter **10** fraternize
forego, forgo: 5 waive **7** abstain, neglect, precede, refrain **8** dispense, renounce
foregoer: 7 example **8** ancestor **10** forerunner **11** predecessor
foregoing: 4 past **5** above **8** anterior, previous **9** preceding **10** antecedent
foregone: 4 past **8** previous
conclusion: **9** certainty
forehanded: 5 early **6** timely **7** prudent, thrifty
forehead: 4 brow **5** frons, front **7** frontes **8** sinciput
pert. to: **7** metopic
prominence: **8** glabella
strap: **4** tump
foreign: 5 alien, fremd **6** exiled, exotic, forane, remote **7** distant, ecdemic, exclude, strange **8** barbaric, peregrin **9** barbarous, extrinsic, peregrine **10** extraneous, irrelevant, outlandish, tramontane **12** adventitious, exallotriote, exterraneous, incompatible, inconsistent
geology: **7** epigene
foreign quarter: 6 barrio, ghetto **7** enclave
foreign service: *official:* **6** consul **7** attache **8** diplomat **10** ambassador
residence: **9** consulate
foreign to: 6 dehors
foreigner: 5 alien, haole **6** gringo, pakeha **7** greener, pardesi **8** outsider, stranger **9** barbarian, estranger, outlander **10** tramontane **12** ultramontane
foreknow: 5 infer **6** divine **7** foresee **8** conclude **9** prescient **11** preconceive
foreknowledge: 10 prescience
forel: 4 case **6** border, sheath **7** selvage **8** slipcase
foreland: 8 headland **10** promontory
forelock: 4 bang **6** cotter **8** linchpin
foreman: 4 boss **5** chief **6** gaffer, ganger, leader **7** capataz, captain, headman, manager, steward **8** overseer **9** chargeman **10** supervisor
foremost: 4 head, high, main **5** chief, first, forme, front, grand **6** banner **7** leading, supreme **9** principal
part: van **5** front
forenoon: 7 morning
forensic: 6 debate **11** disputation **13** argumentative
foreordain: 7 destine, foresay, predoom **8** forecast **9** preordain **10** predestine **12** predestinate, predetermine

forepart: 5 front 9 stomacher
of horse's hoof: toe

forerun: 6 herald, outrun 7 precede, prelude 8 announce 9 forestall, introduce, precourse, prefigure 10 anticipate, foreshadow

forerunner: 4 omen, sign 5 usher 6 augury, herald 8 ancestor, foregoer, fourrier 9 harbinger, messenger, precedent, precursor 10 forefather, foreganger, progenitor, prognostic 11 predecessor

foresee: 4 read 6 divine 8 forecast, foreknow 10 anticipate

foreshadow: 7 forerun 9 adumbrate, prefigure

foreshank: 4 shin

foreshow: 4 bode 5 abode, augur 7 betoken 8 foretell, prophesy 9 auspicate, foretoken 13 prognosticate

foresight: 6 vision 8 prudence 9 prevision 10 prescience, prevoyance, providence 11 forethought 12 anticipation 14 farsightedness

foresighted: 9 prescient, provident 10 farsighted

forest: 4 gapo, wood 5 Arden, glade, gubat, sylva(L.), taiga, waste 6 jungle, timber 7 boscage 8 caatinga, woodland 10 wilderness
deity: 4 faun 5 satyr 7 Aegipan
glade: 5 camas 6 camass, cammas 7 quamash
god: Pan 5 Tapio
love of: 9 hemophily
open place: 5 glade
pert. to: 6 sylvan 7 nemoral 9 forestral
road: 4 ride 5 trail
subarctic: 5 taiga
treeless: 4 wold
warden: 6 ranger

Forest City: 8 Portland, Savannah 9 Cleveland

forest fire locator: 7 alidade

forestall: 5 avert, deter 7 rule out 8 preclude, stave off

forester: 7 montero, treeman, woodman 8 woodsman

foretaste: 4 gust 6 teaser 8 prospect 12 anticipation

foretell: 4 bode, erst, read, spae 5 augur, insee, weird 6 divine 7 bespeak, foresay, portend, predict, presage 8 forebode, forecast, foreshow, prophesy, soothsay 9 predicate, prefigure, prophetic 10 vaticinate 13 prognosticate

foretelling: 9 fatidical, prophetic

forethought: 7 caution 8 prepense, prudence 9 foresight, provident 12 aforethought, anticipation 13 premeditation

foretoken: 4 omen 7 promise 8 forecast, foreshow, foresign 9 auspicate 10 presignify 13 prognosticate

foretold: 10 annunciate

foretooth: 5 biter 6 cutter 7 incisor

forever: aye 4 ever 5 etern 6 always, eterne 7 endless 8 eternity 9 endlessly, eternally, perpetual 10 constantly, invariably 11 ceaselessly, continually, everlasting, incessantly, perpetually, unceasingly 12 interminably, unchangeably 13 everlastingly

forewarn: 5 augur

forewarning: 4 hint 7 portent 11 premonition

foreword: 5 proem 7 preface 8 preamble 12 introduction

for example: 6 such as

forfeit: 4 fine, lose 5 crime, dedit, forgo 6 forego 7 escheat, misdeed, penalty 8 forfault
law: 7 abandum

forfeiture: 4 fine 5 mulct 7 penalty 9 decheance 10 amercement

forfend, forefend: 5 avert 6 secure 7 prevent, protect 8 preserve

forge: 4 mint 5 feign 6 smithy, swinge 7 falsify, fashion 8 bloomery 9 fabricate 11 counterfeit, fabrication, manufacture
nozzle: tew 5 tewel
on: 5 drive
tongs: tew
waste: 5 dross, sprue
wrought iron: 8 bloomery

forged: 10 artificial 11 counterfeit

forger: 5 smith 9 falsifier 10 coachsmith, fabricator

forgery: 4 sham 7 fiction 8 bloomery 11 counterfeit, fabrication 13 falsification

forget: 4 omit 5 fluff 6 ignore 7 neglect 8 overlook 9 disregard 10 draw a blank 11 disremember
one's lines: 5 fluff

forgetful: 6 remiss 7 bemused 8 careless, heedless 9 negligent, oblivious 10 neglectful 11 inattentive

forgetfulness: 7 amnesia, amnesty 8 oblivion
fruit of: 5 lotus
river of: 5 Lethe

forgivable: 6 venial

forgive: 5 remit, spare 6 excuse, pardon 7 absolve, condone 8 overlook 9 exculpate

forgiven: 7 excused

forgiveness: 6 pardon 9 remission 10 absolution 11 condonation

forgiving: 6 humane 7 clement 8 merciful, placable 9 remissive 10 charitable

forgo, forego: 4 quit 5 leave, waive 7 abstain, forbear, forfeit, forsake, neglect, refrain 8 abnegate, forebear, overlook, renounce 9 sacrifice, surrender 10 relinquish

forgoing: 5 above

fork: 4 tine 5 prong 6 bisect, branch, crotch, divide 7 fourche 10 divaricate, fourchette
kind of: 4 croc, evil 5 graip, pikle, glack 7 biprong 9 tormentor

forked: 5 bifid 6 furcal 7 divided, furcate 8 branched 9 furciform 10 bifurcated 11 forficulate

forlorn: 4 lorn, lost, reft 5 alone, stray 6 abject, bereft, ruined 7 forfare 8 deserted, desolate, forsaken, helpless, hopeless, pitiable, wretched 9 abandoned cheerless, desperate, destitute, miserable 10 friendless 11 comfortless 12 disconsolate

form: ame 4 blee, body, make, mode, mold, plan, rite, thew 5 bench, build, frame, guise, image, model, shape 6 adjust, create, figure, invent, manner, ritual, schema, sponge 7 arrange, compose, confect, contour, develop, fashion, outline, pattern, portray, produce, profile 8 ceremony, conceive, likeness, organize, schemata(pl.) 9 construct, etiquette, fabricate, formation, structure 10 appearance, constitute, expression, figuration, observance, similitude 12 conformation 13 configuration, questionnaire
carved: 8 statuary
display: 4 rack 7 manikin 9 mannequin
geometrical: See **figure:** *geometrical*
into arc: 5 embow
into ball: 8 conglobe
into chain: 8 catenate
into fabric: 4 knit
into network: 10 reticulate
literary: ode 5 novel, poesy 6 satire, sonnet 7 romance
liturgical: 6 litany 7 service
lyrical: 6 rondel 7 sestina, sestine(pl.)
of government: 6 polity
of greeting: bow 5 hello, salam 6 salaam, salute 7 curtsey
pert. to: 5 modal

formal: set 4 prim 5 exact, stiff 6 solemn 7 nominal, orderly, precise, regular, solward, starchy, stilted 8 academic, affected, formular, starched 9 essential, officious, reserved 10 ceremonial, methodical, systematic 11 ceremonious, punctilious, superficial 12 conventional

formality: 4 form, rite 8 ceremony 15 conventionality

format: 4 size 5 shape, style 6 makeup 7 pattern

formation: 4 form, rank 5 spread 9 structure 10 procession 11 composition, development 12 construction
bone: 7 ostosis 10 parostosis
cell: 6 tissue
ecological: 5 biome

flesh: 8 sarcosis
geological: lia 4 ione 5 atoll, ledge 6 schist 7 tapeats, terrain, terrane
military: 4 line 5 herse, snail 6 flight 7 echelon
sand: 4 dene, dune

formative: 7 plastic

formed: 5 built 7 decided, matured, settled, wrought 10 constitute
at foot of mountain: 8 piedmont
by law: 9 corporate
crudely: 9 roughhewn
from above: 8 catogene
ingeniously: 5 dedal 6 daedal
of clustered grains (bot.): 7 grumose
on earth's surface: 7 epigene

former: die, old 4 erst, fore, late, once, past 5 forme, gauge, guide, maker, prior 6 whilom 7 ancient, creator, earlier, further, pattern, quondam, templet 8 previous, sometime 9 aforetime, erstwhile 10 antecedent

formerly: ere, nee 4 erst, fore, once, then 5 grave 6 before 7 onetime 8 sometime 9 aforetime, anciently, erstwhile 10 heretofore

formicary: ant 7 anthill, dweller

formicid: ant

formidable: 5 awful, tough 7 fearful 8 alarming, dreadful, menacing, terrible 11 redoubtable, threatening

formless: raw 5 arupa 7 anidian, chaotic 8 deformed, unshaped 9 amorphous, shapeless 13 indeterminate

Formosa: See **Taiwan**

formula: law 4 rule 6 method, recipe, theory 7 receipt

formular: 5 model 6 formal, proper 7 regular

formulate: put 5 draft, frame 6 cook up, devise, draw up, make up 7 dream up, hatch up

formulated: 6 stated 7 written

forsake: 4 deny, drop, flee, quit, shun 5 avoid, forgo, leave, waive 6 beleve, defect, depart, desert, forego, refuse, reject 7 abandon, beleave, discard 8 renounce, withdraw 9 surrender, throw over 10 relinquish

forsaken: 4 lorn 7 forlorn 8 deserted, desolate 9 abandoned, destitute

forswear: 4 deny 6 abjure, reject 7 abandon, perjure 8 abnegate, renounce, take back

forsworn: 8 perjured 11 disaffected

fort: dun, lis, pah 4 liss, shee 5 gotta, redan, sidhe 6 castle, strong 7 bastile, bastion, bulwark, citadel, fortify 8 bastille, castillo, fastness, fortress 10 blockhouse, protection, stronghold
sloping bank of: 6 glacis

forte: bag 5 skill, thing 6 metier 7 calling

8 long suit, strength 9 specialty 11 strong point

forth: out 4 away 6 abroad, manage, onward 7 forward 8 outdoors 10 accomplish

forthright: 7 frankly 9 downright 11 straightway 13 straightforth 5 straightforward

forthwith: now 6 bedene, believe, direct 7 betimes 8 directly 9 extempore, presently, therewith 11 immediately

fortification (see also **defense**): 4 boma, moat, wall 5 redan, tower 6 abatis, castle, glacis, shield 7 bastion, bulwark, citadel, parapet, rampart, ravelin, redoubt 8 fortress 9 barricade 10 stronghold 12 machiolation

kind of: 4 fort 5 redan 6 abatis, sconce 7 lunette, ravelin, redoubt, parados 8 ceinture, demilune, estacade 9 fortalice, bastionet

part: 5 redan 7 bastion, ravelin 8 barbette

fortify: arm, man 4 fort 5 spike 6 abatis, picket 7 bastile, confirm 8 bastille, embattle, fortress, palisade 9 barricade 10 invigorate, strengthen, stronghold

fortitude: 6 mettle 7 bravery, courage, heroism, stamina 8 strength 9 endurance 10 resolution 12 resoluteness 14 impregnability

fortress: 4 fort, keep 5 rocca 6 castle 7 alcazar, barrier, bastile, borough, castlet, castrum, chateau, citadel, fortify 8 alcalzar, alcazava, bastille, chateaux(pl.), fastness 10 stronghold 13 fortification, propugnaculum

outwork of: 6 tenail 8 tenaille

fortuitous: 6 casual, chance, random 9 hazardous 10 accidental, contingent, incidental 12 adventitious

fortuity: 4 luck 6 chance 9 accidence

fortunate: edi, hap, sri 4 good, shri, well 5 faust, happy, lucky, shree 6 dexter 7 favored 8 gracious 9 favorable 10 auspicious, prosperous, successful

fortune: hap, lot 4 bahi, doom, fate, hail, luck 5 weird 6 boodle, bundle, chance, estate, mishap, riches, wealth 7 destiny, success, tidy sum 8 accident, hacienda 9 adventure 10 prosperity 11 king's ransom 13 circumstances

goddess: 5 Tyche

fortune teller: 4 seer 5 gypsy, sibyl, sybil 7 diviner, palmist

forty: 13 quadragesimal

forty days: 4 Lent

forty-five-degree angle: 6 octant

forty-five inches: ell

forty-third asteroid: 4 Eros

43,560 square feet: 4 acre

forty winks: nap 6 snooze

forum: 5 court 8 tribunal

forward: on, to; aid, bog, bug 4 abet, bain, bold, free, help, pert, send, ship, step 5 ahead, along, brash, eager, favor, forth, frack, freck, front, hasty, ready, relay, remit, saucy, serve, spack, ultra 6 afford, ardent, avaunt, before, bright, coming, favour, forthy, hasten, onward, prompt, send on 7 advance, earnest, extreme, further, promote, radical, support 8 adelante, arrogant, champion, immodest, impudent, perverse, petulant, transmit 9 audacious, encourage, forthward, obtrusive, overready 10 accelerate, forritsome, precocious 11 disobedient, progressive

fossa: pit 4 foss, moat 5 canal, ditch, fosse, fovea, graff, grave 6 cavity, trench 10 depression

fossil: 4 fogy 6 dolite 7 antique, lituite 8 calamite, conodont 10 antiquated

egg: 7 ovulite

footprint: 7 ichnite

mollusk: 6 dolite

resin: 5 amber 8 retinite

science: 12 paleontology

shell: 6 dolite

toothlike: 8 conodont

worm track: 7 nereite

fossorial: 9 burrowing

foster: 4 feed, food, help, rear 5 nurse 6 harbor 7 cherish, embosom, gratify, imbosom, indulge, nourish, nursing, nurture, promote, sustain 8 befriend, forester, nursling 9 cultivate, encourage, fosterage, offspring 11 nourishment

foster child: 5 nurry 7 stepson 12 stepdaughter

foudroyant: 8 dazzling, stunning 10 thundering

fougue: 5 ardor 11 impetuosity

foul: 4 base, hory, roil, vile 5 bawdy, black, dirty, grimy, horry, muddy, nasty, sully, weedy 6 clarty, defame, dirten, filthy, impure, malign, odious, putrid, rotten, soiled, unfair 7 abusive, defaced, fulsome, hateful, illegal, noisome, obscene, profane, smeared, squalid, unclean, vicious 8 entangle, indecent, polluted, stinking, wretched 9 dastardly, dishonest, loathsome, nastiness, obnoxious, offensive 10 detestable, disgusting, scurrilous 11 contaminate, unfavorable 12 dishonorable, inauspicious, scatalogical

foulard: tie 11 neckerchief 12 handkerchief

foulmouthed: 7 abusive, obscene, profane 10 scurrilous 11 opprobrious

foulness: 9 feculence

foul play: 5 crime 6 murder 7 killing 8 violence

found: fix, try **4** base, cast, rest **5** board, build, endow, erect **6** attach, depart **8** equipped, practice, provided, supplied **9** establish, institute, originate, supported **10** foundation

foundation: bed **4** base, body, fund, gist, sill **5** basis, bases(pl.), found, stock **6** bottom, legacy, reseau, riprap **7** bedding, bedrock, chantry, roadbed **8** donation, pedestal **9** beginning, endowment **11** corporation **12** substructure

founder: 4 fail **6** author, caster, dismay, dynast **7** stumble **8** miscarry **9** architect, patriarch, supporter, undermine **10** maintainer, originator **11** dumbfounder, establisher

metal: **5** yeter **6** yetter

founding: 8 settling

foundling: oaf **4** waif **6** infant, orphan **8** nursling

fount: 4 fons **6** source **8** fountain **9** reservoir

fountain: jet **4** fond, head, syke, well **5** fount **6** phiale, pirene, source, spring **7** bubbler **8** aganippe **9** reservoir **10** wellspring

god of: **4** Fons

nymph: **5** naiad

Fountain of Youth site: 6 Bimini

fountain pen: 5 stick, stylo

fountainhead: 6 origin, source

four: 6 tetrad **7** quartet

four-footed: 9 quadruped

Four Horsemen: war **5** death **6** famine **8** conquest

four hundred: 5 creme, elect, elite **6** select

four-in-hand: 7 necktie

four inches: 4 hand **7** measure

four-sided: 13 quadrilateral

fourchette: 4 fork **8** wishbone

fourflusher: 9 pretender

fourgon: van **4** cart **5** wagon **7** tumbril

fourpence: 5 groat

fourscore: 6 eighty

foursome: 6 tetrad **7** quartet

foursquare: 7 solidly **8** quadrate **10** forthright

fourth: 5 quart **6** fardel **7** quarter **8** quadrant

fourth estate: 5 press **10** newspapers

foveate: 6 pitted

fowl: hen **4** bird, cock **5** chick, chuck, manoc **7** chicken, rooster **8** volaille

kind of: **4** keel, coot **5** malay, banty, snipe, poult, brant **6** bantam, Houdan, Sussex, rumkin **7** minorca, galeeny

fox: tod **4** fool **5** trick **6** baffle, canine, outwit **7** beguile, confuse, stupefy, vulpine **10** intoxicate, perplexity

foot: pad

hunter's cry: **4** soho **5** yoick

kind of: **4** asse, stag **5** vixen, zorro **6** fennec, corsac **7** reynard, karagan

scent of: **4** drag

young: cub

fox-trot: 5 dance

foxglove: 7 popdock

leaf: **9** digitalis

foxlike: 9 alopecoid

foxtail: 5 brush, grass

foxy: sly **4** wily **5** coony **6** shrewd **7** cunning, vulpine **10** fraudulent

foyer: 5 lobby **6** hearth **8** anteroom, entrance **9** fireplace, greenroom

fra: 4 monk **5** friar **6** priest **7** brother

Fra Diavolo composer: 5 Auber

fracas: 4 bout **5** brawl, melee, set-to **6** rumpus, uproar **7** quarrel **8** fraction **9** commotion **11** disturbance

fraction: bit **4** part **5** break, piece, scrap **6** breach, fracas, little **7** ruction, rupture **8** breaking, fracture, fragment

fractional: 7 partial

fractious: 4 ugly **5** cross **6** unruly **7** crabbed, peevish, waspish **8** perverse, snappish **9** irritable

fracture: 4 flaw, rend **5** break, cleft, crack **6** breach **7** rupture **8** fraction

fragile: 4 fine, frow, weak **5** frail, frowy, light **6** feeble, frough, infirm, slight **7** brickle, brittle, froughy, slender **8** delicate, ethereal **9** frangible

fragility: 8 delicacy **12** delicateness

fragment: bit, ort **4** blad, chip, flaw, grot, part, snip, wisp **5** broke, crumb, flake, groat, piece, relic, scrap, shard, sherd, shred, spall **6** gobbet, morsel, parcel, screed, sheard, sippet, sliver **7** cantlet, flinder, flitter, fritter, oddment, portion, remnant **8** fraction **10** smithereen

biographical: **8** anecdote

diamond: **4** bort

ice afloat: **5** brash

fragmentary: 5 hashy **6** broken

fragments: 5 frush **7** gubbins

literary: ana **7** analect

Fragonard painting: 7 Bathers

fragrance: 4 odor **5** aroma, scent, smell **6** flavor **7** flavour, incense, perfume **9** perfumery, redolence

fragrant: 5 balmy, olent, spicy **7** odorant, odorous, perfumy, scented **8** aromatic, redolent **9** ambrosial **11** odoriferous

fragrant ointment: 4 balm, nard

fragrant wood: 5 aloes, cedar

frail: 4 fine, puny, weak **5** crazy **6** basket, flimsy, infirm, sickly **7** brittle, bruckle, fragile **8** delicate **12** destructible **13** insubstantial

frailty: sin **4** vice **5** fault **6** foible **7** failing **8** weakness **9** frailness, infirmity **10** peccadillo **12** imperfection

fraise: 4 fray, fuss, ream, ruff **6** cajole, defend, praise **7** defense, enlarge, flatter, pancake **8** cajolery **10** strawberry

frame (see also **framework**): bin **4** bunk, form, mold, plan, plot, sill **5** build, cadre, easel, panel, serve, shape, trave **6** abacus, adjust, binder, border, cook up, devise, fabric, invent, manage, profit, redact, resort, tenter **7** arrange, attempt, chassis, fashion, furnish, hatch up, outline, portray, prepare, proceed, prosper **8** contrive, regulate **9** calculate, construct, fabricate, structure

kinds of: ame, mat **4** bier, calm, caum, gill, sash, sess, sime, sley **5** airer, cadar, cader, dekle, easel, grate, herse, knape, trave, scray **6** abacus, deckel, deckle, tenter **7** drosser, hayrack, taboret

frame of mind: 4 bent, mood **5** humor

frame-up: 4 plot **10** conspiracy

framework: 4 rack, sill **5** cadge, cadre, racke **6** replum, stroma **7** chassis, nacelle, trestle **8** skeleton **9** structure

franc: *piece of twenty:* **5** louis

twentieth part of: **7** centime

France: 4 Gaul **6** Gallia

airplane: **5** avion

among: **5** entre

ancient name: **4** Gaul **6** Gallia

and: et

annuity: **5** rente

appellation: nom

architect: **7** LeNotre **9** Corbusier

article: la, le, un; les, une

author: **4** Gide, Hugo, Loti, Sand, Zola **5** Benda, Camus, Dumas, Renan **6** Balzac, Proust, Racine, Sartre **8** Stendhal, Voltaire

axe: **5** hache

baby: **4** bebe **6** enfant

bachelor: **6** garcon

bacteriologist: **7** Pasteur

ball: bal

ballad: lai **7** virelai

bay: **6** Biscay

beach: **5** plage

beast: **4** bete

bed: lit **5** couche

beef: **5** boeuf

billiards: **7** bouchon

bitters: **4** amer

blessed: **4** beni **5** sacre

boat: **6** bateau **8** chaloupe

bond: **5** rente

boxing: **6** savate

boy: **6** garcon

brandy: **8** armagnac, eau de vie

brewery: **9** brasserie

brush: **6** brosse

butcher shop: **11** charcuterie

cafe: **9** estaminet

cape: **5** talma

capital: **5** Paris

card game: **6** ecarte **7** baccara **8** baccarat

cardinal: **7** Mazarin **9** Richelieu

care: **4** soin

cathedral city: **5** Reims, Rouen **6** Nantes, Rheims

chanteuse: **4** Piaf

chaperon: **11** gouvernante

cheese: **4** Brie **9** Camembert, Roquefort

chemist: **5** Curie **7** Pasteur

chestnut: **6** marone, maroon

citizen: **7** citoyen

city: Aix, Pau **4** Caen, Metz, Nice, Vimy **5** Aries, Arles, Arras, Brest, Dijon, Havre, Lille, Lisle, Lyons, Nancy, Nerac, Nesle, Nimes, Paris, Reims, Rouen, Tours, Tulle, Vichy **6** Amiens, Angers, Calais, Lemans, Nantes, Pantin, Perret, Rennes, Rheims, Senlis, Sevres, Tarare, Toulon **7** Limoges, Orleans, Valence **8** Bordeaux, Clermont, Mulhouse, Rochelle, Toulouse **9** Levallois, Marseille

cleric: **4** abbe

cloth: ras **5** toile **8** blancard

cloud: nue

coffeehouse: **9** estaminet

coin: ecu, sol, sou **4** gros **5** agnel, blanc, blank, franc, obole, livre **6** denier, dizain, teston **7** centime, dizaine, testoon **8** cavalier, Louis d'or, Napoleon

commune: Pau **4** Auby, Bron, Dole, Laon, Loos, Orly, Reze, Vimy **5** Ancre, Rodez, Vichy **6** Pessac, Sanvic, Stains, Tarare

composer: **4** Lalo **5** Bizet, Ravel, Thome **6** Gounod, Halevy **7** Debussy

comrade: ami

concrete: **5** beton

conjunction: **4** mais

cordial: **8** anisette

cotton: **7** jasmine

couturier: **4** Dior **5** Patou **6** Chanel **7** Balmain **8** Givenchy **9** Courreges, St. Laurent

cowardly: **5** lache

cowboy: **6** baille **7** gardian

creamcake: **7** dariole

crown: ecu

custom: **9** Gallicism

daffodil: **10** polyanthus

daisy: **10** marguerite

dance: bal **5** gavot **6** branle, canary, cancan **7** bourree, boutade

dash: **4** élan

daughter: **5** fille

dead: **4** mort

dean: **5** doyen

dear: **4** cher

delicatessen: **11** charcuterie

department: Ain, Lot, Var **4** Aube, Aude, Cher, Eure, Gard, Gers, Jura, Nord, Oise, Orne, Tarn **5** Aisne, Corse, Doubs, Drome, Indre, Isere, Loire, Marne, Meuse, Rhone, Seine, Somme,

Yonne **6** Allier, Ariege, Cantal, Creuse, Landes, Loiret, Lozere, Manche, Nievre, Sarthe, Savoie, Vendee, Vienne, Vosges **7** Ardeche, Aveyron, Correze, Dordgne, Gironde, Herault, Mayenne, Meurthe, Moselle

devil: **6** diable

directory: **10** directoire

division: **6** canton **7** commune **10** depart-ment **14** arrondissement

division, ancient: **5** Arles **6** Arelas **7** Are-late **9** Aquitaine

doorkeeper: **9** concierge

dramatist: **5** Piron **6** Halevy, Racine, Sar-dou **7** Moliere

dressmaker: **9** couturier **10** couturiere

duke: duc

dungeon: **6** cachot

dynasty: **5** Capet **6** Valois **7** Bourbon, Or-leans

ecclesiastic: **4** abbe

egg: **4** oeuf

empress: **7** Eugenie **15** Marie Antoinette

essayist: **4** Gide **9** Montaigne

evening: **4** soir

exclamation: **4** hein

FBI: **15** Surete Nationale

farmhouse: **5** ferme

father: **4** pere

finally: **5** enfin

friar: **5** frere

friend: ami

gala: **4** fete

game: jeu **4** jeux(pl.)

god: **4** dieu

good: bon

goodbye: **5** adieu

green: **4** vert

hairdresser: **7** friseur **8** coiffeur

hat: **5** beret **7** chapeau **8** chapeaux

health: **5** sante

heaven: **4** ciel

here: ici

high: **5** haute

horse stable: **6** ecurie

husband: **4** mari

income: **5** rente

inn: **5** hotel **7** auberge

island: ile, yeu **4** Elba **6** Hyeres, Oleron, Ushant **7** Corsica **8** Bellelze

judgment: **5** arret

king: roi **5** Louis, Capet

knife: **7** couteau

lace: **10** colberteen, colbertine **12** Valen-ciennes

lake: **6** Annecy **7** Bourget

language: **7** Catalan **9** Provencal

laugh: ris **4** rire

laundry: **13** blanchisserie

leather: **4** cuir

lenten season: **6** Careme

liqueur: **5** creme **8** anisette **9** Cointreau

lord: **8** seigneur

lover: **5** amant

lyric: **6** rondel **7** descort, rondeau

magistrate: **7** echevin

maidservant: **5** bonne **7** lisette

marshal: Ney **4** Foch, Saxe **5** Murat **6** Pe-tain

mask: **5** loups

mathematician: **5** Borel

me: moi

measure: pot **4** aune, line, mile, mine, muid, pied, sack, velt **5** arpen, carat, lieue, ligne, minot, perch, pinte, point, pouce, toise, velte **6** arpent, hemine, league, perche, quarte, setier **7** chopine, heminee, poisson, septier **8** boisseau, quartaut, roquille **9** decillion, quarteron **12** tonneau de mer

milk: **4** lait

mine: **4** a moi

money: See *coin* above

month: Mai **4** Aout, Juin, Mars, mois **5** Avril **7** Fevrier, Janvier, Juillet, Oc-tobre **8** Decembre, Novembre **9** Sep-tembre

mountain: **4** Alps, Jura **6** Vosges **8** Au-vergne, Cevennes, Cote d'Or, Pyrenees **9** Mont Blanc, Puy de Dome, Vigne-male **10** Puy de Sancy

museum: **5** musee

nail: **4** clou

name: nom

national anthem: **12** Marseillaise

national flower: **4** lily **10** fleur de lis

no: non

noon: **4** midi

nose: nez

nothing: **4** rien

novelist: **4** Gide, Hugo, Loti, Zola **5** Ca-mus, Dumas, Ohnet, Sagan, Verne **6** Halevy, Proust **7** Merimee **8** Flaubert

nursemaid: **5** bonne

of: de

officer: **7** prefect

old money: **6** besant

one: une

opera: **5** Faust, Lakmé, Manon **6** Carmen, Mignon **7** La Juive

painter: **4** Dore **5** Corot, Degas, Manet, Monet **6** Cormon, Legros, Renoir, Seu-rat, Vernet **7** Chardin, Deveria, Lor-rain, Poussin, Utrillo, Watteau **8** Stein-len **9** Deschamps

palace: **6** palais

pancake: **5** crepe

parish priest: **4** cure

Parliament chamber: **5** senat

party: bal

pastry shop: **10** patisserie

patron saint: **5** Denis, Denys **6** Martin

peer: duc **8** seigneur

philosopher: **4** Caro **5** Camus **6** Pascal,

Sartre **8** Rousseau **9** Descartes
physicist: **5** Arago, Binet **6** Ampere
pocket: **5** poche
poem: dit, lai **7** rondeau
poet: **4** Labe **6** Racine **7** Rimbaud, Rostand **8** Verlaine **9** Deschamps, Desportes **10** Beaudelaire
police: **4** flic **6** Surete **8** gendarme
porcelain: **7** Limoges
port: **4** Caen **6** Calais **7** Le Havre **10** Marseilles
preposition: de
president's residence: **6** elysee
pretty: **4** joli **5** jolie
priest: **4** abbe, cure, pere
pronoun: ils, lui, mes, moi **4** elle, nous, vous **6** tienne
psychologist: **5** Binet
pupil: **5** eleve
queen: **5** reine
rabbit: **5** lapin
race course: **7** Auteuil
railroad: **11** chemin de fer
railroad station: **4** gare
read: **4** lire
rear: **7** arrière
region: **6** Alsace
Republic calendar: **6** Nivose **7** Floreal, Ventose **8** Brumaire, Fervidor, Frimaire, Germinal, Messidor, Pluviose, Prairial **9** Fructidor, Thermidor **11** Vendemiaire
resort: Pau **4** Nice **5** Vichy **6** Cannes, Menton **7** Riviera **8** Biarritz **9** Deauville
rest: **5** repos
restaurant: **6** bistro
Revolutionary hero: **6** Danton
Revolutionary leader: **5** Marat
Revolutionary radical: **7** Jacobin
river: Ain, Lot, Lys **4** Aire, Aude, Cher, Eure, Gard, Gers, Loir, Oise, Orne, Saar, Tarn, Yser **5** Adour, Aisne, Drome, Indre, Isere, Loire, Maine, Marne, Meuse, Rance, Rhone, Saone, Sarre, Seine, Seyre, Somme, Veste, Yonne **6** Allier, Ariege, Escaut, Loiret, Nievre, Sambre, Scarpe, Vienne **7** Ardeche, Durance, Garonne, Gironde, Moselle, Scheldt **8** Charente, Dordogne, Nantaise
roast: **4** roti **5** rotir
room: **5** salle
royal family: **5** Capet **6** Valois
saint: **5** Denis, Denys **6** Martin
savant: **7** Diderot
school: **5** ecole, lycee **8** Barbison, Barbizon
scientist: **5** Curie **7** Pasteur
sculptor: **5** Barye, Rodin **9** Bartholdi
sea: mer
seaport: **4** Caen **5** Brest, Havre **6** Calais,

Toulon **8** Bordeaux **9** Dunkerque
shelter: **4** abri
shield: ecu **5** targe
shoe: **9** chaussure
shopgirl: **9** midinette
sister: **5** soeur
slang: **5** argot
soldier: **5** assis, poilu **6** Zouave **8** chasseur
son: **4** fils
song: **5** caira, chant **6** aubade **7** ballade, chanson, Madelon, virelai, virelay
soul: ame
south: sud **4** Midi
spirit: ame **4** elan **6** esprit
stable: **6** ecurie
star: **6** etoile
state: **4** etat
stock exchange: **6** bourse
store: **8** boutique
story: **5** conte
street: rue
stupid: **4** bete
summer: ete
sun king: **8** Louis XIV
symbol: **4** lily **10** Fleur-de-lis
the: la, le; les(pl.)
theater: **5** odeon
then: **5** alors
ticket window: **7** guichet
title: duc **5** comte
tobacco: **5** tabac
town: **4** Agen, Aire, Caen, Sens, Sete **5** Douai, Ernee, Laval, Nerac, Ornes **6** Longwy, Sarlat, Tarbes, Troyes, Verdun **7** Castres **8** Le Perche, Rochelle
true: **4** vrai
Verdun battle: **4** Vaux
verse: **4** vers
verse form: lai **4** alba **6** rondel **7** ballade, virelay
very: **4** tres
vessel: **7** navette
vinegar: **8** vinaigre
vineyard: cru **5** vigne
waiter: **6** garcon
wall: mur
water: eau **4** eaux(pl.)
weight: **4** gros, marc, once **5** carat, livre, pound, tonne, uckia **7** tonneau **8** esterlin **9** esterling
who: qui
wicket: **7** guichet
wind: **7** mistral
wine: vin **4** Bois **8** sauterne **10** Roussillon
wine district: **5** Medoc **8** Bordeaux, Burgundy, Provence **9** Champagne
wine shop: **6** bistro
woman: **5** femme
world: **5** monde
you: **4** vous
Franciscan: **8** Minorite, Capuchin **9** Cordelier

nun: **5** Clare

franchise: soc **5** grant **6** patent **7** license **8** freelage, suffrage **9** privilege

old English: soc **4** soke

francolin: 4 bird **5** titar **9** partridge

frangible: 7 brittle, fragile **9** breakable

frank: 4 free, open, rank **5** bluff, lusty, naive, plain **6** candid, direct, honest **7** artless, genuine, liberal, profuse, sincere **8** carefree, cavalier, generous, vigorous **9** ingenuous, luxuriant, outspoken **10** licentious, unreserved **15** straightforward, unsophisticated

frankincense: 8 olibanum

Frankish hero: 6 Roland

Franklin: *invention:* **5** stove **8** bifocals

pen name: **11** Poor Richard

frankly: 6 freely, openly **7** plainly **8** candidly **9** artlessly, liberally, sincerely, willingly **10** forthright **11** ingenuously **12** unreservedly **13** undisguisedly

frankness: 6 candor **7** freedom **8** openness **9** telltruth, unreserve

Franks: 7 Salians

hero: **6** Roland

king: **5** Pepin **6** Clovis

law of: **5** Salic

peasant: **4** liti(pl.) **5** litus

vassal: **4** leud

frantic: mad **5** rabid **6** insane **7** furious, lunatic, violent **8** deranged, feverish, frenetic, frenzied **9** delirious, desperate, phrenetic **10** distracted, distraught

frap: 5 brace **6** secure, strike **7** tighten **10** strengthen

frappe: ice **4** iced **5** chill **6** cooled, freeze, frozen **9** milk shake

frat: 11 brotherhood

frater: 7 brother, comrade

fraternal: 9 brotherly

fraternity: 4 club **8** sorority **10** sisterhood **11** brotherhood

fraternize: 6 cotton **9** affiliate, associate, forgather **10** foregather

fraud: 4 dole, fake, gaff, gaud, gull, jape, ruse, sham, wile **5** cheat, craft, faker, guile, hocus, quack, trick **6** brogue, deceit, humbug **7** defraud, knavery, roguery, swindle **8** artifice, impostor, subtlety, trickery, trumpery **9** collusion, deception, imposture, stratagem **10** imposition **11** fraudulency **13** bamboozlement, circumvention

fraudulent: 4 fake, wily **5** snide **6** crafty, quacky **7** abusive, crooked, cunning **8** cheating, covinous, guileful, spurious **9** deceitful, deceiving, deceptive, designing, dishonest, horsefair, insidious, underhand **10** fallacious, misleading **11** clandestine, counterfeit, treacherous

fraught: 4 fill, lade, load **5** cargo, equip, laden **6** burden, supply **7** freight **9** freighted, transport

fraxinus: ash **4** tree

fray: 4 feud, fret, riot **5** alarm, brawl, broil, broom, clash, dread, feaze, fight, melee, panic, ravel **6** affray, assail, attack, battle, bustle, combat, fraise, fridge, fright, inroad, terror, tumult **7** contest, frazzle, ruction, terrify **8** disperse, frighten **9** commotion, dissipate **12** apprehension

frayed: 4 worn **7** raveled **10** threadbare

frazzle: 5 upset **7** exhaust, wear out **9** prostrate

freak: 4 bold, flam, lune, mood, whim **5** braid, fancy, fleck, humor, prank, sport **6** frolic, greedy, humour, megrim, mosaic, streak, vagary, whimsy **7** caprice, checker, chimera, crochet, monster, whimsey **8** capricci(pl.), flimflam **9** capriccio, variegate **10** enthusiast **11** monstrosity **12** whimsicality

freakish: odd **6** screwy **7** curious, flighty **9** arbitrary, fantastic, whimsical **10** capricious

fream: 4 roar

freckle: 4 spot **7** ephelis, frecken, lentigo, speckle

remover: **6** adarce

Frederick I's nickname: 10 Barbarossa

Frederick the Great: 6 Alaric

free: lax, rid **4** liss, open, quit, void **5** broad, clear, enode, frank, lisse, loose, ready, siker, slake, spare, untie **6** acquit, adjust, beyond, degage, devoid, exempt, gratis, immune, lavish, loosen, remove, rescue, sicker, unbind **7** absolve, deliver, forward, grivois, inexact, leisure, liberal, manumit, outside, release, relieve, unbound, willing **8** abundant, detached, dispatch, distinct, expedite, familiar, floating, generous, grivoise, indigent, innocent, liberate, overfree, separate, unfasten, unhamper **9** at liberty, discharge, disengage, exculpate, exonerate, expansive, extricate, footloose, guiltless, ingenuous, outspoken, separated, unbridled, unchecked, unimpeded, unleased **10** autonomous, emancipate, gratuitous, immoderate, licentious, openhanded, self-ruling, unattached, uncombined, unconfined, unfettered, unimpaired, unreserved **11** disencumber, disentangle, independent, magnanimous, spontaneous, untrammeled **12** uncontrolled, unencumbered, unrestrained, unrestricted **13** communicative, self-directing, unconstrained

from bacteria: **7** aseptic, sterile

from blame: **5** clear **6** acquit **7** absolve, relieve **9** exonerate

from bondage: **7** manumit **10** emancipate **11** affranchise

from dirt: **7** apinoid
from discount: net
from moisture: dry **9** dehydrate
from restraint: **5** untie
from suspicion: **5** clear, purge **6** acquit **7** absolve **9** exculpate, exonerate
free-for-all: 4 race **5** fight, melee **6** barney **11** competition
free of charge: 8 buckshee
free time: 4 rest **6** recess **7** leisure
freebooter: 5 rider **6** pirate **7** cateran, corsair **8** pillager **9** buccaneer, plunderer **10** filibuster
freed: 8 absolute **13** disencumbered
freedom: 4 ease **7** abandon, content, leisure, liberty, license, release **8** facility, freelage, immunity, latitude, openness **9** exemption, frankness, readiness **10** generosity, liberality, liberation **11** manumission, willingness **12** emancipation, independence **13** outspokenness **14** unreservedness
from activity: **4** rest **6** recess **7** respite
from fraud: **7** honesty **9** bonafides
from pain: **6** aponia
from strife: **5** peace
of access: **6** entree
freehold: 4 alod **5** allod **6** estate, tenure **7** alodium **8** allodium
freeholder: 6 yeoman
freeing: 8 acquital **11** manumission
freeloader: 5 leech **6** sponge **8** hanger-on, parasite **12** lounge lizard
freely: 4 lief **5** noble, nobly **6** gratis **7** frankly, largely, readily **8** heartily **9** beautiful, bounteous, bountiful, copiously, excellent, liberally, voluntary, willingly **10** abundantly, generously **11** beautifully, bounteously, bountifully, excellently, plenteously, plentifully, voluntarily **12** munificently **13** spontaneously **14** unobstructedly **15** unconditionally
freeman: 4 aire **5** ceorl, churl, thane, thegn **6** yeoman **7** burgess, burgher, citizen
Freestone State: 11 Connecticut
freethinker: 7 infidel, skeptic **8** agnostic **10** espritfort, unbeliever
freeze: ice 4 rime **5** chill **6** frappe, harden **7** chilled, congeal, impound **11** conglaciate, refrigerate
freezer: 4 icer
freezing: icy 4 cold **5** gelid, nippy **6** frigid, frosty
freight: 4 load **5** cargo, laden **6** lading **7** fraught **9** transport **10** freightage
freightage: 5 cargo **6** lading **7** freight
freighted: 5 laden **7** fraught
French: See **France**
French-Belgian river: Lys **4** Yser
Frenchman: 4 Gaul **6** Picard **8** Parisian

frenetic, phrenetic: mad **4** wild **5** crazy, fresh, rabid **6** insane, madman **7** fanatic, frantic, madness, violent, zealous **9** delirious **10** distracted, ornamental, passionate **12** absentminded
frenzied: 4 amok, mang **5** amoke, amuck, rabid **6** ramage **7** berserk, frantic, furious **8** frenetic, furibund, maddened **9** delirious
frenzy: mad **4** amok, fury, rage **5** amoke, amuck, furor, mania **7** frantic, madness, oestrus **8** delirium, insanity, maniacal **9** amazement **11** distraction
frequency: 5 crowd **6** throng **7** crebity **9** community, concourse **11** familiarity
unit: **7** fresnel
frequent: 5 haunt, howff, often, usual, visit **6** affect, common, effect, hourly, sundry **7** current, enhaunt, prevail **8** familiar, habitual **9** assiduous, crebrouse, habituate **10** persistent
frequented places: 5 dives **6** haunts **7** resorts
frequenter: 7 denizen, habitue
frequently: oft **5** often **6** hourly **8** ofttimes **10** repeatedly
fresco: 5 mural, shade **8** coolness
fresh: new **4** cool, good, pure, racy **5** brisk, green, ruddy, saucy, sound, sweet, vivid **6** breezy, bright, caller, florid, lively, recent, strong, unused **7** unfaded, untired, untried **9** obtrusive, unspoiled **10** additional, meddlesome, refreshing, unimpaired **11** smart-alecky **12** invigorating, presumptuous
and lively: **4** racy
freshen: 5 renew **6** breeze, revive **7** refresh, sweeten
freshet: 5 flood, spate, stream **9** streamlet **10** inundation
freshly: 5 again
freshman: 4 colt, tyro **5** bejan, frosh, plebe **6** bejant, novice, rookie **8** neophyte, newcomer **10** apprentice
freshness: 4 verd **8** verdancy **9** fraicheur
lose: dry **4** fade, wilt **6** wither
fret: nag, rub, vex **4** care, fray, gall, gnaw, pout, rage, stew **5** chafe, grate, pique, tease, worry **6** abrade, devour, harass, murmur, nettle, plague, rankle, ripple, ruffle, strait **7** agitate, consume, disturb, grizzle, roughen **8** diminish, disquiet, irritate, vexation
fretful: 5 angry, cross **6** repine, sullen **7** carking, frecket, gnawing, peevish, pettish **8** captious, corroded, fretsome, petulant, restless **9** corrosive, impatient, irascible, irritable, plaintive, querulous **10** ill-humored, ill-natured
Freudian term: id; ego **8** superego
Frey: *father:* **5** Njord **6** Njorth
sister: **5** Freya **6** Freyja

wife: 4 Gerd

Freya's husband: 4 Oder

friable: 5 crimp, crisp, crump, loamy, mealy

clay: 4 bole

friar: fra 4 fish, monk 5 frere 6 Bhikku, fraile, frater 7 Bhikshu, brother 8 monastic 9 Carmelite 10 Franciscan 11 Augustinian

black: 9 Dominican

mendicant: 7 Servite

friary: 8 cloister 9 monastery 11 brotherhood

fribble: 4 fool 6 falter, totter, trifle 7 stammer 8 trifling 9 frivolity, frivolous

fricassee: 6 potpie 10 blanquette

friction: rub 5 chafe 9 attrition 10 dissension

air: 7 windage

fridge: rub 4 fray 5 chafe 6 fidget 8 irritate

fried: 4 frit 7 sauteed

fried cake: 7 cruller 8 doughnut

friend: ami(F.), amy, eme, pal 4 ally, amie(F.), chum, kith 5 amigo(Sp.), amiga(Sp.), crony 6 bonami(F.), cummer, gimmer, kimmer 7 comrade, gremial, kinsman 8 cockmate, compadre, paramour, relative 9 associate, attendant, bonne amie(F.), broadbrim, companion, confidant 10 confidante 12 acquaintance

Friend: 6 Quaker

church founder: 9 George Fox

friendless: 7 forlorn

friendliness: 5 amity 8 affinity, amicable, goodwill 10 fellowship 13 companionship

friendly: sib 4 cosh, good, kind 5 chief, howdy 6 blithe, chummy, genial, homely, howdie 7 affable, amiable, amicous, cordial 8 amicable, homelike, intimate, sociable 9 favorable 10 favourable, hospitable 11 warmhearted 12 well-disposed

Friendly island: 5 Tonga

friendship: 5 amity 6 accord 8 relation 9 affection 10 attachment

Friendship author: 6 Cicero

frieze: 4 kelt(Sc.) 5 adorn, chase 8 trimming 9 embroider 10 decoration

band: 6 taenia

frigate (see also **boat, ship**): 5 zabra(Sp.)

frigate bird: iwa 8 alcatras

Frigg: *husband:* 4 Odin

son: 6 Balder

fright: awe, cow 4 fear, fray, funk, gast 5 alarm, gliff, panic, scare, shock 6 affray, dismay, horror, schrik, terror 7 startle 11 trepidation 13 consternation

frighten: awe, cow 4 fray, funk, hare, haze, shoo 5 afear, alarm, appal, gliff, hazen, scare 6 affray, appall, ascare, boggle 7 frecken, startle, terrify 8 affright 10 intimidate

frightened: 4 awed, eery, gast 5 eerie, timid 6 afraid 8 skittish

frightful: 4 grim 5 awful, ferly, scary 6 horrid, ugsome 7 affreux, fearful, gashful, ghastly, hideous 8 alarming, dreadful, fearsome, horrible, horrific, shocking, terrible, terrific 10 horrendous, tremendous

frightfulness: 13 atrociousness 15 schrecklichkeit(Ger.)

frigid: icy 4 cold 5 acold, bleak 6 arctic, frosty 8 freezing

frill: 4 purl 5 jabot, ruche 6 ruffle 7 flounce 8 furbelow 9 balayeuse 11 chitterling

fringe: hem, rim 4 loma 6 border, edging, margin 8 ciliella, trimming

fringed: 9 laciniate 10 frimbriate

frippery: 6 finery 7 regalia 9 full dress 10 Sunday best

frisk: 4 leap, skip, whid 5 brisk, caper, dance, flisk 6 curvet, frisco, frolic, gambol, lively, search 7 disport, friscal 8 caracole 9 shake down 10 frolicsome

frisky: gay 4 pert 6 lively 7 playful 8 frisking, sportive 9 kittenish 10 frolicsome

frisson: 5 chill 6 quiver, shiver, thrill 7 shudder

frith: 4 help 5 firth, hedge 6 hurdle, wattle 7 coppice, estuary, freedom 8 liberate, security 9 brushwood, copsewood, underwood 10 protection

fritter: 5 shred, spend, waste 6 bangle 7 pancake, scatter 8 fragment

frivol: 6 trifle 9 frivolous

frivolity: 6 levity 7 fribble, inanity 8 nonsense 9 lightness

frivolous: gay 5 giddy, inane, petty 6 frivol, futile 7 fatuous, fribble, shallow, trivial 8 gossamer 9 childlike, worthless 11 empty-headed, light-headed 14 featherbrained

frizzed: 5 crepe 6 crispy

fro: 4 away, back, from 5 hence, since 8 backward

frock (see also **dress**): jam 4 grown, slip, wrap 5 tunic 6 cleric, jersey, mantle 7 workman 9 gaberdine

frog: 4 toad 5 frosh, frosk, jakie 6 peeper 7 paddock, quilkin 8 ferreiro 9 amphibian

order of: see *zoological order* below.

pert. to: 6 ranine

rearing place: 7 ranaria(pl.) 8 ranarium

zoological order: 5 anura 6 anoura 9 salientia

frogman: 5 diver 7 swimmer

gear: 5 scuba

frohlich: gay 5 happy 6 joyous

frolic: bum, gay 4 blow, game, gell, jink, lark, orgy, play, ramp, romp 5 caper, freak, frisk, merry, prank, randy, sport, spree 6 curvet, gambol, plisky, prance, rollix, shindy, splore 7 disport, gammock, pliskie, scamper, stashie, wassail 8 carousal 9 gilravage 10 masquerade

frolicsome: gay 4 roid 5 gilpy 6 frisky, gilpey 7 jocular, waggish 8 espiegle, friskful, gamesome, sportive

from: fro
beginning to end: 4 over 7 through
head to foot: 7 capapie
here: 5 hence
that time: 6 thence
the egg: 5 ab ovo
the time that: 5 since
this time: 5 hence

front: bow, van 4 brow, face, fore, head, prow 5 afore 6 before, facade, facing, oppose, sector 7 forward, further, obverse 8 forehead, foremost, forepart, foreside 9 forefront 10 appearance, effrontery 11 countenance
toward the: 8 anterior

frontal: 6 sindon 7 metopic

frontier: 4 face 5 bound, march 6 border, oppose 7 barrier, defense 8 boundary

frontiersman: 4 Cody 5 Boone, Clark 6 Carson 7 pioneer, settler 8 Crockett

fronton: 7 jai-alai

frore: 4 cold 6 frosty, frozen

frost: ice, nip 4 foam, hoar, rime 7 failure

frosted: 4 iced 5 glace 6 frozen

frostfish: 5 smelt 6 tomcod 9 whitefish

frosting: ice, mat 5 icing

frosty: icy 4 cold, rimy 5 chill, frore, gelid, glary 6 frigid, froren 8 chilling, freezing

froth: fob 4 barm, foam, scum, suds 5 spume 6 freath, lather

frow: 4 frau, froe, wife 5 vrouw, woman

froward: 5 balky, cross 7 adverse, awkward, peevish, wayward 8 contrary, perverse, petulant, untoward 9 obstinate 10 refractory, unyielding 11 disobedient, unfavorable 12 ungovernable

frown: 4 lour, pout, sulk 5 gloom, glout, lower, scowl 6 glower, glunch 7 frounce

frowsy, frowzy: 5 musty 6 blowzy 7 raffish, unkempt 8 slovenly 10 disordered

frozen: 4 hard 5 fixed, frore, gelid, glary 6 chilly, frappe, froren 7 chilled, frosted 8 hardened, immobile 9 congealed 10 unyielding 11 coldhearted 12 refrigerated 13 unsympathetic

fructify: 9 fertilize 10 impregnate

frugal: 4 mild 5 chary, roman, spare 6 saving 7 careful, sparing, thrifty 9 economize, provident 10 economical,

unwasteful 12 parsimonious 13 pennypinching

frugality: 6 thrift 7 economy 8 prudence 9 chariness

fruit: fig 4 date, lime, pear, plum, pome 5 apple, berry, drupe, grape, issue, lemon, melon, olive, peach, young 6 cherry, orange, result 7 apricot, azarole, product, progeny 8 dewberry 9 blueberry, nectarine, offspring, pineapple, tangerine 10 grapefruit, production
aggregate: 7 etaerio
apple-like: 4 pome 6 quince
astringent: 4 sloe
baccate: 5 berry
beverage: ade 4 wine
blackthorn: 4 sloe
buttercup: 5 akene 6 achene 7 achenia(pl.) 8 achenium
citrus: 4 lime 5 grape, lemon 6 orange 7 kumquat, tangelo 8 mandarin 9 tangerine 10 grapefruit
collective: 7 syncarp 10 syncarpium
cooked in syrup: 7 compote
decay: 4 blet
desert region: 5 terfa 6 terfez
dish: 7 compote
dried: 5 prune 6 orejon, raisin
drink: ade 5 juice, punch
dry: 5 regma 6 achene, samara
early maturing: 8 rareripe
elm tree: 6 samara
fleshy: 4 pear, plum, pome 5 berry, drupe, melon 6 tomato
fleshy part: 9 sarcocarp
goddess of: 6 Pomona
gourd family: 4 pepo
horseradish tree: ben
husk: 5 lemma
hybrid: 7 tangelo
imperfect: 6 nubbin
juicy: 4 lime, pear, plum 5 grape, lemon, peach 6 orange 7 apricot 9 pineapple 10 grapefruit
layer: 7 epicarp
less: 8 acarpous
lime & lemon: 6 citron
many-seeded: 11 pomegranate
maple: 6 samara
mild acid: 5 guava
multiple: 4 cone
of cactus: 5 sabra
of rose: 11 cynorrhodon
of strawberry: 7 etaerio
oily: 5 olive
one-seeded: 5 akene 6 achene, samara 7 achenis(pl.) 8 achenium
palm tree: 4 date
peach-like: 7 apricot 9 nectarine
pear-shaped: fig 7 avocado
plum-like: 4 sloe 7 carissa
pome: 4 pear 5 apple 7 azarole

preserving: **6** medlar
pulp: pap
pulpy: uva **4** pome **5** drupe, grape, berry
red: **4** plum **5** apple **6** cherry **9** raspberry **10** strawberry
refuse: **4** marc
rind: **7** epicarp
rosebush: hip
science of: **8** pomology
seed: pip, pit
spore: **6** aecium
stalk: **8** peduncle
stone: **4** paip, plum **5** drupe, peach, prune **6** cherry **7** apricot **9** nectarine
study of: **8** pomology **9** carpology
strawberry-family: **7** etaerio
sugar: **7** glucose **8** fructose
tropical: fig **4** date **5** guava, gourd, mango **6** banana, papaya, pawpaw **9** sapodilla
vine: **5** grape
winged: **6** samara
withered; **6** nubbin
yellowish: **5** papaw **6** quince
fruit basket: 6 pottel, pottle
fruit bats: 8 pteropid **10** pteropidae
fruit dealer: 9 frontsman, fruiterer **11** greengrocer
fruit of Jove: 9 persimmon
fruit of paradise: 6 pomelo **10** grapefruit
fruit stone: pit **4** paip **6** pyrene **7** putamen
fruitful: fat **6** fecund **7** fertile **8** abundant, prolific **9** feracious, plenteous, plentiful, procreant **10** productive
fruitgrower: 8 fruitist **10** orchardist, pomologist **14** horticulturist
fruition: joy **8** pleasure **9** enjoyment **11** achievement, fulfillment, realization
fruitless: dry **4** geld, vain **5** addle, blank **6** barren, futile **7** sterile, useless **8** abortive **10** profitless **11** ineffectual **12** unprofitable, unsuccessful
frump: vex **4** mock, snub, sulk **5** dowdy, flout **6** gossip **7** provoke **8** irritate
frustrate: 4 balk, bilk, dash, foil, null, vain, void **5** baulk, blank, block, check, cross, crush, elude **6** baffle, blight, defeat, delude, outwit, scotch, thwart **7** deceive, nullify, prevent, useless **8** confound, infringe, nugatory **9** cancel out, checkmate, discomfit **10** circumvent, counteract, disappoint, disconcert, neutralize **11** countermand, ineffectual **12** unprofitable
frustration: 4 foil, **6** fiasco **12** discomfiture **15** disillusionment
fry: 4 sile **5** brook, roast, saute, young **6** sizzle **9** offspring
fryer: 6 pullet
frying pan: 6 spider **7** griddle, skillet
fuddle: 5 booze **6** muddle, tipple **7** fluster
fuddled: fap, ree **5** bosky, tipsy **7** muddled

fudge: pad **4** fake **5** candy, foist, hunch **6** devise, humbug **8** contrive, nonsense **9** interlope, makeshift **10** substitute **11** counterfeit
fuel: gas, oil **4** coal, coke, peat, wood **5** argal, argol, argul, stoke **6** acetol, elding, firing, petrol **7** pabulum **8** charcoal, gasoline, kerosene, kerosine **9** petroleum **10** exaggerate **11** combustible
fugacious: 6 flying **8** fleeting, volatile **10** evanescent
fuggy: 6 smelly, stuffy
fugitive: 5 exile, fleme **6** emigre, exiled, outlaw **7** fleeing, refugee, roaming, runaway **8** banished, deserter, fleeting, runagate, unstable, vagabond, volatile **9** fugacious, strolling, transient, uncertain **10** evanescent
fugue: 4 fuga **9** ricercare
exponent: **4** Bach **6** Handel
Führer, der: 6 Hitler
Fukien river: Min
fulcrum: 4 bait, prop **5** thole **7** support
fulfill: 4 fill, full, meet **6** effect, finish, occupy **7** achieve, execute, perform, satisfy **8** complete **9** implement **10** accomplish, effectuate
fulfillment, fulfilment: 6 effect **9** execution **10** completion **11** performance, realization **14** accomplishment
fulgent: 6 bright **7** shining **8** dazzling, luminous **9** effulgent
full: bad, big **4** good **5** ample, round, sated, solid, total **6** entire, fulfil, honest **7** baptize, copious, destroy, diffuse, fulfill, fulsome, orotund, perform, plenary, replete, teeming, trample **8** adequate, bouffant, brimming, complete, resonant **9** bouffante, capacious, plentiful **10** consecrate, exhaustive **13** comprehensive
full-blooded: 5 flush, ruddy **6** florid **8** rubicund **12** thoroughbred
full-blown: 4 lush, ripe **5** adult **6** all-out, mature **7** grown-up
full force: 5 brunt
full-grown: 6 mature **9** developed
full of: *cracks:* **6** rimose
glands: **7** adenose
hollows: **8** lacunose
minute openings: **6** porous
sand: **7** arenose
sap or juice: **7** succous **9** succulent
thorns: **6** briary
twists: **5** kinky **7** winding
wrinkles: **6** rugose
fuller: 7 creaser
fuller's grass: 8 soapwort
fullness, fulness: 5 fulth **6** plenty **7** satiety **8** pleonasm **9** abundance, amplitude, plumpness, repletion **10** fleshiness, perfection **12** completeness

fully: 5 amply 6 wholly 7 clearly, largely, utterly 8 entirely, maturely 9 perfectly 10 abundantly, completely, distinctly 11 plenteously, plentifully

fulmar: 4 bird 5 nelly 7 malduck

fulminate: 7 explode, inveigh 8 detonate

fulsome: fat 4 foul, full 5 gross, plump, suave 6 coarse, wanton 7 copious, lustful, overfed 8 abundant, nauseous 9 offensive, overgrown, repulsive, satiating, sickening 10 disgusting, indelicate, nauseating

fumble: paw 4 boot 5 abase, botch, error, grope 6 bobble, bungle, faffle, haffle, huddle, mumble

fume: 4 emit, foam, odor, rage, rant, reek 5 ewder, fumet, smoke, storm, vapor 6 exhale 7 flatter, fumette 8 fumigate, outburst 10 exhalation

fun: gag, gig 4 game, gell, glee, hoax, jest, joke, play 5 mirth, sport 6 gaiety, gayety 9 amusement, diversion, horseplay, merriment 10 pleasantry

function: act, run, use 4 duty, role, work 5 doing 6 action, office 7 calling, operate, service 8 activity, business, ceremony, occasion 9 festivity, gathering, operating, operation 10 occupation, profession, providence 11 performance 13 entertainment

social: tea 4 ball 5 party 6 soiree 9 reception

trigonometrical: 4 sine 6 cosine, secant 7 tangent

fund: 4 fond, pool 5 basis, stock, store 5 endow 6 bottom, ground, supply 7 deposit, reserve 10 foundation, groundwork 12 accumulation

fundamental: 5 basal, basic, vital 7 basilar, organic, primary, radical 8 original, rudiment 9 elemental, essential, important, necessary, paramount, principle 10 elementary

funds: 4 caja, cash 5 money 9 resources

funeral: 6 burial, dismal, exequy 7 cortege, funebre 8 exequial, funereal 9 forthfare, obsequies 10 sepulchral

bell: 5 knell

director: 9 mortician

oration: 5 eloge 6 eulogy 8 encomium 9 panegyric

pile: 4 pyre

song: 5 dirge, elegy, elogy, nenia 6 elegie 7 elogium, epicede 8 threnody 9 epicedium

structure: 10 catafalque

funereal: 5 feral, grave 6 dismal, gloomy, solemn 7 funebre, funeral 8 mournful 9 funebrial, funebrous 10 funebrious

funest: sad 4 dire 5 fatal 7 doleful

fungus: 4 bunt, cepe, mold, rust, smut 5 ergot, fungo, morel, moril, uredo, yeast 6 agaric, fungal, mildew, oidium, telium 7 agarics, amanita, blewits, fungoid, fungous, geaster, truffle 8 amanitin, mushroom, puffball 9 stinkhorn, toadstool 10 fungaceous

disease: rot 5 tinea

edible: 4 cepe 5 morel 7 truffle 8 mushroom

parasitic: 5 ergot

fungus-like: 6 agaric

funk: 4 kick, odor, rage 5 shirk, smell, spark 6 coward, flinch, fright, recoil, shrink 8 frighten 9 cowardice, touchwood

funnel: 4 pipe 6 hopper 7 conduct 8 transmit

funny: odd 5 comic, droll, queer 7 comical, jocular, risible, strange 8 humorous 9 laughable, ludicrous

funny bone: 9 olecranon

funnyman: wit 8 comedian

fur: 4 flix, pell, pelt 5 budge, stole 6 furrow, pelage

coat: 6 pelage

collection of: 5 pelts 6 peltry

kind of: fox 4 mink, paen, scut, seal, vair, woom 5 budge, civet, coney, fitch, lapin, otter, sable 6 ermine, galyac, galyak, marten, martin, moutin, nutria 7 calabar, calaber, caracul, karakul, miniver, platina, sealine 8 karakule, ragondin 9 silver fox

piece: 5 stole

refuse: 4 kemp

fur-bearing animal: fox 4 mink, seal 5 genet, otter, sable 6 marten, martin

furbelow: 5 frill 6 ruffle 7 falbala, falbelo, flounce 8 trimming

furbish: fig, rub 4 fake, vamp 5 clean, scour 6 polish 7 burnish 8 renovate

Furies: 5 Dirae 7 Erinyes

individual: 6 Alecto, Erinys 7 Erinnys, Erinyes, Megaera 9 Tisiphone

furious: mad 5 angry, brain, irate, rabid 6 fierce, furied, insane, stormy 7 frantic, mankind, rushing, violent 8 frenzied, vehement, wrathful 9 impetuous, turbulent 10 boisterous, tumultuous, uproarious

furl: 4 fold, roll, wrap 5 frese 6 enfold, fardel, furdel

furlana: 5 dance, music

furlong: 4 shot 5 stade 7 stadium 10 quarentene

furlough: 5 leave 6 permit 8 passport

furnace: 4 bosh, dome, kiln, oven 5 stove, tisar 6 calcar, cupola, heater 7 athanor, howells, rotator, smelter 8 bloomery, bruckner 9 scorifier 11 incinerator

part: 4 bosh, flue 5 grate

furnish: arm 4 feed, give, lend 5 array, endow, equip, frame, indue 6 afford, graith, insure, render, supply **7** apparel, appoint, garnish, provide **8** hand over, minister, palisade **10** accomplish, administer

crew: man

with battlements: **9** crenelate

with meals: **5** board, cater

furnished: 5 boden, garni **8** equipped, provided, supplied **9** garnished

furnishing: 5 stuff **7** fitment **8** fixtures, muniment, ornament **9** adornment, apparatus, furniture **10** enrichment, habiliment

furniture: 6 graith, outfit **7** fitment, tallboy **8** equipage **9** equipment **10** decoration, encoignure, furnishing **13** embellishment

style: **6** Empire **8** Colonial, Sheraton **11** Chippendale, Hepplewhite, Renaissance

furor: ado, cry, fad **4** fury, rage, to-do **5** craze, mania **6** frenzy **7** madness **10** dernier cri

furrow: fur, rut **4** grip, plow, rout **5** chase, drain, drill, field, rigol, score, stria **6** groove, sulcus, trench **7** channel, crumple, windrow, wrinkle

furrowed: 6 rivose rugose **7** sulcate, porcate **8** porcated **10** corrugated

furry: 5 hairy

further: aid, and, new, yet **4** abet, also, fore, help, more **5** again, front, serve **6** afford, beyond, former **7** advance, earlier, forward, promote, remoter **8** moreover **9** advantage **10** accelerate, additional, in addition

furtherance: 6 assist **8** facility, progress **9** promotion **10** assistance **11** advancement

furthermore: and **4** also **7** besides **8** moreover

furthersome: 4 rash **7** helpful **11** venturesome **12** advantageous

furtive: sly **4** wary, wily **6** secret, sneaky **7** hangdog **8** mystical, sneaking, stealthy **10** creepmouse **11** clandestine **13** under-the-table

fury: ire **4** rage **5** anger, breth, furor, rigor, vixen, wrath **6** beldam, choler, frenzy **7** beldame, madness, oestrus **8** delirium, violence **9** furiosity, vehemence **10** fierceness, turbulence **11** indignation

fuse: 4 flux, frit, melt, weld **5** blend, smelt, unite **6** anneal, mingle, solder **7** liquefy **8** dissolve **10** amalgamate **11** incorporate

fusee: 5 flare, torch **6** signal

fusion: 4 flux **6** fusure, merger **8** alliance, blending **9** coalition **11** coalescence

fuss: ado, row, tew, vex **4** busk, fike, rout, spat, stir, to-do **5** bearm, touse, whaup, worry **6** bother, bustle, caddle, fantad, fantod, fettle, fidget, fissle, fistle, fizzle, fraise, fuffle, fustle, pother, potter, tumult **7** dispute, friggle, fussock, quarrel, sputter, trouble **8** business **9** confusion **10** disconcert

fussy: 6 bustle, fidfad, spruce **7** fidgety, finical **8** overnice **10** fastidious, meticulous **14** overparticular

fustanella: 5 skirt **8** petticoat

fustian: 4 rant **5** tumid **7** bombast, pompous **8** claptrap, inflated **9** bombastic, worthless

fustigate: 4 beat, whip **6** strike

futile: 4 idle, vain **5** empty **6** otiose **7** useless **8** hopeless, trifling **9** frivolous, worthless **11** ineffectual

futility: 11 uselessness **13** frivolousness

future: 5 later **6** coming, onward **9** hereafter

fuzz: nap **4** down, lint, pile **5** fluff **8** puffball

fyke: 7 fishnet

fylfot: 5 cross **6** emblem **8** swastika

G

Gaal's father: 4 Ebed

gab: lie, yap **4** talk **5** boast, mouth, prate, scoff **6** gossip **7** chatter, deceive, prattle

Gabael's son: 5 Aduel

gabardine: 5 cloth **6** fabric

gabbard, gabbart: 4 scow **5** barge **6** vessel **7** lighter

gabble: rai(Sc.), yap **4** cank, chat, talk **6** babble, cackle, gossip, habble, jabber, yabble **7** chatter, clatter, twaddle

gabbro: 4 rock **6** norite

gabelle: tax **4** duty **6** excise, impost

gaberdine: 4 coat, gown **5** frock, smock **6** mantle **7** garment **8** pinafore

gabi: 4 taro

gabirit: 4 mold **5** gauge, model

gable: 4 wall **6** dormer, pinion

Gabon: *capital:* **10** Libreville
city: **4** Oyem **5** Bitam, Kango **10** Port Gentil
ethnic group: **5** Fangs **8** Bapounon
monetary unit: **5** franc **7** centime
mountain: **8** Iboundji
river: **6** Ogooue

Gabriel's instrument: 4 horn **7** trumpet

gad: 4 band, oath, roam, rope, rove **5** prowl, stray **6** ramble, wander **7** traipse **9** gallivant

Gad: *chieftain:* Ahi
descendant: Zia
father: **5** Jacob
mother: **6** Zilpah
son: Eri **5** Ezbon
tribe of: **6** Erites

gadfly: 4 pest **6** bother, critic **7** annoyer **8** busybody

gadget: 4 tool **5** gibbe(Sc.) **6** device, doodad, jigger **9** doohickey **11** contrivance

gadus: 7 codfish

gadwall: 4 duck

gadzooks: 4 egad

Gaea: 6 Tellus
consort: **6** Uranus
offspring: **5** Titan **6** Pontus, Titans, Uranus
parent: **5** Chaos

Gaelic (see also **Irish**)**: 4** Erse **6** Celtic **8** Highland
clan: **4** Sept
hero: **6** Ossian
John: Ian
land distribution: **7** rundale

poem: **4** Duan
spirit: **5** kelpy **6** kelpie **7** banshee
warrior: **5** Dagda **6** Fenian

gaff: 4 hoax, hook, pick, spar, spur, talk **5** fraud, laugh, spear, trick **6** clamor, deceit, fleece, outcry **7** prating **8** raillery

gaffe: 4 goof **5** boner **7** blooper, faux pas

gag: 4 hoax, hush, joke **5** choke, heave, retch **6** be sick, muffle, muzzle **7** prevent, silence **8** obstruct, suppress, throttle **9** wisecrack **13** interpolation

gage (see also **gauge**)**:** bet **4** pawn, risk **5** stake, wager **6** pledge **8** appraise, defiance, security **9** challenge

gaiety: fun, joy **4** glee **5** mirth **7** jollity **8** hilarity **9** festivity, good humor, merriment

gain: buy, get, net, win **4** boot, earn, good, pelf, reap **5** clear, lucre, reach **6** attain, effect, income, obtain, profit, secure **7** achieve, acquire, advance, benefit, conquer, prevail, procure, realize **8** increase **9** accretion, advantage, increment **12** appreciation
ill-gotten: **4** pelf **5** graft, lucre **6** payola

gainsay: 4 deny **6** forbid, impugn, negate, oppose, refute, resist **7** dispute **10** contradict, controvert

Gainsborough painting: 7 Blue Boy

gait: run **4** lope, pace, rack, step, trip, trot, walk **5** amble, strut, tread **6** canter, gallop **7** journey, shamble

gaiter: 4 boot, spat **6** puttee **7** cutikin(Sc.), legging **8** overshoe

gala: gay **4** fete **5** merry **7** festal, fiesta **8** festival **9** glamorous **11** celebration

galago: 5 lemur **6** monkey

Galahad: *father:* **8** Lancelot
mother: **6** Elaine
quest: **5** grail

Galapagos Islands resident: 8 tortoise

Galatea: *lover:* **4** Acis
suitor: **10** Polyphemus

galaxy: 6 nebula

gale: 4 blow, gust, wind **5** blast, storm **7** tempest **8** outburst **9** hurricane, windstorm **11** northeaster, northwester, southeaster, southwester

galea: cap **6** helmet

Galen: 9 physician

galilee: 5 porch **7** portico

Galilee: *ruler:* **5** Herod

town: 4 Cana, Nain 8 Nazareth, Tiberias 9 Capernaum

Galileo's birthplace: 4 Pisa

galimatias: 6 jargon 8 nonsense 9 gibberish

galipot, gallipot: sap 5 rosin 6 barras 10 turpentine

gall: vex 4 bile, fell, flaw, fret 5 annoy, chafe, cheek, spite 6 abrade, harass, injure, poison, rancor 7 blemish 8 acerbity, cecidium, irritate, temerity 9 excoriate, impudence 10 bitterness, effrontery, exasperate

Gallagher's partner: 5 Shean

gallant: gay 4 beau, prow 5 blade, brave, bully, lover, noble, showy, swain 6 escort, polite, suitor 7 amatory, conduct, stately 8 cavalier, handsome, polished, splendid 9 attentive, chevalier, courteous 10 chivalrous, courageous 11 fashionable 12 high-spirited

gallantry: 7 bravery, courage, heroism 8 courtesy 9 attention 11 intrepidity

galled: mad, raw 4 sore 6 peeved

galleon: 4 ship 6 carack, vessel 7 carrack

cargo: oro 4 gold

gallery: 5 porch, salon 6 arcade, loggia, piazza 7 balcony, portico, terrace, veranda 8 audience, catacomb, corridor 9 promenade

galley: 4 boat, ship, tray 5 cuddy, proof 6 bireme, galiot, hearth 7 birling, birlinn, galliot, kitchen, trireme, unireme 8 cookroom, galleass 10 triaconter

galliard: 5 dance

Gallic: 6 French

gallimaufry: 4 hash 6 jumble, medley, ragout 7 melange, mixture 8 pastiche, potpourri 10 hodgepodge

gallinae: 6 grouse, quails 7 rasores, turkeys 8 peafowls 9 curassows, partridge, pheasants

gallinule: hen 4 coot, fowl, rail

gallivant: gad 4 flit, roam 6 travel

galloon: 4 lace 5 braid 7 ribbon 8 trimming

gallop: run 4 gait, pelt 5 chase, speed 6 hasten, sprint 7 mad dash 8 fast clip

galloping dominoes: 4 dice

gallows: 5 bough 6 gibbet 7 potence 8 scaffold

galluses: 10 suspenders

galoot: guy 6 fellow, person 9 screwball, simpleton

galore: 7 profuse 8 abundant 9 plentiful

galosh: 4 boot, 6 arctic, rubber 8 overshoe

galvanize: 4 coat 6 excite 7 startle 9 electrify, stimulate 12 move to action

Galway islands: 4 Aran

galyak: fur

gam: leg 4 chat 5 visit

gamb, gambe: leg 5 shank

gambado: 4 boot 5 antic, caper, prank 6 spring 7 legging

Gambia: *capital:* 6 Banjul

city: 5 Basse 6 Fatoto 7 Kuntaur 10 Georgetown

ethnic group: 4 Fula 5 Wolof 8 Mandinka

monetary unit: 5 butut 6 dalasi

river: 6 Gambia

village in "Roots": 7 Juffure

gambit: 4 move, ploy, ruse 5 trick 7 gimmick, opening 8 maneuver 9 strategem

gamble: bet 4 dice, gaff, game, risk, spec 5 stake, wager 6 chance, hazard, plunge 9 speculate 11 uncertainty

gambler: 5 dicer 6 carrow(Ir.), player 7 plunger, sharper 8 blackleg, gamester 10 speculator

accomplice: 5 shill

gambling (see also **game:** *gambling*):

pert. to: 8 aleatory

place: 4 Reno 6 casino 8 Las Vegas 10 Monte Carlo

stake: pot 4 pool

gambol: hop 4 play 5 caper, frisk, prank 6 cavort, frolic

game: fun, jeu(F.) 4 lame, lark, plan, play, prey 5 brave, dodge, prank, sport, trick 6 course, frolic, gamble, gritty, plucky, quarry, racket, spunky 7 contest, foolery, pastime, project 8 enduring, resolute 9 amusement, diversion 10 courageous

ball: cat, tut 4 golf, polo, pool 5 fives, rugby 6 hockey, pelota, soccer, squash, tennis, tipcat 7 cricket, croquet 8 baseball, football, handball, ping-pong, softball 9 billiards 10 basketball, volleyball

bird: 4 duck 5 quail 6 turkey 7 bustard 8 pheasant 9 partridge

board: 4 keno 5 bingo, chess, Halma, lotto, salta 7 Pachisi 8 checkers, cribbage, Monopoly, Parchesi, Parchisi, Scrabble squails 9 crokinole, Parcheesi 10 backgammon

card: gin, hoc, loo, nap, pam, war 4 bank, brag, faro, hock, jass, ruff, skat, slam, snap, solo, spin, vint 5 beast, chico, cinch, comet, crimp, decoy, gilet, gleek, monte, omber, ombre, pedro, pique, pitch, poker, rummy, stuss, trump, two-up, waist, whist 6 basset, birkie, boston, bridge, casino, commit, ecarte, flinch, hearts, loadum, masset, piquet, rounce, sledge, smudge 7 bezique, canasta, cayenne, Chicago, cooncan, hundred, old maid, primero, reversi, seven-up 8 baccarat(F.), Canfield, commerce, conquian, contract, cribbage, handicap, Michigan, napoleon, patience, penneeck, pinochle 9 cinq-cents, montebank, new market, solitaire, tredrille 11 speculation 14 spite and malice *carnival:* 5 darts 6 hoopla

child's: tag 7 marbles 8 leapfrog 9 hopscotch 13 tiddledy winks

confidence: 4 scam 5 bunco, bunko, sting 6 racket

court: 5 roque 6 pelota, squash, tennis 7 jai alai 8 handball 9 badminton 10 basketball, volleyball

dice: 4 ludo 5 craps 7 pachisi 8 dominoes, trey-trip

gambling: 4 beno, faro, keno, pico 5 beano, bingo, boule, craps, keeno, lotto, monte, pique, pitch, poker, rondo, stuss 6 brelan(F.), fan-tan(Ch.), piquet, policy 7 baccara, barbudi, primero, rondeau(F.) 8 baccarat, crackloo, roulette 9 black-jack, crackaloo, montebank, twenty-one, vingt-et-un(F.) 10 panguingui (Phil. Is.)

goal: run 4 home 5 first, score, spare, tally 6 basket, strike 9 touchdown

kind of: 4 mora(It.) 6 merels, morris, quoits 7 diabolo, loggats, loggets, marbles 9 philopena 10 electronic, jackstraws, spillikins

official: 5 judge, timer 6 umpire 7 referee, starter 8 linesman 10 timekeeper

outdoor: 4 polo 6 tennis 7 cricket, croquet 9 badminton

parlor: 5 jacks 7 matador 8 charades

pin: 7 bowling, kegling, tenpins 8 ninepins, skittles

plan: 8 strategy

racket: 5 bandy 6 squash, tennis 8 lacrosse 9 badminton

rule authority: 5 Hoyle

stewed in wine: 5 salmi 6 ragout

war: 10 kriegspiel

word: 5 ghost, rebus 6 crambo 7 anagram 8 acrostic, scrabble 9 crossword

gamekeeper: 8 warrener

gamester: 5 dicer 6 player 7 gambler

gamete: egg 4 ovum 5 sperm 6 zygote 8 oosphere

gamin: imp, tad 6 urchin

domain: 6 street

gaming cube: die

gammon: leg 4 bosh, dupe, foot, gull 5 bacon, cozen, feign, thigh 6 delude, humbug 7 beguile, deceive, mislead, pretend

gamp: 8 umbrella

gamut: 4 A to Z 5 orbit, range, reach, scale 6 extent, series 7 compass

gamy: 5 spicy 6 smelly 7 lustful 8 spirited 10 malodorous 12 disreputable

ganch: 4 kill 6 impale 7 execute

gander: 4 look 5 goose 6 glance 9 simpleton

Gandhi: *name:* Aba, Abu 4 Abba, Abou, Bapu 7 Mahatma

publication: 7 Harijan

ganef: 5 thief 6 rascal

gang: mob, set 4 band, crew, pack, team 5 group, horde, shift 6 clique, outfit, travel 7 company

member of: 4 b'hoy 5 rowdy, tough

Ganges River city: 7 Benares

gangling: 4 bony 5 lanky 6 skinny 7 awkward 9 spindling

ganglion: 5 tumor

gangplank: 6 bridge 8 platform

gangrene: rot 7 mortify 8 necrosis 9 sphacelus

gangster: 4 goon, hood, thug, yegg 5 rough, thief 6 bandit, gunman 7 mobster, ruffian 8 criminal, hireling

female companion: 4 moll

gangway: 7 couloir 8 corridor 10 passageway

gannet: 4 bird, fowl 5 goose, solan

family: 4 sula

ganoid fish: gar 6 bowfin 8 sturgeon

gaol: 4 brig, jail 6 prison

gaoler: 5 guard 6 warden

gap: col 4 flaw, pass, rent 5 break, breck, chasm, chawn, cleft, clove, meuse, notch, space 6 breach, hiatus, lacuna, ravine 7 fissure, lacunae(pl.), opening 8 aperture, interval, quebrada 10 interstice 12 interruption 13 discontinuity

gape: ope 4 gasp, gawk, gaze, pant, rent, yawn 5 chawn, stare 6 rictus 7 dehisce 8 oscitate 10 rubberneck

gaping: 4 open 7 cracked, yawning 9 cavernous, separated

of plant capsule: 10 dehiscence

garage: 6 hangar, siding 8 building

garb (see also **dress**): 5 array, dress, habit, style 6 attire, bundle, clothe, custom, method 7 apparel, clothes, costume, fashion, raiment, vesture 8 carriage, clothing, vestment 10 appearance, habiliment

garbage: 5 offal, trash, waste 6 debris, litter, refuse, scraps 7 rubbish

garble: 4 sift, 5 twist 6 jumble, mangle, refine, refuse, select 7 distort, pervert 8 disguise, mutilate

garcon: boy, lad 6 waiter

garden: 4 Eden, hall, park, yard 5 arbor, patch, tract 8 outfield 9 cultivate, enclosure 11 commonplace

implement: 4 hoe 4 rake 5 mower, spade 6 scythe, sickle, trowel, weeder

kind of: 4 herb, rock 5 oasis, truck 6 cactus, flower, formal 7 kitchen 8 chinampa 9 botanical, terrarium, vegetable 10 zoological

protector: 7 Priapus

garden plant: See **plant:** *garden*

Garden State: 9 New Jersey

gardener: 8 yardman 9 topiarist 14 horticulturist

garfish: 8 hornbeak, hornfish

Gargantua's son: 10 Pantagruel
gargantuan: 4 huge, vast **5** giant **7** titanic **8** enormous, gigantic **9** monstrous
gargle: 9 mouthwash **11** collutorium
garish: 4 loud **5** cheap, gaudy, showy **6** bright, tawdry **8** dazzling **9** offensive
garland: bay, lei **4** band **5** crown, glory **6** anadem, corona, crants, diadem, laurel, rosary, wreath **7** chaplet, coronal, festoon **9** anthology
garlic: 4 moly, ramp **5** chive, clove **6** ransom
garment (see also **undergarment**): **4** brat, cape, coat, gear, gown, jupe, rail, robe, sari, vest **5** cloak, dress, habit **6** attire, kimono **7** apparel, leotard, raiment **8** vestment **10** investment
ancient: **4** toga **5** palla, stola **6** chiton **7** chlamys **8** himation
ecclesiastical: see **vestment**
infant's: **6** woolly **7** bunting
Malay: **6** cabaya, kabaya, sarong
medieval: **5** simar **6** kirtle, rochet, tabard **8** chausses
mourning: **5** weeds **9** sackcloth
protective: **4** brat **5** apron, armor, chaps, smock **7** cuculla **8** overalls, pinafore **9** coveralls
rain: **6** poncho **7** oilskin, slicker
sleeveless: aba **4** cape, vest **6** mantle **7** sweater **8** slip-over
South Seas: **5** pareu **8** lavalava
upper: **4** coat, vest **5** jupon, shirt, tunic, waist **6** blouse, jersey, peplos, peplus **7** sweater **8** guernsey, slip-over
garner: 4 reap **5** store **6** gather **7** collect, granary **10** accumulate
garnet: 5 jewel, stone **8** essonite
black: **8** melanite
deep-red: **6** pyrope **9** almandine, almandite
green: **7** olivine
garnish: 4 trim **5** adorn, dress, equip **6** set off **7** furnish **8** decorate, ornament **9** embellish
garret: 4 loft **5** attic, solar **6** soller, turret **7** mansard **8** cockloft **10** upper floor, watchtower
garrote, garrotte: 4 kill **7** execute **8** strangle, throttle
garrulous: 5 talky, wordy **7** gossipy, voluble **8** fanfaron **9** talkative **10** longwinded, loquacious
garter: 4 belt **5** snake **7** elastic **9** supporter
garth: dam **4** weir
garvey: 4 boat, scow
gas: 4 fuel, fume, reek, talk **5** steam, vapor **6** gossip, petrol **7** bombast **10** anesthetic, asphyxiate, illuminant
air: **4** neon **5** argon, ozone, xenon **6** oxygen **7** ammonia, krypton, sulfate **8** nitrogen

balloon: **6** helium
blue: **5** ozone
charcoal: **5** oxane
charge with: **6** aerate
colorless: **5** keten, ozone **6** arsine, ethane **7** ammonia
inert: **5** argon, radon, xenon **6** helium **8** nitrogen
inflammable: **6** butane, ethane **7** methane, propane **8** hydrogen
marsh: **7** methane
mustard: **7** yperite
nitrogen and carbon: **8** cyanogen
oxygen: **5** ozone
poisonous: **6** arsine **7** mustard, stibine
gasbag: 7 balloon
gascon: 7 boaster **8** braggart **10** swaggering **12** swashbuckler
gasconade: 7 bluster, bravado **8** boasting
gaseous: 4 thin **5** fluid, light **7** tenuous **8** aeriform, gasiform, volatile **13** unsubstantial
gash: cut **4** bite, chop, slit **5** cleft, gorge, slash, wound **6** pierce **8** incision
gasket: 4 ring, seal
gasoline: gas **6** petrol
gasp: 4 gulp, huff, pant **5** croak **6** wheeze **9** suck in air **13** inhale sharply
gassy: 5 windy **8** inflated **9** flatulent
gastronome: 7 epicure, gourmet **8** gourmand **11** connoisseur
gastropod: 4 slug **5** harpa, oliva, snail **6** nerita, nerite, volute **7** mollusk **8** pteropod
ear-shaped: **7** abalone
marine: **5** cowry, murex **6** cowrie, limpet, tethys **7** aplysia
gat: gun **6** pistol **7** channel, passage **8** revolver
gata: 5 shark
gate: bar, way **4** door, exit, hole, pass, take **5** hatch, valve **6** defile, escape, method, portal, spigot, wicket **7** barrier, opening, postern **8** entrance, receipts **9** box office, threshold, turnstile
flood: **6** sluice
gate money: fee **5** price **9** admission
Gates of Hercules: 9 Gibraltar
gatehouse: bar **5** lodge
gatekeeper: 6 porter, warden **8** guardian, watchman
gateway: 4 arch **5** pylon, toran, torii (Jap.) **6** portal, torana **8** entrance
gather: 4 bale, brew, cull, furl, herd, mass, meet, pick, rake, reap **5** amass, bunch, flock, glean, group, infer, pleat, pluck, raise, shirr **6** bundle, deduce, derive, garner, muster, scrape, summon **7** collect, compile, convene, convoke, harvest, recruit **8** assemble, colonize, compress, conclude, contract, increase **10** accumulate, congregate **11** agglomerate,

concentrate 12 conglomerate

gatherer: 5 miser 7 gleaner 9 collector

gathering: bee, tea 4 bevy, fest, stag 5 crowd, party, troop 6 galaxy, plisse, shivoo, smoker 7 company, meeting, klatsch, turnout 8 assembly, function 9 concourse 10 assemblage, collection, congestion, convention 11 convocation 12 accumulation, congregation

gauche: 5 crude, inept 6 clumsy 7 awkward, uncouth 8 bumbling, plebeian, tactless 9 maladroit 10 left-handed

gaucho: 6 cowboy 8 herdsman

lariat: 5 riata

weapon: 4 bola 7 machete

gaud: 4 bead 6 bauble, gewgaw 7 trinket 8 artifice, ornament

gaudy: 4 loud 5 cheap, feast, showy 6 flashy, garish, tawdry, tinsel 7 brankie(Sc.), glaring 8 festival 9 tasteless 11 pretentious 12 meretricious, ostentatious

gaufre: 5 wafer 6 waffle

gauge, gage: 4 size 5 judge, meter, scale 7 measure 8 estimate, standard 9 criterion, indicator, yardstick

pressure: 9 manometer

rain: 8 udometer

wind: 10 anemometer

Gauguin's island: 6 Tahiti

autobiography: 6 Noa Noa

Gaul: 6 France, Gallia(L.)

chariot: 5 esses 6 esseda, essede

god of thunder and rain: 7 Taranis

god of vegetation: 4 Esus

magistrate: 9 vergobret

people: 4 Remi

priest: 5 druid

river goddess: 8 Belisama

seer: 5 vates

gaulding: 4 bird 5 egret, heron

gaunt: 4 bony, grim, lank, lean, slim, thin 5 spare 6 barren, hollow, meager, wasted 7 haggard, scraggy, scrawny, slender 8 desolate, rawboned 9 emaciated 10 attenuated, cadaverous, forbidding

gauntlet: 4 dare, test 5 glove 6 ordeal 9 challenge, cross fire

Gautama: 6 Buddha 10 Siddhartha

wife: 6 Ahalya

gauze: 4 film, leno 5 crepe, lisse, tulle 6 fabric, tissue 7 bandage, chiffon 11 cheesecloth

gavel: 4 maul 6 hammer, mallet 9 grain pile

gavial: 9 crocodile

Gawain: *brother:* 6 Gareth 7 Gaheris

father: Lot

slayer: 8 Lancelot

son: 5 Lovel 8 Florence, Gyngalyn

uncle: 6 Arthur

gawk: 4 gape, gaze, lout 5 stare 7 bump-

kin 9 simpleton 10 rubberneck

gawky: 6 clumsy 7 awkward 8 bumbling, ungainly 9 lumbering

gay: 4 airy, boon, daft, glad, gleg 5 bawdy, bonny, brisk, happy, jolly, loose, merry, riant, showy 6 blithe, bonnie, bright, flashy, frisky, garish, jocund, jovial, joyful, lively, wanton 7 festive, gleeful, jocular 8 cavalier, cheerful, colorful, mirthful, sportive 9 brilliant, convivial, sprightly, vivacious 10 brilliante, frolicsome, homosexual, licentious 12 lighthearted

gazabo: guy 6 fellow, person

gaze: eye 4 gape, gawk, leer, look, moon, ogle, peer, pore, scan, view 5 glare, gloat, sight, stare 6 behold, glower, regard

gazebo: 6 pagoda 8 pavilion 9 belvedere 11 summerhouse

gazelle: ahu, goa 4 admi, cora, dama, kudu, mohr, oryx 5 ariel, mhorr 7 buffalo, chikara, corinne 8 antelope 9 springbok

kin: 6 impala

gazelle hound: 6 saluki

gazette: 7 courant, journal 9 newspaper

gazetteer: 5 atlas, guide 10 dictionary

Ge: See **Gaea**

gazump: 5 cheat 7 swindle

gean: 6 cherry

gear: 4 cam, cog, rig 4 duds, togs 5 dress, equip, goods, stuff, tools 6 doings, graith(Sc.), outfit, pinion, tackle, things 7 apparel, harness, rigging 8 clothing, cogwheel, garments, materiel, property 9 apparatus, equipment, mechanism, trappings, vestments 10 appliances, belongings, implements 12 appurtenance 13 accoutrements, paraphernalia

Geb: *daughter:* 4 Isis 8 Nephthys

father: Shu

son: Set 6 Osiris

wife: Nut

gecko: 6 lizard 7 tarente

gee: 4 jibe 5 agree 7 command 9 turn right

Gehenna: pit 4 hell 5 hades 7 inferno 10 underworld

geige: 6 fiddle, violin

gel: set 6 harden 7 congeal, thicken 8 solidify 9 coagulate

gelatin, gelatine: 5 jelly 7 sericin 8 agaragar

geld: fix 4 spay 5 alter, prune 6 neuter 8 castrate, multilate 9 expurgate 10 emasculate

gelid: icy 4 cold, iced 6 frozen

gelt: 4 gold 5 money

gem: bud 4 keas, naif, onyx, opal, ruby, sard 5 agate, beryl, cameo, jewel, paste, pearl, stone, topaz 6 amulet, bedeck, garnet, muffin, scarab, spinel **7** diamond, emerald, paragon **8** intaglio, sapphire, tigereye **9** carnelian, germinate **10** aquamarine **11** masterpiece

blue: **8** sapphire **9** turquoise **10** aquamarine

cut: **7** navette **8** baguette, cabachon, marquise **9** brilliant

face: **5** facet

green: **7** emerald, peridot **10** chrysolite

imperfect: **5** loupe

iridescent: **4** opal **5** pearl **7** cat's-eye **8** tigereye **9** moonstone

measure of weight: **5** carat

of fidelity: **5** topaz

of immortality: **7** emerald

of law: **4** ruby

of love: **8** amethyst

of peace: **7** diamond

of purity: **5** pearl

of truth: **8** sapphire

paste: **6** strass

purple: **8** amethyst

rectangular: **6** baguet **8** baguette

red: **4** ruby, sard **5** avena **6** garnet, pyrope **9** carnelian

relief-carved: **5** cameo

setting for: **4** ouch, pave **6** chaton

support: **7** setting

surface: **5** bezel, bezil, facet

Gem State: 5 Idaho

gemel: 4 twin **6** hinged, paired

geminate: 6 binate, double **7** coupled

Gemini: 5 twins **6** Castor, Pollux

gemmule: bud **5** ovule

gemsbok: 4 oryx **8** antelope

gemutlich: 4 cozy **6** genial, kindly **8** cheerful **9** agreeable **11** comfortable, good-natured

gendarme: 7 soldier **9** policeman **10** cavalryman

gender: sex **4** male **5** class, genus **6** female, neuter

genealogy: 7 lineage **8** pedigree **10** family tree **12** descent chart, family record

general: 5 broad, gross **6** common, leader **7** average, officer **8** catholic **9** commander, customary, prevalent, universal **10** prevailing, widespread

Civil War: Lee **5** Grant, Meade **7** Sherman

generalize: 5 widen **6** extend, spread **7** broaden

generate: 4 make **5** beget, breed, steam **6** create **7** develop, produce **8** engender **9** originate, procreate, propagate

generation: age, era **4** kind, race **5** breed, stock **6** family **7** descent, progeny **8** creation **9** genealogy, offspring, posterity **11** descendants, procreation

generative: 8 prolific **10** productive

generator: 6 dynamo, engine **7** creator **8** auto part

generic: 6 common **9** universal **12** encompassing **13** comprehensive

generosity: 7 charity, largess **8** largesse

generous: big **4** free, good, kind, rich **5** ample, frank, noble **6** honest **7** fertile, liberal **8** abundant, gracious, handsome, highborn, spirited **9** bountiful, excellent, honorable, plenteous, unselfish, unstinted **10** altruistic, benevolent, bighearted, charitable, courageous, freehanded, munificent, openhanded **11** magnanimous, stimulating, warmhearted

genesis: 5 birth **6** origin **9** beginning **11** origination

genet: 5 berbe, horse **8** civet fur

genial: 4 bein, bien, warm **5** douce **6** benign, forthy, inborn, jovial, kindly, native **7** cordial, festive **8** cheerful, friendly, pleasant **9** benignant, expansive, gemutlich **10** enlivening

genie: 5 demon, jinni **6** spirit

genitor: 6 parent **7** creator **10** procreator

geniture: 5 birth **8** nativity **9** offspring **10** generation

genius: 5 flair, knack **6** talent, wizard **8** aptitude **9** intellect **10** brilliance

genouillere: 7 kneelet **9** kneepiece

genre: 4 kind, sort, type **5** class, style **7** species **8** category **11** description **14** classification

gens: 4 clan **5** tribe **6** family

genteel: 4 nice **6** polite **7** stylish **8** graceful, lady-like, well-bred **11** fashionable

gentian: 6 flower **7** felwort **9** baldmoney

Gentile: 7 heathen **9** Christian

gentility: 8 breeding **10** refinement

gentle: moy **4** calm, deft, dewy, easy, fair, kind, meek, mild, soft, tame **5** bland, light, milky, quiet, sweet, tamed **6** benign, docile, facile, placid, polite, tender **7** amabile, bonaire, clement, gradual, lenient **8** amenable, dovelike, lenitive, maidenly, mansuete, moderate, peaceful, soothing, tranquil, well-born **9** courteous, excellent, honorable, tractable **10** chivalrous **11** considerate **13** compassionate

gentlemen: don, rye, sir **5** sahib, senor **6** bayard, mister **7** younker **8** cavalier **9** caballero

Gentlemen Prefer Blondes author: 4 Loos

gentlewoman: 4 lady

gentry: 5 elite **7** quality, society **10** gentlefolk, upper class

genty: 5 noble **7** genteel **8** graceful **9** courteous

genu: 4 knee **5** joint

genuflect: 5 kneel **6** kowtow **10** bend the knee

genuine: 4 pure, real, true, vrai(F.) **5** frank, plain, pucka, pukka **6** actual, dinkum, honest **7** germane, gradely, sincere **8** bonafide **9** authentic, heartfelt, intrinsic, simon-pure, true-penny, unalloyed, unfeigned, veridical, veritable **10** legitimate **13** unadulterated **15** unsophisticated

genus: 4 kind, sort **5** class, order **6** gender **8** category **14** classification

pert. to: **7** generic

geode: 5 druse **6** cavity, nodule

geology: 12 earth science

age: **7** Permian **8** Cambrian, cenezoic, Devonian, Jurassic, mesozoic, Silurian, Triassic **9** paleozoic **10** Cretaceous, cryptozoic, Ordovician **13** Mississippian, Pennsylvanian

division: age, era **4** lias, lyas **5** epoch, trias

period: **6** eocene **7** miocene **8** pliocene, tertiary **9** oligocene **10** quaternary **11** pleistocene

remains: **7** fossils

science: **12** paleontology **13** palaeontology

geometric: 8 analytic **9** algebraic **10** arithmetic

geometry: *angle:* **9** incidence

curve: **6** spiral **7** ellipse, evolute **8** parabola, sinusoid

father: **6** Euclid

figure: **4** cone, lune **5** prism, rhomb **6** circle, gnomon, oblong **7** ellipse, rhombus **8** triangle

proposition: **7** theorem

solid: **4** cube **5** prism **7** pyramid

surface: **5** nappe, torus

geoponic: 5 rural **12** agricultural

Georgia: *capital:* **7** Atlanta

city: **5** Macon **6** Albany, Athens, Dalton **7** Augusta **8** Columbus **9** Savannah

county: Lee **4** Bibb, Clay, Cobb, Cook, Dade, Hall, Hart, Long, Pike, Polk, Tift, Ware **5** Bacon, Banks, Burke, Butts, Crisp, Dodge, Dooly, Early, Floyd, Grady, Peach, Rabun, Troup **6** Brooks, Clinch, Coffee, Coweta, De Kalb, Echols, Elbert, Oconee, Sumter, Twiggs, Wilkes **7** Appling, Berrien, Catoosa, Decatur, Jenkins, Lumpkin, Quitman, Screven, Telfair

early explorer: **6** de Soto

island: Sea **6** Amelia, Sapelo **7** Ossabaw, St. Simon **10** Cumberland **11** St. Catherine

lake: **7** Eufaula **8** Seminole, Sinclair **12** Sidney Lanier

mountain: **9** Blue Ridge **13** Brasstown Bald

President Carter's birthplace: **6** Plains

river: **5** Flint **6** Oconee **8** Altamaha, Ocmulgee, Savannah **12** Apalachicola **13** Chattahoochee

state bird: **8** thrasher

state flower: **12** Cherokee rose

state motto: **23** Wisdom, justice, moderation

state nicknames: **5** Peach **18** Empire State of South

state tree: **7** live oak

swamp: **10** Okefenokee

Geraint's wife: 4 Enid

germ: bud, bug **4** seed **5** spore, virus **6** embryo, sprout **7** microbe **8** rudiment **9** bacterium, beginning

germ cell: egg **4** ovum **5** sperm

germane: 4 akin, true **6** allied **7** genuine, related **8** relevant **9** pertinent **11** appropriate

German (see also **East Germany, West Germany**): **4** Goth **5** Boche, Saxon **6** Teuton

ancient tribesman: **4** Jute **6** Teuton **9** Ostrogoth

angry: **4** bose

animal: **4** tier

article: das, der, des, die

artist: **5** Durer

bacteriologist: **4** Koch

beautiful: **5** schon

blue: **4** blau

bread: **4** brot

bright: **4** hell

but: **4** aber

cake: **5** torte **9** lebkuchen **11** pfeffernuss

canal: **4** Kiel

castle: **7** schloss

cheese: **4** kase

chicken: **4** huhn

child: **4** kind

Christmas: **11** Weihnachten

clever: **5** klug

clock: uhr

code: **5** Salic

coin: **4** mark **6** kronen, thaler **7** pfennig **8** groschen

cold: **4** kalt

day: tag

dead: tot

dear: **4** lieb

deep: **4** tief

dog: **4** hund

door: tur

early: **4** fruh

earth: **4** erde

evening: **5** abend

eye: **4** auge

field: **4** feld

forest: **4** wald

forest-keeper: **9** waldgrave

gnome: **6** kobold

good: gut

hair: **4** haar

hall: **4** aula, saal **5** diele

happy: **4** froh

head: **4** kopf

heart: **4** herz

highway: **8** autobahn

home: **4** heim
knight: **6** ritter
lancer: **4** ulan
language: **7** Deutsch
leaf: **5** blatt
letter: **5** brief
measles: **7** rubella
measure: aam, imi **4** last, sack, stab **5** carat, eimer, kanne, kette, maass **6** strich **7** klafter **8** scheffel, schoppen, stubchen **9** masskanne
mister: **4** herr
moon: **4** mond
never: nie
nine: **4** neun
no: **4** nein
nobleman: **4** graf **5** adlig **6** junker, ritter **7** younker
overture: **8** vorspiel
philosopher: **4** Kant **5** Hegel
school: **10** realschule, volkschule **14** oberrealschule
shoe: **5** schuh
singing festival: **10** sangerfest **11** saengerfest
society: **4** bund **6** verein **10** turnverein **12** gesellschaft
son: **4** sohn
song: **4** lied
star: **5** stern
stone: **5** stein
teacher: **6** docent, dozent
tooth: **4** zahn
tower: **4** turm
two: **4** zwei
village: **4** dorf
vowel change: **6** umlaut
weight: lot
white: **5** weiss
wine: **4** hock, wein **5** Rhine **7** Moselle
woman: **4** frau, frow **8** fraulein
world: **4** welt
year: **4** jahr
young: **4** jung
germane: **5** ad rem **7** apropos **8** relevant **9** pertinent
germicide: **5** iodin **6** iodine **10** antiseptic **11** bactericide **12** disinfectant
germinate: bud, gem **6** evolve, sprout **7** develop **10** effloresce
geryon **7** monster
gesso: **5** paste **7** plaster
gest, geste: **4** deed, feat, tale **7** exploit, romance **9** adventure
gestation: **7** bearing **8** breeding, carrying **9** pregnancy
gesture: act, nod **4** sign, wave **6** beckon, motion, salute **8** courtesy **9** formality **10** empty offer **11** gesticulate
get: pen, win **4** earn, find, gain, take, trap **5** annoy, beget, catch, fetch, learn, reach, seize **6** appear, attain, baffle, become, corner, derive, induce, obtain, puzzle, secure, suffer **7** achieve, acquire, capture, conquer, possess, prepare, procure, realize, receive, recover **8** contract, irritate, overcome, persuade, retrieve, vanquish **9** ascertain, determine **10** comprehend, conciliate, understand
get along: **4** fare **5** hurry **7** advance, prosper, succeed **8** progress
get away: lam **4** flee, scat, shoo **6** depart, escape
get back: **6** recoup, redeem, regain **7** recover
get on: **5** board **6** embark
get out: **4** exit **5** leave, scram **6** elicit, escape, reveal **7** publish, take off **8** evacuate
get-together: bee **4** stag **6** social **7** meeting
get up: **5** arise, array, dress, style **6** invent **7** arrange, costume, prepare **9** construct
get well: **4** heal **10** recuperate
gewgaw: toy **4** gaud **6** bauble, fangle, fegary, trifle **7** trinket **8** gimcrack **10** knickknack
geyersite: **4** opal
Ghana: *capital:* **5** Accra
city: **6** Elmina, Kumasi, Tamale **7** Sunyani **9** Cape Coast, Koforidus **10** Bolgatanga
ethnic group: Ewe **4** Akim **7** Akwapim, Ashanti, Dagomba
former name: **9** Gold Coast
monetary unit: **4** cedi **6** pesewa
mountain: **8** Afadjato
region: **5** Upper, Volta **7** Ashanti, Central, Eastern, Western **8** Northern **10** Brong-Ahafo
river: **5** Volta
ghastly: wan **4** grim, pale **5** lurid **6** dismal, grisly, pallid **7** charnel, deathly, fearful, hideous, macabre **8** dreadful, gruesome, horrible, shocking, terrible **9** frightful
ghat: **4** pass **5** range **7** landing **8** mountain
gherkin: **6** pickle **8** cucumber
ghost: hag **4** bhut, hant **5** duppy, shade, spook **6** daemon, spirit, wraith **7** eidolon, haunter, lemures(pl.), phantom, specter **8** guytrash, phantasm, revenant **10** apparition, glimmering **11** poltergeist
ghostly: **4** eery **5** eerie, scary, weird **6** spooky **7** shadowy, spectral, uncanny **9** spiritual
ghoul: **4** ogre **5** fiend **7** monster, vampire **11** grave robber
ghoulish: **9** loathsome
giant: **4** Bara, eten, huge, ogre, rahu, Ymir **5** Argus, Cacus, jumbo, titan, troll **6** ogress **7** Antaeus, Cyclops, Goliath,

monster **8** behemoth, Bellerus, colossus **9** monstrous **10** gargantuan, prodigious, tremendous

gibber: 5 stone **6** pebble **7** boulder, chatter

gibberish: 6 jabber, jargon **7** blather, twaddle **8** claptrap **9** rigmarole **10** double-talk, mumbo jumbo

gibbet: 4 hang **5** noose **7** gallows **8** string up

gibbon: ape, lar **6** monkey, wou-wou **7** hoo-lock, siamang **10** anthropoid

gibbous: 6 convex, humped **7** hunched, rounded **11** hunchbacked, protuberant

gibe 4 gird, jape, jeer, mock, quip, twit **5** fleer, fling, flirt, flout, gleek, scoff, sneer, taunt **6** deride, heckle **7** laugh at, poke fun, sarcasm **8** ridicule

giddy: 4 daft **5** dizzy, faint, silly **6** fickle, volage **7** erratic, flighty, reeling, heedless **9** befuddled, frivolous, **11** harebrained **13** featherheaded

gift: sop **4** bent, boon, dash, dole **5** bonus, bribe, dower, dowry, favor, grant, knack, pilon, power, token **6** bounty, donary, gersum, hansel, legacy, talent **7** aptness, benefit, faculty, handsel, largess, present, subsidy **8** aptitude, bestowal, blessing, donation, gratuity, largesse, offering, pittance, potlatch **9** endowment, gratitude, lagniappe, readiness **10** compliment **11** benefaction, beneficence, serendipity **12** contribution

gifted: 4 deft **5** smart **6** clever **8** talented **9** brilliant, ingenious

gig: job **4** boat, goad, spur **5** rouse, spear, stint **6** chaise **7** demerit, provoke **8** carriage

gigantic: big **4** huge, vast **5** giant, large **7** immense, mammoth, titanic **8** colossal, enormous **9** cyclopean, gigantean, monstrous **10** gargantuan, prodigious

giggle: 5 tehee **6** teehee, titter **7** snicker, snigger

gila: 5 trout **6** lizard **10** woodpecker

Gilbert and Sullivan opera: 7 Thespis **8** Iolanthe, Patience **9** Ruddigore, The Mikado **11** H. M. S. Pinafore

Gilbert island: 5 Makin **6** Tarawa

gild: 5 adorn, tinge **7** overlay **8** brighten, inaurate **9** embellish

Gilda's father: 9 Rigoletto

gilet: 4 vest **6** bodice **9** waistcoat

gill, ghyl: ivy **4** cove, girl, lass **5** brook **6** collar, ravine, stream, tipple, valley, wattle **10** sweetheart
four: **4** pint

gilt: hog, sow **4** gold **5** money **6** gilded, golden

gimcrack: fop, toy **6** bauble, flimsy, gewgaw, trifle **7** trinket, trivial **8** ornament,

trumpery **9** frivolous **10** knickknack **13** unsubstantial

gimlet: 4 tool **8** cocktail

gimme: 6 greedy **11** acquisitive

gimmick: 4 ploy, ruse **5** trick **6** device, gadget **8** maneuver

gimp: vim **4** trim **5** orris **6** spirit **7** cripple **8** lame walk, trimming

gin: net **4** crab, grin, rack, sloe, trap **5** snare, trick **6** device, diddle, liquor, scheme **7** springe **8** artifice, beverage, schnapps **10** intoxicant **11** contrivance

ginger: pep, vim **5** spice, vigor **6** mettle, revive, spirit **8** piquancy, spirited
genus: **8** zingiber
wild: **6** asarum

ginger cookie: 4 snap

ginger root: 4 race

gingerbread: 4 cake **5** money **6** wealth **8** trimming **13** pfefferkuchen(Ger.)

gingerly: 6 warily **7** charily **8** daintily **9** carefully, elegantly, finically, guardedly, mincingly **10** cautiously **12** fastidiously

gingham: 8 chambray

ginseng: 4 herb **5** panax **6** aralia

Gioconda, La: 8 Mona Lisa
painter: **7** da Vinci

giraffe: 5 piano **6** animal, spinet **10** camelopard

girandole: 7 pendant **8** water jet **11** candelabrum

girasol, girasole: 4 opal **5** thorn **9** artichoke

gird, girt: 4 belt, bind, gibe, hasp, hoop, jerk, mock **5** brace, equip, scoff, sneer **6** clothe, fasten, secure **7** besiege, enclose, prepare, provide **8** encircle, surround **9** encompass

girder: 4 beam **6** binder

girdle: obi **4** band, bark, belt, bind, cest, ring, sash, zone **5** girth **6** bodice, cestus, circle, corset, moocha **7** baldric, balteus, environ, equator **8** cincture, cingulum, encircle

girl: gal, sis **4** chit, coed, gill, jill, lass, maid, minx **5** fille, filly, quean(Sc.), skirt, sylph, wench **6** amoret, calico, damsel, female, hoyden, tomboy **7** colleen, flapper, ingenue **9** backfisch, debutante **10** jeune fille, sweetheart **11** maidservant
of song: Amy, Ida, Sue **4** Lucy, Lulu, Mary **5** Daisy, Dinah, Dolly, Laura, Molly, Sally, Susie **6** Louise, Margie **7** Adeline, Jeannie, Mary Lou, Rosalie, Susanna

girlish: 5 sissy **7** artless **8** immature, youthful

girth: 4 band, belt, hoop **5** cinch, cinct, strap, width **6** girdle **7** measure **8** cincture, encircle **13** circumference

gist: nub 4 core, crux, pith **5** heart, point

7 essence, meaning 10 foundation
gitano, gitana: 5 gipsy, gypsy
give: gie(Sc.) 4 cede, dole, emit, hand,
mete 5 apply, endow, grant, serve, yield
6 accord, afford, bestow, commit, confer, denote, devote, donate, impart, render, supply 7 consign, dispose, furnish,
intrust, present, proffer, propose, provide, stretch 8 bequeath 9 vouchsafe
10 administer, contribute, deliquesce,
elasticity
give a hand: aid 4 abet, help
give away: 4 dump 6 betray 7 divulge 8
disclose, get rid of, part with, telltale 9
sacrifice
give back: 4 echo 6 recede, remise, retire,
return 7 replace, restore 8 make good
give forth: 4 emit 6 exhale 8 eradiate
give in: 5 bow to, yield 6 relent 7 succumb 8 back down 9 surrender
give off: 4 emit 5 cease, exude, issue 7
publish
give out: 4 deal, emit, mete 5 exude, issue, print 6 weaken 7 publish, release 9
circulate
give rise: 6 gender 7 produce 8 engender,
occasion 9 originate
give up: 4 cede, drop, quit, stop 5 cease,
demit, forgo, spare, waive, yield 6 devote, forego, resign, retire, reveal, vacate 7 abandon, deliver, despair, present, succumb 8 abdicate, renounce,
swear off 9 lose heart, sacrifice, surrender 10 have no idea, relinquish
given: 5 fixed 6 stated 7 donated, granted
8 addicted, disposed, inclined 9 speci-
fied
givey: 4 soft
glabrous: 4 bald 6 smooth
glace: ice 6 glazed 8 polished
glacial: icy 4 cold 5 gelid 6 arctic, frigid,
frosty, frozen, wintry 7 hostile
glacier: 6 icecap 8 ice sheet
deposit: 5 eskar, esker 6 placer 7 moraine
8 diluvium
direction: 5 stoss
fissure: 8 crevasse
fragment: 5 serac 7 iceberg
hill: 4 paha 7 drumlin
ridge: 4 kame, osar(pl.) 5 eskar, esker
snow: 4 neve
snow field: 4 firn, neve
glacis: 5 slope 7 incline
glad: gay 4 fain 5 eager, happy, merry,
sunny 6 blithe, bright, elated, joyous 7
pleased, willing 8 cheerful 9 delighted,
gratified, satisfied 11 exhilarated, tickled pink 12 lighthearted
gladden: 5 cheer, elate 6 please 7 delight,
gratify, rejoice
glade: 4 vale 5 marsh 8 clearing
gladiator: 5 boxer 6 fencer 7 fighter

competition: 5 ludus
trainer: 7 lanista
gladness: joy 5 bliss, mirth 8 pleasure 9
happiness 12 cheerfulness, exhilaration
glamor, glamour: 5 charm, magic, allure
7 glitter, romance 8 illusion, witchery 9
magnetism 11 enchantment
glamorous, glamourous: 6 exotic 8 alluring, charming, romantic 11 fascinating
glance: 4 peek, peep, scan 5 brush, flash,
graze 6 careen, squint 7 glimpse, rebound 9 quick look
gland: 5 liver, lymph 6 carnel, thymus 7
adrenal, parotid, thyroid 8 exocrine 9
endocrine
edible: 5 liver 6 thymus
enlargement: 7 adenoma
secretion: 5 sebum 7 hormone
swelling: 4 bubo
glandular: 7 adenoid
glare: 4 gaze 5 blaze, flame, scowl, stare 6
glower 7 glitter 8 radiance 9 showiness
glaring: 4 rank 5 clear, gaudy, gross,
plain, vivid 6 brazen, bright, strong 7
blatant, burning, evident, obvious, staring, visible 8 apparent, flagrant, manifest 9 barefaced 11 conspicuous
glary: 6 frosty, frozen 7 intense, shining
8 slippery
glass: 4 lens, pane 6 beaker, bottle, cloche,
cullet, goblet, mirror 7 tumbler 9 barometer, telescope
alcohol: mug 4 pony 5 stein 6 jigger, rummer, seidel 7 snifter 8 schooner
colored: 5 smalt 7 opaline 10 aventurine
container: jar 6 bottle 7 matrass
design: 4 etch
gem: 5 paste 6 strass
molten: 5 metal 7 parison
pert. to: 6 vitric
remove bubbles: 5 plane
glasses: 5 specs 6 shades 7 goggles 8
pince-nez 10 spectacles, binoculars
glassmaking: *device:* 7 ironman
frame: 7 drosser
material: 4 frit
oven: 4 lehr
glassworker: 6 blower, teaser 7 glazier
glasswort: 4 kali 5 plant
glassy: 4 hard 5 sharp 6 shrill 8 strident
9 apathetic 10 forbidding, lackluster,
unwavering, unyielding
Glaucus: *father:* 8 Sisyphus
son: 11 Bellerophon
glaze: 4 blur, coat 5 cover, glare 6 enamel,
finish, polish, veneer 7 burnish, grow
dim, incrust, overlay, vitrify 8 film over
glazier: 11 glassworker
gleam: ray 4 beam, glow 5 blink, blush,
flash, glint, sheen, shine 7 glimmer,
glitter, shimmer, sparkle 8 radiance,

splendor **9** coruscate **10** brightness **11** coruscation, scintillate

gleaming: 6 ablaze, bright

glean: 4 cull, reap **6** garner, gather **7** collect, extract

gleaning: 4 crop

glee: joy **4** song **5** mirth, sport **6** gaiety **7** delight, elation **8** hilarity **9** merriment **10** minstrelsy **12** cheerfulness **13** entertainment

gleeful: gay **5** merry **6** joyous **7** jocular

gleeman: 8 minstrel, musician

glen: 4 dale, dell, vale **5** heuch(Sc.) **6** dingle, valley **10** depression

glib: pat **4** easy, oily **5** quick, ready, slick **6** casual, facile, fluent, smooth **7** offhand, shallow, voluble **8** flippant, slippery, unforced **9** impromptu, talkative, insincere **10** nonchalant, unthinking **11** superficial

glide: 4 flow, sail, sile, skim, slip, soar **5** coast, creep, merge, slide, steal **6** glance **7** slither **8** glissade

gliding over: 6 labile **7** eliding

glim: bit, eye **5** light, watch **12** illumination

glimmer: 4 fire, glow **5** blink, flash, gleam **7** glimpse, glitter, shimmer, sparkle

glimmering: 5 flash, ghost **7** inkling

glimpse: 4 espy, peek, **5** trace **6** glance **7** glimmer **11** view briefly **12** fleeting look

glint: 5 flash, gleam, shine **6** luster **7** glisten, glitter, sparkle **10** brightness

glitch: 5 error **6** mishap **11** malfunction

glitter: 4 fire, glow, pomp, show **5** flash, gleam, sheen, shine **6** glamor, tinsel **7** glamour, glimmer, glisten, spangle, sparkle, twinkle **8** radiance **9** coruscate **10** brilliancy **11** coruscation, scintillate

glittering: 5 gaudy, gemmy **6** bright, fulgid **7** radiant **8** lustrous **9** brilliant, clinquant, sparkling, twinkling

gloaming: eve **4** dusk **8** twilight

gloat: 4 brag **5** exult, vaunt **7** revel in **8** crow over

global: 6 all-out, cosmic **7** general **9** universal, worldwide

globe: orb **4** ball, clew **5** earth, world **6** planet, sphere

half: **10** hemisphere

pert. to: **7** spheric

globular: 5 beady, round **9** orbicular, spherical

globule: 4 bead, blob, drop **6** bubble **7** droplet **8** particle, spherule

glockenspiel: 4 lyra **8** carillon **9** xylophone

glom(sc.): 4 take **5** steal, swipe, watch **10** understand

gloom: 4 dusk, murk **5** cloud, drear, frown **7** despair, dimness, sadness **8** darkness

9 dejection, heaviness, obscurity **10** cloudiness, depression, desolation, melancholy

gloomy: dim, sad, wan **4** blue, dark, dour, eery, glum **5** black, brown, dusky, heavy, moody, murky, stern **6** cloudy, dismal, dreary, morose, somber, sullen **7** clouded, obscure, stygian **8** darkling, darksome, dejected, desolate, downcast, overcast **9** cheerless, darkening, depressed, saturnine, tenebrous **10** depressing, despondent, foreboding, lusterless, melancholy, sepulchral, tenebrific **11** pessimistic **12** disconsolate, disheartened

glop: goo **4** guck, muck **11** thick liquid

glorify: 4 hery, laud **5** adore, adorn, bless, boast, exalt, extol, glory, honor, vaunt **6** praise **7** clarify, elevate, ennoble, magnify **8** emblazon, eulogize **9** celebrate **11** apotheosize

gloriole: 4 aura, halo **7** aureole

glorious: 5 grand, noble **6** bright **7** eminent, haughty, radiant **8** boastful, ecstatic, gorgeous, renowned, splendid **9** wonderful **10** celebrated, delightful **11** illustrious, magnificent, resplendent

glory: 4 fame, halo **5** boast, eclat, exult, honor, kudos, pride **6** beauty, praise, renown **7** aureole **8** ambition, splendor **9** greatness **10** admiration, brilliancy, effulgence, reputation **11** distinction **12** magnificence

gloss: 4 glow **5** dodge, gloze, sheen, shine **6** blanch, enamel, excuse, luster, polish, remark, veneer **7** burnish **8** annotate, flourish, palliate, pretense **9** semblance, sleekness **10** brightness, commentary **14** interpretation

glossal: 7 lingual

glossary: 4 list **7** lexicon

glossy: 5 nitid, silky, sleek **6** bright, smooth **7** shining **8** lustrous, polished, specious **9** plausible

glove: 4 cuff, mitt **6** mitten, sheath **7** chevron, dannock, gantlet **8** gauntlet

fabric: **4** silk, wool **5** nylon **6** cotton

leather: kid **4** napa **5** mocha, suede **7** pigskin

shape: **5** trank

glow: 4 beam, halo **5** ardor, blush, flame, flush, gleam, gloss, shine **6** warmth **7** glimmer **13** incandescence

glower: 4 sulk **5** frown, scowl, stare **9** look black

glowing: hot, red **5** fiery, vivid **6** ardent **7** burning, candent, fervent, radiant, shining **10** candescent

Gluck opera: 5 Orfeo **7** Alceste

glucose: 5 sugar **6** starch **7** sucrose **8** dextrose

glue: fix **5** mount, paste, stick **6** adhere,

attach, cement, fasten, gluten, sizing **7** sericin **8** adhesive, mucilage

glum: 4 dour **5** moody, surly **6** dismal, gloomy, morose, sullen **8** dejected, frowning, overcast **10** melancholy **11** threatening

glume: 4 leaf **5** bract

glut: 4 cloy, fill, gulp, sate **5** draft, gorge **6** englut, excess, pamper **7** engorge, satiate, surfeit, swallow **8** overfeed, overload, plethora, saturate

gluten: gum **4** glue **7** fibrin **8** adhesive

glutethimide: 8 sedative **13** phenobarbitol

glutinous: 4 ropy, sizy **5** gluey, gummy **6** sticky **7** viscous

glutton: hog, pig **8** gourmand **9** overeater, wolverine

gluttonous: 6 greedy **7** hoggish **9** voracious

glyph: 6 symbol **7** channel

gnar, gnarr: 5 growl, snarl

gnarl: 4 knot **5** growl, knurl, snarl, twist **6** tangle **7** contort

gnarled: 6 knotty, rugged, sinewy **7** crabbed, twisted **8** hardened **9** roughened

gnash: 4 bite **5** chomp, grind

gnat: fly **4** pest **5** midge **6** insect

gnaw: eat **4** bite, chew, fret **5** erode **6** harass, nibble **7** corrode, torment **8** wear away

gnome: elf, saw **5** adage, bogey, dwarf, elves(pl.), maxim, motto, pigmy, troll **6** goblin, kobold, sprite **8** aphorism, apothegm

gnomon: 9 indicator **10** sundial pin

gnostic: 4 wise **6** clever, shrewd **7** knowing **12** intellectual

gnu: 5 takin **6** mammal **8** antelope **10** wildebeast

go: act, bet, bid, die, gae, mog, run **4** fall, fare, gang, lead, mosy, move, pass, read, ride, turn, walk, wane, wend, work **5** break, elope, leave, occur, set-to, steal, visit **6** amount, attain, become, belong, betake, depart, elapse, follow, happen, intend, resort, result, retire, travel **7** conduce, operate, proceed, succeed **8** diminish, traverse, withdraw **9** circulate, harmonize, undertake

aboard: **6** embark **7** entrain

ahead: **7** proceed **8** continue, progress

along: **5** agree **6** concur

around: **5** avoid **6** detour **10** circumvent

ashore: **4** land **6** debark **9** disembark

astray: err **8** aberrate, miscarry

away: **4** exit, scat, shoo **5** leave, scram **6** begone, depart, retire

back: ebb **5** recede, return, revert **7** regress, retreat **10** retrogress

back on: **6** betray, renege **7** abandon **10** break faith

before: **4** lead **7** precede **8** antecede

between: **7** mediate **9** interpose

down: sag **4** fall, sink **5** lower **7** decline, descend, founder **8** decrease **11** deteriorate

forward: **4** fare **7** advance **8** progress

into: **5** audit, delve, enter, probe **7** examine

mad: **4** rage, rave, roar **5** erupt

on: **5** enter **7** proceed **8** continue

over: **5** renew **7** retrace **9** backtrack

swiftly: run **5** scoot, speed

through: **6** endure, suffer **9** penetrate **10** experience

to and fro: **5** waver **6** totter, wig-wag **7** stagger **9** fluctuate, vacillate **11** shuttlecock

to pot: die **4** fail **7** decline

up: **4** rise **5** arise, raise **6** ascend

with: **4** date, suit **5** agree **6** escort **9** accompany, harmonize

go-ahead: 4 okay **8** all clear **11** green light **13** authorization

go-between: 5 agent, envoy **6** broker **7** arbiter **8** mediator **10** mouthpiece **11** internuncio **12** intermediary

go-cart: 4 pram **5** wagon **12** perambulator

goa: 6 mugger(Ind.) **7** gazelle

goad: egg, gad, rod **4** brod, dice, edge, move, prod, spur, urge, yerk **5** ankus, decoy, impel, pique, prick, sting, thorn **6** incite **7** inflame **8** irritate, stimulus **9** incentive, instigate, stimulate **10** incitement

goal: aim, end **4** base, butt, dole, hail, mark, mete **5** bourn, finis, score, tally **6** object **7** purpose **8** ambition **9** intention, objective **10** aspiration **11** destination **12** consummation

goat: kid, ram, tur **4** ibex, tahr **5** beden, billy, goral, nanny **6** alpaca, chamal, pasang, victim **7** fall guy, markhor **8** aegagrus, ruminant **9** bouquetin, stambecco, steinbock

constellation: **9** Capricorn

disease: **7** takosis

flesh: **6** chevon

genus: **5** capra

god of: Pan

male: **4** buck **5** billy

pert. to: **6** capric **7** caprine, hircine

wild: **4** ibex **7** markhor

goatee: 5 beard **7** Vandyke

goatherd: 5 Damon

goatish: 4 lewd **6** coarse **7** caprine, hircine, lustful **9** salacious **10** lascivious

goatskin: 9 chevrette

gob: 4 hunk, lump, mass **5** chunk **6** sailor, seaman **7** mariner **8** quantity

gobbet: 4 drip, drop **5** piece **6** morsel **7** driblet, portion **8** fragment, mouthful

gobble: 4 gulp **6** snatch **7** swallow

Gobi Desert site: 4 Asia
goblet: cup **5** glass, hanap **6** beaker, vessel **7** chalice **8** standard
goblin: elf, hag, nis **4** bhut **5** bogey, bogle, bucca, gnome, nisse, ouphe, pooka **6** booger, churel, kobold, sprite **7** brownie
gobs: lots **5** heaps, loads, scads **6** oodles, plenty
god (see also **deity, gods**): Ada, Ani, Asa, Bel, Bes, Geb, Keb, Ler, Min, Pan, Ran, Seb, Tiu, Tyr, Ull, Van **4** aitu, Amen, Amon, Aten, Aton, Baal, deus(L.), deva, dieu(F.), Frey, Hler, idol, Kama, Loke, Loki, Nora, Odin, Orra, Ptah, Rama, Surt, Thor, Vali, Yama, Zeus **5** Aeger, Aegir, Asura, Baldr, Brage, Brama, Donar, Freyr, Hades, image, Othin, Pluto, Shiva, Surtr, Woden **6** Apollo, Brahma, Cronus, Elohim, Ganesa, Hermes, Hoenir, Kronus, Marduk, Njorth, Osiris, Saturn, Vulcan, Yahweh **7** Bacchus, creator, Forsete, godhead, Heimdal, Jehovah, Jupiter, Krishna, Mercury, Serapis, Vitharr **8** Almighty, Dionysus **9** Heindallr, Hlorrithi **11** Ramachandra
false: **4** Baal **6** Mammon
love for: **5** piety **6** amadis, bhakti
God be with you: 5 adieu, adios **7** goodbye
god-fearing: 5 pious **6** devout **9** religious
god-horse: 6 mantis
god-like: 5 pious **6** deific, devout, divine **8** immortal **9** religious
goddess (see also **god**): Bau, Dis, Eir, Eos, Hel, Mut, Nut, Uma **4** Anta, Bast, Devi, Gaia, Hela, Hera, Isis, Juno, Kali, Nina, Norn, Saga, Urth, Wyrd **5** Belit, Ceres, Diana, Durga, Freya, Frigg, Gauri, Nanna, Venus **6** Athena, Aurora, Chandi, Freyja, Frigga, Hecate, Hestia, Shakti, Tiamat **7** Artemis, Asynjur, Demeter, Mylitta, Parvati **9** Aphrodite, Haimavati **10** Persephone, Proserpina
godfather: don **7** sponsor
godforsaken: 6 dismal **8** desolate, wretched **9** miserable, neglected
godless: 6 unholy, wicked **7** impious, profane **9** atheistic
godliness: 5 piety **13** righteousness
godly: 5 pious **6** devout **8** gracious **9** religious, righteous
gods: For gods of specific localities, religions, or functions, see under the specific locality, religion, or function. EXAMPLES: "hindu god": see **Hindu:** *deity;* "god of war": see **war:** *god of.*
gods' abode: 6 heaven **7** Olympus
godsend: 4 boon **8** blessing **9** life saver
Goethe drama: 5 Faust **6** Egmont, Stella **7** Clavigo
gofer: 9 errand boy, messenger
goffer: 4 iron **5** crimp, pleat

go-getter: 6 dynamo **7** hustler **8** live wire
goggle: bug, eye **4** roll **5** stare **6** squint
goggler: 4 scad **5** akule
goggles: 5 specs **7** glasses **8** blinkers
going: run, way **4** exit, fare, gait, gate, path, road **5** bound **6** access **7** current **8** behavior **9** departure **10** passageway
goiter: 6 struma **7** strumae(pl.)
gola: 4 cyma **7** granary **9** storeroom
gold: oro(Sp.) **4** gelt, gilt **5** aurum, metal **6** riches, wealth **7** bullion **9** clinquant
bar: **5** ingot
black: oil
deposit: **6** placer
fool's: **6** pyrite
imitation: **6** ormolu, oroide
measure of weight: **5** carat
pert. to: **4** dore **6** aurous
thin sheet of: **4** foil **6** latten
uncoined: **7** bullion
yielding: **10** auriferous
gold braid: 5 orris
gold-brick: 7 swindle
Gold Bug author: Poe
gold-plate: 4 gild, gilt
golden: 4 gilt, rich **5** auric, blest, blond **6** blonde, mellow, yellow **7** aureate, halcyon, shining **8** precious **9** favorable, Pactolian, yellowish **10** propitious
golden age: 9 siecle d'or(F.)
golden ager: 7 oldster **13** elderly person, senior citizen
golden apple giver: 5 Paris
golden bough: 9 mistletoe
golden chain: 8 laburnum
Golden Fleece: *keeper of:* **6** Aeetes
land of: **7** Colchis
seeker: **5** Jason **8** Argonaut
ship used: **4** Argo
golden oriole: 5 pirol **6** loriot
Golden State: 10 California
goldeneye: cur **9** merrywing
goldenrod: 8 solidago
goldfinch: 8 graypate, greypate **12** yellow-hammer
goldfish: 4 carp **6** calico **9** garibaldi, shubunkin
goldsmith: 7 artisan **9** artificer
crucible: **6** cruset
golem: 5 robot **9** automaton, blockhead
golf: *assistant:* **5** caddy **6** caddie
club: **4** iron, wood **5** baffy, cleek, mashy, spoon **6** brassy, driver, jigger, mashie, putter **7** brassie, midiron, niblick
conceded putt: **5** gimme
course: **5** links
cry: **4** fore
cup: **5** Ryder **6** Walker
hazard: **4** trap **5** stymy **6** bunker, stymie
mound: tee
mulligan: **9** free drive
score: par **5** bogey, bogie, eagle **6** birdie, Nassau

stroke: 4 hook, loft, putt 5 drive, slice
target: cup 4 flag 5 green
term: lie, tee 4 baff, 5 divot, dormy, green 6 dormie, stroke 7 gallery
golfer: 8 linksman
notable men: 4 Ford (Doug), Pate (Jerry) 5 Boros (Julius), Hagen (Walter), Hogen (Ben), Irwin (Hale), Jones (Bobby), Shute (Denny), Smith (Horton), Snead (Sam) 6 Casper (Billy), Miller (Johnny), Nelson (Byron), Ouimet (Francis), Palmer, (Arnold), Player (Gary), Rogers (Bill), Watson (Tom) 7 Sarazen (Gene), Stadler (Craig), Trevino (Lee), 8 Nicklaus (Jack), Weiskopf (Tom) 10 Middlecoff (Cary) 11 Ballesteros (Seve)
notable women: 4 Berg (Patty) 5 Lopez (Nancy), Suggs (Louise) 6 Alcott (Amy), Caponi (Donna), Daniel (Beth), Rankin (Judy), Wright (Mickey) 9 Whitworth (Kathy)
Goliath: 5 giant
home: 4 Gath
place of death: 4 Elah
slayer: 5 David
golly: 4 oath, yell
Gomer: *father:* 7 Japheth
husband: 5 Hosea
gondola: car 4 boat 5 barge, coach
gone: 4 away, left, lost 6 absent 7 missing 8 absorbed, departed, finished, vanished
gone by: ago, o'er 4 over, past
Goneril: *father:* 4 Lear
sister: 5 Regan 8 Cordelia
gonfalon: 4 flag 6 banner, ensign 7 pennant 8 standard
goober: 6 peanut
good: bon(F.), fit 4 able, bein, bien(F.), boon, braw, fine, full, gain, kind, nice, prow 5 ample, brave, bueno(Sp.), bully, moral, nifty, pious, sound, valid 6 benign, devout, expert, profit, proper 7 copious, gradely, helpful, liberal, trained, upright 8 becoming, budgeree, decorous, friendly, gracious, interest, orthodox, pleasant, pleasing, salutary, skillful, suitable, virtuous 9 agreeable, bountiful, competent, dauntless, enjoyable, estimable, excellent, favorable, fortunate, indulgent, reputable, righteous, well-being 10 auspicious, beneficial, benevolent, courageous, gratifying, profitable, sufficient 11 pleasurable, respectable, responsible, well-behaved 12 considerable, satisfactory, stouthearted, well-disposed
good-bye, good-by: 4 tata 5 adieu(F.), adios(Sp.), aloha, ciaou(It.) 6 so-long 7 cheerio 8 farewell
Good Earth author: 4 Buck
good-for-nothing: 4 orra 7 useless, wast-

rel 8 spalpeen(Ir.) 9 worthless 10 ne'er-do-well 11 rapscallion
good health: 5 skoal 6 prosit 7 slainte
good-looking: 4 fair 5 bonny 6 comely, pretty 7 eyesome, winsome 8 handsome 9 beautiful 10 attractive, personable
good luck: 7 fortune
image: 6 alraun
good-natured: 6 genial, jovial 7 amiable 8 cheerful, obliging 9 easy-going, gemutlich
good spirit: 8 eudaemon
goodliness: 5 grace 6 beauty 8 goodness, kindness 10 comeliness, excellence
goodly: 4 kind 5 large 6 comely, portly 8 gracious, handsome 9 capacious, excellent 12 considerable
goodness: 6 bounty, purity, virtue 8 chastity, kindness 10 excellence, generosity, goodliness 11 beneficence, benevolence
goods: 4 gear 5 stock, wares 7 chattel, effects 8 property 11 commodities, merchandise, possessions
cast overboard: 5 lagan, ligan 6 jetsam, lagend
lost in shipwreck: 7 flotsam
smuggled: 10 contraband
stolen: 4 loot, pelf 5 booty 6 spoils
goodwill: 4 love 5 amity, favor 8 kindness, sympathy 9 readiness 10 friendship, heartiness 11 benevolence 12 friendliness
goody: 5 candy 6 bonbon, tidbit 8 goodwife 9 sweetmeat
goof: err 5 gum up, spoil 7 blunder
goofy: 5 silly 6 insane 7 foolish 8 gullible
gook: 4 muck 5 bilge, hooey, trash 6 drival
goon: sap 4 boob, dope, thug 6 mugger 7 hoodlum
gooney bird: 9 albatross
goosander: 9 merganser
goose: 4 bird 5 ninny, solan 7 widgeon 9 screwball, simpleton
cry: 4 honk, yang 5 cronk
flock: 4 raft 6 gaggle
genus: 4 chen 5 anser, brant
mackerel: 9 phalarope
male: 6 gander
pert. to: 8 anserine 9 grossular
snow: 4 chen 5 wavey 9 whitehead
tailor's: 8 flatiron
wild: 5 brant 7 gray-lag 8 barnacle
young: 7 gosling
goose egg: 4 zero 5 zilch 6 cipher, naught 7 nothing
gooseflesh: 5 bumps 7 pimples
goosefoot: 5 blite, plant, shrub
gopher: 4 tuza 6 rodent 8 squirrel, tortoise
Gopher State: 9 Minnesota
Gorboduc's son: 6 Porrex

Gordian: 9 intricate **11** complicated

gore: 4 stab **5** blood, filth, inset, slime **6** gusset, insert, pierce **7** carnage **9** penetrate

gorge: 4 fill, gaum, glut, pass, sate **5** cajon, canon, chasm, flume, gulch, gully, kloof, strid **6** canyon, coulee, defile, englut, nullah, ravine, valley **7** couloir, overeat, pitcher, satiate **8** quebrada **10** gluttonize

gorgeous: 4 vain **5** grand, showy **6** costly **8** dazzling, glorious, splendid **9** beautiful, luxurious **11** magnificent, resplendent

Gorgon: 6 Medusa, Stheno **7** Euryale
watcher for: **4** Enyo **5** Deino **6** Graeae(pl.) **8** Pephredo

gorilla: ape **7** primate **10** anthropoid

gorse: 4 whin **5** furze **7** juniper

gory: 6 bloody **9** murderous **10** sanguinary **12** bloodstained

goshawk: 7 tiercel
keeper: **8** ostreger **10** austringer

gospel: 5 creed **7** tidings **8** doctrine, last word, teaching
harmony of the four: **11** diatessaron

gossamer: 4 airy **5** filmy, gauzy, sheer **10** diaphanous

gossip: gab **4** blab, chat, dirt **5** clack, rumor, snoop **6** babble, gabble, magpie, tattle **7** chatter, hearsay, prattle, scandal **8** busybody, idle talk, informer, quidnunc **9** chatterer **10** newsmonger, talebearer, tattletale **11** scuttlebutt

Goth: 8 Visigoth **9** barbarian, Ostrogoth
hero: **5** Wudga
last: **8** Roderick

Gothamite: 9 New Yorker

Gothic: 4 rude **5** rough **6** fierce **8** barbaric, medieval, Teutonic

Gouda: 6 cheese
kin of: **4** Edam

gouge: 4 tool **5** cheat, fraud **6** cavity, chisel, groove **7** defraud **9** extortion **10** overcharge

goulash: 4 stew **6** jumble **7** mixture **8** mishmash

Gounod opera: 5 Faust

gourd: 4 hole, pepo **5** melon, pepos **6** bottle, vessel **7** anguria **8** calabash, cucurbit **9** colocynth **11** chilacayote
rattle: **6** maraca
sponge: **5** loofa, luffa

gourmand: 7 glutton, gourmet **8** big eater **11** trencherman

gourmet: 7 epicure **8** gourmand **9** bon vivant **10** gastronome **11** connoisseur

gout: 4 clot, drop **5** taste **6** blotch **7** podagra **9** arthritis **11** coagulation, discernment

govern: run **4** curb, rein, rule, sway **5** guide, regle, steer **6** bridle, direct, manage, police **7** command, conduct, control, preside, refrain **8** dominate, regulate, restrain **9** influence, supervise **10** administer, discipline

governance: 7 control **10** government, management

governess: 5 nanny, tutor **6** abbess **8** mistress **9** nursemaid

government: law **4** rule **5** power **6** regime **7** conduct, regency, regimen **8** guidance monarchy, republic **9** authority, autocracy, democracy, hierarchy, oligarchy **10** governance, management, regulation **11** aristocracy
agent: **5** envoy **6** consul **8** diplomat, minister **10** ambassador
art of: **8** politics **13** statesmanship
by a few: **9** oligarchy
by church: **9** hierarchy **10** hierocracy
by one: **8** monarchy **12** dictatorship
by people: **9** democracy
by rich: **10** plutocracy
by three: **8** triarchy **11** triumvirate
by women: **8** gynarchy **11** gynecocracy
head: **4** czar, king **5** queen **7** emperor, empress, premier **8** dictator **9** president **10** presidente
official: **6** syndic **10** bureaucrat
opposition to: **10** antarchism
without: **6** acracy **7** anarchy

governor: bey **4** lord **5** deity, nabob, pilot, ruler **6** rector, regent **7** captain, control, manager, viceroy **8** director **9** president, regulator **10** gubernator, magistrate
castle: **6** alcaid **7** alcaide **9** castellan

gown (see also **dress, garment**): **4** robe, toga **5** frock, habit, manto, toosh **6** clothe, invest, mantua **7** garment **11** formal dress
dressing: **4** robe **6** kimono **8** peignoir
loose: **5** smock **6** banian, camise, chimer **7** cassock, chemise
Moslem: **4** jama **5** jamah

Goya figure: 4 Maja

grab: nab **4** boat, hold, take **5** catch, clasp, grasp, seize **6** arrest, clutch, collar, snatch **7** capture, grapple **11** appropriate

grabble: 5 grope, seize **6** snatch, sprawl **7** grapple **11** appropriate

grace: 4 ease **5** adorn, charm, favor, leave, mercy **6** beauty, become, bedeck, polish, prayer, virtue **7** commend, dignify, gratify **8** beautify, easiness, efficacy, elegance, kindness **9** embellish, privilege **10** comeliness, goodliness, permission, refinement, seemliness **12** dispensation **14** attractiveness

Grace: 6 Aglaia, Charis, Thalia **10** Euphrosyne
mother of: **5** Aegle

graceful: 4 airy, easy **6** comely, gainly,

mignon, seemly **7** elegant, fitting, genteel, tactful **8** charming, debonair, delicate **9** beautiful **11** appropriate

graceless: 4 ugly **5** cruel **7** awkward **8** depraved **9** abandoned, inelegant, merciless **10** ungracious **11** unfortunate

gracenote: 12 appoggiatura

graces: 8 agremens **9** agrements

gracile: 4 thin **6** slight **7** slender **8** graceful

gracious: 4 good, kind, mild **5** civil, godly, happy, lucky, suave **6** benign, goodly, kindly **7** affable **8** benedict, debonair, generous, handsome, merciful, pleasing **9** benignant, courteous

grackle: 9 blackbird

gradation: 4 rank, step **5** scale, stage **6** degree, series **8** position **10** difference

grade: peg **4** mark, rank, rate, size, sort **5** class, level, order, stage **6** ascent, assort, degree, rating, select **7** incline, inspect **8** classify, gradient, graduate **14** classification

grader: 9 bulldozer

gradient: 4 ramp **5** grade, slope

gradine, gradin: 5 shelf **7** retable

gradual: 4 easy, slow **6** gentle **9** leisurely **10** step by step

graduate: 6 alumna **7** alumnus **9** calibrate

Graeae, Graiae: 4 Enyo **5** Deino **8** Pephredo

father: **7** Phorcus, Phorcys

sister: **6** Gorgon, Medusa **7** Gorgons

graff: 5 canal, ditch, fosse **6** trench

graft: dig **4** cion, toil, work **5** ditch, gravy, labor, scion, trade **6** boodle, inarch, payola, trench **7** bribery

grafted: 6 united **8** attached

heraldry: **4** ente

grail: 4 ama, cup **4** bowl **6** vessel **7** chalice, platter **8** sangraal, sangreal

knight of: **4** Bors **7** Galahad **8** Percival

grain: jot, rye **4** corn, grit, meal, oats, rice, seed, wale, whit **5** fiber, grist, maize, scrap, spark, speck, trace, wheat **6** barley, cereal, kernel, russud(Russ.) **7** granule, modicum, texture **8** particle **9** granulate

beard: awn

brewing: **4** malt

bundle: **5** sheaf

chaff: **4** bran, grit

coating: **4** bran

disease: **4** smut **5** ergot

dried: **5** straw **6** groats, rissom, rizzom

ear of: **5** spike **6** ressum

foodstuff: **6** cereal

fungus: **5** ergot

funnel: **6** hopper

goddess of: **5** Ceres **7** Demeter

ground: **4** meal **5** flour, grist

line: **5** swath

measure: **6** thrave

mixture: **6** fodder **7** farrage **9** bullimong

outer membrane: **6** extine

parched: **7** graddan

price: **4** fiar(Sc.)

receptacle: bin **8** elevator

refuse: pug **5** chaff

scoop: **5** shaul

spike: ear

stack: **4** rick

tool: **5** flail

warehouse: **8** elevator

grainy: 6 coarse **8** granular, textured

gram: 6 weight

one-tenth: **8** decigram

molecule: mol **4** mole

gramary: 5 magic **10** necromancy **11** enchantment

grammar: 6 syntax **9** accidence **11** linguistics

case: **6** dative **8** ablative, genitive, vocative **9** objective **10** accusative, nominative, possessive

describe: **5** parse

direct address: **8** vocative

example: **8** paradigm

term: **6** phrase, simile **8** metaphor

grampus: orc **4** ocra **5** whale **7** cetacea, dolphin **8** cetacean, scorpion

granada: 11 pomegranate

granary: bin **4** gola **6** garnel, garner, girnal, girnel, grange **8** cornloft **9** cornhouse **10** repository, storehouse

grand: 4 epic, main **5** chief, great, lofty, noble, showy **6** august, epical, famous, superb, swanky **7** exalted, immense, stately, sublime **8** foremost, glorious, gorgeous, majestic, splendid **9** dignified, grandiose, principal, sumptuous **10** impressive, preeminent **11** ceremonious, illustrious, magnificent **13** comprehensive

Grand Canyon state: 7 Arizona

Grand Duke of Hell: 6 Abogor

grand slam: 4 vole **5** homer **7** home run

grandee: 6 bashaw **7** magnate **8** nobleman **10** clarissimo(It.)

grandeur: 4 pomp **5** state **6** parade **7** majesty **8** elegance, splendor, vastness **9** greatness, immensity, loftiness, nobleness, sublimity **10** augustness **12** magnificence

grandfather: 6 atavus **8** grandfer, gudesire(Sc.)

pert to: **4** aval

grandiloquent: 6 heroic, turgid **7** pompous **9** bombastic

grandiose: 4 epic **5** grand **6** turgid **7** pompous **8** imposing **9** bombastic, expansive, flaunting **10** impressive

grandmother: 6 granny, gudame(Sc.) **7**

grannie **8** babushka(Russ.)
Devil's: **4** Baba
grange: 4 farm **7** granary **9** farmhouse
granger: 6 farmer
granite: 6 aplite **7** haplite, syenite **8** alaskite
Granite State: 12 New Hampshire
granitic: 4 hard **7** austere **10** inflexible
grant: aid **4** boon, cede, gift, give, lend, loan, mise **5** admit, allot, allow, bonus, chart, cowle, spare, yette, yield **6** accede, accord, afford, assent, bestow, betake, beteem, bounty, confer, octroi, patent, permit, remise **7** adjudge, concede, consent, promise, subsidy, tribute **8** bestowal, donation, transfer **9** franchise, undertake **10** concession, permission, relinquish **11** acknowledge
granular: 5 sandy **6** coarse, grainy
granule: 4 pill **5** grain **6** nodule, pellet **8** particle
grape: uva **5** Pinot, Tokay **6** Agawam, Lalang, Malaga, Malage, Muscat **7** Catawba, Concord, Hamburg, Mission, Niagara **8** Delaware, Riesling, Thompson **8** muscadine **11** Scuppernong
acid: **7** racemic
cluster: **10** racemation
conserve: **5** jelly, uvate
cultivation: **11** viniculture, viticulture
dried: **6** raisin
drink: **4** dibs, sapa, wine
fermentation: **6** cuvage(Fr.)
gatherer: **8** vintager
genus of: **5** vitis
juice: **4** dibs, must, sapa, stum
pert. to: **4** uval **10** botryoidal
refuse: **4** marc
residue: **4** marc, rape **6** pomace
seed: **6** acinus
spirit: **4** marc
sugar: **8** dextrose, fructose
grapefruit: 6 pomelo **8** shaddock
Grapes of Wrath: *author:* **9** Steinbeck
family: **4** Joad
people: **5** Okies
grapevine: 4 caro **5** rumor **6** gossip, report
pest: **10** phylloxera
graph: map **5** chart **6** sketch **7** diagram, outline
graphic: 5 lucid, vivid **6** visual **7** precise **8** explicit, incisive **9** pictorial, realistic, well drawn **11** picturesque
graphite: 4 lead **6** carbon
grapnel: 4 drag, hook **6** anchor
grapple: 4 grab, hold **5** grasp **6** clinch, tackle **7** contend, grapnel, seizing, seizure, wrestle **8** struggle
grasp: nap, see **4** clam, fist, grab, grip, hold, take **5** catch, clasp, seize, snare **6** clench, clinch, clutch, snatch **7** control,

embrace, grapple **8** handfast **9** apprehend **10** comprehend, understand **13** comprehension
grasping: 4 avid, hard **6** greedy, grippy **7** miserly **8** covetous **10** avaricious **12** apprehension, parsimonious
adapted for: **10** prehensile, prehensive
grass (see also **cereal**): pot **4** lawn, reed, turf **6** darnel **7** hassock, herbage, pasture **9** colieroot, marijuana, vetiveria **10** greensward
blade of: **7** traneen
dried: hay **6** fodder
fiber: **4** flax **5** istle, ramee, ramie **6** bhabar
fodder: **4** dura, gama **6** millet
forage: **7** setaria
genus of: **4** aira, **5** stipa **6** clover, lygeum **7** setaria
kinds of: eel, fog, hay, poa **4** alfa, bent, cane, diss, leaf, reed, **5** avena, grama, sedge, spart, spike, stipa **6** enalid, marram, quitch, redtop, sesame, sorrel **7** esparto, traneen **8** calfkill **9** bouteloua
tuft: **7** tussock
grasshopper: 4 grig **6** locust
relative: **7** katydid
grassland: lea **4** lawn, rakh(Ind.), vale **5** field, range, veldt **6** meadow, pampas **7** pasture, prairie, savanna
grate: jar **4** fret, grid, grit, rasp **5** grill, grind **6** abrade, basket, offend, prison, scrape **7** grating **8** imprison, irritate
grateful: 8 thankful **9** agreeable **12** appreciative
gratification: 4 gust **6** reward **8** delicacy, gratuity, pleasure **9** enjoyment **10** recompense **11** contentment **12** satisfaction
gratified: 4 glad **5** proud **7** pleased **9** delighted
gratify: 4 feed, sate **5** adorn, amuse, feast, grace, humor, wreak **6** arride, foster, pamper, please **7** appease, content, delight, flatter, gladden, indulge, requite, satisfy
grating: 4 grid, rasp **5** grill, harsh, raspy, rough **6** grille, hoarse **8** gridiron, grinding, strident **9** dissonant **11** latticework
gratitude: 6 thanks **7** tribute **12** appreciation, gratefulness, thankfulness
gratuitous: 4 free **6** gratis, wanton **7** unasked **8** baseless, needless **9** voluntary **10** groundless **11** superfluous, unwarranted
gratuity: fee, tip **4** dole, gift **5** bonus, bribe, pilon **6** bounty **7** cumshaw, pension, present **9** baksheesh, lagniappe, pourboire **10** compliment **11** benefaction
grave: 4 tomb **5** carve, sober, staid **6** sedate, solemn, somber **7** austere, earnest,

engrave, serious **8** decorous, **9** important, momentous, sepulcher

cloth: **8** cerement

robber: **5** ghoul

gravel: 4 dirt, grit **6** bother **7** perplex **8** alluvium **9** embarrass

gravelly: 5 harsh **6** coarse **7** rasping

graven: 6 etched **8** engraved **10** sculptured

graver: 5 burin **8** engraver, sculptor

gravestone: 5 stela, stele **6** cippus, marker **8** monument **9** tombstone

graveyard: 8 cemetery **10** churchyard

gravid: 8 pregnant

graviers: 4 dice

graving tool: 5 burin

gravity: 7 dignity **8** enormity, sobriety **9** heaviness, influence, solemnity **10** importance **11** earnestness, seriousness, weightiness **12** significance **13** momentousness **17** authoritativeness

law discoverer: **6** Newton

without: **7** agravic

gravy: jus(F.) **5** graft, juice, sauce **8** windfall

gravy dish: 9 sauceboat

gray: dim **4** ashy, dull, gris, hoar **5** ashen, bleak, hoary, slate **6** dismal, leaden **7** grizzly, hueless, neutral **9** cheerless **10** achromatic

bluish: **7** cesious

dark: **5** taupe **6** Oxford **8** charcoal

light: **4** ashy **5** pearl

Quaker: **5** acier

Gray's churchyard opus: 5 Elegy

gray matter: 4 head, mind, obex **5** brain **9** intellect **11** thinking cap

gray whale: 7 ripsack

graylag: 5 goose

grayling: 4 fish **9** butterfly

graze: 4 crop, feed, rase, skim **5** brush, shave, touch **6** browse, scrape **7** pasture

grazing ground: 4 colp **5** range **6** collop, meadow **7** pasture

grease: fat, oil **4** lard, soil **5** bribe, cheat, cozen, smear **6** creesh(Sc.) **7** lanolin **9** lubricate

greaser: 6 stoker

greasewood: 5 chico **6** orache **7** chamiso, hopsage **10** iodine bush

greasy fat **4** oily, rich **5** dirty, fatty, gross, porky **7** smeared **8** indecent, slippery, unctuous **10** indelicate **11** threatening

great: big **4** deep, fell, huge, much, rial, unco, vast **5** ample, chief, grand, large, yeder **6** grande(F.), heroic, mickle **7** capital, eminent, extreme, howling, immense, intense, titanic, violent **8** almighty, elevated, enormous, favorite, horrible **9** elaborate, excellent, important, prolonged **10** delightful, omnipotent **11** magnificent

great albacore: 5 tunny **7** bluefin

Great Barrier island: 4 Otea

Great Bear: 9 Big Dipper, Ursa Major

great blue heron: 5 crane

Great Britain: See **England, Ireland, Scotland, Wales**

great deal: 4 gobs, lots

Great Divide: 7 Rockies

Great Expectations hero: Pip

Great Lake: 4 Erie **5** Huron **7** Ontario **8** Michigan, Superior

great many: lac **4** lakh

greaten: 5 exalt **7** enhance, enlarge, magnify **8** increase

greater: 6 better **8** mightier, superior

greatest: 4 arch, best, most **6** utmost **7** extreme, noblest, supreme

greathearted: 5 brave **7** gallant **8** fearless, generous **9** unselfish **10** courageous

greatly: 4 much **6** vastly **8** markedly **9** immensely **10** infinitely

greatness: 8 grandeur **9** magnitude **11** magnanimity

grebe: 8 dabchick **10** diving bird

Grecia: 6 Greece

Grecian: 5 Greek **9** Hellenist

Greece: (see also **Athens, Greek**): *capital:* **6** Athens

city: **4** Elis **6** Candia, Delphi, Nikhia, Patras, Sparta **7** Piraeus **8** Salonika **9** Peristeri

department: **4** Arta, Elis **5** Canea, Chios, Corfu, Drama, Evros, Pella, Samos, Zante **6** Achaea, Attica, Euboea, Kilkis, Kozane, Lesbos, Leukas, Phocis, Pieria, Serrai, Xanthe **7** Aetolia, Arcadia, Argolis, Boeotia, Corinth, Florina, Gravena, Kavalla, Laconia, Larissa, Preveza, Rhodope **8** Cyclades, Ioannina, Karditsa, Kastoria, Magnesia, Messenia, Trikkala

gulf: **7** Argolis, Corinth, Laconia, Saronic **8** Messenia, Salonika, Toronaic **9** Strymonic

island: Ios, Kos **4** Keos, Milo **5** Chios, Corfu, Crete, Delos, Melos, Naxos, Paros, Paxos, Psara, Samos, Syros, Thira, Tenos, Zante **6** Andros, Candia, Cerigo, Ikaria, Ithaca, Lemnos, Lesbos, Leukas, Patmus, Rhodes, Skyros **7** Amorgos, Cimolus, Kythnos, Mykonos, Siphnos **10** Cephalonia, Samothrace

island group: **6** Aegean, Ionian **8** Cyclades, Sporades **10** Dodecanese

monetary unit: **6** lepton **7** drachma

mountain: Ida **4** Oeta, Ossa **5** Athos **6** Othrys, Pelion, Pindus **7** Cyllene, Helicon, Olympus **8** Hymettus, Taygetus **9** Cambunian, Cithaeron, Parnassus **10** Erymanthus **11** Hagios Elias

region: **5** Crete **6** Aegean, Athens, Epirus,

Ionian, Thrace **7** Central **8** Thessaly **9** Macedonia **11** Peloponnese
river: **4** Arta **6** Peneus, Struma **7** Alpheus **8** Achelous, Cephisus **9** Arakhthos, Vistritsa
greed: **7** avarice **8** cupidity, voracity **11** selfishness
greedy: **4** avid **5** eager **6** grabby **7** miserly **8** covetous, grasping **9** rapacious **10** avaricious, gluttonous, insatiable
Greek: **7** Hellene
abode of gods: **7** Olympus
administrator: **10** amphodarch
alphabet: (see *letters* below)
altar: **7** eschara
army corps: **6** evzone
assembly: **5** agora, boule
assembly hill: **4** Pnyx
avenging spirit: **4** Fury **6** Erinys
basin: **6** louter
beauty: **4** Lais
bondman: **6** penest
castanet: **8** crotalum
Catholic: **5** Uniat **6** Uniate
chamber: **12** bouleuterion
chariot: **4** biga
church: **8** Orthodox
citadel: **9** Acropolis
clan: **4** obes **5** genos
cloak: **6** abolla **7** chlamys
coin: **4** mine, obol **5** hecte, nomas **6** lepton, phenix, stater **7** diobolo, drachma
column: **5** Doric, Ionic **10** Corinthian
contest: **4** agon
counselor: **6** Nestor
courtesan: **5** Thais **7** Aspasia
cup: **5** depas
dialect: **5** Doric, Elean, Eolic, Ionic **6** Aeolic
dirge: **5** linos
doom: **4** ker
dramatist: **9** Aeschylus, Euripides, Sophocles **12** Aristophanes
drink: **4** ouzo
enchantress: **5** Circe, Medea
epic: **5** Iliad **7** Odyssey
essence: **5** ousia
fabulist: **5** Aesop
Fate: **6** Clotho **7** Atropos **8** Lachesis
festival: **5** delia, haloa **8** Apaturia
flask: **4** olpe
fleet commander: **7** navarch
flute: **7** hemiope
folk dance: **7** romaika
foot-race course: **6** stadia(pl.) **7** diaulos, stadium
foot soldier: **7** hoplite
Fury: **6** Alecto, Erinys **7** Erinyes, Megaera **9** Tisiphone
galley: **6** bireme **7** trireme, unireme
garment: **5** tunic **6** abolla, chiton, peplos, peplus **7** chlamys

giant: **4** Otus **5** Mimas **7** Aloadae **9** Enceladus, Ephialtes
gift: **6** xenium
god: Dis, Pan **4** Ares, Eros, Zeus **5** Hades, Momus, Pluto, satyr **6** Apollo, Cronus, Hermes, Kronos, Nereus, Triton **7** Bacchus **8** Dionysus, Poseidon
god of love: **4** Eros
god of sea: **6** Triton **8** Poseidon
god of war: **4** Ares
god of wind: **6** Aeolus
goddess: Ara, Ate, Eos, Not, Nyx, Ops **4** Alea, Dice, Dike, Enyo, Gaea, Gaia, Hebe, Hera, Leto, Nike **5** Horae, Irene, Metis, Moera, Niobe, Vesta **6** Athena, Eirene, Hecate, Hekate, Hestia, Selena, Selene, Semele **7** Ariadne, Artemis, Astarte, Demeter, Eunomia, Nemesis **9** Aphrodite **10** Persephone
Gorgon: **4** Enyo **5** Deino **6** Graeae, Graiae, Medusa, Stheno **7** Euryale **8** Pephredo
governor: **6** eparch
gymnasium: **4** xyst **9** palaestra
hero: **4** Aias, Ajax, Idas **5** Jason **7** Cecrops, Theseus **8** Heracles
historian: **7** Ctesias **8** Polybius, Xenophon **9** Herodotus **10** Thucydides
hobgoblin: **6** Empusa
hunter: **5** Orion
huntress: **7** Artemis **8** Atalanta
instrument: **5** aulos **8** barbiton
jar: **7** amphora
judge: **6** dikast **7** heliast
jug: **5** ascos
king: **5** Minos **6** Nestor **9** Agamemnon
lawgiver: **5** Draco, Minos, Solon
legislative council: **5** boule
letters: chi, eta, phi, psi, rho, tau **4** beta, iota, zeta **5** alpha, delta, gamma, kappa, omega, sigma, theta **6** lambda **7** epsilon, omicron, upsilon
letter(primitive): san **5** koppa, sampi **7** digamma
lover: **7** Rhoecus
lyre player: **5** Arion
man of brass: **5** Talos
marker: **5** stela, stele
market place: **5** agora
marriage: **5** gamos
mathematician: **6** Euclid **10** Archimedes
measure: pik **4** bema, piki, pous **5** baril, cados, chous, cubit, diote, doron, pekhe, pygon, xylon **6** acaena, bachel, bacile, barile, cotula, dichas, hemina, koilon, lichas, milion, orgyia, palame, pechys, schene, xestes **7** amphora, choemix, cyathos, diaulos, hekteus, metreta, stadion, stadium, stremma **8** condylos, daktylos, dekapode, dolichos, medimnys, palaiste, plethron, spithame, stathmos **9** hemiekton, oxybaphon

monster: 5 Hydra
musical interval: 6 ditone, meseme
musical note: 4 mese, nete
musical system: 5 neume
mustard: 6 sinapi
nymph: 5 Oread 8 Arethusa
old testament: 10 Septuagint
overseer: 5 ephor
paradise: 7 Elysium
patriarch: 5 Arius
patriot: 6 klepht
people: 5 demos 6 Argive, Cretan, Ionian 7 Hellene, Spartan 8 Athenian
philosopher: 4 Zeno 5 Galen, Plato 6 Thales 8 Diogenes 9 Aristotle 10 Pythagoras
physician: 5 Galen 11 Hippocrates
pilaster: 4 anta
pillar: 5 stela, stele
pitcher: 4 olla, olpe 8 oenochoe
platform: 4 bema 6 logeum
poem: 5 Iliad 7 Odyssey
poet: Ion 5 Arion, Homer 6 Pindar 9 Aeschylus, Euripides, Simonides, Sophocles
poetess: 5 Sapho 6 Sappho 7 Corinna
portico: 4 stoa, xyst
precinct: 7 temenos
priest: 4 papa
priestess: 4 Auge, Hero, Iole 8 Caryatid
promontory: 6 Actium
province: 4 nome 5 nomos 7 eparchy
resistance group: Eam 4 Elas
rose 7 glaieul
sacred place: 6 abaton
sage: 5 Solon 6 Thales 8 Socrates
sanctuary: 5 hiera
sculptor: 5 Myron 7 Phidias
senate: 5 boule
serpent: 4 seps
settler: 5 metic
shield: 5 pelta
ship: 4 saic 5 diota
shrine: 5 secos, sekos
skeptic: 5 Timon
slave: 5 helot 6 penest
slave woman: 5 Baubo, Iambe
soldier: 7 hoplite, palikar
song: ode 5 melos, paeon
soothsayer: 7 Calchas
sorceress: 5 Circe, Medea, Siren
speech: 6 rhesis
statesman: 8 Pericles 9 Aristides 12 Themistocles
statue: 6 xoanon
storm wind: 6 lelaps 7 lealaps
subdivision: 5 phyle
temple: 4 naos 5 cella
theater: 5 odeon, odeum
time: 7 chronos
township: 4 deme
tribal division: 7 phratry

underworld: Dis 5 Hades
vase: 5 dinos
verse: 6 Alcaic
village: obe
weight: mna, oka, oke 4 mina 5 litra, maneh, minah, obole, pound 6 diobol, dramme, kantar, obolos, obolus, stater, talent 7 chalcon, chalque, drachma 8 diobolon, talanton 12 tetradrachma
wine: 7 retsina
wine pitcher: 4 olpe
word: 5 logos
green: new, raw 4 bice, live, verd, vert (Fr.) 5 cedre, crude, fresh, mossy, virid, young 6 callow, recent, unripe 7 untried, verdant 8 blooming, gullible, ignorant, immature, inexpert 9 malachite, undecayed, unskilled, untrained 11 flourishing 13 inexperienced 15 unsophisticated
blue: 4 cyan, saxe 7 sistine 9 turquoise
gray: 5 olive
pale: 7 celadon
shade: 4 lime, nile 5 apple, kelly 6 bottle 7 emerald
woodbine: 7 peridot
yellow: 7 opaline
green light: 4 okay 7 go-ahead 8 approval
Green Mansions author: 6 Hudson
Green Mountain Boys' leader: 10 Ethan Allen
Green Mountain state: 7 Vermont
green peak: 10 woodpecker
greenback: 8 frogskin 10 paper money
greenery: 7 verdure
greengage: 4 plum
greenhorn: 4 hick, jake, rube, tyro 6 novice 8 beginner 9 cheechaco, cheechako 10 tenderfoot 12 apple knocker
Greenland: *base:* 4 Etah
  discoverer: 4 Eric
  Eskimo: Ita
greenlet: 5 vireo
greenroom: 5 foyer 6 lounge
greens: 5 salad
greenstone: 4 jade 7 diorite 8 nephrite 9 malachite
greensward: 4 turf 5 grass
greet: cry 4 hail 6 accost, salute 7 address, receive, welcome
greeting: ave, bow 4 hail 5 aloha, hello, salut (Fr.) 6 salute 7 address, welcome 9 reception 10 salutation
gregarious: 6 social 8 friendly, outgoing, sociable 9 convivial, talkative 11 extroverted
gremlin: imp 5 devil, gnome
Grenada: capital: 9 St. Georges
  Indian: 5 Carib
  Island: 9 Carriacon 16 Petite Martinique
  monetary unit: 4 cent 6 dollar

mountain: **11** St. Catherine
grenade: **4** bomb **5** shell **9** explosive
grenadier: **4** fish **7** rattail, soldier
grenadine: **5** cloth, syrup **6** fabric **9** flavoring
gres: **8** ceramics **9** stoneware
Gretna Green visitor: **6** eloper
Greya's husband: **4** Oder
grid: **5** grate **6** buccan **7** grating, network **8** gridiron
griddle: **5** grill
griddle-cake: **7** crumpet, pancake **8** flapjack
gridiron: **5** field, grill **7** brander, grating, network
grief: woe **4** care, harm, hurt, pain **5** agony, dolor, tears, trial, wrong **6** mishap, regret, sorrow **7** anguish, chagrin, emotion, failure, offense, sadness, trouble **8** disaster, distress, hardship **9** grievance, suffering **10** affliction, desolation, **11** lamentation
Grieg's dancer: **6** Anitra
grievance: **4** beef **5** wrong **6** burden, injury **8** gravamen, hardship **9** complaint, injustice **10** affliction, oppression **11** displeasure
grieve: rue **4** pain, pine, sigh, wail, weep **5** mourn, wound **6** bemoan, lament, sadden, sorrow **7** afflict **8** complain, distress
grievous: sad **4** sore **5** heavy, sorry **6** bitter, severe, tragic, woeful **7** heinous, intense, very bad **8** dolorous, shocking **9** atrocious **10** burdensome, calamitous, deplorable, oppressive **11** distressing
griffon: **7** monster **8** Dutch dog
grifter: **6** con man **8** swindler **12** rip-off artist
henchman: **5** shill **6** come-on
grigri: **5** charm **6** amulet, fetish **8** talisman
grill, grille: **5** broil, grate **7** grating, griddle **8** gridiron, question **11** interrogate, third-degree **12** cross-examine
grilse: **5** trout **6** salmon **7** botcher
grim: **4** dour, sour **5** angry, cruel, gaunt, harsh, stern **6** fierce, grisly, horrid, ragging, savage, sullen **7** furious, ghastly, hideous, ominous **8** horrible, pitiless, ruthless, sinister **9** ferocious, frightful, merciless, repellent **10** forbidding, inexorable, relentless, unyielding
grimace: mop, mow, mug **4** face, mock, moue, **5** fleer, scowl, smirk, sneer **6** glower **9** make a face
grimalkin: cat **6** feline, she-cat
grime: **4** dirt, smut, soil, soot **5** filth, sully
grimp: **5** climb
grimy: **4** foul **5** dingy, dirty **6** grubby, soiled **7** swarthy
grin: **5** fleer, smile

grind: rut **4** chaw, chew, grit, mill, mull, whet **5** chafe, chore, crush, gnash, grate, study **6** abrade, crunch, drudge, harass, polish, powder **7** oppress, sharpen **8** bookworm **9** blackfish, comminute, pulverize, triturate
grinder: **5** molar, tooth **9** submarine **10** flycatcher **12** hero sandwich
grinding: **7** grating, wearing **10** burdensome, oppressive **12** excruciating
grindle: **6** bowfin
grip: bag **4** hold, vise **5** cinch, clamp, clasp, cleat, grasp, rivet, seize **6** clench, clutch, control, handle, valise **7** grapple, handbag, mastery **8** handfast, take hold **9** constrict **12** scene-shifter
gripe: **4** beef, carp, fret, kick, rail **5** annoy **6** grouse, harass, squawk, **7** grumble, protest **8** complain **9** bellyache
grippe, grip: flu **9** influenza
gripper: **6** nipper
gripping device: dog **4** hand, vise **5** tongs **6** pliers
gripsack: **7** handbag
grisly: **4** grim **7** ghastly, hideous **8** dreadful, gruesome, horrible, terrible **10** terrifying
grison: **5** huron **6** weasel
grist: lot **4** malt **5** grain, stint **6** output **8** quantity **9** provision
gristle: **9** cartilage
grit: **4** guts, sand, soil, soot **5** earth, nerve, pluck **6** gravel **7** bravery, courage **8** backbone, decision, tenacity **12** perseverance
gritty: **4** game **5** sandy **6** plucky **7** arenose, arenous **8** resolute, sabulous **10** persistent
grivet: **6** monkey
grivois: **4** bold, free **5** broad **8** indecent
grizzly: **4** bear **7** grayish
groan: **4** moan **5** creak **6** lament **7** whimper
grog: rum **5** drink, **6** liquor **8** beverage
groggery: pub **6** saloon, tavern **7** barroom **8** alehouse
groggy: **5** shaky, tipsy **8** unsteady, wavering **9** tottering
groom: **4** comb, mafu, syce, tend, tidy **5** brush, clean, curry, dress, mafoo, train **7** hostler, marshal, prepare, servant **8** benedict **9** assistant **11** horsekeeper
grooming: **8** toilette
groove: rut **4** dado, rake, slot **5** canal, chase, flute, glyph, regal, rigol, scarf, shaft, stria, sulci(pl.) **6** furrow, gutter, hollow, rabbet, raglet, scrobe, striae(pl.), sulcus **7** channel, striate **10** excavation
groovy: **6** modern **9** excellent, marvelous
grope: **4** feel, poke, test **5** probe **6** fumble, handle **7** examine, fish for, grabble **11** move blindly

grosbeak: 7 warbler 8 hawfinch

gross: big, fat, low, sum 4 bulk, clod, dull, mass, rank, rude 5 amass, broad, brute, bulky, burly, close, crass, dense, heavy, plain, rough, thick, total, whole 6 animal, brutal, coarse, earthy, entire, filthy, greasy, impure, vulgar 7 beastly, brutish, compact, fulsome, general, glaring, massive, obscene, obvious, sensual, swinish, witless 8 cloddish, flagrant, indecent 9 egregious, unlearned, unrefined 10 indefinite, indelicate, scurrilous

grotesque: 5 antic, eerie, weird 7 baroque, bizarre 8 fanciful 9 fantastic, whimsical 11 incongruous 12 preposterous

grotto: den 4 cave, grot, hole 5 crypt, speos, vault 6 cavern, recess

grouch: 4 crab, sulk 5 crank, scold 6 grouse 7 grumble 8 sourpuss 10 crosspatch

ground: 4 base, dirt, fund, land, root, soil 5 earth, field, train 6 bottom, estate, reason 7 country, premise, terrain 8 initiate 9 establish, territory 10 foundation, fundamenta(pl.) 11 fundamentum

break: dig 4 plow 8 excavate 12 start to build

gain: 8 progress 9 move ahead

give: 5 yield 6 retreat

kinds of: bog, lot 4 moor, acre, farm, plat, park 5 arada, glebe, tilth, range, marsh, swale, patch 6 meadow, calade, reseau, maidan 7 pasture, cripple, curragh

raised: 5 ridge 7 hillock, hummock

ground pine: iva

ground squirrel: 6 gopher 8 chipmunk

groundhog: 6 marmot 9 woodchuck

Groundhog Day: 9 Candlemas

groundless: 4 idle 5 false 8 baseless 9 unfounded 10 gratuitous 11 unwarranted

groundnut: 5 chufa, gobbe 6 goober, peanut

grounds: 4 lees 5 basis, dregs, grout 6 bottom 8 sediment 9 settlings

college: 6 campus

military: 4 camp, fort 8 presidio 11 reservation

groundwork: 4 base, root 5 basis 6 bottom, fundus 7 support 8 planning, practice, training 10 foundation 11 preparation 12 underpinning

group: lot, mob, set 4 bevy, gang, herd, mass, ring, sect, team 5 batch, brood, cabal, class, clump, drove, firca, flock, genus, horde, party, squad, suite, tribe 6 bundle, clique, family, galaxy, gather, nation 7 arrange, cluster, collect, company, consort 8 assemble, assembly, classify, division 10 assemblage, assortment, collection, congregate 11 aggregation

pert to: 7 generic

group together: 4 band, meet 7 cluster 8 assemble

grouper: 4 fish, hind, mero 5 guasa

groupies: 4 fans 9 followers, hangers-on

grouse: 5 gripe, quail 6 gorhen, grouch, repine 7 cheeper, gorcock, grumble 8 complain, pheasant, squealer 9 gelinotte, ptarmigan 10 whitebelly 12 capercaillie

grout: 5 dregs 6 mortar 7 grounds, plaster

grouty: 5 cross, sulky 6 sullen

grove: 4 bush, tope, wood 5 copse, hurst, lucus(L.) 6 pinery 7 boscage, boskage, coppice, thicket

pert. to: 7 nemoral

grovel: 4 fawn 5 crawl, toady 6 cringe, kowtow, wallow 7 truckle 9 be servile

groveling: 6 abject 7 hangdog 12 contemptible

grow: age, bud, get, wax 4 come, eche, rise 5 edify, raise, swell 6 accrue, batten, become, expand, extend, thrive 7 augment, develop, distend, enlarge, improve, nourish 8 develope, flourish, increase 9 cultivate 10 accumulate

grow old: age 5 ripen 7 senesce

grower: 6 farmer, raiser 7 rancher 10 orchardist 13 agriculturist 15 arboriculturist

growl: 4 gnar, gurr 5 gnarl, snarl 6 mutter, rumble 7 grumble

grown: 5 adult, risen 6 mature 8 expanded

grownup: man 5 adult

growth: wen 4 rise 5 swell 7 stature 8 increase, swelling 9 accretion, expansion, heterosis 11 development, enlargement 12 augmentation

in clusters: 8 racemose

on another: 8 parasite

on surface: 9 epigenous

organic: 9 accretion

promoting: 8 nutrient 9 nutriment

retarding: 9 paratonic

grub: bob, dig, eat 4 chow, feed, food, moot, plod, root 5 dwarf, larva, stump 6 drudge, larvae(pl.), maggot, search 7 plodder 8 victuals

grubby: 5 dirty, grimy, small 8 dwarfish, slovenly

grudge: 4 envy 5 pique, spite 6 malice, rancor 10 resentment

grue: 6 shiver 7 shudder

gruel: 5 atole 6 burgoo, crowdy 8 porridge

grueling: 4 hard 6 brutal, tiring 7 racking 9 fatiguing, punishing

gruesome: 4 ugly 6 grisly, horrid, sordid

7 fearful, ghastly, hideous, macabre **8** horrible

gruff: 4 curt, rude, sour **5** bluff, harsh, rough, short, surly **6** abrupt, hoarse, morose, severe, sullen **7** brusque, crabbed **8** churlish

grumble: 4 crab, fuss, kick **5** bitch, croak, growl, snarl **6** grouch, grouse, repine, rumble, squawk, yammer **8** begrudge, complain

grumpy: 5 cross, moody, surly

grungy: 5 dirty **10** uncared for

grunt: 4 fish, **5** groan, snork, snort

guacharo: 7 fatbird, oilbird

guaiol: 7 alcohol

Guam: *capital:* **5** Agana
native: **8** Chamorro
port: **4** Apra

guanay: 9 cormorant

guanaco: 5 llama **6** alpaca
relative: **5** camel

guar: 4 bean

guarantee: 4 bail, band, bond, seal **6** assure, avouch, ensure, insure, surety **7** certify, endorse, hostage, warrant **8** guaranty, security, warranty **9** assurance, vouchsafe

guarantor: 5 angel **6** backer, patron **7** sponsor **11** underwriter

guarapucu: 4 fish, peto **5** wahoo

guard: 4 care, curb, herd, hold, keep, rail, tend, ward **5** bless, fence, hedge, watch **6** bantay, bridle, convey, custos, defend, dragon, escort, fender, gaoler, jailer, jailor, keeper, patrol, police, sentry, shield, warden **7** keeping, lineman, protect **8** conserve, preserve, restrain, security, sentinel, watchman **9** attention, custodian, protector **10** cowcatcher, protection
foil: **6** button
line of: **6** cordon
on: **4** wary **5** alert, ready **8** vigilant, watchful **9** observant

guarded: 4 wary **6** manned **7** careful **8** cautious, defended, discreet **9** protected **11** circumspect

guardhouse: 4 brig **5** clink **6** prison **8** hoosegow

guardian: 6 keeper, parent, pastor, patron, warden **7** curator **8** defender, watchdog **9** custodian, protector
church relics: **10** mystagogue
heavenly: **5** angel
legal: **7** trustee
pert. to: **7** tutelar **8** tutelary
subject of: **4** ward
watchful: **5** Argus **8** Cerberus

guardianship: 4 care **5** trust **7** custody, keeping, tuition **8** tutelage

guasa: 7 grouper, jewfish

Guatemala: *capital:* **13** Guatemala City
city: **5** Coban **6** Flores, Jalapa, Salama, Solola **7** Antigua, Jutiapa **9** Escuintla, Tiquisate
department: **5** Peten **6** Izabal, Jalapa, Quiche, Solola, Zacapa **7** Jutiapa **9** Escuintla, San Marcos, Santa Rosa **10** Chiquimula, El Progreso
Indian: **4** Itza, Ixil, Maya **5** Xinca
lake: **6** Izabal **7** Atitlan **9** Peten Itza
measure: **4** vara **6** fanega **7** manzana
monetary unit: **7** centavo, quetzal
mountain peak: **6** Tacana **9** Tajumulco **10** Acatenango, Santa Maria
mountain range: **11** Sierra Madre
river: **5** Dulce **7** Motagua **8** Polochic, Sarstoon **10** Usumacinta
volcano: **4** Agua **5** Fuego **7** Atitlan

Guaycuruan Indian: 4 Toba

gudgeon: pin **4** bait, fish, lure **5** pivot **6** burbot, socket

Gudrun: *brother:* **6** Gunnar
husband: **4** Atli

guenon: 4 mona **6** grivet, monkey

guerdon: 6 reward **8** requital **10** recompense

guerrilla: 8 partisan **11** bush fighter

guess: aim **4** shot **5** fancy, infer, think **6** assume, deduce, divine **7** believe, imagine, opinion, presume, surmise, suspect **8** estimate **9** speculate **10** conjecture

guest: 6 caller, inmate, lodger, patron, roomer **7** visitor

guesthouse: inn **5** hotel **11** caravansary

guff: lip **4** sass **5** hooey **6** humbug **7** hogwash **8** claptrap, nonsense **10** balderdash

guffaw: 5 howl **6** heehaw **10** horselaugh, belly laugh

guidance: 4 helm, help **6** advice **7** auspice, conduct, counsel **8** steerage **9** direction **10** leadership, management **11** instruction

guide: 4 airt, buoy, clue, lead, pole, rein, rule, show **5** model, pilot, reign, steer, teach, treat, tutor, usher **6** beacon, bridle, convey, convoy, direct, escort, govern, leader, manage **7** conduce, conduct, control, marshal, teacher **8** director, instruct, landmark, polestar, regulate, shepherd, textbook **9** catechism, conductor, itinerary, prescribe, regulator **10** instructor **11** superintend **12** show the way to

guidebook: 8 baedeker **9** itinerary **11** tourist's aid

guided missile: ABM, ATA, SAM, SSM **4** Hawk, ICBM, IRBM, Lark, Loki, Loon, Nike, SLBM, Thor, Zuni **5** Atlas, drone, Snark, Titan **6** Bomarc, Falcon, Redeye, Viking **7** Bullpup, Patriot, Po-

laris, Terrier, Tiny Tim **8** Hellfire, Redstone, Tomahawk **9** Minuteman **10** Copperhead, Sidewinder
guideway: 4 slot **5** track **7** channel
Guido: *fifth note:* sol
 first note: ut
 fourth note: fa
 high note: la
 highest note: E; la
 second note: re
 third note: mi
guild: 4 club **5** order, union **6** league **7** society **8** alliance, sodality **10** fellowship **11** association, brotherhood
guile: 4 wile **5** cheat, craft, fraud **6** deceit, humbug **7** cunning **9** duplicity, treachery
guileful: 9 deceitful, insidious **10** fallacious, fraudulent **13** Machiavellian
guileless: 5 naive **6** candid, honest **7** artless **8** innocent **9** ingenuous
guillemot: auk **4** loom, quet **5** murre **7** dovekey, dovekie
guillotine: 6 behead **10** decapitate
 wagon for: **7** tumbrel, tumbril
guilt: sin **5** culpa, fault **6** piacle **7** offense **8** iniquity **10** wickedness **11** criminality, culpability
guiltless: 4 pure **5** clean **8** innocent **9** blameless, righteous
guilty: 6 nocent, wicked **7** correal **8** culpable
Guinea: *capital:* **7** Conakry
 city: **4** Boke, Labe, Pita **5** Fouta **6** Kankan **7** Dubreka
 ethnic group: **4** fula **7** Malinke **8** Soussous
 island: Los **5** Tombo
 monetary unit: **4** kori, syli
 mountain: **5** Nimba
 river: **4** Milo **5** Niger **6** Bafing, Gambia **7** Senegal **8** Konkoure
Guinea-Bissau: *capital:* **6** Bissau
 ethnic group: **4** Fula **7** Balanta **8** Mandyako
 island group: **7** Bijagos
 monetary unit: **4** peso **7** centavo
 river: **4** Geba
guinea fowl: 4 keet
guinea pig: 4 cavy
Guinevere's husband: 6 Arthur
guise: hue **4** form, garb, mask, mien **5** cloak, cover, dress, habit, shape **6** aspect, attire, deceit, manner **7** arrange, fashion **8** behavior, likeness, practice **9** semblance **10** appearance, masquerade
guitar: uke **5** sitar, tiple **6** sancho **7** cittern, ukulele **8** chitarra **10** calascione
 guitarlike instrument: **4** lute, rota **6** citole **7** bandore, pandora, samisen **8** mandolin

 half step in pitch: **5** dital
 key: **5** dital
 of India: **4** vina **5** sitar
 play: **5** pluck, strum
 small: **7** ukelele
 style of playing: **10** bottleneck
guitguit: 4 bird **6** pitpit
gula: 4 cyma, ogee **6** gullet, throat **7** molding
gulch: gorge, gully **6** arroyo, canyon, coulee, ravine, valley
gulf: arm, bay, gap **4** cove, eddy **5** abyss, chasm **6** vorago **9** barathrum, whirlpool **10** separation
Gulf States: 5 Texas **7** Alabama, Florida **9** Louisiana **11** Mississippi
gull: mew **4** dupe, fool, tern **5** cheat, larid **6** sucker, teaser, victim **7** cheater, deceive, defraud, fall guy, mislead **8** dotterel, hoodwink **9** bamboozle, kittiwake **10** mountebank
 kinds of: cob **4** skua **5** allan, annet, pewit **6** larine, teaser, waggel **11** burgomaster
 pert. to: **6** larine, laroid
gullet: maw **6** throat **9** esophagus
gullible: 5 green, naive **9** credulous
Gulliver's Travels: *author:* **5** Swift
 flying island: **6** Laputa
 human beast: **5** Yahoo
 island kingdom: **8** Lilliput
gully: 5 gorge, gulch **6** arroyo, gutter, ravine, valley **7** couloir **11** watercourse
gulp: 4 bolt, glut, swig **5** swill **6** gobble, guzzle **7** swallow
gum: 4 clog, hive, kino **5** cheat, nyssa, stick, trick **6** chicle, gluten, hashab, humbug, impede, tissue, tupelo **7** bilsted, gingiva **8** mucilage **10** eucalyptus **11** masticatory
 derivative: **8** bassorin **10** tragacanth, traganthin **12** tragacanthin
 kinds of: **5** tuart **6** acacia, acacin, balata, touart **7** acacine, dextrin
 resin: **5** elemi, gugal, myrrh **6** salban **9** sagapenum **12** frankincense
gum tree: 5 xylan
gumbo: 4 ocra, okra, soup **7** melange
gumma: 5 tumor
gummy: 6 mastic, sticky **7** viscous **8** adhesive
gumption: 7 courage **8** boldness **10** enterprise, initiative, shrewdness
gums: ula **7** alveoli
 pain in: **7** ulalgia
 pert to: **6** uletic **8** gingival
gumshoe: cop, tec **4** dick **5** skulk, sneak **6** sleuth **9** detective, pussyfoot
gun: gat, rod **5** rifle, tommy **6** cannon, heater, pistol, weapon **7** carbine, shotgun **8** revolver **9** matchlock, surfboard **11** blunderbuss

barrel cleaner: **6** ramrod
kinds of: **4** bore, bren, roer, sten **5** baril **6** ack-ack, archie, barker **7** aerogun, bazooka **8** amusette
mount: **6** turret
part: pin **4** bolt, bore, butt, lock **5** sight, stock **6** barrel, breech, hammer, muzzle, rammer, safety **7** trigger
platform: **11** emplacement
gunfire: **4** rake, shot **5** salvo **6** strafe, volley **7** barrage **8** enfilade **9** fusillade
gunman: **6** killer **7** torpedo **8** assassin
gunner: **7** shooter **8** marksman, rifleman **9** cannoneer **10** bombardier **12** artilleryman
gunny: tat **4** jute **6** burlap
gunpowder: **5** nitro
Gunther's uncle: **5** Hagen
gurgle: **5** plash **6** babble, burble **7** sputter
Gurkha's sword: **5** kukri
gurnard: **4** fish **7** sea robin **8** dragonet
guru: **5** guide **7** teacher
gush: **4** flow, pour, teem **5** issue, smarm, spate, spout, spurt **6** effuse, stream **10** outpouring
gushing: **7** mawkish, prating **8** effusive, unctuous **10** blabbering, flattering
gusset: **4** gore **5** brace **6** insert
gust: **4** puff, scud, waft, wind **5** blast, draft, whiff **6** flurry, squall **8** outburst, paroxysm **9** explosion
gusto: **4** elan, zest **5** taste **6** fervor, liking, relish **7** delight, passion **8** pleasure **9** enjoyment **12** appreciation
gusty: **5** windy **6** savory, stormy **7** squally **8** agitated **11** tempestuous
gut: **5** belly, clean **6** paunch, ravage **7** plunder, stamina, stomach **9** bay window **10** disembowel, eviscerate
gutsy: **4** bold **5** brave, nervy **6** spunky **8** fearless, intrepid **9** audacious **10** courageous
gutta: **8** ornament
gutta-percha: **5** latex **6** balata
gutter: **5** ditch, gully, siver(Sc.) **6** groove, trench, trough, **7** channel, scupper **11** watercourse
guttural: **4** deep **5** burry, harsh, velar **7** rasping, throaty
guy: kid, rod **4** josh, rope, stay twit **5** chain, guide, spoof, tease **6** decamp, fellow, gazabo, gazebo, person **8** ridicule
Guyana: *capital:* **10** Georgetown
  city: **6** Enmore, Suddie **7** Bartica, Charity

8 Mackenzie **10** Enterprise **12** New Amsterdam
district: **7** Berbice **8** Demerara, Rupununi **9** Essequiba, North West
monetary unit: **4** cent **6** dollar
mountain: **6** Acarai **7** Roraima **9** Pacaraima
river: **6** Cuyuni, Potaro **7** Berbice **8** Demerara, Mazaruni **9** Essequibo **10** Courantyne
guy rope: **4** stay, vang
guzzle: **4** bolt, gulp, swig **5** quaff, swill **6** devour, tipple **7** toss off
gymnast: **6** turner **7** acrobat, athlete, tumbler **8** balancer
gymnastic: *stunt:* kip **4** flip **5** vault **9** handstand, headstand **10** handspring, headspring
swing: **7** trapeze
gyp: **5** cheat, steal, sting **6** diddle, rip off **7** defraud, sharper, swindle **8** swindler **9** trickster **10** overcharge
gypsum: **4** geso **6** parget **8** selenite **9** alabaster
resembling: **11** alabastrine
gypsy, gipsy: **4** calo **5** caird, nomad **6** Gitana, Gitano, roamer **7** czigany, tzigany, zincala, zincalo, zingana, zingano, zingara, zingaro **8** Bohemian, brunette, wanderer, zigeuner
boy: **4** chal
camp: tan
dance: **10** zingaresca
devil: **4** beng
dialect: **6** Romany **7** Rommany
fortune: **4** bahi
gentleman: rye
girl: chi **4** chai
horse: gri, gry
husband: rom
nongypsy: **4** gajo
paper: lil
Syrian: **5** Aptal
thief: **4** chor
village: gav
wife: **4** romi
gyrate: **4** spin, turn **5** twirl, whirl **6** rotate **7** revolve
gyrator: top
gyre: **4** ring **6** vortex **7** circuit **10** revolution
gyrfalcon: **6** jerkin
gyve: **4** iron **5** chain **6** fetter **7** shackle

H

H: 5 aitch 8 aspirate
sound of: 8 aspirate
H-shaped: 5 zygal
habeas corpus: 4 writ
haberdashery: hat 5 shirt 6 gloves 7 necktie 8 menswear
habile: 4 able 6 adroit, clever, expert 8 skillful
habiliment (see also **dress, gown**): 4 garb 5 habit 6 attire 7 apparel, clothes, costume, raiment 8 billiment, clothing, equipage, fittings, ornament, vestment 9 equipment, faculties 11 furnishings
habilitate: 5 dress, equip, train 6 clothe, outfit 7 educate
habit (see also **dress**): rut, use 4 coat, garb, gown, suit, vice, wont 5 array, guise, haunt, thews, usage 6 attire, clothe, custom, estate, groove 7 bearing, clothes, costume, garment 8 demeanor, practice, tendency 9 addiction 10 consuetude 11 disposition
habitant: 7 dweller
habitat: 4 home 5 abode, range 6 patria 7 station 8 locality 11 environment
habitation: 4 home, tent 5 abode, house, hovel, igloo 6 colony, harbor, warren 7 lodging 8 domicile, dwelling, tenement 9 chaumiere (F.), residence
habitual: 5 usual 6 common, hectic 7 regular 8 familiar, frequent, ordinary 9 customary 10 accustomed, inveterate
habituate: use 5 enure, inure 6 addict, season 8 accustom, frequent 9 acclimate, 11 acclimatize, familiarize
habitude: 5 habit 6 custom 11 familiarity
habitue: 8 customer 10 frequenter
hachure: 4 line, mark 7 shading
hacienda: 4 farm, 5 ranch 6 estate 10 plantation 13 establishment
proprietor: 9 hacendado
hack: cab, cut, hag, hew 4 chop, taxi 5 coach, cough 6 drudge, fiacre, haggle, mangle 7 butcher, chatter, stammer, stutter 8 carriage, mutilate 9 mercenary
hackee: 8 chipmunk
hackle: 4 bait, comb 6 mangle 7 plumage 8 feathers
hackly: 5 rough 6 broken, jagged
hackney: nag 4 hack, pony 5 horse, noddy 8 carriage

hackneyed: old 4 worn 5 banal, stale, trite 6 common 7 worn out 8 outdated 10 threadbare 11 commonplace, stereotyped
Hades: dis, pit 4 hell 5 Orcus, Sheol 7 Gehenna, inferno 8 Tartarus 11 netherworld
god: 5 Pluto
guard: 8 Cerberus
inhabitant of: 7 hellion
lake to: 7 Avernus
mother: 4 Rhea
pert to: 7 sheolic 8 infernal
river: 4 Styx 5 Lethe 7 Acheron
hadj, hajj: 10 pilgrimage
haff: 6 lagoon
haft: 6 handle
hag: bog, cut 4 bogy, hack, wood 5 copse, crone, demon, ghost, marsh, notch, rudas(Sc.), witch 6 beldam, goblin, harass, spirit 7 beldame, fatigue, pasture, terrify 8 harridan, quagmire 9 cailleach, cailliach, enclosure, hobgoblin
Hagar's son: 7 Ishmael
hagdon: 6 fulmar 7 seabird 10 shearwater
hagfish: 5 borer
haggard: 4 bony, lank, lean, pale, thin, wild 5 drawn, gaunt, spare 6 wasted 7 anxious, untamed 8 careworn, harrowed, 9 exhausted, suffering 10 cadaverous
Haggard novel: She
haggle: cut, hew 4 hack, prig 5 cavil 6 badger, barter, chisel, dicker, higgle, huckle, palter, scotch 7 bargain, chaffer, dispute, stickle, wrangle 8 beat down
haggler: 6 dodger 8 huckster
hagioscope: 6 squint 7 opening
hagride: 6 harass, obsess 7 oppress, torment
hail: ave 4 ahoy, call, goal 5 greet, sleet, sound, whole 6 accost, health, salute 7 address, fortune, graupel 8 greeting 10 salutation 13 precipitation
hailer: 8 bullhorn
hair: fax, fur 4 barb, coma, mane, shag 5 crine, tress 6 crinet, nicety, trifle 7 bristle 8 capillus, filament, finespun 9 chevelure
accessory: 8 barrette
Angora goat: 6 mohair

braid: **5** queue **7** pigtail
coarse: **4** kemp, seta, shag **7** bristle
curl: **7** ringlet
disease: **8** dandruff, psilosis
dye: **5** henna
excessive: **7** pilosis
facial: **5** beard **6** goatee **8** whiskers **9** moustache, sideburns
false: rat, wig **6** peruke, switch, toupee **7** periwig
fringe: **8** frisette, frizette
grooming aid: **4** comb **5** brush **6** pomade
having: **6** pilose **7** barbate, hirsute, villous **8** crinated
horse: **4** mane **5** seton **7** fetlock
intestinal: **6** villus
knot: bun **7** chignon
lock: **4** curl **5** tress **7** cowlick
loss: **8** alopecia, baldness
ornament: bow **4** comb **5** tiara **6** ribbon **7** coronet **8** barrette
pert. to: **6** crinal
plant: **6** villus
remover: **8** epilator **9** depilator, epilatory **10** depilatory
roll: **4** puff **5** twist **7** chignon **9** pompadour
short: **6** setula, setule
soft: **4** down **6** villus
unruly: mop **6** tousle **7** cowlick
white: **4** snow
hairbrained: **5** giddy **8** heedless, volatile
hairbreadth: ace **5** close **10** very narrow
haircloth: aba **6** cilice
haircut: **7** tonsure
hairdo: bob **4** afro, glib(Ir.) **5** braid **6** bubble, marcel **7** beehive, crew cut, pageboy, pigtail, shingle **8** bouffant, ducktail, ponytail **9** pompadour
hairdresser: **6** barber **7** friseur **8** coiffeur **9** coiffeuse
hairless: **4** bald **8** depilous
hairnet: **5** snood
hairpin: **4** bend **6** bodkin **8** bobbypin
hair-raising: **4** eery **5** eerie, weird **10** terrifying
hairy: bushy **6** comate, comous, pilose, shaggy **7** bristly, crinite, hirsute **9** dangerous, difficult, harrowing
Haiti: *capital:* **12** Port-au-Prince
city: **5** Cayes **8** Gonaives **10** Cap Haitien
discoverer: **8** Columbus
island: **5** Vache **6** Gonave **7** Tortuga
monetary unit: **6** gourde **7** centime
mountain: **7** La Selle
national liberator: **9** Toussaint **10** Dessalines
original name: **10** Hispaniola
province: Sud **4** Nord **5** Ouest **9** Nordouest **10** Artibonite
river: **10** Artibonite
hake: **4** fish, idle **5** tramp **6** loiter, trudge

halberd: **6** weapon **8** battle-ax
halcyon: **4** bird, calm **5** happy, quiet **6** golden **8** peaceful, tranquil, affluent **9** unruffled **10** kingfisher, prosperous
Halcyone: *father:* **6** Aeolus
husband: **4** Ceyx
hale: **5** sound **6** hearty, robust, strong, summon **7** healthy **8** vigorous
Halevy opera: **5** Juive
half: **6** moiety **7** partial, portion
half breed: **5** metis **6** mustee **7** mestizo, mestiza, mulatto, mulatta **8** octoroon, quadroon
half circumference: **10** semicircle
half diameter: **6** radius
half-man: **4** faun **6** garuda **7** centaur **8** minotaur
half mask: **4** loup **6** domino
half-month: **9** fortnight
half-moon: **8** crescent **9** semilunar
figure: **4** lune
half-turn: **8** caracole
half-wit: **4** dolt **5** dunce, idiot, moron **8** imbecile **9** blockhead
half-witted: **4** dull **5** dotty, silly **7** foolish **9** senseless
halfbeak: ihi **5** balao
halfhearted: **4** tame **5** faint, tepid **8** listless, lukewarm **10** spiritless
halfway: **4** mid **6** almost, nearly, middle **7** midmost, partial **9** partially **11** equidistant
Halicarnassian: **9** Dionysius, Herodotus
halicore: **6** dugong, sea cow **7** manatee
Halifax citizen: **10** Haligonian
halite: **4** salt **8** rock salt
hall: **4** aula, room, saal(G.) **5** entry, foyer, lobby, manor, odeon, odeum, salle **6** atrium, durbar, saloon **7** chamber, gallery, hallway, passage **8** anteroom, corridor **9** vestibule **10** auditorium, misericord, passageway **11** misericorde
music: **4** gaff **5** odeon, odeum
reception: **5** salon **6** parlor
student residence: **4** dorm **5** bursa **9** dormitory
halloo: **5** shout **6** accost
hallow: **5** bless **8** dedicate **10** consecrate
hallowed: **4** holy
hallowed place: **4** fane **5** altar **6** bethel, chapel, church, shrine, temple **9** cathedral, synagogue
hallucination: d.t.'s **6** mirage **7** fantasy **8** delirium, delusion
hallux: **6** big toe
halo: arc **4** glow, nimb **5** glory **6** areola, areole, brough(Sc.), circle, corona, nimbus **7** aureola, aureole **8** cincture, gloriole
halogen: **6** iodine **7** bromine **8** chlorine **8** cyanogen, fluorine
haloperidal: **10** depressant, **12** tranquilizer

halothane: 10 anesthetic

halt: hop **4** bait, lame, limp, stem, stop **5** cease, hilch, hitch, pause, stand **6** arrest, desist, docked **7** limping **8** lameness, stoppage **9** cessation, mutilated, terminate

halter: 4 rope **5** leash, noose, strap, widdy **6** bridle, hamper **8** cavesson, restrain **9** hackamore

halting: 4 lame **7** limping **8** spavined **9** defective **10** hesitating **11** vacillating

ham: pig **4** hock, pork, **5** actor, thigh **7** amateur, overact

Ham: *brother:* **4** Shem
father: **4** Noah
son: **4** Cush **6** Canaan
son's land: **8** Ethiopia

hamadryad: 5 nymph **6** baboon

hamate: 6 curved, hooked **7** hamular **8** hamiform

Hamilcar: 5 Barca
conquest: **5** Spain
home: **8** Carthage
son: **8** Hannibal

Hamite: *father:* **4** Abel
language: **4** Afar, Agao, Beja **5** Belin, Galla **6** Berber, Kabyle, Shilha, Somali, Zenaga **8** Cushitic, Numidian, Tamashek **9** Ethiopian, Gaetulian **11** Mauretanian
people: **4** Beja, Bogo **5** Fulah **6** Berber, Gallas, Somali

hamlet: 4 dorp **5** aldea(Sp.), casal, hamel, moray, vicus(L.) **6** bustee, casale(It.), thorpe **7** clachan(Sc.), village **10** settlement

Hamlet: *beloved:* **7** Ophelia
castle: **8** Elsinore
character: **7** Laertes, Ophelia **8** Gertrude, Polonius
country: **7** Denmark
dramatist: **11** Shakespeare
friend: **7** Horatio
mother: **8** Gertrude
slayer: **7** Laertes
uncle: **8** Claudius
victim: **7** Laertes **8** Claudius, Polonius

hammer: bit, tup **4** beat, claw, jack, maul, mell, reel, tack, tamp **5** gavel **6** batter, beetle, mallet, martel, pummel, sledge, strike, swinge **7** belabor **8** malleate **11** door-knocker
blacksmith's: **6** fuller, oliver
bricklayer's: **6** scutch
face: **4** trip
firearm: **4** cock **7** doghead
half-round: **6** fuller
head: **4** peen, poll
medical: **6** plexor **7** plessor
stone: **5** kevel, spall
type: air **4** claw **5** sledge **8** ball peen **9** pneumatic

hammerhead: 5 shark **8** numskull **9** hog sucker

hammock: 5 swing **7** machila

hamper: bin, ped **4** beat, clog, curb, load, slow **5** block, cramp, crate, rusky(Sc.), seron(Sp.) **6** basket, burden, fetter, halter, hinder, hopple, impede, panier **7** buffalo, confine, hanaper, manacle, pannier, perplex, shackle, trammel **8** encumber, entangle, obstruct, restrain, restrict **9** container, embarrass

hamstring: hox **4** hock, lame **5** hough **6** hinder, impair **7** cripple, disable

Hananiah: *father:* **4** Azur
son: **8** Zedekiah

hand: fin, paw, pud **4** claw, give, mano, mitt, neif, pass **5** claut(Sc.), grasp, nieve, power, share **6** clunch, daddle, famble, pledge, worker **7** ability, flipper, forepaw, laborer, proffer, workman **8** applause, bestowal, transmit **9** betrothal, craftsman, indicator, operative, signature **11** handwriting
back: **10** opisthenar
by: **8** manually
clenched: **4** fist
covering: **4** mitt, muff **5** glove **6** cestus(L.) **7** gantlet **8** gauntlet
deformity: **11** talipomanus
down: **8** bequeath
hollow: **6** gowpen, gowpin
on hip: **6** akimbo
palm: **6** thenar
part: **4** palm **5** thumb **7** fingers
pert. to: **6** manual
poker: **5** flush **8** straight **9** full house
without: **7** amanous

hand-me-down: 5 cheap **9** ready-made **10** secondhand

hand mill: 5 quern **7** grinder

hand out: 6 donate **7** present **8** give away **10** administer, distribute

hand over: 4 ante, cede **5** yield

hand-picked: 5 elite **8** selected

handbag: bag **4** etui, grip **5** cabas, etwee, purse **6** valise **7** satchel **8** gripsack, pochette, reticule

handball: *game:* **6** pelota **7** jai alai
point: ace

handbarrow: 4 bier

handbill: 5 flyer, libel **6** dodger **13** advertisement

handbook: 6 manual **9** guidebook **11** enchiridion

handcar: 6 gocart **7** go-devil

handcloth: 5 towel **6** napkin **12** handkerchief

handcuff: 4 cuff, iron **5** darby **6** nipper **7** manacle **8** bracelet, handbolt, handlock, restrain

Handel: *composition:* **5** Largo
opera: **4** Nero **6** Almira, Xerxes **7** Ro-

drigo **8** Berenice **9** Agrippina
oratorio: **4** Saul **6** Esther **7** Messiah
handful: 4 grip, wisp **5** claut, gripe **6** gow-pen, gowpin, yaffle **7** maniple **8** quanti-ty
handicap: bar, law **4** edge, lame, lisp, odds **6** burden, hinder, impede **7** stammer, stutter **8** drawback, encumber **9** advan-tage, embarrass, head start **12** disad-vantage
handicapper: 5 rater
handicraft: art **5** trade, metier **8** voca-tion
handicraft goddess: 7 Minerva
handicraftsman: 7 artisan, workman **9** craftsman
handiwork: tat **7** sampler **10** embroidery
handjar: 5 knife **6** dagger **7** khanjar
handkerchief: 5 clout, fogle **6** madras **7** bandana, belcher, sneezer **9** barcelona, handcloth, muckender, neckcloth **11** neckerchief
handle: ear, fan, lug, nob, paw, ply, use **4** ansa, bail, bool, deal, feel, gaum, grip, haft, hank, hilt, knob, name **5** gripe, grope, helve, lever, shaft, swipe, touch, treat, wield **6** behave, direct, finger, manage **7** act upon, control **8** door-knob, handgrip **10** manipulate
ancient: **4** ansa
bucket: **4** bail, bale
cup: ear
equipped with: **6** ansate
pail: **4** bail
printing press: **6** rounce
pump: **5** brake
scythe: **5** snath, snead, thole **6** snathe
shaped: **6** ansate
sword: **4** haft, hilt
whip: **4** crop
handled: 5 dealt **6** ansate
handling: use **4** care **7** control, running **9** treatment **10** management **11** supervi-sion
handout: aid **4** alms, dole, food, gift, meal, mete **5** snack **7** charity
handreading: 9 palmistry
hands: men **4** crew **8** pointers
hands off: 4 tabu **5** taboo
handsome: 4 braw(Sc.), fair, fine, pert **5** ample, belle, bonny, handy, ready **6** bonnie, clever, comely, goodly, heppen, limber **7** elegant, gallant, liberal **8** be-coming, budgeree, generous, gracious, suitable **9** beautiful, dexterous **10** at-tractive, convenient, manageable **11** appropriate, good-looking **12** consider-able
handspring: 6 tumble **9** cartwheel
handwriting: 4 fist, hand **5** ronde **6** script **10** griffonage, manuscript **11** chirography

on the wall: **4** mene **5** tekel **8** graffiti, upharsin
study of: **10** graphology
handy: 4 deft, near **5** adept, ready **6** adroit, clever, heppen **7** close-by **8** adja-cent, dextrous, handsome, skillful **9** available, dexterous, versatile **10** acces-sible, convenient
Handy Andy's catch: 5 Oonah
handyman: 5 fixer **8** factotum, repairer
hang: lag, lop, sag **4** kilt, loll, pend, rest **5** drape, droop, hinge, knack, slope, swing **6** append, dangle, depend, gibbet, talter **7** crucify, execute, stretch, suspend **9** declivity **11** inclination
around: **4** loaf **5** hover **6** loiter **7** frequent
back: lag **6** falter **8** hesitate
down: **5** droop **6** dangle **7** suspend
onto: **5** cling
hang fire: 4 pend **8** hesitate, postpone **13** procrastinate
hangar: 4 shed **6** garage, stable **7** shelter **9** penthouse
hangdog: 4 base **5** cowed **6** shifty **7** ashamed, fawning, furtive **8** cringing, sneaking **9** groveling
hanger-on: bur **5** leech, toady **6** hangby, heeler **7** adjunct, dangler, slinger, sponger **8** bottomer, loiterer, onsetter, parasite **9** appendage, dependent, syco-phant **10** blackguard, free-loader
hanging: 5 arras, drape **6** celure, tippet **7** pendent, pensile, valance **8** inclined **9** declivity, execution, suspended **11** in-clination
Hanging Gardens site: 7 Babylon
hangman: 6 hangie **9** Jack Ketch **11** exe-cutioner
hangout: 5 joint **10** rendezvous
hangover: 8 residuum **11** aftereffect
hang-up: 5 block, **6** phobia **8** fixation **9** obsession
hank: 4 coil, loop **5** skein **6** bundle, han-dle **7** control **9** influence
hanker: yen **4** ache, long **5** crave, yearn **6** desire, hunger, thirst
Hannibal: 7 general
conqueror: **6** Scipio
father: **8** Hamilcar
home: **8** Carthage
place of victory: **6** Cannae
hansom: cab
hap: lot **4** luck **5** check, occur, seize **6** be-fall, chance, snatch **7** fortune, venture **9** happening **10** occurrence, prosperity
haphazard: 6 casual, chance, random **8** careless **10** accidental **11** any which way **13** helter-skelter
hapless: 4 poor **7** unlucky **11** star-crossed, unfortunate
happen: 4 come, fall, fare **5** evene, occur **6** arrive, befall, betide, chance, mayhap **7**

come off, perhaps, stumble **9** eventuate, transpire

happen again: 5 recur

happening: hap **4** case, fact **5** event, thing **6** chance, faring, **7** episode **8** incident, occasion **10** occurrence

happily: 5 fitly, haply **6** gladly **7** luckily **8** joyously **10** gracefully **11** contendedly, fortunately, opportunely **12** felicitously, peradventure, prosperously, successfully **13** appropriately

happiness: joy **4** sele(Sc.), weal **5** bliss, mirth **6** felice, gaiety **7** delight, ecstasy, felicia, rapture **8** felicity, gladness, hilarity **9** beatitude, enjoyment, eudaemony, transport, well-being **10** exaltation, prosperity **11** blessedness

god: **5** Ebisu

incapacity for: **9** anhedonia

happy: apt, gay **4** cosh, glad, gleg **5** blest, lucky, merry, ready, seely, sonsy, sunny **6** elated, sonsie **7** blessed, content, fitting, halcyon, radiant **8** carefree, frohlich, gracious, mirthful **9** contented, fortunate **10** felicitous, propitious, prosperous

happy-go-lucky: 6 casual **8** carefree **9** easygoing

happy hour: 12 cocktail time

happy hunting ground: 6 heaven **8** paradise

Haran: *brother:* **7** Abraham
daughter: **5** Iscah **6** Milcah
father: **5** Terah
son: Lot

harangue: nag **4** rave **5** orate, spiel **6** screed, sermon, speech, tirade **7** address, declaim, oration **8** diatribe, jeremiad, perorate **10** concionate

harass: fag, hag, nag, try, vex **4** bait, fret, gall, hake, hale, haze, jade, rack, raid, tire **5** annoy, beset, bully, chafe, chase, grind, gripe, harry, herry(Sc.), hurry, pique, tease, weary, worry **6** badger, bother, bucket, cumber, hatter, heckle, impede, molest, obsess, pester, plague, pother, scrape **7** afflict, affront, agitate, disturb, exhaust, fatigue, hagride, oppress, perplex, provoke, scourge, torment, trouble **8** distract, distress, irritate **9** exagitate, persecute, tantalize

harbinger: 4 camp, host, omen, sign **5** usher **6** herald, symbol **7** presage, shelter **8** fourrier, harborer **9** messenger, precursor **10** forerunner

spring: **5** robin **6** crocus

harbor, harbour: bay, inn **4** hold, port **5** basin, bayou, haven **6** billet, breach, bunder, covert, foster, refuge **7** fairway, lodging, quarter, retreat, seaport, shelter **9** harborage

entrance: **4** boca
fee: **7** keelage
harbor master: **7** havener

hard: fit **4** acid, cold, dear, dere, dure, firm, iron, mean, oaky, sour **5** champ, close, cruel, hardy, harsh, horny, rigid, rocky, rough, solid, stern, stiff, stony **6** coarse, frozen, knotty, marble, robust, severe, steely, strict, strong **7** adamant, arduous, austere, callous, compact, earnest, intense, onerous, scleral **8** diligent, granitic, grasping, hardened, obdurate, renitent, rigorous, scleroid, toilsome **9** difficult, energetic, fatiguing, inclement, intricate, laborious, petrified, repelling, reprobate, resistant, strenuous, stringent, unfeeling, wearisome **10** inflexible, oppressive, perplexing, persistent, relentless, ungraceful, unyielding **11** at close hand, complicated, distressing, down-to-earth, impregnable, persevering, unremitting **12** blood-and-guts, disreputable, extortionate, impenetrable, incorrigible, unalleviated **13** unsympathetic

to please: **7** finicky

hard-boiled: 5 rough, tough **7** callous **8** obdurate, seasoned **11** down-to-earth **13** unsympathetic

hard coal: 10 anthracite

hard core: 12 intransigent **13** dyed-in-the-wool

hard corn: rye **5** wheat

hard drawn: 4 taut **5** tense

hard-shell: 9 confirmed, extremist

hard times: 9 recession **10** depression

harden: gel, set **4** bake, cake, salt, sear **5** beath, enure, inure, steel **6** endure, freeze, ossify, temper **7** congeal, petrify, stiffen, thicken, toughen **8** concrete, condense, indurate, solidify **10** habituate **11** acclimatize, strengthen

hardened: 4 hard **5** caked **6** frozen, gelled, inured **7** callous, steeled **8** obdurate **9** abandoned, reprobate **10** impenitent, impervious inveterate, solidified **12** impenetrable

hardhat: 7 builder **12** conservative

hardhead: 4 fish **5** whale **7** ribwort **8** knapweed, mackerel, menhaden **9** blockhead **10** niggerhead

hardheaded: 4 keen **6** shrewd **7** willful **8** stubborn **9** sagacious **10** longheaded **11** down-to-earth, sharp-witted **12** matter-of-fact

hardhearted: 4 mean **5** cruel, stern **7** callous **8** obdurate, pitiless **9** unfeeling **13** marblehearted, unsympathetic

hardihood: 5 pluck, vigor **7** bravery, courage **8** audacity, boldness, temerity **9** hardiness, impudence, stoutness **10**

confidence, effrontery, imprudence, resolution, robustness 11 intrepidity 13
audaciousness
hard line: 4 firm 5 fixed 10 determined,
inflexible
hardly: 6 barely 7 faintly, hardily, harshly, roughly 8 forcibly, scarcely, severely,
unfairly 11 unfavorably
hardness: 6 durity 8 asperity, severity,
solidity 9 substance
measuring device: 9 durometer
hardpan: 7 bedrock 8 ortstein
hardship: 5 assay, peril, rigor, trial 6 injury 7 penalty 8 asperity, hardness 9
adversity, endurance, grievance, injustice, privation 10 affliction, difficulty
hardtack: 7 biscuit, galette(F.), pantile
hardwood: ash, oak 4 pelu, teak 5 maple
6 walnut 7 hickory 8 mahogany
genus: 7 quercus
hardy: 4 bold, firm, hard, rash, wiry 5
brave, lusty, manly, stout, tough 6 chisel, daring, robust, rugged, strong, sturdy
7 compact, spartan 8 galliard, intrepid,
resolute, stubborn, vigorous 9 audacious, confident 10 courageous
Hardy heroine: 4 Tess
hare: dol 4 bawd(Sc.), pika 5 harry, lepus,
tease, worry 6 malkin, rabbit 7 leporid,
leveret 8 frighten, leporide 10 jack rabbit
female: doe
genus of: 5 lepus
male: 4 buck
pert. to: 8 leporine
tail: 4 scut
track: 4 file, slot
young: 7 leveret
harem: oda 4 odah 5 serai 6 serail, zenana 8 seraglio
male attendant: 6 eunuch
room: oda
slave: 9 odalisque
haricot: 4 stew 6 ragout
hark: 4 hear, heed, hist 6 attend, listen,
notice 7 whisper
harlequin: 5 clown 7 buffoon 9 fantastic
11 masquerader
harlot: low, pug 4 base, doxy, lewd, slut 5
churl, knave, quean, rogue, whore 6 menial, rascal, wanton 7 buffoon, juggler 8
strumpet, vagabond 10 fricatrice, prostitute
harm: hob, ill, mar, sap 4 bale, bane, evil,
hurt, pain, teen 5 abuse, annoy, grief,
shend, wound, wrong 6 damage, damnum, injure, injury, scathe, sorrow 7
disease, impeach 8 disserve, endamage,
nuisance 10 disservice, misfortune,
wickedness 11 impeachment
harmful: bad 4 evil 5 nasty, toxic 6 no-

cent 7 baneful, hurtful, malefic, noisome, noxious 8 damaging, sinister 9
injurious 10 pernicious 11 contrarious,
deleterious, detrimental, mischievous
harmless: 4 safe 6 dovish 8 innocent,
nontoxic 9 innocuous 11 inoffensive
harmonica: 10 mouth organ
relative of: 7 panpipe
Harmonia: *father:* 4 Ares, Mars
husband: 6 Cadmus
mother: 5 Venus 9 Aphrodite
harmonious: 6 cosmic, dulcet 7 cordial,
musical, spheral, tuneful 8 amicable,
peaceful 9 accordant, agreeable, congruous, consonant, harmonial, melodious,
peaceable 10 compatible, concentive,
concordant 11 harmoniacal, symmetrical 12 proportional
harmonize: gee, key 4 jibe, tone, tune 5
adapt, agree, blend, chime, hitch, rhyme
6 accord, adjust, attune, cotton 7 concent, concord, consist, consort 9 reconcile 10 correspond, sympathize
harmony: 4 tune 5 amity, music, peace 6
cosmos, melody 7 concert, concord,
rapport 9 agreement 10 accordance, atmosphere, conformity, congruence, consonance 11 cooperation 12 together-
ness
bring into: 6 attune
lack: 7 discord
harness: 4 gear, yoke 5 heald 6 fettle,
tackle 7 enclose, hitch-up 9 equipment,
trappings
marker: 7 knacker, lorimer
part: bit, tug 4 hame, rein 5 blind, trace 6
billet, bridle, collar, saddle, terret 7
crouper 9 breeching, circingle, martin-
gal, ridgeband, surcingle 10 breastband,
crownpiece, martingale
harp: 4 arpa, koto, lyre 6 trigon 8 bedlamer 10 instrument 11 clairschach
harper: 4 coin 8 minstrel, musician
harpoon: 5 spear 7 javelin
harpsichord: 6 spinet 8 clavecin, virginal
12 clavicembalo
harpy: 5 leech, scold, vixen 6 virago 8
fishwife, swindler 11 extortioner
Harpy: 5 Aello 7 Celaneo, Ocypete, Po-
darge
harridan: hag 5 crone, horse, vixen, woman 8 strumpet
harrier: dog 4 hawk 5 bully 8 harasser
harrow: vex 4 disk, drag 5 brake, harry,
wound 6 spader 7 oppress, torment 8
distress, lacerate 9 cultivate 10 cultivator
harrowed: 6 pained 7 haggard 8 tortured
harry: rob, vex 4 sack 5 annoy, hound,
hurry, spoil, steal, worry 6 harass, harrow, hector, plague, ravage 7 agitate,

bedevil, despoil, pillage, plunder, torment **9** persecute

harsh: raw **4** grim, hard, hask **5** acerb, acrid, asper, brute, crude, cruel, grill, gruff, raspy, rough, sharp, stern, stiff **6** bitter, brazen, coarse, severe, strict, sullen, unkind **7** austere, braying, drastic, grating, rasping, raucous **8** acerbate, catonian, clashing, croaking, district, guttural, jangling, rigorous, strident, ungentle **9** dissonant, inclement, insensate, repellent, squawking, truculent, unfeeling **10** astringent, discordant, oppressive, relentless **11** acrimonious, disagreeing **12** disagreeable

harshness: **5** rigor **6** duress **7** crudity, raucity **8** acerbity, acrimony, asperity, severity

hart: roe **4** deer, stag **7** red deer, venison
mate: **4** hind

hartebeest: **4** asse, tora **5** caama, kaama **6** lecama **7** bubalis **8** antelope

hartshorn: **6** antler **7** ammonia **11** sal volatile

harum-scarum: **4** rash, wild **7** flighty **8** reckless **11** thoughtless **13** irresponsible

Harun-Al-Rashid's wife: **7** Zobeide

haruspex: **5** augur **7** diviner, prophet **8** foreseer **9** predictor **10** soothsayer **14** prognosticator

harvest: **4** bind, crop, reap **5** amass, cache, hoard **6** foison, gather **8** ingather, stow away
festival: **6** Opalia
fly: **6** cicada
god: **6** Cronus
goddess: Ops **4** Rhea **5** Ceres **7** Demeter

harvest home: **4** kern, kirn(Sc.)

harvester: **8** spalpeen

hash: **4** chop **5** mince, mix-up **6** jumble **7** mixture **9** talk about **11** gallimaufry, olla podrida(Sp.)

hashish: **4** hemp **5** bhang **8** cannabis, narcotic

hashmark: **6** stripe

hasp: **4** gird **5** catch, clasp **7** confine **8** fastener

hassle: row, try **4** talk **6** hustle **7** quarrel, wrestle **8** argument, squabble **9** commotion **10** discussion **11** altercation, controversy

hassock: **4** boss, pess **5** grass, sedge **6** buffet **7** cushion, ottoman, tussock **8** footrest **9** footstool

haste: hie **4** rush **5** hurry, speed **6** bustle, flurry **7** urgency **8** dispatch, rapidity **9** quickness, swiftness **10** expedition, nimbleness **11** festination, impetuosity **12** precipitance **13** impetuousness, precipitation

hasten: hie, run **4** pell, race, rush, trot **5** crowd, drive, fleet, hurry, speed **6** ex-pede, gallop, scurry **7** advance, scamper **8** dispatch, expedite **9** festinate **10** accelerate **11** precipitate

hastily: **6** nimbly **8** speedily **11** impatiently **13** precipitately

hasty: **4** fast, rash **5** brash, fleet, quick, swift **6** abrupt, daring, nimble, speedy, sudden **7** cursory, forward, hurried **8** headlong, pell-mell, succinct **9** hotheaded, hurrisome, impatient, impetuous **10** indiscreet **11** expeditious, precipitate, precipitous

hasty pudding: **4** mush **6** supawn **9** stir-about

hat: cap, dip, fez, lid, nab, tam **4** baku, felt, topi **5** beany, benjy, benny, beret, boxer, cordy, derby, dicer, kelly, terai, topee, toque **6** Alpine, beaver, boater, bonnet, bowler, castor, claque, cloche, fedora, panama, shovel, turban **7** biretta, caubeen, chapeau, homburg, petasus, salacot, shallow **8** capeline, copatain, headgear, sombrero **9** Dunstable, stovepipe, wide-awake **10** belltopper **11** mortarboard
brimless: **7** pillbox
close fitting: **5** toque **6** turban
covering: **8** havelock
crown: **4** poll
ecclesastic: **5** miter **7** biretta
fiber: **4** felt, sola **5** straw
fur used in: **4** mink **5** coney **6** beaver, ermine **8** coonskin
ladies: **5** caddy, cooie **6** Breton, caddie, slouch **7** leghorn **8** duckbill **9** harlequin **12** Gainsborough
maker: **8** milliner
medieval: **6** abacot **7** bycoket
military: **5** shako
oilskin: **5** squam **9** sou'wester
opera: **5** crush, gibus **6** claque, topper
palm-leaf: **7** salacot
pert. to: **9** castorial
pith: **4** topi **5** topee
Quaker: **9** broadbrim
silk: lum(Sc.) **4** tile **5** opera **6** topper **7** catskin **8** gossamer
soft: **6** fedora
straw: **6** boater
tall: **9** stovepipe
three-cornered: **7** tricorn
ventilated: **5** terai
wide-brimmed: **9** sou'wester

hatch: **4** brew, door, gate, sire, vent **5** breed, cleck, clock, cover **6** clutch, wicket **7** concoct **8** contrive, hatchway **9** floodgate
covering: **4** tarp

hatchel: **5** tease, worry **6** heckle **7** torment

hatchet: adz, axe **4** adze, mogo **8** tomahawk

hatchet man: 4 tool 6 critic, killer, stooge 8 assassin, henchman
hatching: 6 cletch 8 breeding
hatchway: 7 scuttle
hate: 4 teen 5 abhor, scorn 6 detest, loathe, rancor, revile 7 contemn, despise, ill will 8 aversion 9 abominate, malignity 11 detestation
hateful: 4 evil, foul 5 black, nasty 6 odious 7 heinous 8 flagrant, infamous 9 abhorrent, invidious, loathsome, malignant, obnoxious, offensive, revolting 10 abominable, detestable, disgusting, malevolent 11 distasteful 12 disagreeable
hatful: 4 lots, many, much 8 quantity
hatred: 5 odium, spite 6 enmity, rancor 8 aversion 9 animosity, hostility, malignity 10 abhorrence, repugnance 11 abomination, detestation, malevolence
 of argument: 8 misology
 of children: 9 misopedia 10 misopaedia
 of mankind: 11 misanthropy
 of marriage: 8 misogamy
 of strangers: 10 xenophobia
hatter: 8 milliner
haughtiness: 4 airs 5 pride 6 morgue 7 hauteur 9 arrogance, insolence
haughty: 4 airy, bold, high 5 aloof, dorty, lofty, noble, proud 6 snooty 7 distant, exalted, fatuous, hontish, paughty, stately 8 arrogant, cavalier, glorious, scornful 9 egotistic, imperious, masterful 10 disdainful, fastidious 11 domineering, magisterial, overbearing 12 contemptuous, presumptuous, supercilious
haul: lug, tow, tug 4 cart, drag, draw, hurl, move, pull, tote 5 bouse, catch, heave, shift, trice 8 cordelle 9 transport
haulage: 6 towage 7 cartage, drayage
hauler: 7 tractor
haulm: 4 culm, stem 5 straw 6 stalks
haunch: hip 4 huck 5 hance 12 hindquarters
haunt: den 4 dive, howf, lair, nest 5 ghost, habit, howff, skill 6 custom, infest, obsess, resort, spirit, wraith 7 hang out, terrify 8 frequent, practice 9 companion 10 fellowship, hang around
haunted: 6 filled, spooky 8 infested
hautboy, hautbois: 4 oboe 9 organ stop 10 strawberry
hauteur: 5 pride 9 arrogance 11 haughtiness
haut monde: 11 high society
have: hae(Sc.), own 4 hold 5 enjoy, ought 6 retain 7 carry on, contain, possess, undergo 10 experience
 on: 4 wear
 to do with: 4 deal
haven: bay, lee 4 hope, port 5 hotel, inlet 6 asylum, harbor, recess, refuge 7 retreat, shelter 9 anchorage, roadstead, sanctuary
haversack: bag
havoc: hob 4 loss, ruin 5 waste 6 ravage 7 destroy 9 devastate 10 desolation 11 destruction, devastation
haw: 4 sloe, yard 5 fence, hedge 6 falter 8 hawthorn
Hawaii: *ballad:* 4 mele
 beach: 7 Waikiki
 beverage: 4 kava 8 kava-kava
 breechcloth: 4 malo
 bush: See *shrub* below
 canoe: 5 waapa
 capital: 8 Honolulu
 channel: 4 Auau
 chant: 4 mele
 city: 4 Hilo 5 Lihue 6 Kailua 7 Kanache, Wailuku
 cloak: 4 mamo 6 ahuula
 cloth: 4 kapa, tapa 5 tappa
 cookout: 4 luau
 county: 4 Maui 5 Kauai 6 Hawaii 8 Honolulu
 cord: aea
 crater: 7 Kilauea
 dance: 4 hula
 discoverer: 4 Cook
 district: 4 Puna, Kona
 farewell, hello: 5 aloha
 feast: 4 luau 7 ahaaina
 fern: 4 heii 5 ekaha, uluhi 6 iwaiwa 7 amaumau
 fiber: 4 pulu
 first settler: 10 Polynesian
 fish: ahi 4 ulua 5 akule
 fish poison: hola 6 auhuhu
 flower: 5 ilima
 food: poi 4 kalo, taro
 game: hei
 garland: lei
 garment: 6 holoku, muumuu 7 holomuu
 god: 4 Kane 5 Wakea
 goddess: 4 Pele
 goose: 4 nene
 grass: 6 emoloa
 greeting: 5 ahola
 harbor: 5 Pearl
 hawk: io
 herb: ape, pia 4 hola 5 awiwi 6 auhuhu
 instrument: uke 7 ukalele, ukelele, ukulele
 island: 4 Maui, Oahu 5 Kauai, Lanai 6 Hawaii, Niihau 7 Molokai 9 Kahoolawe
 lava: aa 8 pahoehoe
 loincloth: 4 malo, maro
 lomilomi: rub 7 massage, shampoo
 love: 5 aloha
 massage: 8 lomilomi
 morning glory: 5 koali
 mountain: 5 Kaala 7 Waianae 8 Mauna Kea, Mauna Loa

native: 6 Kanaka 10 Polynesian
naval base: 11 Pearl Harbor
nickname: 10 Aloha State
octopus: hee
pantheon: 4 Kane
parrot fish: 5 lauia
partnership: hui
pepper: ava
pit for baking: imu
plant: pia 4 hala, taro 5 olona 8 pandanus
poem: 4 mele
porch: 5 lanai
precipice: 4 pali
priest: 6 Kahuna
raven: 5 alala
root: 4 taro
root paste: poi
seaweed: 4 limu
shaman: 6 Kahuna
shrub: 4 akia 5 akala, olona 6 aupaka
song: 4 mele
staple: poi 4 taro
starch plant: pia
starch root: pia 4 taro
state bird: 4 nene 5 goose
state flower: 8 hibiscus
state song: 11 Hawaii Ponoi
state tree: 9 candlenut
temple: 5 heiau
thrush: 4 amao 6 olomao
valley: 5 Manoa
volcano: 7 Kilauea 8 Mauna Kea, Mauna Loa
white man: 5 haole
wind: 4 kona
windstorm: 4 kona
woman: 5 haole
wreath: lei
yam: hoi
hawfinch: 4 kate 8 grosbeak
hawk: io; cry, gos 4 eyas, kite, sell, vend 5 astur, cadge 6 falcon, osprey, peddle, 7 buzzard, harrier, haggard, kestrel, puttock, vulture 8 caracara, jingoist, militant 9 accipiter, swindler, warmonger 11 mortar-board
cage: mew
male: 6 musket, tercel 7 tiercel
leash: 4 jess, lune
nest: 5 aerie
nestling: 4 eyas
pinion feather: 6 sarcel
hawker: 6 badger, cadger, coster, duffer, pedlar, vendor 7 chapman, mercury, packman, peddler 8 falconer, huckster, pitchman 9 colporter 10 colporteur 12 costermonger
hawk-eyed: 12 sharp-sighted
Hawkeye State: 4 Iowa
hawklike: 9 bellicose 11 accipitrine, belligerent
hawser: 4 line, rope

post: 4 bitt 7 bollard
hawthorn: haw, may 5 aglet 6 aiglet 8 cockspur, maybloom, quickset
hay: bed, net 4 park 5 chaff, fence, grass, hedge 9 provender
bundle: mow 4 bale, rick, wisp 5 gavel, stack, truss 7 hayrick
kind of: 6 clover 7 alfalfa, timothy
line: 5 swath 7 windrow
second cutting: 5 rowen
spreader: 6 tedder
storage: mow 4 loft
haycock: 4 coil
hayfork: 4 pike 5 pikel
haymaker: 8 farm hand 10 boxing blow
hayseed: 4 hick 5 yokel 6 farmer, rustic 10 countryman
hazard: die, lay, lot 4 risk 5 peril, stake 6 chance, danger, gamble, menace 7 imperil, venture 8 accident, casualty, endanger, jeopardy 9 adventure 10 jeopardize
hazardous: 5 risky 6 chance, chancy, queasy, unsafe 8 insecure, perilous 9 dangerous, uncertain 10 fortuitous, jeopardous, precarious 11 adventurous
haze: fog 4 beat, film, mist, smog 5 cloud, devil, scold, vapor 6 harass, vapour 7 drizzle, obscure, reverie 8 frighten
hazel: nut 4 bush 6 cobnut 7 filbert 8 noisette 12 reddish brown
Hazor king: 5 Jabin
hazy: dim 5 filmy, foggy, misty, smoky, thick, vague 7 clouded, nebular, obscure, unclear 8 nebulous 9 uncertain 10 indistinct
head: aim, cop, mir, nab, nob, top 4 bean, boro, cape, coco, conk, crop, kopf(G.), lead, mind, pate, poll, tete(F.), turn 5 caput(L.), chief, chump, first, front, froth, start, tibby 6 cabeza(Sp.), cobbra, direct, garret, leader, manage, noggin, noodle, person, sconce, source, spring 7 captain, coconut, costrel, cranium, crumpet, leading, prelate 8 director, foremost, fountain, headland, initiate 9 intercept, president, principal 10 caper-nutie, drug addict, headmaster, promontory 11 caper-noitie 12 intelligence
army camp: 10 commandant
back part: 7 occiput
bald: 9 pilgarlic
boar: 4 hure
bone: 5 skull 7 cranium 8 parietal
crown: 6 cantle
muscle: 11 occipitalis
nautical: 6 toilet 8 lavatory
ornament: hat, wig 4 hair, veil 5 tiara 7 coronet
part: 4 pate 5 scalp 6 earlap, temple 7 cranium

pert. to: 8 cephalic
shaven: 7 tonsure
shrunken: 7 tsantsa
side of: 4 lore 5 lorum 6 temple
skin: 5 scalp
top: 4 pate 5 crown, scalp 7 coxcomb
head cook: 4 chef
head covering (see also **cap, hat**): fez,
tam, wig 4 barb, caul, coif, hair, hood 5
beret, scalp, snood, toque 6 bonnet,
coiffe, peruke, toupee 7 biretta, chapeau, periwig 8 berretta, kerchief, maharmah, sombrero 9 rigolette 10 fascinator
head-shaped: 8 capitate
head to foot: 7 cap-a-pie
headache: 6 megrim 8 headwark, migraine 10 cephalagia
headband: 5 miter, mitre, vitta 6 diadem,
fillet, infula 7 circlet, coronet 8 frontlet
9 sphendone
headcheese: 5 brawn
headdress: 4 caul, coif, pouf 5 ampyx,
crown, cupee, miter, mitre, tiara, toque
6 almuce, bonnet, coiffe, faille, hennin,
mobcap, pinner, turban 7 bandore, bycoket, coronet, topknot 8 biliment, bin-
nogue, capriole, coiffure, stephane, tressure 9 rigolette
medieval: 5 barbe 6 abacot
military: 5 busby, shako 6 casque, helmet
royal: 5 crown, tiara 6 diadem
sacerdotal: 5 miter 7 biretta
sacred: 6 uraeus
Spanish woman's: 8 mantilla
widow's: 7 bandore
headgear: See **headdress**
headily: 6 rashly 9 violently
heading: 5 title, topic 7 caption 8 headline
topical: 5 trope
headland: ras 4 bill, cape, head, nase,
naze, ness, peak 5 Morro, ridge, strip 8
foreland 10 promontory
headless: 4 rash 6 stupid, topless 7 foolish 8 beheaded 10 acephalous, leader-
less
headline: 6 banner 7 feature, 8 streamer
headliner: 4 star 11 personality
headlong: 4 rash 5 hasty, steep 6 abrupt,
sudden 8 reckless 9 desperate, foolhardy, headfirst, impetuous, impulsive 11
precipitate, precipitous
headman: 4 boss 5 chief 6 ataman, cabeza, hetman 7 capitan, captain, foreman
8 alderman, caboceer, capitano 11 executioner
headmaster: 9 principal 11 gymnasiarch
headpiece: See **headdress**
headquarters: 5 depot, yamen 6 center 8
exchange, precinct 9 battalion
headstone: 8 monument 11 grave marker

headstrong: 4 rash 5 cobby 6 mulish, unruly 7 hotspur, violent, willful 8 stubborn 9 obstinate 10 bullheaded, forthright, hotspurred, self-willed 11
intractable, stiff-necked 12 contumacious, ungovernable
heady: 4 rash 7 huffcap, violent, willful 9
impetuous 11 exhilarated, intoxicated,
precipitate 12 intoxicating
heal: 4 cure, hale, knit, mend 5 amend 6
remedy, repair 7 restore 10 recuperate
heal-all: 4 balm 7 figwort, panacea
healer: asa 4 balm 6 doctor 9 naprapath
12 practitioner
healing: 5 balmy 8 covering, curative, remedial, sanative
agent: 6 balsam
goddess: Eir
pert. to: 7 medical 9 medicinal
science: 8 medicine 9 iatrology, latrology
health: 4 hale, hail 5 sante(F.), toast 7
slainte, stamina 8 eucrasia, euphoria,
haleness, vitality 11 disposition
goddess: 7 Minerva
poor: 4 sick 7 illness
resort: spa
healthy: fit 4 hale, sane, well 5 bonny,
hoddy 6 bonnie, hearty, robust 8 salutary, vigorous 9 wholesome 10 healthsome, salubrious
heap: ahu, cob, cop, mow 4 balk, bing,
bulk, deck, dess(Sc.), gobs, hill, lump,
mass, much, pile, pyre, raft, rick, ruck 5
amass, cairn, clump, crowd, spire, stack
6 burrow, hipple, jumble, plenty, throng
7 bourock, cumulus, hurrock 9 congeries, multitude 10 accumulate, collection, congestion, cumulation
hear: ear, see 4 feel, hark, heed, obey 5
learn 6 attend, harken, listen 7 hearken
8 perceive 10 adjudicate
hear ye: 4 oyes, oyez
hearer: 7 audient, auditor 8 disciple, listener
hearing: ear 4 test 5 sound, trial 6 assize,
report 7 earshot, lecture, meeting 8 audience, audition, scolding 9 attention,
audiencia, interview, knowledge 10 attendance, conference, discussion
court: 4 oyer
distance: 7 earshot
judicial: 5 trial 7 retrial
pert. to: 8 acoustic
hearken, harken: 4 hark, hear, heed,
wait 6 attend, listen 7 inquire, whisper
hearsay: 4 buzz, fame, talk 5 on-dit, rumor 6 report 9 grapevine 11 scuttlebutt
hearse: 4 bier, bury, tomb 5 dirge, grave 6
coffin 8 monument, threnody
heart: cor, hub 4 core, gist, hati, love 5
cheer, focus 6 center, centre, depths,

middle, ticker **7** courage, emotion, essence, feeling **9** affection, character **10** compassion
cavity: **6** atrium
chamber: **7** auricle **9** ventricle
contraction: **7** systole
covering: **11** pericardium
disease: **7** cardiac
expansion: **8** diastole
record: **17** electrocardiogram
stimulant: **8** thialdin **9** digitalis, thialdine **10** adrenaline, epinephrin **11** epinephrine
heart-shaped: 7 cordate
heartache: rue, woe **4** pang **5** grief **6** sorrow **7** anguish **10** affliction, cardialgia
heartbeat: 5 pulse, throb **7** systole **9** pulsation
irregular: **10** arrhythmia
heartbreak: 5 grief **6** sorrow **7** tragedy
heartbroken: 12 inconsolable **13** grief-stricken
heartburn: 4 envy **6** enmity **7** pyrosis **8** jealousy **10** cardialgia, discontent, heartscald, heartscaud
hearten: 5 cheer **6** arouse, spirit **7** cheer up, refresh **8** embolden, inspirit, reassure **9** encourage
heartfelt: 4 dear, deep, real, true **6** honest **7** earnest, genuine, sincere **8** bona fide, profound
hearth: 5 cupel, focus, fogon, foyer **8** bloomery, fireside
goddess: **5** Vesta **6** Hestia
line: **6** fettle
heartily: 6 dearly, freely, warmly **8** actively, strongly **9** cordially, earnestly, profusely, sincerely, zealously, zestfully **10** abundantly, completely, vigorously **14** wholeheartedly
heartiness: 4 soul **8** goodwill, strength **9** soundness **10** cordiality
heartless: 5 cruel **7** callous **8** hopeless, listless **9** merciless, unfeeling **10** despairing, despondent, hard-boiled, spiritless **13** unsympathetic
heartsease, heartease: 5 pansy, peace **11** peace of mind **12** tranquillity
heartthrob: 4 dunt, love **5** flame, honey, sweet
heartwood: 4 dura **7** duramen
hearty: 4 firm, hale, real, rich, warm, well **5** cobby, heavy, sound **6** active, cheery, devout, robust, sailor, stanch **7** comrade, cordial, earnest, fertile, healthy, sincere, staunch **8** abundant, cheerful, heartful, vigorous **9** energetic, unfeigned, wholesome **10** full-bodied, nourishing **11** substantial, warmhearted **12** enthusiastic
heat: ire **4** fire, mull, rage, warm, zeal **5** ardor, cauma, chafe, fever, roast, tepor

6 anneal, choler, degree, warmth **7** caloric, ferment, hotness, inflame, passion **8** fervency **9** agitation, animation, chauffage, commotion, vehemence **10** excitement, hot weather **11** temperature **12** exasperation **14** passionateness
measure: **5** therm **6** calory, therme **7** calorie **10** centigrade, fahrenheit **11** calorimeter, pyronometer
pert. to: **7** thermic
quantity: **6** degree **11** temperature
unit of: **5** therm **7** calorie
white: **13** incandescence
heated: 6 ardent **7** excited **8** sizzling, vehement **10** phlogistic **11** acrimonious
heater: 4 etna, oven **5** stove **6** boiler **7** choffer(Sc.), furnace **8** radiator
heath: 4 ling, moor **5** besom, erica, plain
scrub: **9** chaparral
tree: **5** briar, brier
heathen: 5 pagan **6** ethnic, paynim **7** saracen **8** paganist **11** irreligious
deity: **4** idol
non-Jewish: **6** ethnic
non-Muslim: **7** infidel
heather: 4 grig, ling **5** erica
family: **9** ericaceae
heatless: 8 athermic
heautarit: 7 mercury **11** quicksilver
heave: gag **4** cast, haul, heft, hurl, keck, lift, pant, pull, push, quap, toss **5** hoist, pitch, raise, retch, scend, throw, vomit **7** elevate, estuate **8** struggle
heaven: sky **4** Zion **5** dyaus, ether, glory **6** Himmel(G.), utopia, welkin, zodiac **7** Elysium, Nirvana, Valhall, Vahalla **8** devaloka, empyrean, paradise **9** firmament **12** promised land
pert. to: **6** uranic **9** celestial
queen: **7** Astarte
heavenly: 4 lush **5** yummy **6** divine, sacred **7** angelic, olympic, sublime, uranian **8** ethereal, supernal **9** angelical, celestial, celestine
heavenly being: 5 angel **6** seraph
heavenly belt: way **6** galaxy, nebula, zodiac
heavenly body: sun **4** luna, moon, star **5** comet **6** planet **8** luminary
heavenly city: 4 Sion, Zion
heavenly twins: 6 Castor, Gemini, Pollux
heaviness: 5 gloom **6** weight **7** gravity, sadness **10** oppression **12** sluggishness
heavy: 4 clit, deep, dull, logy, loud **5** actor, beefy, burly, dense, grave, gross, hefty, hoggy, massy, thick **6** clayey, cloggy, coarse, gloomy, hearty, leaden, stodgy, strong, stupid **7** big shot, doleful, intense, massive, onerous, porcine, serious, villain, violent, weighty **8** burdened, grievous, inactive, lifeless,

lowering, overcast, pregnant, profound, sluggish **9** heavisome, laborious, lethargic, ponderous, saturnine **10** afflictive, burdensome, cumbersome, encumbered, oppressive **13** consequential

heavy-headed: 4 dull **5** inept **6** drowsy, gauche, stupid **8** bumbling **9** maladroit, ponderous **10** uninspired

heavy-hearted: sad **10** despondent, melancholy

hebdomad: 4 week **5** seven

hebetate: 4 dull **5** blunt

Hebrew (see also **Israel, Judaism**): Jew **6** Semite **7** Semitic **8** Hebraean **9** Israelite

acrostic: **4** agla

alphabet: Mem, Nun, Sin, Taf, Tav, Tet, Vav, Yod, Yud **4** Alef, Ayin, Beth, Caph, Kaph, Koph, Ooph, Resh, Shin **5** Aleph, Cheth, Gimel, Lamed, Sadhe, Tsade, Zayin **6** Daleth, Samekh

ancestor: **4** Eber

clean: **6** kosher

dance: **4** hora

day: yom

eternity: **4** olam

gentile: goi, goy **5** goyim(pl.)

God: El **5** Eloah **6** Adonai, Elohim **7** Jehovah

greeting; **6** shalom

high priest: Eli **5** Aaron

infinity: **6** adalam

Jehovah: **5** Jahve, Yahve, Yahwe **6** Jahvah, Jahveh, Yahveh, Yahweh **7** Jahaveh

juniper: **4** ezel

lawbreaking: **6** averah

lesson: **9** Haphtarah

man: rab **5** bahur, hakam

measure: cab, hin, kab, kor **4** epha, ezba, omer, reed, seah **5** cubit, ephah, homer

month: Ab **4** Adar, Elul **5** Iyyar, Nisan, Tebet **6** Kislew, Shebat, Tammuz, Tishri, Veadar **7** Heshwan

name for God: **6** Adonai, Elohim, Yahweh **7** Jehovah

parchment: **6** mezuza **7** mezuzah

school: **5** heder, schul

scriptures: **4** Tora **5** Torah

son: ben

teacher: **5** rabbi

thief: **5** ganef, ganof, gonof **6** gonoph

title: rab **4** abba

unclean: **4** tref

weight: **4** beka, reba

Hebrides island: 4 Mull, Skye **5** Islay

hecatomb: 9 sacrifice, slaughter

heckle: nag **4** bait, gibe **5** chivy, hound, tease **6** badger, hackle, harass, hector, needle **7** torment **8** bullyrag

hectic: 6 fervid **8** exciting, feverish, habitual, restless **11** consumptive **13** constitutional

hector: nag **4** bait **5** bully, harry, worry **6** harass, heckle, plague **7** bluster, dragoon, torment **8** braggart, bludgeon, browbeat, irritate **9** roisterer, swaggerer **10** intimidate

Hector: *companion:* **8** Diomedes

father: **5** Priam

mother: **6** Hecuba

rescuer: **6** Agenor

slayer: **8** Achilles

wife: **10** Andromache

Hecuba: *daughter:* **6** Creusa **8** Polyxena **9** Cassandra

husband: **5** Priam

son: **5** Paris **6** Hector **7** Helenus, Troilus **9** Deiphobus

victim: **11** Polymestor

hedenbergite: 8 pyroxene

hedge: bar, haw, hem **4** boma, cage, coop **5** beard, evade, fence, frith, guard, skulk **6** hinder, hurdle, privet **6** weasel **7** barrier, enclose, protect **8** boundary, obstruct, quickset, separate, sepiment, sidestep, straddle, surround **14** counterbalance

hedgehog: 6 urchin **7** echinus **8** herisson, hurcheon **9** porcupine

hedonic: 8 cyrenaic

hedonist: 4 rake **7** epicure **9** bon vivant **13** pleasure lover

heed: ear **4** care, cark, cure, gaum, hark, hear, mind, note, obey, reck **5** await, watch **6** attend, beware, harken, listen, notice, regard, remark **7** caution, hearken, observe, respect **8** consider **9** attention, diligence **10** cognizance, solicitude **11** observation

heedful: 4 wary **5** alert, chary **6** attent **7** careful, mindful **8** diligent, watchful **9** advertent, attendant, attentive, observant **10** meticulous, respectful **11** considerate

heedless: 4 rash **5** giddy **6** remiss, unwary **7** languid, witless **8** careless, reckless **9** blindfold, forgetful, negligent, oblivious **10** incautious, indiscreet, insouciant, regardless, unthinking **11** hairbrained, inadvertent, inattentive, indifferent lightheaded, thoughtless, unobservant

heehaw: 4 bray **5** laugh **6** giggle, guffaw **10** horselaugh

heel: cad, end, tip **4** calx, cant, knob, lean, list, tilt **5** knave, rogue, slant, talon **6** careen, rascal **7** incline **12** protuberance

bone: **9** calcaneus

heft: 5 heave, hoist, raise **6** strain, weight **8** exertion **9** heaviness, influence **13** ponderousness

hefty: big **5** beefy, burly, heavy, rough **6** rugged **7** massive, weighty **8** powerful, vehement, vigorous

hegemony: 9 authority, dominance, influence 10 leadership

hegira, hejira: 6 exodus, flight 9 migration

heifer: 4 quey 5 stirk 10 colpindach(Sc.)

height: 4 acme, apex, mote 5 crest 6 climax, summit, zenith 7 stature 8 altitude, eminence, pinnacle 9 celsitude, dimension, elevation, procerity, steepness 11 magnanimity
fear of: 10 acrophobia

heighten: 4 lift 5 elate, exalt, raise 6 accent, bolster 7 advance, augment, elevate, enhance 8 increase 9 aggravate, intensify 10 aggrandize

heinous: 6 crying, malign, odious, wicked 7 hateful 8 flagrant, grievous, shocking 9 atrocious, malicious, nefarious 10 abominable, flagitious, outrageous

heir: son 5 heres, scion 7 heritor, legatee 9 firstborn, inheritor, successor 11 beneficiary

heiress: 5 begum 8 heretrix, heritrix

Hejaz city: 5 Mecca

Hel: *dog:* 4 Garm
father: 4 Loki
mother: 9 Angurboda
realm: 7 Niflhel 8 Niflheim

held: See **hold**

Helen of Troy: *abductor:* 5 Paris
brother-in-law: 9 Agamemnon
daughter: 8 Hermione
half-sister: 12 Clytemnestra 13 Clytaemnestra
husband: 8 Menelaus
mother: 4 Leda

heliacal: 5 solar

helical: 6 spiral

helicon: 4 tuba

helicopter: 4 gyro 7 chopper 8 autogiro 9 eggbeater 10 rotor plane, whirlybird

Helios: 6 Apollo
daughter: 5 Circe 8 Heliadae, Heliades
father: 8 Hyperion
son: 8 Phaethon

heliotrope: 10 bloodstone

heliport: 10 landing pad

helix: 4 coil 6 spiral

hell: 5 hades, limbo 6 prison, tophet 7 dungeon, inferno 9 barathrum

hell-bent: 8 reckless 10 determined

hellebore: 5 plant 7 bugbane

Hellen: *father:* 9 Deucalion
mother: 6 Pyrrha
son: 5 Dorus 6 Aeolus, Xuthus

Hellene: See **Greece**

Hellenistic school: 9 Pergamene

Hellespont: 11 Dardanelles
swimmer: 7 Leander

hellgrammite: 6 dobson 8 fish bait, sialidae

hellish: 6 wicked 7 avernal, stygian 8 devilish, diabolic, infernal, plutonic 9 malignant 10 detestable, diabolical

hello: 8 greeting 10 salutation

helm: 5 helve, steer, wheel 6 direct, tiller 8 guidance
position: 4 alee 5 aport

helmet: cap 4 sola, topi 5 armet, galea, topee 6 casque, heaume, morion, salade, sallet 7 basinet 8 schapska 9 casquetel, headpiece
part: 4 bell 5 crest 7 ventail 8 aventail

helmet-shaped: 7 galeate

helmsman: 5 pilot 9 steersman

Heloise's lover: 7 Abelard

helot: 4 serf 5 slave 6 vassal 7 bondman

help: aid, bot, S.O.S., use 4 abet, boot, bote, cure, lift, mend, rede, tide 5 avail, boost, favor, frith, heeze, serve, speed, stead 6 assist, favour, relief, remedy, repair, succor 7 advance, benefit, forbear, forward, further, improve, promote, relieve, support, sustain 8 befriend, champion, facility 9 adminicle, alleviate, forestall 10 assistance, contribute, facilitate, strengthen 11 cooperation

helper: aid 4 ally 5 aider 6 deputy, server 7 abetter, abettor, ancella, servant, striker 8 adjutant, adjutrix, employee, helpmate 9 adjutrice, assistant, samaritan 10 apprentice, benefactor 11 subordinate

helpful: 4 good 6 aidant, useful 8 adjuvant, helpsome, salutary 9 auxiliary 10 beneficial, profitable 11 furthersome, serviceable 12 advantageous, constructive

helpless: 4 numb, weak 6 feeble, futile, unable 7 forlorn 8 impotent, unaiding 9 destitute, powerless 10 bewildered, unsupplied 11 defenseless, incompetent, unprotected 12 irremediable

helpmate: 4 wife 6 helper 8 helpmeet 9 companion

helter-skelter: 6 random 7 flighty, hotfoot, turmoil 8 pellmell 9 hit-or-miss 11 any which way

helve: 4 haft 5 lever 6 handle

Helvetian: 5 Swiss 6 Suisse

hem: 4 edge, seam 5 hedge 6 border, edging, margin, stitch 7 confine, enclose, environ, inclose 8 surround 9 fimbriate

hem in: 5 beset, limit 6 impale 7 enclose, inclose 8 surround

hematite: 7 iron ore 10 bloodstone 12 black diamond

hemeralopia: 6 defect 9 blindness

hemi: 4 half

hemlock: 4 bunk, herb, tree 5 tsuga 6 conium
drinker: 8 Socrates
poison: 6 conium

hemoglobin: 10 sickle cell

hemophiliac: 7 bleeder

hemp: ife, kef, kif, pua, tow 4 bang, carl, flax, harl, jute, rine, sunn 5 abaca, bhang, istle, ramie, sisal, sizal 6 ambary, banana, cabuja, cabuya, fennel, manila 7 hashish 8 cannabis, nepenthe

hen: pea 4 fowl, rail, wife 5 biddy, chuck, woman 6 gorhen, nester, pullet, towdie 7 chicken 9 gallinule
broody: 6 sitter
coop: 5 caire
spayed: 7 poulard
young: 6 pullet

henbane: 10 nightshade

hence: fro 4 away, ergo(L.), thus 5 since 7 hereout, thither 9 therefore 11 accordingly

henceforth: 9 from now on, hereafter

henchman: 4 page 6 gillie, lackey, minion, squire 7 mobster 8 adherent, disciple, follower 9 attendant, supporter

Hengist: *brother:* 5 Horsa
daughter: 6 Rowena
kingdom: 4 Kent
people: 5 Jutes

henna: dye 6 alcana 7 alcanna

henpeck: Uag 4 carp

Henry II: *adversary:* 6 Becket
drama about: 15 The Lion in Winter
surname: 5 Anjou 11 Plantagenet
wife: 7 Eleanor

Henry V: Hal

Henry VIII:
daughter: 4 Mary 9 Elizabeth
first wife: 9 Catherine
second wife: 4 Anne
third wife: 4 Jane
fourth wife: 4 Anne
fifth wife: 9 Catherine
sixth wife: 9 Catherine
son: 6 Edward
surname: 5 Tudor

hepatitis: 8 jaundice

Hephaestus: 6 Vulcan
father: 4 Zeus 7 Jupiter
mother: 4 Hera, Juno
wife: 5 Venus 6 Charis 8 Charites 9 Aphrodite

heptad: seven 11 septivalent

Hera: 4 Juno
husband: 4 Zeus
mother: 4 Rhea
son: 4 Ares

Heracles: See **Hercules**

herald: 4 bode 5 crier, greet, usher 6 beadle, Hermes, signal 7 declare, forerun, trumpet 8 announce, blazoner, foretell, outrider, proclaim 9 harbinger, introduce, messenger, precursor 10 forerunner, foreshadow

heraldry: 6 armory 9 pageantry
band: 4 fess 5 fesse

bastardy mark: 4 bend 5 baton 7 bendlet 8 sinister
bearing: 4 orle
bell: 7 compane 10 campanella
blood-red: 6 murrey
chaplet: 4 orle
charge: vol 7 boterol, saltier, saltire 8 boteroll, tressour, tressure
circle: 6 bezant
cross: 4 paty 5 patee, patte 6 ermine, moline, pattee 7 erminee, patonce, saltier, saltire
device: 4 ente, orle 5 crest 6 altier
fleur-de-lis: lis, lys
gold: or
grafted: 4 ente
green: 4 vert
keylike: 4 urde
knot: 4 Lacy, Wake 5 Bowen, Dacre 7 Heneage 8 Stafford 9 Bourchier 10 Harrington
leg: 4 gamb, jamb 5 gambe, jambe
line: 4 unde
scattered: 4 seme
shield: 10 escutcheon
tincture: or 5 tenne 6 argent
triangle: 5 giron
winged: 4 aile
wreath: 4 orle 5 torse

herb: iva 4 anet, balm, dill, leek, mint, moly, sage, wort 5 anise, basil, chive, plant, sedge, thyme 6 annual, borage, catnip, clover, lovage, sesame, yarrow 7 caraway, oregano, parsley 8 marjoram, tarragon
aromatic: 4 anet, dill, hemp, mint, nard, sage 5 anise, basil, clary, nondo, tansy, thyme 6 catnip, fennel, hyssop 7 chervil, cudweed, mustard, vetiver 8 wormseed 9 basilmint, spearmint 11 everlasting
bitter: rue 4 aloe, woad 7 aletris, boneset 8 centaury 10 turtlehead
bog: 5 calla 9 steepweed, steepwort
climbing: 4 faba 5 vicia
coarse: 5 tansy 6 eringo, eryngo 7 leafcup 8 pokeweed
flowering: 7 anemone, dittane 8 stapelia 9 celandine
genus: iva 4 ruta 5 ajuga, canna, cicer, cruca, galax, gavra, inula, lemna, loasa, rheum 6 aralia, asarum, cassia, dondia, isatis, mentha, nerine 7 alyssum, anemone, cirsium, hedeoma, torenia 8 psoralea 9 grindelia
medicinal: rue 4 aloe 5 senna, sumac, tansy 6 arnica, lovage, tutsan 7 aconite, boneset
mythical: 4 moly
narcotic: 4 hemp
perennial: pia 4 balm, irid 5 sedum 6 fennel, madder, yarrow 7 bugbane, lopweed

8 sainfoin, soapwort **9** digitalis
poisonous: **4** loco **6** conium **7** hemlock, henbane **9** hellebore
salad: **6** endive **7** chicory **10** watercress
shoot: udo
sweet-scented: **8** woodruff
trinity: **8** hepatica
woody: rue
herbage: 5 grass **7** foliage, pasture
herbicide: 10 weed killer
herculean: 4 huge, vast **5** giant **7** immense, mammoth, titanic **8** colossal, enormous, gigantic **10** superhuman
Hercules: 8 Heracles
captive: **4** Iole
companion: **5** Hylas
friend: **6** Iolaus
lion's home: **5** Nemea
mother: **7** Alcmene
stone: **9** loadstone
sweetheart: **4** Iole
victim: **5** Hydra
wife: **4** Hebe **8** Deianira
herd: mob **4** crew, lead, ruck **5** bunch, crowd, drift, drove, flock, group, guard **6** gather, hirsel, pastor, rabble **7** creaght, shelter **8** guardian **9** associate **10** assemblage, congregate **11** aggregation
herdsman: 5 booly **6** booley, cowboy, drover, gaucho, **7** bucolic, vaquero **8** garthman, ranchero(Sp.), wrangler
god: **5** Pales
here: ici(F.), **5** ready **6** hither **7** on earth, present
hereafter: 5 after, later **6** beyond, future
hereditary: 6 inborn, innate, lineal **8** heirship **9** ancestral, descended **10** congenital **11** inheritable, patrimonial
heredity: 4 line **10** inheritance
factor: **4** gene
heresy: 6 schism **7** dissent **9** defection, misbelief **10** infidelity, radicalism **11** unorthodoxy **13** nonconformism
heretic: 6 bugger **7** infidel, Patarin **8** apostate **9** dissenter, miscreant, sectarian **10** schismatic, unbeliever **13** nonconformist
heretofore: 4 erst **6** before **8** erewhile, formerly, hitherto, previous **9** erstwhile
heritage: 6 legacy **9** patrimony, tradition **10** birthright **11** inheritance
heritor: 4 heir **5** donee **9** inheritor
heritrix, heretrix: 7 heiress
herl: fly **4** barb
hermaphrodite: 5 scrat **9** androgyne **10** androgynus
Hermes: 7 Mercury
birthplace: **7** Cyllene
father: **4** Zeus
mother: **4** Maia
son: **7** Evander **9** Autolycus

staff: **8** caduceus
winged cap: **7** petasos, petasus
winged shoes: **7** talaria
hermetic: 6 sealed, secret **8** airtight **9** alchemist, resistant
Hermione: *father:* **8** Menelaus
husband: **7** Orestes **11** Neoptolemus
mother: **5** Helen
hermit: 4 monk **5** clerk, loner **6** anchor **7** ascetic, eremite, incluse, inclusa, recluse, stylite **8** anchoret, beadsman, bedesman, inclusus, marabout **9** anchorite
hut: **4** cell
hermit crab: 8 pagurian
hermitage: 7 ashrama **8** cloister, hideaway **9** monastery, reclusery
hernia: 6 breach **7** rupture **10** protrusion
hero: ace **4** idol **5** darer **6** knight **7** demigod **8** champion **9** conqueror **10** topnotcher **11** protagonist
deified: **7** demigod
legendary: **6** Amadis, Roland **7** Paladin
Hero's lover: 7 Leander
Herodias: *daughter:* **6** Salome
husband: **5** Herod
heroic: 4 bold, epic, huge **5** brave, great, large, noble **6** daring, epical, mighty **7** extreme, gallant, spartan, valiant **8** colossal, enormous, fearless, intrepid, powerful **9** bombastic **10** courageous **11** extravagant, illustrious, magnanimous, outstanding, venturesome **13** grandiloquent
heroin: 4 drug **5** horse, smack **8** narcotic
heroine: 8 lead role **11** demigoddess, leading lady
heroism: 5 valor **6** valour **7** bravery, courage **8** chivalry, nobility **9** fortitude **13** unselfishness
heron: 4 hern, rail, soco **5** crane, egret, herne, quawk, wader **7** bittern, hernser, quabird **8** aigrette, gaulding, heronsew **9** cormorant, herneshaw, heronsewe, heronshaw
genus: **5** ardea
herpes 6 eczema **8** shingles
herring: 4 raun **7** alewife, anchovy **8** scud-dawn
barrel: **4** cade, cran
catch: **4** tack
family: **8** pilchard
female: **4** raun
fry: **4** sile
genus: **6** clupea
head: **4** cob
lake: **5** cisco
young: **4** brit **5** matie, sprat, sprot
Hersey setting: 5 Adano
Hertha: 4 Erda **7** Nerthus
hesitancy: 10 hesitation, indecision, reluctance

hesitant: shy 4 loth 5 chary, loath 6 averse, wobbly 7 halting 8 timorous 9 reluctant

hesitate: 4 wait 5 delay, demur, doubt, pause, stall, waver 6 boggle, falter, loiter, scotch 7 stammer 8 hang back 10 dillydally 12 shilly-shally, wiggle-waggle 13 procrastinate

hesitating: coy 4 hink 7 halting 8 backward, doubtful 9 ambiguous 10 indecisive 11 vacillating

Hesperides: 5 Aegle 6 Hestia 7 Hespera 8 Arethusa, Erytheia, Erytheis

Hesperus: 5 Venus 11 evening star
father: 8 Astraeus
mother: Eos

hessonite: 6 garnet

Hestia: *father:* 6 Cronus
mother: 4 Rhea

hetaera, hetaira: 8 mistress, paramour 9 companion, concubine 12 demimondaine

heterogeneous: 5 mixed 6 motley, unlike 7 diverse 10 dissimilar 13 miscellaneous 14 indiscriminate

Heteroousian: 5 Arian

hetman: 6 ataman 7 Cossack, headman

hew: cut 4 chip, chop, fell, hack 5 carve, wound 6 haggle, strike, stroke

hex: 4 jinx 6 voodoo 7 bewitch

hexad: 6 sextet

hexadecene: 6 cetene

hexastich: 6 sestet, stanza 7 strophe

heyday: joy, May 4 acme 5 prime 6 spring 8 wildness 14 frolicsomeness

Hezekiah: *father:* 4 Ahaz 7 Neariah
kingdom: 5 Judah
mother: Abi
son: 8 Manasseh
wife: 9 Hephzibah

hiatus: gap 5 break, chasm 6 breach, lacuna 7 opening 8 interval 12 interruption

Hiawatha: *author:* 10 Longfellow
grandmother: 7 Nokomis
mother: 7 Wenonah
wife: 9 Minnehaha

Hibernia: 4 Eire, Erin 7 Ireland

hiccup, hiccough: 4 burp 5 spasm 9 singultus

hick: 4 jake, rube 5 yokel 6 hiccup, rustic 7 bumpkin, hayseed 8 cornball

hickey: 6 pimple 7 pustule

hickory: 5 pecan 9 bitternut, shellbark

hidden: 4 lost 5 inner, perdu 6 arcane, buried, cached, closed, covert, innate, latent, masked, occult, secret, veiled 7 arcanum, covered, cryptic, obscure, recluse 8 screened, secluded, secreted 9 concealed, invisible, recondite 10 mysterious 11 clandestine, delitescent, undisclosed 12 subterranean

hide: bar, kip, lie 4 bury, coat, dern, fell, hill, hood, lurk, pelt, skin, stow, veil 5 cache, cloak, cloud, couch, cover, derne(Sc.), skulk 6 huddle, screen, shroud 7 abscond, conceal, cover up, eclipse, leather, secrete, shelter 8 carucate, disguise, ensconce, hoodwink, palliate, suppress, withhold 9 dissemble 10 camouflage, flagellate
cleaning instrument: 6 slater
measured in: 8 hidation
remove hair from: 4 moon
undressed: kip 4 pelt
worker: 6 tanner

hidebound: 6 narrow 7 bigoted, miserly 9 barkbound, bourgeois, illiberal, niggardly 10 restrained 12 conventional

hideous: 4 fell, grim, ugly 5 awful 6 grisly, horrid, odius, ogrish 7 ghastly, ogreish 8 deformed, dreadful, grewsome, gruesome, horrible, shocking, terrible 9 dismaying, frightful, revolting 10 detestable, discordant, terrifying

hideout: den, mew 4 cave, lair 5 cache 7 retreat 8 hideaway

hides: 4 furs 5 skins 6 peltry

hiding: 7 secrecy 8 flogging 9 coverture

hie: 5 haste, hurry, speed 6 betake, hasten, scurry, strive 8 expedite

hiemal: 6 wintry

hierarch: 4 boss, head 5 chief 6 leader, master, satrap, 10 high priest

hieroglyphic: 7 cryptic 9 illegible

hieroglyphics key: 12 Rosetta stone

higgle: 6 haggle 7 bargain, chaffer

high: alt 4 dear, haut(F.), main, much, tall 5 acute, chief, first, lofty, sharp, steep 6 costly, shrill 7 eminent, exalted, haughty, violent 8 elevated, foremost, hopped up, piercing, towering, turned on 9 admirable, expensive, important, principal, turbulent 10 tumultuous, tripped out 11 mountainous

high and dry: 8 marooned

high-and-mighty: 8 arrogant, insolent, superior 9 imperious 11 overbearing

high-brow: 7 egghead 10 doubledome 14 intelligentsia

high-class: 6 classy 10 first-class

high-flying: 7 icarian 11 pretentious

high-handed: 6 lordly 8 arrogant, cavalier, despotic 9 arbitrary 11 dictatorial, domineering, overbearing

high-hat: 4 snub 8 snobbish 12 aristocratic

high-pitched: 6 shrill 7 shrieky, agitated

high-pressure: 8 forceful, pressing 9 insistent 10 aggressive

high-priced: 4 dear 6 costly 9 expensive

high priest: Eli

high-sea: 4 main

high-sounding: 4 arty 7 fustian, pompous **8** imposing **9** bombastic, overblown **10** altisonant

high-spirited: 5 fiery, jolly, merry **6** lively **7** gallant, gingery, peppery **8** cavalier **10** mettlesome

high-strung: 5 tense **7** nervous, uptight **9** excitable

high-toned: 7 stylish **8** elevated **9** dignified **11** fashionable

highborn: 5 noble **8** generous **12** aristocratic

highbred: 7 genteel, refined

higher: 8 superior

highest: top, 5 first **6** upmost **7** extreme, maximal, supreme **8** bunemost, overmost

highest point: 4 acme **6** zenith

Highland war cry: 6 slogan

Highlander (see also **Scotland**): **4** Celt, Gael, Kelt, Scot **6** Tartan **8** clansman **9** Gluneamie
dance: **4** reel **5** fling
language: **4** Erse
pouch: **6** sporan **7** sporran
weapon: **8** claymore, skeandhu

high-rise: 4 tall **5** lofty **10** multistory

highroad: 7 highway

highway: way 4 bahn(G.), iter(L.), path, pike, road **5** Alcan **6** Appian, artery, causey, course, rumpad, street **7** Lincoln **8** autobahn, causeway, chaussee(F.), highroad, turnpike **9** boulevard **12** thoroughfare

highwayman: pad 5 rider, thief **6** bandit, padder, robber, **7** brigand, footpad, ladrone **8** hightoby **9** bandolero

Highwayman: *author:* **5** Noyes

hijack: rob 6 coerce

hike: 4 jerk, toss, walk **5** march, raise, throw, tramp **6** ramble

hilarious: mad 5 funny, merry, noisy **6** jovial **7** jocular **8** mirthful **9** ludicrous

hilarity: gig, joy 4 glee **5** cheer, mirth **6** gaiety **7** jollity, whoopee **9** happiness, joviality, laughter, merriment **10** joyousness **12** cheerfulness, exhilaration

hill: ben, hoe, kop, pap, tor 4 bank, brae, bult, dagh, dune, fell, heap, hide, knap, knob, loma, mesa, pile **5** bargh, butte, cerro(Sp.), cliff, cover, hurst, morro, mound, mount **6** ascent, barrow, copple, djebel **7** colline, picacho **9** acclivity, elevation, monadnock
D.C.: **7** Capitol
glacial: **4** kame, paha **7** drumlin
Jerusalem: **6** Olivet
range: **5** ridge
sand: **4** dene, dune
top of: tor **4** peak **6** summit

hillbilly: 4 rube **5** yokel **6** rustic **7** bumpkin **12** backwoodsman

hillock: 4 tump **5** croft, hurst, knoll, kop-

je, mound, toman(Sc.) **6** coppet **7** hummock **8** molehill
over grave: **7** tumulus

hillside: 4 brae, cote **5** cleve, cliff, falda(Sp.), slade, slope **6** cleeve

hilly: 5 steep

hilt: 6 handle **8** handgrip

hilum: 4 scar **5** porta **7** nucleus

Himalaya: *animal, bear-like:* **5** panda
antelope: **5** goral, serow
bear: **5** bhalu
bearcat: **5** panda
cedar: **6** deodar
cypress: **6** bhutan
dweller: **8** Nepalese
goat: **4** kras, tahr, tair, thar
oxen: yak
peak: Api **7** Everest
pheasant: **5** monal
sheep: **6** bharal, nahoor
swamp: **5** Terai
tableland: **5** Tibet

Himavat's daughter: 4 Devi

himene, himine: 4 hymn, song

himself: 4 ipse(L.)

Himyarite: 4 Arab **7** Axumite, Sabaean

Hinayana Buddhism: 5 shojo **6** lesser

hind: doe, lad, roe 4 back, chap, stag **5** coney **6** fellow, rustic, worker **7** bailiff, peasant, servant, steward, venison **8** cabrilla, domestic **9** posterior **11** hindquarter

hinder: bar, let 4 slow **5** after, block, cheat, check, choke, cramp, debar, delay, deter, embar, estop, hedge **6** arrest, detain, hamper, harass, impede, impend, injure, retard, scotch **7** bog down, deprive, forelay, impeach, inhibit, prevent **8** encumber, handicap, obstruct, preclude, prohibit **9** embarrass, foreclose, forestall, frustrate, hamstring, interrupt, posterior

hindmost: 4 last, rear **9** aftermost

hindrance: bar, rub 4 clog, curb, snag, stop **5** block, check, delay, hitch **6** arrest **7** barrier **8** drawback, obstacle **9** detention, deterrent, restraint **10** difficulty impediment **11** encumbrance, impeachment, obstruction **12** interruption

Hindu (see also **Indian**): **4** Babu, Koli, Sikh **5** Tamil **6** Gentoo, Hindoo **8** Kolarian
abode of gods: **4** Meru
adherent: Sik **4** Jain, Seik, Sikh **5** Jaina, Seikh
age of world: **4** yuga
alphabet: **6** Sarada
ancestral race: **5** Aryan
apartment: **5** mahal
Aryan race: **4** Swat
ascetic: **4** jogi, sadh, yati, yogi **5** sadhu

atheist: **7** nastika
book: **4** Veda **6** Tantra **11** Yajna-valkya
calendar: Pus **4** Jeth, Asin, Kaur, Magh **5** Asarh, Sawan, Katik, Aghan, Chait **6** Bhadon, Kartik, Phagun **7** Baisakh, Sarawan, Phalgun
call to prayer: **4** azan
caste: Dom, Mal, Meo **4** Dasi, Gola, Koli, Kori, Mali, Pasi, Teli **5** Goala, Palli, Sudra **6** Babhan, Soodra **7** Brahman
caste member: Jat **4** Jain **6** Banian, Banyan, Rajput, Vaisya **7** Rajpoot **9** Kshatriya, Vakkaliga
charm: **6** mantra
chief: mir **6** sirdar
coin: ana, pai, pie **4** anna, pice **5** paisa, rupee
congregation: **5** samaj, somaj
convert to Islam: **6** shaikh
cremation: **4** sati **6** suttee
dancer: **8** devadasi
deity: Dev **4** Deva, Dewa, Maya, Rama, Yama **6** Ganesa, Varuna, Vishnu **7** Ganesha, Krishna **9** Jagannath **10** Jagannatha, Juggernaut **11** Ramachandra
demon: **4** Bali, Bhut, Ketu, Rahu **5** Asura **6** Daitya
devotee: **4** yati
disciple: **4** sikh
divine being: dev **4** deva
doctrine: **5** Karma **6** dharma
drink: **4** soma
duty: **6** dharma
ejaculation: om, um
essence: **4** rasa, rata **5** atman **6** amrita
family: **5** gotra
female energy: **5** Sakti **6** Shakti
festival: **4** Holi, mela **6** Dewali, Hoolee **7** Dashara
flute: bin **5** pungi
garment: **4** sari **5** saree
gentleman: **4** babu **5** baboo, sahib
god (see also *deity* above)*:* **4** Agni, Deva, Kama, Siva, Vayu, Yama **5** Asura, Shiva, Simia **6** Brahma, Ganesa, Skanda, Varuna **7** Ganesha
goddess: Sri, Uma, Vac **4** Devi, Kali, Shri, Vach **5** Durga, Gauri, Sakti, Shree, Ushas **6** Chandi, Shakti **7** Parvati **9** Haimavati
guitar: **5** sitar
headdress: **5** rumal
heaven: **5** dyaus
hermitage: **7** ashrama
hero: **4** Nala, Rama
holy book: **4** Veda **6** Sastra
holy sage: **5** rishi
hymn: **6** mantra
idol worship: **5** arati
incarnation: **6** avatar
Indra: **5** Sakka, Sakra
king: **4** Nala **5** Sesha **6** Shesha

lady: **4** devi, rani **5** ranee
language: **4** Pali, Urdu **5** Hindi, Tamil **8** Sanskrit **10** Hindustani
lawgiver: **4** Manu
leader: **5** Nehru **6** Ghandi, sirdar
life principle: **4** jiva **5** atman, prana
literature: **4** Veda **5** sruti **6** shruti
loincloth: **5** dhoti
magic: **4** jadu, maya **5** jadoo
magician: **5** fakir **6** fakeer
mantra: om, um
master: **5** sahib
mendicant: **4** naga **7** bairagi, vairagi **8** sannyasi
mental discipline: **4** yoga
monastery: **4** math
monkey god: **7** Hanuman
month: see *calendar* above
mother goddess: **6** matris
mystic: **4** yogi
noble: **5** rajah **8** maharaja
non-violence: **6** ahimsa
offering: **4** bali, lepa **5** pinda
paradise: **7** Nirvana
patriarch: **5** pitri
philosophy: **4** yoga **5** tamas
poem: **8** Ramayana **11** Mahabharata **12** Bhagavad-Gita
poet: **6** Tagore
policeman: **5** sepoy
prayer rug: **4** asan **5** asana
priest: **5** hotar
prince: **4** raja, rana **5** rajah **8** maharaja **9** maharajah
princess: **4** rani **5** ranee
pundit: **5** swami
queen: **4** rani **5** ranee **8** maharani **9** maharanee
religion: **5** Prana **7** Jainism, Sivaism **8** Shivaism
rice: **4** boro
rite: **4** puja **5** achar, pooja
ruler: **5** rajah
scripture: Li; rig **4** Veda **5** Sruti **6** Purana, Sastra, Smriti, Tantra **7** Shastra
sect: **4** Sikh, siva **6** Aghori
social division: **5** caste, varna
soldier: **4** Sikh **5** sepoy
soul: **4** atma **5** atman
spirit: **4** Jiva, Mara **5** Asura, Atman, Prana **7** Muktama
supreme being: **6** Vishnu
teacher: pir **4** guru
temple: **4** deul **6** vimana
term of respect: **5** sahib
title: aya, sri **4** mian, raja, shri, sidi **5** rajah, sahib, shree, swami **7** bahadur
tower: **5** stupa
triad god: **4** Siva
tunic: **4** jama **5** jamah
unknown god: Ka
unorthodox: **4** Jain **5** Jaina

Upanishad: 4 Isha, Veda 7 Vedanta
worship: 4 puja 5 pooja
Hindustan: Ind
language: 4 Urdu 5 Hindi
tribesman: 4 toda
hinge: har 4 butt, hang, turn 5 gemel, joint, mount, pivot, stand 6 depend gimmer, gimmor, hingle, lamina, pintle
Hinnom Valley: 7 Gehenna
hint: cue, tip 4 clew, clue, time, turn 5 cheep(Sc.), imply, infer, trace 6 allude, moment 7 inkling, mention, suggest 8 allusion, innuendo, intimate, occasion 9 catchword, insinuate 10 indication, intimation, suggestion 11 insinuation
hip: hop 4 coxa, huck, limp, miss, skip 6 haunch, huckle
pert. to: 7 sciatic
hip boots: 6 waders
hipbone: 5 ileum, ilium
hippie: mod 5 rebel 6 copout 8 bohemian, longhair
Hippocrates: *birthplace:* kos
drug: 5 mecon, opium
hippodrome: 5 arena 6 circus 7 contest
Hippolytus: 9 Greek hero
father: 7 Theseus
mother: 7 Antiope 9 Hippolyne
stepmother: 7 Phaedra
hippopotamus: 6 seacow 8 behemoth 9 pachyderm
hire: buy, fee, let, use 4 rent, sign, wage 5 bribe, lease, put on, price, wages 6 employ, engage, retain, reward, salary 7 charter, conduce, recruit, stipend 9 allowance 12 compensation
hireling: 4 esne, grub, hack, serf 5 slave 8 gangster 9 mercenary
hirsute: 5 hairy, rough 6 coarse, shaggy 7 pileous
hispid: 5 rough, spiny 7 bristly 8 strigose, strigous
hiss: boo 4 hish, sizz, whiz 5 whizz 6 fissle, fistle 8 goose cry, pooh-pooh 9 raspberry 10 assibilate
hissing: 6 fizzle 8 sibilant 9 sibilance
hist: 4 hark, hush 7 be quiet
historian: 8 annalist 9 chronicler
history: 4 tale 5 drama, story 6 annals, memoir, record 7 account 8 relation 9 biography, chronicle, genealogy, narrative
muse: 4 Clio
histrio: 5 actor
histrionics: 6 acting 9 dramatics 11 theatricals 13 theatricality
hit: bat, lam, lob, ram, rap, tap 4 bump, bunt, cast, club, slog, slug, sock, swat, wham 5 clout, flick, knock, smack, smite, smote, throw, touch 6 attain, batted, bingle, strike 7 collide, success 8 bludgeon 10 production, succession
baseball: 4 bunt 5 homer, liner 6 double,

single, triple 7 home run 8 grounder 9 line drive
golf: 5 drive, shank, slice
hit-or-miss: 6 casual, chance, habnab, random 7 aimless 8 careless 9 haphazard
hitch: hop, tie, tug 4 halt, hook, join, knot, limp, pull 5 agree, catch, crick, hotch, marry, thumb, unite 6 attach, enlist, hobble 8 obstacle, stoppage 9 harmonize, hindrance 10 enlistment, impediment 11 contretemps, obstruction
hither: 4 here 6 nearer 11 to this place
hitherto: ago, yet 5 as yet 6 before 7 thus far
Hitler: aerie: 13 Berchtesgaden
chosen race: 5 Aryan
follower: 4 Nazi
hitter: 6 batter 7 batsman, slugger
Hittite: *ancestor:* 4 Heth
capital: 6 Pteria
storm god: 6 Teshub, Teshup
hive: 5 store, swarm 6 apiary 7 store up 9 multitude
hives: 5 uredo 7 allergy 9 urticaria
hoagie, hoagy: 4 hero 9 submarine 13 large sandwich
hoar: 4 cold, gray, rime 5 frost, hoary, musty, stale 6 biting 7 ancient 9 antiquity, venerable 13 venerableness
hoard: 4 save 5 amass, chest, hutch, lay up, stash, stock, store 6 supply 7 husband, reserve 8 quantity, treasure, treasury 10 accumulate, collection
hoarder: 5 miser 6 storer 9 treasurer
hoarfrost: rag 4 rime, rind 9 cranreuch(Sc.)
hoarse: dry, raw 5 gruff, harsh, rocky, rough 7 grating, raucous 10 discordant
hoarseness: 4 frog 5 croup
hoary: old 4 aged, gray, hoar 5 moldy, mossy, musty 7 ancient, hoarish, whitish 9 canescent, venerable
hoax: bam, cod, fun, gyp, hex, kid 4 bilk, dupe, fake, gaff, gegg, gunk, joke, ruse, sell, sham 5 bluff, cheat, spoof, trick 6 canard, diddle, humbug, string 7 deceive 8 artifice 9 bamboozle, deception 11 hornswoggle
hob: elf, peg, pin, tap 4 game, mark, nail, nave 5 clown, fairy, ledge 6 ferret, rustic, sprite 7 mandrel 8 mischief 10 countryman, projection
hobble: tie 4 clog, clop, gimp, limp 5 bunch, cramp, hitch, leash 6 fetter, hamper, hog-tie 7 cramble, perplex, shackle, spancel 9 embarrass 10 difficulty, perplexity 13 embarrassment
hobbledehoy: lad 5 youth
hobbler: 5 pilot 7 boatman, hoveler, laborer 8 retainer 12 longshoreman
hobby: fad 5 horse 6 falcon 7 pastime 9 avocation, diversion

hobgoblin: bug, elf, hag, imp **4** bogy, Puck **5** bogey, bogie, bugan, poker, spook **6** boodie(Sc.), sprite **7** bugaboo **8** bogglebo, worricow(Sc.) **9** coltpixie **10** apparition

hobo: boe, bum **5** tramp **7** drifter, floater, vagrant **8** vagabond

hock: ham, hox **4** pawn **5** ankle, hough, thigh **6** mallow, pledge **8** mortgage **9** hamstring **10** houghsinew

hocket: **6** hiccup **8** obstacle **12** interruption

hockey: **5** bandy **6** shinny
arena: **4** rink
cup: **7** Stanley
disk: **4** puck
goal: net
official: **7** referee **8** linesman
players: Orr (Bobby) **4** Hull (Bobby) **5** Bucyk (John) **6** Mikita (Stan), Parent (Bernie) **7** Ratelle (Jean) **8** Beliveau (Jean), Esposito (Phil) (Tony) **9** Mahovlich (Frank) **10** Delvecchio (Alex)
pro teams (NHL): **4** Jets (Winnipeg) **5** Blues (St. Louis), Kings (Los Angeles) **6** Bruins (Boston), Devils (New Jersey), Flames (Calgary), Flyers (Philadelphia), Oilers (Edmonton), Sabres (Buffalo) **7** Canucks (Vancouver), Rangers (New York), Rockies (Colorado), Whalers (Hartford) **8** Capitals (Washington), Penguins (Pittsburgh), Red Wings (Detroit) **9** Canadiens (Montreal), Islanders (New York), Nordiques (Quebec) **10** Black Hawks (Chicago), Maple Leafs (Toronto), North Stars (Minnesota)
positions: **4** wing **6** center, goalie **7** forward **10** defenseman, goaltender
stick: **6** burley **7** cammock(Sc.)
terms: **7** face-off **8** blue line, empty net **9** backcheck, bodycheck, forecheck, power play **10** center line, penalty box **11** shorthanded **12** box formation **14** penalty killing

hocus: **4** drug **5** cheat, fraud **7** deceive **8** cheating, deceiver, trickery **10** adulterate

hocus-pocus: **5** cheat, trick **6** humbug **7** juggler **8** flimflam, quackery **9** trickster **12** charlatanism

hod: **4** soil, tray **6** barrow **7** scuttle **11** coal scuttle

hodgepodge: ana **4** mess, olio, stew **5** cento **6** medley **7** mixture **8** mishmash **10** hotchpotch, miscellany **11** gallimaufry, olla podrida **12** mingle-mangle

hoe: dig **4** brod, hill, till **5** clean, cliff, paddle, worry **6** sarcle, scrape **7** dogfish, trouble **8** griffaun **9** cultivate **10** promontory

hog (see also **pig**): sow **4** bene, boar, dime, galt, gilt **5** shoat, shote, swine **6** barrow

7 glutton, hogling **8** shilling **9** boschvark **10** backfatter
breed: **5** Essex **9** Hampshire
food: **4** mash **5** slops, swill **6** acorns
genus: sus
young: pig **5** shoat

hog peanut: **8** earthpea

hog plum: **4** amra

hog side: **6** flitch

hog thigh: ham

hogfish: **8** scorpene

hoggish: **5** hoggy **7** selfish, swinish **10** gluttonous

hognut: **5** ouabe **6** pignut **8** earthnut

hogshead: **4** cask **6** barrel, hogget, vessel

hogtie: **4** clog, curb **5** leash **6** fetter, hamper

hogwash: **4** slop **5** draff, swill **7** pigwash

hoi polloi: mob **6** masses, rabble **8** populace, riffraff

hoist: cat, gin **4** jack, lift **5** boost, crane, davit, heave, heeze, horse, lewis, raise, setup, winch **7** derrick, elevate **8** elevator, windlass

hoist sail: **4** swig

hoity-toity: **5** dizzy, giddy, proud **6** snooty **7** flighty, haughty, pompous **8** arrogant **11** harum-scarum, patronizing, thoughtless **13** irresponsible

hokum: **4** blaa, blah, bunk **11** foolishness

hold: own **4** bind, bite, bulk, clip, fill, have, hook, keep, rely, seat, stow, tend **5** avast, carry, catch, grasp, guard, rivet **6** adhere, arrest, behold, cleave, clench, clutch, decree, defend, detain, harbor, occupy, retain **7** adjudge, contain, control, support, sustain **8** consider, interest, maintain, thurrock **9** entertain, mesmerize, spellbind **10** possession, stronghold **11** catch hold of

hold a brief for: **6** defend **8** advocate

hold back: dam **4** curb, stem, stop **5** check, deter **6** detain, retard **7** inhibit, repress **8** restrain **9** hindrance

hold fast: hug **4** hook, nail **5** cling, stick **6** clinch, cohere

hold forth: **5** offer **7** exhibit **8** continue, maintain, propound

hold in custody: **4** jail **6** detain, intern

hold off: **5** avert **7** refrain

hold on: **4** stop, wait **7** forbear **8** continue

hold out: **4** last **6** endure **7** exclude, protend **8** continue

hold up: rob **4** halt, lift, rein **5** boost, check, delay, raise **7** display, exhibit, robbery, support, sustain **8** stoppage **10** overcharge

hold water: **5** sound **10** consistent

holder: **5** haver **6** tenant **9** container **10** receptacle

holding: **4** land **5** asset **6** estate, tenure **8** property
adapted for: **10** prehensile

hole: bay, den, gap, pit **4** bore, cave, cove, deep, dump, flaw, gate, gulf, inlet, leak, mine, nook, peck, rent, vent **5** abyss, chasm, shaft **6** burrow, cavern, cavity, cranny, crater, defect, eyelet, grotto, hollow, pierce, prison, recess **7** dungeon, mortise, opening, orifice, ostiole **8** aperture, bunghole, peephole **9** perforate **10** excavation **11** perforation, predicament
instrument for making: awl **4** bore **5** drill **8** stiletto
wall: **4** muse **5** meuse, niche
Holi, Hoolee: 8 festival
holia: **4** fish **6** salmon
holiday: **4** fete **5** feria, festa, merry **6** fiesta, jovial, outing **7** festive, playday **8** festival, vacation **9** convivial, Mardi Gras
holiness: **5** piety **7** halidom **8** divinity, halidome, sanctity **9** sanctuary **11** saintliness **12** consecration **13** righteousness
Holland: see **Netherlands**
holler: **4** yell **5** shout **6** shriek **7** protest
hollow: den, dip **4** boss, cave, cove, deep, dent, doke, glen, hole, holl, howe, huck, lean, thin, vain, void **5** bight, chase, cuppy, empty, false, gaunt, goyal, goyle, heugh, scoop, sinus, stria **6** cavern, cavity, cirque, groove, hungry, socket, sunken, vacant, valley **7** concave, muffled, unsound **8** alveolus, fossette, not solid, specious **9** cavernous, deceitful, deeply set, depressed, faithless, worthless **10** depression, sepulchral **11** treacherous **12** unsatisfying
out: cut, dig **4** bore **6** excise
hollow-eyed: **7** haggard
hollowed: **7** concave, glenoid, spouted
hollowed out: **6** cavate
hollowness: **6** vanity **7** vacuity
holly: **4** assi, holm, ilex **5** shrub, yapon, yupon **6** hulver, yaupon, youpon
pert to: **6** ilicic
holm oak: **4** ilex **5** holly
Holmes' word: **10** elementary
holobaptist: **12** immersionist
holocaust: **7** inferno **9** sacrifice **11** destruction
holster: **4** case **7** housing **8** scabbard **10** pistol case
holt: den **4** grip, hill, hold, lair, wood **5** copse, grasp **7** retreat **10** wooded hill
holy: **5** pious, sacre(F.), saint, santo **6** devout, divine, hallow, sacred **7** blessed, perfect, sainted, saintly, sinless **8** blissful, hallowed **9** inviolate, sanctuary, spiritual **10** sacrosanct **11** consecrated **13** sanctimonious
Holy City: **4** Kiev, Rome, Zion **5** Mecca, Lhasa, Medina, Moscow **7** Benares **9** Allahabad, Jerusalem
Holy Grail: **8** Sangraal, Sangreal
castle: **9** Monsalvat
knight: **7** Galahad
Holy Joe: **9** clergyman
Holy Land: **9** Palestine
pilgrim: **6** palmer
holy oil: **6** chrism
Holy One: God **6** Christ **7** Jehovah **8** Mohammed **12** Supreme Being
Holy Roman emperor: **4** Otho, Otto
Holy Rood: **5** cross **8** crucifix
holy statue: **4** icon, ikon **5** ikono
holy water: *font:* **5** paten
receptacle: **5** stoup
sprinkler: **11** aspergillum
homage: **5** honor **6** eulogy, fealty, regard **7** loyalty, manrent, ovation, respect **9** adoration, deference, obeisance, reverence **10** allegiance
homager: **6** tenant, vassal
homaloidal: **4** even, flat
hombre: guy, man **6** fellow
homburg: hat **4** felt
home: den **4** nest **5** abode, being, domus, house **6** asylum, estate, maison(F.), **7** habitat, hospice, village **8** domestic, domicile, dwelling **9** homestead, orphanage, residence **10** habitation **11** hearthstone
at: **4** chez(F.)
country: **7** cottage **8** bungalow
wheeled: **7** trailer
home base: den **5** plate
homeborn: **6** native **10** indigenous
homelike: **4** cozy **5** homey **6** homely, homish **8** cheerful, friendly, homesome **11** comfortable
homely: **4** rude, ugly **5** plain **6** hameil, hamelt, hamilt, kindly, simple **7** plainly **8** domestic, familiar, friendly, homelike, intimate **9** unsightly **10** intimately **12** unpretending **13** unpretentious
homemade: **5** plain **6** simple **8** domestic
Homer: *birthplace:* **5** Chios
character: **4** Ajax **6** Nestor **8** Achilles, Odysseus
poem: **5** Iliad **7** Odyssey
Homeric: **4** epic **6** epical
homesickness: **9** nostalgia
homespun: **4** kelt(Sc.), rude **5** plain **6** coarse, folksy **13** unpretentious
homestead: **4** toft, tref(W.) **7** onstead
homicide: **6** murder
homilist: **8** preacher
homily: **5** adage **6** sermon **8** assembly **9** communion, discourse **11** exhortation
hominy: **4** bran, corn, samp **5** grits
Homo sapiens: man
homogeneous: **4** like **5** equal, solid **6** entire **7** similar **10** comparable, compatible, consistent

homologous: 9 identical
homonym: 8 namesake 10 soundalike
homunculus: 5 dwarf 7 manikin
honcho: 4 boss 6 leader 8 in charge
Honduras: *capital:* 11 Tegucigalpa
  city: 7 Gracias, La Ceiba 8 Yuscaran 9 Choluteca, Comayagua, Juticalpa, Santa Rosa 12 San Pedro Sula
  department: 4 Yoro 5 Colon, Copan, La Paz, Valle 6 Cortes 7 Lempira, Olancho 8 Intibuca 9 Atlantida, El Paraiso 10 Ocotepeque
  Indian: 4 Maya, Ulua, Ulva 5 Lenca
  island: 5 Utila 6 Rostan 7 Guanaja
  island group: 5 Bahia
  lake: 5 Yojoa
  measure: 4 vara 5 milla 6 mecate, tercia 7 cajuela, manzana 10 caballeria
  monetary unit: 7 centavo, lempira
  river: 4 Coco, Sico, Ulua 5 Aguan 6 Patuca 9 Choluteca 10 Chamelecon
  weight: 4 caja
hone: 4 long, pine, whet 5 delay, dress, strop 6 lament 7 grumble, sharpen 8 oilstone 9 whetstone
honest: 4 fair, full, just open, pure 5 frank, roman 6 candid, chaste, decent, dexter, dinkum, proper, rustic, square 7 genuine, sincere, upright 8 bonafide, faithful, rightful, reliable, straight, suitable, truthful, upright, virtuous 9 equitable, guileless, honorable, ingenuous, veracious 10 creditable, forthright 11 trustworthy 13 conscientious, dispassionate, incorruptible, unadulterated 15 straightforward
honestly: 5 truly 6 dinkum, justly 8 directly 9 telltruth
honesty: 5 honor 6 equity 7 decency, justice, probity 8 fairness, fidelity, veracity 9 constancy, integrity 10 generosity, liberality 11 uprightness 12 incorruption, suitableness, truthfulness 13 honorableness 15 trustworthiness 19 straightforwardness
honesty plant: 8 moonwort
honey: mel 4 dear, niel(F.) 5 sweet 6 nectar 7 darling, flatter 8 precious
  fermented drink: 4 mead
  source: bee 6 nectar
honey badger: 5 ratel
honey bear: 8 kinkajou
honey buzzard: 4 hawk, pern
honey eater: iao 6 manuao
honeybee: 7 deseret 8 angelito
  disease: 8 sacbrood
honeyberry: 4 tree 5 genep, genip
honeycomb cell: 7 alveola 8 alveolus
honeycombed: 6 favose, pitted 8 alveolar
honeydew: 5 melon 6 mildew, orange
honeyed: 5 sweet 6 sugary 7 candied 11 mellifluous 10 flattering

honeysuckle: 6 azalea, widbin 9 columbine
Hong Kong: *bay:* 4 Mirs 5 Sheko 7 Repulse
  capital: 8 Victoria
  coin: 4 cent 6 dollar 13 British dollar 14 Hong Kong dollar
  peak: 8 Victoria
  peninsula: 7 Kowloon
honor: 4 fame, fete, prow 5 adore, award, exalt, glory, grace, izzat 6 credit, decore, esteem, homage, laurel, praise, regard, repute, revere 7 dignify, dignity, emblaze, ennoble, glorify, honesty, respect, worship 8 accolade 9 celebrate, deference, obeisance, reverence 10 estimation, reputation
  pledge: 6 parole
honorable: 4 dear 5 moral, noble, white 6 gentle, honest 7 upright 8 generous, honorary, sterling 9 dearworth, estimable, reputable 10 creditable 11 commendable, illustrious, magnanimous, meritorious, respectable
honorarium: fee, tip 6 reward, salary 7 douceur, payment 8 gratuity
Honshu: *bay:* Ise
  port: 4 Kobe
hood: cap 4 coif, cowl, hide, thug 5 amice, blind 6 biggin, bonnet, burlet, camail, canopy, chapel, tippet 7 calotte, capuche, surtout 8 capsheaf, caputium, chaperon, covering
  academic: 8 liripipe, liripoop
  monk's: 4 atis, cowl 5 atees
  saddle: 8 tapadera, tapadero
  vehicle: 6 bonnet, capote
hooded: 9 cucullate 10 capistrate
hoodlum: yap 5 rowdy 6 goonda 8 hooligan
hoodoo: 4 jinx 5 Jonah 6 voodoo 7 bewitch, bad luck, unlucky
hoodwink: 4 dupe, fool, hide, wile 5 blear, blind, bluff, cheat, cosen, cover, cozen 6 befool, delude 7 blinder, blinker, deceive, mislead 9 blindfold
hooey: 4 bunk 6 bunkum 7 baloney, boloney, bushwah 8 buncombe, nonsense
hoof: 4 clee, foot, walk 5 cloof, cloot, cluif, dance, tramp 6 ungula
hoofer: 6 dancer, walker
hook: 4 barb, gaff, gore hake, hock, hold, huck, trap 5 catch, cleek, hamus, hitch, larin, seize, snare, steal 6 agrafe, anchor, larree, pilfer, tenter 7 agraffe, capture, grunter, hamulus, hitcher 8 crotchet 10 chatelaine
hooka, hookah: 4 pipe 7 nargile 8 narghile 9 narghileh
hooked: 6 hamate 7 hamular, uncinal 8 addicted, ankyroid, aquiline, uncinate
hooker: 10 prostitute

hooky player: 6 truant
hooligan: 6 loafer 7 hoodlum, ruffian
hoop: 4 bail, band, ring, tire 5 clasp, garth, girth, shout 6 circle, frette 7 circlet, trundle 8 encircle, surround 10 finger ring
hoopskirt: 9 crinoline
hoosegow: jug 4 jail 6 lockup, prison 10 guardhouse
Hoosier State: 7 Indiana
hoot: boo 4 jeer, whoo 5 shout, whoop 6 boohoo 7 ululate
hootch, hooch: 5 house 8 barracks, dwelling 10 thatched hut
Hoover Dam lake: 4 Mead
hop: fly, hip 4 dope, halt, jump, leap, limp, skip 5 bound, dance, hitch 6 flight, gambol, spring 8 jump over 11 supercharge
hop kiln: 4 oast
hop-o'-my-thumb: 5 dwarf, fairy 6 midget
hopbush: 6 akeake
hope: 4 deem, spes(L.), want, wish 5 haven, trust 6 aspire, desire, expect, morale 7 cherish, confide 8 prospect, reliance 9 esperance 10 aspiration 11 expectation 12 anticipation
goddess of: 4 Spes
lack of: 7 despair
symbol of: 4 opal
hopeful: 8 sanguine 9 confident, expectant 10 optimistic
hopeless: 4 gone, vain 6 futile 7 forlorn, useless 8 downcast 9 desperate, heartless, incurable 10 despairing, despondent, desponding, remediless 11 ineffectual 12 disconsolate, irremediable 13 irrecoverable, irretrievable
hophead: 6 addict
Hophni: *brother:* 8 Phinehas
father: Eli
Hopi Indian: 4 Moki 5 Moqui
god: 7 Kachina, Katcina 8 Katchina
prayer stick: 4 paho
hoplite: 7 soldier
hopped up: 4 high 6 stoned, zonked 7 drugged
hopper: box 4 tank 5 chute 6 dancer, leaper 10 freight car, receptacle
hopple: See **hobble**
hopscotch: 7 pallall
stone: 5 potsy 6 peever
Horae: 4 Dike 6 Eirene 7 Euromia
horde: 4 army, camp, clan, pack 5 crowd, group, swarm 6 legion, throng 9 multitude
horehound: 4 mint 6 henbit
Horite chief: 4 Seir
horizon: rim 4 edge, goal 8 prospect
horizontal: 4 flat 5 level
hormigo: 5 quira 7 ant tree

hormone: 8 autacoid 13 cell secretion
female: 8 estrogen
male: 8 androgen
horn: 4 scur, tuba 5 brass, bugle, cornu, drone, siren 6 antler, cornet, rhyton 7 antenna, trumpet 8 oliphant 9 alpenhorn 10 cornucopia
blast: 4 mort, toot 7 fanfare, tantara 9 tantarara
crescent moon: 4 cusp
deer: 4 tine 5 prong 6 antler
drinking: 6 rhyton
Hebrew: 6 shofar 7 shophar
player: 6 bugler 9 cornetist, trumpeter
without: 5 doddy 6 doddie, polled 7 acerous
hornbill: 4 bird, tock 6 homrai
genus of: 7 buceros
hornet: 4 wasp
hornpipe: 4 tune 5 dance 8 matelote
hornswoggle: 4 hoax 5 trick 7 swindle 9 bamboozle
horny: 4 hard 8 ceratoid 9 calloused, toughened 10 semiopaque 15 sexually aroused
hornyhead: 4 chub
horologe: 4 dial 5 clock, watch 9 hourglass, timepiece
horoscope: 4 dial 7 diagram
horrendous: 7 fearful 8 horrible 9 frightful
horrible: 4 dire, grim, ugly 5 great 6 grisly, horrid 7 fearful, ghastly, hideous, horrent, very bad 8 dreadful, gruesome, horrific, shocking, terrible 9 atrocius, excessive, frightful, horrified, nefarious 10 horrendous, tremendous, unpleasant
horrid: 4 grim, ugly 5 awful, rough, shaggy 6 rugged 7 hideous 8 dreadful, grewsome, gruesome, horrible, shocking, terrible 9 bristling, frightful, obnoxious, offensive, revolting 10 detestable, terrifying, unpleasant 13 objectionable
horrific: 5 awful 7 fearful 8 horrible 9 frightful 10 formidable
horrified: 6 aghast 7 ghastly
horrify: 5 shock 6 appall, dismay
horrifying: 8 horrific 9 execrable
horror: 4 fear 5 dread 6 terror 8 aversion 10 abhorrence, repugnance, shuddering 11 abomination, detestation 13 consternation
hors d'oeuvre: 6 canape, relish 7 zakuska 8 aperitif 9 antipasto, appetizer
Horsa's brother: 7 Hengist
horse: gee, nag, pad 4 barb, mare, plug, prad 5 brock, caple, capul, draft, filly, hobby, hoist, mount, pacer, raise, shier, steed, waler 6 cheval, equine, geegee, ladino, pelter, rouncy 7 caballo(Sp.), cavallo(Sp.), cavalry, charger, clipper, courser, hackney, mustang, saddler,

sheltie, sleeper, stepper, trestle **8** bat-
horse, cartaver(Sc.), footrope, jackstay
10 breastband
Achilles': **7** Xanthus
ankle: **4** hock
breastplate: **7** peytrel, poitrel
breed: **4** Arab, Barb **5** Shire **6** hunter,
Morgan **7** Belgian, harness, Suffolk,
trotter **8** Galloway, Normandy, Shetland **9** Percheron **10** Clydesdale
brown: bay **6** sorrel **8** chestnut
buyer: **5** coper **6** trader **7** knacker
calico: **5** pinto
color: bay **4** pied, roan **5** pinto **6** calico,
sorrel **8** chestnut, palomino, schimmel
command: gee, haw, hup **4** whoa **6** giddap
covering: **9** caparison
cry: nie **5** neigh **6** whinny
dappled: **4** roan **5** pinto **7** piebald
dark: **4** zain
dealer: **7** chanter, scorser
disease: **5** surra **6** heaves, lampas **7** lam-
pers, quittor, spavins **9** distemper
docked-tail: **6** curtal **8** cocktail
draft: **4** aver **5** aiver, hairy
dressage: **15** movement control
driver: **6** jockey **7** sumpter **8** coachman
farm: **6** dobbin
feeding box: **6** manger
female: **4** mare, yaud **5** filly
foot: **4** frog, hoof **7** coronet, fetlock, pastern
forehead: **8** chanfrin
gait: run **4** lope, pace, rack, trot, vott,
walk **6** canter, gallop
genus: **5** equus
goddess of: **5** Epona
golden: **8** palomino
gray: **8** schimmel
guide: **4** rein **5** longe
harness: **5** pacer **7** trotter
hired: **4** hack **7** hackney
hybrid: **4** mule
horned: **7** unicorn **9** monoceros
leg: **6** instep **7** fetlock
lover: **10** hippophile
male: **4** stud **6** entire **7** gelding **8** stallion
measure: **4** hand
menage: **6** school **7** academy
pace: **4** lope, trot **5** amble **6** canter
pack: **5** bidet **7** sumpter
pair: **4** span, team
pert. to: **6** hippic
piebald: **5** pinto
prehistoric: **8** Eohippus
races: **8** claiming
racing: **4** turf
rearing: **6** pesade
relay: **6** remuda
round-up: **5** rodeo
saddle: cob **5** mount **7** palfrey
small: cob, nag, tit **4** pony **5** bidet, genet

6 cayuse, jennet(Sp.) **8** galloway, Shetland
sorrel: **4** roan **8** chestnut
spirited: **4** Arab **5** steed **6** rearer **7** courser
stable of: **6** string
talking: **5** Arion
track slope: **6** calade
trainer: **5** valet
trapping: **6** tackle **7** harness **9** caparison
trotting: **6** Morgan
turn: **7** passade
war: **5** steed **7** charger, courser **8** destrier
white-streaked face: **4** shim **5** blaze, reach
wild: **6** bronco, brumby, tarpan **7** mustang **8** warragal, warrigal
winged: **7** Pegasus
working: **4** aver **5** aiver **6** dobbin
worn-out: nag **4** hack, jade, moke, plug **5**
crock, skate **6** garran, garron, gleyde **7**
knacker **8** harridan **9** rosinante
horse-and-buggy: rig **12** old-fashioned
horse collar: **7** bargham(Sc.)
horse mackerel: **4** fish, scad, tuna **5**
atule, tunny **6** bonita, saurel
horse opera: **7** western
horse tackle: **7** harness
horsefly: **4** cleg **5** clegg **6** botfly, gadfly
horsehair: **4** mane **9** haircloth
horsehide: **8** cordovan
horsekeeper: **5** groom **7** hostler
horselaugh: **5** snort **6** guffaw, heehaw
horseman: **5** rider **6** carter, cowboy **7**
centaur, courier, vaquero **8** buckaroo,
chevalier **10** cavalryman, equestrian **12**
broncobuster, equestrienne
horseman goad: **4** spur
horsemanship: **5** skill **6** manege, riding
10 equitation
rearing: **6** pesade
sidewalk: **4** volt
turn: **8** caracole
horseradish: **5** plant **6** relish
horseshoe: *point:* **6** sponge
spur: **4** calk
rim: web
horseshoer: **6** smithy **7** farrier **10** blacksmith
horsewhip: **4** flog **5** quirt **7** chabouk
horticulturist: **8** gardener
Horus: **6** Sun God
brother: **6** Anubis
father: **6** Osiris
mother: **4** Isis
hose: **4** sock, tube, vamp **5** water **6** drench
8 stocking
Hosea: **7** prophet
father: **5** Beeri
wife: **5** Gomer
hospice: inn **5** house **6** asylum, imaret
hospitable: **5** douce **6** cheery **7** cordial **8**
friendly **9** receptive

hospital: 6 creche, refuge, spital 9 infirmary 10 sanatorium 11 xenodochium 12 ambulatorium
attendant: 5 nurse 6 intern 7 orderly
mobile: 9 ambulance
user: 7 patient
hospitality: 7 welcome 10 cordiality
to strangers: 9 xendodochy
host: inn 4 army, here 5 crowd, guest, swarm 6 housel, legion, myriad, throng 7 company, lodging 8 landlord 9 harbinger, multitude, sacrifice 10 assemblage 11 entertainer
receptacle for: pyx 5 paten 8 ciborium
hostage: 4 pawn 5 token 6 pledge 8 security 9 guarantee
hostel: inn 5 hotel, lodge 6 tavern 11 caravansary 12 lodginghouse
hostile: foe 5 black, enemy, fremd 7 adverse, opposed, warlike 8 contrary, inimical 9 resisting 10 malevolent, unfriendly 11 belligerent 12 antagonistic 13 unsympathetic
hostility: 4 feid, feud 6 animus, enmity, hatred, rancor 7 ill-will, warfare 9 animosity, antipathy 10 antagonism, bitterness, opposition, resistance 12 disaffection 14 unfriendliness, vindictiveness
hostler: 5 groom 6 ostler 9 stableman
hot: 5 acrid, angry, calid, eager, fiery, spicy 6 ardent, biting, fervid, recent, strong, sultry, torrid, urgent 7 burning, excited, fervent, flaming, glowing, intense, lustful, peppery, pungent, thermal 8 sizzling, vehement, very warm 9 excitable, impatient, impetuous 10 passionate
hot cakes: 7 pancake 11 griddle cake
hot dog: 6 wiener 7 sausage, show off 11 frankfurter
hot-tempered: 7 iracund 8 choleric 9 irascible
hot-water bottle: pad, pig
hotbed: 4 nest
hotchpotch: 4 stew 6 jumble 9 tripotage(F.) 10 hodgepodge
hotel: inn 5 fonda, haven, house 6 hostel, imaret, tavern 7 auberge, gasthof, hostage 8 building, dwelling, gasthaus 11 caravansary, public house 12 caravanserai, lodginghouse
airport: 6 airtel
auto: 5 motel
keeper: 4 host 7 padrone 8 boniface, hotelier
hotheaded: 5 fiery, hasty 8 reckless 9 impetuous
hothouse: 6 bagnio 10 greenhouse
hot line: 14 emergency phone
hotspur: 4 rash 6 madcap 7 violent 8 reckless 9 impetuous 10 headstrong
Hottentot: *dialect:* 4 Gona, Kora, Nama
garment: 6 kaross
instrument: 4 gora 5 gorah, goura

tribe: 4 Gona, Kora, Nama 6 Damara, Griqua 7 Sandawe, Sandawi
war club: 10 knobkerrie
hound: dog 4 bait, hunt 5 harry 6 addict, talbot 7 devotee, harrier 9 persecute
tail: 5 stern
hour: *canonical:* 4 none, sext
class: 6 period
lights out: 4 taps 6 curfew
hourly 4 soon 5 brief, horal 6 horary, recent 7 quickly 8 frequent 9 continual 10 frequently 11 continually
hourglass: 5 clock 7 shapely
house: cot, hut 4 casa(It.), cote, dorm, dump, firm, flat, flet, haus(G.), home, live, nest 5 abode, bahay, booth, cabin, cover, dacha, domus(L.), hovel, lodge, manor, shack, villa 6 biggin, billet, bottle, camara, casino, duplex, family, grange, harbor, maison(F.), palace, reside, shanty 7 cabildo, chateau, cottage, enclose, mansion, quarter, shelter, theater 8 ancestry, audience, building, bungalow, domicile, dwelling, tenement 9 dormitory, playhouse, residence 10 enterprise, habitation
cluster: 4 dorp 6 hamlet 7 village
commercial: 4 firm 5 store 8 emporium
dog: 6 kennel
eating: inn 4 cafe 6 tavern 9 chophouse 10 restaurant
English royal: 4 York 5 Tudor 6 Stuart 7 Hanover, Windsor 9 Lancaster
guest: inn 5 hotel 11 caravansary
Newfoundland: 4 tilt
Oriental: 5 serai
pert. to: 5 domal
public: inn 5 hotel 6 hostel, tavern 7 hospice 8 hostelry
religious: 4 kirk 6 chapel, church, priory, temple 9 cathedral, synagogue 10 tabernacle
Russian: 4 isba 5 dacha
summer: 6 gazebo 9 belvedere
Upper: 6 Senate
house organ: 8 magazine 10 periodical
house servant: 4 maid 8 domestic
houseboat: 5 barge 6 wangan, wangun 7 wanigan 8 dahabeah, wannigan
housefly: 4 pest 5 musca 8 insect
household: 5 meiny 6 common, family, housal, menage 8 domestic, familiar, ordinary 9 belonging
gods: 5 Lares 7 Penates
regulation: 6 thrift 7 economy 9 husbandry
housekeeper: 6 matron 7 janitor 8 janitrix 9 caretaker, janitress
houseleek: 8 sengreen
houseplant: ivy 5 aphis, calla 6 coleus 7 begonia, violets 11 asphidistra
housewarming: 6 infare
housewife: 8 hausfrau(G.) 9 sewing kit

housework: 5 chore 8 drudgery
housing: box, pad 4 cowl 5 cover, niche 6 garage 7 lodging, shelter 8 covering 10 protection
Houston college: 4 Rice
hove: See **heave**
hovel: hut, sty 4 crib, hole, hulk, hull, shed 5 cabin, hutch, lodge 6 cruive, hemmel, pigpen, pigsty, shanty 7 shelter 10 tabernacle
hover: 4 flit 5 float, pause, waver 7 flitter, flutter
howdy, howdie: 7 midwife 10 salutation
however: but, tho, yet 5 still 6 though 8 after all, although 10 all the same, howsomever 12 nevertheless 15 notwithstanding
howitzer: 6 cannon
howl: bay, cry, wow(Sc.) 4 bawl, gowl, gurl, hurl, wail, wawl, yawl, yell, yowl, yowt 5 whewl 6 lament, scream, squeal, steven 7 ululate 9 complaint 12 sidesplitter
howling: 4 wild 5 great 6 baying, dreary, savage 7 extreme, ululant 10 pronounced
howling monkey: 5 araba 7 guereba, stentor
howsoever: 8 although
howsomever: 8 although 12 nevertheless
hox: 4 hock 5 annoy, worry 6 harass, pester 7 trample 9 hamstring
hoyden, hoiden: 4 romp, rude 6 blowze, tomboy 7 ill-bred 10 roistering
Hreidmar's son: 5 Otter, Regin 6 Fafnir, Reginn
huaca: 4 holy, idol, tomb 6 fetish, sacred, shrine, temple
hub: 4 core, nave 6 center, centre 10 focal point 11 nerve center
Hub: 6 Boston
hubbub: ado, din 4 stir 5 noise 6 clamor, hubble, racket, rumpus, tumult, uproar 7 bobbery 9 commotion, confusion 11 disturbance
hubristic: 4 vain 7 insolent 8 arrogant 12 contemptuous, supercilious 13 high-and-mighty
huckleberry: 9 blueberry
family: 9 ericaceae
Huckleberry Finn: *author:* 9 Mark Twain 13 Samuel Clemens
character: Jim, Tom
river: 11 Mississippi
huckster: 4 sell, vend 5 adman, cheap 6 badger, broker, cadger, cagier(Fr.), hawker 7 haggler, peddler 8 regrater, retailer 9 middleman
huddle: hug 4 hide, raff 5 crowd, hurry 6 bustle, fumble, jumble, mingle 7 conceal, embrace, meeting, scrunch 8 assemble, disorder 9 confusion 10 conference, discussion 14 conglomeration

Hudibras author: 6 Butler
hue: 4 balk, blee, form, tint 5 color, guise, shade, shout, tinge 6 aspect, clamor, depict, figure, outcry 7 clamour 8 shouting 10 appearance, complexion
hueless: 4 gray 9 colorless
huff: dod, pet 4 blow, brag, puff 5 bully, peeve, swell 6 hector 7 bluster, enlarge 8 boasting, offended 11 take offense
huffy: 4 airy 5 fuffy, puffy, windy 6 touchy 7 pettish 8 arrogant 9 conceited 10 swaggering
hug: lug 4 clip, coll 5 carry, clasp, cling, creem, halse, press 6 cuddle, huddle, huggle 7 cherish, embrace, squeeze 9 hold close
huge: big 4 stor(Sc.), vast 5 enorm, giant, great, jumbo, large 6 heroic 7 banging, bumping, immense, massive, monster 8 colossal, enormous, gigantic, titanic 9 monstrous, pyramidal, very large 10 gargantuan, prodigious, tremendous, unmeasured 11 elephantine
hugger-mugger: sly 6 jumble, muddle, secret 7 secrecy 8 confused, hush-hush, in camera, secretly 9 confusion 10 disorderly 11 clandestine 13 clandestinely
hui: 4 firm 5 guild 7 society 8 assembly 11 partnership
huisache: 4 wabe, wabi 5 aromo, shrub 6 cassie 7 popinac 10 spiny plant
huitain: 6 octave, stanza
huke: 4 cape 5 cloak, dress
hulk: 4 bulk, hull, loom, ship 5 hovel 10 disembowel
hulking: 5 bulky, hulky, husky, large 7 loutish, massive 8 unwieldy
hull: hud, hut, pod 4 bulk, hulk, husk, shed 5 shell, strip 6 casing 8 covering 11 decorticate
grain: 4 bran
hullabaloo: ado, din 5 noise 6 clamor, hubbub, racket, tumult, uproar 7 clamour 9 confusion
hum: 4 blur, buzz, huss, huzz, sing, whiz 5 croon, drink, drone, feign, whizz 6 murmur 7 vibrate 9 bombinate 11 bombilation, bombination
human: 6 humane, mortal, person 7 hominid 9 enigmatic
human being: man 6 mortal, person 7 Adamite 8 creature
humane: 4 kind 6 kindly, tender 8 merciful 9 forgiving 10 charitable, civilising 11 sympathetic 13 compassionate, tenderhearted
humanitarian: 14 philanthropist
humanity: 5 flesh, mercy 6 lenity, people 7 mankind 8 kindness 9 mortality 11 human nature
humanize: 6 refine 8 civilize
humble: low 4 mean, meek, mild, poor 5 abase, abash, lower, lowly, plain, stoop

6 debase, deject, demean, demiss, modest, reduce, simple **7** afflict, conquer, degrade, depress, ignoble, mortify **8** contrite, deferent, disgrace, reverent **9** humiliate **10** submissive, unassuming

humbug: gum, kid, pah **4** bosh, flam, guff, hoax, sham **5** cheat, faker, fraud, fudge, guile, trick **6** barney, blague, bunkum, cafard, cajole, gammon **7** deceive, flummer, mislead **8** flimflam, flummery, huckmuck, nonsense, pretense **9** bamboozle, deception, imposture, stratagem **10** flumdiddle **11** flumadiddle

humdinger: **4** oner **5** dandy, doozy, nifty **6** corker **8** jimdandy **11** crackerjack

humdrum: **4** dull **6** boring **7** irksome, prosaic **10** monotonous **11** commonplace, indifferent **13** uninteresting

humerus: **4** bone **8** shoulder, upper arm

humid: wet **4** damp, dank **5** moist **6** sultry **8** humorous, vaporous

humidity: **8** dampness, **9** moistness

humiliate: **5** abase, abash, shame **6** debase, humble **7** degrade, mortify **8** belittle, disgrace

humility: **7** modesty **8** meekness, mildness **9** lowliness **10** diffidence

humming: big **5** brisk, brool **6** lively, strong **7** buzzing, droning **8** frothing, seething **13** extraordinary

hummingbird: ava **5** carib **6** hummer **8** froufrou **9** sheartail

genus of: **6** sappho

hummock: **4** hump **5** knoll **7** hillock

humor, humour: pet, tid, wit **4** baby, mood, whim **5** fancy, fluid, freak, vapor **6** levity, megrim, please, temper **7** caprice, cater to, gratify, indulge **8** drollery, moisture **11** inclination, temperament

humorist: wag, wit **4** card **5** cutup, joker **6** jester

humorous, humourous: **5** comic, droll, funny, humid, moist, witty **6** watery **7** amusive, comical, jocular, playful **8** pleasant **9** facetious, laughable, whimsical **10** capricious

hump: **4** bile, hunk, lump **5** bouge, bulge, bunch, crump, hunch, mound, ridge **6** gibber, gibbus, hummie **7** hummock **12** protuberance

humpback: **5** whale **9** hunchback **10** huckleback

Humperdinck opera: **15** Hansel and Gretel

humus: mor **4** mull, soil

Hun: **6** vandal **9** barbarian

leader: **4** Atli **5** Etzel **6** Attila

Hunan river: **4** Yuan, Yuen

hunch: **4** balk, bend, hump, hunk, lump, push **5** chunk, fudge, shove **6** chilly, frosty, thrust **9** intuition **11** premonition **12** protuberance

Hunchback of Notre Dame: **9** Quasimodo

author: **4** Hugo

hundred: **7** cantred, cantref **11** ten times ten

division into: **12** centuriation

hundred-eyed being: **5** Argus

hundred percent: **6** entire **7** genuine, perfect **9** unalloyed **13** thoroughgoing **14** unquestionable

hundred years: **7** century **9** centenary

hundredfold: **8** centuple **12** centuplicate

hundredweight: cwt **6** cental **7** quintal

hung: See **hang**

Hung Wu: **4** Ming

Hungary: *army:* **6** Honved **9** Honvedseg

capital: Budapest

cavalryman: **6** Hussar

city: **4** Pecs **5** Erlau **6** Szeged **7** Miskolc **8** Debrecen **9** Debreczin, Kecskemet

coin: **6** filler, forint

commune: Mor

composer: **5** Lehar **6** Bartok

county: Vas **4** Pest, Zala **5** Bekes, Fejer, Heves, Tolna **6** Nograd, Somogy

dance: **7** czardas

dog: **4** puli **6** kuvasz

ethnic group: **4** Slav **5** Croat, gypsy **6** Magyar

gyspy: **7** tzigane

lake: **7** Balaton **9** Blaten See

measure: ako **4** hold, joch, yoke **5** antal, itcze, marok, metze **7** huvelyk, merfold

mountain range: **10** Carpathian

poet: **5** Arany

river: **4** Raab **5** Drave, Maros **6** Danube, Poprad, Theiss **7** Vistula

weight: **7** vamfont **8** vammazsa

wine: **5** tokay

hunger: **4** long, want **5** belly **6** desire, famine, starve **7** craving **8** appetite, need food, voracity **9** esurience **10** starvation

abnormal: **7** bulimia **10** polyphagia

hungry: **4** avid, howe, poor **5** eager **6** barren, hollow, jejune **7** craving, uneaten **8** esurient, hungered **10** avaricious

hunk: dad, gob, wad **4** daud, hump, lump **5** chunk, hunch, piece **6** nugget

hunt: dig **4** drag, seek **5** chase, chevy, chivy, delve, drive, hound, probe, quest, stalk, track, trail **6** chivvy, ferret, follow, forage, hunter, pursue, search, shikar **9** persecute, try to find **11** inquisition

god of: **5** Ninip **6** Apollo

hunted: **4** game, prey

hunter: **5** jager, yager **6** chaser, nimrod **7** stalker **8** chasseur **9** sportsman

assistant: **5** gilly, jager

attendant: **5** gilly(Scot.) **6** gillie

constellation: **5** Orion
mythological: **5** Orion
Golden Fleece: **5** Jason
patron saint: **6** Hubert
hunting: *bird:* **6** falcon
  cry: yoi **4** toho **5** chevy, chivy, hoick **6**
    chivvy, hoicks, yoicks
  expedition: **6** safari
  game: **6** shikar, venery
  horn note: **4** mort
  pert. to: **7** venatic
hunting dog: 5 hound **6** basset, beagle,
  setter **7** pointer, spaniel
huntress: 5 Diana **7** Artemis **8** Atalanta
huntsman: 5 jager **6** jaeger **7** catcher,
  venerer **8** chasseur
  changed into stag: **7** Actaeon
hurdle: pen **4** clew, fold, leap **5** bound,
  cover, crate, frith, hedge **6** raddle **7** barrier, confine **8** obstacle, surmount **9** enclosure **10** impediment **11** obstruction
hurdy-gurdy: 4 lira, rota
hurl: 4 cast, dash, haul, howl, hurl, pelt,
  roar, send, toss, turn **5** fling, heave,
  pitch, sling, smite, throw, twist, whang
  6 elance **9** overthrow
hurly-burly: 6 hubbub, tumult, uproar **7**
  turmoil **8** confused **9** confusion
huron: 6 grison
hurrah: joy **5** cheer, huzza, shout **6** tumult **7** triumph **8** applause **9** commotion **13** encouragement
hurricane: 4 wind **5** storm **7** cyclone,
  prester, tempest **8** chubasco **9** hurri-
  cano, windstorm **13** tropical storm
  center of: eye
hurried: See **hurry**
hurry: ado, hie, run **4** pass, pell, race, rese,
  rush, scud, stir, trot, urge, whir **5** drive,
  fight, haste, impel, slide, speed, worry **6**
  convey, harass, hasten, hustle, scurry,
  tumult, urge on **7** agitato(It.), dispute,
  quarrel, quicken **8** dispatch, expedite **9**
  agitation, commotion **10** expedition **11**
  disturbance, festination, precipitate
hurst: 4 hill, wood **5** copse, grove, knoll **7**
  hillock **8** sandbank **11** wooded mound
hurt: 4 harm, maim, pain **5** abuse, blame,
  grief, sorry, wound **6** damage, grieve,
  impair, injure, injury, mittle, offend,
  scathe, strike **7** afflict, collide, hurting
  8 be bad for, distress, mischief, nuisance **9** detriment **12** disadvantage
hurtful: bad **4** evil **6** nocent **7** baneful,
  harmful, malefic, noisome, noxious **10**
  pernicious **11** deleterious, destructive,
  detrimental, prejudicial
hurtle: 4 dash **5** clash, fling, whirl **6** assail, jostle **7** collide **8** brandish
husband: eke, man, rom **4** bond, buck,
  chap, keep, mate, save **5** churl, hoard,
  marry, store **6** manage, spouse, tiller

7 consort, espouse, partner, plowman,
  steward **8** conserve, helpmate **9** cultivate, economize, other half **10** cultivator, husbandman
  more than one: **9** polyandry
  property right: **7** curtesy
husbandman: 4 bond, boor, carl **5** colon
  6 farmer, tiller **7** acre-man **8** agricole
  10 cultivator
husbandry: 6 thrift **7** economy **8** mana-
  gery **9** frugality **11** cultivation **12** conservation
  god: **6** Faunus
hush: tut **4** calm, clam, hist, lull **5** allay,
  quiet, still **6** soothe **7** appease, repress,
  silence
husk: cod, hud **4** bark, bran, coat, hulk,
  hull, leam, peel, rind, skin **5** lemma,
  scale, shack, shell, shuck, straw, strip **6**
  colder **7** envelop, epicarp **8** covering,
  envelope **11** decorticate
Husky: dog **6** Eskimo
huss: 7 dogfish
hussar: 7 soldier **10** cavalryman
  headdress: **5** busby
  uniform jacket: **6** dolman
hussy: 4 jade, minx **5** besom(Sc.), gipsy,
  gypsy, madam, quean **7** drossel **9**
  housewife **11** housekeeper
hustle: 4 push **5** crowd, hurry, shove **6**
  bustle, jostle, thrust **8** activity
hustler: 6 peeler **8** go-getter
hut: cot **4** bari, cote, crib, hulk, shed **5**
  benab, bohio, bothy, cabin, choza,
  house, hovel, humpy, hutch, kraal,
  lodge, scale, shack, toldo, wurly **6** bohawn, canaba, chalet, gunyah, gunyeh,
  lean-to, rancho, shanty **7** balagan, bourock, camalig, cottage, edifice, huddock,
  wickiup **8** barabara, building, chantier
  fisherman's: **4** skeo
  hermit's: **4** cell
  military: **6** Nissen
  mining: coe
  shepherd's: **5** bothy
hutch: ark, bin, box, car, hut, pen **4** coop
  5 chest, hoard, hotch, hovel **6** coffer,
  humped, shanty **7** hunched, shelter **9**
  inclosure
hutzpah: 4 gall **5** nerve
huzza: 5 cheer, shout **6** hurrah
hyacinth: 7 greggle **8** bluebell, harebell
hyalite: 4 opal
hybrid: 4 mule **5** blend, cross **7** mongrel **9**
  composite **10** crossbreed
  bovine: **7** cattalo
  dog: **4** mutt **7** mongrel
  horse and ass: **4** mule **5** hinny
  horse and zebra: **7** zebrula, zebrule **8** ze-
    brinny
  zebra and donkey: **7** zebrass
hydrant: 4 plug **6** faucet **8** fireplug

hydraulic engine: ram
hydrazoate: 4 azid 5 azide
hydrocarbon: 6 butane, carane, nonane, retene 7 benzene, methane, olefine, pentane
 gaseous: 6 ethane, ethene
 liver oil: 8 pristane
 tree: 7 terpene
hydrocyanic acid: 7 prussic
hydrogen: gas 5 arsin 6 arsine
hydroid: 5 polyp 6 obelia 7 acaleph
hydromel: 4 mead 5 aloja 10 melicratum
hydrometer: 9 aerometer
hydromica: 4 mica 9 muscovite
hydrophobia: 5 lyssa 6 rabies
hydrophyte: See **aquatic plant**
hygienic: 4 good 6 healthy 8 sanitary
hymenopteron: ant, bee 4 wasp 6 sawfly 7 gallfly 9 ichneumon
hymn: ode 4 sing, song 5 psalm 6 himene, himine, hirmos, hirmus 7 introit 8 canticle 11 recessional 12 processional
 following psalm: 9 sticheron
 funeral: 5 dirge
 praising: 4 pean 5 paean
 ritual: 8 encomium
 sung in unison: 6 choral 7 chorale 9 plainsong
 tune: 6 choral 7 chorale
 victory: 9 epinicion, epinikion
hyoscyamus: 8 narcotic
hype: 5 boost, put on 6 jack up, promote 7 deceive, mislead
hyperbole: 12 exaggeration 13 overstatement

Hyperborean sage: 6 Abaris
hypercritical: 7 carping 8 captious 10 censorious 12 faultfinding, overcritical, supercilious
Hyperion: *daughter:* Eos 6 Selene
 father: 6 Uranus
 son: 6 Helios
hyphen: 4 band, dash
hypnotic: 6 opiate 8 narcotic 9 soporific 12 somnifacient
hypnotic condition: 4 coma 6 trance 8 lethargy
hypnotize: 5 charm 9 mesmerize, spellbind
hypnum: 4 moss
hypochondria: hyp 6 megrim
hypocrisy: 4 cant 6 deceit 10 simulation
hypocrite: 4 sham 5 faker, phony, quack 6 humbug, poseur 7 Tartufe 9 charlatan, lip server
hypocritical: 5 false 7 bigoted, canting 8 captious, specious 9 deceptive, insincere 11 dissembling, pharisaical 13 sanctimonious, self-righteous
hypostatic: 5 basic 9 elemental
hypotenuse: 5 slant
hypothesis: ism 6 system, theory 9 postulate 10 assumption 11 supposition
hypothetical being: ens 6 entity
hyrax: 5 coney 8 procavia
hyssop: 4 mint 5 plant 11 aspergillum
hysteria: 6 nerves
hysterical: 9 emotional 12 uncontrolled

I

I, Claudius author: 6 Graves
I do not wish to contend: 14 nolo contendere(L.)
I have found it: 6 eureka
I understand: 5 roger
Iago's wife: 6 Emilia
Iasion's father: 4 Zeus
Iberian: 4 Pict
ibex: tur, zac
ibis: 5 guara, stork 9 gourdhead
Ibsen (Henrik): *character:* Ase 4 Gynt, Nora 5 Hedda

 native country: 6 Norway
 play: 5 Ghosts 8 Peer Gynt, Wild Duck 10 Doll's House 11 Hedda Gabler
Icarian: 4 rash 6 daring 9 foolhardy
Icarius' daughter: 7 Erigone 8 Penelope
Icarus' father: 8 Daedalus
ICBM: 5 Atlas 6 weapon 7 missle
ice: 4 cool, geal, grue(Sc.), rime 5 chill, frost glace(F.). 6 freeze, payola 7 congeal, hauteur 8 diamonds 10 confection 11 refrigerant, refrigerate
 crystals: 4 snow 5 frost

floating: **4** berg, floe
fragment: **5** brash
mass: **7** glacier
patch: **4** rone(Sc.)
pendant: **6** icicle
pinnacle of glacier: **5** serac
sea: **6** sludge
sheet: **4** floe
slushy: **4** sish
ice cream dish: 4 soda **6** frappe, sundae **7** parfait
icebox: 6 cooler **12** refrigerator
icecap: 7 calotte
Iceland: *capital:* **9** Reykjavik
city: **8** Akureyri, Keflavik **9** Kopavogur
ethnic group: **4** Celt **5** Norse
measure: fet **4** alin, lina **5** almud, turma **6** almenn, almude, ferfet, pottur **7** fathmur, feralin, fermila, oltunna, sjomila **9** korntunna **10** ferfathmur, kornskeppa, thumlungur
monetary unit: **5** eyrir, krona
notable volcano: **5** Hekla
parliament: **7** Althing
river: **5** Hvita **7** Jokulsa
weight: **4** pund **5** pound **11** tunna smjors
Icelandic epic: **4** Edda **10** Grettisaga
Icelandic Nobel novelist: **7** Laxness (Halldor)
ichneumon: fly **8** mongoose **11** hymenoptera(pl.)
ichnography: map **9** floor plan
ichnolite: 6 fossil **9** footprint
icicle: 10 ice pendent
limestone: **10** stalactite, stalagmite
icing: 7 topping **8** frosting
icky: 6 sticky **7** cloying **10** disgusting **11** distasteful, sentimental
icon, ikon: 5 image **6** eidola(pl.), idolon, symbol **7** eidolon, picture **8** portrait **12** illustration
iconoclast: 5 rebel **7** radical **9** dissenter **13** nonconformist
icterus: 8 jaundice
ictus: fit **4** blow **6** attack, stress, stroke
ICU: 17 intensive care unit
icy: 4 cold **5** gelid **6** arctic, frigid, frosty **8** chilling
Idaho: *capital:* **5** Boise
city: **5** Nampa **6** Burley, Moscow, Rupert **8** Caldwell, Lewiston **9** Blackfoot, Pocatello, Twin Falls
county: Ada, Gem **5** Camas, Latah, Lemhi, Power, Teton **6** Bonner, Cassia, Custer, Oneida, Owyhee **7** Bannock, Benewah, Caribou, Gooding, Payette **8** Kootenai, Minidoka
dam: **8** Brownlee, Dworshak **13** Anderson Ranch
early explorer: **5** Clark (William), Lewis (Meriwether)
gorge: **11** Hell's Canyon
Indian: **7** Bannock **8** Nez Perce, Shosho-

ne **10** Sheepeater
lake: **4** Bear **5** Grays **6** Priest **11** Coeur d'Alene, Pend Oreille
mountain peak: **4** Ryan **5** Borah, Devil, Scott, Waugh **6** Castle, Mormon, Taylor **8** Cape Horn
mountain range: **5** Lemhi **7** Cabinet **8** Sawtooth **9** Lost River **10** Bitterroot
river: **4** Bear **5** Boise, Lemhi, Snake **6** Lochsa, Salmon **7** Big Wood, Payette **10** Clearwater
state bird: **8** bluebird
state flower: **7** syringa
state gem: **10** star garnet
state horse: **9** Appaloosa
state motto: **12** Esto perpetua
state nickname: Gem
state tree: **9** white pine
tourist resort: **9** Sun Valley
Idas' consort: 8 Marpessa
ide: 4 orfe **8** foodfish
idea: 4 idee(F.) **5** fancy, ideal, image **6** design, figure, notion **7** conceit, concept, fantasy, inkling, opinion, project, thought **8** gimcrack **9** archetype **10** appearance, cogitation, conception, impression, reflection
impracticable: **7** chimera **8** chimaera
prompting action: **6** motive
ideal: 5 dream, model **6** mental **7** paragon, perfect, Utopian **8** abstract, fanciful, standard **9** imaginary, visionary **10** aspiration, conceptual
ideal state: 4 Eden **6** Oceana, Utopia
ideate: 5 fancy **7** imagine **8** conceive
idée fixe: 9 fixed idea, obsession
identical: one **4** same, self, twin, very **5** alike, equal, samen(Sc.) **8** selfsame **10** equivalent, tantamount
identify: tag **4** mark, name **5** brand, prove **7** earmark, pick out **9** designate, establish, recognize
identity: 4 name **5** unity **7** oneness **8** sameness **9** exactness **11** homogeneity
crisis: **13** self conflict
false: **5** alias
ideologist: 7 dreamer **8** theorist **9** visionary
ideology: ism **5** credo, dogma **7** beliefs **8** doctrine **10** philosophy
idiasm: 9 mannerism **11** peculiarity **12** idiosyncrasy
idiocy: 7 anoesia, fatuity
idiograph: 9 signature, trademark
idiom: 5 style **6** phrase **7** dialect
idiosyncrasy: way **6** idiasm, manner **11** peculiarity **12** eccentricity
idiot: oaf **4** dolt, fool **5** ament, booby, dunce, moron, **6** cretin, hobbil, nidget **7** dullard, omadawn **8** imbecile, omadhuan **9** blockhead, simpleton **10** changeling
idiotic: 4 daft, zany **5** barmy, inane **7** asi-

nine, fatuous, foolish **9** senseless

idle: 4 lazy loaf, sorn(Sc.), vain **5** dally, empty **6** dawdle, futile, loiter, otiose, unused, vacant **7** aimless, loafing, useless **8** baseless, inactive, indolent, slothful, trifling **9** desultory, unfounded, worthless **10** groundless, unemployed, unoccupied **11** ineffectual

idle talk: 5 rumor **6** gossip

idleness: 5 sloth **7** inertia **8** inaction, laziness **9** indolence **10** inactivity

idler: bum **5** drone **6** loafer **8** faineant, loiterer, sluggard **9** do-nothing, goldbrick, lazybones

Idmon: *father:* **6** Apollo
killer: **4** boar
mother: **6** Cyrene
ship: **4** Argo

idol: god **4** Baal, hero, icon **5** image **6** fetish
matinee: **4** star

idolater: 5 pagan **6** adorer **7** Baalite **9** worshiper

idolatrous: 5 pagan

idolize: 5 adore **6** admire, revere **7** worship **8** venerate

idyl, idyll: 4 poem **7** eclogue

idyllic: 7 bucolic **8** pastoral **9** unspoiled

if: 8 granting, provided **9** supposing

i'faith: 5 truly **6** indeed

iffy: 6 chancy **8** doubtful **9** uncertain

igneous rock: 4 lava **5** magma **6** basalt, gabbro, pumice, scoria **8** porphyry

ignis fatuus: 8 delusion **9** pipe dream **12** will-o'-the-wisp

ignite: 4 fire **5** light **6** kindle **7** inflame

ignoble: low **4** base, mean, vile **6** abject, sordid **8** shameful, wretched **11** disgraceful **12** dishonorable

ignominious: 4 base **5** sorry **6** odious **8** infamous, shameful **9** degrading **10** despicable, inglorious, mortifying **11** disgraceful, humiliating **12** contemptible, dishonorable

ignoramus: 4 dolt **5** dunce **6** nitwit

ignorant: 5 green, naive, young **6** stupid **7** artless, unaware, uncouth **8** nescient, untaught **9** in the dark, unlearned, unskilled, untutored **10** illiterate, unlettered **11** unconscious

ignore: cut **4** omit, snub **5** blink, elide **6** slight **7** neglect **8** overlook **9** disregard, eliminate

Igorot, Igorrote: 6 Bontok **7** Nabaloi **8** Kankanai
chief: Apo

iguana: 6 lizard **7** tuatara

Iguvine: 7 Umbrian **8** Eugubine

ihi: 4 fish **7** skipper **8** halfbeak **9** stichbird

Ihlat: 8 Sunnites

ijolite: 7 apatite, calcite **8** titanite

ilex: 5 holly

Iliad: 4 epic, poem
attributed to: **5** Homer
character: **4** Ajax **5** Helen, Paris, Priam **6** Aeneas, Hector **8** Achilles, Diomedes, Menelaus, Odysseus **9** Agamemnon, Cassandra, Patroclus

ilium: 4 bone

Ilium, Ilion: 4 Troy

ilk: 4 kind, sort, type **5** breed, class, **6** family, nature, stripe

ill: bad **4** evil, harm, poor, sick **5** amiss, badly, wrong **6** ailing, faulty, wicked **7** adverse, ailment, baneful, noxious, trouble, unlucky **8** improper **9** adversity, defective **10** indisposed, iniquitous, misfortune **11** unfortunate

ill-advised: 4 rash **5** hasty **6** unwise **8** reckless **9** imprudent **10** indiscreet **11** thoughtless

ill at ease: 7 awkward **13** uncomfortable

ill-boding: 4 dire **7** ominous, unlucky **12** inauspicious

ill-bred: 4 rude **7** boorish, plebian, uncivil **8** churlish, impolite, malapert **9** bourgeois **11** impertinent **12** discourteous

ill-defined: dim **5** faint, fuzzy, vague **7** unclear **10** indistinct

ill-favored: 4 ugly **9** offensive **10** unpleasant **12** disagreeable

ill-humored: 5 cross **6** cranky, morose **7** fretful, grouchy, peevish

ill-natured: 4 dour **5** nasty, surly **6** crabby

ill-suited: 5 inapt, unfit **8** improper **10** unbecoming **13** inappropriate

ill-tempered: 5 cross, moody **6** crusty **7** bilious **8** choleric, snappish **9** dyspeptic, irritable

ill-treat: 5 abuse **6** misuse

ill will: 4 hate **5** spite, venom **6** animus, enmity, malice, rancor **7** dislike **9** hostility **10** bad feeling
showing: **7** hostile **8** choleric **9** bellicose, irascible, litigious, wrangling **10** pugnacious **11** belligerent, contentious, quarrelsome **12** disputatious

illation: 9 deduction, inference

illegitimate: 7 bastard, bootleg **8** improper, spurious, unlawful, wrongful **9** illogical

illiberal: 6 stingy **7** bigoted **8** partisan **9** hidebound **10** intolerant **11** opinionated **12** narrow-minded

illicit: 7 bootleg, illegal **8** criminal, improper, unlawful **10** contraband, prohibited **12** unauthorized

illimitable: 4 vast **8** infinite **9** boundless **11** measureless **12** immeasurable

Illinois: *capital:* **10** Springfield
city: **5** Cairo, Pekin **6** Galena, Geneva, Joliet, Peoria, Urbana **7** Chicago, Decatur, Wheaton **8** Carthage, Kankakee,

Rockford, Waukegan **10** Belleville,
Rock Island **11** East St. Louis

county: **4** Bond, Cass, Clay, Cook, Kane,
Knox, Ogle, Will **5** Adams, Boone,
Coles, Edgar, Piatt, Stark **6** Bureau, De
Kalb, De Witt, Du Page, Grundy, Har-
din, Massac, Menard, Saline **7** Carroll,
Kendall, La Salle **8** Crawford, Gallatin,
Macoupin, Moultrie, Sangamon

Indian: Fox **4** Sauk **8** Kickapoo

lake: **8** Michigan

river: **4** Ohio, Rock **6** Wabash **8** Illinois,
Kankakee, Mackinaw, Sangamon **9**
Kaskaskia, Vermilion **10** Des Plaines

state bird: **8** cardinal

state flower: **6** violet

state insect: **9** butterfly (Monarch)

state mineral: **8** fluorite

state nickname: **7** Prairie

state slogan: **13** Land of Lincoln

state tree: **8** white oak

illiterate: **6** unread **8** ignorant, untaught
9 barbarous, unlearned, untutored **10**
unlettered

illness: **5** colic **6** malady, morbus **7** ailment, cachexy, disease **8** cachexia, disorder, sickness **9** complaint, distemper
10 affliction, wickedness **13** indisposition

feign: **8** malinger

mental: See **mental disorder**

illogical: **7** invalid, unsound **8** specious **9**
senseless **10** irrational, unreasoned **12**
inconsequent

illuminate: **4** fire **5** adorn, flare, light **6**
inform, kindle **7** clarify, emblaze, ex-
plain **8** brighten, **9** enlighten, irradiate,
make clear **10** illustrate

illumination: *device:* **4** lamp **5** torch **7**
lantern **10** flashlight

in eclipse: **8** penumbra

measure: **4** phot **5** lumen **6** candle

illusion: **5** fancy **6** mirage **7** chimera, fallacy, mockery, phantom **8** delusion **9**
deception **10** appearance

illusive: **4** sham **5** false **6** unreal **7** seeming **8** apparent, illusory **9** deceitful, deceptive, imaginary **10** fallacious, phantasmal

illustrate: **4** show **5** adorn **7** picture,
point up, portray **9** elucidate, exemplify, make clear, represent **10** illuminate

illustration: **4** case **7** example **8** instance,
vignette **13** demonstration **15** exemplification

illustrator: **6** artist

illustrious: **5** famed, grand, noble, noted
6 bright, candid, heroic **7** eminent, exalted **8** glorious, renowned **9** honorable
10 celebrated **11** conspicuous **13** distinguished

ilvaite: **8** silicate

image: god **4** copy, form, icon, idol, ikon **5**
eikon **6** double, effigy, emblem, figure,
statue, symbol **7** phantom, picture **8**
likeness **9** depiction, semblance **10** conception, impression, reflection, similitude, simulacrum

attacker: **10** iconoclast

rainbowlike: **7** spectra(pl.) **8** spectrum

religious: **4** icon

stone: **5** herma **6** hermae(pl.)

pert. to televised: **5** video

wooden: **4** tiki **6** xoanon

worship: **8** idolatry **10** iconolatry

imaginary: **5** ideal **6** unreal **7** fancied,
feigned **8** illusory, mythical, notional **9**
dreamed up, fantastic, visionary **10** artificial, chimerical, fictitious **11** make
believe

imagination: **5** fancy **7** fantasy, thought
9 ingenuity, invention **10** creativity,
enterprise

imaginative: **6** dreamy, poetic **8** fanciful,
original **9** fantastic

imagine: **5** dream, fancy, feign, think **6**
gather **7** picture, suppose, surmise **8**
conceive, envision **9** apprehend **10**
comprehend, conjecture

imago: **12** winged insect

imam: **5** ruler **6** caliph

imaret: inn **7** hospice **11** caravansary

imbecile: **4** dolt, jerk **5** anile, daffy, idiot,
moron **6** cranky, dotard, nitwit **7** fatuous **8** dumbbell **9** driveling **10** changeling, half-witted

imbed: fix **5** embed, inset **6** cement

imbibe: sip **4** soak **5** drink, imbue, steep **6**
absorb **7** swallow **8** saturate **10** assimilate

imbricate: **5** tiled **6** scaled **7** overlap

imbroglio: row **4** spat **7** dispute **8** squabble **9** bickering **11** altercation **12** disagreement **16** misunderstanding

imbrue: wet **4** soak **5** stain **6** drench

imbue: dye **4** soak **5** steep, tinge **6** imbibe,
infuse, leaven **7** animate, ingrain, in-
spire, instill, pervade **8** permeate, saturate **9** inoculate **10** impregnate

imitate: ape **4** copy, echo, mime, mock **5**
mimic **6** follow, repeat **7** copycat, emulate **8** resemble, simulate **9** dissemble
11 counterfeit

imitation: **4** copy, echo, fake, sham **5**
dummy, phony **6** ersatz **7** replica **8**
likeness **9** emulation, facsimile

derisive: **6** parody **7** mockery **9** burlesque

fantastic: **8** travesty

imitation gem: **5** glass, paste

imitation pearl: **6** olivet

immaculate: **4** pure **5** clean **6** candid,
chaste **7** correct, perfect **8** innocent,
spotless, unsoiled **9** faultless, undefiled,
unspotted, unstained, unsullied

immalleable: 5 rigid 10 unyielding

immanent: 8 inherent 9 intrinsic 10 indwelling, subjective

immaterial: 6 slight 8 trifling 9 asomatous, spiritual, unearthly 10 impalpable, intangible 11 unimportant 12 not pertinent 13 insignificant, unsubstantial

immature: 5 crude, green, young 6 callow, unripe 7 puerile, untried 8 childish, youthful 10 incomplete, unfinished 11 undeveloped

immaturity: 5 youth 6 nonage

immeasurable: 7 immense 8 infinite 9 boundless, unlimited 10 indefinite 11 illimitable 12 incalculable

immediate: 4 next 6 direct 7 instant 8 adjacent 9 proximate 10 contiguous, succeeding

immediately: now 4 anon 6 presto 8 directly 9 extempore, forthwith, presently

immemorial: 7 ageless, ancient 8 dateless 11 prehistoric, traditional

immense: 4 huge, vast 5 grand, great, large 7 titanic 8 colossal, enormous, gigantic, infinite 9 extensive, monstrous 10 prodigious, tremendous 12 immeasurable

immerse: dip 4 bury, duck 5 bathe, douse, souse 6 absorb, drench, occupy, plunge 7 baptize, engross 8 submerge

immigrant: 8 newcomer

Israel: 6 halutz 7 chalutz

imminent: 8 expecting 9 impending 10 approaching, threatening

immitigable: 10 implacable

immobile: set 4 firm 5 fixed, inert 6 frozen, laid up, stable 9 immovable 10 motionless, stationary, stock-still

immoderate: 5 undue 7 extreme 9 boundless, excessive, voracious 10 exorbitant, inordinate 11 extravagant, intemperate 12 unreasonable

immodest: 4 bold 6 brazen, coarse 7 forward, obscene 8 indecent, unchaste 9 shameless 10 indecorous

immolation: 8 offering 9 sacrifice

immoral: bad 4 evil 5 loose, wrong 7 corrupt, vicious 8 culpable, depraved, indecent 9 dissolute 10 licentious 11 unwholesome

immortal: 6 divine 7 endless, eternal, godlike, undying 8 enduring 9 ceaseless, deathless 11 amaranthine, everlasting 12 imperishable

immortality: 8 athanasy 9 athanasia 11 endless life

Hindu: 6 amrita

immovable: pat, set 4 fast, firm 5 fixed, rigid 7 adamant 8 constant, immobile, obdurate 9 steadfast 10 adamantine, stationary

immunity: 7 freedom 9 exemption 12 resistance to

immunize: 8 make safe 9 inoculate

immunizer: 5 serum 7 vaccine

immure: 4 wall 7 confine 8 cloister, imprison 11 incarcerate

immutable: 4 firm 7 eternal 10 invariable, unchanging 11 unalterable

Imogen's father: 9 Cymbeline

imp: bud, elf 4 brat, cion, slip 5 child, demon, devil, graft, rogue, scamp, scion 6 sprite, urchin 7 gremlin, progeny 8 devilkin, folletto, folletti(pl.) 9 hobgoblin, offspring 13 mischiefmaker

impact: 4 blow, jolt, pack, slam 5 brunt, crash, force, shock, wedge 6 effect, stroke 7 impulse 9 collision 11 implication

impair: mar 4 harm, hurt 5 spoil, waste 6 damage, debase, hinder, injure, lessen, reduce, sicken, weaken 7 blemish, cripple, vitiate 8 decrease, enfeeble

impaired: 9 afflicted

impala: 7 rooibok 8 rooyebok

impale: 4 spit 5 spear, spike 6 pierce, skewer 8 transfix 10 run through

impalpable: 7 elusive 10 immaterial, intangible

impart: 4 give, lend, tell 5 share, yield 6 bestow, confer, convey, direct, impute, reveal 7 divulge, inspire, instill 8 disclose, discover 10 distribute 11 communicate

impartial: 4 even, fair, just 7 neutral 8 unbiased 9 colorless, equitable, objective 12 unprejudiced 13 disinterested, dispassionate

imparting motion: 7 kinetic

impassable: 5 solid 10 impervious

impasse: box 7 dead end 8 cul-de-sac(F.), deadlock, standoff 9 stalemate 10 blind alley

impassible: 9 impassive, unfeeling 12 invulnerable

impassioned: 5 fiery 6 ardent, fervid 7 fervent 8 eloquent, feverish

impassive: 4 calm 5 stoic 6 serene, stolid 9 apathetic 10 impassible, insensible, phlegmatic 11 emotionless 13 imperturbable

impatient: hot 4 avid, edgy, keen 5 eager, hasty, testy 7 anxious, chafing, fidgety, fretful, peevish 8 choleric, petulant, restless 9 irascible, irritable

impeach: 6 accuse, charge, indict 7 arraign, censure 9 challenge, discredit

impeccable: 5 right 7 correct, perfect 8 flawless 9 exquisite, faultless 11 unblemished

impecunious: 4 poor 5 needy 8 indigent 9 destitute, penniless

impede: 4 clog 5 block, check, choke, delay **6** hamper, harass, hinder, retard, stymie **7** disrupt **8** encumber, handicap, hold back, obstruct

legally: bar **5** debar, estop

impediment: bar, rub **4** clog, flaw, snag **5** hitch **6** defect, malady, remora **8** obstacle **9** detriment, hindrance **10** difficulty

impedimenta: 7 baggage

impel: pat **4** blow, goad, move, send, spur, urge **5** drive, force, hurry **6** compel, excite, incite, induce **7** actuate **8** motivate **9** constrain, encourage, influence, instigate, stimulate

impelling force: 7 impetus **8** momentum

impending: 7 looming **8** imminent, menacing, oncoming **11** approaching, threatening

impenetrable: 4 hard **5** dense **8** airtight **10** impervious, impassable **11** impermeable, inscrutable **12** unfathomable

impenitent: 8 hardened, obdurate **11** remorseless, unrepentant

imperative: 4 duty, rule **5** order, vital **6** urgent **7** crucial **8** pressing, verb form **9** essential, mandatory **10** commanding, compelling, compulsory, peremptory

imperator: 6 leader **7** emperor, general

imperceptible: 10 insensible, intangible **13** inappreciable, indiscernible **17** indistinguishable

imperfect: 4 cull, poor **5** rough **6** faulty, second **9** defective **10** inadequate, incomplete, unfinished

imperfection: 4 flaw, vice **5** fault **6** defect, foible **7** blemish, failing, frailty **8** weakness **10** deficiency **11** shortcoming

imperfectly: 4 half **5** badly

imperial: 5 regal, royal **6** kingly **8** majestic

cap: **5** crown

domain: **6** empery, empire

officer: **8** palatine

imperial woodpecker: 9 ivorybill

imperil: 4 risk **6** expose, hazard **8** endanger **10** jeopardize

imperious: 6 lordly **7** haughty **8** arrogant, despotic, dominant, pressing **10** commanding, imperative, tyrannical **11** dictatorial, domineering, magisterial, overbearing **13** authoritative

imperishable: 7 eternal, undying **8** enduring, immortal **9** continual, deathless **11** everlasting **14** indestructible

impermanent: 8 fleeting **9** ephemeral, temporary, tentative, transient **10** evanescent

impersonal: 4 cold **7** general **8** detached **9** objective **12** matter-of-fact

impersonate: act, ape **4** pose **5** mimic **6** typify

impersonator: 8 imitator, imposter, impostor, **11** entertainer, masquerader

impertinence: 4 sass **8** audacity **9** insolence **10** incivility **11** impropriety, irrelevance

impertinent: 4 rude **5** sassy, saucy **7** illbred **8** arrogant, impudent **9** audacious, officious **10** inapposite **12** inconsequent **13** disrespectful

imperturbability: 8 ataraxia, calmness **9** composure, sangfroid **10** equanimity

imperturbable: 4 cool **6** placid, serene, stable **8** tranquil **9** impassive **10** phlegmatic **11** unexcitable

impervious: 5 tight **8** hardened **10** impassable **11** impermeable **12** impenetrable

impetrate: 7 beseech, entreat, procure

impetuous: hot **4** rash **5** eager, fiery, hasty, heady, sharp **6** abrupt, ardent, fervid, fierce, flashy, sudden **7** furious, rushing, violent **8** forcible, headlong, vehement **9** impulsive, hot-headed **11** precipitate

impetus: 4 prod, push, spur **5** drive, force **6** motive **7** impulse **8** momentum, stimulus **9** incentive

imphee: 5 plant **7** sorghum

impi: 8 soldiers, warriors

impiety: 9 blasphemy **10** disrespect **11** irreverence, ungodliness

impignorate: 4 pawn **6** pledge **8** mortgage

impinge: 6 strike **7** intrude, touch on **8** encroach, trespass

impious: 6 unholy **7** godless, profane, ungodly **9** atheistic, undutiful **10** irreverent **11** irreligious

impish: 6 elfish **7** naughty **11** mischievous

implacable: 6 deadly **10** relentless **11** immitigable **12** unappeasable **14** irreconcilable

implant: sow **4** root **5** embed, infix, inset **6** enroot, infuse **7** impress, inspire, instill **9** inculcate, inoculate, insinuate, introduce **10** impregnate

implausible: 5 fishy **6** flimsy **7** dubious **8** unlikely **9** illogical **10** improbable **12** unbelievable

implement (see also **tool**): **4** gear **6** device, gadget **7** enforce, fulfill, realize, utensil **8** complete, material **9** apparatus, appliance **10** accomplish, instrument

ancient: **4** celt **6** amgarn, eolith **9** paleolith

baker's: **4** peel

barbed: **7** harpoon

cleaning: mop **4** swab **5** broom, brush **6** vacuum **7** sweeper

cutting: **5** knife, mower, razor **6** reaper, scythe, shears **8** scissors **9** jackknife **11** pocketknife

enlarging: **6** reamer **7** dilator
farm: **4** disc, disk, plow, rake **6** seeder, tiller **7** tractor
furcate: **4** fork
garden: hoe **4** rake **5** mower, spade **6** shovel, sickle, weeder
grasping: **5** tongs **6** pliers **8** tweezers
hand printing: **6** brayer, roller
hide cleaning: **6** slater
kind of: **5** dolly **6** fraise, mortar, pestle, rabble **7** mattock, sadiron, scraper
kitchen: pot, pan **5** corer **6** kettle **7** skillet, spatula
lifting: pry **5** lever, tongs
logging: **6** peavey
nap-raising: **6** teasel
pounding: **4** maul **6** hammer, pestle
printer's: **5** biron, press
shovel-like: **5** scoop, spoon **6** trowel
surgical: **7** scalpel **9** tenaculum
threshing: **5** flail
implicate: **5** imply **7** concern, embroil, involve **11** incriminate
implicit: **5** tacit **8** absolute, complete, inherent **9** suggested **10** unshakable
implied: **5** tacit **6** hinted **10** understood
implore: ask, beg **4** coax, pray **5** crave, plead **6** appeal **7** beseech, entreat, solicit **8** petition **10** supplicate
imply: **4** hint **7** connote, involve, presume, signify, suggest **8** comprise, intimate **9** insinuate, presuppose
impolite: **4** rude **5** bluff, crude, rough **7** ill-bred, uncivil **10** indecorous, ungracious, unmannerly, unpolished **12** discourteous **13** disrespectful
impolitic: **6** unwise **10** indiscreet **11** inexpedient, injudicious **12** undiplomatic
import: **5** sense, value **6** convey, denote **7** betoken, bring in, meaning, signify **8** indicate **9** introduce, substance
tax: **4** duty **6** tariff
importance: **4** rank **5** worth **6** moment, weight **7** account, gravity, stature **8** prestige, standing **9** dimension, influence **11** consequence **13** consideration
to be of: **6** matter
important: **4** dear, high **5** grave, great **6** urgent **7** pompous, serious **8** eventful, material **9** momentous, ponderous **10** noteworthy, preeminent **11** influential, significant **12** considerable **13** consequential
important person: VIP **6** bigwig **7** magnate
importunate: **6** urgent **7** teasing **8** pressing **9** demanding, imploring **10** burdensome, persistent
importune: beg, dun, nag, ply, woo **4** urge **5** plead **6** appeal **7** beseech, entreat, solicit **10** supplicate

impose: **4** levy **5** apply **6** create, slap on **7** command, dictate, inflict, obtrude **8** generate **9** institute
impose upon: **4** dupe **5** cheat **7** exploit, palm off
imposing: big **5** burly, proud **6** august **7** stately **9** grandiose, pyramidal **10** commanding, impressive **11** outstanding
imposition: tax **4** duty, fine, levy **5** fraud, gouge, trick **6** burden **7** penalty **9** deception
impossible: **9** insoluble **12** beyond reason, unattainable **13** impracticable
impost: tax **4** duty, levy task, toll **6** annale, avania, custom, excise, surtax, tariff, weight **7** tribute **8** chaptrel
India: **5** abwab
salt: **7** gabelle
impostor: **4** sham **5** cheat, faker, fraud, phony, quack **8** deceiver **9** charlatan, pretender **10** mountebank
imposture: gag **4** sham **5** cheat, fraud, trick **6** deceit, humbug **8** artifice, delusion, quackery **9** deception, falsehood, imitation **10** imposition, simulacrum **11** counterfeit
impotence: **7** acratia **8** weakness **10** feebleness
impotent: **6** barren **7** sterile **8** helpless **9** powerless **11** ineffective
impound: **5** seize, store **6** freeze **7** collect **11** appropriate
impoverish: **4** ruin **6** beggar, weaken **7** deplete, exhaust
impoverished: **4** poor **5** needy **6** bereft **7** drained **8** bankrupt, indigent **9** destitute
impractical: **9** visionary **10** idealistic, starry-eyed, unfeasible **11** unrealistic
imprecation: **4** oath **5** curse **8** anathema **9** blasphemy, profanity **10** execration **11** deprecation, malediction
impregnable: **4** firm, hard **10** unshakable, unyielding **12** inexpugnable
impregnate: **4** soak **6** charge, infuse, leaven **8** fructify, permeate, saturate **9** fecundate, fertilize
impresario: **7** manager **8** director **9** conductor **12** entrepreneur
impress: fix **4** levy, mark, seal, sway **5** affix, brand, delve, print, stamp **6** affect, enlist **7** engrave, implant, imprint **9** inculcate, influence
impressed: **4** awed **8** affected
impression: **4** dent, dint, idea, mark **5** fancy, print, stamp **6** effect, signet **7** opinion **8** reaction **10** conception
printing: **6** macule
impressionable: **7** plastic **9** sensitive **10** responsive **11** susceptible
impressionist painter: **5** Manet, Monet

6 Renoir 8 Pissarro

impressive: 5 grand 6 august, moving, solemn 8 forcible, imposing, majestic, striking 9 arresting, memorable

imprimatur: 7 license 8 approval, sanction

imprint: fix 4 mark 5 press, stamp 6 effect 7 engrave, impress

imprison: 4 cage, jail 5 limit 6 arrest, commit, detain, immure, intern 7 confine, enclose 8 restrain 11 incarcerate

imprisonment: 6 duress 7 durance 9 captivity 11 confinement

improbable: 5 fishy 8 unlikely

impromptu: 7 offhand 9 extempore 10 off the cuff 11 unrehearsed 14 extemporaneous

improper: ill 4 evil 5 amiss, undue, unfit, wrong 6 unjust, naught 7 illegal, illicit 8 indecent, infra dig, shameful, unseemly 9 incorrect 10 inaccurate, indecorous, indelicate, out of place, unbecoming 12 illegitimate

impropriety: 5 gaffe, shame 7 faux pas 8 solecism 9 barbarism 12 impertinence

improve: 4 grow, help, mend 5 amend, edify, emend 6 better, enrich 7 advance, augment, benefit, correct, enhance, perfect, promote, rectify, retouch 9 cultivate, intensify 10 ameliorate

improvident: 8 prodigal, wasteful 9 negligent 10 thriftless 11 extravagant

improvise: 5 ad-lib 6 devise, invent 7 compose 8 contrive 11 extemporize

music: 4 vamp

imprudent: 4 rash 6 unwary, unwise 7 foolish 8 reckless 10 incautious, indiscreet 11 injudicious 12 shortsighted

impudence: lip 4 gall 5 brass, cheek, folly 8 audacity 9 arrogance, assurance, hardihood, insolence 10 confidence, effrontery 11 presumption 13 shamelessness

impudent: 4 bold, pert, rude 5 brash, sassy, saucy 6 brazen 7 forward 8 insolent 9 barefaced, officious 11 impertinent 13 disrespectful

impugn: 4 deny 5 fight 6 assail, resist 7 gainsay 9 challenge, insinuate 10 contradict

impulse: 4 urge 5 drift, force 6 impact, motive 7 impetus 8 instinct, stimulus 9 incentive 11 instigation

blind: ate

characterized by: 7 sensory

divine: 8 afflatus

traveling: 10 wanderlust

impulsive: 5 quick 6 fitful 8 headlong 9 impellent, impetuous

impure: 4 foul, lewd, vile 5 dirty, gross, mixed 6 coarse, filthy, unholy 7 bas-tard, defiled, obscene, unclean, vicious 8 indecent, inferior, unchaste 10 unhallowed 11 adulterated, incongruous, unwholesome

impurity: 5 dross, filth, taint 8 foulness 9 pollution 10 corruption 11 contaminant

impute: 4 give 5 count 6 charge, credit, impart, reckon 7 arraign, ascribe 8 consider 9 attribute

in: 4 amid 5 among 6 corner, entree 7 arrived 9 incumbent

a bad way: 4 sick 5 upset 9 on the spot

a row: 4 arow 6 alined, serial 7 aligned

abeyance: 7 pending

abundance: 6 galore, plenty

accordance with: 5 as per 10 pursuant to

addition: too, yet 4 also, more, plus 7 besides, further 8 moreover

advance: 5 ahead 6 before

another direction: 4 away

any case: 8 however 11 nonetheless

any event: 15 notwithstanding

arrears: 5 owing 6 behind 7 overdue

as much: 5 since 7 because

camera: 7 sub rosa 8 secretly 10 furtively

capacity of: qua

case: 4 lest

common: 5 alike

company of: 4 with

concert: 8 together

due course: 4 soon 11 opportunely

Dutch: 9 disgraced 10 out of favor

every way: 5 fully 6 wholly 7 totally 8 entirely 10 completely, thoroughly

excess: too 4 over

existence: 6 extant

fact: 5 truly 6 indeed 7 de facto(L.)

favor of: for, pro

few cases: 6 rarely, seldom

good season: 5 early 6 betime

great need: 7 straits

manner of: ala

name only: 7 nominal 10 supposedly

place of: for 5 stead 7 instead

reality: 8 actually

regard to: 5 anent 10 concerning

same place: 4 ibid

shape: fit 4 neat, trim 5 ready

spite of: 10 regardless

stitches: 6 amused 8 laughing

store: 8 awaiting

that case: 4 then

the case of: 4 in re(L.)

the center of: 4 amid

the interim: 9 meanwhile

the know: hep, hip

the main: 9 generally

the manner of: a la

the mood: 5 eager 7 willing

the raw: 4 nude 10 dishabille

the red: 5 broke 8 bankrupt, strapped
the same period: 15 contemporaneous
the time of: 6 during
this: 6 herein
this way: 4 thus
toto: all 5 whole 8 complete 10 completely
truth: 6 certes, indeed, verily 8 forsooth
what way: how 7 quomodo(L.)
year of: 4 anno
inability: 9 impotence 10 incapacity 12 incompetence
to articulate: 7 anaudia
to chew: 8 amasesis
to comprehend: 11 acatalepsia
to name correctly: 9 paranomia
to read: 6 alexia
to remember: 7 amnesia
to speak: 6 anepia
to stand erect: 7 astasia
to swallow: 7 aphagia
to understand speech: 7 aphasia
inaccessible: 6 closed 11 unreachable 12 unattainable 14 unapproachable
inaccuracy: 5 error 7 mistake
inaccurate: 5 false, wrong 6 faulty 7 inexact 8 specious 9 defective, erroneous, incorrect, off target
Inachus's daughter: Io
inaction: 8 idleness 9 inertness
temporary: 5 pause 6 recess 7 respite
inactive: lax 4 dead, idle, slow 5 heavy, inert, prone, slack, still 6 latent, otiose, supine 7 dormant, passive 8 dilatory, faineant, indolent, sleeping, slothful, sluggish 9 quiescent, recumbent, sedentary 10 unemployed
inadequate: 5 short 6 scanty 7 wanting 8 below par 9 deficient, imperfect 12 insufficient
perilously: 7 Icarian
inadvertence: 10 negligence 12 carelessness, heedlessness 15 thoughtlessness
inadvisable: 4 rash 6 unwise 10 indiscreet
inalienable: 6 sacred 8 absolute, inherent 10 inviolable
inalterable: 9 steadfast 12 unchangeable
inamorata: 8 mistress 10 sweetheart
inane: 5 empty, silly, vapid 6 vacant 7 fatuous, foolish, idiotic, vacuous 8 trifling 9 doddering, frivolous, pointless, senseless, worthless 11 nonsensical 13 characterless
inanimate: 4 dead, dull, flat 5 inert 6 stolid 8 lifeless 10 insensible, spiritless 11 unconscious
inanition: 7 fasting 8 lethargy 9 emptiness
inanity: 7 vacuity 9 emptiness, frivolity, silliness 10 flimsiness, triviality 11 foolishness 13 senselessness
inapposite: 10 irrelevant

inappreciable: 4 thin 7 tenuous 10 impalpable 11 microscopic 13 imperceptible
inappropriate: 5 inapt 8 improper 9 unfitting 10 out of place, unsuitable
inapt: 5 inept 6 clumsy 7 awkward 8 backward 10 amateurish, unsuitable
inarch: 5 graft
inarticulate: shy 4 dumb, mute 7 blurred 10 tongue-tied
inartistic: 9 tasteless
inasmuch as: for 5 since 7 because 11 considering
inattention: 7 neglect 9 disregard 10 negligence
inattentive: lax 6 absent, remiss 8 careless, heedless 9 forgetful, negligent, unheeding, unmindful 10 abstracted, neglectful 11 inadvertent, thoughtless 13 inconsiderate
inaugurate: 4 open 5 begin, start 6 induct, launch 7 install, usher in 8 initiate 9 auspicate, introduce 10 consecrate
inauspicious: bad 4 foul 7 adverse, ominous 8 sinister 12 unpropitious
inauthentic: 5 false 6 mythic, unreal 8 doubtful, spurious 9 uncertain 10 apocryphal, fictitious
inborn desire: 7 conatus
inbreak: 6 inroad 8 invasion 9 incursion
inbred: 6 inborn, innate, native 7 natural 10 congenital
Inca: 9 Atahualpa
clan: 5 ayllu
empire: 4 Peru
god: 4 Inti 5 Choun, Iraya 6 Chasca 9 Uiracocha, Viracocha 10 Pachacamac
king: 9 Atabalipa, Atahualpa
priests: 6 Amauta
ruler's sister-wife: 5 Ccoya
incalculable: 6 untold 8 infinite 9 boundless, countless, uncertain 11 illimitable 12 immeasurable 13 unpredictable
incandescence: 4 glow, heat
incantation: 5 chant, charm, magic, spell 6 carmen(L.) 7 sorcery 11 conjuration, enchantment
incapable: 5 unfit 6 unable 9 untrained 11 inefficient, unqualified
incapacitate: 4 lame 7 cripple, disable 10 disqualify
incarcerate: 4 jail 6 immure, shut up 7 confine 8 imprison
incarnate: 6 embody 8 make real 10 give form to 11 personified
incarnation: 6 avatar, Christ 10 embodiment
of Vishnu: 4 Rama
incase: 5 cover 7 enclose 8 surround
incautious: 4 rash 6 unwary 8 careless,

heedless, reckless **9** impolitic, imprudent, unguarded **10** indiscreet

incendiarism: 5 arson **9** pyromania

incendiary: 7 firebug **8** agitator **10** pyromaniac **12** inflammatory

incense: 5 anger, aroma **6** arouse, enrage, incite **7** perfume, provoke **8** enkindle, irritate
burner: **6** censer **8** thurible
spice: **6** balsam, stacte

incentive: 4 goad, spur **5** spark **6** motive **7** impetus, impulse **8** stimulus **9** influence **10** incitement, inducement **11** provocation **13** consideration, encouragement

inception: 5 start **6** origin **9** beginning **10** initiation **12** commencement

incertitude: 5 doubt **9** suspicion **10** skepticism, insecurity

incessant: 6 steady **7** endless, eternal **8** constant **9** ceaseless, continual **11** everlasting, unremitting

incessantly: 7 forever **11** continually, unceasingly

inch: 5 creep **7** measure **10** move slowly
one-thousandth: mil
three-quarters of: **5** digit

inch along: 9 worm ahead

inches: *forty-five:* ell
four: **4** hand
nine: **4** span
39.37: **5** meter
two and one-quarter: **4** nail

inchmeal: 9 gradually

inchoate: 8 unformed, unshaped **9** incipient **10** disordered, incomplete

incident: 5 event **7** episode **8** accident, casualty, occasion **9** happening **11** contingency

incidental: minor **6** casual **8** episodic **9** accessory, extrinsic, secondary **10** accidental, contingent, fortuitous, occasional **12** adventitious **14** circumstantial

incidentally: 6 obiter **7** apropos **8** by the way

incinerate: 4 burn **7** combust, consume, cremate

incinerator: 7 furnace **9** crematory

incipient: 7 budding, initial, nascent **8** inchoate **9** beginning **10** commencing

incise: cut **4** chop, etch, rase **5** carve **7** engrave
narrowly: **9** laciniate

incision: cut **4** gash, slit **5** notch, slash

incisive: 5 acute, sharp **6** biting **7** cutting, probing **9** sarcastic, trenchant **10** perceptive **11** penetrating

incisor: 6 cutter **9** foretooth

incite: egg, hie **4** abet, fire, goad, move, prod, spur, urge **5** impel **6** arouse, compel, entice, excite, exhort, foment, induce **7** actuate, agitate, animate, com-

move, provoke **8** motivate **9** encourage, instigate, stimulate

incitement: 6 motive **8** stimulus **9** incentive

incivility: 8 rudeness **9** surliness **10** disrespect, effrontery **11** discourtesy **12** churlishness, impertinence **14** unmannerliness

inclemency: 8 asperity

inclement: raw **4** hard, rude **5** harsh, rough **6** severe, stormy **8** rigorous **10** unmerciful

inclination: 4 bent, bias, broo, hang, love, urge, will **5** fancy, slant, slope, taste, tenor, trend **6** affect, animus, ascent, desire, liking **7** descent, leaning **8** fondness, gradient, penchant, tendency **9** acclivity, affection, direction, proneness **10** attachment, proclivity **11** disposition **12** predilection

incline: bow, dip, tip **4** bend, cant, heel, lean, list, ramp, tend, tilt **5** be apt, grade, pitch, shape, slant, slide, slope, trend **6** prefer **7** upgrade

inclined: apt **4** fain, wont **5** alist, atilt, prone **6** biased, likely, minded **7** hanging **8** addicted **11** predisposed

inclose: 5 hem in, pen in **6** encase **7** contain **8** surround

inclosure: ree(Sc.) **4** wall **5** fence **8** sepiment **10** impalement
animal: pen, sty **4** cage, cote, fold **5** hutch, kraal **6** corral

include: 5 cover **6** entail, take in **7** contain, embrace, involve **8** comprise **9** encompass

incognito: 7 unknown **8** disguised **12** unidentified

incoherent: 6 broken **8** rambling **9** illogical **10** disjointed **11** incongruous **12** disconnected, inconsequent, inconsistent

income: 4 gain **5** rente(F.) **6** profit, return **7** produce, revenue **8** interest, proceeds, receipts **9** emolument

incommensurate: 7 unequal **10** dissimilar **12** insufficient, inconsistent **16** disproportionate

incommode: vex **5** annoy **6** molest, plague **7** trouble **8** disquiet **9** disoblige **10** discommode, **13** inconvenience

incomparable: 8 peerless **9** matchless, unequaled, unrivaled **10** surpassing **11** superlative **15** incommeasurable

incompatible: 8 contrary **9** unmixable **10** discordant **11** conflicting, incongruous **12** inharmonious **13** contradictory, unsympathetic **14** irreconcilable

incompetence: 9 inability, unfitness **10** disability

incompetent: 5 inept, unfit **8** helpless **9** incapable, unskilled **10** untalented **11**

inefficient, unqualified **12** insufficient

incomplete: 5 rough, short **6** broken, undone **7** divided, lacking, partial, wanting **8** immature, inchoate **9** defective, imperfect **10** unfinished **11** fragmentary

incomprehensible: 8 abstruse **9** graspless **10** fathomless, mysterious, unreadable **11** unthinkable **12** unimaginable **13** inconceivable **14** unintelligible

inconceivable: 7 strange **10** improbable, incredible **11** unthinkable **12** beyond belief

inconclusive: 4 open **9** uncertain, undecided **10** indefinite, up in the air **11** ineffective

incondite: 5 crude **9** unrefined **10** unpolished **11** unorganized

incongruity: 9 inharmony **10** dissonance **11** incoherence **12** disagreement **13** inconsistency **14** unsuitableness

incongruous: 5 alien **6** absurd, impure **9** grotesque **10** discordant, unsuitable **12** disagreeable, inconsistent, inharmonious **13** inappropriate

inconsequential: 5 petty, small **6** paltry **7** trivial **8** picayune, piddling, trifling **10** irrelevant **11** unimportant

inconsiderable: 5 petty **7** trivial **8** careless, unworthy **10** negligible

inconsiderate: 4 rash **6** unkind **8** careless **9** imprudent, negligent **10** incautious; indiscreet, neglectful **11** improvident, injudicious, thoughtless

inconsistent: 6 fickle **8** unstable **9** dissonant **10** capricious, discordant, discrepant, inconstant **11** vacillating **13** contradictory **14** irreconcilable

inconsolable: 11 comfortless, heartbroken **12** disconsolate

inconstant: 6 fickle **7** elusive, erratic **8** disloyal, variable **9** desultory, faithless **10** capricious, changeable **12** inconsistent

incontestable: 4 sure **5** valid **7** certain **10** undeniable **11** indubitable, irrefutable

incontrovertible: 7 certain **10** undeniable

inconvenience: 5 annoy **8** disquiet **9** annoyance **10** discomfort, discommode, uneasiness **11** awkwardness, disturbance **12** discomfiture **13** embarrassment

inconvenient: 7 awkward, unhandy **8** annoying **10** unsuitable **11** troublesome **12** unreasonable

incorporate: mix **4** fuse, join **5** blend, merge, unite **6** absorb, embody **7** combine **9** integrate **10** assimilate

incorporation: 10 absorption **11** combination

incorporeal: 4 airy **8** bodiless **9** asomatous, spiritual, sprightly **10** immaterial **13** unsubstantial

incorrect: bad **5** false, wrong **6** faulty, untrue **9** erroneous

incorrect naming of objects: 9 paranomia

incorrigible: 8 hardened **10** beyond help **11** intractable **12** unmanageable

incorruptible: 4 just, pure **6** honest **7** upright

increase: add, eke, wax **4** eche, gain, grow, rise, rist **5** boost, raise, swell **6** accrue, amount, better, dilate, expand, extend, gather, growth **7** amplify, augment, enhance, enlarge, greaten, inflate, magnify **8** addition, flourish, heighten, multiply **9** accession, advantage, aggravate, expansion, extension, increment, intensify **10** accelerate, accumulate, aggrandize, appreciate **11** aggravation, development, enlargement **12** augmentation **13** amplification **15** intensification

in sound: **9** crescendo

possessions: **5** amass **6** enrich

salary: **5** raise

incredible: 6 absurd **7** awesome **10** astounding, far-fetched, impossible **12** preposterous, unbelievable

incredulous: 7 dubious **8** doubting **9** faithless, skeptical **10** mistrustful, unbelieving

increment: 4 gain **6** growth, income **8** increase **12** augmentation

increscent: 6 waxing **7** growing **9** enlarging **10** increasing

incriminate: 6 accuse **7** impeach, involve **9** implicate

incrust: 4 coat **5** glaze **6** barkle

incubate: 5 brood, hatch **7** develop

incubus: 4 load **5** demon **6** burden, spirit **9** hindrance, nightmare **10** impediment **11** encumbrance

inculcate: 5 infix **6** infuse, instil **7** implant, impress, instill

inculpate: 5 blame **11** incriminate

incumbent: 7 binding **8** occupant **9** overlying **11** leaning upon

incunabula: 7 infancy, origins **10** beginnings **11** first stages

incur: 8 contract **9** encounter

incurable: 8 hopeless **11** irreparable **12** irremediable **13** irretrievable

incurious: 9 apathetic **11** unconcerned, uninquiring **12** uninterested

incursion: 4 rade(Sc.), raid **5** foray **6** inroad **7** assault, descent, hosting **8** invasion **10** dragonnade

incurved: 7 concave

incus: ear **5** ambos, anvil

indebted: 8 beholden **9** obligated

indecency: 8 impurity **9** immodesty, in-

decorum, obscenity **10** indelicacy
indecent: 4 foul **5** gross, nasty **6** coarse, greasy, impure **7** immoral, obscene **8** immodest, improper, unseemly **9** dishonest **10** scurrilous
indecipherable: 9 illegible
indecision: 5 doubt **9** hesitancy **10** hesitation **11** uncertainty, vacillation **12** irresolution
indecorous: 4 rude **6** coarse **7** uncivil **8** immodest, impolite, improper, unseemly **10** unbecoming **11** distasteful
indeed: yea **5** truly **6** really **7** in faith, in truth **8** actually, forsooth, honestly **9** certainly **10** positively
indefatigable: 4 busy **8** tireless, untiring **9** assiduous **10** persistent, unwearying **11** persevering
indefensible: 11 inexcusable **12** unpardonable **13** insupportable
indefinite: 5 loose, vague **7** inexact, neutral **8** aoristic **9** ambiguous, equivocal, uncertain, unlimited **10** inexplicit **12** inconclusive
pronoun: any, one **4** some
indehiscent fruit: uva **5** grape, melon
indelible: 4 fast **5** fixed **9** permanent **10** inerasable **12** ineffaceable, ineradicable, inexpungible
indelicate: raw **5** broad, gross **6** coarse, greasy **7** fulsome **8** impolite, improper, unseemly **9** offensive, unrefined **10** indecorous, unbecoming
indemnification: 10 reparation **11** restitution
indemnify: pay **6** recoup **9** reimburse **10** compensate, recompense
indemnity: 7 amnesty **9** exemption **10** protection **12** compensation
indent: jag **4** dent, gimp **5** chase, delve, inlay, notch, press, stamp, tooth **6** bruise, emboss **7** depress
indentation: bay **4** dent, nick **5** notch **6** dimple, recess **10** impression
indenture: 8 contract **9** agreement, inventory
independence: 7 freedom **10** competency
independent: 4 free **5** proud **9** sovereign, uncoerced **11** self-reliant **12** self-centered, uncontrolled, unrestricted **13** self-governing
independently: 5 apart **10** absolutely
indestructible: 7 durable, lasting **9** permanent **10** inviolable **12** imperishable
indeterminate: 5 vague **7** obscure **8** formless **9** uncertain, unlimited
index: 4 file, list **5** table **7** catalog **9** catalogue, repertory
India: *capital:* **8** New Delhi
   city: **4** Agra **5** Delhi, Patna, Poona, Simla **6** Baroda, Bombay, Guntur, Howrah, Imphal, Indore, Jaipur, Kanpur, Madras, Nagpur, Ranchi **7** Lucknow **8** Calcutta, Shillong, Sholapur **9** Ahmadabad, Allahabad, Bangalore, Hyderabad
   desert: **4** Thar
   ethnic stock: **5** Aryan, Munda **6** Mongol **9** Dravidian
   founder of Mogul dynasty: **5** Baber
   island group: **7** Andaman, Minicoy, Nicobar **8** Amindivi **9** Laccadive
   language: **4** Urdu **5** Hindi, Oriya, Tamil **6** Sindhi, Telugu **7** Bengali, Kannada, Marathi, Punjabi **8** Assamese, Gujarati, Kashmiri **9** Kannarese, Malayalam
   monetary unit: **5** paisa, rupee
   mountain range: **5** Ghats **6** Zaskar **7** Satpura, Siwalik **8** Aravalli, Himalaya **9** Hindu Kush
   mountain pass: **5** Bolan, Gumal **6** Khyber
   native: **5** Hindu
   plateau: **6** Deccan **8** Nilgiris
   port: **6** Bombay, Cochin, Madras, Mandvi, Panaji **8** Calcutta **10** Trivandrum
   river: **4** Beas, Luni, Kosi, Ravi, Sind **5** Bhima, Indus, Rapti, Tapti, Tista **6** Chenab, Ganges, Gomati, Jhelum, Sutlej, Yamuna **7** Cauvery, Krishna, Narmada **8** Ghaghara, Godavari, Mahanadi **9** Indravati **11** Brahmaputra
   state: **5** Assam, Bihar, Delhi **6** Kerala, Orissa, Punjab, Sikkim **7** Gujarat, Haryana, Manipur, Tripura **8** Nagaland **9** Karnataka, Meghalaya, Rajasthan, Tamil Nadu **10** West Bengal
   statesman establishing British control: **5** Clive
Indian (see also **Hindu**): *abuse:* **4** gali **5** galee
   acrobat: nat
   agent: **4** amin **5** ameen
   alphabet: **10** Devanagari
   ambassador: **5** vakil **6** vakeel
   ancestor: **4** Manu **5** Pitri
   animal, ox-like: **4** zebu
   antelope: **6** nilgai, nilgau **7** chikara, nilghai
   apartment: **6** zenana
   army officer: **4** naig, naik **6** naique **7** jemadar, jemidar
   astrologer: **5** joshi
   attorney: **6** muktar
   awning: **9** shamianah
   baby: **4** baba
   bandit: **6** dacoit
   bard: **4** bhat
   bathing place: **4** ghat **5** ghaut
   bazaar: **5** chawk, chowk
   bean: urd
   bear: **4** balu **5** baloo
   bearer: **6** sirdar
   bed: **7** charpai, charpoy
   bed cover: **9** palampore

bill of exchange: **5** hundi
bird: **5** shama **8** avadavat
blight: **4** soka
boat: **7** masoola
bodice: **5** choli
body servant: **6** sirdar
boy: **6** chokra, Mowgli
bracelet: **6** sankha
bread: **7** chapati **8** chapatti
breakfast: **5** hazri
brick: **6** soorki, soorky **7** soorkee
buck: **5** sasin
buffalo: **4** arna **5** arnee
bulbul: **4** kala
butter: ghi **4** ghee
buzzard: **4** tesa
cabinet: **7** almirah
calico: **5** saloo **6** salloo
cannabis: **5** ganja
canoe: **5** tanee
cape: **4** divi
carpet: **4** agra
carriage: **4** ekka **5** bandy, tonga **6** gharri, gharry
cashmere: **5** ulwan
caste: **4** Ahir, Mali **5** Dhobi, Lohar, Singh, Sudra **6** Vaisya **7** Agarwal, Brahmin, Harijan **9** Kshatriya
cavalryman: **5** sowar **6** risala
cedar: **6** deodar
chamber: **4** Kiva **8** Tahkhana
charm: **6** mantra
chief: mir **4** raja, rana **5** rajah **6** sirdar
church: **5** samaj
cigarette: **4** biri
civet: **5** rasse, zibet **6** zibeth
clarinet: **4** been
clerk: **4** babu **5** baboo
cloak: **5** choga
cloth: **7** dhurrie
coin: lac, pie **4** anna, dawm, fels, hoon, lakh, pice, tara **5** abidi, crore, paisa, rupee
college: Tol
colonialist: **5** Clive
cook: **8** bawarchi
corn: zea
coronation: **8** abhiseka
court official: **5** nazir
cowrie: **5** zimbi
crane: **5** sarus
crocodile: **6** gavial, mugger
crop: **4** rabi
cymbal: tal
dagger: **5** katar
dais: **8** chabutra
dance: **6** nautch **7** cantico
dancer: nat **8** bayadere
deer: **4** axis **6** chital, chitra, sambar, sambur
demon: **4** bhut **5** asura
deputy: **5** nabob, nawab

devil tree: **4** dita
dignitary: **5** rajah
dill: **4** soya
disease: **5** agrom
dog: **5** dhole **6** pariah
drama: **6** nataka
drink: **4** soma **6** arrack
drinking pot: **5** lotah
drought: **4** soka
drug: **5** bhang
dust storm: **7** shaitan, sheitan
earth: **5** regur
educated man: **4** babu **6** pundit
educated woman: **7** pundita
elephant: **5** hathi
elephant driver: **6** mahout
epic: **8** Ramayana **11** Mahabharata
falcon: **6** shahin **7** shaheen
fan: **5** punka **6** punkah
father: **4** babu
festival: **4** Holi, mela
fiber: **6** ambary
fig tree: **5** pipal **6** peepul
fish: **5** dorab
flower: **5** lotus
fruit: bel
garment: **4** sari **5** burqa, saree
god: **4** Deva, Yama **5** Shiva
goddess: **4** Amma **5** Amman
gossip: gup
government: **6** sircar
governor: **5** nazim
grass: **4** kusa **5** kusha **6** bhabar, darbha
grinding stone: **4** mano **6** metate
grove: **5** Sarna
guard: **7** daloyet
guide: **7** shikari **8** shikaree
hall: **6** durbar
handkerchief: **7** malabar
harem: **6** zenana
harvest: **4** rabi
hemp: **4** bang **5** bhang, ramie
herb: **6** sesame **7** curcuma, tumeric
hero: **4** Rama
holy: sri **4** shri **5** shree
holy man: **5** fakir, sadhu **6** saddhu
house: **5** mahal **8** bungalow
impost: **5** abwab
instrument: **4** vina **5** sarod, sitar **7** sarinda
intoxicant: **4** soma
jungle: **5** shola
justice: **7** adawlut
knife: dah
laborer: **4** toty **7** totyman
lady: **7** sahibah
law opinion: **5** futwa
leader: **5** Nehru **6** Gandhi
legal claim: hak **4** hakh
leopard, hunting: **7** cheetah
loincloth: **5** dhoti
lord: **4** mian

mahogany: **4** toon **5** toona
mail: dak **4** dawk
mangrove: **5** goran
master: **5** saheb, sahib
matting: **5** tatta
meal: ata **4** atta
measure: ady, dha, gaz, gez, guz, jow, kos, lan, ser **4** byee, coss, dain, dhan, hath, jaob, koss, kunk, moot, para, rati, raik, seit, taun, teng, tola **5** bigha, cahar, covid, crosa, danda, denda, drona, garce, gireh, hasta, krosa, pally, parah, ratti, salay, yojan **6** adhaka, amunam, angula, covido, cudava, cumbha, geerah, lamany, moolum, mushti, palgat, parrah, ropani, tipree, unglee, yojana **7** adoulie, dhanush, gavyuti, khahoon, niranga, prastha, vitasti **8** okthabah
merchant: **5** banya **6** banian **8** soudagur **9** brinjaree
millet: **4** joar
mulberry: **6** alroot
muslin: **5** doria **6** gurrah
narcotic: **4** bang **5** bhang **7** hashish
nonviolence: **6** ahimsa
nurse: **4** amah, ayah, dhai
old money: **5** mohur
ox: **4** zebu
peasant: **4** ryot
pheasant: **5** monal **6** monaul, moonal
pipe: **6** hookah
policeman: **4** peon **5** sepoy
priest: **5** mobed, mulla **6** mullah
prince: **4** bana, rana **5** rajah
princess: **4** rani **5** begum, ranee
property: **4** dhan
queen: **4** rani **5** begum, ranee **8** maharani
rainy season: **6** varsha **7** monsoon
religion: **5** Islam **8** Buddhism, Hinduism
religious sect: **4** Sikh
rice: **4** boro
rubber: **10** caoutchouc
rule: raj
sacred grove: **5** Sarna
saffron: **7** zedoary **8** turmeric
sage: **6** pandit, pundit
servant: **4** maty **6** bearer **10** mussalchee
sheep: **5** urial **6** oorial
shirt: **6** banian
shrine: **6** dagaba, dagoba
silk: **4** muga **6** cabeca
silkworm: eri
snake: **5** krait
soldier: **4** peon **5** sepoy
song: **4** raga
spinning wheel: **6** charka **7** charkha
storm: **5** tufan
sun worshiper: **5** parsi **6** parsee
supreme court: **6** Sudder
Taj Mahal site: **4** Agra
tapir: **8** saladang
tariff: **6** zabeta

tax: **10** chaukidari
teacher: **4** guru **5** akhun, mulla **6** akhund, mullah, pandit, pundit **7** akhoond
tenant: **4** ryot
title: sri **5** sahib **6** sirdar **7** sahibah
tower: **5** minar
tree: bel, dar, lin, sal **4** dita, myxa, shoq, teak **5** anjan, pipal, salai **6** banyan, deodar **7** majagua
tribe: Gor, Jat **4** Bhil **6** Badaga **7** Sherani, Shirani
turban: **8** seerband
vessel: **4** doni **6** shibar
viceroy: **5** nabob, nawab
village: **5** abadi **6** mouzah
weight: moo, pai, ser, vis **4** bhar, dhan, drum, kona, myat, pala, pank, pice, raik, rati, ruay, seer, tank, tola, yava **5** adpao, bahar, candy, catty, hubba, masha, maund, pally, pouah, ratti, retti, tical, ticul, tikal **6** abucco, dhurra, karsha, ruttee **7** chittak, peiktha **8** chittack
wheat: **4** suji **5** sujee
wife's cremation: **6** suttee
wild ox: **4** gaur
wine: **5** shrab
wood: eng, sal **4** toon **5** kokra
Indian (Americas): **6** red man **7** Amerind
American: Aht, Kaw, Oto, Sac, Ute **4** Cree, Dene, Erie, Hopi, Ioni, Iowa, Otoe, Pima, Sauk, Tana, Taos, Yuma, Zuni **5** Banak, Caddo, Coree, Creek, Huron, Kania, Kansa, Keres, Kiowa, Miami, Omaha, Osage, Piute, Sioux, Tinne **6** Abnaki, Apache, Dakota, Kansas, Lenape, Mohave, Mojave, Navaho, Navajo, Nootka, Ojibwa, Oneida, Ottawa, Paiute, Pawnee, Sambos, Seneca, Siwash **7** Abenaki, Arikara, Arapaho, Choctaw, Keresan, Mohegan, Shawnee **8** Apalachi, Cherokee, Cheyenne, Chippewa, Comanche, Delaware, Hitchiti, Illinois, Iroquois, Kickapoo, Onondaga, Pokonchi, Sagamore, Seminole, Shoshone **9** Algonquin, Apalachee, Blackfoot, Chickasaw, Tuscarora, Winnebago **10** Muskhogean **12** Narragansett
blanket: **6** stroud **9** strouding
Bolivia: Uro **4** Iten, Moxo **6** Aymara **10** Chiriguano
Brazil: **5** Bravo **7** Tariana
Canadian: **4** Cree, Dene **5** Tinne **6** Micmac, Tinneh **7** Sanetch **9** Athabasca **10** Athabascan
Caribbean: **4** Yaos **5** Arara, Trios **6** Caribs, Oyanas **7** Akawais, Aparais, Chaymas, Macusis **8** Arawakan
ceremonial chamber: **4** kiva
chief: **6** sachem **8** sagamore
child: **7** papoose

corn: zea **4** samp **5** maize
council: **6** powwow
craft: **5** canoe, kayak **6** dugout
female: **5** squaw **6** mahala, mahaly
festival: **8** potlach
fighter: **5** Boone, Miles **6** Custer
flathead: **7** Chinook
game: **6** canute
Great Spirit: **6** manito
guardian spirit: **5** totem
hatchet: **8** tomahawk
headdress: **7** topknot
hut: **5** hogan, toldo **6** wikiup **7** wickiup
leader: **7** Cochise, Pontiac **8** Geronimo, Powhatan, Tecumseh **10** Crazy Horse, Sitting Bull
lodge: **5** tepee
man: **4** buck **5** brave, chief **6** sannup
meal bread: **8** corncake
memorial post: xat **5** totem
moccasin: pac
money: **6** seawan, wampum **7** seawant
Paraguay: **7** Guarani
peace pipe: **7** calumet
Peru: **4** Ande, Cana, Inca, Inka, Peba, Yutu **5** Boros, Campa, Carib, Panos **6** Aymara, Jibaro, Jiyaro, Kechua, Lamano **7** Quechua
pillar: lat, xat
pony: **6** cayuse
porridge: **4** samp
potato: **4** yamp **9** breadroot
prayer stick: **4** paho
Quechuan: **4** Inca
Rio Grande: Tao
Seminole chief: **7** Osceola
snake dancer: **4** Hopi
sorcery: ob; obe, obi
spirit: **5** totem **7** Manitou
tent: **5** tepee **6** wigwam
Tierra del Fuego: Ona **4** Agni
village: **6** pueblo
wampum: **4** peag **5** peage
warrior: **5** brave
weapon: **8** tomahwak
wigwam: **5** tepee
woman: **5** squaw
Indiana: *capital:* **12** Indianapolis
city: **4** Gary, Peru **5** Paoli **6** Brazil, Delphi, Goshen, Kokomo, Marion, Muncie, Warsaw **7** Hammond, La Porte **8** Danville **9** Fort Wayne, Lafayette, South Bend **10** Evansville, Huntington, Terre Haute, Valparaiso
county: Jay **4** Clay, Knox, Lake, Owen, Rush, Vigo **5** Miami, Posey, Wayne **6** Dubois, Fulton, Ripley, Tipton **7** Daviess, Decatur, Hancock, Spencer, Steuben, Warrick, Whitley
Indian: **5** Miami **7** Shawnee
lake: **7** Wawasee **8** Michigan

river: Eel **4** Ohio **5** White **6** Maumee, Pigeon, Wabash **7** Big Blue, St. Marys **8** Kankakee, St. Joseph **10** Tippecanoe
spa: **9** West Baden **10** French Lick
state bird: **8** cardinal
state flower: **5** peony
state motto: **22** the crossroads of America
state nickname: **7** Hoosier
state tree: **5** tulip
indicate: say **4** bode, cite, mark, read, show **5** argue, augur, point **6** allude, denote, evince, import, reveal **7** bespeak, betoken, connote, declare, display, signify, specify **8** decipher, disclose, evidence, manifest, register **9** designate **10** denominate **12** characterize
indicating: *chemical group:* azo
literal transcript: sic
succession: **7** ordinal
indication: **4** clue, hint, mark, note, omen, sign **5** proof, token, trace **6** augury, signal **7** auspice, symptom **8** argument, evidence **10** intimation **11** designation **13** manifestation
indicative: **10** expressive, suggestive
indicator: **4** dial, hand, sign, vane **5** arrow, clock, gauge, index **6** gnomon, marker **7** indices(pl.), pointer **11** annunciator
indict: **6** accuse, charge **7** impeach
indifference: **6** apathy **8** coldness, lethargy **9** aloofness, disregard **10** negligence **11** disinterest **12** carelessness, heedlessness **13** insensibility
indifferent: **4** cold, cool, soso **5** aloof, blase, stoic **6** casual **7** neutral, uneager **8** careless, listless, lukewarm, mediocre **9** apathetic, Laodicean **10** nonchalant **11** adiaphorous, unconcerned, pococurante **12** nonessential
indigene: **6** native
indigenous: **5** natal **6** inborn, innate, native **7** endemic, natural **8** homeborn, inherent **10** aboriginal **13** autochthonous
indigent: **4** free, poor, void **5** needy **7** lacking, wanting **8** beggarly **9** destitute, penniless **11** impecunious, necessitous
indigestion: **9** dyspepsia
indignant: **5** angry, irate, worth **7** annoyed **8** incensed, wrathful, **11** exasperated
indignation: ire **4** fury **5** anger, wrath **7** disdain **8** contempt **11** displeasure
indignity: cut **5** abuse, wrong **6** insult, slight **7** affront, outrage, **9** injustice **13** disparagement
indigo: **4** anil, blue
artificial source: **6** isatin
bale of: **6** seroon
derivative: **5** indol **6** indole

natural source: **4** anil **7** indican
wild genus: **8** baptisia
indigo bunting: 4 bird **5** finch
indirect: 4 side **5** vague **6** shifty, zigzag **7** devious, evasive, oblique **8** circular, rambling **9** dishonest **10** circuitous, collateral, meandering, misleading, roundabout
expense: **8** overhead
indiscernible: 13 imperceptible **17** indistinguishable
indiscreet: 4 rash **5** hasty, silly **6** unwise **7** foolish, witless **8** careless, heedless **9** impolitic, imprudent **10** ill-advised, incautious **11** injudicious **12** undiscerning **13** inconsiderate
indiscretion: 4 slip **5** folly **10** imprudence
indiscriminate: 5 mixed **6** motley, random **7** jumbled, mingled **8** confused, slap-dash **9** haphazard, hit-or-miss, wholesale **13** heterogeneous
indispensable: 5 basic, vital **7** exigent **9** essential, requisite **10** imperative
indisposed: ill **4** sick **6** ailing, averse, unwell **7** opposed **8** hesitant **9** reluctant **11** disinclined
indisposition: 6 malady **7** ailment, illness, malaise **8** disorder, sickness **9** distemper **10** discomfort, reluctance **12** disaffection **13** unwillingness
indisputable: 4 sure **7** certain, evident **8** positive **10** undeniable **11** indubitable **12** irrefragable **13** incontestable **14** unquestionable **16** incontrovertible
indissoluble: 4 firm **6** stable **7** lasting
indistinct: dim **4** dark, hazy **5** faint, misty, vague **6** cloudy, feeble **7** blurred, obscure, shadowy **9** ambiguous, unrefined **10** indefinite **17** indistinguishable
indite: pen **5** write **7** compose **8** inscribe
individual (see also **person**): one **4** oner, self, sole, unit **6** person, single, unique **7** private, special **8** distinct, selfsame, solitary **9** identical **11** inseparable
of compound animal: **4** zoon **5** zooid
selfish: **6** egoist
smug: **4** prig
individuality: 5 seity **7** oneness **9** character **10** uniqueness **11** distinction, personality **14** indivisibility, inseparability
individually: 9 severally **10** personally **14** distributively
Indo-Aryan: Jat **6** khatri, Rajput
deity: **5** Indra
Indo-European: 4 Lett, Serb, Slav **5** Aryan, Croat, Czech
language: **5** Greek, Indic **6** Baltic, Celtic, Italic, Slavic **7** Iranian **8** Albanian, Germanic, Hellenic

indoctrinate: 5 imbue, teach, tutor **7** educate **8** instruct
indolence: 5 scorn, sloth **7** inertia, languor
indolent: 4 idle, lazy **5** inert **6** otiose, supine **7** dronish **8** inactive, slothful, sluggish
indomitable: 6 dogged **8** resolute **9** steadfast **10** invincible **11** intractable **13** unconquerable
Indonesia: *capital:* **7** Jakarta
city: **5** Medan **6** Kupang, Malang, Manado, Padang **7** Bandung **8** Semarang, Surabaja **9** Palembang, Pontianak, Samarinda, Surakarta
ethnic group: **4** Dyak **5** Malay **6** Papuan **7** Chinese **8** Balinese, Javanese **9** Sundanese
island, island group: Aru, Kai, Obi **4** Bali, Batu, Buru, Leti, Nias, Java, Sawu, Sula **5** Ambon, Babar, Ceram, Dolak, Sumba, Timor, Wetar **6** Bangka, Banjak, Batjan, Borneo, Flores, Lombok, Komodo, Tidore **7** Celebes, Sangihe, Sumatra, Sumbawa, Ternate **8** Moluccas, Tanimbar **9** Halmahera **11** Lesser Sunda
lake: **4** Toba **8** Kerintji
monetary unit: sen **6** rupiah
mountain peak: **4** Lawu, Raja **5** Djaja, Raung **6** Leuser, Slamet
mountain range: **4** Iran **5** Maoke **7** Barisan, Tengger
province: **4** Bali, Java, Riau **5** Atjeh **6** Djambi, Maluku **7** Jakarta, Lampung, Sumatra **8** Bengkulu, Sulawesi (Celebes) **10** Irian Barat, Jogiakarta, Kalimantan (Borneo)
river: **4** Deli, Hari, Musi, Solo **6** Asahan, Barito, Kampar, Kapuas, Liwung **7** Brantas, Kahajan, Kali Mas, Mahakam **9** Indragiri
sea: **4** Bali, Java, Savu **5** Banda, Ceram, Timor **6** Flores **7** Arafura, Celebes, Molucca
strait: **4** Sape **5** Sunda **6** Bangka **7** Berhala, Malacca **8** Karimata, Makassar
volcano: Awu **4** Gede **6** Agung, Semeru **7** Sumbing, Tambora **8** Kerintji
volcanic plateau: **5** Idjen
indorse: See **endorse**
Indra: 5 Sakka, Sakra
dragon: **6** Vritra
elephant: **8** Airavata
father: **8** Tvashtri
food: **4** soma
heaven capital: **9** Amaravati
indubitable: 4 sure **7** assured, certain, evident **8** apparent **10** infallible, undeniable **12** irrefragable **13** incontestable **16** incontrovertible

induce: get **4** draw, lure, urge **5** infer, tempt **6** advise, elicit, suborn **7** actuate **8** conclude, convince, persuade **9** encourage, influence

inducement: **4** bait, lure **5** prize **6** motive, reason **9** incentive, influence **10** enticement **13** consideration

induct: **5** enrol **6** enlist, enroll **7** install **8** initiate **9** introduce **10** inaugurate

inductance unit: **5** henry

inductile: **10** inflexible, unyielding

induction: **8** entrance **9** accession, deduction **10** initiation **12** commencement, introduction

indue: **5** endow **6** assume, clothe, invest **7** furnish

indulge: pet **4** baby, feed **5** favor, humor, spoil **6** coddle, cosset, foster, pamper, please **7** cherish, gratify

in antics: **7** skylark

in fault finding: **5** cavil

in recreation: **4** play

to excess: **7** debauch

indulgence: **5** favor, spree **8** clemency, humoring, lenience **9** tolerance **12** dispensation **13** gratification

indulgent: **4** easy, fond, good, kind, mild **7** lenient **8** tolerant **9** compliant **10** charitable

indurate: **5** inure **6** harden **7** callous, scleral **8** obdurate, stubborn

Indus tribesman: Gor

industrial magnate: **6** tycoon

industrious: **4** busy **6** active **7** zealous **8** diligent, sedulous **9** assiduous **11** painstaking **13** indefatigable

industry: **4** toil, zeal **5** labor, skill **6** energy **8** business, hard work **9** assiduity, diligence, ingenuity **10** occupation

indwell: **6** inhere **9** be present

indwelling: **8** immanent, inherent **9** intrinsic

inebriacy: **11** drunkenness **12** intemperance

inebriate: sot **4** lush, soak **6** boozer **7** tippler, tosspot **8** drunkard **11** intoxicated

ineffable: **11** unspeakable, unutterable **13** indescribable, inexpressible **15** unpronounceable

ineffaceable: **9** indelible **12** ineradicable

ineffectively: **6** feebly **9** uselessly

ineffectual: **4** dead, idle, vain, weak **6** futile **7** useless **8** hopeless, impotent, nugatory **9** fruitless **10** inadequate, unavailing **11** inefficient **13** inefficacious

inefficient: **4** poor **5** inept **8** slipshod **9** unskilled **11** incompetent

inelastic: **5** rigid, stiff **9** unbending **10** inflexible, unyielding

inelegant: **5** crass, crude, rough, **6** coarse, vulgar **7** awkward, blatant **9** graceless

ineluctable: **4** sure **5** fated **6** doomed **7** certain **10** inevitable **11** inescapable

inept: **4** dull, slow **5** unfit **6** absurd, clumsy **7** awkward, foolish **8** backward, unsuited **10** unbecoming, unsuitable **11** incompetent **13** inappropriate

inequal: **5** rough **6** uneven

inequality: **4** odds **9** disparity, diversity **10** unevenness **13** disproportion

inequity: **9** injustice **10** unfairness

ineradicable: **7** lasting **9** indelible, permanent **12** ineffaceable

inerrant: **8** unerring **10** infallible

inerratic: **5** fixed **7** settled **11** established

inert: **4** dead, dull, lazy, slow **5** still **6** stupid, supine, torpid **7** passive **8** immobile, inactive, indolent, lifeless, slothful, sluggish **9** apathetic, lethargic **10** motionless, phlegmatic

inertia: **5** sloth **8** idleness **9** indolence

inesculant: **8** inedible

in essence: **9** basically **11** practically **13** fundamentally

inessential: **9** extrinsic **11** unimportant

inestimable: **9** priceless **10** invaluable **12** incalculable

inevitable: due **5** fated **7** certain, fateful **11** ineluctable, inescapable, unavoidable

inexact: **4** free **5** rough **10** inaccurate

inexhaustible: **8** tireless **9** unfailing, unlimited **13** indefatigable

inexorable: **4** grim **5** stony **6** strict **7** ominous **8** rigorous **9** unbending **10** inflexible, relentless, unyielding **11** unrelenting

inexpedient: **6** unwise **9** impolitic, imprudent **10** indiscreet **11** inadvisable, injudicious **12** unprofitable **15** disadvantageous

inexpensive: **5** cheap **6** frugal **9** lowpriced **10** reasonable

inexperienced: raw **5** crude, green, naive, young **6** callow **7** untried **8** inexpert **10** amateurish

inexpert: **5** green **9** unskilled

inexplicable: odd **7** uncanny **8** abstruse, peculiar, puzzling **9** ambiguous, enigmatic **10** mysterious **12** supernatural

inexpressible: **8** nameless **9** ineffable **11** unutterable

inexpressive: **4** dull, dumb **13** unintelligent

infallible: **4** sure **7** certain **8** inerrant, unerring **9** faultless, foolproof, unfailing **11** indubitable

infamous: **4** base **6** bloody, odious **8** shameful **9** nefarious **10** detestable **11** ignominious **12** contemptible

infamy: **5** odium, shame, stain **8** disgrace, dishonor, reproach **10** opprobrium

infancy: **8** babyhood **10** immaturity **11** incunabulum

infant: 4 baby 5 child, minor 7 bambino, chrisom 8 bantling 9 foundling
in law: 5 minor
Indian: 7 papoose
murder: 11 infanticide
infantile 7 babyish, puerile 8 childish 10 sophomoric
infantryman: 6 doggie 7 dogface 8 doughboy
infatuated: mad 4 fond 6 engoue 7 engouee, fatuous 8 enamored, obsessed 9 enamoured 10 captivated 12 enthusiastic
infeasible: 13 impracticable
infect: 5 taint 6 canker, defile, poison 7 pollute 11 contaminate
infection: 6 malady, plague 7 disease, illness
freedom from: 7 asepsis
infectious: 8 catching 9 vitiating 12 demoralizing, pestilential
infelicitous: 7 unhappy 11 unfortunate
infelicity: 6 misery 10 misfortune 11 unhappiness 12 wretchedness
infer: 4 hint 5 drive, educe, guess 6 adduce, deduce, derive, gather 7 surmise 8 conclude, construe
inference: 9 corollary, deduction 10 assumption, conclusion, derivation 11 consequence
inferential: 7 implied 8 illative 9 deductive
inferior: bad 4 base, cull, less, poor 5 baser, below, lower, minor, petit, petty, snide, worst 6 cagmag, common, feeble, impure, lesser, nether 7 cheaper, humbler, unequal 8 mediocre 9 underling 10 inadequate 11 subordinate 12 contemptible 13 insignificant
infernal: 7 avernal, hellish, satanic, stygian 8 all-fired, damnable, devilish, diabolic 9 tartarean 10 acherontic, demoniacal, diabolical
inferno: 4 fire, hell 9 holocaust
infertile: 4 poor 6 barren 7 sterile
infest: 5 beset, haunt 6 plague 7 overrun, 9 swarm over
infidel: 5 pagan 7 atheist, heathen 8 agnostic 10 unbeliever
infiltrate: 4 leak, seep
infinite: 6 Ananta 7 endless, immense 9 boundless, countless, limitless, unlimited 11 everlasting, illimitable, measureless 12 immeasurable, interminable
absorption into: 7 nirvana
infinitesimal: 4 tiny 5 small 6 minute 10 negligible 11 microscopic
infirm: old 4 lame, weak 5 anile, frail 6 cranky, feeble, senile, sickly 7 brittle, failing, fragile 8 decrepit, disabled 9 doddering 10 irresolute 11 debilitated, vacillating

infirmary: 8 hospital
infirmity: 4 vice 7 ailment, disease, failing, frailty 8 debility, sickness, weakness 10 feebleness
infix: 5 inset 6 insert 7 engrave, implant, impress, ingrain, instill 9 inculcate
inflame: 4 boil, fire, goad, heat, stir 5 anger, chafe 6 anneal, arouse, enrage, excite, rankle, redden 7 incense, provoke 8 enkindle, irritate 10 exasperate
with love: 6 enamor
with rage: 6 madden
inflamed: red 5 angry, fiery 6 ablaze
inflammable: 5 fiery 6 ardent, tinder 7 bitumen, piceous 9 excitable, irascible, irritable 10 accendible 11 combustible
inflammation: 4 fire 10 combustion, phlegmasia 13 conflagration
inflate: 4 blow, fill 5 bloat, elate, swell 6 aerify, dilate, emboss, expand, tumefy 7 amplify, distend 8 increase
inflated: 5 wordy 6 turgid 7 bloated, fustian, pompous, swollen 8 expanded 9 bombastic, distended, flatulent, plethoric
inflect: bow 4 bend 5 curve 8 modulate
inflection: 4 tone 6 accent, timbre
of words: 8 paradigm
inflexibility: 8 acampsia
inflexible: 4 dour, hard 5 eager, rigid, stiff, stony 6 strict 7 adamant 8 granitic, obdurate, rigorous 9 immovable, inelastic, unbending 10 implacable, inexorable, relentless 14 uncompromising
inflict: 4 dump 5 wreak 6 impose, unload 7 put upon 10 make suffer, perpetrate
infliction: 7 scourge
inflorescence: 6 raceme
axial circle of: 5 whorl
inflow: 6 influx, inrush
influence: 4 egis, hank, heft, lead, move, pull, rule, sway 5 clout, force, impel 6 affect, aspect, compel, effect, govern, induce, infuse, leaven, motive, weight 7 attract, bearing, command, control, gravity, impress, inspire, mastery 8 hegemony, persuade, pressure, prestige, reaction 9 authority 10 ascendancy, attraction, inducement 13 consideration
by fixed idea: 6 obsess
by reward: 5 bribe
region of: 5 orbit 6 sphere
influence peddling: 8 intrigue, lobbying
influenced: 6 biased 8 affected
easily: 7 pliable
influential: 5 grave 6 potent 8 powerful 9 effective, important, momentous
influenza: flu 5 virus 10 coqueluche
influx: 4 tide 6 inflow 7 arrival, illapse 8 increase 9 inpouring
infold See **enfold**
inform: 4 post, tell 5 train 6 advise, noti-

fy, preach **7** apprise, apprize, educate, lighten **8** acquaint, instruct **9** advertise **11** communicate

informal: 6 casual, simple **7** relaxed **8** sociable **9** easygoing **10** colloquial **13** unceremonious **14** unconventional

conversation: rap **4** chat

information: 4 data(pl.), dope, news, word **5** aviso, datum **6** notice **7** tidings **9** direction, knowledge **11** instruction

condensed: **6** digest, precis **7** summary

detailed: **7** dossier

informative: 11 instructive **12** enlightening

informed: hep, hip **4** told, wise **5** aware **6** posted **7** knowing **8** apprised, notified **11** enlightened

informer: 4 fink, tout **6** canary, gossip, pigeon, snitch, teller **7** stoolie, tipster **8** observer, squealer, telltale **9** informant **10** discoverer, talebearer **11** stoolpigeon

military: spy **5** agent

infraction: 6 breach **8** trespass **9** violation **12** encroachment, infringement **13** transgression

infrequent: 4 rare **6** scarce, seldom, sparse **8** sporadic, uncommon, unwonted **10** occasional

infringe: 6 refute **7** impinge, intrude **8** encroach, overstep, trespass **10** contravene

upon: **6** butt in **7** violate

infringement: 6 breach **8** trespass **9** violation **10** infraction **13** transgression **14** nonfulfillment

infuriate: vex **6** enrage, madden **7** outrage

infuscate: 6 darken **7** obscure

infuse: 4 soak **5** imbue, steep **6** aerify **7** engrain, implant, inspire, instill **9** inculcate, influence, insinuate, introduce

infusion: 7 extract **8** tincture **9** admixture, decoction

malt: **4** wort

Inge play: 6 Picnic **7** Bus Stop

ingeminate: 6 repeat **9** reiterate

ingenious: 4 cute, fine **5** acute, sharp, smart, witty **6** adroit, clever, crafty, daedal, gifted, subtle **7** artless, cunning **8** original, skillful, talented **9** daedalian, deviceful, inventive **11** intelligent, resourceful

ingenuity: art **7** address, cunning **8** artifice **10** adroitness, cleverness **11** originality **13** inventiveness

ingenuous: 4 naif **5** frank, naive, noble, plain **6** candid, honest, simple **7** artless, sincere **8** innocent **9** childlike, guileless **10** unaffected, unreserved **5** unsophisticated

ingenuousness: 7 naivete **9** innocence

ingest: eat **6** absorb **7** consume, swallow

inglorious: 6 shoddy **8** shameful **11** disgraceful, ignominious **12** dishonorable

ingoing: 8 entering

ingot: bar, pig **4** mold

ingrained: 6 imbued, inborn, inbred, innate, native **7** built-in, chronic **8** inherent **9** confirmed **10** congenital, deepseated, inveterate

ingratiating: 4 oily **5** sweet **6** genial, smarmy **7** gushing, likable **8** unctuous **9** appealing **10** flattering, personable **11** sycophantic

ingredient: 7 element **9** component **11** constituent

baking: **4** alum, soda **5** yeast

cough-syrup: **8** glycerin

facial: **5** cream, rouge **6** powder **7** lanolin **8** lanoline

incense: **6** stacte

ink: **6** tannin

varnish: lax **5** drier, resin, rosin

ingress: 4 adit **5** entry **8** entrance

inhabit: 6 live in, occupy, people, settle **7** dwell in, possess **8** populate

inhabitant: 6 inmate, native, tenant **7** citizen, denizen, dweller **8** resident

inhale: 5 sniff **7** respire **9** breathe in

inharmonious: 6 absurd, atonal **7** jarring **9** dissonant, unmusical **10** discordant **11** conflicting **12** antagonistic

inherent: 5 basic **6** inborn, innate **7** infixed **8** immanent **9** essential, ingrained, intrinsic **10** congenital, deeprooted, indwelling

inheritable: 10 hereditary

inheritance: 6 estate, legacy **7** bequest **8** heredity, heritage **9** patrimony **10** birthright

by first-born: **13** primogeniture

portion: **8** legitime

restricted: **10** entailment

Scotch law: **5** annat

seizer: **6** abator

inherited: 6 inborn, native **7** connate, natural **10** handed down

inheritor: 4 heir **7** heiress, legatee

inhibit: ban, bar **4** curb **5** check **6** forbid, hinder **8** prohibit, restrain **9** interdict

inhuman: 4 fell **5** cruel **6** brutal, savage **7** beastly, bestial, brutish **8** devilish **9** barbarous, bloodless, ferocious **10** diabolical

inhumanity: 7 cruelty **9** barbarity

inhume: 4 bury **5** inter **6** entomb **7** deposit

inimical: 6 averse, frosty **7** hostile **8** contrary **9** repugnant **10** unfriendly **11** unfavorable

iniquitous: bad, ill **5** wrong **6** sinful, unjust, wicked **9** nefarious

iniquity: sin **4** evil, vice **5** crime, guilt **8**

darkness 9 injustice 10 wickedness

initial: 5 first 6 letter, maiden 7 opening 8 earliest, monogram, original 9 beginning, incipient 10 commencing, elementary

initial payment: 4 ante 7 deposit

initiate: 4 head, open 5 admit, begin, enrol, found, start 6 enroll, induct, launch 7 install, kick off 8 commence 9 introduce, originate 10 inaugurate

initiation: 7 baptism 8 entrance 9 admission, beginning, induction 10 admittance, 12 commencement

initiative: 4 lead, push 6 energy 8 aptitude, gumption 9 first move 10 creativity, enterprise, get-up-and-go, leadership

inject: put 4 pump 5 force 6 insert, instill 11 interpolate

injection: 4 hypo 5 enema

injudicious: 6 unwise 9 impolitic, imprudent 10 indiscreet 11 inexpedient

injunction: 4 hest, writ 5 order 6 behest, charge 7 mandate, precept, process 9 direction

injure: mar 4 harm, hurt, maim 5 abuse, spoil, sully, wound, wrong 6 impair, insult 7 affront, cripple 8 aggrieve, maltreat 9 disfigure

by bruising: 7 contuse

by scorching: 4 burn, char 5 singe

injury: cut, ill, 4 bane, blow, evil, harm, hurt, loss, risk, stab 5 wound, wrong 6 damage, lesion, trauma 7 scratch 8 hardship 9 contusion, detriment, injustice 10 affliction, aggression, disservice, impairment, laceration, mutilation

causing: 7 malefic 9 traumatic

sense of: 7 umbrage

injustice: 5 wrong 6 injury 8 hardship, inequity, iniquity 9 grievance 10 imposition, unfairness

ink: 4 sign 9 autograph 13 fish secretion

ink fish: 5 squid 6 cuttle

inkling: 4 hint, idea 5 rumor, scent 6 desire, report 7 glimpse 10 glimmering, intimation 11 inclination

inky: 4 dark 5 black 9 cimmerian

inland: 8 domestic, interior

sea: 4 Aral 5 Black

inlay: 5 adorn, couch, set in 6 insert 7 enchase 8 ornament 9 marquetry

work: 6 mosaic 9 certosina, certosino, champleve

inlet: arm, bay, cay, ria 4 cove, gulf, rias(pl.), slew, sloo, slue 5 admit, bayou, bight, creek, fiord, firth, fjord, inlay, sound 6 estero, slough, strait 7 estuary, narrows, orifice, passage 8 entrance

coastline: 5 bight 6 strait

in loco parentis: 8 guardian

inmate: 5 guest, lifer 6 termer 8 domestic,

occupant, prisoner 10 inhabitant

harem: oda

inmost: 8 intimate 10 most secret

inn: pub 4 host, khan 5 fonda, hotel, lodge, serai, tambo, venta 6 fonduk, hostel, imaret, tavern 7 albergo, auberge, boliche, fondaca, fondouk, fonduck, hospice 8 choultry, gasthaus, hostelry, wayhouse 11 caravansary

innamorato(It.): 5 lover 10 sweetheart

innards: 4 guts 7 viscera 8 entrails

innate: 4 born 6 inborn, inbred, native 7 connate, natural 8 inherent 9 ingrained, intrinsic 10 congenital, hereditary 11 instinctive 14 constitutional

inner: ben 5 ental 6 inside, inward 8 esoteric, interior, internal

Innisfail: 4 Eire, Erin 7 Ireland

innkeeper: 4 host 8 boniface, hosteler, publican

innocence: 6 purity 7 naivete 9 ignorance 11 sinlessness 13 guiltlessness

symbol of: 7 diamond

innocent: 4 free, naif 5 naive 6 chaste, dovish, simple 7 artless, upright 9 blameless, childlike, guileless, guiltless, ingenuous, stainless 10 immaculate, unblamable 12 simpleminded 15 unsophisticated

Hebrew: 8 zaccheus 9 zacchaeus

innocent one: 4 babe, lamb 5 child 6 infant

innocuous: 8 harmless, innocent 9 innoxious 11 inoffensive, unoffending

innominate: 7 unnamed 9 anonymous

innovation: 6 change 7 novelty 9 departure 10 new wrinkle

innuendo: 4 clue, hint, slur 8 allusion 10 intimation 11 implication, insinuation

innumerable: 4 many 6 legion, myriad

Ino's grandfather: 6 Agenor

inoculate: 5 imbue 6 infect 7 implant 9 immunize

inoffensive: 8 harmless 9 innocuous

inoperative: 4 dead, idle 10 out of order, unworkable

inopportune: bad 8 ill-timed, untimely 10 malapropos 11 importunate 12 unseasonable, inconvenient

inorb: 8 encircle

inordinate: 5 undue 6 wanton 7 extreme, surplus 8 needless, overmuch 9 excessive 10 disorderly, immoderate 11 unregulated 12 unrestrained

inorganic: 7 mineral

in perpetuum: 4 ever 6 always 7 forever 9 eternally

inquest: 6 search 7 inquiry 11 examination 13 investigation

official: 7 coroner

inquire: ask, esk(Sc.) 4 quiz, seek 5 query 6 demand, search 7 dig into 8 question

11 interrogate, investigate

inquiring: 7 curious

inquiry: 4 hunt 5 audit, check, probe, query 7 inquest 8 question, research, scrutiny 11 examination 13 investigation

for lost goods: 6 tracer

inquisition: 5 trial 8 grilling, tribunal 11 third-degree

inquisitive: 4 nosy 5 nosey 6 prying 7 curious 8 meddling 10 meddlesome

in re(L.): 5 about 9 regarding 10 concerning

inroad: 4 raid 5 foray 6 breach 8 invasion 9 incursion, irruption 12 encroachment

ins and outs: 5 ropes 7 details 11 particulars

insane: mad 4 daft, luny 5 balmy, crazy, daffy, loony, manic 6 cranky, crazed 7 frantic, furious 8 bughouse, demented, deranged, distract, frenetic 9 delirious, phrenetic, psychotic

house for: 6 asylum, bedlam 10 booby hatch, sanitarium

to make: 6 dement 7 derange

insanity: 5 folie, mania 6 frenzy, lunacy 7 madness, vesania 8 delirium, dementia 9 psychosis 10 aberration, alienation 11 derangement

temporary: 7 amentia

insatiable: 6 greedy 9 voracious 11 unsatisfied

inscribe, enscribe: 4 etch 5 delve, enter, stamp, write 6 blazon, enroll, indite, scroll 7 ascribe, engrave 8 dedicate, describe 9 character 12 characterize

inscribed: 8 lettered 9 dedicated

on stone: 10 lapidarian

with Teutonic characters: 5 runed

inscription: 6 legend 7 epigram, writing 8 epigraph

appropriate: 5 motto

end of book: 8 colophon

explanatory: 6 tituli(pl.) 7 titulus

on coins: 5 sigla

tomb: 7 epitaph

inscrutable: 6 secret 10 mysterious 12 impenetrable, inexplorable, unfathomable 16 incomprehensible

insect: ant, bee, bug, fly 4 flea, gnat, lice, mite, moth, tick, wasp 5 emmet, roach 6 beetle, earwig, mantis, spider, weevil 7 cricket, katydid, termite 9 bumblebee, centipede

adult: 6 imago

antenna: 4 palp 6 feeler

back surface: 5 notum

chirping: 7 cricket

destructive: 5 scale 7 termite 8 predator

dipterous: 8 mosquito

eating bird: 5 pewee, vireo 8 redstart 10 flycatcher

eye: 6 ocelli(pl.), stemma 7 ocellus

female: 4 gyne

genus of: 4 nepa 5 emesa 6 acarus, cicada, cicala, mantis, termes

hard covering: 6 chitin

hymenopterous: ant, bee 4 wasp 6 sawfly 7 gallfly 10 ichneumons

immature: 4 grub, pupa 5 larva 6 larvae(pl.) 9 chrysalis 11 caterpillar

long-legged: 5 emesa

molting of: 7 ecdysis

order: 7 diptera

organ: 8 plantula 9 plantulae(pl.)

parasitic: 4 lice 5 louse

part of: 4 nota 5 chirr, media, palps 7 antenna 8 pronotum, tentacle

pert. to: 11 entomologic

plate: 6 scutum

repellant: 4 deet

resin: lac

science: 10 entomology

secretion: lac

small: 4 flea, gnat, mite 5 aphid, aphis, micro, midge 6 garfly 8 bullhead

social: ant, bee 5 emmet

stage: 4 pupa 5 imago, larva 6 instar 9 chrysalis

stinging: ant, bee 4 wasp 6 hornet 7 sciniph 12 yellowjacket

trap: web

winged: bee 4 wasp 6 hornet 7 termite 8 mosquito 12 yellowjacket

wingless: 4 flea 6 aptera(pl.)

insecticide: DDT 6 endrin, ethion 9 hellebore, Malathion, parathion 10 endosulfan

insecure: 5 loose, risky, shaky 6 infirm, unsafe, unsure 7 rickety, unsound 8 doubtful, perilous, unstable 9 dangerous, hazardous 10 precarious

inseminate: sow 7 implant, instill 9 fertilize 10 impregnate

insensate: 4 surd 5 blind, harsh 6 brutal, stupid 7 brutish, fatuous, foolish 9 senseless, unfeeling, untouched 10 insensible

insensibility: 4 coma 6 apathy, torpor, trance 8 lethargy 9 analgesia 10 anesthesia 11 insentience

insensible: 4 dull 7 unaware 8 obdurate 9 inanimate, insensate, unfeeling 10 insentient 11 indifferent, unconscious 13 imperceptible

insensitive: 4 cold, dead, numb 5 blase 7 callous 11 unconcerned

insert: 5 foist, infix, inlay, inset 9 interpose 11 intercalate, interpolate

for growth: 5 graft 7 engraft

triangular: 4 gore 5 wedge

insertion: 5 inset

kind of: 5 shinn 11 parenthesis 13 interpolation, intercalation

of sound in word: 10 epenthesis

inset: 4 gore 5 imbed, infix, panel 6 gusset, insert **7** appoint, engraft, implant **9** insertion

inside: 5 inner **6** lining, within **7** private **8** interior

toward: **5** entad **6** inward

track: **9** advantage

inside out: 7 everted **8** reversed **10** completely, thoroughly

insidious: 4 deep **6** covert **7** cunning **8** guileful **9** concealed, deceitful **10** fallacious, fraudulent **11** disaffected, treacherous

insight: ken **6** acumen, wisdom **9** intuition **10** perception **11** discernment **12** clairvoyance

insignia: 4 mark **5** badge **6** emblem

kind of: tie **7** caducei(pl.), regalia **8** caduceus

insignificance: 10 effacement

insignificant: 4 puny **5** dinky, petit, petty **6** paltry **7** trivial **8** inferior, smallfry, trifling **9** minuscule, senseless **10** immaterial **11** minor-league **12** unimportant

part: bit **4** iota **5** tithe **8** molehill

insincere: 5 false **7** feigned **8** two-faced **9** deceitful, deceptive **12** hypocritical

insinuate: 4 hint **5** imply **6** allude, infuse **7** implant, instill **9** introduce, penetrate **10** ingratiate, serpentine

insinuation: 4 hint **8** innuendo

insipid: dry **4** dead, dull, flat, pale, tame **5** bland, prosy, stale, tepid, vapid, waugh **6** jejune **7** prosaic **8** lifeless **9** pointless, tasteless **10** monotonous, spiritless, unanimated **13** uninteresting

insist: 4 aver **5** claim **6** assert, demand **7** contend **8** maintain **9** reiterate

insistence: 7 command, urgency

insolence: 4 gall **5** nerve **6** insult **8** audacity, contempt **9** arrogance, contumely, impudence **10** effrontery **11** haughtiness, presumption **12** impertinence

insolent: 4 pert, rude **5** saucy **6** brazen **7** abusive, defiant **8** arrogant, impudent **9** audacious, hubristic **11** overbearing **12** contemptuous, contumelious

insolvency: 7 failure **10** bankruptcy

insolvent: 5 broke **6** busted, ruined **8** bankrupt **9** destitute **12** impoverished

insomnia: 7 ahypnia **8** agrypnia

insouciant: 4 calm **8** carefree, heedless **10** unbothered **11** indifferent, unconcerned

inspect: 4 scan, view **5** check, study, **6** peruse **7** examine, observe **8** consider, look over **9** supervise **10** scrutinize

inspection: 4 oyer **6** parade, review **8** scrutiny **11** examination

inspiration: 4 spur **5** flash **6** motive, vision **7** impulse **8** afflatus, stimulus **9** incentive, influence **10** brainstorm

poetic: **7** pierian

pretender to: **6** eolist

inspire: 4 fire, move, stir **5** exalt, imbue **6** arouse, excite, inhale, prompt **7** actuate, animate, enliven, implant **8** motivate **9** encourage, influence, stimulate

inspirit (see also **inspire**): **4** stir **5** cheer, elate, rouse **7** animate, cherish, comfort, hearten, quicken **10** invigorate

inspissate: 7 thicken **8** condense **10** incrassate

instability: 8 fluidity **9** shakiness **10** insecurity **12** irresolution, unsteadiness **13** changeability

install: lay **4** seat, vest **6** induct, invest, locate **7** instate **8** initiate **9** establish **10** inaugurate, set in place

installation: 11 investiture

instance: 4 case, cite, time **7** example, request, symptom **8** occasion **9** exemplify **10** suggestion **12** illustration

instancy: 7 urgency **8** pressure **9** imminence **10** insistence

instant: 4 urge **5** clink, flash, gliff, glisk, trice **6** breath, minute, moment, second, urgent **7** solicit **8** pressing **9** handwhile, immediate **11** importunate

instantly: now **4** just **8** directly

instate: set **6** bestow, confer, **7** install **8** initiate **9** establish **10** inaugurate

instead: 4 else **6** in lieu **10** equivalent, substitute

of: for

instigate: egg **4** abet, goad, move, prod, sick, spur, urge **5** impel **6** compel, excite, foment, incite, prompt, suborn **7** provoke **8** motivate **9** encourage, stimulate

instigator: 6 author **10** ringleader

instill: 5 imbue, infix **6** impart, infuse **7** implant, pervade **9** inculcate, insinuate

instinct: 4 bent, gift, urge **5** knack **7** impulse **8** aptitude

instinctive: 6 innate **7** natural **8** inherent, original **9** automatic, intuitive **11** involuntary, spontaneous

institute: 5 begin, erect, found **6** asylum, ordain **7** academy **8** initiate, organize **9** establish, originate **10** inaugurate

institution: 6 clinic, school **7** academy, college **8** hospital, seminary **10** university **12** constitution

instruct: 4 lead, show **5** breed, coach, drill, edify, guide, teach, train, tutor **6** direct, inform, preach **7** counsel, educate **8** document **9** enlighten **10** discipline **12** indoctrinate

instruction: 6 advice, charge, lesson **7** precept **8** teaching, training, tutelage **9** education, knowledge, schooling **10** directions

art of: **8** pedagogy

period: **4** term, year **7** quarter, session **8**

semester **9** trimester

instructive: 8 didactic, sermonic

instructor: don **5** coach, tutor **6** docent, mentor **7** acharya, teacher, trainer **9** preceptor, professor

instrument (see also **apparatus, device, tool**): **4** deed, writ **5** agent, means **6** medium **7** utensil, writing **9** appliance, implement **11** contrivance

altitude: aba **9** altimeter **10** altazimuth

board: **5** panel

calculating: **6** abacus **8** computer **9** slide rule

copying: **10** hectograph

cutting: **5** knife, razor **6** scythe, shears, sickle **8** scissors

for studying motion: **11** stroboscope

musical: See **musical instrument**

percussion: **12** Glockenspiel

sacred: **4** urim

sealed: **4** deed **5** crypt, vault **6** escrow

surveying: **7** transit **10** theodolite

instrumental: useful **7** helpful **9** conducive, effective **12** of assistance

instrumentalist: 6 oboist **7** flutist, harpist, pianist **8** flautist, minstrel **9** cornetist, violinist **10** trombonist

instrumentality: 5 means **6** agency, medium

insubordinate: 6 unruly **7** defiant, riotous **8** mutinous, perverse **9** fractious, seditious **10** headstrong, rebellious, refractory, unyielding **11** disobedient, intractable **12** contumacious, recalcitrant

insubstantial: 4 airy, thin **5** frail **6** flimsy **10** intangible **12** apparitional

insufferable: 7 hateful, painful **10** unbearable **11** intolerable

insufficient: 4 bare, poor **5** short **6** feeble, scanty, scarce **7** unequal, wanting **9** deficient **10** inadequate **14** incommensurate

insular: 6 biased, narrow **8** isolated **9** parochial, separated **10** provincial

insulate: 6 enisle **7** isolate **9** segregate **10** quarantine

material to: **4** cork **6** Kerite, rubber

insulator: 4 tape **5** cleat **12** nonconductor

insult: 4 slap, slur **5** abuse, flout, scorn, shame **6** offend, revile **7** affront, offense, outrage **9** contumely, indignity, insolence

insulting: 4 rude **8** arrogant, derisive **9** offensive **10** scurrilous **11** opprobrious **12** contumelious, vituperative

insurance: 8 guaranty, warranty **9** assurance **10** protection

computer: **7** actuary **8** adjuster

payee: **11** beneficiary

system: **7** tontine

insurgent (see also **insubordinate**): **5** rebel **8** maverick, mutinous, revolter **9** dissident **10** rebellious

insurmountable: 8 hopeless, too great **10** impassable, invincible **11** insuperable **13** unconquerable

insurrection: 6 mutiny, revolt **8** outbreak, uprising **9** rebellion

insusceptible: 6 immune **9** unfeeling

intact: 5 sound, whole **8** complete, unbroken **9** undefiled, undivided, uninjured, untouched **10** unimpaired

intaglio: cut, gem **9** engraving

intake: net **4** gain, gate **6** profit **8** receipts **11** contraction

intangible: 5 vague **10** immaterial, impalpable **13** imperceptible, unsubstantial

integer: 5 digit **6** figure, number **7** numeral

integral: 4 full **5** basic, total, whole **8** complete **9** component, essential, requisite

integrate: mix **4** join **5** unite **7** combine

integrity: 7 honesty, probity **9** chariness, constancy

integument: 4 aril, coat, skin **5** shell, testa **7** cuticle **8** covering, envelope

intellect: wit **4** mind **5** brain **6** genius, reason **9** mentality **12** intelligence

limited in: **8** retarded

intellection: 6 notion **9** congnition, knowledge **12** apprehension **13** comprehension, understanding

intellectual: 5 ideal **6** brainy, mental, noetic **7** egghead, learned **8** highbrow **9** scholarly

intelligence: 4 chit, mind, news, word **5** sense **6** esprit, notice, wisdom **8** learning **13** understanding

used alone: **6** noesis

without: **4** dull **5** inane **6** stupid

intelligence test deviser: 5 Binet, Simon

intelligencer: spy **9** informant, messenger **10** newsmonger

intelligent: 5 acute, aware, smart **6** bright, mental **7** knowing **8** rational, sensible **9** cognizant **13** understanding

intelligentsia: 8 thinkers **13** intellectuals

intelligible: 5 clear, lucid, plain **10** conceptual **11** perspicuous **14** comprehensible

intemperate: 6 severe **7** extreme, violent **9** excessive, inclement **10** immoderate, inordinate **12** ungovernable, unrestrained

intend: aim **4** mean, plan **6** design **7** destine, propose **9** calculate **10** have in mind **11** contemplate

intended: 5 meant **6** fiance **7** fiancee

intense: hot **4** deep, hard, keen **5** acute, great, heavy, vivid **6** ardent, severe, strong 7 chronic, earnest, extreme, fervent, violent, zealous 8 grievous, powerful, strained, vehement 9 assiduous, excessive, strenuous 11 far-reaching

intensify: 5 exalt 6 deepen 7 enhance, magnify, quicken, sharpen 8 condense, heighten, increase 9 aggravate 10 accentuate 11 concentrate

intensity: 5 depth, force, power, vigor 6 energy, fervor 7 potency 8 severity, strength

of color: 6 chroma

intent: aim 4 rapt 5 eager, fixed, tense 6 design, effect 7 earnest, meaning, purpose 8 absorbed, diligent, sedulous 9 attentive, engrossed, steadfast 10 determined

intention: aim, end 4 goal, plan, will 6 animus, design, motive, object 7 meaning, purpose 11 designation 13 contemplation

intentional: 5 meant 7 planned 8 designed 9 voluntary 10 deliberate 12 premeditated

inter: 4 bury 6 entomb, inhume

interagent: 6 medium 12 intermediary

intercalary month: 4 Adar 6 Veadar

intercalate: 7 insert 9 insinuate, interpose 11 interpolate

intercede: 6 step in 7 mediate 9 arbitrate, interpose, intervene

intercept: nab 4 grab, stop 5 block, catch, seize 7 head off 9 forestall, interrupt

intercessor: 8 advocate, mediator

interchange: 4 vary 7 commute, permute 8 converse, exchange 9 alternate 10 transposal 11 reciprocate 12 conversation

interchangeable: 10 reversible 11 convertible

interconnection: 5 nexus 8 junction

intercourse: 7 dealing 8 business, commerce, converse 9 communion, 10 connection, fellowship 12 conversation 13 communication

interdict: ban 4 veto 5 debar, fence 6 forbid 7 inhibit 8 prohibit 9 proscribe

interdiction: 4 tabu 5 taboo

interest: 4 good, part 5 hobby, share, stake 6 behalf, engage, excite, notice 7 benefit, concern, involve, service, welfare 8 sympathy 9 advantage, attention, fascinate

exorbitant: 5 usury

in law: 5 right, title

lose: 4 tire

rate: 5 yield

without: 6 jejune 9 apathetic

interested: 4 rapt 6 caring

interfere: 5 barge, clash 6 meddle, tamper 7 collide, disturb, intrude 8 obstruct, sabotage 9 interpose, intervene

interference: 6 static

interim: 5 break 6 hiatus 7 stopgap 8 interval, meantime 9 interlude 10 pro tempore 11 provisional

interior: ben 5 ental, inner 6 inland, inside 8 midlands 9 heartland

interject: 5 put in 6 insert, slip in 9 introduce

interjection: boo, hic, rah 4 ahem, alas, amen, egad, ouch, well 6 aroint 7 criminy 11 exclamation

interlace: mat 5 braid, twine, weave 7 entwine 9 interfret, interlink 10 intertwine, interweave 11 interpolate

interlaced: 7 complex

interlock: 4 knit 5 unite 6 clench, engage 9 interlace 11 interrelate

interlocution: 12 conversation 13 communication

interlocutory: 9 mediatory 12 intermediate 14 conversational

interlope: 6 horn in, meddle 7 intrude 8 trespass 9 interfere

interlude: 4 lull 5 let up, pause 6 recess 7 respite 8 breather, entr'acte, interval

intermediary: 5 agent 6 medium 7 referee 8 mediator 9 go-between, middleman 10 ambassador, interagent

intermediate: 5 mense 6 median, middle 7 average, between 8 middling, moderate 10 interposed 11 intervening

interminable: 7 endless, eternal 8 infinite, timeless, unending 9 boundless, limitless, unlimited 10 long-winded

interminably: 7 forever

intermingle: 8 intermix 9 socialize 10 infiltrate

intermission: 4 rest, stop 5 dwell, pause 6 recess 7 respite 8 entr'acte, vacation 9 cessation 10 suspension 13 interposition 14 discontinuance

intermittent: 6 broken, fitful 8 on and off, periodic, sporadic 9 recurrent, spasmodic 10 occasional 11 alternating, interrupted

intermix: 6 mingle 10 interweave

intern: 6 detain, doctor 7 confine, impound, trainee 8 imprison

internal: 5 inner 6 inward, mental 8 domestic, enclosed 9 spiritual

combustion engine part: 5 timer

international: 9 universal, world-wide

international organization: OAS, WHO 4 NATO 5 SEATO 6 UNESCO, UNICEF

internecine: 6 deadly

interpolate: 5 alter 6 insert 9 introduce 11 intercalate

interpose: 6 thrust 7 intrude, mediate 9 intercede, interfere, intervene

interpret: 4 read 6 decode, define, render 7 explain, expound 8 construe 9 elucidate, explicate, make clear, translate **10** paraphrase

interpretation: **5** sense **7** meaning, version **8** exegesis **9** rendering **10** conception **11** translation **12** construction
mystical: **7** anagoge
science of: **12** hermeneutics

interpretive: **10** expository **11** explanatory, hermeneutic **12** constructive

interrogate: ask **4** quiz **5** grill, query **7** examine, inquire **8** question

interrogation: **5** probe **7** inquest **9** catechism

interrogation mark: **7** eroteme

interrogative: how, who, why **4** what, when **5** where **8** question

interrupt: **4** stop **5** break, burst, cease, check, cut in **6** arrest, hinder, thwart **7** disturb, suspend **8** obstruct **9** intercept **11** discontinue

interruption: gap **5** pause **6** breach, hiatus **7** caesura **9** cessation **12** intermission

intersect: cut **4** meet **5** cross **6** divide, pierce **9** decussate

intersection: **6** corner **7** crossing, junction **10** crossroads

interstice: **4** mesh, pore, seam **5** chink, crack, space **6** areola, areole, cranny **7** crevice **8** interval
pert. to: **7** areolar

intertwine: **4** knit, lace **5** twist **9** interlace **10** intertwist

interval: gap **4** rest, span **5** break, space **6** breach, hiatus, recess **7** caesura, respite **8** entracte **9** cessation **12** intermission
at irregular: **12** sporadically
musical: **5** fifth, ninth, sixth, tenth, third **6** fourth, octave, second **7** seventh

intervene: **7** mediate **9** intercede, interpose

intervening: **5** mesne(law) **12** intermediate

interview: see **7** consult, hearing **8** audience, question **9** encounter **10** conference **12** consultation

intervolve: **4** coil, roll, wind **5** twist

interweave: mat **5** braid, plait **6** splice **8** intermix **9** interlace

intestinal fortitude: **4** grit, guts **5** nerve, pluck, spunk **7** courage **8** backbone

intimate: pal **4** boon, chum, dear, hint, homy, near **5** bosom, buddy, close, crony, homey, imply **6** allude, chummy, homely, inmost, secret **7** signify, suggest **8** announce, domestic, familiar, friendly, informal, personal **9** associate, confidant **11** contubernal **12** acquaintance, confidential

intimation: cue **4** clue, hint, wind **5** scent **6** notice **7** inkling **10** suggestion **11** declaration

intimidate: awe, cow **5** abash, bully, daunt, deter, scare **6** hector **7** overawe,

terrify **8** browbeat, dispirit, frighten **9** blackmail, terrorize

into: **4** unto **5** among, until **6** inside

intolerance: **4** bias **6** racism **9** misoneism **10** chauvinism

intolerant: **6** narrow, stuffy **7** bigoted **8** dogmatic **9** hidebound, illiberal, impatient **10** prejudiced

intonation: **5** pitch, sound **7** sonance

intonational: **7** tonetic

intone: **4** cant, sing **5** chant **8** modulate **10** cantillate

in toto: **8** as a whole **10** altogether

intoxicant: (see also **alcoholic drink, liquor**): gin, rum **4** wine **5** booze, drink **6** liquor **7** alcohol, whiskey

intoxicated: **4** high **5** drunk, tight, tipsy **6** boiled, soused, stewed, stoned, zonked **7** excited **8** besotted, glorious, polluted, squiffed **9** crapulous **10** inebriated

intoxicating: **5** heady **12** exhilarating

intracellular: **8** histonal

intractable: **6** mulish, unruly **7** willful **8** indocile, mutinous, obdurate, perverse, stubborn **9** obstinate **10** headstrong, refractory **11** disobedient, unteachable **12** contumacious, ungovernable **14** uncontrollable

intrada: **7** prelude **12** introduction

intranquillity: ado **12** restlessness

intransigent: **8** obdurate **9** unmovable **10** iron-willed, unyielding **14** irreconcilable, uncompromising

intrepid: **4** bold **5** brave, hardy, nervy **6** daring, heroic **7** assured, doughty, gallant, valiant **8** fearless, resolute, valorous **9** dauntless, dreadless, nerveless **10** courageous

intricate: **4** hard **5** dedal **6** daedal, knotty **7** complex, Gordian, sinuous **8** involved **9** Daedalian, difficult, involuted **10** perplexing **11** complicated **12** labyrinthine

intrigue: **4** plot **5** cabal, charm **6** brigue, deceit, design, scheme **7** faction **8** artifice, collogue **9** fascinate **10** concoction, conspiracy **11** machination

intrinsic: **4** real, true **6** inborn, inbred, innate, native **7** genuine, natural **8** immanent, inherent, intimate **9** essential, necessary **11** inseparable **13** indispensable

intrinsically: **5** per se **6** as such

introduce: **5** begin, enter, start, usher **6** broach, herald, infuse, insert **7** forerun, implant, precede, preface, present, sponsor **8** approach, initiate **9** insinuate, institute, originate

introduction: cue **5** debut, proem **7** intrada, introit, isagoge, preface, prelude **8** entrance, exordium, foreword, overture, preamble, prologue, protasis **11** preparation *of new word:* **7** neology

to treatise: **7** isagoge

introductory: 7 initial **8** exordial **9** prefatory, prelusive **11** preliminary

introductory cry: 4 hear, oyes, oyez

introit: 4 hymn **5** psalm **12** introduction

introverted: 8 brooding **9** withdrawn **13** contemplative

intrude: 6 invade, meddle **8** encroach, infringe, muscle in, trespass **9** interfere, interlope, interpose

intruder: 8 outsider **11** gate crasher

intrusion: 10 aggression, infraction

intrusive: 7 curious

intrust: See **entrust**

intuit: 4 feel **5** sense **8** perceive **9** apprehend

intuition: 5 hunch **7** feeling, insight **8** instinct **10** perception, sixth sense

inulase: 6 enzyme

inunction: 7 unguent **8** ointment **9** anointing

pert. to: **7** aliptic

inundate: 4 flow **5** drown, flood **6** deluge **8** overflow, submerge **9** overwhelm **10** overspread

inundation: 8 alluvion

inure, enure: 5 steel **6** harden, season **7** toughen **8** accustom **9** habituate **10** discipline **11** acclimatize

inurn: 4 bury **6** entomb

inutile: bad **7** useless **8** unusable **9** worthless **12** unprofitable

inutterable: See **unutterable**

invade: 4 raid **6** attack, engulf, infest **7** assault, intrude, overrun **8** encroach, trespass **9** march into, penetrate

invalid: 4 null **6** feeble, infirm, sickly **8** nugatory **11** ineffective **14** valetudinarian

invalidate: 4 undo **5** annul, break **7** abolish

invaluable: 8 precious **9** priceless **11** inestimable **13** inappreciable

invariable: 4 same **6** steady **7** uniform **8** constant **9** continual, immutable **10** unchanging **11** determinate **12** unchangeable

invariably: 6 always **7** forever **9** regularly **11** without fail

invasion (see also **invade**): inroad **9** incursion **10** aggression

invective: 5 abuse, venom **6** tirade **7** railing **8** diatribe, reproach **12** vituperation

inveigh: 9 fulminate

inveigle: 4 coax, lure **5** snare **6** allure, entice, entrap **8** persuade

invent: 4 coin, form, make, vamp **5** feign, forge, frame **6** create, design, devise, patent **7** concoct, fashion **8** contrive, discover, engineer **9** fabricate, improvise, originate **11** manufacture

invention: 7 fiction, figment

inventive: 6 adroit **7** fertile **9** ingenious

inventor: 6 author, coiner **7** creator **8** engineer **10** discoverer, originator

airplane: **6** Fokker, Wright

baseball: **9** Doubleday

condensing steam engine: **4** Watt

cotton gin: **7** Whitney

dynamite: **5** Nobel

electric light: **6** Edison

electric motor: **9** Davenport

elevator: **4** Otis

gun: **4** Colt **9** Remington

internal combustion engine: **6** Lenoir **7** Daimler

logarithm: **6** Napier

phonograph: **6** Edison

photography: **6** Niepce, Talbot

power loom: **10** Cartwright

printing: **9** Gutenberg

printing press: Hoe

radio: **7** Marconi **8** de Forest

safety lamp: **4** Davy

sewing machine: **4** Howe **6** Lester

steam locomotive: **10** Stephenson

steamboat: **5** Fitch **6** Fulton, Rumsey

telegraph: **5** Morse

telephone: **4** Bell

television: **6** Nipkow

wireless: **7** Marconi

inventor's right: 6 patent

inventory: 4 list **5** stock, store, tally **7** account, backlog, reserve **8** register, schedule **9** catalogue, stockpile

inveracity: 7 fib, lie **9** falsehood, falseness

inverse: 8 backward, contrary, opposite **11** bottom-to-top

invert: 4 turn **7** reverse

invertebrate: 4 worm **5** polyp **6** insect, sponge **7** mollusk **8** arachnid **12** coelenterate

group: **7** radiata

invest: don **4** belt, gird, gown, robe, vest, wrap **5** allot, array, crown, dress, endow, endue, imbue **6** clothe, confer, embark, ordain **7** envelop, install, instate **8** accredit, enthrone, surround

investigate: pry **4** nose **5** probe, study, trace **6** search **7** examine, explore, inquire **8** research **10** scrutinize

investigator: 6 prober, tracer **9** detective

body: **4** jury **5** panel **9** committee

investiture: 8 clothing **9** induction **10** initiation **12** installation

investment: 4 ante **5** share, stake **6** venture **12** contribution

list: **9** portfolio

investor: 10 capitalist, shareowner **11** stockholder

inveterate: 6 rooted **7** chronic **8** habitual, hardened **9** confirmed, ingrained

invidious: 6 odious **7** envious, hateful **8** spiteful **9** malignant **12** disagreeable

invigorate: 5 cheer, pep up, renew 6 vivify 7 animate, enliven, fortify, refresh 9 stimulate 10 exhilarate, strengthen

invigorating: 7 bracing 9 healthful 10 energizing 12 rejuvenating

invincible: 10 unbeatable 11 indomitable

inviolate: 4 holy 6 sacred 9 undefiled, unstained 10 sacrosanct 13 incorruptible

invisible: hid 6 unseen 10 indistinct, unapparent 13 undiscernible

Invisible Empire: 4 Klan

invitation: bid 4 call, lure 7 request, summons 8 entreaty 9 challenge

initials: 4 RSVP

invite: ask, bid 4 call 5 court 6 allure, entice 7 attract, provoke, request, solicit

invocation: 4 plea 6 prayer, sermon 7 benison 8 entreaty 11 benediction

invoice: 4 bill 5 brief 7 account 8 manifest 9 statement

invoke: 4 call, pray 6 appeal, attest 7 conjure, entreat, provoke, solicit 9 imprecate 10 supplicate

involuntary: 6 forced 9 automatic, unwitting 10 compulsory 11 inadvertent, instinctive, spontaneous

involute: 6 curled, rolled 8 involved 9 intricate

involve: 4 wrap 5 imply, snare 6 bemist, employ, engage, entail 7 concern, embrace, embroil, ensnare, include 8 comprise, encumber, entangle 9 implicate 10 complicate, comprehend

involved: 7 complex 12 labyrinthine

inward: 5 entad, inner 6 inside 8 interior 10 internally

Io: *father:* 7 Inachus

guard: 5 Argus

son: 7 Epaphus

iodine: *compound:* 6 iodide

salt: 6 iodate

source: 4 kelp

substitute: 7 aristal

treat with: 6 iodate

Iolcus king: 6 Pelias

ion: *negative:* 5 anion

positive: 6 cation, kation

Ion: *father:* 6 Apollo

mother: 6 Creusa

iota: bit, jot 4 atom, whit 6 tittle 8 particle

Iowa: *capital:* 9 Des Moines

city: 4 Ames 5 Anita 7 Dubuque, Ottumwa 8 Iowa City, Waterloo 9 Davenport, Oskaloosa, Sioux City 11 Cedar Rapids

county: Ida, Lee, Sac 4 Linn, Lyon, Page, Tama 5 Adair, Emmet, Floyd, Lucas, Mills, Onawa, Story, Worth 6 Bremer, Butler, Hardin, Keokuk, Warren 7 Audubon, Guthrie, Kossuth, Wapello

Indian: Fox 4 Iowa, Sauk 5 Sioux

lake: 5 Storm 6 Spirit 7 Okoboji, Red Rock

President Hoover's birthplace: 10 West Branch

river: 4 Iowa, Rock 5 Boyer, Cedar, Skunk 6 Turkey 7 Nodaway 8 Big Sioux 9 Des Moines 11 Mississippi

state bird: 9 goldfinch

state flower: 8 wild rose

state nickname: 7 Hawkeye

state tree: oak

ipecac: 4 evea

substance: 7 emetine

Iphicles: *brother:* 8 Heracles, Hercules

mother: 7 Alcmene

son: 6 Iolaus

Iphis' daughter: 6 Evadne

ipso facto: 11 by the fact of

irade: 5 edict 6 decree

Iran: (see also **Persia**) *capital:* 7 Teheran

city: Qom 5 Ahvaz 6 Abadan, Kashan, Shiraz, Tabriz 7 Esfahan, Hamadan, Mashhad

ethnic group: 4 Arab, Kurd, Turk 5 Farsi

former name: 6 Persia

governorship: 4 Ilam, Yazd 6 Semnan, Zanjan 7 Hamadan 8 Lorestan

gulf: 4 Oman 7 Persian

island: 5 Kharg, Qeshm 6 Abadan

lake: 5 Niriz, Tashk, Urmia 7 Shahpur

monetary unit: 4 rial 5 dinar

mountain peak: 6 Alwand, Bazman, Sahand, Taftan 8 Damavand, Lalehzar

mountain range: 6 Elburz, Zagros 8 Poshtkuh 9 Hindu Kush

oil center: 6 Abadan

port: 7 Bushire 11 Bandar Abbas

province: 4 Fars 5 Gilan 6 Kerman 7 Esfahan, Teheran 8 Khorasan 9 Khuzestan, Kordestan 10 Azerbaijan

river: 4 Mand 5 Atrek, Karun, Safid 7 Karkheh 9 Kizil Uzen

salt desert: 9 Dasht-e-lut 11 Dasht-e-Kavir

sea: 7 Caspian

strait: 6 Hormuz

Irani, Iranian: 7 Persian

almond: 5 badam

angel: Mah

bazaar: 9 bezooteen

bird: 6 bulbul

cap: taj

coin: pul 4 asar, cran, kran, lari, rial 5 bisti, daric, dinar, larin, shahi, toman 6 shahee, stater 7 ashrafi, kasbeke, pahlavi

comedy: 7 temacha

dynasty: 5 Kajar, Seljuk 7 Pahlavi, Safavid, Safawid 10 Sassanidae

founder of ancient empire: 5 Cyrus

god: 6 Ormazd 7 Mithras

hat: fez 6 turban

javelin: 6 jereed

king: 6 Darius, Xerxes 7 Jamshid, Jamshyd 9 Giamschid 10 Artaxerxes

Koran student: **5** hafiz
language: **5** Farsi **7** Kurdish, Pahlavi
measure: guz, mou, zar, zer **4** cane, foot **5** gareh, jerib, kafiz, makuk, qasab **6** artaba, charac, chebel, gariba, ghalva, ouroub **7** capicha, chenica, farsakh, farsang, mansion, mishara **8** parasang, piamaneh, sabbitha, stathmos **9** collothun, colluthun
moon: **4** Mahi
news agency: **4** IRNA
New Year's Day: **7** Nowroze
people: **4** Kurd, Mede **5** Kajar, Mukri, Tajik **6** Tadjik **7** Hadjemi, Persian
poet: **4** Omar **5** Saadi
religion founder: **9** Zoroaster **11** Zarathustra
religious doctrine: **6** babism
revenue officer: **9** tahsildar **10** tahseeldar
ruler: **4** khan, shah **6** atabeg, atabek, satrap, sultan
screen: **6** purdah
sect: **5** Shiah, Sunni **6** Shiite
tapestry: **7** susanee
tax collector: **9** tahsildar **10** tahseeldar
tent-maker: **4** Omar
throne room: **5** aiwan
tiara: **7** cidaris
title: mir **4** azam **5** mirza
tobacco: **6** tumbak, tumbek **7** tumbaki, tumbeki
traders: **4** sart
trumpet: **6** kerana **7** kerrana
vessel: **6** aftaba
water-pipe: **5** hooka **6** calean, hookah **8** narghile **12** hubble-bubble
water wheel: **5** noria
weight: ser **4** dram, dung, rotl, sang, seer **5** abbas, artal, artel, maund, pinar, ratel **6** batman, dirhem, gandum, karwar, miscal, miskal, nakhod **7** abbassi **8** tcheirek **9** saddirham
Iraq: *capital:* **7** Baghdad
city: **5** Basra, Erbil, Mosul **6** Kirkuk **7** An Najaf, Karbala
desert: **6** Syrian **8** Al Hajara
ethnic group: **4** Arab, Kurd
gulf: **7** Persian
historic site of: **7** Assyria **9** Babylonia
lake: **6** Dalmaj, Sadiya **8** Al Hammar **9** Habbaniya
monetary unit: **4** fils **5** dinar
mountain range: **8** Poshtkuh
port: **5** Basra
river: Zab **6** Diyala, Tigris **7** Hindiya **9** Euphrates **11** Shatt-al-Arab
irascible: **5** irate, testy **6** snappy, touchy **7** fretful, peevish **8** captious, choleric, petulant, snappish **9** impatient, splenetic **10** passionate **11** bad-tempered, belligerent, hot-tempered **13** quick-tempered
irate: mad **5** angry, het up, wroth **6** bitter

7 angered, enraged, furious, teed off **8** incensed, provoked, up in arms, wrathful **9** indignant, irascible
ire: vex **4** fury, heat, rage **5** anger, annoy, wrath **6** choler, dander, temper **8** asperity, vexation **9** vehemence **10** exasperate, resentment **11** displeasure **12** exasperation
Ireland (see also **Irish**): **4** Eire, Erin **5** Ierne **8** Hibernia **9** Innisfail
bay: **4** Clew **5** Sligo **6** Bantry, Dingle, Galway, Mannin, Tralee **7** Donegal, Killala, Youghal **8** Blacksod, Drogheda
capital: **6** Dublin
city: **4** Cobh, Cork **5** Ennis **6** Galway **7** Dundalk **8** Limerick **9** Killarney, Tipperary, Waterford **12** Dun Laoghaire
county: **4** Cork, Mayo **5** Cavan, Clare, Kerry, Louth, Meath, Sligo **6** Carlow, Dublin, Galway, Offaly **7** Donegal, Kildare, Leitrim, Wexford, Wicklow **8** Kilkenny, Laoighis, Limerick, Longford, Monaghan **9** Tipperary, Roscommon, Waterford, Westmeath
early inhabitant: **4** Celt, Pict
island: **4** Aran **5** Clare, Clear, Great **6** Achill, Dursey, Saltee **7** Elasket **8** Scarriff, Valentia
lake: Ree **4** Conn, Derg, Gara, Mask **5** Allen, Foyle, Leane **6** Corrib, Melvin **9** Killarney
monetary unit: **5** penny, pound
port: **4** Bray, Cobh, Cork **6** Arklow, Dublin, Tralee **7** Dundalk, Wexford, Wicklow **8** Drogheda **12** Dun Laoghaire
province: **6** Ulster **7** Munster **8** Connacht, Leinster
river: Lee **4** Erne, Nore, Suir **5** Avoca, Boyne, Foyle **6** Barrow, Liffey, Slaney **7** Shannon **10** Blackwater
irenic: **4** calm **8** pacifist, peaceful **10** nonviolent **12** conciliatory
iridescent: **8** colorful **9** prismatic **10** opalescent **11** rainbow-like
iris: **4** flag **5** orris **7** eye part, rainbow **9** perennial
family: **4** irid, ixia **6** crocus **9** gladiolus
inflammation of: **6** iritis
Irish: **4** Erse **6** Celtic, Gaelic
accent: **6** brogue
ancestor: Mil **6** Miledh **8** Milesius
assembly: **6** aenach, aonach
basket: **7** skeough
battle cry: abu
boat: **7** pookaun **8** pookhaun
cabstand: **6** hazard
cap: **6** barrad
cattle: **5** Kerry
chamber of deputies: **4** Dail
chemist: **5** Boyle
chieftain: **6** Tanist
church: kil
church steward: **7** erenach

clan: 4 sept 5 Cinel
club: 8 shillala 9 shillalah, shillelah 10 shillelagh
coin: rap 4 real
cordial: 10 usquebaugh
coronation stone: 7 Lia Fail
dagger: 5 skean
dance: 10 rinkafadda, rinncefada
dirge: 4 keen
dish: 4 stew
dramatist: see *playwright* below
epic tales: 4 tain, tana(pl.)
exclamation: och 4 arra 5 arrah, ohone
fair: 6 aenach, aonach
fairy: 4 shee 5 sidhe 7 banshee, banshie 10 leprechaun
festival: 4 feis
fort: Lis 4 rath
freebooter: 8 rapparee
freeman: 4 aire
fuel: 4 peat
garment: 4 inar
goblin: 5 pooka
god's mother: Ana, Anu
god of love: 5 Dagda 6 Aengus, Oengus
god of sea: Ler
goddess: 4 Badb, Bodb, Dana
good-for-nothing: 8 spalpeen
groggery: 7 shebeen
harvester: 8 spalpeen
herring: 8 scud-dawn
holiday: 10 Whitmonday
infantryman: 4 kern
king: Rig 5 Ardri
king's home: 4 Tara
lamentation: 6 ochone
landholding system: 7 rundale
lawyer: 6 brehon
legislature: 10 Oireachtas
liquor: 6 poteen 7 potheen
lord: 6 tanist
luck: 4 cess
measure: 4 mile 6 bandle
melody: 7 planxty
militant group: IRA
moccasin: 9 pampootee, pampootie
monk: 6 culdee
monk's cell: kil 4 kill
musical festival: 4 feis
musical instrument: 4 harp, lyre
national emblem: 8 shamrock
nationalist society: 8 Sinn Fein
negative: 5 sorra
novelist: 4 Shaw
oath: 5 bedad
patriot: 5 Emmet 6 Oakboy 7 Parnell
patron saint: 7 Patrick
peasant: 4 kern 5 kerne
peat: gor
person: 4 aire, kern 5 kerne, paddy 7 shoneen 8 spalpeen 10 Eireannach
pig: 5 bonav

playwright: 4 Shaw 5 Synge, Wilde, Yeats 6 O'Casey
poem: 6 amhran
poet: 5 Moore, Wilde, Yeats
priest: 5 druid
princess: 6 Iseult
proprietor: 6 tanist
Protestant: 9 Sassenach
republicanism: 9 Fenianism
revolutionist: 6 Fenian
robber: 8 woodkern
saint: 5 Aidan 7 Patrick
salutation: 6 a chara
servant: 5 biddy 7 gossoon
society: 4 aire
soldier: 6 bonagh 8 rapparee
soldiers' quartering: 7 bonaght 8 bonaught
song: 4 rann
spirit: see *fairy* above
steward: 7 erenach 8 herenach
stock: 4 daer
straw load: 5 barth
surgeon: 6 Colles
sweetheart: gra
symbol: 4 harp 8 shamrock
tax: 7 bonaght 8 bonaught
tenant: 4 saer
tenure: 6 sorren 7 sorehon
term of endearment: 5 aroon, aruin 7 acushla, alannah, asthore 9 avourneen 10 mavoureen
theatre: 5 Abbey
trout: 7 gilaroo
verse: 4 rann
whiskey: 6 poteen 10 usquebaugh
white: 4 bawn
womanhood: 4 emer
writing system: 4 ogam 5 ogham

irk (see also **ire**): vex 4 bore 5 anger, annoy, chafe, peeve, tease, upset, weary 6 nettle 7 trouble 8 irritate 10 exasperate

irksome: 4 dull 7 humdrum, painful, tedious 8 tiresome 9 fatiguing, wearisome 10 burdensome, monotonous, unpleasant 11 displeasing

iron: fer(F.) 4 gyve, hard 5 metal, power, press 6 fetter, smooth, robust, strong 7 manacle, shackle 8 firmness, handcuff, hematite, siderite 10 unyielding
compound: 5 steel
curtain: 7 barrier 8 frontier
dross: 6 sinter
magnet: 8 armature
lump: pig
lung: 10 respirator
marking: 7 brander
meteoric: 8 siderite
pert. to: 6 ferric
sulphate: 7 ilesite
tailor's: 5 goose

Iron City: 10 Pittsburgh
ironclad: 6 strict **7** armored, **9** immutable
ironer: 6 mangle **7** presser
ironhanded: 4 firm **6** strict **8** despotic **11** dictatorial
ironic: 7 satiric **9** sarcastic
iron out: 10 smooth over **11** come to terms
irons: 6 chains **7** fetters **8** shackles
irony: 6 satire **7** asteism, sarcasm **8** ridicule **13** dissimulation
Iroquois tribes: 6 Cayuga, Mohawk, Oneida, Seneca **8** Onondaga **9** Tuscarora
irradiate: ray **4** beam, emit **6** bright **7** diffuse **8** brighten **9** enlighten **10** illuminate
irrational: 4 surd **5** brute **6** absurd, insane, stupid, unwise **7** bestial, brutish, foolish **9** fanatical, illogical, senseless **10** ridiculous **12** preposterous, unreasonable **13** unintelligent
irreclaimable: 4 lost **8** hopeless **9** abandoned **11** irrevocable **12** irredeemable
irreconcilable: 11 conflicting **12** incompatible, inconsistent, intransigent
irrefutable: 10 conclusive, undeniable
irregular: 4 wild **5** erose, false **6** ataxic, fitful, rugged, spotty, uneven, unlike **7** atactic, crabbed, crooked, cursory, devious, erratic, snatchy, unequal, wayward **8** abnormal, atypical, sporadic, unlawful, unstable, unsteady, variable **9** anomalous, desultory, eccentric, unsettled **10** changeable, disorderly, immoderate **11** intemperate **12** uncontrolled, unsystematic **13** extraordinary
irregularity: 4 flaw **5** error **7** anomaly **8** disorder **9** variation **10** unevenness **11** derangement **12** imperfection
irrelevant: 9 unrelated **10** extraneous, immaterial, inapposite **11** unessential **12** inconsequent
irreligious: 5 pagan **6** wicked **7** godless, heathen, impious, profane
irremediable: 6 ruined **8** helpless, hopeless **9** desperate, incurable **11** irreparable **13** irretrievable
irreproachable: 8 spotless **9** blameless, exemplary, faultless **10** impeccable
irresistible: 10 superhuman **11** fascinating, unopposable **12** overpowering, spellbinding
irresolute: 6 fickle, infirm, unsure **8** doubtful, unstable, wavering **9** uncertain, undecided **10** changeable, inconstant **11** fluctuating **12** undetermined
irresponsible: 8 carefree **10** fly-by-night **11** harum-scarum **12** undependable **13** unaccountable
irreverence: 7 impiety **8** dishonor **9** blasphemy, impudence, profanity

irrevocable: 4 firm **5** final **9** immutable **10** conclusive **11** unalterable
irrigate: wet **5** water **6** sluice **7** moisten
irritable: 4 edgy **5** cross, fiery, testy **6** cranky, ornery, tetchy, touchy **7** fretful, peevish, pettish **8** snappish **9** excitable, fractious, impatient, querulent **12** disagreeable
irritate: irk, nag, rub, vex **4** gall, goad, rile, roil **5** anger, annoy, chafe, cross, grate, peeve, pique, spite, sting, tease **6** abrade, badger, bother, burn up, enrage, excite, harass, hector, madden, needle, nettle, put out, ruffle **7** affront, incense, inflame, provoke **8** acerbate, make sore **9** aggravate, displease, stimulate **10** exacerbate, exasperate
irritating: 5 acrid **8** rankling, stinging
irritation: 4 itch, rash, sore **12** inflammation
Isaac's kin: 4 Esau **5** Jacob **7** Abraham
isagoge: 12 introduction
Iseult: *beloved:* **7** Tristan
   husband: **4** Mark
Ishmael: 5 rover **6** pariah **7** outcast
   kin: **5** Hagar **7** Abraham **8** Nebaioth
Ishtar's lover: 6 Tammuz
isinglass: 4 mica
Isis: *kin:* **5** Horus **6** Osiris
   mother: Nut
   shrine: **5** Iseum **6** Iseium
   son: Set **4** Seth
Islam: *adherent:* **6** Moslem, Muslim
   festival: Eed
   founder: **7** Mahomet **8** Mohammed, Muhammad
   god: **5** Allah
   holy city: **5** Mecca **6** Medina
   law: **4** adat **5** sheri **6** sharia, sheria
   paradise: **5** jenna
   pert. to shrine at Mecca: **5** Kaaba
   priest: **4** imam
   scriptures: **5** Koran
island: ait, cay, ile(F.), key **4** holm, inch(Sc.), isle **5** atoll, holme, islet, **6** cut off **7** isolate **8** insulate
   group: **11** archipelago
   pert. to: **7** insular
Isle of Man: *capital:* **7** Douglas
   legislature: **7** tynwald
   lighthouse point: **4** Ayre
   measure: **6** kishen, kishon
   mountain: **8** Snaefell
   tailless cat: **4** Manx
   watering place: **4** Ryde
ism: 5 ology, tenet **6** belief **8** doctrine **10** hypothesis
isolate: 6 detach, enisle, island **7** seclude **8** insulate, separate **9** segregate, sequester **10** quarantine
isolated: 4 sole **5** alone **6** lonely **7** insular **8** singluar, solitary

Isolde's lover: 7 Tristan
isopod: 6 slater 9 wood louse
Israel (see also **Hebrew, Judaism**):
  capital: 9 Jerusalem
  city: Lod 4 Gaza 5 Haifa, Holon, Ramla
    6 Bat Yam 7 Natanya, Rehovot, Tel
    Aviv 8 Ashkelon, Nazareth, Ramat
    Gan 9 Beersheba
  desert: 5 Negev
  district: 5 Haifa 7 Central, Tel Aviv 8
    Northern, Southern 9 Jerusalem
  early name: 5 Judea 9 Palestine
  ethnic group: Jew 4 Arab 5 Druze
  gulf: 5 Aqaba
  lake: 4 Hule 7 Dead Sea 8 Kinneret
  monetary unit: 5 agora 6 shekel
  mountain: 5 Meron, Ramon 6 Carmel,
    Gilboa
  nationalist movement: 7 Zionism
  nationalist pioneer: 5 Herzl (Theodor)
  parliament: 7 Knesset
  plain: 9 Esdraelon
  port: 4 Acre, Gaza 5 Eilat, Haifa 6 Ash-
    dod 7 Tel Aviv
  settlement: 6 moshav 7 kibbutz
  statesman: 4 Meir (Golda) 8 Weizmann
    (Chaim) 9 Ben-Gurion (David)
issuance: 5 issue 6 sortie 7 issuing 9 em-
    anation 12 distribution
issue: 4 emit, flow, gush, pour, send 5
    arise, child, sally, spout, topic, yield 6
    accrue, emerge, source, upshot 7 de-
    scent, dispute, edition, emanate, for-
    tune, outcome, problem, proceed, proge-
    ny 8 question 9 effluence, offspring 10
    distribute
Istanbul: 9 Byzantium 14 Constantinople
  business area: 6 Galata
  foreign quarter: 7 Beyoglu
  patriarch: 9 Nestorius
  suburb: 7 Uskudar
isthmus: 4 neck 6 strait 9 peninsula
istle fiber: 4 pita, pito
it may be: 5 haply 8 possibly
Ita: Ata 4 Aeta 7 Negrito
Italian (see also **Italy**): *actress:* 4 Duse
  astronomer: 6 Secchi 7 Galileo
  bell town: 5 Adano
  bowling game: 5 bocce
  carriage: 7 vettura
  cathedral: 5 duomo
  cereal: 5 arzun
  cheese: 6 Romano 7 riccota 8 Bel paese,
    Parmesan 10 gorgonzola
  chest: 7 cassone
  coin: 4 lira, sudo tari 5 grano, paoli, soldo
    6 ducato, sequin, teston, zequin 8 zec-
    chino 9 centesimo
  composer: 5 Verdi 7 Bellini, Puccini,
    Rossini, Vivaldi 8 Mascagni 9 Donizet-
    ti, Scarlatti

  dance: 5 volta 8 courante 9 rigoletto 10
    tarantella
  dictator: 9 Mussolini
  dough: 5 pasta
  engraver: 8 Raimondi
  entertainment: 5 festa
  family: 4 Asti, Este 5 Amati, Cenci, Sa-
    voy 6 Borgia, Medici, Sforza
  food: 5 pizza 6 scampi 7 lasagna, ravioli,
    tortoni, spumoni 8 linguine 9 manicotti
  gentleman: ser 6 signor 7 signore
  goldsmith: 7 Cellini
  grape: uva 6 verdea
  guessing game: 4 mora
  guitar: 8 chitarra
  hamlet: 5 casal 6 casale
  hello: 4 ciao
  holiday: 5 festa
  house: 4 casa 6 casino
  ice cream: 6 gelato
  infant cupids: 8 amoretti
  inlay work: 6 tarsia
  inn: 7 albergo, locanda, osteria
  innkeeper: 4 oste 7 padrone
  lady: 5 donna 7 signora
  land: 5 paese, terra
  landlord: 7 padrone
  leader: 4 duce
  lover: 6 amante 7 amoroso
  magistrate: 7 podesta
  marble: 7 carrara
  master: 7 padrone
  mayor: 7 sindaco
  measure: pie 4 orna 5 canna, carat, pal-
    ma, piede, punto, salma, staio, stero 6
    barile, miglio, moggio, rubbio, tavola,
    tomolo 7 boccale, braccio, secchio 8
    giornata, polonick, quadrato
  medieval faction: 4 Neri
  millet: 4 buda, moha 5 mohar, tenai
  monk: 5 padre 6 abbate
  month: 4 mese 5 Marzo 6 Agosto, Aprile,
    Giugno, Luglio, Maggio 7 Gennaio, Ot-
    tobre 8 Dicembre, Febbraio, Novembre
    9 Settembre
  musician: 5 Guido
  needlework: 6 ricamo 8 trapunto
  noblewoman: 8 contessa, marchesa
  omelet: 8 frittata
  opera house: 5 Scala
  organization: 7 Balilla
  painter: 4 Reni, Tisi 5 Colle, Lippi, Lot-
    to, Vinci 6 Crespi, Giotto, Guardi,
    Monaco, Sacchi, Titian 7 Amigoni, da
    Vinci, di Credi, di Paolo, Raphael, Ro-
    busti, Strozzi, Tiepolo 8 Angelico,
    Bronzino, Cagliari, Mainardi, Sassetta
    9 Correggio, del Piombo, Giorgione,
    Veneziano 10 Botticelli, Caracciolo,
    Tintoretto
  painting: 9 tenebrosi

patriot: **6** Cavour, Rienzi **7** Mazzini **9** Garibaldi

patron saint: **7** Francis

peasant: **7** paesano **9** contadino

people: **5** Latin, Oscan, Roman **6** Sabine, Tuscan **8** Etruscan, Venetian

philosopher: **5** Croce **7** Aquinas, Rosmini

physicist: see *scientist* below

pie: **5** pizza

plays: **7** Vangeli

poet: **4** Redi, Rota **5** Boito, Dante, Tasso **7** Ariosto, Guarini **8** Petrarch

poetic name: **7** Ausonia

police officer: **6** sbirri, sbirro

policeman: **11** carabiniere, carabinieri

porridge: **7** polenta

pottery: **8** majolica

priest: **5** prete

printer: **6** Bodoni

procession: **5** corso **7** trionfi, trionfo

pronoun: che, chi, lei, mia **4** egli, ella, essa, esse, essi, esso, loro

resort: **4** Como, Lido **5** Capri **6** Ischia, Stresa **7** San Remo **8** Positano, Sorrento, Taormina

rice: **7** risotto

road: **6** strada

rock: **7** scaglia

sausage: **6** salami

scientist: **5** Fermi, Volta **7** Galileo, Galvani, Marconi

sculptor: **6** Pisano **7** Bernini, da Vinci **8** Ghiberti **9** Donatello **12** Michelangelo

secret society: **5** Mafia **7** Camorra **9** Carbonari

shore: **4** riva

soldier: **7** soldato **11** bersagliere

song: **5** canto **7** canzone

soup: **8** minestra **10** minestrone

stream: **4** rivo

summer house: **6** casino

theme: **4** tema

theologian: **7** Aquinas, Peronne

vessel: **9** trabacolo **10** trabascolo

violin maker: **5** Amati **7** Guarner **10** Stradivari

violinist: **7** Corelli, Tartini **8** Paganini

weight: **5** carat, libra, oncia, pound **6** denaro, libbra, ottava **11** chilogrammo

wind: **7** sirocco

wine: **4** Asti **5** Corvo, Soave **6** Barolo, Massic **7** Barbera, Chianti, Marsala **9** Bardolino, Vernaccia

italicize: 6 set off **9** emphasize, underline **10** underscore

Italy: *capital:* **4** Rome

city: **4** Bari, Pisa **5** Genoa, Milan, Parma, Siena **6** Ancona, Foggia, Modena, Naples, Venice **7** Bologna, Catania, Ferrara, Leghorn, Messina, Palermo, Perugia, Ravenna, Trieste **8** Brindisi, Cagliari, Florence

gulf: **5** Gaeta, Genoa **6** Venice **7** Salerno, Taranto

island: **4** Elba **5** Capri, Egadi, Ponza **6** Giglio, Ischia, Lipari, Salina, Sicily, Ustica **7** Capraia **8** Sardinia **9** Stromboli

lake: **4** Como **5** Garda **6** Albano, Lugano **7** Bolsena **8** Maggiore **9** Bracciano, Trasimeno

monetary unit: **4** lira **9** centesimo

mountain pass, tunnel: **4** Cisa, Futa **5** Cenis, Giovi **7** Brenner, Pescara, Simplon **8** Scheggia **9** Bocchetta

mountain peak: Bue **4** Etna, Rosa **5** Corno **6** Gimone, Nerone **7** Miletto, Pollino, Vettore

mountain range: **4** Alps **9** Apennines

port: **4** Bari **5** Genoa **6** Ancona, Naples, Pesaro, Reggio, Rimini, Venice **7** Leghorn, Marsala, Messina, Pescara, Salerno, Taranto, Trieste **8** Brindisi, Cagliari, La Spezia, Syracuse

pre-Roman nation: **7** Etruria

province: **4** Asti, Como, Enna **5** Aosta, Cuneo, Forli, Lecce, Lucca, Nuoro, Parma, Pavia, Rieti, Terni, Udine **6** Aquila, Arezzo, Chieti, Latina, Matera, Modena, Novara, Padova, Ragusa, Rovigo, Savona, Teramo, Trento, Varese, Verona **7** Belluno, Bergamo, Bolzano, Brescia, Caserta, Cosenza, Cremona, Gorizia, Imperia, Isernia, Mantova, Pistoia, Potenza, Sassari, Sondrio, Trapani, Treviso, Vicenza, Viterbo

region: **6** Apulia, Latium, Molise, Sicily, Umbria, Veneto **7** Abruzzi, Campania, Liguria, Marches, Tuscany **8** Calabria, Lombardy, Piedmont, Sardinia

region forming "heel": **6** Apulia

region forming "toe": **8** Calabria

river: **4** Adda, Arno, Liri **5** Adige, Oglio, Piave, Tiber **6** Aterno, Isonzo, Mincio, Panaro, Ticino **7** Pescara **8** Volturno

sea: **6** Ionian **8** Adriatic, Ligurian

volcano: **4** Etna **8** Vesuvius **9** Stromboli

itch: 4 reef, yeuk(Sc.) **6** desire **9** cacoethes, hankering **10** irritation

item (see also **object**): bit **5** entry, scrap, thing, topic **6** detail **7** account, article, product **8** personal **9** paragraph **10** particular **12** circumstance

itemize: 4 list **9** enumerate

Ithaca king: 8 Odysseus

Ithunn's husband: 5 Brage, Bragi

itinerant: 6 errant, roving **7** migrant, nomadic **8** traveler, wanderer **9** migratory, transient, traveling, unsettled, wandering **11** peripatetic

itinerary: 4 plan, tour **5** guide, route **6** record **8** roadbook **9** guidebook

Ivan the Terrible: 4 Tsar
  wife: 9 Anastasia
Ivanhoe: *author:* 5 Scott
  character: 4 Tuck 5 Isaac 6 Cedric, Rowena 7 Rebecca, Wilfred 9 Robin Hood
ivory: die 4 tusk 5 tooth 6 creamy 7 dentine
Ivory Coast: *capital:* 7 Abidjan
  city: Man 5 Daloa 6 Bouake 7 Korhogo
  monetary unit: 5 franc 7 centime
  native: 5 Baule 6 Senufo 7 Malinke

  peak: 5 Nimba
  port: 6 Bassam 9 Sassandra
  river: 7 Bandama 9 Sassandra
ivory tower: 6 dreamy, unreal 7 retreat 8
  escapist 9 visionary 11 impractical
ivy: 4 vine 6 hedera
  poison: 5 sumac
Ixion's descendants: 8 Centaurs
ixtle: 4 pita 5 fiber, istle
izzat: 5 honor 6 credit 8 prestige 10 reputation

J

jaal: 4 goat, ibex 5 beden
jab: hit, jag 4 poke, prod, stab 5 nudge,
  prick, punch 6 thrust
Jabal's father: 6 Lamech
jabber: 4 chat 6 burble, gabble 7 chatter
  9 gibberish
jabberwocky: 8 nonsense 9 gibberish,
  rigmarole
jabiru: 4 ibis 5 stork
jabot: 5 frill 6 ruffle
jacare: 6 caiman 9 crocodile
jack: nob 4 card, lift 5 knave, money 6
  sailor
  group of 4: 8 quatorze
jack-in-the-pulpit: 4 herb 5 plant 7 figwort
jack-of-all-trades: 6 tinker 8 handyman
jack tree: 4 jaca
jackal: 5 diebs
jackanapes: ape, fop 4 beau 5 dandy 6
  monkey 7 coxcomb
jackass: 4 dolt, fool 5 dunce 6 donkey,
  nitwit 9 blockhead
jackdaw: coe 6 caddow 9 blackbird
jacket: 4 bajo, coat, Eton 5 acton, grego,
  wamus 6 anorak, banian(Ind.), bietle,
  blazer, bolero, dolman, reefer, sliver,
  wammus, wampus 7 cassock, doublet,
  pea coat, ristori, spencer 8 camisole,
  chaqueta, hanselin 9 habergeon 10 car-
  magnole(F.), roundabout 11 nightingale
  knitted: 5 gansy 6 gansey, sontag 7
  sweater 8 cardigan, penelope
  sleeveless: 4 vest 6 bolero, jerkin

jackknife: 4 dive 6 barlow
Jack of clubs: pam
jackpot: all 4 pool 5 award 8 windfall
jackrabbit: 4 hare
jackstay: 4 rope 5 staff
jackstones: 4 dibs
Jacob: *brother:* 4 Edom, Esau
  daughters: 5 Dinah
  descendant: 6 Levite 9 Israelite
  father-in-law: 5 Laban
  new name: 6 Israel
  parent: 5 Issac 7 Rebekah
  retreat: 5 Haran
  son: Dan, Gad 4 Aser, Levi 5 Asher, Judah 6 Bononi, Joseph, Reuben, Simeon
  7 Gershon, Zebulun 8 Benjamin, Issachar, Naphtali
  vision(scene): 6 Bethel
  wife: 4 Leah 6 Rachel
jade: fag, nag 4 hack, minx, plug, tire 5
  hussy, weary, wench 6 harass 7 exhaust, fatigue, hilding, pounamu 8
  nephrite 10 greenstone
jaded: 4 worn 5 blase, tired, weary 6
  dulled 7 wearied 9 exhausted, forjaskit,
  forjesket
jaeger: 4 bird, gull, skua 6 hunter 7 diamond 8 huntsman
jag: dag, jab, rag 4 barb, hair, load, mess,
  stab 5 carry, notch, prick, scrap, shred,
  slash, souse, spree, tooth 6 indent, tatter 7 bristle, pendant, portion 8 quantity 13 denticulation
jagged: 5 erose, rough, sharp 6 hackly,
  ragged 7 cutting

jaguar: 5 ounce **8** large cat
jai alai: 4 game **6** pelota
  court: **6** cancha **7** fronton
  racket: **5** cesta
jail: can, jug **4** brig, dump, gaol, keep, stir **5** clink, pokey **6** asylum, carcel, cooler, lockup, prison **7** hoosgow **8** bastille, hoosegaw, hoosegow, imprison **9** calaboose **11** incarcerate
jailer, jailor: 4 caid **5** guard **6** gaoler, keeper, warden **7** alcaide, turnkey
Jairite: Ira
jake: 4 fine, hick, rube **5** dandy **6** rustic **9** first-rate, greenhorn
jako: 6 parrot
jalousie: 5 blind **7** shutter
jam: 4 bind **5** crowd, crush **6** spread **7** squeeze **9** marmalade **10** congestion
Jamaica dogwood: 8 barbasco
  ginger alcohol: **4** jake
James' father: 7 Zebedee
jangle: 4 ring **5** clang, upset **6** bicker, racket **7** quarrel, wrangle **8** irritate **11** altercation
jangling: 5 harsh **7** grating **9** dissonant **10** discordant **11** cacophonous
janitor: 6 porter **9** caretaker, custodian **10** doorkeeper **11** housekeeper
japan: 7 lacquer, varnish
Japan: 6 Nippon
  bay: Ise **5** Mutzu, Osaka **6** Suruga, Toyama, Wakasa **8** Ishikari **9** Kagoshima, Shimabara
  capital: **5** Tokyo
  city: Ome, Usa **4** Kobe, Nara, Ueda **5** Kyoto, Osaka, Otaru, Sakai **6** Nagoya, Sendai **7** Okayama, Okazaki, Sapporo **8** Kawasaki, Nagasaki, Yokohama, Yokosuka **9** Hiroshima
  island: **6** Honshu (mainland), Kyushu **7** Shikoku **8** Hokkaido
  island group: Oki **4** Goto **5** Bonin **6** Marcus, Ryukyu **7** Okinawa, Volcano
  lake: **4** Biwa **8** Chuzenji **10** Inawashiro
  monetary unit: sen, yen
  mountain peak: **4** Kuju **5** Iwaki **6** Ontake **7** Shirane **9** Asahi Dake
  mountain range: **5** Nikko **8** Sakhalin **9** Kirishima
  opened by: **5** Peary
  port: **4** Kobe **5** Chiba, Nanao, Osaka, Tokyo **6** Nagoya, Sasebo **7** Fukuoka, Shimizu, Shimoda **8** Hakodate, Kawasaki, Yokohama
  prefecture: Mie **4** Gifu, Nara, Oita, Saga **5** Aichi, Akita, Chiba, Ehime, Fukui, Gumma, Hyogo, Iwate, Kochi, Kyoto, Osaka, Shiga, Tokyo **6** Aomori, Miyagi, Nagano, Toyama **7** Ibaraki, Okayama, Shimane
  river: **4** Kiso, Tone **5** Iwaki, Shira **6** Sumida, Tashio **7** Shinano

  sea: Suo **6** Harima, Inland, Kumano, Sagami **7** Okhotsk **9** East China
  strait: **5** Bungo, Korea **7** Tsugaru
  volcano: Aso **4** Fuji **5** Asama, Iwate **6** Daisen, On-take
Japanese: *abacus:* **7** soroban
  abalone: **5** awabi
  aborigine: **4** Ainu
  alcoholic beverage: **4** sake, saki
  alloy: **5** mokum
  allspice: **12** chimonanthus
  apricot: ume **4** ansu
  art design: **5** notan
  baron: **6** daimio, daimyo
  battle cry: **6** banzai
  biwa: **6** loquat
  boxes: **4** inro
  brake: **6** warabi
  brazier: **7** hibachi
  brocade: **7** nishiki
  Buddha: **5** Amida
  Buddhist festival: Bon
  Buddhist sect: Zen **4** Jodo, Shin
  bush clover: **4** hagi
  button: **7** netsuke
  calculator: **6** abacus **7** soroban
  calisthenics: **4** judo
  cape: **4** mino
  cherry: **4** fuji
  chess: **5** shogi
  chevrotain: **4** napu
  church: **4** tera
  circle: **4** maru
  clan: **7** Satsuma
  class: eta, roi **6** heimin **7** kwazoku, samurai, shizoku
  clogs: **4** geta
  clover: **4** hagi
  coin: bu; rin, sen, yen **4** oban **5** koban, obang, tempo **6** cobang, ichebu, ichibu, itzebu, itzibu, kobang **7** itzeboo, itziboo
  combine: **8** zaibatsu
  composition: **6** haikai
  costume: **7** netsuke
  court: **5** dairi
  crepe: **8** chirimen
  crest: mon **7** kikumon
  dancing girl: **6** geisha
  deer: **4** sika
  deity: **9** Amaterasu
  dextrose: ame
  dish: **7** sashimi, tempura **8** sukiyaki, teriyaki
  dog: **6** tanate
  door: **6** fusuma
  drama: noh **6** kabuki
  drink: **4** mate, sake, saki
  drum: **5** tarko
  dwarf tree: **6** bonsai
  dye process: **5** yuzen
  earthenware: **5** banko **7** Satsuma **8** rakuware

emperor: 8 Hirohito
emperor's title of old: 6 mikado
ethics: 7 Bushido
explosive: 7 shimose
fabric: 6 birodi 7 habutai, nishiki 8 chirimen, habutaye
family concern: 8 zaibatsu
fan: ogi
festival: Bon 7 Matsuri
fish: ayu, tai, tho 4 fugu, funa
flag: 7 sunflag
flower: 9 nelumbium
flute: 4 fuye
founder of imperial line: 10 Jimmu Tenno
game: 5 goban 6 gobang
garment: 5 haori 6 kimono, mompei
gateway: 5 torii
girdle: obi
girdle receptacle: 4 inro
god: 5 Ebisu, Hotei 6 Benten 7 Daikoku, Jurojin 8 Bishamon 10 Fukurokuju
goddess: 9 Amaterasu
governor's title: 6 shogun, taikun, tycoon
hanging: 8 kakemono
harp: 4 koto
herb: udo
kelp: 4 kome
lacquer: 6 urushi
legislature: 4 Diet
litter: see *palanquin* below
loquat: 4 biwa
lyric: 5 haiku, hokku
magnolia: 5 yulan
measure: bu, jo; boo, cho 4 hiro 5 tsubo 11 kujira-shaku
measure of distance: ri
measure of land: se; tan
measure of weight: mo; fun, kin, kon, rin, shi 4 kati, kwan, niyo 5 carat, catty, momme, picul 6 kwamme 8 hiyak-kin 11 komma-ichida
metalwork: 5 zogan
military ruler: 6 shogun
monastery: 4 tera
music and dancing: 7 san-gaku 8 saru-gaku
musical instrument: 4 fuye, koto 5 tarko 7 samisen, truyume
nautical mile: 5 kairi
news service: 5 Domei
nobility: 7 kwazoku
ornament: 4 inro
outcast: eta 5 ronin
overcoat: 4 mino
pagoda: taa
painting style: 4 kano 7 ukiyoye
palanquin: 4 kago 5 cango 7 norimon
paper-folding art: 7 origami
paper mulberry: 4 kozo
persimmon: 4 kaki 7 Hyakume
pine: 5 matsu

plant: udo 5 kudzu 6 sugamo
plum: 6 kelsey
porcelain: 5 Hizen, Imari 6 Hirado 9 Nabeshima, Sanda ware
porter: 5 akabo
potato: imo
quince: 8 japonica
radish: 6 daikon
receptacle: 4 inro
religion: 6 Shinto 8 Buddhism 9 Shintoism
rice cake: ame
rice wine: 4 sake
robe: 6 kimono
salad plant: udo
salmon: 4 masu
sash: obi
screen: 5 shoji
seaweed: 4 nori
self-defense: 4 judo 6 karate 7 jujitsu, jujutsu
Shinto temple: Sha 5 Jinja 6 Jinsha 7 Yashiro
ship: 4 maro, maru
shoe: 4 geta, zori
shrub: 4 fuji 5 goumi 8 japonica
silk: 7 habutai 8 chirimen, habutaye
silkworm: 7 yamamai
silkworm disease: uji
sock: 4 tabi
song: uta
storm: 7 tsunami
suicide: 7 seppuku 8 hara-kari, hara-kiri, hari-kari, kamikaze
suntree: 7 hinokis
sword: 5 catan 6 cattan 8 wacadash
sword guard: 5 tsuba
tea ceremony: 7 chanoyu
tea girl: 6 mousme 7 mousmee
temple: 4 tera
throne: 6 shinza
title: 4 kami 6 shogun
tortoise shell: 5 bekko
tree: 4 kozo, sugi 5 akeki, kiaki, yeddo 6 urushi 7 camphor 8 akamatsu 10 shirakashi
untouchable: eta
vehicle: 7 ricksha 8 rickshaw 10 jinricksha, jinrikisha
velvet: 6 birodi
verse: 5 tanka
vine: 5 kudzu
wall: 5 shoji
warrior: 7 samurai
windstorm: 5 taifu
winged being: 5 tengu
wrestling: 4 Sumo
writing: 4 kana
zitherharp: 4 koto
Japanese-American: 5 Issei, Kibei, Nisei 6 Sansei
jape: 4 fool, gibe, jeer, jest, joke, mock 5

fraud, trick **6** deride
japery: 10 buffoonery
Japheth: *father:* **4** Noah
  son: **5** Magog, Tubal **7** Meshech
japonica: 4 bush **5** shrub **8** camellia
jar: jug, ola, urn **4** jolt, olla, vase **5** banga,
  clash, cruse, shake, vase **5** banga,
  dria, krater, tinaja **7** agitate, amphora,
  clatter, concuss, discord **10** jardiniere
  fruit: **5** mason
  rubber: **4** lute
  top: lid
  two-handled: **7** amphora
  wide-mouthed: **4** ewer
jardiniere: jar, jug, urn **4** vase **5** stand **7**
  garnish **9** flowerpot
jargon: 4 cant **5** argot, idiom, lingo, slang
  6 pidgin **9** baragouin, gibberish **10** balderdash, vernacular **12** gobbledygook
  lawyer's: **8** legalese
  scholar's: **9** academese
jarl: 4 earl **7** headman **9** chieftain
jarring: 5 rough **9** dissonant **10** discordant
jasmine: 4 vine **6** flower **7** perfume
Jason: *father:* **5** Aeson
  love: **6** Creusa
  men: **9** Argonauts
  ship: **4** Argo
  teacher: **7** Cheiron
  uncle: **6** Pelias
  wife: **5** Medea
jasper: 6 morlop, quartz **10** bloodstone,
  chalcedony
jaundice: 4 bias, envy **7** gulsach, icterus **8**
  jealousy **9** prejudice
jaunt: 4 ride, trip **5** sally, tramp **6** ramble
  7 journey **9** excursion
jaunty: 4 airy **5** cocky, perky, showy,
  smart **7** finical, stylish **8** debonair **9** debonaire, sprightly
java: 6 coffee
Java: see **Indonesia**
Javanese: *almond:* **7** talisay
  arrow poison: **4** upas
  badger: **5** ratel **6** teledu
  berry: **5** cubeb
  carriage: **4** sado **5** sadoo
  civet: **5** rasse
  cotton: **5** kapok
  dancers: **6** bedoyo
  drama: **6** topeng
  Dutchman: **6** blanda
  fabric: **4** ikat
  fig tree: **7** gondang
  grackle: beo
  measure: **4** paal **5** palen
  musical instrument: **5** saron **6** bonang,
  gender **7** gambang, gamelan **8** gamelang
  orchestra: **7** gamelan **8** gamelang
  ox: **7** bantens
  pepper: **5** cubeb

plum: **5** duhal **6** jambul, lomboy **7** jambool
puppet show: **6** wajang, wayang
rice field: **5** sawah
skunk: **6** teledu
speech: **5** krama, ngoko
squirrel: **8** jelerang
straw: **6** peanit
sumac: **6** fuyang
temple: **5** candi **6** chandi, tjandi
tree: **4** upas **6** antiar **7** gondang
village: **5** dessa
weight: **4** amat, pond, tali **5** pound
wild dog: **5** adjag
javelin: 4 dart **5** lance, spear **7** assagai,
  assegai, harpoon
  cord: **7** amentum
jaw: maw **4** chaw, chop, talk **5** scold **6** berate, jabber **7** chatter **8** prattle
  lumpy: **13** actinomycosis
  muscle: **8** masseter
  part: **4** chin
  pert. to: **5** malar **7** gnathic
jawbone: 7 maxilla **8** mandible **13** apply
  pressure
Jayhawker: 6 Kansan
jazz: hot **4** cool, scat **5** funky, swing **6**
  modern **7** ragtime **11** barrelhouse, progressive
jealous: 7 envious **8** watchful **9** green-
  eyed **10** suspicious **11** mistrustful
jeer: bob, boo **4** gibe, hoot, jape, mock **5**
  fleer, flout, scoff, scout, sneer, taunt **6**
  deride **8** ridicule
Jeffersonian: 7 liberal **10** democratic
Jefferson's home: 10 Monticello
Jehiada's wife: 9 Jehosheba **12** Jeho-
  shabeath
Jehoahaz's mother: 7 Hamutal
Jehoiachin's successor: 9 Salathiel
Jehoshaphat: *father:* Asa
  son: **4** Jehu
Jehovah: God **5** Jahve, Yahwe **6** Elohim,
  Jahveh, Yahweh
jehu: 6 driver
jejune: 4 dry **4** arid, dull, flat **5** empty,
  inane, prosy, trite, vapid **6** barren,
  hungry, meager **7** insipid, sterile **8**
  foodless, lifeless **9** innocuous
jell: 7 thicken **9** coagulate **11** crystallize
jelly: gel **6** spread **7** gelatin **8** gelatine
  meat: **5** aspic
  vegetable: **6** pectin
jellyfish: 6 medusa **7** acaleph, milksop **8**
  weakling
  group: **10** discophora
  part: **10** exumbrella
jellylike: 10 gelatinous
je ne sais quoi: 13 I don't know what **14**
  elusive quality
jennet: ass **5** horse **6** donkey
jeopardize: 6 expose **7** imperil **8** endan-

ger **10** compromise
jeopardy: 4 risk **5** peril **6** danger, hazard, menace
Jerahmeel's son: 4 Oren **5** Achia
jeremiad: 6 lament, tirade **9** complaint
jerez: 6 sherry
Jericho: *publican:* **8** Zaccheus **9** Zacchaeus
woman: **5** Rahab
jerk: ass, bob, tic, **4** fool, yank **5** idiot, pluck, twist **6** twitch, wrench
jerkin: 4 coat **6** jacket, salmon **9** blackjack, waistcoat
jerky: 4 meat **5** wagon **7** charqui **8** saccadic, staccato **9** irregular, twitching **10** paroxysmal
jeroboam: 4 bowl **6** bottle, goblet
jerry-built: 5 tacky **6** sleazy **13** unsubstantial
jersey: 6 gansey **7** sweater
Jersey tea: 11 wintergreen **12** checkerberry
Jerusalem: 4 Sion, Zion **5** Salem
captor: **4** Omar
garden: **10** Gethsemane
mosque: **4** Omar
mountain: **4** Sion, Zion **6** Moriah, Olivet
oak: **7** ambrose
pool: **6** Siloam **8** Bethesda
priest: **5** Zadoc, Zadok
prophetess: **4** Anna, Anne
region: **5** Perea
spring: **5** Gihon **6** Siloam
temple treasury: **6** Corban
thorn: **6** retama
Jerusalem artichoke: 5 tuber **7** girasol **8** girasole **10** topinambou
Jerusalem corn: 5 durra
Jerusalem haddock: 4 opah
jess: 5 strap, thong **7** binding
jessamy: fop **5** dandy
Jesse: *father:* **4** Obed
son: **5** David
jest: fun, gag, kid **4** bull, fool, jape, joke, mime, quip **5** chaff, prank, sport, tease **6** banter, japery, trifle **8** drollery **9** burlesque **10** jocularity
jester: 4 fool, mime, zany **5** clown, droll **6** motley **7** buffoon, **8** comedian, humorist **11** merry-andrew
Jesuit: *founder:* **6** Loyola (Ignatius)
motto: **4** A.M.D.G.
saint: **5** Regis
Jesuits' bark: 8 cinchona
jet: 4 ebon, gush **5** black, raven, spout, spurt **6** nozzle **7** lignite **8** aircraft
lag: **7** fatigue
set: **11** social group
jet-assisted takeoff: 4 JATO
Jethro's daughter: 8 Zipporah
jettison: 5 eject, scrap **6** discard **7** abandon **9** throw away

jetty: 4 mole, pier **5** groin, wharf **6** groyne
jeu: 4 game, play **9** diversion
jeune fille: 4 girl, miss
Jew: (see also **Hebrew, Judaism**): **6** Essene, Hebrew, Semite **9** Israelite
jewel: (see also **gem**): gem **5** bijou(F.), ideal, stone **7** paragon **8** ornament
box: **6** casket **7** casquet
case: tye
connoisseur: **10** lapidarist
magnifying lens: **5** loupe
set: **6** parure
weight: **5** carat
jewelry: 10 bijouterie
alloy: **6** oreide, oroide
artificial: **5** paste **6** strass **7** costume
cutting device: dop
piece: pin **4** ring **6** brooch **7** earring **8** bracelet, lavalier, necklace
setting: **4** pave
jezebel: 4 slut **5** hussy, wench **6** virago **7** trollop **8** strumpet
Jezebel: *father:* **7** Ethbaal
husband: **4** Ahab
slayer: **4** Jehu
victim: **6** Naboth
jib: 4 balk, boom, sail **8** crane arm
jibe: 5 agree, shift **6** accord
jiffy: 5 flash, hurry, trice **6** moment, second **7** instant
jig: 4 tool **5** dance, drill **8** fishhook
jigger: cup **4** boat **5** glass **6** gadget
jiggle: jar **5** dance, shake **6** fidget, diddle, teeter **7** agitate
jihad, jehad: war **6** strife **7** contest, crusade **8** campaign
jill: 4 girl **5** woman **10** sweetheart
jilt: 5 leave **6** betray, desert, reject **7** abandon, discard, forsake, let down
jimmy: bar, pry **5** lever **7** crowbar, pry open
Jimsonweed: 6 datura
jingle: 4 ring **5** clank, clink, rhyme, verse **6** tinkle **7** chinkle
jingoist: 10 chauvinist
jinni: 5 genie **6** afreet, Alukah, jinnee, Yaksha, Yakshi(fem.)
jinx: hex **5** jonah **6** hoodoo, whammy **7** evil eye, nemesis
jitters: 5 panic **6** dither, shakes **7** willies
jittery: 5 jumpy **7** fidgety, nervous
jive: kid **5** dance, swing **6** jargon, phoney **7** hot jazz **9** deceitful, jitterbug
Joan of Arc: 7 Pucelle
birthplace: **7** Domremy
counselors: **6** voices
victory: **7** Orleans
Joan's spouse: 5 Darby
job: 4 duty, task **5** chare, cheat, chore, stint, trick **7** farm out **8** position, vocation **10** employment
Job: *daughter:* **5** Kezia **6** Jemima

friend: 5 Elihu 6 Bildad, Zophar 7 Eliphaz

Job's tears: 4 coix 4 adlai, adlay, grass, plant

jobber: 6 dealer 10 wholesaler

Jocasta: *daughter* 6 Ismene 8 Antigone
husband: 5 Laius 7 Oedipus
son: 7 Oedipus 8 Eteocles 9 Polynices 10 Polyneices

jock: 7 athlete

jockey: 4 gull 5 rider, trick 6 driver, outwit 8 maneuver, operator 10 manipulate
kind of: 4 disc

jocose: dry 6 joking 7 playful 9 full of fun

jocular: gay 4 airy 5 droll, funny, jolly, merry, silly, witty 6 blithe, elated, jovial, joyous, lively, ribald 7 comical, festive, gleeful, jesting, playful, waggish 8 animated, cheerful, gladsome, humorous, mirthful, sportive 9 burlesque, convivial, facetious, hilarious, vivacious 10 frolicsome

joculator: 4 mime 6 jester 7 juggler 8 conjurer, jongleur, minstrel 11 entertainer

jocund: gay 6 genial 8 cheerful

jog: run 4 jerk, lope, poke, prod, trot 5 nudge 6 canter 7 refresh 9 stimulate

John: Ian 4 Ivan, Juan, Sean

John Brown's Body author: 5 Benet

John of Gaunt: 9 Lancaster

John the Baptist: *father* 7 Zachary 9 Zachariah, Zacharias
mother: 9 Elizabeth

johnnycake: 4 pone 7 corn bread

Johnson grass: 7 sorghum

join: add, mix, tie, wed 4 ally, fuse, knit, knot, link, mate, meet, seam, team, weld, yoke 5 annex, blend, enrol, enter, graft, hitch, marry, merge, miter, piece, unite 6 attach, cantle, cement, cocket, concur, couple, engage, enlist, enroll, mingle, solder, splice, suture 7 combine, connect, consort, mortise 8 coalesce 9 associate 10 amalgamate 11 consolidate, participate

joint: ell, hip, tee 4 butt, dive, knee, node, seam 5 ankle, cross, elbow, hinge, scarf, wrist 6 arthra(pl.), mutual, rabbet, resort 7 arthron, brothel, calepin, hangout, knuckle, pastern 8 coupling 12 articulation
pert. to: 5 nodal 9 articular
plant stem: 6 phyton 8 phytomer
put out of: 5 upset 9 dislocate
right angle: ell, tee
turned outward: 6 valgus
without: 10 acondylose, acondylous
wooden: 5 tenon

joist: 4 beam 7 sleeper 8 studding

joke: fun, gag, kid, pun 4 fool, gibe, hoax, jape, jest, quip 5 flirt, prank, sally, sport, tease 6 banter 9 wisecrack
old: 6 wheeze 8 chestnut

joker: wag, wit 4 card 5 clown, cutup 6 gagman, jester 7 farceur 11 hidden catch

Joktan: *father:* 4 Eber
son: 5 Ophir

jollity: fun 5 cheer, mirth, revel 6 gaiety, gayety 7 revelry 8 hilarity 9 amusement, festivity, joviality, merriment 11 merrymaking 12 cheerfulness, exhilaration

jolly: 5 buxom, rally 6 cajole, jovial, mellow 7 jocular 9 convivial 11 intoxicated

jolly boat: 4 yawl

jolt: jar 4 blow, bump, butt 5 knock, shake, shock 6 jostle, jounce 7 startle

Jonah: 4 jinx 7 prophet
deliverer: 5 whale

jonquil: 8 daffodil 9 narcissus

Johnson comedy: Fox 7 Epicene, Volpone 9 Alchemist

Jordan: *capital:* 5 Amman
city: 5 Irbid, Zarqa 6 Nablus
ethnic group: 4 Arab, Kurd 8 Armenian
monetary unit: 4 fils 5 dinar
port: 5 Aqaba
river: 6 Jordan

Joseph: *brother:* Dan, Gad 4 Levi 5 Asher, Judah 6 Reuben, Simeon 7 Zebulun 8 Benjamin, Issachar, Naphtali
buyer: 8 Potiphar
father: 5 Jacob
mother: 6 Rachel
son: 4 Igal 7 Ephraim

josh: guy, kid, rib 4 joke 5 chaff, spoof, tease 6 banter 9 poke fun at

Joshua: *associate:* 5 Caleb
burial place: 5 Gaash
father: Nun
place of importance: 7 Aijalon

Joshua tree: 5 yucca

Josiah: *father:* 4 Amon
mother: 7 Jedidah
son: 8 Jehoahaz 9 Jehoiakim

joss: 4 idol 5 image 8 divinity

jostle: jar, jog 4 jolt, push 5 crowd, elbow, shove 6 hurtle, hustle

jot: ace, bit 4 atom, iota, whit 5 grain, minim, point 6 tittle 7 smidgen 8 particle
jotting:

jotting: 4 memo 9 short note

jounce: 4 jolt 5 shake 6 bounce

journal: log 5 diary, paper 6 record 7 daybook, gazette, logbook 8 magazine 10 periodical
keeper: 7 diarist

journalist: 6 editor 8 reporter 9 columnist

journey: run 4 eyre, fare, iter(L.), ride,

sail, tour, trek, trip **5** jaunt, route **6** junket, safari, travel, voyage **7** circuit, odyssey, passage **8** navigate **9** excursion **10** expedition, pilgrimage **13** peregrination
course of: **9** itinerary
division of: lap, leg
pert. to: **6** viatic **11** peripatetic
joust: 4 tilt **6** combat **7** tourney **10** tournament
field: **4** list
ready to: **5** atilt
jovial: gay **5** bully, jolly, merry **6** elated, genial, jocose, jocund, joyous **7** jocular **9** convivial, hilarious
jowl: jaw **4** chop **5** cheek **6** dewlap, wattle **7** jawbone
joy: 4 glee **5** bliss, mirth **6** gaiety, gayety **7** delight, ecstasy, elation, rapture, revelry **8** felicity, gladness, hilarity, pleasure **9** beatitude, festivity, happiness, rejoicing **10** exultation **12** cheerfulness, exhilaration
Muse: **4** Tara
Joyce (James): *character:* **5** Bloom, Rowan **7** Dedalus **9** Earwicker
work: **6** Exiles **7** Ulysses **9** Dubliners **12** Chamber Music **13** Finnegan's Wake, Pomes Penyeach
joyless: 6 dismal **9** cheerless
joyous: gay **4** glad **5** merry **6** blithe, festal **7** blessed, festive, gleeful, jocular **8** cheerful, mirthful **9** blitheful, delighted
Jubal's father: 6 Lamech
jubilant: 6 elated **8** exulting **9** rejoicing **10** triumphant
Judah: *brother:* **4** Levi **6** Joseph, Reuben, Simeon
daughter-in-law: **5** Tamar
descendant: **4** Anub, Boaz **5** David, Jesse **9** Jerahmeel
father: **5** Jacob
mother: **4** Leah
queen: **8** Athaliah
son: Er **4** Onan
Judaism (see also **Hebrew, Israel**):
abode of the dead: **5** Sheol
ascetic: **6** Essene
Bible: **4** Tora **5** Torah
Bible text: **5** miqra
Book of Psalms: **8** Tehillim
bread: **5** echem, matzo **6** hallah, matzos **7** challah, matzoth **8** afikomen
butcher: **6** shohet **8** shochtim
cabalistic book: **5** Zohar
calendar: see *month* below
ceremony: **8** habdalah
community: **6** aljama **8** kehillah
confession of sins: **5** Alhet **7** Ashamnu
convert: ger
Day of Atonement: **9** Yom Kippur
devil: **6** Belial

dietary regulations: **7** kashrut
dispersion: **5** golah **8** diaspora
doctor of law: **6** scribe
doctrine: **6** Mishna **7** Mishnah **8** Kodashim
drum: **4** toph
festival: see *holiday* below
garment: **5** shawl, talis **7** tallith
harp: **5** nebel
healer: Asa
heretical doctrine: **7** Karaism
holiday: **5** Pesah, Purim **6** Pesach, Succos, Sukkos, Yom Tov **7** Sukkoth **8** Chanukah, Hanukkah, Lagbomer, Shabouth **9** Tishahbab, Yom Kippur **11** Rosh Hashana **12** Simhath Torah
horn: **6** shofar **7** shophar
immigrant: **4** oleh **6** halutz **7** chalutz
instrument: **4** asor **5** nebel
instrument player: **9** psalterer, psaltress
judge: **7** shophet
land: **4** Zion
law: **4** Chok, Tora **5** Torah **6** Chukah, Talmud **7** Halacha, Halakah **8** Kashruth
lawgiver: **5** Moses
liturgy: **6** Maarib, Minhah **9** Shaharith
lyre: **4** asor
marriage broker: **8** shadchen
marriage custom: **8** levirate
meat inspection: **7** bedikah
miter: **7** petalon
month: **4** Adar, Iyar, Elul **5** Tebet, Nisan, Sivan **6** Tishri, Kislev, Shebat, Beadar, Tammuz **7** Heshvan
mourning period: **6** Shivah
New Year: **11** Rosh Hashana
Old Testament division **11** Hagiographa
patriarch: **5** Isaac, Jacob **7** Abraham
patriot family: **8** Maccabee
pioneer: **6** halutz **7** chalutz
poems: **6** yigdal **8** Azharoth
prayer: **5** Alenu, Shema **7** Geullah
prayer book: **6** mahzor, siddur
priest: **4** Ezra **5** Aaron, Cohen **6** Levite
priestly caste: **7** Cohanim, Levites
prophet: **4** Amos, Ezra **5** Elias, Hosea, Jonah, Micah, Nahum **6** Daniel, Elijah, Elisha, Haggai **8** Habakkuk, Jeremiah **9** Zechariah
prophetess: **6** Huldah
proselyte: ger
psalm of praise: **6** hallel
redeemer: **4** goel
revelation: **5** Torah
ritual: see *ceremony* above
sabbath: **8** Saturday
sacred objects: **4** urim
sage: **4** Agur
scarf: **5** abnet **7** tallith
scroll: **11** Sepher Torah
sect member: **6** Essene, Hassid

skullcap: **6** kippah **7** yamilke **8** yarmulka
song: **8** hatikvah **9** hattikvah
spirit: **8** Asmodeus
synagogue: **5** schul
tassel: **6** zizith
teacher: **5** amora, rabbi, tanna
temple precentor: **6** cantor
trumpet: **6** shofar **7** shophar
vestment: **5** ephod
women's organization: **8** Hadassah
Judas: **7** traitor **8** betrayer
place of suicide: **8** Aceldama, Akeldama
Judea: *ancient name:* **5** Judah
governor: **6** Pilate
king: Asa **4** Ahaz, Amon **5** Herod **7** Jehoram **8** Manesseh **10** Jehoiachin **11**
Jehoshaphat
place: **5** Berea
judge: try **4** deem, gage, rank, rate **5**
court, gauge, opine **6** assess, critic, decide, reckon, umpire **7** arbiter, believe,
justice, referee, suppose **8** consider, estimate, mediator, sentence **9** criticize,
determine **10** adjudicate, arbitrator,
chancellor, magistrate
bench: **4** banc **6** bancus
chamber: **6** camera
circuit: **4** iter
entry of, after verdict: **6** postea
group: **5** bench
junior or subordinate: **6** puisne
mallet: **5** gavel
of Hades: **5** Minos
of the dead: **6** Osiris
robe: **4** toga
judgment: **5** arret, award, sense, taste **6**
insight, **7** censure, insight, opinion, verdict **8** decision, sentence **9** criticism **10**
astuteness, discretion, horse sense **11**
sensibility
left to one's: **13** discretionary
judicable: **12** determinable
judicial assembly: **5** court
judiciary: **5** bench
document: **4** writ **8** decision
judicious: **4** wise **7** prudent **8** rational,
sensible **9** sagacious **10** discerning
Judith: *husband:* Manasses
victim: **10** Holofernes
judo: **7** jujitsu **10** martial art
rel. of: **9** wrestling
jug: jar **4** ewer, jail, olla **5** crock, cruse **6**
carafe, flagon, lockup, prison, tinaja, ur-
ceus **7** pitcher **9** container **10** bellar-
mine, jardiniere
shaped like a man: **4** Toby
Juggernaut: **6** Vishnu
juggle: **7** falsify, shuffle **10** manipulate
jugglery: **8** trickery **9** deception **10** esca-
motage(F.), hanky-panky **11** legerde-
main **13** sleight-of-hand
juice: jus(F.), oil, sap **4** broo **6** cremor **8**

gasoline **10** succulence **11** electricity
apple: **6** cider
fruit: rob **4** must, stum, wine **5** cider **6**
casiri **7** vinegar
plant: sap **4** milk **5** latex **6** achete
juicy: **4** frim, racy **5** spicy **6** lively **7** piquant **9** succulent
juju: **5** charm **6** amulet, fetish
juke: **4** fake **5** cheat **7** deceive
julep: **5** drink **8** beverage
Juliet: *betrothed:* **5** Paris
father: **7** Capulet
lover: **5** Romeo
jumble: **4** hash, heap, mess **5** mix up **6**
huddle, medley, muddle **7** clutter, mixture **8** disorder, mishmash **9** confusion
10 hodgepodge
jump: hop **4** leap **5** bound, caper, vault **6**
hurdle, prance, spring **7** saltate **8** increase
stick for: **4** pogo, pole
jumper: **5** dress, smock **6** blouse, jacket
jumpsuit: **8** coverall
jumpy: **7** jittery, nervous **12** apprehensive
junco: **5** finch **8** snowbird
junction: **4** axil, seam **5** joint, union **6** suture **7** contact, meeting **8** crossing **10**
confluence, connection
juncture: **4** pass **5** union **6** choice, crisis **8**
exigency **9** emergency **10** crossroads
12 turning point
June bug: **6** beetle **8** figeater
June grass: poa
Jungfrau: **4** peak **8** mountain
site of: **4** Alps
jungle: **4** maze **6** tangle **9** labyrinth **10**
wilderness
junior: **7** student, younger **8** namesake **11**
subordinate
juniper: **4** cade, ezel **5** grose, retem, savin
6 sabine, savine
junk: **4** boat, dope, drug **5** scrap, trash,
waste **6** heroin, refuse **7** discard, rubbish **8** jettison **9** narcotics
junker: **5** crate, noble, wreck **6** German
10 aristocrat
junket: **4** trip **5** feast **6** picnic **9** excursion
13 entertainment
Juno: **4** Hera
consort: **7** Jupiter
special messenger: **4** Iris
junta: **7** council **8** tribunal **9** committee
10 government
junto: **5** cabal **6** clique **7** coterie, faction
Jupiter: **4** Jove, Zeus
angel: **7** Zadkiel
consort: **4** Juno
daughter: **4** Bura **7** Minerva
epithet: **6** Stator
Roman temple: **7** Capitol
satellite: Pan **4** Hera, Leda **5** Hades **6**
Europa, Hestia **7** Demeter **8** Adrastea,

Amalthea, Callisto, Ganymede, Poseidon
son: Castor, Pollux
Jupiter Pluvius: 4 rain
jural: 5 legal **8** juristic
Jurassic division: 4 Lias
jurisdiction: law **5** venue **6** county, domain, sphere **8** dominion, province **9** authority, bailiwick, territory
ecclesiastical: see **6** parish **7** deanery, diocese
jurisprudence: law **14** court decisions
juror: 7 assizer, juryman **8** talesman
group: **4** jury **5** panel
selection list: **6** venire
just: due, fit **4** even, fair, only, true **5** equal, exact, legal, valid **6** candid, honest, merely, normal, purely, simply **7** correct, equable, upright **8** accurate, unbiased **9** equitable, impartial **10** legitimate
justice: law **5** judge **6** equity **7** honesty

god: **7** Forsete, Forseti, Forsite
goddess: **4** Maat
justification: 6 excuse, reason **7** apology, defense **9** authority, rationale
justify: 4 avow **6** adjust, defend, excuse **7** support, warrant **8** maintain, sanction **9** authorize, exculpate, vindicate
jut: 4 butt **5** bulge **6** beetle **7** project **8** overhang, protrude, stick out **10** projection
jute: 4 desi **5** gunny **6** burlap **7** sacking
Jutlander: 4 Dane
jutting: 7 salient **10** protruding **11** overhanging
juvenile: 5 actor, young **6** callow **8** immature, youthful **10** adolescent **11** undeveloped
Juventas: 4 Hebe
juxtaposition: 7 contact **8** nearness **9** adjacence, adjacency, proximity **10** contiguity

K

kaama: 10 hartebeest
kaddish: 6 prayer **8** doxology
kae: 7 jackdaw
kaffeeklatsch: 6 social **9** gathering **11** get-together
Kaffir, Kafir: 5 Bantu
language: **4** Xosa
warriors: **4** Impi
Kafka character: 4 Olga
kaiser: 5 ruler **7** emperor
kaka: 6 parrot
genus: **6** nestor
kakapo: 6 parrot
kaki: 4 bird **5** stilt **9** persimmon
kakkak: 7 bittern
kale: 4 cole **5** green **7** cabbage, collard **8** colewort
kali: 5 plant **6** carpet **8** saltwort
Kali's husband: 4 Siva **5** Shiva
kalinite: 4 alum **7** mineral
Kalmuck, Kalmuk: 6 Mongol
kamias: 7 bilimbi
Kanaka: 8 Hawaiian **10** Melanesian, Polynesian **11** Micronesian
kanari: 6 almond

kangaroo: 'roo **4** euro **5** bilbi, bilby **6** turatt **7** bettong, wallaby **8** bettonga, boongary, forester **11** macropodian
female: doe, gin, roo
male: **6** boomer
young: **4** joey
kangaroo rat: 7 potoroo
Kansas: *capital:* **6** Topeka
city: **4** Iola **5** Lyons, Paola **6** Salina **7** Abilene, Wichita **8** Lawrence **9** Dodge City **10** Hutchinson, Kansas City
county: Elk **4** Gove, Lane, Ness, Reno, Rice **5** Chase, Cloud, Ellis, Geary, Kiowa, Pratt, Riley, Rooks, Trego **6** Barber, Coffey, Finney, Harper, Harvey, Jewell, Kearny, Nemaha, Neosho, Seward, Sumner **7** Bourbon, Greeley, Labette, Rawlins, Stanton
early explorer: **8** Coronado
fort: **5** Riley **6** Larned **11** Leavenworth
Indian: **5** Kiowa **6** Pawnee **7** Wichita **8** Comanche, Kickapoo
President Eisenhower's Library: **7** Abilene
river: **5** Osage **6** Kansas (Kaw), Saline **7**

Solomon **8** Arkansas, Cimarron **9** Smoky Hill **10** Republican
state animal: **7** buffalo
state bird: **10** meadow lark
state flower: **9** sunflower
state motto: **16** Ad astra per aspera
state nickname: **9** Sunflower
state song: **14** "Home on the Range"
state tree: **10** cottonwood
Kant's category: **7** quality **8** modality, quantity, relation
kaolin: **4** clay
kaput: **6** broken, ruined **8** defeated **9** destroyed
karakul: **5** sheep
karate: **10** martial art **14** self-defense art
karma: **4** fate **7** destiny **10** vibrations
karyotin: **9** chromatin
kasha: **4** mush **5** grain **6** cereal
katchung: **6** peanut
kava: ava, awa **6** pepper
bowl: **5** tanoa
kayak: **5** canoe
kayo: **8** knockout
Kazantzakis hero: **5** Zorba
kea: parrot
Keats poem: **5** Lamia
kebbie: **4** club **5** stick **6** cudgel
ked: **4** tick
kedge: **6** anchor
keel: vat **4** ship **5** upset **6** careen, carina **7** capsize, carinae(pl.) **8** flounder, navigate
part: **4** skag, skeg
right angle to: **5** abeam
without: **9** ecarinate
keel over: **5** faint, upset **7** capsize
keel-shaped: **8** carinate
keelbill: ani
keeling: **7** codfish
keen: **4** avid, fell(Sc.), nice, wide **5** acute, awake, eager, sharp **6** ardent, astute, bewail, biting, clever, hearty, lament, severe, shrewd **7** cunning, fervent, intense, parlous, pungent **9** trenchant **10** hardheaded **12** enthusiastic **13** perspicacious
keenly: **6** dearly
keenness: **4** edge **6** acumen, genius, talent
keep: **4** fend, hold **5** board, guard, lodge, place **6** arrest, behold, living, stable **7** confine, contain, husband **8** fortress, maintain, preserve, restrain, withhold **9** celebrate **10** livelihood
going: **7** sustain
keep back: bar, dam **4** save **6** detain **7** reserve **8** withhold **10** stay behind
keep in: **6** retain
keep on: **7** persist **8** continue **9** persevere
keep out: **4** save **5** debar **7** exclude, reserve **8** hold back
keeper: **5** guard **6** pastor, warden **7** cura-

tor, janitor **8** guardian, watchdog **9** caretaker, constable, custodian **10** maintainer
of golden apple: **5** Ithun
of marches: **8** margrave
of park: **6** ranger
keeping: **4** care **5** award, guard, trust **6** charge **7** custody **10** caretaking, possession **11** maintenance **12** guardianship
keepsake: **5** token **7** memento **8** giftbook, souvenir
keest: sap **6** marrow **9** substance
keeve: tub, vat **5** basin
kef: **7** languor, tobacco **8** euphoria **10** dreaminess **12** tranquillity
keg: cag **4** cade, cask **6** barrel **7** barrico
open: **6** unhead
kegler: **6** bowler
keister, keester: **4** rump **7** satchel **8** suitcase
keitloa: **5** rhino
kelly: hat **5** color, derby, green
kelp: **5** algae, varec **6** varech **7** seaweed **8** bellware(Sc.)
kempt: **4** neat, tidy **11** well-groomed
ken: **4** know(Sc.), view **5** admit, sight **7** discern, insight **9** knowledge **10** cognizance, **11** recognition **13** understanding
Kenilworth author: **5** Scott
kennel: **5** drain, sewer **6** cannel, gutter, stable **7** shelter **8** doghouse **9** enclosure
kentledge: **5** metal **7** ballast, pig iron
Kentucky: *capital:* **9** Frankfort
city: **5** Paris **6** Hazard **7** Paducah **8** Richmond **9** Covington, Lexington, Owensboro **10** Louisville
county: **4** Bath, Bell, Boyd, Hart, Pike, Todd **5** Adair, Boone, Boyle, Casey, Floyd, Grant, Knott, Larue, Mason, Rowan, Trigg, Wolfe **6** Estill, Graves, Harlan, Kenton, Laurel, Leslie, Mercer, Oldham, Owsley **7** Bourbon, Bracken, Bullitt, Daviess, Garrard, Greenup, Letcher, Menifee, Trimble, Whitley
gold depository: **8** Fort Knox
horse race: **5** Derby
Indian: **7** Shawnee **8** Cherokee, Iroquois
lake: **5** Dewey **7** Barkley **10** Dale Hollow
mountain peak: **5** Black
plateau: **10** Cumberland
President Lincoln's birthplace: **11** Hodgenville
river: **4** Ohio, Salt **5** Green, Rough **6** Barren **7** Licking, Rolling **8** Big Sandy **10** Cumberland, Tradewater
state bird: **8** cardinal
state flower: **9** goldenrod
state nickname: **9** Bluegrass
state tree: **10** coffee tree
trailblazer: **11** Daniel Boone
Kentucky bluegrass: poa

Kentucky coffee tree: 6 bonduc, chicot
Kenya: *capital:* 7 Nairobi
city: 5 Nyeri 6 Kisumu, Nakuru 7 Mombasa 8 Kakamega
desert: 5 Nyiri
lake: 6 Rudolf 8 Victoria
monetary unit: 4 cent 8 shilling
mountain peak: 5 Elgon, Kenya
native group: Luo 5 Bantu, Kamba, Kisii, Masai, Nandi 6 Kikuyu 7 Swahili, Turkana 8 Kipsigis
province: 5 Coast 6 Nyanza 7 Central, Eastern, Nairobi, Western 10 Rift Valley 12 Northeastern
river: 4 Athi, Tana 5 Ewaso, Tsavo 6 Galana, Sabaki
secret society: 6 Mau Mau
valley: 9 Great Rift
kepi: cap
keratosis: 4 wart
kerchief: 5 curch(Sc.) 6 hankie 7 panuelo 8 bandanna, headrail
kerchoo: 6 sneeze
answer to: 10 gesundheit 11 God bless you
Keresan Indian: Sia
kerf: cut 4 slit 5 notch 6 groove 7 cutting
kermis, kermess: 4 fair 8 carnival 11 celebration
kernel: nut 4 bunt, core, meat, pith, seed 5 acini(pl.), grain 6 acinus, nuclei(pl.) 7 nucleus
kersenneh: ers 5 vetch
kestrel: 6 falcon, fanner 7 stannel 9 windhover
ketch: 4 boat 8 sailboat
ketone: 5 irone 7 acetone, camphor, muscone shogaol 8 acridone, civetone, deguelin 9 heptanone 14 cyclopentanone
kettle: pot, vat 4 cazo(Sp.) 5 lebes 6 hollow 7 caldron 8 cauldron, flambeau 9 teakettle 10 kettledrum
nose: 5 spout
kettledrum: 5 naker, tabor 6 atabal, nagara(Ind.), timbal 7 attabal, timbale, timpano, timpani(pl.), tympani(pl.)
kevel: bar, bit, peg 4 bolt 5 cleat, staff 6 cudgel 7 bollard
key: cay, fin 4 clef, isle, quay, reef 5 dital, islet, pitch 6 claves(pl.), clavis, island, opener, spline, tapper 7 digital 8 clavecin, solution, tonality 11 explanation
notch: 4 ward
part: bit
pert. to: 5 tonal, tonic
skeleton: 4 gilt 5 screw 7 twirler
key chain: 10 chatelaine
keyboard: 6 manual 7 clavier 8 pedalier 10 claviature
keyed up: 4 agog 5 eager 7 excited 10 stimulated
keynote: 5 theme, tonic, topic 7 feature

keynoter: 6 orator 11 main speaker
keystone: 7 support 8 main part 9 principle
Keystone State: 12 Pennsylvania
khan: inn 5 ruler 9 sovereign 11 caravansary
khedive's estate: 5 daira
Khnemu's consort: 6 Anukit
kiang: ass
kibbutz: 4 farm 7 commune 10 collective, settlement
kibble: 5 grind 10 coarse bits
kibitzer: 7 adviser, meddler 9 spectator
kick: 4 boot, funk(Sc.), punt 5 gripe, growl 6 fitter(Sc.), object, recoil, thrill 7 grumble 8 complain 10 calcitrate, enthusiasm
kick off: 5 begin, start 6 launch 8 commence
kick out: 4 fire, sack 5 evict 6 bounce 7 dismiss 9 discharge
kicker: 8 odd twist, surprise 11 hidden point
kickshaw: toy 6 bauble, gewgaw, trifle, tidbit 7 trinket 8 delicacy
kid: guy 4 goat, hoax, joke 5 child, suede, tease 6 banter 7 fatling, leather 8 cheverel, cheveril 9 youngster
kidcote: 6 prison
kidnap: 6 abduct 8 shanghai 10 spirit away
kidney: 4 neer (Sc.) 5 organ
pert. to: 5 renal
kidney-shaped: 8 reniform
kidney stone: 4 jade 8 calculus, nephrite 10 nephrolith
Kilauea goddess: 4 Pele
kilderkin: 4 cask 6 barrel 7 measure
Kilimanjaro peak: 4 Kibo 7 Mawenzi
kill: 4 hang, slay, veto 5 croak, 6 deaden, murder 7 achieve, destroy, execute, 8 dispatch, lapidate 9 finish off, slaughter 11 assassinate
by stoning: 8 lapidate
by strangling: 7 garotte, garrote
killed: 4 slew 5 slain 9 immolated
killer: 6 gunman, hit man, slayer 7 torpedo 8 assassin, murderer 10 triggerman
killer whale: orc 4 orca 7 grampus
killing: 6 murder 7 slaying 8 homicide 9 martyrdom, slaughter 10 euthanasia
of brother or sister: 10 fratricide
of father: 9 patricide
of king: 8 regicide
of mother: 9 matricide
of race: 8 genocide
of self: 7 suicide
of small child: 11 infanticide
killjoy: 8 hinderer, 9 pessimist 10 spoilsport
Kilmer poem: 5 Trees
kiln: 4 oast, oven 5 clamp, stove, tiler

6 cockle 7 furnace

kiloliter: 5 stere

kilt: 4 hang 5 pleat 6 fasten 7 filibag
pouch for: 7 sporran

kilter: 5 order 9 condition

kimono sash: obi

kin: (see also **kinship**): 4 clan, folk, race,
sept 5 flesh, tribe 6 family 7 related 8
affinity, cousinry, relation, relative 12
relationship

kind: ilk, 4 boon, gest, good, kith, mild,
soft, sort, type 5 breed, class, genre, genus, geste, order 6 benign, blithe, gender, genera(pl.), genial, gentle, goodly,
humane, tender 7 amiable, clement,
species, variety 8 amicable, benedict,
friendly, generous, gracious, merciful 9
benignant, brotherly, favorable, indulgent, 10 benevolent, charitable, 11
considerate, description, kindhearted,
sympathetic 13 compassionate
same: 10 homogeneal

kindle: 4 fire, move 5 brood, light, young
6 arouse, decoct, excite, ignite, illume,
incite 7 animate, emblaze, inflame, inspire, provoke

kindling: 5 fagot 6 faggot, sticks, tinder

kindness: 5 aloha 6 bounty 8 benefice 9
benignity 11 beneficence

kindred: kin, sib 5 blood, flesh 6 allied,
family 7 cognate, kinsmen 8 affinity,
kinsfolk 9 congenial 12 relationship

kine: 4 cows 6 cattle

kinetic: 6 active 7 dynamic 9 energetic

king: rex(L.), rey(Sp.), roi(F.) 4 czar, tzar
5 ruler 7 monarch 9 sovereign
title of address: Sir 4 Sire 7 Majesty 8
Highness

King Arthur: *abode:* 6 Avalon
birthplace: 8 Tintagel
court site: 7 Camelot 8 Caerleon
crowner: 6 Dubric
death place: 6 Camlan
father: 5 Uther
fool: 7 Dagonet
forest: 7 Calydon
foster brother: Kay
hound: 6 Cavall
jester: 7 Dagonet
knight: Kay 6 Gareth, Gawain 7 Galahad,
Mordred 8 Lancelot, Tristram 9 Percivale
lady: 4 Enid
lance: Ron
magician: 6 Merlin
mother: 7 Igraine
nephew: 6 Gareth 7 Mordred
queen: 8 Guinever 9 Guinevere
shield: 7 Pridwin
sister: 7 Morgain 11 Morgan le Fay
sword: 9 Excalibur

King Canute's consort: 4 Emma

king clover: 7 melilot

king crab: 7 limulus

King Henry IV character: Hal 5 Blunt,
Henry, Percy, Poins 6 Scroop

King Lear: See **Lear**

king of beasts: 4 lion

king's evil: scrofula

king's yellow: orpiment

kingdom: 5 realm 6 domain, empire 8 dominion

kingfish: 4 barb, haku, opah 6 bagara

kingfisher: 7 halycon

kingly: 5 regal, royal 6 regnal 7 basilic,
leonine 8 imperial, majestic

kinin: 7 adenine, hormone

kink: 4 bend, curl, loop 5 bunch, chink,
cramp, quirk, snarl, twist 6 buckle, tangle 7 caprice 11 peculiarity

kinkajou: 5 potto 6 mammal

kinky: odd 6 far-out 7 bizarre, strange 10
outlandish

kinship (see also **kin**): 5 blood, nasab 8
nearness 9 cognation 10 connection 11
propinquity 13 consanguinity
father's side: 8 agnation
mother's side: 7 enation

kinsman (see also **kin, kindred**): 4 ally
6 friend 8 bandhava 9 rishtadar

kiosk: 5 booth 8 pavilion 9 newsstand

kip: 4 hide, pelt, skin 5 sleep

Kipling: *poem:* 6 L'Envoi
tale: Kim

Kiribati: *capital:* 6 Tarawa
ethnic group: 11 Micronesian
island groups: 4 Line 7 Gilbert, Phoenix
monetary unit: 6 dollar

kirtle: 4 coat, gown 5 dress, skirt, tunic 7
garment 9 petticoat

Kish: *father:* Ner
son: 4 Saul

kismet: 4 fate 7 destiny

kiss: 4 bass, buss 5 smack 6 caress 8 osculate

kiss-me-quick: 6 bonnet

kiss of peace: pax

Kiss sculptor: 5 Rodin

kist: box 4 cist 5 chest 6 locker

kit: bag, box, lot, set 6 outfit 9 container
10 collection
and caboodle: all 10 everything

kitchen: ben(Sc.) 4 chil(Ind.) 5 ca-
lan(P.I.) 6 chilla(Ind.) 7 cuisine 8 scul-
lery
pert. to: 8 culinary
ship's: galley
tool or utensil: 5 corer, ricer 6 beater,
grater, opener, sifter 7 spatula 8 colander, strainer

kite: 4 bird, hawk, sail, soar 6 decamp 10
check, fraud

kith: 6 friend 10 associates 12 acquaintance

kittenish: coy 6 frisky 7 playful 8 childish
kittiwake: 4 gull 5 annet
kitty: 4 bowl, pool 6 stakes
kiwi: 5 fruit 7 Apteryx 14 flightless bird
kleptomaniac: 5 thief 7 filcher 8 pilferer 10 shoplifter
kloof: 4 glen 5 gorge 6 ravine, valley
klutz: oaf 4 lout 6 lummox 9 schlemiel
knack: art 4 ease, gift, hang 5 catch, skill, trick 8 facility 9 dexterity 10 adroitness
knap: cut, rap, top 4 bite, blow, chip, crop, hill, snap 5 break, crest, knock, knoll 6 nibble, strike, summit 7 hilltop, hillock
knapsack: bag 4 case, pack
knarred: 6 knotty 7 gnarled
knave: boy, nob, pam 4 fool, jack 5 cheat, churl, losel, rogue, scamp 6 harlot, rascal, varlet 7 villain 9 miscreant, scoundrel, trickster
knavery: 5 fraud 8 mischief 10 dishonesty 12 sportiveness
knead: elt(Sc.), mix 5 malax 7 massage 8 malaxate 9 masticate 10 manipulate 11 incorporate
knee: bow 5 joint 10 supplicate
  armor: 11 genouillere
  bend: 5 kneel 6 curtsy 9 genuflect
knee breeches: 8 knickers 12 smallclothes
kneecap: 7 patella
knee-jerk: 9 automatic 11 predictable
kneeling desk: 8 prie-dieu
knell: 4 bell, omen, ring, toll 6 stroke, summon 7 warning 8 proclaim
knickers: 7 panties 8 bloomers 9 plus fours
knickknack: toy 6 bauble, bawble, gadget, gewgaw, trifle 7 novelty, trinket 8 gimcrack, kickshaw
knife: cut 4 bolo, dirk, shiv, snee, stab 5 bowie, gully, slash, sword 6 barong, colter, coutel, dagger, worker 7 carving, machete, spatula, whittle, stiletto, yataghan 11 cutting tool, switchblade
  case: 6 sheath
  maker: 6 cutler
  one-bladed: 6 barlow
  plaster and paint: 7 spatula
  sharpener: 4 hone 5 steel, stone
  surgical: 6 catlin 7 catling, scalpel
knight: dub, sir 5 eques 6 equite, Ritter 8 banneret, cavalier 9 caballero, chevalier
  attendant: 6 squire
  banner: 8 gonfanon
  cloak: 6 tabard
  famous: 7 Caradoc, Cradock, Galahad 9 Lohengrin
  fight: 5 joust
  horse: 7 charger, palfrey
  rank above: 7 baronet
  servant: 4 page 6 varlet
  title: sir
  wife: 4 lady
  wreath: 4 orle
knight-errant: 7 paladin
knight of the road: 4 hobo 5 tramp 8 vagabond
knighthood: 8 chivalry
  confer: dub
knightly: 5 brave 9 courteous 10 chivalrous
knit: 4 bind, heal, join, mend, purl 5 plait, unite, woven 6 cement, fasten 7 conjoin, connect, crochet, wrinkle 8 contract, entangle 10 intertwine 11 compaginate, consolidate
knitted blanket: 6 afghan
knitter: 6 legger
knitting: 5 craft 9 handiwork
  rod: 6 needle
  term: 4 purl 7 castoff
knob: bob, bur, nub 4 boss, buhr, burr, club, heel, lump, node, tore, umbo 5 bulge 6 button, croche, emboss, handle, pommel 12 protuberance
  pointed: 6 finial
knobby: 5 gouty, hilly 6 knotty
knobkerrie: 4 club 5 stick
knobstick: 4 cane, club 5 stick 8 blackleg
knock: hit, rap, tap 4 beat, blow, bolt, bump, chop, dash, jolt, rout, slay 5 abuse, pound, thump 6 bounce 7 hillock(Sc.) 8 belittle 9 criticize 12 faultfinding
knock down: 4 fell 5 floor 9 prostrate
knock-kneed: 6 valgus
knock off: rob 4 copy, kill, stop 6 deduct 8 overcome 11 assassinate, discontinue
knock out: 4 daze, stun 6 defeat 7 exhaust 8 paralyze
knockabout: 5 actor, sloop, yacht
knockout: 4 kayo 5 facer 6 eyeful, looker 7 stunner
  blow: 8 haymaker
knoll: 4 knap, knob, lump 5 mound 7 hillock
knop: 5 knosp 6 button 8 ornament
knot: bow, nep, tie 4 bond, burl, burr, harl, knag, knar, knob, knur, loop, lump, node, snag 5 gnarl, hitch, knurl, nodus, snarl 6 finial, granny, nodule, puzzle, tangle 7 bowline, chignon, cockade, laniard, lanyard, rosette 8 entangle 12 entanglement, protuberance
  running: 4 slip 5 noose
  pert. to: 5 nodal
knotted: 5 noded 7 crabbed, nodated 9 intricate
knotted lace: 7 tatting
knotty: 4 hard 5 bumpy, gouty 6 craggy 7 complex, gnarled 9 difficult, intricate 10 perplexing

knout: 4 flog, lash, whip

know: can, con, ken(Sc.), 7 realize 8 perceive 9 recognize 10 comprehend, experience, understand

know-how: 5 knack, skill 7 ability 9 expertise

know-it-all: 6 smarty 8 wiseacre

know-nothing: 8 agnostic 9 ignoramus 11 scissorbill

knowing: 4 able, gash, wise 5 cagey, downy, leery, smart, witty 6 scient, shrewd 7 gnostic, sapient, stylish 8 informed 9 cognitive, conscious, gnostical, wide-awake 10 experience, perceptive 11 intelligent 13 comprehension

knowledge: ken 4 lore 6 wisdom 7 cunning, hearing, science 8 learning, sapience 9 cognition, erudition 10 cognizance, experience 11 information, instruction 12 acquaintance 13 enlightenment, understanding

instrument: 7 organon

lack of: 9 ignorance, nescience

object of: 7 cognita(pl.), scibile 8 cognitum

pert. to: 7 gnostic

seeker: 10 philonoist

slight: 7 inkling, smatter 8 sciolism 10 smattering

summary: 13 encyclopaedia

systematized: 7 science

universal: 9 pantology

known: 5 couth, famed 6 famous 7 notable 8 familiar, renowned 9 notorious

knuckle: 5 joint

head: 5 dunce 8 numbskull

knuckle under: bow 4 cave 5 defer, yield 6 submit 7 succumb 10 capitulate

kobird: 6 cuckoo

kobold: nis 5 gnome 6 goblin 7 Hodeken(G.) 10 nissespire

koel: 4 bird 6 cuckoo

kohl: 8 antimony

kohlrabi: 6 turnip

kokoon: gnu

kokopu: 4 fish, para 5 trout 10 galaxiidae

kola: nut 6 jackal

kooky: 5 crazy 6 far out, insane 7 offbeat 9 fantastic

kopecks (100): 5 ruble

kopje: 4 hill 5 mound 7 hillock

Koran: 10 Islam Bible

division: 4 Sura

interpreter: 5 ulema 7 alfaqui 8 alfaquin

register: 5 sijil 6 sijill

Korea: See **North Korea, South Korea**

kosher: fit 4 pure 5 clean 6 proper 8 Kashruth 9 undefiled

meat maker: 6 porger

opposite of: 4 tref

kowtow: 4 fawn 5 cower, toady 6 tringe, grovel 8 butter up 11 apple polish

kra: ape 7 macaque

kraal: pen 5 crawl 6 corral 9 enclosure

krimmer: fur 4 skin 8 lambskin

Krishna: 6 Vishnu 10 Juggernaut

grandson: 9 Aniruddha

mother: 6 Devaki

paradise: 6 Goloka

kudos: 4 fame 5 award, glory, honor 6 praise, renown 8 prestige 9 extolling

kudu: 8 antelope

kulak: 6 farmer 7 peasant

kumiss: 4 milk 5 drink 8 beverage

kumquat: 5 fruit

relative: 6 orange

kung fu: 10 martial art 14 Chinese defense

kin of: 6 karate

Kurile island: 6 Iturup

Kurland Peninsula inhabitant: 4 Lett

kurrajong: 4 tree 5 shrub 6 calool

kurtosis: arc 9 curvature

Kuwait: *capital:* 8 Al-Kuwait

city: 5 Magwa 7 Hawalli 8 Al Bahrah

dynasty: 7 Al Sabah

island: 7 Bubiyan, Failaka

monetary unit: 4 fils 5 dinar

kvetch (Yid.): 5 gripe, whine 8 complain

kyphosis: 8 humpback 9 curvature, hunchback

L

L: 5 fifty
La Boheme: *composer:* **7** Puccini
  heroine: **4** Mimi
laagte: 6 bottom, valley
Laban's daughter: 4 Leah **6** Rachel
label: tab, tag **4** band, call **5** brand **6** docket, lappet, tassel **8** classify **9** designate, dripstone **10** definition
labellum: lip **5** petal
labile: 8 shifting, unstable **9** adaptable **10** changeable
labium: lip
labor: 4 moil, task, toil, work **5** sweat, yakka **6** effort, labour, stress, strive **7** travail **8** business, drudgery, exertion, industry, struggle **11** lucubration, parturition
labor organization: AFL, CIO, UMW **5** ILGWU, union
labored: 5 heavy **6** forced **8** strained **9** difficult, elaborate
laborer: man, **4** hand, hind, peon, prol **5** cooly, plebe **6** coolie, toiler, worker **7** bracero, dvornik, hobbler, wetback, workman **10** bluecollar
laborious: 4 hard **5** heavy **6** uphill **7** arduous, operose, tedious **8** diligent **9** assiduous, difficult **11** displeasing, hardworking, painstaking
Labrador retriever: 12 Newfoundland
Labrador tea: 5 ledum **8** gowiddie **9** evergreen
labyrinth: web **4** knot, maze, mesh **6** jungle, morass, tangle
  builder: **8** Daedalus
  monster: **8** Minotaur
labyrinthine: 7 complex **8** involved, puzzling, tortuous **9** intricate **10** perplexing **11** complicated
lac: 4 milk **5** resin **6** veneer **10** sealing wax
lace: gin, net, tat **4** band, beat, cord, lash, line **5** braid, lairs, noose, plait, snare, twine, unite **6** fasten, ribbon, string **7** ensnare, entwine, laniard, lanyard **8** biliment, openwork **9** embroider, interlace **10** embroidery, intertwine, shoestring
  barred: **6** grille
  edge: **5** picot
  frilled: **5** jabot, ruche
  front: **5** jabot
  into: **5** abuse **6** attack **7** condemn
  kind: **5** lisle, orris, tulle **7** alencon, allover, guipure, macrame, potlace **9** Alostlace **10** colberteen, colbertine **12** Valenciennes
  knotted: **7** tatting
  loop in: **5** picot
  make: tat
  opening: **6** eyelet
lacerate: cut, rip **4** bite, rend, rive, tear **6** harrow, mangle **8** distress
laceration: rip **4** tear **5** wound
lacework: See **lace**
lachrymose: sad **5** teary, weepy **7** tearful
lack: 4 need, void, want **5** fault, minus **6** dearth **7** absence, failure, in need, paucity, poverty **8** scarcity, shortage **9** indigence **10** deficiency **11** destitution
lackadaisical: 4 blah **7** languid **8** listless **10** spiritless **11** sentimental
lackaday: 4 alas
lackey: 5 toady, valet **7** footman, servant
lacking: shy **5** short **6** absent, barren **7** wanting **8** desolate **9** deficient, destitute
lackluster: 4 dull **6** cloudy **8** dullness
Laconia: *capital:* **6** Sparta
  people: Obe
laconic: 5 brief, pithy, short, terse **7** concise, pointed, summary **8** succinct
lacquer: 5 gloss **7** shellac, varnish
lactate: 4 salt **5** actol, ester
lacteal: 5 milky
lacuna: gap **4** hole **5** break **7** opening **8** interval **10** depression
lacy: 7 weblike **8** delicate
lad: boy, tad **4** carl, dick, hind **5** caddy, youth **6** caddie, shaver **9** stripling **10** adolescent
  on call: **4** page **7** bellboy **9** messenger
  serving: **7** gossoon **8** coistrel, coistril
ladder: run, sty **4** stee **5** scale **6** series **7** scalade
  on fortification: **8** escalade
  step: **7** ratline
ladderlike: 6 scalar
lade: dip **4** bail, draw, lave, load, ship **5** drain, scoop **6** burden, charge, weight **7** fraught, freight
ladies' man: 4 beau **5** dandy **11** philanderer
lading: 4 load **5** cargo **6** burden **7** freight **10** freightage

ladle: dip **4** bail **5** scoop, serve, spoon **6** dipper

ladrone: 5 thief **6** bandit, robber **7** brigand **9** mercenary **10** highwayman

Ladrone island: 4 Guam **6** Saipan **8** Marianas

lady (see also **woman**): **4** burd, dame, dona(Sp.), rani(Ind.) **5** begum(Ind.), donna(It.), madam, ranee(Ind.) **6** domina(L.), female, senora(Sp.) **7** signora (It.) **11** gentlewoman
noble: **5** queen **7** duchess **8** countess, princess
young: **7** damozel **10** demoiselle, jeune fille(F.)

lady-killer: 4 wolf **5** sheik **7** Don Juan **8** Casanova

Lady of the Lake: 5 Ellen, Nimue **6** Vivien
author: **5** Scott

lady's thumb: 5 plant **9** peachwort, persicary

ladybird: bug **6** beetle
genus: **9** epilachna

ladyfish: oio **6** tarpon, wrasse

ladylike: 6 female, polite **7** genteel **8** feminine, mannerly

ladylove: 5 amour, lover **8** mistress **10** sweetheart

Laertes: *father:* **8** Acrisius, Polonius
sister: **7** Ophelia
son: **7** Ulysses, **8** Odysseus
wife: **8** Anticlea

lag: 4 flag, rift, tire **5** delay, stave, tarry, trail, weary **6** dawdle, linger, loiter **8** fall back **9** drawlatch **10** dillydally **11** retardation

lager: ale **4** beer **5** drink **8** beverage

laggard: 4 slow **6** remiss **8** backward, loiterer, sluggish **9** straggler **10** slow person

lagging: 5 tardy **8** backward

lagniappe: tip **4** gift **5** bonus, pilon **7** present **8** gratuity

lagomorph: 4 hare, pika **5** coney **6** rabbit

lagoon: 4 cove, haff, pond, pool **5** liman **6** laguna(Sp.)

Lagoon Islands: 6 Ellice

laic: 6 layman **7** secular **15** nonprofessional

laid-down: 5 posed **6** thetic **8** academic **10** prescribed **11** traditional

lair: den, lie **4** holt, nest **5** haunt **6** cavern **7** hideout, retreat **8** quagmire

Lais: 7 Burmese

laissez-faire: 8 inactive, tolerant **9** donothing, unconcern **11** philosophic **12** indifference, mercantilism **15** individualistic, noninterference

laity: 6 laymen

Laius' son: 7 Oedipus

lake: dye **4** loch, mere, pond, pool, shat, shot, tarn **5** bayou, chott, color, lough, shott **6** lagoon **7** pigment
deposit: **5** trona
highest: **8** Titicaca
Indian: **4** Erie
marshy: **5** liman

Lake State: 8 Michigan

lam: hit **4** bash, beat, flog **6** thrash **7** getaway

Lamaism: *dignitary:* **8** hutukhtu
priest: **6** Getsul
stupa: **7** Chorten

lamasery: 9 monastery

lamb: ean **4** yean **5** agnus(L.) **6** agneau(F.), cosset **7** chilver, fatling, hogling
hand-raised: hob
leg of: **5** gigot
pert. to: **5** ovine
pet: **4** cade **6** cosset

Lamb of God: 8 Agnus Dei

lambaste: 4 drub, flay **5** paste, poynd **6** thrash 7 clobber **8** lash into **10** tonguelash

Lamb's penname: 4 Elia

lambskin: 4 case **5** suede **6** bagdad **7** baghdad

lambent: 7 glowing, radiant **8** wavering **9** brilliant **10** flickering

lame: 4 game, halt **5** gammy **6** feeble **7** halting **8** crippled, decrepit, disabled **9** defective, hamstring **11** handicapped **12** incapacitate

Lamech: *father:* **10** Methuselah
son: **4** Noah **5** Jabal, Jubal **9** Tubalcain
wife: **4** Adah **6** Zillah

lament: cry, rue **4** care, howl, keen, moan, pine, sigh, wail, weep **5** croon, dolor, dirge, elegy, greet, grief, mourn **6** bemoan, bewail, beweep, dolour, grieve, lament, ochone, outcry, plaint, regret, repent, repine, yammer **7** condole, deplore, elegize, wailing **8** jeremiad, mourn for, mourning **9** complaint

lamentable: sad **8** grievous, wretched **10** deplorable **11** distressing

lamia: hag, hex **5** witch **7** vampire **9** sorceress

lamina: 5 blade, flake, hinge, layer

laminated: 5 flaky **6** scaled **7** fissile, spathic, tabular **8** foliated, lamellar

lamp: arc, eye, orb **4** davy, etna **5** light, torch **7** lantern **8** lanthorn **9** veilleuse
hanging: **10** chandelier
safety: **4** davy

lampblack: 4 soot

lamplighter: 5 match, spill, torch

lampoon: 5 squib **6** satire **8** ridicule, satirize **10** caricature, pasquinade

lamprey: eel **6** ramper
migration: **7** eelfare

lanai: 5 patio, porch **7** terrace, veranda

lanate: 5 hairy, wooly 6 woolly
Lancashire section: 6 Eccles
lance: cut 4 dart, hurl 5 joust, spear 6 faucre, lancet, launch, pierce, weapon 7 javelin
  head: 5 morne
Lancelot: *lover:* 6 Elaine 9 Guinevere
  son: 7 Galahad
  victim: 6 Gawain
lancer: 4 ulan 5 uhlan 7 soldier, spearer 10 cavalryman
lancet: 5 fleam, knife
lancinate: 4 stab, tear 5 gouge 6 pierce 8 lacerate
land: erd 4 ager(L.), soil 5 catch, earth, end up, glebe, realm, shore, terra(L.) 6 alight, arrive, debark, estate, ground 7 acreage, capture, country, terrene 9 disembark, territory
  alluvial: 5 delta
  ancestral: 5 ethel
  arid: See **desert**
  barren: See **wasteland**
  body: 9 continent
  church: 5 glebe 8 abadengo
  cultivated: 4 farm 5 arada, arado, ranch, tilth 7 orchard, tillage
  dealer: 7 realtor
  depressed: 6 graben
  elevated: alp 4 hill, mesa 5 mound, ridge 7 plateau 8 mountain
  grazing: 5 field, plain, range 6 meadow 7 pasture
  heritable: 4 alod, fief, odal 5 allod 7 alodium 8 allodium
  hilly: 4 down
  householder's: 6 barton, casate 7 demesne
  in foreign territory: 7 enclave
  living on: 11 terrestrial
  low: 4 vale 5 carse(Sc.) 6 polder, valley 9 intervale
  measure: are, rod 4 acre, mile, rood 5 meter, perch 6 decare
  mythical: 4 Eden 6 Utopia 7 Erewhon, Lemuria 9 Shangri-La
  narrow: 4 neck 6 strake 7 isthmus 9 peninsula
  open: 4 moor, vega, wold 5 field, heath, slash, weald
  owned: see *heritable* above
  pasture: ham 5 grass 6 meadow
  pert. to: 11 continental
  piece: lot 4 acre, farm 5 laine, ranch, range, solum (law) spong 6 estate, parcel
  plowed: 5 arada, arado, field 6 arable, fallow, furrow 7 thwaite
  point of: 4 cape, ness, spit
  profit: 4 crop, rent 7 esplees
  public: 4 parc, park
  reclaimed: 6 polder 7 novalia(Sc.)
  river drained: 5 basin

  sandy: 4 dene
  tilled: see *plowed* above
  treeless: 5 llano 6 steppe 7 prairie, savanna 8 savannah
  triangular: 4 gore
  uncultivated: 5 heath, waste 6 desert, forest
  uplifted: 5 horst
  waste: See **wasteland**
  waterlocked: ile(F.) 4 isle 6 island
  watery: bog 4 flow, moor 5 marsh, swamp 6 morass 7 maremma(It.)
Land of Cakes: 8 Scotland
Land of the Midnight Sun: 6 Norway
Land of Nod: 5 sleep
Land of Plenty: 6 Goshen
Land of Promise: 7 Canaan 9 Palestine
Land of Rising Sun: 5 Japan
land's end guardian: 8 Bellerus
landed: See **estate, land**
landholder: 5 laird 6 coscet, yeoman
landholding: 6 tenure
landing: 7 arrival
  kind: 5 crash 10 three-point
  place: 4 dock, pier 5 wharf 6 runway, stairs 7 airport
landlady: 5 duena 7 hostess 8 mistress 9 concierge
landlord: 4 host 5 laird(Sc.) 6 lessor
landmark: 8 monument 9 milestone 10 guide point 11 classic case
landscape: 4 plan 5 plant, scene 7 scenery, paysage, picture 8 decorate, painting
landslide: 9 avalanche 10 eboulement
  debris: 5 scree, talus
landsman: 6 lubber, sailor 10 compatriot
lane: way 4 char, path, race 5 aisle, alley, byway, chare, tewer 6 boreen, bypath, gullet, street, throat, vennel 7 pathway 8 footpath 10 passageway
language: 4 chib 5 argot, idiom, lingo, slang 6 jargon, speech, tongue 7 dialect, diction
  ancient: 4 Pali 5 Aryan, Greek, Latin 6 Hebrew 7 Chinese 8 Sanskrit 10 vernacular, vocabulary
  artificial: 9 Esperanto
  change: 8 misquote 9 interpret, translate 10 paraphrase
  classical: 5 Greek, Latin
  common: 6 French, German 7 Chinese, English, Italian, Russian, Spanish
  Cretan: 6 Minoan
  dead: 5 Latin
  expert: 8 linguist
  figurative: 7 imagery
  international: od, ro; ido 7 volapuk 9 esperanto
  meaningless: 9 gibberish
  nonmetrical: 5 prose
  pert. to: 8 semantic

pompous: **4** bull, wind **6** hot air **7** bombast, oratory **8** rhetoric
principles: **7** grammar
Romance: **5** Latin **6** French **7** Catalan, Italian, Spanish **8** Rumanian **10** Portuguese
sacred: **4** Pali
secret: **4** cant, code **5** argot
Semitic: **6** Arabic, Hebrew
spoken: **7** diction **13** pronunciation
unintelligible: **9** gibberish
languid: **4** dull, slow, weak **6** dreamy, tender **8** drooping, indolent, listless, lovesick, sluggish **9** lethargic **11** indifferent
languish: die **4** fade, fail, flag, long, pine, wilt **5** droop, dwine, faint, swoon **6** linger, repine **7** decline **12** fail in health
languor: kef **4** kaif, keef, kief **5** ennui **7** boredom **8** debility **9** lassitude **10** stagnation
langur: **6** monkey **8** wanderoo
lanky: **4** lean, slim, tall, thin **5** gaunt, rangy, spare **6** gangly, meager, meagre, skinny **7** haggard, slender **8** gangling, ungainly **9** elongated **12** loose-jointed
lantern: **4** lamp **5** bouet
lanyard, laniard: **4** cord, knot, line, rope
Laocoon: **11** Trojan priest
killer: **7** serpent
Laodamia's father: **7** Acastus
Laodicean: **8** lukewarm **9** apathetic **10** uninvolved **11** indifferent
Laomedon: *father:* **4** Ilus
kingdom: **4** Troy
mother: **8** Eurydice
slayer: **8** Hercules
son: **5** Priam
Laos: *capital:* **9** Vientiane
Communist group: **9** Pathet Lao
language: Lao
monetary unit: kip
religion: **8** Buddhist
river: **6** Mekong, Sabang
supply line: **14** Ho Chi Minh Trail
town: **5** Khong, Pakse **12** Luang Prabang
lap: sip **4** fold, lick, wash **5** bathe, drink, slurp **6** circle, cuddle, enfold, infold **7** circuit
lap robe: rug **5** throw **6** afghan **7** blanket
lapactic: **8** laxative **9** cathartic
lapel: **5** rever **6** revers
lapidary: **7** jeweler **8** engraver **9** gem cutter
instrument: dop **4** dial
lapidate: **4** pelt **5** stone
lapin: **6** rabbit
Lapland: *animal:* **8** reindeer
city or town: **4** Kola **6** Kiruna
sled: **4** pulk **5** pulka
lappet: **4** flap, fold, lobe, moth **5** lapel **6** fabric, revers
lapse: err **5** break, error, fault **6** expire **7**

delapse, escheat, failure, relapse **8** caducity, slipping **9** backslide
lapsed: **4** dead, null, void
laputan: **6** absurd, dreamy **7** utopian **9** visionary **10** unfeasible **11** impractical
lapwing: **5** pewit **6** plover
Lar: god **6** gibbon, spirit
larboard: **4** left, port
larceny: **5** theft **7** looting, robbery **8** burglary, stealage
kind: **5** grand, petty
lard: fat, oil **4** mort **5** add to, adeps(L.), baste, enarm, inarm **6** enrich, fatten, grease **7** garnish **9** embellish
larder: **4** cave **6** pantry, spence, spense **8** cupboard
large: big **4** bold, free, huge, main, vast, waly **5** ample, broad, bulky, burly, enorm, giant, great, hulky, massy, wally **6** goodly, heroic **7** copious, immense, liberal, massive, pompous, titanic, weighty **8** colossal, enormous, generous, gigantic **9** capacious, extensive, plentiful **11** exaggerated, far-reaching **12** considerable **13** comprehensive
largess, largesse: **4** gift **6** bounty **7** charity, present **10** generosity, liberality **11** beneficence
lariat: **4** rope **5** lasso, noose, reata(Sp.), riata(Sp.)
loop: **5** honda, hondo **6** hondoo, hondou
lark: **4** bird, dido **5** spree, pipit **6** frolic **8** carousal **9** make merry
larkspur: **10** delphinium
larrigan: **8** moccasin
larrup: **4** beat, blow, flog, whip
larry: hoe **5** grout, noise **6** mortar **7** mine car **9** confusion **10** excitement
larva: bot, fly, loa **4** bott, grub, worm **5** eruca **6** botfly, woubit **7** atrocha, oestrid **8** cercaria, horsefly **11** caterpillar
aquatic: **12** hellgrammite
beetle: **4** grub
larvate: **6** masked **7** covered **9** concealed
lascar: **6** sailor **12** artilleryman
lascivious: **6** wanton **7** blissom **9** lecherous, salacious, seductive **10** libidinous, licentious
lash: **4** beat, bind, blow, flog, lace, whip, yerk **5** slash **6** berate, fasten, strike, stroke, swinge **7** belabor, eyelash, scourge
lasket: **8** latching
lass: gal **4** gill, girl, maid, miss **5** trull, woman **6** cummer, kimmer, lassie, maiden **7** colleen **10** sweetheart **11** maidservant
lassitude: **5** ennui **7** languor **8** debility, lethargy **10** exhaustion
lasso: See **lariat**
last: **4** dure, tail **5** abide, final, omega **6** endure, latest, newest, utmost **7** der-

nier, extreme, tail-end **8** at the end, continue, eventual, hindmost, rearmost, ultimate **9** aftermost **10** concluding, most recent

but one: **6** penult

long: **7** outwear **9** perendure

word: **8** up-to-date

Last of the Mohicans: 5 Uncas

author: **6** Cooper

Last Supper: *painter:* **7** da Vinci

representation: **4** cena

room: **7** cenacle

lasting (see also **last**): **6** stable **7** chronic, lasting, eternal **8** constant, enduring **9** perennial, permanent, steadfast **11** everlasting

briefly: **9** ephemeral, temporary

latch: 5 catch, sneck **6** fasten **8** fastener

latchet: tab **4** lace **5** thong

late: new **4** dead, sere **5** tardy **6** former, recent **7** belated, overdue **8** neoteric, serotine **10** behindhand

latent: 6 hidden **7** dormant **9** concealed, potential, quiescent, suspended **11** undeveloped

later: 4 anon, soon **5** after, newer **6** behind, future, puisne **7** elderly, neozoic **9** hereafter, posterior, presently **10** subsequent **12** subsequently

lateral: 4 pass, side **8** indirect, sideward, sideways

latest: 4 last **6** newest

latex: 5 juice **6** rubber **9** secretion

lath: 4 slat **5** spale, stave, stick **8** forepole

attachment: **7** setover

operator: **6** turner

part: **7** mandrel

lather: 4 flog, foam, soap, suds **5** froth **6** bustle, freath **10** foamy sweat

Latin (see also **Rome**): **5** Roman **7** Italian, Romanic

always: **6** semper

barracks: **6** canaba

bath, bathhouse: **7** balneum

booth: **7** taberna

bowl: **6** patina

boxing glove: **6** cestus, ceston

boy: **4** puer

breath: **7** halitus

bronze: aes

building: **5** aedes

cape: **5** sagum **6** byrrus

cistern: **9** impluvium

connective: et

contract: **5** nexum

couch: **9** accubitum

deity: **4** deus

dish: **4** lanx **6** lances, pateral, patina

food: **5** cibus

foot: pes

for example: **4** vide

force: vis

friend: **6** amicus

garland: **6** corona

ghosts: **7** lemures

grammar: **5** donat, donet

grammatical case: **6** dative **8** ablative, genitive, vocative **10** accusative, nominative

hope: **4** spes

hour: **4** hora

javelin: **4** pile **5** aclys, pilum

life: **4** vita

ornament: **5** bulla

post: **4** meta

pronoun: tu; ego, hic **4** ille, ipse, iste

ram: **5** aries

rite: **4** orgy **5** sacra

roof opening: **10** compluvium

seat: **5** sella

shelter: **7** taberna

towel: **5** mappa

trumpet: **4** tuba **6** buccin **7** buccina

Latin America: See **Central America, South America**

Latinus's daughter: 7 Lavinia

latite: 4 lava

latitude: 4 room **5** scope, width **6** extent, leeway, margin **7** breadth, freedom **8** distance **9** elbowroom

complement: **10** colatitude

measure: **6** degree **8** parallel

zero degrees: **7** equator

latke: 7 pancake **11** griddle cake

latrant: 7 barking **8** snarling **11** complaining

latrine: 5 privy **6** toilet

latter: 4 last **5** final **6** latest **10** more recent

Latter Day Saints: 7 Mormons

latterly: 4 anew **6** lately **8** recently

lattice: 4 door, gate **6** pinjra(Ind.) **7** trellis **8** espalier

latticework: 5 arbor, grate **6** arbour **7** grating, tracery

Latvia: *city:* **4** Riga(c.) **5** Libau **6** Dvinsk, Libava **8** Dunaburg **10** Daugavpils

coin: lat **6** rublis **7** kapeika **8** santimas

measure: **4** stof **5** kanne, stoff, verst **6** kulmet, sagene, versta, verste **7** verchoc, verchok **8** krouchka, kroushka, pourvete **9** deciatine, lofstelle **10** tonnstelle

parliament: **6** Saeima

people: **5** Letts

river: **4** Ogre **5** Gauga **6** Salaca

university site: **4** Riga

weight: **9** liespfund

laud: 4 lute **5** extol **6** extoll, praise **7** adulate, applaud, cittern, commend, glorify, magnify **8** emblazon, eulogize **9** panegyric **10** compliment

laudable: 9 allowable, exemplary **11** commendable **12** praiseworthy

laugh: 4 gaff, haha **5** fleer, snort **6** cackle, giggle, guffaw, hawhaw, nicker, titter **7** chortle, grizzle, snicker **9** cachinate
disposed to: **7** risible
incipient: **4** grin **5** smile
pert. to: **8** gelastic

laughable: 4 odd **5** comic, droll, funny, merry, queer, witty **7** amusing, comical, risible, strange, waggish **8** gelastic, humorous, sportive **9** burlesque, diverting, facetious, grotesque, ludicrous **10** ridiculous

laughing: 5 riant

laughing bird: 4 gull, loon **5** pewit **10** woodpecker

laughing owl: 5 wekau

laughing stock: 4 butt, jest, joke **5** sport **7** mockery **8** derision, ridicule

laughter: 5 mirth, risus(L.)
pert. to: **7** risible

launch: 4 open, toss **5** begin, fling, leave, set up, start, throw **6** get off **7** propose **9** motorboat **10** inaugurate

launder: tye 4 wash

laundry: 4 wash **10** laundromat **13** blanchisserie(F.)

laureate: 13 distinguished

laurel: 4 bay **4** fame **5** honor **6** daphne, myrtle, tarata, trophy **7** cajuput, garland, taratah **9** spoonwood **11** distinction

lava: 4 slag **5** ashes **6** coulee, latite, scoria, verite **7** clinker **8** pahoehoe
fragment of: **8** lapillus
sheet of: **6** coulee

lavabo: 5 basin **8** washbowl **9** cleansing **11** wall planter

lavaliere, lavalier: 7 pendant **8** necklace

lavation: 4 bath **6** lavage **7** washing **9** cleansing

lavatory: 5 basin **6** toilet **8** washbowl, washroom

lave: 4 bail, lade, pour, soak, wash **5** bathe, rinse

lavender: 6 pastel, purple, violet

laver: 5 basin **6** trough, vessel **7** cistern, seaweed

Lavinia: *father:* **7** Latinus
husband: **6** Aeneas
mother: **5** Amata

lavish: 4 free, lash, rank, wild **5** flush, spend, waste **7** opulent, profuse **8** prodigal, reckless, splendid, squander **9** bountiful, expensive, exuberant, impetuous, luxuriant, sumptuous, unstinted **10** immoderate **11** extravagant, magnificent **12** unrestrained **13** superabundant

law: act, bar, ius(L.), jus(L.), lex(L.) **4** code, doom, rule, Tora **5** canon, edict, mesne, sutra, Torah **6** custom, decree, equity, noetic, sutrah, suttah **7** derecho,

justice, precept, statute **8** handicap **9** enactment, ordinance, principle, regulation **11** commandment, legislation **12** constitution, jurisdiction **13** jurisprudence
action: res **4** suit **5** actus **8** replevin **9** gravamina
body of: **4** code **12** constitution
breaker of: **5** felon **6** sinner **8** criminal
claim: **4** lien
contrary to: **7** illegal, illicit **8** unlawful **16** unconstitutional
decree: **4** nisi **5** edict
degree: LLB, LLD
delay: **4** mora
document: **4** deed, writ **6** capias, elegit
expounder of: **6** jurist
goddess: **4** Maat
male succession: **5** Salic
man of: **5** judge **6** jurist, lawyer **7** counsel, justice **8** attorney **9** barrister
Manu: **5** sutra, sutta
offender: **8** criminal **9** desperado, wrongdoer
offense: **4** tort **5** crime, malum **6** delict
oral: **5** parol **11** nuncupative
order: **4** writ
permitted by: See **lawful**
pert. to: **5** legal **7** canonic **9** canonical, judiciary **11** legislative
philosophy of: **13** jurisprudence
prevent by: **5** estop
violation of: sin **4** tort **5** crime, malum **6** felony
warning: **6** caveat

lawful: due **5** legal, licit, valid **7** canonic, ennomic **10** legitimate

lawgiver: 5 Moses, solon **10** legislator

lawless: 4 lewd **6** unruly **7** illegal **8** anarchic **9** dissolute **10** anarchical, disorderly, tumultuous

lawlessness: 4 riot **5** chaos **6** mutiny, strife **7** anarchy, license **9** mobocracy **10** illegality

lawmaker: 5 solon **7** senator **10** legislator

lawn: 5 arbor, glade, grass, sward **6** arbour **7** batiste **9** grassland, grassplot, grasswork

lawsuit: 4 case **6** action **10** litigation
one engaged in: **8** litigant
subject: res

lawyer: 6 avocat(F.) **7** counsel **8** attorney, commoner **9** barrister, counselor, solicitor **10** counsellor
bad: **7** shyster **11** pettifogger

lax: 4 dull, free, limp, open, pave, slow **5** loose, slack, tardy **6** remiss **7** lenient **8** backward, careless, inactive **9** dissolute, negligent **10** unconfined **11** inattentive **12** unrestrained

lay: bet, put, set **4** bury, cast, cite, hymn,

poem, rest, song **5** allay, carol, ditty, place, quiet, stake, still, wager **6** ballad, entomb, hazard, impose, impute, melody **7** appease, ascribe, deposit, secular, work out **8** suppress **9** knock down, short poem **14** unprofessional **15** nonprofessional

lay aside: 5 table **6** shelve **7** abandon, discard, neglect

lay away: See **lay by**

lay bare: 4 show **5** strip **6** denude, expose, reveal **7** uncover

lay by: 4 hive, save **5** amass, cache, hoard, store **7** deposit, husband, reposit **8** salt away, treasure **10** accumulate

lay down: set **5** posit **6** affirm, give up **9** establish, surrender

lay hold of: 4 grab, grip **5** grasp, gripe, seize **9** apprehend

lay out: 4 plan **5** set up, spend **6** design, expend, extend, invest, make-up **7** arrange **9** residence

lay up: See **lay by**

lay waste: 4 ruin **6** harass, ravage **7** destroy **8** desolate **9** depredate, devastate

layer: bed, hen, ply **4** coat, film, fold, seam, tier, zona **5** paver **6** folium, lamina, veneer **7** bedding, provine, stratum **8** laminate **10** substratum

of coal: **4** seam

of stones: **4** dess

of wood: **4** core **6** veneer

pert. to: **7** stratal

layered: 7 laminal, laminar **8** tunicate

laymen: 4 laic **5** laity

lazar: 5 leper

lazy: 4 idle, laze **5** inert **8** indolent, slothful, sluggard

lea: 6 meadow **7** pasture **9** grassland

leach: wet, **4** soak **7** draw out, moisten **9** lixiviate, percolate **11** bloodsucker

lead: con, van, wad **4** head, lode, star, wadd **5** carry, first, guide, krems, metal, pilot, steer, usher **6** bullet, ceruse, convey, deduce, direct, escort, induce, manage **7** command, conduct, pioneer, plumbum, precede **8** graphite, instruct, outstrip **9** influence **10** show the way

astray: **4** lure **6** allure, delude, entice, seduce **7** deceive, mislead, pervert **8** inveigle

color: **4** dull, gray **5** livid, olive

ore: **6** galena **9** anglesite, cerrusite

paste: **6** strass

pig: **6** fother

sounding: **7** plummet

sulfide: **6** galena

leaden: 4 dull, gray **5** heavy, inert **7** languid, stilted **8** sluggish **9** colorless, plumbous

leader: bo; boh, cob, dux **4** cock, duce, duke, head, line, wire **5** chief, coach, pilot, sinew, snell **6** cantor, Fuhrer(G.), tendon **7** captain, demagog, foreman, Fuehrer(G.) **8** caudillo, choragus, headsman, preceder **9** chieftain, demagogue, drainpipe, principal **10** bellwether **11** condottiere, gymnasiarch

ecclesiastical: fra **4** pope **5** rabbi **6** bishop, father, priest **8** cardinal, minister, preacher **10** evangelist

leadership: 8 guidance, hegemony **9** authority

leading: big **4** duct, head, main **5** ahead, chief, first **6** banner **7** capital, central, guiding, premier, stellar **8** foremost **9** conducive, directing, governing, hegemonic, inductive, principal **11** controlling

leaf: ola, ole, pan **4** foil, olay, olla, page **5** blade, bract, folio, frond, palet, scale, sepal **6** areola, insert, spathe **7** tendril

angle with branch: **4** axil

aperture: **5** stoma

appendage: **6** ligula, stipel **7** stipule

aromatic: See **herb**

circle: **7** corolla

division: **4** lobe

edge: **9** crenation

fern: **5** frond

floating: pad

kind: **5** calxy, petal, sepal **7** corolla

part: pen **4** axil **5** costa, stoma **6** pagina **7** petiole, stomate

secretion on: **4** lerp

set: **5** calxy **7** corolla

vein: rib **5** costa

leafage: 7 foliage, umbrage, verdure

leaflet: 5 pinna, tract **6** folder **7** booklet **8** pamphlet

leafy: 4 lush, **5** green, shady **6** foliar **7** layered, sepaled

league: 4 bond **5** union **7** compact **8** alliance, covenant **9** coalition **10** federation **11** association, combination, confederacy **13** confederation

Leah: *father:* **5** Laban

husband: **5** Jacob

sister: **6** Rachel

son: **6** Simeon

leak: 4 drip, hole, loss, ooze, seep **5** crack **6** escape **7** channel, crevice, fissure

leaky: 6 porous

leal: 4 just, real, true **5** legal, loyal **6** lawful **7** correct, genuine **8** accurate, faithful

leam: 4 husk

lean: 4 bend, cant, lank, mean, poor, rely, slim, tend, thin, tilt **5** gaunt, lanky, scant, spare **6** depend, hollow, meager, meagre, skinny **7** conform, deviate, haggard, incline, recline, scrawny, slender **8** rawboned, scragged **9** deficient, emaciated **10** inadequate **12** unproductive

lean-to: hut **4** shed **5** shack

Leander's sweetheart: 4 Hera, Hero
leaning: 6 desire, **7** pronate **8** aptitude, penchant, tendency, **9** accumbent, prejudice **10** preference
leap: fly, hop **4** dart, dive, jump, loup, skip **5** bound, caper, exult, frisk, lunge, salto, vault **6** bounce, breach, cavort, curvet, gallop, gambol, hurdle, hurtle, spring **7** saltate **8** capriole **9** ballotade, entrechat
leap year: 10 bissextile
leaping: 7 jumping, salient, saltant **9** caprizant, saltation
lear: 4 lore **6** lesson **8** learning
Lear: *daughter:* **5** Regan **7** Goneril **8** Cordelia
 dog: **4** Tray
 follower: **4** Kent
learn: con, get **4** find, here, lere **6** master, pick up **7** acquire, apprise, apprize, realize **8** memorize **9** ascertain
learned: wot **4** blue, read, sage, wise **6** astute, doctus **7** clerkly, cunning, erudite **8** lettered, literary, literose **9** scholarly **10** omniscient **12** well-informed
learner: 5 pupil **7** scholar, trainee **8** disciple, opsimath **10** apprentice
learning: art **4** lear, lore **6** wisdom **7** cunning **8** pedantry **9** education, erudition, knowledge **10** discipline, experience **11** information, scholarship
 display of: **8** pedantry
 love of: **8** philology
 man of: **4** sage **6** pundit, savant **7** scholar, teacher **9** philomath, professor **12** intellectual
lease: let **4** hire, rent **6** demise, engage, rental, tenure **7** charter **8** contract **10** concession
leash: 4 bind, cord, curb, harl, jess, lune **5** strap **6** couple, tether **7** control **8** restrain
least: 6 fewest, little, lowest **7** minimal, minimum **8** shortest, smallest **9** slightest
leather: tan **4** napa, whip, yuft(Russ.) **5** balat, leder, strap **6** thrash
 artificial: **7** keratol
 drying: sam **4** samm **5** sammy
 fine: kid **6** vellum
 finish: **4** buff
 inspector: **6** sealer
 kind: elk, kid, kip **4** bock, buff, calf, doze, napa, roan, seal, vici **5** aluta, basil, mocha, suede, trank **6** castor, levant, oxhide, skiver **7** buffalo, canepin, chamois, morocco, saffian **8** cheverel, cheveril, Cordovan
 napped: **5** suede
 pare: **5** skive
 piece of: **4** rand, welt **5** clout, strap, thong **6** latigo
 prepare: tan, taw **4** mull **5** curry, sammy

 sheepskin: **4** roan **6** skiver
 soft: **5** aluta, mocha, suede **8** cabretta
 tool: **6** skiver
 waste: **6** tanite
 worker: **6** chamar, tanner **8** chuckler
leatherback: 6 turtle
leatherneck: 6 marine
leave: go; let **4** bunk, exit, quit **5** favor, forgo, grace, scram **6** beleve, decamp, depart, desert, entail, favour, forego, forlet, go away, permit, retire, vacate **7** abandon, beleave, forsake, getaway, liberty, license **8** bequeath, emigrate, furlough, vacation **9** allowance **10** permission, relinquish
 behind: **11** outdistance
 in the lurch: **6** desert, maroon, strand
 off: **4** halt, quit, stop **6** desist **8** knock off
 out: **4** omit, skip **5** elide **7** exclude
leave of absence: 5 exeat **8** furlough
leave-taking: 5 adieu, conge **6** congee **7** parting **8** farewell **9** departure
leaven: 5 imbue, yeast **7** lighten **10** impregnate
leaves (see also **leaf, leave**): **7** foliage
 having: see **leafy**
 medicinal: **5** senna
leavings: See **lees, rubbish**
Lebanon: *capital:* **6** Beirut
 dance: **6** dabkeh
 fort: **6** Byblos
 language: **6** Arabic
 monetary unit: **5** pound **7** piaster
 mountain: **4** Mzar **5** Aruba **6** Hermon **7** Sannine
 mountain range: **7** Lebanon **11** Anti-Lebanon
 river: **5** Kebir **6** Litani **7** Orontes
 town: **4** Tyre **5** Sidon, Zahle **7** Tripoli
 valley: **6** El Bika
lech: 4 slab **8** capstone, monument
lecher: 4 rake, roué **7** glutton **8** gourmand, parasite **9** debauchee, libertine
lecherous: 4 lewd **7** boarish, goatish, lustful **9** salacious
lectern: 4 ambo, desk **5** stand **6** podium **10** escritoire
lecture: 5 scold **6** lesson, preach, rebuke, sermon, speech **7** address, hearing, lection, oration, prelect **8** scolding **9** discourse, sermonize **12** dissertation
lecturer: 6 docent, reader **9** prelector, professor
led: See **lead**
Leda: *daughter:* **5** Helen **12** Clytemnestra
 lover: **4** swan, Zeus
 son: **6** Castor, Pollux
ledge: 4 berm, sill **5** bench, berme, shelf **7** retable
ledger: 4 book, tome **6** record
lee: 5 haven **7** shelter **10** protection
 oposite of: **5** stoss **8** windward

leech: 8 parasite 9 blackmail 11 bloodsucker

leer: 4 face, lear, lehr, loin, look, lust, ogle, void 5 empty, flank, fleer, smirk 6 entice, unlade 7 grimace

leery, leary: 4 wary 7 knowing 10 suspicious 11 distrustful 12 on one's guard

lees: 5 draff, dregs, dross, grout 6 bottom, dunder, refuse, ullage 7 grounds 8 leavings, sediment, settling 9 emptyings, excrement, left-overs

leeward: 4 alee

drift: 4 crab

Leeward group island: 5 Nevis 7 Antigua, Barbuda, St. Kitts 8 Anguilla, Dominica, Windward 10 Montserrat

leeway: 4 room 5 space 9 elbowroom

left: 4 port 8 larboard

toward: haw 5 aport 9 sinistrad

left-handed: car 6 clumsy, gauche 7 awkward 8 southpaw 9 portsided

leftist: red 7 liberal, radical 13 revolutionary

leg: gam, run 4 gamb, hoof, limb, prop, walk 5 bough, brace, gambe, shank 6 bender, gammon 8 cabriole

armor: 4 jamb 6 greave

bone: 4 shin 5 femur, ilium, tibia 6 fibula

in heraldry: 4 gamb

muscle: 8 peroneus 9 peronaeus

ornament: 6 anklet

part: 4 calf, crus, knee, shin 5 ankle, thigh 11 anticnemion

pert. to: 6 crural

legacy: 4 gift 6 legate 7 bequest 8 windfall 10 foundation

inheritor: 4 heir 7 legatee

legal (see also **law**): 5 licit, valid 6 lawful 7 juridic 9 juridical 10 authorized, legitimate

legal matter: res

legal right, by: 6 ex jure

legal tender: 4 cash, coin 5 money 6 dollar, specie

legalize: 9 authorize

legate: 5 envoy 6 deputy, legacy, nuncio 8 bequeath, delegate 9 messenger 10 ambassador 14 representative

legatee: 4 heir

joint: 6 coheir

legend: 4 edda, lore, myth, saga, tale 5 fable, story 6 record 7 fiction, proverb 9 tradition

legerdemain: 5 magic 6 deceit 8 trickery 9 conjuring 13 sleight of hand

legging: 4 spat 5 chaps 6 cnemis, cocker, puttie 7 bottine, gambado 8 bootikin, chivarra, chivarro, gamashes 11 galligaskin, spatterdash 12 antigropelos

legible: 8 distinct, readable 14 understandable

legion: 4 army, host 9 multitude

legislate: act 5 elect, enact

legislation: act, law 4 bill 7 statute

legislative body: 4 Dail, diet, rada 5 house, junta 6 senate 7 althing 8 assembly, congress 9 Reichstag 10 parliament

legislator: 5 solon 7 enactor, senator 8 lawmaker 9 statesman 14 representative

legitimate: 4 fair, just, real, true 5 legal, licit, valid 6 cogent, lawful 7 genuine 11 efficacious

legman: 8 reporter

legume: pea, pod, uva 4 bean, soya 5 pulse 6 lentil, loment 9 vegetable

lei: 6 wreath 7 flowers, garland

leisure: 4 case, free, idle, time 5 otium(L.), spare 6 otiose 7 freedom 10 relaxation, unemployed, unoccupied 11 convenience, opportunity 12 unproductive

leisurely: 4 slow 7 gradual 12 deliberately

leitmotiv: 5 theme 6 motive 7 pattern

leman: 5 lover 8 mistress, paramour 10 sweetheart

lemma: 5 bract, theme 7 premise, theorem 8 membrane

lemon: dud 5 fruit 7 failure 9 sour thing

lemonade: 5 drink 6 cooler 8 beverage

lemur: 4 maki, vari 5 avahi, indri, loris, potto 6 aye-aye, colugo, galago, macaco, maholi 7 half-ape, semiape, tarsier 8 kinkajou 9 babacoote 10 angwantibo

lend: 4 give, loan 5 grant, prest 6 afford, impart, settle 7 advance, furnish 11 accommodate

length: 4 pace, term 7 yardage 8 duration 9 dimension

measure: mil 4 foot, inch, yard

lengthen: eke 6 dilate, expand, extend 7 amplify, produce, prolong, stretch 8 elongate, increase, protract

lengthwise: 5 along 7 endlong, endways 14 longitudinally

lengthy: 4 long 8 drawn-out, extended 10 protracted

lenient: lax 4 easy, kind, mild 6 facile, gentle, humane 7 clement 8 lenitive, merciful, mitigant, relaxing, soothing, tolerant 9 assuasive, emollient, softening 10 charitable, forbearing, palliative

Leningrad: 9 Petrograd

lens: 5 glass, optic 7 bifocal 8 meniscus 10 anastigmat

Lent: 6 Careme(F.)

Lenten: 5 plain 6 meager, meagre, somber, sombre 8 meatless 9 cheerless 14 unostentatious

lentigo: 7 freckle

lentil: 6 legume

Leo star: 7 Regulus

leonine: 8 lionlike, powerful
leopard: cat 4 pard 5 ounce 7 cheetah, panther
lepidopter: 4 moth 9 butterfly
leprechaun: elf 5 fairy
leprosy: 5 lepra
lerot: 8 dormouse
lese majesty: 7 treason
Les Miserables author: 4 Hugo
lesion: cut 4 sore 5 ulcer, wound 6 injury 7 fissure
Lesotho: *capital:* 6 Maseru
 former name: 10 Basutoland
 language: 7 Sesotho
 monetary unit: 4 rand
 mountain range: 11 Drakensburg
 people: 7 Basotho
 river: 6 Orange 7 Caledon
 town: 4 Hoek 7 Mohales 8 Mafeteng
less: 5 fewer, minus, under 7 smaller 8 inferior
lessee: 6 leaser, renter, tenant 7 huurder(D.)
lessen: 4 bate, ease, wane 5 abase, abate, decry, lower, peter 6 impair, reduce, soften, shrink, weaken 7 amenuse, assuage, curtail, depress, relieve 8 belittle, condense, contract, decrease, derogate, diminish, minimize, mitigate, palliate, retrench, truncate 9 alleviate, attenuate, disparage, extenuate 10 depreciate 11 deteriorate
lesser: 5 minor 7 reduced 8 inferior 9 small-time 11 minor-league
lesson: 4 lear, task 5 moral, study 6 rebuke 7 example, lecture, precept, reading, reproof, warning 8 exercise 10 assignment 11 composition, instruction
lessor: 8 landlord
lest: 6 in case 11 for fear that
let: 4 hire, rent 5 allow, lease, leave 6 hinder, impede, permit, suffer 7 prevent 8 obstacle 9 hindrance
 fall: 4 drop, slip 5 lower, spill 7 mention
 forth: 4 emit
 in: 5 admit, enter 6 insert
let it stand: sta 4 stet
letdown: 5 slump 8 comedown, drawback 10 anticlimax, relaxation, slackening
lethal: 5 fatal 6 deadly, mortal, poison 9 poisonous 12 death-dealing
lethargic: 4 dull 5 heavy, inert 6 drowsy, sleepy, torpid 8 comatose, sluggish 9 apathetic
lethargy: 5 sopor 6 stupor, torpor 8 hebetude
Lethe: 8 oblivion 13 forgetfulness
Leto: 6 Latona
 daughter: 7 Artemis
 father: 5 Coeus
 mother: 6 Phoebe
 son: 6 Apollo

Lett: 4 Balt 7 Latvian
letter: 4 bull, chit, line, note 5 breve, brief, chain, favor, vowel 6 billet, cartel, charta, favour, screed, symbol 7 collins, courant, epistle, message, missile, missive 9 consonant, precisely, semivowel 12 exact wording 13 communication, semiconsonant
 Anglo-Saxon: edh, eth, wen, wyn 4 wynn
 decorated: fac
 large: 7 capital 9 majuscule, upper case
 sloping: 6 italic
 small: 9 lower case, miniscule
letter carrier: 6 correo(Sp.) 7 mailman, postman 9 messenger
lettered: 7 learned, stamped 8 educated, literate 9 inscribed
lettuce: *kind of:* cos 4 head, leaf 6 butter 7 romaine, simpson
 sea: 4 alga 5 laver
letup: 7 respite 9 abatement, cessation
leucite: 5 lenad 9 amphigene
levant: 5 waver 6 decamp 7 abscond
Levant: 4 East 6 Orient 13 Mediterranean
 garment: 6 caftan
 river: 4 wadi, wady
 ship: 4 jerm, saic
 valley: 4 wady
levee: 4 bank, dike, dyke, pier, quay 6 durbar 9 reception 10 embankment
level: aim, par 4 even, flat, rase, raze, true 5 equal, flush, grade, peavy, plane, point, scalp 6 evenly, peavey, peavie, smooth 7 flatten, mow down, planate, uniform 8 demolish 10 horizontal 12 standardized
 social: 5 caste, class
 tool: 5 plane 6 gimbal
level-headed: 8 sensible
lever: bar, lam, pry 5 helve, jemmy, jimmy, peavy, pedal, prise, swipe 6 binder, garrot, peavey, peavie, tappet, tiller 7 crowbar, treadle 9 rockshaft
 part: 7 fulcrum
leverage: 5 power 9 influence
leveret: 4 hare 8 mistress
Levi: *descendant:* 6 Levite 7 Gershon
 father: 5 Jacob
 son: 6 Kohath
leviathan: 4 ship 5 titan, whale 6 dragon
levigate: 5 grind 6 polish, smooth 9 pulverize
levin: 9 lightning
levitate: 4 rise 5 float
levity: 5 humor 6 gaiety, humour 8 buoyancy 9 frivolity, lightness, silliness 10 fickleness 11 foolishness, instability
levy: tax 4 cess, duty, fine, wage 5 exact, stent 6 assess, extent, impose, impost 7 collect 10 assessment, imposition
lewd: 4 base, rude 5 bawdy 6 carnal,

coarse **7** lustful, obscene, rammish, sensual **8** unchaste **9** debauched, dissolute, lecherous, salacious **10** lascivious, libidinous, licentious **12** pornographic

lexicographer: **6** author **8** compiler **9** onomastic

lexicon: **7** calepin **10** dictionary **11** onomasticon

Leyte capital: **8** Tacloban

liability: **4** debt, loan **5** debit **6** burden **10** obligation

liable: apt **6** likely **8** amenable **10** answerable **11** accountable, responsible **12** legally bound

liaison: **4** bond **6** affair **8** intimacy, intrigue **12** relationship

liana: **4** cipo, vine **5** plant

liang: **4** tael

liar: **5** cheat **6** fibber **7** Ananias, cracker **8** deceiver, fabulist **10** fabricator **11** pseudologue **12** prevaricator, pseudologist **14** misrepresenter

lias: **4** rock **9** limestone

libation: **5** drink **8** potation

libel: **4** bill **6** defame, malign, vilify **7** calumny, lampoon, request, scandal, slander **8** circular, handbill, roorback **10** calumniate, defamation **11** certificate, declaration **12** supplication

libelant: **7** accuser

liberal: **4** free, good, open **5** ample, broad, frank, noble **6** honest **7** electic, profuse **8** abundant, eclectic, generous, handsome **9** benignant, bounteous, bountiful, expansive, expensive, plenteous, plentiful **10** benevolent, charitable, ecumenical, munificent **11** broad-minded, progressive

Liberal: **4** Whig

liberate: rid **4** flee, free **5** clear, loose, remit **6** acquit, redeem, rescue **7** deliver, manumit, release **8** unfetter **9** discharge, disengage, extricate **10** emancipate

Liberia: *boatman:* Kru

capital: **8** Monrovia

city: **8** Buchanan, Marshall **10** Greenville

language: Kwa

measure: **4** kuba

monetary unit: **6** dollar

people: Kru, Kwa, Vai, Vei **4** Kroo, Toma **5** Bassa, Gibbi, Greba **6** Krooby, Kruman **7** Krooboy, Krooman

river: **5** Manna **8** San Pedro

libertine: **4** rake, roue **7** sceptic **9** debauchee, dissolute **10** lascivious, licentious

liberty: may **4** ease, play **5** leave, right **7** freedom, license **9** privilege **11** presumption **12** emancipation

library: **7** archive, bhander **8** atheneum **9** athenaeum **11** bibliotecha, reading room

libretto: **4** book **5** words

Libya: *capital:* **7** Tripoli

chief export: oil

city: **8** Benghasi

gulf: **5** Sidra

language: **6** Arabic

measure: **4** drah **5** bozze, donum, jabia, teman **6** barile **7** mattaro

monetary unit: **5** dinar

mountain: **5** Bette

oasis: **6** Fezzan, Giofra **8** Al-Kufrah, Giarabub

religion: **5** Islam

weight: **4** kele **5** uckia **6** gorraf **7** termino **8** kharouba

wind: **7** sirocco

Libya's child: **5** Belus **6** Agenor

lice: See **louse**

license: tax **5** exeat, leave **6** patent, permit **7** dismiss, freedom, liberty **8** escambio, passport, sanction **9** approbate, authority, authorize, franchise **10** permission **11** imprimateur, unrestraint

licentious: gay, lax **4** free, lewd **5** frank, loose **6** unruly **7** immoral, obscene **9** dissolute **10** lascivious, profligate **12** pornographic, uncontrolled, unrestrained

lichen: **4** moss

derivative: **6** archil, litmus

genus: **5** usnea **7** evernia **10** pertusaria

lich-house: **8** mortuary

licit: **5** legal **6** lawful **9** permitted

lick: bit, dab, lap, win **4** flog **5** slake, taste **6** defeat, thrash **7** clobber, conquer, shellac **8** overcome, vanquish

lickety-split: **4** fast **5** apace **7** quickly, rapidly, swiftly **9** posthaste

licorice: **5** abrin, anise **8** absinthe **9** jequirity

pill: **6** cachou

seed: **9** jequirity

lid: cap, hat, top **4** curb **5** cover **7** shutter **9** operculum, restraint

lie: cog, fib, gab **4** bask, cram, flaw, hide, loll, rest **5** exist **6** covet, extend, grovel, patter, remain, repose **7** cracker, crammer, deceive, falsify, falsity, pronate, untruth **8** position, roorback **9** deception, fabricate, falsehood, fish story, mendacity, prostrate **10** equivocate, inveracity, taradiddle **11** fabrication, prevaricate, tarradiddle **12** song and dance

in ambush: **4** lurk **6** hugger **9** insidiate

Liebestraum composer: **5** Liszt

Liechtenstein: *capital:* **5** Vaduz

monetary unit: **5** rappe

lief: **4** fain, soon **5** leave **6** freely, gladly **7** happily **9** willingly **10** permission

liege: **5** loyal **6** vassal **7** devoted, subject **8** faithful, overlord **9** sovereign

lien: **5** claim **6** charge **8** mortgage **9** trust deed **11** encumbrance, garnishment

lieu: 5 place, stead 7 instead
lieutenant: 7 officer 10 aide-de-camp
life: vie 5 blood, vigor 6 biosis, energy,
spirit 8 vitality, vivacity 9 animation,
biography, existence 11 anilopyrine
animal: 4 bios 5 biota, fauna
god of: 6 Faunus
pert. to: 5 vital 6 biotic, mortal 8 biotical
plant: 4 bios 5 biota, flora
principle: 5 atman, prana, tenet
professional: 6 career
science: 7 anatomy, biology, zoology 12
paleontology
sea: 5 coral 8 halibios, plankton
simple form: 5 ameba 6 amebic, ameoba
7 amoebic, amoebae(pl.)
staff of: 5 bread
without: 4 dead 5 azoic 9 inanimate
life jacket: 7 Mae West
life-like: 9 realistic
lifeless: 4 arid, dead, dull, flat 5 amort,
heavy, inert, vapid 6 anemic, jejune,
torpid 7 anaemic 8 inactive, listless 9
bloodless, examinate, inanimate, powerless, tasteless 10 spiritless, unanimated
lifer: 7 convict 13 career soldier
lifetime: age, day, eon 4 aeon 5 being 8
duration
lift: pry 4 help, jack, perk, rear 5 boost,
crane, exalt, heave, hoick, hoist, hoosh,
raise, scend 6 cleach, cleech 7 derrick,
elevate, enhance 8 elevator, heighten
ligament: 4 band, bind, bond 6 artery 7
bandage
ligan, lagan: 6 debris
ligate: 4 bind 5 tie up 7 bandage
ligature: tie 4 band, bond 6 taenia 7 bandage
light: dey, gay 4 airy, deft, easy, fair, fire,
glim, lamp, mild, moon, neon, soft 5 agile, blond, fanal, filmy, flaky, flame,
flare, happy, merry, torch 6 alight, beacon, bright, candle, floaty, gentle, ignite,
kindle, lively, lumine, nimble, pastel,
volant 7 animate, buoyant, cresset, flyaway, fragile, trivial, whitish 8 bright-
en, cheerful, delicate, ethereal, gossamer, graceful, illumine, luminary,
luminous, trifling 9 frivolous, knowledge, touch down 10 capricious, illuminate
circle: 4 halo 7 aureola, aureole
cloud: 6 nimbus
faint: 7 glimmer, shimmer 9 starlight 10
glimmering, shimmering
globe: 4 bulb
god: 5 Baldr 6 Balder
kind of: arc 4 lamp 5 klieg, torch 7 lantern 9 headlight 10 flashlight 12 incandescent
measure: lux, pyr, rad 5 lumen 6 Hefner
overpower with: 6 dazzle
portable: 4 lamp 5 flare, taper, torch 6

candle 7 lantern 10 flashlight
reflector: 4 lens 6 mirror
refractor: 5 prism
science: 6 optics
source: sun
unit: lux, pyr 4 phot 5 lumen
without: 4 dark 5 blind 7 aphotic
lighten: 4 ease, fade 5 allay, clear 6 alight,
allege, bleach, illume, leaven 7 gladden,
relieve 8 brighten 9 alleviate 10 illuminate
lighter (see also **light**): 5 barge, spill 7
pontoon 8 chopboat
lightheaded: 5 dizzy, giddy 6 fickle 7
flighty, glaiket, glaikit 8 flippant, heedless, unstable, unsteady 9 delirious,
frivolous 10 disordered, inconstant 11
thoughtless
lighthearted: gay 4 glad 5 merry 7 buoyant 8 carefree, cheerful, gleesome, volatile 9 vivacious 12 free from care
lighthouse: 5 phare 6 beacon, pharos 7
seamark, warning
lightness: 6 levity 8 delicacy, mildness
12 cheerfulness
lightning: 4 bolt 5 levin
defier of: 4 Ajax
pert. to: 8 fulgural
protective device: rod 8 arrester
lightning bug: 6 beetle 7 firefly
lightning stone: 9 fulgurite
lights out: 4 taps
ligneous: 5 woody
lignite: 4 coal
ligulate: 11 strap-shaped
likable: 6 genial 7 winning 8 charming,
pleasant 10 attractive
like: 4 love, same 5 alike, enjoy, equal 6
admire, prefer, relish 7 similar 9 analogous, semblance 10 preference, synonymous 11 counterpart, homogeneous
like a: For definitions beginning with
these words, see following important
words. EXAMPLES: "like a cat": see **catlike**; "like a house": see **house:** *pert.
to.*
likelihood: 10 appearance 11 probability
14 verisimilitude
likely: apt 5 prone 6 liable 7 tending 8
credible, feasible, probable, suitable 9
promising 11 verisimilar
liken: 5 apply 7 compare 10 assimilate
likeness: 4 copy, form, twin 5 guise, image 6 effigy, figure, statue 7 analogy,
parable, picture, replica 8 parallel, portrait 9 duplicate, facsimile, imitation,
semblance, simulacre 10 comparison,
photograph, similarity, similitude, simulacrum 11 counterfeit 12 reproduction 14 representation
likewise: and, nor, not, too 4 also 5 ditto
7 besides 8 moreover
liking: goo 4 gust, lust 5 fancy, gusto,

taste **6** comely **7** delight **8** affinity, appetite, fondness, penchant, pleasing, pleasure **9** affection **10** preference, sensuality **12** predilection

lilac: 5 mauve, shrub **6** flower **7** syringa

Lilith's successor: Eve

lilliputian: 4 tiny **5** pretty, small **6** midget **7** dwarfed **10** diminutive, teeny-weeny

lilt: air **4** sing, song, tune **7** cadence

lily (see also **water lily**): **4** aloe, ixia, sego **5** calla, niobe, tiger, water, yucca **6** ti-tree **8** mariposa
family: **9** liliaceae
genus: **7** bessera
sea: **7** crinoid

lily iron: 7 harpoon

lily-livered: 5 timid **6** coward **7** gutless **9** spunkless

Lily Maid of Astolat: 6 Elaine

lily of France: 10 fleur-de-lis

lily of the valley: 6 mugget, mugwet **10** convallily
family: **15** convallariaceae

lima: 4 bean, seed **7** mollusk

liman: bay **5** marsh **6** lagoon **7** estuary

limation: 6 filing **9** polishing

limb: arm, fin, leg **4** edge, wing **5** bough **6** branch, member, rascal, switch **7** flipper, pleopod, support **9** appendage
adapted for swimming: **8** nectopod
flexion: **9** anaclasis

limber: 4 bain, flip, limp **5** lithe **6** pliant, supple, swanky **8** flexible, flippant, handsome, yielding

limbo: 4 hell **5** dance **9** purgatory

lime: 5 color, fruit, green **6** cement, citrus
pendent: **10** stalactite
phosphate: **7** apatite
tree: **4** teil **6** linden, tupelo

limen: 9 threshold

limestone: 4 calp, cauk, malm **5** chalk, ganil, poros(Gr.) **6** clunch, marble, oolite **7** hurlock **8** peastone, pisolite

limey: 6 sailor **7** soldier **10** Engishman

limit: end, fix **4** curb, mete **5** ambit, bound, bourn, check, fence, hedge, scant, stint, verge **6** border, bourne, curfew, define, extent, finish **7** astrict, barrier, closure, confine, environ, extreme **8** boundary, conclude, contract, deadline, restrain, restrict, terminal, terminus **9** condition, constrain, extremity **10** limitation **11** restriction, termination **12** boundary line, circumscribe **13** determination, qualification

limited: few, ltd **5** local, scant **6** finite, narrow, scanty, strait **8** reserved **9** parochial **10** restricted **11** topopolitan

limiting: 5 final **9** bordering, enclosing **10** qualifying, relational

limitless: 4 vast **8** infinite **9** boundless, unbounded, unlimited **11** measureless

limn: 4 draw **5** paint **6** depict, sketch **7** portray **8** describe **9** delineate

limp: hop, lax **4** himp, soft, then **5** hilch, hitch, loose **6** flabby, flimsy, hirple, hobble, limber, wilted **7** flaccid **8** drooping, flexible, hang down **9** inelastic **13** unsubstantial

limpid: 4 pure **5** clear, lucid **6** bright **7** crystal **8** pellucid **11** translucent, transparent

limping: 4 halt **10** claudicant

limy: 6 sticky **7** viscous

Lincoln:
assassin: **5** Booth
debater: **7** Douglas
nickname: **9** Honest Abe **12** Railsplitter
secretary of state: **6** Seward
secretary of war: **7** Stanton
son: Tad
wife: **8** Mary Todd

linden: lin **4** lime, teil **8** basswood
genus of: **5** tilia

line: job, pad, ray, row, wad **4** axis, ceil, cord, dash, etch, face, file, mark, mere, race, rein, rope, rule, seam, wire **5** curve, front, leger, queue, route, serif, snell, steen, stich, stria, swath **6** border, ceriph, cordon, fettle, hawser, isobar, metier, nettle, streak, string, stripe, suture **7** barrier, carrier, contour, outline, radiant, scratch **8** boundary, crossbar, isotherm, wainscot **9** delineate
bottom: **7** net loss **9** net profit
conceptual: **6** agonic, tropic **7** equator, isother **8** latitude, meridian **9** longitude
curved: arc
diagonal: **4** bias
geometrical: arc, ess **4** cant, sine **6** secant **7** tangent **8** parallel **9** asymptote
mathematical: **6** vector
nautical: **6** earing, hawser, ratlin **7** marline, painter, ratline
of soldiers: **4** file, rank **6** column
pert. to: **5** filar **6** linear
raised: **4** weal, welt **5** ridge
with boards: **8** wainscot

lineage: 4 race **5** birth, blood, caste, tribe **6** family, havage, stirps **7** descent, stirpes(pl.) **8** ancestry, heredity, pedigree **9** genealogy **10** progenitor

lineal: 6 direct, racial **9** ancestral **10** hereditary

lineament: 7 feature **14** characteristic

linear: 9 elongated

lineate: 7 striped **8** streaked

lined: 5 ruled **6** notate **7** striate **8** careworn **9** lineolate

lineman: end **5** guard **6** center, tackle **7** wireman

linen: 4 brin, crea(Sp.), lawn **5** toile **6** barras, damask, dowlas, forfar **7** brabant, cambric, dornick **13** linsey-woolsey

fabric: **7** taffeta

household: **6** napery, sheets **10** tablecloth

source: **4** flax

yarn: lea

liner: **4** boat, ship **6** facing, vessel **7** backing, steamer **9** steamship

wrecked: **7** Titanic

lines: net **5** looks **7** harness, network, reticule

ling: **4** fish, hake **5** heath **6** burbot **7** heather **8** chestnut

linger: lag **4** drag, stay, wait **5** dally, delay, dwell, hover, tarry **6** dawdle, loiter, remain, stay on

lingerie: **9** underwear **11** underthings

lingering: **4** slow **7** chronic

lingo: **4** cant **5** argot **6** jargon, patter, tongue **7** dialect **8** language **10** vernacular

lingual: **7** glossal **10** linguistic, tonguelike

linguist: **8** polyglot **9** pantoglot **10** vocabulist **11** interpreter, philologist

linguistics: **7** grammar **9** philology

lingy: **5** agile **6** active, healthy, limber, nimble **8** heathery

liniment: oil **6** lotion **8** ointment **11** embrocation

lining: **5** steen **6** facing, insert **7** backing, ceiling **8** wainscot

link: tie **4** join, joke **5** cleek, nexus, torch, unite **6** braced, catena, copula, couple, course, faster **7** conjoin, connect **8** catenate **10** connection, golf course **11** concatenate

series: **5** chain **13** concatenation

linn, lin: **4** pool **6** linden, ravine **8** cataract **9** precipice, waterfall

linnet: **5** finch, twite **9** gorsebird

linseed: **4** flax

lint: **4** fuzz, pile **5** fluff **7** charpie **8** raveling

lintel: **5** hance **6** clavel **7** transom

lion: **4** puma, star **5** simba **6** cougar, roarer **9** carnivore, celebrity

group: **5** pride

hair: **4** mane

winged, with woman's head: **6** sphinx

young: cub **6** lionet

Lion of God: Ali

lionlike: **7** leonine

lion's share: **8** best part **10** whole thing

lip: rim **4** brim, edge, kiss **5** brink, labia(pl.) **6** labium, margin, **7** labella **8** labellum

ornament: **6** labret

part: **8** philtrum

pert. to: **6** labial **11** labiodental

lipoma: **5** tumor

lipid: fat, wax

liquefy: **4** fuse, melt **6** fusile **7** liquate **8** dissolve, eliquate **10** colliquate, deliquesce, make molten

liqueur: **5** creme, noyau **6** genepi **7** cordial, ratafee **8** anisette, beverage **9** cointreau **10** pousse cafe **11** benedictine

liquid: **5** fluid **6** fluent, watery **8** beverage

colorless: **5** water, **7** alcohol

container: cup, jar, jug, mug, pan, pot **4** etna, ewer, vase, vial **5** cruse, glass, phial **6** boiler, bottle, bucket, goblet, kettle **7** creamer, pitcher, tumbler **8** decanter, demijohn

gasified: **5** steam, vapor

inflammable: see *volatile* below

measure: **4** pint **5** liter, ounce **6** gallon, tierce

oily: **6** cresol, octane **7** aniline, picamar

particle form: **4** mist **5** spray

sweet: **5** sirup, syrup **7** treacle **8** molasses

volatile: gas **5** ether **6** butane **7** alcohol, ligroin **8** gasolene, gasoline, ligroine

liquidate: **5** pay up **6** murder, settle **8** amortize **9** discharge

liquor (see also **liqueur**): ale, bub, dew, gin, rum, rye **4** arak, bang, beer, beno, brew, grog, nipa, raki, sake, saki, soma **5** bhang, booze, budge, drink, hooch, lager, pisco, stout **6** arrack, brandy, porter, pottle, scotch, stingo, strunt, tipple **7** bitters, whiskey **8** beverage **9** aqua vitae, moonshine **10** intoxicant

bad: **5** smoke **6** rotgut **10** balderdash

cabinet: **8** cellaret

crude: **5** hooch, **6** rotgut **9** hoochinoo, moonshine

drugged: **5** hocus **6** mickey **10** mickeyfinn

manufacturer: **6** abkari **9** distiller

measure: **4** dram **5** rouse **7** snifter

mix with: **4** lace

mixture: **5** bogus **7** bragget

residue: **4** must **5** dregs **8** heeltaps

server: **6** barman **7** barmaid, skinker, tapster **9** barkeeper, bartender

shop: bar **6** saloon, tavern **7** shebeen

vessel: ama, keg **4** bowl **5** amula, flask **6** barrel, bottle, flagon **7** bombard, psykter, stamnos **8** cruisken, decanter **9** cruiskeen

lira (one-twentieth): **5** soldo

liripipe, liripoop: **4** hood **5** scarf **6** tippet

lirk: **6** crease **7** wrinkle

lish: **5** agile, quick **6** active, nimble

lisk: **4** loin **5** flank, groin

lisp: **7** prattle

lissome, lissom: **5** agile, lithe **6** limber, nimble, supple **8** flexible

list: tip **4** bill, cant, cast, file, item, keel, leet, memo, ordo, roll, rota, rote, tilt **5** brief, canon, index, panel, scrip, slate **6** careen, docket, roster **7** catalog, incline **8** manifest, register, schedule, tabulate

9 catalogue, inventory, portfolio, repertory **10** repertoire **11** enumeration

listen: ear **4** hark, hear, heed, note **5** audit **6** attend, harken **7** hearken **8** give heed, overhear **9** eavesdrop **10** auscultate, take advice

lister: **4** plow **8** assessor **9** appraiser **10** cataloguer

listing: **5** atilt **7** tilting, tipping **8** register **10** enlistment, enrollment
individual: **4** item **5** entry

listless: **4** dull **5** faint, inert **6** abject, drowsy, supine **7** languid **8** careless, heedless, sluggish **9** apathetic, heartless **10** spiritless **11** indifferent **13** uninteresting

listlessness: **8** doldrums

litany: **6** ectene, ektene, prayer **8** rogation **11** orapronobis

liter: kan(D.) **7** measure

literal: **4** bald, dull, real **5** exact **7** factual, precise, prosaic **8** accurate, verbatim **11** word for word **13** unimaginative

literary: **6** versed **7** bookish, erudite, learned **8** lettered **9** scholarly

literate: **6** reader, writer **8** educated, lettered

literati: **12** men of letters **14** intelligentsia

literator: **6** critic

literature: **7** letters
extracts: **9** anthology
form: **5** novel, prose **6** poetry **7** fiction **9** technical **10** nonfiction, scientific **11** pornography

lithe: **4** bain, slim **6** clever, limber, lissom, pliant, supple, svelte **7** lissome, slender **8** flexible

lithograph: **5** print **6** chromo

Lithuania: *capital:* **7** Vilnius
city: **6** Kaunas **8** Klaipeda
coin: lit **5** litas, marka **6** centas, fennig **7** ostmark **8** auksinas, skatikas
dialect: **5** Zmudz
lowlander: **5** Zhmud **10** Samogitian
people: **4** Balt, Lett **5** Zhmud **6** Litvak **7** Yatvyag
railroad junction: **5** Vilna

litigant: **4** suer **6** suitor **7** accuser

litigation: **4** case, moot, suit **6** action **7** contest, dispute, lawsuit **10** contention, discussion
one involved in: **8** barrater, barrator, litigant

litigious: **10** disputable **11** belligerent, contentious, quarrelsome **14** controvertible

litter: bed, hay **4** bier, mess, raff **5** cabin, couch, dooly, mulch, straw, trash, young **6** doolie, refuse **7** cacolet, clutter, mullock, rubbish, rummage **8** brancard(F.), disorder **9** offspring, stretcher **10** untidiness

litterateur: **7** bookman

little: sma(Sc.), wee **4** poco(It.), puny, tiny **5** crumb, petit, small **6** petite **8** fraction **10** diminutive
by little: **8** inchmeal **9** gradually, piecemeal

Little Dipper: **7** Polaris **9** North Star **13** constellation

little finger: **5** pinky **6** pinkie **7** minimus

little toe: **7** minimus

Little Women: Amy, Meg **4** Beth
author: **6** Alcott
surname: **5** March

littoral: **7** coastal

lituite: **6** fossil

liturate: **7** spotted

liturgy: **4** rite **6** ritual **7** service

livable: **8** bearable **9** endurable, habitable, tolerable

live: **4** fare, room **5** abide, alive, dwell, exist, green, vital, vivid **6** active, reside **7** animate, blazing, breathe, dynamic, subsist **8** animated, continue, converse **9** energetic **10** experience, unexploded
in: **7** inhabit
in the country: **9** rusticate
passively: **8** vegetate
permit to: **5** spare **8** reprieve
with: **7** cohabit

livelihood: **4** keep **5** being **6** living **11** subsistence

liveliness: **6** spirit **8** vitality

lively: gay, vif(F.) **4** airy, cant, fast, pert, racy, vive, yare **5** agile, alert, alive, brisk, canty, chirk, cobby, desto(It.), fresh, peart, peppy **6** active, blithe, bright, cheery, chirpy, cocket, crouse, dapper, frisky, nimble, snappy **7** allegro(It.), animate, animato(It.), buoyant, chipper **8** animated, galliard, spirited, vigorous **9** energetic, sprightly, vivacious

liven: **5** cheer, pep up **7** animate **8** brighten

liver: **4** foie **5** hepar **8** tomalley
disease: **9** cirrhosis, hepatitis
fluid: **4** bile
pert. to: **7** hepatic

liverwort: **4** moss **8** agrimony, hepatica **9** bryophyte
genus: **6** riccia

livery: **7** uniform **8** clothing

livestock: **6** cattle **7** chattel

livid: **4** gray **5** bleak **6** purple **7** deathly **9** colorless **10** discolored **12** black and blue

living: **4** keep **5** alive, being, bread, vivid **6** extant **7** animate **8** animated, benefice **10** livelihood, sustenance **11** subsistence
again: **6** reburn **9** redivivus
correct: **7** regimen **11** orthobiosis
off others: **8** entozoic **9** parasitic, raptorial

together: **11** contubernal
lixiviate: 5 leach
lixivium: lye
lizard: dab, eft **4** adda, dabb, dhab, evet, gila, ibid, newt, seps, uran **5** agama, anole, dhabb, gecko, gekko, goana, scink, skink, varan, waran **6** ameiva, anolis, dragon, goanna, iguana, komodo, lacert, moloch, worral, worrel **7** cheecha, geitjie, monitor, saurian, tuatera **8** basilisk **9** chameleon, galliwasp **10** chuckwalla, horned toad **12** scheltopusik
family: **12** xenosauridae
genus: uta **5** agama **6** ameiva, anolis
mammal similar to: **10** salamander
lizard like: 8 iguanoid
llama: 6 alpaca, vicuna **7** guanaco
habitat: **5** Andes
llanero: 6 cowboy **8** herdsman
llano: 5 plain **7** lowland, prairie
Llyr's son: 4 Bran **7** Branwen
load: jag **4** clog, jagg, lade, onus, pack, tote, stow **5** cargo, weigh **6** burden, charge, hamper, lading, steeve, weight **7** fraught, freight, oppress **8** carriage, encumber **9** aggravate, exonerate **10** adulterate **11** encumbrance
small: jag **4** jagg **5** hurry
loader: 9 stevedore
loadstone: See **lodestone**
loaf: 4 idle, laze **5** bread **6** dawdle, loiter, lounge **10** dilly-dally
loafer: bum **4** hood, shoe **5** idler **7** flaneur, hoodlum, lounger, vagrant **8** hooligan, larrikin, vagabond **11** chairwarmer
loam: rab **4** silt **5** loess, regur(Ind.) **6** cledge **8** dark soil
constituent: **4** clay, lime **5** chalk
deposit: **4** silt **5** loess
loan: 4 dhan(Ind.), lend **5** prest **6** borrow **7** advance **10** obligation, provisions **13** accommodation
loan shark: 6 usurer **11** money-lender
loath, loth: 6 averse, odious **7** hateful **8** backward **9** reluctant, repulsive, unwilling
loathe: 4 hate **5** abhor **6** detest **7** adverse, condemn, despise, dislike **9** abominate
loathsome: 4 foul, ugly, vile **7** carrion, cloying, hateful **8** abhorent, deformed **9** offensive, repellent, repugnant **10** abominable, detestable, disgusting **11** distasteful
lob: hit **4** bowl, lots, lout, lump, step, till, toss, vein **5** droop, stair, throw **6** propel **7** pollack **9** chandelle
lobby: 4 hall, room **5** foyer **8** anteroom, coulisse **9** enclosure, vestibule
lobbyist: 8 promoter **12** propagandist
lobe: 4 flap **5** alula **6** alular, earlap, lappet, lobule
lobelike: 6 lobate

loblolly: 4 mush, pine, tree **5** gruel **6** puddle **7** mudhole
lobo: 4 wolf **10** timber wolf
lobster: *claw:* **5** chela **6** nipper **10** crustacean
female: hen
part: **4** claw **6** pincer, telson, thorax
roe: **5** coral
trap: pot **5** creel **6** bownet
local: 6 narrow, native **7** bucolic, endemic, limited, topical **8** regional, specific **10** restricted
locale: 4 loci(pl.), site **5** locus(L.), place, scene **6** region **9** situation
locality: 4 loci(pl.), seat, site, spot **5** locus, place, situs **6** region **7** habitat **8** district, position **12** neighborhood
localize: 7 situate **8** pinpoint
locate (see also **place**): sat **4** espy, find, seat, show, site, spot **5** stand, trace **6** settle **7** situate, station **8** discover, pinpoint **9** establish
locatio: 7 leasing, letting
locating device: 5 lidar, radar, sonar
location: 4 area, seat, site, spot **5** place, scene, situs **6** ubiety **7** habitat **9** situation
loch: bay **4** lake, pond, pool **5** lough
loci: See **locus**
lock: 4 bolt, curl, frib, hank, hasp, wisp **5** latch, sasse, tress **6** fasten **7** confine, cowlick, ringlet **8** fastener
part: **4** bolt **5** stump **8** cylinder
locker: 5 hutch **6** ascham
locket: 7 jewelry **8** ornament
lockjaw: 7 tetanus, trismus **11** ankylostoma
remedy: **11** antitetanic, antitetanus
lockman: 11 executioner
lockup: jug **4** jail **5** clink **6** cooler **7** hoosgow **8** hoosegaw, hoosegow **9** calaboose
loco: mad **5** crazy **6** insane **8** demented
locomotive: 5 dolly, mogul **6** diesel, dinkey, engine, mallet **8** electric
part: cab **5** pilot
service car: **6** tender **7** coalcar
type: **5** steam **6** diesel **8** electric
Locrine: *daughter:* **7** Sabrina
father: **4** Brut
locus: 4 area, site **5** place **8** locality
locust: 5 bruke, cicad, carob **6** cicada, cicala, cigala, insect **11** grasshopper
wingless: **4** weta
locust bird: 7 grackle **8** starling
locust plant: 5 senna
locust tree: 5 carob **6** acacia
locustberry: 5 drupe, nance **9** glamberry
lode: 4 path, road, vein **5** canal, drain, ledge **6** course **7** deposit, fissure **8** waterway
cavity: vug **4** vugg, vugh
lodestone, loadstone: 6 magnet **7** adamant **8** terrella **9** magnetite

lodge: dig, lie **4** club **5** board, couch, dwell, hogan, motel **6** alight, bestow, encamp, hostel **7** deposit **8** harbinge, domicile **11** brotherhood

lodger: **5** guest **6** roomer, tenant

lodging: bed, hut, inn **4** camp, gite(F.), host, howf, nest, room, tent **5** abode, cabin, hotel, house, hovel, howff **6** billet, tavern, teepee, wigwam **7** mansion **8** barracks, dwelling, hostelry, quarters **9** dormitory, harborage, residence **10** habitation, harbourage
cost: **4** rent **11** maintenance

loess: **4** loam, silt **7** deposit

loft: bin **4** balk **5** attic, raise **6** garret

lofty: **4** aery, epic, high, tall **5** aerie, elate, grand, noble, proud, steep **6** aerial, Andean, andine **7** Andesic, arduous, eminent, haughty, sublime **8** arrogant, assuming, elevated, eloquent, majestic **9** cockhorse, dignified, overproud **11** magisterial, mountainous

log: **4** clog, wood **5** diary **6** billet, loggat, logget, record, timber **7** journal
kind: **4** slab **5** splat **8** puncheon
mass: **5** drive
revolve: **4** birl **7** logroll

log gin: **6** jammer

logarithm: *unit:* bel
inventor: **6** Napier

loge: box **4** room **5** booth, stall

logger: **6** sniper **9** lumberman **10** lumberjack, woodcutter **11** woodchopper
boot: pac **4** pack

loggerhead: **6** turtle **9** blockhead

loggerheads: **4** odds, outs **10** quarreling

loggia: **6** arcade **7** balcony, gallery

logging: *sled:* **4** tode **7** travois **8** travoise
tool: **4** pevy **5** peavy, peevy **6** nigger, peavey

logic: **9** reasoning
inductive: **7** epagoge
specious: **7** sophism
term: **5** ferio, lemma **7** ferison

logical: **4** sane **5** sound, valid **8** coherent, rational **10** consistent, reasonable

logion: **5** maxim, motto **6** saying **11** observation

logograph: **5** rebus **6** puzzle, riddle **7** anagram

logotype: **8** colophon **9** nameplate, signature, trademark

logroll: **4** birl

logy: **4** dull **5** heavy **6** drowsy, groggy **8** sluggish

Lohengrin: *character:* **4** Elsa **8** Parsifal
composer: **6** Wagner

loincloth: **5** pagne

loir: **8** dormouse

loiter: lag **4** idle, loaf **5** dally, delay, drawl, shool, tarry **6** cooter, dawdle, linger **7** saunter **8** hesitate

loiterer: **4** slug **5** drone, idler **7** laggard **8** sluggard

Loki: *child:* Hel **4** Hela, Nare, Nari
mother: **9** Angrbodha
victim: **6** Balder
wife: **5** Sigyn

loll: **4** hang **5** droop, tarry **6** dangle, froust, frowst, lounge, sprawl **7** recline

loma, **4** hill

lombard: **6** cannon

Lombardy: *king:* **6** Alboin
lake: **4** Como

lomilomi: rub **7** massage, shampoo

lomita: **4** hill

London: *bus conductor:* **6** clippy
district: **4** Soho **5** Acton **7** Adelphi, Alsatia, Mayfair
fish market: **12** Billingsgate
monument: Gog **5** Magog **6** Nelson **8** Cenotaph, Victoria
museums and galleries: **4** Tate **8** National **13** Madame Tussaud **17** Victoria and Albert
parks: **4** Hyde **7** Holland, Regent's, St. James **9** Battersea **10** Kew Gardens
promenade: **4** Mall
river: **6** Thames
roisterer: mun
society: **7** Mayfair
square: **9** Leicester **9** Trafalgar
stables: **4** mews
street: **4** Bond **5** Fleet **6** Savile, Strand **7** Downing, Wardour **9** Cheapside, Haymarket, Whitehall **10** Piccadilly
suburb: Kew **8** Finchley
subway: **4** tube **11** underground
timepiece: **6** Big Ben

Londoner: **7** Cockney

lone: **4** sole **5** alone, apart **6** single **7** retired **8** solitary **9** unmarried **12** unfrequented

Lone Ranger's companion: **5** Tonto

Lone Star State: **5** Texas

loneliness: **8** solitude **9** dejection, isolation **10** depression, desolation **12** lonesomeness

lonely: **4** lorn, sole **5** alone, apart **6** dismal, dreary **7** deavely, forlorn **8** deserted, desolate, lonesome, secluded, solitary **11** sequestered **12** unfrequented

long: far **4** hone, hope, pine **5** yearn **6** aspire, hanker, hunger, prolix, thirst **7** lengthy, tedious **8** drawn-out, extended, tiresome **9** elongated, prolonged, wearisome **10** protracted
and slender: **5** lathy, reedy **6** linear **9** elongated
for: **4** miss, want, wish **5** covet, crave **6** aspire, desire

long ago: **4** yore

long dozen: **8** thirteen

long-suffering: **4** meek **7** patient **8** patience **9** endurance **10** forbearing

long-winded: 6 prolix **7** prosaic **9** garrulous

Longfellow hero: 8 Hiawatha

longheaded: 4 wise **6** shrewd **9** sagacious **10** hardheaded **11** foresighted

longing: yen **4** envy, itch **6** desire **7** athirst, craving, wistful **8** appetite, cupidity, homesick, prurient, yearning **9** nostalgia **10** desiderium

longitudinally: 7 endlong **10** lengthwise

longshoreman: 8 dockhand **9** stevedore

loo: pam **6** toilet **8** card game

look: con, pry, see **4** gaze, leer, ogle, peek, peep, peer, pore, scan, seem, skew **5** blush, dekko, fleer, glare, gliff, glime, gloat, gloom, glout, lower, sight, smile, snoop, stare, watch **6** aspect, behold, gander, glance, glower, glunch, notice, regard, search, squint, visage **7** observe **8** demeanor **10** appearance, get a load of

look after: 4 tend **6** attend **7** care for

look at: eye, see **4** glom, ogle, view **6** behold, regard **7** examine, observe

look back: 6 recall, relive, review **7** rethink **8** remember **10** retrospect

look down on: 7 despise

look for: 4 seek **5** await **6** expect **10** anticipate

look forward to: 5 await **6** expect **10** anticipate

look into: 5 study **6** search **7** examine, inspect **8** sound out **11** investigate

look like: 8 resemble

look over: 4 scan **6** ignore, survey **7** examine **8** overlook **9** disregard **11** reconnoiter, reconnoitre

look toward: 4 face

looker-on: 8 audience, beholder **9** bystander, spectator

lookout: 5 scout, watch, worry **6** conner, sentry **7** concern, palaver **8** observer **9** crow's nest **10** watchtower, widow's walk

looks (see also **look**): **4** face **8** features **10** attraction

loom: auk **4** brew, hulk, loon, tool **5** dobby, weave **6** appear, emerge, gather, gentle, impend, puffin, vessel **7** machine **9** guillemot, implement **10** receptacle

part: bar, lam **4** caam, leaf, reed, sley **5** easer, lathe **6** hanger, heddle **7** harness, shuttle, treadle

loon: nut, sap **4** bird, dolt, lout **5** diver, rogue, scamp, wabby **6** cobble, rascal

loony: 5 crazy **8** demented **11** harebrained

loop: eye, tab **4** ansa, coil, fold, hank, kink, knot, oese, ring **5** bight, bride, coque, curve, honda, hondo, noose, picot, terry **6** becket, billet, circle **7** circuit, curette, folding **8** doubling **11** aiguillette

loophole: out **4** muse **5** meuse, oilet **6** escape, eyelet, outlet **7** opening **8** aperture, weakness

loose: gay, lax **4** fast, floa, free, open **5** baggy, bulgy, crank, let up, loose, relax, slack, vague **6** coarse, dangly, random, unlash, wobbly **7** ease off, immoral, movable, relaxed, unbound, unleash **8** insecure, unstable, withdraw **9** desultory, dissolute, unbridled, unchecked **10** incoherent, indefinite, licentious, unattached, unconfined, unfastened **11** untrammeled **12** disconnected, uncontrolled, unrestrained **14** unconventional

loose ends: 4 dags **5** bored **7** details, tagrags **8** restless **9** fragments

loose-jointed: 5 lanky, rangy **6** clumsy, wobbly **7** rickety **10** ramshackle

loosen: pry **4** ease, free, undo **5** relax, untie **7** slacken **8** liberate, unfasten **9** disengage, extricate **10** talk freely **11** disentangle

loot: rob, sum **4** sack, swag **5** booty, money, spoil, strip **6** pilfer, ravage, spoils **7** pillage, plunder

receipt of: **9** theftbote

lop: bob, cut, dod **4** clip, flop, hang, sned(Sc.), snip, trim **5** droop, prune, slice **6** dangle **7** pendant, pendent **8** truncate

lope: job **4** gait **6** canter **7** dogtrot

lopper: 4 clot **6** curdle **7** clabber **9** coagulate

lopsided: 4 alop **6** uneven **7** crooked **10** unbalanced

loquacious: 5 gabby **6** verbal **7** prating **8** cackling **9** garrulous, talkative **10** babblative, chattering

loquacity: 9 garrulity **13** talkativeness

lord: aga **4** agha, earl, peer, rule, tsar **5** liege, ruler **6** domine, master, prince **7** marquis, vavasor **8** domineer, governor, nobleman, seigneur, suzerain, vavasour, viscount **9** dominator

attendant: **5** thane

Lord have mercy upon us: 8 response **10** invocation **12** Kyrie eleison

Lord High Executioner: 4 Koko

Lord Jim author: 6 Conrad

Lord's Prayer: 11 Paternoster

lordly: 5 grand, noble, proud **6** uppish **7** haughty **8** arrogant, despotic **9** imperious, masterful **10** tyrannical **11** dictatorial, domineering, magisterial, overbearing

lordship: 4 rule **7** dynasty **8** dominion **10** allegiance

lore: 4 lear, myth **6** advice, wisdom **7** counsel **8** learning **9** erudition, knowledge, tradition **11** instruction

Lorelei: 5 siren 9 temptress 11 femme fatale
poet: 5 Heine
lorgnette: 8 eyeglass 10 opera glass
lorica: 5 shell 7 cuirass 8 corselet
lorikeet: 6 parrot
loriot: 6 oriole
loris: 5 lemur
lorn: 5 alone 6 bereft 7 forlorn 8 desolate, forsaken, lonesome 9 abandoned
Lorna Doone: 5 novel
author: 9 Blackmore
Lorraine: *capital:* 4 Metz
river: 4 Saar
lose: 4 amit, fail, miss 5 waste 6 defeat, mislay 7 forfeit 9 dissipate, fail to win
losel: bum 6 loafer 10 ne'er-do-well
loss: 4 cost, leak, ruin, toll 5 price, waste 6 damage, damnum, defeat, injury, ullage 7 expense, failure 8 amission, decrease 9 decrement, detriment, privation 10 affliction, bankruptcy 11 bereavement, deperdition, deprivation, destruction
lost: 4 gone, lorn 5 perdu(F.) 6 absent, hidden, ruined, wasted 7 forlorn, mislaid, strayed 8 absorbed, confused, defeated, estrayed, obscured, prodigal 9 abandoned, forfeited, perplexed, reprobate, subverted 10 abstracted, bewildered, dissipated, overthrown 11 preoccupied 13 irreclaimable
Lost Horizon: *author:* 6 Hilton
land: 9 Shangri-La
lot: hap 4 dole, doom, fate, land, luck, much, plat, plot 5 batch, field, grist, group, share, weird 6 amount, bundle, chance, divide, hazard, parcel 7 destiny, fortune, portion 8 caboodle, quantity 9 allotment, apportion, great deal 13 apportionment
appointment by: 9 sortition
miscellaneous: 6 fardel, job lot
Lot: *father:* 5 Haran
grandson: 7 Moabite
nephew: 7 Abraham
place of flight: 5 Sodom
sister: 6 Milcah
son: 4 Moab 5 Ammon
lotion: 4 balm, wash 8 ablution, linament
lots: 4 gobs 5 scads 6 plenty
lottery: 6 raffle 7 drawing 10 sweepstake
lotto: 4 keno 5 bingo, keeno
lotus, lotos: 7 nelumbo 10 chinquapin
lotus bird: 6 jacana
lotus-eater: 7 dreamer
lotus tree: 4 sadr 9 persimmon
loud: 5 gaudy, heavy, noisy, showy, vivid 6 coarse, flashy, vulgar 7 blatant, clamant, obvious, raucous 8 emphatic, strepent, vehement 9 clamorous, insistent, turbulent, unrefined 10 blustering, boisterous, stentorian, tumultuous,

vociferous 11 ear-piercing, thersitical 12 obstreperous
lough: sea 4 lake, loch, pool 5 water
Louisiana:
bird: 7 pelican
capital: 10 Baton Rouge
city: 7 Augusta 9 Biddeford 10 New Orleans, Shreveport
dialect: 6 creole
festival: 9 Mardi Gras
flower: 8 magnolia
mountain: 8 Driskill
native: 5 Cajun 6 Creole 7 Acadian
nickname: 6 Creole 7 Pelican
parish: 4 Winn 5 Allen, Caddo, Union 6 Acadia, De Soto, Iberia, Sabine, Tensas, Vernon
tree: 11 bald cypress
university: LSU 6 Tulane
lounge: 4 idle, loaf, loll, sofa 5 bange, couch, divan, relax 6 froust, frowst, loiter
loup: 4 flee, jump, leap
louse: nit 5 aphid, aphis 6 cootie, slater
lousy: 5 dirty 9 pedicular 10 pediculous
lout: bow, oaf 4 bend, boor, clod, coof, dolt, fool, gaum, gawk, hulk 5 clown, cuddy, stoop, yahoo, yokel 6 curtsy, lubber 7 bumpkin, grobian, palooka 10 clodhopper
loutish: 4 rude 5 crude 6 clumsy, gauche(F.), stupid 7 awkward
lovable, loveable: 4 dear 7 amative, amiable 8 adorable, dovelike 9 endearing 11 captivating, enthralling
love: gra(Ir.), loe(Sc.), 4 dear, dote, like 5 adore, aloha, amore(It.), amour(F.), Cupid, fancy, liebe(G.), lover 6 enamor 7 charity, embrace, idolize 8 fondness, goodwill, idolatry 9 adoration, affection 10 attachment, sweetheart 11 inclination
god of: 4 Amor, Ares, Eros, Frey, Kama 5 Bhaga, Cupid
goddess of: 5 Athor, Freya, Venus 6 Freyja, Hathor, Ishtar 9 Aphrodite
science of: 9 erotology
token of: 6 amoret
love apple: 6 tomato
love feast: 5 agape 7 banquet 9 gathering
love knot: 6 amoret
love potion: 5 charm 7 philter, philtre 11 aphrodisiac
love story: 7 romance
lovebird: 6 parrot
loveliness: 6 beauty 11 pulchritude
lovelock: 4 curl 5 tress 12 heartbreaker
lovely: 5 sweet 6 loving, tender 7 amiable, amorous, angelic 8 adorable, angelina, charming, graceful 9 beautiful 10 attractive
lover: ami(F.), gra(Ir.) 4 beau, chap 5

amant(F.), leman, Romeo **6** adorer, amadis, amante(F.), bon ami(F.) **7** admirer, amateur(F.), amorist, amoroso(It.), Don Juan, gallant **8** belamour, Lothario **9** bonne amie(F.), enamorata (It.) **10** dilettante, innamorata(It.), innamorato(It.), sweetheart **11** philanderer

meeting place: **5** tryst

patron saint: **9** Valentine

rustic: **7** Celadon

lovesick: 6 pining **7** longing **11** languishing

loving: 4 fond **6** erotic, lovely **7** adorant, amative, amatory, amorous, devoted **9** affecting **12** affectionate

loving cup: tyg **5** prize **6** trophy

low: bas(F.), moo **4** base, bass, blue, deep, hill, mean, neap, weak **5** dirty, gross, snide **6** bellow, coarse, common, earthy, feeble, filthy, humble, humbly, slight, sordid, vulgar **7** bestial, cut-rate, ignoble, plebian, shallow, slavish **8** dejected, off-color **9** depressed, earthbred **10** melancholy **11** undignified, unfavorable **12** contemptible, disreputable

lowan: 4 bird **6** leipoa, mallee

Low Country: 7 Belgium, Holland **10** Luxembourg **11** Netherlands

low-lived: 4 mean **10** despicable **12** contemptible

low-necked: 9 decollete

low tide: ebb **4** neap

lowbred: 5 crude **6** coarse, vulgar **11** ill-mannered

lower: 4 alow, bate, drop, sink, vail **5** abase, abate, baser, below, decry, demit, frown, glare, scowl, under **6** bemean, debase, deepen, demean, derate, glower, humble, lessen, meaner, nether, reduce **7** beneath, degrade, depress, descend, subside **8** diminish, downward, inferior, mark down **9** disparage **10** depreciate, nethermore

lowering: 4 dark **5** heavy **6** beetle, cloudy, gloomy, lowery, sullen **8** overcast **11** threatening

lowest: 5 least, nadir **6** bottom **7** bedrock **10** nethermost

lowing (see also **low**): **7** mugient **9** bellowing

lowland: 4 flat, holm, spit, vale **5** terai(Ind.) **6** valley **7** bottoms

Lowlander (see also **Scotland**): **4** Scot **9** Sassenach

language: **6** Lallan **7** Lalland

lowly: 4 base, mean, meek **6** humble, modest **7** ignoble **8** ordinary **11** commonplace **12** unpretending **13** unpretentious

lox: 6 salmon

loy: 4 tool **5** slick, spade

loyal: 4 feal, firm, leal, true **5** liege, pious **6** stanch **7** devoted, staunch **8** constant, faithful

loyalty: 6 homage **10** allegiance **12** faithfulness

Loyalty island: Uea **4** Lifu, Uvea

Loyolite: 6 Jesuit

lozenge: 4 pill **5** candy **6** jujube, pastil, tablet, troche **7** diamond **8** pastille **9** cough drop

lubber: oaf **4** boor, gawk, lout **5** churl, drone, idler **6** sailor **8** landsman

lubricate: oil **4** dope **6** grease **7** moisten

lubricious: 4 lewd **6** shifty, tricky, wanton **7** elusive **8** slippery, unstable **9** lecherous, salacious **10** lascivious

luce: 4 pike

lucent: 5 clear, lucid **6** bright **7** shining **11** translucent, transparent

lucerne, lucern: 7 alfalfa

lucid: 4 sane **5** clear **6** bright, lucent **7** crystal, shining **8** luminous, pellucid, rational **11** clear-headed, resplendent, translucent

lucidity: 6 sanity **7** clarity

Lucifer: 5 devil, Satan

luck: hap, lot, ure **4** cess, eure, fate **5** deuce **6** chance, hansel **7** ambsace, fortune, handsel, success **8** fortuity **9** mischance, advantage **11** good fortune, prosperity

bringer: **5** Jonah **6** clover, mascot **9** horseshoe **10** rabbit-foot

stroke of: **5** fluke

token for: **5** charm **6** amulet, mascot **7** periapt **8** talisman **9** horseshoe

lucky: 5 canny, happy, sonsy **6** sonsie **8** gracious **9** fortunate **10** propitious, prosperous, successful **12** providential

lucrative: 6 paying **7** gainful **10** beneficial, productive, profitable **12** remunerative

lucre: 4 gain, loot, pelf **5** booty, money **6** profit, riches, wealth

ludicrous: 5 antic, awful, comic, droll, funny **6** absurd **7** comical, foolish, risible **8** farcical **9** burlesque, laughable **10** ridiculous

lug: box, ear **4** drag, draw, pull, tote, worm, haul **5** carry **10** projection

luggage: 4 bags **7** baggage **9** suitcases

lugubrious: sad **6** dismal **7** doleful **8** mournful

lukewarm: 5 tepid

lull: 4 calm, hush, rock **5** allay, quiet, still **6** pacify, soothe **7** compose **8** calmness, mitigate **9** cessation **11** tranquilize

lullaby: 4 song **5** baloo, balow(Sc.) **10** cradlesong

lumber: 4 raff, wood **6** refuse, timber

lumbering: 7 awkward **11** heavy footed

lumberman: 6 logger, sawyer, scorer **10** lumberjack

boot: pac
hook: **5** peavy **6** peavey
sled: **4** tode **7** travois **8** travoise
luminary: sun, VIP **4** lion, name, star **5** light **7** notable **12** illumination, intellectual
luminous: 5 clear, lucid **6** bright **7** shining **9** brilliant **11** illuminated, transparent **14** phosphorescent
lummox: 4 boor, lout **5** yahoo **7** bumpkin, bungler
lump: bat, cob, dab, dad, dot, gob, nub, wad **4** beat, blob, burl, cake, clog, clot, daud, heap, hump, hunk, knob, knot, mass **5** bulge, claut, clump, clunk, hunch, wedge **6** dollop, gobbet, nodule, nugget **8** swelling **12** protuberance
lumpfish: 6 paddle
lumpish: 4 dull **5** heavy, inert **6** stodgy, stupid **8** sluggish **9** shapeless
lumpy: 5 heavy, rough **6** choppy, clumsy
lunacy: 5 folly, mania **7** madness **8** delirium, insanity **9** craziness **11** derangement
lunar (see also **moon**): **6** lunate **8** crescent **9** satellite
lunatic: mad **6** insane, madman **7** frantic **8** demoniac **9** bedlamite **10** moonstruck
lune: 5 leash **8** crescent
lung: 5 organ
disease: **11** anthracosis
having: **9** pulmonate
sound: **4** rale
lunge: jab **4** foin, leap, stab **5** barge, longe, lurch, pitch **6** plunge, thrust
lupine: 6 fierce **7** wolfish **8** ravenous, wolflike
lurch: rob **4** jolt, reel, roll **5** barge, cheat, fraud, lunge, pitch, steal, trick **6** careen, career, swerve **7** stagger, stumble
lure: 4 bait, draw, trap **5** decoy, snare, tempt **6** allure, entice, seduce **7** attract, beguile, pitfall **8** inveigle **10** allurement, attraction, enticement
lurer: 4 bait **5** siren **7** trapper
lurid: wan **4** pale **5** gaudy, livid **6** dismal, gloomy **7** ghastly, hideous **8** gruesome, shocking, terrible **9** startling **11** sensational
lurk: 4 hide **5** skulk, slink, sneak **6** ambush **9** lie in wait
luscious: 4 rich, ripe **5** sweet **6** creamy **7** cloying **8** delicate **9** delicious **10** voluptuous
lush: sot **4** rich, soft **5** drunk **6** limber, mellow **7** profuse **9** alcoholic, luxuriant, succulent **11** intoxicated
lusory: 7 playful **8** sportive
lust: 6 desire, liking **7** passion **8** appetite, cupidity **11** inclination **12** sexual desire

luster, lustre: 4 cave, naif **5** sheen, shine, water **6** polish **7** glister **8** radiance, schiller, splendor **10** brightness, brilliance **11** distinction, iridescence
lusterless: mat, wan **4** dead, dull **5** faded, fishy **6** gloomy **9** tarnished
lustful: hot **4** gamy lewd **5** cadgy **7** fulsome, rammish **9** lecherous, salacious
lustrous: 5 nitid **6** bright, glossy, orient **7** radiant **8** nitidous **9** brilliant **11** illustrious, transparent
lusty: 4 cant **5** crank, frack, frank, freck, hardy **6** cranky, gawsie, hearty, robust, strong, sturdy **8** bouncing, vigorous
lute: tar **4** clay, ring **6** cement **7** dyphone **10** instrument
relative of: **8** mandolin
luxe: 8 elegance, richness
Luxembourg: *capital:* **10** Luxembourg
measure: **5** fuder
monetary unit: **5** franc
river: **7** Moselle
luxuriant: 4 lush, rank, rich **5** frank **6** lavish **7** fertile, opulent, profuse, teeming **8** prolific **9** exuberant **10** voluptuous
luxuriate: 4 bask, riot **5** revel **6** wallow
luxurious: 4 posh, rich **5** gaudy **6** costly **7** elegant, opulent **8** gorgeous, sensuous **9** sumptuous **11** comfortable, extravagant
luxury: 6 frills **7** amenity, comfort **8** delicacy, grandeur
lover of: **8** Sybarite
Luzon: *city:* **5** Gapan **6** Ilagan, Manila **10** Cabanatuan
dialect: **6** Itaves
mountain: Iba
people: Ata, Ita **4** Aeta, Atta **5** Tagal **6** Aripas, Arupas, Igorot, Isinay, Itaneg **7** Igorote, Italone, Kalinga, Kankana, Tagalog
seaport: **6** Aparri, Manila
volcano: **5** Mayon
lyam: 5 leash **10** bloodhound
lycanthrope: 8 werewolf
lycee: 6 lyceum, school
lyceum: 11 meeting hall
Lydia: *capital:* **6** Sardis
king: **5** Gyges **7** Croesus
river: **8** Pactolus
lye: 6 potash **7** caustic **8** lixivium
lying: 4 flat **5** awald, awalt, false, prone **6** supine **8** couchant **9** dishonest, mendacity **10** pseudology
lying-in: 11 confinement **12** accouchement
lymph: sap **5** chyle, water **6** plasma, spring
lynch: 4 hang **6** murder **7** execute
Lynette's knight: 6 Gareth
lynx: cat **5** pishu **6** bobcat, lucern **7** cara-

cal **8** carcajou **9** catamount
Lyra star: 4 Vega
lyrate: 9 spatulate
lyre: 4 asor, harp **6** kissar, trigon **7** cithara, kithara, testudo
lye turtle: 11 leatherback
lyric: lai, lay, ode **4** alba, odic, poem **5** epode, gazel, melic, verse **6** ghazel, poetic, rondel **7** cancion, canzone(It.), descort, madrigal, rondeau **9** dithyramb
Muse: **5** Erato **8** Polymnia **10** Polyhymnia
lyrical: 6 epodic **7** sestina
lyrichord: 11 harpsichord
lysogenic: 9 temperate **11** not virulent
lyssa: 6 rabies **11** hydrophobia

M

Maacah: *father:* **6** Talmai **7** Absalom
husband: **5** David **8** Rehoboam
son: Asa **5** Hanan **6** Abijah **7** Absalom
mabolo: 4 plum **7** camagon
macabre: 4 eery, grim **5** eerie **7** ghastly **8** grewsome, gruesome, horrible **9** deathlike
macaca: 5 lemur **6** monkey
macadam: tar **8** pavement
macaque: 4 bruh **6** monkey, rhesus
macaw: ara **4** arra, bird **5** arara **6** parrot **7** maracan **8** aracanga, ararauna, cockatoo
Macbeth: *character:* **5** Angus **6** Banquo
slayer: **7** Macduff
title: **5** Thane
victim: **6** Banquo, Duncan
maccaboy: 5 snuff
mace: dod, rod **4** club, maul, rush **5** spice, staff **6** mallet **7** swindle
bearer: **6** beadle
royal: **7** scepter, sceptre
Macedonia:
capital: **6** Skopje
king: **6** Philip **9** Alexander
last king: **7** Perseus
mountain: **5** Athos **7** Olympus **8** Olympiad
people: **6** Greeks **8** Serbians **9** Albanians **10** Bulgarians
statesman: **9** Antipater
macerate: ret **4** soak **5** steep **8** grow thin
machete: 4 bolo, fish **5** blade, knife **6** guitar, tarpon
Machiavellian: 4 wily **6** crafty **7** cunning **8** guileful **9** deceitful **11** treacherous
Machiavelli's book: 6 Prince **8** Mandrake

machila: 7 hammock
machination: 4 plan, plot **5** cabal **6** scheme **8** artifice, intrigue **10** conspiracy **11** contrivance
machine: car **4** auto **5** robot **6** device, engine **7** vehicle **9** apparatus, appliance, automatic, automaton, mechanism **10** automobile **11** contrivance, machination, stereotyped **12** organization, standardized
hydraulic: **9** telemotor
part: cam **5** rotor, wheel **6** piston, stator, tappet
machine gun: 4 Sten **5** Maxim **7** Gatling **9** Hotchkiss **10** chatterbox
place: **4** nest
machismo: 7 manhood, **14** masculine pride
macilent: 4 lean, thin **9** emaciated
mackerel: 4 scad **5** akule, atule, tunny **7** escolar, tassard **8** hardhead
genus: **7** scomber
net: **7** spiller
young: **5** spike **6** tinker **7** blinker
mackerel bird: 7 wryneck **9** kittiwake
mackle: See **macula**
macle: 7 crystal **11** chiastolite
macrobiotic: 4 diet
macula: 4 blot, blur, spot **5** stain **6** blotch, mackle, macule **7** blemish
maculate: 6 impure **7** defiled **8** speckled, unchaste **10** besmirched
mad: 4 gite, gyte, hute(Sc.) **5** angry, crazy, folle, irate, rabid, vexed **6** frenzy, insane, unwise **7** enraged, foolish, frantic, furious **8** demented, frenetic, incensed, maniacal **9** desperate, fanatical, hilarious, phrenetic, psychotic **10** distracted,

distraught, infatuated, infuriated **11** fantastical, mentally ill **12** arreptitious, unreasonable

Madagascar: *animal:* **6** aye-aye, tanrec, tenrec, **7** tendrac

capital: **12** Antananarivo

city: **7** Mojanga **8** Tamatave **10** Tananarive, Tananarivo

civet: **7** fossane

garment: **5** lamba

island group: **7** Aldabra

language: **8** Malagasy

lemur: **5** avahi, indri **6** aye-aye **9** babacoote

measure: **7** gantang

monetary unit: **5** franc

native: **4** Hova **6** Merina **8** Sakalava

palm: **6** riffia

people: **4** Hova

tree: **11** antankarana

tribe: **4** Bara **5** Hovas **8** Betsileo, Malagasy, Sakalava **13** Betsimasaraka

madam, madame: Mme., Mrs. **4** bawd, lady **5** donna, hussy, woman, title, wench **6** senora **8** mistress **9** courtesan

madcap: **4** wild **7** hotspur **8** reckless **9** impulsive

madder: aal **7** munjeet **8** dyestuff

family: **9** rubiaceae

made: **10** artificial

to-order: **6** custom **11** custom built

up: **8** invented **10** fabricated

Madeira: *capital:* **7** Funchal

wine: **4** bual **5** tinta, tinto **7** malmsey, sercial **8** verdelho

mademoiselle: **4** miss

madhouse: **5** chaos **6** asylum, bedlam **8** bughouse **12** insane asylum

madid: wet **5** moist

madman: **6** maniac **7** furioso, lunatic **8** frenetic **9** phrenetic, psychotic

madness: ire **4** fury **5** folly, furor, mania **6** bedlam, frenzy, lunacy, rabies **7** dewanee, ecstasy, widdrim **8** delirium, dementia, insanity **9** amazement, furiosity, nonsomania, phrenetic **10** great folly **11** derangement

Madras: *present name:* **9** Tamil Nadu

madrepore: **5** coral **6** fossil

Madrid promenade: **5** Prado

madrigal: ode **4** glee, poem **5** lyric **6** verses **8** part-song

Maecenas: **6** patron **10** benefactor

maelstrom: **4** eddy **5** swirl **7** current, turmoil **9** whirlpool

maenad: **9** bacchante

maestro: **6** master **7** teacher **8** composer **9** conductor **10** bandleader **11** choirmaster **13** kapellmeister

di-cappela: **11** choirmaster **13** kapellmeister

maffle: **6** muddle, mumble **7** confuse, stammer, **8** bewilder, squander

mafia: **8** brigands **10** underworld

Magadha king: **9** Bimbisara **10** Ajatasatru

magadis: **5** flute **9** monochord

magazine: **4** pulp **5** depot **7** almacen, arsenal, chamber, journal **9** ephemeris, reservoir, warehouse **10** periodical, repository, storehouse **11** armamentary

magenta: dye **7** fuchsia

maggot: bug **4** grub, mawk, whim **5** larva, mathe **6** gentle, notion **7** caprice **12** eccentricity

magi: **5** Sages **6** Gaspar **8** Melchior **9** Balthasar

gift of: **4** gold **5** myrrh **12** frankincense

magic: art **4** rune **5** fairy, obeah, spell, turgy **6** glamor, voodoo **7** glamour, gramary, sorcery, theurgy **8** brujeria(Sp.), gramarye, wizardry **9** deception, diablerie **10** necromancy, witchcraft **11** conjuration, enchantment, legerdemain, thaumaturgy **12** invultuation

act of: **11** conjuration

lantern: **11** epidiascope **12** stereopticon

perform: hex **6** sorcer **7** conjure

pert. to: **6** goetic

staff: **4** wand **7** rhabdos **8** caduceus

symbol: **5** charm **6** caract **8** pentacle

tree: **13** polemoniaceae

word: **5** selah **6** presto, sesame, shelah **11** abracadabra

Magic Mountain: *author:* **4** Mann

character: **7** Castorp

magical: **6** occult **8** charming **10** bewitching **11** necromantic

magician: **4** mage, magi **5** magus **6** Merlin, wabeno, wizard **7** juggler **8** conjurer, conjuror, mandrake, sorcerer **9** archimage, charlatan, enchanter **11** entertainer, medicine man, necromancer, thaumaturge **13** thaumaturgist **15** prestidigitator

assistant: **6** famuli(pl.) **7** famulus

manual: **8** grimoire

motion: **4** pass

magirist: **4** cook

magisterial: **5** lofty, proud **6** august, lordly **7** haughty, stately **8** arrogant, dogmatic **9** dignified, imperious, masterful **11** dictatorial, domineering, overbearing **13** authoritative

magistrate: **4** beak, doge **5** edile, judge **6** alcade, alcaid, archon, bailie, bailli, syndic **7** alcaide, alcalde, bailiff, burgess, podesta(It.) **8** alderman, governor, mittimus, official **11** burgomaster

orders: **4** acta(pl.) **5** actum

magma: **5** dregs **8** sediment

basalt: **10** limburgite, molten rock

magnanimous: big **4** free **5** lofty, noble **6**
heroic **7** exalted, liberal **8** generous **9**
honorable, unselfish, unstinted **10**
high-minded, high-souled **13** disinterested

magnate: **4** lord **5** baron, mogul, noble **6**
bashaw, tycoon **7** grandee, rich man **10**
clarissimo **11** millionaire

magnesian limestone: **8** dolomite

magnesium: *silicate:* **4** talc
sulfate: **7** loweite

magnet: **7** terella **8** solenoid, terrella **9**
loadstone, lodestone
end: **4** pole
pole: red
type of: bar **9** horseshoe

magnetic: **5** polar **10** attractive, electrical
unit: **5** weber

magnetize: **4** lure **5** charm **7** attract **9**
captivate

magnificence: **4** pomp **8** grandeur, splendor **13** sumptuousness

magnificent: **4** rial, rich **5** grand, great,
noble, regal **6** august, lavish **7** exalted,
stately, sublime **8** glorious, gorgeous,
palatial, splendid, striking **9** beautiful,
excellent, sumptuous **10** munificent

magnify: **4** laud **5** exalt **7** enhance, enlarge greaten **8** increase **9** aggravate,
overstate **10** exaggerate

magniloquent: **6** turgid **8** boastful **9**
bombastic **12** ostentatious **13** grandiloquent

magnitude: **4** bulk, mass, size **6** extent **7**
bigness **9** dimension, greatness

magnolia: **5** yulan

Magnolia State: **11** Mississippi

magnum: **6** bottle

magnum opus: **4** work **11** achievement

magot: ape **6** figure

magpie: **4** bird, pica, piet, piot, pyat **6**
gabber, prater **9** chatterer, haggister
diver: **4** smew
shrike: **7** tanager

magsman: **8** swindler

maguari: **5** stork

maguey: **4** aloe **5** agave, fiber, plant **7**
cantala

magus: **4** magi **6** wizard **7** charmer **8** magician

Magyar: **6** Ugrian **9** Hungarian

maha: **4** deer **6** langur, sambar

mahajan: **11** moneylender

mahala: **5** squaw

mahogany: **4** toon **6** acajou, totara **7** albarco, gunnung **8** bangalay **9** cailcedra
11 reddish brown

maholi: **5** lemur

Mahomet: See **Mohammed**

Mahometan: See **Muslim**

Mahound: **5** devil

mahout: **6** driver, keeper **14** elephant
driver

Maia: **12** Earth Goddess
father: **5** Atlas
sisters: **8** Pleiades
son: **6** Hermes **7** Mercury

maid: **4** ayah, girl, help, lass **5** bonne,
woman **6** damsel, maiden, slavey, virgin
7 Abigail, ancilla, colleen, servant **8** domestic, suivante **9** attendant, camer-
iera, tirewoman
changed to spider: **7** Arachne
mythical: **5** nymph

Maid of Astolat: **6** Elaine

Maid of Orleans: **7** Pucelle **9** Joan of Arc

maiden: deb, new **4** girl, jill, lass **5**
nymph, sylph **6** damsel **7** damosel,
damozel, untried **8** damozell **9** damo-
sella, damoysell, debutante

maiden duck: **8** shoveler

maiden name: nee

maidenhair: **4** fern **8** adiantum
tree: **6** ginkgo

maidenly: **6** gentle, modest, virgin

mail: bag **4** post, send, ship **5** armor **6**
wallet **8** dispatch
boat: **6** packet

maim: **4** hurt **6** mangle **7** cripple, disable
8 mutilate **9** dismember

main: sea **4** duct, high, pipe **5** chief, first,
grand, ocean, prime **7** capital, conduct,
conduit, leading, purpose **8** foremost **9**
principal

Main Street author: **5** Lewis

Maine: *capital:* **7** Augusta
city: **4** Bath **6** Bangor **8** Lewiston, Portland **9** Biddeford, Skowhegan
county: **5** Waldo **9** Penobscot **10** Cumberland
lake: **5** Moose **6** Sebago **8** Rangeley **9**
Moosehead
motto: **6** Dirigo (I direct)
mountain: **5** Kineo **7** Bigelow **8** Cadillac,
Katahdin
nickname: **6** Lumber **8** Pine Tree
port: **6** Bangor **8** Portland
river: **4** Saco **8** Kennebec
state bird: **9** chicadee
state flower: **8** pinecone
state tree: **4** pine

mainland: **8** fastland **9** continent

mainsheet: **4** rope

mainstay: key **7** support

maintain: **4** avow, bear, fend, hold, keep **5**
argue, claim **6** affirm, allege, assert,
avouch, defend, retain, uphold **7** bolster, contend, declare, espouse, justify,
support, sustain **8** conserve, preserve **9**
vindicate **10** provide for
again: **8** reassert

maintainable: **7** tenable

maintenance: 5 batta 6 upkeep 7 alimony, prebend 10 livelihood

maison: 5 house
de sante: 6 asylum 8 hospital 10 sanatorium

maize: 4 corn, samp 5 grain 7 mealies
bread: 4 piki
genus: Zea

majestic: 5 grand, lofty, noble, regal, royal 6 august, kingly 7 leonine, stately, sublime 8 elevated, imperial, splendid 9 dignified, sovereign 11 magnificent

major: big 5 chief 7 capital, greater, officer 8 superior 9 principal
music: dur

majordomo: 6 butler 7 bailiff, manager, servant, steward 9 seneschal

Majorca city: 5 Palma

majority: age 4 body, more, most 6 quorum 7 greater

make: cut, gar(Sc.) 4 coin, form 5 build, force, frame, shape 6 compel, create, invent, render 7 compose, confect, fashion, prepare, produce 8 contrive, generate 9 construct, fabricate 11 manufacture

make-believe: 4 sham 5 feign, magic 7 charade, feigned, fiction, pretend 8 pretense

make do: eke 9 improvise

make fun of: rib 5 scoff 8 ridicule

make known: 6 impart, reveal 7 divulge, publish, uncover 8 disclose, discover, proclaim 9 advertise, publicize

make off: fly, run 4 bolt, flee 7 abscond, run away

make out: see 4 fare 7 succeed 8 copulate

make over: 4 redo 6 revamp 9 refashion

make up: 6 create, devise 7 arrange, compose, typeset 8 assemble, complete, cosmetic 9 fabricate, improvise

make up for: 5 atone 10 compensate

maker: 4 doer 6 author, factor 7 creator 8 declarer, inventor 9 architect 10 originator 12 manufacturer

makeshift: 4 rude 8 resource 9 temporary

mal: bad 4 evil
de mar: 11 seasickness
du pays: 12 homesickness

Malabar: *black:* 5 ochna
canoe: 5 tonee
monkey: 8 wanderoo
palm: 7 talipot
people: 4 Nair

malacca: 4 cane 5 stick

malachite: 4 bice 7 azurite, mineral

maladive: ill 4 sick 6 feeble, sickly, unwell 9 unhealthy

maladroit: 6 clumsy 7 awkward, unhandy 8 bungling, inexpert

malady (see also **disease**)**:** 7 ailment, illness 8 disorder, sickness 9 affection, complaint, distemper 10 affliction 13 indisposition

malanders: 6 eczema

malapropism: 8 solecism, word play 11 error in speech

malapropos: 8 untimely, 10 irrelevant 11 inexpedient, inopportune

malar: 6 zygoma 9 cheek-bone

malaria: 4 agie, ague 5 chill, fever, miasm 6 miasma
antidote: 7 quinine
carrier: 8 mosquito 9 anopheles

malarkey: 6 drivel 8 nonsense

Malawi: *capital:* 8 Lilongwe
export: tea 7 tobacco
former name: 9 Nyasaland
monetary unit: 6 kwacha

malaxate: 5 knead

Malaysia: *almond:* 6 kanari
ape: lar
archipelago: See *island* below
boat: 4 proa 5 praam, prahu 6 praham 7 cougnar
buffalo: 7 carabao 8 seladang
capital: 11 Kuala Lumpur
Christian: 7 Ilokano
condiment: 6 sambal, sambei 7 semball
crane: 5 sarus
disease: 4 amok, lata 5 amuck, latah
export: tin 6 rubber, timber 7 palm oil
form of address: 4 tuan
fruit: 8 rambutan
garment: 6 sarong
island: Aru, Goa, Kei, Oma 4 Bali, Buru, Gaga, Java, Sulu 5 Ambon, Arroe, Arrou, Banca, Banda, Buton, Ceram, Misol, Sangi, Sumba, Timor 6 Boefon, Boeroe, Borneo, Flores, Jilolo, Lombik, Madura, Musool, Sangir, Soemba, Talaur, Waigeu
isthmus: Kra
jacket: 4 baju
knife: 4 cris, kris 5 crise 6 crease, creese, kreese, parang
language: 5 Malay 7 Chinese, English, Tagalog
mammal: 10 chevrotain
measure: 4 tael, wang
monetary unit: 7 ringgit
mountain: 6 Gunong, Gunung
musical instrument: 7 anklong
ox: 5 tsine 7 banteng
palm: 4 ejoo, sago 5 areng 6 arenga, gebang, gomuti, nibong, nibung 7 talipot
parrot: 4 lory 6 lories
people: Ata 5 Bajau, Tagal 6 Aripas, Semang 7 Bisayan, Tagalog, Visayan
pepper: 4 siri 5 sirih
pewter: 4 trah
rice field: 5 sawah
state: 5 Kedah, Perak 6 Johore 7 Malacca

title: **4** tuan

town: **7** Malacca

tree (see also *palm* above): **4** upas **5** kapur, niepa, terap **6** durian, durion

ungulate: **5** tapir

malconformation: 9 imperfect **16** disproportionate

malcontent: reb **5** rebel **6** uneasy **8** agitator, Frondeur **10** discontent, rebellious **12** discontented, dissatisfied

Maldives: 13 Pacific atolls

capital: **4** Male

former name: **14** Maldive Islands

language: **6** Divehi

monetary unit: **5** rupee

people: **7** Islamic

religion: **5** Islam

male: man, mas **4** gent **5** manly **7** mankind, manlike, mannish **9** masculine

animal: tom **4** buck, bull, hart, jack, stag, stud **8** stallion

figure: **7** telamon

gelded: **4** galt **5** steer **6** eunuch **7** gelding

malediction: ban **5** curse **7** malison, slander **8** anathema, evil talk **9** blasphemy **11** imprecation **12** denunciation

malefactor: 5 felon **7** convict, culprit **8** criminal, evildoer, offender **9** wrongdoer

malefic: 4 evil **7** harmful, hurtful **11** mischievous

malevolence: 4 evil, hate **5** pique, spite **6** enmity, hatred, malice, rancor **8** ferocity **9** animosity, hostility, malicious, malignity **10** bitterness

malfeasance: 5 crime, wrong **8** trespass **11** delinquency

malheur: 10 misfortune

Mali: *ancient city:* **8** Timbuktu

capital: **6** Bamako

monetary unit: **5** franc

malice: 5 pique, spite **6** enmity **7** ill will **9** animosity **13** maliciousness

malicious: 4 evil **5** catty, depit **6** bitter **7** heinous **8** sinister, spiteful **9** felonious, green-eyed, malignant, rancorous, resentful **10** calumnious, despiteful, despiteous, malevolent **11** ill-disposed **12** cantankerous, unpropitious

action: **5** arson **8** sabotage **9** vandalism

intention: **6** animus

malign: 4 evil, foul **5** abuse, curse, libel, smear **6** bewray, defame, revile, vilify **7** asperse, baleful, blacken, deprave, hurtful, slander **8** sinister, virulent **10** calumniate, pernicious

malignant: 4 evil **6** wicked **7** hateful, heinous, hellish, noxious, vicious **8** spiteful, venomous, virulent **9** cancerous, felonious, ferocious, invidious, malicious, poisonous, rancorous **10** rebellious **11** deleterious

malikana: fee **4** duty **7** payment

maline: net **4** lace

malinger: 5 dodge, shirk, skulk

malkin: cat, mop **4** drab, hare **6** sponge **8** slattern **9** scarecrow

mall: 4 walk **5** allee, alley **6** arcade, mallet **7** meeting **9** promenade

mallard: 4 duck

genus: **4** anas

malleable: 4 soft **7** ductile, pliable

mallemuck: 6 fulmar, petrel **9** albatross

mallet: tup **4** club, mace, mall, maul, mell(Sc.) **5** gavel, madge **6** beater, beetle, driver, hammer

hatter's: **6** beater

presiding officer's: **5** gavel

wooden: **4** maul **6** beetle

mallow: 4 okra **5** plant **6** escoba **9** hollyhock

malm: 4 loam **5** brick **9** limestone

malmsey: 4 wine **5** grape **7** madeira

malnutrition: 7 cachexy, wasting **8** cachexia

malodorous: 4 rank **5** fetid **6** putrid, smelly **7** noisome **8** stinking **9** odiferous

malt: 8 diastase

beverage: ale **4** beer, brew **5** lager, stout **6** zythem

froth: **4** barm

ground: **5** grist

infusion: **4** wort

vinegar: **6** alegar

worm: **5** toper **7** tippler

Malta: *capital:* **7** Valetta **8** Valletta

hamlet: **5** casal **6** casale

island: **4** Gozo **6** Comino

measure: **4** salm **5** canna, salma **7** caffiso

monetary unit: **5** pound

weight: **4** rotl, salm **5** artal, artel, parto, ratel, salma **6** kantar

wind: **7** gregale **8** levanter

maltreat: 5 abuse **6** defile, defoul, demean, misuse, **9** humiliate

malum: 4 evil **5** wrong **7** offense

malvaceous plant: 4 okra **6** cotton, escoba, mallow **7** althaea

malvasia: 5 grape

mameluke: 5 slave **7** servant

mammal (see also **animal**): cat **5** beast, ovine, swine **6** bovine, equine, feline, monkey, rodent **7** primate **8** edentate, ruminant, ungulant **9** carnivore, marsupial

amphibious: **5** otter

antlered: elk **4** deer **5** moose **7** caribou **8** reindeer

aquatic: **4** seal **5** otter, shark, whale **6** desman, dugong, manati, rytina, walrus **7** dolphin, manatee, sea lion **8** sirenian **12** hippopotamus

aquatic order: **4** cete **7** cetacea

arboreal: ai **5** lemur, sloth **6** fisher, monkey **7** glutton, opossum, raccoon **8** banxring, kinkajou **9** orangutan

armored: **9** armadillo

badgerlike: **5** ratel **8** balisaur

bearlike: **5** panda

bovine: ox; bos, cow **4** bull, calf, zebu **5** bison, steer **7** taurine **8** longhorn

burrowing: **4** mole **6** badger, gopher, wombat **8** squirrel **9** armadillo

camellike: **7** guanaco

caprine: **4** goat

carnivorous: **9** carnivore

cetacean: see *aquatic* above

civetlike: **5** genet

coat: fur **4** hide, skin **6** pelage

cud-chewing: **8** ruminant

deerlike: **10** chevrotain

desert: **5** camel

doglike: **6** jackal

dolphinlike: **4** inia

domestic: cat, cow, dog **5** horse, sheep **6** cattle

edentate: **7** ant bear **8** anteater, pangolin, tamadau

equine: **4** colt, foal, mare **5** filly, horse, zebra **8** stallion

extinct: **6** rytina **8** mastodon

feline: cat **4** lion, lynx, puma **5** ounce, tiger **6** bobcat, cougar, jaguar, ocelot, serval **7** leopard, panther

fish-eating: **5** otter

fleet: **4** deer, hare **8** antelope

flying: bat

fur-bearing: **4** coon, mink **5** coypu, otter, sheep, skunk **6** badger, ermine, marten, martin, nutria, rabbit **7** genette, raccoon **8** squirrel

giraffelike: **5** okapi

gnawing: **6** rodent

hands different from feet: **6** bimana

hedgehog-like: **6** tenrec

herbivorous: **5** daman, tapir **6** bovine, dugong, equine **7** manatee **8** ruminant **9** orangutan **10** rhinoceros **12** hippopotamus

highest order: **7** primate

horned: ox; cow **4** gaur, goat, reem **5** bison **7** buffalo, unicorn **8** antelope, reindeer, seladang **10** rhinoceros

insectivorous: bat **4** mole **6** tenrec **7** tendrac **8** hedgehog

large: **5** whale **7** mammoth **8** behemoth, elephant, mastodon **10** rhinoceros **12** hippopotamus

largest: **5** whale

lemurine: **5** potto

leopardlike: **4** lion, lynx, pard, puma **5** tiger **6** cougar, jaguar, ocelot **7** polecat, wildcat

llamalike: **6** vicuna

lowest order: **9** marsupial **11** marsupialia

marine: see *aquatic* above

marsupial: **4** tait **5** koala **7** opossum **8** kangaroo **9** bandicoot

meat-eating: **9** carnivore

molelike: **6** desman

monkey-like: **5** lemur, loris

mouselike: **5** shrew

musteline: **5** otter, ratel

nocturnal: bat **5** hyena, lemur, ratel, tapir **6** macaco, racoon **7** raccoon, tarsier **8** kinkajou, platypus

omnivorous: hog, pig **5** swine

ovine: **5** sheep

plantigrade: **6** racoon **7** raccoon

porcine: hog, pig **4** boar **5** swine **7** peccary

pouched: **9** marsupial

raccoon-like: **5** coati

retentive: **8** elephant

rhinoceros-like: **5** tapir **14** baluchitherium

ring-tailed: **4** coon **5** lemur

ruminant: ox; yak **4** deer, goat **5** bison, camel, llama, moose, okapi, sheep, steer **6** alpaca, cattle, chewer, vicuna **7** buffalo, giraffe **8** antelope

scaled: **8** pangolin

shelled: **7** armadillo

short-tailed: **7** bobtail

skunk-like: **5** zoril

slow-moving: **5** loris, sloth

smallest: **5** shrew

snake-eating: **8** mongoose

spiny: **6** tenrec **9** porcupine

thick-skinned: **8** elephant **9** pachyderm **10** rhinoceros

toothless: **8** edentate

tropical: **5** coati, rhino **7** peccary **9** coatimodi **10** coati-mundi, rhinoceros

tusked: **6** walrus **7** mammoth **8** elephant, mastodon

ursine: **4** bear **5** panda

viverrine: **8** falanaka

vulpine: fox **4** wolf

web-footed: **5** otter

wing-footed: **6** aliped

winged: bat

zebra-like: **6** quagga

mammock: **4** tear **5** break, scrap **6** mangle

mammogram: **10** breast X ray

mammon: **6** riches, wealth

mammoth: **4** huge **5** large **8** gigantic **10** gargantuan **11** elephantine

man (see also **fellow, person**): guy, vir(L.) **4** aner(Gr.), chal, chap, homo(L.), male, mann(G.), uomo(It.), work **5** bloke, chiel, guard, homme(F.), human, valet **6** andros(Gr.), chield, hombre(Sp.), mensch(Yid.) **7** counter, fortify, homines(L.pl.), husband, laborer, mankind, operate **8** creature **9** anthropos(Gr.)

aged: vet **4** cuff, sire **5** elder, senex(L.), uncle **6** gaffer, geezer, stager **7** grandpa, starets(Russ.) **8** grandpop, old-timer **9** grandsire, graybeard, patriarch **10** golden-ager, Methuselah **11** grandfather **12** octogenarian

bad-tempered: **6** bodach **10** curmudgeon

bald: **9** pilgarlic **10** pillgarlic

big: cob

brass: **5** Talos

brave: **4** hero, lion

castrated: **6** eunuch

coarse: **5** churl, knave **7** ruffian

conceited: **7** coxcomb

cruel: **4** ogre **7** monster, ruffian, villain

cunning: **5** rogue **7** shyster **9** trickster **10** mountebank

dissolute: **4** roue

eccentric: **6** codger

effeminate: **5** fairy, sissy **9** androgyne

elderly: see *aged* above

enlisted: **6** rating, sailor **7** private, soldier **8** sargeant

fashionable: fop **4** dude **5** dandy **10** Corinthian **11** Beau Brummel **12** boulevardier

handsome: **6** Adonis

hard-pressed: Job

hardheaded: **5** boche

henpecked: **10** hoddy-doddy **11** milquetoast

impetuous: **7** hotspur

important: VIP **4** hero, name **5** nabob **7** grandee

ladies': **4** beau **5** beaux(pl.)

learned: PhD **4** bhat **6** doctor, pundit savant **7** erudite, scholar, teacher **8** literati **9** literatus, professor **11** philologist

little: **6** mankin, shrimp, squirt **8** homuncio **10** homunculus

mechanical: **5** robot **9** automaton

medicine: **6** priest, shaman

money: **9** paymaster

mother of: Eve **6** Cybele

newspaper: **6** editor **8** reporter **9** columnist **10** journalist

objectionable: oaf **4** boor **5** bully **8** wiseacre

of all work: **4** joey, mozo **8** factotum, handyman

of letters: **6** savant **11** litterateur

of straw: **6** figure **9** nonentity

of the world: **6** layman **10** secularist **11** cosmopolite **12** sophisticate

old: see *elderly* above

old-clothes: **4** poco

outdoor: **6** camper, hunter **7** athlete **9** fisherman

personifying: **15** anthropomorphic

pert. to: **5** human **6** humane, mortal

political: **7** senator **8** diplomat **9** statesman **10** ambassador **11** assemblyman

14 representative

poor: **6** pauper **7** peasant **8** beadsman, bedesman

primitive: **6** savage **8** urmensch(Yid.)

resembling: **7** android **10** anthropoid

rich: **5** Midas, nabob **6** tycoon **7** Croesus, magnate **9** plutocrat **10** capitalist **11** billionaire, millionaire

science: **9** ethnology **12** anthropology

self-important: **10** cockalorum

shadowless: **6** ascian

single: **4** stag **7** widower **8** bachelor, celibate

unattractive: **4** clod, goon, jerk, lout, rube, slob **5** yokel **6** lummox **7** fathead **10** clodhoppper

undercover: spy **5** agent **9** detective **12** investigator

unemployed: **6** batlan, batlon(Yid.)

unmarried: see *single* above

white: **6** buckra **7** cachila(P.I.) **8** paleface

wicked: **7** villain

wise: **4** sage, seer **5** solon **6** nestor **7** Solomon

worthless: bum **4** hobo **5** idler, tramp

young: boy **5** youth **6** varlet

Man of Destiny: 17 Napoleon Bonaparte

Man of Galilee: 11 Jesus Christ

man of God: 5 rabbi, saint **6** pastor, priest **7** ascetic, prelate **8** minister **12** ecclesiastic

man-of-war: 7 frigate, soldier, warrior

deck: **5** orlop

Man O'War: 5 horse **6** winner

Man Without a Country: *author:* **4** Hale

character: **5** Nolan

manacle: 4 bond, cuff, iron **5** chain, darby **6** fetter, hamper **7** confine, shackle **8** handcuff **9** restraint

manada: 4 herd **5** drove, flock

manage: man, run **4** boss, head, lead, rule **5** dight, frame, get by, guide, order, steer, wield **6** convoy, demean, direct, govern, handle **7** conduct, control, dispose, execute, husband, operate, oversee **8** contrive, dispense, engineer, maneuver **9** supervise **10** accomplish, administer, manipulate

frugally: **6** eke out **7** husband **9** economize

hard to: **6** ornery

manageable: 4 easy, tame, yare **6** docile, wieldy **7** ductile, pliable **8** flexible, maniable, workable **9** compliant, tractable **10** governable

management: 4 care **6** agency, charge, menage **7** address, economy, gestion **8** carriage, demeanor **9** demeanour, governnail, ordinance **10** enterprise, governance **11** generalship

good: **6** eutaxy

manager: 4 doer **6** gerent **7** captain, cura-

tor, foreman, handler, steward **8** director, governor **12** entrepreneur
Manasseh: *father:* **6** Joseph
grandfather: **5** Jacob
son: **4** Amon, Jair **6** Machir
manatee: 6 seacow **8** sirenian
Manchuria: *city:* **5** Hulan, Kirin **6** Harbin, Mukden **8** Shenyang **9** Niuchwang
province: **5** Jehol
river: **4** Amur, Liao, Yalu
manciple: 7 steward **8** purveyor
mandarin: 4 duck, tree **6** orange **7** Chinese **8** official **9** tangerine
residence: **5** yamen
mandate: 4 writ **5** brief, order **6** behest, charge, decree, demand, firman **7** bidding, command, precept **8** warranty **9** direction **10** commission, injunction, referendum
mandatory: 10 imperative, obligatory
mandible: jaw **4** beak **9** chelicera
part: **5** molar
mandrel: bar, rod **4** axle, ball, beam, pick **5** arbor, winch **7** spindle
mandrill: 6 baboon
manducate: eat **4** chew **9** masticate
mane: 4 hair **5** brush **6** grivna **8** encolure
manege: 4 lope, trot **13** riding academy
maneuver: 4 ploy **5** trick **6** deploy, jockey, scheme, tactic **7** echelon **8** artifice, contrive, engineer **9** evolution, stratagem **10** manipulate
aviation: **4** loop, spin **7** echelon, flathat **9** chandelle, Immelmann
military: **6** tactic
manful: See **manly**
mange: eat **4** itch, meal, scab **6** fodder, scurvy
cause of: **4** mite **6** acarid
manger: bin, box **4** crib, meal **5** stall **6** trough **7** banquet
mangle: cut, mar **4** hack, maim **5** botch, spoil **6** bruise, garble, ironer, smooth **8** calender, lacerate, mutilate **9** dismember
mango: 4 tree **5** bauno, fruit
bird: **6** oriole **11** hummingbird
fish: **9** threadfin
tree: **4** tope
mangrove: 4 tree **5** goran, shrub
mangy: 4 mean **5** seedy **6** scurvy, shabby **7** squalid **10** despicable **12** contemptible
manhandle: 4 maul **7** rough up **10** knock about, slap around
mani: 6 peanut
mania: 4 rage **5** craze, furor **6** frenzy, furore, hangup **7** madness, passion **8** delirium, idée fixe(F.) **9** cacoethes, obsession **11** derangement
buying: **9** oniomania
stealing: **11** kleptomania

maniac: 6 crazed, insane madman **7** lunatic **8** demented, deranged **9** psychotic **10** hysterical
manicure: cut **4** clip, pare, trim **6** polish
manifest: 4 open, show **5** argue, clear, index, overt **6** attest, evince, extant, graith, patent, reveal **7** approve, confess, declare, develop, display, evident, exhibit, explain, express, glaring, invoice, obvious, signify, visible **8** apparent, develope, disclose, discover, evidence, indicate, palpable **11** conspicuous, demonstrate, discernible, indubitable, perspicuous **12** indisputable, unmistakable
manifestation: 4 sign **5** phase **6** effect, ostent **7** display **8** epiphany **10** revelation
manifesto: 5 edict **7** placard **8** evidence **9** statement **11** declaration **13** demonstration
manifold: 4 many **7** various **8** multiple, numerous **9** different, multifold, multiplex, replicate **12** multifarious
manikin: 4 puny **5** dwarf, model, pygmy **7** phantom **9** mannequin **10** diminutive, homunculus
Manila: *airfield:* **5** Clark
creek: **6** estero
hemp: **5** abaca, abaka **6** banana
hero: **5** Dewey
nut: **6** peanut
river: **5** Pasig
Manila Bay boat: 6 bilalo
manioc: 7 cassava, tapioca
manipulate: rig, use **4** work **5** treat, wield **6** handle, manage **7** control, operate
manipulator: 9 osteopath
Manitoba: *capital:* **8** Winnipeg
city: **7** Brandon, Portage, St. James **10** St. Boniface
lake: **8** Manitoba, Winnipeg **12** Winnipegosis
national park: **14** Ricing Mountain
province of: **6** Canada
provincial flower: **6** crocus
river: Red **8** Winnipeg **9** Churchill **12** Saskatchewan
mankind: man **4** Adam, male **5** flesh, world **6** humans, people **8** humanity
division: **4** race **5** tribe **6** people
hater: **11** misanthrope
manly: 4 bold, male **5** brave, hardy, noble **6** daring, strong, virile **7** manlike, mannish **8** resolute **9** dignified, honorable, masculine, undaunted **10** courageous
Mann character: 7 Castorp
manna: 4 gift **7** Godsend, support **8** delicacy
mannequin: See **manikin**
manner: air, way **4** cost, form, mien, mode, more, thew **5** guise, trick **6** as-

pect, course, method **7** address, bearing, fashion, quomodo **8** attitude, behavior **9** behaviour, technique **10** appearance, deportment
law: **4** modi(pl.) **5** modus
mannered: 8 affected, stylized **10** artificial **13** self-conscious
mannerism: 4 mode, pose **5** trait **7** bearing **11** affectation, peculiarity
mannerly: 4 nice **5** civil, moral **6** decent, polite, seemly **8** courteous, decorous **11** well-behaved
manners: 5 lates **8** courtesy **9** amenities, etiquette
Mannus' father: 6 Tuisto
manor: 4 hall **5** abode, house **6** estate **7** mansion
land: **6** barton **7** demesne
manse: 7 rectory
manservant: 4 help, mozo, syce **5** gilly(Sc.), groom, valet **6** Andrew, butler, garcon, gillie **8** factotum
manship: 5 honor **6** homage **7** courage, manhood **8** courtesy, humanity **9** manliness
mansion: 4 hall, home **5** abode, house, manor, siege **7** chateau, lodging **8** chateaux(pl.), dwelling **9** residence
papal: **7** Lateran
manslaughter: 6 murder **7** killing, slaying **8** butchery, homicide
mansuete: 4 kind, tame **6** gentle
manta: 4 wrap **5** cloak, cloth **7** blanket, bulwark, shelter **8** mantelet **9** devilfish
mantegar: ape
mantel: 4 arch, beam **5** brace(Sc.), ledge, shelf, stone **6** clavel, lintel **10** manteltree
mantilla: 4 cape **5** cloak, scarf
mantle: 4 brat, capa, cape, coat, cope, hood, mant, robe **5** blush, brain, cover **6** capote, pinken, redden **7** encloak, envelop **8** insignia, mantilla, vestment
mantra: 4 hymn **5** charm, spell
mantua: 4 gown, robe **5** cloak **9** overdress
manual: 4 book, text **7** clavier, didache **8** grimoire, handbook **9** catechism **11** enchiridion
art: **5** craft
religious: **9** catechism
manufacture: 4 fake, make **5** forge **6** invent, make up **7** confect, produce **9** fabricate
manufacturer: 8 employer **9** fabricant, operative **10** fabricator **12** entrepreneur **13** industrialist
manumission: 7 freedom, freeing, release **10** liberation **11** deliverance **12** emancipation
manure: 4 dung **5** addle **7** compost **10** composture
manuscript: 4 copy **5** codex **7** papyrus,

writing **8** document **9** archetype, minuscule **11** composition, handwriting
back: **5** dorso
space: **6** lacuna
copier: **6** scribe
mark: **5** obeli(pl.) **6** obelus
many: 4 fele, raff **6** legion, myriad **7** diverse, several, various **8** manifold, multiple, numerous **9** multifold, multitude, plurality **10** multiplied **11** large number
many-footed: 8 multiped
many-sided: 9 versatile **12** multilateral
mao: 7 peacock
Maori: *bird:* poe, tue, tui
canoe: **4** waka
charm: **7** heitiki
chief: **5** ariki
clan: ati **4** hapu
club: **4** mere, patu, rata
compensation: utu
dance: **4** haka
food: kai
fort: pa; pah
god: **4** tiki
hen: **4** weka
hero: **4** Maui
house: **5** whare **8** wharekai **9** wherekura **12** wharewananga
over: umu
priest: **7** tuhunga
raft: **4** moki **6** moguey
sect: **7** Ringatu
store: **6** pataka
tatooing: **4** moko
tree: **5** mapau **6** manuka **9** tanehakas
tribe: Ati **4** Hapu
village: pah **4** kaik **5** kaika **6** kainga
wages: utu
weapon: **4** mere, patu, rata
map: 4 card, plan **5** carte, chard, chart, image **6** design, set out, sketch, survey **7** diagram, epitome, explore, outline, picture **8** roadbook **9** delineate **10** cartograph, embodiment **14** representation
book: **5** atlas
copier: **10** pantograph
maker: **7** charter **8** Mercator **12** cartographer
townsite: **4** plat
weather line: **6** isobar
maple: 4 acer **5** mazer **7** dogwood **8** sycamore
cup: **5** mazer
derived from: **6** aceric
family: **9** aceraceae
sap: **5** humbo
scale: **10** pulvinaria
seed: **6** samara
spout: **5** spile
mar: 4 amar, blot, scar **5** botch, spoil **6**

damage, deface, deform, impair, injure, mangle **7** blemish **8** obstruct **9** disfigure

marabou: 4 bird, silk **5** stork **6** argala, fabric **8** adjutant **11** feather trim

maral: 4 deer

marasca: 6 cherry **10** maraschino

marasmus: 5 waste **10** emaciation **13** contabescence

marathon: 4 race **7** therapy **10** protracted **13** endurance test

maraud: 4 loot, raid, rove **7** pillage, plunder

marauder: 6 bandit, pirate **7** cateran(Sc.)

marble: 4 cold, hard **5** agate, rance, stone **6** basalt **7** cipolin **8** brocatel, dolomite **9** unfeeling **10** brocatelle

game: taw

mosaic: **7** tessera

playing: mib, pea, taw **4** doby **5** alley, dobie **6** glassy **7** shooter

slab: **5** dalle(F.)

marbled: 7 striped **10** variegated

Marble Faun: *author:* **9** Hawthorne

character: **5** Hilda **6** Kenyon, Miriam **9** Donatello

marc: 6 pomace, refuse **7** residue

march: 4 hike, slog, trek **5** route, troop **6** border, defile, parade **8** boundary, frontier, smallage **9** cavalcade **10** procession

day's: **5** etape

horsemen: **9** cavalcade

spirited: **9** quickstep

March 15: 4 ides

March King: 5 Sousa

March sisters: Jo; Amy, Meg **4** Beth

marchland: 8 frontier **10** borderland

marcid: 4 weak **7** decayed, tabetic **8** withered **9** exhausted **10** emaciating

marcor: 5 decay **7** maramus

Mardi Gras: 8 carnival

king: Rex

mare: yad **4** jade, yade, yaud(Sc.) **5** gilot, horse, meare **6** dobbin, equine, grasni

young: **5** filly

mare's nest: 4 hoax, mess **5** trick **8** disorder **9** confusion

mare's tail: 5 cloud **6** cirrus

margarine: 4 oleo

margin: hem, lip, ori, rim **4** bank, brim, edge, orae(L.), rand, side **5** brink, shore, verge **6** border, fringe, leeway **7** minimum **8** latitude

narrow: **4** hair

note: **7** apostil **8** scholium **10** annotation

set in: **6** indent

marginal: 9 bordering **11** unimportant

Marianas: 4 Guam **6** Saipan

marigold: 5 boots, caper, gools **6** buddle **7** cowslip, elkslip, golland

genus: **7** tagetes

marijuana: boo, hay, pot, tea **4** hemp, weed **5** grass

cigarette: **5** joint, stick **6** greefa, griffo, moocah, reefer **7** mohasky **8** joy-smoke, loco weed, Mary Jane **9** Indian hay **10** bambalacha, Mary Warner, Mary Weaver **11** giggle-smoke

cigarette holder: **6** crutch

user: **7** pothead

marina: 4 dock **5** basin **9** esplanade, promenade

marinade: 5 brine **6** pickle **8** marinate

marinal: 6 marine, sailor, saline **7** mariner **8** nautical

marinara: 11 garlic sauce

marine: tar **5** jolly, naval, water **7** aquatic, marinal, mariner, oceanic, pelagic **8** halimous, maritime, nautical **9** aequoreal **11** leatherneck

crustacean: **8** barnacle

instrument: aba **5** radar **7** pelorus, sextant

plant: **4** alga **5** algae **6** enalid **7** seaweed

science: **10** oceanology **12** oceanography

skeleton: **5** coral

slogan: **6** gung ho

marine animal: orc **4** salp **5** coral, polyp **9** jellyfish

marine fish: 8 menhaden

mariner: gob, tar **5** Jacky **6** galoot, sailor, seaman **7** buscarl **8** buscarle, seafarer, waterman **9** aequoreal

card: **5** chart

compass card: **4** rose

compass points: **6** rhumbs

marionette: 6 puppet **10** bufflehead

marital: 9 connubial **11** matrimonial

maritime: See **marine**

marjoram: 4 herb, mint **6** origan

mark: dot, hob, tag, tee **4** belt, goal, heed, line, note, rate, rist, scar, wale **5** badge, brand, grade, label, score, sign, stamp, track, watch **6** accent, beacon, caract, denote, notice, target **7** betoken, blemish, earmark, impress, imprint, insigne, manifest, observe **8** identify, insignia(pl.), standard **9** character, designate, influence **10** impression, indication **11** distinguish **14** characteristic

bad: **7** demerit

diacritical: **5** breve, tilde **6** macron, umlaut **7** cedilla(F.)

down: **5** lower

out: **6** cancel, define **7** measure **10** obliterate

possessive: **10** apostrophe

printer's: **4** dele, fist, stet **5** caret, obeli **6** dagger, diesis, obelus **7** obelisk

pronunciation: see *diacritical* above

punctuation: **4** dash **5** colon, comma **6** period **8** dieresis **9** diaeresis, semicolon **11** parenthesis, parentheses(pl.)

question: **7** erotema, eroteme

reference: **4** star **6** dagger **8** asterisk

tiny: dot

under letter: **7** cedilla
white: **5** rache, ratch
with critical notes: **8** annotate
Mark Antony's wife: 7 Octavia
Mark Twain's name: 22 Samuel Langhorne Clemens
markaz: 8 district **11** subdivision
marked: 5 fated, noted **7** eminent **9** prominent **10** emphasized **11** conspicuous, outstanding
with lines: **5** ruled **6** gyrose, linear, notate
marker: peg **5** arrow **6** scorer, signal **7** brander, counter, monitor **8** bookmark, recorder **9** indicator, milestone, tombstone **10** gravestone
air course: **5** pylon
floating: **4** buoy
market: 4 gunj(Ind.), mall, mart, sale, sell, shop, sook, vend **5** agora(Gr.), bazar, gunge, halle, plaza, store, tryst(Sc.) **6** bazaar, outlet, rialto, shoppe **8** boutique, debouche(F.), emporium
marketable: 7 salable **8** vendible **10** commercial
markhor: 4 goat
marksman: 4 shot **6** sniper
marl: 4 clay, loam, malm, sand, silt **5** earth **6** manure **10** fertilizer, overspread
marli: 4 lace **5** gauze, tulle
marlin: 6 curlew, godwit **9** spearfish
marlinspike: fid **4** skua, tool **6** Jaeger
marmalade: jam **5** jelly **6** sapote **8** preserve
tree: **6** mammee
marmite: pot **4** soup **6** kettle **9** casserole
marmoset: 4 mico **6** monkey, pinche, sagoin, wistit **7** tamarin, wistiti
marmot: 5 bobac **6** rodent **8** burrower, whistler **9** groundhog, woodchuck
maroon: 6 enisle, strand **7** abandon, cast off, forsake, isolate, reddish **8** cimarron, purplish
marooner: 6 pirate **9** buccaneer
Marapessa's abductor: 4 Idas
marplot: 7 meddler, snooper **8** busybody
Marquand character: 4 Moto **5** Apley, Wayde **6** Pulham **7** Goodwin
marquee: 4 tent **6** awning, canopy
marquetry: 5 inlay
kind of: **8** intarsia
marriage: 5 match, union **6** splice **7** wedding, wedlock **8** nuptials **9** matrimony
absence of: **5** agamy
broker: **9** schatchen(Yid.)
forswearer: **8** celibate
fourth: **9** tetragamy
god: **5** Hymen
goddess: **4** Hera
hater of: **10** misogamist
more than one husband: **9** polyandry
more than one wife: **6** bigamy **8** polygamy
notice: **5** banns

of aged: **8** opsigamy
of gods: **8** theogamy
outside tribe: **7** exogamy
pert. to: **7** marital, nuptial, spousal **8** conjugal, hymeneal **9** connubial, endogamic
portion: dot **5** dowry
second: **6** digamy
secret: **9** elopement
single: **8** monogamy
to promise: **7** betroth **8** affiance
to two people: **6** bigamy
marriageable: 6 nubile
married person: 4 wife **6** spouse **7** husband **8** benedict
marrow: 4 best, pith **5** reest(Sc.) **6** inmost **7** essence, medulla
bones: **5** knees
marry: wed **4** join, mate, wive, yoke **5** cleek, hitch, unite **6** buckle, couple **7** espouse, husband **10** tie the knot
Mars: 4 Ares **6** planet, war god
consort: **10** Rhea Silvia
day: **7** Tuesday
discoverer of satellites: **4** Hall
pert. to: **5** Arean **7** Martian
planet belt: **5** Libya
planet spot: **5** oasis, oases(pl.)
priests of: **5** Salii
region (dark): **4** mare
satellites: **6** Deimos, Phobos
space-craft: **6** Viking **7** Mariner
twin sons: **5** Remus **7** Romulus
Marseillaise author: 13 Rouget de Lisle
marsh: bog, fen, hag **4** jeel, mire, moor, slew, sloo, slue **5** flash, liman, slash, swale, swamp **6** morass, palude, slough **7** cienaga, maremma(It.) **8** quagmire **9** everglade
bird: **4** rail, sora **5** snipe, stilt **7** bittern
crocodile: goa **6** mugger
elder: iva
fever: **7** helodes **8** malaria
gas: **7** methane **8** firedamp
grass: **4** tule **5** sedge, spart
hawk: **7** harrier
marigold: **5** boots **7** cowslip
salt: **6** salina **7** corcass
shrub: **4** reed **7** bulrush, cattail **8** buckbean, moorwort
marsh plant genus: 4 sium **5** calla **6** caltha **7** elatine
marshal: 4 lead **5** align, aline, array, guide, usher **6** direct, parade **7** arrange, officer **8** official
marshwort: 9 cranberry
marshy: wet **5** fenny **6** callow, quaggy **7** helodes, paludal **8** paludous
lake: **5** liman
marsupial: 4 tait **5** coala, koala, tapoa **6** possum, wombat **7** dasyure, opossum **9** bandicoot
Australian: **4** tait **6** cuscus **7** dasyure, wallaby **8** kangaroo **9** phalanger

bearlike: **5** coala, koala **6** wombat
feature: **5** pouch
mart: 4 fair **5** bazar **6** bazaar, market,
rialto **8** emporium
martel: 6 hammer
marten: fur **5** sable **6** animal, fisher
beech: **4** foin
genus: **7** mustela
stone: **4** foin
martial: 7 warlike **8** military
martial art: 4 judo **6** karate, kung fu
Martial's writing: 7 epigram
Martian: 5 Arean
martin: 7 swallow
martinet: 6 tyrant **14** disciplinarian
Martinique: *capital:* **12** Fort-de-France
garment: **4** jupe
volcano: **5** Pelee
martyr: 5 saint **8** sufferer **10** sacrificer
first Christian: **7** Stephen
royal: **7** Charles
martyrdom: 7 killing, passion, torment,
torture **8** butchery, distress **10** affliction
place of: **8** Golgotha
marvel: 5 ferly **6** admire, wonder **7** miracle, portent **8** astonish **9** horehound
12 astonishment
marvelous: 7 strange **8** splendid, wondrous **9** excellent **10** improbable, incredible
Mary Jane: 9 marijuana
Maryland: *bay:* **10** Chesapeake
capital: **9** Annapolis
city: **5** Bowie **8** Baltimore, Frederick **10**
Hagerstown
county: **5** Cecil **7** Hartford **10** Montgomery **12** Prince George
fort: **7** McHenry
founder: **7** Calvert
island: **4** Kent **5** Smith **10** South Marsh
mountain: **8** Backbone, Catoctin **11** Appalachian
nickname: **4** Free **7** Cockade, Old Line
racetrack: **5** Bowie
river: **7** Potomac **8** Patuxent
state bird: **6** oriole
state flower: **14** black-eyed Susan
state tree: oak
masa: 8 cornmeal
Masada: 8 fortress
builder: **5** Herod
defender: **6** zealot
enemy: **4** Rome
historian: **8** Josephus
masculine: 4 male **5** manly **6** strong, virile **7** manlike, mannish
mash: 4 chap, mess, ogle **5** champ, cream,
crush, flirt, smash **6** muddle **7** farrago,
mixture, touble
marshal: 7 parable, proverb
masher: 4 chap **5** flirt, ricer

masjid: 6 mosque
mask: 4 hide, veil **5** cloak, cover, guise, visor **6** screen **7** conceal, curtain **8** defi-
lade, disguise **9** dissemble
half: **4** loup(Fr.) **6** domino(Fr.)
top knot on: **5** onkos
masked: 6 covert **7** larvate, obscure **8** lar-
vated **9** concealed, disguised
masker: 6 domino, mummer
maslin: 5 brass **7** mixture **9** potpourri
mason: 7 builder **11** stoneworker
mixing rod: rab
masonry: 6 ashlar **7** backing, blocage **9**
stonework
masquerade: 5 guise **7** pass for **8** disguise
mass: bat, gob **4** blob, body, bulk, clot,
heap, lump, size, swad **5** amass, batch,
gross, group, store **6** gather, gobbet,
prayer **7** phalanx, service **8** assemble,
majority **9** aggregate, magnitude **10** accumulate, assemblage, congregate,
large-scale **11** agglomerate, composition, compositure, concentrate, consolidate **12** congregation
book: **6** missal
cloudlike: **6** nebula **7** nebulae(pl.)
confused: cot **5** chaos **6** welter **9** imbroglio **10** hotchpotch
directory: **4** ordo
for dead: **7** requiem
musical number: **5** Credo, Kyrie **6** Gloria
7 Sanctus
of particulars: **9** aggregate
pert. to: **5** molar
small: dab, pat, wad **4** floc
tangled: mop **4** shag
mass meeting: 5 rally
Massachusetts: *cape:* Ann, Cod
capital: **6** Boston
city: **8** Brockton **9** Cambridge, Fall River,
Worcester **10** New Bedford **11** Springfield
county: **5** Dukes, Essex **9** Berkshire, Middlesex, Nantucket **10** Barnstable
island: **9** Nantucket **15** Martha's Vineyard
mountain: Tom **6** Brodie **8** Greylock
mountain range: **9** Berkshire
nickname: Bay **6** Old Bay **9** Old Colony
pond: **6** Walden
river: **6** Nashua **7** Charles, Concord **9**
Merrimack **11** Connecticut
state bird: **9** chickadee
state fish: cod
state flower: **9** mayflower
state tree: elm
massacre: 6 pogrom **7** carnage **8** butchery
9 slaughter
massage: rub **5** knead
massager: 7 masseur **8** masseuse
massed: 7 serried
Massenet's opera: 5 Manon, Thais

massive: big **4** bold, huge **5** beamy, bulky, gross, heavy, large, massy **7** hulking, weighty **9** cyclopean, ponderous **10** boisterous

mast: cue **4** spar **5** stick **6** forage **8** beechnut

against: **5** aback

crosspiece: fid

inclination from perpendicular: **4** rake

middle: **8** mainmast

wood for: ash **4** poon

mastaba: **4** tomb **8** platform

master: get, man, rab **4** baas, boss, lord, mian, rule, sire **5** chief, rabbi, sahib(Ind.), tutor **6** artist, bridle, buckra, defeat, doctor, domine, govern, humble, subdue **7** captain, conquer, maestro, padrone(It.) **8** educator, overcome, regulate, surmount, vanquish **9** commander, overpower, preceptor, subjugate **10** proprietor

Eton: **4** beak

fencing: **7** lanista

harbor: **7** havener, havenor

hard: **6** despot, Legree

of house: **13** paterfamilias

pert. to: **6** herile

ship's: **7** captain, skipper

master of ceremonies: **5** emcee

master stroke: **4** coup

masterful: **6** lordly **7** haughty **8** arrogant, masterly **9** arbitrary, imperious **10** commanding **11** dictatorial, domineering, magisterial, overbearing **13** authoritative

mastermind: **4** plan **6** expert **8** wiseacre

masterpiece: **4** coup **6** classic **7** triumph **9** objet d'art **10** masterwork **11** chef d'oeuvre

mastery: **4** gree **5** gripe, skill **7** control, victory **8** conquest, facility **9** influence, supremacy **13** understanding

mastic: **4** tree **5** gummy, resin **8** adhesive

masticate: **4** chaw, chew **5** crush, gnash, grind **6** crunch **9** manducate

mastiff: dog **5** burly **7** massive

mastodon: **5** giant **7** mammoth **9** pachyderm

mat: cot, rug **4** felt **5** doily, platt, snarl **6** carpet, cotter, petate(Sp.), tangle **7** cushion, drugget, gardnap **8** entangle **10** interweave, lusterless

mat grass: **4** nard

Mata Hari: spy **5** agent

Mataco: **4** apar **6** Indian **9** armadillo

matador: **6** torero **8** toreador **11** bullfighter

adversary: **4** bull, toro

garment: **4** cape

staff: **6** muleta

sword: **7** estoque **8** estocada

matagasse: **11** butcherbird

match: go; cap, pit, tir(F.) **4** bout, cope, even, game, mate, pair, peer, side, spar, suit, team, wife **5** amate, equal, fusee(F.), marry, rival, tally, torch, vesta **6** fellow, spouse **7** compare, compeer, contest, husband, lucifer(Eng.) **8** equalize, lampwick, marriage **9** allumette(F.) **10** candlewick, correspond **11** counterpart, countervail, parallelize

matched: **6** paired, teamed

matchless: **5** alone **6** unlike **8** peerless **9** exquisite, unequaled **10** inimitable **12** incomparable

mate: cap, pal, wed **4** fear, fere, join, pair, peer, wife **5** billy, buddy, bully, cully, feere, marry, match **6** bunkle, cobber, couple, fellow, spouse **7** brother, compeer, comrade, consort, espouse, husband, partner **9** associate, companion **10** yokefellow

matelot: **6** sailor

mater: mom **4** mama **6** mother

material (see also **cloth, fabric, substance**): **4** data, gear **5** goods, stuff **6** bodily, carnal, matter **7** apropos, weighty **8** physical, tangible **9** corporeal, essential, important **12** nonspiritual

discard: **4** junk, slag **5** scrap, trash, waste **6** refuse **7** rubbish

raw: ore **6** staple

materialism: **9** carnality, physicism

materialize: **4** loom, rise **6** appear, embody, emerge, show up **8** manifest

materiel: **8** supplies **9** apparatus, equipment

maternal: **8** motherly

relation: **7** enation

matey: **6** chummy **13** companionable

matezite: **7** pinitol **10** caoutchouc

matgrass: **4** nard **8** fogfruit

mathe: **4** grub **6** maggot

mathematician: **5** adder **7** figurer

mathematics: *abbreviation:* Q.E.D.

branch: **7** algebra, geodesy **8** calculus, geometry **9** logarithm **10** arithmetic **12** trigonometry

constant (arbitrary): **9** parameter

deduction: **8** analysis

diagram: **5** graph

equation: **4** surd

exercise: **7** problem

factor: **10** quaternion

function: **4** sine **6** cosine

instrument: **6** sector **7** compass **8** arbalest

irrational number: **4** surd

line: **6** vector

number: **5** digit **12** multiplicand

operation: **7** operand

operator: **5** nabla **10** quaternion

proposition: **7** theorem

quantity: **6** scalar

ratio: pi **4** sine **8** derivate

symbol: **7** faciend, operand **12** multiplicand

term: **4** root, sine **6** cosine

mathemeg: 7 catfish

matie: 7 herring

matin: 4 call, song **6** prayer **9** matutinal

song: **6** aubade

matinee: 5 party **6** soiree **8** negligee **9** reception **13** entertainment

matinee idol: 4 lion, star **5** actor

matka: 4 seal

matrass: 4 tube **5** flask **6** bottle **8** bolthead

matriculate: 5 adopt, enter **6** enroll **8** register **10** naturalize **13** immatriculate

matrimonial: 7 nuptial, spousal **8** conjugal, hymeneal **9** connubial

matrimony: 7 wedlock, **8** marriage

matrix: bed, die, mat **4** form, mold, womb **5** plasm **6** gangue **7** pattern

plate: **6** stereo

matron: 4 dame, wife **5** widow **11** housekeeper

matte: 10 dull finish

matter: pus **4** gear, malm, mass **5** solid, topic **6** affair, behalf **7** article, concern, problem, signify, trouble **8** business, material **11** constituent

law: res

particle: **4** atom

pert. to: **5** hylic

property: **4** mass **7** inertia

rarefied: fog, gas **4** mist **5** vapor **6** miasma

matter of fact: 4 dull **7** literal, prosaic **9** practical, pragmatic **11** utilitarian **12** in plain style

mattock: axe, hoe **4** bill **5** tubal **6** twibil **7** twibill

mattress: pad **4** sack **6** pallet

cover: **4** tick **5** ticking

mature: age, old **4** aged, form, gray, grow, ripe **5** adult, grown, ripen **6** accrue, autumn, decoct, digest, mellow, season **7** develop **8** complete **9** come of age

matutinal: 5 early, matin **10** before noon

Mau Mau land: 5 Kenya

maud: 5 plaid, shawl **7** blanket

maudlin: 5 beery, corny, tipsy **7** tearful, weeping **10** lachrymose **11** sentimental

mauger: 5 spite **7** ill-will **9** unwilling **15** notwithstanding

Maugham: *heroine:* **5** Sadie

play: **4** Rain

maul: paw **4** beat, bung, club, mace, mall, mell, moth **5** abuse, gavel, staff **6** beater, beetle, bruise, hammer, mallet **7** rough up **9** manhandle

maumet: god, guy **4** doll, idol **5** image **6** puppet

maud: beg **6** basket, hamper

maunder: 5 growl, haver **6** beggar, drivel, ramble **7** grumble

Maupassant character: 4 Fifi

Mauritania: *capital:* **10** Novakchott

ethnic group: **5** Arabs, Moors **6** Wolofs **7** Berbers, Poulars **8** Sonunkes

monetary unit: **6** ougiya

language: **6** Arabic, French

neighbor: **4** Mali **7** Algeria, Morocco, Senegal

religion: **5** Islam

river: **7** Senegal

town: **4** Atar **5** Kaldi

Maurois subject: 4 Hugo, Sand **5** Byron, Dumas **6** Proust **8** Disraeli

Mauser: arm, gun **5** rifle **6** weapon **7** firearm

mausoleum: 4 tomb **8** baradari(Ind.)

mauve: 5 lilac **6** purple, violet

maux: 8 slattern, slipshod **10** prostitute

maven: 6 expert **11** connoisseur

mavis: 6 thrush **8** thrasher

maw: 4 craw, crop **6** gullet, mallow **7** stomach

mawk: 6 maggot

mawkish: 5 vapid **6** sickly **8** nauseous **9** squeamish **10** disgusting **11** sentimental

maxilla: jaw **4** bone

maxim: saw **4** dict, rule, word **5** adage, axiom, gnome, logia(pl.), moral, motto **6** logion, saying **7** brocard, precept, proverb **8** aphorism, apothegm, doctrine, moralism **9** erudition, principle **10** apophthegm

maximum: 4 most, peak **5** limit **7** highest, largest **8** greatest

may: can **4** mote **5** might, shall, shrub **8** hawthorn, possible

May: *festival:* **7** Beltane

goddess: **4** Maia

Maya: *day:* **5** uayeb

month: **5** uinal

people: Mam **8** Pokonchi

year: **4** haab

maybe: 6 mayhap **7** perhaps **8** possibly **9** not surely **10** indecision **11** possibility, uncertainty

maybird: 4 knot **6** thrush **8** bobolink

maycock: 5 melon **6** maypop, plover

mayfish: 9 killifish

mayflower: 7 arbutus **8** hawthorn, marigold **10** stitchwort **12** cuckooflower

Mayflower's sister ship: 9 Speedwell

mayfly: dun **6** insect

mayor: 5 maire(F.) **7** alcalde(Sp.) **8** official **10** magistrate **12** burgomeister(G.)

maze: 4 daze **5** amaze, fancy **7** confuse, perplex, stupefy **8** bewilder, confound, delirium, delusion **9** amazement, deception, labyrinth **10** hodgepodge **12** bewilderment

mazer: 4 bowl **6** goblet

mazy: 7 complex **9** intricate **10** circuitous, perplexing **11** bewildering

mea culpa: 10 I am to blame

mead: 5 drink **6** meadow **8** hydromel **9** metheglin

meadow: lea **4** mead, vega, wish, wong **5** field, haugh, marsh **6** saeter **7** pasture **9** grassland, grassplot

piece of: **5** swale

meadowlark: 5 acorn **6** medlar

meadowmouse: 4 vole

meadowsweet: 4 rose **7** spiraea

meager: 4 arid, bare, lank, lean, poor, slim, thin **5** gaunt, scant, spare **6** barren, jejune, lenten, meagre, narrow, pilled, scanty, scarce, sparse **7** scranny, starved, sterile, tenuous **9** emaciated **10** inadequate

meal: tub **4** bite, dune, feed, menu **5** feast, flour, grain, lunch, padar, salep, snack **6** bucket, dinner, morsel, nocake, powder, repast, supper **7** banquet, blowout, potluck, rations **8** sandbank **9** breakfast, collation, pulverize

army: **4** chow, mess

coarse: **5** grout **7** cribble **8** gurgeons

last course: **7** dessert

light: tea **5** lunch, snack **6** tiffin

main dish: **6** entree

wheat: **4** atta(Ind.)

meals: 5 board

mealy: 4 pale **6** floury, spotty, uneven **7** friable, powdery, starchy **8** farinose **9** colorless, personate **11** farinaceous

mean: low **4** base, clam, hard, lean, norm, poor, show **5** argue, augur, footy, nasty, petty, ratty, snide, snivy, sorry **6** abject, chetif, coarse, common, denote, design, dirten, feeble, humble, intend, medial, median, medium, middle, narrow, paltry, pilled, snivey, sordid **7** average, caitiff, ignoble, pitiful, purport, purpose, signify **8** baseborn, beggarly, churlish, recreant, shameful **9** irascible, malicious, niggardly, penurious, truculent **11** disgraceful, hardhearted **12** contemptible, dishonorable, intermediate, narrow-minded, parsimonious

mean line: 9 bisectrix

meander: 4 roam, turn, wind **5** amble, curve, stray, twist **6** wander **7** complex **8** straggle **9** labyrinth

meaning: 5 sense **6** import, intent, spirit **7** anagoge, bearing, purport, purpose **9** intending, intention, knowledge **10** definition, indication **11** designation, implication **12** apprehension, significance **13** signification, understanding

without: **4** null

meanly: 6 humbly, poorly **8** beggarly, shabbily

means: 4 cost, tool **5** agent, funds **6** agency, assets, method **7** quomodo **8** averages, resources **10** instrument **11** wherewithal **12** intermediary

of livelihood: **4** work **5** labor, trade **8** vocation **10** profession

support: **4** hold **6** income **7** aliment **11** maintenance

meantime: 7 interim **8** interval

meanwhile: 9 adinterim

mear: 8 boundary

measles: 7 rubeola

measly: 4 mean **6** skimpy, slight **9** worthless **12** contemptible

measure (see also **measuring instrument**): act, law **4** area, gage, mete, rule, span, tape, time **5** clock, gauge, girth, meter, ruler, scale **6** amount, assize, degree, length, stadia **7** battuta, caliper **8** odometer, tapeline **9** admeasure, calculate, criterion, rotameter

area: are, rod **4** acre **6** decare **7** hectare

astronomical: **7** azimuth

Biblical: cab, hin, kor, log **4** epha **5** cubit, aphah, homer

cable: **4** naut

capacity: **4** cask, gill, orna, peck, pint **5** liter, quart **6** barrel, bushel, gallon

cloth: ell **4** yard

cubic: **4** cord **5** stere **10** hectostere

cut wood: **4** cord

degree of angle: arc

distance: see *length* below

dry: **4** bale, peck **6** bushel

energy: erg **5** ergon, joule

established: **8** standard

fish: vog **4** cran(Sc.) **5** crane, crans

flexible: **4** tape **8** tapeline

heat: **5** term **6** calory, therme **7** calorie **10** centigrade, Fahrenheit

horse: **4** hand

land: ar; are, rod **4** acre, area, mile, rood **6** decare **7** hectare, kiliare

length: dra, ell, pik, rod **4** foot, inch, knot, mile, nail, pace, pole, yard **5** cubit, digit, meter, metre, perch, toise(F.) **6** league, micron, mikron **9** decimeter, kilometer **10** centimeter, hectometer, millimeter

liquid: aam, keg **4** gill, pint **5** lagen, liter, quart **6** barrel, gallon, magnum, minims, runlet, tierce **7** rundlet **8** hogshead **9** hectolite, kiloliter

loudness: **4** phon

medicinal: **4** dram **5** minim, ounce **7** scruple

nautical: **4** knot **6** fathom

paper: **4** page, ream **5** quire, sheet

printer's: **4** pica **5** agate, empen

short: **6** ullage

sound: bel

space: **6** parsec

time: day **4** hour, week, year **5** month **6** decade, minute, moment, second

water depth: **5** sound

weight: ton **4** bale **5** carat, liter, ounce, pound **9** kiloliter **10** hectoliter

wheat: **4** trug
wine: tun **4** butt, pipe
wire: mil **5** stone
work: erg **5** ergon
yarn: lea **4** heer, typp **6** denier **7** spindle
Measure for Measure character: 5 El-
bow, Froth, Lucio **6** Angelo, Juliet
measured: 7 careful, guarded, regular,
uniform **10** deliberate
measureless: 4 vast **7** endless, immense **8**
infinite **9** boundless, limitless, unbounded, unlimited **11** illimitable **12**
immeasurable
measurement: 9 dimension **11** mensura-
tion
pert. to: **6** metric **11** dimensional
measuring instrument: 4 gage, tape **5**
chain, gauge, meter, ruler **7** alidade **8**
measurer, tapeline **9** container, yardstick **13** saccharimeter
acidity: **10** acidimeter
heat: **11** calorimeter
lumber: **6** scaler
surveying: **11** stratameter
thickness: **7** caliper
measuring wheel: 8 odometer **12** perambulator
meat: 4 beef, food, gist, lamb, pork, veal **5**
flesh **6** chevon, mutton **7** chilver, venison **9** nutriment
and-potatoes: **5** basic
ball: **7** rissole **9** croquette, fricandel **11**
fricandelle
bony: **5** scrag **9** spareribs
cured: ham **5** bacon **6** flitch, salame, salami **7** biltong, bultong, sausage **8** pastrami, pastroma **9** biltongue
cut: ham, rib **4** chop, loin, rump **5** flank,
roast, steak **6** cutlet, rasher **7** icebone,
sirloin **9** aitchbone, club steak, rump
roast, short ribs
dish: **5** pasty **6** potpie, ragout **7** goulash,
haricot, ravioli **8** fricando **10** fricandeau
dish with vegetables: **4** olla, stew **8** mulligan **9** lobscouse **10** lobscourse
dried: **5** jerky **7** biltong, bultong, pemican
8 pemmican **9** biltongue
frozen: **5** frigo
ground: **7** rissole, sausage **9** hamburger
jelly: **5** aspic
pie: **5** pasty **7** rissole
pin: **6** skewer
potted: **7** rillett **8** rillette
roasted: **5** brede, cabob, kabob
sauce: **4** A-one **5** caper, gravy **14** Worces-
tershire
slice: **6** collop
smoking place: **5** bucan
unwholesome: **6** cagmag
meatless: 6 lenten, maigre
meatus: 4 butt, duct **5** canal **7** foramen,
passage

meatworks: 8 abattoir **14** slaughterhouse
meaty: 5 heavy, pithy, solid **11** substantial
Mecca (see also **Muslim**): *deity:* **5** Hobal,
Hubal
mosque: **5** Caaba, Kaaba **6** Kaabeh
pilgrim's dress: **5** ihram
pilgrimage: **4** hadj
mechanic: erk(F.) **7** artisan, workman **8**
operator **9** artificer, craftsman, operative
mechanical: 9 automatic **10** uninspired
11 automatical, involuntary, perfunctory, stereotyped
mechanical man: 5 robot **9** automaton
mechanical part: 5 rotor **6** stator, tappet
mechanics branch: 7 statics **8** dynamics
mechanism: 4 gear, tool **5** apron, catch,
slide **7** ratchet, tripper **8** selector, sig-
naler **9** apparatus, machinery
driving: **9** propeller
eccentric: cam
self-moving: **8** antomata(pl.) **9** automaton
medal: 4 disk **5** badge **6** plaque **7** medalet
10 decoration
medallion: 4 coin **8** ornament **11** contor-
niate, contorniato
Medb's consort: 6 Ailill
meddle: 4 nose **5** snoop **6** dabble, finger,
monkey, potter, tamper **7** intrude **9** interfere
meddler: 5 snoop **7** marplot **8** busybody
meddlesome: 4 busy **5** fresh **6** prying **7**
curious **9** intrusive, officious
Mede: 5 Aryan, Mesne **6** Median
caste: **4** magi
king: Evi
Medea: *father:* **6** Aeetes
husband: **5** Jason
rival: **6** Creusa
son: **6** Medeus
media: See **medium**
medial: 6 middle **8** ordinary
median: 4 mean **6** medial, middle **7** average, central **12** intermediate
mediate: 7 referee **8** ruminate **9** arbitrate,
intercede, interpose
mediator: 5 judge **6** broker **7** daysman **9**
go-between, middleman **10** ambocepter,
interagent **12** intermediary
medic: 6 clover, doctor, intern, medico **7**
alfalfa, luterne, student, surgeon **8** resident **9** physician
false: **5** quack **9** charlatan **10** medicaster
medical: 6 iatric **11** aesculapian
medical officer: 7 coroner
medical student: 6 extern, intern **7** ex-
terne, interne **8** resident
medicinal: 6 curing **7** healing **8** salutary
9 relieving **11** aesculapian **12** pharma-
ceutic
bark: **6** cartex
berry: **5** cubeb

capsule: **6** cachet
compound: **4** pill, sera **5** hepar, iodin, serum **6** iodine **7** turpeth
nut: **4** cola
plant (see also *root* below): rue **4** aloe **5** ergot, senna, tansy **6** arnica, cohosh, ipecac **7** chirata **8** valerian
remedy: **8** antidote
root (see also *plant* above): **5** artar, jalap, orris **6** seneca, senega **8** licorice
solution: **8** tincture
tablet: **4** pill **6** troche **7** lozenge
medicine: **4** cure, drug **5** tonic **6** physic, remedy **7** anodyne, nostrum, placebo **10** abirritant, alterative
amount: **4** dose **6** dosage
god of: **11** Aesculapius
institution: **6** clinic **8** hospital
instrument: See **surgery:** *instrument*
mild: **6** tisane
noncuring: **6** ptisan
patent: **7** nostrum
vessel: **4** vial **5** ampul, phial **6** ampule **7** ampoule **8** gallipot
medicine dropper: **7** pipette
medicine man: **4** piay **6** doctor, shaman **8** magician, sorcerer **9** physician
mediety: **4** half, part **6** moiety
medieval: old **6** Gothic
battle: **4** Acre
coin: **9** bracteate
dagger: **6** anlace
fiddle: **4** giga
fort: **11** Carcassonne
gown: **6** cyclas
guild: **5** Hanse
helmet: **5** armet **6** heaume
lyric: **4** alba
prayer book: **7** portass
shield: ecu
weapon: **5** lance, oncin **7** gisarme **8** crossbow
Medina (see also **Muslim**): **8** holy city
citizen: **5** Ansar
mediocre: **4** mean, so-so **6** common, medium **7** average **8** inferior, middling, not so hot, ordinary, passable **11** commonplace, indifferent
meditate: **4** chew, mull, muse, pore **5** brook, study, think, watch, weigh **6** ponder, reason **7** reflect, revolve **8** cogitate, consider, ruminate **10** deliberate **11** contemplate
meditation: **4** yoga **6** prayer **8** inaction **11** engrossment **13** consideration **14** omphaloskepsis
meditative: **7** pensive
mediterranean: **6** inland **7** midland **10** landlocked
Mediterranean: sea **11** mare nostrum
boat: nef **4** saic **5** setee, xebec, zebec **6** galiot, mistic, settee, tartan, zebeck **7** felucca, mistico, polacre

coast: **7** Riviera
country: **5** Italy **6** France, Greece **7** Algeria
Eastern: **6** Levant
falcon: **6** lanner
fish: aco **6** remora
fruit: **5** olive **7** azarole
galley: **6** galiot
grass: **4** diss
gulf: **5** Tunis
island: **4** Elba **5** Capri, Crete, Ibiza, Iviza, Malta **6** Candia, Cyprus, Ebusus, Lesbos, Lipari, Rhodes, Sicily **7** Corsica, Majorca, Panaria **8** Cyclades, Sardinia, Sporades **9** Stromboli **10** Dodecanese
pert. to: **9** Levantine
port: **5** Tunis **7** Tunisia
resort: **4** Nice **6** Menton **7** Mentone
shrub: **7** azarole
storm: **7** borasca, borasco
tree: **5** carob **6** mastic **7** azarole
wind: **6** otesan, solano **7** gregale, mistral, sirocco **8** levanter **10** euroclyden
medium: **4** mean **5** media(pl.), midst, organ **6** degree, medial **7** average, channel, psychic **8** mediator **10** instrument, interagent **11** environment **12** intermediary, intermediate
communication: **4** note **5** cable, phone, radio **6** letter **9** telegraph, telephone **10** television
culture: **4** agar
news: **5** radio **7** journal **8** magazine **9** newspaper **10** periodical, television
medlar: **4** lark, tree **5** fruit **6** loquat
medley: **4** olio **6** jumble **7** farrago, melange, mixture **8** mingling **9** patchwork, potpourri **10** hodgepodge, miscellany, variagated **11** gallimaufry **12** minglemangle
musical: **8** fantasia
medrick: **4** gull, tern
medulla: **4** pith **6** marrow **7** essence, summary **10** compendium **12** adrenal gland
Medusa: **6** Gorgon **7** blubber **9** jellyfish
offspring: **7** Pegasus **8** Chrysaor
representation: **9** Gorgoneum
sister: **6** Stheno **7** Euryale
slayer: **7** Perseus
meed: due **4** gift **5** award, bribe, merit, repay, worth **6** desert, reward **7** bribery **10** excellence, recompense
meek: **4** deft, kind, mild **5** lowly **6** docile, gentle, humble, modest **7** pacific, patient **8** moderate, resigned, sheepish, yielding **9** childlike, spineless **10** spiritless, submissive
meerkat: **6** monkey **8** mongoose, suricate
meerschaum: **4** pipe **7** seafoam **9** sepiolite
meet: fit, kep(Sc.), sit **4** duel, face, join, tidy **5** equal, occur, touch, tryst **6** battle, combat, confer, gather, proper **7**

contact, contend, convene, fitting, fulfill, satisfy **8** assemble, assembly, confront, deal with, moderate, suitable **9** encounter, forgather, gathering, intersect **10** congregate, experience, foregather **11** appropriate, contend with
athletic: **8** gymkhana **10** tournament
meeting: 4 mall, moot **5** gemot, rally, union **6** caucus, gemote, huddle, parley **7** coition, consult, session **8** adjacent, assembly, conclave, congress, junction **10** concurrent, conference, confluence, rendezvous **11** convocation
place: **5** forum
meg: 6 guinea **9** halfpenny
Meg's sisters: Jo; Amy **4** Beth
megalithic chamber: 6 dolmen
megaphone: 8 bullhorn, vamphorn
megapod: 4 bird **5** maleo **6** leipoa **11** large-footed
Megara king: 5 Nisus
megrim: 4 whim **5** blues, fancy, freak, humor, whiff **7** stagger, vertigo **8** flounder, headache **9** dizziness **10** low spirits **12** hypochondria
Mehitabel: cat
companion: **6** Archie **9** cockroach
creator: **7** Marquis
Mekong River: *site:* **4** Asia **7** Vietnam
tribe: Moi
mel: 5 honey
melancholia: 6 athymy **7** athymia
melancholy: sad **4** blue, dram, dull, dump, glum **5** dolar(L.), drear, dusky, gloom **6** dismal, somber, sombre, sorrow, yellow **7** chagrin, doleful, pensive, sadness, unhappy **8** atrabile, downcast, tristful **9** cheerless, dejection, plaintive **10** allicholly, depression, desolation **11** despondency, downhearted **12** disconsolate, heavy-hearted, hypochondria, mournfulness
Melanesia: *language:* **6** Santo
people: **4** Fiji
melange: 4 olio **6** medley **7** mixture **10** hodgepodge
melanic: 5 black
melanous: 4 dark **6** brunet **8** brunette
meld: 4 play **5** blend, merge, unite
mele: 4 poem, song **5** chant, lyric **6** ballad
melee: row **4** fray, riot **5** brawl, fight, foray, mix-up **6** affray, fracas, ruckus **7** ruction, scuffle **8** dogfight, skirmish **9** commotion **10** free-for-all
melilotus: 6 clover
meliorate: 6 better, change, soften **7** improve, get better **10** ameliorate
Melkarth: 4 Baal **6** Moloch
mell: mix **4** maul **5** fight, honey **6** beetle, hammer, mallet, meddle, mingle
mellifluous: 6 sweet **7** honeyed, sugared **8** pleasant **9** melodious

mellow: age **4** aged, rich, ripe, soft **5** loamy, ripen **6** mature, tender **7** matured **8** patinate
melodeon: 6 organ **9** seraphine
melodious: 6 ariose, arioso, dulcet **7** lyrical, melodic, musical, tunable, tuneful **8** canorous **10** harmonious
melodist: 6 singer **8** composer **9** harmonist
melodramatic: 8 dramatic **9** emotional **10** theatrical **11** sensational
melody: air, lay **4** aria, lilt, note, raga (Ind.), solo, song, tune **5** charm, dirge, music, theme **6** strain **7** arietta, harmony, rosalia, sortita **9** cantilena **11** tunefulness
characterization: **6** ariose, arioso
counter: **7** descant
outline: **5** melos
pert. to: **6** plagal
unaccompanied: **4** solo **6** monody
meloid: 6 beetle **9** oil beetle
melon: 4 musk, pepo **5** gourd, water **6** casaba, papaya, spoils **7** Persian **8** honeydew **10** cantaloupe, paddymelon
melon pear: 6 pepino
melongena: 7 mollusk **8** eggplant
melos: 4 song **6** melody
melt: 4 rin(Sc.), run **4** flow, flux, fuse, thaw **5** blend, smelt, sweal **6** render, soften **7** dwindle, liquefy **8** discandy, dissolve, eliquate **10** colliquate, deliquesce **12** disintegrate
down: **6** render **7** liquefy
partly: **4** frit
Melville: *character:* Pip **4** Ahab **5** whale **8** Queequeg, Starbuck
novel: **4** Omoo **5** Typee **8** Moby Dick
member: 4 limb, part **5** organ **6** branch, fellow **7** section **8** district **11** communicant
new: **6** novice **7** entrant **8** neophyte **10** apprentice
oldest: **4** dean
membership: 4 seat **10** fellowship
membrane: web **4** caul, coat, skin, tela **5** layer **6** amnion, amnios, retina, tissue **7** cuticle, eardrum, velamen **8** stiffen
diffusion through: **7** osmosis
fold of: **5** plica
fringe: **4** loma
of bird: **4** cere
spore: **6** intine
weblike: **4** tela
memento: 5 relic, token **6** trophy **8** keepsake, memorial, reminder, souvenir **11** remembrance
memo: 4 chit **8** reminder
memoir: 4 note **5** eloge **6** record, report **7** history **8** memorial **9** biography, narrative **10** commentary
memorabilia: ana **7** history **8** archives

memorable: 7 namable, notable, special 9 reminding 10 remarkable 11 reminiscent 13 distinguished, extraordinary

memorandum: 4 bill, note, stub 5 brief 6 agenda(pl.) 7 agendum, memento, minutes, notanda(pl.), proctol 8 notandum, notation, reminder 9 directive

book: 5 diary 6 agenda 7 tickler 8 calendar

legal: 5 jurat

memorial: ahu 5 facta(pl.), relic 6 factum, memoir, record, trophy 7 memento 8 mnemonic, monument 11 remembrance 12 recollection 13 commemorative

carved: 5 totem

stone: 5 cairn 6 statue 9 mausoleum

memorist: 8 prompter

memory: 4 mind, rote 8 memorial, mind's eye, 9 retention 11 remembrance 12 recollection, reminiscence 13 retrospection

aid: 8 mnemonic, reminder 10 anamnestic

goddess: 9 Mnemosyne

loss: 5 blank, lethe 7 amnesia, aphasia 13 forgetfulness

pattern: 6 engram

pert. to: 6 mnesic 7 mnestic 8 mnemonic

vivid: 7 eidetic

memory book: 5 album, diary 9 scrapbook

Memphis (see also **Egypt**): *chief:* Evi

god: Ra 4 Ptah

men: 4 crew 6 people, troops 9 work force

armed body: 4 army 5 posse

party: 4 stag 6 smoker

section of Greek church: 6 andron

wise: 4 Magi 6 Gaspar 8 Melchior 9 Balthasar, Balthazar

menace: 5 boast, peril 6 danger, impend, threat 8 denounce, forebode, jeopardy, threaten, work evil 9 fulminate

menacing: 10 formidable

menage: 4 club, home 6 family 7 society 8 domicile 9 household 10 management 12 housekeeping

menagerie: zoo 10 collection

mend: fix, sew 4 beet, darn, heal, help, knit 5 amend, botch, clout, emend, moise, patch 6 better, cobble, repair, solder 7 improve, restore 9 get better 10 ameliorate, convalesce

mendacity: lie 5 lying 6 deceit 7 falsity, untruth 9 falsehood

mender: 6 tinker 7 cobbler 9 repairman

mendicant: 4 monk 5 fakir 6 beggar, fakeer, frater

Menelaus: 12 king of Sparta

brother: 9 Agamemnon

daughter: 8 Hermione

father: 6 Atreus

steersman: 7 Canopus

wife: 5 Helen

meng: mix 5 blend 6 mingle

menhaden: 4 fish, pogy 5 pogie, porgy 8 bonyfish 10 mossbunker

young: 7 sardine

menial: fag, low 4 base, mean 6 drivel, harlot, sordid, stocah, varlet 7 servant, servile, slavish 8 coistrel, coistril, servitor 9 degrading underling

meniscus: 4 lens 8 crescent 12 crescent moon

Mennonite: 5 Amish

meno: 4 less

menopause: 12 change of life

Menotti character: 5 Amahl

mental: 5 ideal 6 insane 7 phrenic 9 cognitive 11 intelligent 12 intellectual 13 temperamental

mental aberration: fog 4 daze, haze 5 lapse 6 stupor 7 doldrum, madness 8 insanity

mental defective: 5 idiot, moron 8 imbecile 9 retardate

mental disorder: 6 ataxia 7 aphasia 8 neuritis, neurosis, paranoia 9 melomania, paranomia, psychosis 11 megalomania 12 hypochondria 13 schizophrenia

specialist: 12 psychiatrist

mental faculties: 4 mind, wits

mental image: 4 idea 5 dream 6 idolum 7 fantasy 8 phantasm 10 conception

mental state: 5 blues 6 morale 7 doldrum 8 euphoria

mentality: 4 mind 5 sense 6 acumen, reason 9 endowment, intellect 11 rationality 12 intelligence

mention: 4 cite, hint, mind, name 5 clepe, honor, refer, speak, trace 6 allude, denote, inform, notice, record, remark 7 specify, vestige 8 allusion, citation 9 statement 10 indication

implied: 11 connotation

mentor: 4 guru 7 monitor, teacher 9 counselor 10 instructor

menu: 4 card, meal 5 carte 10 bill of fare

part of: 4 soup 5 salad 6 entree 7 dessert, special 9 appetizer

Mephistophelean: sly 4 evil 6 crafty 7 satanic 8 devilish

mephitic: 4 foul 6 deadly, smelly 7 noxious 8 stinking

mercantile: 7 trading 10 commercial

mercenary: 4 hack 5 venal 6 greedy, sordid 7 Hessian, soldier 8 covetous, hireling, vendible 10 galloglass(Sc.) 11 corruptible, gallowglass 13 stipendiarian

merchandise: 4 sell, ware 5 goods, wares 6 deal in 7 chaffer

cheap: 5 borax 7 camelot, schlock

pert. to: 10 emporeutic

merchant: 4 Seth(Ind.) 5 buyer 6 dealer, seller, sutler, trader, vendor 7 chapman, goladar, howadji, vintner 8 purveyor 9 tradesman 10 shopkeeper 11 storekeeper

group: 5 guild, hansa 6 cartel

ship: 5 oiler 6 argosy, coaler, packet, tanker, trader 7 collier, steamer 8 bilander, Indiaman 9 freighter

wholesale: 6 packer

Merchant of Venice: 7 Antonio

character: 5 Tubal 6 Portia 7 Jessica, Lorenzo, Nerissa, Shylock 8 Bassanio

merciful: 6 benign 7 clement, lenient, sparing 9 benignant, forgiving 10 charitable 13 compassionate

merciless: 4 grim 5 cruel 6 savage 8 pitiless 9 ferocious, graceless, heartless 10 despiteous, implacable, relentless

mercurial: 6 clever, lively, shrewd 8 changing, thievish 9 faithless 10 inconstant

mercury: 5 azoth, guide, thief 6 hawker 9 messenger 11 quicksilver

derivative: 11 quicksilver

Mercury: 6 Hermes, planet

son: 5 Cupid

staff: 8 caduceus

winged cap: 7 petasos, petasus

winged shoes: 7 talaria

mercury chloride: 7 calomel

mercy: law 4 pity, ruth 5 grace, grith 6 lenity 7 charity 8 clemency, humanity, kindness, lenience, leniency, mildness 9 tolerance 10 compassion, indulgence, tenderness 11 forbearance, forgiveness

show: 5 spare 6 pardon 7 forgive 8 reprieve

mercy killing: 10 euthanasia

mere: but, sea 4 bare, club, lake, mear, only, pool, pond, pure, sole 5 bound, limit, plain, sheer, utter 6 divide, entire, famous, scarce, simple 7 unmixed 8 absolute, boundary, glorious, landmark, trifling 9 beautiful, undiluted 11 unqualified

merely: 4 also, just only 5 quite 6 anerly

meretricious: 5 gaudy 6 paltry, vulgar 9 deceptive 10 misleading

merganser: 4 smee, smew 5 harle, robin 7 becscie, bracket, garbill 9 goosander

merge: mix 4 fuse, join, meld 5 blend, unify, unite 6 absorb, mingle 7 combine, conjoin 8 coalesce 9 commingle 10 amalgamate 11 consolidate, incorporate

merger: 5 union 9 coalition 12 amalgamation

mericarp: 8 hemicarp

meridian: 4 apex, noon 6 midday 11 culmination

meringue: 5 icing

merino: 4 wool 5 sheep 6 fabric 7 Delaine

merit: 4 earn, meed 5 worth 6 desert, reward 7 deserve, warrant 10 condignity, excellence

merited: due, fit 7 fitting 8 adequate, suitable

meritorious: 6 worthy 8 laudable, valorous 9 honorable

merkin: mop

merlin: 6 falcon 10 pigeon hawk

Merlin: 4 poem, seer 8 magician 9 alchemist

Merlin's grass: 9 quillwort

mermaid: 5 nymph, siren 6 merrow

meropia: 9 blindness

meros: 5 thigh

merriment: fun 5 deray 9 amusement, diversion, rejoicing, wittiness 11 galliardise 12 cheerfulness, conviviality

merrow: 7 mermaid

merry: gai(F.), gay 4 agog, airy, boon, cant, glad 5 bonny, droll, happy, jolly, sunny 6 blithe, bonnie, cocket, hilary, jocose, jocund, jovial, joyous, lively 7 festive, gleeful, jocular 8 cheerful, chirping, gamesome, gleesome, mirthful, pleasant, sportive 9 hilarious, sprightly 10 blithesome, frolicsome 11 exhilarated 12 lighthearted

merry andrew: 4 zany 5 antic, clown, joker 6 jester 7 buffoon 8 merryman 10 mountebank

merry-go-round: 8 carousel 9 carrousel

Merry Widow composer: 5 Lehar

Merry Wives of Windsor character: Nym 4 Ford 5 Robin 6 Fenton, Pistol 8 Falstaff

merrymaking: 5 jolly, revel 6 splore 7 festive, revelry, wassail 8 carnival 9 festivity, merriment 12 conviviality

merrythought: 8 wishbone

merrywing: 4 duck 9 goldeneye 10 bufflehead

merse: dip 5 marsh 6 plunge 7 immerse

merycism: 10 rumination

mesa: 7 plateau 8 plateaux(pl.) 9 tableland

mescal: 5 cacti(pl.), drink 6 cactus, maguey, peyote, peyotl

mesel: 5 leper 7 leprosy

mesh: net 4 moke 5 snare 6 areola, engage, macula, tangle 7 areolae, ensnare, maculae(pl.), netting, network 8 entangle 9 interlock 10 reticulate

mesial: 6 median, middle

mesmerize: 9 fascinate, hypnotize, spellbind

mesne: 6 middle 11 intervening 12 intermediate

Mesopotamia: 4 Irak, Iraq

ancient city or town: 6 Nippur 7 Babylon

Biblical name: 10 Paddan Aram

capital: **6** Bagdad **7** Baghdad
captives' place: **5** Halah
city: **5** Mosul **7** Edessan, Kerbela
people: **5** Iraki, Iraqi **7** Aramean
river: **6** Tigris **9** Euphrates
wind: **6** shamal
mesquite: **4** tree **5** plant, shrub **9** algarroba
   genus: **8** prosopis
mess: jag, row **4** clat, jagg, meal, mull,
   much, muss, soil **5** batch, botch, cauch,
   dirty, lelee **6** bungle, dabble, jumble, litter, muddle, rumple, tousle **7** crumple,
   mixture, rations, wrinkle **6** disarray, dishevel, disorder, scramble, slaister,
   squabble **9** commotion, confusion,
   mares nest, ugly thing **10** hodgepodge,
   picklement
message: **4** bode, line, memo, news, note,
   wire, word **5** cable **6** brevet, letter **7**
   bodword, depeche, epistle, mission, missive, tidings **9** memoranda **10** communique, memorandum **13** communication
   coded: **10** cryptogram
   good news: **7** evangel
Messalina: **6** wanton **10** prostitute
   husband: **8** Claudius
messenger: **4** bode, page, sand, toty **5** angel, envoy, miler **6** beadle, chiaus, herald, legate, nuncio **7** apostle, carrier,
   courant, courier, hi-carra, mercury,
   prophet, totyman **8** hi-carrah, minister,
   nunciate, portator **9** harbinger **10** ambassador, evangelist, forerunner **11** internuncio
   mounted: **6** cossid(Ind.) **7** courier, estafet
      9 estafette
   of the gods: **6** Hermes **7** Mercury
Messiah: **6** Christ, Savior **7** prophet, Saviour
Messina Strait rock: **6** Scilla, Scylla
messy: **5** dirty **6** sloppy, sticky, untidy
mestizo: **5** cross, metis **7** mixture **9** half-
   breed
metad: rat
metagnomy: **10** divination
metagnostic: **10** unknowable
metal: ore, tin **4** gold, iron, lead, zinc **6**
   cobalt, copper, oroide, pewter, radium,
   silver, sodium, spirit **7** bullion, gallium,
   mercury **9** potassium, substance
   alloy: **5** brass, steel
   bar: gad **5** ingot
   base: **5** dross, sprue
   box: **8** canister
   cake: **4** slag
   clippings: **7** scissel
   containing: **13** metalliferous
   crude: **5** matte
   decorate: **4** etch **6** emboss **9** damascene,
      damaskeen

decorative: **6** chrome, niello
deposit: **4** lode
disc: **5** paten **6** patten
fastener: pin **4** bold, brad, nail **5** rivet,
   screw **6** cotter, solder
filings: **5** lemel
heavy: **6** osmium **7** uranium
impure mass: **7** regulus
layer: **4** seam **5** stope
leaf: **4** foil
lightest known: **7** lithium
lump: pig **4** slug **6** nugget
magnetized: **13** electromagnet
mixture: **5** alloy
nonexpanding: **5** invar
oblong piece: sow
patch: **6** solder
plate: gib
rare: **4** zinc **6** cerium, erbium **7** iridium,
   terbium, uranium, yttrium **8** lutecium,
   platinum
refuse: **4** slag **5** dross **6** scoria
scrap: **6** filing
shaper: **5** swage
sheet: **4** foil **5** lames, plate **6** lamina, latten, tagger
spike: gad
stannic: tin
strip: **6** spline
suit: **4** mail **5** armor
test: **5** assay
tin-like: **7** cadmium
unrefined: ore
vein: **4** lode
waste: **4** slag **5** dross **6** scoria **9** recrement
worker: **5** smith **6** barman **7** riveter **8** tinsmith **9** goldsmith **11** coppersmith, silversmith
metallic: **4** hard **5** tinny **6** brazen **13**
   metalliferous
   content: ory
metamere: **6** somite **8** somatome
metamerism: **12** segmentation
metamorphose: **6** change **9** transform,
   transmute **16** transubstantiate
metamorphosis: **4** pupa **6** change **8** mutation
metaphor: **5** image, trope **6** figure, simile
   8 allegory **10** comparison **11** tralati-
   tion
   faulty or mixed use of: **11** catachresis
metaphorical: **10** figurative
metaphysical: **10** immaterial **12** supernatural, transcendent
metastrophe: **11** interchange
metayer: **6** farmer
mete: **4** dole, give, goal, post **5** allot,
   award, bound, limit, stake **7** measure **8**
   allocate, boundary **9** apportion **10** distribute
meteor: **5** bolis, Cetid, comet, Lyrid **6**
   Antlid, bolide, Lyraid **8** aerolite, fireball

9 Andromede 10 Andromedid 12 heavenly body

August: 8 Perseids

November: 6 Leonid

meteoric: 8 flashing 9 celestial, transient

meteorite: 8 aerolite, aerolith, siderite

meteorological instrument: 6 bolide 9 barometer 11 thermometer

meteorologist: 10 forecaster

meteorology: 14 study of weather

meter: 4 beat, time 5 metre, swing, verse 6 rhythm 7 cadence, measure 8 measurer

cubic: 5 liter, litre, stere

one-hundredth: 10 centimeter

one-millionth: 6 micron

one-tenth: 9 decimeter

one-thousandth: 10 millimeter

square: 7 centare

unit: 4 mora 5 morae(pl.)

meterist: 10 verse-maker

meters: *10:* 9 decameter

100: 10 hectometer

100 square: ar; are

1,000: 9 kilometer

10,000: 10 myriameter

methane hydrocarbon: 8 paraffin 9 paraffine

metheglin: 4 mead 8 beverage

method: way 4 dart, form, garb, mode, rule 5 means, order, style, usage 6 course, manner, system 7 fashion, formula, process 9 procedure, technique 11 orderliness

customary: rut 5 habit 7 routine

methodical: 5 exact 6 severe 7 orderly, precise

methodize: 8 regulate 11 systematize

Methuselah: *father:* 5 Enoch

grandson: 4 Noah

son: 6 Lamech

methyl: *cyanide:* 7 nitrile

ethyl ketone: 8 butanone

ketol: 6 acetol

meticulous: 4 neat, nice, prim 5 fussy, timid 7 careful, fearful, finical 10 fastidious, scrupulous

metier: 4 line 5 trade 7 calling 8 business 10 occupation, profession

metis: 8 octoroon 9 halfbreed

metric: 8 criteria(pl.) 9 criterion

measure: are 5 carat, liter, litre, meter, stere, tonne 6 decare, hectar, micron, miglio 7 centare, deciare, dekiare, hectare, kiliare, manzana, myriare 8 centiare, dekagram, milliare 9 decaliter, decameter, decastere, deciliter, decimeter, decistere, dekaliter, dekameter, dekistere, kiloliter, kilometer, kilostere, megameter 10 centiliter, centimeter, centistere, dekadrachm, hectoliter, hectometer, hectostere, microliter, milliliter, millimeter, millistere, myrialiter, myriameter 15 micromillimeter

metrical beat: 5 ictus

metrical foot: 4 iamb 6 iambic, iambus 7 anapest

accented syllable: 5 arsis

four syllables: 6 syzygy

three short syllables: 8 tribrach

two syllables: 7 spondee, trochee

two together: 6 dipody

metrist: 4 poet 9 metrician

metronome: 5 timer

metropolis: see 4 city, seat 6 center

metropolitan: cit 5 chief, urban 7 bishops, leading 9 principal 10 archbishop

mettle: 4 fire 5 ardor, nerve, pluck, spunk 6 ginger, spirit 7 bravery, courage 9 fortitude

mettlesome: 5 brave, fiery, proud 6 ardent 8 skittish, spirited

Metz's river: 7 Moselle

meuse: gap 4 hole, lurk 7 conceal, opening 8 loophole

mew: den 4 cage, cast, coop, gull, maas(Sp.), molt, shed 5 miaow, miaul 6 change 7 conceal, confine, enclose, garages, stables 8 spicknel 9 enclosure 11 concealment, confinement

mewl: cry 5 whine 6 squall 7 whimper

Mexico: *agave:* 5 datil 6 zapupe

alcoholic beverage: 6 mescal, pulque 7 tepache, tequila

American: 6 gringo

annuity: 5 censo

antelope: 9 pronghorn

bean: 6 fejol, frijol 7 frijole

bedbug: 8 conenose

beverage: 4 chia

bird: 6 jacana, towhee 7 jacamar, tinamou 8 zopilote

blanket: 6 serape

bread: 6 tamale

brigand: 7 ladrone

bull: 4 toro

cactus: 6 bavoso, chaute, chende, mescal 8 alicoche, chichipe 11 alfilerillo

candlewood: 8 ocotillo

capital: 10 Mexico City

cat: 6 margay

chaps(leather): 10 chaparajos, chaparejos

city: 4 Leon, Tula 5 Tepic 6 Colima, Jalapa, Juarez, Merida, Oaxaca, Puebla, Potosi 7 Durango, Orizaba, San Luis, Tampico, Tijuana, Torreon 8 Culiacan, Mazatlan, Mexicali, Saltillo, Vera Cruz, Victoria 9 Chihuahua, Monterrey 10 Hermosillo 11 Guadalajara

cloak: 5 manta 6 serape

cockroach: 9 cucaracha

coin: 4 peso 5 adobe 6 azteca 7 centavo, piaster

conqueror: 6 Cortes, Cortez

cottonwood: **5** alamo
dish: **4** taco **5** atole, tamal **6** tamale **8** tortilla **9** enchilada, guacamole
dollar **4** peso
drug: **7** damiana
early dweller: **4** Maya **5** Aztec
export: **6** coffee, cotton, sulfur **9** petroleum
fiber: **4** pita **5** istle, sisal **6** catena
fish: **6** salema **7** totuava
garment: **5** manga **6** serape **7** chiripa
gopher: **4** tuza **7** quachil
grapefruit: **7** toronja
grass: **5** otate **7** sacaton, zacaton **8** hanequen, hanequin
guardian spirit: **6** nagual
hero: **4** Diaz **6** Juarez
hog: **7** peccary
house: **5** jacal
Indian: see *people* below
ivy: **6** cobaea
laborer: **4** peon **7** bracero, wetback
lake: **7** Chapala
land owner: **8** ranchero
language: **7** Nahuatl, Spanish
laurel: **7** madrona
masonry: **5** adobe
mat: **6** petate
measure: pie **4** alma, vara **5** almud, baril, jarra, labor, legua, linea, sitio **6** almude, fanega **7** pulgada **8** curtillo **9** cuarteron **10** caballeria
measure of weight: bag **4** onza **5** carga, libra, marco **6** adarme, arroba, ochava, tercio **7** quintal
mixed blood: **7** mestizo
mountain: **7** Orizaba **12** Citlaltepetl, Ixtaccihuatl, Popocatepetl
musical instrument: **6** clarin, guiros **7** cabacas, maracas **11** chiapanecas
onyx: **6** tecali
orange: **7** choisya
painter: **6** Orozco, Rivera
pancake: **5** arepa
peasant: **4** peon
peninsula: **7** Yucatan **14** Baja California
people: Mam **4** Cora, Maya, Seri, Xova **5** Aztec, Hauve, Lipan, Nahau, Opata, Otomi, Yaqui, Zoque **6** Indian, Mixtec, Otonia, Toltec **7** Haustec, Nahuatl, Tepanec, Zacatec, Zapotec **8** Totonaco, Zaceteco **9** Campesino **10** Cuitlateca, Cuitlateco
plant: **4** chia **5** agave, amole, datil, jalap, sotol **6** chaute, maguey, slavia **7** tequila **8** acapulco **9** sabadilla
plantation: **8** hacienda
porridge: **5** atole
porter: **5** tamen
ranch: **8** hacienda
resort: **8** Acapulco
river: **6** Penuco **7** Tabasco **9** Rio Grande

rubber tree: ule
sandal: **8** gauracha, guarache, guaracho, huarache, huaracho
sandwich: **4** taco
sauce: **7** tabasco
scarf: **6** rebozo, tapalo
shawl: **6** serape
shrub: **6** anagua, anaqua, colima **7** choisya
state: **6** Colima, Sonora **7** Durango, Hidalgo, Sinaloa, Tabasco, Yucatan **9** Michoacan
sugar: **7** panocha
tea: **6** basote **7** apasote **9** alpasotes
thong: **5** romal
tree: ule **4** sero **5** abeto, amapa, ebano, ocote **6** chacte, colima, mezcal, sabino **7** capulin, colorin **8** chaparro, ulmaceae **9** ahuehuete, canadulce **10** anacahuita
village: **6** ejidos, tecali
volcano: **6** Colima **7** Jorullo **9** Paricutin **12** Popocatepetl
weight: **4** onza
yucca: **5** isote
mezereum: **5** shrub **6** daphne **8** camillia
mezzanine: **5** story **7** balcony **8** entresol
mias: **9** orangutan
miasma: **7** malaria
miaul: mew **4** meow, wraw **5** miaou, miaow **9** caterwaul
mib: **6** marble
mica: **4** talc **5** glist **7** biotite **8** silicate **9** damourite, hydromica, isinglass, muscovite **10** lepidolite
micaceous: **7** talcose
Micah: **7** prophet
son: **5** Abdon
miche: **4** lurk **5** skulk, sneak **6** pilfer **7** conceal, spy upon
Michelangelo work: **5** David, Pieta **12** Last Judgment **13** Sistine Chapel
micher: **5** cheat, thief **6** truant **8** panderer
Michigan: *capital:* **7** Lansing
city: **5** Flint, Ionia **7** Detroit, Pontiac **8** Ann Arbor, Muskegon **9** Marquette **11** Grand Rapids
county: Bay **4** Kent **6** Inghum **7** Berrien, Calhoun, Genesee **9** Kalamazoo
early explorer: **7** La Salle **9** Marquette
Indian: **6** Ottawa
island: **8** Mackinaw
lake: **4** Burt, Erie **5** Huron, Torch **8** Houghton, Michigan
mountain peak: **7** Curwood
nickname: **9** Wolverine
river: **5** Huron **7** Au Sable **8** Manistee, Muskegan **9** Menominee
state bird: **5** robin
state fish: **10** brook trout
state flower: **12** apple blossom
state tree: **9** white pine
mickle: **4** much **5** great

mico: 8 marmoset
micraner: ant
micro: 4 moth
microbe: 4 germ 8 bacillus, organism
microcosm: 5 world 7 village 8 universe 9 community
microfilm sheet: 5 fiche
Micronesia island: 4 Guam, Wake 5 Palau 6 Bikini, Ellice, Saipan
microorganism: 4 germ 5 virus 6 aerobe 7 aerobia 8 aerobium 9 autoblast, spirillum 10 spirochete 11 spirochaete
microphone: bug, 4 mike 8 parabola
microscope: 5 glass 9 magnifier
microscopic: 5 small 6 minute 9 engyscope
microspore: 6 pollen
microsporophyll: 6 stamen
mid: See midst
midday: 4 noon 8 noontide
intermission: 5 lunch 7 nooning 8 noon hour
nap: 6 siesta
middle: 4 mean, part 5 mesne, midst, waist 6 center, centre, centry, median, mesial 7 average, central, centric 9 in between 11 intervening 12 intermediate 13 intermediator
combining form: mes 4 medi, meso
way: 6 midway 7 halfway 10 moderation
Middle Ages: See medieval
Middle East: 6 Levant
country: 4 Iran, Iraq, Oman 5 Egypt, Qatar, Sudan, Syria, Yemen 6 Israel, Jordan, Kuwait 7 Bahrain, Lebanon 11 Saudi Arabia
middleman: 5 agent, butty 6 dealer, trader 8 huckster, retailer 9 go-between 12 interlocutor, intermediary
middling: 4 fair, so-so 6 fairly, medium 7 average 8 mediocre, moderate, ordinary, somewhat 10 moderately 11 indifferent
midge: fly 4 fish, gnat, runt 5 dwarf, stout 6 insect, midget, punkie 8 carriage
midget: 5 dwarf, small 9 miniature
midi: (see also mini) 11 skirt length
Midianite: king: Hur 4 Reba
prince: Evi, Zur
midshipman: 5 cadet 6 reefer
midst: 4 amid, mean 5 among, depth 6 amidst, center, centre, medium, middle, mongst 7 between, halfway, setting 11 surrounding
midwife: 4 baba, dhai(Ind.) 6 cummer, kimmer 9 gracewife 10 accoucheur(F.) 11 accoucheuse(F.), finger-smith
mien: air, eye 4 brow, vult 5 guise 6 aspect, manner, ostent 7 bearing, conduct 8 attitude, behavior, carriage, demeanor 9 behaviour, demeanour 10 appear-

ance, deportment 11 countenance
miffed: 5 sulky, vexed 8 offended 10 displeased
mig: 6 marble 11 sitting duck
migale: 5 mouse, shrew
migeloid fish: 4 bobo
might: arm 4 mote 7 ability 8 strength
mighty: big 4 bulk, fell, vast, very 5 felon, great 6 potent, strong 7 violent 8 enormous, forceful, forcible, powerful, puissant, vigorous 9 extensive, extremely, gigantean 10 omnipotent 11 efficacious
migniard: 6 dainty, minion 7 mincing 8 delicate, mistress
mignon: 5 small 6 dainty, petite 8 delicate, graceful
mignonette: 4 herb 6 reseda
vine: 7 Madeira, tarweed
migraine: 4 whim 8 headache 10 hemicrania
migrant: See migratory
migrate: 4 flee, flit, move, pass, trek 8 colonize, transfer
migration: 5 exode 6 exodus, flight 8 diaspora, movement
of top experts: 10 brain drain
migratory: 6 roving 7 nomadic 9 peregrine, wandering
bird: 4 duck 5 goose, robin
farm worker: 4 Okie
Mikado: 8 operetta 9 sovereign
court: 5 dairi
office 9 mikadoate
milke: 10 microphone
milady: 4 dame 5 madam 10 noblewoman 11 gentlewoman
Milan opera house: 5 Scala
milarite: 8 silicate
mild: moy 4 calm, easy, kind, meek, soft, tame 5 balmy, bland, claro 6 benign, gentle, humble 7 clement, lenient 8 benedict, favonian, gracious, lenitive, merciful, moderate, soothing, tranquil 9 assuasive, forgiving, indulgent, temperate 10 forbearing, mollifying 11 considerate
mildew: 4 mold, rust 5 mould 6 blight, fungus 8 honeydew
genus of: 7 erysibe 8 erysiphe
mildness: 6 comity 8 leniency, meekness 10 good nature, moderation
mile: nautical: 4 knot, naut
one-eighth: 7 furlong
mileage: 8 distance
milepost: 4 mark 5 stela, stele 6 marker, stelae
miler: 6 runner
milestone: 5 event 8 landmark, occasion
milfoil: 6 yarrow 9 ahartalav
milieu: 11 environment 12 surroundings

militant: **7** martial, soldier, warlike **8** fighting **9** combating, combative **10** aggressive

military (see also **army, troop**): **7** martial, warlike

advance: **5** drive **8** anabasis **11** penetration **12** breakthrough

adventurer: **10** filibuster

area: **6** sector

assistant: **4** aide **8** adjutant

base: **4** camp **5** depot, field **7** billets **8** barracks, quarters **10** encampment

call: **6** tattoo

chest: **5** funds

cloak: **5** sagum

command: **4** halt **6** at ease **9** attention

commander: **7** marshal

commission: **6** brevet

engine: ram **6** cannon, onager **7** robinet **8** catapult, mangonel

force: **5** guard **6** legion, troops **7** reserve

formation: **4** file, line **7** echelon

front: **5** lines **6** sector

guard: **6** patrol

hat: **4** kepi **5** shako **6** helmet

hat covering: **8** havelock

horsemen: **7** cavalry, Hussars

informer: spy

inspection: **5** drill **6** parade, review

landing point: **9** beachhead

machine: **4** jeep, tank

maneuver: **6** tactic

messenger: **7** estafet

obstruction: **6** abatis **7** abattis

officer: **5** major **7** captain, colonel, general **9** brigadier, subaltern **10** lieutenant

operations: **8** campaign, strategy

order: **7** command

organization: **5** cadre

pit: **10** trou-de-loup

police: M.P. **9** gendarmes **12** constabulary

prisoner: POW

punishment: **9** strappado

quarters: **4** camp **7** billets **8** barracks

rank: **6** brevet **8** banneret

salute: **5** salvo

signal: **7** chamade

special forces: **10** Green Beret

staff officer: **4** aide

storage place: **5** depot, étape **6** armory **7** arsenal

supplies: **8** materiel, ordnance

survey: **11** reconnoiter

unit: van **4** rear **5** cadre, corps, squad, troop **7** company, platoon **8** division, regiment **9** battalion

vehicle: **4** jeep, tank **6** camion **7** caisson **9** half-track

weapon: **4** croc **6** onager **7** robinet **8** ballista **9** catapult

work: **4** fort

militate: **5** fight, weigh **6** debate **7** contend **8** conflict

milk: lac **4** draw, lait(F.) **5** drain, nurse **6** elicit, suckle **7** exploit

coagulator: **6** rennet

curdled: **6** yogurt **7** clabber, yoghurt, yogourt **8** yoghourt

curdler: **4** ruen **6** rennet

deodorizer: **7** aerator

derived from: **6** lactic

fermented: **5** kefir, kumys **6** koumis, koumys, kumiss **7** koumiss, matzoon

first after delivery: **9** beestings, biestings, colostrum

food: **10** lacticinia

mouse: **6** spurge

pail: soa, soe **5** bowie

pert. to: **6** lactic **7** lactary, lacteal

preparation: **9** lactarene, lactarine

protein: **6** casein

sap: **5** latex

selling place: **5** dairy **9** lactarium

separator: **7** creamer

sour: **4** whig **6** blinky

sugar: **7** lactose

thickened part: **4** curd

watery: **8** blue John

watery part: **4** whey

with: **6** aulait(F.)

milk and honey: **10** prosperity

milk-and-water: **4** weak **7** insipid **10** mamby-pamby, wishy-washy

milk leg: **9** phlebitis

milkfish: awa **6** sabolo

milksop: **4** fool **5** sissy **6** coward **7** cockney **8** weakling **11** mollycoddle

milkweed: *down:* **4** silk

family: **14** asclepiadaceae

fluid: **5** latex

milkwood: **4** tree **5** shrub **9** paperbark

milky: **4** meek, milk, tame **5** timid, white **6** chalky, gentle **7** lacteal, opaline **8** timorous **10** effeminate

Milky Way: **6** galaxy

black spaces in: **9** coalsacks

mill: box **4** beat, nurl **5** crush, dress, fight, grind, knurl, shape, thief **6** finish, powder, thrash **7** factory, machine **8** snuffbox, vanquish **9** comminute, transform **12** housebreaker

end: **7** remnant

run of the: **7** average **8** ordinary

millennium: **6** utopia **8** paradise

millepore: **5** coral

miller: ray **4** moth **5** boxer **7** harrier **8** pugilist **10** flycatcher

miller's thumb: **4** bird, fish **7** warbler **8** cottidae, titmouse **9** goldcrest

millerite: **7** sulfide

millesimal: **10** thousandth

millet: 5 grain 6 cereal
millimeter: *one millionth:* 15 micromillimeter
one thousandth: 6 micron
milliner: 6 hatter
millions of millions: 9 trillions
millpond: dam
millrace: 4 lade(Sc.) 10 millcourse
below wheel: 8 tailrace
millrind: 6 moline
millstone: 6 burden 7 grinder 9 albatross
10 affliction, deadweight
support: 4 rind, rynd
millstream: 5 fleam
milo: 5 grain 7 sorghum
milpa: 5 field 6 chacra 8 clearing
milt: 6 spleen
mim: shy 4 prim 5 quiet 6 demure, modest
mime: ape 4 aper, copy, jest 5 actor,
clown, drama, farce, mimer, mimic 6
comedy, jester 7 buffoon, gesture, imitate 9 represent 11 impersonate
chief: 9 archi-mime
mimeograph: 4 copy 7 stencil
mimesis: 7 mimicry 9 imitation
mimic (see also **mime**): 4 mima,
mimo(G.), mock 6 parrot 7 copy-cat,
copying, mimetic 9 burlesque 11 counterfeit
mimic thrush: 11 mockingbird
mimicry: 4 echo 5 apery, apism 7 mimesis 8 parrotry 9 imitation 10 camouflage
mimidae: 7 catbird 8 thrasher 11 mockingbird
mimmock: 6 dainty 10 fastidious
mimosa: 4 tree 6 acadia 8 turmeric
mimsey: 4 prim 7 prudish
minaret: 5 tower
minatory: 8 menacing 11 threatening
minaway: 6 minuet
mince: cut 4 chop, gait, hash, meat 5
grind 6 affect 7 finnick 9 subdivide 11
affectation
mincemeat: 5 gigot 10 pie filling
minchiate: 5 tarot
mincing: 5 fussy 6 la-di-da, too-too 7 finical 8 affected 11 persnickety
mincingly: 8 gingerly
mind: min(Sc.) 4 care, chit, heed, obey,
reck, tend, will 5 besee, brain, manas
(Ind.), watch 6 animus, burrow, memory, notice, psyche, regard 7 dislike, dispose 9 intellect, mentality 11 inclination, remembrance 12 intelligence,
recollection
keep in: 9 entertain
origin and development: 13 psychogenesis
pert. to: 6 mental, noetic 7 phrenic 13
psychological
split: 13 schizophrenic

state of: 4 mood, tune
Mindanao: *gulf:* 5 Davao
island: 5 Samal
language: Ata
people: Ata 5 Lutao 6 Bagobo, Illano, Lu-
tayo
town: 4 Dapa
volcano: Apo
mind-blowing: 11 psychedelic 12 overwhelming
mindful: 5 aware 7 heedful 9 attentive,
observant, regardful
mine: bal, dig, pit, sap 4 delf, hole, meum
(It.) 5 bargh, delft, delve 6 cavity, gopher, threat 7 gallery, passage 8 colliery
10 excavation 13 treasure trove
basket: 4 corf
ceiling: 5 astel
chisel: gad
coal: rob
deposit: 4 lode, vein
entrance: 4 adit 5 stulm
excavation: 5 stope
extraction: ore, tin 4 gold, lead 6 silver 8
diamonds
partition: 8 brattice
passage: 4 sill 5 stope
platform: 6 sollar, soller
product: ore 4 coal, iron
prop: 5 sprag
refuse: 4 dead 5 attle
reservoir: 4 sump 8 standage
rich: 4 lode 7 bonanza 8 golconda
roof support: nog
shaft: 4 sump
surface: 6 placer
sweeping device: 8 paravane
tunnel: 4 adit 5 stulm
vein: 4 lode
wagon: 4 tram
waste: gob 4 goaf 5 attle 7 rubbish
worker: 5 cager, miner 6 canary 7 cage-
man, trapper 8 onsetter
mine run: 6 common 7 average 11 un-
sorted ore
miner: 6 dammer(Sc.), digger, sapper 7
collier
miner's consumption: 8 phthisis 9 black
lung
mineral (see also **ore, metal**): cal, tin 5
irite 6 barite, iolite 7 alumite, ataxite,
uralite 9 celestite, galactite, inorganic,
uraninite 10 gadolinite, retinalite
amorphous: 6 pinite
black: jet 4 coal 5 irite 6 cerine, yenite 7
knopite, niobite 8 graphite 10 mingue-
tite
blue-green: 5 beryl
brittle: euclase
brown: 6 cerine, egeran, rutile 8 lederite 9
elaterite
calcium and magnesium: 8 diopside

calcium carbonate: **7** calcite **8** calcspar
crystalline: **4** spar **6** yenite **7** apatite, felsite, felspar, knopite **8** boracite, elaterin, felspath
deposit: **4** lode, nest, vein **6** placer
deposit cavity: vug **4** voog, vugg, vugh
earth like: **5** glebe
fibrous: **8** asbestos, oakenite
flaky: **4** mica
gray-green: **7** edenite
gray-white: **5** trona **14** chromiumptrona
green: **7** alalite, apatite, epidote, erinite, prasine, uralian **9** demantoid
gunpowder: **5** niter
hard: **6** spinel **7** adamant **8** corundum, spinelle
lustrous: **4** spar **7** blendes **8** smaltine, smaltite
magnetic: **9** lodestone
mixture: **5** magma
native: ore
non-combustible: **8** asbestos
non-metallic: **4** spar **5** boron **6** gangue, iodine
plaster of paris: **6** gypsum
potash: **4** alum
potassium sulfate: **8** misenite
quartz-like: **4** opal
rare: **7** euclase, thorite
red: **5** balas **6** garnet, rutile
salt: **4** alum
seam: **4** vein
silicate: **4** mica
smelting: ore
soft: **4** talc **6** gypsum
spot: **5** macle
tallow: **11** hatchettine
tar: **4** brea **6** maltha
transparent: **4** mica **5** fluor
vitreous: **4** spar **7** apatite
wax-like: **9** ozocerite
white: **6** barite **8** smaltine, smaltite
yellow: **4** iron **5** topaz **6** pyrite
yellowish green: **7** apidote
mineral jelly: **8** Vaseline
mineral oil: **5** colza **9** petroleum
mineral spring: spa **4** well
mineral water: **6** selter **7** seltzer
Minerva: **6** Athena, Athene
shield: **5** aegis
minestrone: **4** soup
ming: **6** remind **7** mention, recount **8** remember
minge: **5** midge
mingle: mix **4** amix, fuse, join, meng, mool **5** admix, blend, merge, unite **6** huddle **7** blender, combine, compost **8** coalesce, compound, intermix **9** associate, commingle **10** amalgamate, be sociable **11** consolidate
mingle-mangle: **6** medley **7** mixture **10** hodgepodge

mingwort: **8** wormwood
mingy: **4** mean **6** stingy
mini: **8** small car, **9** miniature, **10** short skirt
miniate: **8** decorate, luminate, paint red **9** rubricate
miniature: **4** copy, tiny **5** small, teeny **6** little, minute **8** painting, portrait **9** lineament, miniating **10** diminutive **11** little thing, rubrication **12** illumination **14** representation
minikin: **6** dainty **7** darling, elegant, mincing **8** affected, delicate **10** diminutive
minim: jot **4** drop, fish **6** minnow, minute **7** tiniest **8** smallest **9** miniature **10** diminutive
minimize: **6** reduce **7** detract **8** belittle **9** disparage **10** depreciate
minimum: **5** least **6** lowest
minion: **4** idol, neat **5** lover **6** dainty, pretty **7** darling, elegant **8** creature, delicate, favorite, ladylove, mistress, paramour **9** underling
minister: **4** tend **5** angel, serve **6** afford, attend, cleric, curate, divine, pander, parson, pastor, supply **7** furnish, provide, servant **8** executor, preacher, reverend **9** attendant, clergyman, upstander **10** administer, ambassador
home: **5** manse **9** parsonage
minitant: **11** threatening
Minnesota: *capital:* **6** St. Paul
city: Ely **5** Edina **6** Duluth, Winona **7** St. Cloud **9** Rochester **11** Bloomington, Minneapolis
county: **4** Cass, Clay, Cook, Lake, Pine, Polk, Pope, Rice, Todd **5** Dodge, Swift **6** Atkin, Benton, Carver, Dakota, Ramsey, Roseau, Sibley, Wadena, Wilkin **7** Kanabee, Stearns **8** Hennepin
early explorer: **4** Pike **7** La Salle **8** Hennepin
Indian: **5** Sioux **6** Ojibwa **8** Chippewa
lake: Red **7** Bemidji **8** Superior
motto: **9** North Star
mountain peak: **5** Eagle **7** Misquah
mountain range: **6** Cuyuna, Mesabi **10** Vermillion
nickname: **6** Gopher **9** North Star
river: **5** Rainy **7** St. Croix
state bird: **4** loon
state flower: **11** lady slipper
state tree: **7** red pine
minnow: **5** guppy **6** baggie
minor: **4** less **5** petit, petty, youth **6** infant, lesser, slight **7** smaller **8** inferior **11** subordinate **15** inconsequential
minorate: **7** curtail **8** diminish
minority: few **6** nonage **10** immaturity **11** inferiority
Minos: *child:* **7** Ariadne, Phaedra **9** Androgeus

country: **5** Crete
father: **4** Zeus
lover: **6** Scylla
monster: **8** Minotaur
mother: **6** Europa
slayer: **7** Cocalus
wife: **8** Pasiphae
Minotaur: *father:* **4** bull
home: **9** labyrinth
mother: **8** Pasiphae
owner: **5** Minos
slayer: **7** Theseus
minster: **6** church **9** cathedral, monastery
minstrel: **4** bard, bhat(Ind.), moke, poet **6** harper, jockey, singer **7** gleeman, goliard, Pierrot **8** jongleur, musician **9** blackface, troubador **10** gleemaiden, mountebank, troubadour **11** entertainer
accompanist: **7** harpist
minstrel show: *endman:* **7** Mr. Bones, Mr. Tambo
middleman: **12** interlocutor
part: **4** olio
mint: aim, iva **4** blow, coin, sage **5** basil, feint, money, thyme **6** catnip, hyssop, intend, mentha, ramona **7** attempt, dittany, potherb, purpose, venture **8** bergamot, brand-new, calamint, endeavor, lavender, marjoram **9** fabricate, horehound **12** spick-and-span
charge: see *levy* below
family: **9** lamiaceae
genus of: **7** melissa **10** moluccella
geranium: **8** costmary
herb family: **4** balm **5** basil **6** hyssop
levy: **8** brassage **11** seigniorage
mintage: **5** stamp **7** coinage
minuet: **5** dance
movement: **5** scherzo
minus: **4** lack, less **6** defect, devoid **7** lacking, without **8** negative, subtract **10** deficiency
minuscule: **4** tiny **5** petty, small **6** minute **9** very small **10** diminutive, manuscript **13** insignificant
minute: jot, wee **4** mite, nice, note, time, tiny **5** draft, exact, petty, small **6** atomic, little, moment, record, slight, tittle **7** instant, minutia, precise **8** detailed, trifling **9** memoranda(pl.) **10** blow-by-blow, memorandum **13** imperceptible **14** circumstantial
glass: **9** hourglass
minutely: **7** exactly **9** continual, unceasing
minutes: **4** acta **5** actum **6** record
minutiae: **7** details, trifles **11** particulars
minx: dog **4** girl, jade **5** woman
Minyae king: **7** Athamas
minyan: **6** quorum
mir: **4** head **5** chief **6** leader **9** community
Mira: **4** star

constellation: **5** Cetus
mirabile dictu: **9** wonderful
mirabilia: **7** marvels, wonders **8** miracles
miracle: **4** feat **5** anomy **6** marvel, wonder **8** act of God **10** occurrence, phenomenon
scene of: **4** Cana
worker of: **8** magician **11** thaumaturge
miraculous: **9** marvelous, unnatural, wonderful **12** supernatural
mirador: **5** oriel **6** loggia, turret **7** balcony **10** watchtower
mirage: **5** serab **7** chimera **8** delusion, illusion **10** phenomenon, refraction
Miranda's father: **8** Prospero
mire: bog, mud, wet **4** glar, moil, ooze, slew, slob, sloo, slud, slue **5** addle, embog, glaur(Sc.), marsh, sluig, slush, stall, swamp **6** defile, slough, sludge **7** clabber, sludder **8** entangle, slow down
mire duck: **7** mallard
Miriam: *brother:* **5** Aaron, Moses
father: **5** Amram
mother: **8** Jochebed
mirific: **9** marvelous, wonderful
mirror: **5** glass, model **7** reflect **8** speculum **9** girandole **12** looking glass
pert. to: **9** catoptric **11** catoptrical
mirth: fun, joy **4** glee **5** cheer **6** bawdry, gaiety, levity, spleen **7** delight, jollity **8** gladness, hilarity, laughter **9** festivity, happiness, merriment **10** jocularity, joyousness **12** cheerfulness
god: **5** Comus
mirthful: **5** cadgy, merry
miry: **5** boggy, muddy **6** filthy, swampy **7** guttery
misadventure: **4** slip **5** boner, lapse **6** mishap **7** faux pas **8** accident **9** cataclysm **11** catastrophe
misanthrope: **5** cynic, hater, loner, Timon
misanthropic: **7** cynical **10** antisocial
misapplication: **5** abuse **6** disuse **10** perversion
misappropriate: **5** steal **8** embezzle
misbegotten: **7** bastard **8** spurious **10** fatherless **12** illegitimate
misbehave: **7** disobey, misbear, mislead
misbeliever: **7** heretic, infidel **9** miscreant
misbirth: **8** abortion
miscalculate: err **9** overshoot
miscall: **5** abuse **6** revile **7** misname, slander
miscarriage: **5** lapse **6** mishap **7** failure, misdeed, mistake **8** abortion **9** mischance **11** misdemeanor **13** mismanagement
miscarry: err **4** fail **5** misgo **7** founder **9** fall short
miscegenation: **13** interbreeding
miscellaneous: **5** mixed **6** sundry, varied

8 assorted 13 heterogeneous 14 indiscriminate

miscellany: 4 olio 10 adversaria, hodgepodge

mischance: See **misfortune**

mischief: ate, hob, ill 4 bane, evil, harm, hurt 5 prank, wrack 6 damage, injury 7 cantip, devilry 8 deviltry 9 devilment, diablerie 10 disservice

god: 4 Loki

goddess: Ate 4 Eris

mischiefmaker: elf, imp, wag 5 knave, rogue

mischievous: sly 4 arch, impy 5 elfin, hempy 6 elfish, elvish, impish 7 harmful, knavish, malefic, mocking, naughty, parlous, roguish, teasing, waggish 8 prankish, sportive, venomous 9 injurious

mischievous child: imp 4 brat, limb 5 devil, scamp 6 monkey 7 hellion

miscible: 7 mixable

misconception: 8 abortion 16 misunderstanding

misconduct: 7 offense 8 disorder 9 mismanage 11 delinquency, malfeasance, misbehavior, misdemeanor

mark of: 7 demerit

miscreant: 5 knave 6 rascal, wretch 7 heretic, infidel, villain 8 criminal 9 hereticl, scoundrel 10 unbeliever 11 misbeliever, unbelieving 12 unscrupulous

miscue: 4 miss, slip 5 error 7 mistake

misdeed: sin 4 slip 5 crime, wrong 7 forfeit, offense 8 disorder 11 delinquency 13 transgression

misdemeanor: sin 5 crime, fault, wrong 6 delict 7 misdeed, offense 8 disorder 11 delinquency 12 misdemeanant 13 transgression

misdirect: 7 distort, pervert

mise: 4 levy, pact 5 grant 6 layout, treaty 8 immunity 9 agreement, privilege

misease: 7 poverty 8 distress 10 discomfort

mise-en-scène: set 4 site 7 setting 12 stage setting

miser: 4 cuff 5 churl, flint, hayne, hunks, Nabal 6 codger, huddle, nipper, snudge, wretch 7 hoarder, niggard 8 holdfast 9 collector, skinflint 10 curmudgeon

miserable: bad 4 dawy 6 abject, chetif, elenge, feeble 7 forlorn, pitiful 8 pitiable 10 despicable, discomfort, inadequate 12 disconsolate 13 commiserative

misericord: 4 hall 6 dagger 9 refectory 10 compassion

miserly: 4 mean 5 close, gnede 6 greedy, grippy, stingy 8 covetous, grasping 9 penurious, scrimping 10 avaricious 12 parsimonious

misery: woe 4 ache, pain, ruth 5 agony 6 sorrow 7 anguish, avarice, poverty, sadness, squalor 8 calamity, distress 9 adversity, privation, suffering 10 affliction, depression, misfortune 11 despondency, unhappiness 12 covetousness, wretchedness 13 niggardliness 14 unpleasantness

misfeasance: See **malfeasance**

misfortune: woe 4 dole, evil, harm, slip 5 grief 6 misery, mishap, scathe 7 ill-luck, misfare, reverse, trouble 8 accident, calamity, casualty, disaster 9 adversity, holocaust, infortune, mischance 10 affliction, ill-fortune 11 catastrophe, contretemps, miscarriage 12 misadventure

misgiving: 5 doubt, qualm 7 anxiety 12 apprehension

misguide: 5 abuse 6 injure 7 mislead 8 misteach 9 misbehave, misdirect, misgovern, mismanage

mishandle: 6 bungle 7 rough up

mishap: See **misfortune**

mishmash: 4 olio 6 jumble 10 hodgepodge

Mishnah: 6 Talmud 9 scripture

pert. to: 7 tannaic 8 Mishnaic

section: 4 Moed 5 Aboth

supplement: 8 Toseftas

misinterpret: err 4 warp 7 misread

misjudge: err 12 miscalculate, misinterpret

misky: 5 foggy, misty

mislay: 4 lose 8 misplace

mislead: 4 dupe, fool 5 blear, cheat 6 betray, delude, humbug 7 beguile, debauch, deceive 8 hoodwink, inveigle, misguide 9 duplicate, mismanage

misleading: 5 false 7 crooked 10 fallacious, fraudulent

mismanage: 5 blunk 6 bungle

misplace: 4 lose 6 mislay

misplay: err 5 error 6 renege

mispronunciation: 8 cacology 12 speech defect 13 error in speech

misrepresent: lie 5 belie 6 garble 7 deceive

miss: err, fau, hip 4 balk, chit, fail, girl, lack, lass, lose, muff, omit, skip, slip, snab, want 5 lapse, title 6 escape, lassie, miscue 7 deviate, failure, neglect 8 fraulein(G.), miscarry, mistress, overlook, senorita(Sp.), spinster 9 signorina(It.) 10 desiderate, jeune fille, prostitute 12 mademoiselle(F.) 13 misunderstand

missay: 5 abuse 6 vilify 7 slander

misshapen: 4 ugly 6 clumsy 8 deformed 9 distorted, misformed, monstrous 11 counterfeit

missile: (see also **guided missile**) 4 bola, bolt, dart, shot 5 arrow, shaft, spear 6 bullet, rocket, weapon 7 missive, outcast **8** brickbat **9** boomerang **10** projectile

pert. to: **9** ballistic

missing: out **4** lost **6** absent

mission: **6** charge, errand **7** calling, embassy, message **10** commission, delegation, deputation

missionary: **6** Marist **7** apostle

Mississippi: *capital:* **7** Jackson

city: **6** Biloxi **8** Gulfport, Meridian **10** Greenville

chief product: **6** cotton **8** soybeans

county: **5** Hinds, Jones, Yazoo **7** Neshoba **8** Harrison, Itawamba

early explorer: **6** De Soto

highest point: **9** Woodall Mt.

Indian: **5** Osage **9** Merrimack

lake: **6** Ozarks **9** Tablerock

motto: **14** Virtute et armis (By valor and arms)

nickname: **5** Bayou **8** Magnolia

state bird: **11** mockingbird

state flower: **8** magnolia

Mississippi River: *mouth:* **4** pass

source: **6** Itasca

Mississippian: **15** Eocarboniferous

missive: **4** note **6** billet, letter **7** epistle, message, missile **8** document

love: **9** valentine

Missouri: *capital:* **13** Jefferson City

city: **7** St. Louis **10** Kansas City **11** Springfield **12** Independence

county: **4** Cass, Clay, Cole **5** Adair, Bates, Boone, Lewis, Scott, Taney **6** Pettis **7** Jackson, Pulaski **8** Buchanan **9** Jefferson

dam: **7** Bagnell

early explorer: **6** De Soto **7** La Salle

highest point: **10** Taum Sauk Mt.

Indian: **5** Osage

native: **5** Piker

nickname: **6** Show Me **7** Bullion

plateau: **5** Ozark

river: **5** Osage **9** Merrimack

state bird: **8** bluebird

state flower: **8** hawthorn

state tree: **7** dogwood

Truman library and museum: **12** Independence

misspelling: **10** cacography

misspend: **4** lose **8** squander

misstep: **4** slip, trip **5** error **7** faux pas

miss the mark: **4** fail **9** fall short

mist: dag, dim, fog, hag, rag **4** blur, damp, drow(Sc.), film, haze, scud, smog, soup **5** bedim, brume, cloud, smurr, vapor **6** mizzle, shadow, spirit **7** mystery **9** confusion, obscurity **13** precipitation

mistake: err **4** balk, bull, slip **5** amiss, boner, error, fault, folly **6** astray, erring, escape, miscue, renege **7** blunder, default, erratum, rhubarb **10** inaccuracy **12** inadvertence **13** misconception **15**

misapprehension

mistaken: **5** wrong **9** erroneous, incorrect **13** misunderstood

mister: don, sir **4** herr(G.) **5** senor(Sp.), title **6** signor(It.) **8** monsieur(F.)

mistletoe: **7** allheal, gadbush

family: **12** loranthaceae

mistreat: **5** abuse **6** ill-use **7** violate

mistress: **4** amie, doll, dozy **5** amiga, dolly, donna, duena, leman **7** hostess **8** gudewife(Sc.), ladylove **9** chamberer, concubine, courtesan, courtezan, governess, kept woman **10** chatelaine, proprietor, sweetheart

mistrust: **5** doubt **8** distrust **12** apprehension

misty: dim **5** foggy, musky, vague **6** vapory **7** obscure **10** indistinct **13** unilluminated **14** unintelligible

misunderstanding: **6** breach **7** quarrel **9** imbroglio **12** disagreement

misuse: **5** abuse **6** disuse **7** abusion, pervert **8** maltreat, mistreat **9** misemploy

mite: bit **4** atom, dite, dram, tick **5** acari (pl.), atomy, speck **6** acarid, acarus, minute, smidge **7** acarina, chigger, smidgen, smidgin **8** acaridan, arachnid, particle, smidgeon, smitchin

miter: **4** belt **5** frank, mitre, tiara **6** fillet, girdle, gusset, tavern **7** tall hat **8** headband **9** headdress

flower: **8** cyclamen

Jewish part: **7** Petalon

mithridate: **8** antidote **9** electuary **12** alexipharmic

mitigate: **4** balm, bate, cool, ease, tone **5** abate, allay, delay, mease(Sc.), relax, remit, slake **6** lessen, pacify, soften, temper **7** appease, assuage, mollify, qualify, relieve, sweeten **8** diminish, lenitive, moderate, palliate **9** alleviate, meliorate

mitten: **4** cuff, jilt, mitt **5** glove, hands

mittimus: **4** writ **6** notice **7** quietus, warrant **9** discharge, dismissal **10** magistrate

mittle: **4** hurt **8** mutilate

mix: pug **4** amix, fuse, join, link, meng, stir **5** admix, alloy, blend, cross, knead, merge, unite **6** jumble, mingle, muddle, wuzzle **7** blunder, combine, confect, confuse, shuffle **8** coalesce, compound, confound **9** associate, commingle, hybridize **10** amalgamate **11** incorporate, intermingle

up: **7** confuse, mistake **8** disorder

with water: **5** slake **6** dilute, weaken

mixable: **8** miscible

mixed: **6** impure, motley **7** piebald **11** farraginous **13** heterogeneous **14** indiscriminate

mixed blood: See **hybrid**

person of: **5** metis **6** Baluga, Ladino, mestee, mustee **7** mestizo, metisse, mulatto

mixed metaphor: 11 catachresis
mixed-up: 7 complex, tangled 8 confused 10 disordered
mixer: 5 party, paver 9 bartender
mixture: 4 hash, mash, olio 6 batch, blend 6 medley 7 amalgam, compost, farrage, farrago, melange 8 blendure 9 admixture, potpourri 10 concoction, hodgepodge 11 composition 12 minglemangle
mizmaze: web 4 knot, mesh 5 skein 6 tangle 9 confusion 12 bewilderment
mizzle: 4 mist, rain 5 misle 6 decamp 7 confuse, drizzle, speckle 9 disappear, misinform
mnemonic: 12 recollective 14 memory training
Mnemosyne: 6 Memory
  daughters: 5 Muses
  father: 6 Uranus
  lover: 4 Zeus
  mother: 4 Gaea
moa: 4 bird 6 ratite 8 dinornis
Moab: *city:* Kir
  descendant: 7 Moabite
  famous woman: 4 Ruth
  god: 7 Chemosh
  king: 5 Eglon, Mesha
  mountain: 4 Nebo
  people: 5 Emims
moan: cry 4 sigh, wail 5 groan 6 bemoan, bewail, grieve, lament 7 deplore, whimper 8 complain 9 complaint 11 lamentation
  as the wind: 5 sough
moat: gap 4 foss, lake, pond 5 ditch, fossa, fosse 6 trench 7 barrier
mob: set 4 crew, gang, herd, rout 5 cohue, crowd, drove, flock, group, volge 6 clique, masses, rabble 9 multitude 10 prostitute
  member: 6 rioter 8 gangster
  rule: 7 anarchy 8 violence
  worship: 9 mobolatry
mobbish: 7 lawless 10 disorderly
mobile: 5 fluid 6 fickle, vision 7 movable 8 populace 9 wandering 10 changeable
mobsman: 10 pickpocket
mobster: 7 hoodlum 8 gangster
Moby Dick: 5 whale
  author: 8 Melville
  character: Pip 6 Daggoo, Parsee 7 Ishmael
  pursuer: 4 Ahab
  ship: 6 Pequod
moccasin: pac 4 pack, shoe 5 snake, tegua 6 loafer 7 slipper 8 larrigan 11 cottonmouth
moch: 4 moth
mocha: 6 coffee 7 leather
  stone: 5 agate
mochy: 4 damp 5 misty, moist, muggy
mock: ape, bob, dor, gab 4 gibe, gird, jape, jeer, jibe, leer, sham 5 bourd, elude, false, fleer, flirt, flout, frump, hoker, mimic, scoff, sneer, taunt 6 banter, deride 7 deceive, grimace, imitate 8 ridicule 9 burlesque, imitation 10 disappoint 11 counterfeit
  brawn: 10 headcheese
  cucumber: 5 apple
  nightingale: 7 warbler 8 blackcap
  orange: 7 seringa, syringa, syringe
  ore: 10 sphalerite
  plane: 8 sycamore
mocker: 4 bird 7 flauter 11 mockingbird
  nut: 7 hickory
mockery: 5 bourd, farce, glaik, irony 6 satire, trifle 7 hething, sarcasm 8 futility, illusion, ridicule, travesty 9 burlesque, imitation, indignity 11 insincerity 13 laughingstock
mocking: 8 fleering
mockingbird: 8 imitator, songster
  genus: 5 mimus
mod: 4 bold, free 6 modern 7 offbeat 11 fashionable
mode: cut, fad 4 form, thew 5 modus, order, state, style, vogue 6 course, custom, fangle, manner, method, regime, system 7 fashion 10 convention
model: act, sit 4 form, mold, norm, plan, plot, pose, type 5 canon, ideal, shape 6 design, sitter 7 example, fashion, manikin, paragon, pattern, perfect, templet, typical 8 ensample, exemplar, formular, fugleman, mannikin, paradigm, pattern, specimen, standard, template 9 archetype, construct, exemplary, facsimile, flugelman, mannequin, miniature, precedent, prototype
moderate: 4 bate, calm, ease, easy, even, meek, mild, soft 5 abate, bland, lower, slake, sober 6 ease up, frugal, gentle, lessen, slight, soften, temper 7 average, control 8 attemper, decrease, diminish, tone down 9 abstinent, alleviate, temperate 10 abstemious, reasonable 12 conservative 13 dispassionate
moderating: 9 remissive
moderation: 7 control 9 restraint 10 abstinence, diminution, governance, limitation, mitigation, sedateness 11 restriction 12 middle course 13 temperateness
moderator: 6 umpire 7 arbiter 8 mediator 9 anchorman 10 arbitrator, negotiator
modern: new 4 late 6 latter, recent 8 neoteric
modernize: 8 renovate
modest: coy, mim(Sc.), shy 4 deft, prim 5 douce, lowly, plain 6 chaste, decent, demure, humble 7 bashful 8 decorous, maidenly, moderate, reserved, retiring, verecund, virtuous 9 diffident 10 unas-

suming **13** unpretentious

modicum: bit **6** amount **7** portion, soup-con

modify: **4** edit, tone, vary **5** alter, limit **6** change, master, temper **7** assuage, qualify **8** attemper, mitigate, moderate, modulate **9** influence

modish: **4** chic **7** stylish

modiste: **7** stylist **8** milliner **9** couturier **10** dressmaker

modulated: **5** toned **7** changed, intoned **8** softened, tempered **9** inflected, moderated, regulated

modulation: **9** inflexion **10** inflection

modus: way **5** means **6** manner, method

modus operandi: **12** way of working

mog: jog **4** move, plod, walk **6** depart

moggan: leg **6** sleeve **8** stocking

moggy: cat, cow **4** calf **8** slattern **9** scarecrow

moguey: **4** moki, raft **5** mokhi

mogul: **4** lord, snow **5** nabob, ruler, Tatar **6** Tartar **7** magnate **8** autocrat **9** Mongolian, personage **10** locomotive

Mohammed, Muhammed: **7** Mahomet, Mahound

birthplace: **5** Mecca

daughter: **6** Fatima

descendant: Ali **5** Hasan **6** Hosein, Husain, She-rif **7** Ibrahim, She-reef

father: **8** Abdallah

flight from Mecca: **6** hegira, hejira

follower: **6** Moslem, Muslim, Wahabi **7** Wahabee, Wahabit, Wahhabi **8** Wahabite

horse: **5** Buraq **7** Alborak

nephew: Ali

religion: **5** Islam

son-in-law: Ali

successor: **5** Calif **6** Caliph **7** Abu Bakr

title: **4** Iman

tomb: **6** Medina

uncle: **8** Abu-Talib

wife: **5** Aisha **6** Avesha, Ayesha **7** Khadija

Mohammedan: See **Muslim**

moho: **4** bird, rail **9** gallinule

mohock: **6** attack **8** maltreat

mohr: **7** gazelle

moider: **4** toil **5** worry **6** bother, wander **7** perplex, smother **8** distract, encumber

moiety: **4** half, part **5** piece, share **7** portion **9** community

moil: bar **4** mire, soil, spot, tire, toil, work **5** labor, taint, weary **6** defile, drudge **7** torment, trouble, turmoil **8** drudgery, vexation **9** agitation, confusion **10** defilement

moira: **4** fate **7** destiny

moire: **7** watered

moist: **4** damp, dank **5** humid, rainy **6** clammy **7** maudlin **8** humorous

moisten: dew, dip, ret, wet **4** moil **5** bedew, leach **6** anoint, dabble, dampen, humect, humify, imbrue, sparge **8** irrigate, sprinkle **9** humectate

moisture: fog **4** bree(Sc.), drip, drop **5** humor, vapor, water **6** humour, liquid **8** aquosity, humidity **13** precipitation

excess: **5** edema

remove: dry **4** wipe **5** wring **9** dehydrate

moisture-laden: **6** sodden

moistureless: dry **4** arid, sere **6** burned **7** parched **8** scorched **10** desiccated

mojo: **4** Moxo **5** charm, spell **6** amulet **7** majagua

mokaddam: **5** chief **7** headman

moke: fog, net **4** dolt, mesh, mist **5** horse **6** donkey **7** network **8** minstrel **9** performer

moki: **4** fish, raft **9** trumpeter

moko: **9** tattooing

moko-moko: **6** lizard

mokum: **5** alloy

molar: **5** tooth **7** chopper, grinder

molarimeter: **11** thermometer

molasses: **5** syrup **7** claggum, treacle **8** adherent, theriaca **10** blackstrap, sweetening

molave: **4** tree, wood **5** vitex

mold: die, fen **4** calm, cast, copy, core, form, mull, must, soil **5** decay, frame, humus, knead, model, shape **6** blight, matrix, mildew **7** fashion, matrice, moulage, pattern **9** ceroplast, character, sculpture

opening: **6** ingate

part: **5** nowel, sprue

pert. to: **5** humic

pouring hole: **5** sprue

moldable: **7** fictile

Moldavia: *Rumania capital:* **4** Iasi

department: **4** Iasi **5** Jassy

measure: **7** faltche

molder: rot **5** decay **7** crumble **8** sculptor **9** become old, waste away **12** disintegrate

molding: ess **4** bead, beak, cima, cove, cyma, gula, ogee, reed, tore **5** angle, arris, conge, ogive, ovolo, splay, talon, thumb, torus **6** baguet, baston, fascia, fillet, listel, nebule, reglet, scotia **7** annulet, beading, cavetto, cornice, fingent, reeding, shaping **8** astragal, bageette, bezantee **9** trochilus

case: **5** chape

combination: **9** ledgement

concave: **4** gula **5** oxeye **7** cavetto

convex: **5** torus

curved: **4** ogee **6** nebule

flat: **6** fillet

ogee: **5** talon

pedestal: **7** surbase

rounded: **5** ovolo, torus **6** billet

rule for: **6** screed
moldy: 5 fusty, hoary, mucid, musty, stale
7 foughty **8** mildewed **12** old-fashioned
mole: cob **4** cobb, pier, pile, quay **5** fault,
jetty **6** anicut, burrow, rodent **7** annicut, barrier **8** excavate, starnose, tun-
neler **9** birthmark **10** breakwater **12**
imperfection
cricket: **9** churrworm
genus: **5** talpa
mole-like animal: 4 tape **6** desman
molecule: 4 iota **5** speck **7** modicum **8**
particle
component: **4** atom
gram: mol **4** mole
moleskin: fur **6** fabric
color: **5** taupe
molest: vex **5** annoy, tease **6** assail, bother, harass, heckle, pester **7** disturb, torment, trouble **9** incommode, interfere
10 discommode
moliminous: 7 massive, weighty **9** laborious, momentous **10** cumbersome
moline: 8 millrind
moll: gal **5** wench **8** mistress **9** companion
10 prostitute
mollescent: 9 softening
mollify: 4 bate, calm, ease **5** abate, allay,
relax, sleek **6** lessen, pacify, relent, soft-
en, soothe, temper **7** amolish, appease,
placate, relieve, sweeten **8** mitigate **9**
attempter **10** conciliate **11** tranquilize
mollusk: 5 snail, whelk **6** chiton, limpet **7**
abalone **10** cuttlefish
bivalve: **4** clam, leda, spat **5** chama **6**
cockle, mussel, oyster **7** scallop
cephalopod: **8** argonaut
conical-shaped: **7** limpet
eight-armed: **7** octopus
fresh water: **7** etheria
gastropod: **4** slug **5** snail, whelk **7** abalone
12 taenioglossa
genus: **4** arca, leda(pl.) **5** eolis, ledum
group: **8** pteropod
large: **5** chama
larval: **7** veliger
marine: asi **4** welk **5** murex **7** abalone,
scallop **8** nautilus
one shell: **5** snail **8** univalve
shell: **4** test **5** cowry, testa **6** cowrie, tes-
tae
shell concretion: **5** pearl
shell-less: **4** slug
teeth: **6** radula
ten-armed: **5** squid
used for bait: **5** squid **6** limpet
wrinkled shell: **6** cockle
young: **4** spat
mollycoddle: 6 coddle, pamper **7** indulge
8 weakling **12** spoiled child
moloch: 6 lizard
molt: mew **4** cast, mute, shed **8** exuviate

molten rock: 4 lava **5** magma
molting: 7 ecdysis
Molucca islands: Aru, Kai, Obi **4** Buru **5**
Banda, Ceram **6** Maluku **7** Amboina **9**
Halmahera
moly: 4 herb **6** garlic
momble: 6 jumble, tangle
moment: sec, use **4** gird, hint, tick, tide,
time **5** avail, braid, clink, filip, gliff,
point, stage, trice, value **6** fillip, import,
minute, second, weight **7** instant **8** occasion **9** short time, twinkling **10** importance **11** consequence
critical: **4** inch, nick **6** crisis, crises
particular: **4** then, when
momentary: 5 brief, quick, short **9**
ephemeral, impulsive, transient **10**
transitory **13** instantaneous
momentous: 4 fell **5** grave **7** epochal,
fateful, serious, weighty **8** eventful **9**
important, ponderous **10** chargeable **11**
influential
momentum: 5 force, power **7** impetus
mommy: mom **4** duck **5** mammy **6** mother
momus: 6 critic **11** fault-finder
monachist: 7 monkish
Monaco: *casino:* **10** Monte Carlo
dynasty: **8** Grimaldi
people: **11** Monegasques
prince: **6** Albert **7** Rainier
princess: **8** Caroline
monad: one **4** atom, unit **5** deity, henad **6**
person **7** element **8** particle, zoospore
monarch: 4 csar, czar, tsar, tzar **5** ruler **6**
despot, prince **7** dynasty, emperor **8** autocrat **9** butterfly, potentate, sovereign
monarchal: 5 regal, royal **6** kingly **8** imperial
monarda: tea **4** mint **5** plant **8** bergamot
monastery: 5 abb, badia **6** friary, man-
dra, priory **7** convent, hospice, minster,
nunnery **8** cloister, lamasery **9** sanctuary
Carthusian: **7** certosa
haircut: tonsure
head: **5** abbot, prior **7** hegumen
Hindu: **4** math
officer: **5** prior
room: **4** cell
superior: **5** prior
title: dom
monastic: 4 monk **5** friar **6** oblate **7** ascetic, monkish, recluse **8** abbatial, cenobite **9** cenobitic **10** conventual
monde: 5 globe, mound, world **6** circle **7**
coterie, society
monetary: 9 financial, pecuniary
money (see also **bill, coin**): oof, tin, wad
4 bill, cash, coin, cush, dubs, dump,
gelt, gilt, grig, jack, jake, kale, loot, lour,
mina, moss, pelf **5** blunt, brass, bread,

bunce, chink, clink, dough, funds, livre, lucre, maneh, rhino **6** argent, boodle, change, flimsy, hansel, mazuma, moolah, siller(Sc.), spense, steven, tender, wampum, wealth **7** chattel, handsel, lettuce, ooftish **8** currency **9** spondulix **10** greenbacks, spondulics
ancient: aes
blood: cro **7** breaghe
bag: **4** fels **6** follis, wealth **8** follicle
box: **4** arca, safe, till **5** chest **6** drawer **8** register
bribe: **4** soap **6** boodle
broker: **7** changer
certificate: **5** scrip
changer: **5** saraf, seraf **6** shroff
chest for: **7** brazier
coinage: **4** mint
coined: **6** specie
counterfeit: **5** bogus, queer **6** boodle
cowrie: **6** shells
dealer: **6** broker
depreciation: **4** agio **9** inflation
earnest: **5** arles(Sc.), arrha **6** hansel **7** deposit, handsel **8** handgeld
gambler's: **6** barato
gate: **9** admission
gift: **4** alms **7** bequest, charity **9** endowment
given to lord: **6** farleu, farley
found: **5** trove **8** treasure
hearth: **6** fumage
held: **6** escrow
hole for: **4** slot
hood: **4** lari **5** larin **6** larree
lender: **6** banker, usurer **7** shylock **9** loanshark **10** pawnbroker
lots of: pot **4** heap, mint, pile
maker: **4** mint **7** moneyer
manual of exchange values: **7** cambist
metal: **4** coin **6** change, specie **7** coinage
on the: **12** exactly right
overdue: **7** arrears
oversupply: **9** inflation
paid down: **4** cash **7** deposit **11** downpayment
paper: **4** bill, kale **5** green **6** flimsy **7** cabbage, lettuce
premium: **4** agio
ready: **4** cash **5** asset, darby **9** alcontado(Sp.)
roll of coin: **7** rouleau
sent: **10** remittance
shell: **4** peag **5** cowry, peage, sewan, uhllo **6** cowrie, seawan
small amount: **4** mite **7** peanuts **11** chickenfeed
sorter: **6** teller **7** cashier
standard bank: **5** banco
transactions: **7** banking, finance
unit: ora, yen **4** lira, mark, mina, peso, real, tael **5** franc, krona, krone, maneh,

pound, ruble, rupee **6** dollar, piatre, talent **7** drachma, guilder, milreis, piaster **8** cruzeiro
without: **4** poor **5** broke **11** impecunious
money of account: ora
moneyed: 4 rich **6** heeled **7** opulent, wealthy **8** affluent **10** well-heeled
moneylender: 6 usurer **10** pawnbroker
mong: mix **5** crowd **6** barter, mingle **7** mixture, traffic **8** mingling **11** intercourse
monger: 6 dealer, hawker, trader **7** peddler **8** huckster
Mongolia: *ass:* **8** chigetai
capital: **9** Ulan Bator
caravan leader: **5** bashi
city: **4** Urga **5** Kobdo **7** Kirghiz
conjurer: **6** shaman
conqueror: **9** Tamerland **10** Kublai Khan **11** Genghis Khan
desert: **4** Gobi
dynasty: **4** Yuan
fuel: **5** argal, argol, argul
measure: lan
monetary unit: **5** mungo **6** tugrik
monk: **4** lama
mountain: **5** Altai **8** Tannu-Ola
people: Lai, Rai **4** Garo, Lapp, Shan **5** Asian, Eleut, Tatar **6** Buriat, Tartar **7** Asiatic, Kalmuck, Khalkha **8** Annamese, Oriental **9** Mongoloid
priest: **6** shaman
province: **6** Chahar **7** Suiyuan
religion: **9** Shamanism, Shintoism **12** Confucianism
river: Pei **4** Onon **5** Peiho **7** Kerulen, Selenga **8** Hobdo Gol
tent: **4** yurt
weight: lan
Mongoloid: See **Mongolia:** *people*
mongoose: 4 urva **5** lemur **7** meerkat **9** ichneumon
Kipling's jungle book: **14** Rikki-Tikki-Tavi
mongrel: cur, dog, mut **4** mutt **6** hybrid **7** bastard, piebald **9** crossbred, half-breed, sandpiper
whitefish: **8** tullibee
monial: nun
moniker: 4 name **5** alias **8** nickname
monition: 5 order **6** advice, caveat, notice **7** caution, summons, warning **8** citation **10** admonition, indication, intimation **11** forewarning, instruction **13** animadversion
monitor: mentor, nozzle **7** inciter **8** ironclad, reminder **9** catamaran **10** instigator
bug: **8** conenose
lizard: **4** ibid, uran **5** varan
monk: dom, fra **4** saki **5** clerk, friar, padre(Sp.) **7** devotee **8** anchoret, ceno-

bite, monastic **9** anchorite, baldicoot, bullfinch, hieronach

Buddhist: **4** lama **5** arhat, bonze, goyim, yahan **6** bhikku **7** bhikshu, poongee **8** poonghee, poonghie, talapoin

cap: **5** kulah **6** kullah

Eastern Church: **7** caloyer, starets

haircut: **7** tonsure

hood: **4** cowl

Muslim: **7** dervish

Roman Catholic: **6** Culdee **8** Capuchin, Trappist

room: **4** cell

time in monastery: **9** monachate

monkey (see also **ape**): lar **4** fool, sime **5** burro **6** howler, meddle, nisnas, simian, tamper, trifle, urchin **7** colobin **9** catarrhina, catarhine **10** catarrhina, catarrhine

African: **4** waag **5** jocko, patas, potto **6** grivet, vervet

American: **4** saki **5** acari **6** grison, miriki **7** ouakari **8** marmoset, orabassu **9** beelzebub

Asiatic: **4** douc **5** toque **6** langur **7** macaque

bearded: **8** entellus

beautiful: **7** guereza

bonnet: **4** zati

Callicebus: **5** yapok **6** yapock

capuchin: sai **7** sapajou

cebine: sai

Diana: **7** roloway

entellus: **7** hanuman **10** hoonoo-maun

genus of: **5** cebus **8** alouatta

god: **7** Hanuman

grivet: **4** tota

handsome: **4** mona

howling: **4** mono **5** araba **7** gauriba, stentor **8** alouatta

large: **5** sajou

long-tailed: sai **4** maha **5** patas **6** guenon, langur **7** hanuman, kalasie **8** entellus, telapoin, wanderoo

macaque: **6** rhesus

proboscis: **4** kaha **7** noseape

purple-faced: **8** wanderoo

rhesus: **6** bandar

saki: **6** couxia, couxio

small: **4** titi **6** apelet, teetee **7** apeling **8** marmoset

spider: **6** ateles, coaita **9** belzebuth

squirrel: **6** samiri

tailless: ape

monkey bear: **5** koala

monkey bread: **6** baobab

monkey business: **7** foolish **11** mischievous

monkey flower: **7** figwort, mimulus **8** toadflax

monkey-nut: **6** peanut

monkey pot: **5** fruit

monkey with: **6** meddle **9** interfere

monkey wrench: **7** spanner

monkeyshines: **6** antics, pranks, tricks **7** aperies **12** clownishness

monkish: **7** ascetic **8** monastic

monkshood: **4** atis **5** atees **7** aconite **8** napellus

monoceros: **7** sawfish, unicorn **9** swordfish

monocle: **8** eyeglass

monocleid: **4** desk **7** cabinet

monocracy: **9** autocracy

monodist: **6** singer, writer **8** composer

monody: ode **4** poem, song **5** dirge **7** oration

monogram: **6** cipher, sketch **7** outline **8** initials **9** character

monolith: **6** column, menhir, pillar, statue **7** obelisk **8** colossus, monument

monologue: **9** soliloquy

monomachy: **4** duel **6** combat

monomaniac: **5** crank **12** single-minded

monophone: **9** homophone

Monophysite: **4** Copt **8** Jacobite

monoplane: **5** Taube

monopolize: **5** sew up **6** absorb **7** consume, engross

monopoly: **5** grant, right, trust **6** cartel, corner **7** appalto, charter, control **9** privilege, syndicate **10** consortium

monosaccharide: ose **5** sugar

monostele: **4** root, stem

monotonous: **4** dead, drab, dull, flat, same **6** dreary **7** humdrum, jogtrot, tedious, uniform **8** unvaried **9** wearisome **10** repetitive

monotony: **4** drab **6** tedium **9** treadmill **10** continuity, regularity

monoxylon: **4** boat **5** canoe

monster (see also **beast**): **4** gowl, huge, ogre **5** bilsh, demon, devil, fiend, freak, giant, teras **6** geryon, sphinx **7** centaur, chimera, warlock **12** bandersnatch

fabled: **5** Argus, harpy **6** gorgon, sphinx **8** basilisk, Minotaur **9** bucentaur

female: **5** harpy **6** gorgon, scylla

fire-breathing: **6** dragon **7** chimera

handless: **8** acheirus

headless: **9** acephalus

human: **5** teras **6** terata

medical: **5** teras

nine-headed: **5** hydra

short-limbed: **9** nanomelus

study of: **10** teratology

two-bodied: **7** disomus

two-headed: **10** dicephalus

winged: **5** harpy

without hind limbs: api **4** apus

monster like: **8** teratoid

monstrous: **4** huge, vast **5** enorm, large **6** mortal **7** hideous, immense, massive, strange, titanic **8** colossal, cracking, deformed, enormous, flagrant, gigantic, horrible, shocking **9** atrocious, fantastic, unnatural **10** outrageous, prodigious, stupendous, tremendous **12** overpowering, overwhelming, stupendous **13** extraordinary

Montana: *capital:* **6** Helena

city: **5** Butte **8** Billings, Missoula **10** Great Falls

county: **4** Hill **5** Teton **6** Fergus, Wibaux **7** Big Horn, Cascade, Pondera **8** Missoula

highest point: **11** Granite Peak

Indian: **4** Crow **6** Atsina, Salish **8** Shoshone

lake: **8** Flathead

motto: **9** Oro y Plata (Gold and Silver)

mountain range: **5** Rocky **10** Bittersweet

national park: **7** Glacier **11** Yellowstone

nickname: **6** Big Sky **8** Mountain, Treasure

river: **8** Missouri **11** Yellowstone

state bird: **10** meadowlark

state fish: **5** trout

state flower: **10** bittersweet

state tree: **4** pine

Monte Cristo: *author:* **5** Dumas

hero: **6** Dantes

monteith: **9** punch bowl

montero: cap **6** ranger **8** forester, huntsman

Montezuma's revenge: **8** diarrhea

month: *excess of calendar over lunar:* **5** epact

following: **7** proximo

half: **9** fortnight

preceding: **6** ultimo

present: **7** instant

monticule: **4** hill, rise **5** mount **7** hillock

montilla: **6** sherry

Montmorency: **6** sherry

Montrachet: **8** Burgundy

monument: **4** tomb **5** cairn, relic, vault **6** effigy, record, shrine, statue, trophy **8** cenotaph, cromlech, memorial, reminder **9** antiquity, sepulcher **10** gravestone, testament **11** remembrance

pillar-like: **5** stela, stele **6** stelae

monumental: **4** huge, **5** fatal, heavy **7** epochal, massive **8** enduring, historic

moo: low **6** bellow

mooch: beg, bum **4** loaf **5** cadge, skulk, sneak, steal **6** loiter, pilfer, sponge

moocha: **9** loincloth

mood: tid(Sc.) **4** tune, vein, whim **5** freak, humor **6** strain, temper **7** caprice, feeling **10** atmosphere **11** disposition

assumed: **4** pose

recollection of past: **13** retrospection

moody: sad **4** glum **6** gloomy, grumpy, sullen **7** pensive **8** brooding **9** depressed **10** capricious **11** ill-tempered

mools: **10** chilblains

moon: orb **4** Dian, Luna, lune(F.) **5** Diana, lunar **6** Phoebe **7** Cynthia, selenic **8** satelles, selenian **9** satellite

above: **10** superlunar

age at beginning of calendar year: **5** epact

apogee: **5** apsis

area on: **4** mare

aspect: **5** phase

astronaut: **6** Aldrin **9** Armstrong

crescent: **7** menisci **8** meniscus

crescent point: **4** cusp, horn **6** apogee **7** perigee

distance between apogee and perigee: **5** apsis

festival: **8** neomenia

first quarter: **8** crescent

geographer: **13** selenographer

god: Sin **6** Nannar

goddess: **4** Luna **5** Diana, Tanit **6** Hecate, Hekate, Salena, Selene, Tanith **7** Artemis, Astarte

inhabitant: **8** Selenite

instrument: **11** selenoscope

mock: **10** paraselene

new: **6** phasis

perigee: **5** apsis

pert. to: **5** lunar **7** selenic

phase: new **4** full **11** last quarter **12** first quarter

picture: **11** selenograph

position: **6** octant

spacecraft: **6** Apollo

Uranus's: **5** Ariel

valley: **4** rill **5** cleft, rille

vehicle: LEM

moon-mad: **7** lunatic

moon-shaped: **6** lunate

half: **10** semilunate

moon valley: **5** rille

moonack: **9** woodchuck

moonbeam: ray

moonbill: **4** duck

mooncalf: **4** dolt, mole **7** lunatic, monster **11** monstrosity

mooned: **8** crescent

moonery: **7** madness

moonfish: **4** opah **7** sunfish **9** spadefish

moonflower: **5** daisy, oxeye **6** achete

moonglow: **9** moonlight

moonish: **7** flighty **10** capricious

moonlighting: **4** raid **9** adventure **10** expedition **11** moonshining

moonman: **5** gipsy **6** robber

moonraking: **13** woolgathering

moonshine: **4** idle **5** empty, month, sauce **6** liquor **7** bootleg, eyewash, trivial, whiskey **8** nonsense **10** balsamweed, bathtub gin

moonsick: **7** lunatic

moony: **5** round, silly **6** dreamy **8** listless

moor: bog, fen, fix **4** fell **5** heath, lande,

marsh, swale, swamp **6** anchor, fasten, secure

Moor: 6 Berber, Moslem, Muslim **7** Bedouin, Othello, Saracen **8** Moroccan

moor game: 6 grouse

moor hawk: 7 harrier

moorage: 8 berthage **9** anchorage

moorburn: 7 quarrel **9** ill temper

moorcock: 6 grouse **9** blackcock

moorhen: 4 coot **9** gallinule

Moorish: 8 Moresque

alcazar: **8** Alhambra

garment: **5** jupon **7** burnous **8** albornoz, burnoose

horse: **4** barb

judge: **4** cadi

kettledrum: **5** tabor **6** atabal

opiate: **4** kief

palace: **8** Alhambra

moose: elk **4** alce **5** eland

genus: **5** alces

female: cow

mooseberry: 10 hobblebush **13** cranberry bush

moot: dig **4** grub, plea, root, tell **5** argue, plead, speak **6** debate **7** discuss, meeting **8** argument, assembly, complain, disputed **9** debatable, encounter, gathering, uncertain, undecided **10** discussion, litigation

mop: 4 pout, swab, wash, wipe **5** bunch, clean **6** merkin, moppet, scovel **7** cleanse, grimace

mope: 4 pout, sulk **5** brood, idler **9** sad person

moped: 9 motorbike

moppet: tot **4** baby, doll, tike **5** child **7** darling, toddler **9** youngster

mopsy: son **6** moppet **8** slattern

moquette: 6 carpet, fabric **10** upholstery

mora: 5 delay, stool **7** default **9** footstool **12** postponement

moral: 4 good, pure **5** ethic, noble **6** chaste, decent **7** dutiful, epimyth, ethical, upright **8** priggish, virtuous **9** honorable, righteous **10** principled **11** rightminded

fable: **8** apologue

failure: sin

law: **9** Decalogue

teaching: **5** maxim **7** precept **8** apologue **9** preaching **10** preachment **11** edification

morale: 4 hope, mood, zeal **6** spirit **8** morality **9** condition **10** confidence **13** esprit de corps

morals: 6 ethics **9** standards

morass: bog, fen **4** flow, maze, quag **5** flush, marsh, swamp **8** quagmire

morass weed: 8 hornwort

moratorium: ban **5** delay **10** suspension

Moravian city: 4 Brno, Zlin **5** Brunn

moray: eel **6** conger, hamlet **7** muraena

morbid: 4 sick **6** grisly, morose, sullen **8** diseased, gruesome, horrible **9** debatable, saturnine, unhealthy **11** unwholesome **12** apprehensive, pathological

morbilli: 7 measles

morbus: 7 disease, illness

mordant: 4 keen **5** sharp **6** biting **7** burning, caustic, pungent **8** scathing **9** corrosive, sarcastic

more: piu **4** also, mair, plus **5** again, extra **6** better, custom, manner **7** folkway, further, greater **10** additional, convention

or less: **4** some **6** nearly

than: **4** over **5** above

than enough: too **9** excessive

than one: few **4** many **6** couple, plural **7** several

More opus: 6 Utopia

morel: 8 mushroom **10** nightshade

moreover: and **4** also, then **5** again **7** besides, further **8** likewise **11** furthermore

morepork: 4 peho, ruru **7** boobook, frogmouth

mores: 6 ethics **7** manners **9** amenities **10** civilities

morgue: 7 library **8** mortuary **9** deadhouse, stolidity **11** haughtiness, impassivity

moribund: 5 dying **6** effete **8** decadent, decaying **10** acherontic, terminated **12** at death's door **13** deteriorating

morion: 6 helmet, quartz **8** cabasset

Mormon: 6 Danite

emblem: bee

founder: **5** Smith

officer: **5** elder

priesthood: **7** Aaronic **11** Melchizedek

prophet: **6** Moroni

state: **4** Utah

Mormonweed: 6 flower, mallow

morning: 4 dawn, morn **5** matin **6** aurora **7** sunrise **8** forenoon

concert: **6** aubade

coat: **7** cutaway

moisture: dew

pert. to: **5** matin, wight **7** matinal **9** matutinal

prayer: **5** matin **6** matins

reception: **5** levee

morning glory: nil **7** gaybine, ipomoea

family: **14** convolvulaceae

morning star: 4 Mars **5** Venus **6** Saturn **7** Daystar, Jupiter, Lucifer, Mercury **8** Bartonia

moro: 5 finch

Moro: *chief:* **4** Dato **5** Datto

dialect: **4** Sulu

island: **8** Mindanao

knife: **6** barong

people: **4** Sulu **5** Lanao, Yakan

priest: **4** atli **5** sarip
sailboat: **5** sapit
morocco: 7 leather
imitation: **4** roan
Morocco: *cape:* Nun
capital: **5** Rabat
city (see also *port* below): Fez **4** Assa **5** Oujda **9** Marrakech **10** Casablanca
district: Sus **4** Riff
emperor: **9** Miramolin **11** Miramomolin
government: **7** Maghzen, Makhzan, Machzen
hat: fez
island: **7** Madeira
Jews' quarter: **8** El Millah
measure: **4** sahh **6** fanega, tomini
military expedition: **5** harka
monetary unit: **6** dirham
mountain: Rif **5** Atlas
people: **4** Moor **6** Berber, Kabyle, Moslem, Muslim **7** Maghzen, Makhzan, Makhzen
port: **5** Ceuta, Rabat **6** Agadir, Tetuan **7** Mogador, Tangier **8** El Araish, Laraiche **10** Casablanca
ruler: **6** Hassan, she-rif, sultan **7** she-reef
soldier: **5** askar
tree: **4** arar **5** argan **6** alerse **8** sandarac
weight: **4** rotl **5** artal, artel, gerbe, ratel **6** kintar **7** quintal
morology: 5 folly **8** nonsense
moron: 4 dull, fool **5** ament, idiot **6** stupid **7** dullard **8** imbecile, sluggish
moronic: 4 dull, slow **6** stupid **7** idiotic **8** retarded, sluggish
morose: 4 dour, glum, grum, sour **5** gruff, moody, sulky, surly **6** crusty, gloomy, sullen **7** crabbed, clumpse, clumpst, crooked, unhappy **8** choleric, strounge **9** splenetic **10** embittered, ill-humored
moroseness: 8 asperity
morphine derivative: 6 heroin
morro: 4 hill **5** bluff, point **6** castle **8** headland
Morse code signal: dah, dit
morsel: bit, ort **4** bite, snap **5** crumb, piece, scrap, snack **6** tidbit, titbit **7** morceau, rarebit **8** delicacy, fragment, mouthful
mort: 4 dead, lard **5** death, fatal **6** deadly, grease, salmon
mortacious: 4 very **9** extremely
mortal: 4 dire, grim **5** being, fatal, human **6** deadly, lethal **7** capital, deathly, fleshly **8** grievous **9** extremely **10** implacable **11** destructive
mortality: 5 flesh **8** fatality
mortar: 5 compo, putty **6** cannon, cement, holmos, petard **7** perrier
carrier: hod
mixer: rab
tray: hod

mortarboard: cap **4** hawk
Morte d'Arthur author: 6 Malory
mortgage: 4 bond, deed, hock, lien, pawn **5** trust **6** pledge, wadset(Sc.) **11** encumbrance
giver: **6** lienee
receiver: **6** lienor
mortician: 10 undertaker
mortification: 5 shame **7** chagrin **8** gangrene, necrosis, vexation **11** humiliation **13** embarrassment
mortified: 7 ashamed, decayed **10** distressed, humiliated
mortify: 5 abase, abash, spite **6** humble, offend **7** crucify
mortifying: 8 humbling **11** humiliating, ignominious
mortise: 5 joint **6** cocket
complement of: **5** tenon
law: **8** amortize
machine: **7** slotter
mortuary: 6 morgue **9** dead-house, lich-house, sepulcher **11** funeral home
car: **6** hearse
mosaic: 5 inlay **7** chimera, picture
formed like a: **10** tesselated
tile: **8** abaculus
mosaic gold: 6 ormolu
piece: **7** tessera
Moscow citadel: 7 Kremlin
Moses: 6 leader **8** lawgiver
brother: **5** Aaron
emissary: **5** Caleb
father: **5** Amram
father-in-law: **6** Jethro
law: **4** Tora **5** Torah **10** Pentateuch
mother: **8** Jochebed
mountain: **4** Nebo
sister: **6** Miriam
son: **7** Eliezer, Gershom
successor: **6** Zipporah
mosey: 5 amble, drift **6** depart, ramble, stroll, wander **7** shuffle
Moslem (see also **Muslim**): **7** Islamic, Saracen **9** Moslemite, Mussulman **10** Mohammedan
mosque: 4 jami, mosk **5** Caaba, Kaaba **6** church, dargah, durgah, Kaabeh, Kiblah, masjid, shrine, temple
niche: **4** slab **5** mihrab, **7** chamber
official: **4** imam **5** imaum
student: **5** softa
tower: **7** manarat, minaret **8** minarete
warden: **5** nazir
mosquito: 5 aedes **7** culicid **11** gallinipper
genus of: **5** aedes, Culex **9** Anopheles
killer: **8** culicide
larvae: **8** wigglers
mosquito bee: 5 karbi **8** angelito
mosquito fish: 8 gambusia
mosquito hawk: 9 dragonfly, nighthawk
mosquito plant: 4 mint **10** pennyroyal

Mosquito State: 6 Jersey

moss: bog, fog, rag **5** swamp, usnea **6** lichen, morass **9** bryophyte, treebeard
club: **7** lycoped
edible: **4** agar **8** agaragar
kind: **8** sphagnum

moss cheeper: 5 pipit

moss coral: 8 bryozoan

moss duck: 7 mallard

moss fruit: 11 sporogonium

moss-grown: 10 antiquated **12** old-fashioned

moss hammer: 7 bittern

moss polyp: 8 bryozoan

moss-trouper: 6 raider **8** marauder

mossback: 4 fogy **5** fogey **6** rustic **13** stick-in-the-mud

mossberry: 9 cranberry

mossbunker: 8 menhaden

mosshead: 9 merganser

mosswort: 9 bryophyte

mossy: 4 dull **5** boggy, downy, green, hoary **6** marshy, stupid **7** covered **9** abounding, overgrown

most: 4 best **5** chief **6** utmost **7** maximum **8** majority **9** principal

mostly: 7 chiefly **8** normally **9** generally **10** on the whole

mot: 5 maxim **10** witticism

mote: dot, may **4** atom, hill, iota **5** atomy, match, might, speck, squib, straw **6** barrow, fescue, height, trifle **7** tumulus **8** eminence, impurity, particle **9** lightness **10** stronghold **11** small amount

motel: inn **5** hotel

motet: 4 song **6** anthem **11** composition

moth: 5 tinea **6** bogong, lappet, mallet, miller, tineah, tinean, tineid **7** tineina **8** chloasma, forester **11** yellowshell
clothes: **6** tineid
family: **7** tineina **9** arctiidae
genus of: **5** sesia
larva: **11** caterpillar
spot: **8** chloasma, fenestra
suborder: **10** heterocera

moth-eaten: 4 worn **7** decayed, worn-out **8** decrepit, out-dated
moth hawk: **10** goatsucker
moth hunter: **10** goatsucker

mother: dam **4** dame, womb **5** adopt, dregs, mamma, mater(L.), nurse **6** foster, matron, native, origin, parent, patron **7** nurture, old lady **8** genetrix **10** ancestress, wellspring
of believers: **5** Aisha **6** Ayesha
of gods: **4** Rhea **9** Brigantia
of Gracchi: **8** Cornelia
of Graces: **5** Aegle
of man: **6** Cybele
of months: **4** moon
of presidents: **8** Virginia
of sorrows: **4** Mary **6** Virgin

of states: **8** Virginia
one delivery: **7** unipara
related on side of: **6** enatic
spiritual: **4** amma
three deliveries: **7** tripara
two deliveries: **6** bipara

Mother Carey's chicken: 6 petrel

Mother Hubbard: 4 gown **5** dress

mother-of-pearl: 5 nacre

mother superior: 6 abbess

mother's mark: 9 birthmark

motherland: 4 home **7** country **10** fatherland

motherly: 8 maternal

motion (see also **bodily motion**): **4** fard, idea, move, stir **5** faird **6** signal, unrest **7** gesture, impulse, propose, request, suggest **8** movement, petition, proposal **9** agitation **10** suggestion **11** application, inclination **13** gesticulation
circular: **4** gyre **10** revolution
convulsive: **11** vellication
due to: **7** kinetic
expressive: **7** gesture
impetuous: **6** bensel, bensil **7** bensail, bensall, bensell
pert. to: **7** kinetic **9** kinematic **11** kinematical
producing: **6** motile
quality: **8** momentum
quivering: **6** tremor
rate: R.P.M. **4** time **5** speed, tempo **11** steerageway
science: **10** ballistics, kinematics
transmitter: cog **4** belt, gear
upward: **5** scend **8** upthrust

motion picture: 4 film, show **5** flick, movie, talky **6** cinema **7** flicker **9** photoplay **11** documentary
arc lamp: **5** kleig, klieg
award: **5** Oscar
cowboy and Indian: **5** oater **7** Western
machine: **9** projector **11** kinetoscope **12** animatograph, theatrograph **13** cinematograph **14** cinematographe
outline: **6** script **8** scenario
pert. to: **9** cinematic
prize: **5** Oscar
short: **4** clip **8** newsreel
term: pan **4** shot, take **6** retake **7** reverse

motionless: 4 dead **5** inert, rigid, still **6** asleep **8** becalmed, immobile, stagnant, stagnate, stirless **9** quiescent, sedentary **10** breathless, stock-still

motivate: 4 move **5** impel **6** incite, induce **7** inspire, provoke **9** influence, instigate, stimulate

motive: 4 sake, spur **5** cause **6** object, reason, spring **7** impulse, purpose **8** pressure, stimulus **9** incentive, objective **13** consideration
ostensible: **7** pretext

motley: **4** fool **5** mixed **6** jester **7** diverse, mottled, piebald **9** checkered **10** variegated **11** incongruous **13** heterogeneous, miscellaneous

motmot: **4** bird

motor: car **4** auto, ride **5** drive **6** engine **7** kinetic, machine **8** motorcar **10** automobile

electric: **6** dynamo

hand-powered: **9** baromotor

part: cam **4** coil **5** rotor **6** piston, stator **9** capacitor **10** carburetor

rotary: **7** turbine

motorbike: **5** moped **7** chopper **10** motorcycle

motorboat: **7** cruiser **8** palander, runabout

motor court: inn **5** motel

motor speed control: **8** rheocrat

motorman: **8** engineer, operator

motte: **5** copse, grove

mottled: **4** pied, roed **5** pinto **6** motley **7** brocked, clouded, dappled, piebald, spotted **8** blotched **9** splotched **10** variegated **11** varicolored

motto: mot **4** word **5** adage, axiom, gnome, maxim **6** device, saying, slogan **7** empresa, precept **8** aphorism **9** battle cry **10** shibboleth

mouche: **5** patch

mouchoir: **12** handkerchief

moue: **4** face, pout **7** grimace

mouflon, moufflon: **4** wool **5** sheep

mould: See **mold**

moulding: See **molding**

moult: See **molt**

moulting: See **molting**

mound: ahu, cop, dam, tee **4** balk, bank, butt, dene, dher, doon, dune, heap, hill, hump, pile, terp **5** agger, berry, cairn, dheri, globe, huaca, knoll, stack, toman(Scot.) **6** barrow, bounds, burrow, causey **7** bourock, bulwark, hornito, rampart, tumulus **8** boundary **9** elevation **10** embankment

of sand: **4** dune

of stones: **5** cairn

pert. to: **7** tumular

prehistoric: **4** terp

mound bird: **8** megapode

Mound City: **7** St. Louis

mound of light: **8** kohinoor

mount: **4** glue, hill, pony, rise, seat **5** arise, climb, horse, paste, stage, steed **6** ascend, aspire **8** escalate, increase, mountain **9** intensify **10** promontory **13** fortification

by ladder: **8** escalade

horizontal bar: kip

two-legged: **5** bipod

Mount Etna city: **7** Catania

Mount Everest peak: **6** Lhotse

Mount Helicon fountain: **8** Aganippe

Mount Ida nymph: **6** Oenone

Mount of Olives: **6** Olivet

Mount Parnassus fountain: **8** Castalia

Mount Rainier: **6** Tacoma

mountain: (see also **peak**): alp, ben (Sc.), kop **4** berg, dagh, fell, mesa, mont(F.) **5** onlay **6** barrow, bundoc, sierra **8** bundocks

base of: **8** piedmont

beyond: **10** tramontane **11** transalpine

Biblical: See **Bible:** *mountain*

burning: **7** volcano

crest: tor

depression: col

formation: **7** orogeny **9** orogenesy **10** orogenesis

highest: **7** Everest

lake: **4** tarn

low: **5** butte

mythical: Kaf, Qaf **4** Meru **5** candy, glass **7** Helicon **9** Parnassus

nymph: **5** dryad, oread

pass: col, gap **4** cove, duar, gate, ghat **5** ghaut, gorge, kotal **6** defile

pasture: alp **6** saeter

pert. to: **10** orological

range: **4** Alps, Ghat, Ural **5** Andes, chain, Coast, ridge, Rocky, Teton, White **6** Alatau **7** Rockies, Sierras **8** Cascades, Catskill, Pyrenees **9** Allegheny, Blue Ridge, Himalayas **10** San Jacinto **11** Appalachian, San Gorgonio

ridge: **4** aret, peak, spur **5** arete, crest **6** sierra, summit **7** sawbuck

rocky: **7** nunatak

science: **7** orology

sickness: **4** veta **7** soroche

snow: **5** jokul

study: **7** orology **9** orography

sunset reflection: **9** alpenglow

trail marker: **5** cairn

mountain andromeda: **10** fetterbush

mountain ash: **4** sorb **5** rowan, rowen **8** dogberry, winetree

mountain badger: **6** marmot

mountain balsam: fir

mountain banana: fei

mountain barometer: **8** orometer

mountain beaver: **8** sewellel

mountain bluet: **8** centaury

mountain cat: **4** lynx **6** bobcat, cougar **10** cacomistle

mountain climber: **10** alpestrian

equipment: **4** rope **5** piton **10** alpenstock

mountain climbing: **8** alpinism

equipment: axe **5** piton **7** crampon

mountain cock: **12** capercaillie

mountain curassow: **10** oreophasis

mountain dew: **7** bootleg, whiskey **9** moonshine

mountain duck: **9** harlequin, sheldrake

mountain finch: **9** brambling
mountain flax: **8** centaury
mountain fringe: **8** fumitory, wormwood
mountain goat: **4** ibex **6** mazame
mountain ivy: **6** laurel
mountain leather: **12** palygorskite
mountain lion: **4** puma **6** cougar
mountain magpie: **10** woodpecker **11** butcher-bird
mountain mint: **5** basil **8** calamint
mountain oak: **8** chestnut
mountain panther: **5** ounce **6** cougar **7** leopard
mountain parrot: kea
mountain partridge: **4** dove **5** quail
mountain pheasant: **6** grouse
mountain raspberry: **10** cloudberry
mountain rose: **6** laurel
mountain snow: **4** neve **6** jokul
mountain spinach: **5** orach **6** orache
Mountain State: **7** Montana
Mountain States: **4** Utah **5** Idaho **6** Nevada **7** Arizona, Montana, Wyoming **8** Colorado **9** New Mexico
mountain tea: **11** wintergreen
mountaineer: **5** Aaron **6** rustic **7** climber, hillman **9** hillbilly
 song: **5** yodel
mountainlike: **7** etiolin
mountainous: **4** high, huge **5** alpen **6** alpine, rugged **8** elevated **10** alpestrine, monumental, prodigious
mountaintop: **4** cone, peak **6** summit
mountebank: **4** gull **5** cheat, quack **7** empiric **8** impostor, minstrel, swindler **9** charlatan, pretender
 aid: **4** zany
mounting: **7** setting **9** equipment **13** embellishment
moup: **6** nibble **9** associate
mourn: rue **4** dole, erme, long, sigh, wail, weep **6** bemoan, bewail, grieve, lament, murmur, sorrow **7** deplore **8** mourning
mournful: sad **5** black **6** rueful, woeful **7** doleful, elegiac, pitiful **8** dejected, dirgeful, funereal **9** elegiacal, plaintive, sorrowful, threnodic, woebegone **10** deplorable, lamentable, lugubrious, melancholy **11** distressing **12** heavyhearted
mourning: **4** garb **5** dolor **6** dolour **7** drapery
 bride: **5** plant **8** scabious
 dress: **5** black, crape, crepe, weeds **6** sables
 group: **7** cortege
 song: **5** dirge
mouse: erd, pry **4** girl, hunt, knot **5** snoop, steal **6** bruise, rodent **8** black-eye
 field: **4** vole **7** harvest
 leaping: **6** jerboa
 male: **4** buck

milk: **6** spurge
pert. to: **6** murine
mouse deer: **7** plandok **10** chevrotain
mouse-ear: **8** hawkweed **9** chickweed
mouse hare: **4** pika
mousebird: **4** coly **6** shrike
mouselike: shy **4** drab **5** quiet, timid **6** murine **8** retiring
mouser: cat **8** detective
mouseweb: **6** cobweb **8** gossamer
mousing: **6** prying **7** binding **8** prowling **9** rapacious **11** inquisitive
mousle: **6** rumple
mousse: **7** dessert, messboy
mousy: **4** drab **5** quiet, timid
moutan: **5** peony, plant **6** flower
mouth: gab, gan, gob, mow, mug, mun, ora **4** boca(Sp.), dupe **5** boast, front, orate, stoma **6** cavity, gebbie(Sc.), mumble, rictus **7** flummer, grimace, opening, stomata **8** back talk, entrance **9** impudence, spokesman
 away from: **6** aborad, aboral
 deformity: **7** harelip
 disease: **4** noma **6** canker **10** stomatitis
 muscle: **7** caninus
 of furnace: **5** bocca
 of river: **5** delta, firth
 part: lip **5** uvula **6** palate **7** pharynx
 pert. to: **4** oral **6** rictal **7** oscular, palatal **8** stomatic
 projecting: **5** spout
 roof: **6** palate
 tissue: gum
 toward: **4** orad
 with open: **5** agape
mouth organ: **9** harmonica
mouth-watering: **8** alluring **9** delicious, palatable
mouthful: lot, sup **4** bite, gulp **6** gobbet
mouthpiece: **5** bocal **6** lawyer **8** attorney
mouthwash: **9** collutory **10** antiseptic **11** collutorium
mouthy: **5** talky **9** bombastic, talkative
mouton: fur, spy **4** wool **8** lambskin **9** sheepskin
movable: **5** loose **6** fickle, mobile, motile **8** exorable, floating, unstable, unsteady **10** changeable, inconstant **11** ephelcystic **12** figuratively
move (see also **go**): go; act, gee, mog **4** goad, pass, play, spur, stir **5** budge, cause, clink, impel, rouse, shift, start, sweep **6** affect, arouse, behave, bestir, betake, excite, incite, induce, kindle, motion, prompt, quetch, remble, remove **7** actuate, advance, agitate, animate, attempt, inspire, migrate, propose, provoke, suggest **8** converse, emigrate, maneuver, motivate, transfer **9** influence, instigate, stimulate, stratagem

along: mog **5** mosey, scram **7** maunder

away: shy **8** emigrate

back: ebb **6** recede **7** retreat

back and forth: wag **4** flap, rock, tack **5** dodge, weave **6** falter, teeter, wabble, wiggle, wigwag, zigzag **7** shuttle **9** oscillate

false: **4** balk **5** feint **7** misstep

first: **10** initiative

forward: **4** edge **5** drive, forge, surge **7** advance **8** progress

furtively: **5** skulk, slink, sneak

heaven and earth: try **6** strive

heavily: lug **6** lumber, trudge

in: **6** occupy **7** inhabit

in water: **4** swim, wade

noiselessly: **4** slip **5** creep, glide, skulk, slink, sneak, steal **6** tiptoe **9** pussyfoot

noisily: **6** bustle **7** clatter, rollick

obliquely: **4** edge, joll, skew, slue **5** sidle

on wheels: **4** roll **7** trundle

quickly: fly **4** dart, dash, flit, jump, leap, race, scud, scur, whir **5** bound, hurry, scoot, skirr, spank, start, sweep **6** career, gallop, hurtle, scurry, spring

restlessly: **6** kelter, twitch

rhythmically: bob, jig, jog **5** dance, march

round and round: **4** eddy **5** swirl, twirl

sinuously: **5** snake **6** writhe

slowly: lag, mog **4** edge, inch, worm **5** crawl **6** trudge **7** crowhop

smoothly: **4** slip **5** glide, skate, slide

together: **5** unite **8** converge

movement: act **5** tempo, trend **6** rhythm **7** gesture **8** activity **9** mechanism

biological: **5** taxis

capable of: **6** mobile, motile

music: **6** moto

surface **6** seiche

movie: See **motion picture**

moving: **7** current **8** ambulant, pathetic, poignant, touching **9** affecting, transient **10** ambulatory, impressive

moving about: **8** ambulant **10** ambulatory

moving part: cam, cog **5** rotor, wheel

moving picture: See **motion picture**

moving staircase: **9** escalator

mow: bin, cut, lay, mew **4** barb, clip, heap, mass, pile **5** mouth, scowl, stack **6** scythe, sickle **7** grimace, shorten **8** haystack **9** cornfield

mowana: **6** baobab

Mowgli: *elephant:* **5** Hathi

friend: **5** Akela, Baloo

Mozart opera: **6** Figaro **10** Magic Flute **11** Don Giovanni **12** Cosi fan Tutte

much: **4** fele, high, lots, many **5** great, heaps, scads **6** mickle **7** gaylies, geylies, greatly **8** abundant, uncommon **9** great deal, multitude **10** all kinds of

music: **5** molto

Much Ado About Nothing character: **4** Hero **6** Ursula **7** Antonio, Claudio, Leonato

mucid: **5** moldy, musty, slimy **6** mucous

mucilage: gum **5** paste **6** arabin, mucago **8** adhesive

mucilaginous: **5** gluey, slimy **6** sticky, viscid **8** adhesive

muck: goo **4** dirt, dung, mess **5** botch, filth, money, slime, waste **6** manure, refuse, wealth **7** saunter **10** complicate

mucous: **5** moist, slimy **7** viscous **8** blennoid

mud fen **4** dirt, gore, mire, ooze, roil **5** slime, slush **6** sludge **7** clabber

deposit: **4** silt

hole: pan **6** puddle, wallow **8** quagmire

living in: **10** limicolous

pert to: **7** luteous

mud dab: **8** flounder

mud dabbler: **9** killfish

mud dauber: **4** wasp

mud devil: **10** hellbender

mud eel: **5** siren

mud lark: **5** gamin **6** magpie, urchin

mud mark: **7** mudflow

mud peep: **9** sandpiper

mud puppy: **7** dogfish **10** hellbender, salamander

mud snipe: **8** woodcock

mud sunfish: **4** bass

Mudcat State: **11** Mississippi

muddle: mix **4** ball, daze, doze, mess, roil **5** addle, besot, snafu **6** bemuse, burble, fuddle, jumble, pother **7** bedevil, blunder, confuse, fluster, mystify, perplex, stumble, stupefy **8** befuddle, bemuddle, bewilder, confound, disorder, flounder **9** confusion **10** complicate, intoxicate **12** hugger-mugger

muddled: ree **4** asea **5** beery, crazy, drunk, foggy, tipsy **10** incoherent

muddy: **4** miry, roil, soil **5** dirty, drovy, druvy, slaky, vague **6** claggy, clarty, clashy, cloudy, drubly, lutose, sludgy, slushy, turbid **7** clouded, guttery, obscure, sensual, squalid **8** confused, feculent **9** besmeared, spattered **11** bespattered

mudfish: **6** bowfin **9** killfish

mudhold: **4** slew, sloo, slue **6** slough

mudworm: ipo **9** earthworm

mudwort: **7** mudweed

muezzin's call to prayer: **4** adan, azan

muff: fur, vex **4** flub **5** crest, error **6** bungle, goof up, warmer **8** irritate

muffin: cob, gem **5** bread, scone **7** crumpet, popover

muffle: gag **4** damp, dull, mute, wrap **6** bumble, dampen, deaden, shroud, stifle **7** silence **8** envelope, suppress **10** camouflage

muffled: 6 hollow
muffler: 4 mask, mute 5 scarf 6 tippet 8 silencer
mufflin: 8 titmouse
mufti: 4 alim 8 assessor, civilian, clothing, official 9 expounder
mug: cup 4 cram, dupe, face, fool, toby 5 mouth, mungo, pulse, sheep, stein, study 6 noggin, seidel 7 assault, canette, drizzle, goddard, grimace, tankard 8 schooner 10 photograph
muga: 4 silk 11 caterpillar
mugger: ham 4 thug 6 emoter 7 puncher 9 assailant, crocodile
muggy: 4 damp 5 humid, moist, moldy
mugwet: 4 rose 8 woodruff
muir: 4 moor
mulatto: 5 metis 10 crossbreed, high yellow
mulberry bird: 8 starling
mulberry fig: 8 sycamore
mulch: 5 cover, straw 6 litter 7 compost, sawdust
mulct: 4 balk, fine, scot 5 cheat 6 amerce, defect, fleece, punish 7 blemish, deceive, defraud, forfeit, penalty 8 penalize 10 amercement, forfeiture
mule: 4 mewl, mool, mute 5 coble, hinny 6 hybrid 7 bat-mule, slipper, spinner, tractor 9 chilblain 10 locomotive
cry: 4 bray 6 heehaw
group: 5 atajo, drove
leader in pack train: 8 cencerro
male: 4 jack
spinning: 7 ironman
untrained: 9 shavetail
mule killer: 4 wasp 6 mantis 8 scorpion
muleteer: 4 peon 6 driver 7 arriero(Sp.), skinner 9 almocrebe
mulga: 6 acacia
mulish: 5 balky 6 hybrid, sullen 7 sterile 8 perverse, stubborn 9 obstinate, pigheaded 10 determined
mull: cow 4 crag, dust, heat, mess, mold, muse 5 cloth, crush, grind, snout, spice, think 6 fettle, muslin, muzzle, ponder, powder 7 crumble, failure, rubbish, squeeze, sweeten 8 cogitate, consider, ointment, snuffbox 9 pulverize 10 promontory
mullet: 8 food fish
mulligan: 4 stew
mulligatawny: 4 soup
mulligrubs: 5 blahs, blues, colic, sulks
mulloway: 6 maigre 7 jewfish
multicolored: 4 pied 6 calico 7 dappled, spotted
multifarious: 7 diverse 8 manifold
multifold: 4 many 8 manifold, numerous
multiform: 7 diverse
multiple: 4 many 6 plural 8 numerous
multiplier: 7 facient

multiply: 5 breed 6 spread 7 amplify, augment, magnify 8 increase 9 procreate, reproduce
by eight: 11 octuplicate
by ten: 7 decuple
multitude: mob 4 army, heap, hive, host, many, mass, much, ruck 5 cloud, crowd, drove, flock, horde, shoal, swarm 6 legion, myriad, nation, throng
multitudinous: 4 many 8 manifold, numerous 9 countless 10 numberless
mum: ale 4 beer, dark 5 still 6 mother, silent 7 silence 9 voiceless 10 speechless 13 chrysanthemum
mumble 4 chew, mump 5 mouth 6 chavel, chavle, faffle, fumble, haffle, murmur, mutter, palter, patter 7 flummer, grumble
mumbo-jumbo: 4 idol 6 fetich, fetish 7 bugaboo 9 gibberish
mummer: 4 mime 5 actor 6 guiser, player 7 buffoon 9 performer, puppeteer
mummery: 6 acting 8 puppetry 9 hypocrisy 10 hocus pocus 11 abracadabra
mummy: 5 relic 6 corpse 7 cadaver, carcass
mummy apple: 6 papaya
mump: 5 cheat, sulks 6 mumble, mutter 7 grimace 10 sullenness 11 displeasure
mumper: 6 beggar 8 impostor
mumps: 9 parotitis
munch: eat 4 chew 5 champ 6 growse, growze
mundane: 6 cosmic 7 earthly, prosaic, secular, terrene, worldly 8 temporal 11 terrestrial
municipality: 4 city, town 7 cabildo
pert. to: 5 civic
munificent: 4 free 5 ample 6 lavish 7 liberal 8 generous 9 bounteous, bountiful 10 benevolent
munitions: 7 baggage, weapons 8 armament 10 ammunition
munity: 9 privilege
Munro's penname: 4 Saki
muntjac, muntjak: 4 deer 6 kidang
muraena: 5 moray
mural: 6 fresco 12 wall painting
murder: 4 bane, kill, slay 5 death 7 bump-off, butcher, carnage, killing, murther 8 foul play, homicide 9 slaughter 11 assassinate 12 manslaughter
brother: 10 fratricide
father: 9 patricide
fine: cro 7 wergild 9 bloodfine
infant: 11 infanticide
king: 8 regicide
mother: 9 matricide
own child: 9 prolicide
parent: 9 parricide
prophet: 8 vaticide
sister: 10 sororicide

son or daughter: **8** filicide
spouse: **10** mariticide
wife: **9** uxoricide
woman: **8** femicide
murderous: 4 gory **5** felon **6** bloody, brutal, deadly **7** ruinous **9** ferocious, homicidal **10** sanguinary **12** bloodthirsty
mure: 6 shut up, thrust **7** squeeze **8** imprison
murid: rat **5** mouse **6** rodent
murky: dim **4** dark **5** black, dense, foggy, mirky, misty, mucky, thick **6** cloudy, gloomy **7** obscure **12** impenetrable
murmur: coo, hum, pur **4** curr, fret, huzz, purl, purr, sugh **5** brool, drone, grank, sough **6** babble, grutch, hummer, mumble, mutter, repine, report **7** grumble, whisper **8** complain **9** grumbling
nasal: hum
murphy: 6 potato
Musa: 6 banana
muscadine: 5 grape
muscle: 4 beef, thew **5** brawn, flesh, force, power, sinew, teres **6** lacert **8** strength
affliction: **5** crick **6** abasia, ataxia
bound: **5** rigid, stiff
column: **10** sarcostyle
contracting: **7** agonist
curve: **7** myogram
expansion: **7** dilator
lifting: **7** levator
limb-straightening: **8** extensor
round: **5** teres
segment: **8** myocomma
spasm: **5** tonus
straight: **6** rectus
stretching: **6** tensor
sugar: **7** inosite **8** inositol
trapezius: **10** cucullaris
triangular: **7** deltoid
turning: **7** evertor, rotator
two-headed: **6** biceps
muscovado: 8 raw sugar
Muscovite: Red **4** mica, Russ **7** Russian
mica: **4** talc
prince: **4** Ivan
muscular: 4 ropy, wiry **5** thewy **6** brawny, robust, sinewy, strong, torose, torous **7** fibrous, stringy **8** athletic, vigorous
muse: 4 dump, mull, poet, **5** dream, think **6** loiter, ponder, trifle **7** reflect, reverie **8** cogitate, consider, meditate, ruminate **9** amusement **10** meditation **11** contemplate
Muse: 4 Clio **5** Erato **6** Thalia, Urania **7** Euterpe **8** Calliope, Pierides, Polymnia **9** Melpomene **10** Polyhymnia **11** Terpsichore
birthplace: **6** Pieria
epithet: **7** Pierian
father: **4** Zeus

fountain: **8** Aganippe
home: **5** Aonia **7** Helicon
mother: **9** Mnemosyne
mountain: **9** Parnassus
of astronomy: **6** Urania
of comedy: **6** Thalia
of dancing: **11** Terpsichore
of eloquence: **8** Calliope
of epic poetry: **8** Calliope
of history **4** Clio
of love poetry: **5** Erato
of lyric poetry: **5** Erato
of music: **7** Euterpe
of pastoral poetry: **6** Thalia
of sacred poetry: **8** Polymnia **10** Polyhymnia
of tragedy: **9** Melpomene
seat of worship: **6** Pieria
museful: 6 silent **10** meditative, thoughtful
musery: 4 play **9** amusement
musette: air **4** oboe **7** bagpipe, gavotte
museum: 7 gallery, preserve **10** collection repository
custodian: **7** curator
director: **7** curator
mush: cut **5** atole, crush, gruel, march, notch, sepon **6** indent, sepawn, supawn, travel **7** confuse, journey, pudding, suppawn **8** flattery, porridge, sagamite, umbrella **14** sentimentality
mushroom: 4 grow **6** agaric, spread **7** explode, parvenu, upstart
cap: **6** pileus
disease: **5** flock
edible: **5** morel **10** champignon **11** chanterelle
like: **7** fungous
part of: **4** gill **5** stipe, trama **6** pileus **7** annulus **8** basidium, hymenium, sterigma **12** basidiospore
poisoning: **8** mycetism
poisonous: **7** amanita **9** toadstool
stem: **5** stipe
mushy: 4 hazy, soft, weak **5** gushy, thick **8** effusive, yielding **11** sentimental
music (see also **melody, song,** and entries under **musical**): air, art **4** tune **7** harmony
aftersong: **5** epode
beat: **5** ictus, pulse, tempo **6** rhythm
change to another key: **10** modulation **13** transposition
chord: **5** triad
flourish: **7** roulade
for eight: **5** octet
for five: **7** quintet
for four: **7** quartet
for nine: **5** nonet
for one: **4** soli, solo
for seven: **6** septet
for six: **6** sextet **7** sestole **8** sestolet

for three: **4** trio
for two: duo **4** duet
god: **6** Apollo
half tone: **8** semitone
machine for: **5** radio **7** juke-box, pianola **8** musicbox **10** gramophone, phonograph
major scale: **5** gamut
major third: **6** ditone
mania for: **9** melomania
melodic phrase: **9** leitmotif, leitmotiv
morning song: **6** aubade
muse: **7** Euterpe
notation system: **5** neume
outdoor: **6** aubade **8** serenade
patron saint: **7** Cecilia
pert. to chance elements: **9** aleatoric
simple song: air, lay **4** tune
symbol: bar, key, tie **4** clef, flat, note, rest, slur **5** brace, sharp, staff
syncopated: **4** jazz
theme: **4** tema
timing device: **4** metronome
music hall: **4** gaff, odea(pl.) **5** odeum, odeon
musical: **4** show **5** lyric, revue **7** lyrical, melodic **8** harmonic, rhythmic **9** melodious **10** harmonious
musical composition: **4** glee, opus **5** cento, fugue, opera, rondo **6** ballad, sonata **7** ballade, boutade, cantata, chanson, prelude, scherzo, virelai **8** berceuse, concerto, nocturne, operetta, oratorio, serenata, serenade, sonatina, symphony **9** cabaletta, interlude **10** intermezzo
aria-like: **6** arioso
choral: **5** motet **7** chorale **9** plainsong
dancer's: **10** gymnopedie
dawn: **6** aubade
declamatory: **10** recitative
ending: **4** coda, fine **6** finale
exercise: **5** etude, study
feature: **5** motif, theme
folk song: **4** lied
interlude: **6** verset
jazz: rag **4** jive **5** bebop, blues, swing **7** ragtime **11** rock-and-roll **12** boogie-woogie
opera: **5** scena
poetic: ode
prelude: **6** verset
religious: **4** mass **5** motet, psalm **6** anthem **7** cantata **8** oratorio
round: **5** canon, fugue, troll
suite: **7** partita
musical direction: *above:* **5** sopra
accented: **7** marcato **8** sforzato **9** sforzando
again: DC, DS; bis **6** da capo **8** dal segno
all: **5** tutti
always: **6** sempre
animated: **7** animato **9** spiritoso

ardent: **7** ardente **12** appassionato
as written: sta
begin now: **7** attacca
below: **5** sotto
bold: **6** audace
bowed: **4** arco
bright: **5** anime
cold: **6** freddo
continue: va
devout: **6** divoto
dignified: **8** maestoso
disconnected: **8** staccato
dying away: **7** calando
emotional: **12** appassionato
evenly: **10** eugalmente
everyone: **5** tutti
excited: **7** agitato **9** spiritoso
fast: **4** vivo **5** tosto **6** presto, veloce, vivace **7** allegro **10** tostamente
faster: **7** stretto
freely: **9** ad libitum
furious: **7** furioso
gay: **7** giocoso
gentle: **5** dolce
half: **5** mezzo
heavy: **7** pesante
held: **6** tenuto
hurried: **7** agitato
in the style of: **4** alla
joyous: **7** giocoso
leap: **5** salto
less: **4** meno
little: **4** poco
little by little: **9** poco a poco
lively: **6** vivace **7** allegro, animato, giocoso
loud: **5** forte **10** fortissimo
louder: **9** crescendo
lovingly: **7** amabile, amoroso
lyric: **5** erato
majestic: **8** maestoso
marked: **7** marcato
moderate: **7** andante **8** moderato
more: piu
more rapid: **7** stretta, stretto
much: **5** molto
muted: **5** sorda
passionless: **6** freddo
plaintive: **7** dolente
playful: **7** giocoso **10** scherzando
plucked: **9** pizzicato
proceed: va
quick: **4** vite **5** tosto **6** presto **7** schnell
quick time: **9** alla breve
quickening: **11** affrettando
repeat: bis **6** ancoro **7** ripresa
sadly: **7** dolente **8** doloroso
sharp: **8** staccato **9** sforzando
silent: **5** tacet
singing: **9** cantabile
sliding: **9** glissando
slow: **5** grave, largo, lento, tardo **6** adagio **7** andante **9** larghetto

slower: rit **6** ritard **10** ritardando
slowing: **11** rallentando
smooth: **6** legato **8** grazioso
so much: **5** tanto
soft: **5** dolce, piano **10** pianissimo
softer: **10** diminuendo **11** decrescendo
solemn: **5** grave
somewhat: **4** poco
spirited: **7** animato **9** spiritoso
stately: **7** pomposo **8** maestoso
strong: **5** forte **10** fortissimo
sustained: **6** tenuto **9** sostenuto, sustenuto
sweet: **5** dolce
tempo irregular: **6** rubato
tender: **7** amabile
thrice: ter
throughout: **6** sempre
together: **8** ensemble
too much: **6** troppo
tranquil: **7** calmato
turn: **9** gruppetto
twice: bis
very: tre **4** tres **5** assai, molto **7** dimolto
with: con
musical disc: 6 cymbal, record **9** recording
musical drama: 5 opera **8** operetta, oratorio **9** singspiel
musical event: 5 opera **6** ballet **7** concert, recital **8** musicale, oratorio
musical instrument: 4 drum, fife, gong, harp, horn, lute, lyre, oboe, reed, tuba **5** banjo, flute, organ, piano, viola **6** cornet, guitar, spinet, violin **7** bassoon, ocarina, piccolo, saxhorn, trumpet, ukelele **8** castanet, clarinet, dulcimer, mandolin, trombone **9** euphonium, flageolet, saxophone **11** violoncello
aid: **4** pick **8** diapason, plectrum **9** metronome, pitch pipe
ancient: **4** asor **5** rocta **6** rappel, sebaca **7** cithera, serpent **9** pantaleon
bass: **5** cello **11** violoncello
brass: **4** horn, tuba **5** bugle **6** tromba **7** althorn, helicon, saxhorn, trumpet **8** altohorn, trombone **10** French horn
China: kin
East Indies: **4** bina
Egypt: **7** sistrum
helicon: **4** tuba
Java: **7** gamelon **8** gamelang
keyboard: **5** organ, piano **6** spinet **7** celesta, clavier **8** melodeon **9** accordion **10** clavichord, concertina, pianoforte **11** harpsichord
lute-like: **7** angelot, bandore, cithern, cittern **9** bandurria **10** colascione
lyre-like: **4** asor **6** cither, zither, **7** cithara, kithara
medieval: **5** rebab, rocta **7** chrotta **10** clavichord, hurdy-gurdy

Mexico: **5** guiro **6** clarin **7** cabacas, maracas **11** chiapanecas
mouthpiece: **4** reed **6** fipple
oboe-like: **5** shawm **7** musette
old: **5** rebec **7** cittern, gittern
percussion: **4** drum, gong **5** bells, traps **6** maraca **7** cymbals, marimba timpani, tympani **8** bass drum, castanet, triangle **9** snare drum, xylophone **10** kettledrum, tambourine **12** glockenspiel
piano-like: see *keyboard* above
reed: **4** oboe **7** bassoon **8** clarinet **9** harmonica, saxophone **11** English horn
six-stringed: **6** guitar
stringed: oud, uke **4** asor, bass, harp, lute, lyre, viol, vina **5** banjo, cello, rebec, ruana, viola **6** citole, fiddle, guitar, rebeck, violin, zither **7** bandore, cythara, gittern, pandura, samisen, theorbo, ukelele **8** autoharp, dulcimer, mandolin **11** harpsichord, violoncello
supplementary: **7** theorbo
two-necked: **7** ripieno
viol-like: **5** rebec, ruana **6** rebeck **7** claviol **8** claviole
wind: jub, sax **4** fife, horn, oboe, reed, tuba **5** brass, bugle, flute, organ **6** cornet **7** althorn, bagpipe, bassoon, clarion, ocarina, panpipe, piccolo, saxhorn, serpent, trumpet **8** altohorn, clarinet, recorder, trombone, zampogna **9** flageolet, harmonica, saxophone **10** French horn **11** sarrusphone
xylophone-like: **7** marimba
without electronic sound: **8** acoustic
musical interval: 5 fifth, major, minor, sixth, third **6** ditone, fourth, octave, second, unison **7** perfect, seventh, tritone **9** augmented **10** diminished
musical medley: 4 olio **5** cento
musical note (see also **musical syllable**): **5** breve, minim, neume **6** quaver **9** semibreve
musical piece: See **musical composition, song**
musical program: 5 opera **7** concert, recital **8** musicale
musical rhythm: 4 beat, time **5** ictus, meter, pulse, swing, tempo
measuring device: **9** metronome
musical scale (see also **musical syllable**): **5** gamut
musical sign: 5 segno
entrance: **5** presa
hold: **7** fermata, formata
key: **4** flat **5** sharp **7** natural
pitch level: **4** clef
silence: **4** rest
slur: **8** ligature
smooth: **4** slur
staff: bar
musical syllable: Ela, sol **7** alamire

musical term: *arrangement:* **7** ridotto
ballad style: **8** a ballata
between acts: **8** entracte
cadence: **4** half **6** plagal **7** perfect **9** deceptive, imperfect
chapel-style: **9** a cappella
dance-style: **7** da ballo
embellishment: **8** ornament **9** fioritura **12** appoggiatura
ending: **4** coda
florid: **7** bravura
flourish: **7** cadenza
half note: **5** minim
half tone: **8** semitone
major key: dur
melodic phrase: **5** motif **9** leitmotif, leitmotiv
melos: **4** song **6** melody
minor key: **4** moll
movement: **4** moto
note: **5** breve, neume
refrain: **5** epode **8** repetend
repeat: **5** rondo **7** reprise
run: **6** volata **9** glissando
shake: **5** trill **7** tremolo
soft pedal: VC **7** celeste
third: **6** tierce
thirty-second note: **14** demisemiquaver
three-note chord: **5** triad
time: See **musical rhythm**
tones: **5** chord
tremble: **5** trill **7** tremolo, vibrato
triplet: **6** tercet, triole
two notes: **5** duole
unaccompanied: **9** a cappella
upbeat: **5** arsis
vocal part: **5** canto
musical theme: **4** tema **5** motif **9** leitmotif, leitmotiv
musician: **4** bard **5** piper **6** player, singer **7** drummer, flutist, gleeman, pianist **8** bandsman, composer, flautist, minstrel, organist, virtuoso **9** cornetist, performer, serenader, violinist **10** trombonist **11** clarinetist, saxophonist
group: **4** band, duet, trio **5** choir, nonet **6** chorus, septet, sextet **7** nonetto, quartet **8** ensemble, septette, sextette **9** orchestra, quartette
patron saint: **7** Cecelia
musing: **7** reverie **10** meditation, meditative **13** contemplation
musk: **4** deer **7** perfume
musk beaver: **7** muskrat
musk cat: **5** civet
musk cavy: **5** hutia
musk cucumber: **11** cassabanana
musk deer: **6** cervid **10** chevrotain
musk mallow: **8** abelmosk
musk shrew: **6** desman
muskeg: bog **5** marsh
muskellunge: **4** pike

musket: **4** hawk **5** fusil **6** falcon **7** bundock, bundook, dragoon, firearm **8** biscayen **9** flintlock
Musketeers: See **Three Musketeers**
muskmelon: **6** atimon, casaba **10** cantaloupe
muskrat: **5** shrew **6** desman
Muslim, Moslem (see also **Islam, Mohammed**): **4** Moro **6** Paynim **7** abadite, Islamic, Saracen **9** Mahometan, Mussulman **10** Mohammedan
ablution: **4** widu, wudu, wuzu
Alexandria sect: **6** Senusi
angel: **6** Azrael **7** isrefel, israfil **8** israfeel
annual fast: **7** Ramadan
antenuptial settlement: **4** mahr
ascetic: **4** sufi **5** fakir **6** fakeer
bazaar: **4** sook
beads: **6** tasbih
belt: **5** zonar **6** zonnar
Berber dynasty: **6** Hafsid **7** Hafsite
Bible: **5** Coran, Koran **7** Alcoran
bier: **5** tabut
blood relationship: **5** nasab
calendar: **5** Rabia, Rajab, Safar **6** Jumada, Shaban **7** Ramadan, Shawwal **8** Zu'lhijah, Zu'lkadah **9** Mulharram
call to prayer: **4** adan, azan
cap: taj **5** kulah **6** kullah
caravansary: **6** imaret
caste: **5** mopla **6** moplah
chief: **4** rais, sidi **5** datto, syid, sheik
city (sacred): **5** Mecca **6** Medina
coin: **5** dinar
convert: **5** ansar
council: **5** Ulema
creed: **5** Sunna
crusade: **5** jehad, jihad
decree: **5** irade
deity: **5** Allah, Eblis
demon: **5** afrit, eblis, jinni **6** jinnee
dervish: **6** Sadite, Santon
divorce: **5** ahsan, talak **7** mubarat
fast days: **7** Ramadan
festival: Eed **6** Bairam
freethinker: **7** Saracen **9** Aladinist
garment: **4** izar **6** jubbah
god: **5** Allah
guide (spiritual): pir
headdress: fez, taj **5** kulah **6** kullah, turban
hermit: **8** marabout
holy book: **5** Koran
holy city: **5** Mecca **6** Medina
holy war: **5** jehad, jihad
infidel: **5** kafir **6** kaffir
judge: **4** cadi, cazi, imam, kazi **5** hakim, imaum
kinship: **5** nasab
lady: **5** begum
law: **5** halal **7** sheriat
lawyer: **5** mufti

leader: 4 amir, emir 5 ameer, emeer
men's quarters: 8 selamlik
messiah: 5 Mahdi
minaret crier: 7 muezzin
minister of state: 6 vizier
monastery: 5 tekke
month: see *calendar* above
mosque: 6 masjid
mystic: 4 Sufi
mysticism: 6 Sufism
name: Ali
nymph: 5 houri
officer: aga
official: 5 hajib, mufti
orthodox: 5 hanif 7 Sunnite
people: Laz 4 Lazi, Moro, Sufi, Swat 5 Hanif, Isawa, Salar, Samal, Sunni, Swati 6 Dehgan, Senusi 7 Bazigar, Senoussi, Senussi 8 Senusite 9 Senussian
physician: 5 hakim 6 hakeem
pilgrim: 4 haji 5 hadji, hajji
pilgrimage: 4 hadj
pilgrim's dress: 5 ihram
prayer: 5 namaz, salat
prayer call: 4 adan, azan
priest: 4 imam 5 imaum 6 wahabi
priests (body): 5 ulema
prince: 4 amir, emir, seid 5 ameer, emeer, nawab, sayid
princess: 4 tola 5 begum
religion: 5 Islam
ruler: aga 4 amir, emir 5 ameer, emeer, hakim, nawah 6 hakeem, sultan
saber: 7 yatagan 8 scimitar, scimiter, yataghan
sacred book: see *Bible* above
saint: Pir 5 Abdal 6 Santon 8 Marabout
salutation: 5 salam 6 salaam
sect: 5 Isawa 6 Wahabi 7 Abadite, dervish, Sunnite 8 Ahmadiya, Sifatite
shrine: 5 Kaaba 6 Kaabeh
spirit: 4 jinn(pl.), 5 genie, jinni 7 jinnyeh
spiritual adviser: pir
student: 5 softa
supreme being: 5 Allah
teacher: 4 alim, imam 8 mujtahid
title: sid 4 said, sidi 5 nawab, sayid 6 sayyid
tomb: 5 tabut
warrior: 7 Saracen
washing: 4 widu, wudu, wuzu
women's quarters: 5 harem
muslin: 4 mull 6 cotton 7 organdy 8 nainsook, seerhand, sheeting
muss: See **mess**
mussel: 4 unio 5 naiad 6 mucket, nerita 8 deerhorn
genus of: 8 modiolus
larva: 9 blackhead
part: 6 byssus
mussitate: 6 mutter

Mussolini: 7 Fascist 8 dictator
son-in-law: 5 Ciano
title: 6 Il Duce
Mussulman: See **Muslim**
must: 4 bood, mold, musk, sapa, stum, want 5 juice, ought, shall 6 refuse 9 have got to 10 obligation
mustang: 5 horse, pinto 6 bronco 7 broncho
mustard: 5 nigra, senvy 6 senapi 7 cadlock 8 charlock
chemical: 5 allyl
family: 12 brassicaceae
genus of: 7 sinapis
pod: 7 silicle
mustard plaster: 8 poultice, sinapism
musteline animal: 6 weasel
muster: 4 call 5 erect 6 gather, roster, sample, summon 7 collect, marshal, pattern 8 assemble, generate, mobilize 10 accumulate, congregate
out: 7 disband, release 9 discharge
mustiness: 4 fust, mold
musty: 4 dull, sour 5 dirty, fusty, hoary, moldy, rafty, stale, trite 6 filthy, rancid 7 foughty, spoiled, squalid 10 antiquated
Mut: *child of:* 5 Chons
husband: 4 Amen, Amon
mutable: 6 fickle 8 unstable, variable 9 alterable 10 changeable, inconstant 11 fluctuating, vacillating
mutate: 4 vary 5 alter 6 change, modify 9 transform
mutation: 6 change, revolt 9 posthouse 10 revolution, succession 11 vicissitude
mute: mum 4 dumb, lene, surd 6 deaden, muffle, silent 7 mourner, muffler 8 deadener, silencer 9 voiceless 10 speechless 12 inarticulate
mutilate: mar 4 hack, hurt, maim 6 damage, deface, garble, injure, mangle, mittle(Sc.) 7 cripple, destroy 9 disfigure, dismember, sterilize
mutinous: 6 unruly 9 alienated, seditious, turbulent 10 rebellious, refractory, tumultuous 11 disaffected, disobedient, intractable 12 contumacious 13 insubordinate
mutiny: 6 revolt, strife 9 commotion 12 insurrection
mutt: cur, dog 5 dunce 7 mongrel 9 blockhead
mutter: 5 growl, rumor 6 mumble, murmur, patter 7 channer, grumble, maunder 9 mussitate
mutton: 4 meat 5 sheep 6 candle 10 prostitute
dried: 5 vifda, vivda
leg: 5 cabob, gigot 7 wabbler, wobbler
muttonbird: oii 6 petrel 10 shearwater

muttonchop: 7 whisker 8 burnside, side-burn

muttonfish: 4 sama 5 pargo, porgy 7 eel-pout, mojarra

muttonhead: 5 dunce 9 blockhead, screwball

mutual: 6 common 7 related 10 associated, reciprocal, responsive

mutuality: 13 interrelation

mux: 4 mess 5 botch

muzhik: 7 peasant

muzzle: gag 4 face, grub, nose, root 5 snout 6 clevis, muffle 7 sheathe 8 restrain 10 respirator

muzzy: 4 dull 5 fuzzy 7 blurred, muddled 8 confused 9 befuddled 10 depressive

My Last Duchess author: 8 Browning

mycoid: 7 fungoid

myna: 4 bird 7 grackle

myomorph: rat 5 mouse 6 rodent

myopic: 8 purblind 10 astigmatic 11 nearsighted 12 shortsighted

myriad: 4 host 9 countless 11 innumerable 13 multitudinous

myriapod: 9 centipede

myrmicid: ant

myrmidon: 8 adherent, follower, henchman 9 attendant, underling

myrrh: gum 4 tree 5 resin

myrtle: 6 laurel 8 ramarama 10 periwinkle 11 candleberry

myself: 5 masel(Sc.)

mysterious: dim 4 dark 5 runic 6 arcane, mystic, occult, secret 7 cryptic, strange, uncanny 8 abstruse 9 enigmatic, equivocal, recondite, sphinxine 12 inexplicable, unfathomable

mystery: 4 rune 5 craft, trade 6 cabala, enigma, puzzle, riddle, secret 7 arcanum, esotery, stumper 8 thriller, whodunit 10 closed book 11 brain twister

mystery novel award: 5 Edgar

mystic: 4 seer 5 epopt, magic, runic 6 occult, orphic, secret 7 cryptic, epoptic, obscure 8 anagogic, esoteric, symbolic 9 enigmatic, recondite 10 cabalistic, mysterious

art: 6 cabala

initiate: 5 epopt

Moslem: 4 Sufi

secret sect: 5 cabal

word: 4 evoe 7 abraxas 10 hocus pocus, open sesame 11 abracadabra

mystical: 4 dark 6 occult, secret 8 anagogic, hush-hush, symbolic, telestic 9 spiritual

significance: 7 anagoge

mysticism: 6 cabala 8 cabalism

mystify: 5 befog 6 muddle, puzzle 7 becloud, confuse, perplex 8 befuddle, bewilder 9 bamboozle, obfuscate

myth: 4 saga, tale 5 fable, fancy, story 6 legend 7 parable 9 apocrypha

mythical: 6 famous, unreal 9 imaginary, fabricated 10 fictitious

N

nab: 4 grab 5 catch, seize 6 arrest, clutch, snatch 7 capture 9 apprehend

Nabal: *home:* 4 Maon

wife: 7 Abigail

nabob: 5 nawab 6 bigwig, deputy 7 rich man, viceroy 8 governor 9 personage, plutocrat 10 viceregent 11 billionaire

Nabokov novel: Ada 4 Pnin 6 Lolita

nacelle: 7 shelter 11 compartment

nacket: boy 4 cake 5 lunch

nacre: 8 lustrous 9 shellfish 10 conchiolin, iridescent 13 mother-of-pearl

nadir's opposite: 6 zenith

nag: tit 4 frab, fret, gnaw, jade, plug, pony, twit 5 annoy, cobra, hobby, horse, scold, snake, tease 6 badger, berate, bother, carp at, harass, heckle, hector, padnag, pester, wanton 7 hackney, henpeck 8 harangue, irritate 9 aggravate

naga, nag: 5 cobra, snake

nagor: 8 antelope, reedbuck

Nahor: father: 5 Serug

grandson: 7 Abraham

son: 5 Terah

wife: 6 Milcah

Nahuatlan: 5 Aztec

naiad: 5 nymph **6** mussel
naif: See **naive**
nail: cut, fix, hob **4** brad, brag, brod, claw, cloy, dump, spad, stub, stud, tack, trap **5** affix, catch, clout, grope, seize, spike, sprig, steal **6** clinch, detain, fasten, hammer, secure, strike, unguis, ungula **7** capture **8** fastener, sparable, spikelet **9** finishing, intercept
drive at a slant: toe
headless: **5** sprig
ingrowing: **7** acronyx
marking on: **6** lunule
perforated: **4** spad
shoemaker's: **4** brad **8** sparable
nais: 5 naiad, nymph
naissance: 5 birth
naive: 6 candid, simple **7** artless, natural **8** childish, foolish, gullible, innocent, trusting, untaught **9** childlike, guileless, ingenuous, untutored, unworldly **10** unaffected **13** inexperienced, unphilosophic **15** unsophisticated
naked: 4 bare, nude, open **6** cuerpo **7** evident, exposed, obvious **8** manifest **9** au naturel, disclosed, unadorned, unclothed, uncovered, discovered **11** defenseless, unprotected
namaycush: 5 lunge, togue, trout
namby-pamby: 7 insipid **8** weakling **10** wishy-washy **11** sentimental
name: dub, nom(F.) **4** call, idol, term **5** claim, clepe, count, nemme, nemne, neven, nomen, style, title **6** adduce, appeal, monica, select **7** appoint, baptize, entitle, epithet, mention, moniker **8** christen, delegate, identify, identity, nominate **9** designate, personage **10** denominate, denotation, reputation **11** appellation, designation, give a handle **12** denomination, nomenclature
added: **6** agname **7** agnomen
assumed: **5** alias **6** anonym **9** incognito, pseudonym, sobriquet **10** nom de plume, soubriquet
backwards: **6** ananym
based on location: **7** toponym
Biblical: See **Bible:** *name*
derivation: **7** eponymy
family: **7** eponymy, sirname, surname **8** cognomen
fictitious: **9** pseudonym
first: **9** praenomen
list: **11** onomasticon
maiden: nee
objectionable: **7** caconym
pet: **8** nickname **9** sobriquet
tablet: **5** facia
nameable: 6 famous **7** notable **9** memorable **10** noteworthy
named: 6 yclept
nameless: 7 bastard, obscure **9** anonymous, unnamable **12** illegitimate **13** indescribable, unmentionable
namely: viz **5** id est, noted, to wit **6** famous **8** scilicet **9** expressly, videlicet **10** especially **12** specifically
namesake: 6 junior
Namibia: 15 Southwest Africa
nandu: nandow **4** rhea
nanism: 12 dwarfishness
nanny: 4 goat **5** nurse
nanny plum: 10 sheepberry
Naomi: 4 Mara
daughter-in law: **4** Ruth **5** Orpah
husband: **9** Elimelech
son: **6** Mahlon **7** Chilion
naos: 5 cella **6** shrine, temple
nap: nod **4** calk, doze, fuzz, lint, pile, rest, shag, wink **5** fluff, grasp, let up, seize, sleep, steal **6** siesta, snooze **7** respite **10** forty winks
nape: nod **5** nucha, nuque **6** scruff **7** niddick
napery: 5 linen
Naphtali: *census taker:* **4** Enan
mother: **6** Bilhah
son: **4** Guni **5** Jezer **7** Jahziel, Shallum
naphtha: 9 petroleum
napkin: 5 cloth, doily, towel **6** diaper **8** kerchief **9** handcloth, serviette **11** neckerchief **12** handkerchief
Naples: *biscuit:* **10** ladyfinger
coin: **6** carlin **7** carline
king: **5** Murat
secret society: **7** Camorra
napless: 10 threadbare
napoleon: 4 coin **6** pastry
Napoleon: *battle:* Ulm **4** Acre, Jena, Lodi **7** Dresden, Marengo **8** Borodino, Waterloo **10** Austerlitz
birthplace: **7** Corsica
brother: **5** Louis **6** Jerome, Joseph, Lucien
brother-in-law: **5** Murat
island of exile: **4** Elba
marshal: Ney **5** Murat, Soult **6** Suchet
nickname: **5** Boney
place of victory: **5** Ligny **10** Austerlitz
sister: **5** Elisa, Maria **8** Carlotta, Carolina
wife: **9** Josephine
nappy: ale **4** dish **5** downy, heady, wooly **6** liquor, strong **7** foaming **8** textured **11** intoxicated
napu: 7 deerlet **10** chevrotain
narcissistic: 4 vain **7** stuck-up **9** conceited **12** vainglorious
narcotic (see also **marijuana**)**:** kat **4** bang, dope, junk **5** bhang, dagga, ether, opium **6** heroin, opiate **7** anodyne, cocaine, hashish **8** hasheesh, hypnotic, morphine, takrouri **9** soporific **10** belladonna, hyoscyamus, stramonium
agent: **4** narc

dose: **5** locus
package: **4** deck **6** bindle
plant: kat **4** coca, cuca, hemp, kaat, khat **5** dutra, poppy
seller: **6** pusher **7** peddler
nard: 5 spice **6** anoint **7** rhizome **9** spikenard
nardoo: 5 plant **6** clover
nargileh: 4 pipe **5** hooka **6** hookah
nark: spy, vex **5** annoy **8** informer, irritate **10** spoilsport **11** stool pigeon
narrate: 4 tell **5** state **6** detail, recite, relate, report **7** descant, discuss, recount **8** describe, rehearse **9** chronicle, discourse, expatiate
narrative: 4 epic, myth, saga, tale, yarn **5** conte, drama, fable, story **6** legend **7** account, episode, history, parable **8** allegory, anecdote **9** narration
narrator: 9 reconteur
narrow: 4 mean **5** close, scant, sound, taper **6** biased, linear, little, meager, meagre, strait, strict **7** bigoted, limited **8** condense, contract **9** constrict, hidebound, illiberal, niggardly, parochial **10** inexorable, inflexible, prejudiced, restricted, straighten, ungenerous **11** reactionary **12** parsimonious **13** circumscribed
narrowminded: 6 biased **7** bigoted
narsinga: 7 trumpet
narthex: 5 porch **7** portico **9** vestibule **10** antetemple
nary: 5 never **6** not any
nasal: 6 narine, rhinal, twangy
nascency: 5 birth **6** origin **7** genesis **9** beginning
naseberry: 9 sapodilla
nasi: 9 patriarch
nasicorn: 10 rhinoceros
nasty: bad **4** foul, mean, ugly **5** dirty **6** filthy **7** harmful, obscene, squalid **8** indecent **9** dangerous, malicious, offensive **10** disgusting, ill-natured, malicious, nauseating, unpleasant **12** disagreeable, dishonorable **13** objectionable
natal: 6 inborn, innate, native **7** gluteal **10** congenital
natant: 6 afloat **8** floating, swimming
natator: 7 swimmer
natatorium: 4 bath, pool
natchbone: 7 hipbone **9** aitchbone
nation: 4 host, race **5** caste, class, state **6** people **7** country **9** community, multitude
symbol: **4** flag **5** crest
national: 7 citizen, federal, subject **11** gentilitian
National Guard member: 10 militiaman
native: 5 natal **6** genial, inborn, innate,

normal **7** citizen, endemic, natural **8** domestic, inherent, original, resident **9** aborigine, congenial, ingrained, unbranded, unrefined **10** congenital, indigenous, inhabitant
nativity: 5 birth **8** geniture **9** horoscope
natrium: 6 sodium
natty: 4 chic, neat, tidy, trig, trim **5** smart **6** spruce **10** fastidious
natural: 4 born, easy, open, fool, wild **5** usual **6** candid, common, cretin, inborn, inbred, innate, native, normal **7** general, regular **8** inherent, ordinary, physical **9** primitive, unassumed, unfeigned **10** congenital **13** unenlightened
dice: **5** seven
naturalize: 5 adopt **8** accustom **9** acclimate **11** acclimatize, domesticate, familiarize
nature: 4 kind, sort, type **5** shape **6** figure **7** essence **8** universe **9** character, framework, structure **11** disposition, temperament
divinity: **5** nymph
god: Pan
goddess: **6** Cybele **7** Artemis
same: **10** homogeneal
naught: 4 evil, zero **5** aught, ought **6** cipher, nought, wicked **7** nothing, useless **9** worthless
naughty: bad **4** evil **5** wrong **6** unruly, wicked **7** obscene, wayward, willful **8** improper **10** indelicate **11** disobedient, mischievous
naupathia: 11 seasickness
Nauru: 13 Pacific island
bay: **7** Anibare
capital: **5** Yaren
former name: **15** Pleasant Island
monetary unit: **6** dollar
nausea: 4 pall **7** disgust **8** loathing, sickness **10** queasiness
nauseating: 5 nasty, waugh **7** fulsome **8** brackish **9** loathsome, offensive, sickening **10** disgusting **11** distasteful
nautical (see also **navigation**): **5** naval **6** marine **7** oceanic **8** maritime
cry: **4** ahoy
flag: **6** cornet, pennon
instrument: aba **7** compass, sextant
mile: **4** knot
term: **4** atry **5** abaft, abeam, alist, avast
nautilus: 7 mollusk **9** argonauta
Navaho hut: 5 hogan
naval stores: tar **5** pitch **8** supplies **10** turpentine
nave: hob, hub, nef **4** apse, axle, body, fist **5** aisle, nieve **6** center **10** church part
navel: 6 orange **9** umbilicus **11** belly button
navigate: 4 keel, sail **5** steer **6** direct, manage **7** journey, operate

navigation: 7 nautics, voyage **8** cabotage **10** seamanship
call: **4** ahoy **5** avast, belay
hazard: fog, sub **4** mine **9** submarine
instrument: aba **7** compass, pelorus, sextant
measure: ton **4** knot, seam **6** fathom **7** renning, sea mile **12** cable's length
signal: **4** bell, flag
term: **4** atry **5** abeam, atrip
navigator: 5 flyer, pilot **6** airman **7** aviator, copilot, laborer **8** aeronaut, seafarer, spaceman
navite: 6 basalt
navvy: 4 hand **6** worker **7** laborer **9** navigator
navy: 5 fleet
board: **9** admiralty
depot: **4** base
force: **5** fleet **6** armada **8** squadron
jail: **4** brig
officer: **4** aide, bosh, mate **5** bosun **6** ensign **7** admiral, armorer, captain **8** armourer **9** commander, commodore **10** lieutenant
vessel: PT; sub **7** carrier, cruiser, flattop, gun boat **9** destroyer, submarine, transport **10** battleship
wireless operator: **6** sparks
nawab: 5 nabob, ruler **7** viceroy
nay: nai, not **4** deny, nyet(Russ.) **5** flute, never **6** denial, refuse **7** refusal **8** negative **11** prohibition
naysay: 6 denial **7** refusal
nayword: 6 signal **9** watchword
naze: 8 headland **10** promontory
Nazi: 9 Hitlerite **10** brownshirt
air force: **9** Luftwaffe
armed forces: **9** Wehrmacht
concentration camp: **6** Belsen, Dachau **9** Auschwitz **10** Buchenwald
police: **7** Gestapo
symbol: **6** fylfot **8** swastika
nazim: 7 viceroy **8** governor
neal: 6 anneal, temper
neanic: 8 immature, youthful
neap: 4 tide
near: gin, kin, nar(Sc.) **4** bain, dear, hend, nigh **5** anear, anent, aside, close, equal, handy, hende, match, rival, touch **6** almost, around, beside, climax, narrow, stingy **7** advance, similar, thrifty, vicinal **8** adjacent, approach, intimate **9** niggardly, thriftily **10** contiguous, juxtaposed **11** approximate, closefisted **12** parsimonious **13** propinquitous
nearest: 4 next **5** ewest(Sc.) **7** closest **9** proximate
nearsighted: 6 myopic **12** shortsighted
neat: gim **4** cosh(Sc.), deft, dink, feil(Sc.), nice, prim, pure, snod(Sc.), snug, tidy, tosh, trig, trim **5** clean, compt, dinky,

douce, natty **6** adroit, cattle, clever, dapper **7** concise, orderly, precise, refined, unmixed **8** skillful, tasteful **9** dexterous, ship-shape, undiluted **10** concinnous, meticulous
neath: 5 below **7** beneath
neatherd: 7 cowherd **8** herdsman
neb: nib, tip **4** beak, bill, nose **5** snout
Nebraska: *capital:* **7** Lincoln
city: **5** Omaha **8** Bellevue, Hastings **11** Grand Island
county: **4** Hall, Loup, Otoe **5** Deuel, Sarpy **6** Colfax, Nemalia **7** Douglas, Madison **9** Lancaster
dune: **9** Sand Hills
Indian: **4** Otoe **5** Omaha, Ponca **6** Pawnee
nickname: **4** Beef **10** Blackwater, Cornhusker **12** Tree Planters
river: **6** Platte **8** Missouri, Niobrara **10** Republican
state bird: **10** meadowlark
state flower: **9** goldenrod
state tree: **10** cottonwood
nebbish: 4 meek **5** timid **11** ineffectual
nebris: 8 fawnskin
nebula: sky **5** vapor **6** galaxy **10** atmosphere
nebulize: 7 atomize
nebulous: 4 hazy **5** foggy, misty, vague **6** cloudy **7** obscure, unclear **9** celestial **10** indefinite, indistinct
necessarily: 8 perforce **10** inevitably **12** consequently
necessary: 5 privy, vital **7** needful **8** forcible, integral **9** essential, mandatory, requisite **10** inevitable, undeniable **11** unavoidable, water-closet **13** indispensable
necessitate: 5 force, impel **6** compel, entail, oblige **7** require **9** constrain
necessity: 4 food, must, need, want **5** drink **7** ailment, poverty, urgency **8** distress **9** emergency, essential **11** destitution
neck: pet **4** cape, crag, crop, hals, kiss **5** halse **6** caress, cervix, collum, fondle, strait **7** channel, embrace, isthmus
armor: **6** gorget
artery: **7** carotid
back of: **4** nape **5** nucha, nuque **6** scruff
muscle: **8** scalenus
part: **4** gula **7** withers
pert. to: **7** jugular **8** cervical
piece: bib, boa **5** amice, rabat, scarf, stole **6** collar **8** kerchief
neck and neck: tie **4** even **5** close
neckband: 6 collar, collet **10** collar-band
neckerchief: 4 gimp **7** belcher **8** kerchief, neckatee **12** handkerchief
necklace: 4 rope, torc **5** beads, chain, noose **6** collar, grivna, locket, torque **7**

baldric, chaplet, haltern, necktie, riviere **8** baldrick, carcanet, lavalier **9** esclavage, lavaliere **10** lavalliere

neckpiece: bib, boa **4** ruff **5** amice, choke, jabot, ruche, scarf, stole **6** choker, collar, cravat, dickie **8** kerchief

necktie: bow, tie **4** band **5** ascot, scarf **6** cravat **10** four-in-hand

necktie party: 7 hanging **8** lynching

necrology: 8 obituary

necromancy: art **5** goety, magic **7** grammary, sorcery **8** gramarye, wizardry **11** conjuration, enchantment

necropolis: 8 cemetery

necropsy: 7 autopsy

nectar: 5 honey **8** ambrosia

nee: 4 born **5** named **8** formerly

need: 4 lack, must, want **5** crave **6** behove, demand, desire, hanker, hunger **7** behoove, poverty, require, urgency **8** distress, exigency **9** emergency, extremity, indigence, necessity, requisite **10** compulsion, dependence, obligation, retirement **11** destitution, requirement

needful: 5 vital **8** integral, required **9** essential **13** indispensable

needle: sew **4** acus(L.), darn **5** annoy **6** worry **7** acicula, provoke, spicule **10** strengthen
hole: eye
treatment with: **11** acupuncture
type: **4** sail **5** blunt, style **6** bodkin, stylus **7** darning, obelisk **8** knitting **10** hypodermic, phonograph, upholstery

needlefish: gar **8** pipefish

needlelike: 6 acuate **7** acerate, acerose, acerous, aciform **8** acicular, belonoid

needless: 10 gratuitous **11** superfluous, unnecessary

needlework: 6 sewing **7** sampler, seaming, tatting **8** knitting **9** hemstitch **10** embroidery, crocheting

needy: 4 poor **9** penniless

neep: 6 turnip

ne'er-do-well: bum **5** losel, loser **9** no account, schlemiel, shiftless, worthless **11** incompetent

nef: 5 clock

nefarious: 4 rank **5** gross **6** wicked **7** heinous, impious, vicious **8** flagrant, horrible, infamous **9** atrocious **10** detestable, iniquitous, villainous

nefast: 6 wicked

negate: 4 deny **5** annul **6** refute **7** abolish, nullify **10** neutralize

negation: not **5** empty **6** denial **7** refusal **9** annulment, blankness, nonentity **10** refutation **13** contradiction, nullification

negative: nae(Sc.), nay, non(F.), nor, not **4** film, veto **5** minus, never **7** neutral

neglect: 4 fail, omit, slip **5** fault, forgo,

shirk **6** forego, forget, ignore, slight **7** blink at, default, failure **8** omission **9** disregard, oversight, pay no heed, pretermit **10** negligence **11** inattention **12** inadvertence, indifference

neglectful: lax **6** remiss **8** careless, derelict, heedless **9** dissolute, negligent

negligee: 4 robe **7** undress **8** peignoir **9** nightgown **10** dishabille

negligence: 7 laxness **9** disregard, oversight

negligent: lax **5** slack **6** remiss **8** careless, heedless, slipshod **10** delinquent **11** thoughtless, unconcerned **12** indifferent

negotiable: 12 transferable

negotiate: 4 deal **5** treat **6** dicker, settle **7** arrange, bargain, chaffer, discuss **8** transact **10** accomplish

negotiation: 6 treaty **8** entreaty

negus: 4 king **8** beverage

neigh: 6 whinny

neighbor: 4 abut, line **5** touch, verge **6** adjoin, border **8** border on

neighborhood: 4 area **5** venue **6** locale, region **7** section **8** district, locality, vicinage, vicinity **9** community, proximity, territory **11** propinquity

neighboring: 4 nigh **5** close **6** near-by **7** vicinal **8** adjacent **10** contiguous **11** close-at-hand

neither: not

nema: 7 eelworm **9** roundworm

nemesis: 4 bane **7** avenger

nemoral: 6 sylvan, wooded

neophyte: 4 tyro **5** epopt **6** novice **7** amateur, convert **8** beginner **9** proselyte **10** catechumen

neoteric: new **4** late **6** modern, recent

Nepal: *capital:* **8** Katmandu
city: **5** Palan **8** Bhatgaon **9** Bhaktapur
dynasty: **6** Rajput
language: **6** Bhutia, Nepali, Newari
monetary unit: **4** pice **5** rupee
mountain: **7** Everest
mountain climber: **7** Hillary, Tenzing
mountain range: **8** Himalaya
people: Rai **4** Aoul **5** Bokra, Hindu, Limbu, Murmi, Newar, Tharu **6** Bhotia, Gurkha, Lepcha **7** Kiranti **8** Gorkhall
religion: **5** Hindu **8** Buddhist
river: **4** Kusi **5** Bheri, Tamur **6** Gandak **7** Karnali
sheep: **6** bharal, nahoor, nayaur
tree: sal **4** toon **5** sisoo

nepenthe: 6 opiate **7** anodyne **8** narcotic

nephew: 6 nepote(Sc.)

nephrite: 4 jade **6** pounam **10** greenstone

ne plus ultra: 4 acme **6** summit **9** nth degree

nepotism: 9 patronage **10** favoritism

Neptune: sea 5 ocean 6 seagod
  consort: 7 Salacia
  emblem: 7 trident
Ner's son: 5 Abner
Nereides: *father:* 6 Nereus
  mother: 5 Doris
  steed: 8 seahorse
Nero: 6 tyrant 7 emperor, fiddler
  mother: 9 Agrippina
  successor: 5 Galba
  victim: 5 Lucan 6 Seneca
  wife: 7 Octavia, Poppaea
Nero Wolfe creator: 5 Stout
nerve: 4 grit 5 cheek, pluck, sinew, spunk,
  vigor 6 aplomb, daring, energy, tendon
  7 courage 8 audacity, boldness, coolness, embolden, strength, temerity 9
  encourage, fortitude 10 brazenness, effrontery, invigorate, resolution
  apparatus: 6 sensor
  cell: 6 neuron
  center: 5 brain 8 ganglion
  cranial: 5 optic, vagus
  inflammation: 8 neuritis
  malady: tic 8 neuritis
  network: 4 rete 6 plexus
  operation: 10 neurolysis
  pathway: 4 rete 5 hilum 8 ganglion
  pert. to: 5 neuro 6 neural
  root: 5 radix
  sensory: 8 afferent
  tissue: 8 cinerea
  tumor: 7 neuroma 9 neurinoma 11 neur-
  ocytoma 12 neuromatosis
nerveless: 4 dead, weak 5 brave, inert 8
  unnerved 9 foolhardy, powerless 10
  courageous
nervous: 4 edgy 5 jumpy, timid 6 fidget,
  on edge, sinewy, touchy 7 fearful, fretful, jittery, waspish 8 neurotic, timorous 9 excitable, querulous, sensitive
  10 highstrung 12 apprehensive
nervous disorder: See **mental disorder**
nervous system: *center:* 5 brain
  description of: 11 neurography
  nomenclature: 9 neuronymy
  science: 9 neurology
nervy: 4 bold 5 jerky, tense 6 brazen, sinewy, strong 7 jittery, nervous 8 impudent, vigorous 9 excitable
nescient: 7 infidel 8 agnostic, ignorant
ness: 4 cape 8 headland 10 promontory
nest: den, web 4 aery, bike, dray, drey,
  eyry, home 5 abode, aerie, eyrie, haunt,
  nidus, swarm 6 cuddle, hotbed 7 lodging, retreat 9 residence 10 nidificate
  builder of: ant, bee 4 bird, wasp
  eagle's: 4 aery 5 aerie
  insect's: 5 nidus
  nest egg: 5 hoard, stock 7 reserve 9 reservoir
  squirrel's: 4 drey

nester: 7 settler 8 squatter 11 home-
  steader
nestle: pet 4 nest 6 cuddle, pettle(Sc.) 7
  cherish, shelter, snuggle
nestling: 4 baby, bird, eyas 9 fledgling
nestor: 4 sage 6 parrot 7 adviser, advisor
  9 counselor 10 counsellor
net: bag, gin, web 4 caul, flan, gain, lace,
  lawn, mesh, moke, neat, pure, rete, toil,
  trap, trim, weir 5 clean, clear, gauze, la-
  cis, seize, snare, tulle, yield 6 bright,
  cobweb, entrap, maline, profit 7 dragnet, ensnare, network, protect, rinsing,
  shelter 8 meshwork 9 reticulum 10 reticulate 13 unadulterated
  fishing: lam 4 flew, flue, fyke 5 seine,
  trawl 6 sagene 7 trammel
  hair: 5 snood
  interstice: 4 hole, mesh
nether: 5 lower, under 8 downward, inferior
Netherlands: 7 Holland
  bailiff: 6 schout
  capital: 9 Amsterdam
  cheese: 4 Edam 5 Gouda 6 Leyden 7 cottage
  city: Ede 5 Asten, Breda, Hague 6 Aalten,
  Arnhem, Leiden 7 Commune, Haarlem,
  Utrecht 8 Aalsmeer, The Hague 9 Groningen, Rotterdam 10 Gravenhage
  commune: Ede, Epe 4 Echt 5 Breda,
  Doorn, Hague 6 Dongen, Leyden 9
  Amsterdam, Rotterdam 11 Doniawes-
  tal
  council: 7 heemrad 8 heemraad, heemraat
  fishing boat: 4 tode 6 hooker
  former colony: 4 Java 6 Borneo 7 Celebes, Sumatra, Surinam 9 New Guinea,
  10 East Indies
  gin: 8 schnapps
  inlet: 9 Zuider Zee
  island: 5 Texel 7 Ameland 8 Vlieland 9
  Schelling
  island group: Aru 5 Arroe, Arrou
  lake: 7 Haarlem
  legislative assembly: 4 Raad
  measure: aam, ahm, aum, ell, kan,
  kop(pl.), mud, vat, zak 4 duim, lood,
  mijl, rood, rope, voet 5 anker, carat,
  roede, stoop, wisse 6 bunder, koppen,
  legger, maatje, muddle, mutsje, streep 7
  leaguer, schepel 8 mimgelen, okshoofd,
  steekkan 10 vingerhoed
  monetary unit: 4 cent, doit, raps 5 ryder
  6 florin, gulden, stiver 7 ducaton, esca-
  lan, escalin, guilder, stooter 8 ducatoon
  9 dubbeltje 12 rijksdaalder
  native: 5 Dutch 8 Dutchman
  painter: Lis 4 Hals, Kalf, Neer 5 Helst,
  Steen 6 Leyden 7 De Hoogh, Hobbe-
  ma, Seghers, van Gogh, Vermeer 8
  Kroninck, Mondrian, Mostaert, Ruys-

dael, Ter Borch **9** Rembrandt **10** Van de Velde **11** Van Ruisdael **19** Geertgen Tot Sint Jans
people: **5** Dutch **7** Flemish, Frisian
possessions: **4** Saba **7** Curacao
pottery: **4** delf **5** delft **11** Dutch Guiana, St. Eustacius
province: Epe **7** Brabant, Drenthe, Holland, Limburg, Utrecht, Zeeland **9** Friesland, Groningen **10** Gelderland, Overijssel
reclaimed land: **6** polder
river: Eem **4** Leck, Maas, Rijn, Waal, Ysel **5** Meuse, Rhine, Yssel **6** Ijssel, Kromme **7** Scheldt
scholar: **7** Erasmus
sheriff: **6** schout
town hall: **9** stadhouse
uncle: eme, oom
vessel: **4** koff **5** yanky **6** schuit, schuyt
weight: ons **4** last, lood, pond **5** bahar, grein, pound **6** korrel **7** wichtje **8** esterlin, **9** esterling
woman: **4** frau, frow
netlike: 9 reticular
netop: 5 crony **6** friend **9** companion
netting: 4 lint, mesh **7** network
nettle: vex **4** fret, line **5** annoy, cnida, peeve, pique, sting **6** arouse, henbit, ruffle, splice, stir up **7** affront, blubber, provoke **8** irritant, irritate **9** Urticacea **10** exasperate
nettle cell: 10 nematocyst
family: **10** Urticaceae
genus of: **10** parietaria
network(see also **net**): **4** mesh, rete **5** retia **6** plexus, reseau
neural: 6 dorsal
neurite: 4 axon **5** axone
neurotic: 6 phobic **7** nervous **8** unstable **10** compulsive
neuter: 6 gender **7** neither, neutral, sexless **9** impartial, sterilize
neutral: 4 gray **8** middling, negative **9** colorless **10** achromatic, indefinite, poker-faced **11** adiaphorous, indifferent **12** noncombatant
neutralize: 5 annul **7** abolish, balance, destroy, nullify, vitiate **9** cancel out, frustrate **10** counteract **11** countervail **14** counterbalance
neutralizer: 6 alkali
Nevada: *capital:* **10** Carson City
city: **4** Reno **8** Las Vegas
county: Nye **4** Elko **5** Clark **6** Storey, Washoe
highest point: **12** Boundary Peak
historic site: **9** Hoover Dam **12** Virginia City
industry: **7** divorce **8** gambling
lake: Mud **4** Mead **5** Tahoe **6** Walker **7** Pyramid

mountain range: **4** Ruby **6** Carson **7** Toiyabe
nickname: **6** Silver **9** Sagebrush
plateau: **10** Great Basin
river: **6** Carson **7** Truckee **8** Colorado, Humboldt
state bird: **8** bluebird
state flower: **9** sagebrush
state tree: **5** pinon
neve: 4 firn, snow **7** glacier
never: nay, nie(G.), not **4** nary, ne'er
nevertheless: but, yet **5** still **6** even so **7** how-be-it, however **9** howsoever, natheless **10** howsomever
nevus: 4 mole **5** tumor **7** spiloma **9** birthmark
new: neu(G.) **4** late, nova(L.) **5** fresh, green, novel **6** modern, recent, unused **7** foreign, strange, untried **8** neoteric, original, untested **9** first-hand **10** additional, promethean, unfamiliar **11** fashionable, modernistic **12** unaccustomed **13** inexperienced
New Brunswick: *capital:* **11** Fredericton
city: **6** St. John **7** Moncton
former name: **6** Acadia
island: **10** Campobello
motto: **11** Spem Reduxit
national park: **5** Fundy
province of: **6** Canada
provincial flower: **6** violet
river: **6** St. John **7** St. Croix **9** Miramicki
New Caledonia: *bird:* **4** kagu
capital: **6** Noumea
New Deal agency: CCC, NRA, TVA
New England: *aristocrat:* **7** Brahmin
chair: **6** Carver
inhabitant: **6** Yankee
of the West: **9** Minnesota
settler: **7** Pilgrim, Puritan
New Guinea: *bay:* Oro
capital: **11** Port Moresby
city: Lae **4** Daru **5** Soron **6** Rabaul
export: **5** copra
gulf: **4** Huon **5** Papua
hog: **4** bene
island: Aru **4** Buka **5** Ceram, Papua **6** Mussau
island group: **7** Solomon
mountain: **6** Albert **8** Victoria **9** Carstensz **10** Wilhelmina
parrot: **4** lory
people: **5** Karon **6** Papuan
port: Lae **4** Daru **5** Wewak **6** Madang
river: Fly **5** Sepik **7** Amberno **10** Strickland **15** Kaiserin Augusta
section: **8** Bunagona
New Hampshire: *capital:* **7** Concord
city: **5** Dover, Keene **6** Nashua **10** Manchester, Portsmouth
county: **4** Coos **7** Belknap
explorer: **5** Pring

highest peak: **12** Mt. Washington
lake: **7** Ossipee, Sunapee
motto: **13** Live free or die
mountain: **5** White
nickname: **7** Granite
river: **4** Saco **9** Merrimack **10** Piscataqua
state bird: **5** finch
state flower: **5** lilac
state tree: **5** birch

New Jersey: *capital:* **7** Trenton
city: **6** Camden, Newark **7** Clifton **8** Paterson **9** Elizabeth **12** Atlantic City
county: **5** Essex, Union **6** Bergen, Camden, Mercer, Morris **7** Passaic **8** Monmouth
highest peak: **9** High Point
Indian: **8** Delaware
mountain: **6** Ramapo
nickname: **6** Garden **8** Mosquito
peninsula: **9** Sandy Hook
river: **6** Ramapo **7** Raritan **8** Delaware, Tuckahoe
state bird: **9** goldfinch
state flower: **6** violet
state tree: oak

New Mexico: *capital:* **7** Santa Fe
city: **5** Hobbs **6** Clovis **7** Roswell **9** Las Cruces **10** Farmington **11** Albuquerque
county: **4** Luna, Mora, Quay, Taos, **5** Curry, Otero **6** Catron, Chaves **7** Dona Ana, Hidalgo
highest peak: **7** Wheeler
motto: **12** Crescit eundo (It grows as it goes)
mountain: **14** Sangre de Cresto
mountain range: **6** Chuska **7** Caballo **8** San Mateo **9** San Andres
national park: **15** Carlsbad Caverns
nickname: **8** Sunshine
resort: **4** Taos
river: **4** Gila **5** Pecos **7** San Juan **9** Rio Grande
state bird: **10** roadrunner
state flower: **5** yucca
state tree: **5** pinon

New Testament (see also **Bible**): *book:* **4** Acts, John, Jude, Luke, Mark **5** James, Peter, Titus **6** Romans **7** Hebrews, Matthew, Timothy **8** Philemon **9** Ephesians, Galatians **10** Colossians, Revelation **11** Corinthians, Philippians **13** Thessalonians
gospel: **4** John, Luke, Mark **7** Matthew
letter: **7** epistle

New York: *canal:* **4** Erie
capital: **6** Albany
city: Rye **4** Erie, Rome, Troy **5** Utica **6** Elmira, Ithaca, Malone **7** Buffalo, Yonkers **8** Saratoga, Syracuse **9** Rochester **10** Binghamton
county: **4** Erie **5** Tioga, Wayne, Yates **6** Cayuga, Monroe, Oneida, Oswego, Putnam, Seneca **7** Chemung, Genesee, Niagara, Ontario, Orleans, Steuben, Tompkin, Wyoming **8** Allegheny, Dutchess, Schuyler **11** Westchester
explorer: **6** Hudson **9** Champlain, Verrazano
harbor entrance: **14** Ambrose Channel
island (see also **New York City**): **4** Fire, Long, **7** Fishers, Shelter
Indian: **4** Erie **6** Cayuga, Mohawk, Oneida, Seneca
lake: **5** Keuka **6** Cayuga, Croton, Geneva, Oneida, Seneca **7** Ontario, Saranac **8** Onondago **9** Champlain **11** Canandaigua, Skaneateles
motto: **9** Excelsior (Ever Upward)
mountain: **9** Catskills **11** Adirondacks
nickname: **6** Empire
racetrack: **7** Belmont, Yonkers **8** Aqueduct, Saratoga
river: **5** Tioga **6** Harlem, Hudson **7** Genesee, Niagara **8** Delaware **10** St. Lawrence
state bird: **8** bluebird
state flower: **4** rose
state tree: **5** maple
tourist attraction: **12** Niagara Falls

New York City: **6** Gotham
airports: JFK **7** Kennedy **9** La Guardia
boroughs: **5** Bronx **6** Queens **9** Brooklyn, Richmond **10** Manhattan
island: **5** Ellis **6** Staten **7** Bedloes, Liberty, Welfare **9** Governors, Manhattan **10** Blackwells
nickname: **8** Big Apple
prison: **5** Tombs
river: **4** East **6** Hudson
subway: BMT, IND, IRT

New Zealand: *anteater:* **7** echidna
bird: kea, moa, oii, poe, roa **4** kaka, kiwi, koko, kulu, ruru, titi, weka **6** kakapo **7** apteryx, wrybill **8** morepork, notornis
capital: **10** Wellington
city: see *town* below
clay: **4** papa
dance: **4** haka
fern: **4** weki **5** pitau, wheki
fish: ihi **5** hikus
flax: **8** harakeke
flightless bird: **4** weka **7** apteryx
fort: pa; pah, pau
grass: **6** toetoe
gun: **6** tupara
heron: **6** kotuku
hut: **5** whare
island: **5** North, South **7** Chatham, Stewart
kiwi: moa, roa **7** apteryx
lake: Ada **4** Gunn, Ohau, Rere **5** Hawea, Okaro, Taupo **6** Fergus, Pukaki, Rotoma, Sylvan, Teanau, Tekapo, Wanaka **7** Brunner, Diamond, Kanieri,

Okareka, Rotoiti, Rotoroa, Rotorua **8** Okataina, Paradise, Rotoaira, Tarawera, Wakatipu

mahogany: **6** totara

monetary unit: **6** dollar

mountain: **4** Cook **5** Ohope **6** Egmont **7** Aorangi, Pihanga, Raupehu, Ruapehu, Tauhara, Tauhera **8** Aspiring, Tarawera, Tauranga

national bird: **4** kiwi

ostrich: moa

outlying island: **8** Auckland, Campbell, Kermadec **9** Antipodes

owl: **4** ruru

palm: **5** nikau

parrot: kea **4** kaka **6** kakapo

people: Ati **5** Arawa, Maori **7** Ringatu

pine: **4** rima **6** totara **9** kahikatea

port: Lae **7** Aukland, Dunedin **10** Wellington

reptile: **7** tuatara, tuatera

river: **7** Waikato **8** Wanganui

settlement: pah, pau

shark: **4** mako

shrub: **4** tutu

song: **6** waiata

spa: **5** Aroha **7** Rotorua, Tearoha

storehouse: **5** whata

town: **5** Levin, Otaki, Taupo **6** Foxton, Napier, Nelson, Oamaru Picton, Timaru **7** Dunedin, Raetihi, Rotorua **8** Auckland, Gisborne, Hamilton, Hastings, Tauranga, Wanganui **9** Ashburton, Greymouth, Masterton, Whangarei **10** Dannenirke, Palmerston, Queenstown, Wellington(c.) **12** Christchurch, Invercargill

tree: ake **4** hino, kopi, mako, miro, pelu, puka, rata, rimu, tawa, toro, toru, whau **5** hinau, hinou, karui, mahoe, maire, mapau, ngaio **6** ake-ake, karaka, kowhai, manuka, puriri, tarata, titoki **7** akepiro, taratah, wahahen **8** hiropito, makomako

vine: aka

volcano: **6** Egmont **7** Ruapehu **9** Ngauruhoe

wages: utu

welcome: **8** haeremai

newcomer: 7 settler **8** comeling **9** immigrant

newel: 4 post **6** pillar **7** upright

newfangled: 5 novel **6** latest, modern

Newfoundland: 6 island

airport: **6** Gander

cape: Ray **4** Race **5** Bauld

capital: **8** St. John's

city: **10** Mount Pearl **11** Corner Brook **12** Stephenville

discoverer: **5** Cabot (John)

Indian: **6** Micmac

island: **4** Bell, Fogo

mainland part: **8** Labrador

province of: **6** Canada

provincial flower: **12** pitcher plant

river: **6** Gander, Humber **8** Exploits

newly: 4 anew **5** again **6** afresh, lately **8** recently

news: 4 word **6** notice **7** tidings **11** information, instruction **12** intelligence

agency: DNB, PAP(Pol.), UPI **4** Tass (Russ.) **5** Domei **6** Xinhua(Ch.) **7** Reuters **13** International

gatherer: **8** reporter **13** correspondent

media: **5** radio **7** journal **8** magazine **9** newspaper **10** periodical, television

statement: **8** bulletin

newsboy: 7 carrier

newsmonger: 6 gossip **7** tattler **8** reporter

newspaper: 5 daily, organ **7** gazette, journal, tabloid **10** periodical **11** publication

article: **4** item

collectively: **5** press

employee: **6** editor **7** printer **8** engraver, pressman, reporter **9** columnist, linotyper **10** cartoonist, compositor, journalist, plate maker **12** photographer **13** correspondent

file: **6** morgue

hoax: **6** canard

part of: ear **6** banner **8** obituary **9** editorial

newsstand: 5 booth, kiosk, stall

newt: 4 ask, eft **4** evet **6** lizard, triton **7** axolotl **10** salamander

next: 4 then **5** after, ewest(Sc.), neist(Sc.) **6** coming **7** closest, ensuing, nearest **9** adjoining, following, immediate, proximate **10** contiguous, succeeding **12** conterminous

next to: 6 almost, beside, nearly **8** adjacent

nexus: tie **4** bond, link **10** connection **15** interconnection

nib: pen **4** beak, bill **5** point, prong **8** pen point

nibble: 4 eat, nab **4** bite, gnaw, knap, peck, pick **6** browse **7** chimble, gnabble, gnatter

Nicaragua: *capital:* **7** Managua

city: **4** Leon **6** Massaya **7** Granada **9** Matagalpa

lake: **7** Managua **9** Nicaragua

language: **7** Spanish

measure: **4** vara **5** cahiz, milla **6** suerte, tercia **7** cajuela, estadal, manzana

monetary unit: **7** centavo, cordoba

mountain peak: **6** Madera **9** Momotombo

neighbors: **8** Honduras **9** Costa Rica

river: **4** Coco **7** San Juan **8** Tipitapa

weight: bag **4** caja **8** tonelada

nice: 4 fine, good **5** exact, picky **6** bonita,

dainty, minute, peachy, queasy, subtle
7 correct, elegant, finical, genteel, precise, prudish, refined **8** decorous, delicate, exacting, pleasant, pleasing **9**
agreeable, appealing, exquisite, squeamish **10** appetizing, delightful, discerning, fastidious, old-maidish, particular,
scrupulous **11** considerate, puntilious,
scrumptious **13** hypercritical **14** discriminating

niche: **4** apse, nook **6** alcove, covert, recess **7** edicule, retreat **9** habitacle

nick: cut, nob **4** chip, slit **5** cheat, notch,
tally, trick **6** arrest, record **7** defraud **9**
indenture

nickle compound: **4** zinc **6** copper

nickelodeon: **7** jukebox

nickname (see also **pen name, pseudonym**): tag **6** agname, byword **7** misname, moniker **8** cognomen, monicker
9 sobriquet **10** soubriquet

James Boswell: **5** Bozzy
Winston Churchill: **6** Winnie
Georges Clemenceau: **5** Tiger
Benjamin Disraeli: **5** Dizzy
Thomas Edison: **17** Wizard of Menlo
Park
Dwight Eisenhower: Ike
Elizabeth I: **11** Virgin Queen
Frederick I: **10** Barbarossa
Ernest Hemingway: **4** Papa
Andrew Jackson: **10** Old Hickory
Abraham Lincoln: **9** Honest Abe
Louis XIV: **7** Sun King
Joe Louis: **11** Brown Bomber
Mary I: **10** Bloody Mary
Napoleon I: **14** Little Corporal
Napoleon II: **7** L'Aiglon
Richard Nixon: **10** Tricky Dick
Henry Percy: **7** Hotspur
William Pitt: **13** Great Commoner
Richard I: **11** Lion-Hearted
Richard III: **10** Crouchback
Babe Ruth: **7** Bambino **12** Sultan of
Swat
Joseph Stilwell: **10** Vinegar Joe
Charles Stratton: **8** Tom Thumb

nicknaming: **12** prosonomasia

nictate: **4** wink **5** blink **7** twinkle

nide: **5** brood

nidge: **5** shake **6** quiver

nidget: **4** fool **5** idiot

nidification: **7** nesting

nidor: **4** reek **5** aroma, savor, scent, smell

nidus: **4** nest

nifty: **4** good **5** smart **7** stylish

Niger: *capital:* **6** Niamey
monetary unit: **5** franc
people: **4** Peul **5** Hausa **6** Djerma **7**
Songhai

Nigeria: *capital:* **5** Lagos
city: **4** Kano **6** Ibadan **8** Ogbomosho

monetary unit: **5** naira
people: Ibo **5** Hausa **6** Fulania, Yoruba
port: **5** Lagos **7** Calabar
province: Isa **4** Nupe, Ondo **5** Warri
river: Oli
tree: **5** afara
walled city: **4** Kano

niggard: **5** miser **8** scrimper **9** skinflint
10 curmudgeon

niggardly: **4** mean **5** close **6** narrow,
scanty, stingy **7** miserly **8** churlish,
wretched **10** avaricious **11** closefisted
12 parsimonious

niggle: **6** potter, putter, trifle

nigh: **4** near **5** about, close **6** almost, nearly **8** adjacent, approach **10** contiguous
11 neighboring

night: **4** nuit(F.) **8** darkness
goddess: Nox, Nyx
goddess of: Nyx **6** Hecate
pert. to: **9** nocturnal

night bird: **10** shearwater **11** nightingale

night blindness: **10** nyctalopia

night-wandering: **11** noctivagant

nightcap: **6** biggin

nightchurr: **10** goatsucker

nightclub: **5** boite **7** cabaret

nightfall: eve **4** dusk, even **6** sunset **7**
evening **8** twilight

nightingale: **6** thrush **8** philomel **9** philomela

nightjar: **5** potoo **9** nighthawk **10** goatsucker

nightmare: **5** dream, fancy, fiend **7** incubus **9** cauchemar(F.), ephialtes **12** apprehension

nightshade: **5** morel **7** henbane, morelle
10 belladonna **11** bittersweet

nightstick: bat **4** club **5** baton, billy **6**
cudgel **8** bludgeon

nihil: **7** nothing

nihilist: **8** nihilist **9** anarchist

nil: **4** zero **7** nothing

Nile: **6** Al-Bahr
bird: **4** ibis **7** wryneck
boat: **5** baris **6** nuggar **8** dahabeah
captain: **4** rais, reis
dam: **6** Makwar **9** Aswan High **10** Gebel
Aulia
falls: **5** Ripon
fish: **5** saide **8** mormyrid **9** mormyroid
historic ruins: **4** Giza **5** Luxor **6** Karnak
7 Memphis
houseboat: **8** dahabeah
island: **4** Roda
people: **4** Madi **5** Nilot
plant: **4** sudd **5** lotus
reptile: **9** crocodile
river gauge: **9** nilometer
town: **5** Cairo, Rejaf **7** Rosetta
tributary: **6** Atbara, Kagera

nilgai: **8** antelope, blue bull

nimb: 4 halo
nimble: 4 deft, lish, spry 5 agile, alert, fleet, quick 6 active, adroit, clever, feirie, lissom, lively, prompt, volant 9 dexterous, wide-awake 11 quick-witted
nimbose: 6 cloudy, stormy
nimbus: 4 halo 5 cloud, vapor 6 gloria 7 aureole 10 atmosphere
nimiety: 4 glut 6 excess 10 redundancy
nimmer: 5 thief
nimrod: 5 ruler 6 hunter, tyrant
nincompoop: 4 dolt, fool 5 moron, ninny 9 simpleton
nine: 6 ennead 8 ninefold
  based on: 8 novenary
  days' devotion: 6 novena
  group of: 5 nonet 6 ennead
  inches: 4 span
nine-eyes: 7 lamprey
nine-headed monster: 5 Hydra
nine-killer: 6 shrike
ninepins: 6 kayles 7 bowling, skittle 8 skittles
ninth: 5 nonus(L.)
Niobe: *brother:* 6 Pelops
  father: 8 Tantalus
  husband: 7 Amphion
  sister-in-law: 5 Aedon
nip: cut, sip 4 bite, clip, dram, tang 5 blast, check, clamp, draft, drink, frost, hurry, pinch, seize, sever, steal, sting 6 blight, catnip, snatch, tipple, twitch 7 squeeze 8 compress 10 pickpocket
nipa: 4 atap, palm 5 attap, drink 6 liquor
nipcheese: 5 miser 6 purser
nipper: boy, lad 4 claw, grab 5 biter, child 6 cunner, pliers, urchin 7 forceps, incisor, pincers 8 pincenez 9 handcuffs 10 eyeglasses
Nippon: See **Japan**
nippy: 4 cold 5 brisk, quick, sharp 6 active, biting, chilly, nimble, snappy 7 caustic, pungent 8 vigorous
nisse: 6 goblin, kobold, sprite 7 brownie
nisus: 6 effort 7 impulse 8 endeavor, striving 11 inclination
Nisus' daughter: 6 Scylla
nit: egg, nut 5 speck 6 insect 8 hazelnut
niter, nitre: 5 peter, petre 6 potash 9 saltpeter
nither: 5 blast 6 debase, shiver 7 tremble 9 humiliate
nitid: 6 bright, glossy 7 glowing, radiant 8 lustrous, nitidous
nitpick: 6 niggle
nitrate: 4 salt 5 ester
  sodium: 5 niter, nitre
nitrocotton: 9 guncotton
nitrogen: 5 azote 9 quinoline
  compound: 7 ammonia
nitty-gritty: 10 basic facts
niveau: 5 level 7 plateau

nivenite: 9 uranite
niveous: 5 snowy 8 snowlike
nix: 6 goblin, nobody, sprite 7 nothing, refusal 8 negation
Njorth: *daughter:* 5 Freya 6 Freyja
  son: 4 Frey 5 Freyr
  wife: 6 Skathi
no: nae(Sc.), naw, nay, nea(Sc.), nit, nix, non(F.) 4 nein(G.), nyet(Russ.), play 5 drama 6 denial 7 refusal 8 by no means 12 nothing doing
no-account: 9 worthless
Noah: *dove:* 7 Columba
  father: 6 Lamech
  grandson: 4 Aram
  great-grandson: Hul
  place of debarkation: 6 Ararat
  raven: 6 Corvus
  son: Ham, Sem 4 Shem 7 Japheth
  wine cup: 6 Crater
nob: 4 head, jack, toff 5 swell
nobby: 4 chic 5 swell 7 stylish 9 excellent, first-rate 11 fashionable
noble: 4 epic, fine, free, gent, good, pure, rial 5 burly, ducal, grand, ideal, lofty, manly, moral, proud 6 august, epical, famous, heroic 7 eminent, exalted, gallant, liberal, soulful, stately, sublime 8 elevated, generous, glorious, nobleman, precious, renowned, splendid 9 chevalier, dignified, excellent, honorable 10 idealistic, noblewoman 11 illustrious, magnanimous, magnificent
noble pine: 10 pipsissewa
nobleman: don 4 duke, earl, lord, peer 5 barin(Russ.), baron, count 6 knight, prince, varlet 7 baronet, grandee(Sp.), hidalgo, marquis 8 marquess 10 aristocrat
  pert. to: 5 ducal 6 lordly
noblewoman: 4 lady 7 duchess, peeress 8 baroness, countess, marquise, princess 10 marquisess 11 marchioness
nobody: 4 none 9 nonentity
nocent: 6 guilty 7 harmful, hurtful, noxious 8 criminal
noctambulism: 11 sleep walker 12 somnambulism
noctuad: 4 moth, worm
noctule: bat, owl 9 pipistrel 11 pipistrelle
nocturnal: 5 night 7 nightly 11 nightwalker
nocturnal mammal: bat 5 lemur
nocturne: 7 lullaby 8 serenade
nocuous: 7 harmful 8 damaging
nod: bow 4 beck, bend, doze, wink 5 droop 6 assent, beckon, drowse, nutate, salute 7 signify 8 approval, nutation
nodding: 6 drowsy, nutant, sleepy 8 cernuous 9 pendulous
noddy: auk 4 fool 5 dunce, ninny 7 hackney 9 simpleton

node: bow 4 bump, knob, knot, lump 5 joint, nodus 6 nodule 7 dilemma, granule 8 swelling, tubercle 10 difficulty 12 complication, protuberance

noel: 5 carol 9 Christmas

noetic: 8 abstract 12 intellectual

nog: ale, peg, pin 5 block 6 eggnog, noggin 8 beverage, treenail

no-good: 6 wretch 7 wastrel

noggin: cup, mug, nog 4 head, pate

noir: 5 black

noise: air, din 5 bruit, rumor, sound 6 gossip, norate, report 11 pandemonium

noiseless: 5 quiet, still, tacit 6 silent 7 catlike

noisemaker: 4 bell, horn 6 rattle 7 clapper

noisette: 5 hazel

noisome (see also **noxious**): bad 4 foul 5 fetid 7 harmful, hurtful 8 stinking, unsavory 9 offensive 10 disgusting, malodorous, pernicious 11 destructive, unwholesome

noisy: 4 loud 6 clashy 7 blatant, rackety 8 brawling, clattery, strepent 9 clamorous, hilarious, turbulent 10 boisterous, tumultuous, vociferous 12 obstreperous

nom de plume: 7 pen name 9 pseudonym

noma: 5 ulcer

nomad: 4 Arab, Luri, Moor 5 Alani, gypsy, rover 6 roamer, roving 7 Bedouin, Saracen, scenite 8 wandered

nomadic: 9 itinerant

nomadism: 8 vagrancy 10 wanderlust

nome: 4 Elis 5 nomos 8 nomarchy, province 10 department, prefecture

nomen: 4 gens, name

nomenclature: 4 list, name 8 glossary, register 9 catalogue, designate, recounter 10 dictionary, vocabulary 11 appellation, designation, terminology

nomic: 5 valid 8 ordinary 9 customary 12 conventional

nominal: 4 noun 5 cheap, 6 slight, unreal 7 titular, trivial 8 platonic, so-called 11 theoretical 13 unsubstantial

nominate: tap 4 call, leet(Sc.), name 5 enter, put up, slate 7 appoint, entitle, propose, specify 9 designate 10 denominate

nominee: 9 candidate

non-kosher: 4 tref

non-Mahometan: 5 Kafir

nonage: 7 infancy 10 immaturity 12 youthfulness

nonaspirate: 4 lene

nonbeliever: 5 pagan 7 atheist 8 agnostic

nonce: 7 present 8 occasion

nonchalant: 4 cool, easy 6 casual 8 careless 10 insouciant 11 indifferent 12 lighthearted 13 imperturbable

noncleric: lay 4 laic

noncombatant: 8 chaplain, civilian, observer

noncommittal: 7 neutral 8 reserved

noncompliance: 7 refusal 10 obstinance 13 recalcitrance

non compos mentis: 6 insane 14 not of sound mind

nonconcurrence: 7 dissent

nonconductor: 5 resin

nonconforming: 9 anomalous

nonconformist: 5 rebel 6 hippie 7 beatnik, heretic 8 bohemian 9 dissenter

nonconformity: 6 heresy 7 dissent 9 recusance, recusancy 10 dissidence 13 individualism

nondescript: 13 indescribable 14 indeterminable

none: nane 4 nane(Sc.), neen

nonentity: 4 zero 5 zilch 6 cipher 7 nothing, sad sack 9 small beer

nonessential: 9 extrinsic 10 adiaphoron 11 dispensable, unnecessary 12 adventitious 14 circumstantial

nonesuch: 5 apple, model 7 paragon 8 paradigm 9 matchless, nonpareil, unequaled, unrivaled 13 one in a million

nonexistent: 4 null 8 nonbeing

nonfestal: 6 ferial

nonfulfillment: 6 breach 12 infringement

nongrata: 9 unwelcome

nongypsy: 4 gajo

no-no: 9 forbidden 12 unacceptable

nonobjective: 8 abstract

nonobservance: 9 violation

nonpareil: 4 best 5 ideal 7 paragon, perfect, unequal 8 nonesuch, peerless 9 unrivaled

nonpartisan: 4 fair, just 9 impartial, objective

nonpasserine bird: 4 tody 6 hoopoe, motmot 8 hornbill 10 kingfisher

nonphysical: 7 psychic 9 psychical

nonplus: 5 blank, stump, trump 6 baffle, puzzle 7 perplex, stagger 9 embarrass

nonpositive: 8 negative 9 private

nonproductive: 6 barren 7 sterile 10 unfruitful

nonprofessional: lay 4 laic 7 amateur

nonsense: bah, pah, rot 4 blah, bosh, buff, bunk, flam, tosh 5 blash, folly, fudge, haver, hooey, stite(Sc.) 6 bunkum, drivel, faddle, folder 7 blarney, blather, buncome, inanity, twaddle 8 blahblah, blathery, falderal, folderol, flimflam, trumpery 9 absurdity, fandangle, frivolity, gibberish, moonshine, poppycock, silliness 10 balderdash, flapdoodle, flumdiddle, galimatias, triviality 11 flumadiddle, foolishness, monkeyshine 12 fiddle-dee-dee, flummadiddle, flummydiddle 16 preposterousness

non sequitur: 15 it does not follow
nonsolid: 5 fluid **6** liquid
noodle: 4 bean, fool, head, nizy, noll, pate
5 brain, ninny, nizey, noddy **6** boodle,
noddle, noggin **9** blockhead, simpleton
nook: out, wro **4** cant, cove, glen, hole **5**
angle, herne, niche **6** cantle, corner,
cranny, recess **7** byplace, crevice, retreat
noon: 4 apex **6** midday **8** meridian **11** culmination
noose: tie **4** bond, dull, grin, hang, loop,
trap **5** bight, grane, honda, snare, widdy
6 entrap, halter, lariat **7** ensnare, execute, laniard, lanyard, springe **8** slipknot
　armed with: **10** laquearian
nor: ner **7** neither **8** negative **10** connective
nori: 4 alga **7** amanori, seaweed
noria: 5 wheel
norite: 4 rock **6** gabbro
norm: 4 rule, type **5** gauge, model, norma
7 average, pattern **8** standard, template
normal: 4 sane **5** usual **6** general **7** natural, regular, typical **11** commonplace
12 compos mentis
Normandy: *beach:* **5** Omaha
　capital: **5** Rollo
　conqueror: **5** Rollo
　department: **4** Eure, Orne **6** Manche **8**
　Calvados
　duke: **5** Rollo
　town: **7** Saint-Lo
Norn: 4 fate, Urth, Wyrd **5** Skuld **9**
Verthandi
Norse (see also **Scandinavian**): **4** mink
8 Teutonic **9** Icelandic, Norwegian **12**
Scandinavian
　abode of gods: **6** Asgard
　alphabet: **5** runic
　bard: **5** scald, skald **7** sagaman
　chieftain: **4** jarl, Rolf **5** Rollo
　demigoddess of destiny: Urd
　demon: **4** Mara, Surt **5** Surtr
　epic: **4** Edda
　explorer: **4** Eric **7** Ericson
　fate: **4** Norn
　first man: **4** Askr
　first woman: **5** Embla
　giant: **4** Atli, Loke, Loki, Natt, Norn,
　Nott, Wate, Ymer, Ymir **5** Jotun, Mim-
　er, Mimir, Thrym **6** Fafnir, Jotunn
　god (see also *giant* above): Asa, Ase, Ran,
　Tiu, Tyr, Ull, Zio **4** Frey, Hler, Hoth,
　Loke, Loki, Odin, Surt, Thor, Vali **5**
　Aeger, Aegir, Aesir(pl.), Baldr, Brage,
　Bragi, Donar, Freyr, Gymir, Othin,
　Surtr, Vanir(pl.), Wodan, Woden, Wo-
　tan **6** Balder, Hoenir, Njorth **7** Forsete,
　Forseti, Heimdal, Vitharr **9** Heimdallr,
　Hlorrithi

　goddess: Dis, Eir, Hel **4** Frea, Hela, Nora,
　Saga, Urth, Wyrd **5** Freya, Frigg,
　Nanna **6** Freyja, Frigga **7** Asynjur
　goddess of earth: **4** Erda
　hall of heroes: **8** Valhalla
　king: **4** Atli, Olaf
　mythological wolf: **6** Fenrir
　night: **4** Natt, Nott
　nobleman: **4** yarl
　poem: **4** rune
　poet: **5** scald, skald
　saint: **4** Olaf **5** Olaus
　sea serpent: **6** Kraken **7** Midgard
　tale: **4** saga
　toast: **5** skoal
　viking: **5** Rollo
　watchdog: **4** Garm **5** Garmr
　world tree: **8** Ygdrasil
North Africa: *antelope:* **5** addax **7** gazelle
　country: **5** Libya **7** Algeria, Morocco, Tu-
　nisia
　fruit: fig **4** date
　language: **6** Arabic, Berber
　lyre: **6** kissar
　measure: **4** rotl
　native quarter: **6** casbah, kasbah
　oasis: **4** wadi, wady
　people: **4** Moor **5** Nilot **6** Hamite
　port: **4** Oran, Sfax **6** Annaba **7** Tangier
　10 Casablanca
　sheep: **4** drui **6** aoudad
　valley: **4** wadi, wady
North America: *bird:* **6** fulmar **7** grackle
　8 cardinal, killdeer, kingrail **10** buffle-
　head
　country: **6** Canada, Mexico **9** Greenland
　12 United States
　discoverer: **5** Cabot
　herb: **4** sego
　Indian: see **Indian (Americas)**
　marmoset: **7** tamarin
　orchids: **9** arethusas
　owl: **7** wapacut
　people: **7** Mexican **8** American, Canadian
　reindeer: **7** caribou
　thrush: **5** robin
　tree: lin **4** mabi, sorb, titi **5** balsa, papaw
　6 balsam, pawpaw, redbud, tupelo **7** ca-
　talpa, hickory **8** basswood, oneberry,
　sweetsop **9** sassafras
North Atlantic: *island:* **7** Britain, Ice-
　land, Ireland **9** Manhattan
　seagull: **4** skua
North Britain: 8 Scotland **9** Caledonia
North Carolina: *cape:* **4** Fear **7** Lookout
　8 Hatteras
　capital: **7** Raleigh
　city: **6** Durham **9** Charlotte **10** Greens-
　boro **12** Winston-Salem
　county: **4** Ashe, Dare, Hoke, Wake **5** An-
　son, Avery **6** Lenoir, Onslow **8** Bun-
　combe, Guilford **10** Cumberland

island: 10 Outer Banks
lake: 6 Phelps 8 Waccamaw
mountain: 9 Blue Ridge 10 Great Smoky
mountain range: 11 Appalachian
nickname: 7 Tar Heel 8 Old North 10 Turpentine
river: Haw, Tar 5 Neuse 6 Pee Dee, Yadkin 7 Roanoke
state bird: 8 cardinal
state flower: 7 dogwood
state tree: 4 pine
North Dakota: *capital:* 8 Bismarck
city: 5 Fargo, Minot 9 Jamestown 10 Grand Forks
county: 4 Cass, Ward 6 Morton, Traill 8 Burleigh
Indian: 6 Mandan 7 Arikara
highest peak: 10 White Butte
nickname: 5 Sioux 11 Flickertail
river: Red 8 Missouri
state bird: 10 meadowlark
state flower: 11 prairie rose
state tree: elm
North Korea: *capital:* 9 Pyongyang
monetary unit: won 4 hwan
river: Nam 4 Yalu
North Pole discoverer: 5 Peary
North Sea: *arm:* 9 Skagerrak
canal: 4 Kiel
river: 5 Weser
North Star: 7 polaris 8 loadstar, lodestar, polestar 10 tramontane
North Vietnam (see also **Vietnam**): *capital:* 5 Hanoi
city: 8 Haiphong
gulf: 6 Tonkin
monetary unit: 4 dong
Northwest Territories: *bay:* 5 James 6 Baffin, Hudson, Ungava
capital: 11 Yellowknife
district: 8 Franklin, Keewatin 9 Mackenzie
explorer: 7 Simpson 8 Franklin 9 Frobisher
flower: 13 mountain avens
gulf: 7 Brothia 8 Amundsen 9 Queen Maud 10 Coronation
Indian: 10 Athabascan
industry: 6 mining 7 whaling 8 fur trade
island: 6 Baffin
lake: 9 Great Bear 10 Great Slave
people: 5 Inuit 6 Eskimo
river: 9 Mackenzie 10 Coppermine
territory of: 6 Canada
north wind: 6 boreas
northeaster: 4 blow, gale, wind 5 storm
northern: 6 boreal 13 septentrional
Northern Bear: 6 Russia
Norway: *bird:* 4 rype
boat: 4 pram 5 praam 6 praham
capital: 4 Oslo (formerly Christiania)
cart: 11 stolkjaerre

chieftain: 4 jarl
city: see *town* below
coin: ore 5 krone
counties: 5 amter
county: amt 5 fylke 6 fylker(pl.), Tromso 7 Finmark
dance: 7 halling
embroidery: 9 hardanger
goblin: 5 nisse 6 kobold
governor: 6 amtman
haddock: 8 rosefish
inlet: 5 fiord, fjord
language: 5 Norse 9 Norwegian
measure: fot, mal, pot 4 alen, maal 5 kande 6 fathom 7 skieppe 9 korntonde
mountain: 5 Sogne 6 Kjolen 7 Numedal 8 Telemark, Ustetind 9 Blodfjell, Harteigen, Ramnanosi
parliament: 8 Storting 9 Storthing
plateau: 5 Dovre, velde 6 fjells 9 Hardanger
river: Ena 4 Tana 6 Lougen, Glomma
ruler: 6 hersir
saint: 4 Olaf 5 Olaus
town: Nes 4 Oslo(c.), Voss 5 Bjort, Hamar, Skein, Skjak 6 Bergen, Horten, Larvik, Narvik 7 Alesund, Drammen 9 Stavanger, Trondhjem
traitor: 8 Quisling
weight: lod 4 mark, pund 9 skaalpund 10 bismerpund
nose: neb, nez(F.), pry, spy 4 beak, conk, gift, lora(pl.) 5 lorum, scent, smell, sniff, snoop, snout 6 detect, muffle, muzzle, nozzle, search, socket 7 advance, perfume 8 busybody, discover, informer, perceive 9 proboscis 11 investigate
cartilage: 6 septum
inflammation: 6 coryza 8 rhinitis
kind: pug 5 Roman 8 aquiline
large: 6 nasute
medicine: 7 errhine
muscle: 7 nasalio
opening: 4 nare 7 nostril
partition: 5 vomer
pert to: 5 nasal 6 narial, rhinal
snub: 6 simous
nosebleed: 9 epistaxis
nose-dive: dip 6 plunge 7 plummet
nosegay: 4 posy 7 bouquet, perfume
nosegay tree: 10 frangipani
nosepiece: 5 nasal 6 nozzle
nosh: 4 chew 5 munch, snack
nostalgia: 7 longing 10 melancholy 12 homesickness
Nostradamus: 4 seer 7 prophet 10 forecaster
nostril: 4 nare 5 nares(pl.), naris(pl.) 6 thrill
pert to: 5 naric 6 narial, narine
nostril-shaped: 8 nariform

nosy, nosey: 6 prying 7 curious 8 fragrant 10 malodorous 11 inquisitive

not: nae(Sc.), nay, nor 4 baal, bail, bale, nott 5 shorn 6 nought, polled, shaven 7 neither 8 hornless, negation, negative 11 nothingness

all there: 6 insane

any: nul 4 nane(Sc.), nary, none

at all: 5 never 6 noways, nowise

either: 7 neither

final: 13 interlocutory

otherwise than: 6 merely

the same: 5 other 7 another 9 different

notable: V.I.P. 6 fabled, famous, fat cat 7 eminent, storied 8 big wheel, eventful, historic 9 memorable, notorious 10 noteworthy, remarkable 12 considerable 13 distinguished, extraordinary

notal: 6 dorsal

notandum: 4 note 5 entry 9 memoranda(pl.) 10 memorandum

notarize: 6 attest 7 certify

notary: 5 clerk 8 endorser, observer, official, recorder 9 notorious, scrivener

chief: 11 protonotary 12 prothonotary

notation: 4 memo, note 7 marking 10 annotation 14 representation

phonetic: 5 Romic

notator: 5 noter 8 recorder 9 annotator

notch: cut, dag, gap, hag, jag 4 cope, dent, dint, gash, gimp, hila(pl.), kerf, nick, step 5 crena, grade, hilum, score, tally 6 crenae(pl.), crotch, defile, degree, indent, record, scotch 7 crenate, serrate 8 undercut 9 indenture 10 depression 11 indentation

notched: 5 erose 7 crenate, serrate 8 crenated, serrated

irregularly: 5 erose

note: I.O.U., jot, see 4 bill, call, chit, fame, heed, line, mark, memo, name, sign, sole, song, tone, tune 5 label, sound, token 6 billet, letter, minute, notice, record, regard, remark, renown, report 7 betoken, comment, message, missive, notanda(pl.), observe 8 annotate, breviate, dispatch, eminence, notandum, perceive, reminder 9 character 10 indication, memorandum, prominence, reputation 11 distinction, observation

accompanying: 8 overtone

bank: 6 finnip, flimsy 8 frogskin

bugle: mot

explanatory: 8 scholium 10 annotation

highest: ela

marginal: 6 postil 7 apostil 9 apostille

middle: 4 mese

musical: 4 half 5 breve, gamut, sharp, whole 6 eighth 7 punctus, quarter 8 paramese 9 semibreve

prisoner's: 4 kite

promissory: 11 pledge to pay

writer: 9 annotator

note well: 8 nota bene(L.)

notebook: log 5 diary 6 street 7 journal 10 adversaria

notecase: 10 pocketbook

noted: 9 distingue, well-known 10 celebrated 11 illustrious

notes: *literary:* ana

miscellaneous: 10 adversaria

noteworthy: 6 rubric 7 eminent, notable 9 memorable, red-letter 10 remarkable 11 outstanding 12 considerable

nothing: nil 4 free, luke, nill, zero 5 aught, nihil 6 naught, nought, trifle 7 useless 10 triviality 12 nonexistence, unimportance 14 insignificance

nothing but: all 4 mere, only

notice: ban, see 4 espy, heed, idea, mark, mind, news, note, sign 5 await, quote 6 advice, billet, espial, notion, regard, remark 7 affiche, article, discern, mention, observe, warning 8 appraisal, citation, civility 9 attention, criticism 10 cognizance, intimation, memorandum 11 garnishment 12 announcement, intelligence, notification 13 consideration

advance: 8 heraldry

book: 5 blurb

death: 4 obit 8 obituary

favorable: 4 rave

honorable: 8 citation

leave of: 8 mittimus

legal: 6 caveat

marriage: ban 4 bans 5 banns

official: 5 edict 8 bulletin 12 proclamation

paid: 13 advertisement

Patent Office: 6 caveat

public: 5 edict 8 bulletin

refuse: 6 ignore

noticeable: 7 evident, notable, salient 8 striking 9 prominent 10 noteworthy, remarkable 11 conspicuous, eye-catching, outstanding, significant

notification: 6 notice

notify: bid 4 cite, page, tell, warn 6 inform 7 apprise, declare, frutify, publish 8 acquaint 9 broadcast 10 promulgate

notion: bee 4 buzz, hint, idea, idee, view, whim 5 fancy, image 6 belief, desire, maggot, notice, theory, vagary 7 caprice, conceit, inkling, opinion, thought 9 intention 10 conception 11 inclination

notoriety: 5 eclat 9 publicity

notorious: bad, big 5 known 6 arrant, famous 7 evident 8 apparent, flagrant, infamous 9 acclaimed, well-known 11 conspicuous

notwithstanding: yet 4 even 6 algate, mauger, maugre 7 against, algates, despite, however 8 although 12 nevertheless

nougat: 5 candy 8 nut shell 10 confection

nought: bad, nil 4 zero 5 wrong 7 nothing, useless 9 worthless 10 wickedness

noun: 4 name, word 11 substantive
form: 4 case 6 gender
indeclinable: 6 aptote
kind of: 6 common, proper
verbal: 6 gerund

nourish: 4 feed, grow, rear 5 breed, nurse 6 foison, foster, suckle, supply 7 cherish, support, sustain, develop 9 cultivate, stimulate

nourishing: 4 alma 6 alible, hearty 8 nutrient 9 alimental, nutritive 10 alimentary, nutritious

nourishment: 4 food, keep, meat 5 manna 6 foison, living 7 aliment, pabulum, support 9 nutriment 10 sustenance 13 nutritiveness 14 nutritiousness

nous: 4 mind 6 reason 9 intellect

nova: new 4 star

Nova Scotia: *bay:* 5 Fundy
cape: 5 Canso, Sable 6 Breton, George
capital: 7 Halifax
city: 6 Sydney 8 Glace Bay 9 Dartmouth
county: 10 Cape Breton, Colchester, Cumberland
national park: 7 Fort Ann
native name: 6 Acadia
people: 7 Acadian 8 bluenose
port: 5 Truro
province of: 6 Canada
provincial flower: 7 arbutus 9 mayflower
settler: 10 Highlander, U.S. Loyalist

novel: new, odd 4 book 5 fresh, story 6 recent, unique 7 fiction, romance, strange, unusual 8 original, uncommon 10 newfangled
cut: 11 abridgement 12 condensation

novelette: 5 conte

novelty: fad 6 change 10 innovation, knickknack

novice: cub 4 boot, punk, tyro 5 rooky 6 rookie, tyrone 7 amateur, convert, learner 8 beginner, freshman, neophyte 9 greenhorn 10 apprentice 11 abecedarian

novitiate: 9 probation 14 apprenticeship

now: noo(Sc.) 4 here 5 today 7 because, present 9 forthwith 11 immediately

nowise: 5 navis

noxious: ill 4 evil 5 fetid 6 nocent, putrid 7 baneful, harmful, hurtful, nocuous, noisome, vicious 8 stinking, virulent 9 injurious, miasmatic, poisonous 10 pernicious 11 deleterious, destructive, unwholesome 12 insalubrious

nozzle: 4 nose, vent 5 snout

nuance: 5 shade 7 shading, soupcon 8 subtlety 10 difference, suggestion

nub: 4 core, crux, gist, hang, knob, knot, knub, lump, neck, snag 9 substance 12 protuberance

nubia: 4 wrap 5 cloud, scarf

nubile: 12 marriageable

nubilous: 5 foggy, misty, vague 6 cloudy 7 obscure 8 overcast 10 indefinite

nuclear particle: 6 proton 7 neutron

nucleus: 4 core, seed 5 focus, umbra 6 kernel, fusion 7 fission
pert. to: 8 nucleate
starch: 4 hila(pl.) 5 hilum

nude: 4 bare 5 model, naked 6 statue 7 denuded, picture 8 buff-bare, painting, stripped 9 au naturel, unclothed, uncovered, undressed

nudge: jog, nog 4 knub, lump, poke, push 5 block, elbow

nudibranch: 7 mollusk

nudie: 9 skin flick

nudist: 7 Adamite 12 gymnosophist

nugatory: 4 vain 7 invalid, trivial 8 trifling 9 frustrate, worthless 11 ineffectual

nugget: 4 hunk, lump, mass, slug

nuisance: 4 harm, hurt, pest 6 injury 9 annoyance 12 exasperation 13 inconvenience

null: nil 6 devoid 7 nullify 11 nonexistent 13 insignificant

nullah: 5 gorge, gully 6 ravine

nullifidian: 7 skeptic 10 unbeliever

nullify: 4 flaw, null, undo, void 5 abate, annul, elide 6 cancel, negate, offset, repeal 7 abolish, destroy 8 abrogate, evacuate 9 frustrate 10 counteract, disappoint, invalidate, neutralize

numb: 4 dead, drug, dull 6 asleep, benumb, deaden, stupid, torpid 7 stupefy 8 enfeeble, helpless 9 incapable 10 indifferent, insensible

number: sum 4 curn(Sc.), data(pl.), many, mort, slew, herd, host 5 count, datum, digit, scads, score, total 6 amount, bundle, encore, figure, myriad, reckon, hirsel 7 chiffer, compute, decimal, several 8 numerate, quantity, fraction 9 aggregate, calculate, enumerate, multitude 10 collection, complement, percentage
cardinal: one, two 4 four 5 three
dice: 4 sise
indeterminate: 7 umpteen, zillion
irrational: 4 surd
ordinal: 5 first, third 6 second
prime: one, two 4 five 5 seven, three 6 eleven 8 thirteen
pure: 6 scalar
third power: 4 cube
under ten: 5 digit
whole: 7 integer

numbles: 7 giblets, innards 8 entrails

numen: 5 deity 6 genius, spirit 8 divinity

numerable: 11 enumerative

numeral: 4 word 5 digit 6 figure, letter
style: 5 Roman 6 Arabic

numerate: 4 list, tell 5 count, tally 7 tick off

numerical group: duo 4 trio 5 octet 6 septet, sextet 7 octette, quartet, quintet, twosome 8 foursome, sextette 9 threesome

numerous: 4 lots, many 7 copious, crowded 8 abundant, multiple, thronged 9 multifold, plentiful

Numidia: *bird:* 10 demoiselle
city: 5 Hippo
king: 8 Jugurtha

numskull: 4 dolt 5 dunce 9 blockhead

nun: 4 bird, snew 5 clerk 6 pigeon, sister, vestal 7 confine, devotee 8 titmouse, votaress 9 priestess 10 cloistress
chief: 6 abbess
Franciscan: 5 Clare
headdress: 6 wimple
Latin: 5 Vesta
order: 6 Marist 8 Trappist 9 Dominican, Lorettine

Nun's son: 6 Joshua

nun moth: 7 tussock

nunbird: 6 monase

nuncio: 6 legate 8 delegate 9 messenger 14 representative

nuncupate: 7 declare 8 dedicate, inscribe, proclaim 9 designate

nuncupative: 4 oral 9 unwritten

nunnery: 5 abbey 7 convent 8 cloister 10 sisterhood
head: 6 abbess

nunni: 7 blesbok 8 antelope

nuphar: 9 water lily

nuptial: 6 bridal, genial 7 marital, wedding 11 matrimonial

nurse: 4 amah, ayah, baba, care, feed, rear, tend 5 bonne(F.), mammy, nanny 6 attend, cradle, foster, norice, suckle 7 cherish, nourice, nourish, nurture, promote 10 breast-feed, minister to

nurse shark: 4 gata

nursery: 6 creche 7 brooder

nursling: 4 baby 9 foundling

nurture: 4 diet, feed, food, rear 5 nurse, raise, train 6 cocker, foster 7 bring up, cherish, educate 8 breeding, training 9 education, nutriment

nut: bur, guy, nit 4 burr, cola, core, head, kola, nute, pili, task 5 acorn, betel, crank, hazel, pecan 6 almond, Brazil, cashew, fellow, peanut, pyrene 7 filbert, hickory, lunatic, problem 8 beechnut, chestnut, crackpot 9 eccentric 10 crackbrain, enthusiast 11 undertaking
collective: 4 mast 5 shack
edible part: 6 kernel

ivory: 4 anta

kola: 5 bichy 9 gourou-nut

medicinal: 4 cola, kola

palm: 5 betel, lichi 8 cocoanut

pert. to: 5 nucal

tropical: ben 4 cola, kola

nut-brown: 5 hazel 6 walnut 8 chestnut

nut coal: 10 anthracite

nut grass: 5 sedge

nutant: 7 nodding 8 drooping

nutmeg: *covering:* 4 mace

Nutmeg State: 11 Connecticut

nutramin: 7 vitamin

nutria: fur 5 coypu

nutriment: pap 10 sustenance 11 nourishment

nutrition: 11 nourishment 12 alimentation

nutritious: 9 healthful, wholesome 10 salubrious, nourishing

nutritive: 10 nourishing

nuts-and-bolts: 7 details 12 working parts

nutty: 4 gaga 5 buggy, queer, spicy 7 amorous, piquant 8 demented, pleasant 10 unbalanced 12 crackbrained, enthusiastic

nuzzle: 5 nurse 6 foster, nestle 7 snuggle

nye: 4 eyas, nest, nide 5 brood

nylon: 5 crepe, fiber, ninon, tulle 6 fabric

nymph: 4 doxy 5 Aegle, naiad, siren, oread, sylph 6 nereid 7 Corycia 9 hamadryad
Arcadian: 6 Syrinx
beloved of Narcissus: 4 Echo
Cretan: 8 Cynosura
hills: 5 Oread
laurel tree: 6 Daphne
Messina Strait: 6 Scylla
Mount Ida: 6 Oenone
mountain: 5 Oread
Muslim: 5 houri
ocean: 5 siren 6 Nereid 7 Galatea, Oceanid 10 Callirrhoe
pursued by Apollo: 6 Daphne, Syrinx 8 Arethusa
queen: Mab
sea: 6 Nereid 7 Calypso
water: 4 Nais 5 Naiad 6 Egeria, Lurlei, Undine 7 Apsaras, Hydriad, Lorelei 8 Arethusa
wood: 5 Dryad 6 Nereid 9 Hamadryad

nymphaea: 8 Castalia 9 water lily

nyssa: 6 tupelo 8 black gum

Nyx, Nox: 5 night
brother: 6 Erebus
daughter: Day 4 Eris 5 Light 10 Hesperides
father: 5 Chaos
husband: 5 Chaos 6 Erebus
son: 6 Charon, Hypnos

O

O. Henry: 6 Porter

oaf: 4 boor, dolt, fool, lout **5** clown, dunce, idiot, yoke **6** lummox **8** dumbbell **9** blockhead, foundling, schlemiel, schlemihl, simpleton **10** changeling

oafish: 6 stupid **7** loutish

oak: 5 roble **6** barren, cerris, encina **7** ambrose, durmast, turtosa **8** chaparro **9** blackjack
bark: **4** crut
bitter: **6** cerris
black: **10** quercitron
blight: **5** louse
evergreen: **4** holm
family: **8** fagaceae
fruit: **5** acron **6** camata
fungus: **10** armillaria
gall: **8** oakapple
holm: **4** ilex **5** holly
immature fruit: **6** camata
seed: **5** acorn
tannin: **6** queric **9** quercinic
white: **5** roble
young: **8** flittern

oak beauty: 4 moth

oak fern: 8 polypody

oam: 5 steam

oar: row **4** pole, pull **5** aloof, rower, scull **6** paddle, propel **7** oarsman **9** propeller
blade: **4** palm, peel
collective: **6** oarage
fulcrum: **7** oarlock
part: **4** loom
short: **5** scull
steering: **5** swape, swipe

oarlock: 5 thole **7** rowlock

oarsman: 5 rower **6** stroke **7** sculler

oasis: ojo, spa **4** merv, wadi, wady **6** refuge, relief

oast: 4 kiln, oven **6** cockle

oat: ait(Sc.) **5** grain **6** angora **7** cereal, egilops
genus: **5** avena
head: **7** panicle

oater: 7 western **10** horse opera

oath: vow **4** aith **5** aithe, curse, haith **6** appeal, pledge **7** serment **8** anathema **9** affidavit, expletive, profanity, swearword **10** adjuration, obligation **11** affirmation, imprecation
mild: **4** darn, drat, ecod, egad, gosh **5** golly **7** gee-wizz

take: **5** swear

oatmeal: 6 cereal **7** granola **8** porridge

obclude: 4 hide, **7** conceal

obdurate: 4 firm, hard **5** rough, stony **6** inured, rugged **7** adamant **8** hardened, stubborn **9** calloused, immovable, obstinate, unbending, unfeeling **10** impenitent, inflexible, insensible, persistent, unyielding **11** hardhearted, intractable, stiff-necked, unrepenting **13** unsusceptible

obeah: obi **5** charm **6** fetish, voodoo

Obed: *father:* **4** Boaz
grandson: **5** David
mother: **4** Ruth
son: **4** Jehu **5** Jesse **7** Azariah

obedience: 5 order **7** control **8** docility **10** compliance, conformity, submission **12** jurisdiction

obedient: 7 duteous, dutiful, heedful, mindful, obeying, slavish **8** amenable, biddable, yielding **9** attentive, observing, tractable

obedient plant: 10 dragonhead

obeisance: bow **5** binge, conge, honor, salam **6** congee, curtsy, fealty, homage, salaam **7** curtsey, loyalty **9** abaisance, deference, reference **10** submission **14** respectfulness

obelisk: 4 mark **5** pylon, shaft **6** dagger, guglia, guglio, needle, obelus, pillar **8** monument

Oberon: 4 king, poem **5** fairy, opera
wife: **7** Titania

obese: fat **5** plump, pudgy, pursy, stout **6** fleshy, pyknic, rotund **8** blubbery, liparous

obesity: 7 fatness **10** corpulence **11** avoirdupois
science of: **10** bariatrics

obey: ear **4** hear, mind **6** accept, submit **7** execute

obfuscate: dim **6** darken **7** becloud, confuse, mystify, obscure, perplex, stupefy **8** bewilder **9** obfuscous

obi: 4 sash **6** girdle

obiter dictum: 6 remark **7** comment **11** observation

obituary: 9 necrology **11** death notice

object: aim, end **4** goal, item **5** argue, cavil, demur, thing **6** design, entity, motive, oppose, target **7** dislike, protest, purpose, quarrel **9** challenge, intention, interpose **10** disapprove **11** expostulate, remonstrate

rare: **5** curio **7** antique

sacred: **4** urim

object lesson: 7 example

object to: 4 mind

objection: but **7** defense, protest **8** demurral **9** challenge, exception

legal: **5** demur

objectionable: 4 vile **6** horrid **9** obnoxious, offensive **11** exceptional **12** disagreeable

objective: aim, end **4** goal **6** motive, realty, target **7** purpose **8** detached **9** intention **10** impersonal

objet d'art: 4 vase **5** curio, virtu **6** bauble, gewgaw **7** bibelot **8** figurine

objurgate: 5 abuse, chide, decry **6** berate, rebuke **7** reprove, upbraid **8** execrate **9** castigate

oblate: 4 monk **8** dedicate, monastic

opposite of: **7** prolate

oblation: 4 gift **6** corban **7** charity **8** devotion, offering **9** sacrifice

obligate: 4 bind **6** fasten **7** promise

obligation: vow **4** band, bond, debt, duty, loan, must, oath, onus **6** devoir, pledge **7** promise **8** contract **9** agreement, liability **10** allegiance, commitment, compulsion **11** obstruction **12** indebtedness **14** responsibility

obligato: 13 accompaniment

obligatory: 7 binding, bounden **8** forcible, imposing **9** mandatory

oblige: 4 pawn **5** favor, force **6** engage, please **7** gratify, require **8** mortgage, obligate **9** constrain **11** necessitate

obliged: 8 beholden, grateful, indebted

obliging: 4 kind **5** buxom, civil **6** clever **7** amiable **9** agreeable, courteous **11** complaisant **13** accommodating

oblique: 4 awry, bias, skew **5** askew, bevel, cross, slant **6** aslant, aswash **7** askance, crooked, evasive, scalene **8** inclined, indirect, sidelong, sideways, sidewise, slanting **9** slantways, slantwise, underhand **10** circuitous **12** disingenuous

render: **5** splay

obliterate: 4 blot, dele, rase, raze **5** annul, erase **6** cancel, delete, efface, sponge **7** expunge **10** annihilate, extinguish

obliteration: 7 erasure, removal **10** extinction

oblivion: 5 Lethe, limbo **6** pardon **7** amnesty, nirvana **13** forgetfulness

producer of: **8** nepenthe

oblong: 8 avelonge **9** elongated **11** rectangular

rounded: **7** ellipse

obloquy: 5 abuse, odium **6** infamy **7** calumny, censure **8** disgrace, dishonor **12** reprehension, vituperation **13** animadversion

obnoxious: 4 foul, vile **6** horrid, liable, odious, rancid **7** hateful **9** offensive, repugnant, verminous **13** objectionable

oboe: 4 reed **5** shawm **6** surnai, surnay **7** hautboy, musette **8** szopelka

early relative: **5** shawm

obscene: 4 foul, lewd, nast **5** bawdy, gross, nasty **6** coarse, filthy, impure, vulgar **7** profane **8** immodest, indecent **9** loathsome, offensive, repulsive **10** disgusting, fescennine, licentious **11** foulmouthed **12** pornographic

obscure: dim **4** blot, blur, dark, hazy, hide **5** bedim, befog, blind, faint, foggy, inner, murky, vague **6** bemist, cloudy, darken, darkle, gloomy, mystic, remote **7** becloud, conceal, confuse, cryptic, eclipse, shadowy, unknown, unnoted **8** abstruse, darkling, disguise, mystical, nameless, obstruse, oversile **9** ambiguous, blindfold, difficult, enigmatic, equivocal, mystical, recondite, undefined **10** caliginous, extinguish, indistinct, overshadow **14** uncomprehended

obsecrate: 4 pray **7** beseech, entreat **8** petition **10** supplicate

obsequious: 5 slick **7** devoted, dutiful, fawning, servile, slavish **8** obedient, toadying, toadyish **9** attentive, compliant, parasitic **10** submissive **11** deferential, subservient

obsequy: 4 rite **6** exequy, ritual **7** funeral **8** ceremony **10** compliance

observance: act **4** form, rite, rule **6** custom, notice, regard **8** ceremony, practice **9** attention, deference **11** observation **12** constitution

religious: **6** Novena **9** sacrament

observant: 5 alert **7** careful, mindful **8** watchful **9** attentive **10** perceptive **11** considerate

observation: 4 heed, note **6** notice, remark **7** auspice, autopsy, descant

preliminary: **5** proem

observatory: 4 Lick **5** tower **7** lookout, Palomar **9** astronomy **11** Mount Wilson

observe: eye, see, spy **4** espy, heed, keep, look, nark, note, obey, tout, wait, yeme **5** study, watch **6** behold, descry, follow, notice, regard, remark **7** comment, discern, respect, witness **8** perceive, preserve **9** advertise, celebrate, solemnize **10** animadvert, scrutinize

observer: 8 audience, informer, onlooker **9** bystander, spectator

obsess: 5 beset, haunt **6** harass **9** preoccupy

obsession: 5 craze, mania **6** fetish, hang-up **7** passion **8** idee fixe(F.) **13** preoccupation

obsidian: 5 lapis

obsolescence: 9 desuetude

obsolete: old **4** dead **5** passe **7** ancient, archaic, extinct, outworn **8** out-dated, outmoded **9** discarded, out-of-date **10** antiquated **12** old-fashioned

obstacle: bar, dam, let **4** snag **5** block, hitch **6** bunker, hocket, hurdle **7** barrier **9** hindrance **10** difficulty, impediment **11** Chinese wall, obstruction **12** entanglement

insurmountable: **7** impasse

military: **6** abates

obstetrician: 7 midwife **10** accoucheur

obstetrics: 8 tocology **9** maieutics

obstinate: set **4** dour **5** balky, sulky, tough **6** assish, dogged, mulish, sullen, unruly **7** froward, willful **8** crotched, obdurate, perverse, stubborn **9** foreright, pigheaded **10** bullheaded, determined, headstrong, inflexible, persistent, refractory, selfwilled **11** intractable, opinionated **12** closed-minded, contumacious, pertinacious, recalcitrant

obstreperous: 5 noisy **6** unruly **9** clamorous **10** boisterous, vociferous **11** disobedient

obstruct: bar, dam, dit, gag, mar **4** clog, ditt, fell, stop **5** beset, block, check, choke, delay, hedge **6** arrest, cumber, forbar, hamper, hinder, impede, oppose, retard, screen **7** barrier, forelay, occlude **8** blockade, encumber, incumber **9** barricade, embarrass, interfere, interrupt **10** filibuster **11** fillibuster

obstruction: 4 snag **5** gorce, hitch **7** barrace, barrage, barrier, blinder **8** embolism, obstacle **10** difficulty, impediment **11** impeachment

obtain: beg, bum, eke, get, win **4** earn fang, gain, hent, reap **5** cadge, ettle, reach **6** attain, derive, secure, sponge **7** achieve, acquire, capture, chevise, prevail, procure, receive, succeed

by threat: **6** extort **9** blackmail

obtainable: 9 available

obtest: 6 beg for **7** beseech **10** supplicate

obtrude: 5 eject, expel **6** butt in, impose

obtruncate: lop **6** behead **7** shorten **8** retrench **10** decapitate

obtrusive: 5 fresh, pushy **7** blatant, forward, pushing **9** intrusive **10** aggressive **11** impertinent **12** presumptuous

obtund: 4 dull **5** blunt, quell **6** deaden

obtuse: dim **4** dull **5** blink, blunt, crass, dense **6** stupid **8** boeotian, hebetate, purblind **11** insensitive

obvelation: 7 veiling **10** concealing

obverse: 4 face **5** front **8** converse **10** complement **11** counterpart

obviate: 7 prevent, ward off **8** preclude **9** forestall, interfere, intervene

obvious: 4 open **5** broad, clear, gross, overt, plain **6** patent **7** evident, glaring, visible **8** apparent, distinct, manifest, palpable **11** conspicuous

obvolute: 9 contorted, convolute **11** overlapping

oca, oka: 5 tuber **6** oxalis, sorrel

occasion: 4 hint, sele, time **5** casus, cause, event, nonce, slant **6** excuse, moment **7** instant, pretext **8** ceremony, engender, exigency, function, incident **9** condition, happening **11** opportunity, point in time

festive: **7** holiday

occasional: odd **4** orra **5** stray **6** daimen, random **8** sporadic **10** infrequent

occasionally: 7 betimes **9** sometimes **10** now and then

Occidental: 4 West **6** ponent **7** Western **9** Hesperian, Westerner

occlude: 5 close **6** absorb **7** shut out, take in **8** obstruct

occult: 4 hide **5** eerie, magic **6** hidden, mystic, secret, voodoo **7** alchemy, cryptic **8** esoteric, mystical **9** concealed, recondite **10** mysterious, necromancy **11** supernormal **12** supernatural **13** imperceptible

science: **9** esoterics

occultation: 7 eclipse **13** disappearance

occultism: 5 magic **6** cabala **7** mystery

occupant: 6 inmate, tenant **7** citizen, dweller **10** inhabitant

occupation: job **4** note, toil, work **5** graft, trade **6** career, metier, tenure **7** calling, pursuit **8** business, function, industry, vocation **10** employment, habitation, profession

transient: **5** hobby **9** avocation

occupied: 4 busy, rapt **9** engrossed, inhabited

occupy: sit, use **4** busy, fill, hold, take **6** absorb, employ, engage, expend, fulfil, tenant **7** cohabit, engross, fulfill, inhabit, oversit, pervade, possess **8** interest

occur: be **4** come, meet, pass **5** clash, exist **6** appear, arrive, befall, betide, happen, strike **9** take place

again: **5** recur **6** repeat

occurrence: hap **4** case **5** event, thing **7** episode **8** incident, occasion **9** encounter, happening **12** circumstance

supernatural: **7** miracle

unusual: **6** oddity

ocean (see also **sea**): **4** brim, deep, main **5** brine **6** Arctic, Indian **7** expanse, Pacific **8** Atlantic **9** Antarctic, vastness

approach: **7** seagate

floating matter: **5** algae, lagan **7** flotsam

mammal: **5** whale

periodic motion: **4** tide
swell: sea **4** wave **6** roller

Oceania: 6 Malaya **9** Australia, Melanesia, Polynesia **10** Micronesia, New Zealand **11** archipelago

Oceanid: 5 nymph

Oceanus: *daughter:* **5** Doris **7** Oceanid **8** Eurynome
father: **6** Uranus
mother: **4** Gaea
sister: **6** Tethys
wife: **6** Tethys

ocellus: 6 stemma **7** eyespot

ocelot: cat **7** leopard

ocher: 5 color **7** pigment

ocrea: 6 greave, sheath **7** legging

octave: 4 cask, note, utas **5** eight **8** interval **9** harmonics, organ stop

Octavia: *brother:* **8** Augustus
husband: **6** Antony

octet: 5 group **7** huitain **8** electron

octopus: 5 polyp, poulp **6** poulpe **7** mollusk, polypus **9** devilfish **10** cephalopod
arm: **8** tentacle
kin: **5** squid **10** cuttlefish
secretion: ink
ten arms: **7** decapod

octoroon: 5 metis **7** metisse, mulatto

octose: 5 sugar

octroi: tax **5** grant **9** privilege **10** concession

octuple: 9 eightfold

ocular: eye **5** optic **6** visual

odd: awk **4** fell, left, lone, orra(Sc.), rare **5** droll, extra, funny, impar, outre(F.), queer, weird **6** quaint, uneven **7** azygous, bizarre, curious, strange, unusual **8** fanciful, freakish, peculiar, singular, unpaired **9** burlesque, eccentric, fantastic, grotesque, unmatched, whimsical **10** accidental, occasional **13** extraordinary

oddity: 5 quirk **8** crotchet, quiddity **9** curiosity **12** eccentricity, idiosyncrasy

oddment: ort **5** scrap **7** remnant **8** fragment, leftover

odds: 7 dispute, quarrel **8** variance **9** advantage **10** dissension **13** probabilities

odds and ends: 4 orts **6** refuse, scraps **7** mixture, seconds **8** remnants, sundries **9** leftovers **10** miscellany, remainders

ode: 4 hymn, poem **5** lyric, paean, psalm, verse **7** epicede **8** canticle **9** epicedium
birthday: **12** genethliacon
kind of: **8** pindaric
part: **5** epode **6** strophe
victory: **9** epinicion, epinikion

odeon: 4 hall **5** odeum **7** gallery, theater

Oder tributary: 6 Neisse

odic: 5 lyric

Odin: 5 Wodan, Woden, Wotan **8** Norse god
brother: **4** Vili

daughter-in-law: **5** Nanna
descendant: **5** Scyld
father: Bor
hall: **7** Valhall **8** Valhalla
horse: **8** Sleipner
maiden: **8** Valkyrie
mother: **6** Bestla
raven: **5** Hugin, Munin
ring: **8** Draupnir
ship: **7** Naglfar **11** Skidbladnir
son: Tyr **4** Thor, Vali **5** Baldr **6** Balder
spear: **7** Gungnir
sword: **4** Gram
throne: **10** Hlidskjalf
wife: **4** Fria, Rind **5** Frigg, Rindr **6** Frigga
wolf: **4** Gere, Geri **5** Freki

odious: 4 foul, loth, vile **5** loath **7** hateful, heinous, hideous **8** damnable, flagrant, infamous **9** abhorrent, invidious, obnoxious, offensive, repugnant **10** abominable, detestable, disgusting, forbidding **11** ignominious, opprobrious

odium: 6 stigma **8** aversion, disfavor, disgrace **9** antipathy **14** disapprobation

odograph: 9 pedometer

odontalgia: 9 toothache

odor: 4 fume, funk, nose, olid, tang **5** aroma, ewder, fetor, flair, fumet, nidor, scent, smell, stink **6** breath, flavor, foetor, repute, stench **7** bouquet, essence, flavour, fumette, perfume **9** fragrance, redolence **10** estimation, reputation

odoriferous: 4 gamy **5** balmy **6** smelly **8** fragrant **9** odiferous

Odysseus: See **Ulysses**

Odyssey author: 5 Homer

oeconomus: 7 manager, steward **9** majordomo

Oedipus: *brother-in-law:* **5** Creon
complex: **6** momism
daughter: **6** Ismene **8** Antigone
father: **5** Laius
foster parent: **7** Polybus **8** Periboea
mother: **7** Jocasta
refuge: **7** Colonus
son: **8** Eteocles **9** Polynices **10** Polyneices
victim: **5** Laius **6** Sphinx
wife: **7** Jocasta

oeillade: 4 ogle **6** glance

Oeneus: *father:* **8** Porthaon
kingdom: **7** Claydon, Pleuron
mother: **6** Euryte
wife: **7** Althaea

Oenomaus: *charioteer:* **8** Myrtilus
daughter: **10** Hippodamia
father: **4** Ares
kingdom: **4** Pisa
slayer: **6** Pelops

oeuvre: 4 opus, work

of: 4 from **5** about **10** concerning

off: 4 away, doff, gone **5** aside, wrong **6** absent, cuckoo, remote **7** distant, further, removed **8** launched, postpone

and on: **8** fitfully **10** in snatches **11** irregularly

base: bad **5** wrong **7** illegal **9** incorrect, out-of-line **10** unsuitable

beat: odd **5** kinky **6** far out **7** unusual **9** different **10** unorthodox

camera: **9** privately **13** in private life

chance: **10** likelihood **11** possibility

color: **4** blue, racy **5** spicy **6** risque, unwell **10** discordant, out-of-sorts, suggestive

key: **10** discordant

offal: **5** gurry, waste **6** refuse **7** carrion, garbage, hogwash, leaving, rubbish **8** gralloch

offend: sin, vex **4** hurt, miff **5** abuse, anger, annoy, grate, grill, pique, shock, wrong **6** attack, grieve, insult, revolt **7** affront, default, mortify, outrage, violate **8** trespass **9** disoblige, displease **10** transgress

offended: **4** sore **7** injured **8** insulted

offender: **7** culprit **8** criminal

offense: **5** crime, error, fault, guilt, malum **6** attack, felony, pritch **7** misdeed, umbrage **8** peccancy, trespass **9** indignity **10** aggression, peccadillo, resentment **11** delinquency, misdemeanor

civil: **4** tort **11** stellionate

law: **5** delit **6** delict **8** delictum

moral: **4** evil

offensive: bad **4** foul **5** fetid **6** attack, coarse, horrid **7** beastly, fulsome, hateful, noisome **8** invading **9** loathsome, obnoxious, repugnant **10** aggressive, disgusting, forbidding, ill-favored, scurrilous, ungracious, unpleasant **11** distasteful **12** disagreeable **13** objectionable

offer: bid, try **4** bode, show **6** adduce, allege, tender **7** advance, commend, hold out, present, proffer, propine, propose, suggest **8** bequeath, overture, proposal **9** avertment, volunteer

last: **9** ultimatum

solemn: **6** pledge

offering: **4** gift **6** corban, victim **7** present **9** sacrifice

religious: **5** tithe **7** deodate **8** anathema, oblation **12** contribution

sacrificial: **5** hiera **7** sphagia(pl.) **8** sphagion

offhand: **4** curt **6** casual **7** brusque **8** cavalier, informal **9** impromptu **10** improvised **11** extemporary **14** extemporaneous, unpremeditated **15** autoschediastic **16** extemporaneously

office: job **4** post, wike **5** place, wiken **6** bureau **7** camarin, station **8** function, high sign, position **9** bailiwick, situation **10** commission **11** appointment **13** collectorship

chief: **4** boss **7** manager

deprive of: **6** depose **7** impeach

divine: **9** akoluthia

help: **5** clerk **6** typist **9** secretary **12** stenographer

machine: **5** Xerox **6** copier **8** computer **9** stenotype **10** calculator, mimeograph, typewriter **11** comptometer

paid without work: **8** sinecure

purchase or sale: **8** barratry

put in again: **7** re-elect **9** re-instate

seeker of: **7** nominee **9** candidate **10** politician

officeholder: **6** winner **8** official, placeman **9** incumbent **10** bureaucrat

officer: **4** aide **5** usher **6** direct, ensign, manage, tindal **7** command, conduct, general **8** adjutant **9** executive

army: **5** major **7** captain, colonel, general **10** lieutenant

assistant: **4** aide

college: **4** dean **6** bursar **10** chancellor

future: **5** cadet **10** midshipman

law: cop **7** bailiff, marshal, sheriff **9** constable, detective, patrolman, policeman

naval: **4** mate **5** bosun **6** ensign, yeoman **7** admiral, captain, striper **9** boatswain, commander, commodore **10** lieutenant

noncommissioned: **4** mate **5** chief **8** corporal, sergeant

presiding: **6** archon **7** speaker **8** chairman **9** moderator, president

prison: **5** guard **6** warden

warrant: **5** bosun **9** boatswain

officers: **5** staff

official: **6** formal **9** escribano(Sp.), executive, ex officio **10** authorized, bureaucrat, ex cathedra, magistrate **11** ceremonious **13** authoritative

administrative: **5** reeve **9** executive

assistant: **4** aide

city or town: **5** mayor **7** manager, marshal **8** alderman **9** selectman **10** councilman

civil: **5** judge, mayor **7** bailiff, marshal, sheriff **8** governor **9** constable, patrolman, policeman, president **10** magistrate

corrupt: **7** grafter

despotic: **6** satrap

government: **6** syndic

judicial: **8** assessor, recorder **9** treasurer **11** comptroller

local: **6** bailie(Sc.), grieve **7** burgess

public: **6** notary

state: **8** minister **9** secretary

officiate: act **6** supply, umpire **7** perform, referee **9** celebrate

officious: **4** busy, cool, pert **6** formal **8** arrogant, impudent, informal, official **10** impersonal, meddlesome **11** efficacious, impertinent, pragmatical **12** contemptuous **14** supererogatory **16** superserviceable

offing: 6 future 7 by-and-by, picture 10 background

offset: 6 contra 7 balance 10 compensate, complement 12 counterpoise

offshoot: rod 5 bough, scion 6 branch, sprout 7 spin-off 9 by-product, outgrowth 10 descendant

offspring: fry, imp, kid, son 4 brat, chit, seed 5 brood, child, fruit, issue, scion 6 foster, result 7 outcome, produce, product, progeny 8 children, daughter, geniture 9 genealogy, youngster 10 descendant, generation

off the rack: 9 ready-made 11 ready-to-wear

oficina(Sp.): 5 works 6 office 7 factory 10 laboratory

oflete: 5 wafer 8 oblation, offering

often: 4 much 6 common 8 frequent, repeated 10 frequently 11 continually, over and over

ogdoad: 5 eight

ogee: See **molding**

Ogier: 4 Dane, hero 6 prince 8 Norseman

ogle: eye 4 gaze, leer, look 5 stare 7 examine 10 rubberneck

ogre: 5 demon, giant 6 tyrant, yaksha, yakshi 7 bugaboo, monster

ogress: 5 harpy, vixen 6 virago

ogygian: 7 ancient 8 primeval

oh: ach(G.) 4 ouch

Ohio: *capital:* 8 Columbus
  city: Ada 5 Akron, Berea, Cadiz, Niles, Xenia 6 Canton, Dayton, Lorain, Toledo 9 Sandusky 9 Cleveland 10 Cincinnati, Youngstown 11 Chillicothe 13 Yellow Springs
  county: 4 Lake 5 Allen, Clark 6 Butler, Lorain, Summit 8 Cuyahoga, Franklin, Hamilton
  Indian: 4 Erie 7 Wyandot
  lake: 4 Erie
  mountain range: 9 Allegheny
  nickname: 7 Buckeye
  river: 4 Ohio 5 Miami 6 Maumee, Scioto 7 Portage
  state bird: 8 cardinal
  state flower: 9 carnation
  state tree: 7 buckeye

oil: ben, fat ile 4 balm, fuel 5 bribe, oleum 6 aceite, anoint, chrism, grease 7 lanolin 8 flattery, soft soap 9 lubricate, petroleum
  blasting: 14 nitroglycerine
  bone: 6 olanin
  butter: 4 ghee, oleo
  cedar and juniper: 8 alkitran 9 alchitran
  coal: 8 photogen
  derived from: 5 elaic, oleic
  exporting group: 4 Opec
  in skin: 5 sebum
  linseed: 6 carron

liquid compound: 5 olein
mineral: 7 naphtha
orange-blossom: 6 neroli
pert. to: 5 oleic
plant: 6 sesame
prospector: 10 wildcatter
salt: 7 bittern
ship: 6 tanker
torch: 7 lucigen
vegetable: 8 macassar
vessel: 4 drum, olpe 5 cruet, cruse 6 tanker 7 cresset
well: 6 gusher
whale: 5 sperm

oil beetle: 5 meloe

oilbird: 8 guacharo

oil bottle: 5 cruet

oil fish: 7 escolar

oil lamp: 7 coal-oil 8 kerosene

oil plant: 6 sesame

oil rock: 5 shale 9 limestone

oil tree: 4 eboe, tung 5 mahwa

oil well: 6 gusher

oilcan: 5 oiler

oilcloth: 8 linoleum

oiler: 6 oilcan, tanker

oilseed: til 4 teel 6 sesame 7 linseed 8 rapeseed 10 castorbean, cottonseed

oilskin: 5 squam 7 slicker 8 raincoat

oilstone: 4 hone 5 shale 9 whetstone

oily: fat 4 glib 5 bland, fatty, soapy, suave 6 greasy, oleose, supple 7 fulsome, pinguid 8 slippery, unctuous 9 compliant, plausible 10 oleaginous 11 subservient

ointment: 4 balm, mull, nard 5 cream, salve 6 balsam, cerate 7 unguent 9 spikenard
  application: 11 embrocation
  Biblical: 9 spikenard
  dry: 9 xeromyron, xeromyrum
  hair: 6 pomade 7 pomatum
  oil: 6 carron, cerate 7 oleamen
  veterinary: 8 remolade 9 remoulade
  wax: 6 cerate

Oise tributary: 5 Aisne

Oisin's father: 4 Finn

ojo: 5 oasis

okay: yes 6 ratify 7 approve, consent, correct 10 acceptable

Okie: 7 migrant

Okinawa capital: 4 Naha

Oklahoma: *capital:* 12 Oklahoma City
  city: Ada 4 Enid 5 Tulsa 6 Lawton, Norman 8 Muskegee
  county: Kay 5 Atoka, Caddo 6 Carter 8 Comanche
  highest point: 9 Black Mesa
  Indian: 4 Otoe, Waco 7 Wichita 8 Tawkoni
  lake: 7 Eufaula
  mountain: 5 Ozark 6 Boston 7 Wichita 8 Ouachita

nickname: **6** Sooner
river: Red **4** Blue **5** Grand **7** Washita **8** Arkansas, Cimarron, Salt Fork **9** Verdigris
state bird: **10** flycatcher
state flower: **9** mistletoe
state tree: **6** redbud
okra: **4** soup **5** bendy, gumbo **8** hibiscus
old: agy, ald, eld **4** aged, auld **5** anile, hoary, stale **6** former, infirm, mature, senile, shabby **7** ancient, antique, archaic **8** lifelong, medieval, obsolete **9** doddering, hackneyed, long-lived, senescent, venerable **10** antiquated **11** experienced **12** antediluvian
old age: **10** senescence **11** senectitude
science of: **10** geriatrics
Old Bailey: **4** gaol, jail **6** prison
Old Bay State: **13** Massachusetts
old boy: man **6** alumni(pl.) **7** alumnus
Old Dominion State: **8** Virginia
Old Faithful: **6** geyser
old-fashioned: **5** glass, passe **6** drink, fogram, fogrum, quaint **7** ancient, antique, archaic **8** cocktail, obsolete **9** primitive **10** antiquated **13** horse-and-buggy
Old Franklin State: **9** Tennessee
Old Guard: **13** establishment
old hat: **5** dated, stale, trite **6** cliché **7** vintage **8** shopworn **9** hackneyed, out-of-date
Old Hickory: **13** Andrew Jackson
Old Line State: **8** Maryland
old maid: **8** cardgame, spinster
Old Noll: **14** Oliver Cromwell
Old Rough and Ready: **6** Taylor
Old Sod: **4** Erin **7** Ireland
Old Testament: See **Bible**
old-womanish: **5** anile
Old World: **6** Europe
ape: **6** baboon **10** catarrhina, catarrhine
carnivore: **5** genet
dish: **5** tansy
falcon: **5** saker
goat: **4** ibex
lizard: **5** agama **9** chameleon
mouse: **6** jerboa
olden: **6** bygone **7** ancient
older: **5** elder **6** senior **8** ancestor **11** forefathers **12** predecessors
oldest: **4** dean **6** eldest
olea: **5** olive
oleaginous: **4** oily **5** fatty **7** fulsome
oleander: **5** shrub **9** evergreen **12** rhododendron
olecranon: **5** ancon **9** funny bone
oleo: **9** margarine
oleoresin: **5** anime, elemi, tolus **7** copaiba **10** turpentine
oleum: oil
olfaction: **7** osmesis **8** smelling
olid: **4** gamy **5** fetid

olinda bug: **6** weevil
olio: **4** stew **6** medley **7** melange, mixture **8** mishmash **9** potpourri **10** collection, hodgepodge, miscellany **11** variety show
oliphant: **4** horn **8** elephant
olive: **4** olea **9** appetizer
enzyme: **6** olease
overripe: **5** drupe
pert. to: **9** oleaceous
stuffed: **6** pimola
wild: **8** oleaster
oliver: **6** hammer
olivet: **5** pearl
olla: jar, jug, pot
olivine: **10** chrysolite
ollapodrida: **4** hash, olio, olla, stew **6** medley **9** potpourri
olm: **7** proteus **10** salamander
ology: ism **7** science
oloroso: **6** sherry
olpe: **5** flask **6** vessel **7** pitcher
Olympic cupbearer: **4** Hebe **8** Ganymede
Olympus: *deity:* See **Greek:** *god*
pert. to: **7** exalted, godlike, Olympic **8** heavenly, majestic **9** celestial
Oman: *capital:* Muscat
monetary unit: rial
Omar Khayyam's country: **4** Iran **6** Persia
omber: **8** cardgame
ombudsman: **5** judge **8** mediator
omega: end **4** last **6** letter
omelet: **4** eggs **8** fooyung
omen: **4** bode, omen, sign **5** augur, boder, freet, freit, token **6** augury, handel, hansel **7** auspice, portent, presage, warning **8** bodement, forebode, foresign **9** foretoken **10** foreboding, forerunner, indication, prediction **11** premonition
ominous: **4** dour, grim **5** fatal **6** dismal **7** fateful, fearful **8** menacing, sinister **9** prophetic **10** inexorable, portentous **11** threatening
omission: cut **5** blank, chasm, error **7** default, failure **9** exclusion, oversight
mark of: **5** caret **7** ellipse **10** apostrophe
of vowel: **7** elision
tacit: **7** silence
omit: cut **4** balk, dele, drop, miss, skip, slip **5** abate, elide, spare **6** beleve, cancel, delete, except, forget, ignore **7** beleave, discard, neglect **8** overlook **9** disregard, pretermit
omneity: **7** allness **13** comprehensive
omnibus: **5** barge, whole **11** compilation
omnipotent: God **4** able **5** deity, great **6** arrant, mighty **8** almighty, powerful **9** unequaled, unlimited **11** all-powerful
omnipresent: **7** allover **10** everywhere, ubiquitous
omniscient: **4** wise **7** learned **8** powerful

10 all-knowing, allwitting **11** everpresent

omnitude: 7 allness **8** totality **12** universality

omoplate: 7 scapula

omphalos: hub **4** boss, knob **5** navel, novel **6** center **9** umbilical **10** focal point

Omri: *daughter:* **8** Athaliah
   successor: **4** Ahab

on: 4 atop, upon **5** about, above, ahead, along, anent **6** anenst, within **7** forward **10** concerning
   account of: for
   all sides: **5** about **6** around
   and on: **4** ever **7** endless, forever, tedious
   behalf: for
   other side: **4** over **6** across

on the contrary: 6 rather

on the other hand: but **7** however **8** although **11** nonetheless **12** contrariwise, nevertheless

on time: 6 prompt

on what account: why

Ona: 7 Fuegian

onager: ass **5** kiang **8** catapult

Onam's son: 4 Jada **7** Shammai

once: ane(Sc.) **4** erst, past **5** aince(Sc.) **6** former **7** quondam **8** formerly, one time, whenever
   in a while: **9** sometimes **12** occasionally
   more: **4** anew, echo **5** again **6** encore, repeat
   over: **6** glance, survey **10** inspection
   upon a time: **8** formerly

oncorhynchus: 6 salmon

one: ain(Sc.), ein(G.), tae(Sc.), una, une(F.), yae(Sc.) **4** same, sole, some, unal, unit **5** alone, unity **6** person, single, unique, united **7** numeral, pronoun **8** unbroken **9** singleton, undivided, unmarried **10** individual
   after another: **8** serially, seriatim **11** consecutive **12** successively
   by one: **6** apiece, singly **10** separately

one-chambered: 10 unicameral

one-colored: 13 monochromatic

one-footed: 6 uniped

one-sided: 6 biased, uneven, unfair, unjust **7** bigoted, partial **10** prejudiced, unilateral

one-spot: 4 buck **6** dollar

one tenth: 5 tithe

one thousand: mil

one twenty-fourth: 5 carat

onegite: 8 amethyst

one-horse: 5 petty **6** little

O'Neill, Eugene: 9 dramatist
   character: **4** Anna, Nina, Orin, Yank **5** Brant **7** Christine, Lavinia
   play: Ile **11** The Hairy Ape **12** Ah, Wilderness, Anna Christie, Emperor Jones **15** The Iceman Cometh

oneism: 6 egoism, monism

oneness: 7 concord **8** identity, sameness **9** agreement **11** singularity

onerous: 4 hard **5** heavy **7** arduous, onerose **8** exacting **9** laborious **10** burdensome, cumbersome, oppressive

onetime: 7 quondam **8** formerly

one-upmanship: 7 cunning, **11** competition, superiority

onfall: 5 onset **6** attack

ongoing: 6 course **9** improving, operating **10** progressive

onion: 4 boll, cepa, leek **5** cibol, peral **7** Bermuda, onionet, shallot **8** eschalot, rareripe, scallion
   genus: **6** allium

onlooker: 5 gazer **7** witness **8** audience, beholder **9** bystander, spectator **10** rubberneck

only: 4 just, lone, mere, sole **5** afald **6** anerly, barely, merely, simple, single, singly, solely **9** allenarly, excepting **11** exclusively

onomasticon: 7 lexicon **10** dictionary

onomatopoeic: 5 mimic **6** echoic **9** imitative

onset: 4 dash, dint, fard, rese, rush **5** braid, brunt, faird, frush, start **6** attack, charge **7** assault, attempt, brattle **9** beginning, encounter, onslaught **12** commencement

onslaught: 5 onset **6** attack **7** assault, descent

Ontario: *bay:* **8** Georgian
   capital: **7** Toronto
   city: **6** London, Ottawa **7** Windsor **8** Hamilton **9** Kitchener
   fort: **5** George, Henry
   highest point: **9** Ogidaki Mt.
   lake: **4** Erie, Seul **5** Eagle, Rainy **7** Ontario **8** St. Joseph
   province of: **6** Canada
   provincial flower: **8** trillium
   river: **5** Grand, Moose, Trent **6** Thames

onto: 4 atop **6** aboard

onus: 4 duty, load **6** burden, charge, stigma **10** obligation

onward: 4 away **5** ahead, along, forth **7** forward

onyx: 5 black **10** chalcedony

oodles: 4 heap **5** scads **8** lashings **9** abundance

oolong: tea

oomph: vim **5** drive, verve, vigor **6** energy pizazz, spirit **8** strength, vitality

oopak: tea

oorial: sha **5** sheep

ooze: bog, mud **4** drip, leak, mire, seep, slob **5** exude, gleet, marsh, slime, weeze **6** sludge **8** transude **9** percolate

opah: 4 fish **5** cravo

opal: gem **5** noble, resin **7** girasol, hyalite **8** girasole **10** chalcedony
   girasole: **10** chalcedony

variety: **8** menilite **9** cacholong

opalescent: 7 opaline **8** irisated **10** iridescent

opaque: 4 dark, dull **5** dense **6** obtuse, stupid **7** obscure **8** eyeshade **10** lightproof **14** unintelligible

open: dup, ope **4** ajar, flue, free, undo **5** agape, apert, begin, clear, frank, lance, overt, naked, plain, start, untie **6** candid, direct, expand, expose, honest, liable, patent, unbolt, unfold, unfurl, unlock, unseal, unstop **7** artless, dispart, obvious, sincere, unclose **8** apparent, commence, disclose, disspread, explicit, extended, initiate, manifest, patulous, unfasten **9** disspread, originate, uncovered **10** accessible, forthright, inaugurate, unreserved **11** susceptible, unconcealed, within reach **13** undissembling **15** straightforward

bursting: **10** dehiscence

fully: **4** wide **5** agape **7** yawning **9** dehiscent, full-blown

partly: mid **4** ajar

open-and-shut: 7 evident **10** guaranteed

open air: 8 al fresco

open bar: 10 free drinks

open door: 6 entree **11** hospitality

open-eyed: 5 awake **8** vigilant, watchful **9** receptive **10** astonished, discerning

opener: key **4** knob **5** latch **6** sesame **8** aperient

openhanded: 4 free **7** liberal **8** generous **9** receptive **10** munificent

opening: os; gap, ora(pl.) **4** bore, door, fent, gate, hole, pass, rift, rima, slit, slot, span, vent **5** brack, cleft, debut, mouth, start, width **6** avenue, breach, hiatus, lacuna, outlet, portal, spread **7** crevice, fissure, orifice **8** aperture, overture **11** opportunity

enlarge: **4** ream

escape: **4** muse **5** batch, meuse

having: **10** fenestrate

in chess: **6** gambit

mouth-like: **5** stoma **7** stomata(pl.)

slitlike: **4** rima

small: **4** pore **5** chink **6** cranny, eyelet **7** foramen, pinhole **8** foramina(pl.)

openmouthed: 6 amazed, gaping, greedy **8** ravenous **9** clamorous **10** vociferous

openwork: 7 tracery

opera: 4 Aida **5** Faust **6** Boheme, Carmen, Otello **7** Fidelio **8** Falstaff, Parsifal, Traviata, Walkyrie **9** Lohengrin, Pagliacci, Rheingold, Rigoletto, Trovatore **10** Magic Flute, Tannhauser **11** Don Giovanni **16** Marriage of Figaro

comic: **5** buffa

division: **5** scena

glasses: **9** lorgnette **10** binoculars

horse: **7** Western

kind: **4** soap **5** comic, horse **8** burletta

part: **4** aria

singer: **4** Bori, Pons **5** Eames, Gigli, Melba, Patti, Sills **6** Callas, Caruso, Farrar **8** Flagstad **9** Pavarotti **10** Sutherland

soap: **6** serial **9** melodrama

solo: **4** aria

song: **4** aria **7** sortita **8** cavatina **9** cabaletta

star: **4** diva

opera house: 7 theater

operate: act, man, run, use **4** work **6** affect, effect, manage, open up **7** conduct **10** accomplish

by hand: **10** manipulate

operation: use **4** deed **6** agency **7** process, surgery **8** creation, exercise, function **9** actuation, influence, procedure **10** production **11** maintenance, transaction

operative: 4 hand, open **6** active, artist **7** artisan **8** mechanic **9** detective

beyond itself: **9** transeunt

for past: **11** retroactive

operator: 5 agent, quack **6** dealer, driver **7** manager, operant, surgeon **8** motorist **9** conductor, operative **10** mountebank

operculum: lid **4** flap **8** covering

operose: 4 busy, hard **8** diligent **9** assiduous, laborious **11** industrious

ophidian: asp, eel **5** snake **6** conger **7** reptile, serpent

ophthalmic: 6 ocular

opiate: 4 dope, drug, hemp **5** dwale, opium **6** deaden **7** anodine, anodyne **8** hypnotic, narcotic **9** paregoric

opificer: 7 workman **9** artificer

opine: 4 deem, hold **5** judge, think **6** ponder **7** suppose

opinion: 4 idea, view, ween **5** dicta(pl.), guess, tenet **6** advice, belief, dictum, esteem, notion, repute **7** concept, feeling, thought **8** decision, doctrine, estimate, judgment **9** sentiment **10** conjecture, conviction, deposition, estimation, expression, evaluation, impression, persuasion, point of view **12** apprehension

erroneous: **13** misconception

expression: **4** vote

preconceived: **9** prejudice

united: **9** unanimous

unorthodox: **6** heresy

opinionated: 6 biased **8** dogmatic **9** conceited, obstinate **11** dictatorial

opinions: *collected:* **9** anthology, symposium

professed: **5** credo

opium: 4 dope, drug **10** intoxicant

addiction: **8** thebaism

alkaloid: **6** codein **7** codeine **8** morphine, narcotin **9** narcotine, papaverin **10** papaverine

camphorate tincture: **9** paregoric

concentrated form: 6 heroin
derivative: 7 meconic
Egyptian: 8 thebaine
poppy seed: maw
prepared: 6 chandu 7 chandoo
source: 5 poppy
opossum: 9 marsupial
kin: 8 kangaroo
water: 5 yapok 6 yapock
oppidan: 5 civic, urban 8 townsman
opponent: foe 5 enemy, rival 7 opposer 9 adversary, assailant 10 antagonist
opportune: fit, pat 5 ready 6 timely 8 suitable 9 favorable, well-timed 10 auspicious, convenient, favourable, seasonable 11 appropriate
opportunely: 7 apropos, happily
opportunity: 4 hent, turn 5 break, slant 6 chance, look-in 7 opening 8 occasion 9 advantage 12 circumstance
oppose: pit, vie 4 buck, cope, face, meet, stem, wear 5 argue, block, check, cross, fight, front, match, rebel, rebut, repel 6 breast, combat, object, oppugn, resist 7 contest, counter, gainsay 8 conflict, confront, contrast, frontier, obstruct 9 encounter, withstand 10 calcitrate, contradict, contravene, controvert
opposed: 4 anti 5 alien 6 averse 7 adverse, against, counter, hostile 8 contrary 11 contrariant
opposite: 5 anent, polar 6 across, anenst, averse, contra, facing 7 adverse, counter, inverse, reverse 8 antipode, antipole, contrary, contrast, converse 9 antipodal, repugnant 10 antipodean 12 antagonistic 13 contradictory
opposite to: 7 abreast, subtend
opposition: 5 enemy, atilt 9 animosity, collision, hostility, renitency 10 antagonism, resistance 11 contrariety
oppress 4 load, rape, thew 5 crush, grind, weigh, wrong 6 burden, defoil, defoul, extort, harass, harrow, ravish, subdue 7 afflict, depress, overlay, repress, trample 8 distress, encumber, pressure, suppress 9 constrain, overpower, overthrow, overwhelm, subjugate, weigh down 10 extinguish
oppressed: 5 laden 7 servile 9 debruised 10 heavy-laden 11 downtrodden
oppression: 8 dullness 9 grievance, lassitude 10 affliction 11 obscuration
oppressive: 4 dire, hard 5 close, harsh, heavy 6 gloomy, severe 7 onerous 8 rigorous 10 hardhanded 11 gravaminous, heavyhanded, overbearing 12 extortionate
oppressor: 4 csar, czar, Nero, tsar, tzar 6 tyrant
opprobrium: 5 abuse, odium, scorn 6 infamy, insult 7 calumny, contempt, offense, scandal 8 disgrace, dishonor, reproach 9 contumely 10 disrespect, scurrility
oppugn: 6 oppose 7 contend 10 contradict
oppugnacy: 9 hostility 10 antagonism
Ops (see also **Rhea**): *associate:* 6 Consus
consort: 6 Saturn
daughter: 5 Ceres
festival: 6 opalia
son: 4 Zeus 8 Poseidon
opt: 4 cull, pick 5 elect 6 choose, decide, select
optical: 6 ocular, visual
instrument: 4 lens 7 alidade 9 eriometer, magnifier, optometer, periscope, telescope 10 microscope 11 stereoscope 15 ultramicroscope
organ: eye
optimist: 5 hoper 7 dreamer 8 idealist 9 Pollyanna 10 positivist
optimistic: 4 rosy 6 joyous 7 hopeful, roseate 8 sanguine
option: 5 right 6 choice 9 privilege 10 free choice 11 alternative
optional: 4 free 8 elective 9 voluntary 10 permissive 13 discretionary
opulent: fat 4 rich 5 ample 6 lavish 7 profuse, wealthy 8 abundant, affluent 9 luxuriant, plentiful 11 extravagant
opus: 4 book, work 5 etude, study 11 composition
overlabored: 11 lucubration
oquassa: 5 trout
or: aut(L.), ere 6 either 11 alternative
heraldry: 4 gold 6 yellow
oracle: 4 seer 5 maxim, sibyl 7 prophet, wise man
pert. to: 8 pythonic 9 prophetic
oracular: 4 otic 5 vatic 7 vatical 9 prophetic 10 mysterious 11 dictatorial 13 authoritative
orage: 5 storm 7 tempest
oral: 4 exam 5 aloud, parol, vocal 6 sonant, spoken, verbal 7 uttered 9 unwritten 10 acroamatic 11 word-of-mouth
orange: 4 mock 5 chino, color, hedge, Jaffa, navel, Osage 6 bodock, Temple 7 Seville 8 bergamot, chinotti, mandarin, Valencia 9 tangerine
genus: 6 citrus
heraldry: 5 tenne
membrance: 4 zest
mock: 7 seringa, syringa, syringe
piece: 4 lith(Sc.) 7 segment
red: 7 saffron
seed: pip
seedless: 5 navel
variety: 5 blood, navel, osage 7 Seville
Orange Bowl site: 5 Miami
orange-flower oil: 6 neroli

orange-shaped: 6 oblate
orangeberry: 9 cranberry
orangebird: 7 tanager
orangelike fruit: bel **9** tangerine
orangutan: ape **4** mias **5** pongo, satyr **7** primate
orate: 5 plead, speak, spiel, spout **7** address, declaim, lecture **8** bloviate, harangue **9** discourse, speechify **10** filibuster **11** expostulate
oration: 6 sermon **7** address, concion **9** discourse, panegyric
  funeral: **5** eloge **6** eulogy **7** elogium, encomia(pl.) **8** encomium
orator: 6 rhetor **7** demagog, speaker **8** cicerone, ciceroni(pl.) **9** demagogue, plaintiff **10** petitioner **11** rhetorician, spellbinder
oratorian: 6 priest
oratorical: 8 eloquent **10** articulate, rhetorical
oratorio: 7 Messiah, Seasons
  coda in: **7** stretto
oratory: 6 chapel **8** rhetoric **9** elocution, eloquence
orb: eye, sun **4** ball, moon, star **5** earth, globe **6** circle, planet, sphere **7** circuit, enclose
orbed: 5 lunar, round
orbit: 4 path **5** range, scope, track **6** circle, domain, socket **7** circuit, ellipse, revolve
  point: **5** apsis, syzgy **6** apogee, epigee **7** perigee
orc: 4 orca **5** whale **6** dragon **7** grampus
orchard: 4 farm **5** arbor, grove **6** garden, huerta **8** arbustum **9** enclosure **10** plantation
orchestra: 4 band **5** group **8** ensemble, symphony
  section: **4** wind, wood **5** brass **6** string **7** timpany **8** woodwind **10** percussion
orchestra bells: 12 glockenspiel
orchestra circle: 7 parquet **8** parterre
orchestrate: 5 score **7** arrange, compose **9** harmonize
orchid: 5 faham, petal, vanda **6** flower, praise, purple **7** aerides, calypso, lycaste, pogonia, vanilla **8** arethusa, labellum **10** compliment
  appendage: **8** caudicle
  dried tubers: **5** salep
  genus of: **5** vanda **6** laelia **10** gymnadenia **14** gymnadeniopsis
  leaves: **5** faham
  meal: **5** salep
  petal: lip **8** labellum
  tuber: **5** salep **7** cullion
Orcus: See **Hades**
ordain: 4 deem **5** allot, enact, order **6** decree **7** adjudge, appoint, arrange, behight, command **7** conduct, destine, in-

stall, prepare **9** establish, prescribe **10** adjudicate, commission, constitute
ordeal: 4 gaff, test **5** trial **10** experience **11** tribulation
order: ban, bid **4** boon, fiat, form, ordo, rank, rule, sect, type, will **5** align, array, class, dight, edict, genus, grade, guide **6** billet, charge, cosmos, decree, degree, demand, direct, enjoin, extent, genera(pl.), graith, kilter, manage, method, ordain, police, series, system **7** adjudge, arrange, bespeak, bidding, command, compose, dispose, embargo, mandate, ordines(pl.), precept, process, society **8** decision, neatness, organize, regulate **9** direction, directive, magnitude, procedure **10** injunction, put in shape, succession **11** appointment, arrangement, association, instruction
  back: **6** remand **8** recommit
  connected: **8** seriatim
  cosmic: tao **4** rita
  good: **6** eutaxy **7** eutaxie
  grammar: **5** taxis
  lacking: **5** amiss, chaos, messy, mussy **7** anarchy, chaotic, clutter, unkempt **8** confused **10** disarrayed
  law: **4** writ **7** summons **8** subpoena
  of business: **6** agenda, docket
  of preference: **8** priority
  parliamentary: **9** procedure
  writ: **7** precipe
orderly: 4 aide, neat, tidy, trim **6** batman **7** regular **8** decorous, obedient **9** peaceable, regulated, shipshape **10** law-abiding, methodical, systematic **11** well-behaved
ordinal: 4 book **6** number **7** regular
ordinance: law **4** doom, fiat, rite **5** bylaw, edict **6** assize, decree **7** control, decreta(pl.), statute **8** decretum **9** direction, prescript, sacrament **10** management, regulation **11** appointment
ordinary: 4 lala, ruck, so-so **5** nomic, plain, prose, usual **6** common, normal **7** average, natural, prosaic, trivial, vulgate **8** everyday, familiar, frequent, habitual, mediocre **9** customary, plain Jane **11** commonplace
ordnance: 4 guns **5** armor, orgue **6** petard **7** weapons **8** basilisk, supplies **9** artillery, torpedoes **10** ammunition, serpentine
ordo: 7 almanac
ore (see also **mineral**): tin **4** gold, iron, lead **5** metal **6** copper, silver **7** mineral **8** platinum
  crusher: **5** dolly
  deposit: **4** lode, vein **5** scrin **7** bonanza
  fusing: **8** smelting
  horizontal layer: **5** stope
  impure: **6** speiss **7** halvana

iron: **5** ocher, ochre **8** hematite **9** magnetite

layer: **4** seam **5** stope

lead: **6** galena

loading platform: **4** plat

mercury: **8** cinnabar

refuse: **4** slag **5** dross **6** scoria **8** tailings

separator: **6** vanner

silver: **10** stephanite

sluice: **5** trunk

tin: **5** scove

tungsten: **4** cals

washing trough: **6** strake

worthless: **5** matte

oread: 4 peri **5** nymph

Oregon: *capital:* **5** Salem

 city: **6** Eugene **8** Portland

 county: **4** Coos **5** Cutty **7** Gilliam, Klamath, Hamhill **8** Umatilla

 early explorer: **8** Coronado

 highest peak: **6** Mt. Hood

 Indian: **4** Coos **8** Cherokee

 motto: **8** The Union

 mountain range: **4** Blue **5** Coast **7** Cascade, Wallowa

 nickname: **6** Beaver

 river: **5** Snake **8** Columbia **9** Deschutes

 state bird: **10** meadowlark

 state flower: **5** grape

 state tree: fir

oreortyx: 5 quail

Orestes: *father:* **9** Agamemnon

 friend: **7** Pylades

 mother: **12** Clytemnestra

 sister: **7** Electra **9** Iphigenia

 victim: **9** Aegisthus **12** Clytemnestra

 wife: **8** Hermione

orfe: ide **4** fish **5** dusky

orfevrerie: 7 jewelry

organ: 6 medium **7** journal, vehicle **8** magazine **9** equipment **10** instrument, periodical

 auricular: ear

 barrel: **8** autophon **10** hurdy-gurdy

 bristle-like: **4** seta

 cactus: **7** saguaro

 desk: **7** console

 elongated: **8** tentacle

 essential: **5** brain, heart, liver, lungs **6** viscus **7** viscera(pl.)

 fish: **8** drumfish

 flutter device: **7** tremolo

 footlike: pes

 gallery: **4** loft

 interlude: **6** verset

 lymphoid: **6** tonsil

 mouth: **9** harmonica

 note: **9** tremolant

 of insect: **7** stinger

 of living bodies: **8** organism

 of motion: **6** muscle

 of volition: **5** manas

olfactory: **4** nare, nose

opening: os; ora(pl.)

optical: eye

part: **4** reed, stop

piano: **9** melopiano

pipe: **4** reed **5** flute **7** mixture

portable: **5** regal

prelude: **6** verset

reed: **9** harmonium

respiratory: **4** lung

sawlike: **5** serra

secreting: **5** gland

sensory: ear, eye **4** nose

speech: lip **6** throat, tongue

tactile: **6** feeler

organ stop: 5 quint, viola **7** aeoline, celesta, tertian **8** diapason, dulciana, gemshorn, register **9** philomela, rohrflute **10** quindecima

 adjust: **10** registrate

 bell-like: **8** carillon

 labial: **7** melodia

 reed: **4** oboe **7** bassoon **8** possaune

 storm-imitating: **5** orage

 string: **5** gamba

 two banks of pipes: **7** tertian

organbird: 4 wren **6** magpie

organdy: 6 muslin

organic: 5 vital **6** inborn **7** natural **8** inherent **9** organlike **11** fundamental **14** constitutional

 body: **5** zooid

 compound: **5** amine, ketol

 radical: **5** ethyl

organism: 5 plant **6** aerobe, animal, entity

 bacterial: **4** germ **7** microbe

 body: **4** soma **6** somata(pl.)

 elementary: **5** monad

 minute: **5** ameba, monad, spore

 pelagic: **6** nekton

 process: **6** miosis **7** meiosis

 vegetable: **4** tree **5** plant

organization: 5 setup **11** association, disposition **12** constitution

 business: **4** firm **5** guild **11** cooperative, corporation, partnership **13** establishment

 college: **4** frat **6** alumna, alumni(pl.) **7** alumnus **8** sorority **10** fraternity

 lack of: **5** chaos

 political: **4** bloc **5** party **7** machine

 secret: K.O.P., P.E.O., W.O.W. **4** B.P.O.E., Elks, frat **5** lodge, mafia, Moose **6** apache, maffia, Masons **8** sorority **9** Foresters, Maccabees **10** fraternity, Freemasons **11** underground

 skeleton: **5** cadre

 social: **4** club **5** forum

 veterans: A.V.C., D.A.V., G.A.R., S.A.R., V.F.W. **5** Fidac **6** AMVETS **14** American Legion **21** Veterans of Foreign Wars *women's:* D.A.R., W.A.F., W.R.C. **8** sorority

organize: 4 form, plan **5** edify, set up **6** embody **7** arrange **8** regiment

organized: 7 planned **8** arranged **10** systematic

orgy: 4 lark, romp **5** binge, revel, spree **6** frolic, shindy **7** rampage, revelry, wassail **8** carousal, ceremony **9** bacchanal **10** observance **11** celebration, merrymaking

Oriana: *father:* **8** Lisuarte
  lover: **6** Amadis

oribi: 8 antelope, bleekbok

oriel: bay **6** recess, window **7** balcony, gallery, portico **8** corridor

orient: 4 dawn **5** adapt, place **6** adjust, locate **7** sunrise **11** accommodate

Orient: 4 Asia, East **6** Levant **7** Far East **8** Near East

Oriental: *animal:* **4** zebu
  archangel: **5** Uriel
  bearer: **5** hamal
  beverage: **6** arrack
  bow: **6** salaam
  calculator: **6** abacus
  cap: **7** calpack
  caravansary: **4** khan **5** serai **6** imaret
  carriage: **4** sado **10** jinricksha **11** jinrickshaw
  cart: **5** araba
  chief: **4** khan
  Christian: **4** Uniat
  coin: sen, yen **4** para, yuan **5** dinar, sapek
  commander: ras **4** amir, emir, rais, reis **5** ameer, emeer
  corn: **4** para
  cosmetic: **4** kohl
  council: **5** Divan
  cymbal: tal, zel
  deity: Bel
  destiny: **6** Kismet
  disease: **8** beri-beri
  dish: **5** pilaf, pilau, pilaw
  drug: **4** hemp **6** heroin, opium **7** hashish
  drum: **7** anacara
  dulcimer: **6** santir
  dwelling: dar
  emperor: **6** sultan
  exercise: **4** judo, yoga **8** jiujitsu
  fan: ogi **5** punka
  fish: koi, tai
  food: **4** rice **5** salep **8** beancurd
  garment: aba
  gate: dar
  guitar: **5** sitar
  inn: **5** serai **11** caravansary
  liquor: **4** sake, saki
  litter: **5** dooli, dooly **6** dooley, doolie
  lute: tar
  manservant: **5** hamal
  mansion: **5** yamen

market: **5** bazar **6** bazaar
measure: dra, mao
measure of weight: **4** kati, rotl, tael **5** abbas, bhaar, catty, picul **6** cantar, kantar, miskal
money of account: rin
monkey: **7** macaque
musical instrument: tar **5** sitar, surna, suray **6** santir **7** anacara, samisen
name: Ali
nomad: **5** Tatar **6** Tartar
nurse: **4** amah, ayah
oboe: **5** surna, suray
pagoda: tea
people: Tai, Tho **4** Sere **5** Asian, Tatar **6** Indian, Korean, Muslim, Tartar **7** Chinese, Eastern **8** Japanese **9** Easterner, Levantine **10** Mohammedan
pine: **5** matsu
pipe: **7** nargile **8** harghile, nargileh
plane-tree: **7** cheenar
porter: **5** hamal
rest house: **4** khan **5** serai
rice dish: **5** pilaf, pilau, pilaw
rice paste: ame
ruler: **4** amir, emir, khan, shah **5** ameer, calif, emeer **6** caliph, sultan
saber: **6** tulwar **7** tulwaur **8** scimitar
sailor: **6** calash, lascar
salutation: **5** saheb, salam **6** kowtow, salaam
sash: obi
sauce: soy
sea captain: ras **4** rais, reis
shoe: **6** sandal
shrub: tea **5** henna **9** wineberry
silkworm: **6** tussah, tusseh, tusser **7** tussore
slipper: **7** baboosh **8** babouche
smoking apparatus: **7** nargile **8** narghile, nargileh
sword: **8** scimitar
tale: **7** Ali Baba **13** Arabian Nights
tamarisk: **4** atle **5** atlee
tambourine: **5** daira
taxi: **7** ricksha **8** rickshaw
tea: cha
title: aga **4** amir, baba **5** pasha **6** huzoor
tower: **6** pagoda
tree: **4** atle **5** atlee
vessel: **4** dhow, saic
wagon: **5** araba
weight: **4** mann, tael **5** artal(pl.), catty, liang
whip: **6** chabuk **7** chabouk
wind: **7** monsoon
worker: **5** cooly **6** coolie

oriental: 5 pearl **6** bright, ortive, rising **7** eastern, shining **8** lustrous, pellucid, precious **9** ascending, brilliant **11** resplendent

Oriental rug: 4 Baku, Kali **5** Herez, Ma-

hal, Saruk, Senna, Sumak **6** Kashan, Kerman, Kirman, Meshed, Pamiri, Sarouk, Shiraz, Soumak, Tabriz **7** Bokhara, Bukhara, Chinese, Hamadan, Isfahan, Ispahan, Karajas, Meshhed **8** Lerestan, Sedjadeh **9** Kurdistan **10** Kermanshah
pattern: **7** ainaleh
variation: **6** abrash
orifice: **4** hole, vent **5** inlet, mouth **6** cavity, outlet **7** chimney, opening, ostiole **8** aperture
in brain: **4** lura
origin: nee **4** rise, root, seed **5** birth, cause, start **6** nature, parent, source **7** genesis, lineage **8** ancestry, nascence, nascency **9** beginning, inception, naissance, parentage, paternity **10** extraction, incunabula(pl.) **11** incunabulum, provenience **12** commencement, fountainhead
foreign: **7** ecdemic
of words: **9** etymology
on earth: **7** epigene
original: new **5** first, model, novel **6** fontal, native, primal, primer **7** primary **8** pristine **9** authentic, eccentric, inventive, primitive, prototype **10** aboriginal, innovative **11** fundamental, primigenial
originally: **5** first **9** initially, primarily **10** inherently
originate: **4** coin, make, open, rise **5** arise, begin, breed, cause, found, start **6** create, derive, devise, invent, spring **7** causate, emanate, produce **8** come from, commence, contrive, discover, generate, initiate **9** construct, establish, institute, introduce
originator: **6** author **7** creator **8** inventor **9** architect, innovator
oriole: *golden:* **5** pirol **6** loriot
Orion: **5** Rigel **13** constellation
hound: **6** Aratus
slayer: **5** Diana **7** Artemis
orison: **6** prayer
Orkney Island: *bay:* **9** Scapa Flow
capital: **8** Kirkwall
fishing ground: **4** haaf
hut: **4** skio
inlet: voe
island: Hoy **6** Pomona, Rousay, Sanday **8** Stronsay
land: **4** odal, udal **6** udaler **7** udalman **8** udalborn
largest: **6** Pomona
tower: **5** broch
orle: **6** border, fillet, wreath **7** bearing, chaplet
orlean: **7** annatto
orlop: **4** deck
ormer: **7** abalone

ormolu: **4** gilt, gold **5** alloy **6** mosaic **7** varnish
ornament (see also **decoration**): dub, fob, pin **4** etch, gaud, gear, tool, trim, waly **5** adorn, braid, chase, decor, gutta, inlay, wally **6** amulet, attire, bedaub, bedeck, billet, brooch, edging, emboss, enrich, finery, flower **7** agremen, engrave, enrich, garnish, spangle, trinket **8** agrement, applique, decorate, flourish, lavalier **9** arabesque, billiment, embellish, embroider, lavaliere **10** decorament, furnishing, habiliment, lavalliere
apex: **6** finial
bell-shaped: **9** clochette
Biblical: **4** Urim
boat-shaped: nef
claw-like: **6** griffe
crescent-shaped: **6** lunula **7** lunette, lunulae(pl.)
delicate: **7** tracery
dress: **4** frog, lace **5** jabot **6** bar-pin, sequin, zequin **7** spangle **8** chequeen, zecchino **10** embroidery
flower-like: **6** anadem **7** rosette
hanging: **6** bangle, fringe, tassel **7** earring, pendant
magical: **6** amulet
mantel: **7** bibelot
neck: **5** chain **6** choker, gorget **8** necklace **9** lavaliere
pagoda: tee
protuberant: **4** boss
scroll-like: **6** volute
shoulder: **7** epaulet
silver: **6** tinsel
spiral: **5** helix **7** helices(pl.)
tufted: **6** pompon, tassel **7** rosette
ornamental: **5** fancy **6** chichi, frilly **7** elegant **8** fanciful **10** decorative
ornamented: **6** figury, ornate, tawdry **9** elaborate
ornate: gay **4** fine **5** fancy, showy **6** florid, rococo **7** aureate, baroque, flowery **8** overdone **9** elaborate, unnatural **10** flamboyant **11** overadorned
ornery: **4** mean **7** crabbed **8** contrary, stubborn **9** irritable **12** cantankerous
ornithologist: **7** Audubon, birdman
ornithon: **6** aviary
orogeny: **8** upheaval
orotund: **4** full, loud **5** clear, showy **6** mellow, strong **7** pompous **8** resonant **9** bombastic **10** stentorian
Orozco specialty: **5** mural
orp: **4** fret, weep
orphan: **4** waif **5** Annie **7** cast-off **9** foundling
orpheum: **7** theater
Orpheus: *birthplace:* **6** Pieria
father: **6** Apollo
instrument: **4** lyre

mother: **8** Calliope
wife: **8** Eurydice
orphrey: 4 band **6** border **10** embroidery
orpiment: 7 arsenic
orpit: 7 fretful
orris: 4 gimp, iris, lace **5** braid **7** galloon
ort: bit **5** crumb, scrap **6** morsel, refuse **7** leaving, remnant **8** fragment, leftover
orthodox: 4 good **6** proper **7** canonic, correct **8** accepted, approved, standard **9** canonical, customary **12** conservative, conventional
orthographer: 7 speller
ortolan: 4 bird, rail **7** bunting **8** bobolink, wheatear
ortstein: 7 bedrock, hardpan
oryx: 7 gazelle, gemsbok **8** antelope
os: 4 bone **5** eskar, esker, mouth **7** opening, orifice
Osaka Bay port: 4 Kobe
oscillate: wag **4** rock, sway, vary **5** swing, waver, weave **7** vibrate **9** fluctuate, vacillate
oscitant: 4 dull **6** drowsy, gaping, sleepy, stupid **7** yawning **8** careless, sluggish **9** apathetic
osculate: 4 buss, kiss
osier: rod **4** wand **5** skein **6** basket, sallow, willow **7** dogwood, wilgers
Osiris: *brother:* Set **4** Seth
crown: **4** atef
enemy: Set **4** Seth **7** brother
father: Geb, Keb, Seb
mother: Nut
recorder: **5** Thoth
sister: **4** Isis
son: **5** Horus **6** Anubis
wife: **4** Isis
Osmanli: 4 Turk
osmesis: 8 smelling **9** olfaction
osmosis: 9 diffusion **10** absorption **12** assimilation
osprey: 4 hawk **9** ossifrage **11** feather trim
osseous: 4 bony **6** osteal, spring
ossicle: 4 bone **5** incus **6** stapes **7** bonelet, malleus
ossify: set **6** harden
osso buco: 10 veal shanks
ossuary: urn **4** tomb **5** vault **10** depository, receptacle
ostend: 4 show **6** reveal **7** exhibit **8** manifest **11** demonstrate
ostensible: 7 alleged, seeming **8** apparent, specious **9** pretended, professed
ostensorium: pix, pyx **10** monstrance
ostentation: 4 show **5** eclat, flare **6** parade **7** display, flutter, pageant, portent, presage **8** flourish, pretense **9** showiness, spectacle **10** exhibition **11** fanfaronade
ostentatious: 4 arty, loud **5** gaudy, showy

6 sporty **7** obvious, pompous, splashy **8** fastuous **9** elaborate, flaunting **10** flamboyant **11** pretentious
osteoma: 5 tumor
osteria: inn **6** tavern **10** restaurant
ostiole: 4 pore **5** stoma **7** opening, orifice **8** aperture
ostracize: bar, cut **4** snub **5** exile **6** banish, reject **7** exclude **9** blackball, proscribe **10** expatriate
ostracon: 5 shell **8** fragment, potsherd
ostrich: 4 rhea **5** nandu
extinct: moa
feather: boa, boo **5** plume
ostrichlike bird: emu **4** emeu
otalgia: 7 earache
otary: 4 seal
Othello: 4 Moor
character in play: **6** Bianca, Cassio, Emilia
friend: **4** Iago
wife: **9** Desdemona
other: 4 else, more **5** ither(Sc.) **6** former, second **7** further **8** distinct **9** different, remaining **10** additional
other-worldly: fey **9** imaginary, spiritual **12** supernatural, transmundane
otherness: 8 alterity **9** diversity **13** dissimilarity
others: 4 rest
and: **4** et al **6** et alii
otherwise: 4 else **5** alias **6** aliter **11** differently
otic: 5 aural **8** auditory **9** auricular
otiose: 4 idle, lazy, vain **6** futile, otiant **7** sterile, surplus, useless **8** inactive, indolent, reposing **10** unemployed **11** ineffective, inexcusable, superfluous
otologist: 6 aurist
ottavino: 7 piccolo
otter: fur **4** fish **6** tackle **7** annatto **8** paravane
genus: **5** lutra
sea: **5** kalan
ottoman: 4 pouf, seat **5** couch, divan, stool **6** fabric **9** footstool
Ottoman (see also **Turkey**): **4** Turk **5** Osman **6** Othman
court: **5** porte
governor: **5** pasha
imperial standard: **4** alem
leader of: **5** Osman
poetry couplet: **4** beyt
province: **7** Vilayet
subject: **4** Raia **5** Rayah
ouakari: 6 monkey
relative: **4** saki
oubliette: 7 dungeon
ouch: 5 adorn, bezel, clasp **6** brooch, fibula **7** fibulae(pl.) **8** ornament **11** exclamation
ought: 4 bood, must, want, zero **6** cipher,

naught, nought, should **7** behoove **10** obligation

ouija board part: 10 planchette

ounce: ure **6** weight **7** measure

sixteenth of: **4** dram

ouph, ouphe: elf **6** goblin

our: wir(Sc.) **5** notre(F.) **7** pronoun **10** possessive

ousia: 6 entity, nature **7** essence **9** substance

oust: bar **5** eject, evict, expel **6** banish, remove **7** deprive, dismiss **9** forejudge **10** dispossess

out: 4 away **5** forth **6** absent, begone, issued **8** external **9** published **10** extinguish **12** disadvantage

at elbows: **5** seedy

of control: **4** amok, wild **7** chaotic

of date: old **5** passe **10** antiquated

of kilter: **4** alop, awry **6** broken

of line: **4** awry **5** askew, fresh, wrong **8** improper

of order: **5** amiss, kaput **6** faulty **9** deficient

of place: **5** inept **13** inappropriate

of play: **4** dead, foul

of sight: **5** great **6** hidden **7** extreme

of sorts: **5** cross **7** peevish **9** irritable

of the ordinary: odd **5** novel **6** unique **7** strange, unusual **8** peculiar, uncommon **9** different

of the way: **5** aside **6** afield, remote **10** farfetched

of this world: **4** fine **6** superb

on a limb: **6** in a fix **7** stumped, up a tree **10** vulnerable

out-and-out: 5 sheer, utter **6** arrant, wholly **8** absolute, complete

outage: 4 vent **6** outlet **7** failure **8** blackout **10** suspension **12** interruption

outback: 4 bush **7** country **10** wilderness

outbreak: fit **4** riot **5** burst **6** bust-up, emeute(F.), revolt, ruckus, tumult **7** boutade, ruction **8** eruption, uprising **12** insurrection

new: **13** recrudescence

widespread: **8** epidemic

outbreeding: 7 exogamy

outbuilding: 4 barn, shed **5** privy **6** barton, garage, hemmel **8** outhouse **9** backhouse

outburst: 4 fume, gale, gust, rage, tiff **5** blast, brunt, flare **6** blower, blow-up, tirade **7** tantrum, torrent **8** eruption **9** explosion **10** ebullition

outcast: 5 exile, leper, ronin **6** outlet, pariah **7** refugee **8** banished, castaway, derelict, rejected, vagabond **10** expatriate

outclass: 4 best **5** excel **6** outwit **7** surpass

outcome: 4 fate **5** issue **6** effect, exitus, payoff, result, sequel, upshot **9** after-

math **10** conclusion, denouement **11** consequence

outcrop: 5 ledge **10** break forth

outcry: hue, yip **4** bawl, bray, yell **5** alarm, noise, shout **6** clamor, hubbub, racket, shriek **7** protest, screech, shilloo **9** objection **11** lamentation **12** vociferation

outdate: 7 outmode **9** antiquate, obsolete

outdistance: 7 surpass **11** leave behind, pull ahead of

outdo: cap, cow, top **5** excel **6** defeat, exceed **7** nonplus, surpass **8** overcome **13** steal a march on

outdoors: 8 al fresco **9** in the open

outer: 5 alien, ectad, ectal **6** remote **7** farther, foreign **8** exterior, external **10** extraneous

outermost: 4 last **5** final, utter **6** utmost **7** extreme **8** farthest, remotest

outface: 4 defy **6** resist, subdue **8** overcome **9** stare down

outfit: kit, rig **4** gang, gear, suit, team, unit **5** equip **6** attire **7** furnish **8** equipage **9** equipment, furniture, grubstake **10** enterprise **12** organization **13** paraphernalia

outflow: 4 flux **6** efflux, run-off **8** drainage

outgoing: 4 warm **6** genial **7** exiting, leaving **8** friendly, sociable **9** departing

outgrowth: 4 node **5** issue, shoot **6** result, sequel, sprout **8** offshoot **9** emergence **11** excrescence

outhouse: 4 shed **5** privy **6** biggin **7** latrine

outing: 4 stay, trip **6** junket, picnic **7** holiday **8** vacation **9** excursion

outlandish: 5 alien, queer, weird **6** exotic, remote **7** bizarre, foreign, strange, uncouth **8** peculiar **9** barbarous, fantastic, grotesque, tasteless **10** unorthodox

outlaw: ban **5** exile **6** bandit, banish, forbid **8** criminal, fugitive, prohibit, renegade **9** desperado, proscribe **10** disqualify

outlawed: 7 illegal, illicit

outlay: 4 cost **5** spend **7** expense **11** expenditure **12** disbursement

outlet: 4 exit, vent **5** store **6** egress, escape, exitus **7** opening, release **8** aperture

outline: map **4** form, plan **5** brief, chart, draft, frame, shape, trace **6** border, design, figure, sketch **7** contour, profile, summary **8** describe, skeleton, synopsis **9** delineate, perimeter **10** compendium, silhouette **13** configuration

outlive: 7 survive

outlook: 4 view **5** vista **6** aspect **7** purview **8** frontage, prospect **9** viewpoint **10** perception **11** expectation *medical:* **9** prognosis

outlying district: 6 suburb **7** purlieu **8** environs

outmoded: 5 dated, passe **6** demode **7** antique **8** obsolete, outdated

outpost: 7 station **8** frontier **10** settlement **11** advance base

outpouring: 4 gale, gush **5** flood **6** stream **9** fusillade

output: 5 power, yield **6** energy **7** harvest **10** production **16** computer feedback

outrage: 4 evil, rape **5** abuse **6** insult, offend, ravish **7** affront, offense, violate

outrageous: 4 base, vile **5** gross **6** brutal, far-out **7** heinous, obscene, ungodly **8** flagrant, shocking **9** atrocious, desperate, execrable, fantastic, monstrous **10** exorbitant

outre: 7 bizarre, strange **9** eccentric **11** exaggerated, extravagant

outreach: 6 exceed, extend, **7** project, surpass **8** protrude

outright: 5 total, whole, utter **6** direct, openly, wholly **8** complete, entirely **9** forthwith, instantly **10** thoroughly **15** straightforward

outrival: 5 excel **7** eclipse

outroot: 9 eradicate, extirpate

outrun: 4 beat **6** exceed **7** ski area **10** escape from

outset: 5 start **9** beginning

outside: 5 faint **6** facade, remote, slight **7** surface **8** exterior, external, al fresco **9** apart from **10** unfamiliar

outsider: 5 alien, loner **8** stranger **9** foreigner

outspoken: 4 bold, free **5** bluff, blunt, broad, frank **6** candid, direct **7** artless **8** explicit **10** unreserved **12** unrestrained

outstanding: big **4** arch, rare **5** famed, noted **6** famous, heroic, marked, unpaid **7** eminent **9** principal, prominent, unsettled **10** noticeable, pre-eminent, projecting **11** conspicuous, exceptional, uncollected, unfulfilled **13** distinguished

outstretched: 5 stent(Sc.) **8** extended

outstrip: cap, top, win **4** best, lead, pass **5** excel, **6** exceed **7** surpass **8** distance **9** transcend

outward: 5 ectad, overt **6** exodic, formal **7** extreme, visible **8** apparent, exterior, external, **9** extrinsic **10** ostensible **11** superficial

outweighing: 8 dominant **12** preponderant

outwit: fox **4** balk, best, foil **5** block, check, cross **6** baffle, jockey, thwart **9** checkmate, frustrate **10** circumvent, disappoint

ouzel: 4 piet **5** colly **6** thrush **8** whistler **9** blackbird

ouzo: 7 cordial
flavoring: **7** aniseed

oval: 7 ellipse, stadium **8** avelonge **10** elliptical **11** ellipsoidal

ovate: 9 egg-shaped
inversely: **7** obovate

ovation: 7 acclaim, tribute **8** applause

oven: 4 kiln, oast **5** baker, range, stove **6** calcar **7** furnace
annealing glass: **4** leer, lehr
goddess of: **6** Fornax

over: oer, sur(F.), too **4** also, anew, done, uber(G.), upon **5** above, again, clear, ended, extra, vault **6** across, beyond, excess, on high **7** surplus, through **8** finished **9** completed, excessive **10** terminated **11** consummated, superfluous
and above: **7** besides **8** as well as **11** therewithal

overabundance: 4 glut **6** excess **7** surfeit, surplus **8** plethora

overact: mug **5** emote **7** ham it up **9** burlesque **10** exaggerate

overage: 6 excess **7** surplus

overall: 6 mostly **9** generally **10** throughout **13** comprehensive

overbalance: 7 outweigh **8** dominate

overbearing: 5 proud **6** lordly **7** haughty **8** arrogant, bullying, insolent, snobbish, subduing **9** imperious **10** disdainful, high-handed **11** dictatorial, domineering, magisterial **12** overpowering, supercilious

overburden: 7 oppress **8** encumber, overload **9** surcharge

overcast: dim, sew **4** bind, dark, dull **5** cloud, heavy **6** cloudy, darken, gloomy, lowery **7** accloud, becloud, clouded, obscure

overcharge: gyp, pad **6** excise, fleece **9** extortion

overcoat: 5 benny **6** capote, raglan, slipon(Sc.), ulster **7** paletot(F.), surtout, topcoat **9** balmacaan, greatcoat, inverness **12** chesterfield
close fitting: **7** surtout
loose: **6** raglan **7** paletot
sleeveless: **9** inverness

overcome: awe, get, win **4** beat, best, lick **5** charm, crush, daunt, fordo **6** appall, beaten, craven, defeat, exceed, foredo, master **7** confute, conquer **8** convince, encumber, outstrip, overbear, overturn, suppress, surmount, vanquish **9** overpower, overthrow, overwhelm, prostrate

overcrowded: 6 jammed **9** congested

overdo: 6 exceed **7** exhaust, fatigue **8** go too far, overcook, overwork **9** burlesque **10** caricature, exaggerate

overdue: 4 late **5** tardy **6** behind **7** arrears, belated, delayed **8** expected **10** unpunctual

overeager: 8 feverish

overeat: 5 gorge 7 satiate 8 gourmand 10 gluttonize

overfed: 7 fulsome

overflow: 4 slop, swim, teem, vent 5 excess, float, flood, spate, spill 6 abound, debord, deluge, outlet 7 overrun, surplus 8 alluvion, inundate 9 abundance, cataclysm, ebullient, exuberant

overflowing: 5 awash 7 copious, profuse, teeming

overgrown: 4 lush, rank, 6 jungly 7 fulsome

overhang: jut 5 jetty 6 beetle 7 project, suspend 8 threaten

overhasty: 4 rash 6 daring 8 headlong 11 precipitate

overhaul: 7 examine 8 renovate 9 forereach

overhead: 5 above, aloft 7 expense

overjoyed: 6 elated 8 jubilant 9 delighted

overkill: 9 excessive

overlapping: 5 cover 8 obvolute 9 imbricate

overlay: cap, lap 4 ceil, coat 5 couch, cover, glaze, plate 6 cravat, spread, veneer 7 encrust, oppress, overlie 8 covering 10 overburden 11 superimpose

overload: 4 glut 6 charge 8 encumber

overloaded: 9 plethoric

overlook: 4 balk, miss, omit, skip 5 forgo 6 acquit, excuse, forego, forget, ignore, manage 7 absolve, condone, inspect, neglect 9 disregard, supervise

overlord: 5 liege, ruler 6 despot, satrap, tyrant 8 suzerain

overlying: 8 brochant, superior 9 incumbent

overmatch: 4 best 6 defeat, exceed 7 surpass 8 vanquish

overmodest: 4 prim 7 prudish

overmuch: too 6 excess 7 surplus 9 excessive

overnice: 5 fussy 7 precise 8 dentical, precious 10 fastidious

overpower: awe 4 rout 5 crush, whelm 6 compel, defeat, deluge, master, subdue 7 conquer, convince, entrance, overbear, overcome, vanquish 9 enrapture, overthrow, overwhelm

overpowering: 4 dire 6 fierce 8 dazzling, stunning

overreach: do 5 cheat 6 grease, nobble, outwit 8 go too far 10 circumvent

override: 4 veto 6 defeat 7 nullify 8 vanquish

overrule: 4 veto 7 reverse 8 abrogate

overrun: 5 crush 6 infest, invade, ravage, spread 7 destroy 9 overwhelm

overs: 5 boots

overseas: 5 alien 6 exotic 7 foreign, strange 11 ultramarine

oversee: 5 watch 6 survey 7 examine, inspect 9 supervise 11 superintend

overseer: 4 boss 5 chief, ephor(Gk.), grave, reeve 6 bishop, censor, driver, gaffer, grieve 7 baliff, caporal, curator, foreman, manager 8 banksman, martinet 9 inspector 10 acequiador, supervisor 14 superintendent

agricultural: 8 agronome

spiritual: 6 pastor, priest

overshadow: dim 5 cover, dwarf 6 darken 7 eclipse, obscure 8 dominate 9 adumbrate

overshoe: gum 4 boot 6 arctic, galosh, golosh, patten, rubber 7 flapper

overshoot: 6 exceed 8 go beyond

oversight: 4 care 5 error, lapse, watch 6 charge 7 blunder, control, custody, mistake 8 omission 9 direction 10 inspection, management, negligence 11 supervision 12 surveillance 15 superintendence

overskirt: 6 peplum 7 pannier

oversleeve: 6 armlet

overspread: 4 deck, pall 5 brede, cloud, cover 6 deluge, infest

overstate: 7 magnify 10 exaggerate

overstep: 6 exceed 8 trespass 10 transgress

overt: 4 open 6 patent, public 7 obvious 8 apparent, manifest

overtake: 5 catch 6 attain, detect 7 ensnare 9 apprehend, captivate

overtax: 6 exceed, strain 8 overload

overthrow: tip 4 dash, down, fell, foil, fold, hurl, raze, rout, ruin, rush 5 allay, evert, fling, upset, worst, wrack 6 defeat, topple, tumble, unseat 7 afflict, conquer, destroy, dismiss, ruinate, unhorse 8 confound, demolish, overcome, overturn, reversal, supplant, vanquish 9 discomfit, overpower, overwhelm, prostrate 10 defeasance 11 destruction 12 discomfiture

overtone: 4 hint 7 meaning 9 harmonics 11 implication

overture: 5 offer, proem 7 opening, prelude 8 aperture, proposal 11 proposition 12 introduction

opera: 8 sinfonia

overturn: tip 4 cave, coup, tilt 5 throw, upset 6 topple 7 capsize, destroy, pervert, reverse, subvert 8 overcome 9 overthrow, overwhelm

overweening: 4 rash, vain 8 arrogant, insolent 9 confident, excessive

overwhelm: 4 bury, whip 5 amaze, cover, crush, drouk, swamp 6 defeat, deluge, engulf, quench 7 confute, conquer, engross, oppress 8 astonish, inundate, overturn, submerge 9 overpower, overthrow

overword: 7 refrain
Ovid: *birthplace:* **5** Sulmo
  burial place: **4** Tomi **5** Tomis
  work: **5** Fasti **7** Tristia **13** Metamor-
    phoses
ovine: 5 sheep **9** sheeplike
  female: ewe
ovoid: 5 ovate **7** egglike **8** globular
ovule: egg **4** seed **6** embryo, gamete **7**
  seedlet
  integument: **7** primine
ovum: egg **4** seed **5** spore
owala tree: 4 bobo
owe: due **7** possess **9** attribute
ower: 6 debtor
owl: ule **4** bubo, lulu, momo **5** wekau **7**
  boobook, harfang, woolert **8** billy-wix,
  moreport **10** gillhooter, hob-houchin
  barn: **5** madge
  call: **4** hoot
  genus of: **5** ninox
  light: **7** evening
  pert. to: **8** strigine
  plumed eye area of: **4** disk
  short-eared: **4** momo
  small: **4** utum **6** howlet
  young: **4** utum **5** owlet
Owl and Pussycat author: 4 Lear
own: ain(Sc.), owe **4** avow, have, hold,
  nain(Sc.) **5** admit **7** concede, confess,
  possess **9** recognize **11** acknowledge
ownership: 5 title **7** tenancy **8** dominium
  11 condominium, lawful claim **14** pro-
  prietorship
own up: 11 acknowledge
ox: yak **4** anoa, aver, beef, buff, gaur,
  musk, reem, zebu **5** bison, bugle, gayal,
  steer, tsine **6** bovine **7** banteng, buffalo
  8 seladang **9** quadruped
  extinct: **4** urus
  harness: **4** yoke
  pert. to: **5** bovid **6** bovine **7** taurine
  small: **4** runt
  stall: **5** boose
  wild: **4** gaur **8** seladang
oxalis: oca **5** plant **6** sorrel
oxen: 6 cattle
  yoke: **4** span
oxeye: 5 daisy **14** black-eyed susan

oxford: 4 shoe **5** cloth **10** saddleshoe
Oxford: 10 university
  Earl of: **6** Harley **7** Asquith
  examination: **6** greats
  library: **8** Bodleian
  officer: **5** bedel **6** beadle
  scholar: **4** demy
  scholarship: **6** Rhodes
oxhead: 4 dolt **9** blockhead
oxidation: 4 rust
oxide: *aluminum:* **7** alumina
  barium: **6** baryta
  calcium: **4** lime
  hydrocarbon radical: **5** ether
  iron: **4** rust
  sodium: **4** soda
  strontium: **8** strontia
oxidize: 4 heat, rust **7** calcine, corrode
oxlip: 8 primrose
oxtongue: 7 alkanet, bugloss
oxyacantha: 8 hawthorn
oxygen: gas
  acid: **7** chloric **9** sulphuric
  allotropic: **5** ozone
  binary: **5** oxide
oxygenate: 6 aerate
oyez: 4 hear **6** attend **9** attention
oyster: 5 porte **6** huitre **7** bivalve, mollusk
  bed: **4** park, stew **5** layer **6** clair **9** oyster-
    age
  eggs: **5** spawn
  fossil: **9** ostracite
  gatherer: **7** tongman
  genus: **6** ostrea
  kind of: **6** native **9** bluepoint
  phylum: **8** mollusca
  rake: **5** tongs
  shell: **4** husk, test **5** shuck
  spawn: **5** culch **6** cultch
  tree: **8** mangrove
  young: **4** spat
oyster catcher: 4 bird **5** tirma
oyster grass: 4 kelp **10** sea lettuce
oyster plant: 7 salsify
oysterfish: 6 tautog **8** toadfish
Oz books author: 4 Baum
Ozark State: 8 Missouri
ozone: air

P

pa, pah: dad, paw **4** fort, papa **5** daddy **6** father **7** village **8** stockade **10** settlement

pabulum: 4 food **6** cereal **7** aliment, support **9** nutriment **10** sustenance **11** nourishment

pac, pack: 4 boot **8** moccasin

paca: 4 cavy, lava **5** agout, labba **6** rodent

pace: way **4** clip, gait, lope, pass, rack, rate, step, trot, walk **5** amble, canto, speed, tempo, tread **6** canter, gallop, strait **7** channel, chapter, dogtrot, measure, passage **8** platform **10** passageway

pacer: 5 horse **9** pacemaker

pachisi: 4 game, ludo

pachyderm: 8 elephant **10** rhinoceros **12** hippopotamus

pacific: 4 calm, meek, mild **5** irene **6** irenic, placid, serene **7** amiable **8** peaceful, tranquil **9** appeasing, peaceable **12** conciliatory

Pacific coast state: 6 Oregon **10** California, Washington

Pacific Islands (see also **Oceania**): *archipelago:* Aru **4** Sulu **5** Malay, Samoa **6** Tulagi
  bird: **4** kagu **8** whistler
  cloth: **4** tapa
  collective name: **7** Oceania
  grass: **4** neti
  military base: **4** Guam
  tree: kou **4** ipil, taro **7** dasheen, madrona, madrono **8** eddyroot

Pacific Ocean: *archipelago:* **4** Sulu **5** Malay, Samoa
  discoverer: **6** Balboa
  fish: **5** skate **6** bonito, marlin **7** dolphin **8** albacore **9** barracuda, swordfish **10** yellowtail
  island: Lae, Yap **4** Guam, Truk, Wake **5** Leyte, Samoa **6** Tahiti **8** Tasmania **9** Carolines, Marquesas
  shark: **4** mako
  "stepping stones": **9** Aleutians

pacifier: sop **4** ring **6** nipple **8** sugartit **9** comforter **11** tranquilizer

pacifist: 4 dove **8** appeaser, peacenik

pacify: 4 calm, ease, lull **5** abate, allay, quiet, still **6** serene, soften, soothe **7** appease, assuage, mollify, placate, sweeten **8** mitigate **9** alleviate, reconcile **10** conciliate, propitiate **11** tranquilize

pack: jam, wad **4** bale, cram, gang, load, stow, tamp **5** carry, crowd, flock, horde, steve, store, truss **6** barrel, bundle, duffle, embale, encase, fardel, impact, wallet **8** knapsack
  back: **8** knapsack
  of cards: **4** deck

pack animal: ass **4** mule **5** burro, camel, horse, llama **6** donkey

package: pad **4** bale **6** bundle, packet, parcel

packer: 5 baler, roper **6** canner

packet: 4 boat **6** bundle, parcel **7** fortune

packing: 4 rags **5** gauze, paper, straw, waste **7** stowage
  box: **5** crate
  clay: **4** lute
  material: **6** gasket, baline **9** excelsior
  water-tight: **6** gasket

packing plant: 7 cannery

Pacolet: 5 dwarf, horse

pact: 6 cartel, treaty **7** bargain, compact **8** alliance, contract, covenant **9** agreement **10** settlement

Pactolian: 6 golden

pad: mat, wad, way **4** boss, path, road, walk **5** quilt, stuff, tramp **6** basket, buffer, jockey, pillow, tablet, trudge **7** bolster, bombast, cushion **8** footfall **9** embroider **10** highwayman, protection

padding: 7 packing, robbery, wadding **8** stuffing

paddle: oar, row **4** spud, wade **5** aloof **6** dabble, toddle **8** lumpfish

paddock: lot **4** frog, park **5** field **6** sledge **9** enclosure **10** saddle area

Paddy: 8 Irishman

paddywhack: 4 beat, blow **5** spank **9** thrashing

Paderewski opera: 5 Manru

padlock: 4 lock **6** fasten **7** closing **8** fastener

padre: 4 monk **6** cleric, father, priest **8** chaplain

padrona: 8 landlady, mistress

padrone: 4 boss **5** chief **6** master, patron **8** landlord **9** innkeeper

paean, pean: ode **4** hymn, song **6** praise

pagan: 6 ethnic, paynim **7** heathen, infidel **8** idolator **10** idolatrous, unbeliever **11** nonbeliever *god:* **4** Baal, idol

page: boy **4** call, leaf **5** child, folio, sheet **6** donzel, summon, varlet **7** footboy, servant **8** henchboy, henchman **9** attendant, messenger

beginning: **4** leaf **7** flyleaf

book: **5** folio **6** cahier

lady: **8** escudero

left-hand: **5** verso

number: **5** folio **10** pagination

paper: **5** sheet

reverse: **5** verso

right-hand: **5** recto

title: **5** unwan **6** rubric

pageant: **4** pomp, show **6** parade **7** tableau **8** aquacade, pretense **9** spectacle **10** exhibition, procession

pageantry: **7** display **8** splendor **11** ostentation

Pagliacci: *character:* **5** Nedda, Tonio

composer: **11** Leoncavallo

pagoda: taa **6** alcove, gazebo, temple **10** kryailteyo **11** summerhouse

finial or ornament: tee

pagurian: **4** crab

pah: **5** nasty **6** humbug **8** improper

paha: **4** hill **5** ridge

paideutics: **8** pedagogy

pail: can, cog(Sc.), pan, soa, soe **4** beat, bowk, gawn, meal, trug **5** bowie, cogue (Sc.), eshin, skeel **6** bucket, coggie(Sc.), harass, piggin, situla(L.), thrash, vessel **7** collock, situlae(pl.) **8** cannikin

paillette: **7** spangle **8** ornament

pain: try **4** ache, agra, care, cark, harm, hurt, pang **5** agony, cramp, grief, sting, thraw(Sc.), throe, upset, wound **6** grieve, twinge **7** afflict, algesis, anguish, penalty, torture, travail, trouble **8** disquiet, distress **9** suffering **10** affliction, algophilia, discomfort, punishment

abdominal: **5** colic

back: **7** lumbago

darting: **6** twinge

dull: **4** ache

pert. to: **6** asonal **7** algetic

relayer: **5** nerve

sensitiveness to: **7** algesia

painful: raw **4** sore **5** angry **6** bitter **7** algetic, hurting, irksome **8** exacting **9** difficult, laborious

painkiller: **4** drug **6** opiate **7** anodyne, aspirin **8** morphine, reliever **9** analgesic, paregoric

pains: **4** care, work **5** labor **6** effort **7** trouble **8** exertion

painstaking: **6** loving **7** careful **8** diligent, exacting **9** assiduous, elaborate, laborious **10** meticulous, scrupulous

paint: **4** coat, daub, gaud, limn **5** color, feign, fucus, rouge, stain **6** bedaub, depict, enamel, makeup **7** besmear, portray, pretend **8** decorate, disguise

glossy: **6** enamel

painted: **5** pinto **6** fucate **10** artificial, variegated

painter: **6** artist **7** artiste, workman **9** decorator

painting: oil **5** mural **6** canvas **7** acrylic, picture **10** watercolor

equipment: **5** brush, easel, paint **6** canvas, pallet **7** palette

medium: oil **7** gouache, tempera **10** watercolor

one-color: **8** monotint **10** monochrome

plaster: **5** secco **6** fresco

sacred: **5** pieta

scenic: **5** scape **8** seascape **9** cityscape, landscape

small: **9** miniature

studio: **7** atelier

style: **5** genre

three panels: **8** triptych

wall: **5** mural, panel **6** fresco

pair: duo, two **4** case, diad, duad, dyad, mate, span, team, yoke **5** brace, match, unite **6** couple

paisano: pal **7** comrade, peasant **10** countryman

Paisley: **5** shawl **6** design, fabric **7** pattern

Pakistan: *capital:* **9** Islamabad

city or town: Dir **6** Lahore, Multan, Quetta **7** Karachi **9** Hyderabad **10** Rawalpindi

language: **4** Urdu **6** Sindhi **7** Bengali, Punjabi

leader: Zia **4** Ayub **5** Yahya **6** Bhutto

monetary unit: **5** rupee

mountain: **9** Tirich Mir

mountain range: **8** Himalaya

native: **6** Bengal, Pathan, Sindhi **7** Baluchi, Punjabi

province: **4** Sind, Swat **5** Kalat, Sindh **6** Khelat, Punjab **11** Baluchistan

religion: **5** Hindu, Islam

river: **4** Swat **5** Indus **6** Kundar

weight: **4** seer, tola **5** maund

pal: **4** ally, chum, pard **5** buddy, crony **6** cobber, cohort, digger, friend **7** comrade, partner **9** associate, companion **10** accomplice **11** confederate

palace: **5** court, serai **6** castle, palais(F.) **7** alcazar, edifice, mansion **8** Alcalzar **9** luxurious, pretorium **10** praetorium

officer: **7** paladin **8** palatine

papal: **7** Lateran, Vatican

paladin: **4** hero, peer **6** knight **8** champion, douzeper **11** protagonist

palaestra: **6** school **9** gymnasium

palamate: **9** web-footed

Palamedes: *enemy:* **7** Ulysses

father: **8** Nauplius

mother: **7** Clymene

war: **6** Trojan

Palamon: *rival:* **6** Arcite

wife: **6** Emelye

palanquin, palankeen: 4 kago 5 dooli, dooly, palki, sedan 6 doolee, dooley, doolie, litter, palkee 10 conveyance

palatable: 5 sapid, tasty 6 savory 8 delicate, pleasing 9 agreeable, delicious, toothsome 10 acceptable, appetizing

render: 4 salt 5 spice 6 season

palatal: 5 front, velar 8 gutteral 9 consonant

palate: 5 taste 6 relish 7 gourmet

hard: 11 roof of mouth

pert. to: 6 uranic

soft: 4 cion, vela(pl.) 5 uvula, velum

palatial: 5 large, regal 6 ornate 7 stately 9 luxurious 11 magnificent

palaver: 4 talk 6 debate, glaver, parley 7 chatter, flatter, wheedle 8 business, cajolery, flattery 10 conference 11 terminology 12 conversation

pale: dim, wan 4 ashy, fade, grey, gull, lily, pall, sick 5 ashen, blake, blate, bleak, faint, fence, livid, lurid, stake, stick, white 6 anemic, blanch, chalky, feeble, pallid, pastel, picket, region, sallow, sickly, whiten 7 anaemic, enclose, ghastly, haggard, insipid, obscure, whitish 8 encircle, etiolate 9 colorless 10 pasty-faced

paleness: 6 pallor

Palestinian (see also **Israel**): *guerrillas:* 7 Al Fatah 8 Fedayeen

leader: 6 Arafat

paletot: 8 overcoat 9 greatcoat

palfrey: 5 horse

palimpsest: 6 tablet 9 parchment

palindrome: 5 verse 7 sotadic

paling: 4 pale 5 fence, flake, limit, stake 6 picket 7 fencing 9 enclosure

palinode: 6 abjure 8 take back 10 retraction 11 recantation

Palinurus: 9 steersman

palisade: 5 cliff, fence, stake 6 picket 7 barrier, enclose, fortify, furnish 8 espalier, stockade, surround 9 enclosure, implement

pall: 4 bore, cloy, pale, sate 5 cloak, cloth, faint, stale, weary 6 mantle, 7 disgust, satiate 8 animetta, covering 11 counterpane

Pall Mall site: 7 West End

pallet: bed, cot, pad 5 couch, quilt 7 blanket 8 mattress, plancher 9 headpiece

palliasse: 6 pallet 8 mattress

palliate: 4 ease, hide 5 cloak, cover, gloss, gloze 6 lessen, soften 7 conceal, shelter 8 disguise, mitigate 9 alleviate, exculpate, extenuate, gloss over, sugarcoat, whitewash

pallid: wan 4 ashy, dull, pale, paly 5 bleak, white 7 ghastly 9 colorless

pallion: bit 5 piece 6 pellet

pallium: 4 band 5 cloak 6 mantle 8 himation

palm: 4 hide, tree 5 shrub 6 palmus(L.), thenar, trophy 7 conceal

betel nut: 5 areca, bonga

beverage: 5 assai

cabbage: 8 palmetto

climbing: 6 rattan

coconut: 4 coco

fan-leafed: 7 talipat, talipot, taliput 8 palmetto

feather: 5 howea 6 gomuti 7 urucuri, urucury

fiber: tal 4 buri 6 raffia

food: nut 4 sago 5 fruit

juice: 4 nipa, sura 5 taree, toddy

kind: ti 4 jara 5 assai, royal, tucum 6 bacaba, tucuma 7 babassu, jaggery, tokopat 8 bangalow

leaf: ola, ole 4 olay, olla 5 frond

low: 5 bussu 6 trooly, trouie, ubussu

palmyra: ola, ole, tal 4 brab, olla 6 ronier

pert. to: 6 palmar 8 frondous 10 palmaceous

pith: 4 sago

reader: 7 palmist

sap: 5 toddy

seeds: 4 nipa

spiny: 6 grigri, grugru

starch: 4 sago

stem: 4 cane 5 ratan 6 rattan

stemless: 5 curua

thatch: 4 nipa 9 barriguda

wing-leaved: 6 cohune

palm-leaf mat: 4 yapa

palm off: 5 foist

palma: 5 fiber, yucca

palmary: 5 chief, palmy 6 palmar 8 superior 9 principal 10 pre-eminent, victorious

palmate: 4 flat 5 broad, lobed 6 palmed, webbed 10 hand-shaped

palmer: 5 louse 6 stroll, travel, votary 7 pilgrim 8 wanderer 15 prestidigitator

Palmetto State: 13 South Carolina

palmistry: 10 chirognomy, chiromancy

practicer: 11 chiromancer

palmodic: 5 jerky

palms down: 7 pronate

palmy: 10 prosperous, triumphant 11 flourishing

Palmyra's queen: 7 Zenobia

palmyra tree: 4 brab 7 talipot

palooka: oaf 4 fool

palp: 6 feeler 7 flatter 8 tentacle

palpable: 4 rank 5 plain 6 patent 7 audible, evident, obvious, tactile 8 apparent, distinct, manifest, tangible 10 noticeable 11 perceptible 12 recognizable

palpebra: 6 eyelid

palpebrate: 4 wink

palpitation: 4 beat, pant 7 flicker, flutter 9 pulsation, quivering, throbbing, trembling

palsied: 5 shaky 7 shaking 9 paralyzed,

tottering, trembling
palsy-walsy: 8 intimate
palter: fib, lie **5** trick **6** babble, haggle, mumble, trifle **7** chatter, deceive, quibble **10** equivocate **11** prevaricate
paltock: 5 tunic **6** jacket **7** doublet
paltry: 4 bald, bare, base, mean, puny, vile **5** footy, petty, trash **6** chetif, flimsy, trashy **7** low-down, pitiful, rubbish, trivial **8** picayune, trifling **9** worthless **10** despicable **11** unimportant **12** contemptible **13** insignificant
paludal: 6 marshy
pampas: 6 plains
cat: **6** kodkod, pajero
pamper: pet **4** baby, cram, delt(Sc.), glut **5** humor, spoil **6** caress, cocker, coddle, cosher, cosset, cuddle, dandle, fondle, posset **7** cherish, cockney, gratify, indulge, satiate, forwean
pamphagous: 10 omnivorous
pamphlet: 5 flyer, tract **6** folder **7** booklet, catalog, leaflet **8** brochure **9** catalogue
pan: ape, rap, tab **4** face, part, wash **5** basin **6** frache(F.), lappet, vessel **7** portion, subsoil, utensil **8** ridicule **9** container, criticize **10** acetabulum, receptacle
coal burner: **5** grill **7** brazier
frying: **6** spider **7** skillet
gold-washing: **4** tina **5** batea
Pan: 6 Faunus
father: **6** Hermes
instrument: **4** pipe, reed
place of worship: **7** Arcadia
son: **7** Silenus **8** Seilenos
pan fry: 5 saute
panacea: 4 cure **6** elixir, remedy **7** allheal, cure-all, heal-all, nostrum **8** nepenthe **10** catholicon **11** panchreston
panache: 5 flare, plume, style, verve
panachure: 8 mottling
Panama: hat
capital: **6** Panama
city: **5** Colon, David **8** Santiago **9** Aspinwall, Cristobal
explorer: **6** Balboa
gulf: **6** Darien
island: Rey
highest point: **8** Chiriqui
lake: **5** Gatum
measure: **7** celemin
monetary unit: **6** balboa
port: **5** Colon **6** Balboa **9** Cristobal **10** Portobello
province: **5** Cocle, Colon **6** Panama **8** Chiriqui, Veraguas
river: **5** Chepo, Sambu, Tuira **7** Chagres
tree: **4** yaya **6** alfaje, cativo
Panama Canal: *dam and locks:* **5** Gatun **10** Miraflores
engineer: **9** de Lesseps
lake: **5** Gatun

nickname: **8** Big Ditch
panatela: 5 cigar
panax: 4 herb **7** ginseng
pancake: 5 arepa(Sp.), flawn **6** blintz, fraise, froise **7** blintze, fritter, hotcake **8** flapjack **11** griddlecake
delicate: **5** crepe
panda: 5 wah **6** animal **7** bearcat
pandemonium: din **4** hell, sink **5** noise **6** tumult, uproar **8** disorder **9** confusion
pander: 4 bawd, pimp **5** cater **7** whiskin **8** procurer **9** go-between, procuress
Pandora: *brother:* **10** Prometheus
daughter: **6** Pyrrha
husband: **10** Epimetheus
pandurina: **4** lute
pane: 5 glass **7** section
panegyric: 5 eloge, elogy **6** eulogy, praise **7** encomia(pl.), oration, tribute, writing **8** encomium **9** discourse, laudation
panel: 4 jury **5** group **6** tympan **8** decorate
paneling: 4 wall **7** ceiling **8** covering
panfish: 4 crab, king **9** horseshoe
pang: 4 ache, gird, pain, stab, tang **5** agony, cramp, spasm, throe **6** twinge, twitch, wrench **7** anguish, travail **8** paroxysm **9** heartache
Pangim native: 4 Goan
pangolin: 5 manis **8** anteater, edentate
order: **9** pholidota
panhandle: beg **5** cadge
Panhandle State: 12 West Virginia
panic: 4 fear, fray, funk, wild **5** alarm, chaos, scare **6** frenzy, fright, terror **8** stampede **13** consternation
panjandrum: 7 magnate **9** personage
pannier, panier: bag, ped **5** seron **6** basket, dorsel, dorser, dosser, pantry **9** overskirt
panoply: 4 pomp **5** armor, array **6** armour **7** display
panorama: 4 view **5** range, scene, sweep, vista **7** picture, scenery **9** cyclorama
pan out: 7 succeed
panpipe: 6 syrinx **8** zampogna **10** mouth organ
pansy: 9 heartease **10** heartsease
pant: 4 ache, beat, blow, gasp, puff **5** heave, throb, yearn **7** pulsate **9** palpitate **11** palpitation
Pantagruel: 5 giant
companion: **7** Panurge
father: **9** Gargantua
mother: **7** Badebec
Panthea's husband: 9 Abradatus
pantheon: 6 temple
panther: cat **4** pard, puma **6** cougar, jaguar **7** leopard, painter
pantile: 7 biscuit **8** hardtack
pantomimist: 4 mime **5** actor **7** Marceau
pantry: 4 cave **5** ambry **6** closet, larder **7** buttery, pannier, pantler **8** cupboard

pants: 5 jeans, Levis **6** slacks **7** drawers **8** trousers

leather: **5** chaps **10** chaparajos, chaparteras, chaperejos, lederhosen(G.) **11** chaparreras

pantywaist: 8 weakling **13** characterless

panuelo: 6 collar, ruffle **8** kerchief **9** neckcloth

pap: 4 teat **5** trash **6** nipple **7** garbage, rubbish **8** emulsion, mammilla

papa: dad, paw, pop **6** baboon, father, potato, priest **7** vulture

papal (see also **pope): 9** apostolic **10** pontifical

papal court: 5 curia

papaya: 5 melon, papaw **6** pawpaw

paper: 5 essay, theme, tract **6** cartel, report **7** journal, writing **8** document, treatise **9** monograph, newspaper, wallpaper **10** periodical **11** credentials, examination **12** dissertation **13** unsubstantial

absorbent: **7** blotter **9** towelling

case: **4** file **5** folio **6** binder

collection: **7** dossier

currency: **5** scrip

damaged: **5** broke, casse, salle **6** cassie

design: **9** watermark

detachable: tab **4** stub **6** coupon

fine: **5** linen **6** vellum

folded once: **5** folio

gummed: **5** label, stamp **6** paster **7** sticker

hard: **6** pelure

large-size: **5** atlas

legal: **4** writ

medicinal: **6** charta

official: **5** targe **8** document

pad: **5** block **6** tablet

piece: **5** scrip, scrap, sheet

postage-stamp: **6** pelure

pulp: **4** ulla **9** waterleaf

quantity: **4** page, ream **5** quire, sheet **6** bundle

scroll: **9** parchment

size: cap **4** copy, demi, demy, pott **5** atlas, crown, folio, legal **7** bastard, emperor **8** foolscap, imperial **9** colombier

thin: **6** pelure, tissue **9** onionskin

untrimmed edge: **6** deckle

writing-size: cap **8** foolscap

paper money: 4 bill, cash **7** lettuce **8** frogskin **9** greenback

papier-mache: 7 collage

papilla: bud **6** pimple

papist: 8 Catholic

papoose: 4 baby

pappy: dad, paw **4** papa, soft **5** mushy **6** father **6** spongy **7** squishy **8** yielding **9** succulent

papule: 6 pimple

papyrus: 4 reed **5** sedge **6** biblos, biblus, scroll **7** bulrush **9** parchment

respository: **5** capsa

par: by **5** equal **6** normal **7** average **8** equality, standard **9** enclosure **11** equivalence

par value: 4 face **7** nominal

parable: 4 myth, tale **5** fable, story **6** apolog, byword **7** byspell **8** allegory, apologue, forbysen **10** comparison, similitude

parabola: arc **5** curve **7** antenna

parachute: *material:* **4** silk **5** nylon

part: **4** pack **6** canopy **7** harness, ripcord

paraclete: 5 aider **6** helper **7** pleader **8** advocate, consoler **9** comforter **9** supporter **11** intercessor

parade: 4 pomp, show, walk **5** march, strut **6** flaunt, review, stroll **7** cortege, display, exhibit, marshal **8** ceremony, flourish, grandeur, splendor **9** advertise, pageantry, promenade, strollers **10** callithump, exhibition, pretension, procession **12** magnificence

paradigm: 5 model **7** example, pattern

Paradise: 4 Eden **5** bliss **6** Aidenn, heaven, Utopia **7** Elysium, Nirvana **12** promised land

Buddhist: **4** Jodo

fool's: **5** limbo

Muslim: **5** Jenna

river: **5** Gihon

Paradise Lost angel: 5 Ariel, Uriel

paraffin: 6 alkane **8** kerosene

paragon: gem **4** type **5** ideal, jewel, model **7** pattern **8** last word **9** nonpariel

paragram: pun

paragraph: 4 item, note, sign **5** caput **8** material

Paraguay: *capital:* **8** Asuncion

city: Ita **9** Paraguari, Villa Rica **10** Concepcion, Encarnacion

ethnic group: **8** Mestizos

Indian: **7** Guarani

lake: **4** Ypoa

language: **7** Guarani, Spanish

measure: pie **4** line, lino, vara **5** legua, linea **6** cordel, cuadra, cuarta, fanega, league

money: **7** guarani

river: Apa **6** Parana **8** Paraguay **9** Tibiquare

tea: **4** mate **5** yerba

weight: **7** quintal

parakeet: 6 parrot, wellat **8** lovebird, paraquet, popinjay **10** budgerygay **11** budgereegah

parallel: 4 even **5** along, equal, match **6** equate, line up **8** analogue **10** collateral **11** counterpart

render: **9** collimate

parallelism: 6 simile **10** similarity **11** resemblance **14** correspondence

parallelogram: 5 rhomb **6** oblong, square **9** rectangle

paralogist: 7 sophist

paralysis: 5 cramp, palsy 7 paresis 9 impotence 10 holoplexia 11 monoparesis
with: 7 paretic 9 paralytic
paralyzed: 4 numb 7 palsied 8 benumbed, crippled, immobile
paramnesia: 6 déjàvu
paramount: 5 above, chief, ruler 7 capital, supreme 8 crowning, dominant, superior, suzerain 10 pre-eminent
lord: 5 liege
paramour: 5 leman, lover, wooer 6 amoret, friend, suitor 7 gallant, hetaera 8 mistress 9 concubine, kept woman 10 sweetheart
paranymph: 7 best man 8 advocate 10 bridesmaid
parapet: 4 butt, wall 5 redan 7 bulwark, railing, rampart 10 breastwork 12 embattlement 13 fortification
part of: 5 crete
V-shaped: 5 redan
paraphernalia: 4 gear 9 apparatus, equipment, trappings 10 belongings 11 furnishings 13 appurtenances
paraphrase: 6 reword 7 version 9 interpret, translate 10 transcribe 11 translation
parasite: bug, bur 4 burr, moss 5 leech, toady, virus 6 fungus, sponge 7 sponger 8 hanger-on 9 dependent, mistletoe, sycophant 10 freeloader
animal: 4 flea, mite, tick 8 entozoan
blood: 4 tryp
disease: 7 malaria 11 trichinosis
marine: 6 remora, sponge
plant: 9 entophyte
trout: sug
parasol: 8 sunshade, umbrella 11 bumbershoot
paratrooper cry: 8 Geronimo
paravane: 5 otter
Parcae: See **Fates**
parcel: lot 4 deal, mete, pack, part, wrap 5 bulse, bunch, group, piece 6 bundle, divide, packet 7 package, portion 8 fragment 9 apportion 10 collection, distribute
parch: dry 4 burn, sear 5 roast, toast 6 dry out, scorch 7 bristle, brustle, graddan, shrivel
parched: 4 arid, sere 5 fiery 6 gizzen, torrid
parchment (see also **paper, scroll**): 6 charta 7 diploma
book cover: 5 forel 6 forrel
fine: vel 6 vellum
manuscript: 10 palimpsest
piece: 8 membrane
roll: 4 pell 6 scroll
pard: pal 4 chum 7 partner 9 companion
pardesi: 9 foreigner, outlander
pardo: 7 mulatto
pardon: 4 free 5 mercy, remit, spare 6

assoil, excuse 7 absolve, amnesty, condone, forgive 8 liberate, reprieve, tolerate 9 exculpate, remission 10 absolution, indulgence 11 forgiveness
general: 7 amnesty
stall: 12 confessional
pardonable: 6 venial 9 excusable
pare: cut 4 chip, peel, skin 5 shave 6 reduce, remove, resect 7 curtail, cut back, cut down, whittle 8 diminish, trim back 11 decorticate
paregoric: 7 anodyne 8 sedative
parella, parelle: 6 lichen
parent: dad, dam 4 mama, papa, sire 5 cause, daddy, mater(L.), pater 6 author, father, mother, origin 7 forbear, genitor 8 ancestor, begetter, forebear, generate, guardian, producer 10 forefather, progenitor
parentage: 5 birth 6 family, origin 7 lineage, progeny 8 ancestry 10 extraction, parenthood
parget: 4 coat 6 gypsum 7 plaster 8 decorate 9 whitewash
pariah: 7 Ishmael, outcast
parian: 5 china 6 marble, market 9 porcelain
Paris (Greek god)
beloved: 5 Helen
father: 5 Priam
kin: 7 Troilus 9 Cassandra
mother: 6 Hecuba
slayer: 11 Philoctetes
wife: 6 Oenone
Paris (French capital)
airport: 4 Orly 5 Roissy 8 DeGaulle 9 Le Bourget
bishop: 5 Denis 7 Lombard
boulevard: 8 Rue Royal, St. Honore 11 Rue de la Paix, Rue de Rivoli 13 Champs Elysees
cathedral: 9 Notre Dame
cemetery: 12 Pere-Lachaise
city planner: 9 Hausmann
museum: 5 Cluny 6 Louvre 10 Luxembourg
palace: 6 Elysee, Louvre 9 Tuileries 10 Luxembourg
park: 10 Luxembourg 13 Bois de Boulogne
river: 5 Seine
Roman name: 7 Lutetia
section: 8 Left Bank 9 Right Bank 10 Montmartre, Rive Gauche 12 Montparnasse 15 St. Germain-des-Pres
subway: 5 metro
tower: 6 Eiffel
university: 8 Sorbonne
parish: 4 fold 5 flock 8 diocese 12 congregation
head: 5 vicar 6 pastor, priest 8 minister
official: 9 vestryman 10 borsholder
paristhmion: 6 tonsil

parity: 7 analogy 8 equality 10 similarity 11 resemblance

park: 4 stop 6 refuge 7 commons, paddock, preserve 10 playground

parlance: 4 talk 5 idiom 6 speech 7 diction 9 discourse 11 phraseology 12 conversation

parlay: 5 wager 6 double, paroli 7 build up 8 increase

parley: 5 speak, treat, utter 6 confer 7 discuss, palaver 9 discourse 10 conference, discussion 12 conversation

parliament: 4 diet 5 senat(F.) 7 council 8 assembly, congress 9 gathering 10 conference 11 legislature
  member: 4 lord

parlous: 4 keen 5 risky 6 clever, shrewd 7 cunning 8 critical, perilous 9 dangerous, hazardous 11 exceedingly, excessively, mischievous 13 disconcerting

parnassian: 4 poet

parochial: 5 petty 6 narrow 7 bigoted 9 small-town 10 provincial

parody: 4 skit 6 satire 8 travesty 9 burlesque, imitation 10 caricature

paroemia: 7 proverb

parole: 6 pledge 7 promise

paronomasia: pun 8 word play 12 agnomination

paroxysm: fit 4 pang 5 agony, spasm, throe 6 access, attack, orgasm 8 epitasis, outburst 9 agitation 10 convulsion 12 exacerbation

parrot: ape, ara 4 copy, echo, jako, kaka, lory 5 arara, mimic, polly 6 repeat, tiriba 7 corella, imitate 8 cockatoo, lorikeet, lovebird, parakeet 9 cockateel, cockatiel
  disease: 11 psittacosis
  genus: 9 psittacus
  gray: 4 jako
  green: 5 cagit
  hawk: hia
  like: 5 arine 11 psittaceous
  long-tailed: 5 macaw
  monk: 4 loro
  owl: 4 kaka 6 kakapo
  part of bill: 4 cere
  sheep-killing: kea
  small: 8 lovebird, parakeet

parrot fish: 4 scar 5 lania 6 scarus 8 bluefish 9 labroidea

parry: 4 fend, ward 5 avoid, block, evade 6 thwart 7 deflect, evasion

parse: 7 analyse, analyze, diagram, dissect 8 construe 9 anatomize

Parsee: See **Parsi**

Parsi: 11 Zoroastrian
  holy book: 6 Avesta
  priest: 5 mobed 6 dastur 7 destour, dustoor

parsimonious: 4 mean, near 5 close, scant, spare 6 frugal, meager, narrow,
skimpy, sordid, stingy 7 miserly, sparing 8 covetous, grasping, wretched 9 illiberal, mercenary, niggardly, penurious 10 avaricious, economical, ungenerous 13 penny-pinching 17 narrowheartedness

parsley: herb 5 cumin, garnish 6 eltrot
  derivative: 5 apiol 6 apiole
  genus: 12 petroselinum
  relative: 6 celery

parsley camphor: 6 apiole

parson: 6 pastor, rector 8 minister, preacher 9 clergyman, guidepost

parson bird: poe, tui 4 rook

parson-in-the-pulpit: 10 cuckoopint

parsonage: 5 manse 6 parish 7 rectory 9 pastorium

part (see also **parts**): 4 deal, dole, half, role, rove, side, some, twin 5 chunk, piece, quota, sever, share 6 behalf, canton, cleave, depart, detail, divide, member, parcel, ration, sunder 7 disjoin, element, portion, section, segment 8 alienate, disperse, dissever, disunite, division, estrange, fraction, fragment, separate 9 abteilung(G.), apportion, dismember 10 department, incomplete 11 constituent
  baglike: sac
  basic: 4 core, pith 7 essence
  central: 4 core 5 focus, solar 6 nuclei(pl.) 7 nucleus
  choice: 5 cream, elite 6 marrow 7 essence
  coarse: 5 dregs
  distinct: 4 unit 7 article
  essential: 4 core, gist, pith 6 factor
  final: 5 shank 6 epilog
  hardest: 5 brunt
  highest: top 4 apex 5 crest 6 summit
  inmost: 4 core 5 heart 6 center
  main: 4 body 5 trunk
  minor: bit, cog
  missing: 6 lacuna
  moving: 5 rotor
  narrow: 4 neck
  revolving: 5 rotor 7 rotator
  root-like: 7 radicle
  rounded: 4 bulb
  small: bit, jot 4 atom, iota, mite 5 tithe 6 detail, moiety 7 snippet
  suddenly: 4 rend, snap
  uppermost: top 4 peak 6 upside 7 topside

part with: 4 give, lose, sell 5 leave 6 donate 7 abandon

partage: 4 part 5 share 7 portion 8 division

partake: 4 bite 5 eat of, share 6 divide, join in 11 participate
  of: use

partan: 4 crab

parted: 5 cleft 7 divided, partite 9 separated

Parthian ruler: 7 Arsaces

parti-colored: 4 pied 7 piebald 9 checkered 10 variegated

partial: 4 half, part 6 biased, unfair 7 colored, halfway 8 coloured, inclined, onesided, partisan 10 fractional, incomplete, prejudiced 11 predilected, predisposed

participant: 8 partisan 10 accomplice

participate: 4 join, side 5 enter, share 6 be in on 7 compete, partake 9 cooperate 11 get in the act

particle: ace, bit, dot, gru, jot 4 atom, grue, iota, mite, mote, whit 5 fleck, grain, shred, speck 6 morsel, smidge, tittle 7 driblet, smidgen, smidgin 8 smidgeon, smitchin

affirmative: yes

burnt: 6 cinder

coordinating: or

cosmic: 5 meson

electrified: ion 5 anion 6 cation, proton 7 neutron

icy: 5 sheet

incandescent: 5 spark

minute: jot, ort, ray 4 atom, iota, mite, mote 5 grain, speck 7 granule, ramenta(pl.) 8 molecule, ramentum 9 scintilla

negative: nor, not

negative-charged: ion 8 electron

pluvial: 4 drop

positive-charged: ion 6 proton 8 positron

particular: 4 item, nice 5 fussy, point, thing 6 detail, minute 7 article, careful, correct, precise, special, unusual 8 accurate, concrete, detailed, especial, exacting, itemized, specific 10 fastidious, individual, noteworthy, scrupulous 11 scrumptious 12 circumstance 13 extraordinary 14 circumstantial

opposite: 7 general

particularly: 9 expressly 10 especially

parting: 5 death 8 farewell 11 leavetaking

parting shot: 5 taunt

partisan: 4 pike 5 staff 6 biased, fautor 7 devotee 8 adherent, follower 9 truncheon 10 factionary, factioneer, interested

unwavering: 6 zealot 8 stalwart

partite: 6 parted 7 divided 9 separated

partition: 4 wall 5 septa(pl.) 6 divide, screen, septum 7 enclose, portion, scantle 8 cleavage, close off, division 9 severance 10 distribute, enterclose, separation 11 compartment 13 apportionment

partitioned: 7 septate

partlet: hen 5 woman

partner: pal 4 ally, half, mate, wife 5 butty, crony 6 cohort, fellow, sharer 7 comrade, consort, husband 8 camarada, sidekick 9 associate, coadjutor, colleague, companion 10 accomplice 11 confederate, participant

comedian's: 6 stooge

paid: 6 escort, gigolo

partnership: hui 4 firm 5 tie-up 7 cahoots, company 11 association 14 compagnieschap(D.)

partridge: 4 yutu 5 titar 6 chukar, chukor, seesee 7 tinamou 9 francolin

flock: 5 covey

young: 7 cheeper 8 squealer

parts(see also **part**): 9 genitalia

innermost: 10 penetralia

together: 9 adhesions

totality: 5 unity

two: 6 binary

parturition: 5 birth, labor 7 travail 8 delivery 10 childbirth

party (see also **political party**): bal(F.) 4 clan, drum, orgy, sect, side 5 cabal, group 6 comite, fiesta, person 7 company, faction 9 gathering 10 detachment 11 association, combination 12 participator

afternoon: tea 9 reception

evening: 4 ball 6 soiree

gift: 5 favor

guilty: 7 culprit

men's: 4 stag 6 smoker

reconnaissance: 6 patrol

seashore: 6 picnic 8 clambake

party girl: 4 doxy 10 prostitute

party man: 8 partisan

parure: 5 adorn 6 paring 7 apparel, peeling 8 ornament

parvenu: 4 snob 6 arrive 7 upstart 9 arriviste 11 pig in clover 12 nouveau riche

Pascal work: 7 Pensees

Pasch, Pascha: 6 Easter 8 Passover 10 Good Friday

paschal: 4 lamb 6 supper 8 Passover 11 celebration

pasear: 4 walk 6 airing 9 excursion, promenade

pasha: dey 4 emir

territory: 8 pachalic, pashalic, pashalik

Pashur: *father:* 5 Immer 8 Malchiah

son: 8 Gedaliah

Pasiphae: *children:* 7 Ariadne, Phaedra

husband: 5 Minos

pasqueflower: 6 badger 8 gosling 9 aprilfool 10 badgerweed

pasquinade: 5 squib 6 satire 7 lampoon, pasquil

pass: col, end, gap 4 abra, beal(Sc.), comp, cove, fare, ghat, hand, lane, pace, step, wend 5 canto, enact, ghaut, gorge, hurry, kotal, lapse, lunge, occur, relay, smite, spend, utter, yodel 6 billet, convey, defile, elapse, exceed, expire, happen, passus, permit, ticket, twofer 7 allonge, approve, devolve, passage, surpass, undergo 8 beallach, hand down, surmount 10 abjudicate, permis-

sion **11** Annie Oakley, leave behind **13** complimentary
slowly: **4** drag
without touching: **5** clear
pass around: 5 skirt **6** detour
pass away: die **6** expire, perish, vanish **8** transfer **9** disappear, surrender
pass by: 4 cote, omit, skip **6** forego, forget, ignore **8** overlook **9** disregard
pass off: con **4** pose **5** foist
pass on: die **5** leak **6** convey, impart **7** decease **8** transmit **11** communicate
pass over: die **4** omit, skip **5** cross **6** elapse, expire, excuse, ignore **7** neglect **8** overlook, permeate, transfer, traverse **9** disregard
lightly: **4** skim
quickly: **4** scan, scud
smoothly: **5** elide
pass through: 5 cross **6** divide, pierce **7** pervade **8** permeate, traverse **9** penetrate
pass up: 6 reject **7** decline **9** disregard
passable: fit **4** fair, soso **7** genuine **8** adequate, mediocre, moderate **9** navigable, tolerable **10** admissable, negotiable **11** traversable
passage: gat, gut, wro **4** adit, belt, door, duct, exit, fare, flue, ford, gang, gate, hall, iter, lane, pass, path, pawn, race, ramp, road, slip **5** aisle, allee, alley, alure, atria(pl.), entry, going, gorge, meuse **6** access, arcade, atrium, avenue, burrow, course, defile, egress, strait, travel, tunnel, voyage **7** channel, couloir, estuary, gangway, itinera(pl.), journey, transit **8** aqueduct, corridor, crossing **9** enactment, ventiduct **10** bottleneck, transition **12** thoroughfare **13** accommodation
air: **4** flue **9** ventiduct
between two walls: **5** slype
covered: **6** arcade
literary: **4** text **7** excerpt **9** quotation
mine: **5** stope
musical: bar, cue **4** link **5** break, stave **7** cadenza **8** flourish, spicatto
one outlet: **7** impasse **8** cul-de-sac
roofed: **6** arcade **9** breezeway
scripture: **4** text
subterranean: **4** mine **6** tunnel **8** cuniculi(pl.) **9** cuniculus
passant: 4 past **7** current, cursory, walking **9** ephemeral, excelling **10** proceeding, surpassing, transitory
passe: 4 aged, past, worn **5** faded **7** demoded **8** obsolete, outmoded **9** out-of-date **10** antiquated **12** old-fashioned **13** superannuated
passel: 4 body **5** bunch, group **6** bundle **7** cluster
passementerie: 6 edging **8** trimming
passenger: 4 fare **7** standby **8** ferryman, traveler, wayfarer
passerby: 9 saunterer
passerine bird: 7 sparrow **8** starling
passing: 5 death **7** cursory **8** elapsing, fleeting **9** departing, ephemeral, exceeding **10** pre-eminent, transitory, surpassing
passion (see also **mania**): ire **4** fire, fury, heat, love, lust, raga, rage, zeal **5** anger, ardor **6** affect, choler, desire, fervor, temper **7** emotion, feeling, fervour **8** appetite, distress **9** calenture, martyrdom **10** affliction, enthusiasm, heartthrob
passion flower: 6 maypop **8** bullhoof
family: **14** passifloraceae
passionate: 4 fond **6** fervid, fierce **7** amorous, flaming, peppery **8** frenetic **9** hotheaded, irascible, phrenetic **11** hot-tempered, impassioned **12** affectionate, concupiscent **13** quick-tempered
passionless: 4 calm, cold **6** freddo(It.) **8** detached
passive: 5 inert, stoic **6** latent, stolid **7** patient **8** inactive, yielding **9** apathetic, impassive, lethargic, quiescent **10** phlegmatic, submissive
Passover: 5 Pesah **6** Pesach
bread: **5** matzo **6** matzos **7** matzoth **8** afikomen
festival: **5** Sedar
pert. to: **7** paschal
songs of praise: **6** hallel
story: **7** haggada **8** haggadah
passport: key **5** conge **6** dustuk **7** dustuck, ticket **8** furlough **9** safeguard **10** open sesame
endorsement: **4** visa
passus: 4 pace, part, step **5** canto **8** division
password: 11 countersign
past: ago **4** gone, yore **5** after, agone, ended, since **6** behind, beyond, bygone **8** foregone **9** completed, foregoing **11** antecedents
immediate: **9** yesterday
pert to: **8** historic
tense: **11** perteritive
pasta: 4 orzo **7** ravioli **8** linguine, macaroni **9** fettucini, spaghetti **10** vermicelli
paste: hit, pap **4** beat, blow, cuff, duff, glue, pate **5** cream, dough, false, punch, stick **6** attach, batter, fasten, strass **7** filling **8** adhesive, mucilage **9** imitation
aromatic: **6** pastil **7** pastile **8** pastille
dried: **7** guarana
pasteboard: 4 card, sham **6** flimsy
pastel: 4 pale **6** crayon **7** picture
pastern: 6 hobble, hopple, tether **7** shackle
Pasternak novel: 7 Zhivago
heroine: **4** Lara
pastiche: 4 olio **6** jumble, medley **9** patchwork, potpourri **10** hodgepodge

pastime: 4 game 5 hobby, sport 9 amusement, diversion 10 recreation 13 entertainment

past master: 6 expert

pastor: 4 herd 5 angel, rabbi 6 curate, keeper, priest, rector 7 dominie 8 guardian, minister, shepherd 9 clergyman

pastoral: 4 poem 5 drama, rural 7 bucolic, idyllic, romance 8 agrarian
god: Pan
pert. to: 8 agrestic, geoponic
pipe: 4 reed
place: 7 Arcadia
poem: 4 idyl 5 idyll 7 eclogue, georgic

pastry (see also **cake, pie**): pie 4 baba, cake, flan, huff, tart 5 torte 6 eclair 7 carcake(Sc.), strudel 8 napoleon, turnover 9 cream puff, vol-au-vent 11 petits fours
garnish: 5 cream, fruit 8 meringue
shell: 7 dariole, timbale

pasturage: 4 gang 6 eatage, forage 7 herbage

pasture: lea 5 agist, drift, grass, graze, veldt 6 meadow, saeter 7 grazing, vaccary 9 grassland 10 agostadero
god: Pan

pasty: pie 6 doughy, pallid, sickly 9 unhealthy

pat: apt, dab, tap 4 blow, glib 5 fitly, fixed, impel, throw 6 caress, soothe, strike, stroke, timely 7 apropos, fitting, readily 8 suitable 9 immovable, opportune, pertinent 10 seasonable 12 commendation

Patagonia: *deity:* 7 Setebos
rodent: 4 cavy, mara
tree: 6 alerce, alerse

patch: bit 4 mend, vamp 5 bodge, clout, clump, cover, piece, scrap 6 blotch, cobble, dollop, emblem, parcel, repair, revamp, solder 7 clobber, overlay, remnant
of woods: 5 motte
up: 4 heal, mend

patchwork: 5 cento 6 jumble, scraps 9 fragments 10 hodgepodge, miscellany

pate: pie, top 4 head 5 crown, paste, pasty, patty 6 badger, noggin, spread

patella: pan 4 dish, vase 6 limpet 7 kneecap, kneepan

paten: 4 arca, disc, dish, disk 5 plate 6 vessel

patent: 4 arca, open 5 clear, gross, overt, plain 7 evident, license, obvious 8 apparent, archives, enduring, flagrant, manifest 9 available, franchise 12 unobstructed
medicine: 7 nostrum
notice: 6 caveat

pater: 6 father, priest

paternal: 8 fatherly

kinsman: 6 agnate

paternity: 6 father, origin 10 authorship, fatherhood 12 fatherliness

path: pad, rut, way 4 fare, lane, line, road, walk 5 alley, byway, going, piste, route, track, trail 6 camino, casaun, comino, course, groove 7 footway, highway, towpath
hill: 4 berm 5 berme 6 roddin 7 rodding(Sc.)
math: 5 locus

pathetic: sad 5 sorry, teary 6 moving 7 pitiful 8 stirring 9 affecting

pathic: 6 victim 7 passive, subject 8 catamite 9 suffering

pathological: 4 sick 6 morbid

pathos: 4 pity 9 poignancy

patience: 4 calm 8 stoicism 9 composure, endurance, fortitude 10 submission 11 forbearance, resignation, self-control 12 acquiescence 13 long-suffering

patient: 4 case, meek 6 bovine 13 long-suffering

patina: 5 gloss 6 finish, polish

patio: 5 court 7 terrace 9 courtyard

patisserie: 4 shop 6 pastry

patois: 4 cant 6 Creole, jargon 7 dialect

patriarch: 4 Enos, Levi, Nasi, Noah 5 elder 7 ancient, veteran 9 venerable

patrician: 5 noble 9 gentleman 10 aristocrat 12 aristocratic

patrimony: 6 legacy 8 ancestry, heritage 10 birthright 11 inheritance

patriot: 8 loyalist, partisan 9 flag-waver 10 chauvinist, countryman 11 compatriate, nationalist
song: 6 anthem 7 America

patrol: 5 guard, scout, watch 7 protect 10 detachment

patrolman: cop 5 guard 9 inspector, policeman

patron: 5 buyer, guest 6 client, fautor 7 sponsor 8 advocate, champion, customer, defender, guardian 9 protector, supporter 10 benefactor
stock exchange: 5 buyer 6 seller, trader

patron saint: *of beggars:* 5 Giles
of children: 8 Nicholas
of cripples: 5 Giles
of England: 6 George
of fishermen: 5 Peter
of Ireland: 7 Patrick
of lawyers: 4 Ives, Yves
of musicians: 7 Cecilia
of Norway: 4 Olaf
of sailors: 4 Elmo 8 Nicholas
of Scotland: 6 Andrew
of shoemakers: 7 Crispin
of winegrowers: 7 Vincent
of workers: 6 Joseph

patronage: 5 aegis, favor 6 custom, favour 7 auspice, fomento 8 business 10 assistance 13 encouragement

patronize: use **5** deign **8** frequent **10** condescend

patsy: sap **4** dupe, fool **5** chump **6** sucker, victim **7** fall guy **9** scapegoat

patten: **4** base, clog, foot, shoe **5** skate, stand, stilt **6** sandal **7** support **8** overshoe, snowshoe

patter: **4** cant, talk **5** lingo **6** jargon **7** blatter, chatter

pattern: **4** form, norm, plan **5** bysen, draft, epure, guide, ideal, model, order, plaid **6** checks, design, figure, format, former, sample, stripe **7** example, project, stencil, templet **8** exemplar, forbysen, paradigm, specimen, template **9** archetype, ensampler, precedent **11** arrangement

patulous: **4** open **8** expanded **9** distended, spreading

paucity: **4** lack **6** dearth **7** fewness **8** exiguity, scarcity **13** insufficiency

Paul: **7** apostle
birthplace: **6** Tarsus
companion: **5** Silas, Titus **7** Artemas, Timothy **8** Barnabas
original name: **4** Saul
place of conversion: **8** Damascus
prosecutor: **9** Tertullus
teacher: **8** Gamaliel
tribe: **8** Benjamin

pauldron: **5** armor **6** splint

paunch: **5** belly, rumen **7** abdomen, stomach **8** potbelly **10** disembowel, eviscerate

pauper: **6** beggar **8** indigent **10** down-and-out

pause: **4** halt, lull, rest, stop, wait **5** abide, break, cease, comma, delay, demur, dwell, hover, letup, selah, tarry **6** breach, breath, falter, stance **7** caesura, respite **8** breather, caesurae(pl.), hesitate, intermit **9** cessation **10** hesitation **12** intermission, interruption

paut: paw **4** poke **5** stamp **6** finger

pavane: **5** dance

pave: lay **4** path, stud, tile **5** cover, floor **6** causey, cobble, smooth **7** overlay, prepare **10** facilitate, macadamize

pavid: **5** timid **6** afraid **7** fearful

pavilion: **4** flag, tent **5** kiosk **6** canopy, ensign, litter **8** covering **9** gloriette

paving: **4** flag, sett **5** block, brick, dalle, paver, stone **6** cobble, Tarmac **7** asphalt **9** flagstone

pavis: **5** cover **6** screen, shield **10** protection

pavo: **7** peacock **13** constellation

paw: pud, toe **4** foot, gaum, hand, maul, paty **5** patte, touch **6** fumble, handle, pattee **7** crubeen, flipper **8** forefoot

pawky: sly **4** arch, bold **5** canny, saucy **6** crafty, lively, shrewd **7** cunning, forward, squeamish

pawl: cog, dog **4** bolt, sear, tent, trip **5** catch, click **6** detent, pallet, tongue **7** ratchet

pawn: **4** gage, hock, soak, tool **6** lumber, pledge **7** counter, hostage **8** chessman, guaranty **11** impignorate

pawnbroker: **11** moneylender

Pawnee: **6** Indian
rite: **4** hako

pawpaw: **5** fruit, papaw **6** papaya **7** immoral, naughty **8** indecent **11** bushwhacker

pax: **5** board, peace **6** friend, tablet **10** friendship, osculatory

pay: fee, tip **4** ante, foot, meet, rent, wage **5** clear, repay, spend, yield **6** defray, pony up, reward, salary, satisfy **7** imburse, requite, satisfy, stipend, tribute **9** indemnify, make up for, reimburse **10** compensate, recompense, remunerate **11** retribution **12** compensation
attention: **4** heed **6** listen
back: **6** rebate, refund **9** reimburse, retaliate
extra: **5** batta, bonus **8** kickback
for: buy **4** rent **8** purchase
homage: **5** adore, honor **6** salaam
out: **5** spend **6** expend **8** disburse **10** distribute
up: **4** ante, quit **6** settle **9** liquidate

payable: due **5** owing **11** outstanding

paying: **5** sound **7** solvent **10** profitable **12** advantageous

paymaster: **6** bakshi, bukshi, purser **7** bukshee(Ind.) **8** buckshee **9** treasurer

payment: cro, fee, tax **4** bill, dole, dues, duty, feal, fine, gale, levy, toll **5** gavel, price **6** pledge, rebate, return, reward, tariff **7** alimony, annuity, customs, pension, stipend, trewage, tuition **8** defrayal, requital **9** acquittal, allowance, discharge, honoraria(pl.) **10** honorarium, recompense, remittance **12** compensation, contribution
demand: dun **4** bill
evade: **4** bilk **7** default
failure: **13** nonredemption
illegal: **5** bribe **6** payola **8** kickback
immediate: **4** cash **9** alcontado(Sp.)
on delivery: COD
press for: dun
without: **4** free **6** gratis

payoff: fix **5** bribe **6** climax, profit, return, reward **9** reckoning **10** settlement

payola: **5** bribe

payong: **8** umbrella

paysage: **7** picture **9** landscape

pea: dal **4** gram, seed **5** arhar, chick, cicer, pease **6** gandul, legume, pigeon **7** carmele, catjang **8** garvanro **12** peavetchling
dove: **7** zenaida
early: **8** hastings

family **8** fabaceae
finch: **9** chaffinch
flour: **9** Erbswurst
pod: **5** quash
sausage: **9** Erbswurst
seeds: **5** pulse
shaped: **8** pisiform
peabird: 6 oriole **7** wryneck
peace: pax(L.), paz(Sp.) **4** calm, ease, liss,
rest **5** amity, grith, lisse, quiet **6** repose,
shalom **7** concord, harmony, requiem **8**
ataraxia, security, serenity **9** armistice,
heartease **10** heartsease **11** tranquility
goddess: **5** Irene
symbol: **4** dove, toga **5** olive
peace pipe: 7 calumet
peaceable: 6 gentle **7** amiable, pacific,
solomon **8** amicable **11** undisturbed
peaceful: 4 calm **5** still **6** irenic, placid,
steady **7** halcyon **8** irenical **9** unruffled
11 undisturbed
peach: 4 blab **5** dilly **6** accuse, betray, indict, inform **7** impeach, whittle **8** jimdandy **11** crackerjack
grafted on quince: **9** melocoton
kind: **6** Carman, Crosby, Salwey **7** El-
berta **8** Crawford, quandang, quandong,
quantong **9** freestone, nectarine **10**
clingstone
origin: **5** China
stone: **7** putamen
peachwort: 9 persicary
Peach State: 7 Georgia
peachy: 4 fine, nice **5** dandy **9** beautiful,
excellent
peacock: mao **4** pavo, pawn **5** strut **7**
swagger
fan: **9** flabellum
feather fiber: **4** marl
female: **6** peahen
pert. to: **8** pavonine
tail spot: eye
peacock bittern: sun
peacock fish: 6 wrasse
peacock flower: 8 flambeau **9** poinciana
peacock heron: 7 bittern
peacock ore: 7 bornite **12** chalcopyrite
peag, peage: tax **4** toll **5** beads **6** pedage,
wampum
pea jacket: 11 seaman's coat **13** hip-
length coat
peak: Alp, ben, pic(F.), top, tor **4** acme,
apex, cima, cusp, dent, dolt, pico(Sp.) **5**
crest, crown, point, slink, sneak, steal,
visor **6** shrink, summit **7** epitome, maximum **8** aiguille, headland, mountain,
pinnacle **9** ascendant, ascendent, simpleton **10** promontory
ice: **4** berg **5** serac
ornament: epi **6** finial
rock: alp **4** crag
snow-capped: **7** calotte
peaked: wan **4** pale, thin **5** drawn, sharp

6 picked, sickly **7** pointed **9** emaciated
peal: 4 clap, ring, toll **5** chime **6** appeal,
shovel **7** resound, summons, thunder **8**
carillon
Peale Island: 4 Habe
peanut: 4 mani, mean **5** petty, pinda **6**
goober, pindal **7** beennut **8** earthnut,
earthpea, grassnut, katchung
peanuts: 8 trifling **15** inconsequential
pear: 4 bosc **5** melon **6** beurre, burrel,
warden, winter **7** kieffer, prickly **8** am-
brette, Bartlett, bergamot **9** alligator
10 chaumontel
squash: **5** perry **7** chayote
pear-shaped: 7 bulbous, rounded **8** pyriform
pearl: gem **4** seed, tear **5** nacre, onion **6**
bouton, orient **9** margarite
artificial: **4** blay **6** olivet
of great luster: **8** oriental
seed: **7** aliofar
pearl blush: 7 rosetan
pearl moss: 9 carrageen
Pearl of Antilles: 4 Cuba
pearl opal: 9 cacholong
pearlbird: 6 barbet **11** guinea-fowl
pearlweed: 6 sagina **8** sealwort
pearlwort: 6 sagina **7** poverty
pearly: 8 nacreous, precious
peasant: 4 bond, boor, hind, kopi, peon,
ryot, serf **5** churl, knave, kulak, swain **6**
cotman, cottar, cotter, farmer, fellah,
rascal, rustic **7** bondman, laborer, pai-
sano(Sp.) **9** chopstick, contadino(It.)
10 countryman
Arab: **6** fellah
class: **9** jacquerie
crop sharing: **7** metayer
dress: **7** dirndle
Irish: **4** kern **5** kerne
Russian: **5** kulak **6** muzhik
peashooter: 6 blower, pistol **7** blowgun **9**
slingshot **11** beanshooter
peat: gor(Ir.), pet **4** fuel, turf **6** lawyer,
minion **7** darling **8** favorite **11** combustible
bog: **4** cess, moss **6** yarpha
cutter: **5** piner(Sc.)
spade: **5** slane **6** tuscar
peatwood: 11 loosestrife
peau d'ange: 6 fabric, finish **9** angelskin
peavey, peavy: 4 hook **5** lever
peba: 9 armadillo
pebble: 5 scree, stone **6** gravel, quartz, sy-
cite **7** chuckie, crystal **10** chuckstone
pebble-shaped: 9 calciform **11** calculi-
form
peccadillo: 5 fault **7** offense **8** mischief
peccant: 6 morbid **7** corrupt, sinning **8**
diseased **9** incorrect, unhealthy
peccary: 6 warree **7** musk-hog, tagassu,
tayassu **8** javelina
pech: 4 pant, sigh **6** breath **7** breathe

pecht: 4 pict **5** fairy, gnome, pygmy

peck: dab, dot, nag, nip **4** beak, bill, carp, food, hole, jerk, kiss, nose **5** pitch, prick, throw **6** nibble, stroke **7** chimble, measure **9** great deal
at: nag **4** twit **5** tease **6** attack, harass
four: **6** bushel

pectase: 6 enzyme

peculate: 5 steal **6** misuse **8** embezzle **11** appropriate

peculiar: odd **5** queer **6** unique **7** curious, special, strange, unusual **8** especial, singular **9** eccentric, exclusive **10** particular **11** distinctive **14** characteristic

peculiarity: 4 kink **5** quirk, trait, twist **6** idiasm, oddity **9** attribute **12** idiosyncracy
of expression: **5** idiom **6** idioma, idiome

pecuniary: 8 monetary **9** financial

ped: 6 basket, hamper, panier **7** pannier

pedagogue: 5 tutor **6** pedant **7** dominie, teacher **12** schoolmaster

pedal: 5 lever **7** treadle
coupler: **7** tirasse
piano: **7** celeste

pedant: 4 prig **5** dunce, tutor **6** dorbel, purist, tassel **9** pedagogue **12** bluestocking, schoolmaster

pedantic: 7 bookish **8** teaching **10** didascalic, moralistic
writing: **9** academese

peddle: 4 hawk, sell **5** cadge, cycle, trant **6** higgle, meddle, piddle, retail **7** colport

peddler: 5 faker **6** broker, coster, duffer, hawker, seller, vendor **7** camelot, chapman **8** huckster, pitchman **12** carpetbagger, costermonger

pedestal: 4 anta, base **5** stand **6** pillar, podium **7** support **10** foundation
part: die **4** dado **5** socle **6** plinth, quadra
put on: **7** idolize **8** enshrine

pedestrian: ped **4** dull, slow **6** hoofer, walker **7** footman, plodder, prosaic **8** ordinary **11** commonplace **13** unimaginative

pedicel: ray **4** stem **5** scape, stalk **8** peduncle **9** footstalk
umbel: ray

pedigree: 6 stemma **7** descent, lineage **8** ancestry, purebred, stemmata **9** genealogy

pedometer: 8 odograph, waywiser **12** perambulator

pedum: 5 crook, staff

peek: 4 peep **6** glance **7** glimpse

peekaboo: 4 game **6** bopeep, peep-bo **7** peepeye

peel: 4 bark, harl, hull, pare, rind, skin **5** flipe, scale, slipe, stake, strip **6** shovel **7** undress **8** palisade, stockade **11** decorticate

peeler: 4 crab **5** bobby, corer **7** hustler **8** pillager **9** policeman **11** stripteaser

peeling: 4 rind, skin **6** paring

peep: pry, spy **4** peek, peer, pule, skeg **5** cheep, chirp, dekko, glint, snoop, tweet **6** glance, squeak **9** sandpiper
hawk: **7** kestrel
show: **5** raree

peeper: eye, Tom **4** frog **6** voyeur

peepeye: 8 peekaboo

peephole: 4 hole **6** eyelet **7** crevice, eyehole, opening

peeping: 4 nosy **5** nosey **11** inquisitive

peer: pry **4** duke, earl, fear, fere, gaze, look, lord, mate, peep **5** baron, equal, feere, gloze, noble, snoop, stare, stime(Sc.), styme(Sc.), thane(Sc.) **7** comrade, marquis **8** nobleman, superior, viscount **9** associate, rubberneck **12** contemporary
residence: **6** barony

Peer Gynt: *author:* **5** Ibsen
character: **4** King **6** Anitra
composer: **5** Grieg
mother: Ase

peerage: 4 rank **7** dignity **8** nobility

peerdom: 8 equality

peerless: 9 matchless, nonpareil, unrivaled **11** superlative

peetweet: 9 sandpiper

peeve: irk **6** grudge, nettle **8** irritate **9** annoyance

peevish: 5 cross, techy, testy, wemod **6** crusty, hipped, snarly, sullen, touchy **7** carping, crabbed, frecket, fretful, forward, pettish, spleeny, waspish **8** captious, choleric, contrary, critical, crotched, frampoid, petulant, sawshach, snappish **9** fractious, impatient, irascible, irritable, plaintive, splenetic **10** ill-humored **11** caper-noited, contentious, disgruntled

peewee: 4 bird, lark, tiny **5** dwarf **7** lapwing

peg: fix, hob, nob, nog, pin **4** plug, scob, step **5** cleat, dowel, drink, perch, piton, prong, spill, stake, throw, tooth **6** degree, dowell, marker, reason **7** pretext, support **8** fastener

pega, pegador: 6 remora

pegall: 6 basket

Pegasus: 11 winged horse
rider: **11** Bellerophon
source: **6** Medusa **13** constellation

Peggotty's niece: 5 Emily

peho: 8 morepork

peignoir: 4 gown **5** dress **6** kimono **7** wrapper **8** negligee **9** housecoat **12** dressing-gown

pejorative: 10 derogatory **11** disparaging

pelage: fur **4** hair, pelt

pelagic: 6 marine **7** aquatic, oceanic **9** thalassic

Peleg: *father:* **4** Eber
son: Reu

Peleus: *brother:* **7** Telamon
father: **6** Aeacus
son: **7** Pelides **8** Achilles
wife: **6** Thetis
pelf: rob **4** gain **5** booty, lucre, money, spoil, trash **6** pilfer, refuse, riches, spoils, wealth **7** despoil, rubbish
Pelican State: 9 Louisiana
pelike: jar **4** vase **7** amphora **8** amphorae
pellet: wad **4** ball, pill, shot **5** bolus, stone **6** bullet, pilule **7** granule
pellicle: 4 film, scum, skin **5** crust **7** coating, cuticle **8** membrane
pell-mell 8 confusion, disorder, headlong, stampede **11** impetuously **13** helter skelter
pellock: 8 porpoise
pellucid: 5 clear, sheer **6** bright, limpid **7** crystal **11** crystalline, translucent, transparent
pelmet: 7 cornice, valance
Peloponnesus: *city:* **6** Sparta
people: **7** Moreote
river god: **7** Alpheus
Pelops: *father:* **8** Tantalus
son: **6** Atreus **8** Pittheus, Thyestes
wife: **10** Hippodamia
pelota: 7 jai-alai
pelt: fur **4** beat, blow, cast, dash, fell, hide, hurl, push, skin **5** fitch, flung, hurry, stone **6** gallop, hasten, pelage, refuse, strike, thrust **7** rawhide, rubbish **8** woolfell
dealer: **7** furrier
peludo: 9 armadillo
pelvis: *bone:* **4** ilia **5** ilium, pubes **7** ischium
pert. to: **5** iliac
pen: cot, cub, get, mew, pin, sty **4** bolt, cage, coop, fold, jail, yard **5** bught, crawl, hutch, kraal, quill, write **6** bought, corral, cruive, fasten, hurdle, indite, record, stylus, zareba **7** calamus, compose, confine, enclose, zareeba **9** enclosure **12** penitentiary
kind: ink **8** fountain **9** ball-point **12** stylographic
point: neb, nib **4** stub
seller: **9** stationer
pen-like: 7 styloid
pen name (see also **nickname, pseudonym**): **5** alias **6** anonym **9** pseudonym **10** nom de plume
François Arouet: **8** Voltaire
Isaac Bickerstaff: **9** Dean Swift
Henri Beyle: **8** Stendhal
Eric Blair: **6** Orwell
Charlotte Bronte: **10** Currer Bell
Emily Bronte: **9** Ellis Bell
Samuel Clemens: **9** Mark Twain
Charles Dickens: Boz
Charles Dodgson: **12** Lewis Carroll
Amantine Dupin: **10** George Sand

Mary Ann Evans: **11** George Eliot
Benjamin Franklin: **11** Poor Richard
Charles Lamb: **4** Elia
H. H. Munro: **4** Saki
Alexei Peshkov: **10** Maxim Gorky
Jean Baptiste Poquelin: **7** Moliere
William S. Porter: **6** O. Henry
Jacques Thibault: **13** Anatole France
Louis Viaud: **10** Pierre Loti
penal: 8 punitive, punitory
penalize: 4 fine **5** mulct **6** amerce, punish
penalty: 4 fine, loss, pain **5** mulct **6** amende, amerce **7** forfeit **8** hardship **10** forfeiture, punishment **12** disadvantage
pay: aby **4** abye
penance: 6 sorrow **7** remorse **9** atonement, penitence, suffering **10** contrition, repentance **13** mortification
pencel: 4 flag **6** pennon **8** streamer **9** pennoncel
penchant: 4 bent **5** taste **6** liking **7** leaning **8** fondness **10** attraction **11** inclination
pencil: red, wad **4** blue, lead, wadd **8** charcoal **9** eversharp **10** mechanical
pert. to: **6** desmic
worn-down: **4** stub
pendant, pendent: bob, jab **4** flag, jagg, pend, tail **5** aglet **6** aiglet, tassel **7** pensile, support **8** gamaliel, lavalier **9** lavaliere, pendulous, suspended, undecided **11** counterpart
pending: 6 during
pendulous: lop **6** droopy **7** hanging **8** swinging
Penelope: *father:* **7** Icarius
father-in-law: **7** Laertes
husband: **7** Ulysses **8** Odysseus
suitor: **7** Agelaus
penetralia: 7 privacy **9** sanctuary
penetrate: 4 bore, dive, gore, stab **5** break, enter, imbue, steep **6** fathom, ficche, pierce **7** discern, pervade **8** permeate **9** insinuate, perforate **10** infiltrate, understand
penetrating: 5 acute, sharp **6** astute, shrewd, shrill, subtle **7** knowing **8** incisive **9** sagacious **10** insightful **11** clairvoyant **14** discriminating
penetration: wit **6** acumen **13** understanding
penguin: auk **6** Johnny
genus: **9** eudyptula
home: **4** pole **7** rookery **10** penguinery
large: **7** emperor
small: **6** Adelie
peninsula: 4 neck **6** penile **10** chersonese
penitence: rue **5** qualm **6** regret, sorrow **7** remorse, sadness, scruple **8** distress, humbling **10** contrition, repentance **11** compunction
season of: **4** Lent

penitent: 4 ruer 5 sorry 6 humble 10 remorseful

penitentiary: jug, pen 4 jail, stir 5 tench 6 prison 8 big-house

penman: 6 author, scribe, writer 10 amanuenses, amanuensis 12 calligrapher

penmanship: 4 hand 6 script 7 writing 11 calligraphy, handwriting

pennant: 4 fane, flag, whip 5 roger 6 cornet, banner, pennon, pinion 8 streamer 9 banderole

yacht: 6 burgee

pennate: 6 winged 9 feathered, penniform

penniless: 4 poor 5 broke, needy 8 bankrupt 9 insolvent 11 impecunious

pennon: 4 flag, wing 6 banner, pinion 7 feather, pennant

Pennsylvania: *battlefield:* 10 Gettysburg

capital: 10 Harrisburg

city: 4 Erie 7 Reading, Scranton 9 Allentown 10 Pittsburgh 12 Philadelphia

county: 5 Berks, Bucks 7 Cambria, Chester, Venango, Wyoming

flood: 9 Johnstown

mountain range: 6 Pocono 9 Allegheny

native: 5 Amish 9 Mennonite

nickname: 8 Keystone

river: 4 Ohio 8 Delaware 10 Schuylkill 11 Monongahela, Susquehanna

state bird: 6 grouse

state flower: 14 mountain laurel

state tree: 7 hemlock

valley: 6 Lehigh 7 Lebanon 10 Cumberland

penny: 4 cent 5 brown, pence 6 copper, saltee, stiver

penny-pinching: 6 stingy 7 miserly

penology: 11 criminology

Pensees author: 6 Pascal

pensile: 7 pendent 9 suspended 11 overhanging

pension: 6 retire 7 annuity, payment, stipend, subsidy, tribute 8 gratuity 9 allowance 10 exhibition

pensive: 4 blue 5 sober 6 dreamy, musing 7 wistful 10 meditative, melancholy, reflective, ruminating, thoughtful 13 contemplative

pent: 5 caged 6 shut up 8 confined, enclosed

pentacle: 4 star 8 hexagram

pentastitch: 4 poem 6 stanza 7 strophe

Pentateuch: law 4 tora 5 Bible, torah

first book: 7 Genesis

Pentheus: *grandfather:* 6 Cadmus

mother: 5 Agave

penthouse: 4 roof, shed 5 aerie 6 hangar 7 pentice 8 dwelling 9 apartment, treehouse

pentyl: 4 amyl

penumbra: 5 shade 6 shadow 7 umbrage

penurious: 4 mean, poor 6 barren, frugal, scanty, stingy 7 miserly, wanting 8 indigent 9 destitute 10 avaricious 12 parsimonious

penury: 7 beggary, poverty 9 privation

peon: 4 hand, pawn, serf 5 slave 6 thrall 7 footman, laborer, peasant, soldier 9 attendant, constable, messenger, policeman

state of: 7 peonage

peony: 4 piny 5 plant 6 flower, mouton

people (see also **person**): kin, men 4 folk, gens, herd, pais(law) 5 demos, gentée(Sp.), laity, stock 6 daoine, gentry, settle 7 inhabit, society, tilikum(Ind.) 8 canaglia(It.), canaille(F.), populate, tillicum(Ind.) 11 inhabitants, rank and file

aggregation: 5 tribe

ancient: 4 Seba 5 Itali, Medes 6 Greeks, Romans 7 Sabines 8 Grecians 9 Assyrians, Egyptians, Etruscans

ape-shaped skull: 9 proghathi

body: 4 race 5 tribe 6 nation 7 society 8 assembly, populace 9 citizenry, community 10 electorate, public Rais

group: mob 4 army, band, team 5 corps, crowd, posse 6 chorus, troupe, throng 7 company, coterie 8 assembly 9 orchestra 11 association

headless: 8 Acephali

pert. to: 6 ethnic 7 demotic

present: 5 class, crowd 10 assemblage, attendance 12 congregation

well-bred: 9 gentility

pep: vim 4 dash 5 verve, vigor 6 energy, ginger 7 animate, quicken 9 animation, briskness, encourage, stimulate 10 initiative, invigorate, liveliness

peplos: 5 scarf, shawl

peplum: 9 overskirt

pepo: 5 gourd, melon 6 squash 7 pumpkin 8 cucumber

pepper: ava, hot, red 4 kava, siri 5 betel, green, sirih, sweet 6 speckle 7 paprica, paprika 8 capsicum, kavakava, pimiento

beverage: 4 kava 8 kavakava

grass: 5 cress

hot: 5 chili 7 cayenne, tabasco

package: 6 robin

shrub: 4 cava, kava

species: 5 betel 7 cayenne

pepper-and-salt: 4 gray 7 mottled

pepper picker: 5 Peter, Piper

pepper plant: ava 5 chile, chili 6 chilli

peppermint camphor: 7 menthol

peppery: hot 4 keen 5 alert, fiery 6 lively 7 piquant, pungent 8 choleric, spirited, stinging 9 irascible, irritable 10 passionate

peppy: 4 keen 5 alert 6 lively 8 spirited 9 vivacious

Pequod's captain: 4 Ahab

per: 4 each 6 apiece 7 through

per se: 6 as such, itself 8 directly 11 essentially 13 intrinsically

peradventure: hap 5 doubt, maybe 6 chance, mayhap 7 happily, perhaps 8 possibly 11 uncertainty

perambulate: 4 walk 6 ramble, stroll 8 traverse 9 promenade

perambulator: 5 buggy 12 baby-carriage, pushwainling

per capita: all 4 each 6 apiece

perceive: see 4 feel, hear, know, note, take 5 grasp, scent, sense, smell, taste, touch 6 behold, descry, divine, notice 7 discern, observe, realize, sensate 8 comprise, comprize, identify 9 apprehend, recognize 10 articulate, comprehend, understand 11 distinguish 12 discriminate

perceivable: 11 perceptible

perceiving: 5 acute

percentage: 4 agio, odds, part 5 share 6 profit 7 portion, rake-off 9 advantage 11 probability

perceptible: 5 clear, lucid 7 tactile, visible 8 palpable, sensible, tangible 10 cognizable 11 appreciable, discernible, perceivable 12 intelligible, recognizable

perception: 4 idea 6 acumen 7 insight 9 sensation 13 animadversion, consciousness

capable of: 8 sentient

impaired: 13 acatamathesia

perch: bar, peg, rod, sit 4 fish, jook, mado, okow, pike, pole, pope 5 barse, light, roost, ruffe, staff 6 alight, sauger, settle, weapon, zingel 9 trumpeter

perchance: 5 haply, maybe 7 perhaps 8 possibly

Percheron: 5 horse

percolate: 4 ooze, seep, sift, silt 5 exude, leach 6 filter, strain 7 pervade 8 permeate

percolator: 6 biggin 9 coffeepot

percussion: 5 shock 6 impact 9 collision 10 detonation

percussion instrument: 4 drum, gong, trap 6 cymbal 7 marimba 8 triangle 9 xylophone 10 tambourine 12 glockenspiel

percylite: 7 boleite

perdition: 4 hell, loss, ruin 9 damnation 11 destruction

perdue, perdu: 6 hidden 9 concealed

perdurable: 7 durable, eternal, lasting 8 enduring 9 permanent 11 everlasting

Pere Goriot author: 6 Balzac

peregrinate: 4 roam, walk 6 travel, wander 7 journey, sojourn 8 traverse

peregrine: 4 hawk 5 alien 6 exotic, falcon 7 foreign, pilgrim, strange

peremptory: 5 final, utter 7 decided, express 8 absolute, decisive, dogmatic,

positive 9 arbitrary, imperious, masterful 10 conclusive, imperative 11 dictatorial 13 authoritative

perennial: old, rue 4 tree 5 carex, liana, liane, peony, plant, sedum 6 annual, banana 7 durable 8 enduring, geophyte, toadflax 9 continual, permanent, perpetual, recurrent, unceasing 12 neverfailing

perfect: all 4 fill, fine, holy, pure 5 exact, ideal, right, ripen, sheer, sound, utter, whole 6 entire, expert, finish 7 concoct, correct, improve, plenary, precise, sinless, spheral 8 absolute, accurate, circular, complete, finished, flawless, masterly, thorough 9 blameless, elaborate, exquisite, faultless, righteous 10 accomplish, consummate, immaculate, satisfying

perfecta: 11 betting pool

perfection: 4 acme, pink 5 ideal 7 fulness, paragon 8 fullness, maturity 9 integrity 10 excellence

realm of: 6 Utopia 8 Paradise

perfectly: 4 well 5 quite 10 altogether

perfecto: 5 cigar

perfervid: 6 ardent 7 zealous 11 impassioned

perfidious: 5 false, snaky, venal 8 disloyal, spiteful 9 dishonest, faithless, felonious 10 traitorous 11 dissaffected, treacherous

perfidy: 7 treason 8 apostasy, foul play 9 defection, Judas' kiss, treachery 10 disloyalty, infidelity 13 faithlessness

perforate: eat 4 bore, dock 5 drill, prick, punch 6 pierce, pounce, riddle 8 puncture 9 penetrate, torebrate 10 foraminate

perforation: 4 bore, hole 6 broach, eyelet, tresis 7 stencil 8 aperture

perform: act 4 char, fill, full, play 5 chare, dight, enact, exert 6 effect, fulfil, render, wind up 7 achieve, execute, exhibit, exploit, fulfill, furnish, gesture 8 bring off, transact 9 do up brown 10 accomplish, perpetrate

again: 7 re-enact

inadequately: 5 botch 6 bungle, mess up

while moving about: 11 peripatetic

with ceremony: 9 solemnise, solemnize

performance: act 4 deed, feat, show, test, work 5 stunt 6 acting, action, effect 7 benefit, concert, exploit, matinee 8 feasance, function 9 discharge, execution, rendition 10 completion, efficiency, fulfilment 11 fulfillment 12 consummation 14 accomplishment

daytime: 7 matinee

first: 5 debut 8 premiere

individual: 4 soli, solo

standard: 5 bogey

performer: 4 doer, moke 5 actor, shine 6 artist, worker 7 artiste 8 executor, thespian

company: 6 troupe

diligent: 5 plier 6 drudge 7 plugger 10 workaholic

low-grade: 9 hamfatter

supplementary: 7 ripieno

top-notch: ace 4 star

perfume: 4 atar, aura, balm, nose, otto 5 aroma, attar, cense, irone, myrrh, ottar, scent, smell 6 chypre, flavor, sachet 7 essence, flavour, incense, odorize, sweeten 8 bergamot, fumigate 9 fragrance

base: 4 musk 5 civet 6 neroli 8 bergamot 9 ambergris

container: 4 vial 5 phial 6 censer

medicated: 6 pastil, troche 7 pastile 8 pastille

oriental: 5 myrrh

pad: 6 sachet

powdery: 6 pulvil

shrub source: 8 abelmosk

with burning spice: 5 cense

perfumed cherry: 7 mahaleb

perfumer: 6 censer, sachet 8 atomizer, pomander, thurible

perfunctory: 5 usual 7 routine 8 careless 9 automatic 10 mechanical 11 indifferent, superficial

pergola: 5 arbor, bower 6 arbour 7 balcony, trellis 9 colonnade

perhaps: 5 maybe 6 ablins, belike, theory 7 ablings 8 doubtful, possibly, probably 9 perchance 11 conceivably

peri: elf 5 dwarf, fairy, houri 6 sprite

periapt: 5 charm 6 amulet

pericarp: pod 4 boll 5 berry, shell

Pericles: *consort:* 7 Aspasia

daughter: 6 Marina

disciple: 10 Alcibiades

father: 10 Xanthippus

rival: 10 Thucydides

ward: 10 Alcibiades

periculum: 4 risk 5 peril 6 danger

peril: 4 risk 6 crises, crisis, danger, hazard, menace 7 apperil, imperil 8 endanger, exposure, jeopardy 9 adventure 10 insecurity, subjection

perilous: 6 touchy 7 tottery 8 doubtful, unstable, unsteady 9 dangerous, desperate

perimeter: rim 6 border 7 outline 8 boundary 9 periphery 13 circumference

period: age, dot, end, eon, era 4 aeon, span, stop, term, time 5 avail, close, cycle, epact, epoch, spell, stage 6 season 8 duration, semester 10 conclusion 11 termination

critical: 6 crises, crisis

festive: 7 holiday 8 vacation

holding: 6 tenure

infinite: 8 eternity

penitential: 4 Lent

playing: 4 half, hand 5 frame, round 6 inning 7 chukkar, chukker, quarter

sleep: 6 godown 11 hibernation

tertiary: 6 eocene 7 neocene

time: day 4 hour, week, year 5 month 6 decade, minute, second 7 century 9 fortnight

periodic: 4 eral 6 annual 7 etesian, regular 8 frequent, seasonal 9 recurrent 12 intermittent

periodical: 5 daily, paper 6 annual, review, 7 etesian, journal, tabloid 8 bulletin, magazine 9 ephemeris, newspaper

peripatetic: 8 rambling 9 itinerant, wandering

peripheral: 5 outer 6 distal 7 distant 8 confined, external, marginal

periphery: lip, rim 4 brim, edge 5 ambit, limit 6 areola, areole, border 7 areolae, outside 8 confines, environs 9 perimeter 13 circumference

periphrastic: 14 circumlocutory

perique: 7 tobacco

perish: die 4 fade, fall, ruin 5 decay 6 depart, expire 7 consume, crumble, forfare, go under, succumb 8 pass away

perishable: 6 caduke 7 brittle 9 ephemeral 10 transitory

peristyle: 6 arcade 7 portico 9 colonnade 10 peripteral

perite: 7 skilled

peritomy: 12 circumcision

peritoneum: 8 covering, membrane

fold of: 7 omentum

peritroch: 5 larva 6 embryo

periwig: 6 peruke, toupee

periwinkle: 5 color, snail 6 mussel, myrtle 10 bluebutton

perjink: 4 neat, nice, trim 7 precise

perjure: lie 8 forswear 10 equivocate 11 prevaricate

perk: 5 preen, prink 7 improve, smarten 8 animated, gratuity 9 percolate 10 perquisite

permanent: 5 fixed 6 stable 7 abiding, durable, lasting 8 constant, enduring 9 continual, headdress, perennial 10 continuing, invariable 12 imperishable

permeable: 6 porous

permeate: 4 fill, seep 5 bathe, imbue 6 drench 7 pervade 8 saturate 9 penetrate

permission: 5 leave 7 consent, license 13 authorization

to use: 4 loan

permit: let 4 leve, pass 5 admit, allow, conge, favor, grace, grant, leave 6 accord, beteem, dustuk, entree, favour, suffer 7 consent, dustuck, license, pompano, warrant **8** furlough, tolerate **9** authorize **10** permission

travel: **8** passport

permutation: 6 change **10** alteration **11** interchange **12** modification **13** rearrangement

pern: 7 buzzard

pernicious: bad **4** evil **5** fatal, toxic **6** deadly, malign, mortal, wicked **7** baleful, baneful, harmful, hurtful, malefic, noisome, noxious, ruinous **10** villainous **11** deleterious, destructive, detrimental

pernio: 9 chilblain

peronate: 5 mealy, wooly

perorate: 5 orate **7** address, declaim **8** harangue

perpendicular: 4 sine **5** erect, plumb, sheer **6** abrupt **7** apothem, stand-up, straight, upright **8** binormal, vertical **9** downright

perpetrate: 5 wreak **6** commit, effect **7** perform

perpetual: 7 endless, eternal **8** constant, unending **9** continual, incessant, perennial, permanent, unceasing **10** continuous **11** everlasting

perpetually: 4 ever **6** always **7** forever **11** ad infinitum

perpetuate: 4 keep **8** continue, eternize, maintain, preserve

perplex: cap **4** clog, doze **5** amaze, beset **6** baffle, boggle, bother, cumber, darken, gravel, hamper, harass, hobble, muddle, pother, puzzle, thwart, twitch **7** bedevil, confuse, diffuse, embroil, mystify, nonplus **8** astonish, babulyie, bewilder, confound, distract, distress, entangle **9** bamboozle, obfuscate **10** complicate

perplexed: 4 asea **5** upset **7** anxious **8** confused, troubled **9** intricate **10** distraught

perplexing: 4 hard, mazy **6** crabby **7** carking, complex, crabbed **9** equivocal **11** complicated

perplexity: fox **4** knot **6** tangle **7** anxiety, trouble **9** intricacy **11** encumbrance **13** embarrassment

perquisite: fee, tip **5** right **6** income **7** adjunct, apanage **8** appanage, appenage, gratuity **9** accessory **11** appointment, prerogative **12** appurtenance **13** accompaniment

presidential: **4** veto

perquod: 7 whereby

Perry Mason creator: 7 Gardner

per se: 5 alone **6** as such, solely **8** in itself

Perse: *daughter:* **5** Circe **8** Pasiphae

father: **7** Oceanus

husband: **6** Helios

son: **6** Aeetes, Perses

persecute: vex **4** bait **5** annoy, harry, hound, worry, wrack, wrong **6** harass,

pester **7** afflict, oppress, torment, torture

Persephone: 4 Kore **8** Despoina

daughter: **4** Cora, Kore

father: **4** Zeus

husband: **5** Hades, Pluto

mother: **7** Demeter

Perseus: *father:* **4** Zeus

grandfather: **8** Acrisius

mother: **5** Danae

star of: **4** Atik **5** Algol

victim: **8** Acrisius

wife: **9** Andromeda

perseverance: 4 grit **7** stamina **8** patience, tenacity **9** assiduity, constancy, diligence, endurance **10** insistence, steadiness **11** continuance, persistence, pertinacity **12** continuation **13** indefatigable, steadfastness

persevere: 4 go on **5** abide, stick **7** persist **8** keep at it

persevering: 4 busy **10** persistent **11** unremitting

Persia (see also **Iran**): *ancient inhabitant:* **4** Mede

apple: **6** citron

assembly: **6** majlis, meklis

bug: **5** miana

carpet: see *rug* below

cat: **6** Angora

chief officer: **5** dewan, diwan

deer: **5** maral **6** fallow

elf or fairy: **4** peri

founder: **5** Cyrus

gate: bab

gazelle: **4** cora

goddess: **7** Anahita

lamb: **7** karakul **9** astrakhan

lynx: **7** caracal

measure: gaz, guz, zer

nightingale: **6** bulbul

oil center: **6** Abadan

old coin: **5** daric

poet: **4** Omar, Sadi **5** Hafiz

prophet: **9** Zoroaster

rug: **4** Kali **5** Saruk, Senna **6** Sarouk **7** Isfahan, Ispahan, Teheran **8** Serabend

ruler: **4** shah

scriptures: **5** Koran

sungod: **7** Mithras

tick: **8** miana bug

wheel: **5** noria **7** tympana **8** tympanum

Persian Gulf: *kingdom:* **7** Chaldea

port: **7** Bushire

province: **4** Fars

wind: **6** shamal, sharki **7** shurgee

persiennes: 6 blinds

persiflage: 6 banter **7** mockery **8** chaffing, raillery

persimmon: 7 chapote

family: **5** ebony **9** ebenaceae

persist: 4 go on, last **6** endure, insist, remain **7** carry on, prevail **8** continue **9** persevere

persistent: 4 dree, hard **6** dogged, gritty **7** durable **8** constant, enduring, frequent, holdfast, obdurate, resolute, stubborn **9** assiduous, continued, steadfast, tenacious **10** consistent, continuing, determined, relentless **11** persevering **13** indefatigable

person (see also **people**): guy, man, one, urf **4** body, chap, coot, self, soul **5** being, child, human, wight, woman **6** entity, fellow, galoot **10** individual

admirable: **6** mensch

amusing: **8** comedian, comedien **10** comedienne

bad-luck carrier: **4** jinx **5** jonah

baptized: **10** illuminato **11** illuminatus

base: **7** caitiff, hangdog

bearing the blame: **4** goat

beatified: **6** beatus

betrothed: **6** fiance **7** fiancee

blamed for others: **4** butt, goat **9** scapegoat

brilliant: **6** genius **10** mastermind

callow: **6** gorlin, smarty **7** gosling

canonized: **5** saint

careless: **6** tassel **11** pococurante

charitable: **9** samaritan

cheery: **8** optimist

clumsy: **5** klutz

contemptible: cad, yap **4** heel, toad **7** bauchle

cunning: **8** slyboots

deranged: nut **7** lunatic **10** monomaniac, psychopath

despicable: **5** hound **6** rotter **10** blackguard

detested: **8** anathema

disgruntled: **8** sorehead

dull: **5** dunce, moron **8** imbecile **9** blockhead, defective

eighty-year-old: **12** octogenarian

energetic: **10** ball of fire

enterprising: **8** go-getter

fearless: **10** fearnaught, fearnought **11** dreadnaught, dreadnought

fifty-year-old: **15** quinquagenarian

foolish: sop **4** zany **5** clown **6** dotard **7** halfwit **9** simpleton

forty-year-old: **14** quadragenarian

good-luck carrier: **6** mascot

gray-headed: **7** grisard

guilty: **7** culprit

half-grown: **6** haflin **8** halfling **9** stripling

held as pledge: **7** hostage

holy: ste.(F.) **5** saint

horned: **7** cornute

ill: **7** invalid, patient

indefinite: one **6** anyone **7** anybody, so and so, someone **8** somebody

indifferent to pleasure or pain: **5** stoic

injured: **6** victim **8** casualty

learned: **6** pundit, savant **7** scholar **9** professor **12** intellectual

left-handed: **9** portsider

loud-voiced: **7** stentor

married: **4** wife **6** spouse **7** husband

middle-class: **9** bourgeois **11** bourgeoisie

mischievous: imp **4** pest

named after another: **8** namesake

ninety-year-old: **12** nonagenarian

non-Jewish: **7** gentile

of distinction: VIP **4** star **7** notable

of mixed blood: **7** mestizo, mulatto **8** octoroon **9** half-breed

one-hundred-year-old: **11** centenarian

overnice: **4** prig

perfidious: **5** snake **7** serpent, traitor

proposed for office: **7** nominee

rapacious: **4** wolf **5** harpy, shark

representing another: **5** mimic, proxy **9** alternate

rude: **4** boor **7** caveman

scolding: **9** catamaran

second: you **4** thou

seventy-year-old: **14** septuagenarian

shiftless: bum **7** drifter

sick: **5** ailer **7** invalid, patient **9** aegrotant

sixty-year-old: **12** sexagenarian

skilled: **5** adept **6** artist, master, talent **7** artisan **8** mechanic

small: **4** runt **5** dwarf, sprat **6** midget, poppet

sponsored by another: **7** protege

studious: **5** grind, porer

stupid: ass **4** boob, clod, coot, dolt, fool, gump, moke **5** bucca, clout, moron, stirk, stock, stupe, sumph **6** boodle, duffer, gander, nitwit **7** dullard **8** bonehead, dumbbell, gamphrel **9** boeoetian, simpleton

timid: **11** milquetoast

trustworthy: **7** standby

unmarried: **6** maiden **8** bachelor, celibate, spinster

unusual: **4** oner

wealthy: **5** nabob **9** plutocrat **10** capitalist **11** millionaire **12** millionnaire

white: fay **4** ofay **5** haole **6** albino **7** abiculi, redneck

young: **8** chipling **9** stripling **14** whippersnapper

persona non grata: 12 unacceptable

personable: 6 comely **7** shapely **8** handsome **10** attractive **11** good-looking, well-favored

personage: 6 shogun, tycoon **7** magnate, notable

personal: own **7** private **8** intimate, news item

personality: ego **4** self **8** selfhood **11** disposition **13** individuality

dual: **13** Jekyll and Hyde

split: **13** schizophrenia

personification: 10 embodiment **11** incarnation **14** representation

of rumor: **4** Fama

of truth: Una

personify: 6 embody **9** incarnate, represent **11** impersonate

personnel: 5 staff **9** employees

perspective: 5 vista **7** outlook **9** viewpoint

perspicacious: 4 keen **5** acute **6** shrewd **10** discerning, perceptive **11** penetrating, sharp-witted

perspicacity: wit **6** acumen

perspicuous: 5 clear, lucid, plain **8** manifest **11** conspicuous, translucent, transparent **12** intelligible

perspiration: 5 sudor, sweat **9** exudation **10** ephidrosis

abnormal: **8** hidrosis

pert. to: **7** sudoric

sheep: **5** suint

persuade: get, win **4** coax, gain, sway, urge **5** argue **6** allure, assure, engage, entice, induce **7** convert, entreat, win over **8** convince, inveigle **9** influence

persuaded: 7 pliable **8** gullible **9** credulous

persuasion: 4 cult, mind, view **6** belief **8** judgment, religion

persuasive: 6 cogent **8** eloquent **9** impelling, inductive

pert: 4 bold **5** alert, alive, bardy, brisk, cocky, quick, sassy, saucy, smart **6** active, brazen, clever, cocket, comely, dapper, frisky, lively **7** forward, naughty **8** handsome, impudent, insolent, petulant **9** exquisite, officious, sprightly **11** flourishing

pert girl: 4 minx

pertain: 5 belie **6** bear on, befall, belong, relate **7** concern **9** accessory, associate

pertaining to: For all definitions beginning with this phrase, see under following main word or phrase, EXAMPLES: "pertaining to gold": see **gold:** *pert. to;* "pertaining to the sun": see **sun:** *pert. to.*

pertinacious: 4 firm **6** dogged **8** adhering, stubborn **9** obstinate, tenacious **10** determined, inflexible, persistent, unshakable, unyielding

pertinent: 4 apt, fit, pat **6** proper, timely **7** adapted, apropos, germane, telling **8** apposite, relative, relevant **10** applicable, felicitous **11** appropriate **12** appurtenance

perturb: 5 upset, worry **7** agitate, confuse, derange, disturb, trouble **8** disorder, unsettle **10** discompose, disconcert

perturbation: 6 flight, pother **7** trouble, turmoil **9** agitation, commotion **10** un-

easiness **12** irregularity

pertussis: 5 cough **13** whooping cough

Peru: *animal:* **5** llama **6** alpaca

bark: **8** cinchona

capital: **4** Lima

city: Ica **5** Cuzco, Paita **6** Callao **7** Iquitos **8** Arequipa

conqueror: **7** Pizarro

cormorant: **6** Guanay

dance: **5** cueca

department: Ica, Yca **4** Lima **5** Cusco, Cuzco, Piura, Tacna, Tagna

emblem of nobility: **6** llautu

empire: **4** Inca, Ynca

fog: **5** garua

goddess: **4** Mama

hillock: **4** loma

inn: **5** tambo

king: **7** cacique

lake: **8** Titicaca

liberator: **7** Bolivar

liquor: **5** pisco

llama: **4** paco **6** alpaca

mark of nobility: **6** llautu

measure: **4** topo, vara **5** galon **7** celemin **8** fanegada

monetary unit: sol **5** libra **6** dinero, peseta **7** centavo

partridge: **4** yutu

people: **4** Ande, Cana, Inca, Inka, Peba, Yutu **5** Boros, Campa, Carib, Panos **6** Aymara, Jibaro, Jiyaro, Kechua, Lamano **7** Quechau

plant: oca **6** ulluco **7** rhatany

relic: **5** huaco

river: Ica **5** Rimac, Santa **7** Maranon, Ucayale **8** Apurimac, Huallaga, Urubamba **11** Paucartambo

rodent: **10** chinchilla

ruler: **4** Inca, Inka

shrub: **6** chilca, matico, shansa

skin disease: uta

tableland: **4** puna

tavern: **5** tambo

tinamou: **4** yutu

tree: **6** bucare **8** cinchona

tuber: oca

volcano: **5** Misti

weight: **5** libra **7** quintal

wind: **4** puna **5** sures

peruke: wig **6** toupee **7** periwig

peruse: con **4** read, scan **5** study **6** handle, search, survey **7** examine, inspect **9** supervise

pervade: 4 fill **5** bathe, imbue **6** occupy **8** permeate, traverse **9** penetrate

pervading: 8 profound **9** prevalent, universal **10** widespread

perverse: awk **4** awry, wogh, wraw **6** cranky, divers, wicked, wilful **7** awkward, distort, diverse, forward, froward, vicious, wayward **8** backward, camshach, contrary, crotched, petulant **9** camsteary, camsteery, difficult, fractious, obstinate **10** determined **11** contentious, contrarious, disobedient, intractable **12** cantankerous, contumacious

perversely: auk, awk **7** athwart **8** overwart

pervert: 4 ruin, skew **5** abuse, twist, upset **6** debase, divert, garble, invert, misuse, poison **7** contort, corrupt, deprave, distort, outrage, vitiate **8** apostate, misapply, overturn, renegade **9** misdirect **10** demoralize **12** misinterpret, misrepresent

perverted: bad **6** wicked **7** corrupt, twisted, vicious

pervious: 4 open **6** leachy **9** permeable **10** accessible **11** transparent

pervulgate: 7 publish

Pescadores: *island:* **4** Hoko
town: **4** Mako

peshkar: 5 agent **7** steward **8** minister **10** accountant

peshkash: tax **7** present, tribute **8** offering

pesky: 6 plaguy **8** annoying **9** pestering, vexatious **11** troublesome **12** disagreeable

peso: 4 coin
silver: **4** duro

pessimism: 5 gloom **7** despair **8** cynicism

pessimistic: 6 gloomy **7** alarmed, cynical

pest: 4 bane, weed **5** hound, mouse, worry **6** insect, plague, vermin **7** trouble **8** epidemic, nuisance **9** annoyance **10** pestilence

pester: dun, nag, rib **4** ride **5** annoy, devil, tease, worry **6** badger, bother, harass, molest **7** torment, trouble **9** aggravate **10** drive crazy

pestiferous: 4 evil **10** pernicious **11** mischievous

pestilence: 4 pest **5** death **6** plague **7** disease, scourge **8** epidemic

pestilent: 6 deadly **7** noxious **9** poisonous **10** contagious, infectious

pestle: 4 bray **5** grind **6** beetle, muller
vessel: **6** mortar **10** pulverizer

pet: cat, dog, hug **4** coax, daut(Sc.), dawt(Sc.), dear, duck, huff, neck, sulk, tiff **5** drunt, humor, quiet, spoil **6** caress, coddle, cosher, cuddle, dautie(Sc.), dawtie(Sc.), faddle, fantad, fantod, fondle, pamper, stroke **7** cherish, darling, embrace, indulge, tantrum **8** favorite, fondling **9** cherished, favourite

petal: ala **4** leaf **5** sepal **8** labellum

petals: 7 corolla
without: **9** apetalous

petard: 8 firework **11** firecracker

peteman: 5 thief **7** burglar **9** cracksman **10** safeblower

peter: 4 fade, fail, wane **5** cease **7** dwindle, exhaust **8** decrease, diminish
out: **6** fizzle

Peter: 4 czar, rock **5** saint, Simon
father: **5** Jonas

Peter Pan: *author:* **6** Barrie
character: **4** John **5** Wendy **7** Michael **9** Tiger Lily **10** Tinker Bell
dog: **4** Nana
pirate: **4** Smee

petiole: 4 stem **5** stalk **8** peduncle **9** leafstalk **10** mesopodium

petite: 4 size, trim **5** small **6** demure, little **10** diminutive

petition: ask, beg, sue **4** bill, boon, plea, pray, suit, wish **5** apply, orate, plead **6** appeal, prayer, steven, sue for **7** address, entreat, implore, oration, request, solicit **8** entreaty **10** supplicate **11** application, deprecation **12** supplication **13** contemplation

petitioner: 5 asker **6** beggar, seeker **8** appealer, beadsman, bedesman **9** applicant, suppliant
chancery: **7** relator

peto: 5 wahoo

Petrarch's love: 5 Laura

petrel: 4 titi **5** mitty **7** assilag **8** allamoth **9** albatross, allamonti, allamotti, mallemuck

petrify: 4 daze, numb **6** appall **7** horrify, startle **11** turn to stone

petrifying: 7 numbing **9** deadening, hardening **10** petrescent, terrifying **11** fossilizing

Petrograd: 9 Leningrad

petrol: gas **8** gasoline

petroleum: oil **6** octane **7** naphtha **10** illuminant
by-product: **6** butane, diesel **7** propane **9** propylene
product: wax **4** coke **5** ethyl **6** petrol **7** alcohol, asphalt, canadol, naphtha **8** gasoline, kerosene, paraffin **9** righolene

petrosal: 4 hard **5** stony

petticoat: 4 kilt, slip **5** jupon, pagne **6** kirtle **7** placket, whittle **8** basquine, halfslip, vasquine **9** undercoat, waistcoat **10** fustanella, underskirt **11** farthingale
tails: **7** teacake **9** shortcake

pettifogger: 6 lawyer **7** shyster **8** attorney **10** bush lawyer

pettle: 4 spud **5** spade **6** cuddle, nestle, potter **7** cherish, indulge

petty: 4 base, mean, orra, puny **5** minor, small **6** little, paltry, puisne **7** trivial **8** childish, inferior, nugatory, trifling **9** frivolous, jerkwater, minuscule **10** diminutive **11** Mickey Mouse, subordinate, unimportant **12** contemptible **13** insignificant **14** inconsiderable

fault: **10** peccadillo
matter: **6** fidfad
morel: **9** spikenard **10** nightshade
whin: **10** restharrow
petulant: **4** pert **5** cross, huffy, saucy, short, sulky, testy **6** sullen, wanton, wilful **7** forward, fretful, grouchy, peevish, pettish, wayward **8** contrary, immodest, insolent, perverse **9** impatient, irascible, irritable, plaintive, querulous **10** ill-humored
pew: **4** desk, seat, slip **5** bench, bught, stall **6** bought(Sc.) **10** amen corner
pewee: **10** flycatcher
pewter: tra **5** bidri, bidry **6** bidery, bidree **7** biddery
peyote: **5** plant **6** cactus, mescal, peyotl
Phaedo's school: **5** Elian
Phaedra: *father:* **5** Minos
husband: **7** Theseus
stepson: **10** Hippolytus
phaeton: **8** carriage **10** towing car
phalacrocorax: **4** coot **9** cormorant
phalacrosis: **8** alopecia, baldness
phalanger: **5** ariel, tapoa **6** animal **7** opossum **8** squirrel **9** marsupial
phalera: **4** boss, disk, moth, stud **5** cameo
phantasm: **5** dream, fancy, vapor **6** mirage, shadow **7** phantom **8** delusion
phantasmal: **6** unreal **10** transitory
phantom: **4** idol **5** bogie, ghost, idola, image, shade, umbra **6** eidola(pl.), idolon, idolum, shadow, spirit **7** bugbear, eidolon, fantasy, specter, spectre **8** illusion, **10** apparition
Phaon's consort: **6** Sappho
Pharaoh: **4** king **5** ruler **6** tyrant
Pharaoh's chicken: **7** vulture
Pharaoh's fig: **8** sycamore
Pharaoh's mouse: **9** ichneumon
phare: **6** strait **10** lighthouse
pharisaical: **12** hypocritical
pharmaceutical: dia **7** mellite **9** medicinal
pharmacist: **8** druggist **9** dispenser **10** apothecary
pharmacy weight: **5** obole **6** obolus
pharos: **5** cloak **6** beacon **7** lantern **10** chandelier, lighthouse
phase: **4** hand, side **5** angle, facet, stage **6** aspect **8** passover **13** manifestation
pheasant: **5** argus, cheer, monal **6** monaul, moonal, pukras **7** kallege **8** fireback, tragopan
breeding-place: **4** stew
brood: nid, nye **4** nide
nest: **4** nide
pheasant cuckoo: **6** coucal
pheasant duck: **7** pintail **9** merganser
pheasant finch: **7** waxbill
phenol: **6** orcine, thymol **9** germicide
derivative: **4** anol **5** orcin **6** iresol, thymol

phenomenal: **7** unusual **11** exceptional **13** extraordinary
phenomenon: **4** fact **7** miracle, reality, stunner **9** actuality **10** experience
phenyl salicylate: **5** salol
phial: cup **4** bowl, vial **6** bottle, vessel
philander: **5** dally, flirt **7** opossum **10** flirtation, play around
philanthropic: **6** humane **10** altruistic, benevolent, charitable **11** civic-minded **12** humanitarian
philanthropist: **5** donor **10** benefactor **12** humanitarian
philanthropy: **4** alms **10** almsgiving
universal: **15** omnibenevolence
philippic: **6** screed, tirade **8** diatribe
Philippines: *animal:* **5** civet, lemur
ant: **4** anai, anay
archipelago: **4** Sulu
attendant: **5** alila
banana: **7** lacatan, saguing
barracks: **7** cuartel
beer: **7** pangasi
bird: **4** maya **6** abacay
boat: **5** balsa, banca **8** balangay, barangay
breadfruit: **4** rima **8** casmansi
brigand: **7** ladrone
buffalo: **7** carabao, timarau, timerau
canoe: **5** banca, vinta **6** baroto
capital: **10** Quezon City
carriage: **9** carretela, carromata
chief: **4** dato **5** datto, Iloco **7** Ilocano, Ilokano
Christianized tribe: **5** Bicol, Bikol, Tagal, Vicol **7** Bisayan, Tagalog, Visayan
city: Iba **4** Agoa, Cebu, Naga **5** Albay, Davao **6** Aparri, Baguio, Cavite, Ilagan, Manila **7** Dagupan
coconut meat: **5** copra
cyclone: **6** baguio
dagger: **4** itac **7** balarao
deity: **5** Dagon
discoverer: **8** Magellan
drink: **4** beno, vino **5** bubud **7** pangasi
farmer: lao, tao
fern: **4** nito
fetish: **5** anito
fiber: **4** eruc **6** buntal **9** pineapple
fish: **8** langaray
food: poi **4** baha, taro
forest: **5** gubat
fort: **4** Gota **10** Corregidor
garment: **4** saya
grass: **5** cogon
guerrilla: Huk
gulf: **5** Davao, Ragay
hardwood: **4** ipil **5** narra
hat: **7** salacot
hemp: **5** abaca **6** manila
hero: **5** Rizal
house: **5** bahay
idol: **5** anito

island: 4 Cebu 5 Batan, Bohol, Leyte, Luzon, Panay, Samal, Samar 6 Negros 7 Masbate, Mindora, Palawan, Paragua 8 Mindanao
kitchen: 5 calan
knife: 4 bolo, itac 7 balarao, machete
lake: 4 Taal 5 Lanao
language: 4 Moro 5 Bicol, Tagal 6 Ibanag 7 Ilocano, Tagalog, Visayan
liberator: 9 MacArthur
lighthouse: 4 faro
liquor: 4 beno 7 pangasi
litter: 7 talabon
lizard: 4 ibid
mammal: 7 tarsier
mango: 5 bauno 7 pahutan
market-day: 7 tiangue
measure: 4 loan 5 braza, caban, cavan, chupa, ganta 6 apatan, balita, quinon
measure of weight: 5 catty, fardo, picul, punto 6 lachsa 7 quilate 8 chinanta
monetary unit: peso
mother: ina
mountain: Apo, Iba 5 Mayon, Pulog 7 Banahao
mountaineer: 8 mentesco
mudfish: 5 dalag
muskmelon: 6 atimon
Muslim: 4 Moro
native: see *people* below
nut: 4 pili
oil: 5 cebur
pagan: 6 Italon
palm: 4 nipa 6 anahao, anahau
parrot: 5 cagit
peasant: tao
people: Ata, Ati, Ita, Tao 4 Aeta, Atta, Etas, Moro, Sulu 5 Bicol, Bikol, Tagal, Vicol 6 Igorot, Timaua, Timawa 7 Bisayan, Tagalog, Visayan 8 Filipino, Igorrote 10 Philippino
plant: aga 4 alem 5 abaca, baroi, batad 6 agamid
plum: 6 sapote
port: 4 Cebu 6 Cavite, Iloilo
president: 6 Marcos
priest: 7 pandita
province: 4 Abra 5 Albay, Davao 6 Iloilo, Tarlac
raft: 5 balsa
reptile: 6 python
rice: 4 paga 5 barit, bigas, macan
river: 4 Abra, Agno 5 Pasig 7 Cagayan 8 Mindanao, Pampanga
road: 4 daan
rope tree: 4 nabo 5 anabo
sapodilla: 5 chico
sarong: 8 padadion
sea: 4 Sulu
sentinel: 6 bantay
servant: 4 bata 5 alila
shirt: 4 baro

shrub: 4 alem, nabo 6 anilao
silk: 10 alcaiceria
skirt: 4 saya
slave: 6 alipin
slipper: 7 chinela
soap vine: 4 gogo
spirit: 5 anito
stream: 4 ilog
sword: 6 barong 8 campilan
termite: 4 anai, anay
textile: 4 pina, saba 7 sina-may
thatch: 4 nipa
timber: 5 cahuy
town: 4 Agoa, Cebu 5 Bayan, Pasay, Vigan 6 Iloilo
tree: dao, iba, tua, tui 4 acle, anam, ates, bogo, dita, ifil, ipil, supa 5 almon, amaga, anabo, balao, balau, bayok, betis, bulak, guijo, ligas, tabog, yacal 6 alagao, alagau, alupag, amuyon, anagap, aranga, bancal, banuyo, bataan, batino, botong, dungon, lanete, marang, molave 7 amuguis, amuyong, amabong, apitong, banilad, binukau, hapiton, mambong, tinadalo 8 almaciga, bitanhol, macaasim, malapaho, tanguile 9 alintatad, batikulin, batitinan 10 batikuling 11 alibangbang, balinghasay
tree bark: aga 6 agamid
vine: iyo
volcano: Apo 4 Mayo 7 Canlaon
watchtower: 7 atalaya 8 bantayan
water buffalo: 7 carabao
water-jar: 5 bango
weapon: 4 bolo
weight: 5 catty, fardo, piail, punto 7 quilate
white man: 7 cachila
wine: 4 beno
wood: 4 teak 5 ebony, narra 6 sandal
yam: ubi, uve
Philistine: 6 cretan 7 Babbitt 8 outsider 9 barbarian, bourgeois, hypocrite
city: 4 Gath, Gaza 5 Ekron 8 Ashkelon
foe: 5 David 6 Samson
giant: 7 Goliath
god: 4 Baal 5 Dagan, Dagon
Philomela: 11 nightingale
father: 7 Pandion
ravisher: 6 Tereus
sister: 6 Procne
philosopher: wit 4 sage 5 cynic, stoic 7 scholar, thinker
disciples: 4 sect 6 school
famous: 4 Kant 5 Plato, Renan, Solon 6 Nestor, Seneca 7 Emerson 8 Socrates, Voltaire 9 Epictetus
of Syracuse: 4 Dion
philosophical: 4 wise 8 composed, rational 9 temperate, unruffled 11 level-headed
philosophy: 4 yoga 7 dualism 8 stoicism

9 esoterics 10 empiricism, esthetics, pragmatism 17 transcendentalism
philter, philtre: 4 drug 5 charm 6 potion 7 amatory 9 fascinate
phlebotomize: 5 bleed 8 venesect
phlegm: 6 apathy 10 equanimity 12 indifference
phlegmasia: 12 inflammation
phlegmatic: 4 calm, cool, dull, slow 5 inert 6 watery 7 viscous 8 composed, sluggish 9 apathetic, impassive, lethargic 11 indifferent 13 imperturbable
phloem: 4 bast, flax 6 tissue
phobia: 4 fear 5 dread 12 apprehension
phoca: 4 seal
Phoebad: 7 seeress 9 priestess 10 prophetess
phoebe: 4 bird 5 pewee, pewit 6 peewee 10 flycatcher
Phoebe: 5 Diane 6 Selene 7 Artemis
Phoebus: Sol, sun 6 Apollo
Phoenicia: *city:* 4 Tyre 5 Sidon
colony: 8 Carthage
dialect: 5 Punic
god: 4 Baal 6 Eshmun
goddess: 5 Tanit 6 Baltis, Tanith 7 Astarte
goddess of love: 7 Astarte
king: 6 Agenor
seaport: 5 Sidon
phoenix: 4 bird 7 paragon 8 rara avis
phonetic: 4 oral 5 vocal
notation system: 5 romic
sound: 7 palatal
phonograph: 6 stereo 8 victrola 9 turntable 10 gramophone
inventor: 6 Edison
record: 4 disc, disk 7 platter
phony: 4 fake, sham 5 bogus, false 8 impostor, spurious 9 charlatan 10 fictitious 11 counterfeit
Phorcys: *child:* 5 Ladon 6 Gorgon, Graeae(pl.)
father: 6 Pontus
mother: 4 Gaea
phosphate: 6 ehlite 7 apatite, uranite 9 wavellite
photocopy: 4 stat 5 print
photoengraving: 8 halftone 15 heliotypography
photograph: mug 4 film, snap, X ray 7 picture, tintype 8 likeness, portrait, snapshot 9 ferrotype, pictorial 10 cheesecake, heliograph 13 daguerreotype
bath: 5 fixer, toner 7 reducer 9 developer
book: 5 album
colored: 10 kodachrome
developer: 5 ortol 6 amidol 9 revelator
fixing agent: 4 hypo
instrument: 8 enlarger
inventor: 6 Niepce, Talbot 8 Daguerre
kind: 5 panel, still 6 motion 7 boudoir,

cabinet, diamond 8 imperial, passport, portrait 9 pictorial 10 commercial, scientific 12 composograph 13 carte de visite
negative: 4 film
old-fashioned: 7 tintype 13 daguerreotype
printing: 7 ozotype
photographer: 9 cameraman 10 shutterbug
photology: 6 optics 7 photics
photometric unit: pyr, rad 5 lumen
phrase: mot 4 term, word 5 idiom, state 6 clause, cliche, saving, slogan 7 adjunct, diction, epigram, epithet, thought 8 acrostic, locution 9 catchword, leitmotif 10 expression
phraseology: 7 dialect, diction, wording 8 parlance
phratry: 4 clan 5 curia, tribe
phrenic: 6 mental
Phrixos: *father:* 7 Athamus
mother: 7 Nephele
sister: 5 Helle
Phrygia: *enthusiast:* 9 Montanist
god: 4 Atys 5 Attis 8 Sabazios
king: 5 Midas 7 Gordius
river: 7 Meander
town: 5 Ipsus
phylactery: 5 charm 6 amulet, scroll 8 talisman
phyletic: 6 lineal, racial
phyma: 5 tumor 6 nodule
physic: 5 purge 6 remedy 9 cathartic
physical: 5 lusty 6 bodily, carnal 7 check up, natural, somatic 8 material 9 corporeal, somatical
physician: asa, doc 5 curer, medic, quack 6 doctor, intern, healer, medico 7 interne 8 restorer, sawbones 10 consultant, medicaster 11 aesculapian, philosopher 12 practitioner
association: AMA
group: AMA 5 panel, staff
symbol: 8 caduceus
physicist: 9 hylozoist 10 naturalist
physiognomy: mug 4 face, mien 5 looks 7 feature 8 portrait 10 expression 11 countenance
physique: 4 body 5 build, frame, shape 6 figure 7 anatomy 8 strength 10 appearance 12 constitution
physostigmine: 5 esere 6 eserin 7 eserine
pian: 4 yaws 5 tumor 9 frambesia 10 framboesia
piano: 5 grand 6 softly, spinet 7 clavial, quietly, upright 8 pianette 10 anemochord, pianoforte
dumb keyboard: 9 digitoria 10 digitorium 11 finger board
early: 6 spinet
key: 7 digital

keyboard: **7** clavier
notes: **6** octave
pedal: **7** celeste
pedal keyboard: **8** pedalier
piatti: 7 cymbals
piazza: 5 porch, square **7** balcony, gallery, portico, veranda
pic: 4 peak **5** lance **8** picayune
picacho: 4 hill **5** butte
picador: wit **6** jester **7** debater **11** bullfighter
picadura: 7 tobacco
picaro, picaroon: 5 knave, rogue, tramp **6** bandit, pirate, rascal **7** sharper **8** vagabond **9** hooka-roon **10** adventurer, freebooter
picayune: 4 mean **5** small **6** little, measly, paltry
pichiciago: 9 armadillo
pick: 4 best, gaff, pike, wale **5** adorn, beele, cavil, elect, elite, pluck **6** choice, choose, gather, pickax, select, twitch **7** bargain, diamond **8** plectrum
on: **5** abuse, annoy, tease **9** criticize
out: **4** cull, sort **5** glean **6** assort, choose, select
pickax: 4 bill, pick **6** tubber, twibil **7** mattock, twibill
picked: 5 spiny **8** selected, stripped **10** fastidious
picket: peg **4** pale, post **5** fence, guard, stake **6** fasten, paling, tether **7** enclose, fortify, postern
pickle: 4 alec, dill, mess, peck **5** achar, brine **6** capers, dawdle(Sc.), muddle, nibble, piddle, pilfer(Sc.), trifle(Sc.) **7** chutney, condite, confect, gherkin, vitriol **8** marinate **9** tight spot **11** predicament
mixed: **6** higdon
pickled: 5 drunk, soust **6** soused **9** preserved **11** intoxicated
pickling herb: 4 dill
pickpocket: dip **4** bung, hook, wire **5** diver, filer, ganef, thief **6** buzzer, cannon, dipper, figboy, hooker, ratero(Sp.), robber **7** foister, mobsman, stealer **8** clyfaker **11** fingersmith
helper: **4** duke **5** shill, stall **6** bulker
pickup: 5 tonic, truck **6** arrest, bracer, chippy **8** recovery **9** stimulant **10** hitchhiker **11** improvement, stimulation **12** acquaintance
again: **6** resume
Pickwick Papers author: 7 Dickens
picky: 4 nice **5** fussy **6** choosy **7** finicky
picnic: 4 snap **6** junket, outing
picot: 4 loop **6** edging **8** notching
picotee: 9 carnation
pictograph: 5 glyph
picture (see also **motion picture**): oil **4** copy, draw, icon, idea, ikon **5** ikono,

image, photo, print, scene, vinet **6** chromo, crayon, depict, marine, pastel **7** diorama, etching, explain, imagine, paysage(F.), portray, porture, reflect, tableau **8** describe, likeness, makimono, painting, panorama, portrait, seascape, triptych, vignette **9** delineate, landscape, miniature, represent **10** illustrate, impression, photograph, watercolor **16** chromolithograph
border: mat **5** frame
composite: **7** montage
drawn with heated instrument: **11** pyrogravure
gallery: **5** salon **6** museum
painted on wall: **5** mural
section: **7** gravure
small: **5** cameo **9** miniature **15** microphotograph
stand: **5** easel
viewer: **9** projector **11** alethoscope, stereoscope
Picture of Dorian Gray author: 5 Wilde
picture puzzle: 5 rebus **6** jigsaw
pictured: 11 counterfeit
picturesque: 5 vivid **6** quaint, scenic **7** graphic **8** informal, scenical, striking
picuda: 9 barracuda
piddle: toy **4** pick, play **6** dawdle, putter, trifle
piddling: 5 petty **6** paltry **7** trivial, useless **13** insignificant
pie: 4 mess, snap, tart **5** chaos, flawn, graft, pasty, patty **6** jumble, pastry, tourte **7** cobbler, dessert, mixture **8** crustade, turnover **9** blackbird, confusion
meat: **5** pasty **7** rissole
with ice cream: **7** a la mode
piebald: 4 pied, piet, pyot **5** mixed, motly, pinto **6** bauson, calico **7** mongrel, mottled, dappled **10** variegated **12** multicolored **13** heterogeneous
piece: bat, bit, cob, eke **4** chip, gare, hunk, join, mend, part, slab, slat, snip, stub, tate(Sc.) **5** crumb, flake, patch, pezzo(It.), scrap, sheet, shred, slice, snack, strip **6** cantle, gobbet, morsel, parcel, sliver **7** cantlet, driblet, flinder, flitter, morceau(F.), oddment, portion, section, segment, snippet **8** assemble, dribblet, fraction
tapering: **4** gore, shim **6** gusset
piece de resistance: 8 main dish **9** showpiece **11** centerpiece, chef d'oeuvre, masterpiece
piecemeal: 7 gradual **8** bit by bit **10** in snatches, step-by-step
piece of eight: 4 peso(Sp.) **6** escudo(Sp.)
piece out: eke **8** assemble, complete **10** supplement

piece together: 4 form, make 5 unite
pied: 7 blotchy, mottled, piebald 10 variegated
pied antelope: 8 bontebok
pieplant: 7 rhubarb
pier: cob 4 cobb, dock, mole, pile, quai, quay 5 groin, stilt, wharf 6 bunder, pillar 7 landing, support 8 buttress, pilaster 10 breakwater
  architectural: 4 anta
  base: 5 socle
pierce: cut, dag, rit 4 bear, bite, bore, brod, cloy, dirl, gore, hole, stab, tang 5 break, drill, enter, gride, lance, probe, smite, spear, spike, stick, sting 6 broach, cleave, empale, ficche, impale, riddle, tunnel 7 discern, poniard 8 puncture 9 intersect, lancinate, penetrate, perforate 10 comprehend, run through
  with horn: 4 gore
  with stake: fix 6 impale
pierced: 5 ajour 8 cribrose
piercer: awl 6 gimlet
piercing: 4 fell, high, keen, loud, tart 5 acute, clear, sharp 6 shrill 7 cutting, pungent 8 poignant 9 searching 10 foraminate
Pierus: *consort:* 4 Clio
  son: 10 Hyacinthus
piety: 4 zeal 7 loyalty 8 devotion, fidelity, holiness, religion 9 godliness, reverence 10 compassion, devoutness
pig (see also **hog**): far, ham, hog, sow 4 boar, pork 5 bacon, chuck, crock(Sc.), ingot, shoat, shote, swine 6 farrow, gussie, porker 7 casting, dogboat, glutton, grumphy(Sc.) 8 grumphie(Sc.), pressman, sixpence
  female: sow 4 gilt
  lead: 6 fother
  litter: far 6 farrow
  male: hog 4 boar 6 barrow
  metal: bar 5 ingot
  pert. to: 7 porcine
  pickled feet of: 5 souse
  red variety: 5 Duroc
  tender: 9 swineherd
  young: elt 4 gilt, runt 5 grice(Sc.), piggy, shoat, shote, snork 6 bonham, farrow, piggie, piglet 7 teatman 9 gruntling
pig bed: sty 4 sand
pig deer: 8 babirusa 9 babirussa 10 babiroussa
pig latin: 5 argot
pig potato: 7 cowbane
pig rat: 9 bandicoot
pigboat: sub 9 submarine
piggy bank: 6 pishke 7 knippel, pushkeh
pigeon: 4 barb, bird, dodo, dove, dupe, fool, gull 5 decoy, pluck, squab, wonga 6 coward, culver, cushat, dodlet, fleece,

isabel, pouter, turbit 7 cropper, fantail, jacobin, namaqua, pintado, swallow, tumbler 8 squealer 9 frillback, harlequin 10 sweetheart, turbitteen, turtledove, wongawonga
  call: coo
  carrier: 5 homer 6 homing 8 horseman 10 scandaroon
  clay: 5 skeet 6 target
  domestic: nun 4 barb, ruff, runt, spot 6 pouter 9 satinette, trumpeter
  extinct: 4 dodo 9 passenger
  feed: 7 saltcat
  genus of: 5 goura 7 columba
  hawk: 6 falcon, merlin
  pert. to: 9 columboid 12 peristeronic
  short-beaked: 4 barb
  tooth-billed: 6 dodlet
  young: 5 piper 8 squealer
pigeon blood: red 6 garnet
pigeon grass: 7 foxtail 9 crabgrass 12 bristlegrass
pigeon hawk: 6 merlin
pigeon house: 7 dovecot 9 columbary
pigeon-livered: 4 meek, mild 6 gentle
pigeon pea: dal, tur 4 herb, seed 5 arhar 6 gandul 7 cajanus, catjang
pigeon woodpecker: 7 flicker
pigeonberry: 8 pokeweed 9 Juneberry 11 coffeeberry
pigeonhearted: 5 timid 8 cowardly 14 chickenhearted
pigeonhole: 5 label 6 assort, shelve 7 arrange, catalog, cubicle 8 classify 9 cubbyhole
pigeonry: 7 dovecot 8 dovecote
piggery: 6 pigsty 8 crockery(Sc.)
piggish: 4 mean 6 filthy, greedy 7 selfish 8 stubborn 10 gluttonous
pigheaded: 7 willful 8 perverse, stubborn 9 obstinate 10 determined
piglike animal: 7 peccary
pigment: 5 color, paint 8 colorant
  absence of: 8 achromia, alphosis 9 tacheture
  applied to canvas: 7 impasto
  black: tar 5 sepia 7 melanin 8 india ink
  blood: 10 hemoglobin
  blue: 4 bice 5 azure, smalt 7 cyanine 8 cerulean, verditer
  blue-gray: 4 bice
  blue-white: 4 zinc
  brown: 5 sepia, umber 6 bister, bistre, sienna 7 melanin
  green: 4 bice 7 veriter
  kind: 7 aniline, rubiate 8 alizarin, massicot 9 alizarine
  red: 7 amatito, realgar, turacin
  toxic: 8 gassypol
  yellow: 5 ocher, ochre 7 etiolin 8 orpiment
pigmy: See **pygmy**

pignus: 4 lien, pawn 6 pledge
pigpen: sty
pigskin: 5 glove 6 saddle 8 football
pigsney: eye 4 dear 7 darling 10 sweetheart
pigsticker: 4 sled 5 sword 7 butcher 11 pocketknife
pigtail: 5 braid, pleat, queue
pika: 4 hare 5 mouse 6 rodent
pike: gen(Sc.) 4 dore, fish, gedd(Sc.), luce, pick, road 5 cairn, point, spike, tower 6 beacon, pickax, summit 7 highway 8 poulaine 9 spearhead 11 muskallonge, muskallunge, muskellunge
pike perch: 4 dory 6 sander sauger
pikel, pikle: 7 hayfork 9 pitchfork
pikelet: 7 crumpet
piker: 5 thief, tramp 6 coward 7 gambler, quitter, shirker, vagrant 8 pilferer, tightwad 10 speculator
pilar: 5 downy, hairy
pilaster: 4 anta 5 antae 6 column, pillar
Pilate: 10 procurator
prisoner: 8 Barabbas
tribunal: 8 Gabbatha
wife: 7 Claudia
pilchard: 7 herring, sardine
smoked: 6 fumado
pile: cop, mow, nap 4 bank, bing, cock, dass(Sc.), dess(Sc.), heap, mass, mole, much, pier, rick, sess, shag 5 amass, crowd, spile, stack, stake 6 boodle, bundle, pillar 7 edifice, fortune 8 buttress 10 accumulate, breakwater, coacervate
funeral: 4 pyre 5 mound
hay: 4 cock, rick 5 stack 6 doodle
rubbish: 4 dump
stone: 5 cairn, scree
pile driver: 6 beetle
weight: tup
pileup: 4 heap, mass 5 amass, stack 8 accident 9 collision
pilewort: 4 herb 6 ficary 8 fireweed
pilfer: rob 4 hook, loot, pelf, take 5 filch, sneak, steal, swipe 6 finger, snitch 7 purloin 8 scrounge
pilgrim: 5 ihram 6 palmer 8 crusader, traveler, wanderer, wayfarer 9 sojourner 12 peregrinator
bottle: 7 ampulla, costrel
garb at Mecca: 5 ihram
ship: 9 Mayflower, Speedwell
to Holy Land: 6 palmer
Pilgrim's Progress: 8 allegory
author: 6 Bunyan
character: 5 Demas 9 Christian
pilgrimage: 4 hadj, trip 7 journey
pill: 4 ball, goli, pare, peel, pool 5 bolus, creek, strip 6 pellet, pilule 7 capsule, granule, pitcher, placebo 11 decorticate
pill bug: 5 louse 6 isopod, slater
pillage: 4 flay, loot, prey, sack 5 booty, foray, harry, rifle, spoil, steal, strip 6 maraud, rapine, ravage 7 despoil, plunder 8 expilate, spoliate, trespass 9 depredate, devastate 10 confiscate 11 appropriate
pillager: 6 peeler 8 marauder 10 freebooter
of Rome: 6 Alaric
pillaging: 9 predatory
pillar: lat 4 pile, post, prop 5 cippi(pl.), pylon, shaft, stela, stele 6 cippus, column, stelae(pl.), steles 7 obelisk, osiride, support 8 pedestal, mainstay, pilaster, pillaret 9 stanchion, totem pole
capital: 7 chapter
pert. to: 6 stelar
resembling: 6 stelar
series of: 9 colonnade
without: 7 astylar
pillar saint: 7 stylite
pillar-stone: 8 monument 11 cornerstone
Pillars of Hercules: 5 Abila, Calpe 9 Gibraltar
pillbox: cap, hat 7 shelter 8 brougham 11 emplacement 13 fortification
pilled: 4 bald, bare 6 barked, peeled, shaven 8 tonsured 12 decorticated
pillion: pad 6 saddle 7 cushion
pillory: 4 joug(Sc.) 5 stock, trone 6 cangue, punish
pillow: cod, pad 5 block 7 bolster, cushion, support
stuffing: 5 eider, kapok 6 dacron
pillowcase: 4 sham, slip 5 cover, linen 8 flanerie
pilm: 4 dust
pilon: 4 gift 5 bonus 7 present 8 gratuity, lagnappe 9 lagniappe
pilose: 5 hairy
pilot: ace, fly 4 lead 5 flyer, guide, steer 6 airman, leader 7 aviator, conduct, hobbler 8 chaplain, coxswain, director, governor, helmsman, preacher 9 clergyman, cockswain, steersman 10 cowcatcher
test for: 4 solo
pilot bird: 6 plover
pilot fish: 6 remora, romero 9 whitefish
pilot snake: 4 bull 10 copperhead
pilot whale: 9 blackfish
pilum: 6 pestle 7 javelin
Piman Indian: 5 Opata
pimento: 7 paprika 8 allspice
pimple: 4 blob, burl, flaw 6 burble, papule 7 abscess, bubukle
pin: fed, fix, hob, nog, peg, pen, tit 4 axle, bolt, coak, dart, join, lill, scob 5 affix, arrow, badge, dowel, preen, rivet, spile, stake, style 6 bobbin, broach, brooch, cotter, fasten, pintle, secure, skewer 7 confine, enclose, eyebolt, gudgeon, jewelry, skittle, spindle, trenail 8 fastener,

kingbolt, linchpin, ornament, spilikin, transfix **9** spillikin **10** chatelaine
for fastening meat: **6** skewer
machine: **6** cotter
money: **4** cash **9** allowance
oar: **5** thole
rifle: **4** tige
wooden: fid, peg **5** dowel, thole
pin grass: **7** erodium **9** alfilaria
pin point: **5** tacca
pin-wing: **6** pinion
pinafore: **4** slip **5** apron, dress, smock **6** daidly(Sc.) **8** sundress **9** gaberdine
Pinafore author: **7** Gilbert **8** Sullivan
pince-nez: **5** specs **7** glasses, lorgnon **10** eyeglasses, lorgnette, spectacles
pincers: tew **5** chela, tongs **6** pliers, tenail **7** forceps **8** tenaille
pinch: nip, rob, wry **4** bite, raid **5** cramp, gripe, hinch, steal, stint, theft, tweak **6** arrest, crisis, extort, snatch, snitch, twince **7** confine, squeeze **8** contract, juncture, straiten **9** emergency, vellicate
pinch bar: pry **5** lever
pinchbeck: **4** sham **5** alloy, cheap **8** spurious **11** counterfeit
pinched: **6** wasted **7** haggard
pinch-hitter: sub **6** fill-in **7** stand-in **9** alternate **10** substitute, understudy
pinchpenny: **4** carl **5** miser, stint **9** niggardly
Pindaric: ode
pine: ara, fir, iva, lim **4** ache, flag, fret, hone, mope, tree **5** cedar, droop, dwine, kauri, kaury, larch, mourn, pinon, vacoa, waste, white, yearn **6** balsam, grieve, lament, pandan, repine, spruce, totara, vacona, vacoua, wither **7** agonize, dwindle **8** galagala, languish, Northern **9** evergreen, Norwegian
acid: **5** pinic
exudation: **5** resin, rosin
fruit: **4** cone
grove: **7** pinetum
leaf: **6** needle
mahogany: **6** totara
product: tar **5** resin **10** turpentine
pine bark aphid: **10** phylloxera
pine family: **8** pinaceae
pine gum: **8** sandarac **9** oleoresin
pine knot: **7** dovekie
pine siskin: **5** finch
pine tar: **6** retene
Pine Tree State: **5** Maine
pine tulip: **10** pipsissewa
pineapple: **4** bomb, nana, pina(Sp.) **5** anana(It.) **7** grenade **8** ornament **10** decoration
family: **12** bromeliaceae
genus of: **6** ananas
segment: pip
pineapple weed: **8** marigold

pinecone: **4** clog **8** strobile
pinfold: **4** jail **5** pound **7** confine
ping: **4** push, urge **5** prick
pinguid: fat **5** fatty
pinguin: **7** aguamas
pinguitude: **7** fatness, obesity **8** oiliness **10** greasiness
pinhead: **4** fool **5** clown **6** minnow
pinion: pin, tie **4** bind, gear, wing **5** quill **7** confine, disable, feather, pennant, shackle, trundle **8** cogwheel, restrain
pink: cut **4** deck, rose, rosy, stab, tint **5** adorn, blush, color, coral, prick **6** flower, minnow, pastel, pierce, salmon **7** blossom, radical **8** decorate, grayling **9** carnation, embellish
eye: **14** conjunctivitis
family: **15** caryophyllaceae
genus of: **6** silence
pink needle: **9** alfilaria
pink pill: **7** cure-all
pinkeen: **6** minnow
pinkeye: **14** conjunctivitis
pinnace: **4** boat, ship **5** woman **6** tender **8** mistress
pinnacle: epi, tee, top, tor **4** acme, apex, peak **5** crest, crown, serac **6** finial, needle, summit **8** gendarme
glacial: **5** serac
rocky: tor **8** aiguille
pinnate: **6** winged **9** feathered **11** featherlike
pinniped: **4** seal **6** walrus
Pinocchio author: **7** Collodi **9** Lorenzini
pinochle: **8** card game
term: **4** meld **5** widow **7** auction
two-handed: **7** goulash
pinpoint: aim, dot, fix **5** exact, point **6** trifle **7** precise **8** identify
pintado: **4** cero, fish, sier **6** chintz, pigeon, sierra **7** siering, spotted
pintail: **4** duck, smee **6** grouse
pintle: **4** bolt **5** hinge, dowel
pinto: **4** pied, pony **5** horse **6** calico **7** mottled, painted, piebald
pinxter flower: **6** azalea **11** honeysuckle
pioneer: **5** first, miner **6** digger, open up **7** settler **8** colonist, explorer **9** excavator
pious: **4** good, holy **5** froom, godly, loyal **6** devout, devine, pietic **7** canting, goddard, godlike, piteous **8** faithful, priestly **9** religious **11** reverential **13** sanctimonious
pip: dot **4** lulu, paip, peep, seed, spot **5** cheep, chirp, speck **8** insignia
pipe: oat **4** cask, duct, flue, lead, main, reed, snap, tube **5** briar, canal, drain, spout, stack **6** dudeen, leader, outlet, tubule **7** calumet, conduit, fistula, larigot **8** mirliton(F.)
angle: **5** elbow
bender: **6** hickey

ceremonial: **7** calumet
clay: **4** tile **5** straw **12** churchwarden
closer: **5** valve
connection: ell, tee **5** cross, elbow
end: **4** taft **6** nozzle
joint: ell, tee, wye **5** cross, elbow **7** calepin **8** coupling
Oriental: **5** hooka **6** hookah **7** nargile **8** narghile, nargileh **12** hubble-bubble
part: **4** bowl, stem
pastoral: oat **4** reed
pert. to: **6** tubate
player: **5** fifer **8** shepherd
smoke: **5** tewel
steam: **5** riser
stove: **4** flue **5** tewel **7** chimney
pipe dream: 4 hope **6** bubble **7** chimera, fantasy **8** illusion
pipe wrench: 8 Stillson
pipeline: 7 channel, conduit **9** grapevine
Piper's son: Tom
piperly: 7 trivial **9** worthless
pipette: 4 tube **6** baster, taster **7** burette, dropper
measuring: **11** stactometer
piping: 6 edging, tubing
pipistrel, pipistrelle: bat
pipit: 6 wekeen **7** titlark
pippin: 4 seed **5** apple
pipsqueak: 5 twerp **6** nobody **7** upstart
piquancy: 4 salt **6** flavor, ginger **7** flavour
piquant: 4 racy, tart **5** salty, sharp, spicy, tasty, zesty **6** biting, bitter **7** peppery, pungent, zestful **8** poignant, stinging **11** provocative, stimulating
pique: 4 fret, goad, tick **5** annoy, pride, spite, sting **6** arouse, excite, fabric, grudge, harass, malice, nettle, offend, pritch, strunt **7** chigger, dudgeon, offense, provoke, umbrage **8** irritate, vexation **9** annoyance, displease **10** irritation, resentment **11** displeasure
piqued: 5 pouty
piquet: 8 card game
score: pic
tricks: **5** capot
pirate: 4 Hook, Kidd **5** rover **6** robber, seadog **7** brigand, corsair, omnibus, sea wolf **8** algerine, marauder, picaroon, predator **9** buccaneer, privateer **10** Blackbeard, freebooter, plagiarize
flag: **10** Jolly Roger
gallows: **7** yardarm
piripiri: 4 weed **5** birch, mapau
pirl: 4 spin **5** twine, twist
pirn: 4 reel **5** spool **6** bobbin **7** spindle
pirogue: 5 canoe
pirol: 6 oriole
piscation: 7 fishery, fishing
piscator: 6 angler **9** fisherman
piscina: 4 pool, tank **5** basin **8** fishpond, lavatory **9** reservoir

Pisgah summit: 4 Nebo
pishogue, pishoge: 5 charm, spell **7** sorcery **10** witchcraft
pismire: ant **5** emmet, twerp **9** nonentity
pismo: 4 clam
piste: 4 path **5** spoor, track, trail **8** ski trail
pistil: 6 carpel, umbone
pistle: 4 tale **5** story **7** epistle
pistol: dag, gat, gun, rod **6** barker, buffer **7** dungeon, hand gun **8** bulldoze, revolver **9** automatic, derringer
case: **7** holster
lock: **5** rowet
piston: 4 disk, knob, plug **5** valve **6** roller **7** plunger
pit: 4 butt, delf, foss, hell, hole, mine, pool, seed, sump, trap, weem, well **5** abyss, chasm, delft, delve, fossa, fosse, fovea, grave, shaft, snare, stone **6** cavern, cavity, fossae, hollow, oppose **7** abaddon, cockpit **8** downfall **9** barathron, waterhole **10** depression, excavation **11** indentation
bottomless: **5** abyss **7** Abaddon
of peach: **4** seed **7** putamen
of theater: **7** parquet
small: **6** areole, lacuna **7** foveola **8** alveolus
pit viper: 4 habu **8** lachesis **10** bushmaster, copperhead, fer-de-lance **11** rattlesnake
pitch: dip, key, tar **4** cant, cast, fall, hurl, line, roll, send, tone, toss **5** fling, heave, lunge, lurch, resin, rosin, spiel, throw **6** accent, encamp, patter, plunge, seesaw, totter **7** asphalt, bitumen **8** alkitran **9** alchitran
above: **5** sharp
apple: **5** copei, cupay
baseball: **5** curve **8** knuckler, spitball
below: **4** flat
high in: alt
in: **5** set to **7** get busy **8** get going **10** contribute
pipe: **9** epitonion
relating to: **7** piceous
pitchblende: 6 radium **7** uranium
pitcher: jar **4** ewer, olla, olpe, toby **5** buire, gorge, gotch, ollae, olpae **6** carafe, heaver, hurler, tosser, urceus **7** canette, creamer **8** cruisken, oenochoe **9** container, cruiskeen **10** ballplayer
false move: **4** balk
handle: ear **4** ansa
left-handed: **8** southpaw
motions: **6** windup
place: **5** mound
relief: **7** fireman
pitchfork: 4 evil **5** pikel, pikle **8** sheppeck, sheppick
piteous: 5 pious **6** devout, moving, ruined, tender **7** pitiful, pitying **8** pitiable,

touching **9** imploring **10** beseeching, entreating **13** compassionate

pitfall: **4** lure, trap **5** snare **6** danger **9** booby trap **10** difficulty

pith: jet, nub **4** core, crux, gist, meat, pulp **5** force, vigor **6** center, kernel, marrow **7** essence, medulla, nucleus **8** strength **9** substance

full of: **5** heady, meaty, terse **7** concise

pith helmet: **4** topi **5** topee

pith tree: **7** ambatch

pithy: **5** crisp, meaty, terse **7** compact, concise, laconic **11** sententious **12** apothegmatic **13** short and sweet

plant: **4** sola

saying: mot **5** maxim **9** witticism

pitiful: sad **4** mean **6** rueful, woeful **7** forlorn, piteous **8** pathetic, pitiable **9** miserable, sorrowful **10** despicable, lamentable **12** contemptible

pitiless: **4** grim **5** cruel, stony **6** savage **8** ruthless **9** ferocious, merciless, unfeeling **10** despiteous, dispiteous, relentless **11** hardhearted

pitpit: **8** guitguit

pittance: bit **4** alms, dole, gift, mite, song **5** trace **6** trifle **7** bequest

pitted: **6** etched **7** foveate, opposed, scarred **9** alveolate **10** pockmarked **11** honeycombed

pity: **4** ruth **5** mercy, piety **6** pathos **8** clemency, sympathy **10** compassion, condolence, tenderness **11** commiserate **13** commiseration

Pius: **4** Pope

pivot: toe **4** slew, slue, turn **5** hinge, swing **6** evener, swivel **7** gudgeon

pivot pin: **6** pintle **8** kingbolt

pivotal: **5** polar, vital **7** central, crucial **8** cardinal

pixie, pixy: elf **5** fairy **6** sprite **9** prankster

pixilated: **5** dotty, drunk **9** whimsical **11** intoxicated

placable: **4** calm **8** tolerant **9** agreeable, peaceable, tractable

placard: **4** bill, post, sign **6** poster **7** affiche **9** manifesto **12** proclamation **13** advertisement

placate: **4** calm **5** quiet, sooth **6** pacify, please, soothe **7** appease, comfort **10** conciliate, lay the dust **11** tranquilize

place: lay, put, set **4** area, calm, city, lieu, loci, post, room, seat, site, spot, town **5** being, court, estre, locus, plant, point, posit, siege, situs, space, stead, where **6** bestow, locale, locate, region, repose, square, status **7** allodge, bestead, demesne, deposit, dispose, situate, village **8** dwelling, estimate, identify, location, locality, position **9** collocate, residence, situation

again: **6** reseat **7** restore

apart: **6** enisle **7** isolate **8** separate

before: **6** appose, prefix

beneath: **9** infrapose

between: **6** insert **9** interpose

business: **5** plant, store **6** office

by itself: **7** isolate

camping: **5** etape

end for end: **7** reverse

frequented: **4** dive **5** haunt **6** resort **7** hangout

hiding: mew **4** cave

holy: **6** shrine

in a row: **5** align, aline

in the sun: **5** glory **11** recognition

intermediate: **5** limbo

little hiding: **5** niche

market: **4** mart **5** agora

meeting: **5** tryst **10** rendezvous

one inside another: **4** nest

perfect: **6** heaven, utopia **8** paradise

side by side: **9** collocate, juxtapose

trial: **5** venue

placebo: **5** toady **7** vespers **8** medicine **11** preparation

placid: **4** calm, even, mild **5** downy, quiet, suant **6** gentle, irenic, serene **8** peaceful, tranquil **9** unruffled **11** undisturbed **13** imperturbable

placket: **4** slit **6** pocket **7** opening

plage: **4** zone **5** beach **6** region **7** country **8** transept

plagiarize: rob **4** crib, lift **5** steal **6** borrow, pirate, thieve **7** purloin

plague: dun, pox, vex **4** fret, gall, pest, twit **5** annoy, chafe, harry, tease, worry **6** badger, harass, hector, pester, wanion **7** scourge, torment, trouble **8** calamity, epidemic, irritate, nuisance **9** annoyance **10** affliction, pestilence **11** infestation

carrier: fly, rat

pert. to: **6** loimic

plaice: **5** fluke **8** flatfish, flounder

plaid: **4** maud **5** cloth **6** design, tartan **7** bracken, garment, pattern **9** checkered **11** crossbarred

plain: dry, lea **4** bald, bare, chol, down, even, fair, mead, mere, mesa, moor, open, vega, wold **5** blair, blunt, broad, camas, campo, clear, corah, frank, gross, heath, homey, llano, veldt **6** coarse, graith, homely, humble, lenten, meadow, pampas, simple, steppe, tundra, undyed **7** artless, certain, evident, genuine, glaring, legible, obvious, prairie, quamash, savanna **8** apparent, campagna(It.), campaign, distinct, explicit, flatland, homemade, homespun, ordinary, straight, tailored **9** champaign, downright, outspoken, primitive, unadorned, unfigured, untwilled **10** unaf-

fected **11** perspicuous, transparent, undisguised **12** short on looks, unattractive **13** unembellished **15** straightforward
depression: **5** swale
elevated: **4** mesa **7** plateau
Indian: Ute **5** Caddo, Kiowa, Omaha, Sioux **6** Oneida, Pawnee **9** Algonquin **10** Athapascan
Olympic games: **4** Elis
salt-covered: **5** flats **6** salada
treeless: **5** llano, pampa, veldt **6** tundra **7** prairie, savanna **8** savannah
upland: **4** wold **5** weald
plaint: **6** lament **7** protest **9** complaint **11** lamentation
plaintiff: **4** suer **7** accuser **8** litigant **9** recoverer **10** prosecutor **11** complainant
opposite: **9** defendant
plaintive: sad **5** cross **7** elegiac, fretful, peevish, pettish **7** piteous, pitiful, wailing **8** dolorous, mournful, petulant, repining **9** lamenting, sorrowful **10** melancholy **11** complaining **12** discontented
plait: cue **4** fold, knit **5** braid, crimp, pleat, weave **6** border, gather, goffer, pleach **7** gauffer, pigtail **9** gathering **10** interweave
plaited: **7** browden **10** corrugated
plan: aim, map **4** card, dart, form, game, idea, plat, plot **5** draft, epure, ettle, frame **6** budget, decoct, design, devise, intend, layout, method, policy, scheme, sketch, system **7** arrange, concert, diagram, draught, drawing, outline, program, project, purpose **8** conspire, contrive, engineer, platform, prepense, schedule, strategy **9** blueprint, calculate, machinate, stratagem **10** concoction **11** arrangement, contemplate, contrivance, preconceive, precontrive, premeditate
planate: **5** level **9** flattened
plancher: bed **4** slab **5** board, floor, plank **6** pallet **7** ceiling **8** planking, platform
plane: **4** even, flat, soar **5** glide, level **6** aequor, chinar, smooth **7** surface **8** sycamore
block: **5** stock
handle: **4** toat, tote
inclined: **4** ramp **5** chute, shute
kind of: **4** iron, jack **5** block **6** router **8** grooving, tounging
on same: **8** coplanar
plane figure: *boundary:* **9** perimeter
four angles: **8** tetragon
nine-sided: **7** nonagon
plane iron: bit **5** blade, knife
plane-tree: **8** plantain, sycamore
planer: **4** tool **6** shaper **8** surfacer
planet: orb **4** Mars, moon, star **5** Earth, Pluto, Venus **6** Saturn, sphere, Uranus

7 Jupiter, Mercury, Neptune **8** asteroid, terrella, wanderer **9** satellite
brightest: **5** Venus
cone: **8** strobile
course: **5** orbit
nearest sun: **7** Mercury
newest: **5** Pluto
orbit: **7** ellipse
orbit point: **5** apsis, nadir **6** apogee, zenith **8** parigree
path: **5** orbit
period: **9** alfridary
red: **4** Mars
relation to another: **5** trine **7** sextile **10** opposition **11** conjunction
ringed: **6** Saturn
ruling: **9** dominator
satellite: **4** moon
shadow: **5** umbra
planeta: **5** cloak
planetarian: **10** astrologer
planetarium: **6** orrery **11** observatory
planetary: **4** huge **7** erratic **9** universal, wandering, worldwide **10** astrologer **11** terrestrial
planisphere: **9** astrolabe **11** meteorscope
plank: **4** deal, slab **5** board, slate, stone **6** lumber, timber **8** plancher **9** two-by-four **10** gravestone
breadth: **6** strake
increasing bearing surface: **5** shole
lengthwise: **8** stringer
plank down: pay **7** advance, deposit
planking: **8** flooring
plankton: **4** alga **5** krill **8** organism, protozoa
planner: **9** architect
plant: fix, set, sow, spy **4** arum, bury, bush, fern, herb, hide, rape, root, seed, trap, tree, vine, weed, wort **5** berry, decoy, found, fruit, grain, place, put in, shoot, shrub, sotol, spice, trick, works **6** annual, clover, flower, legume, scheme, settle **7** conceal, creeper, factory, furnish, pungent, sapling **8** building, business, geophyte, radicate **9** detective, equipment, establish, perennial, seasoning, succulent, swindling, vegetable **10** prearrange **13** establishment
acid-juice: **5** ribes **6** nettle **8** knotweed **9** smartweed
aconite: **4** bikh
amaryllis family: **5** agave
ambrosia genus: **7** ragweed
ammoniac: **5** oshac
apiaceous: **4** ache
apoplexy: **4** esca
appendage: **7** stipule
aquatic: See **aquatic plant**
arboreal: **4** tree
aromatic: See **aromatic**
arrowroot-yielding: **7** curcuma

arum family: **4** arad, taro **5** aroid, calla
aster family: **5** oxeye, tansy **8** fleabane
asteraceous: **5** daisy
bayonet: **5** datil
bean family: **6** lupine **8** licorice **9** liquor-
ice
benthonic: **6** enalid
bitter: ers, rue **9** colicroot
blue-blossomed: **6** lupine **8** ageratum
body: **6** cormus
bog genus: **5** abama **10** narthecium
bramble: **5** briar, furze, gorse, thorn
branched: **4** bush, tree **5** shrub
breathing organ: **5** stoma **7** stomata(pl.)
bulbous: **4** lily **5** camas, onion, tulip **7**
jonquil, quamash **8** hyacinth **9** narcissus
cabbage family: **4** rape
cactus family: **5** dildo **6** cereus, mescal **7**
saguaro **11** prickly pear
cactus-like: **8** stapelia **9** xerophyte
capsule: pod
carrot-like: **7** parsnip
cassia genus: **5** senna
catnip family: nep **6** nepeta
celery family: **5** anise
celery-like: udo
cell: **6** gamete
chlorophyll-rich: **4** alga **5** algae(pl.)
chromatophore-lacking: **6** albino
class: **4** alga **5** algae(pl.)
climbing: ive, ivy **4** bine, vine **5** betel, liana, vetch **6** byrony, smilax **7** creeper,
jasmine **8** wisteria **12** morning glory,
philodendron
clover-like: **5** medic **7** calomba
coloring matter: **8** clorofil **10** endochrome
11 chlorophyll
corn lily: **4** ixia
crocus family: **4** irid
crossbred: **6** hybrid
crowfoot family: **5** peony **8** clematis
cruciferous: **5** cress **7** alyssum
cryptogamous: **4** moss
cuticle: **5** cutin
cyperaceous: **5** sedge
decorative: ivy **4** bush, fern **6** flower
desert: **5** agave **6** alhagi, cactus **8** mesquite **11** brittlebush
dipsacus genus: **6** teasel
disease: **4** gall, mold, rust, scab, smut **5**
ergot **6** blight, mildew **7** blister
division: **15** archichlamydeae
dock-like: **6** sorrel
dry-climate: **5** xerad **9** xerophyte **10** om-
brophobe
dwarf: **5** cumin, stunt
dye: **4** anil, weld, woad, wold **5** henna,
woald, would **6** kamala, madder, wurras,
wurrus **7** alhenna, orselle
dye-yielding: **4** anil, woad **5** henna, sumac
6 madder **7** alkanet

ebony family: **6** ebenad
embryo: **8** plantule
environmentally modified: **4** ecad
erica genus: **5** heath **7** heather
Euphorbia genus: **6** spurge
exudation: gum, sap **4** milk **5** latex, resin,
rosin
fabaceous: pea **5** vetch **9** coronippa
family: **7** araceae
fernlike: **8** filicoid
fiber: See **fiber**
flag-family: **4** irid
floating: **5** lotus **7** frogbit **9** water lily
flowering: See **flowering plant**
flowerless: **4** fern, moss **6** fungus, lichen **7**
seaweed
forgetfulness-causing: **5** lotus
fragrant: **5** orris **8** angelica
garden: **4** geum, iris, ixia, rose **5** aster,
calla, canna, daisy, pansy, phlox, poppy,
stock, viola **6** bellis, bletia, celery, cli-
via, cosmos, crocus, lupine, oxalis, zinnia **7** agathea, alyssum, anchusa, anemone, begonia, celosia, clarkia, gazania,
gerbera, godetia, lettuce, lobelia, mus-
cari, petunia, primula, statice, verbena
8 ageratum, arctotis, cyclamen, daffodil, dianthus, herebell, hyacinth, larkspur, marigold, myosotis, scabiosa,
sparaxis, sweet pea, tithonia, watsonia
9 amaryllis, calendula, campanula, candytuft, carnation, centaurea, cinararia,
coreopsis, digitalis, gladiolus, hollyhock,
linararia, narcissus, nicotiana, penste-
mon, portulaca **10** delphinium, gaillar-
dia, gypsophila, marguerite, ranunculus,
snapdragon, sweet basil, wallflower **11**
dusty miller, forget-me-not, helichry-
sum, hunnemannia, Madonna Lily,
shasta daisy **12** nierembergia, rhododendron, salpiglossis, sweet William **13**
chrysanthemum, dimorphotheca, glory
of the sun **14** canterbury bell **15** Star
of Bethlehem **16** spring snowflakes
genus: **4** dion
geography: **14** phytogeography
gourd family: **5** melon
grain: oat, rye **4** corn, teff **5** wheat **6** barley
grass: **5** avena
grass cloth: **5** ramee, ramie
grass-like: **5** sedge
grassland: **6** baccar **7** bacchar
growing from inside: **7** endogen **9** endo-
genae(pl.)
growing from outside: **6** exogen
growth layer: **7** cambium
growth on: **4** gall
habitat: **4** ecad
hawthorn: **7** azarole **9** mayflower
head: bud, bur **4** burr **5** fruit **6** flower
healing: **7** sanicle

heather family: **4** ling **5** erica
hedge: **6** espino
herbaceous: See **herb**
honey-secreting organ: **7** nectary
house: See **houseplant**
interior chaff: **5** palea, palet
iridaceae: **4** irid
iris family: **4** irid, ixia **7** freesia
joined to another: **5** graft
joint: **4** node
juice: see *exudation* above
leafless: **4** ulex **6** dodder **7** restiad, triurid
leguminous: See **legume**
liliaceous: **4** aloe, leek **5** onion **9** birthroot
lily family: **4** aloe, sego **5** lotos, lotus, yuc-
    ca **6** camass
linen-producing: **4** flax
main axis: **4** stem **5** stalk, trunk
male: mas **16** androgametophore
mallow family: **5** altea **6** escoba
manufacturing: **4** mill
marine: See **aquatic plant**
marsh: **4** fern, reed **6** juncus **7** bulrush,
    cattail
masculine: see *male* above
medicinal: hop, oak **4** aloe, dill, flax, herb,
    lime, sage **5** buchu, elder, erica, guaco,
    jalap, peony, poppy, senna, tansy **6** ar-
    nica, carrot, catnep, catnip, fennel, gar-
    lic, ipecac, kousso, laurel, nettle, simple
    7 aconite, boneset, calamus, camphor,
    caraway, catechu, copaiba, ephedra,
    gentian, hemlock, henbane, juniper, lo-
    belia, mullein, mustard, parsley, rhu-
    barb, saffron **8** barberry, camomile,
    crowfoot, foxglove, licorice, plantain,
    rosemary, valerian, wormwood **9** aspar-
    agus, bearberry, buckthorn, chamomile,
    colchicum, coltsfoot, dandelion, liquor-
    ice, monkshood **10** assafetida, penny-
    royal, peppermint, stavesacre **11** assa-
    foetida, bittersweet
microscopic: **5** spore **10** microphyte
millet: **5** hirse
mock orange: **7** syringa
modified by environment: **4** ecad
moss-like: **6** orpine **7** hepatic
mottled leaf: **8** ratsbane
multicellular: **9** metaphyte
mushroom-type: **6** fungus
mustard family: **4** woad **5** cress **6** radish
    7 alyssum
native: **8** indigene
nettle family: **4** hemp
nightshade family: **6** tomato
nursery: **8** seedling
oil-yielding: **4** odal **6** sesame
old-world: **5** lotus
one-seeded fruit: **9** olacaceae
onion family: **4** leek
onion-like: **5** chive **7** shallot
opening: **5** stoma **7** stomata(pl.)

packing: **7** cannery
painful to touch: **5** briar, thorn **6** nettle **8**
    knotweed **9** smartweed
parsley family: **4** dill **5** anise
part: **6** stamen, stipel **7** tendril
pepper: ara
pert. to: **6** agamic **7** botanic, vegetal **9** bo-
    tanical **10** vegetative
pigment-lacking: **6** albino
poaceae: **5** grass
pod: **4** boll
poisonous: **4** atis **6** datura **7** amanita,
    cowbane **8** oleander **10** belladonna
poisonous to cattle: **4** loco **8** calfkill, loco-
    weed
poisonous to fowls: **7** henbane
poppy family: **9** celandine
pore: **8** lenticel
potato-like: oca
potted: **6** bonsai
preserving: **4** dill **7** cannery
prickly: **4** rose **5** briar, brier, cacti(pl.),
    thorn **6** cactus, nettle, teasel **7** thistle **9**
    tearthumb
rat poison: **8** oleander, ratsbane
reproductive organ: **5** spore
root: **5** radix
rope: **4** hemp
rose family: **5** avens
round-leaved: **9** pennywort
salad: **5** cress **6** celery, endive, greens **7**
    lettuce, romaine **8** purslane **10** water-
    cress
scented: **4** mint **6** catnip **7** catmint
science: **6** botany
seasoning: **8** tarragon
sedge family: **5** carex
seed: nut, pip **4** bulb **5** grain **6** button **7**
    putamen
seedless: **4** fern
seller: **7** florist
shoot: rod **4** cion **5** scion, sprig **6** stolon
silk: **5** floss
soap: **5** amole
solanaceous: **7** tobacco
sour-juice: **6** sorrel
starch: pia **4** arum, taro **7** cassava
stem: **4** bine **5** shaft **6** caulis
stem joint: **4** node
stem tissue: **4** pith **6** phloem
submerged: **6** enalid
succulent: **4** aloe, herb **8** gasteria **9** house-
    leek
tanning: **5** sumac
tapioca-yielding: **6** casava, casave, casavi
    7 cassava
tequila-yielding: **5** agave
thistle family: **5** aster
thorny: see *prickly* above
three-leaved: **9** trifolium
tissue: **4** pith **5** xylem **6** phloem **7** cambi-
    um

trailing: **7** arbutus
tropical: **4** arum, palm, taro **5** agave, altea, canna, liana, liane, yucca, zamia **6** pepino **7** dasheen, hamelia **8** mangrove, redwithe
tufted: **4** moss **5** dryas
twining: see *climbing* above
type: **6** exogen
urticaceous: **6** nettle
valerian genus: **4** nard
verbenaceous: **7** lantana
vetch family: ers
vine: ivy **5** liana
wall: ivy
waterside: **5** sedge
wild-growing: **9** agrestial
woody: **4** bush, tree, vine **5** shrub
woody-vine genus: **5** vitis
xyloid: **4** tree
young: **4** cion **5** scion, shoot **6** sprout **7** vinelet **8** seedling
yucca-like: **5** sotol
plant life: 5 flora **10** vegetation
plant louse: 5 aphid
secretion: **4** laap, lerp **5** laarp
plant raising: *pert. to:* **13** floricultural
Plantagenets: 7 Angevin
plantain: 4 weed **6** banana, wabron **8** balisier
plantain eater: 7 touraco **9** splitbeak
plantation: 4 farm **6** estate **8** hacienda
cacti: **7** nopalry
coffee: **5** finca **7** cafetal, fazenda
coniferous tree: **7** pinetum
fictional: **4** Tara
oak tree: **9** quercetum
sugar: **8** trapiche
trees: **5** grove **6** forest **7** orchard
willow: **4** holt **6** osiery
planter: 5 sower **6** farmer, grower, seeder **7** pioneer, settler **8** colonist **13** agriculturist
government by: **11** plantocracy
wall: **6** lavabo
planting stick: 6 dibble
plaque: pin **5** medal **6** broach, brooch **9** nameplate
plash: 4 pool **5** blash, hedge **6** pleach, puddle, splash **9** bespatter
plashy: wet **6** marshy
plasm: 4 mold **6** matrix
plasma: 5 lymph **11** trophoplasm
plaster: 4 coat, daub, harl **5** affix, cover, gatch, gesso, grout, salve, smear **6** cement, mortar, parget **9** slick down
adhesive: **4** tape **7** bandage **8** dressing
artist's: **5** gesso
coarse: **5** grout **6** parget, stucco
of paris: **5** gesso **6** gypsum
patch: **7** spackle
stone: **6** gypsum
support: **4** lath

tool: **7** spatula
wax: **6** cerate
plastered: 5 drunk **6** soused **11** intoxicated
platerer: 5 mason **6** dauber
plastic: 4 soft **7** ductile, fictile, flexile, pliable **8** flexible, unctuous **9** adaptable, formative **14** impressionable
cotton-sizing: **7** viscose
dentist's: **6** cement
plastron: 6 dickey **7** calipee **8** trimming **11** breastplate
plat: lot, map **4** boat, plan **5** braid, chart, plait **6** buffet **7** plateau **9** tableland **10** interweave
plate: cut, gib **4** coat, disc, dish, disk, lame, tile **5** aglet, armor, facia, layer, scute, stove **6** aiglet, discus, lamina, platen, tagger, veneer **7** denture, lamella, laminae, overlay **8** assiette, lamellae, laminate **9** silverize
communion: **5** paten **6** patina
cooking: **4** grid
for throwing: **6** discus
from matrix: **6** stereo **10** stereotype
glass: **4** pane **5** slide
horny: **5** scale, scute
perforated: dog **4** grid **7** stencil **8** hallmark **14** identification
pitcher's: **4** slab **5** mound
ship-shaped: nef
stereotype: **6** cliche
thin: **6** lamina **7** lamella
plateau: 4 dish, mesa, puna, seir **5** fjeld **6** hamada, plaque, salver **7** uplands **9** altiplano, tableland **12** altiplanicie
plateholder: 8 cassette
platen: 6 roller
platform: map **4** bank, bema, dais, deck, plan **5** bench, chart, floor, stage, stand **6** bemata(pl.), podium, pulpit **7** estrade, program, rostrum, tribune **8** chabutra, plancher **9** banquette, gangplank, vestibule
church: **5** solea **6** pulpit
fort: **8** barbette
mining: **6** sollar, soller
nautical: **7** maintop
reloading: **6** staith
salt-manufacturing: **6** hurdle
ship: **7** foretop, maintop **9** gangplank
sleeping: **4** kang
temple: **5** dukan
temporary: **8** scaffold
theater: **7** logeion
wheeled: **5** dolly, float
wooden: **9** boardwalk
platinum: *blond:* **7** towhead
crude: **7** platina
wire: **4** oese
platitude: 6 cliche, truism **7** bromide **8** banality, chestnut, dullness, flatness **9**

rechauffé, staleness, triteness **10** triviality **11** commonplace **15** commonplaceness

Plato: *idea:* **5** eidos
knowledge: **6** noesis
literary form: **8** dialogue
pupil: **9** Aristotle
school: **7** Academe
teacher: **8** Socrates
work: **4** Meno **5** Crito **6** Phaedo **7** Apology, Gorgias, Sophist, Timaeus **8** Republic

platoid: **4** flat **5** broad

platonic: **9** spiritual, visionary **10** idealistic **11** impractical, theoretical
body: **4** cube **10** hexahedron, octahedron **11** icosahedron, tetrahedron **12** dodecahedron
philosophy follower: **9** academist

platoon: set **4** team, unit **5** group, squad **6** volley **7** coterie **8** division **9** formation

platter: **4** dish, lanx(L.) **5** ashet(Sc.), grail, plate **7** charger

platter-shaped: **10** scutellate

platyfish: **8** moonfish

platypus: **8** duckbill **9** mallagong

plaudit: **4** clap, kudo **6** praise **8** applause, approval, encomium **11** acclamation, approbation

plausible: **4** oily **6** glossy **7** colored **8** coloured, credible, specious **10** applausive, believable, creditable ostensible, plauditory

Plautus: **10** playwright
forte: **6** comedy
language: **5** Latin

play: act, fun, jeu(F.), hit, toy **4** game, jeux(F.), move, romp **5** amuse, charm, dally, drama, enact, flirt, sport **6** cavort, divert, engage, fiddle, frolic, gamble, gambol, rollix **7** disport, execute, perform **9** amusement, dalliance, diversion, pantomime **10** manipulate, recreation **13** entertainment
around: **9** philander
badly: err **4** miff **6** bobble
ball: **5** begin **6** resume **9** cooperate
complication: **4** node
down: **9** soft-pedal
festival: **9** festspiel
kind: **4** auto **5** farce **6** comedy, one-act **7** musical, tragedy **8** burletta **9** melodrama, pantomime **13** curtain-raiser
musical: **5** opera **8** burletta, operetta
off: **4** game **6** oppose **8** showdown
on words: pun
outline: **8** scenario
part: act, bit **4** acte(F.), role **5** exode, scene **7** prelude **8** epilogue, epitasis, prologue
possum: **4** sham **5** feign **7** pretend
put on: **5** stage **7** produce

silent: **9** pantomime
up: **6** stress **9** emphasize

playa: **4** lake **5** basin, beach **6** salina

playboy: **4** fool **5** clown, idler **6** madcap **7** buffoon

played out: **5** all in, ended, spent, tired **8** finished, unreeled **9** exhausted

player: man **4** cast, star **5** actor **6** leader **7** enactor, gambler **8** gamester, thespian **9** performer **10** competitor, contestant
card: **4** pone **6** dealer, eldest
leading: **4** star
poor: dub, dud, ham, sub **5** scrub **12** second-string
strolling: **9** serenader, troubador **10** troubadour **11** barnstormer

playful: **5** elfin, merry **6** blithe, frisky, joking, lusory, wanton **7** jocular, larkish, puckish **8** gamesome, humorous, playsome, sportive **10** frolicsome

playground: **4** grid, park, yard **5** field **7** diamond

playhouse: **5** movie **6** casino, cinema **7** theater

playing cards: **4** deck **6** tarots
hand: cat **4** deal

playlet: **4** skit

playmate: pal **6** friend

playroom: bar, den, gym **7** nursery

plaything: die, toy **4** hoop **6** bauble, trifle

playtime: **6** recess

playwright: **6** author **9** dramatist

plaza: **4** park, **5** green **6** common, square **9** carrefour **11** marketplace

plea: sue **4** suit **6** abater, answer, appeal, excuse, prayer **7** apology, pretext, request, solicit **8** argument, entreaty, petition, pretense **12** supplication **14** nolo contendere
defendant's: **4** nolo **6** guilty **9** not guilty

pleach: **5** plait **9** interlace **10** interweave

plead: beg, sue **5** orate **6** allege, assert **7** beseech, entreat, implore, solicit **8** advocate, appealed, petition **9** importune, intercede **10** supplicate

pleading: **4** oyer **6** answer **8** argument, demurrer **9** suppliant **10** litigation **12** supplication

pleasant: gay **4** bien(F.), fair, fine, good, hend, joli, nice, waly **5** bigly, cushy, douce(F.), hende, hoddy, jolie, lepid, merry, sweet, wally **6** genial **7** amiable, amusing, farrand, farrant, jesting, jocular, leesome(Sc.), playful, welcome, winsome **8** delicate, gracious, grateful, humorous, pleasing, sportive **9** agreeable, appealing, congenial, diverting, enjoyable, laughable, sprightly **10** acceptable, delightful, gratifying

pleasantness: **7** amenity **8** goodness, niceness

pleasantry: fun **4** jest, joke **6** banter **7** jesting **10** jocularity **11** gauloiserie **13** facetiousness

please: **4** suit, will **5** agree, amuse, elate, humor **6** arride, humour, tickle **7** aggrate, appease, content, delight, gladden, gratify, indulge, placate, satisfy **9** delectate, titillate

pleased: happy **8** gladsome

pleasing: **4** glad, lief **5** amene, sooth **6** comely, eesome(Sc.), liking **7** roseate **8** fetching, pleasant **9** desirable, favorable, palatable **10** attractive, delectable, delightful, enchanting, favourable

pleasure: fun, joy **4** ease, este, gree, will **5** bliss, mirth, sport, treat **6** gaiety, liking, relish **7** delight, jollity **8** delicacy, fruition, gladness, hilarity **9** amusement, diversion, enjoyment, happiness, merriment **10** beneplacit **11** beneplacity, contentment, delectation **12** cheerfulness **13** gratification

god: Bes

ground: **4** park **9** pleasance

insensitiveness to: **9** anhedonia

pert. to: **7** hedonic

philosophy of: **8** hedonism

seeker: **5** sport **7** epicure, playboy **8** hedonist

pleat: **4** fold, kilt, shir **5** braid, prank **7** plicate

plebe: **5** cadet, **8** commoner, freshman **10** midshipman

plebeian: **5** crude **6** coarse, common, homely, vulgar **7** ignoble, illbred, lowborn **8** baseborn, everyday, ordinary

plebiscite: **4** vote **6** decree **7** mandate **10** referendum

plectrum: **4** pick **5** uvula **6** fescue, tongue **7** malleus

pledge: bet, vas(L.), vow **4** adhi, band, bond, gage, hand, hest, hock, oath, pawn, seal, wage, word **5** siker, skoal, toast, troth **6** arrest, assure, borrow, commit, engage, lumber, parole, plight, **7** betroth, earnest, espouse, hostage, promise, warrant **8** affiance, contract, guaranty, mortgage, security **9** assurance, certainty, sacrament **11** association, impignorate

security for: IOU **4** bond, gage **6** marker

pledget: **4** swab **5** oakum **8** compress

Pleiad of Alexandria: **5** Homer **6** Aratus **8** Nicander **9** Lycophron **10** Apollonius, Theocritus **11** Callimachus

Pleiades: **4** Maia **6** Merope **7** Alcyone, Celaeno, Electra, Sterope, Taygeta, **8** Asterope

constellation: **6** Taurus

father: **5** Atlas

mother: **7** Pleione

Pleione's offspring: **8** Pleiades

plenary: **4** full **6** entire **7** perfect **8** absolute

opposite: **7** summary, complete **11** unqualified

plenipotentiary: **5** agent, envoy **8** minister **10** ambassador

plentiful: **4** full, rich, rife **5** ample, sonsy **6** galore, sonsie **7** copious, fertile, liberal, opulent, profuse **8** abundant, affluent, fruitful, generous, prolific **9** abounding, bounteous, bountiful, exuberant, plenteous **10** productive

plenty: **4** enow, heap, much, raff **5** ample, cheap, fouth **6** enough, foison, scouth **7** copious **8** fullness, opulence **9** abundance, affluence, plenitude **10** exuberance, luxuriance, perfection, sufficient **11** copiousness, sufficiency **12** completeness

goddess: Ops

horn of: **10** cornucopia

plenum: **5** space **8** assembly, fullness, plethora

pleonasm: **7** verbiage **8** fullness **9** tautology **10** redundancy **11** superfluity

plethora: **4** glut **6** excess **8** fullness **9** profusion, repletion **13** overabundance **14** superabundance

plethoric: **6** turgid **7** swollen **8** inflated, overfull **9** bombastic **10** overloaded

pleurapophysis: rib

plexiform: **7** complex, netlike **9** intricate **11** complicated

plexus: **4** rete **5** retia(pl.) **6** tangle **7** network

pliable: **4** easy, limp, soft, waxy **5** lithe **6** docile, limber, pliant, supple **7** bending, ductile, flaccid, flexile, plastic, tensile, willowy **8** amenable, flexible, fluxible, informal, suitable, tractile, workable, yielding **9** adaptable, compliant, malleable, tractable **10** applicable **13** unconstrained

plicate: **4** fold **5** pleat

plight: fix, jam **4** fold, risk **5** array, braid, plait, state **6** engage, pickle, pledge, status **7** betroth, embrace, promise **8** position, quandary **9** betrothal, condition **10** difficulty **11** predicament

plinth: **4** base, orlo **5** block, couch, stone, table **6** course **7** subbase **8** skirting **9** baseboard

flat: **4** orlo

plod: dig, mog, peg **4** grub, plow, slog, toil, tore, vamp, work **5** tramp **6** drudge, trudge

plop: **4** fall **5** plump **8** drop down **10** sit heavily

plot: lot, map **4** land, plan, plat **5** cabal, chart, draft, story, tract **6** design, devise, scheme, secret **7** compact, connive, diagram, outline **8** conspire, con-

trive, engineer, intrigue, scenario **9**
insidiate, machinate **10** conspiracy **11**
machination
garden: bed **5** patch **8** parterre
ground: lot **5** grave **7** terrain
inventor: **8** schemist
play: **4** node
plover: **4** bird, crab, dupe **5** drome, kolea,
oxeye, sandy **6** kildee, piping **7** collier,
killdee, lapwing, maycock, Wilson's **8**
dotterel, killdeer, squealer, toadhead **9**
courtesan, turnstone **10** beetle-head,
blacksmith
relative: **7** wrybill **9** sandpiper
plow, plough: dig, ear **4** farm, mole, rove,
till **5** break **6** cleave, digger, furrow **9**
cultivate **10** cut through
handle: **5** stilt
kind of: **4** snow **5** sulky **6** gopher, lister,
rotary, shovel **7** breaker **8** stirring,
turnplow **9** moldboard **14** prairie-
breaker
knife: **6** colter **7** coulter
part: **4** beam, frog, hale **5** sheth, slade,
stilt **6** sheath **7** pinhead **9** plowshare,
sharebeam
plowhead: **4** beam **5** frame **6** clevis
plowing: **8** aeration
plowshare, ploughshare: lay **5** laver **6**
colter **7** coulter
bone: **5** vomer
ploy: **4** joke **5** sport, trick **6** frolic, gambit,
tactic **7** pastime **8** escapade **11** merrymaking
pluck: rob, tug **4** grit, guts, jerk, pick, pull,
sand, tear **5** cheek, nerve, spunk, strip,
strum, twang **6** daring, finger, fleece,
gather, snatch, spirit, twitch **7** bravery,
courage, deplume, plunder **8** decision,
gameness **9** endurance, fortitude, hardihood **10** resolution
plug: peg, tap, tit **4** blow, bung, calk, cork,
puff, push, slog **5** boost, caulk, estop,
knock, punch, shoot, spile, spill **6** dottle, tampon **7** bouchon, pledget, promote, stopper, stopple **9** advertise, persevere
cannon muzzle: **7** tampion
clay: bod **4** bott
fire: **7** hydrant
medical: **4** clot **7** embolus
wall: **6** outlet
water: **7** hydrant
plug bib: **6** faucet, spigot
plug cock: **6** spigot
plug hat: **4** tile **5** gibus **6** topper
plug-in: **4** jack
plug-ugly: **4** thug **5** rowdy, tough **7** ruffian **8** gangster **9** roughneck
plugboard: **11** switchboard **12** control-
panel
plum: hog **4** amra, coco, find, gage, sloe **5**

catch, drupe, duhat, icaco, prune **6**
damson, jambul, reward, sapote **7** bul-
lace, jambool **8** dividend, windfall **9**
greengage **10** amatungula
dried: **5** prune
seed: pit **7** putamen
wild: **4** skeg, sloe **5** islay
plum-colored: **4** puce **5** mauve **6** purple
plum duff: **7** pudding
plum weevil: **8** curculio
plumage: **4** down **5** dress **6** hackle **7** floc-
cus **8** feathers **9** adornment
plumb: **4** bung, well **5** delve, probe, solve,
sound **6** chunky, fathom, plunge **7** explore, plummet **8** absolute, complete,
entirely, vertical **9** downright **10** absolutely, straighten, understand **13** perpendicular
plumbeous: **6** leaden
plume: **4** tuft **5** crest, egret, preen, pride,
prize, prune **6** aigret, plumet **7** feather,
panache **8** aigrette **9** plumicorn
plummet: dip **4** drop, fall, lead **5** plumb **6**
plunge, tumble, weight **8** nose-dive
plump: fat **4** back, drop, fall, plop, sink,
tidy **5** bonny, buxom, obese, plunk,
stout **6** bonnie, chubby, dilate, flatly,
fleshy, portly, rotund **7** bluntly, distend,
fulsome, support **9** downright
plunder: gut, rob **4** boot, loot, pelf, prey,
raid, sack, swag **5** booty, cheat, harry,
pluck, poach, raven, reave, rifle, spoil,
steal, strip **6** bezzle, boodle, creach(Sc.),
creagh(Sc.), dacoit, maraud, pilfer, pirate, rapine, ravage, ravish, spoils **7** despoil, pillage, ransack **8** spoliate **9** depredate, devastate
plunderer: **5** thief **6** bandit, vandal **8** marauder, predator **10** freebooter
plunge: bet, dig, dip **4** cave, dive, duck,
dump, pool, rush, sink **5** douse, dowse,
drive, fling, lunge, merse, pitch, plumb,
souse **6** absorb, emerge, footer, gamble,
thrust **7** immerge, immerse **8** submerge
plunger: ram **6** risker **10** speculator
plunk: **4** drop, flop, pull, push, sink, toss **5**
drive, pluck, plump, sound, throw **6** dollar, strike
plunther: **4** plod **8** flounder
plurality: **4** most **8** majority **9** multitude
plus: add **4** more, over **5** extra **6** excess **8**
addition, increase, positive
plush: **4** posh **6** deluxe **7** opulent **8** palatial **9** luxurious **11** upholstered
Plutarch work: **5** Lives
Pluto: Dis **5** Hades
kingdom: **5** Hades
wife: **10** Persephone, Proserpina
plutocracy: **13** establishment
plutocrat: **5** nabob **6** fat cat **7** Croesus,
rich man **9** moneybags **10** capitalist
Plutus: *father:* **6** Iasion

mother: **7** Demeter
ply: web **4** bend, fold, mold, sail, urge, work **5** beset, exert, layer, plait, wield **6** double, handle, travel **7** belabor, shuttle **8** belabour, exercise, function **9** importune, thickness
with drink: **5** birle
pneuma: **4** soul **5** neume **6** breath, spirit, **8** ligature **9** breathing, life force
pneumonia: *kind:* **5** lobar, viral **9** bronchial
Po tributary: **4** Adda **5** Oglia **7** Trebba **9** Cispadane
poach: **4** boil, cook **5** shirr, spear, steal, steam **6** pierce, thrust **7** trample **8** encroach, trespass
poacher: pan **5** thief **7** lurcher, stalker, widgeon **8** baldpate
salmon: **7** rebecca, rebekah
Pocahontas: *father:* **8** Powhatan
husband: **5** Rolfe
pochard: **4** duck, **5** scaup **6** dunker
pochette: **6** violin **7** handbag **8** envelope
pock: pit **4** hole, scar **6** hollow **7** pustule
pocket: bin, cly, fob **5** poke, prat, sack **7** cantina, conceal, confine, enclose, isolate, put away **8** cul-de-sac **9** miniature, small area **10** blind alley **11** appropriate
ore: **4** lode **7** bonanza
water: **6** tinaja
pocketbook: bag, fob, lil **4** poke **5** burse, pouch, purse **6** clutch, wallet **8** billfold **12** portemonnaie
poco: **6** little **8** slightly, somewhat
pococurante: **9** apathetic **10** nonchalant **11** indifferent
pocosin, pocoson, pocosen: **5** marsh, swamp
pod: bag, bur, cod, kid, sac **4** aril, boll, hull, swad **5** belly, carob, pouch, shell, shuck **6** legume, loment **7** silicle **8** potbelly
podesta: **5** judge, mayor **8** executor, governor, official **10** magistrate
podgy: fat **5** pudgy, squat
podium: **4** base, dais, wall **7** lectern **8** pedestal, platform **12** substructure
Poe: *bird* **5** raven
house: **5** Usher
poem: **5** Raven **6** Lenore **7** Ulalume
poem: ode **4** duan, epic, raff, rann(Ir.), rime, rune, song, vers(F.) **5** canto, ditty, elegy, ionic, lyric, poesy, raffe, rhyme, stave, verse **6** ballad, carmen, epopee, eulogy, iambic, jingle, poetry, screed, sonnet, tercet **7** ballade, dimeter, sestina, triolet, virelay **8** acrostic, doggerel, hexapody, limerick, madrigal, senarius, trimeter **9** hexameter, hexastich, monometer, octameter, soliloquy **10** tetrameter **11** acatalectic

break in rhythm: **6** cesura **7** caesura
bucolic: **8** pastoral
closing: **5** envoi, envoy
collection: **5** sylva
division of: see *part* below
eight-line: **7** triolet
foot: **4** iamb **6** iambus **7** anapest, spondee
four-line: **8** quatrain
fourteen-line: **6** sonnet
heroic: **4** epic
line: **8** trimeter **9** hexameter **12** decasyllabic
love: **6** erotic **8** madrigal
lyric: lay **4** alba **6** roundel
medieval: lai **4** alba
melodic: **5** lyric
moral: dit
mournful: **5** elegy
narrative: **4** epos
node: **4** plot
nonsensical: **8** doggerel, limerick
part: fit **4** feet, foot, line **5** canto, epode, stich, verse **6** epilog, prolog, stanza **7** refrain **8** epilogue, prologue
pastoral: **4** idyl **7** bucolic, eclogue, georgic
pert. to: **4** odic
religious: **4** hymn **5** psalm
rural: **7** eclogue, georgic
satirical: dit(F.) **6** iambic, kasada, parody
seven-line: **10** heptastich
sort: dit(F.) **5** ditty **6** sonnet **7** epigram **8** rondelet
six-line: **9** hexastich
six-stanza: **7** sestina
ten-line: **6** dizain **7** dizaine **9** decastich
poesy: **4** poem **5** motto, verse **7** nosegay
poet: **4** bard, fili, muse, scop **5** odist, rishi **6** lyrist **7** dreamer, imagist, metrist **8** idyllist, minstrel **9** bucoliast **10** Parnassian **13** cinque-centist
humorous: **4** Lear, Nash
inferior: **5** rimer **6** rhymer **8** rimester **9** poetaster, poeticule, rhymester, versifier
inspiration: **4** Muse
poetic: **4** odic **5** lyric **6** dreamy **8** romantic **9** beautiful, visionary **11** imaginative
poetical: **8** sonnetic
poetry: *accented foot:* **5** arsis
god: **5** Bragi
inspiring to: **7** helicon
muse: **5** Erato **6** Thalia **7** Euterpe **8** Calliope
pogonip: fog
pogrom: **6** attack **7** pillage **8** genocide, massacre **9** slaughter
pogy: **5** perch, trout **8** menhaden
poi: **4** food **5** paste
source: **4** taro
poietic: **8** creative
poignant: **4** keen, tart **5** acute, sharp **6** biting, bitter, moving **7** cutting, pi-

quant, pointed, pungent **8** piercing, pricking, touching

poind: 4 sell **5** seize **7** impound

point: aim, dot, jag, jet, jot, neb, nib, tip **4** apex, barb, cape, crux, cusp, gist, horn, item, peak, pith, pole, show, spit, spot **5** angle, focus, issue, level, prong, punch, refer, sense, taper **6** allude, degree, detail, direct, tip-off, tittle **7** apicula(L.), apiculi(L.), article, element, feature, meaning **8** apiculus(L.), emphasis, indicate, salience, validity **10** particular, promontory

cardinal: **4** east, west **5** north, south

final: dot, end **6** period **7** outcome

finishing: **4** tape

highest: tip **4** acme, apex, noon, peak **6** apices, apogee, maxima, summit, zenith **7** maximum **8** meridian, pinnacle **11** ne plus ultra

land: **4** hook, spit

law: res

lowest: **4** zero **5** nadir **6** bottom, pergee **7** bedrock

pert. to: **6** apical

scoring: ace, run **5** punto **6** sponge

spear: grad

strong: **5** forte

supporting: **5** pivot **7** fulcrum

to the: **6** cogent **8** relevant **9** pertinent

turning: **4** tide **5** cardo, epoch **6** crisis, crises

utmost: **7** extreme, sublime

vibration: **4** node

weak: **4** blot, flaw **5** fault **6** foible

point-blank: 6 direct, wholly **7** bluntly, exactly **8** directly **9** perfectly, precisely **10** completely **13** unqualifiedly

point of view: eye **4** bras **5** angle, sight, slant **7** opinion, outlook **8** attitude

pointed: 5 acute, sharp, tangy, terse **6** acuate, marked, picked **7** actuate, capapie, concise **8** aculeate, piercing, poignant, spicated, stinging **9** acuminate, apiculate, fastigate **10** noticeable **11** conspicuous

pointer: arm, dog, tip **4** clue, hand, hint **5** index **6** fescue, gnomon **7** indices **9** indicator

pointless: 4 dull **5** blunt, inane, silly, vapid **6** stupid **7** insipid **9** senseless

pointsman: 7 flanker, trapper **9** switchman

poise: tee **4** tact **5** carry, grace, weigh **6** aplomb **7** balance, ballast, bearing, support, suspend **8** calmness, carriage, liberate, maintain **9** assurance, elegance, equipoise, stability **10** confidence, equanimity **11** equilibrium **12** counterpoise **14** counterbalance

poison: fig **4** bane, drab, gall **5** atter, taint, venin, venom, virus **6** amarin, debase,

infect, miasma **7** amarine, arsenic, botulin, corrupt, pervert, vitiate **8** empoison, ptomaine **11** contaminate

ant: **10** formmicide **11** formicicide

arrow: **4** haya, inee, upas **5** urali, urare, urari **6** antiar, curare, curari **7** ouabain, woorlai

hexapod: **11** insecticide

kind: **4** bikh **5** abrin, nabee, ricin **6** antiar **7** arsenic, tanghin

pert. to: **9** arsenious

tree: **4** upas

poison ash: 5 sumac **6** sumach **9** torchwood

poison fish: 4 fugu **6** weever **8** scorpion, toadfish

poison flag: 4 iris

poison flower: 11 bittersweet

poison ivy: 5 sumac **6** laurel

poison tobacco: 7 henbane

poisoned: 6 sepsis

poisoning: 6 pyemia **7** jimmies **9** ichthyism, lathyrism

food: **8** botulism

lead: **8** plumbism

poisonous: 5 toxic **6** virose **7** baneful, noxious **8** mephatic, venomous, virulent **9** malignant **11** destructive

fish: **4** fugu

fungus: **7** amanita

gas: **6** arsine **8** phosgene

herb: **8** aconitum

lizard: **4** gila

plant: **8** mandrake **10** nightshade

weed: **4** loco

poisonwood: 5 sumac **8** metopium **10** manchineel

poisson bleu: 7 blue cat, catfish **8** grayling

poitrel: 5 armor, plate **7** pectron **9** stomacher **11** breastplate

poke: bag, dig, hat, jab, jog **4** blow, bore, brod, cuff, prod, root, sack **5** bulge, delay, dunce, nudge, probe, punch, purse, snoop **6** bonnet, dawdle, loiter, meddle, pocket, potter, putter, sleeve, thrust, wallet **7** dawdler, intrude, tobacco

poker: rod **4** dart, game

drawing by: **10** pyrography

forerunner: **7** primero

form: **4** draw, stud

stake: pot **4** ante **5** chips, kitty

poker-faced: 7 neutral, serious

pokeweed: 5 pocan **6** garget **8** inkberry

family: **14** phytolaccaceae

pokey, poky: 4 dull, jail, mean, slow **5** dowdy **6** narrow, shabby, stuffy **7** tedious **8** trifling

Poland: 6 Polska **7** Polonia **8** Sarmatia

astronomer: **10** Copernicus

cake: **4** baba

capital: **6** Warsaw

carriage: **7** britska

city: **4** Lodz **5** Brest, Posen, Vilna **6** Cracow, Gdansk, Gdynia, Grodno, Krakow, Lublin, Poznan, Tarnow **7** Beuthen, Lemberg, Litovsk, Wroclaw **8** Gleiwitz, Katowice, Szczecin, Tarnopol **9** Bialystok, Bielostok, Byelostok

commune: **4** Ruda **5** Plock, Radom

composer: **6** Chopin **10** Paderewski

dance: **5** polka **7** mazurka **9** krakowiak, polonaise **11** cracovienne

dollar: **5** dalar

dynasty: **5** Piast

island: **5** Wolin

labor leader: **6** Walesa

labor union: **10** Solidarity

measure: cal **4** mila, morg, pret **5** linja, morga, sazen, stopa, vloka, wloka **6** cwierc, korzec, kwarta, lokiec **7** garniec **9** kwarterka

monetary unit: **5** ducat, grosz, marka, zloty **6** fennig, halerz, korona

nobleman: **7** starost

parliament: **4** Seim, Sejm, Seym **5** Senat

people: **4** Slav **5** Marur **8** Silesian

premier: **10** Jaruzelski

river: Bug, San **4** Oder, Styr **5** Dwina, Seret **6** Neisse, Niemen, Pripet, Strypa **7** Vistula

scientist: **5** Curie

szlachta: **6** gentry **8** nobility **9** landowner

title of address: **4** Pani

weight: lut **4** funt **5** uncya **6** kamian **7** centner, skrupul

polar: **6** Arctic **7** pivotal **8** opposite

polar explorer: **4** Byrd **5** Peary **6** Wilkes **8** Amundsen

Polaris: **7** missile **9** North Star

pole: bar, pew, poy, rod, xat **4** axis, boom, brog, mast, palo(Sp.), pike, prop, punt, spar, wand **5** caber, guide, nader, perch, sprit, staff, stake, stick, stool, sweep, totem **6** crotch **7** barling

circle: **11** circumpolar

electric: **5** anode **7** cathode, kathode **9** electrode

fishing: rod

tribal: xat **5** totem

vehicle: **4** cope, neap **5** thill

pole fluke: **8** flounder

pole horse: **7** wheeler

pole strip: **8** template

polecat: **5** fitch, skunk, zoril **6** ferret, musang **7** fitchet, fitchew, foumart

polehead: **7** tadpole

polemic: **8** argument **9** disputant **10** discussion **11** disputation **12** disputatious **13** argumentative, controversial

polenta: **4** mush **8** cornmeal, porridge

polestar: **5** guide **8** lodestar **10** tramontane

police: **5** guard, watch **6** govern, patrol **7** protect, rurales **8** officers **11** carabinieri(It.) **12** constabulary

headquarters: **4** tana **7** station **8** bargello, barracks **9** marshalcy

line: **6** cordon

officer: **6** kotwal **8** bargello **10** prefecture

organization: PAL

trap: **7** dragnet

vehicle: car, van **7** cruiser **8** prowl car, squad car

policeman: cop **4** bull **5** bobby, bulky, burly, rural, sepoy **6** bobbie, copper, peeler **7** crusher, gumshoe, officer, trooper **8** flatfoot, gendarme(F.) **9** burkundaz, constable, patrolman **11** burkundauze, carabiniere(It.)

badge: **6** buzzer, shield

club: **5** billy **9** espantoon, truncheon **10** nightstick

policy: wit **4** plan **6** course, wisdom **8** contract, prudence, sagacity **9** diplomacy, principle, procedure **10** artfulness, management, shrewdness **14** administration

polish: rub **4** buff **5** frush, glaze, gloss, grind, rabat, scour, scrub, sheen, shine, slick **6** finish, glance, luster, lustre, rabat, refine, smooth **7** brush up, burnish, culture, furbish, perfect **8** brighten, civilize, elegance, lapidate, levigate, urbanity **10** refinement

polish off: end **4** kill **5** eat up **6** consume, finish

polished: **4** fine **5** compt, suave **6** polite **7** gallant

polisher: **5** brush, emery, rabat(F.) **6** glazer, pumice **8** abrasive

polishing: **7** sanding **8** frottage, limation

polite: **5** civil, suave **6** gentle, smooth, urbane **7** correct, courtly, cunning, gallant, genteel, refined **8** cultured, debonair, decorous, discreet, polished **9** attentive, courteous, debonaire **10** cultivated, debonnaire, thoughtful **11** complaisant, considerate

politesse: **8** courtesy **12** decorousness

politic: **4** wary, wise **5** suave **6** artful, astute, crafty, shrewd **7** prudent **8** discreet **9** expedient, politique, provident, sagacious **10** diplomatic **12** unscrupulous

political: *division:* **4** city, town, ward **5** shire, state **6** county **8** province **9** community

gathering: **5** rally **6** caucus **10** convention

group: **4** bloc, cell, ring **5** cadre, junta, party **6** caucus **7** faction, machine

hanger-on: **10** ward heeler

incumbents: ins

influence: **5** lobby

list: **5** slate

political party: G.O.P. **4** Tory, Whig **5**

Labor **9** Communist, Socialist **10** Democratic, Republican **12** Conservative
principles: **8** platform
program article: **5** plank
unit: **4** city, East, ward, West **5** state **6** county, parish **7** borough, hundred, kingdom **8** district **9** sultanate
politician: pol **4** boss **7** schemer, senator, statist **8** lawmaker **9** intriguer, president, statesman **10** wirepuller **16** congressionalist
polka dot: **4** spot **6** circle
poll: cow **4** clip, coll, head, list, trim **5** count, shave, shear **6** ballot, cut off, fleece, survey **7** canvass, despoil, listing **8** counting, register **9** enumerate
pollack: **4** fish, pool **6** billet, saithe **7** baddock(Sc.) **8** bluefish, coalfish
pollan: **9** whitefish
pollard: cow **4** bran, deer, goat, stag, tree **5** prune, sheep **8** truncate
polled: **8** hornless
pollen: **4** dust, meal **5** flour **6** powder
pollen brush: **5** scopa **6** scopae
pollen grain: *mass:* **8** pollinia **9** pollinium
pollenization: **5** xenia
pollex: **4** inch **5** digit, thumb **6** finger **7** phlange
pollicitation: **7** promise **8** proposal
pollinate: **9** fecundate, fertilize
pollinosis: **8** hay fever
polliwog: **7** tadpole
pollute: **4** foul, soil **5** dirty, smear, stain, sully, taint **6** befoul, defile, ravish **7** corrupt, debauch, profane, violate, vitiate **9** desecrate **11** contaminate
pollution: **4** smog **5** filth **8** impurity **11** desecration, uncleanness
Pollux: *brother:* **6** Castor
father: **4** Zeus
mother: **4** Leda
polo: *division:* **7** chucker, chukker
mount: **4** pony **5** horse
stick: **6** mallet
team: **4** four
Polonius: *daughter:* **7** Ophelia
son: **7** Laertes
Polony: **6** Polish **7** sausage **9** polonaise
polt: **4** blow, club **5** knock, thump
poltergeist: **5** ghost **6** spirit, spook
poltfoot: **8** clubfoot
poltroon: cad **4** idle, lazy **6** coward, craven, wretch **7** dastard **8** cowardly, sluggard **9** dastardly
polverine: **6** potash **8** pearlash
polyandrium: **8** cemetery
polychromatic: **10** variegated **12** multicolored
polygamy: **6** bigamy
polygon: **4** ngon **6** square **7** decagon, hexagon, nonagon, octagon **8** pentagon, triangle

equal sides: **6** isagon
nine sides: **7** nonagon
twelve sides: **9** dodecagon
Polynesia: *apple:* **4** hevi
baking pit: umu
banana: fei
beverage: **4** kava, kawa
breech cloth: **4** malo
burial place: ahu
butterfly: io
chestnut: **4** rata
cloth: **4** tapa
dance: **4** siva
dragon: ati
fern: **4** tara
garment: **5** pareu
god: Oro **4** Tane, Tiki
goddess: **4** Pele
herb: pia
homeland: **7** Havaiki
image: **4** Tiki
island: **4** Cook, Fiji, Line **5** Samoa, Tonga **6** Easter, Ellice **7** Phoenix, Tokelau
language: **7** Tagalog
magical power: **4** mana
memorial: ahu
oven: umu
people: Ati **5** Malay, Maori **6** Kanaka, Samoan, Tongan **8** Hawaiian, Tahitian **9** Marquesan
pepper plant: **4** avas
pigeon: **4** lupe
pine: ara **4** hala
plant: **4** taro
ruler: **7** faipule
sky: **5** langi
sling: ma
spirit: **4** Atua
statue: **4** Tiki
tree: ti **4** ahia, rata
wages: utu
woman: **6** vahine
yam: ube, ubi, uve, uvi
polyp: **5** hydra, tumor **6** seapen **7** anemone, hydroid, octopod
skeleton: **5** coral
polytrophic: **9** versatile
Polyxena: *father:* **5** Priam
lover: **8** Achilles
mother: **6** Hecuba
pomade: **4** balm **5** salve **7** pomatum, unguent **8** cosmetic, ointment
pomander: **4** case **7** pouncet
pome: **4** ball, pear **5** apple, fruit, globe **6** quince, sphere **9** juneberry
pomegranate: **6** granet **7** grenade **8** balausta
syrup: **9** grenadine
pomelo: **8** shaddock **10** grapefruit
Pomerania: *capital:* **7** Stettin
city: **5** Thorn, Torun **6** Anklam
island: **5** Rugen **6** Usedom

province: **7** Pomorze
river: **4** Oder
Pomeranian: dog
pomme de terre: 6 potato
pommel: bat **4** beat, knob **6** finial, handle **12** protuberance
bag: **7** cantina
pomp: 4 fare, form **5** boast, pride, state **6** estate, parade, ritual **7** cortege, display liturgy, pageant **8** ceremony, grandeur, splendor **9** pageantry, spectacle **10** ceremonial **11** ostentation **12** magnificence
Pomp and Circumstance composer: 5 Elgar
pompano: 4 fish **7** alewife, cobbler **8** mackerel **9** poppy fish
Pompeii: *archeologist:* Mau
heroine: **4** Ione
mountain: **8** Vesuvius
pom-pom: 6 gun **6** cannon
pompon: 4 ball, tuft **6** dahlia **8** ornament **13** chrysanthemum
pompous: big **7** bloated, fustian, orotund, stately, stilted **8** arrogant **9** bombastic, flatulent, grandiose **10** altisonant, pontifical, rhetorical **11** altiloquent, dictatorial, magnificent, pretentious, stateliness **12** ostentatious **13** grandiloquent, self-important
Ponchielli opera: 8 Gioconda
pond: dam, lum **4** delf, dike, lake, mere, pool, tarn **6** lagoon, stalina **7** lakelet
fish: **7** pisoina **8** aquarium
frog: **8** ranarium
oyster: **6** claire
pond dogwood: 10 buttonbush
pond duck: 7 mallard
pond hen: 4 coot **6** fulica
ponder: 4 chaw, mull, muse, pore **5** brood, opine, study, think, weigh **6** reason **7** mediate, reflect, revolve **8** appraise, cogitate, consider, evaluate, meditate, ruminate, turn over **10** deliberate **11** contemplate
ponderous: dry **4** dull **5** bulky, grave, heavy, hefty, massy **7** awkward, massive, weighty **8** unwieldy **9** important, momentous **11** elephantine, heavy-footed
pondfish: 7 sunfish
pondokkie: hut **5** hovel
pone: 4 lump, turf **8** swelling **10** johnny-cake
pongee: 4 silk **5** cloth **6** fabric **7** paunche **8** shantung
pongy: 4 monk **6** priest **8** Buddhist
poniard: 4 dirk, kill, stab **6** bodkin, dagger, pierce, stylet **8** stiletto
pont: 5 ferry, float **6** bridge **7** caisson **9** ferryboat
pontiff: 4 pope **6** bishop

pert. to: **5** papal **7** sistine
pontifical: 5 papal **7** pompous **8** dogmatic
pontoon: 4 boat **5** barge, float **6** bridge, vessel **7** caisson
plank: **5** chess
pony: cab, cob, nag **4** crib, trot **5** glass, horse **6** garran, liquor **7** hackney, measure
kind: **5** pinto, tatoo **6** cayuse, Exmoor **8** Shetland
student's: **4** crib, trot
pooch: dog **6** barbet **7** mongrel
pooh-pooh: 7 dismiss, kiss off **8** ridicule **9** denigrate, raspberry
pook: 4 heap, pile, pull **5** pluck, stack
pooka: 6 goblin **7** specter
pool: car, dib(Sc.), dub(Sc.), lin, pit, pot **4** carr, dike, game, jeel, linn, loch, mear, meer, mere, pond, tank, tarn **5** flash, flush, funds, kitty, lough, plash, stake, trunk, trust **6** cartel, charco, flodge, lagoon, plunge, puddle, salina **7** alberca, carline, combine, jackpot, plashet **8** monopoly **9** billabong, billiards, reservoir, resources, syndicate **10** natatorium **11** combination
ball: cue **4** spot **6** ringer
poon: 4 dilo, tree **5** domba, keena **8** mastwood
poonghie: See **pongy**
poop: 4 deck, fool, gulp, seat **5** cheat, cozen, stern **7** exhaust **8** hinddeck **10** nincompoop **11** information
poor: bad, ill **4** bare, base, lean, mean **5** broke, cheap, dinky, naked, needy, seedy **6** abject, barren, feeble, hard up, humble, hungry, in need, paltry, pilled, scanty, shabby **7** hapless, sterile, unlucky **8** dirt poor, indigent, inferior **9** defective, destitute, emaciated, imperfect, infertile, penurious **10** inadequate, ungenerous **11** impecunious, inefficient, unfortunate **12** contemptible, impoverished, insufficient **13** insignificant **14** unsatisfactory
Poor Clare: nun **6** sister
poor joe: 4 bird **5** heron
poor John: cod **4** fish, food, hake
poor man's pepper: 9 stonecrop **11** peppergrass
poor man's soap: 7 spiraea **8** hardhack
poor man's weatherglass: 9 pimpernel
poor soldier: 9 friarbird
poor-spirited: 4 base, mean **8** cowardly
poorer: 5 worse **8** inferior
poorhouse: 6 asylum **9** almshouse, measondue, workhouse
poorly: low **4** mean **6** ailing, sickly, unwell **10** indisposed **13** disparagingly
pop: 4 dart, pawn **5** fling **6** father, strike **8** beverage **9** explosion

popadam: 4 cake 5 wafer 6 cookie
popdock: 8 foxglove
pope: 4 ruff 6 bishop, priest, puffin, shrike 7 pontiff 9 bullfinch, patriarch 10 holy father
  cape: 5 fanon, orale 7 mozetta 8 mozzetta
  court: 5 Curia
  court office: 6 datary 7 dataria
  court officer: 6 datary
  crown: 5 tiara 9 triregnum
  decree: 8 rescript
  envoy: 6 legate 7 nuntius 8 ablegate
  epistle: 8 decretal
  headdress: 5 miter, mitre, tiara
  letter: 4 bull
  line: 6 papacy
  name: Leo 4 John, Pius 5 Peter, Ratti, Urban 6 Adrian 7 Gregory, Zachary 8 Benedict, Innocent
  palace: 7 Lateran, Vatican
  pert. to: 5 papal
  seal: 5 bulla
  secretary: 11 apocrisiary
  veil: 5 orale 6 fannel
Popeye: *baby:* 7 Swee'Pea
  creator: 5 Segar
  girl: 8 Olive Oyl
  occupation: 6 sailor
  rival: 5 Bluto
popinac: 8 huisache
popinjay: 6 parrot 7 papingo 8 parakeet 10 woodpecker
poplar: 4 liar 5 abele, alamo, aspen, bahan, bolle, garab 6 balsam 7 populus 9 tacamahac 10 cottonwood
  white: 4 abele, aspen
Poppaea's husband: 4 Nero
poppy: 5 plant 6 blaver, canker, flower 7 coprose, papaver, ponceau 8 foxglove 10 coquelicot
  herb family: 9 celandine
  seed: maw
poppycock: rot 4 bosh, dung 8 nonsense
populace: mob 4 mass 5 demos, plebs 6 people 10 commonality 11 rank and file, third estate
popular: lay, pop 6 common, simple 7 demotic, favored 8 accepted, favorite 9 prevalent, well-liked 10 democratic, prevailing 11 proletarian 12 nontechnical
popularity: 5 vogue 8 claptrap
populate: 6 occupy, people 7 inhabit
population: 8 universe 9 habitancy 11 inhabitants
  count: 6 census
  study: 10 demography, larithmics
populous: 7 crowded 9 abounding
porbeagle: 5 shark 7 lamnoid
porcelain: 4 frit 5 china 7 biscuit
  ancient: 5 murra
  clay: 6 kaolin 7 kaoline

  furnace: 5 hovel
  kind of: 5 Lenox, Spode 6 Sevres 7 Celadon, Dresden, Limoges, Meissen 8 Haviland 9 Wedgewood
porch: 4 door, stoa 5 lanai, plaza, stoae(pl.), stoop 6 harbor, loggia, piazza 7 balcony, galilee, gallery, portico, terrace, veranda 8 entrance 9 colonnade
  church: 7 galilee, martliex
  sun: 7 solaria(pl.) 8 solarium
  swing: 6 glider
porcine: fat 7 piglike
porcupine: 5 urson 7 cawquaw 8 hedgehog
  disease: 10 ichthyosis
  genus of: 7 hystrix
  spine: 5 quill
porcupine anteater: 7 echidna
porcupine fish: 6 atinga, diodon
porcupine grass: 5 stipa 8 spinefex
  quill: pen
pore: con 4 gaze 5 gloze, stare, stoma, study 6 ponder 7 foramen, opening, orifice, ostiole, stomata(pl.) 8 lenticel, meditate
  plant: 7 ostiole 8 lenticel
porgy: tai(Jap.) 4 fish, scup 6 besugo, pagrus 7 margate, pinfish 8 menhaden 9 spadefish
pork: ham, pig 5 bacon, money, swine 6 hamhog 7 griskin, sausage 8 position
pork-barrelling: 9 patronage
porker: hog, pig 5 swine
porkfish: 4 sisi
porky: fat, pig 6 greasy
pornographic: 4 lewd 7 obscene 10 licentious
porous: 4 open 5 leaky, light 6 leachy 9 permeable 10 penetrable 13 insubstantial
porphyry: 4 rock
porpoise: 4 inia 6 seahog 7 dolphin, pellock(Sc.) 8 cetacean, gairfish
porrect: 6 extend, tender 7 present
porret: 4 leek 5 onion 6 garlic 8 scallion
porridge: 4 samp 5 atole, brose(Sc.), grout, gruel 6 burgoo 7 brochan, burgout, oatmeal, polenta, pottage 9 stirabout 10 miscellany 11 skilligalee
  container: 6 bicker
port: 4 gate, toal, left, wine 5 carry, haven 6 apport, harbor, market, portal, refuge 7 bearing, harbour, meaning, purport, shelter 8 carriage, demeanor, larboard 9 demeanour, transport 10 deportment 11 destination
portable: 5 handy 6 mobile 7 movable 8 bearable 10 convenient, manageable
  bathtub: 4 tosh
  bed: cot 8 rollaway
  chair: 5 sedan
  lamp: 7 lantern

stove: 4 etna
portal: 4 arch, door, gate 7 gateway 8 entrance
portance: 7 bearing, conduct 8 carriage, demeanor
portcullis: bar 4 door, gate, shut 5 grate, herse 7 grating, lattice
porte-monnaie: 5 purse 10 pocketbook
portefeuille: 9 portfolio
portend: 4 bode 5 augur 6 divine 7 betoken, forbode, predict, presage 8 forebode, foretell, prophesy 10 foreshadow
portent: 4 omen, sign 5 event 6 marvel, ostent, wonder 7 meaning, prodigy 8 ceremony 9 foretoken 10 foreboding, prognostic 11 forewarning
portentous: 4 dire 5 fatal, grave 6 solemn 7 fateful, ominous, pompous, weighty 10 impressive 11 significant
porter: ale 4 beer 5 carry, hamal, stout 6 bearer, durwan, hamaul, hammal, khamal, redcap, suisse 7 bailiff, carrier, durwaun, dvornik(Russ.), gateman, hummaul, janitor 8 beverage, cargador, janitrix 9 attendant, concierge, janitress, transport 10 doorkeeper
Portia: *alias:* 9 Balthazar
  husband: 6 Brutus
  lover: 8 Bassanio
  maid: 7 Nerissa
portia tree: 4 maho 5 bendy
portico: 4 stoa(Gr.), xyst 5 porch, stoae(Gr., pl.) 6 atrium, piazza, xystus 7 narthex, pteroma, terrace, veranda 9 colonnade, pteromata(pl.) 10 ambulatory, antetemple
  enclosed: 9 peridrome
  long: 6 xystus 7 veranda
portiere: 5 drape 7 curtain
portion: bit, cut, dab, dot, jag, lot, nip 4 chaw, deal, dole, dunt, fate, jagg, part, some 5 allot, allow, divvy, dower, dowry, endow, piece, quota, ratio, share 6 canton, divide, dowery, gobbet, moiety, parcel, rasher, ration 7 destiny, helping, scruple, section, segment, serving 8 legitime, quantity 9 allotment, allowance, apportion 10 distribute 13 apportionment
portly: fat 5 ample, obese, stout 6 chubby, chunky 7 stately 8 imposing, majestic 9 corpulent, dignified
portmanteau: bag 4 case 6 valise 8 suitcase 9 carpetbag, gladstone
Porto Rico: See **Puerto Rico**
portrait: 4 copy, icon, ikon 5 image 6 effigy 7 picture 8 likeness 10 similitude
  pert. to: 6 iconic
  sitting: 6 seance
portray: act 4 copy, draw, form, limn, mime, show 5 enact, frame, graph, image, paint 6 depict 7 fashion, picture 8

describe 9 delineate, duplicate, pantomime, represent, reproduce 11 demonstrate
portreeve: 5 mayor 7 bailiff, officer
portress, porteress: 6 porter 9 charwoman 10 doorkeeper
Portugal: *brandy:* 10 aguardente
  capital: Lisbon
  city: 4 Ovar 5 Braga, Evora 6 Guarda 7 Coimbra, Opporto 8 Braganca
  commune: 5 Braga
  district: 4 Tete 5 Evora
  explorer: Cao 4 Diaz
  festival: 9 chamarita
  former colony: Diu, Goa 5 Damao, Timor 6 Angola, Guinea 7 Sao Tome 8 Principe 9 Cape Verde 10 Mozambique
  former money: 5 dobra
  guitar: 7 machete
  harbor: 4 Faro, Ovar 5 Macao 6 Aveiro, Lisbon, Oporto, Vianna 7 Setubal 8 Figueira
  island: 6 Angola, Azores 7 Madeira 8 Principe, Sao Thome
  legislature: 6 cortes
  liquid measure: 6 canada
  measure: pe 4 alma, bota, meio, moio, pipa, vara 5 almud, braca, fanga, geira, legoa, linha, milha, palmo 6 almude, covado, quarto 7 alquier, estadio, ferrado, selamin 8 alqueire, tonelada
  monetary unit: 6 escudo 7 centavo
  mountain: 15 Serra d'Estrella
  navigator: 4 Gama 8 Magellan
  news agency: 4 ANOP
  overseas territory: 5 Macao
  people: 7 Iberian
  poet: 7 Camoens
  province: 4 Ovar 5 Beira, Minho 6 Azores 7 Algarve, Madeira 8 Alentejo
  river: 4 Sado 5 Douro, Duero, Minho, Tagus 7 Mondego 8 Guadiana
  saint: Sao
  song: 4 fado
  title: dom 4 dona 6 senhor 7 fidalgo, senhora 9 senhorita
  vessel: 7 caravel
  weight: 4 grao, onca, once 5 libra, marco 6 arroba, oitava 7 arratel, quintal
porwigle: 7 tadpole
posada: inn 5 hotel
posaune: 8 trombone
pose: set, sit 4 airs 5 model, offer, place, strut 6 baffle, puzzle, stance 7 nonplus, posture 8 attitude, confound, position, propound, question 9 mannerism 10 disconcert, expression 11 affectation, impersonate 12 attitudinize
Poseidon: 7 Neptune(L.) 11 earthshaker
  brother: 4 Zeus 5 Hades, Pluto
  father: 6 Cronus
  mother: 4 Rhea

scepter: **7** trident
servant: **7** Proteus
son: **6** Albion, Triton **7** Alebion, Antaeus, Antaios
wife: **10** Amphitrite
poser: 5 facer **6** puzzle **7** problem **8** question
posh: 5 smart **6** spruce, swanky **7** elegant, stylish **9** luxurious
posit: 6 affirm, assert, assume **9** postulate **10** presuppose
position (see also **place**): job, lie, set **4** loci(pl.), pose, post, rank, side, site, view **5** cense, coign, locus, place, situs, stand **6** billet, coigne, estate, locale, office, plight, stance, status **7** calling, posture **8** attitude, doctrine, location, sinecure, statuses(pl.) **9** condition, gradation, situation **10** standpoint **11** affirmation, appointment, disposition **12** circumstance
change: **4** move
correct: **8** oriented
defensive: **4** fort **10** bridgehead
relative: **5** grade **8** standing
troops: **6** deploy
with little work: **8** sinecure
positional: 6 situal
positive: set **4** plus, sure **6** actual, thetic **7** assured, certain, decided **8** absolute, complete, constant, definite, dogmatic, emphatic, explicit **9** assertive, confident, downright, empirical, practical **10** peremptory **11** affirmative, categorical, dictatorial, opinionated, right-handed, unqualified **13** authoritative, overconfident
positively: 5 truly **6** easily, really **8** actually **9** certainly, obviously **11** indubitably
positivism: 7 Comtism **9** certainty, dogmatism **11** materialism
founder: **5** Comte
positure: 7 posture **11** arrangement, disposition **13** configuration
poss: 4 beat, dash, push **5** drive, knock, pound, stamp **6** thrust
posse: 4 band **6** throng
possess: get, owe, own **4** bear, have **5** reach **6** occupy **7** inhabit **8** dominate, maintain
possessed: mad **4** calm **8** demoniac
possession: 4 aver, hold **5** asset, aught **6** havior, seisin, wealth **7** control, dewanee, haviour, mastery **8** property **9** ownership
family: **8** heirloom
legal: **5** title **6** estate
of goods by finding: **6** trover
take: **5** seise
time: **5** lease
possessions: 5 goods **6** graith **8** chattels
possessor: 5 owner **10** proprietor

posset: 4 turn **6** curdle, pamper **8** beverage **9** balductum, coagulate
possibility: 11 contingency, eventuality
possible: may **6** likely **8** feasible, probable **9** expedient, potential **10** contingent **11** practicable
possibly: may **5** maybe **7** perhaps
possum: 4 coon, tait **9** marsupial, phalanger
comic strip: **4** Pogo
play: **4** sham **5** feign **7** pretend
post: set **4** dole, dool, fort, mail, pole, ride, send **5** cippi(pl.), newel, place, stake, stock **6** assign, cippus, column, inform, office, pillar, poster, travel **7** courier, placard, station **8** announce, dispatch, garrison, position **9** advertise, situation
airplane race: **5** pylon
boat rope: **7** bollard, capstan
easy: **4** pipe, snap **8** sinecure
middle: **8** kingpost
post chaise: 4 jack **5** coach **8** carriage
post office: 6 correo(Sp.)
letter box: **8** apartado(Sp.)
postage: 5 stamp
stamp design: **6** burele **8** burelage, spandred
postbox: 7 mailbox
postboy: 7 courier, yamshik(Russ.) **8** horseman yemschik **9** messenger, postilion, yamstchik(Russ.)
postdate: 9 afterdate
poster: 4 bill, clap, sign **6** banner **7** affiche, courier, placard, sticker **9** broadside **10** billposter **12** announcement **13** advertisement
posterior: 4 back, hind, rear **6** behind, caudal, dorsal, hinder **7** adaxial **8** buttocks **10** subsequent
posterity: 6 sequel **9** offspring **10** generation **11** descendants
postern: 4 door, exit, gate, side **7** clocket, private **8** entrance **10** undercover
postfix: add **5** annex **6** append **7** suffix
postiche: wig **4** sham **6** switch, toupee **8** pretense, spurious **9** imitation **14** counterfeiting
postil: 6 homily **7** comment **10** commentary
postilion: 7 courier, postboy
postpone: 4 stay, wait **5** defer, delay, remit, table **6** remand, retard, shelve **7** adjourn, prolong **8** reprieve **10** pigeonhole **11** subordinate **13** procrastinate
postponement: 4 mora, stay **5** delay, morae(pl.) **7** respite **8** reprieve **10** ampliation
postprandial: 11 after-dinner
postscript: 6 sequel **8** footnote
postulant: 9 applicant, candidate **10** petitioner
postulate: 5 claim, posit **6** assume, de-

mand **7** premise, require **10** assumption, hypotheses(pl.), hypothesis, presuppose **11** proposition **12** prerequisite

posture: 4 pose **5** state **6** stance **7** bearing, gesture **8** attitude, carriage, position **9** composure

erect: **11** orthostatic

posy: 5 motto, verse **6** flower, legend **7** bouquet, nosegay **9** anthology, sentiment **11** composition

pot: bag, pan, win **4** dixy, pool **5** abyss, crewe, dixie, drink, kitty, shoot **6** aludel, basket, cruset, posnet, secure, toilet, vessel **7** caldron, capture, cuvette, fortune, notable **8** cauldron, crucible, potation **9** marijuana **11** deteriorate

arch: **4** kiln

earthen: **4** olla **5** crock, cruse **6** chytra

handle: **4** bool

hat: **5** derby **6** bowler

lead: **8** graphite

wheel: **5** noria

pot-au-feu: 4 soup, stew

pot liquid: 6 brewis

pot-rustler: 4 cook

potable: 4 pure **5** clean, drink **8** beverage **9** drinkable

potage: 4 soup **5** broth

potash: 4 kali **5** niter, nitre, salin **6** alkali, saline **8** pearlash

potassium: 6 kalium

compound: **4** alum **6** chrome, potash

sulphate: **4** alum **8** misenite

potation: 4 bout, dram **5** draft, drink **6** liquid, liquor **7** spirits **8** beverage, drinking, libation

potato: 4 ima, oca, yam **4** chat, papa, spud **5** rural, tuber **6** murphy **7** manroot **12** pomme de terre(F.)

beetle: **8** hardback

bud: eye

disease: pox **4** curl

dish: **8** au gratin **9** lyonnaise, scalloped

family: **10** solanaceae

planting ridge: **4** ruck

seed part: eye

starch: **6** farina

state: **5** Idaho, Maine

sweet: yam **6** batata, comote, patata **7** batatas, ocarina

potbank: 7 pottery

potbelly: 5 stove **6** paunch **9** bay window

potboiler: 4 book **8** painting **9** potwaller **10** manuscript

potboy: 8 Ganymede **9** cupbearer

pote: 4 kick, poke, push **5** nudge, shove **6** thrust

poteen, potheen: 6 whisky

potence: 5 cross **6** gibbet **7** gallows

potency: vis **5** force, might, power, vigor **6** energy **8** efficacy, strength, vitality **9** fertility

potent: 4 able **6** cogent, mighty, strong **7** dynamic **8** powerful, puissant, vigorous, virulent **9** effective, efficient **10** convincing **11** influential

potentate: 4 amir, emir, king **5** ameer, emeer, mogul, ruler **6** moghul, prince **7** monarch **9** sovereign

potential: 6 latent, mighty **8** inchoate, possible **10** unrealized **11** influential, possibility, undeveloped

potentiality: 5 power **8** capacity **9** pregnancy

potgun: 6 pistol, popgun **8** braggart

pothead: 9 blackfish

pother: ado, row, vex **4** fuss, stir **5** worry **6** bother, bustle, harass, muddle, uproar **7** fluster, perplex, trouble **9** annoyance, commotion, confusion **11** disturbance **12** perturbation

potherb: 4 kale, mint, wort **5** chard **6** greens **7** mustard, quelite, spinach

pert. to: **7** olitory

pothole: 5 cahot **6** kettle, tinaja

pothook: rod **4** hake, nine **5** crook **6** collar, scrawl

pothouse: bar **6** tavern **8** alehouse

potiche: jar **4** vase

potion: 4 brew, dose, drug **5** draft, drink **6** drench **7** draught, philter, philtre **8** nepenthe

sleeping: **5** dwale **6** opiate **8** narcotic **9** soporific **10** belladonna

potlatch: 4 gift **5** feast

potomania: 10 dipsomania

potpie: 4 stew **9** fricassee

potpourri: jar **4** olio, stew **6** medley **7** mixture **9** anthology **10** miscellany **11** salamagundi

potrero: 6 meadow **7** pasture

potsherd: bit **4** chip **5** shard **8** fragment

potshot: 4 jibe, jeer **5** shoot **6** assail, attack, insult **9** aspersion, sideswipe

potstone: 8 steatite

pottage: 4 soup, stew **6** brewis **8** porridge

potah: 4 deed **5** lease **11** certificate

potted: 5 drunk **9** condensed **11** intoxicated

potter: fad, pry **4** fuss, mess, poke, push **6** cotter, dabble, dacker, daiker, dawdle, dodder, fiddle, footer, footle, loiter, meddle, putter, tamper, tinker, trifle **7** cloamer, fossick, saunter **8** ceramist **10** ceramicist, mess around

potter's clay: 5 argil

potter's field: 8 Aceldama, cemetery

potter's wheel: 4 disk **5** lathe, palet, throw **6** jigger, pallet

pottery: 4 bank, ware **5** china, delft **7** Keramos(F.) **8** ceramics **9** delftware, Keramikos(Gr.), stoneware **11** earthenware

civilization: **6** Minyan

decorating paste: 9 barbotine
dish: 7 ramekin
enameled: 8 majolica
firing box: 6 saggar, sagger 7 saggard
fragment: 5 shard, sherd
kind: uda(Ind.) 4 delf 5 delft 6 basalt 7 aretine, bocraro 8 bucchero, Majolica, vitreous 9 delftware, sigillate 12 buccheronero
maker: 6 potter 8 ceramist
mineral: 8 feldspar
pert. to: 7 ceramic
pottle: 6 liquor 7 tankard 10 half-gallon
potty: 5 crazy, dotty, petty 6 little 7 foolish, haughty, trivial 8 snobbish 9 eccentric 12 supercilious
pouch: bag, cod, pod, sac 4 cyst, sack 5 bulge, bursa, purse 6 budget, gipser, pocket, sporan 7 alforja, gipsire, mailbag, saccule, silicle, sporran 9 spleuchan 10 pocketbook
abdominal: 9 marsupium
Highlander's: 7 sporran
pouch bone: 9 marsupial
pouched: 9 sacculate
dog: 4 wolf
marmot: 8 squirrel 11 spermophile
pouf: 4 bang, puff 5 quilt 7 ottoman 9 hairdress
poule: 6 wanton 10 prostitute
poulp, poulpe: 7 octopus
poultice: 7 plaster 8 compress, dressing 9 cataplasm
poultry: 4 fowl 5 ducks, geese, quail 7 pigeons, turkeys 8 chickens 9 partridge, pheasants 10 guinea fowl
breed: 6 Ancona 7 Dorking, Leghorn 12 Plymouth Rock 14 Rhode-Island Red
dealer: 6 eggler
disease: pip 4 roup
dish: 9 galantine
farm: 7 hennery
yard: 6 barton
pounamu: 4 jade 8 nephrite 10 greenstone
pounce: nab 4 leap, pink, poke, stab 5 pound, prick, punch, stamp, swoop, talon 6 emboss, spring, thrust 8 ornament 9 comminute, perforate
pound: 4 bang, bash, beat, bray, ding, maul, pond, tamp, unit 5 knock, thump 6 bruise, buffet, hammer, powder, wallop, weight 7 contuse 8 malleate 9 enclosure, pulverize
poundage: 6 charge, weight 8 distrain 9 constrain, enclosure 11 confinement
pour: 4 emit, flow, gush, hale, lash, lave, pass, rain, teem, tide, toom(Sc.), vent, well 5 birle, drain, empty, flood, heald, hield, issue, spout, utter 6 affuse, decant, deluge, effuse, libate, sluice, stream 8 downpour 9 discharge

pourboire: fee, tip 7 douceur 8 gratuity 9 buona-mani(pl.), buona-mano
pout: bib, mop 4 moue, sulk 5 boody, bulge, pique 7 catfish, eelpout 8 bullhead 9 sulkiness
poverty: 4 lack, need, want 6 dearth, penury 7 paucity, tenuity 8 scarcity 9 indigence 10 inadequacy, scantiness 11 destitution, inferiority
program: 5 Vista
stricken: 9 penurious
powder: 4 abir(Ind.), dust, kish, mull, talc 5 boral, boron, flour, grind 6 empasm, pollen, pounce, yttria 7 araroba, aristol, malarin, saponin, tripoli 8 cosmetic, sprinkle, tannigen 9 pulverize 10 epiplastic
abrasive: 5 emery
case: 9 bandolier
container: 4 horn 7 arsenal 8 magazine
make: 4 bray 5 grind 7 calcine 9 pulverize
poisonous: 4 antu 5 robin
sachet: 6 pulvil
smokeless: 6 filite, poudre 7 cordite 8 amberite
powdered: 4 seme 5 semee 6 floury
power: arm, art, vis 4 bulk, dint, gift, hand, iron, rial, sway, thew 5 force, might, state, steam, vigor, vires(pl.), wield 6 agency, effort, empire, energy, foison, throne, weight 7 ability, command, control, mastery, potence, potency, stamina 8 capacity, efficacy, function, momentum, strength, virility 9 authority, dominator, influence, intensity, puissance 10 domination, efficiency 11 sovereignty 12 jurisdiction, potentiality
deprive of: 4 maim 7 impeach 8 dethrone 12 deparliament
intellectual: wit 5 brain 6 genius
lack: 5 atony
natural: 4 odyl 5 odyle
partnership: 9 champerty
provide with: 5 endue, endow
reduction: 8 brownout
superior: 10 prepotency 12 predominance
symbol: 5 sword 7 scepter, sceptre
third: 4 cube
unit of: RPM 4 watt
unlimited: 11 omnipotence
power of attorney: 5 agent 10 procurator
powerboat: 5 yacht 9 motorboat
powerful: 4 able, bold, deep 5 stout 6 brawny, cogent, heroic, strong 7 feckful, leonine, weighty 8 puissant 9 effective, effectual 10 dominating 11 efficacious
powerless: 4 weak 6 feeble, supine, unable 7 passive 8 helpless, impotent, inactive, lifeless

Powhatan: *daughter:* 10 Pocahontas

powwow: 4 talk 6 confer, priest 7 meeting 8 assembly, ceremony, congress, conjurer 10 conference

poyou: 6 peludo 9 armadillo

prabble: 7 chatter, quarrel 8 squabble

prabhu: 4 lord 5 chief 6 writer

practic: 6 artful, shrewd 7 cunning, skilled 8 decision(Sc.) 9 practical, practiced

practical: 5 handy, utile 6 actual, beaten, usable, useful 7 practic, working 8 feasible, possible, workable 9 available, practiced, pragmatic, realistic 11 pragmatical, utilitarian
example: 6 praxis
joke: 4 hoax 5 prank, trick 7 waggery

practically: 6 almost, nearly 9 virtually 13 substantially

practice: do; ply, rut, try, use 4 mode, plot, rote 5 apply, canon, cause, drill, habit, trade, train, usage 6 custom, follow, praxic, system 7 perform, process 8 exercise, intrigue, rehearse 9 construct, negotiate, procedure 10 experience
pert. to: 9 pragmatic
sharp: 4 game 5 dodge, fraud, usury 6 deceit 9 chicanery

practiced: 7 skilled, veteran 10 conversant

practitioner: 5 agent 6 artist, doctor, healer, lawyer, novice 7 learner, plotter, schemer 8 civilian 9 assistant

prad: 5 horse

praenomen: 4 name 5 Caius, Gaius, Titus 9 first-name

pragmatic: 7 skilled 8 busybody, dogmatic, meddling 9 conceited, empirical, officious, practical, realistic 10 meddlesome, systematic 11 dictatorial, opinionated, pragmatical

Prague: 4 Prag 5 Praha
river: 6 Moldau, Vltava

prairie: bay 5 camas, llano, plain 6 camass, steppe 7 quamash 9 grassland
clump of trees in: 5 motte
mud: 5 gumbo
plant: 5 camas 6 camass

prairie anemone: 12 pasqueflower

prairie antelope: 9 pronghorn

prairie apple: 9 breadroot

prairie berry: 9 trompillo 10 nightshade

prairie breaker: 4 plow

prairie chicken: 6 grouse

prairie crocus: 12 pasqueflower

prairie dog: 6 gopher, marmot 11 wishton-wish

prairie dog weed: 8 marigold

prairie pigeon: 6 plover 9 sandpiper

prairie potato: 9 breadroot

prairie schooner: ark 12 covered wagon

Prairie State: 8 Illinois

prairie wolf: 6 coyote

prairieweed: 10 cinquefoil

praise: 4 hery, laud, tout 5 adore, allow, alose, bless, cry up, extol, glory, honor, kudos, roosa, roose 6 eulogy, extoll, kudize 7 acclaim, adulate, applaud, commend, encomia(pl.), glorify, hosanna, magnify, plaudit, tribute 8 applause, appraise, blessing, encomium, eulogize, macarism 9 adulation, celebrate, intensify, panegyric 10 compliment, panegyrize 11 approbation 12 commendation 13 glorification
ascription of: 6 Gloria

praiseworthy: 9 exemplary, meritorious 13 complimentary

Prakrit: 4 Pali 7 Bahlika 8 language 11 Dakshinatya

praline: 5 candy 10 confection

pram: 4 cart 5 barge 8 carriage, pushcart, stroller 12 baby carriage, perambulator

prance: 5 brank, caper, dance, strut 6 cavort, frolic, sashay 7 swagger

prank: jig 4 dido, fold, lark, prat, whim 5 adorn, antic, caper, freak, pleat, shine, trick 6 curvet, fegary, frolic, gambol, caprice, dress up 8 capricci(pl.), escapade, mischief 9 capriccio 11 monkeyshine

prase: 6 quartz 10 chalcedony

prat: 4 push 5 nudge, prank, trick 8 buttocks

prate: gab 4 blab, buck, bukh, carp, chat, talk 5 blate, boast, clack, clash 6 babble, claver, tattle, tongue 7 blatter, chatter, deblate, prattle, twaddle 8 harangue 11 deblaterate

prattle: 4 gaff, lisp 5 prate 6 cackle 7 blather, blether, clatter 9 bavardage 11 confabulate

prawn: 6 shrimp 10 crustacean

praxis: 5 habit 6 action, custom 8 practice

pray: ask, beg, bid, sue 5 daven(Heb.) 6 appeal, invite, invoke 7 beseech, conjure, entreat, implore, request 8 petition 10 supplicate

praya: 4 road 5 beach 6 strand 9 esplanade 10 waterfront

prayer: ave 4 bead, bede, bene, boon, plea, suit 5 grace, matin 6 appeal, ectene, ektene, errand, orison 7 Angelus, bidding, collect, complin, gayatri, oration, request, savitri 8 compline, entreaty, petition 9 competory, precation, suppliant 10 paratheses(pl.), parathesis, requiescat 11 application, benediction, paternoster 12 intercession, supplication
beads: 6 rosary
call: 4 adan, azan, bell 5 chime 6 oremus
chancery: 7 relator

day's last: **7** complin **8** compline
for the dead: **7** kaddish, requiem
form of: **5** chant **6** litany
group: **12** comprecation
nine-day: **6** novena
set: **9** akoluthia
short: **5** grace **11** benediction
prayer book: 6 missal, portas, ritual **7** brevary, portass **9** porthouse
prayer desk: 8 prie-dieu
prayer rug: 5 asana
prayer shawl: 5 orale **7** tallith
prayer tower: 7 minaret
praying figure: 5 orant
preach: 4 sugh **5** sough, teach **6** exhort, inform **8** advocate, homilize, instruct, moralize, proclaim **9** discourse, predicate, sermonize **10** concionate, evangelize
preacher: 6 parson, rector **8** minister **9** clergyman, predicant, pulpiteer
preachment: 6 sermon **7** lecture **9** discourse **11** exhortation
preachy: 8 didactic **10** moralistic
preamble: 7 preface **12** introduction
prebend: 4 land **5** tithe **7** stipend **8** benefice **9** allowance
prebendary: 5 canon
precarious: 5 risky **7** assumed, dubious **8** delicate, doubtful, insecure, perilous, unstable **9** dangerous, hazardous, uncertain, unsettled **10** touch-and-go **11** unwarranted
precative: 10 beseeching **12** supplicating
precaution: 4 care **6** cautel **7** caution **8** prudence
precede: 4 lead, pace, rank **5** usher **6** forego **7** forerun, outrank, predate, preface **8** antecede, antedate **9** introduce **10** foreshadow
precedence: pas **8** priority
right: pas
precedent: 5 model, usage **7** example **8** decision, standard
preceding: 5 first **6** before **8** anterior
precentor: 6 cantor
precept: law **4** hest, rule, tora, writ **5** adage, axiom, breve, brief, dogma, maxim, order, sutra, tenet, torah **6** behest, lesson **7** caution, command, mandate **8** doctrine, document, teaching **9** direction, principle **10** injunction **11** commandment, fundamental, instruction
perceptive: 8 didactic **9** mandatory **11** instructive
preceptor: 5 tutor **6** master
precinct: 4 beat **5** ambit, bound **6** hieron **7** temenos **8** boundary, district, environs **9** enclosure
precious: 4 dear, nice, rare, very **5** chere(F.), loved **6** costly, valued **7** beloved, genteel **8** affected, esteemed, fa-

vorite, valuable **9** extremely **10** fastidious **11** inestimable, overrefined
precious stone: See **gem**
precipice: lin **4** crag, drop, linn, pali, scar **5** bluff, brink, cliff, steep **7** clogwyn **8** downfall **9** declivity
precipitate: 4 fall, floc, hurl, rash **5** hasty, heady, hurry, speed, steep, throw **6** abrupt, effect, hasten, madcap, sudden, tumble, unwary **7** hurried, willful **8** headlong, sediment, settling, slapdash **9** desperate, impetuous, impulsive **11** precipitous
precipitation: dew **4** hail, mist, rain, snow **5** haste, sleet **8** downpour **9** hastening **10** deposition **11** impetuosity **12** acceleration
precipitous: 5 sheer, steep **6** steepy **7** prerupt
rock: **4** crag, scar **5** steep
precis: 7 epitome, summary **8** abstract **10** compendium **11** abridgement
precise: 4 even, nice, prim, very **5** exact, rigid, stiff **6** formal, minute, strict **7** buckram, certain, correct, finicky, literal, starchy **8** accurate, definite, delicate, explicit, overnice, priggish, specific **9** faultless, stringent, veracious **10** ceremonial, fastidious, particular, scrupulous **11** ceremonious, on the button, painstaking, punctilious **14** circumstantial
preclude: bar **4** quit, stop **5** avert, close, debar, estop **6** forbid, hinder, impede **7** obviate, prevent **9** foreclose **11** discontinue
precocious: 5 early **6** unripe **7** forward **8** advanced **9** premature
preconceive: 5 dream **6** ideate, scheme **8** foreknow
precursor: 5 usher **6** herald **8** ancestor, foregoer **9** harbinger, messenger **10** forefather, forerunner **11** predecessor
precursory: 11 preliminary, premonitory **12** introductory
predatory: 7 harmful, robbing **8** ravenous **9** pillaging, piratical, rapacious, raptorial **10** plundering, predacious
bird: owl **4** hawk **5** eagle
insect: **6** mantis
predestine: 4 doom, fate **6** decree, ordain **7** destine, predoom **8** foredoom **9** determine, forepoint, preordain **10** foreordain **12** predetermine
predetermine: 4 bias **6** decree **7** destine, predict **8** forecast **9** prejudice **10** preposess
predicament: box, fix **4** hole, stew **5** state **6** pickle, plight, scrape **7** dilemma, in a bind **8** quandary **9** condition, situation
predicant: 5 friar **8** preacher **9** dominican

predicate: cry 4 aver, base 5 imply 6 affirm, assert, preach 7 commend, declare, foresee, involve, predict 8 foretell, proclaim

predict: 4 bode, call, dope, omen 5 augur, guess, weird 6 divine, halsen 7 forbode, presage, presume, suppose 8 forebode, forecast, prophesy, soothsay 9 auspicate, predicate 13 prognosticate

prediction: 5 weird 7 bodword 12 forespeaking, vaticination

predictor: 4 seer 7 prophet

predilection: 4 bent, bias 7 leaning 8 fondness, tendency 9 prejudice 10 partiality, preference, propensity 11 inclination 14 predisposition, susceptibility

predisposed: 5 prone 6 biased 7 partial, willing

predisposition: 7 leaning 12 predilection

predominant: 5 chief 6 ruling 8 dominant, reigning, superior 9 ascendant, ascendent, hegemonic, prevalent 10 dominating, noticeable, prevailing 11 controlling, outstanding 12 preponderant

predominate: 4 rule 6 domine, exceed 8 domineer

preeminent: big 4 star 5 chief, grand 7 capital, palmary, ranking, supreme 8 dominant, superior 9 excellent, prominent 10 surpassing 11 outstanding

preempt: 5 usurp 8 arrogate 9 establish 10 monopolize 11 appropriate

preen: pin, sew 4 perk, trim 5 adorn, clasp, dress, plume, press, pride, primp, prink, prune 6 bodkin, brooch, smooth, spruce, stitch

preface: 5 front, proem 6 herald 7 forerun, precede, prelude 8 exordium, foreword, preamble, prologue 9 introduce 11 preliminary 12 forespeaking, introduction, introductory

prefect, praefect: 4 dean 7 monitor, officer 8 director, minister, official 9 president 10 magistrate

prefecture: 7 eparchy(Gr.) 8 district

prefer: opt 4 like 5 elect, favor 6 choose, desire, favour, rather, select 7 advance, propose

preferable: 6 better

preference: 6 choice 8 appetite, priority 10 partiality 11 advancement, alternative 12 predilection

prefigure: 4 type 6 ideate, typify 7 forerun 8 foretell 9 adumbrate 10 foreshadow

prefix: See list page 825

pregnable: 10 assailable, expugnable, vulnerable 11 conquerable

pregnancy: 6 cyesis 9 fertility, gestation

pregnant: big 5 heavy 6 gravid 7 fertile, teeming, weighty 8 enceinte, fruitful,

prolific 9 abounding, gestating, potential, with child 10 expressive, germinable

prehend: 5 catch, seize

prehistoric: 10 immemorial

preindicate: 7 presage 8 announce, prophesy

prejudice: 4 bent, bias, harm, hurt 6 damage, hatred, impair 7 bigotry, leaning 9 suspicion 10 partiality, prepossess 11 inclination, intolerance 12 disadvantage, jaundiced eye, predetermine, predilection, prejudgement 13 prejudication

prejudicial: 7 harmful 8 contrary 9 injurious 11 contrarious, detrimental 14 discriminatory

prelate: 4 head 5 chief 6 abbess, bishop, priest 7 primate 8 ordinary, superior 9 dignitary 10 archbishop 12 ecclesiastic

prelector: 6 reader 8 lecturer 9 professor 10 discourser

preliminary: 5 basic, prior 7 preface 8 entrance, previous, proemial 9 elemental, inductive, prefatory, threshold 10 antecedent 11 fundamental, preparatory

prelude: 6 verset 7 descant, intrada, opening, preface 8 overture, ritornel 10 ritornelle 12 introduction

premature: 5 early 6 unripe 8 immature, untimely 10 precocious 12 unseasonable

premeditate: See **meditate**

premeditation: 11 forethought 12 aforethought

premier: 5 chief, first 7 leading 8 earliest, foremost 9 principal

premise: 6 ground 9 postulate 10 assumption 11 proposition, supposition

premium: 4 agio 5 bonus, prize, spiff 6 bounty, deport, reward 8 lagnappe, superior 9 lagniappe 10 recompense

premonition: 4 omen 5 hunch 6 notice 7 bodword, warning 9 forescent 10 foreboding 11 forewarning, information 12 apprehension, presentiment

preoccupied: 4 lost, rapt 6 absent, filled 8 absorbed 9 engrossed

preordain: 10 predestine

preparation: 5 array 7 extract, product 8 cosmetic, training 9 condiment, decoction 9 makeready, rehearsal 10 confection 11 arrangement 12 introduction

place of: 10 laboratory, paratorium

without: 5 ad lib 8 careless 9 extempore, impromptu

prepare: arm, fit, fix, get, set 4 bush, busk, gibe, gird, make, pave, suit, tibe 5 adapt, alert, coach, curry, dight, dower, equip, ettle, frame, groom, prime, ready, train 6 adjust, devise, graith, make up 7 address, affaite(F.), apparel, arrange, concoct, confect, dispose, furnish, pro-

vide, qualify **8** accustom, compound, instruct, rehearse **9** calculate, condition, construct **10** concinnate **11** set the stage
for the press: **4** edit **6** redact, revise
prepared: apt **4** yare **5** ready
prepaschal period: **4** Lent
prepense: **8** designed **11** forethought **12** aforethought, premeditated
preponderance: **6** weight **8** majority **9** dominance, supremacy **10** ascendancy, ascendency, prevalence **12** predominance
preponderate: **4** rule, sink **7** incline, surpass
prepossess: **4** bias **7** prevent **12** predetermine
prepossessing: **10** attractive
prepossession: **4** bent, bias **9** prejudice **10** absorption **11** inclination **12** predilection **14** predisposition
preposterous: **6** absurd, screwy **7** foolish **9** grotesque, senseless **10** irrational, ridiculous **11** extravagant, nonsensical
preppy: **6** trendy **7** current **9** the latest
prerequisite: **9** essential, postulate
prerogative: **5** right **8** appanage, immunity, priority **9** exemption, privilege **10** precedence
eldest son's: **6** esnecy
prerupt: **5** steep **11** precipitous
presage: **4** bode, omen, osse, sign **5** augur, token **6** augury, betide, divine, import **7** bespeak, betoken, forbode, meaning, portend, portent, predict, warning **8** announce, forebode, foretell, indicate, prophecy, prophesy **9** foretoken, harbinger **10** foreboding, prediction, prognostic **11** foreknowing, preindicate **12** apprehension, presentiment **13** prognosticate
presbyter: **5** elder **6** priest **7** prester **8** minister **9** clergyman
presbytery: **5** court **7** council, rectory **9** residence
prescience: **9** foresight **11** omniscience **13** foreknowledge
prescind: **6** detach **7** isolate **8** abstract, separate
prescribe: fix, set **5** allot, guide, limit, order **6** assign, define, direct, ordain, outlaw **7** appoint, command, control, dictate, lay down **9** prescript **10** invalidate
prescribed: set **5** basic **6** thetic **9** formulary
prescript: law **7** command, mandate
prescription: **6** recipe **7** formula
presence: **4** mien **5** being **6** aspect, spirit **7** bearing, company, dignity, seeming, spectre **8** assembly **9** influence **10** apparition, appearance, attendance, deportment

present: now **4** boon, gift, give, here **5** adsum(L.), being, bonus, cuddy, grant, nonce, offer, ready, today **6** adduce, allege, bestow, bounty, confer, donate, render, tender **7** cumshaw, display, exhibit, largess, perform **8** donation, gratuity, lagnappe **9** collected, introduce, lagniappe, personate **10** exhibition, here and now **11** benefaction, efficacious
again: **5** rerun
pert. to: **6** modern **7** current **12** contemporary
to guest or stranger: **6** xenium
with another: **8** collocal
presentable: fit **6** decent, proper **11** appropriate, respectable
present-day: **7** current **12** contemporary
presentiment: **10** foreboding **11** disquietude, premonition **12** apprehension
presently: **4** anon, enow, soon **6** by and by **7** shortly **8** directly **9** forthwith **11** immediately
preservation: **6** saving **7** defense **11** safekeeping
preservative: **4** salt **5** borax, brine, spice, sugar **7** alcohol, vinegar **8** creosote **12** conservative
preserve: can, dry, jam, tin **4** corn, cure, keep, salt, save **5** bless, guard, jelly, spare, store, uvate **6** athold, comfit, defend, govern, keep up, retain, secure, shield, uphold **7** compote, condite, confect, forfend, protect, succade, sustain **8** conserve, forefend, maintain **9** confiture, safeguard
preside: run **5** chair **6** direct **7** control, oversee **8** moderate, regulate **9** supervise
president: mir **4** head **5** ruler **8** governor **9** sovereign
successor: **9** designado(Mex.)
President (U.S.): (1, 1789-97) George Washington; (2, 1797-1801) John Adams; (3, 1801-09) Thomas Jefferson; (4, 1809-17) James Madison; (5, 1817-25) James Monroe; (6, 1825-29) John Quincy Adams; (7, 1829-37) Andrew Jackson; (8, 1837-41) Martin Van Buren; (9, 1841) William Henry Harrison; (10, 1841-45) John Tyler; (11, 1845-49) James K. Polk; (12, 1849-50) Zachary Taylor; (13, 1850-53) Millard Fillmore; (14, 1853-57) Franklin Pierce; (15, 1857-61) James Buchanan; (16, 1861-65) Abraham Lincoln, (17, 1865-69) Andrew Johnson; (18, 1869-77) Ulysses S. Grant; (19, 1877-81) Rutherford B. Hayes; (20, 1881) James A. Garfield; (21, 1881-85) Chester A. Arthur; (22, 1885-89) Grover Cleveland; (23, 1889-93) Benjamin Harrison; (24, 1893-97)

Grover Cleveland; (25, 1897-1901) William McKinley; (26, 1901-09) Theodore Roosevelt; (27, 1909-13) William H. Taft; (28, 1913-21) Woodrow Wilson; (29, 1921-23) Warren G. Harding; (30, 1923-29) Calvin Coolidge; (31, 1929-33) Herbert Hoover; (32, 1933-45) Franklin D. Roosevelt; (33, 1945-53) Harry S Truman; (34, 1953-61) Dwight D. Eisenhower; (35, 1961-63) John F. Kennedy; (36, 1963-69) Lyndon B. Johnson; (37, 1969-74) Richard M. Nixon; (38, 1974-77) Gerald R. Ford; (39, 1977-81) Jimmy Carter; (40, 1981-) Ronald Reagan

last name: **4** Ford, Polk, Taft **5** Adams, Grant, Hayes, Nixon, Tyler **6** Arthur, Carter, Hoover, Monroe, Pierce, Reagan, Taylor, Truman, Wilson **7** Harding, Jackson, Johnson, Kennedy, Lincoln, Madison **8** Buchanan, Coolidge, Fillmore, Garfield, Harrison, McKinley, Van Buren **9** Cleveland, Jefferson, Roosevelt **10** Eisenhower, Washington

nickname: Abe, Cal, FDR, Ike **5** Teddy

presignify: 7 presage **8** intimate **9** foretoken

press: hug, jam **4** bale, bear, bind, cram, dint, iron, mash, push, spur, thew, urge **5** brize, brizz, chest, chirt, crowd, crush, drive, force, knead, preen, serry, wring **6** compel, crunch, impact, squash, roller, smooth, throng **7** armoire, embrace, entreat, express, flatten, impress, imprint, scrunge, smasher, squeeze **8** calender, compress, pressure, straiten, wardrobe **9** constrain, embarrass, emphasize, importune **10** constipate, newspapers

corrector: **11** proofreader

critic: **6** censor

press agent: 5 flack

press down: 4 quat, tamp

pressed: 5 dense **7** compact, serried

presser: 5 baler **6** ironer, mangle

of skins: **7** sammier

pressing: 4 dire **5** acute **6** urgent **7** burning, crucial, exigent **8** exacting **9** imperious **10** imperative **11** importunate

pressman: pig **7** printer

pressure: 4 heat, push **5** force **6** duress, stress **7** bearing, squeeze **8** exigency, instancy **10** affliction, constraint, impression, oppression **11** compression

equal: **8** isobaric

gauge: **9** barometer, manometer, manoscope

unit: **4** atmo, dyne **5** barad **7** mesobar

using: **11** arm-twisting

pressure group: 5 lobby

pressure measuring instrument: 10 piezometer

prester: 4 vein **5** snake **6** priest **7** serpent **9** hurricane, presbyter, whirlwind

prestidigitator: 6 palmer **7** juggler **8** conjurer, magician, pythonic

prestige: 4 sway **6** renown, status **7** sorcery **8** eminence, illusion **9** deception, influence **10** importance, prominence

presto: 4 fast **7** passing, quickly **8** suddenly **11** immediately **13** instantaneous

presumably: 6 likely **8** probably **9** assumably **10** ostensibly, supposedly

presume: 5 guess **6** impose **7** daresay, suppose, venture **8** arrogate **9** postulate **10** conjecture, presuppose

presumptuous: 4 bold, smug **5** brash, fresh, pushy **6** uppity **7** forward, haughty, icarian **8** arrogant, assuming, familiar, impudent, insolent **9** audacious, confident, foolhardy **11** adventurous, venturesome

presuppose: 5 posit **6** assume

pretend: act **4** pose, seem, sham **5** claim, feign **6** affect, allege, assume, gammon **7** profess **8** disguise, simulate **10** conjecture **11** dissimulate, make-believe

pretended: 4 fake **5** false **7** alleged, colored, reputed **8** coloured, intended, proposed **10** fictitious, ostensible

pretender: fop **4** fake, idol, snob **5** cowan(Sc.), faker, quack **6** poseur, seemer **8** aspirant, claimant, deceiver, impostor **9** charlatan **10** mountebank **11** fourflusher **12** dissimulator

pretense, pretence: act, peg **4** brag, cant, flam, mask, plea, ruse, sham, show **5** claim, cloak, cover, feint, gloze, study, trick **6** excuse, humbug, tinsel **7** charade, fiction, grimace, pageant, potiche, pretext **8** artifice, disguise, occasion **9** deception, moonshine, semblance **10** appearance, assumption, pretension, subterfuge **11** affectation, fabrication, make-believe, ostentation **13** stalkinghorse

pretentious: big **4** arty **5** gaudy, showy **6** turgid **7** pompous **8** affected, assuming **10** flamboyant **12** highfaluting, ostentatious

pretermit: 4 omit **6** ignore **7** neglect, suspend **8** intermit **9** disregard, interrupt

preternatural: 6 gousty **7** goustie **8** abnormal, uncommon **9** irregular **12** supernatural

pretext: 4 mask **6** excuse **8** pretense

pretty: gay, toy **4** cute, deft, fair, gent, joli **5** bonny, jolie, lindo(Sp.) **6** bonita, bonnie, clever, comely **7** cunning, dollish **8** betcheri, budgeree, handsome, skillful, somewhat **9** beautiful, ingenious **10** attractive, knickknack, moderately

prevail: win **4** rule **5** reign **6** induce, obtain **7** conquer, persist, succeed, triumph **8** dominate **11** predominate

upon: **4** urge **6** allure, induce **7** entreat **8** persuade **9** influence

prevalent: 4 rife **6** common, potent, wonted **7** current, general **8** dominant, powerful **9** extensive **10** prevailing, successful, victorious, widespread **11** efficacious, influential

prevaricate: fib, lie **5** evade **6** garble **7** quibble, shuffle **10** equivocate **12** misrepresent

prevarication: lie **10** subterfuge

prevent: bar, gag, let **4** balk, bind, save, stop, ward, warn **5** avert, debar, deter, estop **6** defend, forlet, hinder, impede, resist, thwart **7** forfend, impeach, obviate, prevent, rule out **8** antevert, forefend, preclude, prohibit, restrain, stave off **9** foreclose, forestall, frustrate **10** anticipate, circumvent

by law: **5** estop

preventive: 12 prophylactic **13** precautionary

previous: ere **4** erst, fore, past **5** early, prior, supra **6** before, bygone, former **7** earlier **8** anterior, foregone, untimely **9** foregoing, preceding, premature **10** antecedent, beforehand, heretofore **11** unwarranted

prevision: 8 forecast **9** foresight **10** prediction, prescience, prevoyance **13** foreknowledge **15** prognostication

prewar: 10 antebellum

prey: 4 feed, game **5** booty, raven, ravin, seize, spoil **6** quarry, ravage, ravine, victim **7** capture, plunder **8** underdog **9** victimize

living on: **9** predatory

prey upon: 4 feed **5** seize **6** devour **9** victimize, depredate

Priam: 10 King of Troy

daughter: **6** Creusa **8** Polyxena **9** Cassandra

grandfather: **4** Ilus

servant: **7** Agelaus

son: **5** Paris **6** Hector **7** Helenus, Troilus

slayer: **7** Pyrrhus

wife: **6** Hecuba

price: fee, tab **4** cost, fare, fiar(Sc.), fier(Sc.), hire, rate **5** cheap, value, worth **6** charge, ransom, reward **7** expense **8** appraise, evaluate **10** estimation, excellence **12** preciousness **13** consideration

maintain: peg

reduced: **4** sale **7** bargain

rising: **4** boom **9** inflation

priceless: 4 rare **6** absurd, costly, unique **7** amusing **8** valuable **9** unsalable **10** invaluable **11** inestimable

prick: dot, jag **4** brod, brog, cloy, drob, goad, jagg, ping, pink, prod, stab, tang, urge **5** briar, point, smart, spine, sting, thorn **6** broach, cactus, incite, nettle, pierce, skewer, tingle **7** bramble, pricker, prickle **8** puncture **9** perforate, stimulate

prick song: 7 descant

pricket: 4 buck **5** spike **11** candlestick

pricking: 8 poignant

prickle: 4 barb, seta **5** setae(pl.), sieve **6** basket **7** acantha, aculeus, spicula(pl.) **8** spiculum

prickly: 5 burry **8** echinate

animal: **8** hedgehog **9** porcupine

plant: **6** cactus, nettle

seed coat: bur **4** burr

shrub: **4** rose **5** briar

prickly heat: 4 rash **6** lichen **8** eruption

prickly pear: 4 tuna **5** nopal **6** cactus **7** opuntia

pride: 5 glory, pique, plume, valor **6** egoism, esteem, spirit, vanity **7** conceit, dignity, disdain, egotism, elation, hauteur, respect **8** nobility, splendor, valiancy **9** arrogance, cockiness, insolence, loftiness **10** lordliness, self-esteem **11** amour propre, haughtiness, self-conceit, self-respect **12** independence **13** self-assurance **15** self-approbation **16** superciliousness

Pride and Prejudice: *author:* **6** Austen

character: **5** Darcy **9** Elizabeth

prier, pryer: 8 busybody **10** inquisitor

priest: fra **4** abbe, club, cura, cure(F.), imam, lama, papa(It.), pere(F.) **5** clerk, druid, hotar(Ind.), imaum, mulla, padre(Sp.), rabbi, sarip, vicar **6** bhikku, bishop, cleric, dastur, divine, father, gallah(Heb.), mullah, oblate, rector, shaman, vestal, wahabi **7** cassock, destour, dustoor, prester, tuhunga, wahhabi **8** minister **9** clergyman, dignitary, oratorian, priesteen **10** chancellor, hierophant, priestling **12** ecclesiastic

army: **5** padre **8** chaplain

assistant: **7** acolyte

cap: **7** biretta

garment: alb **4** cope, robe **5** ephod, habit **8** scapular **9** vestments

habit ornament: **4** urim

headdress: **9** saghavart

high: Eli **5** Aaron **7** pontiff, prelate

neckpiece: **5** amice, stole

pert. to: **10** sacerdotal

scarf: **5** rabat **7** maniple

server: **7** acolyte

surplice: **5** ephod

voodoo: **5** mambu **6** hungan **7** gangang

priestly: 8 hieratic **10** sacerdotal

prig: beg, fop, pan **4** buck, prim **5** dandy, filch, plead, prink, prude, steal, thief **6** haggle, pilfer, purist, tinker **7** bargain, entreat, pitcher **8** pilferer **9** precision **10** pickpocket

priggish: 4 prim, smug **8** thievish **10** complacent **11** overprecise

prill: 4 rill **6** button, nugget, pellet, stream

prim: mim, set **4** neat, nice **5** stiff **6** demure, formal, proper, wooden **7** correct, genteel, precise, prudish **8** accurate, decorous **9** bluenosed **10** ceremonial

prima donna: 4 diva, lead, star **6** singer **7** actress

prima facie: 11 self-evident

primary: 4 main **5** chief, first, prime **6** primal **7** capital, central, initial **8** earliest, original, primeval, pristine **9** elemental, primitive, principal **10** elementary, pre-eminent, primordial **11** fundamental

primate: ape, man **5** lemur, orang **6** bishop, monkey **8** marmoset **9** orangutan **10** anthropoid, archbishop **11** orangoutang

prime: 4 best, size **5** coach **7** morning, prepare, primary, provoke **9** copacetic, excellent, undercoat
of life: **5** bloom **6** heyday

prime minister: 7 premier

primer: 8 hornbook, textbook **11** abecedarium

primeval: 6 primal **7** ancient, ogygian **8** original, pristine **9** primitive

primitive: 5 basic, crude, first, rough **6** simple **7** ancient, archaic, primary, priscan, radical **8** barbaric, original, pristine **9** elemental, underived **10** aboriginal, antiquated **11** uncivilized **12** old-fashioned

primordial: 5 early, first **7** primary **9** elemental **11** fundamental

primordium: bud **6** embryo, origin **8** rudiment

primp: 5 adorn, preen, prink, **7** dress up

primrose: 4 best **5** oxlip, spink(Sc.) **7** cowslip, primula **8** auricula
family: **11** primulaceae

primus: 5 first, stove

prince: bey, ras **4** amir, emir, raja, rial **5** alder, ameer, emeer, ruler **6** despot, dynast, satrap **7** dynasty, monarch **8** archduke **9** potentate, princekin, princelet, sovereign **10** princeling
allowance: **8** appanage
petty: **6** satrap **9** vergobret
pine: **10** pipsissewa
title: **6** serene

Prince Edward Island: *capital:* **13** Charlottetown
city: **8** Sherwood **10** Summerside
discoverer: **7** Cartier
former name: **9** Ile St. John
province of: **6** Canada
provincial flower: **12** lady's slipper

Prince of: *Apostles:* **8** St. Peter
Darkness: **5** devil, Satan **7** Ahriman **9** Beelzebub
Destruction: **6** Timour **9** Tamerlane
Evil Spirits: **7** Sammael
Liars: **5** Pinto
Peace: **7** Messiah
the Ode: **7** Ronsard
the Sonnet: **15** Joachim du Bellay

princedom: 4 rank **11** sovereignty **12** jurisdiction

princely: 5 grand, noble, regal, royal **6** kingly **7** stately **9** sovereign **10** munificent **11** magnificent

princeps: 4 head **5** first **7** headman **8** original

princess: 5 begum(Muslim), ranee(Muslim)
loved by Cupid: **6** Psyche
loved by Zeus: **6** Europa
mythological: **8** Atalanta

Princeton symbol: 5 tiger

principal: top **4** arch, head, high, main, star **5** chief, first grand, major, prime **6** leader, staple **7** capital, captain, chattel, leading, palmary, primary, stellar **8** cardinal, dominant, foremost **9** important, preceptor **10** headmaster **11** outstanding

principle: law **4** rule **5** axiom, canon, dicta(pl.), maxim, prana, tenet **6** dictum **7** brocard, essence, precept, theorum **8** doctrine **9** integrity **11** fundamental, uprightness
accepted: **5** axiom
embodiment: **6** avatar
first: ABC **4** base, seed **5** basis **8** rudiment
general: **9** generalia **12** generalities
statement: **5** credo, creed, motto
vital: **4** soul **5** anima
without: **6** amoral

principles: 5 creed **6** ethics **8** alphabet

princox: fop **7** coxcomb

prink: 4 deck, perk, wink **5** adorn, dress, preen, primp, prune **6** bedeck, glance, sashay

print: 4 copy, film **5** issue, stamp **6** fabric **7** edition, engrave, impress, publish **8** negative **9** engraving, newspaper **10** impression

printer: 4 type **8** letterer, pressman **9** linotyper **10** compositor **11** typographer **12** lithographer
aid: fly **5** devil
cross stroke: **5** serif
direction: cut **6** delete
emblem: **8** colophon

printing: *block:* **4** wood **7** edition **8** linoleum
blurred appearance: **5** macul
color: **17** chromolithography

error: pie **6** errata(pl.) **7** erratum

form: cut, die, mat **5** frame **6** matrix **7** matrice

implement: **5** burin **6** brayer, dabber, dauber

ink spreader: **6** brayer

mark: **4** dash, dele, list, stet **5** caret, obeli, tilde **6** dagger, diesis, obelus **7** obelisk **8** ellipses

measure: **4** pica **5** agate, empen

metal block: **4** quad

plate: **6** stereo **10** stereotype

press part: **6** platen, roller, rounce **7** frisket

process: **6** offset **7** braille, typeset **8** cerotype **10** photolitho **11** letterpress, lithography, rotogravure **14** photoengraving

second: **7** reissue

space block: **4** quad

system for the blind: **7** braille

type for spacing: **4** quad, slug

prion: 6 petrel

prionid: 6 beetle

prior: ere **4** fore, past **5** ahead, elder, until **6** before, former **7** earlier, forward **8** anterior, previous **9** preceding **10** antecedent **11** retroactive

priority: 5 order **8** position **9** privilege **10** ascendancy, precedence, preference **11** superiority

priory: 5 abbey **7** nunnery **8** cloister **9** monastery, sanctuary

priscan: 4 rare **7** ancient **9** primitive

prism: 5 block, nicol **8** cylinder, spectrum, wernicke

prism device: 8 iriscope

prismatic: 5 showy **9** brilliant **10** iridescent **12** orthorhombic

prison: gib, jug **4** brig, cell, gaol, hell, hole, jail, keep, quod, rock, stir **5** bagne, clink, grate **6** bagnio, carcel, carcer, cooler, lockup **7** Atlanta, Bocardo, college, dungeon, Gehenna, hoosgow, kidcote, Ludgate, Newgate, Spandau **8** Alcatraz, Bastille, Dartmoor, hoosegaw, hoosegow, Sing Sing **9** Bridewell, calaboose, enclosure, Old Bailey **10** guardhouse, panopticon, San Quentin **11** Leavenworth **12** penitentiary

guard: **5** screw

keeper: **5** guard **6** gaoler, jailer, jailor, keeper, warden **7** turnkey

naval or ship: **4** brig

room: **4** cell, hole, tank **7** dungeon **8** solitary

sentence: rap

spy: **6** mouton

prisoner: con **5** lifer **6** detenu(F.), inmate **7** caitiff, captive, convict, detenue(F.), parolee **9** collegian **10** emancipist **11** probationer

exchange agreement: **6** cartel

Prisoner of the Vatican: 4 Pope

prisoner of war: PW; P.O.W. **7** kriegie

prissy: 4 prim **5** fussy **7** finicky, precise, prudish **9** sissified **10** effeminate **11** over-refined

pristine: new **4** pure **5** early, fresh **7** ancient, primary **8** original **9** primitive, unspoiled, untouched **11** uncorrupted

pritch: 5 prick, spike, staff **6** pierce **9** perforate

privacy: 7 privity, retreat, secrecy **8** darkness, solitude **9** seclusion **10** penetralia **12** hugger-mugger

privado: 6 friend **8** intimate **9** confidant

private: 5 privy **6** closet, covert, hushed, inside, secret **7** soldier **8** esoteric, homefelt, intimate, personal, secluded, singular, solitary **10** unofficial **12** confidential, unpublicized

private eye: 6 tailer **7** gumshoe **9** detective, operative **12** investigator

privateer: 4 Kidd **5** caper **6** pirate **7** corsair, drumler **8** drumbler

privately: 5 aside **8** inwardly, secretly

privation: 4 loss, want **6** misery **7** absence, poverty **8** hardship **9** suffering **11** deprivation, destitution

privet: 5 hedge, ibota, shrub **7** alatern, ibolium **9** houseleek

privilege: law, soc, use **4** boon, soke **5** favor, grace, grant, right **6** favour, patent **7** charter, liberty **8** easement, immunity **9** advantage, allowance, exemption, franchise, vouchsafe **10** concession **11** prerogative

privy: 4 gong **5** biffy, jakes **6** cloaca, closet, hidden, secret, toilet **7** cloacae(pl.), furtive, private **8** familiar, intimate, out-house **9** backhouse, confidant, necessary **11** clandestine, water-closet **12** confidential **13** surreptitious

prix: 5 prize

prize: cup, pry **4** best, gree(Sc.), prix(F.), tern **5** award, bacon, booty, lever, medal, plate, purse, spoil, stake, value **6** esteem, glaive, reward, trophy **7** capture, premium, seizure **8** estimate, leverage, purchase, treasure **10** appreciate

prizefight: 4 bout, mill **5** match, scrap **7** contest **11** boxing match

ring: **5** arena

prized: 4 dear **5** chary **9** treasured

pro: for **4** with, whiz **6** expert **8** advocate, favoring **9** favouring, in favor of **12** professional

probability: 4 odds **6** chance **8** prospect **10** appearance, likelihood, likeliness **11** credibility

probable: 5 maybe **6** likely **8** apparent, credible, feasible

probably: 6 belike, likely **10** presumably

probation: 4 test 5 trial 6 parole 9 novitiate 11 examination

probe: 4 acus, tent, test 5 grope, query, sound 6 pierce, search seeker, stylet, tracer 7 examine, explore, feel out, inquiry 9 catechize, delve into, penetrate 10 ankylomele, instrument, scrutinize 11 exploration, investigate 13 investigation

probity: 7 honesty 8 goodness 9 integrity, rectitude 11 uprightness

problem: not, sum 4 crux, knot 5 hydra, issue, poser 6 enigma, puzzle, riddle 8 question 9 situation

problematical: 4 moot, open 8 doubtful 9 ambiguous, equivocal, uncertain, unsettled 12 questionable

proboscis: 4 nose 5 snout, trunk

proboscis monkey: 4 kaha

procacious: 4 pert, wise 8 impudent, insolent, petulant

Procas' son: 7 Amulius, Numitor

procavia: 5 hyrax 10 hyracoidea

procedure: 6 course, tactic 7 measure, process, program, routine

proceed: 4 fand, fare, move, pass, wend 5 arise, frame, issue 6 derive, spring 7 advance, emanate, forthgo 8 continue, progress 9 originate

laboriously: mog 4 plod, plow, slog, wade 6 trudge

rapidly: run 5 speed 6 gallop

proceeding: 4 acta(pl.), step 5 actum, doing 6 affair, afflux, course 7 conduct, measure, process 9 affluxion, procedure 11 transaction

proceeds: 4 loot 5 booty 6 income, profit, return 8 stealage

procerity: 6 height 8 tallness

process: 4 cook, writ 5 lapse, order 6 capias, course, manner, method, notice, system 7 advance, mandate, routine, summons 8 progress 9 operation, outgrowth, procedure, sterilize, technique 10 injunction

procession: 4 file 5 march, order 6 course, exequy, litany, parade 7 cortege, pageant 9 cavalcade, formation, recession

prochein: 4 next 7 nearest

proclaim: bid, cry 4 call, deem, show, toot, tout 5 blare, blast, blaze, claim, grede, knell, utter, voice 6 blazon, bounce, defame, herald, indict, outcry, preach 7 declare, divulge, enounce, publish 8 announce, denounce, forspeak 9 advertise, celebrate, enunciate, forespeak, ventilate 10 promulgate

proclamation: ban 4 bans, fiat 5 bando(Sp.), banns, blaze, edict, ukase 6 notice 7 bidding, placard 9 manifesto 11 declaration, publication 12 announce-

ment, annunciation, denunciation, notification, promulgation

proclivity: 4 bent 6 talent 7 leaning 10 propensity 11 disposition, inclination

Procne: *father:* 7 Pandion

husband: 6 Tereus

sister: 9 Philomela

son: 4 Itys

procrastination: 5 delay, stall 9 deferment 10 cunctation, inactivity 12 dilatoriness, postponement

procreant: 8 fruitful 9 producing 10 generating

procreate: 4 sire 5 beget 6 father 7 produce 8 engender, generate 11 give birth to

procreation: 8 virility 9 offspring 10 generation, production

Procris: *father:* 10 Erechtheus

husband and slayer: 8 Cephalus

proctor: 5 agent, proxy 7 monitor 8 advocate, attorney 9 supervise 10 supervisor

procumbent: 5 prone 9 prostate

procurable: 7 parable 10 accessible

procure: get 4 fang, find, gain 5 bring 6 effect, induce, obtain, secure, suborn 7 acquire, chevise, receive 8 contrive 9 impetrate

procurer: 4 bawd, pimp 8 purveyor

procuress: 4 bawd, hack 7 commode

prod: egg, jab 4 brog, goad poke, urge 5 pique 6 excite, incite, thrust 9 instigate, stimulate

prodigal: 5 flush 6 lavish 7 liberal, profuse, spender, wastrel 8 abundant, generous, wasteful 10 profligate, squanderer 11 extravagant, spendthrift, squandering

prodigious: 4 huge 5 giant 7 amazing, immense 8 enormous, gigantic 9 marvelous, monstrous, wonderful 10 portentous, tremendous 11 astonishing 13 extraordinary

prodigy: 4 omen, sign 6 marvel, ostent, wonder 7 miracle, portent 8 ceremony

prodition: 7 treason 8 betrayal 15 treacherousness

prodrome: 7 symptom

produce: 4 bear, form, give, grow, make, show 5 breed, carry, cause, shape, stage, yield 6 create, effect, fruits 7 exhibit, product 8 engender, generate 9 fabricate, offspring, procreate 10 bring about, production, vegetables 11 manufacture

new: 6 create, invent 9 originate

producer: 6 author, farmer, grower, parent 7 creator 8 director 12 manufacturer

product: 4 item 5 fruit, yield 6 number, result 9 offspring, outgrowth

production: 4 work 5 fruit 6 output 11 performance

productive: 4 rich 6 active, parous 7 fertile 8 creative, fruitful, sonorous 10 generative 11 originative

proem: 7 preface, prelude 8 foreword, overture, preamble, prologue 12 introduction

profanation: 9 blasphemy, sacrilege, violation 10 desecration

profane: lay 4 foul 5 abuse 6 debase, defile, defoil, defoul, unholy, vulgar, wicked 7 godless, heathen, impious, obscene, secular, ungodly, violate, worldly 8 temporal 9 desecrate, vulgarize 10 irreverent, unhallowed 11 blasphemous 12 sacrilegious, unsanctified

profanity: 4 oath 5 curse 9 blasphemy

profess: own 4 avow 5 admit, claim 6 affect, affirm, allege, assert 7 confess, declare, pretend, protest 8 proclaim 11 acknowledge

profession: art, job 5 craft, faith, forte, trade 6 avowal, career, metier(F.) 7 calling 8 function, vocation 9 following 10 employment, occupation

professional: pro 4 paid 5 hired 6 expert 7 artiste, skilled, trained 8 finished

professor: don, fly 5 tutor 7 teacher 10 instructor

proffer: bid 4 give, hand 5 offer 6 extend, tender 8 proposal 11 countenance

proficiency: 5 skill 7 ability, advance, aptness 9 adeptness 10 capability, competence, efficiency, expertness 14 accomplishment

proficient: 6 actual, expert, master, versed 8 skillful 9 effective, effectual 10 conversant 11 crackerjack, experienced

profile: 4 form 6 figure 7 contour, drawing, outline 10 silhouette 14 representation

profit: net, pay, use 4 boot, gain, good, help, mend, nett 5 avail, frame, lucre, melon 6 behoof, return 7 account, benefit, bestead, revenue, utility 8 earnings, increase, interest, proceeds 9 advantage, emolument 12 remuneration

receiver of: 6 pernor

undercover: 4 loot 5 booty 6 payola

profitable: fat 8 repaying 9 expedient 12 advantageous

profitless: 9 fruitless 12 unprofitable

profligate: 6 rioter 7 corrupt, riotous, spender, vicious, wastrel 8 depraved, flagrant, prodigal, rakehell, wasteful 9 abandoned, dissolute, reprobate 10 licentious 11 extravagant, spendthrift

profound: low 4 deep, sage, wise 5 heavy 7 abysmal, intense 8 abstruse, unbroken 9 intensive, recondite, sagacious

10 acroamatic, exhaustive 11 far-reaching 12 unfathomable

profuse: 4 lush 5 frank 6 galore, hearty, lavish 7 copious, liberal, opulent, riotous 8 abundant, generous, prodigal, wasteful 9 bountiful, excessive, exuberant, luxuriant, plentiful 10 munificent 11 extravagant, overflowing

prog: 4 food 5 prick, prowl, tramp 6 forage 7 vagrant 8 supplies 9 provender

progenitor: 4 sire 6 parent 8 ancestor 10 forefather, foreparent, forerunner

progeny: imp, son 4 race, seed 5 breed, brood, brook, child, issue, scion, shoot 6 family, strain 8 children, daughter 9 genealogy, offspring 10 generation 11 descendants

prognostic: 4 omen, sign 5 token 8 forecast 10 prediction

prognosticate: 4 bode 5 augur 6 divine 7 betoken, forbode, forerun, portend, predict, presage 8 forebode, forecast, foreshow, foretell, prophesy 9 foretoken, hariolate

prognosticator: 4 seer 5 augur 6 divine 7 augurer, diviner, prophet 9 predictor 10 soothsayer

program: 4 card, list, show, sked 5 draft, edict 6 agenda, course, notice 7 agendum, catalog, outline 8 bulletin, calendar, schedule, syllabus 9 broadcast 10 prospectus 12 proclamation

theater: 8 playbill

programma: 5 edict 6 decree 7 preface 12 prolegomenon

progress: 4 fare, flow, grow, tour, wend 5 march 6 course, growth, motion 7 advance, circuit, develop, headway, improve, journey, passage, proceed 10 betterment, expedition 11 development, furtherance, improvement

planned: 7 telesia, telesis

progression: 5 stage 8 sequence 9 unfolding 10 succession 11 development

progressive: 6 active, onward 7 forward, liberal 9 advancing, ascensive 12 enterprising

prohibit: ban, bar, bid 4 stop, veto 5 debar, estop, fence 6 defend, enjoin, forbid, hinder, outlaw 7 forfend, forwarn, prevent 8 disallow, forefend 9 interdict, proscribe 11 countermand

prohibited: hot 4 tabu 5 taboo 7 illegal, illicit 8 unlawful, verboten(G.)

prohibiting: 8 vetitive

prohibitionist: dry

project: jet, jut, lap 4 abut, apse, barb, butt, game, idea, plan, send, task 5 bulge, filip, shoot, think 6 beetle, design, device, extend, fillip, scheme, wander 7 extrude, imagine, pattern, problem, prolong 8 contrive, lengthen, proposal, protrude **9** intention **10** enterprise **11** contrivance, proposition, undertaking

projectile: 4 bomb, dart, rock, shot **5** arrow, shell **6** bullet, rocket **7** missile, torpedo **8** shrapnel **9** cartridge

curve: **8** parabola

explosive part: **7** warhead, warnose

pert. to: **9** ballistic

submarine: **7** torpedo

projecting: 6 beetle **7** salient

projection: arm, cam, ell, hob, hub, jag, lee, lug, toe **4** apse, barb, croc, fang, lobe **5** bulge, crena, redan, socle, tenon, tooth **6** corbel, crenae(pl.), dormer, lobule, tappet **7** cornice, empathy **8** abutment, ejection, eminence **9** crenation **10** protrusion **12** protuberance

projector: 4 kino **8** bioscope **9** vitascope **12** stereopticon **13** cinematograph, kinematograph

projet: 4 plan **5** draft

prolapse: 7 falling

prolate: 9 elongated

opposite of: **6** oblate

proletarian: 4 mean, rude **6** coarse, vulgar, worker **7** laborer

proletariat: mob **4** mass **6** rabble **11** rank and file **12** working class

prolific: 6 birthy, fecund **7** fertile, teeming **8** fruitful, spawning, swarming **9** abounding, plentiful **10** generative **11** propagative **12** reproductive

prolix: 5 wordy **7** diffuse, irksome, prosaic, tedious, verbose **8** tiresome **9** prolonged, wearisome **10** longwinded, protracted **11** displeasing **13** uninteresting

prolocutor: 6 orator **7** speaker **8** advocate, chairman **9** spokesman **10** mouthpiece

prologue: 7 preface **12** introduction

prolong: 5 defer **6** endure, extend **7** persist **8** continue, lengthen

prolonged: 4 long **5** great **6** prolix **7** chronic, delayed, dilated **8** extended **9** continued, postponed, sostenuto, sustained **10** lengthened, protracted

prom: 4 ball **5** dance

promenade: 4 deck, hall, mall, walf **5** prado(Sp.) **6** avenue, marina, parade, pasear(Sp.) **7** alameda, gallery **9** boardwalk, esplanade

Prometheus: *father:* **7** Iapetus

gift to man: **4** fire

mother: **7** Clymene

prominence: 4 cusp **5** agger **8** eminence, prestige, salience **10** colliculus, promontory **11** distinction

prominent: 5 chief **6** famous, marked, signal **7** capital, eminent, notable, obvious, salient **8** aquiline, manifest **9** egregious, well-known **10** celebrated, noticeable, projecting **11** conspicuous, distinctive **13** distinguished

promiscuous: 6 random, wanton **7** immoral **8** careless **9** haphazard

promise: vow **4** band, hest, hote, oath, pawn, word **5** agree, grant **6** assure, behest, engage, parole, pledge, plight **7** behight, betroth, fianced **8** affiance, contract, covenant **9** assurance, betrothal, foretoken **10** convenable, engagement, obligation **11** declaration, word of honor

Promised Land: 6 Canaan

promissory note: I.O.U. **5** check **6** pledge, ticket

promontory: hoe **4** bill, cape, head, mull, nase, naze, ness, peak, scaw, skaw, spit **5** mount, point **8** headland **10** projection, prominence

promote: aid **4** help, plug, push **5** boost, exalt, nurse, raise, speed **6** better, foster, prefer **7** advance, build up, dignify, elevate, forward, further **9** advantage, encourage, patronize, publicize **10** aggrandize, make much of

promoter: 5 agent **7** abetter, abettor, booster, hustler **8** broacher, lobbyist

promotion: 6 brevet **7** advance **9** publicity **10** graduation, preferment **11** advancement, furtherance

prompt: apt, cue **4** move, urge, yare(Sc.) **5** alert, quick, ready, yeder **6** active, assist, excite, induce, nimble, remind **7** animate, forward **8** punctual, vigilant, watchful **11** expeditious

prompter: aid **4** cuer **7** readier

promptly: 4 soon, tite(Sc.) **8** directly

promptness: 8 alacrity, dispatch

promulgate: 7 declare, publish **8** announce, proclaim **9** advertise

prone: apt **4** bent, flat **5** buxom **6** agroof, agrufe, agruif, liable, supine **7** passive, willing **8** addicted, disposed, inclined, pronated **9** declivous, groveling, lying down, prostrate, reclining, recumbent **10** decubitous

prong: nib, peg **4** fang, fork, horn, tine **5** point, tooth **6** branch

prongbuck: 9 pronghorn, springbok

prong key: 7 spanner

pronghorn: 4 deer **6** cabree **8** antelope, berrendo

pronoun: any, her, him, his, its, one, our she, thy, you **4** mine, ours, that, thee, them, they, this, thou, your **5** their, these, thine, those **6** itself, myself **7** herself, himself, oneself, ourself **8** yourself **9** ourselves **10** themselves, yourselves

demonstrative: **4** that, this **5** these, those

interrogative: who **4** whom **5** whose

substantive: who **7** whoever **9** whosoever

pronounce: 4 pass **5** speak, utter **6** affirm **7** behight, declare, deliver, enounce **8** announce **9** enunciate **10** articulate
free: **7** absolve
guilty: **7** condemn
indistinctly: **4** slur
pronounced: 6 marked **7** decided, howling **12** unmistakable
pronouncement: 4 fiat **5** dicta(pl.) **6** dictum **9** manifesto, statement **11** declaration **12** announcement, proclamation, promulgation
pronto: 4 fast **5** quick **6** at once **7** quickly **8** promptly **11** immediately
pronunciation: 4 burr, lisp, slur **5** drawl, twang
correct: **8** orthoepy **9** phonology
incorrect: **7** cacoepy **8** psellism **9** psellisum
pronunciation mark: 5 tilde **8** dieresis **9** diacritic
proof: 4 test **5** trial **6** reason, result **7** approof, probate, exhibit, outcome **8** argument, evidence **9** testimony **10** indication **11** approbation **12** confirmation, impenetrable, verification **13** certification, demonstration
proofreader mark: cap **4** dele, ital, stet **5** caret, space
prop: leg, nog **4** stay **5** appui, brace, shore, sprag, staff, stell(Sc.), stilt **6** scotch, shorer **7** fulcrum, shore up, support, sustain **8** buttress **10** strengthen
propaganda: 4 hype, plan **5** ideas **6** scheme, system **8** agitprop, doctrine **12** brainwashing
propagation: 12 continuation
propagate: 4 grow **5** breed **6** spread **7** diffuse **8** engender, generate, increase, multiply **9** circulate, procreate **11** disseminate
propel: gun, row **4** flip, move, pole, push, send, urge **5** drive, egg on, flick, force, impel, shove **7** project
propeller: fan, fin, oar **4** vane **5** screw **6** driver, paddle **8** windmill
arm: **4** vane
propensity: yen **4** bent, bias **6** liking **7** aptness, avidity, leaning **8** appetite, tendency **9** affection, proneness **10** proclivity, propension **11** disposition, inclination **12** predilection
proper: due, fit **4** able, fair, fine, good, meet, prim, true **5** right, stiff, utter **6** behove, chaste, comely, decent, honest, modest, sedate, seemly, strict **7** behoove, correct, fitting, seeming **8** accurate, decorous, formular, suitable **9** advisable, allowable, befitting, beseeming, excellent **10** commodious, convenient, scrupulous **11** appropriate, respectable
properly: 6 featly, gladly **8** by rights
property: lot, res **4** acre, alod, aver, bona,
dhan(Ind.), gear **5** addle, allod, asset, aught, glebe, goods, manor **6** domain, estate, havier, realty, wealth **7** acquest, alodium, chattel, haviour, holding, quality **8** allodium **9** acensuada, attribute, homestead, ownership **11** appropriate, possessions **14** characteristic
act to regain: **8** replevin
bride's gift to husband: dos **5** dowry
charge against: **4** lien **8** mortgage
conveyor of: **7** alienor, grantor
deceased wife's gift to husband: **8** courtesy
destruction of: **5** arson **8** sabotage **9** vandalism
found on the thief: **6** mainor
personal: **5** goods **7** chattel
real: **4** land **7** acreage
receiver: **7** alienee
seller: **7** realtor
settle: **6** entail
stolen: **4** loot, pelf **5** booty, lucre, spoil
suit for: **6** trover
transferring party: **7** alienor
property right: 4 lien **5** title **8** easement
prophecy: 5 weird **6** oracle **8** bodement **9** utterance **10** prediction, revelation **11** declaration, foretelling **12** vaticination
pert. to: **9** vatical
prophesy: 4 dope, osse, spae **5** aread, areed, augur **6** divine **7** predict, presage **8** ariolate, forecast, foreshow, foretell **10** vaticinate **11** preindicate **13** prognosticate
prophet: 4 Amos, John, seer **5** augur, Elias, fatal, Hosea, Syrus **6** divine, Elijah, Elisha, leader, mantis, oracle **7** augurer, diviner, Malachi, teacher **8** Mohammed, Muhammed, presager **9** John Smith, predictor **10** soothsayer **11** Nostradamus, vaticinator
prophetess: 5 Sibyl **6** Miriam **7** Deborah, Pythian, seeress **9** Cassandra
prophetic: 5 vatic **6** mantic **7** fateful, fatidic, vatical **8** foretell, oracular **9** prescient, sibylline **10** divinatory, mysterious, predictive, presageful, signifying **11** apocalyptic, fatiloquent, foretelling, nostradamic **12** vaticinatory **14** interpretative
propine: 5 offer **6** pledge **7** present, propose
propinquity: 7 kinship **8** affinity, nearness, vicinity **9** proximity **12** neighborhood, relationship
propitiate: 5 adapt, atone **6** adjust, pacify **7** appease, conform, expiate, satisfy **9** reconcile **10** conciliate
propitious: 4 good, rosy **5** happy, lucky **6** benign, timely **8** benedict **9** benignant, favorable, opportune, promising **10** auspicious, benevolent, prosperous **12** advantageous

proponent: 6 backer 8 advocate 9 supporter
proportion: 4 part, rate, size 5 quota, ratio, share 6 degree 7 analogy, portion,
prorate 8 relation, symmetry 9 dimension
proportional: 5 equal 7 ratable 8 adequate, relative 10 answerable, equivalent, reciprocal 11 symmetrical 12
commensurate
proportionately: 6 fairly 7 prorata 10
adequately
proposal: bid 4 idea, plan 5 offer 6 design, feeler, motion, scheme 7 project 8
overture 10 invitation, nomination,
suggestion 11 proposition
propose: ask, put 4 give, moot, move 5 offer, state 6 allege, design, submit, tender 7 suggest 8 propound 11 contemplate
proposition: 5 axiom, offer, point 6 affair, porism 7 premise, project, theorem
8 offering, overture, proposal, question
9 corollary, postulate, situation, statement 11 affirmation, undertaking
antecedent: 6 premise
preliminary: 5 lemma 7 lemmata(pl.)
propound: 4 pose 5 posit, state 7 propose
proprietor: 5 owner 6 master, tanist 7
lairdie
propriety (see also proper): 4 code, rule
7 customs, manners, quality 8 behavior, elegance, standard 9 attribute, etiquette 13 possessorship
propugnator: 8 defender 10 vindicator
propulsion: jet 5 drift 8 ejection 9 expulsion
prorate: 5 allot 6 assess, divide 9 apportion 10 distribute, proportion
prorogue: 5 defer 6 extend 7 adjourn,
prolong 8 postpone, protract
prosaic: 4 drab, dull, flat 5 prosy 6 common, prolix, stolid, stupid 7 humdrum,
insipid, tedious 8 everyday, tiresome,
unpoetic 9 colorless 10 unexciting 11
commonplace 12 matter-of-fact 13 unimaginative, uninteresting
proscenium: 5 stage
front area: 5 apron
proscribe: ban 4 tabu 5 exile, taboo 6
banish, forbid, outlaw 8 prohibit, sentence 9 interdict, ostracize
prose form: 5 essay, novel, story, tract 7
fiction, romance 8 treatise 9 biography
10 nonfiction
prosecute: sue 4 urge 5 carry, chase,
hound, press 6 accuse, charge, follow,
indict, pursue 7 enforce 8 continue
prosecutor: 7 accuser, relator 8 quaestor
proselyte: 5 alien 7 convert 8 neophyte,
newcomer
to Judaism: ger

Proserpine: See Persephone
perseuche: 7 oratory 9 synagogue
prosit: 5 toast 10 salutation
prosody: 5 meter
prospect: 4 hope, mine, view 5 buyer,
scene, vista 6 aspect 7 explore, outlook
8 customer, exposure 9 applicant, candidate, foretaste 10 contestant
prospective: 5 lofty 6 future, likely 7 eminent 8 expected, prospect 9 provident
11 anticipated, perspective
prospector: 9 sourdough
prosper: dow, hie, wax 4 fare 5 cheve,
edify, frame, speed 6 thrive 7 augment,
blossom, succeed, turn out 8 flourish,
increase
prosperity: hap, ups 4 boom, weal 5 ikbal
6 thrift, wealth 7 fortune, success, welfare 9 abundance, happiness, well-being
god: 4 Frey
goddess: 5 Salus
symbol: 9 turquoise
Prospero: *daughter:* 7 Miranda
servant: 5 Ariel
slave: 7 Caliban
prosperous: 4 bein, bien, boon, rich 5
flush, happy, lucky, palmy, sonsy 6
sonsie, timely 7 halcyon, well-off 8
thriving 9 favorable, fortunate 10 auspicious, propitious, successful, well-
heeled 11 flourishing
prostitute: bat, cat 4 aunt, drab, doxy,
hack, trug 5 abuse, broad, venal, whore
6 callet, debase, harlot, hooker 7 baggage, brothel, corrupt, Cyprian, hackney
8 berdache, call girl, commoner, customer, infamous, occupant 9 courtesan,
courtezan 10 crosha-bell, hobby-horse,
licentious 12 camp follower, streetwalker 13 commercialize
customer: 4 john
reformed: 8 Magdalen
prostitution, house of: 6 bordel 7 brothel 8 bordello
prostrate: bow 4 fell, flat 5 prone 6 fall-
en, supine 7 exhaust 8 dejected, helpless, overcome, paralyze 9 collapsed,
flattened, overthrow, overwhelm, recumbent 10 subjugated, submissive
prosy: dry 4 dull 6 jejune 7 humdrum,
prosaic, tedious 9 colorless 11 commonplace, displeasing 13 unimaginative
protagonist: foe 4 hero, star 5 actor,
agent, enemy 6 leader 7 heroine 8 advocate, champion, defender 9 contender, principal, spokesman
protasis: 8 foreword 11 conditional,
proposition 12 introduction
protean: 9 many-sided 10 changeable
protect: arm 4 bind, hill, save, wear 5
bield, bless, guard, hedge, shade 6 as-

sert, defend, harbor, insure, patent, police, screen, shield **7** bulwark, cherish, forfend, shelter, tuition **8** champion, conserve, forefend, preserve **9** copyright

protecting: 7 tutelar **8** tutelary

protection: bib, lee, pad **4** egis, fort, moat, pass **5** aegis, apron, armor, bribe, frith, graft, guard, shell, smock **6** amulet, armour, patent, safety **7** auspice, defense, parapet, shelter, squeeze, tuition, umbrage **8** passport, security **9** shakedown **12** preservation

protector: 5 guard **6** fautor, patron, shield **8** defender, guardian **9** custodian

name meaning: **5** Edgar **9** Alexander

protectorate: 6 colony **9** territory **10** dependency, possession **11** condominium

protege: 4 ward

proteid: 6 alexin **7** albumin **9** legumelin

Proteida family: olm **7** proteus **8** necturus **11** salamanders, typhlomolge

protein: 6 avidin, casein, fibrin **7** albumin, edestin, mucedin **8** aleurone, creatine, prolamin

group: **8** globulin

poison: **5** abrin, ricin **6** ricine

source of: egg **4** bean, meat, milk **6** cheese, lentil

pro tem: 6 acting **7** interim **9** temporary

protest: 4 aver, beef, deny, kick **5** demur, fight **6** affirm, assert, assure, holler, object, oppose, plaint **7** contest, declare, dissent, testify **8** complain **9** complaint, objection, stipulate **10** asseverate **11** expostulate, remonstrate **12** remonstrance

Protestant: 7 Baptist **8** Anglican, Lutheran **9** Calvinist, dissenter, Methodist **10** Anabaptist **12** Presbyterian

proteus: olm **5** ameba **6** amoeba

Proteus: 6 sea god

friend: **9** Valentine

love: **6** Silvia

wife: **5** Julia

protograph: 7 writing **9** holograph **12** illustration

protoplasm: 5 ameba, spore **6** amoeba **7** sarcode

outer layer: **9** ectoplasm

substance: gel

prototype: 5 model **6** emblem **7** pattern **8** antetype, original **9** archetype **10** forerunner

protozoan: 5 ameba **6** amoeba **7** stentor **8** rhizopod

genus of: **7** arcella

order: **6** lobosa

parasitic: **5** ameba **6** amoeba **8** amoebida

protract: 4 spin **5** defer, delay **6** dilate, extend **7** detract, prolong **8** continue, elongate, lengthen, protrude

protrude: jut **5** blear, bulge **7** extrude,

project **8** stick out **9** interfere

protuberance: nub, wen **4** boll, boss, bulb, bump, heel, hump, knob, knot, lobe, lump, node, snag, umbo **5** bulge, bunch, caput, hunch, torus **8** eminence, swelling **9** gibbosity **10** projection, prominence, protrusion

rounded: **4** hump, umbo

protuberant: 6 convex, extant **7** bottled, gibbous **8** blubbery **9** prominent

proud (see also **pride**)**: 4** ikey, vain **5** brant, chuff **7** haughty, pompous, stately, valiant **8** imposing, splendid **9** cockhorse, hubristic **10** impressive **11** magisterial, overbearing **12** presumptuous, supercilious

prove: try **4** aver, fand, pree, test **5** argue, essay, nurse, prive(Sc.) **6** argify, argufy, attest, evince, verify **7** confirm, justify, probate **8** identify, indicate, manifest **9** ascertain, establish **11** corroborate, demonstrate

provenance: 6 origin, source **10** derivation

provender: hay **4** corn, feed, food, oats, prog **5** grain, straw **6** fodder, forage **7** prebend **10** provisions

proverb: saw **4** word **5** adage, axiom, maxim, motto **6** ballad, byword, enigma, saying **7** byspell, parable **8** allegory, aphorism, forbysen

proverbial: 6 common **9** well-known **11** sententious

provide: 4 give **5** cater, equip, stock, store, yield **6** afford, foison, purvey, ration, render, supply **7** chevise, furnish, support **8** accouter, accoutre **9** stipulate **10** contribute

provided: but **5** boden, found **6** if only, sobeit **8** afforded, equipped, supplied **9** furnished

providence: 6 thrift **7** economy **8** function, guidance, prudence

provident: 4 wise **6** frugal, saving **7** careful, prudent, sparing, thrifty **8** cautious, discreet **9** farseeing **10** economical, farsighted **11** foresighted

providential: 4 kind **5** happy, lucky **9** fortunate **10** auspicious

province: 4 area, nome, work **5** arena, range, realm, shire, tract **6** colony, domain, eparch, region, sphere **7** country, emirate, pursuit **8** district, division, function **9** bailiwick, territory **10** department, palatinate **12** jurisdiction

pert. to: **5** nomic

provincial: 4 rude **5** crude, local, rural **6** narrow, rustic **7** bigoted, insular, limited **9** hidebound, parochial **10** uncultured **11** countrified **15** unsophisticated

provision: 4 fare, food **5** board, cater, grist, stock, store **6** clause, supply, wraith 7 proviso 9 condition

provisional: 4 iffy 7 aeolian 9 makeshift, provisory, temporary, tentative 10 contingent 11 conditional

provisions: 4 cate, chow, fare, food 5 board, bouge, terms 6 forage, stocks, stores, viands 7 rations 9 provender 10 chevisance

search for: 6 forage

stock of: 6 larder 8 magazine

proviso: 5 salvo 6 clause 7 article, caution 9 condition 11 stipulation

provisory: 11 provisional

provocation: 6 appeal 9 annoyance, incentive

provocative: 7 agacant 8 agacante, stimulus 9 provoking 10 aggressive 11 stimulating

provoke: ire, vex 4 bait, move, spur, stir 5 anger, annoy, cause, eager, evoke, frump, pique, start, tease 6 arouse, excite, harass, incite, insult, invite, invoke, madden, nettle, summon 7 affront, incense, outrage, perturb, quicken 8 generate, irritate 9 aggravate, challenge, displease, forthcall, stimulate 10 exasperate

provost: 4 head 5 chief 6 jailer, keeper 7 prefect 8 director, official 10 magistrate 13 administrator 14 superintendent

prow: bow 4 beak, nose, stem 5 brave, prore 6 steven 7 gallant, rostrum, valiant 9 honorable 10 courageous

prowess: 5 skill, valor 6 valour 7 address, bravery, courage, heroism 9 ingenuity 10 excellence

prowl: 4 lurk, roam 6 brevit, ramble, wander

proximate: 4 next 6 direct, nearby 8 imminent 9 immediate 10 near-at-hand

proximity: 8 nearness, nighness, vicinage, vicinity 9 adjacence, closeness, immediacy 10 contiguity 11 propinquity 13 approximation, juxtaposition

proxy: 5 agent, power, vicar 6 agency, deputy 7 proctor 8 assignee, function 9 authority 10 procurator, substitute

prudence: wit 6 acumen 7 economy 10 management 11 calculation

prudent: 4 sage, wary, wise 5 canny, chary, douce, siker 6 frugal, sicker 7 careful, politic 8 cautious, discreet, sensible 9 advisable, cautelous, expedient, provident, sagacious 10 economical, forehanded 11 circumspect, considerate, foresighted 14 forethoughtful

prudish: 4 nice, prim 5 stern 6 severe, stern 7 austere 8 priggish 10 overmodest

prune: cow, cut, lop 4 clip, coll, frog, geld, plum, sned(Sc.), thin, trim 5 brake, dress, dunce, fruit, plume, preen, purge, rasee, razee, shave 6 anoint 7 exclude, tonsure 8 castrate 9 eliminate, simpleton

pruning knife: 8 serpette

prurient: 4 lewd 5 bawdy 6 erotic 7 itching, longing, lustful 10 lascivious

pruritis: 4 itch

Prussia: 11 German state (former)

bay: 4 Kiel 6 Danzig 10 Pomeranian

city: 4 Kiel 5 Essen 6 Aachen, Altena, Berlin, Tilsit 7 Breslau, Hanover, Munster, Stettin 9 Frankfurt, Magdeburg 10 Dusseldorf, Konigsberg 14 Charlottenburg

district: 7 Stettin

island: 5 Rugen 6 Usedom, Wollin 7 Frisian

lagoon: 4 haff 7 Frische 8 Kurische 11 Pommerische

lancer: 4 Ulan 5 Uhlan

land-holding aristocracy: 6 Junker

legislature, upper house: 10 Herrenhaus

measure: 4 fuss, rute, zoll 5 fuder, meile 6 morgen, oxhoft 8 scheffel

mountain: 4 Harz 7 Sudeten 11 Schneekoppe 13 Riesengebirge

province: 5 Posen 6 Berlin, Saxony 7 Hanover, Prussia, Silesia 9 Pomerania, Rhineland 10 Westphalia 11 Brandenburg, East-Prussia, Hesse-Nassau, West-Prussia 12 Hohenzollern 17 Schleswig-Holstein

river: Ems 4 Alle, Eder, Elbe, Oder, Saar 5 Memel 6 Niemen, Pregel 7 Vistula 8 Passarge, Weichsel

seaport: 4 Kiel 5 Emden

spa: Ems

university town: 5 Halle

weight: 4 mark 9 quentchen

prussiate: 4 salt 7 cyanide 12 ferricyanide, ferrocyanide

pry: spy 4 gaze, lift, move, nose, peek, peep, peer 5 jemmy, jimmy, lever, mouse, prize, raise, snoop, twist 6 pick up, potter 7 crowbar 8 leverage, scrounge, separate 10 scrutinize

prying: 4 nosy 5 nosey 7 curious 9 obtrusive, officious 11 inquisitive

psalm: ode 4 hymn, poem, song 6 praise 11 composition

collection: 6 hallel 7 psalter

kind: 4 laud 6 hallel, Venite 7 Cantate, introit 8 Miserere

opening communion: 7 introit

sign: 5 selah

word of punctuation: 5 selah

psalmist: 4 poet 5 David 6 cantor, writer 8 composer 9 precentor

psalterium: 4 bouk, lyra 6 omasum 7 stomach 9 manyplies

psammite: 9 sandstone

pseudo: 4 fake, mock, sham 5 bogus, false, wrong 7 feigned 8 spurious 9 pretended, simulated 11 counterfeit

pseudologist: 4 liar

pseudonym (see also **nickname, pen name**): 5 alias 6 anonym 7 anonyme

Lev Bronstein: 11 Leon Trotsky

Josip Broz: 4 Tito

Iosif Dzhugashvili: 12 Joseph Stalin

Adolf Schicklgruber: 11 Adolf Hitler

Vladimir Ulyanov: 13 Vladimir Lenin

Ehrich Weiss: 7 Houdini

psittaceous: 10 parrotlike

psyche: 4 mind, soul 6 spirit

psychiatrist: 4 Jung 5 Adler, Freud 6 shrink 7 analyst 8 alienist

psychic: 6 mental 7 sensile 9 animistic, spiritual 10 responsive, telepathic 11 impressible

psychic power: ESP

psychotic: mad 5 crazy 6 insane 8 schizoid 10 disordered 12 unreasonable

Ptah's wife: 6 Sekhet

ptarmica: 10 sneezewort

ptarmigan: 4 bird, ripa, rype 6 grouse

PT boat: 11 torpedo boat

pteric: 4 alar 8 winglike

pteroid: 8 fernlike, winglike

ptisan: tea 5 drink 6 coddle, tisane 9 decoction

Ptolemy: *astronomy work:* 8 almagest

wife: 12 Philadelphia

ptomaine: 6 poison

pub: bar, inn 5 hotel 6 tavern

pubble: fat 5 plump

public: 4 open 5 civic, civil, overt, state 6 common, vulgar 7 general, popular, society 8 national, open-door 9 community, following 10 widespread

discussion: 5 forum

record office: 7 archion 8 archives

service: 7 railway, utility 9 telegraph, telephone 10 waterworks

way: 4 road 5 alley 6 bridge, tunnel 7 highway 8 turnpike 9 boulevard

publican: 6 farmer, keeper 9 catchpole, catchpoll, collector 12 saloon keeper, tax collector

publication: 4 book 5 paper 6 annals, blazon, digest 7 booklet 8 pamphlet 9 ephemeris 10 periodical 11 declaration 12 notification, proclamation, promulgation

examiner: 6 censor

list: 12 bibliography

make-up: 6 format

permit: 7 release

preliminary: 9 prodromus

prepare for: 4 edit

regular: 10 periodical

publicist: 5 agent, solon 6 writer 10 journalist

publicity: air 7 buildup, puffery, reclame, write-up 8 ballyhoo 9 promotion 11 advertising, information

publicize: 4 tout 5 extol 7 promote 9 advertise

publish: air 4 blow, edit, vent 5 issue, print 6 blazon, defame, delate, expose, get out, put out 7 declare, diffuse, divulge, release 8 announce, evulgate, forspeak, proclaim, promulge 9 advertise, forespeak 10 promulgate 11 disseminate

without authority: 6 pirated 10 plagiarize

publisher: 6 editor, issuer 7 printer 8 broacher 10 journalist

copy: 5 blurb 8 colophon 12 announcement

Puccini: *heroine:* 4 Mimi

opera: 7 La Tosca 8 La Boheme 12 Manon

puck: elf, imp 4 disk 5 fairy 6 roller, sprite, strike 9 hobgoblin, prankster 10 goatsucker

pucker: 4 fold 5 bulge, purse, reeve, smock 6 cockle, cotter, lucken 7 wrinkle 8 contract

puckered: 7 bullate

puckfist: 8 braggart, puffball

puckish: 7 playful 8 annoying 10 mysterious 11 mischievous

pud: paw 4 hand 7 pudding 8 forefoot

pudding: 4 duff, mush, sago 6 burgoo, hackin, haggis(Sc.), panada 7 burgout, custard, dessert, hacking, sausage, tapioca 8 roly-poly 9 stir-about

puddle: dub 4 plud, pond, pool 5 plash, swamp 6 charco, fiddle, flodge 7 plashet 8 quagmire

pudency: 7 modesty 8 delicacy 11 bashfulness, prudishness 13 embarrassment 14 shamefacedness

pudgy: fat 5 dumpy, plump, squab, squat 6 rotund 7 bulging 8 roly-poly

pueblo: 4 town 7 village 8 dwelling

Pueblo: 4 Hopi, Zuni 6 Indian

assembly hall: 6 estufa

ceremonial chamber: 4 kiva

village: 4 Taos

puerile: 4 weak 5 silly, young 6 jejune 7 babyish, foolish, trivial 8 childish, immature, juvenile, unworthy, youthful 10 unthinking

Puerto Principe: 8 Camaguey

Puerto Rico: *capital:* 7 San Juan

bark: 4 mavi

beverage: 4 mavi

bird: 4 rola 7 yeguita

breadfruit: 7 castana

city: 5 Ponce 6 Dorado 7 Arecibo 8 Mayaguez

conqueror of: 5 Miles

discoverer: 8 Columbus

fish: **4** sama, sisi
island: **4** Mona
measure: **6** cuerda **10** caballeria
person of mixed blood: **6** jibaro
tree: **4** mora **5** yagua, yaray **8** guayroto **9** guaraguao
puff: 4 blow, chug, flam(Sc.), flan, fuff, gust, pant, pegh(Sc.), plug, pouf, waff, waft **5** fluff, quilt, whiff **6** praise
puff up: 5 bloat, swell **6** tumefy **7** distend, inflate
puffball: 4 fist, fuzz **5** smoke **8** fuzzball, snuffbox
puffbird: 6 barbet **8** barbacou
genus: **6** monasa
puffed up: 5 large **6** astrut **7** souffle **8** bouffant, imposing, inflated **9** bombastic, bouffante **11** pretentious
puffer: 6 blower **8** blowfish **9** globefish
puffin: 4 auk **4** bird **9** sea parrot
puffy: 4 soft **5** pursy **6** flabby **7** pompous
pug: dog, elf **4** clay, plug, poke, puck **5** boxer, chaff, churn, dwarf, knead, track **6** harlot, refuse, sprite, thrust **7** trample **8** mistress, pugilist **9** footprint, hobgoblin
pug-nosed: 5 camus
puggy: 6 monkey(Sc.), sweaty **10** sweetheart
pugilist: lug **5** boxer **7** battler, bruiser, fighter
assistant: **6** second **7** handler
pugnacious: 7 defiant, warlike **8** brawling, fighting **9** bellicose, combative **10** aggressive **11** belligerent, contentious, quarrelsome
puisne: 4 puny **5** judge, later, petty **6** feeble, junior **9** associate **10** subsequent **11** subordinate **13** insignificant
puissance: 4 army, host, sway **5** clout, force, might, power, vigor **7** potency **8** strength **9** influence **12** forcefulness
puissant: 6 mighty, strong **8** powerful **10** commanding
puke: 4 snot, wool **5** vomit
pukka, pucka: 4 good, real **7** genuine **8** complete **9** authentic **11** substantial **13** thoroughgoing
pulchritude: 5 grace **6** beauty **10** comeliness, excellence, loveliness
pule: cry **4** peep **5** cheep, whine **6** repine, snivel **7** whimper **8** complain
pull: lug, row, tew, tit, tow, tug, wap **4** claw, drag, draw, duct, hale, haul, jerk, yank, yerk **5** bouse(naut.), heave(naut.), hitch, pluck, tweak **6** arrest, twitch **7** attract, revulse, stretch **9** influence **10** persuasion **12** drawing power
apart: rip **4** rend, tear **8** separate **9** criticize
away: **5** wrest **6** remove **8** withdraw
down: **4** raze **5** wreck **7** destroy **8** demolish

off: pug **6** avulse, manage **7** achieve, succeed **10** accomplish
one's freight: **5** leave **6** depart
one's leg: **4** hoax, joke **7** deceive **8** hoodwink
out: **7** extract **9** extirpate **10** deracinate
through: **7** recover, succeed, survive
up: **4** halt, stop **5** elate, trice
pullet: hen **4** fowl **5** frier **6** earock(Sc.) **7** pollard **8** poullard
pulley: 4 ring **5** fusee, fuzee, wheel **6** sheave
part: **4** arse, drum **6** rigger
Pullman: car **5** coach **7** sleeper
pullulate: bud **4** teem **5** swarm **9** germinate
pulp: pap **4** marc, mash, mass, pith **5** chyme, crush, magma **6** pomace **7** bagasse
machine: **9** macerater
pulpit: 4 ambo, bema, desk **5** chair, stage **7** lectern, rostrum **8** ministry, platform, scaffold
pulpy: 6 flabby, fleshy
pulque: 5 drink **6** liquor, mescal **9** stimulant
pulsate: 4 beat, move, pant **5** pound, throb **6** quiver, strike, thrill **7** vibrate
pulsatory: 8 rhythmic **9** systaltic, throbbing
pulse: mug **7** battuta **8** sphygmus
pulverize: 4 bray, meal, mull, ruin **5** crush, grind **6** bruise **7** atomize, destroy, shatter **8** demolish, levigate **9** comminute, triturate **12** contriturate
pulverized: 4 fine **5** dusty
pulverizer: 7 blender, grinder **13** disintegrator
pulverulent: 5 dusty **7** crumbly, powdery **8** powdered
puma: cat **6** cougar **7** panther **9** carnivore
pumice: 5 stone **8** abrasive
powdered: **4** talc
pummel: fib **4** beat, maul **5** thump **6** batter, hammer
pump: gin, ram **4** jack **5** drain **6** racker **7** draw off, stirrup, syringe **10** pulsometer
handle: **5** sweep, swipe
pumpernickel: 5 bread
pumpkin: 4 pepo **5** clump, gourd **6** citrul, squash
head: **4** dolt **5** dunce **7** Puritan **9** blockhead
pumpkinseed: 7 sunfish **8** bluegill, flatfish, flounder **10** butterfish
pun: mot **4** beat, joke **5** knock, pound **7** quibble **8** paragram **9** calembour, conundrum **11** paronomasia, play on words
punch: ade, jab **4** cuff, glog, poke, prod **5** douse, dowse, drink, negus, paste, point, vigor **6** pierce, strike **7** mattoir **8** bever-

age, puncture **9** perforate

Punch: **5** clown **7** buffoon, journal **8** magazine **10** periodical

first editor of: **5** Lemon

puncheon: die **4** cask, post, snap, stud, tool **5** punch, stamp **6** timber

puncher: **6** cowboy **7** cowpoke **10** cowpuncher, perforator

Punchinello: **5** clown **7** buffoon

punctilious: **4** nice **5** exact **6** formal, proper **7** careful, correct, precise **8** exacting **9** observant **10** ceremonial, scrupulous **11** ceremonious **13** conscientious

punctual: **6** on time, prompt, timely **7** careful

punctuate: **4** mark **5** point **6** divide **8** separate **9** emphasize **11** distinguish

punctuation mark: dot **4** dash, stop **5** colon, comma, quote, slash **6** hyphen, period **7** bracket **8** ellipsis **9** semicolon **10** apostrophe **11** parenthesis

puncture: **4** bite, hole, stab, vent **5** prick, wound **6** pierce, riddle **9** perforate **11** perforation

pundit: **4** sage **5** swami **6** nestor **7** Brahman, scholar, teacher

pung: **4** sled **6** sleigh

pungent: hot **4** fell, keen, racy, rich, tart **5** acrid, acute, cress, minty, salty, sharp, smart, spicy, tangy **6** biting, bitter, pepper, snappy **7** caustic, cutting, peppery, piquant **8** aromatic, incisive, piercing, poignant, stinging **9** trenchant **10** expressive, irritating **11** acrimonious, stimulating

pungi: bin **4** pipe **5** flute

pungled: **8** shrunken **9** shriveled

Punic: **9** faithless **11** treacherous **12** Carthaginian

punish: **4** beat, fine, whip **5** abuse, mulct, scold, slate, smite, spank, strap, wreak **6** amerce, strike **7** chasten, consume, correct, corrige, revenge, scourge **8** chastise, penalize **9** castigate **10** discipline **13** excommunicate

punishing: **8** grueling

punishment: **4** loss, pain **5** peine(law), wrack **6** desert, dirdum, ferule **9** suffering **10** correction, discipline **11** castigation **12** chastisement **13** animadversion

device: rod **6** stocks

freedom from: **8** impunity

spare: **6** acquit **7** absolve **9** exculpate, exonerate

punitive: **5** penal **9** punishing **10** vindictive

Punjab: *East:* **5** India

West: **8** Pakistan

punk: bad **4** fuel, poor **5** conch, tough, tramp **6** amadou, novice, rookie, tinder **8** beginner, elephant, inferior, non-

sense, strumpet **9** beginning, miserable, touchwood, worthless **10** prostitute

punt: **4** boat, kick **6** gamble

punter: **5** poler **6** bettor **7** scalper

puny: **4** weak **5** dawny, frail, petty, small **6** feeble, puisne, sickly, slight **8** droghlin, inferior **9** unskilled **13** inexperienced, insignificant

pupa: **9** chrysalis

case: **5** theca

pupil: **4** tyro **5** cadet, eleve(F.), minor, plebe, youth **6** junior, senior **7** ecolier(F.), learner, scholar, student **8** disciple, neophyte, freshman **9** sophomore

pupilage: **6** nonage **10** immaturity

puppet: **4** baby, doll, dupe, tool **5** image, slave **8** drollery **9** neuropast **10** marionette

show: **6** wajang, wayang **10** shadow-play

puppy: fop **5** twerp, whelp

purblind: **5** blind **6** bisson, myopic, obtuse **12** shortsighted

purchasable: **5** venal **7** corrupt, salable, to be had **9** available **10** marketable

purchase: buy **5** cheap, yield **6** emptio, income, obtain, return **7** acquire, bargain, emption **11** acquisition

back: **6** redeem, regain

purchaser: **4** user **5** buyer **6** emptor, patron, vendee **8** co-emptor, customer **9** acquereur **13** adjudicataire

purdah: **6** screen **7** curtain **9** seclusion

pure: **4** fine, good, mear, meer, mere, neat, nice, pute, true **5** clean, clear, fresh, moral, sheer, utter **6** candid, chaste, simple, vestal, virgin **7** cleanly, genuine, perfect, refined, sincere, sinless, unmixed **8** absolute, complete, dovelike, filtered, innocent, straight, virtuous, zaccheus(Heb.) **9** authentic, blameless, downright, elemental, faultless, guiltless, out-and-out, stainless, unalloyed, undefiled, unsullied **10** immaculate **11** crystalline, unblemished, uncorrupted, unqualified **13** unadulterated **15** unsophisticated

puree: **4** mush, soup **8** porridge

purely: all **4** just **5** quite **6** solely, wholly

purfle: hem **6** border **7** outline **8** decorate, ornament, trimming

purgative: **5** jalap **6** physic **8** cleanser, evacuant **9** cathartic **10** alviducous

purgatory: **5** limbo, swamp

purge: rid **5** clear **6** physic, purify, remove, seethe **7** cleanse, deterge, shut out **8** absterge **9** exculpate, expurgate, liquidate **11** exterminate

purification: **7** baptism **9** catharsis

purify: **5** clean, clear, purge **6** bleach, filter, refine **7** baptize, clarify, cleanse, distill, epurate **8** depurate, lustrate, renovate **9** elutriate

Puritan: 9 Roundhead
puritanical: 4 prim 6 strict 7 genteel, prudish 8 rigorous 9 blue-nosed
purl: rib 4 eddy, knit, spin 5 frill, swirl 6 murmur, purfle, stitch
purlieu: 5 haunt 6 resort 7 environ 12 neighborhood
purloin: 4 crib 5 filch, steal, swipe 6 finger, pilfer, pirate 7 cabbage 8 abstract 10 plagiarize 11 appropriate
purple: 4 plum 5 grape, lilac, mauve, royal 6 blatta, emblem, maroon, ornate, risqué, tyrian, violet 7 cassius 8 amaranth, imperial, lavender 9 cathedral, elaborate 10 rhetorical
  delicate: 5 mauve
  dye: 7 cassius
purple copper ore: 7 bornite
Purple Heart: 5 award, medal, order
purple ragwort: 4 herb 6 jacoby
purport: 4 feck, gist, mean 5 drift, sense, tenor 6 effect, import, intent, object 7 bearing, meaning 9 intention, substance 11 connotation, implication
purpose: aim, end, use 4 bent, goal, main, mean, plan, sake 5 avail, point 6 design, intend, intent, motive 7 mission 8 ambition, proposal 9 intention, objective, predesign 10 aspiration, cogitation, conception, employment, resolution 13 determination
  alleged: 6 excuse 7 pretext
  lacking: 9 driftless
purposive: 5 telic, 6 hormic 12 teleological
purpure: 6 purple 7 mercury
purr: hum 5 noise, sound, thrum, whurl 6 murmur
purse: bag, cly 4 bung, poke 5 bulse, burse, money, pouch 6 pucker, wallet 7 almoner, handbag 8 coco-wort, finances, treasury 9 exchequer 10 pocketbook 12 portemonnaie
purse crab: 5 ayuyu 7 pagurid
purser: 6 bursar 7 boucher, cashier 8 pinchgut 9 paymaster, treasurer
pursue: run 4 bait, hunt, seek 5 chase, chevy, chivy, hound, stalk 6 badger, follow, gallop 7 address, persist, proceed 8 continue 9 prosecute
pursuer: 5 lover 6 hunter 8 huntress 9 plaintiff
pursuit: 4 work 5 quest, scent 7 calling 10 occupation
  means: 7 dragnet
pursy: fat 5 obese, puffy 7 swollen, wealthy 9 asthmatic
purulent: 4 foul, pyic 5 pussy
purvey: tax 5 cater 6 supply 7 foresee, furnish, procure, provide 10 assessment
purveyor: 6 seller, sutler 7 caterer 9 victualer

push: go; pop, por, ram 4 birr, bore, bunt, butt, ding, dush, pelt, ping, pole, porr, poss, prod, urge 5 bevel(Sc.), boost, crowd, drive, elbow, force, heave, hunch, impel, nudge, press, shove, vigor 6 clique, effort, energy, expand, extend, hustle, jostle, launch, potter, propel, thrust 7 advance, promote 8 bulldoze, increase, pressure, stimulus 10 enterprise 14 aggressiveness
  along: 4 prod 5 nudge
  around: 4 bait 5 bully 6 heckle
  down: 7 detrude
  in: 5 stove
pushy: 5 bossy 7 forward 9 officious 10 aggressive 11 presumptuous
pusillanimous: 4 tame 5 timid 6 afraid 8 cowardly 10 irresolute 12 fainthearted
puss: cat 4 face, girl, hare 5 child, mouth, woman 8 baudrons(Sc.)
pustule: 4 blob, burl 5 achor, blain 6 blotch, pimple 7 abscess, blister 8 eruption, swelling 9 carbuncle
put (see also **place**): lay, set 4 cast, push, urge, word 5 clink, drive, fixed, force, impel, place, state, throw 6 appose, attach, bestow, fasten, incite, thrust 7 deposit, express, propose 8 estimate 9 attribute, constrain, translate
  away: 4 kill 5 store 6 murder 7 consume
  back: 6 demote 7 replace, restore
  before: 7 apposed, present
  by: 4 save 5 store 6 reject
  down: 6 humble, record 7 degrade, depress 8 suppress 9 deposited
  forth: 4 show 5 exert, offer 7 extrude, propose, publish 9 circulate
  forward: 7 prepose, propone
  in: 4 ante 5 defer, delay, elude, plant 6 baffle, divert, insert 7 discard, enclose 8 postpone 9 frustrate
  off: fob 4 doff, haft 5 defer, delay, evade, table 6 divert, remove, shelve 7 discard 8 deferred, postpone
  on: act, don 5 apply, endue, indue, stage 6 employ 7 assumed, feigned, pretend 10 exaggerate
  out: irk, vex 4 oust 5 anger, annoy, eject, evict, exert, exile, expel 6 banish, deport, retire 7 publish 8 displace, distress, irritate 9 ostracize 10 discompose, disconcert, expatriate, extinguish 14 discountenance
  over: 4 bilk, hoax 5 cheat, defer, trick 7 deceive
  together: add 5 piece, unite 6 gather, muster 7 collect 8 assemble 9 construct 10 congregate
  up: can 4 post 5 build, erect
  up with: 4 bear, take 5 brook, stand 6 endure 7 stomach 8 tolerate
putrefy: rot 5 decay 6 fester 7 corrupt 9

decompose **12** disintegrate

putrid: bad **4** foul **7** friable, noisome, vicious **8** depraved **10** malodorous, putrescent **11** displeasing **12** disagreeable

puttee: 4 spat **6** gaiter **7** legging

putter: 6 dawdle, fiddle **8** golf club **10** boondoggle

putting area: 5 green

putty: 6 cement

puxy: 5 swamp **8** quagmire

puzzle: cap, get **5** addle, amaze, glaik, griph, pinon, poser, rebus, stick **6** baffle, enigma, fickle, riddle **7** anagram, charade, confuse, foitter, griphus, mystery, mystify, nonplus, paradox, perplex **8** acrostic, bewilder, distract, entangle, intrigue **9** conundrum, dumbfound **10** difficulty, disconcert, palindrome

puzzled: 4 asea

puzzling: 6 knotty **7** knotted **9** difficult, equivocal

pygarg: 5 addax **6** osprey

Pygmalion: *sister:* **4** Dido
offspring: **6** Paphos, Paphus
sister's husband: **8** Sichaeus
statue: **7** Galatea
victim of: **8** Sichaeus

pygmy, pigmy: elf **4** pixy, runt, tiny **5** atomy, dwarf, gnome, minim, short **8** dwarfish **9** dandiprat **10** chimpanzee

pygmy musk deer: 10 chevrotain

pygostyle: 4 bone **5** vomer

pyknic: 5 solid, squat **6** stocky, sturdy **8** muscular **9** endomorph, squatness **11** endomorphic

pylon: 4 post **5** tower **6** marker **7** gateway **8** monument

Pylo's king: 6 Nestor

pyramid: 4 heap, pile, tomb **6** accrue **8** increase
builder of largest: **6** Cheops
inhabitant: **5** Khufu **6** Cheops
site: **4** Giza **7** Cholula

pyramidal: 4 huge **8** enormous, imposing

pyre: 4 bale, bier **6** suttee **7** bonfire

pyrene: pip **4** seed **5** stone

Pyrenees: *bandit:* **8** miquelet
chamois: **5** izard
mountain peak: **5** Aneto
people: **6** Basque
republic: **7** Andorra
resort: Pau

pyriform: 10 pear-shaped

pyromaniac: 7 firebug **8** arsonist

pyrosis: 9 heartburn

pyrotechnics: 9 fireworks

pyrotechnical device: 8 pinwheel

pyroxene: 6 augite **8** diopside **11** schefferite **12** hedenbergite

Pythagoras' birthplace: 5 Samos

Pythias' friend: 5 Damon

python: boa **5** snake **7** serpent
slayer: **6** Apollo

pythonic: 4 huge **8** inspired, oracular **9** monstrous

pyx, pix: box **4** case, test, vase **5** assay, capsa, carry, chest **6** casket, coffer, vessel **8** binnacle, ciborium, preserve **10** tabernacle

Q

Q: cue **5** queue

Qatar's capital: 4 Doha

q.e.d.: 21 quod erat demonstrandum

quaalude: 8 hypnotic, sedative

quabird: 5 heron

quack: cry **4** duck **5** couch, faker, fraud **6** crocus **7** shammer **8** impostor **9** charlatan, pretender **10** mountebank, stimulator **13** counterfeiter

quad: 4 quod, yard **5** block, court **6** campus, person **7** sibling

quadra: 6 fillet, listel, plinth

quadragenarian: 8 fortyish

quadragesimal: 5 forty **6** Lenten

quadrangle: 5 court **6** square **8** tetragon

quadrant: arc, bow **4** gill **6** fourth, radial **8** farthing **9** antimeter **10** instrument

quadrate: 4 suit **5** adapt, agree, ideal **6** square **7** perfect, squared **8** balanced **9** rectangle **10** correspond **13** correspondent

quadriga: 4 cart **6** horses **7** chariot

quadrille: 5 cards, dance 9 cotillion
quadroon: 6 hybrid 7 mixture, mulatto 8 terceron
quadrumane: ape 6 monkey 7 gorilla 10 chimpanzee
quadruped: 6 mammal 10 four-legged
quaff: sip 5 draft, drink 6 tipple, waught
quag: 5 quake 6 quiver 8 quagmire
quagga: 7 wild ass
relative: 5 zebra
quaggy: 4 miry, soft 5 boggy 6 flabby, spongy 7 queachy 8 yielding
quagmire: bog, gog, hag 5 marsh, swamp 6 morass
quahog: 4 clam 10 little neck 11 cherry stone
quail: cow 4 bird 5 colin, cower, quake, shake 6 blench, cringe, curdle, flinch, recoil, shrink, tremor, turnix 7 massena, tremble 8 bobwhite 9 partridge
flock of: 4 bevy 5 covey
young: 7 cheeper 8 squealer
quail snipe: 9 dowitcher
quaint: odd 4 nice 6 crafty 7 antique, curious, strange, unusual 8 fanciful, graceful, peculiar, singular 9 whimsical
quake: 5 quail, shake, waver 6 quiver, shiver, tremor 7 shudder, tremble, vibrate 10 earthquake
Quaker: Fox 4 Penn 6 Friend 9 broadbrim
Quaker City: 12 Philadelphia
Quaker gray: 5 acier
Quaker-ladies: 5 bluet 11 meadowsweet
Quaker State: 12 Pennsylvania
Quaker's founder: 9 George Fox
quaking: 5 aspen, quaky 6 trepid 8 timorous 9 trembling, trepidity
qualification: 7 ability 8 aptitude 9 condition, endowment, knowledge, requisite 10 adaptation, capability, competence, experience 11 acquirement, designation, restriction 12 capacitation, modification
qualified: 4 able 5 ready 8 eligible
qualify: fit 5 abate, adapt, equip, limit 6 enable, modify, soften, temper 7 ascribe, assuage, entitle, prepare 8 diminish, mitigate, moderate, restrain, restrict 9 predicate 10 habilitate 11 characterize
quality: 4 cost, kind, rank, rate, sort, thew, tone 5 class, grade, power, quale, taste, trait 6 nature, status, strain, virtue 7 caliber, calibre, element, feature, stature 8 capacity, nobility, property 9 attribute, character 10 excellence 11 superiority 14 accomplishment, characteristic
of tone: 6 timbre 9 resonance
qualm: 4 drow, pall 5 doubt, spasm 6 attack, nausea, plight, puzzle, regret, twinge 7 scruple 8 sickness 9 faintness, misgiving 10 perplexity 11 compunction 12 apprehension
quandary: fix, jam 4 pass 6 pickle, plight, scrape 7 dilemma, nonplus 11 predicament 12 bewilderment
quantity (see also **amount**): ace, any, bit, jag, jot, lot, sea, sum 4 atom, body, bulk, dash, dose, dram, drop, feck, iota, lick, lots, mass, mort, much, raff, raft, slew, unit 5 batch, bunch, grist, hoard, scads, stack, store 6 amount, capful, degree, extent, hirsel, morsel, number, weight 7 average, driblet, handful, modicum, portion, slather 9 allowance
excessive: 4 glut 5 spate
fixed: 8 constant
full: 10 complement
irrational: 4 surd
per unit: 4 rate
prescribed: 4 dose 6 dosage
small: 4 dram, drop, iota 5 scrap, shred 7 dribble, smidgen
without direction: 6 scalar
Quantrill's men: 7 raiders
quantum: 4 unit 6 amount 7 portion 8 quantity 9 aggregate
quarantine: ban 7 exclude, isolate 8 restrain, sanction 9 interdict, segregate
quaranty: 5 court
quarantene: 4 rood 7 furlong
quark: caw 5 croak, quawk
quarl, quarle: 4 tile 5 brick
quarrel: row 4 feud, fuss, spat, tiff 5 brawl, broil, cavil, flite, flyte, scene, scrap, set to 6 affray, barney, bicker, breach, breeze, fracas, hassle, jangle, ruckus, strife 7 brabble, contend, dispute, faction, rhubarb, wrangle 8 argument, disagree, squabble 9 upscuddle 10 contention 11 altercation, controversy 12 disagreement 16 misunderstanding
quarrelsome: 7 hostile, scrappy 8 brawling, choleric, petulant 9 bellicose, irascible, irritable, litigious 10 discordant, pugnacious 11 belligerent, contentious 12 disputatious 13 argumentative
quarry: pit 4 game, mine, prey 6 object, ravine, victim
quart: 6 fourth 7 measure
four: 6 gallon
metric: 5 liter, litre
one-eighth: 4 gill
two: 6 flagon
quartan: 5 fever 7 malaria
quarter: 4 coin, digs 5 house, lodge, mercy, put up, tract 6 bestow, billet, canton, fourth, harbor, region, supply 7 furnish, harbour, housing, shelter 8 clemency, district, division 9 direction, dismember 11 forbearance

quarters: 4 camp, room 7 billets, lodging, shelter 8 barracks 9 dormitory
nautical: 6 fo'c'sle 7 gunroom 8 steerage, wardroom 10 forecastle
sleeping: 9 dormitory
winter: 10 hibernacle
women's: 5 harem
quarter note: 8 crotchet
quartz: 4 onyx, sand, sard 5 agate, flint, prase, silex, topaz 6 jasper, silica 7 citrine, crystal, rubasse, sinople 8 amethyst 9 carnelian 10 calchedony
quartzite: 9 itabarite, sandstone
quash: 4 cass, drop, void 5 abate, annul, crush, quell 6 cancel, subdue 7 abolish, destroy, shatter 8 abrogate, suppress 9 overthrow
Quasimodo: 9 hunchback
creator: 4 Hugo
occupation: 10 bell ringer
residence: 9 Notre Dame
quaternion: 6 tetrad 7 quartet 8 quatrain
turning factor: 6 versor
quaver: 5 shake, trill, waver 6 falter, quiver 7 tremble, tremolo, vibrate 9 vacillate, vibration
quawk: caw 5 heron 6 squall 7 screech
quay: key 4 bund, dock, mole, pier, wall 5 levee, wharf 7 landing 10 embankment
quean: 4 jade 5 hussy, wench 6 harlot 10 prostitute
queasy: 5 timid 8 delicate, doubtful, qualmish, ticklish, troubled 9 hazardous, nauseated, squeamish, uncertain, unsettled 10 fastidious 11 embarrassed 13 uncomfortable
Quebec: *bay:* 6 Hudson, Ungava
capital: 11 Quebec City
city: 4 Hull 5 Laval 6 Quebec, Verdun 8 Montreal
founder: 9 Champlain
land measure: 6 arpent
patron saint: 4 Anne
peninsula: 5 Gaspe
province of: 6 Canada
provincial flower: 4 lily
river: 10 St. Lawrence
quebrada: gap 5 brook, creek, gorge 6 ravine, stream 7 fissure 8 brooklet
Quechua: 4 Inca 6 Indian
queen: ant, bee 4 card, fers, rani(Ind.) 5 ranee(Ind.), reine(F.) 6 regina 7 monarch 9 sovereign 10 chess piece
fairy: Mab 7 Argante, Titania
widowed: 7 dowager
queen it: 8 domineer 9 put on airs, tyrannize
queen of fairies: Mab, Pam, Una 7 Titania 8 Gloriand
Queen Anne's lace: 10 wild carrot
Queen City: 10 Cincinnati
Queen of the Adriatic: 6 Venice

Queen of the Antilles: 4 Cuba
Queen of the East: 7 Zenobia
queen of gods: 4 Hera, Juno, Sati
Queen of Hearts: 9 Elizabeth
Queen of Heaven: 4 Hera, Mary, moon 7 Astarte
Queen of Isles: 6 Albion
Queen of Palmyra: 7 Zenobia
Queen of Sheba: 6 Balkis
queen of spades: 5 basta
Queen of Thebes: 5 Dirce
queen of underworld: Hel 4 Hela
queen's arm: 6 musket
queen's-delight: oil 4 herb 9 perennial, queenroot
queen's-flower: 6 myrtle 9 bloodwood
queenly: 5 noble, regal, royal 7 haughty, reginal 8 majestic
Queensland: *river:* 8 Brisbane
seaport: 8 Brisbane
queer: odd, rum 4 harm, sham 5 drunk, faint, funny, giddy, rally, spoil 6 banter, insane 7 curious, disrupt, erratic, strange, touched, unusual 8 abnormal, doubtful, fanciful, obsessed, peculiar, qualmish, singular, spurious 9 dishonest, eccentric, fantastic, squeamish 10 homosexual, jeopardize, suspicious 11 counterfeit, intoxicated 12 questionable
queest: 8 ringdove
queet: 4 coot
quell: end 4 calm, cool, dash, kill, quay, sate 5 allay, check, crush, quash, quiet, still 6 obtund, pacify, reduce, soothe, spring, stanch, stifle, subdue 7 assuage, destroy, put down, repress, satisfy 8 fountain, overcome, suppress 9 overpower, overwhelm, subjugate 10 extinguish
quelque-chose: 6 trifle
quench: 5 allay, douse, slake 6 put out 7 satisfy 8 mitigate 10 extinguish
quenelle: 8 meatball 9 forcemeat
quercus: oak 4 tree 9 evergreen
querent: 8 inquirer 9 plaintiff 11 complainant
querist: 8 inquirer 10 questioner
quern: 4 mill 7 grinder 9 millstone
querulous: 7 fretful, peevish, whining 9 irritable, plaintive 11 complaining 12 querimonious
query: ask 5 doubt 6 demand 7 examine, inquire, inquiry 8 question 9 challenge 11 interrogate, uncertainty
quest: ask, bay 4 hunt, seek 6 search 7 examine, inquest, journey, pursuit, seeking 9 adventure 10 enterprise, expedition 13 investigation
question: ask 4 crux, pump, quiz 5 demur, doubt, grill, poser, query, scout, targe(Sc.) 6 appose, cruces(pl.), debate, de-

mand, quaere, riddle, shrive **7** dispute, inquire, inquiry, problem, scruple, stumper **9** catechise, catechize, challenge, interview **10** discussion **11** examination, interrogate, proposition **12** interpellate **13** interrogation, interrogative, investigation

denoting: **15** interrogational

rhetorical: **10** eperotesis

question mark: 7 erotema, eroteme

questionable: 4 moot **7** dubious, suspect **9** ambiguous, equivocal, uncertain **10** improbable, unreliable

questionnaire: 4 form, poll **7** canvass

quetzal: 4 bird, coin **5** dance **6** trogon

queue: cue **4** line **5** braid **7** pigtail

quiaquia: 4 scad **9** cigarfish

quibble: 4 carp **5** cavil, cheat, dodge, evade, hedge **6** bicker **7** evasion, shuffle **8** pettifog **9** find fault **10** equivocate, split hairs **12** equivocation

quica: 7 opossum

quick: apt, yap **4** deft, fast, flit, lish, live, spry, vite(F.), yare **5** acute, agile, alert, alive, apace, brisk, fiery, fleet, hasty, rapid, ready, sharp, swift, tosto(It.), yeder **6** abrupt, active, lively, moving, nimble, prompt, speedy, sudden, volant **7** intense **8** animated, dextrous, shifting, vigorous **9** dexterous, impatient, sensitive, sprightly **10** celeritous, perceptive **11** expeditious **12** invigorating

quick bread: 6 scones **7** muffins, popover **8** biscuits **9** cornbread

quicken: 4 whet **5** hurry, speed **6** arouse, excite, hasten, incite, revive, vivify **7** animate, enliven, provoke, refresh, sharpen **8** expedite, inspirit **9** reanimate, stimulate **10** accelerate **11** resuscitate **12** reinvigorate

quicker than: ere

quick kick: 12 football punt

quicklime: 5 rusma

quickly: 4 fast, rath, soon, vite(F.) **5** alive, apace **6** belive, hourly, presto, pronto **7** rapidly **8** promptly, speedily, vigorous

quickness: 5 speed **6** acumen **7** acidity **8** dispatch, progress, pungency, sagacity **9** acuteness **10** expedition

quicksand: 4 flow, syrt, trap **6** danger, syrtis

quickset: 5 hedge **7** thicket **8** hawthorn

quicksilver: 7 mercury **9** heautarit

quid: cud, fid **4** chaw, chew **5** pound, trade **6** barter, return **8** exchange, quiddity **9** sovereign

quidnunc: 5 frump **6** gossip, tatler **8** busybody

quiescent: 5 quiet, still **6** latent, static **7** dormant, resting **8** inactive, sleeping **10** motionless

quid pro quo: 9 tit-for-tat **10** equivalent **11** interchange

quiet: coy, pet **4** calm, cosh, dead, ease, fair, hush, lull, mild, rest, tame **5** allay, downy, inert, peace, privy, sober, still, tasty **6** gentle, hushed, merely, modest, placid, repose, secret, sedate, serene, settle, silent, smooth, soothe, static, stilly **7** appease, compose, halcyon, restful, retired, silence, subdued, tasteful **8** composed, decorous, inactive, peaceful, secluded, tranquil **9** alleviate, contented, noiseless, peaceable, placidity, quiescent, reposeful, unruffled **10** motionless, silentness, unmolested **11** clandestine, tranquilize, undisturbed

quietus: 5 death **6** repose **8** mittimus **11** acquittance

quiff: 4 girl, puff **5** whiff **8** forelock

quill: cop, pen **5** remex, spina **6** bobbin, pinion **7** remiges(pl.), spindle

porcupine: pen **5** spine

quilt: pad, sew **4** gulp **5** eider **6** caddow, pallet, stitch **7** blanket, comfort, swallow **8** coverlet **9** comforter **11** counterpane

quink: 5 brant

quinoa: 5 seeds **7** pigweed

quinoline derivative: 7 analgen

quintuplets: 6 Dionne **7** Fischer

quip: mot, pun **4** gibe, jest, joke **5** sally, taunt **6** saying **7** quibble

quire: 4 fold **5** choir, paper

quirk: 4 bend, kink, quip, turn **5** clock, crook, knack, sally, trait, twist **6** groove, strike **7** caprice, evasion **8** flourish **9** deviation, mannerism **10** subterfuge **11** peculiarity **12** equivocation

quirquincho: 5 pichi **6** peludo **9** armadillo

quirt: 4 whip **5** romal

quis: 8 woodcock

quisling: rat **7** traitor **8** turncoat

quit: rid **4** free, stop **5** avoid, cease, clear, forgo, leave, repay **6** acquit, depart, desist, forego, resign, vacate **7** abandon, forsake, release, relieve **8** abdicate, absolved, liberate, renounce **9** surrender **10** relinquish **11** discontinue

quitclaim: 5 grant **7** release **12** convey by deed **14** relinquishment

quite: all **4** very, well **5** stark, truly **6** really, wholly **7** totally, utterly **8** entirely **10** altogether, completely, positively **12** considerably

quite so: 7 exactly **9** precisely

quittance: 5 repay **6** return **8** requital **9** discharge, repayment **10** recompense, reparation

quitter: 4 seal, slag **5** piker **6** coward **7** shirker

quiver: 4 beat, case, quag, tirl(Sc.) 5 bever, quake, quick, shake, thirl(Sc.), throb, trill 6 active, arrows, bicker, cocker, dindle, lively, nimble, quaver, sheath, shiver, tremor 7 frisson, pulsate, tremble, vibrate 8 flichter 9 palpitate, vibration

quivering: 5 aspen 6 ashake, didder 7 aquiver 8 blubbery 9 tremulous

quiverleaf: 5 aspen

quixotic: 6 unreal 7 utopian 9 imaginary, visionary 10 chivalrous, idealistic 11 impractical, in the clouds 13 impracticable

quiz: ask 4 exam, hiss, hoax, jest, joke, mock, test, whiz 5 chaff, probe 7 examine 8 instruct, question, ridicule 11 examination, questioning

quizzical: odd 7 amusing, comical, curious, probing, teasing 9 bantering, eccentric, perplexed 11 incredulous

quizzing glass: 7 monocle

quod: jug 4 jail 8 imprison

quodlibet: 6 debate, medley 8 fantasia, question, subtlety

quod vide: 8 which see

quoin: 4 coin 5 angle, wedge 6 corner 8 keystone, voussoir

quoit: 4 disc, ring 5 throw 6 discus 8 cromlech
mark aimed at: tee
pin: hob

quomodo: 5 means 6 manner

quondam: 4 once 6 former 7 onetime 8 sometime

quonset hut: 6 prefab
British type: 6 Nissen

quorum: 5 group 7 council 8 majority

quota: 4 part 5 share 6 divide, ration 8 dividend 9 apportion 10 contingent, proportion

quotation: 5 price, quote

quotation mark: 9 guillemet(F.)

quote: 4 cite, cote, name, note 5 motto, refer 6 adduce, allege, allude, notice, repeat, select 7 excerpt, extract, passage 9 reference, selection 10 memorandum

quoth: 4 said 5 spoke

quotidian: 5 daily 7 trivial 8 everyday, ordinary 9 recurring 11 commonplace

quotient: 5 ratio 6 result 8 fraction

quotity: 5 group 10 collection

R

R: rho 6 letter

Ra: Shu, Tem, Tum 4 Aten 5 Horus 7 Chepera, Khepera, Sokaris 9 Harmachis
bull form: 5 Bacis
child: Mat, Shu 4 Maat 5 Athor
parent: Geb, Keb, Nut, Seb 5 Neith
wife: 4 Mout

raad: 7 catfish

rab: 6 beater

rabato, rebato: 4 ruff 6 collar

rabban: 6 master 7 teacher

rabbet: 4 plow 5 check 6 groove, recess 7 channel 9 fillister

rabbi: 4 lord 5 amora 6 master, rabbin 7 amoraim, tannaim, teacher 8 sabaraim, saboraim 9 clergyman
assistant: 6 cantor
school: 7 yeshiva 8 yeshibah, yeshivah 9 yeshiboth(pl.)

wife: 9 rebbetzin

rabbit: bun, doe 4 buck, cony, hare, tyro 5 bunny, capon, coney, lapin(F.) 6 coward, novice, rodent, tapeti
fictional: 5 Mopsy, Peter 6 Harvey 9 Bugs Bunny
fur: 4 cony, rack, scut 5 coney, lapin
genus: 5 lepus
relative: 4 pika
shelter: 5 hutch 6 burrow, warren 7 clapper
tail: fud(Sc.) 4 scut
young: 4 rack 6 gazabo, gazebo 7 starter

rabbit-ear: 6 aerial, cactus 8 antenna, toadflax

rabbit fever: 9 tularemia

rabbit flower: 8 foxglove, toadflax

rabbit-foot: 5 charm 8 talisman

rabbit-meat: 5 lapin 9 archangel

rabbit tobacco: 10 balsamweed

rabbit vine: 9 groundnut
rabbitfish: 8 chimaera
rabbitmouth: 10 harelipped, snapdragon
rabbitry: 5 hutch **6** warren
rabbit's-root: 12 sarsaparilla
rabble: mob **4** herd, raff, rout, scum **5** crowd **6** polloi, ragtag **7** bobtail **8** canaglia, canaille, riffraff **9** confusion, tag and rag **10** clamjamfry, hubble-shoo, hubble-show **11** commonality, rank and file
rabble-rouser: 6 ragtag **8** agitator **9** demagogue
Rabelaisian: 5 bawdy **6** earthy
rabid: mad **6** raging **7** extreme, frantic, furious, violent, zealous **8** demented, deranged, frenzied, virulent **9** fanatical **12** enthusiastic
rabies: 5 lyssa, lytta **7** madness **11** hydrophobia
raccoon: 5 guara, tejon **6** mapach **7** mapache **9** crabeater
related animal: **5** coati, panda
race: cut, ilk, run **4** dash, gest, herd, kind, lane, line, root, rush, slit, sort, stem, stud, type **5** blood, breed, brood, caste, chevy, chivy, class, corso, creek, flesh, geste, hurry, relay, speed, stock, track, tribe **6** arroyo, bicker, broose, chivvy, course, family, groove, hasten, hurdle, nation, people, slalom, sprint, stirps, strain **7** bombast, channel, contend, contest, dynasty, lineage, regatta, running, scamper, scratch, species **8** marathon **9** holethnos **10** freeforall, generation, passageway **11** competition, descendants, nationality, watercourse
division: **7** Negroid **9** Caucasian, Mongolian
human: man **7** mankind **9** mortality
mixed: See **person:** *of mixed blood*
murder: **8** genocide
pert. to: **6** ethnic
series: **7** regatta
science: **9** athletics, ethnology
starting line: **7** scratch
race board: 9 gangplank
raceabout: 5 sloop **8** roadster
racecourse: 4 heat, oval, ring, turf **6** career, circus, course **8** gymkhana **10** hippodrome
marker: **4** meta **5** pylon
racehorse: 5 pacer **6** maiden, mantis, plater **7** sleeper, trotter
racer: 4 crab **5** miler, snake **6** runner **7** courser, serpent **8** sprinter **9** turntable **10** blacksnake
racetrack: 5 Ascot **7** Belmont, Hialeah **10** Epsom Downs, Gulf Stream, Santa Anita
raceway: 5 canal **7** channel, fishway **8** millrace

Rachel: *children:* **6** Joseph **8** Benjamin
father: **5** Laban
husband: **5** Jacob
sister: **4** Leah
rachis: 4 stem **5** spine **7** spindle **8** backbone
rachitis: 7 rickets
racist: 5 bigot **9** sectarian
rack: bar, fly, gin, jib **4** bink, crib, gait, pace, path, scud, skin, tree **5** airer, brake, creel, flake, horse, stand, touse, trace, track, vapor **6** course, cratch, gantry, harass, strain, wrench **7** afflict, agonize, grating, oppress, pathway, stretch, torment, torture, vestige **9** framework, persecute **10** excruciate, foresaddle
racket: bat, din **4** shoe **5** bandy, dodge, noise, trick, work **6** bustle, clamor, crosse, hubbub, outcry, scheme, strike **7** clangor, clatter, pattern, revelry **8** business, snowshoe **10** battledore, turbulence **11** merrymaking
jai alai: **5** cesta
rack up: 4 gain **5** score **7** achieve **10** accomplish
rackle: 5 clank **6** rattle **7** clatter **8** reckless **9** impetuous **10** headstrong
raconteur: 8 narrator **11** storyteller
racy: 5 brisk, fiery, fresh, smart, spicy, swift **6** lively, risque **7** piquant, pungent, zestful **8** indecent, spirited, stirring, vigorous **10** suggestive **12** exhilarating
rad: 5 eager, quick, ready **6** afraid, elated **11** exhilarated
Radames' love: 4 Aida
radar: 15 detection system
image: **4** blip
screen: **5** scope
raddle: rod **4** beat **5** color, ocher, twist **6** branch, cudgel, thrash **9** separator **10** interweave
radial: ray **8** quadrant
radiance: 4 beam, glow **5** glare, gleam, glory, nitor, sheen, shine **6** luster **7** glitter, glowing, shining **8** lambency, splendor **9** brilliant **10** brightness, brilliancy, effulgence, refulgence
radiant: 6 bright **7** auroral **11** resplendent
radiate: 4 beam, emit **5** shine **6** spread **7** diffuse, emanate **9** coruscate **10** illuminate
radiating: 6 radial **8** stellate **11** centrifugal
radiation detector: 6 geiger
radiator: 6 heater
radical: red **4** root, surd **5** basal, basic, rebel, ultra **7** capital, drastic, extreme, forward, leftist, liberal, organic, support **8** cardinal, complete **9** extremist **10**

foundation, iconoclast **11** fundamental **12** intransigent **13** revolutionary

chemical: ion **4** amyl, aryl **6** acetyl, adenyl, adipyl **7** nitrate, nitrite, sulfate, tartryl **8** aluminyl

political: **9** anarchist, extremist **13** revolutionary

radicate: fix **4** root **5** plant **9** establish

radicle: **7** rootlet **9** hypocotyl

radio: set **8** portable, wireless **9** broadcast, radiogram **10** transistor **12** walkie-talkie

detector: **5** radar

frequency: **5** audio

interference: **6** static

operator: ham **6** sparks **11** broadcaster

part: **5** diode **8** detector, selector

rating: **6** Hooper

signal check: **7** monitor

wave: **5** micro, short

radish: **5** radis(F.) **7** cadlock **9** crossweed

radium: *discoverer:* **5** Curie

emanation: **5** niton, radon

source: **7** uranite

radius: ken **5** orbit, range, spoke, sweep **6** extent, length

pert. to: **6** radial

radix: **4** root **6** etymon **7** radical

raffish: low **4** wild **5** cheap **6** flashy, frowsy, tawdry **7** unkempt **9** worthless **11** disgraceful **12** disreputable

raffle: **4** raff **6** jumble, rabble, refuse, tangle **7** drawing, lottery, rubbish, serrate **8** entangle, riffraff

raft: cow, lot, mat **4** crib, floe, heap, moki, raff, slew, spar **5** balsa, barge, float **6** dinghy, jangar **9** catamaran, transport **10** collection

part: **5** brail

rider: **8** Huck Finn

raft duck: **5** scaup **7** redhead **8** bluebill

rafter: **4** balk, beam, firm, viga **7** carline, chevron

rag: jag, kid, rib **4** mock, rail, rate, tune **5** annoy, dance, scold, scrap, shred, tease **6** banter, harass, rumpus, tatter, uproar **7** quarrel, remnant, wrangle **9** newspaper

ragamuffin: bum **4** hobo, waif **5** tramp **6** loafer, orphan **9** scarecrow **14** tatterdemalion

rage: fad, ire **4** beef, fret, fume, funk, fury, heat, rant, rave, tear **5** anger, chafe, craze, furor, mania, storm, wrath **6** choler, fervor, frenzy, furore, temper **7** amentia, bluster, bombast, emotion, fashion, fervour, passion, thunder **8** acerbity, acrimony, insanity, violence **9** vehemence **10** enthusiasm

ragged: **5** harsh, rough, seedy **6** jagged, shaggy, uneven **7** shreddy, unkempt, worn out **8** strident, tattered **9** defec-

tive, dissonant, imperfect, irregular **10** straggling, threadbare, unfinished **11** dilapidated

ragged jacket: **4** seal

ragged lady: **5** guara **11** love-in-a-mist

ragged sailor: **10** bluebottle, cornflower

raggedy doll: Ann **4** Andy, Anne

raggle-taggle: **6** motley

raging: **4** grim, wild **5** rabid **6** fierce **7** fervent, furious **8** furibund **9** ferocious

raglan: **6** sleeve **8** overcoat

ragout: **4** hash, stew **5** salmi **6** salmis **7** goulash, haricot, terrine **8** salpicon **10** capilotade **11** gallimaufry

ragpicker: **6** bunter **10** chiffonier **11** chiffonnier(F.)

rags: **4** duds **6** shreds **7** clothes, tatters

ragshag: **10** ragamuffin **11** masquerader

ragwort: **5** plant **8** ambrosia **9** groundsel **10** butterweed

rah: **5** cheer **6** hurrah

raid: **4** bust, tala **5** foray **6** attack, creach(Sc.), creagh(Sc.), forage, harass, inroad, invade, maraud, piracy **7** assault, chappow, despoil, hership **8** invasion **9** chevachie, incursion, onslaught, roadstead, cavalcade

rail: bar, jaw **4** coot, flow, gush, jest, rant, rate, slat, sora **5** abuse, array, chide, cloak, crake, dress, guard, heron, plank, scoff, scold, soree, track **6** banter, berate, callet, revile, septum **7** arrange, bidcock, bilcock, clocker, footrest, garment, inveigh **8** decorate, Rallidae(pl.), reproach **9** spectator

genus of: **4** sora **6** rallus

railing: bar **5** fence **7** barrier, parapet **8** balconet, banister, espalier, rabulous **9** bannister, guardrail **10** balconette, balustrade **12** vituperation

raillery: **4** gaff **5** chaff, sport **6** banter, blague, satire **8** badinage, ridicule **10** persiflage

railroad: **4** herd, line, push, rush **5** hurry, track **8** ceinture, monorail **9** transport

branch: **4** spur, stub **6** feeder

bridge: **7** trestle, viaduct

car: **5** coach, diner **6** parlor **7** caboose, coal-car, parlour, Pullman, sleeper

center: **7** station **8** terminal, terminus **10** roundhouse

cross rail: **4** frog

flare: **5** fusee

signal: **5** fusee **9** semaphore

station: **4** gare(F.) **5** depot

switch: **4** frog

tie: **6** timber **7** sleeper

worker: **6** boomer, porter **7** fireman **8** brakeman, engineer, strapper **9** conductor

railway: **5** train **6** subway **8** elevated, jackstay, monorail **9** funicular

raiment: See **dress**

rain: dag, fog 4 mist, pour 5 blizz, blout, misle, plash, spate, storm 6 deluge, mizzle, serein, shower 7 drizzle 8 downpour, sprinkle 10 cloudburst 13 precipitation
check: 4 stub 12 postponement
fine: 4 mist 6 serein 7 drizzle
god: 8 Parjanya
icy: 4 hail, snow 5 sleet
pert. to: 7 pluvial
unit of measure: 4 inch

rain bird: 6 plover 7 tomfool

rain cloud: 5 nimbi(pl.) 6 nimbus

rain forest: 5 selva

rain gauge: 8 udometer 10 hyetometer 11 pluviograph, pluviometer 15 hyetometrograph

rain glass: 9 barometer

rain leader: 9 downspout

rain tree: 5 saman, zaman 6 zamang 8 genisaro 9 monkeypod

rainbow: arc, bow 4 iris
goddess: 4 Iris
measuring device: 12 spectrometer
pert. to: 6 iridal

rainbow chaser: 8 idealist 9 visionary 11 doctrinaire

rainbow-like: 6 iridal 10 iridescent

raincoat: mac 4 mino 6 poncho, ulster 7 slicker 10 mackintosh, trenchcoat

rainfall: *pert. to:* 6 hyetal

rainfowl: 6 cuckoo 10 woodpecker 11 channelbill

rainspout: 4 rone(Sc.)

rainy: wet 4 damp 5 moist 7 flooded 8 cluttery
season: 7 monsoon

raise: end 4 buoy, grow, hain, heft, hike, levy, lift, rear, rise, stir 5 arear, boost, breed, build, crane, dight, elate, erect, exalt, hance, heave, heeze, hoist, horse, rouse, set-up, start, trice 6 arouse, ascend, assume, awaken, cantle, create, emboss, excite, gather, incite, leaven, muster, obtain, remove, uplift 7 address, advance, bring up, chevise, collect, elevate, enhance, ennoble, lighten, present, procure, produce, promote 8 addition, heighten, increase 9 cultivate, establish, institute, intensify, originate, propagate, resurrect 10 aggrandize, appreciate, invigorate

raised: 4 hove 6 arrect, enleve(F.) 8 elevated

raisin: 5 lexia, zibeb 7 currant, sultana 8 muscatel

raison d'être: 14 reason for being

raj: 4 rule 5 reign 11 sovereignty

rajah: 4 king 5 chief 6 prince 9 dignitary
wife: 4 rani 5 ranee

Rajmahal creeper: 4 jiti, vine

rake: gad, rue, rut 4 path, raff, roue, rove, trip 5 claut, glean, scour, track 6 gather, groove 7 collect, gleaner, scratch 8 enfilade, rakehell 9 debauchee 11 inclination
with gunfire: 8 enfilade

rakehell: 4 wild 7 immoral 9 debauched, debauchee, dissolute 10 profligate

rake-off: 4 take 6 profit, rebate 10 commission, percentage

rakish: 4 lewd, pert 7 roguish 9 dissolute

rale: 6 rattle

rally: 4 drag, mock, stir 5 chaff, noise, rouse 6 arouse, attack, banter, deride, revive 7 recover, restore, reunite 8 assemble, mobilize, raillery, ridicule 10 recuperate, strengthen 11 concentrate

rallying cry: 5 motto 6 slogan 9 battle cry

ram: hit, pun, tup, wad 4 buck, butt, cram, tamp, teap 5 Aries, crash, sheep, stuff 6 batter, beetle, chaser, rancid, strike, thrust, wether 7 collide, plunger 8 bulldoze

ram cat: tom 4 male

ramage: 4 wild 5 bough, rough 6 unruly 7 untamed 8 branches, frenzied, wildness

ramage hawk: 8 brancher

Rama's bride: 4 Sita

ramate: 8 branched

ramble: gad 4 roam, rove, walk 5 jaunt, prowl, range 6 sprawl, stroll, travel, wander 7 digress, saunter 8 straggle 9 excursion

rambling: 7 cursory, devious 9 desultory, scattered, wandering 10 circuitous, discursive 11 peripatetic 12 disconnected

rambunctious: 4 wild 5 rough 6 unruly 9 turbulent 10 boisterous, disorderly, rampageous 12 obstreperous 14 uncontrollable

ramekin: pan 4 dish 9 casserole

ramentum: 5 palea, palet 6 paleae(pl.), scales 7 shaving 8 particle

ramie, ramee: 4 hemp, rhea 5 fiber 6 ortiga

ramification: arm 4 rami(pl.) 5 ramus 6 branch, spread 8 division, offshoot 9 branching 10 divergence 12 embranchment

rammish: 4 lewd, rank 7 violent

Ramona author: 7 Jackson

ramose: 7 cladose 8 branched 9 branching

ramp: rob 4 bank, rage, walk 5 apron, crawl, creep, slope, storm 6 dupery, unruly 7 incline, swindle 8 gradient, platform 9 helicline 10 cuckoopint

rampage: 5 binge, spree, storm 6 uproar 7 turmoil

rampageous: 4 wild 6 unruly 7 riotous 10 boisterous

rampant: 4 rife 6 fierce 7 violent 9 excessive, unchecked 10 immoderate, prevailing, rampageous, widespread 11 extravagant, flourishing, threatening, 12 unrestrained 14 uncontrollable

rampart: 4 wall 5 agger, mound, redan 6 vallum 7 barrier, bastion, bulwark, parapet, ravelin 10 embankment 13 fortification

part: 4 spur

ramper: 7 lamprey

rampire: dam 7 fortify, rampart 10 embankment, strengthen

Ramses' goddess: 4 Anta

ramshackle: 4 rude 5 loose, shaky 7 rickety 10 disorderly, dissipated, tumbledown

ramus: 6 branch 10 branchlike

rancel: 6 search 7 ransack

ranch: 4 casa, farm, tear 5 finca, pluck 7 acreage, scratch 8 estancia, hacienda 9 estantion

worker: 4 hand 5 owner 6 cowboy, farmer, gaucho 7 cowpoke, rancher 8 herdsman, ranchero(Sp.), ranchman

rancid: 4 rank, sour 5 musty, stale 6 frowsy, putrid 7 spoiled 8 stinking 9 obnoxious, offensive, repulsive 10 malodorous, unpleasant

rancor, rancour: ire 4 gall, hate 5 spite 6 enmity, grudge, hatred, malice 8 rankling 9 animosity, antipathy, hostility, virulence 10 bitterness

randan: row 4 boat 5 spree 6 uproar 7 rampage

random: 5 loose, stray 6 casual, chance 7 aimless 9 desultory, haphazard, hit-or-miss 10 accidental, fortuitous 11 purposeless

randy: 5 crude, revel, shrew 6 beggar, coarse, frolic, virago, vulgar 7 canvass 8 carousal 9 festivity 10 disorderly, licentious 12 unmanageable

range: ken, row 4 ally, area, farm, line, rank, roam, rove 5 align, aline, ambit, blank, class, field, gamut, orbit, order, reach, ridge, scope, space, stove, stray, sweep 6 extent, ramble, series, sphere, stroll, tether, wander 7 arrange, compass, explore, habitat, saunter 8 classify, distance 9 cookstove, grassland 11 systematize

range-finder: 6 stadia 9 mekometer, telemeter 10 trekometer

ranger: 4 seal 5 rover, sieve 6 keeper, warden 8 commando, wanderer

rangy: 8 gangling, spacious

rank: row 4 army, file, foul, line, rate, sort, tier 5 array, caste, cense, class, fetid, frank, genus, grade, gross, order, proud, range, space, utter 6 barony, coarse, degree, estate, gentry, mighty, rancid, rating, series, status, strong 7 caliber, calibre, calling, compeer, copious, corrupt, dignity, extreme, fertile, froward, glaring, haughty, noisome, obscene, overfed, peerage, precede, quality, rammish, rampant, station, stratum, swollen, violent 8 absolute, abundant, classify, division, eminence, estimate, flagrant, gentrice, headlong, indecent, palpable, position, powerful, vigorous 9 condition, downright, egregious, excessive, exuberant, formation, gradation, hierarchy, luxuriant, offensive, overgrown, plentiful 10 coordinate, malodorous 11 arrangement, distinction 14 classification

deprive of: 4 bust 5 break 6 depose 7 cashier

mark of: 6 stripe

military: PFC 5 major 7 captain, colonel, general, private 8 banneret, corporal, sergeant 10 lieutenant

rank and file: 6 member, plebes 9 common man 11 commonality

rankle: irk, vex 4 fret, gall 6 fester, obsess, plague 7 inflame 8 irritate, ulcerate

rann: 5 verse 6 stanza, strain

ransack: 4 loot, rake, sack 5 rifle, steal 6 search 7 pillage, rummage

ransom: buy, fee 5 atone, price 6 redeem, rescue 7 deliver, expiate, release 8 liberate, retrieve 13 consideration

money: 10 redemptory

rant: 4 fume, huff, rage, rail, rand, rave, riot, song, tune 5 dance, orate, revel, scold, spout 6 frolic, speech, steven 7 bluster, bombast, carouse, declaim, fustian 9 discourse 11 merrymaking, rodomontade 13 jollification

rantipole: 4 wild 6 rakish, unruly 9 termagant

ranula: 4 cyst 8 swelling

rap: bob, box, con, hit, tap 4 blow, chap, chat, grab, knap, talk, tirl 5 blame, clink, clout, knock, seize, smite, steal, utter 6 rebuke, snatch, strike, thwack 7 deliver 8 sentence 9 criticize, criticism, enrapture, transport 10 conference, punishment

rapacious: 6 fierce, greedy 8 covetous, grasping, ravening, ravenous 9 ferocious, voracious 10 avaricious, predacious

rapacity: 5 claim, ravin 7 edacity 8 appetite, cupidity, exaction 9 extortion

rape: 4 file, rasp 5 abuse, haste, hasty, hurry, quick, seize, spoil 6 defile, pomace, ravish, turnip 7 despoil, hastily, outrage, pillage, plunder, robbery, scratch, violate 9 violation 10 plundering, spoliation

rapeseed: 5 colza 7 ravison

Raphael: 5 angel 7 painter 9 archangel

raphe: 4 line, seam 5 joint 6 suture

rapid: 4 fast 5 agile, brisk, chute, fleet, quick, steep, swift 6 abrupt, moving, nimble, speedy 10 fastmoving 11 expeditions

rapidity: 5 haste, speed 8 celerity, velocity 9 quickness

rapidly: 4 fast 5 apace

rapier: 5 bilbo, sword 6 verdun 7 ricasso
blade heel: 7 ricasso
part of: 5 forte 6 foible

rapine: 7 pillage, plunder 10 spoliation

rapparee: 6 robber 8 vagabond 9 plunderer 10 freebooter

rappee: 5 snuff

rapport: 6 accord 7 harmony 8 affinity, relation 9 agreement 12 relationship

rapscallion: 5 rogue, scamp 6 rascal, wretch 7 villain 8 vagabond 11 ne'er-do-well 14 good-for-nothing

rapt: 4 deep 5 tense 6 intent 8 absorbed, ecstatic 9 comprised, enchanted, engrossed, entranced, transport 10 enraptured 11 preoccupied, transported

raptorial: 9 rapacious 11 accipitrine

raptorial bird: owl 4 hawk 5 eagle 7 vulture

rapture: 5 bliss 6 trance 7 delight, ecstasy 8 rhapsody 9 enrapture, happiness, transport 10 exultation

rara avis: 6 rarity, wonder 7 phoenix

rare: odd, raw 4 fine, good, nice, thin 6 choice, dainty, geason, scarce, seldom, unique 7 antique, capital, curious, extreme, special, tenuous, unusual 8 precious, uncommon, unwonted 9 beautiful, excellent, exclusive, exquisite, scattered, underdone 10 infrequent 11 distinctive, exceptional 13 distinguished, extraordinary

rarefied: 4 thin 7 diluted, ethered, gaseous, refined 8 aethered 10 attenuated

rarely: 5 extra 6 seldom 10 hardly ever

rarity: 5 curio, relic 6 geason, oddity 7 antique

ras: 4 cape 6 fabric, prince 7 fascist 8 headland 9 commander

rascal: boy, cad, imp 4 file, loon 5 foist, gipsy, gypsy, knave, rogue, scamp 6 ablach, budzat, coquin, harlot 7 budzart, glutton, villain 8 hosebird, scalawag, sealpeen, widdifow 9 miscreant, reprobate, scallawag, scoundrel, trickster 11 rapscallion

rascally: 4 base, mean 6 arrant 9 dishonest, worthless 11 furciferous, mischievous

rash: cut, mad 4 bold 5 brash, erase, hardy, hasty, heady, hives, scamp, shave, slash, uredo 6 daring, eczema, scrape,

unwary 7 foolish, hotspur, icarian, scratch 8 careless, epidemic, eruption, headlong, heedless, reckless, temerous 9 desperate, exanthema, foolhardy, foreright, hotheaded, impetuous, imprudent, overhasty, urticaria, venturous 10 headstrong, hotspurred, incautious, indiscreet, unthinking 11 adventurous, furthersome, harum-scarum, precipitate, precipitous, temerarious, thoughtless, venturesome 13 adventuresome, efflorescence

rasher: 5 slice 6 collop 7 portion 8 rockfish

rashness: 4 rage, rese 5 folly 6 acrisy 8 temerity 9 headiness

rasorial: 7 gnawing 10 scratching

rasp: rub 4 file 5 belch, eruct, grate 6 scrape 8 irritate

rasping: 5 harsh, raspy, rough 6 hoarse, rasion 7 raspish, raucous 8 guttural 9 offensive

rasse: 5 civet 6 weasel

rat: pad 4 scab, snot 6 defect, inform, rodent, vermin 8 betrayer, deserter, informer, renegade, squealer 9 councilor, counselor 11 stool-pigeon 13 double-crosser
catcher: 9 pied piper
genus: 6 spalax
kind: kok 5 metad, zemmi, zemni 6 tosher 7 hamster
poison: 7 arsenic 8 ratsbane

ratafia: 4 noyau 7 biscuit, cordial, liqueur 8 macaroon

rataplan: 8 drumbeat

ratch: bar 4 rend 7 stretch 8 distance

ratchet: 4 pawl 5 click 6 bobbin, detent

rate: fee, tax 4 earn, fare, file, pace, rank 5 abuse, blame, chide, class, grade, price, scold, score, tempo, value 6 assess, assize, charge, degree, reckon, regard, tariff 7 account, censure, chasten, despise, quality, reprove 8 appraise, classify, consider, estimate, evaluate 10 proportion 14 classification

rate of exchange: 4 agio 5 batta

ratel: 6 badger, burier

ratfish: 8 chimaera

rathe, rath: 4 soon 5 eager, early, quick 6 prompt, speedy 7 betimes 8 promptly, speedily

rather: 5 prior 6 before, choice, enough, in lieu, pretty, sooner 7 earlier, instead, quickly 8 somewhat 10 preferably, preference 11 immediately

rather than: ere 6 before

ratify: 4 amen, pass, seal 6 affirm, enseal, verify 7 approve, confirm, endorse, license 8 roborate, sanction 9 authorize, establish

rating: 4 rank 5 cense, class, grade 6 rebuke **8** estimate, scolding, standing **9** reprimand **10** evaluation **14** classification

ratio: cos **4** rate, sine **5** quota, share **6** cosine, degree, ration **7** average, portion **8** relation **10** percentage, proportion **11** capacitance

ratiocination: 5 logic **7** thought **8** argument **9** inference, reasoning

ration: 4 dole, food, meed, mete **5** allot, quota, ratio, share **6** divide **7** portion **8** relation **9** allotment, allowance, apportion **10** distribute **11** calculation

rational: 4 sane **5** sober, sound **7** logical, prudent **8** sensible **10** reasonable **11** intelligent, level-headed **13** philosophical

rational integer: 4 norm

rational principle: 5 logos

rationale: 6 reason **11** explanation

rations: 8 buckshee **10** provisions

ratite: emu, moa **4** bird, emeu **7** ostrich **9** cassowary
genus: **7** apteryx **8** dinornis

ratoon: 5 shoot, stalk **6** spring, sprout

rattail: 4 file **5** braid **7** pigtail

rattan: 4 cane, lash, palm, sega, whip **5** noose, thong **6** punish, switch, wicker

ratter: cat, dog **8** betrayer

rattle: din **4** birl, chat, rale, rick, stun, tirl **5** addle, annoy, clack, rouse, scold, upset **6** assail, bicker, maraca, racket, uproar **7** agitate, chatter, clapper, clatter, clitter, confuse, fluster, gnatter, shatter **9** crepitate, embarrass **10** disconcert

rattlebrained: 5 dizzy, giddy, silly **7** flighty **9** frivolous **11** empty-headed, harebrained

rattlepate: ass **4** dolt **9** chatterer

rattleroot: 7 bugbane

rattlesnake: 8 cascavel, crotalus **9** sistrurus **10** massasauga

rattlesnake fern: 9 sporangia

rattlesnake herb: 9 baneberry

rattlesnake pilot: 10 copperhead

rattle-top: 7 bugbane

rattletrap: 5 ratty **7** gewgaws, rickety **10** ramshackle **11** knickknacks

ratty: 4 mean **6** shabby **7** unkempt **11** dilapidated

ratwa: 7 muntjac

raucous: dry **4** loud **5** gruff, harsh, noisy, rough **6** coarse, hoarse **7** braying, brusque, rasping **8** strident **9** turbulent **11** cacophonous

raun: roe **5** spawn

raupo: 7 cattail

ravage: eat **4** loot, prey, ruin, sack **5** foray, harry, havoc, spoil, waste **6** forage **7** despoil, destroy, overrun, pillage, plunder, scourge, violate **8** deflower, desolate, lay waste **9** devastate **10** depopulate, desolation **11** despoilment, devastation

rave: 4 rage, rant **5** blurb, crush, orate, storm **7** bluster, bombast, declaim, enthuse **8** harangue **11** infatuation **12** commendation

ravel: run **4** comb, fray, rail **5** snarl **6** runner, sleave, tangle, unwind **7** crumble, involve, perplex, railing, untwist, unweave **8** entangle, separate **10** complicate **11** disentangle

ravelin: 8 demilune **13** fortification

raveling: 4 lint **6** thread

raven: 4 crow **5** black **9** blackbird
genus: **5** corvus
of Odin: **5** Hugin

Raven: *author:* Poe
character: **6** Lenore
refrain: **9** Nevermore

ravenous: 6 greedy, hungry, lupine, toothy **7** starved **8** edacious, famished **9** cormorant, ferocious, rapacious, voracious **10** catawampus, gluttonous

ravine: cut, den, gap, lin **4** dell, ghyl, gill, linn, sike, wadi, wady **5** abyss, canon, chasm, chine, clove, ditch, flume, glack, gorge, goyal, goyle, griff, grike, gulch, gully, kloof, notch, strid **6** arroyo, canyon, cleuch, clough, coulee, gulley, hollow, nullah **7** crevice, dry wash **8** barranca, barranco, quebrado **10** depression

raving: 8 frenzied **9** delirious **10** incoherent, irrational **12** arreptitious

ravish: rob **4** rape **5** abuse, charm, force, harry, seize **6** defile, snatch **7** afforce, corrupt, delight, despoil, enchant, plunder, violate **8** deflower, entrance **9** captivate, constrain, enrapture, transport

ravishment: 7 ecstasy, rapture **9** transport

raw: 4 cold, damp, dazy(Sc.), lash, nude, rare, rude **5** bawdy, bleak, chill, crude, green, harsh, naked **6** abrade, chilly, coarse, unfair **7** cutting, natural, obscene **8** immature, indecent, uncooked **9** inclement, unexposed, unrefined, unskilled, untrained **10** indelicate, unfinished, unprepared, unseasoned **11** uncivilized, unpracticed, unprocessed **12** uncultivated **13** inexperienced

rawboned: 4 lean **5** gaunt **7** angular, scrawny

rawhide: 4 pelt, whip **5** knout, quirt, thong

ray: 4 beam, beta, dorn, soil **5** array, dress, flair, gleam, gleed, light, manta, order, shaft, shine, sight, skate **6** defile, glance, obispo, radial, streak, stripe, vision **7** besmear, homelyn, radiate, raiment **9** irradiate, selachian **10** perception, vertebrate **11** arrangement, irradiation

fish: **4** dorn **5** skate
penetrating: **5** gamma
rayon: 5 moire, ninon, tulle **6** faille, pongee **7** taffeta
yarn size: **6** denier
raze, rase: cut, rub **4** rage, ruin, tear **5** erase, graze, growl, level, shave, wreck **6** efface, incise, scrape **7** destroy, scratch, subvert **8** demolish, dismantle **9** deprecate, overthrow, prostrate **10** obliterate
razee: cut **5** prune **6** reduce **7** abridge
razor: 4 clam **6** shaver
kind: **7** rattler **8** electric
sharpen: **4** hone **5** strop
razorback: hog **5** ridge **10** roustabout
razorbill: auk **7** skimmer
razor stone: 10 novaculite
razz: 5 chaff, tease **6** banter, deride, heckle **8** ridicule
razzle-dazzle: 5 spree **7** confuse **8** hilarity **9** confusion
re: 5 anent **9** regarding **10** concerning
Re: See **Ra**
reach: ken, run, toe **4** come, gain, hawk, hent, ryke(Sc.), seek, span, spit **5** get to, grasp, retch, scope, vomit **6** advene, affect, amount, arrive, attain, extend, extent, strive **7** achieve, contact, expanse, possess, stretch **8** approach, make up to **9** culminate, penetrate **10** accomplish
under: **7** subtend
reachable: 10 accessible
reaching: 6 effort **8** profound
reaction: 4 kick **5** start **6** answer **7** tropism **8** response **9** influence **10** impression, opposition
adverse: **8** backlash
read: con **4** lire(F.), pore, scan, show, skim, tell **5** aread, areed, drone, guess, solve, study **6** advise, browse, peruse, relate **7** counsel, declare, discern, foresee, learned **8** decipher, describe, foretell, indicate **9** interpret, supervise
ability to: **8** literacy
inability to: **6** alexia **8** dyslexia
metrically: **4** scan
superficially: **4** skim
readable: 7 legible
reader: 6 lector, lister, primer **7** reciter **8** bookworm, lectrice, lecturer **9** anthology, **10** instructor **11** proofreader **12** elocutionist
readily: 4 well **6** easily, freely **7** lightly
readiness: art **4** ease, gift **6** graith **7** address, freedom **8** alacrity, facility, goodwill, volition **9** dexterity, eagerness, quickness **10** promptness, volubility **12** preparedness
reading: 6 lesson **7** lection, lecture, perusal, recital, version **9** collation, rendition **10** prelection

ready; apt, fit **4** free, gird, glib, here, pret(F.), ripe **5** alert, apert, bound, eager, handy, happy, point, quick **6** active, adroit, facile, fluent, prompt **7** forward, prepare, willing **8** cheerful, dextrous, handsome, prepared, skillful **9** agreeable, available, dexterous **10** convenient **11** expeditious **12** unhesitating
real: 4 very, true, vrai(F.) **5** being, loyal **6** actual, hearty **7** certain, cordial, factual, genuine, gradely, literal, sincere **8** existent, faithful, tangible **9** authentic, effective, heartfelt, intrinsic, unfeigned, veritable **10** unaffected
real estate: 4 alod **5** allod, lands **6** realty **8** allodium, freehold, premises, property **13** hereditaments
claim: tax **4** lien **8** mortgage **9** trust deed **11** encumbrance
pert. to: **7** predial
realistic: 5 vivid **6** shrewd **7** prudent **8** lifelike **11** down-to-earth **12** matter-of-fact
realization: 8 fruition **9** awakening
realize: get **4** gain, know **5** sense, think **6** effect, obtain **7** achieve, acquire, convert, fulfill **8** complete, conceive **9** apprehend **10** accomplish, appreciate, understand
really: aru **4** very, well **5** quite, sooth **6** indeed **8** actually
realm: 4 land **5** bourn, clime, range **6** bourne, circle, domain, empire, region, sphere **7** country, demesne, dynasty, kingdom, terrene **8** division, dominion, province **9** territory **10** department **11** sovereignty **12** jurisdiction
realty: 7 honesty, loyalty, royalty **8** fidelity, property **10** possession
ream: 4 bore, draw, foam, scum **5** bevel, cheat, cream, froth, widen **7** enlarge, stretch **8** quantity **11** countersink
reamer: 4 tool **5** borer, drift **6** broach
reanimate: 5 rally, renew **6** revive **11** resuscitate **12** reinvigorate
reap: cut **4** crop, rake **5** glean **6** garner, gather **7** acquire, collect, harvest
rear: aft, end, fix **4** back, buck, cave, grow, last, lift, rere, tail **5** abaft, breed, build, erect, nurse, raise, stern, train **6** astern, behind, foster, nursle **7** arriere(F.), bring up, buttocks, educate, elevate, nurture **9** construct, establish, posterior **10** background, forthbring
toward: aft **5** abaft **6** astern
rearing by horse: 5 stend **6** pesade
rearhorse: 6 insect, mantis
rearward: 8 backward **9** posterior **10** retrograde
reason: peg, why, wit **4** mind, nous **5** argue, brain, cause, logic, sense, think **6** debate, ground, motive, ponder, sanity

7 meaning **8** argument, converse **9** discourse, intellect, rationale, wherefore **10** moderation, understand **11** explanation, expostulate, ratiocinate, rationality, rationalize **12** plausibility **13** consideration, understanding

alleged: **7** pretext

deprived of: **8** demented

pert. to: **6** noetic

want of: **5** folie **7** amentia, madness **8** insanity

reasonable: 4 fair, just **5** cheap **8** feasible, moderate, rational **9** equitable **11** inexpensive

reasoning: 5 logic **8** argument **10** conclusion **13** argumentation

basis of: **7** premise

reassure: 5 cheer **7** comfort, hearten **9** encourage

reata, riata: 4 rope **5** lasso **6** lariat

reave: rob **4** tear **5** burst, seize, split **7** bereave, pillage, plunder, unravel

rebate: 5 check **6** lessen, reduce, refund, weaken **8** diminish, discount, kickback **9** abatement, deduction, reduction, remission

rebato: See **rabato**

rebec: 4 lyre **5** sarod, rebab **6** fiddle, violin

Rebekah: *brother:* **5** Laban

father: **7** Bethuel

husband: **5** Isaac

mother: **6** Milcah

son: **4** Esau **5** Jacob

rebel: 4 rise **6** oppose, revolt, rise up **8** renegade **9** adversary, insurgent **10** antagonist

rebellion: 6 mutiny, putsch, revolt **8** defiance, sedition, uprising **10** resistance, revolution **12** disobedience, insurrection, renunciation **15** insubordination

rebellious: 9 estranged **10** refractory **12** contumacious, recalcitrant **13** insubordinate

rebirth: 7 revival **10** conversion, renascence **11** renaissance **13** reincarnation

reboant: 7 echoing **13** reverberating

rebound: dap **4** echo, stot **5** bound, carom **6** bounce, carrom, recoil, re-echo, resile, return, spring **7** recover, reflect, resound **8** ricochet, snap back **9** boomerang **11** reverberate

rebuff: cow **4** scat, slap, snub **5** check, chide, fling, repel, scold, spurn **6** lesson **7** censure, fend off, refusal, reprove, repulse **9** rejection, reprimand

rebuke: nip, rap, tsk, tut, wig **4** beat, snub, tush **5** barge, blame, check, chide, scold **6** berate, dirdum, lesson, rating **7** downset, lecture, repress, reproof, reprove **8** admonish, chastise, reproach, restrain **9** criticism, criticize, repre-

hend, reprimand, talking-to **10** correction **11** comeuppance, reprobation

rebus: 6 enigma, puzzle, riddle

rebut: 5 reply **6** oppose, rebuff, refute, revile **7** fend off, repulse **8** disprove **10** contradict

recalcitrant: 5 rebel **6** unruly **7** defiant **8** stubborn **9** obstinate, resisting **10** rebellious, refractory

recall: 5 annul **6** abjure, cancel, encore, memory, remind, repeal, revoke **7** abolish, bethink, rescind, restore, retrace, retract, summons **8** remember, withdraw **9** recollect, reminisce **11** countermand

recant: 6 abjure, revoke **7** abandon, disavow, retract **8** renounce, take back, withdraw **9** repudiate **10** contradict

recapitulate: sum **5** essay **6** repeat, review **7** restate **8** argument **9** enumerate, reiterate, summarize

recapture: 6 recall, regain, retake **7** recover **9** reacquire

recede: ebb **6** depart, retire **7** deviate, regress, retreat **8** decrease, fall back, withdraw **10** retrograde

receipt: 4 chit, stub, take **6** acquit, apocha, binder, recipe **7** formula **11** acquittance **14** acknowledgment **15** acknowledgement

receipts: 6 income **7** revenue **8** payments

receive: get **4** take **5** admit, adopt, greet, **6** accept, assume, derive, obtain, take in **7** acquire, procure

receiver: 4 host **5** donee, fence **6** pernor, porter **7** breaker, catcher, hostess, rentier **8** cymaphen, receptor **9** collector, condenser, treasurer **12** receptionist

of property in trust: **6** bailee **7** trustee

of stolen goods: **5** fence

recension: 6 review **8** revision **9** reviewing **11** enumeration, examination

recent: new **4** late **5** fresh **6** modern **7** current **8** neoteric

recently: 4 anew **8** latterly

receptacle: bin, box, can, cup, fat, pan, pot, tub, urn, vat **4** case, cell, cist, crib, font, pail, tray, vase, well, tank **5** basin, chest, torus **6** basket, bottle, bucket, carton, holder, hopper, trough **7** cistern, humidor, pitcher **8** canister, receiver **9** container, reservoir

reception: tea **5** levee, party **6** accoil, durbar, soiree **7** accueil, ovation, receipt, welcome **8** greeting **9** admission, collation **10** admittance **13** entertainment

morning: **5** levee

place: **4** hall **5** atria(pl.), foyer, salon **6** atrium, parlor **7** parlour **9** vestibule

receptive: 8 amenable **9** acceptant **10** hospitable, open-minded **11** sympathetic

receptor: 5 basin 8 receiver 10 dispositor, sense organ 11 nerve ending

recess: ala, bay 4 apse, cave, cove, grot, hole, nook 5 ambry, cleft, crypt, niche, sinus 6 alcove, closet, grotto, rabbet, retire 7 adjourn, conceal, retreat, seclude 8 dissolve, interval, vacation 9 cessation, embrasure, suspension

recessive: 8 backward, receding

Rechab's son: 7 Jonadab

recherché: new 4 rare 5 fresh, novel 6 choice, exotic 7 unusual 8 uncommon 9 exquisite 10 farfetched

recidivation: 7 relapse 8 apostasy 11 backsliding

recipe: 7 formula, pattern, receipt 12 prescription

recipient: 4 heir 5 donee 7 alienee, devisee, legatee 8 receiver 9 receiving, receptive

reciprocal: 4 mate, twin 6 mutual 9 alternate 11 convertible, correlative

reciprocate: 5 bandy, repay 6 return 7 requite 8 exchange, give back 9 alternate 10 recompense 11 countervail, interchange

recital: 4 saga, tale 5 story 6 report 7 account, concert, program 8 relation 9 narration, narrative, rehearsal, statement 10 recitation, repetition 11 declamation, description, enumeration

recitation: 7 reading

recitative: 5 scena 9 narrative

recite: say 4 carp, scan, tell 5 chant, spout 6 intone, relate 7 recount 9 enumerate 10 cantilate 12 recapitulate

reciter: 6 anteri, diseur(F.) 7 diseuse(F.) 8 narrator 12 elocutionist

reck: 4 care, deem, heed, mind 7 concern 8 consider, estimate

reckless: 4 bold, rash 5 blind, folle, perdu 6 madcap, perdue 7 hotspur 8 careless, headlong, heedless 9 blindfold, bodacious, daredevil, desperate, dissolute, hotheaded, imprudent 10 neglectful, regardless 11 adventurous, extravagant, harum-scarum, indifferent, thoughtless 13 inconsiderate, irresponsible

reckon: 4 aret, date, deem, rate, rely, tell 5 audit, count, guess, think 6 arette, impute, number, regard, repute 7 account, ascribe, compute, include, suppose, surmise 8 consider, estimate, numerate 9 calculate, enumerate 10 adjudicate, understand 11 connumerate

reckoner: 5 abaci, brain 6 abacus 9 tabulator 10 calculator 11 comptometer

reckoning: 4 bill, rate, scot, shot 5 chalk, score 6 compot, esteem 11 computation

machine: I.B.M. 5 adder, brain 6 abacus 9 tabulator 10 calculator

reclaim: 4 save, tame 5 train 6 ransom, recall, redeem, reform, repair, rescue, revoke 7 recover, restore, salvage 8 civilize, empolder 10 regenerate 11 domesticate

reclaimed land: 6 polder

recline: lay, lie, sit 4 lean, loll, rest 5 slant 6 repose 7 incline

reclining: 5 lying, prone 6 supine 7 leaning, lolling, passive, resting 8 reposing 9 accumbent, recumbent

recluse: nun 4 monk 6 hermit, hidden, secret 7 eremite 8 anchoret, secluded, solitary 9 anchoress, anchorite, cloistral 10 cloistered 11 sequestered

recognition: 4 fame 6 credit 9 awareness

recognize: ken, own, see 4 avow, know, note, spot 5 admit, greet 6 accept, acknow, agnize, beknow, notice, recall, remark, review, revise, salute 7 consent, correct, recover 8 identify, perceive 9 apprehend 10 appreciate 11 acknowledge, distinguish

recoil: shy 4 kick 5 quail, wince 6 blanch, flinch, shrink 7 rebound, retreat, reverse, squinch 8 withdraw

recollect: 4 cite 5 waken 6 recall 7 bethink 8 remember 9 remininisce

recollection: 4 mind 6 memory 8 memorial 9 anamnesis 11 remembrance 12 reminiscence

recommence: 5 renew 6 resume 7 reprise

recommend: 4 tout 5 refer 6 advise, commit, denote 7 commend, consign, counsel, entrust 8 advocate

recommit: 6 remand

recompense: fee, pay 5 repay 6 amends, bounty, reward, salary 7 premium, requite 8 requital 9 gratulate, indemnify, reimburse, repayment 10 compensate, remunerate, reparation 11 reciprocate, restitution, retribution 12 compensation, remuneration 13 consideration, gratification

without: 4 free 6 gratis

reconcile: 4 wean 5 adapt, agree, atone 6 accord, adjust, pacify, regain, settle, shrive, square 7 absolve, conform, expiate, explain, restore, reunite, satisfy 9 harmonize, make peace 10 conciliate, propitiate

recondite: 4 dark, deep 6 heavy, hidden, mystic, occult, secret 7 cryptic, obscure 8 abstract, abstruse, esoteric, profound 9 concealed

reconnaissance: 5 recce 6 survey

reconnoiter: spy 5 scout 6 recall, survey 7 examine, explore, inquire 8 discover

record: log, tab 4 acta(pl.), book, dope, file, memo, note, past, roll, show 5 actum, album, annal, chart, diary, enrol, enter, entry, graph, score 6 agenda, enroll, legend, memoir, postea, report **7** account, archive, blotter, calends, catalog, dossier, estreat, history, journal, kalends, rotulet **8** calendar, document, memorial, register **9** catalogue, chronicle, itinerary, narration **10** background, chronology, memorandum, transcribe, transcript

historical: **6** annals

holder: **4** file **6** binder **7** cabinet

keeper: **8** recorder **9** registrar

of arrest: **7** blotter

of meeting: **7** minutes

of proceedings: **4** acta(pl.) **7** minutes

of ship: log

of travel: **9** itinerary

official: **4** acta(pl.) **5** actum

personal: **5** diary **7** journal

recorder: **5** flute, judge **8** greffier, register **9** cartulary, registrar **10** chartulary

recording: **5** album, label **7** cutting

recording device: **4** tape **5** meter

recount: **4** deem, tell **5** count **6** recite, reckon, relate, repeat, retail **7** account, include, narrate **8** describe, rehearse **9** enumerate

recoup: **7** recover **9** indemnify, reimburse **10** compensate, recuperate

recover: get **5** amend, rally, upset **6** obtain, recoup, reform, regain, rescue, resume, retake **7** balance, get back, reclaim, recruit, restore, salvage **8** overcome, retrieve, snap back **9** repossess **10** bounce back, compensate, convalesce, recuperate

recovery: **4** cure **8** comeback **13** convalescence

law: **6** trover

recreant: **5** false **6** coward, craven, crying, wretch, yellow **7** traitor **8** apostate, betrayer, cowardly, deserter, disloyal, renegade, yielding **9** faithless **10** traitorous, unfaithful **11** disaffected **12** mean-spirited

recreation: **4** meal, play **5** dance, hobby, sport **6** picnic **7** renewal **9** amusement, avocation, diversion **10** relaxation **11** delassement, refreshment **12** regeneration **13** divertisement, entertainment

time: **6** recess **7** holiday **8** vacation

recrement: **4** scum, slag **5** dregs, dross, spume **6** refuse, scoria

recruit: **4** bleu(F.), boot **5** raise, renew, rooky **6** gather, muster, novice, revive, rookie, supply **7** draftee, private, recover, refresh, restore, soldier **8** assemble, bezonian, inductee, renovate **9** reinforce, replenish **10** recuperate, strengthen

rectangle: **6** oblong, square

rectifier: **5** diode

rectify: **5** amend, emend, right **6** adjust,

better, purify, refine, reform, remedy, repair **7** correct, distill, rebuild **8** emendate, regulate **10** straighten

rectitude: **6** equity, virtue **7** fitness, honesty **8** goodness **10** straitness **11** uprightness **12** straightness

rector: **4** head **5** chief, ruler **6** leader, priest **7** proctor **8** director, governor, minister **9** clergyman, conrector **10** headmaster, proproctor

rectory: **5** manse **8** benefice **9** parsonage

recumbent: **4** idle **5** lying, prone **7** leaning, resting **8** inactive, reposing **9** reclining

recuperate: **4** heal, rest **5** rally **6** perk up, regain **7** improve, recover **10** convalesce

recur: **6** advert, repeat, resort, return **7** iterate, rearise, **8** reappear

recurrent, recurring: **6** cyclic **7** chronic **9** returning **10** isochronal **11** reappearing **12** intermittent

recusant: **9** dissenter **11** dissentient **12** non-conformer

red: **4** lake, puce, rosy, ruby **5** canna, color, coral, fiery, gules, peony, roset, ruddy **6** cerise, cherry, claret, garnet, maroon, rubric, sienna, titian **7** carmine, crimson, glowing, leftist, magenta, nacarat, radical, roseate, Russian, scarlet **8** amaranth, blushing, inflamed, rubicund **9** anarchist, bloodshot, Bolshevik, communist, Muscovite, vermilion **10** erubescent **11** incarnadine **12** bloodstained

antique: **5** canna

brown: **5** sepia **6** russet, sorrel

dye: aal, lac **4** chay, choy **5** aurin, eosin **6** aurine **8** morindin

marked with: **6** rubric

purplish: **4** lake **6** claret

Venetian: **5** siena **6** sienna

yellow: **4** lama **5** aloma, brass, ochre, tenne **6** alesan, orange **7** saffron **9** alabaster, peachblow

red ape: **9** orangutan

red arsenic: **7** realgar

red-backed sandpiper: **6** dunlin

red bell: **9** columbine

red-bellied snipe: **9** dowitcher

red benjamin: **9** birthroot

red-blooded: **8** vigorous

red blotch: **10** adustiosis

red box: **8** official **12** bureaucratic

red bug: **7** chigger

red cedar: **5** savin **6** sabine, savine **7** juniper **8** flindosa

red cell: **11** erythrocyte

red chalk: **4** bole **6** ruddle

red cobalt: **9** erythrite

red copper ore: **7** cuprite

red corpuscle deficiency: **6** anemia

Red Cross founder: 6 Barton
Red Cross Knight: 6 George
wife: Una
red deer: roe **4** hart, hind, spay, stag
red-faced: 7 blowzed, flushed **8** blushing
red fever: 10 erysipelas
red fir: 4 pine **6** spruce **7** Douglas
red gum: 10 eucalyptus, strophulus
red-handed: 6 openly
red honeysuckle: 5 sulla
red-hot: 8 up-to-date
red lead ore: 8 corcoite
red-letter: 10 noteworthy
red man: 6 Indian
red-neck: 4 hick, rube **5** yokel **6** rustic
red pepper: 5 chile, chili **6** chilli
red perch: 8 rosefish
Red Planet: 4 Mars
Red Sea: 9 Erythrean
gulf: **4** Suez **5** Aqaba
island: **5** Perim
peninsula: **5** Sinai
red viper: 10 copperhead
red willow: 5 osier **6** cornel
redact: 4 edit **5** draft, frame **6** reduce, revise
redan: 7 rampart **8** fortress **10** breastwork **13** fortification
redbelly: 4 char **7** grouper **8** terrapin
redbird: 7 tanager **8** cardinal **9** bullfinch
redbird cactus: 7 jewbush
redbreast: 5 robin
redbud tree: 5 judas
redcap: 6 porter **7** carrier, specter, spectre **8** tarboosh **9** goldfinch, policeman
redden: 5 blush, flush, rouge
redeem: buy **4** free, save **6** ransom, regain, rescue **7** deliver, fulfill, reclaim, recover, release, restore **8** liberate **10** compensate, repurchase
redeye: 4 rudd **5** vireo **6** whisky **7** sunfish, whiskey **8** rock bass **10** copperhead
redhead: 5 finch **7** pochard **10** woodpecker
redmouth: 4 fish **5** grunt
redolence: 4 balm, odor **5** aroma, odour, scent, smell, **7** bouquet, perfume **9** fragrance, sweetness
redouble: 6 reecho, repeat **7** reprise, retrace **9** intensify **10** ingeminate
redoubt: 4 fort **6** schanz **10** breastwork, stronghold **13** fortification
redoubtable: 5 dread **6** famous **7** fearful **8** fearsome **10** formidable
redound: 5 react **6** accrue, recoil **7** conduce, resound **10** contribute **11** reverberate
redress: 5 amend, emend **6** adjust, relief, remedy **7** correct, relieve **10** compensate, reparation **12** compensation, satisfaction

redshank: 4 bird, clee **9** sandpiper
redshirt: 9 anarchist **11** Garibaldian **13** revolutionist
reduce: cut **4** bant, bate, bust, diet, ease, pare, raze, thin **5** abase, abate, annul, break, level, lower, scale, slash, smelt **6** appall, change, debase, demote, depose, derate, dilute, equate, humble, impair, lessen, rebate, refine, subdue, weaken **7** abridge, assuage, commute, conquer, curtail, cut back, degrade, deplete, whittle **8** attemper, condense, contract, decrease, diminish, discount, emaciate, minimize, retrench, slim down **9** subjugate **10** annihilate, bantingize, depreciate
to half: **9** dimidiate
sail: **4** reef
reduction: cut **5** slice **6** rebate **7** cut back, cutting, meiosis **8** analysis, discount **9** attrition **11** contraction, degradation **12** annihilation
redundancy: 7 nimiety **8** pleonasm, verbiage **8** plethora **9** verbosity **10** flatulence **11** periphrasis, superfluity
redundant: 5 wordy **6** lavish, prolix **7** copious, diffuse, verbose **9** excessive, exuberant **10** pleonastic **11** overflowing, superfluous **12** overabundant, tautological **13** superabundant **17** circumlocutionary
redwing: 6 thrush **7** gadwall **9** blackbird, francolin
redwood: 4 tree **7** Sequoia **9** evergreen
Ree: 7 Arikara
re-echo: rebound, resound **8** resonate **11** reverberate
reed: sag **4** dart, junk, pipe, sley, stem **5** arrow, grass, spear, stalk **7** bulrush, calamus, fistula
loom: **4** sley
reed organ: 8 melodeon **9** harmonium
reedbird: 7 warbler **8** bobolink
reedbuck: kob **4** koba **5** bohor, nagor **7** reitbok **8** antelope **9** waterbuck
reeder: 8 thatcher
reedy: 4 thin, weak **11** arundineous
reef: bar, cay, key **4** cayo, itch, lode, vein **5** atoll, mange, shoal **6** boiler **7** bioherm, shorten **8** eruption
mining: **4** lode, vein
sail: **4** furl **7** shorten
reefer: 4 coat, eton **5** miner **6** jacket, oyster **9** cigarette **10** midshipman
reek: rig **4** emit, fume, heap, pile, vent **5** equip, exude, smell, smoke, steam, vapor **6** exhale, stench **7** seaweed **8** mountain **10** exhalation
reel: 4 drum, pirn(Sc.), roll, spin, sway, swim, wind **5** dance, lurch, spool, swift, swing, waver, whirl, wince **6** bobbin, careen, hammer, teeter, totter, wintle **7**

stagger, stumble 8 titubate, windlass
fishing: 4 pirn
reem: 4 moan, uris 7 unicorn
reeve: pen 4 pass, wind 5 twist 6 pucker,
thread 7 bailiff, provost, steward, wrinkle 8 overseer 9 enclosure, sheepfold
refection: 4 food, meal 5 drink, lunch 6
repast 11 refreshment
refectory: 4 mess 10 dining hall
monastery: 6 frater
refer: 4 cite, harp, send 5 recur 6 advert,
allude, appeal, assign, charge, commit,
direct, impute, regard, relate, return,
submit 7 ascribe, bring up, consult,
mention, specify 8 identify 9 affiliate,
appertain, attribute
referee: 5 judge 6 decide, umpire 7 arbiter 8 mediator 10 arbitrator
decision: nod
reference: 5 quote 6 aspect 7 respect 9
relevance 10 connection, pertinence 11
credentials 12 relationship 13 recom-
mendance 14 recommendation
mark: 4 star 6 dagger 8 asterisk
reference book: 5 atlas 7 almanac 8
handbook, syllabus 9 thesaurus 10 dictionary 12 encyclopedia
referendum: 4 poll, vote 7 mandate 10
plebiscite
refine: 4 edit 5 exalt, smelt 6 decoct, filter, finish, polish, purify 7 clarify,
cleanse, concoct, elevate, improve, perfect 8 chastise, separate 9 cultivate,
elaborate, subtilize 12 spiritualize
refined: 4 nice 5 civil 6 artful, chaste, polite, urbane 7 courtly, elegant, genteel 8
delicate, graceful, highbred 9 courteous,
exquisite 10 fastidious
refinement: 5 grace 6 polish 7 culture,
dignity, finesse
refining cup: 5 cupel
reflect: 4 echo, muse, pore 5 glass, image,
study, think, weigh 6 divert, mirror,
ponder 7 bethink, deflect 8 cogitate,
consider, meditate, ruminate 9 reproduce 10 deliberate 11 contemplate, reverberate
reflected: 7 derived 8 mirrored, specular
reflection: 4 idea 5 image 6 musing 7
thought 8 likeness 10 cogitation, meditation, rumination 12 deliberation 13
consideration, contemplation
measuring device: 11 albedograph
reflective: 7 pensive 11 thoughtful
reflex: 4 bend, fold, turn 11 involuntary
reflux: ebb 6 ebbing, euripi(pl.), reflow 7
euripus 9 refluence, returning
reform: 4 mend, trim 5 amend, emend,
prune, renew 6 better, direct, punish,
remass, repair, revise 7 censure, correct,
improve, rebuild, reclaim, rectify, redress, reprove, reshape, restore 8 in-

struct 10 regenerate 11 reformation
refract: 6 impair 7 deflect, reflect 8 diminish 9 break down
refraction: *device:* 4 lens 5 prism 9 telescope
pert. to: 10 anaclastic
refractory: 6 immune, unruly 7 froward,
restive 8 contrary, perverse, stubborn 9
camsteary, camsteery, obstinate 10
headstrong rebellious, unyielding 11
contrarious, disobedient, intractable,
stiff-necked 12 contumacious, ungovernable, unmanageable, unresponsive
13 insusceptible
refrain: bob 4 curb, deny, shun 5 avoid,
cease, check, epode, forgo 6 chorus,
forego, govern 7 abstain, forbear, inhibit 8 response, restrain, withhold
music: 4 aria, song 5 ditty
refresh: 4 rest 5 bathe, cheer, renew,
slake 6 caudle, revise, revive, vivify 7
comfort, enliven, freshen, hearten,
quicken, restore 8 recreate, renovate 9
reanimate, replenish 10 invigorate, rejuvenate, strengthen 12 reinvigorate
refreshing: 4 dewy 5 balmy, tonic 11 re-
fectorial, refrigerant
refreshment: 8 refresco 9 collation
refrigerant: ice 5 freon 6 cooler 7 ammonia, coolant, cooling 13 carbon dioxide
refrigerate: ice 4 cool 5 chill 6 freeze
refuge: ark 4 home, port, rock 5 haven 6
asylum, bilbie, covert, harbor, resort,
shield 7 crannog(Sc.), harbour, retreat,
shelter 8 crannoge(Sc.), hospital, immunity, resource 9 sanctuary 10 protection, rendezvous, subterfuge
refugee: 5 exile, 6 emigre 8 fugitive
refulgent: 6 bright 7 glowing, radiant,
shining 8 splendid 9 brilliant 11 resplendent
refund: 5 repay 6 rebate 8 kickback 9 reimburse, repayment
refurbish: 5 renew, 6 polish, revamp 7
freshen 8 brighten, renovate
refusal: nay 6 denial
refuse: nay, ort 4 balk, coom, culm, deny,
dirt, dreg, junk, marc, nite, pelf, pelt,
veto 5 chaff, coomb, crawm, debar,
drast, drest, dross, grith, offal, renig, repel, scrap, trash, waste, wrack 6 debris,
forbid, garble, litter, lumber, reject, renege 7 backing, baggage, decline, disavow, forsake, garbage, gubbins, leaving, mullock, rubbish, repulse 8
disclaim, renounce, withhold 9 excrement, repudiate
coffee beans: 6 triage
grape: 4 marc
metal: 4 slag 5 dross 6 scoria
table: ort 5 scrap

wine: 4 lees

refute: 4 deny, meet 5 avoid, rebut, refel 6 assoil 7 confute 8 disprove, infringe, redargue 9 overthrow 10 contradict
serving to: 8 elenctic 10 elenctical

regain: 4 save 6 recoup 7 get back, recover 8 retrieve

regal: 5 jewel, royal 6 august, kingly 7 channel, stately 8 imperial, imposing, majestic, splendid

regale: 4 dine, fete 5 feast, treat, 6 dinner, spread 7 delight, gratify 9 entertain

regalia: kit 5 crown, dress 6 finery 7 emblems, ensigns, scepter, symbols 8 costumes, insignia 9 full dress 11 decorations 13 paraphernalia

Regan: *father:* 4 Lear
sister: 7 Goneril 8 Cordelia

regard: air, awe, con, eye 4 care, deem, gaze, heed, hold, look, mind, note, rate, sake, view, yeme 5 assay, honor, think, treat, value, watch 6 admire, aspect, assess, attend, behold, esteem, glance, homage, notice, remark, repute, revere, 7 adjudge, concern, observe, respect 8 consider, estimate, interest, relation 9 adoration, affection, attention, deference, reference 10 admiration, appearance, attendance, estimation, veneration 11 contemplate 13 consideration, contemplation

regarding: 4 as to, in re 5 about, anent 6 anenst 7 apropos

regardless: 9 negligent 10 neglectful

regatta: 4 race 8 boat race

regency: 4 rule 8 dominion 10 government

regenerate: 5 renew 6 reborn, redeem, reform, revive 7 convert, newborn, reclaim, refresh, restore 8 gracious, recreate, renovate 9 reproduce

regent: 5 ruler 6 ruling 7 regnant, teacher 8 governor 9 governing
of sun: 5 Uriel

regimen: 4 diet, rule 6 system 7 control, hygiene 10 government, regulation 14 administration

regiment: 4 alai 5 cadre, order 11 systematize 12 military unit
flag: 6 pennon
member: 9 grenadier
nucleus: 5 cadre
officer: 5 boots 7 colonel

regina: 5 queen

region: des, erd, gay 4 area, belt, part, zone 5 clime, field, place, realm, space, tract 6 locale, sector, sphere 7 climate, country, demesne, kingdom 8 district, division, latitude, province, vicinity 9 territory 12 neighborhood 13 neighbourhood
elevated: 8 highland

infernal: 5 Hades 7 Avernus 8 Tartarus 10 underworld
pert. to: 5 areal
surrounded by alien power: 7 enclave
upper: 5 ether
warm: 7 tropics
wooded: 5 taiga 6 forest
woodless: 4 wold 5 llano, plain, weald 6 desert, meadow, steppe 7 pasture, savanna 8 savannah

regional: 5 local 9 sectional 10 provincial

register: lid 4 book, list, roll, rota, show 5 album, annal, diary, enter, entry, slate 6 agenda, docket, enlist, enroll, record, roster 7 ascribe, calends, catalog, certify, coucher, kalends, license, stopper 8 archives, bookmark, calendar, indicate, recorder, registry, schedule 9 catalogue, chronical, inventory, registrar
cash: 6 damper
legal: 6 docket
of deaths: 9 necrology

registrar: 5 clerk 7 actuary 8 greffier, recorder, register

reglet: 5 strip 7 molding

regnal: 5 royal 6 kingly

regnant: 6 regent, ruling 8 dominant, reigning 9 prevalent 10 widespread 11 predominant

regorge: 5 vomit 8 disgorge

regress: 6 egress, return, revert 9 backslide, throwback 10 retrograde, withdrawal

regret: rew, rue 4 miss, ruth 5 demur, grief, mourn, qualm, sorry, spurn 6 lament, repent, repine, sorrow 7 bethink, deplore, dislike, remorse, scruple 8 aversion, distress, forthink 9 penitence 10 misgivings, repentance 11 compunction, lamentation 14 disappointment

regular: 4 even 5 exact, sober, usual, utter 6 formal, normal, proper, serial, stated, steady 7 amiable, correct, general, habitue, ordered, orderly, typical, uniform 8 complete, constant, decorous, formular, habitual, ordinary, ordinate, periodic, pleasant, rhythmic, rotative, standard, thorough 9 continual, customary, isometric 10 consistent, dependable, methodical, systematic 11 symmetrical

regulate: set 4 pace, rule, time 5 frame, guide, order 6 adjust, behave, direct, govern, police, settle 7 arrange, compose, conduct, control, correct, dispose, rectify 8 attemper, modulate 9 establish 10 discipline 11 standardize

regulation: law 5 bylaw, canon, regle 6 assize, normal 7 precept, regimen, repulse, statute 8 ordinary 9 ordinance 14 administration

regulator: 5 valve

electricity: **9** rheometer

regulus: 4 king, star **5** matte, ruler

rehabilitate: 7 reclaim, recover, restore **9** reinstate

rehash: 7 restate **9** rechauffe

rehearse: say **4** cite, tell **5** drill, quote, speak, train **6** detail, recite, relate, repeat **7** mention, narrate, prepare, recount **8** describe, instruct, practice **9** enumerate **12** recapitulate

Rehoboam: *father:* **7** Solomon
kingdom: **5** Judah **6** Israel
son: **6** Abijah

reign: raj **4** rule, sway **5** guide, power, realm **6** empire, govern **7** kingdom, prevail **8** dominate **9** authority, dominance **10** prevalence **11** predominate
pert. to: **6** regnal

reimburse: pay **5** repay **6** defray, offset, recoup, refund **7** recover, replace **9** indemnify **10** compensate, recompense, remunerate

rein: 4 curb, slow, stop, turn **5** check, guide, leash, strap **6** bridle, direct, govern, haunch, kidney **7** compose, control, repress **8** restrain **9** hindrance

reindeer: 6 tarand **7** caribou, cervine
genus: **8** rangifer
Santa's: See **Santa Claus's reindeer**

reinforce: 4 back **5** brace, reman **6** second **7** afforce, augment, support **8** buttress, multiply **10** strengthen

reinforcement: 4 sput **9** accession

reinstate: 6 recall, revest **7** put back

reinvigorate: 7 quicken, refresh

reiterate: 4 drum, harp **6** repeat, resume **8** rehearse **10** ingeminate **12** recapitulate

reject: 4 defy, snub **5** eject, repel, scorn, scout, spurn, vomit **6** abjure, disown, rebuff, recuse, refuse **7** cashier, decline, discard, dismiss, disobey, forsake, shut out **8** abnegate, castaway, disallow, forswear, relegate, renounce **9** blackball, eliminate, ostracize, reprobate, repudiate **10** disapprove, disbelieve **13** excommunicate

rejoice: 5 cheer, elate, exult, glory **6** please **7** delight, gladden **8** jubilate **10** exhilarate, tripudiate

rejoin: 5 reply **6** answer **7** respond, reunite

rekindle: 6 revive **7** relight

relapse: 4 fall, sink, slip **7** setback, subside **9** backslide **10** recurrence **12** recidivation

relate: 4 ally, tell **5** apply, refer, state **6** allude, detail, recite, report **7** connect, declare, narrate, pertain, recount, restore **8** describe, rehearse **9** appertain, associate, correlate, enumerate **10** make public

related: kin **4** akin **7** cognate, connate,

germane, kindred **9** affiliate, connected **10** becousined **11** appropriate
on father's side: **6** agnate
on mother's side: **5** enate **6** enatic **7** cognate

relation: sib **5** blood, ratio **6** degree, family, status **7** account, bearing, history, kinship **8** affinity, standing **10** connection, friendship **12** relationship **13** consanguinity
mutual: **11** correlation
on father's side: **6** agnate
on mother's side: **5** enate

relative: eme, kin, sib **4** aunt, mama, papa **5** aunty, niece, uncle **6** auntie, cousin, father, friend, mother, nephew, sister **7** brother, kindred, kinsman, sibling **8** ancestor, apposite, relation, relevant **9** connected, kinswoman, pertinent **10** pertaining **11** comparative **13** corresponding, proportionate
maternal: **5** enate

relative amount: 5 ratio **6** ration

relatives: 7 kinfolk **8** cousinry, kinsfolk
favoritism to: **8** nepotism

relax: 4 ease, open, rest **5** abate, loose, remit **6** divert, lessen, loosen, reduce, soften, unbend **7** cool off, mollify, release, relieve, slacken **8** be at ease, calm down, mitigate **10** feel at home

relaxation: 4 ease, rest **6** repose **7** detente(F.), relache **9** amusement, diversion **10** recreation **11** delassement

relaxed: 4 lash **7** lenient **8** flexuous

relay: 4 post, race **5** spell **6** remuda(Sp.), supply **7** forward, relieve, station **8** avantlay, transmit

release: 4 bail, drop, emit, free, liss, trip, undo, vent **5** let go, lisse, relay, remit, slake, untie, yield **6** acquit, assoil, demise, exempt, loosen, parole, remise, rescue, spring **7** absolve, deliver, disband, freedom, manumit, publish, relieve, unleash, unloose **8** cut loose, liberate, mitigate, unfasten **9** acquittal, discharge, disengage, eliminate, exculpate, extricate **10** emancipate, liberation, relinquish **11** acquittance, deliverance **12** emancipation

relegate: 5 exile, refer **6** banish, charge, commit, deport, remove **7** consign, dismiss **8** accredit, turn over

relent: 4 melt **5** abate, let up, yield **6** soften **7** abandon, liquefy, mollify, slacken **8** dissolve, moderate **10** deliquesce

relentless: 4 grim, hard **5** harsh, stern, stony **6** fierce, strict **8** pitiless, rigorous **9** ferocious, immovable, merciless **10** inexorable, inflexible, persistent **11** unremitting

relevant: apt **5** ad rem **6** timely **7** apropos, germain, germane **8** apposite **9** connected, pertinent **10** applicable, to the point **11** appropriate, referential

reliable: 4 safe, true **5** tried **6** dinkum, honest, secure, steady, trusty **7** certain **9** authentic **10** dependable **11** trustworthy

reliance: 4 hope **5** faith, trust **6** belief **8** affiance **10** confidence, dependence

relic: 5 curio, mummy **6** corpse, hallow, remain **7** antique, leaving, memento, remnant, residue, vestige **8** memorial, souvenir **11** remembrance

pert. to: **9** reliquary

relic cabinet: 6 etager **7** etagere, whatnot

relict: 5 widow **7** widower **8** residual, survivor

relief: bot **4** alms, boot, bote, dole, ease, help **15** indemnification

ornamental: **4** fret **7** relievo

relieve: aid **4** beet, ease, free, help, liss **5** abate, allay, beete, erase, lisse, raise, relay, slake, spare, spell **6** assist, lessen, remedy, remove, succor **7** assuage, comfort, console, deliver, lighten, redress, release, support, sustain, unloose **8** diminish, mitigate **9** alleviate, debarrass, disburden, discharge, exonerate

religieuse: nun **6** sister

religieux: 4 monk **5** pious **9** religious

religion (see also next entry): **4** cult, sect **5** faith, piety **6** voodoo **7** service, worship **8** devotion, doctrine, fidelity **9** adoration, voodooism **10** conformity, observance, persuasion **17** conscientiousness

sect: **5** alogi

study of: **8** theology

system of: **5** faith

religion: See also under specific religions. Example: "Islamic priest," see **Islam:** *priest*

religious: 4 holy **5** exact, godly, pious **6** devout, divine **7** fervent, godlike, zealous **8** faithful, monastic **9** pietistic, spiritual **10** devotional, scrupulous **13** conscientious

belief: **5** credo, creed

brotherhood: **8** sodality

denomination: **4** sect

devotion: **6** novena

directory: **4** ordo **7** ordines(pl.)

festival: **5** Purim **6** Easter **8** Passover

formally: **5** rigid **6** strict **8** orthodox **9** pharisaic

image: **4** icon

military order member: **7** Templar

observance: **4** fast, Lent

offering: **5** tithe **7** deodand **8** oblation

reformer: Hus **4** Huss, Knox **6** Luther

sayings: **5** logia

relinquish: 4 cede, drop, quit **5** demit, forgo, grant, leave, waive, yield **6** desert, forego, give up, remise, resign **7** abandon, dispose, forsake, lay down **8** abdi-

cate, abnegate, disgorge, renounce **9** surrender

reliquary: box **4** apse, arca **5** apsis, chest **6** casket, chasse, shrine **7** chorten

reliquiae: 6 relics **7** remains

relish: 4 dash, gust, like, tang, zest **5** achar, enjoy, gusto, sauce, savor, taste **6** admire, canape, degust, flavor, palate, savour **7** delight, flavour **8** appetite, hautgout **9** appetizer, degustate, enjoyment, seasoning **11** inclination

kind: **5** achar, curry **6** catsup, caviar **7** botargo, chutney, mustard

relucent: 6 bright **7** radiant, shining **9** refulgent

reluct: 5 fight **6** revolt **8** struggle

reluctance: 6 revolt **8** aversion **9** aversion, antipathy, hesitancy **10** opposition, repugnance, resistance **13** indisposition, unwillingness **14** disinclination

reluctant: 4 loth **5** loath **6** averse, forced **7** adverse **8** backward, grudging, hesitant, opposing **9** resisting, unwilling **11** disinclined

rely: 4 bank, base, hold, hope, lean, rest **5** count, rally, trust **6** belong, cleave, depend, expect, lippen, reckon, repose **7** believe, confide, count on

Remagen's river: 5 Rhine

remain: lie **4** bide, last, rest, stay, wait **5** abide, dwell, hover, stand, tarry, thole **6** endure, linger, reside **7** persist, survive **8** continue **11** stick around

remainder: 4 rest, stub **5** stump **6** excess **7** balance, remanet, remnant, residue, surplus **8** leavings, residual, residuum **9** leftovers

remains: 4 dust **5** ashes, relic, ruins, trace **6** corpse, fossil **7** vestige

remand: 6 commit **7** consign **8** recommit, send back

remanent: 7 further **8** enduring **10** additional **13** supplementary

remark: say, see **4** barb, heed, note, word **5** aside, gloss, state, write **6** notice, postil, regard **7** comment, descant, express, observe **8** indicate, perceive **9** aspersion, platitude **10** animadvert, annotation, commentary, expression **11** distinguish, observation

embarrassing: **5** boner, break **7** blooper, faux pas

incidental: **12** obiter dictum

witty: gag, mot **4** quip **5** sally **7** sarcasm **9** witticism

remarkable: 7 notable, strange, unusual **8** uncommon **9** egregious, wonderful **10** noticeable **11** exceptional **12** considerable **13** extraordinary

remble: 4 move, stir

remedy: aid, bot **4** balm, boot, bote, cure, drug, gain, hale, heal, help **5** amend,

salve, topic **6** arcana(pl.), elixir, physic, relief, repair **7** arcanum, correct, cure-all, nostrum, panacea, placebo, rectify, redress, relieve **8** antidote, curative, medicine **9** treatment **10** assistance, catholicon, chevisance, corrective, reparation **13** counteractive
imaginary: **6** elixir **7** panacea
quack: **7** nostrum, placebo
soothing: **4** balm **6** balsam
remember: 4 cite **6** ideate, recall, record, remind, reward **7** bethink, mention **9** recollect, reminisce **10** look back on **11** commemorate
remembrance: 4 gift, mind **5** relic, token **6** memory, minnie, notice, trophy **7** memento, mention **8** allusion, keepsake, memorial, souvenir **9** discourse, reference **10** impression **11** inscription **12** recollecting, recollection
remex: 5 quill **7** feather
remind: 4 hint **6** recall **7** suggest
reminder: cue **4** hint, memo, note, prod, twit **7** memento, monitor **10** admonition, expression
reminiscence: act **4** fact **5** power **6** memory **9** anamnesis, recalling **10** experience **11** memorabilia, remembering, remembrance **12** recollection
remiss: lax **4** lazy, mild, pale **5** slack, tardy **6** gentle **7** diluted, languid, lenient, relaxed **8** careless, derelict, dilatory, faineant, heedless, indolent, moderate, slothful **9** dissolved, liquefied, negligent **10** neglectful, **11** inattentive, thoughtless **13** irresponsible
remission: 6 rebate **9** abolition, cessation, lessening **10** diminution
remit: pay **4** bate, send **5** abate, defer, enter, refer, relax, spend **6** cancel, excuse, insert, pardon, resign, return, submit **7** abandon, absolve, forgive, forward, readmit, release, restore, slacken, suspend **8** abrogate, liberate, mitigate, moderate, postpone, recommit, transmit **9** exculpate, surrender
remittance: 9 allowance
remnant: bit, end, ort, rag **4** dreg, fent, left, part, rest, stub **5** crumb, piece, relic, scrap, trace, wrack **7** leaving, portion, remains, residue **8** fragment **9** remainder **10** suggestion
remodel: 6 change, recast **7** rebuild **11** reconstruct
remolade, remoulade: 5 sauce **8** dressing, ointment
remonstrance: 5 demur **7** protest **10** benedicite **13** expostulation
remonstrate: 5 fight, argue **6** combat, object **7** declare, profess, protest **8** complain **11** demonstrate, expostulate
remora: 4 clog, drag, fish, pega **5** delay **7**

pegador **9** hindrance **10** impediment **11** sucking fish
remorse: rue **4** pity, ruth **5** grief, qualm **6** regret, sorrow **7** penance **8** distress **9** penitence **10** compassion, contrition, repentance **11** compunction
remote: far, off **4** afar, back, cool **5** alien, aloof, faint, vague **6** forane, slight **7** distant, faraway, foreign, obscure, removed **8** secluded, separate **10** abstracted, impersonal, unfriendly **11** indifferent **12** inaccessible
goal or end: **5** Thule
more: **7** endmost, further **8** ulterior
most: **6** ultima **9** diametric **11** ultima Thule
place: **9** backwoods, boondocks
remove: rid **4** bate, dele, doff, fire, free, kill, move, oust, pare, raze, rend, sack, void, weed **5** amove, apart, avoid, elide, eloin, erase, evict, expel, strip **6** betake, cancel, change, convey, deduct, delete, depose, disbar, distal, eloign, recall, remble, retire, uproot **7** cast off, deprive, despoil, dismiss, extract, take off, uncover, whittle **8** abstract, disclose, discover, dislodge, displace, relegate, separate, supplant, transfer **9** clear away, eliminate, eradicate, translate **10** disconnect **11** assassinate
by surgery: **6** ablate
clothing: **5** strip **7** disrobe, undress
from office: **4** oust **6** depose, recall **7** dismiss
hair: **5** shave **8** depilate
ice: **7** defrost
impurities: **5** smelt **6** filter, refine
legally: **4** oust **6** disbar
seeds: **5** stone
skin: **4** hull, husk
to another place: **8** transfer
removed: off **4** away, move **5** alone, aloof, apart **6** remote **7** distant, obscure **10** abstracted
remuneration: pay **5** wages **6** reward **7** payment, stipend **8** requital **9** emolument, repayment **10** recompense **12** compensation, satisfaction **13** consideration, gratification, reimbursement
remunerative: 10 beneficial, profitable **12** advantageous
Remus: *father:* **4** Mars
foster mother: **4** wolf
mother: **4** Rhea
slayer: **7** Romulus
twin brother: **7** Romulus
renaissance: 7 rebirth, revival
renal: 7 nephric **9** nephritic
Renard: See **Reynard**
rend: cut, rip **4** pull, rent, rive, slit, tear **5** break, burst, sever, split, wrest **6** breach, cleave, divide, enrive, pierce, re-

move, screed, sunder **7** abscind, dispart, disrupt, rupture **8** fracture, lacerate, separate **9** dismember **12** disintegrate

render: pay, put, try **4** emit, give, make, melt **5** treat, yield **6** depict, recite, repeat, return, submit **7** clarify, deliver, exhibit, extract, furnish, inflict, payment, perform, present, requite, restore **8** transmit **9** interpret, represent, surrender, translate **10** administer, contribute

rendezvous: **4** date, meet **5** place, tryst **6** gather, refuge **7** hangout, meeting, retreat **8** assemble, mobilize **9** agreement, gathering **11** appointment

rendition: **8** delivery **9** surrender **11** deliverance, performance, translation **14** interpretation

renegade: rat **5** rebel **6** bolter **7** traitor **8** apostate, deserter, fugitive, renegado, turncoat **10** changeling

renege, renig: **4** deny **5** welsh **6** desert, refuse, revoke **7** decline **8** back down, renounce

renew: **4** beet **5** beete **6** extend, refill, repair, repeat, resume, revamp, revive **7** freshen, rebuild, refresh, replace, restore **8** make over, reassume, re-create, renovate **9** modernize, replenish **10** invigorate, recommence, regenerate, rejuvenate **11** re-establish, resuscitate **12** redintegrate

renitent: **7** opposed **8** opposing **9** obstinate, resistant **12** recalcitrant

rennet: lab **5** apple **6** curdle, keslop **7** earning(Sc.) **8** earnings(Sc.), membrane **9** cheeselip, coagulate

ferment: **6** enzyme, rennin

renounce: **4** cede, defy, deny **5** cease, forgo, renay, renig, waive **6** abjure, defect, desert, disown, forego, forlet, forsay, recant, reject, renege, repeal, resign **7** abandon, disavow, forsake, retract **8** abdicate, abnegate, disclaim, forspeak, forswear, renounce **9** repudiate, surrender **10** abrenounce, relinquish **12** abrenunciate

renovate: **4** redo **5** alter, clean, renew **6** purify, repair, resume, revive **7** cleanse, furbish, refresh, replace, restore **10** invigorate, regenerate

renown: rap **4** fame, note **5** eclat, glory, kudos, rumor **6** report **7** acclaim **8** eminence **9** celebrity **10** reputation **11** celebration, distinction

renowned: **5** known **6** famous **11** illustrious

rent: (see also **rend**): let, pay **4** gape, hire, hole, rime, toll **5** censo, chink, cleft, crack, cuddy, gavel, gorge, lease, share, split, yield **6** breach, engage, income, profit, return, reward, schism **7** fissure,

opening, revenue, rupture, tribute **9** lacerated

high: **8** rackrent

transfer: **6** attorn

rental: **4** cost, flat, list **5** house **8** lodgings, schedule **9** apartment

rente: **6** income(Fr.) **7** annuity, revenue

renter: **6** lessee, tenant **8** occupant

reopen: **6** resume **10** recommence

rep: **4** fame **5** cloth **6** fabric, **10** reputation

repair: fix **4** darn, heal, help, mend **5** amend, order, patch, piece, refit, renew **6** remedy, return, revamp, revive **7** correct, rebuild **8** overhaul, renovate

repairman: **6** tinker **7** cobbler **8** mechanic

repand: **4** bent, wavy **6** uneven

reparation: **4** bote **6** amende, amends, reward **7** damages, redress **8** requital **9** amendment, atonement, indemnity, quittance, repairing **10** recompense **11** restitution **12** compensation, distribution, partitioning **14** redistribution

repartee: wit **5** reply **6** banter, retort **7** riposte, sarcasm **8** badinage

repast: tea **4** bait, feed, food, meal **5** bever, feast, snack, treat **6** dinner **7** banquet **9** collation, refection **11** refreshment

pert. to: **8** prandial

repatriation: **6** return **11** restoration

repay: pay **4** meed **5** appay, award **6** avenge, offset, profit, punish, refund, return, reward **7** balance, deserve, requite, restore **9** gratulate, reimburse, retaliate **10** compensate, recompense, remunerate **11** reciprocate

repeal: **4** lift, void **5** amend, annul, emend **6** appeal, cancel, recall, revoke **7** abolish, rescind, retract, reverse **8** abrogate, derogate, renounce, withdraw

repeat: bis(It.), din **4** cite, echo, rame **5** ditto, quote, recap, recur **6** encore, parrot, resume, retell **7** iterate, recount, reprise, restate **8** redouble **9** duplicate, reiterate **10** ingeminate, repetition **11** battologize **12** recapitulate

music: bis

performance: **6** encore

sign in music: **5** segno

repeatedly: oft **5** often **10** frequently **11** continually, day after day **12** continuously

repeater: gun **5** rifle, watch **6** pistol **7** firearm **8** holdover **10** recidivist

repel: **4** beat, stop **5** check, debar, force **6** combat, defend, oppose, rebuff, refuse, reject, remove, resist **7** decline, disgust, fend off, repulse **8** vanquish **10** extinguish

repellent: **4** grim **5** harsh **9** offensive, repugnant **10** forbidding **12** antipathetic

repent: rue **5** atone **6** grieve, lament, regret **7** reptant **8** crawling, creeping, forthink, penitent

repentance: 4 pity, ruth **5** shame **7** penance, remorse **9** attrition, penitence **10** contrition **11** compunction

repentant: 9 regretful **10** remorseful **11** penitential

repercussion: 4 blow, echo **5** tenor **6** impact, recoil **7** rebound **8** backwash, reaction **10** reflection **11** reiteration **12** ballottement **13** reverberation

repertory: 4 list **5** index **7** theater, theatre **8** calendar, magazine, treasury **9** catalogue **10** collection, storehouse

repetition: bis **4** copy, echo, rote **5** rondo **6** dilogy, encore **7** replica, tremolo **8** iterance **9** iteration, rehearsal **10** redundancy **12** reproduction

mechanical: **4** rote **8** anaphora

of homologous parts: **6** merism

of idea: **8** pleonasm **9** tautology

of others: **7** echolia, mimicry **9** echolalia

of sound: **4** echo

repine: 4 fail, fret, wane **5** mourn **6** grouse, lament, regret, weaken **7** grumble, whimper **8** complain, languish

replace: 5 alter, change, reset, stead **6** follow **7** relieve, restore, succeed **8** supplant **9** reimburse, supersede **10** substitute

replacement: 6 ersatz **9** successor **10** substitute

replenish: 4 feed, fill **5** renew, stock **7** restore

replete: fat **4** full, rife **5** alive, sated, stout **6** filled, gorged **7** bloated, implete, stocked, stuffed **8** complete **9** abounding, surfeited

replica: 4 copy **5** image **6** carbon, ectype **8** likeness **9** facsimile **10** repetition **12** reproduction

replicate: 4 bend, copy, fold **5** reply **6** repeat **8** manifold, repeated **9** duplicate, multifold

reply: 4 echo, fold, sass **5** rebut **6** answer, oracle, re-echo, rejoin, repeat, retort, return **7** respond, retract, riposte **8** repartee, response **9** rejoinder **11** replication

report: pop **4** fame, tell, word **5** bruit, noise, rumor, state, story **6** breeze, cahier(F.), delate, digest, recite, relate, repeat, return, rumour **7** account, crackle, hansard, hearing, hearsay, inkling, narrate, recital, summary **8** announce, describe **9** circulate, grapevine, narration, narrative **10** reputation

false: fib, lie **6** canard **7** slander **8** tall-tale **12** misstatement

reporter: cub **6** legman, writer **7** newsman **9** columnist **10** journalist

symbol: **6** thirty

young: cub

repose: lie, set, sit **4** calm, ease, rely, rest, seat **5** peace, place, quiet, sleep **6** relief **7** compose, confide, deposit, dignity, recline, replace, restore, support **8** calmness, serenity **9** composure, quietness **10** relaxation, stretch out **12** requiescence, tranquillity

repository: ark, box **4** bank, file, safe, shop **5** ambry, capsa, chest, depot, vault **6** closet, museum **7** arsenal, capsule, granary, storage **8** magazine, treasury **9** confidant, reliquary, sepulcher, warehouse **10** depository, storehouse

reposoir: 5 altar

repossess: 6 regain **7** recover, retrieve, take back

reprehend: 4 warn **5** blame, chide, scold **6** rebuke **7** censure, reprove, upbraid **8** admonish, disprove **9** criticize, reprimand

reprehensible: 8 criminal, culpable **11** blameworthy

represent: act **4** show **5** enact, image **6** clothe, denote, depict, embody, typify **7** exhibit, express, picture, portray, produce, profess **8** describe, simulate **9** delineate, designate, exemplify, reproduce, symbolize **10** illustrate, substitute **11** impersonate **12** characterize

representation: map **4** icon, idol, ikon **5** chart, graph, image, model **6** avowal, blazon, sample **7** account, diagram, picture **8** likeness, notation **9** portrayal, statement **10** similitude **11** histrionics, performance, portraiture

favorable: **14** recommendation

graphic: **5** chart **6** bisect

representative: 4 heir **5** agent, envoy **6** consul, deputy, legate **7** tribune, typical **8** delegate, executor, exponent, instance, salesman **10** ambassador **12** illustrating, illustrative **13** administrator

repress: 4 bury, curb, hush, rein, stop **5** check, choke, crush, daunt, press, quell **6** bridle, deaden, reduce, stifle, subdue **7** compose, depress **8** compress, restrain, suppress, withhold **9** constrain, overpower

reprieve: 5 defer, delay, grace **6** escape **7** respite, suspend **8** postpone **12** postponement

reprimand: rap, wig **4** call **5** check, chide, slate **6** rebuff, rebuke **7** censure, chapter, chasten, repress, reproof, reprove **8** admonish, call down **9** reprehend **12** reprehension

reprint: 4 copy

reprisal: 8 requital **9** tit for tat **11** retaliation

reprise: 6 repeat **8** reassume **10** compensate, recommence, repetition

reproach: 4 blot, slur, twit 5 abuse, blame, braid, chide, shame, shend, sully, taunt 6 accuse, infamy, rebuke, revile, stigma, vilify 7 censure, condemn, reprove, traduce, upbraid 8 besmirch, disgrace, dishonor 9 bespatter, challenge, contumely, discredit, disrepute, invective 10 correction, exprobrate, opprobrium, scurrility 11 impeachment 12 vilification 13 animadversion 15 discommendation
old word of: 4 raca

reprobate: 4 hard 5 Satan, scamp, wrong 6 disown, rascal, reject 7 abandon, condemn, corrupt, decline, vicious 8 blamable, castaway, denounce, hardened 9 abandoned, blameable, criticize, reprehend, scoundrel 10 censurable, condemned, disallowed 11 blameworthy, disapproved 12 unprincipled 13 reprehensible

reproduce: 4 copy, draw 6 repeat 7 imitate 8 multiply 9 duplicate, procreate, propagate, represent 11 reconstruct
asexually: 5 clone

reproduction: 6 ectype 7 fission, replica 8 likeness 9 facsimile, photostat 10 carbon copy 11 counterpart 13 proliferation

reproductive: 8 prolific

reproductive cell: 6 gamete

reprove: 4 flay, rate, slam 5 blame, check, chide, roast, scold, shame 6 berate, rebuff, rebuke, refute, reject 7 censure, confute, correct, lecture, upbraid 8 admonish, carritch, chastise, disgrace, disprove, lambaste, redargue, reproach 9 castigate, challenge, criticize, objurgate, reprehend, reprimand, reprobate 10 administer, animadvert, carritches, take to task 11 epostulate

reptant: 8 crawling, creeping

reptile: 4 croc, worm 5 snake 6 turtle 8 dinosaur, tortoise 9 alligator, crocodile, pterosaur 11 pterodactyl
age: 8 Mesozoic
edible: 6 iguana, turtle
group: 6 sauria
legless: 4 apod 5 snake
pert. to: 7 saurian 8 ophidian
scale: 5 scute
study of: 11 herpetology

reptilian: low 4 mean 5 snaky 6 lizard, sneaky 7 reptant, saurian, serpent 8 crawling, creeping, ophidian 9 groveling, malignant 10 despicable

republic: 5 state 6 nation 9 democracy 10 commonweal, government 12 commonwealth
imaginary: 7 Oceania
world's smallest: 5 Nauru

Republic author: 5 Plato

repudiate: 4 defy, deny 6 abjure, defect, disown, recant, refuse, reject 7 abandon, decline, disavow, discard, divorce, forsake, retract 8 abrogate, disclaim, renounce 9 disaffirm

repugn: 6 oppose, resist

repugnance: 5 odium 6 enmity, hatred 7 disgust, dislike 8 aversion, distaste, loathing 9 antipathy, hostility, repulsion 10 abhorrence, antagonism, opposition, reluctance 11 abomination, contrariety, incongruity 13 inconsistency

repugnant: 4 foul, vile 8 inimical 9 offensive, repellent 10 refractory 12 disagreeable

repulse: 4 deny, foil, rout 5 check, fling, rebut, refel, repel 6 defeat, denial, rebuff, refuse, reject 7 disgust, exclude, refusal 8 fend off 9 rejection

repulsive: 4 dain, evil, loth, ugly, vile 5 loath, toady 6 odious 7 fulsome, hateful, loathly 9 offensive, repellent, repugnant 10 disgusting, forbidding 11 distasteful, gorgonesque

repurchase: 6 redeem

reputable: 4 good 8 credible 10 creditable 11 respectable, responsible

reputation: 4 fame, name, note, odor 5 eclat, glory, honor, izzat, odour, stamp 6 credit, honour, renown, repute 7 respect 8 standing 9 attribute, character 11 distinction 13 consideration
loss of: 7 scandal

reputed: dit 8 putative, supposed 11 conjectural 12 hypothetical

request: ask, beg, sue 4 plea, pray, suit, wish 5 apply, crave, order 6 appeal, behest, demand, invite 7 entreat, prithee, solicit 8 entreaty, petition, rogation 11 application 12 solicitation, supplication
for help: SOS
formal: 8 rogation

requiem: 4 hymn, mass, rest, song 5 chant, dirge, peace, quiet 7 service

requiescat: 4 wish 6 prayer
in pace: 11 rest in peace

requiescence: 4 rest 6 repose

requin: 5 shark 8 man-eater

require: ask 4 lack, need 5 claim, crave, exact, force 6 behove, compel, demand, enjoin, entail, expect, oblige 7 behoove 9 postulate 11 necessitate

requirement: 4 duty 9 essential, formality, requisite

requisite: 4 just, need 7 needful 9 condition, essential 11 requirement 13 indispensable

requisition: 5 order 6 billet, demand 9 embargo, request 11 application, requirement

requital: 7 guerdon 8 reprisal 9 vengeance 11 retaliation, retribution

requite: pay 5 atone, repay 6 acquit, avenge, defray, return, reward 7 content, deserve, gratify, revenge, satisfy 9 retaliate 10 compensate, recompense, 11 reciprocate

reredos: 4 wall 6 screen 7 brazier, drapery 9 backplate, partition

rerun: 6 replay, reshow

res: 5 point, thing 6 matter 7 subject

rescind: 4 lift, void 5 annul 6 cancel, repeal, revoke 7 abolish, retract, reverse 8 abrogate 11 countermand

rescript: 5 edict, order 6 answer, decree, letter 9 rewriting 11 counterpart

rescue: 4 free, save 6 ransom, redeem, succor 7 deliver, reclaim, recover, release, salvage 8 delivery, liberate 9 extricate 11 deliverance

research: 7 inquiry 11 examination 13 investigation 5 experimentation

reseau: net 6 ground 7 network 10 foundation 11 filter screen

reseda: 5 plant 10 mignonette

resemblance: 5 image 6 simile, symbol 7 analogy 8 affinity, likeness, parallel, vicinity 9 agreement, imitation, semblance 10 comparison, similarity, similitude 12 assimilation 14 representation

one bearing: 6 ringer, 9 lookalike

resemble: 5 favor 8 look like 9 take after

resentment: ire 4 gall 5 anger, depit, pique, spite 6 animus, choler, enmity, grudge, hatred, malice, rancor, spleen 7 dudgeon, ill will, offense, umbrage 8 acrimony 9 animosity, annoyance, hostility, malignity 10 irritation 11 displeasure, indignation

reserve: 4 book, cash, cave, fund, keep, save 5 spare, stock, store 6 assets, retain, supply 7 backlog, bespeak, caution, modesty, shyness, silence, surplus 8 coldness, distance, forprise, nest egg, preserve, withhold 9 exception, reservoir, restraint, retention, reticence 10 constraint, diffidence, discretion, limitation, substitute 11 reservation, taciturnity

reserved: coy, shy 4 cold 5 aloof, staid, taken 6 sedate 7 bashful, distant 8 backward, cautious 9 qualified 10 unsociable 15 incommunicative, uncommunicative

reservoir: vat 4 font, pond, pool, sump, tank 5 basin, fount, stope, store 6 cenote, supply 7 cistern, favissa, forebay, piscina, reserve 8 favissae(pl.), fountain

reset: 4 help 5 abode, alter 6 harbor, refuge, resort, succor 7 receipt, receive, replace, secrete, shelter 9 receiving 10 receptacle

reside: lie 4 bigg, live, room, stay 5 abide, dwell, habit, lodge 6 remain, settle 7 consist, hang out, inhabit, sojourn, subside 8 habitate

residence: 4 digs, home, seat, shed 5 abode, house, villa 6 biding, castle, palace 7 habitat, mansion 8 domicile, residuum, sediment 9 apartment 10 habitation, villanette 13 collectorship

resident: cit 6 lessee, tenant 7 burgess, citizen 8 inherent, occupant 10 inhabitant

residue: ask 4 dreg, lees, marc, orts, rest, silt, slag 5 ashes, dregs 6 cinder, excess, relics, sludge, sordes 7 balance, remains, remnant 8 leavings, remanent, residuum, sediment 9 remainder

residuum: 7 deposit 8 hangover 9 remainder

resign: 4 cede, quit 5 demit, remit, yield 6 devote, submit 7 abandon, consign, deliver 8 abdicate, renounce 9 surrender 10 relinquish

resignation: 7 modesty 8 meekness, patience 9 endurance 12 acquiescence

resile: 6 recede, return 7 rebound, retract, retreat 8 back down, withdraw

resilient: 5 toned 7 buoyant, elastic, springy 8 bouncing, flexible, stretchy, volatile 9 recoiling 10 rebounding

resin, rosin: alk, gum, lac, tar 4 aloe, balm, tolu 5 amber, anime, animi, copal, damar, elemi, gugal, gugul, loban, myrrh, pitch, roset, syrup 6 balsam, charas, dammar, derrid, elemin, googul, salban, storax 7 acouchi, acrylic, ambrite, arioera, copaiba, copaiva, derride, exudate, fluavil, galipot, hartite, ladanum, retinol 8 alkitran, bdellium, fluavile, gedanite, glessite, guaiacum, labdanum, retinite, sandarac 9 alchitran, colophony, elaterite 11 colophonium 12 frankincense

fossil: 5 amber 8 glessite, retinite

gum: 5 gugal, myrrh 6 mastic 8 bdellium

incense: 8 sandarac

purified: 7 shellac

varnish: 5 anime, copal

resinous tree: fir 4 pine 6 balsam

resist: 4 buck, fend 5 rebel, repel 6 baffle, combat, defeat, defend, impugn, oppose, wither 7 contest, counter, dispute, prevent 8 obstruct, traverse 9 frustrate, gainstand, withstand

resistance: 6 rebuff 7 defense 9 hostility, renitence 10 antagonism, oppugnance 13 recalcitrance

resistance box: 8 rheostat

resistant: 4 hard 8 obdurate, renitent, stubborn

resolute: 4 bold 5 fixed 7 animose, animous 8 faithful, positive, resolved, stalwart, stubborn, unshaken **9** unbending **10** unwavering

resolution: vow **4** grit, thew **5** heart, nerve **7** courage, purpose, resolve, verdict **8** analysis, backbone, decision, firmness, proposal, strength **9** assurance, certainty, constancy, fortitude, hardihood, statement, sternness, stoutness **10** conviction, separation, steadiness **11** intrepidity, persevering **12** deliberation, faithfulness, perseverance, resoluteness **13** determination, inflexibility, steadfastness **14** simplification **15** disentanglement

resolve: **4** free, melt **5** relax, solve, untie **6** answer, assoil, decide, dispel, inform, loosen, reduce, remove, settle **7** analyze, appoint, dispose, explain, liquefy, scatter, unravel **8** conclude, decision, dissolve, enfeeble, persuade, separate

resonant: **4** deep, full, rich **5** round **6** mellow, rotund **7** ringing, vibrant **8** sonorous, sounding **10** resounding **11** reverberant

resort: spa, use **4** howf **5** crowd, haunt, howff, joint, place, visit **6** betake, casino, refuge, return, revert, throng **7** company **8** frequent, habitual, recourse **10** assemblage, fall back on

health: spa **10** sanatorium

place of: **5** haunt **7** purlieu

resound: **4** echo, peal, ring **5** clang **6** re-echo **11** reverberate

resounding: **7** vibrant **8** emphatic, plangent

resource: **5** shift **6** device **7** stopgap

resourceful: apt **5** sharp **6** clever, facile **7** fertile

resources: **5** funds, means, money **6** assets, riches, stocks, stores **7** capital, fortune, resorts **8** property, reserves, supplies, supports **10** expedients **12** contrivances

guardian: **15** conservationist

respect: awe **4** heed **5** defer, honor, value **6** admire, esteem, homage, regard, revere **7** concern, observe, respite, tribute, worship **8** postpone, venerate **9** attention, deference, reference, reverence **10** admiration

act of: **6** devoir

pay: **5** greet, kneel, toast **6** salute **9** genuflect

respectable: **4** good **6** decent, honest, proper **7** fausant **8** decorous **9** estimable, honorable, reputable **10** creditable **11** presentable

respectful: **5** civil **6** polite **7** careful, duteous **8** gracious **9** courteous **11** ceremonious

respective: **4** each **6** sundry **7** partial, several **9** regardful **10** individual, particular

respiration: **6** breath **7** eupnoea **9** breathing

difficulty: **4** rale **5** cough **7** dyspnea **8** dyspnoea

normal: **7** eupnoea

respire: **4** live, sigh **6** exhale, inhale **7** breathe

respite: **4** lull, rest **5** break, delay, pause **6** recess **7** leisure **8** interval, reprieve, surcease **9** cessation **10** suspension **12** intermission, postponement

resplendent: **6** bright **7** aureate, blazing, flaming, glowing, radiant, shining **8** dazzling, glorious, gorgeous, lustrous, splendid **9** brilliant, refulgent **10** epiphanous, flamboyant

respond: **4** echo, feel **5** react, reply, write **6** accord, answer, pillar, rejoin, retort return **8** response **10** correspond

response: **4** word **5** verse **6** anthem, chorus, phrase **7** introit, refrain **8** sentence

involuntary: **6** reflex **7** tropism

responsibility: **4** care, duty, onus **6** burden, charge **9** liability **10** obligation **11** reliability **14** accountability **15** trustworthiness

responsible: **6** liable **8** amenable **9** accordant, reputable **10** answerable, dependable, sufficient **13** correspondent

responsive: **6** mutual, tender **8** amenable, sentient **9** sensitive **11** sympathetic

res publica: **5** state **8** republic **10** commonweal **12** commonwealth

rest: lay, lie, set, sit **4** clam, ease, hang, lair, lean, liss, prop, rely, seat, slip, stay, stop **5** abide, cease, found, let up, lie down, lisse, pause, peace, quiet, relax, renew, repos(F.), sleep, stand **6** alight, cesura, depend, desist, ease up, remain, repose, settle **7** balance, caesura, comfort, leisure, refresh, remains, remnant, reposal, residue, respite, shelter, support, surplus **8** breather, interval, slack off, vacation **9** cessation, establish, quietness, remainder, stillness **10** immobility, inactivity, relaxation **11** refreshment **12** intermission, peacefulness, tranquillity

noonday: nap **6** siesta

poetic: **7** caesura

rest house: inn **4** chan, khan **5** hotel, serai **6** abalam, hostel, tavern **7** chhatri

restate: **6** reword **8** reassert **10** paraphrase

restaurant: inn **4** cafe **5** diner, grill, hotel **6** bistro, tavern **7** automat, beanery, cabaret, tearoom **9** brasserie, cafeteria, chophouse, hashhouse, trattoria **10** rotisserie, steakhouse **11** rathskeller(G).

restful: **5** quiet **6** placid **8** peaceful, tranquil

resting: **4** abed **6** asleep, latent **7** dormant

restitution: **6** amends, return **8** recovery

10 recompense, reparation **11** restoration **12** compensation **13** reimbursement

restive: 5 balky, tense **6** uneasy, unruly **7** fidgety, nervous **8** contrary, perverse, restless, stubborn **9** impatient **10** refractory **12** unmanageable

restless: 5 itchy, jumpy **6** fidget, fitful, haunty, hectic, roving, uneasy **7** agitato(It.), fidgety, fretful, inquiet, jittery, nervous, restive, unquiet **8** agitated, feverish, stirring **9** disturbed, impatient, sleepless, unsettled, wandering **10** disquieted, reposeless **12** discontented

restoration: 7 renewal **10** reparation **11** restitution

restorative: 5 tonic **7** anodyne **8** salutary **9** analeptic

restore: 4 cure, heal, mend **5** amend, atone, renew, repay, right **6** redeem, refund, repair, return, revive **7** convert, get back, put back, rebuild, recover, replace **8** renovate **9** reinstate, resurrect **10** regenerate **11** reconstruct, re-establish, resuscitate **12** redintegrate, rehabilitate

printer's mark: **4** stet

restrain: bar, dam, gag **4** bate, bind, calm, clog, curb, hold, rein, rule, stay, stop **5** chain, check, cramp, deter, guard, limit, still, stint **6** arrest, behave, bridle, coerce, detain, fetter, forbid, govern, halter, hamper, hinder, pinion, tether **7** abridge, abstain, chasten, command, compose, confine, contain, control, deprive, forbear, inhibit, prevent, repress, shackle, trammel **8** attemper, compesce, compress, conclude, imprison, moderate, prohibit, restrict, suppress, withhold **9** constrain **12** circumscribe

restrained: 5 quiet **6** severe **8** reserved **9** hidebound **11** disciplined

restraint: bit **5** force **7** barrier, durance, reserve **9** avoidance, reticence **10** internment

legal: **5** estop

of trade: **7** embargo

restrict: bar, tie **4** curb **5** bound, cramp, limit, scant, shrink, stint **6** censor, coerce, hamper, modify, ration **7** confine, repress, tighten **8** contract, derogate, prohibit, restrain, straiten **9** constrict **12** circumscribe

restricted: 5 local **6** closed, finite, narrow, strait **9** parochial **10** provincial

restriction: 5 cramp **9** restraint **10** regulation **11** reservation **12** ball and chain **13** qualification

restrictive: 7 binding **8** limiting **9** confining, stringent

result: end, sum **4** leap, rise **5** close, ensue, event, fruit, issue, score, total **6** accrue, answer, effect, finish, follow, sequel, spring, upshot **7** outcome, proceed, redound **8** aftering, decision **9** aftermath, eventuate, terminate **10** conclusion **11** achievement, consequence, termination

result in: 5 cause

resume: 4 go on **5** renew **6** pick up, reopen, repeat, review **7** epitome, summary **8** continue, reoccupy, return to, synopsis **9** epitomize, reiterate, summarize **10** abridgment, recommence **12** recapitulate **14** recapitulation

resurrection: 7 rebirth, revival **11** restoration

resuscitate: 6 revive **7** quicken, restore **8** revivify

ret: rot, sop **4** soak **5** steep **6** dampen

retable: 5 ledge, shelf **6** gradin **9** framework

retail: 4 hawk, sell, vent **5** trade **6** barter, peddle, relate, repeat

retailer: 6 dealer **8** clothier, huckster, merchant

retain: 4 have, hire, hold, keep, save **6** adhere, athold, behold, employ **7** contain, prevent, reserve **8** maintain, preserve, remember, restrain, withhold **9** entertain, recollect

retainer: fee **4** cage, hewe **5** frame **6** menial, minion, vassal **7** hobbler **8** follower **9** burkundaz

retaining: 9 retentive

retaliate: 5 repay **6** avenge, punish, retort **7** requite, revenge

retaliation: 6 talion **8** reprisal, requital **11** retribution

retard: 4 slow **5** brake, catch, defer, delay, deter, trash **6** belate, deaden, detain, fetter, hamper, hinder, impede **8** encumber, obstruct, postpone, restrain **10** decelerate

retardation: lag **4** drag **5** delay

retch: gag **4** hawk, keck, spit **5** heave, reach, vomit **6** expand, extend, strain **7** stretch

rete: 6 plexus **7** network

retem: 7 juniper

retention: 6 memory **7** holding, keeping, storage **11** maintenance, remembering

retiarius: 9 gladiator

retiary: 6 meshed, telary **7** netlike

reticent: 4 dark **6** silent **7** sparing **8** discreet, reserved, retiring, taciturn **9** secretive **10** mysterious **15** uncommunicative

reticule: bag **4** etui **5** cabas, etwee **6** pocket, sachet **7** handbag, reticle, workbag **8** carryall

reticulum: net **7** network, stomach **8** meshwork

retinaculum: 6 frenum

retinue: 4 band, crew, ging, rout, suit, tail **5** harem, meiny, suite, train **6** attend, escort **7** cortege, service **8** equipage **9**

entourage, following, retainers **10** attendants

retire: ebb **5** leave **6** depart, recede, recess, remove, vanish **7** pension, retreat **8** withdraw **9** disappear, sequester **10** hit the sack

retired: 4 abed, lone **5** quiet **6** secret **7** obscure, private, recluse **8** abstruse, emeritus, reserved, secluded, solitary **9** recondite

retiring: shy **5** timid **6** modest **7** bashful, fugient **8** reserved **9** diffident **11** unobtrusive

retort: mot **4** quip, turn **5** facer, repay, reply, sally **6** answer, recoil, return **7** alembic, cornute, respond, riposte **8** blizzard, repartee, take back **9** retaliate

retortion, retorsion: 7 bending **8** reprisal, twisting **10** reflection

retract: 4 bend **6** abjure, cancel, disown, recall, recant, remove, repeal, retire, revoke **7** disavow, prevent, rescind, retreat **8** restrain, withdraw **9** repudiate

retraction: 8 palinode

retral: 8 backward **9** posterior **10** retrograde

retreat: den **4** abri, cave, holt, lair, nest, nook, rout **5** arbor, bower **6** arbour, asylum, harbor, recede, recess, refuge, retire **7** harbour, privacy, pull out, retiral, shelter **8** fall back, solitude, withdraw **9** departure, hibernate, sanctuary, seclusion **10** rendezvous, retirement, sanitarium, withdrawal

religious: **5** asram

underground: **4** abri, cave

retrench: cut **4** bate, omit, pare **6** delete, excise, lessen, reduce, remove **7** abridge, curtail, cut back, repress, shorten **8** decrease, diminish **9** economize, intercept

retrenchment: 5 ditch **7** parapet, rampart **8** traverse **10** breastwork **12** entrenchment

retribution: pay **6** return, reward **7** nemesis, revenge, tribute **8** requital **9** vengeance **10** punishment, recompense **11** retaliation

goddess of: Ate **4** Fury **7** Nemesis

retrieve: 6 recall, regain, revive **7** recover, restore **8** discover **10** recuperate

retrograde: 4 slow **5** lapse **6** recede, retral, worsen **7** decline, inverse, opposed, regress **8** backward, contrary, decadent, inverted, rearward, withdraw **9** backslide, catabolic, reversely **10** degenerate, retrogress **11** deteriorate

retrogress: 4 sink **6** revert, **9** backslide **10** degenerate

retrospective: 6 review **8** backward **11** retroactive **13** contemplative

return: lob **4** bend, turn **5** recur, remit, repay, yield **6** advert, answer, come in,

profit, render, report, retort, revert **7** put back, regress, replace, reprise, requite, respond, restore, revenue, reverse **8** give back, requital, response, take back **9** repayment, repercuss, retaliate, reversion **10** recompense, recurrence **11** reciprocate, replacement, restoration **12** reappearance **13** reciprocation

Return of the Native author: 5 Hardy

Reuben: *brother:* **6** Joseph

father: **5** Jacob

mother: **4** Leah

Reuel's father: 4 Esau

reunite: 6 rejoin **9** reconcile

reus: 9 defendant

rev: 10 accelerate, give the gun, race a motor

revamp: 5 renew **7** restyle, rewrite

reveal: bid **4** bare, blab, jamb, open, show, tell, wray **5** exert **6** betray, bewray, descry, detect, expose, impart, unveil **7** confide, develop, display, divulge, exhibit, give out, let slip, publish, uncover **8** announce, decipher, develope, disclose, discover, evidence, manifest, revelate **11** communicate

reveille: 4 call, dian **5** diana, levet, rouse **6** signal

revel: joy **4** orgy, riot, wake **5** feast, let go, randy, spree, watch **6** bezzle, gavall, high-go **7** carouse, delight, revelry, roister **8** carnival, carousal, cut loose, domineer, festival **9** celebrate, festivity **11** celebration, merrymaking **12** conviviality

revelation: 4 tora **5** torah **6** vision **8** epiphany, prophecy **9** discovery **10** apocalypse, disclosure **13** manifestation

reveler, reveller: 6 ranter, rioter **8** bacchant **9** bacchanal, roisterer **10** merrymaker

cry: **4** evoe

revenant: 5 ghost **7** specter **9** recurring **10** apparition

revenge: 6 avenge, defend **7** requite **8** requital **9** retaliate **11** retaliation, retribution

revenue: 4 rent **5** yield **6** income, profit, rental, return, salary **7** finance **8** earnings, interest

reverberate: 4 echo, ring **6** return **7** reflect, resound

reverberating: 7 reboant **8** resonant **12** repercussive

revere: 4 love **5** adore, honor, prize, value **6** admire, esteem, regard, repute **7** respect, worship **8** venerate

reverence: awe **4** fear **5** dread, honor, piety **6** homage **8** devotion **9** deference, obeisance, solemnity

gesture of: **8** kneeling **11** genuflexion **12** genuflection

reverend: sri 4 holy 5 abbot 6 clergy, sacred 9 clergyman, monsignor, venerable

reverent: 6 devout, humble 7 awesome, dutiful

reverie: 5 dream 6 musing, trance, vision 7 fantasy 8 daydream

revers: 5 lapel

reverse: 5 annul, upset 6 defeat, invert, regard, repeal, revoke 7 abolish, backset, convert, subvert 8 backward, contrary, converse, disaster, opposite, overturn 9 about face, disaffirm, overthrow, transpose 10 misfortune 11 countermand

reversion: 6 return 7 relapse 9 throwback, volte-face

to state: 7 escheat

to type: 7 atavism

revert: 5 lapse, react 6 advert, return, revive 7 escheat, recover, reverse 9 backslide, throw back 11 antistrophe

review: 4 edit 5 recap 6 parade, resume, survey 7 account, journal 8 ceremony, critique, revision 9 criticise, criticism, criticize, re-examine 10 certiorari, inspection, periodical, reconsider, retrospect 11 examination

revile: 4 hate, rail 5 abuse, blame, brawl, libel, scold 6 debase, malign, vilify 7 chew out, slander 8 reproach 9 blaspheme 10 calumniate

revise: 4 edit 5 alter, amend, emend 6 change, polish, redact 7 correct, improve, recense, rewrite 8 readjust, work over 9 castigate, reexamine, supervise

reviser, revisor: 8 redactor, reformer

revival: 6 recall 7 rebirth 8 wakening 11 renaissance 12 reproduction 13 recrudescence

revive: daw 4 gain, wake 5 rally, renew, rouse 6 return 7 enliven, freshen, quicken, recover, refresh, restore 8 reawaken, recreate, rekindle, remember, revivify 9 reanimate, refreshen, resurrect 10 recuperate, regenerate, rejuvenate 11 resuscitate 12 reinvigorate

revoice: 4 echo 5 refit 7 restore

revoke: 4 lift, void 5 adeem, annul, check, renig 6 cancel, recall, recant, renege, repeal 7 abolish, fenagle, finagle, prevent, repress, rescind, retract, reverse 8 abrogate, remember, restrain, withdraw 9 fainaigue 11 countermand

revolt: 5 rebel, repel 6 mutiny, offend 7 disgust, retreat 8 renounce, sedition, uprising 9 rebellion 11 rise against 12 insurrection, renunciation

revolting: 4 ugly 6 horrid 7 hateful, hideous 8 shocking 9 loathsome, offensive, repellent, repulsive 10 disgusting, nauseating

revolution: 4 gyre, turn 5 cycle 7 circuit, shake-up 8 disorder, rotation, uprising 9 overthrow, rebellion 12 renunciation

revolutions per minute: RPM 4 revs

revolve: con 4 birl, roll, spin, turn, whir 5 recur, swing, trend, twirl, wheel, whirl, whirr 6 circle, gyrate, ponder, rotate 7 agitate, reflect, trundle 8 consider, meditate 10 deliberate

revolver: gat, gun 6 pistol 7 firearm

revolving: 4 orby 6 rotary

part: 5 rotor 7 rotator

revue: 4 show 6 follies 9 burlesque 13 entertainment

revulsion: 4 fear 6 change 8 reaction 9 reversion 10 withdrawal 11 abomination

reward: fee, pay, utu 4 heed, hire, meed, plum, rent 5 ameed, award, bonus, check, crown, merit, medal, prize, repay, wages, yield 6 bounty, carrot, gersum, notice, profit, regard, return, salary, trophy 7 guerdon, premium, success 8 requital 9 honoraria(pl.) 10 compensate, honorarium, recompense, remunerate 11 retribution 12 compensation, remuneration 13 gratification

rewarding: 7 helpful 10 beneficial

rewrite: See **revise**

rex: 4 king

Reynard: fox

rezai: 8 coverlet, mattress

rhamn: 9 buckthorn

rhapsodic: 8 ecstatic, effusive 9 emotional

rhea: emu 4 emeu 5 nandu 6 ratite 7 ostrich 8 avestruz(Sp.)

Rhea: Ops

child: 4 Hera, Zeus 5 Hades 6 Hestia 7 Demeter 8 Poseidon

father: 6 Uranus

husband: 6 Cronus, Saturn

rhema: 4 term, verb, word

rheoscope: 12 galvanoscope

rheostat: 6 dimmer 8 resistor 9 regulator

rheotome: 11 interrupter

rhesus: 6 monkey 7 macaque

rhetor: 6 master, orator 7 teacher

rhetoric: 6 speech 7 bombast 9 eloquence

rhetorical: 6 florid 8 forensic 9 highflown 10 figurative, oratorical

rhetorician: 6 master, orator, writer 7 speaker, teacher

rhetorics: *digression:* 6 ecbole

diminution: 7 litotes

figure of speech: 6 aporia, simile 7 epandos 8 metaphor 10 apostrophe 12 alliteration, onomatopoeia 15 personification

rheum: 4 cold 7 catarrh 8 rhinitis

rhexis: 7 rupture

rhinal: 5 nasal 6 narial

Rhine: 5 river

city: 4 Bonn, Koln 5 Mainz 7 Cologne 8 Mannheim 9 Wiesbaden
magic hoard: 9 Rheingold, Rhinegold
nymph: 7 Lorelei
pert. to: 7 Rhenish
tributary: Aar, Ill 4 Aare, Lahn, Main, Ruhr, Waal
wine: 7 Moselle
rhino: 4 cash 5 money 10 rhinoceros
rhinoceros: 5 abada, topan 6 borele, umhofo 7 keitloa, upeygan
black: 6 borele
cousin of: 5 tapir
feature: 4 horn
rhinoceros beetle: 4 uang
rhinoceros bird: 9 beefeater
rhizoid: 7 rootlet 8 rootcell
rhoda: 4 rose
Rhode Island: *bay:* 12 Narragansett
capital: 10 Providence
city: 7 Warwick 8 Cranston 9 Pawtucket 10 Woonsocket
founder: 13 Roger Williams
island: 5 Block 8 Prudence 9 Aquidneck
motto: 4 Hope
nickname: 5 Ocean 11 Little Rhody
resort: 7 Newport
river: 9 Pawcaduck 10 Woonsocket
state flower: 6 violet
state tree: 5 maple
Rhodes: *ancient wonder:* 8 Colossus
festival: 10 Chelidonia
Rhodesia: See **Zimbabwe**
rhoeadales: 5 poppy
rhomboid: 13 parallelogram
rhonchus: 4 rale 7 snoring 8 croaking 9 whistling
Rhone: *town:* 5 Arles
tributary: 5 Isere, Saone
rhubarb: 5 error 6 hassle 7 mistake, quarrel, yaw-weed 8 argument, pieplant 9 butterbur, rhapontic 10 discussion
derived from: 5 rheic
genus: 5 rheum
rhus tree: 5 sumac 6 sumach
rhyme: 5 agree, verse 6 poetry 9 harmonize
rhymester: 4 poet 6 rhymer 8 rimester 9 poetaster
rhythm: 4 beat, lilt, time 5 clink, meter, pulse, swing, tempo 7 cadence, measure
break in: 7 caesura 8 caesurae(pl.)
instrument: 4 drum 7 cymbals 8 triangle 10 tambourine
monotonous: 8 singsong
rhythmic: 6 poetic 8 metrical 9 recurrent
ria: bay 5 creek, inlet
rialto: 4 mart 6 bridge, market 8 district, exchange
riant: gay 6 bright, merry 8 cheerful, laughing, smiling
riata: See **reata**

rib: 4 bone, hair, purl, stay, wale, wife 5 costa, ridge, tease 6 banter, costae(pl.), lierne 7 bristle, support 9 cotelette, tierceron
pert. to: 6 costal 7 costate
ribald: low 5 rogue, scamp 6 coarse, rascal, vulgar 7 obscene 9 offensive 10 irreverent, scurrilous 11 blasphemous
ribband: bar 4 spar 5 plank, strip 6 bridge, timber 9 scantling
ribbed: 6 barred, corded 7 costate
fabric: rep 5 twill 6 faille
ribbon: bow 4 tape 5 braid, corse, padou, reins, shred, snood, strip, taste 6 cordon, fillet, riband, silver, taenia, tatter 7 bandeau, binding, taeniae(pl.) 8 banderol, decorate, tressour, tressure 9 banderole
badge: 6 cordon
binding: 6 lisere
ribbon-fish: 7 cutlass, oarfish 8 bandfish, dealfish
ribbon gum: 8 eucalypt
ribbon-like: 8 taeniate, taenioid
ribbon worm: 9 nemertean
ribless: 8 ecostate 9 decostate
ribwort: 8 hardhead, plantain
rice: 4 boro, chit, paga, twig 5 arroz(Sp.), bigas, canin, macan, pilaf, pilau, stick 6 branch 7 risotto 9 brushwood
boiled with meat: 5 pilaf, pilau
drink: 4 sake 5 bubud 7 pangasi
field: 4 padi 5 paddy
husk: 4 shud 5 shood
inferior: 4 chit
long-stemmed: 4 aman
milk: 5 gruel 7 pudding 8 porridge
paste: ame
polishings: 5 darac
rice rail: 4 sora
ricebird: 7 bunting, sparrow 8 bobolink 9 gallinule
rich: fat 4 dear, oofy 5 ample, heavy, opime 6 absurd, costly, creamy, daedal, fruity, greasy, hearty, mellow, mighty, oofier, ornate, potent 7 copious, fertile, moneyed, opulent, orotund, pinguid, wealthy 8 abundant, affluent, generous, luscious, powerful, valuable, well-to-do 9 abounding, bountiful, elaborate, laughable, luxuriant, plentiful, sumptuous 10 in the money, productive 12 concentrated, preposterous
man: 5 Midas, nabob 7 Croesus 9 plutocrat
Richelieu's successor: 7 Mazarin
riches: 4 gold, pelf, weal 5 lucre, worth 6 wealth 7 fortune 8 treasure
demon of: 6 Mammon
region of: 8 Eldorado
worship of: 10 plutomania
rick: 4 goaf, heap, pile 5 noise, scold,

stack, twist **6** jingle, rattle, sprain, wrench **7** chatter

rickety: 4 weak **5** crazy, shaky **6** feeble, senile **7** unsound **8** unstable **9** tottering **10** ramshackle

ricksha, rickshaw: 6 samlor **8** carriage

ricochet: 4 skip **5** carom **6** bounce, glance **7** rebound

rictus: 4 gape, grin, mask **7** grimace

rid: 4 free **5** clear, empty **6** assoil, remove, rescue **7** deliver, relieve **8** dispatch, liberate, throw off **9** eradicate **11** disencumber

ridder: 4 sift **5** sieve

riddle: ree **4** crux, sift **5** aread, areed, griph, rebus, sieve **6** enigma, pierce, puzzle **7** griphus, mystery, perplex **8** disprove, separate **9** conundrum, criticize, perforate

ride: 4 bait, dosa **5** drift, drive, float, motor, tease **6** harass **7** hagride, journey, torment **8** ridicule **9** carrousel, cavalcade, excursion **10** go for a spin **12** merry-go-round

to hounds: **4** hunt

without power: **5** coast, glide

rider: 6 clause, cowboy, jockey, knight **7** allonge **8** addition, appendix, bucaayro, buckaroo, cavalier, desultor, horseman **9** amendment, performer, straddler **10** equestrian, freebooter, highwayman, horsewoman **11** endorsement, mosstrooper **12** bronco-buster, equestrienne(fem.)

ridge: aas, rib, top **4** aret, asar, back, balk, bank, barb, bult, dene, dune, gold, kame, lira, loma, osar(pl.), rand, reef, ring, ruck, ruga, seam, spur, wale, wave, weal, welt **5** arete, arris, bargh, chine, costa, crest, eskar, esker, hause, oesar(pl.), rugae(pl.), serac, spine, stria, varix, wheal, whelk **6** costae(pl.), crista, rideau, striae(pl.) **7** annulet, costula, cristae(pl.), hogback, porcate, varices(pl.), wrinkle, yardang **8** costulae(pl.), headland, sastrugi, shoulder, zastrugi **9** elevation, razorback

anatomical: **5** spine, stria

cloth: **4** wale

glacial: **5** esker

pert. to: **7** cardinal

shell: **5** varix **7** varices(pl.)

skin: **4** wale, welt

ridge oak: 9 blackjack

ridged and furrowed: 7 porcate

ridicule: guy, pan **4** gibe, jeer, lout, mock, quiz, razz, twit **5** borak, chaff, irony, roast, scout, sneer, taunt **6** banter, deride, expose, satire **7** asteism, buffoon, lampoon, mockery, pillory, sarcasm **8** derision, raillery, satirize **9** burlesque, make fun of, poke fun at

deity: **5** Momus

object of: **4** butt **13** laughingstock

ridiculous: 5 droll **6** absurd **7** amusing, foolish **8** farcical **9** laughable, ludicrous **10** indecorous, irrational, outrageous **12** preposterous

riding: 8 shivaree **9** chevachie **10** equitation

costume: **5** habit

pants: **8** jodhpurs

shoe: **8** solleret

riding school: 6 manege

riding whip: 4 crop **5** quirt

ridotto: 6 resort **7** redoubt, retreat **8** festival **9** gathering **10** masquerade **11** abridgement, arrangement **12** entertainment

riem: 5 strap, strip, thong

Rienzi composer: 6 Wagner

rife: 5 alive, brief **7** current, replete **8** abundant, numerous **9** abounding, plentiful, prevalent **10** prevailing, widespread

riff: 4 scan, skim **6** browse, riffle, ripple **7** midriff **9** diaphragm

Riff: 6 Berber

riffle: 4 plow, reef **5** rapid, shoal **6** rattle, ripple **7** shallow, shuffle **11** obstruction

riffraff: mob **4** raff, scum **5** trash **6** rabble, refuse **7** rubbish **9** sweepings

rifle: arm, gun, rob **4** tige **5** reeve, steal **6** furrow, groove, weapon **7** bundock, carbine, despoil, escopet, firearm, pillage, plunder, ransack **8** bandhook **9** chassepot, escopette

accessory: **6** ramrod

ball: **5** minie

instrument: **7** bayonet

kind of: **6** Garand, Mauser **7** Enfield **9** Remington **10** Winchester **11** Springfield

magazine: **6** Mauser

pin: **4** tige

rifleman: 5 jager, yager

rift: lag **4** flaw, rive **5** belch, break, chasm, cleft, crack, rapid, split **6** breach, cleave, divide **7** blemish, fissure, opening, shallow **8** crevasse, division

rig: fig, fit, fix **4** dupe, fool, gear, hoax, wind **5** dress, equip, prank, rifle, storm, trick **6** lateen, outfit, square, tackle **7** arrange, costume, derrick, furnish, ransack, swindle, turnout **8** accouter, accoutre, carriage, equipage **9** apparatus, equipment, imposture **10** manipulate **11** contraption

riga: 6 balsam

Riga Gulf island: 5 Oesel

Riga native: 4 Lett **7** Latvian

rigadoon: 5 dance

rigescence: 8 numbness **9** stiffness

rigging: 4 gear, spar 5 ropes 6 tackle 7 clothes

right: due, fit, gee, hak 4 mend, fair, good, real, sane, soke, true 5 droit, sound 6 angary, dexter, equity, excuse, lawful, normal, patent, proper 7 correct, diehard, fitting, genuine, liberty, rectify, redress 8 appanage, becoming, courtesy, directly, easement, interest, straight, suitable, usufruct, virtuous 9 authority, equitable, faultless, franchise, privilege 10 obligation, perquisite 11 appropriate, certificate, prerogative

exclusive: 7 patents 10 concession

law: ius, jus 5 droit

of way: 8 easement

proprietary: 8 interest

royal: 7 regalia

widow's: 5 terce

right-angled: 10 orthogonal, rectangled 11 rectangular

right hand: 6 dextra 7 dextera

right-hand page: 5 recto

right-handed: 7 dextral 8 dextrous, positive 9 clockwise dexterous

right-minded: 5 moral 7 ethical 10 principled

right-winger: 7 diehard 11 bitter-ender 12 conservative

righteous: 4 good, holy, just 5 godly, moral, pious, zadoc, zadok 6 devout, worthy 7 perfect, sinless, upright 8 virtuous 9 blameless, equitable, guiltless

righteousness: 6 dharma 9 rectitude

rightful: due, fit 4 fair, just, true 5 legal 6 honest, lawful, proper 7 fitting, upright 9 equitable 11 appropriate

rightist: 4 Tory 11 reactionary 12 conservative

rigid: set 4 firm, hard, taut 5 fixed, stark, stern, stiff, stony, tense 6 marbly, severe, strait, strict 7 austere 8 hard-line, rigorous 9 immovable, stringent, unbending 10 inflexible, ironhanded, motionless, unyielding

rigmaree: 4 coin 6 trifle

rigmarole: 8 nonsense 10 balderdash

Rigoletto: *composer:* 5 Verdi

role: 5 Gilda

rigor, rigour: 4 fury 5 trial 7 cruelty 8 asperity, hardship, rigidity, severity, violence 9 austerity, harshness, rigidness, sharpness, stiffness 10 difficulty, exactitude, puritanism, strictness, visitation 13 inflexibility

rigorous: 5 angry, rigid, stern, stiff 6 severe, strait, strict 7 ascetic, correct, drastic, onerous, precise 8 accurate 9 inclement 10 inexorable, oppressive, relentless

rikk: 10 tambourine

rile: vex 4 roil 5 anger, annoy, upset 7 ag-

itate, disturb 8 irritate 9 turbidity

rill: 5 brook, creek, crick, ditch 6 course, furrow, groove, runnel, trench 7 rillock, rivulet 8 brooklet 9 arroyuelo(Sp.), streamlet

rim: lip 4 bank, brim, edge, orle, ring, tire 5 basil, bezel, bezil, brink, somma, verge 6 border, flange, margin, shield 7 enclose, horizon 8 boundary 9 perimeter

external: 6 flange

horseshoe: web

wheel: 4 tire 5 felly 6 felloe

rima: 5 cleft, crack 7 fissure 8 aperture 10 breadfruit

rimate: 7 cracked 8 fissured

rime: ice 4 hoar, poem, rent, rung, step 5 chink, crack, frost, rhyme, verse 6 freeze 7 fissure, versify 8 aperture 9 cranreuch(Sc.), hoarfrost 10 incrustate

rimple: 4 fold 6 crease, ripple, rumple 7 wrinkle

rimption: lot 4 scad 9 abundance

Rinaldo's steed: 6 Bayard 7 Bajardo

rind: 4 bark, husk, melt, peel, skin 5 crust, waste 6 cortex 7 clarify, epicarp, peeling 8 cortices(pl.)

rindle: 5 brook, creek 6 runnel 7 rivulet

ring: bee, cut, rim, set 4 bail, band, cric, ding, dirl, echo, gyre, halo, hank, hoop, link, lute, peal, toll, tore 5 anlet, arena, bague, bezel, chime, clang, group, knell, longe, ridge, rigol 6 arenae, border, boxing, brough(Sc.), chaton, circle, circus, clique, collar, collet, corona, dindle, dingle, famble, gasket, girdle, terret, tingle, tinkle, toroid 7 annulet, annulus, circlet, coterie, curette, ferrule, grommet, resound, ringlet, tanbark, vibrate 8 bracelet, cincture, encircle, surround 9 archivolt, enclosure, encompass, telephone 10 racecourse 11 combination, reverberate 14 tintinnabulate

carrier: 9 go-between

gem setting: 5 bezel 6 chaton

of chain: 4 link

of rope: 7 grommet

pert. to: 7 annular

stone: gem

to hold reins: 6 terret

to tighten joint: 6 washer

wedding: 4 band

ring finger: 5 third

ring ouzel: 5 amsel 6 thrush 8 whistler

ring plover: 5 sandy

ring-shaped: 7 annular 8 annulate, circular 9 annulated

ring-worm: 5 tinea 6 kerion, tetter 7 serpigo 8 milleped 9 millepede

ringdove: 6 cushat, pigeon

ringed: 6 wedded 7 engaged, married 8 annulate, circular 9 annulated, decorat-

ed, encircled **10** surrounded
ringed worm: **7** annelid
ringent: **6** gaping
ringing: **4** clam **6** bright **7** orotund **8** resonant
ringleader: **10** instigator
ringlet: **4** curl, lock, ring **5** tress
rings: *interlocking:* **6** gimmal
  series: **4** coil
rink: man **4** hero, race, ring **9** encounter
rinse: **4** lave, sind(Sc.), wash **5** douse, swill **6** douche, gargle, sluice **7** cleanse
riot: din, wow **4** clem, howl **5** brawl, feast, melee, revel **6** affray, bedlam, clamor, excess, pogrom(Russ.), tumult, uproar **7** dispute, quarrel, revelry **8** carousal, debauche, disorder, outburst, sedition, uprising **9** commotion, confusion, luxuriate **10** donnybrook **11** dissolution, disturbance
riotous: **4** loud, wild **5** loose **6** wanton **7** profuse **10** boisterous, profligate **11** saturnalian **12** contumacious, unrestrained
rip: hag, rit **4** rend, rent, rive, tear **6** sunder **7** sputter **8** disunite, harridan, lacerate **9** debauchee **10** laceration
roaring: **5** noisy **6** lively **8** exciting **9** hilarious **10** boisterous, uproarious
ripa: **4** bank **5** beach, shore **6** strand
ripe: fit, rob **4** aged, bank, rife **5** adult, ready **6** addled, august, mature, mellow **7** grown-up, matured, plunder **8** complete, finished, seashore **9** developed, full-grown, perfected, riverbank **10** consummate, seasonable **11** intoxicated
  early: **8** rareripe
ripen: age **4** grow **6** mature, mellow, season **7** develop, enhance, improve, perfect, prepare **8** heighten
ripost, riposte: **5** reply **6** retort, return, thrust **8** repartee
ripper: **5** dilly **6** corker **7** bobsled **8** jimdandy **9** humdinger **10** crackerjack
rippet: **4** fuss, romp **6** uproar **7** quarrel
ripping: **4** fine **8** splendid **9** admirable, excellent, marvelous **10** remarkable
rippit: **5** fight
ripple: cut, lap **4** curl, fret, purl, riff, tear, wave **5** acker, graze **6** cockle, dimple, riffle, rimple **7** crinkle, scratch, wavelet, wrinkle **8** undulate
ripple grass: **7** ribwort
rise: **4** flow, grow, hulk, loom, rare, rear, soar, stem, well **5** arise, begin, climb, get up, issue, mount, reach, rebel, stand, start, surge, swell, tower **6** amount, appear, ascend, ascent, aspire, assume, attain, derive, emerge, growth, mature, revolt, spring, thrive **7** adjourn, advance, elevate, emanate, prosper, roll out, stand up, succeed **8** addition, eminence,

flourish, increase, levitate **9** ascension, beginning, elevation, originate
above: **8** surmount
again: **7** resurge **9** resurrect
against: **5** rebel **6** mutiny **9** insurrect
and fall: **4** tide **5** heave **6** welter
up: **4** fume **5** tower **6** ascend
riser: **4** pipe, step
risible: **5** funny **7** amusing **9** laughable, ludicrous
rising: **5** arise **6** orient, ortive, revolt **7** montant, nearing **8** gradient, uprising **9** ascendant, ascension **11** approaching **12** extumescence, insurrection
risk: **4** dare, defy, face, gage, wage **5** peril, stake **6** chance, danger, expose, gamble, hazard, injury, plight, plunge **7** imperil, venture **8** endanger, exposure, jeopardy **9** adventure, liability **12** disadvantage
risky: **5** hairy **6** chancy **7** parlous **8** ticklish **9** hazardous
risqué: **4** racy **5** salty, spicy **6** daring **8** off-color **9** audacious, hazardous, salacious **10** suggestive
rissle: **4** pole **5** staff, stick
rist: **4** mark **5** wound **6** ascent **7** engrave, scratch
risus: **5** laugh **8** laughter
ritardando: **9** retarding **11** rallentando
rite: **4** cult, form, orgy **5** sacra **6** augury, exequy, novena, prayer, ritual **7** liturgy, obsequy **8** accolade, ceremony, occasion **9** formality, ordinance, procedure, sacrament, solemnity **10** ceremonial, initiation, observance
Ritter: **6** knight
ritual: **4** cult, form, rite **7** liturgy, obsequy **8** ceremony **9** obsequies(pl.) **10** ceremonial
ritus: **5** usage **6** custom
ritzy: **6** modish **7** elegant, haughty **9** expensive, luxurious **11** fashionable
rivage: **4** bank, duty **5** coast, shore
rival: try, vie **4** even, peer **5** equal, match **6** amount **7** compete, emulate, feuding **8** corrival, emulator, opponent, struggle **9** adversary, competing **10** antagonist, competitor, contending **11** comparative
rivalry: **7** contest **8** tug-of-war **11** competition
rive: rip, rob **4** bank, chop, plow, pull, rend, rent, rift, tear **5** break, cleft, shore, split, steal **6** arrive, cleave, pierce, sunder, thieve, thrust **7** dispart, shatter **8** lacerate **9** disembark
rivel: **6** shrink **7** shrivel, wrinkle
river: ree, ria(Sp.), rio(Sp.), run **4** wadi, wady **5** bayou, waddy **6** stream **7** channel **8** effluent **9** abundance **11** watercourse
arm: **4** fork **7** estuary **9** tributary
bank: **4** rand, ripa **5** levee

channel: bed **6** alveus
current: **4** eddy **6** rapids
dam: **4** weir
gauge: **9** nilometer
god: **7** Alpheus, Inachus **8** Achelous
horse: **5** hippo, rhino **12** hippopotamus
ice: **7** glacier
inlet: **5** bayou **6** slough
island: ait **4** holm
Kubla Khan's: **4** Alph
land: **5** carse(Sc.), flats **7** bottoms
living in: **9** amphibian, rheophile
long run: **9** sluiceway
longest: **4** Nile
mouth: **4** beal(Sc.), lade **5** delta **7** estuary
mythical: **4** Styx
nymph: **4** nais **5** naiad
obstruction: **4** snag **5** gorce
of oblivion: **5** Lethe
passage: **4** ford **7** estuary
pert. to: **5** amnic **7** fluvial, potamic **8** riverine **9** fluminose, fluminous
sacred: **5** Ganga **6** Ganges
siren: **7** Lorelei
small: **5** brook, creek, tchai **6** stream **7** rivulet **8** riverlet **9** streamlet
thief: **6** ackman
underworld: **4** Styx **5** Lethe **7** Acheron, Cocytus
winding part: ess
river dog: **10** hellbender
river duck: **4** teal **7** mallard, widgeon
river mussel: **4** unio
River of Forgetfulness: **5** Lethe
River of Hate: **4** Styx
River of Sorrows: **7** Acheron
riverbed: **4** wadi, wady **5** waddy **7** batture
riverboat: ark **5** barge **6** pulwar **7** rowboat, towboat **8** flatboat
riverside: **4** bank **5** shore
riverweed family: **13** podostemaceae
rivet: fix **4** bolt, brad **6** clinch, fasten **8** fastener
riviere: **8** necklace
rivulet: **4** burn, rill **5** bache, bayou, bourn, brook, creek **6** bourne, rindle(Sc.), runlet, runnel, stream **7** channel **9** streamlet
rixatrix: **5** scold **6** virago
rixy: **4** tern
roach: bug, cut **4** fish, hill, rock, roll, soil, spot **6** braise **7** sunfish **9** cockroach
road: way **4** fare, gang, iter, path, raid, ride **5** agger, bargh, going, itero(pl.), route **6** avenue, camino, career, causey, chemin, course, street **7** calzada(Sp.), estrada, gangway, highway, itinera(pl.), journey, passage, railway **8** beallach, causeway, chaussee(F.), cul-de-sac, pavement, railroad **9** direction, incursion, roadstead **10** expedition

bend: **7** hairpin
character: **4** hobo **5** tramp **10** hitchhiker
country: **4** lane **6** boreen (Ir.)
edge: **4** berm **8** shoulder
machine: **4** harl **5** paver **6** grader **9** bulldozer
menace: **7** speeder
military: **5** agger
surface: tar **6** bricks, gravel, stones **7** macadam **8** concrete, pavement
roadblock: bar **7** barrier **8** blockade
road book: map **9** gazetteer, itinerary
roadhouse: inn **5** hotel, lodge **6** tavern
roadman: **7** drummer, peddler **8** salesman **9** canvasser
road runner: **6** cuckoo **7** paisano(Sp.)
roadster: **5** horse **7** bicycle **8** runabout
roam: err, gad **4** roil, rove **5** prowl, range, stray **6** bangle, ramble, stroll, travel, wander **7** meander **8** straggle **9** gallivant
roamer: **5** gipsy, gypsy, nomad, rover **8** fugitive **12** peregrinator
roan: bay **5** color, horse **9** sheepskin
Roanoke bell: **7** cowslip
roar: cry, din **4** bawl, beal, bell, bere, boom, bray, clap, hurl, rote, rout, yell **5** blart, brool, fream, laugh, shout **6** bellow, buller, clamor, outcry, steven **7** bluster, thunder **8** shouting
roaring: **4** loud **5** aroar, brisk, noisy **7** riotous **10** boisterous, disorderly, stentorian **11** flourishing
roaring game: **7** curling
roaring Meg: **6** cannon
roast: fry **4** bake, burn, cook, razz, roti(F.) **5** asado(Sp.), brede, grill, parch **6** assate, banter **7** torrefy, torrify **8** lambaste, ridicule **9** criticize
meat on stick: **5** cabob, kabob
prepare: **5** truss
roasting stick: **4** spit **6** skewer
rob: cop **4** fake, flap, loot, pelf, take **5** bribe, filch, harry, heist, pilch, pinch, pluck, raven, reave, rifle, spoil, steal, strip, touch **6** burgle, hold up, pilfer, pirate, ravish, shrive, snatch, snitch, thieve **7** bereave, defraud, deprive, despoil, pillage, plunder, purloin **10** burglarize, housebreak, plagiarize
Rob Roy: **5** canoe
robber: **4** goul, yegg **5** ghoul, thief **6** arrant, bandit, cat-man, dacoit, pirate **7** brigand, corsair, footpad, ladrone, yeggman **8** marauder **9** bandolero, buccaneer, privateer **10** depredator, highwayman
robe (see also **dress, gown**): aba **4** skin, vest, wrap **5** array, camis, camus, cloak, cover, cymar, habit, simar, talar, tunic **6** caftan, chimer, clothe, dolman, invest, kimono, mantle, revest **7** chimere,

costume, garment, manteau, vesture **8** clothing, covering, vestment **10** sticharion

robin: 4 lout, tody **6** oriole, thrush **7** bumpkin, chewink, warbler **8** trimming **10** cuckoopint, toxalbumin

Robin Goodfellow: elf **4** Puck **5** fairy **6** sprite **9** hobgoblin

Robin Hood: *chaplain:* **9** Friar Tuck
follower: **4** John **9** Friar Tuck
sweetheart: **6** Marian **10** Maid Marian

robin sandpiper: 4 knot **9** dowitcher

robinet: 6 cannon **9** chaffinch

Robinson Crusoe: *author:* **5** Defoe
companion: **9** Man Friday

roborant: 4 drug **5** tonic **13** strengthening

roborean: 5 oaken, stout **6** strong

robot: 5 droid, golem **7** android **9** androides, automaton
drama about: RUR

robust: 4 hale, hard, iron, rude **5** hardy, lusty, rough, sound, stout, wally **6** brawny, coarse, hearty, rugged, sinewy, strong, sturdy **7** healthy **8** athletic, muscular, vigorous **10** boisterous, flourishing

roc: 4 bird **6** simurg **7** simurgh, soldier

rocca: 4 hold, keep **6** donjon **8** fortress

rochet: 5 cloak, frock **7** camisia, garment, gurnard **8** vestment
relative: alb

rock: dag, ore, tor **4** clay, crag, lull, peak, reef, reel, roll, scar, shog, spar, sway, toss, trap, tufa, tuff, wash **5** agate, brack, candy, chert, cliff, earth, flint, geest, hurry, lytta, prase, scree, shake, shale, shaul, slate, stane(Sc.), stone, swing, wacke **6** aplite, basalt, dacite, egeran, gneiss, gravel, issite, oolite, pebble, refuge, rognon, schist, silica, sinter, teeter, totter **7** adinole, akerite, alunite, defense, diamond, gondite, granite, griesen, support, tremble, vibrate **8** andesite, banakite, dolomite, laterite, obsidian, porphyry, psephite, rhyolite, undulate **9** epidosite, flagstone, oscillate, phanerite **10** greenstone, promontory **11** petrography
boring tool: **6** trepan
cavity: vug **4** vugg **5** druse, geode
clay: **8** ganister
debris: **5** talus **8** detritus, xenolith
decomposed: **6** gossan
discarded: **5** attle
finely broken: **4** sand
fissile: **5** shale
flintlike: **5** chert **6** quartz
fold: **8** syncline **9** anticline
fragments: see *debris* above
glacier deposit: **7** moraine
glacier-transported: **7** erratic

igneous: **4** boss, sial, sima, trap, tufa **5** trass **6** basalt, domite, latite **7** diabase, diorite, felsite, ijolite, peridot **8** extaxite, ijussite, porphyry **11** agglomerate
laminated: **4** mica **5** shale, slate
liquid: **4** lava
mythical: **6** Scylla
nodule: **5** geode
pert. to: **6** petric **7** petrean
point: **4** crag, peak
science: **9** petrology
strata: see *fold* above
volcanic: **4** lava, tufa, tuff

rockabilly: 12 country music

rock badger: 4 cony **5** hyrax

rock bass: 6 red-eye **8** cabrilla

rock bottom: 6 lowest **7** essence **8** cheapest

rock dove: 6 pigeon **9** guillemot

rock eel: 6 gunnel

rock falcon: 6 merlin

rock geranium: 8 alumroot

rock goat: 4 ibex

rock grouse: 9 ptarmigan

rock hind: 7 grouper

rock hopper: 7 penguin

rock kangaroo: 7 wallaby

rock oak: 8 chestnut **10** California, chinquapin

rock oil: 9 petroleum

rock plant: 4 moss **6** lichen

rock rabbit: 5 hyrax

rock snake: 5 krait **6** python

rock starling: 5 ouzel

rock tar: 9 petroleum

rock tripe: 6 lichen

rock wren: 4 bird

rockaway: 8 carriage

rockbell: 9 columbine

rockbird: 5 murre **9** sandpiper

rocker: 5 chair, skate **6** cradle **7** shoofly

rocket: 4 weld, wold **5** slate, woald, would **9** satellite **11** firecracker
end of combustion: **7** burnout
landing: **7** reentry **10** splashdown
launcher: **7** bazooka
launching: **4** shot **8** blastoff
launching postponement: **5** abort

rockfish: 4 bass, rena **5** perch, reina, viuva **6** gopher, tambor **7** grouper **9** killifish **10** priestfish

rockling: 4 fish, gade

rockrose: 6 cistus

rocky: 4 hard, weak **5** dizzy, shaky, stony **6** cliffy **7** obscene, petrean **8** obdurate, unsteady **9** unfeeling **10** insensible

Rocky Mountain: *goat:* **6** mazame **8** antelope
park: **5** Estes
peak: **5** Logan, Pikes
range: **5** Teton **7** Wasatch
sheep: **7** bighorn

wind: **7** chinook
rococo: **4** arty **6** ornate **9** fantastic **10** flamboyant
rod: bar, gad, guy, rab, rib **4** axle, bolt, came, cane, crop, goad, I-bar, lath, pole, prod, race, scob, spit, wand, wire **5** arrow, baton, board, lytta, osier, perch, power, scion, spoke, staff, stick, stock, strip, tribe **6** baculi(pl.), batten, broach, carbon, etalon, eyebar, ferule, needle, pistol, piston, pontil, raddle, skewer, switch, toggle **7** baculus, caliper, crowbar, distaff, measure, scepter, sceptre, spindle, stemmer, support, tringle, tyranny **8** arrester, offshoot, revolver **9** authority **10** oppression, punishment **12** chastisement
bundle: **6** fasces
divination by: **7** dowsing **11** rhabdomancy
movable: **6** piston
square: **5** perch
rod-like: **6** rhabdo **7** virgate
rodd: **8** crossbow, stonebow
rodent: jap, rat **4** cavy, cony, cypu, degu, hare, mole, paca, pica, pika, utia, vole **5** aguti, hutia, jutia, lerot, mouse, ratel, zokor **6** agouti, agouty, beaver, biting, cururo, gerbil, gopher, gundie, jerboa, marmot, murine, rabbit, weasel **7** chincha, hamster, leveret, muskrat, pack rat **8** capibara, capybara, dormouse, gerbille, leporide, sewellel, squirrel, viscacha, vizcacha **9** porcupine **10** chinchilla
aquatic: **6** beaver **7** muskrat
genus: Mus **5** Lepus
jumping: **6** jerboa
pert. to: **8** rosorial
rodeo: **7** roundup **9** enclosure **10** exhibition
rodge: **7** gadwall
rodman: **4** thug **10** highwaymen
rodomontade: **4** brag, rant **5** boast, empty, pride **6** vanity **7** bluster, bombast **8** boastful, boasting, braggart
roe: ova, pea **4** deer, eggs, hart, hind **5** coral, spawn **6** caviar
roebuck: **4** girl **9** chevreuil
Roentgen's discovery: **4** X ray
roestone: **6** oolite
rogation: law **6** decree, litany, prayer **7** inquiry **12** supplication
rogue: boy, gue, imp, wag **4** hemp, kite **5** catso, cheat, crank, decry, gipsy, gypsy, hempy, knave, scamp, shark, tramp **6** beggar, canter, coquin, harlot, pirate, rascal, wander **7** corsair, culprit, erratic, hellion, sharper, vagrant, villain, waggish **8** picaroon, swindler, vagabond **9** scoundrel, trickster **10** delinquent, frolicsome, stigmatize **11** rapscallion
pert. to: **10** picaresque

roguery: **5** fraud **8** mischief, trickery **15** mischievousness
roguish: coy, sly **4** arch **5** pawky **6** wanton **7** playful, puckish **8** espiegle, sportive **9** dishonest, fun-loving **12** unscrupulous
roid: **5** rough **6** severe **7** riotous, roguish **10** frolicsome **12** unmanageable
roil: mud, vex **4** foul, rile, roam, romp, rust, stir **5** anger, annoy, muddy, rouse **6** cloudy, fidget, ruffle, wander **7** blunder, disturb, pollute **8** irritate **9** displease, unsettled **10** exasperate **11** contaminate
roily: **6** turbid
roister: **4** brag, rude **5** bully, revel, spree **7** bluster, boorish, carouse, reveler, swagger, violent **9** gilravage
roistering: **6** hoiden, hoyden
rojo: **6** Indian **7** redskin
roke: fog **4** mist, stir **5** smoke, steam, vapor **8** moisture
roker: ray **8** rockling **9** thornback
roky: **4** damp **5** foggy, misty, smoky **6** hoarse
Roland: **7** Orlando
beloved: **4** Aude
emperor: **11** Charlemagne
enemy: **4** Gano **7** Ganelon
friend: **6** Oliver
horn: **7** Olivant
horse: **10** Veillantif
sword: **8** Durendal
uncle: **11** Charlemagne
role: bit **4** cast, duty, part **5** cameo, heavy **6** office **8** business, function **9** character, soubrette **13** impersonation **16** characterization
leading: **4** star
roll: bun, gad, rob **4** bolt, coil, file, flow, furl, list, pell, pour, roam, rota, seel, sway, toss, turn, wind, wrap **5** bagel, cadre, frisk, lurch, shift, surge, swing, trill, troll, wheel **6** bundle, enroll, enwrap, goggle, grovel, ponder, roster, rotate, rumble, scroll, spiral, swathe, tumble, wallow, wander, welter, whelve, wintle **7** biscuit, brioche, fortune, revolve, rissole, stagger, swagger, trundle **8** cylinder, flounder, register, undulate
of hair: bun **7** chignon
sweet: **6** danish **9** schnecken
roll back: **5** lower **6** reduce **7** repulse
roll in: **4** flow **6** arrive, wallow, welter
roll up: **4** furl **5** amass **6** arrive, gather **10** accumulate
roller: **4** band, wave **5** finer, inker, swath **6** canary, caster, fascia, fillet, pigeon, platen, rowlet, sponge **7** bandage, breaker, presser, sirgang, tumbler **8** cylinder **9** surcingle

rolleyway: 4 road 5 track 7 gangway, tramway

rollick: 4 romp 5 sport 6 frolic, gambol, wallow 8 escapade

rollicking: gay 5 antic, happy 6 jovial, lively 8 careless 9 hilarious 12 lighthearted

rolling stock: 4 cars 6 trucks 7 coaches, engines 8 cabooses, Pullmans, sleepers, trailers 11 locomotives

rolling stone: 5 rover 7 drifter 8 wanderer

rolling weed: 10 tumbleweed

rolltop: 4 desk

roly-poly: 5 dumpy, pudgy, round 6 portly, rotund 7 pudding

rom: 5 gipsy, gypsy

romaine: cos 5 plant 7 lettuce

romal: 5 thong

Roman: 5 brave, Latin 6 frugal, honest, simple 7 Italian

Roman Catholic: *cassock:* 7 soutane, zimarra

  church: 7 lateran

  ecclesiastic: 7 Rosmini

  priest: 4 abbe(F.) 6 father 8 sacerdos 9 monsignor

  skullcap: 9 zucchetto

  society: 7 Jesuits

romance: woo 4 gest, tale 5 court, dream, fable, fancy, feign, geste, novel, story 6 affair 7 chimera, fantasy, fiction, romanza 9 falsehood, sentiment 10 exaggerate, love affair 12 exaggeration

Romance language: 6 French 7 Catalan, Italian, Spanish 8 Rumanian 9 Provencal 10 Portuguese

Romania: See **Rumania**

romantic: 6 exotic, poetic, unreal 8 quixotic 9 imaginary, visionary 10 idealistic 11 extravagant, sentimental

Romany, Rommany: 5 gipsy, gypsy

  tongue: 7 Romanes

romanza: 7 fiction, romance

Rome (see also **Latin**): 4 Roma

  abode of gods: 7 Olympus

  adviser to king: 6 Egeria

  airport: 8 Ciampino 9 Fiumicino 15 Leonardo da Vinci

  amphitheater: 9 colosseum

  apostle: 4 Neri, Paul

  army unit: 6 cohort

  army wing: ala

  assembly: 5 forum 6 senate 7 comitia

  attendant: 7 aliptes 8 aleiptes

  augur: 6 auspex

  author (see also *biographer, historian, poet,* below): 5 Pliny, Varro

  authority symbol: 6 fasces

  basilica: 7 lateran

  battle array: 5 acies

  biographer: 5 Nepos 9 Suetonius

  brothers: 5 Remus 7 Romulus

  burial site: 9 Catacombs

  Caesar's title: 9 imperator

  captain: 9 centurion

  carriage: 5 essed

  chapel: 7 Sistine

  chief god: 4 Jove 7 Jupiter

  citadel: arx

  clans: 4 gens

  cloak: 4 toga

  coin: aes 5 assis(pl.), aurei(pl.), semis 6 aureus, dinder, solidu, triens 7 denarii(pl.), siliqua 8 decussis, denarius, sesterce, sesteria(pl.) 9 sesterium 10 sestertius, victoriate 11 victoriatus

  comedy: 5 exode

  comedy writer: 6 Cicero 7 Plautus, Terence

  concert hall: 5 odeum

  conqueror: 6 Alaric

  conspirator: 8 Catiline

  court: 5 atria(pl.) 6 atrium

  custodian: 10 neocorates

  date: 4 Ides 5 Nones

  district: 5 Pagus 7 Pontine 8 Pomptine

  diviner: 5 augur 6 auspex

  division: 5 curia

  earthwork: 5 agger

  emperor: 4 Nero, Otho, Otto 5 Galba, Nerva, Titus 6 Caesar, Julian, Trajan 7 Hadrian 8 Augustus, Claudius, Domitian, Tiberius 9 Vespasian 10 Elagabalus 11 Constantine

  empress: 7 Eudocia

  encampment: 7 castrum

  entrance hall: 5 atria(pl.) 6 atrium

  epic: 6 Aeneid

  family: 7 familia

  farmer: 7 colonus 8 agricola

  Fate: 4 Nona 5 Morta, Parca 6 Decuma, Parcae(pl.)

  fighter: 9 gladiator

  fortress: 7 castrum

  founder: 5 Remus 7 Romulus

  fountain: 5 Trevi

  galley: 6 bireme 7 trireme

  garment: 4 toga 5 palla, sagum, stola, stole, togae(pl.), tunic

  general: 5 Sulla, Titus 6 Antony, Marius, Scipio 8 Agricola

  god: Dis, Lar, Sol 4 Amor, Jove, Mars 5 Comus, Cupid, Fauns, Janus, Lares, manes, Orcus, Pluto 6 Faunus, Vulcan 7 Jupiter, lemures, Neptune, penates, Phoebus, Vatican 8 Dispater, Morpheus, Quirinus 11 Aesculapius

  god of dead: 5 Orcus

  god of death: 4 Mors

  god of fire: 6 Vulcan

  god of love: 4 Amor

  god of mirth: 5 Comus

  god of sea: 7 Neptune

  god of sleep: 8 Morpheus

god of sun: Sol
god of underworld: Dis **5** Pluto
god of war: **4** Mars
god of wind: **5** Eurus **6** Boreas
god of wine: **7** Bacchus
goddess: dea(L.), Lua, Nox, Ops, Pax **4**
 Caca, Juno, Luna, Maia, Paca **5** Ceres,
 Diana, Epona, Terra, Venus, Vesta **6**
 Aestas, Annona, Aurora, Lucina, Rumi-
 na, Tellus, Vacuna **7** Bellona, Fortuna,
 Minerva **8** Libitina **9** Abudantia, Discordia, Felicitas
goddess of agriculture: Ops **5** Ceres
goddess of beauty: **5** Venus
goddess of flowers: **5** Flora
goddess of hearth: **5** Vesta **6** Hestia
goddess of hope: **4** Spes
goddess of hunting: **5** Diana
goddess of love: **5** Venus
goddess of marriage: **4** Juno
goddess of moon: **4** Luna
goddess of night: Nox
goddess of peace: Pax **5** Irene
goddess of plenty: Ops
goddess of underworld: **10** Proserpina
goddess of vegetation: **5** Ceres
goddess of victory: **6** Vacuna
goddess of war: **7** Bellona, Minerva
goddess of wisdom: **7** Minerva
greeting: ave
guard: **6** lictor
hall: **5** atria(pl.) **6** atrium
hat: **7** petasos, petasus
helmet: **5** galea **6** galeae(pl.)
highway: via **4** iter **6** Appian **8** itiner-
 es(pl.)
hill: **7** Caelian, Viminal **8** Aventine, Palatine, Quirinal **9** Esquiline **10** Capitoline
historian: **4** Livy **5** Nepos
holiday: **5** feria **6** feriae(pl.)
judge: **5** edile **6** aedile
jurist: **5** Gaius
king: **7** Romulus, Servius, Tullius **12** An-
 cus Martius **13** Numa Pompilius **15**
 Tullus Hostilius **18** Tarquinius Super-
 bus
lake: **4** Nemi
language: **5** Latin
law: fas, lex **4** cern
leader: dux
magistrate: **5** edile **6** aedile, censor, pretor
 7 praetor, tribune
marble: **7** cipolin
measure: pes, urn **4** mile, pace, urna **5** actus, clima, cubit, juger **6** culeus, dolium,
 gradus, hemina, modius, palmus, passus, saltus, versus **7** amphora, congius,
 cyathus, digitus, stadion, stadium **8**
 centuria, hereduim, quadrant **9** decem-
 peda, millarium, sextarius **10** acetabulum, quartarius
measure of weight: bes **4** pood **5** assis(pl.),

libra, uncia **6** duella **7** dodrans, sextula,
 solidus **8** sicilium **9** scrupulus, scrupu-
 lum
military formation: ala **6** alares(pl.) **7**
 phalanx
military machine: **7** terebra
military unit: **6** cohort, legion **7** maniple
military vessel: **6** bireme **7** trireme
naturalist: **5** Pliny
nymph: **6** Egeria
official: **5** augur, edile **6** aedile, lictor **7**
 prefect, tribune **8** irenarch **9** nestorian
ox: **4** urus
palace: **5** chigi **7** lateran
palace troops: **9** palatines
people: **5** Laeti **7** Sabines **8** plebians **10**
 patricians
pert. to: **9** classical
philosopher: **4** Cato **6** Seneca
physician: **9** archiater **11** Aesculapius
pillager: **6** Alaric
pin: **4** acus
poet: **4** Ovid **5** Cinna, Lucan **6** Horace,
 Vergil, Virgil **7** Juvenal, Terence **8** Ca-
 tullus, Tibullus **10** Propertius
port: **5** Ostia
praenomen: **5** Aulus, Caius, Gaius, Titus
 6 Appius **7** Quintus, Spurius **8** Tiberius
priest: **5** epulo **6** flamen **7** luperci
priestess: **6** vestal
procurator: **5** Felix **6** Pilate
province: **5** Dacia **7** Cilicia
queen of goddesses: **4** Juno
racecourse: **6** circus
regulator: **6** censor
religious law: fas
river: **5** Tiber
road: **4** iter
room: ala **5** atria(pl.) **6** atrium **7** tablin-
 a(pl.) **8** fumarium, tablinum
rural deity: **6** Faunus
saint: **4** Neri
senate division: **5** curia
senate emblem: **9** laticlave
senate house: **5** curia
shield: scuta(pl.) **6** ancile, scutum **7** anci-
 lia(pl.), clypeus
slave: **9** Spartacus
spirits of dead: **5** manes
standard: **7** labarum, vexilla(pl.) **8** vexillum
standard-bearer: **9** vexillary
statesman: **4** Cato **5** Pliny **6** Caesar, Cicero, Seneca **7** Agrippa **8** Maecenas
tax gatherer: **8** publican
temple: **4** naos **5** cella **8** pantheon
treasurer: **8** quaestor
veteran: **7** emeriti(pl.) **8** emeritus
weight: see *measure of weight* above
writing tablet: **7** diptych
Romeo: **7** gallant
 beloved: **6** Juliet

enemy: **6** Tybalt
father: **8** Montague
friend: **8** Mercutio
rival: **5** Paris
romp: 4 hoit, play, roil **6** cavort, frolic, gambol, hoiden, hoyden **7** carouse, courant, gammock **8** carousal, courante **9** cut capers
Romulus: *brother:* **5** Remus
father: **4** Mars
rondure: orb **4** ball **5** globe, round **6** circle, sphere **9** plumpness, roundness
rood: 5 cross **7** measure **8** crucifix
roodebok: 6 impala
roof: top **5** cover **6** harbor **7** palate, shelter **8** covering
border: **4** eave
of mouth: **6** palate
style: hip **4** dome, flat, nave, sark **5** gable, spire **6** cupola **7** cricket, gambrel, mansard **9** penthouse pyramidal **10** jerkinhead
support: **6** rafter
window: **6** dormer
roofing material: tar, tin **4** tile **5** paper, slate, straw, terne **6** copper, gravel, shakes, thatch **7** pantile **8** shingles
rook: 4 bird, crow **5** cheat, raven, steal **6** castle, fleece **7** defraud, sharper, swindle **8** swindler
rookery: 5 roost **8** building
rookie: 4 tyro **6** novice **7** recruit, trainee **8** beginner **10** apprentice
rooky: 5 foggy **6** untidy **10** disheveled
room: ala, ben, den **4** aula, cell, digs, hall, loge, play, sala(Sp.), seat **5** atria(pl.), aulae(pl.), cubby, divan, kiosk, lodge, place, salle(F.), salon, scope, space **6** atrium, casino, harbor, leeway, margin, reside, saloon, scouth **7** boudoir, cabinet, chamber, cubicle, expanse, gallery, lodging, rotunda, theater **9** apartment, garderobe **10** auditorium
conversation: **6** exedra **7** exedrae(pl.) **11** drawing room
eating: **4** nook **7** cenacle, kitchen **8** cenacula(pl.) **9** cenaculum, refectory
on a ship: **5** cabin **6** galley
private: **7** boudoir
provision: **4** ewry **5** ewery **6** larder **7** pantry **8** cupboard
reading: den **5** study **7** library **8** Atheneum
sleeping: **5** lodge **6** dormer **7** barrack, bedroom **8** roomette **9** dormitory
storage: **4** loft, shed **5** attic **6** cellar **9** storeroom
room and board: 14 accommodations
roomer: 5 guest **6** lodger, tenant **7** boarder
rooms: 4 flat **5** suite **9** apartment
roomy: 5 ample, broad, spacy **8** spacious

9 capacious **10** commodious
roorback, roorbach: lie **4** hoax **6** canard **7** fiction **9** falsehood
roose: 5 boast, extol, vaunt **6** praise
Roosevelt, F. D.: *dog:* **4** Fala
mother: **4** Sara
wife: **7** Eleanor
roost: sit **4** nest, pole, rest **5** abode, perch, sleep **6** alight, garret **7** lodging, support
rooster: 4 cock **5** gallo(Sp.) **11** chanticleer
root: dig **4** base, bulb, core, grub, moot, rout, stem **5** basis, cheer, grout, plant, radix, shout, tuber **6** bottom, center, etymon, ground, origin, settle **7** applaud, essence, radical, radices(pl.), rootlet, support **8** entrench **9** beginning, establish **10** foundation
dyeing: **6** madder
edible: oca, roi, rue, uva, yam **4** beet, eddo, taro **5** orris, tania **6** carrot, ginger, orrice, radish, turnip **7** parsnip **8** rutabaga **9** sassafras
fragrant: **4** khus **5** orris
medicinal: **5** jalap, lappa **7** ginseng
outer layer: **7** exoderm
pert. to: **7** radical
principal: **7** taproot
pungent: **11** crinkleroot
starch: **4** arum
root out: 4 stub **6** evulse **7** destroy **8** demolish **9** eradicate, extirpate **10** annihilate, deracinate
rooted: 10 inveterate
rooter: fan **10** enthusiast
rootlet: 7 radicle, rhizoid
rootstock: 5 orris **6** ginger, pannum, stolon **7** rhizome
rope: gad, guy, tie, tow **4** bind, cord, hemp, line, stay **5** cable, longe, riata, sheet, widdy **6** binder, fasten, halter, hawser, lariat, shroud, tether **7** aweband, binding, bobstay, bollard, cordage, halyard, marline, painter **8** inveigle, prolonge
animal's: **5** leash **6** halter, tether
fiber: **4** coir, flax, jute **5** istle, sisal **6** cotton, Manila
holder: **6** becket
loop: **5** bight, noose **6** becket, parral, parrel
restraining: **6** tether
ship's: tye **4** colt, lift, rode, stay, vang **5** brace, braid, sheet **6** hawser, inhaul, parral, parrel, ratlin, shroud **7** halyard, lanyard, painter, ratline
splice pin: fid
throwing: **5** lasso, reata, riata **6** lariat
ropedancer: 7 acrobat **9** funambulo **11** funambulist
roper: 6 cowboy, packer
ropery: 6 banter **7** roguery

ropes: 8 minutiae 10 ins and outs
roque: 7 croquet
roric: 4 dewy
rosary: 4 bede 5 beads 7 chaplet, garland 8 beadroll
rose (see also **rise**): ris 5 blush, delta, flush 6 flower, nozzle 7 rambler, rosette 9 hellebore
  family: 8 rosaceae
  kind of: dog 4 moss, musk
  oil: 4 atar, otto 5 attar, ottar
  part: 5 petal
Rose City: 8 Pasadena, Portland
rose of Sharon: 6 althea 11 shrubby plant
rose parakeet: 7 rosella
rose pogonia: 10 snakemouth
rosebay: 8 oleander
rosemary: 4 herb, mint 8 moorwort
rosette: 4 chou, knot 7 cockade 8 ornament
rosilla: 9 rockbrush 10 sneezeweed
rosin: See **resin**
Rosinante: nag 4 jade, plug 5 horse, steed
rosiness: 5 blush, flush
ross: 4 bark, peel 5 waste 8 exterior
roster: 4 list, roll, rota 5 slate 6 muster 7 catalog
rostrum: 4 beak, dais 5 snout, stage 6 pulpit 7 lectern, tribune 8 platform 9 proboscis
rosy: red 4 pink 5 ruddy 6 bright, florid 7 auroral, flushed, hopeful, roseate 8 blooming, blushing, cheerful, rubicund 9 favorable, promising, rosaceous 10 favourable, optimistic
rot: ret 4 bosh, dote, doze, joke 5 chaff, decay, spoil, tease, trash 6 banter, fester, perish 7 corrupt, putrefy, rubbish, twaddle 8 nonsense 9 decompose, poppycock 10 degenerate 13 decomposition
rota: 4 list, roll 5 court, round 6 course, roster 8 register
rotate: 4 pass, roll, spin, turn 5 twirl, wheel, whirl 6 gyrate 7 perform, revolve, trundle 8 rotiform 9 alternate, take turns
rotation: 4 eddy 6 torque, vortex 9 pirouette 10 revolution
  part: cam 4 axle 5 rotor, wheel
rote: 4 list 5 learn 6 course, custom, memory, repeat, system 7 routine 8 practice 9 automatic 10 memorizing, repetition
rotiform: 6 rotate 11 wheel-shaped
rotor: 7 spinner 8 impeller
rotten: bad 4 evil, foul 5 fetid, nasty 6 putrid 7 carrion, corrupt, decayed, spoiled, tainted, unsound, vicious 8 depraved, unstable 9 offensive, putrefied 10 abdominable, decomposed, putrescent, undermined 12 disagreeable 13 disintegrated 14 unsatisfactory

rotter: cad 7 shirker, slacker 10 blackguard
rotula: 5 round 6 troche 7 kneepan, lozenge, patella
rotund: 5 beefy, chunky, obese, plump, round, stout 6 chubby, portly 7 rounded 8 rolypoly, sonorant, sonorous 9 spherical
roturier: 7 freeman, upstart 8 commoner
roué: rip 4 rake 9 debauchee, libertine
rouge: red 5 blush, color, flush, paint, score 6 redden, ruddle 8 cosmetic
rough: 4 hard, rude, wild 5 acrid, brute, crude, gross, hairy, harsh, husky, lumpy, raggy, rowdy, seamy, stern, surly, tight, tough, uncut 6 abrupt, broken, choppy, coarse, crabby, craggy, hoarse, jagged, rugged, severe, shaggy, uneven 7 austere, boorish, bristly, brusque, grating, hirsute, inexact, jarring, raucous, ruffian, ruffled, uncivil 8 churlish, clownish, gangster, impolite, obdurate, unplaned 9 imperfect, inclement, turbulent, unrefined 10 boisterous, discordant, incomplete, indecorous, tumultuous, unpleasant, unpolished 11 approximate, tempestuous
rough-and-ready: 9 makeshift 10 unpolished
roughen: 4 chap, fret, shag 5 feaze 7 engrail 10 exasperate
roughneck: 4 boor 5 rowdy, tough
roughness: 7 crudity 8 acrimony, asperity, inequality
rough out: 6 sketch
rough up: 9 manhandle
rouky: 5 foggy, misty
roulade: 8 arpeggio, division, flourish
roulette: 10 epicyloid 11 epitrochoid 12 gambling game, hypotrochoid
  bet: bas 4 noir 5 carre, rouge 6 milieu 7 dernier, encarre, enplein
rounceval: 5 giant, large 6 virago 7 monster 8 gigantic 9 termagant
round: 4 ball, beat, bout, full, rung 5 group, large, orbed, plump 6 circle, curved, nearly, period, polish, rotund 7 bulbous, circuit, liberal, through 8 circular, complete, globular, resonant, rolypoly 9 outspoken, spherical 11 cylindrical
round clam: 6 quahog
round dance: hay, ray 5 polka, waltz 7 roundel 9 roundelay, schottish 11 schottische
round robin: 6 letter, series 7 contest 8 document, petition, sequence 9 cigarfish 10 tournament
Round Table knight: Kay 4 Bors, Owen 6 Gawain 7 Caradoc, Cradock, Gaheris, Galahad 8 Lancelot, Tristram 9 Percivale

roundabout: 4 tour **5** dance **6** detour **7** devious **8** circular, indirect, tortuous, verbiage **9** excursion **10** circuitous, farfetched **13** approximately **14** circumlocution, circumlocutory

rounded: 4 oval **5** bombe, ovate **6** convex, curved, rotund **7** arrondi, bunting, gibbous **8** circular **10** curvaceous, labialized

roundel: 4 guze, hurt **5** plate **6** circle, pellet, shield

rounder: 4 roue **5** sport **7** wastrel **8** criminal, drunkard, preacher **11** spendthrift

roundhead: 5 Swede **7** Puritan

roundup: 5 rodeo **7** summary **9** gathering

roundworm: 4 nema **7** ascaris **8** nematode

roup: 4 sale **6** clamor **7** auction **8** shouting

rouse: daw, hie **4** call, move, stir, wake, whet **5** alarm, awake, raise, rally, start, toast, upset, waken **6** arouse, awaken, bestir, excite, foment, frolic, revive, stir up **7** actuate, agitate, animate, disturb, enliven, provoke, startle **8** inspirit **9** intensify, stimulate

Rousseau hero: 5 Emile

roussette: 5 shark **7** dogfish

roust: 4 roar, stir, tide **5** rouse **6** bellow, tumult **7** current, provoke, roaring **9** bellowing

roustabout: 4 hand **6** worker **7** laborer **8** floorman

rout: mob **4** band, beat, bray, dart, fuss, roar, root **5** crowd, drive, expel, knock, noise, scoop, shout, snore, snort, troop **6** bellow, clamor, defeat, furrow, rabble, search, strike, throng, tumult, uproar **7** company, confuse, debacle, repulse, retinue, retreat, rummage, slumber, trouble **8** assemble, assembly, confound, disperse, reversal, shouting, stampede, vanquish **9** discomfit, multitude, overpower, overthrow, overwhelm **11** disturbance, put to flight **12** discomfiture

route: way **4** gest, lane, line, path, road, send **5** geste, guide, march, trail **6** course, skyway **7** circuit, journey **9** direction, itinerary

circuitous: **6** detour

ocean: **4** lane

straight: **7** beeline

routh: 6 plenty **8** abundant **9** abundance, plentiful

routine: rut **4** pace, rote **5** grind, habit, round, troll, usual **6** course, groove, system **8** habitual, ordinary **9** treadmill

rove: gad **4** move, part, pass, plow, roam, turn **5** prowl, range, stray **6** maraud, pierce, ramble, stroll, wander **8** straggle

rover: 5 nomad **6** pirate **7** corsair, drifter, floater, Ishmael, migrant, vagrant **8** gadabout **9** itinerant

roving: 6 errant **7** cursory, devious **9** desultory, itinerant **10** discursive

row: air, oar **4** bank, dust, file, fuss, line, list, pull, rank, sail, scud, spat, tier **5** align, aline, brawl, broil, garry, mouth, noise, scold, scull, swath **6** barney, clamor, paddle, pother, propel, rumpus, swathe **7** dispute, quarrel, ruction **8** argument, squabble **9** catalogue, commotion, excursion **11** disturbance **13** collieshangie

form in: **4** line **5** align, aline

rowan tree: ash **4** sorb

rowboat: 4 cog, gig **4** dory, skif **5** canoe, cobil, coble, scull, skiff, skift **6** caique, galley, randan, wherry

stern: **7** transom

rowdy: 4 b'hoy, punk, rude **5** rough, tough **6** roarer, trickly **7** hoodlum, vicious **8** larrikin, plug-ugly **9** obstinate, roughneck **10** boisterous

rowel: 4 spur **5** wheel **6** circle

rowen: 4 crop **5** field **9** aftermath

rower: oar **6** punter **7** oarsman

rowing: 6 randan **8** sculling

royal: 4 easy, real, rial, stag, true **5** basil, grand, regal **6** august, kingly, superb **7** stately **8** imperial, imposing, majestic, princely, splendid **9** excellent, sovereign **11** magnificent, monarchical

royal agaric: 8 mushroom

Royal Canadian Mounted Police: 7 Mountie

royal rock snake: 6 python

royal standard: 4 flag **6** banner, emblem

royalist: 4 Tory **8** Cavalier **11** reactionary

royalty: 5 share **6** emblem **7** kingdom **8** dividend, kingship, nobility **10** kingliness, percentage **11** sovereignty

denoting: **5** crown **6** ermine, purple **7** scepter

symbol: **6** ermine

rub: irk, vex **4** bark, bray, buff, fret, rasp, wear, wipe **5** chafe, dight, feeze, grind, peeve, scour, smear **6** abrade, anoint, fridge, nettle, polish, scrape, smooth, stroke **7** burnish, massage **8** friction, irritate, obstacle **9** hindrance, triturate **10** difficulty, impediment

rub down: 4 comb, wipe **5** curry, groom **7** massage

rub elbows: 6 jostle **9** associate **10** fraternize

rub out: 4 kill **5** elide, erase **6** cancel, efface, murder **7** expunge **10** obliterate

rubber: 4 band **5** brick **6** caucho, cutter, eraser **7** ebonite, masseur **8** busybody, masseuse, overshoe, polisher **9** vulcanite **10** caoutchouc

juice: **6** achete

source: 5 latex
substitute: 7 factice
synthetic: 4 buna 5 butyl
tree: 7 seringa
Rubber City: 5 Akron
rubberneck: 4 gape 5 stare 6 butt-in 7 meddler, tourist 8 busybody, kibitzer, quidnunc
rubber tree: ule 4 para 6 caucho 7 seringa 10 caoutchouc
rubbish: ket(Sc.), pap 4 flam, gear, junk, mull, pelf, pelt, raff, rose 5 crawm, dross, offal, trash, waste, wrack 6 colder, debris, garble, litter, refuse, rubble, trashy 7 baggage, beggary, mullock, rùmmage 8 nonsense, trumpery 9 worthless 10 clamjamfry 11 foolishness
rube: 4 hick, jake 6 rustic 7 bumpkin, hayseed 9 hillbilly 10 countryman
rubellite: 10 tourmaline
rubeola: 7 measles, rubella
rubescent: red 4 pink 8 blushing, flushing 9 reddening 10 erubescent
rubicund: red 4 rosy, ruby 5 ruddy 6 florid 7 flushed, reddish, redness 8 sanguine 11 fullblooded
rubor: 9 hyperemia
rubric: red 4 name 5 title 6 redden 7 concept, heading 8 category
book: 4 ordo 7 ordines(pl.)
ruby: gem, red 5 balas, jewel, stone 6 spinel 7 rubasse
ruck: rut, sit 4 fold, heap, mass, pile, rake, rick 5 cower, crowd, squat, stack 6 crease, crouch, furrow, pucker 7 crumple, wrinkle 9 gathering, multitude
ruckus: ado, row 6 rumpus, uproar 7 ruction 9 confusion 11 disturbance
ruction: 4 fray 5 fight, melee 6 uproar 7 quarrel 8 fraction, outbreak 11 disturbance
rudder: *control:* 4 helm 6 tiller
edge: 8 bearding
part: 4 yoke
ruddle: 5 rouge 6 redden
ruddy: red 4 rosy 5 fresh 6 florid, tanned 7 reddish 8 blushing
rude: 4 bold, curt, lewd 5 bluff, crude, harsh, rough, rowdy 6 bloody, borrel, brutal, clumsy, coarse, crusty, fierce, rugged, rustic, savage, severe, vulgar 7 artless, boorish, brutish, country, jarring, loutish, uncivil, uncouth, violent 8 churlish, clownish, homespun, ignorant, impolite, impudent, insolent, ungentle, untaught 9 barbarian, barbarous, dissonant, ferocious, imperfect, impetuous, inclement, inelegant, insulting, makeshift, truculent, turbulent, unskilled, untrained 10 boisterous, discordant, tumultuous, uncultured, ungracious, un-

mannerly, unpolished 11 acrimonious, impertinent, uncivilized 12 contumelious, discourteous 13 inexperienced
rudeness: 4 gaff 6 ferity
rudiment: 4 germ 7 vestige 9 beginning
rudimentary: 5 basic 7 initial 9 elemental, vestigial 10 elementary 11 abecedarian, fundamental
rue: rew 4 pity, rake 5 dolor, grief, mourn 6 bewail, grieve, lament, regret, repent, sorrow, street, suffer 7 afflict, deplore, remorse, sorrow 8 penitent 10 bitterness, compassion, repentance 14 disappointment
rueful: 5 sorry 6 woeful 8 penitent, wretched 10 despondent, melancholy
ruff: ree 4 bird, fish 5 perch, plait, reeve, stamp, trump 6 collar, fraise, hackle, pigeon, rabato, rebato, ruffle, tippet 7 applaud, sunfish 8 disorder, drumbeat 9 sandpiper
female: ree 5 reeve
ruffian: 4 hood, pimp, rage, thug 5 bully, cruel, rowdy, tough 6 brutal, cutter, cuttle, pander, roarer, stormy 7 lawless, lustful, violent 8 assassin, gangster, hooligan, paramour 9 cutthroat, desperado
ruffle: vex 4 beat, blow, fret, roil, rool 5 annoy, crimp, frill, jabot, ruche, shake 6 abrade, nettle, riffle, ripple, tousel, tousle, tumult 7 agitate, derange, disturb, flounce, flutter, panuelo, roughen, wrinkle 8 brandish, dishevel, disorder, drumbeat, furbelow, irritate 9 balayeuse, carfuffle, commotion, confusion 10 disarrange, discompose, intimidate 12 irregularity
neck: 5 jabot, ruche
ruffler: 5 bully, tramp 6 beggar 7 boaster, ruffian 8 braggart 9 swaggerer 10 attachment
rufous: 5 color, rusty, tawny 7 reddish
rug: dog, mat, tug 4 Agra, cozy, haul, pull, snug, tear, wrap 5 Herat 6 afghan, carpet, frieze, kaross, liquor, runner, wrench 7 bargain, blanket, drugget, laprobe 8 Akhissar, Amritsar, covering, portiere 9 Samarkand 11 comfortable
Persian: See **Oriental rug**
ruga: 4 fold 6 crease 7 wrinkle 8 membrane
rugby: 8 football
formation: 5 scrum
player: 6 center, hooker, winger 8 standoff 9 scrum half
score: try 4 goal 10 conversion
rugged: 4 hard, rude, sour 5 asper, hardy, harsh, rough, stern, surly, tough 6 craggy, fierce, horrid, robust, seamed, severe, shaggy, stormy, strong, sturdy, uneven 7 arduous, austere, crabbed,

gnarled, uncivil, unkempt **8** obdurate, vigorous, wrinkled **9** difficult, irregular, turbulent **10** ungracious, unpolished **11** tempestuous

rugose: 6 ridged **8** wrinkled **10** corrugated

ruin: gin **4** bane, bust, dash, do in, doom, fall, fate, fell, harm, loss, undo **5** blast, break, decay, exile, fordo, havoc, spoil, waste, wrack, wreck **6** beggar, blight, damage, deface, defeat, diddle, dismay, foredo, impair, injure, perish, ravage **7** decayed, despoil, destroy, pervert, ruinate, subvert **8** bankrupt, calamity, demolish, desolate, disaster, downfall **9** confusion, crumbling, decadence, desecrate, disfigure, overthrow, perdition, ruination **10** bankruptcy, desolation, subversion **11** destruction, devastation, dissolution, ecroulement, play hob with **12** dilapidation

ruined: 4 dead **5** kaput **6** shabby, forlorn **8** bankrupt, desolate **10** tumbledown **11** dilapidated

ruinous: 5 fatal **10** pernicious **11** destructive

rule: law **4** lead, lord, norm, sway **5** axiom, by-law, canon, guide, maxim, order, regle, reign **6** course, decide, decree, direct, domine, empire, govern, manage, method, regime, screed **7** alidade, brocard, command, conduct, control, counsel, formula, precept, prevail, regency, regimen, theorem **8** behavior, decision, doctrine, domineer, dominion, persuade, practice, regulate, standard **9** authority, criterion, direction, enactment, influence, principle **10** convention, government, regulation **11** aristocracy, be number one, predominate **12** prescription **14** administration

absolute: **8** autarchy

pert. to: **5** rutic

rule out: bar **5** debar **6** forbid, refuse **7** exclude, prevent, scratch **8** preclude, prohibit

ruler: dey, min **4** amir, czar, emir, king, lord, tsar, tzar **5** alder, ameer, emeer, prior, queen **6** archon, author, despot, dynast, ferule, gerent, prince, regent, satrap, sultan, tyrant **7** emperor, monarch, regulus, viceroy **8** autocrat, dictator, governor, hierarch, interrex **9** dominator, governail, imperator, matriarch, potentate, sovereign, yardstick **10** interreges(pl.) **12** straightedge

family: **7** dynasty

former: Nhu **4** czar, Diem, tsar, tzar **5** Lenin **6** Fuhrer, Hitler, Stalin **7** Batista, Fuehrer, Leopold **8** Napoleon, Nicholas **9** Alexander, Mussolini

one of three: **7** triarch **8** triumvir

one of two: **6** duarch

wife: **4** rani **5** queen, ranee **7** czarina, empress, tsarina

rules: 4 code

infraction: **4** foul **8** cheating

ruling: law **5** edict **7** average, central, current, inkling, regnant, statute **8** decision, dominant **9** ascendant, ascendent, hegemonic, prevalent **10** prevailing **11** predominant **13** predominating

rum: bad, odd **4** good, grog, poor **5** queer, tafia **6** liquor **7** Bacardi, cachaca, strange **8** beverage, peculiar **9** excellent

rumal: 8 kerchief(Ind.)

Rumania: *capital:* **9** Bucharest

coin: ban, lei, leu, ley **4** bani(pl.)

Communist leader: **9** Ceausescu

conservative: **5** boyar

king: **5** Carol **7** Michael

mountain: **5** Negoi **10** Carpathian

old name: **5** Dacia

queen: **5** Marie

river: Alt, Jiu **4** Prut **5** Aluta, Arges, Schyl, Siret **6** Danube, Sereth

river port: **6** Galati, Galatz

town: **4** Arad, Iasi **5** Bacau, Jassy, Neamt, Turnu **6** Braila, Brasov, Galati, Galatz **7** Craiova, Focsani, Ploesti, Severin **8** Cernauti, Irongate, Kishenef, Kolsovar, Temesvar

rumble: 4 clap, peal, roll, seat **5** crack, crash, growl, rumor **6** murmur, polish, ramble, report, ripple, uproar **7** grumble **9** complaint **11** disturbance

rumbo: 4 grog **6** liquor

rumen: cud **6** paunch **7** stomach

ruminant: yak **4** deer, goat **5** bison, camel, llama, moose, okapi, sheep, steer **6** alpaca, cattle, vicuna **7** buffalo, chewing, giraffe **8** antelope **10** meditative, thoughtful

female: cow, doe, ewe **5** nanny

genus: bos **5** capra

male: ram **4** buck, bull

stomach: **4** read, reed **5** rumen **6** omasum **8** abomasum, abomasus, roddikin **9** reticulum

ruminate: 4 chaw, chew, mull, muse **5** think, weigh **6** ponder **7** reflect **8** cogitate, consider, meditate

rummage: 4 grub, rout, stow **6** gather, litter, search **7** clutter, collect, derange, examine, fossick, ransack, rubbish, stowage, turmoil **8** disorder, upheaval **9** confusion, ferret out, searching **10** disarrange **11** derangement

rummer: cup **5** glass

rummy: 4 chap, game **5** drunk **7** bizarre, strange **8** drunkard

rumor: 4 buzz, sugh, talk, tell, word **5** bruit, noise, sough, story, voice **6** clamor, furphy, gossip, murmur, norate, report, spread, uproar **7** hearsay, message, tidings, whisper **9** grapevine, statement **10** reputation **11** scuttlebutt

personification: **4** Fama

rump: 4 dock **6** behind, insult **7** hurdies, plunder, remnant **8** bankrupt, buttocks **11** legislature

rump bone: 6 sacrum **8** edgebone **9** aitchbone

rumple: 4 fold, muss, rool, rump, tail **5** plait, touse **6** crease, frowse, tousle **7** crinkle, crumple, wrinkle

rumpus: row **5** brawl **6** barney, fracas, hubbub, uproar **8** argument **9** commotion, confusion **11** disturbance

rumshop: bar **6** saloon, tavern **7** barroom, taproom

run: fly, gad, ply, rin(Sc.), sew **4** butt, cast, dart, dash, emit, flow, fuse, gait, grow, hare, hunt, melt, mold, move, pass, pour, race, roam, rove, sail, scud, tear, tend, trip, trot, turn, work **5** blend, brook, carry, climb, cover, creek, creep, dog it, drive, enter, going, hurry, range, ravel, reach, recur, river, route, scoot, score, scour, speed, stand, trace, treat **6** ascend, become, bicker, career, charge, course, elapse, extend, gallop, govern, hasten, manage, output, pursue, refine, resort, rotate, scurry, spread, spring, sprint, stream, thrust **7** conduct, contend, descend, develop, diffuse, journey, liquefy, make off, migrate, operate, proceed, process, roulade, scamper, scutter, scuttle, smuggle, stretch, trickle **8** continue, dissolve, duration, function, sequence, stampede, traverse **9** discharge, suppurate, take flight, transport **11** watercourse

run across: 4 meet **8** discover **9** encounter **10** transverse

run aground: 7 founder

run away: 4 bolt, flee **5** elope **6** decamp, desert, escape

run down: hit **4** kill, sink, stop **5** crush, decry, seedy **6** pursue **7** capture, decline, traduce **8** overbear **9** disparage, exhausted, overthrow **11** dilapidated

run for office: 5 stand

run-in: 4 tiff **5** fight **7** quarrel **11** altercation

run-of-the-mill: 6 common, medium **7** average, general **8** ordinary

run off: 5 print, waste **7** impress

run out: 4 fail, flow **5** expel, lapse, peter, spill, spilt, waste **6** banish, elapse, expire, spread **8** squander

run over: 6 exceed, strike **8** overflow, rehearse

run through: 4 stab **5** use up **6** browse, pierce **7** examine, inspect, pervade **8** transfix

run up: 4 grow, rise **5** erect **7** enlarge, throw up **8** increase **9** construct **10** accumulate

runagate: 7 runaway **8** apostate, deserter, fugitive, renegade, vagabond, wanderer

runaway: 7 escapee **8** fugitive, runagate

rundle: 4 ball, drum, rung, step **5** orbit, round **6** circle, sphere

rundlet: keg, tun **4** cask **6** barrel

rune: wen **5** charm, magic **6** secret **7** mystery

rung: rod **4** spar, step **5** round, spoke, staff, stair, stake, stave, tread **6** cudgel, degree, rundle **7** girdled

runnel: 4 rill **5** brook, creek, rhine **6** runlet, stream **7** channel, rivulet **9** streamlet **11** watercourse

runner: rug, ski **5** agent, miler, racer, ravel, scarf **6** cursor, stolon **8** operator, smuggler, sprinter **9** collector, detective, messenger, solicitor

running: 4 care, easy, trip **6** active, attack **7** contest, current, cursive, journey **8** skirmish, together **9** oversight **10** management, successive

running birch: 9 snowberry

running board: 9 footboard

running knot: 5 noose

running toad: 10 natterjack

runt: 4 chit, wrig **5** dwarf, pygmy **6** durgan, durgen, titman

runty: 4 puny **5** small **7** stunted **8** dwarfish **10** diminutive, undersized **12** contemptible

runway: 4 file, path, ramp, road **5** chute, strip, track, trail **6** bridge, groove, trough **7** channel **8** platform **10** passageway

rupia: 8 eruption

rupture: 4 open, part, rend, rent **5** break, burst, split **6** breach, hernia, rhexis **7** divorce, parting, ruction, ruption **8** division, fraction, fracture **10** disruption, separating

rural: 6 rustic **7** bucolic, country, idyllic, outland **8** agrestic, Arcadian, geoponic, pastoral **11** countrified

life: **7** bucolic, georgic **8** pastoral

ruse: 4 fall, hoax, slip, wile **5** dodge, feint, fraud, shift, trick **6** deceit **8** artifice **9** stratagem **10** subterfuge

rush: sag **4** birr, dart, dash, flow, junk, race, rout, scud, tear **5** break, brook, chute, feeze, haste, hurry, onset, press, sally, scoot, spate, sprat, sprot, straw, surge **6** attack, bustle, charge, combat, course, defeat, fescue, hasten, hurtle, hustle, plunge, runlet, sortie, trifle **7** assault, bulrush, cattail, destroy, rampage, repulse, tantivy **8** eruption, stampede, vanquish **9** overthrow **11** undergrowth **13** precipitation

family: **9** juncaceae
rush hour: 4 peak
rush nut: 5 chufa
rush toad: 10 natterjack
rusk: 4 cake **5** bread, crisp, toast **7** biscuit **8** zweiback
Russia (Soviet Union): 4 USSR **6** Soviet **7** Muscovy
administrative committee: **9** presidium
alcoholic beverage: **5** kvass, quass, vodka **9** slivovitz
antelope: **5** saiga
apple: **9** astrachan
aristocrat: **5** Boyar **6** Boyard
automobile: Zis
beer: **4** kvas **5** kvass
bondman: **4** serf
braid: **8** soutache
cabinet member: **9** commissar
cactus: **7** thistle
calendar: **6** Julian
cap: **4** aska
capital: **6** Moscow
carriage: **6** drosky, troika **8** tarantas
cathedral: **5** sobor
caviar: **4** ikra **5** ikary
citadel: **7** Kremlin
city: **4** Kiev, Omsk, Orel, Perm **5** Gomel, Kasan, Kazan, Minsk, Pensa, Pskov **6** Kertch, Moskva, Nizhni, Odessa, Rostov, Samara, Sartov **7** Bataisk, Ivanovo, Kalinin, Rybinsk **8** Kostroma, Orenburg, Smolensk, Taganrog, Tashkent, Vladimir, Voronezh, Yaroslaf **9** Archangel, Astrakhan, Kuibishev, Petrograd
coal area: **6** Donets
coin: **5** altin, copec, kopek, ruble **6** copeck, grivna, kopeck **9** altininck, poltinnik **10** chervonets
collective farm: **6** kolhoz **7** kolkhos
commune: **6** kolhoz **7** kolkhos, kolkhoz
composer: Cui **9** Prokofiev **10** Stravinsky **12** Tschaikovsky **13** Shostakovitch **14** Rimsky-Korsakov
cossack: **6** Tartar
council: **4** Duma
country house: **5** dacha
dance: **7** ziganka
decree: **5** ukase
delicacy: **6** caviar **7** caviare
despot: **4** czar, tsar
devil: **5** chort
diplomat: **5** Malik, Zorin **6** Stalin **7** Gromyko, Molotov, Sobolev **8** Malenkov **9** Kuznetzov, Tsarapkin, Vishinsky **11** Shcherbakov
district: **7** Karelia
dog: **4** alan **6** borzoi **7** owtchah **9** wolfhound
dress; **7** sarafan
emperor: **4** czar, Ivan, tsar, tzar **5** Peter

empress: **7** czarina, tsarina, tzarina **8** tsaritza, tzaritza
exclamation: **7** nichevo **8** nitchevo
farmer: **5** kulak
fish: **6** beluga
flax: **6** bobbin
folk song: **6** bylina
forest: **6** tundra
former ruler: **4** czar, tsar
fortress: **7** Kremlin
fox: **6** corsac **7** karagan
gambling game: **6** coocoo
general: **10** Timoshenko **14** Tukhashchevski
government farm: **7** sovkhos, sovkhoz
government group: **4** duma, rada, tsik **6** soviet **7** zemstvo **9** Comintern, Politburo, Presidium **10** Praesidium **11** Politbureau
grandmother: **8** babushka
gulf: **4** Azov
hood: **7** bashlik, bashlyk
horse: **6** tarpan
house: **4** isba **5** dacha
image: **4** icon, ikon **5** ikono
imperial order: **5** ukase
kerchief: **6** analav
labor association: **5** artel
lagoon: **5** liman
lake: **4** Aral, Neva, Sego **5** Elton, Ilmen, Onega
leader: **5** Lenin **6** Stalin **7** Molotov **8** Andropov, Brezhnev **10** Khrushchev
measure: fut, lof **4** duim, fass, loof, stof **5** duime, foute, korec, ligne, osmin, pajak, stoff, vedro, verst **6** arshin, charka, liniya, osmina, paletz, sagene, tchast, versta, verste **7** arsheen, botchka, chkalik, garnetz, verchoc, verchok **8** boutylka, chetvert, krouchka, kroushka **9** chetverik **10** dessiatine **11** polugarnetz
mile: **5** verst
money: **5** ruble
monk: **7** starets **8** Rasputin
mountain range: **4** Alai, Ural **8** Caucasus
musical instrument: **5** gudok, gusla, gusle **9** balalaika
name: **4** Igor, Ivan, Olga **5** Peter, Sonya
naval academy: **6** Frunze
negative: **4** nyet
news agency: **4** Tass
newspaper: **6** Pravda **8** Izvestia
novelist: **5** Gorki **7** Chekhov, Tolstoy **10** Dostoevsky
peasant: **5** kulak **6** muzhik, muzjik
peninsula: **4** Kola **6** Crimea **7** Karelia
people: Red **4** Lett, Russ, Slav **5** Ersar **7** Cossack, Russine **9** Muscovite **12** Byelorussian
plain: **6** steppe
poet: **6** Jehuda **7** Pushkin **9** Aleksandr, Pasternak, Sholokhov **11** Sergyeevich,

Voznesensky, Yevtushenko
port: 4 Eisk 5 Anapa 6 Odessa 9 Archangel 10 Sebastopol, Sevastopol 11 Vladivostok
prince: 4 knez 5 knais, knyaz
republic: 5 Uzbek 6 Latvia 7 Armenia, Georgia, Kirghiz, Turkmen, Ukraine
revolutionist: 5 Lenin, Rykov 6 Stalin, Tomsky 7 Trotsky
river: Don, Ili, Ner, Oka, Ros, Ufa 4 Amur, Duna, Kara, Lena, Neva, Orel, Sura, Svir, Ural 5 Dnepr, Dvina, Onega, Terek, Tobol, Volga 6 Donets, Irtish, Irtysh 7 Dnieper
saint: 4 Olga 8 Vladimir
satellite: 7 sputnik
sea: 4 Aral, Azof, Azov 6 Baikal
secret police: KGB 4 NKVD, OGPU
soup: 5 shchi 6 borsch 7 borscht
spa: Ems
stockade: 5 etape
tavern: 6 caback
tax: 5 obrok
urn: 7 samovar
villa: 5 dacha
village: mir
violinist: 5 Elman
weight: 4 dola, pood
whip: 5 knout
wind: 5 buran
worker: 7 dvornik 12 Stakhanovite
youth organization: 8 Comsomol, Komsomol
russud: 5 grain 6 forage
rust: eat 5 erode 6 aerugo, blight, canker, patina 7 corrode, erosion, oxidize 9 corrosion, oxidation, verdigris
rustic: hob 4 boor, carl, dull, hick, hind, jake, rube, rude 5 bacon, carle, chuff, churl, clown, doric, hodge, plain, rough, rural, swain, yokel 6 coarse, gaffer, honest, simple, sturdy, sylvan 7 artless, awkward, boorish, bucolic, bumpkin, bushman, Corydon, country, georgic, hayseed, peasant, plowboy, plowman, uncouth 8 agrestic, churlish, clownish, pastoral 9 agrestian, campesino, chawbacon, greenhorn, unadorned 10 clodhopper, countryman, unaffected, unpolished 12 backwoodsman
rustle: 5 haste, steal 6 fissle, fistle, scroop 7 crinkle
Rustum: *father:* Zal
  son: 6 Sohrab
rut: rat, rit 4 brim 5 ditch, grind, track 6 furrow, groove, strake 7 channel, routine, wrinkle
rutabaga: 6 turnip
ruth: woe 4 pity 5 grief, mercy 6 regret, sorrow 7 remorse, sadness 8 penitence 10 compassion, repentance, tenderness 17 compassionateness
Ruth: *husband:* 4 Boaz
  mother-in-law: 5 Naomi
  son: 4 Obed
ruthless: 4 grim 5 cruel 6 savage 8 pitiless 9 cutthroat, ferocious
rutter: 4 plow 5 guide 7 trooper 8 horseman
ruttle: 6 gurgle, rattle
Rwanda: *capital:* 6 Kigali
  former name: 12 Ruanda-Urundi
  lake: 4 Kivu
  language: 7 Swahili 11 Kinyarwanda
  monetary unit: 5 franc
  mountain: 7 Virunga 9 Karisimbi
rye: ree, rie 5 grain, grass 6 whisky 7 whiskey 9 gentleman
  disease: 5 ergot
ryot, raiyat (Ind.): 6 farmer, tenant 7 peasant 10 cultivator
Ryukyu island: 7 Okinawa

S

S-shaped: 4 ogee **7** sigmate, sigmoid
sabana: See **savanna**
sabbat: 8 assembly
sabbath: 6 Sunday **7** sabaoth, shabbat, shabbos
saber, sabre: 8 scimitar, scimiter, yataghan
Sabine: *goddess:* **6** Vacuna
  people: **7** Vestini
sable: sad **4** dark, ebon **5** black, brush, saber **6** dismal, gloomy, marten, pellet **8** antelope, darkened **10** mysterious **11** threatening
  genus of: **7** mustela
  pert. to: **8** zibeline **9** zibelline
sablefish: cod **6** beshow **10** candlefish
sabot: 4 shoe
sabotage: 5 block, wreck **7** destroy, subvert **9** undermine **10** impairment **11** destruction
sabre: See **saber**
Sabrina River: 6 Severn
sabulous: 5 dusty, sandy **6** floury, gritty **10** arenaceous
sabutan: 5 fiber, straw
sac: bag, pod **4** cyst, sack **5** ascus, bursa, pouch, theca **6** cavity **7** cistern, utricle, vesicle
Sacar's son: 5 Ahiam
sacaton: 5 grass
saccadic: 5 jerky **9** twitching
saccharine: 5 sweet **7** gluside **10** sweetening **12** ingratiating
saccos: See **sakkos**
sacculated: 7 pouched
sacerdotal: 8 clerical, hieratic, priestly
sachem: 4 boss **5** chief **8** sagamore
sachet: bat, pad **4** oris **5** pouch, scent **8** reticule
sack: (see also **sac**): bag, bed **4** base, fire, loot, poke, ruin **5** bursa, gunny, harry, pouch, purse, waste **6** budget, burlap, jacket, ravage, wallet **7** boucher, dismiss, musette, pillage, plunder, ransack **8** desolate **9** container, discharge, dismissal **11** send packing
  fiber: **4** jute **5** gunny **6** burlap
sackbut: 8 trombone
sackless: 4 weak **7** bashful **8** harmless, innocent **9** guiltless, peaceable **10** dispirited, unmolested
sacque: 6 jacket

sacrament: 4 sign **5** token **6** pledge, symbol **7** baptism, mystery, penance, promise, unction **8** ceremony, covenant **9** communion, Eucharist, matrimony **12** confirmation
sacrarium: 5 ambry **6** chapel, shrine **7** oratory **9** sanctuary **10** tabernacle
sacred: 4 holy **5** godly, huaca, santo **6** divine **7** blessed, saintly **8** hallowed, reverend **9** cherished, geistlich(G.), inviolate, venerated **10** inviolable, sacrosanct **11** consecrated **13** sanctimonious
  make: **8** enshrine
  most: **10** sacrosanct
sacred bean: 5 lotus
sacred beetle: 10 scarabaeus
sacred fig: 5 pipal
sacred place: 6 chapel, church **7** sanctum
sacred weed: 7 vervain
sacrifice: 4 host, loss **5** forgo **6** corban, homage, korban, victim **8** hecatomb, immolate, oblation, offering, part with **9** holocaust, martyrdom, privation, surrender **10** immolation **11** destruction, kiss goodbye
sacrilege: 9 blasphemy **11** desecration, profanation
sacristy: 6 vestry
  pert. to: **7** vestral
sacrosanct: 6 sacred **8** esteemed, regarded **9** respected
sad: bad **4** blue, dark, dram(Sc.), dull **5** dusky, grave, sober, sorry, trist **6** dismal, dreary, gloomy, solemn, somber, sombre, triste(F.), wicked, woeful **7** doleful, dolente(It.), pensive, serious, unhappy **8** dejected, desolate, dolorous, downcast, grievous, mournful, pathetic, pitiable **9** afflicted, cheerless, depressed, plaintive, sorrowful **10** calamitous, deplorable, despondent, lugubrious **11** distressing, melancholic **12** disconsolate, heavyhearted
sadden: 7 attrist, depress **8** make blue
saddle: 4 load **5** ridge **6** burden, howdah **7** aparéjo, pillion, restrict **8** encumber
  blanket: **6** corona, tilpah
  bow: **6** pommel
  maker: **7** knacker, saddler
  pad: **5** panel **7** housing
  part: **4** horn, tore **5** arson, cinch, croup,

girth, panel, pilch, skirt **6** cantle, corona, crutch, latigo, pommel **7** stirrup **8** sudadero **9** saddlebow

rear part: **6** cantle

saddle horse: 4 pony **5** mount

saddle rock: 6 oyster

saddle strip: 5 cindi, girth **6** latigo **7** harness

saddleback: 4 hill **5** ridge

saddlebag: sag(Sc.) **4** jagg(Sc.) **7** alforja, pannier

saddlecloth: 5 panel **7** housing **8** shabrack **9** shabraque

saddler: 4 seal **5** horse **7** cobbler, knacker, lorimer, loriner **9** shoemaker **11** saddlemaker

sadness: 4 funk **5** blues, dumps **7** anguish, megrims

saeter: 6 meadow **7** pasture

safari: 4 hunt, trek **7** caravan, journey **9** excursion **10** expedition

safe: box **4** sure **5** chest, siker, sound, vault **6** armory, closet, coffer, holder, secure, sicker, unhurt **8** cautious, cupboard, harmless, unharmed **9** strongbox, untouched **10** depository **11** gardeviance, trustworthy

safe-conduct: 4 pass **5** cowle, guard **6** convoy **10** permission, protection

safecracker: 4 yegg **7** peteman

safeguard: 4 pass **5** guard **6** convoy, escort, safety **7** defense, protect **10** protection

safekeeping: 4 care **7** custody, storage **10** protection **12** preservation

safety: 8 security **9** assurance, touchback

place of: ark **4** port **5** haven **6** asylum, refuge **7** retreat, sanctum

zone: **6** island

safety lamp: 4 Davy

safety pin: 5 clasp **6** fibula

safety rail: 9 guardrail

safety zone: 5 islet **6** island, refuge

saffron: 6 crocus, yellow **9** safflower

sag: 4 bend, flag, reed, rush, sink, wilt **5** drift, droop, sedge, slump **6** settle, weaken **7** deflate

saga: 4 edda, epic, myth, tale **5** story **6** legend **7** history, recital **9** narrative

narrator: **7** sagaman

sagaciate: 4 fare **6** thrive

sagacious: 4 sage, wise **5** acute, quick **6** argute, astute, shrewd **7** knowing, politic, prudent, sapient **9** far-seeing, judicious **10** discerning, farsighted, hardheaded **11** clairvoyant, penetrating, wise as an owl **13** perspicacious

sagacity: 6 acumen, wisdom **8** sapience

sagamore: 5 chief **6** sachem

sage: 4 herb, mint, seer, wise **5** clary, grave, rishi(Ind.), solon, spice **6** pundit, salvia, savant, shrewd, solemn **7**

learned, prudent, sapient, wise man **8** sagebush **9** counselor, judicious, venerable **10** counsellor, discerning, perceptive **11** philosopher

Sage: *of Chelsea:* **13** Thomas Carlyle

of Concord: **17** Ralph Waldo Emerson

of Emporia: **17** William Allen White

of Ferney: **8** Voltaire

of Monticello: **15** Thomas Jefferson

of Pylos: **6** Nestor

sage cheese: 7 cheddar

sage cock: 6 grouse

sage hen: 6 grouse **7** Nevadan

Sagebrush State: 6 Nevada

saginate: 6 fatten, pamper

Sagittarius: 6 archer, bowman **13** constellation

sago: 6 starch

sago palm: 7 coontie

sagoin: 8 marmoset

saguaro: 6 cactus

sagum: 5 cloak

Sahara: 6 desert

people: **4** Arab **5** nomad **6** Berber, Tuareg

plateau: **6** hamada **7** hammada

wind: **5** leste **6** gibleh

saic: 4 boat **5** ketch

said (see also **say**): dit(F.) **4** such **5** quoth **6** spoken, stated **7** reputed, uttered **8** supposed

saiga: 4 coin **8** antelope

sail: awe, awn, fly, rig, van **4** dart, duck, haul, keel, luff, move, scud, skim, soar, swim, trip **5** fleet, float, glide, sheet **6** canvas, depart, embark, voyage **7** journey **8** go easily, navigate **9** excursion **11** get underway

kind of: jib **5** royal **6** lateen, mizzen, square **7** balloon, lugsaid, skysail, spanker, topsail, trysail **8** foresail, mainsail, staysail, studding **9** crossjack, foreroyal, spinnaker **10** topgallant **12** forestaysail

nearer wind: **4** luff

part: **4** bunt, clew, yard **5** leach, leech, sheet **6** earing **7** earring, yardarm

pert. to: **5** velic

prepare to: **4** trim

triangular: jib

sailboat: 4 bark, yawl **5** ketch, skiff, sloop, yacht **7** caravel **9** caravelle

sailcloth: 4 duck **6** canvas

sailfish: 6 woohoo **8** billfish

sailing: 4 asea

sailing ship: cog, **4** bark, brig, saic, yawl **5** sloop **6** barque, cutter, galley, sampan, vessel **7** frigate, galleon **8** schooner **10** barkentine, brigantine **11** barquentine

scoop: **5** skeet

sailor: gob, hat, tar, tot **4** salt, swab **5** Jacky **6** hearty, lascar, ratiny, seaman **7**

mariner **8** coxswain, seafarer, waterman **10** bluejacket, lobscouser
assent: aye
associate: **8** messmate
British: **5** limey
call: **4** ahoy
carving: **9** scrimshaw
chapel: **6** bethel
fictional: **6** Sinbad
group: **4** crew **5** hands
jacket: **6** reefer
mess tub: kid
old: **4** salt
patron saint: **4** Elmo
patroness: **11** Mother Carey
potion: **4** grog
song: **6** chanty **7** chantey **9** barcarole
saint (see also **patron saint**): Sao(Port.), Ste. **4** holy **5** santa(Sp.), santo **6** hallow **7** beatify **8** canonize, enshrine
biography: **11** hagiography
image: **5** santo
invocation of: **10** hagiolatry
worship: **10** hagiolatry, hierolatry
Saint Andrew's cross; 7 saltier, saltire
Saint Anthony's cross: tau **4** ankh
Saint Catherine's home: 5 Siena
Saint Elmo's fire: 5 flame **6** furole **9** corposant
Saint John's bread: 5 carob
Saint Paul: *birthplace:* **6** Tarsus
companion: **4** Luke
Saint Peter: 5 Simon **7** apostle
Saint-Saens opera: 16 Samson and Delilah
Saint Vitus' dance: 6 chorea
saintly: 4 holy **5** godly, pious **6** devout **7** angelic **9** angelical **10** God-fearing **13** sanctimonious
sake: end **4** good **5** cause, drink **6** behalf, motive, regard **7** account, benefit, concern, purpose **8** beverage **9** advantage, intention **13** consideration
saker: 6 falcon
saki: 5 drink, yarke **6** monkey, yarkee **8** beverage **9** cup bearer
sakkos, saccos: 7 tunicle **8** vestment
sal: 4 salt
sala: 4 hall
salaam, salam: bow **4** bend **6** salute **8** greeting **9** obeisance **10** compliment, salutation
salacious: 4 lewd **7** lustful, obscene **8** scabrous **9** lecherous **10** licentious **12** pornographic
salad: 5 aspic **6** Caesar, tossed **7** melange
ingredient: **5** cress **6** celery, endive, greens, tomato **7** cabbage, lettuce, parsley, romaine **8** scallion **9** dandelion **10** watercress
meal-size: **5** chef's
Saladin's foes: 9 Crusaders

salamander: eft, olm **4** evet, newt **6** spirit, triton **7** axoloti, axolotl, caudata, urodela, urodele **9** amphibian, fireplace **10** hellbender
order: **7** caudata, urodela
salami: 7 sausage
Salammbo author: 8 Flaubert
salary: fee, pay **4** hire **5** wages **6** reward **7** stipend **8** pittance **9** allowance, emolument **10** exhibition, honorarium, recompense **12** compensation, remuneration **13** consideration
sale: net **4** deal, hall, vend **5** bower **6** market, palace, vendue, willow **7** auction, bargain, rummage **8** contract, transfer **9** utterance, vendition **10** conveyance **11** transaction
kind: **4** yard **5** white **6** garage
sales talk: 4 line **5** pitch, spiel **6** patter
salesman: 5 agent, clerk **6** hawker, pedlar, seller, sutler, vendor **7** drummer, hustler, peddler **8** pitchman, vendeuse (fem.) **9** solicitor **14** representative
salience: 5 point **7** agility **8** emphasis **9** high-light **10** notability, prominence **12** protuberance
salient: 4 line **5** redan **6** marked, moving, signal, trench **7** jumping, leaping **8** bounding, extended, striking **9** arresting, important **10** noticeable **11** conspicuous
salient angle: 5 arris
salient point: 5 heart **6** detail, source **7** feature
salientia: 5 anura, frogs, toads **7** aglossa, costata **8** Amphibia, linguata
salina: 4 lake, pond **5** marsh **9** saltworks
saline: 4 tear **5** briny, salty **8** brackish **10** saliferous
Salisbury steak: 9 hamburger
saliva: 4 spit **5** water **7** spittle
salix: 5 genus **6** osiers **7** sallows, willows
salle: 4 room
sallet: 6 helmet
sallow: wan **4** pale, twig **5** muddy, osier, shoot **6** pallid, willow **9** colorless, yellowish
sally: 4 leap, quip, rush, trip **5** dance, issue, jaunt, start **6** attack, emerge, escape, retort, sortie, spring **7** darting, journey, rushing **8** escapade, outbreak, outburst **9** excursion, witticism **10** liveliness
salmagundi: 4 hash, olio **5** salad **6** medley **7** mixture **9** potpourri **10** hodgepodge
salmi: 6 ragout
salmon: gib **4** chum, kelt, keta, pike, pink **5** color, haddo, holia, smolt, tecon **6** jumper, laurel, sauqui, taimen **7** gilling, saumont, shedder **8** schoodic, springer, weakfish **9** ceratodus **10** barramunda

enclosure: **4** weir, yair
female: **4** raun **6** baggit
male: **6** kipper
pool: **5** stell
silver: **4** coho
smoked: lox
trap: **4** slap
young: **4** parr
salmon trout: 5 sewen **9** steelhead
Salome: *mother:* **8** Herodias
stepfather: **5** Herod
salon: 4 hall, room **5** group **6** museum **7** gallery **9** apartment, reception **10** assemblage, exhibition **11** drawing room
saloon: bar **4** hall, room **5** cabin, coach, cuddy, divan, sedan **6** tavern **7** barroom, cantina(Sp.) **8** alehouse, groggery
salpa, salp: 8 tunicate
salse: 7 volcano
salt: sal, tar, wit **4** alum, corn, cure **5** brine, briny, ester, salic, sharp, witty **6** alkali, flavor, halite, harden, lively, sailor, saline, seaman, season **7** bromate, piquant, pungent, seadust **8** brackish, halinous **9** seasoning
deposit: **6** saline
oleic acid: **6** oleate
resembling: **5** halid **6** halide, haloid
rock: pig
working: **7** halurgy
salt-like: 6 haloid
salt marsh: 6 salina **9** grassland
salt pit: vat
salt tree: 4 atle **8** tamarisk
salt water: 5 brine
saltate: 4 jump, leap **5** bound, dance
saltcellar: 5 saler
salted: 4 alat **5** cured **6** corned
saltpeter, saltpetre: 5 niter, nitre
saltworks: 7 saltern, saltery
salty: 4 racy **5** witty **8** indecent, nautical
salubrious: 4 good **7** bracing, healthy **8** salutary **9** benignant, healthful, wholesome **10** beneficial
salutary: 4 good **6** benign **7** healthy, helpful **8** curative **9** desirable, healthful, medicinal, wholesome **10** beneficial **11** restorative
salutation: ave, bow **4** beck, hail **5** aloha, hello, howdy, skoal **6** curtsy, kowtow, Mizpah, Mizpeh, prosit, salaam, salute **7** address, welcome, slainte **8** accolade, chin-chin, encomium, farewell, greeting
salute: nod **4** hail **5** greet, halse, salvo **6** accost, praise, signal **7** address **9** obeisance **11** pay homage to
salvage: 4 save **6** rescue **7** reclaim **12** compensation
salvation: 6 rescue **10** redemption **12** conservation, preservation
pert. to: **8** soterial **9** soterical
salve: 4 balm, nard **6** anoint, cerate,

soothe **7** assuage, unguent **8** flattery, gratuity, ointment, palliate **9** alleviate
salver: 4 tray
salvo: 4 shot **6** excuse, salute **7** gunfire, pretext, proviso, quibble **9** exception **11** reservation, testimonial
samadh: 4 tomb **6** shrine
samaj: 6 church **7** society **12** congregation
samaritan: 6 helper, **8** welldoer **10** benefactor
Samaritan: *alphabet:* jud, mim, nun, phi, sen, tav, tit **4** alaf, bith, goph, kaph, rish, sadi, shan **5** dalat, gaman, labad **6** simcat
god: **6** Tartak
people: **8** Assyrian **9** Israelite
sambar, sambur: elk **4** deer, maha, rusa
same: ilk, one **4** ibid, idem, like, meme(F.), self, very **5** alike, ditto, equal, exact **7** identic **9** identical, unchanged **10** invariable
sameness: 8 identity, monotony **10** similarity **11** equivalence, resemblance **14** correspondence
Samhain Eve: 9 Halloween
Samian philosopher: 10 Pythagoras
samisen: 5 banjo
samlet: 4 parr **6** salmon **10** fingerling
sammy: 5 ninny **6** clammy, sodden, watery **9** simpleton
Samoa (see also **Polynesia**): *capital:* **4** Apia **8** Pago Pago
fish: **6** ataata, sesele
hostess: **5** taupo **6** taupou
island: **5** Upolu **6** Savaii
mollusk: asi
mudworm: ipo
owl: **4** lulu
red: **4** mumu
spirit: **4** aitu
warrior: toa
samovar: urn **6** teapot
samp: 4 meal, mush, soup **6** cereal, hominy **8** porridge
sampaloc: 8 tamarind
sampan: 4 boat **5** skiff
sample: 4 test **5** taste **6** swatch **7** example, pattern **8** instance, specimen **12** illustration
sampleman: 6 taster **12** demonstrator
sampler: 5 model **6** taster **7** example, hanging, pattern **8** original, specimen **9** archetype
Samson: *betrayer:* **7** Delilah
deathplace: **4** Gaza
vulnerable place: **4** hair
Samuel: *home:* **5** Ramah
mentor: Eli
parent: **6** Hannah **7** Elkanah
son: **5** Abiah
victim: **4** Agag, Agog

Samurai: 7 soldier, warrior
ostracized: **5** Ronin
San Francisco hill: Nob
San Simeon name: 6 Hearst
sanative: 6 curing **7** healing **8** curative **9** healthful
sanatorium: spa **8** hospital
Sancho Panza: *island:* **9** Barataria
master: **10** Don Quixote
mule: **6** Dapple
sanctify: 8 dedicate **10** consecrate
sanctimonious: 4 holy **5** pious **6** devout, sacred **7** prudish, saintly, zealous **10** sanctified **12** hypocritical
sanction: 4 amen, fiat **5** allow **6** assent, avouch, permit, placet, ratify **7** approve, confirm, consent, endorse, indorse, support **8** accredit, approval, legalize **9** allowance, approbate, authority, authorize, encourage, subscribe **10** imprimatur **11** approbation, countenance, countersign, endorsement **12** ratification **13** authorization, encouragement
sanctity: 5 piety, rites **6** purity **7** halidom **8** halidome, holiness, recesses **9** godliness, solemnity **10** sacredness **11** obligations, saintliness **13** inviolability
place of: **4** fane **5** altar, hiera **6** chapel, church, hieron, shrine, temple **7** chaitya **9** synagogue
sanctuary: ark **4** bema, fane, holy, naos **5** abbey, adyta(pl.), bamah, grith, haven **6** adytum, asylum, bemata, chapel, church, haikal, priory, refuge, shrine, temple **7** alsatia, chancel, convent, halidom, preserve, retreat, sanctum, shelter **8** cloister, halidome, holiness **9** monastery **10** penetralia, protection, tabernacle **11** hiding place, reservation **12** holy of holies
sanctum: den **5** study **6** adytum, office **7** retreat **9** sanctuary
sand: rub **4** grit **5** nerve **6** abrade, desert, gravel, smooth **7** courage **8** alluvium, asbestic
and clay: **4** loam
particle: **5** grain
particles: **4** silt
resembling: **7** arenoid
sand dune: 4 hill, sand **5** towan
sand eel: 4 grig **5** lance **6** launce
sand flea: 6 chigoe **7** chigger
sand flounder: 5 fluke **10** windowpane
sand hill: 4 dune
sandal (see also **moccasin**)**: 4** clog, shoe, zori **6** buskin, caliga, charuk **7** rullion, slipper, talaria **8** huarache **9** alpargata **10** espadrille
winged: **7** talaria(pl.)
wooden: **6** patten
sandalwood: 5 algum, almug, maire

Sandalwood Island: 5 Sumba
sandarac: 4 tree **5** resin **7** realgar
tree: **4** arar
wood: **6** alerce, alerse
sandbank: 4 dune, meal
sandbar: 4 dene, dune, reef, spit **5** beach, shelf, shoal
sandpiper: ree **4** bird, knot, ruff **5** reeve, terek **6** dunlin, teeter, tiltup **7** brownie, chorook, fiddler, haybird **8** triddler, redshank **10** canderling
sandstone: 4 grit **5** hazel **6** arkose **8** ganister **9** gritstone
block: **6** sarsen
pert. to: **10** arenilitic
sandy: dry **6** gritty, plucky **7** arenose **8** granular, sabuline, shifting, unstable **13** uninteresting
pert. to: **6** eremic
sane: 4 wise **5** lucid, sober, sound **6** normal **7** healthy, sapient **8** all there, rational, sensible **10** reasonable
sangfroid: 8 calmness, coolness **9** composure, stability **16** imperturbability **10** equanimity
Sangraal: See **Holy Grail**
sanguinaria: 6 yarrow **9** bloodroot
sanguine: red **4** fond, gory, warm **5** cruel, ruddy **6** ardent, bloody, crayon, savage, yarrow **7** buoyant, hopeful **8** cheerful, hematite **9** confident, expectant, ferocious, murderous **10** bloodstone, ensanguine, optimistic, sanguinary **12** bloodthirsty
sanitarium: See **sanatorium**
sanitary: 5 clean **8** hygienic
sanitize: 8 clean out
sanity: 6 reason **7** balance **8** lucidity, saneness **9** soundness **13** wholesomeness
sans: 7 without
Sanskrit: *dialect:* **4** Pali
dictionary: **10** amara-kosha
division of literature: **5** Sruti **6** Shruti
epic: **8** Ramayana
epic character: **4** Sita
school: tol
soul: **5** atman
verse: **5** sloka
sans souci: 12 free from care
Santa Barbara island: 8 Catalina
Santa Claus's reindeer: 5 Comet, Cupid, Vixen **6** Dancer, Dasher, Donder, Donner **7** Blitzen, Prancer
santon: 4 monk **5** image, saint **6** hermit **7** dervish
sap: lac **4** dupe, fool, milk, mine, seve(F.), upas **5** drain, fluid, juice, latex, lymph, vigor **6** energy, impair, trench, weaken **7** exhaust, saphead **8** enervate, knock out, vitality, weakling **9** exudation, schlemiel, schlemihl, screwball, under-

mine **10** debilitate, devitalize
dried: gum
lose: **5** bleed
spout: **5** spile
sapajou: 6 monkey
sapanwood, sappanwood: 4 tree **10** brazilwood
saphead: See **sap**
saphie: 5 charm **6** amulet **8** talisman
sapid: 5 tasty **6** savory **7** savoury **8** engaging **9** palatable **10** flavorable **11** fit for a king
sapient: 4 sage, sane, wise **6** shrewd **7** erudite, knowing, learned **9** sagacious **10** discerning
sapiutan: 4 anoa
sapless: dry **7** insipid **8** withered **9** exsuccous **11** devitalized
sapling: 5 plant, youth
sapo: 4 soap **8** toadfish
sapodilla: 5 chico **7** nispero **9** naseberry
saponaceous: 5 soapy **7** elusive **8** slippery
sapor: 5 gusto, savor, taste **6** flavor, relish **7** flavour
sapper: 5 miner **6** digger
Sappho: 7 poetess
consort: **5** Phaon
home: **6** Lesbos
sappy: 5 juicy, moist, pithy, plump, silly **6** sodden **7** fatuous, foolish **8** vigorous **9** energetic, succulent **11** sentimental
sapsago: 6 cheese
sapsucker: 10 woodpecker
sapwood: 8 alburnum
Saracen: 4 Arab **5** nomad **6** Moslem, Muslim **7** corsair
knight: **6** Rogero **8** Ruggiero
leader: **7** Saladin
Sarah: *husband:* **7** Abraham
slave: **5** Hagar
son: **5** Isaac
sarcasm: 4 gibe, jeer **5** fling, humor, irony, taunt **6** attack, rebuke, satire **7** mockery **8** acerbity, acridity, reproach, ridicule **9** criticism
pert. to: **8** ironical
sarcastic: dry **6** biting **7** cutting, mordant **8** incisive, sardonic **9** corrosive, trenchant
sarcenet, sarsenet: 4 silk, soft **6** gentle, smooth **8** tempered
sarcina: 8 bacteria
sarcophagus: 4 tomb **6** coffin, cooler
sardine: 4 bang, sild **8** pilchard
Sardinia: 6 island
capital: **8** Cagliari
language: **7** Catalan
sardonic: 8 derisive **9** sarcastic
sargo: 5 grunt **7** pinfish **10** sheepshead
sarkinite: 8 arsenate
sarong: 5 skirt **6** comboy **7** garment
sarrazin: 9 buckwheat

sarsen: 5 block **8** monument **9** sandstone
sartor: 6 tailor
sash: obi **4** band, belt, benn(Sc.) **5** scarf **6** fascia, girdle **8** casement **9** waistband **10** cummerbund
sasin: 8 antelope **9** black buck
Saskatchewan: *capital:* **6** Regina
city: **8** Moose Jaw **9** Saskatoon **12** Prince Albert
Indian: **4** Cree
lake: **5** Rouge **8** Reindeer **9** Athabaska, Wollaston
national park: **12** Prince Albert
province of: **6** Canada
provincial bird: **6** grouse
provincial flower: **4** lily
river: **7** Red Deer **9** Qu'Appelle **11** Assiniboine
sasquatch: 4 omah **7** big boot **13** manlike animal
sassaby: 8 antelope
sassafras: tea **6** saloop
Satan: 4 liar, Nick **5** demon, devil, eblis, fiend **6** Belial **7** Lucifer, tempter **8** diabolus **9** archenemy, archfiend **14** Mephistopheles
associate: **9** Beelzebub
son: Imp
satanic: 4 evil **5** cruel **6** wicked **8** devilish, diabolic, infernal, terrible **10** diabolical
satchel: bag **4** case, grip **5** cabas **6** valise
sate: 4 cloy, cram, glut **5** gorge, stuff **7** gratify, surfeit
satellite (see also **Jupiter, Saturn** and **Uranus): 4** luna, moon, vein **6** minion, planet **7** Iapetus, Japetus **8** follower, hanger-on **9** attendant, dependent **11** concomitant
man-made: Oso **4** Anna, Echo, Luna, Mars, Zond **5** Ariel, Faith, Lunik, Midas, Relay, Samos, Tiros **6** Cosmos, Flight, Ranger, Skylab, Syncom, Venera, Viking, Vostok **7** Courier, Mariner, Pioneer, Sputnik, Telstar, Transit, Voyager **8** Alouette, Explorer, Telestar, Vanguard **9** Vela-Hotel **10** Discoverer **12** Mercury-Atlas, Project-Score
pert. to: **9** aerospace
weather: **5** Tiros
satiny: 5 sleek **6** glossy, smooth **8** lustrous
satire: 5 grind, irony, spoof **6** banter, parody **7** lampoon, mockery, sarcasm **8** ridicule, travesty
satiric: dry **6** bitter, ironic **7** abusive, atellan, caustic, cutting, mocking **8** ironical, poignant, spoofing **10** censorious, lampooning **11** reproachful
satirize: 4 lash, mock **5** grind, spoof **6** attack, expose **7** lampoon **8** denounce, ridicule **9** criticize
satisfaction: 4 ease, gree **6** amends **7** content, payment **8** pleasure **9** atone-

ment, enjoyment **10** bloodmoney, recompense, reparation, settlement **11** complacence, contentment, restitution **12** compensation, propitiation, remuneration **13** gratification **15** indemnification.
  combat for: **4** duel
  payment for killing: cro
satisfactory: pat **4** good, okay **5** valid **6** decent, enough **8** adequate **9** allowable, expiatory **10** acceptable, sufficient
satisfied: fed **4** paid, smug **5** proud **9** contented, gratified **10** complacent
satisfy: pay **4** cloy, feed, fill, free, meet, sate, suit **5** appay, atone, clear, repay, serve, slake **6** assure, defray, please, supply **7** appease, assuage, content, expiate, fulfill, gratify, requite, satiate, suffice, surfeit **8** convince, make good, reparate **9** discharge **10** compensate, remunerate
satrap: **5** ruler **6** prince, tyrant **7** viceroy **8** governor, official, overlord
sattva: **5** truth **6** purity, wisdom **8** goodness **12** tranquillity
saturate: ret, sog, sop, wet **4** fill, glut, soak **5** imbue, souse, steep **6** dampen, drench, imbibe, imbrue, seethe, sodden **7** ingrain, satiate, satisfy **8** permeate **9** penetrate **10** impregnate
Saturday: **7** Sabbath
  pert. to: **9** sabbatine
Saturday night special: **7** handgun
Saturn: **6** Cronus, planet
  in alchemy: **4** lead
  ring part: **4** ansa **5** ansae(pl.)
  satellite: **4** Rhea **5** Dione, Mimas, Titan **6** Phoebe, Tethys **7** Iapetus, Japetus **8** Hyperion **9** Enceladus
  temple treasury: **8** aerarium
  wife: Ops
saturnalia: **4** orgy **5** feast **7** revelry **8** carnival, festival
saturnine: **4** dull **5** grave, heavy, staid **6** gloomy, morose, silent, somber, sullen **8** sluggish, taciturn
satyr: **4** faun, idol **5** deity **7** demigod **9** butterfly
sauce: dip **5** gravy **6** flavor, liquor, relish **8** back talk, dressing, matelote **9** condiment
  kind: soy **4** alec, hard, lear **5** garum **6** catsup **7** catchup, gascony, ketchup, mustard **8** chawdron, remolade **9** genevoise, matelote, remoulade **10** Bordelaise, mayonnaise **11** Hollandaise, vinaigrette
  thickener: **4** roux
saucy: **4** bold, coxy, pert, rude **5** brash, fresh **6** bantam, cocket **7** defiant, forward **8** impudent, malapert **9** audacious, sprightly **11** impertinent

Saudi Arabia (see also **Arabian**): *capital:* **6** Riyadh
  city: **5** Jidda, Mecca **6** Jeddah
  coin: **5** qursh, riyal
  desert: **5** Nefud
  gulf: **5** Aqaba
  port: **5** Jidda **6** Jeddah
  religious center: **5** Mecca **6** Medina
  state: **4** Asir, Nejd
sauger: **4** fish **5** perch
Saul: *concubine:* **6** Rizpah
  daughter: **6** Michal
  father: **4** Kish
  grandfather: Ner
  herdsman: **4** Doeg
  son: **8** Jonathan
  successor: **5** David
  uncle: Ner
  wife: **7** Ahinoam
Saul of Tarsus: **4** Paul
Sault Sainte Marie: Soo
saumont: **6** salmon
sauna: **4** bath **9** bathhouse **12** bathing place
saunter: lag **4** idle, roam, rove, walk **5** amble, mosey, range, shool, stray **6** dander, dawdle, go slow, loiter, lounge, potter, ramble, stroll, wander **8** ruminate
saurel: **4** fish, scad **5** xurel
saurian: **6** lizard **8** dinosaur
saury: **4** fish
sausage: **5** gigot, wurst **6** salami, wiener **7** balloon, baloney, bologna, saveloy **8** cervelate, drisheen, rollejee, rolliche **9** andouille, bratwurst, rollichie **11** wienerwurst **12** andouillette
  casing: **4** bung
  poisoning: **11** allantiasis
sausage-shaped: **9** allantoid **10** botuliform
savage: **4** fell, grim, rude, wild **5** brute, crude, cruel, feral, rabid, rough **6** brutal, ferine, fierce **7** brutish, furious, howling, inhuman, untamed **8** pitiless, ruthless, work evil **9** aborigine, atrocious, barbarian, barbarous, ferocious, merciless, murderous, primitive, truculent **10** unpolished **11** uncivilized **12** uncultivated, unrestrained
Savage Island people: **5** Niuan
savanna, savannah: **5** plain **9** grassland
savant: **4** sage **5** Solon **6** expert, pedant **7** scholar, wise man **9** scientist
savarin: **7** brioche **10** coffeecake
save: aid, bar, but **4** hain, keep, only **5** amass, catch, guard, hoard, salve, spare, store **6** defend, except, redeem, rescue, retain, scrimp, unless **7** deliver, husband, protect, reclaim, reserve, salvage **8** conserve, maintain, preserve **9** economize, excepting **10** accumulate
savin, savine: **7** juniper **9** evergreen

saving: 6 frugal, rescue, thrift 7 thrifty 9 frugality 10 economical

savings: 7 account, addlins 8 addlings

savoir faire: 4 tact 7 know-how 10 adroitness 11 worldliness 12 mannerliness 14 sophistication

savor, savour: eat 4 odor, zest 5 sapor, scent, smack, smell, taste, tinge 6 degust, fervor, flavor, relish, season 9 degustate

savory: 5 gusty, salty, sapid, tasty 7 piquant 8 delicacy, flavored, fragrant, pleasing 9 agreeable, palatable 10 appetizing, delightful

saw: cut, hew 4 talk, word 5 adage, axiom maxim, motto, rumor, sever 6 cliche, saying 7 proverb 8 aphorism, apothegm 9 platitude 10 apophthegm
kind: 5 briar, edger, serra 6 stadda, trapan, trepan 8 trephine
part: 4 tine 5 redan, tooth
surgical: 6 trapan, trepan 8 trephine

saw-like: 8 serrated

sawbelly: 7 alewife

sawbones: 7 surgeon

sawbuck: 7 ten spot 13 ten-dollar bill

sawder: 7 flatter

sawfish: ray

sawhorse: 4 buck 7 sawbuck

sawyer: 6 beetle, logman 9 lumberman 10 woodcutter

saxhorn: 4 alto, tuba

Saxon: 9 Sassenach
chief: 5 Horsa
city: Ave
king: Ine 6 Harold
lady: 6 Godiva, Rowena
serf: 4 esne
swineherd: 5 Gurth
warrior: 5 Thane

Saxony city: 7 Dresden

say: 4 aver, call, deem, show, silk, tell 5 put it, speak, state, utter, voice 6 advise, allege, answer, assert, bucket, direct, fabric, nearly, recite, relate, remark, repeat, report 7 declare, dictate, express, iterate, speak up, testify 8 announce, indicate 9 pronounce 10 asseverate, put in words
again: 6 repeat 9 reiterate
further: add

saying: mot, saw 4 quip, word 5 adage, axiom, logia, maxim, motto 6 byword, phrase 7 epigram, proverb 8 aphorism, apothegm 9 statement 11 declaration
apt: 6 bon mot
collection: ana 9 gnomology
distinguishing: 10 shibboleth

scab: 4 sore 5 crust, mange 6 eschar, ratter 7 blemish 8 blackleg 9 scoundrel 13 strike-breaker

scabbard: 4 case 6 sheath, tsubas 7 holster
put in: 7 sheathe
tip: 7 crampit

scabby: low 4 base, mean 5 flaky, mangy 6 scurvy, shabby, stingy 7 blotchy 9 blemished 12 contemptible

scabies: 4 itch 5 mange 11 skin disease

scads: 4 lots 6 oodles

scaffold: 4 cage, loft 5 easel, stage 7 gallery, support 8 platform

scalar: 10 ladderlike

scalawag, scallawag: 4 pony, runt 5 scamp 6 rascal 10 scapegrace

scald: vex 4 burn 5 worry 6 blanch, excite, scorch 7 inflame, torment

scale: cup, hut 4 bowl, film, husk, peel, rate, rule, scut, shed, size, skin 5 climb, flake, gamut, lepis, palea, scute, shive, weigh 6 ascend, degree, lamina, rament, spread, vessel, weight 7 balance, clamber, coating, compare, lamella, measure, scatter, vernier 8 covering, disperse, flake off, separate 9 gradation, steelyard 12 incrustation
bony: 6 scutum
earthquake: 7 Richter
graduated: 7 Vernier
having: 7 leprose, scutate
temperature: 6 Kelvin 7 Celsius 10 centigrade, Fahrenheit

scale-like: 6 scurfy 7 leprose

scallion: 4 leek 5 onion 7 shallot

scallop: 4 quin 5 crena, notch, twist 7 crenate, mollusk

scalp: rob 4 peel, skin 5 cheat 6 defeat, denude, profit, trophy 9 speculate
disease: 5 favus, scurf 8 dandruff

scalpel: 5 knife 6 lancet 8 bistoury

scalper: 6 punter, trader 10 speculator

scaly: low 4 mean 5 flaky 6 stingy 7 powdery 8 squamous 10 despicable

scam: 7 swindle 11 con man's ploy

scamble: 6 sprawl 7 collect, shamble, trample 8 scramble

scamp: imp 5 cheat, knave, rogue 6 rascal 8 scalawag, spalpeen, widdifow 9 scallawag, scoundrel 10 highwayman 13 mischief-maker

scamper: run 4 race 5 speed 6 frolic, hasten, scurry 7 brattle, skitter 9 hurry away, skedaddle

scan: eye 5 study, watch 6 behold, peruse, survey 7 examine, observe, poetize 8 skim over 10 scrutinize 11 contemplate

scandal: 5 eclat, odium, shame 6 gossip, malign 7 calumny, outrage, slander 8 disgrace, ignominy, iniquity 9 discredit 10 backbiting, defamation, detraction, opprobrium

scandalize: 5 shock 6 malign, offend, vilify

scandalous: 6 unholy 8 libelous, shocking

9 offensive 10 flagitious, outrageous 11 furciferous

scandent: 13 climbing plant

Scandinavian (see also **Norse, Teutonic**): **4** Dane, Lapp **5** Norse, Swede **8** Norseman, Suigoth **9** Icelandic, Norwegian

alphabetical character: **4** rune

bard: **5** scald **7** sagaman

country: **6** Norway, Sweden **7** Denmark, Finland, Iceland

division: amt

drink: **4** glog **7** aquavit

explorer: **4** Eric

hero's place: **8** Valhalla

king: **4** Atli

land: **4** odal

legend: **4** edda, saga

legendary creature: nis **5** nisse, troll **6** Kraken

measure: ass, lod, ort, vog **4** last, mark, pund, sten, untz **5** carat **6** nylast **7** centner, lispund **8** lispound, skalpund, skeppund, skippund **9** shippound, skaalpund, skibslast **10** bismerpund

minstrel: See *bard* above

money: **5** krone

navigator: **4** Eric

nobleman: **4** jarl

pert. to: **5** Norse

plateau: **5** fjeld

rulers: Ros **10** Varangians

ship: **4** aesc

small bay: **5** fjord

trumpet: **4** lure

scant: few **4** lean **5** chary, short, stint **6** geason, meager, meagre, narrow, scrimp, slight, sparse **7** limited, sparing, wanting **9** not enough **12** parsimonious

scantling: 4 beam, size, stud **5** grade **6** timber **7** caliber **8** standard

scape: 4 slip, stem, view **5** fault, shaft **7** picture **8** escapade, peduncle

scapegoat: 4 dupe **6** victim **9** sacrifice **10** substitute

scapegrace: 5 rogue, scamp **6** madcap, rascal **7** wastrel **8** scalawag **9** reprobate, scallawag **10** profligate

scar: arr, mar, shy **4** mark, rock, seam, slit, wild **5** chink, cliff, crack, wound **6** cinder, damage, deface, scared **7** blemish, catface, clinker **8** cicatrix, mountain, pockmark **9** disfigure, precipice **13** disfigurement

pert. to: **5** uloid

tissue: **6** keloid

scarab: 5 charm **6** beetle

scaramouch: 4 fool **5** scamp **6** rascal **7** buffoon **8** braggart, poltroon

scarce: few, shy **4** dear, just, rare **5** scant, short **6** geason, meager, meagre, scanty, sparse **8** uncommon **9** deficient **10** in-frequent **12** insufficient

scarcely: 6 barely, hardly, merely

scarcity: 4 lack, need, want **6** dearth, famine, penury, rarity **7** failure, paucity, poverty **8** rareness, sparsity **9** parsimony **10** deficiency, scarceness **11** infrequency, sparingness **12** uncommonness **13** insufficiency, niggardliness

scare: awe, shy **4** fear, fleg **5** alarm, dread, gliff, gloff, panic, spook **6** fright **7** scarify, startle, terrify **8** affright, frighten

scarecrow: 5 bogle **6** figure **10** frightener

scarf: boa, tie **4** gand, sash, wrap **5** adorn, ascot, barbe, cloud, cover, orale, shawl, stole, unite **6** cravat, groove, rebozo, runner, tapalo, tippet **7** dopatta(Ind.), muffler, necktie **8** liripipe, neckwear **9** comforter, cormorant **10** fascinator **11** comfortable, neckerchief

feathered: boa

head: **8** babushka

scarfskin: 7 cuticle **9** epidermis

scarify: See **scare**

scarlet: red **4** lewd **5** bawdy **8** flagrant **10** prostitute

Scarlett O'Hara: *home:* **4** Tara

husband: **5** Rhett

scarp: cut **5** cliff, slope **7** descent, incline **8** fragment **9** declivity, precipice

scary: 4 eery **5** eerie, timid, weird **6** spooky **7** fearful, ghostly, uncanny **8** alarming **11** frightening

scat: bop, tax **4** beat, riff, shoo **5** smash **6** begone, go away, rebuff, shower **7** getaway, scatter, tribute, vamoose **8** nonsense

scathe: 4 harm, hurt, sear **5** blast **6** assail, damage, injure, scorch, wither **8** denounce, lash into, work evil **9** castigate

scathing: 6 biting, severe **7** mordant **8** blasting, injuring, wounding **9** scorching, truculent, withering

scatological: 5 fecal **7** obscene, raunchy

scatter: sow, ted **4** cast, deal, rout **5** fling, spray, strew, waste **6** dispel, shower, splash, spread **7** bestrew, confuse, diffuse, disband, fritter, radiate **8** dishevel, disperse, distract, separate, sprinkle, squander **9** bespatter, circulate, discomfit, dissipate **10** disconnect, distribute **11** disseminate

scatter-gun: 7 shotgun

scatterbrained: 5 giddy **7** flighty **9** frivolous

scattered: 6 sparse **7** erratic, strawed **8** rambling, sporadic **9** irregular **10** straggling

scatula: 7 pill box

scaup: 4 duck **8** grayback **10** canvasback

scavage: tax **4** duty, toll

scavenger: rat **7** sweeper, vulture

scenario: 4 plot 6 script 7 outline 10 continuity

scend: 4 lift 5 heave, pitch

scene: act 4 site, view 5 arena, sight, vista 6 blow-up, locale 7 diorama, display, episode, picture, quarrel, setting, tableau 8 prospect 9 landscape, spectacle, way of life
last: 6 finale

scenery: 4 view 5 decor, props 8 stage set 9 landscape 14 representation

sceneshifter: 4 grip

scenic: 8 dramatic 9 panoramic 10 theatrical 11 picturesque

scenite: 5 nomad

scent: 4 clue, nose, odor 5 aroma, odour, savor, smell, sniff, spoor, track 6 breath, flavor 7 bouquet, essence, flavour, inkling, perfume 8 effluvia 9 emanation, fragrance

scented: 5 olent 8 perfumed

scepter, sceptre: rod 4 mace 5 baton, staff 6 emblem 7 trident 8 caduceus 9 authority 11 sovereignty

schedule: 4 card, list, plan, time 5 slate, table 6 tariff 7 catalog, program, routine, writing 8 calendar, document, register, tabulate 9 catalogue, inventory, timetable

schefferite: 8 pyroxene

schelm: 5 rogue 6 rascal

schema: 4 plan 6 figure 7 diagram, outline

scheme: aim, gin, web 4 dart, list, plan, plot 5 angle, cabal, cadre, draft, drift, table, trick 6 design, device, devise, figure, racket 7 concoct, diagram, epitome, outline, program, project, purpose 8 conspire, contrive, forecast, gimcrack, intrigue, maneuver 9 statement, stratagem 10 concoction, conspiracy 11 contrivance, machination, proposition

schemer: 7 plotter, traitor 9 con artist

scheming: 6 artful, crafty, tricky 8 fetching 9 designing 10 intriguing

schism: 4 rent 5 split 6 breach, heresy 8 division 10 separation

schist: 5 slate

schizocarp: 5 fruit, regma

schizophrenia: 8 catatony, insanity 9 psychosis 16 split personality

schlemiel: dub, oaf 4 clod, goof 5 chump 7 saphead

schlepp: 4 jerk, drag, pull

schmaltz: 4 corn 14 sentimentality

scholar: 4 sage 5 clerk, pupil 6 pedant, savant 7 bookman, learner, student 8 disciple 11 academician, philologist
day: 6 extern
servant: 7 famulus

scholarly: 7 erudite, learned 8 studious 10 scholastic

scholarship: 7 bursary 8 learning 9 allowance, education, erudition, knowledge 10 fellowship 11 instruction

scholiast: 6 critic 9 annotator 10 glossarist 11 commentator 13 glossographer

school: gam, pod 4 cult, lead, sect 5 drill, ecole(F.), flock, group, lycee(F.), shoal, teach, train 6 manege 7 academy, advance, college, company, convent, educate, seminar 8 atheneum, document, exercise, instruct, seminary 9 athenaeum, cultivate 10 realschule(G.), university 11 institution
grounds: 6 campus
group: PTA
kind: 4 high, prep 5 grade 7 primary 8 military 9 finishing, secondary 10 elementary, vocational 11 preparatory
of fish: 5 shoal
of whales: gam
official: 9 principal, scholarch 10 headmaster 14 superintendent
pert. to: 8 academic
religious: 5 heder 6 cheder 8 seminary
riding: 6 manege
task: 6 lesson 7 problem 10 assignment 11 composition
term: 7 quarter 8 semester 9 trimester

schoolbook: 4 text 5 atlas 6 primer, reader 7 speller 9 geography

schoolmaster: 4 caji, head 7 dominie, manager, pedagog 9 pedagogue

schooner: 4 boat, brig, tern 5 glass 6 vessel 7 measure
builder: 14 Andrew Robinson

schottische: 5 dance, polka

schout: 7 bailiff, sheriff

schrik: 5 panic 6 fright

science: art, sci 5 ology 9 education, knowledge 10 technology
of agriculture: 8 agronomy
of animals: 7 zoology
of crop production: 8 agronomy
of enviroment: 7 ecology
of healing: 9 iatrology
of heredity: 8 genetics
of human behavior: 6 ethics 10 psychology
of motion: 8 kinetics
of mountains: 7 orology
of plants: 6 botany
of projectiles: 10 ballistics
of words: 9 semantics
principle: 5 logic

sciential: 4 able 7 capable 9 competent

scientific: 5 exact 8 skillful 9 practical, technical

scilicet: 5 to wit 6 namely 9 videlicet

scimitar, scimiter: 4 snee 5 saber, sword 8 billhook

scintilla: 4 atom, iota 5 spark, trace 8 particle 10 least trace

scintillate: 5 flash, gleam, spark 7 glitter, sparkle, twinkle 9 coruscate

scion, cion: bud, son 4 heir, twig 5 shoot, sprig 6 sprout 8 offshoot 9 offspring 10 descendant

scissor: cut 4 clip, trim 5 shear

scleroid: 4 hard 8 hardened 9 indurated

scoff: 4 food, gibe, gird, jeer, leer, meal, mock, rail 5 fleer, flout, gleek, scout, sneer, steal, taunt 6 deride 7 mockery, plunder 8 ridicule 9 indignity

scoffer: 5 clown 6 jester, mocker 10 unbeliever

scold: nag, yap 4 haze, jump, rail, rant, rate 5 abuse, barge, boast, brawl, chide, score, shrew, slate 6 berate, bounce, rebuff, rebuke, revile, virago 7 bawl out, chew out, reprove, upbraid 8 chastise, lambaste 9 criticize, objurgate 10 vituperate

scolding: 6 dirdum, rating, rebuke 7 combing, hearing, reproof 8 dressing 9 complaint

scombroid fish: 4 tuna 6 bonito 8 mackerel

sconce: 4 fine, fort, head 5 cover, skull 7 bracket, bulwark, lantern, penalty, shelter 8 entrench 10 protection 11 candlestick

scone: 4 farl 5 farle 7 biscuit

scoop: dig 4 bail, beat, lade, news 5 didle, empty, gouge, ladle, skeet, spoon 6 bucket, chisel, dipper, dredge, gather, hollow, shovel, vessel 7 curette 8 excavate

scoot: run 4 bolt, dart, dray, scud 5 hurry, scram, shoot, slide 6 begone, decamp, scurry 9 skedaddle

scooter: toy 4 boat, plow 6 glider

scop: 4 bard, poet

scope: 4 area, goal, room 5 range, reach, theme, tract 6 domain, extent, import, intent, length, object, sphere, target 7 breadth, liberty 8 distance, latitude 9 dimension, extension, intention

having: 13 comprehensive

large: 7 general

scopic: 6 visual 9 extensive

scorch: cut, dry 4 burn, char, flay, sear, skin 5 adust, be hot, parch, score, singe, slash, speed, sting, toast 6 birsle, scathe, wither 7 blister, scratch, shrivel 8 lambaste

score: cut, run, tab, taw 4 goal, line, mark, rate 5 chalk, chase, corge, count, judge, notch, scold, slash, tally 6 abrade, barter, berate, furrow, grudge, number, reason, record, scotch, twenty, weight 7 account, arrange, scratch, upbraid 8 incision 9 criticize, grievance, reckoning 10 obligation 11 enumeration, orchestrate 12 indebtedness

scoria: 4 lava, rock, slag 5 ashes, dross 6 refuse 7 residue

scoring point: ace, hit, run 4 down, goal 5 tally 6 basket

scorn: 4 geck, jeer, mock 5 flout, scoff 6 deride, reject, slight 7 condemn, despise, despite, disdain 8 contempt, derision 9 contumely

scornful: 5 aloof 7 haughty, stuckup 8 arrogant, insolent 9 rejecting 10 disdainful, fastidious

scorpion: 4 nepa 6 onager, weapon 7 scourge, stinger 8 arachnid, catapult 10 vinegaroon

stinger: 6 telson

Scorpion's Heart: 7 Antares

scot: tax 4 levy 6 assess 7 payment 9 reckoning 10 assessment 12 contribution

Scot: 4 Gael, Pict 10 Caledonian, Highlander

scotch (see also **Scotland**): cut 4 stop 5 check, chock, notch, score, wedge 6 hinder, stingy, whisky 7 scratch, scruple, sparing 8 hesitate 9 frustrate

Scotchman: Mac 4 Gael, Scot 7 bluecap, Scottie 10 Highlander

scoter: 4 coot, duck, fowl

genus: 7 oidemia 9 melanitta

scot-free: 4 safe 5 clear 6 unhurt 7 untaxed

Scotland: *accent:* 4 birr, burr

askew or awry: 4 agee 5 agley

at all: ava

author: 5 Scott 6 Barrie

bay: 5 Scapa

beg: 4 sorn

bird: gae 4 hern 6 grouse, snabby 7 snabbie 8 throstle 9 swinepipe

blessing: 6 rebuke 8 scolding

blood money: cro

boat: 4 zulu 6 scaffy, sexern 7 coracle, skaffie

bonfire: 6 tandle

brain: 4 harn

bread: 5 briar 6 tammie 7 bannock

bread dish: 4 saps

briar: 4 rose

brook: 4 sike

broth: 4 soup

bucket: 5 stoop, stoup

bull: 4 stot

bushel: fou

buxom: 6 sonsie

cake: 5 scone

camp follower: 6 gudget

cap: tam 6 bonnet, tassel, toorie 8 Balmoral 9 Glengarry 11 Tam O'Shanter

capital: 9 Edinburgh

cap tassel: 6 toorie

cascade: lin 4 linn 5 force

cat: 6 malkin

cattle: **8** Ayrshire
celebration: **4** kirn
chafing dish: **7** choffer
chair: **5** regal
chief: **5** thegn
child: **4** dalt **5** bairn **6** scuddy **8** smatchet
church: **4** kirk
city: Ayr **5** Alloa, Leith, Perth, Troon **6** Dundee **7** Glasgow, Grunock, Paisley **8** Aberdeen, Stirling **9** Edinburgh, Inverness, St. Andrews **10** Kilmarnock
cloth: **4** kelt **6** tartan
coin: **4** demy **5** bodle, groat **6** baubee, bawbee
colt: **4** stag
congress: Mod
corner: **4** neuk
county: Ayr **4** Bute, Fife, Ross **5** Angus, Banff, Moray, Nairn, Perth **6** Argyll, Lanark, Orkney **7** Berwick, Kinross, Peebles, Renfrew, Selkirk, Wigtown **8** Aberdeen, Ayrshire, Dumfries, Roxburgh, Shetland, Stirling
court officer: **5** macer
cross: **8** crantara **9** crostarie
cuddy: **6** draper **7** peddler
cup: **4** tass
curlies: **4** kale
dagger: **5** skean
dance: bob **4** reel **7** walloch **9** ecossaise **10** strathspey **13** Highland-fling
destiny: **5** weird
devil: **4** deil
district: Ayr **5** Rinns **6** Atholl **7** Lothian **8** Galloway **9** Tweeddale **11** Breadalbane
donkey: **5** cuddy
drapery: **4** pand
drinking bout: **6** screed
drinking vessel: **4** tass **6** quaich, quaigh
duck: **10** bufflehead
elm: **4** wych
ember: **5** aizle
endure: **4** dree
excuse: **6** sunyie
explorer: Rae
eye: ee
fairy: **4** fane
farmer: **6** cottar, cotter **7** crofter
fashion: **7** Scotice
festival: Mod **7** Uphelya
fiddle: **4** itch
fingering: **4** wool, yarn
fireplace: **5** ingle
firth: Tay **4** Loch, Lorn **5** Clyde, Forth, Moray **6** Linnhe **8** Cromarty
fish: **4** sile **7** sillock **8** spalding
fish trap: **4** yare **5** yaire
fishing expedition: **5** drave
fog: **4** haar
fool: **4** gype
fort: **4** dune **10** roundabout

game: **6** shinty
garment: tam **4** kilt, maud **5** toosh **6** fecket, tartan **7** arisard **8** Balmoral **11** Tam o' Shanter
garter: **8** wooer-bab
ghost: **6** taisch
girl: **4** jill, lass **5** quean **6** lassie, towdie **7** winklot
give: gie
grandchild: oe, oy; oye
grandfather: **8** gudesire
grandmother: **6** gudame
granite: **5** gowan
guess: **4** rede
gutter: **5** siver
hands: **8** paddling
have: hae
hazelnut: nit
heater: **7** choffer
heath: **7** heather
heavy: **5** tharf
hill: **4** brae **6** strone
hillside: **4** brae
historian: **4** Hume **5** Skene
hoppers: **9** hopscotch
icicle: **7** shoggle
inlet: gio
island: **4** Iona **5** Arran **6** Orkney **8** Hebrides, Shetland
kale: **8** borecole
kelp: **8** bellware
king: **6** Robert
kiss: **8** smoorich
lake: dee **4** loch
lament: **6** ochone
land: **6** carses
land tax: **4** cess
landholder: **5** laird, thane
language: **4** Erse **6** Lallan **7** Lalland
liquor: **5** scour **6** athole **8** whittier
lord: **5** laird
loyal: **4** leal
marauder: **7** cateran
measure: cop **4** cran, fall, mile, peck, pint, rood, rope **5** crane, crans, lippy **6** firlot, lippie **7** auchlet, chalder, choppin **8** mutchkin, stimpart, stimpert **9** particate, shaftment, shaftmont
mist: ure
money: **6** siller
monk: **6** culdee
mountain: **8** Ben Nevis **9** Grampians
muddled: ree
music festival: Mod
musical instrument: **5** pipes **7** bagpipe
muscian: **5** piper
must: **4** maun
native: **4** Gael, Pict, Scot
naval base: **9** Scapa Flow
negative: nae
oath: **4** aith
odd: **4** orra

pastry: **5** scone **7** carcake
patron saint: **6** Andrew
payment: cro
peasant: **6** cottar, cotter
peninsula: **5** Rinns
people: **8** Damnonii **9** Dammonian
physicist: **4** Watt
plaid: **4** maud
poet: **4** Hogg, Moir **5** Burns
pole: **5** caber
pool: lin **4** linn
porridge: **5** brose
proprietor: **5** laird
pouch: **6** sporan **7** sporran
pudding: **6** haggis
queen: **4** Mary
refuge: **6** bilbie
ridge: run
river: Ayr, Dee, Don, Esk, Tay **4** Doon, Find, Norn, Nith, Spey **5** Afton, Annan, Clyde, North, Tweed **6** Teviot **7** Deveron
sausage: **9** whitehass **10** whitehawse
schoolmaster: dux
scurvy grass: **8** seabells
seaport: **4** Leth **5** Alloa **6** Dundee
sect: **9** Buchanite
self: sel
servant: **5** gilly **6** gillie
sheepfold: ree
small: sma
snow: sna **4** snaw
soldier: **7** cateran
song: **6** strowd
student: **5** bejan **6** nejant
sweetheart: **4** jill
tenure: **6** sorren **7** sorehon
tinker: **5** caird
tithe: **5** teind
title: **5** laird
to: tae
toad: ted **4** taed
tobacco: **5** elder
toe: tae
toil: **4** darg
topaz: **6** tassel **9** cairngorm
tourist resort: **4** Oban
tower: **7** toorock
town hall: **8** tolbooth **9** tollbooth
tree: arm
trousers: **5** trews
uncle: eme
unit: ane
vigor: vir
warrior: **4** kemp
water spirit: **5** kelpy **6** kelpie
waterfall: lin **4** linn **5** force
weakling: **4** ribe **5** shilp **7** shilpit
weapon: **5** skean **8** claymore, skeandhu
weight: **4** boll, drop **5** trone **6** bushel
whine: **4** yirn
whirlpool: **7** swilkie **8** swelchie

whisky: **6** athole **9** Glenlivat, Glenlivit **10** Usquebaugh
whitefish: **7** vendace
window: **7** winnock
woman: **4** burd
woodcock: **4** eggs
world: **4** warl
yell: **4** gowl
youth: **5** chiel **7** callant
Scott: *character:* **5** Norma **7** Ivanhoe **9** Lochinvar
novel: **6** Rob Roy **7** Ivanhoe **8** Talisman **10** Kenilworth
poem: **7** Marmion
Scottish: See **Scotland**
scoundrel: cad **4** scab **5** cheat, filth, knave, scamp **6** rascal, varlet **7** glutton, villain, warlock **8** bezonian **9** miscreant, reprobate **10** blackguard
scour: eat, rub, run **4** beat, rake, rush, wash **5** clean, hurry, purge, scrub, sweep **6** decamp, polish, punish, remove **7** cleanse, roister **8** brighten, traverse
scourge: **4** bane, flay, flog, lash, whip **5** harry, shoot, slash **6** plague, punish, ravage, swinge, switch **7** afflict, torment **8** chastise, epidemic, lambaste **9** devastate **10** affliction, discipline, flagellate, infliction, punishment
Scourge of God: **6** Attila
scout: guy, spy **4** chap, jeer, look **5** scoff, spurn, watch **6** fellow, search **7** despise, explore, lookout, observe **8** emissary, informer, ridicule, watchman **9** search out **11** reconnoiter, reconnoitre
unit: den **4** pack **5** troop
scouth: **4** room **5** range, scope **6** plenty
scow: **4** acon(F.), boat **5** barge, float **6** garvey **7** lighter
scowl: **5** frown, glare, glout, lower **6** glower
scraggly: **6** jagged, ragged **7** unkempt **9** irregular **10** splintered
scraggy: **4** bony, lean, thin **5** rough, weedy **6** meager, rugged, skinny **7** knotted, scrawny **8** slovenly
scram: **4** flee, shoo **6** beat it, benumb, depart, go away **7** vamoose **8** paralyze, withered
scramble: mix **4** push **5** climb, crowd, crush, fight, haste **6** hustle, jostle, sprawl, spread, strive **7** clamber, pushing, scatter **8** struggle
scrambled: **4** pied **5** mixed **11** meaningless
scrap: bit, end, jag, ort, rag **4** chip, item, junk **5** brawl, fight, grain, piece, shred, waste **6** cullet, morsel, refuse **7** cutting, discard, extract, oddment, quarrel, remnant **8** fraction, fragment **11** small amount
scrape: bow, hoe, row, rub, saw **4** claw, grit, harl, rake, rasp, scud, trap **5** claut, erase,

grate, graze, gride, hoard, order, shave **6** abrade, dredge, fiddle, gather, harass, refine, remove, sclaff **7** collect, corrode, scratch **9** situation **10** difficulty **11** predicament **12** touch lightly

scraper: 4 tool **6** barber, rasper, xyster **7** fiddler, strigil **8** grattoir

scraping: 6 rasion, rasure

scrapper: 5 boxer **7** fighter **8** pugilist **9** combatant

scratch: dig, mar, rat, rit, rub, wig **4** claw, draw, feed, heap, line, mark, race, rake, rist, tear **5** break, claut, clawk, erase, expel, fluke, frush, money, score, wound **6** cancel, furrow, gather, injury, rasure, scotch, scrape, scrawl **7** expunge, roughen, scarify **8** abrasion, incision, scribble, scrobble, withdraw

scratchy: 6 uneven **10** irritating

scrawl: 4 teem **5** crawl **7** scratch, writing **8** scribble

scrawny: 4 lean, poor, thin **6** meager **7** scraggy, scranny, scrubby **8** rawboned

screak: 4 rasp **5** creak, grate

scream: cry **4** wail, yarm, yaup, yawl, yell, yowt **6** shriek, squall, yammer **7** screech **10** funny story

screamer: 5 chaja, error **7** caption

scree: 5 stone, talus **6** pebble **7** deposit

screech: cry **4** yell **5** quawk **6** outcry, scream, shriek **7** ululate

screed: say **4** land, rend, rent, tear **5** board, shred, strip **6** scrape, smooth, tirade **7** leveler **8** diatribe, fragment, harangue **9** discourse

screen: 4 cage, hide, mask, mesh, reja, sept, sift, veil **5** arras, blind, chick-(Ind.), cloak, cover, grill, purda, scarf, shade, sieve, speer, spier **6** defend, filter, grille, purdah, settle, shield **7** conceal, curtain, protect, reredos, shelter, shut out **8** block out, covering, separate **9** breakwind, partition

architectural: 5 spier

chancel: 4 jube **7** reredos

chimney: 6 bonnet

Japanese: 5 shoji

mesh: 4 laun **5** sieve

wind: 8 paravent

screw: key, pay **4** turn, wind, worm **5** cheat, guard, horse, miser, twist **6** extort, gimlet, keeper, salary, scrimp, spiral **7** contort, crumple, distort, robbery, squeeze, tighten, turnkey **9** bargainer, propeller, skinflint **10** contortion, crustacean, instructor

screw pine: 5 vacoa **6** vacona, vacoua **8** pandanus

screw-pine family: 11 pandanaceae

screwball: nut, sap **5** crank, crazy, dippy, goose **6** galoot **7** fanatic, saphead **8** crackpot, dumbbell **9** blockhead, eccen-

tric **10** crackbrain, muttonhead

screwed: 5 drunk **11** intoxicated

screw up: 5 spoil **6** fasten

screwy: 5 crazy, wacky **6** absurd, insane, whacky **7** winding **8** freakish, peculiar **9** eccentric, fantastic **10** irrational, misleading, unbalanced **11** impractical **12** crackbrained, preposterous

scribble: 5 write **6** scrawl **7** jot down, scratch **8** scrabble

scribe: 5 clerk, write **6** author, copier, doctor, notary, penman, writer **7** copyist, graffer, teacher **9** draftsman, scenarist, scrivener, secretary **10** amanuensis, journalist **11** transcriber **13** bibliographer

scriggle: 5 twist **6** squirm, wiggle **7** wriggle **8** curlicue

scrimmage: 4 play **5** fight **6** battle, splore, tussle **8** football, practice **10** free-for-all

scrimp: 4 save **5** stint **6** meager, save up, scanty **9** economize **12** pinch pennies

scrimping: 7 miserly, sparing **9** niggardly

scrip: 4 list **5** token **7** writing **8** currency, schedule **10** paper money **11** certificate

script: 5 ronde **8** scenario **10** penmanship **11** chirography, handwriting

Arabic: 5 neski

round: 5 ronde

Syriac: 5 serta

scriptor: See **scribe**

scriptural: 8 Biblical

scrivello: 4 tusk

scrivener: 6 notary, writer **8** recorder

scrofula: 4 evil **6** struma **9** king's evil

scrofulous: 7 corrupt **10** degenerate **12** contaminated

scroll: 4 curl, list, roll **5** draft **6** amulet, legend, record, scrawl, spiral, volute **7** outline, papyrus, writing **8** enscribe, inscribe, schedule, streamer

Hebrew: 6 mezuza **7** mezuzah

writing: 8 makimono

scrouge: 5 crowd, press **7** squeeze

scrounge: beg **5** cadge, steal **6** pilfer, search, sponge

scrub: mop, rub **4** mean, poor, runt, stop, wash **5** clean, dwarf, scour, small **6** drudge, paltry, shabby **7** call off, cleanse **8** inferior **10** brushwood, shrubbery, undersized **14** undernourished

scrub turkey: 6 leipoa **8** megapode

scrubby: 5 runty, small **6** shabby **7** stunted **8** inferior

scruff: 4 film, nape, scum **5** crust, dross **6** refuse **7** coating **8** covering, dandruff

scrumptious: 4 fine, nice **5** dandy, tasty **7** capital, elegant **8** splendid **9** delicious, excellent

scrunch: 5 crush **6** crunch, huddle **7** squeeze

scruple: 4 part 5 demur, doubt, qualm 6 amount, boggle, weight 7 anxiety, portion 8 question 9 disbelief, misgiving 10 uneasiness 11 compunction

scrupulous: 4 nice 5 chary, exact 6 honest, proper, strict 7 careful, correct, precise, upright 8 accurate, cautious 9 honorable, reluctant 11 punctilious 13 conscientious

to excess: 7 finicky, prudish 10 fastidious

scrutinize: eye, pry 4 scan, sift 5 probe 6 survey 7 examine, inspect, observe 8 look over

scrutiny: 4 gaze, look 8 overview

scryer: 4 seer

scuba diver: 7 frogman 8 aquanaut

scud: ale, fly, run 4 beer, gust, mist, move, skim 5 cloud, hurry, spray 6 scrape, shower 10 crustacean

scuff: 4 blow, cuff, drag, gust, toss, wipe 5 brush, evade, graze, rowdy, slare, touch, tread 6 buffet, rabble, scrape, scruff, shower, slight 7 scatter, shuffle, slipper 8 scramble 9 roughened, scratched

scuffle: row 4 cuff 5 amble, fight, melee, set-to 6 affray, bustle, clinch, combat, sclaff, strive, tussle 7 contend, shamble, shuffle 8 struggle

scug: 5 shade 6 shadow 7 protect, shelter 8 pretense, squirrel 9 schoolboy

scull: oar, row 4 boat 6 basket, propel, wherry 7 rowboat 8 scullion

scullion: 6 menial 7 servant

sculptor: 6 artist, graver, imager

famous: Arp 4 Gabo 5 Moore, Rodin, Smith 6 Calder, Robbia, Zorach 7 Cellini, daVinci, Epstein, Maillol, Noguchi, Pevsner, Phidias, Picasso, Zadkine 8 Brancusi, Hepworth, Nevelson 9 Lipschitz, Mestrovic 10 Giacometti, Praxiteles 11 Polycleitus 12 Michelangelo

tool: 6 graver

sculpture: 4 bust, form, head 5 carve, grave, torso 6 clusel, emboss, relief, statue 7 engrave, relievo

framework: 8 armature

pert. to: 7 glyphic, glyptic 9 glyptical

slab: 6 metope

scum: 4 brat, foam, scud, silt, skim 5 dregs, dross, froth, range, scour, slime, sperm, spume, sweep 6 bubble, rabble, refuse, scoria 10 impurities 12 offscourings

scumfish: 5 choke 9 discomfit, overpower, suffocate

scup: 4 fish 5 bream, porgy

scuppernong: 4 wine 5 grape 9 muscadine

scurrilous: low 4 foul, vile 5 gross 6 ribald, vulgar 7 abusive, obscene 8 indecent 9 insulting, offensive 11 disparaging, foulmouthed, opprobrious

scurry: hie, run 4 race, rush 5 harry, scoot, scour, skirr, speed 6 flurry, hasten 7 scamper, scuttle, skelter 9 skedaddle

scurvy: bad, low 4 mean 6 shabby, vulgar 7 disease 8 scorbute 12 contemptible, discourteous

preventative: 6 citrus 13 antiscorbutic

scutage: fee, tax 4 levy 6 impost

scuttle: hod, run 4 dish, ruin, rush, sink, veto 5 scoot 6 basket, bucket, scotch, scurry, shovel 7 octopus, platter 8 bankrupt, hatchway 10 cuttlefish

scuttlebutt: 5 rumor 6 gossip 7 hearsay

scutum: 5 plate, scute 6 shield

Scylla: 4 rock

father: 5 Nisus

lover: 5 Minos

scythe: 6 sickle

handle: 5 snath, thole 6 snathe

sweep: 5 swath

sea: mer(F.) 4 blue, deep, meer(G.), much 5 ocean

anemone: 5 polyp 7 actinia

approach: 7 seagate

arm: bay 4 gulf 5 bayou, firth, fjord, frith, inlet, lough 7 estuary

at: 4 asea

bottom: bed

current: 4 tide 8 undertow

deity: Ler, Ran 5 Aegir, Doris 6 Nereus, Triton 7 Neptune, Phorcus, Phorcyn, Phorcys, Phorkys, Proteus 8 Palaemon, Poseidon

delicacy: roe 4 nori

description: 11 haliography

god: 7 Neptune, Proteus 8 Poseidon

goddess: Ran 4 Nina 8 Eurynome 9 Leucothea 10 Amphitrite

king: Ler 5 chief 6 pirate, viking

land in: 6 island

life of: 8 halibios

little: 6 sealet

mammal: 4 seal 5 whale

open: 6 midsea

periodic motion: 4 tide

pert. to: 4 vast 5 naval 6 marine 7 oceanic, pelagic 8 maritime, nautical 9 aequoreal, thalassic

plant: 6 enalid

roughness: 5 swell, waves 6 lipper

route: 4 lane

spray: 9 spindrift 10 spoondrift

swell: 4 surf

term: 4 ahoy 5 avast, belay, trice

sea cow: 6 dugong, rytina, walrus 7 manatee 8 sirenian 12 hippopotamus

sea cucumber: 6 pedata 7 trepang 11 holothurian

sea dog: tar 4 seal 6 pirate, sailor 7 breaker, dogfish 9 privateer

sea duck: 5 eider 6 scoter

sea eagle: ern **4** erne, tern **6** osprey
sea-ear: 7 abalone
sea-foam: 5 froth **9** sepiolite **10** meer-schaum
sea hog: 8 porpoise
sea horse: 6 walrus **8** whitecap **11** hippocampus
sea kale: 4 cole **7** potherb
sea lettuce: 5 algae, laver **7** seaweed
sea nettle: 6 medusa **9** jellyfish
sea nympth: 5 siren **6** Nereid **7** Galatea, Oceanid
sea raven: 7 sculpin **9** cormorant **10** squaretail
sea robber: 6 jaeger, pirate **7** corsair **9** buccaneer, privateer
sea rover: 6 pirate, viking **7** scummer
sea slug: 6 trepan **8** cucumber **10** nudibranch
sea soldier: 6 marine **10** hermit crab
sea squirt: 5 salpa **8** ascidian, tunicate
sea swallow: 4 tern **6** petrel
sea unicorn: 7 narwhal
sea urchin: 6 repkie **7** echinid, echinus **8** echinoid **10** echinoderm
rock hole: **5** geode
sea wall: 7 bulwark **10** embankment
sea wolf: 4 seal **6** pirate **9** privateer, submarine
seabird: auk, ern **4** duck, erne, gull, smew, tern **5** solan, yager **6** gannet, petrel **7** pelican **9** albatross **10** shearwater
seaboard: 5 coast **9** coastland, tidewater
seafarer: gob, tar **4** salt **6** sailor, seaman **7** mariner **9** navigator
seagoing: 8 maritime, nautical **9** seafaring **13** weatherbeaten
seal: cap, fix, hem, set, wax **4** bind, bull, cere, lute, rope, shut, sign **5** bulla, chain, close, sigil, stamp, token, wafer **6** attest, cachet, clinch, fasten, pledge, ranger, ratify, scarab, secure, signet **7** closure, confine, confirm, leather, sticker **8** breloque, document, guaranty, imprison, sealskin, validate **9** assurance, carnivore, guarantee, sigillate, wax wafer **10** obligation **12** authenticate **14** authentication
bearded: **5** ursuk **6** makluk
decorated with: **9** sigillate
eared: **5** otary
eared genus: **8** zalophus
female fur: **5** matka
letter: **6** cachet
limb: **7** flipper
official: **6** signet
pelt: **5** sculp
pert. to: **7** phocine
place: **7** rookery
polar: **5** otary, phoca, Ross's, ursal, ursuk **6** makluk **8** bedlamer, seecatch **9** sterrinck

school: pod
young: pup **6** beater, hopper **7** quitter, saddler **11** flipperling, holluschick
sealing wax: lac
seam: sew **4** bond, fash, fold, join, line, load, mark, scar **5** cleft, joint, layer, raphe, ridge, strip, unite **6** groove, streak, suture **7** crevice, fissure, stratum, wrinkle **8** cicatrix **10** packsaddle
pert. to: **7** sutural, suturic
seaman: See **sailor, seafarer**
seamark: 6 beacon **8** landmark **10** lighthouse
seamer: 5 sewer **8** stitcher **10** dressmaker, seamstress
seamless: 5 whole **7** unsewed **12** araphorostic
seamy: 5 rough **6** sordid **8** degraded, wrinkled **12** disreputable
seance: 7 meeting, session, sitting
holder: **6** medium
seaport: 4 port **6** habor
sear (see also **sere**): dry **4** burn, cook, mark, scar **5** brand, brown, catch, parch, singe **6** braise, deaden, scorch, sizzle, wither **9** cauterize
search: 4 comb, grub, hunt, look, nose, rout, seek **5** delve, frisk, probe, quest, scour **6** brevit, ferret, forage, pierce, sphere, survey **7** canvass, examine, explore, inquire, inquiry, inspect, ransack, rummage **8** research, scrounge, scrutiny **9** penetrate, shake down **10** scrutinize **11** exploration, investigate
searching: 4 hard, keen **5** acute, sharp **6** shrewd **7** groping **10** discerning
seascape: 4 view **7** picture
seashell: 4 clam **5** conch, snail **7** scallop
seashore: 5 beach, coast, shore **7** seaside **8** seabeach, seacoast
pert. to: **8** littoral
season: age, dry, tid, ver **4** beek, fall, salt, sele, tide, time **5** devil, imbue, inure, ripen, savor, spice, taste, tinge, train **6** autumn, embalm, flavor, harden, mature, period, school, soften, spring, summer, temper, winter **7** condite, flavour, weather **8** accustom, marinate **9** habituate **10** impregnate **11** acclimatize, opportunity
religious: **4** Lent **6** careme
seasonable: apt, pat **4** ripe **6** timely **7** apropos **8** suitable **9** opportune **11** appropriate
seasonal: 8 periodic
seasoned: 7 veteran **8** finished, flavored **11** experienced
seasoning: 4 herb, mace, sage, salt **5** cumin, onion, spice, thyme **6** celery, cloves, cummin, garlic, nutmeg, pepper, relish **7** caraway, cuminos, mustard, oregano, paprika, vinegar **8** allspice, cardamom,

marjoram, rosemary, turmeric **9** condiment, coriander **10** experience

seat: fix, pew, put, see **4** apse, bank, base, form, hold, home, loge, room, site **5** asana, bench, chair, floor, place, sella(L.), siege, stool, usher **6** exedra, center, grange, howdah, locate, sedile, settee, settle, throne **7** capital, install, ottoman, situate, station, taboret, tendoor, tendour **8** bleacher, buttocks, locality, location, tabouret **9** banquette, establish, residence, situation **10** foundation **11** nerve center
chancel: **6** sedile
high: **5** roost
of judgment: **8** tribunal
of justice: **4** banc
on elephant: **6** houdah, howdah
tier of: **6** gradin
seat bone: 7 ischium
seat worm: 7 pinworm
seaweed: ore **4** agar, alga, kelp, nori **5** algae, dulse, laver, varec, vraic, wrack **6** delisk, desmid, fucoid, varech **7** oreweek **8** agar-agar, hempweed, sargasso **9** desmidian
culture medium: **4** agar
edible: **4** limu, ulva **5** dulse
extract: **4** agar
genus of: **6** alaria
pert. to: **6** algous
purple: **4** nori **5** laver **9** carrageen, Irish moss
red: **5** dulse **6** delisk
study: **6** algology
sebaceous: 5 fatty
sec: dry
secant: 5 chord **7** cutting **12** intersecting
secede: 5 leave **6** desert **7** dissent **8** withdraw
secern: 11 distinguish **12** discriminate
seckel: 4 pear
seclude: bar **4** deny, hide **5** debar, expel **6** recess, remove, retire, screen **7** exclude, isolate, protect, retreat **8** cloister, prohibit, separate, withdraw **9** segregate, sequester **10** quarantine
secluded: 5 aloof, apart **6** remote, secret **7** private, retired **8** excepted, solitary **9** quiescent
second: aid **4** abet, back, echo, time **5** other **6** assist, attend, backer, handle, moment, ratify **7** another, confirm, endorse, forward, further, instant, succeed, support, sustain **8** inferior **9** assistant, encourage, imperfect, prototype, reinforce, secondary, supporter, viscosity **10** additional **11** corroborate, subordinate **13** supplementary
second childhood: 6 dotage **8** senility
second-rate: 6 shabby **8** inferior, mediocre

second sight: ESP **9** intuition **12** clairvoyance
second-story man: 5 thief **7** burglar
second team: 6 scrubs **9** yannigans **11** substitutes
secondary: bye **5** minor **6** deputy **8** delegate, inferior **9** auxiliary, satellite **10** accidental **11** subordinate, unessential
color: **5** green **6** orange, purple
proposition: **5** lemma
secondary school: 4 high, prep **5** lycee(F.) **7** academy **10** realschule(G.), vocational
secondhand: old **4** used, worn **6** resold **7** derived **8** borrowed **10** unoriginal
dealer: **6** ragman **7** junkman
secret: 4 dark, dern, hide, rune **5** blind, cabal, close, inner, privy **6** arcane, arcana, closet, covert, hidden, occult, remote, stolen **7** arcanum, cryptic, furtive, mystery, obscure, privacy, private, privity, retired, unknown **8** discreet, esoteric, eyes-only, intimate, mystical, reticent, secluded, stealthy **9** clancular, concealed, intrinsic, recondite, seclusion, secretive, underhand **10** confidence **11** clandestine, concealment **12** confidential, hugger-mugger **13** surreptitious, under-the-table
secret agent: spy **8** emissary, saboteur **10** counterspy
secret place: 6 adytum **7** retreat, sanctum
secretaire: 4 desk **10** escritoire
secretary: 4 desk **5** clerk **8** recorder **9** confidant **10** amanuensis
secrete: 4 bury, hide, ooze, stow **5** exude **7** conceal, store up
secretion: 3 gum, sap **4** bile, laap, lerp, milk **5** juice, latex, mucus, resin, sudor, sweat **6** saliva **9** exudation
sect: 4 clan, cult, part **5** class, group, order, party **6** school **7** faction **8** religion **9** following **10** philosophy **12** denomination
distinguishing word: **10** shibboleth
sectarian: 7 bigoted, heretic **8** apostate **9** dissenter **12** narrow-minded **13** nonconformist **17** denominationalist
section: 4 area, pane, part **5** piece, slice **6** canton **7** portion, segment **8** division **9** signature **11** subdivision
concluding: **8** epilogue
section hand: 6 worker **7** crewman, laborer
sector: 4 area, part **8** division **10** semicircle
secular: lay **4** laic **5** civil **6** carnal, laique(F.), vulgar **7** earthly, profane, worldly **8** temporal **9** temporary **17** nonecclesiastical
secure: buy, get, pot, tie **4** bail, bind, bolt,

easy, fast, firm, gird, moor, nail, safe, sure, tape **5** chain, guard, siker, spike, trice, truss **6** anchor, assure, clinch, defend, fasten, obtain, sicker, stable, strong **7** acquire, assured, certain, procure, protect **8** à couvert, conserve **9** confident, constrain, guarantee **10** batten down, dependable **11** trustworthy, undisturbed **13** overconfident

security: 4 bail, bond, ease, gage **5** guard **6** pledge, safety, surety **7** defense, hostage, shelter **8** guaranty, warranty **9** assurance, certainty, guarantee, insurance, stability **10** confidence, protection

sedan: car **4** auto, limo **5** chair **10** automobile

sedate: 4 calm, cool, dope, drug **5** douce, grave, quiet, sober, staid **6** demure, proper, serene, solemn **7** earnest, serious, settled **8** composed, decorous **9** dignified, unruffled **10** put to sleep **12** tranquillize **13** contemplative, dispassionate, imperturbable

sedative: 6 remedy **7** aconite, bromide, chloral, nervine **8** barbital, lenitive **9** paregoric **10** palliative **12** sleeping pill **13** tranquillizer, sleep-inducing

sedent: 6 seated **7** sitting
opposite: **9** analeptic

sedentary: 5 inert **7** settled, sitting **8** inactive, slothful, tranquil **10** deliberate, motionless, stationary

sederunt: 7 session, sitting **8** assembly

sedge: sag **5** brood, flock **7** bulrush, hassock
genus of: **5** carex **7** scirpus

sediment: lee **4** crap, silt **5** dregs, magma, waste **6** bottom, refuse **7** deposit, grounds, residue **8** settling

sedition: 4 coup **6** revolt, strife, tumult **7** treason **9** coup d'etat, rebellion **10** dissension, dissention, turbulence **12** insurrection

seduce: 4 lure **5** charm, decoy, tempt **6** allure, betray, enamor, entice **7** corrupt, debauch, mislead **8** inveigle

seducer: 4 beau **7** Don Juan **8** Casanova, Lothario **11** philanderer

sedulous: 4 busy **8** diligent, untiring **9** assiduous, laborious, unwearied **10** persistent **11** industrious, painstaking, persevering, unremitting

see: spy **4** espy, hear, ibid, look, meet, rank, scry, seat, view **5** chair, power **6** attend, behold, descry, detect, escort, notice, office, throne **7** diocese, discern, examine, inspect, observe, undergo, witness **8** cathedra, consider, discover, perceive **9** accompany, apprehend, authority, bishopric, encounter, interview, visualize **10** comprehend, experience, scrutinize, understand

seed: ben, egg, pea, pip, pit, sow **4** germ, milt, tare **5** acorn, drupe, grain, ovule, plant, spore, sperm, stock **6** acinus, bubble, kernel, origin, samara, source **7** capsule, progeny, seedlet **8** ancestry **9** beginning, inoculate, offspring, posterity **10** descendant
apple: pip
aromatic: **5** anise **6** fennel, nutmeg
cell: **4** cyst
coat: pod **4** aril, bran, burr **5** testa
container: bur, pod **6** carpel, legume, loment
flavoring: **5** anise, cumin **6** sesame **7** caraway
immature: **5** ovule
organ: **6** pistil
part: pod **4** aril **5** testa **6** tegman, tunica **9** endosperm
part with: **4** core
poisonous: **7** calabar **9** jequirity **10** castor bean
remove: gin, pit **5** picul
scar: **4** hila(pl.) **5** hilum
vessel: pod **6** carpel, legume

seed leaf: 9 cotyledon

seedless: 7 agamous

seedy: 4 worn **5** tacky **6** shabby **7** scruffy **8** slovenly **11** debilitated

seek: beg, sue try, woo **4** busk, fand, hunt, sick **5** court, crave, essay, probe, quest, scout, trace **6** aspire, follow, fraist, pursue, search **7** attempt, beseech, entreat, examine, explore, inquire, request, solicit **8** endeavor **9** cast about, importune, search out **11** investigate

seeker: 6 hunter, prober, tracer **7** pursuer, zetetic **9** applicant **10** petitioner

seel: 5 blind **8** hoodwink

seem: 4 look **5** feign **6** appear **7** pretend **8** manifest

seeming: 5 false **8** apparent, illusory

seemingly: 5 quasi **10** apparently, supposedly

seemly: fit **5** right **6** comely, decent, proper, rather, suited **7** fitting **8** decently, decorous, graceful, handsome, passably, suitable, suitably **10** becomingly **13** appropriately

seen (see also **see**): **7** visible

seep: run **4** leak, ooze **5** exude **7** trickle **8** transude **9** percolate **10** infiltrate

seer: 4 sage **5** augur, sybil **6** mystic, oracle, scryer **7** augurer, diviner, prophet, wise man **9** predictor, spectator **10** forecaster, foreteller, soothsayer **11** clairvoyant, Nostradamus **14** prognosticator

seesaw: 6 teeter, tilter, totter **9** alternate, crossruff, vacillate **10** reciprocal

seethe: hum **4** boil, fume, soak, stew, teem

5 steep 6 bubble, buller, decoct 7 blubber 8 saturate

segment: arc 4 part 5 piece, tmema 6 cantle, divide, set off, somite 7 isomere, portion, section 8 division, fragment, metamere, separate
body: 8 somatome
of crustacean: 6 telson

segregate: 4 part 5 sever 6 divide, select 7 exclude, isolate, seclude 8 classify, separate

seine: net 5 trawl

Seine tributary: 4 Aube, Eure, Oise 5 Marne

seism: 10 earthquake

seity: 8 selfhood 13 individuality

seize: bag, cap, cly, cop, hap, nab, net 4 bind, bite, claw, fang, grab, grip, hent, hook, prey, take, trap 5 annex, catch, clink, grasp, reave, ravin, usurp, wrest 6 affect, arrest, attach, attack, betake, clinch, clutch, collar, fasten, kidnap, ravene, snatch, strike 7 afflict, capture, grabble, grapnel, possess, prehend 8 arrogate 9 apprehend, deprehend, lay hold of, raptorize 10 comprehend, confiscate, understand 11 appropriate
for debt: 6 attach 8 distrain 9 garnishee

seizure: fit 6 attack, stroke 10 androlepsy 11 androlepsia, manucapture

Sekhet's husband: 4 Ptah

seladang: 4 gaur 6 animal 7 buffalo

seldom: 4 rare 6 rarely 10 infrequent 12 infrequently

select: opt 4 cull, draw, name, pick, wale 5 allot, elect, elite 6 assign, choice, choose, chosen, exempt, picked, prefer 7 the best 8 eximious 9 excellent, exclusive, segregate 10 fastidious, particular 11 outstanding

selection: 5 piece 7 analect, excerpt, passage 10 collection

selective: 5 fussy, picky 6 choosy 8 eclectic 9 demanding

Selene: 4 Luna, moon

selenium: *compound:* 7 selenid 8 selenide
soft acid: 8 selenate

self: ego, own, sel(Sc.), soi(F.) 4 same, very 5 being 6 myself 7 himself 8 personal 9 identical 10 particular 11 personality
killing of: 7 suicide 8 felo-de-se
pert. to: 8 personal

self-acting: 9 automatic

self-assertion: 6 egoism, vanity

self-centered: 6 stable 7 selfish 9 egotistic 10 egocentric

self-confidence: 5 poise 6 aplomb 8 presence 9 composure

self-contained: 4 calm, cool 8 composed, reserved 9 collected 11 independent 15 uncommunicative

self-control: 4 will 8 calmness 10 equanimity, moderation 11 forbearance

self-defense: 4 judo 6 boxing, karate 7 fencing, j(i)ujitsu, j(i)ujutsu 8 fighting

self-denial: 10 abstinence, asceticism, puritanism 11 forbearance

self-esteem: 5 pride 6 egoism, vanity 7 egotism 9 assurance

self-evident: 5 clear 7 certain, obvious 8 truistic 9 axiomatic

self-examination: 13 introspection

self-generated: 11 spontaneous

self-government: 8 autonomy 11 self-control 12 independence

self-important: 7 pompous

self-love: 6 vanity 7 conceit, egotism

self-possessed: 4 calm, cool 6 cooler 8 composed 11 undisturbed 12 strong-willed

self-reproach: rue 6 regret 7 remorse 9 penitence 10 contrition

self-respect: 5 pride 6 vanity

self-righteous: 11 pharisaical

self-satisfied: 4 smug, vain 6 jaunty 10 complacent

self-subsistence: 12 independence

selfish: 6 stingy 7 hoggish 9 dissocial, egotistic 10 egocentric, egomaniacal 12 self-centered

selfsame: 9 identical

sell: 4 bilk, cant, deal, dump, dupe, give, gull, hand, hawk, hoax, vend 5 cheat, trade, trick, yield 6 barter, betray, impose, market, peddle, retail 7 auction, bargain, deceive, deliver, dispose 8 convince, persuade, transfer 9 negotiate, wholesale
out: 6 desert, betray 8 inform on
over official rate: 5 scalp

seller: 6 dealer, seller, sutler, trader, vender, vendor 7 peddler 8 salesman 9 tradesman 10 saleswoman, saltcellar

selling place: See **market**

selvage: 4 edge, list 5 gouge 6 border, margin 8 sticking

semblance: air 4 copy, face, form, look, mask 5 guise, image 6 aspect, figure 7 pretext 8 likeness, pretense 10 apparition, appearance, conformity, likelihood, similarity, similitude, simulacrum 11 countenance, presumption, resemblance 14 representation

Semele: *brother:* 9 Polydorus
father: 6 Cadmus
sister: 3 Ino 5 Agave
son: 7 Bacchus 8 Dionysos 9 Dionysius

semester: 4 half, term 6 course, period

semi: 4 half

semiape: 5 lemur

semidiameter: 6 radius

seminar: 6 course, school 7 meeting 10 conference, discussion

seminary: 6 school 7 academy, college 11 institution
Seminole Indian chief: 7 Osceola
Semiramis: *husband:* 5 Ninus
kingdom: 7 Babylon
Semite: Jew 4 Arab 6 Hebrew 7 Moabite 8 Aramaean, Assyrian 9 Canaanite 10 Babylonian, Phoenician
god: 4 Baal 5 Anath, Hadad 6 Moloch 7 Shamash
language: 4 Geez 6 Arabic, Hebrew, Syrian 7 Hebraic, Maltese
people: 6 Shagia 7 Shaigia 9 Shaikiyeh
semolina: 4 meal, suji 5 flour, sujee 6 groats
semper: 6 always
semper fidelis: 14 always faithful
sempiternal: 4 ever 7 endless, eternal 11 everlasting
senate: 5 boule, divan 7 council 8 assembly 11 legislature
senator: 5 solon 8 lawmaker 10 legislator
send: 4 haul, mail, ship 5 drive, grant, impel, issue, relay, speed, thrill 6 bestow, commit, convey, depute, ordain, propel 7 address, consign, delight, deliver, dismiss, forward, inflict, project 8 delegate, dispatch, transmit 9 broadcast, discharge, vouchsafe 10 commission
back: 5 remit 6 remand, return
down: 5 demit
for: 5 order 6 summon
forth: 4 emit 6 effuse 7 emanate
out: 4 beam, emit 5 exile 6 depot, export
to obscurity: 8 relegate
packing: 7 dismiss 9 discharge
up: 4 jail 6 parody, satire 7 take-off 8 imprison
Senegal: *capital:* 5 Dakar
gazelle: 5 korin
language: 5 Serer, Wolof 6 French
monetary unit: 5 franc
mountain: 6 Gounou
religion: 5 Islam
river: 6 Gambia 7 Senegal
timber: 9 cailcedra
senescent: 5 aging
senile: old 4 aged, weak 5 aging 6 daffle, dotard, infirm 7 ancient, elderly, rickety 8 decrepit 9 doddering 12 feebleminded 13 deteriorating
senility: 6 dotage 8 caducity
senior: 4 aine, dean 5 doyen, elder, older 7 ancient, student 8 alderman, superior 13 undergraduate
senior citizen: 10 golden-ager
seniority: age 5 state 6 status 7 quality 8 priority 9 authority 10 precedence
by birth: 13 primogeniture
Sennacherib: *father:* 6 Sargon
son: 8 Sharezer
sensation: 5 sense 6 marvel, thrill 7 emo-

tion, feeling 8 interest 10 appearance, experience, perception 11 sensibility 12 great success
lacking: 4 numb
sensational: 5 lurid 6 superb, yellow 8 eloquent, exciting 9 emotional, startling, thrilling 12 melodramatic
sense: 4 feel, mind, pith 5 touch 6 import, intuit, reason, sanity, wisdom 7 feeling, meaning 8 judgment, perceive, prudence 9 apprehend, awareness, sensation, sentience, soundness, substance 10 appreciate, brainpower, cognizance, comprehend, perception 11 sensibility 12 intelligence 13 consciousness, sensitiveness, understanding 14 susceptibility
Sense and Sensibility author: 6 Austen
sense organ: 3 ear, eye 4 nose, skin 5 nerve 6 tongue 8 receptor
senseless: mad 4 dumb, numb 5 blind, inane 6 simple, stupid, unwise 7 foolish, idiotic 9 insensate, unfeeling 10 half-witted, insensible, irrational 11 meaningless, nonsensical, purposeless, unconscious 12 unreasonable 13 unintelligent
sensible: 5 aware, privy 7 prudent 8 rational 10 reasonable, responsive 11 cognizant of
sensitive: raw 4 nice, sore 5 acute, alive 6 pliant, tender, touchy 8 delicate 9 receptive 10 compatible, responsive 11 susceptible 14 impressionable
plant: 6 mimosa
sensual: 4 lewd 5 alive, gross 6 carnal, coarse, fleshy, sexual 7 bestial, brutish, fleshly, lustful, worldly 9 seductive 10 lascivious, licentious, voluptuous 13 materialistic
sentence: rap 4 doom 5 award, axiom, maxim, motto 6 decide, decree, saying 7 adjudge, condemn, opinion, passage, proverb 8 aphorism, decision, judgment 9 destinate, proscribe, statement 12 adjudication, pass judgment 13 determination
consisting of one word: 7 monepic
construction: 6 syntax
describe: 5 parse
part: 6 clause, phrase, object 7 subject 9 predicate
same backwards and forwards: 10 palindrome
type: 6 simple 7 complex 8 compound
sententious: 5 pithy, short, terse 7 compact, concise, laconic 10 meaningful, moralistic, proverbial
sentient: 5 alive, aware 6 living 7 feeling 8 sensible 9 conscious
sentiment: 4 idea, love 5 maxim, toast 6 lyrics, saying 7 emotion, feeling, lean-

ing, meaning, opinion **9** sensation, substance **10** perception **11** sensibility **14** susceptibility

sentimental: 5 gushy, loving **7** maudlin, mawkish, schmalz **8** romantic, schmaltz **9** fantastic **10** idealistic, lovey-dovey, moonstruck **11** susceptible, tear-jerking **13** lackadaisical

sentinel: 5 guard, vedet(Sp.), videt(Sp.), watch **6** bantay(P.I.), sentry, warder **7** soldier **8** watchman **10** factionary, watchtower

sepal: 4 leaf

separate: 4 bolt, cull, deal, free, know, part, rend, rift, shed, sift, slay, sley, sort **5** alone, aloof, apart, aside, break, hedge, ravel, sever, space, strip **6** assort, breach, cleave, decide, deduct, depart, detach, divide, refine, remove, secede, single, sleave, sleeve, sunder, winnow **7** break up, disjoin, dispart, diverse, divorce, expanse, isolate, segment **8** abstract, alienate, detached, discrete, disperse, dissolve, distinct, disunite, secluded, solitary, withdraw **9** demarcate, different, discharge, disengage, dismember, disparate, eliminate, segregate, withdrawn **10** disconnect, dispossess, dissociate, distribute, individual, quarantine, sejunctive **11** disembodied, distinctive, distinguish, fractionate, independent, part company, precipitate, unconnected **12** disassociate, disconnected, disintegrate

separation: 4 gulf **6** schism, tmesis **7** diacope, divorce **8** distance **9** apartheid, cessation, partition **14** discontinuance

separatist: 8 apostate **9** dissenter

separatists: 8 Pilgrims, Zoarites **9** Bimmelers

Sephardim: 4 Jews
country of origin: **5** Spain **8** Portugal
dialect: **6** Ladino

sepia: dun **5** color **7** pigment **9** red-yellow **10** cuttlebone, cuttlefish

sepiment: 5 hedge **7** defense **9** enclosure

sepiolite: 10 meerschaum

sepoy: 9 policeman

seps: 5 snake **6** lizard **7** serpent

sept: 4 clan, fine **5** seven, tribe **8** ancestry

septic: 6 putrid, rotten **8** diseased **9** infective

septum: 4 wall **9** partition

sepulcher: 4 bury, tomb **5** grave, inter, vault **6** entomb **8** monument **10** repository
subterranean vault: **8** catacomb

sepulchral: 4 deep **6** gloomy, hollow **7** charnel **8** funereal

sequacious: 6 pliant **7** ductile, servile **9** attendant, compliant, dependent, following, malleable

sequel (see also **sequence**): **4** next **5** issue **6** effect, result, upshot **7** outcome **8** follower, follow up, sequitur **9** aftermath, following, inference **10** conclusion **11** consequence, continuance **12** continuation

sequence (see also **sequel**): run, set **5** gamut, order, suite **6** course, series, tenace **8** straight **10** succession **11** progression

sequential: 9 following **10** continuous, processive, succeeding **11** consecutive

sequester: 5 seize **6** enisle **7** isolate, seclude **8** separate **10** appropriate **11** confiscate

sequestered: 5 alone **6** lonely, seized **7** private, recluse, removed, retired **8** isolated, secluded, solitary, withdrew **9** concealed, renounced, separated, withdrawn **10** cloistered, disclaimed, segregated **11** confiscated **12** appropriated

sequin: 4 disk **7** spangle

sequoia: 7 redwood

serac: 5 block **11** ice pinnacle

seraglio: 5 harem, serai **6** zenana **7** brothel **8** lodgings **9** enclosure, warehouse

serai: 8 lodgings, seraglio **9** rest house **11** caravansary **12** caravanserai

serape: 5 cloak, shawl **7** blanket

seraph: 5 angel **6** cherub

seraphic: 4 pure **5** pious **7** angelic, lovable, refined, sublime **8** beatific, cherubic **9** unworldly

Serb: 4 Slav

Serbia: See **Yugoslavia**

sere, sear: dry, wax **4** worn **5** dried, talon **6** yellow **7** parched, several, various **8** scorched, separate, withered **10** desiccated, threadbare

serenade: 6 aubade **8** nocturne, serenata
burlesque: **8** shivaree **9** charivari **10** callithump

serene: 4 calm, cool, damp **5** clear, light, quiet **6** bright, placid, sedate, serein, steady **7** pacific **8** composed, decorous, peaceful, tranquil **9** collected, impassive, unruffled **10** unobscured **11** undisturbed **13** dispassionate, imperturbable

serenity: 4 calm **5** peace **6** repose **7** balance **10** equanimity

serf: 4 esne, peon **5** churl, helot, slave **6** servus, thrall, vassal **7** bondman, peasant, villein **8** bondsman, hireling
female: **5** neife **6** colona

serge: 7 worsted

sergeant: 6 chiaus, noncom **7** topkick **9** attendant

sergeant fish: 5 cobia **6** robalo

series: set **4** list **5** chain, gamut, suite, train **6** catena, course **8** beadroll, cate-

gory, sequence, seriatim **9** gradation **10**
continuity, succession

arranged in: **6** serial **7** seriate **11** install-
ment

serious: 4 deep, grim, hard, keen **5** grave,
heavy, sober, staid **6** demure, sedate, severe, solemn **7** austere, capital, earnest,
weighty **9** important, momentous **10**
no-nonsense, poker-faced, thoughtful
11 considerate

serment: 4 oath **9** sacrament

sermon: 4 talk **5** psalm, speak **6** homily **7**
address, lecture **8** harangue **9** collation,
discourse, preaching **10** admonition

study of: **10** homiletics

subject: **4** text

sermonic: 5 grave **8** didactic

sermonize: 6 advise, preach **8** admonish,
moralize **9** discourse

seroon: 4 bale **7** package

serotine: bat

serous: 4 thin **6** watery

serow: 5 goral, jagla **8** antelope

serpent (see also **snake**): **5** devil, fiend **7**
entwine, reptile

elapine: **4** naia, naja

mythological: Ahi **5** Apepi, Dahak, Hydra
6 ellops, dragon **8** basilisk **11** Amphis-
baena

nine-headed: **5** Hydra

pert. to: **5** anguine

thousand-headed: **5** Sesha **6** Ananta

victim: **7** Laocoon

worship of: **6** ophism

serpentine: 4 file, wily, worm **5** snaky **7**
devious, sinuous, turning, winding **8**
fiendish, tempting **10** circuitous, convoluted, meandering

variety: **10** antigorite

serpigo: 5 tinea **6** herpes, tetter **8** ringworm

serrate: 7 notched, toothed **11** denticu-
late

serried: 5 dense **6** massed, packed **7** compact, crowded **10** continuous

serum: 4 whey **5** fluid **9** antitoxin

servable: 6 usable **10** functional

servant: 4 amah, bata, cook, dasi, esne,
girl, help, hewe, hind, maid, maty,
mozo, syce **5** alila, biddy, boots, chela,
gilly, groom, hamal, nurse, scout, slave,
usher, valet **6** batman, bearer, bildar,
butler, chakar, ewerer, flunky, garcon,
gillie, hamaul, hammal, harlot, helper,
khamal, menial, tenant, varlet, vassal **7**
bondman, famulus, flunkey, footman,
hummaul **8** chasseur, domestic, retainer, sergeant, servitor **9** atriensis **11**
chamberlain, subordinate

female: **4** amah, maid **5** wench **6** slavey

garment: **5** apron **6** livery **7** uniform

head: **6** butler

male: **5** valet **6** butler, lackey

of God: **4** monk, pope **5** friar, rabbi **6**
bishop, priest **8** chaplain, minister,
preacher **10** Holy Father, missionary

of nobleman: **7** equerry

pert. to: **8** famulary

retired: **8** emeritus

serve: act, aid **4** abet, give, help, mess,
pass, suit, tend, wait **5** avail, cater,
frame, ladle, treat **6** answer, assist, attend, do good, succor **7** advance, benefit, be of use, bestead, deliver, forward,
further **8** do a hitch, function, minister
9 officiate **10** distribute

server: urn **4** tray **6** salver, waiter **7** caterer **9** assistant, lazy-Susan

Servia: See **Serbia**

service: use **4** mass, rite **5** favor, throw **6**
employ, repair, supply **7** chakari, reti-
nue, utility **8** ceremony, kindness, ministry **11** maintenance **12** installation,
ministration

military: **4** duty **5** hitch **7** stretch **10** enlistment **12** conscription

public: **7** utility

service charge: fee, tip

serviceable: 4 kind **6** useful **7** durable,
helpful, lasting **8** obliging **9** available,
practical **10** beneficial, commodious

serviette: 6 napkin

servile: 4 base, bond, mean **6** abject, menial, sordid **7** fawning, slavish **8** cringing, enslaved **9** dependent, parasitic,
truckling **10** obsequious, sequacious,
submissive **11** subservient, sycophantic

Servite: 5 friar **9** mendicant

servitor: 6 beadle, menial, squire **7** servant, soldier **8** adherent, follower **9** assistant, attendant **10** apprentice **12** ex-
hibitioner

servitude: 4 yoke **7** bondage, peonage,
serfdom, service, slavery **8** sentence **9**
captivity, vassalage **10** subjection

sesame: til **4** herb, teel **5** benne **7** passkey
8 ajonjoli, password

seed: **7** gingili, tilseed

session: 4 term **6** assize **7** meeting, sitting
8 sederunt **10** assemblage, conference

set: fix, gel, lay, put, sit **4** bent, clan, club,
cock, crew, gang, jell, laid, park, port,
pose, prim, ring, seat, stud, suit **5** align,
aline, brood, elect, elite, embed, fixed,
group, imbed, place, plant, posit, range,
ready, rigid, scene, staid, stake, stand,
suite **6** adjust, assign, cement, circle,
clique, define, direct, formal, harden,
impose, impost, ordain, series, settle **7**
appoint, arrange, bearing, company,
confirm, congeal, coterie, decline, deposit, dispose, instate, platoon, station,
stiffen **8** attitude, decorate, exchange,
immobile, moveless, regulate, solidify **9**

coagulate, collocate, designate, determine, establish, immovable, obstinate, prescribe, stabilize **10** assortment, collection, constitute, stationary

about: **5** begin, start

afloat: **6** launch

apart: **5** elect **6** exempt **7** isolate, reserve, seclude **8** allocate, dedicate, separate **9** segregate, sequester

aside: **4** void **5** annul, table **6** except, reject **7** discard, dismiss, earmark, exclude, reserve **8** overrule, separate

at naught: **4** defy **7** despise **9** disregard

back: **4** loss **5** check, delay **6** defeat, hinder **7** relapse, reverse, setback

down: fix **4** land, seat **5** abase, enter, place, write **6** alight, depose, encamp, ordain, reckon, record, regard, relate **7** appoint, descend, resolve, slacken **8** consider, estimate, register **9** attribute, determine, establish, humiliate, prescribe

forth: **5** adorn, offer, state **6** expone, expose **7** arrange, commend, display, enounce, exhibit, explain, expound, present, promote, propone, publish **8** announce, decorate, manifest **9** interpret, translate **10** promulgate

free: See **liberate**

fresh: **5** relay

in motion: **5** start **6** excite **8** activate

in operation: **4** jump, move, skip **5** slide, start **6** launch, plunge, spring

in order: **4** file, tidy **5** align, aline **6** adjust **7** arrange

of players: **4** team **5** squad

of rules: **4** code

off: **5** start **8** mobilize **10** compensate

on end: **5** upend **10** topsyturvy

on fire: **4** tind **5** light **6** kindle

out: **4** head, plan **5** adorn, allot, equip, extol, issue, limit, start **6** design, embark, escort, outfit, recite **7** present, publish **8** describe, proclaim **9** embellish **10** promulgate

right: **4** file **5** align, aline, amend, order **6** adjust, repair **7** arrange, correct, redress, take off **11** systematize

thickly: **4** stud

to: **4** bout **5** fight **6** fracas **7** contest **8** struggle

TV: box **8** boob tube

up: **4** post **5** build, erect, exalt, found, hoist, raise, treat **7** appoint, arrange, elevate **8** organize **9** establish

Set: **5** deity **9** god of evil

brother: **6** Osiris

father: Geb

mother: Nut

victim: **6** Osiris

wife: **8** Nephthys

seta: **6** chaeta **7** bristle

setaceous: **7** bristly

seth: **6** banker **8** merchant

Seth: *brother:* **4** Abel, Cain

descendant: **4** Enos **7** Sethite

father: **4** Adam

son: **4** Enos

seton: **6** suture

setout: **4** fuss **5** get-up **6** outfit **7** costume, display, exhibit **9** beginning **10** excitement **13** entertainment

settee: **4** seat, sofa **5** bench, divan

setter: dog **5** Irish **6** Gordon **7** English **10** compositor

setting: **4** eggs, trap, pave **5** decor, scene, snare, scena(It.) **6** locale **7** scenery **8** mounting **9** hardening **10** background, thickening **11** environment, mise-en-scene **12** surroundings

settle: fix, pay, sag, set **4** calm, firm, lend, nest, root, seat, sink, toit **5** affix, agree, audit, bench, clear, couch, lodge, order, perch, plant, quiet, serve, solve **6** accord, adjust, alight, assign, decide, locate, purify, reduce, render, secure, soothe, wind up **7** appoint, arrange, clarify, compone, compose, confirm, conform, deposit, depress, dispose, privide, resolve, silence, subside **8** colonize, compound, conclude, ensconce, regulate **9** designate, determine, establish, habituate, liquidate, touch down **10** adjudicate, administer, strengthen **11** accommodate, tranquilize

strike: **7** mediate

settled: **4** alit, fast, firm **5** ended, fixed, staid **6** formed, sedate **7** certain, decided, peopled, statary, testate **8** decorous **9** inerratic, sedentary, steadfast **10** consistent, contracted, determined, inveterate, unchanging **11** established

in advance: **13** predetermined

settlement: dos **4** camp, lees **5** abode, dregs **6** colony, hamlet **7** payment, village **8** decision, disposal, fixation, sediment **9** aldeament, community, residence **10** adjustment, compromise, conclusion, habitation, occupation, regulation **11** arrangement **12** colonization, satisfaction **13** clarification, determination, establishment

arrange: **9** negotiate

study of: **8** ekistics

settler: **6** sooner, vessel **7** planter, pioneer **8** colonist, emigrant **9** colonizer, immigrant **10** forehearth, receptacle

American: **7** Pilgrim, Puritan

seven: **4** zeta

days and nights: **8** sennight

deadly sins: **4** envy, lust **5** anger, pride, sloth **8** gluttony **12** covetousness

dice roll: **7** natural

group of: **6** heptad, septet **8** hebdomad

Seven Against Thebes: 6 Tydeus **8** Adrastus, Capaneus, Eteocles **10** Amphiaraus, Hippomedon, Polyneices **13** Parthenopaeus

Seven Churches: 6 Sardis, Smyrna **7** Ephesos **8** Laodicea, Pergamos, Thyatira **12** Philadelphia

Seven Dwarfs: Doc **5** Dopey, Happy **6** Grumpy, Sleepy, Sneezy **7** Bashful

seven-fold: 8 septuple

seven hills: See **Rome:** *hill*

seven-sided: 10 heptagonal

seventh heaven: 7 ecstasy

sever: cut **4** deal, know, part, rend, slit **5** break **6** breach, cleave, depart, detach, divide, sunder **7** dispart, divorce **8** disunite, separate **9** dismember **10** disconnect, dissociate **12** disassociate

from neck: **6** behead **9** decollate **10** decapitate

several: few **4** many, some **6** divers, single, sundry **7** diverse, not a few, various **8** distinct, peculiar **9** different **10** individual, respective

minimum: **5** three

severe: bad **4** cold, dear, dere, dour, dure, grim, hard, keen, sore, tart **5** acute, cruel, grave, gruff, harsh, rethe, rigid, rough, sharp, sober, stark, stern, stiff **6** biting, bitter, chaste, coarse, sedate, simple, solemn, strict, trying, unkind **7** ascetic, austere, caustic, chronic, condign, crucial, cutting, drastic, extreme, intense, painful, serious, spartan, violent **8** captious, exacting, grievous, rigorous, scathing **9** difficult, draconian, inclement, strenuous, stringent, unsparing **10** afflictive, astringent, censorious, forbidding, iron-willed, methodical, oppressive, restrained **12** unornamented

severity: 8 acerbity, acrimony, asperity **10** simplicity, unkindness

Seville cathedral tower: 7 Giralda

sew: hog, sow **4** bind, darn, join, mend, seam **5** baste, broth, drain, sewer, shirr, smock, unite **6** fasten, needle, stitch, suture **7** pottage

up: end **6** settle **7** exhaust **8** conclude **10** monopolize

with gathers: **4** full **5** shirr

sewan: 5 beads, money **6** wampum

Seward's Folly: 6 Alaska

sewer: 5 drain **6** tunnel **7** channel, conduit, servant **10** seamstress

opening: **7** manhole

sewing machine: *inventor:* **9** Elias Howe

part: **8** plicator **10** zipperfoot

sex: 6 gender **10** copulation

hormone: **7** steroid

sexless: 6 neuter **7** epicene

sexton: 6 shamus, verger, warden **7** sacrist **9** sacristan **12** underofficer

sextuplet: 7 sestole **8** sestolet

sexual: 5 gamic **6** carnal, erotic, loving **7** amatory **10** lascivious

continence: **8** chastity

inclination: **4** urge **6** libido

sexy: 4 racy **5** spicy **6** carnal, erotic **7** amatory, earthly

Seychelles Islands: 4 Mahe **7** La Digue, Praslin

capital: **8** Victoria

sha: 5 sheep, urial **6** nahoor, oorial

shabby: old **4** base, mean, worn **5** dowdy, faded, seedy **6** paltry, ragged, scurvy **7** outworn, unkempt **8** beggarly, dogeared, shameful, tattered, unworthy **10** despicable, gone to seed, threadbare **11** disgraceful **12** contemptible, deteriorated

shack: coe **4** plug **5** cabin, catch, chase, hovel **6** lean-to, refuse, wander

shackle: tie **4** band, bind, bolt, bond, curb, gird, gyve, idle, iron, loaf, ring **5** chain, gyves **6** fetter, hamper, hinder, hobble, pinion, secure **7** confine, manacle, trammel **8** coupling, restrain **10** fetterlock

shad: 4 fish **5** alose **6** allice **7** crappie, herring, mojarra

shaddock: 5 fruit **6** pomelo **10** grapefruit

shade: bar, dim, hue **4** dark, dull, hint, tint, tone, veil **5** color, cover, ghost, hatch, tinge, trace, umbra, vault **6** awning, canopy, darken, degree, nuance, screen, shadow, spirit, sprite, shield **7** curtain, eclipse, foliage, obscure, parasol, phantom, protect, shelter, specter, shutter, umbrage, vestige **8** clearing, darkness, ornament, penumbra **9** adumbrate, gradation, variation **10** apparition, difference, overshadow, protection, silhouette **11** small amount

light: **6** pastel

lines: **5** hatch

of cap: **5** visor

of meaning: **6** nuance

shaded: 7 shadowy **8** screened **10** umbrageous

shaded walk: 4 mall **6** arcade **8** cloister

shadetail: 8 squirrel

shadow (see also **shade**): dog **4** blot, lurk, omen, tail **5** cleek, cloud **6** attend, follow, shroud, symbol **7** remnant, suggest, vestige **8** penumbra **9** adumbrate **10** apparition, indication, overspread **13** prefiguration

dark cone of: **5** umbra

dispelling: **9** scialytic

figure: **10** silhouette

of death: **5** gloom, Sheol

outline: **10** silhouette

person without: **6** ascian

shadowbox: 4 spar

shadowy: dim 5 faint, vague 6 opaque, umbral, unreal 7 ghostly, obscure, retired 8 adumbral 9 imaginary 10 impalpable, indistinct, overspread, transitory 12 inaccessible 13 unsubstantial

Shadrach: *companion:* 7 Meshach 8 Abednego
persecutor: 14 Nebuchadnezzar

shady: 6 risque 7 shadowy, umbrous 9 dishonest 11 underhanded 12 disreputable, questionable

shaffle: 4 limp 5 shirk 6 hobble, loiter 7 shuffle

shaft: bar, pit, ray, rod 4 axle, beam, bolt, cone, fust, hole, pole, stem, tige, tole 5 arbor, arrow, helve, heuch, heugh, irony, lance, scape, shank, spear, spire, stalk, stele, thill, trunk 6 arbour, column, groove, handle, pillar, tongue, upcast 7 chamber, chimney, Maypole, missile, obelisk, spindle 8 gatepost, monolith 9 flagstaff 10 air passage
column: 4 fust 5 scape, verge
feather: 5 scape
part: 4 orlo
plant: 4 axis
vehicle: 5 thill

shag: mat, nap 4 hair, mane, mass, pile, toss, wool 5 chase, fetch, fiber, shake 6 follow, rascal, refuse 7 garment, thicket, tobacco 9 cormorant 10 blackguard

shaggy: 5 bushy, furry, hairy, nappy, rough 7 hirsute, scrubby, unkempt, villous 8 straggly, textured 10 unpolished

shagreen: 4 skin 7 leather, rawhide 8 galuchat

shaitan, sheitan: 5 devil, fiend

shake: bob, jar, jog, wag 4 free, jolt, move, pass, rese, rock, shog, stir, sway, toss, wave 5 churn, drink, eject, greet, quake, shock, steal, swing, trill 6 depart, dither, dodder, goggle, hustle, joggle, quaver, quiver, rattle, shiver, totter, tremor, weaken 7 agitate, chatter, concuss, disturb, fluster, tremble, unnerve, vibrate 8 brandish, convulse, dislodge, enfeeble, flourish 10 earthquake
down: bed, con 5 dance 6 extort, search, settle, try out 9 blackmail
off: 4 shed 6 excuss 8 disagree
up: 6 jumble 7 agitate 10 clean-sweep

Shaker: 4 sect
founder: Lee

Shakespeare: *actor:* 4 Ward 5 Booth 6 Burton 7 Garrick, Gielgud, Olivier, Sothern 8 Modjeska 9 Barrymore
alternate author: 5 Bacon
character: 4 Bone, Iago, Iras, Lear, Snug 5 Biron, Cleon, Henry, Regan, Romeo, Speed, Timon 6 Banquo, Hamlet, Juliet, Oberon, Portia, Simple 7 Antonio, Cas-

sius, Othello, Richard, Salerio, Shylock, Silence, Slender, Titania 8 Falstaff
elf: 4 Puck
forest: 5 Arden
home: 4 Avon
play: 4 Lear 6 Hamlet 7 Macbeth, Othello 9 Cymbeline 10 The Tempest 11 As You Like It 12 Julius Caesar, Twelfth Night
theater: 5 Globe
wife: Ann

shaking: 4 ague 7 jittery 9 tremulant, tremulous 10 concussion

shako: cap 9 headdress
decoration: 6 pompon

shakti: 5 force, power

shaky: 4 weak 6 groggy, infirm, wabbly, wobbly 7 rickety, unsound 8 insecure 9 tottering, trembling, tremulous, uncertain 10 unreliable 12 questionable

shale: 4 bone, husk, rock 5 metal, slate 8 impurity

shall: may 4 must, will 5 would 7 obliged

shallop: 4 boat 6 dinghy, vessel

shallot: 4 herb, tube 5 onion 8 eschalot

shallow: hat 4 cart, idle, tray, vain, weak 5 shoal 6 basket, flimsy, slight 7 cursory, trivial 9 depthless, frivolous 11 superficial

shalom: 5 peace 8 farewell, greeting

sham: 4 fake, hoax, mock 5 bogus, cheat, dummy, false, feign, fraud, trick 6 assume, bunyip, chouse, deceit, delude, device, duffer, humbug, shoddy 7 deceive, feigned, forgery, grimace, mockery, pretend 8 imposter, pretense, trickery 9 brummagem, deception, hypocrisy, imitation, imposture, pretended, trickster 10 artificial, fictitious, simulacrum, substitute 11 counterfeit, make-believe

shamal: 4 wind

shaman: 4 monk 6 beggar, priest 8 conjurer 11 medicine man

Shamash: 6 sun god
consort: Aya
messenger: 6 Bunene
worship center: 5 Larsa 6 Sippar

shamble: 5 stall, table 7 bauchle, butcher, shuffle 9 malformed, slaughter

shambles: 4 mess 5 mix-up 8 wreckage 9 confusion

shame: 5 abase, abash 6 assume, bemean, bismer 7 degrade, mortify 8 contempt, disgrace, dishonor 9 embarrass, humiliate 10 repentance 11 degradation, shortcoming 12 illegitimacy 13 embarrassment, mortification

shamefaced: shy 6 humble, modest 7 bashful 9 diffident, regretful

shameful: 4 base, mean 5 gross, wrong 7 ignoble 8 flagrant, improper, indecent, infamous **9** degrading, dishonest **10** outrageous, scandalous, slanderous **11** disgraceful, ignominious, opprobrious **12** contumelious, dishonorable, disreputable, vituperative **13** dishonourable

shameless: 6 arrant, brazen **8** immodest, impudent **9** abandoned, audacious, barefaced **10** unblushing **11** bold as brass

shampoo: 4 lave, wash **5** clean

shamrock land: 4 Eire, Erin **5** Irena **7** Ireland

Shang dynasty: Yin

shanghai: 4 drug, ship **5** seize **6** abduct, coerce, kidnap

Shangri-la: 6 utopia **8** paradise

shank: leg **4** gamb, meat, shin, stem, tang **5** gambe, knife, ladle, ridge, tibia

pert. to: **6** crural

shantung: 4 silk **6** fabric, pongee, tussah

Shantung's capital: 6 Tsinan

shanty: hut **5** cabin, hovel, hutch, lodge, shack **6** leanto **8** chantier, dwelling

shape: fit, hew **4** bend, cast, form, knap, make, mold, plan, tool, trim **5** block, boast, build, carve, feign, frame, guise, image, model, mould, order, state, torus **6** create, decree, design, devise, figure, format, happen, ordain **7** appoint, arrange, conform, contour, fashion, incline, phantom, posture, whittle **8** attitude, contrive **9** condition, determine, structure **10** apparition, appearance, figuration **11** arrangement **13** configuration

different: **8** variform

garden: **7** topiary

in: **4** trim

up: **9** get better

shapeless: 6 deform **8** deformed, formless **9** amorphous, contorted, distorted, misshapen, unshapely

shapely: fit **4** neat, trim **6** decent, gainly **8** suitable **9** beautiful **10** curvaceous **11** symmetrical

shaping machine: 5 edger, lathe **6** shaper

shard: 5 scale, shell **8** fragment, potsherd

share: cut, lot **4** cant, deal, dole, hand, part, rent **5** divvy, enter, quota, ratio, shear, split **6** cleave, divide, impart, moiety, ration **7** partake, portion **8** dividend, division, interest **9** allotment, allowance, apportion, communion, plowshare **10** distribute **11** participate

widow's: **5** dower, dowry, terce, third **6** dowery

sharecropper: 7 metayer **12** tenant farmer

Shari River: See **Cameroon**

shark: 4 gata, haye, mako, tope **5** adept **6** expert, lawyer, usurer **7** dogfish, sharper, sponger **8** drunkard, hybodont, man-

eater, parasite, predator, swindler, thrasher, thresher **9** porbeagle, selachian, trickster **10** hammerhead

blue pointer: **4** mako

genus of: **11** carcharodon

nurse: **4** gata

pilot: **6** remora

small: **4** tope **5** lamia

young: **8** sharklet

sharkskin: 12 cotton fabric

sharp: 4 acid, cold, cute, edgy, fell, gash, gnib, high, keen, nice, sour, tart, wise **5** acrid, acute, adept, alert, brisk, crisp, eager, edged, fiery, harsh, salty, steep, tangy, witty **6** abrupt, active, acuate, astute, barbed, biting, bitter, clever, crafty, crispy, expert, peaked, severe, shrewd, shrill, snelly(Sc.) **7** angular, austere, caustic, cunning, cutting, gingery, grating, intense, lyncean, nipping, painful, piquant, pointed, pungent, rasping, violent, waspish **8** aculeate, distinct, handsome, incisive, piercing, poignant, vigilant, vigorous **9** attentive, beautiful, designing, impetuous, merciless, penetrant, sagacious, sarcastic, trenchant **10** discerning, ungracious **11** acrimonious, intelligent, penetrating, quick-witted, underhanded

to taste: **4** acid **5** acrid

sharp-sighted: 6 astute

sharpen: nib, ted **4** edge, hone, whet **5** grind, point, reset, strop **6** acuate **7** enhance, quicken **9** aggravate, intensify, stimulate **10** cacuminate

sharper: gyp **4** bite **5** cheat, rogue **6** cogger, keener **7** cheater, gambler **8** deceiver, swindler **9** trickster **12** double-dealer

sharpness: 4 edge **6** acumen **8** acrimony, keenness

sharpshooter: 6 sniper **8** marksman

shastra class: 5 sruti **6** purana, smriti, tantra

shatter: 4 blow, dash **5** blast, break, burst, crash, smash, split, wreck **6** batter, damage, impair **7** clatter, derange, destroy, disable, scatter **8** demolish, disorder, disperse, splinter **9** dissipate

shattered: 6 broken **7** damaged **8** broozled, doddered

shave: ace, cut **4** pare, poll, trim **5** cheat, graze, skive **6** glance, rasure, reduce, scrape **7** tonsure, whittle

shaveling: boy **4** monk **5** youth **6** priest **9** hypocrite, stripling **10** cut it close

shavetail: 4 mule **10** lieutenant

shaving: 5 flake, piece **8** ramentum

shawl (see also **vestment**): **4** maud, wrap **5** manta, orale **6** serape(Mex.) **7** amlikar, paisley **8** epiblema

Shawnee Indian chief: 8 Tecumseh, Tecumtha

Shea player: Met
sheaf: 5 bunch 6 bundle 7 cluster
shear: cut 4 clip, gnaw, reap, rend, snip, trim 5 carve, force, mince, prune, sever, shave, strip 6 cleave, divest, fleece, nibble, pierce, remove 7 deprive, scissor, whittle 10 circumcise
shearing machine: 7 cropper
shears: 6 forfex 8 scissors, secateur
sheartail: 4 tern 11 hummingbird
shearwater: 4 crew 6 hagdon, haglet, petrel, puffin
sheatfish: 4 wels 7 catfish
sheath: cot 4 boot, case, skin 5 dress, ocrea, theca, stall 6 forrel, spathe 8 covering, envelope, scabbard
sheathe: 4 bury, case, ceil, dull 5 blunt, cover, glove 6 clothe 7 enclose, envelop
sheave: 5 wheel 6 pulley 9 back water
sheaves: See **sheaf**
shebang: hut 4 deal 6 affair, outfit 7 concern 8 business 11 contrivance 13 establishment
shed: cut, hut 4 abri(F.), byre, cast, cote, drop, emit, hull, lair, molt, nest, part, pour 5 booth, cabin, hovel, repel, scale, spill, tease 6 belfry, dingle, divest, divide, effuse, hangar, hemmel, impart, lean-to, slough 7 cast off, cottage, diffuse, emanate, radiate, scatter, shelter, testudo, take off 8 disperse, jettison, outhouse, separate, sprinkle, throw out, workshop 9 irradiate, penthouse 11 intersperse, out-building
skin: 7 ecdysis
shedder: 4 crab 6 peeler, salmon 7 lobster
sheen: 4 fair 5 gleam, gloss, shine, shoes 6 bright, finish, glossy, luster 7 exalted, glisten, glitter, radiant, shimmer, shining 8 lustrous, splendid, splendor 9 beautiful, shininess 10 brightness, glittering 11 illustrious, resplendent
sheep: mug, sha 5 argal, dumba, ovine, urial 6 aoudad, argali, wether 7 bighorn, bleater, karakul, mouflon 8 karakule, moufflon, ruminant 9 blackface
breed: 4 Horn 6 Dorset, Exmoor, Merino, Romney 7 Cheviot, Delaine, Lincoln, Suffolk 8 Cotswold, Dartmoor 9 Leicester, Southdown, Teeswater 10 Corriedale, Oxford Down, Shropshire
caretaker: 8 shepherd
coat: 4 wool 6 fleece
cry: maa 5 bleat
dead: 5 braxy, traik
disease: coe, gid, rot 5 braxy 6 sturdy
feed: 5 graze 7 pasture
female: ewe
male: ram, tup 6 wether 10 bellwether
mark: 4 smit 5 brand
meat: 6 mutton
pathway: 6 roddin 7 rodding

pen: 5 bught(Sc.) 6 bought(Sc.)
pert. to: 5 ovine
wild: sha 4 arui, udad 5 argal, audad, urial 6 aoudad, argali, bharal, nahoor, nayaur 7 mouflon 8 moufflon
young: hog, teg 4 lamb, tegg 5 heder 6 bident, gimmer, hogget, sheder 7 twinter 8 hoggerel, shearhog 9 four-tooth, shearling
sheep dog: 6 collie 8 shepherd
sheep-like: 4 meek 5 ovine 6 docile
sheepfaced: See **sheepish**
sheepheaded: 5 silly 6 stupid 12 simpleminded
sheepish: shy 4 meek 5 blate, silly, timid 7 abashed, awkward, bashful, daffish 11 embarrassed
sheepskin: 4 bond, cape 5 basil 6 mouton 7 diploma 9 parchment
leather: 4 roan
sheepwalk: run 5 range, slait 7 pasture
sheer: 4 fine, mere, pure, thin, turn 5 brant, clear, steep, utter 6 abrupt, bright, swerve 7 deviate, shining, unmixed, utterly 8 absolute, outright 9 deviation, downright, undiluted 10 diaphanous 11 transparent, unqualified 12 change course 13 perpendicular
sheet: air 4 fine, page, rope, sail 5 chain, daily, linen, paper, plate, white 6 expand, lamina, shroud 7 tabloid 8 handbill, pamphlet 9 baking tin, newspaper
twelvemo: 9 duodecimo
sheeting: 5 linen 6 cotton 7 percale
shelf: 4 bank, berm, bink, reef, sill 5 altar, berme, layer, ledge, shoal 6 gradin, mantel 7 bedrock, bracket, gradine, retable, sandbar, stratum 8 credence, credenza, sandbank 9 banquette 10 pigeonhole
shell: hud, pod 4 boat, bomb, coin, hull, husk, lyre, shot, swad, test 5 balat, cameo, conch, cowry, crust, frame, money, murex, scale, shuck, spoon, testa, troca 6 coffin, concha, cowrie, crusta, dolite, dugout, lamina, lorica, strafe 7 abalone, admiral, bombard, capsule, caracol, dariole, grenade 8 caracole, carapace, covering, exterior, frustule 9 cartridge 10 open fire on, projectile, schoolroom
beads: 4 peag 6 wampum
casing: 5 gaine
defective: dud
explosive: 4 bomb 7 grenade
hole: 6 crater
large: 5 conch
measuring device: 11 conchometer
money: 4 peag 5 cowry, peage, sewan, uhllo 6 cowrie, seawan, wampum
protected with: 8 loricate
ridge: 4 lira 5 varix 7 varices(pl.)

unexploded: dud

shellac: lac 4 whip 5 resin 6 defeat 7 trounce

shellacking: 6 defeat 7 beating 8 flogging, whipping

Shelley: 4 poet
alias: 5 Ariel
poem: 7 Adonais, Alastor 8 Queen Mab 10 Ozymandias, To a Skylark

shellfire: 6 strafe 7 barrage

shellfish: 5 nacre 6 limpet 7 mollusk 10 crustacean

shell out: pay 4 give 5 spend 8 disburse

shelter: cot, hut, lee 4 abri, barn, camp, cote, fold, gite(F.), herd, howf, port, roof, shed, skug, tent 5 benab, bield, boist, bower, cloak, cover, embay, haven, house, hovel, howff, hutch, shack 6 asylum, burrow, covert, defend, garage, hangar, harbor, hostel, refuge, sconce, sconce, screen, shield, trench 7 carport, cottage, defense, embosom, foxhole, harbour, hospice, imbosom, nacelle, pillbox, protect, retreat, trailer, umbrage 8 bescreen, ensconce, mantelet, quarters, security 9 coverture, harbinger, harborage, sanctuary 10 harbourage, protection

sheltered side: 7 leeward
on: 4 alee

shelve: tip 4 tilt 5 defer, ledge, shelf, table 6 mantel, retire 7 dismiss, project, put away 8 overhang, platform, postpone 10 pigeonhole

Shem: *father:* 4 Noah
son: Lud 4 Aram, Elam 6 Asshur

shenanigan: 5 prank, trick 7 evasion, foolery 8 goings-on, mischief, nonsense, trickery 12 clownishness

Sheol: 4 hell 5 grave, Hades 10 underworld

shepherd: 4 herd, lead, tend 5 drive, guard, guide, watch 6 attend, escort, feeder, gather, herder, leader, pastor, shadow 7 care for 8 guardian, minister
band of: 10 pastoureau
dog: 6 Collie 8 Cebalrai
god: Pan 5 Pales
pert. to: 8 pastoral
pipe: 4 reed 7 musette 11 flageolette
purse: 4 herb 9 blindweed
staff: 4 kent 5 crook

shepherdess: 7 bergere 9 Amarillis, Amaryllis

sherbet: ice 5 glace

sherd: See **shard**

Sheridan play: 6 Critic, Rivals

sheriff: 6 grieve 7 bailiff, marshal, officer
aides: 5 posse
deputy: 6 elisor 7 bailiff
jurisdiction: 9 bailiwick

Sherlock Holmes: *companion:* 6 Watson

creator: 5 Doyle

sherry: 4 wine 5 tokay 6 Solera 7 oloroso 11 amontillado

Shetland Island: *capital:* 7 Lerwick
inlet: voe
land: 4 odal, udal 6 udaler 7 udalman
measure: ure
musical instrument: gue
ounce: ure
tax: 4 scat

shibboleth: 4 test 6 phrase 8 password 9 criterion, watchword

shield: ecu(F.), rim 4 egis, hide, umbo 5 aegis, armor, avert, badge, board, cloak, cover, guard, pavis, shade, targe 6 blazon, brooch, canopy, defend, forbid, screen, target 7 buckler, clypeus, conceal, defense, lirelle, prevent, protect, rotella, shelter, testudo 8 conserve, rondache 9 protector, safeguard 10 escutcheon, protection
band across: 4 fess
boss: 4 umbo
Minerva's: 4 egis 5 aegis
part of: 4 boss, ente, orle, umbo 6 pointe 7 bordure, impresa
rim: 4 orle
small: ecu
strap: 6 enarme

shield-bearer: 8 escudero

shield-shaped: 7 peltate, scutate 9 clypeolar

shift: yaw 4 deal, eddy, fend, jibe, move, quit, ruse, stir, tour, turn, veer 5 avoid, dodge, evade, feint, hours, order, shunt, slide, spell 6 assign, bestir, change, device, divide, period 7 arrange, convert, dispose, evasion, replace, shuffle 8 artifice, clothing, exchange, mutation, transfer 9 apportion, expedient, vacillate 10 equivocate, subterfuge, transition, transplant 11 contrivance 12 redistribute 13 transposition

shifting: 8 ambulant, drifting, floating 9 deviation

shiftless: 4 lazy 8 feckless, indolent 10 thriftless 11 inefficient

shifty: 4 haft 6 fickle, tricky 7 cunning, devious, evasive, hangdog 8 sneaking 9 faithless, underhand 10 changeable

shikar: 4 hunt 5 sport 7 hunting

shikari, shikaree: 5 guide 6 hunter 9 sportsman

shill: 5 decoy 10 accomplice 11 confederate

shillelagh: 4 club 6 cudgel 7 sapling

shillibeer: 6 hearse 7 omnibus

shilling: bob

shilly-shally: 5 hedge, waver 6 dawdle, trifle 8 hesitate 9 fluctuate, vacillate

shim: hoe 5 image, level, wedge 6 streak, washer 7 glimpse, shingle

Shimeil's father: 4 Gera
Shimel's father: Ela
shimmer: 5 flash, light **7** glimmer, glisten
shimmy: 5 dance, shake **6** quiver **7** chemise, tremble, vibrate
shin: run **4** kick, walk **5** climb, ridge, shank, tibia **6** ascend
pert. to: **7** cnemial
shindig: 4 basli, fete **6** shiono **7** shebang
shindy: row **4** jump, lark, orgy, romp **5** brawl, dance, noise, party, revel, spree **6** fracas, frolic, rumpus, uproar **7** quarrel, wassail **8** carousal **9** commotion **11** disturbance, merrymaking
shine: ray, rub **4** beam, beek(Sc.), glow, star **5** black, blaze, blink, excel, glaik, gleam, glent, glint, gloss, gloze, light, prank, sheen **6** liking, polish **7** glimpse, glisten, glister, glitter, radiate, touch up **8** fondness, illumine **9** coruscate, irradiate
shiner: hat **4** chub **6** bruise **8** blackeye **9** bootblack
shingle: 4 sign, whip, wood **7** haircut **9** hair style, signboard
splitting tool: **6** prower
shingles: 4 zona **6** herpes **11** skin disease
shining: 4 glad, gold **5** aglow, glary, lucid, nitid, sleek **6** ardent, argent, bright, fulgid, glossy, lucent **7** beaming, eminent, fulgent, glowing, radiant **8** flashing, gleaming, gorgeous, luminous, lustrous, radiance, splendid **9** brilliant, effulgent, refulgent, sparkling, unclouded **10** glistening, glittering, remarkable **11** illustrious, irradiating, resplendent
shinplaster: 5 scrip
Shinto: *deity:* **8** Hachiman
gateway: **5** torii
temple: sha **5** Jinja **6** Jinsha **7** Yashiro
shiny: See **shining**
ship: 4 boat, pink, send **5** shift **7** hagboat **8** balinger
abandoned: **8** derelict
ancient: **5** knorr **7** galleon, trireme
Arabian: **6** boutre
arctic: **6** sealer
Argonaut's: **4** Argo
armored: **7** carrack, cruiser **9** destroyer, ironsides, submarine
ascent: **5** scend
attendant: **7** steward
auxiliary: **6** tender
beak: bow, ram **4** prow
beam: **7** carling, keelson
berth: **4** dock, slip
boarding device: **6** ladder **9** gangplank
boat: **4** dory, life **5** barge, dingy **6** dingey, dinghy, tender **7** pinnace
body: **4** hull
breadth of: **4** beam
brutally disciplined: **8** hell ship

burden: **5** cargo
cabin: **9** stateroom
canvas: **4** sail
capacity: **7** tonnage
capacity unit: ton
cargo: **7** gaiassa
cargo invoice: **8** manifest
carpenter: **5** Chips
channel: gat **5** canal **6** narrow, strait
clean: **6** careen
clock: nef
coast guard: **6** cutter
coastal: hoy **4** dhow, grab **6** droger, trader **7** drogher
codfishing: **6** banker **8** walloper
commercial: **6** trader
company of: **4** crew **5** fleet, hands **6** armada
compass housing: **8** binnacle
cook: **6** slushy
course: **7** sealane
crane: **5** davit
crew member: **4** hand, mate **5** bosun **6** purser, sailor
curved planking: sny
desert: **5** camel
deserter: rat
drain: **7** scupper
enemy watching: **7** vedette
employee: **5** oiler **6** purser, sailor **7** steward **8** deckhand, engineer, helmsman, steerman **9** navigator
fishing: **5** smack **6** hooker, lugger **7** trawler
flat-bottom: **4** keel **5** barge
fleet of: **6** armada
floor: **4** deck
fuel: **5** barge, oiler **6** coaler, tanker **7** collier
fur-hunting: **6** sealer
group: **4** navy **5** fleet **6** armada
hoist: **4** boom **5** crane, davit **7** capstan
jail: **4** brig
kitchen: **6** galley
lateral movement: **6** leeway
left side: **4** port
line: **7** marline, ratline
merchant: **6** argosy
middle: **9** amidships
mortgage: **8** bottomry
movement: **6** leeway
oar: **6** bireme, galley, sampan **7** pinnace, rowboat, trireme
officer: **4** mate **5** bosun **6** purser **7** steward **9** boatswain
part: bow **4** beam, brig, deck, helm, hold, hull, keel, mast, prow **5** bilge, stern, waist, wheel **6** bridge, galley, rudder, steven **7** lazaret, scupper **8** binnacle **9** lazarette, lazaretto, sternpost
partition: **7** bulwark **8** bulkhead
personnel: **4** crew **5** hands

pirate: **8** gallivat
planking: sny **6** strake
prison: **4** brig
privateer: **10** brigantine
prow: **5** prore
quarters: **6** fo'c'sle **8** steerage **10** forecastle
record: log
repair: **6** careen
repairing device: **7** drydock
rescue: ark
riglet side: **9** starboard
room: **4** brig **5** cabin, salon **6** galley **7** caboose **10** forecastle
rope: **4** line **6** hawser **7** halyard, lanyard, painter, ratline
sailing: **4** brig, buss, dhow, proa, yawl **5** ketch, sloop, smack, xebec **6** caique, chebec, hooker, lugger, mistic, saltie **7** caravel, galleon, Geordie, polacre **8** schooner
shovel: **5** skeet
side: **5** abeam
station: **5** berth
structure frame: **7** carcass
table frame: **6** fiddle
tender: **7** collier, pinnace
tiller: **4** helm
timber: rib **4** bitt, keel, mast, spar **5** stick **7** bollard
twin-hulled: **9** catamaran
unseaworthy: **4** hulk **5** wreck **8** ballahoo, ballahou, derelict
upward movement: **5** scend
Venetian: **9** frigatoon
voyage record: log
war (see also **warship**): sub **7** cruiser, flattop **8** corvette **9** destroyer, submarine **11** dreadnaught
wheel: **4** helm
windlass: **7** capstan
window: **4** port **8** porthole
wood for: **4** teak
worm: **5** borer **6** teredo
Ship of Fools author: 5 Brant **6** Porter
ship out: 6 enlist, export
shipment: 5 cargo **7** carload, freight **8** delivery
shipping center: 7 seaport
shipshape: 4 neat, taut, tidy, trim **7** orderly
shipwright: 6 fairer, plater, shorer, wayman **10** woodworker
shire: 5 derby, horse **6** county, region **8** district, province **11** subdivision
shirk: 4 duck, funk **5** avoid, dodge, evade, slack **6** desert **7** neglect **9** fainaigue **11** leave undone
shirker: 6 loafer, truant **7** slacker **8** embusque
shirr: 4 cook **6** gather **7** wrinkle
shirt: tee **4** jupe, polo, sark **5** dress, haire,

kamis, parka, sport **6** camisa, camise, cilice, parkee
button: **4** stud
hair: **6** cilice
shirtfront: 5 dicky **6** dickey
shirtwaist: 6 blouse **9** garibaldi
shiver: 4 grue **5** chill, quake, shake **6** dither, quiver, tremor, twitch **7** flicker, frisson, shatter, shudder, tremble, vibrate **8** fragment, splinter
fit: **4** ague **6** chills **10** goosebumps
shivoo: 7 banquet, shindig **9** gathering **13** entertainment
shoal: bar **4** bank, fish, mass, reef **5** barra, crowd, flock **6** school, throng **7** shallow **9** coral reef, multitude
shoat: hog, pig
shock: jar, lot **4** blow, bump, heap, jolt, pile, stun **5** appal, brunt, bunch, bushy, gliff, gloff, scare, shake **6** excite, fright, impact, offend, parcel, shaggy, stroke, trauma **7** astound, collect, disgust, horrify, startle, terrify **8** paralyze **9** agitation, collision **10** assemblage, concussion, head of hair
mental: **6** trauma
to reality: **5** sober
shock absorber: 6 spring **7** snubber
shocking: 5 awful, lurid **6** horrid, unholy **7** fearful, ghastly, hideous **8** dreadful, horrible **9** egregious, revolting **10** disgusting, outrageous
shod: 5 soled **6** booted **7** ensoled
shoddy: 4 bad **4** poor **5** cheap **6** shabby **8** inferior, slovenly
shoe (see also **overshoe**): **4** boot, clog, flat, pump **5** gilly, sabot, scuff **6** brogan, brogue, buskin, caliga, crakow, gaiter, galosh, gillie, loafer, oxford, patten, sandal **7** blucher, flattie, slipper, sneaker **8** colonial, Congress, mocassin, mocasin, solleret **9** brodequin, pampootee **10** clodhopper, veldschoen
aid: **4** horn
baby: **6** bootee
form: **4** last, tree
grip: **5** cleat
gym: **7** sneaker
house: **4** mule **7** slipper
mule's: **6** planch
part: box, cap, tip, toe, top **4** heel, lace, lift, pull, rand, vamp, welt **5** shank, strap **6** insole, tongue **7** counter, outsole **8** backstay, slipsole
paste: **7** clobber
piked: **6** cleats, crakow
repair: tap **5** retap **6** reheel, resole, stitch
rolling: **5** skate
rubber: **6** arctic, galosh **7** galoshe **8** overshoe
winged: **7** talaria
wooden: **5** sabot **6** patten

worker: **6** laster **7** cobbler
worn: **7** bauchle
shoebill: 5 stork
shoelace: tie **5** lacet **7** latchet
tip: **5** aglet **6** aiglet
shoemaker: 5 soler, sutor(L.) **7** cobbler,
crispin, farrier **10** cordonnier(F.)
apprentice: **4** snob
patron saint: **7** Crispin
tool: **4** butt **5** elsin **6** elshin
shoeshine: 9 bootblack
shofar, shophar: 4 horn
shog: jog **4** jerk, jolt, push, rock **5** shake **6**
jostle
shole: 5 plank, plate
shoneen: 4 snob **5** toady
shoo: 4 scat **10** do away with
in: **6** victor **9** sure thing **11** sure success
shooi: 4 bird, skua **6** jaeger
shook: See **shake**
shoot: bud, pot **4** bine, cast, chit, cion,
dart, emit, film, fire, grow, hunt, move,
plug, push, rush, twig **5** bough, chute,
drive, eject, plant, scion, snipe, spear,
spout, spray, sprig, spurt, throw, tuber,
utter, wound **6** branch, inject, propel,
sprout, stolon, strike, thrust, twinge **7**
burgeon, project **9** discharge **10** photograph **11** inject a drug, precipitate
objective: **6** target
shooting match: tir(F.) **5** skeet **6** affair
shooting star: 5 comet **6** meteor **8** fireball
shop: 5 store **6** market, office, prison,
tienda **7** bottega, factory **8** boutique,
emporium, workshop **9** workplace
coffee: **4** cafe **6** bistro **9** estaminet
dairy: **8** cremerie
kind: **6** smithy, stithy **7** mercery **8** saddlery, smithery **12** haberdashery
meat: **7** shamble **10** rotisserie **11** charcuterie
wine: **4** cafe **6** bistro
shopkeeper: cit **8** merchant, retailer **9**
tradesman **11** businessman, storekeeper
shoplift: cop **5** boost, pinch, steal, swipe **6**
rip off
shopper: 5 buyer **8** customer
shopworn: 5 trite **6** cliche **8** overused **9**
hackneyed
shore: 4 bank, edge, land, prop, side **5**
beach, brink, coast, drain, offer, scold,
sewer **6** border, rivage, strand **7** seaside,
support **8** buttress, threaten **9** foreshore
pert to: **8** littoral
poetic: **6** strand
recess: bay **4** cove **5** bayou, inlet
shore up: 4 prop **7** bolster, support **10**
strengthen
shorebird: ree **4** ruff **5** snipe **6** curlew,
plover **9** sandpiper

shorn: See **shear**
short: 4 curt, rude **5** bluff, brief, brusk,
crisp, harsh, scant, spare, terse **6**
abrupt, scanty, scarce **7** briefly,
brusque, concise, crisply, curtail, friable,
summary **8** abruptly, succinct, unawares **9** concisely, crumbling, deficient, shortstop **10** to the point **11**
compendious **12** insufficient
and stout: **5** bunty, dumpy **6** stocky,
stodgy, stubby **8** rolypoly, thickset
short-breathed: 5 pursy **6** winded **7** puffing
short-lived: 9 ephemeral, transient
short-spoken: 4 curt **5** gruff **7** laconic
shortage: 4 need **7** deficit, failure **10** deficiency **13** insufficiency
shortcoming: 4 flaw **5** fault **6** defect, foible **7** failure **9** weak point **10** deficiency, inadequacy **12** imperfection
shortcut: 5 alley, route **6** byroad **8** diagonal
shorten: bob, cut, lop **4** clip, furl, reef **5**
check **6** lessen, reduce **7** abridge, curtail, curtate, deprive **8** condense, contract, decrease, diminish **9** apocopate,
decurtate **10** abbreviate **11** encapsulate
short fuse: 11 quick temper
shorthand: 11 stenography **12** brachygraphy, speedwriting
system: **5** Gregg **6** Pitman
shortly (see also **short**): **4** soon **7** quickly
9 presently
shortness: 7 brevity
shortsighted: 4 dull **6** myopic, obtuse **11**
nearsighted **12** narrow-minded **13** opportunistic
Shoshone Indian: Ute **4** Hopi, Otoe,
Utah **5** Piute **6** Paiute **8** Comanche
shot (**see also shoot**): pop, try **4** dram **5**
blank, carom, drink, fling, guess, masse,
photo, range, reach, sally, tired, weary **6**
bullet, pellet, stroke **7** attempt, missile
8 marksman, snapshot **9** exhausted,
reckoning **10** conjecture, projectile **11**
intoxicated, opportunity
size: BBB **4** dust **8** air-rifle, buckshot
should: 4 want **5** ought
shoulder: 4 berm, edge, push **5** bough, elbow, raise **6** axilla, hustle, jostle **7** bulwark, support
angle: **6** epaule
belt: **4** sash **7** baldric
bone: **7** scapula **8** clavicle
muscle: **7** deltoid
ornament: tab **7** epaulet **9** epaulette
pain: **7** omalgia
pert to: **4** alar **7** humeral **8** scapular
protection for: **8** pauldron
to shoulder: **7** serried
shoulder blade: 7 scapula **8** acromion
shout: boo, cry, hoy, hue **4** bark, bawl, call,

crow, hoot, howl, roar, root, scry, yell, yelp **5** cheer, huzza, noise, whoop, yodel, yodle **6** clamor, halloo, hurrah, outcry, yammer **7** acclaim **10** vociferate **11** acclamation

hunting: **5** hallo, holla **6** yoicks **7** tallyho **9** view-haloo

shove: 4 cast, push **5** drive, eject, elbow, hunch, shunt **6** hustle, jostle, propel, thrust

shovel: dig **4** pale, peel **5** scoop, skeet, spade **7** shuffle **8** excavate

shoveler: 9 broadbill, river duck

shovelfish: 9 spadefish **10** paddlefish

shovelhead: 5 shark **7** catfish **8** flathead, sturgeon

show: 4 bosh, come, dash, fair, lead, look, mask, pomp **5** coach, farce, gloss, guide, movie, plead, prove, raree, revue, stage, teach, train **6** accuse, afford, allege, appear, assign, bestow, blazon, cinema, circus, confer, denote, detect, escort, evince, expose, flaunt, gaiety, gayety, inform, locate, parade, reveal, tinsel, turn up, unveil, veneer **7** bespeak, betoken, bravura, declare, display, divulge, exhibit, explain, perform, present, produce, trot out **8** ceremony, disclose, evidence, flourish, indicate, instruct, manifest **9** barnstorm, burlesque, designate, establish, rareeshow, represent, semblance **10** appearance, exhibition, exposition, expression **11** countenance, demonstrate, opportunity, performance **12** motion picture **13** demonstration

false: **9** tinsel

forth: **7** publish **8** manifest, proclaim **9** publicize

stylized: **4** mime **6** parade **7** pageant **9** cavalcade, pantomime

way: **5** guide, usher **6** direct, escort **7** conduct

show up: 5 strip **6** appear, arrive, expose **7** display

showcase: 7 vitrine, cabinet, exhibit

shower: wet **4** bath, rain, sump, wash **5** bathe, party, spray, water **6** bestow, deluge **7** barrage, drizzle, scatter **8** revealer, sprinkle **9** exhibitor

meteor: **6** Leonid

showery: wet **4** damp **5** moist **7** tearful

showing: 4 sign **6** aspect **7** account **10** apocalypse, appearance

first: **8** premiere

showy: gay **4** arty, loud **5** dashy, gaudy, grand **6** flashy, garish, ornate, swanky **7** dashing, gallant, pompous **8** gorgeous, splendid, striking **9** brilliant, flaunting, sumptuous **10** pretensive **11** pretentious **12** ostentatious **13** grandiloquent

shrapnel: 8 fragment **10** projectile

shred: bit, cut, hew, jag, rag **4** fell, jagg, snip, tear, twig, wisp **5** blype, grate, piece, prune, rip up, scrap, sever, shard, strip **6** divide, screed, sliver, tailor, tatter **7** fritter, parings, vestige **8** fragment, particle **9** pulverize, tear apart **12** make confetti

shrew: 5 curse, harpy, scold, vixen **6** mammal, tartar, virago **7** muskrat, villain **9** scoundrel, termagant, Xanthippe

long-tailed: **5** sorex

shrewd: bad, sly **4** cagy, cute, evil, foxy, hard, keen, sage, wily, wise **5** acute, canny, harsh, sharp, smart, stern **6** argute, artful, astute, biting, clever, crafty, subtle, wicked **7** abusive, cunning, gnostic, hurtful, knowing, parlous, politic, sapient **8** depraved, grievous, piercing, shrewish **9** gnostical, ingenious, injurious, sagacious **10** discerning, farsighted, hardheaded **11** distressing, intelligent, mischievous, penetrating, sharpwitted **13** perspicacious

shrewish: 7 nagging **8** vixenish **9** termagant **10** ill-humored **11** quarrelsome

shriek: cry, yip **4** yell **6** holler, outcry, scream, squeal **7** screech

shrift (see also **shrive**): **10** absolution, confession, disclosure **12** confessional **14** acknowledgment

shrill: 4 high, keen **5** acute, sharp **6** argute, biting, piping, shriek, squeak **7** screech **8** piercing, poignant, strident **9** dissonant **11** highpitched, penetrating

shrimp: kid **5** dwarf **6** shaver **7** seafood **9** stripling **10** crustacean

large: **5** prawn

shrine: box **4** case, naos, tomb **5** altar, caaba, chest, kaaba, huaca **6** abaton, adytum, chapel, chasse, dagaba(Ind.), dagoba(Ind.), entomb, hallow, temple **7** chaitya, enclose, memoria **8** canonize, enshrine, memorial **9** container, holy place, reliquary, sanctuary **10** receptacle

goddesses: **9** anaktoran

visitor: **7** pilgrim

shrink: shy **4** fawn, funk, shun, wane **5** cling, cower, quail, rivel, shrug, wizen **6** blench, boggle, cotter, cringe, flinch, gizzen, huddle, humble, lessen, recoil, retire, wither **7** atrophy, dwindle, retract, shrivel **8** condense, contract, decrease, pull back, withdraw **9** constrict **10** depreciate **15** psychotherapist

shrinking: shy **5** timid **6** afraid, modest **8** reticent **9** diffident

shrive: rob **4** free **5** purge **6** acquit, pardon **7** absolve, confess **8** disclose **9** reconcile

shrivel: age **5** blast, crine, parch, rivel, wizen **6** cotter, scrump, shrink, weazen, wither **9** deteriorate

shroff: 6 banker, expert **7** changer, inspect **8** separate **12** moneychanger

shroud: lop **4** hide, trim, veil, wrap **5** array, cloak, cover, crypt, dress, shade, sheet, vault **6** branch, clothe, enfold, screen, shadow **7** conceal, curtain, envelop, foliage, garment, plumage, protect, shelter **8** cerement, clothing, covering, envelope **9** cerecloth **10** protection

shrub: lop, tea, tod **4** bago, bush, cade, coca, gumi, majo, nabo, olea, sida, sola **5** elder, lilac, prune, punch, salal **6** cudgel, frutex **7** arboret, buckeye, chamise, chamiso, heather, scratch, tarbush **8** abelmosk, barberry, beverage, huisache, **9** chaparral, manzanita

aromatic: tea **4** mint, sage **5** batis, thyme **8** rosemary

bean family: **4** ulex

collection: **10** fruticetum

desert: **5** retem **6** alhagi, raetam

evergreen: box **4** ilex, moss, titi **5** furze, heath, salal, savin **6** laurel, myrtle **7** jasmine, juniper **8** oleander **9** mistletoe

fence: box **5** hedge

flowering: **5** lilac, tiara, wahoo **6** azalea, laurel, myrtle, spirea **7** lantana, rhodora, spiraea, syringa **8** japonica, oleander, oleaster **9** mistletoe **10** mignonette

fruit: **5** salal

genus of: **4** inga **5** erica, ledum **6** aralia

hardy: **7** althaea, heather

indigo: **4** anil

Mexican: **8** bluebush

myrtle-like: **7** cajeput, cajuput

ornamental: **6** privet

parasitic: **9** mistletoe

pert. to: **9** fruticose, fruticous

poisonous: **5** sumac **6** sumach

prickly: **4** whin **5** briar, brier, caper, gorse **7** bramble **8** allthorn, hawthorn

rubber: **7** guayule

stunted: **5** scrag, scrub

tea-like: kat **4** coca

tropical: **5** henna **6** olacad **7** lantana **10** frangipani

shruff: 5 dross **7** rubbish

shrug: don, tug **5** hitch **6** fidget, shiver, shrink **7** gesture, shudder **8** contract, hitching **9** handshake **10** convulsion

off: **7** dismiss, not care **13** underestimate

shrunken (see also **shrink**)**: 4** lank **9** atrophied, shriveled

Shu: *parent:* Ra **6** Hathor

sister: **6** Tefnut

wife: **6** Tefnut

shuck: pod **4** husk, sham **5** fraud, shell, strip **6** recoil, remove **7** discard, mislead, swindle

shudder: 4 grue **5** quake, shake **6** quiver,

shiver **7** frisson, tremble

shuffle: mix **4** gait, plod, walk **5** dance, scuff **6** huddle, juggle, jumble, mingle, remove, sclaff **7** evasion, quibble, scuffle, shamble **8** artifice **9** confusion **10** equivocate **11** prevaricate **12** equivocation

shuffling: 6 shifty **7** evasive **9** deceitful **13** opportunistic

shun: 4 balk, flee, hide, snub **5** avert, avoid, evade, evite **6** eschew **7** abstain, forbear, forsake, refrain **8** forebear

shunt: 4 push **5** shift, shove **6** divert, remove, switch **9** conductor, rechannel, sidetrack, turn aside

shut: bar, rid **4** free **5** close **6** climax, fasten, forbid **7** confine, exclude, turn off **8** prohibit **10** portcullis

in: hem, pen **4** cage, pent, wall **5** embar, embay, fence **6** bottle, hemmed **7** bottled, confine, enclose, impound **8** imprison **10** quarantine, surrounded

shut-in: 7 invalid, recluse **12** convalescent

shut out: bar **6** screen **7** exclude **8** preclude

shut up: end, gag **7** seclude **8** be silent, conclude **9** terminate

shutter: 5 blind, cover **6** screen **7** buckler **8** jalousie

shuttle: 4 loom **5** shunt, train **6** looper **9** air travel

shuttlecock: 4 bird **6** birdie

shy: coy, mim **4** balk, jump, shun, wary **5** aloof, avoid, chary, dodge, scant, start, throw, timid **6** boggle, demure, escape, modest, recoil, shrink **7** bashful, lacking, potshot **8** farouche, hesitant, reserved, retiring, secluded, sheepish, skittish **9** diffident, reluctant, shrinking **10** incomplete, shamefaced, suspicious, unassuming **11** distrustful, unobtrusive **13** self-conscious **14** unostentatious

Shylock: 6 usurer **9** loan shark **11** money lender

coin: **5** ducat

daughter: **7** Jessica

friend: **5** Tubal

shyster: 11 pettifogger

si: yes

Siam: See **Thailand**

Siamese twin: Eng **5** Chang

sib: kin **4** akin **5** ayllu **6** allied, sister **7** brother, kindred, kinship, kinsman, related **8** friendly, relation, relative **9** congenial, kinswoman **12** well-disposed

Siberia: *antelope:* **5** saiga

carnivore: **5** sable

city: **4** Enna, Omsk **5** Chita, Tomsk **7** Barnaul, Irkutsk

dog: **7** Samoyed **8** Samoyede

Eskimo: **4** Yuit

fish: **5** nelma

forest: 5 Urman
fur: 7 calabar
hunters and fishers: 6 Giliak, Gilyak 7 Samoyed 8 Samoyede
hut: 8 barabara, barabora
leopard: 5 ounce
mountains: 4 Ural 5 Altai
peninsula: 6 Taimir 9 Kamchatka
people: 5 Sagai, Tatar, Yakut 6 Kirgiz, Tartar 7 Kirghis, Kirghiz, Yukagir 8 Yukaghir 9 Mongolian
plain: 6 steppe, tundra
region: 5 taiga
river: Ili, Tom 4 Amur, Lena, Maya, Onon, Yana 5 Sobol, Tobol 6 Anadyr, Olenek 7 Yenisei
squirrel: 7 miniver
squirrel-skin: 7 calabar
storm: 5 buran
tanning plant: 5 badan
tent: 4 yurt 5 yurta
wild cat: 5 manul
wild sheep: 6 argali
sibilant: ess 7 hissing
sibling (see also **sib**): 6 sister 7 brother
sibyl: 4 seer 5 witch 6 Libyan, Samian, Trojan 7 Cumaean, prophet, seeress 8 Delphian, Phrygian 9 Cimmerian, Erythrean, sorceress, Tiburtine 10 prophetess 13 fortuneteller, Hellespontine
sibylline: 6 occult 7 cryptic, obscure 8 oracular 9 ambiguous, equivocal, prophetic 10 exorbitant, mysterious 11 prophetical
sic: set 4 seek, thus, urge 5 chase, egg on 6 attack, incite
Sicilian: 10 Trinacrian
Sicily: *cape:* 4 Boeo, Faro 7 Passaro
capital: 7 Palermo
city: 4 Gela 5 Aetna, Bidis, Nakos 6 Alcamo, Modica, Ragusa 7 Catania, Marsala, Messina, Trapani 8 Girgenti, Monreale, Taormina 9 Agrigento 13 Caltanissetta
composer: 7 Bellini
crime society: 5 Mafia
god: 7 Adranus
harbor: 7 Palermo
island: 11 Pantelleria
king: 4 Eryx
measure: 5 salma 7 caffiso
mountain: 4 Etna
people: 5 Elymi, Sicel
river: 5 Salso 6 Belice, Simeto 7 Platani
seaport: Aci 7 Messina
secret society: 5 Mafia
volcano: 4 Etna
whirlpool: 9 Charybdis
youth: 4 Acis
sick: bad, ill, set, wan 4 abed, pale, seek, urge, weak 5 badly, chase, crank, cronk,

fed-up, unfit, weary 6 ailing, attack, incite, insane, unwell 7 unsound 8 impaired 9 corrupted, crapulous, depressed, disgusted, instigate, nauseated, surfeited, unhealthy 10 indisposed 11 exasperated 12 disconsolate
deathly: 5 amort 7 alamort
person: 7 invalid, patient
sickbay: 6 clinic 8 hospital 9 infirmary 10 dispensary
sicken: 5 upset 6 affect 8 get worse, languish
sickening: 7 fulsome 9 offensive, revolting 10 disgusting, nauseating
sickle: 6 scythe
sickly: ill, wan 4 fue, pale, puny, weak cothy, faint, frail 6 ailing, cranky, feeble, infirm, morbid, weakiy 7 cothish, insipid, invalid, languid, mawkish, queechy 8 diseased 9 colorless, sickening, unhealthy 10 unwholesome
sickness: 6 malady, nausea 7 ailment, disease, disgust, illness, insanity 9 distemper, infirmity, weariness 12 qualmishness 13 indisposition
feign: 8 malinger
mental: See **mental disorder**
side: far 4 edge, face, line, part, team, wall, wide 5 agree, ample, costa, facet, flank, latus, party, phase, place, proud, shore, slope, space, width 6 aspect, behalf, border, margin, region, severe 7 conceit, distant, faction, lateral, sheathe, support, surface 8 district, position, spacious 9 declivity, direction, outskirts, viewpoint 10 collateral, occasional 15 pretentiousness
on the: 5 apart
pain in: 6 stitch
pert. to: 7 lateral
piece: rib 5 stave
sheltered: lee
side arm: 5 sword 6 pistol, weapon 7 bayonet 8 revolver
side by side: 8 parallel, together 12 cheek to cheek
side view: 7 profile
sideboard: 6 buffet 8 credence, credenza, cupboard
sidekick: pal 4 chum 6 friend 7 partner 8 follower 9 assistant, companion, satellite 11 confederate
sideline: 5 bench 7 put away 9 avocation
sidepiece: rib 6 border
sidereal: 6 astral, starry 7 stellar 8 starlike
siderite: ore
sideroad: 5 byway 10 digression
siderolite: 9 meteorite
sideshow: 10 attraction
attraction: 5 freak
sideslip: 4 skid 5 slide 10 digression

sidestep: 4 duck 5 avoid, dodge, evade

sidetrack: 4 spur 5 shunt 6 divert, switch

sidewalk: 6 causey 9 banquette, board-walk

part: 4 curb, kerb 5 crack 6 paving

sideways: 5 aside 6 askant 7 askance, athwart, lateral 8 indirect 9 laterally, obliquely

Sidi's wife: 5 Amine

sidle: 4 edge 6 loiter 7 saunter

Sidon's modern name: 5 Saida

siege: see 4 bout, rank 5 bench, beset, flock, place, privy 6 attack 7 sitting 8 blockade 9 onslaught 13 beleaguerment

Siegfried: *mother:* 9 Sieglinde

slayer: 5 Hagen

sword: 7 Balmung

vulnerable spot: 4 back 8 shoulder

wife: 9 Kriemhild

sierra: 4 fish 5 range, ridge

Sierra Leone: *capital:* 8 Freetown

coin: 5 leone

language: 5 Mende, Temne 6 Creole

Sierra Nevada: *fog:* 7 pogonip

peak: 4 Dana 7 Whitney

siesta: nap 4 lull, rest 5 sleep

sieve: 4 lawn, sift 5 tamis, temse 6 basket, bolter, filter, gossip, ranger, riddle, screen, sifter, strain 7 chaffer, cribble, measure 8 colander, separate, strainer

for clay: 4 laun

sift: 4 bolt, cull, scry, sort 5 sieve, temse 6 dredge, filter, refine, riddle, screen, strain, winnow 7 analyze, canvass, examine, inspect, scatter 8 look into, separate 10 scrutinize

sifter: 5 sieve 6 bolter 8 strainer

sigh: sob 4 moan, wail 5 mourn, sough, yearn 6 bemoan, grieve, lament 7 deplore 11 respiration

sight: aim, ken, see 4 espy, gaze, look, mess, show, vane, view 5 scene 6 behold, descry, glance, vision 7 discern, display, eyesore, glimpse 9 spectacle 10 exhibition, inspection, perception 11 examination, observation

defect: 7 anopsia

gun: 4 bead

loss: 9 amaurosis

obscurity: 6 caligo

offending: 7 eyesore

out of: 11 disappeared

pert. to: 6 ocular, visual

second: ESP, fey 7 psychic

sightless: 5 blind 6 unseen 9 invisible

sightseer: 7 tourist 10 rubberneck

sigil: 4 seal, sign, word 6 device, signet 9 signature

sigmoid: ess

Sigmund: *father:* 7 Volsung

son: 6 Sigurd

sword: 4 Gram

wife: 7 Hiordis

sign (see also **signal**): cue, nod 4 hint, hire, mark, note, omen 5 badge, image, segno(It.), sigil, spoor, token, trace 6 banner, beacon, beckon, effigy, emblem, engage, ensign, figure, motion, notice, poster, signet, symbol, wigwag 7 auspice, endorse, gesture, initial, message, picture, portent, prodigy, vestige, warning 8 evidence, password, pretense, standard 9 autograph, character, semaphore, semblance, subscribe, watchword 10 denotation, expression, forerunner, indication, prognostic, suggestion, underwrite 11 countersign 13 advertisement, constellation, demonstration, foreshadowing

diacritical: 5 hamza, tilde 6 hamzah, tittle, umlaut 7 cedilla

direction: 5 arrow

illuminated: 4 neon 6 lights

liturgical: 5 selah 6 shelah

magic: 5 sigil

music: 5 presa, segno

pert. to: 5 semic 8 semantic

Zodiac: See **zodiac sign**

sign language: 11 dactylology

sign off: end, out 6 thirty 8 withdraw

sign on: 4 hire, ship 6 engage, enlist, enroll 8 register

signal (see also **sign**): 4 flag 5 alarm, siren 6 buzzer, ensign, notify, sennet, tocsin 7 betoken, eminent, lantern, notable, presage, signify 9 memorable, prominent, semaphore, symbolize 10 noticeable, remarkable 11 communicate, conspicuous 13 extraordinary

distress: SOS 6 mayday

electric: 8 teleseme

system: 4 code

warning: 5 alarm, alert, flare, siren 6 alarum, beacon, tocsin 7 blinker

signature: ink 4 hand, mark, name, sign, visa, vise 5 sigil, stamp 9 allograph, autograph 10 directions, impression 11 bookbinding, countersign

signet: 4 mark, seal, sign 5 sigil, stamp 10 impression 12 authenticate

significance: 6 repute 7 bearing, meaning, purport 13 signification

significant: 4 sign 5 grave, token 6 symbol 7 ominous, weighty 8 eloquent, sinister 9 important, momentous, prominent 10 expressive, indicative, meaningful, portentous, suggestive 13 consequential

signify: nod 4 mean, show, sign 5 augur, imply, spell, utter 6 amount, denote, import, inform, matter, signal 7 add up to, betoken, compare, declare 8 announce, foreshow, indicate, intimate, manifest 11 communicate

signor: man 4 lord 5 title 9 gentleman
signpost: 5 guide 6 beacon 7 pointer 9 guidepost
signum: 4 bell, mark, sign 9 signature
Sigurd: *father:* 7 Sigmund
foster father: 5 Regin 6 Reginn
horse: 5 Grani
slayer: 5 Hogni
victim: 6 Fafnir
wife: 6 Gudrun
Sigyn's husband: 4 Loki
Sikkim (see also **India**): *capital:* 7 Gangtok
people: 4 Rong 6 Bhotia, Lepcha
silage: 4 feed, fodder
Silas Marner author: 5 Eliot
silence: gag 4 hush, mute, rest, stun 5 choke, death, floor, quiet, still, tacet 6 muffle, refute 7 confute, destroy, repress, secrecy 8 muteness, suppress 9 obscurity, reticence, stillness 10 silentness
goddess: 8 Angerona
music: 5 tacet
silencer: 4 mute 5 gavel 7 muffler 8 sourdine
silene: 7 campion 8 catchfly
silent: mum 4 dumb, flat, mute 5 quiet, still, tacit 8 inactive, overcome, reserved, reticent, taciturn, unspoken 9 noiseless, secretive, unuttered 10 flavorless, speechless, unrecorded 11 unexpressed, unmentioned 15 uncommunicative
silex: 5 flint 6 quartz, silica 7 mineral
silhouette: 6 shadow 7 outline 9 lineation 10 figuration
silicate: 4 mica 6 cerite, iolite 7 epidote 8 calamine, severite, wellsite
silk: 5 pekin, surah, tulle 6 fabric 7 foulard 8 florence, sarcenet, sarsenet
corded: 6 faille
embroidery thread: 5 floss 8 arrasene
fabric: 4 gros 5 caffa, China, crepe, moire, ninon, pekin, satin, surah, tabby, tulle 6 cendal, faille, mantua, pongee, samite, sendal, tussah, tusser, tussur 7 alamode, marabou, sarsnet, taffeta, tsatlee, tussore 8 sarcenet, sarsenet
fishline: 4 gimp
hank: 4 hasp
hat: 6 topper
Indian moth: 4 muga
raw: 5 grege 8 marabout
refuse: 6 strass
source: 6 cocoon
thread: 4 filo
unspun: 6 sleave
waste: 4 noil 5 floss 6 frison
watered: 5 moire
wild: 6 tussah 7 tussore
worker: 7 thrower 9 throwster
yarn: 4 tram 7 schappe

yarn size: 6 denier
silk-stocking: 5 elite 7 elegant, wealthy 9 exclusive, luxurious 10 Federalist 12 aristocratic
silken: 4 fine, soft 5 quiet, silky, sleek, suave, sweet 6 gentle, glossy, smooth, tender 7 elegant 8 delicate, lustrous, silklike 9 luxurious, sericeous 10 effeminate 12 ingratiating
silkworm: eri 4 eria 6 bombyx, tussah 8 bombycid
silkworm rot: 7 calcino
sill: 4 beam, seat, sile 5 bench, frame, ledge, shelf, stone 6 timber 9 threshold 10 foundation
silliness: 5 folly 6 betise(F.) 11 foolishness
silly: mad 4 bete, daft, fond, fool, idle, simp, weak 5 anile, apish, barmy, dazed, dense, frail, giddy, goofy, goose, inane, plain 6 absurd, cranky, cuckoo, dotard, dottle(Sc.), feeble, footle, humble, infirm, paltry, rustic, sickly, simple, stupid, unwise 7 asinine, fatuous, foolish, foppish, shallow, trivial, witless 8 childish, fopperly, ignorant, imbecile, innocent 9 brainless, childlike, ludicrous, pointless, senseless, simpleton 10 half-witted, indiscreet 12 simpleminded 15 unsophisticated
silt: 4 scum 5 dregs 7 deposit, moraine, residue 8 sediment 9 percolate
silver: 4 coin, pale 5 money, plate, sweet 6 argent, gentle 7 bullion 8 argentum, eloquent, lustrous, peaceful, precious, sterling 9 tableware 11 resplendent 13 argentiferous
containing: 5 lunar
lace: 8 filigree
pert. to: 9 argentine, argentous
reducing kettle: 4 cazo(Sp.)
silver thaw: 10 glitter ice
silver thistle: 8 acanthus
silver-tongued: 4 glib 8 eloquent 10 persuasive
silverfish: 6 insect, tarpon
silversmith: 5 sonar 9 artificer
silverware: 5 vases 6 dishes 8 platters 9 ornaments, tableware
ornament: 7 gadroon
silverweed: rue 5 tansy 9 jewelweed 10 cinquefoil
silvery: 7 frosted 9 artentine 10 argenteous, shimmering
silviculture: 8 forestry
s'il vous plait: 6 please
simar: 4 robe 6 jacket 7 garment 12 undergarment
Simeon: *father:* 5 Jacob
mother: 4 Leah
son: 4 Ohad 6 Nemuel
simian: ape 6 monkey 7 apelike 10 anthropoid

similar: sib **4** akin, like, such **5** alike **6** evenly **7** uniform **8** analogic, parallel **9** semblance **9** analogous, resembling **11** approximate, counterpart, homogeneous, resemblance **13** correspondent

simile: **10** comparison **14** figure of speech

similitude: **4** form **5** image **6** simile, symbol **7** analogy, parable, replica **8** allegory, likeness **9** facsimile, semblance **10** similarity **11** counterpart, resemblance **14** representation

similize: **5** liken **7** compare

simmer: **4** boil, stew **6** braise

simmon: **9** persimmon

simnel: **5** bread **7** biscuit **8** cracknel **9** fruitcake

Simon: **5** Peter **7** apostle

Simon Legree: **10** taskmaster **11** slave driver

simon-pure: **4** real, true **6** simple **7** genuine **9** authentic **11** unqualified

simony: **8** barratry

simoom, simoon: **4** wind **5** storm **6** tebbad **9** dust storm

simper: **5** mince, smile, smirk **7** whimper

simple: **4** bald, bare, dull, easy, fond, mere, poor, pure, real, true, weak **5** folly, lowly, naive, naked, plain, Roman, silly **6** common, Dorian, homely, humble, oafish, rustic, severe, single, stupid **7** artless, austere, babyish, foolish, genuine, idyllic, natural, onefold, sincere, Spartan, unmixed **8** absolute, arcadian, childish, complete, gullible, homemade, ignorant, innocent, modestly, ordinary, retarded, tailored, trifling **9** childlike, elemental, ingenuous, primitive, unadorned **10** elementary, unaffected, uninvolved **11** homogeneous, undesigning, unimportant **12** inartificial, uncompounded, unpretending **13** insignificant, plain speaking, uncomplicated, unconstrained, unembellished **15** straightforward, undistinguished, unsophisticated

simple-minded: **6** simple, stupid **7** artless **12** feeble-minded, moronic, unsuspecting **13** simple-hearted **15** unsophisticated

simpleton: ass, daw **4** boob, dolt, fool, gaby, gawk, gawp, gowk, lout, simp, tony, zany **5** dunce, goose, idiot, ninny, noddy, sammy **6** dawkin, gander, gawney, gulpin, nincom, nincum, nitwit, noodle **7** gomeral, gomerel, gomeril, muggins, widgeon **8** Abderite, fondling, numskull, omadhaun **10** changeling, nincompoop **11** ninnyhammer

simplify: **6** clean up, cut down **7** clarify, expound **9** elucidate, interpret

simulacrum: **4** copy, fake, sham **5** image **6** aspect **7** phantom **8** likeness, pretense, travesty **9** imposture, semblance **11** assemblance, counterfeit

simulate: act, ape **4** fake, mock, sham **5** feign, feiut **6** affect, assume **7** feigned, imitate, pretend **8** make like, resemble **9** dissemble, personate, pretended **10** fictitious **11** counterfeit

simulation: **9** hypocrisy **10** sanctimony

simurg, simurgh: roc

sin: err **4** debt, envy, evil, lust, vice **5** anger, blame, crime, error, fault, folly, guilt, pride, sloth, wrong **6** acedia, felony **7** do wrong, offense, violate **8** gluttony, iniquity, peccancy **9** deviation **10** immorality, peccadillo, transgress, wickedness, wrongdoing **11** misdemeanor, ungodliness, viciousness **12** covetousness **13** transgression

canonical: **6** heresy, murder **8** adultery, idolatry

deadly: **4** envy, lust **5** anger, pride, sloth **8** gulttony **12** covetousness

Sinai mountain: **5** Horeb

sinapis: **4** herb **7** mustard

Sinbad's bird: roc

since: ago, for, fro, now **4** ergo, gone, past, sith, syne(Sc.) **5** after, hence, later **7** already, because, whereas **8** inasmuch, until now **9** afterward, therefore, thereupon **11** considering **12** continuously, subsequently

sincere: **4** open, pure, real, true **5** frank, whole **6** candid, devout, hearty, honest **7** artless, cordial, correct, earnest, genuine, unmixed, upright **8** faithful, truthful, virtuous **9** authentic, blameless, heartfelt, unfeigned, veracious **10** unaffected **11** unvarnished **12** wholehearted **13** unadulterated **15** straightforward

sinciput: **8** forehead

sind: **5** rinse **6** drench, quench

sine qua non: **13** indispensable

sinecure: **4** pipe, snap **5** cinch, gravy

sinew: **5** power, snare **6** tendon **8** potency

sinewy: **4** firm, wiry **5** thewy, tough **6** brawny, robust, strong **7** fibrose, nervous stringy **8** foreceful, muscular, powerful, vigorous **9** tendinous

sinful (see also **sin**): bad **4** evil **5** wrong **6** wicked **7** immoral, ungodly, vicious **10** iniquitous **11** blameworthy, unrighteous

sing: hum **4** cant, lilt, pipe, ring, talk **5** carol, chant, chirl, croon, ditty, yodel, yodle **6** betray, inform, intone, warble **7** chortle, confess, descant, divulge, rejoice, roulade, tweedle

as a round: **5** troll

softly: hum **5** croon

with trills: **6** warble **7** roulade

singable: **7** lyrical, melodic, tuneful **9** cantabile

singe: 4 burn, char, sear 6 scorch 7 blemish
fiber: 6 genapp
singer: 4 alto, bard, bass, diva 5 basso,
buffa, buffo, tenor 6 artist, cantor 7 artiste, chanter, crooner, soloist, songman, soprano 8 baritone, minstrel, vocalist 9 chanteuse, chorister, contralto,
descanter 10 cantatrice 11 entertainer
12 mezzo-soprano
comic opera: 5 buffa
female: 9 chanteuse 10 cantatrice
opera: 4 diva
singerie: 6 design 7 picture 10 decoration 11 monkeyshine
singing: 4 cant 5 charm 9 cantation
group: 4 duet, trio 5 choir, octet 6 chorus,
sextet 7 octette, quartet 8 chanters,
sextette 9 quartette
pert. to: 6 choral 9 cantative
trio: 9 tricinium
voice: 4 alto, bass 5 tenor 7 soprano 8
baritone 9 contralto 12 mezzo-soprano
single: one 4 lone, only, part, sole, unit 5
alone, unwed 6 unique 7 base hit, onefold, unusual 8 celibate, separate, singular, solitary, withdraw 9 sequester, unmarried 10 individual, particular 11
unsupported
single out: 6 choose
singlet: 5 shirt 6 jersey 9 waistcoat 10
undershirt
singly: 4 once 5 alone, apart 6 merely,
solely 7 unaided 8 honestly 9 severally,
sincerely 12 individually, particularly,
single-handed
singsong: 5 chime 7 tedious 11 repeti-
tious
singular: odd, one 4 each, rare, sole 5
queer 6 single, unique 7 eminent, private, several, unusual 8 isolated, peculiar, separate, superior, uncommon 9
eccentric, fantastic, whimsical 10 individual, one and only, remarkable, unexampled 11 exceptional 12 unparalleled
13 extraordinary, unprecedented
singultus: 7 hiccups
sinister: car(Sc.) 4 dark, dire, evil, grim,
left 7 adverse, baleful, corrupt, ominous
9 dishonest, injurious, malicious, underhand 10 disastrous, portentous 11
apocalyptic, prejudicial, unfortunate 12
inauspicious
sink: bog, dip, ebb, sag, pet 4 cave, drop,
fail, fall, ruin, wane 5 avale, drain,
droop, embog, heald, hield, lower,
plump, sewer, slope, stoop 6 debase, do-
lina, doline, drench, extend, gutter,
humble, plunge, settle, thrust 7 decline,
degrade, depress, descend, destroy, immerse, relapse, subside 8 decrease, diminish, submerge, suppress 9 penetrate
11 come to grief

below horizon: set
ship: 7 scuttle
sinker: 5 pitch 6 weight 8 doughnut
Sinkiang: *capital:* 7 Urumchi
river: 5 Tarim
sinking: 7 descent 10 depression
sinless: 4 pure 7 perfect 8 innocent 9
righteous
sinner: 5 scamp 8 evildoer, offender, penitent 9 bad person, reprobate, wrongdoer 10 backslider, trespasser 12 transgressor
sinning: 7 peccant
sinuous: 4 wavy 5 snaky 7 bending,
crooked, curving, devious, winding 9
deviating, intricate 10 circuitous, serpentine 11 anfractuous
sinus: bay 4 bend, fold 5 bosom, curve 6
cavity, hollow, recess 7 channel, opening 10 depression
pert. to: 5 sinal 7 sinusal
Sioux: Kaw, Oto 4 Crow, Iowa, Otoe 5
Brule, Omaha, Osage, Sioux 6 Dakota,
Santee, Tutelo 8 Catawba 9 Winnebago
division: 5 Teton
sip: bib, lap, sup 5 draft, drink, quaff, taste
6 tipple 8 toothful 11 small amount
sipper: 4 tube 5 straw
sir: 4 lord 5 title 6 knight, master 9 gentleman
sirdar: 5 chief, noble 6 bearer 7 officer,
servant
sire: 4 lord 5 title 6 father, master, parent
8 ancestor, begetter, generate 10 forefather, procreator, progenitor
siren: 5 alarm, lurer 7 charmer, foghorn,
Lorelei, mermaid 8 water god 9 Cleopatra 10 attractive, bewitching 11 fascinating, femme fatale
Siren: 5 Ligea 8 Leucosia 10 Parthenope
siriasis: 9 sunstroke
Sirius' master: 5 Orion
sirocco: 4 wind
sisal: 4 hemp 5 fiber
Sisera: *enemy:* 5 Barak
murderer: 4 Jael
siskin: 5 finch, tarin 9 small bird
sissy: 6 coward 7 girlish 8 weakling 10
effeminate 11 mollycoddle
sister: nun, sis 4 girl 5 soror(L.) 7 sibling
murder: 10 sororicide
pert. to: 5 soral 8 sororate, sororial
younger: 7 cadette(F.)
Sister Superior: 6 abbess
sisterhood: 8 sorority
sistrum: 6 rattle 10 noisemaker
sit: lie, set 4 meet, pose, rest, seat 5 brood,
dwell, model, perch, press, roost, squat
6 occupy, remain, repose 7 convene 8
incubate
carelessly: 4 loll 6 sprawl

sit in: 6 attend, object **7** protest **11** participate

sit on: 6 confer, hush up, rebuke **7** repress, squelch **8** suppress **9** reprimand **11** appropriate, investigate

site: 4 ruin, seat, spot **5** arena, locus(L.), place, scene, venue **6** locale, locate **8** location, position **9** situation

sitfast: 5 fixed, stone **8** crowfoot **9** immovable **10** stationary

sithe: lot **6** chance, mishap

Sitsang: 5 Tibet

sitting: 4 seat **5** abode, place **6** clutch, posing, seance, sedent, sejaul **7** meeting, sejeant, session **8** sederunt
court: **6** assize **7** session

Sitting Bull: *enemy:* **6** Custer
tribe: **5** Sioux

sitting duck: 4 dupe **5** decoy **6** target

situated: 4 seat **5** basal **6** nether, placed, plight **7** located, station **8** marginal **13** circumstanced
between folds: **11** interplical
in the middle: **6** medial, median
on membrane enveloping the brain: **8** epidural
on right: **6** dexter
toward rear: **6** astern **7** postern **9** posterior

situation: job **4** case, need, post, seat, site **5** berth, place, siege, situs(L.), state **6** estate, locale, morass, plight, scrape, strait **7** bargain, dilemma, station, vantage **8** locality, location, position, quandary **9** condition, emergency, imbroglio, pregnancy **11** predicament, whereabouts **12** circumstance

situla: 4 pail, vase **6** bucket **10** receptacle

situs: 5 place **8** location, position **9** situation

Siva: 8 Hindu god
consort: Uma **4** Devi
son: **6** Skanda
trident: **6** trisul **7** trisula
wife: **4** Sati

six: 6 senary, sestet **7** digamma, sestole **8** senarius
group: **5** hexad **6** hexade, senary, sextet **8** sextette
pert. to: **6** senary
series of: **5** hexad **6** hexade

six on dice: 4 sice

six sheets: 7 sextern

six-eyed: 9 senocular

sixfold: 8 sextuple

six-footed: 7 hexaped **9** hexapodal, hexapodan

six-line stanza: 6 sestet

six-shooter: gun **6** weapon **8** revolver

size: 4 area, bore, bulk, mass **5** cover, glaze, grade **6** adjust, amount, candle, extent, format, volume **7** arrange, examine, measure, stiffen **8** classify, standard **9** dimension, magnitude **11** measurement
book page: **9** duodecimo
indefinite: nth
paper: cap **4** copy, demi, demy, pott **5** atlas, crown, felic, folio, legal **6** bagcap **7** bastard, emperor **8** foolscap, imperial **9** colombier
separation device: **6** grader
type: **4** pica, ruby **5** agate, canon, elite, pearl **6** minion, primer **7** brevier, diamond, English, paragon **9** bourgeois, columbian, nonpareil
yarn: lea **5** forty **6** denier

sizing: 4 glue **6** starch **9** allotment

sizy: 7 viscous **9** glutinous

sizz: 4 hiss

sizzle: fry **4** burn, sear, siss **7** shrivel

sizzling: hot **6** torrid

sjambok: 4 flog, whip

skate: jag, man, ray **4** fish, plug, shoe, skid **5** flair, glide, horse
kind: **6** figure, hockey

skate blade: 6 runner

skating arena: 4 rink

skean: 4 dirk **5** sword **6** dagger

skedaddle: 4 bunk, flee **5** leave, scoot **6** go away, scurry **7** scamper **8** clear out, hightail

skeesicks: 6 rascal **9** skinflint **14** good-for-nothing

skeet: 12 trapshooting

skegger: 4 fish, parr **6** salmon

skein: rap **4** hank, maze, wind **5** flock **6** flight, hurdle, sleeve **7** spireme, thimble **8** filament, wild fowl

skelder: 5 cheat **7** vagrant **9** panhandle

skeletal: 4 bony **9** emaciated

skeleton: 4 past **5** atomy, bones, coral, ilium, mummy **6** sketch **7** outline, remains **9** framework
disease: **7** rickets
hiding place: **6** closet
organization: **5** cadre
sea animal: **5** coral, shell **6** sponge

skeleton key: 4 gilt **5** screw **7** twirler

skelly: 4 chub **6** squint **9** chaffinch

skelp: say **4** beat, blow, kick, pare, push, rain, slap, walk **5** write **6** basket, colony, squall, stride, strike **7** beehive, measure, perform, quickly, scratch, scuttle **8** splinter, suddenly

skeppist: 8 apiarist **9** beekeeper

skeptic, sceptic: 7 doubter, infidel **10** pyrrhonist, unbeliever **11** disbeliever, freethinker, nullifidian

skeptical, sceptical: 8 doubting **9** faithless **11** incredulous, questioning

skerry: 4 isle, punt, reef, rock **6** potato

sketch: dot, jot, map **4** draw, limn, plan, play, skit **5** draft, paint, skate, story, trace **6** apercu, design, layout, pastel **7** cartoon, croquis, drawing, outline, schizzo(It.) **8** describe **9** delineate, summarize **10** compendium **11** composition, delineation, description

sketchy: 5 rough, vague **10** inadequate, unfinished **11** superficial

skew: cup, cut, set **4** awry, fail, make, shun, slip, turn **5** askew, avoid, flunk, slant, stone, throw, twist **6** coping, escape, eschew, gauche, glance, offset, squint, swerve **7** blunder, distort, drizzle, oblique, pervert **8** slanting **9** deviating, distorted **12** misrepresent

skewer: pin, rod **5** prick, truss **6** fasten, pierce **7** hairpin **8** puncture **9** brochette

ski: 5 glide, slide
 fall marker: **8** sitzmark
 lift: **4** j-bar, t-bar **5** chair **7** gondola
 race: **6** slalom **8** down-hill
 run: **6** schuss

skid: bar **4** clog, curb, drag, hook, rail, scud, shoe, slip, trig **5** brake, check, slide **6** fender, runner, timber, twitch **7** plummet, protect, skidpan, support **8** platform, sideslip

skid row: 4 slum **6** bowery

skiff: 4 boat, skim **5** canoe, glide, graze, touch **6** caique, flurry **7** currane, rowboat

skiing salutation: 4 heil

skill: art, can **5** craft, haunt, knack, virtu **7** ability, address, aptness, cunning, finesse, justice, mastery, science **8** artifice, capacity, deftness, facility, industry, rhetoric, training **9** adeptness, dexterity, knowledge, readiness **10** adroitness, artfulness, astuteness, capability, cleverness, competence, efficiency, experience, expertness **11** information, proficiency **12** skillfulness

skillet: 6 spider **9** frying pan

skillful: apt **4** able, deft, fine, good, hend **5** adept, handy **6** adroit, artful, aufait, clever, crafty, daedal, expert, habile **7** capable, cleanly, cunning **8** dextrous, tactical **9** daedalian, dexterous, ingenious, righteous **10** proficient **11** intelligent **12** accomplished

skim: cut **4** film, flit, sail, scud, scum, skip **5** clear, cover, fleet, float, glide, graze, ready, study, throw **6** browse, glance, refuse **7** examine

skim over: 5 skirr **6** passim

skimp: 6 meager, scanty, scrimp **7** neglect **9** economize

skimpy: 5 chary, spare **6** scanty, stingy **9** niggardly **12** parsimonious

skin: 4 bark, best, derm, dole, fell, film, flay, hide, pare, peel, pell, pelt, rack, rind, scum **5** balat, cheat, cutis, derma, fraud, layer, plica, purse, scalp, shell,

strip, sweep **6** abrade, callus, dermis, escape, fleece, scrape, spoils **7** callous, coating, cuticle, defraud, plating, profits, sharper, sheathe, surface, swindle **8** covering, exterior, membrane, pellicle, planking **9** epidermis, skinflint **10** integument, overcharge, pocketbook **11** decorticate, outdistance

 animal: fur **4** coat, hide, pelt, plew, rack, robe, vair **5** coney, sculp **6** hackle, peltry
 beaver: **4** plew
 blemish: wen **4** mole, wart **7** freckle
 burning sensation: **5** uredo
 decoration: **6** tattoo
 deeper layer: **5** cutis
 depression: **6** dimple
 disease: **4** acne **5** hives, mange, psora, rupia, tinea **6** eczema, tetter
 dressed: fur
 dryness: **7** xerosis
 excessive pigment: **8** melanism
 exudation: **5** sudor, sweat **12** perspiration
 fold: **5** plica **7** dewlaps
 fruit: **7** epicarp
 layer: **4** derm **5** cutis, derma
 oil: **5** sebum
 opening: **4** pore
 pert. to: **5** deric **6** dermal **9** cuticular, epidermal
 piece: **5** blype
 prepare: taw
 presser: **7** sammier
 protuberance: **4** mole, wart **6** pimple
 remover: **5** parer
 resembling: **7** dermoid
 sensitive layer: **5** cutis **7** enderon
 spot: **7** freckle
 tan: taw
 tumor: wen
 unsheared pelt: **8** woolfell
 without: **8** apellous

skin-deep: 7 shallow **9** cutaneous **13** insignificant

skin game: 5 bunco, bunko, fraud **7** swindle

skinflint: 5 miser **6** huddle **7** niggard

skink: 4 adda, draw, hock, shin **5** drink, serve **6** liquor, lizard

skinker: 7 tapster

skinned: *dark:* **7** melanic, swarthy
 thick: **9** pachyderm **11** pachydermic
 thin: **9** sensitive

skinner: bet, gyp **5** cheat **6** driver **8** swindler

skinny: 4 bony, lean, thin **5** scant, spare **6** meanly, stingy **9** emaciated, niggardly **10** membranous
 dip: **8** nude swim

skip: dap, hip, hop **4** balk, flee, gait, jump, leap, miss, omit, trip **5** bound, caper, elide, frisk, leave, scout, vault **6** basket,

bucket, escape, gambol, glance, lackey, spring **7** abscond, captain, footman, servant **8** be absent, ricochet
along a surface: **7** skitter
school: tib **9** play hooky
skip over: **5** elide
lightly: **4** skim
water: dap
skipjack: fop **4** dish **6** bonito, elater **7** upstart **8** sailboat **9** stripling **10** butterfish **11** V-bottom boat
skipper: ihi **5** saury **6** leader, master **7** captain **9** butterfly, commander
East Indian: **6** serang
skippet: box **4** boat **5** skiff **8** envelope
skirl: fly **4** pipe, rain, snow **5** sweep, whirl **6** scream, shriek
skirling: **5** trout **6** salmon
skirmish: **5** brush, clash, fence, fight, melee **6** action, battle, bicker, combat, effort **7** contend, contest **8** conflct, flourish **9** encounter **10** velitation
skirr: fly, run **4** move, skim, tern **5** scour, whirr **6** scurry
skirt: lie, rim **4** edge, flap, girl, maxi, mini, slit **5** dress, evade, trend, woman **6** border, fringe **8** envelope, environs, go around **9** outskirts, periphery, petticoat **10** wraparound
ballet: **4** tutu
coat: **6** lappet
divided: **7** culotte
hoop: **6** peplum **9** crinoline, krinoline **11** farthingale
section: **4** gore **5** panel
short: **4** kilt, mini
steel: **5** tasse **7** lamboys
velvet: **4** base
skit: act **4** gibe, girl, gust, hoax, jeer, jest, slap **5** caper, pound, revue, story, taunt, trick **6** parody, shower, sketch, splash **7** asperse, flounce **8** ridicule **9** enclosure, stage show **10** caricature, reflection
skitter: hop **4** pass, skim, skip **5** glide **7** scamper, scatter **8** sprinkle
skittish: coy, shy **5** jumpy **6** fickle, frisky, lively **7** nervous, playful, restive **8** spirited **9** excitable, frivolous, sensitive **10** capricious **12** undependable
skittle: **4** play **5** trash **7** ninepin **8** nonsense, squander **9** enjoyment
skive: **4** dart, pare, skim **5** shave, wheel
skiver: **6** impale, skewer **7** leather, scatter
skivvy: **9** underwear **10** undershirt
skoal: **5** drink, toast **10** salutation **11** exclamation
skua: **4** gull **5** jager **6** jaeger
skulduggery: **8** foul play, trickery **10** craftiness, wickedness
skulk: **4** hide, lurk **5** dodge, evade, hedge, shirk, slink, sneak **8** malinger
skull: **4** bean, head, mind **5** brain **6** cob-

bra, crania(pl.) **7** cranium, harnpan
back part: **7** occiput
bone: **5** vomer **6** zygoma **7** frontal, maxilla **8** mandible, sphenoid, temporal
cavity: **5** fossa **7** foramen
pert. to: **5** inial **7** cranial
protuberance: **5** inion
soft spot: **8** fontanel
skullcap: **5** calot **6** beanie **7** calotte **8** capeline, yarmelke, yarmulke **9** zucchetto
Arabian: **7** chechia
cardinal's: **10** berrettino
defensive: **4** coif **9** coiffette
ecclesiastical: **6** callot **7** calotte **9** zucchetto
felt: **6** pileus
Jewish: **8** yarmelke, yarmulke
skunk: **5** snipe **6** putois(F.) **7** polecat, stinker **8** betrayer **9** overwhelm
skunk-like animal: **5** civet **7** zorillo
sky: **4** blue **5** azure, ether **6** summit, welkin **7** heavens **9** firmament
god: Anu **4** Anat **5** Dyaus
goddess: **5** Frigg **6** Frigga
highest point: **6** zenith
pert. to: **6** coelar **9** celestial
sky-blue: **5** azure **7** celeste **8** cerulean
sky pilot: **5** padre **8** chaplain, preacher **9** clergyman **10** missionary
skylark: run **4** bird, jump, lark, play, skip, yerk **5** pipit **6** frolic
genus: **6** alauda
skylight: **6** dormer, window **8** abatjour(F.)
skyline: **7** horizon
skyscraper: **5** tower **8** building **9** structure
slab: **4** tile, wood **5** dalle, plate, slice, stela, stele **6** tablet
slab-like: **6** stelar **7** stelene
slack: **4** lax **5** dull, idle, lull, slow, soft **5** chaff, evade, loose, relax, shirk, slake, tardy **6** abated, ease up, loosen, remiss **8** careless, dilatory, inactive, listless, sluggish, unsteady **9** dissolute, impudence, looseness, negligent **10** diminished, inadequate, neglectful **11** inattentive, indifferent
slacken: **4** ease, slow **5** abate, delay, relax **6** loosen reduce, relent, retard **8** decrease, moderate
slackening: **7** detente(F.), slowing
slacker: **4** spiv **7** coucher, shirker **8** embusque **9** goldbrick
slacks: **8** trousers
slade: den **4** cave, glen **5** glade, glide, slide **6** ravine, valley **7** peat bog **8** hillside
slag: **4** lava **5** ashes, dross, waste **6** cinder, debris, refuse, scoria **7** residue, scoriae(pl.) **9** recrement **11** agglomerate
slain: **4** dead **6** fallen, killed **8** murdered **11** slaughtered **12** assassinated

slainte: 5 toast 6 health 8 greeting 10 salutation

slake: mud, wet 4 cool, daub, flag, free, lick, mire, sate 5 abate, algae, allay, gully, loose, relax, slack, slime, smear, yield 6 aslake, deaden, lessen, quench, ravine, reduce 7 appease, assuage, crumble, gratify, refresh, relaxed, release, relieve, satisfy, slacken 8 decrease, mitigate, moderate 10 extinguish 12 disintegrate

slam: hit 4 bang, beat, blow, cuff, dash, gibe, push, shut, vole 5 abuse, clash, close, noise, throw 6 impact 7 collide, flounce 9 criticize

in cards: 4 vole

slammer: 4 jail 6 prison

slander: 4 tale 5 belie, libel, shame 6 defame, malign, report, vilify 7 asperse, blacken, distort, scandal, traduce 8 derogate, disgrace, dishonor, reproach, tear down 10 defamation, depreciate, detraction, scandalize 12 misrepresent

slang: 4 cant 5 abuse, argot 6 jargon, rakish, vulgar 7 dialect, license, swindle 10 vernacular

slant: tip 4 bend, bias, cant, skew, slab, tilt, turn, view 5 aside, bevel, point, slope 6 biased, breeze, falsify, glance, sklent 7 incline, opinion 8 attitude, diagonal, occasion 9 prejudice, viewpoint 10 hypotenuse 11 inclination, opportunity

slanted angle: 5 bevel

slap: box, hit, lap 4 blow, clap, cuff, nick, scud, snub, spat 5 break, click, clink, cluff, plump, skelp, smack 6 buffet, insult, rebuff, slight, strike 7 attempt 8 haymaker 9 castigate

slapdash: 5 abuse, hasty 8 careless, reckless 9 impetuous, roughcast 10 abruptness 11 haphazardly 12 carelessness 13 precipitately

slapjack: 7 pancake 11 griddlecake

slapstick: 4 joke 5 farce 6 comedy

slash: cut 4 dash, gash, lash, slit 5 crack, slosh, wound 6 attack, defeat, lessen, reduce, splash, strike, stripe 7 censure, scourge, slitter 8 diagonal, mark down 9 criticize, light into

slasher: 5 knife, sword 6 dagger 8 billhook 9 swordsman 12 swashbuckler

slashing: 4 huge 6 severe 7 dashing, driving, immense, violent 8 spirited 9 merciless 10 tremendous 11 criticizing

slat: bar, dab, rib 4 blow, flap, hide, hurl, lath, slap 5 strip, throw 6 louver 8 fragment, splinter

slate: rag 4 gray, list, rock, tile 5 board, color, flesh, hound, plank, scold 6 ballot, berate, pummel, punish, pursue, record, roster, tablet, thrash, ticket 7 censure, roofing 8 nominate, register,

schedule 9 criticize, reprimand, thrashing

clean: 10 tabula rasa

tool: sax, zax

slater: 6 critic 9 wood louse

slath: 6 basket

slattern: daw 4 drab, frow, slut 5 dolly, idler, moggy, waste 6 blowze, faggot, sloppy 7 trifler, trollop 8 careless, slovenly

slatternly: 5 dirty, dowdy 6 blowzy, sordid, untidy 8 slovenly

slaty: 6 clayey 7 grayish 9 argillous 12 argillaceous

slaughter: 4 gash, kill, slay 6 battue, murder, pogrom, reduce 7 butcher, carnage, destroy, killing 8 butchery, hecatomb, massacre, violence 9 bloodshed, reduction 10 butchering 11 destruction

slaughterhouse: 8 abattoir, butchery, matadero(Sp.)

waste: 7 tankage

Slav: 4 Pole, Serb, Sorb, Wend 5 Croat, Czech 6 Slovak 7 Russian, Serbian, Servian 8 Bohemian, Croatian, Moravian, Silesian 9 Bulgarian, Ukrainian 12 Czechoslovak

slave: 4 bond, esne, neif, peon, serf, toil 5 chela, helot, thane 6 addict, cumhal, drudge, penest(Gr.), thrall, toiler, vassal, wretch 7 bondman, captive, chattel, enslave, odalisk, servant, work hard 9 gallerian, hierodule, odalisque, sycophant

block: 7 catasta

comedy: 5 Davus(L.)

dealer: 5 bichy

fugitive: 6 maroon

pen: 5 crawl

ship: 6 slaver

The Tempest: 7 Caliban

traveling group: 6 coffle

slave driver: 6 despot, tyrant 8 martinet 11 Simon Legree

Slave States: 5 Texas 7 Alabama, Florida, Georgia 8 Arkansas, Delaware, Kentucky, Maryland, Missouri, Virginia 9 Carolinas, Louisiana, Tennessee 11 Mississippi 13 North Carolina, South Carolina

slaver: 5 drool, smear 6 drivel, saliva 7 flatter, slabber, slobber 8 be insane

slavery: 7 bondage, service 8 drudgery 9 captivity, servitude thralldom, vassalage 10 subjection 11 enslavement 12 enthrallment

release from: 7 manumit 8 liberate 10 emancipate 11 affranchise, enfranchise

Slavic: See **Slav**

slavish: low 4 base, bond, hard, vile 6 abject, menial 7 servile 8 despotic, enslaved 9 barbarous, dependent, imitative **10** oppresive, tyrannical **11** down-trodden, subservient

slay: 4 do in, kill **5** amuse, smite **6** murder, strike **7** butcher, delight, destroy, execute **9** slaughter **10** annihilate **11** assassinate, exterminate

by suffocation: **5** burke

slayer: 4 bane **6** killer **8** criminal, genocide, murderer, regicide, vaticide **9** matricide, patricide, regicidal **10** fratricide, sororicide

sleazy: 4 mean, thin **5** tacky **6** flimsy

sled: 4 pung **6** jumper, sleigh **7** clipper, coaster, travois, vehicle **8** toboggan **10** conveyance

Russian: **6** troika

sledge: 4 dray, sled **5** break **6** hammer, hurdle, sleigh, strike

sleek: nap **4** chic, oily **5** gloss, preen, shiny, slick, smart, suave **6** finish, glossy, polish, smooth, soigne **7** flatter, mollify, soignee **8** polished, unctuous **10** flattering **11** insinuating

sleep: nap **4** doss, doze **5** death, sopor **6** drowse, repose, snooze, stupor **7** bed down, slumber **8** lethargy **10** somnipathy **11** hibernation **15** unconsciousness

deep: **4** coma **5** sopor **6** stupor

god: **4** Soma **6** Hypnos **8** Morpheus

inability to: **8** insomnia

inducer of: **6** opiate **7** sandman, sopient **8** sedative

midday: **6** siesta

pert. to: **7** somnial

sleeper: bet, tie **4** beam **5** horse, shark **6** rafter, rester, timber **7** dormant, earmark, Pullman, reposer **8** dormouse, long shot **9** dowitcher, slumberer **11** stringpiece

sleepiness: 10 drowsiness, somnolence

sleeping: 4 abed **6** latent **7** dormant **8** inactive **9** quiescent

place: bed **4** bunk, doss **5** berth, couch **6** pallet **7** cubicle **9** cubiculum, dormitory

sickness: **12** encephalitis

sleepless: 5 alert **7** unquiet, wakeful **8** restless, vigilant, watchful **9** ceaseless **11** industrious, persevering

sleepwalker: 12 noctambulist, somnambulist

sleepy: 4 dull **5** tired **6** drowsy **7** languid **8** sluggish, soporose, soporous **9** lethargic, somnolent **10** phlegmatic, slumberous

Sleepy Hollow author: 6 Irving

sleet: ice **5** glaze

sleeve: 6 armlet, moggan **7** bushing, cathead

bar on: **7** chevron

leg-of-mutton: **5** gigot

sleigh: 4 pung, sled **6** cutter **7** cariole **8** carriole, toboggan

runner: **4** shoe

sleight: sly **5** craft, knack, skill, trick **6** crafty, wisdom **7** address, agility, conjure, cunning **8** artifice, deftness, prudence, trickery **9** chicanery, deception, dexterity, dexterous, quickness, stratagem **10** nimbleness

sleight-of-hand: 11 legerdemain

performer: **4** mage **8** conjurer, magician **15** prestidigitator

slender: 4 lean, slim, thin, weak **5** exile, guant, lanky, lithe, petit, reedy, short, small, sylph, wispy **6** feeble, lissom, meager, narrow, slight, svelte **7** gracile, lissome, tenuous, trivial, willowy **8** ethereal **9** attenuate, elongated **10** abstemious

slenderize: 4 slim **6** reduce

slenderness: 7 exility, tenuity

sleuth: tec **6** tracer **7** gumshoe, tracker, trailer **9** detective, operative **10** private eye **12** investigator

slew (see also **slough**)**:** lot **4** much, slue, turn **5** bunch, twist **6** slough

sley: 4 reed **8** guideway

slice: cut, saw **4** jerk, part **5** carve, piece, share, shave, slash, whang **6** cantle, divide, rasher, shiver, sliver **7** portion **8** separate, splinter

of bacon: **6** rasher

of meat: **6** collop

slick: mag **4** fine, neat, oily, tidy **5** alert, preen, sleek, slide **6** adroit, chisel, clever, crafty, glossy, paddle, polish, smooth **7** cunning, dress up, smarten, thicket **8** slippery **9** enjoyable, excellent, ingenious **10** attractive, glistening **12** accomplished

slicker: 4 dude **5** cheat **6** gypper **7** gambler **8** raincoat, swindler **9** trickster

slide: 4 fall, skid, sled, slew, slip, slue **5** chute, coast, creep, glide, hurry, scoot, steal **6** sledge **7** decline, incline, slither, sluther **8** glissade, ornament **9** avalanche, backslide, landslide

fastener: **6** zipper

slideway: 8 guideway

slight: cut **4** fine, slap, snub, thin **5** flout, frail, leger(L.), light, minor, scant, scorn, sleek, small **6** flimsy, ignore, meager, remote, scanty, simple, slight, smooth **7** distain, fragile, gracile, neglect, nominal, shallow, slender, trivial **8** careless, delicate **9** disesteem, disparage, disregard, indignity **10** immaterial **11** discourtesy, superficial, unimportant **12** contemptuous **13** disparagement, imperceptible, insignificant, unsubstantial

sound: **4** peep

variation: **6** nuance **7** shading

slightest: 5 least
slighting remark: 4 slur
slim: sly 4 lean, slur, thin 5 gaunt, small, spare 6 adroit, crafty, meager, meagre, scanty, slight, sparse, svelte 7 cunning, slender, tenuous 9 worthless 10 slenderize
slime: mud 4 gore, ooze, slop 5 cover, filth, gleet, smear 6 mucous
slimer: 8 toadfish
slimy: 4 vile 6 filthy, vulgar 7 viscous 9 glutinous, offensive, repulsive 10 disgusting
sling: 4 cast, hurl 5 drink, fling, throw 6 weapon 7 bandage 9 slingshot
slink: 4 lurk 5 cower, crawl, sneak, steal
slip: err, imp 4 balk, clay, fall, omit, pier, quay, shed, skid, slue 5 chute, elude, error, fault, glide, lapse, leash, scion, shoot, slide 6 elapse, harbor, miscue 7 blunder, cutting, delapse, descend, faux pas, illapse, misstep, mistake, neglect, slither, sluther 8 lingerie, pinafore 9 anchorage, gaucherie 12 undergarment 13 transgression
slip away: die 4 pass 5 steal 6 elapse, escape
slip back: 6 revert 7 relapse 8 get worse
slip by: 4 pass 6 elapse
slip-up: 5 error 6 miscue 7 failure 9 oversight
slipknot: 5 noose
slipper: 4 mule, shoe 5 moyle, scuff 6 juliet, pliant, sandal 7 bauchle, scuffer, shuffle, willowy 8 babouche, slippery
slippery: 4 eely, glib, oily 5 slick 6 crafty, shifty, tricky, wanton 7 elusive, evasive, glidder 8 glibbery, unstable 9 deceitful, uncertain 10 unreliable 11 treacherous 13 untrustworthy
slipshod: 8 careless, slommack, slovenly, slummock 10 disorderly
slipslop, slip-slop: 5 inane, slops 6 gabble 7 blunder, twaddle 10 wishy-washy 11 malapropism
slit: cut, rit 4 fent, gash, kerf, nick, open, race, rent, tear 5 break, crack, sever, slash, split, unrip 6 cleave 7 fissure, opening 8 aperture, incision
slither: 4 slip 5 glide, slide 6 rubble 7 rubbish 8 slippery
sliver: cut 5 shred, slice, slops, split 6 strand 7 slobber 8 fragment, splinter
slob: ice, mud 4 mire, ooze, snow 5 slime 6 sloven, sludge 7 bungler
slobber: 4 gush, kiss 5 drool, slime, smarm 6 drivel, slaver, sloven 7 blubber, moisten, slabber
sloe: haw 4 plum 10 blackthorn
slog: hit 4 blow, plod, plug, slam, slug, toil, work 5 drive 6 drudge, strike 9 persevere

slogan: cry 4 word 5 motto 6 phrase 9 catchword
sloop: 4 boat, dray 8 sailboat
slop: mud 4 gulp, gush, mash, plod 5 slush, smock, spill, swill, waste 6 puddle, refuse, splash 7 cassock, clothes, garment, slobber 8 breeches, clothing, trousers
slope: dip, lie 4 bank, brae(Sc.), brow, cant, hang, ramp, rise, tilt 5 bevel, cliff, grade, scarp, slant, talus 6 ascent, aslant, aslope, bajada, depart, escarp, glacis 7 descent, incline, terrace, versant 8 gradient, hillside 9 acclivity, declivity, obliquely 10 declension 11 inclination
angle-measuring device: 10 clinometer
protective: 6 glacis
sloping: 6 aslant 7 oblique 8 downhill, inclined, slanting 9 declivous, inclining
sloppy: 5 messy 6 slushy 7 splashy 8 careless, effusive, slipshod, slovenly 11 intoxicated 12 disagreeable
slosh: mud 4 blow, gulp 5 slime, slush, spill, throw 6 splash, wallow 8 flounder
slot: bar, cut 4 bolt, slat, stab 5 crack, track, trail 6 groove, hollow, keyway, spline 7 keyhole, opening 8 aperture, guideway 10 depression
sloth: ai 4 idle, lazy, pack, slow, unau 5 delay 6 acedia, animal, apathy, torpor 7 accidie, inertia, neglect 8 edentate, idleness, laziness, slowness 9 indolence, tardiness 11 sleuthhound 12 sluggishness, wastefulness
two-toed: 4 anau
slothful: 4 argh, idle, lazy 5 inert 8 inactive, indolent, sluggish 9 sedentary
slouch: hat 4 gait, idle, loll, lout, pipe 5 droop 6 bonnet, loafer, lubber 7 posture 8 drooping, laziness 9 pendulous 13 shiftlessness
slough, slew, slue: bog, mud 4 fall, hull, husk, mire, molt, ooze, plod, road, shed, skin, turn, veer 5 bayou, inlet, pivot, swamp, swing, twist 6 sheath, strike, swerve 7 channel, discard, mudhole 8 imprison
of despond: 7 despair 10 depression
sloughing: 7 ecdysis
sloven: 4 slob 5 besom, clart 6 loafer 7 hallion 9 scoundrel 11 undeveloped 12 uncultivated
slovenly: 4 lazy 5 dowdy, messy 6 blowzy, frouzy, frowsy, frowzy, grubby, sloppy, untidy 7 unkempt 8 careless, slattern, slipshod, sluttish 9 negligent 10 disorderly, slatternly
slow: lax 4 dull, late, poky 5 brosy, delay, grave, hooly, inert, pokey, slack, tardy 6 boring, hamper, hinder, retard, stolid, strike, stupid 7 dronish, gradual, lag-

gard, slacken **8** boresome, dilatory, diminish, inactive, retarded, sluggard, sluggish **9** leisurely, lingering, slowgoing, unhurried **10** decelerate, deliberate, phlegmatic, retrograde **13** unprogressive

music: **5** largo, lento, tardo **6** adagio

slow down: lap **4** idle **5** delay, relax **6** retard **7** decline **10** decelerate, deliberate

slow loris: **5** kokam

slow-witted: **4** bull **6** stupid

slowness: **5** delay **6** lentor

slowpoke: **5** snail **7** dawdler **9** straggler

sludge: ice, mud **4** mire, ooze, slob **5** slime, waste **7** deposit, mixture **8** sediment **9** settlings

slue: See **slough**

sluff: **7** discard

slug: bat, hit **4** blow, dose, dram, slam, slow, snag, stud **5** delay, drink, limax, snail **6** bullet, hinder, loiter, nugget, strike **7** draught, mollusk, trepang **9** gastropod **11** caterpillar

genus of: **4** doto **5** limax **6** elysia

pert. to: **8** limacine

sea: **7** trepang **10** nudibranch

sluggard: daw **4** idle, lazy, slug **5** drone, idler **8** faineant

slugger: bat **4** goon **5** boxer **6** hitter, mauler **7** batsman **8** operator

sluggish: **4** dull, lazy, logy, slow **5** brosy, faint, heavy, inert **6** bovine, drowsy, leaden, supine, torpid **7** dronish, languor, lumpish **8** dilatory, inactive, indolent, slothful, sluggard, stagnant **9** apathetic, lethargic **10** tardigrade **15** procrastinating

sluice: **4** gash, gote, gout, pipe, pour, race **5** flume, flush, swill, valve **6** breach, stream, trough **7** channel, launder, opening, passage **8** irrigate **9** floodgate

sluit: **5** ditch, gulch, gully

slum: **4** dump, junk, room **5** alley **6** barrio, ghetto **7** skid row

slumber: **4** coma, doze **5** sleep **6** drowse, repose **8** lethargy

slumberous: **4** calm **5** quiet **6** drowsy, sleepy **8** peaceful, tranquil **9** lethargic, somnolent, soporific

slump: sag **4** drop, fall, sink, slip **5** droop **6** cave in, slouch **7** decline **8** collapse **10** depreciate, depression

slur: **4** blot, blur, slip, soil **5** cheat, decry, elide, glide, slare, slide, smear, stain, sully, trick **6** insult, macule, slight, smirch, stigma **7** blemish, calumny, dimness, traduce **8** besmirch, disgrace, innuendo, reproach **9** aspersion, criticize, discredit, disparage, indignity **10** calumniate **11** contaminate **12** imperfection

slush: mud, wet **4** gush, mire, pulp, slud,

wash **5** grout **6** drench, drivel, sluice, splash **7** mixture, sludder **14** sentimentality

slut: **4** jade, minx **5** bitch, filth, quean **6** harlot, wanton **8** slattern **9** dratchell

sluttish: **4** lewd **5** gross **6** filthy, sordid **8** slovenly **10** disorderly

sly: **4** arch, cagy, foxy, ruse, slee, wily **5** coony, snaky, sneak **6** artful, clever, crafty, feline, secret, shrewd, slinky, sneaky, subtle, tricky **7** cunning, evasive, furtive, roguish **8** skillful, sneaking **9** cautelous, deceitful, secretive, underhand **10** fallacious **11** clandestine, dissembling, mischievous, underhanded **12** hugger-mugger

look: **4** leer, ogle

slyly spiteful: **5** catty

smack: bit, hit **4** bash, belt, blow, boat, buss, kiss, slap, tang **5** crack, savor, sloop, taste, touch, trace **6** cutter, flavor, heroin, strike, vessel **7** vestige **8** mouthful, sailboat **10** suggestion

smacking: **5** brisk, sharp **6** lively **8** spanking, vigorous

small: dab, sma(Sc.), tot, wad, wee(Sc.) **4** base, cute, lite, mean, puny, thin, tiny, whit, wisp **5** dawny, minim, minor, petty, scant **6** atomic, dapper, grubby, humble, little, mignon, minute, modest, petite(F.), remote, slight **7** minimal, selfish, slender, trivial **8** atomical, picayune, trifling **9** miniature, minuscule, thumbnail **10** diminutive **12** narrow-minded **13** insignificant

amount: mot **4** atom, chip, drop, iota, mote, tate **5** speck **6** detail, morsel **7** driblet, handful, modicum, morceau(F.), snippet **8** modecule

bunch: **4** wisp

coin: **4** mite

small-fry: **4** kids, tots **8** children **10** youngsters

small-minded: **4** mean **5** petty **6** narrow **7** bigoted, selfish **10** prejudiced, ungenerous, vindictive

small talk: **6** babble **7** prattle **8** badinage, chitchat

smallage: **6** celery **7** parsley

smallness: **7** elixity, paucity

smallpox: **7** variola

smaragd: **7** emerald

smarm: **4** gush **7** slobber

smarmy: **8** unctuous

smart: **4** bite, braw, chic, neat, pain, posh, smug, tidy, trig, wily, wise **5** acute, alert, brisk, clean, fresh, natty, nifty, quick, sharp, sting, witty **6** active, astute, bright, cheesy, clever, dressy, jaunty, lively, shrewd, spruce, suffer, swanky **7** capable, elegant, knowing, pungent, stylish **8** spirited, talented, vigorous **9**

competent, dexterous **10** precocious,
suffer pain **11** fashionable, intelligent

smarten: 6 spruce **7** improve **8** brighten,
titivate

smash: hit **4** bash, blow, bung, dash, ruin
5 break, crash, crush, stave, wreck **6**
defeat, impact **7** destroy, shatter,
smash-up, success **8** collapse, stra-
mash(Sc.) **9** collision, pulverize **10**
bankruptcy

smashed: 5 drunk **11** intoxicated

smashup: 4 ruin **5** wreck **6** defeat, impact
7 failure **8** collapse **9** collision **10**
bankruptcy **11** destruction

smatter: 5 break **6** babble, dabble **7** chatter, clatter, crackle, shatter **9** fragments, small bits

smatterer: 7 dabbler **8** sciolist

smear: dab, rub **4** blot, blur, daub, gaum,
soil, spot, stop, whip **5** clart, cleam,
slake, slare, stain, sully, taint **6** anoint,
bedaub, blotch, defame, defeat, defile,
grease, malign, smirch, smudge, spread,
stigma, thwart **7** besmear, plaster, pollute, slander, splatch **8** besmirch, ointment, slaister **9** overwhelm **10** overspread

smearcase: 6 cheese

smectic: 9 detergent, purifying

smell: 4 funk, fust, odor, olid, reek **5** aroma, fetor, flair, scent, sniff, trace **6**
breath **7** hircine, noisome, perfume **9**
fragrance **10** suggestion **11** get a whiff
of, graveolence

having a disagreeable: bad **4** foul, olid, **5**
fetid **10** malodorous

loss of sense: **7** anosmia

offensive: **4** reek **5** fetor, nidor, stink **6**
stench

pert. to: **9** olfactory

pleasant: **5** aroma **7** perfume

stale: **5** fusty, musty

smell-feast: 7 sponger **8** parasite

smeller: 4 nose **6** feeler **7** antenna, bristle

smelling salts: 9 hartshorn

smelt: 4 fish, flux, fuse, melt, prim **6** iuan-
ga(N.Z.), reduce, refine **7** process, scor-
ify

smelting: *by-product:* **4** slag

cone: **4** pina

smew: 4 duck **9** merganser

smidge, smidgen: bit **4** mite **8** particle

smile: 4 beam, grin **5** smirk, sneer **6** arride, simper

smirch: 4 blot, soil **5** smear, stain, sully,
taint **6** blotch, smudge, smutch **7** begrime, blacken, blemish, tarnish **8** besmirch, discolor, dishonor

smirk: 4 leer, trim, yirn **5** quick, smart,
smile, sneer **6** simper, spruce **7** grimace,
smiling

smite: hit **4** blow, clap, cuff, dash, gird,

hurl, kill, pass, slap, slay, swat **5** blast,
knock, skite **6** attack, buffet, defeat,
hammer, pierce, punish, strike **7** afflict,
chasten, clobber, collide, destroy, disease, impress, inspire **8** distress

smith: 6 forger **7** farrier **10** blacksmith
11 metalworker

smithereens: 4 bits **5** atoms **6** pieces **8**
flinders **9** fragments, particles

smithy: 6 forger **7** farrier **10** blacksmith

smitten: 6 fond of **8** affected, enamored,
stricken **9** afflicted, enamoured

smock: 5 kamis, shift, tunic **6** camise **7**
chemise **11** overgarment

smog: fog **4** mist

smoke: 4 floc, fume, funk, haze, mist,
pipe, smog **5** cigar, cubeb, segar,
smook(Sc.), vapor **6** smudge **7** cheroot,
cigaret **9** cigarette

fragrant: **7** incense

outlet: **7** chimney **8** fumeduct, fumiduct

wisp: **4** floc

smoke out: 5 flush **6** reveal **8** discover

smokejack: 4 flue **6** funnel

smoker: car **4** stag **5** party

smokestack: 4 pipe **6** funnel **7** chimney

smoky: 4 hazy **5** dingy, fumid **6** fumish,
smudgy **9** fumacious

smolder, smoulder: 5 choke, smoke **6**
smudge **7** smother **9** fulminate, suffocate

smooth: 4 calm, ease, easy, even, gleg, glib,
iron, lene, mild, pave, sand **5** bland,
brent, furry, glace, glary, gloze, level,
plane, preen, press, quiet, silky, sleek,
slick, soapy, suave **6** creamy, evenly,
fluent, gentle, glassy, glossy, mangle, serene, sleeky **7** amiable, equable, erugate,
flatten, plaster **8** explicit, friendly, glabrous, hairless, levigate, palliate, pleasant, polished, soothing **9** courteous, unruffled **10** flattering **11** alabastrine **12**
frictionless, ingratiating **13** mellifluent-
ly, uninterrupted

phonetically: **4** lene

smoother: 7 abraser

smorgasbord: 8 mishmash **9** appetizer
10 restaurant **12** hors d'oeuvres

smother: 5 choke **6** stifle, welter **7** overlie, repress, smolder, turmoil **8** suppress
9 suffocate

smudge: 4 blot, blur, smug, smut, soil,
soot **5** laugh, prink, smear, smile, stain
6 smutch **7** begrime, chuckle, smolder
10 blackening

smug: 4 neat, prig, tidy, trim, vain **5**
clean, grind, smart, steal, suave **6** pilfer,
spruce **7** correct **9** confident **10** blacksmith, complacent **13** selfsatisfied

smuggler: 6 runner **10** bootlegger

smurr, smur: 4 mist **5** cloud **7** drizzle

smut: 4 bunt, coom, mark, soil, spot **5**

coomb, grime, stain, sully, taint **6** blight, defile, smudge **8** besmirch, discolor **9** obscenity

smutch: 4 blot, dirt, smut, soot, spot **5** grime, stain, sully, taint, tinge, touch, trace **6** defile, smudge **7** blacken

smutty: 5 dirty, dusky, sooty **6** soiled, sordid **7** obscene, spoiled, tainted **8** indecent

Smyrna: 5 Izmir
fig: **5** eleme, elemi

snack: bit, sip **4** ball, bite, jibe, nosh, part, snap **5** acute, alert, chack, lunch, quick, seize, share, smack, taste **6** adroit, morsel, repast, snatch **7** portion, quickly, sharply, teatime **8** grasping, snappish **9** light meal

snaffle: bit **4** loot **5** check, steal **6** pilfer **7** saunter, snuffle **8** restrain **9** bridle bit, restraint

snafu: 4 awry **5** mix-up **6** muddle **8** disorder, entangle **9** confusion

snag: cut, hew, nag, nub **4** base, carp, knot, part, slug, tear, tine, tree, trim, unit **5** break, catch, fault, point, snail, stump, tooth **6** branch, damage, hazard, tongue **8** obstacle **9** hindrance **10** difficulty, impediment **11** obstruction **12** protuberance

snagger: 8 billhook

snail: 4 slug, snag, wilk **5** drone, mitra **6** dodman, tritou, winkle **7** driller, mollusk, testudo **8** escargot, neritine, sluggard **10** hoddy-doddy
clam-killing: **6** winkle
genus of: **5** fusus **6** nerita **9** clausilla
pond: **5** coret
shell: **7** cochlea

snailflower: 7 caracol

snake: asp, boa, nag **4** bind, curl, drag, draw, naga, skid, snot, tail, turn, wind, worm **5** aboma, adder, arrow, braid, cobra, coral, crawl, creep, cribo, filch, kriat, mamba, racer, sneak, steal, viper **6** katuka, python **7** bokadam, camoodi, elapine, hagworm, ingrate, meander, rattler, reptile, serpent, slither **8** anaconda, bungarum, camoodie, moccasin, ophidian, ringhals **9** whipsnake **10** blacksnake, bushmaster, copperhead, massasauga, sidewinder **11** cottonmouth, rattlesnake **12** schaapsteker
big: boa **6** python **8** anaconda **11** constrictor
expert: **13** herpetologist
genus of: boa **7** ophidia
horned: **8** cerastes
killer: **7** mongoos **8** mongoose
marine: **6** chital
movement: **7** slither
mythological: See **serpent**
poison: **5** venom

resembling: **8** viperine
sea: **6** kerril
sound: **4** hiss **6** rattle

snake charmer's flute: 5 pungi

snake dancers: 4 Hopi, Taos **5** Moqui

snake-haired woman: 6 Gorgon, Medusa, Stheno **7** Euryale

snake in the grass: 4 evil **7** traitor **12** hidden danger

snake killer: 8 mongoose **10** road runner

snake-shaped: 9 anguiform

snakeberry: 6 byrony **9** baneberry **11** bittersweet **14** partridge-berry

snakebird: 6 darter **7** anhinga, wryneck

snakebite antidote: 5 guaco

snakeflower: 7 campion **8** blueweed **10** starflower, stitchwort

snakehead: 7 figwort **10** turtlehead

snakelike: 8 ophidian **9** colubrine **10** anguineous
fish: eel

snakemouth: 6 orchid **7** pogonia

snakeroot: 6 seneca, senega **7** bugbane, sangrel **9** birthwort **10** bitter-bush

snakeskin: 6 exuvia

snaky: sly **4** evil, wavy **5** angry **6** touchy **7** anguine, sinuous, winding, wriggly **8** spiteful, twisting, venomous **9** snakelike **10** perfidious, serpentine **11** exasperated, treacherous

snap: rod **4** bark, easy, knap, pass, shut **5** break, catch, chack, cheat, cinch, close, crack, filip, flask, flick, ganch, grasp, hanch, quick, seize, sever, smart, snack, spell, stamp, steal, vigor, wafer **6** biting, cookie, energy, fillip, report, retort, snatch **7** capture, crackle, project, sharper, sparkle **8** interval, particle, puncheon, sinecure, snapshot **9** crackling, crispness, elasticity, fastening, handcuffs, interrupt, smartness, snatching **10** photograph **11** scintillate
with finger: **6** fillip

snap back: 7 rebound, recover

snape: nip **4** snub **5** bevel, check, stint, taper **6** rebuke **8** beveling **10** disappoint

snapper: 4 bean **5** error **6** beetle, bonbon, turtle **7** cosoque, stumble, whopper **8** cachucho, fastener **9** castanets **10** stitchwort, woodpecker **11** firecracker, glassworker, phainopepla

snappish: 4 edgy, tart **5** cross, short, testy **7** cutting, peevish, uncivil **8** petulant **9** fractious, irascible, irritable **12** sharp-tongued

snappy: 4 cold **5** brisk, quick, sharp, smart **6** spiffy, strong, sudden **7** pungent, stylish **9** energetic, copacetic

snapshot: 7 picture, tintype **10** photograph

snare: bag, gin, net, pit, web **4** fang, grin,

lure, mesh, toil, trap **5** benet, brake, catch, grasp, noose, steal **6** ambush, cobweb, entice, entoil, entrap, gilder, tangle, trapan, trepan **7** involve, overnet, pitfall **8** entangle, inveigle **9** deception **12** entanglement

snark: 5 snore **6** boojum

snarl: arr **4** carl, girn, gnar, harl, hurr, knot, maze, snap, yarr, yirr **5** anvil, catch, ganch, gnarl, gnarr, growl, scold **6** hamper, tangle **7** confuse, grizzle, grumble, involve, quarrel **8** complain, entangle **9** confusion **10** complicate **12** complication

snarly: 5 cross, surly **7** peevish, snarled, tangled **8** confused, snarling **10** illnatured **11** bad-tempered

snash: 5 abuse **6** gibing **9** insolence

snatch: bit, get, hap, nab **4** grab, snap, take, trap, yerk **5** braid, catch, clawk, cleek, erept, grasp, gl=ebe, nip up, pluck, seize, snare, spell, stint, swipe, wrest **6** abduct, clutch, kidnap, remove, twitch **7** excerpt, grabble **8** fragment

snatchy: 9 irregular, spasmodic **11** interrupted **12** disconnected

snath, snathe: lop **5** prune, shaft, snead **6** handle

sneak: 4 lurk **5** cower, creep, filch, miche, peach, skulk, slink, snoop, steal **6** coward, cringe, pilfer, rascal, secret, snudge, tattle **9** fefnicute

sneaking: sly **4** mean, poor **6** craven, hidden, paltry, secret **7** furtive, hangdog **8** cowardly, stealthy **9** dastardly, niggardly, underhand **12** contemptible **12** surreptitious

sneap: spy **5** sneak **7** reprove

sneb: bar **4** bolt, snub **6** fasten, rebuke **9** reprimand

sneer: 4 gibe, gird, grin, jeer, mock, snub **5** fleer, fling, flird, flout, flurn, scoff, slare, snirl, snort **7** disdain, grimace, snicker **8** belittle, ridicule

sneeze: 5 neese(Sc.) **7** kerchoo **12** sternutation

pert. to: **7** errhine **12** sternutatory

sneezewort: 8 ptarmica, ptarmite

snell: 4 hard, keen **5** acute, eager, harsh, sharp, smart, snood, swift **6** active, biting, clever, leader, severe **7** caustic, extreme, pungent, quickly, swiftly **8** piercing **10** vigorously

snick: cut, hit **4** blow, draw, kink, knot, move, nick, snip **5** click, notch, share, shoot, snack **6** pierce, strike

snicker: 5 knife, laugh, neigh, sneer, snirl **6** giggle, hee-haw, titter, whinny **7** chortle, chuckle

snide: low, sly **4** base, mean **6** tricky **7** crooked **8** inferior, spurious **9** malicious **11** counterfeit

sniff: 4 nose **5** scent, smell, snuff **6** detect, inhale **7** sniffle **8** perceive, sibilate **9** recognize

sniffy: 8 scornful **10** disdainful **12** contemptuous, supercilious

snifter: 4 blow, dram, good **5** drink, sniff, snort, storm **6** goblet, moment, snivel **7** dilemma, reverse **9** excellent

snit: eel, lop **4** chop, drag, jerk **5** snake, sneak **6** pilfer

sniggle: 4 trap **5** catch **7** broggle

snip: bit, cut **4** clip, curb, minx, snap **5** check, filch, notch, piece, shred, snack **6** snatch, stripe, stroke, tailor **8** fragment, incision, particle **9** disfigure

snipe: 4 bird, butt, fool **5** skunk **8** fire upon **9** criticize **10** sharp-shoot

cry: **5** scape

flock: **5** whisp

snipe hawk: 7 harrier

sniper: 8 ambusher

snippy: 4 curt, mean, tart **5** bluff, brief, gruff, sharp **6** sniffy, stingy **8** snappish, snippety **11** closefisted, fragmentary **12** supercilious

snit: 5 pique **8** angry fit

snitch: 4 nose, tell **5** catch, peach, pinch, steal, thief **6** betray, inform, pilfer, smitch, snatch **8** informer, inform on, particle

snivel: cry **4** cant, fret, weep **5** sniff, whine **6** pathos **7** emotion, snuffle **8** complain

snob: cut, sob **4** aper, scab **5** toady **6** flunky, poseur **7** cobbler, cricket, flunkey, parvenu, plebian, shoneen, upstart **8** blackleg, bluenose, commoner, parvenue, townsman **9** pretender, shoemaker **10** fivestones

snobbish: 7 high-hat **11** overbearing

snood: hat, tie **4** bind **5** braid **6** fasten, fillet, ribbon **7** hairnet

snook: pry **5** smell, sneak, sniff **6** follow, robalo, search **7** snuffle **9** barracuda

snoop: pry **4** look, nose, peek, peep **5** sneak **6** search **8** busbody

snooper: 7 marplot, meddler **8** busybody

snoot: 4 face, nose, snub **7** grimace

snooty: 7 haughty, upstage **8** snobbish **10** hoity-toity **12** contemptuous, supercilious

snooze: nap **4** doze **5** sleep **6** drowse, siesta **7** snoozle

snoozle: 4 doze **5** sleep **6** cuddle, nuzzle **7** snuggle

snore: 4 rout **5** snork, snort **7** saw wood

snoring: 5 stiff **7** roaring, stertor **10** stertorous

snork: pig **5** grunt, snore, snort

snort: 4 rout **5** drink, grunt, laugh, snirl, snore, snork **11** inhale a drug

snotty: 5 dirty, nasty, slimy **6** offish,

snooty **7** haughty, viscous **8** impudent, snotlike **9** offensive **12** contemptible, supercilious

snout: neb **4** mull, nose **5** groin, spout, trunk **6** nozzle **7** conduit, rostrum, tobacco

snout-nose: 7 gruntle **9** proboscis

snow: ice, sna **4** grue, snaw(Sc.) **5** blizz, cover, opium **6** heroin **7** cocaine, deceive **8** obstruct **9** whiteness

glacial: **4** firn, neve

granular: **4** corn

half-melted: **5** slush

house: **4** iglu **5** igloo

living in: **5** neval

mushy: **4** slob

pellet: **7** graupel

resembling: **7** niveous

slide: **8** glissade **9** avalanche

vehicle: **4** pung, sled **6** sleigh

wedding: **4** rice

snow and rain: 5 sleet

snow flurry: 5 skirl

snow goose: 4 chen **5** brant, wavey

snow grouse: 9 ptarmigan

snow mass: 9 avalanche

snow ridges: 8 sastrugi, zastrugi

snow runner: ski **4** skee

snowflake: 4 bird **5** finch **7** crystal

snowshoe: pac, ski **4** skee

snowstorm: 8 blizzard

snowy: 4 pure **5** nival, white **6** chaste **8** spotless, unsoiled

snub: cut, nip **4** chip, curb, slap, stop **5** check, frump, quell, scold, snool, snoot **6** hinder, ignore, rebuff, rebuke, remark, retort, slight, tauten **7** affront, neglect, repress, upbraid **8** restrain, send away **9** interrupt, ostracize, reprimand

snuff: 4 odor **5** pinch, pique, scent, smell, sniff, snort **6** detect, inhale **7** offense, tobacco, umbrage **8** sibilate **10** extinguish

kind of: **5** musty **6** rappee **8** bergamot, Maccaboy **10** blackguard, Copenhagen

snuffbox: 4 mill, mull **9** tabatiere

snuffy: 5 dirty, sulky, vexed **6** horrid **7** annoyed **10** displeased **12** disagreeable, unattractive **13** short-tempered

snug, 4 bein, bien, cosh, cozy, neat, safe, tidy, trim, warm **5** close, quiet, tight **6** modest, secure, silent **7** compact, snuggle **8** reticent, secreted, taciturn **9** concealed, seaworthy, secretive **10** prosperous **11** comfortable

snuggery: den **4** nook **7** cottage

snuggle: 4 nest **6** cuddle, nestle

snugly: 6 cosily

so: sae, sic, sua **4** ergo, thus, very **5** hence **7** because **9** in this way, similarly, therefore **11** accordingly **12** consequently

so be it: 4 amen

so far: yet **4** thus

soak: dip, hit, ret, sog, sop, sot, wet **4** bate, blow, bowk, buck, hurl, ooze, pawn, sock **5** binge, drink, drouk, imbue, punch, souse, spree, steep **6** drench, engage, imbibe, imbrue, seethe, tipple **8** drunkard, macerate, permeate, saturate **9** distemper, percolate **10** impregnate, instructor, overcharge

flax: ret

in brine: **4** corn, salt **8** marinate

soaked: wet **6** sodden **7** drenched

soap: 4 sape, sapo, wash **5** money, savon **6** lather **7** cleanse, flatter **8** flattery **9** detergent **14** television show

convert into: **8** saponify

frame bar: **4** sess

ingredient: lye

mottled: **7** castile **8** eschwege

parmaceutical: **4** sapo

plate: **4** sess

substitute: **5** amole, borax

soap plant: 5 amole

soapstone: 4 talc **8** steatite

full of: **7** talcose

soapy: 4 oily, soft **5** suave **6** smooth **7** saponic **8** lathered, unctuous **9** soapsuddy **10** latherable **11** saponaceous **12** ingratiating

soar: fly **4** lift, rise, sail **5** float, glide, hover, mount, plane **6** ascend, aspire **7** take off **9** transcend

Soave: 12 dry white wine

sob: cry **4** sigh, wail, weep **6** boohoo **7** whimper **8** frighten

sober: 4 calm, cool, dark, gray, poor, sane **5** douce, grave, quiet, staid **6** ailing, feeble, gentle, humble, sedate, severe, simple, solemn, somber, steady, subdue, temper **7** chasten, earnest, regular, serious, subdued, weighty **8** composed, decorous, moderate, peaceful, rational **9** abstinent, collected, realistic, temperate **10** abstemious **11** indifferent **13** unimpassioned, unpretentious

sobol: 5 sable **6** marten

soboles: 5 shoot **6** stolen, sucker

sobriety: 7 gravity **9** restraint, soberness, solemnity, soundness **10** abstinence, moderation, sedateness, temperance **11** seriousness **14** reasonableness

sobriquet, soubriquet: 4 name **5** alias, chuck, title **6** byname **7** affront, epithet **8** nickname **11** appellation

so-called: 7 alleged, nominal **10** ostensible

soccer player: 6 booter, goalie, kicker, winger

sociability: 10 affability

sociable: 4 cozy, sofa **6** chummy, social **7** affable **8** carriage, familiar, friendly, informal, tricycle **9** aeroplane, agreeable, reception, talkative **10** accessible, gregarious **13** communicative, companionable

social: tea **4** stag **5** party **6** genial, smoker **9** agreeable, convivial, gathering **10** gregarious **13** companionable

affair: tea **4** ball **6** soiree **9** reception

career beginning: **5** debut

climber: **4** snob **7** parvenu, upstart

gathering: bee, tea **4** club, stag **5** party **6** smoker **7** reunion **9** reception

group: **4** clan, club **5** caste, class, lodge, tribe **6** estate, family, jet set **7** coterie **8** sorority **9** fraternity

insect: bee

outcast: **5** leper **6** pariah

person: **4** host **5** mixer **7** hostess

system: **6** feudal, modern, regime, tribal **11** traditional

worker: **7** almoner, analyst **8** do-gooder **9** clinician

socialism: **7** etatism **9** Communism **10** utopianism

socialist: Red **6** Fabian **9** anarchist, Bolshevik, communist **10** Bolshevist **11** nationalist **12** collectivist

socialize: mix **6** mingle **9** associate

society (see also **organization**): **4** bund, clan, gild **5** guild, order, union **6** menage, jet set **7** academy, company, hetaera, hetaira **8** academie, alliance **9** accademie, community **10** connection, upper crust **11** aristocracy, association, cooperation, intercourse, partnership **12** denomination, relationship **13** companionship, confederation, confraternity, participation

girl: deb

high: **9** beau monde, haut monde

low (member): **4** raff **8** riff-raff

kind of: **4** SPCA, frat, tong **5** elite, order, choir **7** societe **8** sorority **10** fraternity

secret: Hui **4** tong, egbo **5** mafia, lodge **6** mafia, ogboni **7** Camorra **9** Carbonari

symbol: **7** regalia

Society Islands: **5** Tahaa **6** Moorea, Tahiti **7** Huahine, Maupiti, Raiatea **8** Bora Bora

capital: **7** Papeete

explorer: **4** Cook

people: **10** Polynesian

Society of Friends: **7** Quakers

founder: Fox

sociology: **8** demotics

sock: hit, sew **4** beat, blow, hurl, shoe, sigh, vamp **5** drive **6** anklet, buskin, comedy, sandal, strike **7** hosiery, slipper socking **8** drainage, stocking **9** plowshare

sockdolager: **4** oner **8** finisher

socket: **5** lance, spear **6** cavity, collet, hollow **7** opening **9** plowshare

kind of: pan **4** birn **5** orbit **8** alveolus

Socrates: *biographer:* **5** Plato

birthplace: **6** Athens

dialogue: **4** Meno **6** Phaedo **8** Apologia

escape plotter: **5** Crito

love: **10** philosophy, Alcibiades

method: **8** maieutic

poison: **7** hemlock

wife: **8** Xantippe **9** Xanthippe

sod: **4** delf, dove, flag, peat, soak, soil, turf **5** delft, divot, glebe, soggy, sward **6** saddle, sodden **7** stratum **9** fermented

pert. to: **8** alkaline

soda: sal **8** beverage **9** saleratus

sodalite: **5** lenad **7** mineral

sodality: **5** union, unity **6** chapel **10** fellowship, fraternity **11** association, brotherhood **13** companionship

sodden: wet **5** drunk, heavy, moist, sammy, soggy **6** boiled, dulled, soaked, stewed, stupid **7** bloated, drunken, steeped **8** spirited **9** saturated **11** intoxicated

sodium: **7** natrium

carbonate: **4** soda **5** borax, trona **6** natron **7** salsoda

chlorate: **5** NaClO$_3$

chloride: sal, tar **4** NaCl, salt **7** saltcat

compound: **4** soda

nitrate: **5** niter

tetraborate: **5** borax

Sodom: *king:* **4** Bera

neighbor: **8** Gomorrah

sodomite: **6** bugger

sofa: **5** boist, couch, divan **6** lounge, settee **7** bergere, dosados, ottoman **8** causeuse **9** banquette, davenport **12** chesterfield

soft: coy, low **4** easy, feil, fine, limp, mild, waxy, weak **5** bland, cushy, downy, dolce, dulce, faint, givey, hooly, light, mushy, piano, sooth **6** clammy, dreamy, fluffy, gentle, gently, placid, silken, simple, smooth, tender **7** clement, ductile, lenient, lightly, quietly, squashy, subdued **8** delicate, feminine, flexible, tranquil **9** temperate, tractable, untrained **10** effeminate, peacefully **11** comfortable, sympathetic **12** nonalcoholic **13** compassionate

and smooth: **5** furry, silky, soapy **6** mellow, supple **7** cottony

and sweet: **5** dolce **6** dulcet

and wet: **5** mushy **7** squashy

food: pap

mass: **4** pulp

music: **5** dulce, piano

palate: **4** cion **5** uvula, velum

pedal: **6** hush-up **7** silence **8** play down

soap: **4** gush **7** blarney, flatter, wheedle **8** flattery, sweet-talk, wheedling

soft drink: ade, pop **4** soda **5** tonic

softa: 7 student 8 beginner

soften: 4 ease, melt 5 allay, malax, relax, yield 6 affect, anneal, gentle, pacify, relent, soother, subdue, temper, weaken 7 amolish, appease, assuage, mollify 8 attemper, enervate, enfeeble, lenitive, macerate, mitigate, modulate 9 alleviate, emolliate, meliorate 10 emasculate, depreciate, intenerate 11 tranquilize

softening: 7 lenient 8 emulsive 9 demulcent 10 moderation 11 melioration
of brain: 8 dementia
of decayed fruit: 4 blet

soft-spoken: 4 mild 5 bland, suave 6 gentle, smooth 12 ingratiating

softhearted: 6 tender 13 compassionate

soft touch: 4 snap 6 sucker 8 easy mark, pushover

sog: 4 doze, soak 6 drowse 8 saturate

soggy: wet 4 damp 5 heavy, humid 6 soaked, sodden, watery 9 saturated

soigne, soignee: 4 chic, neat, tidy 5 sleek 7 stylish 9 dressed up 11 well-groomed

soil: mud 4 blot, blur, daub, dirt, foil, grit, land, moil, mool, slur, spot 5 dirty, earth, filth, glebe, grime, smear, solum, stain, sully, taint 6 assoil, bedaub, befile, befoul, bemire, defile, grease, ground, refuse, sewage, smirch, smudge, vilify 7 begrime, benasty, besmear, corrupt, country, pollute, tarnish 8 alluvium, besmirch, disgrace 9 bedraggle, bespatter, droppings, excrement 11 contaminate
claylike: 4 marl
goddess of: 7 Demeter
kind of: 4 clay, loam, marl, lair, malm, moss 5 adobe, loess, groot, humus
organic: 5 humus

soiled: 4 foul 5 dingy, grimy 6 smeary 7 sullied 8 unchaste 9 blemished

soilure: 5 satin 6 smirch

soiree: 5 party 6 affair

sojourn: 4 bide, howf, rest, stay, stop 5 abide, abode, delay, dwell, howff, lodge, tarry, visit 6 reside, travel 7 allodge, mansion 8 abidance 9 residence, tarriance 11 peregrinate

sojourner: 7 boarder 8 comeling, resident 9 transient

sol: sun 4 gold 6 sun-god 7 Phoebus

solace: 5 allay, amuse, cheer 6 lessen, relief, soothe 7 assuage, comfort, console 9 alleviate, diversion, entertain 10 recreation, relaxation 11 alleviation, consolation

solan: 4 fowl 5 goose 6 gannet

solar, soler, sollar: 4 loft, roof, room 5 floor, story 6 garret, heliac, tropic 7 chamber 8 heliacal 9 apartment
deity: Shu
disk: 4 aten, aton

excess over lunar year: 5 epact

solar system: *member:* 6 planet
beyond: 9 deep space
model: 6 orrery

sold (see also **sell**): 8 marketed

solder: 4 fuse, heat, join, mend, weld 5 braze, patch, unite 6 cement 9 sculpture

soldering: *flux:* 5 resin, rosin
piece: lug

soldier: man, vet 4 fogy, swad 5 fogey, guffy, poilu, sammy, shirk 6 galoot, marine, Zouave 7 brigand, feedman, fighter, hobbler, hotspur, palikar, private, regular, trooper, veteran, warrior 8 bear arms, buffcoat, cavalier, gendarme, malinger, servitor, tolpatch, shackman 9 grenadier, musketeer 10 serviceman
cavalry: 6 hussar 8 chasseur
detachment: 4 file
drinking flask: 7 canteen
female: 4 WAAC
foreign: 4 peon, kern 5 nezam, poilu, sepoy, kerne, spahi 6 askari, lascar, sapper 7 cateran, hoplite, Billjim 8 grognard, miquelet 10 base wallah, carmagnole, carabineer
group of: 4 band, file 5 corps, force, squad, troop 7 brigade, caterva, company, platoon 8 division 9 battalion
irregular: 9 guerrilla
mercenary: 7 Hessian, Swisser, Switzer
newly trained: 5 cadet, plebe, rooky 6 rookie 7 chicken, recruit, trainee 8 bezonian 11 replacement
of fortune: 10 adventurer
old: vet 7 veteran 8 grognard
overcoat: 6 capote
quarters: 7 billets 8 barracks
special functions: 6 lancer, sapper 7 velites, dragoon, trooper 8 fencible, fugleman 9 fantassin, targeteer, flugelman 10 cuirassier, velitation, carabineer, carabinier 12 antesignanus
trenching tools: 8 burgoyne
vacation: 4 pass 5 leave, R and R 8 furlough

soldierly: 5 brave 6 heroic 7 martial

sole: one 4 dish, fish, foot, lone, mere, only, yoke 5 afald, alone, floor, plate, slade 6 bottom, entire, furrow, halter, hearth, lonely, single, unique, valley 7 outsole, subsoil 8 desolate, flatfish, isolated, solitary, unshared 9 exclusive, threshold, unmarried, unmatched 10 foundation, one and only, underframe, unsharable, windowsill
foot: 4 vola 5 pelma
part: 5 shank
pert. to: 7 plantar

solecism: 5 error 9 barbarism, deviation 11 impropriety

solely: all 4 only 5 alone 6 merely, simply, singly 8 entirely 9 allenarly 11 exclusively

solemn: sad 5 budge, grave, sober, usual 6 august, devout, formal, gloomy, ritual, sacred, severe, somber 7 earnest, serious, stately, weighty 8 eloquent, funereal, splendid 9 customary, dignified, sumptuous 10 ceremonial, devotional, noteworthy 11 reverential 13 distinguished

solemnize: 5 exalt, marry 7 dignify, glorify, observe 9 celebrate 11 commemorate

soler: 7 cobbler 9 shoemaker

solicit: ask, beg, woo 4 bark, plea, seek, tout 5 court, crave, mooch, tempt 6 accost, demand, entice, incite, invite, manage 7 beseech, canvass, entreat, forward, implore, request 8 campaign, disquiet, petition 9 importune, panhandle, prosecute 10 supplicate 12 make advances

solicitor: 4 tout 6 barker, lawyer 8 attorney 10 petitioner

chambers: 4 inns

solicitous: 5 eager 7 anxious, careful 8 desirous, troubled 9 attentive, concerned 10 thoughtful 11 considerate 12 apprehensive

solicitude: 4 care, coda, ease, fear, heed, yeme 7 anxiety, concern 8 business 11 carefulness 12 apprehension 13 consideration

solid: 4 cone, cube, firm, full, hard 5 cubic, dense, level, sound, stiff, valid 6 bodily, sphere, stable, strong 7 bedrock, compact, uniform, weighty 8 constant, reliable, sterling, unbroken 9 estimable, unanimous 10 consistent, dependable, inflexible 11 homogeneous, responsible, substantial, trustworthy

geometrical: 4 cone, cube 5 prism 7 pyramid 8 cylinder 11 heptahedron, pentahedron 12 dodecahedron

solidify: gel, set 4 cake 6 cement, cohere, harden 7 compact 8 concrete, condense, contract 9 coagulate 11 consolidate, crystallize

solidity: 5 unity 8 firmness, hardness 9 solidness, soundness, stability 11 compactness, consistency 13 dependability

solidum: sum 4 dado

soliloquy: 4 poem 9 discourse, monologue, utterance

solitaire: 4 game 6 hermit 7 diamond, recluse 8 Canfield, patience 9 neckcloth

solitary: 4 hole, lone, monk, only, sole 5 alone 6 hermit, lonely, remote, simple, single 7 dungeon, eremite, recluse 8 derelict, desolate, lonesome, solitary 9 withdrawn 10 antisocial, individual 12 unfrequented

solitude: 6 dearth, desert 7 expanse, privacy, retreat 8 soleness 9 isolation, seclusion 10 loneliness, quarantine, remoteness, retirement, uniqueness, wilderness 12 solitariness

solo: air 4 aria 5 alone, scena, radel 6 strain 9 monologue 13 unaccompanied

accompaniment: 8 obligato 9 obbligato

soloist: 6 cantor, singer 7 aviator

Solomon: 7 wise man

ally: 5 Hiram

father: 5 David

gold obtained from: 5 Ophir

mother: 9 Bathsheba

son: 8 Rehoboam

temple: 6 shamir

Solomon Islands: 4 Buka, Gizo, Savo 7 Malaita 10 New Georgia 11 Guadalcanal

capital: 7 Honaira

discoverer: 9 de Mendana

gulf: 4 Huon, Kula

monetary unit: 6 dollar

volcano: 5 Balbi

Solon: 4 sage 7 senator 8 lawmaker 9 publicist, statesman 10 legislator

soluble: 4 frim 6 solute 11 liquefiable

solus: 5 alone

solute: 4 free 5 loose, solve 7 arrange, soluble 8 dissolve, separate 9 dissolved 13 disintegrated

solution: key 6 answer, result 8 analysis 9 discharge, releasing 10 denouement, resolution 11 deliverance, explanation 14 disintegration 15 disentanglement

kinds of: lye 5 brine, eusol, iodin, titer, sirup, syrup 6 iodine, phenol

strength of: 5 titer

solve: 4 free, undo 5 break 6 assoil, fathom, have it, unfold 7 explain, resolve, unravel, work out 8 dissolve 9 interpret 11 disentangle

solvent: 8 solution 9 detergent

Somalia: *capital:* 9 Mogidishu

division: 6 Hawiya

measure: top 4 caba 5 chela, darat, tabla 6 cubito

monetary unit: 8 shilling

river: 4 Juba 7 Shebeli

somatic: 6 bodily, carnal 8 parietal, physical 9 corporeal 13 somatopleuric

somber, sombre: sad 4 dark, dern, dull 5 dusky, gloom, grave, sober 6 dismal, gloomy, lenten, severe, solemn 7 austere, ominous 9 depressed 10 depressing, lackluster, melancholy

sombero: hat 8 headgear, sunshade

some: any, few, one 4 part 5 about 6 nearly 7 certain, portion, several 13 approximately

somersault: 4 flip

something: 5 drink 6 entity, liquor 7 aliquid, whatnot **8** beverage, somewhat

sometime: 4 late, once **6** former, whilom **7** quondam **8** formerly **12** occasionally

somewhat: 6 rather **7** aliquid **9** something, to a degree **10** moderately

Somme city: 6 Amiens **9** Abbeville

sommelier: 6 butler **9** cellarman **11** wine steward

somnambulism: 12 noctambulism, sleepwalking

somnolent: 6 drowsy, sleepy **7** languid

son: ben, boy **4** fils **5** child, scion **6** filius, Jesuit, native **8** disciple, follower, relative **9** offspring **10** descendant

pert. to: **6** filial

Scot.: Mac

youngest: **5** cadet

son-in-law: 5 gener **8** beau-fils

Son of God: 6 Savior **7** Saviour

sonance: 4 tune **5** sound

sonant: 4 oral **5** tonic, vocal **6** voiced **8** sounding **9** intonated

sonata: *closing:* **4** coda

part: **5** rondo **7** scherzo

song: dit, lay, uta **4** aria, call, cant, dite, duan, fuss, glee, hymn, lied, lilt, noel, poem, tune **5** blues, canto, carol, chant, charm, ditty, lyric, melos, music, psalm, verse **6** ballad, cantic, cantus, canzon, carmen, chanty, clamor, himene, himine, melody, poetry, shanty, sonnet, strain, trifle **7** cancion, cantion, canzone, chantey, descant, shantey **8** canticle, pittance **9** cabaletta **11** composition

baby's: **7** lullaby

choral muse: **11** Terpischore

Christmas: **4** noel **5** carol

college: **4** glee

collection: **9** anthology **10** cancionero

evening: **6** vesper **8** serenade

folk: **5** blues **6** ballad

funeral: **5** dirge, elegy, elogy **6** elegie, lament, threne **7** elogium, epicede **8** epicedia, threnody **9** epicedium

gay: **4** lilt

German: **4** lied **6** lieder(pl.)

gypsy: **10** zingaresca

love: **6** amoret, ballad, serena **8** serenade

mountaineeer's: **5** yodel

mourning: see *funeral* above

obscure: **4** rune

of joy: **5** paean

operatic: **4** aria

part: **5** canon, round **8** madrigal

pert. to.: **5** melic

sacred: **4** hymn **5** chant, motet, psalm **6** anthem **7** polymny

sailor's: **6** chanty, shanty **7** chantey, shantey **8** rumbelow **9** barcarole **10** barcarolle

simple: **5** ditty

solo: **4** glee

triumphal: **5** paean

wedding: **5** hymen

song-like: 6 ariose, arioso **7** lyrical

Song of Bernadette author: 6 Werfel

songbird: 4 lark, wren **5** mavie, mavis, robin, veery, vireo **6** canary, linnet, mocker, oriole, oscine, thrush **7** mocking, warbler **8** redstart, vocalist

songman: 6 singer **7** gleeman **8** minstrel

songwriter: 8 composer, lyricist

sonnet: 4 poem, song **5** octet, verse **6** sestet

conclusion: **6** sestet

sonority: 8 loudness **9** resonance

sonorous: 7 ringing **8** imposing, resonant **10** impressive, rhetorical

sook: 4 call **5** booth **6** market

soon: ere **4** anon, fast, yern **5** early, later, quick, yerne **6** belive, rather, speedy **7** betimes, by-and-by, erelong, quickly, readily, shortly **8** directly, promptly, speedily **9** presently, willingly **10** beforetime **11** immediately, in the future

sooner: 4 erst **6** before **9** Oklahoman **10** preferably

Sooner State: 8 Oklahoma

soot: 4 coom, smut, stup **5** black, colly, coomb, grime, sweet, smoke **6** carbon, gentle, smudge **7** blacken, residue **9** melodious

particle: **4** isel, izle

pert. to: **10** fuliginous

sooth: 4 fact, real, soft, true **5** being, sweet, truly **6** augury, in fact, smooth **7** comfort, genuine, present, proverb, pleasing, pleasure, soothing, truthful **10** delightful **11** soothsaying, trustworthy

soothe: coy, pat, pet **4** balm, calm, dill, ease, lull **5** accoy, allay, charm, dulce, quiet **6** pacify, soften, solace, stroke **7** appease, assuage, comfort, compose, console, demulce, flatter, mollify, placate, relieve **8** mitigate, palliate **9** alleviate, attemper **10** demulceate **11** tranquilize

soother: 4 balm **5** salve **7** anodyne **9** emollient, flatterer

soothing: 4 mild **5** balmy, downy, dulce **6** dreamy, dulcet, gentle **7** anodyne, calming **8** lenitive, sedative **9** appeasing, assuasive, demulcent **13** tranquilizing

soothsay: 4 omen **7** portent, predict, proverb **8** foretell

soothsayer: 4 seer **5** augur, weird, vates **6** ariole, mantis **7** augurer, diviner, prophet, seeress **8** haruspex, chaldean **10** forecaster, hariolizer **14** prognosticator

sooty: 4 dark **5** black, colly, dingy, dirty, dusky **6** brokie **9** blackened **10** fuliginous

sop: wet **4** dunk, gift, heap, lump, mass, mess, soak, tuft **5** bribe, cloud, clump, steep **7** advance, milksop **8** saturate, weakling

sophist: **7** casuist, teacher, thinker **8** reasoner **10** paralogist **11** philosopher

sophistical: **7** cunning **8** captious **9** deceptive, insincere **11** adulterated

sophisticate: **5** alter, spoil **6** debase, garble **7** corrupt, falsify, mislead **10** adulterate **11** disillusion

sophisticated: **4** chic, wise **7** amended, refined, worldly **8** tasteful **11** adulterated, worldly-wise

sophistry: **6** deceit **7** fallacy, quibble **8** argument, trickery **9** deception **11** insincerity

Sophocles play: **4** Ajax **7** Electra, Oedipus **8** Antigone

sopor: **5** sleep **6** apathy, stupor

soporific: **5** dwale **6** drowsy, opiate, sleepy **8** hypnotic, narcotic **9** apathetic **11** somniferous **12** somnifacient, somnivolency

soppy: wet **5** rainy **6** soaked **7** mawkish **8** drenched **11** sentimental

soprano: **6** singer, treble **9** high voice

operatic: **4** Lind, Pons **5** Freni, Melba, Moffo, Patti, Price, Sills **6** Arroyo, Callas, Peters, Resnik, Scotto **7** Crespin, Farrell, Kirsten, Lehmann, Nilsson, Stevens, Tebaldi, Traubel **8** Flagstad, Ponselle **10** Sutherland, Tetrazzini **11** Schwarzkopf **12** de los Angeles

sora: **4** bird, rail

sorcerer: **4** mage, magi **5** boyla, brujo, Goeta **6** boolya, wizard **7** charmer, warlock **8** conjurer, magician **9** occultist **11** necromancer, thaumaturge **13** thaumaturgist

sorceress: hag, hex **5** Circe, Lamia, sibyl, witch **6** Gorgon **11** enchantress

sorcery: **5** magic, obeah, spell **6** fetich, fetish, voodoo **8** pishogue, prestige **9** diablerie, diabolism **10** necromancy, witchcraft **11** enchantment

sordellina: **7** bagpipe

sordid: low **4** base, mean, vile **5** dirty, gross **6** chetif, filthy, greedy, menial **7** ignoble, selfish, servile, squalid **8** churlish, covetous, grasping, grewsome, gruesome, sluttish, wretched **9** mercenary, niggardly **10** avaricious, despicable, slatternly **12** contemptible

sordor: **5** dregs **6** refuse **10** sordidness

sore: raw **4** boil, buck, evil, harm, kibe, pain, sair **5** angry, blain, botch, grief, ulcer, vexed, wound, wrong **6** bitter, bruise, fester, severe, sorrel, sorrow, tender, touchy **7** angered, annoyed, disease, extreme, grieved, hostile, painful, penance, trouble, violent **8** abrasion, grievous, inflamed, offended, sickness **9** detriment, irritated, sensitive, suffering, ulcerated, vexatious **10** affliction, afflictive, contrition, difficulty, distressed, unpleasant **11** disgruntled, distressing **13** temperamental, oversensitive

sorehead: **5** loser **6** griper, grouch **10** malcontent

sorely: **7** greatly **8** severely, urgently **9** extremely, painfully, violently **10** grievously **12** distressingly **13** unpleasantly

soreness: **4** ache, pain **8** severity, vexation, violence **10** bitterness **11** painfulness **12** irritability

sorghum: **4** cush, dura, milo **5** batad, darso, durra, sorgo **7** shallu **8** feterita

sorite: **4** heap **10** collection

sorority: **4** club **7** society **10** sisterhood

sorrel: oca **5** brown, color, horse, plant **6** oxalis **7** roselle

sorrow: rue, woe **4** bale, care, dole, harm, loss, sigh, teen, weal **5** devil, dolor, grief, mourn, rogue, scamp **6** grieve, lament, misery, plague, regret **7** sadness, trouble, waeness **8** calamity, distress, egrimony, mourning **9** adversity, penitence, suffering **10** affliction, compassion, contrition, discomfort, melancholy **11** lamentation, tribulation, unhappiness **12** wretchedness

over: **6** bemoan, bewail, lament **7** deplore

sorrowful: sad **4** teen **5** drear, sadly **6** dismal, dolent, dreary, rueful, woeful **7** doleful, grieved, unhappy **8** contrite, dolesome, dolorous, grievous, mournful **9** afflicted, plaintive **10** lamentable, melancholy **11** distressing **12** disconsolate

sorry: bad, sad **4** hurt, mean, poor **5** vexed **6** dismal, gloomy, regret, repent, vulgar **7** chagrin, painful, pitiful, unhappy **8** contrite, grievous, mournful, penitent, wretched **9** afflicted, chagrined, miserable, mortified, regretful, worthless **10** apologetic, melancholy, remorseful **12** contemptible, disappointed

sort: ilk, set, way **4** cull, gere, kind, part, race, rank, sift, suit, type **5** adapt, allot, batch, befit, breed, class, genus, grade, group, order **6** adjust, assign, garble, gender, manner, nature, punish, screen, select **7** arrange, conform, fashion, quality, species, stripes, variety **8** classify, separate **9** character **10** collection, distribute **11** accommodate, description

sorted: **6** chosen **8** assorted, selected **9** separated **10** classified

sortie: **4** knot **5** foray, sally **6** attack

sortilege: **7** sorcery **8** witchery **11** enchantment

sosh: jag **4** dash **5** drunk **11** intoxicated
soso: bad **4** poor **6** medium, unwell **8** mediocre, middling, passable **9** tolerable **11** indifferent
sot: 4 fool, lush **5** fixed, toper, waste **6** befool, guzzle, tipple **7** dastard, stupefy, tippler, tosspot **8** drunkard, squander, stubborn **9** immovable, inebriate, obstinate, simpleton, swillbowl **10** winebibber
sottish: 4 dull **6** stupid **7** doltish, drunken, foolish **9** senseless
sotto: 5 below, under
sotto voce: 5 aside **6** weakly **7** faintly **9** privately **13** in an undertone
soubise: 5 sauce
soubrette: 4 maid, role **7** actress **11** entertainer, maidservant
soucar: 6 banker **8** merchant, straight **9** honorable
souchong: tea
sough: die, sob **4** moan, sigh, whiz **5** chant, ditch, drain, rumor, whizz **6** murmur, report **7** breathe, moaning, whistle **8** singsong **9** murmuring
soul: ame, God, ker **4** alma **5** atman, being, force, heart, human, psyche, saint **6** dibbuk, esprit, fervor, leader, pneuma, spirit **7** courage, essence **8** inspirer **10** embodiment, heartiness, individual **11** anilopyrine **15** personification
   loss: **9** perdition
   personification: **6** Psyche
soulless: 5 brute
sound: cry, din **4** birr, blow, bray, firm, good, hail, hale, rime, safe, sane, seem, test, tone, true **5** alarm, blare, bruit(F.), chang, clang, fresh, grope, hoddy, inlet, legal, loyal, noise, plumb, probe, rhyme, solid, valid, whole **6** bedlam, bratte, clamor, entire, fathom, hearty, honest, hubbub, intact, measure, outcry, racket, report, robust, secure, stable, steven, strong, sturdy, tumult, uproar **7** bluster, clamour, clangor, clatter, clitter, clutter, declare, earshot, examine, explore, feel out, healthy, hearing, measure, perfect, sonance, sputter **8** complete, flawless, orthodox, profound, rational, reliable, shouting, splutter, thorough **9** honorable, undamaged **10** dependable, hullabaloo, scrutinize **11** arm of the sea, trustworthy, undisturbed
   amorous: coo
   atonic: **4** surd
   beating drum: **8** rataplan
   bell-like: **4** ding **5** clang, knell **6** tinkle
   breathing: **4** rale **5** snore
   bullet: zip **4** ping
   buzzing: **4** whiz **5** whirr, whizz
   cat's: mew **4** meow, mewl, purr
   contemptuous: **5** snort

   contented: **4** purr
   derisive: boo **7** catcall
   detection instrument: **10** hydrophone
   discordant: **6** jangle **9** cacophony
   distinctive: **6** timbre
   donkey's: **4** bray **6** heehaw
   dove's murmuring: **4** curr
   drum: **4** roll, tuck
   dry leaves: **6** rustle
   dull: **4** thud **5** clonk
   elephant's: **4** roar **7** trumpet
   engine: **4** chug, ping
   explosive: pop **4** bang, boom, clap, roar **5** blast **6** report
   guttural: **4** burr **5** grunt
   harsh: **4** bray **5** creak, twang **9** cacophony
   high-pitched: **4** ping, ting
   hissing: zip **4** siss
   hoarse: caw **4** bray
   in doctrine: **8** orthodox
   in mind: **4** sane
   insect's: **5** chirr
   jingling: **16** tintinnabulation
   light: **5** swish **7** pitapat
   loud: **4** boom, peal **5** blare, clang
   magnifying device: **9** megaphone **11** loudspeaker
   measurement of: bel
   menacing: **5** growl, snarl
   mentally: **4** sane **5** lucid **6** normal
   metallic: **4** ping, ting **5** clang, clank **6** tinkle
   monotonous: hum **4** moan **5** drone
   mournful: sob
   murmuring: **4** purr **5** groan
   musical: **4** note
   nasal: **5** snore, whine **7** stridor
   of bell: **4** ding
   of disapproval: bah, boo **4** hiss **7** catcall
   of drinking: **4** glub
   of hoofbeat: **4** clop
   of horn: **7** tantara
   of pain: **4** moan, ouch, yell **5** groan
   or rising birds: **5** whirr
   of surf: **4** rote
   pert. to: **5** tonal **6** sonant **10** acoustical
   pleasing in: **8** euphonic
   repeated: **4** echo
   respiratory: **4** rale
   ringing: **5** clang **8** tinnitus
   rustling: **8** froufrou
   shallow: **6** lagoon, laguna, lagune
   shrill: **5** reedy, skirl
   sibilant: **4** hiss, siss
   small: **4** peep
   solemn: **4** peal
   speech: **5** vowel **8** phonetic
   splashing: **5** swash
   syllabic: **6** sonant
   throat: **8** guttural
   transposition: **10** spoonerism
   trumpet: **5** blare **7** clarion

unvaried: **8** monotone
vibrant: **4** birr
vocal: **4** tone **6** hiccup **8** hiccough
warning: **5** alarm **6** alarum, tocsin
water: **4** klop, rote **5** plash, swish **6** splash
whispering: **8** susurrus
whizzing: **4** ping **5** swish
yelping: yip
sounded: **4** blew, rang, rung **5** oaten **6** tooted **7** clanged **8** syllabic
sounding: **6** sonant **8** plangent, resonant, snorous, strident **9** bombastic **11** mellisonant **12** grandisonant, grandisonous
soundless: **4** deep **5** quiet **6** silent **9** noiseless **10** bottomless **12** unfathomable
soundly: **6** deeply **7** healthy **8** securely **9** violently **10** completely, forcefully, profoundly, thoroughly
soundness: wit **5** truth **6** sanity **8** lucidity, solidity, strength **9** integrity, rectitude, stability **10** heartiness **11** healthiness
sound off: **7** speak up **8** speak out
sound out: **5** study **7** explore **11** investigate
sounds: *having melody and rhythm:* **5** music
succession of: **4** peal
vocal symbols: **6** sonant
soup: **5** broth, puree, shchi, slash, stchi **6** borsch, borsht, oxtail **7** chowder, garbure, shtchee **8** consomme, gazpacho **11** predicament **12** mulligatawny **13** bouillabaisse
dish: **6** tureen
ingredient: **4** lalo, okra **7** noodles
spoon: **5** ladle
thick: **4** bisk **5** hoosh, puree **6** bisque, burgoo **7** burgout, pottage **8** minestra **10** minestrone
thickener: **7** tapioca
thin: **5** broth **8** consomme
soupcon: **4** hint **5** taste, trace **7** modicum, portion **8** particle **9** suspicion **10** suggestion
sour: bad, wry **4** acid, dour, grim, hard, tart **5** acerb, acrid, cross, eager, gruff **6** acetic, bitter, cruety, morose, sullen **7** acetose, acetous, acidify, austere, crabbed, painful, peevish **8** acerbate, acescent, embitter **9** acidulate, acidulent, acidulous, fermented **10** afflictive, astringent, ill humored, unpleasant **11** distasteful **12** disagreeable
source: **4** fons, font, germ, head, rise, root, seed **5** fount **6** ascent, origin, parent, spring **7** edition **8** fountain, wellhead **9** beginning **10** wellspring **12** fountainhead
of contrary action: **7** reagent
of gum arabic: **6** acacia

of income: **7** revenue
of indigo: **4** anil
of inspiration: **4** Muse
of iodine: **4** kelp
of knowledge: **7** organon
of metal: ore
of phosphorus: **7** apatite
of vitamin C: **6** citrus, orange
of vitamin E: **5** grain
primary: **4** root **5** radix
sourdine: **5** muted **7** subdued
sourdough: **6** leaven **7** settler **10** prospector
sourness: **7** acidity **8** acerbity, acrimony, asperity **10** moroseness **16** disagreeableness
sourpuss: **5** crank **6** grouch **8** sorehead **10** complainer
soursop: **4** tree **9** guanabana
souse, souce, sowce, sowse: ear, jag, wet **4** blow, cuff, duck, fall, prop, soak, wash **5** bathe, brine, douse, drink, swoop, thump **6** drench, pickle, plunge, pounce, strike, thwack **7** heavily, immerse, tippler **8** clumsily, drunkard, saturate, steeping, submerge **9** drenching
soutache: **5** braid **8** trimming
soutane: **5** cloak **7** cassock, zimarra
South: (see also **Confederacy**): **5** Dixie
crop: **6** cotton **7** tobacco
dish: **4** okra **5** gumbo **7** hoecake
inlet: **5** bayou
novelist: **5** Welty **8** Faulkner
South Africa: *animal:* das **5** nenta **8** suricate
antelope: gnu **5** eland, leche, oribi, peele **6** lechee, lechwe, rhebok **7** blaubok, blesbok, boshbok, grysbok, rheeboc, rheebok, sassaby **8** blesbuck, bontebok, boschbok
armadillo: **4** para
ass: **6** quagga
assembly: **4** raad
aunt: **5** tanta
bay: **5** Algoa, False
blaubok: **5** etaac
breastwork: **6** scherm
bushman: **4** Qung
camp: **5** lager **6** laager
capital: **8** Cape Town, Pretoria
caterpillar: **6** risper
cattle enclosure: **5** kraal
city: **6** Durban **9** Germiston **12** Bloemfontein, Johannesburg
cliff: **4** klip
club: **10** knobkerrie
coin: **4** cent, pond, rand **6** florin
colonist: **4** Boer
conference: **6** indaba
cony: das
corn: **5** mealy **6** mealie
council: **4** raad

criminal: **8** amalaita
desert: **8** Kalahari
dialect: **4** Taal
diamond: **4** jager **9** schlenter
Dutch: **4** Boer, Taal
Dutch speech: **9** Afrikaans
ferry: **4** pont
foreigner: **9** uitlander
fox: **4** asse **5** caama
garment: **6** caross, kaross
gazelle: **9** springbok
goldfield: **4** rand
government: **8** republic
grass country: **4** veld **5** veldt
greenhorn: **5** ikona
gully: **5** donga
gun: **4** roer
hill: kop **8** spitzkop
hillock: **5** kopje
hippopotamus: **6** zeekoe
hog: **9** boschvark
hut: **8** rondavel, rondawel
javelin: **7** assagai
laborer: **4** togt
leader: **5** Botha, Smuts **7** Vorster **8** Ver-
woerd
legislative assembly: **4** raad
lowland: **4** vlei, vley
monetary unit: **4** rand
monkey: **4** vervet **8** talapoin
mountain: kop **9** Swartberg
native: **5** Bantu **7** Swahili **9** Hottentot
pass: nek
pasture: **5** veldt
people: **4** Xosa **5** Bantu, Namas, Pondo **6**
Damara **7** Swahili **8** Bechuana **9** Hottentot
plain: **5** veldt
plant: **4** aloe
plot: erf
polecat: **6** musang
policeman: **4** zarp
province: **4** Cape **5** Natal **9** Transvaal
race: see *people* above
racial policy: **9** apartheid
region: **5** congo
river: **4** Vaal **6** Molopo, Orange **7** Limpopo
rodent: **5** ratel
settler: **4** Boer
shrub: **6** protea
simpleton: **5** ikona
snake: **5** elaps **8** eggeater
spirit: **8** tikolosh
starling: **5** sprew **7** spreeuw
stream: aar
sumac: **6** karree
throng: **4** reim **7** riempie
tick: **6** tampan
tract: **9** zuurveldt
trader: **7** Swahili
tree: **5** tenio **7** assagai **8** gamdeboo

tribe: see *people* above
village: **5** kraal
warrior: **4** impi
weaverbird: **4** taha
whip: **7** sjambok
South African: 4 Boer **9** Afrikaner **10**
Afrikander
South America: *animal:* **4** paca **5** coati,
coypu, llama, sloth, tapir **6** alpaca, jaguar, nutria, vicuna **8** anteater **9** armadillo
ant: **5** sauba, sauva
anteater: **7** tamandu
arbor: **6** ramada
armadillo: **4** apar **7** tatouay **10** pichiciago
arrow poison: **6** curara, curare
balsam: **4** tolu
beast of burden: **5** llama
beef: **6** tasajo
beverage: **4** mate
bird: **4** aura, guan, mitu, myna, rara, taha,
yeni **5** agami, arara, chaja, mynah **6**
barber, barbet **7** aracari, jacamar, oilbird, seriema, tinamou **8** bellbird, boatbill, curassow, guacharo, puffbird,
screamer, terutero
blanket: **6** serape
boat: **6** cayuco
cactus: **7** airampo
catfish: **5** dorad
cattle ranch: **8** estancia **9** estantion
country: **4** Peru **5** Chile **6** Brazil, Guyana
7 Bolivia, Ecuador, Surinam, Uruguay
8 Colombia, Paraguay **9** Argentina,
Patagonia, Venezuela
cowboy: **6** gaucho **7** llanero, planero
cowboy's weapon: **5** bolas
dance: **5** mambo, samba **6** cha-cha
deer: **6** guemal, guemul
dove: **9** talpacoti
duck: **7** muscovy
estuary: **4** para **5** Plata
fish: **4** paru **6** aimara, carbie **7** scalare **8**
arapaima
fox: **4** asse
game: **6** pelota
garment: **6** serape
gold: oro
griddle cake: **5** arepa
hare: **6** tapeti
hawk: **8** caracara
herb: **9** romerillo
herdsman: **7** llanero
Indian: Ges, Ona **5** Auca, Inca, Tama **5**
Carib, Tapas **6** Arawak, Jivaro **7** Caya-
pos, Goyanas, Guatoan, Pampero, Tapuyan **8** Camacans, Coroados, Timbiras
9 Caingangs, Chavantes **10** Patagonian
Indian hut: **5** toldo
Indian medicine man: **4** peai **6** shaman
Indian poison: **6** curara, curare, curari
island: **5** Aruba

knife: **7** machete **8** machette
language: Ona **7** Spanish **9** Portugese
lapwing: **8** terutero
liberator: **7** Bolivar
limestone: **5** tosca
liquor: **6** chicha
lizard: **4** teju **5** coati
lowlands: **6** llanos, pampas, selvas
mammal: ai **4** paca **5** coati, llama, tapir **6** alpaca, guanco **8** kinkajou, pacarana **10** coati-mondi, coati-mundi
marmoset: **7** tamarin
measure: **4** vara **7** manzana
mineral: **4** urso
monkey: sai **4** saki, titi **5** acari, araba **6** grison, teetee **7** ouakari, sapajou **8** marmoset, orabassu **9** barrigudo, beelzebub
mountains: **5** Andes **6** Acarai, Parima
native: **5** Carib
opossum: **5** quica **7** sarigue
ostrich: **4** rhea
palm: **5** assai, bussu, datil, troly **6** tooroo, ubussu **7** troolie
parrot: **5** macaw
plain: **5** llano, pampa
plains dweller: **7** llanero
plant: **6** ipecac **8** crassula **10** tillandsia
porridge: **5** atole
rabbit: **6** tapeti
raccoon: **5** coati **10** coatimundi
rain forest: **5** selva
rancher: **10** estanciero
river: **4** Para **5** Plata **6** Amazon **7** Orinoco
rodent: **4** degu, mara, paca **5** coypu **6** agouti, agouty **8** viscacha, vizcacha **10** chinchilla
root: oca
rubber tree: **4** para
ruminant: **5** llama **6** alpaca
scarf: **5** manta
serpent: **5** aboma
shrub: **4** coca
slaughterhouse: **11** frigorifico
snake: bom **4** lora **5** aboma **8** anaconda **10** bushmaster
sorrel: oca
stock: Ona
strait: **8** Magellan
tapir: **5** danta
tiger cat: **5** chati
toucan: **4** toco **7** aracari
tree: **4** fotu, lana, mora, para, vera **5** balsa, cacao, cebil, couma, pekea **6** chicha, simaba, yachan **7** bebeeru, quayabi **9** balaustre, couvatari **11** chichicaste
tribe: Ona
trumpeter: **5** agami
tuber: oca
turtle: **8** matamata
vulture: **6** condor
walnut: **9** conacaste

weapon: **4** bola **5** bolas
wild cat: **4** eyra
wind: **7** pampero
South American: 5 Latin
South Australia: See **Australia**
South Carolina: *capital:* **8** Columbia
city: **8** Rock Hill **10** Charleston, Greenville **11** Spartanburg
county: Lee **4** York **5** Horry, Union **6** Dillon, Oconee
dam: **6** Santee **9** Pinopolis
fort: **6** Sumter
island: **4** Bull **6** Edisto, Klawah, Parris **10** Hilton Head
motto: **13** Dum spiro spero (While I breathe, I hope)
mountain: **9** Sassafras
nickname: **8** Palmetto
resort: **10** Hilton Head
river: **6** Peedee, Saluda, Santee
state bird: **4** wren
state flower: **7** jasmine
state tree: **8** palmetto
South Dakota: *capital:* **6** Pierre
city: **8** Aberdeen **9** Rapid City **10** Sioux Falls
county: Day **4** Clay, Hand, Hyde, Lake, Todd **5** Bruel, Deuel, Tripp
Indian: **5** Brule, Sioux **6** Dakota
lake: **4** Oahe **8** Bigstone, Traverse
mine: **9** Homestake
mountain: **10** Black Hills
national monument: **10** Mt. Rushmore
river: **5** James **7** Big Bend, Randall **8** Missouri
state bird: **8** pheasant
state flower: **12** pasqueflower
state tree: **6** spruce
South India: See **India**
South Korea: *capital:* **5** Seoul
city: **5** Pusan, Taegu **6** Inchon
monetary unit: Won
South Pacific: See **South Sea**
South Pole: See **Antarctica**
South Sea: *canoe:* **4** proa
island: **4** Bali, Fiji, Sulu **5** Samoa, Tonga **6** Tahiti **7** Society **8** Pitcairn **9** New Guinea
island drink: ava
island money: **6** wakiki
islander: **5** Maori **6** Kanaka, Samoan **10** Melonesian, Polynesian **11** Micronesian
plant: **4** taro
product: **5** copra
sea: **5** Coral **6** Tasman
staple: **4** taro
South Vietnam (see also **Vietnam**): *capital:* **6** Saigon
guerillas: **8** Vietcong
holiday: Tet
monetary unit: **7** piastre

river: **6** Mekong
woman's garb: **5** aodai
south wind: 5 notus **6** auster
South Wind author: 7 Douglas
Southeast Asia (see also **Asia**)**: 4** Laos, Siam **5** Burma **6** Ceylon **7** Vietnam **8** Cambodia, Malaysia, Pakistan, Thailand **9** Indonesia **10** Bangladesh **11** Philippines
southeast wind: 5 eurus
southern: 7 austral
Southern dish: See **South:** *dish*
Southern France: 4 Midi
Southwest: *cowboy:* **7** llanero
   Indian: **4** Cree
southwest wind: 8 libeccio
southwester: *hat* **4** gale **5** squam, storm
souvenir: 5 curio, relic **6** memory **7** memento **8** keepsake, reminder **11** remembrance **12** recollection
sovereign: 4 coin, free, king **5** chief, liege, queen, royal, ruler **6** couter, Mikado, prince **7** emperor, empress, highest, monarch, supreme **8** autocrat, greatest, princely, reigning, superior, suzerain **9** effectual, excellent, governing, paramount, potentate **10** omnipotent **11** controlling, efficacious, independent
   petty: **8** tetrarch
sovereign power: 6 throne
sovereign prerogative claim: 11 seigniorage
sovereignty: 4 rule, sway **5** realm **6** diadem, empery, empire, status, throne **7** dynasty, majesty, scepter, sceptre **8** dominion **9** supremacy **10** ascendancy, ascendency, domination
   absolute: **8** autarchy
   joint: **11** condominium
soviet: 7 council, Russian **9** committee
Soviet Union (see also **Russia**)**: 4** USSR
   administrative committee: **9** presidium
   founder: **5** Lenin
   government farm: **7** sovkhos, sovkhoz **8** sovkhose
   hero: **5** Lenin **6** Stalin
   money: **5** ruble
   news agency: **4** Tass
   newspaper: **5** Pravda **8** Izvestia
   republic: **5** Uzbek **6** Latvia **7** Armenia, Georgia, Kirghiz, Turkmen, Ukraine
   secret police: KGB **4** NKVD, OGPU
sow: *hog, pig* **4** heap, seed, shed **5** ditch, drain, drill, plant, stack, strew, swine **6** runner, sluice, spread **7** channel, furnish, grumphy, implant, scatter **8** disperse, grumphie **9** broadcast, inoculate **10** salamander **11** disseminate
   wild: **8** javelina
   young: elt **4** gilt
sower: 7 seedman
   of dragon's teeth: **6** Cadmus

soy bean: 4 soja, soya
soya: 4 dill **6** fennel **7** soybean
spa: 5 oasis, oases **6** resort, spring **8** Saratoga **10** sanatorium **12** health resort
   place: Ems **4** Bath **5** Baden **8** Karlsbad
space: gap **4** area, path, rank, roam, room, rove, void, walk **5** ambit, plena(pl.), range, track **6** course, divide, extent, plenum, region **7** areolae, arrange, expanse **8** capacity, distance, duration, interval, quantity **11** reservation **14** accommodations
   agency: **4** NASA
   architectural: **8** pediment
   between eyes: **4** lore
   between two intersecting lines: **5** angle
   between two points: **8** distance
   blank: **6** lacuna **7** lacunae(pl.)
   breathing: **6** recess
   cleared: **5** glade
   coin: **7** exergue
   docking: **6** linkup
   empty: **4** void **5** blank, inane **6** vacuum
   forest: **5** glade
   hallowed: **7** mortice, mortise
   included: **8** contents
   limitless: **8** infinite
   occupied: **6** volume
   of time: **8** interval
   on surface: **4** area
   partitioned: **4** room
   pert. to: **5** areal
   portion of: **5** place
   safekeeping: **7** storage
   secluded: **6** alcove
   small: **6** areola, areole **7** aerolae
   storage: **4** shed **5** attic **6** cellar **9** storeroom, warehouse
   void: **5** chasm **7** inanity
   wall: **5** niche
   white: **6** margin
space full of matter: 6 plenum
space theory: 7 plenism
spacecraft: 6 rocket **9** satellite
   decision: **6** go-no-go
   first: **7** Sputnik
   part: **6** module **7** capsule
   to moon: **6** Apollo
   slowdown: **7** deboost
spaced out: 4 high **5** doped **6** stoned, zonked **7** drugged
spaceman: 9 astronaut, cosmonaut
spacer: bar
spacious: 4 vast **5** ample, broad, great, large, rangy, roomy **9** capacious, expansive, extensive **13** comprehensive
spad: 4 nail
spadassin: 5 bravo **7** duelist **9** swordsman
spade: dig **5** graft **6** shovel **11** playing card
   Irish: **5** slane
   kind of: **6** scavel

narrow: loy
plasterer's: **6** server
sharp: **4** spud
triangular: **5** didle
turf: **5** slane
spaghetti: 5 pasta
spahi, spahee: 7 cavalry
Spain: 6 Espana, Iberia
adventurer: **9** almogaver
ancient name: **8** Hispania
article: las, los, una
aunt: tia
author: **9** Cervantes
bayonet: **5** yucca
beach: **5** playa
belle: **4** maja
blanket: **6** serape
boat: **5** aviso
brandy: **11** aguardiente
bull: **4** toro
cape: **9** Trafalgar
capital: **6** Madrid
cart: **7** carreta **8** carretta
cathedral city: **7** Seville
cedar: **6** acajou
celery: **4** apio
cellist: **6** Casals
champion: Cid
channel: **4** Cano
chaperone: **6** duenna
cheer: ole
city: **6** Bilbao, Malaga **7** Granada, Seville **8** Valencia **9** Barcelona, Saragossa
clerk: **11** escribiente
cloak: **4** capa **5** manta **6** mantle
coat: **7** zamarra, zamarro
coin: **5** dobla **6** cuarto, doblon, peseta **7** Alfonso, centimo, piaster **8** cuartino **9** cuartillo
conqueror: Cid **7** Pizarro **12** conquistador
contract: **7** asiento **8** assiento
council: **5** junta
count: **5** conde
dance: **4** jota **5** danza, tango **6** bolero, gitano **8** fandango, saraband **9** zapateado **10** seguidilla
dish: **6** posole
district: **5** Xeres
dollar: **4** duro, peso, pezo **7** piaster, piastre
dumpling: **6** tamale
earth: **6** tierra
exclamation: **6** carajo **7** caramba
execution: **7** garotte, garrote **8** garrotte
explorer: **7** Mendoza **8** Coronado
fabric: **5** tiraz
fleet: **6** armada
former leader: **6** Franco
friend: **5** amigo
frigate: **5** zabra
game: **5** omber **6** pelota **7** jai-alai
gentleman: don **5** senor **9** caballero

god: **4** dios
goddess: **5** Diosa
gold: oro
governor: **10** idelantado
grass: **5** spart **7** esparto
greeting: **4** hola
griddlecake: **5** arepa
gunboat: **5** barca
gypsy: **7** zincalo
hall: **4** sala
head covering: **8** mantilla
herdsman: **8** ranchero
hero: Cid **8** Palmerin
hill: **5** cerro, morro
holiday: **6** fiesta
horse: **7** caballo
hotel: **5** venta **6** posada
house: **4** casa
instrument: **8** castanet, zambomba
island: **5** Ibiza **7** Majorca, Minorca
island group: **6** Canary **8** Balearic
judge: **7** alcalde
kettle: **4** cazo
king: rey
kingdom: **4** Leon **6** Aragon **7** Castile
lady: **4** dona **6** senora
lagoon: **6** laguna
lake: **4** lago
lariat: **5** reata, riata
leather: **8** cordovan
legislature: **6** cortes
letter: **5** carta
letter carrier: **6** correo
linen cloth: **4** crea
lute: **7** vihuela
magic: **8** brujeria
man: don **6** hombre
mausoleum: **8** Escorial
mayor: **6** alcade **7** alcalde
measure: pie **4** codo, copa, dedo, moyo, paso, vara **5** aroba, braza, cafiz, cahiz, legua, linea, medio, milla, palmo, sesma **6** cordel, cuarta, estado, fanega, league, racion, yugada **7** azumbre, cantara, celemin, estadel, pulgada **8** aranzada, fanegada **9** cuarteron, cuartilla, cuartillo **10** caballeria
miss: **8** senorita
monetary unit: **6** peseta
monk: **5** padre
mountain: **8** Asturian, Pyrenees **9** Mulahacem **10** Cantabrian, Guardarrama, Pic de Netou **11** La Maladetta **12** Sierra Morena, Sierra Nevada **14** Sierra de Toledo
mouth: **4** boca
muleteer: **7** arriero
native: **7** Catalan, Iberian
nobleman: don **7** grandee, hidalgo
now: **5** ahora
nun: **6** Teresa
officer: **8** alguacil, alguazil

operetta: **8** zarzuela
other: **4** otro
oyster: **5** pinna
painter: **4** Cano, Dali, Goya, Miro, Sert **6** Ribera **7** El Greco, Murillo, Picasso, Zuloaga **9** Velasquez
palace: **8** Escorial
pancake: **5** arepa
parliament: **6** cortes
pear: **7** avocado
peasant: **7** paisano
peninsula: **6** Iberia
pepper: **5** chili **7** pimento
pickpocket: **6** ratero
plant: aji
poet: **6** Encina
porridge: **5** atole
port: **5** Palos
post office: **6** correo
pot: **4** olla
priest: **4** cura **5** padre
promenade: **5** paseo
pronunciation mark: **5** tilde
province: **4** Jaen, Leon, Lugo, Vigo **5** Alava, Avila, Cadiz, Soria **6** Burgos, Coruna, Cuenca, Gerona, Huelva, Huesca, Lerida, Madrid, Malaga, Murcia, Orense, Oviedo, Teruel, Toledo, Zamora **7** Almeria, Badajoz, Caceres, Cordoba, Granada, Logrono, Navarra, Segovia, Seville, Vizcaya **8** Albacete, Alicante, Palencia, Valencia **9** Barcelona, Guipuscoa, Salamanca, Santander, Saragossa, Tarragona **10** Ciudad Real, Pontevedra, Valladolid **11** Guadalajara **15** Balearic Islands **18** Castellon de la Plana
raisin: **4** pasa
rice: **5** arroz
rider: **8** herisson
river: ria, rio **4** Ebro **5** Douro, Tagus **8** Guadiana **12** Guadalquivir
road: **6** camino
room: **4** sala
seaport: **4** Adra **5** Palos
sentinel: **5** vedet, videt **7** vedette, vidette
shawl: **5** manta **6** serape
sherry: **5** Xeres **11** Amontillado
silk: **5** tiraz
sorcerer: **5** brujo
south: sur
stanza: **10** seguidilla
street: **5** calle
sword: **5** bilbo
tax: **8** alcabala
title: don **5** senor **6** senora **7** hidalgo **8** senorita
tomorrow: **6** manana
town: **4** Irun, Jaen, Leon, Olot **5** Cadiz, Gijon, Lorca, Ronda, Siero, Xeres **6** Murcia, Toledo **7** Cordoba, Cordova, Granada **8** Zaragoza **9** Cartagena, Sala-

manca, Santander **10** Carthagena, Valladolid **17** Jerez de la Frontera
trail: **6** camino
trefoil: **7** alfalfa, lucerne
uncle: tio
vase: **4** urna
vehicle: **7** tartana
very: muy
victory cry: ole
watchword: **6** alerta
water: **4** agua
watercourse: **6** arroyo
weight: **4** onza **5** frail, grano, libra, marco, tomin **6** adarme, arroba, dinero, dracma, ochava **7** arienzo, quilate, quintal **8** caracter, tonelada **9** escrupulo **10** castellano
white: **6** blanco
wind: **6** solano
window: **7** ventana
witchcraft: **8** brujeria
woman: **6** senora
spalpeen: boy, fop, lad **5** scamp **6** rascal **7** laborer, workman **8** braggart **9** youngster
spall: **4** chip, fall **5** break **6** reduce **7** breakup, crumble **8** fragment, shoulder
spalt: **4** chip, tear **5** crisp, split **7** brittle
span: **4** arch, cock, pair, rope, swim, team, time **5** cover, grasp, reach, seize **6** attach, bridge, extend, fasten, fetter, hobble, length, period, spread **7** confine, matched, measure, stretch **8** distance, duration, encircle **9** encompass, perfectly **10** completely
spancel: tie **4** clog **6** fetter, hobble
spang: **4** bang, hurl, jump, kick, leap, yoke **5** clasp, crack **6** stride **7** ·spangle **8** abruptly, directly, ornament, straight
spangle: set **4** boss **5** adorn, aglet, gleam, plate **6** aiglet, sequin, zequin **7** glisten, glitter, sparkle **8** ornament, sprinkle, zecchino
Spaniard: **5** Latin **7** Espanol **9** Castilian
imaginary: **9** Espriella
spaniel: **5** trasy **6** cocker, punish **8** springer **9** sycophant
spank: **4** prat, slap, whip **6** strike **7** reprove **8** chastise
spanker: **4** sail
spanking: new **4** fine **5** brisk, fresh, large, stout **6** lively, strong **7** dashing **8** vigorous
spanner: **6** wrench
spar: bar, box, rod **4** beam, bolt, boom, gaff, mast, pole, raft, rung, shut, yard **5** close, fight, lever, lunge, sprit, steve **6** barite, bicker, charge, fasten, rafter, strike, thrust, timber **7** contend, contest, dispute, enclose, quarrel, wrangle, yardarm **8** dolomite, lazulite
end: **7** yardarm

spare: 4 bear, free, gain, hain, lean, part, save, slim, slit, slow, stop, thin **5** avoid, chary, extra, favor, gaunt, grant, lanky, stint **6** desist, endure, exempt, favour, frugal, let off, meager, scanty, scrimp **7** deprive, forbear, forgive, haggard, leisure, opening, placket, refrain, relieve, reserve, sparing **8** dilatory, forebear, preserve, tolerate **9** duplicate, parsimony **10** substitute **11** replacement, superfluous **12** parsimonious

spare time: 7 leisure

sparge: 6 splash **7** moisten **8** sprinkle **9** bespatter

sparing: 5 chary, gnede, scant **6** frugal, meager, saving, scanty **7** careful, limited, thrifty **8** merciful, reticent, stinting **9** scrimping **11** tightfisted **12** parsimonious

spark: arc, woo **4** beau, funk, soil **5** aizle, belle, blade, court, flash, grain, light, lover **7** diamond, gallant, sparkle, spatter **8** motivate, sparklet **9** scintilla **10** sweetheart **11** scintillate

igniting property: **11** incendivity

sparked: 5 arced **7** courted, spotted **8** streaked **10** variegated

sparker: 5 lover **7** gallant **8** firework

sparkle: 5 blink, flash, gleam, glent, glint, shine, spark, strew, trace **6** bubble **7** diffuse, glisten, glitter, radiate, reflect, scatter, showing, spangle **8** disperse, sprinkle, vivacity **9** coruscate **10** effervesce, illuminate, liveliness **11** coruscation, scintillate **13** scintillation

sparkling: 4 dewy **5** crisp, witty **6** bright, lively, starry **7** shining **8** animated, eloquent, flashing, gleaming **9** brillante, brilliant, twinkling **10** glittering, reflecting **12** effervescent, effervescing

sparoid fish: 4 scup **5** porgy **10** sheepshead

sparrer: 5 boxer **7** sparrow

sparrow: 7 chanter

sparse: 4 thin **5** scant **6** meager, meagre, scanty **7** scatter **8** disperse **9** scattered **10** distribute, infrequent

Sparta: *army:* **4** mora

bondman: **5** helot

commander: **7** lochage

country: **7** Laconia

dog: **10** bloodhound

enemy: **6** Athens

festival: **6** Carnea **7** Carneia

governor: **7** harmost

king: **8** Leonidas, Menelaus **9** Tyndareus

lawgiver: **8** Lycurgus

magistrate: **5** ephor

method of cipher writing: **7** scytale

native: **8** Laconian

queen: **4** Leda **5** Helen

serf: **5** helot

tyrant: **5** Nabis

spartan: 5 brave, hardy **6** frugal, heroic, severe **7** laconic **9** undaunted **10** courageous

spasm: fit, tic **4** grip **5** crick **6** frenzy **7** seizure **8** paroxysm **10** convulsion **11** contraction

muscle: **5** cramp

of distress: **4** pang

of pain: **5** throe

spasmodic: 6 fitful, sudden **7** snatchy, violent **9** excitable **12** intermittent

disease: **7** tetanus

spat: row **4** blow, clap, fuss, slap, tiff **5** eject **6** gaiter, oyster, splash, strike **7** dispute, legging, quarrel

spate: 4 gush, rain **5** flood **6** throng **7** freshet, outflow, torrent **8** cataract **9** overwhelm, rainstorm **10** waterspout

spatial: 5 areal **6** steric **8** sterical

spatter: jet **4** dash, drop, soil, spot **5** slart, spurt **6** dabble, defame, injure, splash, spread **7** scatter, spatule, sputter **8** splutter, sprinkle

spatterdash: 6 gaiter **7** legging

spatula: 4 tool **5** spade **6** thible

spatulate: 6 lyrate **11** spoon-shaped

spawn: roe **4** eggs, germ, seed, sire, spot **5** fungi **6** bulbis, source **7** cormels, deposit, produce **8** generate, mycelium **9** procreate

ascending river to: **10** anadromous

spay: 4 geld **8** castrate **9** sterilize

speak: say **4** carp, chat, hail, talk, tell **5** extol, honor, orate, utter **6** remark, reveal **7** address, bespeak, declaim, declare, deliver, express, publish **8** converse, harangue, manifest, proclaim **9** celebrate, discourse, pronounce **10** articulate

affectedly: **4** mimp **5** mince

against: **6** oppose

at length: **7** dissert **9** expatiate

curtly: **4** snap, birk

evasively: **5** hedge, stall

for: **6** defend **7** testify

foolishly: **5** prate **6** drivel

from memory: **6** recite

hesitantly: **7** stammer

imperfectly: **4** lisp **7** stutter

impulsively: **5** blurt

in undertone: **6** mumble, murmur

inability to: **6** alalia, mutism **7** aphasia **8** aglossia

incoherently: **6** gabble, gibber

noisily: **4** fume, rant, rave

of: **4** call **7** mention

offhand: **11** extemporize

oracularly: **11** pontificate

out: **6** affirm

pert. to: **10** oratorical

profusely: **6** dilate **7** palaver

rapidly: **5** troll **6** patter **8** splutter
rhetorically: **5** orate **7** declaim
slightingly: **8** backbite **9** disparage
slowly: **5** drawl
softly: **7** whisper
thoughtlessly: **4** blat **8** splutter
through nose: **9** nasillate
to: **5** greet **6** accost **7** address
under breath: **6** mumble, mutter
with interruption: haw, hem
speaker: **5** drone, sayer **6** lisper, orator, proser, ranter, talker **7** demagog, utterer **8** lecturer **9** demagogue, spokesman **10** mouthpiece, prolocutor **11** entertainer, spellbinder
inspired: **7** prophet
of many languagues: **8** linguist, polyglot
speaker's hammer: **5** gavel
speaking: *style:* **8** staccato, fluently
without preparation: **13** extemporizing
spear: gad, rod **4** dart, fram, reed, shut, spar, stab **5** apine, blade, lance, shoot, stalk **6** aprout, glaive, impale, pierce, strike **7** feather, harpoon, javelin, missile, trident **9** penetrate
grass: **5** blade
kind of: **4** gaff **5** gidia, gidya **6** bident, fizgig, gidgea, gidgee, gidjee, gidyea **7** assagai, assegai, bourdon, harpoon, leister, trident
three-pronged: **7** trident
spear-shaped: **7** hastate
spearfish: **8** billfish **9** swordfish
spearhead: **4** gaff, lead **6** direct **7** advance, precede
spearwort: **8** crowfoot
special: **4** dear, rare **5** chief, extra, local **6** unique **7** express, limited, notable, unusual **8** concrete, detailed, favorite, intimate, paramour, peculiar, personal, specific, uncommon **9** specially **10** especially, individual, noteworthy, particular, restricted **11** distinctive, exceptional **12** particularly **13** distinguished, extraordinary
ability: **6** talent
edition: **5** extra
specialist: *atomic:* **9** physicist
city planning: **8** urbanist
medical: (see also **doctor**): **7** oculist, surgeon **9** internist, otologist **11** neurologist, orthopedist **12** gynecologist, obstetrician, pediatrician **15** ophthalmologist
mineral: **12** mineralogist
money management: **9** economist
surgical: see **doctor**
specialty: bag **5** forte, skill **8** aptitude **13** particularity
specie: **4** cash, coin **5** money
species: **4** kind, race, sort, type **5** breed, brood, class, genre, image **7** mankind,

variety **8** category, humanity **9** spectacle **10** exhibition, reflection
modified by environment: **4** ecad
spider: **5** acera
various: **5** genus **6** genera
specific: **5** exact **7** precise, special **8** clearcut, concrete, definite, detailed, explicit, peculiar **10** particular, restricted, specifying **11** determinate
specifically: **6** namely **9** expressly, specially
specify: **4** name, tell **5** allot, state **6** assign, define, detail **7** itemize, mention **8** describe, nominate **9** designate, stipulate, enumerate **10** articulate
specimen: **4** mark **5** model, relic, token **6** cotype, sample, swatch **7** example, pattern **8** instance **11** examination **12** illustration
specious: gay **4** fair **5** false, showy **6** glossy, hollow **7** colored **8** coloured, illusory **9** colorable, plausible **10** ostensible **12** hypocritical
speck: bit, dot, nit **4** blot, iota, mark, mite, mote, spot, whit **5** glebe, stain **7** blemish, blubber **8** impurity, particle
speckle: dot **5** fleck **7** stipple
speckled: **6** menald **7** bracket
specs: **10** eyeglasses, spectacles
spectacle: **4** show **5** bysen, model, scene, sight **6** marvel, mirror **7** display, diorama, example, pageant, pattern **8** panorama, spyglass **9** cyclorama **10** exhibition **14** representation
structure for: **5** arena **7** stadium, theater, theatre **8** coliseum
spectacles: **7** glasses
part of: **6** bridge, temple
spectator: **4** eyer **6** espier **7** witness **8** beholder, kibitzer, looker-on, observer, onlooker
specter, spectre: **4** bogy **5** bogey, bogie, bogle, ghost, shade, spook **6** boggle, spirit, wraith **7** boggard, boggart, bugaboo, bugbear, phantom **8** boggle-bo, guytrash, illusion, phantasm, revenant **10** apparition
spectral: **6** ghosty, spooky **7** ghostly, phantom **12** apparitional **13** insubstantial
spectrum: **8** infrared **11** ultraviolet
colors: red **4** blue **5** green **6** indigo, violet, yellow
speculate: **5** guess, think **6** gamble, mirror, ponder, wonder **7** predict **8** consider, meditate, ruminate, theorize **10** conjecture, deliberate, philosophy **11** contemplate
speculation: **4** risk **6** bubble, vision **7** surmise **8** decision **9** guesswork, intuition **10** conclusion, conjecture
speculative: **5** risky **9** uncertain **11** theoretical

speculator: 7 gambler, lookout, scalper 8 explorer, observer, theorist 12 contemplator, investigator

speculum: 6 mirror 7 diopter

speech: 4 talk 5 idiom, voice, slang 6 dilogy, epilog, orison, steven, tongue 7 address, dialect, oration, oratory, vinegar 8 colloquy, epilogue, harangue, language 9 utterance 12 vocalization

abusive: 6 tirade

art: 8 rhetoric

bitter: 8 diatribe

blunder: 8 solecism

boastful: 7 bluster

bombastic: 8 harangue

conclusion: 10 peroration

defect: 4 lisp 6 alogia 7 stammer, stutter

denunciation: 5 frump 6 tirade 8 filippic 9 philippic

difficulty: 9 baryphony 10 baryphonia

element: 4 surd

expert: 9 phonetist

figure of: 5 irony, trope 6 aporia, simile 7 imagery 8 metaphor

goddess: Vac

hesitation: haw 7 stammer, stutter

impassioned: 6 tirade 9 dithyramb

insane: 9 bedlamism

local: 6 patois 7 dialect

long: 5 spiel

loss: 6 alalia 7 aphasia 8 muteness

part: 4 noun, verb 6 adverb 9 adjective 11 conjunction, preposition 12 interjection

peculiar: 5 idiom

provincial: 6 patois 7 dialect

readiness: 9 fecundity

religious: 6 sermon 9 preaching

representing: 8 phonetic

reserved: 8 reticent

summary: 5 notes

violent: 6 tirade

voiceless element: 4 surd 7 spirate

world language: 7 volapuk 9 esperanto

speechless: mum 4 dumb, mute 6 silent 9 voiceless

speed: hie, rip 4 drug, fare, flee, help, race, rate 5 haste, hurry 6 assist, career, gallop, hasten, profit, succor 7 execute, prosper 8 celerity, dispatch, expedite, rapidity, velocity 9 advantage, discharge, quickness, swiftness 10 accelerate, expedition, facilitate 12 precipitance

full: 5 amain

great: 4 zoom 5 haste, spurt, amain 6 career 9 posthaste

measuring device: 5 radar 8 odometer 10 tachymeter 11 speedometer, velocimeter

note: 4 time 5 clock

rate of: RPM 4 pace 5 tempo

ratio: 4 Mach

up: 6 hasten 8 catalyze

speeder: 5 racer 6 driver 11 accelerator

speedily: 4 fast, soon 5 apace 6 presto 7 betimes, hastily, quickly, rapidly 8 promptly 13 expeditiously

speedy: 4 fast 5 fleet, hasty, quick, rapid, swift 6 active, prompt 7 helpful 11 expeditious

spell: bar, peg 4 chip, form, lath, mean, rest, rung, save, tale, talk, tell, trap, turn, snap 5 brief, charm, curse, magic, relay, shift, spare, speak, spell, story, utter, weird, while 6 glamor, gospel, import, period, relate, relief, splint, trance, voodoo 7 bewitch, cantrip, compose, glamour, relieve, shaving, signify, sorcery, drought, syncope 8 pishogue, splinter 9 discourse 10 constitute, demonifuge 11 abracadabra, conjuration, enchantment, fascination 12 entrancement 13 orthographize, prognosticate, substitute for

in another alphabet: 13 transliterate

out: 7 clarify, develop, explain 9 interpret

spellbind: 5 orate 7 enchant, engross 8 enthrall 9 fascinate

speller (according to pronunciation): 9 phonetist 11 phoneticist

poor: 11 cacographer

spelt: 5 grain, wheat 6 cereal

spelter: 4 zinc

spencer: wig 4 coat 6 butler, jacket, pantry 7 buttery, steward, trysail

spend: run, use 4 blow, dash, flow, give, jump, pass, span 5 beset, exert, grasp, waste 6 attach, bestow, beware, devote, elapse, expend, fasten, lavish, lay out, manage, spread, spring, weaken 7 consume, exhaust, fatigue, perform 8 confound, disburse, squander 9 dissipate, sacrifice 10 distribute

wisely: 7 husband

spend the summer: 8 estivate

spendthrift: 6 waster 7 wastrel 8 prodigal, wasteful 10 dingthrift, profligate, squanderer

Spenserian character: Una

spent: 4 beat, paid, used 5 all in, weary 6 effete, wasted 7 worn out 8 lavished 9 exhausted 10 squandered

speos: 4 cave, tomb 6 grotto, temple

sperm: 4 germ, seed 5 semen

sperm whale: 8 cachalot

spet: 9 barracuda

spew, spue: bog 4 gush, ooze, spit 5 eject, exude, strew, vomit 7 extrude, flow out, scatter 8 disgorge

sphacelate: 7 decayed, mortify 8 withered

sphenic: 11 wedge-shaped

spheral: 7 perfect 10 harmonious 11 symmetrical

sphere: orb, sky 4 ball, rank, star 5 ambit,

arena, class, field, globe, orbit, order, range, scope **6** domain, orblet, planet **7** circuit, compass, heavens, stratum, station, theatre, terella **8** idiosome, position, province **9** idioblast **10** atmosphere, department, occupation **12** jurisdiction

of action: **5** arena

of influence: **5** orbit **14** balance of power

perforated: **4** bead

spheric: 8 globular **11** globe-shaped

spherical: 5 orbic, round **6** rotund **7** globate, globose, spatial **8** globated, globular, obrotund **9** globulous, orbicular

spheroid: 4 ball **5** earth

spherule: 7 globule, variole

sphinx: 6 enigma **7** monster, prophet **8** colossus, hawkmoth

land of: **5** Egypt

mother: **7** Echidna

query of: **6** riddle

site of: **4** Giza **5** Luxor

sphinxian: 10 mysterious **11** enigmatical, inscrutable

sphygmus: 5 pulse

spica: 4 star **7** bandage

spice: 4 dash, hint, kind, mace, mull, nard, odor, sort, vein **5** aroma, taste, touch **6** embalm, flavor, relish, season **7** modicum, perfume, portion, species, variety **8** quantity, specimen **9** admixture, condiment, fragrance, seasoning **10** appearance

kind of: **4** mace, mull, sage **5** anise, cumin, curry, thyme **6** cloves, fennel, ginger, nutmeg, pepper, stacte, tamara **7** caraway, cayenne, mustard, oregano, paprika, pimento **8** allspice, cinnamon, marjoram, pimiento, turmeric

mill: **5** quern

package for: **6** robbin

Spice Islands: See **Molucca islands**

spick-and-span: 4 neat, trim **5** clean, fresh **6** spruce **8** brand-new **11** well-groomed

spicknel: mew **8** bearwort

spicule: rod **4** dart, nail, toxa **5** aster, spine **6** actine **7** prickle, rhabdus **8** sclerite, spikelet

sponge: **5** cymba

spicy: hot **4** keen, racy **5** balmy, natty, showy, smart, sweet **6** active, risque **7** gingery, peppery, piquant, pungent **8** aromatic, fragrant, spirited **11** interesting

spider: bug, cob, cop, hub, pan **5** arain **6** eresid, epeira, snarer, tripod, trivet **7** pokomoo, skillet, retiary **8** arachnid, attercop, telarian **9** frying pan, tarantula **12** candleholder

family of: **7** attidae **9** drassidae **10** citigradae

genus of: **6** aranea, epeira

three-legged: **6** trivet

venomous: **9** tarantula **10** black widow

web-spinning organ: **9** spinneret

spider bug: 5 emesa

spider crab: 4 maia

spider monkey: 9 belzebuth

spider nest: web **5** nidus

spider web: 8 attercop

resembling: **9** arachnoid

spinner: **9** spinneret

spiel: 5 pitch

spieler: 5 crier **6** barker, talker **7** sharper, showman, speaker **8** lecturer, swindler **9** announcer **11** spellbinder

spiffy: 4 chic, neat **5** smart **6** spruce

spiflicate, spifflicate: 4 beat, kill **6** stifle **8** astonish, bewilder, confound

spigot: peg, pin, tap **4** cock, plug **5** spile, spout **6** dossil, faucet, pierce **7** stopper

spike: cut, cob, ear, gad **4** brob, chat, nail, stab, tine, umbo **5** ament, block, prong **6** antler, cereal, earlet, fasten, finish, impale, pierce, secure, thwart **7** bayonet, disable, fortify, trenail **8** mackerel, puncture **9** frustrate, merganser **10** spadix-tine **13** inflorescence

spikenard: 4 nard **8** ointment

spile: pin, rod, tap **4** bung, heap, pile, plug, rule, tube **5** spill, spout, stake **6** spigot **7** stopper **8** forepole, splinter

spill: die, mar, peg, pin rod **4** disk, fail, fall, flow, kill, roll, ruin, shed, slip, slop, tell **5** flosh, spile, spoil, spool, waste **6** betray, injure, perish, punish, reveal, sheath, tumble, wasted **7** confess, correct, destroy, divulge, scatter **8** chastise, downpour, gratuity, overflow, spillway, splinter, squander **11** deteriorate

Spillane's detective: 6 Hammer

spiloma: 5 nevus **9** birthmark

spin: 4 birl, burl, gyre, pirl, reel, ride, turn **5** drive, spurt, swirl, twirl, twist, whirl **6** gyrate, rotate **7** prolong, revolve **8** protract

spin a yarn: 7 narrate

spina: 4 wall **8** backbone

spinach: 7 epinard, potherb

spinal: 5 balas

area: **6** dorsal, lumbar, sacral **8** cervical

column: **6** rachis **8** backbone **9** vertebrae

cord: **4** alba **6** myelon

disease: **5** polio **8** myelitis

layer: **4** dura

muscle: **5** psoas

spindle: pin, rod **4** axis, axle, hasp, stem **5** arbor, fusee, shaft, stalk, xeres **6** arbour, broach, fuseau, rachis **7** mandrel

spindling: 4 weak **5** leggy **7** slender **11** ineffectual

spine (see also **spinal**): awn **4** back, seta **5** chine, ridge, thorn **6** chaeta, needle, spirit **7** acantha, acicula, courage, prickle, spicule **8** backbone, spiculum **9** vertebrae

spine bone: 6 sacrum

spineless: 4 weak **7** slavish **11** ineffectual

spine-tingling: 4 eery **5** eerie **7** ghostly

spinet: 5 piano **7** giraffe **11** harpsichord

spinnaker: 4 sail

spinner: cap, top **5** spoon **6** spider, weaver **8** narrator **10** goatsucker

spinney: 5 copse, grove **7** thicket

spinning: 5 areel **6** rotary **8** whirling **9** revolving

device: **7** distaff

machine: **4** mule **5** jenny **8** throstle

rod: **7** distaff

spinning wheel: 6 charka **7** charkha

spin-off: 9 byproduct, outgrowth

Spinoza work: 6 Ethics

spinster: 7 old maid **10** maiden lady

spiny: 6 picked, thorny **7** prickly **9** acanthoid, difficult

spiny-footed: 10 acanthopod **13** acanthopodous

spiny shrub: 4 ulex

spiracle: 4 hole, pore, vent **6** breath **7** orifice **8** aperture, blowhole

spiral: 4 coil, curl **5** curve, helix **7** coiling, curving, helical, winding **8** circling, helicoid **9** corkscrew **11** anfractuous

spire: 4 coil, curl **5** blade, stalk, tower, twist, whorl **6** fleche, sprout **7** sapling, steeple

finial: epi **4** epis

ornament: **6** finial

spirit: hag, pep, vim **4** aitu, alma, dash, dook, elan, fire, gimp, life, mood, soul, wind **5** angel, ardor, bugan, dhoul, ethos, fairy, fling, ghost, haunt, metal, pluck, shade, spook, verve, vigor **6** ardour, asuang, breeze, elixir, energy, esprit, ginger, mettle, morale, pneuma, temper, yaksha (mas.), yakshi(fem.) **7** animate, bravery, courage, entrain, hearten, loyalty **8** folletto, phantasm, vivacity **9** animation, encourage **10** apparition, enterprise, enthusiasm, getup-and-go **11** disposition, inspiration **12** cheerfulness, entrainement

air: **5** Ariel

animating: **6** animus

animation: pep **4** dash

avenging: Ate **6** alecto, erinys **7** megaera, nemesis **9** tisiphine

away: **6** abduct, kidnap, snatch

evil: Ate, imp, Ker **4** baka, beng, boko, drow, gyre **5** bugan, demon, devil **6** animus, asuang, daemon, daitya, dibbuk, Erynes, Lilith **9** cacodemon **10** cacodaemon

female: **6** undine **7** banshee, banshie

fire: **4** Agni

good: **5** genie, genus **7** eudemon **8** eudaemon

heralding death: **7** banshee, banshie

kinds of: akh, imp, lar, nat **4** arac, gimp, Kuei, Kwei, soul **5** angel, Ariel, duffy, duppy, dusio, ethos, genie, jinni, manes, rakee, shade **6** animus, fulgja, jinnee, mammon, tangie, Undine **7** banshee

lose: **7** despond

mischievous: imp **4** Puck **6** goblin **7** gremlin **11** poltergeist

of censure: **5** Momus

of people: **5** ethos

spirit-land: 9 fairyland

spirit-leaf: 8 manyroot

spirited: gay **4** fell, gamy, bold **5** brisk, eager, fiery **6** active, audace, birkie, ginger, lively, spunky **7** animato, dashing, zealous **8** animated, desirous, eloquent, frampoid, generous, vigorous **9** audacious, energetic, spiritoso, sprightly **10** mettlesome

horse: **5** steed **7** charger

spiritless: 4 cold, dead, meek **5** amort, blate, vapid **6** flashy **7** daviely, hilding, languid **8** dejected, feckless, flagging, lifeless, listless, thewless **9** apathetic, depressed, exanimate, heartless **10** dispirited

spiritlike: 8 ethereal

spirits: 4 mood **5** booze **6** liquor **7** alcohol

dash of: **5** lacer

dead: **5** manes

dwelling place of: Po **5** Hades **7** Elysium

kinds of: **6** furies, uplift **7** elation, Sammael **9** firewater **13** aquacaelestis

lift: **5** elate **7** gladden

low: **5** blues, dumps, gloom **6** gloomy **8** doldrums

spirits and water: 4 grog

spiritual: 4 holy, pure, song **6** devout, divine, sacred **7** ghostly **8** churchly, internal, platonic, spirited **9** animastic, geistlich, unworldly **10** devotional, immaterial **11** animastical, disembodied, incorporeal **14** ecclesiastical

apathy: **6** acedia

being: ens **5** angel, entia(pl.) **6** seraph

darkness: **4** Hell **5** tamas

spiritualistic meeting: 6 seance

spiritualize: 5 endow **6** purify, refine **7** animate **8** idealize **11** etherealize

spirituous: gay **4** airy, hard **5** vivid **6** active, ardent, lively **7** tenuous **8** ethereal **9** alcoholic **10** immaterial **11** incorporeal

spiry: 4 tall **6** coiled, curled, spiral **7** slender **8** tapering, wreathed **10** serpentine

spit: dig, fix, rod **4** emit, hang, rain, reef, snow **5** eject, image, light, plant, reach, retch, shoal, spade, stick, sword, utter **6**

broach, dagger, impale, saliva, skewer, sputum, thrust **7** spindle, spittle, sputter **8** broacher, likeness, sandbank, spadeful, sprinkle **9** brochette, secretion **11** counterpart, expectorate

spital: den **6** refuge, resort **7** shelter **8** hospital **9** lazaretto

spite: vex **4** hate, hurt, mood **5** annoy, depit, pique, shame, venom **6** enmity, grudge, hatred, injury, malice, mauger, maugre, rancor, thwart **7** chagrin, despite, dislike, ill-will, mortify **8** disgrace, dishonor **9** animosity, frustrate, hostility, humiliate **10** resentment **11** disposition, malevolence **12** spitefulness **13** mortification

spiteful: 4 mean **5** catty, snaky **6** sullen **7** hostile, waspish **8** annoying, venomous **9** malicious, malignant **10** dispiteous, irritating, malevolent, vindictive **11** troublesome

spitfire: 6 virago **7** sulphur **9** brimstone

spitter: 4 deer **5** spade **7** brocket **8** spitball **12** expectorater

spitting: 6 saliva **10** exspuition

spitting image: 4 twin **6** double, ringer

spittle: 4 peel, spit **6** saliva

spittle insect: 10 froghopper

spittoon: 8 crachoir, cuspidor

spiv: 7 slacker **8** parasite

splash: lap **4** dash, daub, gout, lave, mark, plop, pond, pool, spot **5** bathe, blash, slart, slash, spray **6** blotch, dabble, flouse, floush, strike **7** display, feature, scatter, spatter **8** splatter **9** dashingly **10** appearance, excitement **14** ostentatiously

splashboard: 4 gate, trap **5** board, plank **6** fender, screen **8** mudguard

splashy: wet **5** muddy, showy **6** blashy, slushy, watery **8** striking **11** sensational, spectacular **12** ostentatious

splat: 4 open, plot, spot **5** patch **6** blotch **7** flatten

splatter: dab **4** dash, rush **6** hubbub, splash **7** cluster

splay: hem **4** awry, turn **5** adorn, bevel, carve, slant, slope **6** clumsy, expand, spread **7** awkward, display, diverge, sloping **8** ungainly **9** dislocate, expansion, obliquely, slopingly, spreading **10** slantingly **11** enlargement

spleen: 4 fire, milt **5** anger, ardor, freak, mirth, organ, spite **6** malice **7** dislike, impulse **8** ill-humor, laughter **9** lienculus, merriment **10** melancholy **11** impetuosity

pert. to: **6** lienal

spleeny: 5 angry **7** fretful, peevish **9** irritable **10** melancholy

splendent: 6 glossy **7** beaming, shining **8** lustrous, splendid **9** brilliant **11** conspicuous, illustrious, magnificent, resplendent

splendid: gay **4** braw, fine, good, rial **5** grand, regal, showy, tinny **6** bright, candid, costly, superb **7** gallant, ripping, shining, sublime **8** glorious, gorgeous **9** brilliant, excellent, grandiose, sumptuous **11** illustrious, magnificent, resplendent

splendor, splendour: 4 gite, pomp **5** blaze, eclat, gleam, glory, sheen **6** bright, fulgor, luster, parade **7** display, fulgour **8** elegance, grandeur, radiance, richness **9** pageantry, showiness **10** brightness, brilliance, brilliancy, effulgence **12** gorgeousness, magnificence, resplendence **14** impressiveness

splenetic: 6 sullen, vapory **7** fretful, peevish, splenic **8** spiteful **9** depressed, irritable, malicious, spleenful **10** melancholy

splice: 4 join **5** marry, unite **6** fasten **7** wedding **8** marriage **10** interweave

splint: 4 coal, lath, tace, scob **5** brace, plate, split, strip, tasse **6** fasten **7** confine

splinter: 4 chip, rend **5** break, broom, slice, smash, spale, split **6** fasten, shiver, sliver **7** confine, flinder, shatter **8** fragment

split: cut, rit **4** chap, rend, rent, rive, ruin, tear **5** break, burst, clave, cleft, crack, peach, reave, riven, share, wedge **6** betray, bisect, bottle, breach, broken, cleave, cloven, dilute, divide, rifted, schism, sliver, sunder **7** destroy, dispart, divided, fissure, portion, rupture, shatter **8** fragment, informer, separate, splinter **9** fractured, separated **10** separation

in two parts: **5** bifid **6** cloven, halved **8** bisected **9** bipartite

up: **10** separation

split pea: dal

splitting: 5 funny **6** severe **7** comical, fission, rending **8** piercing

of mind: **13** schizophrenia

splotch: dab **4** blob, blot, dash, daub, mark, spot **5** smear, stain **6** blotch, mottle, splash **7** blemish

splurge: 5 spend **6** effort, splash **7** display **11** ostentation **13** demonstration

splutter: 4 fuff **5** hurry, noise, stuff **6** bustle, splash **7** dispute, glutter, quarrel, scatter, spatter, stammer **8** nonsense **9** confusion

Spode: 5 china **9** porcelain

Spohr opera: 8 Jessonda

spoil: mar, rob, rot **4** baby, blad, boot, loot, pelf, prey, rape, ruin, swag **5** bitch, blend, booty, carve, cheat, decay, harry, prize, seize, strip, taint, waste **6** coddle, damage, deface, divest, forage, impair, infuse, injure, pamper, perish, ravage, thwart **7** connach, corrupt, estrepe, deprive, despoil, destroy, indulge, pillage, plunder, violate, vitiate **8** confound, unclothe **10** chevisance, corruption, impairment

eggs: **5** addle

spoiled: bad **5** dazed, musty **6** addled, marred, molded, petted, preyed, rotted **7** botched, decayed, damaged, tainted **8** pampered, pillaged **9** plundered

spoiler: **6** robber **7** marplot **8** marauder, pillager **9** despoiler, plunderer **10** depredator

spoilsport: **7** killjoy **10** wet-blanket

spoke: bar **4** clog, grip, rung, tale, talk **5** block, check, drone, round, spake, stake, stick **6** radius, speech **7** mention, uttered **8** handhold **10** impediment **11** enchantment

spoken: **4** oral, said **5** parol, vocal **7** uttered **9** declaimed

spoliate: rob **6** ravage **7** despoil, pillage, plunder

spoliation: **4** loss **6** rapine **7** pillage, plunder, robbery **8** pillaged **11** destruction **12** despoliation

spondyl: **8** vertebra

sponge: bum, wet **4** form, swab, wipe **5** ascon, cadge, dough, erase, mooch **6** absorb, ascula, efface, rhagon **7** badiaga, cleanse, destroy, drinker, scrunge, zimocca **8** drunkard, parasite, scrounge **10** freeloader

calcareous: **6** leucon

orifice: **6** oscula(pl.) **7** osculum

pen: **5** kraal

pert. to: **9** poriferal

spicle: **4** toxa

vegetable: **5** loofa, luffa **6** loofah

sponge tree: **8** huisache

sponger: **5** leech **6** cadger **8** parasite

spongewood: **4** sola

spongy: **4** fozy, soft **5** rainy **6** porous, quaggy **9** absorbent

sponsor: **4** back **5** angel **6** backer, gossip, patron, surety **9** godfather, godmother, introduce

sponsorship: **4** egis **5** aegis **7** backing **8** auspices

spontaneous: **4** free, wild **6** native **8** careless, untaught **9** automatic, impulsive **10** indigenous, self-acting **11** instinctive, involuntary, unpremeditated

spontoon: **4** club, pike **6** cudgel **7** halberd, pantoon **9** truncheon

spoof: guy **4** fool, hoax, joke **5** trick **7** deceive, swindle **8** nonsense **9** deception

spook: spy **5** annoy, ghost, haunt **6** spirit, wraith **7** specter, startle **8** frighten **9** hobgoblin **10** apparition, make nervous

spooky: **4** eery **5** eerie, weird **6** creepy **7** ghostly, haunted, uncanny **8** spectral

spool: **4** reel, wind **6** bobbin, broach, holder **7** spindle **8** cylinder

spoon: pet, woo **4** neck **5** ladle, labis, lover, ninny **6** nestle, shovel, spoony **7** student **8** cochlear, golf club, make love **9** simpleton

spoon-fed: **7** coddled **8** pampered

Spoon River poet: **7** Masters

spoon-shaped: **8** cochlear, spatular

spoonbill: **5** ajaja **8** shoveler **10** paddlefish

spoor: **4** clue, hint, odor **5** piste, scent, trace, track, trail

spore: **4** cyst, germ, seed

spore sac: **5** ascus **7** capsule

sport (see also **game:** *official*): bet, fun, gig, toy **4** game, gaud, glee, jest, joke, mock, play, polo, romp **5** dally, freak, mirth, wager **6** frolic, gamble, racing, shikar **7** contest, gambler, jesting, mockery, pastime **8** derision, raillery **9** amusement, diversion, plaything **10** pleasantry, recreation **13** entertainment

attendance: **4** gate

event: **4** game, meet, race **5** match

shirt: tee **4** polo

shoe: **6** loafer **7** sneaker

site: gym **4** grid, oval, pool, ring, rink **5** arena, court, field, links, track **6** course **7** diamond, stadium **8** coliseum **10** hippodrome

summer: **6** diving, hiking, quoits, rowing, skiing **7** fishing, sailing **8** swimming

water: **6** diving, rowing **7** sailing, surfing **8** canoeing, swimming, yachting

winter: **6** hockey, skiing **7** curling, skating **8** sledding **11** tobogganing

sportive: gay **5** merry **6** frisky, lusory, wanton **7** amorous, festive, jocular, playful **8** frolicky, gamesome, playsome, pleasant **9** lecherous **10** frolicsome

sportiveness: **7** devilry, roguery, waggery

sportsman: **6** hunter **7** shikari **8** shikaree

sportula: **4** gift **7** largess, present

sporty: **4** loud **5** showy **6** casual, flashy

spot: bit, dab, dot, job, see **4** blot, blur, find, fish, flaw, mark, site, soil **5** blaze, fault, fleck, nevus, patch, place, point, ready, speck, stain, sully, tache, taint **6** blotch, defect, detect, locate, macula, macule, naevus, random, remove, stigma **7** asperse, blemish, freckle, splotch **8** discolor, disgrace, handicap, identify, locality, location, maculate, particle, position, quantity, reproach **9** bespatter, recognize **11** predicament

kinds of: ace, dot, pip, tee **4** blet, fret, gall, rone, spil, wems **5** macle, oasis **6** alcove, bethel, mascle, mottle, mouche **7** freckle **8** bethesda, fenestra, fontanel *on animal's face:* 4 star 5 blaze

on playing card: pip

spotless: 5 clean, snowy **6** chaste **9** blameless, unspotted, unsullied **10** immaculate **11** unblemished, untarnished **14** irreproachable

spotlight: arc **4** beam **9** emphasize, publicity **10** illuminate

spotted: 6 bauson, calico, espied, marked, notate, sanded, ticked **7** bracket, dappled, guttate, mottled, noticed, stained, sullied **9** blemished, suspected, tarnished

animal: 4 paco, pard 6 chital, ocelot 7 cheetah, leopard

fever: 6 typhus

spotter: 7 watcher **9** detective

spotty: few **5** dotty **6** uneven **9** irregular

spousal: 7 wedlock **8** ceremony, marriage, nuptials

spouse: 4 mate, wife **5** bride **6** fiance **7** consort, fiancee, husband, partner **9** companion **10** bridegroom

spout: jet, jut, lip **4** dale, flow, geat, gush, lift, pawn, pipe, rant **5** chute, eject, issue, orate, shoot, speak, spile, spurt, utter **6** pledge, recite, spigot, spring, squirt, stream, trough **7** conduit, declaim **8** downpour, gargoyle **9** discharge, waterfall **10** waterspout

sprack: 4 deft **5** alert **6** active, lively, nimble, shrewd

sprag: 4 prop **6** billet

sprain: 4 pull, tear, turn **5** chink **6** weaken, wrench **10** overstrain

sprat: 5 bleak **6** garvie **7** herring **8** sixpence

sprattle: 6 sprawl **8** scramble, struggle

sprawl: 4 loll **5** slump **7** grabble **8** struggle **9** sprauchie

spray: jet **4** chap, hose, twig **5** bough, shoot, spree, sprig, water **6** boquet, branch, sparge, spread, volley **7** atomize, bouquet, scatter **8** sprinkle **9** aspersion, discharge, sprindrift

spread: fan, jam, ted **4** emit, meal, oleo, open, span, taft **5** cover, feast, flare, jelly, reach, smear, splay, strew, widen **6** anoint, dilate, dinner, expand, extend, extent, ramify, unfold, unfurl **7** broaden, compass, diffuse, distend, diverge, divulge, enlarge, exhibit, expanse, overlay, overrun, prolong, protect, publish, radiate, scatter, slather, stretch **8** coverlet, diffused, dispense, disperse, expanded, extended, increase, multiply, permeate, straddle **9** broadcast, circulate, dispersed, displayed, expansion, expatiate, propagate **10** distribute, generalize **11** disseminate

abroad: 4 toot 5 bruit, noise, libel, rumor 6 delate, rumour, spring 7 divulge, radi-

ate **9** broadcast, publicize **11** disseminate

as plaster: 4 teer

for drying: ted

loosely: 5 strew 7 scatter

on: 5 apply

out: fan, lap, ted 4 bray, open, span 5 flare, widen 6 deploy, flange, sprawl, unfold

spreader: 5 knife **6** tedder

spreading of light: 8 halation

spreading out: 6 radial

spree: bat, jag **4** bout, bust, gell, lark, orgy, romp, toot, jagg **5** beano, binge, booze, revel **6** bender, buster, bust-up, frolic, high-go, shindy **7** carouse, debauch, wassail **8** carousal **10** indulgence

sprig: 4 brad, nail, trim, twig **5** bough, ꜱcion, shoot, smart, spray, youth **6** active, branch, sprout, spruce **7** tendril **9** stripling, youngster

sprightly: gay, tid **4** airy, pert **5** agile, alive, antic, brisk, canty, crank, desto, elfin, peart **6** active, blithe, clever, lively **7** briskly, buoyant, chipper, ghostly, quickly **8** animated, vigorous **10** enlivening, spiritedly, spiritlike **11** incorporeal, quick-witted

spring: ain, fly, hop, spa **4** bend, dart, font, head, jump, leap, lilt, rise, warp, well **5** arise, begin, bound, flirt, issue, lymph, shoot, spurt, start, therm, tower, vault **6** accrue, bounce, emerge, season, therme, venero **7** estuary, thermae **8** fountain **10** intoxicate

abruptly: 4 bolt

back: 6 recoil, resile 7 rebound

deposit: 4 urao 5 trona

hot: 7 balneum, thermae, gipsies

kind of: ain, cee, spa, ver, hop, ojo 4 font 5 lymph 6 geyser, charco, source, saline 7 gambado 9 Castalian

pert. to: 6 vernal

up: 5 arise 6 sprout

spring-like: 6 vernal

springboard: 5 wagon **6** batule **8** tremplin **10** trampoline

springbok: 7 gazelle

springe: gin, set **4** trap **5** agile, catch, noose, snare **6** supple **7** pitfall **9** booby trap

springer: 5 fryer **7** grampus, spaniel **9** springbok

springing back: 7 elastic **9** renascent

springtime: May **8** germinal

springy: wet **6** pliant, spongy **7** elastic **8** flexible **9** resilient

sprinkle: deg, dot, wet **4** dart, rain, spot **5** color, flour, spray, strew, twist, water **6** affuse, bedrop, dabble, dredge, sparge **7** asperge, asperse, baptize, drizzle, moisten, scatter, spairge, sparkle, spatter,

speckle 8 disperse 9 bespangle, bespatter 10 besprinkle, intoxicate
with flour: 6 dredge
with grains of mustard: 8 sinapize
with grit: 4 sand
with moisture: 5 bedew
with mud: 9 bespatter
with powder: 4 dust
with water: deg
sprinkler: 7 dredger 11 aspergillum 12 extinguisher
sprinkling: 4 seme 7 baptism 9 aspersion
sprint: run 4 dash, race 5 snare, speed 6 bicker 7 springe
sprinter: 5 racer 6 runner 7 athlete
sprit: bud 4 dart, rush, spar 5 shoot, speck, sprat 6 sprint, sprout, squirt 8 bowsprit 9 germinate
sprite: elf, fay, hob, imp 4 elve, life, mind, mood, peri, soul 5 Ariel, bucca, fairy, genie, ghost, gnome, nisse, pixie, shade, vital 6 goblin, person, spirit 7 essence 9 germinate, hobgoblin 10 apparition, woodpecker 11 disposition, inspiration
kind of: nix 5 ariel, demon, Holda, naiad, nixie 6 Kelpie 8 coltpixy 9 coltpixie 10 leprechaun, shoopiltie
sprocket: cam 5 tooth, whelp
sproil: 6 active, energy 7 agility 8 activity 9 energetic
sprout: bud, eye, son 4 brod, chit, chun, cion, germ, malt 5 achar, brode, chine, shoot, spire, spout, sprig, spurt 6 braird, expand, germen, growth, ratoon 7 burgeon 8 offshoot, seedling 9 germinate
spruce: gim 4 chic, deft, neat, posh, smug, tidy, trig, trim 5 compt, fussy, natty, Picea, smart, sprig 6 dapper, picked 7 dandify, dress up, finical, smarten 8 overnice, titivate 11 well-groomed
tree: 5 larch 8 epinette
spruce: 4 hole 5 dross 7 opening 8 psilosis 9 asparagus
sprunt: 4 hill, leap 5 steep 6 spring 8 struggle
spry: 5 agile, brisk, quick, smart 6 active, clever, lively, nimble, spruce 7 knowing 8 vigorous 9 sprightly
spud: dig, man 4 hand 5 child, dough, drill, money, spade, tater 6 paddle, potato, reamer, remove, shovel 10 projection
spume: 4 foam, scum 5 froth 6 lather
spun: See **spin**
spunk, sponk: vim 4 punk 5 anger, flame, gleam, match, nerve, pluck, spark 6 kindle, mettle, spirit, sponge, tinder 7 courage, passion 9 fortitude, touchwood 10 doggedness
spunky: 4 game 5 brave, quick 6 plucky, touchy 8 spirited 9 irritable 10 coura-

geous, mettlesome
spur: egg 4 calk, gaff, goad, move, peak, prod, prop, urge 5 arete, brace, drive, hurry, impel, press, prick, range, ridge, rowel, spine, spoor, strut, tower 6 arouse, broach, calcar, digger, excite, foment, griffe, hasten, incite, motive, urge on 7 gablock, provoke, publish 8 buttress, stimulus 9 incentive, instigate, stimulate 10 blockhouse 11 publication
having: 7 spicate
of mountain: 5 arete
on gamecock: 4 gaff
railroad: 6 siding
wheel: 5 rowel
spur wheel: 5 rowel
spurge: 4 weed 6 balsam, purify 8 milkweed 9 euphorbia
spurious: 4 fake 5 bogus, false, phony, snide 6 forced 7 bastard 10 adulterate, apocryphal, artificial, fictitious, fraudulent 11 counterfeit, superficial 12 illegitimate 14 supposititious
spurn: hit 4 blow, dash, kick, rush, snub, spur 5 flout, haste, scorn 6 affray, incite, pillar, rebuff, refuse, reject, scrape, strike 7 contemn, decline, despise, disdain, scratch, stumble 10 engagement
spurt: jet, jut 4 dart, gush 5 expel, spell, spout 6 sprout, squirt 8 increase, outbreak
Sputnik: 9 satellite
dog: 5 Laika
sputter: ado 4 fuss, spit 7 bluster
sputum: 4 spit 6 saliva 7 spittle
spy: pry, see 4 case, espy, keek, note, tout 5 scout, sneak, snoop, spook, watch 6 behold, descry, detect, espial, gaycat, mouton, search 7 discern, examine, hicarra, inspect, observe, snooper 8 discover, emissary, hi-carrah, informer, perceive, stake out 10 discoverer, scrutinize 11 secret agent 13 intelligencer
famous: 4 Hari 5 Andre, Caleb, Fuchs 6 Arnold, Cavell 8 Mata Hari
spying: 9 espionage 12 surveillance 16 counter-espionage
Spyri's heroine: 5 Heidi
squab: coy, fat, shy 4 drop, sofa 5 couch, piper, plump, press, short, spill, thick 6 callow, pigeon, stocky 7 cushion, ottoman 8 nestling 9 fledgling, unfledged, upholster
squabble: 5 argue, brawl 6 bicker, jangle 7 bobbery, contend, dispute, quarrel, wrangle 13 collie-shangie
squad: 4 team 5 group, troop
leader of: 8 sergeant
squadron: 6 armada 10 escadrille
squalid: 4 base, foul, mean, poor, ugly, vile 5 dirty, nasty 6 filthy, shabby, sor-

did **7** unclean **8** wretched **9** miserable, repellant, repellent, repulsive **10** broken-down

squall: cry, pet **4** bawl, dear, drow, gush, gust, wawl **5** storm **6** flurry, scream, shower, squawk, wretch **7** borasca, borasco, dispute, quarrel, trouble **8** borasque **9** windstorm **11** disturbance

squalor: mud **4** dirt, mire **5** filth **9** roughness **10** filthiness **11** squalidness **12** wretchedness

squander: **4** burn, lash **5** spend, waste **6** befool, lavish, wander **7** consume, debauch, dispend, scatter **8** disperse, embezzle, misspend **9** dissipate **10** trifle away **12** extravagance

squanderer: **5** loser **7** wastrel

square: **4** even, parc, park, true **5** agora, carre, clear, exact, hunky, plaza **6** dinkum, direct, honest, settle **7** commons, quarrel, upright **8** justness, quadrate, **9** carre-four, criterion, principle **11** unequivocal **12** conventional **13** parallelogram **15** straightforward

public: **5** plaza **6** common

square dance: **4** reel **7** hoedown, lancers **9** quadrille

squared circle: **4** ring **5** arena

squarehead: **4** dolt **5** dunce, Swede **6** German **8** numskull **9** screwball **12** Scandinavian

squaring tool: **5** edger

squarish: **4** boxy

squarrose: **5** rough, scaly

squash: **4** beat, fall, ooze, pepo, stop **5** crowd, crush, press **6** stifle **7** cymling, flatten, pumpkin, squeeze, squelch **8** suppress **9** discomfit **10** disconcert

kind of: **5** acorn **6** banana, cushaw, simnel, summer, turban **7** cymling, Hubbard, Italian **8** cymbling, patty pan, zucchini **9** crookneck

squashy: wet **4** soft **5** boggy, muddy, mushy, pulpy **8** overripe

squat: sit **5** cower, dumpy, pudgy, stoop **6** bruise, crouch, fodgel, hurkle, settle, splash, stocky, stubby **8** thickset

squatter: **4** flap **5** squat **6** crouch, nester, plunge **7** bywoner, confuse, flutter, nestler, scatter, settler **8** bewilder, squander **9** sandpiper

Squatter State: **6** Kansas

squaw: **4** wife **5** woman **6** mahala, coween **10** klootchman

husband: **4** buck **6** sannup

squawbush: **5** sumac **6** shoval

squawfish: **4** chub **8** chappaul **9** surfperch

squeak: cry, wee **4** peep, talk **5** cheep, creak, noise, speak **6** betray, escape, inform, shrill **7** confess, disturb **11** opportunity

squeal: yip **4** blab, sing **5** broil, frail, weary **6** betray, inform, scream **7** dispute, protest, quarrel **8** complain

squealer: **4** duck, fink **5** quail, swift **6** grouse, pigeon, plover **7** traitor **8** informer **9** partridge

squeamish: shy **4** helo, nice, stir **5** dizzy, heloe **6** bustle, dainty, dauncy, modest, queasy **7** finical, prudish **8** overnice, qualmish **9** dizziness, giddiness, nauseated, reluctant, sensitive **10** fastidious, scrupulous **13** oversensitive

squeeze: eke, hug, jam **4** gain, mull, neck, silk **5** chirt, creem, crowd, crush, force, pinch, press, wring **6** corner, eke out, escape, extort, scrump, scruze, thrust, twitch **7** embrace, extract, oppress, procure, scrunch, scrunge **8** compress, condense, pressing, pressure, scrounge **9** constrict, influence **10** commission, constraint **11** compression, predicament

squeezer: **5** drier, noose **6** juicer, reamer **7** wringer **8** squeegee **9** extractor

squeezy: **7** cramped **8** confined

squelch: **4** blow, fall **5** crush, quash, quell, stamp **6** rebuke, subdue **7** silence **8** suppress **9** discomfit **10** disconcert

squib: jet **4** ball, bomb, mote, pipe, skit, tube **5** candy, match, throw **6** filler, squirt, writer **7** dispute, explode, lampoon, pasquil, torpedo, writing **9** bespatter **10** pasquinade **11** firecracker

squid: **6** loligo **7** mollusk, octopus **8** calamary **10** cuttlefish

arm: **8** tentacle

pen: **5** quill

secretion: ink

shell: pen

squiffer (Br.): **10** concertina

squiggle: **4** curl, line **5** shake, twist **6** squirm, writhe **7** wriggle **8** curlicue, scribble

squilla: **5** prawn **6** shrimp **8** sea onion

squinch: **4** arch **5** twist **6** lintel, quince, recoil, squint, wrench **7** squeeze, squench **9** corbeling

squint: **4** bent, cast, glee, gleg, skew **5** glent, trend **6** gledge, goggle **7** deviate **10** hagioscope, strabismus

squint-eyed: **5** gleed, gleyd

squire: **4** beau **5** lover, title **6** donzel, escort **7** gallant **8** henchman, servitor **9** accompany, attendant, gentleman, landowner

squirrel: bun **5** hoard, sisel, stash, xerus **6** chippy, gyrate **7** assapan **8** archilla, jelerang **9** assapanic, chickaree, shadetail

burrowing: **6** gopher

flying: **7** assapan

genus of: **7** sciurus

nest: **4** dray, drey

shrew: **4** tana
skin: **4** vair
squirrellike: 8 sciuroid
animal: **8** dormouse
squirt: jet **5** chirt, eject, skite, slirt, spout, spurt **14** whippersnapper
sri: 4 holy **7** Lakshmi **8** glorious, reverend **9** fortunate
Sri Lanka: See **Ceylon**
stab: dab, jab, jag, try **4** gore, jagg, pink, yerk **5** chive, drive, knife, knive, lunge, prick, sound, stake, stick, stool, stump, wound **6** attack, broach, dagger, pierce, strike, stroke, thrust **7** attempt, poniard, roughen **8** puncture **9** penetrate
in fencing: **4** pink **8** stoccado
stability: 5 poise **7** balance **8** firmance, firmness, strength **9** constancy, fixedness **10** permanence, stableness, steadiness **12** immovability, immutability **13** steadfastness **15** indissolubility
stabilize: fix, set **4** calm **5** poise **6** steady **8** regulate
stabilizer: 7 ballast
stable: 4 barn, fast, firm, mews, shed, sure **5** fixed, set-up, solid, sound, stall **6** hangar, secure, steady, strong, sturdy **7** durable, equerry, lasting **8** constant, enduring, immobile **9** confirmed, establish, permanent, resistant, steadfast, unabashed, unvarying **10** stationary, unwavering **11** established, trustworthy **12** unchangeable
royal: **4** mews
stableman: 5 groom **6** ostler **7** hostler
stack: set **4** bike, flue, heap, pike, pile, rick, stow, tier **5** group, hovel, mound, scroo, shock **7** chimney, conduit **9** fireplace
stacked: 10 curvaceous
stad: 4 town **7** village
staddle: row **4** tree **5** stain, swath **7** sapling, support
stadium: 4 oval **5** arena, stade, stage **7** furlong **8** coliseum
staff: bar, gad, rod **4** cane, club, line, mace, maul, pole, prod, rung, wand **5** aides, baton, crook, equip, lance, pedum, perch, spear, stave, stick, suite **6** baston, cudgel, stanza **7** attache, bailiff, caducei(pl.), scepter, sceptre, support **8** caduceus **9** constable, entourage, personnel **10** assistants, associates **12** quarter-staff
bearer: **5** macer
kinds of: **4** kent, wand **5** filch **6** croche, muleta **7** baculus, bourdon, cambuca, crosier, crozier, distaff, rhabdos **10** alpenstock
officers: **5** aides, cadre
staff of life: 5 bread
stag: 4 colt, deer, hart **5** party **7** pollard,

shorten **8** informer
horn: **4** rial **9** bezantler
stage: era **4** dais, gest, step, tier **5** arena, board, coach, floor, grade, level, phase, shelf, stair, story **6** degree, stadia **7** display, exhibit, produce, rostrum, stadium, theater **8** platform, scaffold **9** condition, dramatize, gradation **10** proscenium, stagecoach **11** subdivision
extra: **4** supe **5** super
hanging: **7** scenery **8** backdrop
on: **7** en scene
part: **4** role
pert. to: **6** scenic
raised: **4** dais **7** estrade
signal: cue
stage direction: 4 exit, sola **5** aside, enter, manet, omnes, solus **6** exeunt, sennet **8** loquitur
stage whisper: 5 aside
stagger: 4 reel, rock, stun, sway **5** lurch, shake, waver **6** hobble, totter, wintle (Sc.) **7** startle, tremble, vibrate **8** flounder, hesitate, titubate, unsettle
stagnant: 4 dull, foul **5** inert, stale, still **7** languid **8** sluggish, standing **10** motionless **13** unprogressive
stagnate: 4 dull **5** inert **8** vegetate **10** motionless
stagnation: 6 stases, stasis, torpor **10** depression
stagy: 8 affected **10** theatrical **12** ostentatious
staid: set **5** fixed, grave, sober **6** demure, sedate, solemn, steady **7** earnest, serious, settled **8** decorous **9** dignified, steadfast **10** coolheaded
stain: dye **4** blot, blur, soil, spot, tint **5** cloud, color, paint, smear, sully, tache, taint, tinge, trace **6** blotch, debase, infamy, macula, smirch, smudge, stigma, vilify **7** blemish, corrupt, tarnish **8** discolor, disgrace, dishonor, maculate, tincture **9** bespatter, pollution **10** attainture **11** contaminate
stainless: 4 pure **6** chaste, honest
stair: 4 step **5** stage, stile **6** degree
face: **5** riser
post: **5** newel
series of: **6** flight
staircase: 5 grece, grice **6** griece, ladder
handrail: **8** banister **9** bannister
moving: **9** escalator
on ship: **12** companionway
outdoor: **6** perron
part of: **4** rung **5** newel, riser, tread
portable: **6** ladder
spiral: **8** caracole
stake: bet, peg, pin, pot, set **4** ante, back, gage, pale, pile, pole, pool, post, risk, spit, stob **5** anvil, prize, spile, stick, teest, wager **6** chance, gamble, hazard,

picket **7** venture **8** interest **9** horse race **10** capitalize
driver: **4** maul
pert. to: **5** palar
stale: old **4** flat, hoar, lure, rung, worn **5** banal, blown, corny, decoy, frowy, moldy, musty, shaft, trite, vapid, waugh(Sc.) **7** insipid, tainted **9** hackneyed, tasteless **10** flavorless, prostitute **11** commonplace, overtrained **13** uninteresting
stalemate: **4** draw **7** impasse **8** deadlock, standoff **10** standstill
stalk: bun **4** axis, halm, hunt, mote, prey, risp, seta, stem **5** chase, haulm, spear, stipe, straw **6** pursue, ratoon, stride **7** pedicel, petiole **8** peduncle
having: **9** petiolate
remove: **5** strig
stalker: **6** hunter
stalking-horse: **4** mask **5** blind, decoy **7** pretext **8** pretense
stalkless: **7** sessile
stall: bin, cot, pew **4** crib, loge, mire, seat, stop **5** boose, boosy, booth, check, crame, decoy, delay, stand **6** manger, stable **7** pretext, station **8** hesitate **9** enclosure **10** dilly-dally **11** compartment, confederate **13** procrastinate
stallion: **5** horse **6** cooser(Sc.)
stalwart: **4** firm **5** brave, stout **6** brawny, robust, strong, sturdy **7** valiant **8** partisan, resolute **10** unyielding
stamina: gut **4** grit **5** vigor **7** courage, essence **8** backbone, capacity, strength **9** endurance, fortitude
stammer: **6** falter, hacker, jabber **7** stumble, stutter **8** hesitate
stamp: die **4** beat, coin, form, kind, mark, seal, tool, type **5** brand, class, crush, drive, label, pound, press, print, stomp **6** signet, strike, thresh **7** impress, imprint, postage, sticker, trample **8** inscribe **9** character **10** impression **11** distinguish
collecting: **9** philately
fencing: **5** appel
madness for: **11** timbromania
paper: **6** pelure
space: **8** spandrel
stampede: **4** bolt, rout, rush **5** blitz, panic **6** flight **7** debacle
stamping plate: die
stance: **4** pose **7** posture, station **8** position
stanch, staunch: **4** firm, stem, stop, true **5** allay, check, close, loyal, quell, sound **6** hearty, quench, steady, strong, trusty **7** zealous **8** constant, faithful, resolute, suppress **9** steadfast **10** extinguish, unswerving, unwavering, watertight **11** substantial, trustworthy

stanchion: bar **4** beam, post, prop **5** brace, piton **7** confine, support, upright
stand: set **4** bear, dais, ease, halt, hold, last, rack, stop **5** abide, arise, booth, cease, erect, pause, table **6** afford, endure, hack it, podium, remain, resist, tripod, trivet **7** etagere, station, sustain, support, taboret, undergo **8** attitude, continue, hesitate, maintain, position, tabouret, tolerate **9** withstand **10** resistance
candles: **7** epergne **10** candelabra
cuplike: **4** zarf
for: **4** mean **8** tolerate **9** represent
for election: run
in awe of: **4** fear **5** dread **7** respect
on end: **5** upend
on hind legs: **4** ramp, rear
opposite: **4** face
ornamental: **7** atagere, etagere
out: jut **6** beetle **7** project **8** overhang, protrude
painter's: **5** easel
small: **7** taboret **8** tabouret
still: **4** stop, whoa
three-legged: **6** tripod, trivet
stand-in: **9** surrogate **10** substitute
standard: cup, par, set **4** fiar(Sc.), flag, mark, norm, suit, type, unit **5** canon, gauge, grade, ideal, level, model **6** assize, banner, beacon, ensign, goblet, normal, sample, signal **7** classic, example, labarum(L.), pattern, support, upright **8** accepted, brattach(Sc.), gonfalon, orthodox, vexillum **9** criterion, oriflamme, yardstick **10** touchstone **11** candlestick, rule of thumb
bearer: **11** gonfalonier
of measurement: **6** metric
Turkish: **4** alem, toug
standardize: **9** calibrate, normalize
standing: **4** rank, term **5** being, erect, fixed **6** estate, stable, stance, status **7** lasting, settled, statant, station, upright **8** constant, duration, location, position, stagnant **9** permanent, situation **10** reputation, stationary
upright: **11** orthostatic
standing room only: S.R.O.
standoff: tie **4** draw **10** unsociable
standstill: **4** halt, rest, stop **5** state **8** deadlock **9** cessation, stalemate
stanhope: **5** buggy
stank: **4** pond, pool **5** ditch **9** reservoir
stanze: **5** envoi, stave, verse **7** strophe **8** division **9** apartment
eight line: **6** huitan, octave **7** triolet
five line: **8** cinquain
four line: **8** quatrain
irregular: **13** alloeostropha
six line: **6** sestet
ten line: **6** dizain **7** dizaine

three line: **8** tristich

staple: 4 city, town **5** chief, fiber, shaft **6** fasten **7** chaplet, support **8** fastener **9** commodity, principal **10** foundation

star (see also **constellation**): ace, orb, sun **4** hero, lead **5** actor, badge, chief, shine **6** etoile **7** actress, estoile, heroine, ingenue, stellar **8** asterisk, luminary, pentacle, twinkler **9** bespangle, headliner, principal **10** preeminent, topnotcher

apple: **7** caimito

brightest in constellation: **5** alpha

difference in direction: **8** parallax

divination: **9** astrology

evening: **5** Venus **6** Hesper, Vesper **7** Evestar **8** Hesperus

evil: **8** sidereal

exploding: **4** nova

five-pointed: **8** pentacle

group: **6** galaxy **13** constellation

in Aquila: **6** Altair

in Bootes: **8** Arcturus

in Canis Major: **6** Sirius

in Carina: **7** Canopus

in Centaurus: **5** Agena

in Cetus: **4** Mira

in Cygnus: **5** Deneb **7** Albireo

in Draco: **6** Alsafi **7** Al Rakis, Eltanin

in Gemini: **5** Wasat **6** Alhena, Castor, Polux

in Leo: **7** Regulus

in Lyra: **4** Vega

in Orion: **5** Rigel, Saiph

in Perseus: **5** Algol

in Scorpius: **7** Antares

in Taurus: **8** Pleiades

in Ursa Major: **5** Alcor, Mizar **6** Alkaid

in Ursa Minor: **7** Polaris

in Virgo: **5** Spica

morning: **4** Mars **5** Venus **6** Saturn **7** Daystar, Jupiter, Mercury **8** Phosphor

north: **7** polaris **8** loadstar, lodestar, polestar

pert. to: **6** astral **7** astrean, stellar **8** sidereal, stellate

representation: **6** etoile

shooting: **5** comet **6** Leonid, meteor

six-pointed: **8** hexagram

suddenly flaring: **4** nova

two: **9** bistellar

variable: **4** Mira

worshiper: **7** sabaist

star cluster: 6 nebula

star-crossed: 7 unlucky **11** unfortunate

star facet: 4 pane

star-like: 8 stellate

Star-Spangled Banner author: 15 Francis Scott Key

Star Wars: 5 force

characters: Han **4** C3PO, Ewok, Jedi, Leia, Luke, R2D2, Solo, Yoda **5** Jabba **7** Han Solo **8** Boba Fett **9** Chewbacca **10** Darth Vader **12** Obi-Wan Kenobi, Princess Leia **13** Luke Skywalker

starch: vim **4** arum, sago **5** tikor, vigor **6** amylum, energy, farina, strong **7** cassava, precise, stiffen **8** activity, glycogen, strength, vitality **9** arrowroot, formality, stiffness **12** carbohydrate

starchy: 5 rigid, stiff **6** formal **7** precise **9** unbending

stare: 4 gape, gaup, gawk, gawp, gaze, gouk, gowk, gype, look, ogle, peer **5** glare, glaze, glore **6** glower, goggle **7** bristle **8** starling **10** rubberneck

starfish: 7 sun star **8** asteroid

limb: ray

stargazer: 4 fish **10** astrologer, astronomer

staring: 6 gazing **7** glaring **8** wide-eyed

stark: 4 bare, firm, hard, nude, pure **5** bleak, harsh, plain, quite, rigid, rough, sheer, stern, stiff, tense, utter **6** barren, severe, strong, wholly **7** violent **8** absolute, complete, desolate, entirely, metallic, obdurate, powerful, stalwart, stripped, vigorous **9** downright, unadorned **10** absolutely, unyielding **11** intractable

starnose: 4 mole

starry: 6 astral, bright **7** shining, stellar **8** luminous, sidereal, starlike, stellate **9** celestial, sparkling

start: fit, run, shy **4** dart, head, jerk, jump, lead, rush **5** alarm, begin, dodge, enter, flush, found, glent, lever, onset, rouse, sally, shock, wince **6** boggle, broach, flinch, fright, loosen, recoil, outset, spring, twitch **7** disturb, get away, impulse, kickoff, provoke, retreat, startle **8** commence, displace, draw back, embark on, handicap, outburst **9** advantage, dislocate, introduce, originate **10** inaugurate

starter: 5 drill, punch **7** entrant **8** official **10** controller

startle: 5 alarm, rouse, scare, shock, start **6** excite **8** affright, frighten, surprise **9** electrify

startling: 7 rousing **8** alarming, restless, skittish **10** surprising **11** astonishing

starvation: 4 lack **6** famine

starve: 4 fast **6** famish, hunger

starveling: 4 lean **6** hungry, pining, wasted

starwort: 5 aster **9** chickweed, colicroot

stash: end **4** hide, stop **5** hoard, store **7** secrete

state: say **4** acme, aver, etat(F.), mode, pomp, rank, seat, tell, term, weal **5** chair, posit, style, utter **6** affirm, allege, assert, avouch, degree, empire, estate, height, nation, polity, recite, relate, report, status, throne **7** account, country, declare, dignity, enounce, express, narrate **8** ceremony, eminence, grandeur, position, property, propound, set forth, standing **9** community, condition, enunciate, pronounce, situation, territory **10** asseverate, possession **11** body politic, stateliness **12** circumstance, commonwealth

based on honor: **9** timocracy

bound by treaty: **4** ally

emotional: **5** fever **7** feeling

explicitly: **6** define **7** itemize, specify **13** particularize

ideal: **6** Utopia

member: **7** citizen

of balance: **9** equipoise

of excitement: **7** ferment

of mind: **4** mood **5** humor **6** fettle, morale

office of: **11** secretariat

pert. to: **7** federal

relating to: **6** statal

subdivision: **6** county

under foreign control: **12** protectorate

State Fair author: **5** Stong

state police: **7** trooper

stated: **4** firm **5** fixed **6** avowed **7** regular **8** declared **10** formulated **11** established

statehouse: **7** capitol

stately: **5** grand, lofty **6** august, formal, superb **7** courtly, gallant, haughty **8** imperial, imposing, majestic **9** dignified **10** deliberate **11** ceremonious, magisterial, magnificent

music: **5** largo

woman: **4** Juno

statement: **4** bill, word **5** audit, dicta **6** dictum, precis, remark, report, resume **7** account, address, article, bromide, epitome, invoice, recital, summary **8** abstract, averment(law), relation, sentence, schedule **9** affidavit, agreement, manifesto, narrative **10** abridgment, allegation, deposition, expression **11** abridgement, affirmation, assertation, certificate, declaration **12** presentation **13** prevarication **14** circumspection

assumed true: **7** premise

authoritative: **6** dictum

defamatory: **5** libel

false: lie

financial: **6** budget **12** balance-sheet

formal: **9** affidavit **10** deposition

introductory: **5** proem **7** preface, prelude **8** foreword, prologue

mathematical: **7** theorem

of belief: **5** credo, creed

of facts: **4** case

self-contradictory: **7** paradox

self-evident: **6** truism

stateroom: **5** cabin

statesman: **7** statist **8** minister, diplomat **10** politician

static: **7** resting **8** inactive **9** quiescent **10** stationary **11** electricity

station: fix, run, set **4** camp, halt, post, rank, seat, spot, stop **5** berth, depot, field, place, serai, siege **6** assign, church, degree, region, stance, status **7** appoint, calling, cuartel(Sp.), dignity, habitat, posture **8** attitude, location, position **9** condition, homestead, situation **10** constitute **11** equilibrium, institution

stationary: set **4** fast **5** fixed **6** stable, static **8** immobile, inactive, moveless **9** immovable, permanent, sedentary **10** motionless, stock-still, unchanging

stationer: **9** publisher **10** bookseller

stationery: ink, pen **5** blank, paper **6** pencil **10** blank book, papeteries

statist: **9** statesman **10** politician

statistician: **7** analyst, statist

statue: **4** bust, icon, ikon, nude **5** image, orant **6** bronze **7** Madonna **8** Colossus, figurine, likeness, monument **9** sculpture

at Thebes: **6** Memnon

base: **6** plinth

gigantic: **8** colossus

in London Guildhall: Gog **5** Magog

praying: **5** orant

primitive: **6** xoanon

small: **8** figurine

that came to life: **7** Galatea

upper part of: **4** bust **5** torso

weeping: **5** Niobe

Statue of Liberty: *poet:* **7** Lazarus

sculptor: **9** Bartholdi

statuesque: **4** tall **7** shapely, stately **8** graceful

statuette: **8** figurine

stature: **6** height **8** prestige

status: **4** rank **5** state **6** aspect, classe(F.) **8** position, relation, standing **9** condition

status quo: **4** as is **13** existing state

statute: act, law **4** rule **5** edict **6** assize, decree **9** enactment, ordinance **10** regulation

heading of: **5** title

volume of: **4** code **5** codex **7** codices

staunch: See **stanch**

stave: bar **4** rung, slat, stap(Sc.) **5** break, lathi, staff, stick **6** stanza, verse **7** baculus **8** puncture

bundle of: **5** shook

off: **7** ward off **8** postpone **9** drive away

stavesacre: **8** larkspur

stay: dam, guy, lie, rib **4** base, bide, calm, curb, halt, hold, live, prop, rely, rest, rope, stem, stop, tack, wait **5** abide, allay, avast, await, brace, cable, cease, check, defer, delay, demur, dwell, pause, quell, stand, stare, tarry, visit **6** arrest, corset, depend, detain, endure, fasten, linger, pacify, remain, reside, resist, secure, shroud, status **7** appease, control, incline, refrain, satisfy, sojourn, support, sustain, triatic **8** continue, restrain **9** anchorage, cessation, hindrance, residence **10** impediment, permanence, standstill **12** postponement

staying power: 7 stamina **9** endurance

stead: 4 farm, help, lieu, site, spot **5** avail, beset, place, trace, track **6** assist, behalf **7** benefit, bestead, impress, involve, replace, service, support **8** bedstead, locality, position **9** advantage, farmstead, situation, successor **10** substitute

steadfast, stedfast: 4 fast, firm, sure, true **5** fixed, staid **6** stable, stanch, steady **7** certain, settled, staunch **8** constant, enduring, faithful, resolute **9** immovable **10** inflexible, unchanging, unswerving **11** established, unalterable

steadiness: 5 nerve **7** balance **8** firmness **9** constancy, stability

steading: 4 site **9** farmhouse, homestead

steady: 4 calm, even, firm, sure **5** fixed, grave, sober, staid **6** direct, stable, sturdy **7** assured, equable, regular, uniform **8** constant, diligent, faithful, reliable, resolute **9** boyfriend, incessant, stabilize, steadfast **10** continuous, controlled, girlfriend, invariable, sweetheart, unswerving, unwavering **11** unfaltering, unmitigated **13** unfluctuating, uninterrupted

steak: 4 club **5** chuck, flank, round, shell, t-bone **7** griskin, New York, sirloin **9** entrecote, hamburger **10** tenderloin **11** porterhouse **13** chateaubriand

steal: bag, cly, cop, gyp, nim, rap, rob **4** crib, gain, glom, hook, lift, stem, take **5** bribe, creep, fetch, filch, harry, pinch, poach, shaft, sneak, stalk, swipe, theft **6** abduct, burgle, convey, divert, extend, handle, kidnap, pilfer, pirate, rustle, snitch **7** bargain, purloin **8** embezzle, peculate **9** condiddle **10** plagiarize **11** appropriate **14** misappropriate

stealer: 5 thief **6** robber **7** burglar **10** plagiarist **11** biblioklept

cattle: **7** abactor, rustler

stealthy: sly **6** artful, secret **7** catlike, cunning, furtive **11** clandestine **13** surreptitious

walk: **5** stalk

steam: 4 boil, fume, heat, reek **5** force, power, smoke, vapor, water **6** energy **8** vaporize, vexation **10** exhalation, irritation

bath: **5** sauna

jet: **5** stufa **8** soffione

pipe: **5** riser

steamer: 4 boat, clam, ship **5** liner **6** vessel **9** steamship

cabin: **5** texas

steamroller: 4 whip **5** crush **8** override

steamship: 5 liner **7** steamer

route: **4** lane

smokestack: **6** funnel

steatite: 4 talc **9** soapstone

steed: 4 Arab **5** horse **7** charger, courser

steel: 4 gird, rail **5** acier(F.), inure, press **6** damask, harden, smooth, toledo **8** Bessemer, Damascus **9** encourage **10** strengthen

process: **8** Bessemer **11** cementation

steelhead: 5 trout

steely: 10 unyielding

steelyard: 7 balance

steep: ret **4** bate, bath, bold, bowk, brew, buck, high, soak, stew, tall **5** bathe, brant, brent, heavy, hilly, imbue, lofty, proud, sharp, sheer **6** abrupt, bright, clifty, decoct, drench, imbibe, imbrue, infuse, seethe **7** arduous, extract, extreme, immerse **8** elevated, headlong, macerate, saturate, solution **9** difficult, distemper, excessive, expensive, precipice **10** exorbitant, impregnate **11** precipitous **13** perpendicular

steeper: 6 vat **6** teapot, vessel **7** cistern

steeple: 5 spire, tower **6** cupola **8** pinnacle **9** campanile

steer: con, tip **4** bull, conn, helm, lead, stot **5** guide, pilot **6** bovine, direct, govern, manage **7** bullock, control, operate, oversee

close to wind: **4** luff

steerage: 8 guidance **9** direction **10** management, regulation

steering: aim **9** direction **10** government, management

apparatus: **4** helm **6** wheel **6** rudder, tiller

part: **10** rudderhead

superintend: con **4** conn

steeve: 4 pack, stow **5** store, stuff

stein: mug **4** toby

steinbock: 8 antelope

stela, stele: 4 slab **6** pillar **8** monument **10** gravestone

stelar: 10 columnlike

stellar: 5 chief **6** astral, major, starry **7** leading **8** starlike, stellate **9** principal **10** preeminent **11** outstanding

Steller's sea cow: 6 rytina

stem: bow, bun, dam, leg, ram **4** axis, base, body, bole, cane, culm, halt, load, prow, race, reed, risp, root, stop, tamp **5** check, haulm, orise, shaft, stalk, stipe, stock, trunk **6** branch, derive, oppose, spring, stanch **7** lineage, pedicel, petiole, spindle **8** ancestry, contract, peduncle, restrain **9** originate, petiolule **10** derive from

bulblike: 4 corm 5 tuber 7 rhizome
climbing: 4 bine 7 tendril
fungus: 5 stipe
joint: 4 node
part: 4 pith 5 stele
pert. to: 7 cauline 8 stipular
sheath: 5 ocrea
stemma: 7 descent, lineage 8 ancestry, pedigree 9 genealogy
stemmer: bar
stench: 4 fogo, odor, reek 5 fetor, smell, stink 6 foetor
Stendhal hero: 5 Sorel
stenographer: 8 recorder
stenography: 9 shorthand 12 brachygraphy
stent: 5 tight 6 extend, extent 7 stretch 12 outstretched
stentor: 6 roarer
stentorian: 4 loud 10 resounding
step: act, sty, way 4 gait, pace, rank, rest, rung, walk 5 break, crush, dance, grade, ledge, level, plane, round, shelf, space, stage, stair, stalk, strut, stufe(G.), tread 6 action, degree, manner, squash, stride 7 advance, deprive, measure 8 distance, footfall, foothold, footrest, footstep, movement 9 footprint, gradation, procedure, promotion 10 proceeding, stepladder 11 translation
dance: pas 5 coule 6 chasse 8 glissade
introductory: 8 rudiment 10 initiative
ladder's: 4 rime, rung
measuring device: 10 passimeter
over fence: 5 stile
part: 5 riser, tread 6 nosing
recording device: 8 odograph
rope ladder: 7 ratline
series of raised: 6 gradin 7 gradine
step up: rev 8 increase 10 accelerate
step-by-step: 7 in order, gradual 9 piecemeal
step-in: 4 shoe 7 slipper
step-ins: 10 underpants
stepbrother: 9 beau-frere(F.) 11 beaux-freres
stepdame: 10 stepmother
steppe: 5 plain, space 7 prairie 9 grassland, wasteland
storm: 5 buran
stepper: 5 horse 6 dancer
steps: See **step, staircase**
stepson: 8 beau-fils(F.) 9 beaux-fils
stere: 9 kiloliter
stereotyped: 5 trite 7 routine 9 hackneyed
sterile: dry 4 arid, dead, geld 6 barren, meager, meagre, otiose 7 aseptic, useless 8 impotent, sanitary 9 fruitless, infertile 10 unfruitful, unoriginal 11 ineffective 12 unproductive
sterility: 7 asepsis 10 barrenness

sterilize: fix 4 geld, spay 5 unsex 6 change, neuter 9 disinfect
sterling: 5 penny 7 genuine 9 excellent
stern: 4 back, dour, firm, grim, hard, helm, rear 5 harsh, rough, steer, stout 6 fierce, gloomy, mighty, rudder, savage, severe, strict, strong, sturdy, sullen, tiller, unkind 7 austere, massive, tail end 8 buttocks, exacting, resolute, rigorous 9 unbending, unfeeling 10 astringent, forbidding, inexorable, inflexible, relentless, uninviting, unyielding 11 hardhearted 14 uncompromising
toward: aft 5 abaft 6 astern
Sterne character: 4 Slop, Toby, Trim 6 Shandy, Yorick 8 Tristram
sternforemost: 7 awkward 8 backward
sternness: 5 rigor 7 cruelty 8 hardness, severity 9 austerity, harshness, rigidness, stiffness 10 strictness 12 exactingness 13 inflexibility
sternum: 8 skeleton 10 breastbone
sternutation: 6 sneeze 8 sneezing
sterol: 7 alcohol
stertor: 5 snore
stevedore: 6 loader, stower 8 cargador 12 longshoreman
Stevenson: *character:* 4 Hyde 6 Jekyll 10 Jim Hawkins 14 Long John Silver
home: 5 Samoa
novel: 9 Kidnapped 14 Treasure Island
stew: 4 boil, cook, dive, fret, mess, olio, slum, snit 5 anger, cloud, imbue, steep, study, sweat, worry 6 burgoo, dither, ragout, seethe, simmer 7 brothel, goulash, haricot, swelter 8 hothouse 9 Brunswick, commotion, confusion 10 capilotade, excitement, hodgepodge, hotchpotch, miscellany 11 predicament
steward: 5 dewan, diwan, graff, grave 6 factor, grieve, waiter 7 bailiff, curator, foreman, granger, manager, officer, proctor 8 bhandari, employee, guardian 9 custodian, dispense, seneschal 10 magistrate 11 chamberlain
monastery: 8 cellarer
ship: 6 flunky 7 flunkey
stewed: 5 drunk 10 inebriated 11 intoxicated
sthenic: 6 active, strong
stib: 6 dunlin 9 sandpiper
stich: 4 line 5 verse
stick: bar, bat, bow, cue, gad, gum, put, rod, set 4 bind, cane, clag, clam, club, fife, glue, kill, mast, poke, pole, push, spit, stab, stem, stop, twig, wand 5 affix, baton, cheat, cleam, cling, decoy, delay, demur, flute, mount, paste, place, prick, shoot, shove, staff, stalk, stall, stave, trunk 6 adhere, attach, baffle, ballow, billet, branch, cement, cleave, cohere, cudgel, endure, ferule, fescue,

fleece, impale, mallet, pierce, puzzle, rammer, strike, thrust **7** defraud, drummer, nonplus **8** bludgeon, clarinet, hesitate, puncture, revolver, tolerate **9** crabstick, drumstick **10** overcharge

bamboo: **5** lathi **6** lathee

bundle of: **5** fagot **6** fasces **7** fascine

conductor's: **5** baton

crooked: **5** caman **7** cammock, gambrel

jumping: **4** pogo

measuring: **5** ruler **7** ellwand **8** yardwand **9** yardstick

mountain climbing: **10** alpenstock

stick out: **7** extrude **8** protrude

stick up: rob **6** hold up **7** plunder, ransack

sticker: bur **4** burr, seal **5** knife, label, poser, stamp, thorn **6** paster, puzzle, weapon **7** bramble

sticking: **6** viscid **8** adhering, cohesive **12** stonewalling

stick-in-the-mud: **4** fogy **6** square **10** fuddy-duddy

stickleback: **4** fish **6** bandie(Sc.)

stickler: **6** purist, second, umpire **7** arbiter, meddler **8** mediator

sticky: **4** clit, hard **5** gluey, gooey, humid, messy **6** claggy, clammy, clarty, slushy, viscid, wooden **7** viscous **8** adhesive **9** difficult, glutinous **10** saccharine **11** sentimental **13** uncomfortable

stiff: bum **4** dead, deep, firm, hard, high, hobo, taut **5** brave, budge, clung, dense, drunk, fixed, grave, harsh, horse, miser, rigid, steep, tense, thick, tramp, woody **6** clumsy, corpse, formal, loafer, proper, robust, severe, stanch, strong, sturdy **7** awkward, buckram, cadaver, precise, starchy **8** absorbed, drunkard, exacting, resolute, rigorous, stalwart, starched, stubborn **9** difficult, excessive, laborious, obstinate, unbending **10** ceremonial, consistent, inflexible, unyielding **11** intoxicated **12** pertinacious **14** uncompromising

stiff-necked: **5** proud **8** stubborn **9** obstinate **12** contumacious

stiffen: set **5** brace **6** benumb, harden, starch **10** inspissate

stiffness: **5** rigor **8** rigidity **10** constraint **11** starchiness

stifle: gag **4** stop **5** check, choke **6** muffle, quench **7** repress, silence, smother **8** strangle, stultify, suppress, throttle **9** suffocate **10** extinguish

stigma: **4** blot, mark, scar, spot **5** brand, cloud, odium, stain, taint **6** defect **7** blemish **9** disgrace, dishonor

stigmatize: **5** brand **7** censure **8** denounce

stile: **4** post, step **8** entrance **9** turnstile

stiletto: **4** kill, stab **6** bodkin, dagger, stylet **9** eyeleteer

still: but, een, low, mum, tho, yet **4** also, calm, cosh, drip, even, ever, hush, lull, stop **5** allay, check, inert, quiet **6** always, distil, gentle, hushed, pacify, serene, soothe **7** appease, however, silence, subdued **8** habitual, inactive, restrain, suppress, tranquil **9** noiseless, uniformly **10** constantly, distillery, motionless, photograph, stationary, uneventful **11** continually **12** nevertheless

stillicide: **4** drip, drop **9** eavesdrop

stilt: **4** bird, limp, pile, pole, post **5** shaft **6** crutch **8** longlegs

stilted: **6** formal, wooden **7** awkward, pompous **8** affected **9** bombastic, dignified **10** rhetorical **11** sententious

Stilton: **6** cheese

feature: **4** mold

Stilwell's nickname: **10** Vinegar Joe

stimulant: kat **4** drug **5** drink, tonic **6** bracer **8** beverage **9** incentive, sassafras

heart: **8** cardiant, thialdin **9** digitalis, thialdine **10** adrenaline, epinephrin **11** epinephrine

in coffee: **7** caffein **8** caffeine

in tea: **5** thein

stimulate: fan, jog, pep **4** goad, move, spur, stir, urge, whet **5** brace, elate, filip, impel, rouse, sting **6** affect, arouse, excite, fillip, incite **7** animate, enliven, inspire, provoke, quicken **8** irritate, motivate **9** encourage, galvanize, instigate **10** exhilarate, invigorate

stimulating: **5** brisk **7** pungent **8** exciting **9** innerving **12** invigorating

stimulus: **4** goad, spur **5** cause, filip, sting **6** fillip, motive **7** impetus **9** incentive

threshold: **5** limen

sting: gyp **4** bite, dupe, goad, mast, pain, pike, pole, post, tang, urge **5** cheat, prick, shaft, smart, wound **6** impale, incite, nettle, pierce, tingle **7** stimuli **8** irritate, stimulus **9** stimulate **10** incitement **11** double cross

stinger: **4** blow **5** drink

stinginess: **9** closeness, frugality, parsimony **13** niggardliness

stinging: **6** biting, bitter **7** caustic, piquant, pungent **8** piercing **10** irritating **11** acrimonious

stingo: ale, vim, zip **4** beer, zest **6** energy

stingy: **4** dree(Sc.), hard, mean **5** cheap, light, sharp, stint, tight **6** biting, greedy, meager, scanty **7** miserly, niggard, nipping, selfish **8** covetous **9** illiberal, penurious **10** avaricious **11** closefisted **12** parsimonious **13** pennypinching

stinking: bad **4** foul, rank **5** drunk, fetid **6** putrid, rancid **7** noisome **8** unsavory **9** offensive **10** malodorous

stint, stent: **4** duty, stay, stop, task **5**

bound, cease, check, chore, limit, scant, serve, spare, spell, stunt **6** assign, desist, divide, scrimp **7** confine **8** quantity, restrain, restrict **9** economize, restraint **10** assignment, limitation, proportion **11** restriction

stipe: 4 stem **5** stalk **6** caudex **7** petiole

stipend: ann, fee, pay **4** hire, wage **5** annal **6** income, salary **7** payment, prebend **9** allowance, emolument **12** compensation, remuneration

stipendiary: 4 beak **7** soldier, teacher **9** clergyman, mercenary **10** magistrate **11** beneficiary

stipple: dot **5** fleck **6** render **7** engrave, speckle

stipulate: 5 agree **7** bargain, provide, specify **8** contract, covenant

stipulation: 4 bond, item **6** clause, demand, detail **7** article, bargain, compact, proviso **8** contract, covenant **9** agreement, condition, situation **11** arrangement, undertaking

stir: ado, fan, gog, jog, mix, sir **4** busk, fuss, jail, move, plow, poke, roil, to-do **5** awake, budge, churn, doing, hurry, rally, rouse, shake, shift, shove, stoke, waken **6** arouse, awaken, bestir, bustle, excite, flurry, foment, hubbub, incite, motion, muddle, pother, prison, quetch, seethe, tumult **7** agitate, animate, blunder, disturb, flutter, inflame, provoke, trouble **8** activity, brandish, displace, movement **9** commotion, stimulate **10** manipulate **12** penitentiary

stirabout: 8 porridge

stirk: cow **4** bull **6** heifer **7** bullock

stirless: 10 motionless

stirps: 4 race **5** stock **6** branch, family

stirring: 5 afoot, astir **6** moving, tumult, uproar **7** rousing **8** activity, eloquent, exciting, movement **9** agitation, animating, inspiring, thrilling **10** incitement **11** stimulating

stirrup: bar **4** ring, rope **5** clamp, strap **6** stapes **7** support **8** footrest
hood: **8** tapadera(Sp.)
straps: **8** chapelet

stitch: bit, hem, sew **4** loop, pain, purl **5** baste, picot, ridge, unite **6** feston, suture, tailor **8** distance **9** embroider
knitting: **4** purl **6** feston
zigzag: **8** bargello

stitchbird: ihi

stitcher: 5 sewer **6** seamer **10** dressmaker

stitchwort: 9 chickweed

stithy: 5 anvil, forge **6** smithy **8** smithery

stive: 5 pen up **6** stifle **9** suffocate

stiver: 4 coin **5** money **7** bristle, stagger **8** struggle

stivy: 5 close **8** stifling

stoa: 7 portico **9** colonnade

stoat: 6 ermine, weasel **8** clubster **9** clubstart

stob: 4 post, stab **5** stake **6** pierce

stock: cop, log **4** band, bond, butt, fund, hive, line, post, race, rail, soup, stem **5** banal, block, blood, brace, breed, broth, flesh, frame, hoard, stake, stick, store, stump, swell, trite, trunk, trust **6** budget, common, cravat, family, handle, holder, pillar, strain, supply **7** capital, descent, extract, lineage, provide, reserve, rhizome, support **8** ancestry, bitstock, colewort, material, ordinary **9** hackneyed, livestock, provision, replenish **10** estimation, foundation **11** commonplace, certificate **12** accumulation
framed on: **5** ramed
of food: **5** foray
of goods: **4** line
preliminary: **5** scrip
racial: **8** pedigree

stockade: pen **4** jail **5** etape, pound **6** corral, kennel, prison **7** barrier, fortify, protect **8** hoosegow, poundage **9** enclosure
Africa: **4** boma **5** kraal **6** keddah, zareba **7** zareeba

stock exchange: 6 bourse(F.)
business: **9** arbitrage
patron: **5** buyer **6** seller, trader

stockfish: cod **4** hake, ling **5** torsk **7** haddock

stock-in-trade: 4 tool, ware **5** goods **7** capital **8** material **9** equipment **11** merchandise

stocked: 7 replete

stockholder: 8 investor, stockman

stocking: bas(F.) **4** hose **7** hosiery
bishop's: **6** buskin, caliga
cotton: **5** lisle
footless: **7** hushion
ornament: **5** clock
run: **6** ladder
soleless: **7** traheen
worsted: **7** scogger

stockjobbing: 8 agiotage

stockman: 6 herder **7** rancher **8** beastman

stockpile: 5 amass, hoard, lay up **7** backlog, reserve **9** inventory, reservoir

stocky: fat **4** stub **5** cobby **6** chumpy, stubby, sturdy **7** bunting, defiant **8** thickset **9** corpulent **10** boisterous, headstrong

stodge: 4 plod **6** trudge **7** satiate, satisfy

stodgy: 4 dull **5** bulky, heavy, tacky, thick **6** packed, sticky **7** crammed, lumpish, stuffed, tedious **8** thickset **9** out-of-date, satiating **10** uninspired **13** uninteresting

stogy: 4 boot, shoe **5** cigar **6** brogan, clumsy, coarse

stoic: 5 porch 6 stolid 7 ascetic, passive, patient 9 impassive 10 phlegmatic 11 unconcerned

stoicism: 6 apathy 8 patience 11 impassivity 13 impassiveness
founder: 4 Zeno

stoke: 4 feed, fire, fuel, poke, tend 5 stick 6 supply

stoker: 5 firer 7 fireman, greaser
glassworks: 6 teaser

stole: fur 5 scarf 7 garment, orarion 8 vestment 13 epitrachelion

stolen property: 4 loot, pelf
buyer of: 5 fence

stolid: 4 dull, firm, slow 5 beefy 6 stupid 7 brutish, clumpse, clumpst, passive 9 impassive, inanimate, unfeeling 10 impassable 12 unexciteable

stolon: 5 shoot 6 branch, runner 7 rhizome

stoma: 4 pore 5 mouth 7 opening, orifice

stomach: gut, maw 4 bear, craw, crop, kyte, vell 5 belly, bingy, brook, pride, rumen 6 bingey, desire, endure, gebbie(Sc.), resent, spirit 7 abdomen, gizzard, gizzern 8 appetite, tolerate 9 arrogance 11 inclination
acidity: 4 acor
bird's maw 4 craw, crop
enzyme: 6 pepsin, rennin
lower opening of: 7 pylorus
muscle: 7 pylorus
pert. to: 7 gastric
ruminant's first: 5 rumen
ruminant's fourth: 4 read, reed 8 abomasum, roddikin(Sc.)
ruminant's second: 6 bonnet 9 reticulum
ruminant's third: 6 omasum 9 manyplies 10 psalterium
used as food: 5 tripe

stomach-ache: 5 colic 7 gullion 12 collywobbles

stomacher: 4 gimp 7 echelle 8 forepart

stomachy: 5 proud 8 paunched, spirited 9 irascible, irritable, obstinate, resentful 10 potbellied

stomp: See **stamp**

stone (see also **rock**): gem, pit, rub 4 bone, buhr, pelt, rock 5 block, brick, lapis(L.), scour, scrub 6 chaton, cobble, domino, marble 7 diamond, dornick, scruple, sharpen 8 lapidate, memorial, monolith, testicle 9 hailstone, hemachate, milestone, millstone, whetstone 10 gravestone, grindstone
abrasive: 5 emery
and clay: 4 sere
artificial: 8 albolite, albolith 9 granolith
base: 6 plinth
Biblical: 4 ezel
broken: 6 rubble
carved: 5 cameo

chip of: 5 spall 6 gallet
convert into: 7 petrify
druid: 6 sarsen
drupe: 6 nutlet
eagle: 5 etite
engraving: 8 intaglio
famous: 4 Hope, Pitt 5 Green, Mogul, Sancy, Scone 6 Jonker, Nassak, Orloff, Regent, Vargas 7 Blarney, Dresden, Jubilee, Kohinur, Rosetta, Stewart, Tiffany 8 Braganza, Cullinan, Kohinoor 9 Excelsior, Polar Star 10 Florentine, Great Mogul 12 Plymouth Rock, Star of Africa 14 Star of the South
fruit: pit 4 paip 5 drupe 6 pyrene 7 putamen
gem cutting: 6 adamas
granitic: 6 gneiss
grave: 5 stela, stele 6 marker, stelae, steles 8 memorial, monument
grinding: 6 metate
hammering: 8 lapstone
hand grinding: 4 mano
hard: 5 flint 6 quartz 7 adamant 9 chatoyant
heap: 4 karn 5 cairn
hoist: 5 lewis
hollow: 5 druse, geode
hurling device: 9 trebucket
implement: 4 celt 5 arrow 7 neolith
kidney: 8 calculus
loose: 6 gibber
maize grinding: 4 mano
meteoric: 8 aerolite, aerolith
monumental: 4 lech 6 menhir 8 megalith
of arch: 8 keystone
paving: 4 flag, slab, slat
pert. to: 7 lithoid
philosopher's: 6 carmot, elixir
precious: gem 4 keas, onyx, opal, ruby 5 beryl, pearl, topaz 6 garnet, jasper, lazuli, ligure 7 diamond, peridot 8 astroite, sapphire, tigereye 9 aromatite
pyramid-shape: 6 benben
shaped into pillars: 7 obelisk 9 monoliths
sharpening: oil 4 hone, whet
seam: dry
semiprecious: 4 jade, onyx, sard 5 agate, lapis 6 garnet, lazule, lazuli 7 olivine 8 murrhine 11 lapis lazuli
small: 6 pebble
squared: 6 ashlar
to death: 8 lapidate
uncut: 4 naif
upright: 5 bauta 6 menhir
used for cameos: 4 onyx
woman turned into: 5 Niobe
worker: 5 mason 6 slater
writing: 5 slate

Stone Age tool: 4 celt 6 eolith 7 neolith 10 palaeolith

stonecrop: 5 orpin, sedum 6 orpine

stonecutter: 6 jadder
chisel: **5** drove
disease: **9** silicosis
wooden receptacle of: **7** sebilla
stoned: 5 doped, drunk **6** zonked **7** drugged **8** turned on **9** spaced-out **11** intoxicated
stonelike: 7 lithoid
stoneman: 5 cairn
stonewall: 5 evade **8** obstruct, stubborn **9** obstinate **10** determined, filibuster
stoneware: 4 gres **7** ceramic, pottery **11** earthenware
stonework: 7 masonry
stoneworker: 5 mason
stony: 4 cold, card, poor **5** fixed, rigid, rocky, rough, still **7** adamant **8** obdurate, pitiless **9** petrified, unfeeling **10** inexorable, inflexible, petrifying, relentless, stupefying, unyielding **14** expressionless **15** uncompassionate
stood: 5 arose **7** endured
stooge: 4 foil, tool
stookie: 4 fool
stool: 4 base, mora, pole, seat, thew **5** bench, decoy, morae, stand, stump **6** buffet, growth, tiller, tripod **7** commode, creepie, taboret, trestle **8** kingship, platform, standard, tabouret **9** footstool **10** foundation **11** chieftaincy
stoolpigeon: spy **4** fink, sing **5** decoy, narks, shill **6** inform, snitch, squeal **7** peacher **8** betrayer, informer, observer
stoop: bow, lay **4** bend, bode, duck, lean, post, sink, tilt **5** deign, lower, porch, slant, souse, stake, stump, swoop, yield **6** alight, boggle, coorie, crouch, debase, gamble, huckle, humble, patron, pillar, pounce, submit **7** decline, degrade, descend, subject, succumb, veranda **8** overcome, platform, stairway **9** prostrate, supporter **10** condescend **11** humiliation **13** condescension
stop: bar, dam, end, inn, pug **4** bait, bode, bung, call, calk, clog, drop, fill, halt, mend, pawl, plug, quit, stay, stem, stum, wear, weir, whoa **5** avast, basta, block, break, catch, caulk, cease, check, choke, close, delay, embar, estop, holla, hollo, parry, pause, point, repel, stall, tarry **6** alight, anchor, arrest, behold, boggle, defeat, desist, detain, draw up, finish, gravel, hinder, period, reside, scotch, stanch, stench **7** caesura, counter, prevent, sojourn, station, staunch, stopper, suspend **8** caesurae(pl.), obstacle, obstruct, obturate, pinblock, preclude, prohibit, restrain, stoppage, suppress, withhold **9** barricade, cessation, hindrance, intercept, interrupt, punctuate **11** countermand, discontinue, obstruction **12** intermis-

sion, interruption, lodginghouse
blood: **6** stanch
legally: **5** estop
organ: **5** orage, viola **7** posaune **8** dulciana, gemshorn **9** rohrflote
short: **5** delay, pause **7** respite **8** interval **9** cessation **12** intermission
temporary: **5** pause
up: **4** cork, plug **7** occlude
stop watch: 5 timer
stopcock: 5 valve **6** faucet
stope: 8 excavate **10** excavation
stopgap: 4 plug **5** shift **6** resort **9** expedient, makeshift **10** substitute
stoppage: end **4** halt **5** block, choke, hitch **6** arrest, devall, strike **7** embargo, seizure **9** cessation, detention **10** arrestment, congestion **11** obstruction
body fluid: **6** stasis
debate: **7** cloture
temporary: **5** delay, pause **6** arrest, recess **10** arrestment **12** interception, intermission, interruption
stopper: wad **4** bung, cork, fill, plug **7** bouchon
stopping: 4 halt **5** block, check **7** seizure **9** detention **11** obstruction, punctuation
device: **5** brake
stopple: 4 bung, cork, plug **7** stopper
storage: 4 dump **11** safekeeping
battery plate: **4** grid
bin: **4** mow **4** loft **7** granary **8** elevator
charge: **9** demurrage
place: bin **4** shed, silo **5** attic, depot **6** cellar, closet **7** arsenal, granary **8** cupboard, elevator **9** blood bank, reservoir, warehouse
prepare for: can
room: **6** closet, larder **7** lastage, lazaret **9** lazarette, lazaretto
storax: 5 resin **6** balsam
store: bin **4** cave, deck, deep, dose, fond, fund, hold, mass, save, shop, stow **5** amass, breed, cache, depot, hoard, stock **6** amount, budget, garner, market, repair, shoppe, supply **7** bhandar, collect, deposit, furnish, husband, provide, put away, reserve, restore **8** emporium, reserves, supplies, treasure **9** abundance, chandlery, livestock, replenish, reservoir, resources, sweetshop, warehouse **10** accumulate, collection, provisions, storehouse **12** accumulation
candle: **9** chandlery
fodder: **6** ensile **8** ensilate
food: **6** market **9** sweetshop **12** delicatessen
fruit: **12** greengrocery
hidden: **5** cache
Hindu: **7** bhandar
in ground: **5** cache

in silo: **6** ensile
military: **7** canteen **10** commissary
milk: **5** dairy
shoe: **7** bootery
slang: **5** stash
up: **4** hive **6** garner **8** squirrel
storehouse: 4 barn, bike, crib, shed, silo **5** cache, depot, etape **7** arsenal, bhandar, camalig, camarin, granary **8** building, magazine, treasury **9** repertory, warehouse **10** commissary **11** chalkotheke
military: **5** depot **7** arsenal **10** commissary
public: **5** depot, etape
rural: mow **4** barn, crib, shed, silo **7** granary
wool: **6** lanary
storekeeper: 6 grocer **8** bhandari, merchant, storeman **10** shopkeeper **11** almacenista, stockkeeper
storeroom: 4 cave, gola, loft **5** attic **6** bodega, cellar, pantry **7** buttery, genizah, granary **8** basement **10** repository
stork: 4 ibis **6** simbil **7** marabou **12** xenorhynchus
kin of: **4** ibis **5** heron **10** hammerhead
storken: 6 thrive **7** congeal, stiffen
storklike: 8 pelargic
storm: wap **4** birr, blow, bura, fume, gale, gust, hail, rage, raid, rain, rand, rant, rave, snow, wind **5** anger, blizz, brash, buran, orage **6** attack, expugn, shamal, shower, simoom, simoon, tumult, Wester **7** assault, barrage, bluster, borasca, borasco, bravado, cyclone, rampage, tempest, tornado, trouble **8** calamity, eruption, outburst, upheaval, violence **9** agitation, bourasque, commotion, hurricane **10** hurly-burly **11** disturbance
dust: **6** simoom
god: **5** Rudra
revolving: **7** cyclone
sand: **6** tebbad
snow: **5** buran
stormcock: 6 petrel, thrush **9** fieldfare **10** woodpecker
stormy: 4 dark, foul, wild **5** dirty, gusty **6** raging **7** furious, riotous, violent **8** agitated, cluttery **9** inclement, turbulent **10** blustering, passionate, tumultuous **11** tempestuous
story: fib, lie **4** myth, news, plot, saga, tale, tier, yarn **5** etage, fable, floor, rumor, solar, soler **6** fabula, gossip, legend, record, report, solar **7** account, article, episode, history, narrate, parable, recital **8** anecdote, intrigue **9** falsehood, happening, narration, narrative, statement, tradition **11** description
complication in: **4** node **5** nodus
continued: **6** serial, sequel

correspondent's: **8** dispatch
exclusive: **4** beat **5** scoop
heroic: **4** gest, saga **5** geste
involved: **8** megillah
kind of: **4** epic, saga, tale, yarn **5** conte, fable **6** canard, legend, script **7** mystery, novella, parable, romance **8** allegory, scenario, whodunit
short: **5** conte **8** anecdote
traditional: **4** myth **6** legend
upper: **5** attic **6** garret
storyteller: 4 liar **5** Aesop **6** disour, fibber **8** narrator **9** raconteur
stot: 4 bull **5** bound, lurch, steer **6** bounce **7** rebound, stagger, stammer, stumble, stutter
stound: 4 ache, beat, blow, pain, pang, stun, time **5** grief, shock, sight, smart, swoon, throb **6** attack, benumb, bruise, moment, period, season, sorrow, thrill, twinge **7** assault, instant, stupefy **8** astonish, occasion **10** apparition **12** astonishment, stupefaction
stoup: cup **4** cask, font, pail **5** basin **6** bucket, flagon, vessel **7** measure, tankard **10** aspersoria **11** aspersorium
holy water: **8** benitier, canthari(pl.) **9** cantharus, kantharos, kantharoi(pl.)
stoush: 4 beat, blow **6** attack, strike, tirade **7** assault
stout: ale, fat **4** beer, bold, firm, gnat, hard **5** brave, bulky, burly, cobby, frack, freck, hardy, heavy, obese, plump, proud, shock, solid, tough **6** active, flagon, fleshy, liquor, porter, portly, robust, rotund, stable, stanch, stocky, stouty, strong, sturdy **7** defiant, haughty, violent, weighty **8** arrogant, bouncing, enduring, forceful, forcible, horsefly, insolent, powerful, resolute, stalwart, stubborn, thickset, vigorous **9** corpulent, energetic, obstinate **10** courageous, overweight **11** substantial
and rough: **5** burly
and short: **6** stocky **8** thickset
stout-hearted: 4 bold, good **5** brave **7** doughty **8** unafraid **9** dauntless **10** courageous
stove: 4 dent, etna, kiln **5** grate, plate, range, stave **6** cockle, heater **7** furnace **8** potbelly **10** calefactor, glasshouse **12** conservatory
alcohol: **4** etna
charcoal: hod
grated: **8** chauffer
part: **4** oven **7** firebox, griddle
stovepipe: hat **4** flue **7** silk hat
stow: box, cut **4** cram, crop, hide, hold, mass, pack, stop, trim **5** cease, crowd, douse, dowse, lodge, place, shoot, slice, stack, store, stump **7** arrange, contain, secrete

cargo: 5 steve 6 steeve
stowage: 6 charge 7 packing
Stowe novel: 14 Uncle Tom's cabin
character: 5 Topsy 8 Little Eva, Uncle Tom 11 Simon Legree
stower: 9 stevedore
strabismus: 6 squint 8 cock-eye, cross-eye
Strad, Stradivarius: 6 violin
straddle: 5 hedge 6 option, sprawl 7 astride, bracket 8 bestride 11 noncommital, spread-eagle
strafe: 5 shell 6 punish 7 bombard 8 fire upon 9 castigate
straggle: 4 rove 5 stray 6 ramble, sprawl, wander 7 meander
straight: 4 neat 5 brant, erect, euthy, frank, ortho, plain, recti, rigid, stern 6 aright, candid, direct, graith, honest, severe 7 rightly, sincere, stretch, through, unmixed, upright 8 accurate, directly, honestly, reliable, rigorous, sequence, unbroken, virtuous 9 correctly, honorably, undiluted 10 continuous, conventional, methodical, unmodified 11 immediately, straightway, undeviating, unqualified 12 continuously, heterosexual, unswervingly 13 unaccompanied, uninterrupted
straight course: 7 beeline
straight edge: 5 ruler
straight-faced: 7 deadpan 9 impassive
straight-haired: 12 leiotrichous 13 lissotrichous
straight man: 4 foil 6 stooge
partner: 8 comedian
straight-out: 5 utter 6 direct 8 outright 11 unqualified 12 unrestrained 13 thorough-going
straight up and down: 15 perpendicularly
straighten: 5 align, aline, level, order, plumb 7 compose, rectify, unravel 11 disentangle
up: 4 tidy
straightforward: 4 even, open 5 apert, frank 6 aright, candid, dexter, direct, honest, simple 7 sincere 8 directly, outright, straight 9 foreright, outspoken 10 forthright, unaffected 11 undeviating
straightway: 4 anon 6 aright, bedene 8 directly 9 downright, forthwith 10 forthright 11 immediately
strain: air, hug, sie, sye, tax, try 4 balk, barb, bend, bind, curb, dash, gain, heft, kind, line, mood, note, ooze, race, sift, solo, sort, tone, tune, turn, urge, vein 5 breed, clasp, class, demur, exert, force, music, press, raise, shade, sieve, stock, style, tenor, touch, trace, track, trail, wield 6 burden, colate, effort, extend,

extort, family, fasten, filter, injure, manner, melody, obtain, sprain, strand, streak, stress, strive, temper, thread, weaken, wrench 7 anxiety, confine, descent, element, embrace, lineage, overtax, progeny, quality, squeeze, stretch, strophe, tension, trickle, variety 8 ancestry, brandish, compress, eliquate, exertion, restrain, tendency 9 begetting, character, constrain, constrict, percolate 10 distortion, generation 11 deformation, disposition
blood: 4 race 5 breed, stock 6 family 7 lineage
chief: 5 brunt
great: tax, tug 5 tense 6 stress 7 tension 8 exertion, overbear 11 tenterhooks
measuring device: 9 telemeter
strained: 4 taut 5 tense, tight 6 forced 7 intense 8 weakened, wrenched 9 distorted, laborious 10 farfetched
strainer: 4 cage, sile 5 sieve, strum, tamis 6 filter, milsey, milsie, sifter 8 colander, colature, huckmuck 10 colatorium
strait: 4 area, bind, neck, pass 6 crisis, narrow 7 channel, isthmus 11 predicament
between Labrador and Newfoundland: 9 Belle Isle
Strait of Gibraltar: 17 Pillars of Hercules
Strait of Messina rock: 6 Scylla
straiten: 5 hem in, limit 6 hamper 7 confine, enclose 8 contract, distress, restrict 9 embarrass
strait-jacket: 8 camisole 9 restraint
strait-laced: 4 prim 5 stiff 6 severe, strict 8 stubborn 9 obstinate, puritanic 10 restricted 11 constrained 12 narrowminded 14 overscrupulous
straits: 5 pinch, rigor 7 narrows, poverty 8 extremes 10 difficulty
Straits Settlement: 6 Penang 8 Malacca 9 Singapore
island: 5 Cocos 6 Labuan 9 Christmas
native state: 5 Perak 6 Johore, Pahang 8 Selangor 11 Sungei Ujong 13 Negri Sembilan
strake: rut 4 band 5 crack 6 loiter, streak, stripe, stroll, trough, wander 7 stretch
strand: sea 4 bank, quay, wire 5 beach, fiber, shore, wharf 6 gutter, maroon, region, stream, thread 7 channel, current 8 filament 9 shipwreck
stranded: 6 ashore 7 aground, beached 8 castaway, marooned 10 high and dry
strange: new, odd 4 fell, rare, unco 5 alien, droll, eerie, fremd, novel, queer 6 exotic, quaint 7 bizarre, curious, distant, erratic, foreign, oddball, uncanny, unknown, unusual 8 abnormal, estrange, fanciful, peculiar, reserved, sin-

gular, uncommon **9** couthless, different, eccentric, unnatural, wonderful **10** mysterious, outlandish, unfamiliar, unfriendly **11** exceptional **12** unaccustomed, unacquainted **13** extraordinary, inexperienced, preternatural

language: **4** cant **5** lingo **6** jargon **7** dialect

stranger: 5 alien, guest, odder **6** ganger, novice **7** comical, visitor **8** emigrant, estrange, intruder, newcomer, outsider **9** auslander, foreigner, outlander **10** tramontane **12** intermeddler

strangle: 4 kill, slay **5** choke, grane **6** stifle **7** garrote, repress **8** garrotte, suppress, throttle **9** constrict, suffocate

stranglehold: 4 grip **8** chancery, monopoly

strangulate: 5 choke **8** compress, obstruct, **9** constrict

strap: bar, fit, tie **4** band, beat, belt, bind, hang, rein, riem, whip **5** girth, groom, strip, strop, thong **6** billet, chaser, credit, enarme, fillet, halter, latigo, ligule, punish, secure **7** furnish, laniard, lanyard, sharpen **8** chastise

kind of: **4** jess, taws **5** guige, leash, strop, tawse, thong **6** chaser, enarme **8** bretelle **10** boondoggle

strap-shaped: 6 lorate **7** ligular **8** ligulate

strapping: 6 robust, strong **7** beating **9** thrashing

strass: 5 glass, paste

strata (see also **stratum**): *geological:* **4** lias

later: **7** neozoic

social: **7** classes

stratagem: 4 coup, ruse, wile **5** cheat, fetch, fraud, trick **6** blench, device, humbug, scheme **7** finesse **8** artifice, intrigue, maneuver **9** chicanery, deception, execution, expedient, slaughter **10** artfulness

smart: **8** liripipe, liripoop

strategic: 9 favorable **12** advantageous

strategy: 8 artifice, game plan, intrigue, maneuver

stratification: 7 bedding

stratum: bed **5** class, layer, level **6** couche **7** section **8** division

thin: **4** seam

Strauss opera 6 Salome **7** Electra **10** Fledermaus **13** Rosenkavalier

Stravinsky work: 8 Firebird **10** Petrouchka

straw: hat, wap **4** gloy, mote, pipe, rush **5** chaff **6** fescue, litter, trifle **9** worthless, yellowish **11** meaningless **12** churchwarden

bed: **6** pallet

bundle of: **6** batten **8** windling

coat: **4** mino

color: **6** flaxen

colored: **11** stramineous

for hats: **6** sennit **7** leghorn, sabutan

half rotten: **5** mulch

load of: **5** barth

man: **9** scarecrow

plaited: **6** sennit

threshing floor: **6** bhossa

to protect plants: **5** mulch

waxed: **6** strass

weaving: **5** rafia

straw in the wind: 4 clue, omen, sign **7** portent, warning

straw vote: 4 poll

strawberry: 6 fraise, runner **8** fragaria

strawlike: 11 stramineous

stray: err, gad, odd **4** cavy, roam, rove, waif **5** range **6** casual, course, errant, random, stroll, swerve, wander **7** decline, deviate, digress, forlorn, go wrong, habitat, runaway, saunter **8** detached, distract, isolated, straggle **9** straggler, unrelated **10** incidental, occasional **12** unenumerated

calf: **4** dogy **5** dogie

straying: 6 astray, errant **7** erratic **8** aberrant **9** deviation, erroneous

streak: 4 hint, line, vein, wale **5** fleck, freak, garle, hurry, layer, lined, round, spell, trace, trait **6** period, smooth, strain, strake, stripe, stroke **7** stratum, striped **8** discolor **10** suggestion

mottled: roe

narrow: **5** stria **6** striae

regular: **6** stripe

streaked: 4 liny **6** marked **7** alarmed, brindle, striped, worried **8** brindled **10** variegated

streaking: 12 frosted hair

streaky: 4 liny **5** liney, mixed **6** uneven **8** variable

stream: run **4** burn, flow, flux, ford, gote, gush, pour, rill, rush **5** bache, bayou, bourn, brook, creek, fleam, floss, flume, fluor, force, issue, river, speed, trend **6** amount, bourne, course, fluent, runnel **7** channel, current, rivulet **8** affluent **9** anabranch **11** watercourse

diminutive: run **4** race **5** brook **6** rillet **7** rivulet **9** streamlet

dry bed: **6** arroyo

lava: **6** coulee

living in: **9** amphibian, rheophile

ravine: **4** ghyl, gill

rushing: jet **7** torrent

small: run **4** rill, sike **5** brook, siket **6** rillet, runlet

sound: **4** purl **6** murmur

underground: aar

upper part of: **6** source **9** headwater

streamer: jet **4** flag **5** strip **6** guidon, ribbon **7** feather, pendant, pennant **8** banderol, headline **9** banderole

streamlet: 4 rill 5 brook 6 rillet, runlet, runnel 7 freshet, rivulet

streamlined: 6 modern 8 straight 10 simplified

street: rew(Sc.), way 4 lane, road 5 calle, chare 6 avenue, causey, ruelle, spread 7 highway, roadway, strasse(G.) 8 chaussee, contrada 9 boulevard 12 thoroughfare
Chinese: 6 hutung
degraded: 4 slum
ditch: 6 gutter
India: 5 chawk, chowk
narrow: 4 wynd 5 alley, place
street urchin: 4 arab 5 gamin
streetcar: 4 tram 7 trolley
driver: 8 motorman
streetwalker: 5 whore 6 hooker, wanton 7 cruiser 10 prostitute

strength: arm 4 beef, iron, thew 5 brawn, force, might, power, vigor 6 energy, foison 7 ability, potency, stamina, sthenia 8 capacity, firmness, solidity, validity 9 coherence, endurance, fortitude, intensity, lustiness, puissance, stability, stoutness, substance, toughness, vehemence 10 heartiness, robustness 14 impregnability
deprive of: 7 unnerve 8 enervate
diminish: 6 dilute
electric current: 8 amperage
liquor: 5 proof
loss: 8 asthenia
military: 8 armament
of character: 4 guts, sand 9 fortitude
of will: 8 backbone
poetic: 9 puissance
regain: 5 rally
solution: 5 titer, titre
source of: 5 asset

strengthen: add 4 back, bind, frap, gird, help, prop 5 brace, nerve, steel 6 clench, deepen, endure 7 afforce, comfort, confirm, educate, fortify, nourish, support, sustain, toughen 8 roborate 9 encourage, reinforce 10 invigorate 11 consolidate
with alcohol: 5 spike 7 fortify

strenuous: 4 hard 5 eager 6 active, ardent, severe 7 arduous, zealous 8 vigorous 9 energetic

strepitant: 5 noisy 9 clamorous

stress: try 4 pain 5 brunt, force, labor, press 6 accent, strain 7 afflict, amplify, overtax, tension, urgency 8 ampliate, distrain, distress, emphasis, exertion, pressure 9 emphasize, intensity 10 constraint, importance, overstrain, resistance 12 significance 13 inconvenience
free from: 4 calm 6 anneal
mechanical: 8 erossure

metrical: 5 ictus
music: 6 accent
voice: 5 arsis 6 accent

stretch: run 4 span, walk 5 range, reach, retch, space, tract, while 6 course, dilate, eke out, effort, expand, extend, period, spread, strain 7 distend, elastic, enlarge, expanse, tension 8 distance, elongate, sentence 9 direction, embroider, extension 10 exaggerate
injuriously: 6 sprain
out: lie 4 rest 6 repose
the neck: 5 crane
the truth: lie 10 exaggerate
stretched: 6 craned 7 porrect 8 extended, prolated 9 elongated
tight: 4 taut 5 tense
while drying: 8 tentered
stretcher: 5 dooly 6 litter, racker 8 ringhead
neck: 6 craner

strew: 6 litter, spread 7 diffuse, scatter 8 disperse, sprinkle 9 bespatter, broadcast 10 besprinkle 11 disseminate

strewing: 4 seme

stria: 4 band, line, vein 5 ridge 6 fillet, furrow, groove, hollow, streak, stripe 7 channel

stricken (see also **strike**): 7 smitten, worn out, wounded 13 incapacitated

strickle: 5 rifle 7 pattern 8 template

strict: 4 blue, hard, true 5 close, exact, harsh, rigid, stern, tense, tight 6 entire, severe 7 ascetic, austere, binding, correct, perfect, precise 8 absolute, acurate, intimate, limiting, rigorous, straight 9 confining, puritanic, stringent 10 compressed, forbidding, hardboiled, inexorable, inflexible, iron-handed, relentless, scrupulous 11 punctilious, puritanical, restricting, straitlaced, undeviating 14 uncompromising
disciplinarian: 8 martinet
discipline: 13 regimentation
strictness: 5 rigor 9 closeness
in law: 8 legalism

stricture: 4 sign 5 spark, touch, trace 7 binding, censure, closing 9 criticism 11 contraction 13 animadversion

strid: 5 gorge 6 ravine

stride: 4 step, walk 5 stalk 7 advance 8 bestride, progress, straddle 11 advancement

strident: 5 harsh 6 shrill 7 grating, raucous, yelling 11 acrimonious, cacophonous

stridulate: 5 cheep, chirk, chirp, creak, crick 7 clitter

strife: war 4 bait, bate, feud 5 fight, flite, flyte, noise, strow 6 combat, debate, estrif 7 contest, discord, hurling, quarrel

8 conflict, endeavor, exertion, struggle **9** emulation **10** contention **11** altercation, competition, controversy

about mere words: **9** logomachy

civil: **6** stasis

striffen: **8** membrane, thin skin

strigil: **7** scraper

strigose, strigous: **5** rough, sharp **6** hispid **7** bristly

strike: bat, bob, box, cob, cop, dab, dad, hew, hit, lam, pat, ram, rap, wap **4** baff, bang, bash, bean, beat, biff, bill, bump, bunt, chap, cope, coup, cuff, dash, daub, daud, dint, dunt, fist, flap, flog, frap, gird, give, gowf, hurl, hurt, knap, lash, pelt, rout, slam, slap, slay, swat **5** clash, clink, clout, douse, dowse, dunch, filch, gowff, impel, knock, occur, punch, skelp, skite, slash, smear, smite, spank, swipe, trend, whang **6** assail, attack, attain, bounce, buffet, fettle, hammer, hartal, punish **7** afflict, collide, impress, walkout **8** discover, struggle

a balance: **5** agree **6** settle **10** compromise

a mean: **7** average

against: ram **4** bump **5** crash **7** assault, collide

and rebound: **5** carom **6** carrom **9** carambole

demonstrator: **6** picket

down: **4** fell, kill **5** floor **7** disable

dumb: **4** stun

feature: **7** lockout

gently: dab, pat **4** bump, putt

heavily: lam, ram **4** bash, slog, slug

obliquely: **5** carom

on head: **4** bean

out: fan **4** dele, head **5** elide, erase **6** cancel, delete **9** eliminate

prepare to: **4** coil

producing musical sound: **5** chime

series of blows: **4** pelt

settler: **8** mediator

together: **5** clash, crash **7** collide

up: **5** begin, start **8** commence

violently: ram **4** bash, slam

with fist: **4** plug **5** pound, punch

with head: **4** butt

with wonder: awe **7** astound **8** surprise

strikebreaker: rat **4** fink, goon, scab **8** blackleg(Br.)

striker: **4** tern **6** batman, batter, helper, hitter, smiter **7** batsman, clapper, mobster **9** assistant, harpooner

striking: **4** dint **5** showy **6** cogent **7** salient, telling **8** stunning **9** arresting, effective **10** noticeable, remarkable, surprising **11** conspicuous

effect: **5** eclat

string: **4** band, cord, hoax, josh, line **5** bound, braid, chain, jolly, strip, twine **6** series, thread **8** resource **10** conditions, succession **14** qualifications

course: **6** guidon

kinds of: **4** wire **5** lacet, snare **6** amenta, hypate, lachet **7** amentum, langate

of beads: **6** rosary **8** necklace

up: **4** hang, lace **5** lynch, scrab, gibbet

string along: toy **4** fool **5** dally **6** lead on **7** deceive, flatter

string instrument: uke **4** harp, lute, lyre **5** banjo, cello, piano, viola **6** fiddle, guitar, spinet, violin, zither **7** ukelele, ukulele **8** mandolin **11** harpsichord

old: **4** lute, lyre **6** spinet **8** psaltery **11** harpsichord

stringent: **4** grim, hard, ropy **5** rigid, tense, tight **6** cogent, severe, strict **7** binding, extreme **10** convincing **11** restrictive

stringer: tie **4** rope, vein **6** timber **8** filament

stringy: **4** ropy **5** gluey **6** sinewy, viscid **7** fibrous, viscous **8** muscular **11** filamentous

strip: bar, rob, tab, tag, top **4** band, bare, bark, belt, doff, flay, hull, husk, peel, pull, skin, tear **5** clear, flake, fleck, pluck, shred, spoil, swath, unrig **6** border, denude, devest, divest, expose, flense, length, ravage, reduce, remove, runway, swathe **7** bandage, bandeau, bereave, degrade, deprive, despoil, disrobe, pillage, plunder, uncloak, uncover, undress, unleave **8** bandeaux(pl.), denudate, disarray, headland, separate **9** dismantle, excoriate **10** disfurnish, dispossess **11** debenzolize, decorticate

blubber: **6** flense

kinds of: **4** came, cove, lead, rand, riem, tirr **5** cleat, ridge, stave **6** inwale, reglet **7** gunwale

leather: **4** welt **5** thong **6** latigo **7** belting

narrow: **4** slat, tape **5** reeve, strap **7** bandeau **8** bandeaux(pl.)

wooden: rib **4** lath, slat **5** stave **6** reglet

strip tease dancer: **9** ecdysiast

stripe: bar, ilk, roe **4** band, beat, belt, blow, kind, lash, line, mark, sort, type, wale, weal, welt, zone **5** chest, stria **6** border, frenum, streak, strike, stroke **7** chevron, lineate, pattern, rivulet **8** division **9** character

striped: **5** bandy **6** banded, barred **7** lineate, vittate **8** bayadere, streaked

animal: **5** bongo, zebra

cloth: **6** madras

stripling: boy, lad **5** chiel, youth **6** chield

stripped: **4** bare, nude **6** picked **10** deprived of

by trickery: **7** buncoed, bunkoed, fleeced

strive: aim, hie, tew, try, tug, vie **4** seek, toil **5** bandy, ensue, fight, labor, rival **6** battle, buffet, resist, strain **7** attempt, compete, contend, contest, emulate **8** contrast, endeavor, struggle

striving: 5 nisus **7** attempt, contest
strobile: 4 chat **8** pine cone
strockle: 6 shovel
stroke: bat, coy, fit, hew, hit, pat, pet, rub **4** baff, beat, blow, chap, coup, dash, ding, dint, flip, gowf, hurt, lash, mark, milk, oner, shot, walk, whet **5** chare, douse, dowse, flack, fluke, gowff, ictus, knock, power, pulse, rower, strut, throb, trait **6** attack, caress, effort, fondle, ictuse, impact, injury, soothe, stride **7** seizure, sharpen, whample **8** apoplexy, disaster **9** influence
brilliant: ace **4** coup
cutting: **4** chop **5** slice
kinds of: **5** eagle, cerif, serif, wedge **6** birdie **7** virgule
of luck: hit **5** fluke **6** strike **8** windfall
short: **4** flip, putt **5** whisk
stroll: 4 gait, mosy, roam, rove, walk **5** mosey, range, stray, tramp **6** dacker, daiker, dander, ramble, soodle, wander **7** saunter
stroller: 4 cart, pram **5** actor, sulky, tramp **6** beggar, gocart, player, shuler **7** peddlar, pedler, shuiler, vagrant **8** bohemian, carriage, wanderer **9** saunterer
Stromboli: 6 island **7** volcano
stromming: herring
strong: fit, hot **4** able, bold, dure, elon, fere, firm, fort, hale, hard, rank, sure, warm, wiry **5** bonny, clear, eager, frack, freck, fresh, great, gross, hardy, heavy, large, lusty, solid, sound, stout, tough, yauld **6** active, ardent, bonnie, brawny, cogent, feckle, mighty, potent, robust, rugged, sinewy, stable, sturdy **7** buirdly, durable, fertile, greatly, humming, intense, sthenic, violent, zealous **8** accented, athletic, distinct, flagrant, forceful, forcible, muscular, powerful, puissant, resonant, severely, stalwart, strongly, vehement, vigorous **9** Atlantean, difficult, effective, impetuous, important, strapping, tenacious, violently **10** boisterous, forthright, malodorous, nourishing, outrageous, passionate, persuasive, productive, pronounced, remarkable, spirituous **11** excessively **12** concentrated
upward movement: **5** surge
strong man: 6 tyrant **10** powerhouse
Biblical: **6** Samson **7** Sampson
legendary: **5** Atlas **8** Herakles, Hercules
strong point: 5 forte
strong-arm: rob **4** beat, thug **5** force, power **7** assault **8** violence **9** terrorize **10** intimidate
man: **4** goon **7** bouncer
strongbox: 4 case, safe **5** chest, vault **6** coffer
stronghold: 4 fort, hold, keep **5** tower **6** castle **7** citadel, fortify, redoubt **8** fast-hold, fastness, fortress **13** fortification
strong-smelling: 4 foul, rank **5** fetid **8** mephitic, stinking
strop: 4 hone, whet **7** sharpen
strophe: 6 stanza **10** heptastich
stroygood: 7 wastrel **11** spendthrift
struck: 4 smit **5** smote **7** shocked, smitten **8** punished
with amazement: **6** aghast
with small missiles: **6** pelted
with sudden fear: **7** alarmed
with terror: **6** aghast **7** shocked
with wonder: **6** aghast
struck out: 5 deled **6** elided, erased, fanned **7** deleted
structural quality: 7 texture
structure: dam **4** form **5** frame, house **6** bridge, format, make-up, syntax **7** edifice, texture **8** building, bulkhead **9** formation, framework **11** arrangement, composition, fabricature **12** constitution, construction
abnormal: **12** malformation
calcareous: **5** coral
conical: **7** pyramid
crown-like: **6** corona
curved: **4** arch
filamentous: **4** hair
floating: **4** roar
funeral: **10** catafalque
grammatical: **6** syntax
hallowed: **6** bethel, chapel, church, temple **8** basilica **9** cathedral, synagogue **10** tabernacle
high: **5** tower
human: **8** physique
keel-like: **6** carina
latticework: **7** trellis
looplike: **4** ansa
monumental: **5** pylon **7** pyramid
on roof: **6** cupola, dormer **9** penthouse
Oriental: **6** pagoda
original: **6** isogen
osseous: **4** bone
over obstacles: **6** bridge
pergola-like: **6** ramada
pert. to: **8** tectonic
projecting into water: **4** jiti **5** jetty **6** jettee
raised: **4** dais **5** altar, stage **8** platform
sacrificial: **5** altar
sheltering: cot **4** cote
supporting: **4** pier
tall: **5** tower **7** steeple **9** campanile
tent-like: **10** tabernacle
white: **6** albedo
strudel: 6 pastry
struggle: try, tug, vie **4** agon, cope, frab, wade **5** fight, heave, labor **6** battle, buckle, bustle, combat, effort, Peniel, strife, strike, strive, throes, tussle, widdle **7** attempt, bargain, barrace, contend, contest, flounce, scuffle, warfare,

wrestle **8** conflict, endeavor, exertion, flounder, scraffle, scramble **10** contention, difficulty
a deux: **4** duel
helplessly: **8** flounder
struma: **6** goiter, goitre
strummed: **8** thrummed
strumpet: **4** brim **5** belie, wench **6** blowen, harlot, wanton **7** cocotte, debauch, slander **8** harridan **10** prostitute
strung: **6** beaded
highly: **5** tense **7** nervous
strut: **4** brag, cock, gait, step, walk **5** brace, bulge, swell **6** flaunt, parade, sashay, stride, strife, strunt, thrust **7** distend, peacock, provide, stiffen, stretch, support, swagger, wrangle **8** protrude **10** contention **11** protuberant
struthious: **4** emus **5** rheas **6** ratite **9** ostriches
stub: pen **4** beat, dolt, snag **5** crush, drive, guard, hinge, squat, stumb **6** coupon, nubbin, stocky **7** feather, remnant **8** thickset **9** blockhead, extirpate **11** counterfoil
stubble: bun **6** strunt **8** eelgrass
field: **5** rowen
stubborn: set **4** rude **5** fixed, hardy, harsh, rough, tough **6** coarse, dogged, mulish, sturdy **7** restive **8** obdurate, perverse, resolute, starkish, vigorous **9** camsteary, camsteery, difficult, obstinate, pigheaded **10** bullheaded, calcitrant, determined, hardheaded, headstrong, inflexible, refractory, unyielding **11** intractable, persevering **12** pertinacious
stubby: **5** squat **6** stocky, stumpy **8** thickset
stuck: See **stick**
stuck in the mud: **7** bemired
stuck-up: **4** vain **7** haughty **8** arrogant, snobbish **9** conceited **12** supercilious **13** self-important
stud: dot, pin, rod **4** boss, knob, male, spot, stub **5** adorn, aglet, beset, brace haras, study, stump **6** aiglet, button, pillar **7** chaplet, sprinkle, support **9** studhorse
farm: **5** haras
for shoe: **7** hobnail
with jewels: **5** engem
with radiating bodies: **6** enstar
student: **5** eleve(F.), pupil **6** bursar **7** educand, learner **8** disciple, observer
according to grade: **6** termer
agricultural college: **5** Aggie
college: **4** soph **6** junior, senior **7** protege, scholar **8** freshman **9** sophomore **13** undergraduate
divinity: **9** theologue **10** theologian
fellow: **9** classmate

first-year: **5** Fuchs(G.) **8** freshman
former: **7** dropout **8** graduate
fourth-year: **6** senior
girl: **4** coed
group: **5** class
hall: **5** burse **9** dormitory
in charge: **7** monitor
law: **8** stagiary
medical: **6** intern **7** interne
military: **5** cadet, plebe
naval academy: **5** cadet **10** midshipman
of birds: **13** ornithologist
of crime: **10** penologist **13** criminologist
of heavens: **13** uranographist
of proverbs: **14** paroemiologist
of punishment: **10** penologist
of relics: **13** archaeologist
of reptiles: **13** herpetologist
of spiders: **13** arachnologist
Oxford: **8** commoner
probationary: **8** stibbler
residence: **5** house **6** hostel **9** dormitory
room: **7** seminar
second-year: **9** sophomore
stipend paid: **6** bursar
talmudic: **5** bahur
third-year: **6** junior
West Point: **5** cadet, plebe
studied: **5** pored **6** intent **7** learned, planned **8** affected, designed, inclined, reasoned **10** ceremonial, deliberate **12** premeditated
studies: *academic:* **4** arts **7** science **10** humanities
advanced: **7** seminar **8** graduate
chosen by students: **9** electives
series of: **6** course
studio: **7** atelier, bottega **8** workshop **11** ergasterion
studious: **5** booky **7** bookish, devoted, studied **8** diligent, sedulous **9** assiduous, scholarly **10** deliberate **13** contemplative
study: con, den, mug **4** bone, muse, muzz, pore, read, scan **5** grind **6** lesson, peruse, ponder **7** analyse, analyze, canvass, croquis, examine, reverie **8** consider, exercise, meditate **9** attention **10** scrutinize **11** contemplate **13** consideration, contemplation
animals: **9** zoography
bees: **8** apiology
Bible: **9** isagogics
by lamplight: **9** lucubrate
closely: con **4** pore **7** examine
course: **7** seminar
fingerprints: **13** dactylography
fixed course: **4** rote
flowers: **12** anthoecology
group: **7** seminar
handwriting: **10** graphology
hard: **4** bone, cram

horses: **9** hippology
human generations: **15** anthropogenesis
insect's habits: **10** entomology
laborious: **11** lucubration
mountains: **7** orology
musical: **5** etude
optional: **8** elective
population: **10** larithmics
preliminary: **6** sketch
punishment: **8** penology
sacred edifices: **7** naology
sacred images: **9** iconology
sermons: **10** homiletics
wines: **7** enology
words: **9** etymology
stuff: jam, pad, ram, wad **4** copy, cram,
fill, gaum, junk, pang **5** crowd, farce,
force, grain, pulse, steve **6** fabric,
graith, matter, refuse, stifle **7** bombast,
element, essence, filling, mixture, portion **8** material, medicine, nonsense,
overload **9** character, principle, substance, suffocate
full: **4** glut **5** gorge **6** stodge **7** satiate
harvested grain: **7** stubble
sticky: goo
worthless: **4** gear **7** hogwash
stuffed: **6** bourre, stodgy **7** bombast, replete **8** farctate
stuffing: **7** padding, viscera **8** dressing **9**
forcemeat
stuffy: fat **4** dull, prim **5** angry, close,
fubsy, fuggy, humid, stout, sulky **6**
froust, frowst, stodgy **7** airless, pompous **8** resolute, stifling **9** obstinate **10**
mettlesome, old-fogyish **11** strait-laced
12 conservative, old-fashioned
Stuka: **6** bomber
stulm: **4** adit **8** entrance **10** passageway
stultiloquy: **6** babble **11** foolish talk
stumble: err **4** fall, slip, trip **5** lurch **6**
boggle, chance, faffle, falter, happen, offend, puzzle, teeter, wallow **7** blunder,
failure, founder, perplex, scrupple, stagger, stammer **8** confound, flounder
stumbling block: **8** obstacle **9** hindrance
10 impediment **11** obstruction
stump: cob, end, lop **4** butt, dare, foil,
grub, plod, snag, stab, stub **5** block,
clump **6** baffle, corner, hobble, lumber,
pillar, puzzle, strunt, thwart, travel **7**
blunted, canvass, nonplus, perplex, rostrum, stumble **8** defiance, platform **9**
challenge **11** electioneer
stumps: **4** legs
stumpy: **5** bunty, money **6** stubby **8**
thickset
stun: **4** bowl, daze, tear **5** amaze, daunt,
daver, dizzy, dover, shock **6** appall, benumb, bruise, crease, deaden, deafen **7**
astound, dammish, scratch, startle, stupefy **8** astonish, bewilder **9** dumbfound,

overpower, overwhelm **10** strike dumb
stunned: **10** astonished
stunning: **7** stylish **8** dazzling, gorgeous **9**
beautiful, excellent **10** foudroyant
stunt: act **4** feat **5** angry, blast, blunt,
check, cramp, crowl, dwarf, stamp,
trick, whale **6** abrupt, hinder **7** curtail,
exploit, shorten **8** stubborn, suppress
10 undersized **11** performance
gymnastic: kip **4** kipp **10** handspring
stunty: **5** short **6** flashy, stocky **7** dwarfed
stupa: **5** mound, tower **6** shrine
lamaism: **7** chorten
stupefacient: **4** drug **8** narcotic
stupefy: fox, sot **4** baze, daze, dope, doze,
drug, dull, dunt, numb, stun **5** amaze,
aston, besot, blunt, daunt, daver, deave,
shock **6** astone, bedaze, bemuse, benumb, muddle **7** astound, confuse **8** astonish, bewilder, confound **10** incrassate
with drink: **6** fuddle
stupendous: **4** huge **5** great, large **7** amazing, immense **8** enormous **9** marvelous,
monstrous, wonderful **10** astounding
11 astonishing **12** overpowering, overwhelming **13** extraordinary
stupid: **4** bete, clod, dull, dumb, dunt,
guam, lewd, slow **5** besot, blunt, booby,
crass, dazed, dense, dizzy, dunce, goosy,
heavy, inane, sumph **6** assish, barren,
beetle, boring, bovine, dawkin, doiled,
doited, drowsy, goosey, hebete, lurdan,
oafish, obtuse, simple, stolid, torpid **7**
asinine, brutish, buzzard, calvish, daffish, doldrum, doltish, duffing, dullard,
fatuous, foolish, foppish, glaiket, glaikit,
gomerel, goosish, gullish, lurdane, prosaic, stunned, vacuous, witless **8** anserine, anserous, backward, bayardly,
blockish, boeotian, cloddish, deadened,
footless, headless, retarded, sluggish **9**
blocklike, bourgeois, brainless, cod-
headed, inanimate, insensate, insipient,
lethargic, plumbeous, pointless, senseless, stupefied **10** hardwitted, hulver-
head, irrational, slow-witted **11** claybrained, heavy-headed **12** buffleheaded
13 unintelligent, uninteresting
person: ass, sap **4** clod, clot, coot, dolt,
dope, fool, jerk, loon **5** dunce, goose,
idiot, moron, ninny **7** dullard, fathead **8**
numskull **9** blockhead
stupor: fog **4** coma, damp, dote **5** sopor **6**
apathy, trance **7** languor **8** lethargy
pert. to: **7** carotic, narcose
sturdy: gid, set **4** buff, firm **5** felon, hardy,
harsh, lusty, sound, stern, stiff, stout **6**
brawny, robust, rugged, rustic, stable,
steady, strong **7** violent **8** obdurate, resolute, stalwart, stubborn, vigorous **9**
rigidness, obstinate **10** courageous, de-

termined, unyielding **11** substantial
sturdy and stout: 5 burly
sturgeon: 6 beluga
  small: **7** sterlet
  white: **6** beluga
  roe: **6** caviar
Sturm und Drang: 6 unrest **7** ferment, turmoil
stutter: 7 stammer
stuttering: 8 psellism **9** psellisum
sty, stye: pen **4** boil, dump, sink **5** lodge, stair, steps, stile **6** ladder, pigpen **8** swelling **9** enclosure
stygian: 6 gloomy **7** hellish **8** infernal
style: air, dub, pen, pin, ton, way **4** call, garb, gere, kind, mode, name, sort, term, tone, type **5** vogue **6** format, gnomon, graver, manner, method, needle, phrase, stylus **7** alamode, diction, entitle, fashion, variety **8** demeanor **9** designate, execution **10** denominate **12** characterize, construction
  architecture: **5** Doric, Greek, Ionic, Roman, Saxon **6** Gothic, Norman **7** Italian **8** Colonial, Georgian, Monterey **9** Byzantine **10** Corinthian, Romanesque **11** Elizabethan, Renaissance **13** Mediterranean
  art: **5** genre
  artistic: **5** gusto
  dress: **5** get-up, guise
  fantastic: **6** rococo **7** baroque
  furniture: **6** Empire
  hair: **4** Afro, coif **8** coiffure
  lofty: **4** epic
  oratorical: **10** rhetorical
  out of: **5** dated, passe
  painting: **5** genre
  penmanship: **4** hand
  performance: **9** execution
stylet: pro **5** organ, probe **6** dagger **7** poniard **8** stiletto **9** appendage
  sugrical: **6** trocar
stylish: 4 chic, posh, tony **5** dashy, nifty, smart, swell **6** chichi, classy, dressy, jaunty, modish, spiffy, swanky **7** alamode, dashing, doggish, genteel, knowing, swagger **11** fashionable
stylist: 7 modiste
stylites: 7 hermits **8** ascetics
styloid: 8 belonoid
stymie, stymy: 5 block **6** hinder, impede **8** obstruct
styptic: 4 alum **10** astringent, tannic acid
Styx: 5 nymph, river
  father: **7** Oceanus
  ferryman: **6** Charon
  locale: **5** Hades
  mother: **6** Tethys
  pert. to: **7** stygian
suant: 4 even **5** grave, quiet **6** demure, placid, smooth, steady **7** equable, regu-

lar **9** agreeable, following
suave: 4 easy, oily, smug **5** bland, civil, soapy, sweet **6** polite, smooth, urbane **7** fulsome **8** gracious, mannered, pleasant, polished, tactful, unctuous **9** agreeable **12** ingratiating
suavity: 6 comity **7** amenity **8** urbanity **10** politeness **12** complaisance
sub: 6 fill-in **9** alternate, auxiliary, submarine **11** replacement
sub rosa: 8 covertly, secretly
subbase: 6 plinth
subdivide: 5 carve, mince **8** separate
subdivision: 4 part **6** sector **8** category **10** department
  lateral: **5** aisle
  rocks: **5** range
subdue: cow **4** bend, quay, tame **5** accoy, allay, amate, atill, break, charm, crush, daunt, dompt, lower, quell, sober **6** adaunt, bridle, disarm, dismay, evince, master, mellow, reduce, soften, steady, subact **7** affaite, chasten, conquer, control, put down, repress, squelch **8** convince, diminish, overcome, suppress, surmount, vanquish **9** captivate, castigate, overpower, subjugate
suber: 4 cork **10** cork tissue
subjacent: 8 inferior **10** underlying
subject: try **4** text **5** basis, cause, prone, theme, topic **6** liable, motive, phrase, reason, submit, vassal **7** article, citizen, conquer, exposed, reality **8** disposed, incident, inferior, obedient **9** dependent, subjugate **10** contingent, predispose, submissive, substratum **11** conditional, subordinate
  of discourse: **5** theme, topic
  of disease: **4** case **7** patient
  of lawsuit: res
  of verb: **4** noun
  to abuse: **6** revile
  to argument: **4** moot
  to authority: **6** master
  to be taught: **10** didascalic
  to change: **7** mutable
  to choice: **8** elective
  to control: **7** rulable
  to death: **6** mortal
  to depression: **5** moody
  to discussion: **4** moot **9** debatable
  to dislike: **8** aversion
  to ill treatment: **6** misuse
  to mistakes: **7** erratic
  to taxation: **8** reteable
  to whirling action: **11** centifugate
subjection: 7 slavery **8** thirling **9** captivity
subjoin: add **5** affix, annex **6** append, attach
subjugate: 6 compel, master, reduce, subdue **7** conquer, depress, overawe **8** overcome

sublate: 4 deny 5 annul 6 cancel, lift up, negate, remove 9 eliminate, take away

sublime: 5 exalt, grand, great, lofty, noble, proud 6 purify, refine 7 emotion, exalted, haughty, supreme 8 elevated, empyreal, heavenly, heighten, majestic, splendid, upraised

sublimity: 4 apex 7 majesty 8 grandeur 12 magnificence

submarine: 4 boat 5 diver 9 periscope 11 submersible

detector: 5 sonar

group: 8 wolf-pack

projectile: 7 missile, Polaris, torpedo

submerge: dip 4 bury, dive, hide, sink 5 souse 6 deluge, drench, engulf, plunge 7 immerse 8 inundate, suppress

submerged: 4 sunk 5 awash, latent 6 sunken 10 underwater

continent: 8 Atlantis

submission: 5 offer 8 meekness 9 deference, obedience, surrender 10 compliance, confession 11 resignation 12 acquiescence 13 nonresistance

act of: 5 kneel 6 curtsy 7 curtsey

to destiny: 8 fatalism

submissive: 4 meek, tame 5 buxom 6 docile, humble 7 dutiful, passive, servile 8 obedient, resigned, yielding 9 childlike, compliant

to wife: 8 uxorious

submit: bow 4 bend, fall, obey 5 abide, agree, avale, defer, heald, hield, lower, stoop, yield 6 assent, comply, delate, hand in, resign, soften, subdue, suffer, temper 7 exhibit, knuckle, propose, succumb, suggest 8 moderate 9 acquiesce, surrender 10 condescend

for consideration: 5 remit

proposal to: 4 move

to: 4 obey 6 suffer

subordinate: 5 minor, under 6 puisne, subdue 7 control, subject 8 inferior, obedient, servient 9 ancillary, assistant, auxiliary, dependent, secondary, underling 10 accidental, collateral, incidental, submissive 11 subservient

activity: 8 parergon

adjunct: 9 appendage

officer: 4 exon

suborn: 5 bribe, foist 6 father, incite, induce 7 procure 9 instigate

subpoena: 4 writ 6 summon 7 summons

subrogate: 10 substitute

subscribe: 5 agree, favor 6 adhere, assent, attest 7 ascribe, consent, support 8 sanction 10 contribute, underwrite

subscription to newspaper: 10 abonnement

subsequent: 5 after, later 6 puisne 7 ensuing 8 retainer 9 attendant, companion, following 11 consecutive

to birth: 9 postnatal

subsequently: 5 after, later, since 10 afterwards, thereafter

subservient: 6 menial, vassal 7 duteous, servile 8 obeisant 9 accessory, ancillary, auxiliary, truckling 10 obsequious, submissive 11 subordinate

subside: ebb 4 bate, fall, lull, sink, wane 5 abate, cease, lower, quiet 6 settle 7 descend, flatten, relapse 8 decrease, withdraw

subsidiary: 6 back-up 7 reserve 9 accessory, assistant, auxiliary, tributary 10 collateral 12 nonessential 13 supplementary

subsidy: aid 4 gift, help 5 bonus, grant 6 bounty 7 pension, reserve, support, tribute 10 assistance, subvention 13 appropriation

subsist: 4 feed, hold, live, stay 5 abide, exist, stand 6 obtain, remain 7 support, survive 8 continue, maintain

subsistence: 6 living 9 allowance, inherency, substance 10 livelihood, provisions 11 persistence

subsoil: bed, pan 4 sole 7 stratum

animal: 4 mole

substance: sum 4 body, core, gist, mass, meat 5 basis, metal, stuff, tenor, thing 6 estate, ground, import, matter, realty, spirit, supply, wealth 7 aliment, content, essence, meaning, purport 8 hardness, majority, material, property, solidity, sum total 9 actuality, affluence, resources, solidness 11 consistency

amorphous: 5 resin, rosin 7 ferrite

animal: 7 gelatin

bitter: 4 acid 5 aloes, aloin, linin 6 ilicin 7 amarine, emetine 8 elaterin

dissolving: 9 resolvent

drying: 9 desiccant

expansive: gas

reaction-inducing: 7 reagent

rubber-like: 5 gutta

simple: 7 element

sour: 4 acid 7 vinegar

starch-like: 6 inulin, olivil 8 alantine

sticky: goo, gum, tar 4 glue 5 paste

transparent: 6 hyalin 7 hyaline 9 celluloid

unctuous: oil 6 grease

vegetable: 4 peat 5 resin, rosin

white: 4 alba 6 inulin 7 alanine 8 elaterin

substantial: big 4 firm, real, true 5 ample, large, meaty, solid, sound, stout 6 actual, bodily, hearty, stable, strong, sturdy 7 genuine, wealthy 8 material, tangible 9 corporeal, important 10 meaningful 12 considerable

substantiality: See **substance**

substantiate: try 4 test 5 prove 6 assure, embody, verify 7 confirm 9 establish 11 corroborate

substantive: 4 noun 5 vital 6 actual, entity 7 pronoun 9 essential 13 self-contained

substitute: 5 extra, fill-in, fudge, proxy, vicar 6 backup, deputy, ersatz(G.), ringer 7 commute, replace 8 exchange, nominate, resource 9 alternate, makeshift, surrogate 10 understudy, viceregent 11 succedaneum 13 succenturiate

for a name: 6 dingus, doodad, widget 9 doohickey 11 thingamabob

temporary: 7 stopgap 9 expedient

substructure: 4 base 6 podium 10 foundation

subsume: 7 contain, include 8 classify 9 encompass

subterfuge: 4 plan, ruse 5 blind, trick 6 device, escape, refuge 7 evasion, secrecy 8 artifice, pretense 9 chicanery, deception 13 prevarication 14 tergiversation

subterranean: 4 cave 6 cavern, grotto, hidden, secret 11 underground

subtile: See **subtle**

subtilize: 5 exalt 6 rarefy, refine 9 sublimate

subtle: sly 4 deft, fine, keen, nice, thin wily 5 acute 6 artful, clever, crafty, expert, shrewd 7 cunning, elusive, logical, refined, tenuous 8 abstruse, analytic, delicate, rarefied, skillful 9 beguiling, designing, ingenious, intricate 10 mysterious, perceptive 11 penetrating 14 discriminating

emanation: 4 aura

variation: 6 nuance

subtlety: 7 exility, finesse 8 delicacy

subtract: 5 minus 6 deduct, remove 7 detract 8 withdraw, withhold

suburb: 7 purlieu 8 environs 9 outskirts, periphery

subvention: aid 4 help 5 grant 7 subsidy, support 9 endowment, provision 10 assistance 11 maintenance 13 appropriation

subvert: sap 4 ruin 5 evert, upset 6 change, uproot 7 corrupt, destroy, pervert 8 alienate, overturn, sabotage 9 overthrow, undermine

subway: 4 tube 5 metro 6 tunnel 11 underground

entrance: 5 kiosk

succeed: win 4 fare 5 fadge 6 attain, follow, make it, thrive 7 achieve, catch on, come off, inherit, prevail, prosper, replace 8 approach, flourish 10 accomplish

succeeding: 7 ensuing, sequent 10 subsequent, successful 11 consecutive

success: hit, wow 4 luck 7 arrival, fortune 8 accolade 9 happiness 11 consequence

succession: row, run 5 cycle, order 6 course, series 7 dynasty 8 sequence 9 gradation

next in line: 4 heir

succin: 5 amber

succinct: 4 curt 5 brief, short, terse 6 girded 7 compact, concise, laconic, summary 10 compressed

succor: aid 4 abet, cure, help 5 serve 6 assist, refuge, relief, rescue 7 comfort, deliver, provide, sustain 8 befriend, mitigate 9 alleviate 10 strengthen

succory: 7 chicory

succulent: 4 aloe, lush 5 fresh, juicy, sappy, tasty, vital 6 cactus, tender

fruit: uva

succumb: die 4 fall 5 yield 6 perish, submit 8 pass away 10 capitulate

succursal: 6 branch 8 offshoot 9 auxiliary 10 subsidiary

such: sic(L.) 4 kind, like, some 7 certain, similar

suck: rob, sip 4 draw, lick, swig 5 bleed, draft, drain, drink, nurse 6 absorb, imbibe, inhale, take in 7 consume, extract, suction

sucker: 4 dupe, fool 5 leech 6 victim 8 lollipop, parasite, pushover 9 simpleton

sucking fish: 6 remora 7 lamprey

suckle: 4 feed, rear, suck 5 nurse 6 foster 7 nourish 10 breast-feed 11 honeysuckle

sucrose: 5 sugar 10 saccharose

suction: 6 intake 7 drawing, lifting

Sudan: *animal:* 4 dama 6 oterop

beer: 4 dolo

capital: 8 Khartoum

city: 7 Kassala 8 Omdurman 9 Port Sudan

conqueror: 11 Mohammed Ali

desert: 6 Nubian

language: Ewe, Ibo, Kru 4 Efik, Mole, Tshi 6 Yoruba 8 Mandingo 10 Kordofaman

monetary unit: 5 pound

mountain: 4 Nuba

people: 4 Beri, Daza, Fula, Golo, Nuer, Sere 5 Fulah, Hausa, Mossi 7 Nubiyan

province: 6 Darfur 8 Kordofan

river: 4 Nile

stockade: 6 zareba 7 zareeba

stretcher: 7 angareb

weapon: 8 trombash, trumbash

weight: 5 habba

sudarium: 6 napkin 8 veronica 10 sweat cloth 12 handkerchief

sudden: 4 rash, soon 5 early, ferly, hasty, short, swift 6 abrupt, speedy 7 prerupt, violent 8 headlong, meteoric, unawares 9 alertness, impetuous, impromptu 10 unexpected, unforeseen, unprepared 11 precipitate, precipitous

suddenly: 6 presto

Sudra caste member: 5 palli

suds: bog 4 beer, foam 5 dregs, filth, froth 6 lather, refuse 7 bubbles, sadness

sue: beg, woo 4 seek, urge 5 chase, court, ensue, plead 6 appeal, guided 7 address, beseech, contest, entreat, proceed, request, solicit 8 litigate, petition, practice 9 prosecute

suer: 9 plaintiff

suet: fat 6 tallow

Suez Canal: *builder:* 9 de Lesseps
port: 4 Said 7 Ismalia

suffer: get, let 4 bear, bide, dree(Sc.), hurt 5 admit, allow, groan, thole 6 endure, grieve, permit, submit 7 agonize, undergo 8 tolerate 10 experience

sufferance: 4 pain 6 misery 7 consent 8 patience, sanction 9 endurance 10 permission 11 forbearance

sufferer: 6 martyr, victim

suffering: ill 4 bale, dree(Sc.), loss, pain 5 agony 6 ailing, injury, misery 7 passion 8 distress, sickness 9 adversity 10 affliction 11 tribulation
reliever of: 9 Samaritan

suffice: 5 serve 6 answer 7 appease, content, satisfy

sufficiency: 4 fill 6 enough 7 ability, conceit 8 adequacy, capacity 9 abundance 10 capability, competency

sufficient: due, fit 4 able, enow, good 5 ample, valid 6 decent, enough, plenty 7 suffice 8 abundant, adequate 9 competent, effectual, efficient, qualified 11 responsible, substantial 12 satisfactory 13 well-qualified

suffix: See list page 826

suffocate: 4 kill 5 burke, choke, stive 6 stifle 7 destroy, smother 8 compress, strangle, suppress, throttle 10 asphyxiate, extinguish

suffrage: aid 4 help, vote 5 right, voice 6 assent, ballot, prayer 7 witness 8 petition 9 franchise, testimony 10 assistance 12 intercession, supplication

suffuse: 4 fill, pour 5 embay 7 diffuse 9 interject, introduce 10 overspread

sugar: gur, ose 4 cane 5 biose, candy, maple, money, oside 6 acrose, aldose, fucose, gulose, hexose, ketose, talose, triose, xylose 7 caramel, chitose, glucide, maltose, sucrose, sweeten, tetrose, threose 8 rhodeose 9 muscovado, raffinose, sweetness 10 digitoxose, endearment, piloncillo, saccharose, sweetening 12 carbohydrate, disaccharide 14 monosaccharide
artificial: 6 allose 7 glucose 9 saccharin
boiling kettle: 8 flambeau
burnt: 7 caramel
crystals: 5 candy
daddy: 4 beau 6 patron

fruit: 8 fructose, levulose
liquid: 5 sirup, syrup
lump: 4 cube, loaf
measure: 13 saccharimeter
milk: 7 lactose
mixture: 5 syrup
preparation device: 10 granulator
raw: 9 cassonade
source: sap 4 beet, cane, corn 5 maple
substitute: 5 honey 9 saccharin
syrup: 7 treacle 8 molasses

sugar apple: 6 biriba 8 sweetsop

sugarcane: *disease:* 5 sereh
pulp: 4 marc 6 megass 7 bagasse
refuse: 4 marc 7 bagasse
stalk: 6 ratoon

sugarloaf: 4 hill 8 conoidal, mountain

sugarplum: sop 6 bonbon 9 juneberry, sweetmeat

sugary: 5 sweet 7 honeyed 8 pleasant 10 flattering, saccharine 11 mellifluous

suggest: 4 hint, move 5 imply 6 advise, allude, broach, prompt 7 connote, inspire, mention, propose 8 indicate, intimate 9 adumbrate, insinuate 11 bring to mind

suggestion: 4 hint, idea 5 tinge, touch, trace 6 advice 7 inkling, remnant, soupcon 8 proposal 9 complaint 10 accusation, incitement, intimation, temptation 11 information

sui generis: 6 unique 8 peculiar

sui juris: 5 adult 11 responsible

suicidal: 4 rash 5 fatal 6 deadly, lethal 8 dejected, wretched

suidae: hog 5 swine

suing: 6 wooing 11 prosecution

suint: 5 sweat 6 grease 12 perspiration

suit: fit 4 case(law), plea 5 adapt, agree, apply, cards, dress, fadge, group, habit, match, serve, tally 6 accord, adjust, answer, appeal, attire, behove, outfit, please, prayer, series, trover, wooing 7 arrange, behoove, clothes, comport, conform, costume, flatter, request, satisfy, uniform 8 courting, entreaty, petition 9 harmonize 10 correspond, litigation 11 accommodate 12 solicitation
maker: 6 sartor, tailer
type: 4 zoot 6 monkey 9 paternity 10 pinstriped 11 class action

suitable: apt, due, fit, pat 4 able, fair, good, just, meet 5 right 6 comely, gainly, proper 7 a propos, seeming 8 adequate, apposite, becoming, coherent, eligible, feasible, idoneous, matching 9 competent, congruent, congruous, consonant, expedient 10 commodious, compatible, consistent, convenient, equivalent 11 appropriate 12 commensurate
render: 5 adapt 7 prepare

suitcase: bag 4 grip 6 valise 9 gladstone

suite: set 4 band 5 abode, group, music, staff, train 6 series 7 retinue 8 equipage 9 apartment, entourage 10 collection

member of: 7 attache

musical: See **musical composition**

suited: See **suitable**

suiting: 4 wool 5 serge 6 fabric 9 gabardine, gaberdine

suitor: 4 beau 5 lover, wooer 7 gallant 8 follower, litigant 10 petitioner

sulcate: 4 plow 6 fluted 7 grooved 8 furrowed

sulfate: 5 treat 7 convert, sulphur 9 brimstone 10 impregnate

kind: 4 alum 5 hepar, matte 6 barite, blende 7 ilesite, loweite

sulfur: 9 brimstone

substance containing: 5 hepar

sulfuric acid: 7 vitriol

sulk: 4 dort(Sc.), mope, pout 5 brood, frown, grump 6 glower, grouch

sulky: 4 cart, dull, weak 5 chuff, dorty, inert 6 gloomy, gocart, grouty, sullen 7 doggish, peevish 8 carriage, inactive 10 unyielding

sullage: mud 4 silt 5 filth 6 refuse, scoria, sewage 8 drainage 9 pollution 10 filthiness

sullen: sad 4 dour, dull, glum, grim, sour 5 alone, black, cross, felon, gruff, heavy, moody, pouty, stern, sulky, surly 6 crusty, dismal, dogged, gloomy, grouty, morose, silent, somber 7 baleful, boorish, crabbed, fretful, hostile, peevish, serious 8 churlish, lowering, petulant, solitary 9 obstinate, saturnine 10 depressing, ill-humored, ill-natured, refractory, unsociable 11 intractable, threatening 12 unpropitious

Sullivan's collaborator: 7 Gilbert

sully: See **soil**

sulphate: See **sulfate, sulfur**

sultan: 5 ruler 8 padishah 9 sovereign

decree: 5 irade

sultry: hot 5 close, fiery, humid, lurid 6 coarse, smutty, torrid 7 obscene, sensual 8 inflamed, stifling 10 oppressive, sweltering 13 uncomfortable

sum: add, end, tot 4 gist, host 5 count, gross, issue, total, whole 6 amount, degree, extent, height, number, result, summit 7 integer, numeral, problem, summary 8 addition, assembly, entirety, perorate, quantity 9 aggregate, calculate, epitomize, gathering, magnitude, substance, summarize, summation 11 epilogation 12 recapitulate

forfeited: 5 dedit

large: gob, pot

small: 4 drab 7 driblet, peanuts 8 pit-

tance 11 chickenfeed

subtracted: 9 deduction

unexpended: 7 savings

up: add 9 summarize 12 recapitulate

sumac: 4 rhus 8 shoemake 11 balinghasay

Sumatra: 6 island

animal: 4 balu, tanu 5 orang

ape: 5 orang 6 ourang 9 orangutan

city: 5 Achin, Jambi, Medan 6 Padang 8 Bonkulin 9 Bencoolen, Indrapoor, Palembang

country: 9 Indonesia

deer: 4 napu

fiber: 6 caloee

highest peak: 8 Kerintji

lake: 4 Toba

language: 4 Nias

measure: 4 paal

mountain: 7 Barisan

raft: 5 rakit

river: 4 Musi 5 Jambi, Rokan 9 Indragiri

wildcat: 4 balu

summarize: sum 5 recap 6 digest, review 7 abridge, shorten 8 abstract 9 epitomize

summary: sum 4 gist 5 brief, recap, short 6 digest, precis, resume, summit 7 concise, epitome, extract, general, medulla 8 abstract, argument, breviate, succinct, synopsis 9 condensed, inventory 10 compendium, run-through 11 abridgement 13 comprehension 14 recapitulation

summation: See **sum**

summer: ete(F.) 6 lintel 8 estivate

ailment: 8 heat rash

beverage: ade

pass: 8 estivate

pert. to: 7 estival

summerhouse: 5 kiosk 6 alcove, casino, gazebo 7 cottage, pagoda 8 pavilion 9 belvedere

summery: 4 warm 5 light 7 estival 8 delicate

summing up: See **sum**

summit (see also **mountain, peak**): bow, cap, tip, top, van 4 acme, apex, knap, roof 5 crest, crown, ridge 6 climax, comble, height, vertex, zenith 8 pinnacle 9 fastigium(L.) 10 conference 11 culmination

pert. to: 6 apical

summon: ban, bid 4 call, page 5 charm, evoke, rally, rouse 6 accite, appeal, arouse, compel, demand, gather, muster 7 call for, collect, command, convoke, provoke

to court: 4 cite, sist

summoner: 6 beadle 9 apparitor

summons: 4 call, writ 6 venire 7 command, warning 8 citation, subpoena 9 challenge **12** notification

sump: mud, pit **4** dirt, pool, pump, tank, well **5** drain, march, swamp **6** puddle, slough **7** cistern, depress **8** cesspool **9** reservoir **10** depression, excavation, receptacle

sumpter: 4 pack **6** burden **7** baggage

sumptuous: 4 rich **5** grand **6** costly, lavish, superb **8** splendid **9** expensive, grandiose, luxurious **11** magnificent

sun: orb, sol **4** bask, star **5** Titan **6** bleach **7** daystar, Phoebus **8** luminary **9** Harmachis

crossing equator: **7** equinox

god: Tem, Utu **4** Baal, Lleu, Llew, Utug **6** Apollo, Helios **7** Chepera, Khepara, Shamash, Sokaris **8** Hyperion

luminous envelope of: **6** corona

measuring device: **13** pyrheliometer

mock: **9** parhelion

near: **6** heliac

outer layer: **6** corona

part: **6** corona

path: **8** ecliptic

pert. to: **5** solar **6** heliac

protective devices: **7** parasol **8** blindage, havelock

satellite: **6** planet

worshiper: **5** Parsi **6** Parsee **10** heliolater

sun disk: 4 Aten

sun dog: 4 halo **7** rainbow **9** parhelion

Sun King: 8 Louis XIV

sun room: 7 solaria(pl.) **8** solarium

sun watch: 7 sundial **9** timepiece

sunburn: tan **8** heliosis

sunburst: 6 brooch, ensign

sun-clock: 7 sundial

Sunda Island: 4 Bali, Java, Nias **6** Borneo, Lombok **7** Celebes, Sumatra

Sunday: *following Easter:* Low **9** Quasimodo

mid-Lent: **7** Laetare

pert. to: **9** dominical

special: **4** Palm **6** Easter

sunder: cut, rip **4** part, rend, rive **5** break, sever, split **6** divide **7** disjoin, disrupt, divorce **8** demolish, dissever, disunite, separate

sundial part: 6 gnomon

sundown: See **sunset**

sundowner: 5 drink, tramp **7** captain **8** nightcap

sundry: 4 many **5** apart **6** divers **7** asunder, diverse, several, various **8** distinct, frequent, manifold, numerous, separate, sundered **9** different, disunited **10** all sorts of, respective, separately **12** multifarious **13** miscellaneous

companion of: all

sunfall: See **sunset**

sunfish: 4 opah **5** bream **8** bluegill, pondfish

genus of: **4** mola

sunflower: 4 marigold, rockrose **10** balsamroot, heliotrope

maid turned into: **6** Clytie

Sunflower State: 6 Kansas

sunk (see also **sink**): pad **4** bank, seat, turf **5** couch **6** abject, hollow **8** absorbed, downcast, overcome **9** depressed

sunken: 6 hollow **9** depressed

fence: **4** ha-ha

sunless: 4 dark

sunny: gay **4** fair, warm **5** clear, happy, merry **6** bright, golden, sunlit **8** cheerful, luminous **9** sparkling, vivacious

sunrise: 4 dawn, east

song: **6** aubade

sunset: e'en, eve **4** dusk **7** evening **8** twilight

pert. to: **9** acronical

reflection: **9** alpenglow

Sunset State: 6 Oregon **7** Arizona

sunshade: 5 visor **6** awning **7** parasol **8** umbrella

sunshine: 5 cheer, light **6** warmth **8** daylight, sunburst **9** happiness, sunniness **11** fairweather **12** cheerfulness

Sunshine State: 9 New Mexico **11** South Dakota

sunspot: 4 flaw **6** facula **7** blemish, freckle

sunstroke: 8 siriasis **9** calenture

sunwise: 6 deasil **9** clockwise

Suomi: 7 Finland

sup: eat, sip **4** dine **5** drink, feast, taste **6** tipple **7** swallow **8** mouthful, quantity, spoonful

supawn: 4 mush **12** hasty pudding

super: 5 actor, watch **6** square **7** janitor **9** excellent, marvelous, first-rate

superable: 12 surmountable

superabundance: 5 flood **6** excess, plenty **8** plethora, quantity **10** exuberance **11** diffuseness, superfluity

superabundant: 4 rank **6** lavish **9** redundant **11** overflowing

superannuate: 6 retire **7** outdate, outlast **8** obsolete **9** antiquate, out-of-date **10** disqualify

superb: 4 fine, rich **5** grand, noble, proud **6** lordly **7** elegant, haughty, stately **8** enormous, majestic, opulent, splendid, very best **9** excellent, grandiose, luxurious, sumptuous **13** extraordinary

superbity: 5 pride **9** arrogance **11** haughtiness

supercilious: 5 lofty, proud **6** uppish **7** haughty **8** arrogant, cavalier, snobbish **9** arbitrary **10** disdainful **11** overbearing **12** contemptuous **13** hypercritical

superficial: 4 glib **5** hasty **6** casual, flimsy, slight **7** cursory, outward, shallow, surface **8** apparent, external

superfine: 4 luxe, nice, rich 5 extra, plush, prime 6 choice, subtle, superb 8 delicate, overnice 9 excellent, grandiose

superfluity: 6 excess, luxury 9 abundance, profusion 11 prodigality

superfluous: 4 over 5 spare 6 de trop(F.) 7 surplus, useless 8 abnormal, needless, wasteful 9 excessive, redundant, worthless 10 gratuitous, inordinate 11 extravagant, unnecessary 12 nonessential 13 superabundant

superhuman: 6 divine 7 demigod, uncanny 9 herculean 13 extraordinary

superhumeral: 5 amice, stole

superimpose: 7 overlay

superintend: 4 boss 5 guide 6 direct, manage 7 conduct, control, inspect, oversee 8 engineer 9 supervise 10 administer

superintendence: 4 care 8 guidance 9 authority, oversight 14 responsibility

superintendent: 4 boss 5 super 6 bishop 7 captain, curator, manager 8 director, minister, overseer 9 inspector 10 supervisor 11 chamberlain

superior: 4 fine, head, lord, over, peer 5 above, chief, eigne, extra, liege, upper 6 better, choice, higher, senior 7 exalted, greater, haughty, palmary, prelate, ranking 8 alderman, arrogant, assuming, dominant, elevated, masterly 9 ascendant, ascendent, excellent, marvelous, paramount, spiritual 10 preeminent, surpassing 11 predominant 12 supercilious, supernatural 13 comprehensive

superiority: 4 gree(Sc.) 8 priority 9 advantage, meliority, seniority 13 preponderance

position of: 10 domination

superlative: 4 acme, best, peak 6 utmost 7 supreme 8 peerless 9 excessive, consummate 11 exaggerated

absolute: 7 elative

Superman's friend: 8 Lois Lane

supernal: 4 high 6 divine 8 ethereal, heavenly 9 celestial

supernatural: 5 magic 6 divine, occult 7 ghostly 9 marvelous 10 miraculous, superhuman 13 preternatural

supernatural being: elf, god 4 atua 5 angel, deity, demon, fairy, gnome, nymph, troll 6 cherub, seraph, spirit 7 banshee, goddess 10 leprechaun

Moslem: 4 jinn

Persian: 4 peri

supernatural happening: 6 vision 7 miracle

supernumerary: 5 actor, extra

superpower: USA 4 USSR

superscribe: 5 write 6 direct 7 address, engrave

superscription: 5 title 7 caption 9 direction 11 description, inscription

supersede: 7 replace, succeed 8 displace, override, set aside, supplant

supersonic noise: 4 boom

superstition: 5 freet, freit, magic 6 fetish, voodoo 8 idolatry

supervene: 5 ensue 6 follow, happen 7 succeed

supervise: 4 boss, edit, read, scan 5 check 6 direct, govern, manage, peruse, revise 7 conduct, correct, inspect, oversee 11 superintend

supervisor: 7 foreman 8 alytarch(G.) 9 spectator 10 roadmaster

supine: 5 inert, prone 6 abject, drowsy 7 languid, leaning, passive, sloping, unalert 8 inactive, inclined, indolent, listless, sluggish 9 apathetic, negligent, reclining 10 submissive 11 inattentive, indifferent

supper: tea 4 meal

supplant: 4 oust 5 usurp 6 follow, remove, uproot 7 replace, succeed 8 displace 9 extirpate, supersede, undermine

supple: sly 4 bain, oily 5 agile, lithe 6 limber, lissom, nimble, pliant, swanky 7 cunning, elastic, fawning, lissome, plastic, pliable, servile 8 flexible, yielding 9 adaptable, compliant, resilient, versatile 10 obsequious, responsive 11 complaisant

supplement: add 8 addendum, addition, appendix 9 accessory 10 complement 13 reinforcement

supplemental: 7 special 12 adscititious 13 succenturiate

suppliant: 5 asker 6 beggar, suitor 10 beseeching, entreating, petitioner

supplicate: beg, sue 4 pray 5 crave, plead 6 appeal, invoke, obtest 7 beseech, conjure, entreat, implore, request, solicit 8 petition 9 importune, obsecrate

supplication: 6 litany, prayer 8 rogative

supply: aid, fit 4 feed, fill, fund, give, help, load 5 cache, cater, equip, hoard, relay, stock, store, yield 6 afford, employ, foison, purvey, relief, succor 7 fraught, furnish, granary, nourish, plenish, provide, replace, reserve, satisfy 8 minister, ordnance, turn over 9 profusion, provision, reinforce, replenish, reservoir, temporary 10 administer, assistance, compensate, contribute 4 accumulation

support: aid, arm, guy, leg, peg, rib 4 back, base, beam, bear, bibb, fend, help, keep, limb, pier, prop, stay 5 boost, brace, carry, cheer, cleat, easel, favor, found, hinge, shore, sling, staff, strut, truss 6 anchor, assent, behalf, better, defend, endure, lintel, living, pillar, second, shield, splint, spring, suffer, tripod, trivet, uphold, upkeep, verify **7** bolster, cherish, comfort, confirm, console, endorse, espouse, fulcrum, nourish, nurture, protect, provide, reserve, shore up, subsidy, sustain, trestle **8** advocate, approval, baluster, befriend, evidence, maintain, pedestal, sanction, tolerate, underlie **9** adminicle, encourage, financing, reinforce, stanchion, vindicate **10** assistance, foundation, strengthen **11** corroborate, countenance **12** alimentation, substantiate

for statue: **5** socle **8** pedestal

one-legged: **6** unipod

slab: **4** tray **6** planch

supporter: **4** ally, knee **5** brace **6** bearer, patron, rooter **7** abetter, abettor, booster, founder **8** adherent, advocate, assertor, exponent, follower, henchman, partisan **9** auxiliary, suspender

suppose: **4** deem, trow, ween **5** allow, imply, judge, opine, think **6** assume, expect, repute, theory **7** believe, imagine, incline, opinion, presume, suspect **8** conceive, conclude, consider, obligate, supposal **9** apprehend, intention **10** conjecture, presuppose, substitute, understand **11** expectation, supposition

supposed: **7** alleged, assumed

supposition: **4** idea **6** notion, theory **7** forgery, surmise **9** postulate **10** alteration, assumption, conjecture, estimation, hypothesis **11** expectation, implication, proposition, uncertainty

supposititious: **7** assumed, feigned **8** fabulous, putative, spurious, supposed **9** imaginary, pretended **10** artificial, chimerical, fictitious **11** counterfeit **12** hypothetical, illegitimate

suppress: **4** hide, keep, kill, stop **5** check, choke, crush, elide, quash, quell, stunt **6** arrest, bridle, censor, harass, hush up, ravish, retard, stifle, subdue **7** abolish, compose, conceal, destroy, exclude, oppress, prevent, refrain, repress, silence, smother, squelch **8** compress, prohibit, restrain, withhold **9** interdict, overpower, overthrow **10** dissolving, extinguish

suprarenal: **7** adrenal

supremacy: **4** sway **5** power **7** control, mastery **8** dominion **9** authority, autocracy, dominance, influence **10** ascendancy, domination **11** sovereignty **12** predominance **13** preponderance

supreme: **4** best, last **5** alone, chief, final **6** superb, utmost **7** crucial, highest, maximum **8** foremost, greatest, loftiest, peerless, ultimate **9** excellent, paramount **10** preeminent

supreme being: God **5** Allah, monad **7** creator, Jehovah

surcease: end **4** rest, stay, stop **5** defer,

delay **6** desist, relief **7** refrain, respite, suspend **8** postpone **9** cessation

surcharge: tax **4** cost, fill, load **6** burden, impost **7** surfeit **8** overload, surprint **9** overcrowd, overprint, overstock **10** impregnate, overburden, overcharge

surcingle: **4** band, belt **6** girdle **8** cincture

surcoat: **5** jupon **6** cyclas **7** garment

surd: **4** deaf **7** radical **9** insensate, voiceless **10** irrational

sure: **4** fast, firm, safe, true **5** siker(Sc.) **6** indeed, secure, sicker(Sc.), stable, steady, strong **7** assured, certain **8** enduring, positive, reliable, unerring **9** authentic, betrothed, confident, convinced, steadfast, undoubted, unfailing **10** dependable, infallible, inevitable **11** indubitable, trustworthy, unfaltering **12** indisputable **13** incontestable **14** unquestionable

surely: **6** atweel(Sc.), really

sureness: **9** certitude

sure thing: **6** shoo-in, winner **9** certainty

surety: **4** bail **6** backer, pledge **7** engager, sponsor **8** bailsman, bondsman, security **9** assurance, certainty, guarantee, guarantor **10** confidence

post: **4** bond

surf: **4** foam, wave **5** spray, swell **7** breaker

sound of: **4** rote

surface: top **4** area, face, pave, side, skin **5** facet, plane **6** come up, facing, finish, patina **7** outside **8** boundary, exterior **11** superficial

flat: **4** area **5** plane, sheet **7** lateral

geometrical: **5** nappe **6** sphere, toroid

inclined: **4** cant, ramp **7** descent

mellowed: **6** patina

pert. to: **6** facial

rounded: **9** concavity, convexity

toward: **5** ectad

surfacing: **6** gravel **7** asphalt, macadam **8** emerging

surfeit: **4** cloy, feed, glut, sate **6** excess, nausea, supply **7** disgust, replete, satiate, satiety, satisfy **8** disorder **9** satiation **10** discomfort **11** extravagant, overindulge, superfluity **13** overabundance **14** overindulgence

surge: **4** pour, rise, rush, tide, wave **5** gurge, swell **6** billow **7** estuate, rolling **8** sweeping, swelling

surgeon: **8** sawbones **10** chirurgeon

surgeonfish: **4** tang

surgery: **9** operation, resection

appliance: **5** brace **6** crutch, splint

compress: **5** stupe

instrument: **5** fleam, lance, probe, scala **6** bilabe, gorget, lancet, splint, stylet, trapan, trepan, trocar, vectis **7** forceps, levator, ligator, rongeur, scalpel, trilabe,

trochar **8** bistoury, ecraseur, trephine, tweezers **9** goosebill, heart tenaculum, vulsellum **10** abaptiston, adaptistum, terebellum, tourniquet
perform: **7** operate
plug: **6** tampon
puncture: **8** centesis
roller: **6** fascia **7** fasciae
stitch: **5** seton **6** suture
thread: **6** catgut
Surinam, Suriname: *capital:* **10** Paramaribo
formerly: **11** Dutch Guiana
hut: **5** benab
language: **5** Dutch
measure: **7** ketting
monetary unit: **7** guilder
mountain: **10** Tumuc-Humac
river: **5** Itany **6** Maroni **8** Suriname **9** Corantijn
toad: **4** pipa **5** pipal
tribe: **4** Boni **5** Djuka
surly: **4** glum, grum, rude **5** bluff, chuff, cross, gruff, gurly **6** abrupt, grumpy, morose, sullen **7** boorish, crabbed, haughty, uncivil, waspish **8** arrogant, churlish, growling **9** fractious **10** ill-natured **11** intractable
surmise: **4** deem **5** guess, infer, trace **6** charge **7** believe, imagine, presume, suppose **9** suspicion **10** allegation, assumption, conclusion, conjecture **11** supposition
surmount: top **4** pass, rise, tide **5** clear, climb, crown, excel, outdo, total **6** ascend, exceed, hurdle, subdue **7** conquer, surpass **8** overcome **9** negotiate, transcend
surmountable: **8** possible **9** superable
surmounting: **4** atop
surname: **6** byname **7** agnomen **8** cognomen **11** appellation
surpass: cap, cob, top **4** beat, flog **5** amend, excel, outdo **6** better, exceed, outvie **7** eclipse, outrank, outsoar **8** outclass, outreach, outstrip, surmount **9** transcend
surpassing: **4** fine **6** banner **7** supreme **9** excellent **10** inimitable, preeminent
surplice: **5** cotta, ephod **8** vestment
surplus: **4** over, rest **5** extra **6** excess **7** backlog, reserve **8** overplus **9** remainder **10** redundancy
surprise: awe, cap **5** alarm, amaze, catch, seize, shock **6** ambush, dazzle, detect, strike, waylay, wonder **7** astound, capture, gloppen, perplex, startle, uncover **8** astonish, bewilder, confound, dumfound, overcome **9** amazement, overwhelm **11** flabbergast
surprised: **5** agape
surprising: **6** sudden **9** startling **10** unex-

pected **13** extraordinary
surrender: **4** cede, fall, give **5** remit, yield **6** remise, resign, tender, waiver **7** abandon, cession, concede, deliver, forsake **8** dedition, remittal **9** rendition **10** abdication, capitulate, compromise, relinquish **11** divestiture **12** cancellation
surreptitious: sly **6** covert, secret **7** bootleg **8** sneaking, stealthy **9** underhand **11** clandestine
surrey: **8** carriage
surrogate: **6** deputy **8** delegate, resource **9** subrogate **10** substitute
surround: bar, hem **4** belt, fold, gird, ring, span, wrap **5** beset, embay, flood, hedge **6** border, circle, corral, encase, enring, invest **7** besiege, embosom, enclose, environ, imbosom **8** encircle, envelope, inundate, overflow **9** beleaguer, encompass **12** circumscribe **14** circumnavigate
with water: **4** isle **6** enisle
surrounded: **4** amid **5** among **6** amidst **7** between, bounded
surrounding: **5** about, midst **7** context, setting **8** ambiance **9** entourage **11** environment **12** circumjacent, circumstance
surtax: **4** agio, levy **5** extra
surtout: **4** coat, hood **7** garment **8** overcoat
survey: **4** pool, scan, view **5** study **6** regard, review, search **7** examine, history, inspect, oversee **8** consider, estimate, traverse **9** delineate, determine, supervise, treatment **10** compendium, exposition, scrutinize **11** description, examination, reconnoiter, superintend **13** triangulation **14** reconnaissance
surveyor: **6** gauger **9** arpenteur, inspector **14** superintendent
helper: **6** rodman **7** lineman, poleman **8** chainman
instrument: **11** stratameter
nail: **4** spad
tool: **6** alidad **7** alidade, transit **10** theodolite **12** perambulator
survival: **5** relic
survive: **6** endure **7** outlast, outlive **11** pull through
Susanna: *accusers:* **6** elders
husband: **7** Joachim
susceptible: **4** easy, open **6** liable **7** exposed, subject **8** allergic, sensible, sentient **9** receptive, sensitive **10** responsive, vulnerable **11** softhearted, unresistant **13** tenderhearted **14** impressionable
to error: **8** fallible
susceptibility: **5** sense **7** emotion, feeling **11** sensibility **13** affectibility
suscitate: **5** rouse **6** excite **7** animate,

provoke **9** stimulate

suslik: 5 sisel **8** squirrel **11** spermophile

suspect: 4 fear **5** doubt, guess **7** accused, believe, dubious, imagine, inkling, presume, suppose, surmise **8** conceive, distrust, doubtful, mistrust **9** discredit **10** disbelieve, intimation, suspicious, understand **12** apprehension

suspend: bar **4** hang, hold, oust, stop **5** cease, debar, defer, demur, expel **6** dangle, recess, repeal **7** adjourn, exclude **8** intermit, postpone, withhold **9** pretermit

suspended: 4 hung **6** latent **7** abeyant, pendent, pensile **8** dangling, inactive **11** inoperative

suspender: 5 brace **6** gallus, garter, hanger **9** supporter

suspense: 5 worry **6** unease **7** anxiety **8** cautious, hesitant, withheld **11** tenterhooks, uncertainty **12** apprehension **14** indecisiveness

in: **7** pending

suspension: 4 stop **5** delay, pause **7** failure **8** abeyance, buoyancy, stoppage **9** remission **11** withholding **12** intermission, interruption

in air: **5** vapor

of court sentence: **9** probation

of hostilities: **5** truce **9** armistice, ceasefire

suspicion: 4 hint **5** doubt, hunch, touch, trace **7** askance, caution, inkling **8** distrust, jealousy, mistrust **9** misgiving **10** diffidence, intimation, suggestion, uneasiness **11** expectation, uncertainty **12** apprehension

suspicious: 4 wary **5** fishy, leery **8** doubtful **9** equivocal **11** mistrustful **12** questionable

suspire: 4 sigh **7** long for, respire

sustain: 4 abet, back, bear, buoy, dure, feed, help, prop **5** abide, carry **6** assist, endure, foster, second, succor, suffer, supply, uphold **7** comfort, confirm, console, contain, nourish, prolong, provide, stand by, support, undergo **8** befriend, continue, maintain **9** encourage, withstand **10** experience, strengthen **11** corroborate

sustenance: 4 food, meat **5** bread, viand **6** living, upkeep **7** aliment, support **9** nutrition, provision **10** exhibition **11** maintenance, nourishment, subsistence **12** alimentation

susurrus: 6 murmur, rustle **7** whisper

sutler: 7 provant **9** vivandier **10** vivandiere

suttee: 7 suicide **10** immolation

suture: 4 line, seam **6** stitch **9** arthrosis **12** articulation

suzerain: 8 overlord **9** paramount, sovereign **10** feudal lord

svelte: 4 slim **5** lithe **6** lissom **7** lissome, slender **8** graceful

swab: gob, mop **4** lout, wash, wipe **5** brush, clean **7** epaulet, officer, plunger **8** medicate

swack: 4 blow, cuff **5** whack **6** nimble, pliant, supple

swaddle: 4 beat, bind, wrap **6** clothe, cudgel, swathe **7** bandage **8** restrict, surround

swag: pit, sag, tip **4** list, loot, sway **5** booty, lurch, money, spoil, swing, tramp **6** bundle, hollow **7** plunder **10** decoration

swagger: 4 brag, lord **5** bluff, boast, bully, lurch, strut, swank, swell **6** cuttle, hector, prance **7** bluster, gauster, panache, quarrel, roister, ruffler, stagger, stylish **8** vagabond **11** braggadocio, fanfaronade **16** ultrafashionable

swaggering: 6 gascon **7** huffcap

swagman: 5 fence **7** bushman **9** sundowner

bundle: **5** bluey

swain: boy **5** lover, youth **6** escort, rustic, suitor **7** admirer, gallant, peasant, servant **8** shepherd **9** attendant, boyfriend **10** countryman

swale: fen **4** moor, sway **5** marsh, shade, slash, sweal, swing, swirl **6** hollow, meadow, valley **8** coolness **10** depression

swallow: eat, sip, sup **4** bear, bolt, down, gaup, gawp, glut, gulp, take, tern **5** drink, merge, quilt, swift **6** absorb, accept, englut, engulf, go-down, gullet, imbibe, ingest, martin, mumble, recant, resorb, throat, vanish **7** believe, consume, engorge, retract **8** aperture, suppress, tolerate, withdraw **9** esophagus

swamp: bog, fen **4** mire, moor, muck, ruin, sink, slew, sloo, slue, thin, wham **5** clear, empty, flood, marsh **6** deluge, engulf, hollow, morass, slough **7** cienaga, pocosin, pocoson, slender **8** overcome, quagmire, submerge **9** marshland, overwhelm **10** Everglades

gas: **6** miasma **7** methane

grass: **5** sedge

pert. to: **7** miasmal, paludal

swan: cob, elk, pen **5** swear **6** cygnet **7** declare, whooper **8** surprise **9** trumpeter

female: pen

genus: **6** cygnus

male: cob

young: **6** cygnet

Swan river: 4 Avon

swank: 5 showy **6** active, lively **7** stylish, swagger **12** ostentatious

swanky: 4 chic **9** grandiose

Swann's Way author: 6 Proust

swap: 5 trade **6** barter, dicker **8** exchange

sward: sod **4** lawn, skin, turf **8** covering

swarm: 4 bike(Sc.), byke(Sc.), host, move, shin, swim, teem **5** climb, cloud, crowd, flock, group, horde, mount **6** abound, rabble, throng **7** migrate **8** assemble **9** multitude **10** congregate

swarming: 6 aswarm **10** emigration

swarthy: dun **4** dark **5** dusky **8** blackish

swash: bar **4** blow, move **5** noise, slosh, sound **6** splash, strike **7** bluster, channel, dashing, swagger **9** splashing

swashbuckler: 5 bravo **6** gascon **7** ruffian, slasher, soldier **9** combatant, daredevil, swaggerer

swashy: 4 weak **6** watery **7** insipid

swastika: 5 cross **6** fylfot **7** insignia **9** Gammadion

swat: bat, hit **4** blow **5** clout **6** strike

swatch: 5 swash **6** sample **7** channel

swath, swathe: row **4** band, bind, crop, wrap **5** strip, sweep **6** clothe, stroke **7** enfold, swaddle, windrow

sway: 4 bend, bias, lean, move, reel, rock, rule, veer **5** force, grace, guide, lurch, power, shake, swing, waver, wield **6** direct, divert, govern, swerve, totter, waddle **7** affect, command, control, deflect, shoggie **8** dominion, rotation **9** dominance, influence, oscillate, vacillate **10** ascendancy, ascendency **11** fluctuation, inclination, sovereignty **13** lithesomeness

Swaziland: *capital:* **7** Mbabane
language: **7** Siswati
monetary unit: **9** lilangeni
people: **4** Zulu **5** Bantu
river: **5** Usutu **6** Komati, Umbuluzi
town: **7** Manzini, Mbabane

swear: vow **4** bind **5** curse, utter **6** adjure, affirm, assert, pledge, threat **7** declare, promise, testify **8** execrate **9** blaspheme **10** administer, asseverate, vituperate
falsely: **7** perjure, slander
to secrecy: **4** tile

sweat: dry **4** emit, ooze, work **5** bleed, exude, hoist, labor, sudor(L.) **6** drudge, fleece **7** excrete, extract, ferment, putrefy, soldier **8** condense, overwork, perspire, transude

sweater: 5 shell **8** cardigan, pullover, slipover

Sweden: *artist:* **4** Zorn
botanist: **5** Fries **9** Bromelius
bread: **10** knackebrod
capital: **9** Stockholm
city and town: **5** Boras, Edane, Falun, Gavle, Malmo, Ystad **6** Orebro, Upsala **7** Uppsala **8** Goteborg, Nykoping **9** Falkoping, Jonkoping, **10** Eskilstuna, Gothenburg, Norrkoping **11** Halsingborg
clover: **6** alsike

coin: ore **5** krona **8** skilling
county: lan
dance: **6** polska
division: amt **4** Laen **5** Skane **8** Gotaland, Gothland, Norrland, Swealand
dynasty: **4** Vasa
explorer: **5** Hedin
farm: **4** torp
gulf: **7** Bothnia
highest peak: **10** Kebnekaise
island: **5** Oland **8** Gotaland
king: **4** Eric, Wasa **5** Oscar **10** Bernadotte
lake: **5** Asnen, Malar, Wener **6** Siljan, Vanern, Vatter, Wennen, Wetter **7** Hielmar, Malaren, Vattern
manual training: **5** sloyd
match: **12** taendstikker
measure: aln, fot, mil, ref, tum **4** famn, last, stop **5** carat, foder, kanna, kappe, linje, nymil, spann, stang, tunna **6** fathom, jumfru **7** kollast, oxhuvud, tunland **8** fjarding, kappland, koltunna, tunnland
monetary unit: **5** krona
motion-picture director: **7** Bergman
mountain: **6** Kjolen Sarjek
noble title: **4** graf
parliament: **7** Riksdag
philologist: **5** Ihre
physicist: **5** Dalen
province: **6** Kalmar, Orebro, Upsala **7** Gotland, Halland **8** Blekinge, Elfsborg, Jamtland, Malmohus, Wermland
river: Dal **4** Gota, Klar, Umea **5** Indal, Kalix, Lulea, Pitea, Ranea, Torne **6** Lainio, Ljusne, Tornea, Windel **7** Ljungan
soprano: **7** Nilsson **9** Jenny Lind
sour milk: **8** tatmjolk
state religion: **8** Lutheran
tribe: **6** Geatas
weight: ass, lod, ort **4** last, mark, pund, sten, untz **5** carat **6** nylast **7** centner, lispund **8** lispound, skalpund, skeppund **9** ship pound
writer: **6** Carlen **7** Bellman **8** Lagerlof **10** Strindberg

Swedish Nightingale: 4 Lind **5** Jenny

sweep: fly, oar **4** line **5** besom, broom, brush, clean, clear, drive, range, scope, scour, strip, surge, swath **6** extend, remove **7** contour, stretch **8** traverse

sweeping: 6 all-out **8** complete **9** extensive, out-and-out **13** comprehensive, thoroughgoing

sweepings: 6 fulyie(Sc.), fulzie(Sc.), refuse

sweet: 4 dear, fair **5** bonny, candy, dolce, douce(F.), fresh, soave **6** dulcet, gentle, lovely, pretty, sugary, syrupy **7** beloved, caramel, darling, honeyed, musical, winning **8** aromatic, fetching, fragrant, pleasant, pleasing, preserve **9** agreeable, ambrosial, melodious **10** attractive, confection, harmonious **11** good-natured, mellisonant

sweet flag: 4 arum **7** calamus

sweet potato: yam **6** batata **7** ocarina

sweetbread: 4 meat, veal **9** ris de veau

sweetbrier: 4 rose **9** eglantine

sweeten: 4 mull **5** sugar **6** pacify, purify, refine, soften, solace **7** appease, cleanse, freshen, mollify, perfume, relieve **9** disinfect, sugarcoat **10** edulcorate

sweetfish: ayu

sweetheart: gra **4** agra, beau, dear, doll, doxy, gill, girl, jill, lass, love **5** bully, court, flame, leman, lover, **6** adorer, fellow, orpine **8** paramour, truelove **9** good thing

sweetmeat: 4 cake **5** candy, goody **6** comfit, dragee, pastry **7** caramel, dessert **8** confetti, conserve, hardbake, marzipan, preserve **9** marchpane, sugarplum **10** confection

sweetsop: 4 ates

swell: nob, sea **4** bell, bulb, bulk, grow, huff, lord, rise, surf, toff, wave **5** bloat, bulge, grand, surge **6** billow, dilate, expand, extend, roller, tiptop, tumefy **7** augment, distend, enlarge, inflate, seagate, stylish **8** increase **9** elevation, excellent, first-rate, intumesce, marvelous, wonderful **10** prominence, thickening **11** fashionable **12** protuberance **16** ultrafashionable

swelled head: 6 egoist **7** conceit

swellfish: 6 puffer **8** puff-fish

swelling: sty **4** bleb, bubo, node **5** blain, botch, bouge, bunch, edema, tumor **6** aswell, gather, growth **7** gibbous, turgent **8** windgall **9** gibbosity **10** rhetorical

on plants: **4** gall

pert. to: **5** nodal **9** edematose, edematous

swelter: 4 burn, fret, heat, rush **5** exude, faint, roast, sweat **6** wallow, welter **8** perspire

swerve: bow **4** skew, turn, veer **5** stray, yield **6** totter **7** deflect, deviate, digress

swift: 4 cran(Sc.), fast, reel **5** alert, fleet, hasty, quick, rapid, ready **6** lizard, prompt, speedy, winged

Swift: 8 Jonathan, satirist

brute: **5** Yahoo

flying island: **6** Laputa

hero: **8** Gulliver

lady friend: **6** Stella

pen name: **11** Bickerstaff

swig: 4 gulp, rock, sway **5** booze, draft, drink, hoist, snort, swash **6** guzzle, imbibe, tackle

swile: 4 seal

swill: 4 fill, wash **5** drink, flood, rinse, swash, waste **6** basket, drench, guzzle, refuse **7** garbage, hogwash

swim: 4 reel, spin **5** float, swoon, whirl **9** dizziness **13** forgetfulness **15** unconsciousness

pert. to: **8** natatory

swimmer: 7 natator

of the English Channel: **6** Ederle

of the Hellespont: **7** Leander

of Tiber river: **7** Cloelia

swimming: 6 filled, naiant, natant **7** flooded, vertigo **9** dizziness

swimming pool: 4 tank **10** natatorium

swimming stroke: 4 back, side **5** crawl **6** breast **7** trudgen **9** butterfly, dogpaddle

swindle: con, gyp **4** bilk, dupe, fake, mace, rook **5** bunco, bunko, cheat, foist, fraud, spoof, trick **6** diddle, trepan **7** defraud **8** flimflam **10** overcharge

swindler: fob **5** biter, cheat, crook, knave, rogue, shark **6** chiaus, chouse, shaver **7** sharper **8** blackleg

swine: hog, pig, sow **4** boar **7** peccary

breed of: **8** Cheshire, Tamworth **9** Berkshire, Hampshire, Yorkshire **11** Duroc-Jersey, Poland China **12** Chester White

feeding of: **7** pannage **8** slopping

female: sow **4** gilt

fever: **6** rouget **7** cholera

flesh: **4** pork

litter of: **6** farrow

male: **4** boar

pert. to: **7** porcine

young: pig **5** shoat **6** piglet

swing: 4 beat, bent, blow, hang, hurl, lilt, slew, slue, sway, turn, whip **5** fling, lurch, power, shake, throw, trend, waver **6** dangle, handle, manage, rhythm, stroke, totter **7** flutter, shoggie(Sc.), suspend, trapeze, vibrate **8** brandish, undulate **9** fluctuate, oscillate

swing around: jib **4** slue

swinger: 8 party man **9** bon vivant

swinish: 5 gross **6** coarse **7** beastly, boarish, brutish, piggish, sensual

swipe: 4 blow, glom **5** draft, drink, lever, steal, swape, sweep **6** pilfer, snatch, strike

swirl: ess **4** curl, eddy, purl **5** curve, gurge, twist, whirl, whorl

swish: 4 cane, flog, hiss, lash, whip **5** birch, smart, sound **6** rustle, strike **9** exclusive

Swiss: See **Switzerland**

switch: gad, rod, wag **4** beat, flog, lash, turn, twig, wand, whip **5** shift, shunt, swing **6** change, divert, strike **7** scourge **8** exchange, transfer **10** disconnect, substitute

switchboard: 5 panel

switchman: 7 shunter

Switzerland: 6 Suisse(F.) 7 Schweiz(G.)
8 Helvetia
archer: 11 William Tell
ax: 6 piolet
bay: 3 Uri
canton: Uri, Zug 4 Bern, Genf, Vaud 5
Basel, Basle, Waadt 6 Aargau, Geneva,
Geneve, Glaris, Glarus, Luzern, St.
Gall, Schwyz, Tessin, Ticino, Valais,
Wallis, Zurich 7 Grisons, Lucerne,
Schwytz, Soleure, Thurgau 8 Freiberg
9 Appenzell, Neuchatel, Neuenberg, So-
lothurn 10 Graubunden 11 Sankt Gallen, Schaffhouse, Unterwalden 12
Schaffhausen
capital: 4 Bern
card game: 4 jass
cheese: 7 Gruyere, sapsago 9 schweizer
10 Emmentaler 13 schweizer-kase
city: 4 Bale, Chur, Genf, Sion 5 Basel,
Basle, Berne 6 Geneva, Schwyz, Zurich
7 Fyzabad, Locarno, Lucerne 8 Faiz-
abad, Lausanne, Montreux, St. Gallen
9 Constance, Neuchatel 10 Farukha-
bad, Winterthur
coin: 5 franc, rappe 6 rappen 7 angster,
centime, duplone 8 blaffert
commune: Zug 4 Biel, Wald 5 Aarau,
Morat
composer: 4 Raff 5 Bloch 6 Martin
district: 6 canton
food: 12 bernerplatte
herdsman: 4 senn
hero: 11 Wilhelm Tell
highest peak: 9 Monte Rosa 12 Dufour-
spitze
lake: Uri, Zug 4 Joux, Thon 5 Leman 6
Bienne, Brienz, Geneva, Lugano, Sar-
nen, Wallen, Zurich 7 Lucerne, Lun-
gern 8 Viervald 9 Constance, Neuchatel, Sarnersee, Thunersee 10 Stattersee
11 Brienzersee
language: 5 Ladin 6 French, German 7
Italian, Romansh 8 Romansch, Roumansh 14 Switzerdeutsch
legislature: 8 grossrat 9 grosserat, gross-
rath
measure: imi, pot 4 aune, elle, fuss, immi,
muid, pied, saum, zoll 5 lieue, ligne,
linie, maass, moule, pouce, schuh, staab,
toise 6 perche, setier, strich 7 juchart,
klafter, viertel 9 quarteron 11 holz-
klafter
monetary unit: 5 franc
mountain: 4 Alps, Jura, Rigi, Rosa 5
Blanc, Cenis, Genis 7 Pilatus 8 Jungfrau 10 Matterhorn, St. Gotthard 11
Burgenstock
mountain pass: 5 Furka 7 Grimsel, Simplon 8 Gotthard, Lotschen 13 Saint
Gotthard
officer: 5 amman

painter: 4 Klee
people: 4 muff 5 French, German 7 Italian, Romansh 8 Rhaetian, Romansch,
Roumansh 9 Helvetian
pine: 6 arolla
psychologist: 4 Jung
river: Aar, Inn 4 Aare 5 Doubs, Reuss,
Rhine, Rhone
sled: 4 luge 5 luger
song: 5 yodel
tunnel: 5 Cenis 7 Simplon 8 Gotthard 11
Loetschberg
valley: Aar 7 Zermatt 8 Engadine
weight: 5 pfund 7 centner, quintal
wind: 4 bise
wine: 7 Dezaley
swivel: 4 turn 5 swing
swollen: 4 blub 5 blown, pursy, tumid 6
turgid 7 blubber, bulbous, bulging,
pompous 8 enlarged, inflated, varicose
9 distended, increased, tumescent 10
rhetorical
swoon: fit 4 coma, dwam 5 dwalm(Sc.),
faint, sleep, spell 6 attack, stupor 7 ecstasy, syncope 8 black out, languish
swoop: cut 5 seize, sweep 6 pounce 7 descend
sword: sax 4 dirk, epee, foil, pata 5 bilbo,
brand, estoc, glawe, gully, kukri, saber,
sabre 6 barong, creese, cutlas, Damask,
dusack, espada, floret, parang, rapier,
spatha, Toledo 7 ascalon, askelon, bas-
lard, curtana, curtein, cutlass, espadon,
estoque, shabble, simitar 8 acinaces,
camplian, claymore, Damascus, fal-
chion, flamberg, scimitar, schlager,
whinyard 9 achiavone, flamberge
blade of: 5 forte
cross guard: 7 quillon
curved: 5 saber, sabre 8 scimitar
fencing: 4 epee, foil
handle: 4 haft, hilt
of the Cid: 6 Colada
shaped: 6 ensate 8 ensiform
short: 4 dirk
two-edged: 4 pata
two-handed: 7 espadon 8 claymore
sword lily: 9 gladiolus
swordfish: 6 espada 7 espadon 9 broadbill
swordlike: 5 xypho 6 ensate 8 ensiform,
gladiate
swordsman: 6 fencer 7 epeeist 8 thruster
sworn: 6 avowed 7 devoted 8 affirmed,
attested 9 confirmed 10 determined,
inveterate
swot (see also **swat**): 4 cram 5 grind, labor, sweat
syagush: 7 caracal
sybarite: 7 epicure 8 hedonist 10 volup-
tuary
Sybil: See **sibyl**

sycophant: 5 toady 6 lackey 7 fawning, spaniel 8 informer, parasite 9 charlatan, flatterer 10 footlicker, talebearer

syllable: bit 4 whit 5 shred 7 modicum 8 particle
added: 6 prefix, suffix
deletion: 7 apocope
final: 6 ultima
lacking at end: 10 catalectic
next to last: 6 penult
second before last: 10 antepenult
short: 4 mora 5 breve
shortening: 7 apocope, elision, systole
stressed: 5 arsis
unaccented: 6 atonic

syllabus: 6 digest, precis, sketch 7 outline, summary 8 abstract, headnote, synopsis 9 statement 10 compendium

sylloge: 10 collection, compendium

syllogism: 5 logic 7 Sorites 8 argument 9 reasoning 10 epichirema 11 epicheirema

sylph: elf, fay 5 fairy 6 spirit, undine

sylphlike: 4 thin 7 lissome, slender 8 graceful

sylvan: 5 woody 6 rustic, wooded 8 woodsman 10 forestlike

sylvan deity: Pan 4 faun 6 Faunus

symbol (see also **element**): 4 icon, ikon, sign, type, word 5 badge, creed, crest, cross, image, token, totem 6 caract, emblem, ensign, figure, letter 7 diagram 9 character, hierogram, trademark 10 expression, indication, similitude, substitute 12 abbreviation, contribution
achievement: 5 medal 6 ribbon
comedy: 4 sock
early Christian church: 5 orant
immortality: 6 phenix 7 phoenix
mourning: 5 crepe 7 cypress
peace: 4 dove
put into: 6 notate
saintliness: 4 halo
servitude: 4 yoke
victory: 4 palm 6 laurel
wisdom: owl

symbolical: 7 typical 8 mystical 11 allegorical 12 emblematical, sacramental 14 representative

symbolize: 5 agree 6 concur, mirror, typify 7 betoken, combine, express, signify 9 harmonize, represent 10 illustrate

symmetrical: 5 equal 7 regular, spheral 8 balanced 13 commensurable

symmetry: 7 balance, harmony 9 congruity 10 conformity, consistency, proportion

sympathetic: 4 soft 6 humane, tender 7 pietoso, piteous 8 affected 9 condolent, congenial, consonant, expansive, sensitive 10 responsive 13 compassionate, understanding

sympathize: 4 pity 6 bemoan 7 condole, feel for 11 commiserate

sympathy: 4 pity 6 accord, liking 7 harmony 8 interest 9 agreement 10 compassion, condolence, kindliness, tenderness 13 commiseration, understanding
expression of: 8 clemency 10 condolence
lack of: 8 dyspathy

symphony: 5 music 7 concord, harmony 9 orchestra
division: 8 movement
for Napoleon: 6 Eroica
form: 6 sonata

symposium: 4 talk 7 banquet 8 dialogue, potation 10 conference, discussion 11 compotation

symptom: 4 mark, note, sign 5 token 8 evidence 10 indication

synagogue: 4 shul 5 group 8 assembly, building, religion 9 communion, community 12 congregation
officer: 6 parnas
platform: 7 almemar
pointer: yad
Sephardic: 5 anoga
singer: 6 cantor, chazan 7 chazzan

synaxis: 7 meeting, service 12 congregation

synchronize: 6 concur 7 arrange 8 coincide, regulate 12 contemporize

synchronous: 8 existing 10 concurrent 11 concomitant 12 contemporary, simultaneous 15 contemporaneous

syndetic: 10 connective

syndic: 5 agent, judge, mayor 7 manager, officer, trustee 8 advocate, official 10 magistrate

syndicate: 4 sell 5 chain, group, trust, union, unite 6 cartel 7 censure, combine, council 8 monopoly 9 committee 11 association 12 conglomerate, organization

syndrome: 6 malady 7 ailment, disease 8 disorder

synod: 4 body 5 court 7 council, meeting 8 assembly 10 convention 11 convocation

synonym: 7 metonym

synonymous: 4 like 5 alike 10 equivalent

synopsis: 4 plan 5 brief 7 summary 8 abstract 9 statement 10 compendium, conspectus 11 abridgement

syntax: 5 order 6 system 7 grammar 9 structure 11 arrangement
analyze: 5 parse
mistake: 8 solecism

synthesis: 5 blend, summa 7 complex 11 combination, composition 13 incorporation

synthetic: 6 ersatz 7 man-made 10 artificial, fabricated

syphilis: pox 4 lues 7 disease

lesion: **7** chancre
old remedy: **9** Salvarsan
Syracuse: *conqueror:* **4** Rome
founder: **7** Archias
tyrant: **5** Gelon
Syria: *ancient name:* **4** Aram
animal: **5** addax, daman
bear: **4** dubb
bishop: **4** abba
buried city: **4** Dura
capital: **8** Damascus
church plan: **8** triconch
city and town: **4** Homs **5** Calno, Derra **6** Aleppo, Balbec, Calneh **7** Antioch, Latakia **8** Seleucia
coin: **6** talent **7** piaster
deity: **4** Baal **5** Allat **6** Mammon **7** Resheph
district: **6** Aleppo, Hauran
goat: **6** angora
grass: **7** Johnson
gypsy: **5** Aptal
lake: **5** Merom **7** Djeboid **8** Tiberias
mallow: **4** okra
measure: **5** makuk **6** garava
monetary unit: **5** pound
mountain: **6** Carmel, Hermon **7** Libanus
peasant: **6** fellah
people: **5** Druse **7** Ansarie, Saracen

plant: **5** cumin
religious sect: **5** Druse
river: Asi **6** Barada, Jordan **7** Orontes
script: **5** serta
silk: **4** acca
tetrarchy: **7** abilene
weight: oke **4** cola, rotl **5** artal, artel, ratel **6** talent
wind: **6** simoon
syringa: **5** lilac, shrub **10** mock orange
syrup: **4** karo, sapa **6** orgeat **7** glucose, sarghum **10** sweetening
system: ism **4** code **5** group, setup, whole **6** circle, method, regime, theory **7** regimen **8** religion, treatise, universe **9** procedure **10** assemblage, hypothesis, philosophy, regularity **11** aggregation, arrangement, orderliness
of rules: **4** code
of weights: **4** troy
of worship: **4** cult
of writing: **7** braille **8** alphabet
systematic: **4** neat **7** orderly, regular **9** organized **10** methodical
systematics: **8** taxonomy
systematize: **5** order **6** adjust **7** arrange, catalog, marshal **8** organize, regiment **9** catalogue
Szechwan capital: **7** Chengtu

T

t-shaped: tau
taa: **6** pagoda
Taal: **9** Afrikaans
tab: eye, pan, tag **4** bill, drop, flap, loop **5** aglet, check, index, label, price, score, strap, strip **6** aiglet, eartab, record **7** account, latchet, officer **9** appendage, reckoning **10** accounting
tabac: **5** snuff **7** tobacco
tabanid: **6** gadfly **8** horsefly
tabard: inn **4** cape, coat **5** cloak, tunic **6** chimer, jacket, mantle **7** pendant
tabasco: **5** sauce
tabatiere: **8** snuffbox
tabby: cat, pad **4** gown, silk **5** dress **6** fabric, gossip, moreen **7** old maid, padding, taffeta **8** brindled, spinster

tabella: **6** tablet **7** lozenge
tabernacle: **4** tent **5** abode, dwell, hovel, niche **6** church, recess, reside, temple **7** deposit, shelter, support **8** enshrine **9** sanctuary, structure **10** habitation, house of God, receptacle **13** house of prayer
table: hem **4** fare, feed, food, slab, wash **5** bench, board, canon, index, panel, plate, treat **6** indius, lamina, record, repast, tablet **7** console, counter, plateau, surface **8** credence, feasting, postpone, schedule, synopsis, tabulate **9** sideboard **10** collection **11** concentrate **12** stringcourse
centerpiece: **7** epergne
communion: **5** altar **8** credence, credenza

cover: **5** baize, cloth, tapis
decorative cloth: **6** runner
d'hote: **6** dinner **12** complete meal
dish: **6** tureen
dressing: **6** toilet, vanity
game: **4** pool **8** Ping-Pong **9** billiards
linen: **6** napery **7** napkins **11** tablecloths
philosophers: **14** deipnosophists
small: **5** stand, wagon **6** teapoy **7** taboret, tendoor, tendour
working: **5** bench
writing: **4** desk **10** escritoire
tableau: **7** picture **8** register, schedule **14** representation
tableland: **4** mesa **5** karoo **6** karroo **7** plateau **8** balaghat, plateaus, plateaux **9** balaghaut **12** altiplanicie
tablet: pad **4** bred, pill, slab **5** facia, panel **6** troche **7** lozenge **10** receptacle
medicine: **4** disc **6** troche
sculptured: **5** stela, stele
stone: **4** slab **5** stele
three-leaved: **8** triptych
two-leaved: **7** diptych
writing: pad **5** slate
tableware: cup **4** bowl, dish, fork **5** china, glass, knife, plate, spoon **6** saucer **8** flatware
tabloid: **5** short **9** condensed **11** sensational **12** concentrated
taboo, tabu: ban **5** debar **6** forbid **8** prohibit **9** forbidden, ineffable **12** interdiction
opposed to: noa
tabor, tabour: **4** drum **6** atabal **7** attabal, eardrum, timbrel
taboret, tabouret: **4** drum, seat **5** stand, stool, tabor **6** tabour **7** cabinet
tabu: See **taboo**
tabulate: **4** list **7** arrange **8** schedule
tabulation: **5** table, tally
grammatical: **8** paradigm
of the year: **8** calendar
tache: tie **5** clasp **6** attach, buckle
tacit: **6** silent **7** implied **8** implicit, unspoken, wordless **9** noiseless **10** understood
taciturn: **6** silent **7** laconic **8** reserved, reticent **9** saturnine **15** uncommunicative
tack: **4** beat, busk, clap, gear, haul, join, link, nail, rope, slap, trim, turn **5** baste, catch, fetch, rider, shift, spell, strip, tying, unite **6** attach, course, fasten, handle, method, secure, tackle **7** clothes, connect, payment **8** contract, saddlery **9** agreement, endurance, fastening **10** deflection, digression, stickiness, supplement **12** adhesiveness
glazier: **4** brad
nautical: **5** board
to: **4** jibe

to windward: **4** trip
two pointed: **6** staple
tackle: rig **4** arms, food, gear, tack **5** angle, drink, seize, stuff **6** attack, collar, secure, take on **7** grapple, harness, rigging, weapons **8** mistress, windlass **9** apparatus, encounter, equipment, undertake **13** accoutrements, paraphernalia
football: **4** stop **5** throw
fishing: tew
single and double block: **6** burton
strong: cat
tacky: **5** crude, dowdy, seedy **6** frowsy, frumpy, shabby, sticky, untidy **8** adhesive, slovenly
tact: **5** poise, touch **6** stroke **7** address, feeling **8** delicacy, graceful **9** appendage, diplomacy **10** adroitness, cleverness, discretion, perception **11** discernment **14** discrimination
tactful: **8** discreet, graceful **10** diplomatic
tactical: **9** expedient
tactics: **6** method, system **9** procedure
tactless: **5** brash
tactlessness: **9** gaucherie
tad: bit, boy, lad, son **5** child **6** urchin
tadpole: **8** polliwog
taenia: **4** band **6** fillet **8** headband
taffy: **5** candy, gundy **7** glaggum **8** flattery
Taffy: **8** Welshman
tag: dog, end, tab **4** flap, game, join, lock **5** aglet, label, shred, strip, touch **6** aiglet, append, attach, eartab, fasten, follow, rabble, ticket **7** refrain, taglock **9** appendage, catchword, shibboleth **11** aiguillette, commonplace
metal: **5** aglet **6** aiglet
Tagalog (see also **Philippines**): **8** Filipino, Pilipino
taha: **4** baya, **10** weaverbird
Tahiti: *canoe:* **4** pahi
capital: **7** Papeete
centipede: **4** veri
coronation robe: **4** maro
food plant: **4** taro
god: Oro **6** Taaroa
loincloth: **4** malo, maro
mountain: **7** Orohena
mulberry: **4** aute
neighboring islands: **6** Moorea **7** Huahine, Maupiti, Raiatea **8** Bora Bora
old name: **8** Otaheite
people: **10** Polynesian
resident painter: **7** Gauguin
seaport: **7** Papeete
woman: **6** vahine, wahine
Tai, Thai: **7** Siamese
tail: bun, cue, end, eye **4** arse, back, bunt, last, rear **5** cauda **6** follow, pursue, shadow, switch **7** limited, pendant, reduced **8** abridged, buttocks, encumber,

entailed **9** appendage, curtailed, extremity, fundament
having a: **7** caudate
kinds of: bob, bun, fud **4** bunt, scut **5** cauda, plume, stern, twist **6** strunt, wreath **8** streamer **9** empennage
pert to: **6** caudal
plane: **10** stabilizer
short: bun **4** scut
tailed: 7 caudate
tailing: 5 chaff, waste **6** refuse
tailless: 7 acaudal, anurous **8** acaudate, ecaudate **9** excaudate
tailor: 4 snip **5** adapt, alter, style **6** darzee, draper, sartor **7** cabbage **9** bushelman **11** bushelwoman
goose: **8** flatiron
iron: **5** goose
lap board: **5** panel
pert to: **9** sartorial
tailspin: 7 flicker
taint: dip, dye, hit, hue **4** blow, blur, evil, hogo, hurt, spot, tint **5** cloud, color, imbue, prove, spoil, stain, sully, tinge, touch, trace, wound **6** accuse, damage, defile, infect, poison, stigma **7** attaint, blemish, convict, corrupt, debauch, deprave, pollute, vitiate **8** disgrace, empoison, hautgout, tincture **10** conviction, corruption, impregnate **11** contaminate
tainted: bad **5** blown
taipo: 5 demon, devil **10** theodolite
tait: 9 marsupial
Taiwan: *capital:* **6** Taipei
city: **7** Chilung **8** Taichung
island group: **5** Matsu **6** Penghu, Quemoy
mountain: **6** Tzukao, Yushan
other name: **7** Formosa
river: **5** Wuchi **6** Tachia **7** Choshui, Tanshui
seat of: **10** Kuomintang (Chinese Nationalists)
taj: cap **8** Taj Mahal
Taj Mahal site: 4 Agra
take: act, buy, eat, get, hit, win **4** bear, doff, fang, glom, grip, haul, lead, trap **5** adopt, atone, avail, carry, catch, charm, cheat, check, fetch, glaum, grasp, infer, seize, snare, spell, steal, swear, touch, treat, trick **6** absorb, accept, affirm, amount, arrest, assume, attach, attack, borrow, choose, convey, deduce, deduct, derive, employ, endure, engage, number, obtain, profit, remove, secure, select, strike, submit, tenure **7** attract, capture, conduct, detract, extract, promise, receive, swallow, undergo **8** abstract, contract, proceeds, quantity, receipts, subtract **9** apprehend, interrupt **11** appropriate

aback: **5** check **7** startle **8** astonish, confound, surprise
account of: **6** notice, regard
advantage of: **5** abuse **6** misuse **7** exploit
advice: **4** hear, heed, mind **6** listen
after: **6** follow **8** resemble
aim: **4** bead **5** level
another's place: sub **9** alternate **10** substitute
apart: **4** ruin **7** analyze, destroy, dissect **9** dismantle
as actual: **5** posit
as one's own: **5** adopt **6** borrow
away: **5** decry, reave **6** adempt, deduct, divest, recant, remove **7** deprive, detract, retract **8** derogate, diminish, subtract
back: **6** abjure, recall, recant **7** retract **8** withdraw **9** repossess
beforehand: **7** pre-empt
bold attitude: **5** brisk
by craft: **6** entoil
by force: **5** erept **8** ereption
by storm: **5** seize **6** attack
by stratagem: **4** trap
care: **4** mind, reck **5** nurse, watch **6** beware, cuiado
care of: fix **4** tend **5** nurse
chair: sit
cognizance of: **4** note **6** notice
comb from beehive: **4** geld
delight: **5** revel
direction: **5** steer
down: **5** abase, lower **6** escort, humble, record, reduce **7** swallow **8** dismount, emaciate, withdraw **10** distribute
evening meal: sup **4** dine
exception: **5** demur **6** object
fire: **5** spunk
first: **7** preempt
five: **4** rest
for granted: **6** assume **7** presume
forcibly: **5** seize
from: **5** wrest **6** deduct, divest **7** deprive, derived, detract **8** derogate, subtract
heed: **4** mind, reck, ware
hold: **5** grasp **6** obtain
in: **4** furl, open **5** admit, annex, brail, cheat, fence, trick, visit **6** absorb, attend, escort **7** deceive, embrace, enclose, explore, include, observe, receive **8** commence, comprise, contract **9** apprehend, encompass **10** comprehend, understand
in hand: **5** seize **7** attempt **9** undertake
in sail: **4** reef
into custody: **6** arrest **9** apprehend
it ill: **6** resent
it easy: **4** rest **5** relax
leave: **6** decamp, depart
legal possession of: **5** seise, seize
liberties: **7** presume

meals for pay: **5** board
no notice of: **9** disregard
notice: see **7** witness
off: **4** copy, doff, lift, soar **5** abate, begin, deter, mimic, start **6** deduct, depart, get out, lessen, remove **7** detract **8** discount, distract, subtract, withdraw **9** burlesque, calculate, determine, reproduce
off suspended list: **9** reinstate
offense of: **6** resent
on: add, don **4** hire **5** start **6** assume, employ, engage, oppose, tackle **7** consort, receive **8** arrogate **9** associate, undertake
on cargo: **4** lade
one's way: **4** wend
orders: **4** obey **5** yield
out: **4** copy, dele, kill, omit **5** elide **6** deduct, delete, efface, escort, except, remove **7** excerpt, extract, scratch, unhitch **8** airbrush, overall, separate **9** eliminate
out by roots: **9** extirpate
out curves and bends: **10** straighten
out of pawn: **6** redeem
over: **5** seize **6** assume, convey **7** relieve
part: **4** join **5** share **11** participate
part in contest: **7** compete
part of: **4** side **5** enact
place: **5** occur **6** happen
place again: **5** recur
place of: **4** else **8** supplant **9** supersede
pleasure in: **5** enjoy, fancy **6** admire
positive opinion: **4** side
possession of: **5** enter, seise, seize
root: **4** grow **6** settle
service as seaman: **4** ship
shape: **4** form, jell **11** cyrstallize
shelter: **6** nestle, shroud
some of: **7** partake
stock: **5** count **6** survey **8** appraise, estimate **9** inventory
the stick: **5** steer
to court: sue
turns: **9** alternate
umbrage at: **6** resent
unawares: **5** seize **7** astound, capture, startle **8** astonish, confound, overcome, surprise **9** overwhelm
unlawfully: rob **5** steal, usurp **6** pilfer
up: buy **4** fill, lift **5** adopt, allow, begin, check, enter, exact, mount, raise, seize, set to **6** absorb, accept, arrest, assume, borrow, employ, gather, occupy, remove, resume **7** collect, dissent, elevate, engross, receive **8** commence, initiate **9** extirpate, reprimand **10** comprehend, understand
up again: **5** renew **6** reopen, resume
up weapons: arm **4** rise

with: **4** like **5** brook **6** accept **7** confess **11** acknowledge
without authority: **5** usurp
taken: **8** occupied
in all: **7** overall **9** inclusive
taker: **5** thief **6** captor **7** catcher **8** pilferer, purveyor **10** plagiarist
of court action: **4** suer
of income or profits: **6** pernor
takin: **7** gazelle **8** antelope
relative of: **6** musk ox
taking: **4** take **5** catch, palsy **6** arrest, attack, blight, plight **7** capture, malefic, seizing, seizure **8** alluring, captious, catching, engaging, grasping, receipts **9** accepting, rapacious, receiving, reception **10** attachment, attractive, contagious, infectious **11** captivating **12** apprehension
different form: **7** protean **11** metamorphic
precedence: **7** ranking
unauthorized leave: **4** A.W.O.L.
takt: **4** beat **5** beats, pulse, tempo **7** measure
talapoin: **6** monkey
talc: **4** mica **6** powder, talcum **7** agalite **8** steatite **9** soapstone
tale: lie **4** gest, myth, saga, talk, tell, yarn **5** count, fable, geste, speak, story, tally, total, whole **6** esteem, gossip, legend, reckon, report, speech **7** account, fiction, history, parable, recital **8** anecdote, category, consider, counting, relation **9** discourse, falsehood, narration, narrative, numbering, reckoning **10** detraction **11** declaration, enumeration, information **12** conversation
adventure: **4** gest **5** geste
kind of: lai **4** epic, gest, saga, yarn **5** bourd, geste, roman **6** legend **7** romance **8** allegory, jeremiad **9** storiette
medieval: lai, lay
Tale of Two Cities: *author:* **7** Dickens
characters: **5** Lucie (Manette) **6** Carton (Sidney), Darnay (Charles)
talebearer: **6** buzzer, gossip **7** tattler **8** informer, talepyet, telltale **10** newsmonger **13** scandalmonger
talent: **4** gift **5** anger, dowry, flair, gifts, knack, money, skill, talon **6** custom, desire, flavor, genius, powers, riches, wealth **7** ability, betters, faculty, feature, longing, passion **8** appetite, aptitude, capacity, charisma, gamblers, property **9** abilities, abundance, attribute, expertise **10** endowments **11** disposition, inclination **14** accomplishment
special: **5** forte
talented: **4** able **5** smart **6** clever, gifted **8**

addicted, disposed, inclined
talesman: 5 juror 8 narrator
taletelling: 4 blab
taliation: 5 tally 10 adjustment
taliera: 4 tara
talion: 11 retaliation
talipot: 4 palm
talisman: 4 tara 5 charm, saffi, safie 6 amulet, fetich, fetish, grigri, saphie, scarab, telesm 8 greegree 10 lucky piece
talk: yap 4 buck, bukh, carp, chat, gaff, knap, talk, word 5 bazoo, lingo, parle, prate, rumor, speak, theme, utter 6 confer, debate, gabble, gossip, reason, report, speech, steven, tongue 7 address, chatter, consult, council, dialect, express, meeting, mention, palabra 8 causerie, chitchat, collogue, colloquy, converse, parlance, verbiage 9 dalliance, discourse 10 conference, discussion 11 communicate 12 conversation
about: 6 gossip 7 discuss
abusive: 5 hoker
back: 4 sass 6 retort, ripost 7 riposte 8 repartee
big: 4 brag 5 boast
boastful: 4 gaff, rant
ceremonious: 8 chin-chin
chatty: gab 6 gossip
common: 7 hearsay
complaining: 4 carp
confused: 10 galimatias
desultorily: 6 ramble
deliriously: 4 rave
down: 7 outtalk, silence
down to: 9 patronize 10 condescend
effusively: 4 gush, rave
familiar: 6 confab
fast and idly: 7 gnatter
flattering: 7 palaver
flippant: 10 persiflage
fluent: 7 verbose, voluble
foolish: gab, gas 4 bosh, buff, bunk, gash 5 spiel 6 babble, bunkum, claver, fraise, patter 7 blabber, palaver, twaddle 8 buncombe, wishwash 9 poppycock, rigmarole 11 goosecackle, stultiloquy
formal: 7 address, lecture
from pulpit: 6 homily, sermon
glib: 6 patter 7 palaver
idly: gab, gas 5 prate 6 tattle 7 chatter, twaddle
imperfectly: 4 lisp 7 stutter
in sleep: 15 somniloquacious
indiscreetly: 4 blab
indistinctly: 6 mumble, mutter 7 sputter
into: 6 induce
irrationally: 4 rant, rave
light: 5 chaff 6 banter 8 raillery
over: 7 discuss
persuasively: 6 reason

pert: lip 4 sass
profuse: 4 chat 6 patter 7 palaver 10 persiflage
slowly: 5 drawl
small: gab 4 chat, chin 7 prattle 8 chitchat
table: ana 9 symposiac
tediously: 5 prose
to no purpose: 4 blat
together: 4 chat 8 converse
turgid; 4 cant, rant
unintelligible: 6 drivel, jargon, patter 9 gibberish
wildly: 4 rant, rave
talkative: 4 cozy, gash, glib 5 gabby 6 chatty, clashy, fluent 7 verbose, voluble 8 flippant 9 garrulous 10 babblative, loquacious
talker: 6 proser, ranter, rhetor 7 babbler, spieler 17 conversationalist
incessant: 6 gasbag, magpie 10 chatterbox 12 blabbermouth
talkfest: 6 confab 9 gathering 10 discussion, bull session
talking iron: gun 5 rifle
tall: 4 bold, deft, fine, high, lank, long 5 brave, grand, great, lanky, large, lofty, quick, rangy, ready, steep, tally 6 comely, docile, seemly 7 doughty, skyhigh, unusual 8 obedient, towering, yielding 9 excellent 10 courageous, incredible 11 exaggerated 13 grandiloquent
tallow: fat 4 suet 5 sevum, smear 6 fatten, grease
pert to: 7 stearic
pot: 7 fireman
refuse: 9 crackling
sediment: 7 greaves
tally: run, tab, tag 4 deal, goal, jibe, mark, mate, suit 5 agree, check, count, grade, label, match, notch, score 6 accord, reckon, record 7 account, compare, loftily 8 estimate, numerate 9 agreement, reckoning 10 correspond 11 counterpart
tallyho: cry 5 coach
crier of: 6 hunter
talma: 4 cape, coat 6 cloak
Talmud: 9 Jewish law
commentary: 6 Gemara
text: 6 Mishna
Talmudic academy: 7 Yeshiva 8 Yeshibah, Yeshivah 9 Yeshiboth
student: 5 bahur
talon: 4 claw, fang, heel, sere 6 clutch, hallux 7 molding 11 certificate
Talos' slayer: 8 Daedalus
talus: 5 ankle, scree, slope 6 debris 8 clubfoot 9 anklebone 11 knucklebone
tam: cap, hat 5 beret 8 headgear
tamarack: 5 larch
tamarind: 8 sampaloc

tamarisk: sal 4 atle, jhow 5 atlee
tambo: inn 6 corral, stable, tavern 7 station
tambour: cup 4 desk, drum 5 frame 7 drummer 8 buttress, ornament 9 embroider 10 embroidery, projection
tambourin: 4 drum 5 dance, tabor
tambourine: 4 dove, drum, taar 5 daira 7 timbrel, travale
tame: cut 4 bust, dead, dull, meek, mild 5 accoy, begin, break, daunt, prune 6 broach, docile, gentle, humble, soften, subdue 7 affaite, crushed, insipid, servile 8 amenable, cicurate, civilize, familiar, harmless 9 deficient, tractable 10 accustomed, cultivated, submissive 11 domesticate, housebroken, ineffectual 12 domesticated 13 pusillanimous
animal: pet 4 cade 6 cosset
tamed: 6 broken, gentle
tameness: 10 mansuetude
Tamil: 8 language
caste member: 7 Vellala
race: 9 Dravidian
Taming of the Shrew character: Sly 4 Kate 6 Bianca, Tranio 8 Baptista
tamis: 5 sieve, tammy 8 strainer
Tammany Society: *boss:* 5 Tweed
leader: 6 sachem
officer: 8 Wiskinky 9 Wiskinkie
Tammuz: *love:* 6 Ishtar
sister: 6 Belili
tamp: ram 4 cram 5 drive 6 plug up 11 concentrate
tamper: fix 4 fool, plot, tool 5 bribe 6 dabble, meddle, potter, scheme 7 machine 9 influence, interfere
Tampico fiber: 5 istle
tampon: 4 plug 6 tympan 9 drumstick
nasal: 9 rhinobyon
tan: dun, sun, taw 4 beat, camp, ecru, flog, tent, whip 5 brown, color, toast 6 almond, bronze, switch, tannin, thrash 7 embrown, imbrown, sunburn, tanbark
derived from: 6 tannic
tanager: 4 bird, yeni 8 cardinal
genus of: 7 piranga
tang: nip 4 bite, butt, capt, fang, foil, odor, pang, pike, ring, root, spur, tine, zest 5 aroma, knife, prick, prong, shank, smack, sting, taste, tinge, trace, twang 6 branch, flavor, pierce, tangle, tongue 7 flavour, seatang, seaweed 8 rockweed 10 suggestion 11 surgeonfish
Tanganyika: See **Tanzania**
tangelo: 4 ugli
tangent: 5 slope 8 adjacent, touching
tangible: 4 real 6 actual 7 tactile 8 definite, material, palpable 9 objective, touchable 11 perceptible, substantial
Tangiers: *feature:* 6 casbah

measure: 4 kula, mudd
tangle: bar, cot, mat 4 fank, harl, kink, knot, mesh, trap 5 catch, frame, gnarl, ravel, snare, snarl 6 balter, entrap, icicle, medley, muddle, sleave 7 ensnare, involve 8 obstruct, quandary, scrobble 9 embarrass 10 complicate, intertwine, perplexity
of thread: 5 snarl
tangle-foot: 5 drink 6 liquor, whisky
tangled: 11 complicated
tango: 5 bingo, dance
tania: 4 taro 6 yautia
Tanis: 4 Zoan
tank: hit, vat 4 bang, lake, pond, pool 5 basin, knock, trunk 7 cistern, cuvette, drinker, pachuca, piscina, stomach 9 container, reservoir
part: 5 tread 6 turret
tankard: mug 5 facer, hanap, stoup 6 flagon, pottle 7 goddard
tanked: 11 intoxicated
tanker: 4 ship 5 oiler
tanned: 5 brown, tawny 8 sixpence, sunburnt
tanner: 6 barker 8 sixpence
Tannhauser composer: 6 Wagner
tannic acid salt: 7 tannate
tannin: 10 astringent
tanning: 7 pasting 8 browning, flogging, whipping
extract: 5 cutch 7 amaltas, catechu
material: 5 sumac 6 sumach
method: 4 napa
pert to: 11 scytodepsic
plant: 5 alder, sumac 6 sumach
tansy: 4 weed 9 tanacetum
tantalize: 4 grig 5 taunt, tease 6 harass 7 torment
Tantalus: *children:* 5 Niobe 6 Pelops
father: 4 Zeus
tantamount: 4 same 5 equal 9 identical 10 equivalent
tantara, tantarara: 5 blare 7 fanfare
tantieme: 5 bonus, share 10 percentage
tantrum: fit, pet 4 rage
tantum: 5 stint 9 allowance
Tanzania: *capital:* 11 Dar es Salaam
island: 5 Pemba
lake: 5 Nyasa, Rukwa 8 Victoria 10 Tanganyika
language: 7 Swahili
monetary unit: 8 shilling
mountain: 4 Meru 11 Kilimanjaro
part: 8 Zanzibar 10 Tanganyika
people: 4 Goma 5 Bantu 6 Sukuma, Wagogo, Wagoma 7 Swahili, Wabinga
river: 6 Kagera, Rufija 7 Pangane
title: 5 sahid
town: 5 Moshi, Tanga 6 Arusha, Mwanza
weight: 8 farsalah
Taoism: 8 religion 12 cosmic reason

founder: **6** Lao Tzu

tap: bar, bob, cut, hit, hob, pat, rap, tit, vat **4** beat, blow, cock, flip, heat, hole, open, pipe, plug **5** break, fever, flirt, knock, leach, spile, touch, valve **6** broach, faucet, repair, signal, spigot, strike, tapnet **7** censure, connect, penance, reprove **8** nominate **9** designate

down: **4** tamp

tape: gin, tie **4** band, bind, mole **5** scale, strip **6** fillet, liquor, ribbon, secure **7** bandage, binding

kind of: **4** lear, wick **5** inkle **6** ferret

machine: **8** recorder

needle: **6** bodkin

taper: **4** ream, wick **5** light, point, snape **6** candle, cierge, lessen, narrow, trowel **7** conical, dwindle, trindle **8** decrease, diminish **9** acuminate **11** pyramidical

tapering: **5** conic **6** terete **7** conical **9** acuminate

blades: **6** spires

four-sided pillar: **7** obelisk

piece: **4** gore, shim **5** miter **6** gusset

tapestry: **5** arras **6** bayeux, dorser, dosser **7** dossier, gobelin **8** dossiere

hanging: **5** tapis

kind: **5** Arras **7** Gobelin **8** Aubusson

warp thread: **5** lisse

tapeworm: **6** taenia **8** parasite

embryonic form: **10** oncosphere

segments: **8** strobila

head: **6** scolex

taphouse: bar, inn **6** saloon, tavern **7** taproom

tapioca-like food: **5** salep

source: **7** cassava

tapir: **4** anta **5** danta **8** anteater, ungulate

taproom: bar, pub **6** saloon, tavern

tapster: **7** barmaid, skinker **9** barkeeper, bartender

Tapuyan: **8** S.A. Indian

tribe: Ges **5** Gesan **6** Cayapo, Goyana, Timbra **7** Camacan, Coroado **8** Botocudo, Caingang, Chavante

tar: gob **4** brea, salt **5** black, pitch, taint, tease **6** cresol, incite, sailor, seaman **7** blacken, mariner, provoke **8** alkitran, irritate, seafarer, telegram **9** alchitran **10** bluejacket

tar and feathers: **12** plumeopicean

taradiddle: fib, lie **8** nonsense

Taranaki volcano: **6** Egmont

tarantula: **6** spider

tarboosh: cap, fez

tardigrade: **8** sluggish **9** slow-paced

tardy: lag, lax **4** late, slow **5** delay, slack **6** remiss, retard **7** belated, lagging, overdue **8** dilatory **10** behindhand, unprepared **11** cunctatious

tare: **4** weed **5** vetch, weigh **6** darnel **7**

leakage **9** allowance **13** counterweight

target: cut, tee, use **4** butt, coin, mark, vane **5** shred, sight, slice **6** cymbal, object, shield, tassel, tatter **7** buckler, pendant **8** ambition, bullseye, ornament, ridicule **9** indicator, objective, criticism

center: eye **5** clout **8** bull's-eye

shotting gallery: **4** duck

target finder: **5** radar, sonar

Tarheel State: **13** North Carolina

tariff: tax **4** duty, list, rate **5** price, scale **6** charge, scheme, system **7** average, tribute **8** schedule

favorer: **13** protectionist

Tarkington title: **6** Penrod **9** Seventeen

tarn: **4** lake, pool

tarnish: dim **4** blot, dull, soil, spot **5** cloud, dirty, spoil, stain, sully, taint **6** canker, darken, defile, injure, smirch **7** asperse, blemish, destroy, distain, obscure **8** besmirch, diminish, discolor

taro: **4** coco, eddo, gabi **5** aroid, cocgo, eddoe, tania **7** dasheen **8** caladium

paste: poi

tarpaulin: hat, tar **4** coat **5** cover **6** sailor **7** sea-bred **10** sailorlike

tarpon: **6** sabalo **9** savanilla **10** silverfish

relative of: **5** chiro

tarriance: **5** delay **7** sojourn **8** awaiting, tarrying **9** hindrance, lingering

tarrock: **4** gull, tern

tarry: lag, vex **4** bide, loll, rest, stay, stop, wait **5** abide, await, black, dally, defer, delay, demur, dwell, lodge, pause, visit, weary **6** arrest, bundle, hinder, linger, loiter, remain, retard, soiled, tarred, tarrow **7** fatigue, outstay, sojourn, unclean **8** irritate

tarrying: **6** arrest

tarsus: **5** ankle

fore: **4** pala

tart: pie **4** acid, doxy, flan, girl, keen, sour **5** acerb, acrid, acute, bowla, sharp **6** pastry, pielet, severe, tender, tourte **7** caustic, cutting, painful, piquant, pungent **8** piercing, poignant, turnover **9** acidulous, endearing, sensitive **10** astringent, prostitute

tartan: **4** sett, ship **5** plaid

tartar: **5** argol **12** incrustation

Tartar: See **Tatar**

tartarean: **8** infernal

Tartarus: **4** hell **5** Hades

Tartary prince: **4** Agib

Tartuffe: **9** hypocrite, pretender

author: **7** Moliere

tarweed: **5** Madia

Tarzan's mate: **4** Jane

task: job, tax **4** busk, char, darg, duty, lade, load, test, toil, work **5** chare, chore, labor, stent, stint, study **6**

amount, burden, dargue, devoir, effort, impost, lesson, strain **7** aufgabe, censure, oppress, overtax **8** quantity **10** accounting, assignment, employment **11** undertaking

easy: **4** pipe, snap **5** cinch **8** sinecure

taskmaster: 6 driver **8** overseer **11** slave driver

Tasmania: 6 island

animal: **6** wombat

cape: **4** Grim

capital: **6** Hobart

devil: **7** dasyure

discoverer: **6** Tasman

lake: **4** Echo **6** Sorell **12** Westmoreland

location: **12** South Pacific

mountain: **4** Grey **5** Brown, Drome, Nevis **6** Barrow **8** Humboldt **9** Ben Lomond **10** Wellington

original name: **14** Van Dieman's Land

phalanger: **5** tapoa

river: **4** Huon **5** Tamar **6** Arthur, Jordan **7** Derwent

thylacine: **5** tiger

town: **6** Hobart **9** Devontown **10** Launceston

wolf: **9** thylacine

tass: cup, mow **4** bowl, heap **5** draft **6** goblet **10** small draft

tassel: 4 tuft **5** adorn, label **6** fringe, toorie, zizith **7** pendant **8** ornament

taste: bit, eat, gab, goo, sip, try **4** bent, dash, feel, gout, gust, heed, hint, rasa, tang, test **5** drink, flair, gusto, prove, sapor, savor, scent, shade, smack, smell, spice, touch, trace **6** degust, flavor, liking, little, palate, relish, relush, ribbon, sample, savour **7** flavour, soupcon, thought **8** appetite, delicacy, elegance, fondness **9** attention, degustate, judgement **10** experience, suggestion **11** discernment, inclination **14** discrimination

absence of: **7** ageusia

fundamental: **4** acid, salt, sour **5** sweet **6** bitter

kind of: nip, sip **4** tang **5** prose, sapor, savor, smack **8** penchant

lacking in: **4** rude **8** ungentle **9** inelegant **10** unpolished **11** inaesthetic

pert. to: **7** palatal **9** gustative, gustatory

perversion: **7** malacia

refined: **7** elegant

strong: **4** tang

tasteful: 4 neat **5** tasty **6** savory **7** elegant

tasteless: 4 dull, flat **5** vapid **7** insipid **8** barbaric, lifeless **9** savorless **10** inartistic **11** unpalatable

tasty: 5 quiet, sapid **6** savory **7** palatal **9** flavorful, palatable, toothsome **10** delectable

tat: rag, tap **4** pony **5** touch **6** tangle **7** crochet **8** absolute

Tatar, Tartar: Hun **6** ataman, hetman **7** Cossack

dynasty: Kin, Wei

horseman: **7** Cossack

king: **4** khan

militiaman: **4** Ulan **5** Uhlan

mounted band: **4** ulan **5** horde, uhlan **7** chambul

nobleman: **5** murza

principality: **7** Khanate

republic capital: **5** Kazan

tribe: Hun **5** Alani, Alans **7** Shortzy

tatou, tatu: 9 armadillo

tatter: jag, rag, rip **4** jagg, stir, tear **5** hurry, scold, scrap, shred, testy **6** bustle, gabble, ribbon, tattle **7** chatter, flitter, peevish **8** guenille **14** tatterdemalion

tatterdemalion: 8 vagabond **10** ragamuffin

tattered: 4 torn **6** broken, jagged, ragged, shabby, shaggy **7** slashed **9** disrupted **10** disheveled **11** dilapidated

tattle: 4 blab, chat, gash, talk, tell **5** cheep, clash, clype, prate **6** gossip, report **7** chatter, clatter, prattle, stammer

tattler: 6 gossip **8** informer, telltale **9** sandpiper **10** talebearer

Taube: 9 monoplane

taught: See **teach**

taunt: bob **4** dare, gibe, jeer, jibe, mock, quip, tall, twit **5** check, fleer, glaik, reply, slare, slart, sneer, tease, tempt **6** banter, deride, flaunt, insult, offend, rejoin **7** provoke, upbraid **8** reproach, ridicule **9** aggravate

taurine: 4 bull **6** bovine

Taurus: 4 bull

tant: 4 firm, neat, snug, tidy, trim **5** rigid, stiff, tense, tight, tough **6** severe, strict **9** distended, shipshape

tauten: 5 tense **7** tighten

tautog: 9 blackfish **10** oysterfish

tautology: 8 pleonasm, verbiage **10** redundancy

tavern: bar, hut, inn, pub **4** bush, howf **5** booth, hotel, house, howff **6** saloon **7** cabaret, gasthof **8** alehouse, gasthaus, hostelry

tavert: (Sc.) **5** tired **6** stupid **8** confused

taw: tan, tew **4** beat, whip **5** agate, stake **6** harass, marble **7** scourge, shooter, torment, toughen

tawdry: 5 cheap, gaudy, showy **6** sleazy, tinsel

tawny, tawney: tan **5** brown, dusky, olive, swart, tenne **6** Indian, tanned **7** fulvous, tigrine **8** brindled **9** bullfinch

tawse, taws: 4 whip **5** strap

tax: 4 cess, duty, feel, fine, levy, load, rate,

scat, scot, task, toll **5** abuse, agist, exact, order, scatt, stent, stint, tithe, touch, value **6** accuse, assess, avania, burden, charge, demand, excise, extent, handle, hidage, impose, impost, settle, strain **7** censure, dispute, finance, gabelle, license, tailage, tallage, tollage, tribute **8** estimate, exaction, overtire, reproach **9** prescribe **10** assessment, imposition **12** contribution

agency: IRS
assessment: **7** doomage
church: **5** tithe
feudal: **7** scutage, tailage, tallage
gatherer: **9** catchpole, catchpoll
hide: **6** hidage
kind of: cro, soc **4** cess, geld, scat **5** finta, tithe **6** abkari, excise, pavage, surtax, taille, vinage **7** boscage, chevage, patente, prisage, scewing, tailage **8** auxilium, carucage **9** surcharge **10** chaukidari
rate: **10** assessment
salt: **7** gabelle
taxable: 10 assessable, censurable
taxation: tax **6** charge **7** finance, reproof, revenue **9** valuation **10** accusation, assessment
degree of: **5** ratal
taxi: cab **4** hack **5** jixie **6** litter **7** vehicle
parking place: **5** stand
taximeter: 5 clock
taxing: 5 tough **6** trying **7** onerous **9** demanding **10** accusation
taxman: 8 publican
taxpayer: 9 ratepayer
tazza: cup **4** bowl, vase
tea: 5 party **6** repast, supper **8** beverage, function **9** collation, decoction, marijuana, reception
black: **5** bohea, oopak, pekoe **8** souchong
cake: **5** scone **6** cookie
constituent: **8** caffeine
container: **8** canister
drug: see *stimulant* below
expert: **6** taster
family: **8** Theaceae
genus: **4** thea
Indian: **10** Darjeeling
kind of: cha **4** chaa, chia, tsia **5** assam, black, bohea, congo, chias, Emesa, green, hyson, Ledum, oopak, pekoe, salop **6** congue, oolong, saloop **7** cambric **8** bouillon, go-widdie **9** gunpowder
plant: **4** thea
receptacle: **8** canister
room: **5** kiosk
serve: **4** pour
stimulant: **5** thein **6** theine
table: **5** tepoy **6** teapoy
urn: **7** samovar
weak: **5** blash

Tea House location: 4 Naha **7** Okinawa
teach: 4 show **5** coach, edify, endue, guide, point, train, tutor **6** commit, direct, lesson, preach, school **7** apprise, apprize, beteach, conduct, educate **8** accustom, amaister, document, instruct **9** enlighten **10** discipline **11** demonstrate **12** indoctrinate
teachable: apt **6** docile, pliant **7** fitting **8** amenable
teacher: 4 guru, prof **5** coach, guide, Plato, tutor **6** docent, doctor, mentor, pedant, pundit, reader, regent **7** adjunct, edifier, maestro, sophist, trainer **8** civilian, director, educator, gamaliel, moralist, preacher **9** pedagogue, preceptor **10** instructor **12** schoolmaster
Alexandria: **6** Origen
association: NEA
fee: **8** minerval
Hindu: **5** swami
Indian religion: **4** guru
Jewish: **5** rabbi
Mohammedan: pir **5** molla, mulla **6** mollah, mullah
of eloquence: **6** rhetor **7** sophist
of the deaf: **7** oralist
Russia: **7** starets
teaching: 5 moral **6** docent **7** precept **9** education **10** discipline **11** instruction
of a fable: **5** moral
of the Twelve: **7** Didache
pert. to: **9** pedagogic
teak: 4 wood **5** djati
teakettle: 4 suke, suky **5** sukey, sukie
teal: 4 duck **8** garganey
team: 4 crew, gang, join, pair, race, span, yoke **5** brood, chain, flock, group, wagon **6** convey, couple, number **7** lineage, progeny, vehicle **8** carriage **9** associate
baseball: **4** nine
basketball: **4** five
football: **6** eleven
kinds of: duo **4** crew **6** jayvee, scrubs **7** varsity
supporter: fan **6** rooter
two animals: **4** pair, yoke
teamster: 6 carter, driver **7** carrier
tear: ram, rip, rit, run **4** claw, drag, fine, pull, rage, rend, rent, rive, rush, skag, snag, weep **5** binge, break, claut, larme, reave, split, spree, touse, unrip, waste **6** cleave, course, dainty, damage, divide, flurry, lament, pierce, remove, screed, tatter, wrench **7** agitate, chatter, consume, destroy, disrupt, extract, fritter, passion, shatter, torment **8** carousal, delicate, lacerate, lachryma, separate
apart: **4** rend **9** dismember
down: **4** rase, raze **6** malign **7** destroy **8** demolish **10** scandalize **11** disassemble
into: rip **6** attack

limb from limb: 9 dismember
off: rip, run 4 rush 5 start
to pieces: 6 tatter 10 dilacerate
up by the roots: 6 arache 9 eradicate, extirpate
teadrop design: 5 larme
tearful: sad 6 watery 7 flebile, snively, weeping 8 lacrimal 10 lachrymose
mother: 5 Niobe
tearing: 4 rage 5 hasty, hurry 7 furious, violent 8 splendid 9 furiously, harrowing, impetuous 10 impressive 12 excruciating
tear-jerking: 5 mushy 6 sticky 7 maudlin 8 bathetic
tearpit: 7 larmier
tears: 5 grief
inducing: 9 rheumatic
pert. to: 8 lacrimal
poetic: 5 rheum
tease: beg, guy, irk, nag, rag, tew, vex 4 card, coax, comb, drag, fret, hare, razz, stir, tear, twit 5 annoy, chevy, chivy, devil, taunt, worry, wrack 6 badger, bother, caddle, chivvy, harass, heckle, molest, pester, plague, teasel 7 disturb, hatchel, provoke, scratch, torment 8 irritate, separate 9 aggravate, importune, tantalize 11 disentangle
wool: tum 4 comb, toom
teasel: 4 comb 5 plant
teaser: 4 gull 6 carder, curler, sniper, stoker, willow 7 curtain, fireman, problem 8 operator, pesterer, willower
teasing: 5 chaff 6 banter 11 importunate
teaty: 5 cross 7 fretful, peevish
tebbad: 6 simoom 9 sandstorm
tebeldi: 6 baobab
teched: 4 daft 5 batty 6 insane 7 cracked 8 demented
technology of agriculture: 10 agrotechny
techy: 4 spot 5 habit 6 touchy, vexing 7 blemish, fretful, peevish, quality 9 irascible, irritable
teck: 6 cravat 10 four-in-hand
tectonic: 7 builder, plastic 9 carpenter 10 structural 13 architectural
ted: 4 toad, turn 5 waste 6 spread 7 scatter
tedge: 6 ingate, runner
tedious: dry 4 arid, dead, dree, dull, long, slow 5 bored, prosy 6 boring, borish, elenge, prolix 7 irksome, noxious, peevish, prosaic 8 dilatory, slowness, tiresome 9 exhausted, irritable, laborious, prolixity, wearisome 10 monotonous 11 displeasing, everlasting 13 uninteresting
tedium: 5 ennui 7 boredom, doldrum 8 monotony 11 irksomeness, tediousness 13 wearisomeness

tee: 5 mound
off: 5 drive, scold 9 reprimand
teem: 4 bear, fill, gush, lead, pour, rain, swim 5 bring, drain, empty, fetch, swarm 6 abound, resort, seethe, summon 7 produce 8 abundant, conceive, generate, prolific
teeming: 4 full 5 agush, alive 7 pouring, replete 8 crowding, prolific 9 abounding, bristling 11 overflowing 13 overabounding
teeny: wee 4 tiny 5 small 7 fretful, peevish 9 malicious
teeny-weeny: 4 tiny 5 small 6 minute
teeter: 4 rock, sway 5 lurch, waver 6 jiggle, quiver, seesaw 7 rocking, rolling, tremble 9 sandpiper, vacillate
teeter board: 6 seesaw
teeth: 5 tines 7 canines 8 choppers, crackers, grinders
decay of: 6 caries
false: 5 plate 8 dentures
grinding of: 7 bruxism
hard tissue: 7 dentine
having all alike: 7 isodont
incrustation on: 6 tartar
large: 4 buck 5 snags
long: 5 fangs 6 tushes
outer covering of: 6 enamel
pert. to: 5 molar 6 dental
serpent: 5 fangs
socket: 7 alveoli (pl.) 8 alveolus
sower of dragon's: 6 Cadmus
without: 10 edentulate, edentulous
teethy (Sc.): 5 cross 6 biting 7 crabbed 9 irritable
teeting: 7 titlark
teetotal: dry 6 entire 7 abstain 8 complete
teetotaller: dry 7 nonuser 9 abstainer, rechabite, refrainer
teetotum: top, toy
teg: doe 4 deer 5 sheep, woman 6 fleece
tegmen: 5 cover, plate 6 elytra 7 tympani 8 covering, fore-wing
tegua: 6 sandal
tegula: 4 tile
tegument: 4 coat 5 cover, testa 6 thatch
tegurium: hut 5 cabin 6 shrine
tehee: 5 laugh 6 giggle, titter 7 snicker
Tehuantepec Gulf Indian: 5 Huave
teiidae: 4 teju 7 lizards
teju: 6 lizard 8 teguexin
tekke: rug 6 carpet 7 convent 9 monastery
tela: web 6 tissue 7 bristle 8 membrane
telamon: 8 atlantes, caryatid
Telamon: 5 Atlas
brother: 6 Peleus
father: 6 Aeacus
friend: 8 Heracles, Hercules
son: 4 Ajax 6 Teucer

teledu: 6 badger
telega: 4 cart 5 wagon
telegraph: 4 wire 5 cable
  code: 5 Morse
  inventor: 5 Morse
  key: 6 tapper
  signal: dot 4 dash 9 semaphore
telegraphic communication: 10 letter-
  gram
Telemachus: *father:* 7 Ulysses 8 Odysseus
  mother: 8 Penelope
teleost fish: eel 5 apoda
telephone: 4 buzz, call, dial, ring 6 ring
  up
  book: 9 directory
  inventor: 4 Bell
  receiver: 8 cymaphen
Telephus: *father:* 8 Hercules
  mother: 4 Auge
telescope: jam 5 glass 7 shorten 8 collapse, condense, simplify
  object seen with: 11 debilissima
  site: 7 Palomar
telescopic: 9 farseeing
television: TV 4 tube 5 telly, video 8
  boob tube, idiot box
  award: 4 Emmy
  broadcast: 8 telecast
  cable: 7 coaxial
  camera platform: 5 dolly
  commercial: 4 spot 7 message
  commercial cat: 6 Morris
  dragon: 5 Ollie
  frequency: UHF, VHF
  interference: 4 snow 5 ghost
  lens: 4 zoom
  network: ABC, CBS, NBC, NET, PBS
  picture tube: 9 kinescope
  type of show: 4 live, news, quiz, talk 5
    movie, panel, rerun 6 serial, sitcom,
    sudser 9 soap opera
telic: 9 purposive 10 purposeful 12 teleological
tell: bid, say 4 chat, deem, hill, know, tale,
  talk, tole, toll 5 aread, areed, breve,
  count, mound, order, speak, state, utter,
  value, weigh 6 decide, direct, impart,
  inform, number, recite, reckon, regard,
  relate, repeat, report, reveal, tattle 7 account, command, dictate, discern, divulge, express, mention, narrate, publish, recount, request 8 acquaint,
  announce, disclose, rehearse 9 calculate,
  discourse, enumerate, recognize 11
  communicate 12 discriminate
  confidentially: 7 confide
  in advance: 4 warn
  on: 4 sing 5 peach 6 snitch, squeal
  revelatory facts: 6 debunk
  romances: 4 gest 5 geste
  secrets: 5 clype

stories: 4 yarn 6 tattle
thoughtlessly: 4 blab, blat
without authority: 5 rumor
Tell's home: Uri
teller: 4 blow 5 shoot 6 remark, sprout 7
  cashier 8 informer, narrator 9 bank
  clerk, describer 11 annunciator
telling: 5 valid 6 cogent 8 forceful, relation, striking 9 effective, pertinent 10
  convincing, satisfying
telltale: 4 blab, hint 6 gossip 7 tattler 8
  betrayer, informer 9 betraying, indicator 10 indication, talebearer
telltruth: 7 honesty 9 frankness
telluride: 7 altaite
telson: 6 somite 7 segment
  of king crab: 5 pleon
temblor: 5 shake, shock 6 tremor 10
  earthquake
temerarious: 4 rash 6 chance 8 heedless,
  reckless 9 venturous 10 fortuitous,
  headstrong 11 adventurous, venturesome
temerity: 4 gall 5 cheek, nerve 8 audacity, boldness, rashness 9 assurance, hardihood 10 effrontery 12 recklessness
  13 foolhardiness 15 venturesomeness
temper: fit, ire, mix 4 bait, bate, coll,
  curb, cure, ease, heal, mean, mood, neal,
  rage, tone 5 adapt, anger, birse, blend,
  delay, humor 6 adjust, animus, anneal,
  attune, church, dander, dilute, direct,
  govern, harden, manage, medium, mingle, modify, puddle, reduce, season, soft-
  en, soothe, steady 7 assuage, chasten,
  control, moisten, mollify, passion, qualify, restore, toughen 8 chastise, compound, mitigate, moderate, modulate,
  regulate, restrain 9 composure 10 equanimity, irritation 11 accommodate, disposition, state of mind
  display: 5 scene 7 tantrum
  even: 4 calm 5 staid 6 sedate
  kind of: ire 4 huff, mood 6 choler, spleen
temperament: 4 mood 5 gemut, humor 6
  crasis, nature 7 caprice, climate, emotion 10 adjustment 11 disposition,
  temperature 12 constitution
temperance: 7 measure 8 sobriety 10 abstinence, continence, moderation
temperate: 4 calm, cool, mild 5 sober 6
  soften 8 moderate 9 continent 10 abstemious, restrained 12 conservative
  13 dispassionate
temperature: 4 heat 5 fever, state 6 temper, warmth 7 mixture 8 compound,
  mildness 9 intensity 10 moderation,
  proportion 11 disposition, temperament 12 constitution
tempest: 4 gale, rage, wind 5 orage, storm
  6 tumult 7 agitate, borasca, borasco,
  turmoil 9 agitation, bourasque, commo-

tion, hurricane **12** thunderstorm

Tempest characters: 5 Ariel **7** Caliban, Miranda **8** Prospero

tempestuous: 4 wild **5** galey, gusty **6** stormy **7** violent **9** turbulent

template, templet: 4 beam, lute, mold **5** bezel, bezil, gauge **7** pattern

temple: 4 fane, naos, rath **5** candi, cella, edile, huaca, kovil, ratha, speos **6** aedile, chandi, church, haffet, haffit, hieron **10** house of God, tabernacle
basin: **5** laver
for all gods: **8** pantheon
kind of: sha, taj, wat **4** deul, Rath **5** jinjua, Ratha **6** church, jinsha, pagoda **7** capitol **8** pantheon **9** Parthenon
part: **5** cella
sanctuary: **10** penetralia

tempo: 4 pace, rate, time **5** speed **6** rhythm, timing
pert. to: **6** agogic
rapid: **6** presto **7** allegro
slow: **5** lento **6** adagio
very slow: **5** grave

temporal: 4 laic **5** civil, scale **6** carnal, muscle **7** earthly, profane, secular, worldly **9** ephemeral, political, temporary **10** transitory **11** impermanent **13** chronological, materialistic

temporary: 6 acting, pro tem, timely **7** interim, secular, topical **8** temporal **9** ad interim, ephemeral, transient **10** transitory **11** provisional
contrivance: **9** makeshift

temporize: 5 delay, humor, yield **6** demand, parley, soothe **9** negotiate **13** procrastinate

tempt: try **4** defy, fand, lead, lure, test **5** decoy, probe, prove, taunt **6** allure, assail, entice, incite, induce, seduce **7** assault, attempt, attract, provoke **8** endeavor, persuade **9** endeavour, seduction **10** inducement

temptation: 4 bait **5** trial **7** testing **9** seduction **10** allurement, enticement, inducement

tempter: 5 devil, Satan **6** baiter

tempting: 8 alluring, enticing, inviting **9** seductive **10** attractive

temptress: 4 vamp **5** Circe, siren **7** Delilah, Lorelei, mermaid **10** Parthenope **11** enchantress

tempus fugit: 9 time flies

ten: 4 iota (Gk.) **5** decad **6** decade, denary
ares: **6** decare
decibels: bel
dollars: **7** sawbuck
group of: **6** decade
prefix: dec **4** deca

Ten Commandments: 9 Decalogue

ten-footed: 7 decapod

ten-gallon hat: 8 sombrero

ten-sided figure: 7 decagon

ten-stringed: 9 decachord

ten-year periods: 7 decades **9** decenniad, decennium

tenable: 8 credible **9** plausible **10** defensible **11** justifiable **12** maintainable

tenacious: 4 fast, firm **5** tough **6** cledgy, dogged, grippy, sticky, strong **7** gripple, miserly, viscous **8** adhesive, cohesive, holdfast, sticking, stubborn **9** glutinous, niggardly, retentive **10** persistent **11** closefisted **12** pertinacious

tenacity: 7 courage **8** firmness **9** toughness **11** miserliness, persistence **12** adhesiveness, cohesiveness, perseverance

tenancy: 6 estate, tenure **7** holding **9** occupancy **10** possession

tenant: 4 leud **5** ceile, dreng **6** border, drengh, geneat, holder, leaser, lessee, occupy, renter, vassal **7** chakdar, cottier, dweller, inhabit **8** occupant **9** bordarius, collibert **10** inhabitant
feudal: **4** leud **6** vassal **7** socager

tend: 4 burn, care, lead, mind, move, till, wait, work **5** apply, await, guard, nurse, offer, reach, see to, serve, swing, treat, watch **6** attend, direct, expect, extend, foster, intend, kindle, listen, manage, supply **7** care for, conduce, hearken, incline, oversee, provide, purpose, stretch, tending **8** minister, tendency **9** accompany, attentive, co-operate, cultivate, gravitate, look after **10** contribute
a fire: **5** stoke
to rise: **8** levitate
toward one point: **8** converge

tendency: run, set **4** bent, bias, tide **5** drift, drive, tenor, trend **6** course, effect, object, result **7** aptness, bearing, leaning **8** appetite, movement, relation **9** affection, direction, proneness, readiness **10** proclivity, propension, propensity **11** disposition, inclination
structural: **7** peloria

tender: bid, tid **4** boat, dear, fond, gift, keen, kind, mild, nice, soft, sore, thin, warm, weak **5** chary, frail, light, offer, young **6** delate, feeble, gentle, humane, loving, submit, touchy, vessel, waiter **7** amabile, amatory, amorous, careful, fragile, pitiful, present, proffer, slender, sparing, steamer, subdued, suggest, tenuous, vehicle **8** delicate, feminine, immature, merciful, precious, proposal, ticklish, tolerant **9** brotherly, sensitive, succulent **10** charitable, effeminate, scrupulous **11** considerate, kindhearted, softhearted, susceptible, sympathetic, warmhearted **12** affectionate **13** compassionate **14** impressionable
animals: **6** herder **10** husbandman
cattle: **6** cowboy, herder **7** byreman **8**

neatherd **9** byrewoman
for cloth: **9** stenterer
horse: **5** groom **6** ostler **7** hostler, stabler
music: **7** amoroso
ship: gig **5** barge **6** dingey, dinghy **7** collier, pinnace
tenderfoot: 6 novice **7** greenie **8** beginner, neophyte, newcomer **9** cheechaco, cheechako, greenhorn
tenderhearted: 6 humane **11** sympathetic
tenderloin: 5 steak **11** filet mignon
tenderness: 4 love, pity **6** cherte **8** kindness, softness, sympathy, weakness **9** affection **10** compassion, gentleness **13** sensitiveness
tendon: 4 band, cord **5** chord, nerve, sinew **11** aponeurosis
Achilles: **9** hamstring
tendril: 4 curl **5** clasp, sprig **6** branch, cirrus **7** ringlet, stipule
tenebrous: 4 dark **5** dusky **6** gloomy **7** obscure **8** darkness
tenement: 5 abode **8** building, dwelling **9** apartment **10** habitation
tenet: ism **4** view **5** adoxy, canon, creed, dogma, maxim **6** belief, decree **7** opinion, paradox **8** doctrine **9** principle
tenfold: 6 denary **7** decuple
tengere: sky **7** heavens
teniente: 6 deputy **7** headman **10** lieutenant
tenne: 5 brown, color, tawny
Tennessee: *capital:* **9** Nashville
city: **7** Jackson, Memphis **9** Knoxville **11** Chattanooga
county: **4** Clay, Dyer, Knox, Lake, Polk, Rhea **6** Blount, Greene, Shelby **8** Davidson, Hamilton, Sullivan
dam: **6** Norris
explorer: **6** de Soto, Joliet **7** Jolliet, LaSalle **9** Marquette
federal agency: TVA
lake: **8** Reelfoot
mountain **5** Unaka **7** Lookout **12** Great Smokies
national park: **6** Shiloh
nickname: **9** Volunteer
pioneer: **12** Davy Crockett
plateau: **10** Cumberland
state bird: **11** mockingbird
state flower: **4** iris
state tree: **11** tulip poplar
tennis: *between four persons:* **7** doubles
between two persons: **7** singles
champion: **4** Ashe (Arthur), Betz (Pauline), Borg (Bjorn), Hard (Darlene), Hart (Doris), King (Billie Jean), Wade (Virginia) **5** Budge (Don), Bueno (Maria), Court (Margaret Smith), Evert (Chris), Laver (Rod), Lloyd (Chris Evert), Perry (Fred), Riggs (Bobbie),

Vilas (Guillermo), Wills (Helen) **6** Austin (Tracy), Fraser (Neale), Gibson (Althea), Kramer (Jack), Marble (Alice), Parker (Frank), Tilden (Bill) **7** Connors (Jimmy), Emerson (Roy), Lacoste (Rene), McEnroe (John), Nastase (Ilie), Sedgman (Frank) **8** Connolly (Maureen), Gonzalez (Pancho), Newcombe (John), Rosewall (Ken)
game series: set
no score: **4** love
old form: **5** bandy
points: **4** aces
prize cup: **5** Davis
racket: bat
related game: **6** squash **8** handball **9** badminton
score: ace **4** love **5** deuce
shoe: **7** sneaker
shot: cut, lob **4** chop, dink **8** backhand, forehand
term: ace, cut, let, lob, set **4** love **5** deuce, fault, serve **6** volley **7** receive, service **9** advantage
Tennyson: 11 English poet
character: **4** Enid **5** Arden **6** Hallam
poem: **4** Maud **10** In Memoriam **11** The Princess **12** Locksley Hall
tenon: cog **4** coak **8** dovetail
tenor: 4 body, copy, feck, gist **5** drift, stamp, trend **6** course, intent, nature, singer **7** holding, meaning, purport, writing **8** tendency **9** character, condition, direction, discourse, procedure, substance **10** transcript
falsetto: **8** tenorino
tens of thousands: 7 myriads
tense: 4 edgy, rapt, taut, time **5** rigid, stiff, tight **6** intent, queasy, tauten **7** intense, uptight **8** strained **9** stretched **10** breathless
past: **9** preterite
verb: **4** past **6** aorist, future **7** perfect, present **9** preterite **10** pluperfect **11** conditional
tensile: 6 pliant **7** ductile, elastic
tension: 4 bent **6** strain, stress **7** closure **8** pressure
releasing of: **7** detente
tent: hut **4** camp, care, heed, show, stop, tend, test, wine **5** cover, crame, frame, lodge, probe, teach, tempt **6** attend, beware, encamp, hinder, intent, pulpit, tender **7** observe, prevent, proffer, shelter **9** attention, attentive **10** habitation
dweller: **4** Arab **5** nomad **6** camper, Indian **7** scenite, tourist
flap: fly
kind: pup **4** pawl, yurt **5** darry, shool, tepee, toldo, yurta **6** abbacy, teepee, tienda, wigwam **7** balagan, kibitka, marquee, sparver **8** pavilion **9** pretor-

ium **10** praetorium
large: **8** pavilion
maker: **4** Omar
tentacle: **6** feeler **7** tendril
animal with: **5** squid **7** octopus **10** cuttle-fish
without: **7** acerous
tentage: **5** camps
tentamen: **5** trial **7** attempt
tentative: **9** temporary **11** conditional, impermanent, provisional, vacillating **12** experimental
tenter: **5** frame
tenterhooks: **4** nail **6** strain **8** suspense
tenth: **5** tithe **6** decima **7** decimae **8** decimate
part: **5** tithe
tenuity: **6** rarity **7** exility, poverty **8** delicacy, fineness, rareness, thinness **9** faintness, indigence **10** meagerness, slightness **11** slenderness
tenuous: **4** fine, rare, slim, thin, weak **6** flimsy, slight, subtle **7** gaseous, slender, subtile **8** delicate, ethereal **11** implausible **13** insignificant, unsubstantial
tenure: **4** hold, term **5** lease **6** manner **8** courtesy **9** condition
tepee, teepee: **6** wigwam
tepid: **4** mild, warm **8** lukewarm **11** halfhearted
tequila: **5** drink **6** liquor, mescal
tera: **6** church **9** monastery
Terah: *father:* **5** Nahor
son: **5** Haran **7** Abraham
teraph: **4** idol **5** image **8** talisman
teras: **7** monster
tercet: **5** rhyme **7** triplet
terebene: **9** deodorant **10** antiseptic **12** disinfectant
terebra: **5** auger, drill
terebrate: **4** bore **9** perforate
teredo: **7** mollusk **8** shipworm
terete: **7** centric, tapered **8** columnar **11** cylindrical
Tereus: *sister-in-law:* **9** Philomela
son: **4** Itys **6** Itylus
wife: **6** Procne
tergal: **4** back **6** dorsal
tergiversate: lie **5** shift **6** defect, weasel **7** shuffle **10** apostatize, equivocate
tergiversation: **6** deceit **7** evasion **8** apostasy **10** subterfuge
tergum: **4** back
term: end **4** call, date, half, name, span, time, word **5** bound, limit, state **6** period, tenure **7** article, entitle, epithet, session **8** boundary, duration, semester **9** condition, extremity **10** definition, expression **11** appellation, termination
cricket: off, ons **6** yorker
fencing: hai, hay **4** bind **5** coupe **6** touche **8** tacautac

golf: lie, par, tee **4** baff, fore, hook **5** bogey, bogie, divot, eagle, green, slice **6** birdie, stroke, stymie **7** gallery
grammar: **6** phase, simile, syntax
heraldry: **4** ente, urde
Hindu, of respect: sri
jail: lag **4** jolt **7** stretch
Jewish, of reproach: **4** raca
mathematics: **4** nome, root, sine **6** cosine
of address: sir **4** sire **6** milady, milord, sirrah
of endearment: **5** astor **8** ashtore
of life: age **5** sands
of office: **6** regime, tenure
printer: **4** dele, stet
rugby: try **5** scrum
school: **7** quarter **8** semester **9** trimester
science: ame, azo **4** beta **5** stoss
sea: **4** ahoy **5** avast, belay
termagant: **5** shrew **6** Amazon, tartar, virago **7** furious **8** scolding **9** turbulent **10** boisterous, tumultuous **11** quarrelsome
termed: **5** named **6** called, styled, yclept
terminable: **6** finish, finite **9** limitable **12** determinable **13** discontinuing
terminal: end **4** last **5** anode, depot, final, limit **6** finish **7** cathode, closing, limital, station **8** desinent, ultimate **9** electrode, extremity **10** concluding
negative: **7** cathode, kathode
positive: **5** anode
terminate: end **4** call, halt, quit, stop **5** bound, cease, close, limit **6** define, direct, expire, finish, result **7** achieve, adjourn, confine, destine, dismiss, perfect **8** complete, conclude, restrict
terminating: **5** final **6** ending
distinct point: **9** apiculate
trefoil: **6** botone
termination: end **4** amen **5** bound, close, event, limit **6** ending, expiry, finale, finish, period, result, upshot **7** outcome, purpose **8** boundary, decision, finality, terminus **9** extremity **10** completion, concluding, conclusion, expiration **13** determination
malady: **5** lysis
terminative: **8** absolute, bounding, definite **10** concluding **11** determining
termite: ant **4** anai, anay
termless: **8** infinite, nameless, unending **9** boundless, limitless **13** indescribable, inexpressible, unconditional
terms: **9** agreement **10** conditions, provisions **11** limitations **12** propositions **13** circumstances
come to: **5** agree
make: **5** treat **9** negotiate
tern: **4** darr, gull **10** sea swallow
genus: **5** anous **6** sterna
ternary: **6** treble, triple **7** ternion, trinity **9** threefold

ternate: 12 trifoliolate

terra: 5 earth

terra alba: 4 clay **6** gypsum, kaolin **8** magnesium

terra cotta: 4 clay **6** statue **7** pottery **11** earthenware

terra firma: 5 earth **6** estate **8** mainland **11** solid ground

terrace: 4 bank, dais, mesa, step **5** bench **7** balcony, gallery, portico **8** chabutra, platform **9** colonnade

in series: **8** parterre

wall: **6** podium

terrain: 4 form, turf **5** tract **6** milieu, region **7** contour, demesne **11** environment

terrapin: 4 emyd, emys **6** coodle, heifer, potter, slider, turtle

terrestrial: 6 earthy, layman, mortal **7** earthly, mundane, terrene, worldly **9** planetary

terret: 4 ring **7** cringle

terrible: 4 dire, gast, hard **5** awful, lurid **6** severe, tragic **7** direful, extreme, fearful, ghastly, hideous, intense, painful, very bad **8** almighty, dreadful, horrible, terrific **9** appalling, atrocious, excessive, frightful **10** formidable, terrifying, tremendous, unpleasant **12** disagreeable

Terrible one: 4 Ivan

terrier: dog, fox **4** Bull, Skye **5** cairn, Irish, Welsh **6** Boston **8** Airedale, Scottish, Sealyham **9** Yorkshire **10** Bedlington, Clydesdale

terrific: 7 extreme, fearful **8** dreadful, exciting, terrible **9** appalling, excessive, frightful, marvelous **10** terrifying, tremendous

terrified: 4 awed **6** afraid, aghast, frozen **7** ghastly

terrify: awe, cow, hag **4** bree, fray, stun **5** alarm, annoy, appal, daunt, deter, drive, haunt, impel, scare, shock, tease **6** affirm, afread, agrise, appall, bother, dismay, injure **7** stupefy, torment **8** affright, frighten **9** importune

terrifying: 6 horrid **7** ghastly, hideous **8** terrible

terrigenous: 9 earthborn **13** autochthonous

terrine: jar **4** dish, stew **6** ragout

territorial division: amt **6** canton **7** commune **10** department **14** arrondissement

territory: 4 area, land **5** field, scope, state, tract **6** extent, ground, region, sphere **7** country, portion, terrain **8** district, environs, province **9** bailiwick **12** neighborhood

kind of: **5** banat **6** canton **7** banlieu, enclave **8** banlieue, Pashalic **10** palatinate

shut in: **7** enclave

terror: awe **4** fear, fray, pest **5** alarm, dread, panic **6** affray, dismal, fright, horror **8** dreddour **11** trepidation **12** terribleness **13** consternation

terrorism: 11 subjugation **12** intimidation

terrorist: 5 rebel **6** bomber **8** alarmist **11** scaremonger

terrorize: awe **5** abash, appal, scare **6** appall, coerce **8** frighten **9** embarrass **10** intimidate

terry: 4 loop **5** cloth

terse: 4 curt, neat **5** brief, pithy **6** abrupt, claret, rubbed, smooth **7** compact, concise, laconic, pointed, refined **8** clearcut, incisive, polished, succinct, unprolix **11** sententious, tightlipped **12** accomplished

tertiary period: 5 third **7** neocene

tertulia: 4 club **5** party **7** meeting

terzina: 6 tercet **7** triplet

tessellated: 5 tiled **6** mosaic **9** checkered

tessera: 4 cube, tile **5** glass, label, token **6** billet, marble, pledge, tablet, ticket **7** voucher **8** password **9** rectangle **11** certificate

test: pot, try **4** exam, fand, feel, will **5** assay, check, cupel, grope, proof, prove, shell, taste, testa, trial, weave **6** ordeal, refine, sample **7** approof, approve, examine, witness **8** cupeling, evidence, potsherd, standard **9** construct, criterion, determine, testament, testimony **10** experience, experiment, touchstone **11** examination, performance **12** authenticate

in fineness and weight: pyx

kind: **4** acid

operation: **9** shakedown

ore: **5** assay

series: **7** gantlet

testa: 7 coating **8** covering, episperm, tegument **10** integument

testament: Job **4** will **8** covenant, landbook **9** testimony **12** confirmation

testator: 7 legator, witness **9** testatrix

beneficiary of: **4** heir **7** heiress, heritor **9** inheritor

tester: 5 crown, frame **6** canopy, conner, helmet, prover, teston **7** assayer, candler, sparver **8** denierer **9** chauffeur, headpiece

testicle: cob **6** testis, testes(pl.) **7** genitor

deer: **6** doucet, dowcet, dowset

testified under oath: 7 deponed

testifier: 7 witness **8** deponent

testify: 5 swear **6** affirm, attest, depone, depose **7** declare, express, profess, protest **8** indicate, manifest, proclaim

testimonial: 4 sign **5** salvo, token **7** tribute, warrant, writing **8** evidence **9** testimony **10** credential **11** certificate

testimony: say **6** attest, avowal **7** witness

8 evidence 10 deposition, profession 11 affirmation, attestation, certificate, declaration 14 recommendation

testudo: 4 lyre, shed 5 cover, talpa, tumor, vault 6 screen 7 ceiling

testy: 6 touchy 7 crabbed, fretful, grouchy, peevish, waspish 8 petulant, snappish 9 impatient, irascible, irritable, obstinate 10 headstrong

tetanus: 7 lockjaw 9 holotonia

tetchy: 6 touchy 7 peevish 9 irascible, irritable, sensitive

tête-a-tête: 4 chat, seat, sofa 7 vis-a-vis 8 causeuse 12 conversation

tetel: 5 torah

tether: tie 4 band, rope 5 cable, chain, leash, limit, noose 6 fasten, picket 7 confine 8 restrain

Tethys: 5 Titan 8 Titaness
  brother: 6 Cronus
  father: 6 Uranus
  husband: 7 Oceanus

tetrad: 4 four 7 quartet 8 fourfold

tetragon: 6 square 7 rhombus 10 quadrangle

tetric: 5 harsh 6 gloomy, sullen 7 austere

tetter: 4 fret 6 eczema, herpes, lichen

Teutonic: 5 Dutch 6 German, Gothic 7 English 12 Scandinavian
  alphabet character: 4 rune
  barbarian: 4 Goth
  deity: Eir, Hel, Tiu, Tyr, Ull 4 Erda, Frea, Frig, Norn, Odin, Thor 5 Aesir, Baldr, Brage, Bragl, Donar, Othin, Tiwaz, Wodin, Wotan 6 Balder, Frigga, Saeter 7 Forseti 8 Heimdall
  homicide: 5 morth
  land: 4 odal
  law: 5 Salic
  legendary hero: 4 Offa
  race: 4 Ubii 5 Danes, Goths, Jutes 6 Angles, Franks, Saxons 7 Germans, Vandals 8 Lombards 10 Norwegians 11 Burgundians 13 Scandinavians
  water nymph: nis

tew: taw, tow, vex 4 beat, fuss, pull, work 5 knead, tease, tools 6 incite, strive, tackle, tuyere 7 fatigue 8 struggle

tewit: 7 lapwing

Texas: *battle:* 5 Alamo 10 San Jacinto
  bronco, broncho: 7 mustang
  capital: 6 Austin
  city: 4 Waco 6 Dallas, El Paso, Laredo, Odessa 7 Abilene, Denison, Houston, Lubbock 8 Amarillo 9 Fort Worth 10 San Antonio
  cottonwood: 5 alamo
  county: Bee 4 Leon, Polk, Rusk 5 Nolan, Starr, Tyler 6 Harris, Sutton, Walker 7 Houston, Madison, Navarro, Trinity 8 Anderson, Angelina, Cherokee 9 Freestone, Limestone

cowboy jacket: 8 chaqueta
fever carrier: 4 tick
fortress: 5 Alamo
founder: 6 Austin
island: 5 Padre 9 Galveston, Matagorda
massacre site: 5 Alamo
motto: 10 Friendship
national park: 7 Big Bend
nickname: 8 Lone Star
river: Red 5 Pecos 6 Brazos, Neches, Nueces 9 Rio Grande
shrine: 5 Alamo
shrub: 6 anagua, anaqua
state bird: 11 mockingbird
state flower: 10 bluebonnet
state police: 6 ranger
state tree: 5 pecan
U.S. president: LBJ 10 Eisenhower 14 Lyndon B. Johnson

text: 4 copy 5 theme, topic 7 passage, subject 11 handwriting 13 subject matter
  operatic: 8 libretto
  pen: 5 ronde
  pert. to: 7 textual
  revision: 9 recension
  set to music: 8 oratorio
  variation: 7 lection

textbook: 6 manual, primer

textile: 6 fabric
  dealer: 6 mercer
  goods: 7 mercery
  ornament: 8 fagoting
  plant refuse: 5 hurds
  ring device: 6 poteye
  worker: 4 dyer 6 reeder

texture: web 4 wale 5 fiber, grain 6 cobweb, fabric, tissue 7 essence, textile 9 structure 11 composition, fabrication
  cloth: 4 wale, warp, woof

tez: 7 pungent, violent

tezkirah: 7 license 8 passport 11 certificate

Thackeray: 8 novelist
  novels: 9 Pendennis 10 Vanity Fair 11 Henry Esmond

Thailand: 4 Siam
  cab: 5 samlo 6 samlaw, samlor
  canal: 5 klong
  capital: 7 Bangkok
  city: 7 Ayuthia, Ayuthya, Bangkok 9 Sukhothai
  coin: att 4 baht 5 fuang, tical 6 pynung, salung, satang
  demon: nag
  dialect: Lao
  dress: 6 panung
  fabric: 8 siamoise
  island: 6 Phuket
  isthmus: Kra
  king: 4 Rama
  measure: ken, niu, nmu, rai, sat, sen, sok,

wah, yot **4** keup, ngan, tang, yote **5** kwien, laang, sesti, tanan **6** kabiet, kam meu **6** kanahn **7** chai meu, roeneng **8** chang awn **9** anukabiet

monetary unit: **4** baht

mountain: **5** Khies **8** Maelamun

native: Lao

people: Tai **4** Thai **7** Siamese

provincial capital: **5** Muang

river: **6** Mekong, Meping **7** Meklong **10** Chaophraya

spirit: nat

state: **6** Patani

temple: wat

town: **5** Puket **7** Ayuthia, Bangkok, Lopburi, Singora, Songkla **8** Kiangmai **9** Chiengmai

weight: hap, pai, sen, sok **4** baht, haph, klam, klom **5** catty, chang, coyan, picul, tical **6** fluang, salung, sompay **7** tamlung

Thais composer: 8 Massenet

thalassic: 6 marine **7** oceanic, pelagic **8** maritime

Thalia: See **Grace, Muse**

thalidomide: 8 sedative **12** hypnotic drug

Thames: 4 Isis **5** river

city and town: **4** Eton **6** Henley, London, Oxford

tributary: **6** Tyburn

Thanatopsis author: 6 Bryant

Thanatos: 5 death

brother: **6** Hypnos

mother: Nyx

thane: 5 churl **7** servant, warrior **8** follower **9** attendant

estate: **5** manor

thank: 5 blame **11** acknowledge

thankful: 8 grateful **11** meritorious **12** appreciative

thankless: 10 ungrateful **13** unappreciated

person: **7** ingrate

thanks: 7 cumshaw **8** gramercy **9** because of, gratitude **11** gratulation **12** appreciation **15** acknowledgement

that: yon **4** such **6** yonder **7** because

that is: 5 id est, to wit **6** namely

that not: 4 lest

thatch: 4 nipa, roof **5** cover

peg: **4** scob

support: **6** wattle

thatcher: 6 reeder **7** crowder, hellier

thaumaturgists: 6 Goetae **7** wizards **9** magicians, sorcerers

thaumaturgy: 5 magic **11** legerdemain

thaw: 4 melt **6** unbend **7** liquefy **8** dissolve

the: 7 article

French: les

German: der, die, das

Italian: **4** egli, ella

Spanish: las, los

the same: 4 idem **5** ditto **8** likewise **9** identical

theater, theatre: 5 arena, drama, house, odeon, odeum, stage **8** coliseum **9** playhouse

audience: **5** house

award: **4** Tony

box-office sign: SRO

curtain: **4** drop **6** teaser

district: **6** Rialto

Elizabethan: **5** Globe

entrance hall: **5** foyer, lobby

full: SRO

Greek: **5** odeon, odeum

group: **4** ANTA

low-class: **4** gaff

motion-picture: **5** movie **6** cinema **8** bioscope **13** cinematograph, kinematograph

outdoor: **5** arena **7** drive-in, open-air

part: box, pit **4** loge **5** foyer, stage **7** balcony, gallery, parquet **8** parterre **9** orchestra **10** proscenium

pit: **6** circle **7** parquet **8** parterre

sports: **5** arena

theater-in-the-round: 5 arena

theatrical: 5 showy, stagy **6** scenic **7** pompous **8** affected, dramatic **10** artificial, histrionic **11** declamation **12** melodramatic

company: **6** troupe

extra: **4** supe **5** super

profession: **5** stage

sign: SRO

spectacle: **7** pageant

star: **4** hero, lead **7** heroine

valet: **7** dresser

Thebes: *acropolis:* **6** Cadmea

blind soothsayer: **8** Tiresias

deity: **4** Amon **5** Ament

district: **7** Thebiad

founder: **6** Cadmus

king: **5** Laius **7** Amphion, Oedipus **8** Eteocles, Pentheus

poet: **6** Pindar

prince: **7** Oedipus

queen: **5** Aedon, Niobe **7** Jocasta

statue: **6** Memnon

wicked queen: **5** Dirce

theca: sac, sad **4** case **7** capsule

theft: 5 pinch, steal **6** furtum, piracy **7** bribery, larceny, robbery **8** burglary **9** pilferage **10** conveyance, plagiarism **12** embezzlement

theft-like: 7 piratic

thelium: 6 nipple **7** papilla

them: 5 hemen

thema: 5 topic **6** thesis **7** subject **12** dissertation

theme: 4 base, text **5** ditty, essay, motif, topic **6** matter, theses, thesis **7** subject

9 discourse 11 composition, proposition 12 dissertation 13 subject matter
hackneyed: 6 cliche
literary: 5 motif
musical: 4 tema
title: 5 lemma
Themis: *concern of:* law 7 harmony
father: 6 Uranus
mother: 4 Gaea
then: 4 next 5 again, alors(F.) 6 before 7 besides 8 formerly, moreover 9 therefore 11 accordingly
music: poi
then too: 5 again
thence: 4 away 9 elsewhere, therefore, therefrom 10 henceforth 11 thenceforth
theodolite: 7 alidade
theologian: 6 cleric, divine 9 churchman
authority: 4 imam 5 ulema
famous: 5 Arius 6 Calvin, Luther 7 Erasmus 13 Thomas Aquinas
study of unity: 7 irenics
theorbo: 4 lute
theorem: 4 rule 5 axiom 9 principle
theoretical: 5 ideal 8 abstract, platonic 11 speculation, speculative, unpractical 12 hypothetical
theorist: 10 ideologist
theorize: 7 suggest 9 postulate, speculate
theory: ism 4 plan 5 guess 6 scheme 7 formula 8 analysis, doctrine 9 principle 10 assumption, conjecture, hypothesis 11 explanation, speculation 13 contemplation
kind of: 7 plenism 9 Platonism 13 phenomenalism
therapy: 9 treatment 10 psychiatry
there: ibi(L.), yon 4 able 5 ready, voila 6 yonder 7 thither 8 equipped, reliable 10 dependable
thereafter: 9 afterward 11 accordingly 12 subsequently
therefore: 4 ergo, then, thus 5 hence, since 6 frothy, thence 9 wherefore 11 accordingly 12 consequently
therewith: mit 6 withal 7 besides, thereat 8 moreover 9 forthwith, thereupon
therm, therme: 4 bath, pool 7 calorie
thermal: hot 4 warm
thermal unit: btu 6 degree 7 calorie
thermometer: 7 Celsius, Reaumur 8 pyrostat 9 pyrometer 10 Centigrade, Fahrenheit
thesaurus: 5 Roget 7 lexicon 8 treasury 10 dictionary, repository, storehouse 12 encyclopedia
Thesaurus compiler: 5 Roget
Theseus: 12 King of Athens
father: 6 Aegeus
lover: 7 Ariadne
mother: 6 Aethra

slayer of: 8 Minotaur
wife: 7 Antiope, Phaedra 9 Hippolyte
thesis: 5 essay, point, theme 7 premise 9 discourse, postulate, statement 10 assumption, conception 11 affirmation, proposition 12 dissertation
opposed to: 5 arsis
thespian: 5 actor 6 player 7 actress 8 dramatic 9 tragedian
Thessaly: *king:* 7 Admetus
mountain: Ida, Osa 4 Ossa 6 Othrys, Pelion, Pindus 7 Olympus 9 Psiloriti
valley: 5 Tempe
witch: 7 Aganice
thetic: 8 positive 9 arbitrary 10 prescribed
Thetis: 6 Nereid
husband: 6 Peleus
son: 8 Achilles
theurgy: 5 magic 7 miracle, sorcery 9 occultism
thew: 4 form, mode 5 habit, power, press, sinew, stool, trait 6 custom, manner, muscle, virtue 7 oppress, pillory, quality 8 strength 10 discipline, resolution
thewless: 4 lazy 6 feeble 10 spiritless
thick: fat 4 dull, hazy 5 broad, brosy, burly, close, crass, dense, gross, heavy, husky, plump, solid 6 coarse, filled, greasy, hoarse, obtuse, shaggy, stodgy, stupid 7 blubber, compact, crowded, grumous, muffled, thicket, viscous 8 abundant, familiar, friendly, guttural, intimate, profound, thickset 9 excessive, luxuriant 10 indistinct 11 inspissated, marticulate, thickheaded 12 impenetrable
and short: 5 squat 6 chunky
soup: 5 puree 7 pottage
thick-skinned: 4 cold 7 callous 9 pachyderm 11 pachydermic
thicken: gel 4 clot, crud, curd 5 cloud, crowd, flock 6 curdle, deepen, harden 7 confirm, congeal, stiffen 8 condense 9 intensify 10 incrassate, inspissate, strengthen
thicket: 4 bosk, bush, rone, shaw 5 brake, clump, copse, grove, hedge, shola 6 bosket, covert, greave 7 boscage, boskage, bosquet, coppice, spinney 9 brushwood 10 underbrush
kind: 5 brake, hedge, shola 7 chamise, chamiso, coppice, spinney 8 chamisal 9 chaparral
thickheaded: 4 dull 5 dense 6 stupid 7 doltish 11 blockheaded
thickness: ply 5 layer, sheet 8 diameter 9 curdiness, denseness, dimension, heaviness 10 corpulence 11 consistency
thickset: 4 stub 5 squat, stout 6 chumpy, chunky, fleshy, portly, stocky, stodgy, stubby

thickskulled: 4 dull, slow **5** heavy **6** obtuse, stupid **11** thickheaded

thief (see also **stealer**): **4** chor, gilt, prig **5** budge, scamp **6** ackman, arrant, bandit, cannon, cloyer, hooker, looter, nimmer, rascal, robber, sucker, waster **7** bramble, brigand, burglar, filcher, grifter, sneaker, stealer **8** cutpurse, gangster, larcener **9** larcenist, scoundrel **10** cat burglar, depredator, freebooter, highwayman, plagiarist

crucified beside Christ: **6** Desmas, Dismas, Dysmas

kind of: gun **5** ganef, ganof, gonof, snoop **6** ackman, angler, gonoph, pirate, swiper **7** gorilla, mercury, rustler **9** drawlatch **10** pickpocket

thieveless(Sc.): **4** cold **5** bleak **6** frigid **7** aimless **8** bootless, listless **10** forbidding

thieves' Latin: 5 slang

thievish: sly **7** furtive, kleptic **8** stealthy **9** larcenous

thigh: ham **4** hock **5** carve, femur, flank, meros, merus **6** femora(pl.), gammon

armor: **5** cuish

bone: **5** femur, ilium

muscle: **9** sartorius

pains: **8** sciatica

pert. to: **6** crural

thill: 4 sill **5** plank, shaft **6** thwart **8** planking, wainscot

thimble: cup **5** cover

conjurer: **6** goblet

machine: **6** sleeve

thimblerigger: 5 cheat **8** imposter, swindler

thin: dim **4** bony, flue, lank, lean, pale, poor, rare, slim, weak **5** acute, exile, faint, gaunt, lanky, lathy, scant, sheer, spare, washy, wizen **6** dilute, flimsy, hollow, meager, meagre, papery, rarefy, reduce, scanty, scarce, skinny, slight, slinky, sparse, watery, weaken, weazen **7** gracile, haggard, scrawny, slender, tenuous **8** araneous, gossamer, rarefied, scantily **9** attenuate, emaciated, extenuate, infertile, subtilize **10** inadequate **11** high-pitched, transparent, watered down **12** unbelievable, unconvincing **13** unsubstantial

and delicate: **8** araneous

and haggard: **5** gaunt

and slender: **4** lean **5** lanky

and vibrant: **5** reedy

and weak: **6** watery

and withered: **5** wizen **6** weezen

coating or layer: **4** film **6** veneer

disk: **5** wafer

out: **5** peter

plate: **4** leaf, shim **5** wedge **6** lamina, tegmen

scale: **5** flake **6** lamina **7** lamella

Thin Man: *dog* **4** Asta

wife: **4** Nora

thin-skinned: 6 tender, touchy **9** sensitive

thine: 4 tuum

thing: act **4** deed, idea, item **5** cause, chose, court, event, point, stuff **6** action, affair, detail, entity, matter, notion, object, reason, wealth **7** article, council **8** assembly, incident, property **9** happening **10** occurrence **11** transaction **12** circumstance

accomplished: **4** acta, deed **5** actum, actus

added: ell **6** insert **7** addenda(pl.) **8** addendum, addition, appendix **9** insertion **10** additament, complement, supplement

admitted: **4** fact **5** datum **7** element **9** principle

aforesaid: **5** ditto

assumed: **7** premise, premiss **9** postulate **11** implication, stipulation **14** presupposition

brought into existence: **8** creation

capable of spontaneous motion: **8** automata **9** automaton

complete in itself: **5** unity

consecrated to a deity: **6** hieron, sacrum **8** anathema

cursed: **8** anathema

extra: **5** bonus **6** bounty, lanyap **7** premium **8** lagnappe **9** lagniappe

following: **6** sequel

forfeited to crown: **7** deodand

found: **5** trove

given as security: **4** gage **6** pledge

indefinite, unnamed: **7** so and so **11** nondescript

invariable: **8** constant

known by reasoning: **7** noumena **8** noumenon

known by senses: **9** phenomena **10** phenomenon

of no value: **4** bean, junk **5** nihil, waste **6** fillip, nought, stiver, trifle **7** bauchle, nothing, pinhead, trinket **8** picayune **9** nonentity, resnihili **10** resnullius

of remembrance: **5** token

personal property law: **5** chose

precious: **4** oner **5** curio, relic **6** pippin, rarity **8** treasure

small: dot, jot **4** atom, iota, whit **6** tittle **8** particle, scuddick

to be done: **5** chore **6** agenda **7** agendum

unusual: **5** freak **6** oddity **11** monstrosity **12** malformation

thingamajig: 6 device, doodad, gadget, widget **9** doohickey, doohickus, doohinkey, doohinkus, thingummy **10** thingumbob

things: res **4** duds, gear, togs **5** goods,

point **6** fetish **7** clothes, effects **10** belongings **13** appurtenances
between extremes: **13** intermediates
done: **9** res gestae
for sale: **5** goods, wares **8** services **11** merchandise
gained by purchase: **10** acquirenda **12** acquisitions
hidden: **10** penetralia
holy: **5** hagia
jumble of: **4** mess, muss **14** conglomeration
linked in nature: **8** cognates
movable: **8** chattels **10** resmobiles
obtained from other things: **11** derivatives
prohibited: **7** vetanda
suitable for eating: **9** esculents
to see: **6** sights
worth remembering: **11** memorabilia
thingumbob: See **thingamajig**
think: wis **4** deem, feel, muse, seem, trow, ween **5** judge, opine **6** appear, esteem, expect, intend, reason, repute, scheme **7** believe, bethink, concoct, imagine, purpose, reflect, resolve, suppose, surmise, suspect **8** cogitate, conceive, consider, meditate, ruminate **9** calculate, determine, speculate **10** conjecture, deliberate, reconsider, understand **11** contemplate
alike: **5** agree
logically: **6** reason
out: **4** plan **5** solve **6** devise **7** develop, perfect **8** cogitate, contrive, discover **10** excogitate
over: **5** brood **10** reconsider
think tank: **14** research center
thinker: **4** mind **5** brain **7** sophist, student **9** meditator **11** philosopher
Thinker sculptor: **5** Rodin
thinking: **7** opinion **9** judgement **10** cogitation, reflection **13** ratiocination **17** intellectualizing
marked by exact: **13** ratiocinative
thinly: **6** airily **8** sparsely **14** insufficiently
metallic: **5** tinny
scattered: **6** sparse
thinner: **5** rarer **7** sheerer **10** turpentine
thinness: **6** rarity **7** exility, tenuity **11** attenuation
third: *figure mood:* **7** ferison
in number: **8** tertiary
music: **6** tierce
power of number: **4** cube
third estate: **10** commonalty **11** rank and file
Third Man author: **6** Greene
third world: **17** nonaligned nations
thirlage: fee, pay **4** dues **5** right **7** multure, service **8** mortgage **9** servitude, thralldom

thirling: **7** bondage **10** subjection
thirst: **4** long, wish **5** covet, crave, dryth **6** desire **7** aridity, craving, longing
absence of: **7** adipsia
excessive: **9** anadipsia
thirsty: dry **4** adry, arid, avid **5** eager **6** desire, drouth **7** athirst, craving, drought, longing, parched, wild for **8** droughty
thirty: end **6** lambda(Gr.), trente(F.)
thirty-nine and thirty-seven hundredths inches: **5** meter
this: yis **4** esta(Sp.), haec(L.)
this and that: **8** sundries **11** odds and ends
this way: **4** here
Thisbe's love: **7** Pyramus
thistle: **4** weed **7** bedegar, caltrop **8** bedeguar **10** acanaceous
genus of: **5** layia
thistle-like plants: **7** carlina
thistledown: **6** pappus
thither: end, yon **5** hence, there **6** yonder **7** farther, thereat **8** ulterior
tho: **5** still
thole: peg, pin **4** bear **5** allow **6** endure, remain, suffer **7** oarlock, undergo **8** tolerate
Thomas' opera: **6** Mignon
thong: **4** lace, lash, rein, riem **5** lasso, leash, romal, strap, strip, whang **6** twitch **7** amentum, laniard, lanyard, latchet **8** whiplash
thong-shaped: **6** lorate
Thor: *father:* **4** Odin
god of: **7** thunder
hammer: **8** Mjollnir
stepson: Ull
wife: Sif
thorax: **5** chest, trunk **6** breast
thorn: **4** brod, goad **5** briar, brier, spine, worry **7** acantha **8** vexation **9** annoyance **10** irritation
apple: **5** metel **6** datura
Egyptian: **5** babul **6** gonake **7** gonakie
full of: **6** briery
small: **7** spinule
thorny: **5** sharp, spiny **6** spinal **7** brambly, bristly, prickly **8** spinated **9** acanthoid, difficult, vexatious **10** nettlesome **11** contentious
thorough: **4** deep, full **5** utter **6** arrant **7** through **8** absolute, accurate, complete, finished **9** downright, intensive **10** exhaustive, throughout **11** painstaking **13** thoroughgoing
thoroughbred: **5** horse **7** trained **8** cultured, educated, pedigree, purebred, well-bred **11** full-blooded
thoroughfare: way **4** road **5** alley **6** artery, avenue, street **7** highway, passage, transit **8** waterway **9** boulevard

thoroughgoing: 6 arrant 7 radical 13 dyed-in-the-wool
thoroughly: all 4 inly, well 6 deeply 9 downright, intensive 10 absolutely, altogether
thoroughwort: 7 boneset 9 hoarhound
thorp, thorpe: 4 dorp 6 hamlet 7 village 9 community
Thoth: god 6 Tehuti
head: 4 ibis
though: 4 when 5 while 7 however, whereas 12 nevertheless
thought: 4 care, hope, idea, mind, view 5 trace 6 deemed, musing, opined 7 anxiety, concept, judging, opinion 9 brainwork, cogitated, reasoning 10 cogitation, conception, meditation, melancholy, reflection 11 cerebration, expectation, imagination, speculation 12 deliberation, recollection 13 concentration, consideration, ratiocination 16 intellectualized
continuous: 10 meditation
deep in: 10 cogitabund
form: 6 ideate
inability to express: 6 asemia
reader: 8 telepath
transference: 9 telepathy
thoughtful: 4 kind 5 moody 7 careful, earnest, heedful, mindful, pensive, prudent, serious 9 attentive, designing, regardful 10 cogitabund, meditative, melancholy, reflective, ruminative, solicitous 11 circumspect, considerate
thoughtless: 4 dull, rash 5 hasty, short 6 remiss, stupid 7 glaiket, glaikit 8 careless, heedless, reckless 9 brainless 10 unthinking 11 harum-scarum, inadvertent, inattentive, lightheaded 13 inconsiderate
thousand: *dollars:* 5 grand
one: mil 5 grand 7 chiliad
years: 10 millennium
thousand-headed snake: 5 Sesha 6 Shesha
thousandth: 10 millesimal
of an inch: mil
Thrace: *goddess:* 6 Bendis
king: 6 Tereus
modern name: 8 Bulgaria
mountaineers: 5 Bessi
musician: 7 Orpheus
people: 6 Satrae 8 Bisaltae
river: 6 Hebrus 7 Maritsa
town: 6 Sestos
thrall: 4 esne, serf, thew 5 slave 7 bondage, bondman, captive, enslave, slavery, subject 8 enslaved, enthrall 9 servitude, suffering 10 oppression, subjugated
thrash: lam, tan 4 bang, beat, bray, ding, drub, flax, flog, lash, rush, sail, whip,

yerk 5 array, baste, bless, flail, pound, swing, threp, whang 6 anoint, defeat, fettle, raddle, strike, threap, threep, threip, threpe, thresh, thwack 7 trounce 8 belabour, blathery, vanquish 9 triturate 10 flagellate
out: 5 argue 6 debate 7 discuss 10 kick around
thrashing: 4 bean 6 defeat 7 beating, milling 8 drubbing, flogging, whipping
thrave: 4 bind 5 crowd 6 bundle, number, throng 8 quantity
thread: ray 4 filo, line, vein, yarn 5 fiber, reeve, weave 6 strata, stream, string 7 quality, stratum 8 filament, fineness, raveling 9 ravelling 11 composition
a needle: 5 reeve
ball of: 4 clew, clue
bits of: 4 lint 9 ravelings
cell: 5 cnida
cone: cop
dental: 5 floss
division of: 4 beer
holder: 6 bobbin
in weaving shuttle: 4 weft
inserted beneath skin: 5 seton
kind of: 4 bast, bave, film, silk, yarn 5 floss, linen, lisle, rayon, seton, trame 6 cotton, lingel, lingle 8 arrasene
knot in: 4 burl
like: 6 filose
on spindle: cop
pert. to: 5 filar
raveled: 6 sleave
shoemaker's: 6 lingel
silk: bur 4 bave, burr 5 floss, trame 9 filoselle
skein of: 4 hasp
surgical: 5 seton 6 catgut, suture
tape: 5 inkle
tester: 9 serimeter
used as core for tinsel: 4 poil
winding tube: cop
threadbare: 4 bare, sere, worn 5 banal, corny, stale, trite 6 frayed, pilled, shabby 7 napless 9 hackneyed
threads: 4 beer, weft, woof 6 filler 8 clothing
threadworm: 7 filaria 8 nematode
threat: vex 4 fail, lack, urge, want, warn 5 chide, crowd, peril, press, troop 6 compel, menace, misery, throng 7 oppress, reprove, trouble, warning 8 maltreat, threaten 10 compulsion
threaten: cow 4 brag 5 augur, boast, lower, utter 6 charge, menace 7 portend, promise 8 denounce 10 intimidate
threatening: big 6 greasy, lowery 7 ominous 8 lowering, menacing 9 impending 10 formidable
three: 4 drei(G.) 5 crowd, gamma(Gr.), trias 7 Trinity

combination of: **7** triplet, ternary
consisting of: **7** ternate
group of: tre **4** trio **5** triad, trine **7** ternion
8 triumvir
months: **7** quarter **9** trimester
ruling group: **11** triumvirate
Three B's (in music): **4** Bach **6** Brahms **9**
Beethoven
three-card monte: 9 montebank
three-cleft: 6 trifid
three-dimensional: 5 cubic **6** stereo **7**
cubical
three-flowered: 9 trifloral
Three Graces: job **5** bloom **6** Aglaia,
Thalia **10** brilliance, Euphrosyne
three-headed goddess: 6 Hecate
three-hundredth anniversary: 13 ter-
centennial, tricentennial
three in one: 6 triune **7** trinity
Three Kingdoms: Wu, Shu, Wei
three-layered: 10 trilaminar
three-legged stand: 6 tripod, trivet
three-lined: 9 trilinear
three L's: 4 lead **7** lookout **8** latitude
three-masted vessel: 5 xebec **8** schooner
Three Musketeers: 5 Athos **6** Aramis **7**
Porthos
author: **5** Dumas
friend: **9** D'Artagnan
three-piled: 4 best **6** costly **11** extravagant
three-pointed: 11 tricuspidal
three-score: 5 sixty
three-seeded: 11 trispermous
three-sided figure: 6 trigon **8** triangle
three-spot: 4 trey
three-square: 5 cross **9** irritable, threefold
three-styled: 10 trystylous
Three Wise Men: 6 Gaspar **8** Melchior **9**
Balthasar
threefold: 4 tern **5** trine **6** ternal, thrice,
treble, trinal, triple, triply
threescore: 5 sixty
threesome: 4 trio **5** triad **11** triumvirate
threnody: 4 song **5** dirge **6** hearse
thresh (see also **thrash**): cob **4** beat, flog,
lump, rush **5** berry, flail
thresh out: 5 argue **6** debate **7** discuss
threshed grain husks: 5 straw
thresher: 5 flail, shark **6** beater **7** combine
thresher shark: 6 sea fox **7** foxfish **8**
whiptail
genus: **7** alopias
threshold: eve **4** gate, sill **5** limen, verge **6**
outset **8** doorsill, entrance **9** beginning
thribble: 6 triple **9** threefold
thrice: 4 very **6** highly **7** greatly **9** threefold
thrift: 4 work **5** labor **7** economy **9** austerity, frugality, husbandry, parsimony

10 employment, occupation, prosperity, providence **14** forehandedness
thriftless: 6 lavish **8** prodigal, wasteful
11 extravagant, improvident
thrifty: 4 near **5** fendy, small **6** frugal,
narrow, proper, saving, useful, worthy **7**
careful, sparing **8** thriving **9** befitting,
estimable, provident **10** economical,
forehand, prospering **11** flourishing,
serviceable
thrill: 4 bang, bore, cast, dirl, girl, hurl,
kick **5** drill, elate, flush, thirl, throw **6**
dindle, pierce, quiver, tremor, wallop **7**
frisson, tremble, vibrate **8** fremitus,
transfix **9** penetrate, perforate, throbbing, vibration
thrilly: 8 stirring **11** sensational
thrive: dow **4** boom, gain, grow **5** addle,
moise **6** batten, fatten **7** improve, prosper, succeed **8** flourish, increase
in shade: **11** sciophilous
thrivingly: 5 gaily, gayly **7** bravely
throat: maw **4** crag, crop, gowl, hals, lane,
tube **5** halse **6** groove, gullet, guzzle,
weason **7** channel, orifice, weasand **8**
guttural
armor: **6** gorget
covering: **4** barb
infection: **5** croup **6** angina, quinsy **8** cyn-
anche **9** squinancy **10** laryngitis **11**
strep throat
irritation: **4** frog
lozenge: **6** pastil, troche **7** pastile **8** pastille
part: **7** glottis
pert. to: **5** gular **7** jugular **8** guttural
protector: **5** scarf **7** muffler
sore: **6** housty
swelling: **6** goiter
to clear: hem **4** hawk
upper: **4** gula
warmer: **5** scarf
throat skin: 6 dewlap
throaty: 5 husky **6** hoarse **8** guttural **9**
voracious
throb: 4 ache, beat, drum, pant **5** flack,
pulse, thump **7** flacker, pulsate, vibrate
8 resonate **9** palpitate, pulsation
throbbing: 4 beat **7** pitapat
throe: 4 pain, pang **5** agony **6** attack, effort **7** anguish **8** struggle **10** convulsion
thrombus: 4 clot **6** fibrin
throne: see **4** apse, seat **5** asana, chair, exalt, gaddi, gadhi, power, siege **6** toilet **7**
anguish, dignity **8** cathedra, enthrone
11 sovereignty
remove from: **6** depose
throng: 4 busy, crew, heap, host, push,
rout **5** bunch, close, crowd, flock, group,
horde, peril, press, swarm **6** busily, bustle, strain, stress **7** company, hurried **8**
distress, familiar, hardship, intimate **9**

confusion, frequency, multitude **10** assemblage

thronged: 5 alive **7** peopled **8** crawling **10** celebrious

throttle: gun **5** check, choke **6** throat **7** garrote **8** compress, garrotte, strangle, suppress, windpipe **9** suffocate **11** accelerator

open: gun

through, thru: per, via **4** over **5** about, athro, ended **6** across, coffin, direct **7** by way of, perpend **8** athrough, finished, washed-up **9** completed, tombstone **11** sarcophagus **12** thoroughfare, unobstructed

the agency of: per

the mouth: **7** peroral

throughgan(Sc.): **5** labor **6** energy **11** overhauling **12** thoroughfare

throughgoing: 9 reprimand **11** examination, overhauling **12** thoroughfare

throughout: 5 about **6** bedene, during, sempre **7** perfect **8** thorough **10** completely, everywhere

throw: boa, cob, don, hit, lob, pat, peg, put, shy, wap **4** bail, bear, blow, bung, cast, dash, fall, form, hike, hove, hurl, pelt, rack, risk, shed, time, toss, turn, yerk **5** check, chuck, chunk, crank, drive, exert, flick, fling, flirt, force, frame, heave, impel, pitch, place, scarf, sling, start, strip, trice, twist, whang, while, whirl **6** change, defeat, divest, hinder, retard, sprain, spread, spring, strike, stroke, thrust, thwart, wrench, writhe **7** address, advance, discard, fashion, present, produce, project, revolve, venture **8** catapult, coverlet, distance, obstruct **9** prostrate **10** flagellate

a fit: **5** angry **7** excited **9** disturbed, irritated

a scare into: **5** scare **7** terrify

about: **4** tack **5** slosh **6** thrash

at quoits: **6** leaner, ringer

away: **5** waste **6** refuse, reject **7** discard, leaflet **8** handbill, squander

back: **5** check, delay, repel **6** refuse, reject, retort, revert **8** reversal **9** reversion

dice: **4** cast, main, roll

double one at dice: **7** ambsace

down: **4** cast, fell **5** fling **6** defeat, reject **7** refusal, subvert **9** overthrow, rejection **11** precipitate

down the gauntlet: **4** defy **9** challenge

dust in one's eyes: **7** deceive, mislead

from saddle: **7** unhorse

in: add **4** join **6** inject **9** introduce **10** contribute

in the towel: **4** cede, quit **5** yield **6** give up **9** surrender

into confusion: **4** riot **5** snafu **7** disturb **8** stampede **10** demoralize

into disorder: pif **4** pied **7** derange

into ecstasy: **6** enrapt

into shade: **7** eclipse

lazily: lob

light upon: **6** illume

lightly: **4** toss

obliquely: **4** deal, skew, toss

off: rid **4** cast, emit, free, molt, shed **5** abate, expel, moult, shake **6** reject **7** abandon, deflect, discard **8** discount **10** disconnect

off the track: **6** derail

one's weight around: **4** push, urge **8** domineer

out: say **4** emit, lade **5** egest, eject, evict, expel, utter **6** extend, reject **7** confuse, discard, excrete, project **8** distance **9** eliminate

out of order: **7** derange

over: **4** jilt **7** abandon

overboard: **8** jettison

six at dice: **4** sise **5** sises

stones at: **8** lapidate

together: **7** collect **8** assemble

underhand: lob

up: **4** rise **5** demit, vomit **10** jerry-build, relinquish

water upon: **5** douse

with force: **4** bung

throwing rope: 5 lasso, reata, riata **6** lariat

throwing-stick: 6 atlatl **9** boomerang

thrown: 4 cast **6** hurled **7** twisted **8** unseated

thrum: bit **4** birr, drum, lout, purr, tuft **5** strum, waste **6** fringe, recite, repeat, tangle, thatch **8** particle **10** threepence

thrush: 5 mavie, mavis, ouzel, robin, veery **6** missel, oriole, shrike **7** bearing **8** bluebird, throstle **9** blackbird

disease: **4** soor **5** aptha **6** aphtha

European: **4** osel **5** mavis, ossel, ousel, ouzel **6** missel, shrike

ground: **5** pitta

migratory: **5** robin

thrust: dig, jab, ram, run **4** bear, birr, bore, butt, dush, gird, jerk, pelt, poke, prop, push, stab **5** barge, clash, crowd, drive, force, hunch, impel, longe, lunge, onset, press, shove **6** attack, detude, extend, hustle, pierce, plunge, repost, ripost, spread, stress, throng **7** allonge, assault, collide, extrude, intrude, riposte **8** estocade, pressure, protrude **9** interject, interpose, substance

against the wall: **5** crush, mured

aside: **5** shove, shunt

back: **4** rout **6** defeat **7** repulse

thud: 4 baff, blow, gust, move, push **5** clonk, clunk, press, thump **6** strike **7** tempest **9** windstorm

thug: 4 hood **5** rough **6** attack, cuttle,

gunman **7** gorilla, hoodlum, ruffian **8** assassin, gangster **9** cutthroat

thumb: 6 pollex, thenar **9** hitchhike, peachwort

part: **6** thenar

through: **6** browse **7** dip into **8** glance at

Thummim's partner: 4 Urim

thump: cob, dad, dub, hit **4** bang, beat, blow, brace, clash, ding, dird, drub, dunt, polt, whip, yerk **5** blaff, bunch, clour, crump, knock, pound, throb **6** bounce, cudgel, hammer, pummel, strike, thrash, thunge

thumping: 5 large **6** tattoo **7** bumping **8** whopping

thunder: 4 bang, peal, rage, roar **6** bronte **7** fouldre **9** fulminate

god: **4** Thor, Zeus

witch: **4** baba

thunder and lightning: 8 ceraunic **9** fulminous

thunder-smitten goddess: 6 Semele

thunderbolt: 6 fulmen **7** fouldre **9** fulminant, lightning

thunderhead: 4 omen **5** cloud **7** warning

thundering: 5 large **8** thumping, whopping **10** foudroyant

thunderstorm: *Cuba:* **6** bayamo

West Indies: **7** houvari

thunge: 4 bang **5** sound, thump

thurible: 6 censer

Thuringia: *castle:* **8** Wartburg

city: **4** Gera, Jena **5** Gotha **6** Erfurt, Weimar

Thursday: *god of:* **4** Thor

Holy: **5** Skire

thus: sae, sic **4** fiat **5** hence **9** therefore **12** consequently

thwack: rap **4** bang, blow, pack **5** crump, crush, drive, force, knock, whack **6** defeat, strike, thrash **7** belabor **8** belabour

thwart: 4 balk, foil, pert, seat **5** bench, block, brace, clash, cross, parry, saucy, spite, zygon **6** across, baffle, defeat, hinder, oppose, outwit, resist **7** athwart, oblique, prevent, quarrel **8** contrair, obstruct, perverse, stubborn, thwartly **9** frustrate, interpose **10** contravene, disappoint, opposition, transverse **11** intractable, obstruction

Thyestes: *brother:* **6** Atreus

father: **6** Pelops

mother: **10** Hippodamia

son: **9** Aegisthus

thylacine: 4 wolf **5** tiger, yabbi

thyme: 8 hillwort

thymus: 5 gland

thyroid enlargement: 6 goiter

thyrsus: 5 staff, stick

tiara: 5 crown, miter **6** diadem, fillet **7** cidares, cidaris, coronet **8** frontlet **9** headdress

Tibet: 7 Sitsang

animal: **5** panda

antelope: goa, sus

ass: **5** kiang

banner: **5** tanka

beast of burden: yak

beer: **5** chang

capital: **5** Lassa, Lhasa

coin: **5** tanga

deer: **4** shou

dialect: **9** Bhutanese

ecclesiastic: **4** lama **5** dalai

food: **6** tsamba

gazelle: goa

goat fleece: **5** pashm

kingdom: **5** Nepal

lama: **5** Dalai

language: **7** Bodskad

leopard: **5** ounce

monastery: **8** lamasery

monk: **4** lama

mountain range: **5** A-ling **6** Kunlun **8** Himalaya

ox: yak

oxlike animal: **4** zebu

people: **6** Bhotia **7** Bhotiya

pony: **6** tangum, tangun **7** tanghan

priest: **4** lama

religion: Bon

river: **5** Indus **7** Salween

ruminant: **5** takin

sheep: sha **6** bharal, nahoor, nayaur

town: Noh **5** Ka-erh

wild ass: **5** kiang

wildcat: **5** manul

Tibetan: 6 Tangut

tibia: 5 flute **6** cnemis **8** shinbone

pert. to: **7** cnemial

tiburon: 5 shark

Tiburon Island Indian: 4 Seri

tic: 4 jerk **5** spasm **8** fixation **9** twitching **11** vellication

tick: 4 dot, fag, ked, pat, tag, tap **4** beat, case, dash, kade, mark, mite, note, pest **5** acari, chalk, click, count, cover, flirt, speck, touch, trust **6** acarid, acarus, credit, fondle, insect, moment, record, second, tampon, talaje **7** acarina, instant **8** acaridan, arachnid, garapata, indicate, mattress, parasite **10** pajahuello, pajaroello

fowl: **5** argas

genus of: **5** argas

sheep: ked

ticker: 4 bomb **5** clock, heart, watch

ticket: bid, tag **4** book, card, list, note, slip, tick **5** check, ducat, fiche, label, score, sight, slate, token **6** ballot, billet, notice, permit, record **7** license, placard, voucher, warrant **8** document, passport **9** cardboard, discharge, etiquette **10** memorandum **11** certificate

complimentary: **4** comp, pass **11** Annie Oakley
of leave: **6** parole
receiver of free: **8** deadhead
season: **6** abonne **10** abonnement
sell above cost: **5** scalp
speculator: **7** scalper
tickle: 4 beat, nice, play, stir, take, whip **5** amuse, annoy, frail, tease, touch **6** arouse, cuitle, divert, excite, kittle, please, thrill, tingle, touchy, wanton **7** capture, cuittle, delight, gratify, operate, passage, portray, provoke, tickler **8** chastise, delicate, insecure, tickling, ticklish, unstable, unsteady **9** difficult, squeamish, titillate, vellicate **10** insecurely
tickled: 4 glad **6** amused **7** pleased **9** gratified
tickler: pad, sip **4** book, cane, file **5** flask, knife, prong, strap **6** pistol, puzzle, record, weapon **7** problem
tickling: 7 craving **13** gratification
ticklish: 4 nice **5** risky **6** fickle, queasy, touchy **7** comical **8** critical, delicate, unstable, unsteady **9** uncertain **10** changeable, inconstant, precarious, unreliable **13** oversensitive
tick off: 4 list **6** rebuke **8** reproach **9** make angry
tidal: *creek:* **5** firth **6** estero
current: **8** tiderace
flow: **4** bore **5** eagre
wave: **4** bore **5** aigre, eagre
tidbit, titbit: 5 goody **7** saynete **8** beatille, delicacy
tide: sea **4** fair, flow, hour, pass, time **5** carry, drift, drive, flood, point, space, surge, tidal **6** befall, betide, endure, happen, moment, period, season, stream **7** current, freshet, proceed **8** continue, festival, occasion, surmount, tendency **11** anniversary, opportunity
lowest: **4** neap
type: ebb, low **4** high **5** flood **6** spring
tidewater: 5 shore **6** strand **8** seaboard
tidily: 5 fitly **7** smartly **8** cleverly, suitable **9** shipshape
tiding, tidings: ebb **4** flow, news **5** event **6** advice, gospel **7** account, message **9** happening **11** information **12** intelligence
tidy: 4 cosh, fair, good, meet(obs.), neat, redd, smug, tosh, trig, trim **5** clean, douce, great, groom, large, natty, plump, sleek **6** comely, fettle, sleeky, spruce, tidily, timely, worthy **7** healthy, orderly, upright **8** diligent, pinafore, skillful **9** shipshape **10** receptacle, seasonable **12** antimacassar, considerable, satisfactory
tie: rod, sag, wed **4** band, beam, beat, bind, bond, cord, draw, duty, even, join, knot, lace, link, post, rope, teck **5** angle, as-

cot, brace, cadge, chain, equal, hitch, marry, nexus, sheaf, trice, union, unite **6** attach, cement, connex, couple, cravat, enlace, fasten, hamper, pledge, string, tether, tiewig **7** confine, connect, necktie, oxfords, sleeper **8** alligate, restrain, restrict, shoelace **9** constrain, constrict, influence, stalemate **10** allegiance, obligation
down: **7** confine **8** restrain, restrict
fast: **5** belay
off: **4** snub **5** belay
ornament: pin **4** clip
securely: **4** lash **5** truss **7** shackle, trammel
tightly: **4** bind, lash
up: **4** bind, moor, stop **5** truss **6** hinder, tether **8** obstruct
tie-up: 5 delay **6** strike **7** mooring **10** connection
tied: 4 even **5** bound **8** knotted
up: **5** busy **8** occupied **10** encumbered
tier: row **4** bank, line, rank **5** class, layer, place, stack, story **6** degree **7** antenna, arrange **8** pinafore
tierce: 4 cask **5** lunge, parry, third **7** measure **8** sequence
Tierra del Fuego Indian: Ona **4** Agni
tiff: fit, pet, row, sip **4** huff, mood, spat **5** draft, dress, drink, humor, lunch, order, run-in, scent, smell, sniff, spell, state, taste **6** liquor **7** quarrel **8** outburst **9** condition **11** altercation
tiffin: 5 lunch **6** eating, repast **8** drinking
tiger: cat, cub **4** howl, rake, yell **5** bully, groom **6** feline, jaguar **7** leopard **9** carnivore, swaggerer, thylacine **12** organization
family: **7** felidae
young: cub
tiger finch: 8 amadavat
tiger-hunting dog: 5 dhole
tigerish: 5 cruel **6** fierce, flashy **9** ferocious **10** swaggering **12** bloodthirsty
tigers-mouth: 8 foxglove, toadflax **10** snapdragon
tight: 4 fast, firm, hard, held, neat, snug, taut, tidy, trim **5** alert, bound, cheap, close, dense, drawn, drunk, fixed, ready, smart, solid, tense, tipsy **6** climax, comely, firmly, packed, severe, steady, stingy, strait, strict **7** capable, compact, concise, quickly, shapely, soundly, unmoved **8** constant, exacting, faithful **9** competent, condensed, energetic, mercenary, niggardly **10** impervious, vigorously **11** close-fisted, intoxicated, restraining **12** parsimonious
tight-fisted: 6 stingy **12** parsimonious
tight-laced: 4 prim
tight-lipped: 5 terse **6** silent **8** taciturn **9** secretive
tighten: 5 tense **6** tauten **9** constrict

10 excellency **11** monseigneur

feminine: **4** dame, lady **5** hanum, madam **6** hanoum, milady, missis, missus **8** mistress

foreign: aga, aya, Dan, don, mir, sha, sri **4** baba, Herr, lars, sidi, shri **5** basha, mirza, mpret, pasha, sayid, senor, shree, sieur **6** bashaw, madame, shogun, squire **7** dominus, effendi, mynheer **8** monsieur

holder: **4** peer **5** noble **8** champion

of Athena: **4** Alea

pert. to: **7** titular

royal: hon., sir **4** sire **5** Grace **8** banneret **9** honorable

titmouse: mag, nun, tit **4** bird **6** fuffit, puffer, titmal, tomtit, verdin **7** jacksaw, titmall, tomnoup **8** heckimal **9** chickadee, mumruffin

pert. to: **6** parine

titter: **5** laugh **6** giggle, rather, seesaw, sooner, totter, wobble **7** tremble

tittered: **7** giggled, teeheed **9** snickered

tittle: dot, jot **4** iota, sign, whit **5** fleck, point, tilde **6** accent, gossip, tattle **7** cedilla, snippet, whisper **8** particle

tittup: **5** caper, frisk

titubate: **4** reel **6** totter **7** stagger **8** unsteady **11** vacillating

titular: **7** nominal **8** so-called

Titus Andronicus: *daughter:* **7** Lavinia
  queen: **6** Tamora

Tivoli's ancient name: **5** Tibur

tizzy: **4** snit **6** dither **7** anxiety

TNT: **6** trotyl **8** dynamite **14** trinitrotoluol **15** trinitrotoluene

to (see also next entries): tae **4** till, unto **5** until **6** before, toward **7** against, ahead of, forward

a conclusion: out

a place on: **4** onto

a point on: **4** onto

an end: out

be: **4** esse(L.), etre(F.), sein(G.) **5** einai(Gk.) **6** essere(It.)

be sure: **4** even **6** indeed **9** certainly

no extent: not

one side: **5** abeam

position into: **4** into

sheltered side: **4** alee

that time: **5** until

the left: haw **5** aport

the opposite side: **6** across

the point that: **5** until

the rear: **5** abaft **6** astern

the victor: **4** aboo

this: **6** hereto

this place: **4** here **6** hither

which: **7** whereto

wit: viz. **6** namely **8** scilicet **9** videlicet

your health: **5** skoal **6** prosit

to-do: ado **4** fuss, stir **6** bustle **9** commotion

toa: **7** warrior

toad: ted **4** agua, bufo, hyla, pipa, scum, snot, tade **6** anuran, peeper **7** crapaud, paddock, quilkin **9** amphibian, spadefoot, sycophant

genus of: **4** bufo, hyla **6** alytes

larva: **7** tadpole **8** polliwog

tongueless suborder: **7** aglossa

toadfish: **4** sapo **6** angler, grubby, puffer, slimer **8** frogfish **10** midshipman

toadflax: **8** gallwort, ramstead **13** butter-and-eggs

toady: **4** fawn, snob, ugly, zany **6** flunky **7** flunkey, hideous, shoneen, truckle **8** bootlick, hanger-on, parasite, truckler **9** dependent, flatterer, repulsive, sycophant, toadeater

toast: dry, tan **4** soak, warm **5** brede, brown, drink, melba, parch, roast, skoal, worst **6** birsle, pledge, prosit, salute **7** bristle, carouse, drinker, propose, swindle, tippler, wassail **8** cinnamon

kind of: **4** rusk **5** melba **8** zwieback

toasted bread: **6** sippet

toastmaster: **5** emcee

tobacco: **4** leaf, weed

chewing: **4** quid

coarse: **7** caporal

disease: **6** calico **7** walloon

flavor mixture: **6** petune

holder: **4** pipe **7** humidor

hookah smoking: **7** goracco

ingredient: **8** nicotine

in pipe-bowl: **6** dottel, dottle

juice: **6** ambeer, ambier

kind of: **4** capa, shag **5** bogie, fogus, tabac **6** Burley, cowpen **7** caporal, henbane, Latakia, perique, Turkish **8** domestic, Virginia **9** salvadora

leaf moistener: **5** caser

low grade: **4** shag

paste: **7** goracco

pile: **4** bulk

pulverized: **5** snuff

receptacle: **4** pipe **7** humidor

roll: **5** cigar, segar **7** carotte **9** cigarette

small portion: cud, fid, fig **4** quid **6** dottel, dottle **7** carotte

Tobacco Road: *author:* **8** Caldwell
  character: **5** Pearl **6** Jeeter

tobacco smoke hater: **11** misocapnist

Tobias: *father:* **5** Tobit
  wife: **4** Sara

toboggan: **4** sled **7** coaster, decline

toby: cup, jug, mug, way **5** cigar, stein **6** street **7** highway, pitcher, robbery

toby-man: **6** robber **10** highwayman

tocology: **9** midwifery **10** obstetrics

tocsin: **4** bell, sign **5** alarm **6** alarum, signal

tod: fox, mat **4** bush, load, pack **5** clump, shrub **6** bundle, weight

---

ropes: **4** frap

tightwad: **4** fist **5** miser, piker **7** niggard **9** skinflint **10** cheapskate

Tigris River city: Kut **5** Ashur, Calah **7** Nineveh

til: **5** plant **6** sesame

tile: hat **5** brick, drain, plate, slate **6** tegula **7** carreau, quarrel

composed of: **7** tegular **9** tessellar

curved: **7** pantile

malting floor: **6** pament **7** pamment

mosaic: **7** tessera **8** abaculus

pert. to: **7** tegular

roofing: **7** pantile

used in game: **6** domino

tiler: cat **4** kiln **5** field, thief **7** hellier **10** doorkeeper

tilery: **4** kiln

tiles: **8** ceramics

till: box, far, for, get, hoe, sow **4** draw, earn, farm, gain, plow, tend, tray, up to, work **5** charm, dress, labor, train, while **6** casket, drawer, entice, strive, whilst **7** develop, prepare **9** cultivate **10** concerning

tillable: **6** arable **7** earable

tillage: **4** farm, land **7** aration, culture **11** cultivation

fit for: **6** arable

tilled land: **5** arada

tiller: bar, bow **4** helm, hoer **5** lever, stalk, stick **6** farmer, handle, rudder, sprout **7** husband, rancher **10** cultivator, husbandman

tilt: tip **4** cant, duel, heel, lean, list, rush, tent **5** argue, fight, forge, heald, hield, joust, pitch, poise, slant, slope, speed, upend, upset **6** awning, canopy, careen, combat, hammer, oppose, seesaw, stroke, thrust, topple **7** contest, dispute, incline **8** covering, tiltyard **10** tournament **1** altercation

hammer: **6** oliver

skyward: **5** upend

tilter: **5** sword **6** avocet, seesaw **7** jouster **9** sandpiper

tilting: **5** alist **7** swaying **8** inclined, jousting, slanting

timbal: **10** kettledrum

timber: log, rib **4** balk, beam, fuel, gate, land, raff, stay, wood **5** build, cahuy, cover, fence, frame, gripe, spile, stile, trees **6** forest, girder, lumber, rafter **7** support **8** building, contrive **9** construct, structure, underpier

bend: sny **6** camber, rafter

central portion: **7** duramen **9** heartwood

cut: **4** bunk **6** lumber **7** fallage **8** teakwood

decay: **4** conk, dote, doze

end: **5** tenon

estimator: **6** scaler **7** cruiser

joining peg: **7** trenail, trunnel **8** treenail

parts of building: rib **4** sill **5** joist, spale **6** purlin, rafter **7** purline **8** stringer

peg: **4** coak

ship: bao, rib **4** bibb, bitt, keel, mast, spar, wale **5** snape, spale **7** stemson **8** sternson

sloping: **6** rafter

standing: **4** stud **5** spile **6** forest, purlin **8** puncheon, studding, stumpage

tree: ash, fir **4** pine **5** birch, cedar, maple **6** walnut **7** redwood **8** mahogany

wolf: **4** lobo

timberman: **6** sawyer **7** cruiser **8** woodsman **9** carpenter, lumberman

timbre: **4** mood, tone **5** crest, miter **6** spirit, temper **7** coronet, quality, timbrel **9** character

timbrel: **4** drum **5** tabor **10** tambourine

time: age, day, eld, era, tid **4** book, date, fuss, hint, hour, sele, term, week, year **5** clock, epoch, month, set up, spell, tempo, tense, watch **6** during, indeed, minute, moment, period, season, second, steven **8** duration, occasion, regulate, schedule, yuletide **11** opportunity **13** demonstration

ahead of: **5** early **9** premature

allowed for payment: **6** usance

and again: **5** often **10** frequently

another: **5** again

at no: **5** never **9** nevermore

before: eve

blossom: **9** blutezeit

break in: **6** hiatus

brief: **4** span **6** moment

Christmas: **8** yuletide

devoted to religion: **8** holytide

error in order of: **11** anachronism

fast: **4** Lent

gone by: **4** past, yore **10** yesteryear

granted: **4** stay **5** delay, frist **8** reprieve

happy: **4** bust, lark **5** revel, spree **6** soiree **8** jamboree

intervening: **7** interim **8** meantime **9** meanwhile

length: age, eon, era **6** moment, period

long ago: **4** yore

music: **6** presto

music marker: **9** metronome

of great depression: **5** nadir

of highest strength: **6** heyday

olden: eld **4** syne (Sc.), yore

period of: age, day, eon, era **4** aeon, date, hour, span, term, week, year **5** epoch, month, spell, trice **6** decade, ghurry, minute, moment, recess, season, second **7** century, instant **8** azoic age **9** fortnight

pert. to: **4** eral **8** temporal

present: **5** nonce

right: tid (Sc.)

single: **4** once

to come: **5** tabor **6** future

waste: **4** idle, loaf **5** dally **6** dawdle, diddle, loiter **8** flanerie
wrong: **13** anachronistic
time being: 5 nonce
time clock: 8 recorder
Time Machine author: 5 Wells
time out: 5 break **6** recess **10** rest period
timeless: 4 true **5** valid **6** eterne **7** ageless, eternal, undated **8** dateless, unending, untimely **9** co-eternal, continual, premature **11** everlasting **12** interminable
timely: apt, pat **4** soon **5** early **6** prompt, proper **8** relevant, temporal **9** favorable, opportune, pertinent **10** auspicious, forehanded, seasonable
timepiece: 4 dial **5** clock, watch **8** sunwatch **9** horologue **11** chronometer **17** chronothermometer
water: **9** clepsydra
times: *many:* oft **5** often **10** frequently
olden: eld **9** yesterday **10** yesteryear
prosperous: ups **5** booms
timetable: 7 program **8** schedule
timid: shy **4** argh, eery **5** arghe, bauch, blate, eerie, faint, mousy, pavid, scary **6** afraid **7** bashful, fearful, gastful, nervous **8** cowardly, fearsome, ghastful, hesitant, retiring, timorous, undaring **9** diffident, shrinking **11** vacillating **12** fainthearted **13** pusillanimous **14** chicken-hearted
timor: 5 dread
Timor: *capital:* **4** Dili
coin: avo **6** pataca
island: **4** Leti
language: **5** Tetum
part of: **9** Indonesia
timorous: 5 faint, timid **6** afraid, cowish, sheepy **7** fearful **8** fearsome, hesitant, quailing, terrible **9** shrinking **10** shuddering **12** fainthearted
timpani: 11 kettledrums
tin: box, can, pan **5** metal, money, terne **6** latten **7** element, stannic, stannum **8** preserve, prillion **9** container
pert. to: **7** stannic, stranic
rubbish: **5** stent
sheet: **6** latten
symbol: Sn
tin and copper alloy: 6 pewter
Tin Can Island: 7 Niuafoo
tin foil: 4 tain
Tin Pan Alley group: 5 ASCAP
tin-pot: 4 poor **6** paltry **8** inferior, wretched
tinamou: 4 bird, yutu **6** ynambu **7** ostrich
tincal: 5 borax
tincture: or **4** cast, tint **5** color, gules, imbue, myrrh, smack, stain, taint, tenne, tinge, trace **6** elixir, imbrue **7** pigment, vestige **8** coloring **9** admixture, suspicion **10** extraction **12** modification

for sprains: **6** arnica
of opium: **9** paregoric
tinder: 4 punk **6** amadou **8** kindling
tine: tub, vat **4** fork, lose, pain, teen **5** grief, point, prong, spike, tooth **6** harrow, perish **7** destroy, trouble
tinea: 8 ringworm **11** skin disease
tinean: 4 moth
tineoidea: 5 moths
tinge: dye, hue **4** cast, hint, odor, tint **5** color, imbue, savor, shade, smack, stain, touch, trace **6** affect, flavor **7** glimpse, quality **8** coloring, discolor, tincture **9** influence **10** suggestion
tinged with purple: 10 violaceous
tingle: 4 dirl, girl, nail, ring, tack **5** alive, chime, patch, sting **6** dindle, jingle, tinkle **7** support, tremble, vibrant **9** fastening, sensation, stimulate
tinker: auk **4** fuss, mend, work **5** caird, gypsy, murre, patch, rogue, skate, tramp **6** fiddle, mender, mugger, potter, putter, rascal, repair, wander **7** botcher, bungler, vagrant **8** mackerel **10** play around **11** silversides
tinkle: 5 clink **6** dindle, dingle, tingle
tinner: 6 canner **8** tinsmith
tinny: 4 hard, rich, thin **5** cheap, harsh **6** bright **7** brittle, wealthy **8** metallic, tinsmith
tinplate: 5 terne
tinsel: 4 sham **5** gaudy, showy **6** tawdry **8** specious, splendor **9** clinquant **10** forfeiture, glittering
tinstone: 11 cassiterite
tint: dye, hue **5** blush, color, stain, taste, tinge, trace **6** nuance **9** foretaste **10** complexion
cheeks: **5** rouge
tinter: 4 dyer
tintinnabulum: 4 bell **5** rhyme **6** rhythm **8** rhymster
tintype: 9 ferrotype
tiny: wee **5** small, teeny **6** atomic, infant, minute **9** miniature **10** diminutive, pocket-size **11** lilliputian, microscopic **13** infinitesimal
tip: cap, cue, end, fee, neb, tap, toe, top **4** apex, barb, blow, cant, cave, clue, dump, fall, heel, hint, keel, lean, list, pile, tilt, vail **5** aglet, alist, chape, crown, drink, empty, point, slant, snick, spire, steer, touch, upset **6** aiglet, apices, arista, careen, corona, nozzle, summit, topple, unload **7** crampit, crumshaw, ferrule, incline **8** bakshish, bonamano, gratuity, overturn **9** baksheesh, buona-mano, buona-mani, extremity, overthrow, pourboire, protector **10** intoxicate
near to: **6** apical
off: **4** hint, tell, warn **5** alarm **8** forewarn **10** indication

over: **5** upset **8** overturn
tippet: boa, fur **4** barb, cape, hood, rope, ruff **5** amice, scarf, snell **6** almuce, sindon **7** hanging, muffler, patagia(pl.) **8** liripipe, liripoop, palatine, patagium **9** comforter, victorine
tipping: 5 alist **7** ripping, topping
up: **5** atilt
tipple: bib, nip, sip, tip **4** drip, gill, lose, suck, whet **5** drink, spend, upset **6** fuddle, liquor, sipple, tumble **8** overturn
tippled: 5 drank **6** beered
tippler: sot **4** lush, soak **5** souse, toper, winer **6** boozer, bubber **7** drinker, whetter **8** drunkard **9** draftsman **11** draughtsman
tippy: 5 smart **6** wobbly **7** stylish **8** unsteady
tipstaff: 7 bailiff **9** attendant, constable
tipster: 4 tout **8** dopester, informer **10** forecaster
tipsy: ree **4** awry **5** bosky, drunk, shaky **6** bungfu, groggy **7** crooked, ebriose, ebrious, foolish, fuddled, muddled, puddled **8** unsteady **10** staggering **11** intoxicated
tiptoe: 5 alert, eager, steal **6** roused, warily **7** eagerly, exalted, gumshoe, quietly **8** cautious, stealthy **9** pussyfoot **10** cautiously **11** expectantly
tiptop: 4 best **9** first-rate **11** galumptious
tirade: 6 screed, speech **7** censure **8** diatribe, harangue, jeremiad **9** philippic
tirailleur: 5 tease **8** skirmish **12** sharpshooter
tire: fag, lag, rim **4** band, bore, gnaw, hoop, jade, pall, prey, pull, shoe, tear, tier **5** recap, seize, spare, weary **6** casing, harass, satiate, tucker **7** exhaust, fatigue, frazzle, vesture **8** decorate, enervate, enfeeble, enginery, overwork, pinafore, wear down
burst: **4** flat **7** blowout
casing: **4** shoe
kind: **4** bias, snow **6** radial **7** retread **9** whitewall
saver: **5** recap **7** retread
tired: 5 all in, blown, spent, weary **6** aweary, fagged, sleepy **7** wearied **8** fatigued **9** exhausted **10** tuckered out
out: **5** jaded, spent
tireless: 4 busy **6** active **8** untiring **10** unwearying **12** enthusiastic **13** indefatigable
Tiresias: 4 seer **10** soothsayer
blinded by: **6** Athena, Athene
home: **6** Thebes
tiresome: dry **4** dull, tame **6** boring, borish, dreary, prolix **7** irksome, onerous, prosaic, tedious **8** annoying, ennuyant **9** fatiguing, wearisome **10** irritating, monotonous **13** uninteresting

tiro: See **tyro**
tissue: gum, web **4** mesh, tel gauze, sheer, telae, weave **6** bon **7** network **8** meshwork der, gauzelike **10** interweave
animal: fat, gum **4** bone, seur, su wax **7** keratin **8** gelatine
connective: **6** stroma, tendon **9** c
horny: **7** keratin
human: fat, gum **4** suet, tela **5** fib bedo, diploe, keloid, stroma, te tonsils **8** ligament, stromata **10** chyma
layer of: **6** dermis, strata **7** stratum
nerve: **8** ganglion
oily: fat
pert. to: **5** telar
resembling: **7** histoid
vegetable: **4** bast **5** xylem **6** lignin **7** darch **8** meristem
wasting away of: **8** phthisis
tit: nag, pap, pin, tap, tee, tug **4** bird, bl draw, girl, hade, jerk, plug, pull, te tite, twit **5** horse, woman **6** nipp twitch
Titan: 4 Bana, Leto, Maia, Rhea **5** Atla Coeus, Creus, Dione, giant, Theia Cronus, Kronos, Pallas, Phoebe, Te thys, Themis **7** Iapetus, Oceanus **8** gi gantic, Hyperion **9** extensive, Mnemos yne
father: **6** Uranus
mother: **4** Gaia
Titania's husband: 6 Oberon
titanic: 4 huge **5** great **7** immense **8** c lossal, gigantic
titanite: 6 sphene **7** ijolite
tite: 4 soon **7** quickly **8** promptly **11** i mediately
tithe: tax **4** levy **5** tenth **6** decima
pert. to: **7** decimal
titi: 6 monkey **8** marmoset
titillate: 6 excite, tickle **9** stimulate, cate
titlark: 4 bird **5** pipit
title: Bey, sir **4** Czar, dame, deed, I Earl, Emir, Khan, King, name, Shah **5** Baron, claim, Count, friar jor, Mayor, Noble, right **6** assign sign, Kaiser, Knight, legend, ma Mikado, notice, Prince, record, Sultan **7** Admiral, ascribe, Ba Captain, caption, Emperor, epith quire, General, heading, Justice dive, Marquis, placard, Viceroy duke, cognomen, document, Go Viscount **9** Commander, Comm designate, President **10** appela pitulate, Lieutenant **11** designa championship, denomination eralissimo
ecclesiastic: dom, fra **4** abba **8**

today: now **4** here, oggi(It.) **7** present **8** nowadays
pert. to: **7** diurnal **9** hodiernal
toddle: **4** walk **5** dance **6** daddle, diddle, stroll, waddle **7** saunter
toddler: tot **4** trot **5** child
toe: paw, tip **5** digit, pivot, reach, touch **7** journal **10** projection
great: **6** hallux
little: **7** minimus
pert. to: **7** digital
thickening of skin: **4** corn **6** callus
without: **10** adactylous
toehold: **7** footing
toga: **4** gown, robe **5** tunic **7** garment
togated: **7** stately **9** dignified
together: mix **5** along, chain, on end, union **6** at once, bedene, fasten, unison **7** alongst, concert, contact, harmony, jointly **8** ensemble **9** cojointly, collision, courtship **11** association **12** cohabitation **13** companionship, consecutively **14** coincidentally, simultaneously
toggle, toggel: pin, rod **4** bolt, mend **5** screw **6** cotter **10** crosspiece
Togo: *capital:* **4** Lome
language: Ewe **4** Mina **6** French
tribe: Ewe **4** Mina **6** Cabrai
togs: **6** attire **7** clothes, raiment **8** clothing
togue: **9** namaycush
toil: fag, net, tug **4** drag, mesh, moil, plod, pull, rend, roll, task, trap, work **5** broil, cloth, graft, labor, slave, snare, sweat **6** battle, drudge, effort, entrap, harass, strife **7** contend, ensnare, travail, turmoil **8** distress, drudgery, industry, overwork, struggle **10** accomplish, contention, employment, occupation
toiler: **5** slave **7** laborer, plodder, workman
toilet: can **4** head, john **5** cloth, dress **6** attire **7** costume, latrine **8** bathroom, grooming, toilette **9** cleansing
case: **4** etui **5** etwee
toilsome: **4** hard **7** arduous **9** laborious, wearisome
toise: eye **4** look **6** extend **7** stretch
toit: **6** dawdle, settle, totter **7** saunter
Tokay: **4** wine **5** grape
token: **4** gift, mark, omen, sign **5** badge, check, medal, merit, proof **6** amulet, emblem, hansel, ostent, pledge, signal, symbol **7** betoken, betroth, feature, handsel, memento, portent, presage, signify **8** accolade, evidence, forbysen, keepsake, souvenir, tessella **9** character, symbolize **10** denotation, expression, indication, prognostic **11** remembrance **14** characteristic
affection: **6** amoret, mascot **7** handsel **8** accolade
officer: **5** badge

servitude: **4** yoke
victory: **4** palm **6** laurel
tokus: **8** buttocks
Tokyo: Edo **4** Yedo
tolbooth, tollbooth: **4** city, hall, jail, town **5** burgh **6** prison **9** tollhouse **11** customhouse
toldo: hut **4** tent
tole: **5** decoy **6** allure, entice
tolerable: gey **4** fair, so-so **6** decent **8** bearable, passable **9** allowance, endurable **10** good enough, sufferable **11** comportable, respectable, supportable, translation **13** entertainment
tolerance: **7** stamina **9** allowance, endurance, variation **10** indulgence **11** forbearance **13** understanding
tolerant: **5** broad **7** lenient, liberal, patient **8** enduring **9** indulgent **10** ecumenical, open-minded **11** forebearing
tolerate: **4** bear, bide **5** abide, allow, broad, brook, stand **6** accept, endure, permit, resist, suffer
Tolkien creature: Ent **7** Hobbit
toll: due, tax **4** chum, drag, draw, duty, lure, peal, pull, rent, ring **5** annul, decoy, knell, sound **6** allure, charge, custom, entice, excise, impost, invite, vacate **7** expense, scatter, trewage **8** announce, exaction **10** assessment **12** compensation
gatherer: **8** customer, publican **9** collector
kind of: **6** caphar **7** tronage **9** chiminage **10** ballastage
weight: **7** tronage
tolls: **4** dues
tolly: **4** cane **5** spire **6** candle
Toltec: **7** Nahuatl **9** Nahuatlan
site of ruins: **4** Tula **6** Mexico
tolu: **6** blasam
tolypeutine: **4** apar **9** armadillo
Tom Sawyer: *aunt:* **5** Polly
author: **5** Twain **7** Clemens
brother: Sid
girl friend: **5** Becky
pal: **15** Huckleberry Finn
Tom Thumb: **4** runt **5** dwarf **6** midget, peewee
Tom Tulliver's river: **5** Floss
tomahawk: ax; axe, cut **4** kill **6** assail, attack, strike **7** hatchet **9** criticize
toman: **4** coin **6** weight **8** division
tomato: **9** loveapple **10** prostitute
relish: **6** catsup **7** ketchup
sauce: **6** catsup **7** ketchup
soup: **6** bisque **8** gazpacho
tomb: **4** bury **5** grave, house, huaca, speos, vault **6** burial, hearse **7** chamber **8** catacomb, cenotaph **9** mausoleum, sepulcher
empty: **8** cenotaph
for bones: **7** ossuary

kind of: 4 cist 7 tritaph 8 cistvaen, kist-
vaen 9 mausoleum 11 sarcophagus
saint's: 6 shrine
tombe: 4 drum
tomboy: meg 5 rowdy 6 gamine, harlot,
hoyden 8 strumpet
tombstone: 5 stele 8 memorial, monument 11 grave marker
Tombstone marshal: 4 Earp 5 Wyatt
tomcat: gib
tome: 4 book 5 atlas 6 ledger, letter, volume 12 encyclopedia
tomfool: ass 5 clown 6 stupid 7 buffoon,
doltish, foolish, half-wit 8 rainbird 9
blockhead 10 flycatcher, nincompoop
11 harebrained
tomfoolery: 5 prank 8 nonsense 9 silliness
tommyrot: 7 hogwash, rubbish 8 nonsense 9 silliness
tomorrow: 6 domani(It.), manana(Sp.)
ton: 4 lots, mode 5 heaps, style, tunny,
vogue 6 weight 7 fashion
tonant: 7 blatant 10 boisterous
tone: 4 mood, note, tint, vein 5 color,
pitch, shade, sound, trend, vigor 6 accent, effect, intone, modify, temper,
timbre 7 quality 8 coloring, mitigate,
modulate, strength 9 character, harmonize 10 atmosphere, elasticity, inflection, intonation, modulation 12 modification
down: 4 mute, tame 6 soften, subdue 8
modulate
nasal: 5 twang
of cord: 8 concento
quality: 6 timbre
rapid: 7 tremolo
sharp: 4 tang
single: 8 monotone
singsong: 4 sugh 5 sough
succession: 5 melos
system of: 6 tonart
thin: 7 sfogato
third of diatonic scale: 7 mediant
vibrant: 5 twang
tone arm: 6 pickup
tone color: 6 timbre
toneless: 5 atony
tones: *combination of:* 5 chord
series of: 5 scale
Tonga: *also called:* 15 Friendly Islands
capital: 9 Nukualofa
island group: 5 Vavau 6 Haajai 9 Tonga-
tapu
monetary unit: 6 paanga
town: 6 Neiafu
tongs: 5 clamp 6 tenail 7 forceps, pincers,
tueiron 8 scissors, tenaille
tongue: gab 4 bark, chib, fame, flap, howl,
pole, sole, vote 5 chide, clack, lingo,
prate, scold, speak, utter 6 report 7

beeweed, dialect, feather, lingula 8 language, lingulae, reproach 9 pronounce
bone: 5 hyoid
classical: 5 Greek, Latin 6 Hebrew
click of: tch
disease: 5 agrom 9 lichenoid
Jesus': 7 Aramaic
mother: 10 vernacular
of land: 4 spit 5 reach
oxcart: 4 cope
pert. to: 7 glossal, lingual
pivoted: 4 pawl
projection: 7 papilla 8 papillae(pl.)
sacred: 4 Pali
seam: 5 raphe
serpent: 4 fang
tied: 4 dumb, mute 5 quiet 8 taciturn 12
inarticulate
tip of: 6 corona
wagon: 4 neap, pole 5 shaft
tongue-lash: 5 baste, scold 6 berate 7 tell
off
tongue-like: 7 lingual
tongued: 6 prated
tongueless: 4 dumb, mute 10 speechless
tonic: 5 aloes 6 bracer 7 bracing 8 medicine, pick-me-up, roborant 9 sassafras,
stimulant 10 astringent, refreshing 11
corroborant 12 invigorating
kind of: 4 dope 6 catnip 7 boneset, nervine
tonic leaf: 4 coca
tonsil: 5 gland 8 amygdala
inflammation: 6 quinsy
operation: 13 tonsillectomy
tonsorialist: 6 barber
tonsure: 5 crown, shave 7 haircut
tonsured: 4 bald 5 shorn 6 pilled, shaven
7 clipped
tony: 5 smart 7 stylish
too: and, tae 4 also, ever, over, very 6 as
well, overly 7 besides 8 likewise 9 extremely 11 exceedingly, excessively,
furthermore 13 superfluously
bad: 4 alas
late: 5 tardy 7 belated 8 untimely
little: 6 scanty, skimpy 12 insufficient
much: 7 nimiety
small to matter: 13 inappreciable
soon: 9 premature
tool (see also **instrument**): adz, axe, saw,
zax 4 adze, draw, dupe, file, form, ride
5 drive, plane, shape, sword 6 convey,
device, finish, hammer, manage, puppet, weapon 7 cat's-paw, hatchet, utensil 8 ornament 9 appliance, implement
10 manipulate
abrading: 4 file
biting edge: bit
bookbinding: 5 gouge
boring: awl, bit 5 auger, drill 6 gimlet,
reamer 7 bradawl

box: see *chest* below

bricklayer: **4** hock **5** float, level **6** hammer, trowel

butcher: saw **5** knife, steel **6** skewer, skiver **7** cleaver

carpenter: bit, saw **4** rasp **5** auger, level, plane, punch **6** chisel, gimlet, hammer, pliers, square **7** handsaw, hatchet, scriber

chest: kit

chopping: **7** dolabra

cobbler's: awl **6** hammer

cultivating: **4** plow **6** harrow, plough **7** leveler

cutting: adz, axe, bit, hob, saw **4** adze **5** bezel, bezil, gouge, knife, plane, razor **6** chisel, graver, reamer, shears

edged: axe **4** adze **5** knife, razor **6** chisel, reamer

engraver's: **5** burin **7** scouper

excavating: **4** pick **6** pickax, shovel

flat: **7** spatula

garden: hoe **4** rake **5** edger, mower, spade **6** sickel, trowel, weeder

gripping: **4** vise **5** clamp, tongs **7** pincers **8** tweezers

hole-making: **6** dibble

kind of: awl, fid, fro, loy, tap, zax **4** celt, file, lute, sley **5** burin, edger, flail, lathe, loper, peavy, peevy, punch **6** chisel, cranny, eolith, flange, lifter, peavey, peevey, pommel, taster, trepan, trowel **7** setiron **8** burgoyne **12** straightedge

marble worker's: **6** fraise

mason's: **6** chisel

mining: gad **4** pick

molding: die

pointed: awl, fid, gad **4** barb, brod, brog, pick **6** gimlet, stylet

pounding: **6** hammer, mallet, pestle

prehistoric: **4** celt **5** flint **6** eolith **9** paleolith **10** palaeolith

set: kit

shaping: **5** lathe, swage

slate-measuring: **7** scantle

smoothing: **4** file **5** plane **7** sleeker

splitting: axe **4** frow **7** hatchet

temperer: **8** hardener

trimming: ax; axe, saw **6** shears **8** clippers, scissors

woodworking: adz **4** adze **7** edgeman, grainer, scauper, scriber **10** spokeshave

tool handle: *end* **4** butt

fitted part: **4** tang

tools: tew **4** gear **7** gibbles(Sc.)

toot: pry, spy **4** blow, fool, gaze, peep **5** binge, blast, draft, drink, shout, sound, spree **6** bender, spread, sprout **7** carouse, declare, trumpet, whistle **8** carousal, eminence, proclaim **9** elevation

tooter: spy **7** lookout **8** watchman **9** trumpeter

tooth (see also **teeth**): cog, jag **4** bite, dent, fang, jagg, snag, tine, tusk **5** molar, point, prong **6** cuspid, indent **7** consume, grinder, incisor, snaggle **10** projection

canine: **4** tush **6** cuspid, holder **7** laniary

cap: **5** crown

coat: **6** enamel

diminutive: **8** denticle **13** denticulation

doctor: **7** dentist

edge: **7** dentate

fore: **5** biter **6** cutter

gear wheel: cog **4** dent, tine

grinding surface: **5** mensa

having but one: **8** monodont

tooth decay: **6** caries **8** cavities **11** saprondontia

tooth for tooth: **6** talion

toothache: **4** worm(Sc.) **8** dentagra **10** odontalgia

toothed: *irregularly:* **5** erose

on edge: **8** serrated

toothless: **4** weak **6** futile **7** edental **8** decrepit, edentate **9** infantile **10** agomphious, edentulate

toothsome: **5** sapid, tasty **6** savory **8** pleasing **9** agreeable, delicious, palatable

top: ace, cap, fid, lid, tip, toy **4** acme, apex, crop, head, knap, lead, peak, pick, tent, tilt, tuft **5** caput, cream, crest, crown, drain, drink, equal, excel, outdo, prune, ridge, upset **6** apices(pl.), better, capote, culmen, exceed, finial, summit, swells, topple, tumble, upside, vertex, zenith **7** gyrator, highest, maximum, surpass, topmost **8** covering, dominate, forelock, foremost, pinnacle, surmount, vertexes(pl.), vertices(pl.) **9** excellent, uppermost **10** pre-eminent **11** aristocrats

altar: **5** mensa

head: **4** pate **5** scalp

of card suit: ace

of wave: **5** crest

toy: **8** teetotum

wooden stand: **5** criss

top-drawer: **7** exalted

top-hole: **6** tiptop **9** excellent, first-rate **10** first-class

top kick: **8** sergeant

top-notch: **4** best **6** tiptop **7** highest **9** excellent, first-rate **11** unsurpassed

topaz: gem **5** stone **7** pycnite **11** hummingbird

symbol of: **8** fidelity

topcoat: **6** reefer **8** siphonia **12** chesterfield

tope: **4** butt, wren **5** clump, drink, grove, shark, stupa **6** guzzle **7** dogfish, orchard

topee, topi: cap, hat **6** helmet

toper: sot **5** shark **6** boozer, bouser **7** tippler, tosspot **8** drunkard

tophaceous: 5 rough, sandy, stony 6 gritty

tophet, topheth: 4 hell 5 chaos 8 darkness 9 confusion

topic: 4 item, text 5 issue, theme 6 reason, remedy 7 heading, subject, themata 8 argument 11 proposition 13 consideration

topical: 5 local 9 temporary

topknot: 4 hair, head, tuft 5 crest, onkos 7 commode 8 flounder 9 headdress

toplofty: 5 proud 7 haughty 8 inflated 9 egotistic 10 disdainful 12 contemptuous, supercilious

topmost: 6 apical 7 highest, maximum 9 uppermost

topnotcher: ace 4 hero, star 8 jimdandy, knockout

topography: 7 terrain

topper: hat 5 cover, float 6 stower 7 cheater, snuffer, topcoat 10 high-rigger 11 high-climber

toppiece: 4 head 6 toupee 11 masterpiece

topping: 4 bran, fine, good 5 icing, proud 6 refuse, tiptop 7 forlock, gallant, highest, topknot, topmost 8 arrogant, pleasant, superior 9 excellent, first-rate, skimmings 11 pretentious

topple: tip 4 fall, tilt 5 pitch, upset 6 teeter, totter, tumble 7 overset 8 overhang, overturn 9 overthrow 10 somersault 11 overbalance

tops: 4 A-one, aces, best 7 supreme 8 topnotch

topsman: 5 chief 6 drover 7 hangman, headman

topsy-turvy: 8 cockeyed, confused 10 disordered, upside-down 11 withershins

toque: hat 6 bonnet 9 headdress

tor: taw 4 crag, hill, peak 5 mound 8 pinnacle

tora, torah: law 5 tetel 7 precept 10 hartebeest, Pentateuch, revelation 11 instruction

torch: 4 lamp 5 blaze, brand, flare, fusee 7 lucigen 8 flambeau 9 flambeaux(pl.) 10 flashlight, incendiary
frame: 7 cresset

tore: 4 knob, plod 5 grass 6 pommel 9 persevere

toreador: 6 torero 7 matador 11 bullfighter

torii: 7 gateway

torment: rib, vex 4 bait, hurt, pain, rack 5 agony, annoy, chevy, chivy, devil, force, grill, harry, tease, wrack 6 badger, chivvy, harass, harrow, hector, misery, molest, pester, plague, strain 7 afflict, agitate, anguish, bedevil, crucify, distort, hagride, hatchel, tempest, torture, travail 8 distress, vexation 9 martyrdom, suffering, tantalize 10 cruciation 11 persecution

tormenting: 6 plaguy, vexing 9 harassing 11 troublesome 12 excruciating

tormina: 5 colic, pains 6 cramps, gripes

torn: 4 rent 5 riven 6 broken, ripped 7 mangled 9 lacerated

tornado: 4 wind 6 squall 7 cyclone, thunder, twister 9 hurricane, whirlwind, windstorm 12 thunderstorm

Tornado Junction: 8 Trinidad

toro: 4 bull, tree 7 cavalla, cowfish

torous, torose: 6 brawny 7 bulging, knobbed, swollen 8 muscular 11 protuberant

torpedinous: 9 benumbing 10 stupefying

torpedo: 4 mine, ruin 5 wreck 6 attack, benumb, damage, gunman 7 destroy, explode, shatter 8 assassin, firework, gangster, numbfish, paralyze 9 crampfish, detonator
front end: 4 nose

torpedo fish: ray

torpid: 4 boat, dull, numb 5 inert 6 leaden, static, stupid 7 dormant 8 benumbed, inactive, lifeless, sluggish 9 apathetic, lethargic

torpor: 4 coma 5 sleep 6 acedia, apathy, stupor 7 accidie 8 dormancy, dullness, lethargy 10 inactivity, stagnation 12 sluggishness 13 insensibility

torque: bee 5 chain, sarpe, twist 6 collar 8 necklace

torrefy, torrify: dry 5 parch, 6 scorch

torrent: 4 flow, rush 5 flood, parch, roast, spate 6 stream 7 burning, channel consume, current, niagara, roaring, rushing 8 downpour 9 impetuous

torrential: 10 outpouring 12 overwhelming

torrid: hot 4 arid 5 dried 6 ardent, sultry 7 burning, parched, zealous 8 inflamed, parching, scorched 9 scorching 10 oppressive, passionate 11 impassioned

tort: 4 evil 5 libel, wrong 6 damage, injury 8 iniquity

tortoise: 6 turtle 8 terrapin 9 chelonian
genus: 4 emys
kind: 4 emyd 5 giant 9 Galapagos
marsh: 6 gopher 7 elodian
shell: 8 carapace

tortuous: 5 snaky 6 cranky, spiral 7 crooked, devious, immoral, sinuate, sinuous, winding, wriggly 8 wrongful 9 deceitful, injurious, twisting 10 circuitous, roundabout 11 anfractuous 12 labyrinthine

torture: 4 hurt, maim, pain, rack 5 agony, twist, wheel 6 deform, punish, wrench 7 afflict, agonize, anguish, crucify, distort, torment 8 distress, mutilate, twisting 9 martyrdom 10 affliction, cruciation, distortion, excruciate, perversion, punishment *device:* **4** rack

torus: 6 baston **7** molding **9** elevation **10** anchor ring, receptacle **12** protuberance

torvous: 4 grim **5** stern **6** severe

tory: 6 Papist **8** loyalist, marauder, Royalist **11** reactionary **12** conservative

Tosca's love: 5 Mario

tosh: 4 bath, bosh, neat, tidy **5** souse, trash **6** drench, neatly **7** bathtub **8** familiar, intimate, nonsense **10** intimately

toss: cob, cup, lob **4** cast, cave, flip, hike, hurl, rear, roll **5** chuck, flick, fling, flirt, heave, pitch, raise, serve, throw, wager **6** buffet, chance, fillip, harass, tossup, totter, uplift **7** agitate, disturb **8** disquiet **9** agitation, commotion **10** excitement

a coin: **4** flap, flip

about: **5** bandy **6** thrash, thresh **7** discuss

carelessly: **4** flip

head in derision: **4** geck

side to side: **6** careen

together confusedly: **8** scramble

tosspot: sot **5** toper **7** drinker **8** drunkard

bottle: **6** flagon

tosticate: 6 harass **8** distract **10** intoxicate

tosto: 4 fast **5** quick

tosy: 4 snug **10** comforting **11** intoxicated

tot: add, cup **4** dram, item, note **5** child, count, drink, total, totum **6** amount, toddle, totter **7** jotting, toddler

tota: 6 grivet, monkey

total: add, all, sum, tot **4** full **5** gross, run to, utter, whole **6** abrupt, all-out, amount, entire **7** concise, overall, perfect, plenary, summary **8** absolute, complete, entirety **9** aggregate, full-scale, undivided **10** accumulate

totalitarian: 7 fascist **8** absolute, despotic **9** arbitrary **10** tyrannical **13** authoritarian

tote: all, lug, tot **4** bear, haul, lead, load **5** carry, count, total **6** handle, reckon **7** conduct **9** abstainer, transport

totem: 6 emblem, fetich, fetish, figure

totem pole: xat

toto: all **4** baby **5** young

totter: 4 fall, hang, reel, rock, sway, toss **5** lurch, pitch, shake, swing, waver **6** dodder, falter, quiver, seesaw, staver(Sc.), toddle **7** fribble, stagger, tremble **8** titubate, unstable, unsteady **9** vacillate

tottle: 4 boil, purl **5** count, total **6** reckon, simmer, toddle, topple

toty(Ind.)**: 7** laborer **9** messenger

toucan: 4 bird, toco **7** aracari **8** hornbill **13** constellation

touch: dab, hit, paw, rap, rob, tag, tap, tig, toe, use **4** abut, blow, feel, hint, meet, rape **5** equal, reach, rival, steal, taste,

trait **6** accuse, adjoin, affect, amount, attain, border, borrow, extend, handle, molest, rebuke, strike, stroke **7** attinge, censure, contact, impinge, palpate, partake **8** perceive **9** mishandle, tactility

boundary line: **4** abut

closely: **8** osculate

clumsily: paw

for medical diagnosis: **7** palpate

lightly: **5** brush, graze **7** attinge, twiddle

measuring device: **10** haptometer

off: **4** fire **5** start

organ of: **4** palp **6** feeler **7** antenna

perceptible by: **7** tactile **8** palpable

pert. to: **6** haptic **7** tactile, tactual

touching: 4 upon **6** moving **7** against, apropos, contact, meeting, piteous, tangent **8** adjacent, pathetic **9** affecting, attingent, conjoined **10** contacting, contiguous, contingent, responsive **13** compassionate

a single point: **7** tangent

touchstone: 4 test **8** basanite, standard **9** barometer, criterion

touchwood: 4 funk, punk **5** sponk, spunk **6** amadou, tinder **8** punkwood

touchy: 4 sore **5** cross, risky, snaky, techy, testy **7** peevish **8** ticklish **9** irascible, irritable, sensitive **10** precarious **11** inflammable **13** over-sensitive

tough: 4 thug, wiry **5** bully, hardy, rigid, rough, rowdy, stiff **6** brutal, flinty, robust, rugged, sinewy, sticky, strong **7** hickory, onerous, ruffian, violent, viscous **8** cohesive, enduring, hardened, hard-line, leathery, rowdyish, stubborn, sturdily, toilsome, vigorous **9** difficult, glutinous, obstinate, ruffianly **10** aggressive, unyielding

and lean: **5** scrag **6** sinewy

tough-minded: 6 shrewd **7** willful **8** stubborn **9** practical, realistic **10** hardheaded **13** unsentimental

toughen: 5 inure **6** anneal, endure, harden, temper

toupee: rug, wig **5** doily **6** peruke **7** periwig

tour: 4 trip, turn **5** cover, drive, range, round, shift, spell, trick, watch **6** course, travel **7** circuit, compass, journey, proceed **9** barnstorm, excursion **10** appearance, revolution

tourbillion: 5 whirl **6** vortex **8** firework, karrusel **9** whirlwind

tour de force: 4 feat **7** classic, exploit **11** masterpiece

tourelle: 5 tower **6** turret

tourist: 8 traveler **9** sightseer **10** rubberneck

tourmaline: 6 schorl **7** mineral **8** achroite, siberite **9** rubellite

tournament: 4 tilt **5** joust, sport, trial **6**

battle **7** contest, tourney **9** encounter

tournure: pad **5** poise **6** bustle **7** contour, outline

touse: **4** pull, rack, tear **5** worry **6** handle, rumple **8** dishevel

tousle, tousel: **4** drag, muss, pull, tear **5** touse **6** ruffle, rumple, tussle **7** rummage **8** dishevel, disorder **9** mop of hair

tout: spy, vex **4** peep, peer, puff, toot **5** tease, thief, watch **6** herald, praise **7** canvass, lookout, solicit, tipster, touting, trumpet **8** ballyhoo, informer, proclaim, smuggler **9** importune, recommend

tout a fait: **5** quite **10** altogether

tow: tew, tug **4** drag, draw, flax, haul, lead, pull, rope **5** barge, chain **6** hawser, propel **7** towboat, towrope, tugboat **8** cordelle

tow-row: **6** rumpus, uproar **9** racketing

toward: tae(Sc.) **4** near **5** anent **6** coming, facing, future, onward **7** apropos, forward, willing **8** imminent, obliging **9** compliant, promising, regarding, tractable **10** concerning **11** approaching

center: **5** entad

exterior: **5** ectad

mouth: **4** orad

stern: aft **5** abaft **6** astern

towardly: **6** docile, gentle, kindly **7** affable **9** compliant, favorable, friendly, tractable **10** propitious

towel: dry, rub **5** cloth **6** napkin **8** vesperal **9** handcloth

fabric: **4** huck **5** linen, terry

tower: **4** rise, silo, soar **5** broch, exalt, mount, pylon, raise, reach, sikar, spire, stupa **6** ascend, belfry, castle, donjon, pagoda, prison, turret **7** bastile, bulwark, citadel, clocher, defense, elevate, mansion, minaret, mirador, overtop, shikara, steeple, surpass, zikurat **8** bastille, domineer, fortress, look down, overlook, ziggurat, zikkurat **9** campanile **10** protection, stronghold

bell: **6** belfry **8** carillon **9** campanile

castle: **6** donjon

church: **5** spire **7** steeple

famous: **4** Pisa **5** Babel, Minar **6** Eiffel, London

glacier ice: **5** serac

kind of: **5** ivory

mosque: **7** minaret

over: **5** dwarf **7** command **8** dominate

signal: **6** beacon

small: **6** turret

towering: **4** high, tall **5** great, lofty, steep **7** eminent, intense, supreme, violent **9** monstrous **11** overweening

towhee: **7** bunting, chewink

town: **4** burg, city, dorp, farm, stad, vill, yard **5** bourg, burgh, court, derby, house, manor, ville(F.), voter **6** ciudad(Sp.), garden, hamlet, parish, podunk, staple **7** borough, village **8** bourgade **9** enclosure, farmstead

Attica: **4** deme

official: **5** mayor **6** grieve **8** alderman

pert. to: **5** civic, urban **7** oppidon

plan: **4** plat

small: **8** one-horse **10** dullsville **11** whistle-stop

witch: **5** Salem

townsman: cit **7** burgher, citizen, oppidan

township: **4** area, dorp **8** district

toxic: **9** poisonous

toxophilite: **6** archer

toy: pet, top **4** ball, daff, doll, fool, play, whim **5** antic, dally, fancy, flirt, panda, sport **6** bauble, cosset, finger, frolic, gewgaw, hoople, rattle, trifle **7** caprice, conceit, disport, pastime, trinket **8** aversion, flirting, gimcrack, interest, mistress, ornament, teetotum, weakling **9** bandalore, dalliance, headdress, plaything, rattlebox, teddybear **10** knickknack

toyish: **6** wanton **7** playful, trivial, useless **8** sportive, trifling **9** fantastic, frivolous, whimsical **13** unsubstantial

trabant: **9** attendant, bodyguard

trabea: **4** toga

trabeation: **11** entablature

trabuco: **5** cigar **11** blunderbuss

trace: **4** clew, clue, copy, draw, fall, file, hint, line, mark, nose, path, road, seek, sign, step, tang, walk **5** grain, march, probe, route, shade, spoor, tinge, token, track, trail, tread **6** amount, deduce, derive, detect, follow, locate, ramble, sketch, trudge **7** conduct, glimpse, impress, imprint, inquire, outline, remnant, soupcon, uncover, vestige **8** discover, evidence, quantity, traverse **9** ascertain, attribute, delineate, establish, footprint, scintilla **10** indication, procession **11** investigate

tracer: **5** horse **6** bullet, gilder, seeker, stylus **7** stainer **8** outliner, searcher **9** draftsman

trachea: **4** duct **8** windpipe

trachyte: **4** rock **6** domite

tracing: **4** copy **6** record **8** ergogram **10** cardiogram

track: rut, way **4** drag, draw, hunt, line, mark, oval, path, rail, road, wake **5** march, route, scent, sight, spoor, trace, trail, tread **6** course, follow, infuse, pursue, shadow, teapot, travel **7** circuit, conduct, vestige **8** guideway, sequence, speedway, trackage, traverse **9** ascertain, footprint, spectacle **10** beaten path, cinder path, succession

animal: run **4** slot **5** spoor

down: 4 hunt 6 pursue, search
official: 5 judge, timer 7 referee, starter
race: 4 mile 5 relay 6 sprint
running: 4 flat 7 cinders
ship: 4 wake
train: 4 rail, spur 6 siding
tracker: 5 guide, tower 7 tugboat
tract (see also **land**): lot 4 area, mark, path, zone 5 campo, clime, essay, lapse, range, trace, track 6 course, estate, extent, region 7 country, expanse, leaflet, portion, quarter, stretch 8 brochure, district, duration, pamphlet, sequence, treatise 9 lineament, narrative, territory 10 exposition 11 subdivision 12 dissertation
tractable: 4 easy 5 buxom 6 docile, gentle, pliant 7 ductile, flexile, pliable 8 amenable, flexible, obedient, workable 9 adaptable, complaint, malleable 10 governable
tractate: 5 essay, tract 8 handling, treatise 9 discourse, treatment 10 discussion 12 dissertation
tractile: 6 pliant 7 ductile, tensile
traction 5 power 7 drawing, utility 8 friction 9 influence 10 attraction
tractor: rig 9 agrimotor
trade: buy, way 4 chap, chop deal, fuss, path, sell, swap, work 5 cheap, craft, habit, track, trail, tread 6 action, barter, bother, course, employ, manner, method, metier, scorse 7 bargain, calling, dealing, pursuit, traffic 8 activity, business, commerce, exchange, practice, purchase 9 patronage 10 handicraft, occupation, profession 11 intercourse, nundination
association: NAM 5 hansa, hanse
combination: 4 gild 5 guild, hanse 6 cartel, merger
pert. to: 10 emporeutic
unlawful: 10 contraband 11 black market
votes: 7 logroll
trademark: 4 logo 5 brand 8 logotype
trader: 4 ship 6 dealer, monger, seller, slaver, sutler 7 chapman 8 barterer, merchant 9 tradesman 10 shopkeeper 11 stockbroker
tradesman: 5 buyer 7 artisan, workman 8 merchant 9 craftsman 10 shopkeeper 11 storekeeper
supply: 4 line 5 stock 9 inventory
tradition: 4 code, lore 6 belief, custom, legend 8 heritage, practice 9 surrender 10 convention
traduce: 4 slur 5 abuse, belie 6 debase, defame, malign, vilify 7 asperse, blacken, detract, pervert, slander 8 disgrace 10 calumniate
traffic: buy 4 coup, sell 5 trade 6 barter, market 7 chaffer, dealing 8 business,

commerce, exchange 9 patronage 11 intercourse
in holy offices: 6 simony
violator: 7 speeder 9 jaywalker
trafficker: 6 dealer, trader 8 merchant
in narcotics: 6 pusher
tragacanth: gum 4 tree 5 shrub
tragedy: lot, woe 6 buskin, misery 8 calamity, disaster 10 misfortune
Muse: 9 Melpomene
tragic: sad 4 dire 5 fatal 7 doleful 8 dreadful, mournful, pathetic, terrible
tragopan: 8 pheasant
tragule: 4 deer 10 chevrotain
trail: lad 4 drag, draw, halt, hang, hunt, mark, path, plod, slot, tail, wake 5 blaze, delay, drail, piste, route, scent, spoor, trace, track, train, tramp, troll 6 camino(Sp.), course, follow, trapse, trudge 7 draggle, dwindle, traipse 8 footpath, straggle
blazer: 7 pioneer
marker: 5 cairn
trailer: 4 vine
truck: 4 semi
train: row 4 bait, drag, draw, file, form, gait, lead, line, lure, rack, rank, rear, tail, trap 5 breed, coach, decoy, drawl, drill, flier, guide, local, seine, shape, snare, suite, teach, trace, trail 6 allure, coffle, convoy, cradle, direct, entice, ground, harden, scheme, school, season, series, shaped 7 caravan, conduct, cortege, educate, prepare, retinue 8 accustom, artifice, equipage, instruct protract, rehearse, sequence, trickery 9 condition, cultivate, entourage, following, stratagem, treachery 10 attendants, conveyance, discipline, procession, succession 11 streamliner 13 accommodation
end car of: 7 caboose
fast: 7 express, limited
horses: 6 manege
men: 4 crew
of attendants: 5 suite 7 cortege, retinue 9 entourage
overhead: 8 elevated, monorail
slow: 5 local
underground: 4 tube 5 metro(F.) 6 subway
trained: 4 bred 5 aimed 8 educated
trainee: 4 boot 5 cadet, pupil 6 novice 10 apprentice
trainer: 5 tamer 7 lanista 11 gymnasiarch
training: 4 diet 5 drill 8 breeding, exercise 9 education 10 background, discipline 11 supervision
lack of: 11 inappetence
manual: 5 sloid, sloyd
traipse, trapes: gad 4 drag, walk 5 trail,

tramp, tread **6** trudge, wander **8** gadabout, slattern

trait: 4 line, mark, note, thew **5** touch **6** streak, stroke **7** feature, quality **9** attribute, lineament, mannerism **11** peculiarity **14** characteristic

traitor: 5 Judas **8** betrayer, Iscariot, renegade

Norwegian: **8** Quisling

traitorous: 5 false **9** faithless, felonious **11** disaffected, treacherous, treasonable

traject: way **4** cast **5** ferry, route, throw **6** course, trajet **7** conduct, passage **8** transmit

tralatitious: 10 handed down **12** metaphorical

tram: car, leg **4** beam, haul, limb **5** bench, shaft, wagon **6** thread **7** tramcar, trammel, tramway, trolley **9** streetcar **10** conveyance

tier: **4** deck

trammel: net, tie **4** clog, lock **5** check, gauge **6** braids, fasten, fetter, hamper, impede **7** compass, confine, pothook, prevent, shackle, tresses **8** entangle, restrain, stultify **9** intercept, plaitings **10** instrument

tramontane: 4 boor **5** alien **7** foreign **8** stranger **9** barbarous **10** outlandish **11** transalpine

tramp: bo; boe, bum, vag **4** hike, hobo, hoof, plod, prog, step, tart, vamp, walk **5** caird, jaunt, tread **6** gaycat, trapes, travel, trudge, waffie, wander, wanton **7** steamer, traipse, vagrant **8** vagabond **9** excursion **10** prostitute **11** bindle stiff

baggage: **6** bindle

offering to: **7** handout

trample: 4 foil, hurt **5** crush, stamp, stomp, tread **6** injure **7** destroy, tread on, violate

trance: 4 coma, daze **5** spell, swoon **6** prance, raptus, stupor **7** ecstasy, enchant, passage, reverie **8** entrance **9** catalepsy, enrapture, transport

tranquil: 4 calm, cool, easy, even, mild **5** equal, quiet, still **6** gentle, placid, serene, steady **7** equable, pacific, restful **8** composed, peaceful **9** sedentary **10** motionless **11** undisturbed **13** imperturbable

tranquility, tranquillity: kef, kif **5** peace, quiet **8** ataraxia, serenity **10** equanimity **12** peacefulness

tranquilize: 4 calm, lull **5** allay, quiet **6** sedate, settle, soften, soothe, subdue **7** appease, assuage **9** alleviate

transact: 5 treat **7** conduct, perform **8** complete, transfer **9** negotiate

transaction: 4 deal, sale **6** affair **7** bargain **8** business, contract, covenant **10** proceeding **11** proposition

unlawful: **10** chevisance

Transcaspian capital: 9 Ashkhabad

Transcaucasia: See **Armenia, Azerbaijan**

transcend: 4 pass, soar **5** climb, excel, mount, raise **6** ascend, exceed **7** elevate, surpass **8** outstrip, overstep, surmount **9** rise above

transcendent: 8 superior **13** extraordinary

transcendental: 5 ideal **7** eternal, supreme **8** abstract, ethereal **10** superhuman **12** metaphysical, otherworldly, supersensual, supranatural

transcribe: 4 copy **5** write **6** impute, record **7** ascribe, imitate **9** reproduce, translate **10** paraphrase

transcript: 6 record **8** apograph **9** duplicate **12** reproduction

transfer: 4 cede, deed, give, move, pass, sale, send **5** carry, grant, shift **6** assign, attorn, change, convey, decant, demise, depute, remove **7** dispose **8** alienate, delegate, make over, sign over, transmit **9** transform, translate, transport **10** abalienate **12** transmission **13** transposition

bus or train: **6** ticket **8** add-a-ride

design: **5** decal

of court suit: **7** remover

property: **4** deed **5** grant **6** convey

transference: 7 passage **10** conveyance

transfigure: 5 exalt **7** glorify **8** idealize **9** transform **12** metamorphose

transfix: fix, pin **5** spear, stick **6** fasten, impale, pierce, thrill **11** transpierce

transform: 4 turn **5** alter **6** change **7** convert **9** transmute **11** transfigure **12** metamorphose, transmogrify

into human form: **16** anthropomorphize

transfuse: 5 imbue **6** infuse **7** instill **8** permeate, transfer, transmit

transgress: err, sin **5** break, cross **6** offend **7** disobey, violate **8** overstep, trespass

transgression: 5 crime, fault **6** breach **7** misdeed **8** trespass **10** infraction **12** infringement **13** contravention

transient: 7 flighty, passing **8** fleeting, fugitive **9** ephemeral, itinerant, migratory, momentary, temporary, transeunt **10** evanescent, shortlived, transitory **11** impermanent

transit: 6 change **7** passage **9** transport **10** conveyance, transition **12** thoroughfare

coach: bus

transition: 5 phase, shift **7** passage **9** metabasis **10** alteration, conversion

transitive: 7 flowing **12** transitional

transitory: 5 brief, fleet **8** caducous, temporal **9** ephemeral, short-term, temporary **10** evanescent

translate: put **4** read, rede **6** change, decode, remove, render **7** convert **8** construe, decipher, entrance, transfer **9** enrapture, interpret **10** paraphrase

translation: 4 pony, trot **7** version **9** rendition **10** paraphrase **14** interpretation **15** transliteration

translucent: 5 clear **6** limpid **7** obvious **9** alabaster **11** perspicuous, transparent

transmigration: 7 samsara

transmit: 4 emit, hand, send **5** carry, relay **6** convey, render **7** conduct, devolve, forward **8** bequeath, dispatch **9** pass along **11** communicate

transmutation: 9 evolution

transom: 5 trave **6** louver, window

transparent: 4 open **5** clear, filmy, frank, gauzy, lucid, plain, sheer **6** candid, limpid, lucent **7** obvious, pelucid **8** luminous, lustrous **9** colorless **10** diaphanous **11** crystalline, perspicuous, translucent **12** clear as glass

transpierce: 6 impale **8** transfix **9** penetrate

transpire: 6 get out, happen, result **9** eventuate

transport: dak **4** bear, boat, buss, haul, move, send, ship, tote **5** bring, carry, ferry, flute, truck **6** banish, convey, deport, ravish **7** convict, ecstasy, emotion, fraught, freight, passion, portage, rapture, smuggle, transit, vehicle **8** entrance, horsecar, overcome, palander, transfer **9** captivate, enrapture, happiness

transportation: *business:* **4** mail **7** air line, express **8** shipping, trucking **9** steamship **11** railroading

transpose: 5 shift **6** change, remove **7** convert, disturb, reverse **8** exchange, transfer **9** rearrange, transform, translate, transmute **11** interchange

transposition: 7 anagram **10** spoonerism **11** permutation

Transvaal: *capital:* **8** Pretoria
city: **12** Johannesburg
goldfield: **13** Witwatersrand
native: **4** Zulu **7** Bushman **9** Hottentot
province of: **11** South Africa (which also see)
resource: **4** gold

transverse: bar, way **4** bank, over, pass, rung, turn **5** argue, cross, pivot, route, shift, trace **6** across, denial, stripe, survey, swivel, thwart, travel **7** barrier, discuss, examine, impeach, oblique, pervade, quarrel **8** diagonal **9** alternate, crossbeam, crosswise **10** crosspiece

Transylvania: *city:* **4** Cluj
fabled resident: **7** Dracula, vampire

trap: bag, get, gin, net, pit **4** cage, lure, nail, snag **5** brake, buggy, catch, goods, mouth, rocks, snare, steps, trick **6** ambush, corner, detect, enmesh **7** capture, cunning, ensnare, luggage, pitfall, springe **8** carriage, confound, covering, deadfall, separate, trapball **9** caparison, detective, policeman, stratagem **10** belongings, stepladder
animal: pot, web **4** weir **5** creel **6** bownet, eelpot **8** deadfall
police: **7** dragnet **9** roadblock

trapdoor: 4 drop, slot

trapes: See **traipse**

trapeze: bar

trapping: 4 gear **5** cloth **7** harness **8** catching, covering, ornament **9** adornment, caparison, coverture **10** decoration **12** accouterment, accoutrement **13** embellishment, paraphernalia
theatrical: **4** prop **7** scenery **8** property

Trappist: 4 monk
cheese: oka
writer: **6** Merton

traps: 5 bells, drums **7** cymbals

trapshooting: 5 skeet
target: **10** clay pigeon

trash: jog, lop **4** bosh, clog, crop, dirt, jade, pelf, plod, raff, tosh **5** leash, money, tramp, waste, wrack **6** bushwa, debris, halter, hinder, rabble, refuse, retard, rubble, trudge **7** baggage, beggary, blather, rubbish **8** encumber, flummery, nonsense, restrain, riffraff, trumpery, vandalize **10** balderdash **11** sleuthhound

trashy: 4 mean **5** cheap **6** common **9** worthless

trauma: 5 shock, wound **6** injury, stress **8** collapse

travail: 4 pain, pang, task, toil, work **5** agony, drive, labor **6** effort, travel **7** journey, torment, trouble **8** exertion **9** suffering **10** birth throe **11** parturition

trave: 9 crossbeam

travel: run **4** fare, move, mush, post, ride, tour, trek, trip, walk, wend **5** coast **6** motion **7** commute, journey, migrate, passage, proceed, sojourn, travail **8** traverse **9** gallivant, itinerate **10** locomotion **11** peregrinate
company: **7** caravan
pert. to: **6** viatic
schedule: **9** itinerary
yen for: **10** wanderlust

traveler: 5 farer, tramp **6** viator **7** drummer, pilgrim, swagman, tourist, voyager **8** salesman, vagabond, wanderer, wayfarer **9** intinerant **12** globe-trotter
aid of: **5** guide **7** courier **8** cicerone
commercial: **5** agent **6** bagman **7** drummer **8** salesman
refuge: inn **5** oasis, motel **7** hospice

travels: 7 odyssey
traverse: 4 deny, ford, pass 5 cross, range, rebut 6 oppose, patrol, refute, swivel, thwart
travesty: 5 mimic 6 parody, satire 8 disguise 9 burlesque, imitation 10 caricature
writer: 8 parodist
trawl: net 4 fish, line 5 seine 7 boulter, dragnet
tray: hod 4 font 6 hurdle, salver, server 7 coaster
treacherous: 5 false, punic, snaky 6 fickle, hollow, tricky 8 disloyal, insecure, plotting, unstable 9 dangerous, faithless, insidious 10 fraudulent, perfidious, precarious, traitorous, unreliable 11 disaffected 12 Machiavelian 13 Machiavellian, untrustworthy
treachery: 5 guile 6 deceit 7 perfidy, treason, untruth 8 betrayal 9 dirty pool 10 infidelity
treacle: 4 cure 5 syrup 6 remedy 7 claggum 8 molasses
treaclewort: 4 herb 10 pennycress
tread: rut 4 gait, mark, pace, rung, step, volt, walk 5 clump, crush, dance, labor, march, press, stair, stamp, trace, track, trail, tramp 6 balter, course, quench, stride, subdue, trapes 7 conquer, repress, traipse, trample 8 copulate, footfall 9 footprint 10 employment, occupation
treadle: 5 pedal 7 chalaza
treason: 7 perfidy 8 betrayal, sedition 9 treachery
treasure: 4 find, plum, roon 5 cache, hoard, pearl, prize, store, trove, value 6 gersum, riches, supply, wealth 7 cherish, finance 8 hold dear 9 thesaurus(L.) 10 appreciate, collection 12 accumulation
Treasure State: 7 Montana
treasured: 4 dear 5 chary 7 precious
treasurer: 7 cashier, curator 8 bhandari, cofferer, deftedar, guardian, receiver 11 chamberlain
college: 6 bursar
treasury: 4 fisc, fund 5 chest, hoard 6 coffer 7 bonanza, bursary, revenue 9 exchequer 10 repository, storehouse
Roman: 6 fiscus
treat: use 4 blow, deal, dose, lead, urge 5 argue, besee, Dutch, feast, guide, serve, stand, touch 6 attend, confer, demean, doctor, govern, handle, parley, regale, regard, repast 7 address, bargain, control, discuss, entreat, expound 8 consider, deal with, delicacy, transact, treatise 9 discourse, entertain, negotiate 10 manipulate
improperly: 4 snub 5 flout, scout, spite 6

ill-use, misuse 8 dishonor
leather: tan, taw 7 chamois
tenderly: 5 spare 6 coddle, pamper
treatise: 5 essay, tract 6 thesis, treaty 7 account, grammar 8 brochure 9 discourse, narration, treatment 10 commentary, discussion, exposition 11 description 12 dissertation
elementary: 6 primer 7 grammar
opening part: 8 exordium
preface: 7 isagoge
treatment: 4 care 5 usage 7 therapy 8 demeanor, entreaty, handling 10 management 13 entertainment
before doctor's arrival: 8 first aid
compassionate: 5 mercy
harsh: 5 abuse 8 misusage, severity
treaty: 4 pact 7 article, concord, entente 8 contract, treatise 9 agreement, discourse 10 convention, discussion 11 arrangement, negotiation 13 understanding
treaty-bound: 6 allied
treble: 4 high 5 acute 6 shrill, triple 7 soprano 9 threefold 11 high-pitched
tree (see also next entry)**:** ach, ber, dal, dao, ebo, elm, fir, hur, iba, kou, lin, mee, oak 4 acle, alan, alof, anam, asak, asok, ates, ausu, bael, biti, bogo, bola, dali, dhak, dita, ipil, mabi, mora, odal, palm, pole, post, ship, toon, trap, wood, yaya 5 areca, asoka, betis, bongo, bulak, bumbo, cacao, carob, catch, cebil, couma, dadap, dalli, fulwa, genip, ligas, mahua, neeba, nepal, niepa, nitta, oodal, rohan, roman, salai, sassy, shaft, shift, siman, sissu, spade, staff, stake, stick, tikur, yacca 6 bahera, banyan, barbas, bariba, brauna, bucare, cativo, cedron, chalta, chogak, chupon, cocuyo, colima, corner, cudgel, design, gibbet, gomart, illupi, jarrah, locust, marane, marara, ramoon, sabino, simaba, sissoo, stemma, tikoor, timber 7 anubing, araraba, arboret, assagai, assegai, azarole, capture, champac, champak, cocullo, dhamnoo, diagram, gallows, guaraba, gumihan, hautboy, hollong, madrona, madrono, malpaho, mambong 8 ahueuete, cockspur, gamdeboo, ironbark, magnolia, mangrove, mokihana, phulwara, seedling, tamarack 9 bandoline, betel-palm, bitanhole, canadulce, couratari, currajong genealogy, sassywood 10 bunyabunya, chaulmugra 11 balinghasay, chaulmaugra, chaulmoogra, guachipilin, hursinghair
alder: arn 5 alnus, birch 12 ament-bearing
algarroba: 5 carob 6 calden
allspice: 7 pimento
apple: 4 sorb

aromatic: **9** sassafras
balsam: fir **9** torchwood
bark: **4** ross, tapa
basswood: **6** linden
bead: nim
bean: **5** sapan
bearing samara: ash
beefwood: **5** belah, belar
betel: **5** areca
bignoniacious: **7** catalpa
blinding sap: **7** alipata
boxwood: **5** seron
breadnut: **6** capomo
buckthorn: **7** cascara
buckwheat: **4** titi **6** teetee
Buddha's: **6** botree
bully: see *gum* below
burned, broken: **7** rampick, rampike
buttonball: **5** plane **8** sycamore
cabbage: **7** angelin
camphor: **5** kapur
candlenut: ama
caoutchouc: ule **6** rubber
caucho-yielding (see also *rubber* below)*:*
    ule
cemetery: yew
chestnut: **10** chinqua pin
chocolate: **5** cacao
cinchona: **7** quinine **9** quinidine
cinnamon family: **6** cassia
citrus: **4** lime **5** lemon **6** orange **8** berga-
    mot **10** calamondin
clump: **4** tump **5** motte
coconut: **4** coco
coffee: **6** chicot
conebearing: fir, yew **4** pine **5** alder, ce-
    dar, larch **6** spruce **7** conifer, cypress,
    hemlock, juniper, redwood **8** gnetales
coral: **6** gabgab
cottonwood: **5** alamo
covering: **4** bark
cranberry: **7** pembina
derivative: **5** pinic
devil: **4** dita
drumstick: **11** canafistolo, canafistula,
    canafistulo
drupe bearing: **4** bito
dwarf: **5** scrub **7** abuscle **10** chinquapin
dwelling: **4** nest
dye yielding: tua, tui **4** mora **7** annatto
    10 hursinghar
ebony: **9** diospyros
elder: **7** trammon
eucalyptus: **4** yati **6** mallee
evergreen: fir, yew **4** pine, tawa, titi **5** car-
    ob, cedar, holly, larch, ocote, olive **6**
    balsam, carobe, cazaba, coigue, tarata **7**
    bebeery, juniper, madrona, madrono,
    taratah
exudation: gum, lac, sap, tar **5** resin, ros-
    in, xylan
fabacious: **5** agati

fiber: **5** bulak, simal, terap **7** bentang
fig family: **4** upas **5** pipal **6** botree **7** gon-
    dang
flowering: **5** agati, elder, sumac, titis **6**
    mimosa, redbud **7** dogwood **8** cleaster,
    oleaster
fodder: **5** mahoe **9** tagasaste
food: **4** akee
fruit: bel, fig, gab **4** gaub, lime **5** araca,
    lemon, mahis, olive, papaw, topes **6** an-
    nona, banana, bearer, biriba, litchi,
    medlar, pawpaw, sapota **7** avocado, cap-
    ulin, genipap, tangelo **8** bakupari, tama-
    rind **9** tangerine **12** custard apple
gaucho: ule
group: **4** bosk **5** copse, grove, woods **6** for-
    est **7** coppice, orchard
grower: **8** arborist
gum: **5** babul, balta **6** balata, sapota, sa-
    pote, tupelo, zapote **8** banildad **9** sapo-
    dilla, sapotilha, sapotilla **10** bansalague,
    eucalyptus
gum genus: **6** owenia
hardwood: **4** poon **5** aalii, gidia, gidya,
    mabee, maple, narra, ngaio **6** gidgea,
    gidgee, gidjee, gidyea, walnut **7** hickory,
    tindalo **8** macaasin, mahogany **9** que-
    bracho
heartwood: **7** duramen
health: **5** briar, brier
hickory: **5** pecan
holly: **4** ilex
honeberry: **5** genip
horseradish: **4** behn **5** behen
jobber: **10** woodpecker
juniper: **4** cade **5** cedar
kino: **4** bija
koranic: **6** zaggum
laurel: bay **7** tarairi
limb: **5** bough **6** branch
lime: lin **5** linn, teil **6** linden **9** tilicetum
linden: **4** lime, teil **8** basswood
locust: **6** acacia **9** courbaril
lotus: sad **6** jujube
mafurra: **6** elcaja
magnolia: **5** yulan
mahogany: **4** toon
maple: **4** acer
margosa: **4** neem
marmalade: **6** mammee, mammey, sapote
medicinal: **5** sumac **6** sumach, wahahe
mimosaceous: **5** siris
monkeybread: **6** baobob
mountain ash: **4** sorb **5** rowan **7** service
mulberry: **5** osage **8** sycamine
nut: **4** cola **5** hazel, pecan, pinon **6** akh-
    rot, chicha **9** almendron, pistachio
nymph turned into: **6** Daphne
oil: **5** mahua, mahwa **9** candlenut
oil-yielding: bel, ben **4** eboe, shea
olive: **4** olea
olive family: ash

palm: tal **4** coco, nipa **5** ratan **6** arengs
paradise: **8** aceituna
part: **4** bark, bole, knot, leaf, root, twig **5** trunk **6** branch
pert. to: **8** arboreal
pine: see *evergreen* above
plane: **8** sycamore **10** buttonwood
plantain: **4** pala
pod-bearing: **7** catalpa
poisonous: **4** upas **5** ligas **7** tanquen
poon: **4** dilo **5** keena
poplar: **5** abele, alamo, aspen, tulip **10** cottonwood
pottery: **7** caraipe, caraipi
rain: **5** saman, zaman **6** zamang **8** genisaro **9** algarroba
rare: **6** Joshua
resin: **4** arar
ribbon: **6** akaroa **7** houhere
rowan: see *mountain ash* above
rubber: ule **4** para **6** caucho **7** seringa **10** caoutchouc
rutaceous: **4** lime
salt: **4** atle **5** atlee
sandarac: **4** arar
sandbox: **6** assacu
science: **7** silvics
shade: ash, elm, oak **5** guama, maple **6** linden, poplar **7** catalpa **8** sycamore
smoke: **6** fustet **9** zante-wood
soft-wood: lin **5** ambay, balsa, linde
sour gum: **5** nyssa **6** tupelo
sprout: **5** sprig **7** sapling
streaked wood: **5** baria
stunted: **5** scrub
tallow: **4** cera
tamarisk: see *salt* above
tea: **6** manuka
teak: **4** teca
thorny: bel **4** bael, bito, brea **7** colorin **9** barriguda **11** chichicaste
timber: ash, dar, eng, koa, saj, sal, yew **4** coco, cuya, ipil, pelu, pine, poon, rata, tala, teak, toon, ulmo **5** acana, almon, amate, balao, balau, bayok, beech, birch, cedar, culla, dalli, ebano, fotui, guijo, icica, kauri, kaury, maple, narra, pekea, penda, rauli, tenio, timbo, uadal, yacal, zorro **6** alerce, alerse, alfaje, ausubo, bacury, banaba, banago, banaki, bancal, banuyo, bataan, batino, dagame, dungon, lanete, molave, satine, totara, walnut **7** batulin, becuiba, billian, camagon, capulin, cypress, gateado, gomavel, guacimo, hapiton, redwood **8** flindosa, flindosy, mahogany, zapetero **9** balaustre, guaraguao **10** batikuling
treatise: **5** silva
tropical genus: **8** bauhinia
trunk: **4** bole **5** shaft
tulip: **6** poplar
Turkey oak: **6** cerris

turpentine: **6** tarata **7** taratah **9** terebinth
walnut see *nut* above: **6** akhrot
wattle: **5** boree
wide-spreading: **5** cedar **7** juniper
willow: **5** osier, saugh **6** poplar
worship: **11** dendrolatry
yellow alder: **8** sagerose
young: **7** sapling
tree: For trees of specific countries or regions, see under that country or region.
tree bear: **7** raccoon
tree runner: **8** nuthatch
tree toad: **4** hyla **6** peeper
treeless: **6** barren
plain: **5** llano, pampa **6** steppe **7** prairie, savanna **8** savannah
treelike: **11** arborescent
treen: **6** wooden
treenail: nog, peg, pin **5** spike **7** trunnel
trefoil: **4** leaf **6** clover
treillage: **5** grill **7** trellis **8** espalier **11** laticework
trek: **4** draw, pull **5** march **6** travel **7** journey, migrate **10** expedition
trellis: **5** bower, cross **7** lattice, pergola **8** espalier **10** interweave **11** latticework
trematode: **8** cercaria, flatworm, parasite
tremble: **5** bever, quake, shake **6** didder, dither, dodder, falter, quaver, quiver, shiver, totter, tremor **7** flacker, flicker, shudder, vibrate **9** trepidate
trembling: **7** fearful, twitter **9** tremulous
tremendous: big **4** huge **5** awful, giant, great, large **7** amazing, fearful **8** dreadful, enormous, great big, horrible, powerful, terrific **9** frightful, momentous, monstrous **10** terrifying **13** extraordinary
tremolo: **6** quaver **7** vibrato
tremor: **5** quake, shake **6** quiver, shiver, thrill **7** tremble **9** vibration **10** earthquake
tremplin: **11** springboard
tremulous: **5** aspen, timid **7** aquiver, fearful, nervous, palsied **8** timorous, unsteady, wavering **9** quavering, sensitive **11** palpitating
trench: cut, gaw **4** bury, gash, moat, sike **5** carve, ditch, drain, fosse, fossa(L.), graff, graft, slash, slice **6** border, furrow, groove, gutter **7** acequia **8** encroach, entrench, infringe **10** excavation
digger: **6** sapper
digging: sap
trenchant: **4** keen **5** acrid, acute, sharp **6** biting, caustic **7** cutting **8** clear-cut, distinct, forceful, incisive, vigorous **9** energetic **11** penetrating
trencher: **5** board, plate **7** platter **9** parasitic **11** sycophantic
trencherman: **7** glutton, gormand, sponger **8** gourmand, hanger-on, parasite **11**

gormandizer **12** gourmandizer

trend: run **4** bend, bent, tone, turn, vein **5** drift, swing, tenor **6** extend, strike **7** fashion, incline **8** movement, tendency **9** direction **11** inclination

trepan: **4** lure, tool, trap **5** snare, trick **6** entrap **7** deceive, ensnare, swindle **9** perforate, stratagem

trepang: **8** teatfish **10** beche-de-mer **22** holothurian-sea-cucumber

trepid: **7** quaking **8** timorous **9** trembling

trepidation: **4** fear **5** alarm, dread **6** dismay, tremor **7** quaking **9** agitation, confusion **11** disturbance **12** perturbation **13** consternation

trespass: sin **5** poach **6** breach, invade, offend **7** intrude **8** encroach, entrench, infringe **9** do wrong by, interlope **10** infraction, transgress **11** misfeasance

tress: **4** curl, hair, lock **5** braid, plait **7** ringlet, wimpler

tressure: **4** band, caul **6** border, fillet, ribbon **9** headdress

trestle: leg **5** bench, horse, stand, stool **6** tripod, trivet **7** support, viaduct **8** sawhorse **9** framework

tret: **9** allowance

trews: **8** breeches, trousers **9** stockings

triad: **5** three, trine **6** triune **7** trinity **9** threesome, trivalent **11** triumvirate

trial: try **4** bout, case, pain, test **5** assay, cross, essay, grief, proof **6** assize, effort, ordeal, sample **7** approof, attempt, calvary, contest, hearing, inquiry **8** crucible, endeavor, evidence, hardship **10** affliction, experience, experiment, tournament, visitation **11** examination, tribulation **13** investigation
and error: **10** experiment
inconclusive: **8** mistrial
pert. to: **7** empiric
scene of: **5** court

trial balloon: **4** kite, test **6** feeler

triangle: **5** delta **6** trigon **7** scalene, trigone **9** isosceles **11** equilateral
draw circle touching: **7** escribe
in heraldry: **5** giron
side: leg **10** hypotenuse
unequal sided: **7** scalene

triangular: **7** cunate, deltoid, hastate **13** three-cornered
piece: **4** gore **5** miter, mitre, wedge **6** gusset
sail: jib **6** lateen **9** spinnaker

triangular muscle: **7** deltoid

triarchy: **11** triumvirate

tribe: (for tribe of specific country see *tribe, native* or *people* under that country) rod **4** band, clan, kind, race, sept **5** class, firca(Ind.), group **6** family **9** community
emblem: **5** totem

head: **5** chief **9** patriarch

tribulation: **5** agony, trial **6** misery, sorrow **8** distress **9** suffering **10** affliction, oppression, wrongdoing **11** persecution

tribunal: bar **4** banc, seat **5** bench, court, forum **7** tribune **8** assembly **10** consistory

tribune: **4** dais **6** throne **8** platform **10** magistrate

tributary: **5** ruler, state **6** feeder **7** subject **9** auxiliary **10** subsidiary **11** subordinate **12** contributory

tribute: fee, tax **4** cain, dues, duty, gift, levy, rent, scat **5** grant **6** assign, eulogy, impost, praise, tariff **7** chevage, ovation, payment, respect **8** encomium **9** attribute, gratitude, laudation, panegyric **10** obligation **11** testimonial

trice: **4** bind, gird, haul, lash, pull **5** jiffy **6** moment, secure **7** instant **9** twinkling

trichome: **4** hair **7** bristle, prickle

trichord: **4** lyre

trick: bob, boy, cog, dor, fob, fox, fub, gag, gum, toy **4** bilk, dupe, feat, flam, fool, gaff, gaud, girl, gull, hoax, jest, joke, prat, ruse, trap, turn, wile **5** catch, child, cully, dodge, feint, fraud, gleek, guile, hocus, knack, prank, shift, skite, spell, stunt **6** begunk, chouse, delude, humbug, palter, trepan, trifle **7** beguile, cantrip, deceive, defraud, finesse, gimmick, pretext, sleight, swindle **8** artifice, flimflam, illusion, maneuver **9** bamboozle, capriccio, chicanery, diablerie, imposture, mannerism, stratagem **10** subterfuge **11** hornswoggle, legerdemain

trickery: art **5** fraud, hocus **6** cautel, deceit, japery **7** knavery, roguery, slyness **8** cheating, trumpery **9** deception, duplicity **10** hanky-panky **11** doublecross

trickle: **4** drip, flow, sipe(Sc.) **5** exude **6** distil **7** distill, dripple

trickster: **5** cheat **6** rascal **7** slicker **8** swindler **9** gyp artist

tricksy: **5** smart, tight **6** spruce **7** evasive, playful, quirksy, roguish **8** prankish, sportive **9** deceiving, deceptive, uncertain **11** embellished, mischievous

tricky: sly **5** dodgy **6** artful, catchy **7** devious **8** delicate, ticklish, unstable **9** deceitful, intricate

tricycle: **6** tricar

trident: **5** spear **7** scepter
bearer: **7** Neptune

tried: **6** ettled(Sc.), proved, select, tested **7** staunch **8** faithful, reliable **9** steadfast **11** trustworthy

trier: **5** judge **7** refiner **8** examiner, renderer **12** experimenter, investigator

trifle: bit, fig, rap, sou, toy **4** bean, doit,

fike, hint, jest, mock, mote, play **5** dally, flirt, straw, trick, use up, waste **6** bauble, burn up, coquet, dabble, dawdle, delude, dibble, doodle, fiddle, fidget, footer, footle, frivol, gewgaw, misuse, potter **7** deceive, dessert, fribble, nothing, traneen **8** flimflam, gimcrack, raillery **9** bagatelle **10** equivocate, knick-knack, triviality

trifling: 4 airy, idle, mere **5** banal, inane, petty **6** futile, little **7** shallow, wasting **8** badinage, frippery **9** dalliance, small talk **10** immaterial **11** unimportant **13** insignificant

trifolium: 6 clover **8** shamrock

trig: run **4** chic, cram, deck, fill, firm, full, line, neat, prim, prop, stop, tidy, trim, trot **5** brisk, dandy, natty, smart, sound, stiff, stone, stuff, wedge **6** active, lively, spruce, steady, strong, trench **7** distend, foppish, precise, stylish, support **10** methodical

triggerman: gun **6** hit man **8** assassin

trigo: 5 wheat

trigon: 4 harp, lyre **5** trine **8** triangle

trigonometry function: 4 sine **6** cosine, secant **7** tangent

Trilby: *author:* **9** du Maurier
character: **8** Svengali

trill: 4 drip, flow, move, turn **5** shake, twirl **6** gruppo, quaver, quiver, warble **7** mordent, trickle, vibrate

trim: bob, cut, gay, lop **4** beat, chic, clip, crop, deft, dink, edge, fine, firm, neat, nice, snod(Sc.), snug, tidy, trig, whip **5** adorn, braid, cheat, chide, dress, equip, fitty, natty, nifty, order, preen, prune, ready, shave, shear, whack **6** adjust, dapper, defeat, modify, petite, punish, spruce, thrash **7** balance, compact, defraud, furnish, orderly, shapely **8** chastise, decorate, ornament, pleasant, tailored **9** condition, embellish, excellent, shipshape **10** commission, compromise **11** disposition
a tree: **5** prune **7** pollard
coin: nig
dress: **4** gimp **5** ruche **6** sequin
lace: **5** jabot **6** ruffle

trimmer: 5 finer

trimming: 4 gimp, lace **5** braid, ruche **6** frieze, fringe, piping **7** falbala, ruching **8** furbelow, ornament, rick-rack **9** garniture **10** decoration **13** passementerie

trindle: 4 roll **5** wheel **7** trundle

trine: 4 hang **5** march, triad **6** trigon, trinal, triple, triune **7** Trinity **9** favorable, threefold **10** auspicious

Trinidad-Tobago: *capital:* **11** Port-of-Spain
gulf: **5** Paria
music: **7** calypso, goombay

point: **6** Galera
seaport: **11** San Fernando

trinitrotoluene: TNT **6** trotyl **13** high explosive

trinity: 5 three, triad **6** triune **9** threeness **10** spiderwort

trinket: 4 bead, gaud, ring **5** bijou, jewel **6** bangle, bauble, gewgaw, tinsel, trifle **7** bibelot **8** gimcrack, intrigue, ornament **9** plaything, showpiece **10** knick-knack

trio: 5 triad **9** threesome

trip: run **4** gait, halt, hike, pawl, skip, slip, spin, tour **5** brood, caper, catch, danse, drive, error, flock, jaunt, lapse, tread, wedge **6** cruise, error, falter, voyage **7** blunder, failure, journey, misstep, mistake, release, stumble **8** obstruct **9** excursion **10** expedition

tripe: 5 trash **7** rubbish **8** nonsense

triple: 5 triad, trine **6** treble **9** threefold

triplet: 4 trin, trio

tripletail: 9 berrugate, spadefish

triplicate: 6 treble, triple **9** threefold

tripod: cat **5** easel, stand **6** trivet

Tripoli ruler: dey

trippet: cam

tripping: 5 quick **6** nimble **7** walking

triptych: 7 picture **10** altarpiece
wing: **5** volet

trismus: 7 lockjaw, tetanus

Tristram, Tristan: *beloved:* **5** Isolt **6** Iseult, Isolde
uncle: **4** Mark
villain: **5** Melot

Tristram Shandy author: 6 Sterne

triste: sad **4** dull **6** dismal **8** mournful **9** sorrowful **10** depressing, melancholy

trite: 4 dull, flat, hack, worn **5** banal, corny, stale, vapid **6** common, jejune, old hat **7** bromide, trivial **9** hackneyed **10** threadbare, unoriginal, warmed-over **11** commonplace, stereotyped **12** conventional **13** platitudinous

trite expression: 6 cliche **7** bromide

triton: eft **4** newt **7** demigod **10** salamander

triturate: rub **5** crush, grind **6** bruise **9** comminute, pulverize

triumph: win **4** gain **5** exult, glory **6** defeat, hurrah **7** conquer, prevail, rejoice, success, victory **8** flourish **10** exultation **11** achievement, celebration

triumvirate: 5 junta **6** troika
first: **6** Caesar, Pompey **7** Crassus
second: **6** Antony **7** Lepidus **8** Octavius

trivet: 4 rack **5** stand **6** tripod **7** support

trivial: 5 banal, fluff, inane, petty, small, trite **6** common, little, paltry, slight **7** nominal, piperly **8** doggerel, ordinary, trifling **9** frivolous **10** negligible **11** unimportant **13** insignificant, no great shakes **14** inconsiderable

troche: **4** pill **6** pastil, rotula, tablet **7** lozenge, pastile **8** pastille **9** small ball

trochilus: **7** warbler **9** goldcrest **11** hummingbird

trod: **4** path, walk **5** trace, track, tread **8** footpath, footstep

trogon: **4** bird **7** quetzal

troika: **5** triad **8** carriage **11** triumvirate

Troilus: *beloved:* **8** Cressida

  father: **5** Priam

  mother: **6** Hecuba

  slayer: **8** Achilles

Trojan: **9** Dardanian

  epic: **5** Iliad

  king: **5** Priam

  prince: **5** Eneas, Paris **6** Aeneas, Hector

  prisoner: **5** Sinon

  serpent victim: **7** Laocoon

  soothsayer: **7** Helenus **9** Cassandra

Trojan horse: **4** ruse, trap **6** ambush **8** saboteur **10** subversive

  builder: **5** Epeus

Trojan War: *cause:* **5** Helen

  hero: **4** Ajax **5** Eneas **6** Aeneas, Agenor, Hector **9** Agamemnon, Palamedes

troll: run, wag **4** bowl, fish, lure, reel, roll, sing, song, turn **5** angle, catch, chant, dwarf, giant, gnome, round, spoon **6** trolly **7** revolve, trolley, trollop **9** circulate

trolley: car **4** cart, tram **5** block **6** barrow, sledge **8** handcart **9** streetcar

trollop: **4** hang **5** slump **6** dangle, slouch, wanton **8** slattern **10** bedraggled, prostitute

trombone: **7** sackbut

trommel: **5** sieve **6** screen

troop: lot **4** army, band, ging, line, rout, walk, wave **5** crowd, group **6** number, troupe **7** battery, cavalry, company, echelon, militia, phalanx **8** quantity, soldiers **9** associate, gathering **10** combatants, congregate **11** armed forces

  Anglo-Indian: **6** risala **7** ressala, risalah

  arrangement: **7** echelon

  assembling: **6** muster

  concealed: **6** ambush

  German: **6** Panzer

  quarters: **4** camp **5** etape **8** barracks

  raise: **4** levy **5** draft **9** conscript

  sellers to: **6** sutler **10** vivandiere

trooper: **6** hussar **7** soldier **9** policeman, troopship **10** cavalryman

trop: too **4** many

trope: **5** irony **6** simile **8** metaphor

trophy: cup **4** palm **5** prize **6** laurel, reward **7** memento **8** memorial, ornament **11** remembrance

tropic: **5** limit **8** boundary

tropical: hot **6** steamy, torrid

  animal: **4** alco, eyra **5** agama, coati, potto

6 agouti, iguana **7** peccary

  bird: ani **4** tody **5** jalap **7** jacamar

  fish: **4** toro **6** salema **7** squetee

  fruit: **4** date **5** guava, mango, papaw **6** banana, papaya **8** tamarind

  genus of herb: **4** evea, sida **5** tacca, urena **8** laportea

  helmet: **4** topi

  plant: dal **4** aloe, arum, sida, taro **5** agave **6** alacad **7** cowhage, lantana **8** gardenia

  plant genus: **5** rhoeo **6** cannas **7** bomarea, geonoma, hamelia

  storm: **7** typhoon

  tree: ebo **4** ceba, coco, dali, eboe, etua, guao, mabi, palm **5** acapu, amate, artar, assai, balsa, banak, bongo, cacao, dalli, guama, guava, icica, nepal, nitta, njave, papaw, seron, zorro **6** baboen, bacury, banana, barbas, cazaba, chupon, dagame, espave, mammee, pawpaw, sapota **7** anubing, gateado, guacimo **8** amarillo, mangrove, sweetsop, tamarind **9** huamuchli, quebracho, sapodilla, sapotilha, sapotilla **10** frangipane, frangipani, manchineel **11** guachipilin

trot: hag, jog, run, tot **4** gait, pony **5** child, hurry **6** hasten **7** toddler **11** translation

trot out: **4** show **6** expose **7** display, show off

troth: **5** certy, faith **6** certie, pledge **8** fidelity **9** betrothal **10** engagement

trottoir: **8** footpath, pavement, sidewalk

troubadour, troubador: **4** bard, poet **6** rhymer, singer **8** minstrel, musician

trouble: ado, ail, irk, try, vex, woe **4** busy, care, cark, fike, fuss, harm, pain, sore, stir **5** anger, annoy, grief, labor, tease, upset, worry **6** bother, burble, caddle, cumber, dither, effort, harass, impair, matter, mishap, molest, pester, plague, pother, sorrow, unrest **7** afflict, agitate, anxiety, chagrin, concern, disease, disturb, embroil, illness, perturb, travail **8** aggrieve, calamity, disorder, disquiet, distress, exertion **9** adversity, incommode, interfere **10** difficulty, disarrange, discomfort, discommode, misfortune, perplexity, uneasiness **11** displeasure, encumbrance **13** inconvenience

troubled: **6** queasy **10** distraught **12** heart-scalded

troublemaker: **6** gossip **8** agitator, bad actor

troublesome: **4** mean, ugly **5** pesky **6** wicked **8** fashious **9** pestilent, turbulent, wearisome **10** burdensome, oppressive

troublous: **6** stormy, turbid **7** unquiet **8** restless **9** unsettled

trough: bin **4** bosh, bowl, dale, tank, tomb **5** bakie, basin, chute **6** buddle, coffin, dugout, gutter, sluice **7** channel, conduit

between waves: **6** valley

inclined: **5** chute

trounce: sue **4** beat, flog, whip **5** scold, tramp **6** cudgel, defeat, indict, punish, ramble, thrash **7** censure, journey **11** walk all over

troupe: **4** band **5** group **7** company **9** cuadrilla(Sp.)

trouper: **5** actor **11** entertainer

troupial: **6** oriole **7** cacique, cowbird **9** blackbird **10** meadowlark

trousers: **5** pants **6** skilts, slacks **8** breeches, culottes **9** pantalets, shintiyan **10** pantaloons

foreign: **7** shalwar **9** shaksheer, shulwaurs **10** calzoneras(Sp.)

trout: sea **4** char, peal **5** brook, brown, river, sewen **6** finnac, grilse **7** gilaroo, rainbow **8** finnacle, speckled **9** steelhead **10** squeteague

lake: **9** namaycush

trovatore: **10** troubadour

trove: **9** discovery **12** accumulation

trow: **4** boat, hope **5** faith, fancy, smack, think, troll, trust **6** belief, expect **7** believe, imagine, suppose **8** covenant **9** catamaran

Troy (see also **Trojan, Trojan horse, Trojan War**): **5** Iliac, Ilian, Ilion, Ilium, Troad, Troas **8** Teucrian

defender: **6** Aeneas

excavator: **10** Schliemann

founder: **4** Ilus, Tros

king: **5** Priam

mountain: Ida

pert. to: **5** Iliac **6** Trojan

region: **5** Troad

troy weight: **5** grain, ounce, pound **11** pennyweight

truant: **4** idle **5** stray **6** beggar, errant **7** shirker, vagrant **8** straying, vagabond, wanderer **9** shiftless

play: **5** miche

truce: **5** pause, treve(F.) **7** respite **9** armistice, cease-fire, cessation **12** intermission

truck: van **4** deal, dray **5** lorry, trade, trash **6** barrow, barter, camion, peddle, potter **7** bargain, rubbish, traffic, trundle **8** business, commerce, exchange, handcart **9** negotiate, transport, vegetable **10** handbarrow **11** association, intercourse

with trailer: **4** semi

truckle: **4** fawn **5** toady, wheel **6** caster, cheese, cringe, submit **7** trundle **8** bootlick **11** apple-polish **12** knuckle under

truckling: **7** servile

truculent: **4** mean, rude **5** cruel, harsh **6** fierce, savage **7** abusive **8** ruthless,

scathing **9** barbarous, ferocious **11** belligerent, destructive

trudge: pad **4** plod, slog, trek, walk **5** stoge, tramp **6** trapes **7** traipse

true: **4** just, leal(Sc.), pure, real, vera(L.), vrai(F.) **5** align, aline, exact, level, loyal, plumb, right, valid **6** actual, adjust, honest, lawful, proper, steady **7** certain, correct, devoted, factual, genuine, germane, precise, sincere, staunch, upright **8** accurate, bonafide, constant, faithful, reliable, unerring, virtuous **9** authentic, steadfast, truepenny, unfeigned, veracious, veritable **10** legitimate **11** unfaltering

true blue: **5** loyal **7** staunch **8** faithful

truelove: **10** girl friend, sweetheart

truffle: **5** tuber **8** earthnut

truism: **5** axiom, maxim **8** veracity **11** commonplace

Truk island: Tol **4** Moen, Udot, Uman **6** Dublon

trull: **4** dell, girl, lass **5** demon, fiend, giant, wench **6** blowze, callet, wanton **7** trollop **8** strumpet **10** prostitute

truly: **4** iwis, very, well **6** atweel, dinkum, indeed, verily **13** realistically

trump: cap, pam **4** beat, ruff **5** outdo, pedro **7** nonplus, surpass **8** jew's-harp

trumpery: **5** fraud, showy, trash, weeds **6** deceit, paltry **7** rubbish **8** gimcrack, nonsense, trickery **9** worthless

trumpet: **4** horn, tout **5** blare **6** bucina(L.), funnel, kerana, summon **7** begonia, clarion, publish **8** denounce, proclaim

belt: **7** baldric

blare: **6** sennet **7** fanfare, tantara

caller: **7** Gabriel

muffler: **4** mute

ram's horn: **6** shofar

stage direction: **6** sennet

trumpet creeper: **5** plant **6** tecoma

trumpet shell: **6** triton

trumpeter: **4** bird, swan **6** herald, pigeon, tooter **7** yakamik

truncate: cut, lop, top **6** lessen **7** shorten **10** abbreviate

truncheon: **4** club, stem **5** baton, staff **6** cudgel **8** fragment, splinter **9** billy club **10** nightstick

trundle: bed **4** bowl, cart, hoop, roll **5** truck, twirl, wheel, whirl **6** barrow, caster, pinion, rotate **7** revolve **11** wheelbarrow

trunk: box **4** body, bole, pipe, runt, stem, tank, tube **5** chest, snout, stock, torso **6** caudex, coffer, corpse, thorax **7** baggage, carcass **9** proboscis

animal: **4** soma **5** torso, snout

truss: tie, wap **4** bind, furl, gird, hang, lade, pack **6** bundle, fasten **7** arrange, bracket, enclose, package, support, tighten **10** strengthen

trust: 4 affy, care, duty, hope, task **5** faith **6** belief, cartel, charge, credit, depend, merger, rely on **7** believe, confide, consign, custody, keeping, loyalty **8** affiance, commenda, credence, reliance, security **9** assurance, coalition, fiduciary, syndicate **10** commission, confidence **11** combination

trustee: 6 bailee **7** sindico **8** director, guardian **9** fiduciary, garnishee **13** administrator

trustful: 7 devoted **9** confiding **13** unquestioning

trustworthy: 4 safe, true **5** siker, solid, tried **6** honest, sicker **7** certain **8** credible, fiducial, reliable **9** authentic, confiding **10** dependable **12** confidential

trusty: 8 faithful **9** confiding **12** tried and true

truth: 4 fact **5** sooth, troth **6** certes, verity **7** honesty, loyalty **8** accuracy, fidelity, veracity **9** agreement, constancy, integrity, principle, sincerity, veracity **11** correctness, genuineness, uprightness **12** faithfulness **14** verisimilitude
goddess: **4** Maat
personification of: Una
seeming: **14** verisimilitude
self-evident: **5** axiom **6** truism

truthful: 6 honest **7** correct **9** veracious, veridical

try: 4 cull, sift, test **5** annoy, assay, essay, ettle(Sc.), fling, found, prove, trial **6** choose, effort, hansel, harass, purify, refine, render, sample, screen, select, strain, strive **7** adjudge, afflict, approve, attempt, contest, extract, handsel, subject, torment, venture **8** audition, endeavor, irritate, separate, struggle **9** ascertain, undertake **10** experience, experiment **11** demonstrate, investigate

trying: 5 tight **6** severe **7** irksome, onerous, painful **8** annoying **12** exasperating

tryst: 4 fair **5** visit **6** market **7** bespeak, meeting **9** agreement, gathering **10** engagement, rendezvous **11** appointment, assignation

tsar: 4 czar, Ivan, tzar **5** Peter **6** despot **8** autocrat

tsetse fly: 4 kivu **6** muscid **8** glossina

tsine: 6 wild ox **7** banteng

tuatara, tuatera: 6 iguana, lizard

tub (see also **barrel, cistern, vat, vessel**): box, kid, soe, vat **4** bath, boat, cask, cool, ship, tram **5** barge, bathe, bowie(Sc.), eshin, fatty, keeve, skeel **6** bucket, pulpit, vessel **7** bathtub, cistern, tubfish **9** container

wooden: soe

tuba: 7 helicon
mouthpice: **5** bocal

tubal: 8 pipelike

Tubalcain's father: 6 Lamech

Tubal's father: 7 Japheth

tubber: 6 cooper, pickax

tubby: 5 plump, squat **6** chubby, portly, rotund

tube: 4 duct, hose, lull, pipe **5** chute, diode **6** cannon, siphon, tremie, triode, tunnel **7** cannula, conduit, fistula, pipette, tetrode **8** adjutage, bombilla(Sp.), cylinder **9** telescope
anatomical: **7** salpinx
flexible: **4** hose
for winding silk: cop
glass: **6** sipper **7** pipette
remove by: **6** siphon, syphon
system of: **6** pipage
underground: **6** subway, tunnel

tuber: oca, yam **4** beet, bulb, clog, eddo, root, taro, yamp **5** jalap, salep **6** potato **8** swelling **9** tubercule **10** tuberosity **12** protuberance
orchid: **5** salep

tubercle: 6 nodule **10** prominence

tuberculosis: 8 phthisis **11** consumption

Tubuai island: 4 Rapa **6** Rurutu **8** Rimatara

tubular: 4 pipy **5** round **11** cylindrical

tuck: eat, nip **4** draw, fold, hang, poke **5** cramp, feast, pinch, scold, stuff, sword **6** energy, gather, hamper, rapier **7** consume, shorten, tighten

tucked up: 7 cramped, worn out **8** hampered **9** exhausted

tucker: bib **4** food, meal, tire, wilt **5** board, weary **6** ration **7** fatigue **10** chemisette

Tuesday: 5 mardi(F.)
god of: Tiu, Tyr
Shrove: **9** Mardi Gras

tuft: 4 beat, coma, disk **5** beard, bunch, clump, crest, mound **6** button, comose, dollop, goatee, pompon, tassel **7** cluster, fetlock, scopula **8** imperial
of feathers: **7** panache
of hair: **4** tate
ornamental: **6** pompon
vascular: **6** glomus

tuft-hunter: 4 snob

tug: lug, tit, tow **4** drag, draw, haul, maul, pull, rope, toil, yank **5** chain, exert, hitch, labor, strap, trace **6** drudge, effort, strain, strife, strive, tussle **7** contend, contest, tugboat, wrestle **8** struggle **11** counterpull

tuition: 4 care **5** watch **6** charge **7** custody **8** teaching **10** protection **11** instruction **12** guardianship

tule: 7 bulrush

tumble: 4 fall, leap, roll, trip, veer 5 pitch, slope, spill, whirl 6 happen, rumple, spring, tousle 7 clutter, plummet, stumble 8 collapse, discover, dishevel, disorder 9 confusion, overthrow 10 disarrange, handspring, somersault 11 precipitate
down: 10 dilapidate
tumbler: dog 4 cart, pupa 5 glass 6 dunker, pigeon, roller, vessel 7 acrobat, gymnast, tippler, tumbrel
tumbrel, tumbril: 4 cart 5 wagon 8 dumpcart
tumefy: 4 puff 5 swell 7 inflate
tumid: 6 turgid 7 bloated, bulging, fustian, pompous, swollen, teeming 8 bursting, enlarged, inflated 9 bombastic, distended, plethoric, 10 rhetorical 11 protuberant
tumor: wen 4 beal, wart 5 edema, gumma 6 ambury, anbury, glioma, lipoma 7 bombast 8 blastoma, ganglion, hepatoma, neoplasm, papiloma, sarocele, swelling 10 distending 12 adamantinoma, protuberance
benign: 7 fibroid, fibroma
brain: 6 glioma
hard: 8 scirrhus
operation: 8 ancotomy
small: wen 7 papilla
soft: 5 gumma
study of: 8 oncology
tumult: din, mob 4 fray, fuss, riot 5 babel, brawl, broil, noise 6 affray, babble, bedlam, bustle, dirdum(Sc.), emeute, hubbub, uproar 7 bluster, bobbery, ferment, tempest, turmoil 8 disorder, outbreak, outburst, paroxysm, uprising 9 agitation, commotion, confusion, distemper, hurlement, maelstrom 10 convulsion, excitement, hullabaloo, turbulence 11 disturbance
tumultuous: 4 high, wild 5 rough 6 stormy 7 furious, violent 9 termagant, turbulent 10 boisterous, hurly-burly
tumulus: 4 tump 5 mound 6 barrow 7 hillock
tun: cup, jar, tub, vat 4 cask 5 drink 6 barrel, guzzle, vessel 7 chimney
tuna: 8 albacore, skipjack 11 prickly pear
tune: air, fix, key, pat 4 lilt, port, song, tone 5 dirge, drant, sound 6 choral, draunt, melody, string 7 chorale, concord, harmony, sonance 8 anglaise, regulate 9 agreement 10 adjustment
in: 4 dial
out: 6 detune
tuneful: 7 musical, tunable 9 melodious 10 concordant, euphonious, harmonious
tungsten 7 wolfram 8 scheelin
alloy: 8 carboloy

tunic: 4 coat, jamah, jupe, robe, toga, vest 5 acton, frock, gippo, jamah 6 kirtle 8 colobium 10 cote-hardie, sticharion 11 houppelande
tunicate: 4 salp 5 salpa 12 marine animal
Tunisia: *cape:* bon
capital: 5 Tunis
gulf: 5 Gabes, Tunis 8 Hammamet
island: 6 Djerba
lake: 7 Bizerte 10 Sida al-Hani
measure: saa, sah 4 saah 5 cafiz, whiba 6 mettar 9 millerole
mettar 9 millerole
monetary unit: 5 dinar
mountain range: 5 Atlas
river: 8 Medjerda
ruins: 8 Carthage
ruler: bey, dey
town: 4 Sfax 6 Sousse 7 Bizerte 8 Kairouan
weight: saa 4 rotl 5 artal, artel, ratel, uckia 6 kantar
tunk: rap, tap 5 thump
tunnel: net 4 adit, bore, flue, tube 6 burrow, funnel 10 smokestack
long: 5 Otira 6 Hoosac, Severn, Spiral 7 Arlberg, Detroit, Holland, Lincoln, Mont D'Or, St. Clair, Simplon 8 Gotthard, Gunnison 9 Baltimore, Cascade Mt., Connaught, Gallitzin, Montcenis, Mt. Roberts 10 Bitterroot, Cumberland, Lotschberg, St. Gotthard, Wasserfluh 11 Busk-Ivanhoe, Loetschberg, Trans-Andine
tunny: 4 tuna 7 bluefin 8 albacore
tupelo: gum 4 tree 5 nyssa
tur: pea 4 goat
turban: cap, fez, hat 4 pata 5 scarf 6 fillet, mandil 7 bandana 9 headdress
turbid: 4 dark, dull 5 dense, gumly(Sc.), muddy, riley, roily, thick 6 cloudy, grumly(Sc.), impure 7 muddled, obscure 8 confused, polluted 9 perplexed
render: 4 roil
turbine: 6 engine
part: 6 stator
wheel: 5 rotor
turbot: 5 brill 8 flatfish
turbulence: 4 fury 5 babel, fight 6 fracas, tumult, uproar 7 bluster, ferment, rioting 8 disorder 9 agitation, commotion 11 disturbance, pandemonium
turbulent: 4 wild 5 rough 6 stormy, unruly 7 furious, violent 9 clamorous 10 boisterous, rip-roaring, tumultuous 11 tempestuous
turdine bird: 6 thrush
turf: sod 4 area, flag, peat, vell 5 divot, grass, sward 6 region, sphere 7 terrain
Turgenev character: 5 Elena
turgid: 5 tumid 7 bloated, pompous, swollen, turgent 8 inflated, swelling 9 bom-

bastic, distended, flatulent, grandiose, tumescent **10** rhetorical **12** magniloquent **12** grandiloquent
Turk: aga **5** Tatar **7** Osmanli, Ottoman **9** Kizilbash
Turkestan: See **Turkistan**
turkey: tom **4** flop **5** poult **7** bustard, failure, gobbler
 buzzard: **7** vulture
 young: **5** poult
Turkey: *agent:* **6** Kehaya
 army corps: **4** ordu **8** seraglio
 army regiment: **4** alai
 bath: **6** hamman
 boat: **4** sail **6** mahone
 cabinet: **5** divan
 camp: **7** palanka
 cap: **6** calpac
 capital: **6** Ankara
 cavalryman: **5** spahi **6** spahee
 chief (see also *ruler* below): aga **6** kehaya **7** chambul
 city: bir **4** Homs, Sert, Urfa **5** Adana, Bursa, Izmir, Konya, Siirt, Sivas **6** Aintab, Edessa, Edirne, Elaziz, Marash, Samsun, Smyrna **7** Broussa, Erzurum, Kayseri, Scutari, Skutari, Uskudar **8** Istanbul, Stamboul **9** Eskisehir **10** Adrianople, Diyarbekir
 coin: (see *money* below)
 commander: **4** amir, emir **5** ameer, emeer, pacha, pasha **6** sirdar **9** seraskier
 council: **5** divan, diwan
 court: **5** porte
 decree: **5** irade **11** hatti-sherif **12** hatti-humaiun, hatti-humayum
 deputy: **6** kahaya
 dignitary: **5** pasha
 district: **4** Pera **7** Beyoglu, Cilicia
 division: **4** caza **5** adana **6** eyalet **7** vilayet **8** villayet
 drink: **5** airan
 dynasty: **6** seljuk
 empire: **7** Ottoman
 fig: **5** eleme, elemi
 flag: **4** alem, toug **9** horsetail
 general: **5** kamal
 gold coin: **4** lira **6** mahbub
 gulf: Cos **7** Antalya
 hat: fez **6** calpac
 infidel: **6** giaour
 inn: **6** imaret **7** cafenet
 javelin: **5** jerid **6** jeered
 judge: **4** cadi
 liquor: **4** raki **5** rakee **6** mastic
 man-of-war: **6** carvel **7** caravel **9** caravelle
 measures: dra, oka, oke, pic, pik **4** alma, draa, hatt, khat, kile, zira **5** almud, berri, donum, kileh, zirai **6** almude, arshin, chinik, djerib, fotin, halebi, parmak **7** arsheen, arshine, nocktat, parmack **9** pik halebi

 military camp: **4** ordu
 military rank: **6** chiaus **7** chaoush **8** bimbashi, binbashi
 minister: **5** vizir **6** vizier
 money: **4** lira, lire, para **5** akcha, asper, atun, pound, rebia **6** akcheh, sequin, zequin **7** altilik, beshlik, chequin, chiquin, pataque, piaster **8** medjidie, zecchino **9** medjidieh
 mosque: **4** jami
 mountain: **6** Ararat
 mountain range: **6** Taurus
 musical instrument: **5** canum, kanum **7** kussier
 musket: **8** tophaike
 oak: **6** cerris
 official: **4** amir, emir **5** ameer, emeer **6** vizier **7** osmanli, subashi **8** subbassa
 palace: **5** serai
 policeman: **7** zaptiah, zaptieh
 prayer rug: **5** kulah, melas, meles
 province: **4** Sert **5** Bursa, Siirt **6** Angora, Eyalet
 religious war: **11** crescentade
 reservist: **5** redif
 river: Gok **5** Mesta, Sarus **6** Delice, Seihun, Seyhan, Tigris **7** Maritsa
 rug: **5** riconia **6** Smyrna **9** Kurdistan (see also **Oriental rug**)
 ruler: bey, dey **4** khan **5** mudir **6** sultan **7** chambul **9** president
 saber: **6** odolus
 sailor: **8** galionji **9** galiongee
 seaport: **4** Enos
 slave: **8** mameluke
 soldier: **6** nizami **8** janizary **9** janissary **11** bashi-bazouk
 statue: **8** tanzimat
 storage place: **5** ambar
 sultan: Ali **5** Ahmed, calif, Selim **6** caliph **7** Ilderim, Saladin
 sword: **7** yatagan **8** yataghan
 tambourine: **5** daira
 tax: **5** vergi **6** caphar, avania
 title: ali **4** amir, baba **5** ameer, basha, pasha **6** bashaw **7** effendi
 tobacco: **7** chibouk, Latakia **9** chibouque
 treasurer: **8** deftedar
 tribe: **4** Kurd
 veil: **7** yashmac, yashmak **8** maharmah
 weight: oka, oke **4** dram, kile, ocha, rotl **5** artal, artel, cequi, cheke, kerat, kileh, maund, obolu, ratel **6** batman, dirhem, kantar, miskal **7** drachma, quintal, yusdrum
 wheat: **6** bulgar
 woman's clothing: **6** jelick **8** charshaf
turkey buzzard: **4** aura **9** gallinazo
Turkish: **7** Osmanli
 toweling: **10** terrycloth
Turkistan: *cities:* **6** Kokand **7** Andijan, Bukhara **8** Tashkent **9** Samarkand

highland: **6** Pamirs
land: **5** takyr
moslem: **5** salar
mountain: **4** Alai
peoples: **4** Sart **5** Tatar, Uigur, Usbeg, Usbek, Uzbeg, Yakut **6** Tartan
regiment: **4** alai
river: Ili
salt lake: **4** Shov
sea: **4** Aral
Turkmen: *capital:* **9** Ashkhabad
carpet: **5** Tekke, Yomud **6** Afghan **7** Bokhara
tribe: **5** Ersar **7** Viddhal
turmeric: rea **4** herb **5** spice **7** curcuma **9** bloodroot
turmoil: ado, din **4** hurl, toil, toss **5** hurly, labor, touse, upset, worry **6** harass, tumult, unrest, uproar, welter **7** ferment, quarrel, tempest, trouble **8** disquiet, drudgery **9** agitation, commotion, confusion **10** turbulence **11** disturbance **12** perturbation
turn: bow, lap, rev **4** airt, bend, bent, bout, cant, char, head, plow, roll, slew, slue, spin, veer, vert **5** alter, avert, cramp, crook, curve, hinge, pivot, quirk, screw, shunt, spell, tarve, upset, wheel, whirl, whorl **6** bought, change, curdle, direct, divert, gyrate, invert, ponder, rotate, sprain, swerve, swivel, wimple(Sc.), zigzag **7** convert, derange, ferment, meander, rebound, reverse, revolve **8** exchange, nauseate, persuade **9** cinclamen, influence, pirouette, transform, translate **11** disposition **12** metamorphose
about: **9** alternate
another way: **6** obvert
inside out: **5** evert **6** invert
inward: **9** introvert
left: haw **4** port, wynd, wyne
outward: **5** evert, splay **8** extrorse **9** extrovert
rapidly: **4** spin **5** twirl, whirl
right: gee **9** starboard
sour: **5** blink, spoil **8** acescent
to one side: **4** awry, skew
to stone: **8** lapidify
turn around: **4** gyre, slue, spin **9** about-face, volte-face
turn aside: **4** skew, veer **5** shunt **6** detour, divert, swerve
turn away: shy **5** avert, avoid, deter, evade, repel, shunt **6** depart, desert, divert **7** abandon, decline, deflect, deviate, dismiss, diverge, swerve
turn back: **4** fold **5** repel **6** return, revert **7** evolute, retrace **9** inversion **10** recrudesce, retroverse
turn down: **4** fold, veto **6** invert, refuse, reject **7** decline **9** repudiate

turn in: **5** rat on **6** betray, retire **7** deliver, produce **8** hand over, inform on
turn off: **4** hang **5** marry, shunt **6** detour, divert **7** consign, deflect, dismiss, putrefy **9** discharge
turn out: **4** bear, oust, trig **5** array, evert, expel, prove **6** outfit, output, siding **7** abandon, costume, dismiss, produce, reverse, striker **8** equipage, withdraw **9** discharge, equipment, eventuate **12** lose interest
turn over: **4** keel **5** spill, upset **6** invert, ponder, reform **7** evolute **8** delegate, overturn, transfer **10** relinquish
turn up: **6** appear, arrive
turnabout: **8** reversal **9** about-face, volte-face
turncoat: **8** apostate, renegade **10** changeling
turned up: **9** retrousse
turner: **7** gymnast, tumbler
turning point: **6** crisis **8** decision, juncture, landmark
turnip: **4** neep(Sc.) **5** dunce, watch **8** rutabaga **9** blockhead
turnip-shaped: **8** napiform
turnkey: **5** screw **6** jailer, warder
turnover: **4** tart **7** shake-up
turnpike: **4** road **7** highway **8** tollgate
gatekeeper: **7** pikeman
turnstile: **4** tirl **5** stile
turnstone: **4** bird **6** pover, redleg
turpentine: **4** thus **5** resin, rosin **7** galipot **9** oleoresin
residue: **5** resin, rosin
tree: **4** pine **6** tarata **9** terebinth
turpitude: **6** fedity **8** baseness, vileness **9** depravity
turquoise: **5** color, stone **10** chalchuite **12** greenish-blue
turret: **5** tower **8** gunhouse, turricle
turtle: **5** arrau, caret, torup **6** cooter, emydea, jurara **7** snapper **8** chelonia, matamata, shagtail, terrapin, tortoise **10** loggerhead, thalassian **11** leatherback
genus of: **4** emys **7** caretta, testudo **9** chelodina
giant: **5** arrau
part: **7** calipee
shell: **8** carapace
Tuscany: *city:* **4** Pisa **8** Florence
commune: **5** Greve
island: **4** Elba
river: **4** Arno
wine: **7** chianti
tusk: **4** fang **5** ivory, tooth **9** scrivello
tussis: **5** cough
tussle: **4** spar **5** fight **6** tousel, tousle **7** contend, contest, scuffle, wrestle **8** skirmish, struggle **9** scrimmage
tussock: **4** tuft **5** bunch, clump **7** hassock
tut: **4** hush **6** rebuke

tutelage: 7 nurture 8 guidance, teaching 9 tutorship 11 instruction 12 guardianship

tutelary: 10 protecting
gods: 5 Lares

tutor: 5 coach, drill, guide, teach, train, watch 6 ground, mentor, school 7 grinder, pedagog, teacher 8 guardian, instruct 9 pedagogue, preceptor 10 discipline

tutta: all 5 whole 6 entire

tuyere: tew 4 pipe 5 tewel 6 nozzle

TV: See **television**

twaddle: rot 4 bunk, chat 5 haver, prate 6 babble, drivel, fottle, gabble 8 nonsense 9 poppycock 10 balderdash

twangy: 5 nasal

tweak: 4 jerk, pull 5 pinch, twist 6 twitch

tweet: 4 peep 5 chirp 7 chirrup

tweezers: 7 pincers 9 merganser

twenty: 5 corge, kappa, score

twenty-faced: 11 icosahedral

twerp: 4 brat, jerk 5 sprat 6 squirt 7 big shot

twibil: axe 6 chisel 7 mattock

twice: bis(L.) 6 doubly 7 twofold

twig: see 4 beat, mode, pull 5 birch, bough, scion, shoot, spray, sprig, style, tweak, withe 6 branch, fescue, notice, sallow, switch, twitch, wattle 7 fashion, observe 8 perceive 9 apprehend 10 comprehend, understand
bundle: 5 fagot 6 barsom

twiggy: 4 thin 6 slight 7 slender 8 delicate

twilight: 4 dusk 5 gloam 6 dimmet 7 decline, evening 8 gloaming, glooming 9 cocklight 10 crepuscule
of the Gods: 8 Ragnarok 17 Goetterdaemmerung
pert. to: 11 crepuscular

twill: rib 5 cloth, quill, weave

twin: two 4 dual, pair, part 5 gemel, sever, twain 6 couple, double, sunder 7 twofold 8 didymous 11 counterpart
crystal: 5 macle
kind of: 9 fraternal, identical
one: 5 gemel
Siamese: Eng 5 Chang
stars: 6 Castor, gemini, Pollux

twinge: 4 ache, pain, pang 5 pinch, qualm, tweak 6 stitch, twitch

twine: ran 4 coil, turn, vine, warp, wind, wrap 5 braid, snarl, twist 6 encurl, enfold, enlace, infold, string, tangle, thread 7 anamite, embrace, wreathe 8 encircle, undulate 9 interlace 10 interweave 11 convolution, intermingle

twink: 6 punish, thrash 9 chaffinch

twinkle: 4 wink 5 blink, flash, gleam, shine 7 flicker, flutter, glimmer, glitter, instant, light up, sparkle 11 scintillate

twinkler: 4 star 8 sparkler

twirl: 4 coil, curl, gyre, move, spin, turn 5 querl, twist, whirl 6 gyrate 7 revolve, twizzle 8 flourish, rotation 9 pirouette, whirligig 11 convolution

twist: 4 bend, coil, cord, curl, skew, slew, slue, spin, tirl(Sc.), turn, wind, yarn 5 crink, crook, curve, gnarl, hinge, quirk, screw, tweak, twine, wring 6 hankle, spiral, sprain, squirm, thread, torque, wrench, writhe 7 confuse, contort, distort, entwine, flexure, meander, perplex, pervert, revolve, scatter, tendril, torment, torsion, torture 8 appetite, squiggle 9 constrain, corkscrew, deviation, insinuate 10 intertwine, interweave 11 convolution, misrepresent, peculiarity

twisted: cam, wry 6 warped 7 complex, tortile

twister: 4 roll, turn 7 cruller, cyclone, mallard, tornado 8 doughnut 10 somersault, waterspout

twit: guy 4 gibe, jive, josh 5 blame, chirp, taunt, tease 7 upbraid 8 reproach, ridicule

twitch: nip, tic, tie, tug 4 draw, jerk, pick, pull, skid, yank 5 grasp, pluck, start, thong, tweak 6 clutch, fasten, snatch 9 vellicate 11 contraction

twitter: 4 chat 5 chirp, run on, shake 6 giggle, titter, tremor 7 chatter, chitter, flutter, tremble 9 agitation

two: duo, twa(Sc.) 4 beta(Gr.), both, duet, dyad, pair 5 twain, twins 6 couple 7 twosome
chambered: 9 bicameral
edged: 5 sharp 9 ancipital
handed: 8 bimanual 12 ambidextrous
headed: 11 dicephalous
metrical feet: 6 dipody
months: 8 bi-mester
parts: 6 bident 9 bifurcate 11 dichotomous
pert. to: 4 dual 6 dyadic
winged: 7 bialate 8 dipteral 9 dipterous

two-bit: 5 cheap

two-faced: 5 false 9 deceitful 11 treacherous 12 hypocritical
god: 5 Janus

two-fisted: 6 virile 8 vigorous

two-foot: 5 biped 7 bipedal

two-pronged: 6 bident

two-sided: 9 bilateral

two-spot: 5 deuce

two-time: 5 cheat 7 deceive 11 double-cross

two-tone: 7 bicolor

twofold: 4 dual 5 duple 6 bifold, binary, double, duplex 9 bifarious, duplicate

twopenny: ale 4 mean 5 cheap 9 worthless

twosome: 4 duet, pair 6 couple

tycoon: 7 magnate 9 financier 13 industrialist
tydie: 4 bird, wren 8 titmouse
tyee: 5 chief
tyke, tike: cur, dog 5 child 6 shaver 7 bumpkin
tylopod: 5 camel
tympan: 4 drum
tympanum: 6 tympan 7 eardrum 10 kettledrum
tympany: 7 bombast, conceit 9 inflation 10 distention, turgidness
Tyndareus: *kingdom:* 6 Sparta
  wife: 4 Leda
typal: 8 symbolic
type: gem, ilk, lot 4 font, form, kern, kind, mark, mold, norm, pica, sign, slug, sort 5 agate, class, doric, elite, genre, group, ideal, ionic, metal, model, order, pearl, roman, stamp, token 6 emblem, italic, minion, nature, rubric, stripe, symbol 7 brevier, example, impress, paragon, pattern, species 8 boldface, classify 9 bourgeois, character, condensed, nonpareil 10 persuasion 11 Baskerville
  block: 4 quad 7 quadrat
  frame: 5 chase
  line: 4 slug
  mold: 6 matrix
  size: 4 pica, ruby 5 elite, pearl 6 minion 7 brevier, diamond 9 nonpareil
  slanting: 6 italic
  stroke: 5 serif
  tray: 6 galley
typeset: 7 compose

typesetter: 8 linotype, monotype 10 compositor
typewriter part: key 6 platen, spacer 9 tabulator
typhoon: 4 wind 5 storm 7 cyclone 9 hurricane
typical: 5 ideal, model, typal 6 classic, normal 7 regular 9 exemplary, schematic 10 emblematic, figurative 13 prefigurative 14 characteristic, representative
typify: 6 embody 9 epitomize, prefigure, represent, symbolize
typographer: 7 printer 10 compositor
tyrannical: 5 cruel, harsh 6 brutal, lordly, unjust 7 slavish 8 absolute, despotic 9 arbitrary, imperious 10 oppressive 11 domineering
tyrannosaurus: 8 dinosaur
tyranny: 5 rigor 7 fascism 8 iron heel, severity 9 despotism, harshness
tyrant: 4 czar, tsar, tzar 6 despot 7 fuehrer, monarch, usurper 8 dictator, martinet 9 oppressor, strong man
  murder: 11 tyrannicide
Tyre: *king:* 5 Belus, Hiram
  noble: 7 Acerbas
  prince: 8 Pericles
  princess: 4 Dido
tyro: 4 tiro 5 pupil 6 novice 7 amateur 8 beginner, neophyte 9 commencer 10 apprentice 11 abecedarian
tzar, czar, tsar: 4 king 5 ruler 6 tyrant
tzigane: 5 gypsy

U

U-boat: sub 9 submarine
ubermensch: 8 superman
uberous: 7 copious 8 abundant, fruitful
ubiety: 8 location, position, relation 9 whereness
ubiquitous: 10 everywhere 11 omnipresent
uca: 4 crab
udder: bag 5 gland
Uffizi site: 8 Florence
Uganda: *capital:* 7 Kampala
  cattle: 6 ankoli

  lake: 5 George, Kyoga 6 Edward 8 Victoria
  language: Luo 5 Atero 7 Luganda, Swahili
  leader: 5 Obote 7 Idi Amin, Muwanga
  monetary unit: 8 shilling
  mountain: 5 Elgon 9 Ruwenzori
  people: 5 Lango 7 Bunyoro
  river: 4 Aswa, Kafu 5 Pager
  town: 5 Jinja, Mbale 7 Entebbe
ughten: 4 dawn, dusk 7 evening, morning 8 twilight

ugli: 5 fruit **7** tangelo
ugliness symbol: 4 toad
ugly: bad **4** base, vile **5** awful, cross, grave, snivy, toady **6** cranky, homely, snivey, sullen **7** crabbed, hideous, ominous **8** grewsome, gruesome, horrible, terrible, unlovely **9** dangerous, fractious, frightful, graceless, loathsome, offensive, repulsive, unsightly **10** ill-favored, ill-natured, unpleasant **11** ill-tempered, quarrelsome, threatening, troublesome **12** cross-grained, disagreeable **13** objectionable
Ugrian: *language:* **6** Ostyak
 people: **4** Avar
ugsome: 6 horrid **9** abhorrent, frightful, loathsome
uhlan: 6 lancer **7** soldier **10** cavalryman
uitlander: 5 alien **9** foreigner, outlander
ukase: 5 edict, order **6** decree **7** command **12** proclamation
ukelele, ukulele: uke
Ukraine: *assembly:* **4** rada
 capital: **4** Kiev
 coin: **6** grivna **7** schagiv
 dance: **5** gopak
 holy city: **4** Kiev
 Mother of Cities: **4** Kiev
 river: Bug **6** Donets **7** Dnieper
 seaport: **6** Odessa
 town: **7** Donetsk, Kharkov
Ulalume author: Poe
ulcer: 4 noma, sore **7** egilops **8** aegilops, fossette **9** cacoethes
 kind of: **6** peptic **8** duodenal
ulceration: 7 bedsore **8** helcosis
ule: 4 tree **6** caucho **10** rubber ball
uliginous: wet **4** oozy **5** moist, muddy **6** swampy
ullage: 7 wantage **8** shortage **10** deficiency
ulna: 4 bone **5** elbow **7** cubitus, forearm
 end of: **5** ancon
ulster: 8 overcoat
ulterior: 5 later, privy **6** future **7** further, guarded, remoter **9** concealed **10** subsequent, succeeding, under wraps **11** undisclosed
ultimate: end **4** dire, last **5** final, telos(Gr.) **6** remote **7** extreme, maximum, primary **8** eventful, eventual, farthest **9** elemental **10** apotheosis, conclusive **11** fundamental
ultimatum: 5 order **6** demand, threat
ultra: 5 kinky, outré **6** beyond **7** extreme, forward, radical **9** excessive, extremist, fanatical **10** outlandish **11** extravagant **14** uncompromising
ulu: 5 knife
ululate: bay **4** hoot, howl, wail, yelp **6** lament **7** screech
Ulysses: 8 Odysseus

 antagonist: **4** Irus
 author: **5** Joyce
 character: **5** Bloom, Molly **7** Dedalus
 dog: **5** Argos
 enchantress of: **5** Circe
 enemy: **8** Poseidon
 father: **7** Laertes
 friend: **6** Mentor
 kingdom: **6** Ithaca
 mother: **8** Anticlea
 plant: **4** moly
 son: **9** Telegonus **10** Telemachus
 swineherd: **7** Eumaeus
 temptress: **5** Circe
 voyage: **7** odyssey
 wife: **8** Penelope
umber: 5 brown, shade, visor **6** darken, shadow **7** protect, umbrere **8** grayling, umbrette
umbilicus: 4 core **5** heart, navel
umbra: 4 fish **5** ghost, shade **6** shadow **7** phantom, vestige **10** apparition
umbrage: 5 anger, cloak, doubt, pique, shade, trace **6** offend, shadow **7** foliage, offense, pretext, shelter **8** disfavor, disgrace, disguise **9** disesteem, semblance, suspicion **10** overshadow, protection, resentment **11** displeasure
umbrageous: 5 shady **6** shaded
umbrella: 4 gamp **5** blind, guard, shade **6** brolly, chatta, payong, pileus, screen **7** parasol, protect, shelter **8** disguise **11** bumber-shoot
umbrella tree: 8 magnolia
umbrette: 9 hammerkop **10** hammerhead
umbrous: 5 shady
umiak: 4 boat **6** oomiac, oomiak
umpire: 5 judge **6** decide, oddman **7** arbiter, daysman, oddsman, referee **9** supervise **10** arbitrator
Una boat: 7 catboat
unable: 6 cannot **7** disable **8** helpless, impotent **9** incapable **11** incompetent, inefficient, unqualified **13** incapacitated
unaccented: 4 lene **6** atonic
unaccompanied: 4 bare, solo **5** alone
unacountable: 7 strange **9** countless **10** mysterious **12** inexplicable, unfathomable **13** irresponsible
unaccustomed: new **7** strange **8** uncommon, unwonted **10** unfamiliar
unacquainted: 7 strange, unusual **8** ignorant **10** unfamiliar **13** inexperienced
unadorned: 4 bald, bare **5** naked, plain, stark **6** rustic **7** austere
unadulterated: 4 pure **5** clean **6** honest **7** genuine, sincere, unmixed **8** straight **9** immutable
unaffected: 4 easy, naif, real **5** naive, plain **6** rustic, simple **7** artless, genuine, natural, sincere, unmoved **8** unbiased **9**

ingenuous, unaltered, untouched **12** uninfluenced

Unalaska native: 5 Aleut

unalike: 9 different

unalleviated: 4 hard

unalloyed: 4 pure **7** genuine, unmixed **11** unqualified

unambiguous: 5 clear **8** explicit

unanchored: 6 adrift

unanimous: 5 solid **6** united **8** agreeing **9** of one mind **11** consentient

unanimously: 7 una voce

unanswerable: 5 final **10** conclusive

unappeasable: 10 implacable

unapproachable: 5 aloof **7** distant **10** unsociable **12** inaccessible

unarmed: 4 bare **5** inerm **11** defenseless

unaspirated: 4 lene

unassailable: 10 invincible **12** invulnerable

unassuming: shy **6** humble, modest **7** natural **8** retiring **9** diffident **14** unostentatious

unattached: 4 free **5** loose **6** single **9** unmarried **11** independent **13** noncollegiate

unattractive: 4 rude, ugly **5** plain **10** ungracious

unau: 5 sloth

unavailing: 6 futile **8** bootless, gainless

unavowed: 6 secret **8** ulterior

unaware: 6 unwary **8** heedless, ignorant **11** thoughtless

unbalanced: 6 insane, uneven **8** deranged, lopsided, one-sided

unbecoming: 4 rude **5** inept **6** clumsy, gauche **8** improper, unseemly, unworthy **10** indecorous, unsuitable **11** disgraceful **12** unattractive

unbefitting: 5 below **8** improper **10** unsuitable

unbelief: 10 skepticism **11** agnosticism, incredulity

unbelievable: 4 thin, weak **5** thick **8** fabulous **9** fantastic **10** incredible **11** implausible **13** inconceivable

unbeliever: 5 pagan **7** atheist, doubter, heretic, infidel, scoffer, skeptic **8** agnostic **11** freethinker

unbend: 4 rest, thaw **5** relax, untie, yield **6** loosen, uncock **7** slacken **8** unfasten

unbending: 5 rigid, stern, stiff **8** obdurate, resolute **10** inexorable, inflexible, unsociable

unbiased: 4 fair, just **8** detached **9** impartial **12** unprejudiced

unbind: 4 free, undo **5** untie **6** detach, loosen **7** absolve, deliver, release **8** dissolve, unfasten

unbleached: 4 blae, ecru **5** beige **7** natural

unblemished: 4 pure **5** whole **6** chaste **8** spotless

unblushing: 9 shameless

unbolt: 4 open **5** unbar, unpin **6** unlock **8** unfasten

unbosom: 4 tell **6** reveal

unbound: 4 free **5** loose **10** unconfined

unbounded: 4 open **9** limitless, unchecked, unlimited **11** measureless **12** uncontrolled, unrestrained

unbrace: 4 free, undo **5** carve, relax **6** loosen, reveal, weaken **8** disjoint, enfeeble

unbridled: 4 free **5** loose **7** violent **9** dissolute, unchecked **10** licentious, ungoverned **12** uncontrolled, unrestrained

unbroken: one **4** flat **5** undug, whole **6** entire, intact **7** untamed **8** unplowed **9** continual, undivided, unsubdued **10** continuous **13** uninterrupted

unburden: rid **4** ease **5** empty, untax **6** unload **7** disload, relieve

unbury: 6 exhume

uncanny: 4 eery **5** eerie, scary, weird **6** spooky **7** awkward, ghostly, strange **8** careless **9** dangerous, unnatural **10** mysterious **11** supernatural

uncanonical: 10 apocryphal

unceasing: 6 eterne **7** endless, eternal **9** continual, incessant, perennial **11** everlasting **14** unintermittent

unceremonious: 4 curt **5** bluff, blunt, short **6** abrupt **8** familiar, informal **14** unconventional

uncertain: 4 asea, dark, hazy, moot **5** fluky, vague **6** chancy, fitful, queasy **7** at a loss, dubious **8** aleatory, doubtful, unsteady, variable **9** ambiguous, equivocal, hazardous, undecided **10** changeable, inconstant, indefinite, precarious **11** vacillating **12** questionable **13** indeterminate, problematical, untrustworthy

uncertainty: 4 were **5** doubt, query **6** gamble, wonder **7** dubiety **8** suspense **9** dubiosity **10** skepticism

unchanging: 4 same **6** steady **7** eternal, forever, settled, uniform **9** immutable, steadfast, unvarying **10** invariable, stationary

unchaste: 4 lewd **5** bawdy **6** coarse, impure **7** haggard, obscene **8** immodest

unchecked: 4 free **5** loose **7** rampant **9** unbounded, unbridled

uncia: 4 coin, inch **5** ounce **7** twelfth

uncivil: 4 rude **5** bluff, crass, crude **7** ill-bred **8** clownish, impolite **9** barbarous **10** indecorous, ungracious, unsuitable **11** uncivilized **12** discourteous **13** disrespectful

uncivilized: 4 rude, wild **5** feral **6** brutal, ferine, savage **7** boorish **8** barbaric **9** barbarian, barbarous, primitive **10** outrageous, unmannerly **13** unenlightened

uncle: eme, oom **10** pawnbroker
pert. to: **9** avuncular
Uncle Remus: *author:* **6** Harris
rabbit: **4** Brer
Uncle Tom's Cabin author: 5 Stowe
character: **5** Eliza, Topsy **6** Legree **9** Little Eva
unclean: 4 foul, tref, vile **5** black, dirty **6** common, filthy, impure **7** defiled, obscene **8** polluted, unchaste **11** unwholesome
unclose: ope **4** open **6** reveal **10** unreserved
unclothe: 5 spoil, strip **6** divest, expose **7** despoil, uncover, undress
unclothed: 4 bare, nude **5** naked
unclouded: 4 fair, open **5** clear, sunny
uncoil: 6 unlink, unwind
uncombined: 4 free **5** frank, loose **10** elementary
uncomfortable: 5 harsh **6** uneasy **7** prickly **8** scratchy
uncommon: odd **4** rare **5** extra, novel **6** choice, scarce, unique **7** special, strange, unusual **8** especial, unwonted **10** infrequent, remarkable **11** exceptional **12** unaccustomed **13** extraordinary, preternatural
uncommunicative: 6 silent **8** reserved, reticent **10** unsociable
uncompassionate: 5 stony **9** unfeeling
uncomplaining: 5 stoic **7** patient, stoical
uncomplicated: 5 plain **6** honest, simple
uncompromising: 4 firm **5** rigid, stern, tough **6** strict **9** unbending **10** determined, inflexible, unyielding **12** intransigent
unconcealed: 4 bare, open **5** frank, overt
unconcerned: 4 cool, easy **8** careless, detached **9** apathetic **10** insouciant, nonchalant **11** indifferent **12** uninterested
unconditional: 4 free **5** frank **8** absolute, explicit
unconfined: lax **4** free **5** loose **9** boundless, limitless, unlimited
unconfused: 4 calm **5** clear **6** steady
unconnected: 5 gappy **6** abrupt **8** detached, rambling, separate **10** incoherent **12** disconnected
unconscionable: 5 undue **7** extreme **9** excessive **10** outrageous
unconscious: out **6** asleep, torpid **7** stunned, unaware **8** comatose, ignorant, mindless **9** inanimate, lethargic **10** insensible
render: **4** stun
state: **5** swoon **8** apsychia
unconsciousness: 4 coma **5** faint **6** torpor
unconstrained: 4 easy, free **7** natural **8** familiar **9** easygoing **11** spontaneous **12** unrestrained **13** demonstrative

uncontrollable: 4 wild **5** unruly **11** intractable
uncontrolled: 4 free, wild **5** loose **9** irregular, unbounded, unmanaged **10** hysterical, licentious, ungoverned **11** unregulated **12** unrestrained
unconventional: 5 loose, outre, queer **6** casual **7** devious, offbeat **8** Bohemian, informal **13** unceremonious
uncooked: raw
uncorrupted: 4 pure **5** naive **6** virgin **8** pristine **9** unspoiled
uncouple: 5 loose **6** detach **8** unfasten **10** disconnect
uncouth: odd **4** rare, rude **5** crude **6** clumsy, coarse, dismal, rugged **7** awkward, boorish, loutish, strange, uncanny, unknown **8** derelict, desolate, dreadful, ignorant, uncommon, ungainly, yokelish **9** unrefined **10** mysterious, outlandish, uncultured, unpolished **11** comfortless **12** discourteous, uncultivated
uncouth person: oaf **4** boor, lout **5** yokel **6** bumkin, rustic **7** bumpkin
uncover: 4 bare, open, tirl(Sc.), tirr(Sc.) **6** denude, detect, divest, expose, remove, reveal, unveil **7** display, divulge, undrape, unearth **8** disclose, discover
uncovered: 4 bald, nude, open **5** naked **6** cuerpo **9** developed **10** bareheaded
uncrystallized: 9 amorphous
unction: oil **7** suavity, unguent **8** ointment
give extreme: **5** anele
unctuous: fat **4** oily **5** bland, fatty, soapy, suave **6** fervid, greasy **7** fulsome, gushing, pinguid, plastic **10** oleaginous
uncultivated: 4 arid, wild **5** feral **6** coarse, desert, fallow **7** deserty **9** barbarous
uncultured: 4 rude **6** coarse **7** artless, boorish **9** unrefined
uncurbed: 9 audacious **12** uncontrolled
undamaged: 5 whole **6** intact
undaunted: 4 bold **5** brave **7** spartan **8** fearless, intrepid, undashed **9** confident, turbulent, unbridled, unchecked **10** courageous, undismayed **11** unconquered
undecayed: 5 fresh, green
undeceive: 8 disabuse **11** disillusion
undecided: 4 moot, pend **7** pending **8** doubtful, wavering **9** unsettled **10** inconstant, irresolute, unresolved **13** problematical
undefiled: 4 pure **6** chaste **8** innocent, virtuous **9** unlimited **10** immaculate
undemonstrative: 4 calm, cold, cool **7** aseptic, laconic **8** reserved **10** restrained
undeniable: 4 true **7** certain **12** indisputable **13** incontestable

undependable: 5 trick 6 unsafe 7 erratic 10 fly-by-night 13 irresponsible

under: 4 alow 5 below, neath, sotto(It.) 6 nether 7 beneath 8 inferior 10 underneath 11 subordinate

cover: 9 sheltered

obligation: 5 owing 8 beholden, indebted

the weather: 4 sick 5 drunk 6 ailing

under-set: 4 prop 6 sublet 7 provide, support 8 maintain, underlet 10 strengthen

undercover: 6 secret 13 surreptitious

man: spy 5 agent 9 detective 10 counterspy

underdog: 6 victim 9 dark horse

underdone: 4 rare

underestimate: 8 minimize 9 underrate 10 undervalue

undergarment: bra 4 slip 5 teddy 6 bodice, briefs 6 cilice, corset, flimsy, shorts, stepin 7 chemise, panties, step-ins 9 brassiere, chemilonn, hairshirt, petticoat, teddybear, underwear 10 foundation 11 camiknicker, combination

undergo: bow 4 bear, pass 5 carry, defer, yield 6 endure, suffer 7 sustain 8 tolerate 10 experience

undergraduate: 4 coed 6 junior, senior 7 student 8 freshman 9 sophomore

underground: 5 train 6 hidden, secret, subway 7 beneath 10 undercover 12 subterranean 13 surreptitious

burial place: 5 crypt 8 catacomb

dweller: 5 dwarf, gnome, troll

fighter: 6 marquis 8 partisan

fungus: 7 truffle 8 earthnut

railway: 6 subway

worker: 5 miner 6 mucker, pitman, sapper

undergrowth: 4 rush 5 brush 10 hypotrophy, underbrush

underhanded: sly 4 dern, mean 5 shady 6 byhand, secret, sneaky, unfair 8 sneaking, unfairly 9 deceitful 10 circuitous, fraudulent 11 clandestine, shorthanded, unobtrusive 13 unobtrusively 15 surreptitiously

underlie: 4 bear 7 support

underline: 4 mark 6 stress 9 emphasize

underling: 6 menial, minion 8 inferior 11 subordinate

underlying: 5 basic 7 obscure 8 cardinal 9 elemental 11 fundamental

undermine: sap 4 cave 5 drain, erode 6 impair, weaken 7 corrupt, founder, subvert 8 discover, enfeeble, excavate, sabotage 10 demoralize

underneath: 5 below, under 6 bottom, secret 7 beneath 13 surreptitious

underpin: 7 justify, support 8 maintain 9 vindicate 12 substantiate

underprop: 6 uphold 7 support 8 underpin

underrate: 5 decry 7 devalue 8 discount 9 extenuate 10 depreciate, undervalue 13 underestimate

underscore: 9 emphasize, italicize

undersea boat: sub 5 U-boat, wreck 9 submarine 11 submersible

eye: 9 periscope

undershirt: 4 vest 7 chemise

undershrub: 4 bush 7 heather

undersized: 4 puny 5 runty, small 7 scrubby

underskirt: 4 slip 9 petticoat

understand: con, dig, get, ken, see 4 know, sabe, twig 5 grasp, infer, sabby, savey, savvy, sense 6 follow, reason, savvey 7 discern, realize 8 conceive, perceive 9 apprehend, interpret, penetrate 10 comprehend, conjecture 12 get the hang of

understandable: 5 clear, lucid 6 simple 8 exoteric

understanding: ken 4 feets, idea, news 5 amity, brain 6 humane, kindly, reason, treaty 7 compact, concept, empathy, entente, knowing, meaning 8 attitude, contract, footwear, judgment, skillful, sympathy 9 agreement, diagnosis, knowledge, tolerance 10 acceptance 11 intelligent, sympathetic 12 intelligence

understatement: 7 litotes

understood: 5 clear, lucid, tacit 8 implicit

undertake: try 4 dare, fand, fang 5 chide, grant, seize 6 accept, assume, engage, incept, take on 7 attempt, emprise, emprize, execute, perform, promise, receive, reprove 8 contract, covenant, endeavor, overtake 9 guarantee

undertaker: 5 cerer 6 surety 7 rebuker, sponsor 8 embalmer 9 mortician 12 entrepreneur

undertaking: 4 task 6 charge, pledge 7 attempt, calling, project, promise, venture 8 covenant 9 adventure, guarantee 10 enterprise 11 proposition

written: 6 cautio

undertone: 5 aside 6 murmur 11 association

undertow: 4 eddy 6 vortex 7 current, riptide

undervalue: 5 decry 8 disprize, disvalue 10 depreciate

underwater: *apparatus:* 6 tremie 7 caisson

breathing equipment: 5 scuba

captain: 4 Nemo

chamber: 4 cave 7 caisson

craft: sub 5 U-boat 7 pigboat 9 submarine

missile: torpedo

sound detector: 5 sofar, sonar

underwear: 6 skivvy 7 dessous(F.), stepins 8 lingerie, skivvies 12 underclothes

(see also **undergarment**)

underwood: 5 frith 7 boscage, coppice 8 gangland 10 underbrush 11 undergrowth

underworld: 4 hell 5 Hades, Orcus, Sheol 6 Amenti, Erebus 7 xibalba 8 gangland 9 antipodes

boatman: 6 Charon

deity: Dis 4 Bran 5 Hades, Pluto 6 Osiris 8 Dispater 9 Enmeshara 11 Ningishzida

goddess: 6 Allatu, Belili, Hecate, Trivia

organization: 5 Mafia

pert. to: 8 chthonic 9 chthonian

river: 4 Styx 5 Lethe 7 Acheron

watchdog: 8 Cerberus

underwrite: 4 sign 6 insure 7 assure, endorse, finance, sponsor 9 subscribe

undesigning: 6 simple 7 artless, genuine, sincere

undetermined: 5 vague 7 dubious, pending 8 aoristic, doubtful 9 equivocal

undeveloped: 5 crude 6 latent 8 backward, immature, primitive

undeviating: 4 even 6 direct 8 straight

undigested: 5 crude

undiluted: 4 neat, pure 8 straight

undiminished: 6 entire

undine: nix 4 wave 5 nymph 11 water spirit

undisciplined: 4 wild 6 unruly, wanton 9 untrained

undisclosed: 6 hidden, sealed, secret 8 ulterior 12 confidential

undisguised: 4 bald, open 5 frank, plain, overt 9 barefaced

undisturbed: 4 calm 5 quiet, sound 6 placid, secure, serene 8 tranquil 9 unruffled

undivided: one 5 total, whole 6 entire, intact 8 complete, unbroken 10 continuous

undo: 4 open, ruin 5 annul, fordo, loose, solve, untie 6 betray, cancel, defeat, diddle, foredo, outwit, unlash, unwrap 7 abolish, defease, destroy, disjoin, explain, nullify, release, uncover, unravel 8 unfasten 9 bring down 10 disappoint, disconnect, invalidate

undoing: 4 ruin 8 downfall 9 overthrow

undomesticated: 4 wild 5 feral 6 ferine

undone: raw 6 ruined 9 disgraced, neglected 10 defeasible

undoubted: 4 sure 7 certain 8 accepted, admitted 9 authentic 11 indubitable

undraped: 4 bare, nude

undress: 4 doff 5 strip 6 devest, divest, expose 7 disrobe 8 unclothe 10 dishabille

undressed skin: kip 4 pelt

undue: 7 extreme 8 improper 9 excessive 10 exorbitant, immoderate, inordinate,

unsuitable 11 unwarranted 12 unreasonable 13 inappropriate

undulant: 7 aripple, sinuous

fever: 11 brucellosis

undulate: 4 roll, wave 5 swell, swing 6 billow 9 fluctuate

undutiful: 7 impious

undying: 6 eterne 7 ageless, endless, eternal 8 immortal, unending 9 continual, deathless 10 continuing, persistent 12 imperishable

unearth: dig 4 show 5 learn 6 exhume, expose 7 uncover 8 disclose, discover

unearthly: 4 eery 5 eerie, weird 7 awesome, foolish, uncanny, ungodly 8 terrific 9 appalling, fantastic 10 mysterious, outlandish 12 preposterous, supernatural 13 preternatural

uneasiness: 4 care 5 worry 6 unrest 7 anxiety, disease, trouble 8 disquiet 10 constraint, discomfort, discontent 11 displeasure, disturbance 12 apprehension 13 embarrassment, inconvenience 15 dissatisfaction

uneasy: 5 stiff, tense 7 anxious, awkward, fidgety, unquiet, restive 8 doubtful, restless 9 difficult, perturbed, unsettled 13 uncomfortable

uneducated: 8 ignorant 10 illiterate, unlettered, unschooled

unemotional: 4 cold 5 stony, stoic 7 stoical 9 unfeeling 10 phlegmatic

unemployed: 4 idle 6 otiant, otiose 7 jobless, laid off 8 inactive, leisured 9 at liberty

unencumbered: 4 free

unending: 7 endless, eternal, undying 8 timeless 9 ceaseless, continual 11 everlasting 12 interminable

unendurable: 10 impassible, unbearable 11 intolerable 12 insufferable

unenthusiastic: 4 cool 5 tepid 9 apathetic 12 uninterested

unequal: 6 uneven, unfair, unjust 8 lopsided, variable 9 different, disparate, irregular 11 fluctuating 16 disproportionate

condition: 4 odds

unequaled: 5 alone 7 supreme 9 matchless, unmatched, unrivaled 10 surpassing 12 unparalleled

unequivocal: 5 clear, plain 7 sincere 8 definite, explicit, positive 9 certainly 11 categorical 15 straightforward

unerring: 4 sure, true 5 exact 7 certain 8 inerrant 9 inerrancy, unfailing 10 infallible

unethical: 5 wrong 6 amoral 7 corrupt

uneven: odd 5 erose, gobby, haggy, rough 6 hobbly, rugged, spotty, unfair, unjust, unlike 7 unequal, varying 8 lopsided 9 disparate, irregular 10 ill-matched 11 fluctuating, ill-assorted **12** inconsistent

unexamined: 7 apriori

unexcelled: 8 champion, superior, top-notch

unexceptional: 5 usual **6** common, decent **7** regular **8** ordinary

unexcited: 4 calm **5** level **7** stoical

unexciting: 4 dead, dull, tame **6** boring **7** prosaic **13** uninteresting

unexpected: 5 eerie **6** abrupt, sudden **9** inopinate, unguarded **10** accidental, unforeseen

unexpended: 6 saving **7** reserve, surplus **8** left over

unexpired: 5 alive, valid **9** operative, remaining

unexpressed: 5 tacit **6** silent **7** implicit

unfadable: 4 fast **9** memorable

unfaded: 5 fresh **6** bright

unfading flower: 8 amaranth

unfailing: 4 same, sure **7** certain **8** reliable, unerring **10** infallible, unflagging, unyielding **13** inexhaustible

unfair: 4 foul, hard **5** wrong **6** biased, uneven, unjust **8** unseemly, wrongful **9** dishonest, unethical **11** inequitable, underhanded, unfavorable **12** dishonorable

unfaithful: 7 infidel, traitor **8** derelict, disloyal, recreant, turncoat **9** dishonest, faithless **10** adulterous, inaccurate, traitorous **13** untrustworthy

unfaltering: 4 sure, true **5** brave **6** steady

unfamed: 5 lowly **6** humble **7** obscure

unfamiliar: new **7** strange, unknown **8** ignorant **12** unaccustomed

unfashionable: 5 dated **9** distorted, unshapely

unfasten: 4 free, open, undo **5** loose, unbar, unfix, unpin, untie **6** detach, loosen, unlace, unlock **8** untether

unfathomable: 10 bottomless **12** impenetrable

unfavorable: bad, ill **4** evil, foul **6** averse **7** adverse **8** contrary **15** disadvantageous

unfeeling: 4 dull, hard, numb **5** cruel, harsh, stern, stony **6** brutal, marble, stolid **7** callous **8** numbness, obdurate, pitiless **9** apathetic, bloodless, heartless, insensate, senseless **10** impassible, insensible **11** cold-blooded, hardhearted, insensitive **13** unsusceptible **16** unimpressionable

unfeigned: 4 real, true **6** hearty **7** genuine, natural, sincere

unfermented grape juice: 4 stum

unfertile: 4 arid **6** barren

unfettered: 4 free **5** broad, loose

unfilled: 5 blank, empty **6** vacant **7** vacuous

unfilled cavity: 4 vugg

unfinished: raw **4** rude **5** crude, rough **7**

sketchy **8** immature **9** imperfect **10** amateurish, incomplete

unfit: bad **4** sick **5** inept, pasul(Heb.) **6** faulty **8** disabled, improper **9** ill-suited, maladroit **10** out of place, unsuitable **11** handicapped, incompetent, unqualified **12** disqualified **13** incapacitated

unfix: 6 detach, loosen **8** dissolve, unfasten, unsettle

unflagging: 6 steady **8** constant, tireless

unflappable: 4 calm, cool **7** relaxed

unflattering: 4 open **5** blunt, frank **6** candid **10** derogatory, unbecoming

unfledged: 5 green, young **6** callow **8** immature **11** undeveloped, unfeathered

bird: **4** eyas **8** nestling

unflinching: 4 firm, grim **6** stanch **8** resolute **9** steadfast **10** unwavering, unyielding

unfold: ope **4** open **5** break, solve **6** deploy, evolve, expand, explat, flower, reveal, spread, unfurl, unwrap **7** develop, display, divulge, evolute, explain, explate, release **8** disclose **9** explicate

unforced: 4 easy **7** natural, willing **9** voluntary

unforeseen: 6 casual, sudden **10** accidental

unformed: 4 rude **6** callow **9** shapeless, uncreated **11** undeveloped

unfortunate: bad, ill, sad **4** poor **5** worst **6** dismal, wretch **7** hapless, malefic, unhappy, unlucky **8** luckless, wretched **9** graceless, miserable **10** calamitous, deplorable, prostitute, ungracious **12** inauspicious, infelicitous, unsuccessful

unfounded: 4 idle, vain **8** baseless **10** chimerical, groundless

unfrequented: 6 lonely **8** isolated, solitary

unfriendly: 4 cool **6** remote **7** asocial, hostile **8** inimical, unsocial **9** dissocial

terms: **4** outs

unfruitful: 5 blunt **6** barren, wasted **7** sterile, useless **8** impotent, infecund **9** fruitless, infertile **12** unproductive, unprofitable

unfurl: 4 open **5** enrol **6** enroll, expand, spread, unfold, unroll **7** develop

unfurnished: 4 bare **6** vacant

ungainly: 5 lanky **6** clumsy **7** awkward, boorish, uncouth **8** clownish, slammock, slummock **9** maladroit **11** elephantine

ungenerous: 4 mean **5** harsh, nasty, petty **6** stingy

ungirt: 5 loose, slack **7** unbound

ungodly: 6 impure, sinful, wicked **7** impious, profane **8** dreadful **9** atheistic, atrocious, unearthly **10** indecorous, outrageous **11** unbelieving **12** hypocritical

ungovernable: 4 wild **6** unruly **7** froward

9 unbridled 10 disorderly, headstrong, licentious, rebellious 11 intractable 13 irrepressible 14 uncontrollable

ungraceful: 6 clumsy 7 angular, awkward 9 inelegant

ungracious: 4 hard, rude 5 short 8 churlish, impolite 9 offensive 10 unmannerly, unpleasant 11 unfortunate 12 discourteous, unattractive

ungrateful: 9 offensive, thankless

ungrounded: 8 baseless 9 unfounded 10 uninformed 12 uninstructed

ungrudging: 8 cheerful

unguarded: 6 unwary 8 careless 9 imprudent 10 incautious 11 defenseless, thoughtless, unprotected

unguent: 4 balm 5 salve 6 cerate, ceroma, chrism 8 ointment 9 lubricant

ungula: 4 claw, hoof, nail

ungulate: hog, pig 4 deer 5 horse, tapir 6 hoofed 8 elephant 10 rhinoceros

unhallowed: 6 impure, unholy, wicked 7 impious, profane 10 desecrated

unhandsome: 4 mean, rude 5 plain 6 homely, stingy 10 unbecoming

unhandy: 6 clumsy 7 awkward 12 inconvenient

unhappiness: woe 5 blues, dolor, grief, worry 6 misery, unrest 7 sadness

unhappy: sad 4 evil 6 dismal 7 unlucky 8 dejected, ill-fated, wretched 9 miserable, sorrowful, woebegone 10 calamitous 11 melancholic, mischievous, unfavorable, unfortunate 12 inauspicious, unsuccessful 13 inappropriate

unharmed: 4 safe 6 unhurt 8 harmless 10 scatheless

unharmonious: 9 dissonant

unharness: 6 disarm, divest, ungear 7 unhitch, unhorse

unhealthy: ill 4 sick 6 sickly 7 vicious 9 dangerous 11 unwholesome

unheard of: 7 obscure, strange, unknown 13 unprecedented

unheated: 4 cold

unheeding: 4 deaf 8 careless 11 inattentive 12 disregarding

unhesitating: 5 ready

unhidden: 5 overt

unholy: See **ungodly**

unhorse: 5 throw 8 dislodge, dismount 9 overthrow, unharness

unhurried: 4 easy, slow 10 deliberate

unhurt: 4 safe 5 whole 8 unharmed 9 uninjured

unicellular animal: 5 ameba 6 amoeba 9 protozoan 10 paramecium

unicellular plant: 5 spore

unicorn: 4 reem

unicorn fish: 4 unie 7 narwhal 8 filefish

unidentified flying object: UFO

uniform: 4 even, flat, like, suit 5 equal, level 6 livery, outfit, steady 7 orderly, regular, similar 8 constant, equiform 9 continual, equitable, unvarying 10 compatible, consistent, equiformal, invariable, monotonous, unchanging 11 homogeneous

cord: 11 aiguillette

in color: 4 flat, flot

prisoner's: 7 stripes

servant's: 6 livery

shoulder ornament: 7 epaulet 9 epaulette

uniformly: 6 always, evenly

unify: 5 merge, unite 8 coalesce 9 correlate, harmonize, integrate 11 consolidate

unimaginative: 4 dull 7 literal, prosaic 10 pedestrian

unimpaired: 4 free 5 fresh, whole 6 entire, intact

unimpassioned: 6 steady 10 phlegmatic 12 matter-of-fact

unimpeachable: 6 decent 9 blameless, faultless 14 irreproachable, unquestionable 15 unexceptionable

unimpeded: 4 free 8 expedite

unimportant: 5 minor, petty, small 6 little, paltry 7 trivial 10 negligible

uninformed: 8 ignorant

uninhabited: 5 empty 6 vacant 8 deserted, desolate

uninspired: 4 dull 6 stodgy 9 ponderous

unintelligent: 4 dumb 5 brute 6 obtuse, simple, stupid, unwise 7 foolish 8 ignorant 9 senseless 10 irrational

unintentional: 9 haphazard, unwitting 10 accidental 11 inadvertent

uninteresting: dry 4 arid, drab, dull, flat 5 stale 6 boring, jejune, prolix, stupid 7 humdrum, insipid, prosaic, tedious 8 tiresome 9 colorless 10 unexciting

uninterrupted: 6 direct 7 endless, eternal 9 continual 10 continuous 11 everlasting

unio: 6 mussel

union: AFL, CIO, one, UAW 4 bloc 5 artel, joint, ILGWU, unity 6 accord, copula, fusion, gremio(Sp.), league, merger, unicum 7 amalgam, concord, contact, entente, meeting, oneness, society 8 alliance, junction, marriage 9 coalition, coherence, composure 10 connection, copulation, federation, fellowship 11 association, coalescence, combination, concurrence, confederacy, conjunction, consistency, unification

political: 4 bloc 9 coalition

trade: 5 guild, hanse

union jack: 4 flag

Union of South Africa: See **South Africa**

Union of Soviet Socialist Republics (see also **Russia, Soviet Union**): 4 USSR 6 Russia, Soviet

unique: odd, one 4 only, rare, sole 5 alone,

queer **6** single **7** notable, special, unequal, unusual **8** peculiar, singular **9** matchless **11** exceptional **13** extraordinary

unison: 5 union **6** accord **7** concord, harmony **9** agreement, consonant, homophony, identical, unanimity, unisonous **10** concordant, consonance

unit: ace, one **4** item **5** digit, group, monad, whole **6** entity **10** individual
conductivity: mho
discord: **4** word
fluidity: rhe
flux density: **5** gauss
force: **4** dyne, volt **5** kinit, tonal **6** newton **7** poundal
hypothetical: **5** idant **6** pangen **7** pangene
illumination: **4** phot
inductance: **5** henry
light: lux, pyr **5** lumen
magnetic: **5** weber
measure: are, mil, rod **4** pint **5** meter, stere
measuring sound: **7** decibel
metrical: **4** dyne, mora **5** liter, morae
military: **4** army **5** corps, squad **7** brigade, company, platoon **8** division, regiment **9** battalion
physical: erg **7** atomerg
power: bel **4** watt **5** dynam, horse
pressure: **5** barad, barye **10** atmosphere
reluctance: rel
resistance: ohm
social: **4** clan, sect **5** tribe **6** family **7** chapter
speed: **4** velo
stellar: **6** parsec
tale: **4** rees
telegraphic: **4** baud
thermal: **6** calory **7** calorie
time: day **4** bell, hour, week, year **5** month **6** minute, season, second
ultimate: **5** monad
velocity: kin **4** kine, velo
volume: cwt, ton **5** ounce, pound **13** hundredweight
weight: ton **4** dram, gram, tael **5** carat, grain, ounce, pound
work: erg **5** ergon, joule **6** kilerg

unite: ass, fay, mix, pan, sew, tie, wed **4** ally, band, bind, club, fuse, hasp, join, knit, link, meld, pair, seam, weld **5** affix, annex, blend, graft, hitch, marry, merge, piece, rally, unify **6** adhere, adjoin, attach, cement, cohere, concur, couple, embody, mingle, solder, splice **7** combine, conjoin, connect, consort, convene **8** assemble, coalesce, compound, concrete, condense, conspire, continue, federate, regulate **9** affiliate, aggregate, associate **10** amalgamate, articulate, consociate, federalize, hook

up with, join forces **11** concentrate, consolidate, incorporate **12** conglutinate

united: one **9** concerted, conjugate, corporate

United Nations Organization: UNO

United Provinces: 7 Holland, Utrecht, Zeeland **9** Friesland, Groningen **10** Gelderland, Overijssel

United States: *coin:* bit **4** cent, dime **5** eagle, penny **6** dollar, nickel **7** quarter
falls: **7** Niagara **8** Yosemite **9** Multnomah
flagmaker: **9** Betsy Ross
frontiersman: **4** Cody **5** Boone, Clark, Lewis **8** Crockett
measure: lea, mil, rod, ton, tub, vat **4** acre, bolt, cord, drum, foot, gill, hand, hank, heer, inch, iron, last, line, link, mile, nail, pace, palm, peck, pint, pipe, pole, pool, roll, sack, span, typp, vara, yard **5** block, carat, chain, labor, minim, perch, point, prime, quart, skein, stran **6** barrel, basket, bushel, fathom, gallon, league, pottle, square, strand, thread **7** quarter, section, spindle **8** hogshead, quadrant, standard, township **9** board foot, decillion, fluid dram **10** fluid ounce **11** teaspoonful **13** tablespoonful **16** Winchester bushel
measure of weight: bag, keg, kip, ton **5** carat, flask, grain, ounce, pound **6** denier **7** long ton, quarter, quintal **9** troy ounce, troy pound **11** metric carat **13** hundredweight
mountain: **4** Hood **5** Rocky **6** Cumbre, Elbert, Helena, Shasta **7** Massive, Rainier, Whitney **8** Katahdin, McKinley **10** Laurentian **11** Appalachian
pioneer: see *frontiersman* above
President: see **President (U.S.)**
racetrack: **5** Bowie **6** Goshen, Laurel **7** Hialeah, Jamaica, Pimlico **8** Aqueduct **10** Meadowland, Santa Anita
river: see under individual states
Vice President: see **Vice President (U.S.)**

unity: one **5** union **6** accord **7** concord, harmony, oneness **8** alliance, identity **9** agreement, communion, congruity **10** singleness, solidarity, uniformity **11** conjunction, unification

universal: all **5** local, total, whole **6** common, cosmic, entire, public **7** general **8** catholic, constant **9** continual, unlimited **11** omnipresent **12** all-pervading
language: ido **9** Esperanto
military training: **5** draft

universe: 5 earth, monad, world **6** cosmos, nature, system **8** creation, megacosm
controlling principle: **4** tien **5** logos

pert to: **6** cosmic
science: **9** cosmology
university (see also **college**): **7** academy, college **8** academie **9** accademie
division: **6** school **7** college
grounds: **6** campus
Ivy League: **4** Yale **5** Brown **7** Cornell, Harvard **8** Columbia **9** Dartmouth, Princeton **12** Pennsylvania
official: **4** dean **6** regent
rank: **9** professor **10** instructor
team: **7** varsity
univocal: **5** clear **7** uniform **9** unanimous, unisonous **11** indubitable **12** unmistakable
unjust: **5** cruel **6** unfair **8** improper, wrongful **9** dishonest, faithless **10** inaccurate, iniquitous, unfaithful **11** inequitable
unkempt: **5** crude, messy, rough **6** frouzy, frowsy, frowzy, shaggy, untidy **7** ruffled, squalid, tousled **8** slovenly **9** unrefined **10** disarrayed, disheveled, unpolished
unkind: bad, ill **4** mean, vile **5** cruel, harsh, rough, stern **6** severe, wicked **7** foreign, strange **8** ungenial **9** inclement, undutiful, unnatural **10** degenerate, ungenerous, ungracious, ungrateful, unsuitable **11** unfavorable
unknit: **4** undo **5** ravel, relax, untie **6** unknot **7** unravel **8** disperse, dissolve, disunite
unknowable: **6** sealed **8** mystical **9** enigmatic
unknown: **4** unco **7** inconnu(F.), obscure, strange **9** anonymous, incognito **10** unfamiliar **12** incalculable **13** inexpressible
unlace: **4** undo **5** loose **6** carver **7** undress, unravel **8** unfasten, untangle
unlawful: **7** bastard, illegal, illicit **8** criminal, wrongful **9** irregular **10** contraband **12** illegitimate
hunting: **8** poaching
intrusion: **8** trespass
unlearned: **4** lewd **5** gross **6** borrel **7** natural **8** ignorant, untaught **9** ututored **10** illiterate, uneducated **11** instinctive, instinctual, unscholarly
unleashed: **4** free **5** loose **8** released
unleavened: **4** flat **7** azymous
bread: **4** azym **5** azyme, matzo **7** matzoth(pl.)
unless: **4** lest, nisi(L.), save **6** except **9** excepting
unlettered: **4** lewd **8** ignorant **9** barbarian **10** illiterate, uneducated
unlike: **6** uneven **7** difform, diverse **8** unlikely **9** different, irregular **10** dissimilar, improbable **13** heterogeneous
unlikely: **5** unfit **10** improbable, unsuitable **11** unpromising **12** disagreeable,

unattractive **13** objectionable
unlikeness: **8** contrast **12** disagreement **13** dissimilarity
unlimited: **4** vast **5** total **9** boundless, limitless, unbounded, undefined, universal **10** indefinite, unconfined **11** illimitable, untrammeled **12** immeasurable, unrestricted **13** indeterminate
unload: **4** dump, land **5** empty, trash **6** decant, remove **7** deplete, discard, lighten, relieve **9** disburden, discharge, jettison, liquidate, sacrifice
unlock: ope **4** open **5** solve **6** reveal
unlooked for: **6** chance **10** unexpected
unlucky: bad, fey, ill **7** hapless **8** ill-fated **9** ill-omened **11** apocalyptic, starcrossed unfortunate
unman: **5** crush **7** monster, unnerve **8** castrate
unmanageable: **5** randy **6** unruly **8** churlish **10** disorderly
unmanly: **8** childish
unmannerly: **4** rude **7** boorish, uncivil **8** impolite **10** ungracious **12** discourteous
unmarried: one **4** lone **6** chaste, single
in law: **4** sole
woman: **7** old maid **8** spinster **12** bachelorette
unmask: **6** expose, reveal, unface **7** uncloak **8** disclose **9** dismantle
unmatched: odd **5** alone **9** matchless
unmeasured: **4** huge, vast **7** immense **9** boundless **12** incalculable, unrestrained
unmelodious: **9** dissonant **11** cacophonous
unmerciful: **5** cruel **8** pitiless, ruthless **9** inclement **10** relentless
unmethodical: **7** cursory, erratic **9** desultory
unmindful: **8** careless, heedless **9** forgetful, negligent **10** neglectful
unmistakable: **4** open **5** clear, plain **6** patent **7** evident, obvious **8** apparent, definite
unmitigated: **4** mere, pure **5** sheer, utter **6** arrant **8** absolute, clearcut **10** unmodified
unmixed: **4** deep, mear, mere, pure **5** blank, sheer, utter **7** sincere **8** straight
unmoved: **4** calm, cool, firm **5** stony **6** serene **7** adamant **8** obdurate, stubborn, unshaken **9** apathetic
unmoving: **5** inert **6** static
unnatural: **4** eery **5** eerie **7** strange, uncanny **8** abnormal, affected, farcical **9** irregular **10** artificial, factitious **11** counterfeit **12** supernatural
unnecessary: **6** excess **7** useless **8** needless **8** prodigal **9** redundant **10** gratuitous **11** superfluous, uncalled-for
unnerve: **5** unman **6** weaken, castrate **8** enervate **10** dishearten, emasculate

unobservant: 8 heedless 11 inattentive

unobstructed: 4 free, open 9 panoramic

unobtrusive: 5 quiet 6 modest 8 retiring

unobtrusively: 9 underhand

unoccupied: 4 free, idle, void 5 empty 6 vacant 7 leisure 10 unemployed

unofficial: 7 private 8 informal

unorganized: 5 messy 7 chaotic 10 disorderly, incoherent

unoriginal: 4 arid, copy 5 trite 7 sterile 10 secondhand

unorthodox: 9 heretical

unostentatious: 5 plain, quiet 6 lenten, modest 10 restrained

unpaid: due 6 arrear 10 unrevenged 11 outstanding

unpaired: odd

unpalatable: 4 flat, thin, weak 8 nauseous 10 unpleasant 11 distasteful

unparalleled: 5 alone 6 unique 7 unequal 8 peerless 9 matchless, unmatched 10 inimitable

unpleasant: bad 7 irksome 9 offensive 10 abominable, forbidding, ill-favored, ungracious 11 displeasing, distasteful 12 disagreeable

most: 5 worst

unplowed: lea 6 fallow 8 untilled

unpolished: 4 rude 5 bruit, crude, rough 6 coarse, rugged 7 boorish 8 agrestic, impolite 9 barbarous 10 agrestical

unpopularity: 5 odium

unprecedented: new 5 novel 9 unheard-of 10 unexampled

unprejudiced: 4 fair 9 impartial 13 dispassionate

unpremeditated: 6 casual 9 extempore 10 accidental 11 spontaneous

unprepared: raw 5 unfit 6 asleep 11 unorganized

unprepossessing: 4 ugly 5 plain 6 homely 11 unappealing 12 unattractive

unpretentious: 5 plain 6 homely, humble, modest, simple 10 unaffected

unprincipled: 4 lewd 7 corrupt 9 abandoned 10 perfidious 12 unscrupulous

unprocessed: raw 5 crude

unproductive: 4 arid, dead, lean 6 barren, futile, geason 7 sterile 8 impotent 10 unfruitful

unprofessional: lay 6 laical 7 amateur 9 unskilled 15 nonprofessional

unprofitable: dry 4 dead 6 barren 7 inutile, useless 8 bootless, gainless 9 fruitless, frustrate 10 unfruitful 12 frustraneous 15 disadvantageous

unpropitious: 4 evil 7 adverse, counter, ominous, opposed 12 antagonistic, inauspicious

unprotected: 6 unsafe 7 exposed 8 helpless, insecure 9 unguarded

unqualified: 4 bare, mear, meer, mere, sure 5 sheer, unfit, utter 6 entire, unable 7 plenary 8 absolute, complete, definite 9 categoric, downright, incapable 11 categorical, incompetent

unquestionable: 7 certain, decided, evident 8 implicit, positive 9 authentic, downright 12 indisputable

unravel: 4 undo 5 feaze, ravel, solve 6 unfold, unlace 8 disorder, disunite, separate, untangle 9 disengage, extricate, figure out 11 disentangle

unready: 4 slow 5 unfit 6 clumsy 7 awkward 8 hesitant 9 undressed 10 unprepared

unreal: 5 false, ideal 6 aerial 7 fancied, fatuous, nominal 8 aeriform, fanciful, illusive, illusory, spurious 9 deceptive, fantastic, imaginary, pretended, visionary 10 apocryphal, artificial, barmecidal, fictitious, mendacious 11 counterfeit, imaginative 13 insubstantial, unsubstantial

unreasonable: mad 6 absurd 9 excessive, illogical, senseless 10 exorbitant, immoderate, irrational 11 extravagant, impractical

unrecognized: 6 unsung 7 unknown 13 unappreciated

unrefined: raw 4 dark, loud, rude 5 broad, crass, crude, gross 6 coarse, common, earthy, native, vulgar 7 uncouth 8 ungraded 12 uncultivated

unregenerate: 6 carnal, sinful 9 obstinate, shameless 10 impenitent 11 unrepentant 12 recalcitrant

unrelated: 5 fremd 8 separate 9 disjoined

unrelaxed: 4 taut 5 tense

unrelenting: 4 grim, hard, iron 5 cruel, stern 6 severe 8 rigorous 9 merciless 10 inexorable, inflexible, relentless, unyielding

unreliable: 5 fishy 6 fickle, shifty, unsafe 7 casalty 10 capricious, fly-by-night 12 undependable 13 irresponsible, untrustworthy

unremitting: 4 busy, hard 9 assiduous, continual, incessant 10 persistent 11 persevering

unrepentant: 10 impenitent 11 remorseless 12 unregenerate

unreserved: 4 free 5 frank 6 candid 9 outspoken, unlimited 13 demonstrative

unresponsive: 4 cold, cool 6 frigid

unrest: 5 alarm 6 bustle, motion 7 anarchy, ferment 8 disquiet 9 commotion 10 uneasiness

unrestrained: lax 4 free, wild 5 bluff, blunt, broad, loose 6 wanton 7 riotous 9 abandoned, audacious, dissolute, excessive, expansive, unbounded, unbridled, unlimited 10 licentious, unmeasured 11 extravagant 12 uncontrolled

unrestraint: 7 abandon, license **8** immunity **11** spontaneity

unrevealed: 6 hidden, latent, masked, untold **7** covered **9** concealed

unripe: 5 crude, green, young **6** callow **7** uncured, unready **8** immature **9** premature **10** precocious, unseasoned **12** unseasonable **13** inexperienced

unroll: 6 evolve, unfold **7** develop, display, open out **8** disclose

unruffled: 4 calm, cool **5** quiet **6** placid, poised, sedate, serene, smooth **8** decorous **11** undisturbed **13** dispassionate, philosophical

unruly: 6 haunty, ramage **7** froward, lawless, restive **9** fractious, obstinate, out of hand, turbulent **10** disorderly, headstrong, licentious, refractory **11** disobedient, intractable **12** recalcitrant, ungovernable, unmanageable

unsafe: 5 risky, shaky **7** exposed **8** insecure, perilous **9** dangerous, hazardous **10** unreliable

unsatisfactory: bad 9 defective, imperfect **10** inadequate **11** inefficient

unsavory: 7 insipid **9** offensive, tasteless **10** unpleasant **11** distasteful, unpalatable **12** disagreeable, unappetizing

unscrupulous: 5 shady, venal **6** crafty **7** corrupt **8** rascally **9** dishonest, miscreant **12** unprincipled **13** untrustworthy

unseal: 4 open **8** disclose

unseasonable: 6 unripe **8** ill-timed, improper, untimely **9** premature **11** inopportune

unseasoned: raw 5 bland, green **8** untimely

unseat: 6 depose, remove **7** unhorse **9** overthrow

unseemly: 5 crude, inept **6** coarse **8** improper, indecent, unworthy **10** indecorous, unbecoming **13** inappropriate

unseen: 9 invisible, unnoticed **10** unobserved **11** unperceived **12** undiscovered

unselfish: 6 heroic **8** generous **10** altruistic, benevolent

unserviceable: 7 useless **11** impractical

unsettle: 5 upset **7** commove, derange, disturb **8** disorder, displace, disquiet **10** disarrange, discompose

unsettled: 4 back, moot **6** fickle, queasy, unpaid **7** dubious, pending **8** restless, unstable **9** ambiguous, desultory, itinerant, uncertain, unquieted **10** changeable, precarious, unoccupied **11** unpopulated **12** undetermined **13** problematical

unshaken: 4 firm, sure **6** steady

unshapely: 8 deformed

unsheathe: 4 draw **6** remove **7** pull out

unsightly: 4 drab, ugly **5** messy **6** homely

unskilled: 4 rude **5** green **6** puisne **7** artless **8** ignorant, malapert **10** amateurish

unskillful: 5 inept **6** bungly, clumsy **7** awkward **10** inexpertly **13** inexperienced

unskillfully: 5 badly

unsociable: shy 4 cool **5** aloof **6** sullen **8** reserved **9** withdrawn **11** standoffish

unsoiled: 5 clean **10** immaculate

unsophisticated: 4 naif, pure **5** frank, green, naive **6** callow, simple **7** artless, genuine, natural **8** bona fide, innocent **9** ingenious, untutored

unsound: bad 4 evil, sick, weak **5** crazy, dotty, false, frail, risky, shaky **6** addled, fickle, flawed, hollow, insane, rotten, weakly **7** decayed, wracked **8** diseased, impaired, insecure, weakened **9** dangerous, defective, imperfect, tottering **10** ill-founded

unspeakable: bad 4 vile **6** wicked **7** heinous **9** ineffable **10** outrageous **11** unutterable

unspoiled: 4 racy **5** fresh **6** virgin

unspoken: 4 mute **5** tacit **6** silent **9** ineffable, unuttered

unspotted: 5 clear **8** spotless **10** immaculate

unstable: 5 loose, sandy **6** fickle, fitful, flitty, labile **7** astatic, dwaible, dwaibly, erratic, flightly, mutable, plastic **8** doubtful, insecure, ticklish, unhinged, unsteady, variable **9** eccentric, faithless, irregular, unsettled **10** changeable, inconstant, precarious, unreliable **11** fluctuating, vacillating

unsteady: 5 dizzy, fluky, shaky, tippy **6** fickle, flicky, fluffy, groggy, wabbly, wobbly **7** erratic, movable, quavery, rickety, unsound, wayward **8** titubate, unstable, variable, wavering **9** desultory, irregular, uncertain **10** capricious, changeable, flickering, inconstant **11** fluctuating, lightheaded, vacillating

unstinted: 5 ample **6** lavish **7** endless **8** generous

unstudied: 7 natural **8** careless, unforced, unversed **9** unlearned **10** colloquial, unaffected **11** extemporary, spontaneous

unsubstantial: 4 airy, slim, thin, weak **5** filmy, light, paper **6** aerial, flimsy, papery, slight, unreal **7** folious, gaseous, nominal, shadowy, tenuous **8** filigree, footless **9** visionary **10** immaterial **11** implausible

unsuccessful: 6 losing **7** failing, unlucky **8** abortive **9** fruitless **10** disastrous **11** ineffectual, unfortunate

unsuitable: bad 5 inapt, inept, undue, unfit **8** improper **10** unbecoming **13** inappropriate

unsullied: 4 pure 5 clean 6 chaste 8 spotless 10 immaculate

unsure: 4 weak 5 timid 6 infirm 8 doubtful 9 dangerous, hazardous 10 precarious, unreliable 11 vacillating 13 untrustworthy

unsusceptible: 6 immune 8 obdurate

unsweetened: dry, sec 4 sour

unswerving: 4 firm, true 5 fixed, loyal 6 steady 8 straight 9 steadfast

unsymmetrical: 8 lopsided 9 irregular 15 disproportional

unsympathetic: 4 cold, cool, hard 5 stony 6 frozen 7 hostile 9 heartless, unfeeling, unlikable 11 hardhearted 12 unresponsive

untainted: 4 free, good, pure 8 innocent 9 unsullied

untalented: 8 mediocre 11 incompetent

untamed: 4 wild 5 feral 6 ferine, ramage, ramish, savage 9 unsubdued

untangle: 4 free 6 sleave, unlace 9 extricate 11 disentangle

untanned skin: kip 4 hide, pelt 8 shagreen

untarnished: 5 clean 8 spotless

untaught: 5 naive 7 natural 8 ignorant 9 unlearned 10 illiterate, uneducated 11 spontaneous 12 uninstructed

untenanted: 5 empty 6 vacant

untended: 7 run-down 9 neglected

untested: new 5 green 7 untried

unthinking: 4 rash 5 brute 6 casual 8 careless, feckless, heedless 9 impetuous 11 thoughtless 13 inconsiderate

unthrifty: 6 wanton 7 foolish, profuse 8 prodigal 10 profitless, profligate 11 extravagant, improvident

untidy: 5 dowdy, messy 7 bunting 8 careless, littered, slipshod, slovenly 10 disheveled, disordered, slatternly 11 disarranged

untidy person: pig 4 slob 6 sloven 8 slattern

untie: 4 free, undo 5 loose 6 loosen, unbind, unlash 8 disunite, unfasten 9 disengage, extricate

until: til 4 till, unto
  now: 5 as yet

untimely: 5 early 8 immature 9 premature 11 inopportune 12 unseasonable

untiring: 4 busy 8 sedulous, tireless 13 indefatigable

untold: 4 huge, vast 9 boundless, unrelated 10 uninformed, unrevealed 13 innumerable 12 immeasurable, incalculable

untouchable: 7 outcast 8 chandala, déclassé 10 intangible

untouched: 5 whole 6 intact, virgin 9 insensate

untoward: 6 unruly 7 awkward, froward,

unlucky 8 improper, perverse, stubborn, unseemly 9 vexatious 10 indecorous, ungraceful 11 troublesome, unfavorable, unfortunate 12 inconvenient, unpropitious

untrained: raw 4 wild 5 green 7 awkward, untamed 8 undocile 9 unskilled 10 amateurish, unprepared

untrammeled: 4 free 5 loose 9 audacious, unlimited 10 unhampered

untransferable: 11 inalienable

untraversed: 6 untrod

untried: new 5 fresh, green 8 immature, untested 13 inexperienced

untrue: 4 flam 5 false, wrong 8 disloyal, perjured 9 erroneous, faithless, incorrect 10 fallacious, unfaithful 11 disaffected

untrustworthy: 6 tricky, unsafe 8 slippery 9 dishonest, uncertain 10 perfidious, unreliable 12 undependable

untruth: lie 5 fable 7 fallacy, falsity 9 falsehood, mendacity, treachery 11 fabrication, tarradiddle

untutored: 5 naive 6 simple 7 artless, natural 8 clownish, ignorant, untaught 9 barbarian, unlearned 10 illiterate 15 unsophisticated

untwine: 4 free, undo 5 frese, untie 6 unwind 9 extricate 11 disentangle

unused: new 4 idle 5 fresh 6 vacant 8 unwonted 12 unaccustomed

unusual: odd 4 rare 5 novel, queer, weird 6 quaint, unique 7 strange 8 abnormal, uncommon, unwonted 9 anomalous, different, eccentric 10 remarkable 11 exceptional 12 illegitimate 13 extraordinary

unusual person or thing: 4 oner

unutterable, inutterable: 7 extreme 9 ineffable 11 unspeakable 13 inexpressible 15 unpronounceable

unvaried: 5 alike 7 uniform 10 monotonous

unvarnished: 4 bald 5 frank, plain 6 simple 8 unglazed 9 unadorned, unglossed 13 unembellished

unveil: 4 open 6 reveal 7 uncover 8 disclose

unvoiced: 4 surd 5 tacit 6 secret 8 unspoken 9 unuttered

unwarranted: 5 undue 8 baseless 11 unjustified 12 unreasonable

unwary: 4 rash 7 unaware 8 careless, heedless 9 credulous, unguarded 10 groundless, incautious 11 precipitate

unwavering: 4 firm, pure 5 solid 6 stable 8 constant 9 steadfast

unwearied: 4 busy 8 tireless 9 assiduous 13 indefatigable

unweave: 4 undo 5 ravel 6 unfold

unwed: 6 single

unwelcome: 8 non grata, unwanted 9 intruding, intrusive 13 objectionable

unwell: ill 4 evil, sick 5 badly 6 ailing 8 off-color 9 squeamish 10 out-of-sorts

unwholesome: 4 evil 6 impure 7 corrupt, harmful, immoral, noisome, noxious, unclean 9 offensive 11 unhealthful

unwieldy: 5 bulky, heavy 6 clumsy 7 awkward, hulking 8 cumbrous, ungainly 9 ponderous 10 cumbersome 12 hippopotamic, unmanageable

unwilling: 4 loth 5 loath 6 averse, mauger, maugre 7 loathly 8 backward 9 eschewing, reluctant 11 disinclined

unwind: 5 ravel, relax 6 uncoil 8 untangle 11 disentangle

unwise: 5 inane, naive 6 simple 7 foolish, witless 9 brainless, impolitic, imprudent, senseless 10 indiscreet, irrational 11 injudicious 12 undiplomatic 13 unintelligent

unwonted: 4 rare 6 unused 7 unusual 8 uncommon 10 infrequent 11 exceptional 12 unaccustomed

unworldly: 4 eery 5 eerie, naive, weird 6 dreamy, natural 9 spiritual, unearthly

unworthy: 4 base 7 beneath 8 shameful, unseemly 9 no-account, worthless 10 despicable, unbecoming 12 contemptible, dishonorable

unwrinkled: 5 brent(Sc.) 6 smooth

unwritten: 4 oral 5 blank, vocal 6 verbal 11 word-of-mouth

unwrought: 8 unworked

unyielding: set 4 fast, firm, grim, hard, iron 5 fixed, rigid, stern, stiff, stith, stony, tough 6 frozen, steely 7 adamant 8 obdurate, stubborn 9 inelastic, obstinate, unbending 10 determined, inexorable, inflexible, relentless 11 immalleable 12 contumacious, unsubmissive 14 uncompromising

unyoke: 4 free, part 5 loose 6 remove 7 disjoin, release 8 separate 10 disconnect

up: 4 busy, rise 5 aloft, astir, raise 6 active 7 success 8 familiar 9 according

up and down: 5 erect 6 direct, uneven 7 upright 8 vertical 9 downright, irregular 10 thoroughly, undulating 13 perpendicular

up to: 4 able 5 until
date: new 6 modern 7 stylish 11 fashionable
this time: 6 hereto 8 hitherto

upas tree gum: 6 antiar 11 arrow poison

upbeat: 5 arsis 10 optimistic

upbraid: 4 draw, rail, twit 5 abuse, blame, braid, chide, scold, score, taunt, twist 6 accuse, charge 7 censure, reprove 8 denounce, reproach 9 exprobate 10 denunciate

upbuilding: 8 increase 11 edification

update: 5 renew 7 restore 9 modernize

upgrade: 5 raise, slope 6 ascent 7 incline

upheaval: 5 storm 6 revolt 7 rummage 9 agitation, cataclysm, commotion

upheave: 4 lift, rear, rise

uphill: 4 hard 6 rising, tiring 7 arduous, labored 9 ascending, difficult, laborious

uphold: aid 4 abet, back, bear, lift, stay 5 favor, raise 6 assert, defend, favour, second 7 confirm, support, sustain 8 conserve, maintain 9 encourage, vindicate 11 countenance

upholder: 6 dealer 8 adherent 9 tradesman 10 undertaker 11 upholsterer

upholstered: fat 9 cushioned, luxurious

upkeep: 4 cost 6 repair 7 support 8 overhead 11 maintenance

upland: 4 wold 6 coteau 7 plateau

uplift: 4 head, lift, rock 5 erect, raise, tower 7 collect, elevate, ennoble, improve 8 upheaval 9 elevation 10 illuminate

Upolu: *city:* 4 Apia
island group: 5 Samoa

upon: oer, sur(law) 4 atop, over 5 about, above 8 touching 10 concerning
that: 7 threat 9 thereupon
which: 7 whereat 9 whereupon

upper: 4 bunk, drug, over, vamp 5 above, berth 8 superior 9 stimulant 11 amphetamine

upper case: 7 capital

upper crust: 5 elite 7 segment, society

upper lips part: 5 flews

upperclassman: 6 junior, senior

uppermost: top 5 first 6 apical 7 highest, topmost 8 farthest, foremost, loftiest 9 outermost 11 predominant

uppish: 5 brash, proud 6 elated 7 haughty, peevish 8 arrogant, assuming, snobbish 12 presumptuous

upraised: 5 atilt 6 lifted, raised 7 erected 8 elevated, extolled, improved 10 encouraged

uprear: 5 build, erect, exalt, raise

upright: 4 good, just, true 5 erect, moral, piano, right, stela, stele, stile 6 honest, square 7 endwise, sincere 8 straight, vertical, virtuous 9 elevation, equitable, honorable, righteous 10 pianoforte, scrupulous 11 unambiguous 13 perpendicular
support: 4 jamb, stud

uprightness: 6 equity 7 probity 9 rectitude

uprising: 4 riot 6 ascent, mutiny, putsch, revolt, tumult 7 ensuing 8 reaction 9 ascending, commotion, rebellion 10 increasing, insurgency, revolution 12 insurrection 17 counterrevolution

uproar: din 4 riot, rout 5 brawl, chaos,

hurly, melee, noise **6** bedlam, bustle, clamor, dirdum, fracas, habble, hubble, hubbub, rattle, tumult **7** clamour, ferment, turmoil **8** outbreak **9** commotion, confusion **10** convulsion, donnybrook, hurlyburly, rumbullion, tintamarre **11** disturbance, pandemonium

uproot: 4 move **5** shift **7** destroy **8** supplant **9** eradicate, extirpate **10** annihilate, transplant **11** exterminate

upset: irk **4** cave, coup, keel, rile, turn **6** defeat, refund, topple **7** capsize, confuse, derange, disturb, outcome, pervert, quarrel, reverse, subvert **8** capsized, overturn **9** discomfit, embarrass, overthrow, perturbed **10** debilitate, discompose, disconcert, disordered, distressed, overturned **11** disorganize

upshot: end **5** issue, limit **6** effect, finish, result, sequel **7** outcome **9** aftermath, substance **10** conclusion **11** termination **12** consummation

upside-down: 7 chaotic, jumbled **8** inverted **10** topsy-turvy

upstage: shy **5** aloof **6** offish **8** backward, outshine, snobbish **9** conceited **12** supercilious

upstart: 4 snob **6** origin **7** dalteen, parvenu, saffron **8** parvenue **9** cockhorse

upstir: 6 incite **7** agitate **9** stimulate

upsurge: 4 boom **9** inflation

upstake: 4 flue, tube **5** shaft **6** upcast **10** collection, comprehend **13** comprehension, understanding

uptight: 4 edgy **5** tense **6** uneasy

up-to-date: 6 modern **7** abreast **9** au courant

upupoid bird: 6 hoopoe

upward: 4 more, over **5** above, aloft, lofty **7** airward, skyward **8** airwards **9** ascending

uraeus: asp **6** symbol **8** ornament **10** decoration

uralite: 9 amphibole

Urania's son: 5 Hymen

uranian: 8 heavenly **9** celestial, homosexual **12** astronomical

uranium: 15 chemical element
dioxide: **10** ianthinite
source: **11** pitchblende

Uranus: *children:* **4** Rhea **5** Titan **7** Cyclops
moon: **5** Ariel **6** Oberon **7** Titania, Umbriel
mother: **4** Gaea, Gaia
satellite: **5** Ariel **6** Oberon **7** Miranda, Titania, Umbriel
wife: **4** Gaea, Gaia

urban: 5 civic **7** oppidan **8** citified **9** inner city

urban division: 4 ward

urbane: 5 bland, civil, suave **6** poised, polite, smooth **7** affable, elegant, genteel, refined **8** polished **9** courteous **12** cosmopolitan **13** sophisticated

urchin: boy, cub, elf, imp, tad **4** arab, brat **5** child, elfin, gamin **8** cylinder, hedgehog, hurcheon **9** hunchback, youngster **10** ragamuffin, street arab

ure: 4 haze, mist

urease: 6 enzyme

uredo: 5 hives **9** urticaria **11** burning itch

urge: dun, egg, ert(Sc.), hie, ply, sue **4** brod, coax, goad, prod, push, spur **5** broad, drive, filip, force, hurry, impel, plead, press **6** allege, compel, demand, desire, excite, exhort, fillip, incite, induce, insist, motive, needle **7** animate, augment, entreat, impulse, provoke, solicit **8** advocate, persuade **9** flagitate, importune, incentive, influence, stimulate **10** exasperate

urgency: 4 need **5** haste, hurry **6** crisis, stress **8** exigency, pressure **10** insistence **11** importunity

urgent: hot **5** grave **7** clamant, driving, exigent **8** critical, pressing **9** demanding, impelling, important **10** solicitous **11** importunate

Uriah's wife: 9 Bathsheba

urial, oorial: sha **5** sheep

Uriel: 5 angel **9** archangel

Urim's partner: 7 Thummim

Uris novel: 5 QBVII **6** Exodus

urisk: 7 brownie

urn: jar, run **4** bury, ewer, urna, vase **5** grave, inurn, steen, theca **6** spring **7** capsule, cistern, pitcher, samovar, vaselet **8** fountain **9** container **10** jardiniere **11** watercourse
for bones: **7** ossuary
tea: **7** samovar

urn-shaped: 9 urceolate

urodela: 5 newts, order **7** Caudata **8** amphibia **10** salamander

Ursa: 4 Bear
Major: **9** Great Bear
Minor: **10** Little Bear

ursine: 7 arctoid **8** bearlike

urticaria: 5 hives, uredo

urubu: 7 vulture

Uruguay: *capital:* **10** Montevideo
city: **4** Melo **5** Minas **6** Rivera
discoverer: **5** Solis
estuary: **5** Plata
lake: **5** Merin, Mirim
measure: **4** vara **6** cuadra, suerte
monetary unit: **4** peso
river: **4** Malo **5** Negro **6** Ulimar **7** Uruguay **9** Cebollary **10** Tacaurembo
weight: **7** quintal

urus: tur **7** aurochs

us: uns(Gr.) **4** nous(Fr.)

usable: fit **4** open **8** servable **9** available,

practical **10** convenient, functional **11** serviceable, utilitarian

usage: use **4** form, wont **5** habit, haunt, idiom **6** custom, method **7** conduct, manners, utility **8** behavior, interest, practice **9** treatment **10** convention, employment, experience

use: try **4** boot, duty, hire, vail, wont **5** apply, avail, guide, habit, right, spend, stead, treat, trope, usage, value, wield **6** behoof, custom, employ, expend, handle, hansel, occupy, target **7** benefit, consume, exhaust, exploit, utility, utilize **8** accustom, deal with, exercise, frequent, function, handling, practice **9** habituate, privilege, treatment **10** employment, fall back on, manipulate **11** application, consumption, utilization

as example: **4** cite

refrain from: **7** boycott

to be of: **5** avail

up: eat **4** tire **5** drain, spend **7** consume, deplete, exhaust, outwear

wastefully: **5** spill **7** fritter **8** squander **9** dissipate

used: **8** shopworn **10** secondhand **11** experienced

useful: **4** good **5** utile **7** helpful, thrifty **9** practical **10** beneficial, commodious, profitable **11** serviceable **12** advantageous

usefulness: **5** avail, value **6** profit **7** utility

useless: **4** idle, null, vain **6** futile, otiose **7** inutile **8** bootless, hopeless **9** fruitless, worthless **11** ineffectual, inefficient, superfluous **12** unprofitable **13** impracticable, unserviceable **14** good-for-nothing

user: **6** addict **7** pothead **8** consumer

usher: **4** lead, page **5** guide **6** beadle, escort, herald **7** chobdar, conduct, officer, precede, preface, servant, teacher **9** announcer, assistant, attendant, harbinger, introduce, precursor **10** doorkeeper, forerunner, inaugurate

in: **6** launch **9** introduce **10** inaugurate

usings: **8** property **10** belongings

U.S.S.R.: See **Union of Soviet Socialist Republics**

usual: **4** rife **6** common, normal, wonted **7** average, chronic, general, regular, routine, typical **8** familiar, frequent, habitual, ordinary, orthodox **9** customary **10** accustomed, prevailing **11** stereotyped **12** conventional

usurer: **5** shark **6** loaner **9** loan shark **11** moneylender

usurp: **4** take **5** seize, wrest **6** assume **8** accroach, arrogate

usury: **7** gombeen

Utah: *canyon:* **5** Bryce

capital: **12** Salt Lake City

city: **4** Orem **5** Logan, Ogden, Provo **6** Murray

county: **4** Juab **5** Cache, Davis, Wayne, Weber **6** Uintah

highest peak: **5** Kings

Indian: Ute

lake: **4** Swan, Utah **6** Sevier **9** Great Salt

motto: **8** Industry

mountain range: **5** Uinta

national park: **4** Zion

nickname: **6** Mormon **7** Beehive

people: **6** Mormon

plateau: **7** Wasatch

river: **5** Grand, Green, Weber **6** Jordan, Sevier **8** Colorado

state bird: **7** seagull

state flower: **8** sego lily

state tree: **6** spruce

town: **4** Lehi **5** Delta, Heber, Kanab **6** Beaver, Eureka, Payson, Tooele **7** Milford

utensil: pan, pot, wok **4** tool **5** sieve **6** grater, vessel **7** skillet **8** strainer **9** collander, implement **10** instrument

cleaning: mop **5** broom, brush **6** Hoover, ramrod, vacuum **7** Bissell, sweeper

Uther's son: **10** King Arthur

utile: **6** useful **9** practical **10** profitable **12** advantageous

utilitarian: **5** plain **6** useful **8** economic **9** practical, realistic **10** functional **12** matter-of-fact

utility: use **5** avail **6** profit **7** benefit, service

utilize: use **6** employ, enlist **7** consume, exploit, harness, husband **9** economize

utmost: end **4** best, last **5** final **7** extreme, maximum **8** farthest, greatest **9** uttermost

Uto-Aztecan Indian: **4** Pima **7** Nahuatl **8** Shoshone

Utopia: **4** Eden **9** Shangri La

author: **4** More

Harrington's: **6** Oceana

Utopian: **5** ideal **8** idealist, Quixotic **9** visionary **10** chimerical

utricle: sac **7** vesicle

Uttar Pradesh: *capital:* **7** Lucknow

country: **5** India

utter: add, say **4** blat, bray, dang, darn, emit, gasp, pipe, pray, rail, roar, tell, vent **5** blurt, clack, croak, drawl, final, issue, mince, sheer, speak, spill, spout, stark, state, total, trill, voice **6** assert, direct, entire, mumble, reveal, warble **7** bluster, deliver, divulge, enounce, express, extreme, iterate, publish **8** abnormal, absolute, complete, disclose **9** downright, enunciate, out-and-out, pronounce **10** articulate, peremptory **11** unqualified **13** unconditional

utterance: gab **4** osse, word **5** aside, dicta, ditty **6** dictum, oracle, speech **7** calling **8** effusion, monotone, phonesis, rhapsody **9** phonation **10** expression, forthgoing **12** articulation, vocalization
soft: **6** breath, murmur **7** whisper
voiced: **6** sonant
voiceless: **4** surd **7** spirate
uttered: **4** oral **6** spoken
utterly: all **4** well **5** fully, stark **6** in toto, merely **7** totally **8** entirely **10** absolutely, allutterly, completely **11** diametrally **13** diametrically **17** straightforwardly
uttermost: **5** final **6** utmost **7** extreme, outmost
utu: **6** reward **12** compensation, satisfaction
uva: **5** fruit, grape
uxorial: **6** wifely
Uzbek: *capital:* **8** Tashkent
country: **4** USSR

V

V: vee **4** five
symbol of: **7** victory
V-shaped piece: **5** wedge
vacancy: gap **5** break, chasm, space **6** cavity, hollow **7** interim, vacuity **10** hollowness, interstice **11** vacuousness
vacant: **4** free, idle, open, void **5** blank, empty, fishy, inane, silly **6** barren, devoid, hollow, lonely **7** foolish, lacking, leisure, vacuous, wanting **8** unfilled **9** destitute **10** disengaged, unemployed, unoccupied, untenanted **12** unencumbered, unreflecting **14** expressionless
vacate: **4** quit, void **5** annul, avoid, clear, empty, leave **6** repeal **7** abandon, abolish, rescind **8** abdicate, abrogate, evacuate
vacation: **4** rest **5** leave, spell **6** outing, recess **7** holiday, leisure, nonterm, respite, time off **8** furlough **9** justitium **12** intermission
place: spa **4** city, lake, park **5** beach, ocean **6** forest, resort **7** seaside **9** mountains
vaccinate: **9** inoculate
vaccination: *inventor:* **6** Jenner
vaccine: **4** sera, shot **5** serum
discoverer of: **4** Salk **6** Jenner
vacillate: **4** sway **5** dally, waver **6** dacker, daiker, dawdle, seesaw, teeter, totter **7** flutter, stagger **8** hesitate, titubate **9** fluctuate, hem and haw, oscillate
vacillation: **5** doubt **7** halting, swaying **8** wavering **9** faltering, hesitancy, infirmity **10** fickleness, indecision, unsureness
11 uncertainty **12** irresolution **13** dillydallying **14** changeableness
vacuity: **4** hole, void **6** hollow **7** inanity, vacancy **11** nothingness
vacuous: **4** dull, idle **5** blank, empty **6** stupid **8** unfilled **9** evacuated, senseless **11** purposeless **13** unintelligent
vacuum: **4** void **5** space **9** emptiness
opposite of: **6** plenum
vacuum pump: **10** pulsometer
vacuum tube: **5** diode **7** tetrode **9** electrode
vade mecum: **6** manual **8** handbook
vadimonium: **4** bond **6** pledge **8** bailment, contract, security
vadium: **4** bail, pawn **6** pledge
vagabond: bum **4** rove **5** scamp, stray, tramp **6** beggar, canter, jockey, rascal, rogue, wander **7** erratic, gadling, nomadic, vagrant, wayward **8** bohemian, brodyaga, drifting, fugitive, wanderer **9** itinerant, shiftless, straggler, wandering, worthless **10** blackguard, ne'er-do-well **11** bindle stiff **12** hallanshaker **14** good-for-nothing
vagarious: **5** kinky **7** erratic **9** arbitrary **13** unpredictable
vagary: **4** roam, whim **5** caper, fancy, freak, jaunt, prank, quirk, stray, trick, waver **6** action, breach, notion, oddity, ramble, totter, whimsy **7** caprice, conceit **8** flagarie, rambling **9** departure, excursion, procedure, wandering **10** digression, divergence **12** passing fancy **13** manifestation

vagrant: See **vagabond**

vague: dim **4** dark, hazy **5** faint, loose, misty, stray **6** bleary, blurry, dreamy, vagary **7** obscure, shadowy, sketchy, unfixed, vagrant **8** confused, nebulous, vagabond, wanderer **9** ambiguous, uncertain, unsettled, wandering **10** ill-defined, indefinite, indistinct, intangible **13** indeterminate

vail: tip, use **4** doff, dole **5** bribe, lower, yield **6** humble, submit **7** benefit, subside **8** gratuity **9** advantage **10** beneficial

vain: **4** idle **5** empty, flory, petty, proud, silly **6** flimsy, futile, hollow, otiose, snooty **7** foolish, foppish, stuckup, trivial, useless **8** gorgeous, hopeless, ignorant, nugatory, peacocky **9** conceited, fruitless, worthless **10** chimerical, evanescent, unavailing, unrewarded **11** empty-headed, ineffectual, overweening, unimportant **12** unprofitable, vainglorious

vain boasting: **11** fanfaronade

vain person: fop **5** dandy **7** coxcomb

vainglorious: **8** boastful, insolent **9** conceited

vair: fur

Vaishnavas: *deity:* **6** Vishnu
priest: **6** gosain, gusain

Vaisya caste: **6** Aroras

vakass: **5** amice

valance: **5** drape **6** pelmet **7** curtain, drapery, hanging

vale: **4** dale, dean, dell, dene, glen **5** bache, combe, glade **6** dingle, valley **8** farewell

valediction: **5** adieu **7** address, good-bye **8** farewell

Valence's river: **5** Rhone

valence: **5** power, value **7** atomism **10** importance

valentine: **4** card, gift, love **8** greeting **10** sweetheart

valerian: **4** drug **5** plant **7** allheal, panacea, setwall

valet: man **4** goad **5** stick **6** andrew, tartar **7** dresser **9** attendant, cameriere, chamberer **10** manservant

Vali's parents: **4** Odin, Rind **5** Rindr

valiant: **4** bold, prow **5** aught, brave, proud, stout **6** heroic, robust, strong, sturdy **7** doughty **8** galliard, intrepid, powerful, stalwart, vigorous, virtuous **9** bounteous, excellent, steadfast **10** chivalrous, courageous **11** meritorious **12** stouthearted

valid: **4** good, just, true **5** legal, solid, sound **6** cogent, lawful, robust, strong **7** binding, healthy, telling, weighty **8** forcible, powerful **9** authentic, effective, efficient **10** conclusive, convincing, sufficient **11** efficacious **12** satisfactory, well-grounded

opposite of: **4** null, void

validate: **7** confirm **9** establish **11** rubber-stamp

valise: bag **4** case, grip **7** baggage, satchel **8** suitcase

valium: **4** drug **12** tranquilizer

Valjean: *pursuer:* **6** Javert
friend: **6** Marius
protege: **7** Cosette

Valkyrie: **6** maiden **8** Brynhild **10** Brunnhilde

vallecula: **6** furrow, groove **7** channel **10** depression

Valletta people: **7** Maltese

valley: dip **4** brae, comb, coom, cove, dale, dean, dell, dene, ghyl, gill, glen, rill, vale, wadi, wady **5** atrio, basin, combe, coomb, dhoon, glack, gorge, goyal, goyle, gully, kloof, swale, waddy **6** bolson, canada, canyon, clough, coombe, coulee, dingle, gutter, hollow, ravine, rincon, strath, trough **7** blowout **10** depression
between volcanic cones: **5** atrio
deep: **5** canon **6** canyon

vallum: **4** wall **7** rampart

valor, valour: **4** guts, sand **5** arete, merit, value, worth **6** bounty, spirit, virtue **7** bravery, courage, heroism, prowess **8** position **9** valuation **10** importance **11** distinction **12** fearlessness

valuable: **4** dear **5** asset **6** costly, prized, useful, worthy **8** precious **9** estimable, excellent, expensive, respected, treasured **10** worthwhile **11** serviceable

valuable discovery: **4** find

value: use **4** cost, feck(Sc.), rate **5** avail, cheap, price, prize, worth **6** assess, assize, esteem, extend, moment **7** account, apprise, apprize, care for, cherish, compute, opinion, quality, respect, utility **8** appraise, estimate, evaluate, treasure **9** inventory, valuation **10** appreciate, estimation, importance
anything of little: **5** plack(Sc.) **6** trifle
equal: **6** parity
full: **11** money's worth
mathematical limit of: **8** derivate
mean: **7** average
net: **7** reserve
nominal: par
reduction: **12** depreciation
relative: **9** ad valorem
without: **5** waste **6** trashy **7** useless **9** worthless

valve: tap **4** cock, gate **6** faucet, outlet, piston, spigot **7** petcock
heart: **6** mitral **8** bicuspid
sliding: **6** piston

vamoose: lam **4** scat **5** leave, scram **6** decamp, depart, get out

vamp: **4** hose, mend, plod, sock **5** fix up,

flirt, patch, tramp 6 invent, repair, seduce 7 beguile, concoct, fireman 8 contrive 9 fabricate, improvise

vampire: bat 5 lamia 6 alukah, corpse, usurer 7 seducer 11 blackmailer, bloodsucker, extortioner 12 extortionist
famous: 7 Dracula

van: fan 4 fore, lead, wing 5 front, truck, wagon 6 shovel, summit, winnow 7 fourgon, vehicle 9 forefront

Van Gogh town: 5 Arles

vandal: hun 6 looter 7 hoodlum, ruffian, wrecker 8 hooligan 9 plunderer

vandalize: mar 6 deface, rip off 7 destroy

Vandyke: 5 beard 6 artist 7 picture

vane: arm 5 blade 7 feather 9 indicator 11 weathercock
feather: web 8 vexillum

vanguard: 9 forefront 10 avantgarde

vanilla: 5 bland 7 extract

vanilla substance: 8 coumarin

vanish: 4 fade, melt 5 clear 8 disperse, evanesce 9 disappear

vanity (see also **vain**): 4 airs 5 pride 6 egoism 7 compact, conceit, egotism, falsity, foppery 8 futility, idleness 9 dizziness, emptiness 10 hollowness 11 fatuousness, foolishness, self-conceit
symbol of: 7 peacock

vanity case: 4 etui 7 compact

Vanity Fair: *author:* 9 Thackeray
character: 10 Becky Sharp

vanquish: get, win 4 beat, best, rout 5 expel, floor 6 defeat, expugn, humble, master, subdue 7 confute, conquer, subvert 8 confound, overcome, suppress, surmount 9 overthrow

vanquisher: 6 victor 8 champion

vantage: See **advantage**

vapid: dry 4 dull, flat, pall, weak 5 inane, stale, trite 7 insipid, mawkish 8 lifeless 9 milk-toast, pointless, tasteless 10 flavorless, spiritless, unanimated, unexciting 13 uninteresting

vapor: fog, gas 4 fume, haze, idea, mist 5 boast, brume, cloud, ewder, fancy, humor, smoke, steam 6 breath, bubble, humour, nimbus, notion 7 halitus 8 contrail, humidity, phantasm 9 evaporate 10 blustering 11 braggadocio
frozen: 4 hail, rime, snow 5 frost, sleet
pressure indicator: 9 tonometer

vaporize: 5 steam 7 boil off 9 evaporate

vaporous: 4 hazy 8 fleeting, volatile 13 unsubstantial

vaquero: 6 cowboy 8 herdsman, horseman 10 equestrian

varec, varech: 4 kelp 5 ashes, wrack 7 seaweed

variable (see also **vary**): 6 fickle, fitful 7 mutable, protean, unequal, variant, varying 8 floating, unstable, unsteady 9 irregular, uncertain 10 capricious, changeable, inconstant

variance (see also **vary**): 7 discord, dispute 10 contention, difference 11 discrepancy

variation (see also **vary**): 8 heterism, mutation 9 tolerance 10 aberration, deflection 11 distinction

varicose: 7 dilated, swollen 8 enlarged

varied: 6 daedal 7 several 13 miscellaneous

variegated: 4 pied, shot 5 lyard(Sc.), lyart(Sc.) 6 daedal, menald, motley, varied 7 dappled, flecked, mottled, painted, piebald, tissued 8 speckled 9 different, enamelled 11 diversified

variety: 4 kind, sort, type 5 breed, class 7 species 9 diversity, variation 10 assortment, difference

variola: 6 cowpox 8 horsepox, smallpox

various: 4 many 6 divers, sundry 7 certain, diverse, several 8 distinct, manifold, variable 9 different, uncertain, versatile 10 changeable, inconstant

varlet: boy 4 page 5 gippo, knave, noble, youth 6 menial, rabble, rascal, vassal 7 bailiff, footman, servant 8 coistrel, coistril 9 attendant, scoundrel

varnish: 4 spar 5 japan 7 lacquer 8 brighten, palliate 9 embellish
ingredient: lac 5 copal, elemi, resin, rosin 6 dammar

vary: 4 part 5 alter, range, shift 6 change, depart, differ, divide, modify, swerve 7 deviate, dispute, dissent, diverge, qualify, quarrel, variate 8 disagree, modulate, separate 9 alternate, diversify, fluctuate, oscillate

vas: 4 duct 6 pledge, surety, vessel

vase: jar, urn 4 asci, olla, vaso 5 ascus, askos, echea, tazza 6 crater, deinoi, deinos, krater 7 amphora, urceole 8 lekythose 10 cassolette, jardiniere
handle: 4 ansa

vasectomy: 13 sterilization

vassal: man 4 bond, esne, lend, rule, serf 5 ceile, helot, liege, slave 6 geneat, varlet 7 bondman, feedman, feodary, homager, peasant, servant, servile, subject 8 dominate 9 dependent, feudatory 11 beneficiary, subordinate
pert. to: 6 feudal

vast: 4 huge 5 ample, broad, great, large, vasty 6 cosmic, lonely, mighty, untold 7 immense 8 colossal, enormous, farflung, gigantic, spacious 9 boundless, capacious, cyclopean, extensive 11 farreaching, illimitable

vastness: 7 expanse 8 enormity, grandeur 9 magnitude

vat (see also **barrel, tub, vessel**): bac, fat, pit, tub, tun, wit 4 back, beck, cask,

coom, gyle, keel, kier, tank **5** coomb, keeve, kieve, press **6** barrel, kettle, vessel **7** caldron, chessel, cistern **8** cauldron, chessart
bleaching: **4** kier
cheese: **7** chessel
vatic: **8** inspired, oracular **9** prophetic
Vatican: *basilica:* **8** St. Peter's
chapel: **7** Sistine
guards' nationality: **5** Swiss
official: **6** datary
palace: **7** Lateran
ruler: **4** Pope
site: **4** Rome
vaticinate: **5** augur **7** predict **8** foretell
vaudeville: **5** revue
act: **4** skit, song, turn **5** dance
vaudevillian: **5** actor **6** dancer, hoofer, singer **7** acrobat, juggler **9** performer
vaudy: gay **5** gaudy, showy **6** elated, sturdy **8** cheerful
vault: box, pit **4** arch, bend, cave, cope, dome, jump, leap, over, roof, room, safe, soar, tomb **5** bound, clear, croft, crypt, curve, floor, groin, mount, shade **6** cavern, cellar, crater, cupola, curvet, flaunt, grotto, hurdle, spring, welkin **7** ceiling, chamber, dungeon, glorify, testudo **8** flourish **9** concavity, staircase **10** depository, repository, testudines(pl.)
vaunt: van **4** brag, font **5** boast, roose **6** avaunt **7** display, exhibit, show off **11** ostentation
veal: **4** calf, meat, veau(F.)
cutlet: **9** schnitzel
larded: **8** fricando **10** fricandeau
shank: **8** osso buco
vector: **4** host **7** carrier **8** gradient
opposite of: **6** scalar
vedette: **5** vigil, watch **8** sentinel
Vedic: *artisans of gods:* **6** Ribhus
cosmic order: **4** Rita
fire god: **4** Agni
god: **6** Aditya
hymn: **6** mantra
language: **4** Pali **8** Sanskrit
sky serpent: ahi
sun god: **7** Savitar
text: **5** Sakha, Shaka
veer: yaw **4** slue, sway, turn **5** alter, shift **6** broach, careen, change, depart, swerve **7** deviate, digress **8** angle off **9** fluctuate
veery: **6** thrush
vega: **5** tract **6** meadow
Vega's constellation: **4** Lyra
vegetable: pea, yam **4** bean, beet, corn, kale, leek, ocra, okra, soya **5** onion, plant **6** carrot, celery, lentil, pepper, radish, squash, tomato, turnip **7** brocoli, cabbage, lettuce, parsley, parsnip,

peascod, rhubarb, spinach **8** broccoli, cucumber, eggplant, peasecod, rutabaga **9** artichoke **11** cauliflower **14** Brussels sprout
dealer: **8** huckster **11** greengrocer **12** costermonger
decayed: **4** duff **5** humus
dish: **6** zimmis **10** chiffonade
exudation: lac, sap **5** resin
ferment: **5** yeast
green: **5** sabzi
onionlike: **4** leek **7** shallot
pepsin: **6** caroid
pod: **4** hull **8** peasecod
purple: **8** eggplant
salad: **4** leek **5** chard **6** endive **7** cabbage, lettuce, romaine, shallot **8** scallion
sponge: **5** loofa, luffa **6** loofah
spread: **4** oleo **9** margarine
stunted: **5** scrub
vegetable caterpillar: **5** aweto
vegetable pear: **7** chayote
vegetate: **4** idle **8** languish, stagnate **9** hibernate
vegetation: **6** growth **7** verdure
floating: **4** sadd, sudd **8** pleuston
god: **4** Atys, Esus **5** Attis
vegete: **6** lively **7** healthy **11** flourishing
vehement: hot **4** wild **5** angry, eager, fiery, hefty, irked, rabid, yeder **6** ardent, fervid, flashy, heated, raging, urgent **7** animose, animous, fervent, furioso, furious, intense, violent **8** emphatic, forceful, vigorous **9** impetuous, pronounced **10** boisterous, passionate
vehicle (see also **aircraft, ship**): ark, bus, car, van **4** auto, shay, taxi, tool, wain **5** araba, brake, break, buggy, dilly, means, sedan, sulky, wagon **6** barrow, charet, device, hansom, landau, troika, vector **7** chariot, kibitka(Russ.), tallyho **8** carriage, charette **9** buckboard, implement, velociman **10** automobile, conveyance
army: **4** jeep, tank **9** ambulance
child's: **4** pram **5** buggy **6** walker **7** scooter **8** carriage, stroller, tricycle **10** velocipede
display: **5** float
hauling: van **4** dray, lory, sled **5** truck **7** tractor, trailer
parade: **5** float
passenger: bus, cab **4** hack, taxi, tram **5** train **6** hansom **7** minibus, omnibus, tramcar, trolley **9** charabanc
public: bus, cab, car **4** taxi, tram **5** train **7** omnibus, ricksha **8** rickshaw **10** jinricksha, jinrikisha
snow: **4** pung, sled **6** sleigh
two-wheeled: **4** cart **5** sulky, tonga **6** cisium **7** bicycle, caleche **9** carromata (Fil.) **11** vinaigrette

wheelless: **4** ship, sled **6** cutter, sledge, sleigh

veil: dim **4** caul, film, hide, mask **5** cloak, cover, orale, velum, volet **6** bumble, enfold fannel, masque, screen, shroud, soften **7** conceal, cover up, curtain, secrete, watcher **8** calyptra, disguise, headrail **11** amphithyron
in botany: **5** velum
Moslem: **7** yashmak

veiling: **5** tulle, voile **6** purdah **7** curtain **10** obvelation

vein: bed, rib **4** dash, hilo, hint, lode, mood, seam, tang, tone, vena, wave **5** costa, crack, scrin, shade, smack, spice, style, tinge, touch, trend, venae **6** cavity, costae, manner, nature, strain, streak **7** bonanza, channel, crevice, fashion, fissure, stratum **8** tendency **9** character **11** inclination, variegation
arrangement of: **9** neuration
enlarged: **5** varix
fluid: **4** icor **5** blood, ichor
inflammation: **9** phlebitis
leaf: rib **5** costa
mining: **4** lode
pert. to: **6** veinal, venous
small: **6** venule
throat: **7** jugular

veinstone: **6** gangue, matrix **9** lodestuff

velamen: **5** velum **8** membrane

velar: **7** palatal **8** guttural

velarium: **6** awning **8** covering

veldt, veld: **6** meadow, plains **9** grassland

velitation: **5** brush, run-in **7** contest, dispute **8** skirmish **9** encounter

velleity: **4** hope, will, wish **6** desire **8** volition **11** inclination

vellicate: nip **4** jerk, pull **5** pinch, pluck **6** fidget, tickle, twitch **9** titillate

velocious: **4** fast **6** speedy

velocipede: **4** bike **7** bicycle, dicycle **8** tricycle **11** quadricycle

velocity: **4** pace **5** speed **7** headway, impetus **8** celerity, rapidity **9** quickness, swiftness
instrument: **11** cinemograph

velum: **4** veil **6** awning, palate **8** membrane

velutinous: **7** velvety

velvet: **4** gain **5** drink **6** birodo(Jap.), profit **7** surplus **8** winnings
fabric like: **5** panne **6** velour, velure

velvet dock: **6** mullen **7** mullein **10** elecampane

velvetbreast: **9** merganser

venal: **6** venous **7** corrupt, crooked, salable **8** infamous, saleable, vendible **9** mercenary

vend: **4** hawk, sell **5** utter **6** market, peddle **7** declare, publish **8** transfer

vendetta: **4** feud

vendeuse: **9** salesgirl **10** saleswoman

vendible: **5** venal **7** salable **8** saleable **9** mercenary **10** marketable

vendition: **4** sale

vendor, vender: **6** seller **7** alienor, butcher, peddler **8** merchant, salesman

vendue: **4** sale **7** auction

veneer: lac **4** coat, face, mask, show **5** glaze, gloss, layer, plate **6** enamel, facing **7** overlay **8** palliate

venerable: old **4** aged, hoar, sage **5** hoary **6** august **7** ancient, antique, classic **8** honorable

veneration: awe **4** fear **6** esteem **7** respect, worship **8** devotion, idolatry **9** adoration, reverence
of saints and angels: **5** dulia

venerer: **6** hunter **8** huntsman

venery: **5** chase **7** coition, hunting

Venetian: See **Italy, Venice**

Venezuela: *capital:* **7** Caracas
city: **7** Cabimas **8** Valencia **9** Maracaibo
coin: **4** real **5** medio **6** fuerte **7** bolivar, centimo **8** morocota **10** venezolano
dam: **4** Guri
fiber: **5** erizo
gulf: **5** Paria
Indian: **6** Timote
island: **9** Margarita
lake: **7** Valencia **9** Maracaibo, Tacarigua
language: **4** Pume **7** Spanish
liberator: **7** Bolivar
measure: **5** galon, milla **6** fanega **7** estadel
measure of weight: bag **5** libra
monetary unit: **7** bolivar
mountain: **5** Andes, Icutu **6** Concha, Cuneva, Parima **7** Imutaca, Roraima
people: **5** Carib **6** Timote **7** Timotex **8** Guarauno
plain: **5** llano
port: **8** La Guaira, La Guayra **9** Maracaibo **13** Ciudad Bolivar, Puerto-Cabello
revolutionist: **7** Miranda
river: **4** Meta **5** Apure, Caura **6** Arausa, Caroni **7** Orinoco, Ventuar
snake: **4** lora
state: **4** Lara **5** Apure, Sucre, Zulia **6** Aragua, Falcon, Merida, Zamora **7** Bolivar, Cojedes, Guarico, Monagas, Tachira, Yaracuy **8** Carabobo, Trujillo
town: **4** Aroa, Coro **6** Atures, Cumana, Merida **7** Barinas, Guaware, Maracay, Maturin
tree: **6** balata

vengeance: **5** wrack **6** wanion **7** revenge **8** reprisal, requital **10** punishment **11** retaliation, retribution
god of: **6** Erinys **7** Alastor
goddess of: Ara, Ate **7** Nemesis

venial: **7** trivial **9** allowable, excusable, tolerable **10** forgivable, pardonable **13** insignificant

Venice: *beach:* 4 Lido
  boat: 7 gondola 9 bucentaur
  bridge: 6 Rialto
  coin: 5 betso, bezzo, ducat 6 sequin 8 ba-
    gatino, gazzetta
  court: 8 quaranty
  district: 6 Rialto
  island: 6 Rialto 8 San Marco 9 San Gior-
    gio
  magistrate: 4 doge
  medal: 5 osela, osele 6 osella, oselle 7 os-
    cella
  old silver coin: 5 betso
  painter: 6 Titian 7 Bellini 8 Veronese 9
    Giorgione 10 Tintoretto
  resort: 4 Lido
  river: 6 Brenta
  traveler and writer: 5 Conti 9 Marco Polo
  wine measure: 6 anfora
Venice of the North: 9 Stockholm
venin: 6 poison
venireman: 5 juror
venison: 4 deer
venomous: 5 snaky, toxic 6 attern, deadly
  7 baleful, baneful, noxious 8 poisoned,
  spiteful, virulent 9 malicious, malignant, poisonous, rancorous 11 mischievous
vent: 4 draw, emit, exit, hole, slit 5 brand,
  eject 6 go into, outlet 7 cast out, express, fissure, opening, release 8 aperture, disgorge, emission 9 discharge,
  embrasure 10 escapement, expression
ventilate: air, fan 6 aerate, aerify, broach,
  winnow 8 talk over 9 broadcast, oxygenate
ventilation: 6 aerage 9 breathing 10 conference
ventilator: 6 blinds, funnel, louver 8 air-
  shaft
ventral: 7 sternal
ventriloquist: 12 engastrimyth 13 gas-
  triloquist
venture: hap, try 4 dare, face, luck, risk,
  wage 5 brave, essay, stake 6 chance,
  danger, feeler, gamble, hazard 7 attempt, courage, flutter, fortune, risking
  8 trespass 9 adventure, speculate 10
  enterprise 11 contingency, presumption, speculation, undertaking
venturesome: 4 bold, rash 5 hardy, risky
  6 heroic 8 fearless, heedless, reckless 9
  audacious, dangerous, foolhardy, hazardous, venturous 11 adventurous,
  furthersome, temerarious
venue: hit 4 bout, site 5 lunge, match, onset, place 6 coming, ground, locale,
  thrust 7 arrival, assault 9 encounter
Venus (see also **Aphrodite**): 6 Hesper,
  planet, Vesper 8 Hesperus
  as morning star: 7 Lucifer
  girdle: 6 cestus

  island: 5 Melos
  mother: 5 Dione
  son: 5 Cupid
  sweetheart: 6 Adonis
  tree sacred to: 6 myrtle
Venus flytrap: 5 plant 7 dionaea 10
  swamp plant
venust: 6 comely 7 elegant 8 graceful 9
  beautiful
veracious: 4 true 6 direct 8 truthful 9
  measuring, veridical
veracity: 5 truth 6 gospel, truism 7 honesty 8 accuracy, trueness 9 judgement,
  precision, sincerity 11 correctness 12
  faithfulness, truthfulness
veranda: 5 lanai, porch, stoop 6 loggia,
  piazza 7 gallery, portico
verb: *auxiliary:* can, had, has, may, was 4
  hast, have, must, will 5 might, shall,
  shalt, would
  form: 5 tense
  table: 8 paradigm
  tense: 4 past 6 aorist 7 present 11 conditional
verbal: 4 oral 5 wordy 7 verbose 9 talkative 10 articulate
verbatim: 6 orally 7 literal 8 verbally 11
  word for word
verbena: 4 tree 5 plant 7 aloysia, lantana
verbiage: 4 talk 7 chatter, diction, fustian, wording 9 verbosity, wordiness 10
  redundancy 11 purple prose
verbose: 5 windy, wordy 6 prolix 7 diffuse 9 redundant 10 long-winded 11
  tautologous
verboten: 4 tabu 5 taboo 6 banned 9 forbidden 10 prohibited
verdant: raw 5 fresh, green 6 grassy 8 immature, innocent 13 inexperienced 15
  unsophisticated
Verdi: *opera:* 4 Aida 6 Ernani, Otello 7
  Othello 8 Falstaff, Traviata 9 Rigoletto
  9 Trovatore
verdict: 4 word 6 ruling 7 finding, opinion 8 decision, judgment
verdigris: 4 rust 6 aerugo
Verdun river: 5 Meuse
verdure: 4 odor 5 scent, smell 6 flavor 7
  foliage 8 greenery, strength, tapestry,
  tartness 9 freshness, greenness
verecund: shy 6 modest 7 bashful
Verein: 7 society 11 association 12 organization
verge: lip, rim, rod 4 edge, tend, twig,
  wand 5 bound, brink, limit, marge,
  range, scope, shaft, staff, stick, watch 6
  border, margin, point 7 incline, touch
  on, virgate 8 approach, boundary, yardland 9 extremity, threshold, timepiece
  13 circumference
verger: 4 dean 6 garden 7 justice, orchard
  8 official 9 attendant

Vergil: See **Virgil**

veridical: 4 real, true 7 genuine 8 accurate, truthful 9 veracious 12 truthtelling

verification: 5 proof 7 checkup 8 averment 12 confirmation 14 authentication

verify: 4 aver, back, test 5 audit, check, prove 6 affirm, ratify, second 7 certify, collate, confirm, support 8 maintain 9 establish 11 certificate 12 authenticate, substantiate

verily: yea 4 amen, even 5 parde, pardi, pardy, truly 6 certes, indeed, pardie, really 9 certainly 11 confidently

verisimilitude: 5 color, truth 10 likelihood 11 probability

veritable: 4 real, true 6 actual, gospel, honest 7 factual, genuine 9 authentic, veracious

verity: 8 veracity 12 faithfulness

verjuice: 7 acidity 8 sourness, tartness

vermiform: 4 long, thin 7 sinuous, slender 8 wormlike 10 vermicular

vermifuge: 4 drug 12 anthelmintic

vermilion: red 8 cinnabar

vermin: 4 lice, mice, rats 5 filth, fleas, flies 7 bedbugs, rodents, weasels

verminous: 5 dirty 6 filthy 7 noxious 9 offensive

Vermont: *capital:* 10 Montpelier
city: 5 Barre 7 Rutland 10 Bennington, Burlington, Montpelier 11 Brattleboro
county: 5 Essex 6 Orange 7 Addison, Windsor 8 Lamoille
explorer: 9 Champlain
highest peak: 11 Mt. Mansfield
island: 5 Grand 7 LaMotte 9 North Hero
lake: 7 Caspian, Dunmore, Seymour 9 Champlain
motto: 15 Freedom and Unity
mountain range: 5 Green 7 Taconic
nickname: 13 Great Mountain
river: 8 Lamoille, Poultney, Winooski 10 Otter Creek
ski resort: 5 Stowe 9 Sugarbush
state bird: 6 thrush
state flower: 6 clover
state tree: 5 maple

vernacular: 4 cant 5 argot, idiom, lingo 6 jargon, patois 7 dialect

vernal: 4 mild, warm 5 fresh, young 6 spring 8 youthful 10 springlike

Verne: *character:* 4 Fogg (Phileas), Nemo 12 Passepartout
submarine: 8 Nautilus

verneuk: 5 cheat 6 humbug 7 swindle

versatile: 5 handy 6 mobile 7 flexile 8 flexible, variable 9 all-around, many-sided 10 changeable, reversible

verse (see also **poem**): 4 turn 5 meter, stave, stich 6 stanza 7 revolve, stichos 8 consider 11 familiarize
Bible: 4 text
foot: 4 iamb
pert. to: 6 poetic
stress: 5 ictus

versed: 5 adept 6 beseen 7 abreast, erudite, learned, skilled 8 familiar 9 au courant, competent, practiced 10 acquainted, conversant, proficient 11 experienced

versifier: 4 poet 5 rimer 6 verser 7 poetess 9 poetaster

versify: 6 berime 7 berhyme

version: 7 account, edition, turning 9 rendition 10 conversion, paraphrase 11 translation 14 interpretation, transformation

versipel: 8 werewolf

versus: con 6 contra 7 against, vis-a-vis

vertebra: 4 axis, bone 7 spondyl

vertebrae: 4 back 5 spine

vertebrate: ray 7 animal 9 backboned
class: 4 aves
division: 6 somite
feathered: 4 bird
group: 9 amnionata

vertex: top 4 apex 6 apogee, summit, tiptop, zenith 11 culmination

vertical: 4 acme 5 apeak, erect, plumb, sheer 6 abrupt, height, summit, vertex 7 upright 8 up-and-down 10 straight-up 13 perpendicular

verticil: 5 whorl

vertiginous: 5 dizzy, giddy 6 rotary 8 rotating, spinning, unstable, whirling 9 dizziness, giddiness, revolving 10 inconstant 11 vacillating

vertigo: 6 megrim 9 dizziness, giddiness

verve: pep 4 dash, elan, fire, zest 5 ardor, gusto, vigor 6 bounce, spirit, talent 7 ability 8 aptitude, vivacity 9 animation 10 enthusiasm, resiliency

vervet: 6 monkey

very: too 4 bare, fell, mere, real, same, tres(F.), true, unco(Sc.) 5 assai(It.), molto(It.), truly, utter 6 actual, lawful, mighty, really 7 dimolto(It.), exactly, genuine, precise 8 absolute, complete, especial, peculiar, rightful, truthful 9 authentic, extremely, identical, precisely, veracious, veritable 10 legitimate, mortacious 11 exceedingly
French: 4 tres
German: 4 sehr

vesicle: sac 4 bleb, cell, cyst 5 bulla 6 cavity, vessel 7 bladder, blister, utricle
air: 8 aerocyst

Vesper: 4 star 5 Venus 8 Hesperus

vespers: 6 prayer 7 service 8 ceremony, evensong

vessel (see also **aircraft, boat, container, pail, ship**): can, cog, cup, jar, pan, tub, urn, vas **4** bell, cadi, drum, duct, ewer, olla, olpe, tank, tube, vase **5** bocal, cadus, canoe, cogue, craft, cruse, laver, liner, paten **6** aftaba, aludel, barrel, cootie, crater, cutter, firkin, funnel, goblet, goulah, holmos, krater, patera, situla, yetlin **7** aleyard, blickey, blickie, cistern, cresset, gabbard, gabbart, paterae, pinnace, pitcher, situlae, steamer, utensil, yetling **8** aiguiere, ciborium **9** alcarraza **10** receptacle

anatomical: vas **4** vasa(pl.), vein **6** artery

assaying: **5** cupel

drinking: cup, mug **4** toby **5** flask, glass, gourd, jorum, stein, stoup **6** dipper, flagon, seidel **7** tankard, tumbler **8** schooner

earthen: **5** crock

oil: **5** cruse, cruet

pert. to: **5** vasal

sacred: ama, pix, pyx

small: nog **4** pony, shot **6** dinghy, jigger, noggin,

wooden: soe **5** cogue, skeel **6** barrel, piggin

vest: 4 robe **5** dress, endow, gilet **6** accrue, clothe, jacket, jerkin, linder, weskit **7** furnish, garment **9** waistcoat **10** undershirt

Vesta: 5 match **6** Hestia

vestal: nun **4** pure **6** chaste, virgin

vestibule: 4 hall **5** entry, foyer, lobby, porch **7** chamber, narthex, passage **8** anteroom, entrance, vestible **10** antechapel

vestige: bit **4** mark, path, sign **5** relic, scrap, shred, smack, trace, track, umbra **8** footstep, tincture **9** vestigium

vestiture: 4 garb **5** dress **8** clothing

vestment (see also **dress**): **4** garb, gear, gown, hood, robe **5** cotta, dress, orale **6** chimer, chimre, gloves, rochet, tippet **7** cassock, garment, sandals **8** cincture, clothing, covering **10** habiliment

ecclesiastical: alb, cap **4** alba, cope **5** albae, amice, ephod, fanon, miter, orale, stole **6** lappet, palium, saccos **7** cassock, maniple, tunicle **8** chasuble, dalmatic, surplice

pert. to: **8** vestiary

vestry: 4 room **7** meeting **8** sacristy

vesture: 4 corn **5** cover, crops, grass **6** clothe, seizin **7** apparel, envelop, raiment, stubble, wrapper **8** garments, vestment **9** underwood **11** investiture

vesuvian: 5 fusee, match **8** volcanic

vetch: ers **4** akra, tare, weed **5** fetch **7** arvejon

bitter: ers **5** ervil

veteran: old **7** oldster **8** old-timer, seasoned **9** practiced **10** past master **11** experienced

veterinarian: 7 farrier **12** animal doctor

vetiver: 5 grass **6** cuscus **8** khuskhus

veto: nix **4** kill **6** forbid **7** message **8** disallow, document, negative, overrule, prohibit **11** disapproval, forbiddance, prohibition **12** interdiction

vettura: 5 coach **8** carriage

veuve: 4 bird **5** widow **6** whydah

vex: ire, irk, tew **4** cark, chaw, fret, fuss, gall, miff, rile, roil, toss **5** anger, annoy, chafe, harry, shake, spite, tease, worry, wrack **6** bother, cumber, harass, madden, molest, nettle, offend, plague, pother, ruffle **7** afflict, agitate, discuss, dispute, disturb, perplex, provoke, torment, trouble **8** disquiet, irritate, vexation **9** annoyance, displease, infuriate **11** disturbance

vexation: 5 pique, thorn **7** fatigue **9** annoyance, weariness **13** mortification

vexatious: 4 chaw, sore **5** pesky **8** annoying, cumbrous, frampoid, untoward **9** disturbed, pestilent **10** afflictive **11** contrarious, troublesome

vexed: 5 sorry **7** grieved

vexillum: web **4** flag, vane **6** banner **8** standard

via: way **4** road **5** right **7** by way of, passage, through **9** by means of

viable: 6 doable **8** feasible, possible, workable **11** practicable

viaduct: 6 bridge **7** trestle

vial: 5 ampul, cruet, phial **6** bottle, caster, vessel **7** ampoule

viand: 4 fare, food **6** edible **7** aliment **8** victuals **10** provisions

choice: **4** cate

viaticum: 5 money **8** supplies **9** allowance **10** provisions

viator: 8 traveler, wayfarer

Viaud's pen name: 4 Loti

vibrant: 5 alive, ringy **8** resonant, sonorous, vigorous **9** vibrating

vibrate: jar, wag **4** beat, cast, dirl, rock, whir **5** pulse, quake, shake, swing, throb, throw, trill, waver, whirr **6** dindle, launch, quaver, quiver, shimmy, shiver, thrill **7** agitate, resound, tremble **8** brandish, flichter(Sc.), resonate **9** fluctuate, oscillate, vacillate

vibration: 4 dirl(Sc.), tirl(Sc.) **5** thirl(Sc.) **6** dingle, quaver, quiver, thrill, tremor **7** flutter **8** fremitus, stirring **9** trembling **11** oscillation, vacillation

musical: **5** trill **7** sonance, tremolo, vibrato **8** overtone

point without: **4** node

vicar: 5 proxy **6** deputy, priest **8** minister **9** clergyman **10** substitute, vicegerent

assistant: **6** curate

of christ: **4** Pope

Vicar of Wakefield author: 9 Goldsmith

vicarage: 4 dues 5 house 6 salary, tithes 8 benefice 9 household, pastorate, rectorate, residence

vice: sin 4 evil, grip, hold, turn 5 crime, fault, force, grasp, place, proxy, stead, taint 6 defect 7 blemish, failing, squeeze, stopper 8 iniquity, stairway 9 deformity, depravity 10 corruption, immorality, wickedness 11 harmfulness, viciousness 12 imperfection

Vice President (U.S.): 4 Burr, Ford, King 5 Adams, Agnew, Dawes, Gerry, Nixon, Tyler 6 Arthur, Colfax, Curtis, Dallas, Garner, Hamlin, Hobart, Morton, Truman, Wilson 7 Barkley, Calhoun, Clinton, Johnson, Sherman, Wallace, Wheeler 8 Coolidge, Fillmore, Marshall, Tompkins, Van Buren 9 Fairbanks, Hendricks, Jefferson, Roosevelt, Stevenson 11 Rockefeller 12 Breckinridge

Adams, J.: 9 Jefferson
Adams, J.Q.: 7 Calhoun
Arthur: none
Buchanan: 12 Breckinridge
Carter: 7 Mondale
Cleveland: 9 Hendricks(1), Stevenson(2)
Coolidge: 5 Dawes
Eisenhower: 5 Nixon
Fillmore: none
Ford: 11 Rockefeller
Garfield: 6 Arthur
Grant: 6 Colfax(1), Wilson(2)
Harding: 8 Coolidge
Harrison, B.: 6 Morton
Harrison, W.H.: 5 Tyler
Hayes: 7 Wheeler
Hoover: 6 Curtis
Jackson: 7 Calhoun(1) 8 Van Buren(2)
Jefferson: 4 Burr(1) 7 Clinton(2)
Johnson, A.: none
Johnson, L.B.: 8 Humphrey
Kennedy: 7 Johnson
Lincoln: 6 Hamlin(1) 7 Johnson(2)
Madison: 5 Gerry(2) 7 Clinton(1)
McKinley: 6 Hobart(1) 9 Roosevelt(2)
Monroe: 8 Tompkins
Nixon: 4 Ford(2) 5 Agnew(1)
Pierce: 4 King
Polk: 6 Dallas
Reagan: 4 Bush
Roosevelt, F.D.: 6 Garner(1), Truman(3) 7 Wallace(2)
Roosevelt, T.: 9 Fairbanks
Taft: 7 Sherman
Taylor: 8 Fillmore
Truman: 7 Barkley
Tyler: none
Van Buren: 7 Johnson
Washington: 5 Adams
Wilson: 8 Marshall

viceroy: 5 nabob, nazim 6 exarch, satrap 7 khedive, provost 8 governor 9 butterfly

vice versa: 5 again 10 conversely

vicinity: 6 region 8 locality, nearness 9 proximity 11 propinquity, resemblance 12 neighborhood

vicious: bad, ill 4 evil, foul, lewd, mean, vile 5 wrong 6 faulty, savage, severe, wicked 7 corrupt, immoral, intense, noxious 8 debasing, depraved, infamous, spiteful 9 dangerous, defective, dissolute, malicious, malignant, nefarious, perverted 10 corrupting, iniquitous, villainous

vicissitude: 6 change 8 mutation, reversal 10 difficulty, revolution, succession 11 alternation, interchange

victim: 4 dupe, fool, goat, gull, prey 6 sucker 8 easy mark, offering, underdog 9 sacrifice
list: 4 toll

victor: 6 captor, master, winner 7 conquer 8 bangster, unbeaten 9 conqueror 10 vanquisher, victorious

victory: win 7 mastery, success, triumph 8 conquest 9 landslide, supremacy 11 superiority
celebrating: 9 epinician
crown: bay 6 laurel
easy: 6 breeze
goddess: 4 Nike
memorial: 4 arch 6 spoils, trophy
ruinous: 7 Pyrrhic
sign: vee
song: 9 epinicion
symbol: 4 palm 5 scalp 6 trophy
unexpected: 5 upset

Victory heroine: 4 Lena

victrola: 9 turntable 10 phonograph 12 record player

victualler: 6 sutler 9 innkeeper

victuals: bit 4 bite, chow, eats, food, grub, meat 6 viands 7 vittles 11 comestibles, nourishment

videlicet: viz 5 to wit 6 namely 8 scilicet

vie: bet, run 4 cope 5 bandy, rival, stake, wager 6 endure, hazard, oppose, strive 7 compete, contend, contest, emulate 8 panorama, prospect, struggle 9 challenge

Vienna: 4 Wien
palace: 10 Schonbrunn
park: 6 Prater

Vietnam (See also North Vietnam and South Vietnam): *capital:* 5 Hanoi
city: Hue 6 Da Nang 8 Haiphong, Nha Trang 13 Ho Chi Minh City (formerly Saigon)
Communist leader: 9 Ho Chi Minh
former division: 5 North, South
French defeated at: 11 Dien Bien Phu
independence movement: 8 Vietminh

monetary unit: **4** dong
region: **5** Annam **6** Tonkin **11** Cochin-China
river: Red **6** Mekong
view: aim, eye, ken, see, vue(F.) **4** goal, look, scan **5** aview, scape, scene, sight, slant, tenet, vista, watch **6** admire, apercu(F.), aspect, behold, belief, object, regard, sketch, survey, vision **7** concept, examine, inspect, observe, opinion, picture, profile, summary, thought, witness **8** attitude, consider, panorama, prospect, scrutiny, synopsis **9** apprehend **10** appearance, inspection, perception, photograph, scrutinize, standpoint **11** contemplate, examination, expectation **13** contemplation
extended: **8** panorama
mentally: **8** envision
obstruct: **4** hide **7** conceal
open to: **4** bare **5** overt **6** expose
pleasing: **6** eyeful
viewer: **9** spectator **11** eyewitness, stereoscope
viewing instrument: **5** scope **9** telescope **10** binoculars
viewy: **5** showy **8** fanciful **9** visionary **11** spectacular, unpractical **12** ostentatious
vigil: eve **4** wake **5** guard **7** lookout, prayers, service **8** devotion, watchman
vigilant: **4** agog, wary **5** alert, awake, aware **7** careful, wakeful **8** cautious, watchful **9** attentive, observant, sharp-eyed, sleepless, wide-awake **11** circumspect, on one's guard
vigilant person: **5** Argus
vigilantes: **5** posse
vigneron: **10** winegrower **13** viticulturist
vignette: **5** scene **6** sketch **7** picture
vigor, vigour: pep, vim, vir(Sc.), vis **4** bang, birr, zeal **5** drive, flush, force, nerve, power **6** energy, foison, growth, health, spirit **7** impetus, potency, stamina **8** activity, boldness, strength, virility, vitality **9** animation, fraicheur, hardihood, intensity, vehemence **10** get-up-and-go, invigorate
deprive of: sap **6** deaden **8** enervate
lose: fag, sag **4** fail, flag, pine **6** weaken **7** decline
period of: **6** heyday
vigoroso: **8** vigorous **9** direction, energetic
vigorous: yep **4** able, cant, fell, hale, spry, yepe **5** eager, frank, hardy, hefty, lusty **6** florid, hearty, lively, robust, rugged, strong, sturdy **7** cordial **8** athletic, muscular **9** effective, energetic, strenuous **11** efficacious, hard-hitting **13** rough-and-ready
Viking: **4** Dane, Eric **5** rover **6** pirate **8**

Norseman, Northman **12** Scandinavian
vile: bad, low **4** base, evil, foul, mean **5** cheap, lowly, nasty **6** abject, coarse, drasty, filthy, impure, odious, sinful, sordid, wicked **7** bestial, carrion, corrupt, debased, ignoble, unclean, vicious **8** baseborn, befouled, depraved **9** abandoned, degrading, loathsome, nefarious, obnoxious, offensive, repulsive, worthless **10** abominable, despicable, disgusting, flagitious **12** contaminated
vileness: **6** fedity **9** turpitude
vilify: **5** abuse, avile, libel **6** bemean, berate, debase, defame, malign, revile, slight **7** asperse, blacken, cheapen, debauch, degrade, despise, detract, slander, traduce **8** belittle, disgrace, dishonor, mistreat, reproach, vilipend **9** blaspheme, disparage **10** calumniate, depreciate
villa: **5** aldea, dacha(Russ.), house **6** castle, estate **8** villakin **9** residence, villaette **10** villanette
village: gav, mir(Russ.), rew(Sc.) **4** burg, dorp, home, stad(African), town, vici **5** aldea, bourg, kraal, thorp, vicus **6** bustee, castle, hamlet, pueblo, thorpe **7** borough, caserio(Sp.), endship **8** bourgade **9** aldeament **10** settlement **11** aggregation **12** municipality
villain: **4** boor, heel, Iago, lout, serf **5** churl, demon, devil, heavy, knave, rogue, scamp **6** rascal **8** scelerat **9** miscreant, scoundrel **10** blackguard, villainous
mythological: **4** ogre **5** giant **6** dragon
nemesis of: **4** hero
villainous: bad, low **4** base, evil, mean, vile **6** common, slight, vulgar, wicked **7** boorish, vicious **8** clownish, criminal, depraved, flagrant, wretched **9** dastardly, dissolute, felonious **10** detestable, flagitious, iniquitous, outrageous **12** disagreeable **13** objectionable
villainy: **5** crime **7** knavery **9** depravity
villatic: **5** rural **6** rustic
villein: **4** carl, serf **5** ceorl, churl **7** bondsman, cottier
vim: zip **4** gimp, kick, push **5** force, vigor **6** energy, ginger, pepper, spirit **8** strength
vina: **10** instrument
vinaigrette: box **5** sauce **6** bottle **7** vehicle **8** carriage
vincible: **11** conquerable **12** surmountable
vinculum: tie **4** band, bond **5** brace, union **6** frenum
vindicate: **4** free **5** clear **6** acquit, assert, avenge, defend, excuse, uphold **7** absolve, bear out, deliver, justify, propugn, revenge, support, sustain **8** advocate,

maintain, plead for **9** exculpate, exonerate

vindication: 7 apology

vindictive: 7 hostile **8** punitive, spiteful, vengeful **10** revengeful **11** retaliatory, retributive

vine: hop, ivy **4** akas, bine, gogo, odal, soma **5** betel, buaze, bwazi, guaco, liana, liane **6** maypop **7** creeper, cupseed, trailer **8** clematis **9** grapevine **10** chilicothe

covered with: **5** ivied **7** lianaed

fruit-bearing: **5** grape **7** cupseed

parasite: **5** aphid, aphis

twining: **4** bine

vinegar: vim **4** acid **5** eisel **6** acetum, alegar, eisell **8** vinaigre(F.)

bottle: **5** cruet

dregs: **6** mother

ester: **7** acetate

pert. to: **6** acetic

preserve in: **6** pickle

salt: **7** acetate

spice: **8** tarragon

vinegary: 4 sour **7** acetose, crabbed **9** unamiable **11** ill-tempered **12** cantankerous

vineyard: cru

protector: **7** Priapus

vinous: 4 winy **9** vinaceous

vintage: 4 crop, wine **5** cuvee, yield **6** demode, classic **7** antique **12** old-fashioned

vintner: 8 merchant

viol: 5 gigue, rebec **6** fiddle, rebeck, vielle **7** quinton **9** violaalta

progenitor: **5** rebec

violate: err, sin **4** flaw, rape **5** abuse, break, force, harry, spoil, wrong **6** betray, broach, defile, defoil, defoul, injure, insult, invade, offend, ravage, ravish **7** corrupt, debauch, disturb, falsify, outrage, pollute, profane **8** deflower, dishonor, infringe, mistreat, trespass **9** constrain, desecrate, disregard **10** contravene, transgress

violation: 5 crime, error **6** breach **10** infraction **11** delinquency, profanation **13** nonobservance

sentence structure: **11** anacoluthon

violence: 4 fury **5** ardor, force **6** bensel, bensil, fervor, frenzy, hubris, hybris **7** assault, bensail, bensall, bensell, outrage **8** ferocity, foul play **9** bloodshed **11** desecration, profanation **12** infringement

violent: 4 high, loud **5** acute, fiery, great, heady, heavy, hefty, rabid, rough, sharp, vivid **6** fierce, mighty, raging, savage, severe, stormy, strong **7** extreme, furious, hotspur, intense, rammish **8** flagrant, forceful, forcible, frenetic, vehe-

ment **9** atrocious, explosive, impetuous, phrenetic, turbulent **10** headstrong, hotspurred, immoderate, inordinate, passionate, tumultuous **11** tempestuous

violently: 4 hard **5** amain **8** like fury, slambang

violet: 5 mauve **6** blaver, flower, purple

perfume: **5** irone

violet root: 5 orris **6** iridin

violet tip: 9 butterfly

violin: kit **4** alto, bass **5** Amati, cello, Rocta, Strad **6** fiddle **7** Cremona **8** Guarneri **10** Guadagnini, Guarnerius, Stradivari **11** violincello **12** Stradivarius

city: **7** Cremona

direction: **4** arco **9** pizzicato

forerunner: **5** rabab

part: peg **4** hole, neck **6** string **7** eclisse

rare: **5** Amati, Strad **10** Guarnerius

violin-shaped: 7 waisted

violinist (first): 13 concertmaster **14** concertmeister

comic: **5** Benny

fabled: **4** Nero

famous: **4** Auer **5** Elman, Stern, Ysaye **7** Heifetz, Milstein, Menuhin **8** Kreisler, Spalding **9** Zimbalist

V.I.P.: 4 lion **6** bigwig **7** big shot, notable

viper: asp **5** adder, snake **8** cerastes **10** bushmaster, copperhead, fer-de-lance **11** rattlesnake

genus of: **5** echis

viperish: 8 spiteful, venomous **9** malicious

virago: 5 harpy, randy, scold, vixen, woman **6** Amazon, beldam, callet **7** beldame **8** fishwife **9** brimstone, termagant

vireo: 7 grasset **8** greenlet, songbird

Virgil: 9 Roman poet

birthplace: **6** Mantua

character: **5** Amata, Damon **7** Corydon

family name: **4** Maro

friend: **8** Maecenas

hero: **6** Aeneas

language: **5** Latin

poem: **4** epic **6** Aeneid

queen: **4** Dido

virgin: new **4** maid, pure **5** first, fresh **6** chaste, intact, maiden, modest, vestal **7** initial **8** maidenly, spinster **9** unalloyed, undefiled, unsubdued, unsullied, untouched **10** uncaptured **11** undisturbed **12** uncultivated, unfertilized **13** unadulterated

Virgin Islands (of U.S.): **6** St. John **7** St. Croix **8** St. Thomas

Virgin Mary: *flower:* **7** cowslip **8** marigold

image: **5** Pieta

Virgin Queen: 10 Elizabeth I

virginal: 6 spinet **11** harpsichord

Virginia: *aristocracy:* FFV
capital: **8** Richmond
city: **7** Hampton, Norfolk **8** Richmond
10 Chesapeake **11** Newport News
colonist: **7** Fairfax
county: **4** Bath **5** Bland, Floyd **7** Bedford,
Fairfax, Henrico **9** Arlington
estuary: **12** Hampton Roads
highest point: **8** Mt. Rogers
Indian: **6** Tutelo **7** Monacan **8** Powhatan
lake: **7** Claytor **8** Drummond **13** Smith
Mountain
motto: **17** Sic semper tyrannis
mountain: **9** Allegheny, Blue Ridge
mountain range: **11** Appalachian
national park: **10** Shenandoah
nickname: **11** Old Dominion
river: Dan **5** James **9** Potomac, Rapidan,
Roanoke **10** Shenandoah
state bird: **8** cardinal
state flower: **7** dogwood
state tree: **7** dogwood
surrender site: **8** Yorktown **10** Appomat-
tox
swamp: **6** Dismal
town: **5** Luray **8** Danville
Virginia creeper: ivy **5** plant **8** woodbine **10** ampelopsis
Virginia goat's rue: **6** catgut
Virginia snakeroot: **7** sangrel **9** birthwort **11** sangree-root
Virginia willow: iva **4** itea
Virginian author: **6** Wister
virgularian: **6** searod
viridity: **5** youth **7** verdure **8** verdance **9**
freshness, greenness **10** liveliness
virile: **4** male **5** manly **6** potent, robust **7**
lustful **8** forceful, powerful, vigorous **9**
masculine, masterful
virose: **5** fetid **8** virulent **9** poisonous **10**
malodorous
virtu: **5** curio **7** antique
virtually: **6** almost, nearly **7** morally, totally **8** in effect **9** in essence **11** practically
virtue: **4** thew **5** arete, grace, piety, power
6 bounty, purity **7** probity, quality **8**
chastity, efficacy, goodness, morality **9**
rectitude, excellence **11** uprightness **13**
righteousness
cardinal: **4** hope **5** faith **7** charity, justice
8 prudence **9** fortitude **10** temperance
paragon of: **5** saint
virtuoso: **4** whiz **6** expert, savant **7** scholar **8** aesthete, esthetic **10** dilettante,
empiricist **11** connoisseur, philosopher
12 professional
virtuous: **4** good, pure **5** brave, moral **6**
chaste, honest, potent **7** goddard,
thrifty, upright, valiant **8** valorous **9** effective, righteous **11** efficacious, industrious

virulent: **5** acrid, rabid **6** bitter, deadly,
potent **7** cutting, hateful, hostile, noxious **8** spiteful, venomous **9** festering,
injurious, malignant, poisonous **10** infectious **12** antagonistic
virus: **5** taint, venom **6** poison **8** acrimony **10** corruption
vis: **5** force, power, vigor **7** potency **8**
strength
vis-a-vis: **4** seat, sofa **6** versus **7** against **8**
carriage, opposite **9** tete-a-tete **10** face
to face
visage: **4** face, look, show **5** image **6** aspect **8** features, portrait **9** semblance
10 appearance, expression **11** countenance
viscera: **4** guts **6** vitals **8** entrails **10** in-
testines
visceral: gut **5** inner **9** intuitive **11** instinctive
viscid: **7** viscous
viscount: **4** peer **6** deputy **7** sheriff **8** nobleman
viscous: **4** limy, ropy, sizy **5** gobby, gummy, tarry, thick, tough **6** mucous, sir-
upy, sticky, viscid **7** stringy **8** adhering,
sticking **9** glutinous, semisolid, tenacious
vise: **5** clamp, winch
part: jaw
Vishnu: *bearer:* **6** Garuda
consort: Sri **7** Lakshmi
epithet: **8** Bhagavat
incarnation: **4** Rama **6** avatar **7** Krishna
8 Balarama **11** Ramachandra
serpent: **4** Naga
visible: **4** seen **6** extant **7** evident, glaring,
obvious **8** apparent, manifest **9** available **11** conspicuous, discernible, perceivable, perceptible
Visigoth king: **6** Alaric
vision: eye **5** dream, fancy, image, sight,
think **6** beauty, seeing **7** fantasy, imagine **9** nightmare **10** apparition, revelation
defect: **6** anopia, myopia **14** metamor-
phopsae, metamorphopsia
double: **8** diplopia
illusory: **6** mirage
instrument of: **6** retina
lacking in: **8** purblind
measuring device: **9** optometer
pertaining to: **5** optic **6** ocular, visual
without: **5** blind
visionary: fey **4** aery, airy, wild **5** ideal,
lofty, noble **6** unreal **7** dreamer, fantast,
laputan, utopian **8** delusive, idealist,
quixotic, romantic **9** fantastic, imaginary **10** chimerical, ideologist **11** imaginative, impractical, speculative
visit: gam, see, vis **4** call, chat, hawk,
slum, stay **5** apply, haunt **6** assail, at-

tend, avenge **7** afflict, ceilidh(Sc.), inflict, sojourn **8** converse **10** inspection, visitation **12** conversation

visitation: **5** trial **7** calvary **8** disaster **9** migration **10** affliction

visitor: **5** guest **6** caller **7** company

vison: **4** mink

visor: **4** bill, peak **8** eyeshade

vista: **4** view **5** scene **7** outlook **8** long view, panorama, prospect

Vistula tributary: Bug, San

visual: **5** optic **6** ocular, scopic **7** optical, visible **11** perceptible

visualize: **5** think **6** ideate **7** foresee, imagine, picture **8** envisage **13** conceptualize

vita: **4** life **9** biography

Vita Nuova author: **5** Dante

vital: **4** live **5** basic, chief, fatal **6** deadly, lively, living, needed, souled, viable **7** animate, capital, exigent, supreme **8** integral, vigorous **9** breathing, elemental, energetic, essential, important, necessary, requisite **10** imperative **11** fundamental **13** indispensable

vital fluid: sap **5** blood, lymph

vital signs: **5** pulse **11** respiration, temperature

vitality: sap, vim **5** vigor **6** foison

vitalize: **5** pep up **7** animate **8** activate **11** put life into

vitals: **7** viscera

vitamin: **6** citrin, niacin **7** choline **8** ascorbic, carotene, inositol, thiamine **10** calciferol, pyridoxine, riboflavin, tocopherol

vitellus: **4** yolk **7** egg yolk

vitiate: **5** pical, spoil, taint **6** debase, faulty, impair, impure, injure, poison, weaken **7** abolish, corrupt, deprave, envenom, pervert, pollute **9** defective **10** adulterate, invalidate, neutralize **11** contaminate

viticulturist: **8** vigneron **10** winegrower

vitrella: **11** retinophore

vitrify: **5** glaze

vitrine: **8** showcase

vitriol: **4** acid, sory **5** venom **7** caustic

vitriolic: **5** sharp **6** biting, bitter **7** caustic **8** scathing, virulent **9** sarcastic

vituperate: **4** rail **5** abuse, curse, scold **6** berate, revile, rip into **7** censure, chew out **8** lambaste

vituperative: **7** abusive **8** critical **10** scurrilous **11** opprobrious

vivacious: gay **4** airy **5** brisk, merry **6** active, breezy, lively, vivace(It.) **7** buoyant, zestful **8** animated, cheerful, spirited, sportive **9** exuberant, long-lived, sprightly **12** lighthearted

vivacity: **4** fire, zeal **5** ardor, force, verve, vigor **6** esprit, gaiety, gayety **7** gayness,

sparkle **9** longevity **10** liveliness

vivarium: box, zoo **4** cage **6** warren **9** enclosure

viva voce: **5** vocal **6** orally **11** word of mouth

vive: **5** brisk, vivid **6** lively, living **8** forcible, lifelike **9** perceived

vivid: **4** keen, live, rich **5** clear, fresh, sharp **6** active, bright, lively, living, strong **7** eidetic, flaming, glaring, glowing, graphic, intense **8** animated, colorful, distinct, dramatic, spirited, striking, vigorous **9** brilliant

vivificate: **7** quicken

vivify: **5** endue **6** revive **7** animate, enliven, quicken **10** give life to, invigorate

vivres: **9** foodstuff **10** provisions

vixen: fox, nag **4** fury **5** scold, shrew, woman **6** virago **9** termagant

viz: **5** to wit **6** namely **9** videlicet

vizard: **4** mask **5** guise, visor **8** disguise

vizcacha, viscacha: **6** rodent

vocabulary: **5** words **7** diction, lexicon **8** glossary, wordbook **10** dictionary **11** terminology

vocabulist: **13** lexicographer

vocal: **4** oral **5** vowel **9** outspoken, unwritten **10** articulate

vocalist: **4** alto **5** basso, tenor **6** artist, singer **7** soprano **8** baritone, songster **9** performer **10** coloratura

vocalization: **6** speech **7** diction **11** melismatics

vocation: **4** call **5** trade **6** career **7** calling, mission, summons **8** business **9** following **10** employment, occupation, profession

vociferate: cry **4** bawl, call, roar **5** shout, utter **6** assert, bellow, clamor, holler **7** clamour

vociferous: **4** loud **5** noisy **7** blatant **8** brawling, strident **9** turbulent **10** boisterous **11** loud-mouthed, openmouthed **12** obstreperous

voe: bay **5** creek, inlet

vogue: cut, ton(F.) **4** mode **5** style **6** bon ton, custom **7** fashion **8** practice **10** dernier cri, popularity

in: **4** chic **5** smart **10** prevailing

voice: say, vox(L.) **4** emit, voce(It.), vote, wish **5** rumor, say-so, speak, utter **6** choice, report, speech, steven, tongue **7** divulge, express, opinion **8** announce, falsetto, proclaim **9** utterance **10** articulate, expression

handicap: **4** lisp **7** stutter

loss of: **7** anaudia, aphonia

loud: **12** megalophonic **13** megalophonous

male: **4** bass **5** basso, tenor **8** baritone, barytone **12** countertenor

natural singing: **7** dipetto

pert. to: **5** vocal **8** phonetic
principal: **6** cantus
quality: **5** pĭtch **6** timbre
quiet: **5** sotto **7** whisper
sound: **5** vowel **6** symbol
stop: **9** affricate
stress: **5** arsis
voice box: 6 larynx
voiced: 4 oral **6** sonant, spoken **11** articulated
voiceless: mum **4** dumb, mute, surd **6** atonic, flated, silent **7** aphonic, spirate **8** aphonous **10** speechless
void: gap **4** free, hole, idle, lack, null, vain, want **5** abyss, annul, blank, drain, egest, eject, empty, leave, space **6** devoid, hollow, remove, vacant, vacate, vacuum **7** invalid, lacking, leisure, nullify, opening, useless, vacuity, wanting **8** evacuate, throw out **9** destitute, discharge, emptiness, frustrate **10** unemployed, unoccupied **11** ineffective, ineffectual
voila tout: 8 that's all
voile: 5 ninon
voir dire: 10 juror's oath
voiture: 5 wagon **8** carriage
volage: 5 giddy **6** fickle **7** flighty **8** fleeting
volant: 5 agile, light, quick **6** flying, nimble **7** flounce **8** volitant
volary: 4 cage **6** aviary **8** bird cage
volatile: 4 airy, bird **5** ether **6** fickle, figent, flying, lively, volage, volant **7** alcohol, ammonia, buoyant, elastic, essence, gaseous, volatic **8** fleeting, fugitive, vaporous **9** excitable, fugacious, transient **10** capricious, changeable, inconstant, transitory **11** hairbrained **12** lighthearted
volcano: Apo, Aso **4** Etna **5** Askja, Pelee **6** Ranier, Shasta **8** Cotopaxi, Krakatao, Krakatau, Mauna Loa, Vesuvius **9** Stromboli **10** Mt. St. Helens **12** Popocatepetl
matter: ash **4** lava, tufa **6** pumice, scoria
mud from: **5** salse
opening: **5** mouth **6** crater **8** fumarole
rock: **5** trass **6** dacite **8** tephrite
slag: **6** cinder, scoria
steam from: **5** stufa
vole: 6 craber, rodent
Volga: Rha
volition: 4 will **6** choice desire, option **13** determination
volley: 6 shower **7** barrage **8** blizzard, drumfire
volplane: 5 coast, glide
Volsunga Saga: *dragon:* **6** Fafnir
  characters: **4** Atli **6** Sigurd **7** Gunther **8** Brunhild **9** Siegfried
Voltaire: *character:* **8** Pangloss
  estate: **6** Ferney

novel: **5** Zadig **7** Candide
  real name: **6** Arouet
volte face: 8 reversal **9** about-face
voluble: 4 glib **5** wordy **6** fickle, fluent **8** rotating, unstable **9** garrulous, revolving, talkative **10** changeable, loquacious
volume: 4 body, book, bulk, coil, mass, roll, tome, turn **6** amount, cubage, scroll **7** content **8** capacity, document, fullness, loudness, quantity, strength **9** aggregate **10** crassitude **11** convolution
large: **4** tome
measure: **11** stereometer
voluminous: 4 full, many **5** bulky, large
Volund's brother: 4 Egil **5** Egill
voluntary: 4 free **6** freely **7** willful, willing **8** elective, optional, unforced **9** volunteer, willingly **10** deliberate, unimpelled **11** intentional, spontaneous **13** unconstrained
volunteer: 5 offer **6** enlist, worker **7** proffer
Volunteer State: 9 Tennessee
voluptuous: 4 lush **6** wanton **7** sensual **8** sensuous **9** luxurious **11** pleasurable
volute: 4 turn **5** whorl **6** cilery, scroll, spiral **7** cillery
volution: 4 coil, turn **5** twist, whorl **7** rolling **9** revolving **11** convolution
vomit: 4 barf, boke, bolk, puke, spew **5** braid, brake, reach, retch **6** emetic **7** throw up **8** disgorge **10** egurgitate **11** regurgitate
voodoo: obe, obi **5** Jonah, magic, obeah **6** fetish **7** bewitch **8** magician, sorcerer
charm: **4** mojo
voracious: 5 eager **6** greedy, hungry **8** esurient, ravening, ravenous **9** cormorant, rapacious **10** gargantuan, gluttonous, immoderate, insatiable
voracity: 7 edacity **10** greediness **12** ravenousness
vorago: 4 gulf **5** abyss, chasm
vortex: 4 apex, eddy, gyre **5** spout, whirl **6** spiral **7** tornado **9** waterpool, whirlpool, whirlwind **10** waterspout
votary: 5 freak **6** addict, zealot **7** amateur, devoted, devotee **8** adherent, follower, promised **10** enthusiast
vote: aye, con, nay, pro, vow, yes **4** anti, poll, wish **5** elect, grant **6** assign, ballot, choice, confer, prayer **7** declare, opinion **8** dedicate, suffrage **10** plebiscite, referendum
group: **4** bloc
method: **4** hand **5** proxy, straw, voice **6** ballot, secret **7** write-in **10** plebiscite, referendum
of assent: aye, nod, yea **6** placet
of dissent: nay
receptacle: **6** situla **7** situlae
right to: **8** suffrage **9** franchise

solicitation of, for bill: **5** lobby

voter: 6 poller **7** elector **8** balloter, chooser **11** constituent

kind: **8** absentee

illegal: **8** repeater, underage **11** nonresident

voters (body of): **10** electorate

vouch: vow **4** aver, back, bail, call, pray **6** affirm, allege, assure, attest, second, summon **7** certify, confirm, declare, resolve, support, warrant **8** accredit, maintain, sanction **9** assertion, establish, guarantee **11** attestation **12** authenticate

voucher: 4 chit **7** receipt **9** debenture, statement **10** credential

vouchsafe: 4 give **5** design, grant, yield **6** assure, bestow, beteem **7** concede **9** guarantee **10** condescend

voussoir: 5 wedge **8** keystone

projection: ear

vow: vum **4** bind, hote, oath, wish **5** swear **6** behest, devote, pledge, plight **7** behight, declare, promise **8** dedicate **9** assertion **10** consecrate, obligation **12** asseveration, supplication

dedicated by: **6** votive

vowel: 5 vocal **6** letter

contraction: **6** crases, crasis **9** diphthong

gradation: **6** ablaut

group of two: **6** digram **7** digraph

mark: **5** breve, tilde **6** umlaut **8** dieresis **10** circumflex

omission: **7** aphesis

sound: **6** dental, labial **7** palatal

unaspirated: **4** lene

vox: 5 voice

voyage: 4 tour, trip **6** cruise, travel **7** journey, passage, passing, project **8** proceeds **9** excursion **10** enterprise, expedition, pilgrimage **11** undertaking

voyageur: 7 boatman, trapper **8** traveler, woodsman

voyaging: 4 asea

vraic: 7 seaweed

vrouw: 4 frow **5** woman **8** mistress **9** housewife

vug, vugg, vugh: 6 cavity, hollow

Vulcan: 5 smith **10** blacksmith, Hephaestus

consort: **4** Maia **5** Venus

epithet: **8** Mulciber

parents: **4** Juno **7** Jupiter

son: **5** Cacus **8** Caeculus

workshop: **4** Etna

vulcanite: 7 ebonite

vulcanize: 4 burn, cure

vulgar: 4 base, lewd, rude **5** crude, gross **6** coarse, common, public, slangy **7** boorish, general, obscene, popular, profane **8** barbaric, churlish, ordinary **9** customary, earthbred, inelegant, unrefined

vulgarism: 4 cant **9** barbarism

vulgate: 6 patois **10** colloquial, vernacular

vulnerable: 6 liable **7** exposed **9** pregnable, untenable **10** assailable **11** defenseless, susceptible

point: **12** Achilles heel

vulpine: fox, sly **4** foxy **6** artful, clever, crafty, tricky **7** cunning **9** alopecoid

vulture: 4 papa **5** arend, grape, gripe, griph, urubu **6** condor, griphe **8** aasvogel, zopilote **9** gallinazo **11** lammergeier

W

waag: 6 grivet, monkey

wabble: See **wobble**

wabby: 4 loon

wabeno: 6 shaman **8** magician

wachna: cod **7** codfish

wacky, whacky: 5 crazy **6** insane, screwy **7** erratic, foolish **9** eccentric **10** irrational

wad: bat, gag, pad, ram **4** cram, heap, lead, line, lump, mass, plug, roll, tuft **5**
crowd, money, stuff, trace, track, would **6** bundle, insert, pledge, wealth **7** fortune, stopper **8** bankroll, compress, graphite

of paper money: **4** roll

Wadai Muslim: 4 Maba

wadding: 4 hemp **5** kapok **6** cotton

waddle: 5 tread **6** hoddle, toddle, widdle **7** trample

waddy: peg **4** beat, cane, club **5** stick **6**

attack, cowboy **7** rustler

wade: 4 ford, pass, plod **6** paddle **7** proceed **8** struggle

wader: 4 boot, coot, hern, ibis, rail **5** crane, heron, snipe, stork **6** jacana **9** sandpiper

wadi, wady: bed **4** wash **5** gully, oasis, river **6** ravine, stream, valley **7** channel **11** watercourse

wading bird: See **bird:** *wading*

wadset: 4 pawn **6** pledge **8** mortgage

wafer: 4 cake, disk, ring, seal, snap **5** close **6** fasten, matzoh **7** biscuit, cracker

container for: pix, pyx

waffle: 4 cake **6** babble **10** equivocate

waft: 4 blow, buoy, flag, gust, odor, puff, turn, wave, weft **5** carry, drift, float, gleam, sound, taste, whiff **6** beckon, breath, direct, propel, signal, wraith **7** glimpse, pennant **9** transport

wag: wit **4** card, move, stir, sway, zany **5** joker, leave, nudge, rogue, shake, swing **6** beckon, depart, signal **7** farceur, vibrate **8** brandish, flourish, humorist, jokester **9** comedian, oscillate, prankster

wage (see also **wager**): fee, pay, utu **4** hire, levy, pawn **5** bribe, fight, incur **6** employ, engage, reward, salary **7** attempt, conduct, contend, stipend **9** emolument **10** recompense **12** compensation

deduct: **4** dock

insurance: **7** chomage

wage earner: 6 worker **7** laborer **8** employee, mechanic **11** proletarian

wager: bet, bid, lay, vie **4** gage, risk **5** prize, sport, stake **6** gamble, hazard, parlay, pledge **7** venture

made in bad faith: **6** levant

waggery: 4 jest, joke **7** foolery **10** pleasantry **11** waggishness

waggish: 4 arch, pert **5** droll, merry, saucy **7** jesting, jocular, parlous, playful, roguish **8** humorous, sportive **10** frolicsome **11** mischievous

waggle: 4 sway **6** switch, waddle, wobble

Wagner: *character:* Eva **4** Elsa, Erda **5** Hagen, Senta, Wotan **8** Parsifal

father-in-law: **5** Liszt

opera: **6** Rienzi **9** Lohengrin **10** Tannhauser **12** Das Rheingold **15** Gotterdammerung

wife: **6** Cosima

wagon: bin, van **4** cart, dray, tram, wain **5** araba, aroba, dilly, gilly, lorry, lurry, tonga **6** camion, telega **7** caisson, chariot, fourgon, vehicle **8** carryall **12** perambulator

maker: **10** wainwright

part: **4** neap, pole, rave **5** thill **6** tongue

shaft: **5** thill

wagon-lit: 7 sleeper

wagonload: 5 cargo **6** fother

wah: 5 panda

wahine: 4 wife **5** woman **8** mistress **10** girl surfer, sweetheart

wahoo: elm **4** fish, peto, tree **8** nonsense, tommyrot **9** buckthorn, guarapucu

waif: 4 flag **5** stray **7** pennant, vagrant, wastrel **8** castaway, homeless, wanderer **9** foundling

wail: cry, wow **4** bawl, howl, moan, waul, weep, yarm **5** croon, mourn **6** bemoan, bewail, grieve, lament, plaint **7** deplore, ululate **8** complain **9** complaint **11** lamentation

wain: 4 cart **5** fetch, wagon **6** convey **7** chariot, vehicle

wainscot: 4 ceil, dado, line **6** lining **7** ceiling **8** paneling **10** wall lining

waist: 4 belt, wasp **5** shirt **6** basque, blouse, bodice, camisa, girdle **7** corsage **8** camisole **10** mid-section

circumference: **5** girth

waistband: obi **4** sash **6** girdle **8** ceinture, cincture

waistcoat: 4 vest **5** benjy, gilet **6** fecket, jacket, jerkin, weskit

wait: 4 bide, rest, stay, stop, tend **5** await, cater, court, dally, defer, delay, guard, serve, tarry, watch **6** ambush, attend, escort, expect, follow, harken, linger, remain **7** hautboy, hearken, observe **8** hesitate, inactive, postpone **9** accompany **10** anticipate, minister to **11** stick around **12** watchfulness

waiter: spy **4** tray **6** garcon, salver, server, vessel **7** messboy, messman, servant, steward, watcher **8** servitor, watchman, waylayer **9** attendant

waive: put **4** cast, turn **5** allow, cease, defer, forgo, grant, leave, swing, yield **6** desert, forego, refuse, reject, vacate **7** abandon, forbear, forsake, neglect **8** postpone **9** disregard **10** relinquish

waka: 5 canoe

wake: 4 call, stir, wauk(Sc.) **5** guard, revel, rouse, track, trail, vigil, waken, watch **6** arouse, awaken, excite, revive **7** passage

wakeful: 5 alert **8** restless, vigilant **9** sleepless

Walden author: 7 Thoreau

Waldensian: 7 Leonist

wale: rib **4** best, flog, mark, pick, weal, welt **5** ridge, wheal **6** choice, choose, select, streak, strip **7** timber **8** choicest

Wales (see also **Welsh**): **5** Cymru **7** Cambria

bard: **5** ovate

boat: **7** coracle

capital: **7** Cardiff

city: **6** Amlweh, Bangor **7** Rhondda, Swansea **8** Hereford, Holyhead, Pem-

broke **9** Carnarvon, Worcester
cheese: **10** Caer-philly
county: **5** Clwyd, Dyfed, Gwent
deity: **4** Bran **5** Dylan
dog: **5** corgi
emblem: **4** leek
fine: **6** saraad
island: **8** Anglesey
lake: **4** Bala
language: **6** Cymric, Kymric **7** Cymraeg
law: **7** galanas
legendary prince: **5** Madoc
marriage fee: **6** amober
measure: **5** cover **7** cantred, cantref, lestrad, listred **8** crannock
mountain: **6** Berwyn **7** Snowdon **8** Cambrian
musical instrument: **7** pibcorn
patron saint: **5** David
people: **5** Cymry, Kymry
person: **5** Taffy **8** Welshman
poet: **6** Thomas
port: **7** Cardiff
river: Dee, Wye **4** Teme **5** Teifi **6** Conway, Severn
walk: mog, pad, wag **4** foot, gait, hike, hoof, limp, mall, pace, path, plod, ramp, reel, roam, roll, step, turn, wade **5** allee, amble, field, haunt, mince, scuff, stalk, stram, stray, strut, stump, trail, tramp, tread **6** airing, arcade, foot it, hobble, loiter, lumber, pasear, prance, ramble, resort, stride, stroll, toddle, totter, trapes, trudge, wander **7** alameda, saunter, shuffle, stretch, traipse **8** ambulate, frescade, traverse **9** esplanade, promenade, tilicetum **11** perambulate **12** somnambulate **14** constitutional
a beat: **6** patrol
affectedly: **5** mince
inability to: **6** abasia
lamely: **4** limp
public: **4** mall **6** arcade **7** alameda **9** esplanade, promenade
reeling: **5** lurch
walk off: **5** leave **6** depart
walk off with: win **5** steal
walk-out: **6** strike
walk out on: **5** leave **6** desert **7** abandon
walkaway: **4** rout **7** victory
walker: **6** ganger **7** footman **8** stroller **10** pedestrian
walking: **7** passant(her.) **8** ambulant **10** ambulation **11** peripatetic
like a bear: **11** plantigrade
walking meter: **9** pedometer
walking stick: **4** cane **5** kebby, staff, stilt, waddy **6** kebbie
walkway: **4** path **7** catwalk, passage **8** sidewalk
wall: bar **4** dike, ha-ha **5** fence, levee, redan, scarp **6** bailey, cashel, escarp, haw-

haw, paries, podium, septum **7** barrier, bastion, curtain, defense, enclose, parapet, rampart **9** barricade, enclosure, encompass, partition, revetment **13** fortification
bracket: **6** corbel, sconce
covering: **4** tile **5** cloth, paint, paper **8** paneling **9** calcimine, draperies, kalsomine
dividing: **5** septa(pl.) **6** septum **9** partition
enclose within: **4** mure **6** immure
hanging: **5** arras
lining: **8** wainscot
masonry: **9** revetment
on: **5** mural
opening: **4** bole, door **6** window **7** scupper
ornament: **4** dado **6** mirror, plaque **7** hanging, molding, picture, placque **8** moulding, tapestry
part: **4** dado, pier **5** bahut, gable **6** coping, plinth **7** cornice
pert. to: **5** mural **8** parietal
plug: **6** outlet
protective: **7** parapet
up: **6** immure
wallaba tree: apa
wallaby: **8** kangaroo
wallah, walla: **5** agent, owner **6** fellow, master, person, worker **7** servant
wallet: bag, jag **4** jagg, pack, poke, sack **5** purse, scrip **6** budget **8** billfold, knapsack **10** pocketbook
wallop: **4** beat, blow, flog, lick, whip, whop **6** defeat, impact, strike, thrash, thrill
walloping: **5** large **6** strong **8** enormous
wallow: pit **4** bask, fade, mire, roll **5** surge **6** billow, grovel, hollow, trough, welter, wither **7** founder, stumble **8** flounder, kommetje **10** depression
wallowish: **4** flat **7** insipid
wallpaper measure: **4** bolt
walnut: **6** bannut
skin: **4** hull, zest **5** shell
walrus: **5** morse **6** mammal, seacat **8** mustache **9** rosmarine
flock: pod
limb: **7** flipper
order: **5** bruta
tooth: **4** tusk
waltz: zip **5** dance, valse **6** breeze
kind of: **6** Boston, Vienna
wampum: **4** peag **5** beads, money, shells **7** roanoke
wamus: **6** jacket **7** doublet **8** cardigan
wan: dim, one, sad **4** dark, fade, pale, sick, weak, worn **5** dusky, faint, livid **6** anemic, dismal, feeble, gloomy, pallid, pallor, peaked, sickly **7** ghastly, haggard, languid, wanness **8** paleness **9** bloodless, colorless, sorrowful, washed out **10** lusterless

wand: rod 4 pole, twig 5 baton, shoot, staff, stick 6 switch 7 pointer, rhabdos, scepter, sceptre 8 caduceus 9 horsewhip
royal: 4 mace 7 scepter
wand-shaped: 7 virgate
wander: bat, err, gad 4 haik, hake, prog, rave, roam, roil, rove, wind 5 amble, drift, mooch, prowl, range, shift, stray 6 cruise, dander, depart, ramble, stroll, trapes, travel 7 deviate, digress, meander, saunter, traipse 8 divagate, straggle, traverse 11 peregrinate
aimlessly: gad 5 slosh, stray 7 meander traipse
wanderer: vag 4 Arab, waif 5 gypsy, nomad, rover 6 truant 7 migrant, pilgrim, vagrant 9 itinerant, meanderer 11 extravagant
religious: 6 palmer
wandering: 5 vagus(anat.) 6 astray, errant 7 devious, erratic, journey, odyssey 8 aberrant 9 aberrance, delirious, planetary 10 circuitous, incoherent 11 noctivigant, perambulant
wandering Jew: ivy 5 plant 7 zebrina 10 spiderwort
wanderlust: 8 nomadism 9 itchy-foot 12 restlessness
wane: ebb 4 fail, lack, sink, want 5 abate, decay, peter 6 absent, defect, repine 7 decline, dwindle, subside 8 decrease, diminish 10 defervesce
opposite of: wax
wang: 4 king 5 ruler 6 prince
wanga: 5 charm, spell 6 voodoo 7 philter, sorcery
wangle: 4 fake 5 shake 6 adjust, change, juggle, totter, wiggle 7 falsify, finagle, wriggle 8 contrive, engineer 9 extricate 10 manipulate
want: gap 4 hole, lack, lose, miss, mole, must, need, void, wish 5 crave, fault, ouglet 6 besoin, choose, dearth, desire, forget, hunger, penury 7 absence, beggary, blemish, craving, lacking, missing, poverty, require, straits, vacancy 8 exigency, scarcity, shortage 9 deficient, fall short, indigence, necessary, necessity, privation 10 deficiency, inadequacy 11 deprivation, destitution, requirement 12 difficulties
wanting: 4 less 5 minus, short 6 absent, devoid 7 without, witless 9 deficient 12 feeble-minded
wanton: gay 4 fast, lewd 5 cadgy, dally, frisk, merry, revel 6 frisky, frolic, giglet, harlot, lavish, trifle, unruly 7 fulsome, haggard, ill-bred, immoral, lustful, playful, sensual, wayward 8 arrogant, flagrant, inhumane, insolent, prodigal, spiteful, sportive, unchaste 9 dissolute, lecherous, luxuriant, luxurious, mali-

cious, merciless 10 capricious, effeminate, frolicsome, gratuitous, lascivious, licentious, prostitute, refractory, voluptuous 11 extravagant, mollycoddle 12 disregardful, supererogant, unmanageable, unrestrained 13 undisciplined, unjustifiable
wantwit: 4 fool 5 dunce
wap: 4 beat, bind, blow, whop, wrap 5 blast, fight, knock, storm, truss 6 bundle, strike 8 wrapping
wapiti: elk 4 deer, stag 8 wampoose
war: 4 feud 5 blitz, fight 6 battle, combat, strife 7 contend, crusade 8 struggle
alarm: 4 flap
club: 4 mace 5 nulla 6 nullah
fleet: 6 armada
god of: Ira, Tyr 4 Ares, Coel, Mars, Odin, Thor 5 Woden 6 Nergal
goddess: 4 Alea 5 Anath, Bella 6 Anunit, Ishtar 7 Bellona
instrument: 7 caltrap, caltrop 9 relocator
machine: ram 4 bomb, tank 6 rocket 7 missile 8 catapult
religious: 5 jehad, jihad 7 crusade
restriction: 8 blockade
trophy: 4 star 5 medal, scalp 6 ribbon
vehicle: 4 jeep, tank
vessel: sub 6 corvet 7 cruiser 8 corvette 9 destroyer, submarine 11 dreadnaught
War and Peace author: 7 Tolstoy
war chest: 8 treasury
war hawk: 5 jingo
war-horse: 5 steed 6 leader 7 charger, standby, veteran 8 partisan 10 campaigner, politician
warbird: 7 aviator, tanager 8 airplane
warble: 4 sing 5 carol, chant, chirl, shake, trill, yodel 6 melody 7 descant, twitter, vibrate
warbler: 4 wren 5 pipit, robin 6 singer, thrush 8 blackcap, grosbeak, redstart, songbird, songster 9 beccafico 10 bluethroat 11 whitethroat
ward: 4 care, jail, rule, warn 5 guard, parry, watch 6 charge, defend, govern, prison, warden, warder 7 counsel, custody, defense, deflect, enclose, fortify, keeping, protege 8 district, garrison, guardian, watchman 9 safeguard 10 protection 11 confinement 12 guardianship 14 arrondissement(F.)
pert. to: 9 pupillary
ward off: end 4 fend 5 avert, guard, parry, repel 7 forfend, prevent
warden: 4 caid 5 guard, nazir 6 disdar, dizdar, jailer, jailor, keeper, ranger, regent, sexton 7 alcaide, alcayde, turnkey, viceroy 8 director, governor, guardian, overseer, watchman 9 castellan, concierge, constable, custodian 10 doorkeeper, gatekeeper, supervisor

warder (see also **warden**): 5 staff 7 bulwark 8 sentinel 9 caretaker, truncheon 10 stronghold

wardrobe: 4 room 5 privy, trunk 6 closet 7 apparel, armoire, bedroom, cabinet, chamber, clothes 8 costumes 9 garderobe 12 clothespress

ware: 4 host, sage, shun, wary, wise 5 avoid, aware, china, goods, ready, spend, stuff, waste 6 people, shrewd 7 careful, chaffer, heedful, pottery, prudent, seaweed 8 cautious, products, squander, vigilant 9 cognizant, commodity, porcelain

warehouse: 4 silo, stow 5 depot, etape, guard, store 6 fonduk, godown 7 almacen, fonduk, funduck, protect, shelter, storage 8 elevator, entrepot, magazine 10 storehouse 11 accommodate

fee: 7 storage

warfare: See **war**

warily (see also **wary**): 6 tiptoe 8 gingerly

warlike: 7 hostile, martial 8 militant, military 9 bellicose, Bellonian, soldierly 10 battailous, pugnacious 11 belligerent

warlock: 6 wizard 8 conjuror, magician, sorcerer 9 enchanter

warm (see also **hot**): 4 avid, beek, heat, keen, kind, mild 5 angry, brisk, calid, chafe, eager, fiery, fresh, tepid, toast 6 ardent, devout, genial, hearty, heated, kindly, lively, loving, strong, tender, toasty 7 affable, amorous, clement, cordial, earnest, enliven, excited, fervent, glowing, irksome, sincere, thermal, zealous 8 animated, friendly, generous, gracious, grateful, vehement, vigorous 9 harassing, irascible, irritated, sprightly, strenuous 10 overheated, passionate, responsive 11 sympathetic 12 affectionate, disagreeable, enthusiastic 13 uncomfortable

warmth: 4 elan, glow, heat, zeal, zest 6 spirit 7 passion

pert. to: 7 thermal

warn: tip 4 rede 5 alarm, alert 6 advise, exhort, inform, notify 7 apprise, apprize, caution, counsel 8 admonish, threaten 9 reprehend

warning: 4 omen 5 knell 6 alarum, beware, caveat, lesson, signal 7 caution, sematic 10 admonition 13 animadversion

sound of: 4 bell 5 alarm, siren 6 alarum, tocsin

warp: abb, end, hit, mud, wry 4 beat, bend, bias, cast, emit, hurl, kink, line, rope, silt, sway, turn, warf 5 eject, expel, fling, quirk, throw, twist 6 buckle, debase, deform, devise, fasten, swerve 7 contort, deflect, distort, falsify, pervert 8 sediment 9 fabricate 10 aberration, intertwine 12 misinterpret, misrepresent

thread for loom: 6 stamen

warragal, warrigal: 5 dingo, horse

warrant: act 4 earn, save, write 5 berat, guard, merit, order, right 6 assert, defend, ensure, ground, permit, reason, refuge, safety 7 behight, command, defense, justify, precept, protect, voucher, writing 8 document, guaranty, maintain, mittimus, sanction 9 authority, authorize, guarantee, protector, safeguard 10 commisssion, foundation, instrument, obligation, protection 11 certificate, stand behind 13 authorization, justification

warranty: 8 guaranty, sanction, security, 9 assurance, guarantee 13 authorization, justification

warren: 5 hutch 8 rabbitry, tenement

warrior: toa 4 hero, impi 5 brave 6 Amazon 7 fighter, martial, soldier 10 serviceman

group: 4 army

mythical: 6 Amazon 7 Aslauga

professional: 7 Hessian 9 gladiator, mercenary

Trojan: 6 Agenor, Hector

warship: sub 5 razee 6 bireme 7 cruiser, dromond, frigate, onebank, trireme 8 corvette 9 destroyer, submarine 10 battleship 11 dreadnaught

deck: 5 orlop

fleet: 6 armada

pert. to: 5 naval

quarters: 7 gunroom

squadron: 10 escadrille

three-bank: 7 trireme

two-bank: 6 bireme

wart: 5 tumor 7 verruca 9 subaltern 10 midshipman

wary: shy 5 alert, cagey, canny, chary, leery 7 careful, guarded, knowing, prudent, sparing 8 cautious, discreet, stealthy, watchful 9 cautelous, provident 10 economical 11 circumspect, on one's guard

wase: pad 4 wisp 6 bundle

wash: lap, mud, pan 4 lave, silt, soap 5 bathe, clean, creek, drift, float, leach, rinse, scour, scrub, slosh 6 buddle, debris, purify, sperge 7 cleanse, launder, shampoo 8 ablution, alluvium 9 lixiviate

away: 5 erode, purge

out: 4 fail 5 elute, erase, flush 7 discard, launder

up: 6 finish 7 discard, dismiss

washbowl: 4 sink 5 basin 6 lavabo 8 lavatory 9 aljofaina

washed-out: wan **4** pale **5** all in, faded, tired **6** effete **8** depleted **9** exhausted **10** dispirited, spiritless

washer: 4 rove **5** clove

washing: 8 ablution, lavation
chemical: **6** eluate

Washington, D.C.: 7 capital
art gallery: **5** Freer **8** National **8** Corcoran
nickname: **11** Foggy Bottom
original planner: **7** L'Enfant
river: **7** Potomac

Washington, George: *home:* **11** Mount Vernon
portraitist: **6** Stuart
wife: **6** Martha

Washington, State of: *capital:* **7** Olympia
city: **6** Tacoma, Yakima **7** Everett, Seattle, Spokane **10** Walla Walla
county: **4** King **5** Adams, Clark, Ferry, Lewis **6** Pierce
dam: **11** Grand Coulee
explorer: **4** Gray **6** Hecate **9** Vancouver **13** Lewis and Clark
Indian: **7** Chinook **8** Sahaptin
island: **5** Orcas **7** San Juan
motto: **4** Alki (By and By)
mountain peak: **5** Adams, Baker **7** Rainier **8** St. Helens
mountain range: **6** Kettle **7** Cascade, Olympic
nickname: **7** Chinook **9** Evergreen
river: **5** Snake **6** Yakima **8** Columbia
sound: **5** Puget
state bird: **9** goldfinch
state flower: **12** rhododendron
state tree: **7** hemlock
strait: **4** Haro **7** Georgia, Rosario **10** Juan de Fuca

washout: 4 flop **5** gulch, gully **6** fiasco **7** erosion, failure

washy: 4 oozy, thin, weak **5** loose **6** feeble, watery **7** diluted, insipid **8** slippery **9** frivolous, worthless

wasp: 5 whamp **6** dauber, hornet, insect, vespid **12** hymenopteron, yellow jacket
genus of: **5** sphex
pert. to: **6** vespal **7** vespine

waspish: 5 testy **7** peevish, slender **8** choleric, petulant, snappish, spiteful **9** fractious, irascible, irritable **11** bad-tempered **12** cantankerous

wassail: 4 lark, orgy, romp **5** binge, drink, revel **6** frolic, shindy **7** carouse **8** carousal **9** festivity, high jinks, merriment **10** salutation **11** celebration

waste (see also **refuse, wasteland**)**: 4** bush, fail, idle, loss, pine, ruin, sack **5** decay, dwine, havoc **6** barren, bezzle, devour, molder, ravage, refuse **7** atrophy, badland, consume, corrode, destroy, dwindle, exhaust, fritter **8** con-

found, decrease, demolish, desolate, emaciate, enfeeble, misspend, squander **9** condiddle, devastate, dissipate **11** consumption, destruction, devastation, dissipation, fritter away, prodigality, superfluous, uninhabited **12** extravagance, improvidence, uncultivated
allowance: **4** tret
from a mine: **7** mullock
lay: **4** sack **5** havoc, spoil **6** ravage

waste away: age, rot **4** pine, wilt **5** decay **6** molder **7** atrophy

waste matter: 5 ashes, dregs, dross **6** debris **7** garbage

wasted: 7 haggard, wizened **8** impaired phthisic **9** emaciated, shriveled

wasteful: 6 lavish **8** prodigal **10** thriftless **11** extravagant, improvident

wasteland: fen **4** burn, moor **5** heath, marsh, swamp, wilds **6** desert, morass **8** badlands

wastrel: 4 rake, roué, waif **5** idler **6** waster **8** vagabond **10** profligate **11** spendthrift **13** good-for-nothing

wat: 6 temple

watch: eye, see, spy **4** espy, glom, heed, look, mark, mind, tend, view, wait **5** await, guard, timer, vigil **6** ambush, behold, defend, patrol, police, regard, sentry **7** bivouac, lookout, observe **8** horologe, meditate, sentinel **9** ambuscade, timepiece **11** keep an eye on, observation **13** sleeplessness
crystal rim: **5** basil, bezel, bezil
maker: **10** horologist
part: fob **7** crystal

watchdog: 6 keeper, warden **8** guardian **9** custodian
Hel's: **4** Garm **5** Garmr
underworld: **8** Cerberus

watcher: spy **5** scout **8** watcher, watchman **9** spectator

watchful: 4 wary **5** alert, aware **7** careful, wakeful **8** cautious, open-eyed **9** attentive, wide-awake **10** unsleeping **11** circumspect

watchman: 5 guard, scout **6** sentry, warder **8** sentinel **10** gatekeeper

watchtower: 6 beacon, garret **7** lookout, mirador **8** bantayan **10** lighthouse, widow's walk

watchword: 5 motto **6** ensign, signal, parole **8** consigne **10** shibboleth **11** countersign

watchworks: 8 movement
arrangement: **7** caliper
mechanism: **10** escapement

water: eau(F.), wet **4** agua(Sp.), aqua(L.), brim, broo, burn, hose, pani **5** brine, fluid, flume, laver, lough, lymph, spray **6** dilute, liquid **7** moisten **8** calender, beverage, irrigate, sprinkle **10** citronelle *body:* (see also **watercourse**): bay, sea **4** deep, gulf, lake, mear, mere, pind, pool, tank, well **5** oasis, ocean **6** lagoon, strait **7** springs **9** reservoir

carrier: **4** duct, pipe **5** barge, canal, flume, zanja **7** aguador **8** aqueduct

congealed: ice **5** glace **6** icicle

covered by: **5** awash **7** flooded

down: **4** thin

draw: **4** lade

element: **6** oxygen **8** hydrogen

French: eau

goddess: **4** Nina **7** Anahita, Anaitis

hog: **8** capybara

hole: **5** oasis **7** alberca

Latin: **4** aqua

living in: **9** amphibian

mineral: **5** Vichy **6** selter, Shasta **7** seltzer

neck: **6** strait

obstruction: bar, dam **4** reef

pert. to: **6** marine **7** aquatic

play in: **5** plash

pure: **8** aqua pura(L.)

raising apparatus: **4** pump **5** sweep **6** siphon **7** shadoof **10** water wheel

rough: rip, sea **4** eddy **5** waves **6** rapids **8** breakers

search for: **5** dowse

soapy: **4** suds **6** graith

sound: **4** drip **5** plash **6** murmur, splash

Spanish: **4** agua

still: **6** lagoon

surface: **4** ryme

vessel: jug **4** cowl, ewer, lota, pail **5** cruse, flask, lotah **6** bottle, bucket, goblet **7** pitcher, stamnos **8** decanter

Water Bearer: 8 Aquarius

water bird: 4 coot, loon **5** diver **8** alcatras **9** waterfowl

water bottle: 4 lota, olla **6** tinaja

water buffalo: ox **7** carabao

water carrier: 4 pipe **7** aguador(Sp.), bheesty(Ind.), channel **8** bheestie(Ind.)

water cavy: 6 rodent **8** capybara

water centipede: 12 hellgrammite

water chicken: 9 gallinule

water clock: 6 ghurry **9** clepsydra

water cooler: 4 icer, olla, tank **11** refrigerant

water cow: 7 manatee

water crow: 4 coot **9** snakebird

water crowfoot: 4 herb **9** buttercup

water cure: 10 hydropathy **12** hydrotherapy **17** hydrotherapeutics

water deer: 10 chevrotain

water eagle: 6 osprey

water elephant: 12 hippopotamus

water gate: 6 sluice **9** floodgate **11** watercourse

water germander: 4 mint

water glass: 6 goblet **7** tumbler **9** clepsydra

water grampus: 12 hellgrammite

water hog: 7 bushpig **8** capybara

water hole: pit **4** lake, pond, pool **5** oasis **7** alberca

water horse: 6 kelpie **11** hippocampus **12** hippopotamus

water ice: 7 sherbet

water lily: 5 lotos, lotus **6** bobbin, nuphar **7** nelumbo **8** nenuphar

water meter: 7 venturi

water moccasin: 5 snake, viper

water mole: 6 desman **8** duckbill, platypus

water nymph: nix **4** lily **5** Ariel, naiad, nixie **6** flower, kelpie, nereid, Undine **7** goddess, hydriad, Oceanid **9** dragonfly

water on the brain: 13 hydrocephalus

water ouzel: 4 bird **6** dipper, thrush

water pig: 7 gourami **8** capybara

water pipe: 4 duct, hose, tube **6** hookah **8** nargileh

water plant: 7 aquatic **10** hydrophyte

water plug: tap **6** spigot **7** hydrant

water pocket: 6 tinaja

water rat: 4 vole **6** rodent **7** muskrat

water sprite: See **water nymph**

water thief: 6 pirate

watercourse (see also **water:** *body*): run **4** dike, dyke, race, wadi, wady **5** brook, canal, chute, creek, drain, gully, river **6** arroyo(Sp.), course, gutter, nullah, ravine, sluice, stream **7** channel, trinket **8** barranca(Sp.)

watercraft: See **boat, ship**

watercress: 9 brooklime

watered: 5 moire

waterfall: lin **4** linn **5** force **7** cascade, chignon, Niagara **8** cataract, Victoria, Yosemite **9** multnomah

waterfowl: 4 coot, loon **5** diver **8** game bird

waterfront worker: 5 navvy **9** stevedore

Watergate judge: 6 Sirica

waterhead: sap **5** booby **6** source **9** headwater **12** fountainhead **13** hydrocephalus

watering device: 4 hose, pump **5** spray **6** nozzle

watering place: bar, spa **4** pool **5** oasis **6** aguada(Sp.), battis, resort, spring **9** nightclub

waterless: dry **4** arid

waterlog: 4 soak **5** swamp **8** saturate

watermelon: 5 gourd **6** citrul, sandia **7** anguria

waters: See **watering place**

primeval: **4** Apsu

watershed: 5 ridge **6** divide

waterspout: 5 canal, spate **7** tornado **8** gargoyle **9** hurricane, whirlwind

waterwheel: 5 noria, sakia **6** sakieh **7** sakiyeh **8** tympanum

watery: wet **4** pale, soft, thin, weak **5** fluid, sammy, soggy **6** blashy, dilute, serous, soaked, sweaty **7** aqueous, insipid, tearful, weeping **8** humorous **11** transparent

wattle: rod **4** beat, bind, flog, gill, jowl, twig, wand **5** cooba, fence, stick, twist, withe **6** acacia, coobah, dewlap, hurdle, lappet **9** boobyalla, framework, hackthorn **10** interwine, interweave

wave: ola(Sp.), sea, set, wag **4** bore, curl, flap, surf, sway, tide, vein **5** bless, crimp, curve, eager, eagre, float, flood, ridge, shake, surge, swell, swing, tilde, water, waver **6** beckon, billow, comber, fickle, flaunt, marcel, ripple, roller, signal **7** breaker, flutter, ripplet, seagate, tsunami, vibrate, wavelet **8** brandish, flourish, undulate, whitecap **9** fluctuate, permanent, vibration **10** undulation, unevenness

largest: **7** decuman

top: **5** crest

upward motion: **5** scend

waver: **4** reel, sway, trim, twig **5** quake, swing **6** change, falter, seesaw, teeter, totter, wiggle **7** flicker, flitter, flutter, sapling, stagger, tremble, vibrate **8** hesitate **9** fluctuate, hem and haw, oscillate, vacillate **11** back and fill

wavering: **4** weak **6** fickle **7** lambent **8** doubtful, flexuous, unsteady **9** desultory **10** hesitating, irresolute **11** vacillating

wavy: **4** ente(her.), onde(her.), unde(her.), undy(her.) **5** crisp, curly, snaky, undee(her.) **6** flying **7** billowy, sinuate, sinuous **8** squiggly, undulant **9** undulated **10** undulating

wax: **4** cere, grow, pela, rise **5** putty **6** become **7** cerumen, suberin **8** adhesive, increase, paraffin **11** zietriskite

candle: **5** taper **6** cierge

cobbler's: **4** code

figure: **9** ceroplast

match: **5** vesta

mixture: **6** cerate

myrtle: **8** bayberry

ointment: **6** cerate

opposite of: **4** wane

pert. to: **5** ceral

preparation: **6** cerate

substance: **5** cerin

used for skis: **7** klister

yellow: **7** ceresin

waxbill: **7** astrild

waxen: **4** ashy, pale **6** pallid, viscid **7** cerated, pliable **8** yielding **11** impressible **14** impressionable

waxwing: **9** cedarbird **10** weaverbird

waxy: **5** angry, vexed **7** pliable **8** yielding

way: via **4** cost, door, drag, fore, gait, lane, mode, path, plan, road, room **5** alley, going, habit, milky, route, space, style, track **6** ambage, arcade, artery, avenue, career, causey, chemin, course, detour, device, manner, method, scheme, street **7** advance, fashion, highway, opening, passage **8** causeway, contrada, distance, progress **9** banquette, boulevard, direction, procedure **12** idiosyncrasy

in: **7** contact **8** entrance

on: **7** en route

open: **7** pioneer

out: **4** exit **6** egress, escape

waybill: **8** manifest **9** itinerary

wayfarer: **6** viator **8** traveler **9** itinerant

waygate: **4** path **9** departure **10** passageway

waylay: **5** awiat, belay, beset, prowl, skulk, slink **6** ambush **7** forelay **8** surprise **9** ambuscade

waymark: ahu **5** arrow **9** guidepost, milestone

wayward: **6** fickle, unruly **7** erratic, froward, naughty, willful **8** contrary, perverse, stubborn, unsteady, untoward **9** arbitrary, irregular **10** capricious, headstrong, inconstant, refractory, selfwilled **11** disobedient, fluctuating, intractable **13** unpredictable

we: nos(L.) **8** ourselves

weak: wan **4** puny, soft, thin, worn **5** anile, bauch, chirp, crank, crimp, dicky, faint, frail, seely, washy, waugh, young **6** caduke, debile, dickey, dilute, dotish, faulty, feeble, flabby, flaggy, flimsy, foible, infirm, sickly, squeak, tender, unwise, watery **7** brittle, dwaibly, fragile, pliable, rickety **8** asthenic, childish, decrepit, feckless, flagging, helpless, impotent **9** childlike, dissolute, enfeebled, nerveless, powerless, spineless **10** effeminate, inadequate **11** implausible, ineffective **12** unconvincing

weaken: sap **4** thin, tire **5** appal, blunt, break, craze, delay **6** appall, deaden, defeat, dilute, impair, lessen, rebate, reduce, soften **7** cripple, decline, depress, disable, exhaust, unnerve **8** enervate, paralyze **9** attenuate, extenuate, undermine **10** debilitate, demoralize

weakling: **5** puler, sissy **6** softie, sucker **7** crybaby, sad sack **8** mama's boy, pushover **10** weak sister

weakness: **4** flaw **6** defect, foible **7** acratia, ailment, failing **8** appetite, debility, fondness **9** inability **11** attenuation **12** imperfection

of organ or muscle: **5** atony

weal: **4** line, mark, pomp, wale, welt **5** ridge, state **6** choice, choose, riches, stripe, wealth **7** welfare **9** happiness, wellbeing **10** commonweal, prosperity

wealth: **4** dhan, gear, gold, good, mean,

pelf, weal **5** goods, money **6** assets, graith, mammon, riches **7** capital, fortune, welfare **8** opulence, property, treasure **9** abundance, affluence, wellbeing **10** prosperity **11** possessions

gained: **8** chevance **9** chievance

god of: **6** Plutus

income from: **6** usance

person of: **5** Midas, nabob **7** Croesus, magnate **9** moneybags, plutocrat

wealthy: 4 full, rich **5** ample, pursy

wean: 4 baby **5** child **6** detach, infant **8** alienate, estrange **9** reconcile

weapon: arm, dag, gun **4** beak, bola, bolo, celt, claw, dart, dirk, epee, foil, pike **5** arrow, bolas, glave, knife, lance, rifle, saber, sabre, shaft, sling, spear, sword, talon, vouge **6** bomber, dagger, eolith, glaive, mortar, pistol, poleax, rapier **7** bayonet, bazooka, carbine, gisarme, halberd, halbert, machete, missile, poleaxe, trident **8** catapult, crossbow, fauchard, leeangle, revolver, stiletto, tomahawk **9** artillery, derringer **11** blunderbuss

lay down: **6** disarm **9** surrender

storage place: **7** arsenal

without: **7** unarmed

wear: don, rub **4** fray, tire **5** chafe, erode, grind, sport, weary **6** abrade, attire, batter, endure, impair **7** apparel, clothes, consume, corrode, display, exhaust, exhibit, fatigue, frazzle **8** diminish **11** deteriorate

away: eat **5** erode **6** abrade **7** corrode

down: **4** tire **5** drain **7** exhaust, fatigue

out: **4** whip **6** tucker **7** exhaust **8** knock out

weariness (see also **weary**): **4** arid **5** ennui **6** tedium **7** fatigue **8** vexation **9** lassitude

weary: bad, fag, irk, sad **4** bore, jade, puny, tire, weak, worn **5** annoy, bored, curse, spent, timid, tired **6** harass, plague, sickly **7** exhaust, fatigue, irksome, tedious **8** fatigued, grievous, tiresome **9** forjaskit, forjesket, surfeited **10** defatigate, disastrous **11** unfortunate

Weary Willie: 5 tramp **7** shirker, vagrant **8** vagabond **13** featherbedder

weasand: 6 gullet, throat **7** trachea **8** windpipe **9** esophagus

weasel: 4 cane, stot, vare **5** ratel, sneak, stoat **6** ermine, ferret **9** pussyfoot **10** equivocate

family: **6** ermine, ferret, marten **9** musteline

weather: dry **4** hail, rain, snow, wind **5** erode, sleet **7** climate **8** discolor, windward **12** disintegrate

weather map line: 6 isobar

weather satellite: 5 Tiros

weathercock: 4 fane, vane

weathered: 5 faded **6** tanned **7** bronzed, stained **8** bleached, hardened **9** roughened, toughened

weatherman: 13 meteorologist

weave: 4 darn, knit, lace, spin **5** braid, drape, lurch, plait, unite **6** devise, enlace, wattle **7** canille, entwine, fashion, stagger **8** cannelle, contrive **9** fabricate, interlace, interwind **10** intertwine, intertwist

twigs: **6** wattle

weaverbird: 4 baya, taha **5** finch **6** whidah

weaver's tool: 4 loom, reed, sley

weaving: *cylinder:* **4** beam

goddess: **6** Ergane

machine: **4** loom **6** carder **8** jacquard

product: **5** cloth **7** textile

weazen: See **wizen**

web: mat, net, ply **4** caul, maze, mesh, trap, veil, warp **5** snare **6** fabric, morass, tangle, tissue **7** ensnare, network, texture, webbing **8** entangle, gossamer, membrane, vexillum **9** labyrinth **11** fabrication **12** entanglement

pert. to: **6** telary **7** retiary

web-footed: 7 palmate **11** totipalmate

web-like: 4 lacy **7** spidery

half: **11** semi-palmate

webbing: 7 binding

Weber opera: 6 Oberon **13** Der Freischutz

wed: 4 join **5** elope, marry, mated, unite **6** joined, pawned **7** espouse, pledged, spliced **9** mortgaged

pert. to: **7** marital

wedding: 6 splice **8** ceremony, espousal, marriage, nuptials **11** anniversary

anniversary: see **wedding anniversary**

attendant: **5** usher **10** bridesmaid

canopy: **5** chupa **6** huppah **7** chuppah

celebration: **8** shivaree

party: **9** breakfast, reception

proclamation: **5** banns

ring: **4** band

wedding anniversary: *fifteenth:* **7** crystal

fifth: **4** wood

fiftieth: **6** golden

first: **5** paper

kind of: tin **4** ruby **5** candy, china, coral, linen, paper, pearl, straw **6** floral, golden, silver, wooden **7** crystal, diamond, emerald, leather

seventy-fifth: **7** diamond

tenth: tin

thirtieth: **5** pearl

twentieth: **5** china

twenty-fifth: **6** silver

wedge: jam **4** club, heel, lump, shim, shoe **5** cleat, crowd, ingot, piece, split **6** cleave, sector, wedgie **7** niblick **8** separate, triangle, voussoir **9** formation

wedge-shaped: **6** cuneal **7** cuneate, sphenic **8** cuneated, cuniform **9** cuneiform

wedgie: **4** shoe

wedlock (see also **wedding**): **4** wife **8** marriage **9** matrimony **11** conjugality

Wednesday (source of name): **5** Woden

wee: **4** tiny **5** bitty, small, teeny **6** little, minute **9** miniature **10** diminutive **11** lilliputian

weed: **4** band, garb, loco, milk, sida, tare **5** armor, cheat, dress, horse, vetch **6** darnel, datura, nettle, remove, sarcle, spurge **7** allseed, clothes, costume, garment, illness, mallows, purloin, ragweed, relapse, thistle, tobacco **8** clothing, plantain, purslane, sealwort, toadflax, trumpery **9** alfilaria, dandelion, eradicate, marijuana **11** undergrowth

weed killer: **8** paraquat **9** herbicide

weeds: **8** mourning

weedy: **4** foul, lean **5** lanky **7** scraggy **8** ungainly **9** overgrown

week: **8** hebdomad

weekday: **5** feria

weekly: **5** aweek **10** hebdomadal, periodical **11** hebdomadary, publication

weeks (two): **9** fortnight

weel: **4** eddy, pool, trap **6** basket **9** whirlpool

ween: **4** hope **5** fancy, think **6** expect **7** believe, imagine, suppose **8** conceive

weep: cry, sob **4** drip, leak, tear, wail **5** exude, greet, mourn **6** bewail, beweep, boohoo, lament **7** blubber, deplore

Weeping Philosopher: **10** Heraclitus

weeping statue: **5** Niobe

weepy: **5** moist, seepy **6** oozing **7** tearful, weeping **8** mournful

weevil: **4** boll, lota **7** billbug **8** circulio

weft: web **4** film, warp, woof, yarn **5** shoot, shute **7** filling **12** crossthreads

weigh: tax **4** bear, lift, tare, test **5** carry, hoist, poise **6** burden, esteem, matter, ponder, regard **7** balance, examine, measure, portion, support **8** consider, dispense, meditate, militate **9** apportion **14** counterbalance

weigh down: sit **4** lade, load, sway **5** beset **7** depress, oppress **8** encumber

weigher: **5** trone **6** potdar, scaler **7** balance, trutine **8** computer **9** steelyard

weighing machine: **5** scale, trone **7** balance **9** steelyard

weight: bob, CWT, keg, lot, mol, tod, tom, ton, tup **4** beef, dram, gram, heft, lade, last, load, mina, onus, pari, rati, shot, tola **5** carat, clove, flask, grain, ounce, pfund, poise, pound, power, ratti, rider, scale, stein **6** barrel, burden, cental,

charge, denier, fother, fotmal, gramme, grivna, import, moment **7** centner, drachma, gravity, oppress, plummet, quarter, quintal, scruple, tonnage **8** decagram, encumber, kilogram, pressure, vamfront, vammazsa, vierling **9** authority, centigram, heaviness, hectogram, influence, liespfund, microgram, milligram, myriagram, quentchen, zollpfund **10** importance **11** consequence **12** significance **13** hundredweight, ponderability

allowance: **4** tare, tret **7** scalage

gem: **5** carat

inspector: **6** sealer

of container: **4** tare

of 100 pounds: **6** cental

of 2000 pounds: ton

official: **6** metage

pert. to: **5** baric **8** ponderal

system of: net **4** troy **5** avoir **6** metric **8** jeweler's **11** avoirdupois **12** apothecaries

weighted: **4** bias **5** laden **6** loaded **8** burdened **9** evaluated, oppressed

weightiness: **4** pomp **7** dignity, gravity **9** solemnity **10** importance

weighty: fat **5** bulky, heavy, hefty, large, massy, obese, solid **6** severe, solemn **7** capital, massive, onerous, serious, telling **8** forcible, grievous, powerful **9** corpulent, important, momentous, ponderous **10** burdensome, chargeable, cumbersome, impressive, oppressive

weir: dam **4** bank **5** fence, garth, levee **7** barrier, milldam **11** obstruction

weird: lot, odd **4** eery, fate, unco, wild **5** charm, eerie, queer, scary, spell **6** creepy, kismet, spooky **7** awesome, curious, destine, destiny, fortune, ghostly, macabre, predict, strange, uncanny, unusual **8** foretell, prophecy **9** unearthly **10** mysterious, prediction, soothsayer

weka: **4** bird, rail

welcome: **4** hail **5** adopt, greet **7** acclaim, cordial, embrace **8** greeting, pleasant **9** agreeable, bienvenue, desirable **10** acceptable, salutation, satisfying

weld: **5** unite **6** solder **11** consolidate

welding gas: **9** acetylene

welfare: **4** dole, good, sele, weal **7** benefit **10** prosperity

goddess: **5** Salus

welkin: air, sky **10** atmosphere

well: fit, pit **4** bene(It., L.), bien (F.), fair, flow, gush, hole, sump **5** aweel(Sc.), fitly, fount **6** gusher, hearty, indeed, justly, source, spring **7** cistern, gaylies, geylies, gradely, healthy **8** artesian, expertly, fountain **9** correctly **10** gratifying, prosperous **11** excellently **12** satisfactory

drill device: jar
lining: **5** steen
pit: **4** sump
pole: **5** sweep
well-behaved: 4 good
well-being: 4 good, weal **6** health **7** comfort, welfare **8** eucrasia, felicity **9** eudaemony, happiness **10** prosperity
well-bred: 5 civil **6** polite **7** genteel, refined **8** cultured, wellborn **9** pedigreed **10** cultivated **11** gentlemanly **12** thoroughbred
well-defined: 8 distinct **11** distinctive
well-developed: 5 curvy **7** rounded **10** curvaceous
well-founded: 4 firm, good, just **6** cogent
well-groomed: 4 neat **5** clean, sleek **6** dapper, soigne **7** soignee
well-grounded: 4 firm **5** valid
well-heeled: 4 rich **7** moneyed **10** prosperous
well-known: 5 noted **6** famous **7** eminent, leading **8** familiar **9** notorious
well-liked: 7 popular **8** favorite **9** preferred
well-made: 5 solid **6** sturdy **9** affabrous
well-nigh: 6 almost, nearly
well-off: 5 lucky **8** thriving **10** prosperous
well-timed: 6 timely **9** opportune **10** propitious
well-versed: 7 erudite **13** knowledgeable
Welland: 4 city **5** canal, river
wellaway: woe **4** alas **5** alack **6** regret **9** alackaday
wellborn: 4 rich **5** noble **7** eugenic
wellhead: 6 source, spring **8** fountain **12** fountainhead
welsh, welch: 5 cheat, evade, renig **6** renege **7** swindle **8** back down
Welsh, Welch (see also **Wales**): **6** Cymric **8** Cambrian
welsh drake: 7 gadwall
Welsh onion: 5 cibol
Welsh Rabbit: 7 rarebit
welt: 4 blow, mark, turn, wale **5** ridge, upset, wheal **6** stripe, thrash **8** overturn
welter: 4 reel, roll, toss, wilt **5** upset **6** grovel, tumble, wallow, wither **7** stagger, turmoil **8** overturn **9** confusion
wem: 4 flaw, scar, spot **5** stain
wen: 4 cyst, rune **5** tumor **6** growth **7** blemish **11** excrescence **12** imperfection, protuberance
wench: 4 dell, doxy, drab, gill, girl **5** child, gouge, trull, woman **6** blowen, blowze, damsel, maiden, wanton **7** consort, servant **8** strumpet **11** maidservant
wend: bow **4** fare, pass **5** alter, shift **6** depart, push on, travel **7** circuit, journey, proceed
Wend: 4 Slav, Sorb **7** Sorbian

wenzel: 4 jack **5** knave
werewolf: 8 turnskin, versipal **11** lycanthrope
West: 8 frontier, Occident
West Africa: See **Africa**
West Germany capital: 4 Bonn
West Indies: 7 Bahamas **8** Antilles
bird: **4** arar, tody **6** mucaro
boat: **7** drogher **9** catamaran
dance: **5** limbo
fiber: **5** cajun
fish: **4** paru, pega, sesi **5** pelon **6** testar **7** pegador **8** scirenga **9** picudilla
fleas: **7** chigoes
fruit: **4** tuna **5** papaw **6** papaya, pawpaw **7** genipap
handkerchief: **7** malabar
herb: **4** ocra **6** vanglo **7** vangloe
island: **4** Cuba **5** Aruba, Haiti, Nevis **6** Bahama **7** Grenada, Jamaica **8** Antilles, Barbados, Trinidad **10** Martinique, Puerto Rico, Santa Lucia **13** Virgin Islands
language: **6** Creole, French **7** English, Spanish
liquor: **5** mobby, tafia **6** mobbie, taffia
lizard: **6** arbalo
mistletoe: **7** gadbush
palm: **5** yagua, yaray **6** grigri, grugru
people: Ebo **4** Eboe **5** Cuban **6** Creole
pert. to: **9** Antillean
plum: **4** jobo
republic: **5** Haiti
rodent: **5** hutia, jutia **6** agouti
shrub: **4** anil **7** joewood
snuff: **8** maccaboy, maccoboy
sorcery: obe, obi **6** voodoo
sugar work: **5** usine
taro: **5** tania
tortoise: **7** hicatee **8** hiccatee
tree: **4** ausu, cera **5** acana, acapu, ebony, genip, papaw, yacca **6** aralie, ausubo, balata, cocuyo, gomart, pawpaw, ramoon **7** cocullo **8** aceituna, cockspur, drumwood **9** cocuswood, sapodilla
treewood: **5** galba
volcano: **5** Pelee
West Point: *mascot:* **4** mule
student: **4** pleb **5** cadet, plebe **8** yearling
West Virginia: *capital:* **10** Charleston
chief product: **4** coal
city: **7** Weirton **8** Wheeling
county: **4** Clay, Wood **5** Mingo, Roane **6** Cabell **7** Fayette, Kanawha
highest point: **10** Spruce Knob
nickname: **8** Mountain **9** Panhandle
river: Elk **4** Ohio
state bird: **8** cardinal
state flower: **12** rhododendron
state tree: **5** maple
western: 5 oater **10** horse opera
Western Samoa: *capital:* **4** Apia

monetary unit: **4** tala
Western treaty alliance: 4 NATO
Westminster clock: Ben
Westphalian city: 7 Munster
wet: lax, off **4** damp, dank, dewy, dram, lash, mire, rain, soak **5** bedew, bewet, dabby, foggy, humid, leach, misty, moist, mushy, rainy, soggy, soppy, sweat, wrong **6** clashy, dampen, drench, humect, imbrue, jarble, liquor, shower, soaked, sodden, watery **7** flotter, moisten, splashy, squashy **8** dampened, irrigate, moisture, sprinkle **9** misguided **11** intoxicated **18** anti-prohibitionist
wet blanket: 6 dampen **7** depress, killjoy **8** deadhead, dispirit **10** discourage, spoilsport
wet flax: ret
wet one's whistle: 5 drink
weta: 6 insect, locust
wetbird: 9 chaffinch
wether: ram **4** wool **5** sheep **6** eunuch **7** dinmont
whack: hit, try **4** bang, beat, belt, blow **5** fling, share, thump, trial, whang **6** chance, strike, stroke, thwack **7** attempt, portion **8** division **9** allowance, condition
whacking: 4 huge, very **5** large **8** whopping **10** tremendous
whale: hit, orc **4** beat, cete, drub, lash, orca, wale, whip, whop **5** giant, poggy, sperm, whack **6** baleen, beluga, blower, killer, strike, thrash **7** Cetacea, grampus, marwheel, rorqual, ripsack **8** cachalot, hardhead **9** blackfish, mysticete, mysticeti, zeuglodon **10** bottlehead, zeuglodont **13** sulphur-bottom
blue: **9** sibbaldus
carcass: **5** kreng
constellation: **5** Cetus
fat: **7** blubber
female: cow
food: **4** brit
iron: **7** harpoon
order: **4** cete **7** Cetacea
pert. to: **5** cetic
school: gam, pod
secretion: **9** ambergris
skin: **6** muktuk
strip blubber from: **6** flense
tail part: **5** fluke
young: **4** calf **5** stunt **9** shorthead
whale oil: 10 spermaceti
cask: **4** rier
whaleback: 9 steamship **10** turtleback **12** grain-carrier
whalebird: 4 gull **6** petrel **9** phalarope, turnstone
whalebone: 5 stiff **6** baleen, severe **10** inflexible
whalehead: 8 shoebill

whaler: 4 ship **7** bushman, swagman, whopper **8** whaleman **9** sundowner, whaleboat
visit: gam
whaling: 4 huge **8** whopping
cask: **4** rier **6** cardel
profit: lay
spear: **7** harpoon
whaling ship: 6 Pequod, whaler
wham: 4 bang **5** crack, smash
whammy: hex **4** jinks **6** hoodoo, voodoo **10** Indian sign
whang: 4 bang, blow, chop **5** chunk, slice, thong, throw, whack **6** assail, strike **7** leather, rawhide
whangee, wanghee: 4 cane **5** stick **6** bamboo
wharf: 4 dock, pier, quai(F.), quay **5** jetty, levee **7** landing
space: **7** quayage
worker: **9** stevedore
whatnot: 7 etagere **10** knickknack
wheal: 4 mark, mine, wale, weal **5** whelk **6** strake, streak, stripe **7** pustule **9** suppurate
wheat: 5 durum, spelt, trigo **6** imphee **7** einkorn, semoule
beard: awn
chaff: **4** bran
disease: **4** bunt, rust, smut **5** ergot **6** aecium, fungus
gritty part: **8** semolina
head: ear
outer coal: **4** bran
processed: **4** suji **5** grits **6** bulgur **9** middlings
repository: bin **8** elevator
state: **4** Ohio **5** Idaho **6** Dakota, Kansas **7** Indiana, Montana **8** Illinois, Missouri, Nebraska, Oklahoma **9** Minnesota **10** Washington **12** Pennsylvania
stubble: **6** arrish
wheat duck: 7 widgeon **8** baldpate
wheat louse: 5 aphid
wheat smut: 4 bunt **8** colbrand
wheatbird: 4 lark **9** chaffinch
wheater: 4 bird **5** chack **8** chickell **10** gorsehatch
wheedle: cog **4** cant, coax **5** carny, tease, whine **6** banter, butter, cajole, carney, fleech, whilly **7** blarney, cuittle, flatter **8** persuade, soft-soap **9** influence, sweet-talk
wheel (see also **gear**)**:** cam, cog **4** bike, disk, helm, reel, roll, turn **5** cycle, drive, pivot, rotor, rowel, skeif, skive **6** caster, circle, league, roller, rotate, sheave **7** bicycle, chukkar, chukker, pedrail, revolve **10** revolution, waterwheel
furniture: **6** caster
part: cam, cog, hub, rim **4** tire **5** felly, spoke, sprag **6** felloe **8** sprocket

pert. to: **5** rotal
potters: see **potter's wheel**
rim: **5** felly **6** felloe
shaft: **4** axle
spinning: see **spinning wheel**
spoke: **6** radius
spurred: **5** rowel
stopper: **5** brake
toothed: cog **4** gear
water-raising: see **waterwheel**
wheel-shaped: 6 rotate **8** circular, rotiform
wheelbarrow: hod **10** hurlbarrow
wheeler (see also **wheelman**): **7** cyclist, vulture **11** wheelwright
wheeler-dealer: 7 shrewdy **8** go-getter, operator, promoter
wheelman: 5 pilot **7** cyclist, steerer, wheeler **8** helmsman, pedalist **9** bicyclist
wheeze: gag **4** hint, hiss, joke **5** adage, dodge, hoose, hooze, prank, trick **6** cliche, coghle(Sc.), device, saying **9** witticism
relative of: **4** rale
wheezy: 9 asthmatic
whelk: 4 acne **5** snail **6** papule, pimple, winkle **7** pustule
whelm (see also **overwhelm**): **5** cover, crush **6** deluge **9** drainpipe
whelp: cub, dog, pup **4** bear, fawn, lion, wale, welt, wolf **5** child, puppy, tiger, youth **7** leopard **11** give birth to
when: 5 until **6** though **7** whereas **8** although, whenever
where: 5 place **7** whither
whereas: 5 since **7** because
wherefore: 5 cause **6** reason **9** therefore **11** accordingly
whereness: 6 ubiety
wherewithal: 5 funds, means, money **9** resources
wherry: 4 boat **5** barge, carry, scull **7** lighter, rowboat, vehicle **9** transport
whet: 4 hone, stir **5** grind, rouse, strop **6** excite **7** quicken, sharpen **9** appetizer, stimulate
whetstone: bur **4** buhr, burr, hone **8** strickle **9** sharpener
whey: 4 pale **5** serum **6** watery
which: who **4** that, whom
which was to be shown: QED
whicker: 5 neigh **6** whinny
whiff: fan **4** flag, fuff, guff, gust, hint, odor, puff, waft, wave **5** expel, fluff, jiffy, smell **6** breath, exhale, inhale, stench **7** instant **10** inhalation
whiffle: 4 blow, emit, idle, turn, veer, wave **5** expel, shake, shift **6** change, trifle **7** flicker, flutter, scatter **8** disperse, hesitate **9** vacillate
while: yet **5** until **6** albeit, effort **7** where-

as **8** although, occasion
whilom: 4 erst, once, past **6** former **8** erewhile
whim: fad, fit, gig **4** idea, mood **5** fancy, humor, winch **6** megrim, notion, trifle, vagary, vision, whimsy **7** boutade, caprice, capstan, fantasy, whimsey **8** crotchet
whimper: cry, sob **4** mewl, moan, pule, weep **5** whine **6** murmur, yammer **7** grizzle, sniffle
whimsical: odd **5** droll, queer **6** cockle **7** bizarre, comical **8** fanciful, freakish, notional **9** arbitrary, conceited, eccentric, fantastic, grotesque, uncertain **10** capricious **11** fantastical
whimsy: See **whim**
whin: 4 rock **5** furze, gorse
whinchat: 8 songbird **9** gorsechat, grasschat
whine: wow **4** cant, girn, moan, pule **5** croon, whewl **6** snivel, yammer **7** whimper **8** complain
whinny: 4 bray **5** hinny, neigh
whinyard: 5 sword
whip: cat, gad, tan **4** beat, cane, crop, flay, flog, hide, jerk, lace, lash, urge, wind, wrap **5** birch, flick, knout, outdo, quirt, spank, strap, swish **6** defeat, punish, stitch, strike, swinge, switch, thrash **7** belabor, chicote, conquer, overlay, rawhide, scourge, sjambok **8** chawbuck, coachman, huntsman **9** bullwhack, flagellum **10** discipline, flagellate **13** cat-o-nine-tails
mark: **4** wale, weal, welt
part: **4** crop **5** snead **6** handle, socket
whippersnapper: 6 squirt **9** nonentity
whir: bur, fly **4** birl, burr, move, whiz, zizz **5** hurry, skirr, swirl, whizz **6** bustle, hurtle **7** revolve, vibrate **9** commotion
whirl: 4 eddy, reel, spin, stir, tirl, turn **5** drill, fling, hurry, swirl, twirl **6** bustle, circle, gyrate, rotate, swinge, tumult, uproar, vortex **7** revolve **9** commotion, pirouette **10** hurly-burly, revolution
whirlbone: 7 kneepan, patella **10** hucklebone
whirlpool: 4 eddy **5** gorce, swirl **6** gurges, vortex **9** Charybdis, maelstrom
whirlwind: 4 dust, fuss, stir **7** cyclone, tornado **9** hurricane, maelstrom
whirr: See **whir**
whisk: 4 tuft, whip, wisp **5** flisk, hurry
whiskers (see also **beard**): **6** growth **7** stubble **9** sideburns, vibrissae **11** muttonchops
fish: **7** barbels
whiskey, whisky: rye **4** corn **6** poteen, redeye, rotgut, Scotch **8** blockade, busthead **9** moonshine **10** usquebaugh
maker: **9** distiller

punch: 5 facer

whisper: 4 buzz, hint 5 rumor 6 breeze, murmur 7 confide

whisperer: 7 tattler 9 backbiter, slanderer 10 talebearer

whist: 4 game, hush, mute 5 cards, quiet, still 6 silent 7 silence 8 silently

declaration: 6 misere

dummy: 4 mort

hand: 6 tenace 10 Yarborough

whistle: 4 hiss, pipe, sugh, toot 5 flute, siren, sough 6 signal

whistle duck: 9 goldeneye

whistlewing: 9 goldeneye

whit: bit, jot 4 atom, doit, haet, hate, iota 5 speck 8 particle

white: wan 4 ashy, bawn, hoar, pale, pure 5 ashen, happy, hoary, ivory 6 albino, argent, blanch, chalky, grayed, honest, pallid, pearly 7 ivorine, silvery 8 harmless, innocent, palliate, spotless 9 colorless, fortunate, honorable 10 auspicious

becoming: 9 canescent

egg's: 5 glair 7 albumen

with age: 4 hoar 5 hoary

white ant: 4 anai, anay 7 termite

white cell: 9 leucocyte

white cliffs' site: 5 Dover

white-collar: 5 clerk 6 typist 8 salesman 9 secretary 10 bookkeeper

white crow: 7 vulture

white elephant (land of): 4 Siam 5 Burma, India 6 Ceylon 8 Thailand

white feather: 4 fear 9 cowardice

white flag: 5 truce 9 surrender

white gentian: 9 feverroot

white-haired: 8 favorite

white heat: 13 incandescence

White House: *designer:* 5 Hoban

first resident: 5 Adams

white Indian hemp: 8 milkweed

white iron pyrites: 9 marcasite

white jade: 9 alabaster

white lead: 6 ceruse

white lead ore: 9 cerussite

white-lightning: 9 moonshine

white livered: 8 cowardly 13 pusillanimous

white merganser: 4 smew

white mica: 9 muscovite

White Monk: 10 Cistercian

White Mountain: 5 Adams

white mule: gin 6 liquor, whisky 7 whiskey 9 moonshine

white mundic: 12 arsenopyrite

white nun: 4 smew

white plague: 8 phthisis 11 consumption 12 tuberculosis

white plantain: 9 pussytoes

white pyrite: 9 marcasite

white sanicle: 9 snakeroot

white snipe: 6 avocet 10 sanderling

white walnut: 8 shagbark, sycamore 9 butternut

white whale: 6 beluga

white widgeon: 4 smew

whitebelly: 6 grouse, pigeon

whitecap: 4 wave 5 crest

whitefish: 5 cisco 6 beluga 8 menhaden

whiten: 4 pale 5 chalk 6 blanch, bleach 8 etiolate, palliate

whitetail: 4 deer

whitewash: 6 blanch, defeat, parget 7 absolve, conceal, palliate

whiteweed: 5 daisy

whitewing: 4 sail 6 scoter 7 sweeper 9 chaffinch

whither: 5 where 8 wherever

whiting: 4 fish, hake 5 chalk

whitlow: 4 sore 5 felon 6 fetlow 12 inflammation

Whitsunday: 9 Pentecost

whitterick: 6 curlew

whittle: cut 4 pare, whet 5 carve, knife, shape, shave 6 reduce, remove

whiz: hum 4 buzz, hiss, pirr, whir 5 hurry 6 corker, expert, rotate 7 bargain

who: quo(L.), Wer(G.), wha(Sc.) 4 what 5 which 13 interrogative

whoa: 4 halt, stop

whole: all, sum 4 full, hail, hale, sole, unit 5 gross, total 6 entire, healed, intact, wholly 7 perfect 8 absolute, complete, ensemble, entirely, entirety, integral, thorough, totality, unbroken 9 aggregate, unanimous, undamaged, undivided 10 unimpaired

whole note: 9 semibreve

whole number: 7 integer

wholehearted: 6 hearty 7 devoted, earnest, sincere 8 bona fide, complete 10 unreserved 11 unmitigated

wholesale: 4 bulk, lots 7 massive 8 abundant, sweeping 9 extensive

wholesome: 4 safe 5 sound 6 benign, hearty, robust 7 healthy 8 benedict, clean cut, curative, halesome, salutary, vigorous 9 favorable, healthful 10 beneficial, healthsome, propitious, salubrious

wholly: all 4 well 5 quite 7 algates 10 altogether 11 exclusively

whoop: 4 hoot, urge, yell 5 cheer, shout 6 halloo

whooping cough: 9 pertussis

whop: 4 beat, blow, bump, flop 5 knock, throw 6 strike, stroke

whopper: lie 5 story 6 bender, bumper 7 bouncer

whopping: 4 huge, much, very 5 great, large 7 banging

whore: 4 drab 5 wench 6 harlot 8 strumpet 9 courtesan 10 prostitute

whorl: 5 spire, swirl

why: 5 proof 6 enigma, reason 7 mystery 9 wherefore

whyo: 6 robber 7 footpad 8 gangster

wick: bay 4 bend, town 5 creek, inlet 6 corner, hamlet 7 borough 9 farmstead

wicked: bad, ill 4 evil, vile, wrong 6 fierce, guilty, horrid, risqué, sinful, unjust 7 beastly, harmful, heinous, hellish, painful, playful, profane, vicious 8 criminal, depraved, devilish, diabolic, felonous, fiendish, flagrant, indecent, skillful, spiteful 9 atrocious, dangerous, difficult, malicious, nefandous, nefarious, perverted 10 diabolical, flagitious, impassable, iniquitous, outrageous, villainous 11 mischievous, troublesome

wicker: 4 twig 5 osier, withe

wicket: 4 arch, door, gate, hoop 5 hatch 6 window 7 guichet, opening

wickiup: hut 7 shelter

wide: 5 ample, broad, loose, roomy 6 opened 7 liberal 8 expanded, spacious 9 capacious, distended, expansive, extensive 12 farspreading 13 comprehensive

wide-awake: hat 4 keen, tern 5 alert, aware 7 knowing 8 watchful 10 interested

widely: far 4 afar 6 abroad

widen: 4 ream 6 dilate, expand, extend, spread 7 amplify, broaden, enlarge 10 generalize

widespread: 4 rife 7 allover, diffuse, general 8 diffused, sweeping 9 extensive, pervasive, prevalent, universal 10 prevailing 13 comprehensive

widgeon: 4 duck 5 goose 8 baldpate 9 simpleton

  genus: 6 mareca

widow: 5 widdy 6 relict 7 dowager 8 bereaved

  in cards: 4 skat

  in printing: 9 short line

  right: 5 dower 10 quarantine

  suicide: 6 suttee

widow monkey: 4 titi

widowhood: 7 viduage

widowman: 7 widower

width: 5 girth, range 7 breadth 8 diameter, latitude, wideness

wield: ply 4 bear, cope, deal, rule 5 exert, power, swing 6 direct, employ, handle, manage, ordain 7 conduct, control 8 brandish 9 determine 10 manipulate

wife: ux(L.); hen 4 frau, frow, mate, uxor(L.) 5 donna, mujer, squaw 6 gammer, spouse 7 consort 8 helpmate, helpmeet 10 better half

  bequest to: dot 5 dowry

  clergyman's: 8 curatess

  killer: 9 uxoricide

  lord's: 4 lady

  pert. to: 7 uxorial

  rajah's: 4 rani 5 ranee

  slave's: 9 broadwife

wig: 4 gizz 5 busby, caxon, jasey, judge, scold 6 baguio, peruke, rebuke, toupee 7 censure, periwig, spencer 8 Chedreux 9 dignitary, Gregorian, reprimand

  repair: 6 careen

wiggle: 5 shake 6 waggle, wobble 7 stagger, wriggle

wight: man 4 loud 5 brave, human, swift, witch 6 active, nimble, strong 7 swiftly, valiant 8 creature, powerful, strongly

wigwag: 6 signal

wigwam: 4 home, tipi 5 tepee

wild: mad, ree 4 daft, wowf(Sc.) 5 feral, rough, waste, weird 6 desert, ferine, native, ramage, savage, stormy, unruly 7 bestial, furious, haggard, riotous, untamed, wilsome 8 aberrant, agrestal, desolate, dramatic, farouche, frenetic, reckless, untilled 9 agrestial, barbarian, barbarous, dissolute, disturbed, ferocious, hellicate, imprudent, primitive, turbulent, unbridled, visionary 10 chimerical, dissipated, irrational, licentious, tumultuous, wilderness 11 extravagant, harumscarum, uncivilized, uninhabited 12 obstreperous, uncontrolled, uncultivated 13 irresponsible 14 uncontrollable

wild alder: 8 goutweed

wild arum: 10 cuckoopint

wild ass: 5 kiang 6 onager

wild banana: 5 papaw 6 pawpaw

wild coffee: 9 buckthorn, feverroot

wild crocus: 12 pasqueflower

wild dog: 5 dhole, dingo

wild flower: See **flower**

wild goat: 4 ibex

wild goose: 7 greylag 8 Jacobite

wild hog: 4 boar

wild horse: 7 mustang

wild Irishman: 10 tumatakura

wild kale: 6 radish 8 charlock

wild masterwort: 8 goutweed

wild musk: 9 alfilaria

wild mustard: 8 charlock

wild passionflower: 6 maypop

wild pineapple: 7 pinguin

wild plum: 4 sloe

wild pumpkin: 11 calabazilla

wild sage: 5 clary

wild sago: 7 coontie

wild sheep: See **sheep**

wild succory: 7 chicory

wild sweet potato: 7 manroot

wild turnip: 6 radish 8 rutabaga 9 breadroot

wildcat: cat 4 balu, eyra, lynx 6 ocelot, serval 7 panther 9 promotion

wildbeest: gnu

wilderness: 5 waste 6 desert, forest 10

hinterland 12 back of beyond

wildfowl: 4 duck **6** goose, quail **8** pheasant **9** partridge

flock: **5** skein

wildness: 5 waste **6** ramage **8** ferocity **12** extravagance

wile: art **4** lure, ruse **5** fraud, guile, trick **6** allure, deceit, entice **7** attract, beguile, cunning **8** artifice, trickery **9** stratagem

will: 4 lust, wish **5** elect, fancy **6** animus, choose, decree, desire, devise, prefer, see fit **7** command, longing **8** appetite, pleasure, volition **9** intention, testament **11** disposition, inclination, self-control **13** determination

appendix: **7** codicil

having no: **9** intestate

maker of: **8** testator **9** testatrix

proof of: **7** probate

valid: **7** testacy

willful: mad **4** rash **5** heady **7** wayward **8** stubborn **9** camsteary, camsteery, impetuous, obstinate, voluntary **10** hard-headed **11** intentional

willies: 6 creeps **7** jitters

William Tell: *canton:* Uri

composer: **7** Rossini

hero: **4** Egil

William the Conqueror's burial place: 4 Caen

willing: apt **4** fair **5** prone, ready **6** minded **7** tending **8** desirous, disposed, unforced **9** agreeable, voluntary **10** volitional

willingly: 4 fain, lief **5** lieve **6** freely, gladly

willingness: 7 consent **8** alacrity

willow: iva **4** itea **5** osier, salix **6** teaser

willow wren: 10 chiffchaff

willowy: 5 lithe **6** pliant, supple **7** slender **8** flexible, graceful

willpower: 7 purpose **10** resolution **11** self-control **12** resoluteness **13** determination

loss of: **6** abulia **7** aboulia

willy-nilly: 8 perforce **11** whether or no

Wilson's thrush: 5 veery

wilt: sag **4** fade, flag **5** droop, quail **6** wither **8** collapse, anguish

wily: sly **4** foxy **5** canny, smart **6** artful, astute, crafty, shrewd, subtle **7** cunning, subtile **9** cautelous, sagacious

wimble: awl **4** bore **5** auger, brace, scoop, twist **6** active, gimlet, pierce **9** penetrate, sprightly, whimsical

Wimbledon event: 6 tennis

wimple: 4 bend, fold, turn, veil, wind **5** curve **6** ripple **7** meander, wriggle **9** headdress

win: get, pot **4** beat, earn, gain, take **5** charm **6** allure, attain, defeat, entice, obtain, secure **7** achieve, acquire, capture, conquer, prevail, succeed, triumph, victory **8** vanquish **9** captivate, influence **10** accomplish, conciliate

all tricks: **4** slam

back: **7** recover **8** retrieve

over: **6** defeat, disarm, induce **8** persuade, talk into **10** conciliate

wince: 4 crab, reel **5** start **6** cringe, flinch, recoil, shrink **8** windlass

wind: air **4** birr, bise, blow, bora, coil, flaw, gale, gust, hint, kona, reel, wend, wrap **5** belay(naut.), blast, buran, crank, curve, foehn, noser, reeve, samum, siroc, storm, trade, twine, twist, wield **6** boreas, bought, breath, breeze, buster, deform, gibleh, simoom, simoon, solano, squall, writhe, zephyr **7** chamsin, chinook, cyclone, entwine, entwist, etesian, gregale, khamsin, meander, monsoon, nothing, pampero, revolve, sirocco, tempest, tornado, typhoon, wreathe, wriggle, wulliwa **8** blizzard, entangle, khamseen, libeccio, williwaw, willywaw **9** harmattan, hurricane, libecchio, noreaster **10** euroclydon, tramontana, tramontane

desert: **6** simoon **7** sirocco

down: **5** relax **10** deescalate

god of: **4** Adad, Adda, Vayu **5** Eolus **6** Aeolus, Eecatl

periodic: **7** etesian, monsoon

personification: **6** Caurus **7** Caecias **8** Favonius

pert. to: **6** eolian **7** aeolian

scale: **8** Beaufort

summer: **6** breeze, zephyr

wind gauge: 4 vane **10** anemometer **11** weathercock

wind instrument: sax **4** fife, horn, oboe, tuba **5** flute, organ **6** cornet **7** hautboy, trumpet **8** clarinet, trombone

wind up: end **4** coil **5** close **6** finish, settle **8** conclude

windbreaker: 6 jacket

windfall: 4 boon, vail **5** manna **7** bonanza, fortune **8** buckshee

windflower: 7 anemone

windhover: 7 kestrel

windiness: 7 conceit **9** puffiness, verbosity **11** verboseness **12** boastfulness

winding: 4 wily **6** screwy, spiral, tricky **7** coiling, crinkle, devious, pliable, sinuous, twining, wriggly **8** flexible, rambling, tortuous, twisting **9** deceitful, intricate, meandrous, sinuosity **10** anfracyure, circuitous, convoluted, meandering, serpentine **11** amortisseur, anfractuous

winding device: 4 reel **7** capstan **8** windlass

winding sheet: 6 shroud

windjammer: 4 ship **6** bugler, sailor,

talker **8** musician **9** trumpeter
windlass: 4 crab, reel **5** hoist, winch **7** capstan
windle: 7 measure, redwing
windmill: *blade:* **4** vane
fighter of: **7** Quixote
pump: gin
sail: awe, ban
window: bay **5** gable, glaze, oriel **6** dormer **7** balcone, fenetre, lucarne, mirador, opening, winnock(Sc.) **8** aperture, casement, fenestra, jalousie
arrangement: **12** fenestration
bay: **5** oriel
frame: **4** sash
leading: **4** came
ledge: **4** sill
part: **4** came, sill
pert. to: **9** fenestral
recess: **6** exedra
roof: **6** dormer **8** skylight
sash weight: **5** mouse
ship's: **4** port **8** porthole
ticket: **6** wicket **7** guichet
worker: **7** glazier
windpipe: 6 artery, gullet, throat, weason **7** trachea, weasand, weazand **9** esophagus
pert. to: **8** trachean
windrow: 4 pile **5** swath **6** furrow, swathe
windshake: 8 anemosis
windstorm (see also **storm, wind**): **4** gale **7** cyclone, typhoon **9** hurricane
windward: 5 aloof **8** aweather
Windward Island: 7 Grenada **9** Martinique
windy: 4 airy **5** blowy, empty, gusty, huffy, swift, wordy **6** breezy, stormy **7** gustful, pompous, verbose **8** boastful, skittish **9** aeolistic, bombastic, inflated **10** boisterous, changeable, intangible **11** harebrained, tempestuous **13** unsubstantial
Windy City: 7 Chicago
wine: vin(F.) **4** alac, Asti, Bual, cote, deal, port, tent **5** Baden, Casel, drink, liane, Medoc, merum(L.), Rhine, tinta, tokay, Yquem **6** Barolo, Barsac, Beaune, canary, claret, Malaga, Massic, Muscat, Saumur, sherry **7** Alicant, Banyals, Bastard, Chablis, chacoli, Chateau, Chianti, Conthey, Dezaley, Falerno, hollock, Madeira, Margaux, Marsala, Medeira, Moselle, Orvieto **8** Alicante, Ambonnay, beverage, Bordeaux, Bucellas, Burgundy, Florence, Marsalla, muscadel, Muscatel, Riesling, Ruchelle, Rulander, sauterne **9** Gladstone, hermitage, teneriffe, Zeltinger, zinfandel **10** Beaujolais, Calon-Segur, Hockheimer, Roussillon **11** Niersteiner,

scuppernong **12** Geisenheimer **15** scharlachberger
apple: **5** cider
bag: **8** wineskin
bibber: sot **5** toper **7** tippler **8** drunkard
bottle: **6** fiasco, magnum **8** decanter, jeroboam
cask: tun, vat **4** pipe
cask deposit: **6** tartar
cellar: **6** bodega
comb. form: oen **4** oeno
cruet: **7** burette
cup: ama **5** amula **6** goblet **7** chalice
deposit: **6** tartar
discoverer: **4** Noah
disorder: **5** casse
drink: kir **5** clary, mulse, negus, punch
dry: sec **4** brut
film: **8** beeswing
fragrance: **7** bouquet
god: **4** Soma **7** Bacchus **8** Dionysus
list: **4** card
lover: **11** oenophilist
maker: **6** abkari, abkary **7** vintner
measure: aam, aum **4** orna, orne
medicinal preparation: **5** mosto
merchant: **6** bistro(F.) **7** vintner **8** gourmand
new: **4** must
pert. to: **5** vinic **6** vinous
pitcher: **4** olpe **5** olpae **8** oenochoe
punch: **7** sangria
residue: **4** marc
rice: **4** sake
scene of miracle: **4** Cana
shop: **6** bistro, bodega
spiced: **9** hippocras
steward: **9** sommelier
stock: **6** cellar
study of: **7** enology **8** oenology
strength: **4** seve
sweet: **4** port **5** lunel, tokay **7** malmsey, Moselle **8** Alicante, muscatel
unfermented: **4** must
vessel: ama **5** amula **7** chalice
year: **7** vintage
wine and dine: 4 fete **6** regale
wineberry: 5 grape **7** currant **8** billberry, makomako **9** raspberry **10** gooseberry
winegrower: 8 vigneron **13** viticulturist
Winesburg Ohio author: 8 Anderson
wineshop: bar **6** bistro, bodega
wineskin: 5 askos
wing: ala, arm, ell, fin, fly, van **4** limb **5** aisle, alula, annex, pinna, shard, speed, volet, wound **6** hasten, pennon, pinion **7** flutter
arrangement: **7** alation
building: ell
pert. to: **4** alar **6** pteric
under: **8** subalary
vestigial: **5** alula

wing cover: 7 elytron
wing-footed: 5 fleet, swift **6** aliped **9** mercurial
wing-like: 4 alar **5** alary, alate **6** pteric **7** aliform, pteroid
part: ala **4** alae **7** aileron
winged: 4 aile, alar **5** alary, alate, lofty, rapid, swift **6** alated **7** bialate, sublime, wounded **9** aliferous, aligerous, feathered
in heraldry: **4** aile
Winged Horse: 7 Pegasus
wingless: 7 apteral **8** apterous
wingless locust: 4 weta
wings: *being with:* **5** angel **6** cherub, seraph **7** Mercury
conjoined: vol(her.)
wink: bat, nap, nod **4** hint **5** blink, flash, gleam, prink, sleep **6** signal **7** connive, flicker, instant, nictate, slumber, sparkle, twinkle **9** nictation, nictitate, twinkling **10** periwinkle
winking: 13 blepharospasm
winks (forty): nap **6** catnap
winner: 6 earner, reaper, victor **7** faceman, sleeper **8** bangster **9** conqueror
Winnie-the-Pooh: *author:* **5** Milne
character: Owl, Roo **5** Kanga **6** Piglet, Rabbit, Tigger
winning (see also **win, winsome**): **5** shaft, sweet **6** profit **7** victory
winning three numbers: 4 tern
winnow: fan, van **4** beat, blow, flap, sift, sort **5** dight **6** assort, select **7** analyze, examine, scatter **8** brandish, disperse, separate **9** eliminate, screen out
winsome: gay **5** bonny, merry, sweet **6** blithe, bonnie **7** likable, lovable, winning **8** adorable, charming, cheerful, engaging, pleasant **9** agreeable **10** attractive **11** captivating **12** lighthearted
winter: 9 hibernate
French: **5** hiver
pear: **6** seckel, warden
pert. to: **6** brumal, hiemal
Spanish: **8** invierno
winter quarters: 10 hibernacle **12** hibernaculum
winter teal: 9 greenwing
winterbloom: 6 azalea
wintergreen: 10 pipsissewa
Winter's Tale character: 4 Dion **5** Mopsa **6** Dorcas **7** Camillo, Leontes, Perdita
wintle: 4 reel, roll **7** stagger, wriggle
wintry: icy **4** aged, cold **5** hoary, snowy, white **6** frigid, hiemal, stormy **8** chilling, hibernal, wintered **9** cheerless
wipe: dry, hit, mop, rub **4** beat, blow, draw, gibe, jeer, pass **5** brand, cheat, clean, dight, erase, stain, swipe, towel, trick **6** defeat, remove, sponge, strike,

stroke **7** abolish, defraud, exhaust, sarcasm **8** disgrace **10** annihilate, obliterate **11** exterminate **12** handkerchief
off: **4** dust **5** scuff
out: **5** erase, scrub **6** cancel **7** destroy
up: **4** swab, swob
wire: 4 coil **5** cable **6** fasten **8** telegram **9** cablegram, telegraph
bundle of: **5** cable
cutters: **6** pliers
for teeth: **6** braces
measure: mil **5** stone
system: **7** network, reticle
wire cutter: 6 pliers **8** secateur
wiredraw: 4 thin **5** wrest **7** distort, prolong, spin out **8** protract **9** attenuate **10** overrefine
wireless: 5 radio
wirework: 7 netting **8** filigree
wireworm: 8 myriapod **9** millepede
wiry: 4 lean **5** hardy, stiff, tough **6** sinewy, strong **8** muscular
wis: 4 deem, know **5** think **7** believe, imagine, suppose
Wisconsin: *capital:* **7** Madison
city: **6** Racine **7** Kenosha **8** Green Bay **9** Milwaukee
county: **4** Dane, Polk, Rusk, Sauk **5** Brown, Dodge, Pepin, Vilas **6** Barron **7** Ozaukee **8** Bayfield, Walworth, Waushara
explorer: **7** Nicolet
falls: **10** Big Manitou
lake: **7** Mendota **9** Winnebago
motto: **7** Forward
native: **6** Badger
nickname: **6** Badger
river: **4** Wolf **5** Black **7** St. Croix **8** Chippewa **9** Wisconsin **11** Mississippi
state bird: **5** robin
state flower: **6** violet
state tree: **5** maple
wisdom (see also **wise**): **4** lore **5** sense **8** judgment, sagacity **9** knowledge
god of: **4** Nabu, Nebo **6** Ganesa **7** Ganesha
goddess of: **6** Athena, Pallas **7** Minerva
man of: **6** Nestor
wisdom tooth: 5 molar
wise: hep **4** mode, sage, sane, show, wary **5** aware, canny, smart, sound, witty **6** advise, crafty, direct, inform, manner, method, shrewd, subtle, versed, witful **7** beguile, cunning, erudite, explain, fashion, gnostic, heedful, knowing, learned, politic, prudent, sapient, skilled **8** discreet, informed, instruct, persuade, profound, sensible, skillful **9** cognizant, dexterous, expedient, judicious, on the beam, provident, sagacious **10** discerning, omniscient **11** calculating, circumspect, enlightened, intelligent, well-advised **13** sophisticated

infinitely: **10** omniscient
up: **5** learn **6** advise, inform
wise man: 4 sage **5** magus, solon **6** Casper, Gasper, Nestor, savant, wizard **7** scholar **8** magician, Melchior **9** Balthasar, Balthazar, councilor
Wise Men: 4 Magi
wise saying: saw **5** adage, maxim
wiseacre: 5 dunce **7** prophet **9** simpleton **10** mastermind, smart aleck **11** wisenheimer
wisecrack: gag **4** joke, quip **9** witticism
wiselike: 6 decent **7** fitting **8** becoming, sensible **9** judicious **11** appropriate
wish: 4 hope, long, want **5** crave, fancy, yearn **6** behest, desire, expect, impose, invoke **7** longing, propose, request **8** petition, yearning **10** aspiration, invocation **11** imprecation
grammatical mood expressing: **8** optative
wishbone: 8 furculum **10** fourchette
wishful: 7 longing **8** desirous **9** desirable **10** attractive
wishy-washy: 4 pale, sick, thin, weak **5** tepid **6** feeble, trashy, watery **7** insipid **13** unsubstantial
wisp: 4 band, lock, ring, wase **5** broom, brush, bunch, clean, flock, shred, torch, whisk **6** bundle, parcel, rumple, strand, wreath **7** crumple, handful **8** fragment
wispy: 5 filmy, frail **6** slight **7** slender **8** gossamer, nebulous
wisteria: 4 bush, fuji **6** purple, violet
wistful: 6 intent **7** longing, pensive **8** yearning **9** attentive, nostalgic
wistfulness: rue **6** regret
wit: wag **4** know, mind **5** humor, irony, learn **6** acumen, esprit(F.), namely, reason, satire, widsom **7** cunning, faculty, punster **8** comedian, drollery, funnyman, prudence, repartee **9** intellect **12** intelligence, perspicacity **13** understanding
low form of: pun
witch: hag, hex **4** baba **5** biddy, bruja, charm, crone, lamia, woman **6** cummer, kimmer, wizard **8** magician, sorcerer **9** fascinate, sorceress
cat: **9** grimalkin
city: **5** Endor, Salem
doctor: **6** goofer
famous: **5** Circe **6** Lilith
gathering: **5** coven
male: **7** warlock
means of transportation: **5** broom
witch hazel: 4 tree **5** shrub **6** lotion **8** hornbeam **10** astringent
witchcraft: 5 charm, magic **7** cunning, hexerei, sorcery **8** brujeria(Sp.), pishogue, witchery, wizardry **9** sortilege **11** enchantment, fascination **12** invultuation

goddess of: **5** Obeah **6** Hecate
practice: hex **7** bewitch
witchman: 6 shaman, wizard **8** sorcerer
with: wi(Sc.); con(It.), cum(L.), mit(G.) **4** avec(F.), near **5** along **7** against **9** alongside **12** accompanying
with respect to: 4 as to **5** as for **7** apropos
withdraw: 4 void **5** avoid **6** absent, abjure, depart, detach, divert, recall, recant, recede, remove, retire, secede, shrink **7** abscond, decline, detract, extract, forbear, forsake, give way, refrain, retract, retreat, subduce, subside **8** abstract, alienate, derogate, distract, evacuate, fall back, renounce, restrain, withhold **9** disengage, sequester **10** relinquish, retrograde
from reality: **6** autism
withdrawn: shy **5** aloof **6** remote **8** detached **10** unsociable **11** indifferent
withe: 4 band, bind, herb, rope, twig **5** osier, snare, withy **6** branch, fasten, halter, wattle, willow
wither: age, die, dry **4** fade, pine, sear, sere, wilt **5** blast, cling, daver, decay, wizen **6** blight, cotter, shrink, weaken **7** shrivel, wrinkle **8** languish
withered: 4 arid, sere **7** sapless **10** marcescent **11** sphacelated
withershins: 10 topsy-turvy **12** contrariwise
withhold: 4 curb, deny, hide, keep **5** check **6** desist, detain, refuse, retain **7** abstain, forbear, prevent, refrain, repress, reserve **8** maintain, postpone, restrain
within: in, on; ben **4** inly, into **5** among **6** during, herein, inside **7** indoors **8** interior, inwardly **10** underneath
without: 4 bout, sans, sine(L.) **6** beyond **7** lacking, outside **9** outwardly **10** externally, out-of-doors
without this: 7 sine hoc
withstand: 4 bear, bide, defy **5** abide **6** combat, endure, oppose, resist **7** gainsay **8** confront, tolerate **9** gainstand **10** contradict, controvert
withy: 4 turn, twig, wind, wiry **5** agile, braid, tough **6** branch, willow **8** flexible
witless: mad **5** crazy, gross **6** insane, simple, stupid **7** foolish, unaware **8** heedless **9** brainless, pointless, unknowing **10** dullwitted, indiscreet
witness: eye, see, wit **4** know **5** teste **6** attest, beheld, behold, martyr **7** certify, endorse, observe, sponsor, testify **8** beholder, evidence, indicate, observer, onlooker **9** spectator, subscribe, testifier, testimony **11** attestation **13** understanding
witticism: mot, pun **4** gibe, jeer, jest, joke,

quip **5** sally **11** gauloiserie

witting: 5 aware **7** tidings **8** judgment **9** knowledge, voluntary **10** deliberate **11** information, intentional **12** intelligence

witty: 4 gash, wise **5** comic **6** bright, clever, facete, jocose, jocund, versed **7** amusing, comical, jocular, knowing **8** humorous, informed **9** facetious **11** intelligent

witty reply: 7 riposte **8** repartee

wivern: 6 dragon

wizard: 4 mage, sage **5** fiend **6** expert, genius, Merlin **7** magical, prodigy, warlock **8** charming, conjurer, magician, sorcerer **10** enchanting **11** necromancer, thaumaturge

wizardry: art **5** magic **7** sorcery **10** witchcraft

wizen, weazen: dry **6** whither **7** shrivel

woad: 6 indigo **8** dyestuff

wobble, wabble: 4 boil **5** lurch, shake, waver **6** quaver, teeter **7** tremble **9** vacillate

wobbly: 5 loose, shaky **7** rickety

woe: 4 bale, bane **5** grief **6** misery, sorrow **7** trouble **8** calamity, disaster **9** dejection **10** affliction, desolation, melancholy, misfortune

tale of: **8** jeremiad **11** lamentation

woebegone: 4 worn **6** gloomy, shabby **8** downcast **10** lugubrious, melancholy

woeful: sad **4** dire **6** paltry **7** direful, pitiful, unhappy **8** mournful, wretched **9** miserable, sorrowful, woebegone **10** deplorable, dispirited **12** disconsolate

wolaba: 8 kangaroo

wold: lea **5** plain **6** meadow

wolf: 4 lobo **6** canine, chanco, coyote **7** Don Juan **8** Casanova **9** thylacine **10** ladykiller **11** philanderer, skirt chaser

cry: **4** howl

gait: **4** lope

genus: **5** canis

pert. to: **6** lupine

timber: **4** lobo

young: pup **5** whelp

wolf-like: 6 lupine **9** rapacious

wolfhound: 4 alan **6** borzoi

wolfsbane: 7 aconite **9** monkshood

Wolsey's birthplace: 7 Ipswich

wolverine: 7 glutton **8** carcajou

genus of: **4** gulo

Wolverine State: 8 Michigan

woman (see also **girl, mother**): gin, hen **4** bint, dame, dona, lady, maid, rani, wife **5** begum, broad, chick, donna, femme, madam, mujer, ranee, skirt, squaw **6** calico, cummer, domina, female, heifer, kimmer, maness, senora **7** alewife, servant, signora **8** mistress, senorita **10** klootchman, sweetheart **11** gentlewoman

advisor: **6** egeria

attractive: **4** doll, peri **5** belle, filly, pin-up, siren, sylph, Venus **6** beauty, looker **7** charmer, Zenobia **8** Musidora

beloved: **9** inamorata

brave: **7** hellcat, heroine

celibate: **7** agapeta

domain: **7** distaff

dowdy: **5** frump

kept: **8** mistress **9** concubine **12** demimondaine

lawyer: **6** Portia

learned: **4** blue **7** basbleu(F.), seeress **12** bluestocking

little: Mrs. **4** wife **7** ladykin

loose: tib **4** drab, flap, jilt, slut **5** hussy, quean, queen **6** chippy, giglet, giglot, harlot, wanton **7** cocotte, Jezebel, trollop **9** courtesan, courtezen, dratchell

married: **4** frau, frow, wife **5** vrouw **6** matron

mythical: **6** Gorgon, Medusa

objectionable: hag **5** fagot, shrew, witch **6** faggot, gorgon, virago **8** harridan **9** grimalkin, termagant

old: gib, hag **4** baba, dame, trot **5** crone, frump **6** carlin, gammer, granny **7** carline, dowager, grandam **8** grandame, spinster **9** cailleach, cailliach

organization: DAR, WAC, WSP **4** AMVS, WAAC, WAVE, Wren **5** Ebell **6** circle **7** sorosis **8** sorority **10** sisterhood

pert. to: **7** gynecic **8** gynaecic **9** muliebral

patient: **8** Griselda

physicist: **5** Curie **7** Meitner

pregnant: **7** gravida

ruler: **5** queen **9** matriarch

sailor: **4** Spar, Wave

serving: see **servant**

single (see also **maiden**): **6** virgin **8** mistress, spinster

soldier: Wac **4** Waac

staid: **4** lady **6** beldam, matron **7** beldame

state of: **10** muliebrity

strong: **6** Amazon, virago **8** titaness

suffragist: **4** Mott **5** Stone **7** Anthony, Stanton

talkative: cat, gad, hen **5** dolly, flirt, scold, shrew, vixen **6** fizgig, virago **7** hellcat **9** termagant

theater: **6** dancer **7** actress, chorine, ingenue **9** soubrette

unattractive: bag, dog **4** drab **5** crone, dowdy, witch **8** slattern

young (see also **girl**): tib **4** burd, dell, drab, lass **5** filly, trull, wench **6** lassie **7** damozel **10** demoiselle

woman chaser: 4 wolf **8** lothario **10** sheepbiter **11** philanderer

woman hater: 10 misogynist

womanish: 5 anile **6** effete, female **8** feminine **10** effeminate

womb: bag **5** belly **6** uterus

wombat: 6 badger **9** marsupial

won (see also **win**): **4** live **5** abide, dwell **7** inhabit

wonder: awe **4** evil, fear, harm, sign **5** grief, shock, wrong **6** esteem, marvel **7** curious, miracle, prodigy **8** surprise **9** amazement, reverence, speculate, uncertain **10** admiration, wonderment **11** destruction, uncertainty **12** astonishment

of the world: **6** Pharos **8** pyramids, Colossus

performance: see **magic**

worker of: see **wizard**

Wonder State: 8 Arkansas

wonderful: 4 fine, good **5** super **6** lovely **7** amazing, amusing, corking, mirific, strange **8** wondrous **9** admirable, excellent, marvelous **10** miraculous, surprising **11** astonishing, interesting **13** extraordinary

wonky: off **4** awry **5** shaky **6** feeble **7** tottery **8** unsteady **9** tottering

wont: use **5** dwell, habit, usage, usual **6** custom, reside **8** inclined, practice **10** accustomed

woo: beg, sue **4** coax, seek **5** court, spark **6** assail, invite, splunt(Sc.) **7** address, beseech, entreat, solicit **9** importune **10** bill and coo

wood: hag, keg, mad **4** bois(F.), bosk, bowl, cask, holt, wold **5** angry, cahuy, grove, hurst, trees, xylem **6** forest, insane, lumber, timber **7** enraged, furious, violent **8** woodland

ash: **6** potash

black: **5** ebony

bundle of: **5** fagot

burned: ash **4** brae **8** charcoal

core: ame

dealer: **10** xylopolist

decayed: **4** punk

derivative: tar **5** turps **6** balsam **10** turpentine

distillation from: tar **5** turps **10** turpentine

eater: **7** termite

edge: **8** woodrime, woodside

fine-grained: yew **6** brauna

firing easily: **4** punk **5** sponk, spunk **6** tinder **8** kindling, punkwood **9** touchwood

flexible: **5** edder, osier **6** willow

fragrant: **5** aloes, cedar

god: see **woodland:** *deity*

growth: **7** coppice

gum: **5** resin, xylan

hard: ash, elm, eng, oak **4** lana, poon, rata, teak **5** ebony, maple, zante **6** walnut **7** hickory **8** mahogany

juice: sap

kind: see **tree**

knot: nur **4** burl, knag, knar **5** gnarl

light: **4** cork **5** balsa

overlaying: **6** veneer

part: fid, nog, peg, rib **4** lath, shim, slat **5** dowel, spile, sprag, stave, tenon **6** batten, billet, reglet, splint **7** dingbat

pert. to: **5** treen **6** xyloid

steward: **9** woodreeve

strip: **4** lath, slat **6** batten, spline

striped: roe

supporting: **5** cleat

valuable: sal **4** teak

worker: **6** joiner, sawyer **7** paneler **9** carpenter

wood alcohol: 6 methyl **8** methanol

wood-ash salt: 6 potash

wood nymph: 4 moth **5** dryad **8** grayling **11** hummingbird

wood pigeon: 4 dove **6** cushat **8** ringdove

wood pussy: 5 skunk

wood sorrel: oca **6** oxalis **7** begonia **8** haremeat

wood stork: 4 ibis

woodbine: 11 honeysuckle

woodchuck: 6 marmot **9** groundhog

woodcock: 4 dupe, fool **5** pewee **7** becasse(F.) **9** simpleton **10** woodpecker

woodcutter: 6 axeman, logger, sawyer **7** chopper **8** woodsman **9** lumberman

wooded: 5 bosky **6** sylvan

wooden: dry **4** dull, wood **5** heavy, oaken, stiff, treen **6** clumsy, stolid **7** awkward **8** lifeless **9** ponderous **10** spiritless **11** insensitive **14** expressionless

wooden-headed: 4 dull **6** stupid **8** blockish

Wooden Horse: See **Trojan Horse**

wooden shoe: 4 clog, geta **5** sabot **6** patten

woodland: 5 weald **6** forest **10** timberland

burnt over: **6** brulee

deity: Pan **4** faun **5** Diana, satyr, Silen **7** Silenus **8** Seilenos

landscape: **7** boscage

woodpecker: 4 chab **5** picus **6** picule, yaffle, yockel, yuckle, yukkel **7** flicker, piculet, whetile, wryneck, yaffler **8** hickwall, woodcock, woodhack **9** sapsucker, woodchuck, woodspite **10** carpintero, woodhacker, woodjobber **11** hickoryhead, woodknacker

genus: **5** picus

type: **5** downy, hairy **8** imperial, pileated **9** redheaded

pert. to: **6** picine **8** piciform

woodsman: 5 scout **6** hunter **7** bushman, trapper **8** forester

woodwind: 4 oboe **5** flute **7** bassoon, piccolo **8** clarinet **9** saxophone

woodworker: 6 joiner, turner **9** carpenter **12** cabinetmaker *machine:* saw **5** edger, lathe **6** planer, router, shaper **7** sticker

tool: adz, saw **4** adze **5** plane **6** hammer

woody: 4 bosky **6** sylvan, xyloid **8** ligneous

woody fiber: 4 bast, hemp **5** xylem

wooer: 4 beau **6** suitor **8** courtier, paramour

woof: abb **5** cloth, weave **6** fabric **7** filling, texture **9** essential

wool: fur **4** coat, hair, lamb **5** llama, sheep **6** fleece, mohair **8** barragan, barragon **9** cordillas

blemish: **4** mote

clean: **7** garnett

cloth: **5** baize, duroy, tweed **6** alpaca, angora, baline, duffel, frieze, hodden, kersey, melton, merino, mohair, vicuna **7** flannel, ratteen, stammel **8** cashmere, casimire **9** cassimere, gabardine, hauberget **10** broadcloth, fearnaught, fearnought **11** dreadnaught, dreadnought

fat: **5** suint **7** lanolin **8** lanoline

fibers: nep **4** noil

grower: **5** sheep **7** rancher

implement: **6** carder, shears, teaser **7** distaff, spindle

inferior: **7** cleamer

kind: **4** noil, shag **8** mortling **9** downright, shearling

lock: **5** flock

mixed hues: tum

nap-raising plant: **5** tease

package: **5** fadge

piece: **4** frib, tate(Sc.) **7** cleamer

pulled: **5** slipe

reclaimed: **5** mungo **6** shoddy

refuse: **6** pinion **7** backing

source: **4** goat, lamb **5** camel, llama, sheep

spun: **4** yarn

tease: tum **4** card

texture: nap

twisted roll: **4** slub

unravel: **5** tease

waste: fud

weight: tod **5** clove

worker: **8** shedhand

yarn: abb, eis **7** eiswool

wool-colored: 5 beige, camel

wool-dryer: 5 fugal

woolly: 5 hairy **6** fleecy, lanate, lanose **7** lanated **8** peronate

woozy: 5 dazed, dizzy, drunk, shaky **7** muddled, sickish, strange, trembly **9** befuddled

word: 4 fame, news, talk, term **5** adage, couch, honor, maxim, motto, order, parol, state, voice **6** assent, avowal, phrase, pledge, remark, report, repute, saying, signal, speech **7** account, adjunct, command, comment, dispute, express, message, promise, proverb, tidings **8** acrostic, language, password **9** direction, discourse, statement, watchword **10** expression **11** affirmation, declaration, information **12** intelligence **13** communication

battle: **9** logomachy

colorful: **5** slang

complex of ideas: **10** holophrase **11** holophrasis

connective: **11** conjunction

containing all vowels: **6** oiseau(F.) **7** eulogia, miaoued, sequoia **12** ambidextrous **14** undiscoverably **15** uncopyrightable

containing all vowels in reverse sequence: **10** duoliteral

containing all vowels in sequence: **8** caesious

containing four letters: **9** tetragram

containing no vowels: cwm, nth **5** crwth

containing uu: **6** mutuum, vacuum **7** duumvir, triduum **8** residuum **9** continuum, menstruum, perpetuum, zuurveldt **10** duumvirate

contraction: **9** haplology

corresponding: **8** analogue

derived from another: **7** paronym

figurative use: **5** trope **7** metonym

group: **6** clause, phrase **8** sentence

hard to pronounce: **10** jawbreaker

imitative: **9** onomatope

improper use: **8** solecism

inventor: **6** coiner **9** neologist

last sound omitted: **7** apocope

longest: **45** pneumonoultramicroscopicsilicovolcanokoniosis

magical: **6** presto, sesame **11** abracadabra

meaning: **9** semantics

misuse of: **11** catachresis, malapropism

mystical: **7** anagoge

new: **9** neologism, neoterism

of action: **4** verb

of naming: **4** noun

of opposite meaning: **7** antonym

of same meaning: **7** synonym

pretentious: **10** lexiphanic

root: **6** etymon

sacred: **5** selah **6** sesame, shelah

same backword and forward: **10** palindrome

same sound: **7** homonym **9** homophone

same spelling: **9** homograph

scrambled: **7** anagram

separation: **6** tmesis **7** diacope

square: **10** palindrome

substituted: **5** trope **7** metonym

transposition: **7** anagram

use of imitative: **12** onomatopoeia

use of new: **7** neology

use of unnecessary: **8** pleonasm

very long: **13** sesquipedalia(pl.)

word blindness: 6 alexia

word for word: 7 exactly **8** verbatim **9** literally

Word of God: 5 Logos

word of honor: 4 oath 6 parole 7 promise

word puzzle: 5 rebus 7 anagram, charade 8 acrostic 9 crossword

word-sign: 8 ideogram, logogram 10 hieroglyph, pictograph

wordbook: 7 lexicon, speller 8 libretto 9 thesaurus 10 cyclopedia, dictionary, vocabulary

wordiness: 8 verbiage

wording: 8 phrasing 9 wrangling 10 expression

wordless: 5 tacit 6 silent 8 unspoken

words: 4 text 6 lyrics 7 quarrel 8 libretto
depiction in: 8 vignette
excessive interest in: 10 verbomania
meaningless: 6 drivel 9 gibberish
misuse: 11 catachresis, heterophemy
put into: 5 state 6 phrase 7 express
written: 4 copy, text

wordy: 6 prolix 7 diffuse, verbose 9 garrulous, redundant 10 long-winded

wore: See **wear**

work: act, job, tew 4 beat, duty, feat, move, opus, plan, task, till, worm 5 chore, craft, draft, ergon, exert, graft, grind, knead, labor, solve, stint, trade 6 arbeit(G.), design, effort, puddle, strive 7 belabor, ferment, operate, pattern, perform, travail 8 activity, belabour, business, drudgery, exertion, function, industry, struggle 10 accomplish, employment, manipulate, occupation, profession 11 achievement, performance, undertaking
agreement: 4 code, pact 8 contract
aimlessly: 6 fiddle, potter, putter
aversion to: 10 ergophobia
by day: 4 char 5 chare
defensive: see **fortification**
divine: 7 theurgy
excess: 6 overdo
evade: 4 snib 9 goldbrick
hard: peg, ply 4 char, moil, plod, plug, toil 5 chare, delve, drill, labor, sweat 6 drudge 7 travail 8 scrabble 9 lucubrate
incomplete: 7 ebauche
labored: 11 lucubration
lover of: 9 ergophile
musical: see **musical composition**
period: day 4 hour, turn, week 5 month, shift, spell, trick, watch 8 schedule
steadily: ply
together: 4 team 5 co-act 9 co-operate 11 collaborate
unit: erg 5 ergon, joule 7 calorie
women's: 7 distaff

work-a-day: 7 prosaic 8 everyday, ordinary 11 commonplace

work for: 4 earn 5 serve 7 benefit

work of art: 4 song 6 statue 7 classic, etching, picture 8 painting

work on: 6 affect 9 influence

work out: fix 5 erase, solve 6 efface 7 arrange, develop, exhaust 8 exercise 9 calculate, elaborate 10 accomplish

work over: 4 redo 6 recast, rehash, revamp, revise 8 persuade 9 brainwash, elaborate, influence

work up: irk 5 raise, rouse 6 arouse, excite, expend 7 advance, develop 8 generate 9 elaborate 10 manipulate

workable: 4 ripe 6 mellow, pliant 8 feasible, possible 9 practical 11 practicable

workaholic: 5 grind

workbag: 8 reticule

worker: 4 arry, doer, hand, hind 5 navvy 6 earner, toiler 7 artisan, laborer 8 operator 9 artificer, craftsman, operative, performer 11 breadwinner
fellow: 5 buddy 7 comrade 8 confrere 9 colleague
group: 4 crew, gang, team 5 corps, shift, staff, union 9 personnel
hard: 6 beaver, drudge, fagger
head: 4 boss 5 super 6 ganger 7 foreman, manager 8 employer, overseer 10 supervisor 14 superintendent
kind: 5 diver, mason, miner, smith, tuner 6 barman, cocker, hopper, joiner, laster, sapper, sawyer, slater, smithy, tanner, warper, wright 7 analyst, cobbler, collier, geordie, glazier, paneler, plumber, reedman, riveter, sandhog, spinner 8 chaffman, chuckler, enameler, mechanic, shedhand, strapper 9 carpenter, groundhog, machinist, stevedore
migrant: 4 hobo, Okie 5 Arkie 6 boomer 7 floater, wetback
objectionable: 4 scab 7 botcher, bungler 11 scissorbill 13 featherbedder
skilled: 7 artisan
unskilled: 4 peon 6 coolie 7 laborer

workhorse: 4 peon, serf 5 slave 6 drudge, toiler 7 trestle 8 sawhorse

workhouse: 6 prison 8 workshop 9 almshouse, poorhouse

working (see also **work**): 4 busy 5 alert 6 active, decree, effort 7 halurgy 8 employed, endeavor 9 ordinance, practical 10 contortion
not: off 4 idle 5 kaput 6 broken 10 unemployed

working class: 7 laborer 11 proletariat

workman: See **worker**

workman-like: 4 deft 5 adept 8 skillful 10 proficient

workroom: den, lab 4 mill, shop 5 plant, study 6 studio 7 atelier, bottega, factory, library 10 laboratory 11 ergasterion

works: 5 plant

worktable: 5 bench

world: 5 earth, globe, realm 6 cosmos, domain, people, public 7 kingdom, mankind 8 creation, humanity, universe
antedating creation of: 10 premundane

bearer of: **5** Atlas
external: **6** nonego
lower: see **underworld**
miniature: **9** microcosm
pert. to: **7** mundane, secular **11** terrestrial
World War I: *battle:* **5** Marne, Somme, Ypres **6** Verdun **7** Jutland
general: **8** Pershing
hero: **5** York **12** Rickenbacker
marshal: **4** Foch
treaty: **10** Versailles
World War II: *alliance:* **4** Axis **6** Allies
battle: **4** Orel **5** Anzio, Bulge **6** Bataan, Sicily, Tarawa, Warsaw **7** Cassino, Iwo Jima, Okinawa **8** Normandy
general: **6** Patton, Rommel **7** Bradley **10** Eisenhower, Montgomery
worldly: **6** carnal, laical **7** earthen, earthly, mundane, secular, sensual, terrene **11** terrestrial **13** materialistic, sophisticated
worldwide: **6** global **8** ecumenic, pandemic **9** planetary, universal **10** ecumenical **13** international
worm: bob, eel, eri, ess ipo, loa, lug, pin **4** grub, nais, nema **5** borer, larva, tinea **6** looper, maggot, palolo, teredo, wretch **7** annelid, ascarid, ipomoea, reptile, sagitta, serpent, tagtail, wriggle **8** cercaria, helminth **9** angleworm, earthworm, insinuate, nemertina, nemertine, nemertini, trematode **10** nemertinea, serpentine **13** platyhelminth
aquatic: sao **4** nais, nema **5** cadew, leech **6** nereis **7** achaeta, annelid
bait: mad **4** lurg **7** tagtail
eye-infecting: loa
genus of: **6** nereis **8** geoplana
parasitic: **5** fluke, leech **7** ascarid, cestode, pinworm **8** tapeworm, trichina **9** roundworm
segment: **6** somite **8** metamere
threadlike: **7** filaria
worm-eaten: old **6** pitted, ragged, shabby **7** decayed, worn-out **8** decrepit **9** out-of-date, worthless **10** antiquated
worm-eating mammal: **4** mole
wormlike: **7** vermian **11** helminthoid
wormweed: **8** pinkroot
wormwood: **4** moxa **7** cudweed **8** mingwort
wormy: **6** earthy, rotten **8** diseased, crawling
worn: See **wear**
worn down: **5** erose, tired **6** eroded **7** abraded, attrite **8** attrited
worn-out: **4** sere, used **5** jaded, passe, seedy, spent, stale, trite **6** effete, frayed, shabby **7** haggard **8** consumed, decrepit, impaired, weakened **9** enfeebled, exhausted, hackneyed **10** bedraggled, threadbare **11** commonplace
worry: dun, hox, nag, vex **4** bait, care, cark, faze, fear, fike, fret, fuss, gnaw, hare, stew **5** annoy, brood, choke, gally, harry, hurry, touse, trial, upset **6** badger, bother, caddle, fidget, harass, hatter, hector, pester, plague, pother **7** anxiety, bedevil, chagrin, concern, despair, disturb, perturb, torment, trouble **8** distress, strangle **9** worriment **10** disconcert, uneasiness
without: **8** carefree
worsen: **8** pejorate **7** decline, descend **10** retrogress **11** deteriorate
worship: **4** cult, fame, love **5** adore, dulia, honor, worth **6** credit, homage, latria, renown, repute, revere **7** dignity, idolism, idolize, liturgy, respect **8** blessing, devotion, hierurgy, idolatry, venerate **9** adoration, deference, monolatry, reverence, theolatry **10** admiration, allotheism, hagiolatry, hierolatry, hyperdulia, reputation, veneration, worthiness
form of: **4** rite **6** ritual
house of: dom **6** chapel, church, mosque, shrine, temple **9** cathedral, synagogue **10** tabernacle
nature: **11** physiolatry
of angels and saints: **5** dulia
object of: **4** icon, idol **5** totem **6** fetich, fetish
pert. to: **8** liturgic **10** liturgical
place of: **5** altar
system of: **4** cult **6** cultus
worshiper: **6** adorer, bhakta, votary **7** devotee **8** disciple, idolater
worshipful: **4** good **5** proud **7** notable **8** esteemed **9** honorable, respected **10** venerating **11** worshipping **13** distinguished
worst: bad **4** beat, best **6** defeat **9** discomfit, overthrow
worsted: **4** garn, yarn **5** serge **6** fabric, tamine **8** whipcord **9** gabardine
yarn: **6** caddis, crewel **7** caddice, genappe **9** fingering
wort: **4** herb, root **8** fleabane
worth: **4** mark, note **5** merit, price, value **6** bounty, desert, esteem, riches, virtue, wealth **7** account, fitting, quality, stature **8** eminence **9** deserving, desirable, substance **10** excellence, importance, possession, usefulness
sense of: **5** pride **7** dignity, respect
thing of little: rap **6** stiver, trifle
worthless: bad, rap **4** base, evil, idle, vain, vile **5** inane **6** cheesy, drossy, futile, hollow, no-good, paltry, putrid, rotten, trashy **7** fustian, inutile, useless **8** feckless, unworthy **9** frivolous, no-account, valueless **11** undeserving **12** contemptible **14** good-for-nothing
worthy: **4** dear, good **7** condign **8** deserved, eligible, laudable, meriting, valuable **9** competent, deserving, estimable,

excellent, honorable, qualified **11** appropriate, meritorious

wound: cut **4** gore, harm, hurt, pain, stab, wing **5** break, ganch, sting **6** breach, damage, grieve, harrow, injury, trauma **7** afflict, attaint **8** distress, puncture
discharge from: pus **5** ichor, serum
dressing: **7** bandage, pledget
in heraldry: **4** vuln
lint to dilate: **4** tent
mark: **4** scab, scar, welt **7** blister

woundwort: **6** betony **7** allheal

wove: See **weave**

woven (see also **weave**): **4** lacy **7** damasse
raised figures: **6** broche **7** brocade

wow: hit, mew **4** howl, rave, wail **5** smash, whine **7** success

wrack: **4** kelp, rack, ruin **5** goods, trash, weeds, wreck **6** avenge, defeat, injury **7** destroy, seaweed, torment, unsound **8** calamity, mischief, wreckage **9** overthrow, shipwreck, vengeance **10** punishment **11** destruction, persecution

wraith: **5** ghost, spook **7** phantom, specter **10** apparition

wrangle (see also **quarrel**): **4** spar **5** argue, brawl, chide **6** bicker, debate, haggle **7** contend, dispute, quarrel **11** altercation, controversy **12** disagreement

wrangler: **6** cowboy, hafter **7** student **8** herdsman, opponent **9** disputant **10** antagonist

wrap: hap, rug, wap **4** cere, coil, fold, furl, hide, mask, roll, wind **5** cloak, cover, nubia, twine **6** afghan, encowl, enfold, infold, invest, swathe **7** blanket, conceal, enclose, envelop, package **8** enshroud, enswathe, surround **9** encompass **10** camouflage

wrapper: **4** gown **5** cover **6** fardel **8** galabeah

wrapping: wap **8** cerement, covering

wrasse: **4** fish **6** ballan

wrath: ire **4** fury, rage **5** anger **6** choler, felony **7** offense, passion **8** acerbity, violence **10** turbulence **11** indignation **12** exasperation

wrathful: **5** wroth **8** choleric, incensed **9** malignant

wreak: **5** exact **6** avenge, punish **7** gratify, indulge, inflict, revenge **9** vengeance

wreath, wreathe: lei **4** bank, coil, orle, roll, turn **5** crown, drift, torse(her.), twine, twist, whorl **6** anadem, corona, crants, crease, laurel, spirea, wrench **7** chaplet, contort, coronet, crownal, entwine, festoon, garland, spiraea, wrinkle **8** encircle, surround
in heraldry; **5** torse

wreck: **4** hulk, ruin **5** crash, ruins, smash, total, wrack **6** damage, defeat, jalopy, thwart **7** destroy, disable, founder, shatter **8** collapse, demolish, derelict, sabotage **9** overthrow, shipwreck, vandalize **11** destruction

wreckage: **7** flotsam **8** driftage **9** driftwood

wrench (see also **wrest**): wry **4** jerk, pipe, pull, rack, tear, tool, turn **5** twist, wring **6** injury, monkey, sprain, strain, twinge **7** distort, spanner **8** Stillson **9** alligator, epitonion **10** distortion

wrest: **4** rend, ruse **5** exact, force, fraud, seize, trick, usurp, wring **6** elicit, extort, snatch **7** pervert, wrestle **10** confiscate

wrestle: tug **6** squirm, strive, tussle, wraxle **7** contend, grapple, wriggle **8** struggle

wrestler: **6** mauler

wrestling: *ceremonial:* **4** sumo
hold: **6** nelson **8** headlock, scissors
pad: mat
place: **4** ring **5** arena **8** palestra **9** palaestra
score: **4** fall
term: pin **8** takedown
throw: **4** hipe

wretch: bum, dog **4** worm **5** exile, loser **6** beggar, pauper **7** hilding, ingrate, sad sack, scroyle **8** derelict, recreant **9** miscreant **11** rapscallion

wretched: **4** base, foul, lewd, mean, poor **5** dawny **6** abject, dismal, paltry, pilled, woeful **7** baleful, caitiff, forlorn, unhappy **8** dejected, grievous, inferior, pitiable **9** afflicted, execrable, miserable, niggardly **10** calamitous, deplorable, depressing, despicable, distressed **11** unfortunate **12** contemptible, parsimonious **14** unsatisfactory

wriggle: **4** frig, turn, wind **5** dodge, evade, snake, twist **6** fitter, squirm, widdle, wintle, writhe **7** meander **10** equivocate

wring: **4** fret, rack **5** press, twist **6** elicit, extort, squirm, wrench **7** afflict, extract, squeeze, wrestle **8** compress, struggle

wrinkle: fad, rut **4** fold, idea, knit, line, lirk, ruck, ruga, seam **5** crimp, fancy, knack, reeve, ridge, rivel **6** cockle, crease, device, furrow, notion, pucker, rimple **7** crimple, crinkle, crumple, frumple, novelty, winding **8** contract **9** crow's foot, corrugate **10** prominence

wrinkled: **6** crepey, rugate, rugose, rugous **7** savoyed **8** rugulose
free from being: **6** smooth **7** erugate

wrist: **5** joint **6** carpus
bone: **4** ulna **6** carpal **7** carpale
mark: **7** rasceta
ornament: **4** band **8** bracelet
pert. to: **6** carpal

wristlet: **4** band **5** strap **8** bracelet, handcuff **9** wristband

writ: **5** breve, brief, tales **6** capias, elegit, extent, venire **7** exigent, process, writing **8** detainer, document, mittimus, replevin, subpoena **10** certiorari, distringas, injunction, instrument **11** fieri-facias

of execution: **5** outre **6** elegit

write: pen **4** note **5** chalk, clerk, enrol **6** direct, enface, enroll, indite, record, scrawl, scribe **7** compose, engross, scratch **8** inscribe, scribble **9** character

letters: **10** correspond

write down: **4** list, note **6** record **10** depreciate

write off: **4** drop **5** decry **6** cancel, deduct, remove

writer: **4** hack, poet **5** clerk, odist **6** author, critic, glozer, lawyer, penman, scribe **7** copyist, glosser, hymnist, penster, realist, tropist **8** annalist, composer, essayist, gazeteer, literate, lyricist, novelist, parodist, prefacer, reviewer, scriptor **9** annotater, columnist, craftsman, dramatist, glossator, scrivener, solicitor **10** amanuensis, chronicler, glossarist, journalist **12** calligrapher, epistolarian **13** glossographer

inferior: **4** hack **8** rhymster **9** poetaster, scribbler

prose: **8** prosaist

unscrupulous: **10** plagiarist

verse: **4** bard, poet **5** odist **7** elegist **9** sonneteer

writhe: **4** bend, bind, curl, toss, turn **5** twist, wrest, wring **6** squirm **7** agonize, contort, distort, shrivel, wriggle **8** encircle, enswathe **9** convolute, insinuate **10** contortion, intertwine

writhing: **4** eely **9** wriggling

writing: ola **4** book, deed, olla, poem, writ **5** diary, essay, print, prose, verse **6** script **7** epistle, pothook **8** contract, covenant, document, makimono, pleading, spelling **9** allograph, cerograph, enrolment, esoterics **10** enrollment, instrument, literature, penmanship **11** chirography, composition, handwriting, inscription, orthography, pornography, publication

alternate: **13** boustrophedon

ancient manuscript: **6** uncial

character: (see also **word-sign**)*:* **4** sign **6** letter, symbol **9** cuneiform **10** hieroglyph

desk: **9** secretary **10** escritoire

excessive interest in: **11** graphomania

inferior: **9** potboiler

master: **7** stylist

material: pad **5** board, paper, slate **6** tablet **7** papyrus **9** parchment **10** stationery

on the wall: **4** mene **5** tekel **8** upharsin

pert. to: **7** scribal

sacred: **5** Bible, Koran **6** psalms, Talmud **9** hagiology, testament **10** scriptures

secret: **4** code **6** cipher **10** cryptogram **12** cryptography

tool: pen **5** chalk, stick **6** pencil, stylus **8** computer **9** ballpoint **10** typewriter

wrong: bad, car, ill, off, out, sin **4** awry, evil, harm, tort **5** abuse, agley, amiss, crime, error, false, grief, malum, unfit **6** astray, faulty, injure, injury, malign, seduce, sinful, unfair, unjust, wicked **7** crooked, defraud, immoral, misdeed, twisted, vicious, violate **8** dishonor, improper, iniquity, mistaken, tortuous, wrongful, wrongous **9** erroneous, incorrect, injurious, injustice, reprobate, violation **10** dispossess, inaccurate, iniquitous, unsuitable **11** malfeasance, misfeasance **12** illegitimate **13** inappropriate **14** unsatisfactory

civil: **4** tort

wrongdoer: **5** felon **6** sinner **8** criminal, violator **9** miscreant **10** malefactor, tort-feasor, trespasser **12** transgressor

wroth: **5** angry, irate **7** violent **8** incensed, wrathful **9** turbulent

wrought (see also **work**)*:* **4** agog, made **5** eager **6** formed, shaped, worked **7** excited, operose **9** decorated, disturbed, fashioned, processed **10** elaborated, ornamented, stimulated **11** embroidered **12** manufactured

up: **7** excited, stirred

wrung: See **wring**

wry: **4** awry, bend, bias, sour, tend, turn **5** avert, pinch, twist, wring **6** swerve, warped, wrench **7** contort, crooked, cynical, deflect, deviate, distort, incline **8** contrary, perverse, sardonic

wryneck: **5** loxia **9** snakebird **10** woodpecker **11** torticollis

genus: **4** jynx

Wurttemberg: *capital:* **9** Stuttgart

city: Ulm **9** Esslingen, Heilbronn

river: **6** Danube, Neckar

Wuthering Heights author: **6** Bronte

Wycliffe disciple: **7** Lollard

Wyoming: *capital:* **8** Cheyenne

city: **6** Casper **7** Laramie **8** Sheridan **11** Rock Springs

county: **4** Park **5** Teton **6** Albany, Carbon **7** Fremont

highest point: **11** Gannett Peak

Indian: **4** Crow **7** Arapaho

motto: **11** equal rights

mountain range: **8** Absaroka **9** Wind River

national park: **10** Grand Teton **11** Yellowstone

nickname: **8** Equality

river: **5** Green, Snake **6** Powder **7** Bighorn **11** North Platte

state bird: **10** meadowlark

state flower: **16** Indian paintbrush

state tree: **10** cottonwood

X

X: chi, ten **4** mark **5** cross, error **7** mistake **9** signature
X-shaped: 8 cruciate
Xanadu's river: 4 Alph
xanthic: 6 yellow **9** yellowish
Xanthippe: 5 scold, shrew **6** nagger, virago **9** termagant
  husband: **8** Socrates
xanthous: 6 yellow **9** Mongolian
xebec: 4 boat, ship **6** vessel
xema: 4 gull
xenium: 4 gift **7** present **8** delicacy
xenogamy: 13 fertilization
xenon: 7 element
Xenophanean: 7 eleatic
Xenophon: 14 Greek historian
  teacher: **8** Socrates
  work: **8** Anabasis **9** Hellenica
Xeres: 4 wine **5** Jerez **6** sherry
xerophyte: 6 cactus
xerosis: 7 dryness
xerotic: dry, sec
Xerox: 4 copy **6** copier **9** duplicate, reproduce
xerus: 8 squirrel

Xerxes: *composer:* **6** Handel
  kingdom: **6** Persia
  parent: **6** Atossa, Darius
  wife: **6** Esther
Xhosa, Xosa: 5 Bantu, tribe **8** language
xiphoid: 8 ensiform **9** sword-like
Xmas: 4 Noel, Yule **9** Christmas
X-ray: *inventor:* **8** Roentgen
  measuring device: **11** quantimeter
  science: **9** radiology **13** roentgenology
  source: **6** target
  treatment: **11** radiotherapy
  type: **8** grenzray
xurel: 4 scad **6** saurel
xylograph: 5 print **7** woodcut **9** engraving **10** impression
xyloid: 5 woody **8** ligneous
Xylonite: 9 celluloid
xylophone: 5 saron **6** gender **7** gambang, gamelan, marimba **8** gamalang, gigelira, sticcado
xyrid: 4 iris
xyst, xystos, xystus: 4 stoa, walk **5** porch **7** portico, terrace

Y

yabber: 4 talk **6** jabber **8** language **12** conversation
yabby, yabbie: 8 crayfish
yacht: 4 boat, race, sail, ship **5** craft **6** cruise, sonder
yacht basin: 6 marina
yacht flag: 6 burgee
yaffle: 10 woodpecker
yahoo: 4 lout **5** brute, tough **6** savage **7** bumpkin **9** roughneck
  creator: **5** Swift

Yahweh: God **4** YHVH, YHWH **5** Yahwe **7** Jehovah
yak: 4 joke, zobo **6** sarlak, sarlyk **7** buffalo, chatter
yakamik: 9 trumpeter
yaksha: god **4** jinn, ogre **5** angel, demon, dryad, fairy, gnome **6** spirit
Yakut river: 4 Lena
Yale: Eli **4** lock **10** University
Yalta: *conference member:* **6** Stalin **9** Churchill, Roosevelt

location: 6 Crimea

yam: ube, ubi 5 tugui 6 buckra, igname, potato, uviyam 7 boniata 8 cush-cush 9 posthouse 11 sweet potato

yamen: 6 office 7 mansion 9 residence 12 headquarters

yammer: cry 4 chat, yell 5 crave, gripe, shout, whine, yearn 6 clamor, desire, lament, scream 7 chatter, grumble, stammer, whimper 8 complain

yamp: 5 tuber

yang: cry 4 honk

yang-kin: 8 dulcimer

Yangtze River tributary: Han, Kan, Min

yank: tug 4 blow, jerk, pull 5 hoick 6 snatch, twitch 7 extract

Yank, Yankee: 8 American 10 Northerner

yap: apt, cur, dog, gab 4 bark, keen, talk, yelp 5 cheep, clown, eager, mouth, quick, ready, rowdy, scold 6 active, hungry, jabber, rustic 7 bumpkin, chatter, hoodlum 9 greenhorn

Yap Island money: fei 5 stone

yapock, yapok: 6 monkey 7 opossum

Yaqui: 5 river 6 Indian

yard: rod 4 lawn, spar, wand 5 court, garth, staff, stick 7 confine 9 courtyard, curtilage, enclosure 10 correction, playground, quadrangle

enclosed: 5 garth, patio

part of: 4 foot, inch

sixteenth of: 4 nail

yards: *five and one-half:* rod

119.6 square: ar

600: 4 heer

two hundred twenty: 7 furlong

yardage: 6 length 8 distance

yardland: 7 virgate

yardstick: 5 gauge 7 measure 8 standard

yarn: abb, eis, tow 4 chat, garn, sley, tale 5 fiber, story 6 caddis, crewel 7 caddice, eiswool, genappe, schappe 8 converse 9 fingering

ball: 4 clew

holder: cop

quantity: cop, lea 4 clew, clue, hank, hasp 5 skein 7 spangle

reel: 4 pirn

size: 6 denier

spindle: 4 hasp

waste: 5 thrum

yarr: 5 growl, snarl 7 spurrey

yarrow: 4 herb 7 allheal, milfoil

yashmak, yasmak: 4 veil

yataghan: 5 knife, saber 8 scimitar

yaupon: 5 holly 7 cassena, cassina 9 evergreen

yaw: 4 turn, veer 5 steer 6 seesaw, swerve 7 deviate

yawl: 4 boat, howl 6 scream, vessel

yawn: nap 4 galp, gant(Sc.), gape, yaup, yawp 5 chasm 6 tedium 7 opening 8 oscitate

yawp: bay, cry, yap 4 bawl, call, gape, yelp 5 gripe 6 bellow, scream, squall 8 complain

yaws: 7 disease 9 frambesia

yawweed: 7 rhubarb

yclept: 5 named 6 called

ye: you 4 thee, thou

yea: aye, yes 4 also, even 5 truly 6 assent, indeed, verily 11 affirmative

yean: ean 4 bear, lamb 7 produce

yeanling: kid 4 lamb 7 newborn

year: 5 annus(L.)

designation: 4 leap 5 lunar, solar 6 fiscal 7 natural 8 calendar, sidereal, tropical 12 astronomical

difference between lunar and solar: 5 epact

division: 5 month, raith(Sc.) 6 season

of plenary indulgence: 7 jubilee

one-fourth of calendar: 9 trimester

one-half of academic: 8 semester

one-third of academic: 9 trimester

record: 5 annal 8 calendar

yearbook: 6 annual 7 almanac

yearling: 4 colt 9 hornotine

Yearling: *author:* 8 Rawlings

boy: 4 Jody

yearly: 6 annual 7 etesian 8 annually

yearn: beg, vex, yen 4 ache, long, pine, sigh, wish 5 covet, crave 6 desire, grieve, hanker, yammer 7 request

yearning: 4 wish 5 eager 7 anxious 8 ambition 10 aspiration

years: age, eon, era 4 time

eight: 9 octennial

fifteen: 9 indiction

five: 6 pentad 7 lustrum

four: 11 quadrennial

hundred: 9 centenary 10 centennial

ninety: 10 nonagenary

seventy: 12 septuagenary

ten: 6 decade 8 decenary 9 decennary, decenniad, decennium

thousand: 7 chiliad 10 millennium

two: 8 biennium

yeast: bee 4 barm, foam, rise 5 froth 6 leaven 7 ferment 9 agitation

brewer's: 4 barm

yeasty: 5 giddy, light 8 restless 9 frivolous, unsettled 11 superficial

yegg: 5 thief 6 robber 7 burglar 8 criminal 11 safebreaker, safecracker

yell: cry 4 call, gowl, howl, roar, yarm, yowl 5 cheer, shout, whoop 6 outcry, scream, shriek, yammer 7 yelloch

yelling: 8 strident 9 clamorous

yellow: 4 gull, mean, sere, turn, yolk 5 amber, blake, color, favel, lemon, ochre, tinge 6 butter, canary, fallow, flavic, flavid, flaxen, golden, sallow 7 unmanly, xanthic **8** cowardly, recreant **9** flavicant, jaundiced, lutescent **10** flavescent, melancholy **11** lily-livered, sensational, treacherous **12** contemptible, dishonorable **13** dishonourable, untrustworthy

brown: dun **4** bran **5** aloma, amber, pablo, straw **6** manila

dyestuff: **5** morin **6** orlean **7** annatto, annotto, arnatto

egg's: **4** yolk

gray: **4** drab

green: **5** olive **6** acacia, privet **8** glaucous, tarragon **10** chartreuse, serpentine

lemon: **8** generall

orange: **9** grenadine

red: **4** lava, roan **5** sandy **6** orange **7** nacarat

yellow alloy: **5** brass

yellow bird: **6** canary **7** warbler **9** goldfinch

yellow copper ore: **12** chalcopyrite

yellow copperas: **9** copiapite

yellow jacket: **4** wasp **6** hornet **8** eucalypt

yellow mustard: **8** charlock

yellow ocher: sil

yellow pigment: **7** etiolin **8** orpiment

yellow race: **6** Mongol **9** Mongolian

Yellow River: **7** Hwang Ho

yellow star: **10** sneezeweed

yellow starwort: **10** elecampane

yellowback: **9** dime novel

yellowbelly: rat **4** funk **6** coward

yellowhammer: **4** bird, yite **5** ammer, finch, skite **6** gladdy **7** yeldrin **8** yeldrine, yeldring, yeldrock, yoldring **10** woodpecker

Yellowhammer State: **7** Alabama

yellowlegs: **4** bird **7** tattler **8** redshank **9** sandpiper

Yellowstone Park attraction: **4** deer **5** bears **6** geyser **11** Old Faithful

yelp: cry, yip **4** bark, brag **5** boast, cheep, shout **6** greedy, outcry, shriek, squeal **7** ululate **8** complain **9** criticize

Yemen (People's Democratic Republic of): *capital:* **4** Aden

gulf: **4** Aden

island: **5** Perim **7** Kamaran, Socotra

monetary unit: **5** dinar

town: **7** Mukalla

Yemen Arab Republic: *capital:* **4** San'a

desert: **10** Rub 'al-Khali

monetary unit: **4** rial

seaport: **4** Moka **5** Mocha **7** Hodeida

town: **5** Damar, Ta'izz **6** Dhamar

yen: **4** coin, long, urge **5** yearn **6** desire **7** longing **10** propensity

one-hundredth: sen

yenta (Yid.): **6** gossip

yeoman: **5** clerk **6** butler **8** retainer **9** assistant, attendant **10** freeholder, journeyman, manservant **11** subordinate

of guard officer: **4** exon

U.S. Navy: **12** petty officer

yes: aye, iss, oui(F.), yeh, yep **4** okay, yeah **5** agree **6** assent **7** exactly **8** all right **9** assuredly **11** affirmation, affirmative

yet: but **4** also **5** still **6** even so, though **7** algates, besides, further, however **9** after all, sometime **10** eventually **11** nonetheless **12** nevertheless **15** notwithstanding

yeti: **7** monster, snowman

yew: **4** tree **5** shrub **7** conifer **9** evergreen

genus: **5** taxus

Yiddish: **6** Jewish **8** language

prayer: **5** daven

synagogue: **4** shul

yield: bow, net, pay, sag **4** bear, bend, cave, cede, cess, elde, fold, give, obey, vail **5** addle, admit, agree, allow, avale, defer, grant, heald, hield, repay, stoop, waive **6** accede, afford, comply, impart, output, profit, relent, render, return, reward, soften, submit, supply **7** abandon, bring in, concede, consent, deliver, produce, revenue, succumb **9** acquiesce, surrender **10** capitulate, recompense, relinquish **11** acknowledge **12** knuckle under

yielding: **4** meek, soft, waxy **5** buxom **6** feeble, flabby, pliant, supple **7** flaccid, passive **8** flexible, recreant **9** tractable **10** manageable

yip: **4** yell, yelp

Ymer, Ymir: **5** giant

slayer: **4** Odin, Vili

yodel: **4** call, sing **5** carol, shout **6** warble **7** refrain

yogi: **5** fakir, yogin **6** fakeer **7** ascetic

sitting posture: **5** asana

yoke: tie **4** bail, bond, join, link, pair, span, team **5** bangy, fight(Sc.), hitch, marry, seize(Sc.) **6** attack(Sc.), banghy, couple, inspan, tackle(Sc.) **7** bondage, carrier, enslave, harness, oppress, service, slavery **8** restrain **9** associate, servitude

yoked: **9** conjugate

yokefellow: **4** mate, wife **6** spouse **7** husband, partner **9** associate, companion

yokel: oaf **4** boor, clod, lout, rube **6** obtuse, rustic **7** bumpkin, hayseed, plowboy **8** Abderite, gullible **10** countryman, slowwitted

yolk: **6** center, yellow **7** essence **8** vitellus

yon: See **yonder**

yonder: **4** away **5** there **6** beyond **7** distant, farther, further, thither

yore: **4** past **7** long ago

Yorkshire: *district:* **5** Otley, Selby

river: Ure

town: **5** Leeds

you: sie(G.), yez **4** thee, thou

young: fry, raw **4** tyro, weak **5** brood, fetus, fresh, green **6** active, callow, foetus, litter, strong, tender **7** pliable **8** childish, ignorant, immature, juvenile, newcomer, vigorous, workable, youthful **9** offspring, succulent **13** inexperienced
bring forth: ean **4** yean **5** calve, whelp
with: **6** gravid **8** pregnant
young animal: cub, kid, pup **4** calf, colt, fawn, joey **5** chick, puppy **6** kitten **7** tadpole
young hare: 7 leveret
young herring: 4 brit
younger: 6 junior
younger son: 5 cadet
youngster (see also **child**): boy, cub, lad, tad, tot **4** baby, calf, colt, girl, lass, tike **5** chick, child, filly, youth **6** moppet, shaver, urchin **9** stripling **10** midshipman
youth: bud **4** chap **5** chiel(Sc.), chabo **6** hoiden, hoyden **7** callant(Sc.), ephebos, ephebus, gossoon, puberty **8** teenager **9** youngster **10** adolescent **11** adolescence, hobbledehoy
goddess of: **4** Hebe
mythological: **5** Etana **6** Adonis, Apollo, Icarus
time of: **9** salad days
youth shelter: 6 hostel
youthful: new **5** early, fresh, young **6** active **7** puerile **8** immature, juvenile, vigorous, virginal
yowl: cry **4** bawl, howl, wail, yell
yo-yo: top **9** fluctuate, vacillate
Yucatan: 12 Mexican state
capital: **6** Merida
people: **4** Maya **5** Mayan
tree: **5** yaxche
yucca: 5 palma

Yugoslavia: *capital:* **8** Belgrade
city: **6** Skopje, Zagreb **7** Skoplje **8** Sarajevo
island: Rab, Vis **4** Cres, Hvar **5** Solta, Susak
language: **10** Macedonian
leader: **4** Broz, Tito **10** Mihajlovic
measure: rif **4** akov, ralo **5** donum, khvat, lanaz, stopa **6** motyka, palaze, ralico
monarch: **5** Peter **9** Alexander
monetary unit: **5** dinar
mountain: **7** Triglav **8** Durmitor
mountain range: **6** Julian **7** Dinaric, Velebit
people: **4** Serb **5** Croat **7** Slovene
plateau: **5** Karst
republic: **6** Serbia **7** Croatia **8** Slovenia **9** Macedonia **10** Montenegro
river: **4** Sava **5** Drava, Tisza **6** Marava, Vardar
seaport: **5** Split **7** Spalato **9** Dubrovnik
town: Pec **4** Stip **5** Veles
weight: oka, oke **5** dramm, tovar, wagon **7** satlijk
Yukon Territory: *capital:* **10** Whitehorse
explorer: **4** Bell (John) **9** Campbell (Robert)
flower: **8** fireweed
gold rush region: **8** Klondike
gold rush town: **10** Dawson City
highest peak: **7** Mt. Logan
lake: **6** Kluane
mountain range: **5** Rocky **7** St. Elias, Ogilvie, Stikine **9** Mackenzie
river: **5** Lewes, Liard, Pelly, White, Yukon **8** Klondike
territory of: **6** Canada
town: **4** Faro, Mayo
yule: 9 Christmas **13** Christmastide

Z

Z: zed **6** izzard
zac: 4 goat, ibex
zacate: hay **5** grass **6** forage
Zacchaeus, Zaccheus: 4 pure **8** innocent
Zadok: 4 just **9** righteous
  son: **7** Ahimaaz
zaftig: 5 buxom, juicy, plump **10** full-bodied
Zagreb: See **Yugoslavia**
zaguan: 4 gate **8** entrance **11** entranceway
Zaire: *animal:* **5** okapi
  capital: **8** Kinshasa
  city: **7** Kananga **10** Luluabourg
  cool season: **7** cacimba
  formerly: **12** Belgian Congo
  lake: **5** Tumba
  official language: **6** French
  people: **5** Bantu, Pygmy **7** Hamitic, Ni-
  lotic **8** Sudanese
  river: **4** Uele **5** Congo, Dengi, Zaire **6** Li-
  kati **7** Aruwimi
  snake: **8** amphiuma
  wet season: **6** kundey
Zambia: *capital:* **6** Lusaka
  falls: **8** Victoria
  former name: **15** Northern Rhodesia
  lake: **5** Niveru **9** Bangweulu
  leader: **6** Kuanda
  monetary unit: **6** kwacha
  religion: **5** Hindu, Islam **7** animist
  town: **5** Kitwe, Ndola **8** Chingola
zamia: 4 tree **5** cycad, shrub
zampogna: 7 bagpipe, panpipe
zanja: 5 canal, ditch, gully **6** arroyo
zanni: 5 clown
zany: wag **4** dolt, fool **5** clown, crazy, dotty, nutty, toady **7** acrobat, buffoon, idiotic **8** clownish, follower, imitator **9**
  simpleton **11** merry-andrew
Zanzibar: See **Tanzania**
zap: hit, pep **4** kill **5** verve **6** defeat, energy
zarf: cup **5** stand **6** holder
zarzuela: 11 seafood stew
zati: 6 monkey **7** ascetic, devotee
zeal: 4 fire **5** ardor, gusto, fervor,
  spirit **7** passion **8** devotion, interest **9**
  eagerness **10** enthusiasm, fanatacism
Zealand: *city:* **10** Copenhagen
zealot: bug, nut **5** bigot **6** votary **7** devotee, fanatic **8** disciple, partisan, votaress **10** enthusiast

zealous: 4 warm **5** rabid **6** ardent, fervid,
  hearty **7** devoted, earnest, fervent **8** frenetic, vigorous, wild-eyed **9** phrenetic,
  strenuous **12** enthusiastic
Zebedee's son: 4 John **5** James
zebra: 4 dauw **9** butterfly
  extinct: **6** quagga
  resembling: ass **5** horse
zebrawood: 7 arariba **9** nakedwood **10**
  marblewood
zebu: 12 Brahmany bull
Zebulon, Zebulun: *brother:* **4** Levi **5** Judah **6** Simeon
  father: **5** Jacob
  mother: **4** Leah
zecchino: 6 sequin
Zelus: *brother:* Bia **6** Cratus
  father: **6** Pallas
  mother: **4** Styx
  sister: **4** Nike
zemi: 5 charm
zenana: 5 harem **8** seraglio
zenith: 4 acme, apex, peak **6** summit **11**
  culmination
  opposite of: **5** nadir
Zeno: *city:* **4** Elea
  follower: **5** Stoic
Zenobia: *country:* **7** Palmyra
  husband: **9** Odenathus
zephyr: 4 aura, wind **6** breeze
zeppelin: 5 blimp **7** balloon **9** dirigible
zero: nil **5** aught, zilch **6** cipher, naught,
  nought **7** nothing **9** nonentity
Zeruiah's son: 7 Abishai
zest: 4 tang **5** gusto, savor, taste **6** flavor,
  relish **8** piquancy **9** enjoyment **10** enthusiasm
zestful: 4 racy **6** hearty **7** pungent
Zeus: 7 Alastor, Jupiter
  attendant: **4** Nike
  beloved of: Io **6** Europa
  brother: **5** Hades **8** Poseidon
  cupbearer: **4** Hebe **8** Ganymede
  daughter: Ate **4** Hebe, Kore **5** Irene **6**
  Athena, Athene **7** Artemis, Astraea **8**
  Despoina **9** Aphrodite **10** Persephone,
  Proserpina, Proserpine **11** Persephassa
  epithet: **5** soter **7** Alastor
  form assumed by: **4** bull, swan
  messenger: **4** Iris **6** Hermes
  nurse: **4** goat **8** Amalthea, Cynosura
  oracle: **6** Dodona

parent: 4 Rhea 6 Cronus, Kronos
shield: 5 aegis
sister: 4 Hera
son: Gad 4 Ares 5 Arcas, Argus 6 Aeacus, Apollo, Hermes, Tityus 7 Perseus 8 Dardanus, Dionysos, Dionysus, Heracles, Herakles, Hercules, Tantalus 10 Hephaestus
victim: 4 Idas
wife: 4 Hera, Juno 5 Danae, Metis 6 Semele
ziarat, ziara: 4 tomb 6 shrine
ziggurat: 5 tower 7 pyramid
zigzag: 4 tack, turn 5 angle, crank, weave 8 flexuous
zilch: 4 zero 7 nothing 8 goose egg
Zillah: *husband:* 6 Lamech
son: 9 Tubal-cain
Zilpah's son: Gad 5 Asher
zimarra: 5 cloak 7 cassock, soutane
zimb: bug, fly 6 insect
Zimbabwe: *capital:* 6 Harare (formerly Salisbury)
former name: 8 Rhodesia
language: 5 Shona 7 Ndebele
leader: 5 Nkomo 6 Mugabe
monetary unit: 6 dollar
town: 8 Bulawayo
zinc: 7 adamine, adamite, spelter, tutenag 9 galvanize, tutenague
ore: 6 blende 10 splialerite
sulphate: 7 ilesite
zing: pep, vim, zip 4 dash, snap 5 force, vigor 6 energy, spirit, stingo 9 animation, eagerness 10 enthusiasm
zingaro: 5 gypsy, nomad
zingel: 4 fish 5 perch
zinger: 6 retort 9 punch line
zinnia: 5 aster 6 flower
Zion: 4 hill 6 heaven 7 Utopia
Zionism founder: 5 Herzl
zip: 4 zing 5 hurry 6 breeze
zipper: 8 fastener
Zipporah's kin: 5 Moses, Reuel 6 Jethro 7 Eliezer, Gershom
zippy: 5 agile, brisk 6 snappy
zizith: 7 fringes, tassels
zizz: 4 whir, whiz
Zoan: 5 Tanis
zodiac sign: Leo Ram 4 Bull, Crab, Fish, Goat, Lion 5 Aries, decan, Libra, Scale, Twins, Virgo 6 Archer, Cancer, Fishes, Gemini, Pisces, Taurus, Virgin 7 Balance, Scorpio 8 Aquarius, Scorpion 9 Capricorn 11 Capricornus, Sagittarius, Waterbearer
Zola: *defender of:* 7 Dreyfus
work: 4 Nana 6 Verite 7 J'accuse 8 Germinal
zombie: 5 drink, dunce, snake 9 eccentric
zone: 4 area, band, belt, path, zona (L.) 5 layer, tract 6 course, girdle, region, sector, stripe 7 circuit, segment 8 cincture, encircle, engirdle
geological succession: 6 assise
marked by: 6 zonate
zonked: 4 high 5 doped 6 stoned 7 drugged 8 turned on 9 spaced-out 11 intoxicated
zoom: 5 speed 9 chandelle
zoo: 8 vivarium 9 menagerie
floating: ark
zoophyte: 5 coral 9 ectoproct
zoril: 5 skunk 6 weasel 7 polecat
Zoroaster's works: 6 Avesta
Zoroastrian: 5 Parsi 6 gheber, ghebre, Parsee
demon: 4 deva
god: 5 Ahura, Mazda 10 Ahura-Mazda
zoster: 4 belt 6 girdle
Zouave: 4 Zuzu 7 soldier
zounds: 4 egad 8 mild oath
zoysia: 5 grass
zucchetto: 7 calotte 8 skullcap
zucchini: 5 gourd 6 squash
zufolo: 5 flute 9 flageolet
zuisin: 4 duck 7 widgeon 8 baldplate
Zulu: *boy:* 6 umfaan
headman: 6 induna
language: 5 Bantu
regiment: 4 impi
spear: 7 assegai
Zuni: 6 Indian, Pueblo
zwieback: 4 rusk 5 toast 7 biscuit
zygomatic bone: 5 malar 9 cheekbone
zygote: 7 oosperm
zymase: 6 enzyme
source: 5 yeast
zymogen activating substance: 6 kinase
zymosis: 7 disease 12 fermentation
zythum: 4 beer

Prefixes, Suffixes and Combining Forms

Prefixes, suffixes and combining forms are listed alphabetically rather than by number of letters. The endings given in parentheses may be added on to the affix given, or the affix may be used on its own. For example, the prefix for **accessory** may be either *par* or *para*.

PREFIXES

abnormal: dys
about: ambi
above: hyper, super, supra, sur
accessory: par(a)
across: di(a), trans
additional: super
advocating: pro
after: meta, post
again: an(a)
against: ant(h) (i), cat(a) (h) (o), contra, kat(a) (h) (o)
ahead: pre
almost: pen(e)
alongside: par(a)
alternate: counter
among: inter
anew: an(a)
apart: dis
around: ambi, circum, peri
asunder: dis
at the front: pre
away from: ap(h) (o)
back: an(a), retro
before: ante, pre, pro
beforehand: pre
beside: par(a)
between: inter, intra
beyond: extra, praeter, preter, sur, trans, ultra
both: ambi
chemical: ox(a)
chief: arch(i)
combating: ant(h) (i)
complementary: counter

corresponding: counter
deprived of: dis
detached: ap(h) (o)
different: ap(h) (o)
difficult: dys
diseased: dys
down: cat(a) (h) (o), kat(a) (h) (o)
dwarf: nan(o)
earlier: ante
excess: hyper
excessive: sur
extreme: arch(i)
faulty: par(a)
forward: ante
front: pro
great: arch(i)
half: hemi, semi
higher: super, supra
improper: mis
in advance: pre
incorrect: mis
later: meta
less than: hypo
low-pitched: contra
lower: hypo
mistaken: mis
near: pros
nearer: cis
near to: ep(h) (i)
negative: dis
not: non
one: uni
opposed: dis
opposing: ant(h) (i)
opposite: counter
outer: ep(h) (i)

outside: extra
over: ep(h) (i), extra, hyper, super, supra, sur
partial: demi, semi
prime: arch(i)
principal: arch(i)
prior: ante, pro
resembling: par(a)
retaliatory: counter
reverse: dis, dys
rival: ant(h) (i)
round: peri
ruler: arch
secondary: sub
single: uni
subsequent: post
substituting: pro
succeeding: meta
surrounding: circum, peri
through: di(a), per
throughout: per
together: co(l) (m) (n) (r), sy(m) (n), sym(n)
toward: pros
transcending: meta, supra
transformation: meta
two: twi
under: hypo, sub
underneath: intra
unfavorable: dys
up: an(a), sur
upon: ep(h) (i)
upward: ano
with: co(l) (m) (n) (r), sym(n)
within: intra
wrong: mis

SUFFIXES

abundance: ose
accomplishing: ive
act: ade, ance, ion, ure
act (upon): ate
action: age, ance, ence, ing, ization
adherent: ist, ite
adjective: ular
agency: ator, eer
agent: ator, eer, facient, fic, ier
alcohol: itol
approximately: ish
art: ery
becoming: escence, escent
beginning: escent
being: ant, ent, ical, ure
belonging to: an, ean, ian, ish
capable of: ile
capable: able, ible
caused by: ical
causing: able, facient, fic, ible
character: ery
characteristic: ism
characteristic of: ical, ish, ist, istic(al)
characterized by: ful, ial, ical, in(a) (e), ory, ous
chemical: ane, ein(e), ene, idin, ile, ine, ite, ole, olic, ose, ylene
citizen: ese, ian, ist, ite
city: polis
collection: ery
collection of: age
compound: ate
condition: ance, ate, ence, ency, hood, ile, ism, ment, osis
cult: ism
degree: ity
descendant: ite
diminutive: cle, cular, ette, ole, ule
direction: ling
disease: itis, oma
doctrine: ism

doer: ast, ator, eer, facient, ier, ist, ster
existing: ent
expert: ician, ist
female: ine
feminine: ette
fit: able, ible
form: ify
formation: osis
full of: ous
function: ate, ure
group: ery, ome
group of: ette
imitation: ette
inferior: ling
inflammation: itis
inhabitant: ese, ite
instrument: tron
language: ese
like: ose
little: ette
little one: el, elle, ium, kin(s), ock
make: ify
marked by: ling
mineral: ite
musical instrument: in(a) (e)
native: ite
object: ment
office: ate, dom, ship, ure
offspring: ite
old: ster
ordinal: eth, th
participant: ster
pertaining to: ese, ile
place: arium, ary, ery, orium
place for: ory
place of: age
places: aria
plant: acea
plants: aceae, ales
practice: ery, ics, ism
practitioner: ician
process: age, ence, ing, ion, ization, ment, osis, ure
product: ade

profession: ship
quality: ance, ancy, ence, ency, hood, ice, ity, ness, ship
rank: ate
realm: dom
reflecting: escent
related to: in(a) (e)
relating to: ative, ean, ese, ial, ical, ile, ine, ist, istic(al), itious, ory
resembling: ular
result: ization, ment
serving for: ory
skill: ics, ship
small: ling
small one: ula, ule, ulum, ulus
specialists: ician
specialized in: an, ean, ian
state: age, ance, ancy, ate, ation, dom, ence, ency, ery, hood, ion, ism, ity, ization, ment, ness, osis, ship
stem: ome
study: ics
style: esque
substitute: ette
sugar: ose, ulose
superlative: est
supporter: ite
sweet drink: ade
system: ism
tendency: itis
tending toward: ive
theory: ism
thing: ant, orium
things: oria
trace of: ish
trade: ery
trait: ism
tumor: oma
user: ster
vacuum tube: tron
worthy: able, ible
young: ster
youngster: ling

COMBINING FORMS

abdomen: ventr(i) (o)
abounding: poly
above: supero
accelerating: auxo
acid: acet(o), oxy
acorn: balan(o)

action: praxia
adhesion: anchyl(o), ancyl(o), ankyl(o)
affinity: phily
again: pali
against: cat(h) (a), kat(a)

agricultural: agro
air: atm(o), pneumo
aldehyde: ald(o)
alike: hom(o), is(o)
all: omn(i), pan(o)
alone: mon(o), soli

alternative: allelo
amber: succin(o)
ancient: archae(o), archeo, palae(o), pale(o)
angle: anguli, angulo, gon
animal: zoic
ankle: tars(o)
ant: myrmec(o)
antimony: stib(i) (o)
ape: pithec(o) (us)
apex: apic(i) (o)
appear: phaner(o)
appearance: phany
appetite: orexia
archetypal: prot(o)
arising: genous
arm: brachi(o)
armed: hoplo
around: amph(i)
arrangement: tax(i) (o)
art: techn(o)
ass: ono
asunder: dich(o)
atlas: atlant(o), atlo
aviation: aer(o)
avoidance: phob(o)
back: dors(i) (o), not(o) (us), opisth(o)
bad: cac(o), mal
balance: stato
beautiful: cali(o), calli(o)
bed: clin(o)
bee: api, avi
beginning: acr(o), akr(o)
berry: bacci, cocc(i) (o)
best: aristo
billionth: nano
bitter: picr(o)
black: atro, mel(a) (o), melan(o)
blind: typhl(o)
blood: haem(o), hem(a) (i) (o)
blue: cyan(o)
boat: scaph(o)
body: dema, soma, somat(o)
bone: oste(o)
book: biblio
both: amph(i) (o), bis
brain: cerebr(i) (o)
branched: cladous
breast: mast(o)
brief: brevi
bright: lampro
bristle: chaet(o), seti
broad: lati
broom: scopi
brush: scopi
bud: blast(o)
bulk: onc(h) (o)

bulky: hadr(o)
bull: taur(i) (o)
butter: butyr(o)
cat: aelur(o), ailur(o)
cattle: bovi
caudal: ur(o)
cause: aetio, aitio, etio
cavity: antr(o)
cecum: typhl(o)
cell: blast, cyt(e) (o), gamet(o), phag(e)
cement: lith
chain: strept(o)
chamber: thalam(o)
cheek: bucco, mel(o)
cheese: case(o), tyr(o)
chemical: amid(o), amin (o)
chest: stern(o), steth(o), thorac(i) (o)
chief: prot(o)
child: paed(o), ped(o)
chin: genio, mento
China: sino
Chinese: sinic(o)
church: ecclesi(o)
clay: argill(i) (o), argillaceo, pel(o)
cleft: fissi, schisto, schiz(o)
climate: meteor(o)
close: sten(o)
closed: cleist(o), clist(o)
closure: cleisis, clisis
clot: thromb(o)
cloud: cirr(hi) (i) (o) (ho), nephel(o), nepho, nimbo
cluster: cym(o), kym(o)
coal: anthrac(o)
cold: cry(o), frigo, psychro
color: chrom(o)
colorless: leuc(o), leuk(o)
combination: hapt(o)
compact: pycn(o)
complete: hol(o), tel(e) (o)
concealed: adel(o)
condition: ance, ancy, blasty
contact: hapt(o)
contemporary: ne(o)
contest: machy
copper: chalc(o), chalk(o), cupr(o)
correct: orth(o)
counterfeit: pseud(o)
counterpart: pseud(o)
covered: crypt(o), krypt(o)
craft: techn(o)
creeping: herpet(o)

crooked: anchyl(o), ancyl(o), ankyl(o)
crown: corono, stephan(o)
crystal: hedron
cup: cotyl(i) (o), cyath(o), scyph(i) (o)
current: rheo
dark: melan(o), nyct(i) (o)
dead: abio
decomposition: lysis
deep: bathy
deer: cervi
defective: atel(o)
deficiency: penia
deficient: privic
dense: pycn(o)
depth: bath(o)
descendant: ite
desire: orexia
development: plasia
devouring: vorous
diaphragm: phren(i) (o)
difficult: mogi
disease: agra, pathia, pathic, pathy
diseased: cac(o)
disintegration: lysis
dislike: mis(o)
distant: tel(e) (o)
distinct: idio
diver: dyt(a) (es)
diverse: vari(o)
divided: fid, fissi, schisto
doctrine: logy
doer: ist
dog: cyn(o)
donkey: ono
double: bis
down: cat(h) (a), kat(a)
dream: oneir(o), onir(o)
drug: pharmaco
dry: xer(o)
dull: ambly(o), brady
dwarf: nano
eagle: aet(o)
ear: aur(i), ot(o)
earnest: serio
earth: geo
earthquake: seismo
eat: phag(o)
eating: vore
egg: ov(i) (o)
empty: ken(o)
end: acr(o), akr(o), tel(e) (o)
entire: hol(o), integri, toti
environment: ec(o), oeco, oiko
equal: aequi, equi, is(o), pari

era: zoic
eruption: anthema
even: homal(o)
everywhere: omni
evil: mal
exam'nation: opsy
existence: ont(o)
external: ect(o), exo
extremity: acr(o), akr(o)
eye: irid(o), ocul(o), opto,
 opy
eyelid: blephar(o)
false: pseud(o)
fat: adip(o), lip(o), seb(i)
 (o), steat(o)
fatty: lipar(o)
fear: phob(o)
fearful: din(o)
feather: penn(i) (o),
 pinn(i), pter(o)
feeling: pathia, pathy
feigned: pseud(o)
female: gyn(e) (o)
few: olig(o), pauci
fewer: meio, mi(o)
fictitious: pseud(o)
fifth: quint(i)
fight: machy
fin: pinn(i)
fine: lept(o)
finger: dactyl(o), digit(i)
fire: igni, pyr(o)
first: prot(o)
fish: ichthy(o), pisci
fixed: aplano, stato
flagellum: mastig(o)
flat: homal(o), plan(i)
flute: aul(o)
fon lness: phily
food: sito, troph(o)
foot: ped(i) (o), pod(e) (o)
footprint: ichn(o)
foreign: xen(o)
forest: hyl(o)
form: morph(o)
four: tessar(a), tesser(a),
 tetr(a)
freezing: cry(o)
front: antero
fruit: carp(ia) (ium) (us),
 fructi
fungus: myc(o),
 mycete(e) (o)
gas: aer(o), pneumo
gate: pyl(e) (o)
ghost: sci(a) (o), skia
giant: megal(o)
gill: branch
gilled: branchia
gland: aden(o), adren(o)
glandular: aden(o)
glass: hyal(o), vitr(o)

glue: coll(o)
gnat: culic(i)
goat: capri
gold: auro
good: agath(o)
goose: chen(o)
government: archy, cracy
grain: cocc(i) (o), sito
grape: botry(o)
grave: serio
grease: seb(i) (o)
great: macr(o), meg(a),
 megal(o)
growth: auxo
guest: xen(o)
guiding: agogue
gums: ulo
habitat: ec(o), oeco, oiko
hand: cheir(o), chir(o),
 man(i) (u)
hard: scler(a) (o), stere(o)
hardening: scler(a) (o)
hare: lag(o)
hatred: mis(o), phobia
head: cephal(o) (us),
 crani(o)
healing: iatric(s), iatro(y)
heap: cumul(i) (o)
hearing: acou(o), acousia,
 audio, oto
heart: cardi(a) (o)
heavens: uran(o)
heavy: bary, gravi, hadr(o)
heel: calcaneo
height: acr(o), akr(o), alt,
 hyps(i) (o)
hidden: adel(o), crypt(o),
 krypt(o)
hide: derm(a) (o)
high: alti
hollow: cel(o), coel(o)
holy: hagi(o), hier(o),
 sacr(o)
homogeneous: is(o)
honey: meli, mell(i)
horn: cerat(o), corn,
 kerat(o)
horned: cera
horse: equi, hipp(o)
human: anthrop(o)
hundred: centi, hect(o)
hundredth: centi
idea: ideo
illness: agra
image: eidolo, idolo, typ(o)
imperfect: atel(o)
incomplete: atel(o)
increase: auxo
individual: idio
inner: ent(o)
insect: entom(o)
instrument: labe

intermediate: mes(o)
intestine: enter(o)
iris: irid(o)
iron: ferr(i) (o), sider(o)
irregular: anom(o),
 anomal(i) (o)
irregularly: mal
jackass: ono
jaw: gnath(o)
joint: arthr(o), condyl(o)
juice: opo
kernel: cary(o), kary(o)
key: cleid(o)
kidney: nephr(o),
 ren(i) (o)
killer: cide
kind: gen(o)
knee: gon
knob: tyl(o)
knowledge: gnosia,
 gnosis, gnosy, ics
lake: limn(i) (o)
land: chor(o), gaea, geo
language: gloss(o),
 glott(o), lingu(a) (i) (o)
large: macr(o), meg(a),
 megal(o)
law: nom(o)
layer: cline
lead: molybd(o), plumb(o)
leaf: phyll(o)
level: plan(i) (o)
lifeless: abio
ligament: desm(o)
light: luci, lumin(i) (o),
 phos, phot(o)
like: home(o), homoe(o),
 homoi(o)
lily: crinus
line: lineo, stich
lip: labio
listening: acou(o)
living: ont(o), vivi
lizard: saur(o)
local: top(o)
love: eroto
loving: phil(e) (o)
lung: pneum(o), pulmo
maiden: partheno
male: andr(o)
man: anthrop(o)
manifest: phaner(o)
many: mult(i), pluri, poly
marriage: gamy
marrying: gamous
mass: onc(h) (o)
master: arch
matter: hyl(o)
measuring: metry
medical treatment:
 iatric(s), iatro(y)
memory: mnem(o)

middle: mes(o)
milk: lact(i) (o)
million: meg(a)
millionth: micr(o)
mind: menti, noo, phren(i) (o), psych(o)
mineral: lite, lyte
mite: acar(i) (o)
modern: ne(o)
moisture: hygr(o)
monster: terat(o)
moon: selen(i) (o)
mosquito: culic(i)
mother: matr(i) (o)
motley: part(i) (y)
mouse: my(o) (s)
mouth: or(i) (o), stom(a) (e) (o)
mouths: stomat(a) (o)
much: mult(i), poly
mud: pel(o)
muscle: my(o)
name: omato, onym
narrow: sten(o)
native: ite
navel: omphal(o)
near: juxta
neck: cervic(i) (o)
nerve: neur(o)
nerve tissue: gangli(o)
new: ne(o)
night: nyct(i) (o)
nine: ennea
ninth: non(a)
nipple: mast(o), papilli(o)
nitrogen: az(a) (o)
nose: nas(i) (o), rhin(o) (us)
novel: caen(o), cen(o)
nucleus: cary(o), kary(o)
number: arithmo
nut: cary(o), kary(o)
nutrition: troph(o)
occult: crypt(o), krypt(o)
odd: azygo
offspring: gen(o), ped(o)
oil: elaeo, elaio, eleo, ole(i) (o)
oily: lipar(o)
old age: geront(o)
one: mon(o)
opening: pora, pore, pyle, stom(a) (o)
organ (internal): viscer(i) (o)
organism: ont(o)
other: all(o), heter(o)
out of: ect(o)
outside: ect(o), exo
ox: bovi
oyster: ostre(i) (o)
pain: agra, alg(o), algia

paralysis: plegia, plegy
part: mer(o)
particle: plast
parturition: toky
path: ode
peak: acr(o), akr(o)
peculiar: idio
people: dem(o), ethn(o)
perfect: tel(e) (o)
person: idio
phenomena: ics
physician: iatrist, iatro(y)
picture: picto, pinac(o)
pig: choerus
pillar: styl(o)
pipe: aul(o), siphon(i) (o), solen(o)
pit: bothr(o)
place: chor(o), gaea, gea, loco, top(o)
plant: chore, phyt(a)
pleasant: hedy
poem: stich
poison: toxic(o)
pond: limn(i) (o)
pool: limn(i) (o)
pouch: cyst(i) (is) (o)
poverty: penia
power: dynam(o)
practice: ics
practitioner: path
pressure: baro, piezo, tono
prickly: echin(o)
primary: prot(o)
producer: gen(e)
producing: genetic
qualities: ics
quinine: chin(o)
race: ethn(o), gen(o), phyl(o)
radiating: actin(i) (o)
rain: hyet(o), ombro, pluvi(a) (o)
rainbow: irid(o)
raven: corax
ray: actin(i) (o)
recent: caen(o), cen(o), ne(o)
reciprocal: allelo
recital: logue
recognition: gnosia, gnosis, gnosy
record: gram, graph
recurring: ennial
red: erythr(o), pyrrh(o), rhod(o)
reduction: lysis
remote: dist(i) (o), palae(o), pale(o), tel(e) (o)
repetition: pali
representation: graphy

reptile: herpet(o)
resembling: form
respiration: pneumo
resting: stato
rib: cost(i) (o), pleur(i) (o)
ribbon: taen(i) (o)
rice: oryz(i) (o)
right: dextr(o), orth(o), rect(i)
river: potam(o)
rock: clast, ite, lite, lith, lyte, petr(i) (o), phyre
rod: rhabd(o)
roof: steg(o)
root: rhiz(o)
rose: rhod(o)
rotten: sapr(o)
rough: trachy
round: globo, troch(o), ventr(i) (o)
rule: archy
ruler: arch
running: drom(o), dromous
sac: cyst(i) (o)
sacred: hagi(o), sacr(o)
saints: hagi(o)
salt: hal(o), ite, sali
same: hom(o), is(o)
saw: serri
science: ics, logy, ology, onomy, sophy
sea: mer, pelag(o)
second: deuter(o), deut(o)
seed: sperm(a) (i) (o), spermat(o)
seizure: agra
self: aut(o)
separate: idio
serpent: ophi(o)
seven: hept(a), sept(i)
sex: gen(o)
shadow: sci(a) (o), skia
shaggy: dasy
shape: morph(o)
sharp: oxy
sheet: pallio
shell: conch(o), oeco, ostrac(o)
shield: aspid(o), aspis, scut(i)
shoot: blast(o), thall(i) (o)
short: brachy, brevi
shoulder: om(o)
shrub: thamn(o)
side: ali, later(i) (o), pleur(i) (o)
sides: ali
sight: opsia, opsy
silver: argent(i) (o), argyr(o)

similar: hol(o), home(o), hom(o), homoe(o), homoi(o)
simple: apl(o), hapl(o)
single: apl(o), hapl(o), mon(o)
six: hex(a), sex(i), sexti
skill: ics, techn(o)
skin: derm(a) (o), dermis
slant: clin(o)
sleep: hypn(o)
slope: cline
slow: brady
small: lept(o), micr(o), olig(o), parv(i) (o)
smaller: meio, mi(o)
smell: brom(o)
smooth: leio, lio, liss(o)
snake: ophi(o)
snow: chio, chion(o)
sodium: natr(o)
soil: agro, geo
solid: stere(o)
solitary: erem(o)
song: melo
soul: psych(o), thym(o)
sound: audio, phon(e) (o) (y), phonia
south: austr(o), not(o)
sow: choerus
specialist: ician, ist, logue
speech: lalo, log(o), phon(o)
spherical: globo
spider: arachn(o)
spiral: helic(o)
spirit: psych(o), thym(o)
spot: macul(i) (o)
spring: cren(o)
sprout: blast(o), clad(o)
sprouting: blastic
stain: macul(i) (o)
star: astr(o)
starch: amyl(o)
steam: atmid(o)
stem: caul(i) (o)
stick: rhabd(o)
stomach: gaster(o), gastr(i) (o)
stone: lith(o)
stoppage: stasis
straight: lineo, orth(o), rect(i)
strain: tono
strange: xen(o)
stranger: xen(o)
stream: fluvio
stroke: plegia
structure: morph(o)
stupor: narc(o)
substance: hyl(o), phane, state

suffering: path(o), pathia, pathy
sugar: gluc(o), glyc(o), sacchar(i) (o), sucr(o)
sulfur: thi(o)
summit: acr(o), akr(o), apic(i) (o)
sun: heli(o)
supporter: crat, ist, ite
surface: hedron
surgical removal: ectomy
sweat: hidr(o)
sweet: glyc(o)
swine: hyo
swollen: phys(o)
tablet: pinac(o), plac(o)
talk: logue
tallow: seb(i) (o), stear(o), steat(o)
tapeworm: taen(i) (o)
taste: geusia
teeth: odontia
ten: dec(a), decem, dek(a)
tendency: philia, phily
tendon: teno
tenth: deci
terrible: din(o)
theft: klept(o)
theory: logy
therapy: pathia, pathic, pathy
thick: dasy, hadr(o), pachy
thigh: mer(o), merus
thin: lept(o)
third: tri, trit(o)
thorn: acanth(o) (us), spini(o)
thought: ideo, log(o)
thousand: kilo
thread: nem(a) (o), nemat(o)
three: ter, tri
throat: bronch(o)
thunder: bront(o), ceraun(o), kerauno
tick: acar(i) (o)
time: chron(o), chronous
tin: stann(i) (o)
tip: acr(o), akr(o), apic(i)(o)
tissue: hist(o), hypho
toe: dactyl(o)
tone: phon(o)
tongue: gloss(o), lingu(a) (i) (o)
tooth: dent(i) (o), odont(o)
top: acr(o), akr(o), apic(i)(o)

total: hol(o)
touch: hapt(o), thigmo
track: ichn(o)
translucent: hyal(o)
transmission: phoresis
transparent: hyal(o)
treatise: logy
tree: dendr(o), dendron
trench: bothr(o)
triangular: trigon(o)
tribe: phyl(o)
trillion: treg(a)
trillionth: pico
trough: bothr(o)
true: orth(o)
tube: siphon(i) (o), solen(o), syring(o)
tumor: cele, gangli(o), myom(o), onc(h) (o)
twice: bis
twin: didym(o)
twist: spir(i) (o)
twisted: strept(o)
two: bin, duo
twofold: diphy(o), dipl(o)
type: morph(o)
umbilicus: omphal(o)
unarmed: anopl(o)
unequal: anis(o)
uniform: is(o)
union: gamous, gamy, zyg(o)
united: gam(o)
universal: cosm(o), omni
universe: cosm(o)
unpleasant: cac(o)
unreal: pseud(o)
untrue: pseud(o)
unusual: anom(o)
upright: orth(o)
urchin: echin(o)
usage: nom(o)
vapor: atm(o)
variation: all(o)
various: part(i) (y)
vehicle: mobile
vein: phleb(o), ven(i) (o)
vertebra: spondyl(o) (us)
vessel: angi(o), arteri(o), vas(i) (o), vascul(o)
viewing instrument: scope
vine: ampel(o), viti
vinegar: acet(o)
virgin: parthen(o)
viscera: splanchn(o)
visible: phaner(o)
vision: opia, opsy, opto, opy

voice: phon(e) (o) (y)
war: machy
water: hydr(o)
wave: cym(o), kym(o)
wax: cer(o)
way: ode
weak: asthen(o), lept(o)
wealth: plut(o)
weather: meteor(o)
web: hypho
weight: bar(o)
well: agath(o)
wet: hygr(o)
whale: cet(o)
wheel: troch(o)
whip: mastig(o), mastix
white: alb(o), cali(o), calli(o), leuc(o), leuk(o)

whole: hol(o), integri, pan(o), toti
wholly: toti
wide: eury, lati
wild: agrio
wild beast: ther(o)
wind: anem(o), venti, vento
windpipe: bronchi(o), trache(o)
wing: ali, pter(o)
within: end(o), ent(o), eso
wolf: lyc(o)
woman: gyn(e) (o), gynaec(o), gynec(o)
womb: hyster(o), metr(a) (o), uter(o)
wood: hyl(o), lign(i) (o),

xyl(o)
wool: erio, lan(i) (o)
word: log(o)
work: erg(o) (y)
worker: ergat(o)
world: cosm(o)
worm: helminth(o), vermi
worship: latry
wound: traumat(o)
wrist: carp(o)
writer: grapher
writing: grapho
year: ennial
yellow: chrys(o), flav(o), lute(o), xanth(o)
yoke: zyg(o)
yolk: vitell(o)